Collins

Portuguese
Dictionary
& Grammar

HarperCollins Publishers
Westerhill Road
Bishopbriggs
Glasgow
G64 2QT

First Edition 2013

Reprint 10 9 8 7 6 5 4 3 2 1 0

© HarperCollins Publishers 2013

ISBN 978-0-00-749676-1

Collins® is a registered trademark of
HarperCollins Publishers Limited

www.collinslanguage.com

A catalogue record for this book is
available from the British Library

HarperCollins Publishers,
10 East 53rd Street,
New York, NY 10022

COLLINS PORTUGUESE DICTIONARY
& GRAMMAR
First US Edition 2013

Library of Congress cataloging-in-
Publication Data has been applied for

ISBN 978-0-06-227802-9
www.harpercollins.com

HarperCollins books may be
purchased for educational,
business, or sales promotional use.
For information, please write to:
Special Markets Department,
HarperCollins Publishers,
10 East 53rd Street,
New York, NY 10022

Typeset by Davidson Publishing
Solutions, Glasgow

Printed in India by
Gopsons Papers Ltd

Acknowledgements
We would like to thank those authors
and publishers who kindly gave
permission for copyright material to be
used in the Collins Corpus. We would
also like to thank Times Newspapers Ltd
for providing valuable data.

SUMÁRIO		CONTENTS	

GERÊNCIA DE PROJETO/PROJECT MANAGEMENT
Teresa Álvarez García
Carol McCann

COLABORADORES/CONTRIBUTORS
Gaëlle Amiot-Cadey
Susie Beattie
Gerard Breslin
Vitoria Davies
Carla Gaspar
Daniel Grassi
Orin Hargraves
Mike Harland
Jane Horwood
Cordelia Lilly
Amos Maidantchik
Helio Leoncio Martins
Dr Euzi Rodrigues Moraes
Helen Newstead
Nelly Wanderley Fernandes Porto
Carlos Ramires
Adriana Ceschin Rieche
Maggie Seaton
Ana Maria de Mello e Souza
Daniel Veloso
John Whitlam
Lígia Xavier

**GRAMÁTICA PORTUGUESA/
PORTUGUESE GRAMMAR GUIDE**
Manuela Cook

COMPUTAÇÃO/COMPUTING
Agnieszka Urbanowicz

PARA A EDITORA/FOR THE PUBLISHER
Lucy Cooper
Kerry Ferguson
Elaine Higgleton
Ruth O'Donovan

INTRODUÇÃO

PARA COMPREENDER O INGLÊS

A nova edição atualizada deste dicionário oferece ao leitor uma cobertura ampla e prática dos usos linguísticos mais comuns, incluindo terminologia da área de negócios e da informática, além de uma seleção abrangente de abreviaturas, siglas e topônimos de uso frequente. As formas irregulares de verbos e substantivos ingleses também foram incluídas na nomenclatura, com remissão à forma de base, onde se encontra a tradução. As notas adicionais ajudam a entender algumas referências culturais.

PARA EXPRESSAR-SE EM INGLÊS

A fim de ajudar o leitor a expressar-se de forma correta e idiomática em inglês, foram incluídas várias indicações para orientá-lo quanto à tradução mais apropriada em um determinado contexto. Todas as palavras mais frequentes receberam um tratamento detalhado, com muitos exemplos de uso típicos.

UM COMPANHEIRO DE TRABALHO

Todo o cuidado foi tomado para fazer deste dicionário da editora Collins uma obra totalmente confiável, fácil de ser usada e útil para o trabalho e os estudos do leitor. Esperamos que ele seja de grande ajuda na compreensão e no uso do inglês.

NOVOS SUPLEMENTOS DE GRAMÁTICA

Uma das características mais importantes deste dicionário é a inclusão de suplementos de gramática para aprendizes tanto do inglês quanto do português, que trazem explicações claras dos principais pontos gramaticais e exemplos reais de seu uso.

INTRODUCTION

UNDERSTANDING PORTUGUESE

This new, updated edition of the dictionary provides the user with wide-ranging, practical coverage of current usage, including business and IT terminology, and a comprehensive selection of common abbreviations, acronyms and geographical names. You will also find irregular forms of Portuguese verbs and nouns with a cross-reference to the basic form where a translation is given. Additional notes are given to help you understand some cultural references.

EXPRESSING YOURSELF IN PORTUGUESE

To help you express yourself correctly and idiomatically in Portuguese, numerous labels or signposts guide you to the most appropriate translation for your context. All the most commonly used words are given detailed treatment, with many examples of typical usage.

A WORKING COMPANION

Much care has been taken to make this Collins dictionary thoroughly reliable, easy to use and relevant to your work and study. We hope it will help you understand and communicate better.

NEW HELPFUL GRAMMAR SUPPLEMENTS

A key feature of this dictionary is the addition of grammar supplements for learners of both English and Portuguese. These give clear explanations of the main grammatical issues and provide real examples to demonstrate their use.

ABREVIATURAS   ABBREVIATIONS

abreviatura	AB(B)R	abbreviation
adjetivo	ADJ	adjective
administração	Admin	administration
advérbio, locução adverbial	ADV	adverb, adverbial phrase
aeronáutica	Aer	flying, air travel
agricultura	Agr	agriculture
anatomia	Anat	anatomy
arquitetura	Arq, Arch	architecture
artigo definido	ART DEF	definite article
artigo indefinido	ART INDEF	indefinite article
uso atributivo do substantivo	ATR	compound element
Austrália	Aust	Australia
automobilismo	Aut(o)	the motor car and motoring
auxiliar	AUX	auxiliary
aeronáutica	Aviat	flying, air travel
biologia	Bio	biology
botânica, flores	Bot	botany
português do Brasil	BR	Brazilian Portuguese
inglês britânico	BRIT	British English
química	Chem	chemistry
linguagem coloquial	col	colloquial
comércio, finanças, bancos	Com(m)	commerce, finance, banking
comparativo	compar	comparative
computação	Comput	computing
conjunção	CONJ	conjunction
construção	Constr	building
uso atributivo do substantivo	CPD	compound element
cozinha	Culin	cookery
artigo definido	DEF ART	definite article
economia	Econ	economics
educação, escola e universidade	Educ	schooling, schools and universities
eletricidade, eletrônica	Elet, Elec	electricity, electronics
especialmente	esp	especially
exclamação	excl	exclamation
feminino	f	feminine
ferrovia	Ferro	railways
uso figurado	fig	figurative use
física	Fís	physics
fisiologia	Fisiol	physiology
fotografia	Foto	photography
(verbo inglês) do qual a partícula é inseparável	FUS	(phrasal verb) where the particle is inseparable
geralmente	gen	generally
geografia, geologia	Geo	geography, geology
geometria	Geom	geometry
geralmente	ger	generally
impessoal	IMPESS, IMPERS	impersonal
artigo indefinido	INDEF ART	indefinite article
linguagem coloquial	inf	colloquial
infinitivo	infin	infinitive
invariável	INV	invariable

irregular	*irreg*	irregular
jurídico	*Jur*	law
gramática, linguística	*Ling*	grammar, linguistics
masculino	*m*	masculine
matemática	*Mat(h)*	mathematics
medicina	*Med*	medicine
masculino ou feminino, dependendo do sexo da pessoa	*m/f*	masculine/feminine
militar, exército	*Mil*	military matters
música	*Mús, Mus*	music
substantivo	N	noun
navegação, náutica	*Náut, Naut*	sailing, navigation
adjetivo ou substantivo numérico	NUM	numeral adjective or noun
Nova Zelândia	NZ	New Zealand
	o.s.	oneself
pejorativo	*pej*	pejorative
fotografia	*Phot*	photography
física	*Phys*	physics
fisiologia	*Physiol*	physiology
plural	*pl*	plural
política	*Pol*	politics
particípio passado	*pp*	past participle
preposição	PREP	preposition
pronome	PRON	pronoun
psicologia, psiquiatria	*Psico, Psych*	psychology, psychiatry
português de Portugal	pt	European Portuguese
pretérito	pt	past tense
química	*Quím*	chemistry
religião e cultos	*Rel*	religion, church services
	sb	somebody
educação, escola e universidade	*Sch*	schooling, schools and universities
singular	*sg*	singular
	sth	something
sujeito (gramatical)	*su(b)j*	(grammatical) subject
subjuntivo, conjuntivo	*sub(jun)*	subjunctive
superlativo	*superl*	superlative
também	*tb*	also
técnica, tecnologia	*Tec(h)*	technical term, technology
telecomunicações	*Tel*	telecommunications
tipografia, imprensa	*Tip*	typography, printing
televisão	*TV*	television
tipografia, imprensa	*Typ*	typography, printing
inglês americano	US	American English
ver	V	see
verbo	VB	verb
verbo intransitivo	VI	intransitive verb
verbo reflexivo	VR	reflexive verb
verbo transitivo	VT	transitive verb
zoologia	*Zool*	zoology
marca registrada	®	registered trademark
equivalente cultural	≈	cultural equivalent
linguagem ofensiva	!	offensive

PRONÚNCIA INGLESA

Em geral, damos a pronúncia de cada entrada em colchetes logo após a palavra em questão. Todavia, quando a entrada for composta de duas ou mais palavras, e cada uma delas aparecer em outro lugar no dicionário, o leitor encontrará a pronúncia de cada palavra na sua posição alfabética.

VOGAIS

	Exemplo Inglês	Explicação
[aː]	father	Entre o a de padre e o o de nó; como em fada
[ʌ]	but, come	Aproximadamente como o primeiro a de cama
[æ]	man, cat	Som entre o a de lá e o e de pé
[ə]	father, ago	Som parecido com o e final do português de Portugal
[əː]	bird, heard	Entre o e aberto e o o fechado
[ɛ]	get, bed	Como em pé
[ɪ]	it, big	Mais breve do que em si
[iː]	tea, see	Como em fino
[ɔ]	hot, wash	Como em pó
[ɔː]	saw, all	Como o o de porte
[u]	put, book	Som breve e mais fechado do que em burro
[uː]	too, you	Som aberto como em juro

DITONGOS

	Exemplo Inglês	Explicação
[aɪ]	fly, high	Como em baile
[au]	how, house	Como em causa
[ɛə]	there, bear	Como o e de aeroporto
[eɪ]	day, obey	Como o ei de lei
[ɪə]	here, hear	Como ia de companhia
[əu]	go, note	[ə] seguido de um u breve
[ɔɪ]	boy, oil	Como em boia
[uə]	poor, sure	Como ua em sua

CONSOANTES

	Exemplo Inglês	Explicação
[d]	men**d**ed	Como em *dado*, an*d*ar
[g]	**g**et, bi**g**	Como em *g*rande
[dʒ]	**g**in, **j**udge	Como em ida*d*e
[ŋ]	si**ng**	Como em ci*n*co
[h]	**h**ouse, **h**e	*h* aspirado
[j]	**y**oung, **y**es	Como em *i*ogurte
[k]	**c**ome, mo**ck**	Como em *c*ama
[r]	**r**ed, t**r**ead	*r* como em pa*r*a, mas pronunciado no céu da boca
[s]	**s**and, ye**s**	Como em *s*ala
[z]	ro**s**e, **z**ebra	Como em *z*ebra
[ʃ]	**sh**e, ma**ch**ine	Como em *ch*apéu
[tʃ]	**ch**in, ri**ch**	Como *t* em *t*imbre
[w]	**w**ater, **wh**ich	Como o *u* em ág*u*a
[ʒ]	vi**s**ion	Como em *j*á
[θ]	**th**ink, my**th**	Sem equivalente, aproximadamente como um *s* pronunciado entre os dentes
[ð]	**th**is, **th**e	Sem equivalente, aproximadamente como um *z* pronunciado entre os dentes

b, f, l, m, n, p, t, v pronunciam-se como em português.

O sinal [*] indica que o r final escrito nâo se pronuncia em inglês britânico, exceto quando a palavra seguinte começa por uma vogal. O sinal ['] indica a sílaba acentuada.

BRAZILIAN PORTUGUESE PRONUNCIATION

CONSONANTS

c	[k]	café	c before a, o, u is pronounced as in cat
ce, ci	[s]	cego	c before e or i, as in receive
ç	[s]	raça	ç is pronounced as in receive
ch	[ʃ]	chave	ch is pronounced as in shock
d	[d]	data	as in English EXCEPT
de, di	[dʒ]	difícil	d before an i sound or final unstressed
		cidade	e is pronounced as in judge
g	[g]	gado	g before a, o, u as in gap
ge, gi	[ʒ]	gíria	g before e or i, as s in leisure
h		humano	h is always silent in Portuguese
j	[ʒ]	jogo	j is pronounced as s in leisure
l	[l]	limpo, janela	as in English EXCEPT
	[w]	falta, total	l after a vowel tends to become w
lh	[ʎ]	trabalho	lh is pronounced like the lli in million
m	[m]	animal, massa	as in English EXCEPT
	[ãw]	cantam	m at the end of a syllable preceded by a
	[ĩ]	sim	vowel nasalizes the preceding vowel
n	[n]	nadar, penal	as in English EXCEPT
	[ã]	cansar	n at the end of a syllable, preceded by a
	[ẽ]	alento	vowel and followed by a consonant, nasalizes the preceding vowel
nh	[˜]	tamanho	nh is pronounced like the ni in onion
q	[k]	queijo	qu before i or e is usually pronounced as in kick
q	[kw]	quanto	qu before a or o, and sometimes before
		cinquenta	e or i, is pronounced as in queen
-r-	[r]	compra	r preceded by a consonant (except n) and followed by a vowel is pronounced with a single trill
r-, -r-	[h]	rato, arpão	inital r, r followed by a consonant and
rr	[h]	borracha	rr are pronounced like h in house
-r	[r]	pintar, dizer	word-final r can sometimes be heard as a single trill, but usually it is not pronounced at all in colloquial speech
s-	[s]	sol	as in English EXCEPT
		escada	
		livros	
-s-	[z]	mesa	intervocalic s and s before b, d, g, l, m, n,
		rasgar,	r, and v, as in rose
		desmaio	
-ss-	[s]	nosso	double s is always pronounced as in boss
t	[t]	todo	as in English EXCEPT
te, ti	[tʃ]	amante	t followed by an i sound or final
		tipo	unstressed e is pronounced as ch in cheer
x-	[ʃ]	xarope	initial x is pronounced like sh in ship
-x-	[s]	exceto	x before a consonant is pronounced
		explorar	like s in sail
ex-	[z]	exame	x in the prefix ex before a vowel is pronounced as z in squeeze
-x-	[ʃ]	relaxar	x in any other position may be
	[ks]	fixo	pronounced as in ship, axe or sail
	[s]	auxiliar	

| z | [z] | **z**angar | as in English |
| | | carta**z** | |

b, f, k, p, v, w are pronounced as in English.

VOWELS

a,á,à,â	[a]	m**a**ta	*a* is normally pronounced as in f*a*ther
ã	[ã]	irm**ã**	*ã* is pronounced approximately as in s*u*ng
e	[e]	v**e**jo	unstressed (except final) *e* is pronounced like *e* in th*e*y, stressed *e* is pronounced either as in th*e*y or as in b*e*t
-e	[i]	fom**e**	final *e* is pronounced as in mon*ey*
é	[ɛ]	mis**é**ria	*é* is pronounced as in b*e*t
ê	[e]	p**ê**lo	*ê* is pronounced as in th*e*y
i	[i]	v**i**da	*i* is pronounced as in m*ea*n
o	[o]	loc**o**motiva	unstressed (except final) *o* is pronounced as in l*o*cal;
	[ɔ]	l**o**ja	stressed *o* is pronounced either as in
	[o]	gl**o**bo	l*o*cal or as in r*o*ck
-o	[u]	livr**o**	final *o* is pronounced as in f*oo*t
ó	[ɔ]	**ó**leo	*ó* is pronounced as in r*o*ck
ô	[o]	col**ô**nia	*ô* is pronounced as in l*o*cal
u	[u]	l**u**va	*u* is pronounced as in r*u*le
	[w]	ling**u**iça	it is usually silent as in *gue, gui, que, qui*
		freq**u**ente	but in some words it is pronounced as a *w* sound in this position

DIPHTHONGS

ãe	[ãj]	m**ãe**	nasalized, approximately as in fl*y*ing
ai	[aj]	v**ai**	as is r*ide*
ao, au	[aw]	**ao**s, a**u**xílio	as is sh*out*
ão	[ãw]	v**ão**	nasalized, approximately as in r*ound*
ei	[ej]	f**ei**ra	as is th*ey*
eu	[ew]	d**eu**sa	both elements pronounced
oi	[oj]	b**oi**	as is t*oy*
ou	[o]	cen**ou**ra	as is l*ocal*
õe	[õj]	avi**õe**s	nasalized, approximately as in 'b*oing*!'

STRESS

The rules of stress in Portuguese are as follows:

(a) when a word ends in *a, e, o, m* (except *im, um* and their plural forms) or *s*, the second last syllable is stressed;
camar*a*da; camar*a*das
p*a*rte; p*a*rtem

(b) when a word ends in *i, u, im* (and plural), *um* (and plural), *n* or a consonant other than *m* or *s*, the stress falls on the last syllable:
ven*di*, al*gum*, al*guns*, fa*lar*

(c) when the rules set out in (a) and (b) are not applicable, an acute or circumflex accent appears over the stressed vowel:
*ó*tica, *â*nimo, ingl*ê*s

In the phonetic transcription, the symbol ['] precedes the syllable on which the stress falls.

EUROPEAN PORTUGUESE PRONUNCIATION

The pronunciation of Brazilian Portuguese differs quite markedly from the
Portuguese spoken in Portugal itself and in the African and island states.
The more phonetic nature of Brazilian means that words nearly always retain
their set pronunciation; in European Portuguese, on the other hand, vowels can
often be unpronounced or weakened and consonants can change their sound,
all depending on their position within a word or whether they are being elided
with a following word. The major differences in pronunciation of European
Portuguese are as follows:-

CONSONANTS: as in Brazilian, except:

-b-	[β]	cuba	*b* between vowels is a softer sound, closer to have
d	[d]	dança, difícil	as in English EXCEPT *d* between vowels is softer,
-d-	[ð]	fado, cidade	approximately as in the
-g-	[ɣ]	saga	*g* between vowels is a softer sound, approximately as in lager
gu	[ɣw]	aguentar	in certain words *gu* is pronounced as in Gwent
qu	[kw]	tranquilo	in certain words *qu* is pronounced as in quoits
r-, rr	[R]		initial *r* and double *r* are pronounced either like the
	[rr]		French *r* or strongly trilled as in Scottish Rory; pronunciation varies according to region
-r-, -r	[r]	rato, arma	*r* in any other position is slightly trilled
t	[t]	todo, amante	*t* is pronounced as in English
z	[ʒ]	zangar	as in English EXCEPT final *z* is pronounced as *sh* in flash
	[ʃ]	cartaz	

VOWELS: as in Brazilian, except:

a	[a]	falar	stressed *a* is pronounced either as in father or as
	[ɐ]	cama	*u* in further
-a-, -a	[ə]	falar, fala	unstressed or final *a* is pronounced as *e* in further
e	[ə]	medir	unstressed *e* is a very short *i* sound as in rabbit
-e	[ə]	arte, regime	final *e* is barely pronounced; these would sound like English art and regime
o	[u]	poço, poder	unstressed or final *o* is pronounced as in foot

PORTUGUESE SPELLING

In 2009, a spelling reform was introduced in all the Portuguese-speaking countries with the aim of eliminating the differences which existed between Brazilian and European Portuguese spelling. The following table summarizes these differences, which you will come across in texts written before the 2009 reform:

Description	Brazilian spelling pre-2009	European Portuguese spelling pre-2009	Universal spelling post-2009
The combinations -gue-, -gui-, -que-, -qui- when u is pronounced	With trema, e.g. *lingüiça, freqüente* etc.	Without trema, e.g. *linguiça, frequente* etc.	Without trema, e.g. *linguiça, frequente* etc.
Stressed -ei- and -oi- in penultimate syllables	With acute accent, e.g. *idéia, heróico*	Without acute accent, e.g. *ideia, heroico*	Without acute accent, e.g. *ideia, heroico*
Stressed o followed by unstressed o	First o has circumflex accent, e.g *vôo, abençôo*	No written accent, e.g. *voo, abençoo*	No written accent, e.g. *voo, abençoo*
First person plural preterite tense of -ar verbs	Without accent, e.g. *amamos, jogamos*	With acute accent, e.g. *amámos, jogámos*	Without accent, e.g. *amamos, jogamos*
comum + mente	*comumente*	*comummente*	*comumente*
com + nós	*conosco*	*connosco*	*conosco*
(h)úmido and derivatives	*úmido, umidade*	*húmido, humidade*	*úmido, umidade*
Latin consonant group -ct-	Simplified to -c-/-ç- or -t-, e.g. *acionar, ação, ator*	Silent -c- retained, e.g. *accionar, acção, actor*	Simplified spelling, e.g. *acionar, ação, ator*
Latin consonant group -pt-	Simplified to -ç- or -t-, e.g. *exceção, ótimo*	Silent -p- retained, e.g. *excepção, óptimo*	Simplified spelling, e.g. *exceção, ótimo*
Months of the year	e.g. *janeiro, dezembro*	e.g. *Janeiro, Dezembro*	e.g. *janeiro, dezembro*

One important difference between Brazilian and Portuguese spelling which still applies even after the reform is that, when a written accent is required on stressed *e* and *o* before *m* or *n*, Brazilian uses the circumflex while European uses the acute accent, reflecting the difference in the way the sounds are pronounced, e.g. *tênis* (BR), *ténis* (PT); *econômico* (BR), *económico* (PT). In addition, there are cases where two different spellings are permitted in European Portuguese to reflect two possible pronunciations, e.g. *súdito/súbdito, sutil/subtil, anistia/amnistia*.

VERBOS IRREGULARES EM INGLÊS

PRESENT	PT	PP	PRESENT	PT	PP
arise	arose	arisen	**find**	found	found
awake	awoke	awoken	**fling**	flung	flung
be (am, is, are; being)	was, were	been	**fly**	flew	flown
			forbid	forbad(e)	forbidden
bear	bore	born(e)	**forecast**	forecast	forecast
beat	beat	beaten	**forget**	forgot	forgotten
begin	began	begun	**forgive**	forgave	forgiven
bend	bent	bent	**freeze**	froze	frozen
bet	bet, betted	bet, betted	**get**	got	got, (US) goten
bid (at auction)	bid	bid	**give**	gave	given
bind	bound	bound	**go** (goes)	went	gone
bite	bit	bitten	**grind**	ground	ground
bleed	bled	bled	**grow**	grew	grown
blow	blew	blown	**hang**	hung	hung
break	broke	broken	**hang** (execute)	hanged	hanged
breed	bred	bred	**have**	had	had
bring	brought	brought	**hear**	heard	heard
build	built	built	**hide**	hid	hidden
burn	burnt, burned	burnt, burned	**hit**	hit	hit
			hold	held	held
burst	burst	burst	**hurt**	hurt	hurt
buy	bought	bought	**keep**	kept	kept
can	could	(been able)	**kneel**	knelt, kneeled	knelt, kneeled
cast	cast	cast			
catch	caught	caught	**know**	knew	known
choose	chose	chosen	**lay**	laid	laid
cling	clung	clung	**lead**	led	led
come	came	come	**lean**	leant, leaned	leant, leaned
cost	cost	cost			
creep	crept	crept	**leap**	leapt, leaped	leapt, leaped
cut	cut	cut			
deal	dealt	dealt	**learn**	learnt, learned	learnt, learned
dig	dug	dug			
do (does)	did	done	**leave**	left	left
draw	drew	drawn	**lend**	lent	lent
dream	dreamed, dreamt	dreamed, dreamt	**let**	let	let
			lie (lying)	lay	lain
drink	drank	drunk	**light**	lit, lighted	lit, lighted
drive	drove	driven			
eat	ate	eaten	**lose**	lost	lost
fall	fell	fallen	**make**	made	made
feed	fed	fed	**may**	might	–
feel	felt	felt	**mean**	meant	meant
fight	fought	fought	**meet**	met	met

PRESENT	PT	PP	PRESENT	PT	PP
mistake	mistook	mistaken	speed	sped,	sped,
mow	mowed	mown,		speeded	speeded
		mowed	spell	spelt,	spelt,
must	(had to)	(had to)		spelled	spelled
pay	paid	paid	spend	spent	spent
put	put	put	spill	spilt,	spilt,
quit	quit,	quit,		spilled	spilled
	quitted	quitted	spin	spun	spun
read	read	read	spit	spat	spat
rid	rid	rid	spoil	spoiled,	spoiled,
ride	rode	ridden		spoilt	spoilt
ring	rang	rung	spread	spread	spread
rise	rose	risen	spring	sprang	sprung
run	ran	run	stand	stood	stood
saw	sawed	sawed,	steal	stole	stolen
		sawn	stick	stuck	stuck
say	said	said	sting	stung	stung
see	saw	seen	stink	stank	stunk
sell	sold	sold	stride	strode	stridden
send	sent	sent	strike	struck	struck
set	set	set	swear	swore	sworn
sew	sewed	sewn	sweep	swept	swept
shake	shook	shaken	swell	swelled	swollen,
shear	sheared	shorn,			swelled
		sheared	swim	swam	swum
shed	shed	shed	swing	swung	swung
shine	shone	shone	take	took	taken
shoot	shot	shot	teach	taught	taught
show	showed	shown	tear	tore	torn
shrink	shrank	shrunk	tell	told	told
shut	shut	shut	think	thought	thought
sing	sang	sung	throw	threw	thrown
sink	sank	sunk	thrust	thrust	thrust
sit	sat	sat	tread	trod	trodden
sleep	slept	slept	wake	woke,	woken,
slide	slid	slid		waked	waked
sling	slung	slung	wear	wore	worn
slit	slit	slit	weave	wove	woven
smell	smelt,	smelt,	weep	wept	wept
	smelled	smelled	win	won	won
sow	sowed	sown,	wind	wound	wound
		sowed	wring	wrung	wrung
speak	spoke	spoken	write	wrote	written

PORTUGUESE VERB FORMS

1 Gerund. **2** Imperative. **3** Present. **4** Imperfect. **5** Preterite. **6** Future.
7 Present subjunctive. **8** Imperfect subjunctive. **9** Future subjunctive.
10 Past participle. **11** Pluperfect. **12** Personal infinitive.

etc indicates that the irregular root is used for all persons of the tense, e.g. **ouvir 7** ouça *etc* = ouça, ouças, ouça, ouçamos, ouçais, ouçam.

abrir 10 aberto

acudir 2 acode **3** acudo, acodes, acode, acodem

aderir 3 adiro **7** adira

advertir 3 advirto **7** advirta *etc*

agir 3 ajo **7** aja *etc*

agradecer 3 agradeço **7** agradeça *etc*

agredir 2 agride **3** agrido, agrides, agride, agridem **7** agrida *etc*

AMAR 1 amando **2** ama, amai **3** amo, amas, ama, amamos, amais, amam **4** amava, amavas, amava, amávamos, amavéis, amavam **5** amei, amaste, amou, amamos, amastes, amaram **6** amarei, amarás, amará, amaremos, amareis, amarão **7** ame, ames, ame, amemos, ameis, amem **8** amasse, amasses, amasse, amássemos, amásseis, amassem **9** amar, amares, amar, ámarmos, amardes, amarem **10** amado **11** amara, amaras, amara, amáramos, amáreis, amaram **12** amar, amares, amar, amarmos, amardes, amarem

ameaçar 5 ameacei **7** ameace *etc*

ansiar 2 anseia **3** anseio, anseias, anseia, anseiam **7** anseie *etc*

arrancar 7 arranque *etc*

arruinar 2 arruína **3** arruíno, arruínas, arruína, arruínam **7** arruíne, arruínes, arruíne, arruínem

atribuir 3 atribuo, atribuis, atribui, atribuímos, atribuís, atribuem

bulir 2 bole **3** bulo, boles, bole, bolem

caber 3 caibo **5** coube *etc* **7** caiba *etc* **8** coubesse *etc* **9** couber *etc*

cair 2 cai **3** caio, cais, cai, caímos, caís, caem **4** caía *etc* **5** caí, caíste **7** caia *etc* **8** caisse *etc*

cobrir 3 cubro **7** cubra *etc* **10** coberto

compelir 3 compilo **7** compila *etc*

crer 2 crê **3** creio, crês, crê, cremos, credes, creem **5** cri, creste, creu, cremos, crestes, creram **7** creia *etc*

cuspir 2 cospe **3** cuspo, cospes, cospe, cospem

dar 2 dá **3** dou, dás, dá, damos, dais, dão **5** dei, deste, deu, demos, destes, deram **7** dê, dês, dê, demos, deis, deem **8** desse *etc* **9** der *etc* **11** dera *etc*

deduzir 2 deduz **3** deduzo, deduzes, deduz

denegrir 2 denigre **3** denigro, denigres, denigre, denigrem **7** denigre *etc*

despir 3 dispo **7** dispa *etc*

dizer 2 diz (dize) **3** digo, dizes, diz, dizemos, dizeis, dizem **5** disse *etc* **6** direi *etc* **7** diga *etc* **8** dissesse *etc* **9** disser *etc* **10** dito

doer 2 dói **3** doo, dóis, dói

dormir 3 durmo **7** durma *etc*

emergir 3 emirjo **7** emirja *etc*

escrever 10 escrito

ESTAR 2 está **3** estou, estás, está, estamos, estais, estão **4** estava *etc* **5** estive, estiveste, esteve, estivemos, estivestes, estiveram **7** esteja *etc* **8** estivesse *etc* **9** estiver *etc* **11** estivera *etc*

extorquir 3 exturco **7** exturca *etc*

FAZER 3 faço **5** fiz, fizeste, fez, fizemos, fizestes, fizeram **6** farei *etc* **7** faça *etc* **8** fizesse *etc* **9** fizer *etc* **10** feito **11** fizera *etc*

ferir 3 firo **7** fira *etc*

fluir 3 fluo, fluis, flui, fluímos, fluís, fluem

fugir 2 foge **3** fujo, foges, foge, fogem **7** fuja *etc*

ganhar 10 ganho
gastar 10 gasto
gerir 3 giro **7** gira *etc*
haver 2 há **3** hei, hás, há, havemos, haveis, hão **4** havia *etc* **5** houve, houveste, houve, houvemos, houvestes, houveram **7** haja *etc* **8** houvesse *etc* **9** houver *etc* **11** houvera *etc*
ir 1 indo **2** vai **3** vou, vais, vai, vamos, ides, vão **4** ia *etc* **5** fui, foste, foi, fomos, fostes, foram **7** vá, vás, vá, vamos, vades, vão **8** fosse, fosses, fosse, fôssemos, fôsseis, fossem **9** for *etc* **10** ido **11** fora *etc*
ler 2 lê **3** leio, lês, lê, lemos, ledes, leem **5** li, leste, leu, lemos, lestes, leram **7** leia *etc*
medir 3 meço, **7** meça *etc*
mentir 3 minto **7** minta *etc*
ouvir 3 ouço **7** ouça *etc*
pagar 10 pago
parir 3 pairo **7** paira *etc*
pecar 7 peque *etc*
pedir 3 peço **7** peça *etc*
perder 3 perco **7** perca *etc*
poder 3 posso **5** pude, pudeste, pôde, pudemos, pudestes, puderam **7** possa *etc* **8** pudesse *etc* **9** puder *etc* **11** pudera *etc*
polir 2 pule **3** pulo, pules, pule, pulem **7** pula *etc*
pôr 1 pondo **2** põe **3** ponho, pões, põe, pomos, pondes, põem **4** punha *etc* **5** pus, puseste, pôs, pusemos, pusestes, puseram **6** porei *etc* **7** ponha *etc* **8** pusesse *etc* **9** puser *etc* **10** posto **11** pusera *etc*
preferir 3 prefiro **7** prefire *etc*
prevenir 2 previne **3** previno, prevines, previne, previnem **7** previna *etc*
prover 2 provê **3** provejo, provês, provê, provemos, provedes, proveem **5** provi, proveste, proveu, provemos, provestes, proveram **7** proveja *etc* **8** provesse *etc* **9** prover *etc*
querer 3 quero, queres, quer **5** quis, quiseste, quis, quisemos, quisestes, quiseram **7** queira *etc* **8** quisesse *etc* **9** quiser *etc* **11** quisera *etc*
refletir 3 reflito **7** reflita *etc*
repetir 3 repito **7** repita *etc*
requerer 3 requeiro, requeres, requer **7** requeira *etc*
reunir 2 reúne **3** reúno, reúnes, reúne, reúnem **7** reúna *etc*
rir 2 ri **3** rio, ris, ri, rimos, rides, ridem **5** ri, riste, riu, rimos, ristes, riram **7** ria *etc*
saber 3 sei, sabes, sabe, sabemos, sabeis, sabem **5** soube, soubeste, soube, soubemos, soubestes, souberam **7** saiba *etc* **8** soubesse *etc* **9** souber *etc* **11** soubera *etc*
seguir 3 sigo **7** siga *etc*
sentir 3 sinto **7** sinta *etc*
ser 2 sê **3** sou, és, é, somos, sois, são **4** era *etc* **5** fui, foste, foi, fomos, fostes, foram **7** seja *etc* **8** fosse *etc* **9** for *etc* **11** fora *etc*
servir 3 sirvo **7** sirva *etc*
subir 2 sobe **3** subo, sobes, sobe, sobem
suster 2 sustém **3** sustenho, sustens, sustém, sustendes, sustêm **5** sustive, sustiveste, susteve, sustivemos, sustivestes, sustiveram **7** sustenha *etc*
ter 2 tem **3** tenho, tens, tem, temos, tendes, têm **4** tinha *etc* **5** tive, tiveste, teve, tivemos, tivestes, tiveram **6** terei *etc* **7** tenha *etc* **8** tivesse *etc* **9** tiver *etc* **11** tivera *etc*
torcer 3 torço **7** torça *etc*
tossir 3 tusso **7** tussa *etc*
trair 2 trai **3** traio, trais, trai, traímos, traís, traem **7** traia *etc*
trazer 2 (traze) traz **3** trago, trazes, traz, **5** trouxe, trouxeste, trouxe, trouxemos, trouxestes, trouxeram **6** trarei *etc* **7** traga *etc* **8** trouxesse *etc* **9** trouxer *etc* **11** trouxera *etc*
UNIR 1 unindo **2** une, uni **3** uno, unes, une, unimos, unis, unem **4** unia, unias, uníamos, uníeis, uniam **5** uni, uniste, uniu, unimos, unistes, uniram **6** unirei, unirás, unirá, uniremos,

unireis, unirão **7** una, unas, una,
unamos, unais, unam **8** unisse,
unisses, unisse, uníssemos, unísseis,
unissem **9** unir, unires, unir, unirmos,
unirdes, unirem **10** unido **11** unira,
uniras, unira, uníramos, uníreis,
uniram **12** unir, unires, unir, unirmos,
unirdes, unirem

valer 3 valho **7** valha *etc*

ver 2 vê **3** vejo, vês, vê, vemos, vedes,
veem **4** via *etc* **5** vi, viste, viu, vimos,
vistes, viram **7** veja *etc* **8** visse *etc*
9 vir *etc* **10** visto **11** vira

vir 1 vindo, **2** vem **3** venho, vens, vem,
vimos, vindes, vêm **4** vinha *etc* **5** vim,
vieste, veio, viemos, viestes, vieram

7 venha *etc* **8** viesse *etc* **9** vier *etc*
10 vindo **11** viera *etc*

VIVER 1 vivendo **2** vive, vivei **3** vivo,
vives, vive, vivemos, viveis, vivem
4 vivia, vivias, vivia, vivíamos, vivíeis,
viviam **5** vivi, viveste, viveu, vivemos,
vivestes, viveram **6** viverei, viverás,
viverá, viveremos, vivereis, viverão
7 viva, vivas, viva, vivamos, vivais,
vivam **8** vivesse, vivesses, vivesse,
vivêssemos, vivêsseis, vivessem
9 viver, viveres, viver, vivermos,
viverdes, viverem **10** vivido **11** vivera,
viveras, vivera, vivêramos, vivêreis,
viveram **12** viver, viveres, viver,
vivermos, viverdes, viverem

NÚMEROS

NUMBERS

NÚMEROS CARDINAIS

CARDINAL NUMBERS

Português		English
um (uma)	1	one
dois (duas)	2	two
três	3	three
quatro	4	four
cinco	5	five
seis	6	six
sete	7	seven
oito	8	eight
nove	9	nine
dez	10	ten
onze	11	eleven
doze	12	twelve
treze	13	thirteen
catorze	14	fourteen
quinze	15	fifteen
dezesseis (BR), dezasseis (PT)	16	sixteen
dezessete (BR), dezassete (PT)	17	seventeen
dezoito	18	eighteen
dezenove (BR), dezanove (PT)	19	nineteen
vinte	20	twenty
vinte e um (uma)	21	twenty-one
trinta	30	thirty
quarenta	40	forty
cinquenta	50	fifty
sessenta	60	sixty
setenta	70	seventy
oitenta	80	eighty
noventa	90	ninety
cem	100	a hundred
cento e um (uma)	101	a hundred and one
duzentos(-as)	200	two hundred
trezentos(-as)	300	three hundred
quinhentos(-as)	500	five hundred
mil	1.000/1,000	a thousand
um milhão	1.000.000/1,000,000	a million

NÚMEROS

FRAÇÕES ETC
zero vírgula cinco	**0,5/0.5**	zero point five
três vírgula quatro	**3,4/3.4**	three point four
dez por cento	**10%**	ten per cent
cem por cento	**100%**	a hundred per cent

NÚMEROS ORDINAIS
primeiro	**1°/1st**	first
segundo	**2°/2nd**	second
terceiro	**3°/3rd**	third
quarto	**4°/4th**	fourth
quinto	**5°/5th**	fifth
sexto	**6°/6th**	sixth
sétimo	**7°/7th**	seventh
oitavo	**8°/8th**	eighth
nono	**9°/9th**	ninth
décimo	**10°/10th**	tenth
décimo primeiro	**11°/11th**	eleventh
vigésimo	**20°/20th**	twentieth
trigésimo	**30°/30th**	thirtieth
quadragésimo	**40°/40th**	fortieth
quinquagésimo	**50°/50th**	fiftieth
centésimo	**100°/100th**	hundredth
centésimo primeiro	**101°/101st**	hundred-and-first
milésimo	**1000°/1000th**	thousandth

NUMBERS

FRACTIONS ETC

ORDINAL NUMBERS

English – Portuguese
Inglês – Português

Aa

A, a [eɪ] N (letter) A, a m; (Mus): **A** lá m; **A for Andrew** (BRIT) or **Able** (US) A de Antônio; **A road** (BRIT Aut) via expressa; **A shares** (BRIT Stock Exchange) ações fpl preferenciais

(KEYWORD)

a [eɪ, ə] INDEF ART (before vowel or silent h: **an**)
1 um(a); **a book/girl/mirror** um livro/uma menina/um espelho; **an apple** uma maçã; **she's a doctor** ela é médica
2 (instead of the number "one") um(a); **a year ago** há um ano, um ano atrás; **a hundred/ thousand** etc **pounds** cem/mil etc libras
3 (in expressing ratios, prices etc): **3 a day/week** 3 por dia/semana; **10 km an hour** 10 km por hora; **30p a kilo** 30p o quilo

a. ABBR = **acre**
AA N ABBR (= Alcoholics Anonymous) AA m; (BRIT: = Automobile Association) ≈ TCB m (BR), ≈ ACP m (PT); (US: = Associate in/of Arts) título universitário; (= anti-aircraft) AA
AAA N ABBR (= American Automobile Association) ≈ TCB m (BR), ≈ ACP m (PT); (BRIT) = **Amateur Athletics Association**
AAUP N ABBR (= American Association of University Professors) sindicato universitário
AB ABBR (BRIT) = **able-bodied seaman**; (CANADA) = **Alberta**
abaci ['æbəsaɪ] NPL of **abacus**
aback [ə'bæk] ADV: **to be taken ~** ficar surpreendido, sobressaltar-se
abacus ['æbəkəs] (pl **abaci**) N ábaco
abandon [ə'bændən] VT abandonar ▶ N (wild behaviour): **with ~** com desenfreio; **to ~ ship** abandonar o navio
abandoned [ə'bændənd] ADJ (child, house) abandonado; (unrestrained) desenfreado
abase [ə'beɪs] VT: **to ~ o.s. (so far as to do)** rebaixar-se (até o ponto de fazer)
abashed [ə'bæʃt] ADJ envergonhado
abate [ə'beɪt] VI (lessen) diminuir; (calm down) acalmar-se
abatement [ə'beɪtmənt] N see **noise abatement**
abattoir ['æbətwɑ:'] (BRIT) N matadouro
abbey ['æbɪ] N abadia, mosteiro
abbot ['æbət] N abade m
abbreviate [ə'bri:vɪeɪt] VT (essay) resumir; (word) abreviar
abbreviation [əbri:vɪ'eɪʃən] N (short form) abreviatura; (act) abreviação f
ABC N ABBR (= American Broadcasting Company) rede de televisão
abdicate ['æbdɪkeɪt] VT abdicar, renunciar a ▶ VI abdicar, renunciar ao trono
abdication [æbdɪ'keɪʃən] N abdicação f
abdomen ['æbdəmən] N abdômen m
abdominal [æb'dɔmɪnl] ADJ abdominal
abduct [æb'dʌkt] VT sequestrar
abduction [æb'dʌkʃən] N sequestro
Aberdonian [æbə'dəunɪən] ADJ de Aberdeen ▶ N natural m/f de Aberdeen
aberration [æbə'reɪʃən] N aberração f; **in a moment of mental ~** num momento de desatino
abet [ə'bɛt] VT see **aid**
abeyance [ə'beɪəns] N: **in ~** (law) em desuso; (matter) suspenso
abhor [əb'hɔ:'] VT detestar, odiar
abhorrent [əb'hɔrənt] ADJ detestável, repugnante
abide [ə'baɪd] VT aguentar, suportar; **I can't ~ him** eu não o soporto
▶ **abide by** VT FUS (promise, word) cumprir; (law, rules) ater-se a
ability [ə'bɪlɪtɪ] N habilidade f, capacidade f; (talent) talento; (skill) perícia; **to the best of my ~** o melhor que eu puder or pudesse
abject ['æbdʒɛkt] ADJ (poverty) miserável; (coward) desprezível, vil; **an ~ apology** um pedido de desculpa humilde
ablaze [ə'bleɪz] ADJ em chamas; **~ with light** resplandecente
able ['eɪbl] ADJ capaz; (skilled) hábil, competente; **to be ~ to do sth** poder fazer algo
able-bodied [-'bɔdɪd] ADJ são/sã; **~ seaman** (BRIT) marinheiro experimentado
ably ['eɪblɪ] ADV habilmente
ABM N ABBR = **anti-ballistic missile**
abnormal [æb'nɔ:məl] ADJ anormal
abnormality [æbnɔ:'mælɪtɪ] N anormalidade f
aboard [ə'bɔ:d] ADV a bordo ▶ PREP a bordo de; (train) dentro de
abode [ə'bəud] N (old) residência, domicílio; (Law): **of no fixed ~** sem domicílio fixo

abolish [ə'bɔlɪʃ] vt abolir
abolition [æbə'lɪʃən] n abolição f
abominable [ə'bɔmɪnəbl] adj abominável, detestável
aborigine [æbə'rɪdʒɪnɪ] n aborígene m/f
abort [ə'bɔːt] vt (Med) abortar; (plan) cancelar
abortion [ə'bɔːʃən] n aborto; **to have an ~** fazer um aborto
abortive [ə'bɔːtɪv] adj (failed) fracassado; (fruitless) inútil
abound [ə'baund] vi: **to ~ (in or with)** abundar (em)

(KEYWORD)

about [ə'baut] adv 1 (approximately) aproximadamente; **it takes about 10 hours** leva mais ou menos 10 horas; **at about 2 o'clock** aproximadamente às duas horas; **it's just about finished** está quase terminado
2 (referring to place) por toda parte, por todo lado; **to run/walk etc about** correr/andar etc por todos os lados
3: **to be about to do sth** estar a ponto de fazer algo
▶ prep 1 (relating to) acerca de, sobre; **a book about London** um livro sobre Londres; **what is it about?** do que se trata?, é sobre o quê?; **we talked about it** nós falamos sobre isso; **what or how about doing this?** que tal se fizermos isso?
2 (place) em redor de, por; **to walk about the town** andar pela cidade

about face n (Mil) meia-volta; (fig) reviravolta
about turn n = **about face**
above [ə'bʌv] adv em or por cima, acima
▶ prep acima de, por cima de; **mentioned ~** acima mencionado; **costing ~ £10** que custa mais de £10; **~ all** sobretudo
aboveboard [ə'bʌv'bɔːd] adj legítimo, limpo
abrasion [ə'breɪʒən] n (on skin) esfoladura
abrasive [ə'breɪzɪv] adj abrasivo; (fig: person) cáustico; (: manner) mordaz
abreast [ə'brɛst] adv lado a lado; **to keep ~ of** (fig) estar a par de
abridge [ə'brɪdʒ] vt resumir, abreviar
abroad [ə'brɔːd] adv (be abroad) no estrangeiro; (go abroad) ao estrangeiro; **there is a rumour ~ that ...** (fig) corre o boato de que ...
abrupt [ə'brʌpt] adj (sudden) brusco; (curt) ríspido
abruptly [ə'brʌptlɪ] adv bruscamente
abscess ['æbsɪs] n abscesso (BR), abcesso (PT)
abscond [əb'skɔnd] vi: **to ~ with** sumir com; **to ~ from** fugir de
absence ['æbsəns] n ausência; **in the ~ of** (person) na ausência de; (thing) na falta de
absent ['æbsənt] adj ausente; **~ without leave** ausente sem permissão oficial; **to be ~** faltar
absentee [æbsən'tiː] n ausente m/f
absenteeism [æbsən'tiːɪzəm] n absenteísmo

absent-minded adj distraído
absent-mindedness [-'maɪndɪdnɪs] n distração f
absolute ['æbsəluːt] adj absoluto
absolutely [æbsə'luːtlɪ] adv absolutamente; **oh, yes, ~!** claro que sim!
absolve [əb'zɔlv] vt: **to ~ sb (from)** (sin etc) absolver alguém (de); (blame) isentar alguém (de); **to ~ sb from** (oath) desobrigar alguém de
absorb [əb'zɔːb] vt absorver; (group, business) incorporar; (changes) assimilar; (information) digerir; **to be ~ed in a book** estar absorvido num livro
absorbent [əb'zɔːbənt] adj absorvente
absorbent cotton (US) n algodão m hidrófilo
absorbing [əb'zɔːbɪŋ] adj (book, film etc) absorvente, cativante
absorption [əb'zɔːpʃən] n absorção f; (interest) fascinação f
abstain [əb'steɪn] vi: **to ~ (from)** abster-se (de)
abstemious [əb'stiːmɪəs] adj abstinente
abstention [əb'stɛnʃən] n abstenção f
abstinence ['æbstɪnəns] n abstinência, sobriedade f
abstract [adj, n 'æbstrækt, vt æb'strækt] adj abstrato ▶ n resumo ▶ vt (remove) abstrair; (summarize) resumir; (steal) surripiar
absurd [əb'səːd] adj absurdo
absurdity [əb'səːdɪtɪ] n absurdo
ABTA ['æbtə] n abbr = **Association of British Travel Agents**
Abu Dhabi ['æbuː'dɑːbɪ] n Abu Dabi (no article)
abundance [ə'bʌndəns] n abundância
abundant [ə'bʌndənt] adj abundante
abuse [n ə'bjuːs, vt ə'bjuːz] n (insults) insultos mpl; (misuse) abuso; (ill-treatment) maus-tratos mpl ▶ vt insultar; maltratar; abusar; **open to ~** aberto ao abuso
abusive [ə'bjuːsɪv] adj ofensivo
abysmal [ə'bɪzməl] adj (ignorance) profundo, total; (very bad) péssimo
abyss [ə'bɪs] n abismo
AC n abbr (US) = **athletic club** ▶ abbr (= alternating current) CA
a/c abbr (Banking etc: = account) c/
academic [ækə'dɛmɪk] adj acadêmico; (pej: issue) teórico ▶ n universitário(-a)
academic freedom n liberdade de cátedra
academic year n ano letivo
academy [ə'kædəmɪ] n (learned body) academia; (school) instituto, academia, colégio; **military/naval ~** academia militar/escola naval; **~ of music** conservatório
ACAS ['eɪkæs] (BRIT) n abbr (= Advisory, Conciliation and Arbitration Service) ≈ Justiça do Trabalho
accede [æk'siːd] vi: **to ~ to** (request) consentir em, aceder a; (throne) subir a
accelerate [æk'sɛləreɪt] vt, vi acelerar
acceleration [æksɛlə'reɪʃən] n aceleração f

accelerator [æk'sɛləreɪtəʳ] N acelerador *m*

accent ['æksɛnt] N (*written*) acento; (*pronunciation*) sotaque *m*; (*fig: emphasis*) ênfase *f*

accentuate [æk'sɛntjueɪt] VT (*syllable*) acentuar; (*need, difference etc*) ressaltar, salientar

accept [ək'sɛpt] VT aceitar; (*responsibility*) assumir

acceptable [ək'sɛptəbl] ADJ (*offer*) bem-vindo; (*risk*) assumir, aceitável

acceptance [ək'sɛptəns] N aceitação *f*; **to meet with general ~** ter aprovação geral

access ['æksɛs] N acesso ▶ VT (*Comput*) acessar; **to have ~ to** ter acesso a; **the burglars gained ~ through a window** os ladrões conseguiram entrar por uma janela

accessible [æk'sɛsəbl] ADJ acessível; (*available*) disponível

accession [æk'sɛʃən] N acessão *f*; (*of king*) elevação *f* ao trono; (*to library*) aquisição *f*

accessory [æk'sɛsərɪ] N acessório; (*Law*): **~ to** cúmplice *m/f* de; **toilet accessories** (BRIT) artigos de toalete

access road N via de acesso

accident ['æksɪdənt] N acidente *m*; (*chance*) casualidade *f*; **to meet with** or **have an ~** sofrer or ter um acidente; **~s at work** acidentes de trabalho; **by ~** (*unintentionally*) sem querer; (*by coincidence*) por acaso

accidental [æksɪ'dɛntl] ADJ acidental

accidentally [æksɪ'dɛntəlɪ] ADV (*by accident*) sem querer; (*by chance*) casualmente

Accident and Emergency Department N (BRIT) pronto-socorro

accident insurance N seguro contra acidentes

accident-prone ADJ com tendência para sofrer or causar acidente, desastrado

acclaim [ə'kleɪm] VT aclamar ▶ N aclamação *f*; **to be ~ed for one's achievements** ser aclamado por seus fatas

acclamation [æklə'meɪʃən] N (*approval*) aclamação *f*; (*applause*) aplausos *mpl*

acclimate [ə'klaɪmət] (US) VT = **acclimatize**

acclimatize [ə'klaɪmətaɪz] (BRIT) VT: **to become ~d (to)** aclimatar-se (a)

accolade ['ækəleɪd] N louvor *m*, honra

accommodate [ə'kɔmədeɪt] VT alojar; (*reconcile: subj: car, hotel, etc*) acomodar, conciliar; (*oblige, help*) comprazer a; (*adapt*): **to ~ one's plans to** acomodar seus projetos a; **this car ~s 4 people** este carro tem lugar para 4 pessoas

accommodating [ə'kɔmədeɪtɪŋ] ADJ complacente, serviçal

accommodation [əkɔmə'deɪʃən] (BRIT) N, (US) **accommodations** [əkɔmə'deɪʃənz] NPL alojamento; (*space*) lugar *m* (BR), sítio (PT); **he's found ~** ele já encontrou um lugar para morar; **"~ to let"** "aluga-se (apartamento *etc*)"; **they have ~ for 500** têm lugar para 500 pessoas; **seating ~** lugares *mpl* sentados

accompaniment [ə'kʌmpənɪmənt] N acompanhamento

accompanist [ə'kʌmpənɪst] N acompanhador(a) *m/f*, acompanhante *m/f*

accompany [ə'kʌmpənɪ] VT acompanhar

accomplice [ə'kʌmplɪs] N cúmplice *m/f*

accomplish [ə'kʌmplɪʃ] VT (*task*) concluir; (*goal*) alcançar

accomplished [ə'kʌmplɪʃt] ADJ (*person*) talentoso; (*performance*) brilhante

accomplishment [ə'kʌmplɪʃmənt] N (*bringing about*) realização *f*; (*achievement*) proeza; **accomplishments** NPL (*skills*) talentos *mpl*

accord [ə'kɔ:d] N tratado ▶ VT conceder; **of his own ~** por sua iniciativa; **with one ~** de comum acordo

accordance [ə'kɔ:dəns] N: **in ~ with** de acordo com, conforme

according [ə'kɔ:dɪŋ] PREP: **~ to** segundo; (*in accordance with*) conforme; **~ to plan** como previsto

accordingly [ə'kɔ:dɪŋlɪ] ADV (*thus*) por conseguinte; (*appropriately*) do modo devido

accordion [ə'kɔ:dɪən] N acordeão *m*

accost [ə'kɔst] VT abordar

account [ə'kaunt] N conta; (*report*) relato; **accounts** NPL (*books, department*) contabilidade *f*; **"~ payee only"** (BRIT) "cheque não endossável (*a ser creditado na conta do favorecido*)"; **to keep an ~ of** anotar, registrar; **to bring sb to ~ for sth/for having done sth** chamar alguém a contas por algo/por ter feito algo; **by all ~s** segundo dizem todos; **of little ~** sem importância; **on his own ~** por sua conta; **to pay £50 on ~** pagar £50 por conta; **to buy sth on ~** comprar algo a crédito; **of no ~** sem importância; **on ~** por conta; **on no ~** de modo nenhum; **on ~ of** por causa de; **to take into ~, take ~ of** levar em conta ▶ **account for** VT FUS (*explain*) explicar; (*represent*) representar; **all the children were ~ed for** nenhuma das crianças faltava; **4 people are still not ~ed for** 4 pessoas ainda não foram encontradas

accountability [əkauntə'bɪlɪtɪ] N responsabilidade *f*

accountable [ə'kauntəbl] ADJ: **~ (to)** responsável (por)

accountancy [ə'kauntənsɪ] N contabilidade *f*

accountant [ə'kauntənt] N contador(a) *m/f* (BR), contabilista *m/f* (PT)

accounting [ə'kauntɪŋ] N contabilidade *f*

accounting period N exercício

account number N número de conta

account payable N conta a pagar

account receivable N conta a receber

accredited [ə'krɛdɪtɪd] ADJ (*agent*) autorizado

accretion [ə'kri:ʃən] N acreсção *f*

accrue [ə'kru:] VI aumentar; (*mount up*) acumular-se; **to ~ to** advir a

accrued interest [ə'kru:d-] N juros *mpl* acumulados

accumulate [ə'kju:mjuleɪt] VT acumular ▶ VI acumular-se

accumulation [əkju:mju'leɪʃən] N acumulação f

accuracy ['ækjurəsɪ] N exatidão f, precisão f

accurate ['ækjurɪt] ADJ (number) exato; (description) correto; (person, device) preciso; (shot) certeiro

accurately ['ækjurətlɪ] ADV com precisão

accusation [ækju'zeɪʃən] N acusação f; (instance) incriminação f

accusative [ə'kju:zətɪv] N (Ling) acusativo

accuse [ə'kju:z] VT: **to ~ sb (of sth)** acusar alguém (de algo)

accused [ə'kju:zd] N: **the ~** o/a acusado/a

accustom [ə'kʌstəm] VT acostumar; **to ~ o.s. to sth** acostumar-se a algo

accustomed [ə'kʌstəmd] ADJ (usual) habitual; **~ to** acostumado a

AC/DC ABBR (= alternating current/direct current) CA/CC

ACE [eɪs] N ABBR = **American Council on Education**

ace [eɪs] N ás m; **to be** or **come within an ~ of doing** (BRIT) não fazer por um triz

acerbic [ə'sə:bɪk] ADJ (also fig) acerbo

acetate ['æsɪteɪt] N acetato

ache [eɪk] N dor f ▶ VI doer; (yearn): **to ~ to do sth** ansiar por fazer algo; **I've got (a) stomach ~** eu estou com dor de barriga; **my head ~s** dói-me a cabeça; **I'm aching all over** estou todo dolorido

achieve [ə'tʃi:v] VT (reach) alcançar; (realize) realizar; (victory, success) obter

achievement [ə'tʃi:vmənt] N (of aims) realização f; (success) proeza

acid ['æsɪd] ADJ, N ácido

acidity [ə'sɪdɪtɪ] N acidez f

acid rain N chuva ácida

acknowledge [ək'nɔlɪdʒ] VT (fact) reconhecer; (person) cumprimentar; (also: **acknowledge receipt of**) acusar o recebimento de (BR) or a receção de (PT)

acknowledgement [ək'nɔlɪdʒmənt] N (of letter) notificação f de recebimento; **acknowledgements** NPL (in book) agradecimentos mpl

ACLU N ABBR (= American Civil Liberties Union) associação que defende os direitos humanos

acme ['ækmɪ] N acme m

acne ['æknɪ] N acne f

acorn ['eɪkɔ:n] N bolota

acoustic [ə'ku:stɪk] ADJ acústico

acoustics [ə'ku:stɪks] N, NPL acústica

acquaint [ə'kweɪnt] VT: **to ~ sb with sth** (inform) pôr alguém ao corrente de alguma coisa; **to be ~ed with** (person) conhecer; (fact) saber

acquaintance [ə'kweɪntəns] N conhecimento; (person) conhecido(-a); **to make sb's ~** conhecer alguém

acquiesce [ækwɪ'ɛs] VI: **to ~ (to)** condescender (a); (request) ceder (a)

acquire [ə'kwaɪə^r] VT adquirir; (interest, skill) desenvolver

acquired [ə'kwaɪəd] ADJ adquirido; **an ~ taste** um gosto cultivado

acquisition [ækwɪ'zɪʃən] N aquisição f

acquisitive [ə'kwɪzɪtɪv] ADJ cobiçoso

acquit [ə'kwɪt] VT absolver; **to ~ o.s. well** desempenhar-se bem

acquittal [ə'kwɪtəl] N absolvição f

acre ['eɪkə^r] N acre m (= 4047m²)

acreage ['eɪkərɪdʒ] N extensão f (em acres)

acrid ['ækrɪd] ADJ (smell) acre; (fig) mordaz

acrimonious [ækrɪ'məunɪəs] ADJ (remark) mordaz; (argument) acrimonioso

acrobat ['ækrəbæt] N acrobata m/f

acrobatic [ækrə'bætɪk] ADJ acrobático

acrobatics [ækrə'bætɪks] NPL acrobacia

Acropolis [ə'krɔpəlɪs] N: **the ~** a Acrópole

across [ə'krɔs] PREP (from one side to the other of) de um lado para outro de; (on the other side of) no outro lado de; (crosswise) através de ▶ ADV de um lado ao outro; **to walk ~ (the road)** atravessar (a rua); **to run/swim ~** atravessar correndo/a nado; **the lake is 12 km ~** o lago tem 12 km de largura; **~ from** em frente de; **to get sth ~ (to sb)** conseguir comunicar algo (a alguém)

acrylic [ə'krɪlɪk] ADJ acrílico ▶ N acrílico

ACT N ABBR (= American College Test) ≈ vestibular m

act [ækt] N ação f; (Theatre) ato; (in show) número; (Law) lei f ▶ VI tomar ação; (behave, have effect) agir; (Theatre) representar; (pretend) fingir ▶ VT (part) representar; **in the ~ of** no ato de; **~ of God** (Law) força maior; **to catch sb in the ~** apanhar alguém em flagrante, flagrar alguém; **it's only an ~** é só encenação; **to ~ Hamlet** (BRIT) representar Hamlet; **to ~ the fool** (BRIT) fazer-se de bobo; **to ~ as** servir de; **it ~s as a deterrent** serve para dissuadir; **~ing in my capacity as chairman, I ...** na qualidade de presidente, eu ...

▶ **act on** VT FUS: **to ~ on sth** agir de acordo com algo

▶ **act out** VT (event) representar; (fantasy) realizar

acting ['æktɪŋ] ADJ interino ▶ N (performance) representação f, atuação f; (activity): **to do some ~** fazer teatro

action ['ækʃən] N ação f; (Mil) batalha, combate m; (Law) ação judicial; **to bring an ~ against sb** (Law) intentar ação judicial contra alguém; **killed in ~** (Mil) morto em combate; **out of ~** (person) fora de combate; (thing) com defeito; **to take ~** tomar atitude; **to put a plan into ~** pôr um plano em ação

action replay (BRIT) N (TV) replay m

activate ['æktɪveɪt] VT (mechanism) acionar; (Chem, Phys) ativar

active ['æktɪv] ADJ ativo; (volcano) em atividade

active duty (US) N (Mil) ativa

actively ['æktɪvlɪ] ADV ativamente

active partner N (*Comm*) comanditado(-a)
active service (*BRIT*) N (*Mil*) ativa
activist ['æktıvıst] N ativista *m/f*, militante *m/f*
activity [æk'tıvıtı] N atividade *f*
actor ['æktər] N ator *m*
actress ['æktrıs] N atriz *f*
actual ['æktjuəl] ADJ real
actually ['æktjuəlı] ADV realmente; (*in fact*) na verdade; (*even*) mesmo
actuary ['æktjuərı] N atuário(-a)
actuate ['æktjueɪt] VT atuar, acionar
acuity [ə'kju:ıtı] N acuidade *f*
acumen ['ækjumən] N perspicácia; **business ~** tino para os negócios
acupuncture ['ækjupʌŋktʃər] N acupuntura
acute [ə'kju:t] ADJ agudo; (*person*) perspicaz
ad [æd] N ABBR = **advertisement**
A.D. ADV ABBR (= *Anno Domini*) d.C. ▶ N ABBR (*US Mil*) = **active duty**
adamant ['ædəmənt] ADJ inflexível
Adam's apple ['ædəmz-] N pomo-de-Adão *m* (*BR*), maçã-de-Adão *f* (*PT*)
adapt [ə'dæpt] VT adaptar ▶ VI: **to ~ (to)** adaptar-se (a)
adaptability [ədæptə'bılıtı] N adaptabilidade *f*
adaptable [ə'dæptəbl] ADJ (*device*) ajustável; (*person*) adaptável
adaptation [ædæp'teıʃən] N adaptação *f*
adapter [ə'dæptər] N (*Elec*) adaptador *m*
ADC N ABBR (*Mil*) = **aide-de-camp**; (*US*: = *Aid to Dependent Children*) auxílio a crianças dependentes
add [æd] VT acrescentar; (*figures: also:* **add up**) somar ▶ VI: **to ~ to** (*increase*) aumentar
▶ **add on** VT acrescentar, adicionar
▶ **add up** VT (*figures*) somar ▶ VI (*fig*): **it doesn't ~ up** não faz sentido; **it doesn't ~ up to much** é pouca coisa
adder ['ædər] N víbora
addict ['ædıkt] N viciado(-a); **heroin ~** viciado(-a) em heroína; **drug ~** toxicômano(-a)
addicted [ə'dıktıd] ADJ: **to be/become ~ to** ser/ficar viciado em
addiction [ə'dıkʃən] N (*Med*) dependência
addictive ADJ que causa dependência
adding machine ['ædıŋ-] N máquina de somar
Addis Ababa ['ædıs'æbəbə] N Adis-Abeba
addition [ə'dıʃən] N (*adding up*) adição *f*; (*thing added*) acréscimo; **in ~** além disso; **in ~ to** além de
additional [ə'dıʃənl] ADJ adicional
additive ['ædıtıv] N aditivo
address [ə'drɛs] N endereço; (*speech*) discurso ▶ VT (*letter*) endereçar; (*speak to*) dirigir-se a, dirigir a palavra a; **form of ~** tratamento; **to ~ (o.s. to)** (*problem, issue*) enfocar
addressee [ædrɛ'si:] N destinatário(-a)
Aden ['eɪdən] N Áden (*no article*); **Gulf of ~** golfo de Áden
adenoids ['ædınɔıdz] NPL adenoides *fpl*
adept ['ædɛpt] ADJ: **~ at** hábil *or* competente em

adequate ['ædıkwıt] ADJ (*enough*) suficiente; (*suitable*) adequado; (*satisfactory*) satisfatório; **to feel ~ to the task** sentir-se à altura da tarefa
adequately ['ædıkwıtlı] ADV adequadamente
adhere [əd'hıər] VI: **to ~ to** aderir a; (*abide by*) ater-se a
adhesion [əd'hi:ʒən] N adesão *f*
adhesive [əd'hi:zıv] ADJ, N adesivo
adhesive tape N (*BRIT*) durex® *m*, fita adesiva; (*US*) esparadrapo
ad hoc [-hɔk] ADJ (*decision*) para o caso; (*committee*) ad hoc
ad infinitum [-ınfı'naıtəm] ADV ad infinitum
adjacent [ə'dʒeısənt] ADJ: **~ (to)** adjacente (a)
adjective ['ædʒɛktıv] N adjetivo
adjoin [ə'dʒɔın] VT ser contíguo a
adjoining [ə'dʒɔınıŋ] ADJ adjacente
adjourn [ə'dʒə:n] VT (*postpone*) adiar; (*session*) suspender ▶ VI encerrar a sessão; (*go*) deslocar-se; **they ~ed to the pub** (*BRIT inf*) deslocaram-se para o bar
adjournment [ə'dʒə:nmənt] N (*period*) recesso
Adjt ABBR (*Mil:* = *adjutant*) Ajte
adjudicate [ə'dʒu:dıkeıt] VT, VI julgar
adjudication [ədʒu:dı'keıʃən] N julgamento
adjust [ə'dʒʌst] VT (*change*) ajustar; (*clothes*) arrumar; (*machine*) regular ▶ VI: **to ~ (to)** adaptar-se (a)
adjustable [ə'dʒʌstəbl] ADJ ajustável
adjuster [ə'dʒʌstər] N *see* **loss adjuster**
adjustment [ə'dʒʌstmənt] N ajuste *m*; (*of engine*) regulagem *f*; (*of prices, wages*) reajuste *m*; (*of person*) adaptação *f*
adjutant ['ædʒətənt] N ajudante *m*
ad-lib [-lıb] VT, VI improvisar ▶ N improviso; (*Theatre*) caco ▶ ADV: **ad lib** à vontade
adman ['ædmæn] (*inf*) (*irreg: like* **man**) N publicitário
admin ['ædmın] (*inf*) N ABBR = **administration**
administer [əd'mınıstər] VT administrar; (*justice*) aplicar; (*drug*) ministrar
administration [ədmınıs'treıʃən] N administração *f*; (*US: government*) governo
administrative [əd'mınıstrətıv] ADJ administrativo
administrator [əd'mınıstreıtər] N administrador(a) *m/f*
admirable ['ædmərəbl] ADJ admirável
admiral ['ædmərəl] N almirante *m*
Admiralty ['ædmərəltı] (*BRIT*) N (*also:* **Admiralty Board**) Ministério da Marinha, Almirantado
admiration [ædmə'reıʃən] N admiração *f*
admire [əd'maıər] VT (*respect*) respeitar; (*appreciate*) admirar
admirer [əd'maıərər] N (*suitor*) pretendente *m/f*; (*fan*) admirador(a) *m/f*
admission [əd'mıʃən] N (*admittance*) entrada; (*fee*) ingresso; (*enrolment*) admissão *f*; (*confession*) confissão *f*; **"~ free", "free ~"** "entrada gratuita", "ingresso gratuito"; **by his own ~ he drinks too much** ele mesmo reconhece que bebe demais

admit [əd'mɪt] vt admitir; (*acknowledge*) reconhecer; (*accept*) aceitar; (*confess*) confessar; **"children not ~ted"** "entrada proibida a menores de idade"; **this ticket ~s two** este ingresso é válido para duas pessoas; **I must ~ that ...** devo admitir *or* reconhecer que ...
  ▶ **admit of** vt fus admitir
  ▶ **admit to** vt fus confessar
admittance [əd'mɪtəns] N entrada; **"no ~"** "entrada proibida"
admittedly [əd'mɪtədlɪ] ADV evidentemente
admonish [əd'mɒnɪʃ] vt admoestar
ad nauseam [æd'nɔːsɪæm] ADV sem parar
ado [ə'duː] N: **without further** *or* **(any) more ~** sem mais cerimônias
adolescence [ædəu'lɛsns] N adolescência
adolescent [ædəu'lɛsnt] ADJ, N adolescente *m/f*
adopt [ə'dɒpt] vt adotar
adopted [ə'dɒptɪd] ADJ adotivo
adoption [ə'dɒpʃən] N adoção *f*
adoptive [ə'dɒptɪv] ADJ adotivo
adorable [ə'dɔːrəbl] ADJ encantador(a)
adoration [ædə'reɪʃən] N adoração *f*
adore [ə'dɔːʳ] vt adorar
adoring [ə'dɔːrɪŋ] ADJ devotado
adoringly [ə'dɔːrɪŋlɪ] ADV com adoração
adorn [ə'dɔːn] vt adornar, enfeitar
adornment [ə'dɔːnmənt] N enfeite *m*, adorno
ADP N ABBR = **automatic data processing**
adrenalin [ə'drɛnəlɪn] N adrenalina
Adriatic [eɪdrɪ'ætɪk], **Adriatic Sea** N (mar *m*) Adriático
adrift [ə'drɪft] ADV à deriva; **to come ~** desprender-se
adroit [ə'drɔɪt] ADJ hábil
ADSL N ABBR (= *asymmetric digital subscriber line*) ADSL *m*
ADT (*US*) ABBR (= *Atlantic Daylight Time*) *hora de verão de Nova Iorque.*
adult ['ædʌlt] N adulto(-a) ▶ ADJ adulto; (*literature, education*) para adultos
adult education N educação *f* para adultos
adulterate [ə'dʌltəreɪt] vt adulterar
adulterer [ə'dʌltərəʳ] N adúltero
adulteress [ə'dʌltərɪs] N adúltera
adultery [ə'dʌltərɪ] N adultério
adulthood ['ædʌlthud] N idade *f* adulta
advance [əd'vɑːns] N avanço; (*money: payment in advance*) adiantamento; (: *loan*) empréstimo; (*Mil*) avançada ▶ ADJ antecipado ▶ vt (*develop*) desenvolver, promover; (*money*) adiantar ▶ vi (*move forward*); (*progress*) progredir; **in ~** com antecedência; **to make ~s to sb** (*gen*) fazer propostas a alguém; (*amorously*) fazer propostas amorosas a alguém
advanced [əd'vɑːnst] ADJ avançado; (*studies, country*) adiantado; **~ in years** de idade avançada
advancement [əd'vɑːnsmənt] N (*improvement*) progresso; (*in rank*) promoção *f*
advance notice N aviso prévio

advantage [əd'vɑːntɪdʒ] N vantagem *f*; (*supremacy*) supremacia; (*advantage*) benefício; (*Tennis*) vantagem *f*; **to take ~ of** (*use*) aproveitar, aproveitar-se de; (*gain by*) tirar proveito de; **it's to our ~ (to do)** é vantajoso para nós (fazer)
advantageous [ædvən'teɪdʒəs] ADJ: **~ (to)** vantajoso (para)
advent ['ædvənt] N advento, chegada; **A~** (*Rel*) Advento
Advent calendar N calendário do Advento
adventure [əd'vɛntʃəʳ] N aventura
adventurous [əd'vɛntʃərəs] ADJ aventureiro
adverb ['ædvəːb] N advérbio
adversary ['ædvəsərɪ] N adversário(-a)
adverse ['ædvəːs] ADJ (*effect*) contrário; (*weather, publicity*) desfavorável; **~ to** contrário a
adversity [əd'vəːsɪtɪ] N adversidade *f*
advert ['ædvəːt] (*BRIT*) N ABBR = **advertisement**
advertise ['ædvətaɪz] vi anunciar, fazer propaganda; (*in newspaper etc*) anunciar ▶ vt (*event, job*) anunciar; (*product*) fazer a propaganda de; **to ~ for** (*staff*) procurar
advertisement [əd'vəːtɪsmənt] N (*classified*) anúncio; (*display, TV*) propaganda, anúncio
advertiser ['ædvətaɪzəʳ] N anunciante *m/f*
advertising ['ædvətaɪzɪŋ] N publicidade *f*
advertising agency N agência de publicidade
advertising campaign N campanha publicitária
advice [əd'vaɪs] N conselhos *mpl*; (*notification*) aviso; **piece of ~** conselho; **to ask (sb) for ~** pedir conselho (a alguém); **to take legal ~** consultar um advogado
advice note (*BRIT*) N aviso
advisable [əd'vaɪzəbl] ADJ aconselhável
advise [əd'vaɪz] vt aconselhar; (*inform*): **to ~ sb of sth** avisar alguém de algo; **to ~ sb against sth** desaconselhar algo a alguém; **to ~ sb against doing sth** aconselhar alguém a não fazer algo; **you would be well/ill ~d to go** seria melhor você ir/você não ir
advisedly [əd'vaɪzɪdlɪ] ADV de propósito
adviser, advisor [əd'vaɪzəʳ] N conselheiro(-a); (*consultant*) consultor(a) *m/f*; (*political*) assessor(a) *m/f*
advisory [əd'vaɪzərɪ] ADJ consultivo; **in an ~ capacity** na qualidade de assessor(a) *or* consultor(a)
advocate [vt 'ædvəkeɪt, n 'ædvəkɪt] vt defender; (*recommend*) advogar ▶ N advogado(-a); (*supporter*) defensor(a) *m/f*
advt. ABBR = **advertisement**
AEA (*BRIT*) N ABBR (= *Atomic Energy Authority*) ≈ CNEN *f*
AEC (*US*) N ABBR (= *Atomic Energy Commission*) ≈ CNEN *f*
Aegean [iː'dʒiːən] N: **the ~ (Sea)** o (mar) Egeu
aegis ['iːdʒɪs] N: **under the ~ of** sob a égide de

aeon ['i:ən] N eternidade f
aerial ['ɛərɪəl] N antena ▸ ADJ aéreo
aerobatics [ɛərəu'bætɪks] NPL acrobacias fpl aéreas
aerobics [ɛə'rəubɪks] N ginástica
aerodrome ['ɛərədrəum] (BRIT) N aeródromo
aerodynamic [ɛərəudaɪ'næmɪk] ADJ aerodinâmico
aerodynamics [ɛərəudaɪ'næmɪks] N, NPL aerodinâmica
aeronautics [ɛərə'nɔ:tɪks] N aeronáutica
aeroplane ['ɛərəpleɪn] (BRIT) N avião m
aerosol ['ɛərəsɔl] N aerossol m
aerospace industry ['ɛərəuspeɪs-] N indústria aeroespacial
aesthetic [i:s'θɛtɪk] ADJ estético
aesthetics [i:s'θɛtɪks] N, NPL estética
afar [ə'fɑ:ʳ] ADV: **from ~** de longe
AFB (US) N ABBR = **Air Force Base**
AFDC (US) N ABBR (= *Aid to Families with Dependent Children*) auxílio-família m
affable ['æfəbl] ADJ afável; (*behaviour*) simpático
affair [ə'fɛəʳ] N (*matter*) assunto; (*business*) negócio; (*question*) questão f; (*also:* **love affair**) caso; **~s** (*matters*) assuntos mpl; (*personal concerns*) vida; **that is my ~** isso é comigo; **the Watergate ~** o caso Watergate
affect [ə'fɛkt] VT afetar; (*move*) comover
affectation [æfɛk'teɪʃən] N afetação f
affected [ə'fɛktɪd] ADJ afetado
affection [ə'fɛkʃən] N afeto, afeição f
affectionate [ə'fɛkʃənət] ADJ afetuoso, carinhoso
affectionately [ə'fɛkʃənətlɪ] ADV carinhosamente
affidavit [æfɪ'deɪvɪt] N (*Law*) declaração f escrita e juramentada
affiliated [ə'fɪlɪeɪtɪd] ADJ: **~ (to)** afiliado (a); **~ company** filial f
affinity [ə'fɪnɪtɪ] N afinidade f; **to have an ~ with** (*rapport*) ter afinidade com; (*resemblance*) ter semelhanca com
affirm [ə'fə:m] VT afirmar
affirmation [æfə'meɪʃən] N afirmação f
affirmative [ə'fə:mətɪv] ADJ afirmativo ▸ N: **in the ~** afirmativamente
affix [ə'fɪks] VT (*signature*) apor; (*stamp*) colar
afflict [ə'flɪkt] VT afligir; **to be ~ed with** sofrer de
affliction [ə'flɪkʃən] N aflição f; (*illness*) doença
affluence ['æfluəns] N riqueza
affluent ['æfluənt] ADJ rico; **the ~ society** a sociedade de abundância
afford [ə'fɔ:d] VT (*provide*) fornecer; (*goods etc*) ter dinheiro suficiente para; (*permit o.s.*): **I can't ~ the time** não tenho tempo; **can we ~ a car?** temos dinheiro para comprar um carro?; **we can ~ to wait** podemos permitir-nos esperar
affordable [ə'fɔ:dəbl] ADJ acessível
affray [ə'freɪ] (BRIT) N (*Law*) desordem f, tumulto

affront [ə'frʌnt] N ofensa
affronted [ə'frʌntɪd] ADJ afrontado, ofendido
Afghan ['æfgæn] ADJ, N afegão(-gã) m/f
Afghanistan [æf'gænɪstæn] N Afeganistão m
afield [ə'fi:ld] ADV: **far ~** muito longe
AFL-CIO N ABBR (= *American Federation of Labor and Congress of Industrial Organizations*) confederação sindical
afloat [ə'fləut] ADV (*floating*) flutuando; (*at sea*) no mar; **to stay ~** continuar flutuando; **to keep/get ~** (*business*) manter financeiramente equilibrado/estabelecer
afoot [ə'fut] ADV: **there is something ~** está acontecendo algo
aforementioned [ə'fɔ:mɛnʃənd] ADJ acima mencionado
aforesaid [ə'fɔ:sɛd] ADJ supracitado, referido
afraid [ə'freɪd] ADJ (*frightened*) assustado; (*fearful*) receoso; **to be ~ of/to** ter medo de; **I am ~ that** lamento que; **I'm ~ so/not** receio que sim/não
afresh [ə'frɛʃ] ADV de novo
Africa ['æfrɪkə] N África
African ['æfrɪkən] ADJ, N africano(-a)
Afrikaans [æfrɪ'kɑ:ns] N (Ling) afrikaan m
Afrikaner [æfrɪ'kɑ:nəʳ] N africânder m/f
Afro-American ['æfrəu-] ADJ afro-americano
AFT N ABBR (= *American Federation of Teachers*) sindicato dos professores
aft [ɑ:ft] ADV a ré
after ['ɑ:ftəʳ] PREP (*time*) depois de ▸ ADV depois ▸ CONJ depois que; **~ dinner** depois do jantar; **the day ~ tomorrow** depois de amanhã; **day ~ day** dia após dia; **time ~ time** repetidas vezes; **a quarter ~ two** (US) duas e quinze; **what are you ~?** o que você quer?; **who are you ~?** quem procura?; **~ having done** tendo feito; **the police are ~ him** a polícia está atrás dele; **to ask ~ sb** perguntar por alguém; **~ all** afinal (de contas); **~ you!** passe primeiro!
afterbirth ['ɑ:ftəbə:θ] N placenta
aftercare ['ɑ:ftəkɛəʳ] (BRIT) N (*Med*) assistência pós-operatória
after-effects NPL (*of illness etc*) efeitos mpl secundários
afterlife ['ɑ:ftəlaɪf] N vida após a morte
aftermath ['ɑ:ftəmæθ] N consequências fpl; **in the ~ of** no período depois de
afternoon [ɑ:ftə'nu:n] N tarde f; **good ~!** boa tarde!
afters ['ɑ:ftəz] (BRIT inf) N (*dessert*) sobremesa
after-sales service (BRIT) N serviço pós-vendas; (*of computers etc*) assistência técnica
after-shave, after-shave lotion N loção f após-barba
aftershock ['ɑ:ftəʃɔk] N abalo secundário
aftersun ['ɑ:ftəsʌn] N loção f pós-sol
afterthought ['ɑ:ftəθɔ:t] N reflexão f posterior or tardia
afterwards ['ɑ:ftəwədz] ADV depois; **immediately ~** logo depois

again [ə'gɛn] ADV (once more) outra vez; (repeatedly) de novo; **to do sth ~** voltar a fazer algo; **~ and ~** repetidas vezes; **now and ~** de vez em quando

against [ə'gɛnst] PREP contra; (compared to) em contraste com; **~ a blue background** sobre um fundo azul; **(as) ~** (BRIT) em contraste com

age [eɪdʒ] N idade f; (old age) velhice f; (period) época ▸ VT, VI envelhecer; **he's 20 years of ~** ele tem 20 anos de idade; **at the ~ of 20** aos 20 anos de idade; **under ~** menor de idade; **to come of ~** atingir a maioridade; **it's been ~s since I saw him** faz muito tempo que eu não o vejo; **~d 10** de 10 anos de idade

aged ['eɪdʒɪd] ADJ idoso ▸ NPL: **the ~** os idosos

age group N faixa etária; **the 40 to 50 ~** a faixa etária dos 40 aos 50 anos

ageless ['eɪdʒlɪs] ADJ (eternal) eterno; (ever young) sempre jovem

age limit N idade f mínima/máxima

agency ['eɪdʒənsɪ] N agência; (government body) órgão m; **through** or **by the ~ of** por meio de

agenda [ə'dʒɛndə] N ordem f do dia

agent ['eɪdʒənt] N agente m/f; (spy) agente m/f secreto(-a)

aggravate ['ægrəveɪt] VT agravar; (annoy) irritar

aggravation [ægrə'veɪʃən] N irritação f

aggregate ['ægrɪgət] N (whole) conjunto; **on ~** (Sport) no total dos pontos

aggression [ə'grɛʃən] N agressão f

aggressive [ə'grɛsɪv] ADJ agressivo

aggressiveness [ə'grɛsɪvnɪs] N agressividade f

aggrieved [ə'griːvd] ADJ aflito

aggro ['ægrəu] N (inf: physical) porrada; (: hassle) chateação f

aghast [ə'gɑːst] ADJ horrorizado

agile ['ædʒaɪl] ADJ ágil

agitate ['ædʒɪteɪt] VT agitar; (trouble) perturbar ▸ VI: **to ~ for/against** fazer agitação a favor de/contra de

agitation [ædʒɪ'teɪʃən] N agitação f

agitator ['ædʒɪteɪtər] N agitador(a) m/f

AGM N ABBR (= annual general meeting) AGO f

agnostic [æg'nɔstɪk] N agnóstico

ago [ə'gəu] ADV: **2 days ~** há 2 dias (atrás); **not long ~** há pouco tempo; **as long ~ as 1960** já em 1960; **how long ~?** há quanto tempo?

agog [ə'gɔg] ADJ (eager) ávido; (impatient): **~ to** ansioso para; (excited): **(all) ~** entusiasmado

agonize ['ægənaɪz] VI: **to ~ over sth** agoniar-se or angustiar-se com algo

agonizing ['ægənaɪzɪŋ] ADJ (pain) agudo; (wait) angustiante

agony ['ægənɪ] N (pain) dor f; (distress) angústia; **to be in ~** sofrer dores terríveis

agony column N correspondência sentimental

agree [ə'griː] VT (price, date) combinar ▸ VI concordar; (correspond) corresponder; (statements etc) combinar; **to ~ (with)** (person, Ling) concordar (com); **to ~ to do** aceitar fazer; **to ~ to sth** consentir algo; **to ~ that** (admit) concordar or admitir que; **it was ~d that ...** foi combinado que ...; **they ~ on this** concordam or estão de acordo nisso; **garlic doesn't ~ with me** não me dou bem com o alho

agreeable [ə'griːəbl] ADJ agradável; (willing) disposto; **are you ~ to this?** você concorda or está de acordo com isso?

agreed [ə'griːd] ADJ (time, place) combinado; **to be ~** concordar, estar de acordo

agreement [ə'griːmənt] N acordo; (Comm) contrato; **in ~** de acordo; **by mutual ~** de comum acordo

agricultural [ægrɪ'kʌltʃərəl] ADJ (of crops) agrícola; (of crops and cattle) agropecuário

agriculture ['ægrɪkʌltʃər] N (of crops) agricultura; (of crops and cattle) agropecuária

aground [ə'graund] ADV: **to run ~** encalhar

ahead [ə'hɛd] ADV adiante; **go right** or **straight ~** siga em frente; **go ~!** (fig) vá em frente! (: speak) pode falar!; **~ of** na frente de; (fig: schedule etc) antes de; **~ of time** antes do tempo; **to go ~ (with)** prosseguir (com); **to be ~ of sb** (fig) ter vantagem sobre alguém

AI N ABBR = **Amnesty International**; (Comput) = **artificial intelligence**

AIB (BRIT) N ABBR (= Accident Investigation Bureau) comissão de inquérito sobre acidentes.

AID N ABBR = **artificial insemination by donor**; (US) = **Agency for International Development**

aid [eɪd] N ajuda ▸ VT ajudar; **with the ~ of** com a ajuda de; **in ~ of** em benefício de; **to ~ and abet** (Law) ser cúmplice de; see also **hearing aid**

aide [eɪd] N (person) assessor(a) m/f

AIDS [eɪdz] N ABBR (= acquired immune deficiency syndrome) AIDS f (BR), SIDA f (PT)

AIH N ABBR = **artificial insemination by husband**

ailing ['eɪlɪŋ] ADJ enfermo

ailment ['eɪlmənt] N achaque m

aim [eɪm] VT: **to ~ sth (at)** (gun, camera, blow) apontar algo (para); (missile, remark) dirigir algo (a) ▸ VI (also: **take aim**) apontar ▸ N (skill) pontaria; (objective) objetivo, meta; **to ~ at** (with weapon) mirar; **to ~ to do** pretender fazer

aimless ['eɪmlɪs] ADJ sem objetivo

aimlessly ['eɪmlɪslɪ] ADV à toa

ain't [eɪnt] (inf) = **am not**; **aren't**; **isn't**

air [ɛər] N ar m; (appearance) aparência, aspecto ▸ VT arejar; (grievances, ideas) discutir ▸ CPD (currents, attack etc) aéreo; **to throw sth into the ~** jogar algo para cima; **by ~** (travel) de avião; (send) por via aérea; **to be on the ~** (Radio, TV: programme, station) estar no ar

air base N base f aérea

air bed ['ɛəbɛd] (BRIT) N colchão m de ar

airborne ['ɛəbɔːn] ADJ (*in the air*) no ar; (*plane*) em voo; (*troops*) aerotransportado

air cargo N frete *m* aéreo

air-conditioned [-kən'dɪʃənd] ADJ com ar condicionado

air conditioning [-kən'dɪʃənɪŋ] N ar-condicionado

air-cooled [-kuːld] ADJ refrigerado a ar

aircraft ['ɛəkrɑːft] N INV aeronave *f*

aircraft carrier N porta-aviões *m inv*

air cushion N almofada de ar

airfield ['ɛəfiːld] N campo de aviação

Air Force N Força Aérea, Aeronáutica

air freight N frete *m* aéreo

air freshener [-'frɛʃnəʳ] N perfumador *m* de ar

air gun ['ɛəgʌn] N espingarda de ar comprimido

air hostess (BRIT) N aeromoça (BR), hospedeira (PT)

airily ['ɛərɪlɪ] ADV levianamente

airing ['ɛərɪŋ] N: **to give an ~ to** arejar; (*fig: ideas, views*) discutir

air letter (BRIT) N aerograma *m*

airlift ['ɛəlɪft] N ponte aérea

airline ['ɛəlaɪn] N linha aérea

airliner ['ɛəlaɪnəʳ] N avião *m* de passageiros

airlock ['ɛəlɔk] N (*blockage*) entupimento de ar

airmail ['ɛəmeɪl] N: **by ~** por via aérea

air mattress N colchão *m* de ar

airplane ['ɛəpleɪn] (US) N avião *m*

air pocket N bolsa de ar

airport ['ɛəpɔːt] N aeroporto

air raid N ataque *m* aéreo

airsick ['ɛəsɪk] ADJ: **to be ~** enjoar-se (no avião)

airspace ['ɛəspeɪs] N espaço aéreo

airstrip ['ɛəstrɪp] N pista (de aterrissar)

air terminal N terminal *m* aéreo

airtight ['ɛətaɪt] ADJ hermético

air traffic control N controle *m* de tráfego aéreo

air traffic controller N controlador(a) *m/f* de tráfego aéreo

airy ['ɛərɪ] ADJ (*room*) arejado; (*manner*) leviano

aisle [aɪl] N (*of church*) nave *f*; (*of theatre etc*) corredor *m*, coxia

ajar [ə'dʒɑːʳ] ADJ entreaberto

AK (US) ABBR (*Post*) = **Alaska**

aka ABBR (= *also known as*) vulgo

akin [ə'kɪn] ADJ: **~ to** parecido com

AL (US) ABBR (*Post*) = **Alabama**

ALA N ABBR = **American Library Association**

à la carte [ælaː'kɑːt] ADJ, ADV à la carte

alacrity [ə'lækrɪtɪ] N alacridade *f*; **with ~** prontamente

alarm [ə'lɑːm] N alarme *m*; (*anxiety*) inquietação *f* ▶ VT alarmar, inquietar

alarm call N (*in hotel etc*) sinal *m* de alarme

alarm clock N despertador *m*

alarming [ə'lɑːmɪŋ] ADJ alarmante

alarmist [ə'lɑːmɪst] ADJ, N alarmista *m/f*

alas [ə'læs] EXCL ai, ai de mim

Alaska [ə'læskə] N Alasca *m*

Albania [æl'beɪnɪə] N Albânia

Albanian [æl'beɪnɪən] ADJ albanês(-esa) ▶ N albanês(-esa) *m/f*; (*Ling*) albanês *m*

albeit [ɔːl'biːɪt] CONJ embora

album ['ælbəm] N (*for stamps etc*) álbum *m*; (*record*) elepê *m*

albumen ['ælbjumɪn] N albumina; (*of egg*) albume *m*

alchemy ['ælkɪmɪ] N alquimia

alcohol ['ælkəhɔl] N álcool *m*

alcohol-free ADJ sem álcool

alcoholic [ælkə'hɔlɪk] ADJ alcoólico ▶ N alcoólatra *m/f*

alcoholism ['ælkəhɔlɪzəm] N alcoolismo

alcove ['ælkəuv] N alcova

Ald. ABBR = **alderman**

alderman ['ɔːldəmən] (*irreg: like* **man**) N vereador *m*

ale [eɪl] N cerveja

alert [ə'ləːt] ADJ atento; (*to danger, opportunity*) alerta; (*sharp*) esperto; (*watchful*) vigilante ▶ N alerta *m* ▶ VT: **to ~ sb (to sth)** alertar alguém (de *or* sobre algo); **to be on the ~** estar alerta; (*Mil*) ficar de prontidão

Aleutian Islands [ə'luːʃən-] NPL ilhas *fpl* Aleútas

A levels NPL ≈ ENEM *m*

Alexandria [ælɪg'zɑːndrɪə] N Alexandria

alfresco [æl'freskəu] ADJ, ADV ao ar livre

Algarve [æl'gɑːv] N: **the ~** o Algarve

algebra ['ældʒɪbrə] N álgebra

Algeria [æl'dʒɪərɪə] N Argélia

Algerian [æl'dʒɪərɪən] ADJ, N argelino(-a)

Algiers [æl'dʒɪəz] N Argel

algorithm ['ælgərɪðəm] N algoritmo

alias ['eɪlɪəs] ADV também chamado ▶ N (*of criminal*) alcunha; (*of writer*) pseudônimo

alibi ['ælɪbaɪ] N álibi *m*

alien ['eɪlɪən] N estrangeiro(-a); (*from space*) alienígena *m/f* ▶ ADJ: **~ to** alheio a

alienate ['eɪlɪəneɪt] VT alienar

alienation [eɪlɪə'neɪʃən] N alienação *f*

alight [ə'laɪt] ADJ em chamas; (*eyes*) aceso; (*expression*) intento ▶ VI (*passenger*) descer (de um veículo); (*bird*) pousar

align [ə'laɪn] VT alinhar

alignment [ə'laɪnmənt] N alinhamento

alike [ə'laɪk] ADJ semelhante; (*identical*) igual ▶ ADV similamente, igualmente; **to look ~** parecer-se

alimony ['ælɪmənɪ] N (*payment*) pensão *f* alimentícia

alive [ə'laɪv] ADJ vivo; (*lively*) alegre; **to be ~ with** fervilhar de; **~ to** sensível a

alkali ['ælkəlaɪ] N álcali *m*

(KEYWORD)

all [ɔːl] ADJ (*singular*) todo(-a); (*plural*) todos(-as); **all day/night** o dia inteiro/a noite inteira; **all men** todos os homens; **all five came** todos os cinco vieram; **all the books/food** todos os livros/toda a comida;

all the time/his life o tempo todo/toda a sua vida
▶ PRON 1 tudo; **I ate it all, I ate all of it** comi tudo; **all of us/the boys went** todos nós fomos/todos os meninos foram; **we all sat down** nós todos sentamos; **is that all?** é só isso?; (*in shop*) mais alguma coisa?
2 (*in phrases*): **above all** sobretudo; **after all** afinal (de contas); **not at all** (*in answer to question*) em absoluto, absolutamente não; **I'm not at all tired** não estou nada cansado; **anything at all will do** qualquer coisa serve; **all in all** ao todo
▶ ADV todo, completamente; **all alone** completamente só; **it's not as hard as all that** não é tão difícil assim; **all the more** ainda mais; **all the better** tanto melhor, melhor ainda; **all but** quase; **the score is 2 all** o jogo está empatado em 2 a 2

allay [ə'leɪ] VT (*fears*) acalmar; (*pain*) aliviar
all clear N sinal *m* de tudo limpo; (*after air raid*) sinal de fim de alerta aérea
allegation [ælɪ'geɪʃən] N alegação *f*
allege [ə'lɛdʒ] VT alegar; **he is ~d to have said** afirma-se que ele disse
alleged [ə'lɛdʒd] ADJ pretenso
allegedly [ə'lɛdʒɪdlɪ] ADV segundo dizem
allegiance [ə'li:dʒəns] N lealdade *f*
allegory [ælɪgərɪ] N alegoria
all-embracing [-ɪm'breɪsɪŋ] ADJ universal
allergic [ə'lə:dʒɪk] ADJ: **~ (to)** alérgico (a)
allergy [ælədʒɪ] N alergia
alleviate [ə'li:vɪeɪt] VT (*pain*) aliviar; (*difficulty*) minorar
alley [ælɪ] N (*street*) viela; (*in garden*) passeio
alliance [ə'laɪəns] N aliança
allied [ælaɪd] ADJ aliado; (*related*) afim, aparentado
alligator [ælɪgeɪtə'] N aligátor *m*; (*in Brazil*) jacaré *m*
all-important ADJ importantíssimo
all-in (BRIT) ADJ, ADV (*charge*) tudo incluído
all-in wrestling (BRIT) N luta livre
alliteration [əlɪtə'reɪʃən] N aliteração *f*
all-night ADJ (*café*) aberto toda a noite; (*party*) que dura toda a noite
allocate [æləkeɪt] VT (*earmark*) destinar; (*share out*) distribuir
allocation [ælə'keɪʃən] N (*of money*) repartição *f*; (*distribution*) distribuição *f*; (*money*) verbas *fpl*
allot [ə'lɔt] VT distribuir, repartir; **to ~ to** designar para; **in the ~ted time** no tempo designado
allotment [ə'lɔtmənt] N (*share*) partilha; (*garden*) lote *m*
all-out ADJ (*effort etc*) máximo; (*attack etc*) irrestrito ▶ ADV: **all out** com toda a força
allow [ə'lau] VT (*practice, behaviour*) permitir; (*sum to spend etc*) dar, conceder; (*claim, goal*) admitir; (*sum, time estimated*) calcular; (*concede*): **to ~ that** reconhecer que; **to ~ sb to do** permitir a alguém fazer; **he is ~ed to**

do é permitido que ele faça, ele pode fazer; **smoking is not ~ed** é proibido fumar; **we must ~ 3 days for the journey** temos que calcular três dias para a viagem
▶ **allow for** VT FUS levar em conta
allowance [ə'lauəns] N ajuda de custo; (*welfare, payment*) pensão *f*, auxílio; (*Tax*) abatimento; **to make ~s for** levar em consideração
alloy [ælɔɪ] N liga
all right ADV (*well*) bem; (*correctly*) corretamente; (*as answer*) está bem!
all-round ADJ (*view*) geral, amplo; (*person*) consumado
all-rounder (BRIT) N: **to be a good ~** ser homem/mulher para tudo
allspice [ɔ:lspaɪs] N pimenta da Jamaica
all-time ADJ (*record*) de todos os tempos
allude [ə'lu:d] VI: **to ~** aludir a
alluring [ə'ljuərɪŋ] ADJ tentador(a)
allusion [ə'lu:ʒən] N alusão *f*
alluvium [ə'lu:vɪəm] N aluvião *m*
ally [*n* ælaɪ, *vt* ə'laɪ] N aliado ▶ VT: **to ~ o.s. with** aliar-se com
almighty [ɔ:l'maɪtɪ] ADJ onipotente; (*row etc*) maior
almond [ɑ:mənd] N (*fruit*) amêndoa; (*tree*) amendoeira
almost [ɔ:lməust] ADV quase
alms [ɑ:mz] NPL esmolas *fpl*, esmola
aloft [ə'lɔft] ADV em cima
alone [ə'ləun] ADJ só, sozinho ▶ ADV só, somente; **to leave sb ~** deixar alguém em paz; **to leave sth ~** não tocar em algo; **let ~ ...** sem falar em ...
along [ə'lɔŋ] PREP por, ao longo de ▶ ADV: **is he coming ~?** ele vem conosco?; **he was hopping/limping ~** ele ia pulando/coxeando; **~ with** junto com; **all ~** (*all the time*) o tempo tudo
alongside [əlɔŋ'saɪd] PREP ao lado de ▶ ADV (*Naut*) encostado
aloof [ə'lu:f] ADJ afastado, altivo ▶ ADV: **to stand ~** afastar-se
aloofness [ə'lu:fnɪs] N afastamento, altivez *f*
aloud [ə'laud] ADV em voz alta
alphabet [ælfəbet] N alfabeto
alphabetical [ælfə'betɪkəl] ADJ alfabético; **in ~ order** em ordem alfabética
alphanumeric [ælfənju:'mɛrɪk] ADJ alfanumérico
alpine [ælpaɪn] ADJ alpino
Alps [ælps] NPL: **the ~** os Alpes
already [ɔ:l'rɛdɪ] ADV já
alright [ɔ:l'raɪt] (BRIT) ADV = **all right**
Alsatian [æl'seɪʃən] (BRIT) N (*dog*) pastor *m* alemão
also [ɔ:lsəu] ADV também; (*moreover*) além disso
altar [ɔltə'] N altar *m*
alter [ɔltə'] VT alterar ▶ VI modificar-se
alteration [ɔltə'reɪʃən] N (*to plan*) mudança; (*to clothes*) conserto; (*to building*) reforma;

timetable subject to ~ horário sujeito a mudanças

alternate [adj ɔl'təːnɪt, vi 'ɔltəːneɪt] ADJ alternado; (US: alternative) alternativo ▸ VI: **to ~ with** alternar-se (com); **on ~ days** em dias alternados

alternately [ɔl'təːnɪtlɪ] ADV alternadamente

alternating ['ɔltəːneɪtɪŋ] ADJ: **~ current** corrente f alternada

alternative [ɔl'təːnətɪv] ADJ alternativo ▸ N alternativa

alternatively [ɔl'təːnətɪvlɪ] ADV: **~ one could ...** por outro lado se podia ...

alternator ['ɔltəːneɪtər] N (Aut) alternador m

although [ɔːl'ðəu] CONJ embora; (given that) se bem que

altitude ['æltɪtjuːd] N altitude f

alto ['æltəu] N (female) contralto f; (male) alto

altogether [ɔːltə'geðər] ADV (completely) totalmente; (on the whole) no total; **how much is that ~?** qual é a soma total?

altruistic [æltruˈɪstɪk] ADJ (person) altruísta; (behaviour) altruístico

aluminium [ælju'mɪnɪəm] (BRIT) N alumínio

aluminum [ə'luːmɪnəm] (US) N = **aluminium**

always ['ɔːlweɪz] ADV sempre

Alzheimer's ['æltshaɪməz], **Alzheimer's disease** N mal m de Alzheimer

AM ABBR = **amplitude modulation**

am [æm] VB see **be**

a.m. ADV ABBR (= ante meridiem) da manhã

AMA N ABBR = **American Medical Association**

amalgam [ə'mælgəm] N amálgama m

amalgamate [ə'mælgəmeɪt] VI amalgamar-se ▸ VT amalgamar, unir

amalgamation [əmælgə'meɪʃən] N (Comm) amalgamação f, união f

amass [ə'mæs] VT acumular

amateur ['æmətər] ADJ, N amador(a) m/f

amateur dramatics N teatro amador

amateurish ['æmətərɪʃ] (pej) ADJ amador(a)

amaze [ə'meɪz] VT pasmar; **to be ~d (at)** espantar-se (de or com)

amazement [ə'meɪzmənt] N pasmo, espanto; **to my ~** para o meu espanto

amazing [ə'meɪzɪŋ] ADJ (surprising) surpreendente; (fantastic) fantástico; (incredible) incrível

amazingly [ə'meɪzɪŋlɪ] ADV (surprisingly) surpreendentemente; (incredibly) incrivelmente

Amazon ['æməzən] N (Geo) Amazonas m; (Mythology) amazona f ▸ CPD amazônico, do Amazonas; **the ~ basin** a bacia amazônica; **the ~ jungle** a selva amazônica

Amazonian [æmə'zeunɪən] ADJ (of river, region) amazônico; (of state) amazonense ▸ N amazonense m/f

ambassador [æm'bæsədər] N embaixador/embaixatriz m/f

amber ['æmbər] N âmbar m; **at ~** (BRIT Aut) em amarelo

ambidextrous [æmbɪ'dɛkstrəs] ADJ ambidestro

ambience ['æmbɪəns] N ambiente m

ambiguity [æmbɪ'gjuɪtɪ] N ambiguidade f

ambiguous [æm'bɪgjuəs] ADJ ambíguo

ambition [æm'bɪʃən] N ambição f

ambitious [æm'bɪʃəs] ADJ ambicioso; (plan) grandioso

ambivalent [æm'bɪvələnt] ADJ ambivalente; (pej) equívoco

amble ['æmbl] VI (also: **amble along**) andar a furta-passo

ambulance ['æmbjuləns] N ambulância

ambush ['æmbuʃ] N emboscada ▸ VT emboscar

ameba [ə'miːbə] (US) N = **amoeba**

ameliorate [ə'miːlɪəreɪt] VT melhorar

amen ['ɑːmɛn] EXCL amém

amenable [ə'miːnəbl] ADJ: **~ to** (advice etc) receptivo a

amend [ə'mɛnd] VT (law, text) emendar; (habits) corrigir; see also **amends**

amendment [ə'mɛndmənt] N (to law etc) emenda; (text) correção f

amends [ə'mɛndz] N: **to make ~ (for)** compensar; **to make ~ to sb for sth** compensar alguém por algo

amenity [ə'miːnɪtɪ] N amenidade f; **amenities** NPL (features, facilities) atrações fpl, comodidades fpl

America [ə'mɛrɪkə] N (continent) América; (USA) Estados Unidos mpl

American [ə'mɛrɪkən] ADJ americano; (from USA) norte-americano, estadunidense ▸ N americano(-a); (from USA) norte-americano(-a)

Americanize [ə'mɛrɪkənaɪz] VT americanizar

amethyst ['æmɪθɪst] N ametista

Amex ['æmɛks] N ABBR = **American Stock Exchange**

amiable ['eɪmɪəbl] ADJ amável

amicable ['æmɪkəbl] ADJ amigável; (person) amigo

amid [ə'mɪd], **amidst** [ə'mɪdst] PREP em meio a

amiss [ə'mɪs] ADV: **to take sth ~** levar algo a mal; **there's something ~** aí tem coisa

ammo ['æməu] (inf) N ABBR = **ammunition**

ammonia [ə'məunɪə] N (gas) amoníaco; (liquid) amônia

ammunition [æmju'nɪʃən] N munição f; (fig) argumentos mpl

ammunition dump N depósito de munições

amnesia [æm'niːzɪə] N amnésia

amnesty ['æmnɪstɪ] N anistia; **to grant an ~ to** anistiar

amoeba, (US) **ameba** [ə'miːbə] N ameba

amok [ə'mɔk] ADV: **to run ~** enlouquecer

among [ə'mʌŋ], **amongst** [ə'mʌŋst] PREP entre, no meio de

amoral [æ'mɔrəl] ADJ amoral

amorous ['æmərəs] ADJ amoroso; (in love) apaixonado, enamorado

amorphous [ə'mɔːfəs] ADJ amorfo
amortization [əmɔːtaɪ'zeɪʃən] N amortização f
amount [ə'maunt] N quantidade f; (of money etc) quantia, importância, montante m ▶ VI: **to ~ to** (reach) chegar a; (total) montar a; (be same as) equivaler a, significar; **this ~s to a refusal** isto equivale a uma recusa; **the total ~** (of money) o total
amp ['æmp], **ampère** ['æmpɛəʳ] N ampère m; **a 13 ~ plug** um plugue com fusível de 13 ampères
ampersand ['æmpəsænd] N "e" m comercial
amphibian [æm'fɪbɪən] N anfíbio
amphibious [æm'fɪbɪəs] ADJ anfíbio
amphitheatre, (US) **amphitheater** ['æmfɪθɪətəʳ] N anfiteatro
ample ['æmpl] ADJ amplo; (abundant) abundante; (enough) suficiente; **this is ~** isso é mais do que suficiente; **to have ~ time/room** ter tempo/lugar de sobra
amplifier ['æmplɪfaɪəʳ] N amplificador m
amplify ['æmplɪfaɪ] VT amplificar
amply ['æmplɪ] ADV amplamente
ampoule, (US) **ampule** ['æmpuːl] N (Med) ampola
amputate ['æmpjuteɪt] VT amputar
Amsterdam ['æmstədæm] N Amsterdã (BR), Amsterdão (PT)
amt ABBR = **amount**
amuck [ə'mʌk] ADV = **amok**
amuse [ə'mjuːz] VT divertir; (distract) distrair; **to ~ o.s. with sth/by doing sth** divertir-se com algo/em fazer algo; **to be ~d at** achar graça em; **he was not ~d** ele ficou sem graça
amusement [ə'mjuːzmənt] N diversão f; (pleasure) divertimento; (pastime) passatempo; (laughter) riso; **much to my ~** para grande diversão minha
amusement arcade N fliperama m
amusement park N parque m de diversões
amusing [ə'mjuːzɪŋ] ADJ divertido
an [æn, ən, n] INDEF ART see **a**
ANA N ABBR = **American Newspaper Association**; **American Nurses Association**
anachronism [ə'nækrənɪzəm] N anacronismo
anaemia, (US) **anemia** [ə'niːmɪə] N anemia
anaemic, (US) **anemic** [ə'niːmɪk] ADJ anêmico
anaesthetic, (US) **anesthetic** [ænɪs'θɛtɪk] ADJ, N anestésico; **under ~** sob anestesia; **local/general ~** anestesia local/geral
anaesthetist, (US) **anesthetist** [æ'niːsθɪtɪst] N anestesista m/f
anagram ['ænəgræm] N anagrama m
analgesic [ænæl'dʒiːsɪk] ADJ anaalgésica ▶ N analgésico
analog, analogue ['ænələg] ADJ (watch, computer) analógico
analogy [ə'nælədʒɪ] N analogia; **to draw or make an ~ between** fazer uma analogia entre
analyse, (US) **analyze** ['ænəlaɪz] VT analisar

analyses [ə'næləsiːz] NPL of **analysis**
analysis [ə'næləsɪs] (pl **analyses**) N análise f; **in the last or final ~** em última análise
analyst ['ænəlɪst] N analista m/f; (psychoanalyst) psicanalista m/f
analytic [ænə'lɪtɪk], **analytical** [ænə'lɪtɪkəl] ADJ analítico
analyze ['ænəlaɪz] (US) VT = **analyse**
anarchic [ə'nɑːkɪk] ADJ anárquico
anarchist ['ænəkɪst] ADJ, N anarquista m/f
anarchy ['ænəkɪ] N anarquia
anathema [ə'næθɪmə] N: **it is ~ to him** ele tem horror disso
anatomical [ænə'tɔmɪkəl] ADJ anatômico
anatomy [ə'nætəmɪ] N anatomia
ANC N ABBR (= African National Congress) CNA m
ancestor ['ænsɪstəʳ] N antepassado
ancestral [æn'sɛstrəl] ADJ ancestral
ancestry ['ænsɪstrɪ] N ascendência, ancestrais mpl
anchor ['æŋkəʳ] N âncora ▶ VI (also: **to drop anchor**) ancorar, fundear ▶ VT (boat) ancorar; (fig): **to ~ sth to** firmar algo em; **to weigh ~** levantar âncoras; **to drop ~** fundear
anchorage ['æŋkərɪdʒ] N ancoradouro
anchor man (irreg: like man), **anchor woman** (irreg: like woman) N (TV, Radio) âncora m/f
anchovy ['æntʃəvɪ] N enchova
ancient ['eɪnʃənt] ADJ antigo; (person, car) velho; **~ monument** monumento antigo
ancillary [æn'sɪlərɪ] ADJ auxiliar
and [ænd] CONJ e; **~ so on** e assim por diante; **try ~ come** tente vir; **he talked ~ talked** ele falou sem parar; **better ~ better** cada vez melhor
Andes ['ændiːz] NPL: **the ~** os Andes
anecdote ['ænɪkdəut] N anedota
anemia [ə'niːmɪə] (US) N = **anaemia**
anemic [ə'niːmɪk] (US) ADJ = **anaemic**
anemone [ə'nɛmənɪ] N (Bot) anêmona
anesthetic [ænɪs'θɛtɪk] (US) ADJ, N = **anaesthetic**
anesthetist [æ'niːsθɪtɪst] (US) N = **anaesthetist**
anew [ə'njuː] ADV de novo
angel ['eɪndʒəl] N anjo
anger ['æŋgəʳ] N raiva ▶ VT zangar
angina [æn'dʒaɪnə] N angina (de peito)
angle ['æŋgl] N ângulo; (viewpoint): **from their ~** do ponto de vista deles ▶ VI: **to ~ for** (fish, compliments) pescar
angler ['æŋgləʳ] N pescador(a) m/f de vara (BR) or à linha (PT)
Anglican ['æŋglɪkən] ADJ, N anglicano(-a)
anglicize ['æŋglɪsaɪz] VT anglicizar
angling ['æŋglɪŋ] N pesca à vara (BR) or à linha (PT)
Anglo- ['æŋgləu] PREFIX anglo-
Anglo-Brazilian ADJ anglo-brasileiro
Anglo-Portuguese ADJ anglo-português(-esa)
Anglo-Saxon [-'sæksən] ADJ anglo-saxão(-xôni(c)a) ▶ N anglo-saxão(-xôni(c)a) m/f; (Ling) anglo-saxão m

Angola [æŋ'gəʊlə] N Angola (*no article*)
Angolan [æŋ'gəʊlən] ADJ, N angolano(-a)
angrily ['æŋgrɪlɪ] ADV com raiva
angry ['æŋgrɪ] ADJ zangado; **to be ~ with sb/ at sth** estar zangado com alguém/algo; **to get ~** zangar-se; **to make sb ~** zangar alguém
anguish ['æŋgwɪʃ] N (*physical*) dor *f*, sofrimento; (*mental*) angústia
angular ['æŋgjʊlə^r] ADJ (*shape*) angular; (*features*) anguloso
animal ['ænɪməl] N animal *m*, bicho ▶ ADJ animal
animate [*vt* 'ænɪmeɪt, *adj* 'ænɪmɪt] ADJ animado ▶ VT animar
animated ['ænɪmeɪtɪd] ADJ animado
animation [ænɪ'meɪʃən] N animação *f*
animosity [ænɪ'mɒsɪtɪ] N animosidade *f*
aniseed ['ænɪsiːd] N erva-doce *f*, anis *f*
Ankara ['æŋkərə] N Ancara
ankle ['æŋkl] N tornozelo
ankle sock N soquete *f*
annex [*n* 'ænɛks, *vt* ə'nɛks] N (*BRIT: building*) anexo ▶ VT anexar
annexation [ænɛks'eɪʃən] N anexação *f*
annexe ['ænɛks] (*BRIT*) N = **annex**
annihilate [ə'naɪəleɪt] VT aniquilar
anniversary [ænɪ'vəːsərɪ] N aniversário
annotate ['ænəʊteɪt] VT anotar
announce [ə'naʊns] VT anunciar; **he ~d that he wasn't going** ele declarou que não iria
announcement [ə'naʊnsmənt] N anúncio; (*official*) comunicação *f*; (*in letter etc*) aviso; **to make an ~** anunciar alguma coisa
announcer [ə'naʊnsə^r] N (*Radio, TV*) locutor(a) *m/f*
annoy [ə'nɔɪ] VT aborrecer; **to be ~ed (at sth/ with sb)** aborrecer-se (com algo/alguém); **don't get ~ed!** não se aborreça!
annoyance [ə'nɔɪəns] N aborrecimento; (*thing*) moléstia
annoying [ə'nɔɪɪŋ] ADJ irritante; (*person*) importuno
annual ['ænjʊəl] ADJ anual ▶ N (*Bot*) anual *f*; (*book*) anuário
annual general meeting (*BRIT*) N assembleia geral ordinária
annually ['ænjʊəlɪ] ADV anualmente
annual report N relatório anual
annuity [ə'njuːɪtɪ] N anuidade *f or* renda anual; **life ~** renda vitalícia
annul [ə'nʌl] VT anular; (*law*) revogar
annulment [ə'nʌlmənt] N anulação *f*; (*of law*) revogação *f*
annum ['ænəm] N *see* **per annum**
Annunciation [ənʌnsɪ'eɪʃən] N Anunciação *f*
anode ['ænəʊd] N anodo
anoint [ə'nɔɪnt] VT ungir
anomalous [ə'nɒmələs] ADJ anômalo
anomaly [ə'nɒməlɪ] N anomalia
anon [ə'nɒn] ADV daqui a pouco
anon. [ə'nɒn] ABBR = **anonymous**
anonymity [ænə'nɪmɪtɪ] N anonimato

anonymous [ə'nɒnɪməs] ADJ anônimo; **to remain ~** ficar no anonimato
anorak ['ænəræk] N anoraque *m* (*BR*), anorak *m* (*PT*)
anorexia [ænə'rɛksɪə] N (*Med: also:* **anorexia nervosa**) anorexia
another [ə'nʌðə^r] ADJ: **~ book** (*one more*) outro livro, mais um livro; (*a different one*) um outro livro, um livro diferente ▶ PRON outro; **~ drink?** outra bebida?, mais uma bebida?; **in ~ 5 years** daqui a 5 anos; *see also* **one**
ANSI N ABBR (= *American National Standards Institute*) instituto de padrões
answer ['ɑːnsə^r] N resposta; (*to problem*) solução *f* ▶ VI responder ▶ VT (*reply to*) responder a; (*problem*) resolver; **in ~ to your letter** em resposta *or* respondendo à sua carta; **to ~ the phone** atender o telefone; **to ~ the bell** *or* **the door** atender à porta
▶ **answer back** VI replicar, retrucar
▶ **answer for** VT FUS responder por, responsabilizar-se por
▶ **answer to** VT FUS (*description*) corresponder a; (*needs*) satisfazer
answerable ['ɑːnsərəbl] ADJ: **~ (to sb/for sth)** responsável (perante alguém/por algo); **I am ~ to no-one** não tenho que dar satisfações a ninguém
answering machine ['ɑːnsərɪŋ-] N secretária eletrônica
answerphone ['ɑːnsərfəʊn] N (*esp BRIT*) secretária eletrônica
ant [ænt] N formiga
ANTA N ABBR = **American National Theater and Academy**
antacid [ænt'æsɪd] ADJ antiácido
antagonism [æn'tægənɪzəm] N antagonismo
antagonist [æn'tægənɪst] N antagonista *m/f*, adversário(-a)
antagonistic [æntægə'nɪstɪk] ADJ antagônico, hostil; (*opposed*) oposto, contrário
antagonize [æn'tægənaɪz] VT contrariar, hostilizar
Antarctic [ænt'ɑːktɪk] ADJ antártico ▶ N: **the ~** o Antártico
Antarctica [æn'tɑːktɪkə] N Antártica
Antarctic Circle N Círculo Polar Antártico
Antarctic Ocean N oceano Antártico
ante ['æntɪ] N: **to up the ~** apostar mais alto
ante... ['æntɪ] PREFIX ante..., pré...
anteater ['æntiːtə^r] N tamanduá *m*
antecedent [æntɪ'siːdənt] N antecedente *m*
antechamber ['æntɪtʃeɪmbə^r] N antecâmara
antelope ['æntɪləʊp] N antílope *m*
antenatal ['æntɪ'neɪtl] ADJ pré-natal
antenatal clinic N clínica pré-natal
antenna [æn'tɛnə] (*pl* **antennae**) N antena
antennae [æn'tɛniː] NPL *of* **antenna**
anthem ['ænθəm] N motete *m*; **national ~** hino nacional
ant hill N formigueiro
anthology [æn'θɒlədʒɪ] N antologia

anthropologist [ænθrə'pɒlədʒɪst] N antropologista m/f, antropólogo(-a)
anthropology [ænθrə'pɒlədʒɪ] N antropologia
anti... [ænti] PREFIX anti...
anti-aircraft ADJ antiaéreo
anti-aircraft defence N defesa antiaérea
anti-ballistic missile ['æntɪbə'lɪstɪk-] N míssil m antimíssil
antibiotic [æntɪbaɪ'ɔtɪk] ADJ, N antibiótico
antibody ['æntɪbɒdɪ] N anticorpo
anticipate [æn'tɪsɪpeɪt] VT (foresee) prever; (expect) esperar; (forestall) antecipar; (look forward to) aguardar, esperar; **this is worse than I ~d** isso é pior do que eu esperava; **as ~d** como previsto
anticipation [æntɪsɪ'peɪʃən] N (expectation) expectativa; (eagerness) entusiasmo; **thanking you in ~** antecipadamente grato(s), agradeço (or agradecemos) antecipadamente a atenção de V.Sª
anticlimax [æntɪ'klaɪmæks] N desapontamento
anticlockwise [æntɪ'klɔkwaɪz] (BRIT) ADV em sentido anti-horário
antics ['æntɪks] NPL bobices fpl; (of child) travessuras fpl
anticyclone [æntɪ'saɪkləun] N anticiclone m
antidote ['æntɪdəut] N antídoto
antifreeze ['æntɪfri:z] N anticongelante m
antiglobalization N antiglobalização m; **~ protesters** manifestantes antiglobalização
antihistamine [æntɪ'hɪstəmi:n] N anti-histamínico
Antilles [æn'tɪli:z] NPL: **the ~** as Antilhas
antipathy [æn'tɪpəθɪ] N antipatia
Antipodean [æntɪpə'di:ən] ADJ australiano e neozelandês
Antipodes [æn'tɪpədi:z] NPL: **the ~** a Austrália e a Nova Zelândia
antiquarian [æntɪ'kwɛərɪən] ADJ: **~ bookshop** livraria de livros usados, sebo (BR) ▶ N antiquário(-a)
antiquated ['æntɪkweɪtɪd] ADJ antiquado
antique [æn'ti:k] N antiguidade f ▶ ADJ antigo
antique dealer N antiquário(-a)
antique shop N loja de antiguidades
antiquity [æn'tɪkwɪtɪ] N antiguidade f
anti-Semitic [-sɪ'mɪtɪk] ADJ (person) antissemita; (views, publications etc) antissemítico
anti-Semitism [-'sɛmɪtɪzəm] N antissemitismo
antiseptic [æntɪ'sɛptɪk] ADJ, N antisséptico
antisocial [æntɪ'səuʃəl] ADJ insociável; (against society) antissocial
antitank ['æntɪ'tæŋk] ADJ antitanque inv
antitheses [æn'tɪθɪsi:z] NPL of **antithesis**
antithesis [æn'tɪθɪsɪs] (pl **antitheses**) N antítese f
antitrust legislation ['æntɪ'trʌst-] N legislação f antitruste

antivirus ['ænti'vaɪərəs] ADJ antivírus m inv; **~ software** software antivírus
antlers ['æntləz] NPL esgalhos mpl, chifres mpl
Antwerp ['æntwə:p] N Antuérpia
anus ['eɪnəs] N ânus m
anvil ['ænvɪl] N bigorna
anxiety [æŋ'zaɪətɪ] N (worry) inquietude f; (eagerness) ânsia f; (Med) ansiedade f; **~ to do** ânsia de fazer
anxious ['æŋkʃəs] ADJ (worried) preocupado, apreensivo; (worrying) angustiante; (keen) ansioso; **~ to do/for sth** ansioso para fazer/por algo; **to be ~ that** desejar que; **I'm very ~ about you** estou muito preocupado com você
anxiously ['æŋkʃəslɪ] ADV ansiosamente

(KEYWORD)

any ['ɛnɪ] ADJ **1** (in questions etc) algum(a); **have you any butter/children?** você tem manteiga/filhos?; **if there are any tickets left** se houver alguns bilhetes sobrando
2 (with negative) nenhum(a); **I haven't any money/books** não tenho dinheiro/livros
3 (no matter which) qualquer; **choose any book you like** escolha qualquer livro que quiser
4 (in phrases): **in any case** em todo o caso; **any day now** qualquer dia desses; **at any moment** a qualquer momento; **at any rate** de qualquer modo; **any time** a qualquer momento; (whenever) quando quer que seja
▶ PRON **1** (in questions etc) algum(a); **have you got any?** tem algum?; **can any of you sing?** algum de vocês sabe cantar?
2 (with negative) nenhum(a); **I haven't any (of them)** não tenho nenhum (deles)
3 (no matter which one(s)): **take any of those books (you like)** leve qualquer um desses livros (que você quiser)
▶ ADV **1** (in questions etc) algo; **do you want any more soup/sandwiches?** quer mais sopa/sanduíches?; **are you feeling any better?** você está se sentindo melhor?
2 (with negative) nada; **I can't hear him any more** não consigo mais ouvi-lo

anybody ['ɛnɪbɔdɪ] PRON qualquer um, qualquer pessoa; (in interrogative sentences) alguém; (in negative sentences) **I don't see ~** não vejo ninguém
anyhow ['ɛnɪhau] ADV (at any rate) de qualquer modo, de qualquer maneira; (haphazard) de qualquer jeito; **I shall go ~** eu irei de qualquer jeito; **she leaves things just ~** ela deixa as coisas de qualquer maneira
anyone ['ɛnɪwʌn] PRON (in questions etc) alguém; (with negative) ninguém; (no matter who) quem quer que seja; **I can't see ~** não vejo ninguém; **can you see ~?** você pode ver alguém?; **if ~ should phone ...** se alguém telefonar; **~ could do it** qualquer um(a)

poderia fazer isso; I could teach ~ to do it eu poderia ensimar qualquer um(a) a fazer isso

anyplace ['ɛnɪpleɪs] (US) ADV em qualquer parte; (negative sense) em parte nenhuma; (everywhere) em or por toda a parte

anything ['ɛnɪθɪŋ] PRON (in questions etc) alguma coisa; (with negative) nada; (no matter what) qualquer coisa; **can you see ~?** você pode ver alguma coisa?; **if ~ happens to me ...** se alguma coisa me acontecer ...; **I can't see ~** naõ posso ver nada; **you can say ~ you like** você pode dizer o que quiser; **~ will do** qualquer coisa serve

anytime ['ɛnɪtaɪm] ADV (at any moment) a qualquer momento; (whenever) não importa quando

anyway ['ɛnɪweɪ] ADV (at any rate) de qualquer modo; (besides) além disso; **I shall go ~** eu irei de qualquer jeito; **~, I couldn't come even if I wanted to** além disso, mesmo se eu quisesse, não poderia vir

anywhere ['ɛnɪwɛəʳ] ADV (in questions etc) em algum lugar; (with negative) em parte nenhuma; (no matter where) não importa onde, onde quer que seja; **can you see him ~?** você pode vê-lo em algum lugar?; **I can't see him ~** não o vejo em parte nenhuma; **~ in the world** em qualquer lugar do mundo; **put the books down ~** colegue os livros em qualquer lugar

Anzac ['ænzæk] N ABBR (= Australia-New Zealand Army Corps) soldado da tropa ANZAC

apart [ə'pɑːt] ADV à parte, à distância; (separately) separado; **10 miles ~** a uma distância de 10 milhas um do outro; **to take ~** desmontar; **they are living ~** estão separados; **~ from** além de, à parte de

apartheid [ə'pɑːteɪt] N apartheid m

apartment [ə'pɑːtmənt] (US) N apartamento

apartment building (US) N prédio or edifício (de apartamentos)

apathetic [æpə'θɛtɪk] ADJ apático

apathy ['æpəθɪ] N apatia, indiferença

APB (US) N ABBR (= all points bulletin) expressão usada pela polícia significando "descubram e prendam o suspeito"

ape [eɪp] N macaco ▸ VT macaquear, imitar

Apennines ['æpənaɪnz] NPL: **the ~** os Apeninos

aperitif [ə'pɛrɪtɪv] N aperitivo

aperture ['æpətʃuəʳ] N orifício; (Phot) abertura

APEX ['eɪpɛks] N (BRIT: = Association of Professional, Executive, Clerical and Computer Staff) sindicato de funcionários comerciais; (Aviat: = advance passenger excursion) tarifa aérea com desconto por compra antecipada

apex ['eɪpɛks] N ápice m

aphid ['eɪfɪd] N pulgão m

aphrodisiac [æfrəʊ'dɪzɪæk] ADJ afrodisíaco ▸ N afrodisíaco

API N ABBR = **American Press Institute**

apiece [ə'piːs] ADV (for each person) cada um, por cabeça; (for each item) cada

aplomb [ə'plɔm] N desenvoltura

APO (US) N ABBR (= Army Post Office) serviço postal do exército

apocalypse [ə'pɔkəlɪps] N apocalipse m

apolitical [eɪpə'lɪtɪkl] ADJ apolítico

apologetic [əpɔlə'dʒɛtɪk] ADJ cheio de desculpas

apologetically [əpɔlə'dʒɛtɪklɪ] ADV (say) desculpando-se; (smile) como quem pede desculpas

apologize [ə'pɔlədʒaɪz] VI: **to ~ (for sth to sb)** desculpar-se or pedir desculpas (por or de algo a alguém)

apology [ə'pɔlədʒɪ] N desculpas fpl; **please accept my apologies for ...** peço desculpas por ...; **to send one's apologies** apresentar desculpas

apoplectic [æpə'plɛktɪk] ADJ (Med) apopléctico; (inf): **~ with rage** enraivecido

apoplexy ['æpəplɛksɪ] N (Med) apoplexia

apostle [ə'pɔsl] N apóstolo

apostrophe [ə'pɔstrəfɪ] N apóstrofo

app [æp] (inf) N ABBR (= application program) aplicativo (BR), aplicação f (PT)

appal [ə'pɔːl] VT horrorizar

Appalachian Mountains [æpə'leɪʃən-] NPL: **the ~** os montes Apalaches

appalling [ə'pɔːlɪŋ] ADJ (shocking) chocante; (awful) terrível; **she's an ~ cook** ela é uma péssima cozinheira

apparatus [æpə'reɪtəs] N aparelho; (in gym) aparelhos mpl; (organization) aparato

apparel [ə'pærl] (US) N vestuário, roupa

apparent [ə'pærənt] ADJ aparente; (obvious) claro, patente; **it is ~ that ...** é claro or evidente que ...

apparently [ə'pærəntlɪ] ADV aparentemente, pelo(s) visto(s)

apparition [æpə'rɪʃən] N aparição f; (ghost) fantasma m

appeal [ə'piːl] VI (Law) apelar, recorrer ▸ N (Law) recurso, apelação f; (request) pedido; (plea) súplica; (charm) atração f; **to ~ (to sb) for** suplicar (a alguém); **to ~ to** (subj: person) suplicar a; (be attractive to) atrair; **to ~ to sb for mercy** pedir misericórdia a alguém; **it doesn't ~ to me** não me atrai; **right of ~** direito a recorrer or apelar

appealing [ə'piːlɪŋ] ADJ (attractive) atraente; (touching) comovedor(a), comovente

appear [ə'pɪəʳ] VI (come into view) aparecer; (be present) comparecer; (Law) apresentar-se, comparecer; (publication) ser publicado; (seem) parecer; **it would ~ that ...** pareceria que ...; **to ~ in "Hamlet"** trabalhar em "Hamlet"; **to ~ on TV** (person, news item) sair na televisão; (programme) passar na televisão

appearance [ə'pɪərəns] N (coming into view) aparecimento; (presence) comparecimento; (look, aspect) aparência; **to put in or make an ~** comparecer; **in order of ~** (Theatre) por ordem de entrar em cena; **to keep up ~s** manter as aparências; **to all ~s** ao que tudo indica

appease [ə'piːz] VT (*pacify*) apaziguar; (*satisfy*) satisfazer

appeasement [ə'piːzmənt] N apaziguamento

append [ə'pɛnd] VT anexar

appendage [ə'pɛndɪdʒ] N apêndice *m*

appendices [ə'pɛndɪsiːz] NPL *of* **appendix**

appendicitis [əpɛndɪ'saɪtɪs] N apendicite *f*

appendix [ə'pɛndɪks] (*pl* **appendices**) N apêndice *m*; **to have one's ~ out** tirar o apêndice

appetite ['æpɪtaɪt] N apetite *m*; (*fig*) desejo; **that walk has given me an ~** essa caminhada me abriu o apetite

appetizer ['æpɪtaɪzəʳ] N (*food*) tira-gosto; (*drink*) aperitivo

appetizing ['æpɪtaɪzɪŋ] ADJ apetitoso

applaud [ə'plɔːd] VI aplaudir ▸ VT aplaudir; (*praise*) admirar

applause [ə'plɔːz] N aplausos *mpl*

apple ['æpl] N maçã *f*; (*also*: **apple tree**) macieira; **she's the ~ of his eye** ela é a menina dos olhos dele

apple tree N macieira

apple turnover N pastel *m* de maçã

appliance [ə'plaɪəns] N (*Tech*) aparelho; **electrical** *or* **domestic ~s** eletrodomésticos *mpl*

applicable [ə'plɪkəbl] ADJ aplicável; (*relevant*) apropriado; **the law is ~ from January** a lei entrará em vigor a partir de janeiro; **to be ~ to** valer para

applicant ['æplɪkənt] N: **~ (for)** (*for post*) candidato(-a) (a); (*Admin: for benefit etc*) requerente *m/f* (de)

application [æplɪ'keɪʃən] N aplicação *f*; (*for a job, a grant etc*) candidatura, requerimento; (*hard work*) empenho; (*Comput*) aplicativo (BR), aplicação *f* (PT); **on ~** a pedido

application form N (formulário de) requerimento

applications package N (*Comput*) pacote *m* de aplicativos

applied [ə'plaɪd] ADJ aplicado

apply [ə'plaɪ] VT (*paint etc*) usar; (*law etc*) pôr em prática ▸ VI: **to ~ to** apresentar-se a; (*be suitable for*) ser aplicável a; (*be relevant to*) valer para; (*ask*) pedir; **to ~ for** (*permit, grant*) solicitar, pedir; (*job*) candidatar-se a; **to ~ the brakes** frear (BR), travar (PT); **to ~ o.s. to** aplicar-se a, dedicar-se a

appoint [ə'pɔɪnt] VT (*to post*) nomear; (*date, place*) marcar

appointed [ə'pɔɪntɪd] ADJ: **at the ~ time** à hora marcada

appointee [əpɔɪn'tiː] N nomeado(-a)

appointment [ə'pɔɪntmənt] N (*engagement*) encontro, compromisso; (*at doctor's etc*) hora marcada; (*act*) nomeação *f*; (*post*) cargo; **to make an ~ (with sb)** marcar um encontro (com alguém); (*with doctor, hairdresser etc*)

marcar hora (com alguém); **"~s (vacant)"** (*Press*) "ofertas de emprego"; **by ~** com hora marcada

apportion [ə'pɔːʃən] VT repartir, distribuir; (*blame*) pôr; **to ~ sth to sb** atribuir algo a alguém

appraisal [ə'preɪzl] N avaliação *f*

appraise [ə'preɪz] VT avaliar

appreciable [ə'priːʃəbl] ADJ apreciável, notável

appreciate [ə'priːʃɪeɪt] VT (*like*) apreciar, estimar; (*be grateful for*) agradecer; (*understand*) compreender ▸ VI (*Comm*) valorizar-se; **I ~ your help** agradeço-lhe a *or* pela sua ajuda

appreciation [əpriːʃɪ'eɪʃən] N apreciação *f*, estima; (*understanding*) compreensão *f*; (*gratitude*) agradecimento; (*Comm*) valorização *f*

appreciative [ə'priːʃɪətɪv] ADJ (*person*) agradecido; (*comment*) elogioso

apprehend [æprɪ'hɛnd] VT (*understand*) perceber, compreender; (*arrest*) prender

apprehension [æprɪ'hɛnʃən] N apreensão *f*

apprehensive [æprɪ'hɛnsɪv] ADJ apreensivo, receoso

apprentice [ə'prɛntɪs] N aprendiz *m/f* ▸ VT: **to be ~d to** ser aprendiz de

apprenticeship [ə'prɛntɪsʃɪp] N aprendizado, aprendizagem *f*; **to serve one's ~** fazer seu aprendizado

appro. ['æprəu] (BRIT *inf*) ABBR (*Comm*) = **approval**

approach [ə'prəutʃ] VI aproximar-se ▸ VT aproximar-se de; (*be approximate*) aproximar-se a; (*ask, apply to*) dirigir-se a; (*subject, passer-by*) abordar ▸ N aproximação *f*; (*access*) acesso; (*proposal*) proposição *f*; (*to problem, situation*) enfoque *m*; **to ~ sb about sth** falar com alguém sobre algo

approachable [ə'prəutʃəbl] ADJ (*person*) tratável; (*place*) acessível

approach road N via de acesso

approbation [æprə'beɪʃən] N aprovação *f*

appropriate [*adj* ə'prəuprɪɪt, *vt* ə'prəuprɪeɪt] ADJ (*apt*) apropriado; (*relevant*) adequado ▸ VT (*take*) apropriar-se de; (*allot*): **to ~ sth for** destinar algo a; **it would not be ~ for me to comment** não seria conveniente eu comentar

appropriately [ə'prəuprɪɪtlɪ] ADV adequadamente

appropriation [əprəuprɪ'eɪʃən] N (*confiscation*) apropriação *f*; (*of funds for sth*) dotação *f*

approval [ə'pruːvəl] N aprovação *f*; (*permission*) consentimento; **on ~** (*Comm*) a contento; **to meet with sb's ~** (*proposal etc*) ser aprovado por alguém, obter a aprovação de alguém

approve [ə'pruːv] VT (*publication, product*) autorizar; (*motion, decision*) aprovar
▸ **approve of** VT FUS aprovar

approved school [ə'pruːvd-] (BRIT) N reformatório

approvingly [ə'pru:vɪŋlɪ] ADV com aprovação
approx. ABBR = **approximately**
approximate [adj ə'prɔksɪmɪt, vt ə'prɔksɪmeɪt] ADJ aproximado ▶ VT aproximar
approximately [ə'prɔksɪmɪtlɪ] ADV aproximadamente
approximation [əprɔksɪ'meɪʃən] N aproximação f
apr N ABBR (= annual percentage rate) taxa de juros anual
Apr. ABBR = **April**
apricot ['eɪprɪkɔt] N damasco
April ['eɪprəl] N abril m; see also **July**
April Fool's Day N Primeiro-de-abril m
apron ['eɪprən] N avental m; (Aviat) pátio de estacionamento
apse [æps] N (Arch) abside f
APT (BRIT) N ABBR = **advanced passenger train**
apt [æpt] ADJ (suitable) adequado; (appropriate) a propósito, apropriado; (likely): ~ **to do** sujeito a fazer
Apt. ABBR (= apartment) ap., apto.
aptitude ['æptɪtju:d] N aptidão f, talento
aptitude test N teste m de aptidão
aptly ['æptlɪ] ADV (express) acertadamente; ~ **named** apropriadamente chamado
aqualung ['ækwəlʌŋ] N aparelho respiratório autônomo
aquarium [ə'kwɛərɪəm] N aquário
Aquarius [ə'kwɛərɪəs] N Aquário
aquatic [ə'kwætɪk] ADJ aquático
aqueduct ['ækwɪdʌkt] N aqueduto
AR (US) ABBR (Post) = **Arkansas**
ARA (BRIT) N ABBR = **Associate of the Royal Academy**
Arab ['ærəb] ADJ, N árabe m/f
Arabia [ə'reɪbɪə] N Arábia
Arabian [ə'reɪbɪən] ADJ árabe
Arabian Desert N deserto da Arábia
Arabian Sea N mar m Arábico
Arabic ['ærəbɪk] ADJ árabe; (numerals) arábico ▶ N (Ling) árabe m
Arabic numerals NPL algarismos mpl arábicos
arable ['ærəbl] ADJ cultivável
ARAM (BRIT) N ABBR = **Associate of the Royal Academy of Music**
arbiter ['ɑ:bɪtər] N árbitro
arbitrary ['ɑ:bɪtrərɪ] ADJ arbitrário
arbitrate ['ɑ:bɪtreɪt] VI arbitrar
arbitration [ɑ:bɪ'treɪʃən] N arbitragem f; **the dispute went to** ~ o litígio foi submetido a arbitragem
arbitrator ['ɑ:bɪtreɪtər] N árbitro
ARC N ABBR = **American Red Cross**
arc [ɑ:k] N arco
arcade [ɑ:'keɪd] N arcada; (round a square) arcos mpl; (passage with shops) galeria
arch [ɑ:tʃ] N arco; (of foot) curvatura ▶ VT arquear, curvar ▶ ADJ malicioso ▶ PREFIX: ~(-) arce..., arqui...; **pointed** ~ ogiva
archaeological, (US) **archeological** [ɑ:kɪə'lɔdʒɪkl] ADJ arqueológico

archaeologist, (US) **archeologist** [ɑ:kɪ'ɔlədʒɪst] N arqueólogo(-a)
archaeology, (US) **archeology** [ɑ:kɪ'ɔlədʒɪ] N arqueologia
archaic [ɑ:'keɪɪk] ADJ arcaico
archangel ['ɑ:keɪndʒəl] N arcanjo
archbishop [ɑ:tʃ'bɪʃəp] N arcebispo
arch-enemy N arqui-inimigo(-a)
archeology [ɑ:kɪ'ɔlədʒɪ] (US) N = **archaeology**
archer ['ɑ:tʃər] N arqueiro(-a)
archery ['ɑ:tʃɪrɪ] N tiro de arco
archetypal ['ɑ:kɪtaɪpəl] ADJ arquetípico
archetype ['ɑ:kɪtaɪp] N arquétipo
archipelago [ɑ:kɪ'pɛlɪgəu] N arquipélago
architect ['ɑ:kɪtɛkt] N arquiteto(-a)
architectural [ɑ:kɪ'tɛktʃərəl] ADJ arquitetônico
architecture ['ɑ:kɪtɛktʃər] N arquitetura
archives ['ɑ:kaɪvz] NPL arquivo
archivist ['ɑ:kɪvɪst] N arquivista m/f
archway ['ɑ:tʃweɪ] N arco
ARCM (BRIT) N ABBR = **Associate of the Royal College of Music**
Arctic ['ɑ:ktɪk] ADJ ártico ▶ N: **the** ~ o Ártico
Arctic Circle N Círculo Polar Ártico
Arctic Ocean N oceano Ártico
ARD (US) N ABBR (Med) = **acute respiratory disease**
ardent ['ɑ:dənt] ADJ (admirer) ardente; (discussion) acalorado; (fervent) fervoroso
ardour, (US) **ardor** ['ɑ:dər] N (passion) ardor m; (fervour) fervor m
arduous ['ɑ:djuəs] ADJ árduo
are [ɑ:r] VB see **be**
area ['ɛərɪə] N (zone) zona, região f; (part of place) região; (in room, of knowledge, experience) área; (Math) superfície f, extensão f; **dining** ~ área de jantar; **the London** ~ a região de Londres
area code (US) N (Tel) (código) DDD (BR), indicativo (PT)
arena [ə'ri:nə] N arena; (of circus) picadeiro (BR), pista (PT); (for bullfight) arena (BR), praça (PT)
aren't [ɑ:nt] = **are not**
Argentina [ɑ:dʒən'ti:nə] N Argentina
Argentinian [ɑ:dʒən'tɪnɪən] ADJ, N argentino(-a)
arguable ['ɑ:gjuəbl] ADJ discutível
arguably ['ɑ:gjuəblɪ] ADV possivelmente
argue ['ɑ:gju:] VI (quarrel) discutir; (reason) argumentar; **to** ~ **about sth** (**with sb**) discutir sobre algo (com alguém); **to** ~ **that** sustentar que
argument ['ɑ:gjumənt] N (reasons) argumento; (quarrel) briga, discussão f; (debate) debate m; ~ **for/against** argumento a favor de/contra
argumentative [ɑ:gju'mɛntətɪv] ADJ (person) que gosta de discutir
aria ['ɑ:rɪə] N (Mus) ária
ARIBA (BRIT) N ABBR = **Associate of the Royal Institute of British Architects**

arid ['ærɪd] ADJ árido
aridity [ə'rɪdɪtɪ] N aridez f
Aries ['ɛərɪz] N Áries m
arise [ə'raɪz] (pt **arose**, pp **arisen**) VI (rise up) levantar-se, erguer-se; (emerge) surgir; **to ~ from** resultar de; **should the need ~** se for necessário
arisen [ə'rɪzn] PP of **arise**
aristocracy [ærɪs'tɔkrəsɪ] N aristocracia
aristocrat ['ærɪstəkræt] N aristocrata m/f
aristocratic [ærɪstə'krætɪk] ADJ aristocrático
arithmetic [ə'rɪθmətɪk] N aritmética
arithmetical [ærɪθ'mɛtɪkl] ADJ aritmético
ark [ɑːk] N: **Noah's A~** arca de Noé
arm [ɑːm] N braço; (of clothing) manga; (of organization etc) divisão f ▶ VT armar; **arms** NPL (weapons) armas fpl; (Heraldry) brasão m; **~ in ~** de braços dados
armaments ['ɑːməmənts] NPL (weapons) armamento
armband ['ɑːmbænd] N faixa de braço, braçadeira; (for swimming) boia de braço
armchair ['ɑːmtʃɛəʳ] N poltrona
armed [ɑːmd] ADJ armado; **the ~ forces** as forças armadas
armed robbery N assalto à mão armada
Armenia [ɑː'miːnɪə] N Armênia
Armenian [ɑː'miːnɪən] ADJ armênio ▶ N armênio(-a); (Ling) armênio
armful ['ɑːmful] N braçada
armistice ['ɑːmɪstɪs] N armistício
armour, (US) **armor** ['ɑːməʳ] N armadura; (also: **armour plating**) blindagem f
armoured car, (US) **armored car** ['ɑːməd-] N carro blindado
armoury, (US) **armory** ['ɑːmərɪ] N arsenal m
armpit ['ɑːmpɪt] N sovaco
armrest ['ɑːmrɛst] N braço (de poltrona)
arms control N controle m de armas
arms race N corrida armamentista
army ['ɑːmɪ] N exército
aroma [ə'rəumə] N aroma
aromatherapy N aromaterapia
aromatic [ærə'mætɪk] ADJ aromático
arose [ə'rəuz] PT of **arise**
around [ə'raund] ADV em volta; (in the area) perto ▶ PREP em volta de; (near) perto de; (fig: about) cerca de; **is he ~?** ele está por aí?
arouse [ə'rauz] VT despertar; (anger) provocar
arrange [ə'reɪndʒ] VT arranjar; (organize) organizar; (put in order) arrumar ▶ VI: **we have ~d for a car to pick you up** providenciamos um carro para buscá-lo; **it was ~d that ...** foi combinado que ...; **to ~ to do sth** combinar em or ficar de fazer algo
arrangement [ə'reɪndʒmənt] N (agreement) acordo; (order, layout) disposição f; **arrangements** NPL (plans) planos mpl; (preparations) preparativos mpl; **to come to an ~ (with sb)** chegar a um acordo (com alguém); **home deliveries by ~** entregas a domicílio por convênio; **I'll make all the necessary ~s** eu vou tomar todas as providências necessárias

array [ə'reɪ] N: **~ of** (of things, people) variedade f de; (Math, Comput) tabela
arrears [ə'rɪəz] NPL atrasos mpl; **to be in ~ with one's rent** estar atrasado com o aluguel
arrest [ə'rɛst] VT prender, deter; (sb's attention) chamar, prender ▶ N detenção f, prisão f; **under ~** preso
arresting [ə'rɛstɪŋ] ADJ (fig: beauty) cativante; (: painting, novel) impressionante
arrival [ə'raɪvl] N chegada; **new ~** recém-chegado; (baby) recém-nascido
arrive [ə'raɪv] VI chegar
▶ **arrive at** VT FUS (fig) chegar a
arrogance ['ærəgəns] N arrogância
arrogant ['ærəgənt] ADJ arrogante
arrow ['ærəu] N flecha; (sign) seta
arse [ɑːs] (BRIT!) N cu m (!)
arsenal ['ɑːsɪnl] N arsenal m
arsenic ['ɑːsnɪk] N arsênico
arson ['ɑːsn] N incêndio premeditado
art [ɑːt] N arte f; (craft) ofício; (skill) habilidade f, jeito; **Arts** NPL (Sch) letras fpl; **work of ~** obra de arte
artefact ['ɑːtɪfækt] N artefato
arterial [ɑː'tɪərɪəl] ADJ (Anat) arterial; **~ road** estrada mestra
artery ['ɑːtərɪ] N (Med) artéria; (fig) estrada principal
artful ['ɑːtful] ADJ ardiloso, esperto
art gallery N museu m de belas artes; (small, private) galeria de arte
arthritis [ɑː'θraɪtɪs] N artrite f
artichoke ['ɑːtɪtʃəuk] N (globe artichoke) alcachofra; (also: **Jerusalem artichoke**) topinambo
article ['ɑːtɪkl] N artigo; **articles** NPL (BRIT Law: training) contrato de aprendizagem; **~s of clothing** peças fpl de vestuário; **~s of association** (Comm) estatutos mpl sociais
articulate [adj ɑː'tɪkjulɪt, vt ɑː'tɪkjuleɪt] ADJ (speech) bem articulado; (writing) bem escrito; (person) eloquente ▶ VT expressar
articulated lorry [ɑː'tɪkjuleɪtɪd-] (BRIT) N caminhão m or camião m (PT) articulado, jamanta
artifice ['ɑːtɪfɪs] N ardil m, artifício
artificial [ɑːtɪ'fɪʃəl] ADJ artificial; (limb) postiço; (person, manner) afetado
artificial insemination [-ɪnsɛmɪ'neɪʃən] N inseminação f artificial
artificial intelligence N inteligência artificial
artificial respiration N respiração f artificial
artillery [ɑː'tɪlərɪ] N artilharia
artisan ['ɑːtɪzæn] N artesão(-sã) m/f
artist ['ɑːtɪst] N artista m/f; (Mus) intérprete m/f
artistic [ɑː'tɪstɪk] ADJ artístico
artistry ['ɑːtɪstrɪ] N arte f, mestria
artless ['ɑːtlɪs] ADJ (innocent) natural, simples; (clumsy) desajeitado

art school N = escola de artes
ARV N ABBR (= *American Revised Version*) *tradução norte-americana da Bíblia*
AS (US) N ABBR (*Sch*: = *Associate in/of Science*) *título universitário* ▶ ABBR (*Post*) = **American Samoa**

(KEYWORD)

as [æz, əz] CONJ **1** (*referring to time*) quando; **as the years went by** no decorrer dos anos; **he came in as I was leaving** ele chegou quando eu estava saindo; **as from tomorrow** a partir de amanhã
2 (*in comparisons*) tão ... como, tanto(s) ... como; **as big as** tão grande como; **twice as big as** duas vezes maior que; **as much/many as** tanto/tantos como; **as much money/many books as** tanto dinheiro quanto/tantos livros quanto; **as soon as** logo que, assim que
3 (*since, because*) como; **as you can't come, I'll go without you** como você não pode vir, eu vou sem você
4 (*referring to manner, way*) como; **do as you wish** faça como quiser; **as she said** como ela disse
5 (*concerning*): **as for** *or* **to that** quanto a isso
6: **as if** *or* **though** como se; **he looked as if he was ill** ele parecia doente
▶ PREP (*in the capacity of*): **he works as a driver** ele trabalha como motorista; **he gave it to me as a present** ele me deu isso de presente; *see also* **long, such, well**

ASA N ABBR (= *American Standards Association*) *associação de padronização*
a.s.a.p. ABBR = **as soon as possible**
asbestos [æz'bɛstəs] N asbesto, amianto
ascend [ə'sɛnd] VT subir; (*throne*) ascender
ascendancy [ə'sɛndənsɪ] N predomínio, ascendência
ascendant [ə'sɛndənt] N: **to be in the ~** estar em alta
Ascension [ə'sɛnʃən] N (*Rel*): **the ~** a Ascensão
Ascension Island N ilha da Ascensão
ascent [ə'sɛnt] N subida; (*slope*) rampa; (*promotion*) ascensão f
ascertain [æsə'teɪn] VT averiguar, verificar
ascetic [ə'sɛtɪk] ADJ ascético
asceticism [ə'sɛtɪsɪzəm] N ascetismo
ASCII ['æskiː] N ABBR (= *American Standard Code for Information Interchange*) ASCII m
ascribe [ə'skraɪb] VT: **to ~ sth to** atribuir algo a
ASCU (US) N ABBR = **Association of State Colleges and Universities**
ASE N ABBR = **American Stock Exchange**
ASH [æʃ] (BRIT) N ABBR (= *Action on Smoking and Health*) liga antitabagista
ash [æʃ] N cinza; (*tree, wood*) freixo
ashamed [ə'ʃeɪmd] ADJ envergonhado; **to be ~ of** ter vergonha de; **to be ~ (of o.s.) for having done** ter vergonha de ter feito

ashen ['æʃn] ADJ cinzento
ashore [ə'ʃɔːʳ] ADV em terra; **to go ~** descer à terra, desembarcar
ashtray ['æʃtreɪ] N cinzeiro
Ash Wednesday N quarta-feira de cinzas
Asia ['eɪʃə] N Ásia
Asia Minor N Ásia Menor
Asian ['eɪʃən] ADJ, N asiático(-a)
Asiatic [eɪsɪ'ætɪk] ADJ asiático(-a)
aside [ə'saɪd] ADV à parte, de lado ▶ N aparte m; **~ from** além de
ask [ɑːsk] VT perguntar; (*invite*) convidar; **to ~ sb sth** perguntar algo a alguém; **to ~ sb for sth** pedir algo a alguém; **to ~ sb to do sth** pedir para alguém fazer algo; **to ~ sb the time** perguntar as horas a alguém; **to ~ sb about sth** perguntar a alguém sobre algo; **to ~ about the price** perguntar pelo preço; **to ~ (sb) a question** fazer uma pergunta (a alguém); **to ~ sb out to dinner** convidar alguém para jantar
▶ **ask after** VT FUS perguntar por
▶ **ask for** VT FUS pedir; **it's just ~ing for it** *or* **trouble** é procurar encrenca
askance [ə'skɑːns] ADV: **to look ~ at sb/sth** olhar alguém/algo de soslaio
askew [ə'skjuː] ADV torto
asking price ['ɑːskɪŋ-] N preço pedido
asleep [ə'sliːp] ADJ dormindo; **to fall ~** dormir, adormecer
ASLEF ['æzlɛf] (BRIT) N ABBR (= *Associated Society of Locomotive Engineers and Firemen*) sindicato dos ferroviários
asp [æsp] N áspide m *or* f
asparagus [əs'pærəgəs] N asparago (BR), espargo (PT)
asparagus tips NPL aspargos mpl
ASPCA N ABBR = **American Society for the Prevention of Cruelty to Animals**
aspect ['æspɛkt] N aspecto; (*direction in which a building etc faces*) direção f
aspersions [əs'pəːʃənz] NPL: **to cast ~ on** difamar, caluniar
asphalt ['æsfælt] N asfalto
asphyxiate [æs'fɪksɪeɪt] VT asfixiar ▶ VI asfixiar-se
asphyxiation [æsfɪksɪ'eɪʃən] N asfixia
aspirations [æspə'reɪʃəns] N (*hopes*) esperança; (*ambitions*) aspirações fpl
aspire [əs'paɪəʳ] VI: **to ~ to** aspirar a
aspirin ['æsprɪn] N aspirina
ass [æs] N jumento, burro; (*inf*) imbecil m/f; (US !) cu m (!)
assail [ə'seɪl] VT assaltar, atacar
assailant [ə'seɪlənt] N (*attacker*) assaltante m/f, atacante m/f; (*aggressor*) agressor(a) m/f
assassin [ə'sæsɪn] N assassino(-a)
assassinate [ə'sæsɪneɪt] VT assassinar
assassination [əsæsɪ'neɪʃən] N assassinato, assassínio
assault [ə'sɔːlt] N assalto; (*Law*): **~ (and battery)** vias fpl de fato ▶ VT assaltar, atacar; (*sexually*) agredir, violar

assemble [ə'sɛmbl] vt (*people*) reunir; (*objects*) juntar; (*Tech*) montar ▶ vi reunir-se

assembly [ə'sɛmblɪ] n (*meeting*) reunião f; (*institution*) assembleia; (*people*) congregação f; (*construction*) montagem f

assembly language n (*Comput*) linguagem f de montagem

assembly line n linha de montagem

assent [ə'sɛnt] n aprovação f ▶ vi: **to ~ (to sth)** consentir or assentir (em algo)

assert [ə'sə:t] vt afirmar; (*claim etc*) fazer valer; **to ~ o.s.** impor-se

assertion [ə'sə:ʃən] n afirmação f

assertive [ə'sə:tɪv] adj (*vigorous*) enérgico; (*forceful*) agressivo; (*dogmatic*) peremptório

assess [ə'sɛs] vt avaliar

assessment [ə'sɛsmənt] n avaliação f

assessor [ə'sɛsəʳ] n avaliador(a) m/f; (*of tax*) avaliador(a) do fisco

asset ['æsɛt] n (*property*) bem m; (*quality*) vantagem f, trunfo; **assets** npl (*property, funds*) bens mpl; (*Comm*) ativo

asset-stripping [-'strɪpɪŋ] n (*Comm*) venda em parcelas do patrimônio social

assiduous [ə'sɪdjuəs] adj assíduo

assign [ə'saɪn] vt (*date*) fixar; **to ~ (to)** (*task*) designar (a); (*resources*) destinar (a); (*cause, meaning*) atribuir (a)

assignment [ə'saɪnmənt] n tarefa

assimilate [ə'sɪmɪleɪt] vt assimilar; (*absorb: immigrants*) integrar

assimilation [əsɪmɪ'leɪʃən] n assimilação f

assist [ə'sɪst] vt ajudar; (*progress etc*) auxiliar; (*injured person etc*) socorrer

assistance [ə'sɪstəns] n ajuda, auxílio; (*welfare*) subsídio; (*to injured person*) socorro

assistant [ə'sɪstənt] n assistente m/f, auxiliar m/f; (brit: also: **shop assistant**) vendedor(a) m/f

assistant manager n subgerente m/f

assizes [ə'saɪzɪz] npl sessão f de tribunal superior

associate [*adj* ə'səuʃɪɪt, *vt, vi* ə'səuʃɪeɪt] adj associado; (*professor, director etc*) adjunto ▶ n (*colleague*) colega m/f; (*at work, member*) sócio(-a); (*in crime*) cúmplice m/f ▶ vi: **to ~ with sb** associar-se com alguém ▶ vt associar; **~ company** companhia ligada; **~ director** diretor(a) m/f associado(-a)

associated company [ə'səuʃɪeɪtɪd-] n companhia ligada

association [əsəusɪ'eɪʃən] n associação f; (*link*) ligação f; (*Comm*) sociedade f; **in ~ with** em parceria com

association football (brit) n futebol m

assorted [ə'sɔ:tɪd] adj sortido; **in ~ sizes** em vários tamanhos

assortment [ə'sɔ:tmənt] n (*of shapes, colours*) sortimento; (*of books, people*) variedade f

Asst. abbr = **assistant**

assuage [ə'sweɪdʒ] vt (*grief, pain*) aliviar, abrandar; (*thirst*) matar

assume [ə'sju:m] vt (*suppose*) supor, presumir;

(*responsibilities etc*) assumir; (*attitude, name*) adotar, tomar

assumed name [ə'sju:md-] n nome m falso

assumption [ə'sʌmpʃən] n (*supposition*) suposição f, presunção f; **on the ~ that** na suposição or hipótese que; (*on condition that*) com a condição de que

assurance [ə'ʃuərəns] n garantia; (*confidence*) confiança; (*insurance*) seguro

assure [ə'ʃuəʳ] vt assegurar; (*guarantee*) garantir; **to ~ sb that** garantir or assegurar a alguém que

AST (us) abbr (= *Atlantic Standard Time*) hora de inverno de Nova Iorque

asterisk ['æstərɪsk] n asterisco

astern [ə'stə:n] adv à popa; (*direction*) à ré

asteroid ['æstərɔɪd] n asteroide m

asthma ['æsmə] n asma

asthmatic [æs'mætɪk] adj, n asmático(-a)

astigmatism [ə'stɪgmətɪzəm] n astigmatismo

astir [ə'stə:ʳ] adv em agitação

astonish [ə'stɔnɪʃ] vt assombrar, espantar

astonishing [ə'stɔnɪʃɪŋ] adj espantoso, surpreendente

astonishingly [ə'stɔnɪʃɪŋlɪ] adv surpreendentemente

astonishment [ə'stɔnɪʃmənt] n assombro, espanto; **to my ~** para minha grande surpresa

astound [ə'staund] vt pasmar, estarrecer

astray [ə'streɪ] adv: **to go ~** (*person*) perder-se; (*letter etc*) extraviar-se; **to go ~ in one's calculations** cometer um erro em seus cálculos; **to lead ~** (*morally*) desencaminhar

astride [ə'straɪd] prep montado or a cavalo sobre

astringent [ə'strɪndʒənt] adj adstringente ▶ n adstringente m

astrologer [əs'trɔlədʒəʳ] n astrólogo(-a)

astrology [əs'trɔlədʒɪ] n astrologia

astronaut ['æstrənɔ:t] n astronauta m/f

astronomer [əs'trɔnəməʳ] n astrônomo(-a)

astronomical [æstrə'nɔmɪkəl] adj astronômico

astronomy [əs'trɔnəmɪ] n astronomia

astrophysics ['æstrəu'fɪzɪks] n astrofísica

astute [əs'tju:t] adj astuto

asunder [ə'sʌndəʳ] adv: **to put ~** separar; **to tear ~** rasgar

ASV n abbr (= *American Standard Version*) tradução da Bíblia

asylum [ə'saɪləm] n (*refuge*) asilo; (*hospital*) manicômio; *see also* **political asylum**

asylum seeker [-si:kəʳ] n solicitante m/f de asilo

asymmetric [eɪsɪ'mɛtrɪk], **asymmetrical** [eɪsɪ'mɛtrɪkl] adj assimétrico

(KEYWORD)

at [æt] prep **1** (*referring to position*) em; (*referring to direction*) a; **at the top** em cima; **at home/school** em casa/na escola; **at the baker's**

na padaria; **to look at sth** olhar para algo
2 (referring to time): **at 4 o'clock** às quatro
horas; **at night** à noite; **at Christmas** no
Natal; **at times** às vezes
3 (referring to rates, speed etc): **at £1 a kilo** a uma
libra o quilo; **two at a time** de dois em dois
4 (referring to manner): **at a stroke** de um
golpe; **at peace** em paz
5 (referring to activity): **to be at work** estar no
trabalho; **to play at cowboys** brincar de
mocinho; **to be good at sth** ser bom em algo
6 (referring to cause): **to be shocked/
surprised/annoyed at sth** ficar chocado/
surpreso/chateado com algo; **I went at his
suggestion** eu fui por causa da sugestão
dele
▶ N (symbol @) arroba

ate [eɪt] PT of **eat**
atheism ['eɪθɪɪzəm] N ateísmo
atheist ['eɪθɪɪst] N ateu/ateia m/f
Athenian [ə'θiːnɪən] ADJ, N ateniense m/f
Athens ['æθɪnz] N Atenas
athlete ['æθliːt] N atleta m/f
athletic [æθ'lɛtɪk] ADJ atlético
athletics [æθ'lɛtɪks] N atletismo
Atlantic [ət'læntɪk] ADJ atlântico ▶ N: **the ~
(Ocean)** o (oceano) Atlântico
atlas ['ætləs] N atlas m inv
Atlas Mountains NPL: **the ~** os montes Atlas
ATM ABBR (= automated teller machine) caixa
eletrônico m
atmosphere ['ætməsfɪər] N atmosfera; (fig)
ambiente m
atmospheric [ætməs'fɛrɪk] ADJ atmosférico
atmospherics [ætməs'fɛrɪks] NPL (Radio)
estática
atoll ['ætɔl] N atol m
atom ['ætəm] N átomo
atom bomb, atomic bomb N bomba atômica
atomic [ə'tɔmɪk] ADJ atômico
atomic bomb N = **atom bomb**
atomizer ['ætəmaɪzər] N atomizador m,
pulverizador m
atone [ə'təun] VI: **to ~ for** (sin) expiar;
(mistake) reparar
atonement [ə'təunmənt] N expiação f
ATP N ABBR (= Association of Tennis Professionals)
Associação f de Tenistas Profissionais
atrocious [ə'trəuʃəs] ADJ atroz; (very bad)
péssimo
atrocity [ə'trɔsɪtɪ] N atrocidade f
atrophy ['ætrəfɪ] N atrofia ▶ VT atrofiar ▶ VI
atrofiar-se
attach [ə'tætʃ] VT (fasten) prender; (document,
letter) juntar, anexar; (importance etc) dar;
(employee, troops) adir; **to be ~ed to sb/sth**
(like) ter afeição por alguém/algo; **to ~ a file
to an email** anexar um arquivo a um
e-mail; **the ~ed letter** a carta junta or
anexa
attaché [ə'tæʃeɪ] N adido(-a)
attaché case N pasta

attachment [ə'tætʃmənt] N (tool) acessório;
(to email) anexo; (love): **~ (to)** afeição f (por)
attack [ə'tæk] VT atacar; (subj: criminal)
assaltar; (task etc) empreender ▶ N ataque m;
(mugging etc) assalto; (on sb's life) atentado;
heart ~ ataque cardíaco or de coração
attacker [ə'tækər] N agressor(a) m/f; (criminal)
assaltante m/f
attain [ə'teɪn] VT (also: **attain to**: happiness,
results) alcançar, atingir; (: knowledge) obter
attainments [ə'teɪnmənts] NPL feito
attempt [ə'tɛmpt] N tentativa ▶ VT tentar;
to make an ~ on sb's life atentar contra a
vida de alguém; **he made no ~ to help** ele
não fez nada para ajudar
attempted [ə'tɛmptɪd] ADJ: **~ theft** etc (Law)
tentativa de roubo etc
attend [ə'tɛnd] VT (lectures) assistir a; (party)
presenciar; (school) cursar; (church) ir a;
(course) fazer; (patient) tratar; **to ~ (up)on**
acompanhar, servir
▶ **attend to** VT FUS (matter) encarregar-se de;
(speech etc) prestar atenção a; (needs, customer)
atender a; (patient) tratar de
attendance [ə'tɛndəns] N (being present)
comparecimento; (people present) assistência
attendant [ə'tɛndənt] N servidor(a) m/f;
(Theatre) arrumador(a) m/f ▶ ADJ
concomitante
attention [ə'tɛnʃən] N atenção f; (care)
cuidados mpl ▶ EXCL (Mil) sentido!; **at ~** (Mil)
em posição de sentido; **for the ~ of**
(Admin) atenção ...; **it has come to my ~
that ...** constatei que ...
attentive [ə'tɛntɪv] ADJ atento; (polite) cortês
attentively [ə'tɛntɪvlɪ] ADV atentamente
attenuate [ə'tɛnjueɪt] VT atenuar ▶ VI
atenuar-se
attest [ə'tɛst] VI: **to ~ to** atestar
attic ['ætɪk] N sótão m
attire [ə'taɪər] N traje m, roupa
attitude ['ætɪtjuːd] N atitude f; (view): **~ (to)**
atitude (para com)
attorney [ə'təːnɪ] N (US: lawyer) advogado(-a);
(having proxy) procurador(a) m/f
Attorney General N (BRIT) procurador(a) m/f
geral da Justiça; (US) Secretário de Justiça
attract [ə'trækt] VT atrair, chamar
attraction [ə'trækʃən] N atração f; (good point)
atrativo; **~ towards sth** atração por algo
attractive [ə'træktɪv] ADJ atraente; (idea, offer)
interessante
attribute [n 'ætrɪbjuːt, vt ə'trɪbjuːt] N atributo
▶ VT: **to ~ sth to** atribuir algo a
attrition [ə'trɪʃən] N: **war of ~** guerra de atrição
Atty. Gen. ABBR = **Attorney General**
ATV N ABBR (= all terrain vehicle) veículo
todo-terreno
aubergine ['əubəʒiːn] N beringela
auburn ['ɔːbən] ADJ castanho-avermelhado
auction ['ɔːkʃən] N (also: **sale by auction**)
leilão m ▶ VT leiloar; **to sell by ~** vender em
leilão; **to put up for ~** pôr em leilão

auctioneer [ɔːkʃəˈnɪəʳ] N leiloeiro(-a)
auction room N local m de leilão
audacious [ɔːˈdeɪʃəs] ADJ audaz, atrevido; (pej) descarado
audacity [ɔːˈdæsɪtɪ] N audácia, atrevimento; (pej) descaramento
audible [ˈɔːdɪbl] ADJ audível
audience [ˈɔːdɪəns] N (in theatre, concert etc) plateia; (of TV, radio programme) audiência; (of speech etc) auditório; (of writer, magazine) público; (interview) audiência
audio-typist [ˈɔːdɪəu-] N datilógrafo(-a) (de textos ditados em fita)
audiovisual [ɔːdɪəuˈvɪzjuəl] ADJ audiovisual
audiovisual aid [ˈɔːdɪəuvɪzjuəl-] N recursos mpl audiovisuais
audit [ˈɔːdɪt] VT fazer a auditoria de ▶ N auditoria
audition [ɔːˈdɪʃən] N audição f
auditor [ˈɔːdɪtəʳ] N auditor(a) m/f
auditorium [ɔːdɪˈtɔːrɪəm] (pl **auditoria**) N auditório
Aug. ABBR = **August**
augment [ɔːgˈmɛnt] VT, VI aumentar
augur [ˈɔːgəʳ] VI: **it ~s well** é de bom augúrio ▶ VT (be a sign of) augurar, pressagiar
August [ˈɔːgəst] N agosto; see also **July**
august [ɔːˈgʌst] ADJ augusto, imponente
aunt [ɑːnt] N tia
auntie [ˈɑːntɪ] N titia
aunty [ˈɑːntɪ] N titia
au pair [ˈəuˈpɛəʳ] N (also: **au pair girl**) au pair f
aura [ˈɔːrə] N (of person) ar m, aspecto; (of place) ambiente m
auspices [ˈɔːspɪsɪz] NPL: **under the ~ of** sob os auspícios de
auspicious [ɔːsˈpɪʃəs] ADJ favorável; (occasion) propício
austere [ɔsˈtɪəʳ] ADJ austero; (manner) severo
austerity [ɔsˈtɛrətɪ] N simplicidade f; (Econ) privação f
Australasia [ɔːstrəˈleɪzɪə] N Australásia
Australia [ɔsˈtreɪlɪə] N Austrália
Australian [ɔsˈtreɪlɪən] ADJ, N australiano(-a)
Austria [ˈɔstrɪə] N Áustria
Austrian [ˈɔstrɪən] ADJ, N austríaco(-a)
AUT (BRIT) N ABBR (= Association of University Teachers) sindicato universitário
authentic [ɔːˈθɛntɪk] ADJ autêntico
authenticate [ɔːˈθɛntɪkeɪt] VT autenticar
authenticity [ɔːθɛnˈtɪsɪtɪ] N autenticidade f
author [ˈɔːθə] N autor(a) m/f
authoritarian [ɔːθɔrɪˈtɛərɪən] ADJ autoritário
authoritative [ɔːˈθɔrɪtətɪv] ADJ (account) autorizado; (manner) autoritário
authority [ɔːˈθɔrɪtɪ] N autoridade f; (government body) jurisdição f; (permission) autorização f; **the authorities** NPL (ruling body) as autoridades; **to have ~ to do sth** ter autorização para fazer algo
authorization [ɔːθəraɪˈzeɪʃən] N autorização f
authorize [ˈɔːθəraɪz] VT autorizar
authorized capital [ˈɔːθəraɪzd-] N (Comm)

capital m autorizado
authorship [ˈɔːθəʃɪp] N autoria
autistic [ɔːˈtɪstɪk] ADJ autista
auto [ˈɔːtəu] (US) N carro, automóvel m ▶ CPD (industry) automobilístico
autobiographical [ɔːtəbaɪəˈgræfɪkl] ADJ autobiográfico
autobiography [ɔːtəbaɪˈɔgrəfɪ] N autobiografia
autocratic [ɔːtəˈkrætɪk] ADJ autocrático
autograph [ˈɔːtəgrɑːf] N autógrafo ▶ VT (photo etc) autografar
automat [ˈɔːtəmæt] N (vending machine) autômato; (US: restaurant) restaurante m automático
automata [ɔːˈtɔmətə] NPL of **automaton**
automated [ˈɔːtəmeɪtɪd] ADJ automatizado
automatic [ɔːtəˈmætɪk] ADJ automático ▶ N (gun) pistola automática; (washing machine) máquina de lavar roupa automática; (BRIT: car) carro automático
automatically [ɔːtəˈmætɪklɪ] ADV automaticamente
automatic data processing N processamento automático de dados
automation [ɔːtəˈmeɪʃən] N automação f
automaton [ɔːˈtɔmətən] (pl **automata**) N autômato
automobile [ˈɔːtəməbiːl] (US) N carro, automóvel m ▶ CPD (industry, accident) automobilístico
autonomous [ɔːˈtɔnəməs] ADJ autônomo
autonomy [ɔːˈtɔnəmɪ] N autonomia
autopsy [ˈɔːtɔpsɪ] N autópsia
autumn [ˈɔːtəm] N outono
auxiliary [ɔːgˈzɪlɪərɪ] ADJ, N auxiliar m/f
AV N ABBR (= Authorized Version) tradução inglesa da Bíblia ▶ ABBR = **audiovisual**
Av. ABBR (= avenue) Av., Avda.
avail [əˈveɪl] VT: **to ~ o.s. of** aproveitar, valer-se de ▶ N: **to no ~** em vão, inutilmente
availability [əveɪləˈbɪlɪtɪ] N disponibilidade f
available [əˈveɪləbl] ADJ disponível; (time) livre; **every ~ means** todos os recursos à sua (or nossa etc) disposição; **is the manager ~?** o gerente pode me atender?; (on phone) queria falar com o gerente; **to make sth ~ to sb** pôr algo à disposição de alguém
avalanche [ˈævəlɑːnʃ] N avalanche f
avant-garde [ˈævɑ̃ˈgɑːd] ADJ de vanguarda
avarice [ˈævərɪs] N avareza
avaricious [ævəˈrɪʃəs] ADJ avarento, avaro
Ave. ABBR (= avenue) Av., Avda.
avenge [əˈvɛndʒ] VT vingar
avenue [ˈævənjuː] N avenida; (drive) caminho; (means) solução f
average [ˈævərɪdʒ] N média ▶ ADJ (mean) médio; (ordinary) regular ▶ VT alcançar uma média de; (calculate) calcular a média de; **on ~** em média; **above/below (the) ~** acima/abaixo da média
▶ **average out** VT calcular a média de ▶ VI: **to ~ out at** dar uma média de

averse [ə'vəːs] ADJ: **to be ~ to sth/doing sth** ser avesso or pouco disposto a algo/a fazer algo; **I wouldn't be ~ to a drink** eu aceitaria uma bebida

aversion [ə'vəːʃən] N aversão f

avert [ə'vəːt] VT prevenir; *(blow, one's eyes)* desviar

aviary ['eɪvɪərɪ] N aviário, viveiro de aves

aviation [eɪvɪ'eɪʃən] N aviação f

avid ['ævɪd] ADJ ávido

avidly ['ævɪdlɪ] ADV avidamente

avocado [ævə'kɑːdəu] N (BRIT: *also:* **avocado pear**) abacate m

avoid [ə'vɔɪd] VT evitar

avoidable [ə'vɔɪdəbl] ADJ evitável

avoidance [ə'vɔɪdəns] N evitação f

avowed [ə'vaud] ADJ confesso, declarado

AVP (US) N ABBR = **assistant vice-president**

AWACS ['eɪwæks] N ABBR (= *airborne warning and control system*) AWACS m (*sistema aerotransportado de alerta e de controle*)

await [ə'weɪt] VT esperar, aguardar; **~ing attention/delivery** (*Comm*) a ser(em) atendido(s)/entregue(s); **long ~ed** longamente esperado

awake [ə'weɪk] ADJ acordado ▶ VT, VI (*pt* **awoke,** *pp* **awoken**) despertar, acordar; **~ to** atento a; **to be ~** estar acordado; **he was still ~** ele ainda estava acordado

awakening [ə'weɪkənɪŋ] N despertar m

award [ə'wɔːd] N (*prize*) prêmio, condecoração f; (*Law: damages*) sentença; (*act*) concessão f ▶ VT outorgar, conceder; (*damages*) determinar o pagamento de

aware [ə'wɛəʳ] ADJ: **~ of** (*conscious*) consciente de; (*informed*) informado de or sobre; **to become ~ of** reparar em, saber de; **politically/socially ~** conscientizado politicamente/socialmente; **I am fully ~ that ...** eu compreendo perfeitamente que ...

awareness [ə'wɛənɪs] N consciência; (*knowledge*) conhecimento; **to develop people's ~ (of)** conscientizar o público (de)

awash [ə'wɔʃ] ADJ: **~ with** (*also fig*) inundado de

away [ə'weɪ] ADV fora; (*faraway*) muito longe; **two kilometres ~** a dois quilômetros de distância; **two hours ~ by car** a duas horas de carro; **the holiday was two weeks ~** faltavam duas semanas para as férias; **~ from** longe de; **he's ~ for a week** está ausente uma semana; **he's ~ in Miami** ele foi para Miami; **to take ~** levar; **to work/pedal** *etc* **~** trabalhar/pedalar *etc* sem parar; **to fade ~** (*colour*) desbotar; (*enthusiasm, sound*) diminuir

away game N (*Sport*) jogo de fora

away match N (*Sport*) jogo de fora

awe [ɔː] N temor m respeitoso

awe-inspiring ADJ imponente

awesome ['ɔːsəm] ADJ ≈ awe-inspiring

awestruck ['ɔːstrʌk] ADJ pasmado

awful ['ɔːfəl] ADJ terrível, horrível; (*quantity*): **an ~ lot of** um monte de

awfully ['ɔːfəlɪ] ADV (*very*) muito

awhile [ə'waɪl] ADV por algum tempo, um pouco

awkward ['ɔːkwəd] ADJ (*person, movement*) desajeitado; (*shape*) incômodo; (*problem*) difícil; (*situation*) embaraçoso, delicado

awkwardness ['ɔːkwədnəs] N (*embarrassment*) embaraço

awl [ɔːl] N sovela

awning ['ɔːnɪŋ] N toldo

awoke [ə'wəuk] PT *of* **awake**

awoken [ə'wəukən] PP *of* **awake**

AWOL ['eɪwɔl] ABBR (*Mil*) = **absent without leave**

awry [ə'raɪ] ADV: **to be ~** estar de viés or de esguelha; **to go ~** sair mal

axe, (US) **ax** [æks] N machado ▶ VT (*employee*) despedir; (*project etc*) abandonar; (*jobs*) reduzir; **to have an ~ to grind** (*fig*) ter interesse pessoal, puxar a brasa para a sua sardinha (*inf*)

axes[1] ['æksɪz] NPL *of* **axe**

axes[2] ['æksiːz] NPL *of* **axis**

axiom ['æksɪəm] N axioma m

axiomatic [æksɪəu'mætɪk] ADJ axiomático

axis ['æksɪs] (*pl* **axes**) N eixo

axle ['æksl] N (*Aut*) eixo

ay, aye [aɪ] EXCL (*yes*) sim ▶ N: **the ayes** os votos a favor

AYH N ABBR = **American Youth Hostels**

AZ (US) ABBR (*Post*) = **Arizona**

azalea [ə'zeɪlɪə] N azaleia

Azores [ə'zɔːz] NPL: **the ~** os Açores

Aztec ['æztɛk] ADJ, N asteca m/f

azure ['eɪʒəʳ] ADJ azul-celeste *inv*

Bb

B, b [biː] N (*letter*) B, b m; (*Mus*): **B** si m; **B for Benjamin** (*BRIT*) *or* **Baker** (*US*) B de Beatriz; **B road** (*BRIT Aut*) via secundária

b. ABBR = **born**

BA N ABBR = **British Academy**; (*Sch*) = **Bachelor of Arts**

babble ['bæbl] VI balbuciar; (*brook*) murmurinhar ▸ N balbucio

baboon [bəˈbuːn] N babuíno

baby ['beɪbɪ] N neném m/f, nenê m/f, bebê m/f; (*US inf*) querido(-a)

baby carriage (*US*) N carrinho de bebê

baby food N papinha de bebê

baby grand N (*also*: **baby grand piano**) piano de ¼ de cauda

babyhood ['beɪbɪhud] N primeira infância

babyish ['beɪbɪɪʃ] ADJ infantil

baby-minder (*BRIT*) N ≈ babá f

baby-sit (*irreg: like* **sit**) VI tomar conta da(s) criança(s)

baby-sitter N baby-sitter m/f

baby wipe N lenço umedecido

bachelor ['bætʃələʳ] N solteiro; (*Sch*): **B~ of Arts** ≈ bacharel m em Letras; **B~ of Science** ≈ bacharel m em Ciências

bachelorhood ['bætʃələhud] N celibato

bachelor party (*US*) N despedida de solteiro

back [bæk] N (*of person*) costas fpl; (*of animal*) lombo; (*of hand*) dorso; (*of car, train*) parte f traseira; (*of house*) fundos mpl; (*of chair*) encosto; (*of page*) verso; (*of book*) lombada; (*of crowd*) fundo; (*of coin*) reverso; (*Football*) zagueiro (*BR*), defesa m (*PT*) ▸ VT (*financially*) patrocinar; (*candidate: also:* **back up**) apoiar; (*horse: at races*) apostar em; (*car*) dar ré com ▸ VI (*car etc: also:* **back up**) dar ré (*BR*), fazer marcha atrás (*PT*) ▸ CPD (*payment*) atrasado; (*Aut: seats, wheels*) de trás ▸ ADV (*not forward*) para trás; (*returned*) de volta; **throw the ball ~** devolva a bola; **he called ~** (*again*) chamou de novo; **to have one's ~ to the wall** (*fig*) estar acuado; **to break the ~ of a job** (*BRIT*) fazer o mais difícil de um trabalho; **at the ~ of my mind was the thought that ...** no meu íntimo havia a ideia que ...; **~ to front** pelo avesso, às avessas; **~ garden/room** jardim m / quarto dos fundos; **to take a ~ seat** (*fig*) colocar-se em segundo plano; **when will you be ~?** quando você estará de volta?; **he ran ~** voltou correndo; **can I have it ~?** pode devolvê-lo?

▸ **back down** VI desistir

▸ **back on to** VT FUS: **the house ~s on to the golf course** a casa dá fundas para o campo de golfe

▸ **back out** VI (*of promise*) voltar atrás, recuar

▸ **back up** VT (*support*) apoiar; (*Comput*) fazer um backup de

backache ['bækeɪk] N dor f nas costas

backbencher [bæk'bentʃəʳ] (*BRIT*) N *membro do parlamento sem pasta*

backbiting ['bækbaɪtɪŋ] N maledicência

backbone ['bækbəʊn] N coluna vertebral; (*fig*) esteio; **he's the ~ of the organization** ele é o pilar *or* esteio da organização

backchat ['bæktʃæt] (*BRIT inf*) N insolências fpl

backcloth (*BRIT*) N pano de fundo

backcomb ['bækkəʊm] (*BRIT*) VT encrespar

backdate [bæk'deɪt] VT (*letter*) antedatar; **~d pay rise** aumento de vencimento com efeito retroativo

backdrop ['bækdrɔp] N = **backcloth**

backer ['bækəʳ] N (*supporter*) partidário(-a); (*Comm: in partnership*) comanditário(-a); (*: financier*) financiador(a) m/f

backfire [bæk'faɪəʳ] VI (*Aut*) engasgar; (*plan*) sair pela culatra

backgammon [bæk'gæmən] N gamão m

background ['bækgraund] N fundo; (*of events*) antecedentes mpl; (*basic knowledge*) bases fpl; (*experience*) conhecimentos mpl, experiência ▸ CPD (*noise, music*) de fundo; **~ reading** leitura de fundo; **family ~** antecedentes mpl familiares

backhand ['bækhænd] N (*Tennis: also:* **backhand stroke**) revés m

backhanded ['bækhændɪd] ADJ (*fig*) ambíguo

backhander ['bækhændəʳ] (*BRIT*) N (*bribe*) propina, peita (*PT*)

backing ['bækɪŋ] N (*fig*) apoio; (*Comm*) patrocínio; (*Mus*) fundo (musical)

backlash ['bæklæʃ] N reação f

backlog ['bæklɔg] N: **~ of work** atrasos mpl

back number N (*of magazine etc*) número atrasado

backpack ['bækpæk] N mochila

backpacker ['bækpækə^r] N excursionista *m/f* com mochila

back pay N salário atrasado

backpedal ['bækpɛdl] VI (*fig*) recuar, voltar atrás

backside [bæk'saɪd] (*inf*) N traseiro

backslash ['bækslæʃ] N contrabarra

backslide ['bækslaɪd] (*irreg: like* **slide**) VI ter uma recaída

backspace ['bækspeɪs] VI (*Typing*) retroceder

backstage [bæk'steɪdʒ] ADV nos bastidores

back-street ADJ (*abortion*) clandestino; ~ **abortionist** aborteiro(-a)

backstroke ['bækstrəuk] N nado de costas

backtrack ['bæktræk] VI (*fig*) = **backpedal**

backup ['bækʌp] ADJ (*train, plane*) reserva *inv*; (*Comput*) de backup ▶ N (*support*) apoio; (*Comput: also:* **backup file**) backup *m*; (*US: congestion*) congestionamento

backward ['bækwəd] ADJ (*movement*) para trás; (*person, country*) atrasado; (*shy*) tímido; ~ **and forward movement** movimento de vaivém

backwards ['bækwədz] ADV (*move, go*) para trás; (*read a list*) às avessas; (*fall*) de costas; **to know sth ~** (*BRIT*) *or* ~ **and forwards** (*US*) (*inf*) saber algo de cor e salteado

backwater ['bækwɔ:tə^r] N (*fig: backward place*) lugar *m* atrasado; (: *remote place*) fim-do-mundo *m*

backyard [bæk'jɑ:d] N quintal *m*

bacon ['beɪkən] N toucinho, bacon *m*

bacteria [bæk'tɪərɪə] NPL bactérias *fpl*

bacteriology [bæktɪərɪ'ɔlədʒɪ] N bacteriologia

bad [bæd] ADJ mau/má, ruim; (*child*) levado; (*mistake, injury*) grave; (*meat, food*) estragado; **his ~ leg** sua perna machucada; **to go ~** estragar-se; **to have a ~ time of it** passar um mau pedaço; **I feel ~ about it** (*guilty*) eu me sinto culpado (por isso); **in ~ faith** de má fé

bad debt N crédito duvidoso

bade [bæd] PT *of* **bid**

badge [bædʒ] N (*of school etc*) emblema *m*; (*policeman's*) crachá *m*

badger ['bædʒə^r] N texugo ▶ VT acossar

badly ['bædlɪ] ADV mal; ~ **wounded** gravemente ferido; **he needs it ~** faz-lhe grande falta; **things are going ~** as coisas vão mal; **to be ~ off (for money)** estar com pouco dinheiro

bad-mannered [-'mænəd] ADJ mal-educado, sem modas

badminton ['bædmɪntən] N badminton *m*

bad-tempered ADJ mal humorado; (*temporary*) de mau humor

baffle ['bæfl] VT (*puzzle*) deixar perplexo, desconcertar

baffled ['bæfld] ADJ perplexo

baffling ['bæflɪŋ] ADJ desconcertante

bag [bæg] N saco, bolsa; (*handbag*) bolsa; (*satchel, shopping bag*) sacola; (*case*) mala; (*of hunter*) caça ▶ VT (*inf: take*) pegar; (*game*)

matar; (*Tech*) ensacar; ~**s of …** (*inf: lots of*) … de sobra; **to pack one's ~s** fazer as malas; ~**s under the eyes** olheiras *fpl*

bagful ['bægful] N saco cheio

baggage ['bægɪdʒ] N bagagem *f*

baggage allowance N franquia de bagagem

baggage checkroom [-'tʃɛkru:m] (*US*) N depósito de bagagem

baggage claim N (*at airport*) recebimento de bagagem

baggy ['bægɪ] ADJ folgado, largo

Baghdad [bæg'dæd] N Bagdá *f*

bagpipes ['bægpaɪps] NPL gaita de foles

bag-snatcher [-'snætʃə^r] (*BRIT*) N trombadinha *m*

bag-snatching [-'snætʃɪŋ] (*BRIT*) N roubo de bolsa

Bahamas [bə'hɑ:məz] NPL: **the ~** as Bahamas

Bahrain [bɑ:'reɪn] N Barein *m*

bail [beɪl] N (*payment*) fiança; (*release*) liberdade *f* sob fiança ▶ VT (*prisoner: grant bail to*) libertar sob fiança; (*boat: also:* **bail out**) baldear a água de; **on ~** sob fiança; **to be released on ~** ser posto em liberdade mediante fiança; *see also* **bale** ▶ **bail out** VT (*prisoner*) afiançar; (*fig: help out*) socorrer

bailiff ['beɪlɪf] N (*Law: BRIT*) oficial *m/f* de justiça (*BR*) *or* de diligências (*PT*); (: *US*) funcionário encarregado de acompanhar presos no tribunal

bait [beɪt] N isca, engodo; (*for criminal etc*) atrativo, chamariz *m* ▶ VT iscar, cevar; (*person*) apoquentar

bake [beɪk] VT cozinhar ao forno; (*Tech: clay etc*) cozer ▶ VI assar; (*be hot*) fazer um calor terrível

baked beans [beɪkt-] NPL feijão *m* cozido com molho de tomate

baked potato N batata assada com a casca

baker ['beɪkə^r] N padeiro(-a)

bakery ['beɪkərɪ] N (*for bread*) padaria; (*for cakes*) confeitaria

baking ['beɪkɪŋ] N (*act*) cozimento; (*batch*) fornada

baking powder N fermento em pó

baking tin N (*for cake*) fôrma; (*for meat*) assadeira

baking tray N tabuleiro

balaclava [bælə'klɑ:və] N (*also:* **balaclava helmet**) capuz *f*

balance ['bæləns] N equilíbrio; (*scales*) balança; (*Comm*) balanço; (*remainder*) resto, saldo ▶ VT equilibrar; (*budget*) nivelar; (*account*) fazer o balanço de; (*compensate*) contrabalançar; (*pros and cons*) pesar; ~ **of trade/payments** balança comercial/ balanço de pagamentos; ~ **carried forward** transporte; ~ **brought forward** transporte; **to ~ the books** fazer o balanço dos livros

balanced ['bælənst] ADJ (*report*) objetivo; (*personality, diet*) equilibrado

balance sheet N balanço geral

balcony ['bælkənɪ] N (open) varanda; (closed) galeria; (in theatre) balcão m
bald [bɔːld] ADJ calvo, careca; (tyre) careca
baldness ['bɔːldnɪs] N calvície f
bale [beɪl] N (Agr) fardo
  ▶ **bale out** VI (of a plane) atirar-se de para-quedas ▶ VT (Naut: water) baldear; (: boat) baldear a água de
Balearic Islands [bælɪ'ærɪk-] NPL: **the ~** as ilhas Baleares
baleful ['beɪlful] ADJ (look) triste; (sinister) funesto, sinistro
balk [bɔːk] VI: **to ~ (at)** (subj: person) relutar (contra); (: horse) refugar, empacar (diante de); **to ~ at doing** relutar em fazer
Balkan ['bɔːlkən] ADJ balcânico ▶ N: **the ~s** os Balcãs
ball [bɔːl] N bola; (of wool, string) novelo; (dance) baile m; **to play ~ with sb** jogar bola com alguém; (fig) fazer o jogo de alguém; **to be on the ~** (fig: competent) ser competente or batuta (inf); (: alert) estar alerta; **to start the ~ rolling** (fig) dar começo, dar o pontapé inicial; **the ~ is in their court** (fig) é a vez deles de agir
ballad ['bæləd] N balada
ballast ['bæləst] N lastro
ball bearings NPL rolimã m
ball cock N torneira com boia
ballerina [bælə'riːnə] N bailarina
ballet ['bæleɪ] N balé m
ballet dancer N bailarino(-a)
ballistic [bə'lɪstɪk] ADJ balístico
ballistics [bə'lɪstɪks] N balística
balloon [bə'luːn] N balão m; (hot air balloon) balão de ar quente ▶ VI (sails etc) inflar(-se); (prices) disparar
balloonist [bə'luːnɪst] N aeróstata m/f
ballot ['bælət] N votação f
ballot box N urna
ballot paper N cédula eleitoral
ballpark ['bɔːlpɑːk] (US) N estádio de beisebol
ballpark figure (inf) N número aproximado
ballpoint ['bɔːlpɔɪnt], **ballpoint pen** N (caneta) esferográfica
balls [bɔːlz] (!) NPL colhões mpl (!), ovos mpl (!)
balm [bɑːm] N bálsamo
balmy ['bɑːmɪ] ADJ (breeze, air) suave, fragrante; (BRIT inf) = **barmy**
BALPA ['bælpə] N ABBR (= British Airline Pilots' Association) sindicato dos aeronautas
balsa ['bɔːlsə], **balsa wood** N pau-de-balsa m
balsam ['bɔːlsəm] N bálsamo
Baltic ['bɔːltɪk] N: **the ~ (Sea)** o (mar) Báltico
balustrade [bæləstreɪd] N balaustrada
bamboo [bæm'buː] N bambu m
bamboozle [bæm'buːzl] (inf) VT embromar, trapacear
ban [bæn] N proibição f, interdição f; (suspension, exclusion) exclusão f ▶ VT proibir, interditar; (exclude) excluir; **he was ~ned from driving** (BRIT) cassaram-lhe a carteira de motorista

banal [bə'nɑːl] ADJ banal
banana [bə'nɑːnə] N banana
band [bænd] N (group) bando, banda; (gang) quadrilha; (at a dance) orquestra; (Mil) banda; (strip) faixa, cinta
  ▶ **band together** VI juntar-se, associar-se
bandage ['bændɪdʒ] N atadura (BR), ligadura (PT) ▶ VT enfaixar
Band-Aid® ['bændeɪd] (US) N esparadrapo
B & B N ABBR = **bed and breakfast**
bandit ['bændɪt] N bandido
bandstand ['bændstænd] N coreto
bandwagon ['bændwægən] N: **to jump on the ~** (fig) entrar na roda, ir na onda
bandy ['bændɪ] VT (jokes, insults) trocar
  ▶ **bandy about** VT usar a torto e a direito
bandy-legged ADJ cambaio, de pernas tortas
bane [beɪn] N: **it** (or **he** etc) **is the ~ of my life** é a maldição da minha vida
bang [bæŋ] N estalo; (of door) estrondo; (of gun, exhaust) explosão f; (blow) pancada ▶ EXCL bum!, bumba! ▶ VT bater com força; (door) fechar com violência ▶ VI produzir estrondo; (door) bater; (fireworks) soltar ▶ ADV (BRIT inf): **to be ~ on time** chegar na hora exata; **to ~ at the door** bater à porta com violência; **to ~ into sth** bater em algo
banger ['bæŋər] N (BRIT: car: also: **old banger**) calhambeque m, lata-velha; (inf: sausage) salsicha; (firework) bomba (de São João)
Bangkok [bæŋ'kɔk] N Bangcoc
Bangladesh [bæŋglə'dɛʃ] N Bangladesh m (no article)
bangle ['bæŋgl] N bracelete m
bangs [bæŋz] (US) NPL (fringe) franja
banish ['bænɪʃ] VT banir
banister ['bænɪstər] N, **banisters** ['bænɪstəz] NPL corrimão m
banjo ['bændʒəu] (pl **banjoes** or **banjos**) N banjo
bank [bæŋk] N banco; (of river, lake) margem f; (of earth) rampa, ladeira ▶ VI (Aviat) ladear-se; (Comm): **they ~ with Pitt's** eles têm conta no banco Pitt's
  ▶ **bank on** VT FUS contar com, apostar em
bank account N conta bancária
bank card N cartão m de garantia de cheques
bank charges (BRIT) NPL encargos mpl bancários
bank draft N saque m bancário
banker ['bæŋkər] N banqueiro(-a); **~'s card** (BRIT) cartão m de garantia de cheques; **~'s order** (BRIT) ordem f bancária
bank giro N transferência bancária
Bank holiday (BRIT) N feriado nacional
banking ['bæŋkɪŋ] N transações fpl bancárias; (job) profissão f de banqueiro
banking hours NPL horário de banco
bank loan N empréstimo bancário
bank manager N gerente m/f de banco
banknote ['bæŋknəut] N nota (bancária)
bank rate N taxa bancária

bankrupt ['bæŋkrʌpt] N falido(-a), quebrado(-a) ▶ ADJ falido, quebrado; **to go ~** falir; **to be ~** estar falido/quebrado

bankruptcy ['bæŋkrʌptsɪ] N falência; *(fraudulent)* bancarrota

bank statement N extrato bancário

banner ['bænəʳ] N faixa

bannister ['bænɪstəʳ] N, **bannisters** ['bænɪstəz] NPL = **banister**

banns [bænz] NPL proclamas *fpl*

banquet ['bæŋkwɪt] N banquete *m*

bantamweight ['bæntəmweɪt] N peso-galo

banter ['bæntəʳ] N caçoada

baptism ['bæptɪzəm] N batismo

Baptist ['bæptɪst] N batista *m/f*

baptize [bæp'taɪz] VT batizar

bar [bɑːʳ] N *(gen, of chocolate)* barra; *(rod)* vara; *(of window etc)* grade *f*; *(fig: hindrance)* obstáculo; *(: prohibition)* impedimento; *(pub)* bar *m*; *(counter: in pub)* balcão *m* ▶ VT *(road)* obstruir; *(window)* trancar; *(person)* excluir; *(activity)* proibir ▶ PREP: **~ none** sem exceção; **~ of soap** sabonete *m*; **behind ~s** *(prisoner)* atrás das grades; **the B~** *(Law: profession)* a advocacia; *(people)* o corpo de advogados

Barbados [bɑː'beɪdɔs] N Barbados *m (no article)*

barbaric [bɑː'bærɪk] ADJ bárbaro

barbarous ['bɑːbərəs] ADJ bárbaro

barbecue ['bɑːbɪkjuː] N churrasco

barbed wire ['bɑːbd-] N arame *m* farpado

barber ['bɑːbəʳ] N barbeiro, cabeleireiro

barbiturate [bɑː'bɪtjurɪt] N barbitúrico

Barcelona [bɑːsə'ləunə] N Barcelona

bar chart N gráfico de barras

bar code N código de barras

bare [bɛəʳ] ADJ despido; *(head)* descoberto; *(trees, vegetation)* sem vegetação; *(minimum)* básico ▶ VT *(body, teeth)* mostrar; **the ~ essentials** o imprescindível

bareback ['bɛəbæk] ADV em pelo, sem arreios

barefaced ['bɛəfeɪst] ADJ descarado

barefoot ['bɛəfut] ADJ, ADV descalço

bareheaded [bɛə'hɛdɪd] ADJ, ADV de cabeça descoberta

barely ['bɛəlɪ] ADV apenas, mal

Barents Sea ['bærənts-] N: **the ~** o mar de Barents

bargain ['bɑːgɪn] N *(deal)* negócio; *(agreement)* acordo; *(good buy)* pechincha ▶ VI *(trade)* negociar; *(haggle)* regatear; *(negotiate)* **to ~ (with sb)** pechinchar (com alguém); **into the ~** ainda por cima
▶ **bargain for** *(inf)* VT FUS: **he got more than he ~ed for** ele conseguiu mais do que pediu

bargaining ['bɑːgənɪŋ] N *(haggling)* regateio; *(talks)* negociações *fpl*

barge [bɑːdʒ] N barcaça
▶ **barge in** VI irromper
▶ **barge into** VT FUS *(collide with)* atropelar; *(interrupt)* intrometer-se em

baritone ['bærɪtəun] N barítono

barium meal ['bɛərɪəm-] N contraste *m* de bário

bark [bɑːk] N *(of tree)* casca; *(of dog)* latido ▶ VI latir

barley ['bɑːlɪ] N cevada

barley sugar N maltose *f*

barmaid ['bɑːmeɪd] N garçonete *f* (BR), empregada (de bar) (PT)

barman ['bɑːmən] *(irreg: like* **man***)* N garçom *m* (BR), empregado (de bar) (PT)

barmy ['bɑːmɪ] (BRIT *inf*) ADJ maluco

barn [bɑːn] N celeiro

barnacle ['bɑːnəkl] N craca

barometer [bə'rɔmɪtəʳ] N barômetro

baron ['bærən] N barão *m*; *(of press, industry)* magnata *m*

baroness ['bærənɪs] N baronesa

barracks ['bærəks] NPL quartel *m*, caserna

barrage ['bærɑːʒ] N *(Mil)* fogo de barragem; *(dam)* barragem *f*; *(fig)*: **a ~ of questions** uma saraivada de perguntas

barrel ['bærəl] N barril *m*; *(of gun)* cano

barrel organ N realejo

barren ['bærən] ADJ *(sterile)* estéril; *(land)* árido

barricade [bærɪ'keɪd] N barricada ▶ VT barricar; **to ~ o.s. (in)** basrricar-se (em)

barrier ['bærɪəʳ] N barreira; *(fig: to progress etc)* obstáculo; (BRIT: *also*: **crash barrier**) cerca entre as pistas

barrier cream (BRIT) N creme *m* protetor

barring ['bɑːrɪŋ] PREP exceto, salvo

barrister ['bærɪstəʳ] (BRIT) N advogado(-a), causídico(-a)

barrow ['bærəu] N *(wheelbarrow)* carrinho (de mão)

bar stool N tamborete *m* de bar

bartender ['bɑːtɛndəʳ] (US) N garçom *m* (BR), empregado (de bar) (PT)

barter ['bɑːtəʳ] N permuta, troca ▶ VT: **to ~ sth for sth** trocar algo por algo

base [beɪs] N base *f* ▶ VT *(troops)*: **to be ~d at** estar estacionado em; *(opinion, belief)*: **to ~ sth on** basear *or* fundamentar algo em ▶ ADJ *(thoughts)* sujo, baixo, vil; **coffee-~d** à base de café; **a Rio-~d firm** uma empresa sediada no Rio; **I'm ~d in London** estou sediado em Londres

baseball ['beɪsbɔːl] N beisebol *m*

baseboard ['beɪsbɔːd] (US) N rodapé *m*

base camp N base *f* de operações

Basel ['bɑːzl] N = **Basle**

basement ['beɪsmənt] N *(in house)* porão *m*; *(in shop etc)* subsolo

base rate N taxa de base

bases¹ ['beɪsɪz] NPL *of* **base**

bases² ['beɪsiːz] NPL *of* **basis**

bash [bæʃ] *(inf)* VT *(with fist)* dar soco *or* murro em; *(with object)* bater em ▶ N (BRIT): **I'll have a ~ (at it)** vou tentar (fazê-lo); **~ed in** amassado
▶ **bash up** *(inf)* VT *(car)* arrebentar; (BRIT: *person)* dar uma surra em, espancar

bashful ['bæʃful] ADJ tímido, envergonhado

bashing ['bæʃɪŋ] *(inf)* N surra; **Paki-~** (!) *espancamento de asiáticos por motivos racistas*; **queer-~** (!) espancamento de homossexuais

BASIC ['beɪsɪk] N (*Comput*) BASIC *m*
basic ['beɪsɪk] ADJ básico; (*facilities*) mínimo; (*vocabulary, rate*) de base
basically ['beɪsɪkəlɪ] ADV basicamente; (*really*) no fundo
basic rate N (*of tax*) alíquota de base
basics ['beɪsɪks] NPL: **the ~** o essencial
basil ['bæzl] N manjericão *m*
basin ['beɪsn] N (*vessel*) bacia; (*dock, Geo*) bacia; (*also:* **washbasin**) pia
basis ['beɪsɪs] (*pl* **bases**) N base *f*; **on a part-time ~** num esquema de meio-expediente; **on a trial ~** em experiência; **on the ~ of what you've said** com base no que você disse
bask [bɑːsk] VI: **to ~ in the sun** tomar sol
basket ['bɑːskɪt] N cesto; (*with handle*) cesta
basketball ['bɑːskɪtbɔːl] N basquete(bol) *m*
basketball player N jogador(a) *m/f* de basquete
basketwork ['bɑːskɪtwəːk] N obra de verga, trabalho de vime
Basle [bɑːl] N Basileia
Basque [bæsk] ADJ, N basco(-a)
bass [beɪs] N (*Mus*) baixo
bass clef N clave *f* de fá
bassoon [bə'suːn] N fagote *m*
bastard ['bɑːstəd] N bastardo(-a); (!) filho da puta *m* (!)
baste [beɪst] VT (*Culin*) untar; (*Sewing*) alinhavar
bastion ['bæstɪən] N baluarte *m*
bat [bæt] N (*Zool*) morcego; (*for ball games*) bastão *m*; (BRIT: *for table tennis*) raquete *f* ▶ VT: **he didn't ~ an eyelid** ele nem pestanejou; **off one's own ~** por iniciativa própria
batch [bætʃ] N (*of bread*) fornada; (*of papers*) monte *m*; (*lot*) remessa, lote *m*
batch processing N (*Comput*) processamento batch
bated ['beɪtɪd] ADJ: **with ~ breath** contendo a respiração
bath [bɑːθ] N (*pl* **baths** [bɑːðz, baθs]) banho; (*bathtub*) banheira ▶ VT banhar; **to have a ~** tomar banho (de banheira); **baths** NPL (*also:* **swimming baths**) banhos *mpl* públicos
bath chair N cadeira de rodas
bathe [beɪð] VI banhar-se; (US: *have a bath*) tomar banho (de banheira) ▶ VT banhar; (*wound*) lavar
bather ['beɪðər] N banhista *m/f*
bathing ['beɪðɪŋ] N banho
bathing cap N touca de banho
bathing costume, (US) **bathing suit** N (*woman's*) maiô *m* (BR), fato de banho (PT)
bath mat N tapete *m* de banheiro
bathrobe ['bɑːθrəub] N roupão *m* de banho
bathroom ['bɑːθrum] N banheiro (BR), casa de banho (PT)
bath towel N toalha de banho
bathtub ['bɑːθtʌb] N banheira
batman ['bætmən] (BRIT) (*irreg: like* **man**) N ordenança *m*

baton ['bætən] N (*Mus*) batuta; (*Athletics*) bastão *m*; (*truncheon*) cassetete *m*
battalion [bə'tælɪən] N batalhão *m*
batten ['bætn] N (*Carpentry*) caibro ▶ **batten down** VT (*Naut*): **to ~ down the hatches** correr as escotilhas
batter ['bætər] VT espancar; (*subj: wind, rain*) castigar ▶ N massa (mole)
battered ['bætəd] ADJ (*hat, pan*) amassado, surrado; **~ wife/child** mulher/criança seviciada
battering ram ['bætərɪŋ] N aríete *m*
battery ['bætərɪ] N bateria; (*of torch*) pilha
battery charger N carregador *m* de bateria
battery farming N criação *f* intensiva
battle ['bætl] N batalha; (*fig*) luta ▶ VI lutar; **that's half the ~** (*fig*) é meio caminho andado; **it's a** *or* **we're fighting a losing ~** estamos lutando em vão
battle dress N uniforme *m* de combate
battlefield ['bætlfiːld] N campo de batalha
battlements ['bætlmənts] NPL ameias *fpl*
battleship ['bætlʃɪp] N couraçado
bauble ['bɔːbl] N bugiganga
baud [bɔːd] N (*Comput*) baud *m*
baud rate N (*Comput*) índice *m* de baud, taxa de transmissão
baulk [bɔːlk] VI = **balk**
bauxite ['bɔːksaɪt] N bauxita
bawdy ['bɔːdɪ] ADJ indecente; (*joke*) imoral
bawl [bɔːl] VI gritar; (*child*) berrar
bay [beɪ] N (*Geo*) baía; (*Bot*) louro; (BRIT: *for parking*) área de estacionamento; (: *for loading*) vão *m* de carregamento ▶ VI ladrar; **to hold sb at ~** manter alguém a distância; **the B~ of Biscay** o golfo de Biscaia
bay leaf (*irreg: like* **leaf**) N louro
bayonet ['beɪənɪt] N baioneta
bay tree N loureiro
bay window N janela saliente
bazaar [bə'zɑːr] N bazar *m*
bazooka [bə'zuːkə] N bazuca
BB (BRIT) N ABBR (= *Boys' Brigade*) movimento de meninos
BBB (US) N ABBR (= *Better Business Bureau*) organização de defesa ao consumidor
BBC N ABBR (= *British Broadcasting Corporation*) companhia britânica de rádio e televisão
B.C. ADV ABBR (= *before Christ*) a.C. ▶ ABBR (CANADA) = **British Columbia**
BCG N ABBR (= *Bacillus Calmette-Guérin*) BCG *m*
BD N ABBR (= *Bachelor of Divinity*) título universitário
B/D ABBR = **bank draft**
BDS N ABBR (= *Bachelor of Dental Surgery*) título universitário

---

KEYWORD

be [biː] (*pt* **was** *or* **were**, *pp* **been**) AUX VB **1** (*with present participle: forming continuous tense*) estar; **what are you doing?** o que você está fazendo? (BR) *or* a fazer (PT)?; **it is raining** está chovendo (BR) *or* a chover (PT); **I've been**

waiting for you for hours há horas que eu espero por você

2 (*with pp: forming passives*): **to be killed** ser morto; **the box had been opened** a caixa tinha sido aberta; **the thief was nowhere to be seen** tinha sumido o ladrão

3 (*in tag questions*): **it was fun, wasn't it?** foi divertido, não foi?; **she's back again, is she?** ela voltou novamente, é?

4 (+ *to* + *infin*): **the house is to be sold** a casa está para ser vendida; **you're to be congratulated for all your work** você devia ser cumprimentado pelo seu trabalho; **he's not to open it** ele não pode abrir isso

▶ VB + COMPLEMENT **1** (*gen*): **I'm English** sou inglês; **I'm tired** estou cansado; **I'm hot/cold** estou com calor/frio; **he's a doctor** ele é médico; **2 and 2 are 4** dois e dois são quatro; **she's tall/pretty** ela é alta/bonita; **be careful!** tome cuidado!; **be quiet!** fique quieto!, fique calado!; **be good!** seja bonzinho!

2 (*of health*) estar; **how are you?** como está?; **he's very ill** ele está muito doente

3 (*of age*): **how old are you?** quantos anos você tem?; **I'm twenty (years old)** tenho vinte anos

4 (*cost*) ser; **how much was the meal?** quanto foi a refeição?; **that'll be £5.75, please** são £5.75, por favor

▶ VI **1** (*exist, occur etc*) existir, haver; **the best singer that ever was** o maior cantor de todos os tempos; **is there a God?** Deus existe?; **be that as it may …** de qualquer forma …; **so be it** que seja assim

2 (*referring to place*) estar; **I won't be here tomorrow** eu não estarei aqui amanhã; **Edinburgh is in Scotland** Edinburgo é *or* fica na Escócia; **it's on the table** está na mesa

3 (*referring to movement*) ir; **where have you been?** onde você foi?; **I've been to the post office/to China** fui ao correio/à China; **I've been in the garden** estava no quintal

▶ IMPERS VB **1** (*referring to time*) ser; **it's 8 o'clock** são 8 horas; **it's the 28th of April** é 28 de abril

2 (*referring to distance*) ficar; **it's 10 km to the village** o lugarejo fica a 10 km de distância

3 (*referring to the weather*) estar; **it's too hot/cold** está quente/frio demais

4 (*emphatic*): **it's only me** sou eu!; **it's only the postman** é apenas o carteiro; **it was Maria who paid the bill** foi Maria quem pagou a conta

B/E ABBR = **bill of exchange**

beach [biːtʃ] N praia ▶ VT puxar para a terra *or* praia, encalhar

beachcomber [ˈbiːtʃkəʊməʳ] N vagabundo(-a) de praia

beachwear [ˈbiːtʃwɛəʳ] N roupa de praia

beacon [ˈbiːkən] N (*lighthouse*) farol *m*; (*marker*) baliza; (*also:* **radio beacon**) radiofarol *m*

bead [biːd] N (*of necklace*) conta; (*of sweat*) gota; **beads** NPL (*necklace*) colar *m*

beady [ˈbiːdɪ] ADJ: ~ **eyes** olhinhos vivos

beagle [ˈbiːgl] N bigle *m*

beak [biːk] N bico

beaker [ˈbiːkəʳ] N copo com bico

beam [biːm] N (*Arch*) viga; (*of light*) raio; (*Naut*) través *m*; (*Radio*) feixe *m* direcional ▶ VI brilhar; (*smile*) sorrir; **to drive on full** *or* **main ~** (BRIT), **to drive on high ~** (US) transitar com os faróis altos

beaming [ˈbiːmɪŋ] ADJ (*sun, smile*) radiante

bean [biːn] N feijão *m*; (*of coffee*) grão *m*; **runner/broad ~** vagem *f*/fava

bean shoots NPL brotos *mpl* de feijão

bean sprouts NPL brotos *mpl* de feijão

bear [bɛəʳ] (*pt* **bore**, *pp* **borne**) N urso; (*Stock Exchange*) baixista *m/f* ▶ VT (*carry, support*) arcar com; (*tolerate*) suportar; (*fruit*) dar; (*name, title*) trazer; (*traces, signs*) apresentar, trazer; (*children*) ter, dar à luz; (*Comm: interest*) render ▶ VI: **to ~ right/left** virar à direita/à esquerda; **to ~ the responsibility of** assumir a responsabilidade de; **to ~ comparison with** comparar-se a; **I can't ~ him** eu não o aguento; **to bring pressure to ~ on sb** exercer pressão sobre alguém

▶ **bear out** VT (*theory, suspicion*) confirmar, corroborar

▶ **bear up** VI aguentar, resistir

▶ **bear with** VT FUS (*sb's moods, temper*) ter paciência com; **~ with me a minute** só um momentinho, por favor

bearable [ˈbɛərəbl] ADJ suportável, tolerável

beard [bɪəd] N barba

bearded [ˈbɪədɪd] ADJ barbado, barbudo

bearer [ˈbɛərəʳ] N portador(a) *m/f*; (*of title*) detentor(a) *m/f*

bearing [ˈbɛərɪŋ] N porte *m*, comportamento; (*connection*) relação *f*; **bearings** NPL (*also:* **ball bearings**) rolimã *m*; **to take a ~** fazer marcação; **to find one's ~s** orientar-se

beast [biːst] N bicho; (*inf*) fera

beastly [ˈbiːstlɪ] ADJ horrível

beat [biːt] (*pt* **beat**, *pp* **beaten**) N (*of heart*) batida; (*Mus*) ritmo, compasso; (*of policeman*) ronda ▶ VT (*hit*) bater em; (*eggs*) bater; (*defeat*) vencer, derrotar; (*better*) superar, ultrapassar; (*drum*) tocar; (*rhythm*) marcar ▶ VI (*heart*) bater; **to ~ about the bush** falar com rodeios (BR), fazer rodeios (PT); **to ~ it** (*inf*) cair fora; **off the ~ track** fora de mão; **to ~ time** marcar o compasso; **that ~s everything!** isso é o cúmulo!

▶ **beat down** VT (*door*) arrombar; (*price*) conseguir que seja abatido; (*seller*) conseguir que abata o preço ▶ VI (*rain*) cair a cântaros; (*sun*) bater de chapa

▶ **beat off** VT repelir

▶ **beat up** VT (*inf: person*) espancar; (*eggs*) bater

beaten [ˈbiːtn] PP *of* **beat**

beater ['biːtə^r] N (for eggs, cream) batedeira
beating ['biːtɪŋ] N batida; (thrashing) surra;
to take a ~ levar uma surra
beat-up (inf) ADJ (car) caindo aos pedaços;
(suitcase etc) surrado
beautician [bjuːˈtɪʃən] N esteticista m/f
beautiful ['bjuːtɪful] ADJ belo, lindo, formoso
beautify ['bjuːtɪfaɪ] VT embelezar
beauty ['bjuːtɪ] N beleza; (person) beldade f,
beleza; **the ~ of it is that ...** o atrativo disso
é que ...
beauty contest N concurso de beleza
beauty queen N miss f, rainha de beleza
beauty salon [-sælɔn] N salão m de beleza
beauty spot N sinal m (de beleza na pele); (BRIT
Tourism) lugar m de beleza excepcional
beaver ['biːvə^r] N castor m
becalmed [bɪˈkɑːmd] ADJ parado devido a
calmaria
became [bɪˈkeɪm] PT of **become**
because [bɪˈkɔz] CONJ porque; **~ of** por causa de
beck [bɛk] N: **to be at sb's ~ and call** estar às
ordens de alguém
beckon ['bɛkən] VT (also: **beckon to**) chamar
com sinais, acenar para
become [bɪˈkʌm] (irreg: like **come**) VT (suit)
favorecer a ▶ VI (+n) virar, fazer-se, tornar-se;
(+adj) tornar-se, ficar; **to ~ fat/thin** ficar
gordo/magro; **to ~ angry** zangar-se, ficar
com raiva; **it became known that** soube-se
que; **what has ~ of him?** o que é feito dele?,
o que aconteceu a ele?
becoming [bɪˈkʌmɪŋ] ADJ (behaviour) decoroso;
(clothes) favorecedor(a), elegante
BEd N ABBR (= Bachelor of Education) habilitação ao
magistério
bed [bɛd] N cama; (of flowers) canteiro; (of coal,
clay) camada, base f; (of sea, lake) fundo; (of
river) leito; **to go to ~** ir dormir, deitar(-se)
▶ **bed down** VI dormir
bed and breakfast N (place) pensão f; (terms)
cama e café da manhã (BR) or pequeno
almoço (PT)
bedbug ['bɛdbʌg] N percevejo
bedclothes ['bɛdkləuðz] NPL roupa de cama
bed cover N colcha
bedding ['bɛdɪŋ] N roupa de cama
bedevil [bɪˈdɛvl] VT (harass) acossar; **to be ~led
by** ser vítima de
bedfellow ['bɛdfɛləu] N: **they are strange ~s**
(fig) eles formam uma dupla estranha
bedlam ['bɛdləm] N confusão f
bedpan ['bɛdpæn] N comadre f
bedpost ['bɛdpəust] N pé m de cama
bedraggled [bɪˈdrægld] ADJ molhado,
ensopado; (dirty) enlameado
bedridden ['bɛdrɪdn] ADJ acamado
bedrock ['bɛdrɔk] N (fig) fundamento,
alicerce m; (Geo) leito de rocha firme
bedroom ['bɛdrum] N quarto, dormitório
Beds (BRIT) ABBR = **Bedfordshire**
bedside ['bɛdsaɪd] N: **at sb's ~** à cabeceira de
alguém ▶ CPD (book, lamp) de cabeceira

bedsit ['bɛdsɪt], **bedsitter** ['bɛdsɪtə^r] N (BRIT)
conjugado

Um **bedsit** é um quarto mobiliado cujo
aluguel inclui uso de cozinha e banheiro
comuns. Esse sistema de alojamento é
muito comum na Grã-Bretanha entre
estudantes, jovens profissionais liberais
etc.

bedspread ['bɛdsprɛd] N colcha
bedtime ['bɛdtaɪm] N hora de ir para cama
bee [biː] N abelha; **to have a ~ in one's
bonnet (about sth)** estar obcecado (por
algo)
beech [biːtʃ] N faia
beef [biːf] N carne f de vaca; **roast ~** rosbife m
▶ **beef up** (inf) VT (support) reforçar; (essay)
desenvolver mais
beefburger ['biːfbəːgə^r] N hambúrguer m
beefeater ['biːfiːtə^r] N alabardeiro (da guarda da
Torre de Londres)
beehive ['biːhaɪv] N colmeia
bee-keeping ['biːkiːpɪŋ] N apicultura
beeline ['biːlaɪn] N: **to make a ~ for** ir
direto a
been [biːn] PP of **be**
beer [bɪə^r] N cerveja
beer can N lata de cerveja
beet [biːt] (US) N beterraba
beetle ['biːtl] N besouro
beetroot ['biːtruːt] (BRIT) N beterraba
befall [bɪˈfɔːl] (irreg: like **fall**) VT acontecer a
befit [bɪˈfɪt] VT convir a
before [bɪˈfɔː^r] PREP (of time) antes de; (of space)
diante de ▶ CONJ antes que ▶ ADV antes,
anteriormente; à frente, na dianteira;
~ going antes de ir; **~ she goes** antes dela
sair; **the week ~** a semana anterior; **I've
seen it ~** eu já vi isso (antes); **I've never
seen it ~** nunca vi isso antes
beforehand [bɪˈfɔːhænd] ADV antes
befriend [bɪˈfrɛnd] VT fazer amizade com
befuddled [bɪˈfʌdld] ADJ atordoado, aturdido
beg [bɛg] VI mendigar, pedir esmola ▶ VT (also:
beg for) mendigar; (favour) pedir; (entreat)
suplicar; **to ~ sb to do sth** implorar a
alguém para fazer algo; **that ~s the
question of ...** isso dá por resolvida a
questão de ...; see also **pardon**
began [bɪˈgæn] PT of **begin**
beggar ['bɛgə^r] N (also: **beggarman,
beggarwoman**) mendigo(-a)
begin [bɪˈgɪn] (pt **began**, pp **begun**) VT, VI
começar, iniciar; **to ~ doing** or **to do sth**
começar a fazer algo; **~ning (from) Monday**
a partir de segunda-feira; **I can't ~ to thank
you** não sei como agradecer-lhe; **to ~ with**
em primeiro lugar
beginner [bɪˈgɪnə^r] N principiante m/f
beginning [bɪˈgɪnɪŋ] N início, começo; **right
from the ~** desde o início
begrudge [bɪˈgrʌdʒ] VT: **to ~ sb sth** (envy)
invejar algo de alguém; (give grudgingly) dar
algo a alguém de má vontade

beguile [bɪ'gaɪl] vt (*enchant*) encantar
beguiling [bɪ'gaɪlɪŋ] adj (*charming*) sedutor(a), encantador(a)
begun [bɪ'gʌn] pp *of* **begin**
behalf [bɪ'hɑ:f] n: **on** *or* **in** (*us*) **~ of** (*as representative of*) em nome de; (*for benefit of*) no interesse de; (*in aid of*) em favor de; **on my/his ~** em meu nome/no nome dele
behave [bɪ'heɪv] vi comportar-se; (*well: also:* **behave o.s.**) comportar-se (bem)
behaviour, (*us*) **behavior** [bɪ'heɪvjə^r] n comportamento
behead [bɪ'hɛd] vt decapitar, degolar
beheld [bɪ'hɛld] pt, pp *of* **behold**
behind [bɪ'haɪnd] prep atrás de ▶ adv atrás; (*move*) para trás ▶ n traseiro; **~ (time)** atrasado; **to be ~ (schedule) with sth** estar atrasado *or* com atraso em algo; **~ the scenes** nos bastidores; **to leave sth ~** (*forget*) esquecer algo; (*run ahead of*) deixar algo para trás
behold [bɪ'həuld] (*irreg: like* **hold**) vt contemplar
beige [beɪʒ] adj bege
Beijing [beɪ'ʒɪŋ] n Pequim
being ['bi:ɪŋ] n (*state*) existência; (*entity*) ser *m*; **to come into ~** nascer, aparecer
Beirut [beɪ'ru:t] n Beirute
belated [bɪ'leɪtɪd] adj atrasado
belch [bɛltʃ] vi arrotar ▶ vt (*also:* **belch out**: *smoke etc*) vomitar
beleaguered [bɪ'li:gəd] adj (*city, fig*) assediado; (*army*) cercado
Belfast ['bɛlfɑ:st] n Belfast
belfry ['bɛlfrɪ] n campanário
Belgian ['bɛldʒən] adj, n belga *m/f*
Belgium ['bɛldʒəm] n Bélgica
Belgrade [bɛl'greɪd] n Belgrado
belie [bɪ'laɪ] vt (*contradict*) contradizer; (*disprove*) desmentir; (*obscure*) ocultar
belief [bɪ'li:f] n (*opinion*) opinião *f*; (*trust, faith*) fé *f*; (*acceptance as true*) crença, convicção *f*; **it's beyond ~** é inacreditável; **in the ~ that** na convicção de que
believe [bɪ'li:v] vt: **to ~ sth/sb** acreditar algo/em alguém ▶ vi: **to ~ in** (*God, ghosts*) crer em; (*method, person*) acreditar em; **I ~ (that) ...** (*think*) eu acho que ...; **I don't ~ in corporal punishment** não sou partidário de castigos corporais; **he is ~d to be abroad** acredita-se que ele esteja no exterior
believer [bɪ'li:və^r] n (*Rel*) crente *m/f*, fiel *m/f*; (*in idea, activity*): **~ in** partidário(-a) de
belittle [bɪ'lɪtl] vt diminuir, depreciar
Belize [bɛ'li:z] n Belize *m* (*no article*)
bell [bɛl] n sino; (*small, doorbell*) campainha; (*animal's, on toy*) guizo, sininho; **that rings a ~** (*fig*) tenho uma vaga lembrança disso; **the name rings a ~** o nome não me é estranho
bell-bottoms npl calça boca-de-sino
bellboy ['bɛlbɔɪ] (*brit*) n boy *m* (de hotel) (*br*), groom *m* (*pt*)

bellhop ['bɛlhɔp] (*us*) n = **bellboy**
belligerent [bɪ'lɪdʒərənt] adj (*at war*) beligerante; (*fig*) agressivo
bellow ['bɛləu] vi mugir; (*person*) bramar ▶ vt (*orders*) gritar, berrar
bellows ['bɛləuz] npl fole *m*
bell pepper n (*esp us*) pimentão *m*
bell push (*brit*) n botão *m* de campainha
belly ['bɛlɪ] n barriga, ventre *m*
bellyache ['bɛlɪeɪk] (*inf*) n dor *f* de barriga ▶ vi bufar
belly button ['bɛlɪbʌtn] n umbigo
belong [bɪ'lɔŋ] vi: **to ~ to** pertencer a; (*club etc*) ser sócio de; **the book ~s here** o livro fica guardado aqui
belongings [bɪ'lɔŋɪŋz] npl pertences *mpl*
beloved [bɪ'lʌvɪd] adj querido, amado ▶ n bem-amado(-a)
below [bɪ'ləu] prep (*beneath*) embaixo de; (*lower than, less than*) abaixo de; (*covered by*) debaixo de ▶ adv em baixo; **see ~** ver abaixo; **temperatures ~ normal** temperaturas abaixo da normal
belt [bɛlt] n cinto; (*of land*) faixa; (*Tech*) correia ▶ vt (*thrash*) surrar ▶ vi (*brit inf*): **to ~ along** ir a toda, correr; **industrial ~** zona industrial
  ▶ **belt out** vt (*song*) cantar a plenos pulmões
  ▶ **belt up** (*brit inf*) vi calar a boca
beltway ['bɛltweɪ] (*us*) n via circular
bemoan [bɪ'məun] vt lamentar
bemused [bɪ'mju:zd] adj bestificado, estupidificado
bench [bɛntʃ] n banco; (*work bench*) bancada (de carpinteiro); (*brit Pol*) assento num Parlamento; **the B~** (*Law*) o tribunal; (*people*) os magistrados, o corpo de magistrados
bench mark n referência
bend [bɛnd] (*pt, pp* **bent**) vt (*leg, arm*) dobrar; (*pipe*) curvar ▶ vi dobrar-se, inclinar-se ▶ n curva; (*in pipe*) curvatura; **bends** npl mal-dos-mergulhadores *m*
  ▶ **bend down** vi abaixar-se; (*squat*) agachar-se
  ▶ **bend over** vi debruçar-se
beneath [bɪ'ni:θ] prep (*position*) abaixo de; (*covered by*) debaixo de; (*unworthy of*) indigno de ▶ adv em baixo
benefactor ['bɛnɪfæktə^r] n benfeitor(a) *m/f*
benefactress ['bɛnɪfæktrɪs] n benfeitora
beneficial [bɛnɪ'fɪʃl] adj: **~ (to)** benéfico (a)
beneficiary [bɛnɪ'fɪʃərɪ] n (*Law*) beneficiário(-a)
benefit ['bɛnɪfɪt] n benefício, vantagem *f*; (*as part of salary etc*) benefício; (*money*) subsídio, auxílio; (*also:* **benefit performance**) apresentação *f* beneficente ▶ vt beneficiar ▶ vi: **to ~ from sth** beneficiar-se de algo
benefit performance n apresentação *f* beneficente
Benelux ['bɛnɪlʌks] n Benelux *m*
benevolent [bɪ'nɛvələnt] adj benévolo

BEng N ABBR (= *Bachelor of Engineering*) título universitário

benign [bɪ'naɪn] ADJ (*person, smile*) afável, bondoso; (*Med*) benigno

bent [bɛnt] PT, PP *of* **bend** ▶ N inclinação f ▶ ADJ (*wire, pipe*) torto; (*inf: dishonest*) corrupto; **to be ~ on** estar empenhado em; **to have a ~ for** ter queda para

bequeath [bɪ'kwi:ð] VT legar

bequest [bɪ'kwɛst] N legado

bereaved [bɪ'ri:vd] NPL: **the ~** os enlutados ▶ ADJ enlutado

bereavement [bɪ'ri:vmənt] N luto

beret ['bɛreɪ] N boina

Bering Sea ['beɪrɪŋ-] N: **the ~** o mar de Bering

Berks (*BRIT*) ABBR = **Berkshire**

Berlin [bə:'lɪn] N Berlim

berm [bə:m] (*US*) N acostamento (*BR*), berma (*PT*)

Bermuda [bə:'mju:də] N Bermudas *fpl*

Bermuda shorts NPL bermuda

Bern [bə:n] N Berna

berry ['bɛrɪ] N baga

berserk [bə'sə:k] ADJ: **to go ~** perder as estribeiras

berth [bə:θ] N (*bed*) beliche *m*; (*cabin*) cabine f; (*on train*) leito; (*for ship*) ancoradouro ▶ VI (*in harbour*) atracar, encostar-se; (*at anchor*) ancorar; **to give sb a wide ~** (*fig*) evitar alguém

beseech [bɪ'si:tʃ] (*pt, pp* **besought**) VT suplicar, implorar

beset [bɪ'sɛt] VT (*pt, pp* **beset**) (*subj: problems, difficulties*) acossar ▶ ADJ: **a policy ~ with dangers** uma política cercada de perigos

besetting [bɪ'sɛtɪŋ] ADJ: **his ~ sin** seu grande vício

beside [bɪ'saɪd] PREP (*next to*) junto de, ao lado de, ao pé de; (*compared with*) em comparação com; **to be ~ o.s. (with anger)** estar fora de si; **that's ~ the point** isso não tem nada a ver

besides [bɪ'saɪdz] ADV além disso ▶ PREP (*as well as*) além de; (*except*) salvo, exceto

besiege [bɪ'si:dʒ] VT (*town*) sitiar, pôr cerco a; (*fig*) assediar

besotted [bɪ'sɔtɪd] (*BRIT*) ADJ: **~ with** gamado em, louco por

besought [bɪ'sɔːt] PT, PP *of* **beseech**

bespectacled [bɪ'spɛktɪkld] ADJ de óculos

bespoke [bɪ'spəuk] (*BRIT*) ADJ (*garment*) feito sob medida; **~ software** software *m* sob medida; **~ tailor** alfaiate *m* que confecciona roupa sob medida

best [bɛst] ADJ melhor ▶ ADV (o) melhor; **the ~ part** of (*quantity*) a maior parte de; **at ~** na melhor das hipóteses; **to make the ~ of sth** tirar o maior partido possível de algo; **to do one's ~** fazer o possível; **to the ~ of my knowledge** que eu saiba; **to the ~ of my ability** o melhor que eu puder; **he's not exactly patient at the ~ of times** mesmo nos seus melhores momentos ele não é muito paciente; **the ~ thing to do is ...** o melhor é ...

best-before date N validade f

best man N padrinho de casamento

bestow [bɪ'stəu] VT (*affection*) dar, oferecer; (*honour, title*): **to ~ sth on sb** outorgar algo a alguém

bestseller ['bɛst'sɛlə'] N (*book*) best-seller *m*

bet [bɛt] (*pt, pp* **bet** *or* **betted**) VT: **to ~ sb sth** apostar algo com alguém ▶ N: **to ~ (on)** apostar (em) ▶ N aposta; **to ~ money on sth** apostar dinheiro em algo; **it's a safe ~** (*fig*) é coisa segura, é dinheiro ganho

Bethlehem ['bɛθlɪhɛm] N Belém

betray [bɪ'treɪ] VT trair; (*denounce*) delatar

betrayal [bɪ'treɪəl] N traição f

better ['bɛtə'] ADJ, ADV melhor ▶ VT melhorar; (*go above*) superar ▶ N: **to get the ~ of sb** vencer alguém; **you had ~ do it** é melhor você fazer isso; **he thought ~ of it** pensou melhor, mudou de opinião; **to get ~** melhorar; **you'd be ~ off this way** seria melhor para você assim; **that's ~!** isso!

betting ['bɛtɪŋ] N jogo

betting shop (*BRIT*) N agência de apostas

between [bɪ'twi:n] PREP no meio de, entre ▶ ADV no meio; **the road ~ here and London** a estrada daqui a Londres; **we only had 5 ~ us** juntos só tínhamos 5; **~ you and me** cá entre nós

bevel ['bɛvəl] N (*also*: **bevel edge**) bisel *m*

beverage ['bɛvərɪdʒ] N bebida

bevy ['bɛvɪ] N: **a ~ of** um grupo *or* bando de

bewail [bɪ'weɪl] VT lamentar

beware [bɪ'wɛə'] VT, VI: **to ~ (of)** precaver-se (de), ter cuidado (com) ▶ EXCL cuidado!; **"~ of the dog"** "cuidado com o cachorro"

bewildered [bɪ'wɪldəd] ADJ atordoado; (*confused*) confuso

bewildering [bɪ'wɪldərɪŋ] ADJ atordoador(a), desnorteante

bewitching [bɪ'wɪtʃɪŋ] ADJ encantador(a), sedutor(a)

beyond [bɪ'jɔnd] PREP (*in space, exceeding*) além de; (*exceeding*) acima de, fora de; (*date*) mais tarde que; (*above*) acima de ▶ ADV além; (*in time*) mais longe, mais adiante; **~ doubt** fora de qualquer dúvida; **to be ~ repair** não ter conserto

b/f ABBR = **brought forward**

BFPO N ABBR (= *British Forces Post Office*) serviço postal do exército

bhp N ABBR (*Aut*: = *brake horsepower*) potência efetiva ao freio

bi... [baɪ] PREFIX bi...

biannual [baɪ'ænjuəl] ADJ semestral

bias ['baɪəs] N (*prejudice*) parcialidade; (*preference*) prevenção f

biased, biassed ['baɪəst] ADJ parcial; **to be bias(s)ed against** ter preconceito contra

bib [bɪb] N babadouro, babador *m*

Bible ['baɪbl] N Bíblia

bibliography [bɪblɪ'ɔgrəfɪ] N bibliografia

bicarbonate of soda [baɪ'kɑːbənɪt-] N bicarbonato de sódio
bicentenary [baɪsɛn'tiːnərɪ] N bicentenário
bicentennial [baɪsɛn'tɛnɪəl] N bicentenário
biceps ['baɪsɛps] N bíceps *m inv*
bicker ['bɪkəʳ] VI brigar
bicycle ['baɪsɪkl] N bicicleta
bicycle path N ciclovia
bicycle pump N bomba de bicicleta
bicycle track N ciclovia
bid [bɪd] N oferta; (*at auction*) lance *m*; (*attempt*) tentativa ▶ VI (*pt, pp* **bid**) fazer uma oferta; fazer lance; (*Comm*) licitar, fazer uma licitação ▶ VT (*pt* **bade** [bæd], *pp* **bidden** ['bɪdn]) (*price*) oferecer; (*order*) mandar, ordenar; **to ~ sb good day** dar bom dia a alguém
bidder ['bɪdəʳ] N (*Comm*) licitante *m/f*; **the highest ~** quem oferece mais
bidding ['bɪdɪŋ] N (*at auction*) lances *mpl*; (*Comm*) licitação *f*; (*order*) ordem *f*
bide [baɪd] VT: **to ~ one's time** esperar o momento adequado
bidet ['biːdeɪ] N bidê *m*
bidirectional ['baɪdɪ'rɛkʃənl] ADJ bidirecional
biennial [baɪ'ɛnɪəl] ADJ bienal ▶ N (*plant*) planta bienal
bier [bɪəʳ] N féretro
bifocals [baɪ'fəuklz] NPL óculos *mpl* bifocais
big [bɪg] ADJ grande; (*bulky*) volumoso; **~ brother/sister** irmão/irmã mais velho/a; **to do things in a ~ way** fazer as coisas em grande escala
bigamy ['bɪgəmɪ] N bigamia
big dipper [-'dɪpəʳ] N montanha-russa
big end N (*Aut*) cabeça de biela
bigheaded ['bɪg'hɛdɪd] ADJ convencido
big-hearted ['bɪg'hɑːtɪd] ADJ magnânimo
bigot ['bɪgət] N fanático, intolerante *m/f*
bigoted ['bɪgətɪd] ADJ fanático, intolerante
bigotry ['bɪgətrɪ] N fanatismo, intolerância
big toe N dedão *m* do pé
big top N tenda de circo
big wheel N (*at fair*) roda gigante
bigwig ['bɪgwɪg] (*inf*) N mandachuva *m*
bike [baɪk] N bicicleta
bikini [bɪ'kiːnɪ] N biquíni *m*
bilateral [baɪ'lætrəl] ADJ bilateral
bile [baɪl] N bílis *f*
bilingual [baɪ'lɪŋgwəl] ADJ bilíngue
bilious ['bɪlɪəs] ADJ bilioso
bill [bɪl] N conta; (*invoice*) fatura; (*Pol*) projeto de lei; (*US: banknote*) bilhete *m*, nota; (*in restaurant*) conta, notinha; (*notice*) cartaz *m*; (*of bird*) bico ▶ VT (*item*) faturar; (*customer*) enviar fatura a; **may I have the ~ please?** a conta *or* a notinha, por favor?; **"stick *or* post no ~s"** "é proibido afixar cartazes"; **to fit *or* fill the ~** (*fig*) servir; **~ of exchange** letra de câmbio; **~ of lading** conhecimento de carga; **~ of sale** nota de venda; (*formal*) escritura de venda
billboard ['bɪlbɔːd] N quadro para cartazes

billet ['bɪlɪt] N alojamento ▶ VT alojar, quartelar
billfold ['bɪlfəuld] (*US*) N carteira
billiards ['bɪlɪədz] N bilhar *m*
billion ['bɪlɪən] N (= 1,000,000,000) bilhão *m* (*BR*), mil milhão *m* (*PT*)
billow ['bɪləu] N (*of smoke*) bulcão *m* ▶ VI (*smoke*) redemoinhar; (*sail*) enfunar-se
billy goat ['bɪlɪ-] N bode *m*
bin [bɪn] N caixa; (*BRIT: also:* **dustbin, litter bin**) lata de lixo; *see also* **breadbin**
binary ['baɪnərɪ] ADJ binário
bind [baɪnd] (*pt, pp* **bound**) VT atar, amarrar; (*wound*) enfaixar; (*oblige*) obrigar; (*book*) encadernar ▶ N (*inf*) saco
  ▶ **bind over** VT (*Law*) pôr em liberdade condicional
  ▶ **bind up** VT (*wound*) enfaixar; **to be bound up with** estar vinculado a
binder ['baɪndəʳ] N (*file*) fichário
binding ['baɪndɪŋ] ADJ (*contract*) sujeitante ▶ N (*of book*) encadernação *f*
binge [bɪndʒ] (*inf*) N: **to go on a ~** tomar uma bebedeira
bingo ['bɪŋgəu] N bingo
binoculars [bɪ'nɔkjuləz] NPL binóculo
bio ... [baɪəu] PREFIX bio ...
biochemistry [baɪə'kɛmɪstrɪ] N bioquímica
biodegradable ['baɪəudɪ'greɪdəbl] ADJ biodegradável
biodiesel ['baɪəudiːzl] N biodiesel *m*
biodiversity ['baɪəudaɪ'vəːsɪtɪ] N biodiversidade *f*
biofuel ['baɪəufjuəl] N biocombustível *m*
biographer [baɪ'ɔgrəfəʳ] N biógrafo(-a)
biographic [baɪə'græfɪk], **biographical** [baɪə'græfɪkl] ADJ biográfico
biography [baɪ'ɔgrəfɪ] N biografia
biological [baɪə'lɔdʒɪkəl] ADJ biológico
biologist [baɪ'ɔlədʒɪst] N biólogo(-a)
biology [baɪ'ɔlədʒɪ] N biologia
biometric ['baɪəu'mɛtrɪk] ADJ biométrico
biophysics ['baɪəu'fɪzɪks] N biofísica
biopsy ['baɪɔpsɪ] N biopsia
biotechnology ['baɪəutɛk'nɔlədʒɪ] N biotecnia
birch [bəːtʃ] N bétula; (*cane*) vara de vidoeiro
bird [bəːd] N ave *f*, pássaro; (*BRIT inf: girl*) gatinha
birdcage ['bəːdkeɪdʒ] N gaiola
bird flu N gripe *f* aviária
bird's-eye view N vista aérea; (*overview*) vista geral
bird watcher [-'wɔtʃəʳ] N ornitófilo(-a)
Biro® ['baɪərəu] N caneta esferográfica
birth [bəːθ] N nascimento; (*Med*) parto; **to give ~ to** dar à luz, parir
birth certificate N certidão *f* de nascimento
birth control N controle *m* de natalidade; (*methods*) métodos *mpl* anticoncepcionais
birthday ['bəːθdeɪ] N aniversário (*BR*), dia *m* de anos (*PT*) ▶ CPD de aniversário; *see also* **happy**

birthmark ['bə:θmɑːk] N nevo
birthplace ['bə:θpleɪs] N lugar m de nascimento
birth rate N índice m de natalidade f
Biscay ['bɪskeɪ] N: **the Bay of ~** o golfo de Biscaia
biscuit ['bɪskɪt] N (BRIT) bolacha, biscoito; (US) pão m doce
bisect [baɪ'sɛkt] VT dividir ao meio
bishop ['bɪʃəp] N bispo
bit [bɪt] PT of **bite** ▶ N pedaço, bocado; (of tool) broca; (of horse) freio; (Comput) bit m; **a ~ of** (a little) um pouco de; **a ~ mad/dangerous** um pouco doido/perigoso; **~ by ~** pouco a pouco; **to come to ~s** (break) cair aos pedaços; **bring all your ~s and pieces** traz todos os teus troços; **to do one's ~** fazer sua parte
bitch [bɪtʃ] N (dog) cadela, cachorra; (!: woman) cadela (!), vagabunda (!)
bite [baɪt] VT, VI (pt **bit**, pp **bitten**) morder; (insect etc) picar ▶ N mordida; (insect bite) picada; (mouthful) bocado; **to ~ one's nails** roer as unhas; **let's have a ~ (to eat)** (inf) vamos fazer uma boquinha
biting ['baɪtɪŋ] ADJ (wind) penetrante; (wit) mordaz
bit part N (Theatre) ponta
bitten ['bɪtn] PP of **bite**
bitter ['bɪtə^r] ADJ amargo; (wind, criticism) cortante, penetrante; (battle) encarniçado ▶ N (BRIT: beer) cerveja amarga; **to the ~ end** até o fim
bitterly ['bɪtəlɪ] ADV (complain, weep) amargamente; (criticize) asperamente; (oppose) implacavelmente; (jealous, disappointed) extremamente; **it's ~ cold** faz um frio glacial
bitterness ['bɪtənɪs] N amargor m; (anger) rancor m
bittersweet ['bɪtəswiːt] ADJ agridoce
bitty ['bɪtɪ] (BRIT inf) ADJ sem nexo
bitumen ['bɪtjumɪn] N betume m
bivouac ['bɪvuæk] N bivaque m
bizarre [bɪ'zɑː^r] ADJ esquisito
bk ABBR = **bank; book**
BL N ABBR (= Bachelor of Laws, Bachelor of Letters) título universitário; (US: = Bachelor of Literature) título universitário
bl ABBR = **bill of lading**
blab [blæb] VI dar or bater com a língua nos dentes ▶ VT (also: **blab out**) revelar, badalar
black [blæk] ADJ preto; (humour) negro ▶ N (colour) cor f preta; (person): **B~** negro(-a) ▶ VT (shoes) lustrar (BR), engraxar (PT); (BRIT Industry) boicotar; **to give sb a ~ eye** esmurrar alguém e deixá-lo de olho roxo; **~ and blue** (bruised) contundido; **there it is in ~ and white** (fig) aí está preto no branco; **to be in the ~** (in credit) estar com saldo credor
▶ **black out** VI (faint) desmaiar
black belt (US) N zona de negros

blackberry ['blækbərɪ] N amora(-preta) (BR), amora silvestre (PT)
blackbird ['blækbə:d] N melro
blackboard ['blækbɔːd] N quadro(-negro)
black box N (Aviat) caixa preta
black coffee N café m preto
Black Country (BRIT) N: **the ~** zona industrial na região central da Inglaterra
blackcurrant [blæk'kʌrənt] N groselha negra
black economy (BRIT) N economia invisível
blacken ['blækən] VT enegrecer; (fig) denegrir
Black Forest N: **the ~** a Floresta Negra
blackhead ['blækhɛd] N cravo
black ice N gelo negro
blackjack ['blækdʒæk] N (Cards) vinte-e-um m; (US: truncheon) cassetete m
blackleg ['blæklɛg] (BRIT) N fura-greve m/f
blacklist ['blæklɪst] N lista negra ▶ VT colocar na lista negra
blackmail ['blækmeɪl] N chantagem f ▶ VT fazer chantagem a
blackmailer ['blækmeɪlə^r] N chantagista m/f
black market N mercado or câmbio negro
blackout ['blækaut] N blecaute m; (fainting) desmaio; (of radio signal) desvanecimento
Black Sea N: **the ~** o mar Negro
black sheep N (fig) ovelha negra
blacksmith ['blæksmɪθ] N ferreiro
black spot N (Aut) lugar m perigoso; (for unemployment etc) área crítica
bladder ['blædə^r] N bexiga
blade [bleɪd] N folha; (of knife, sword) lâmina; (of oar, rotor) pá f; **a ~ of grass** uma folha de relva
blame [bleɪm] N culpa ▶ VT: **to ~ sb for sth** culpar alguém por algo; **to be to ~** ter a culpa
blameless ['bleɪmlɪs] ADJ (person) inocente
blanch [blɑːntʃ] VI (person, face) empalidecer ▶ VT (Culin) escaldar
bland [blænd] ADJ suave; (taste) brando
blank [blæŋk] ADJ em branco; (shot) sem bala; (look) sem expressão; (of memory): **to go ~** dar um branco ▶ N (on form) espaço em branco; (cartridge) bala de festim; **we drew a ~** (fig) chegamos a lugar nenhum
blank cheque, (US) **blank check** N cheque m em branco; **to give sb a ~ to do ...** dar carta branca a alguém para fazer ...
blanket ['blæŋkɪt] N (for bed) cobertor m; (for travelling etc) manta; (of snow, fog) camada ▶ ADJ (statement, agreement) global, geral; **to give ~ cover** (subj: insurance policy) dar cobertura geral
blare [blɛə^r] VI (horn, radio) clangorar
blasé ['blɑːzeɪ] ADJ indiferente
blasphemous ['blæsfɪməs] ADJ blasfemo
blasphemy ['blæsfɪmɪ] N blasfêmia
blast [blɑːst] N (of wind) rajada; (of whistle) toque m; (of explosive) explosão f; (shock wave) sopro; (of air, steam) jato ▶ VT (blow up) fazer voar; (blow open) abrir com uma carga explosiva ▶ EXCL (BRIT inf) droga!; **(at) full ~**

(*play music etc*) no volume máximo; (*fig*) a todo vapor
▸ **blast off** vi (*Space*) decolar
blast-off N (*Space*) lançamento
blatant ['bleɪtənt] ADJ descarado
blatantly ['bleɪtəntlɪ] ADV (*lie*) descaradamente; **it's ~ obvious** é de toda a evidência, está na cara
blaze [bleɪz] N (*fire*) fogo; (*in building etc*) incêndio; (*flames*) chamas fpl; (*fig: of colour*) esplendor m; (: *of glory, publicity*) explosão f ▸ vi (*fire*) arder; (*guns*) descarregar; (*eyes*) brilhar ▸ vt: **to ~ a trail** (*fig*) abrir (um) caminho; **in a ~ of publicity** numa explosão de publicidade
blazer ['bleɪzə'] N casaco esportivo, blazer m
bleach [bliːtʃ] N (*also*: **household bleach**) água sanitária ▸ vt (*linen*) branquear
bleached [bliːtʃt] ADJ (*hair*) oxigenado; (*linen*) branqueado, alvejado
bleachers ['bliːtʃəz] (*us*) NPL (*Sport*) arquibancada descoberta
bleak [bliːk] ADJ (*countryside*) desolado; (*prospect*) desanimador(a), sombrio; (*weather*) ruim; (*smile*) sem graça, amarelo
bleary-eyed ['blɪərɪ'aɪd] ADJ de olhos injetados
bleat [bliːt] vi balir ▸ N balido
bled [blɛd] PT, PP of **bleed**
bleed [bliːd] (*pt, pp* **bled**) vt, vi sangrar; **my nose is ~ing** eu estou sangrando do nariz
bleeper ['bliːpə'] N (*of doctor etc*) bip m
blemish ['blɛmɪʃ] N mancha; (*on reputation*) mácula
blend [blɛnd] N mistura ▸ vt misturar ▸ vi (*colours etc: also*: **blend in**) combinar-se, misturar-se
blender ['blɛndə'] N (*Culin*) liquidificador m
bless [blɛs] (*pt, pp* **blessed**) vt abençoar; **~ you!** (*after sneeze*) saúde!
blessed¹ [blɛst] PT, PP of **bless**; **to be ~ with** estar dotado de
blessed² ['blɛsɪd] ADJ (*Rel: holy*) bendito, bento; (*happy*) afortunado; **it rains every ~ day** chove cada santo dia
blessing ['blɛsɪŋ] N bênção f; (*godsend*) graça, dádiva; (*approval*) aprovação f; **to count one's ~s** dar graças a Deus; **it was a ~ in disguise** Deus escreve certo por linhas tortas
blest [blɛst] PT, PP of **bless**
blew [bluː] PT of **blow**
blight [blaɪt] vt (*hopes etc*) frustrar, gorar ▸ N (*of plants*) ferrugem f
blimey ['blaɪmɪ] (*BRIT inf*) EXCL nossa!
blind [blaɪnd] ADJ cego ▸ N (*for window*) persiana; (*also*: **Venetian blind**) veneziana ▸ vt cegar; (*dazzle*) deslumbrar; **the blind** NPL (*blind people*) os cegos; **to turn a ~ eye (on** *or* **to)** fazer vista grossa (a)
blind alley N beco sem saída m
blind corner (*BRIT*) N curva sem visibilidade
blind date N encontro às cegas

blindfold ['blaɪndfəuld] N venda ▸ ADJ, ADV com os olhos vendados, às cegas ▸ vt vendar os olhos a
blindly ['blaɪndlɪ] ADV às cegas; (*without thinking*) cegamente
blindness ['blaɪndnɪs] N cegueira
blind spot N (*Aut*) local m pouco visível; (*fig*) ponto fraco
blink [blɪŋk] vi piscar ▸ N (*inf*): **the TV's on the ~** a TV está com defeito
blinkers ['blɪŋkəz] NPL antolhos mpl
blinking ['blɪŋkɪŋ] (*BRIT inf*) ADJ: **this ~ …** este danado …
bliss [blɪs] N felicidade f
blissful ['blɪsful] ADJ (*event, day*) maravilhoso; (*sigh, smile*) contente; **in ~ ignorance** numa bendita ignorância
blissfully ['blɪsfulɪ] ADV (*smile*) ditosamente; (*happy*) maravilhosamente
blister ['blɪstə'] N (*on skin*) bolha; (*in paint, rubber*) empola ▸ vi (*paint*) empolar-se
BLit, BLitt N ABBR (= *Bachelor of Literature*) título universitário
blithe [blaɪð] ADJ alegre
blithely ['blaɪðlɪ] ADV (*unconcernedly*) tranquilamente; (*joyfully*) alegremente
blithering ['blɪðərɪŋ] (*inf*) ADJ: **this ~ idiot** esta besta quadrada
blitz [blɪts] N bombardeio aéreo; (*fig*): **to have a ~ on sth** dar um jeito em algo
blizzard ['blɪzəd] N nevasca
BLM (*us*) N ABBR = **Bureau of Land Management**
bloated ['bləutɪd] ADJ (*swollen*) inchado; (*full*) empanturrado
blob [blɔb] N (*drop*) gota; (*stain, spot*) mancha; (*indistinct shape*) ponto
bloc [blɔk] N (*Pol*) bloco
block [blɔk] N (*of wood*) bloco; (*of stone*) laje f; (*in pipes*) entupimento; (*toy*) cubo; (*of buildings*) quarteirão m ▸ vt obstruir, bloquear; (*pipe*) entupir; (*progress*) impedir; **~ of flats** (*BRIT*) prédio (de apartamentos); **3 ~s from here** a três quarteirões daqui; **mental ~** bloqueio; **~ and tackle** (*Tech*) talha
▸ **block up** vt (*hole*) tampar; (*pipe*) entupir; (*road*) bloquear
blockade [blɔ'keɪd] N bloqueio ▸ vt bloquear
blockage ['blɔkɪdʒ] N obstrução f
block booking N reserva em bloco
blockbuster ['blɔkbʌstə'] N grande sucesso
block capitals NPL letras fpl de forma
blockhead ['blɔkhɛd] N imbecil m/f
block letters NPL letras fpl maiúsculas
block release (*BRIT*) N licença para fins de aperfeiçoamento profissional
block vote (*BRIT*) N voto em bloco
blog ['blɔg] N blogue m ▸ vi blogar
blogger ['blɔgə'] N (*person*) blogueiro(-a)
blogosphere ['blɔgəsfɪə'] N blogosfera
bloke [bləuk] (*BRIT inf*) N cara m (*BR*), gajo (*PT*)
blond, blonde [blɔnd] ADJ, N louro(-a)

b

blood [blʌd] N sangue *m*
bloodcurdling ['blʌdkə:dlɪŋ] ADJ horripilante, de fazer gelar o sangue nas veias
blood donor N doador(a) *m/f* de sangue
blood group N grupo sanguíneo
bloodhound ['blʌdhaund] N sabujo
bloodless ['blʌdlɪs] ADJ (*victory*) incruento; (*pale*) pálido
bloodletting ['blʌdletɪŋ] N (*Med*) sangria; (*fig*) derramamento de sangue
blood poisoning N toxemia
blood pressure N pressão *f* arterial *or* sanguínea
bloodshed ['blʌdʃed] N matança, carnificina
bloodshot ['blʌdʃɔt] ADJ (*eyes*) injetado
bloodstained ['blʌdsteɪnd] ADJ manchado de sangue
bloodstream ['blʌdstri:m] N corrente *f* sanguínea
blood test N exame *m* de sangue
bloodthirsty ['blʌdθə:stɪ] ADJ sanguinário
blood transfusion N transfusão *f* de sangue
blood vessel N vaso sanguíneo
bloody ['blʌdɪ] ADJ sangrento; (*nose*) ensanguentado; (*BRIT !*): **this ~** ... essa droga de ..., esse maldito ...; **~ strong/good** forte/ bom pra burro (*inf*)
bloody-minded ['blʌdɪ'maɪndɪd] (*BRIT inf*) ADJ espírito de porco *inv*
bloom [blu:m] N flor *f*; (*fig*) florescimento, viço ▶ VI florescer
blooming ['blu:mɪŋ] (*inf*) ADJ: **this ~** ... esse maldito ..., esse miserável ...
blossom ['blɔsəm] N flor *f* ▶ VI florescer; (*fig*) desabrochar-se; **to ~ into** (*fig*) tornar-se
blot [blɔt] N borrão *m*; (*fig*) mancha ▶ VT borrar; (*ink*) secar; **a ~ on the landscape** um aleijão na paisagem; **to ~ one's copy book** (*fig*) manchar sua reputação
▶ **blot out** VT (*view*) tapar; (*memory*) apagar
blotchy ['blɔtʃɪ] ADJ (*complexion*) cheio de manchas
blotter ['blɔtə^r] N mata-borrão *m*
blotting paper ['blɔtɪŋ-] N mata-borrão *m*
blouse [blauz] N blusa
blow [bləu] (*pt* **blew**, *pp* **blown**) N golpe *m*; (*punch*) soco ▶ VI soprar ▶ VT (*subj: wind*) soprar; (*instrument*) tocar; (*fuse*) queimar; (*glass*) soprar; **to ~ one's nose** assoar o nariz; **to come to ~s** chegar às vias de fato
▶ **blow away** VT levar, arrancar ▶ VI ser levado pelo vento
▶ **blow down** VT derrubar
▶ **blow off** VT levar ▶ VI ser levado
▶ **blow out** VI (*candle*) apagar-se; (*tyre*) estourar ▶ VT (*candle*) apagar
▶ **blow over** VI passar
▶ **blow up** VI explodir; (*fig*) perder a paciência ▶ VT explodir; (*tyre*) encher; (*Phot*) ampliar
blow-dry N escova ▶ VT fazer escova em
blowlamp ['bləulæmp] (*BRIT*) N maçarico
blown [bləun] PP *of* **blow**

blow-out N (*of tyre*) furo; (*inf: big meal*) rega-bofe *m*
blowtorch ['bləutɔ:tʃ] N = **blowlamp**
blowzy ['blauzɪ] (*BRIT*) ADJ balofa
BLS (*US*) N ABBR = **Bureau of Labor Statistics**
blubber ['blʌbə^r] N óleo de baleia ▶ VI (*pej*) choramingar
bludgeon ['blʌdʒən] VT bater em
blue [blu:] ADJ azul; (*depressed*) deprimido; **blues** N (*Mus*): **the ~s** o blues; **to have the ~s** (*inf: feeling*) estar na fossa, estar de baixo astral; (**only**) **once in a ~ moon** uma vez na vida e outra na morte; **out of the ~** (*fig*) de estalo, inesperadamente
blue baby N criança azul
bluebell ['blu:bel] N campainha
bluebottle ['blu:bɔtl] N varejeira azul
blue cheese N queijo tipo roquefort
blue-chip ADJ: **~ investment** investimento de primeira ordem
blue-collar worker N operário(-a)
blue film N filme picante
blue jeans NPL jeans *m* (*BR*), jeans *mpl* (*PT*)
blueprint ['blu:prɪnt] N anteprojeto; (*fig*): **~ (for)** esquema *m* (de)
bluff [blʌf] VI blefar ▶ N blefe *m*; (*crag*) penhasco ▶ ADJ (*person*) brusco; **to call sb's ~** pagar para ver alguém
blunder ['blʌndə^r] N gafe *f* ▶ VI cometer *or* fazer uma gafe; **to ~ into sb/sth** esbarrar com alguém/algo
blunt [blʌnt] ADJ (*knife*) cego; (*pencil*) rombudo; (*person*) franco, direto ▶ VT embotar; **~ instrument** (*Law*) arma imprópria
bluntly ['blʌntlɪ] ADV sem rodeios
bluntness ['blʌntnɪs] N (*of person*) franqueza, rudeza
blur [blə:^r] N borrão *m* ▶ VT borrar, nublar; (*vision*) embaçar
blurb [blə:b] N (*for book*) dizeres *mpl* de propaganda
blurred [blə:d] ADJ indistinto, borrado
blurt out [blə:t-] VT (*reveal*) deixar escapar; (*say*) balbuciar
blush [blʌʃ] VI corar, ruborizar-se ▶ N rubor *m*, vermelhidão *f*
blusher ['blʌʃə^r] N blusher *m*
bluster ['blʌstə^r] N fanfarronada, bazófia ▶ VI fanfarronar
blustering ['blʌstərɪŋ] ADJ (*person*) fanfarrão(-rona)
blustery ['blʌstərɪ] ADJ (*weather*) borrascoso, tormentoso
Blvd ABBR = **boulevard**
BM N ABBR = **British Museum**; (*Sch*: = *Bachelor of Medicine*) título universitário
BMA N ABBR = **British Medical Association**
BMJ N ABBR = **British Medical Journal**
BMus N ABBR (= *Bachelor of Music*) título universitário
BO N ABBR (*inf*: = *body odour*) fartum *m*, c.c. *m*; (*US*) = **box office**
boar [bɔ:^r] N javali *m*

board [bɔːd] N (*wooden*) tábua; (*blackboard*) quadro; (*notice board*) quadro de avisos; (*for chess etc*) tabuleiro; (*committee*) junta, conselho; (*in firm*) diretoria, conselho administrativo; (*Naut, Aviat*): **on** ~ a bordo ▶ VT embarcar em; **full** ~ (BRIT) pensão f completa; **half** ~ (BRIT) meia-pensão f; ~ **and lodging** casa e comida; **above** ~ (*fig*) limpo; **across the** ~ *adj* geral; *adv* de uma maneira geral; **to go by the** ~ ficar abandonado, dançar (*inf*)
▶ **board up** VT (*door*) entabuar
boarder ['bɔːdəʳ] N hóspede m/f; (*Sch*) interno(-a)
board game N jogo de tabuleiro
boarding card ['bɔːdɪŋ-] N = **boarding pass**
boarding house ['bɔːdɪŋ-] N pensão m
boarding pass ['bɔːdɪŋ-] (BRIT) N (*Aviat, Naut*) cartão m de embarque
boarding school ['bɔːdɪŋ-] N internato
board meeting N reunião f da diretoria
board room N sala da diretoria
boardwalk ['bɔːdwɔːk] (US) N passeio de tábuas
boast [bəust] VI contar vantagem ▶ VT ostentar ▶ N jactância, bazófia; **to** ~ (**about** *or* **of**) gabar-se (de), jactar-se (de)
boastful ['bəustful] ADJ vaidoso, jactancioso
boastfulness ['bəustfulnɪs] N bazófia, jactância
boat [bəut] N barco m; (*ship*) navio; **to go by** ~ ir de barco; **to be in the same** ~ (*fig*) estar no mesmo barco
boater ['bəutəʳ] N (*hat*) chapéu m de palha
boating ['bəutɪŋ] N passeio de barco
boatman ['bəutmən] (*irreg: like* **man**) N barqueiro
boatswain ['bəusn] N contramestre m
bob [bɔb] VI (*boat, cork on water: also*: **bob up and down**) balouçar-se ▶ N (BRIT *inf*) = **shilling**
▶ **bob up** VI aparecer, surgir
bobbin ['bɔbɪn] N bobina, carretel m
bobby ['bɔbɪ] (BRIT *inf*) N policial m/f (BR), polícia m (PT)
bobsleigh ['bɔbsleɪ] N bob m, trenó m duplo
bode [bəud] VI: **to** ~ **well/ill (for)** ser de bom/mau agouro (para)
bodice ['bɔdɪs] N corpete m
bodily ['bɔdɪlɪ] ADJ corporal; (*pain*) físico; (*needs*) material ▶ ADV (*lift*) em peso
body ['bɔdɪ] N corpo m; (*corpse*) cadáver m; (*of car*) carroceria; (*of plane*) fuselagem f; (*fig: group*) grupo m; (: *organization*) organização f; (: *quantity*) conjunto; (: *of wine*) corpo; **in a** ~ todos juntos
body-building N musculação f
bodyguard ['bɔdɪgɑːd] N guarda-costas m inv
body language N linguagem f corporal
body repairs NPL lanternagem f
bodywork ['bɔdɪwəːk] N lataria
boffin ['bɔfɪn] (BRIT) N cientista m/f
bog [bɔg] N pântano, atoleiro ▶ VT: **to get** ~**ged down (in)** (*fig*) atolar-se (em)

bogey ['bəugɪ] N (*worry*) espectro; (BRIT *inf*: *dried mucus*) meleca
boggle ['bɔgl] VI: **the mind** ~**s** (*wonder*) não dá para imaginar; (*innuendo*) nem quero pensar
bogie ['bəugɪ] N (*Rail*) truque m
Bogotá [bɔgə'tɑː] N Bogotá
bogus ['bəugəs] ADJ falso; (*workman etc*) farsante
Bohemia [bəu'hiːmɪə] N Boêmia
Bohemian [bəu'hiːmɪən] ADJ, N boêmio(-a)
boil [bɔɪl] VT ferver; (*eggs*) cozinhar ▶ VI ferver ▶ N (*Med*) furúnculo; **to bring to the** (BRIT) *or* **a** (US) ~ deixar ferver; **to come to the** (BRIT) *or* **a** (US) ~ começar a ferver
▶ **boil down to** VT FUS (*fig*) reduzir-se a
▶ **boil over** VI transbordar
boiled egg [bɔɪld-] N ovo cozido
boiled potatoes [bɔɪld-] NPL batatas fpl cozidas
boiler ['bɔɪləʳ] N caldeira; (*for central heating*) boiler m
boiler suit (BRIT) N macacão m (BR), fato macaco (PT)
boiling ['bɔɪlɪŋ] ADJ: **it's** ~ (*weather*) está um calor horrível; **I'm** ~ (**hot**) (*inf*) estou morrendo de calor
boiling point N ponto de ebulição
boisterous ['bɔɪstərəs] ADJ (*noisy*) barulhento; (*excitable*) agitado; (*crowd*) turbulento
bold [bəuld] ADJ corajoso; (*pej*) atrevido, insolente; (*outline, colour*) forte
boldness ['bəuldnɪs] N arrojo, coragem f; (*cheek*) audácia, descaramento
bold type N (*Typ*) negrito
Bolivia [bə'lɪvɪə] N Bolívia
Bolivian [bə'lɪvɪən] ADJ, N boliviano(-a)
bollard ['bɔləd] (BRIT) N (*Aut*) poste m de sinalização; (*Naut*) poste de amarração
bolster ['bəulstəʳ] N travesseiro
▶ **bolster up** VT sustentar
bolt [bəult] N (*lock*) trinco, ferrolho; (*with nut*) parafuso, cavilha ▶ ADV: ~**upright** direito como um fuso ▶ VT (*door*) fechar a ferrolho, trancar; (*food*) engolir às pressas ▶ VI fugir; (*horse*) disparar; **to be a** ~ **from the blue** (*fig*) cair como uma bomba, ser uma bomba
bomb [bɔm] N bomba ▶ VT bombardear
bombard [bɔm'bɑːd] VT bombardear
bombardment [bɔm'bɑːdmənt] N bombardeio
bombastic [bɔm'bæstɪk] ADJ bombástico
bomb disposal N: ~ **expert** perito(-a) em desmontagem de explosivos; ~ **unit** unidade f de desmontagem de explosivos
bomber ['bɔməʳ] N (*Aviat*) bombardeiro; (*terrorist*) terrorista m/f
bombing ['bɔmɪŋ] N bombardeio; (*by terrorists*) atentado a bomba
bomb scare N ameaça de bomba
bombshell ['bɔmʃɛl] N granada de artilharia; (*fig*) bomba
bomb site N zona bombardeada
bona fide ['bəunə'faɪdɪ] ADJ genuíno, autêntico

b

bonanza [bə'nænzə] N boom m
bond [bɔnd] N (binding promise) compromisso; (link) vínculo, laço; (Finance) obrigação f; (Comm): **in ~** (goods) retido sob caução na alfândega
bondage ['bɔndɪdʒ] N escravidão f
bonded warehouse ['bɔndɪd-] N depósito da alfândega, entreposto aduaneiro
bone [bəun] N osso; (of fish) espinha ▶ VT desossar; tirar as espinhas de
bone china N porcelana com mistura de cinza de ossos
bone-dry ADJ completamente seco
bone idle ADJ preguiçoso
boner ['bəunəʳ] (US) N gafe f
bonfire ['bɔnfaɪəʳ] N fogueira
Bonn [bɔn] N Bonn
bonnet ['bɔnɪt] N toucado; (BRIT: of car) capô m
bonny ['bɔnɪ] (SCOTLAND) ADJ bonito
bonus ['bəunəs] N (payment) bônus m; (fig) gratificação f; (on salary) prêmio, gratificação f
bony ['bəunɪ] ADJ (arm, face, Med: tissue) ossudo; (meat) cheio de ossos; (fish) cheio de espinhas
boo [bu:] VT vaiar ▶ N vaia ▶ EXCL ruuh!, bu!
boob [bu:b] (inf) N (breast) seio; (BRIT: mistake) besteira, gafe f
booby prize ['bu:bɪ-] N prêmio de consolação
booby trap ['bu:bɪ-] N armadilha explosiva
booby-trapped ['bu:bɪtræpt] ADJ que tem armadilha explosiva
book [buk] N livro; (of stamps, tickets) talão m; (notebook) caderno ▶ VT reservar; (driver) autuar; (football player) mostrar o cartão amarelo a; **books** NPL (Comm) contas fpl, contabilidade f; **to keep the ~s** fazer a escrituração or contabilidade; **by the ~** de acordo com o regulamento, corretamente; **to throw the ~ at sb** condenar alguém à pena máxima
▶ **book in** (BRIT) VI (at hotel) registrar (BR), registar (PT)
▶ **book up** VT reservar; **all seats are ~ed up** todos os lugares estão tomados; **the hotel is ~ed up** o hotel está lotado
bookable ['bukəbl] ADJ: **seats are ~** lugares podem ser reservados
bookcase ['bukkeɪs] N estante f (para livros)
book ends NPL suportes mpl de livros
booking ['bukɪŋ] (BRIT) N reserva
booking office (BRIT) N (Rail, Theatre) bilheteria (BR), bilheteira (PT)
book-keeping N escrituração f, contabilidade f
booklet ['buklɪt] N livrinho, brochura
bookmaker ['bukmeɪkəʳ] N book(maker) m (BR), agenciador m de apostas (PT)
bookmark ['bukmɑːk] N (for book) marcador m de livro; (Comput) favorito, bookmark m
bookseller ['buksɛləʳ] N livreiro(-a)
bookshop, bookstore N livraria
bookstall ['bukstɔːl] N banca de livros
bookstore ['bukstɔːʳ] N = **bookshop**

book token N vale m para livro
book value N valor m contábil
boom [bu:m] N (noise) barulho, estrondo; (in sales etc) aumento rápido; (Econ) boom m, fase f or aumento de prosperidade ▶ VI (sound) retumbar; (business) tomar surto
boomerang ['bu:məræŋ] N bumerangue m
boom town N cidade f de rápido crescimento econômico
boon [bu:n] N dádiva, benefício
boorish ['buərɪʃ] ADJ rude
boost [bu:st] N estímulo ▶ VT estimular; **to give a ~ to sb's spirits** or **to sb** dar uma força a alguém
booster ['bu:stəʳ] N (Med) revacinação f; (TV) amplificador m (de sinal); (Elec) sobrevoltador m; (also: **booster rocket**) foguete m auxiliar
booster seat N (Aut: for children) assento de carro para crianças maiores
boot [bu:t] N bota; (for football) chuteira; (for walking) bota (para caminhar); (ankle boot) botina; (BRIT: of car) porta-malas m (BR), mala (BR inf), porta-bagagem m (PT) ▶ VT (kick) dar pontapé em; (Comput) iniciar; **to ~ ...** (in addition) ainda por cima ...; **to give sb the ~** (inf) botar alguém na rua
booth [bu:ð] N (at fair) barraca; (telephone booth, voting booth) cabine f
bootleg ['bu:tlɛg] ADJ de contrabando; **~ recording** gravação f pirata
booty ['bu:tɪ] N despojos mpl, pilhagem f
booze [bu:z] (inf) N bebida alcoólica ▶ VI embebedar-se
boozer ['bu:zəʳ] (inf) N (person) beberrão/beberrona m/f; (BRIT: pub) pub m
border ['bɔːdəʳ] N margem f; (for flowers) borda; (of a country) fronteira; (on cloth etc) debrum m, remate m ▶ VT (also: **border on**) limitar-se com ▶ CPD (town, region) fronteiriço; **the B~s** a região fronteiriça entre a Escócia e a Inglaterra
▶ **border on** VT FUS (fig) chegar às raias de
borderline ['bɔːdəlaɪn] N (fig) fronteira
borderline case N caso-limite m
bore [bɔːʳ] PT of **bear** ▶ VT (hole) abrir; (well) cavar; (person) aborrecer ▶ N (person) chato(-a), maçante m/f; (of gun) calibre m; **what a ~!** que chato! (BR), que saco! (BR), que maçada! (PT)
bored [bɔːd] ADJ entediado; **to be ~ to tears** or **~ to death** or **~ stiff** estar muito entediado
boredom ['bɔːdəm] N tédio, aborrecimento
boring ['bɔːrɪŋ] ADJ chato, maçante
born [bɔːn] ADJ: **to be ~** nascer; **I was ~ in 1990** nasci em 1990; **~ blind** cego de nascença; **a ~ leader** um líder nato
born-again [bɔːnə'gɛn] ADJ: **~ Christian** evangélico(-a), crente m/f
borne [bɔːn] PP of **bear**
Borneo ['bɔːnɪəu] N Bornéu
borough ['bʌrə] N município

borrow ['bɔrəu] VT: **to ~ sth (from sb)** pedir algo emprestado a alguém; **may I ~ your car?** você pode me emprestar o seu carro?

borrower ['bɔrəuə^r] N tomador(a) m/f de empréstimo

borrowing ['bɔrəuɪŋ] N empréstimo(s) m(pl)

borstal ['bɔːstl] (BRIT) N reformatório (de menores)

bosom ['buzəm] N peito

bosom friend N amigo(-a) íntimo(-a) or do peito

boss [bɔs] N chefe m/f; (employer) patrão(-troa) m/f; (in agriculture, industry etc) capataz m ▶ VT (also: **boss about, boss around**) mandar em

bossy ['bɔsɪ] ADJ mandão(-dona)

bosun ['bəusn] N contramestre m

botanical [bə'tænɪkl] ADJ botânico

botanist ['bɔtənɪst] N botânico(-a)

botany ['bɔtənɪ] N botânica

botch [bɔtʃ] VT (also: **botch up**) estropiar, atamancar

both [bəuθ] ADJ, PRON ambos(-as), os dois/as duas ▶ ADV: **~ A and B** tanto A como B; **~ of us went, we ~ went** nós dois fomos, ambos fomos

bother ['bɔðə^r] VT (worry) preocupar; (irritate) incomodar, molestar; (disturb) atrapalhar ▶ VI (also: **bother o.s.**) preocupar-se ▶ N (trouble) preocupação f; (nuisance) amolação f, inconveniente m ▶ EXCL bolas!; **to ~ about** preocupar-se com; **I'm sorry to ~ you** lamento incomodá-lo; **please don't ~** por favor, não se preocupe, não se dê ao trabalho; **don't ~** não vale a pena; **to ~ doing** dar-se ao trabalho de fazer; **it's no ~** não tem problema

Botswana [bɔt'swaːnə] N Botsuana

bottle ['bɔtl] N garrafa; (of perfume, medicine) frasco; (baby's) mamadeira (BRIT), biberão m (PT) ▶ VT engarrafar

▶ **bottle up** VT conter, refrear

bottle bank N depósito de vidro para reciclagem, vidrão m (PT)

bottleneck ['bɔtlnɛk] N (traffic) engarrafamento; (fig) obstáculo, problema m

bottle-opener N abridor m (de garrafas) (BRIT), abre-garrafas m inv (PT)

bottom ['bɔtəm] N (of container, sea) fundo; (buttocks) traseiro, bunda (inf); (of page, list) pé m; (of class) nível m mais baixo; (of mountain, hill) sopé m ▶ ADJ (low) inferior, mais baixo; (last) último; **to get to the ~ of sth** (fig) tirar algo a limpo

bottomless ['bɔtəmlɪs] ADJ sem fundo; (fig) insondável; (funds) ilimitado

bough [bau] N ramo

bought [bɔːt] PT, PP of **buy**

boulder ['bəuldə^r] N pedregulho, matacão m

bounce [bauns] VI (ball) saltar, quicar; (cheque) ser devolvido (por insuficiência de fundos) ▶ VT fazer saltar ▶ N (rebound) salto; **he's got plenty of ~** (fig) ele tem pique

bouncer ['baunsə^r] (inf) N leão de chácara m

bound [baund] PT, PP of **bind** ▶ N (leap) pulo, salto; (gen pl: limit) limite m ▶ VI (leap) pular, saltar ▶ VT (border) demarcar; (limit) limitar ▶ ADJ: **~ by** (law, regulation) limitado por; **to be ~ to do sth** (obliged) ter a obrigação de fazer algo; (likely) na certa ir fazer algo; **~ for** com destino a; **out of ~s** fora dos limites

boundary ['baundrɪ] N limite m, fronteira

boundless ['baundlɪs] ADJ ilimitado

bountiful ['bauntɪful] ADJ (person) generoso; (supply) farto

bounty ['bauntɪ] N (generosity) generosidade f; (wealth) fartura

bouquet ['bukeɪ] N (of flowers) buquê m, ramalhete m; (of wine) buquê m, aroma m

bourbon ['buəbən] (US) N (also: **bourbon whiskey**) uísque m (BR) or whisky m (PT) (norte-americano)

bourgeois ['buəʒwaː] ADJ burguês(-guesa)

bout [baut] N período; (of malaria etc) ataque m; (of activity) explosão f; (Boxing etc) combate m

boutique [buːˈtiːk] N butique f

bow^1 [bəu] N (knot) laço; (weapon, Mus) arco

bow^2 [bau] N (of the body) reverência; (of the head) inclinação f; (Naut: also: **bows**) proa ▶ VI curvar-se, fazer uma reverência; (yield): **to ~ to** or **before** ceder ante, submeter-se a; **to ~ to the inevitable** curvar-se ao inevitável

bowels ['bauəlz] NPL intestinos mpl, tripas fpl; (fig) entranhas fpl

bowl [bəul] N tigela; (for washing) bacia; (ball) bola; (of pipe) fornilho; (US: stadium) estádio ▶ VI (Cricket) arremessar a bola

▶ **bowl over** VT (fig) impressionar, comover

bow-legged ADJ cambaio, de pernas tortas

bowler ['bəulə^r] N jogador(a) m/f de bolas; (Cricket) lançador m (da bola); (BRIT: also: **bowler hat**) chapéu-coco m

bowling ['bəulɪŋ] N (game) boliche m

bowling alley N boliche m

bowling green N gramado (BR) or relvado (PT) para jogo de bolas

bowls [bəulz] N jogo de bolas

bow tie [bəu-] N gravata-borboleta

box [bɔks] N caixa; (crate) caixote m; (for jewels) estojo; (for money) cofre m; (Theatre) camarote m ▶ VT encaixotar; (Sport) boxear contra ▶ VI (Sport) boxear

boxer ['bɔksə^r] N (person) boxeador m, pugilista m; (dog) boxer m

boxer shorts NPL cueca samba-canção

boxing ['bɔksɪŋ] N (Sport) boxe m, pugilismo

Boxing Day (BRIT) N Dia de Santo Estevão (26 de dezembro)

boxing gloves NPL luvas fpl de boxe

boxing ring N ringue m de boxe

box number N (for advertisements) caixa postal

box office N bilheteria (BR), bilheteira (PT)

boxroom ['bɔksrum] N quarto pequeno

boy [bɔɪ] N (young) menino, garoto; (older) moço, rapaz m; (son) filho; (servant) criado

boycott ['bɔɪkɔt] N boicote m, boicotagem f
▶ VT boicotar
boyfriend ['bɔɪfrɛnd] N namorado
boyish ['bɔɪɪʃ] ADJ (man) jovial; (looks) pueril;
(woman) como ares de menino
Bp ABBR = **bishop**
BPOE (US) N ABBR (= Benevolent and Protective
Order of Elks) associação beneficente
BR ABBR = **British Rail**
Br. ABBR (Rel: = brother) Fr.
bra [brɑː] N sutiã m (BR), soutien m (PT)
brace [breɪs] N reforço, braçadeira; (on teeth)
aparelho; (tool) arco de pua; (Typ: also: **brace
bracket**) chave f ▶ VT firmar, reforçar; (knees,
shoulders) retesar; **braces** NPL (BRIT)
suspensórios mpl; **to ~ o.s.** (for weight, fig)
preparar-se
bracelet ['breɪslɪt] N pulseira
bracing ['breɪsɪŋ] ADJ tonificante
bracken ['brækən] N samambaia (BR), feto (PT)
bracket ['brækɪt] N (Tech) suporte m; (group)
classe f, categoria; (range) faixa; (also: **brace
bracket**) chave f; (also: **round bracket**)
parêntese m; (also: **square bracket**) colchete
m ▶ VT pôr entre parênteses; (fig: also:
bracket together) agrupar; **in ~s** entre
parênteses (or colchetes)
brackish ['brækɪʃ] ADJ (water) salobro
brag [bræg] VI gabar-se, contar vantagem
braid [breɪd] N (trimming) galão m; (of hair)
trança
Braille [breɪl] N braile m
brain [breɪn] N cérebro; **brains** NPL (Culin)
miolos mpl; (intelligence) inteligência, miolos;
he's got ~s ele é inteligente
brainchild ['breɪntʃaɪld] N ideia original
brainless ['breɪnlɪs] ADJ estúpido, desmiolado
brainstorm ['breɪnstɔːm] N (fig) momento de
distração; (US: brainwave) ideia luminosa
brainwash ['breɪnwɔʃ] VT fazer uma lavagem
cerebral em
brainwave ['breɪnweɪv] N inspiração f, ideia
luminosa or brilhante
brainy ['breɪnɪ] ADJ inteligente
braise [breɪz] VT assar na panela
brake [breɪk] N freio (BR), travão m (PT) ▶ VT, VI
frear (BR), travar (PT)
brake fluid N óleo de freio (BR) or dos travões (PT)
brake light N farol m do freio (BR), farolim m
de travagem (PT)
brake pedal N pedal m do freio (BR), travão m
de pé (PT)
bramble ['bræmbl] N amora-preta
bran [bræn] N farelo
branch [brɑːntʃ] N ramo, galho; (road) ramal
m; (Comm) sucursal f, filial f; (: bank) agência
▶ VI bifurcar-se
▶ **branch out** VI (fig) diversificar suas
atividades; **to ~ out into** estender suas
atividades a
branch line N (Rail) ramal m
branch manager N gerente m/f de sucursal or
filial

brand [brænd] N marca; (fig: type) tipo ▶ VT
(cattle) marcar com ferro quente; (fig: pej):
to ~ sb a communist etc estigmatizar
alguém de comunista etc
brandish ['brændɪʃ] VT brandir
brand name N marca de fábrica, griffe f
brand-new ADJ novo em folha, novinho
brandy ['brændɪ] N conhaque m
brash [bræʃ] ADJ (rough) grosseiro; (forward)
descarado
Brasilia [brəˈzɪlɪə] N Brasília
brass [brɑːs] N latão m; **the ~** (Mus) os metais;
the top ~ as altas patentes
brass band N banda de música
brassiere ['bræsɪər] N sutiã m (BR), soutien m (PT)
brass tacks NPL: **to get down to ~** passar ao
que interessa, entrar no assunto principal
brat [bræt] (pej) N pirralho(-a), fedelho(-a)
bravado [brəˈvɑːdəʊ] N bravata
brave [breɪv] ADJ valente, corajoso ▶ N
guerreiro pele-vermelha ▶ VT (face up to)
desafiar; (resist) encarar
bravery ['breɪvərɪ] N coragem f, bravura
bravo [brɑːˈvəʊ] EXCL bravo!
brawl [brɔːl] N briga, pancadaria ▶ VI brigar
brawn [brɔːn] N força; (meat) patê m de carne
brawny ['brɔːnɪ] ADJ musculoso, carnudo
bray [breɪ] N zurro, ornejo ▶ VI zurrar,
ornejar
brazen ['breɪzn] ADJ descarado ▶ VT: **to ~ it
out** defender-se descaradamente
brazier ['breɪzɪər] N braseiro
Brazil [brəˈzɪl] N Brasil m
Brazilian [brəˈzɪljən] ADJ, N brasileiro(-a)
Brazil nut N castanha-do-pará f
breach [briːtʃ] VT abrir brecha em ▶ N (gap)
brecha; (estrangement) rompimento;
(breaking): **~ of contract** inadimplência (BR),
inadimplemento (PT); **~ of the peace**
perturbação f da ordem pública
bread [brɛd] N pão m; (inf: money) grana;
to earn one's daily ~ ganhar o pão or a vida;
**to know which side one's ~ is buttered
(on)** saber o que lhe convém
bread and butter N pão m com manteiga; (fig)
ganha-pão m
breadbin ['brɛdbɪn] (BRIT) N caixa de pão
breadboard ['brɛdbɔːd] N tábua de pão
breadbox ['brɛdbɔks] (US) N caixa de pão
breadcrumbs ['brɛdkrʌmz] NPL migalhas fpl;
(Culin) farinha de rosca
breadline ['brɛdlaɪn] N: **to be on the ~** viver
na miséria
breadth [brɛtθ] N largura; (fig) amplitude f
breadwinner ['brɛdwɪnər] N arrimo de
família
break [breɪk] (pt broke, pp broken) VT quebrar
(BR), partir (PT); (split) partir; (promise)
quebrar; (word) faltar a; (fall) amortecer;
(journey) interromper; (law) violar,
transgredir; (record) bater; (news) revelar
▶ VI quebrar-se, partir-se; (storm) estourar;
(weather) mudar; (dawn) amanhecer;

(*story, news*) revelar ▶ N (*gap*) abertura; (*crack*) fenda; (*fracture*) fratura; (*breakdown*) ruptura, rompimento; (*rest*) descanso; (*interval*) intervalo; (*at school*) recreio; (*chance*) oportunidade *f*; **to ~ one's leg** *etc* quebrar a perna *etc*; **to ~ with sb** romper com alguém; **to ~ the news to sb** dar a notícia a alguém; **to ~ even** sair sem ganhar nem perder; **to ~ free** *or* **loose** soltar-se; **to ~ open** (*door etc*) arrombar; **to take a ~** (*few minutes*) descansar um pouco, fazer uma pausa; (*holiday*) tirar férias para descansar; **without a ~** sem parar
  ▶ **break down** VT (*door etc*) arrombar; (*figures, data*) analisar; (*resistance*) acabar com ▶ VI (*go awry*) desarranjar-se; (*machine, Aut*) enguiçar, pifar (*inf*); (*Med*) sofrer uma crise nervosa; (*person: cry*) desatar a chorar; (*talks*) fracassar
  ▶ **break in** VT (*horse etc*) domar; (*US: car*) fazer a rodagem de ▶ VI (*burglar*) forçar uma entrada; (*interrupt*) interromper
  ▶ **break into** VT FUS (*house*) arrombar
  ▶ **break off** VI (*speaker*) parar-se, deter-se; (*branch*) partir ▶ VT (*talks*) suspender; (*relations*) cortar; (*engagement*) terminar, acabar com
  ▶ **break out** VI (*war*) estourar; (*prisoner*) libertar-se; **to ~ out in spots/a rash** aparecer coberto de manchas/brotoejas
  ▶ **break through** VI: **the sun broke through** o sol apareceu, o tempo abriu ▶ VT FUS (*defences, barrier*) transpor; (*crowd*) abrir passagem por
  ▶ **break up** VI despedaçar-se; (*ship*) partir-se; (*partnership*) acabar; (*marriage*) desmanchar-se; (*friends*) separar-se, brigar, falhar ▶ VT (*rocks*) partir; (*biscuit etc*) quebrar; (*journey*) romper; (*fight*) intervir em; (*marriage*) desmanchar; **you're ~ing up** sua voz está falhando
breakable ['breɪkəbl] ADJ quebradiço, frágil ▶ N: **~s** artigos *mpl* frágeis
breakage ['breɪkɪdʒ] N quebradura; (*Comm*) quebra; **to pay for ~s** pagar indenização por quebras
breakaway ['breɪkəweɪ] ADJ (*group etc*) dissidente
breakdown ['breɪkdaun] N (*Aut*) enguiço, avaria; (*in communications*) interrupção *f*; (*of marriage*) fracasso, término; (*machine*) enguiço; (*Med: also:* **nervous breakdown**) esgotamento nervoso; (*of figures*) discriminação *f*, desdobramento
breakdown service (*BRIT*) N autossocorro (*BR*), pronto socorro (*PT*)
breakdown van (*BRIT*) N reboque *m* (*BR*), pronto socorro (*PT*)
breaker ['breɪkə'] N onda grande
breakeven ['breɪk'iːvn] CPD: **~ chart** gráfico do ponto de equilíbrio; **~ point** ponto de equilíbrio
breakfast ['brɛkfəst] N café *m* da manhã (*BR*), pequeno-almoço (*PT*)

breakfast cereal N cereais *mpl*
break-in N roubo com arrombamento
breaking point ['breɪkɪŋ-] N limite *m*
breakthrough ['breɪkθruː] N ruptura; (*fig*) avanço, novo progresso
break-up N (*of partnership, marriage*) dissolução *f*
break-up value N (*Comm*) valor *m* de liquidação
breakwater ['breɪkwɔːtə'] N quebra-mar *m*
breast [brɛst] N (*of woman*) peito, seio; (*chest, meat*) peito
breast-feed (*irreg: like* **feed**) VT, VI amamentar
breast pocket N bolso sobre o peito
breaststroke ['brɛststrəuk] N nado de peito
breath [brɛθ] N fôlego, respiração *f*; **to go out for a ~ of air** sair para tomar fôlego; **out of ~** ofegante, sem fôlego
Breathalyser® ['brɛθəlaɪzə'] N bafômetro
breathe [briːð] VT, VI respirar; **I won't ~ a word about it** não vou abrir a boca, eu sou um túmulo
  ▶ **breathe in** VT, VI inspirar
  ▶ **breathe out** VT, VI expirar
breather ['briːðə'] N pausa
breathing ['briːðɪŋ] N respiração *f*
breathing space N (*fig*) descanso, repouso
breathless ['brɛθlɪs] ADJ sem fôlego; (*Med*) ofegante
breathtaking ['brɛθteɪkɪŋ] ADJ comovedor(a), emocionante
bred [brɛd] PT, PP *of* **breed**
-bred [brɛd] SUFFIX: **well/ill~** bem-/mal-educado
breed [briːd] (*pt, pp* **bred**) VT (*animals*) criar; (*plants*) multiplicar; (*hate, suspicion*) gerar ▶ VI acasalar-se ▶ N raça
breeder ['briːdə'] N (*person*) criador(a) *m/f*; (*Phys: also:* **breeder reactor**) reator *m* regenerador
breeding ['briːdɪŋ] N reprodução *f*; (*raising*) criação *f*; (*upbringing*) educação *f*
breeze [briːz] N brisa, aragem *f*
breezy ['briːzɪ] ADJ (*person*) despreocupado, animado; (*weather*) ventoso
Breton ['brɛtən] ADJ bretão(-tã) ▶ N bretão(-tã); (*Ling*) bretão *m*
brevity ['brɛvɪtɪ] N brevidade *f*
brew [bruː] VT (*tea*) fazer; (*beer*) fermentar; (*plot*) armar, tramar ▶ VI (*tea*) fazer-se, preparar-se; (*beer*) fermentar; (*storm, fig*) armar-se
brewer ['bruːə'] N cervejeiro(-a)
brewery ['bruːərɪ] N cervejaria
briar ['braɪə'] N (*thorny bush*) urze-branca *f*; (*wild rose*) roseira-brava
bribe [braɪb] N suborno ▶ VT subornar; **to ~ sb to do sth** subornar alguém para fazer algo
bribery ['braɪbərɪ] N suborno
bric-a-brac ['brɪkəbræk] N bricabraque *m*
brick [brɪk] N tijolo
bricklayer ['brɪkleɪə'] N pedreiro
brickwork ['brɪkwəːk] N alvenaria

brickworks ['brɪkwɔːkz] N fábrica de tijolos
bridal ['braɪdl] ADJ nupcial
bride [braɪd] N noiva
bridegroom ['braɪdgrum] N noivo
bridesmaid ['braɪdzmeɪd] N dama de honra
bridge [brɪdʒ] N (Arch, Dentistry) ponte f; (Naut) ponte de comando; (Cards) bridge m; (of nose) cavalete m ▶ VT (river) lançar uma ponte sobre; (gap) transpor
bridging loan ['brɪdʒɪŋ-] (BRIT) N empréstimo a curto prazo
bridle ['braɪdl] N cabeçada, freio ▶ VT enfrear; (fig) refrear, conter
bridle path N senda
brief [briːf] ADJ breve ▶ N (Law) causa; (task) tarefa ▶ VT (inform) informar; (instruct) instruir; **briefs** NPL (for men) cueca (BR), cuecas fpl (PT); (for women) calcinha (BR), cuecas fpl (PT); **in ~ ...** em resumo ...; **to ~ sb about sth** informar alguém sobre algo
briefcase ['briːfkeɪs] N pasta
briefing ['briːfɪŋ] N instruções fpl; (Press) informações fpl
briefly ['briːflɪ] ADV (glance) rapidamente; (say) em poucas palavras; **to glimpse ~** vislumbrar
briefness ['briːfnɪs] N brevidade f
Brig. ABBR (= brigadier) Brig.
brigade [brɪ'geɪd] N (Mil) brigada
brigadier [brɪgə'dɪər] N general m de brigada, brigadeiro
bright [braɪt] ADJ claro, brilhante; (weather) resplandecente; (person: clever) inteligente; (: lively) alegre, animado; (colour) vivo; (future) promissor(a), favorável; **to look on the ~ side** considerar o lado positivo
brighten ['braɪtən], **brighten up** VT (room) tornar mais alegre; (event) animar, alegrar ▶ VI (weather) clarear; (person) animar-se, alegrar-se; (face) iluminar-se; (prospects) tornar-se animado or favorável
brightly ['braɪtlɪ] ADV brilhantemente
brightness ['braɪtnɪs] N claridade f
brilliance ['brɪljəns] N brilho, claridade f
brilliant ['brɪljənt] ADJ brilhante; (clever) inteligente; (inf: great) sensacional
brim [brɪm] N borda; (of hat) aba
brimful ['brɪmful] ADJ cheio até às bordas; (fig) repleto
brine [braɪn] N (Culin) salmoura
bring [brɪŋ] (pt, pp **brought**) VT trazer; **to ~ sth to an end** acabar com algo; **I can't ~ myself to fire him** não posso me resolver a despedi-lo
▶ **bring about** VT ocasionar, produzir
▶ **bring back** VT (restore) restabelecer; (return) devolver
▶ **bring down** VT (price) abaixar; (Mil: plane) abater, derrubar; (government, plane) derrubar
▶ **bring forward** VT adiantar; (Bookkeeping) transportar
▶ **bring in** VT (person) fazer entrar; (object) trazer; (Pol: legislation) introduzir; (: bill)

apresentar; (Law: verdict) pronunciar; (produce: income) render; (harvest) recolher
▶ **bring off** VT (task, plan) levar a cabo; (deal) fechar
▶ **bring out** VT (object) tirar; (meaning) salientar; (new product, book) lançar
▶ **bring round** VT (unconscious person) fazer voltar a si; (convince) convencer
▶ **bring to** VT (unconscious person) fazer voltar a si
▶ **bring up** VT (person) educar, criar; (carry up) subir; (question) introduzir; (food) vomitar
brink [brɪŋk] N beira; **on the ~ of doing** a ponto de fazer, à beira de fazer; **she was on the ~ of tears** ela estava à beira de desatar em prantos
brisk [brɪsk] ADJ vigoroso; (tone, person) enérgico; (speedy) rápido; (trade, business) ativo
bristle ['brɪsl] N (of animal) pelo rijo; (of beard) pelo de barba curta; (of brush) cerda ▶ VI (in anger) encolerizar-se; **to ~ with** estar cheio de
bristly ['brɪslɪ] ADJ (beard, hair) eriçado
Brit [brɪt] (inf) N ABBR (= British person) britânico(-a)
Britain ['brɪtən] N (also: **Great Britain**) Grã-Bretanha; **in ~** na Grã-Bretanha
British ['brɪtɪʃ] ADJ britânico ▶ NPL: **the ~** os britânicos
British Isles NPL: **the ~** as ilhas Britânicas
British Rail N (Hist) companhia ferroviária britânica
Briton ['brɪtən] N britânico(-a)
Brittany ['brɪtənɪ] N Bretanha
brittle ['brɪtl] ADJ quebradiço, frágil
Bro. ABBR (Rel: = brother) Fr.
broach [brəʊtʃ] VT (subject) abordar, tocar em
broad [brɔːd] ADJ (street, range) amplo; (shoulders, smile) largo; (distinction, outline) geral; (accent) carregado ▶ N (US inf) sujeita; **~ hint** indireta transparente; **in ~ daylight** em plena luz do dia
broadband ['brɔːdbænd] N banda larga
broad bean N fava
broadcast ['brɔːdkɑːst] (pt, pp **broadcast**) VT (Radio, TV) transmitir ▶ VI transmitir ▶ N transmissão f
broadcasting ['brɔːdkɑːstɪŋ] N radiodifusão f, transmissão f
broadcasting station N emissora
broaden ['brɔːdən] VT alargar ▶ VI alargar-se; **to ~ one's mind** abrir os horizontes
broadly ['brɔːdlɪ] ADV em geral
broad-minded ADJ tolerante, liberal
broccoli ['brɒkəlɪ] N brócolis mpl (BR), brócolos mpl (PT)
brochure ['brəʊʃjʊər] N folheto, brochura
brogue [brəʊg] N (accent) sotaque m regional; (shoe) chanca
broil [brɔɪl] (US) VT grelhar
broke [brəʊk] PT of **break** ▶ ADJ (inf) sem um vintém, duro; (: company) falido; **to go ~** quebrar
broken ['brəʊkən] PP of **break** ▶ ADJ quebrado; (marriage) desfeito; **~ leg** perna quebrada;

a ~ **home** um lar desfeito; **children from ~ homes** filhos de pais separados; **in ~ English** num inglês mascavado

broken-down ADJ (car) enguiçado; (machine) com defeito; (house) desmoronado, caindo aos pedaços

broken-hearted ADJ com o coração partido

broker ['brəukə'] N corretor(a) m/f

brokerage ['brəukrɪdʒ] N corretagem f

brolly ['brɔlɪ] (BRIT inf) N guarda-chuva m

bronchitis [brɔŋ'kaɪtɪs] N bronquite f

bronze [brɔnz] N bronze m; (sculpture) estátua feita de bronze

bronzed ['brɔnzd] ADJ bronzeado

brooch [brəutʃ] N broche m

brood [bru:d] N ninhada; (children) filhos mpl; (pej) prole f ▶ VI (hen) chocar; (person) cismar, remoer

broody ['bru:dɪ] ADJ (fig) taciturno, melancólico

brook [bruk] N arroio, ribeiro

broom [brum] N vassoura; (Bot) giesta-das-vassouras f

broomstick ['brumstɪk] N cabo de vassoura

Bros. ABBR (Comm: = brothers) Irmãos

broth [brɔθ] N caldo

brothel ['brɔθl] N bordel m

brother ['brʌðə'] N irmão m

brotherhood ['brʌðəhud] N (association, Rel) confraria

brother-in-law (pl **brothers-in-law**) N cunhado

brotherly ['brʌðəlɪ] ADJ fraternal, fraterno

brought [brɔ:t] PT, PP of **bring**

brow [brau] N (forehead) fronte f, testa; (rare: gen: eyebrow) sobrancelha; (of hill) cimo, cume m

browbeat ['braubi:t] (irreg: like **beat**) VT intimidar, amedrontar

brown [braun] ADJ marrom (BR), castanho (PT); (hair) castanho; (tanned) bronzeado, moreno; (rice, bread, flour) integral ▶ N (colour) cor f marrom (BR) or castanha (PT) ▶ VT tostar; (tan) bronzear; (Culin) dourar; **to go ~** (person) bronzear-se, ficar moreno; (leaves) secar

brown bread N pão m integral

Brownie ['braunɪ] N (also: **Brownie Guide**) fadinha de bandeirante

brownie ['braunɪ] (US) N (cake) docinho de chocolate com amêndoas

brown paper N papel m pardo

brown sugar N açúcar m mascavo

browse [brauz] VI (in shop) dar uma olhada; (among books) folhear livros; (animal) pastar; **to ~ through a book** folhear um livro

browser ['brauzə'] N (Comput) browser m

bruise [bru:z] N hematoma m, contusão f ▶ VT machucar; (fig) magoar ▶ VI (fruit) amassar

Brum [brʌm] (inf) N ABBR = **Birmingham**

Brummagem ['brʌmədʒəm] (inf) N = **Birmingham**

Brummie ['brʌmɪ] (inf) N natural m/f de Birmingham

brunch [brʌntʃ] N brunch m

brunette [bru:'nɛt] N morena

brunt [brʌnt] N: **the ~ of** (greater part) a maior parte de

brush [brʌʃ] N escova; (for painting, shaving etc) pincel m; (Bot) mato rasteiro; (quarrel) bate-boca m ▶ VT (sweep) varrer; (groom) escovar; (also: **brush past, brush against**) tocar ao passar, roçar; **to have a ~ with sb** bater boca com alguém; **to have a ~ with the police** ser indiciado pela polícia
▶ **brush aside** VT afastar, não fazer caso de
▶ **brush up** VT (knowledge) retocar, revisar

brushed [brʌʃt] ADJ (Tech: steel, chrome etc) escovado; (nylon, denim etc) felpudo

brush-off (inf) N: **to give sb the ~** dar o fora em alguém

brushwood ['brʌʃwud] N (bushes) mato; (sticks) lenha, gravetos mpl

brusque [bru:sk] ADJ ríspido; (apology) abrupto

Brussels ['brʌslz] N Bruxelas

Brussels sprout N couve-de-bruxelas f

brutal ['bru:tl] ADJ brutal

brutality [bru:'tælɪtɪ] N brutalidade f

brute [bru:t] N bruto; (person) animal m ▶ ADJ: **by ~ force** por força bruta

brutish ['bru:tɪʃ] ADJ grosseiro, bruto

BS (US) N ABBR = **Bachelor of Science**

bs ABBR = **bill of sale**

BSA N ABBR = **Boy Scouts of America**

BSc N ABBR = **Bachelor of Science**

BSI N ABBR (= British Standards Institution) instituto britânico de padrões

BST ABBR (= British Summer Time) hora de verão

btu N ABBR (= British thermal unit) BTU f (1054.2 joules)

bubble ['bʌbl] N bolha (BR), borbulha (PT)
▶ VI borbulhar

bubble bath N banho de espuma

bubble gum N chiclete m (de bola) (BR), pastilha elástica (PT)

Bucharest [bu:kə'rest] N Bucareste

buck [bʌk] N (rabbit) macho; (deer) cervo; (US inf) dólar m ▶ VI corcovear; **to pass the ~** fazer o jogo de empurra
▶ **buck up** VI (cheer up) animar-se, cobrar ânimo ▶ VT: **to ~ one's ideas up** tomar jeito

bucket ['bʌkɪt] N balde m ▶ VI (BRIT inf): **the rain is ~ing down** está chovendo a cântaros

buckle ['bʌkl] N fivela ▶ VT afivelar ▶ VI torcer-se, cambar-se
▶ **buckle down** VI empenhar-se

Bucks [bʌks] (BRIT) ABBR = **Buckinghamshire**

bud [bʌd] N broto; (of flower) botão m ▶ VI brotar, desabrochar; (fig) florescer

Budapest [bju:də'pest] N Budapeste

Buddha ['budə] N Buda m

Buddhism ['budɪzəm] N budismo

Buddhist ['budɪst] ADJ (person) budista; (scripture, thought etc) budístico ▶ N budista m/f

budding ['bʌdɪŋ] ADJ (flower) em botão; (passion etc) nascente; (poet etc) em ascensão

buddy ['bʌdɪ] (US) N camarada m, companheiro

budge [bʌdʒ] VT mover ▶ VI mexer-se

budgerigar ['bʌdʒərɪgɑːʳ] N periquito

budget ['bʌdʒɪt] N orçamento ▶ VI: **to ~ for sth** incluir algo no orçamento; **she works out her ~ every month** ela calcula seu orçamento todos es meses; **I'm on a tight ~** estou com o orçamento apertado

budgie ['bʌdʒɪ] N = **budgerigar**

Buenos Aires ['bwɛnə'saɪrɪz] N Buenos Aires

buff [bʌf] ADJ (colour) cor de camurça ▶ N (inf: enthusiast) aficionado(-a)

buffalo ['bʌfələu] (pl **buffalo** or **buffaloes**) N (BRIT) búfalo; (US: bison) bisão m

buffer ['bʌfəʳ] N para-choque m; (Comput) buffer m

buffering ['bʌfərɪŋ] N (Comput) buffering m, armazenamento intermediário

buffer state N estado-tampão m

buffet¹ ['bufeɪ] (BRIT) N (in station) bar m; (food) bufê m

buffet² ['bʌfɪt] VT (subj: wind etc) fustigar

buffet car (BRIT) N vagão-restaurante m

buffet lunch N almoço americano

buffoon [bə'fuːn] N bufão m

bug [bʌg] N (esp US: insect) bicho; (fig: germ) micróbio; (spy device) microfone m oculto; (tap) escuta clandestina; (Comput: of program) erro; (: of equipment) defeito ▶ VT (inf: annoy) apoquentar, incomodar; (room) colocar microfones em; (phone) grampear; **I've got the travel ~** peguei a mania de viajar

bugbear ['bʌgbɛəʳ] N pesadelo, fantasma m

bugger ['bʌgəʳ] (!) N filho-da-puta m (!) ▶ VT: **~ (it)!** merda! (!); **~ all** (nothing) chongas (!) ▶ **bugger off** (!) VI: **~ off!** vai a merda! (!)

buggy ['bʌgɪ] N (for baby) carrinho (desdobrável) de bebê

bugle ['bjuːgl] N trompa, corneta

build [bɪld] (pt, pp **built**) VT construir, edificar ▶ N (of person) talhe m, estatura ▶ **build on** VT FUS (fig) explorar, aproveitar ▶ **build up** VT (Med) fortalecer; (stocks) acumular; (business) desenvolver; (reputation) estabelecer

builder ['bɪldəʳ] N (contractor) construtor(a) m/f, empreiteiro(-a); (worker) pedreiro

building ['bɪldɪŋ] N (act, industry) construção f; (residential, offices) edifício, prédio

building contractor N empreiteiro(-a) de obras; (company) construtora

building industry N construção f

building site N terreno de construção

building society (BRIT) N sociedade f de crédito imobiliário, financiadora

building trade N construção f

build-up N (of gas etc) acumulação f; (publicity): **to give sb/sth a good ~** fazer muita propaganda de alguém/algo

built [bɪlt] PT, PP of **build** ▶ ADJ: **~-in** (cupboard) embutido; (device) incorporado, embutido

built-up area N zona urbanizada

bulb [bʌlb] N (Bot) bulbo; (Elec) lâmpada

bulbous ['bʌlbəs] ADJ bojudo

Bulgaria [bʌl'gɛərɪə] N Bulgária

Bulgarian [bʌl'gɛərɪən] ADJ búlgaro ▶ N búlgaro(-a); (Ling) búlgaro

bulge [bʌldʒ] N bojo, saliência; (in birth rate, sales) disparo ▶ VI inchar-se; (pocket etc) fazer bojo; **to be bulging with** estar abarrotado de

bulimia [buː'lɪmɪə] N bulimia

bulk [bʌlk] N (mass) massa, volume m; **in ~** (Comm) a granel; **the ~ of** a maior parte de

bulk buying [-'baɪɪŋ] N compra a granel

bulkhead ['bʌlkhɛd] N anteparo

bulky ['bʌlkɪ] ADJ volumoso; (person) corpulento

bull [bul] N touro; (Stock Exchange) altista m/f; (Rel) bula

bulldog ['buldɔg] N buldogue m

bulldoze ['buldəuz] VT arrasar (com buldôzer); **I was ~d into doing it** (fig: inf) fui forçado or obrigado a fazê-lo

bulldozer ['buldəuzəʳ] N buldôzer m, escavadora

bullet ['bulɪt] N bala

bulletin ['bulɪtɪn] N noticiário; (journal) boletim m

bulletin board N (US) quadro de anúncios; (Comput) fórum m

bulletproof ['bulɪtpruːf] ADJ à prova de balas; **~ vest** colete m à prova de balas

bullet wound N ferida de bala

bullfight ['bulfaɪt] N tourada

bullfighter ['bulfaɪtəʳ] N toureiro

bullfighting ['bulfaɪtɪŋ] N (art) tauromaquia

bullion ['buljən] N ouro (or prata) em barras

bullock ['buləok] N boi m, novilho

bullring ['bulrɪŋ] N praça de touros

bull's-eye N centro do alvo, mosca (do alvo) (BR)

bully ['bulɪ] N fanfarrão m, valentão m ▶ VT intimidar, tiranizar

bullying ['bulɪɪŋ] N provocação f, implicância

bum [bʌm] N (inf: backside) bumbum m; (esp US: tramp) vagabundo(-a), vadio(-a) ▶ **bum around** (inf) VI vadiar

bumblebee ['bʌmblbiː] N mamangaba

bumf [bʌmf] (inf) N (forms etc) papelada

bump [bʌmp] N (blow) choque m, embate m, baque m; (in car: minor accident) batida; (jolt) sacudida; (on head) galo; (on road) elevação f; (sound) baque ▶ VT (strike) bater contra, dar encontrão em ▶ VI dar sacudidas ▶ **bump along** VI mover-se aos solavancos ▶ **bump into** VT FUS chocar-se com or contra, colidir com; (inf: person) dar com, topar com

bumper ['bʌmpəʳ] N (BRIT) para-choque m ▶ ADJ: **~ crop/harvest** supersafra

bumper cars NPL carros mpl de trombada

bumph [bʌmf] N = **bumf**

bumptious ['bʌmpʃəs] ADJ presunçoso

bumpy ['bʌmpɪ] ADJ (road) acidentado, cheio de altos e baixos; (journey) cheio de solavancos; (flight) turbulento

bun [bʌn] N pão *m* doce (BR), pãozinho (PT); (*in hair*) coque *m*

bunch [bʌntʃ] N (*of flowers*) ramo; (*of keys*) molho; (*of bananas, grapes*) cacho; (*of people*) grupo; **bunches** NPL (*in hair*) cachos *mpl*

bundle ['bʌndl] N trouxa, embrulho; (*of sticks*) feixe *m*; (*of papers*) maço ▸ VT (*also*: **bundle up**) embrulhar, atar; (*put*): **to ~ sth/sb into** meter *or* enfiar algo/alguém correndo em
▸ **bundle off** VT (*person*) despachar sem cerimônia
▸ **bundle out** VT expulsar sem cerimônia

bung [bʌŋ] N tampão *m*, batoque *m* ▸ VT (*also*: **bung up**: *pipe, hole*) tapar; (*BRIT inf: throw*) jogar; **my nose is ~ed up** estou com o nariz entupido

bungalow ['bʌŋɡələu] N bangalô *m*, chalé *m*

bungle ['bʌŋɡl] VT estropear, estragar

bunion ['bʌnjən] N joanete *m*

bunk [bʌŋk] N beliche *m*

bunk beds NPL beliche *m*, cama-beliche *f*

bunker ['bʌŋkəʳ] N (*coal store*) carvoeira; (*Mil*) abrigo, casamata; (*Golf*) bunker *m*

bunny ['bʌnɪ] N (*also*: **bunny rabbit**) coelhinho

bunny girl (BRIT) N coelhinha

bunny hill (US) N (*Ski*) pista para principiantes

bunting ['bʌntɪŋ] N bandeiras *fpl*

buoy [bɔɪ] N boia
▸ **buoy up** VT fazer boiar; (*fig*) animar

buoyancy ['bɔɪənsɪ] N flutuabilidade *f*

buoyant ['bɔɪənt] ADJ flutuante; (*person*) alegre; (*market*) animado; (*currency, prices*) firme

burden ['bə:dn] N (*responsibility*) responsabilidade *f*, fardo; (*load*) carga ▸ VT carregar; (*oppress*) sobrecarregar; (*trouble*): **to be a ~ to sb** ser um estorvo para alguém

bureau [bjuə'rəu] (*pl* **bureaux**) N (BRIT: *desk*) secretária, escrivaninha; (US: *chest of drawers*) cômoda; (*office*) escritório, agência

bureaucracy [bjuə'rɔkrəsɪ] N burocracia

bureaucrat ['bjuərəkræt] N burocrata *m/f*

bureaucratic [bjuərə'krætɪk] ADJ burocrático

bureau de change [-də'ʃɑ̃ʒ] (*pl* **bureaux de change**) N casa de câmbio

bureaux [bjuə'rəuz] NPL *of* **bureau**

burgeon ['bə:dʒən] VI florescer

burger ['bə:ɡəʳ] N hambúrguer *m*

burglar ['bə:ɡləʳ] N ladrão/ladrona *m/f*

burglar alarm N alarma de roubo

burglarize ['bə:ɡləraɪz] (US) VT assaltar, arrombar

burglary ['bə:ɡlərɪ] N roubo

burgle ['bə:ɡl] VT assaltar, arrombar

Burgundy ['bə:ɡəndɪ] N (*wine*) borgonha *m*

burial ['bɛrɪəl] N enterro

burial ground N cemitério

burly ['bə:lɪ] ADJ robusto, forte

Burma ['bə:mə] N Birmânia

Burmese [bə:'mi:z] ADJ birmanês(-esa) ▸ N INV birmanês(-esa) *m/f*; (*Ling*) birmanês *m*

burn [bə:n] (*pt, pp* **burned** *or* **burnt**) VT queimar; (*house*) incendiar ▸ VI queimar-se, arder; (*sting*) arder, picar ▸ N queimadura; **the cigarette ~t a hole in her dress** o cigarro fez um buraco no vestido dela; **I've ~t myself!** eu me queimei!
▸ **burn down** VT incendiar
▸ **burn out** VT (*subj: writer etc*): **to ~ o.s. out** desgastar-se

burner ['bə:nəʳ] N (*on cooker, heater*) bico de gás, fogo

burning ['bə:nɪŋ] ADJ ardente; (*hot: sand etc*) abrasador(a); (*ambition*) grande

burnish ['bə:nɪʃ] VT polir, lustrar

burnt [bə:nt] PT, PP *of* **burn**

burnt sugar (BRIT) N caramelo

burp [bə:p] (*inf*) N arroto ▸ VI arrotar

burrow ['bʌrəu] N toca, lura ▸ VI fazer uma toca, cavar; (*rummage*) esquadrinhar

bursar ['bə:səʳ] N tesoureiro(-a); (BRIT: *student*) bolsista *m/f* (BR), bolseiro(-a) (PT)

bursary ['bə:sərɪ] (BRIT) N (*Sch*) bolsa

burst [bə:st] (*pt, pp* **burst**) VT (*balloon, pipe*) arrebentar; (*banks etc*) romper ▸ VI estourar; (*tyre*) furar; (*bomb*) estourar, explodir ▸ N estouro; (*of shots*) rajada; **to ~ into flames** incendiar-se de repente; **to ~ into tears** desatar a chorar; **to ~ out laughing** cair na gargalhada; **to be ~ing with** (*emotion*) estar tomado de; (*subj: room, container*) estar abarrotado de; **to be ~ing with health/energy** estar esbanjando saúde/energia; **the door ~ open** a porta abriu-se de repente; **a ~ of applause** una salva de palmas; **a ~ of energy/speed/enthusiasm** uma explosão de energia/velocidade/entusiasmo
▸ **burst into** VT FUS (*room etc*) irromper em
▸ **burst out of** VT FUS sair precipitadamente de

bury ['bɛrɪ] VT enterrar; (*at funeral*) sepultar; **to ~ one's head in one's hands** cobrir o rosto com as mãos; **to ~ one's head in the sand** (*fig*) bancar avestruz; **to ~ the hatchet** (*fig*) fazer as pazes

bus [bʌs] N ônibus *m inv* (BR), autocarro (PT)

bus conductor N cobrador(a) *m/f* de ônibus

bush [buʃ] N arbusto, mata; (*scrubland*) sertão *m*; **to beat about the ~** ser evasivo

bushel ['buʃl] N alqueire *m*

bushy ['buʃɪ] ADJ (*thick*) espesso

busily ['bɪzɪlɪ] ADV atarefadamente

business ['bɪznɪs] N (*matter*) negócio; (*trading*) comércio, negócios *mpl*; (*firm*) empresa; (*occupation*) profissão *f*; (*affair*) assunto; **to be away on ~** estar fora a negócios; **he's in the insurance ~** ele trabalha com seguros; **to do ~ with sb** fazer negócios com alguém; **it's my ~ to …** encarrego-me de …; **it's none of my ~** eu não tenho nada com isto; **that's my ~** isso é cá comigo; **he means ~** fala a sério

business address N endereço profissional

business card N cartão *m* de visita

business class N (*on plane*) classe *f* executiva

businesslike ['bɪznɪslaɪk] ADJ eficiente, metódico, sério

businessman ['bɪznɪsmən] (*irreg: like* **man**) N homem *m* de negócios

business trip N viagem *f* de negócios

businesswoman ['bɪznɪswumən] (*irreg: like* **woman**) N mulher *f* de negócios

busker ['bʌskər] (BRIT) N artista *m/f* de rua

bus lane N pista reservada aos ônibus (BR) *or* autocarros (PT)

bus shelter N abrigo

bus station N rodoviária

bus-stop N ponto de ônibus (BR), paragem *f* de autocarro (PT)

bust [bʌst] N (*Anat*) busto ▶ ADJ (*inf: broken*) quebrado ▶ VT (*inf: Police: arrest*) prender, grampear; **to go ~** falir

bustle ['bʌsl] N animação *f*, movimento ▶ VI apressar-se, andar azafamado

bustling ['bʌslɪŋ] ADJ (*town*) animado, movimentado

bust-up (BRIT *inf*) N bate-boca *m*

busy ['bɪzɪ] ADJ (*person*) ocupado, atarefado; (*shop, street*) animado, movimentado; (*US Tel*) ocupado (BR), impedido (PT) ▶ VT: **to ~ o.s. with** ocupar-se em *or* de

busybody ['bɪzɪbɒdɪ] N intrometido(-a)

busy signal (US) N sinal *m* de ocupado (BR) *or* impedido (PT)

---

but [bʌt] CONJ **1** (*yet*) mas, porém; **he's not very bright, but he's hard-working** ele não é muito inteligente mas é trabalhador; **he's tired but Paul isn't** ele está cansado mas Paul não; **the trip was enjoyable but tiring** a viagem foi agradável porém cansativa

2 (*however*) mas; **I'd love to come, but I'm busy** eu adoraria vir, mas estou ocupado

3 (*showing disagreement, surprise etc*) mas; **but that's far too expensive!** mas isso é caro demais!

▶ PREP (*apart from, except*) exceto, menos; **he was/we've had nothing but trouble** ele só deu problema/nós só tivemos problema; **no-one but him** só ele, ninguém a não ser ele; **who but a lunatic would do such a thing?** quem, exceto um louco, faria tal coisa?; **but for** sem, se não fosse; **but for you** se não fosse você; **(I'll do) anything but that** (eu faria) qualquer coisa menos isso

▶ ADV (*just, only*) apenas; **she's but a child** ela é apenas uma criança; **had I but known** se eu soubesse; **I can but try** a única coisa que eu posso fazer é tentar; **all but finished** quase acabado

---

butane ['bju:teɪn] N butano

butcher ['bʊtʃər] N açougueiro (BR), homem *m* do talho (PT) ▶ VT (*prisoners etc*) chacinar, massacrar; (*cattle etc for meat*) abater e carnear

butcher's, butcher's shop N açougue *m* (BR), talho (PT)

butler ['bʌtlər] N mordomo

butt [bʌt] N (*cask*) tonel *m*; (*for rain*) barril *m*; (*thick end*) cabo, extremidade *f*; (*of gun*) coronha; (*of cigarette*) toco (BR), ponta (PT); (BRIT *fig: target*) alvo ▶ VT (*subj: goat*) marrar; (*: person*) dar uma cabeçada em
▶ **butt in** VI (*interrupt*) interromper

butter ['bʌtər] N manteiga ▶ VT untar com manteiga

butter bean N fava

buttercup ['bʌtəkʌp] N botão-de-ouro *m*, ranúnculo

butter dish N manteigueira

butterfingers ['bʌtəfɪŋgəz] (*inf*) N mão-furada *m/f*

butterfly ['bʌtəflaɪ] N borboleta; (*Swimming: also:* **butterfly stroke**) nado borboleta

buttocks ['bʌtəks] NPL nádegas *fpl*

button ['bʌtn] N botão *m*; (US: *badge*) emblema *m* ▶ VT (*also:* **button up**) abotoar ▶ VI ter botões

buttonhole ['bʌtnhəul] N casa de botão, botoeira; (*flower*) flor *f* na lapela ▶ VT obrigar a ouvir

buttress ['bʌtrɪs] N contraforte *m*

buxom ['bʌksəm] ADJ (*baby*) saudável; (*woman*) rechonchudo

buy [baɪ] (*pt, pp* **bought**) VT comprar ▶ N compra; **to ~ sb sth/sth from sb** comprar algo para alguém/algo a alguém; **to ~ sb a drink** pagar um drinque para alguém
▶ **buy back** VT comprar de volta; (*Comm*) recomprar
▶ **buy in** (BRIT) VT (*goods*) comprar, abastecer-se com
▶ **buy into** (BRIT) VT FUS (*Comm*) comprar ações de
▶ **buy off** VT (*partner*) comprar a parte de; (*business*) comprar o fundo de comércio de
▶ **buy up** VT comprar em grande quantidade

buyer ['baɪər] N comprador(a) *m/f*; **~'s market** mercado de comprador

buzz [bʌz] N zumbido; (*inf: phone call*): **to give sb a ~** dar uma ligada para alguém ▶ VI zumbir ▶ VT (*call on intercom*) chamar no interfone; (*Aviat: plane, building*) voar baixo sobre
▶ **buzz off** (*inf*) VI cair fora

buzzard ['bʌzəd] N abutre *m*, urubu *m*

buzzer ['bʌzər] N cigarra, vibrador *m*; (*doorbell*) campainha

buzz word N modismo

---

by [baɪ] PREP **1** (*referring to cause, agent*) por, de; **killed by lightning** morto por um raio; **a painting by Picasso** um quadro de Picasso

2 (*referring to method, manner, means*) de, com; **by bus/car/train** de ônibus/carro/trem; **to pay by cheque** pagar com cheque; **by moonlight/candlelight** sob o luar/à luz de vela; **by saving hard, he ...**

economizando muito, ele …
3 (*via, through*) por, via; **we came by Dover** viemos por *or* via Dover
4 (*close to*) perto de, ao pé de; **the house by the river** a casa perto do rio; **a holiday by the sea** férias à beira-mar; **she sat by his bed** ela sentou-se ao lado de seu leito
5 (*past*) por; **she rushed by me** ela passou por mim correndo
6 (*not later than*): **by 4 o'clock** antes das quatro; **by this time tomorrow** esta mesma hora amanhã; **by the time I got here it was too late** quando eu cheguei aqui, já era tarde demais
7 (*during*): **by daylight** durante o dia
8 (*amount*) por; **by the kilometre** por quilômetro; **paid by the hour** pago por hora
9 (*Math, measure*) por; **to divide/multiply by 3** dividir/multiplicar por 3; **it's broader by a metre** tem um metro a mais de largura
10 (*according to*) segundo, de acordo com; **it's all right by me** por mim tudo bem
11: (**all**) **by oneself** *etc* (completamente) só, sozinho; **he did it (all) by himself** ele fez tudo sozinho
12: **by the way** a propósito; **this wasn't my idea, by the way** a propósito, essa não era a minha ideia

▶ ADV **1** *see* **go, pass** *etc*
2: **by and by** logo, mais tarde; **by and large** (*on the whole*) em geral; **Britain has a poor image abroad, by and large** de uma maneira geral, a Grã-Bretanha tem uma imagem ruim no exterior

bye ['baɪ], **bye-bye** ['baɪ'baɪ] EXCL até logo! (BR), tchau! (BR), adeus! (PT)
bye-law N lei *f* de município
by-election (BRIT) N eleição *f* parlamentar complementar
bygone ['baɪgɔn] ADJ passado, antigo ▶ N: **let ~s be ~s** o que passou passou
by-law N = **bye-law**
bypass ['baɪpɑːs] N via secundária, desvio; (*Med*) ponte *f* de safena ▶ VT evitar
by-product N subproduto, produto derivado; (*of situation*) subproduto
byre ['baɪəʳ] (BRIT) N estábulo (de vacas)
bystander ['baɪstændəʳ] N circunstante *m/f*; (*observer*) espectador(a) *m/f*; **a crowd of ~s** um grupo de curiosos
byte [baɪt] N (*Comput*) byte *m*
byway ['baɪweɪ] N caminho secundário
byword ['baɪwəːd] N: **to be a ~ for** ser sinônimo de
by-your-leave N: **without so much as a ~** sem mais aquela

b

Cc

C¹, c [si:] N (*letter*) C, c *m*; (*Sch: mark*) ≈ 5, 6; (*Mus*): **C** dó *m*; **C for Charlie** C de Carlos

C² ABBR (= *Celsius, centigrade*) C

c ABBR (= *century*) séc.; (= *circa*) ca.; (US: = *cent*) cent

CA N ABBR = **Central America**; (BRIT) = **chartered accountant** ▶ ABBR (US Post) = **California**

ca. ABBR (= *circa*) c.

c/a ABBR = **capital account**; **credit account**; (= *current account*) c/c

CAA N ABBR (BRIT) = **Civil Aviation Authority**; (US: = *Civil Aeronautics Authority*) ≈ DAC *m*

CAB (BRIT) N ABBR (= *Citizens' Advice Bureau*) serviço de informação do consumidor

cab [kæb] N táxi *m*; (*of truck etc*) boleia; (*of train*) cabina de maquinista; (*horse-drawn*) cabriolé *m*

cabaret ['kæbəreɪ] N cabaré *m*

cabbage ['kæbɪdʒ] N repolho (BR), couve *f* (PT)

cabbie, cabby ['kæbɪ], **cab driver** N (*inf*) taxista *m/f*

cabin ['kæbɪn] N cabana; (*on ship*) camarote *m*; (*on plane*) cabina de passageiros

cabin crew N (*Aviat*) tripulação *f*

cabin cruiser N lancha a motor com cabine

cabinet ['kæbɪnɪt] N (*Pol*) gabinete *m*; (*furniture*) armário; (*also*: **display cabinet**) armário com vitrina; **~ reshuffle** reforma ministerial

cabinet-maker N marceneiro(-a)

cabinet minister N ministro(-a) (*integrante do gabinete*)

cable ['keɪbl] N cabo; (*telegram*) cabograma *m* ▶ VT enviar cabograma para

cable-car N bonde *m* (BR), teleférico (PT)

cablegram ['keɪblgræm] N cabograma *m*

cable railway (BRIT) N funicular *m*

cable television N televisão *f* a cabo

cache [kæʃ] N esconderijo; **a ~ of arms** *etc* um depósito secreto de armas *etc*

cackle ['kækl] VI gargalhar; (*hen*) cacarejar

cacti ['kæktaɪ] NPL *of* **cactus**

cactus ['kæktəs] (*pl* **cacti**) N cacto

CAD N ABBR (= *computer-aided design*) CAD *m*

caddie ['kædɪ] N corregador *m* de tracos

caddy ['kædɪ] N = **caddie**

cadet [kə'dɛt] N (*Mil*) cadete *m*

cadge [kædʒ] (*inf*) VT: **to ~ (from** *or* **off)** filar (de)

cadre ['kɑːdəʳ] N funcionários *mpl* qualificados

Caesarean, (US) **Cesarean** [siː'zɛərɪən] ADJ, N: **~ (section)** cesariana

CAF (BRIT) ABBR (= *cost and freight*) custo e frete

café ['kæfeɪ] N café *m*

cafeteria [kæfɪ'tɪərɪə] N lanchonete *f*

caffein, caffeine ['kæfiːn] N cafeína

cage [keɪdʒ] N (*bird cage*) gaiola; (*for large animals*) jaula; (*of lift*) cabina ▶ VT engaiolar; enjaular

cagey ['keɪdʒɪ] (*inf*) ADJ cuidadoso, reservado, desconfiado

cagoule [kə'guːl] N casaco de náilon

CAI N ABBR (= *computer-aided instruction*) CAI *m*

Cairo ['kaɪərəu] N o Cairo

cajole [kə'dʒəul] VT lisonjear

cake [keɪk] N (*large*) bolo; (*small*) doce *m*, bolinho; **it's a piece of ~** (*inf*) é moleza *or* sopa; **he wants to have his ~ and eat it (too)** (*fig*) ele quer chupar cana e assoviar ao mesmo tempo; **a ~ of soap** um sabonete

caked [keɪkt] ADJ: **~ with** encrostado de

cake mix N massa pronta de bolo

cake shop N confeitaria

calamitous [kə'læmɪtəs] ADJ calamitoso

calamity [kə'læmɪtɪ] N calamidade *f*

calcium ['kælsɪəm] N cálcio

calculate ['kælkjuleɪt] VT calcular; (*estimate: chances, effect*) avaliar
▶ **calculate on** VT FUS: **to ~ on sth/on doing sth** contar com algo/em fazer algo

calculated ['kælkjuleɪtɪd] ADJ (*insult, action*) intencional; **a ~ risk** um risco calculado

calculating ['kælkjuleɪtɪŋ] ADJ (*scheming*) maquinador(a), calculista; (*clever*) matreiro

calculation [kælkju'leɪʃən] N cálculo

calculator ['kælkjuleɪtəʳ] N calculador *m*

calculus ['kælkjuləs] N cálculo; **integral/differential ~** cálculo integral/diferencial

calendar ['kæləndəʳ] N calendário

calendar month N mês *m* civil

calendar year N ano civil

calf [kɑːf] (*pl* **calves**) N (*of cow*) bezerro, vitela; (*of other animals*) cria; (*also*: **calfskin**) pele *f* or couro de bezerro; (*Anat*) barriga da perna

caliber ['kælɪbəʳ] (US) N = **calibre**

calibrate ['kælɪbreɪt] VT calibrar

calibre, (US) **caliber** ['kælɪbər] N (of person) capacidade f, competencia, calibre m
calico ['kælɪkəu] N (BRIT) morim m; (US) chita
California [kælɪ'fɔ:nɪə] N Califórnia
calipers ['kælɪpəz] (US) NPL = **callipers**
call [kɔ:l] VT chamar; (label) qualificar, descrever; (Tel) telefonar a, ligar para; (summon: witness) citar; (announce: flight) anunciar; (meeting, strike) convocar ▶ VI chamar; (shout) gritar; (Tel) telefonar; (visit: also: **call in, call round**) dar um pulo ▶ N (shout, announcement) chamada; (also: **telephone call**) chamada, telefonema m; (of bird) canto; (visit) visita; (fig: appeal) chamamento, apelo; **to be ~ed** chamar-se; **she's ~ed Suzanna** ela se chama Suzanna; **to ~ (for)** passar (para buscar); **who is ~ing?** (Tel) quem fala?; **London ~ing** (Radio) aqui fala Londres; **on ~** (nurse, doctor etc) de plantão; **please give me a ~ at 7** acorde-me às 7.00 por favor; **to make a ~** telefonar; **to pay a ~ on sb** visitar alguém, dar um pulo na casa de alguém; **there's not much ~ for these items** não há muita procura para esses artigos
▶ **call at** VT FUS (subj: ship) fazer escala em; (: train) parar em
▶ **call back** VI (return) voltar, passar de novo; (Tel) ligar de volta ▶ VT (Tel) ligar de volta para
▶ **call for** VT FUS (demand) requerer, exigir; (fetch) ir buscar
▶ **call in** VT (doctor, expert, police) chamar
▶ **call off** VT (cancel) cancelar
▶ **call on** VT FUS (visit) visitar; (appeal to) pedir; (turn to) recorrer a; **to ~ on sb to do** pedir para alguém fazer
▶ **call out** VI gritar, bradar ▶ VT (doctor, police, troops) chamar
▶ **call up** VT (Mil) chamar às fileiras; (Tel) ligar para
call box (BRIT) N cabine f telefônica
call centre (BRIT) N (Tel) central f de chamadas
caller ['kɔ:lər] N visita m/f; (Tel) chamador(a) m/f
call girl N call girl f, prostituta
call-in (US) N (Radio) programa com participação dos ouvintes; (TV) programa com participação dos espectadores
calling ['kɔ:lɪŋ] N vocação f; (trade) profissão f
calling card (US) N cartão m de visita
callipers, (US) **calipers** ['kælɪpəz] NPL (Math) compasso de calibre; (Med) aparelho ortopédico
callous ['kæləs] ADJ cruel, insensível
callousness ['kæləsnɪs] N crueldade f, insensibilidade f
callow ['kæləu] ADJ inexperiente
calm [kɑ:m] ADJ calmo; (peaceful) tranquilo; (weather) estável ▶ N calma ▶ VT acalmar; (fears, grief) abrandar
▶ **calm down** VT acalmar, tranquilizar ▶ VI acalmar-se

calmly ['kɑ:mlɪ] ADV tranquilamente, com calma
calmness ['kɑ:mnɪs] N tranquilidade f
Calor gas® ['kælər-] N butano
calorie ['kælərɪ] N caloria
calve [kɑ:v] VI parir
calves [kɑ:vz] NPL of **calf**
CAM N ABBR (= computer-aided manufacture) CAM m
camber ['kæmbər] N (of road) abaulamento
Cambodia [kæm'bəudjə] N Camboja
Cambodian [kæm'bəudɪən] ADJ, N cambojano(-a)
Cambs (BRIT) ABBR = **Cambridgeshire**
camcorder ['kæmkɔ:dər] N filmadora, máquina de filmar
came [keɪm] PT of **come**
camel ['kæməl] N camelo
cameo ['kæmɪəu] N camafeu m
camera ['kæmərə] N máquina fotográfica; (Cinema, TV) câmera; **in ~** (Law) em câmara
cameraman ['kæmərəmən] (irreg: like **man**) N cinegrafista m
camera phone N celular m com câmera
Cameroon [kæmə'ru:n] N Camarões m
Cameroun [kæmə'ru:n] N = **Cameroon**
camouflage ['kæməflɑ:ʒ] N camuflagem f ▶ VT camuflar
camp [kæmp] N campo, acampamento; (Mil) acampamento; (for prisoners) campo; (faction) facção f ▶ VI acampar ▶ ADJ (inf) afeminado
campaign [kæm'peɪn] N (Mil, Pol etc) campanha ▶ VI fazer campanha
campaigner [kæm'peɪnər] N: **~ for** partidário(-a) de; **~ against** oponente m/f de
campbed (BRIT) N cama de campanha
camper ['kæmpər] N campista m/f; (vehicle) reboque m
camping ['kæmpɪŋ] N camping m (BR), campismo (PT); **to go ~** acampar
camping site N camping m (BR), parque m de campismo (PT)
campsite ['kæmpsaɪt] N camping m (BR), parque m de campismo (PT)
campus ['kæmpəs] N campus m, cidade f universitária
camshaft ['kæmʃɑ:ft] N eixo de ressaltos
can¹ [kæn] N (of oil, food) lata ▶ VT enlatar; (preserve) conservar em latas; **to carry the ~** (BRIT inf) assumir a responsabilidade

(KEYWORD)

can² [kæn] (negative **can't** or **cannot**, pt, conditional **could**) AUX VB (be able to) poder; **you can do it if you try** se você tentar, você consegue fazê-lo; **I'll help you all I can** ajudarei você em tudo que eu puder; **she couldn't sleep that night** ela não conseguiu dormir aquela noite; **I can't go on any longer** não posso continuar mais; **can you hear me?** você está me ouvindo?; **I can see you tomorrow, if you're free** posso vê-lo amanhã, se você estiver livre

2 (know how to): saber; **I can swim** sei nadar; **can you speak Portuguese?** você fala português?

3 (may): **can I use your phone?** posso usar o telefone?; **could I have a word with you?** será que eu podia falar com você?; **you can smoke if you like** você pode fumar se quiser; **can I help you with that?** posso ajudá-lo?

4 (expressing disbelief, puzzlement): **it CAN'T be true!** não pode ser verdade!; **what CAN he want?** o que é que ele quer?

5 (expressing possibility, suggestion etc): **he could be in the library** ele talvez esteja na biblioteca; **they could have forgotten** eles podiam ter esquecido

Canada ['kænədə] N Canadá m
Canadian [kə'neɪdɪən] ADJ, N canadense m/f
canal [kə'næl] N canal m
Canaries [kə'nɛərɪz] NPL = **Canary Islands**
canary [kə'nɛərɪ] N canário
Canary Islands NPL: **the ~** as (ilhas) Canárias
Canberra ['kænbərə] N Canberra
cancel ['kænsəl] VT cancelar; (contract) anular; (cross out) riscar, invalidar; (stamp) contrasselar
  ▶ **cancel out** VT anular; **they ~ each other out** eles se anulam
cancellation [kænsə'leɪʃən] N cancelamento; (of contract) anulação f
cancer ['kænsə^r] N câncer m (BR), cancro (PT); **C~** (Astrology) Câncer
cancerous ['kænsrəs] ADJ canceroso
cancer patient N canceroso(-a)
cancer research N pesquisa sobre o câncer (BR) or cancro (PT)
candid ['kændɪd] ADJ franco, sincero
candidacy ['kændɪdəsɪ] N candidatura
candidate ['kændɪdeɪt] N candidato(-a)
candidature ['kændɪdətʃə^r] (BRIT) N = **candidacy**
candied ['kændɪd] ADJ cristalizado; **~ apple** (US) maçã f do amor
candle ['kændl] N vela; (in church) círio
candle holder N (single) castiçal m; (bigger, more ornate) candelabro, lustre m
candlelight ['kændllaɪt] N: **by ~** à luz de vela; (dinner) à luz de velas
candlestick ['kændlstɪk] N (plain) castiçal m; (bigger, ornate) candelabro, lustre m
candour, (US) **candor** ['kændə^r] N franqueza
C & W N ABBR = **country and western**
candy ['kændɪ] N (also: **sugar candy**) açúcar m cristalizado; (US) bala (BR), rebuçado (PT)
candy-floss [-flɔs] (BRIT) N algodão-doce m
candy store (US) N confeitaria
cane [keɪn] N (Bot) cana; (stick) bengala; (for chairs etc) palhinha ▶ VT (BRIT Sch) castigar (com bengala)
canine ['kænaɪn] ADJ canino
canister ['kænɪstə^r] N lata

cannabis ['kænəbɪs] N (also: **cannabis plant**) cânhamo; (drug) maconha
canned [kænd] ADJ (food) em lata, enlatado; (inf: music) gravado; (BRIT inf: drunk) bêbado; (US inf: worker) despedido
cannibal ['kænɪbəl] N canibal m/f
cannibalism ['kænɪbəlɪzəm] N canibalismo
cannon ['kænən] (pl **cannon** or **cannons**) N canhão m
cannonball ['kænənbɔːl] N bala (de canhão)
cannon fodder N bucha para canhão
cannot ['kænɔt] = **can not**
canny ['kænɪ] ADJ astuto
canoe [kə'nuː] N canoa
canoeing [kə'nuːɪŋ] N (Sport) canoagem f
canoeist [kə'nuːɪst] N canoísta m/f
canon ['kænən] N (clergyman) cônego; (standard) cânone m
canonize ['kænənaɪz] VT canonizar
can opener N abridor m de latas (BR), abre-latas m inv (PT)
canopy ['kænəpɪ] N dossel m; (Arch) baldaquino
cant [kænt] N jargão m
can't [kɑːnt] = **can not**
Cantab. (BRIT) ABBR = **cantabrigiensis; of Cambridge**
cantankerous [kæn'tæŋkərəs] ADJ rabugento, irritável
canteen [kæn'tiːn] N cantina; (bottle) cantil m; (BRIT: of cutlery) jogo (de talheres)
canter ['kæntə^r] N meio galope ▶ VI ir a meio galope
cantilever ['kæntɪliːvə^r] N cantiléver m
canvas ['kænvəs] N (material) lona; (for painting) tela; (Naut) velas fpl; **under ~** (camping) em barracas
canvass ['kænvəs] VI (Pol): **to ~ for** fazer campanha por ▶ VT (Pol: district) fazer campanha em; (: person) angariar; (investigate: opinions) sondar
canvasser ['kænvəsə^r] N cabo eleitoral
canvassing ['kænvəsɪŋ] N (Pol) angariação f de votos; (Comm) pesquisa de mercado
canyon ['kænjən] N canhão m, garganta, desfiladeiro
CAP N ABBR (= Common Agricultural Policy) PAC f
cap [kæp] N gorro; (peaked) boné m; (of pen, bottle) tampa; (contraceptive: also: **Dutch cap**) diafragma m; (for toy gun) cartucho; (BRIT Football): **he won his England ~** ele foi escalado para jogar na seleção inglesa ▶ VT (outdo) superar; (put limit on) limitar; **and to ~ it all, he ...** (BRIT) e para completar or culminar, ele ...
capability [keɪpə'bɪlɪtɪ] N capacidade f
capable ['keɪpəbl] ADJ (of sth) capaz; (competent) competente, hábil; **~ of** (interpretation etc) susceptível de, passível de
capacious [kə'peɪʃəs] ADJ vasto
capacity [kə'pæsɪtɪ] N capacidade f; (of stadium etc) lotação f; (role) condição f, posição f; **filled to ~** lotado; **in his ~ as**

em sua condição de; **this work is beyond my ~** este trabalho está além das minhas limitações; **in an advisory ~** na condição de consultor; **to work at full ~** trabalhar com máximo rendimento

cape [keɪp] N capa; (*Geo*) cabo

Cape of Good Hope N Cabo da Boa Esperança

caper ['keɪpər] N (*Culin: gen pl*) alcaparra; (*prank*) travessura

Cape Town N Cidade f do Cabo

capita ['kæpɪtə] *see* **per capita**

capital ['kæpɪtl] N (*also:* **capital city**) capital f; (*money*) capital m; (*also:* **capital letter**) maiúscula

capital account N conta de capital

capital allowance N desconto para depreciação

capital assets NPL bens mpl imobilizados, ativo fixo

capital expenditure N despesas fpl or dispêndio de capital

capital gains tax N imposto sobre ganhos de capital

capital goods NPL bens mpl de capital

capital-intensive ADJ intensivo de capital

capitalism ['kæpɪtəlɪzəm] N capitalismo

capitalist ['kæpɪtəlɪst] ADJ, N capitalista m/f

capitalize ['kæpɪtəlaɪz] VT capitalizar ▶ VI: **to ~ on** (*fig*) aproveitar, explorar

capital punishment N pena de morte

capital transfer tax (*BRIT*) N imposto sobre transferências de capital

Capitol ['kæpɪtl] N *ver nota*

O Capitólio (**Capitol**) é a sede do Congresso dos Estados Unidos, localizado no monte Capitólio (*Capitol Hill*), em Washington.

capitulate [kə'pɪtjuleɪt] VI capitular

capitulation [kəpɪtju'leɪʃən] N capitulação f

capricious [kə'prɪʃəs] ADJ caprichoso

Capricorn ['kæprɪkɔːn] N Capricórnio

caps [kæps] ABBR = **capital letters**

capsize [kæp'saɪz] VT, VI emborcar, virar

capstan ['kæpstən] N cabrestante m

capsule ['kæpsjuːl] N cápsula

Capt. ABBR (= *captain*) Cap.

captain ['kæptɪn] N capitão m ▶ VT capitanear, ser o capitão de

caption ['kæpʃən] N (*heading*) título; (*to picture*) legenda

captivate ['kæptɪveɪt] VT cativar

captive ['kæptɪv] ADJ, N cativo(-a)

captivity [kæp'tɪvɪtɪ] N cativeiro

captor ['kæptər] N capturador(a) m/f

capture ['kæptʃər] VT prender, aprisionar; (*person*) capturar; (*place*) tomar; (*attention*) atrair, chamar ▶ N captura; (*of place*) tomada; (*thing taken*) presa

car [kɑː] N carro, automóvel m; (*Rail*) vagão m; **by ~** de carro

Caracas [kə'rækəs] N Caracas

carafe [kə'ræf] N garrafa de mesa

caramel ['kærəməl] N (*sweet*) caramelo; (*burnt sugar*) caramelado

carat ['kærət] N quilate m; **18 ~ gold** ouro de 18 quilates

caravan ['kærəvæn] N reboque m (*BR*), trailer m (*BR*), rulote f (*PT*); (*in desert*) caravana

caravan site (*BRIT*) N parque m de campismo

caraway ['kærəweɪ] N: **~ seed** sementes fpl de alcaravia

carb [kɑːb] (*inf*) N ABBR (= *carbohydrate*) carboidrato

carbohydrate [kɑːbəu'haɪdreɪt] N hidrato de carbono; (*food*) carboidrato

carbolic acid [kɑː'bɔlɪk-] N ácido carbólico, fenol m

car bomb N carro-bomba m

carbon ['kɑːbən] N carbono

carbonated ['kɑːbəneɪtɪd] ADJ (*drink*) gasoso

carbon copy N cópia de papel carbono

carbon dioxide [-daɪ'ɔksaɪd] N dióxido de carbono

carbon footprint N pegada de carbono

carbon monoxide [-mə'nɔksaɪd] N monóxido de carbono

carbon-neutral [kɑːbn'njuːtrəl] ADJ sem emissão de carbono

carbon offset N compensação f de emissão de carbono

carbon paper N papel m carbono

carbon ribbon N fita carbono

carburettor, (*US*) **carburetor** [kɑːbju'rɛtər] N carburador m

carcass ['kɑːkəs] N carcaça

carcinogenic [kɑːsɪnə'dʒɛnɪk] ADJ carcinogênico

card [kɑːd] N (*also:* **playing card**) carta; (*visiting card, postcard etc*) cartão m; (*membership card etc*) carteira; (*thin cardboard*) cartolina; **to play ~s** jogar cartas

cardamom ['kɑːdəməm] N cardamomo

cardboard ['kɑːdbɔːd] N cartão m, papelão m

cardboard box N caixa de papelão

card-carrying member [-'kærɪɪŋ-] N membro ativo

card game N jogo de cartas

cardiac ['kɑːdɪæk] ADJ cardíaco

cardigan ['kɑːdɪgən] N casaco de lã, cardigã m

cardinal ['kɑːdɪnl] ADJ cardeal; (*Math*) cardinal ▶ N (*Rel*) cardeal m; (*Math*) número cardinal

card index N index m fichário

Cards (*BRIT*) ABBR = **Cardiganshire**

cardsharp ['kɑːdʃɑːp] N batoteiro(-a), trapaceiro(-a)

card vote (*BRIT*) N votação f de delegados

CARE [kɛər] N ABBR (= *Cooperative for American Relief Everywhere*) associação beneficente

care [kɛər] N cuidado; (*worry*) preocupação f; (*charge*) encargo, custódia ▶ VI: **to ~ about** (*person, animal*) preocupar-se com; (*thing, idea*) ter interesse em; **would you ~ to/for ...?** você quer ...?; **I wouldn't ~ to do it** eu não gostaria de fazê-lo; **~ of** (*on letter*) aos cuidados de; **in sb's ~** a cargo de alguém; **"with ~"** "frágil"; **to take ~ (to do)**

cuidar-se or ter o cuidado (de fazer); **to take ~ of** (*person*) cuidar de; (*situation*) encarregar-se de; **the child has been taken into ~** a criança foi entregue aos cuidados da Assistência Social; **I don't ~** não me importa; **I couldn't ~ less** não dou a mínima
▸ **care for** VT FUS cuidar de; (*like*) gostar de

careen [kə'ri:n] VI (*ship*) dar de quilha, querenar ▸ VT querenar

career [kə'rɪəʳ] N carreira ▸ VI (*also:* **career along**) correr a toda velocidade

career girl N moça disposta a fazer carreira

careers officer N orientador(a) *m/f* vocacional

career woman (*irreg: like* **woman**) N mulher *f* com profissão liberal

carefree ['kɛəfri:] ADJ despreocupado

careful ['kɛəful] ADJ (*thorough*) cuidadoso; (*cautious*) cauteloso; **(be) ~!** tenha cuidado!

carefully ['kɛəfulɪ] ADV cuidadosamente; cautelosamente

careless ['kɛəlɪs] ADJ descuidado; (*heedless*) desatento

carelessly ['kɛəlɪslɪ] ADV sem cuidado; (*without worry*) sem preocupação

carelessness ['kɛəlɪsnɪs] N descuido, falta de atenção

carer ['kɛərəʳ] N (*professional*) acompanhante *m/f*; (*unpaid*) cuidador(a) *m/f*

caress [kə'rɛs] N carícia ▸ VT acariciar

caretaker ['kɛəteɪkəʳ] N zelador(a) *m/f*

caretaker government (*BRIT*) N governo interino

car-ferry N barca para carros (*BR*), barco de passagem (*PT*)

cargo ['kɑːgəu] (*pl* **cargoes**) N carga; (*freight*) frete *m*

cargo boat N cargueiro

cargo plane N avião *m* de carga

car hire (*BRIT*) N aluguel *m* (*BR*) or aluguer *m* (*PT*) de carros

Caribbean [kærɪ'bi:ən] ADJ caraíba ▸ N: **the ~ (Sea)** o Caribe

caricature ['kærɪkətjuəʳ] N caricatura

caring ['kɛərɪŋ] ADJ (*person*) bondoso; (*society*) humanitário

carnage ['kɑːnɪdʒ] N carnificina, matança

carnal ['kɑːnl] ADJ carnal

carnation [kɑː'neɪʃən] N cravo

carnival ['kɑːnɪvəl] N carnaval *m*; (*US: funfair*) parque *m* de diversões

carnivorous [kɑː'nɪvərəs] ADJ carnívoro

carol ['kærəl] N: **(Christmas) ~** cântico de Natal

carouse [kə'rauz] VI farrear

carousel [kærə'sɛl] (*US*) N carrossel *m*

carp [kɑːp] N INV (*fish*) carpa
▸ **carp at** VT FUS criticar

car park (*BRIT*) N estacionamento

carpenter ['kɑːpɪntəʳ] N carpinteiro

carpentry ['kɑːpɪntrɪ] N carpintaria

carpet ['kɑːpɪt] N tapete *m* ▸ VT atapetar; (*with fitted carpet*) acarpetar; **fitted ~** (*BRIT*) carpete *m*

carpet slippers NPL chinelos *mpl*

carpet sweeper [-'swi:pəʳ] N limpador *m* de tapetes

car rental (*US*) N aluguel *m* (*BR*) or aluguer *m* (*PT*) de carros

carriage ['kærɪdʒ] N carruagem *f*; (*BRIT Rail*) vagão *m*; (*of goods*) transporte *m*; (: *cost*) porte *m*; (*of typewriter*) carro; (*bearing*) porte *m*; **~ forward** frete a pagar; **~ free** franco de porte; **~ paid** frete or porte pago

carriage return N retorno do carro

carriageway ['kærɪdʒweɪ] (*BRIT*) N (*part of road*) pista

carrier ['kærɪəʳ] N transportador(a) *m/f*; (*company*) empresa de transportes, transportadora; (*Med*) portador(a) *m/f*; (*Naut*) porta-aviões *m inv*

carrier bag (*BRIT*) N saco, sacola

carrier pigeon N pombo-correio

carrion ['kærɪən] N carniça

carrot ['kærət] N cenoura

carry ['kærɪ] VT carregar; (*take*) levar; (*transport*) transportar; (*a motion, bill*) aprovar; (*involve: responsibilities etc*) implicar; (*Math: figure*) levar; (*Comm: interest*) render ▸ VI (*sound*) projetar-se; **to get carried away** (*fig*) exagerar
▸ **carry forward** VT transportar
▸ **carry on** VI (*continue*) seguir, continuar; (*inf: complain*) queixar-se, criar caso ▸ VT prosseguir, continuar
▸ **carry out** VT (*orders*) cumprir; (*investigation*) levar a cabo, realizar; (*idea, threat*) executar

carrycot ['kærɪkɔt] (*BRIT*) N moisés *m inv*

carry-on (*inf*) N alvoroço, rebuliço

cart [kɑːt] N carroça, carreta; (*US: for luggage*) carrinho ▸ VT transportar (em carroça)

carte blanche ['kɑːt'blɔ̃ʃ] N: **to give sb ~** dar carta branca a alguém

cartel [kɑː'tɛl] N (*Comm*) cartel *m*

cartilage ['kɑːtɪlɪdʒ] N cartilagem *f*

cartographer [kɑː'tɔgrəfəʳ] N cartógrafo(-a)

cartography [kɑː'tɔgrəfɪ] N cartografia

carton ['kɑːtən] N (*box*) caixa (de papelão); (*of yogurt*) pote *m*; (*of milk*) caixa; (*packet*) pacote *m*

cartoon [kɑː'tuːn] N (*drawing*) desenho; (*Press*) charge *f*; (*satirical*) caricatura; (*BRIT: comic strip*) história em quadrinhos (*BR*), banda desenhada (*PT*); (*film*) desenho animado

cartoonist [kɑː'tuːnɪst] N caricaturista *m/f*, cartunista *m/f*; (*Press*) chargista *m/f*

cartridge ['kɑːtrɪdʒ] N cartucho; (*of record player*) cápsula

cartwheel ['kɑːtwiːl] N pirueta, cabriola; **to turn a ~** fazer uma pirueta

carve [kɑːv] VT (*meat*) trinchar; (*wood, stone*) cinzelar, esculpir; (*initials, design*) gravar
▸ **carve up** VT dividir, repartir

carving ['kɑːvɪŋ] N (*object*) escultura; (*design*) talha, entalhe *m*

carving knife (*irreg: like* **knife**) N trinchante *m*, faca de trinchar

car wash N lavagem *f* de carros
cascade [kæs'keɪd] N cascata ▶ VI cascatear, cair em cascata
case [keɪs] N (*instance, investigation, Med*) caso; (*for spectacles etc*) estojo; (*Law*) causa; (*BRIT: also*: **suitcase**) mala; (*of wine etc*) caixa; (*Typ*): **lower/upper ~** caixa baixa/alta; **to have a good ~** ter bons argumentos; **there's a strong ~ for ...** há bons argumentos para ...; **in ~ (of)** em caso (de); **in any ~** em todo o caso; **just in ~** *conj* se por acaso; *adv* por via das dúvidas
case history N (*Med*) anamnese *f*
case study N (*Med*) caso clínico; (*Sociology*) estudo sociológico
cash [kæʃ] N dinheiro (em espécie) ▶ VT descontar; **to pay (in) ~** pagar em dinheiro; **~ on delivery** pagamento contra entrega; **to be short of ~** estar sem dinheiro
▶ **cash in** VT (*insurance policy etc*) resgatar
▶ **cash in on** VT FUS lucrar com, explorar
cash account N conta de caixa
cash-book N livro-caixa *m*
cash box N cofre *m*
cash card (*BRIT*) N cartão *m* de saque
cash desk (*BRIT*) N caixa
cash discount N desconto por pagamento à vista
cash dispenser N caixa automática *or* eletrônica
cashew [kæ'ʃuː] N (*also*: **cashew nut**) castanha de caju
cash flow N fluxo de caixa
cashier [kæ'ʃɪər] N caixa *m/f* ▶ VT (*Mil*) exonerar
cashmere [kæʃmɪər] N caxemira, cachemira
cash payment N (*in money*) pagamento em dinheiro; (*in one go*) pagamento à vista
cash point N caixa *m* eletrônico
cash price N preço à vista
cash register N caixa registradora
cash sale N venda à vista
casing [keɪsɪŋ] N invólucro; (*of boiler etc*) revestimento
casino [kə'siːnəu] N cassino
cask [kɑːsk] N barril *m*
casket [kɑːskɪt] N cofre *m*, porta-joias *m inv*; (*US*: *coffin*) caixão *m*
Caspian Sea [kæspɪən-] N: **the ~** o mar Cáspio
casserole [kæsərəul] N panela de ir ao forno; (*food*) ensopado (*BR*) no forno, guisado (*PT*) no forno
cassette [kæ'sɛt] N fita-cassete *f*
cassette deck N toca-fitas *m inv*
cassette player N toca-fitas *m inv*
cassette recorder N gravador *m*
cassock [kæsək] N sotaina, batina
cast [kɑːst] (*pt*, *pp* **cast**) VT (*throw*) lançar, atirar; (*skin*) mudar, perder; (*metal*) fundir; (*Theatre*): **to ~ sb as Hamlet** dar a alguém o papel de Hamlet ▶ VI (*Fishing*) lançar ▶ N (*Theatre*) elenco; (*mould*) forma, molde *m*;

(*also*: **plaster cast**) gesso; **to ~ loose** soltar; **to ~ one's vote** votar
▶ **cast aside** VT rejeitar
▶ **cast away** VT desperdiçar
▶ **cast down** VT abater, desalentar
▶ **cast off** VI (*Naut*) soltar o cabo; (*Knitting*) rematar os pontos ▶ VT (*Knitting*) rematar
▶ **cast on** VT (*Knitting*) montar ▶ VI montar os pontos
castanets [kæstə'nɛts] NPL castanholas *fpl*
castaway [kɑːstəwəɪ] N náufrago(-a)
caste [kɑːst] N casta
caster sugar [kɑːstər-] (*BRIT*) N açúcar *m* branco refinado
casting vote [kɑːstɪŋ-] (*BRIT*) N voto decisivo, voto de minerva
cast iron N ferro fundido ▶ ADJ: **cast-iron** (*fig*: *will*) de ferro; (: *alibi*) forte
castle [kɑːsl] N castelo; (*Chess*) torre *f*
castor [kɑːstər] N (*wheel*) rodízio
castor oil N óleo de rícino
castor sugar (*BRIT*) N = **caster sugar**
castrate [kæs'treɪt] VT castrar
casual [kæʒjul] ADJ (*by chance*) fortuito; (*irregular*: *work etc*) eventual; (*unconcerned*) despreocupado; (*informal*: *clothes etc*) descontraído, informal; **~ wear** roupas *fpl* esportivas
casual labour N mão-de-obra *f* ocasional
casually [kæʒjulɪ] ADV (*in a relaxed way*) casualmente; (*dress*) informalmente
casualty [kæʒjultɪ] N (*wounded*) ferido(-a); (*dead*) morto(-a); (*of situation*: *victim*) vítima; (*Med*: *department*) pronto-socorro; (*Mil*) baixa; **casualties** NPL perdas *fpl*
casualty ward (*BRIT*) N setor *m* de emergência, pronto-socorro
cat [kæt] N gato
catacombs [kætəkuːmz] NPL catacumbas *fpl*
Catalan [kætəlæn] ADJ catalão(-lã) ▶ N catalão(-lã) *m/f*; (*Ling*) catalão *m*
catalogue, (*US*) **catalog** [kætəlɔg] N catálogo ▶ VT catalogar
Catalonia [kætə'ləuniə] N Catalunha
catalyst [kætəlɪst] N catalisador *m*
catapult [kætəpʌlt] (*BRIT*) N catapulta; (*sling*) atiradeira
cataract [kætərækt] N (*also Med*) catarata
catarrh [kə'tɑːr] N catarro
catastrophe [kə'tæstrəfɪ] N catástrofe *f*
catastrophic [kætə'strɔfɪk] ADJ catastrófico
catcall [kætkɔːl] N assobio
catch [kætʃ] (*pt*, *pp* **caught**) VT (*ball, train, illness*) pegar (*BR*), apanhar (*PT*); (*fish*) pescar; (*arrest*) prender, deter; (*person*: *by surprise*) flagrar, surpreender; (*attention*) atrair; (*hear*) ouvir; (*understand*) compreender; (*get entangled*) prender; (*also*: **catch up**) alcançar ▶ VI (*fire*) pegar; (*in branches etc*) ficar preso, prender-se ▶ N (*fish etc*) pesca; (*act of catching*) captura; (*game*) manha, armadilha; (*of lock*) trinco, lingueta; **to ~ sb's attention** *or* **eye** chamar a atenção de alguém; **to ~ fire** pegar fogo;

(*building*) incendiar-se; **to ~ sight of** avistar
▶ **catch on** vi (*understand*) entender (BR),
perceber (PT); (*grow popular*) pegar
▶ **catch out** (BRIT) vt (*with trick question*)
apanhar em erro
▶ **catch up** vi equiparar-se; (*make up for lost
time*) recuperar o tempo perdido ▶ vt (*also:*
catch up with) alcançar
catch-22 [-twentɪ'tu:] N: **it's a ~ situation** é
uma situação do tipo se correr, o bicho pega,
se ficar, o bicho come
catching ['kætʃɪŋ] ADJ (*Med*) contagioso
catchment area ['kætʃmənt-] N (BRIT) *área
atendida por um hospital, uma escola etc*
catch phrase N clichê *m*, slogan *m*
catchy ['kætʃɪ] ADJ (*tune*) que pega fácil, que
gruda no ouvido
catechism ['kætɪkɪzəm] N (*Rel*) catecismo
categoric [kætɪ'gɔrɪk], **categorical**
[kætɪ'gɔrɪkəl] ADJ categórico, terminante
categorize ['kætɪgəraɪz] vt classificar
category ['kætɪgərɪ] N categoria
cater ['keɪtər] vi preparar comida
▶ **cater for** vt FUS (*needs*) atender a;
(*consumers*) satisfazer
caterer ['keɪtərər] N (*service*) serviço de bufê
catering ['keɪtərɪŋ] N serviço de bufê; (*trade*)
abastecimento
caterpillar ['kætəpɪlər] N lagarta ▶ CPD
(*vehicle*) de lagartas
caterpillar track N lagarta
cathedral [kə'θi:drəl] N catedral *f*
cathode ['kæθəud] N cátodo
cathode ray tube N tubo de raios catódicos
Catholic ['kæθəlɪk] ADJ, N (*Rel*) católico(-a)
catholic ['kæθəlɪk] ADJ eclético
cat's-eye (BRIT) N (*Aut*) catadióptrico
catsup ['kætsəp] (US) N ketchup *m*
cattle ['kætl] NPL gado
catty ['kætɪ] ADJ malicioso
catwalk ['kætwɔːk] N passarela
Caucasian [kɔː'keɪʒn] ADJ, N caucasoide *m/f*
Caucasus ['kɔːkəsəs] N Cáucaso
caucus ['kɔːkəs] N (*Pol: group*) panelinha (de
políticos); (: US) comitê *m* eleitoral (para
indicar candidatos)
caught [kɔːt] PT, PP *of* **catch**
cauliflower ['kɔlɪflauər] N couve-flor *f*
cause [kɔːz] N causa; (*reason*) motivo, razão *f*
▶ vt causar, provocar; **there is no ~ for
concern** não há motivo de preocupação;
to ~ sth to be done fazer com que algo seja
feito; **to ~ sb to do sth** fazer com que
alguém faça algo
causeway ['kɔːzweɪ] N (*road*) calçada;
(*embankment*) banqueta
caustic ['kɔːstɪk] ADJ cáustico; (*fig*) mordaz
caution ['kɔːʃən] N cautela, prudência;
(*warning*) aviso ▶ vt acautelar, avisar
cautious ['kɔːʃəs] ADJ cauteloso, prudente,
precavido
cautiously ['kɔːʃəslɪ] ADV com cautela
cautiousness ['kɔːʃəsnɪs] N cautela, prudência

cavalier [kævə'lɪər] ADJ arrogante ▶ N (*knight*)
cavaleiro
cavalry ['kævəlrɪ] N cavalaria
cave [keɪv] N caverna, gruta
▶ **cave in** vi dar de si; (*roof etc*) ceder
caveman ['keɪvmæn] (*irreg: like* **man**) N
troglodita *m*, homem *m* das cavernas
cavern ['kævən] N caverna
caviar, caviare ['kævɪɑːr] N caviar *m*
cavity ['kævɪtɪ] N cavidade *f*; (*in tooth*) cárie *f*
cavort [kə'vɔːt] vi cabriolar
cayenne [keɪ'ɛn] N (*also:* **cayenne pepper**)
pimenta-de-caiena
CB N ABBR = **Citizens' Band (Radio)**; (BRIT:
= *Companion of (the Order of the Bath*)) título
honorífico
CBC N ABBR = **Canadian Broadcasting
Corporation**
CBE N ABBR (= *Companion of (the Order of) the
British Empire*) título honorífico
CBI N ABBR (= *Confederation of British Industry*)
federação de indústria
CBS (US) N ABBR = *Columbia Broadcasting System*)
emissora de televisão
CC (BRIT) ABBR = **County Council**
cc ABBR (= *cubic centimetre*) cc; (*on letter etc*)
= **carbon copy**
CCA (US) N ABBR (= *Circuit Court of Appeals*)
tribunal de recursos itinerante
CCTV N ABBR (= *closed-circuit television*) CFTV
CCTV camera N câmera de segurança
CCU (US) N ABBR (= *coronary care unit*) unidade de
cardiologia
CD N ABBR = **compact disc**; (*Mil: BRIT*) = **Civil
Defence (Corps)**; (US) = **Civil Defense** ▶ ABBR
(BRIT: = *Corps Diplomatique*) CD
CD burner, CD writer N gravador *m* de CD
CDC (US) N ABBR = **center for disease control**
CD player N toca-discos *m inv* laser
Cdr. ABBR (= *commander*) Com.
CD-ROM N ABBR (= *compact disc read-only
memory*) CD-ROM *m*
CDT (US) N ABBR (= *Central Daylight Time*) hora de
verão do centro
cease [si:s] vt, vi cessar
ceasefire [si:s'faɪər] N cessar-fogo *m*
ceaseless ['si:slɪs] ADJ contínuo, incessante
ceaselessly ['si:slɪslɪ] ADV sem parar, sem
cessar
CED (US) N ABBR = **Committee for Economic
Development**
cedar ['si:dər] N cedro
cede [si:d] vt ceder
cedilla [sɪ'dɪlə] N cedilha
CEEB (US) N ABBR (= *College Entry Examination
Board*) *comissão de admissão ao ensino superior*
ceiling ['si:lɪŋ] N (*also fig*) teto
celebrate ['sɛlɪbreɪt] vt celebrar ▶ vi celebrar;
(*birthday, anniversary etc*) festejar; (*Rel: mass*)
rezar
celebrated ['sɛlɪbreɪtɪd] ADJ célebre
celebration [sɛlɪ'breɪʃən] N (*act*) celebração *f*;
(*party*) festa

celebrity [sɪˈlɛbrɪtɪ] N *(person, fame)* celebridade *f* ▶ CPD *(couple, magazine)* de celebridades; ~ **guests** celebridades convidadas
celeriac [səˈlɛrɪæk] N aipo-rábano
celery [ˈsɛlərɪ] N aipo
celestial [sɪˈlɛstɪəl] ADJ *(of sky)* celeste; *(divine)* celestial
celibacy [ˈsɛlɪbəsɪ] N celibato
cell [sɛl] N cela; *(Bio)* célula; *(Elec)* pilha, elemento; *(US: cellphone)* celular *m* (BR), telemóvel *m* (PT)
cellar [ˈsɛləʳ] N porão *m*; *(for wine)* adega
'cellist [ˈtʃɛlɪst] N violoncelista *m/f*
'cello [ˈtʃɛləʊ] N violoncelo
cellophane [ˈsɛləfeɪn] N celofane *m*
cellphone [ˈsɛlfəʊn] N (telefone) celular *m* (BR), telemóvel *m* (PT)
cell tower *(US)* N *(Tel)* torre *f* de celular
cellular [ˈsɛljuləʳ] ADJ celular
cellulose [ˈsɛljuləʊs] N celulose *f*
Celsius [ˈsɛlsɪəs] ADJ Célsius *inv*
Celt [kɛlt] ADJ, N celta *m/f*
Celtic [ˈkɛltɪk] ADJ celta ▶ N *(Ling)* celta *m*
cement [səˈmɛnt] N cimento ▶ VT cimentar; *(fig)* cimentar, fortalecer
cement mixer N betoneira
cemetery [ˈsɛmɪtrɪ] N cemitério
cenotaph [ˈsɛnətɑːf] N cenotáfio
censor [ˈsɛnsəʳ] N *(person)* censor(a) *m/f*; *(concept)*: **the ~** a censura ▶ VT censurar
censorship [ˈsɛnsəʃɪp] N censura
censure [ˈsɛnʃəʳ] VT criticar
census [ˈsɛnsəs] N censo
cent [sɛnt] N *(US: of dollar)* centavo; *(of euro)* cêntimo; *see also* **per cent**
centenary [sɛnˈtiːnərɪ] N centenário
centennial [sɛnˈtɛnɪəl] N centenário
center [ˈsɛntəʳ] *(US)* = **centre**
centigrade [ˈsɛntɪgreɪd] ADJ centígrado
centilitre, *(US)* **centiliter** [ˈsɛntiliːtəʳ] N centilitro
centimetre, *(US)* **centimeter** [ˈsɛntimiːtəʳ] N centímetro
centipede [ˈsɛntɪpiːd] N centopeia
central [ˈsɛntrəl] ADJ central
Central African Republic N República Centro-Africana
Central America N América Central
Central American ADJ centroamericano
central heating N aquecimento central
centralize [ˈsɛntrəlaɪz] VT centralizar
central processing unit N *(Comput)* unidade *f* central de processamento
central reservation *(BRIT)* N *(Aut)* canteiro divisor
centre, *(US)* **center** [ˈsɛntəʳ] N centro; *(of room, circle etc)* meio ▶ VT centrar ▶ VI *(concentrate)*: **to ~ (on)** concentrar (em)
centrefold, *(US)* **centerfold** [ˈsɛntəfəʊld] N poster *m* central
centre-forward N *(Sport)* centroavante *m*, centro

centre-half N *(Sport: centro)* médio
centrepiece, *(US)* **centerpiece** [ˈsɛntəpiːs] N centro de mesa
centre spread *(BRIT)* N páginas *fpl* centrais
centrifugal [sɛntrɪˈfjuːgl] ADJ centrífugo
centrifuge [ˈsɛntrɪfjuːʒ] N centrífuga
century [ˈsɛntjurɪ] N século; **20th ~** século vinte
CEO N ABBR = **chief executive officer**
ceramic [sɪˈræmɪk] ADJ cerâmico
ceramics [sɪˈræmɪks] N cerâmica
cereal [ˈsiːrɪəl] N cereal *m*
cerebral [ˈsɛrɪbrəl] ADJ cerebral; *(intellectual)* intelectual
ceremonial [sɛrɪˈməʊnɪəl] N cerimonial *m*; *(rite)* rito
ceremony [ˈsɛrɪmənɪ] N cerimônia; *(ritual)* rito; **to stand on ~** fazer cerimônia
cert [səːt] *(BRIT inf)* N: **it's a dead ~** é barbada, é coisa certa
certain [ˈsəːtən] ADJ *(sure)* seguro; *(person)*: **a ~ Mr Smith** um certo Sr. Smith; *(particular)*: **~ days/places** certos dias/lugares; *(some)*: **a ~ coldness/pleasure** uma certa frieza/um certo prazer; **to make ~ of** assegurar-se de; **for ~** com certeza
certainly [ˈsəːtənlɪ] ADV certamente, com certeza
certainty [ˈsəːtəntɪ] N certeza
certificate [səˈtɪfɪkɪt] N certidão *f*, diploma *m*
certified mail [ˈsəːtɪfaɪd-] *(US)* N correio registrado
certified public accountant [ˈsəːtɪfaɪd-] *(US)* N perito-contador *m*/perita-contadora *f*
certify [ˈsəːtɪfaɪ] VT certificar ▶ VI: **to ~ to** atestar
cervical [ˈsəːvɪkl] ADJ: **~ cancer** câncer *m* (BR) *or* cancro (PT) do colo do útero; **~ smear** exame *m* de lâmina, esfregaço
cervix [ˈsəːvɪks] N cerviz *f*
Cesarean [sɪˈzɛərɪən] *(US)* ADJ, N = **Caesarean**
cessation [səˈseɪʃən] N cessação *f*, suspensão *f*
cesspit [ˈsɛspɪt] N fossa séptica
CET ABBR *(= Central European Time)* hora da Europa Central
Ceylon [sɪˈlɔn] N *(old)* Ceilão *m*
cf. ABBR *(= compare)* cf.
c/f ABBR *(Comm: = carry forward)* a transportar
CFC N ABBR *(= chlorofluorocarbon)* CFC *m*
CG *(US)* N ABBR = **coastguard**
cg ABBR *(= centigram)* cg
CH *(BRIT)* N ABBR *(= Companion of Honour)* título honorífico
ch *(BRIT)* ABBR = **central heating**
ch. ABBR *(= chapter)* cap.
Chad [tʃæd] N Chad *m*
chafe [tʃeɪf] VT *(rub)* roçar; *(wear)* gastar; *(irritate)* irritar ▶ VI *(fig)*: **to ~ at sth** irritar-se com algo
chaffinch [ˈtʃæfɪntʃ] N tentilhão *m*
chagrin [ˈʃægrɪn] N desgosto
chain [tʃeɪn] N corrente *f*; *(of islands)* grupo; *(of mountains)* cordilheira; *(of shops)* cadeia;

(*of events*) série *f* ▶ VT (*also*: **chain up**) acorrentar

chain reaction N reação *f* em cadeia

chain-smoke VI fumar um (cigarro) atrás do outro

chain store N magazine *m* (BR), grande armazem *f* (PT)

chair [tʃɛəʳ] N cadeira; (*armchair*) poltrona; (*of university*) cátedra; (*of meeting*) presidência, mesa ▶ VT (*meeting*) presidir; **the ~** (US: *electric chair*) a cadeira elétrica

chairlift ['tʃɛəlɪft] N teleférico

chairman ['tʃɛəmən] (*irreg*: *like* **man**) N presidente *m*

chairperson ['tʃɛəpə:sn] N presidente *m/f*

chairwoman ['tʃɛəwumən] (*irreg*: *like* **woman**) N presidenta, presidente *f*

chalet ['ʃæleɪ] N chalé *m*

chalice ['tʃælɪs] N cálice *m*

chalk [tʃɔ:k] N (*Geo*) greda; (*for writing*) giz *m* ▶ **chalk up** VT escrever a giz; (*fig: success*) obter

challenge ['tʃælɪndʒ] N desafio ▶ VT desafiar; (*statement, right*) disputar, contestar; **to ~ sb to sth/to do sth** desafiar alguém para algo/a fazer algo

challenger ['tʃælɪndʒəʳ] N (*Sport*) competidor(a) *m/f*

challenging ['tʃælɪndʒɪŋ] ADJ desafiante; (*tone*) de desafio

chamber ['tʃeɪmbəʳ] N câmara; (BRIT Law: *gen pl*) sala de audiências

chambermaid ['tʃeɪmbəmeɪd] N arrumadeira (BR), empregada (PT)

chamber music N música de câmara

chamber of commerce N câmara de comércio

chamber pot N urinol *m*

chameleon [kə'mi:lɪən] N camaleão *m*

chamois ['ʃæmwɑ:] N camurça

chamois leather ['ʃæmɪ-] N camurça

champagne [ʃæm'peɪn] N champanhe *m or f*

champion ['tʃæmpɪən] N campeão(-peã) *m/f*; (*of cause*) defensor(a) *m/f* ▶ VT defender, lutar por

championship ['tʃæmpɪənʃɪp] N campeonato

chance [tʃɑ:ns] N (*luck*) acaso, casualidade *f*; (*opportunity*) oportunidade, ocasião *f*; (*likelihood*) chance *f*; (*risk*) risco ▶ VT arriscar ▶ ADJ fortuito, casual; **there is little ~ of his coming** é pouco provável que ele venha; **to take a ~** arriscar-se; **it's the ~ of a lifetime** é uma chance que só se tem uma vez na vida; **by ~** por acaso; **to ~ it** arriscar-se; **to ~ to do** fazer por acaso ▶ **chance on, chance upon** VT FUS dar com, encontrar por acaso

chancel ['tʃɑ:nsəl] N coro, capela-mor *f*

chancellor ['tʃɑ:nsələʳ] N chanceler *m*; **C~ of the Exchequer** (BRIT) Ministro da Economia (Fazenda e Planejamento)

chandelier [ʃændə'lɪəʳ] N lustre *m*

change [tʃeɪndʒ] VT (*alter*) mudar; (*wheel, bulb, money*) trocar; (*replace*) substituir; (*clothes, house*) mudar de, trocar de; (*nappy*) mudar, trocar; (*transform*): **to ~ sb into** transformar alguém em ▶ VI mudar(-se); (*change clothes*) trocar-se; (*trains*) fazer baldeação (BR), mudar (PT); (*be transformed*): **to ~ into** transformar-se em ▶ N mudança; (*exchange*) troca; (*difference*) diferença; (*of clothes*) muda; (*modification*) modificação *f*; (*transformation*) transformação *f*; (*coins: also*: **small change**) trocado; **to ~ gear** (*Aut*) trocar de marcha; **to ~ one's mind** mudar de ideia; **for a ~** para variar; **she ~d into an old skirt** ela (trocou de roupa e) vestiu uma saia velha; **a ~ of clothes** uma muda de roupa; **to give sb ~ for** or **of £10** trocar £10 para alguém

changeable ['tʃeɪndʒəbl] ADJ (*weather*) instável; (*mood*) inconstante

change machine N máquina que fornece trocado

changeover ['tʃeɪndʒəuvəʳ] N (*to new system*) mudança

changing ['tʃeɪndʒɪŋ] ADJ variável

changing room (BRIT) N (*Sport*) vestiário; (*in shop*) cabine *f* de provas

channel ['tʃænl] N (*TV*) canal *m*; (*of river*) leito; (*for boats*) canal; (*of sea*) canal, estreito; (*groove*) ranhura; (*fig: medium*) meio, via ▶ VT (*money, resources*): **to ~ (into)** canalizar (para); **to go through the usual ~s** seguir os trâmites normais; **green/red ~** (*Customs*) canal verde/vermelho; **the (English) C~** o Canal da Mancha

Channel Islands NPL: **the ~** as ilhas Anglo-Normandas

chant [tʃɑ:nt] N (*of crowd*) canto; (*Rel*) cântico ▶ VT cantar; (*word, slogan*) entoar

chaos ['keɪɔs] N caos *m*

chaotic [keɪ'ɔtɪk] ADJ caótico

chap [tʃæp] N (BRIT *inf: man*) sujeito (BR), tipo (PT); (*term of address*): **old ~** meu velho ▶ VT (*skin*) rachar

chapel ['tʃæpəl] N capela

chaperon, chaperone ['ʃæpərəun] N mulher *f* acompanhante ▶ VT acompanhar

chaplain ['tʃæplɪn] N capelão *m*

chapped [tʃæpt] ADJ ressecado

chapter ['tʃæptəʳ] N capítulo

char [tʃɑ:ʳ] VT (*burn*) tostar, queimar ▶ VI (BRIT) trabalhar como diarista ▶ N (BRIT) = **charlady**

character ['kærɪktəʳ] N caráter *m*; (*in novel, film*) personagem *m/f*; (*role*) papel *m*; (*eccentric*): **to be a (real) ~** ser um número; (*letter*) letra; **a person of good ~** uma pessoa de bom caráter

character code N (*Comput*) código de caráter

characteristic [kærɪktə'rɪstɪk] ADJ característico ▶ N característica

characterize ['kærɪktəraɪz] VT caracterizar

charade [ʃə'rɑ:d] N charada

charcoal ['tʃɑ:kəul] N carvão *m* de lenha; (*Art*) carvão *m*

charge [tʃɑ:dʒ] N (*of gun, electrical, Mil: attack*) carga; (*Law*) encargo, acusação *f*; (*fee*) preço, custo; (*responsibility*) encargo; (*task*) incumbência ▶ VT (*battery*) carregar; (*Mil: enemy*) atacar; (*price*) cobrar; (*customer*) cobrar dinheiro de; (*sb with task*) incumbir, encarregar; (*Law*): **to ~ sb (with)** acusar alguém (de) ▶ VI precipitar-se; (*make pay*) cobrar; **charges** NPL: **bank ~s** taxas *fpl* bancárias; **labour ~s** custos *mpl* de mão-de-obra; **free of ~** grátis; **is there a ~?** se tem que pagar?; **there's no ~** é de graça; **extra ~** sobretaxa; **to reverse the ~s** (*BRIT Tel*) ligar a cobrar; **how much do you ~?** quanto você cobra?; **to ~ an expense (up) to sb's account** pôr a despesa na conta de alguém; **to take ~ of** encarregar-se de, tomar conta de; **to be in ~ of** estar a cargo de *or* encarregado de; **they ~d us £50 for the dinner** cobraram £50 pelo jantar; **to ~ in/out** precipitar-se para dentro/fora

charge account N conta de crédito

charge card N cartão *m* de crédito (*emitido por uma loja*)

chargé d'affaires ['ʃɑːʒeɪdæ'fɛəʳ] N encarregado(-a) de negócios

chargehand ['tʃɑːdʒhænd] (*BRIT*) N capataz *m*

charger ['tʃɑːdʒəʳ] N (*also:* **battery charger**) carregador *m*; (*old: warhorse*) cavalo de batalha

charisma [kə'rɪzmə] N carisma *m*

charitable ['tʃærɪtəbl] ADJ caritativo; (*organization*) beneficente

charity ['tʃærɪtɪ] N caridade *f*; (*organization*) obra de caridade; (*kindness*) compaixão *f*; (*money, gifts*) donativo

charlady ['tʃɑːleɪdɪ] (*BRIT*) N diarista

charlatan ['tʃɑːlətən] N charlatão *m*

charm [tʃɑːm] N (*quality*) charme *m*; (*attraction*) encanto, atrativo; (*spell*) feitiço; (*talisman*) amuleto; (*on bracelet*) berloque *m* ▶ VT encantar, deliciar

charm bracelet N pulseira de berloques

charming ['tʃɑːmɪŋ] ADJ encantador(a)

chart [tʃɑːt] N (*table*) quadro; (*graph*) gráfico; (*diagram*) diagrama *m*; (*map*) carta de navegação; (*weather chart*) carta meteorológica *or* de tempo ▶ VT fazer um gráfico de; (*course, progress*) traçar; **charts** NPL (*hit parade*) paradas *fpl* (de sucesso); **to be in the ~s** (*record, pop group*) estar nas paradas (de sucesso)

charter ['tʃɑːtəʳ] VT fretar ▶ N (*document*) carta, alvará *m*; **on ~** (*plane*) fretado

chartered accountant ['tʃɑːtəd-] (*BRIT*) N perito-contador/perita-contadora *m/f*

charter flight N voo charter *or* fretado

charwoman ['tʃɑːwumən] (*irreg: like* **woman**) N = **charlady**

chase [tʃeɪs] VT (*pursue*) perseguir; (*hunt*) caçar, dar caça a; (*also:* **chase away**) enxotar ▶ VI: **to ~ after** correr atrás de ▶ N perseguição *f*, caça

▶ **chase down** (*US*) VT = **chase up**

▶ **chase up** (*BRIT*) VT (*person*) ficar atrás de; (*information*) pesquisar

chasm ['kæzəm] N abismo

chassis ['ʃæsɪ] N chassi *m*

chaste [tʃeɪst] ADJ casto

chastened ['tʃeɪsnd] ADJ: **to be ~ by an experience** aprender uma lição com uma experiência

chastening ['tʃeɪsnɪŋ] ADJ: **it was a ~ experience** foi uma lição

chastise [tʃæs'taɪz] VT castigar

chastity ['tʃæstɪtɪ] N castidade *f*

chat [tʃæt] VI (*also:* **have a chat**) conversar, bater papo (*BR*), cavaquear (*PT*); (*on the Internet*) bater papo, conversar ▶ N conversa, bate-papo *m* (*BR*), cavaqueira (*PT*)

▶ **chat up** (*BRIT inf*) VT (*girl*) paquerar

chatroom N sala *f* de bate-papo (*BR*), sala *f* de conversação (*PT*)

chat show (*BRIT*) N programa *m* de entrevistas

chattel ['tʃætl] N: **goods and ~s** bens móveis

chatter ['tʃætəʳ] VI (*person*) tagarelar; (*animal*) emitir sons; (*teeth*) tiritar ▶ N tagarelice *f*; emissão *f* de sons; (*of birds*) chilro

chatterbox ['tʃætəbɔks] N tagarela *m/f*

chatty ['tʃætɪ] ADJ (*style*) informal; (*person*) conversador(a)

chauffeur ['ʃəufəʳ] N chofer *m*, motorista *m/f*

chauvinism ['ʃəuvɪnɪzəm] N (*also:* **male chauvinism**) machismo; (*nationalism*) chauvinismo

chauvinist ['ʃəuvɪnɪst] N (*also:* **male chauvinist**) machista *m*; (*nationalist*) chauvinista *m/f*

ChE ABBR = **chemical engineer**

cheap [tʃiːp] ADJ barato; (*ticket etc*) a preço reduzido; (*poor quality*) barato, de pouca qualidade; (*behaviour*) vulgar; (*joke*) de mau gosto ▶ ADV barato; **a ~ trick** uma sujeira, uma sacanagem

cheapen ['tʃiːpən] VT baixar o preço de, rebaixar; **to ~ o.s.** rebaixar-se

cheaply ['tʃiːplɪ] ADV barato, por baixo preço

cheat [tʃiːt] VI trapacear; (*at cards*) roubar (*BR*), fazer batota (*PT*); (*in exam*) colar (*BR*), cabular (*PT*) ▶ VT defraudar, enganar ▶ N fraude *f*; (*person*) trapaceiro(-a); **to ~ sb out of sth** defraudar alguém de algo; **to ~ on sb** (*inf: husband, wife etc*) trair alguém

cheating ['tʃiːtɪŋ] N trapaça

check [tʃɛk] VT (*examine*) controlar; (*facts*) verificar; (*count*) contar; (*halt*) conter, impedir; (*restrain*) parar, refrear ▶ VI verificar ▶ N (*inspection*) controle *m*, inspeção *f*; (*curb*) freio; (*US: bill*) conta; (*Chess*) xeque *m*; (*token*) ficha, talão *m*; (*pattern: gen pl*) xadrez *m*; (*US*) = **cheque** ▶ ADJ (*also:* **checked**): *pattern, cloth* xadrez *inv*; **to ~ with sb** perguntar a alguém; **to keep a ~ on sb/sth** controlar alguém/algo

▶ **check in** VI (*at hotel*) registrar-se; (*at airport*) apresentar-se ▶ VT (*luggage*) entregar

▶ **check off** VT checar

▶ **check out** VI (*of hotel*) pagar a conta e sair ▶ VT (*story*) verificar; (*person*) investigar;

~ **it out** (*see for yourself*) confira
▶ **check up** VI: **to ~ up on sth** verificar algo; **to ~ up on sb** investigar alguém
checkbook ['tʃɛkbuk] (US) N = **chequebook**
checkered ['tʃɛkəd] (US) ADJ = **chequered**
checkers ['tʃɛkəz] (US) N (jogo de) damas *fpl*
check guarantee card (US) N cartão *m* (de garantia) de cheques
check-in, check-in desk N (*at airport*) check-in *m*
checking account ['tʃɛkɪŋ-] (US) N conta corrente
checklist ['tʃɛklɪst] N lista de conferência
checkmate ['tʃɛkmeɪt] N xeque-mate *m*
checkout ['tʃɛkaut] N caixa
checkpoint ['tʃɛkpɔɪnt] N (ponto de) controle *m*
checkroom ['tʃɛkrum] (US) N depósito de bagagem
checkup ['tʃɛkʌp] N (*Med*) check-up *m*; (*of machine*) revisão *f*
cheek [tʃiːk] N bochecha; (*impudence*) folga, descaramento; **what a ~!** que folga!
cheekbone ['tʃiːkbəun] N maçã *f* do rosto
cheeky ['tʃiːkɪ] ADJ insolente, descarado
cheep [tʃiːp] N (*of bird*) pio ▶ VI piar
cheer [tʃɪəʳ] VT dar vivas a, aplaudir; (*gladden*) alegrar, animar ▶ VI gritar com entusiasmo ▶ N (*gen pl*) gritos *mpl* de entusiasmo; **cheers** NPL (*of crowd*) aplausos *mpl*; **~s!** saúde!
▶ **cheer on** VT torcer por
▶ **cheer up** VI animar-se, alegrar-se ▶ VT alegrar, animar
cheerful ['tʃɪəful] ADJ alegre
cheerfulness ['tʃɪəfulnɪs] N alegria
cheerio [tʃɪərɪ'əu] (BRIT) EXCL tchau! (BR), adeus! (PT)
cheerleader ['tʃɪəliːdəʳ] N animador(a) de torcida *m/f*
cheerless ['tʃɪəlɪs] ADJ triste, sombrio
cheese [tʃiːz] N queijo
cheeseboard ['tʃiːzbɔːd] N (*in restaurant*) sortimento de queijos
cheesecake ['tʃiːzkeɪk] N queijada, torta de queijo
cheetah ['tʃiːtə] N chitá *m*
chef [ʃɛf] N cozinheiro-chefe/cozinheira-chefe *m/f*
chemical ['kɛmɪkəl] ADJ químico ▶ N produto químico
chemist ['kɛmɪst] N (BRIT: *pharmacist*) farmacêutico(-a); (*scientist*) químico(-a)
chemistry ['kɛmɪstrɪ] N química
chemist's, chemist's shop (BRIT) N farmácia
cheque [tʃɛk] (BRIT) N cheque *m*; **to pay by ~** pagar com cheque
chequebook ['tʃɛkbuk] (BRIT) N talão *m* (BR) or livro (PT) de cheques
cheque card, cheque guarantee card N (BRIT) cartão *m* (de garantia) de cheques
chequered, (US) **checkered** ['tʃɛkəd] ADJ (*fig*) variado, acidentado
cherish ['tʃɛrɪʃ] VT (*person*) tratar com carinho; (*memory*) lembrar (com prazer); (*love*)

apreciar; (*protect*) cuidar; (*hope etc*) acalentar
cheroot [ʃə'ruːt] N charuto
cherry ['tʃɛrɪ] N cereja; (*also:* **cherry tree**) cerejeira
Ches (BRIT) ABBR = **Cheshire**
chess [tʃɛs] N xadrez *m*
chessboard ['tʃɛsbɔːd] N tabuleiro de xadrez
chessman ['tʃɛsmæn] (*irreg: like* **man**) N peça, pedra (de xadrez)
chess player N xadrezista *m/f*
chest [tʃɛst] N (*Anat*) peito; (*box*) caixa, cofre *m*; **to get sth off one's ~** (*inf*) desabafar algo
chest measurement N medida de peito
chestnut ['tʃɛsnʌt] N castanha; (*also:* **chestnut tree**) castanheiro; (*colour*) castanho ▶ ADJ castanho
chest of drawers N cômoda
chew [tʃuː] VT mastigar
chewing gum ['tʃuːɪŋ-] N chiclete *m* (BR), pastilha elástica (PT)
chic [ʃɪk] ADJ elegante, chique
chick [tʃɪk] N pinto; (*inf: girl*) broto
chicken ['tʃɪkɪn] N galinha; (*food*) galinha, frango; (*inf: coward*) covarde *m/f*, galinha ▶ **chicken out** (*inf*) VI agalinhar-se
chicken feed N (*fig*) dinheiro miúdo
chickenpox ['tʃɪkɪnpɔks] N catapora (BR), varicela (PT)
chickpea ['tʃɪkpiː] N grão-de-bico *m*
chicory ['tʃɪkərɪ] N chicória
chide [tʃaɪd] VT repreender, censurar
chief [tʃiːf] N (*of tribe*) cacique *m*, morubixaba *m*; (*of organization*) chefe *m/f* ▶ ADJ principal; **C~ of Staff** (*Mil*) chefe *m* do Estado-Maior
chief constable (BRIT) N chefe *m/f* de polícia
chief executive (BRIT), **chief executive officer** N diretor(a) *m/f* geral
chiefly ['tʃiːflɪ] ADV principalmente
chiffon ['ʃɪfɔn] N gaze *f*
chilblain ['tʃɪlbleɪn] N frieira
child [tʃaɪld] (*pl* **children**) N criança; (*offspring*) filho(-a); **do you have any ~ren?** você tem filhos?
childbirth ['tʃaɪldbəːθ] N parto
childcare ['tʃaɪldkɛəʳ] N serviço de cuidado infantil
childhood ['tʃaɪldhud] N infância
childish ['tʃaɪldɪʃ] ADJ infantil
childless ['tʃaɪldlɪs] ADJ sem filhos
childlike ['tʃaɪldlaɪk] ADJ infantil, ingênuo
child minder (BRIT) N cuidadora de crianças
children ['tʃɪldrən] NPL *of* **child**
Chile ['tʃɪlɪ] N Chile *m*
Chilean ['tʃɪlɪən] ADJ, N chileno(-a)
chili ['tʃɪlɪ] (US) N = **chilli**
chill [tʃɪl] N frio, friagem *f*; (*Med*) resfriamento ▶ VT (*Culin*) semi-congelar; (*person*) congelar ▶ ADJ frio, glacial; **"serve ~ed"** "servir fresco"
chilli, (US) **chili** ['tʃɪlɪ] N pimentão *m* picante
chilling ['tʃɪlɪŋ] ADJ (*wind*) gelado; (*look*) arrepiante; (*smile, thought*) horripilante

chilly ['tʃɪlɪ] ADJ frio; (*person*) friorento; **to feel ~** estar com frio

chime [tʃaɪm] N (*of bell*) repique *m*; (*of clock*) soar *m* ▶ VI repicar; soar

chimney ['tʃɪmnɪ] N chaminé *f*

chimney sweep N limpador *m* de chaminés

chimpanzee [tʃɪmpæn'zi:] N chimpanzé *m*

chin [tʃɪn] N queixo

China ['tʃaɪnə] N China

china ['tʃaɪnə] N porcelana; (*crockery*) louça fina

Chinese [tʃaɪ'ni:z] ADJ chinês(-esa) ▶ N INV chinês(-esa) *m/f*; (*Ling*) chinês *m*

chink [tʃɪŋk] N (*opening*) fenda, fissura; (*noise*) tinir *m*

chip [tʃɪp] N (*gen pl*: BRIT *Culin*) batata frita; (US: *also*: **potato chip**) batatinha frita; (*of wood*) lasca; (*of glass, stone*) lasca, pedaço; (*at poker*) ficha; (*Comput*: *also*: **microchip**) chip *m* ▶ VT (*cup, plate*) lascar; **when the ~s are down** (*fig*) na hora H
▶ **chip in** (*inf*) VI interromper; (*contribute*) compartilhar as despesas

chipboard ['tʃɪpbɔ:d] N compensado

chipmunk ['tʃɪpmʌŋk] N tâmia *m*

chippings ['tʃɪpɪŋz] NPL: **"loose ~"** "projeção de cascalho"

chiropodist [kɪ'rɔpədɪst] (BRIT) N pedicuro(-a)

chiropody [kɪ'rɔpədɪ] (BRIT) N quiropodia

chirp [tʃə:p] VI chilrar, piar; (*cricket*) chilrear ▶ N chilro

chirpy ['tʃə:pɪ] ADJ alegre, animado

chisel ['tʃɪzl] N (*for wood*) formão *m*; (*for stone*) cinzel *m*

chit [tʃɪt] N talão *m*

chitchat ['tʃɪttʃæt] N conversa fiada

chivalrous ['ʃɪvəlrəs] ADJ cavalheiresco

chivalry ['ʃɪvəlrɪ] N cavalheirismo

chives [tʃaɪvz] NPL cebolinha

chloride ['klɔ:raɪd] N cloreto

chlorinate ['klɔrɪneɪt] VT clorar

chlorine ['klɔ:ri:n] N cloro

chock [tʃɔk] N cunha

chock-a-block ADJ abarrotado, apinhado

chock-full ADJ = **chock-a-block**

chocolate ['tʃɔklɪt] N chocolate *m*

choice [tʃɔɪs] N (*selection*) seleção *f*; (*option*) escolha; (*preference*) preferência ▶ ADJ seleto, escolhido; **by** or **from ~** de preferência; **a wide ~** uma grande variedade

choir ['kwaɪə'] N coro

choirboy ['kwaɪəbɔɪ] N menino de coro

choke [tʃəuk] VI sufocar-se; (*on food*) engasgar ▶ VT estrangular; (*block*) obstruir ▶ N (*Aut*) afogador *m* (BR), ar *m* (PT)

choker ['tʃəukə'] N (*necklace*) colar *m* curto

cholera ['kɔlərə] N cólera *m*

cholesterol [kə'lɛstərɔl] N colesterol *m*

choose [tʃu:z] (*pt* **chose**, *pp* **chosen**) VT escolher ▶ VI: **to ~ between** escolher entre; **to ~ to do** optar por fazer

choosy ['tʃu:zɪ] ADJ exigente

chop [tʃɔp] VT (*wood*) cortar, talhar; (*Culin*: *also*: **chop up**) cortar em pedaços; (*meat*) picar ▶ N golpe *m*; (*Culin*) costeleta; **chops** NPL (*inf*: *jaws*) beiços *mpl*; **to get the ~** (BRIT *inf*: *project*) ser cancelado; (: *person*: *be sacked*) ser posto na rua
▶ **chop down** VT (*tree*) abater, derrubar

choppy ['tʃɔpɪ] ADJ (*sea*) agitado

chopsticks ['tʃɔpstɪks] NPL pauzinhos *mpl*, palitos *mpl*

choral ['kɔ:rəl] ADJ coral

chord [kɔ:d] N (*Mus*) acorde *m*

chore [tʃɔ:'] N tarefa; (*routine task*) trabalho de rotina; **household ~s** afazeres *mpl* domésticos

choreographer [kɔrɪ'ɔɡrəfə'] N coreógrafo(-a)

choreography [kɔrɪ'ɔɡrəfɪ] N coreografia

chorister ['kɔrɪstə'] N corista *m/f*

chortle ['tʃɔ:tl] VI rir, gargalhar

chorus ['kɔ:rəs] N (*group*) coro; (*song*) coral *m*; (*refrain*) estribilho

chose [tʃəuz] PT *of* **choose**

chosen ['tʃəuzn] PP *of* **choose**

chowder ['tʃaudə'] N sopa (de peixe)

Christ [kraɪst] N Cristo

christen ['krɪsn] VT batizar; (*nickname*) apelidar

christening ['krɪsnɪŋ] N batismo

Christian ['krɪstɪən] ADJ, N cristão(-tã) *m/f*

Christianity [krɪstɪ'ænɪtɪ] N cristianismo

Christian name N prenome *m*, nome *m* de batismo

Christmas ['krɪsməs] N Natal *m*; **Happy** or **Merry ~!** Feliz Natal!

Christmas card N cartão *m* de Natal

Christmas cracker N *ver nota*

> Um **Christmas cracker** é um cilindro de papelão que ao ser aberto faz estourar uma bombinha. Contém um presente surpresa e um chapéu de papel que cada convidado coloca na cabeça durante a ceia de Natal.

Christmas Day N dia *m* de Natal

Christmas Eve N véspera de Natal

Christmas Island N ilha de Christmas

Christmas tree N árvore *f* de Natal

chrome [krəum] N = **chromium**

chromium ['krəumɪəm] N cromo

chromosome ['krəuməsəum] N cromossomo

chronic ['krɔnɪk] ADJ crônico; (*fig*: *drunkenness*) inveterado

chronicle ['krɔnɪkl] N crônica

chronological [krɔnə'lɔdʒɪkəl] ADJ cronológico

chrysanthemum [krɪ'sænθəməm] N crisântemo

chubby ['tʃʌbɪ] ADJ roliço, gorducho

chuck [tʃʌk] VT jogar (BR), deitar (PT); (BRIT: *also*: **chuck up, chuck in**: *job*) largar; (: *person*) acabar com
▶ **chuck out** VT (*thing*) jogar (BR) or deitar (PT) fora; (*person*) expulsar

chuckle ['tʃʌkl] VI rir

C

chuffed [tʃʌft] (inf) ADJ: ~ **(about sth)** encantado (com algo)

chug [tʃʌg] VI mover-se fazendo ruído de descarga; (car, boat: also: **chug along**) ir indo

chum [tʃʌm] N camarada m/f

chump [tʃʌmp] (inf) N imbecil m/f, boboca m/f

chunk [tʃʌŋk] N pedaço, naco

chunky ['tʃʌŋkɪ] ADJ (furniture) pesado; (person) atarracado; (knitwear) grosso

church [tʃəːtʃ] N igreja; **the C~ of England** a Igreja Anglicana

churchyard ['tʃəːtʃjɑːd] N adro, cemitério

churlish ['tʃəːlɪʃ] ADJ (silence) constrangedor(a); (behaviour) grosseiro, rude

churn [tʃəːn] N (for butter) batedeira; (also: **milk churn**) lata, vasilha ▶ VT bater, agitar ▶ **churn out** VT produzir em série

chute [ʃuːt] N rampa; (also: **rubbish chute**) despejador m

chutney ['tʃʌtnɪ] N conserva picante

CIA (US) N ABBR (= Central Intelligence Agency) CIA f

CID (BRIT) N ABBR = **Criminal Investigation Department**

cider ['saɪdə^r] N sidra

CIF ABBR (= cost, insurance and freight) CIF

cigar [sɪ'gɑː^r] N charuto

cigarette [sɪgə'rɛt] N cigarro

cigarette case N cigarreira

cigarette end N ponta de cigarro, guimba (BR)

cigarette holder N piteira (BR), boquilha (PT)

C-in-C ABBR = **commander-in-chief**

cinch [sɪntʃ] (inf) N: **it's a ~** é sopa, é moleza

Cinderella [sɪndə'rɛlə] N Gata Borralheira

cinders ['sɪndəz] NPL cinzas fpl

cine-camera ['sɪnɪ-] (BRIT) N câmera (cinematográfica)

cine-film ['sɪnɪ-] (BRIT) N filme m cinematográfico

cinema ['sɪnəmə] N cinema m

cine-projector ['sɪnɪ-] (BRIT) N projetor m cinematográfico

cinnamon ['sɪnəmən] N canela

cipher ['saɪfə^r] N cifra; **in ~** cifrado

circa ['səːkə] PREP cerca de

circle ['səːkl] N círculo; (in cinema) balcão m ▶ VI dar voltas ▶ VT (surround) rodear, cercar; (move round) dar a volta de

circuit ['səːkɪt] N circuito; (tour, lap) volta; (track) pista

circuit board N placa

circuitous [səː'kjuɪtəs] ADJ tortuoso

circular ['səːkjulə^r] ADJ circular ▶ N (carta) circular f

circulate ['səːkjuleɪt] VT, VI circular

circulation [səːkju'leɪʃən] N circulação f; (of newspaper, book etc) tiragem f

circumcise ['səːkəmsaɪz] VT circuncidar

circumference [sə'kʌmfərəns] N circunferência

circumflex ['səːkəmflɛks] N (also: **circumflex accent**) (acento) circunflexo

circumscribe ['səːkəmskraɪb] VT circunscrever

circumspect ['səːkəmspɛkt] ADJ prudente, cauteloso

circumstances ['səːkəmstənsɪz] NPL circunstâncias fpl; (conditions) condições fpl; (financial condition) situação f econômica; **in the ~** em tais circunstâncias, assim sendo, neste caso; **under no ~** de modo algum, de jeito nenhum

circumstantial [səːkəm'stænʃl] ADJ (report) circunstanciado; **~ evidence** prova circunstancial

circumvent [səːkəm'vɛnt] VT (rule etc) driblar, burlar

circus ['səːkəs] N circo; (also: **Circus**: in place names) praça

cistern ['sɪstən] N tanque m; (in toilet) caixa d'água

citation [saɪ'teɪʃən] N (commendation) menção f; (US Law) intimação f; (quotation) citação f

cite [saɪt] VT citar; (Law) intimar

citizen ['sɪtɪzn] N (of country) cidadão(-dã) m/f; (of town) habitante m/f

citizenship ['sɪtɪznʃɪp] N cidadania

citric acid ['sɪtrɪk-] N ácido cítrico

citrus fruit ['sɪtrəs-] N citrino

city ['sɪtɪ] N cidade f; **the C~** centro financeiro de Londres

city centre N centro (da cidade)

City Hall N (US) ≈ a Prefeitura

civic ['sɪvɪk] ADJ cívico, municipal

civic centre (BRIT) N sede f do município

civil ['sɪvɪl] ADJ civil; (polite) delicado, cortês

civil disobedience N resistência passiva

civil engineer N engenheiro(-a) civil

civil engineering N engenharia civil

civilian [sɪ'vɪliən] ADJ, N civil m/f

civilization [sɪvɪlaɪ'zeɪʃən] N civilização f

civilized ['sɪvɪlaɪzd] ADJ civilizado

civil law N direito civil

civil rights NPL direitos mpl civis

civil servant N funcionário(-a) público(-a)

Civil Service N administração f pública

civil war N guerra civil

cl ABBR (= centilitre) cl

clad [klæd] ADJ: ~ **(in)** vestido (de)

claim [kleɪm] VT exigir, reclamar; (rights etc) reivindicar; (responsibility) assumir; (assert): **to ~ that/to be** afirmar que/ser ▶ VI (for insurance) reclamar ▶ N reclamação f; (Law) direito; (pretension) pretensão f; (assertion) afirmação f; (wage claim etc) reivindicação f; **(insurance) ~** reclamação f; **to put in a ~ for** (pay rise etc) reivindicar

claimant ['kleɪmənt] N (Admin, Law) requerente m/f

claim form N formulário de requerimento; (Insurance) formulário para reclamações

clairvoyant [klɛə'vɔɪənt] N clarividente m/f

clam [klæm] N molusco ▶ **clam up** (inf) VI ficar calado

clamber ['klæmbə^r] VI subir; (up hill etc) escalar

clammy ['klæmɪ] ADJ (hands, face) úmido e pegajoso; (sticky) pegajoso

clamour, (US) **clamor** ['klæmə^r] N clamor m
▶ VI: **to ~ for** clamar

clamp [klæmp] N grampo ▶ VT prender
▶ **clamp down on** VT FUS reprimir

clan [klæn] N clã m

clandestine [klæn'dɛstɪn] ADJ clandestino

clang [klæŋ] N retintim m, som metálico ▶ VI retinir

clansman ['klænzmən] (irreg: like **man**) N membro de um clã escocês

clap [klæp] VI bater palmas, aplaudir ▶ VT (performer) aplaudir ▶ N (of hands) palmas fpl; **to ~ one's hands** bater palmas; **a ~ of thunder** uma trovoada

clapping ['klæpɪŋ] N aplausos mpl, palmas fpl

claret ['klærət] N clarete m

clarification [klærɪfɪ'keɪʃən] N esclarecimento

clarify ['klærɪfaɪ] VT esclarecer

clarinet [klærɪ'nɛt] N clarinete m

clarity ['klærɪtɪ] N clareza

clash [klæʃ] N (fight) confronto; (disagreement) desavença; (of beliefs) divergência; (of colours, styles) choque m; (of dates) coincidência; (of metal) estridor m ▶ VI (gangs, beliefs) chocar-se; (disagree) entrar em conflito, ter uma desavença; (colours) não combinar; (dates, events) coincidir; (weapons, cymbals etc) ressoar

clasp [klɑːsp] N fecho; (embrace) abraço ▶ VT (hold) prender; (hand) apertar; (embrace) abraçar

class [klɑːs] N classe f; (lesson) aula; (type) tipo ▶ CPD de classe ▶ VT classificar

class-conscious ADJ que tem consciência de classe

class consciousness N consciência de classe

classic ['klæsɪk] ADJ clássico ▶ N (author, work, race etc) clássico; **classics** NPL (Sch) línguas fpl clássicas

classical ['klæsɪkl] ADJ clássico

classification [klæsɪfɪ'keɪʃən] N classificação f

classified ['klæsɪfaɪd] ADJ (information) secreto

classified advertisement N classificado

classify ['klæsɪfaɪ] VT classificar

classmate ['klɑːsmeɪt] N colega m/f de aula

classroom ['klɑːsrum] N sala de aula

classy ['klɑːsɪ] (inf) ADJ (person) classudo; (flat, clothes) chique, incrementado

clatter ['klætə^r] N ruído, barulho; (of hooves) tropel m ▶ VI fazer barulho or ruído

clause [klɔːz] N cláusula; (Ling) oração f

claustrophobia [klɔːstrə'fəubɪə] N claustrofobia

claw [klɔː] N (of animal) pata; (of bird of prey) garra; (of lobster) pinça; (Tech) unha ▶ VT arranhar
▶ **claw at** VT FUS arranhar; (tear) rasgar

clay [kleɪ] N argila

clean [kliːn] ADJ limpo; (clear) nítido, bem definido ▶ VT limpar; (hands, face etc) lavar
▶ ADV: **he ~ forgot** ele esqueceu completamente; **to come ~** (inf: own up) abrir o jogo; **to ~ one's teeth** (BRIT) escovar os dentes; **~ driving licence** (BRIT), **~ record** (US) carteira de motorista sem infrações
▶ **clean off** VT tirar
▶ **clean out** VT limpar
▶ **clean up** VT limpar, assear ▶ VI (fig: make profit): **to ~ up on** faturar com, lucrar com

clean-cut ADJ (person) alinhado

cleaner ['kliːnə^r] N (person) faxineiro(-a); (product) limpador m

cleaner's ['kliːnəz] N (also: **dry cleaner's**) tinturaria

cleaning ['kliːnɪŋ] N limpeza

cleaning lady N faxineira

cleanliness ['klɛnlɪnɪs] N limpeza

cleanly ['kliːnlɪ] ADV perfeitamente; (without mess) limpamente

cleanse [klɛnz] VT limpar; (purify) purificar

cleanser ['klɛnzə^r] N limpador m; (for face) creme m de limpeza

clean-shaven [-'ʃeɪvn] ADJ sem barba, de cara raspada

cleansing department ['klɛnzɪŋ-] (BRIT) N departamento de limpeza

clean technology N tecnologia limpa

clean-up N limpeza geral

clear [klɪə^r] ADJ claro; (footprint, photograph) nítido; (obvious) evidente; (glass, water) transparente; (road, way) limpo, livre; (conscience) tranquilo; (skin) macio; (profit) líquido; (majority) absoluto ▶ VT (space) abrir; (desk etc) limpar; (room) esvaziar; (Law: suspect) absolver; (fence, wall) saltar, transpor; (obstacle) salvar, passar sobre; (debt) liquidar; (woodland) desmatar; (cheque) compensar; (Comm: goods) liquidar ▶ VI (weather) abrir; (sky) clarear; (fog etc) dissipar-se ▶ ADV: **~ of** a salvo de ▶ N: **to be in the ~** (out of debt) estar sem dívidas; (out of suspicion) estar livre de suspeita; (out of danger) estar fora de perigo; **to ~ the table** tirar a mesa; **to ~ one's throat** pigarrear; **to ~ a profit** fazer um lucro líquido; **let me make myself ~** deixe-me explicar melhor; **do I make myself ~?** entendeu?; **to make o.s. ~** fazer-se entender bem; **to make it ~ to sb that …** deixar bem claro para alguém que …; **I have a ~ day tomorrow** (BRIT) não tenho compromisso amanhã; **to keep ~ of sb/sth** evitar alguém/algo
▶ **clear off** (inf) VI (leave) cair fora
▶ **clear up** VT limpar; (mystery) resolver, esclarecer

clearance ['klɪərəns] N (of trees, slums) remoção f; (permission) permissão f

clearance sale N (Comm) liquidação f

clear-cut ADJ bem definido, nítido

clearing ['klɪərɪŋ] N (in wood) clareira; (BRIT Banking) compensação f

clearing bank (BRIT) N câmara de compensação

clearly ['klɪəlɪ] ADV (*distinctly*) distintamente; (*obviously*) claramente; (*coherently*) coerentemente

clearway ['klɪəweɪ] (*BRIT*) N *estrada onde não se pode estacionar*

cleavage ['kli:vɪdʒ] N (*of dress*) decote *m*; (*of woman*) colo

cleaver ['kli:və] N cutelo (de açougueiro)

clef [klɛf] N (*Mus*) clave *f*

cleft [klɛft] N (*in rock*) fissura

clemency ['klɛmənsɪ] N clemência

clement ['klɛmənt] ADJ (*weather*) ameno

clench [klɛntʃ] VT apertar, cerrar; (*teeth*) trincar

clergy ['klə:dʒɪ] N clero

clergyman ['klə:dʒɪmən] (*irreg*: *like* **man**) N clérigo, pastor *m*

clerical ['klɛrɪkəl] ADJ de escritório; (*Rel*) clerical

clerk [klɑ:k, (*US*) klə:rk] N auxiliar *m/f* de escritório; (*US*: *sales person*) balconista *m/f*; **C~ of Court** (*Law*) escrivão(-vã) *m/f* (do tribunal)

clever ['klɛvə^r] ADJ (*mentally*) inteligente; (*deft, crafty*) hábil; (*device, arrangement*) engenhoso

clew [klu:] (*US*) N = **clue**

cliché ['kli:ʃeɪ] N clichê *m*, frase *f* feita

click [klɪk] VT (*tongue*) estalar; (*heels*) bater; (*Comput*) clicar em ▶ VI (*make sound*) estalar; (*Comput*) clicar

client ['klaɪənt] N cliente *m/f*

clientele [kli:a:n'tɛl] N clientela

cliff [klɪf] N penhasco

cliffhanger ['klɪfhæŋə^r] N (*TV, fig*) história de suspense

climactic [klaɪ'mæktɪk] ADJ culminante

climate ['klaɪmɪt] N clima *m*

climate change N mudanças *fpl* climáticas

climax ['klaɪmæks] N clímax *m*, ponto culminante; (*sexual*) clímax

climb [klaɪm] VI subir; (*plant*) trepar; (*plane*) ganhar altitude; (*prices etc*) escalar; (*move with effort*): **to ~ over a wall/into a car** passar por cima de um muro/entrar num carro ▶ VT (*stairs*) subir; (*tree*) trepar em; (*hill*) escalar ▶ N subida; (*of prices etc*) escalada
▶ **climb down** VI descer; (*BRIT fig*) recuar, ceder

climb-down (*BRIT*) N retração *f*

climber ['klaɪmə^r] N alpinista *m/f*; (*plant*) trepadeira

climbing ['klaɪmɪŋ] N alpinismo

clinch [klɪntʃ] VT (*deal*) fechar; (*argument*) decidir, resolver

cling [klɪŋ] (*pt, pp* **clung**) VI: **to ~ to** pegar-se a, aderir a; (*hold on to: support, idea*) agarrar-se a; (*clothes*) ajustar-se a

Clingfilm® ['klɪŋfɪlm] N papel *m* filme

clinic ['klɪnɪk] N clínica; (*consultation*) consulta

clinical ['klɪnɪkl] ADJ clínico; (*fig*) frio, impessoal

clink [klɪŋk] VI tinir

clip [klɪp] N (*for hair*) grampo (*BR*), gancho (*PT*); (*also*: **paper clip**) mola, clipe *m*; (*TV, Cinema*)

---

clipe; (*on necklace etc*) fecho; (*Aut: holding hose etc*) braçadeira ▶ VT (*cut*) aparar; (*also*: **clip together**: *papers*) grampear

clippers ['klɪpəz] NPL (*for gardening*) podadeira; (*for hair*) máquina; (*also*: **nail clippers**) alicate *m* de unhas

clipping ['klɪpɪŋ] N recorte *m*

clique [kli:k] N panelinha

cloak [kləuk] N capa, manto ▶ VT (*fig*) encobrir

cloakroom ['kləukrum] N vestiário; (*BRIT: WC*) sanitários *mpl* (*BR*), lavatórios *mpl* (*PT*)

clock [klɔk] N relógio; (*in taxi*) taxímetro; **round the ~** (*work etc*) dia e noite, ininterruptamente; **30,000 on the ~** (*BRIT Aut*) 30.000 milhas rodadas; **to work against the ~** trabalhar contra o tempo
▶ **clock in, clock on** (*BRIT*) VI assinar o ponto na entrada
▶ **clock off, clock out** (*BRIT*) VI assinar o ponto na saída
▶ **clock up** VT (*miles, hours etc*) fazer

clockwise ['klɔkwaɪz] ADV em sentido horário

clockwork ['klɔkwə:k] N mecanismo de relógio ▶ ADJ de corda

clog [klɔg] N tamanco ▶ VT entupir ▶ VI (*also*: **clog up**) entupir-se

cloister ['klɔɪstə^r] N claustro

clone [kləun] N clone *m*

close [*adj, adv* kləus, *vb, n* kləuz] ADJ próximo; (*print, weave*) denso, compacto; (*friend*) íntimo; (*connection*) estreito; (*examination*) minucioso; (*watch*) atento; (*contest*) apertado; (*weather*) abafado; (*atmosphere*) sufocante; (*room*) mal arejado ▶ ADV perto
▶ VT (*shut*) fechar; (*end*) encerrar ▶ VI (*shop, door etc*) fechar; (*end*) concluir-se, terminar-se ▶ N (*end*) fim *m*, conclusão *f*, terminação *f*; **~ by, ~ at hand** perto, pertinho; **how ~ is Edinburgh to Glasgow?** qual é a distância entre Edimburgo e Glasgow?; **to have a ~ shave** (*fig*) livrar-se por um triz; **at ~ quarters** de perto; **~ to** perto de; **to bring sth to a ~** dar fim a algo
▶ **close down** VT, VI fechar definitivamente
▶ **close in** VI (*hunters*) apertar o cerco; (*night, fog*) cair; **the days are closing in** os dias estão ficando mais curtos; **to ~ in on sb** aproximar-se de alguém, cercar alguém
▶ **close off** VT (*area*) isolar

closed [kləuzd] ADJ fechado

closed-circuit ADJ: **~ television** televisão *f* de circuito fechado

closed shop N *estabelecimento industrial que só admite empregados sindicalizados*

close-knit ADJ (*family, community*) muito unido

closely ['kləuslɪ] ADV (*exactly*) fielmente; (*carefully*) rigorosamente; (*watch*) de perto; **we are ~ related** somos parentes próximos; **a ~ guarded secret** um segredo bem guardado

closet ['klɔzɪt] N (*cupboard*) armário; (*walk-in*) closet *m*

close-up [kləus-] N close m, close-up m

closing ['kləuzɪŋ] ADJ (stages, remarks) final; **~ price** (Stock Exchange) cotação f de fechamento

closing-down sale (BRIT) N liquidação f (por motivo de fechamento)

closure ['kləuʒər] N (of factory etc) fechamento

clot [klɔt] N (gen: blood clot) coágulo; (inf: idiot) imbecil m/f ▶ VI (blood) coagular-se

cloth [klɔθ] N (material) tecido, fazenda; (rag) pano; (also: **tablecloth**) toalha

clothe [kləuð] VT vestir; (fig) revestir

clothes [kləuðz] NPL roupa; **to put one's ~ on** vestir-se; **to take one's ~ off** tirar a roupa

clothes brush N escova (para a roupa)

clothes line N corda (para estender a roupa)

clothes peg, (US) **clothes pin** N pregador m

clothing ['kləuðɪŋ] N = **clothes**

clotted cream ['klɔtɪd-] (BRIT) N creme m coalhado

cloud [klaud] N nuvem f ▶ VT (liquid) turvar; **to ~ the issue** confundir or complicar as coisas; **every ~ has a silver lining** (proverb) Deus escreve certo por linhas tortas ▶ **cloud over** VI (also: fig) fechar

cloudburst ['klaudbə:st] N aguaceiro

cloud computing N computação f em nuvem

cloud-cuckoo-land (BRIT) N: **to live in ~** viver no mundo da lua

cloudy ['klaudɪ] ADJ nublado; (liquid) turvo

clout [klaut] VT dar uma bofetada em ▶ N (blow) bofetada; (fig) influência

clove [kləuv] N cravo

clove of garlic N dente m de alho

clover ['kləuvər] N trevo

cloverleaf ['kləuvəli:f] (irreg: like **leaf**) N (Aut) trevo rodoviário

clown [klaun] N palhaço ▶ VI (also: **clown about**, **clown around**) fazer palhaçadas

cloying ['klɔɪɪŋ] ADJ (taste, smell) enjoativo, nauseabundo

club [klʌb] N (society) clube m; (weapon) cacete m; (also: **golf club**) taco ▶ VT esbordoar ▶ VI: **to ~ together** cotizar-se; **clubs** NPL (Cards) paus mpl

club car (US) N (Rail) vagão-restaurante m

clubhouse ['klʌbhaus] N sede f do clube

cluck [klʌk] VI cacarejar

clue [klu:] N indício, pista; (in crossword) definição f; **I haven't a ~** não faço ideia

clued up, (US) **clued in** (inf) [klu:d-] ADJ entendido

clueless ['klu:lɪs] (inf) ADJ burro

clump [klʌmp] N (of trees etc) grupo

clumsy ['klʌmzɪ] ADJ (person) desajeitado; (movement) deselegante, mal-feito; (attempt) inábil

clung [klʌŋ] PT, PP of **cling**

cluster ['klʌstər] N grupo; (of flowers) ramo ▶ VI agrupar-se, apinhar-se

clutch [klʌtʃ] N (grip, grasp) garra; (Aut) embreagem f (BR), embraiagem f (PT); (pedal) pedal m de embreagem (BR) or embraiagem

(PT) ▶ VT empunhar, pegar em ▶ VI: **to ~ at** agarrar-se a

clutter ['klʌtər] VT (also: **clutter up**) abarrotar, encher desordenadamente ▶ N bagunça, desordem f

CM (US) ABBR (Post) = **North Mariana Islands**

cm ABBR (= centimetre) cm

CNAA (BRIT) N ABBR (= Council for National Academic Awards) órgão não universitário que outorga diplomas

CND N ABBR = **Campaign for Nuclear Disarmament**

CO N ABBR (= commanding officer) Com.; (BRIT) = **Commonwealth Office** ▶ ABBR (US Post) = **Colorado**

Co. ABBR = **county**; (= company) Cia.

c/o ABBR (= care of) a/c

coach [kəutʃ] N (bus) ônibus m (BR), autocarro (PT); (horse-drawn) carruagem f, coche m; (of train) vagão m; (Sport) treinador(a) m/f, instrutor(a) m/f; (tutor) professor(a) m/f particular ▶ VT (Sport) treinar; (student) preparar, ensinar

coach station (BRIT) N rodoviária

coach trip N passeio de ônibus (BR) or autocarro (PT)

coagulate [kəu'ægjuleɪt] VI coagular-se ▶ VT coagular

coal [kəul] N carvão m

coal face N frente f de carvão

coalfield ['kəulfi:ld] N região f carbonífera

coalition [kəuə'lɪʃən] N coalizão f, coligação f

coalman ['kəulmæn] (irreg: like **man**) N carvoeiro

coal merchant N = **coalman**

coalmine ['kəulmaɪn] N mina de carvão

coal miner N mineiro de carvão

coal mining N mineração f de carvão

coarse [kɔ:s] ADJ grosso, áspero; (vulgar) grosseiro, ordinário

coast [kəust] N costa, litoral m ▶ VI (Aut) ir em ponto morto

coastal ['kəustəl] ADJ costeiro

coaster ['kəustər] N embarcação f costeira, barco de cabotagem; (for glass) descanso

coastguard ['kəustgɑ:d] N (service) guarda costeira; (person) guarda-costeira m/f

coastline ['kəustlaɪn] N litoral m

coat [kəut] N (jacket) casaco; (overcoat) sobretudo; (of animal) pelo; (of paint) demão f, camada ▶ VT cobrir, revestir

coat hanger N cabide m

coating ['kəutɪŋ] N camada

coat of arms N brasão m

co-author [kəu-] N coautor(a) m/f

coax [kəuks] VT persuadir com meiguice

cob [kɔb] N see **corn**

cobbler ['kɔblər] N sapateiro

cobbles ['kɔblz] NPL pedras fpl arredondadas

cobblestones ['kɔblstəunz] NPL = **cobbles**

COBOL ['kəubɔl] N COBOL m

cobra ['kəubrə] N naja

cobweb ['kɔbwɛb] N teia de aranha

cocaine [kɔ'keɪn] N cocaína
cock [kɔk] N (rooster) galo; (male bird) macho
▶ VT (gun) engatilhar; **to ~ one's ears** (fig)
prestar atenção
cock-a-hoop ADJ exultante, eufórico
cockerel ['kɔkərəl] N frango, galo pequeno
cock-eyed [-aɪd] ADJ (crooked) torto; (fig: idea)
absurdo
cockle ['kɔkl] N berbigão m
cockney ['kɔknɪ] N londrino(-a) (nativo dos
bairros populares do leste de Londres)
cockpit ['kɔkpɪt] N (in aircraft) cabina
cockroach ['kɔkrəutʃ] N barata
cocktail ['kɔkteɪl] N coquetel m (BR),
cocktail m (PT)
cocktail cabinet N móvel-bar m
cocktail party N coquetel m (BR), cocktail m (BR)
cocktail shaker [-ʃeɪkəʳ] N coqueteleira
cocoa ['kəukəu] N cacau m; (drink)
chocolate m
coconut ['kəukənʌt] N coco
cocoon [kə'ku:n] N casulo
COD ABBR (BRIT) = **cash on delivery**; (US)
= **collect on delivery**
cod [kɔd] N INV bacalhau m
code [kəud] N cifra; (dialling code, post code)
código
codeine ['kəudi:n] N codeína
code of practice N deontologia
codicil ['kɔdɪsɪl] N codicilo
codify ['kəudɪfaɪ] VT codificar
cod-liver oil N óleo de fígado de bacalhau
co-driver [kəu-] N (in race) co-piloto; (in lorry)
segundo motorista m
co-ed ['kəu'ɛd] ADJ ABBR = **coeducational** ▶ N
(US: female student) aluna de escola mista; (BRIT:
school) escola mista
coeducational ['kəuɛdju'keɪʃənl] ADJ misto
coerce [kəu'ə:s] VT coagir
coercion [kəu'ə:ʃən] N coerção f
coexistence ['kəuɪg'zɪstəns] N coexistência
C. of C. N ABBR = **chamber of commerce**
C of E ABBR = **Church of England**
coffee ['kɔfɪ] N café m; **white ~** (BRIT) or **~ with
cream** (US) café com leite
coffee bar (BRIT) N café m, lanchonete f
coffee bean N grão m de café
coffee break N hora do café
coffee cake (US) N pão m doce com passas
coffee cup N xícara (BR) or chávena (PT) de café
coffee grounds NPL borras fpl de café
coffee plant N pé m de café
coffeepot ['kɔfɪpɔt] N cafeteira
coffee table N mesinha de centro
coffin ['kɔfɪn] N caixão m
C of I ABBR = **Church of Ireland**
C of S ABBR = **Church of Scotland**
cog [kɔg] N (tooth) dente m; (wheel) roda
dentada
cogent ['kəudʒənt] ADJ convincente
cognac ['kɔnjæk] N conhaque m
cognitive ['kɔgnɪtɪv] ADJ cognitivo
cogwheel ['kɔgwi:l] N roda dentada

cohabit [kəu'hæbɪt] VI (formal): **to ~ (with sb)**
coabitar (com alguém)
coherent [kəu'hɪərənt] ADJ coerente
cohesion [kəu'hi:ʒən] N coesão f
cohesive [kəu'hi:sɪv] ADJ coeso
COI (BRIT) N ABBR (= Central Office of Information)
serviço de informação governamental
coil [kɔɪl] N rolo; (rope) corda enrolada; (of
smoke) espiral f; (Elec) bobina; (contraceptive)
DIU m ▶ VT enrolar ▶ VI enrolar-se,
espiralar-se
coin [kɔɪn] N moeda ▶ VT (word) cunhar, criar
coinage ['kɔɪnɪdʒ] N moeda, sistema m
monetário
coin box (BRIT) N telefone m público
coincide [kəuɪn'saɪd] VI coincidir
coincidence [kəu'ɪnsɪdəns] N coincidência
coin-operated [-'ɔpəreɪtɪd] ADJ (machine,
laundry) automático, que funciona com
moedas
Coke® [kəuk] N coca
coke [kəuk] N (coal) coque m
Col. ABBR (= colonel) Cel.
COLA (US) N ABBR (= cost-of-living adjustment)
≈ URP f
colander ['kɔləndəʳ] N coador m, passador m
cold [kəuld] ADJ frio ▶ N frio; (Med) resfriado
(BR), constipação f (PT); **it's ~** está frio; **to be
or feel ~** (person) estar com frio; (object) estar
frio; **to catch ~** pegar friagem; **to catch a ~**
ficar resfriado (BR), apanhar uma
constipação (PT); **in ~ blood** a sangue frio;
to have ~ feet (fig) estar com medo; **to give
sb the ~ shoulder** tratar alguém com frieza,
dar um gelo em alguém (inf)
cold-blooded [-'blʌdɪd] ADJ (Zool) de sangue
frio; (murder) a sangue frio
cold cream N creme m de limpeza
coldly ['kəuldlɪ] ADV friamente
cold-shoulder VT tratar com frieza
cold sore N herpes m labial
coleslaw ['kəulslɔ:] N salada de repolho cru
colic ['kɔlɪk] N cólica
collaborate [kə'læbəreɪt] VI colaborar
collaboration [kəlæbə'reɪʃən] N colaboração f
collaborator [kə'læbəreɪtəʳ] N
colaborador(a) m/f
collage [kɔ'lɑ:ʒ] N colagem f
collagen ['kɔlədʒən] N colágeno
collapse [kə'læps] VI cair, tombar; (roof) dar de
si, desabar; (building) desabar; (Med)
desmaiar ▶ N desabamento,
desmoronamento; (of government) queda;
(Med) colapso
collapsible [kə'læpsəbl] ADJ dobrável
collar ['kɔləʳ] N (of shirt) colarinho; (of coat etc)
gola; (for dog) coleira; (Tech) aro, colar m ▶ VT
(inf: person) prender
collarbone ['kɔləbəun] N clavícula
collate [kɔ'leɪt] VT cotejar
collateral [kə'lætrəl] N garantia subsidiária
or pignoratícia
collation [kə'leɪʃən] N colação f

colleague ['kɔliːg] N colega *m/f*
collect [kə'lɛkt] VT reunir; *(as a hobby)* colecionar; *(gather)* recolher; *(wages, debts)* cobrar; *(donations, subscriptions)* colher; *(mail)* coletar; *(BRIT: call for)* (ir) buscar ▶ VI *(people)* reunir-se; *(dust, dirt)* acumular-se ▶ ADV: **to call ~** *(US Tel)* ligar a cobrar; **to ~ one's thoughts** refletir; **~ on delivery** *(US Comm)* pagamento na entrega
collected [kə'lɛktɪd] ADJ: **~ works** obra completa
collection [kə'lɛkʃən] N coleção *f*; *(of people)* grupo; *(of donations)* arrecadação *f*; *(of post, for charity)* coleta; *(of writings)* coletânea
collective [kə'lɛktɪv] ADJ coletivo
collective bargaining N negociação *f* coletiva
collector [kə'lɛktəʳ] N colecionador(a) *m/f*; *(of taxes etc)* cobrador(a) *m/f*; **~'s item** *or* **piece** peça de coleção
college ['kɔlɪdʒ] N *(of university)* faculdade *f*; *(of technology, agriculture)* escola profissionalizante; **to go to ~** fazer faculdade; *ver nota*

> Além de "universidade", **college** também se refere a um centro de educação superior para jovens que terminaram a educação obrigatória, *secondary school*. Alguns oferecem cursos de especialização em matérias técnicas, artísticas ou comerciais, outros oferecem disciplinas universitárias.

college of education N faculdade *f* de educação
collide [kə'laɪd] VI: **to ~ (with)** colidir (com)
collie ['kɔlɪ] N collie *m*
colliery ['kɔlɪərɪ] *(BRIT)* N mina de carvão
collision [kə'lɪʒən] N colisão *f*; **to be on a ~ course** estar em curso de colisão
colloquial [kə'ləukwɪəl] ADJ coloquial
collusion [kə'luːʒən] N colusão *f*, conluio; **in ~ with** em conluio com
cologne [kə'ləun] N *(also:* **eau-de-cologne**) (água de) colônia
Colombia [kə'lɔmbɪə] N Colômbia
Colombian [kə'lɔmbɪən] ADJ, N colombiano(-a)
colon ['kəulən] N *(sign)* dois pontos; *(Med)* cólon *m*
colonel ['kəːnl] N coronel *m*
colonial [kə'ləunɪəl] ADJ colonial
colonize ['kɔlənaɪz] VT colonizar
colony ['kɔlənɪ] N colônia
color ['kʌləʳ] *(US)* = **colour**
Colorado beetle [kɔlə'rɑːdəu-] N besouro da batata, dorífora
colossal [kə'lɔsl] ADJ colossal
colour, *(US)* **color** ['kʌləʳ] N cor *f* ▶ VT colorir; *(with crayons)* colorir, pintar; *(dye)* tingir; *(fig: account)* falsear ▶ VI *(blush)* corar; **colours** NPL *(of party, club)* cores *fpl*; **in ~** *(photograph etc)* a cores
　▶ **colour in** VT *(drawing)* colorir

colour bar, *(US)* **color bar** N discriminação *f* racial
colour-blind, *(US)* **color-blind** ['kʌləblaɪnd] ADJ daltônico
coloured, *(US)* **colored** ['kʌləd] ADJ colorido; *(old: person)* de cor
coloureds, *(US)* **coloreds** ['kʌlədz] NPL *(old)* gente *f* de cor
colour film, *(US)* **color film** N filme *m* a cores
colourful, *(US)* **colorful** ['kʌləful] ADJ colorido; *(account)* vívido; *(personality)* vivo, animado
colouring, *(US)* **coloring** ['kʌlərɪŋ] N colorido; *(complexion)* tez *f*; *(in food)* corante *m*
colourless, *(US)* **colorless** ['kʌlələs] ADJ sem cor, pálido
colour scheme, *(US)* **color scheme** N distribuição *f* de cores
colour supplement *(BRIT)* N *(Press)* revista, suplemento a cores
colour television, *(US)* **color television** N televisão *f* a cores
colt [kəult] N potro
column ['kɔləm] N coluna; *(of smoke)* faixa; *(of people)* fila; **the editorial ~** o editorial
columnist ['kɔləmnɪst] N cronista *m/f*
coma ['kəumə] N coma *m*; **to be in a ~** estar em coma
comb [kəum] N pente *m*; *(ornamental)* crista; *(of cock)* crista ▶ VT *(hair)* pentear; *(area)* vasculhar
combat ['kɔmbæt] N combate *m* ▶ VT combater
combination [kɔmbɪ'neɪʃən] N combinação *f*; *(of safe)* segredo
combination lock N fechadura de combinação
combine [vt, vi kəm'baɪn, n 'kɔmbaɪn] VT combinar; *(qualities)* reunir ▶ VI combinar-se ▶ N *(Econ)* associação *f*; *(pej)* monopólio; **a ~d effort** um esforço conjunto
combine harvester N ceifeira debulhadora
combo ['kɔmbəu] N *(Jazz etc)* conjunto
combustible [kəm'bʌstɪbl] ADJ combustível
combustion [kəm'bʌstʃən] N combustão *f*

(KEYWORD)

come [kʌm] *(pt* **came,** *pp* **come**) VI **1** *(movement towards)* vir; **come here!** vem aqui!; **I've only come for an hour** eu só vim por uma hora; **come with me** vem comigo; **are you coming to my party?** você vem à minha festa?; **to come running** vir correndo
2 *(arrive)* chegar; **he's just come from Aberdeen** ele acabou de chegar de Aberdeen; **she's come here to work** ela veio aqui para trabalhar; **they came to a river** eles chegaram num rio; **to come home** chegar em casa
3 *(reach)*: **to come to** chegar a; **the bill came to £40** a conta deu £40; **her hair came to her waist** o cabelo dela batia na cintura; **to come to power** chegar ao poder; **to come to a decision** chegar a uma decisão

4 (occur): **an idea came to me** uma ideia me ocorreu
5 (be, become) ficar; **to come loose/undone** soltar-se/desfazer-se; **I've come to like him** passei a gostar dele
▶ **come about** VI suceder, acontecer
▶ **come across** VT FUS (person) topar com; (thing) encontrar
▶ **come away** VI (leave) ir-se embora; (become detached) desprender-se, soltar-se
▶ **come back** VI (return) voltar
▶ **come by** VT FUS (acquire) conseguir
▶ **come down** VI (price) baixar; (tree) cair; (building) desmoronar-se
▶ **come forward** VI (volunteer) apresentar-se
▶ **come from** VT FUS (place, source etc: subj: person) ser de; (: thing) originar-se de
▶ **come in** VI (visitor) entrar; (on deal etc) participar; (be involved) estar envolvido
▶ **come in for** VT FUS (criticism etc) receber
▶ **come into** VT FUS (money) herdar; (fashion) ser; (be involved) estar envolvido em
▶ **come off** VI (button) desprender-se, soltar-se; (attempt) dar certo
▶ **come on** VI (pupil, work, project) avançar; (lights, electricity) ser ligado; **come on!** vamos!, vai!
▶ **come out** VI (fact) vir à tona; (book) ser publicado; (stain, sun) sair
▶ **come round** VI (after faint, operation) voltar a si
▶ **come to** VI (regain consciousness) voltar a si
▶ **come up** VI (sun) nascer; (problem, subject) surgir; (event) acontecer
▶ **come up against** VT FUS (resistance, difficulties) enfrentar, esbarrar em
▶ **come upon** VT FUS (find) encontrar, achar
▶ **come up with** VT FUS (idea) propor, sugerir; (money) contribuir

comeback ['kʌmbæk] N (of film star etc) volta; (reaction) reação f; (response) resposta
comedian [kə'mi:dɪən] N cômico, humorista m
comedienne [kəmi:dɪ'ɛn] N cômica, humorista
comedown ['kʌmdaun] (inf) N revés m, humilhação f
comedy ['kɔmɪdɪ] N comédia; (humour) humor m
comet ['kɔmɪt] N cometa m
comeuppance [kʌm'ʌpəns] N: **to get one's ~ (for sth)** pagar (por algo)
comfort ['kʌmfət] N comodidade f, conforto; (well-being) bem-estar m; (solace) consolo; (relief) alívio ▶ VT consolar, confortar; **comforts** NPL (of home etc) conforto
comfortable ['kʌmfətəbl] ADJ confortável; (financially) tranquilo; (walk, climb etc) fácil; **I don't feel very ~ about it** não estou completamente conformado com isso
comfortably ['kʌmfətəblɪ] ADV confortavelmente

comforter ['kʌmfətəʳ] (US) N edredom m (BR), edredão m (PT)
comfort station (US) N banheiro (BR), lavatórios mpl (PT)
comic ['kɔmɪk] ADJ (also: **comical**) cômico ▶ N (person) humorista m/f; (BRIT: magazine) revista em quadrinhos (BR), revista de banda desenhada (PT), gibi m (BR inf)
comical ['kɔmɪkl] ADJ engraçado, cômico
comic strip N história em quadrinhos (BR), banda desenhada (PT)
coming ['kʌmɪŋ] N vinda, chegada ▶ ADJ que vem, vindouro; **in the ~ weeks** nas próximas semanas
coming and going N, **comings and goings** NPL vaivém m, azáfama
Comintern ['kɔmɪntə:n] N Comintern m
comma ['kɔmə] N vírgula
command [kə'mɑ:nd] N ordem f, mandado; (control) controle m; (Mil: authority) comando; (mastery) domínio; (Comput) comando ▶ VT (troops) mandar; (give orders to) mandar, ordenar; (dispose of) dispor de; (deserve) merecer; **to ~ sb to do** mandar alguém fazer; **to have/take ~ of** ter/assumir o controle de; **to have at one's ~** (money, resources etc) dispor de
commandeer [kɔmən'dɪəʳ] VT requisitar
commander [kə'mɑ:ndəʳ] N (Mil) comandante m/f
commander-in-chief N (Mil) comandante-em-chefe m/f, comandante-chefe m/f
commanding [kə'mɑ:ndɪŋ] ADJ (appearance) imponente; (voice, tone) autoritário, imperioso; (lead, position) dominante
commanding officer N comandante m/f
commandment [kə'mɑ:ndmənt] N (Rel) mandamento
command module N (Space) módulo de comando
commando [kə'mɑ:ndəu] N (group) comando; (soldier) soldado
commemorate [kə'mɛməreɪt] VT (with monument) comemorar; (with celebration) celebrar
commemoration [kəmɛmə'reɪʃən] N comemoração f
commemorative [kə'mɛmərətɪv] ADJ comemorativo
commence [kə'mɛns] VT, VI começar, iniciar
commend [kə'mɛnd] VT (praise) elogiar, louvar; (entrust) encomendar; (recommend) recomendar
commendable [kə'mɛndəbl] ADJ louvável
commendation [kɔmɛn'deɪʃən] N elogio, louvor m
commensurate [kə'mɛnʃərɪt] ADJ: **~ with** compatível com
comment ['kɔmɛnt] N comentário ▶ VI comentar; **to ~ on sth** comentar algo; **to ~ that** observar que; **"no ~"** "sem comentário"
commentary ['kɔməntərɪ] N comentário

commentator ['kɔmənteɪtəʳ] N comentarista m/f

commerce ['kɔmə:s] N comércio

commercial [kə'mə:ʃəl] ADJ comercial ▶ N anúncio, comercial m

commercial bank N banco comercial

commercial break N intervalo para os comerciais

commercial college N escola de comércio

commercialism [kə'mə:ʃəlɪzəm] N mercantilismo

commercialize [kə'mə:ʃəlaɪz] VT comercializar

commercial radio N rádio f comercial

commercial television N televisão f comercial

commercial traveller N caixeiro/a-viajante m/f

commercial vehicle N veículo utilitário

commiserate [kə'mɪzəreɪt] VI: **to ~ with** comiserar-se de, condoer-se de

commission [kə'mɪʃən] N (body, fee) comissão f; (act) incumbência; (order for work of art etc) empreitada, encomenda ▶ VT (Mil) dar patente oficial a; (work of art) encomendar; (artist) incumbir; **out of ~** (Naut) fora do serviço ativo; (not working) com defeito; **to ~ sb to do sth** mandar alguém fazer algo; **to ~ sth from sb** encomendar algo a alguém; **~ of inquiry** (BRIT) comissão de inquérito

commissionaire [kəmɪʃə'nɛəʳ] (BRIT) N porteiro

commissioner [kə'mɪʃənəʳ] N comissário(-a)

commit [kə'mɪt] VT (act) cometer; (money, resources) alocar; (to sb's care) entregar; **to ~ o.s. (to doing)** comprometer-se (a fazer); **to ~ suicide** suicidar-se; **to ~ to writing** pôr por escrito, pôr no papel; **to ~ sb for trial** levar alguém a julgamento

commitment [kə'mɪtmənt] N (obligation) compromisso; (political etc) engajamento; (undertaking) promessa

committed [kə'mɪtɪd] ADJ (writer, politician etc) engajado

committee [kə'mɪtɪ] N comitê m; **to be on a ~** ser membro de um comitê

committee meeting N reunião f de comitê

commodity [kə'mɔdɪtɪ] N mercadoria; **commodities** NPL (Comm) commodities mpl

commodity exchange N bolsa de mercadorias

common ['kɔmən] ADJ comum; (vulgar) ordinário, vulgar ▶ N área verde aberta ao público; **Commons** NPL (BRIT Pol): **the (House of) C~s** a Câmara dos Comuns; **to have sth in ~ (with sb)** ter algo em comum (con alguém); **in ~ use** de uso corrente; **it's ~ knowledge that** todos sabem que; **to the ~ good** para o bem comum

common denominator N (fig) elemento comum

commoner ['kɔmənəʳ] N plebeu(-beia) m/f

common ground N (fig) consenso

common law N lei f consuetudinária ▶ ADJ: **common-law wife** concubina

commonly ['kɔmənlɪ] ADV geralmente

Common Market N Mercado Comum

commonplace ['kɔmənpleɪs] ADJ vulgar, trivial ▶ N lugar-comum m

common room N sala comum; (Sch) sala dos professores (or estudantes)

common sense N bom senso

Commonwealth ['kɔmənwɛlθ] N: **the ~** a Comunidade Britânica

commotion [kə'məuʃən] N tumulto, confusão f

communal ['kɔmju:nl] ADJ (life) comunal; (shared) comun

commune [n 'kɔmju:n, vi kə'mju:n] N (group) comuna ▶ VI: **to ~ with** comunicar-se com

communicate [kə'mju:nɪkeɪt] VT comunicar ▶ VI: **to ~ (with)** comunicar-se (com)

communication [kəmju:nɪ'keɪʃən] N comunicação f; (letter, call) mensagem f

communication cord (BRIT) N sinal m de alarme

communications network N rede f de comunicações

communications satellite N satélite m de comunicações

communicative [kə'mju:nɪkətɪv] ADJ comunicativo

communion [kə'mju:nɪən] N (also: **Holy Communion**) comunhão f

communiqué [kə'mju:nɪkeɪ] N comunicado

communism ['kɔmjunɪzəm] N comunismo

communist ['kɔmjunɪst] ADJ, N comunista m/f

community [kə'mju:nɪtɪ] N comunidade f; (within larger group) sociedade f

community centre N centro social

community chest (US) N fundo de assistência social

community health centre N centro de saúde comunitário

community service N serviços mpl comunitários

community spirit N espírito comunitário

commutation ticket [kɔmju'teɪʃən-] (US) N passe m, bilhete m de assinatura

commute [kə'mju:t] VI viajar diariamente ▶ VT comutar

commuter [kə'mju:təʳ] N viajante m/f habitual

compact [adj kəm'pækt, n 'kɔmpækt] ADJ compacto; (style) conciso ▶ N (pact) pacto; (also: **powder compact**) estojo

compact disc N disco laser

compact disc player N som cd m

companion [kəm'pænɪən] N companheiro(-a)

companionship [kəm'pænɪənʃɪp] N companhia, companheirismo; (spirit) camaradagem f

companionway [kəm'pænɪənweɪ] N (Naut) escada de tombadilho

company ['kʌmpənɪ] N companhia; (Comm) sociedade f, companhia; **he's good ~** ele é uma boa companhia; **we have ~** temos visita; **to keep sb ~** fazer companhia a alguém; **to part ~ with** separar-se de; **Smith and C~** Smith e Companhia

company car N carro da companhia

company director N administrador(a) m/f de companhia

company secretary (BRIT) N (Comm) secretário(-a) geral (de uma companhia)

comparable ['kɔmpərəbl] ADJ comparável

comparative [kəm'pærətɪv] ADJ (study) comparativo; (peace, safety) relativo

comparatively [kəm'pærətɪvlɪ] ADJ (relatively) relativamente

compare [kəm'pɛəʳ] VT comparar; (contrast): **to ~ (to/with)** comparar (a/com) ▶ VI: **to ~ with** comparar-se com; **how do the prices ~?** qual é a diferença entre os preços?; **~d with** or **to** em comparação com

comparison [kəm'pærɪsn] N comparação f; **in ~ (with)** em comparação (com), comparado (com)

compartment [kəm'pɑ:tmənt] N (Rail, of fridge) compartimento; (of wallet) divisão f

compass ['kʌmpəs] N bússola; **within the ~ of** no âmbito de

compasses ['kʌmpəsɪz] NPL compasso

compassion [kəm'pæʃən] N compaixão f

compassionate [kəm'pæʃənət] ADJ compassivo; **on ~ grounds** por motivos humanitários

compatibility [kɔmpætɪ'bɪlɪtɪ] N compatibilidade f

compatible [kəm'pætɪbl] ADJ compatível

compel [kəm'pɛl] VT obrigar

compelling [kəm'pɛlɪŋ] ADJ (fig: argument) convincente

compendium [kəm'pɛndɪəm] N compêndio

compensate ['kɔmpənseɪt] VT (employee, victim) indenizar ▶ VI: **to ~ for** compensar

compensation [kɔmpən'seɪʃən] N compensação f; (damages) indenização f

compère ['kɔmpɛəʳ] N apresentador(a) m/f

compete [kəm'pi:t] VI (take part) competir; (vie): **to ~ (with)** competir (com), fazer competição (com)

competence ['kɔmpɪtəns] N competência, capacidade f

competent ['kɔmpɪtənt] ADJ competente

competition [kɔmpɪ'tɪʃən] N (contest) concurso; (Econ) concorrência; (rivalry) competição f; **in ~ with** em competição com

competitive [kəm'pɛtɪtɪv] ADJ competitivo; (person) competidor(a)

competitive examination N concurso

competitor [kəm'pɛtɪtəʳ] N (rival) competidor(a) m/f; (participant, Econ) concorrente m/f; **our ~s** (Comm) a (nossa) concorrência

compile [kəm'paɪl] VT compilar, compor

complacency [kəm'pleɪsnsɪ] N satisfação f consigo mesmo

complacent [kəm'pleɪsənt] ADJ relaxado, acomodado

complain [kəm'pleɪn] VI queixar-se; (in shop etc) reclamar; **to ~ of** (pain) queixar-se de

complaint [kəm'pleɪnt] N (objection) objeção f; (criticism) queixa; (in shop etc) reclamação f; (Law) querela; (Med) achaque m, doença

complement ['kɔmplɪmənt] N complemento; (esp ship's crew) tripulação f ▶ VT complementar

complementary [kɔmplɪ'mɛntərɪ] ADJ complementar

complete [kəm'pli:t] ADJ completo; (finished) acabado ▶ VT (finish: building, task) acabar; (set, group) completar; (a form) preencher; **a ~ disaster** um desastre total

completely [kəm'pli:tlɪ] ADV completamente

completion [kəm'pli:ʃən] N conclusão f, término; (of contract etc) realização f; **to be nearing ~** estar quase pronto; **on ~ of contract** na assinatura do contrato; (for house) na escritura

complex ['kɔmplɛks] ADJ complexo ▶ N (Psych, of ideas etc) complexo; (of buildings) conjunto

complexion [kəm'plɛkʃən] N (of face) cor f, tez f; (fig) aspecto

complexity [kəm'plɛksɪtɪ] N complexidade f

compliance [kəm'plaɪəns] N (submission) submissão f; (agreement) conformidade f; **in ~ with** de acordo com, conforme

compliant [kəm'plaɪənt] ADJ complacente, submisso

complicate ['kɔmplɪkeɪt] VT complicar

complicated ['kɔmplɪkeɪtɪd] ADJ complicado

complication [kɔmplɪ'keɪʃən] N problema m; (Med) complicação f

compliment [n 'kɔmplɪmənt, vt 'kɔmplɪmɛnt] N (formal) cumprimento; (praise) elogio ▶ VT elogiar; **compliments** NPL cumprimentos mpl; **to pay sb a ~** elogiar alguém; **to ~ sb (on sth/on doing sth)** cumprimentar or elogiar alguém (por algo/por ter feito algo)

complimentary [kɔmplɪ'mɛntərɪ] ADJ lisonjeiro; (free) gratuito

complimentary ticket N entrada de favor or de cortesia

compliments slip N memorando

comply [kəm'plaɪ] VI: **to ~ with** cumprir com

component [kəm'pəunənt] ADJ componente ▶ N (part) peça; (element) componente m

compose [kəm'pəuz] VT compor; **to be ~d of** compor-se de; **to ~ o.s.** tranquilizar-se

composed [kəm'pəuzd] ADJ calmo

composer [kəm'pəuzəʳ] N (Mus) compositor(a) m/f

composite ['kɔmpəzɪt] ADJ composto

composition [kɔmpə'zɪʃən] N composição f

compost ['kɔmpɔst] N adubo

composure [kəm'pəuʒəʳ] N serenidade f, calma

compound [n, adj 'kɔmpaund, vt kəm'paund] N (Chem, Ling) composto; (enclosure) recinto ▶ ADJ composto; (fracture) complicado ▶ VT (fig: problem etc) agravar

compound interest N juro composto

comprehend [kɔmprɪ'hɛnd] vt compreender
comprehension [kɔmprɪ'hɛnʃən] N compreensão f
comprehensive [kɔmprɪ'hɛnsɪv] ADJ abrangente; (Insurance) total
comprehensive insurance policy N apólice f de seguro com cobertura total
comprehensive school (BRIT) N escola secundária de amplo programa

> Criadas na década de 1960 pelo governo trabalhista da época, as **comprehensive schools** são estabelecimentos de ensino secundário polivalentes concebidos para acolher todos os alunos sem distinção e lhes oferecer oportunidades iguais, em oposição ao sistema seletivo das *grammar schools*.

compress [vt kəm'prɛs, n 'kɔmprɛs] vt comprimir; (text, information etc) reduzir ▶ N (Med) compressa
compression [kəm'prɛʃən] N compressão f
comprise [kəm'praɪz] vt (also: **be comprised of**) compreender, constar de; (constitute) constituir
compromise ['kɔmprəmaɪz] N meio-termo ▶ vt comprometer ▶ vi chegar a um meio-termo ▶ CPD (decision, solution) de meio-termo
compulsion [kəm'pʌlʃən] N compulsão f; (force) coação f, força; **under ~** sob coação, à força
compulsive [kəm'pʌlsɪv] ADJ compulsório; **he's a ~ smoker** ele não pode deixar de fumar
compulsory [kəm'pʌlsərɪ] ADJ obrigatório; (retirement) compulsório
compulsory purchase N compra compulsória
compunction [kəm'pʌŋkʃən] N compunção; **to have no ~ about doing sth** não hesitar em fazer algo
computer [kəm'pju:tər] N computador m
computer game N game m
computerize [kəm'pju:təraɪz] vt informatizar, computadorizar
computer language N linguagem f de máquina
computer literate ADJ capaz de lidar com um computador
computer peripheral N periférico
computer program N programa m de computador
computer programmer, computer programer N programador(a) m/f
computer programming, computer programing N programação f
computer science N informática, computação f
computer scientist N cientista m/f da computação
computing [kəm'pju:tɪŋ] N computação f; (science) informática
comrade ['kɔmrɪd] N camarada m/f

comradeship ['kɔmrɪdʃɪp] N camaradagem f
comsat® ['kɔmsæt] N ABBR = **communications satellite**
con [kɔn] vt enganar; (cheat) trapacear ▶ N vigarice f; **cons** NPL see **convenience, pro**; **to ~ sb into doing sth** convencer alguém a fazer algo (por artimanhas)
concave [kɔn'keɪv] ADJ côncavo
conceal [kən'si:l] vt ocultar; (information) omitir
concede [kən'si:d] vt (admit) reconhecer, admitir ▶ vi ceder
conceit [kən'si:t] N presunção f
conceited [kən'si:tɪd] ADJ vaidoso
conceivable [kən'si:vəbl] ADJ concebível; **it is ~ that** é possível que
conceivably [kən'si:vəblɪ] ADV: **he may ~ be right** é possível que ele tenha razão
conceive [kən'si:v] vt conceber ▶ vi conceber, engravidar; **to ~ of sth/of doing sth** conceber algo/fazer ideia de fazer algo
concentrate ['kɔnsəntreɪt] vi concentrar-se ▶ vt concentrar
concentration [kɔnsən'treɪʃən] N concentração f
concentration camp N campo de concentração
concentric [kɔn'sɛntrɪk] ADJ concêntrico
concept ['kɔnsɛpt] N conceito
conception [kən'sɛpʃən] N (idea) conceito, ideia; (Bio) concepção f
concern [kən'sə:n] N (matter) assunto; (Comm) empresa; (anxiety) preocupação f ▶ vt (worry) preocupar; (involve) envolver; (relate to) dizer respeito a; **to be ~ed** (about) preocupar-se (com); **"to whom it may ~"** "a quem interessar possa"; **as far as I'm ~ed** no que me diz respeito, quanto a mim; **to be ~ed with** (person: involved with) ocupar-se de; (book: be about) tratar de; **the department ~ed** (under discussion) o departamento em questão; (relevant) o departamento competente
concerning [kən'sə:nɪŋ] PREP sobre, a respeito de, acerca de
concert ['kɔnsət] N concerto; **in ~** de comum acordo
concerted [kən'sə:tɪd] ADJ (joint) conjunto; (strong) sério
concert hall N sala de concertos
concertina [kɔnsə'ti:nə] N sanfona ▶ vi engavetar-se
concert master (US) N primeiro violino de uma orquestra
concerto [kən'tʃə:təu] N concerto
concession [kən'sɛʃən] N concessão f; **tax ~** redução no imposto
concessionaire [kənsɛʃə'nɛər] N concessionário(-a)
concessionary [kən'sɛʃənrɪ] ADJ (ticket, fare) a preço reduzido
conciliation [kənsɪlɪ'eɪʃən] N conciliação f
conciliatory [kən'sɪlɪətrɪ] ADJ conciliador(a)
concise [kən'saɪs] ADJ conciso

conclave ['kɔnkleɪv] N conclave m
conclude [kən'kluːd] VT (finish) acabar, concluir; (treaty etc) firmar; (agreement) chegar a; (decide) decidir ▶ VI terminar, acabar; **to ~ that** chegar à conclusão de que
conclusion [kən'kluːʒən] N conclusão f; **to come to the ~ that** chegar à conclusão de que
conclusive [kən'kluːsɪv] ADJ conclusivo, decisivo
concoct [kən'kɔkt] VT (excuse) fabricar; (plot) tramar; (meal) preparar
concoction [kən'kɔkʃən] N (mixture) mistura
concord ['kɔŋkɔːd] N (harmony) concórdia; (treaty) acordo
concourse ['kɔŋkɔːs] N (hall) saguão m; (crowd) multidão f
concrete ['kɔnkriːt] N concreto (BR), betão m (PT) ▶ ADJ concreto
concrete mixer N betoneira
concur [kən'kəː'] VI estar de acordo, concordar
concurrently [kən'kʌrntlɪ] ADV ao mesmo tempo, simultaneamente
concussion [kən'kʌʃən] N (Med) concussão f cerebral
condemn [kən'dɛm] VT (denounce) denunciar; (prisoner, building) condenar
condemnation [kɔndɛm'neɪʃən] N condenação f; (blame) censura
condensation [kɔndɛn'seɪʃən] N condensação f
condense [kən'dɛns] VI condensar-se ▶ VT condensar
condensed milk [kən'dɛnst-] N leite m condensado
condescend [kɔndɪ'sɛnd] VI condescender, dignar-se; **to ~ to do sth** condescender a fazer algo
condescending [kɔndɪ'sɛndɪŋ] ADJ condescendente
condition [kən'dɪʃən] N condição f; (health) estado de saúde; (Med: illness) doença ▶ VT condicionar; **conditions** NPL (circumstances) circunstâncias fpl; **on ~ that** com a condição (de) que; **in good/poor ~** em bom/mau estado (de conservação); **a heart ~** um problema no coração; **weather ~s** condições fpl meteorológicas
conditional [kən'dɪʃənl] ADJ condicional; **to be ~ upon** depender de
conditioner [kən'dɪʃənə'] N (for hair) condicionador m; (for fabrics) amaciante m
condo ['kɔndəu] (US inf) N ABBR = **condominium**
condolences [kən'dəulənsɪz] NPL pêsames mpl
condom ['kɔndɔm] N preservativo, camisinha
condominium [kɔndə'mɪnɪəm] (US) N (building) edifício; (rooms) apartamento
condone [kən'dəun] VT admitir, aceitar
conducive [kən'djuːsɪv] ADJ: **~ to** conducente para a
conduct [n 'kɔndʌkt, vt, vi kən'dʌkt] N conduta, comportamento ▶ VT (research etc)

fazer; (heat, electricity) conduzir; (manage) dirigir; (Mus) reger ▶ VI (Mus) reger uma orquestra; **to ~ o.s.** comportar-se
conducted tour [kən'dʌktɪd-] N viagem f organizada; (of building etc) visita guiada
conductor [kən'dʌktə'] N (of orchestra) regente m/f; (on bus) cobrador(a) m/f; (US Rail) revisor(a) m/f; (Elec) condutor m
conductress [kən'dʌktrɪs] N (on bus) cobradora
conduit ['kɔndɪt] N conduto
cone [kəun] N cone m; (Bot) pinha; (for ice-cream) casquinha; **pine ~** pinha
confectioner [kən'fɛkʃənə'] N confeiteiro(-a) (BR), pasteleiro(-a) (PT)
confectioner's, confectioner's shop N confeitaria (BR), pastelaria (PT); (sweet shop) confeitaria
confectionery [kən'fɛkʃnərɪ] N (sweets) balas fpl; (sweetmeats) doces mpl
confederate [kən'fɛdrɪt] ADJ confederado ▶ N cúmplice m/f; (US History) confederado(-a) (sulista)
confederation [kənfɛdə'reɪʃən] N confederação f
confer [kən'fəː'] VT: **to ~ on** outorgar a ▶ VI conferenciar
conference ['kɔnfərns] N (meeting) congresso; **to be in ~** estar em conferência
conference room N sala de conferência
confess [kən'fɛs] VT confessar ▶ VI (admit) admitir
confession [kən'fɛʃən] N admissão f; (Rel) confissão f
confessional [kən'fɛʃənl] N confessionário
confessor [kən'fɛsə'] N confessor m
confetti [kən'fɛtɪ] N confete m
confide [kən'faɪd] VI: **to ~ in** confiar em, fiar-se em
confidence ['kɔnfɪdns] N confiança; (faith) fé f; (secret) confidência; **to have (every) ~ that** ter certeza de que; **motion of no ~** moção de não confiança; **in ~** em confidência
confidence trick N conto do vigário
confident ['kɔnfɪdnt] ADJ confiante, convicto; (positive) seguro
confidential [kɔnfɪ'dɛnʃəl] ADJ confidencial; (secretary) de confiança
confidentiality ['kɔnfɪdɛnʃɪ'ælɪtɪ] N sigilo
configuration [kən'fɪgju'reɪʃən] N (also Comput) configuração f
confine [kən'faɪn] VT (shut up) encarcerar; (limit): **to ~ (to)** confinar (a); **to ~ o.s. to (doing) sth** limitar-se a (fazer) algo
confined [kən'faɪnd] ADJ (space) reduzido
confinement [kən'faɪnmənt] N (imprisonment) prisão f; (enclosure) reclusão f; (Med) parto
confines ['kɔnfaɪnz] NPL confins mpl
confirm [kən'fəːm] VT confirmar
confirmation [kɔnfə'meɪʃən] N confirmação f; (Rel) crisma
confirmed [kən'fəːmd] ADJ inveterado

confiscate ['kɔnfɪskeɪt] VT confiscar
confiscation [kɔnfɪs'keɪʃən] N confiscação f
conflagration [kɔnflə'greɪʃən] N
conflagração f
conflict [n 'kɔnflɪkt, vi kən'flɪkt] N
(disagreement) divergência; (of interests,
loyalties) conflito; (fighting) combate m ▶ VI
estar em conflito; (opinions) divergir
conflicting [kən'flɪktɪŋ] ADJ (reports)
divergente; (interests) oposto; (account)
discrepante
conform [kən'fɔːm] VI conformar-se; **to ~ to**
ajustar-se a, acomodar-se a
conformist [kən'fɔːmɪst] N conformista m/f
confound [kən'faund] VT confundir; (amaze)
desconcertar
confounded [kən'faundɪd] ADJ maldito
confront [kən'frʌnt] VT (problems) enfrentar;
(enemy, danger) defrontar-se com
confrontation [kɔnfrən'teɪʃən] N
confrontação f
confrontational [kɔnfrən'teɪʃənl] ADJ
agressivo
confuse [kən'fjuːz] VT (perplex) desconcertar;
(mix up) confundir, misturar; (complicate)
complicar
confused [kən'fjuːzd] ADJ confuso; (person)
perplexo, confuso
confusing [kən'fjuːzɪŋ] ADJ confuso
confusion [kən'fjuːʒən] N (mix-up) mal-
entendido; (perplexity) perplexidade f;
(disorder) confusão f
congeal [kən'dʒiːl] VI (freeze) congelar-se;
(coagulate) coagular-se
congenial [kən'dʒiːnɪəl] ADJ simpático,
agradável
congenital [kən'dʒɛnɪtl] ADJ congênito
conger eel ['kɔŋger-] N congro
congested [kən'dʒɛstɪd] ADJ congestionado
congestion [kən'dʒɛstʃən] N (Med) congestão f;
(traffic) congestionamento
conglomerate [kən'glɔmərɪt] N (Comm)
conglomerado
conglomeration [kənglɔmə'reɪʃən] N
conglomeração f, aglomeração f
Congo ['kɔŋgəu] N (state) Congo
congratulate [kən'grætjuleɪt] VT
parabenizar; **to ~ sb (on)** felicitar or
parabenizar alguém (por)
congratulations [kəngrætju'leɪʃənz] NPL
parabéns mpl ▶ EXCL parabéns!
congregate ['kɔŋgrɪgeɪt] VI reunir-se
congregation [kɔŋgrɪ'geɪʃən] N (in church)
fiéis mpl; (assembly) congregação f, reunião f
congress ['kɔŋgrɛs] N congresso; (US): **C~**
Congresso

O Congresso (**Congress**) é o Parlamento
dos Estados Unidos. Consiste na House of
Representatives e no Senado Senate. Os
representantes e senadores são eleitos
por sufrágio universal direto. O
Congresso se reúne no Capitol, em
Washington.

congressman ['kɔŋgrɛsmən] (US) (irreg: like
man) N deputado
congresswoman ['kɔŋgrɛswumən] (irreg:
like **woman**) N deputada
conical ['kɔnɪkl] ADJ cônico
conifer ['kɔnɪfəʳ] N conífera
coniferous [kə'nɪfərəs] ADJ (forest) conífero
conjecture [kən'dʒɛktʃəʳ] N conjetura ▶ VT, VI
conjeturar
conjugal ['kɔndʒugl] ADJ conjugal
conjugate ['kɔndʒugeɪt] VT conjugar
conjugation [kɔndʒu'geɪʃən] N conjugação f
conjunction [kən'dʒʌŋkʃən] N conjunção f;
in ~ with junto com
conjunctivitis [kəndʒʌŋktɪ'vaɪtɪs] N
conjuntivite f
conjure ['kʌndʒəʳ] VI fazer truques ▶ VT fazer
aparecer
▶ **conjure up** VT (ghost, spirit) fazer aparecer,
invocar; (memories) evocar
conjurer ['kʌndʒərəʳ] N mágico(-a),
prestidigitador(a) m/f
conjuring trick ['kʌndʒərɪŋ-] N mágica
conker ['kɔŋkəʳ] (BRIT) N castanha-da-índia
conk out [kɔŋk-] (inf) VI pifar
con man ['kɔn-] (irreg: like **man**) N vigarista m
connect [kə'nɛkt] VT (Elec, Tel) ligar; (fig:
associate) associar; (join): **to ~ sth (to)** juntar
or unir algo (a) ▶ VI: **to ~ with** (train) conectar
com; **to be ~ed with** estar relacionado com;
I'm trying to ~ you (Tel) estou tentando
completar a ligação
connecting flight N conexão f
connection [kə'nɛkʃən] N ligação f; (Elec, Rail)
conexão f; (Tel) ligação f; (fig) relação f; **in ~
with** com relação a; **what is the ~ between
them?** qual é a relação entre eles?;
business ~s contatos de trabalho
connexion [kə'nɛkʃən] (BRIT) N = **connection**
conning tower ['kɔnɪŋ-] N torre f de comando
connive [kə'naɪv] VI: **to ~ at** ser conivente em
connoisseur [kɔnɪ'səʳ] N conhecedor(a) m/f,
apreciador(a) m/f
connotation [kɔnə'teɪʃən] N conotação f
connubial [kə'njuːbɪəl] ADJ conjugal
conquer ['kɔŋkəʳ] VT conquistar; (enemy)
vencer; (feelings) superar
conqueror ['kɔŋkərəʳ] N conquistador(a) m/f
conquest ['kɔŋkwɛst] N conquista
cons [kɔnz] NPL see **convenience**
conscience ['kɔnʃəns] N consciência; **in all ~**
em sã consciência
conscientious [kɔnʃɪ'ɛnʃəs] ADJ
consciencioso; (objection) de consciência
conscientious objector N aquele que faz uma
objeção de consciência à sua participação nas forças
armadas
conscious ['kɔnʃəs] ADJ: **~ (of)** consciente
(de); (deliberate: insult, error) intencional; **to
become ~ of** tornar-se consciente de,
conscientizar-se de
consciousness ['kɔnʃəsnɪs] N consciência; **to
lose/regain ~** perder/recuperar os sentidos

conscript ['kɔnskrɪpt] N recruta m/f
conscription [kən'skrɪpʃən] N serviço militar obrigatório
consecrate ['kɔnsɪkreɪt] VT consagrar
consecutive [kən'sɛkjutɪv] ADJ consecutivo
consensus [kən'sɛnsəs] N consenso; **the ~ (of opinion)** o consenso (de opiniões)
consent [kən'sɛnt] N consentimento ▶ VI: **to ~ to** consentir em; **age of ~** maioridade; **by common ~** de comum acordo
consequence ['kɔnsɪkwəns] N consequência; (*significance*): **of ~** de importância; **in ~** por consequência
consequently ['kɔnsɪkwəntlɪ] ADV por conseguinte
conservation [kɔnsə'veɪʃən] N (*of energy, paintings etc*) conservação f; (*of the environment*) preservação f; (*also:* **nature conservation**) proteção f do meio ambiente; **energy ~** conservação da energia
conservationist [kɔnsə'veɪʃənɪst] N conservacionista m/f
conservative [kən'sə:vətɪv] ADJ conservador(a); (*cautious*) moderado; (*BRIT Pol*): **C~** conservador(a) ▶ N (*BRIT Pol*) conservador(a) m/f
conservatory [kən'sə:vətrɪ] N (*Mus*) conservatório; (*greenhouse*) estufa
conserve [kən'sə:v] VT conservar; (*preserve*) preservar; (*supplies, energy*) poupar ▶ N conserva
consider [kən'sɪdə'] VT considerar; (*believe*) acreditar; (*take into account*) levar em consideração; (*study*) estudar, examinar; **to ~ doing sth** pensar em fazer algo; **~ yourself lucky** dê-se por sortudo; **all things ~ed** afinal de contas
considerable [kən'sɪdərəbl] ADJ considerável; (*sum*) importante
considerably [kən'sɪdərəblɪ] ADV consideravelmente
considerate [kən'sɪdərɪt] ADJ atencioso
consideration [kənsɪdə'reɪʃən] N consideração f; (*deliberation*) deliberação f; (*factor*) fator m; (*reward*) remuneração f; **out of ~ for** em consideração a; **to be under ~** estar em apreciação; **my first ~ is my family** minha maior preocupação é a minha família
considering [kən'sɪdərɪŋ] PREP em vista de ▶ CONJ: **~ (that)** apesar de que, considerando que
consign [kən'saɪn] VT consignar; **to ~ to** (*to a place*) relegar para; (*to sb's care, to poverty*) confiar a
consignee [kɔnsaɪ'ni:] N consignatário(-a)
consignment [kən'saɪnmənt] N consignação f
consignment note N (*Comm*) guia de remessa
consignor [kən'saɪnə'] N consignador(a) m/f
consist [kən'sɪst] VI: **to ~ of** (*comprise*) consistir em
consistency [kən'sɪstənsɪ] N (*of policies etc*) coerência; (*thickness*) consistência

consistent [kən'sɪstənt] ADJ (*person*) coerente, estável; (*argument, idea*) sólido; (*even*) constante; **~ with** compatível com, de acordo com
consolation [kɔnsə'leɪʃən] N conforto
console [vt kən'səul, n 'kɔnsəul] VT confortar ▶ N consolo
consolidate [kən'sɔlɪdeɪt] VT consolidar
consols ['kɔnsɔlz] (*BRIT*) NPL (*Stock Exchange*) consolidados mpl
consommé [kən'sɔmeɪ] N consomê m, caldo
consonant ['kɔnsənənt] N consoante f
consort [n 'kɔnsɔ:t, vi kən'sɔ:t] N consorte m/f ▶ VI: **to ~ with** ter ligações com, conviver com; **prince ~** príncipe m consorte
consortia [kən'sɔ:tɪə] NPL of **consortium**
consortium [kən'sɔ:tɪəm] (*pl* **consortiums** or **consortia**) N consórcio
conspicuous [kən'spɪkjuəs] ADJ (*noticeable*) conspícuo; (*visible*) visível; (*garish*) berrante; (*outstanding*) notável; **to make o.s. ~** fazer-se notar
conspiracy [kən'spɪrəsɪ] N conspiração f, trama
conspiratorial [kən'spɪrə'tɔ:rɪəl] ADJ conspirador(a)
conspire [kən'spaɪə'] VI conspirar
constable ['kʌnstəbl] (*BRIT*) N policial m/f (*BR*), polícia m/f (*PT*); **chief ~** chefe m/f de polícia
constabulary [kən'stæbjulərɪ] N polícia (distrital)
constant ['kɔnstənt] ADJ constante; (*loyal*) leal, fiel
constantly ['kɔnstəntlɪ] ADV constantemente
constellation [kɔnstə'leɪʃən] N constelação f
consternation [kɔnstə'neɪʃən] N consternação f
constipated ['kɔnstɪpeɪtəd] ADJ com prisão de ventre
constipation [kɔnstɪ'peɪʃən] N prisão f de ventre
constituency [kən'stɪtjuənsɪ] N (*Pol*) distrito eleitoral; (*people*) eleitorado
constituency party N partido local
constituent [kən'stɪtjuənt] N (*Pol*) eleitor(a) m/f; (*component*) componente m
constitute ['kɔnstɪtju:t] VT (*represent*) representar; (*make up*) constituir
constitution [kɔnstɪ'tju:ʃən] N constituição f; (*health*) compleição f
constitutional [kɔnstɪ'tju:ʃənl] ADJ constitucional
constrain [kən'streɪn] VT obrigar
constrained [kən'streɪnd] ADJ: **to feel ~ to ...** sentir-se compelido a ...
constraint [kən'streɪnt] N (*compulsion*) coação f, pressão f; (*restriction*) limitação f; (*shyness*) constrangimento
constrict [kən'strɪkt] VT apertar, constringir
construct [kən'strʌkt] VT construir
construction [kən'strʌkʃən] N construção f; (*structure*) estrutura; (*fig: interpretation*) interpretação f; **under ~** em construção

construction industry N construção f
constructive [kən'strʌktɪv] ADJ construtivo
construe [kən'stru:] VT interpretar
consul ['kɔnsl] N cônsul m/f
consulate ['kɔnsjulɪt] N consulado
consult [kən'sʌlt] VT, VI consultar
consultancy [kən'sʌltənsɪ] N consultoria
consultancy fee N honorário de consultor
consultant [kən'sʌltənt] N (Med) (médico(-a))
especialista m/f; (other specialist) assessor(a)
m/f, consultor(a) m/f ▶ CPD: ~ **engineer**
engenheiro-consultor/engenheira-
consultora m/f; ~ **paediatrician** pediatra
m/f; **legal/management** ~ assessor
jurídico/consultor em administração
consultation [kɔnsəl'teɪʃən] N (Med)
consulta; (discussion) discussão f; **in ~ with**
em consulta com
consulting room [kən'sʌltɪŋ-] (BRIT) N
consultório
consume [kən'sju:m] VT (eat) comer; (drink)
beber; (fire etc, Comm) consumir
consumer [kən'sju:mə^r] N consumidor(a) m/f
consumer credit N crédito ao consumidor
consumer durables NPL bens mpl de consumo
duráveis
consumer goods NPL bens mpl de consumo
consumerism [kən'sju:mərɪzəm] N (Econ)
consumismo; (consumer protection) proteção f
ao consumidor
consumer society N sociedade f de consumo
consummate ['kɔnsəmeɪt] VT consumar
consumption [kən'sʌmpʃən] N consumo;
(Med) tuberculose f; **not fit for human ~**
impróprio para consumo
cont. ABBR = **continued**
contact ['kɔntækt] N contato ▶ VT entrar or
pôr-se em contato com; **to be in ~ with sb**
estar em contato com alguém; **he has
good ~s** tem boas relações
contact lenses NPL lentes fpl de contato
contagious [kən'teɪdʒəs] ADJ contagioso; (fig:
laughter etc) contagiante
contain [kən'teɪn] VT conter; **to ~ o.s.**
conter-se
container [kən'teɪnə^r] N recipiente m; (for
shipping etc) container m, cofre m de carga
containerize [kən'teɪnəraɪz] VT containerizar
contaminate [kən'tæmɪneɪt] VT contaminar
contamination [kəntæmɪ'neɪʃən] N
contaminação f
cont'd ABBR = **continued**
contemplate ['kɔntəmpleɪt] VT (idea)
considerar; (person, painting etc) contemplar;
(expect) contar com; (intend) pretender,
pensar em
contemplation [kɔntəm'pleɪʃən] N
contemplação f
contemporary [kən'tɛmpərərɪ] ADJ
contemporâneo; (design etc) moderno ▶ N
contemporâneo(-a)
contempt [kən'tɛmpt] N desprezo
contemptible [kən'tɛmptəbl] ADJ desprezível

contempt of court N (Law) desacato à
autoridade do tribunal
contemptuous [kən'tɛmptjuəs] ADJ
desdenhoso
contend [kən'tɛnd] VT (assert): **to ~ that**
afirmar que ▶ VI: **to ~ with** (struggle) lutar
com; (difficulty) enfrentar; (compete): **to ~ for**
competir por; **to have to ~ with** arcar com,
lidar com; **he has a lot to ~ with** ele tem
muito o que enfrentar
contender [kən'tɛndə^r] N contendor(a) m/f
content [adj, vt kən'tɛnt, n 'kɔntɛnt] ADJ (happy)
contente; (satisfied) satisfeito ▶ VT contentar,
satisfazer ▶ N conteúdo; (fat content, moisture
content etc) quantidade f; **contents** NPL (of
packet, book) conteúdo m; **(table of) ~s** índice m
das matérias; **to be ~ with** estar contente or
satisfeito com; **to ~ o.s. with sth/with
doing sth** contentar-se com algo/em fazer
algo
contented [kən'tɛntɪd] ADJ contente,
satisfeito
contentedly [kən'tɛntɪdlɪ] ADV
contentemente
contention [kən'tɛnʃən] N (assertion) asserção f;
(disagreement) contenda; **bone of ~** pomo da
discórdia
contentious [kən'tɛnʃəs] ADJ controvertido
contentment [kən'tɛntmənt] N
contentamento
contest [n 'kɔntɛst, vt kən'tɛst] N contenda;
(competition) concurso ▶ VT (dispute) disputar;
(legal case) defender; (Pol) ser candidato a;
(competition) disputar; (statement, decision)
contestar
contestant [kən'tɛstənt] N competidor(a) m/f;
(in fight) adversário(-a)
context ['kɔntɛkst] N contexto; **in/out of ~**
em/fora de contexto
continent ['kɔntɪnənt] N continente m; **the
C~** (BRIT) o continente europeu; **on the C~**
na Europa (continental)
continental [kɔntɪ'nɛntl] ADJ continental
▶ N (BRIT) europeu(-peia) m/f
continental breakfast N café m da manhã
(BRIT), pequeno almoço (PT de pão, geleia e café)
continental quilt (BRIT) N edredom m (BR),
edredão m (PT)
contingency [kən'tɪndʒənsɪ] N contingência
contingency plan N plano de contingência
contingent [kən'tɪndʒənt] N contingente m
▶ ADJ contingente; **to be ~ upon** depender
de
continual [kən'tɪnjuəl] ADJ contínuo
continually [kən'tɪnjuəlɪ] ADV
constantemente
continuation [kəntɪnju'eɪʃən] N
prolongamento; (after interruption)
continuação f, retomada
continue [kən'tɪnju:] VI prosseguir,
continuar ▶ VT continuar; (start again)
recomeçar, retomar; **to be ~d** (story) segue;
~d on page 10 continua na página 10

continuity [kɒntɪˈnjuɪtɪ] N (also Cinema, TV) continuidade f

continuity girl N (Cinema) continuista

continuous [kənˈtɪnjuəs] ADJ contínuo; ~ **performance** (Cinema) sessão f contínua; ~ **stationery** (Comput) formulários mpl contínuos

continuously [kənˈtɪnjuəslɪ] ADV (repeatedly) repetidamente; (uninterruptedly) continuamente

contort [kənˈtɔːt] VT contorcer

contortion [kənˈtɔːʃən] N contorção f

contortionist [kənˈtɔːʃənɪst] N contorcionista m/f

contour [ˈkɒntuəʳ] N (outline: gen pl) contorno; (also: **contour line**) curva de nível

contraband [ˈkɒntrəbænd] N contrabando ▶ ADJ de contrabando, contrabandeado

contraception [kɒntrəˈsɛpʃən] N anticoncepção f

contraceptive [kɒntrəˈsɛptɪv] ADJ anticoncepcional ▶ N anticoncepcional m

contract [n, cpd ˈkɒntrækt, vt, vi kənˈtrækt] N contrato ▶ CPD (price, date) contratual; (work) de empreitada ▶ VI (become smaller) contrair-se, encolher-se; (Comm): **to ~ to do sth** comprometer-se por contrato a fazer algo ▶ VT contrair; ~ **of employment** or **service** contrato de trabalho, ≈ vínculo empregatício
  ▶ **contract in** VI comprometer-se por contrato
  ▶ **contract out** VI desobrigar-se por contrato; (from pension scheme) optar por não participar

contraction [kənˈtrækʃən] N contração f

contractor [kənˈtræktəʳ] N contratante m/f

contractual [kənˈtræktʃuəl] ADJ contratual

contradict [kɒntrəˈdɪkt] VT contradizer, desmentir

contradiction [kɒntrəˈdɪkʃən] N contradição f; **to be in ~ with** contradizer

contradictory [kɒntrəˈdɪktərɪ] ADJ contraditório

contralto [kənˈtræltəu] N contralto

contraption [kənˈtræpʃən] (pej) N engenhoca, geringonça

contrary¹ [ˈkɒntrərɪ] ADJ contrário ▶ N contrário; **on the ~** muito pelo contrário; **unless you hear to the ~** salvo aviso contrário; ~ **to what we thought** ao contrário do que pensamos

contrary² [kənˈtrɛərɪ] ADJ teimoso

contrast [n ˈkɒntrɑːst, vt kənˈtrɑːst] N contraste m ▶ VT comparar; **in ~ to** or **with** em contraste com, ao contrário de

contrasting [kənˈtrɑːstɪŋ] ADJ contrastante

contravene [kɒntrəˈviːn] VT infringir

contravention [kɒntrəˈvɛnʃən] N contravenção f, infração f

contribute [kənˈtrɪbjuːt] VT contribuir ▶ VI dar; **to ~ to** (charity) contribuir para; (newspaper) escrever para; (discussion) participar de

contribution [kɒntrɪˈbjuːʃən] N (donation) doação f; (BRIT: for social security) contribuição f; (to debate) intervenção f; (to journal) colaboração f

contributor [kənˈtrɪbjutəʳ] N (to newspaper) colaborador(a) m/f

contributory [kənˈtrɪbjutərɪ] ADJ: **it was a ~ factor in ...** era um fator que contribuiu para ...

contributory pension scheme (BRIT) N sistema m de pensão contributária

contrite [ˈkɒntraɪt] ADJ arrependido, contrito

contrivance [kənˈtraɪvəns] N (scheme) maquinação f; (device) aparelho, dispositivo

contrive [kənˈtraɪv] VT (invent) idealizar; (carry out) efetuar; (plot) tramar ▶ VI: **to ~ to do** chegar a fazer

control [kənˈtrəul] VT controlar; (traffic etc) dirigir; (machinery) regular; (temper) dominar ▶ N controle m; (of car) direção f (BR), condução f (PT); (check) freio, controle; **controls** NPL (of vehicle) comandos mpl; (on radio, television etc) controle; **to take ~ of** assumir o controle de; **to be in ~ of** ter o controle de; (in charge of) ser responsável por; **to ~ o.s.** controlar-se; **out of/under ~** fora de/sob controle; **through circumstances beyond our ~** por motivos alheios à nossa vontade

control key N (Comput) tecla de controle

controller [kənˈtrəuləʳ] N controlador(a) m/f

controlling interest [kənˈtrəulɪŋ-] N (Comm) controle m acionário

control panel N painel m de instrumentos

control point N ponto de controle

control room N sala de comando; (Radio, TV) sala de controle

control tower N (Aviat) torre f de controle

control unit N (Comput) unidade f de controle

controversial [kɒntrəˈvəːʃl] ADJ controvertido, polêmico

controversy [ˈkɒntrəvəːsɪ] N controvérsia, polêmica

conurbation [kɒnəˈbeɪʃən] N conurbação f

convalesce [kɒnvəˈlɛs] VI convalescer

convalescence [kɒnvəˈlɛsns] N convalescença

convalescent [kɒnvəˈlɛsnt] ADJ, N convalescente m/f

convector [kənˈvɛktəʳ] N (heater) aquecedor m de convecção

convene [kənˈviːn] VT convocar ▶ VI convocar-se

convener [kənˈviːnəʳ] N organizador(a) m/f

convenience [kənˈviːnɪəns] N (easiness) facilidade f; (suitability) conveniência; (comfort) comodidade f; (advantage) vantagem f, conveniência; **at your ~** quando lhe convier; **at your earliest ~** (Comm) o mais cedo que lhe for possível; **all modern ~s** (also: BRIT inf: **all mod cons**) com todos os confortos

convenience foods NPL alimentos mpl semiprontos

convenient [kən'vi:nɪənt] ADJ conveniente; (*useful*) útil; (*place*) acessível; (*time*) oportuno, conveniente; **if it is ~ to you** se isso lhe convier, se isso não lhe for incômodo
conveniently [kən'vi:nɪəntlɪ] ADV convenientemente
convent ['kɔnvənt] N convento
convention [kən'vɛnʃən] N (*custom*) costume m; (*agreement*) convenção f; (*meeting*) assembleia
conventional [kən'vɛnʃənl] ADJ convencional
convent school N colégio de freiras
converge [kən'və:dʒ] VI convergir; (*people*): **to ~ on** convergir para
conversant [kən'və:snt] ADJ: **to be ~ with** estar familiarizado com
conversation [kɔnvə'seɪʃən] N conversação f, conversa
conversational [kɔnvə'seɪʃənl] ADJ de conversa; (*familiar*) familiar; (*talkative*) loquaz
conversationalist [kɔnvə'seɪʃnəlɪst] N conversador(a) m/f; **she's a good ~** ela tem muita conversa
converse [n 'kɔnvə:s, vi kən'və:s] N inverso ▶ VI conversar
conversely [kɔn'və:slɪ] ADV pelo contrário, inversamente
conversion [kən'və:ʃən] N conversão f; (BRIT: of house) transformação f
conversion table N tabela de conversão
convert [vt kən'və:t, n 'kɔnvə:t] VT converter ▶ N convertido(-a)
convertible [kən'və:təbl] ADJ convertível ▶ N conversível m
convex [kɔn'vɛks] ADJ convexo
convey [kən'veɪ] VT transportar, levar; (*thanks*) expressar; (*information*) passar
conveyance [kən'veɪəns] N (*of goods*) transporte m; (*vehicle*) meio de transporte, veículo
conveyancing [kən'veɪənsɪŋ] N (*Law*) transferência de bens imóveis
conveyor belt [kənveɪəʳ-] N correia transportadora
convict [vt kən'vɪkt, n 'kɔnvɪkt] VT condenar; (*sentence*) declarar culpado ▶ N presidiário(-a)
conviction [kən'vɪkʃən] N condenação f; (*belief*) convicção f; (*certainty*) certeza
convince [kən'vɪns] VT (*assure*) assegurar; (*persuade*) convencer; **to ~ sb of sth/that** convencer alguém de algo/de que
convinced [kən'vɪnst] ADJ: **~ of/that** convencido de/de que
convincing [kən'vɪnsɪŋ] ADJ convincente
convincingly [kən'vɪnsɪŋlɪ] ADV convincentemente
convivial [kən'vɪvɪəl] ADJ jovial, alegre
convoluted ['kɔnvəlu:tɪd] ADJ (*shape*) curvilíneo; (*argument*) complicado
convoy ['kɔnvɔɪ] N escolta
convulse [kən'vʌls] VT convulsionar; **to be ~d with laughter/pain** morrer de rir/dor

convulsion [kən'vʌlʃən] N convulsão f; (*laughter*) ataque m, acesso
coo [ku:] VI arrulhar; (*person*) falar suavemente
cook [kuk] VT cozinhar; (*meal*) preparar ▶ VI cozinhar ▶ N cozinheiro(-a)
▶ **cook up** (*inf*) VT (*excuse, story*) bolar
cookbook ['kukbuk] N livro de receitas
cooker ['kukəʳ] N fogão m
cookery ['kukərɪ] N (*dishes*) cozinha; (*art*) culinária
cookery book (BRIT) N = **cookbook**
cookie ['kukɪ] (US) N bolacha, biscoito
cooking ['kukɪŋ] N cozinha ▶ CPD (*apples, chocolate*) para cozinhar; (*utensils, salt*) de cozinha
cookout ['kukaut] (US) N churrasco
cool [ku:l] ADJ fresco; (*not hot*) tépido; (*calm*) calmo; (*unfriendly*) frio ▶ VT resfriar ▶ VI esfriar; **it's ~** (*weather*) está fresco
▶ **cool down** VI esfriar; (*fig: person, situation*) acalmar-se
cool box (BRIT) N mala frigorífica
cooler ['ku:ləʳ] (US) N mala frigorífica
cooling tower ['ku:lɪŋ-] N torre f de esfriamento
coolly ['ku:lɪ] ADV (*calmly*) calmamente; (*audaciously*) descaradamente; (*unenthusiastically*) friamente
coolness ['ku:lnɪs] N frescura; (*hostility*) frieza; (*indifference*) indiferença
coop [ku:p] N (*for poultry*) galinheiro; (*for rabbits*) capoeira
▶ **coop up** VT (*fig*) confinar
co-op ['kəuɔp] N ABBR = **cooperative**
cooperate [kəu'ɔpəreɪt] VI colaborar; (*assist*) ajudar
cooperation [kəuɔpə'reɪʃən] N cooperação f, colaboração f
cooperative [kəu'ɔpərətɪv] ADJ cooperativo ▶ N cooperativa
coopt [kəu'ɔpt] VT: **to ~ sb onto a committee** cooptar alguém para fazer parte de um comitê
coordinate [vt kəu'ɔ:dɪneɪt, n kəu'ɔdɪnət] VT coordenar ▶ N (*Math*) coordenada; **coordinates** NPL (*clothes*) coordenados mpl
coordination [kəuɔ:dɪ'neɪʃən] N coordenação f
coot [ku:t] N galeirão m
co-ownership [kəu-] N co-propriedade f, condomínio
cop [kɔp] (*inf*) N policial m/f (BR), polícia m/f (PT), tira m (inf)
cope [kəup] VI sair-se, dar-se; **to ~ with** poder com, arcar com; (*problem*) estar à altura de
Copenhagen ['kəupn'heɪgən] N Copenhague
copier ['kɔpɪəʳ] N (*also: photocopier*) copiador m
co-pilot [kəu-] N co-piloto(-a)
copious ['kəupɪəs] ADJ copioso, abundante

copper ['kɔpə^r] N (*metal*) cobre *m*; (*BRIT inf: policeman/woman*) policial *m/f* (BR), polícia *m/f* (PT); **coppers** NPL (*coins*) moedas *fpl* de pouco valor

coppice ['kɔpɪs] N bosquete *m*

copse [kɔps] N = **coppice**

copulate ['kɔpjuleɪt] VI copular

copulation [kɔpju'leɪʃən] N cópula

copy ['kɔpɪ] N cópia; (*duplicate*) duplicata; (*of book etc*) exemplar *m*; (*of writing*) originais *mpl* ▶ VT copiar; (*imitate*) imitar; **to make good ~** (*Press*) fazer uma boa matéria ▶ **copy out** VT copiar

copycat ['kɔpɪkæt] (*inf*) N macaco

copyright ['kɔpɪraɪt] N direitos *mpl* autorais, copirraite *m*; **~ reserved** todos os direitos reservados

copy typist N datilógrafo(-a)

copywriter ['kɔpɪraɪtə^r] N redator(a) *m/f* de material publicitário

coral ['kɔrəl] N coral *m*

coral reef N recife *m* de coral

Coral Sea N: **the ~** o mar de Coral

cord [kɔːd] N corda; (*Elec*) fio, cabo; (*fabric*) veludo cotelê; **cords** NPL (*trousers*) calça (BR) or calças *fpl* (PT) de veludo cotelê

cordial ['kɔːdɪəl] ADJ cordial ▶ N cordial *m*

cordless ['kɔːdlɪs] ADJ sem fio

cordon ['kɔːdn] N cordão *m* ▶ **cordon off** VT isolar

corduroy ['kɔːdərɔɪ] N veludo cotelê

CORE [kɔː^r] (US) N ABBR = **Congress of Racial Equality**

core [kɔː^r] N centro, núcleo; (*of fruit*) caroço; (*of problem*) âmago ▶ VT descaroçar; **rotten to the ~** completamente podre

Corfu [kɔː'fuː] N Corfu *f* (*no article*)

coriander [kɔrɪ'ændə^r] N coentro

cork [kɔːk] N rolha; (*tree*) cortiça

corkage ['kɔːkɪdʒ] N taxa cobrada num restaurante pela abertura das garrafas levadas pelo cliente

corked [kɔːkt] (BRIT) ADJ que tem gosto de rolha

corkscrew ['kɔːkskruː] N saca-rolhas *m inv*

corky ['kɔːkɪ] (US) ADJ que tem gosto de rolha

cormorant ['kɔːmərnt] N cormorão *m*, corvo marinho

corn [kɔːn] N (BRIT: *wheat*) trigo; (US: *maize*) milho; (*cereals*) grão *m*, cereal *m*; (*on foot*) calo; **~ on the cob** (*Culin*) espiga de milho

cornea ['kɔːnɪə] N córnea

corned beef ['kɔːnd-] N carne *f* de boi enlatada

corner ['kɔːnə^r] N (*outside*) esquina; (*inside*) canto; (*in road*) curva; (*Football etc: also:* **corner kick**) córner *m* ▶ VT (*trap*) encurralar; (*Comm*) açambarcar, monopolizar ▶ VI (*in car*) fazer uma curva; **to cut ~s** (*fig*) matar o serviço

corner flag N (*Football*) bandeira de escanteio

corner kick N (*Football*) córner *m*

cornerstone ['kɔːnəstəun] N pedra angular; (*fig*) base *f*, fundamento

cornet ['kɔːnɪt] N (*Mus*) cornetim *m*; (BRIT: *of ice-cream*) casquinha

cornflakes ['kɔːnfleɪks] NPL flocos *mpl* de milho

cornflour ['kɔːnflauə^r] (BRIT) N farinha de milho, maisena®

cornice ['kɔːnɪs] N cornija

Cornish ['kɔːnɪʃ] ADJ de Cornualha ▶ N (*Ling*) córnico

corn oil N óleo de milho

cornstarch ['kɔːnstɑːtʃ] (US) N = **cornflour**

cornucopia [kɔːnju'kəupɪə] N cornucópia

Cornwall ['kɔːnwəl] N Cornualha

corny ['kɔːnɪ] (*inf*) ADJ velho, gasto

corollary [kə'rɔlərɪ] N corolário

coronary ['kɔrənərɪ] N: **~ (thrombosis)** trombose *f* (coronária)

coronation [kɔrə'neɪʃən] N coroação *f*

coroner ['kɔrənə^r] N *magistrado que investiga mortes suspeitas*

coronet ['kɔrənɪt] N coroa aberta, diadema *m*

Corp. ABBR = **corporation**

corporal ['kɔːpərl] N cabo ▶ ADJ: **~ punishment** castigo corporal

corporate ['kɔːpərɪt] ADJ (*finance*) corporativo; (*action*) coletivo; (*image*) da empresa

corporate identity N imagem *f* da empresa

corporate image N imagem *f* da empresa

corporation [kɔːpə'reɪʃən] N (*of town*) município, junta; (*Comm*) sociedade *f*

corporation tax N imposto sobre a renda de sociedades

corps [kɔː^r] (*pl* **corps** [kɔːz]) N (*Mil*) unidade *f*; (*diplomatic*) corpo; **the press ~** a imprensa

corpse [kɔːps] N cadáver *m*

corpuscle ['kɔːpʌsl] N corpúsculo

corral [kə'rɑːl] N curral *m*

correct [kə'rɛkt] ADJ exato; (*proper*) correto ▶ VT corrigir; **you are ~** você tem razão

correction [kə'rɛkʃən] N correção *f*; (*erasure*) emenda

correlate ['kɔrɪleɪt] VT correlacionar ▶ VI: **to ~ with** corresponder a

correlation [kɔrɪ'leɪʃən] N correlação *f*

correspond [kɔrɪs'pɔnd] VI (*write*): **to ~ (with)** corresponder-se (com); (*be equal to*): **to ~ to** corresponder a; (*be in accordance*): **to ~ (with)** corresponder (a)

correspondence [kɔrɪs'pɔndəns] N correspondência; (*relationship*) relação *f*

correspondence course N curso por correspondência

correspondent [kɔrɪs'pɔndənt] N correspondente *m/f*

corresponding [kɔrɪs'pɔndɪŋ] ADJ correspondente

corridor ['kɔrɪdɔː^r] N corredor *m*

corroborate [kə'rɔbəreɪt] VT corroborar

corrode [kə'rəud] VT corroer ▶ VI corroer-se

corrosion [kə'rəuʒən] N corrosão *f*

corrosive [kə'rəuzɪv] ADJ corrosivo

corrugated ['kɔrəgeɪtɪd] ADJ corrugado

corrugated iron N chapa ondulada or corrugada
corrupt [kə'rʌpt] ADJ corrupto; (*Comput*) corrupto, danificado ▶ VT corromper; (*bribe*) subornar; (*data*) corromper, destruir; **~ practices** corrupção f
corruption [kə'rʌpʃən] N corrupção f
corset ['kɔːsɪt] N espartilho; (*Med*) colete m
Corsica ['kɔːsɪkə] N Córsega
Corsican ['kɔːsɪkən] ADJ, N córsico(-a)
cortège [kɔː'teɪʒ] N séquito, cortejo
cortisone ['kɔːtɪzəun] N cortisona
coruscating ['kɔrəskeɪtɪŋ] ADJ cintilante
c.o.s. ABBR (= *cash on shipment*) pagamento na expedição
cosh [kɔʃ] (*BRIT*) N cassetete m
cosignatory ['kəu'sɪgnətərɪ] N cossignatário(-a)
cosiness, (*US*) **coziness** ['kəuzɪnɪs] N conforto; (*atmosphere*) aconchego, conforto
cos lettuce [kɔs-] N alface m (cos)
cosmetic [kɔz'mɛtɪk] N cosmético ▶ ADJ (*preparation*) cosmético; (*fig: measure, improvement*) simbólico, superficial; **~ surgery** cirurgia plástica embelezadora
cosmic ['kɔzmɪk] ADJ cósmico
cosmonaut ['kɔzmənɔːt] N cosmonauta m/f
cosmopolitan [kɔzmə'pɔlɪtn] ADJ cosmopolita
cosmos ['kɔzmɔs] N cosmo
cosset ['kɔsɪt] VT paparicar
cost [kɔst] (*pt, pp* **cost**) VI custar ▶ VT custar; (*determine cost of*) determinar o custo de ▶ N (*gen*) custo; (*price*) preço; **costs** NPL (*Comm*) custos *mpl*; (*Law*) custas *fpl*; **how much does it ~?** quanto custa?; **it ~s £5/too much** custa £5/é muito caro; **to ~ sb time/effort** custar tempo/esforço a alguém; **it ~ him his life/job** custou-lhe a vida/o emprego; **at the ~ of** à custa de; **the ~ of living** o custo de vida; **at all ~s** custe o que custar
cost accountant N contador(a) m/f de custos
co-star [kəu-] N coestrela m/f
Costa Rica ['kɔstə'riːkə] N Costa Rica
Costa Rican ['kɔstə'riːkən] ADJ, N costarriquenho(-a)
cost centre N centro de custo
cost control N controle m dos custos
cost-effective ADJ rentável
cost-effectiveness N rentabilidade f
costly ['kɔstlɪ] ADJ (*expensive*) caro, custoso; (*valuable*) suntuoso
cost-of-living ADJ: **~ allowance** ajuda de custo; **~ index** índice m de preços ao consumidor
cost price (*BRIT*) N preço de custo
costume ['kɔstjuːm] N traje m; (*BRIT: also:* **swimming costume**: *woman's*) maiô m (*BR*), fato de banho (*PT*); (: *man's*) calção m (de banho) (*BR*), calções *mpl* de banho (*PT*)
costume jewellery N bijuteria

cosy, (*US*) **cozy** ['kəuzɪ] ADJ cômodo; (*atmosphere*) aconchegante; (*life*) folgado, confortável
cot [kɔt] N (*BRIT: child's*) cama (de criança), berço; (*US: campbed*) cama de lona
Cotswolds ['kɔtswəuldz] NPL: **the ~** região de colinas em Gloucestershire
cottage ['kɔtɪdʒ] N casa de campo; (*rustic*) cabana
cottage cheese N queijo tipo cottage (*BR*), queijo creme (*PT*)
cottage industry N indústria artesanal
cottage pie N prato de carne picada com batata
cotton ['kɔtn] N algodão m; (*thread*) fio, linha ▶ CPD de algodão
  ▶ **cotton on** (*inf*) VI: **to ~ on (to sth)** sacar (algo)
cotton bud (*BRIT*) N cotonete® m
cotton candy (*US*) N algodão m doce
cotton wool (*BRIT*) N algodão m (hidrófilo)
couch [kautʃ] N sofá m; (*doctor's*) cama; (*psychiatrist's*) divã m ▶ VT formular
couchette [kuː'ʃɛt] N leito
cough [kɔf] VI tossir ▶ N tosse f
  ▶ **cough up** VT expelir; (*inf: money*) desembolsar
cough drop N pastilha para a tosse
cough mixture N xarope m (para a tosse)
cough syrup N xarope m (para a tosse)
could [kud] PT, CONDITIONAL *of* **can²**
couldn't ['kudnt] = **could not**
council ['kaunsl] N conselho; **city** or **town ~** câmara municipal; **C~ of Europe** Conselho da Europa
council estate (*BRIT*) N conjunto habitacional
council house (*BRIT*) N casa popular
councillor ['kaunslə'] N vereador(a) m/f
counsel ['kaunsl] N (*advice*) conselho; (*lawyer*) advogado(-a) ▶ VT: **to ~ sth/sb to do sth** aconselhar algo/alguém a fazer algo; **~ for the defence/the prosecution** advogado(-a) m/f de defesa/promotor(a) m/f público(-a)
counsellor, (*US*) **counselor** ['kaunslə'] N conselheiro(-a); (*US Law*) advogado(-a)
count [kaunt] VT contar; (*include*) incluir ▶ VI contar ▶ N (*of votes etc*) contagem f; (*of pollen, alcohol*) nível m; (*nobleman*) conde m; (*sum*) total m, soma; **not ~ing the children** sem contar as crianças; **10 ~ing him** 10 contando com ele; **it ~s for very little** conta muito pouco; **~ yourself lucky** considere-se sortudo; **that doesn't ~!** isso não vale!
  ▶ **count on** VT FUS contar com; **to ~ on doing sth** contar em fazer algo
  ▶ **count up** VT contar
countdown ['kauntdaun] N contagem f regressiva
countenance ['kauntɪnəns] N expressão f ▶ VT tolerar
counter ['kauntə'] N (*in shop*) balcão m; (*in post office etc*) guichê m; (*in games*) ficha ▶ VT contrariar; (*blow*) parar ▶ ADV: **~ to** ao

contrário de; **to buy under the ~** (*fig*) comprar por baixo do pano *or* da mesa

counteract [kauntər'ækt] VT neutralizar

counterattack ['kauntərətæk] N contraataque *m* ▶ VI contra-atacar

counterbalance [kauntə'bæləns] N contrapeso

counter-clockwise ADV ao contrário dos ponteiros do relógio

counter-espionage N contraespionagem *f*

counterfeit ['kauntəfɪt] N falsificação *f* ▶ VT falsificar ▶ ADJ falso, falsificado

counterfoil ['kauntəfɔɪl] N canhoto (BR), talão *m* (PT)

counterintelligence ['kauntərɪn'tɛlɪdʒəns] N contrainformação *f*

countermand ['kauntəmɑːnd] VT revogar

countermeasure ['kauntəmɛʒər] N contramedida

counteroffensive ['kauntərə'fɛnsɪv] N contraofensiva

counterpane ['kauntəpeɪn] N colcha

counterpart ['kauntəpɑːt] N (*opposite number*) homólogo(-a); (*equivalent*) equivalente *m/f*

counterproductive ['kauntəprə'dʌktɪv] ADJ contraproducente

counterproposal ['kauntəprə'pəuzl] N contraproposta

countersign ['kauntəsaɪn] VT autenticar

countersink ['kauntəsɪŋk] (*irreg: like* **sink**) VT escarear

counterterrorism [kauntə'tɛrərɪzəm] N antiterrorismo

countess ['kauntɪs] N condessa

countless ['kauntlɪs] ADJ inumerável

countrified ['kʌntrɪfaɪd] ADJ bucólico, rústico

country ['kʌntrɪ] N país *m*; (*nation*) nação *f*; (*native land*) terra; (*as opposed to town*) campo; (*region*) região *f*, terra; **in the ~** no campo; (*esp in Brazil*) no interior; **mountainous ~** região montanhosa

country and western, country and western music N música country

country dancing (BRIT) N dança folclórica

country house N casa de campo

countryman ['kʌntrɪmən] (*irreg: like* **man**) N (*national*) compatriota *m*; (*rural*) camponês *m*

countryside ['kʌntrɪsaɪd] N campo

country-wide ADJ em todo o país; (*problem*) de escala nacional ▶ ADV em todo o país

county ['kauntɪ] N condado

county town (BRIT) N capital *f* do condado

coup [kuː] N golpe *m* de mestre; (*also*: **coup d'état**) golpe (de estado)

coupé ['kuːpeɪ] N (*Aut*) cupê *m*

couple ['kʌpl] N (*of things, people*) par *m*; (*married couple, courting couple*) casal *m* ▶ VT (*ideas, names*) unir, juntar; (*machinery*) ligar, juntar; **a ~ of** um par de; (*a few*) alguns/algumas

couplet ['kʌplɪt] N dístico

coupling ['kʌplɪŋ] N (*Rail*) engate *m*

coupon ['kuːpɒn] N cupom *m* (BR), cupão *m* (PT); (*pools coupon*) talão *m*; (*voucher*) vale *m*

courage ['kʌrɪdʒ] N coragem *f*

courageous [kə'reɪdʒəs] ADJ corajoso

courgette [kuə'ʒɛt] (BRIT) N abobrinha

courier ['kurɪər] N correio; (*diplomatic*) mala; (*for tourists*) guia *m/f*, agente *m/f* de turismo

course [kɔːs] N (*direction*) direção *f*; (*process*) desenvolvimento; (*of river, Sch*) curso; (*of ship*) rumo; (*of bullet*) trajetória; (*fig*) procedimento; (*Golf*) campo; (*part of meal*) prato; **of ~** naturalmente; (*certainly*) certamente; **of ~!** claro!, lógico!; **(no) of ~ not!** claro que não!; **in due ~** oportunamente, no devido tempo; **first ~** entrada; **in the ~ of the next few days** no decorrer dos próximos dias; **the best ~ would be to do ...** o melhor seria fazer ...; **we have no other ~ but to ...** não temos nenhuma outra opção senão ...

course of action N atitude *f*

court [kɔːt] N (*royal*) corte *f*; (*Law*) tribunal *m*; (*Tennis etc*) quadra ▶ VT (*woman*) cortejar, namorar; (*danger etc*) procurar; **out of ~** (*Law: settle*) extrajudicialmente; **to take to ~** demandar, levar a julgamento; **~ of appeal** tribunal de recursos

courteous ['kɜːtɪəs] ADJ cortês(-esa)

courtesan [kɔːtɪ'zæn] N cortesã *f*

courtesy ['kɜːtəsɪ] N cortesia; **(by) ~ of** com permissão de

courtesy coach N ônibus *m* (BR) *or* autocarro (PT) gratuito

courtesy light N (*Aut*) luz *f* interior

court-house (US) N palácio de justiça

courtier ['kɔːtɪə'] N cortesão *m*

court martial N (*pl* **courts martial**) conselho de guerra ▶ VT submeter a conselho de guerra

courtroom ['kɔːtrum] N sala de tribunal

court shoe N escarpim *m*

courtyard ['kɔːtjɑːd] N pátio

cousin ['kʌzn] N primo(-a) *m/f*; **first ~** primo-irmão/prima-irmã *m/f*

cove [kəuv] N angra, enseada

covenant ['kʌvənənt] N convênio ▶ VT: **to ~ £2000 per year to a charity** comprometerse a doar £2000 por ano para uma obra de caridade

Coventry ['kɒvəntrɪ] N: **to send sb to ~** (*fig*) relegar alguém ao ostracismo

cover ['kʌvə'] VT (*gen, Press, costs*) cobrir; (*with lid*) tampar; (*chairs etc*) revestir; (*distance*) percorrer; (*include*) abranger; (*protect*) abrigar; (*issues*) tratar ▶ N (*gen, Press, Comm*) cobertura; (*lid*) tampa; (*for chair etc*) capa; (*for bed*) cobertor *m*; (*envelope*) envelope *m*; (*of book, magazine*) capa; (*shelter*) abrigo; (*Insurance*) cobertura; **to take ~** abrigar-se; **under ~** (*indoors*) abrigado; **under ~ of** sob o abrigo de; (*fig*) sob capa de; **under separate ~** (*Comm*) em separado; **£10 will ~ everything** £10 vão dar para tudo

▶ **cover up** VT (*person, object*): **to ~ up (with)** cobrir (com); (*fig: truth, facts*) abafar, encobrir ▶ VI: **to ~ up for sb** (*fig*) cobrir alguém

coverage [ˈkʌvərɪdʒ] N (*Press, Insurance*) cobertura
cover charge N couvert *m*
covering [ˈkʌvərɪŋ] N cobertura; (*of snow, dust etc*) comada
covering letter, (US) **cover letter** N carta de cobertura
cover note N (*Insurance*) nota de cobertura
cover price N preço de capa
covert [ˈkʌvɜːt] ADJ (*threat*) velado; (*action*) oculto, secreto
cover-up N encobrimento (dos fatos)
covet [ˈkʌvɪt] VT cobiçar
cow [kau] N vaca ▶ CPD fêmea ▶ VT intimidar
coward [ˈkauəd] N covarde *m/f*
cowardice [ˈkauədɪs] N covardia
cowardly [ˈkauədlɪ] ADJ covarde
cowboy [ˈkaubɔɪ] N vaqueiro
cower [ˈkauəʳ] VI encolher-se (de medo)
cowshed [ˈkauʃɛd] N estábulo
cowslip [ˈkauslɪp] N (*Bot*) primavera
cox [kɔks] N ABBR = **coxswain**
coxswain [ˈkɔksn] N timoneiro(-a)
coy [kɔɪ] ADJ tímido
coyote [kɔɪˈəutɪ] N coiote *m*
coziness [ˈkəuzɪnɪs] (US) N = **cosiness**
cozy [ˈkəuzɪ] (US) ADJ = **cosy**
CP N ABBR (= *Communist Party*) PC *m*
cp. ABBR (= *compare*) cp.
c/p (BRIT) ABBR = **carriage paid**
CPA (US) N ABBR = **certified public accountant**
CPI N ABBR (= *Consumer Price Index*) IPC *m*
Cpl. ABBR = **Corporal**
CP/M N ABBR (= *Central Program for Microprocessors*) CP/M *m*
c.p.s. ABBR (= *characters per second*) c.p.s
CPSA (BRIT) N ABBR (= *Civil and Public Services Association*) sindicato dos funcionários públicos
CPU N ABBR = **Central Processing Unit** (*of PC*) torre *f*
cr. ABBR = **credit; creditor**
crab [kræb] N caranguejo
crab apple N maçã ácida
crack [kræk] N rachadura; (*gap*) brecha; (*noise*) estalo; (*joke*) piada; (*drug*) crack *m*; (*inf: attempt*): **to have a ~ (at sth)** tentar (fazer algo) ▶ VT quebrar; (*nut*) partir, descascar; (*wall*) rachar; (*safe*) arrombar; (*whip etc*) estalar; (*knuckles*) estalar, partir; (*joke*) soltar; (*mystery*) resolver; (*code*) decifrar ▶ ADJ (*expert*) de primeira classe; **to get ~ing** (*inf*) pôr mãos à obra
  ▶ **crack down on** VT FUS (*crime*) ser linha dura com; (*spending*) cortar
  ▶ **crack up** VI (*Psych*) sofrer um colapso nervoso
crackdown [ˈkrækdaun] N: **~ (on)** (*on crime*) repressão (contra); (*on spending*) arrocho (a)
cracked [krækt] (*inf*) ADJ doido
cracker [ˈkrækəʳ] N (*biscuit*) biscoito; (*Christmas cracker*) busca pé surpresa *m*; (*firework*) busca-pé *m*; **a ~ of a ...** (BRIT inf) um(a) ... sensacional

crackers [ˈkrækəz] (BRIT inf) ADJ: **he's ~** ele é maluco
crackle [ˈkrækl] VI crepitar
crackling [ˈkræklɪŋ] N (*of fire*) crepitação *f*; (*of leaves etc*) estalidos *mpl*; (*of pork*) torresmo
cradle [ˈkreɪdl] N berço ▶ VT (*child*) embalar; (*object*) segurar com cuidado
craft [krɑːft] N (*skill*) arte *f*; (*trade*) ofício; (*cunning*) astúcia; (*boat*) barco
craftsman [ˈkrɑːftsmən] (*irreg: like* **man**) N artífice *m*, artesão *m*
craftsmanship [ˈkrɑːftsmənʃɪp] N acabamento
craftsmen [ˈkrɑːftsmɛn] NPL *of* **craftsman**
crafty [ˈkrɑːftɪ] ADJ astuto, malandro, esperto
crag [kræg] N penhasco
cram [kræm] VT (*fill*): **to ~ sth with** encher *or* abarrotar algo de; (*put*): **to ~ sth into** enfiar algo em ▶ VI (*for exams*) estudar na última hora
cramming [ˈkræmɪŋ] N (*for exams*) virada final
cramp [kræmp] N (*Med*) cãibra; (*Tech*) grampo ▶ VT (*limit*) restringir; (*annoy*) estorvar
cramped [kræmpt] ADJ apertado, confinado
crampon [ˈkræmpən] N gato de ferro
cranberry [ˈkrænbərɪ] N oxicoco
crane [kreɪn] N (*Tech*) guindaste *m*; (*bird*) grou *m* ▶ VT, VI: **to ~ forward, to ~ one's neck** espichar-se, espichar o pescoço
crania [ˈkreɪnɪə] NPL *of* **cranium**
cranium [ˈkreɪnɪəm] (*pl* **crania**) N crânio
crank [kræŋk] N manivela; (*person*) excêntrico(-a)
crankshaft [ˈkræŋkʃɑːft] N virabrequim *m*
cranky [ˈkræŋkɪ] ADJ (*eccentric*) excêntrico; (*bad-tempered*) irritadiço
cranny [ˈkrænɪ] N *see* **nook**
crap [kræp] (!) N papo furado; **to have a ~** cagar (!)
crappy [ˈkræpɪ] (!) ADJ fuleiro
crash [kræʃ] N (*noise*) estrondo; (*of car*) batida; (*of plane*) desastre *m* de avião; (*Comm*) falência, quebra; (*Stock Exchange*) craque *m* ▶ VT (*car*) bater com; (*plane*) jogar ▶ VI (*car*) bater; (*plane*) cair; (*two cars*) colidir, bater; (*Comm*) falir, quebrar; (*fall noisily*) cair (com estrondo); (*fig*) despencar; **to ~ into** bater em; **he ~ed into a wall** ele bateu com o carro num muro
crash barrier (BRIT) N (*Aut*) cerca de proteção
crash course N curso intensivo
crash helmet N capacete *m*
crash landing N aterrissagem *f* forçada (BR), aterragem *f* forçosa (PT)
crass [kræs] ADJ grosseiro
crate [kreɪt] N caixote *m*; (*inf: old car*) lata-velha; (*for bottles*) engradado
crater [ˈkreɪtəʳ] N cratera
cravat, cravate [krəˈvæt] N gravata
crave [kreɪv] VT, VI: **to ~ for** ansiar por
craving [ˈkreɪvɪŋ] N (*of pregnant woman*) desejo
crawl [krɔːl] VI arrastar-se; (*child*) engatinhar; (*insect*) andar; (*vehicle*) andar a passo de

tartaruga ▶ N rastejo; (*Swimming*) crawl *m*;
to ~ to sb (*inf*) puxar o saco de alguém
crayfish ['kreɪfɪʃ] N INV (*freshwater*) camarão-
d'água-doce *m*; (*saltwater*) lagostim *m*
crayon ['kreɪən] N lápis *m* de cera, crayon *m*
craze [kreɪz] N mania; (*fashion*) moda
crazed [kreɪzd] ADJ (*look, person*) enlouquecido;
(*pottery, glaze*) craquelê
crazy ['kreɪzi] ADJ (*person*) louco, maluco,
doido; (*idea*) disparatado; **to go ~**
enlouquecer; **to be ~ about sb/sth** (*inf*) ser
louco por alguém/algo
crazy paving (BRIT) N pavimento irregular
creak [kri:k] VI ranger
cream [kri:m] N (*of milk*) nata; (*artificial,
cosmetic*) creme *m*; (*élite*) **the ~ of** a fina flor
de ▶ ADJ (*colour*) creme *inv*
▶ **cream off** VT (*fig*) tirar
cream cake N bolo de creme
cream cheese N ricota (BR), queijo creme (PT)
creamery ['kri:məri] N (*shop*) leiteria; (*factory*)
fábrica de laticínios
creamy ['kri:mi] ADJ (*colour*) creme *inv*; (*taste*)
cremoso
crease [kri:s] N (*fold*) dobra, vinco; (*in trousers*)
vinco; (*wrinkle*) ruga ▶ VT (*fold*) dobrar, vincar;
(*wrinkle*) amassar, amarrotar ▶ VI (*wrinkle up*)
amassar-se, amarrotar-se
crease-resistant ADJ: **a ~ fabric** um tecido
que não amarrota
create [kri:'eɪt] VT criar; (*produce*) produzir
creation [kri:'eɪʃən] N criação *f*
creative [kri:'eɪtɪv] ADJ criativo; (*inventive*)
inventivo
creativity [kri:er'tɪvɪti] N criatividade *f*
creator [kri:'eɪtər] N criador(a) *m/f*; (*inventor*)
inventor(a) *m/f*
creature ['kri:tʃər] N (*animal*) animal *m*, bicho;
(*living thing*) criatura
crèche [krɛʃ] N creche *f*
credence ['kri:dns] N: **to lend** or **give ~ to** dar
crédito a
credentials [krɪ'dɛnʃlz] NPL credenciais *fpl*
credibility [krɛdɪ'bɪlɪti] N credibilidade *f*
credible ['krɛdɪbl] ADJ acreditável;
(*trustworthy*) digno de crédito
credit ['krɛdɪt] N (*gen, Comm*) crédito; (*merit*)
mérito ▶ VT (*believe: also*: **give credit to**)
acreditar; (*Comm*) creditar ▶ CPD creditício;
credits NPL (*Cinema, TV*) crédito; **to ~ sb with
sth** (*fig*) atribuir algo a alguém; **to ~ £5 to sb**
creditar £5 a alguém; **to be in ~** (*person, bank
account*) ter fundos; **on ~** a crédito; **to one's ~**
honra lhe seja; **to take the ~ for sth**
atribuir-se o mérito de; **it does him ~** é
motivo de honra para ele; **he's a ~ to his
family** ele é um orgulho para a família
creditable ['krɛdɪtəbl] ADJ louvável
credit account N conta de crédito
credit agency (BRIT) N agência de crédito
credit balance N saldo credor
credit bureau (US) (*irreg: like* **bureau**) N = **credit
agency**

credit card N cartão *m* de crédito
credit control N controle *m* de crédito
credit crunch N contração *f* do crédito
credit facilities NPL crediário
credit limit N limite *m* de crédito
credit note N nota de crédito
creditor ['krɛdɪtər] N credor(a) *m/f*
credit transfer N transferência
creditworthy ['krɛdɪtwə:ðɪ] ADJ merecedor(a)
de crédito
credulity [krɪ'dju:lɪti] N credulidade *f*
creed [kri:d] N credo
creek [kri:k] N enseada; (US) riacho
creel [kri:l] N cesto de pescador
creep [kri:p] VI (*pt, pp* **crept**) (*animal*) rastejar;
(*person*) deslizar(-se); (*plant*) trepar ▶ N (*inf*)
puxa-saco *m*; **to ~ up on sb** pegar alguém de
surpresa; **it gives me the ~s** me dá arrepios
creeper ['kri:pər] N trepadeira; **creepers** NPL
(US: *for baby*) macacão *m* (BR), fato macaco (PT)
creepy ['kri:pi] ADJ (*frightening*) horripilante
creepy-crawly [-'krɔ:li] (*inf*) N bichinho
cremate [krɪ'meɪt] VT cremar
cremation [krɔ'meɪʃən] N cremação *f*
crematoria [krɛmə'tɔ:riə] NPL *of*
crematorium
crematorium [krɛmə'tɔ:riəm] (*pl* **crematoria**)
N crematório
creosote ['krɪəsəut] N creosoto
crêpe [kreɪp] N (*fabric*) crepe *m*; (*paper*) papel
crepom *m*
crêpe bandage (BRIT) N atadura de crepe
crêpe paper N papel *m* crepom
crêpe sole N sola de crepe
crept [krɛpt] PT, PP *of* **creep**
crescendo [krɪ'ʃɛndəu] N crescendo
crescent ['krɛsnt] N meia-lua; (*street*) rua
semicircular
cress [krɛs] N agrião *m*
crest [krɛst] N (*of bird*) crista; (*of hill*) cimo,
topo; (*of helmet*) cimeira; (*of coat of arms*)
timbre *m*
crestfallen ['krɛstfɔ:lən] ADJ abatido,
cabisbaixo
Crete [kri:t] N Creta
crevasse [krɪ'væs] N fenda
crevice ['krɛvɪs] N (*crack*) fenda; (*gap*) greta
crew [kru:] N (*of ship etc*) tripulação *f*; (*gang*)
bando, quadrilha; (*Mil*) guarnição *f*; (*Cinema*)
equipe *f*
crew-cut N corte *m* à escovinha
crew-neck N gola arredondada
crib [krɪb] N manjedoira, presépio; (US: *cot*)
berço ▶ VT (*inf*) colar
cribbage ['krɪbɪdʒ] N *jogo de cartas*
crick [krɪk] N cãibra; **~ in the neck** torcicolo
cricket ['krɪkɪt] N (*insect*) grilo; (*game*)
criquete *m*, cricket *m*
cricketer ['krɪkɪtər] N jogador(a) *m/f* de
criquete
crime [kraɪm] N (*no pl: illegal activities*) crime *m*;
(*offence*) delito; (*crime in general*)
criminalidade *f*; (*fig*) pecado, maldade *f*

crime wave N onda de criminalidade

criminal ['krɪmɪnl] N criminoso ▶ ADJ criminal; (*law*) penal; (*morally wrong*) imoral; **the C~ Investigation Department** (*BRIT*) a Brigada de Investigação Criminal

crimp [krɪmp] VT (*hair*) frisar

crimson ['krɪmzn] ADJ carmesim *inv*

cringe [krɪndʒ] VI encolher-se

crinkle ['krɪŋkl] VT amassar, enrugar

cripple ['krɪpl] N aleijado(-a) ▶ VT aleijar; (*ship, plane*) inutilizar; (*industry, exports*) paralisar

crippling ['krɪplɪŋ] ADJ (*disease*) devastador(a); (*taxation, debts*) excessivo

crises ['kraɪsiːz] NPL *of* **crisis**

crisis ['kraɪsɪs] (*pl* **crises**) N crise *f*

crisp [krɪsp] ADJ (*crunchy*) crocante; (*vegetables, fruit*) fresco; (*bacon etc*) torrado; (*manner*) seco

crisps [krɪsps] (*BRIT*) NPL batatinhas *fpl* fritas

crispy ['krɪspɪ] ADJ crocante

criss-cross [krɪs-] ADJ (*design*) entrecruzado; (*pattern*) em xadrez ▶ VT entrecruzar; **~ pattern** padrão *m* em xadrez

criteria [kraɪ'tɪərɪə] NPL *of* **criterion**

criterion [kraɪ'tɪərɪən] (*pl* **criteria**) N critério

critic ['krɪtɪk] N crítico(-a)

critical ['krɪtɪkl] ADJ crítico; (*illness*) grave; **to be ~ of sth/sb** criticar algo/alguém

critically ['krɪtɪkəlɪ] ADV (*examine*) criteriosamente; (*speak*) criticamente; (*ill*) gravemente

criticism ['krɪtɪsɪzm] N crítica

criticize ['krɪtɪsaɪz] VT criticar

critique [krɪ'tiːk] N crítica

croak [krəuk] VI (*frog*) coaxar; (*bird*) crocitar; (*person*) falar lugubremente ▶ N grasnido

Croatia [krəu'eɪʃə] N Croácia

crochet ['krəuʃeɪ] N crochê *m*

crock [krɔk] N jarro; (*inf: also:* **old crock**: *person*) caco velho; (*: car*) calhambeque *m*

crockery ['krɔkərɪ] N louça

crocodile ['krɔkədaɪl] N crocodilo

crocus ['krəukəs] N açafrão-da-primavera *m*

croft [krɔft] (*BRIT*) N pequena chácara

crofter ['krɔftər] (*BRIT*) N arrendatário

croissant ['krwasã] N croissant *m*

crone [krəun] N velha encarquilhada

crony ['krəunɪ] (*inf, pej*) N camarada *m/f*, compadre *m*

crook [kruk] N (*inf: criminal*) vigarista *m/f*; (*of shepherd*) cajado; (*of arm*) curva

crooked ['krukɪd] ADJ (*bent*) torto; (*path*) tortuoso; (*dishonest*) desonesto

crop [krɔp] N (*produce*) colheita; (*amount produced*) safra; (*riding crop*) chicotinho; (*of bird*) papo ▶ VT cortar
  ▶ **crop up** VI surgir

cropper ['krɔpər] N: **to come a ~** (*inf*) dar com os burros n'água, entrar pelo cano

crop spraying [-'spreɪɪŋ] N pulverização *f* das culturas

croquet ['krəukeɪ] (*BRIT*) N croquet *m*, croquê *m*

croquette [krə'kɛt] N croquete *m*

cross [krɔs] N cruz *f*; (*hybrid*) cruzamento ▶ VT cruzar; (*street etc*) atravessar; (*thwart: person, plan*) contrariar ▶ VI atravessar ▶ ADJ zangado, mal-humorado; **to ~ o.s.** persignar-se; **they've got their lines ~ed** eles têm um mal-entendido
  ▶ **cross out** VT riscar
  ▶ **cross over** VI atravessar

crossbar ['krɔsbɑːr] N travessa; (*Sport*) barra transversal

crossbreed ['krɔsbriːd] N raça cruzada

cross-Channel ferry N barca que faz a travessia do Canal da Mancha

cross-check N conferição *f* ▶ VT conferir

cross-country, cross-country race N corrida pelo campo

cross-examination N interrogatório; (*Law*) repergunta

cross-examine VT interrogar; (*Law*) reperguntar

cross-eyed [-aɪd] ADJ vesgo

crossfire ['krɔsfaɪər] N fogo cruzado

crossing ['krɔsɪŋ] N (*road*) cruzamento; (*rail*) passagem *f* de nível; (*sea passage*) travessia; (*also:* **pedestrian crossing**) faixa (para pedestres) (*BR*), passadeira (*PT*)

crossing guard (*US*) N guarda *m/f* para pedestres

cross-purposes NPL: **to be at ~ (with sb)** não entender-se (com alguém); **we're (talking) at ~** não falamos da mesma coisa

cross-reference N referência remissiva

crossroads ['krɔsrəudz] N cruzamento

cross section N (*of object*) corte *m* transversal; (*of population*) grupo representativo

crosswalk ['krɔswɔːk] (*US*) N faixa (para pedestres) (*BR*), passadeira (*PT*)

crosswind ['krɔswɪnd] N vento costal

crosswise ['krɔswaɪz] ADV transversalmente

crossword ['krɔswəːd] N palavras *fpl* cruzadas

crotch [krɔtʃ] N (*of garment*) fundilho

crotchet ['krɔtʃɪt] N (*Mus*) semínima

crotchety ['krɔtʃɪtɪ] ADJ (*person*) rabugento

crouch [krautʃ] VI agachar-se

croup [kruːp] N (*Med*) crupe *m*

croupier ['kruːpɪə] N crupiê *m/f*

crouton ['kruːtɔn] N crouton *m*

crow [krəu] N (*bird*) corvo; (*of cock*) canto, cocoricó *m* ▶ VI (*cock*) cantar, cocoricar; (*fig*) contar vantagem

crowbar ['krəubɑːr] N pé-de-cabra *m*

crowd [kraud] N multidão *f*; (*Sport*) público, galera (*inf*); (*unruly*) tropel *m*; (*common herd*) turba, vulgo ▶ VT (*fill*) apinhar ▶ VI (*gather*) amontoar-se; (*cram*): **to ~ in** apinhar-se; **~s of people** um grande número de pessoas

crowded ['kraudɪd] ADJ (*full*) lotado; (*well-attended*) concorrido; (*densely populated*) superlotado

crowd scene N (*Cinema, Theatre*) cena de multidão

crown [kraun] N coroa; (of head, hill) topo; (of hat) copa ▶ VT coroar; (tooth) pôr uma coroa artificial em; (fig) rematar
crown court (BRIT) N Tribunal m de Justiça
crowning ['kraunɪŋ] ADJ (achievement, glory) supremo
crown jewels NPL joias fpl reais
crown prince N príncipe m herdeiro
crow's-feet NPL pés-de-galinha mpl
crow's-nest N (on ship) cesto de gávea
crucial ['kru:ʃl] ADJ (decision) vital; (vote) decisivo; **~ to** vital para
crucifix ['kru:sɪfɪks] N crucifixo
crucifixion [kru:sɪ'fɪkʃən] N crucificação f
crucify ['kru:sɪfaɪ] VT crucificar
crude [kru:d] ADJ (materials) bruto; (fig: basic) tosco; (: vulgar) grosseiro ▶ N (also: **crude oil**) petróleo em bruto
crude oil N petróleo em bruto
cruel ['kruəl] ADJ cruel
cruelty ['kruəltɪ] N crueldade f
cruet ['kru:ɪt] N galheta
cruise [kru:z] N cruzeiro ▶ VI (ship) fazer um cruzeiro; (aircraft) voar; (car): **to ~ at ... km/h** ir a ... km por hora
cruise missile N míssil m Cruise
cruiser ['kru:zəʳ] N cruzador m
cruising speed ['kru:zɪŋ-] N velocidade f de cruzeiro
crumb [krʌm] N (of bread) migalha; (of cake) farelo
crumble ['krʌmbl] VT esfarelar ▶ VI (building) desmoronar-se; (plaster, earth) esfacelar-se; (fig) desintegrar-se
crumbly ['krʌmblɪ] ADJ farelento
crummy ['krʌmɪ] (inf) ADJ mixa; (unwell) podre
crumpet ['krʌmpɪt] N bolo leve
crumple ['krʌmpl] VT (paper) amassar; (material) amarrotar
crunch [krʌntʃ] VT (food etc) mastigar; (underfoot) esmagar ▶ N (fig): **the ~** o momento decisivo
crunchy ['krʌntʃɪ] ADJ crocante
crusade [kru:'seɪd] N cruzada; (campaign) campanha ▶ VI (fig): **to ~ for/against** batalhar por/contra
crusader [kru:'seɪdəʳ] N cruzado; (fig): **~ (for)** batalhador(a) m/f (por)
crush [krʌʃ] N (people) esmagamento; (crowd) aglomeração f; (love): **to have a ~ on sb** ter um rabicho por alguém; (drink): **lemon ~** limonada ▶ VT (press) esmagar; (squeeze) espremer; (paper) amassar; (cloth) enrugar; (army, opposition) aniquilar; (hopes) destruir; (person) arrasar
crushing ['krʌʃɪŋ] ADJ (burden) esmagador(a)
crust [krʌst] N côdea; (of bread) casca; (of snow, earth) crosta
crustacean [krʌs'teɪʃən] N crustáceo
crusty ['krʌstɪ] ADJ cascudo
crutch [krʌtʃ] N muleta; (of garment: also: **crotch**) fundilho
crux [krʌks] N ponto crucial

cry [kraɪ] VI chorar; (shout: also: **cry out**) gritar ▶ N grito; (of bird) pio; (of animal) voz f; **to ~ for help** gritar por socorro; **it's a far ~ from ...** (fig) é totalmente diferente de ...
▶ **cry off** VI desistir
crying ['kraɪɪŋ] ADJ (fig) flagrante
crypt [krɪpt] N cripta
cryptic ['krɪptɪk] ADJ enigmático
crystal ['krɪstl] N cristal m
crystal-clear ADJ cristalino, claro
crystallize ['krɪstəlaɪz] VT cristalizar ▶ VI cristalizar-se
CSA N ABBR = **Confederate States of America**
CSC N ABBR (= Civil Service Commission) comissão de recrutamento de funcionários públicos
CSE (BRIT) N ABBR = **Certificate of Secondary Education**
CS gas (BRIT) N gás m CS
CST (US) N ABBR (= Central Standard Time) fuso horário
CT (US) ABBR (Post) = **Connecticut**
ct ABBR = **carat**
cu. ABBR = **cubic**
cub [kʌb] N filhote m; (also: **cub scout**) lobinho
Cuba ['kju:bə] N Cuba
Cuban ['kju:bən] ADJ, N cubano(-a)
cubbyhole ['kʌbɪhəul] N esconderijo
cube [kju:b] N cubo ▶ VT (Math) elevar ao cubo
cube root N raiz f cúbica
cubic ['kju:bɪk] ADJ cúbico; **~ metre** etc metro cúbico etc
cubicle ['kju:bɪkl] N cubículo; (shower cubicle) boxe m
cuckoo ['kuku:] N cuco
cuckoo clock N relógio de cuco
cucumber ['kju:kʌmbəʳ] N pepino
cud [kʌd] N: **to chew the ~** ruminar
cuddle ['kʌdl] VT abraçar ▶ VI abraçar-se
cuddly ['kʌdlɪ] ADJ fofo
cudgel ['kʌdʒəl] N cacete m ▶ VT: **to ~ one's brains** quebrar a cabeça
cue [kju:] N (Snooker) taco; (Theatre etc) deixa
cuff [kʌf] N (of shirt, coat etc) punho; (US: on trousers) bainha; (blow) bofetada ▶ VT esbofetear; **off the ~** de improviso
cuff links NPL abotoaduras fpl
cu. in. ABBR = **cubic inches**
cuisine [kwɪ'zi:n] N cozinha
cul-de-sac ['kʌldəsæk] N beco sem saída
culinary ['kʌlɪnərɪ] ADJ culinário
cull [kʌl] VT (flowers) escolher; (story, idea) escolher, selecionar; (kill) matar seletivamente ▶ N (of animals) matança seletiva
culminate ['kʌlmɪneɪt] VI: **to ~ in** terminar em; (lead to) resultar em
culmination [kʌlmɪ'neɪʃən] N (of career) auge m; (of process) conclusão f
culottes [kju:'lɔts] NPL saia-calça
culpable ['kʌlpəbl] ADJ culpável
culprit ['kʌlprɪt] N culpado(-a)
cult [kʌlt] N culto

cult figure N ídolo
cultivate ['kʌltɪveɪt] VT (*also fig*) cultivar
cultivation [kʌltɪ'veɪʃən] N cultivo; (*fig*) cultura
cultural ['kʌltʃərəl] ADJ cultural
culture ['kʌltʃəʳ] N (*also fig*) cultura
cultured ['kʌltʃəd] ADJ culto
cumbersome ['kʌmbəsəm] ADJ pesado, desajeitado; (*person*) lente, ineficiente
cumin ['kʌmɪn] N cominho
cumulative ['kju:mjulətɪv] ADJ cumulativo
cunning ['kʌnɪŋ] N astúcia ▶ ADJ astuto, malandro; (*device, idea*) engenhoso
cup [kʌp] N xícara (BR), chávena (PT); (*prize, of bra*) taça
cupboard ['kʌbəd] N armário; (*for crockery*) guarda-louça
cup final (BRIT) N final f
Cupid ['kju:pɪd] N Cupido
cupidity [kju:'pɪdɪtɪ] N cupidez f
cupola ['kju:pələ] N cúpula
cuppa ['kʌpə] N (BRIT *inf*): **a ~** um chá
cup tie (BRIT) N jogo eliminatório
curable ['kjuərəbl] ADJ curável
curate ['kjuərɪt] N coadjutor m
curator [kjuə'reɪtəʳ] N diretor(a) m/f
curb [kə:b] VT refrear ▶ N freio; (US) = **kerb**
curdle ['kə:dl] VI coalhar
curds [kə:dz] NPL coalho
cure [kjuəʳ] VT curar ▶ N tratamento, cura; **to be ~d of sth** sarar(-se) de algo
cure-all N (*fig*) panaceia
curfew ['kə:fju:] N toque m de recolher
curio ['kjuərɪəu] N antiguidade f
curiosity [kjuərɪ'ɔsɪtɪ] N curiosidade f
curious ['kjuərɪəs] ADJ (*interested*) curioso; (*nosy*) abelhudo; (*unusual*) estranho
curiously ['kjuərɪəslɪ] ADV curiosamente; **~ enough, ...** por estranho que pareça, ...
curl [kə:l] N (*of hair*) cacho ▶ VT (*hair: loosely*) frisar; (: *tightly*) encrespar; (*paper*) enrolar; (*lip*) torcer ▶ VI (*hair*) encaracolar ▶ **curl up** VI frisar-se; (*person*) encaracolar-se
curler ['kə:ləʳ] N rolo, bobe f
curlew ['kə:lu:] N maçarico
curling ['kə:lɪŋ] N (*Sport*) curling m
curling tongs, (US) **curling irons** NPL ferros mpl de frisar cabelo
curly ['kə:lɪ] ADJ cacheado, crespo
currant ['kʌrnt] N passa de corinto; (*blackcurrant, redcurrant*) groselha
currency ['kʌrnsɪ] N moeda; **foreign ~** câmbio, divisas; **to gain ~** (*fig*) consagrar-se
current ['kʌrnt] N corrente f; (*in river*) correnteza ▶ ADJ corrente; (*present*) atual; (*accepted*) corrente; **in ~ usage** de uso corrente
current account (BRIT) N conta corrente
current affairs NPL atualidades fpl
current assets NPL (*Comm*) ativo corrente
current liabilities NPL (*Comm*) passivo corrente
currently ['kʌrntlɪ] ADV atualmente

curricula [kə'rɪkjulə] NPL *of* **curriculum**
curriculum [kə'rɪkjuləm] (*pl* **curriculums** *or* **curricula**) N programa m de estudos
curriculum vitae [-'vi:taɪ] N currículo
curry ['kʌrɪ] N caril m ▶ VT: **to ~ favour with** captar simpatia de
curry powder N pós mpl de caril, curry m
curse [kə:s] VI xingar (BR), praguejar (PT) ▶ VT (*swear at*) xingar (BR), praguejar a (PT); (*bemoan*) amaldiçoar ▶ N maldição f; (*swearword*) palavrão m (BR), baixo calão m (PT); (*problem*) castigo
cursor ['kə:səʳ] N (*Comput*) cursor m
cursory ['kə:sərɪ] ADJ rápido, superficial
curt [kə:t] ADJ seco, brusco
curtail [kə:'teɪl] VT (*freedom, rights*) restringir; (*visit etc*) abreviar, encurtar; (*expenses etc*) reduzir
curtain ['kə:tn] N cortina; (*Theatre*) pano
curtain call N (*Theatre*) chamada à ribalta
curtain ring N argola
curtsy, curtsey ['kə:tsɪ] N mesura, reverência ▶ VI fazer reverência
curvature ['kə:vətʃəʳ] N curvatura
curve [kə:v] N curva ▶ VT encurvar, torcer ▶ VI encurvar-se, torcer-se; (*road*) fazer (uma) curva
curved [kə:vd] ADJ curvado, curvo
cushion ['kuʃən] N almofada; (*Snooker*) tabela ▶ VT (*seat*) escorar com almofada; (*shock, fall etc*) amortecer
cushy ['kuʃɪ] (*inf*) ADJ: **a ~ job** uma boca; **to have a ~ time** estar na moleza
custard ['kʌstəd] N (*for pouring*) nata, creme m
custard powder (BRIT) N pó m para fazer creme
custodian [kʌs'təudɪən] N guarda m/f
custody ['kʌstədɪ] N custódia; (*for offenders*) prisão f preventiva; **to take into ~** deter
custom ['kʌstəm] N (*tradition*) tradição f; (*convention*) costume m; (*habit*) hábito; (*Comm*) clientela
customary ['kʌstəmərɪ] ADJ costumeiro; **it is ~ to do it** é costume fazê-lo
custom-built ADJ feito sob encomenda
customer ['kʌstəməʳ] N cliente m/f; **he's an awkward ~** (*inf*) ele é um cara difícil
customize ['kʌstəmaɪz] VT personalizar
customized ['kʌstəmaɪzd] ADJ personalizado, feito sob encomenda
custom-made ADJ (*car*) feito sob encomenda; (*clothes*) feito sob medida
customs ['kʌstəmz] NPL alfândega
Customs and Excise (BRIT) N autoridades fpl alfandegárias
customs duty N imposto alfandegário
customs officer N inspetor(a) m/f da alfândega, aduaneiro(-a)
cut [kʌt] (*pt, pp* **cut**) VT cortar; (*price*) baixar; (*record*) gravar; (*reduce*) reduzir; (*inf: class*) matar ▶ VI cortar; (*intersect*) interceptar-se ▶ N corte m; (*in spending*) redução f; (*of garment*) tacho; **cold cuts** NPL (US) frios mpl sortidos;

to ~ a tooth estar com um dente nascendo;
to ~ one's finger cortar o dedo; **to get one's
hair ~** cortar o cabelo; **to ~ sth short**
abreviar algo; **to ~ sb dead** fingir que não
conhece alguém
▶ **cut back** VT (*plants*) podar; (*production,
expenditure*) cortar
▶ **cut down** VT (*tree*) derrubar; (*reduce*) reduzir;
to ~ sb down to size (*fig*) abaixar a crista de
alguém, colocar alguém no seu lugar
▶ **cut in** VI: **to ~ in (on)** interromper; (*Aut*)
cortar
▶ **cut off** VT (*piece, Tel*) cortar; (*person, village*)
isolar; (*supply*) suspender; (*retreat*) impedir;
(*troops*) cercar; **we've been ~ off** (*Tel*) fomos
cortados
▶ **cut out** VT (*shape*) recortar; (*activity etc*)
suprimir; (*remove*) remover
▶ **cut through** VI abrir caminho
▶ **cut up** VT cortar em pedaços
cut-and-dried ADJ (*also:* **cut-and-dry**) todo
resolvido
cutaway ['kʌtəweɪ] ADJ, N: **~ (drawing)** vista
diagramática
cutback ['kʌtbæk] N redução *f*, corte *m*
cute [kju:t] ADJ bonitinho; (*shrewd*) astuto
cut glass N cristal *m* lapidado
cuticle ['kju:tɪkl] N cutícula
cuticle remover N produto para tirar as
cutículas
cutlery ['kʌtlərɪ] N talheres *mpl*
cutlet ['kʌtlɪt] N costeleta
cutoff ['kʌtɔf] N (*also:* **cutoff point**) ponto de
corte
cutoff switch N interruptor *m*
cutout ['kʌtaut] N (*shape*) figura para recortar;
(*switch*) interruptor *m*
cut-price, (US) **cut-rate** ADJ a preço reduzido
cut-throat N assassino(-a) ▶ ADJ feroz
cutting ['kʌtɪŋ] ADJ cortante; (*remark*) mordaz
▶ N (BRIT: *from newspaper*) recorte *m*; (: *Rail*)
corte *m*; (*Cinema*) corte *m*; (*from plant*) muda
cutting edge N (*of knife*) fio de corte; **on** *or* **at
the ~ of** na ponta de
cutting-edge ADJ (*technology, research*) de ponta
cuttlefish ['kʌtlfɪʃ] N sita
cut-up ADJ arrasado, aflito
CV N ABBR = **curriculum vitae**
cwo ABBR (*Comm*) = **cash with order**

cwt ABBR = **hundredweight**
cyanide ['saɪənaɪd] N cianeto
cyber attack ['saɪbərətæk] N ciberataque *m*
cyberbullying ['saɪbəbulɪɪŋ] N cyberbullying,
bullying *m* cibernético
cybercafé ['saɪbəkæfeɪ] N cibercafé *m*
cybernetics [saɪbə'nɛtɪks] N cibernética
cybersecurity [saɪbəsɪ'kjʊrɪtɪ] N
cibersegurança
cyberspace ['saɪbəspeɪs] N ciberespaço
cyclamen ['sɪkləmən] N cíclame *m*
cycle ['saɪkl] N ciclo; (*bicycle*) bicicleta ▶ VI
andar de bicicleta
cycle lane, cycle path N ciclovia *f*
cycle race N corrida de bicicletas
cycle rack N engradado para guardar
bicicletas
cycling ['saɪklɪŋ] N ciclismo
cyclist ['saɪklɪst] N ciclista *m/f*
cyclone ['saɪkləun] N ciclone *m*
cygnet ['sɪgnɪt] N cisne *m* novo
cylinder ['sɪlɪndəʳ] N cilindro; (*of gas*) bujão *m*
cylinder capacity N capacidade *f* cilíndrica,
cilindrada
cylinder head N cilíndrico
cylinder-head gasket N culatra
cymbals ['sɪmblz] NPL pratos *mpl*
cynic ['sɪnɪk] N cínico(-a)
cynical ['sɪnɪkl] ADJ cínico, sarcástico
cynicism ['sɪnɪsɪzəm] N cinismo
CYO (US) N ABBR = **Catholic Youth
Organization**
cypress ['saɪprɪs] N cipreste *m*
Cypriot ['sɪprɪət] ADJ, N cipriota *m/f*
Cyprus ['saɪprəs] N Chipre *f*
cyst [sɪst] N cisto
cystitis [sɪs'taɪtɪs] N cistite *f*
CZ (US) N ABBR (= *Canal Zone*) zona do canal do
Panamá
czar [zɑ:ʳ] N czar *m*
Czech [tʃɛk] ADJ tcheco ▶ N tcheco(-a); (*Ling*)
tcheco
Czechoslovak [tʃɛkə'sləuvæk] ADJ, N
= **Czechoslovakian**
Czechoslovakia [tʃɛkəslə'vækɪə] N
Tchecoslováquia
Czechoslovakian [tʃɛkəslə'vækɪən] ADJ, N
tchecoslovaco(-a)
Czech Republic N: **the ~** a República Tcheca

Dd

D¹, d [di:] N (letter) D, d m; (Mus): **D** ré m; **D for David** (BRIT) or **Dog** (US) D de dado

D² (US) ABBR (Pol) = **democrat; democratic**

d (BRIT) ABBR (old) = **penny**

d. ABBR = **died**

DA (US) N ABBR = **district attorney**

dab [dæb] VT (eyes, wound) tocar (de leve); (paint, cream) aplicar de leve ▶ N (of paint) pincelada; (of liquid) gota; (amount) pequena quantidade f

dabble ['dæbl] VI: **to ~ in** interessar-se por

dachshund ['dækshund] N bassê m

dad [dæd] (inf) N papai m

daddy ['dædɪ] N = **dad**

daddy-long-legs N INV pernilongo

daffodil ['dæfədɪl] N narciso-dos-prados m

daft [dɑːft] ADJ bobo, besta; **to be ~ about** ser louco por

dagger ['dægə'] N punhal m, adaga; **to look ~s at sb** olhar feio para alguém; **to be at ~s drawn with sb** andar às turras com alguém

dahlia ['deɪljə] N dália

daily ['deɪlɪ] ADJ diário ▶ N (paper) jornal m, diário; (BRIT: domestic help) diarista (BR), mulher f a dias (PT) ▶ ADV diariamente; **twice ~** duas vezes por dia

dainty ['deɪntɪ] ADJ delicado; (tasteful) elegante, gracioso

dairy ['dɛərɪ] N leiteria ▶ ADJ (industry) de laticínios; (cattle) leiteiro

dairy cow N vaca leiteira

dairy farm N fazenda de gado leiteiro

dairy products NPL laticínios mpl

dairy store (US) N leiteria

dais ['deɪɪs] N estrado

daisy ['deɪzɪ] N margarida

daisy wheel N (on printer) margarida

daisy-wheel printer N impressora margarida

Dakar ['dækə'] N Dacar

dale [deɪl] (BRIT) N vale m

dally ['dælɪ] VI vadiar

dalmatian [dæl'meɪʃən] N (dog) dálmata m

dam [dæm] N represa, barragem f ▶ VT represar

damage ['dæmɪdʒ] N (physical) danos mpl; (harm) prejuízo; (dents etc) avaria ▶ VT (spoil, break) danificar; (harm) prejudicar; **damages** NPL (Law) indenização f por perdas e danos; **to pay £5,000 in ~s** pagar £5,000 de indenização; **~ to property** danos materiais

damaging ['dæmɪdʒɪŋ] ADJ: **~ (to)** prejudicial (a)

Damascus [də'mɑːskəs] N Damasco

dame [deɪm] N (title) título honorífico dado a uma membra da Ordem do Império Britânico; título honorífico dado à esposa de um cavalheiro ou baronete; (US inf) dona; (Theatre) dama

damn [dæm] VT condenar; (curse) maldizer ▶ N (inf): **I don't give a ~** não dou a mínima, estou me lixando ▶ ADJ (inf: also: **damned**) danado, maldito; **~ (it)!** (que) droga!

damnable ['dæmnəbl] (inf) ADJ (behaviour) condenável; (weather) horrível

damnation [dæm'neɪʃən] N (Rel) danação f ▶ EXCL (inf) droga!

damning ['dæmɪŋ] ADJ (evidence) prejudicial; (criticism) condenador(a)

damp [dæmp] ADJ úmido ▶ N umidade f ▶ VT (also: **dampen**: cloth, rag) umedecer; (: enthusiasm etc) jogar água fria em

dampcourse ['dæmpkɔːs] N impermeabilização f

damper ['dæmpə'] N (Mus) abafador m; (of fire) registro; **to put a ~ on** (fig: atmosphere) criar um mal-estar em; (: party) acabar com a animação de; (: enthusiasm) cortar

dampness ['dæmpnɪs] N umidade f

damson ['dæmzən] N ameixa pequena

dance [dɑːns] N dança; (party etc) baile m ▶ VI dançar; **to ~ about** saltitar

dance hall N salão m de baile

dancer ['dɑːnsə'] N dançarino(-a); (professional) bailarino(-a)

dancing ['dɑːnsɪŋ] N dança

D and C N ABBR (Med: = dilation and curettage) dilatação f e curetagem f

dandelion ['dændɪlaɪən] N dente-de-leão m

dandruff ['dændrəf] N caspa

dandy ['dændɪ] N dândi m ▶ ADJ (US inf) bacana

Dane [deɪn] N dinamarquês(-esa) m/f

danger ['deɪndʒə'] N perigo; (risk) risco; (possibility): **there is a ~ of ...**; **"~!"** (on sign) "perigo!"; **to be in ~ of** correr o risco de; **in ~** em perigo; **out of ~** fora de perigo

danger list N (Med): **on the ~** na lista dos pacientes graves

dangerous [ˈdeɪndʒərəs] ADJ perigoso
dangerously [ˈdeɪndʒərəslɪ] ADV
perigosamente; **~ ill** gravemente doente
danger zone N zona de perigo
dangle [ˈdæŋgl] VT balançar ▸ VI pender
balançando
Danish [ˈdeɪnɪʃ] ADJ dinamarquês(-esa) ▸ N
(Ling) dinamarquês m
Danish pastry N doce m (de massa com frutas)
dank [dæŋk] ADJ frio e úmido
Danube [ˈdænjuːb] N: **the ~** o Danúbio
dapper [ˈdæpəʳ] ADJ garboso; (appearance)
esmerado
dare [dɛəʳ] VT: **to ~ sb to do sth** desafiar
alguém a fazer algo ▸ VI: **to ~ (to) do sth**
atrever-se a fazer algo, ousar fazer algo;
I ~ say (I suppose) acho provável que; **I ~n't
tell him** (BRIT) eu não ouso dizê-lo a ele;
I ~ say he'll turn up acho provável que ele
venha
daredevil [ˈdɛədɛvl] N intrépido, atrevido
Dar-es-Salaam [ˈdɑːrɛssəˈlɑːm] N Dar-es-
Salaam
daring [ˈdɛərɪŋ] ADJ (audacious) audacioso;
(bold) ousado ▸ N atrevimento, audácia,
ousadia; (courage) coragem f, destemor m
dark [dɑːk] ADJ (gen, hair) escuro; (complexion)
moreno; (cheerless) triste, sombrio; (fig)
sombrio ▸ N escuro; **in the ~** no escuro;
in the ~ about (fig) no escuro sobre; **after ~**
depois de escurecer; **it is/is getting ~** está
escuro/está escurecendo
dark chocolate N chocolate m amargo
darken [ˈdɑːkən] VT escurecer; (colour) fazer
mais escuro ▸ VI escurecer(-se)
dark glasses NPL óculos mpl escuros
darkly [ˈdɑːklɪ] ADV (gloomily) sombriamente;
(in a sinister way) sinistramente
darkness [ˈdɑːknɪs] N escuridão f
darkroom N câmara escura
darling [ˈdɑːlɪŋ] ADJ querido ▸ N querido(-a);
(favourite): **to be the ~ of** ser o queridinho de
darn [dɑːn] VT cerzir
dart [dɑːt] N dardo; (in sewing) alinhavo ▸ VI
precipitar-se; **to ~ away/along** ir-se/seguir
precipitadamente
dartboard [ˈdɑːtbɔːd] N alvo (para jogo de
dardos)
darts N (game) jogo de dardos
dash [dæʃ] N (sign) hífen m; (: long) travessão m;
(rush) corria; (small quantity) pontinha ▸ VT
(throw) arremessar; (hopes) frustrar ▸ VI
precipitar-se, correr
▸ **dash away** VI sair apressado
▸ **dash off** VT (letter, essay) escrever a toda ▸ VI
= **dash away**
dashboard [ˈdæʃbɔːd] N painel m de
instrumentos
dashing [ˈdæʃɪŋ] ADJ arrojado
dastardly [ˈdæstədlɪ] ADJ vil
data [ˈdeɪtə] NPL dados mpl
database [ˈdeɪtəbeɪs] N banco de dados
data capture N entrada de dados

data processing N processamento de dados
data transmission N transmissão f de dados
date [deɪt] N (day) data; (with friend) encontro;
(fruit) tâmara; (tree) tamareira ▸ VT datar;
(person) namorar; **what's the ~ today?** que
dia é hoje?; **~ of birth** data de nascimento;
closing ~ data de encerramento; **to ~** até
agora; **out of ~** desatualizado; **up to ~**
(correspondence etc) em dia; (dictionary, phone
book etc) atualizado; (method, technology)
moderno; **to bring up to ~** (correspondence,
person) pôr em dia; (method) modernizar;
letter ~d 5th July (BRIT) or **July 5th** (US)
carta de 5 de julho
dated [ˈdeɪtɪd] ADJ antiquado
dateline [ˈdeɪtlaɪn] N meridiano or linha de
data
date rape N estupro cometido pelo
acompanhante da vítima, geralmente após
encontro romântico
date stamp N carimbo datador
daub [dɔːb] VT borrar
daughter [ˈdɔːtəʳ] N filha
daughter-in-law (pl **daughters-in-law**) N
nora
daunt [dɔːnt] VT desalentar, desencorajar
daunting [ˈdɔːntɪŋ] ADJ desanimador(a)
dauntless [ˈdɔːntlɪs] ADJ intrépido, destemido
dawdle [ˈdɔːdl] VI (waste time) fazer cera;
(go slow) vadiar
dawn [dɔːn] N alvorada, amanhecer m;
(of period, situation) surgimento, início ▸ VI
(day) amanhecer; (fig): **it ~ed on him that ...**
começou a perceber que ...; **at ~** ao
amanhecer; **from ~ to dusk** de manhã à
noite
dawn chorus (BRIT) N canto dos pássaros na
alvorada
day [deɪ] N dia m; (working day) jornada, dia
útil; **the ~ before/after** a véspera/o dia
seguinte; **the ~ before yesterday**
anteontem; **the ~ after tomorrow** depois
de amanhã; **the following ~** o dia seguinte;
(on) **the ~ that ...** (n)o dia em que ...; **~ by ~**
dia a dia; **by ~** de dia; **paid by the ~** pago
por dia; **these ~s, in the present ~** hoje
em dia
daybook [ˈdeɪbuk] (BRIT) N diário
day boy (Sch) N externo
daybreak [ˈdeɪbreɪk] N amanhecer m
day-care centre [ˈdeɪkɛə-] N (for elderly etc)
centro de convivência; (for children) creche f
daydream [ˈdeɪdriːm] N devaneio ▸ VI
devanear
day girl (Sch) N externa
daylight [ˈdeɪlaɪt] N luz f (do dia)
Daylight Saving Time (US) N hora de verão
day release N: **to be on ~** ter licença de um
dia por semana para fins de
aperfeiçoamento profissional
day return (BRIT) N (ticket) bilhete m de ida e
volta no mesmo dia
day shift N turno diurno

daytime ['deɪtaɪm] N dia *m* ▸ ADJ de dia, diurno

day-to-day ADJ (*life, expenses*) cotidiano; **the ~ routine** o dia-a-dia; **on a ~ basis** dia a dia, diariamente

day trip N excursão *f* (de um dia)

day tripper N excursionista *m/f*

daze [deɪz] VT (*stun*) aturdir ▸ N: **in a ~** aturdido

dazzle ['dæzl] VT (*bewitch*) deslumbrar; (*blind*) ofuscar

dazzling ['dæzlɪŋ] ADJ deslumbrante, ofuscante

DC ABBR (*Elec*) = **direct current**; (*US Post*) = **District of Columbia**

DD N ABBR (= *Doctor of Divinity*) título universitário

dd. ABBR (*Comm*: = *delivered*) entregue

D/D ABBR = **direct debit**

D-day ['di:deɪ] N o dia D

DDS (*US*) N ABBR (= *Doctor of Dental Science, Doctor of Dental Surgery*) títulos universitários

DDT N ABBR (= *dichlorodiphenyltrichloroethane*) DDT *m*

DE (*US*) ABBR (*Post*) = **Delaware**

DEA (*US*) N ABBR (= *Drug Enforcement Administration*) ≈ Conselho Nacional de Entorpecentes

deacon ['di:kən] N diácono

dead [dɛd] ADJ morto; (*deceased*) falecido; (*numb*) dormente; (*telephone*) cortado; (*Elec*) sem corrente ▸ ADV (*very*) totalmente; (*completely*) completamente; (*exactly*) absolutamente ▸ NPL: **the ~** os mortos; **to shoot sb ~** matar alguém a tiro; **the line has gone ~** (*Tel*) caiu a ligação; **~ tired** morto de cansado; **to stop ~** estacar; **~ on time** na hora em ponto

deaden ['dɛdn] VT (*blow, sound*) amortecer; (*pain*) anestesiar

dead end N beco sem saída ▸ ADJ: **a dead-end job** um emprego sem perspectivas

dead heat N (*Sport*) empate *m*; **to finish in a ~** (*race*) ser empatado

dead-letter office N seção *f* de cartas não reclamadas

deadline ['dɛdlaɪn] N prazo final; **to work to a ~** trabalhar com prazo estabelecido

deadlock ['dɛdlɔk] N impasse *m*

dead loss (*inf*) N: **to be a ~** não ser de nada

deadly ['dɛdlɪ] ADJ mortal, fatal; (*weapon*) mortífero ▸ ADV: **~ dull** tediosíssimo, chatíssimo

deadpan [dɛd'pæn] ADJ sem expressão

Dead Sea N: **the ~** o mar Morto

deaf [dɛf] ADJ surdo

deaf-aid (*BRIT*) N aparelho para a surdez

deaf-and-dumb ADJ surdo-mudo; **~ alphabet** alfabeto de surdos-mudos

deafen ['dɛfn] VT ensurdecer

deafening ['dɛfnɪŋ] ADJ ensurdecedor(a)

deaf-mute N surdo-mudo/surda-muda

deafness ['dɛfnɪs] N surdez *f*

deal [di:l] (*pt, pp* **dealt**) N (*agreement*) acordo; (*business*) negócio ▸ VT (*cards, blows*) dar;

to strike a ~ with sb fechar um negócio com alguém; **it's a ~!** (*inf*) negócio fechado; **he got a fair/bad ~ from them** ele foi/não foi bem tratado por eles; **a good** *or* **great ~ (of)** bastante, muito

▸ **deal in** VT FUS (*Comm*) negociar em *or* com

▸ **deal with** VT FUS (*people*) tratar com; (*problem*) ocupar-se de; (*subject*) tratar de; (*Comm*) negociar com; (*punish*) castigar

dealer ['di:lə'] N negociante *m/f*; (*for cars*) concessionário(-a); (*for products*) revendedor(a) *m/f*; (*Cards*) carteador(a) *m/f*, banqueiro(-a)

dealership ['di:ləʃɪp] N concesionária

dealings ['di:lɪŋz] NPL transações *fpl*

dealt [dɛlt] PT, PP *of* **deal**

dean [di:n] N (*Rel*) decano; (*Sch*: *BRIT*) reitor(a) *m/f*; (: *US*) orientador(a) *m/f* de estudos

dear [dɪə'] ADJ querido, caro; (*expensive*) caro ▸ N: **my ~** meu querido/minha querida ▸ EXCL: **~ me!** ai, meu Deus!; **D~ Sir/Madam** (*in letter*) Prezado Senhor/Prezada Senhora (*BR*), Exmo. Senhor/Exma. Senhora (*PT*); **D~ Mr/Mrs X** Prezado Sr. X/Prezada Sra. X

dearly ['dɪəlɪ] ADV (*love*) ternamente; (*pay*) caro

dearth [də:θ] N escassez *f*

death [dɛθ] N morte *f*; (*Admin*) óbito

deathbed ['dɛθbɛd] N leito de morte

death certificate N certidão *f* de óbito

death duties NPL (*BRIT*) impostos *mpl* sobre inventário

deathly ['dɛθlɪ] ADJ (*colour*) pálido; (*silence*) profundo ▸ ADV (*quiet*) completamente

death penalty N pena de morte

death rate N (índice *m* de) mortalidade *f*

death row (*US*) N corredor *m* da morte

death sentence N sentença de morte

death toll N número de mortos (*en acidentes*)

deathtrap ['dɛθtræp] N perigo

deb [dɛb] (*inf*) N ABBR = **debutante**

debacle [deɪ'ba:kl] N fracasso

debar [dɪ'ba:'] VT (*exclude*) excluir; **to ~ sb from doing sth** proibir a alguém fazer algo *or* que faça algo

debase [dɪ'beɪs] VT degradar; (*value*) desvalorizar; (*quality*) piorar

debatable [dɪ'beɪtəbl] ADJ discutível

debate [dɪ'beɪt] N debate *m* ▸ VT debater ▸ VI (*consider*): **to ~ whether** perguntar-se se

debauchery [dɪ'bɔ:tʃərɪ] N decadência

debenture [dɪ'bɛntʃə'] N (*Comm*) debênture *f*

debilitate [dɪ'bɪlɪteɪt] VT debilitar

debit ['dɛbɪt] N débito ▸ VT: **to ~ a sum to sb** *or* **to sb's account** lançar uma quantia ao débito de alguém *or* à conta de alguém; *see also* **direct debit**

debit balance N saldo devedor

debit card N cartão *m* de débito

debit note N nota de débito

debrief [di:'bri:f] VT interrogar

debriefing [di:'bri:fɪŋ] N interrogatório

debris ['dɛbri:] N escombros *mpl*

debt [dɛt] N (*sum*) dívida; (*state*) endividamento; **to be in ~** ter dívidas, estar endividado; **bad ~** dívida incobrável

debt collector N cobrador(a) *m/f* de dívidas

debtor [ˈdɛtəʳ] N devedor(a) *m/f*

debug [ˈdiːˈbʌg] VT (*Comput*) depurar

debunk [diːˈbʌŋk] VT (*myths, ideas*) desmascarar

début [ˈdeɪbjuː] N estreia

debutante [ˈdɛbjutænt] N debutante *f*

Dec. ABBR (= *December*) dez.

decade [ˈdɛkeɪd] N década

decadence [ˈdɛkədəns] N decadência

decadent [ˈdɛkədənt] ADJ decadente

decaf [ˈdiːkæf] (*inf*) N descafeinado *m*

decaffeinated [dɪˈkæfɪneɪtɪd] ADJ descafeinado

decamp [dɪˈkæmp] (*inf*) VI safar-se

decant [dɪˈkænt] VT (*wine*) decantar

decanter [dɪˈkæntəʳ] N garrafa ornamental

decarbonize [diːˈkɑːbənaɪz] VT (*Aut*) descarbonizar

decathlon [dɪˈkæθlən] N decatlo

decay [dɪˈkeɪ] N decadência; (*of building*) ruína; (*fig*) deterioração *f*; (*rotting*) podridão *f*; (*also:* **tooth decay**) cárie *f* ▶ VI (*rot*) apodrecer-se; (*fig*) decair

decease [dɪˈsiːs] N falecimento, óbito

deceased [dɪˈsiːst] N: **the ~** o falecido/a falecida

deceit [dɪˈsiːt] N engano; (*duplicity*) fraude *f*

deceitful [dɪˈsiːtful] ADJ enganador(a)

deceive [dɪˈsiːv] VT enganar

decelerate [diːˈsɛləreɪt] VT moderar a marcha de, desacelerar ▶ VI diminuir a velocidade

December [dɪˈsɛmbəʳ] N dezembro; *see also* **July**

decency [ˈdiːsənsɪ] N decência; (*kindness*) bondade *f*

decent [ˈdiːsənt] ADJ (*proper*) decente; (*kind, honest*) honesto, amável

decently [ˈdiːsəntlɪ] ADV (*respectably*) decentemente; (*kindly*) gentilmente

decentralization [ˈdiːsɛntrəlaɪˈzeɪʃən] N descentralização *f*

decentralize [diːˈsɛntrəlaɪz] VT descentralizar

deception [dɪˈsɛpʃən] N engano; (*deceitful act*) fraude *f*

deceptive [dɪˈsɛptɪv] ADJ enganador(a)

decibel [ˈdɛsɪbɛl] N decibel *m*

decide [dɪˈsaɪd] VT (*person*) convencer; (*question, argument*) resolver ▶ VI decidir; **to ~ to do/that** decidir fazer/que; **to ~ on sth** decidir-se por algo; **to ~ on doing** decidir fazer; **to ~ against doing** decidir não fazer

decided [dɪˈsaɪdɪd] ADJ (*resolute*) decidido; (*clear, definite*) claro, definido

decidedly [dɪˈsaɪdɪdlɪ] ADV (*distinctly*) claramente; (*emphatically*) decididamente

deciding [dɪˈsaɪdɪŋ] ADJ decisivo

deciduous [dɪˈsɪdjuəs] ADJ decíduo

decimal [ˈdɛsɪməl] ADJ decimal ▶ N decimal *m*; **to 3 ~ places** com 3 casas decimais

decimalize [ˈdɛsɪmələaɪz] (BRIT) VT decimalizar

decimal point N vírgula de decimais

decimate [ˈdɛsɪmeɪt] VT dizimar

decipher [dɪˈsaɪfəʳ] VT decifrar

decision [dɪˈsɪʒən] N (*choice*) escolha; (*act of choosing*) decisão *f*; (*decisiveness*) resolução *f*; **to make a ~** tomar uma decisão

decisive [dɪˈsaɪsɪv] ADJ (*action*) decisivo; (*person*) decidido; (*manner, reply*) categórico

deck [dɛk] N (*Naut*) convés *m*; (*of bus*) **top ~** andar *m* de cima; (*of cards*) baralho; **to go up on ~** subir ao convés; **below ~** abaixo do convés principal; **record/cassette ~** toca-discos *m inv*/toca-fitas *m inv*

deck chair N cadeira de lona, espreguiçadeira

deck hand N taifeiro(-a)

declaration [dɛkləˈreɪʃən] N declaração *f*; (*public announcement*) pronunciamento

declare [dɪˈklɛəʳ] VT (*intention*) revelar; (*result*) divulgar; (*income, at customs*) declarar

declassify [diːˈklæsɪfaɪ] VT tornar público

decline [dɪˈklaɪn] N declínio; (*lessening*) diminuição *f*, baixa ▶ VT recusar ▶ VI diminuir; (*fall*) baixar; **~ in living standards** queda dos padrões de vida; **to ~ to do sth** recusar-se a fazer algo

declutch [ˈdiːˈklʌtʃ] (BRIT) VI debrear

decode [diːˈkəud] VT decifrar; (*TV signal etc*) decodificar

decoder [diːˈkəudəʳ] N decodificador *m*

decompose [diːkəmˈpəuz] VI decompor-se

decomposition [diːkɔmpəˈzɪʃən] N decomposição *f*

decompression [diːkəmˈprɛʃən] N descompressão *f*

decompression chamber N câmara de descompressão

decongestant [diːkənˈdʒɛstənt] N descongestionante *m*

decontaminate [diːkənˈtæmɪneɪt] VT descontaminar

decontrol [diːkənˈtrəul] VT (*prices etc*) liberar

décor [ˈdeɪkɔːʳ] N decoração *f*; (*Theatre*) cenário

decorate [ˈdɛkəreɪt] VT (*adorn*): **to ~ (with)** adornar (com); (*give medal to*) condecorar; (*paint*) pintar; (*paper*) decorar com papel

decoration [dɛkəˈreɪʃən] N decoração *f*, adorno; (*on tree, dress etc*) enfeite *m*; (*act*) decoração; (*medal*) condecoração *f*

decorative [ˈdɛkərətɪv] ADJ decorativo

decorator [ˈdɛkəreɪtəʳ] N (*painter*) pintor(a) *m/f*

decorum [dɪˈkɔːrəm] N decoro

decoy [ˈdiːkɔɪ] N engodo, chamariz *m*

decrease [n ˈdiːkriːs, vt, vi diːˈkriːs] N: **~ (in)** diminuição *f* (de) ▶ VT reduzir ▶ VI diminuir; **to be on the ~** estar diminuindo

decreasing [diːˈkriːsɪŋ] ADJ decrescente

decree [dɪˈkriː] N decreto ▶ VT: **to ~ (that)** decretar (que); **~ absolute** sentença final de divórcio

decree nisi N ordem *f* provisória de divórcio

decrepit [dɪˈkrɛpɪt] ADJ decrépito; (*building*) (que está) caindo aos pedaços

decry [dɪ'kraɪ] VT execrar; (*disparage*) denegrir

decrypt [di:'krɪpt] VT (*Comput, Tel*) desencriptar

dedicate ['dɛdɪkeɪt] VT dedicar

dedicated ['dɛdɪkeɪtɪd] ADJ (*person, Comput*) dedicado; **~ word processor** processador *m* de texto dedicado

dedication [dɛdɪ'keɪʃən] N (*devotion*) dedicação *f*; (*in book*) dedicatória; (*on radio*) mensagem *f*

deduce [dɪ'dju:s] VT deduzir

deduct [dɪ'dʌkt] VT deduzir; (*from wage etc*) descontar

deduction [dɪ'dʌkʃən] N (*deducting*) redução *f*; (*amount*) subtração *f*; (*deducing*) dedução *f*; (*from wage etc*) desconto; (*conclusion*) conclusão *f*, dedução *f*

deed [di:d] N feito; (*Law*) escritura, título

deed of covenant N escritura de transferência

deem [di:m] VT julgar, estimar; **to ~ it wise to do** julgar prudente fazer

deep [di:p] ADJ profundo; (*in measurements*) de profundidade; (*voice*) baixo, grave; (*person*) fechado; (*breath*) fundo; (*colour*) forte, carregado ▶ ADV: **the spectators stood 20 ~** havia 20 fileiras de espectadores; **knee-~ in water** com água até os joelhos; **to be 4 metres ~** ter 4 metros de profundidade; **he took a ~ breath** ele respirou fundo

deepen ['di:pən] VT aprofundar ▶ VI (*mystery*) aumentar

deep-freeze N congelador *m*, freezer *m* (BR)

deep-fry VT fritar em recipiente fundo

deeply ['di:plɪ] ADV (*breathe*) fundo; (*interested, moved*) profundamente

deep-rooted [-'ru:tɪd] ADJ (*prejudice*) enraizado; (*affection*) profundo

deep-sea diver N escafandrista *m/f*

deep-sea diving N mergulho com escafandro

deep-sea fishing N pesca de alto-mar

deep-seated [-'si:tɪd] ADJ (*beliefs etc*) arraigado

deep-set ADJ (*eyes*) fundo

deer [dɪər] N INV veado, cervo

deerskin ['dɪəskɪn] N camurça, pele *f* de cervo

deerstalker ['dɪəstɔ:kər] N *tipo de chapéu como o de Sherlock Holmes*

deface [dɪ'feɪs] VT desfigurar

defamation [dɛfə'meɪʃən] N difamação *f*

defamatory [dɪ'fæmətrɪ] ADJ difamatório

default [dɪ'fɔ:lt] VI (*Law*) inadimplir; (*Sport*) não comparecer ▶ N (*Comput*) default *m*, padrão *m*; **by ~** (*win*) por desistência; (*Law*) à revelia; (*Sport*) por ausência; **to ~ on a debt** deixar de pagar uma dívida

defaulter [dɪ'fɔ:ltər] N (*in debt*) devedor(a) *m/f* inadimplente

default option N (*Comput*) opção *f* padrão

defeat [dɪ'fi:t] N derrota; (*failure*) malogro ▶ VT derrotar, vencer; (*fig: efforts*) frustrar

defeatism [dɪ'fi:tɪzm] N derrotismo

defeatist [dɪ'fi:tɪst] ADJ, N derrotista *m/f*

defect [*n* 'di:fɛkt, *vi* dɪ'fɛkt] N defeito ▶ VI: **to ~ to the enemy** desertar para se juntar

ao inimigo; **physical/mental ~** defeito físico/mental

defective [dɪ'fɛktɪv] ADJ defeituoso

defector [dɪ'fɛktər] N trânsfuga *m/f*

defence, (US) **defense** [dɪ'fɛns] N defesa; **in ~ of** em defesa de; **witness for the ~** testemunha de defesa; **the Ministry of D~** (BRIT), **the Department of Defense** (US) o Ministério da Defesa

defenceless [dɪ'fɛnslɪs] ADJ indefeso

defend [dɪ'fɛnd] VT defender; (*Law*) contestar

defendant [dɪ'fɛndənt] N acusado(-a); (*in civil case*) réu/ré *m/f*

defender [dɪ'fɛndər] N defensor(a) *m/f*; (*Sport*) defesa

defending champion [dɪ'fɛndɪŋ-] N (*Sport*) atual campeão(-peã) *m/f*

defending counsel [dɪ'fɛndɪŋ-] N (*Law*) advogado(-a) de defesa

defense [dɪ'fɛns] (US) N = **defence**

defensive [dɪ'fɛnsɪv] ADJ defensivo ▶ N: **on the ~** na defensiva

defer [dɪ'fə:r] VT (*postpone*) adiar ▶ VI (*submit*): **to ~ to** submeter-se a

deference ['dɛfərəns] N deferência; **out of** or **in ~ to** por or em deferência a

defiance [dɪ'faɪəns] N desafio; (*rebellion*) rebeldia; **in ~ of** sem respeito por; (*despite*) a despeito de

defiant [dɪ'faɪənt] ADJ (*insolent*) desafiante, insolente; (*challenging*) desafiador(a)

defiantly [dɪ'faɪəntlɪ] ADV desafiadoramente

deficiency [dɪ'fɪʃənsɪ] N (*lack*) deficiência, falta; (*defect*) defeito; (*Comm*) déficit *m*

deficiency disease N doença de carência

deficient [dɪ'fɪʃənt] ADJ (*inadequate*) deficiente; (*incomplete*) incompleto; (*defective*) imperfeito; (*defective*): **~ in** falto de, carente de

deficit ['dɛfɪsɪt] N déficit *m*

define [dɪ'faɪl] VT (*memory*) desonrar; (*statue etc*) profanar ▶ VI desfilar ▶ N desfile *m*

define [dɪ'faɪn] VT definir

definite ['dɛfɪnɪt] ADJ (*fixed*) definitivo; (*clear, obvious*) claro, categórico; (*certain*) certo; (*Ling*) definido; **he was ~ about it** ele foi categórico

definitely ['dɛfɪnɪtlɪ] ADV sem dúvida

definition [dɛfɪ'nɪʃən] N definição *f*

definitive [dɪ'fɪnɪtɪv] ADJ conclusivo

deflate [di:'fleɪt] VT esvaziar; (*person*) fazer perder o rebolado; (*Econ*) deflacionar

deflation [di:'fleɪʃən] N (*Econ*) deflação *f*

deflationary [di:'fleɪʃənrɪ] ADJ (*Econ*) deflacionário

deflect [dɪ'flɛkt] VT desviar

defog ['di:'fɔg] (US) VT desembaçar

defogger ['di:'fɔgər] (US) N (*Aut*) desembaçador *m*

deform [dɪ'fɔ:m] VT distorcer

deformed [dɪ'fɔ:md] ADJ deformado

deformity [dɪ'fɔ:mɪtɪ] N deformidade *f*

defraud [dɪ'frɔːd] VT: **to ~ sb (of sth)** trapacear alguém (por causa de algo)

defray [dɪ'freɪ] VT (*costs, expenses*) correr com

defriend [diː'frɛnd] VT (*on social network*) excluir (*em rede social*)

defrost [diː'frɔst] VT descongelar

deft [dɛft] ADJ (*hands*) destro; (*movement*) hábil

defunct [dɪ'fʌŋkt] ADJ extinto

defuse [diː'fjuːz] VT tirar o estopim *or* a espoleta de; (*situation*) neutralizar

defy [dɪ'faɪ] VT desafiar; (*resist*) opor-se a; (*order*) desobedecer

degenerate [vi dɪ'dʒɛnəreɪt, adj dɪ'dʒɛnərɪt] VI deteriorar ▶ ADJ degenerado

degradation [dɛgrə'deɪʃən] N degradação f

degrade [dɪ'greɪd] VT degradar

degrading [dɪ'greɪdɪŋ] ADJ degradante

degree [dɪ'griː] N grau m; (*Sch*) diploma m, título; **~ in maths** formatura em matemática; **10 ~s below (zero)** 10 graus abaixo de zero; **a considerable ~ of risk** um grau considerável de risco; **by ~s** (*gradually*) pouco a pouco; **to some ~, to a certain ~** até certo ponto

dehydrated [diːhaɪ'dreɪtɪd] ADJ desidratado; (*milk*) em pó

dehydration [diːhaɪ'dreɪʃən] N desidratação f

de-ice VT (*windscreen*) descongelar

de-icer [-'aɪsər] N descongelador m

deign [deɪn] VI: **to ~ to do** dignar-se a fazer

deity ['diːɪtɪ] N divindade f, deidade f

dejected [dɪ'dʒɛktɪd] ADJ (*depressed*) deprimido; (*face*) triste

dejection [dɪ'dʒɛkʃən] N desânimo

del. ABBR = **delete**

delay [dɪ'leɪ] VT (*decision etc*) retardar, atrasar; (*train, person*) atrasar ▶ VI hesitar ▶ N demora; (*postponement*) adiamento; **to be ~ed** estar atrasado; **without ~** sem demora *or* atraso

delayed-action [dɪ'leɪd-] ADJ de retardo, de ação retardada

delectable [dɪ'lɛktəbl] ADJ (*person*) gostoso; (*food*) delicioso

delegate [n 'dɛlɪgɪt, vt 'dɛlɪgeɪt] N delegado(-a) ▶ VT (*person*) autorizar; (*task*) delegar; **to ~ sth to sb/sb to do sth** delegar algo a alguém/alguém para fazer algo

delegation [dɛlɪ'geɪʃən] N (*group*) delegação f; (*by leader*) autorização f

delete [dɪ'liːt] VT eliminar, riscar; (*Comput*) deletar, excluir

Delhi ['dɛlɪ] N Délhi

deliberate [adj dɪ'lɪbərɪt, vi dɪ'lɪbəreɪt] ADJ (*intentional*) intencional; (*slow*) pausado, lento ▶ VI deliberar; (*consider*) considerar

deliberately [dɪ'lɪbərɪtlɪ] ADV (*on purpose*) de propósito; (*slowly*) lentamente

deliberation [dɪlɪbə'reɪʃən] N deliberação f

delicacy ['dɛlɪkəsɪ] N delicadeza; (*of problem*) dificuldade f; (*choice food*) iguaria

delicate ['dɛlɪkɪt] ADJ delicado; (*health*) frágil; (*skilled*) fino

delicately ['dɛlɪkɪtlɪ] ADV delicadamente

delicatessen [dɛlɪkə'tɛsn] N delicatessen m

delicious [dɪ'lɪʃəs] ADJ delicioso; (*food*) saboroso

delight [dɪ'laɪt] N (*feeling*) prazer m, deleite m; (*person*) encanto; (*experience*) delícia ▶ VT encantar, deleitar; **to take (a) ~ in** deleitar-se com

delighted [dɪ'laɪtɪd] ADJ: **~ (at** or **with sth)** encantado (com algo); **to be ~ to do sth/ that** ter muito prazer em fazer algo/ficar muito contente que; **I'd be ~** eu adoraria

delightful [dɪ'laɪtful] ADJ encantador(a), delicioso

delimit [diː'lɪmɪt] VT delimitar

delineate [dɪ'lɪnɪeɪt] VT delinear; (*fig: describe*) descrever, definir

delinquency [dɪ'lɪŋkwənsɪ] N delinquência

delinquent [dɪ'lɪŋkwənt] ADJ, N delinquente m/f

delirious [dɪ'lɪrɪəs] ADJ delirante; **to be ~** delirar

delirium [dɪ'lɪrɪəm] N delírio

deliver [dɪ'lɪvər] VT (*distribute*) distribuir; (*hand over*) entregar; (*message*) comunicar; (*speech*) proferir; (*free*) livrar; (*Med*) partejar; **to ~ the goods** (*fig*) dar conta do recado

deliverance [dɪ'lɪvrəns] N libertação f, livramento

delivery [dɪ'lɪvərɪ] N entrega; (*of mail*) distribuição f; (*of speaker*) enunciação f; (*Med*) parto; **to take ~ of** receber

delivery note N guia *or* nota de entrega

delivery van, (*US*) **delivery truck** N furgão m de entrega

delta ['dɛltə] N delta m

delude [dɪ'luːd] VT iludir, enganar; **to ~ o.s.** iludir-se

deluge ['dɛljuːdʒ] N dilúvio; (*fig*) enxurrada ▶ VT (*fig*): **to ~ (with)** inundar (de)

delusion [dɪ'luːʒən] N ilusão f; **to have ~s of grandeur** ter mania de grandeza

de luxe [də'lʌks] ADJ de luxo

delve [dɛlv] VI: **to ~ into** (*subject*) investigar, pesquisar; (*cupboard etc*) vasculhar

Dem. (*US*) ABBR (*Pol*) = **democrat**; = **democratic**

demagogue ['dɛməgɔg] N demagogo(-a)

demand [dɪ'mɑːnd] VT exigir; (*rights*) reivindicar, reclamar ▶ N exigência; (*claim*) reivindicação f; (*Econ*) procura; **to ~ sth (from** or **of sb)** exigir algo (de alguém); **to be in ~** estar em demanda; **on ~** à vista

demanding [dɪ'mɑːndɪŋ] ADJ (*boss*) exigente; (*work*) absorvente

demarcation [diːmɑː'keɪʃən] N demarcação f

demarcation dispute N (*Industry*) dissídio coletivo

demean [dɪ'miːn] VT: **to ~ o.s.** rebaixar-se

demeanour, (*US*) **demeanor** [dɪ'miːnər] N conduta, comportamento

demented [dɪ'mɛntɪd] ADJ demente, doido

demilitarized zone [diː'mɪlɪtəraɪzd-] N zona desmilitarizada

demise [dɪ'maɪz] N falecimento
demist [di:'mɪst] (BRIT) VT desembaçar
demister [di:'mɪstə^r] (BRIT) N (Aut) desembaçador m de para-brisa
demo ['dɛməu] (inf) N ABBR (= demonstration) passeata
demobilize [di:'məubɪlaɪz] VT desmobilizar
democracy [dɪ'mɔkrəsɪ] N democracia
democrat ['dɛməkræt] N democrata m/f
democratic [dɛmə'krætɪk] ADJ democrático
demography [dɪ'mɔgraəfɪ] N demografia
demolish [dɪ'mɔlɪʃ] VT demolir, derrubar; (fig: argument) refutar, contestar
demolition [dɛmə'lɪʃən] N demolição f; (of argument) contestação f
demon ['di:mən] N demônio ▶ CPD: **a ~ squash player** um(a) craque em squash
demonstrate ['dɛmənstreɪt] VT demonstrar ▶ VI: **to ~ (for/against)** manifestar-se (a favor de/contra)
demonstration [dɛmən'streɪʃən] N (Pol) manifestação f; (: march) passeata; (proof) demonstração f; (exhibition) exibição f; **to hold a ~** realizar uma passeata
demonstrative [dɪ'mɔnstrətɪv] ADJ demonstrativo
demonstrator ['dɛmənstreɪtə^r] N (Pol) manifestante m/f; (Comm: sales person) demonstrador(a) m/f; (: car, computer etc) modelo de demonstração
demoralize [dɪ'mɔrəlaɪz] VT desmoralizar
demote [dɪ'məut] VT rebaixar de posto
demotion [dɪ'məuʃən] N rebaixamento
demur [dɪ'mə:^r] VI: **to ~ (at sth)** objetar (a algo), opor-se (a algo) ▶ N: **without ~** sem objeção
demure [dɪ'mjuə^r] ADJ recatado
demurrage [dɪ'mʌrɪdʒ] N sobre-estadia
den [dɛn] N (of animal) covil m; (of thieves) antro, esconderijo; (room) aposento privado, cantinho
denationalization ['di:næʃnəlaɪ'zeɪʃən] N desnacionalização f, desestatização f
denationalize [di:'næʃnəlaɪz] VT desnacionalizar, desestatizar
denial [dɪ'naɪəl] N refutação f; (refusal) negativa, (of report etc) desmentido
denier ['dɛnɪə^r] N denier m; **15 ~ stockings** meias de 15 denieres
denigrate ['dɛnɪgreɪt] VT denegrir
denim ['dɛnɪm] N brim m, zuarte m; **denims** NPL jeans m (BR), jeans mpl (PT)
denim jacket N jaqueta de brim
denizen ['dɛnɪzn] N habitante m/f
Denmark ['dɛnmɑːk] N Dinamarca
denomination [dɪnɔmɪ'neɪʃən] N valor m, denominação f; (Rel) confissão f, seita
denominator [dɪ'nɔmɪneɪtə^r] N denominador m
denote [dɪ'nəut] VT (indicate) denotar, indicar; (represent) representar; (mean) significar
denounce [dɪ'nauns] VT denunciar
dense [dɛns] ADJ (crowd) denso; (smoke, foliage etc) denso, espesso; (inf: stupid) estúpido, bronco

densely ['dɛnslɪ] ADV: **~ populated** com grande densidade de população; **~ wooded** coberto de florestas densas
density ['dɛnsɪtɪ] N densidade f
dent [dɛnt] N amolgadura, depressão f ▶ VT (also: **make a dent in**) amolgar, dentar; **to make a ~ in** (fig) reduzir
dental ['dɛntl] ADJ (treatment) dentário; (hygiene) dental
dental floss [-flɔs] N fio dental
dental surgeon N cirurgião(-giã) m/f dentista
dentist ['dɛntɪst] N dentista m/f; **~'s surgery** (BRIT) consultório dentário
dentistry ['dɛntɪstrɪ] N odontologia
dentures ['dɛntʃəz] NPL dentadura
denunciation [dɪnʌnsɪ'eɪʃən] N denúncia
deny [dɪ'naɪ] VT negar; (report) desmentir; (refuse) recusar; **he denies having said it** ele nega ter dito isso
deodorant [di:'əudərənt] N desodorante m (BR), desodorizante m (PT)
depart [dɪ'pɑːt] VI ir-se, partir; (train etc) sair; **to ~ from** (fig: differ from) afastar-se de
department [dɪ'pɑːtmənt] N (Sch) departamento; (Comm) seção f; (Pol) repartição f; **that's not my ~** (fig) este não é o meu departamento; **D~ of State** (US) Departamento de Estado
departmental [di:pɑːt'mɛntl] ADJ departamental; **~ manager** chefe m/f de serviço
department store N magazine m (BR), grande armazém m (PT)
departure [dɪ'pɑːtʃə^r] N partida, ida; (of train etc, of employee) saída; (fig): **~ from** afastamento de; **a new ~** uma nova orientação
departure lounge N sala de embarque
departures board, (US) **departure board** N horário de saídas
depend [dɪ'pɛnd] VI: **to ~ (up)on** depender de; (rely on) contar com; **it ~s** depende; **~ing on the result …** dependendo do resultado …
dependable [dɪ'pɛndəbl] ADJ (person) de confiança, seguro; (watch, car) confiável
dependant [dɪ'pɛndənt] N dependente m/f
dependence [dɪ'pɛndəns] N dependência
dependent [dɪ'pɛndənt] ADJ: **to be ~ (on)** depender (de), ser dependente (de) ▶ N = **dependant**
depict [dɪ'pɪkt] VT (in picture) retratar, representar; (describe) descrever
depilatory [dɪ'pɪlətrɪ] N (also: **depilatory cream**) depilatório
depleted [dɪ'pli:tɪd] ADJ esgotado
deplorable [dɪ'plɔːrəbl] ADJ (disgraceful) deplorável; (regrettable) lamentável
deplore [dɪ'plɔː^r] VT (condemn) deplorar; (regret) lamentar
deploy [dɪ'plɔɪ] VT dispor; (missiles) instalar
depopulate [di:'pɔpjuleɪt] VT despovoar

d

depopulation ['di:pɔpju'leɪʃən] N despovoamento
deport [dɪ'pɔ:t] VT deportar
deportation [dɪpɔ:'teɪʃən] N deportação f
deportation order N ordem f de deportação
deportment [dɪ'pɔ:tmənt] N comportamento; (way of walking) modo de andar
depose [dɪ'pəuz] VT depor
deposit [dɪ'pɔzɪt] N (Comm, Geo) depósito; (Chem) sedimento; (of ore, oil) jazida; (down payment) sinal m; (for hired goods etc) caução f ▸ VT depositar; (luggage) guardar; **to put down a ~ of £50** pagar um sinal de £50
deposit account N conta de depósito a prazo
depositor [dɪ'pɔzɪtər] N depositante m/f
depository [dɪ'pɔzɪtərɪ] N (person) depositário(-a); (place) depósito
depot ['dɛpəu] N (storehouse) depósito, armazém m; (for vehicles) garagem f, parque m; (US) estação f
depraved [dɪ'preɪvd] ADJ depravado, viciado
depravity [dɪ'prævɪtɪ] N depravação f, vício
deprecate ['dɛprɪkeɪt] VT desaprovar
deprecating ['dɛprɪkeɪtɪŋ] ADJ desaprovador(a)
depreciate [dɪ'pri:ʃɪeɪt] VT depreciar ▸ VI depreciar-se, desvalorizar-se
depreciation [dɪpri:ʃɪ'eɪʃən] N depreciação f
depress [dɪ'prɛs] VT deprimir; (press down) apertar
depressant [dɪ'prɛsnt] N (Med) depressor m
depressed [dɪ'prɛst] ADJ (person) deprimido; (area, market, trade) em depressão
depressing [dɪ'prɛsɪŋ] ADJ deprimente
depression [dɪ'prɛʃən] N (also Econ) depressão f; (hollow) achatamento
deprivation [dɛprɪ'veɪʃən] N privação f; (loss) perda
deprive [dɪ'praɪv] VT: **to ~ sb of** privar alguém de
deprived [dɪ'praɪvd] ADJ carente
dept. ABBR (= department) depto.
depth [dɛpθ] N profundidade f; (of feeling) intensidade f; (of room etc) comprimento; **in the ~s of despair** no auge do desespero; **at a ~ of 3 metres** a uma profundidade de 3 metros; **to be out of one's ~** (BRIT: swimmer) estar sem pé; (fig) estar voando; **to study sth in ~** estudar algo em profundidade
depth charge N carga de profundidade
deputation [dɛpju'teɪʃən] N delegação f
deputize ['dɛpjutaɪz] VI: **to ~ for sb** substituir alguém
deputy ['dɛpjutɪ] ADJ: **~ chairman** vice-presidente(-a) m/f ▸ N (assistant) adjunto; (replacement) substituto(-a), suplente m/f; (Pol: MP) deputado(-a); (second in command) vice m/f
deputy head (BRIT) N (Sch) diretor adjunto/diretora adjunta m/f
deputy leader (BRIT) N (Pol) vice-líder m/f
derail [dɪ'reɪl] VT descarrilhar; **to be ~ed** descarrilhar

derailment [dɪ'reɪlmənt] N descarrilhamento
deranged [dɪ'reɪndʒd] ADJ (person) louco, transtornado
derby ['də:bɪ] (US) N chapéu-coco
deregulate [dɪ'regjuleɪt] VT liberar
deregulation [dɪ'regju'leɪʃən] N liberação f
derelict ['dɛrɪlɪkt] ADJ abandonado
deride [dɪ'raɪd] VT ridicularizar, zombar de
derision [dɪ'rɪʒən] N irrisão f, escárnio
derisive [dɪ'raɪsɪv] ADJ zombeteiro
derisory [dɪ'raɪsərɪ] ADJ (sum) irrisório; (person, smile) zombeteiro
derivation [dɛrɪ'veɪʃən] N derivação f
derivative [dɪ'rɪvətɪv] N derivado ▸ ADJ derivado; (work) pouco original
derive [dɪ'raɪv] VT: **to ~ (from)** obter or tirar (de) ▸ VI: **to ~ from** derivar-se de
dermatitis [də:mə'taɪtɪs] N dermatite f
dermatology [də:mə'tɔlədʒɪ] N dermatologia
derogatory [dɪ'rɔgətərɪ] ADJ depreciativo
derrick ['dɛrɪk] N (crane) guindaste m; (oil derrick) torre f de perfurar
derv [də:v] (BRIT) N gasóleo
DES (BRIT) N ABBR (= Department of Education and Science) Ministério da Educação e das Ciências
desalination [di:sælɪ'neɪʃən] N dessalinização f
descend [dɪ'sɛnd] VT, VI descer; **to ~ from** descer de; **to ~ to** descambar em; **in ~ing order** em ordem decrescente
▸ **descend on** VT FUS (subj: enemy, angry person) cair sobre; (: misfortune) abater-se sobre; (: gloom, silence) invadir; **visitors ~ed (up)on us** visitas invadiram nossa casa
descendant [dɪ'sɛndənt] N descendente m/f
descent [dɪ'sɛnt] N (descida); (slope) declive m, ladeira; (origin) descendência
describe [dɪs'kraɪb] VT descrever
description [dɪs'krɪpʃən] N descrição f; (sort) classe f, espécie f; **of every ~** de toda a sorte, de todo o tipo
descriptive [dɪs'krɪptɪv] ADJ descritivo
desecrate ['dɛsɪkreɪt] VT profanar
desert [n 'dɛzət, vt, vi dɪ'zə:t] N deserto ▸ VT (place) desertar; (partner, family) abandonar ▸ VI (Mil) desertar
deserter [dɪ'zə:tər] N desertor m
desertion [dɪ'zə:ʃən] N (Mil) deserção f; (Law) abandono do lar
desert island N ilha deserta
deserts [dɪ'zə:ts] NPL: **to get one's just ~** receber o que merece
deserve [dɪ'zə:v] VT merecer
deservedly [dɪ'zə:vɪdlɪ] ADJ merecidamente
deserving [dɪ'zə:vɪŋ] ADJ (person) merecedor(a), digno; (action, cause) meritório
desiccated ['dɛsɪkeɪtɪd] ADJ dessecado
design [dɪ'zaɪn] N (sketch) desenho, esboço; (layout, shape) plano, projeto; (pattern) desenho, padrão m; (of dress, car etc) modelo; (art) design m; (intention) propósito, intenção f ▸ VT desenhar; (plan) projetar; **to have ~s on** ter a mira em; **well-~ed** bem projetado; **to**

be ~ed for sb/sth (*intended*) ser destinado a alguém/algo

designate [*vt* 'dɛzɪgneɪt, *adj* 'dɛzɪgnɪt] VT (*point to*) apontar; (*appoint*) nomear; (*destine*) designar ▶ ADJ designado

designation [dɛzɪg'neɪʃən] N (*appointment*) nomeação f; (*name*) designação f

designer [dɪ'zaɪnəʳ] N (*Art*) artista m/f gráfico(-a); (*Tech*) desenhista m/f, projetista m/f; (*fashion designer*) estilista m/f

desirability [dɪzaɪrə'bɪlɪtɪ] N necessidade f

desirable [dɪ'zaɪərəbl] ADJ (*proper*) desejável; (*attractive*) atraente

desire [dɪ'zaɪəʳ] N anseio; (*sexual*) desejo ▶ VT querer; (*lust after*) desejar, cobiçar; **to ~ to do sth/that** desejar fazer algo/que

desirous [dɪ'zaɪərəs] ADJ: **~ of** desejoso de

desk [dɛsk] N (*in office*) mesa, secretária; (*for pupil*) carteira f; (*at airport*) balcão m; (*in hotel*) recepção f; (*BRIT: in shop, restaurant*) caixa

desk-top publishing N editoração f eletrônica, desktop publishing m

desolate ['dɛsəlɪt] ADJ (*place*) deserto; (*person*) desolado

desolation [dɛsə'leɪʃən] N (*of place*) desolação f; (*of person*) aflição f

despair [dɪs'pɛəʳ] N desesperança ▶ VI: **to ~ of** desesperar-se de; **to be in ~** estar desesperado

despatch [dɪs'pætʃ] N, VT = **dispatch**

desperate ['dɛspərɪt] ADJ desesperado; (*situation*) desesperador(a); **to be ~ for sth/to do** estar louco por algo/para fazer

desperately ['dɛspərɪtlɪ] ADV desesperadamente; (*very: unhappy*) terrivelmente; (*: ill*) gravemente

desperation [dɛspə'reɪʃən] N desespero, desesperança; **in (sheer) ~** desesperado

despicable [dɪs'pɪkəbl] ADJ desprezível

despise [dɪs'paɪz] VT desprezar

despite [dɪs'paɪt] PREP apesar de, a despeito de

despondent [dɪs'pɔndənt] ADJ abatido, desanimado

despot ['dɛspɔt] N déspota m/f

dessert [dɪ'zəːt] N sobremesa

dessertspoon [dɪ'zəːtspuːn] N colher f de sobremesa

destabilize [diː'steɪbɪlaɪz] VT desestabilizar

destination [dɛstɪ'neɪʃən] N destino

destine ['dɛstɪn] VT destinar

destined ['dɛstɪnd] ADJ: **to be ~ to do sth** estar destinado a fazer algo; **~ for** com destino a

destiny ['dɛstɪnɪ] N destino

destitute ['dɛstɪtjuːt] ADJ indigente, necessitado; **~ of** desprovido de

destroy [dɪs'trɔɪ] VT destruir; (*animal*) sacrificar

destroyer [dɪs'trɔɪəʳ] N (*Naut*) contratorpedeiro

destruction [dɪs'trʌkʃən] N destruição f

destructive [dɪs'trʌktɪv] ADJ (*capacity, criticism*) destrutivo; (*force, child*) destruidor(a)

desultory ['dɛsəltərɪ] ADJ (*reading, conversation*) desconexo; (*contact*) irregular

detach [dɪ'tætʃ] VT separar; (*unstick*) desprender

detachable [dɪ'tætʃəbl] ADJ separável; (*Tech*) desmontável

detached [dɪ'tætʃt] ADJ (*attitude*) imparcial, objetivo; (*house*) independente, isolado

detachment [dɪ'tætʃmənt] N distanciamento; (*Mil*) destacamento; (*fig*) objetividade f, imparcialidade f

detail ['diːteɪl] N detalhe m; (*trifle*) bobagem f; (*Mil*) destacamento ▶ VT detalhar; (*Mil*): **to ~ sb (for)** destacar alguém (para); **in ~** pormenorizado, em detalhe; **to go into ~(s)** entrar em detalhes

detailed ['diːteɪld] ADJ detalhado

detain [dɪ'teɪn] VT deter; (*in captivity*) prender; (*in hospital*) hospitalizar

detainee [diːteɪ'niː] N detido(-a)

detect [dɪ'tɛkt] VT perceber; (*Med, Police*) identificar; (*Mil, Radar, Tech*) detectar

detection [dɪ'tɛkʃən] N descoberta; (*Med, Police*) identificação f; (*Mil, Radar, Tech*) detecção f; **to escape ~** evitar ser descoberto; **crime ~** investigação f de crimes

detective [dɪ'tɛktɪv] N detetive m/f; **private ~** detetive particular

detective story N romance m policial

detector [dɪ'tɛktəʳ] N detetor m

detention [dɪ'tɛnʃən] N detenção f, prisão f; (*Sch*) castigo

deter [dɪ'təːʳ] VT (*discourage*) desanimar; (*dissuade*) dissuadir; (*prevent*) impedir

detergent [dɪ'təːdʒənt] N detergente m

deteriorate [dɪ'tɪərɪəreɪt] VI deteriorar-se

deterioration [dɪtɪərɪə'reɪʃən] N deterioração f

determination [dɪtəːmɪ'neɪʃən] N determinação f; (*resolve*) resolução f

determine [dɪ'təːmɪn] VT determinar; (*facts*) descobrir; (*limits etc*) demarcar; **to ~ to do** resolver fazer, determinar-se de fazer

determined [dɪ'təːmɪnd] ADJ (*person*) resoluto; (*quantity*) determinado; (*effort*) grande; **~ to do** decidido a fazer

deterrence [dɪ'tɛrəns] N dissuasão f

deterrent [dɪ'tɛrənt] N dissuasivo

detest [dɪ'tɛst] VT detestar

detestable [dɪ'tɛstəbl] ADJ detestável

detonate ['dɛtəneɪt] VI explodir, estalar ▶ VT detonar

detonator ['dɛtəneɪtəʳ] N detonador m

detour ['diːtuəʳ] N desvio

detract [dɪ'trækt] VI: **to ~ from** (*merits, reputation*) depreciar; (*quality, pleasure*) diminuir

detractor [dɪ'træktəʳ] N detrator(a) m/f

detriment ['dɛtrɪmənt] N: **to the ~ of** em detrimento de; **without ~ to** sem detrimento de

detrimental [dɛtrɪ'mɛntl] ADJ: **~ (to)** prejudicial (a)

deuce [dju:s] N (*Tennis*) empate *m*, iguais
devaluation [dɪvælju'eɪʃən] N
desvalorização *f*
devalue [dɪ'vælju:] VT desvalorizar
devastate ['dɛvəsteɪt] VT devastar; (*fig*): **to be
~d by** estar arrasado com; **he was ~d by the
news** as notícias deixaram-no desolado
devastating ['dɛvəsteɪtɪŋ] ADJ devastador(a);
(*fig*) assolador(a)
devastation [dɛvəs'teɪʃən] N devastação *f*
develop [dɪ'vɛləp] VT desenvolver; (*Phot*)
revelar; (*disease*) contrair; (*resources*) explotar;
(*engine trouble*) começar a ter ▶ VI desenvolver-
se; (*advance*) progredir; (*evolve*) evoluir;
(*appear*) aparecer
developer [dɪ'vɛləpə^r] N (*Phot*) revelador *m*;
(*also*: **property developer**) empresário(-a) de
imóveis
developing country [dɪ'vɛləpɪŋ-] N país *m* em
desenvolvimento
development [dɪ'vɛləpmənt] N
desenvolvimento; (*advance*) progresso; (*of
land*) urbanização *f*
development area N zona a ser urbanizada
deviate ['di:vɪeɪt] VI desviar-se
deviation [di:vɪ'eɪʃən] N desvio
device [dɪ'vaɪs] N (*scheme*) estratagema *m*,
plano; (*apparatus*) aparelho, dispositivo;
explosive ~ dispositivo explosivo
devil ['dɛvl] N diabo
devilish ['dɛvlɪʃ] ADJ diabólico
devil-may-care ADJ despreocupado
devious ['di:vɪəs] ADJ (*means*) intricado,
indireto; (*person*) malandro, esperto
devise [dɪ'vaɪz] VT (*plan*) criar; (*machine*)
inventar
devoid [dɪ'vɔɪd] ADJ: **~ of** destituído de
devolution [di:və'lu:ʃən] N (*Pol*)
descentralização *f*
devolve [dɪ'vɔlv] VI: **to ~ (up)on** passar a ser
da competência de
devote [dɪ'vəut] VT: **to ~ sth to** dedicar algo a
devoted [dɪ'vəutɪd] ADJ (*friendship*) leal;
(*partner*) fiel; **to be ~ to** (*love*) estar devotado
a; **the book is ~ to politics** o livro trata de
política
devotee [dɛvəu'ti:] N adepto(-a), entusiasta
m/f; (*Rel*) devoto
devotion [dɪ'vəuʃən] N devoção *f*; (*to duty*)
dedicação *f*
devour [dɪ'vauə^r] VT devorar
devout [dɪ'vaut] ADJ devoto
dew [dju:] N orvalho
dexterity [dɛks'tɛrɪtɪ] N destreza
dexterous, dextrous ['dɛkstrəs] ADJ destro
dg ABBR (= *decigram*) dg
diabetes [daɪə'bi:ti:z] N diabete *f*
diabetic [daɪə'bɛtɪk] ADJ (*person*) diabético;
(*chocolate, jam*) para diabéticos ▶ N
diabético(-a)
diabolical [daɪə'bɔlɪkl] ADJ diabólico; (*inf*:
dreadful) horrível
diagnose [daɪəg'nəuz] VT diagnosticar

diagnoses [daɪəg'nəsi:z] NPL *of* **diagnosis**
diagnosis [daɪəg'nəusɪs] (*pl* **diagnoses**) N
diagnóstico
diagonal [daɪ'ægənl] ADJ diagonal ▶ N
diagonal *f*
diagram ['daɪəgræm] N diagrama *m*,
esquema *m*
dial ['daɪəl] N disco ▶ VT (*number*) discar (BR),
marcar (PT); **to ~ a wrong number** discar
(BR) *or* marcar (PT) um número errado; **can I
~ London direct?** é possível discar direto
para Londres?
dial. ABBR = **dialect**
dial code (US) N = **dialling code**
dialect ['daɪəlɛkt] N dialeto
dialling code ['daɪəlɪŋ-] (BRIT) N código de
discagem
dialling tone ['daɪəlɪŋ-] (BRIT) N sinal *m* de
discagem (BR) *or* de marcar (PT)
dialogue, (US) **dialog** ['daɪəlɔg] N diálogo;
(*conversation*) conversa
dial tone (US) N = **dialling tone**
dialysis [daɪ'ælɪsɪs] N diálise *f*
diameter [daɪ'æmɪtə^r] N diâmetro
diametrically [daɪə'mɛtrɪklɪ] ADV: **~ opposed
(to)** diametralmente oposto (a)
diamond ['daɪəmənd] N diamante *m*; (*shape*)
losango, rombo; **diamonds** NPL (*Cards*) ouros
mpl
diamond ring N anel *m* de brilhante
diaper ['daɪəpə^r] (US) N fralda
diaphragm ['daɪəfræm] N diafragma *m*
diarrhoea, (US) **diarrhea** [daɪə'ri:ə] N diarreia
diary ['daɪərɪ] N (*daily account*) diário;
(*engagements book*) agenda; **to keep a ~** ter
um diário
diatribe ['daɪətraɪb] N diatribe *f*
dice [daɪs] NPL *of* **die** ▶ N INV dado ▶ VT (*Culin*)
cortar em cubos
dicey ['daɪsɪ] (*inf*) ADJ: **it's a bit ~** é um pouco
arriscado
dichotomy [daɪ'kɔtəmɪ] N dicotomia
Dictaphone® ['dɪktəfəun] N ditafone® *m*,
máquina de ditar
dictate [dɪk'teɪt] VT ditar ▶ VI: **to ~ to** (*person*)
dar ordens a; **I won't be ~d to** não vou
acatar ordens
dictates ['dɪkteɪts] NPL ditames *mpl*
dictation [dɪk'teɪʃən] N ditado; **at ~ speed**
com a velocidade de ditado
dictator [dɪk'teɪtə^r] N ditador(a) *m/f*
dictatorship [dɪk'teɪtəʃɪp] N ditadura
diction ['dɪkʃən] N dicção *f*
dictionary ['dɪkʃənrɪ] N dicionário
did [dɪd] PT *of* **do**
didactic [daɪ'dæktɪk] ADJ didático
didn't ['dɪdnt] = **did not**
die [daɪ] N (*pl* **dice**) dado; (*pl* **dies**) cunho,
molde *m* ▶ VI morrer; (*fig: fade*) murchar; **to ~
of** *or* **from** morrer de; **to be dying for sth/
to do sth** estar louco por algo/para fazer algo
▶ **die away** VI (*sound, light*) extinguir-se
lentamente

▶ **die down** VI (*fire*) apagar-se; (*wind*) abrandar; (*excitement*) diminuir

▶ **die out** VI desaparecer; (*animal, bird*) extinguir-se

diehard ['daɪhɑːd] N reacionário(-a), reaça *m/f* (*inf*)

diesel ['diːzl] N diesel *m*; (*also*: **diesel fuel, diesel oil**) óleo diesel

diesel engine ['diːzəl-] N motor *m* diesel

diesel fuel N óleo diesel

diet ['daɪət] N dieta; (*restricted food*) regime *m* ▶ VI (*also*: **be on a diet**) estar de dieta, fazer regime; **to live on a ~ of** alimentar-se de

dietician [daɪə'tɪʃən] N dietista *m/f*

differ ['dɪfəʳ] VI (*be different*): **to ~ from sth** ser diferente de algo, diferenciar-se de algo; (*disagree*): **to ~ (about)** discordar (sobre)

difference ['dɪfərəns] N diferença; (*disagreement*) divergência; (*quarrel*) desacordo; **it makes no ~ to me** não faz diferença para mim, para mim dá no mesmo; **to settle one's ~s** resolver as diferenças

different ['dɪfərənt] ADJ diferente

differential [dɪfə'rɛnʃəl] N (*Aut*) diferencial *m*; **wage/price ~s** diferenças de salário/preço

differentiate [dɪfə'rɛnʃɪeɪt] VT diferenciar, distinguir ▶ VI: **to ~ (between)** distinguir (entre)

differently ['dɪfərəntlɪ] ADV de outro modo, de forma diferente

difficult ['dɪfɪkəlt] ADJ difícil; **~ to understand** difícil de (se) entender

difficulty ['dɪfɪkəltɪ] N dificuldade *f*; **to have difficulties with** ter problemas com; **to be in ~** estar em dificuldade

diffidence ['dɪfɪdəns] N timidez *f*

diffident ['dɪfɪdənt] ADJ tímido

diffuse [*adj* dɪ'fjuːs, *vt* dɪ'fjuːz] ADJ difuso ▶ VT difundir

dig [dɪg] (*pt, pp* **dug**) VT (*hole, garden*) cavar; (*coal*) escavar; (*nails etc*) cravar ▶ N (*prod*) pontada; (*archaeological*) excavação *f*; (*remark*) alfinetada; **to ~ into one's pockets for sth** enfiar as mãos nos bolsos à procura de algo; **to ~ one's nails into** cravar as unhas em

▶ **dig in** VI (*Mil*) cavar trincheiras; (*inf: eat*) atacar ▶ VT (*compost*) misturar; (*knife, claw*) cravar; **to ~ in one's heels** (*fig*) bater o pé; **~ in!** vai lá!

▶ **dig into** VT FUS (*savings*) gastar

▶ **dig out** VT escavar

▶ **dig up** VT (*plant*) arrancar; (*information*) trazer à tona

digest [*vt* daɪ'dʒɛst, *n* 'daɪdʒɛst] VT (*food*) digerir; (*facts*) assimilar ▶ N sumário

digestible [dɪ'dʒɛstəbl] ADJ digerível

digestion [dɪ'dʒɛstʃən] N digestão *f*

digestive [dɪ'dʒɛstɪv] ADJ digestivo

digit ['dɪdʒɪt] N (*Math*) dígito; (*finger*) dedo

digital ['dɪdʒɪtəl] ADJ digital

digital camera N câmara digital

digital computer N computador *m* digital

digital TV N televisão *f* digital

dignified ['dɪgnɪfaɪd] ADJ digno

dignitary ['dɪgnɪtərɪ] N dignitário(-a)

dignity ['dɪgnɪtɪ] N dignidade *f*

digress [daɪ'grɛs] VI: **to ~ from** afastar-se de

digression [daɪ'grɛʃən] N digressão *f*

digs [dɪgz] (BRIT *inf*) NPL pensão *f*, alojamento

dike [daɪk] N = **dyke**

dilapidated [dɪ'læpɪdeɪtɪd] ADJ arruinado

dilate [daɪ'leɪt] VT dilatar ▶ VI dilatar-se

dilatory ['dɪlətərɪ] ADJ retardio

dilemma [daɪ'lɛmə] N dilema *m*; **to be in a ~** estar num dilema

diligent ['dɪlɪdʒənt] ADJ (*worker*) diligente; (*research*) cuidadoso

dill [dɪl] N endro, aneto

dilly-dally ['dɪlɪ'dælɪ] VI (*loiter*) vadiar; (*hesitate*) vacilar

dilute [daɪ'luːt] VT diluir ▶ ADJ diluído

dim [dɪm] ADJ (*light, eyesight*) fraco; (*outline*) indistinto; (*memory*) vago; (*room*) escuro; (*inf: person*) burro ▶ VT (*light*) diminuir; (US *Aut*) baixar; **to take a ~ view of sth** desaprovar algo

dime [daɪm] (US) N (*moeda de*) *dez centavos*

dimension [dɪ'mɛnʃən] N dimensão *f*; (*measurement*) medida; (*also*: **dimensions**: *scale, size*) tamanho

-dimensional [dɪ'mɛnʃənl] SUFFIX: **two~** bidimensional

diminish [dɪ'mɪnɪʃ] VT, VI diminuir

diminished [dɪ'mɪnɪʃt] ADJ: **~ responsibility** (*Law*) responsabilidade *f* reduzida

diminutive [dɪ'mɪnjutɪv] ADJ diminuto ▶ N (*Ling*) diminutivo

dimly ['dɪmlɪ] ADV fracamente; (*not clearly*) indistintamente

dimmers ['dɪməz] (US) NPL (*Aut: headlights*) faróis *mpl* baixos

dimple ['dɪmpl] N covinha

dim-witted [-'wɪtɪd] (*inf*) ADJ burro

din [dɪn] N zoeira ▶ VT: **to ~ sth into sb** (*inf*) meter algo na cabeça de alguém, repisar algo a alguém

dine [daɪn] VI jantar

diner ['daɪnəʳ] N (*person*) comensal *m/f*; (*Rail*) vagão-restaurante *m*; (US: *eating place*) lanchonete *f*

dinghy ['dɪŋgɪ] N dingue *m*, bote *m*; **rubber ~** bote de borracha; (*also*: **sailing dinghy**) barco a vela

dingy ['dɪndʒɪ] ADJ (*room*) sombrio, lúgubre; (*clothes, curtains etc*) sujo; (*dull*) descolorido

dining car ['daɪnɪŋ-] (BRIT) N (*Rail*) vagão-restaurante *m*

dining room ['daɪnɪŋ-] N sala de jantar

dinkum ['dɪŋkəm] (AUST *inf*) ADJ (*also*: **fair dinkum**) de verdade

dinner ['dɪnəʳ] N (*evening meal*) jantar *m*; (*lunch*) almoço; (*banquet*) banquete *m*; **~'s ready!** está na mesa!

dinner jacket N smoking *m*

dinner party N jantar *m*

dinner time N (*midday*) hora de almoçar; (*evening*) hora de jantar

dinosaur ['daɪnəsɔːʳ] N dinossauro

dint [dɪnt] N: **by ~ of** à força de

diocese ['daɪəsɪs] N diocese *f*

dioxide [daɪ'ɔksaɪd] N dióxido

dip [dɪp] N (*slope*) inclinação *f*; (*in sea*) mergulho; (*Culin*) pasta para servir com salgadinhos ▶ VT (*in water*) mergulhar; (*ladle etc*) meter; (*BRIT Aut: lights*) baixar ▶ VI (*ground, road*) descer subitamente

Dip. (*BRIT*) ABBR = **diploma**

diphtheria [dɪf'θɪərɪə] N difteria

diphthong ['dɪfθɔŋ] N ditongo

diploma [dɪ'pləumə] N diploma *m*

diplomacy [dɪ'pləuməsɪ] N diplomacia

diplomat ['dɪpləmæt] (*BRIT*) N diplomata *m/f*

diplomatic [dɪplə'mætɪk] ADJ diplomático; **to break off ~ relations (with)** romper relações diplomáticas (com)

dipstick ['dɪpstɪk] N (*Aut*) vareta medidora

dipswitch ['dɪpswɪtʃ] (*BRIT*) N (*Aut*) interruptor *m* de luz alta e baixa

dire [daɪəʳ] ADJ terrível; (*very bad*) péssimo

direct [daɪ'rɛkt] ADJ direto; (*route*) reto; (*manner*) franco, sincero ▶ VT dirigir; (*order*): **to ~ sb to do sth** ordenar alguém para fazer algo ▶ ADV direto; **can you ~ me to ...?** pode me indicar o caminho a ...?

direct cost N (*Comm*) custo direto

direct current N (*Elec*) corrente *f* contínua

direct debit (*BRIT*) N (*Banking*) débito direto

direct dialling N (*Tel*) discagem *f* direta (*BR*), marcação *f* directa (*PT*)

direct hit N (*Mil*) acerto direto

direction [dɪ'rɛkʃən] N (*way*) indicação *f*; (*TV, Radio, Cinema*) direção *f*; **directions** NPL (*to a place*) indicação *f*; (*instructions*) instruções fpl; **~s for use** modo de usar; **to ask for ~s** pedir uma indicação, perguntar o caminho; **sense of ~** senso de direção; **in the ~ of** na direção de

directive [dɪ'rɛktɪv] N diretriz *f*

direct labour N mão-de-obra direta

directly [dɪ'rɛktlɪ] ADV (*in a straight line*) diretamente; (*at once*) imediatamente

direct mail N mala direta

direct mailshot (*BRIT*) N mailing *m*

directness [daɪ'rɛktnɪs] N (*of person, speech*) franqueza

director [dɪ'rɛktəʳ] N diretor(a) *m/f*; **D~ of Public Prosecutions** (*BRIT*) ≈ procurador(a) *m/f* de República

directory [dɪ'rɛktərɪ] N (*Tel*) lista (telefônica); (*also*: **street directory**) lista de endereços; (*Comm*) anuário comercial; (*Comput*) diretório

directory enquiries, (*US*) **directory assistance** N (*serviço de*) informações fpl

dirt [dəːt] N sujeira (*BR*), sujidade (*PT*); **to treat sb like ~** espezinhar alguém

dirt-cheap ADJ baratíssimo

dirt road N estrada de terra

dirty ['dəːtɪ] ADJ sujo; (*joke*) indecente ▶ VT sujar

dirty trick N golpe *m* baixo, sujeira

disability [dɪsə'bɪlɪtɪ] N incapacidade *f*

disability allowance N pensão *f* de invalidez

disable [dɪs'eɪbl] VT (*subj: illness, accident*) incapacitar; (*tank, gun*) inutilizar

disabled [dɪs'eɪbld] ADJ deficiente ▶ NPL: **the ~** os deficientes

disadvantage [dɪsəd'vɑːntɪdʒ] N desvantagem *f*; (*prejudice*) inconveniente *m*

disadvantaged [dɪsəd'vɑːntɪdʒd] ADJ (*person*) menos favorecido

disadvantageous [dɪsædvɑːn'teɪdʒəs] ADJ desvantajoso

disaffected [dɪsə'fɛktɪd] ADJ: **~ (to** or **towards)** descontente (de)

disaffection [dɪsə'fɛkʃən] N descontentamento

disagree [dɪsə'griː] VI (*differ*) diferir; (*be against, think otherwise*): **to ~ (with)** não concordar (com), discordar (de); **garlic ~s with me** o alho me faz mal, o alho não me convém

disagreeable [dɪsə'griəbl] ADJ desagradável

disagreement [dɪsə'griːmənt] N desacordo; (*quarrel*) desavença

disallow ['dɪsə'lau] VT não admitir; (*Law*) vetar, proibir; (*BRIT: goal*) anular

disappear [dɪsə'pɪəʳ] VI desaparecer, sumir; (*custom etc*) acabar

disappearance [dɪsə'pɪərəns] N desaparecimento, desaparição *f*

disappoint [dɪsə'pɔɪnt] VT (*cause to regret*) desapontar; (*let down*) decepcionar; (*hopes*) frustrar

disappointed [dɪsə'pɔɪntɪd] ADJ decepcionado

disappointing [dɪsə'pɔɪntɪŋ] ADJ decepcionante

disappointment [dɪsə'pɔɪntmənt] N decepção *f*; (*cause*) desapontamento

disapproval [dɪsə'pruːvəl] N desaprovação *f*

disapprove [dɪsə'pruːv] VI: **to ~ of** desaprovar

disapproving [dɪsə'pruːvɪŋ] ADJ desaprovativo, de desaprovação

disarm [dɪs'ɑːm] VT desarmar

disarmament [dɪs'ɑːməmənt] N desarmamento

disarming [dɪs'ɑːmɪŋ] ADJ (*smile*) encantador(a)

disarray [dɪsə'reɪ] N desordem *f*; **in ~** (*troops*) desbaratado; (*organization*) desorganizado, caótico; (*thoughts*) confuso; (*clothes*) em desalinho; **to throw into ~** (*troops*) desbaratar; (*government etc*) deixar em polvorosa

disaster [dɪ'zɑːstəʳ] N (*accident*) desastre *m*; (*natural*) catástrofe *f*

disastrous [dɪ'zɑːstrəs] ADJ desastroso

disband [dɪs'bænd] VT dispersar ▶ VI dispersar-se, desfazer-se

disbelief [dɪsbə'liːf] N incredulidade *f*; **in ~** com incredulidade, incrédulo

disbelieve ['dɪsbə'liːv] VT não acreditar em

disc [dɪsk] N disco; (*Comput*) = **disk**

disc. ABBR (*Comm*) = **discount**

discard [dɪs'kɑːd] VT (*old things*) desfazer-se de; (*fig*) descartar

disc brake N freio de disco (BR), travão *m* de discos (PT)

discern [dɪ'səːn] VT perceber; (*identify*) identificar

discernible [dɪ'səːnəbl] ADJ perceptível; (*object*) visível

discerning [dɪ'səːnɪŋ] ADJ perspicaz

discharge [vt dɪs'tʃɑːdʒ, n 'dɪstʃɑːdʒ] VT (*duties*) cumprir, desempenhar; (*settle: debt*) saldar, quitar; (*patient*) dar alta a; (*employee*) despedir; (*soldier*) dar baixa em, dispensar; (*defendant*) pôr em liberdade; (*waste etc*) descarregar, despejar ▶ N (*Elec*) descarga; (*dismissal*) despedida; (*of duty*) desempenho; (*of debt*) quitação *f*; (*from hospital*) alta; (*from army*) baixa; (*Law*) absolvição *f*; (*Med*) secreção *f*; (*also:* **vaginal discharge**) corrimento; **to ~ one's gun** descarregar a arma, disparar; **~d bankrupt** falido(-a) reabilitado(-a)

disciple [dɪ'saɪpl] N discípulo(-a)

disciplinary ['dɪsɪplɪnərɪ] ADJ disciplinar; **to take ~ action against sb** mover ação disciplinar contra alguém

discipline ['dɪsɪplɪn] N disciplina; (*self-discipline*) auto-disciplina ▶ VT disciplinar; (*punish*) punir; **to ~ o.s. to do sth** disciplinar-se para fazer algo

disc jockey N (*on radio*) radialista *m/f*; (*in discotheque*) discotecário(-a)

disclaim [dɪs'kleɪm] VT negar

disclaimer [dɪs'kleɪmə^r] N desmentido; **to issue a ~** publicar um desmentido

disclose [dɪs'kləuz] VT revelar

disclosure [dɪs'kləuʒə^r] N revelação *f*

disco ['dɪskəu] N ABBR = **discotheque**

discolour, (US) **discolor** [dɪs'kʌlə^r] VT descolorar; (*fade: fabric*) desbotar; (*yellow: teeth*) amarelar; (*stain*) manchar ▶ VI (*fabric*) desbotar; (*teeth etc*) amarelar

discolouration, (US) **discoloration** [dɪskʌlə'reɪʃən] N (*of fabric*) desbotamento; (*stain*) mancha

discoloured, (US) **discolored** [dɪs'kʌləd] ADJ descolorado; (*teeth etc*) amarelado

discomfort [dɪs'kʌmfət] N (*unease*) inquietação *f*; (*physical*) desconforto

disconcert [dɪskən'səːt] VT desconcertar

disconnect [dɪskə'nekt] VT desligar; (*pipe, tap*) desmembrar; (*gas, water*) cortar

disconnected [dɪskə'nektɪd] ADJ (*speech, thoughts*) desconexo, incoerente

disconsolate [dɪs'kɔnsəlɪt] ADJ desconsolado, inconsolável

discontent [dɪskən'tɛnt] N descontentamento

discontented [dɪskən'tɛntɪd] ADJ descontente

discontinue [dɪskən'tɪnjuː] VT interromper; (*payments*) suspender; **"~d"** (*Comm*) "fora de linha"

discord ['dɪskɔːd] N discórdia; (*Mus*) dissonância

discordant [dɪs'kɔːdənt] ADJ dissonante

discotheque ['dɪskəutɛk] N discoteca

discount [*n* 'dɪskaunt, *vt* dɪs'kaunt] N desconto ▶ VT descontar; (*idea*) ignorar; **to give sb a ~ on sth** dar *or* conceder um desconto a alguém por algo; **~ for cash** desconto por pagamento à vista; **at a ~** com desconto

discount house N (*Finance*) agência corretora de descontos; (*Comm: also:* **discount store**) loja de descontos

discount rate N taxa de desconto

discourage [dɪs'kʌrɪdʒ] VT (*dishearten*) desanimar; (*dissuade*) dissuadir; (*deter*) desincentivar; (*theft etc*) desencorajar; (*advise against*): **to ~ sth/sb from doing** desaconselhar algo/alguém a fazer

discouragement [dɪs'kʌrɪdʒmənt] N (*depression*) desânimo, desalento; **to act as a ~ to sb** dissuadir alguém

discouraging [dɪs'kʌrɪdʒɪŋ] ADJ desanimador(a)

discourteous [dɪs'kəːtɪəs] ADJ descortês

discover [dɪs'kʌvə^r] VT descobrir; (*missing person*) encontrar; (*mistake*) achar

discovery [dɪs'kʌvərɪ] N (*act*) descobrimento, descoberta; (*of object etc*) achado; (*thing found*) descoberta

discredit [dɪs'krɛdɪt] VT desacreditar; (*claim*) desmerecer ▶ N descrédito

discreet [dɪ'skriːt] ADJ discreto; (*careful*) cauteloso

discreetly [dɪ'skriːtlɪ] ADV discretamente

discrepancy [dɪ'skrɛpənsɪ] N (*difference*) diferença; (*disagreement*) discrepância

discretion [dɪ'skrɛʃən] N discrição *f*; **at the ~ of** ao arbítrio de; **use your ~** aja segundo o seu critério

discretionary [dɪ'skrɛʃənrɪ] ADJ (*powers*) discricionário

discriminate [dɪ'skrɪmɪneɪt] VI: **to ~ between** fazer distinção entre; **to ~ against** discriminar contra

discriminating [dɪ'skrɪmɪneɪtɪŋ] ADJ (*public, audience*) criterioso

discrimination [dɪskrɪmɪ'neɪʃən] N (*discernment*) discernimento; (*bias*) discriminação *f*; **racial/sexual ~** discriminação racial/sexual

discus ['dɪskəs] N disco; (*event*) arremesso do disco

discuss [dɪ'skʌs] VT discutir; (*analyse*) analisar

discussion [dɪ'skʌʃən] N discussão *f*; (*debate*) debate *m*; **under ~** em discussão

disdain [dɪs'deɪn] N desdém *m* ▶ VT desdenhar

disease [dɪ'ziːz] N doença

diseased [dɪ'ziːzd] ADJ doente

disembark [dɪsɪm'bɑːk] VT, VI desembarcar

disembarkation [dɪsembɑːˈkeɪʃən] N desembarque m

disembodied [ˈdɪsɪmˈbɔdɪd] ADJ desencarnado

disembowel [ˈdɪsɪmˈbauəl] VT estripar, eviscerar

disenchanted [ˈdɪsɪnˈtʃɑːntɪd] ADJ: **~ (with)** desencantado (de)

disenfranchise [ˈdɪsɪnˈfræntʃaɪz] VT privar do privilégio do voto; (Comm) retirar a concessão de

disengage [dɪsɪnˈgeɪdʒ] VT soltar; (Tech) desengrenar; (Aut): **to ~ the clutch** desembrear

disentangle [dɪsɪnˈtæŋgl] VT (from wreckage) desvencilhar; (wool, wire) desembaraçar

disfavour, (US) **disfavor** [dɪsˈfeɪvər] N desfavor m

disfigure [dɪsˈfɪgər] VT (person) desfigurar; (object) estragar, enfear

disgorge [dɪsˈgɔːdʒ] VT descarregar, despejar

disgrace [dɪsˈgreɪs] N ignomínia; (downfall) queda; (shame) vergonha, desonra ▶ VT (family) envergonhar; (name, country) desonrar

disgraceful [dɪsˈgreɪsful] ADJ vergonhoso; (behaviour) escandaloso

disgruntled [dɪsˈgrʌntld] ADJ descontente

disguise [dɪsˈgaɪz] N disfarce m ▶ VT disfarçar; **to ~ o.s. (as)** disfarçar-se (de); **in ~** disfarçado; **there's no disguising the fact that …** não há como esconder o fato de que …

disgust [dɪsˈgʌst] N repugnância ▶ VT repugnar a, dar nojo em

disgusting [dɪsˈgʌstɪŋ] ADJ (revolting) repugnante; (unacceptable) inaceitável

dish [dɪʃ] N prato; (serving dish) travessa; **to do** or **wash the ~es** lavar os pratos or a louça
▶ **dish out** VT repartir
▶ **dish up** VT servir; (facts, statistics) apresentar

dishcloth [ˈdɪʃklɔθ] N pano de prato or de louça

dishearten [dɪsˈhɑːtn] VT desanimar

dishevelled, (US) **disheveled** [dɪˈʃevəld] ADJ (hair) despenteado; (clothes) desalinhado

dishonest [dɪsˈɔnɪst] ADJ (person) desonesto; (means) fraudulento

dishonesty [dɪsˈɔnɪstɪ] N desonestidade f

dishonour, (US) **dishonor** [dɪsˈɔnər] N desonra

dishonourable, (US) **dishonorable** [dɪsˈɔnərəbl] ADJ (person) desonesto, vil; (behaviour) desonroso

dish soap (US) N detergente m

dishtowel [dɪʃˈtauəl] (US) N pano de prato

dishwasher [ˈdɪʃwɔʃər] N máquina de lavar louça or pratos

dishy [ˈdɪʃɪ] ADJ (BRIT inf) bonitão

disillusion [dɪsɪˈluːʒən] VT desiludir ▶ N desilusão f; **to become ~ed** ficar desiludido, desiludir-se

disillusionment [dɪsɪˈluːʒənmənt] N desilusão f

disincentive [dɪsɪnˈsentɪv] N desincentivo; **to be a ~ to sb** desincentivar alguém

disinclined [ˈdɪsɪnˈklaɪnd] ADJ: **to be ~ to do** estar pouco disposto a fazer

disinfect [dɪsɪnˈfekt] VT desinfetar

disinfectant [dɪsɪnˈfektənt] N desinfetante m

disinflation [dɪsɪnˈfleɪʃən] N desinflação f

disinherit [dɪsɪnˈherɪt] VT deserdar

disintegrate [dɪsˈɪntɪgreɪt] VI desintegrar-se

disinterested [dɪsˈɪntrəstɪd] ADJ imparcial

disjointed [dɪsˈdʒɔɪntɪd] ADJ desconexo

disk [dɪsk] N (Comput) disco; (removable) disquete m

disk drive N unidade f de disco

diskette [dɪsˈket] (US) N (Comput) disquete m

disk operating system N sistema m operacional residente em disco

dislike [dɪsˈlaɪk] N desagrado ▶ VT antipatizar com, não gostar de; **to take a ~ to sb/sth** tomar antipatia por alguém/algo; **I ~ the idea** não gosto da ideia

dislocate [ˈdɪsləkeɪt] VT deslocar; **he has ~d his shoulder** ele deslocou o ombro

dislodge [dɪsˈlɔdʒ] VT mover, deslocar; (enemy) desalojar

disloyal [dɪsˈlɔɪəl] ADJ desleal

dismal [ˈdɪzml] ADJ (dull) sombrio, lúgubre; (depressing) deprimente; (very bad) horrível

dismantle [dɪsˈmæntl] VT desmontar, desmantelar

dismay [dɪsˈmeɪ] N consternação f ▶ VT consternar; **much to my ~** para minha grande consternação

dismiss [dɪsˈmɪs] VT (worker) despedir; (pupils) dispensar; (soldiers) dar baixa a; (official) demitir; (Law, possibility) rejeitar ▶ VI (Mil) sair de forma

dismissal [dɪsˈmɪsəl] N (of worker) despedida; (of official) demissão f

dismount [dɪsˈmaunt] VI (from horse) desmontar; (from bicycle) descer

disobedience [dɪsəˈbiːdɪəns] N desobediência

disobedient [dɪsəˈbiːdɪənt] ADJ desobediente

disobey [dɪsəˈbeɪ] VT desobedecer a; (rules) transgredir, desrespeitar

disorder [dɪsˈɔːdər] N desordem f; (rioting) distúrbios mpl, tumulto; (Med) distúrbio; **stomach ~** problema estomacal

disorderly [dɪsˈɔːdəlɪ] ADJ (untidy) desarrumado; (meeting) tumultuado; (behaviour) escandaloso

disorderly conduct N (Law) perturbação f da ordem, ofensa à moral

disorganized [dɪsˈɔːgənaɪzd] ADJ desorganizado

disorientated [dɪsˈɔːrɪenteɪtəd] ADJ desorientado

disown [dɪsˈəun] VT repudiar; (child) rejeitar

disparaging [dɪsˈpærɪdʒɪŋ] ADJ depreciativo; **to be ~ about sb/sth** fazer pouco de alguém/algo, depreciar alguém/algo

disparate [ˈdɪspərɪt] ADJ (groups) diverso; (levels) desigual

disparity [dɪs'pærɪtɪ] N desigualdade f
dispassionate [dɪs'pæʃənət] ADJ (calm) calmo, controlado; (impartial) imparcial
dispatch [dɪs'pætʃ] VT (person, business) despachar; (send: parcel etc) expedir; (: messenger) enviar ▶ N (sending) remessa; (speed) rapidez f, urgência; (Press) comunicado; (Mil) parte f
dispatch department N (serviço de) expedição f
dispatch rider N (Mil) estafeta m/f
dispel [dɪs'pɛl] VT dissipar
dispensary [dɪs'pɛnsərɪ] N dispensário, farmácia
dispense [dɪs'pɛns] VT (give out) dispensar; (medicine) preparar (e vender); **to ~ sb from** dispensar alguém de
▶ **dispense with** VT FUS prescindir de
dispenser [dɪs'pɛnsər] N (device) distribuidor m automático
dispensing chemist [dɪs'pɛnsɪŋ-] (BRIT) N farmácia
dispersal [dɪs'pə:sl] N dispersão f
disperse [dɪs'pə:s] VT (objects) espalhar; (crowd) dispersar ▶ VI dispersar-se
dispirited [dɪs'pɪrɪtɪd] ADJ desanimado
displace [dɪs'pleɪs] VT (shift) deslocar
displaced person [dɪs'pleɪst-] N (Pol) deslocado(-a) de guerra
displacement [dɪs'pleɪsmənt] N deslocamento
display [dɪs'pleɪ] N (in shop) mostra; (exhibition) exposição f; (Comput: information) apresentação f visual; (: device) display m; (Mil) parada; (of feeling) manifestação f; (pej) ostentação f; (show, spectacle) espetáculo ▶ VT mostrar; (goods) expor; (feelings, tastes) manifestar; (ostentatiously) ostentar; (results, departure times) expor; **on ~** (visible) à mostra; (goods, paintings etc) em exposição
display advertising N anúncios mpl
displease [dɪs'pli:z] VT desagradar, desgostar; (offend) ofender; (annoy) aborrecer
displeased [dɪs'pli:zd] ADJ: **~ with** descontente com; (disappointed) aborrecido
displeasure [dɪs'plɛʒər] N desgosto
disposable [dɪs'pəʊzəbl] ADJ descartável; (income) disponível
disposable nappy (BRIT) N fralda descartável
disposal [dɪs'pəʊzl] N (availability, arrangement) disposição f; (of rubbish) destruição f; (of property etc: by selling) venda, traspasse m; (: by giving away) cessão f; **at sb's ~** à disposição de alguém; **to put sth at sb's ~** pôr algo à disposição de alguém
dispose [dɪs'pəʊz]: **to ~ of** VT FUS (time, money) dispor de; (unwanted goods) desfazer-se de; (throw away) jogar (BR) or tirar (PT) fora; (Comm: stock) vender; (problem, task) lidar; (argument) derrubar
disposed [dɪs'pəʊzd] ADJ: **~ to do** disposto a fazer; **to be well ~ towards sb** estar predisposto a favor de alguém

disposition [dɪspə'zɪʃən] N (inclination) disposição f; (temperament) índole f
dispossess ['dɪspəzɛs] VT: **to ~ sb (of)** despojar alguém (de)
disproportion [dɪsprə'pɔ:ʃən] N desproporção f
disproportionate [dɪsprə'pɔ:ʃənət] ADJ desproporcionado
disprove [dɪs'pru:v] VT refutar
dispute [dɪs'pju:t] N disputa; (verbal) discussão f; (domestic) briga; (also: **industrial dispute**) conflito, disputa ▶ VT disputar; (argue) discutir; (question) questionar; **to be in** or **under ~** (matter) estar em discussão; (territory) estar em disputa, ser disputado
disqualification [dɪskwɔlɪfɪ'keɪʃən] N (Law) inabilitação f, incapacitação f; (Sport) desclassificação f; **~ (from driving)** (BRIT) cassação f da carteira (de motorista)
disqualify [dɪs'kwɔlɪfaɪ] VT (Sport) desclassificar; **to ~ sb for sth/from doing sth** desqualificar alguém para algo/de fazer algo; **to ~ sb (from driving)** (BRIT) cassar a carteira (de motorista) a alguém
disquiet [dɪs'kwaɪət] N inquietação f
disquieting [dɪs'kwaɪətɪŋ] ADJ inquietante, alarmante
disregard [dɪsrɪ'gɑ:d] VT ignorar ▶ N (indifference): **~ (for)** (feelings) desconsideração f (por); (danger) indiferença (a); (money) menosprezo (por)
disrepair [dɪsrɪ'pɛər] N: **to fall into ~** ficar dilapidado
disreputable [dɪs'rɛpjutəbl] ADJ (person) de má fama; (behaviour) vergonhoso
disrepute ['dɪsrɪ'pju:t] N descrédito, desonra; **to bring into ~** desacreditar, desprestigiar
disrespect [dɪsrɪ'spɛkt] N: **~ (for)** desrespeito (por)
disrespectful [dɪsrɪ'spɛktful] ADJ desrespeitoso
disrupt [dɪs'rʌpt] VT (plans) desfazer; (conversation, proceedings) perturbar, interromper
disruption [dɪs'rʌpʃən] N (interruption) interrupção f; (disturbance) perturbação f
disruptive [dɪs'rʌptɪv] ADJ (influence) maléfico; (strike) perturbador(a)
dissatisfaction [dɪssætɪs'fækʃən] N descontentamento
dissatisfied [dɪs'sætɪsfaɪd] ADJ: **~ (with)** descontente (com)
dissect [dɪ'sɛkt] VT dissecar
disseminate [dɪ'sɛmɪneɪt] VT divulgar
dissent [dɪ'sɛnt] N dissensão f
dissenter [dɪ'sɛntər] N (Rel, Pol etc) dissidente m/f
dissertation [dɪsə'teɪʃən] N (also Sch) dissertação f, tese f
disservice [dɪs'sə:vɪs] N: **to do sb a ~** prejudicar alguém
dissident ['dɪsɪdnt] ADJ, N dissidente m/f
dissimilar [dɪ'sɪmɪlər] ADJ: **~ (to)** dessemelhante (de), diferente (de)

dissipate ['dɪsɪpeɪt] VT dissipar; *(money, effort)* desperdiçar ▶ VI dissipar-se

dissipated ['dɪsɪpeɪtɪd] ADJ *(person)* dissoluto

dissociate [dɪ'səʊʃɪeɪt] VT dissociar, separar; **to ~ o.s. from** desassociar-se de, distanciar-se de

dissolute ['dɪsəluːt] ADJ dissoluto

dissolution [dɪsə'luːʃən] N dissolução f

dissolve [dɪ'zɔlv] VT dissolver ▶ VI dissolver-se; *(fig: problem etc)* desaparecer; **to ~ in(to) tears** debulhar-se em lágrimas

dissuade [dɪ'sweɪd] VT: **to ~ sb (from)** dissuadir alguém (de)

distance ['dɪstns] N distância; **in the ~** ao longe; **what's the ~ to London?** qual é a distância daqui a Londres?; **it's within walking ~** pode-se ir a pé, dá para ir a pé *(inf)*

distant ['dɪstnt] ADJ distante; *(manner)* afastado, reservado

distaste [dɪs'teɪst] N repugnância

distasteful [dɪs'teɪstful] ADJ repugnante

Dist. Atty. *(US)* ABBR = **district attorney**

distemper [dɪs'tempə^r] N *(paint)* tinta plástica; *(of dogs)* cinomose f

distended [dɪs'tendɪd] ADJ inchado

distil, *(US)* **distill** [dɪs'tɪl] VT destilar

distillery [dɪs'tɪlərɪ] N destilaria

distinct [dɪs'tɪŋkt] ADJ *(different)* distinto; *(clear)* claro; *(unmistakable)* nítido; **as ~ from** em oposição a

distinction [dɪs'tɪŋkʃən] N *(difference)* diferença; *(honour)* honra; *(in exam)* distinção f; **to draw a ~ between** fazer distinção entre; **a writer of ~** um escritor de destaque

distinctive [dɪs'tɪŋktɪv] ADJ distintivo

distinctly [dɪs'tɪŋktlɪ] ADV claramente, nitidamente

distinguish [dɪs'tɪŋgwɪʃ] VT distinguir; *(differentiate)* diferenciar; *(identify)* identificar ▶ VI: **to ~ between** *(concepts)* distinguir entre, fazer distinção entre; **to ~ o.s.** distinguir-se

distinguished [dɪs'tɪŋgwɪʃt] ADJ *(eminent)* eminente; *(in appearance)* distinto; *(career)* notável

distinguishing [dɪs'tɪŋgwɪʃɪŋ] ADJ *(feature)* distintivo

distort [dɪs'tɔːt] VT distorcer

distortion [dɪs'tɔːʃən] N detorção f; *(of sound)* deturpação f

distract [dɪs'trækt] VT distrair; *(attention)* desviar; *(bewilder)* aturdir

distracted [dɪs'træktɪd] ADJ distraído; *(anxious)* aturdido

distraction [dɪs'trækʃən] N distração f; *(confusion)* aturdimento, perplexidade f; *(amusement)* divertimento; **to drive sb to ~** deixar alguém louco

distraught [dɪs'trɔːt] ADJ desesperado

distress [dɪs'tres] N *(anguish)* angústia; *(misfortune)* desgraça; *(want)* miséria; *(pain)* dor f ▶ VT *(cause anguish)* afligir; **in ~** *(ship)* em perigo; **~ed area** *(BRIT)* área de baixo nível socioeconômico

distressing [dɪs'tresɪŋ] ADJ angustiante

distress signal N sinal m de socorro

distribute [dɪs'trɪbjuːt] VT distribuir; *(share out)* repartir, dividir

distribution [dɪstrɪ'bjuːʃən] N distribuição f; *(of profits etc)* repartição f

distribution cost N custo de distribuição

distributor [dɪ'strɪbjutə^r] N *(Aut)* distribuidor m; *(Comm)* distribuidor(a) m/f; *(: company)* distribuidora

district ['dɪstrɪkt] N *(of country)* região f; *(of town)* zona; *(Admin)* distrito

district attorney *(US)* N promotor(a) m/f público(-a)

district council *(BRIT)* N ≈ município *(BR)*, câmara municipal *(PT)*

district nurse *(BRIT)* N enfermeiro/a do Serviço Nacional que visita os pacientes em casa

distrust [dɪs'trʌst] N desconfiança ▶ VT desconfiar de

distrustful [dɪs'trʌstful] ADJ desconfiado

disturb [dɪs'təːb] VT *(disorganize)* perturbar; *(upset)* incomodar; *(interrupt)* atrapalhar; **sorry to ~ you** desculpe incomodá-lo

disturbance [dɪs'təːbəns] N perturbação f; *(upheaval)* convulsão f; *(political, violent)* distúrbio; *(of mind)* transtorno; **to cause a ~** perturbar a ordem

disturbed [dɪs'təːbd] ADJ perturbado; *(child)* infeliz; **to be mentally/emotionally ~** ter problemas psicológicos/emocionais

disturbing [dɪs'təːbɪŋ] ADJ perturbador(a)

disuse [dɪs'juːs] N: **to fall into ~** cair em desuso

disused [dɪs'juːzd] ADJ abandonado

ditch [dɪtʃ] N fosso; *(irrigation ditch)* rego ▶ VT *(inf: partner)* abandonar; *(: car, plan etc)* desfazer-se de

dither ['dɪðə^r] VI vacilar

ditto ['dɪtəʊ] ADV idem

divan [dɪ'væn] N *(also: **divan bed**)* divã m

dive [daɪv] N *(from board)* salto; *(underwater, of submarine)* mergulho; *(Aviat)* picada; *(pej: café, bar etc)* espelunca ▶ VI mergulhar; picar; **to ~ into** *(bag, drawer etc)* enfiar a mão em; *(shop, car etc)* enfiar-se em

diver ['daɪvə^r] N *(Sport)* saltador(a) m/f; *(underwater)* mergulhador(a) m/f

diverge [daɪ'vəːdʒ] VI divergir

divergent [daɪ'vəːdʒənt] ADJ divergente

diverse [daɪ'vəːs] ADJ diverso; *(group)* heterogêneo

diversification [daɪvəːsɪfɪ'keɪʃən] N diversificação f

diversify [daɪ'vəːsɪfaɪ] VT, VI diversificar

diversion [daɪ'vəːʃən] N *(BRIT Aut)* desvio; *(distraction, Mil)* diversão f; *(of funds)* desvio

diversity [daɪ'vəːsɪtɪ] N diversidade f

divert [daɪ'vəːt] VT desviar; *(amuse)* divertir

divest [daɪ'vest] VT: **to ~ sb of sth** privar alguém de algo

divide [dɪ'vaɪd] VT *(Math)* dividir; *(separate)* separar; *(share out)* repartir ▶ VI dividir-se;

(*road*) bifurcar-se; **to ~ (between** or **among)** dividir or repartir (entre); **40 ~d by 5** 40 dividido por 5
▶ **divide out** VT: **to ~ out (between** or **among)** distribuir or repartir (entre)
divided [dɪˈvaɪdɪd] ADJ (*fig*) dividido
divided highway (US) N pista dupla
divided skirt N saia-calça
dividend [ˈdɪvɪdɛnd] N dividendo; (*fig*) lucro; **to pay ~s** valer a pena
dividend cover N cobertura para pagamento de dividendos
dividers [dɪˈvaɪdəz] NPL compasso de ponta seca; (*between pages*) divisórias fpl
divine [dɪˈvaɪn] ADJ (*also fig*) divino ▶ VT (*future, truth*) adivinhar; (*water, metal*) descobrir
diving [ˈdaɪvɪŋ] N (*Sport*) salto; (*underwater*) mergulho
diving board N trampolim m
diving suit N escafandro
divinity [dɪˈvɪnɪtɪ] N divindade f; (*Sch*) teologia
division [dɪˈvɪʒən] N divisão f; (*sharing out*) repartição f; (*disagreement*) discórdia; (*Football*) grupo; (BRIT Pol) votação f; **~ of labour** divisão do trabalho
divisive [dɪˈvaɪsɪv] ADJ que causa divisão
divorce [dɪˈvɔːs] N divórcio ▶ VT divorciar-se de; (*dissociate*) dissociar
divorced [dɪˈvɔːst] ADJ divorciado
divorcee [dɪvɔːˈsiː] N divorciado(-a)
divulge [daɪˈvʌldʒ] VT (*information*) divulgar; (*secret*) revelar
DIY (BRIT) ADJ ABBR, N ABBR = **do-it-yourself**
dizziness [ˈdɪzɪnɪs] N vertigem f, tontura
dizzy [ˈdɪzɪ] ADJ (*person*) tonto; (*height*) vertiginoso; **to feel ~** sentir-se tonto, sentir-se atordoado; **to make sb ~** dar vertigem a alguém
DJ N ABBR = **disc jockey**
Djakarta [dʒəˈkɑːtə] N Jacarta
DJIA (US) N ABBR (*Stock Exchange*) = **Dow Jones Industrial Average**
dl ABBR (= *decilitre*) dl
DLit, DLitt N ABBR (= *Doctor of Literature, Doctor of Letters*) títulos universitários
DLO N ABBR = **dead-letter office**
dm ABBR (= *decimetre*) dm
DMus N ABBR (= *Doctor of Music*) título universitário
DMZ N ABBR = **demilitarized zone**
DNA N ABBR (= *deoxyribonucleic acid*) ADN m

(KEYWORD)

do [duː] (*pt* **did**, *pp* **done**) AUX VB **1** (*in negative constructions*): **I don't understand** eu não compreendo
2 (*to form questions*): **didn't you know?** você não sabia?; **what do you think?** o que você acha?
3 (*for emphasis, in polite expressions*): **people do make mistakes sometimes** é impossível não cometer erros de vez em quando; **she**

does seem rather late ela está muito atrasada; **do sit down/help yourself** sente-se/sirva-se; **do take care!** tome cuidado!; **oh do shut up!** cale a boca!
4 (*used to avoid repeating vb*): **she swims better than I do** ela nada melhor que eu; **do you agree? — yes, I do/no, I don't** você concorda? — sim, concordo/não, não concordo; **she lives in Glasgow — so do I** ela mora em Glasgow — eu também; **who broke it? — I did** quem quebrou isso? — (fui) eu
5 (*in question tags*): **you like him, don't you?** você gosta dele, não é?; **he laughed, didn't he?** ele riu, não foi?
▶ VT **1** (*gen: carry out, perform etc*) fazer; **what are you doing tonight?** o que você vai fazer hoje à noite?; **to do the washing-up/cooking** lavar a louça/cozinhar; **to do one's teeth/nails** escovar os dentes/fazer as unhas; **to do one's hair** (*comb*) pentear-se; (*style*) fazer um penteado; **we're doing Othello at school** (*studying*) nós estamos estudando Otelo na escola; (*performing*) nós vamos encenar Otelo na escola
2 (*Aut etc*): **the car was doing 190** o carro andava a 190 por hora; **we've done 200 km already** já percorremos 200 km; **he can do 190 km/h in that car** ele consegue chegar a 190 km/h naquele carro
▶ VI **1** (*act, behave*) fazer; **do as I do** faça como eu faço
2 (*get on, fare*) ir; **how do you do?** como você está indo?
3 (*suit*) servir; **will it do?** serve?
4 (*be sufficient*) bastar; **will £10 do?** £10 dá?; **that'll do** é suficiente; **that'll do!** (*in annoyance*) basta!, chega!; **to make do (with)** contentar-se (com)
▶ N (*inf: party etc*) festa; **we're having a little do on Saturday** nós vamos dar uma festinha no sábado; **it was rather a do** foi uma festança
▶ **do away with** VT FUS (*kill*) matar; (*abolish: law etc*) abolir; (*withdraw*) retirar
▶ **do up** VT (*laces*) atar; (*zip*) fechar; (*dress, skirt*) abotoar; (*renovate: room, house*) arrumar, renovar
▶ **do with** VT FUS (*be connected*) ter a ver com; (*need*): **I could do with a drink/some help** eu bem que gostaria de tomar alguma coisa/eu bem que precisaria de uma ajuda; **what has it got to do with you?** o que é que isso tem a ver com você?
▶ **do without** VI: **if you're late for tea then you'll do without** se você chegar atrasado ficará sem almoço ▶ VT FUS passar sem; **I can do without a car** eu posso ficar sem um carro; **we'll have to do without a holiday this year** não poderemos ter férias esse ano

do. ABBR = **ditto**
DOA ABBR (= *dead on arrival*) ≈ já era cadáver

d.o.b. ABBR = **date of birth**
docile ['dəʊsaɪl] ADJ dócil
dock [dɔk] N (Naut) doca; (wharf) cais m; (Law) banco (dos réus) ▶ VI (arrive) chegar; (Naut: enter dock) atracar; (Space) unir-se no espaço ▶ VT (pay etc) deduzir; **docks** NPL docas fpl
dock dues NPL direitos mpl portuários
docker ['dɔkə'] N portuário, estivador m
docket ['dɔkɪt] N (of delivery etc) guia
dockyard ['dɔkjɑːd] N estaleiro
doctor ['dɔktə'] N médico(-a); (PhD etc) doutor(a) m/f ▶ VT (fig) tratar, falsificar; (drink etc) falsificar; (cat) castrar; **~'s office** (US) consultório
doctorate ['dɔktərɪt] N doutorado
Doctor of Philosophy N (degree) doutorado; (person) doutor(a) m/f
doctrine ['dɔktrɪn] N doutrina
document [n 'dɔkjumənt, vt 'dɔkjumɛnt] N documento ▶ VT documentar
documentary [dɔkju'mɛntərɪ] ADJ documental ▶ N documentário
documentation [dɔkjumɛn'teɪʃən] N documentação f
DOD (US) N ABBR = **Department of Defense**
doddering ['dɔdərɪŋ] ADJ (senile) caquético, caduco
Dodecanese [dəʊdɪkə'niːz] N, **Dodecanese Islands** NPL (ilhas fpl do) Dodecaneso
dodge [dɔdʒ] N (of body) evasiva; (trick) trapaça ▶ VT esquivar-se de, evitar; (tax) sonegar; (blow) furtar-se a ▶ VI: **to ~ out of the way** esquivar-se; **to ~ the traffic** ziguezaguear por entre os carros
dodgems ['dɔdʒəmz] (BRIT) NPL carros mpl de choque
dodgy ['dɔdʒɪ] ADJ arriscado
DOE N ABBR (BRIT) = **Department of the Environment**; (US) = **Department of Energy**
doe [dəʊ] N (deer) corça; (rabbit) coelha
does [dʌz] VB see **do**
doesn't ['dʌznt] = **does not**
dog [dɔg] N cachorro, cão m ▶ VT (subj: person) seguir; (: bad luck) perseguir; **to go to the ~s** (nation etc) degringolar
dog biscuits NPL biscoitos mpl para cachorro
dog collar N coleira de cachorro; (of priest) gola de padre
dog-eared [-ɪəd] ADJ surrado
dog food N ração f para cachorro
dogged ['dɔgɪd] ADJ tenaz, persistente
doggy bag ['dɔgɪ-] N quentinha
dogma ['dɔgmə] N dogma m
dogmatic [dɔg'mætɪk] ADJ dogmático
do-gooder [-'gudə'] (pej) N bom/boa samaritano(-a)
dogsbody ['dɔgzbɔdɪ] (BRIT inf) N faz-tudo m/f
doing ['duɪŋ] N: **this is your ~** foi você que fez isso; **doings** NPL (events) acontecimentos mpl; (activities) atividades fpl
do-it-yourself N sistema m faça-você-mesmo ▶ ADJ do tipo faça-você-mesmo

doldrums ['dɔldrəmz] NPL: **to be in the ~** (person) estar abatido; (business) estar parado or estagnado
dole [dəʊl] (BRIT) N (payment) subsídio de desemprego; **on the ~** desempregado ▶ **dole out** VT distribuir
doleful ['dəʊlful] ADJ triste, lúgubre
doll [dɔl] N boneca; (US inf: woman) gatinha ▶ **doll up** VT: **to ~ o.s. up** embonecar-se (BR), ataviar-se (PT)
dollar ['dɔlə'] N dólar m
dollar area N zona do dólar
dolled up [dɔld-] (inf) ADJ embonecado
dolphin ['dɔlfɪn] N golfinho
domain [də'meɪn] N domínio; (fig) campo
dome [dəʊm] N (Arch) cúpula; (shape) abóbada
domestic [də'mɛstɪk] ADJ doméstico; (national) nacional; (home-loving) caseiro; (strife) interno
domesticated [də'mɛstɪkeɪtɪd] ADJ domesticado; (home-loving) prendado; **he's very ~** ele é muito prendado (no lar)
domesticity [dɔmɛs'tɪsɪtɪ] N vida caseira
domestic servant N empregado(-a) doméstico(-a)
domicile ['dɔmɪsaɪl] N domicílio
dominant ['dɔmɪnənt] ADJ dominante
dominate ['dɔmɪneɪt] VT dominar
domination [dɔmɪ'neɪʃən] N dominação f
domineering [dɔmɪ'nɪərɪŋ] ADJ dominante, mandão(-dona)
Dominican Republic [də'mɪnɪkən-] N República Dominicana
dominion [də'mɪnɪən] N domínio; (territory) império
domino ['dɔmɪnəʊ] (pl **dominoes**) N peça de dominó; **dominoes** N (game) dominó m
don [dɔn] N (BRIT) professor(a) m/f universitário(-a) ▶ VT vestir
donate [də'neɪt] VT doar
donation [də'neɪʃən] N doação f; (contribution) contribuição f
done [dʌn] PP of **do**
dongle ['dɔŋgl] N ABBR (Comput: for internet access) modem USB m; (protecting software) dongle m
donkey ['dɔŋkɪ] N burro
donkey-work (BRIT inf) N labuta
donor ['dəʊnə'] N doador(a) m/f
donor card N cartão m de doador
don't [dəʊnt] = **do not**
doodle ['duːdl] N rabisco ▶ VI rabiscar
doom [duːm] N (fate) destino; (ruin) ruína ▶ VT: **to be ~ed to failure** estar destinado or fadado ao fracasso
doomsday ['duːmzdeɪ] N o Juízo Final
door [dɔː'] N porta; (entry) entrada; **next ~** na casa ao lado; **to go from ~ to ~** ir de porta em porta
doorbell ['dɔːbɛl] N campainha
door handle N maçaneta (BR), puxador m (PT); (of car) maçaneta
door knocker N aldrava

doorman ['dɔːmæn] (*irreg: like* **man**) N porteiro
doormat ['dɔːmæt] N capacho
doormen ['dɔːmɛn] NPL *of* **doorman**
doorpost ['dɔːpəust] N batente *m* de porta
doorstep ['dɔːstɛp] N degrau *m* da porta, soleira
door-to-door ADJ: ~ **selling** venda de porta em porta
doorway ['dɔːweɪ] N vão *m* da porta, entrada
dope [dəup] N (*inf: person*) imbecil *m/f*; (: *drugs*) maconha; (: *information*) dica, macete *m* ▶ VT (*horse etc*) dopar
dopey ['dəupɪ] (*inf*) ADJ (*groggy*) zonzo; (*stupid*) imbecil
dormant ['dɔːmənt] ADJ inativo; (*latent*) latente
dormer ['dɔːmə^r] N (*also:* **dormer window**) água-furtada, trapeira
dormice ['dɔːmaɪs] NPL *of* **dormouse**
dormitory ['dɔːmɪtrɪ] N dormitório; (*US*) *residência universitária*
dormouse ['dɔːmaus] (*pl* **dormice**) N rato (de campo)
DOS [dɔs] N ABBR (= *disk operating system*) DOS *m*
dosage ['dəusɪdʒ] N dosagem, posologia; (*on label*) posologia
dose [dəus] N dose *f*; (*BRIT: bout*) ataque *m* ▶ VT: **to ~ o.s.** medicar-se; **a ~ of flu** uma gripe
doss house ['dɔs-] (*BRIT*) N pensão *f* barata *or* de malta (*PT*)
dossier ['dɔsɪeɪ] N dossiê
DOT (*US*) N ABBR = **Department of Transportation**
dot [dɔt] N ponto; (*speck*) pontinho ▶ VT: **~ted with** salpicado de; **on the ~** em ponto
dotcom [dɔt'kɔm] N empresa pontocom
dote [dəut]: **to ~ on** VT FUS adorar, idolatrar
dotted line ['dɔtɪd-] N linha pontilhada; **to sign on the ~** (*fig*) firmar o compromisso
dotty ['dɔtɪ] (*inf*) ADJ lelé, doido
double ['dʌbl] ADJ duplo ▶ ADV (*twice*): **to cost ~ (sth)** custar o dobro (de algo) ▶ N dobro; (*person*) duplo(-a); (*Cinema*) substituto(-a) ▶ VT dobrar; (*efforts*) duplicar ▶ VI dobrar; (*have two uses*): **to ~ as** servir também de; **~ five two six (5526)** (*BRIT Tel*) cinco cinco dois meia; **it's spelt with a ~ "l"** escreve-se com dois ls; **at the ~** (*BRIT*), **on the ~** em passo acelerado; *see also* **doubles**
▶ **double back** VI (*person*) voltar atrás
▶ **double up** VI (*bend over*) dobrar-se; (*share room*) dividir o quarto
double bass N contrabaixo
double bed N cama de casal
double bend (*BRIT*) N curva dupla, curva em "s"
double-breasted [-'brɛstɪd] ADJ trespassado
double-check VT, VI verificar de novo
double-click VI (*Comput*) clicar duas vezes
double-clutch (*US*) VI fazer embreagem dupla
double cream (*BRIT*) N creme *m* de leite

double-cross [dʌbl'krɔs] VT (*trick*) enganar; (*betray*) atraiçoar
double-decker [dʌbl'dɛkə^r] N ônibus *m* (*BR*) *or* autocarro (*PT*) de dois andares
double-declutch (*BRIT*) VI fazer embreagem dupla
double exposure N (*Phot*) dupla exposição *f*
double glazing [-'gleɪzɪŋ] (*BRIT*) N (janelas *fpl* de) vidro duplo
double room N quarto de casal
doubles N (*Tennis*) dupla
double whammy [-'wæmɪ] N (*inf*) baque *m* duplo
doubly ['dʌblɪ] ADV duplamente
doubt [daut] N dúvida ▶ VT duvidar; (*suspect*) desconfiar de; **without (a) ~** sem dúvida; **beyond ~** *adv* sem dúvida alguma; *adj* indubitável; **there is no ~ that** não há dúvida que; **to ~ that ...** duvidar que ...; **I ~ it very much** duvido muito
doubtful ['dautful] ADJ duvidoso; **to be ~ about sth** ter dúvidas *or* estar em dúvida sobre algo; **I'm a bit ~** duvido
doubtless ['dautlɪs] ADV sem dúvida
dough [dəu] N massa; (*inf: money*) grana
doughnut, (*US*) **donut** ['dəunʌt] N sonho (*BR*), bola de Berlim (*PT*)
dour [duə^r] ADJ austero
douse [daus] VT (*with water*) encharcar; (*flames*) apagar
dove [dʌv] N pomba
dovetail ['dʌvteɪl] VI (*fig*) encaixar-se ▶ N: **~ joint** sambladura em cauda de andorinha
dowager ['dauədʒə^r] N *mulher que herda o título do marido falecido*
dowdy ['daudɪ] ADJ desalinhado; (*inelegant*) deselegante, pouco elegante
Dow-Jones average ['dau'dʒəunz-] (*US*) N índice *m* da bolsa de valores de Nova Iorque
down [daun] ADV abaixo; (*downwards*) para baixo; (*on the ground*) por terra ▶ PREP por, abaixo ▶ VT (*inf: drink*) tomar de um gole só; (: *food*) devorar ▶ N (*fluff*) lanugem *f*; (*feathers*) penugem *f*; (*hill*) colina; **Downs** NPL (*BRIT*): **the ~** chapada gredosa do sul da Inglaterra; **~ there** lá em baixo; **~ here** aqui em baixo; **the price of meat is ~** o preço da carne baixou; **I've got it ~ in my diary** já o anotei na minha agenda; **to pay £2 ~** pagar £2 de entrada; **England are two goals ~** a Inglaterra está perdendo por dois gols; **to ~ tools** (*BRIT*) cruzar os braços; **~ with X!** abaixo X!
down-and-out N (*tramp*) vagabundo(-a)
down-at-heel ADJ descuidado, desmazelado; (*appearance*) deselegante
downbeat ['daunbiːt] N (*Mus*) tempo forte ▶ ADJ sombrio, negativo
downcast ['daunkɑːst] ADJ abatido
downer ['daunə^r] (*inf*) N (*drug*) calmante *m*; **to be on a ~** (*depressed*) estar na fossa, estar de baixo astral
downfall ['daunfɔːl] N queda, ruína

downgrade ['daʊngreɪd] VT (*reduce*) reduzir; (*devalue*) desvalorizar, depreciar

downhearted [daʊn'hɑːtɪd] ADJ desanimado

downhill ['daʊn'hɪl] ADV para baixo ▶ N (*Ski: also*: **downhill race**) descida; **to go ~** descer, ir morro abaixo; (*fig: business*) degringolar

Downing Street ['daʊnɪŋ-] (BRIT) N *ver nota*

> Downing Street é a rua de Westminster (Londres) onde estão localizadas as residências oficiais do Primeiro-ministro (número 10) e do Ministro da Fazenda (número 11). O termo **Downing Street** é frequentemente utilizado para designar o governo britânico.

download ['daʊnləʊd] VT (*Comput*) baixar, fazer o download de

downloadable ADJ (*Comput*) baixável

down-market ADJ destinado a consumidores de renda baixa

down payment N entrada, sinal *m*

downplay ['daʊnpleɪ] (US) VT minimizar

downpour ['daʊnpɔː'] N aguaceiro

downright ['daʊnraɪt] ADJ (*lie*) patente; (*refusal*) categórico ▶ ADV francamente

downsize [daʊn'saɪz] VT enxugar, reestruturar

Down's syndrome [daʊnz-] N síndrome *f* de Down

downstairs ['daʊn'stɛəz] ADV (*below*) lá em baixo; (*direction*) para baixo; **to come** *or* **go ~** descer

downstream ['daʊn'striːm] ADV água *or* rio abaixo

downtime ['daʊntaɪm] N (*of machine, person*) tempo ocioso

down-to-earth ADJ prático, realista

downtown ['daʊn'taʊn] ADV no centro da cidade ▶ ADJ (US): **~ Chicago** o centro comercial de Chicago

downtrodden ['daʊntrɒdn] ADJ oprimido

down under ADV na Austrália (*or* Nova Zelândia)

downward ['daʊnwəd] ADJ, ADV para baixo; **a ~ trend** uma tendência para a baixa

downwards ['daʊnwədz] ADV = **downward**

dowry ['daʊrɪ] N dote *m*

doz. ABBR (= *dozen*) dz.

doze [dəʊz] VI dormitar
▶ **doze off** VI cochilar

dozen ['dʌzn] N dúzia; **a ~ books** uma dúzia de livros; **80p a ~** 80p a dúzia; **~s of times** milhares de vezes

DPh N ABBR (= *Doctor of Philosophy*) título universitário

DPhil N ABBR = **DPh**

DPP (BRIT) N ABBR = **Director of Public Prosecutions**

DPT N ABBR (*Med*: = *diphtheria, pertussis, tetanus*) espécie de vacina

Dr ABBR (= *doctor*) Dr(a).

dr ABBR (*Comm*) = **debtor**

Dr. ABBR (*in street names*) = **drive**; (= *doctor*) Dr(a).

drab [dræb] ADJ sombrio

draft [drɑːft] N (*first copy*) rascunho; (*Pol: of bill*) projeto de lei; (*bank draft*) saque *m*, letra; (US: *call-up*) recrutamento ▶ VT (*plan*) esboçar; (*speech, letter*) rascunhar; *see also* **draught**

draftsman ['drɑːftsmən] (US) N = **draughtsman**

drag [dræg] VT arrastar; (*river*) dragar ▶ VI arrastar-se ▶ N (*inf*) chatice *f* (BR), maçada (PT); (*of cigarette*) tragada; (*Aviat, Naut*) resistência; (*women's clothing*): **in ~** em travesti
▶ **drag away** VT: **to ~ away (from)** desgrudar (de)
▶ **drag on** VI arrastar-se

dragnet ['drægnet] N rede *f* de arrasto; (*by police*) diligência policial

dragon ['drægən] N dragão *m*

dragonfly ['drægənflaɪ] N libélula

dragoon [drə'guːn] N (*cavalryman*) dragão *m*
▶ VT: **to ~ sb into doing sth** (BRIT) forçar alguém a fazer algo

drain [dreɪn] N (*drain pipe*) cano de esgoto; (*underground*) esgoto; (*in street*) bueiro; (*source of loss*) sorvedouro ▶ VT (*land, marshes, Med*) drenar; (*reservoir*) esvaziar; (*vegetables*) coar; (*fig*) esgotar ▶ VI (*water*) escorrer, escoar-se; **to feel ~ed** sentir-se esgotado *or* estafado

drainage ['dreɪnɪdʒ] N (*act*) drenagem *f*; (*Med, Agr*) dreno; (*system*) esgoto

drainboard ['dreɪnbɔːd] (US) N = **draining board**

draining board ['dreɪnɪŋ-] (BRIT) N escorredor *m*

drainpipe ['dreɪnpaɪp] N cano de esgoto

drake [dreɪk] N pato (macho)

dram [dræm] N (*drink*) trago

drama ['drɑːmə] N (*art*) teatro; (*play, event*) drama *m*

dramatic [drə'mætɪk] ADJ dramático; (*theatrical*) teatral

dramatically [drə'mætɪklɪ] ADV dramaticamente

dramatist ['dræmətɪst] N dramaturgo(-a)

dramatize ['dræmətaɪz] VT dramatizar

drank [dræŋk] PT *of* **drink**

drape [dreɪp] VT ornar, cobrir ▶ VI cair

draper ['dreɪpə'] (BRIT) N fanqueiro(-a)

drapes [dreɪps] (US) NPL cortinas *fpl*

drastic ['dræstɪk] ADJ drástico

drastically ['dræstɪklɪ] ADV drasticamente

draught, (US) **draft** [drɑːft] N (*of air*) corrente *f*; (*drink*) trago; (*Naut*) calado; (*beer*) chope *m*; **on ~** (*beer*) de barril

draughtboard ['drɑːftbɔːd] (BRIT) N tabuleiro de damas

draughts (BRIT) N (jogo de) damas *fpl*

draughtsman, (US) **draftsman** ['drɑːftsmən] (*irreg: like* **man**) N desenhista *m/f* industrial

draughtsmanship, (US) **draftsmanship** ['drɑːftsmənʃɪp] N (*art*) desenho industrial; (*technique*) habilidade *f* de desenhista

draughtsmen, (US) **draftsmen** ['drɑːftsmɛn] NPL *of* **draughtsman**

draw [drɔ:] (pt **drew**, pp **drawn**) VT (picture) desenhar; (cart) puxar; (curtain) fechar; (gun) sacar; (attract) atrair; (money) tirar; (: from bank) sacar; (wages) receber; (comparison, distinction) fazer ▶ VI (Sport) empatar ▶ N (Sport) empate m; (lottery) sorteio; (attraction) atração f; **to ~ to a close** tender para o fim; **to ~ near** aproximar-se
▶ **draw back** VI (move back): **to ~ back (from)** recuar (de)
▶ **draw in** VI (BRIT: car) encostar; (: train) entrar na estação ▶ VT (involve) envolver
▶ **draw on** VT FUS (resources) recorrer a, lançar mão de; (person, imagination) recorrer a
▶ **draw out** VI (car, train) sair ▶ VT (lengthen) esticar, alargar; (money) sacar; (confession, truth) arrancar; (shy person) desacanhar, desinibir
▶ **draw up** VI (stop) parar(-se) ▶ VT (chair etc) puxar; (document) redigir; (plans) esboçar
drawback ['drɔ:bæk] N inconveniente m, desvantagem f
drawbridge ['drɔ:brɪdʒ] N ponte f levadiça
drawee [drɔ:'i:] N sacado
drawer[1] [drɔ:[r]] N gaveta
drawer[2] ['drɔ:ə[r]] N (of cheque) sacador(a) m/f, emitente m/f
drawing ['drɔ:ɪŋ] N desenho
drawing board N prancheta
drawing pin (BRIT) N tachinha (BR), pionés m (PT)
drawing room N sala de visitas
drawl [drɔ:l] N fala arrastada
drawn [drɔ:n] PP of **draw** ▶ ADJ (haggard) abatido
drawstring ['drɔ:strɪŋ] N cordão m
dread [drɛd] N medo, pavor m ▶ VT temer, recear, ter medo de
dreadful ['drɛdful] ADJ terrível
dream [dri:m] (pt, pp **dreamed** or **dreamt**) N sonho ▶ VT, VI sonhar; **to have a ~ about sb/sth**, **to ~ about sb/sth** sonhar com alguém/algo; **sweet ~s!** sonha com os anjos!
▶ **dream up** VT inventar, bolar (inf)
dreamer ['dri:mə[r]] N sonhador(a) m/f
dreamt [drɛmt] PT, PP of **dream**
dreamy ['dri:mɪ] ADJ (expression, person) sonhador(a), distraído; (music) sentimental
dreary ['drɪərɪ] ADJ (talk, time) monótono; (weather) sombrio
dredge [drɛdʒ] VT dragar
▶ **dredge up** VT tirar do fundo; (fig: unpleasant facts) trazer à tona, descobrir
dredger ['drɛdʒə[r]] N (ship) draga; (BRIT: also: **sugar dredger**) polvilhador m
dregs [drɛgz] NPL lia; (of humanity) escória, ralé f
drench [drɛntʃ] VT encharcar; **to get ~ed** encharcar-se
dress [drɛs] N vestido; (no pl: clothing) traje m ▶ VT vestir; (wound) fazer curativo em; (Culin) preparar, temperar ▶ VI vestir-se; **to ~ o.s.**, **to get ~ed** vestir-se; **to ~ a shop window** adornar uma vitrina
▶ **dress up** VI vestir-se com elegância; (in fancy dress) fantasiar-se
dress circle (BRIT) N balcão m nobre
dress designer N estilista m/f
dresser ['drɛsə[r]] N (Theatre) camareiro(-a); (also: **window dresser**) vitrinista m/f; (BRIT: cupboard) aparador m; (US: chest of drawers) cômoda de espelho
dressing ['drɛsɪŋ] N (Med) curativo; (Culin) molho
dressing gown (BRIT) N roupão m; (woman's) peignoir m
dressing room N (Theatre) camarim m; (Sport) vestiário
dressing table N penteadeira (BR), toucador m (PT)
dressmaker ['drɛsmeɪkə[r]] N costureiro(-a)
dressmaking ['drɛsmeɪkɪŋ] N (arte f da) costura
dress rehearsal N ensaio geral
dress shirt N camisa social
dressy ['drɛsɪ] (inf) ADJ (clothes) chique
drew [dru:] PT of **draw**
dribble ['drɪbl] VI gotejar, pingar; (baby) babar ▶ VT (ball) driblar
dried [draɪd] ADJ seco; (eggs, milk) em pó
drier ['draɪə[r]] N = **dryer**
drift [drɪft] N (of current etc) força; (of snow, sand etc) monte m; (distance off course) deriva; (meaning) sentido ▶ VI (boat) derivar; (sand, snow) amontoar-se; **to ~ apart** (friends, lovers) afastar-se um do outro; **I get** or **catch your ~** eu entendo mais ou menos o que você está dizendo
drifter ['drɪftə[r]] N nômade m/f
driftwood ['drɪftwud] N madeira flutuante
drill [drɪl] N furadeira; (bit, of dentist) broca; (for mining etc) broca, furadeira; (Mil) exercícios mpl militares ▶ VT furar, brocar; (Mil) exercitar ▶ VI (for oil) perfurar
drilling ['drɪlɪŋ] N (for oil) perfuração f
drilling rig N torre f de perfurar
drink [drɪŋk] (pt **drank**, pp **drunk**) N bebida ▶ VT, VI beber; **to have a ~** tomar uma bebida; **a ~ of water** um copo d'água; **would you like something to ~?** você quer beber or tomar alguma coisa?; **to ~ to sb/sth** brindar alguém/algo
▶ **drink in** VT embeber-se em
drinkable ['drɪŋkəbl] ADJ (not dangerous) potável; (palatable) bebível
drinker ['drɪŋkə[r]] N bebedor(a) m/f
drinking ['drɪŋkɪŋ] N (drunkenness) alcoolismo
drinking fountain N bebedouro
drinking water N água potável
drip [drɪp] N gotejar m; (one drip) gota, pingo; (Med) gota a gota m; (inf: person) mané m, banana m ▶ VI gotejar, pingar
drip-dry ADJ (shirt) de lavar e vestir
drip-feed (irreg: like **feed**) VT alimentar intravenosamente
dripping ['drɪpɪŋ] N gordura ▶ ADJ: **~ wet** encharcado

d

drive [draɪv] (*pt* **drove**, *pp* **driven**) N passeio (de automóvel); (*journey*) trajeto, percurso; (*also:* **driveway**) entrada; (*energy*) energia, vigor *m*; (*Psych*) impulso; (*Sport*) drive *m*; (*campaign*) campanha; (*Tech*) propulsão *f*; (*Comput*) drive *m* ▶ VT conduzir; (*car*) dirigir (BR), guiar (PT); (*urge*) fazer trabalhar; (*by power*) impelir; (*push*) empurrar; (*Tech: motor*) acionar; (*nail*): **to ~ sth into** cravar algo em ▶ VI (*Aut: at controls*) dirigir (BR), guiar (PT); (: *travel*) ir de carro; **to go for a ~** dar um passeio (de carro); **it's 3 hours' ~ from London** fica a 3 horas de carro de Londres; **left-/right-hand ~** direção à esquerda/direita; **front-/rear-wheel ~** (*Aut*) tração dianteira/traseira; **to ~ sb to do sth** impelir alguém a fazer algo; **to ~ sb mad** deixar alguém louco

▶ **drive at** VT FUS (*fig: intend, mean*) querer dizer; **what are you driving at?** onde é que voce queria chegar?

▶ **drive on** VI seguir adiante ▶ VT impelir

drive-in ADJ drive-in ▶ N (*cinema*) drive-in *m*

drive-in window (US) N balcão *m* drive-in

drivel ['drɪvl] (*inf*) N bobagem *f*, besteira

driven ['drɪvn] PP *of* **drive**

driver ['draɪvər] N motorista *m/f*; (*Rail*) maquinista *m*

driver's license (US) N carteira de motorista (BR), carta de condução (PT)

driveway ['draɪvweɪ] N entrada

driving ['draɪvɪŋ] N direção *f* (BR), condução *f* (PT) ▶ ADJ: **~ rain** chuva torrencial

driving force N (*fig*) mola

driving instructor N instrutor(a) *m/f* de autoescola (BR) *or* de condução (PT)

driving lesson N aula de direção (BR) *or* de condução (PT)

driving licence (BRIT) N carteira de motorista (BR), carta de condução (PT)

driving mirror (BRIT) N retrovisor *m*

driving school N autoescola *f*

driving test N exame *m* de motorista

drizzle ['drɪzl] N chuvisco ▶ VI chuviscar

droll [drəʊl] ADJ engraçado

dromedary ['drɒmədərɪ] N dromedário

drone [drəʊn] N (*sound*) zumbido; (*male bee*) zangão *m* ▶ VI (*bee, engine*) zumbir; (*also:* **drone on**) falar monotonamente

drool [druːl] VI babar(-se); **to ~ over sth** babar por algo

droop [druːp] VI pender

drop [drɒp] N (*of water*) gota; (*lessening*) diminuição *f*; (*fall: distance*) declive *m*; (: *in prices*) baixa, queda; (: *in salary*) redução *f*; (*also:* **parachute drop**) salto ▶ VT (*allow to fall*) deixar cair; (*voice, eyes, price*) baixar; (*set down from car*) deixar (saltar/descer); (*omit*) omitir ▶ VI cair; (*price, temperature*) baixar; (*wind*) parar; **drops** NPL (*Med*) gotas *fpl*; **cough ~s** pastilhas para tosse; **a ~ of 10%** uma queda de 10%; **to ~ sb a line** escrever (umas linhas) para alguém

▶ **drop in** (*inf*) VI (*visit*): **to ~ in (on)** dar um pulo (na casa de)

▶ **drop off** VI (*sleep*) cochilar ▶ VT (*passenger*) deixar

▶ **drop out** VI (*withdraw*) retirar-se; (*student etc*) largar tudo

droplet ['drɒplɪt] N gotícula

drop-out N pessoa que abandona o trabalho, os estudos etc

dropper ['drɒpər] N conta-gotas *m inv*

droppings ['drɒpɪŋz] NPL fezes *fpl* (de animal)

dross [drɒs] N escória

drought [draʊt] N seca

drove [drəʊv] PT *of* **drive** ▶ N: **~s of people** uma quantidade de gente

drown [draʊn] VT afogar; (*also:* **drown out**: *sound*) encobrir ▶ VI afogar-se

drowse [draʊz] VI dormitar

drowsy ['draʊzɪ] ADJ sonolento; **to be ~** estar com sono

drudge [drʌdʒ] N burro-de-carga *m*

drudgery ['drʌdʒərɪ] N trabalho enfadonho

drug [drʌg] N remédio, medicamento; (*narcotic*) droga; (: *Med, Admin*) entorpecente *m* ▶ VT drogar; **to be on ~s** (*an addict*) estar viciado em drogas; (*Med*) estar sob medicação; **hard/soft ~s** drogas pesadas/leves

drug addict N toxicômano(-a)

druggist ['drʌgɪst] (US) N farmacêutico(-a)

drug peddler N traficante *m/f* de drogas

drugstore ['drʌgstɔː] (US) N drogaria

drum [drʌm] N tambor *m*; (*large*) bombo; (*for oil, petrol*) tambor, barril *m* ▶ VI (*with fingers*) tamborilar ▶ VT: **to ~ sth into sb** incutir algo em alguém; **drums** NPL (*kit*) bateria

▶ **drum up** VT (*enthusiasm, support*) angariar

drummer ['drʌmər] N baterista *m/f*

drum roll N rufo de tambor

drumstick ['drʌmstɪk] N (*Mus*) baqueta; (*of chicken*) perna

drunk [drʌŋk] PP *of* **drink** ▶ ADJ bêbado ▶ N (*drunkard*) bêbado(-a); **to get ~** ficar bêbado, encher a cara (*inf*)

drunkard ['drʌŋkəd] N beberrão(-beberrona) *m/f*

drunken ['drʌŋkən] ADJ (*laughter*) de bêbado; (*party*) com muita bebida; (*person*) bêbado; **~ driving** embriaguez *f* no volante

drunkenness ['drʌŋkənnɪs] N embriaguez *f*

dry [draɪ] ADJ seco; (*day*) sem chuva; (*uninteresting*) insípido; (*humour*) irônico ▶ VT secar, enxugar; (*tears*) limpar ▶ VI secar; **on ~ land** em terra firme; **to ~ one's hands/hair/eyes** enxugar as mãos/o cabelo/as lágrimas

▶ **dry up** VI secar completamente; (*supply*) esgotar-se; (*in speech*) calar-se; (*dishes*) enxugar (a louça)

dry-clean VT lavar a seco

dry-cleaner N tintureiro(-a)

dry-cleaner's N tinturaria, lavanderia

dry-cleaning N lavagem *f* a seco

dry dock N (*Naut*) dique *m* seco

dryer ['draɪə^r] N secador *m*; (*also*: **spin-dryer**) secadora

dry goods NPL (*Comm*) fazendas *fpl* e artigos *mpl* de armarinho

dry goods store (US) N armarinho

dry ice N gelo seco

dryness ['draɪnɪs] N secura

dry rot N putrefação *f* fungosa

dry run N (*fig*) ensaio, prova

dry ski slope N pista de esqui artificial

DSc N ABBR (= *Doctor of Science*) título universitário

DSS (BRIT) N ABBR (= *Department of Social Security*) ≈ INAMPS *m*

DST (US) ABBR (= *Daylight Saving Time*) hora de verão

DT N ABBR (*Comput*) = **data transmission**

DTI (BRIT) N = **Department of Trade and Industry**

DTP N ABBR (= *desktop publishing*) DTP *m*

DT's (*inf*) NPL ABBR (= *delirium tremens*) delirium tremens *m*

dual ['djuəl] ADJ dual, duplo

dual carriageway (BRIT) N pista dupla

dual-control ADJ de duplo comando

dual nationality N dupla nacionalidade *f*

dual-purpose ADJ de duplo uso

dubbed [dʌbd] ADJ (*Cinema*) dublado; (*nicknamed*) apelidado

dubious ['djuːbɪəs] ADJ duvidoso; (*reputation, company*) suspeitoso; **I'm very ~ about it** eu tenho muitas dúvidas a respeito

Dublin ['dʌblɪn] N Dublin

Dubliner ['dʌblɪnə^r] N natural *m/f* de Dublin

duchess ['dʌtʃɪs] N duquesa

duck [dʌk] N pato ▶ VI (*also*: **duck down**) abaixar-se repentinamente ▶ VT mergulhar

duckling ['dʌklɪŋ] N patinho

duct [dʌkt] N conduto, canal *m*; (*Anat*) ducto

dud [dʌd] N (*shell*) bomba falhada; (*object, tool*): **it's a ~** não presta ▶ ADJ (BRIT: *coin, note*) falso; **~ cheque** cheque *m* sem fundos, cheque *m* voador (*inf*)

due [djuː] ADJ (*proper*) devido; (*expected*) esperado; (*fitting*) conveniente, oportuno ▶ N: **to give sb his/her ~** ser justo com alguém ▶ ADV: **~ north** exatamente ao norte; **dues** NPL (*for club, union*) quota; (*in harbour*) direitos *mpl*; **in ~ course** no devido tempo; (*eventually*) no final; **~ to** devido a; **the rent is ~ on the 30th** o aluguel vence no dia 30; **the train is ~ at 8** o trem deve chegar às 8; **I am ~ 6 days' leave** eu tenho direito a 6 dias de folga

due date N (*data de*) vencimento

duel ['djuəl] N duelo; (*fig*) batalha

duet [djuː'ɛt] N dueto

duff [dʌf] (BRIT *inf*) ADJ de nada

duffel bag ['dʌfl-] N mochila

duffel coat ['dʌfl-] N casaco de baeta

duffer ['dʌfə^r] (*inf*) N zero (à esquerda)

duffle bag ['dʌfl-] N = **duffel bag**

duffle coat ['dʌfl-] N = **duffel coat**

dug [dʌg] PT, PP *of* **dig**

duke [djuːk] N duque *m*

dull [dʌl] ADJ (*light*) sombrio; (*intelligence, wit*) lento; (*boring*) enfadonho; (*sound, pain*) surdo; (*weather, day*) nublado, carregado; (*blade*) embotado, cego ▶ VT (*pain, grief*) aliviar; (*mind, senses*) entorpecer

duly ['djuːlɪ] ADV devidamente; (*on time*) no devido tempo

dumb [dʌm] ADJ mudo; (*pej: stupid*) estúpido; **to be struck ~** (*fig*) ficar pasmo

dumbbell ['dʌmbɛl] N (*Sport*) haltere *m*

d

dumbfounded [dʌm'faundɪd] ADJ pasmado

dummy ['dʌmɪ] N (*tailor's model*) manequim *m*; (*mock-up*) modelo; (BRIT: *for baby*) chupeta; (*Cards*) morto ▶ ADJ falso

dummy run N prova, ensaio

dump [dʌmp] N (*heap*) montão *m*; (*also*: **rubbish dump**) depósito de lixo; (*inf: place*) chiqueiro; (*Mil*) depósito ▶ VT (*put down*) depositar, descarregar; (*get rid of*) desfazer-se de; (*Comm: goods*) fazer dumping de; **to be (down) in the ~s** (*inf*) estar na fossa

dumping ['dʌmpɪŋ] N (*Econ*) dumping *m*; (*of rubbish*): **"no ~"** "proibido jogar lixo" (BR), "proibido deitar lixo" (PT)

dumpling ['dʌmplɪŋ] N bolinho cozido

dumpy ['dʌmpɪ] ADJ gorducho

dunce [dʌns] N burro, ignorante *m/f*

dune [djuːn] N duna

dung [dʌŋ] N estrume *m*

dungarees [dʌŋgə'riːz] NPL macacão *m* (BR), fato macaco (PT)

dungeon ['dʌndʒən] N calabouço

dunk [dʌŋk] VT mergulhar

duo ['djuːəu] N (*gen*) dupla; (*Mus*) duo

duodenal [djuːə'diːnl] ADJ duodenal

dupe [djuːp] N (*victim*) otário(-a), trouxa *m/f* ▶ VT enganar

duplex ['djuːplɛks] (US) N (*house*) casa geminada; (*also*: **duplex apartment**) duplex *m*

duplicate [N 'djuːplɪkət, VT 'djuːplɪkeɪt] N (*of document*) duplicata; (*of key*) cópia ▶ VT duplicar; (*photocopy*) multigrafar; (*repeat*) reproduzir; **in ~** em duplicata; **~ key** cópia de chave

duplicating machine ['djuːplɪkeɪtɪŋ-] N duplicador *m*

duplicator ['djuːplɪkeɪtə^r] N duplicador *m*

duplicity [djuː'plɪsɪtɪ] N falsidade *f*

durability [djuərə'bɪlɪtɪ] N durabilidade *f*, solidez *f*

durable ['djuərəbl] ADJ durável; (*clothes, metal*) resistente

duration [djuə'reɪʃən] N duração *f*

duress [djuə'rɛs] N: **under ~** sob coação

during ['djuərɪŋ] PREP durante

dusk [dʌsk] N crepúsculo, anoitecer *m*

dusky ['dʌskɪ] ADJ (*sky, room*) sombrio; (*person, complexion*) moreno

dust [dʌst] N pó *m*, poeira ▶ VT (*furniture*) tirar o pó de; (*cake etc*): **to ~ with** polvilhar com ▶ **dust off** VT (*dirt*) tirar

dustbin ['dʌstbɪn] N (BRIT) lata de lixo
duster ['dʌstər] N pano de pó
dust jacket N sobrecapa
dustman ['dʌstmən] (BRIT) (irreg: like **man**) N lixeiro, gari m (BR inf)
dustpan ['dʌstpæn] N pá f de lixo
dusty ['dʌstɪ] ADJ empoeirado
Dutch [dʌtʃ] ADJ holandês(-esa) ▶ N (Ling) holandês m ▶ ADV: **let's go ~** (inf) cada um paga o seu, vamos rachar; **the Dutch** NPL (people) os holandeses
Dutch auction N leilão m em que os ertantes oferecem cada vez menos
Dutchman ['dʌtʃmən] (irreg: like **man**) N holandês m
Dutchwoman ['dʌtʃwumən] (irreg: like **woman**) N holandesa
dutiable ['dju:tɪəbl] ADJ (taxable) tributável; (by customs) sujeito a impostos alfandegários
dutiful ['dju:tɪful] ADJ (child) respeitoso; (husband, wife) atencioso; (employee) zeloso, consciente
duty ['dju:tɪ] N dever m; (tax) taxa; (customs) taxa alfandegária; **duties** NPL funções fpl; **to make it one's ~ to do sth** dar-se a responsabilidade de fazer algo; **to pay ~ on sth** pagar imposto sobre algo; **on ~** de serviço; (at night etc) de plantão; **off ~** de folga
duty-free ADJ livre de impostos; **~ shop** duty-free f
duty officer N (Mil etc) oficial m de serviço
duvet ['du:veɪ] (BRIT) N edredom m (BR), edredão m (PT)
DV ABBR (= Deo volente) se Deus quiser
DVD N ABBR (= digital versatile or video disc) DVD m

DVD burner N gravador m de DVD
DVD player N DVD player m
DVD writer N gravador m de DVD
DVM (US) N ABBR (= Doctor of Veterinary Medicine) título universitário
dwarf [dwɔ:f] N (pl **dwarves**) anão/anã m/f ▶ VT ananicar
dwarves [dwɔ:vz] NPL of **dwarf**
dwell [dwɛl] (pt, pp **dwelt**) VI morar ▶ **dwell on** VT FUS estender-se sobre
dweller ['dwɛlər] N habitante m/f
dwelling ['dwɛlɪŋ] N residência
dwelt [dwɛlt] PT, PP of **dwell**
dwindle ['dwɪndl] VI diminuir
dwindling ['dwɪndlɪŋ] ADJ descrescente, minguante
dye [daɪ] N tintura, tinta ▶ VT tingir; **hair ~** tintura para o cabelo
dyestuffs ['daɪstʌfs] NPL corantes mpl
dying ['daɪɪŋ] ADJ moribundo, agonizante; (moments) final; (words) último
dyke [daɪk] (BRIT) N (embankment) dique m, represa
dynamic [daɪ'næmɪk] ADJ dinâmico
dynamics [daɪ'næmɪks] N, NPL dinâmica
dynamite ['daɪnəmaɪt] N dinamite f ▶ VT dinamitar
dynamo ['daɪnəməu] N dínamo
dynasty ['dɪnəstɪ] N dinastia
dysentery ['dɪsntrɪ] N disenteria
dyslexia [dɪs'lɛksɪə] N dislexia
dyslexic [dɪs'lɛksɪk] ADJ, N dislético(-a), disléxico(-a)
dyspepsia [dɪs'pɛpsɪə] N dispepsia
dystrophy ['dɪstrəfɪ] N distrofia; see also **muscular dystrophy**

Ee

E', e [i:] N (letter) E, e m; (Mus): **E** mi m; **E for Edward** (BRIT) or **Easy** (US) E de Eliane

E² ABBR (= east) E

E111 N ABBR (also: **form E111**) formulário E111

ea. ABBR = **each**

E.A. (US) N ABBR (= educational age) idade educacional

each [i:tʃ] ADJ cada inv ▶ PRON cada um(a); **~ one** cada um; **~ other** um ao outro; **they hate ~ other** (eles) se odeiam; **you are jealous of ~ other** vocês têm ciume um do outro; **~ day** cada dia; **they have 2 books ~** eles têm 2 livros cada um; **they cost £5 ~** custam £5 cada; **~ of us** cada um de nós

eager ['i:gə'] ADJ ávido; (hopeful) desejoso; (ambitious) ambicioso; (pupil) empolgado; **to be ~ to do sth** ansiar por fazer algo; **to be ~ for** ansiar por

eagle ['i:gl] N águia

E and OE ABBR (= errors and omissions excepted) SEO

ear [ɪə'] N (external) orelha; (inner, fig) ouvido; (of corn) espiga; **to play by ~** tocar de ouvido; **up to one's ~s in debt** endividado até o pescoço

earache ['ɪəreɪk] N dor f de ouvidos

eardrum ['ɪədrʌm] N tímpano

earl [ə:l] N conde m

earlier ['ə:lɪə'] ADJ (date etc) mais adiantado; (edition etc) anterior ▶ ADV mais cedo

early ['ə:lɪ] ADV cedo; (before time) com antecedência ▶ ADJ (sooner than expected) prematuro; (reply) pronto; (Christians, settlers) primeiro; (man) primitivo; (life, work) juvenil; **to have an ~ night/start** vá para cama cedo/saia de manhã cedo; **in the ~ or ~ in the spring/19th century** no princípio da primavera/do século dezenove; **as ~ as possible** o mais cedo possível; **you're ~!** você chegou cedo!; **~ in the morning** de manhã cedo; **she's in her ~ forties** ela tem pouco mais de 40 anos; **at your earliest convenience** (Comm) o mais cedo que lhe for possível

early retirement N aposentadoria antecipada

early warning system N sistema m de alerta antecipado

earmark ['ɪəmɑ:k] VT: **to ~ sth for** reservar or destinar algo para

earn [ə:n] VT ganhar; (Comm: interest) render; (praise, reward) merecer; **to ~ one's living** ganhar a vida

earned income [ə:nd-] N rendimento do trabalho individual

earnest ['ə:nɪst] ADJ (wish) intenso; (manner) sério ▶ N (also: **earnest money**) sinal m em dinheiro; **in ~** a sério

earnings ['ə:nɪŋz] NPL (personal) vencimentos mpl, salário, ordenado; (of company) lucro

ear nose and throat specialist N otorrinolaringologista m/f, otorrino m/f

earphones ['ɪəfəunz] NPL fones mpl de ouvido

earplugs ['ɪəplʌgz] NPL borrachinhas fpl (de ouvido)

earring ['ɪərɪŋ] N brinco

earshot ['ɪəʃɔt] N: **out of/within ~** fora do/ao alcance do ouvido or da voz

earth [ə:θ] N terra; (BRIT Elec) fio terra ▶ VT (BRIT Elec) ligar à terra; **what on ~!** que diabo!

earthenware ['ə:θənwɛə'] N louça de barro ▶ ADJ de barro

earthly ['ə:θlɪ] ADJ terrestre; **~ paradise** paraíso terrestre; **there is no ~ reason to think …** não há a mínima razão para se pensar que …

earthquake ['ə:θkweɪk] N terremoto (BR), terramoto (PT)

earth-shattering ['ə:θʃætərɪŋ] ADJ bombástico

earth tremor N tremor m, abalo sísmico

earthworks ['ə:θwə:ks] NPL trabalhos mpl de terraplenagem

earthworm ['ə:θwə:m] N minhoca

earthy ['ə:θɪ] ADJ (fig: vulgar) grosseiro; (: natural) natural

earwax ['ɪəwæks] N cerume m

earwig ['ɪəwɪg] N lacrainha

ease [i:z] N facilidade f; (relaxed state) sossego ▶ VT facilitar; (relieve: pressure) afrouxar; (: pain, tension) aliviar; (help pass): **to ~ sth in/out** meter/tirar algo com cuidado ▶ VI (situation) abrandar; **at ~!** (Mil) descansar!; **to be at ~** estar à vontade; **with ~** com facilidade

▶ **ease off** VI acalmar-se; (at work) deixar de trabalhar tanto; (wind) baixar; (rain) moderar-se

▶ **ease up** VI = **ease off**

easel ['i:zl] N cavalete m
easily ['i:zɪlɪ] ADV facilmente, fácil (inf)
easiness ['i:zɪnɪs] N facilidade f; (of manner) desenvoltura
east [i:st] N leste m ▸ ADJ (region) leste; (wind) do leste ▸ ADV para o leste; **the E~** o Oriente; (Pol) o leste
Easter ['i:stəʳ] N Páscoa ▸ ADJ (holidays) da Páscoa; (traditions) pascal
Easter egg N ovo de Páscoa
Easter Island N ilha da Páscoa
easterly ['i:stəlɪ] ADJ (to the east) para o leste; (from the east) do Leste
Easter Monday N Segunda-Feira da Páscoa
eastern ['i:stən] ADJ do leste, oriental; **E~ Europe** a Europa Oriental; **the E~ bloc** (Pol) o Bloco Oriental
Easter Sunday N Domingo da Páscoa
East Germany N Alemanha Oriental
eastward ['i:stwəd], **eastwards** ['i:stwədz] ADV ao leste
easy ['i:zɪ] ADJ fácil; (comfortable) folgado, cômodo; (relaxed) natural, complacente; (victim, prey) desprotegido ▸ ADV: **to take it** or **things ~** (not worry) levar as coisas com calma; (go slowly) ir devagar; (rest) descansar; **payment on ~ terms** (Comm) pagamento facilitado; **that's easier said than done** é mais fácil falar do que fazer; **I'm ~** (inf) para mim, tanto faz
easy chair N poltrona
easy-going ADJ pacato, fácil
eat [i:t] (pt **ate**, pp **eaten**) VT, VI comer
  ▸ **eat away** VT corroer
  ▸ **eat away at** VT FUS corroer
  ▸ **eat into** VT FUS = **eat away at**
  ▸ **eat out** VI jantar fora
  ▸ **eat up** VT (food) acabar; **it ~s up electricity** consome eletricidade demais
eatable ['i:təbl] ADJ comestível
eau de Cologne [əudə-] N (água de) Colônia
eaves [i:vz] NPL beira, beiral m
eavesdrop ['i:vzdrɔp] VI: **to ~ (on)** escutar às escondidas
ebb [ɛb] N refluxo ▸ VI baixar; (fig: also: **ebb away**) declinar; **the ~ and flow** o fluxo e refluxo; **to be at a low ~** (fig: person) estar de maré baixa; (: business, relations etc) ir mal
ebb tide N baixa-mar f, maré f vazante
ebony ['ɛbənɪ] N ébano
e-book ['i:buk] N livro eletrônico
ebullient [ɪ'bʌlɪənt] ADJ vivo, enérgico
EC N ABBR (= European Community) CE f
e-card ['i:ka:d] N cartão m eletrônico
ECB N ABBR (= European Central Bank) BCE m, Banco Central Europeu
eccentric [ɪk'sɛntrɪk] ADJ, N excêntrico(-a)
ecclesiastic [ɪkliːzɪ'æstɪk], **ecclesiastical** [ɪkliːzɪ'æstɪkəl] ADJ eclesiástico
ECG N ABBR (= electrocardiogram) eletro
ECGD N ABBR (= Export Credits Guarantee Department) serviço de garantia financeira para exportações

echo ['ɛkəu] N (pl **echoes**) eco ▸ VT (sound) ecoar, repetir ▸ VI ressoar, repetir
éclair [eɪ'klɛəʳ] N (Culin) bomba
eclipse [ɪ'klɪps] N eclipse m ▸ VT eclipsar
ECM (US) N ABBR = **European Common Market**
eco-friendly [i:kəu'frɛndlɪ] ADJ ecológico
ecological [i:kə'lɔdʒɪkəl] ADJ ecológico
ecologist [ɪ'kɔlədʒɪst] N ecologista m/f
ecology [ɪ'kɔlədʒɪ] N ecologia
e-commerce N ABBR (= electronic commerce) comércio eletrônico
economic [i:kə'nɔmɪk] ADJ econômico; (business etc) rentável
economical [i:kə'nɔmɪkəl] ADJ econômico; (proposition etc) rentável
economically [i:kə'nɔmɪklɪ] ADV economicamente
economics [i:kə'nɔmɪks] N economia ▸ NPL aspectos mpl econômicos
economist [ɪ'kɔnəmɪst] N economista m/f
economize [ɪ'kɔnəmaɪz] VI economizar, fazer economias
economy [ɪ'kɔnəmɪ] N economia; **economies of scale** economias de escala
economy class N (Aviat) classe f econômica
economy size N tamanho econômico
ecosystem ['i:kəusɪstəm] N ecossistema m
ECSC N ABBR (= European Coal and Steel Community) CECA f
ecstasy ['ɛkstəsɪ] N êxtase m; **to go into ecstasies over** extasiar-se com
ecstatic [ɛks'tætɪk] ADJ extasiado
ECT N ABBR = **electroconvulsive therapy**
ECU N ABBR (= European Currency Unit) ECU f
Ecuador ['ɛkwədɔːʳ] N Equador m
Ecuadorian [ɛkwə'dɔːrɪən] ADJ, N equatoriano(-a)
ecumenical [i:kju'mɛnɪkl] ADJ ecumênico
eczema ['ɛksɪmə] N eczema m
eddy ['ɛdɪ] N rodamoinho
edge [ɛdʒ] N (of knife etc) fio; (of table, chair etc) borda; (of lake etc) margem f ▸ VT (trim) embainhar ▸ VI: **to ~ forward** avançar pouco a pouco; **on ~** (fig) = **edgy**; **to have the ~ on** (fig) levar vantagem sobre; **to ~ away from** afastar-se pouco a pouco de
edgeways ['ɛdʒweɪz] ADV lateralmente; **he couldn't get a word in ~** não pôde entrar na conversa
edging ['ɛdʒɪŋ] N (Sewing) debrum m; (of path) borda
edgy ['ɛdʒɪ] ADJ nervoso, inquieto
edible ['ɛdɪbl] ADJ comestível
edict ['i:dɪkt] N édito
edifice ['ɛdɪfɪs] N edifício
edifying ['ɛdɪfaɪɪŋ] ADJ edificante
Edinburgh ['ɛdɪnbərə] N Edimburgo
edit ['ɛdɪt] VT (be editor of) dirigir; (cut) cortar, redigir; (Comput, TV) editar; (Cinema) montar
edition [ɪ'dɪʃən] N (gen) edição f; (number printed) tiragem f
editor ['ɛdɪtəʳ] N redator(a) m/f; (of newspaper) diretor(a) m/f; (of column) editor(a) m/f;

(*of book*) organizador(a) *m/f* da edição; (*also:* **film editor**) montador(a) *m/f*

editorial [ɛdɪˈtɔːrɪəl] ADJ editorial ▶ N editorial *m*; **the ~ staff** a redação

EDP N ABBR = **electronic data processing**

EDT (*US*) ABBR (= *Eastern Daylight Time*) *hora de verão de Nova Iorque*

educate [ˈɛdjukeɪt] VT educar; **~d at ...** que cursou ...

education [ɛdjuˈkeɪʃən] N educação *f*; (*schooling*) ensino; (*science*) pedagogia; **primary** (*BRIT*) *or* **elementary** (*US*) ~ ensino de 1°/2° grau

educational [ɛdjuˈkeɪʃənl] ADJ (*policy, experience*) educacional; (*teaching*) docente; (*toy etc*) educativo; **~ technology** tecnologia educacional

Edwardian [ɛdˈwɔːdɪən] ADJ da época do rei Eduardo VII, dos anos 1900

EE ABBR = **electrical engineer**

EEC N ABBR (= *European Economic Community*) CEE *f*

EEG N ABBR (= *electroencephalogram*) eletro

eel [iːl] N enguia

EENT (*US*) N ABBR (*Med*) = **eye, ear, nose and throat**

EEOC (*US*) N ABBR = **Equal Employment Opportunity Commission**

eerie [ˈɪərɪ] ADJ (*strange*) estranho; (*mysterious*) misterioso

EET N ABBR (= *Eastern European Time*) *hora da Europa Oriental*

effect [ɪˈfɛkt] N efeito ▶ VT (*repairs*) fazer; (*savings*) efetuar; **effects** NPL (*Theatre*) efeitos *mpl*; (*property*) bens *mpl* móveis, pertences *mpl*; **to take ~** (*law*) entrar em vigor; (*drug*) fazer efeito; **to put into ~** (*plan*) pôr em ação *or* prática; **to have an ~ on sb/sth** produzir efeito em alguém/algo; **in ~** na realidade; **his letter is to the ~ that ...** a carta dele informa que ...

effective [ɪˈfɛktɪv] ADJ (*successful*) eficaz; (*striking*) impressionante; (*actual*) efetivo; **to become ~** (*Law*) entrar em vigor; **~ date** data de entrada em vigor

effectively [ɪˈfɛktɪvlɪ] ADV (*successfully*) eficazmente; (*in reality*) efetivamente

effectiveness [ɪˈfɛktɪvnɪs] N eficácia

effeminate [ɪˈfɛmɪnɪt] ADJ efeminado

effervescent [ɛfəˈvɛsnt] ADJ efervescente

efficacy [ˈɛfɪkəsɪ] N eficácia

efficiency [ɪˈfɪʃənsɪ] N eficiência; (*of machine*) rendimento

efficiency apartment (*US*) N kitchenette *f*

efficient [ɪˈfɪʃənt] ADJ eficiente; (*machine*) rentável

efficiently [ɪˈfɪʃəntlɪ] ADV eficientemente

effigy [ˈɛfɪdʒɪ] N efígie *f*

effluent [ˈɛfluənt] N efluente *m*

effort [ˈɛfət] N esforço; **to make an ~ to** esforçar-se para

effortless [ˈɛfətlɪs] ADJ fácil

effrontery [ɪˈfrʌntərɪ] N descaramento

effusive [ɪˈfjuːsɪv] ADJ efusivo; (*welcome*) caloroso

EFL N ABBR (*Sch*) = **English as a foreign language**

EFTA [ˈɛftə] N ABBR (= *European Free Trade Association*) AELC *f*

e.g. ADV ABBR (= *exempli gratia*) p. ex.

egalitarian [ɪgælɪˈtɛərɪən] ADJ igualitário

egg [ɛg] N ovo; **hard-boiled/soft-boiled ~** ovo duro/mole
▶ **egg on** VT incitar

eggcup [ˈɛgkʌp] N oveiro

eggplant [ˈɛgplɑːnt] (*esp US*) N beringela

eggshell [ˈɛgʃɛl] N casca de ovo

egg white N clara (de ovo)

egg yolk N gema

ego [ˈiːgəu] N ego

egoism [ˈiːgəuɪzəm] N egoísmo

egoist [ˈiːgəuɪst] N egoísta *m/f*

egotism [ˈɛgəutɪzəm] N egotismo *m*

egotist [ˈɛgəutɪst] N egotista *m/f*

Egypt [ˈiːdʒɪpt] N Egito

Egyptian [ɪˈdʒɪpʃən] ADJ, N egípcio(-a)

eiderdown [ˈaɪdədaun] N edredom *m* (*BR*), edredão *m* (*PT*)

eight [eɪt] NUM oito; *see also* **five**

eighteen [ˈeɪˈtiːn] NUM dezoito; *see also* **five**

eighteenth [ˈeɪˈtiːnθ] NUM décimo oitavo

eighth [eɪtθ] NUM oitavo; *see also* **fifth**

eightieth [ˈeɪtɪɪθ] NUM octogésimo

eighty [ˈeɪtɪ] NUM oitenta; *see also* **fifty**

Eire [ˈɛərə] N (República da) Irlanda

EIS N ABBR (= *Educational Institute of Scotland*) *sindicato dos professores escoceses*

either [ˈaɪðəʳ] ADJ (*one or other*) um ou outro; (*each*) cada; (*any*) qualquer; (*both*) ambos
▶ PRON: **~ (of them)** qualquer (dos dois)
▶ ADV: **no, I don't ~** eu também não ▶ CONJ: **~ yes or no** ou sim ou não; **on ~ side** de ambos os lados; **I don't like ~** não gosto nem de um nem do outro; **I haven't seen ~ one or the other** eu não vi nem um nem o outro

ejaculation [ɪdʒækjuˈleɪʃən] N (*Physiol*) ejaculação *f*

eject [ɪˈdʒɛkt] VT expulsar ▶ VI (*pilot*) ser ejetado

ejector seat [ɪˈdʒɛktəʳ-] N assento ejetor

eke [iːk]: **to ~ out** VT (*money*) economizar; (*food*) economizar em; (*add to*) complementar

EKG (*US*) N ABBR (= *electrocardiogram*) eletro

el [ɛl] (*US inf*) N ABBR = **elevated railroad**

elaborate [*adj* ɪˈlæbərɪt, *vt, vi* ɪˈlæbəreɪt] ADJ complicado; (*decorated*) rebuscado ▶ VT elaborar; (*expand*) expandir; (*refine*) aperfeiçoar ▶ VI: **to ~ on** acrescentar detalhes a

elapse [ɪˈlæps] VI transcorrer

elastic [ɪˈlæstɪk] ADJ elástico; (*adaptable*) flexível, adaptável ▶ N elástico

elastic band (*BRIT*) N elástico

elasticity [ɪlæsˈtɪsɪtɪ] N elasticidade *f*

elated [ɪˈleɪtɪd] ADJ: **to be ~** rejubilar-se

e

elation [ɪ'leɪʃən] N exaltação f
elbow ['ɛlbəu] N cotovelo ▶ VT: **to ~ one's way through the crowd** abrir passagem pela multidão com os cotovelos
elbow room N (fig) liberdade f
elder ['ɛldə^r] ADJ mais velho ▶ N (tree) sabugueiro; (person) o/a mais velho(-a); (of tribe) ancião; (of church) presbítero
elderly ['ɛldəlɪ] ADJ idoso, de idade ▶ NPL: **the ~** as pessoas de idade, os idosos
eldest ['ɛldɪst] ADJ mais velho ▶ N o/a mais velho(-a)
elect [ɪ'lɛkt] VT eleger ▶ ADJ: **the president ~** o presidente eleito; **to ~ to do** (choose) optar por fazer
election [ɪ'lɛkʃən] N (voting) votação f; (installation) eleição f; **to hold an ~** realizar uma eleição
election campaign N campanha eleitoral
electioneering [ɪlɛkʃə'nɪərɪŋ] N campanha or propaganda eleitoral
elector [ɪ'lɛktə^r] N eleitor(a) m/f
electoral [ɪ'lɛktərəl] ADJ eleitoral
electoral college N colégio eleitoral
electoral roll (BRIT) N lista de eleitores
electorate [ɪ'lɛktərɪt] N eleitorado
electric [ɪ'lɛktrɪk] ADJ elétrico
electrical [ɪ'lɛktrɪkəl] ADJ elétrico
electrical engineer N engenheiro(-a) eletricista
electrical failure N pane f elétrica
electric blanket N cobertor m elétrico
electric chair (US) N cadeira elétrica
electric cooker N fogão m elétrico
electric current N corrente f elétrica
electric fire (BRIT) N aquecedor m elétrico
electrician [ɪlɛk'trɪʃən] N eletricista m/f
electricity [ɪlɛk'trɪsɪtɪ] N eletricidade f
electricity board (BRIT) N empresa de energia elétrica
electric light N luz f elétrica
electric shock N choque m elétrico
electrify [ɪ'lɛktrɪfaɪ] VT (fence, Rail) eletrificar; (audience) eletrizar
electro... [ɪ'lɛktrəu] PREFIX eletro...
electrocardiogram [ɪ'lɛktrəu'kɑːdɪəgræm] N eletrocardiograma m
electroconvulsive therapy N eletrochoques mpl
electrocute [ɪ'lɛktrəkjuːt] VT eletrocutar
electrode [ɪ'lɛktrəud] N eletrodo (BR), eléctrodo (PT)
electroencephalogram [ɪ'lɛktrəuɛn'sɛfələgræm] N eletroencefalograma m
electrolysis [ɪlɛk'trɔlɪsɪs] N eletrólise f
electromagnetic [ɪlɛktrəumæg'nɛtɪk] ADJ eletromagnético
electron [ɪ'lɛktrɔn] N elétron m (BR), electrão m (PT)
electronic [ɪlɛk'trɔnɪk] ADJ eletrônico
electronic data processing N processamento de dados eletrônico

electronic mail N correio eletrônico
electronics [ɪlɛk'trɔnɪks] N eletrônica
electron microscope N microscópio eletrônico
electroplated [ɪ'lɛktrəu'pleɪtɪd] ADJ galvanizado
electrotherapy [ɪ'lɛktrəu'θɛrəpɪ] N eletroterapia
elegance ['ɛlɪgəns] N elegância
elegant ['ɛlɪgənt] ADJ (person, building) elegante; (idea) refinado
element ['ɛlɪmənt] N elemento; **to brave the ~s** enfrentar intempérie
elementary [ɛlɪ'mɛntərɪ] ADJ (gen) elementar; (primitive) rudimentar; (school, education) primário
elementary school (US) N ver nota

> Nos Estados Unidos e no Canadá, uma **elementary school** (também chamada de grade school ou grammar school nos Estados Unidos) é uma escola pública onde os alunos passam de seis a oito dos primeiros anos escolares.

elephant ['ɛlɪfənt] N elefante m
elevate ['ɛlɪveɪt] VT elevar; (in rank) promover
elevated railroad (US) N ferrovia elevada
elevation [ɛlɪ'veɪʃən] N elevação f; (land) eminência; (height) altura
elevator ['ɛlɪveɪtə^r] (US) N elevador m
eleven [ɪ'lɛvn] NUM onze; see also **five**
elevenses [ɪ'lɛvənzɪz] (BRIT) NPL refeição leve da manhã
eleventh [ɪ'lɛvnθ] NUM décimo-primeiro; **at the ~ hour** (fig) no último momento, na hora H; see also **fifth**
elf [ɛlf] (pl **elves**) N elfo, duende m
elicit [ɪ'lɪsɪt] VT: **to ~ (from)** (information) extrair (de); (response, reaction) provocar (de)
eligible ['ɛlɪdʒəbl] ADJ elegível, apto; **to be ~ for sth** (job etc) ter qualificações para algo; (pension etc) ter direito a algo
eliminate [ɪ'lɪmɪneɪt] VT (poverty, smoking) erradicar; (candidate, team) eliminar; (strike out) suprimir; (suspect) eliminar, excluir
elimination [ɪlɪmɪ'neɪʃən] N eliminação f; **by a process of ~** por eliminação
élite [eɪ'liːt] N elite f
élitist [eɪ'liːtɪst] (pej) ADJ elitista
elixir [ɪ'lɪksə^r] N elixir m
Elizabethan [ɪlɪzə'biːθən] ADJ elisabetano
ellipse [ɪ'lɪps] N elipse f
elliptical [ɪ'lɪptɪkl] ADJ elíptico
elm [ɛlm] N olmo
elocution [ɛlə'kjuːʃən] N elocução f
elongated ['iːlɔŋgeɪtɪd] ADJ alongado
elope [ɪ'ləup] VI fugir
elopement [ɪ'ləupmənt] N fuga do lar paterno
eloquence ['ɛləkwəns] N eloquência
eloquent ['ɛləkwənt] ADJ eloquente
El Salvador [el'sælvədɔː^r] N El Salvador
else [ɛls] ADV outro, mais; **something ~** outra coisa; **somewhere ~** em outro lugar (BR),

noutro sítio (PT); **everywhere ~** por todo o lado (menos aqui); **everyone ~** todos os outros; **where ~?** onde mais?; **what ~ can we do?** que mais podemos fazer?; **or ~** senão; **there was little ~ to do** não havia outra coisa a fazer; **nobody ~ spoke** ninguém mais falou

elsewhere [ɛls'wɛəʳ] ADV (be) em outro lugar (BR), noutro sítio (PT); (go) para outro lugar (BR), a outro sítio (PT)

ELT N ABBR (Sch) = **English Language Teaching**

elucidate [ɪ'lu:sɪdeɪt] VT esclarecer, elucidar

elude [ɪ'lu:d] VT (pursuer) escapar de, esquivar-se de; (subj: fact, idea) evadir

elusive [ɪ'lu:sɪv] ADJ esquivo; (quality) indescritível; (answer) evasivo

elves [ɛlvz] NPL of **elf**

emaciated [ɪ'meɪsɪeɪtɪd] ADJ emaciado, macilento

email ['i:meɪl] N e-mail m, correio eletrônico ► VT (person) enviar um e-mail a

email account N conta de e-mail, conta de correio eletrônico

email address N e-mail m, endereço eletrônico

emanate ['ɛmaneɪt] VI: **to ~ from** emanar de

emancipate [ɪ'mænsɪpeɪt] VT libertar; (women) emancipar

emancipated [ɪ'mænsɪpeɪtɪd] ADJ emancipado

emancipation [ɪmænsɪ'peɪʃən] N emancipação f

emasculate [ɪ'mæskjuleɪt] VT emascular

embalm [ɪm'bɑ:m] VT embalsamar

embankment [ɪm'bæŋkmənt] N aterro; (of river) dique m

embargo [ɪm'bɑ:gəu] N (pl **embargoes**) (Naut) embargo; (Comm) proibição f ► VT boicotear; **to put an ~ on sth** proibir algo

embark [ɪm'bɑ:k] VI embarcar ► VT embarcar; **to ~ on** (fig) empreender, começar

embarkation [ɛmbɑ:'keɪʃən] N (of people, goods) embarque m

embarkation card N cartão m de embarque

embarrass [ɪm'bærəs] VT (politician) embaraçar; (emotionally) constranger

embarrassed [ɪm'bærəst] ADJ (laugh, silence) descomfortável; **to be financially ~** estar com dificuldades financeiras

embarrassing [ɪm'bærəsɪŋ] ADJ embaraçoso, constrangedor(a)

embarrassment [ɪm'bærəsmənt] N embaraço, constrangimento; (financial) dificuldades fpl

embassy ['ɛmbəsɪ] N embaixada

embed [ɪm'bɛd] VT embutir; (teeth etc) cravar

embedded [ɪm'bɛdɪd] ADJ encravado

embellish [ɪm'bɛlɪʃ] VT embelezar; (fig: story) florear

embers ['ɛmbəz] NPL brasa, borralho, cinzas fpl

embezzle [ɪm'bɛzl] VT desviar

embezzlement [ɪm'bɛzlmənt] N desvio (de fundos)

embezzler [ɪm'bɛzləʳ] N malversador(a) m/f

embitter [ɪm'bɪtəʳ] VT (person) amargurar; (relations) azedar

embittered [ɪm'bɪtəd] ADJ amargurado

emblem ['ɛmbləm] N emblema m

embodiment [ɪm'bɔdɪmənt] N encarnação f

embody [ɪm'bɔdɪ] VT (features) incorporar; (ideas) expressar

embolden [ɪm'bəuldn] VT encorajar, animar

embolism ['ɛmbəlɪzəm] N embolia

embossed [ɪm'bɔst] ADJ realçado; **~ with** ornado com relevos de

embrace [ɪm'breɪs] VT abraçar, dar um abraço em; (include) abarcar, abranger; (adopt: idea) adotar ► VI abraçar-se ► N abraço

embroider [ɪm'brɔɪdəʳ] VT bordar; (fig: story) florear

embroidery [ɪm'brɔɪdərɪ] N bordado

embroil [ɪm'brɔɪl] VT: **to become ~ed (in sth)** ficar envolvido (em algo)

embryo ['ɛmbrɪəu] N (fig) embrião m

emend [ɪ'mɛnd] VT emendar

emerald ['ɛmərəld] N esmeralda

emerge [ɪ'mə:dʒ] VI sair; (from sleep) acordar; (fact, idea) emergir; **it ~s that ...** (BRIT) veio à tona que ...

emergence [ɪ'mə:dʒəns] N surgimento, aparecimento; (of a nation) nascimento

emergency [ɪ'mə:dʒənsɪ] N emergência; **in an ~** em caso de urgência; **state of ~** estado de emergência

emergency cord (US) N sinal m de alarme

emergency exit N saída de emergência

emergency landing N aterrissagem f forçada (BR), aterragem f forçosa (PT)

emergency lane (US) N (Aut) acostamento (BR), berma (PT)

emergency meeting N reunião f extraordinária

emergency road service (US) N autossocorro (BR), pronto socorro (PT)

emergency services NPL serviços mpl de emergência

emergency stop (BRIT) N (Aut) parada de emergência

emergent [ɪ'mə:dʒənt] ADJ (nation) em desenvolvimento; (group) emergente

emery board ['ɛmərɪ-] N lixa de unhas

emery paper ['ɛmərɪ-] N lixa or papel m de esmeril

emetic [ɪ'mɛtɪk] N emético

emigrant ['ɛmɪgrənt] N emigrante m/f

emigrate ['ɛmɪgreɪt] VI emigrar

emigration [ɛmɪ'greɪʃən] N emigração f

émigré ['ɛmɪgreɪ] N emigrado(-a)

eminence ['ɛmɪnəns] N eminência

eminent ['ɛmɪnənt] ADJ eminente

eminently ['ɛmɪnəntlɪ] ADV eminentemente

emirate ['ɛmɪrɪt] N emirado

emission [ɪ'mɪʃən] N emissão f

emit [ɪ'mɪt] VT (gen) emitir; (smoke) soltar; (smell) exalar; (sound) produzir

emolument [ɪ'mɔljumənt] N (often pl: formal: fee) honorário; (salary) remuneração f
emoticon [ɪ'məutɪkən] N (Comput) emoticon m
emotion [ɪ'məuʃən] N emoção f
emotional [ɪ'məuʃənəl] ADJ (needs, exhaustion) emocional; (person) sentimental, emotivo; (scene) comovente; (tone) emocionante
emotionally [ɪ'məuʃənəlɪ] ADV (disturbed, involved) emocionalmente; (behave) emotivamente; (speak) com emoção
emotive [ɪ'məutɪv] ADJ que sensibiliza; **~ power** capacidade f de comover
empathy ['ɛmpəθɪ] N empatia; **to feel ~ with sb** ter afinidade com alguém
emperor ['ɛmpərə'] N imperador m
emphases ['ɛmfəsi:z] N PL of **emphasis**
emphasis ['ɛmfəsɪs] (pl **emphases**) N ênfase f; (stress) acentuação f; **to lay** or **place ~ on sth** dar ênfase a; **the ~ is on reading** a leitura ocupa um lugar de destaque
emphasize ['ɛmfəsaɪz] VT (word, point) enfatizar, acentuar; (feature) salientar
emphatic [ɛm'fætɪk] ADJ (statement) vigoroso, expressivo; (person) convincente; (manner) enfático
emphatically [ɛm'fætɪkəlɪ] ADV com ênfase; (certainly) certamente
empire ['ɛmpaɪə'] N império
empirical [ɛm'pɪrɪkl] ADJ empírico
employ [ɪm'plɔɪ] VT empregar; (tool) utilizar; **he's ~ed in a bank** ele trabalha num banco
employee [ɪmplɔɪ'i:] N empregado(-a)
employer [ɪm'plɔɪə'] N empregador(a) m/f, patrão(-troa) m/f
employment [ɪm'plɔɪmənt] N (gen) emprego; (work) trabalho; **to find ~** encontrar um emprego; **without ~** sem emprego, desempregado; **place of ~** local de trabalho
employment agency N agência de empregos
employment exchange (BRIT) N bolsa de trabalho
empower [ɪm'pauə'] VT: **to ~ sb to do sth** autorizar alguém para fazer algo
empress ['ɛmprɪs] N imperatriz f
emptiness ['ɛmptɪnɪs] N vazio, vácuo
empty ['ɛmptɪ] ADJ vazio; (place) deserto; (house) desocupado; (threat) vão/vã ▶ N (bottle) vazio ▶ VT esvaziar; (place) evacuar ▶ VI esvaziar-se; (place) ficar deserto; **on an ~ stomach** em jejum, com o estômago vazio; **to ~ into** (river) desaguar em
empty-handed [-'hændɪd] ADJ de mãos vazias
empty-headed [-'hɛdɪd] ADJ de cabeça oca
EMS N ABBR (= European Monetary System) SME m
EMT N ABBR = **emergency medical technician**
emulate ['ɛmjuleɪt] VT (person) emular com
emulsion [ɪ'mʌlʃən] N emulsão f; (also: **emulsion paint**) tinta plástica
enable [ɪ'neɪbl] VT: **to ~ sb to do sth** (allow) permitir que alguém faça algo; (prepare) capacitar alguém para fazer algo
enact [ɪn'ækt] VT (law) pôr em vigor, promulgar; (play) representar; (role) fazer

enamel [ɪ'næməl] N esmalte m
enamel paint N esmalte m
enamoured [ɪ'næməd] ADJ: **to be ~ of** (person) estar apaixonado por; (activity etc) ser louco por; (idea) encantar-se com
enc. ABBR (in letters etc) = **enclosed**; **enclosure**
encampment [ɪn'kæmpmənt] N acampamento
encased [ɪn'keɪst] ADJ: **~ in** (enclosed) encaixado em; (covered) revestido de
enchant [ɪn'tʃɑ:nt] VT encantar
enchanted [ɪn'tʃɑ:ntɪd] ADJ encantado
enchanting [ɪn'tʃɑ:ntɪŋ] ADJ encantador(a)
encircle [ɪn'sə:kl] VT cercar, circundar; (waist) rodear
encl. ABBR (in letters etc) = **enclosed**; **enclosure**
enclave ['ɛnkleɪv] N: **an ~ of** um encrave de
enclose [ɪn'kləuz] VT (land) cercar; (with letter etc) anexar (BR), enviar junto (PT); **please find ~d** segue junto
enclosure [ɪn'kləuʒə'] N cercado; (Comm) documento anexo
encoder [ɪn'kəudə'] N (Comput) codificador m
encompass [ɪn'kʌmpəs] VT abranger, encerrar
encore [ɔŋ'kɔ:'] EXCL bis!, outra! ▶ N bis m
encounter [ɪn'kauntə'] N encontro ▶ VT encontrar, topar com; (difficulty) enfrentar
encourage [ɪn'kʌrɪdʒ] VT (activity) encorajar; (growth) estimular; (person): **to ~ sb to do sth** animar alguém a fazer algo
encouragement [ɪn'kʌrɪdʒmənt] N estímulo
encouraging [ɪn'kʌrɪdʒɪŋ] ADJ animador(a)
encroach [ɪn'krəutʃ] VI: **to ~ (up)on** invadir; (time) ocupar
encrusted [ɪn'krʌstəd] ADJ: **~ with** incrustado de
encrypt [ɪn'krɪpt] VT (Comput, Tel) criptografar
encumber [ɪn'kʌmbə'] VT: **to be ~ed with** (carry) estar carregado de; (debts) estar sobrecarregado de
encyclopaedia, encyclopedia [ɛnsaɪkləu'pi:dɪə] N enciclopédia
end [ɛnd] N (gen, also aim) fim m; (of table, line, rope etc) ponta; (of street, town) final m; (Sport) ponta ▶ VT acabar, terminar; (also: **bring to an end, put an end to**) acabar com, pôr fim a ▶ VI terminar, acabar; **from ~ to ~** de ponta a ponta; **to come to an ~** acabar; **to be at an ~** estar no fim, estar terminado; **in the ~** ao fim, por fim, finalmente; **on ~** (object) na ponta; **to stand on ~** (hair) arrepiar-se; **for hours on ~** por horas a fio; **at the ~ of the day** (BRIT fig) no final das contas; **to this ~, with this ~ in view** a este fim ▶ **end up** VI: **to ~ up in** terminar em; (place) ir parar em
endanger [ɪn'deɪndʒə'] VT pôr em perigo; **an ~ed species** uma espécie ameaçada de extinção
endear [ɪn'dɪə'] VT: **to ~ o.s. to sb** conquistar a afeição de alguém, cativar alguém
endearing [ɪn'dɪərɪŋ] ADJ simpático, atrativo

endearment [ɪn'dɪəmənt] N: **to whisper ~s** sussurrar palavras carinhosas; **term of ~** palavra carinhosa

endeavour, (US) **endeavor** [ɪn'dɛvər] N esforço; (attempt) tentativa; (striving) empenho ▶ VI: **to ~ to do** esforçar-se para fazer; (try) tentar fazer

endemic [ɛn'dɛmɪk] ADJ endêmico

ending ['ɛndɪŋ] N fim m, conclusão f; (of book) desenlace m; (Ling) terminação f

endive ['ɛndaɪv] N (curly) chicória; (smooth, flat) endívia

endless ['ɛndlɪs] ADJ interminável; (possibilities) infinito

endorse [ɪn'dɔːs] VT (cheque) endossar; (approve) aprovar

endorsee [ɪndɔː'siː] N endossado(-a), endossatário(-a)

endorsement [ɪn'dɔːsmənt] N (BRIT: on driving licence) descrição f das multas; (approval) aval m; (signature) endosso

endorser [ɪn'dɔːsər] N endossante m/f, endossador(a) m/f

endow [ɪn'dau] VT (provide with money) dotar; (: institution) fundar; **to be ~ed with** ser dotado de

endowment [ɪn'daumənt] N dotação f

endowment assurance N seguro dotal

end product N (Industry) produto final; (fig) resultado

end result N resultado final

endurable [ɪn'djuərəbl] ADJ suportável

endurance [ɪn'djuərəns] N resistência

endurance test N teste m de resistência

endure [ɪn'djuər] VT (bear) aguentar, suportar ▶ VI (last) durar; (resist) resistir

end user N (Comput) usuário(-a) (BR) or utente m/f (PT) final

enema ['ɛnɪmə] N (Med) enema m, clister m

enemy ['ɛnəmɪ] ADJ, N inimigo(-a); **to make an ~ of sb** fazer de alguém um inimigo

energetic [ɛnə'dʒɛtɪk] ADJ energético

energy ['ɛnədʒɪ] N energia; **Department of E~** Ministério da Energia

energy crisis N crise f de energia

energy drink N energético, bebida energética

energy-saving ADJ (policy) de economia de energia; (device) que economiza energia

enervating ['ɛnəveɪtɪŋ] ADJ enervante

enforce [ɪn'fɔːs] VT (Law) fazer cumprir

enforced [ɪn'fɔːst] ADJ forçoso

enfranchise [ɪn'fræntʃaɪz] VT conferir o direito de voto a; (set free) emancipar

engage [ɪn'geɪdʒ] VT (attention) chamar; (interest) atrair; (lawyer) contratar; (clutch) engrenar ▶ VI (Tech) engrenar; **to ~ in** dedicar-se a, ocupar-se com; **to ~ sb in conversation** travar conversa com alguém

engaged [ɪn'geɪdʒd] ADJ (BRIT: phone) ocupado (BR), impedido (PT); (: toilet) ocupado; (betrothed) noivo; **to get ~** ficar noivo; **he is ~ in research** dedica-se à pesquisa

engaged tone (BRIT) N (Tel) sinal m de ocupado (BR) or de impedido (PT)

engagement [ɪn'geɪdʒmənt] N (appointment) encontro; (booking) contrato; (battle) combate m; (to marry) noivado; **I have a previous ~** já tenho compromisso

engagement ring N aliança de noivado

engaging [ɪn'geɪdʒɪŋ] ADJ atraente, simpático

engender [ɪn'dʒɛndər] VT engendrar, gerar

engine ['ɛndʒɪn] N (Aut) motor m; (Rail) locomotiva

engine driver (BRIT) N maquinista m/f

engineer [ɛndʒɪ'nɪər] N engenheiro(-a); (US Rail) maquinista m/f; (BRIT: for repairs) técnico(-a); (: for domestic appliances) consertador(a) m/f (de aparelhos domésticos)

engineering [ɛndʒɪ'nɪərɪŋ] N engenharia ▶ CPD: **~ works** or **factory** fábrica de construção de máquinas

engine failure N falha do motor

engine trouble N enguiço

England ['ɪŋglənd] N Inglaterra

English ['ɪŋglɪʃ] ADJ inglês(-esa) ▶ N (Ling) inglês m; **the English** NPL (people) os ingleses; **an ~ speaker** uma pessoa de língua inglesa

English Channel N: **the ~** o Canal da Mancha

Englishman ['ɪŋglɪʃmən] (irreg: like **man**) N inglês m

English-speaking ADJ de língua inglesa

Englishwoman ['ɪŋglɪʃwumən] (irreg: like **woman**) N inglesa

engrave [ɪn'greɪv] VT gravar

engraving [ɪn'greɪvɪŋ] N gravura

engrossed [ɪn'grəust] ADJ: **~ in** absorto em

engulf [ɪn'gʌlf] VT (subj: fire, water) engolfar, tragar; (: panic, fear) tomar conta de

enhance [ɪn'hɑːns] VT (gen) ressaltar, salientar; (beauty) realçar; (position) melhorar; (add to) aumentar

enigma [ɪ'nɪgmə] N enigma m

enigmatic [ɛnɪg'mætɪk] ADJ enigmático

enjoy [ɪn'dʒɔɪ] VT (like) gostar de; (have: health, privilege) desfrutar de; (food) comer com gosto; **to ~ o.s.** divertir-se

enjoyable [ɪn'dʒɔɪəbl] ADJ (pleasant) agradável; (amusing) divertido

enjoyment [ɪn'dʒɔɪmənt] N (joy) prazer m; (use) gozo

enlarge [ɪn'lɑːdʒ] VT aumentar; (broaden) estender, alargar; (Phot) ampliar ▶ VI: **to ~ on** (subject) desenvolver, estender-se sobre

enlarged [ɪn'lɑːdʒd] ADJ (edition) ampliado; (Med: organ, gland) dilatado, hipertrofiado

enlargement [ɪn'lɑːdʒmənt] N (Phot) ampliação f

enlighten [ɪn'laɪtn] VT (inform) informar, instruir

enlightened [ɪn'laɪtnd] ADJ (cultured) culto; (knowledgeable) bem informado; (tolerant) compreensivo

enlightening [ɪn'laɪtnɪŋ] ADJ esclarecedor(a)

enlightenment [ɪn'laɪtənmənt] N
esclarecimento; (History): **the E~** o Século
das Luzes

enlist [ɪn'lɪst] VT alistar; (support) conseguir,
aliciar ► VI alistar-se; **~ed man** (US Mil)
praça m

enliven [ɪn'laɪvn] VT animar, agitar

enmity ['ɛnmɪtɪ] N inimizade f

ennoble [ɪ'nəʊbl] VT (with title) nobilitar

enormity [ɪ'nɔːmɪtɪ] N enormidade f

enormous [ɪ'nɔːməs] ADJ enorme

enormously [ɪ'nɔːməslɪ] ADV imensamente

enough [ɪ'nʌf] ADJ: **~ time/books** tempo
suficiente/livros suficientes ► PRON: **have
you got ~?** você tem o suficiente? ► ADV:
big ~ suficientemente grande; **will 5 be ~?**
com 5 dá?; **~!** basta!, chega!; **that's ~,
thanks** chega, obrigado; **I've had ~!** não
aguento mais!; **I've had ~ of him** estou
farto dele; **he has not worked ~** não tem
trabalhado o suficiente; **it's hot ~ (as it is)!**
já está tão quente!; **he was kind ~ to lend
me the money** ele teve a gentileza de me
emprestar o dinheiro; **which, funnily or
oddly ~ ...** o que, por estranho que pareça ...

enquire [ɪn'kwaɪəʳ] VT, VI = **inquire**

enrage [ɪn'reɪdʒ] VT enfurecer, enraivecer

enrich [ɪn'rɪtʃ] VT enriquecer

enrol, (US) **enroll** [ɪn'rəʊl] VT inscrever; (Sch)
matricular ► VI inscrever-se; matricular-se

enrolment, (US) **enrollment** [ɪn'rəʊlmənt] N
inscrição f; (Sch) matrícula

en route [ɔn-] ADV (on the way) no caminho;
~ for or to a caminho de

ensconced [ɪn'skɒnst] ADJ: **~ in** acomodado
em

enshrine [ɪn'ʃraɪn] VT (fig) conservar,
resguardar

ensign ['ɛnsaɪn] N (flag) bandeira; (Mil)
insígnia; (US Naut) guarda-marinha m

enslave [ɪn'sleɪv] VT escravizar

ensue [ɪn'sjuː] VI seguir-se; (result) resultar;
(happen) acontecer

ensure [ɪn'ʃʊəʳ] VT assegurar; **to ~ that**
verificar-se que

ENT N ABBR (= Ear, Nose & Throat)
otorrinolaringologia

entail [ɪn'teɪl] VT (involve) implicar; (result in)
acarretar

entangle [ɪn'tæŋgl] VT enredar, emaranhar;
to get ~d in sth (fig) ficar enrolado em algo

enter ['ɛntəʳ] VT (room) entrar em; (club) ficar
or fazer-se sócio de; (army) alistar-se em;
(competition) inscrever-se em; (sb for a
competition) inscrever; (write down) completar;
(Comput) digitar ► VI entrar
► **enter for** VT FUS inscrever-se em
► **enter into** VT FUS (relations) estabelecer;
(plans) fazer parte de; (debate, negotiations)
entrar em; (agreement) chegar a, firmar
► **enter on** VT FUS (career) entrar para
► **enter up** VT lançar
► **enter upon** VT FUS = **enter on**

enteritis [ɛntə'raɪtɪs] N enterite f

enterprise ['ɛntəpraɪz] N empresa;
(undertaking) empreendimento; (initiative)
iniciativa; **free/private ~** livre-empresa/
empresa privada

enterprising ['ɛntəpraɪzɪŋ] ADJ
empreendedor(a)

entertain [ɛntə'teɪn] VT (amuse) divertir,
entreter; (invite: guest) receber (em casa);
(idea, plan) estudar

entertainer [ɛntə'teɪnəʳ] N artista m/f

entertaining [ɛntə'teɪnɪŋ] ADJ divertido ► N:
to do a lot of ~ receber com frequência

entertainment [ɛntə'teɪnmənt] N
(amusement) entretenimento, diversão f;
(show) espetáculo

entertainment allowance N verba de
representação

enthralled [ɪn'θrɔːld] ADJ encantado, cativado

enthralling [ɪn'θrɔːlɪŋ] ADJ cativante,
encantador(a)

enthuse [ɪn'θuːz] VI: **to ~ about** or **over**
entusiasmar-se com or por

enthusiasm [ɪn'θuːzɪæzəm] N entusiasmo

enthusiast [ɪn'θuːzɪæst] N entusiasta m/f;
a jazz etc **~** um(-a) aficionado(a) de jazz etc

enthusiastic [ɪnθuːzɪ'æstɪk] ADJ
entusiasmado; **to be ~ about** entusiasmar-
se por

entice [ɪn'taɪs] VT atrair, tentar; (seduce)
seduzir

enticing [ɪn'taɪsɪŋ] ADJ sedutor(a), tentador(a)

entire [ɪn'taɪəʳ] ADJ inteiro

entirely [ɪn'taɪəlɪ] ADV totalmente,
completamente

entirety [ɪn'taɪərətɪ] N: **in its ~** na sua
totalidade

entitle [ɪn'taɪtl] VT: **to ~ sb to sth** dar a
alguém direito a algo; **to ~ sb to do** dar a
alguém direito de fazer

entitled [ɪn'taɪtld] ADJ (book etc) intitulado;
to be ~ to sth/to do sth ter direito a algo/de
fazer algo

entity ['ɛntɪtɪ] N ente m

entourage [ɔntu'rɑːʒ] N séquito

entrails ['ɛntreɪlz] NPL entranhas fpl

entrance [n 'ɛntrəns, vt ɪn'trɑːns] N entrada;
(arrival) chegada ► VT encantar, fascinar;
to gain ~ to (university etc) ser admitido em

entrance examination N exame m de
admissão

entrance fee N joia; (to museum etc) (preço da)
entrada

entrance ramp (US) N (Aut) entrada (para a
rodovia)

entrancing [ɪn'trɑːnsɪŋ] ADJ encantador(a),
fascinante

entrant ['ɛntrənt] N participante m/f; (BRIT: in
exam) candidato(-a)

entreat [ɛn'triːt] VT: **to ~ sb to do** suplicar
con alguém para fazer

entreaty [ɛn'triːtɪ] N rogo, súplica

entrée ['ɔntreɪ] N (Culin) entrada

entrenched [ɛn'trɛntʃd] ADJ (*position, power*) fortalecido; (*idea*) arraigado

entrepreneur [ɔntrəprə'nə:ʳ] N empresário(-a)

entrepreneurial [ɔntrəprə'nə:rɪəl] ADJ empreendedor(a)

entrust [ɪn'trʌst] VT: **to ~ sth to sb** confiar algo a alguém

entry ['ɛntrɪ] N entrada; (*permission to enter*) acesso; (*in register*) registro, assentamento; (*in account*) lançamento; (*in dictionary*) verbete *m*; **"no ~"** "entrada proibida"; (*Aut*) "contramão" (*BR*), "entrada proibida" (*PT*); **single/double ~ book-keeping** escrituração por partidas simples/dobradas

entry form N formulário de inscrição

entry phone (*BRIT*) N interfone *m* (*em apartamento*)

entwine [ɪn'twaɪn] VT entrelaçar

enumerate [ɪ'nju:məreɪt] VT enumerar

enunciate [ɪ'nʌnsɪeɪt] VT pronunciar; (*principle etc*) enunciar

envelop [ɪn'vɛləp] VT envolver

envelope ['ɛnvələup] N envelope *m*

enviable ['ɛnvɪəbl] ADJ invejável

envious ['ɛnvɪəs] ADJ invejoso; (*look*) de inveja

environment [ɪn'vaɪərnmənt] N meio ambiente *m*; **Department of the E~** (*BRIT*) Ministério da Habitação, Urbanismo e Meio Ambiente

environmental [ɪnvaɪərn'mɛntl] ADJ ambiental; **~ studies** (*Sch*) ecologia

environmentalist [ɪnvaɪərn'mɛntəlɪst] N ecologista *m/f*

Environmental Protection Agency (*US*) N ≈ Secretaria Especial do Meio Ambiente

envisage [ɪn'vɪzɪdʒ] VT (*foresee*) prever; (*imagine*) conceber, imaginar

envision [ɪn'vɪʒən] (*US*) VT = **envisage**

envoy ['ɛnvɔɪ] N enviado(-a)

envy ['ɛnvɪ] N inveja ▶ VT ter inveja de; **to ~ sb sth** invejar alguém por algo, cobiçar algo de alguém

enzyme ['ɛnzaɪm] N enzima

EPA (*US*) N ABBR (= *Environmental Protection Agency*) ≈ SEMA

ephemeral [ɪ'fɛmərl] ADJ efêmero

epic ['ɛpɪk] N epopeia ▶ ADJ épico

epicentre, (*US*) **epicenter** ['ɛpɪsɛntəʳ] N epicentro

epidemic [ɛpɪ'dɛmɪk] N epidemia

epilepsy ['ɛpɪlɛpsɪ] N epilepsia

epileptic [ɛpɪ'lɛptɪk] ADJ, N epilético(-a)

epilogue ['ɛpɪlɔg] N epílogo

episcopal [ɪ'pɪskəpl] ADJ episcopal

episode ['ɛpɪsəud] N episódio; (*instalment*) capítulo

epistle [ɪ'pɪsl] N epístola

epitaph ['ɛpɪtɑːf] N epitáfio

epithet ['ɛpɪθɛt] N epíteto

epitome [ɪ'pɪtəmɪ] N epítome *m*

epitomize [ɪ'pɪtəmaɪz] VT epitomar, resumir

epoch ['iːpɔk] N época

epoch-making ADJ que marca época, marcante

eponymous [ɪ'pɔnɪməs] ADJ epônimo

equable ['ɛkwəbl] ADJ (*climate*) uniforme; (*temper, reply*) equânime; (*character*) tranquilo, calmo

equal ['iːkwl] ADJ igual; (*treatment*) equitativo, equivalente ▶ N igual *m/f* ▶ VT ser igual a; **to be ~ to** (*task*) estar à altura de; **~ to doing** capaz de fazer

equality [iː'kwɔlɪtɪ] N igualdade *f*

equalize ['iːkwəlaɪz] VT, VI igualar; (*Sport*) empatar

equalizer ['iːkwəlaɪzəʳ] N gol *m* (*BR*) *or* golo (*PT*) de empate

equally ['iːkwəlɪ] ADV igualmente; (*share etc*) por igual

Equal Opportunities Commission, (*US*) **Equal Employment Opportunity Commission** N comissão para a não-discriminação no trabalho

equal sign, equals sign N sinal *m* de igualdade

equanimity [ɛkwə'nɪmɪtɪ] N equanimidade *f*

equate [ɪ'kweɪt] VT: **to ~ sth with** equiparar algo com; **to ~ sth to** igualar algo a

equation [ɪ'kweɪʒən] N (*Math*) equação *f*

equator [ɪ'kweɪtəʳ] N equador *m*

equatorial [ɛkwə'tɔːrɪəl] ADJ equatorial

Equatorial Guinea N Guiné *f* Equatorial

equestrian [ɪ'kwɛstrɪən] ADJ equestre; (*sport*) hípico ▶ N (*man*) ginete *m*; (*woman*) amazona

equilibrium [iːkwɪ'lɪbrɪəm] N equilíbrio

equinox ['iːkwɪnɔks] N equinócio

equip [ɪ'kwɪp] VT equipar; (*person*) prover, munir; **to ~ sb/sth with** equipar alguém/algo com, munir alguém/algo de; **to be well ~ped** estar bem preparado *or* equipado

equipment [ɪ'kwɪpmənt] N equipamento; (*machines etc*) equipamentos *mpl*, aparelhagem *f*

equitable ['ɛkwɪtəbl] ADJ equitativo

equities ['ɛkwɪtɪz] (*BRIT*) NPL (*Comm*) ações *fpl* ordinárias

equity capital N capital *m* próprio

equivalent [ɪ'kwɪvəlnt] ADJ equivalente ▶ N equivalente *m*; **to be ~ to** ser equivalente a

equivocal [ɪ'kwɪvəkl] ADJ equívoco; (*open to suspicion*) ambíguo

equivocate [ɪ'kwɪvəkeɪt] VI sofismar

equivocation [ɪkwɪvə'keɪʃən] N sofismas *mpl*

ER (*BRIT*) ABBR (= *Elizabeth Regina*) *a rainha Elisabete*

ERA (*US*) N ABBR (Pol: = *equal rights amendment*) *emenda sobre a igualdade das mulheres*

era ['ɪərə] N era, época

eradicate [ɪ'rædɪkeɪt] VT erradicar, eliminar

erase [ɪ'reɪz] VT apagar

eraser [ɪ'reɪzəʳ] N borracha (de apagar)

e-reader ['iːriːdəʳ] N leitor *m* de livros digitais

erect [ɪ'rɛkt] ADJ (*posture*) ereto; (*tail, ears*) levantado ▶ VT erigir, levantar; (*assemble*) montar; (*tent*) armar

erection [ɪˈrɛkʃən] N construção f; (assembly) montagem f; (structure) edifício; (Physiol) ereção f

ergonomics [əːgəˈnɒmɪks] N ergonomia

ERISA (US) N ABBR (= Employee Retirement Income Security Act) lei referente às aposentadorias

ermine [ˈəːmɪn] N arminho

ERNIE [ˈəːnɪ] (BRIT) N ABBR (= Electronic Random Number Indicator Equipment) computador que serve para o sorteio dos "premium bonds"

erode [ɪˈrəud] VT (Geo) causar erosão em; (confidence) minar; (salary) corroer

erosion [ɪˈrəuʒən] N erosão f; (fig) corrosão f

erotic [ɪˈrɒtɪk] ADJ erótico

eroticism [ɪˈrɒtɪsɪzm] N erotismo

err [əːʳ] VI errar, enganar-se; (Rel) pecar

errand [ˈɛrnd] N recado, mensagem f; **to run ~s** fazer incumbências; **~ of mercy** missão f de caridade

errand boy N mensageiro

erratic [ɪˈrætɪk] ADJ imprevisível

erroneous [ɪˈrəunɪəs] ADJ errôneo

error [ˈɛrəʳ] N erro; **typing/spelling ~** erro de datilografia/ortografia; **in ~** por engano; **~s and omissions excepted** salvo erro ou omissão

error message N (Comput) mensagem f de erro

erstwhile [ˈəːstwaɪl] ADJ antigo

erudite [ˈɛrjudaɪt] ADJ erudito

erupt [ɪˈrʌpt] VI entrar em erupção; (fig) explodir, estourar

eruption [ɪˈrʌpʃən] N erupção f; (fig) explosão f

ESA N ABBR (= European Space Agency) AEE f

escalate [ˈɛskəleɪt] VI intensificar-se; (costs, prices) disparar

escalation [ɛskəˈleɪʃən] N escalada, intensificação f

escalation clause N cláusula de reajustamento

escalator [ˈɛskəleɪtəʳ] N escada rolante

escapade [ɛskəˈpeɪd] N peripécia

escape [ɪˈskeɪp] N fuga; (from duties) escapatória; (from chase) fuga, evasão f; (of gas) escapatória ▶ VI escapar; (flee) fugir, evadir-se; (leak) vazar, escapar ▶ VT evitar, fugir de; (consequences) fugir de; (elude): **his name ~s me** o nome dele me foge à memória; **to ~ from** (place) escapar de; (person) escapulir de; (clutches) livrar-se de; **to ~ to** fugir para; **to ~ to safety** salvar-se; **to ~ notice** passar despercebido

escape artist N ilusionista m/f

escape clause N cláusula que permite revogação do contrato

escape key N (Comput) tecla de saída

escape route N (from fire) saída de emergência; (of prisoners) roteiro da fuga

escapism [ɪˈskeɪpɪzəm] N escapismo, fuga à realidade

escapist [ɪˈskeɪpɪst] ADJ (person) que foge da realidade; (literature) de evasão

escapologist [ɛskəˈpɒlədʒɪst] (BRIT) N ilusionista m/f

escarpment [ɪsˈkɑːpmənt] N escarpa

eschew [ɪsˈtʃuː] VT evitar

escort [n ˈɛskɔːt, vt ɪˈskɔːt] N acompanhante m/f; (Mil, Naut) escolta ▶ VT acompanhar; (Mil, Naut) escoltar

escort agency N agência de escorte

Eskimo [ˈɛskɪməu] ADJ esquimó ▶ N esquimó m/f; (Ling) esquimó m

ESL N ABBR (Sch) = **English as a Second Language**

esophagus [iːˈsɒfəgəs] (US) N = **oesophagus**

esoteric [ɛsəˈtɛrɪk] ADJ esotérico

ESP N ABBR = **extrasensory perception**

esp. ABBR = **especially**

especially [ɪˈspɛʃlɪ] ADV (gen) especialmente; (above all) sobretudo; (particularly) em particular

espionage [ˈɛspɪənɑːʒ] N espionagem f

esplanade [ɛspləˈneɪd] N (by sea) avenida beira-mar, esplanada

espouse [ɪˈspauz] VT (policy, idea) adotar; (cause) abraçar

Esq. (BRIT) ABBR (= Esquire) Sr.

Esquire [ɪˈskwaɪəʳ] (BRIT) N (abbr Esq.): **J. Brown, ~** Sr. J. Brown

essay [ˈɛseɪ] N (Sch, Literature) ensaio

essence [ˈɛsns] N essência; **in ~** em sua essência; **speed is of the ~** a rapidez é fundamental

essential [ɪˈsɛnʃl] ADJ (necessary) indispensável; (basic) essencial ▶ N elemento essencial; **it is ~ that** é indispensável que (+sub)

essentially [ɪˈsɛnʃəlɪ] ADV essencialmente

EST (US) ABBR (= Eastern Standard Time) hora de inverno de Nova Iorque

est ABBR = **estimated; established**

establish [ɪˈstæblɪʃ] VT estabelecer; (facts) verificar; (proof) demonstrar; (reputation) firmar

established [ɪˈstæblɪʃt] ADJ consagrado; (staff) fixo

establishment [ɪˈstæblɪʃmənt] N estabelecimento; **the E~** a classe dirigente

estate [ɪˈsteɪt] N (land) fazenda (BR), propriedade f (PT); (property) propriedade; (Law) herança; (Pol) estado; (BRIT: also: **housing estate**) conjunto habitacional

estate agency (BRIT) N imobiliária, corretora de imóveis

estate agent (BRIT) N corretor(a) m/f de imóveis (BR), agente m/f imobiliário(-a) (PT)

estate car (BRIT) N perua (BR), canadiana (PT)

esteem [ɪˈstiːm] N estima ▶ VT estimar; **to hold sb in high ~** estimar muito alguém

esthetic [ɪsˈθɛtɪk] (US) ADJ = **aesthetic**

estimate [n ˈɛstɪmət, vb ˈɛstɪmeɪt] N (assessment) avaliação f; (calculation) cálculo; (Comm) orçamento ▶ VT estimar, avaliar, calcular ▶ VI (BRIT Comm): **to ~ for a job** orçar uma obra; **at a rough ~** numa estimativa aproximada

estimation [ɛstɪˈmeɪʃən] N opinião f; (calculation) cálculo; (esteem) apreço; **in my ~** na minha opinião

Estonia [ɛ'stəunɪə] N Estônia

estranged [ɪ'streɪndʒd] ADJ (couple) separado; (husband, wife) de quem se separou

estrangement [ɪ'streɪndʒmənt] N separação f

estrogen ['iːstrəudʒɛn] (US) N = **oestrogen**

estuary ['ɛstjuərɪ] N estuário

ET (US) ABBR (= Eastern Time) hora de Nova Iorque

ETA N ABBR = **estimated time of arrival**

et al. ABBR (= et alii) e outras pessoas

etc. ABBR (= et cetera) etc.

etch [ɛtʃ] VT gravar com água-forte

etching ['ɛtʃɪŋ] N água-forte f

ETD N ABBR = **estimated time of departure**

eternal [ɪ'təːnl] ADJ eterno; (unchanging) absoluto

eternity [ɪ'təːnɪtɪ] N eternidade f

ether ['iːθəʳ] N éter m

ethereal [ɪ'θɪərɪəl] ADJ etéreo

ethical ['ɛθɪkl] ADJ ético; (honest) honrado

ethics ['ɛθɪks] N ética ▸ NPL moral f

Ethiopia [iːθɪ'əupɪə] N Etiópia

Ethiopian [iːθɪ'əupɪən] ADJ, N etíope m/f

ethnic ['ɛθnɪk] ADJ étnico; (culture) folclórico; (food) exótico

ethnology [ɛθ'nɔlədʒɪ] N etnologia

ethos ['iːθɔs] N sistema m de valores

e-ticket ['iːtɪkɪt] N bilhete m eletrônico

etiquette ['ɛtɪkɛt] N etiqueta

ETV (US) N ABBR (= Educational Television) TV f educativa

etymology [ɛtɪ'mɔlədʒɪ] N etimologia

EU ABBR (= European Union) UE f

eucalyptus [juːkə'lɪptəs] N eucalipto

euphemism ['juːfəmɪzm] N eufemismo

euphemistic [juːfə'mɪstɪk] ADJ eufêmico

euphoria [juː'fɔːrɪə] N euforia

Eurasia [juə'reɪʃə] N Eurásia

Eurasian [juə'reɪʃən] ADJ (person) eurasiático; (continent) eurásio ▸ N eurasiático(-a)

Euratom [juə'rætəm] N ABBR (= European Atomic Energy Community) EURATOM f

euro ['juərəu] N (currency) euro m

Eurocheque ['juərəutʃɛk] N eurocheque m

Eurocrat ['juərəukræt] N eurocrata m/f, funcionário(-a) da CEE

Eurodollar ['juərəudɔləʳ] N eurodólar m

Europe ['juərəp] N Europa

European [juərə'piːən] ADJ, N europeu(-peia)

European Court of Justice N Tribunal m Europeu de Justiça

European Union N: **the ~** a União Europeia

euthanasia [juːθə'neɪzɪə] N eutanásia

evacuate [ɪ'vækjueɪt] VT evacuar

evacuation [ɪvækju'eɪʃən] N evacuação f

evade [ɪ'veɪd] VT (person) evitar; (question, duties) esquivar-se de; (tax) sonegar

evaluate [ɪ'væljueɪt] VT avaliar; (evidence) interpretar

evangelist [ɪ'vændʒəlɪst] N evangelista m/f; (preacher) evangelizador(a) m/f

evangelize [ɪ'vændʒəlaɪz] VT evangelizar

evaporate [ɪ'væpəreɪt] VI evaporar-se ▸ VT evaporar

evaporated milk [ɪ'væpəreɪtɪd-] N leite m desidratado

evaporation [ɪvæpə'reɪʃən] N evaporação f

evasion [ɪ'veɪʒən] N evasão f, fuga; (of tax) sonegação f; (fig) evasiva

evasive [ɪ'veɪsɪv] ADJ evasivo

eve [iːv] N: **on the ~ of** na véspera de

even ['iːvn] ADJ (level) plano; (smooth) liso; (speed, temperature) uniforme; (equal, Sport) igual; (number) par; (nature) equilibrado ▸ ADV até, mesmo; **~ if** mesmo que; **~ though** mesmo que, embora; **~ more** ainda mais; **~ faster** ainda mais rápido, mais rápido ainda; **~ so** mesmo assim; **never ~** nem sequer; **not ~** nem; **~ he was there** até ele esteve ali; **~ on Sundays** até nos domingos; **to get ~ with sb** ficar quite com alguém; **to break ~** sair sem lucros nem prejuízos ▸ **even out** VI nivelar-se

evening ['iːvnɪŋ] N (early) tarde f; (late) noite f; (before six) tarde f; (event) noitada f; **in the ~** à noite; **this ~** hoje à noite; **tomorrow/ yesterday ~** amanhã/ontem à noite

evening class N aula noturna

evening dress N (man's) traje m de rigor (BR) or de cerimónia (PT); (woman's) vestido de noite

evenly ['iːvnlɪ] ADV uniformemente; (space) regularmente; (divide) por igual

evensong ['iːvnsɔŋ] N oração f da tarde

event [ɪ'vɛnt] N acontecimento; (Sport) prova; **in the course of ~s** no decorrer dos acontecimentos; **in the ~ of** no caso de; **in the ~** de fato, na realidade; **at all ~s** (BRIT), **in any ~** em todo o caso

eventful [ɪ'vɛntful] ADJ cheio de acontecimentos; (game etc) cheio de emoção, agitado

eventing [ɪ'vɛntɪŋ] N (Horseriding) concurso completo (hipismo)

eventual [ɪ'vɛntʃuəl] ADJ (outcome) final; (resulting) definitivo

eventuality [ɪvɛntʃu'ælɪtɪ] N eventualidade f

eventually [ɪ'vɛntʃuəlɪ] ADV (finally) finalmente; (in time) por fim

ever ['ɛvəʳ] ADV já, alguma vez; (in negative) nunca, jamais; (always) sempre; (at any time) em qualquer momento; (in question): **why ~ not?** por que não, ora?; **the best ~** o melhor que já se viu; **have you ~ seen it?** você alguma vez já viu isto?; **better than ~** melhor que nunca; **for ~** para sempre; **hardly ~** quase nunca; **~ since** adv desde então; conj depois que; **~ so pretty** tão bonitinho; **thank you ~ so much** muitíssimo obrigado, obrigadão (inf); **yours ~** (BRIT: in letters) sempre seu/sua

Everest ['ɛvərɪst] N (also: **Mount Everest**) o monte Everest

evergreen ['ɛvəgriːn] N sempre-verde f

everlasting [ɛvə'lɑːstɪŋ] ADJ eterno, perpétuo

every ['ɛvrɪ] ADJ 1 (each) cada; **every one of them** cada um deles; **every shop in the town was closed** todas as lojas da cidade estavam fechadas

2 (all possible) todo(-a); **I gave you every assistance** eu lhe dei toda assistência; **I have every confidence in her** tenho absoluta confiança nela; **we wish you every success** desejamos-lhe o maior sucesso; **he's every bit as clever as his brother** ele é tão inteligente quanto o irmão

3 (showing recurrence) todo(-a); **every day/week** todo dia/toda semana; **every other car had been broken into** cada dois carros foram arrombados; **she visits me every other/third day** ele me visita cada dois/três dias; **every now and then** de vez em quando

everybody ['ɛvrɪbɔdɪ] PRON todos, todo mundo (BR), toda a gente (PT); ~ **knows about it** todo o mundo já sabe; ~ **else** todos os outros

everyday ['ɛvrɪdeɪ] ADJ (daily) diário; (usual) corrente; (common) comum; (routine) rotineiro

everyone ['ɛvrɪwʌn] PRON = **everybody**

everything ['ɛvrɪθɪŋ] PRON tudo; ~ **is ready** tudo está pronto; **he did ~ possible** ele fez todo o possível

everywhere ['ɛvrɪwɛəʳ] ADV (be) em todo lugar (BR), em toda a parte (PT); (go) a todo lugar (BR), a toda a parte (PT); (wherever): ~ **you go you meet …** aonde quer que se vá, encontra-se …

evict [ɪ'vɪkt] VT despejar

eviction [ɪ'vɪkʃən] N despejo

eviction notice N notificação f de despejo

evidence ['ɛvɪdəns] N (proof) prova(s) f(pl); (of witness) testemunho, depoimento; (indication) sinal m; (facts) dados mpl, evidência; **to give ~** testemunhar, prestar depoimento; **in ~** (obvious) em evidência, evidente

evident ['ɛvɪdənt] ADJ evidente

evidently ['ɛvɪdəntlɪ] ADV evidentemente; (apparently) aparentemente

evil ['iːvl] ADJ mau/má; (person) perverso; (system, influence) nocivo; (smell) horrível ▸ N mal m, maldade f

evildoer ['iːvldʊːəʳ] N malfeitor(a) m/f

evince [ɪ'vɪns] VT evidenciar

evocative [ɪ'vɔkətɪv] ADJ evocativo, sugestivo

evoke [ɪ'vəuk] VT evocar

evolution [iːvə'luːʃən] N evolução f; (development) desenvolvimento

evolve [ɪ'vɔlv] VT desenvolver ▸ VI desenvolver-se

ewe [juː] N ovelha

ex- [ɛks] PREFIX (former) ex-; (out of): **the price ~works** o preço na porta da fábrica

exacerbate [ɛks'æsəbeɪt] VT (pain, illness) exacerbar; (fig) agravar

exact [ɪg'zækt] ADJ exato; (person) meticuloso ▸ VT: **to ~ sth (from)** exigir algo (de)

exacting [ɪg'zæktɪŋ] ADJ exigente; (conditions) difícil

exactitude [ɪg'zæktɪtjuːd] N exatidão f

exactly [ɪg'zæktlɪ] ADV exatamente; (time) em ponto; (indicating agreement) isso mesmo

exaggerate [ɪg'zædʒəreɪt] VT, VI exagerar

exaggeration [ɪgzædʒə'reɪʃən] N exagero

exalted [ɪg'zɔːltɪd] ADJ exaltado

exam [ɪg'zæm] N ABBR = **examination**

examination [ɪgzæmɪ'neɪʃən] N (Sch, Med) exame m; (Law) inquirição f; (inquiry) investigação f; **to sit** (BRIT) or **take an ~** submeter-se a um exame; **the matter is under ~** o assunto está sendo examinado

examine [ɪg'zæmɪn] VT examinar; (inspect) inspecionar; (Law: person) interrogar; (at customs: luggage) revistar; (: passport) controlar

examiner [ɪg'zæmɪnəʳ] N examinador(a) m/f

example [ɪg'zɑːmpl] N exemplo; **for ~** por exemplo; **to set a good/bad ~** dar um bom/mau exemplo

exasperate [ɪg'zɑːspəreɪt] VT exasperar, irritar

exasperating [ɪg'zɑːspəreɪtɪŋ] ADJ irritante

exasperation [ɪgzɑːspə'reɪʃən] N exasperação f, irritação f

excavate ['ɛkskəveɪt] VT escavar

excavation [ɛkskə'veɪʃən] N escavação f

excavator ['ɛkskəveɪtəʳ] N (machine) escavadeira

exceed [ɪk'siːd] VT exceder; (number) ser superior a; (speed limit) ultrapassar; (limits) ir além de; (powers) exceder-se em; (hopes) superar

exceedingly [ɪk'siːdɪŋlɪ] ADV extremamente

excel [ɪk'sɛl] VI sobressair, distinguir-se ▸ VT superar; **to ~ o.s.** (BRIT) destacar-se

excellence ['ɛksələns] N excelência

Excellency ['ɛksələnsɪ] N: **His/Her ~** Sua Excelência

excellent ['ɛksələnt] ADJ excelente

except [ɪk'sɛpt] PREP (also: **except for, excepting**) exceto, a não ser ▸ VT: **to ~ sb from** excluir alguém de; ~ **if/when** a menos que, a não ser que; ~ **that** exceto que

exception [ɪk'sɛpʃən] N exceção f; **to take ~ to** ressentir-se de; **with the ~ of** à exceção de; **to make an ~** fazer exceção

exceptional [ɪk'sɛpʃənl] ADJ excepcional

excerpt ['ɛksəːpt] N trecho

excess [ɪk'sɛs] N excesso; (Comm) excedente m; **in ~ of** mais de

excess baggage N excesso de bagagem

excess fare (BRIT) N sobretaxa de excesso

excessive [ɪk'sɛsɪv] ADJ excessivo

excess supply N oferta excedente

exchange [ɪks'tʃeɪndʒ] N troca; (of teachers, students) intercâmbio; (also: **telephone exchange**) estação f telefônica (BR), central f telefónica (PT) ▸ VT: **to ~ (for)** trocar (por);

in ~ for em troca de; **foreign ~** (*Comm*) divisas *fpl*, câmbio

exchange control N controle *m* de câmbio

exchange market N mercado cambial *or* de câmbio

exchange rate N (taxa de) câmbio

Exchequer [ɪks'tʃɛkə^r] (*BRIT*) N: **the ~** ≈ o Tesouro Nacional

excisable [ɪk'saɪzəbl] ADJ tributável

excise [*n* 'ɛksaɪz, *vt* ɛk'saɪz] N imposto de consumo ▶ VT cortar (fora)

excise duties NPL impostos *mpl* indiretos

excitable [ɪk'saɪtəbl] ADJ excitável; (*edgy*) nervoso

excite [ɪk'saɪt] VT (*stimulate, arouse*) excitar; (*awaken*) despertar; (*move*) entusiasmar; **to get ~d** entusiasmar-se

excitement [ɪk'saɪtmənt] N emoções *fpl*; (*anticipation*) expectativa; (*agitation*) agitação *f*

exciting [ɪk'saɪtɪŋ] ADJ emocionante, empolgante

excl. ABBR = **excluding; exclusive**

exclaim [ɪk'skleɪm] VI exclamar

exclamation [ɛksklə'meɪʃən] N exclamação *f*

exclamation mark N ponto de exclamação

exclude [ɪk'sklu:d] VT excluir; (*except*) excetuar

excluding [ɪk'sklu:dɪŋ] PREP: **~ tax** imposto excluído

exclusion [ɪk'sklu:ʒən] N exclusão *f*; **to the ~ of** a ponto de excluir

exclusion clause N cláusula de exclusão

exclusive [ɪk'sklu:sɪv] ADJ exclusivo; (*club, district*) privativo; (*item of news*) com exclusividade; **~ of tax** sem incluir os impostos; **~ of postage** tarifas postais excluídas; **from 1st to 15th March ~** entre o dia 1° e 15 de março; **~ rights** (*Comm*) exclusividade *f*

exclusively [ɪk'sklu:sɪvlɪ] ADV unicamente

excommunicate [ɛkskə'mju:nɪkeɪt] VT excomungar

excrement ['ɛkskrəmənt] N excremento

excrete [ɪk'skri:t] VI excretar

excruciating [ɪk'skru:ʃɪeɪtɪŋ] ADJ (*pain*) doloroso, martirizante

excursion [ɪk'skə:ʃən] N excursão *f*

excursion ticket N passagem *f* de excursão

excusable [ɪk'skju:zəbl] ADJ perdoável, excusável

excuse [*n* ɪk'skju:s, *vt* ɪk'skju:z] N desculpa; (*evasion*) pretexto ▶ VT desculpar, perdoar; **to ~ sb from doing sth** dispensar alguém de fazer algo; **~ me!** (*attracting attention, apology*) desculpe!; (*asking permission*) (com) licença; **if you will ~ me ...** com a sua licença ...; **to make ~s for sb** apresentar desculpas por alguém; **to ~ o.s. for sth/for doing sth** desculpar-se de algo/de fazer algo

ex-directory (*BRIT*) ADJ: **~ (phone) number** número que não figura na lista telefônica

execute ['ɛksɪkju:t] VT (*plan*) realizar; (*order*) cumprir; (*person, movement*) executar

execution [ɛksɪ'kju:ʃən] N realização *f*; (*killing*) execução *f*

executioner [ɛksɪ'kju:ʃənə^r] N verdugo, carrasco

executive [ɪg'zɛkjutɪv] N (*Comm, Pol*) executivo(-a) ▶ ADJ executivo

executive director N diretor(a) *m/f* executivo(-a)

executor [ɪg'zɛkjutə^r] N executor(a) *m/f* testamentário(-a), testamenteiro(-a)

exemplary [ɪg'zɛmplərɪ] ADJ exemplar

exemplify [ɪg'zɛmplɪfaɪ] VT exemplificar; (*illustrate*) ilustrar

exempt [ɪg'zɛmpt] ADJ: **~ from** isento de ▶ VT: **to ~ sb from** dispensar *or* isentar alguém de

exemption [ɪg'zɛmpʃən] N (*from taxes etc*) isenção *f*; (*from military service*) dispensa; (*immunity*) imunidade *f*

exercise ['ɛksəsaɪz] N exercício ▶ VT exercer; (*right*) valer-se de; (*dog*) levar para passear ▶ VI (*also*: **to take exercise**) fazer exercício

exercise bike N bicicleta ergométrica

exercise book N caderno

exert [ɪg'zə:t] VT exercer; **to ~ o.s.** esforçar-se, empenhar-se

exertion [ɪg'zə:ʃən] N esforço

ex gratia [-'greɪʃə] ADJ: **~ payment** gratificação *f*

exhale [ɛks'heɪl] VT, VI expirar

exhaust [ɪg'zɔ:st] N (*Aut: also*: **exhaust pipe**) escape *m*, exaustor *m*; (*fumes*) escapamento (de gás) ▶ VT esgotar; **to ~ o.s.** esgotar-se; **~ manifold** (*Aut etc*) cano de descarga

exhausted [ɪg'zɔ:stɪd] ADJ esgotado

exhausting [ɪg'zɔ:stɪŋ] ADJ exaustivo, estafante

exhaustion [ɪg'zɔ:stʃən] N exaustão *f*

exhaustive [ɪg'zɔ:stɪv] ADJ exaustivo

exhibit [ɪg'zɪbɪt] N (*Art*) obra exposta; (*Law*) objeto exposto ▶ VT (*courage etc*) manifestar, mostrar; (*quality, emotion*) demonstrar; (*film*) apresentar; (*paintings*) expor

exhibition [ɛksɪ'bɪʃən] N exposição *f*

exhibitionist [ɛksɪ'bɪʃənɪst] N exibicionista *m/f*; (*of talent etc*) mostra

exhibitor [ɪg'zɪbɪtə^r] N expositor(a) *m/f*

exhilarating [ɪg'zɪləreɪtɪŋ] ADJ estimulante, tônico

exhilaration [ɪgzɪlə'reɪʃən] N euforia

exhort [ɪg'zɔ:t] VT exortar

exile ['ɛksaɪl] N exílio; (*person*) exilado(-a) ▶ VT desterrar, exilar; **in ~** em exílio, exilado

exist [ɪg'zɪst] VI existir; (*live*) viver

existence [ɪg'zɪstəns] N existência; (*life*) vida; **to be in ~** existir

existentialism [ɛgzɪs'tɛnʃlɪzəm] N existencialismo

existing [ɪg'zɪstɪŋ] ADJ (*laws*) existente; (*system, regime*) atual

exit ['ɛksɪt] N saída ▶ VI (*Comput, Theatre*) sair

exit ramp (*US*) N (*Aut*) saída da rodovia

exit visa N visto de saída

exodus ['ɛksədəs] N êxodo
ex officio [-ə'fɪʃɪəʊ] ADJ, ADV ex-officio, por dever do cargo
exonerate [ɪg'zɒnəreɪt] VT: **to ~ from** (*responsibility*) desobrigar; (*guilt*) isentar
exorbitant [ɪg'zɔːbɪtənt] ADJ exorbitante
exorcize ['ɛksɔːsaɪz] VT exorcizar
exotic [ɪg'zɒtɪk] ADJ exótico
expand [ɪk'spænd] VT (*widen*) ampliar; (*number*) aumentar; (*influence etc*) estender ▶ VI (*population, business*) aumentar; (*trade, gas etc*) expandir-se; (*metal*) dilatar-se; **to ~ on** (*notes, story etc*) estender-se sobre
expanse [ɪk'spæns] N extensão f
expansion [ɪk'spænʃən] N (*of town*) desenvolvimento; (*of trade*) expansão f; (*of population*) aumento; (*of metal*) dilatação f
expansionism [ɪk'spænʃənɪzəm] N expansionismo
expansionist [ɪk'spænʃənɪst] ADJ expansionista
expatriate [n ɛks'pætrɪət, vt ɛks'pætrɪeɪt] N expatriado(-a) ▶ VT expatriar
expect [ɪk'spɛkt] VT (*gen*) esperar; (*count on*) contar com; (*suppose*) supor; (*require*) exigir ▶ VI: **to be ~ing** estar grávida; **to ~ sb to do** (*anticipate*) esperar que alguém faça; (*demand*) esperar de alguém que faça; **to ~ to do sth** esperar fazer algo; **as ~ed** como previsto; **I ~ so** suponho que sim
expectancy [ɪks'pɛktənsɪ] N expectativa; **life ~** expectativa de vida
expectant [ɪk'spɛktənt] ADJ expectante; **~ mother** gestante f
expectantly [ɪk'spɛktəntlɪ] ADV cheio de expectativa
expectation [ɛkspɛk'teɪʃən] N (*hope*) esperança; (*belief*) expectativa; **in ~ of** na expectativa de; **against** or **contrary to all ~(s)** contra todas as expectativas; **to come** or **live up to one's ~s** corresponder à expectativa de alguém
expedience [ɛk'spiːdɪəns] N = **expediency**
expediency [ɛk'spiːdɪənsɪ] N conveniência; **for the sake of ~** por ser mais conveniente
expedient [ɛk'spiːdɪənt] ADJ conveniente, oportuno ▶ N expediente m, recurso
expedite ['ɛkspədaɪt] VT acelerar
expedition [ɛkspə'dɪʃən] N expedição f
expeditionary force [ɛkspə'dɪʃənrɪ-] N força expedicionária
expeditious [ɛkspə'dɪʃəs] ADJ eficiente
expel [ɪk'spɛl] VT expelir; (*from place, school*) expulsar
expend [ɪk'spɛnd] VT gastar; (*use up*) consumir
expendable [ɪk'spɛndəbl] ADJ prescindível
expenditure [ɪk'spɛndɪtʃəʳ] N gastos mpl; (*of energy*) consumo
expense [ɪk'spɛns] N gasto, despesa; (*high cost*) custo; (*expenditure*) despesas fpl; **expenses** NPL (*Comm: costs*) despesas fpl; (*: paid to employee*) ajuda de custo; **at the ~ of**

à custa de; **to go to the ~ of** fazer a despesa de; **to meet the ~ of** arcar com a despesa de
expense account N relatório de despesas
expensive [ɪk'spɛnsɪv] ADJ caro
experience [ɪk'spɪərɪəns] N experiência ▶ VT (*situation*) enfrentar; (*feeling*) sentir; **to learn by ~** aprender com a experiência
experienced [ɪk'spɪərɪənst] ADJ experiente
experiment [ɪk'spɛrɪmənt] N experimento, experiência ▶ VI: **to ~ (with/on)** fazer experiências (com/em)
experimental [ɪkspɛrɪ'mɛntl] ADJ experimental
expert ['ɛkspəːt] ADJ hábil, perito ▶ N perito(-a); (*specialist*) especialista m/f; **~ in** or **at doing sth** perito em fazer algo; **an ~ on sth** um perito em algo
expertise [ɛkspəː'tiːz] N perícia
expert witness N (*Law*) perito(-a)
expire [ɪk'spaɪəʳ] VI (*gen*) expirar; (*end*) terminar; (*run out*) vencer
expiry [ɪk'spaɪərɪ] N expiração f, vencimento
explain [ɪk'spleɪn] VT explicar; (*clarify*) esclarecer; (*demonstrate*) expor ▶ **explain away** VT justificar
explanation [ɛksplə'neɪʃən] N explicação f; **to find an ~ for sth** achar uma explicação para algo
explanatory [ɪk'splænətrɪ] ADJ explicativo
explicit [ɪk'splɪsɪt] ADJ explícito
explode [ɪk'spləʊd] VI estourar, explodir; (*fig*) explodir ▶ VT detonar, fazer explodir; (*fig: theory*) derrubar; (*: myth*) destruir
exploit [n 'ɛksplɔɪt, vt ɪk'splɔɪt] N façanha ▶ VT explorar
exploitation [ɛksplɔɪ'teɪʃən] N exploração f
exploration [ɛksplə'reɪʃən] N exploração f
exploratory [ɪk'splɒrətrɪ] ADJ (*talks*) exploratório, de pesquisa; (*Med: operation*) exploratório
explore [ɪk'splɔːʳ] VT explorar; (*fig*) examinar, pesquisar
explorer [ɪk'splɔːrəʳ] N explorador(a) m/f
explosion [ɪk'spləʊʒən] N explosão f
explosive [ɪk'spləʊsɪv] ADJ explosivo ▶ N explosivo
exponent [ɪk'spəʊnənt] N (*of theory etc*) representante m/f, defensor(a) m/f; (*of skill*) expoente m/f; (*Math*) expoente m
export [vt ɛk'spɔːt, n, cpd 'ɛkspɔːt] VT exportar ▶ N exportação f ▶ CPD de exportação
exportation [ɛkspɔː'teɪʃən] N exportação f
exporter [ɛk'spɔːtəʳ] N exportador(a) m/f
export licence N licença de exportação
expose [ɪk'spəʊz] VT expor; (*unmask*) desmascarar
exposed [ɪk'spəʊzd] ADJ exposto; (*house etc*) desabrigado; (*wire*) descascado; (*pipes, beams*) aparente
exposition [ɛkspə'zɪʃən] N exposição f
exposure [ɪk'spəʊʒəʳ] N exposição f; (*publicity*) publicidade f; (*Phot*) revelação f; (*: shot*) fotografia; **to die from ~** (*Med*) morrer de frio

exposure meter N fotômetro
expound [ɪk'spaund] VT expor, explicar
express [ɪk'sprɛs] ADJ (definite) expresso, explícito; (BRIT: letter etc) urgente ▶ N (train) rápido ▶ ADV (send) por via expressa ▶ VT exprimir, expressar; (quantity) representar; **to ~ o.s.** expressar-se
expression [ɪk'sprɛʃən] N expressão f
expressionism [ɪk'sprɛʃənɪzəm] N expressionismo
expressive [ɪk'sprɛsɪv] ADJ expressivo
expressly [ɪk'sprɛslɪ] ADV expressamente
expressway [ɪk'sprɛsweɪ] (US) N rodovia (BR), autoestrada (PT)
expropriate [ɛks'prəuprɪeɪt] VT expropriar
expulsion [ɪk'spʌlʃən] N expulsão f; (of gas, liquid) emissão f
exquisite [ɛk'skwɪzɪt] ADJ requintado
ex-serviceman (irreg: like **man**) N veterano (de guerra)
ext ABBR (Tel: extension) r. (BR), int. (PT)
extemporize [ɪk'stɛmpəraɪz] VI improvisar
extend [ɪk'stɛnd] VT (visit, street) prolongar; (building) aumentar; (offer) fazer; (hand) estender; (Comm: credit) conceder; (: period of loan) prorrogar ▶ VI (land) estender-se
extension [ɪk'stɛnʃən] N (Elec) extensão f; (building) acréscimo, expansão f; (of rights) ampliação f; (Tel) ramal m (BR), extensão f (PT); (of deadline, campaign) prolongamento, prorrogação f
extension cable N cabo de extensão
extensive [ɪk'stɛnsɪv] ADJ extenso; (damage) considerável; (broad) vasto, amplo; (frequent) geral, comum
extensively [ɪk'stɛnsɪvlɪ] ADV (altered, damaged etc) amplamente; **he's travelled ~** ele já viajou bastante
extent [ɪk'stɛnt] N (breadth) extensão f; (of damage etc) dimensão f; (scope) alcance m; **to some** or **to a certain ~** até certo ponto; **to the ~ of ...** a ponto de ...; **to a large ~** em grande parte; **to what ~?** até que ponto?; **to such an ~ that ...** a tal ponto que ...; **debts to the ~ of £5,000** dívidas da ordem de £5,000
extenuating [ɪks'tɛnjueɪtɪŋ] ADJ: **~ circumstances** circunstâncias fpl atenuantes
exterior [ɛk'stɪərɪəʳ] ADJ externo ▶ N exterior m; (appearance) aspecto
exterminate [ɪk'stə:mɪneɪt] VT exterminar
extermination [ɪkstə:mɪ'neɪʃən] N extermínio
external [ɛk'stə:nl] ADJ externo; (foreign) exterior ▶ N: **the ~s** as aparências; **for ~ use only** (Med) exclusivamente para uso externo
externally [ɛk'stə:nəlɪ] ADV por fora
extinct [ɪk'stɪŋkt] ADJ extinto
extinction [ɪk'stɪŋkʃən] N extinção f
extinguish [ɪk'stɪŋgwɪʃ] VT extinguir
extinguisher [ɪk'stɪŋgwɪʃəʳ] N (also: **fire extinguisher**) extintor m

extol, (US) **extoll** [ɪk'stəul] VT (merits) exaltar; (person) elogiar
extort [ɪk'stɔ:t] VT: **to ~ sth (from sb)** extorquir algo (a or de alguém)
extortion [ɪk'stɔ:ʃən] N extorsão f
extortionate [ɪk'stɔ:ʃnət] ADJ extorsivo, excessivo
extra ['ɛkstrə] ADJ adicional; (excessive) de mais, extra; (bonus: payment) extraordinário ▶ ADV (in addition) adicionalmente ▶ N (surcharge) extra m, suplemento; (Cinema, Theatre) figurante m/f; (newspaper) edição f extra; **the wine will cost ~** o vinho não está incluído no preço; **~ large sizes** tamanhos extra grandes
extra... ['ɛkstrə] PREFIX extra...
extract [vt ɪk'strækt, n 'ɛkstrækt] VT tirar, extrair; (tooth) arrancar; (mineral) extrair; (money) extorquir; (promise) conseguir, obter; (confession) arrancar, obter ▶ N extrato
extraction [ɪk'strækʃən] N extração f; (of tooth) arrancamento; (descent) descendência
extracurricular ['ɛkstrəkə'rɪkjuləʳ] ADJ (Sch) extracurricular
extradite ['ɛkstrədaɪt] VT (from country) extraditar; (to country) obter a extradição de
extradition [ɛkstrə'dɪʃən] N extradição f
extramarital [ɛkstrə'mærɪtl] ADJ extramatrimonial
extramural [ɛkstrə'mjuərl] ADJ (course) de extensão universitária
extraneous [ɛk'streɪnɪəs] ADJ: **~ to** alheio a
extraordinary [ɪk'strɔ:dnrɪ] ADJ extraordinário; (odd) estranho
extraordinary general meeting N assembleia geral extraordinária
extrapolation [ɛkstræpə'leɪʃən] N extrapolação f
extrasensory perception ['ɛkstrə'sɛnsərɪ-] N percepção f extrassensorial
extra time N (Football) prorrogação f
extravagance [ɪk'strævəgəns] N extravagância; (no pl: spending) esbanjamento
extravagant [ɪk'strævəgənt] ADJ (lavish) extravagante; (wasteful) gastador(a), esbanjador(a); (price) exorbitante; (praise) excessivo; (odd) excêntrico, estranho
extreme [ɪk'stri:m] ADJ extremo; (case) excessivo ▶ N extremo; **the ~ left/right** (Pol) a extrema esquerda/direita; **~s of temperature** temperaturas extremas
extremely [ɪk'stri:mlɪ] ADV muito, extremamente
extremist [ɪk'stri:mɪst] ADJ, N extremista m/f
extremity [ɪk'strɛmətɪ] N extremidade f; (need) apuro, necessidade f
extricate ['ɛkstrɪkeɪt] VT: **to ~ sb/sth (from)** (trap) libertar alguém/algo de; (situation) livrar alguém/algo de
extrovert ['ɛkstrəvə:t] N extrovertido(-a)
exuberance [ɪg'zju:bərəns] N exuberância
exuberant [ɪg'zju:bərənt] ADJ (person) eufórico; (style) exuberante

exude [ɪg'zjuːd] VT exsudar; (confidence)
esbanjar; **the charm** etc **he ~s** o charme que
emana dele etc
exult [ɪg'zʌlt] VI: **to ~ (in)** regozijar-se (em)
exultant [ɪg'zʌltənt] ADJ exultante,
triunfante
exultation [ɛgzʌl'teɪʃən] N exultação f,
regozijo
eye [aɪ] N olho; (of needle) buraco ▶ VT olhar,
observar; **as far as the ~ can see** a perder de
vista; **to keep an ~ on** vigiar, ficar de olho
em; **to have an ~ for sth** ter faro para algo;
in the public ~ conhecido pelo público;
with an ~ to doing (BRIT) com vista a fazer;
there's more to this than meets the ~ a
coisa é mais complicada do que parece
eyeball ['aɪbɔːl] N globo ocular
eyebath ['aɪbɑːθ] (BRIT) N copinho (para lavar
o olho)
eyebrow ['aɪbrau] N sobrancelha
eyebrow pencil N lápis m de sobrancelha
eye-catching ADJ chamativo, vistoso

eye cup (US) N copinho (para lavar o olho)
eyedrops NPL gotas fpl para os olhos
eyeglass ['aɪglɑːs] N monóculo; **eyeglasses**
NPL (US) óculos mpl
eyelash ['aɪlæʃ] N cílio
eyelet ['aɪlɪt] N ilhós m
eye-level ADJ à altura dos olhos
eyelid ['aɪlɪd] N pálpebra
eyeliner ['aɪlaɪnəʳ] N delineador m
eye-opener N revelação f, grande surpresa
eye shadow N sombra de olhos
eyesight ['aɪsaɪt] N vista, visão f
eyesore ['aɪsɔːʳ] N monstruosidade f
eyestrain ['aɪstreɪn] N cansaço ocular
eyetooth ['aɪtuːθ] (irreg: like **tooth**) N dente m
canino superior; **to give one's eyeteeth for
sth/to do sth** (fig) dar tudo por algo/para
fazer algo
eyewash ['aɪwɔʃ] N colírio; (fig) disparates
mpl, maluquices fpl
eye witness N testemunha f ocular
eyrie ['ɪərɪ] N ninho de ave de rapina

F¹, f [ɛf] N (letter) F, f m; (Mus): **F** fá m; **F for Frederick** (BRIT) or **Fox** (US) F de Francisco

F² ABBR = **Fahrenheit**

FA (BRIT) N ABBR (= Football Association) confederação de futebol

FAA (US) N ABBR = **Federal Aviation Administration**

fable ['feɪbl] N fábula

fabric ['fæbrɪk] N tecido, pano; (of building) estrutura

fabricate ['fæbrɪkeɪt] VT inventar

fabrication [fæbrɪ'keɪʃən] N invencionice f

fabric conditioner N amaciante m de pano

fabulous ['fæbjuləs] ADJ fabuloso; (inf: super) sensacional

façade [fə'sɑːd] N fachada

face [feɪs] N (Anat) cara, rosto; (grimace) careta; (of clock) mostrador m; (side, surface) superfície f; (of building) frente f, fachada ▶ VT (facts, problem) enfrentar; (particular direction, building) dar para; **~ down** (person) de bruços; (card) virado para baixo; **to lose ~** perder o prestígio; **to save ~** salvar as aparências; **to make** or **pull a ~** fazer careta; **in the ~ of** (difficulties etc) diante de, à vista de; **on the ~ of it** a julgar pelas aparências, à primeira vista; **~ to ~** face a face; **we are ~d with serious problems** estamos enfrentando sérios problemas, temos sérios problemas pela frente
▶ **face up to** VT FUS enfrentar

face cloth (BRIT) N pano de rosto

face cream N creme m facial

face lift N (operação f) plástica; (of façade) remodelamento

face pack (BRIT) N máscara facial

face powder N pó m de arroz

face-saving ADJ para salvar as aparências

facet ['fæsɪt] N faceta

facetious [fə'siːʃəs] ADJ jocoso

face-to-face ADV face a face, cara a cara

face value N (of coin, stamp) valor m nominal; **to take sth at ~** (fig) tomar algo em sentido literal

facia ['feɪʃə] N = **fascia**

facial ['feɪʃəl] ADJ facial

facile ['fæsaɪl] ADJ superficial

facilitate [fə'sɪlɪteɪt] VT facilitar

facilities [fə'sɪlɪtɪz] NPL facilidades fpl, instalações fpl; **credit ~** crediário

facility [fə'sɪlɪtɪ] N facilidade f; (factory) usina; (for sports, research) espaço

facing ['feɪsɪŋ] PREP de frente para ▶ N (of wall etc) revestimento; (Sewing) forro

facsimile [fæk'sɪmɪlɪ] N (copy, machine, document) fac-símile m

fact [fækt] N fato; **in ~** realmente, na verdade; **to know for a ~ that ...** saber com certeza que ...; **~s and figures** dados e números

fact-finding ADJ: **a ~ tour** or **mission** uma missão de pesquisa

faction ['fækʃən] N facção f

factor ['fæktəʳ] N fator m; (Comm) comissário financiador, empresa que compra contas a receber; (: agent) corretor(a) m/f ▶ VI comprar contas a receber; **safety ~** fator de segurança

factory ['fæktərɪ] N fábrica

factory farming (BRIT) N criação f intensiva

factory ship N navio-fábrica m

factual ['fæktjuəl] ADJ real, fatual

faculty ['fækəltɪ] N faculdade f; (US: teaching staff) corpo docente

fad [fæd] (inf) N mania, modismo

fade [feɪd] VI (colour, cloth) desbotar; (sound, hope) desvanecer-se; (light) apagar-se; (flower) murchar
▶ **fade in** VT (sound) subir; (picture) clarear
▶ **fade out** VT (sound) abaixar; (picture) escurecer

faeces, (US) **feces** ['fiːsiːz] NPL fezes fpl

fag [fæg] (inf) N (cigarette) cigarro; (US: homosexual) bicha; (chore): **what a ~!** que saco!

fag end (BRIT inf) N ponta de cigarro, guimba

fagged out [fægd-] (BRIT inf) ADJ estafado

fail [feɪl] VT (candidate) reprovar; (exam) não passar em, ser reprovado em; (subj: leader) fracassar; (: courage) carecer; (: memory) falhar ▶ VI (candidate, attempt) fracassar; (business) falir; (supply) acabar; (engine, brakes, voice) falhar; (patient) enfraquecer-se; **to ~ to do sth** (neglect) deixar de fazer algo; (be unable) não conseguir fazer algo; **without ~** sem falta

failing ['feɪlɪŋ] N defeito ▶ PREP na or à falta de; **~ that** senão

failsafe ['feɪlseɪf] ADJ (*device etc*) de segurança contra falhas
failure ['feɪljəʳ] N fracasso; (*in exam*) reprovação *f*; (*of crop*) perda; (*mechanical etc*) falha; **his ~ to turn up** o fato dele não ter vindo; **heart ~** parada cardíaca
failure rate N taxa de reprovados
faint [feɪnt] ADJ fraco; (*recollection*) vago; (*mark*) indistinto; (*smell, trace*) leve; (*dizzy*) tonto ▶ N desmaio ▶ VI desmaiar; **to feel ~** sentir tonteira
faint-hearted ADJ pusilânime
faintly ['feɪntlɪ] ADV indistintamente, vagamente
faintness ['feɪntnɪs] N fraqueza
fair [fɛəʳ] ADJ justo; (*hair*) louro; (*complexion*) branco; (*weather*) bom; (*good enough*) razoável; (*sizeable*) considerável ▶ ADV: **to play ~** fazer jogo limpo ▶ N (*also*: **trade fair**) feira; (*BRIT: funfair*) parque *m* de diversões; **a ~ amount of time** bastante tempo; **it's not ~!** não é justo!
fair copy N cópia a limpo
fair-haired ADJ (*de cabelo*) louro
fairly ['fɛəlɪ] ADV (*justly*) com justiça; (*share*) igualmente; (*quite*) bastante; **I'm ~ sure** tenho quase certeza
fairness ['fɛənɪs] N (*justice*) justiça; (*impartiality*) imparcialidade *f*; **in all ~** com toda a justiça
fair play N jogo limpo
fair trade N comércio justo
fairy ['fɛərɪ] N fada
fairy godmother N fada-madrinha
fairy lights (*BRIT*) NPL lâmpadas *fpl* coloridas de enfeite
fairy tale N conto de fadas
faith [feɪθ] N fé *f*; (*trust*) confiança; (*denomination*) seita; **to have ~ in sb/sth** ter fé *or* confiança em alguém/algo
faithful ['feɪθful] ADJ fiel; (*account*) exato
faithfully ['feɪθfulɪ] ADV fielmente; **yours ~** (*BRIT: in letters*) atenciosamente
faith healer N curandeiro(-a)
fake [feɪk] N (*painting etc*) falsificação *f*; (*person*) impostor(a) *m/f* ▶ ADJ falso ▶ VT fingir; (*painting etc*) falsificar; **his illness is a ~** sua doença é fingimento *or* um embuste
falcon ['fɔːlkən] N falcão *m*
Falkland Islands ['fɔːlklənd-] NPL: **the ~** as (ilhas) Malvinas *or* Falkland
fall [fɔːl] (*pt* **fell**, *pp* **fallen**) VI cair; (*price*) baixar ▶ N queda; (*US: autumn*) outono; **falls** NPL (*waterfall*) cascata, queda d'água; **to ~ flat** (*on one's face*) cair de cara no chão; (*plan*) falhar; (*joke*) não agradar; **to ~ short of** (*sb's expectations*) não corresponder a, ficar abaixo de; **a ~ of snow** (*BRIT*) uma nevasca
▶ **fall apart** VI cair aos pedaços; (*inf: emotionally*) descontrolar-se completamente
▶ **fall back** VI retroceder
▶ **fall back on** VT FUS (*remedy etc*) recorrer a
▶ **fall behind** VI ficar para trás

▶ **fall down** VI (*person*) cair; (*building*) desabar; (*hopes*) cair por terra
▶ **fall for** VT FUS (*trick*) cair em; (*person*) enamorar-se de
▶ **fall in** VI (*roof*) ruir; (*Mil*) alinhar-se
▶ **fall in with** VT FUS (*sb's plans etc*) conformar-se com
▶ **fall off** VI cair; (*diminish*) declinar, diminuir
▶ **fall out** VI (*hair, teeth*) cair; (*friends etc*) brigar; (*Mil*) sair da fila
▶ **fall over** VI cair por terra, tombar
▶ **fall through** VI (*plan, project*) furar
fallacy ['fæləsɪ] N (*error*) erro; (*lie*) mentira, falácia
fallback ['fɔːlbæk] ADJ: **~ position** alternativa
fallen ['fɔːlən] PP *of* **fall**
fallible ['fæləbl] ADJ (*person*) falível; (*memory*) falha
falling-off ['fɔːlɪŋ-] N declínio
fallopian tube [fə'ləupɪən-] N (*Anat*) trompa de Falópio
fallout ['fɔːlaut] N chuva radioativa
fallout shelter N refúgio contra chuva radioativa
fallow ['fæləu] ADJ alqueivado, de pousio
false [fɔːls] ADJ falso; (*impression, hair, teeth etc*) postiço; (*disloyal*) desleal, traidor(a)
false alarm N alarme *m* falso
falsehood ['fɔːlshud] N (*lie*) mentira; (*falseness*) falsidade *f*
falsely ['fɔːlslɪ] ADV falsamente
false pretences NPL: **under ~** sob falsos pretextos
false teeth (*BRIT*) NPL dentadura postiça
falsify ['fɔːlsɪfaɪ] VT falsificar
falter ['fɔːltəʳ] VI (*engine*) falhar; (*person*) vacilar
fame [feɪm] N fama
familiar [fə'mɪlɪəʳ] ADJ (*well-known*) conhecido; (*tone*) familiar, íntimo; **to be ~ with** (*subject*) estar familiarizado com; **to make o.s. ~ with sth** familiarizar-se com algo; **to be on ~ terms with sb** ter intimidade com alguém
familiarity [fəmɪlɪ'ærɪtɪ] N familiaridade *f*
familiarize [fə'mɪlɪəraɪz] VT: **to ~ o.s. with** familiarizar-se com
family ['fæmɪlɪ] N família
family allowance (*BRIT*) N abono-família *m*
family business N negócio de família
family doctor N médico(-a) da família
family life N vida familiar
family planning N planejamento familiar; **~ clinic** clínica de planejamento familiar
family tree N árvore *f* genealógica
famine ['fæmɪn] N fome *f*
famished ['fæmɪʃt] ADJ faminto; **I'm ~!** (*inf*) estou morrendo de fome
famous ['feɪməs] ADJ famoso, célebre
famously ['feɪməslɪ] ADV (*get on*) maravilhosamente
fan [fæn] N (*hand-held*) leque *m*; (*Elec*) ventilador *m*; (*person*) fã *mf*; (*Sport*)

torcedor(a) *m/f* (BR), adepto(a) (PT) ▶ VT abanar; (*fire, quarrel*) atiçar
▶ **fan out** VI espalhar-se

fanatic [fəˈnætɪk] N fanático(-a)

fanatical [fəˈnætɪkəl] ADJ fanático

fan belt N correia do ventilador (BR) or da ventoinha (PT)

fancied [ˈfænsɪd] ADJ imaginário

fanciful [ˈfænsɪful] ADJ (*notion*) irreal; (*design*) extravagante

fan club N fã-clube *m*

fancy [ˈfænsɪ] N (*whim*) capricho; (*taste*) inclinação *f*, gosto; (*imagination*) imaginação *f*; (*fantasy*) fantasia ▶ ADJ (*decorative*) ornamental; (*luxury*) luxuoso; (*as decoration*) como decoração ▶ VT (*feel like, want*) desejar, querer; (*imagine*) imaginar; (*think*) acreditar, achar; **to take a ~ to** tomar gosto por; **it took** *or* **caught my ~** gostei disso; **when the ~ takes him** quando lhe dá na veneta; **to ~ that …** imaginar que …; **he fancies her** (*inf*) ele está a fim dela

fancy dress N fantasia

fancy-dress ball N baile *m* à fantasia

fancy goods NPL artigos *mpl* de fantasia

fanfare [ˈfænfeəʳ] N fanfarra

fanfold paper [ˈfænfəuld-] N formulários *mpl* contínuos

fang [fæŋ] N presa

fan heater (BRIT) N aquecedor *m* de ventoinha

fanlight [ˈfænlaɪt] N (*window*) basculante *f*

fantasize [ˈfæntəsaɪz] VI fantasiar

fantastic [fænˈtæstɪk] ADJ (*enormous*) enorme; (*strange, wonderful*) fantástico

fantasy [ˈfæntəsɪ] N (*dream*) sonho; (*unreality*) fantasia; (*imagination*) imaginação *f*

FAO N ABBR (= *Food and Agriculture Organization*) FAO *f*

FAQ ABBR (= *free at quay*) posto no cais

far [fɑːʳ] ADJ (*distant*) distante ▶ ADV (*also:* **far away, far off**) longe; **the ~ side/end** o lado de lá/a outra ponta; **the ~ left/right** (*Pol*) a extrema esquerda/direita; **is it ~ to London?** Londres é longe daqui?; **it's not ~ (from here)** não é longe (daqui); **~ better** muito melhor; **~ from** longe de; **by ~** de longe; **go as ~ as the farm** vá até à (BR) or à (PT) fazenda; **as ~ as I know** que eu saiba; **as ~ as possible** na medida do possível; **how ~?** até onde?; (*fig*) até que ponto?

faraway [ˈfɑːrəweɪ] ADJ remoto, distante

farce [fɑːs] N farsa

farcical [ˈfɑːsɪkəl] ADJ farsante

fare [feəʳ] N (*on trains, buses*) preço (da passagem); (*in taxi: cost*) tarifa; (: *passenger*) passageiro(-a); (*food*) comida ▶ VI sair-se; **half/full ~** meia/inteira passagem

Far East N: **the ~** o Extremo Oriente

farewell [feəˈwɛl] EXCL adeus ▶ N despedida ▶ CPD (*party etc*) de despedida

far-fetched [-ˈfɛtʃt] ADJ inverossímil

farm [fɑːm] N fazenda (BR), quinta (PT) ▶ VT cultivar

▶ **farm out** VT (*work etc*) dar de empreitada

farmer [ˈfɑːməʳ] N fazendeiro(-a), agricultor *m*

farmhand [ˈfɑːmhænd] N lavrador(a) *m/f*, trabalhador(a) *m/f* rural

farmhouse [ˈfɑːmhaus] (*irreg: like* **house**) N casa da fazenda (BR) or da quinta (PT)

farming [ˈfɑːmɪŋ] N agricultura; (*tilling*) cultura; (*of animals*) criação *f*; **intensive ~** cultura intensiva; **sheep ~** criação de ovelhas, ovinocultura

farm labourer N lavrador(a) *m/f*, trabalhador(a) *m/f* rural

farmland [ˈfɑːmlænd] N terra de cultivo

farm produce N produtos *mpl* agrícolas

farm worker N = **farmhand**

farmyard [ˈfɑːmjɑːd] N curral *m*

Faroe Islands [ˈfɛərəu-] NPL: **the ~** as (ilhas) Faroë

Faroes [ˈfɛərəuz] NPL = **Faroe Islands**

far-reaching [-ˈriːtʃɪŋ] ADJ de grande alcance, abrangente

far-sighted ADJ presbita; (*fig*) previdente

fart [fɑːt] (!) N peido (!) ▶ VI soltar um peido (!), peidar (!)

farther [ˈfɑːðəʳ] ADV mais longe ▶ ADJ mais distante, mais afastado

farthest [ˈfɑːðɪst] SUPERL *of* **far**

FAS (BRIT) ABBR (= *free alongside ship*) FAS

fascia [ˈfeɪʃə] N (*Aut*) painel *m*

fascinate [ˈfæsɪneɪt] VT fascinar

fascinating [ˈfæsɪneɪtɪŋ] ADJ fascinante

fascination [fæsɪˈneɪʃən] N fascinação *f*, fascínio

fascism [ˈfæʃɪzəm] N fascismo

fascist [ˈfæʃɪst] ADJ, N fascista *m/f*

fashion [ˈfæʃən] N moda; (*fashion industry*) indústria da moda; (*manner*) maneira ▶ VT modelar, dar feitio a; **in ~** na moda; **out of ~** fora da moda; **in the Greek ~** à grega, à maneira dos gregos; **after a ~** (*finish, manage etc*) até certo ponto

fashionable [ˈfæʃənəbl] ADJ da moda, elegante; (*writer, café*) da moda

fashion designer N estilista *m/f*

fashion show N desfile *m* de modas

fast [fɑːst] ADJ rápido; (*dye, colour*) firme, permanente; (*Phot: film*) de alta sensibilidade; (*clock*): **to be ~** estar adiantado ▶ ADV rápido, rapidamente, depressa; (*stuck, held*) firmemente ▶ N jejum *m* ▶ VI jejuar; **my watch is 5 minutes ~** meu relógio está 5 minutos adiantado; **~ asleep** dormindo profundamente; **as ~ as I can** o mais rápido possível; **to make a boat ~** (BRIT) amarrar um barco

fasten [ˈfɑːsn] VT fixar, prender; (*coat*) fechar; (*belt*) apertar ▶ VI prender-se, fixar-se
▶ **fasten on, fasten upon** VT FUS (*idea*) agarrar-se a

fastener [ˈfɑːsnəʳ] N presilha, fecho; (*of door etc*) fechadura; **zip ~** (BRIT) fecho ecler (BR) or éclair (PT)

fastening ['fɑ:snɪŋ] N = **fastener**
fast food N fast food f
fastidious [fæs'tɪdɪəs] ADJ (fussy) meticuloso; (demanding) exigente
fast lane N (Aut) pista de velocidade
fat [fæt] ADJ gordo; (meat) com muita gordura; (greasy) gorduroso; (book) grosso; (wallet) recheado; (profit) grande ▶ N (on person, Chem) gordura; (lard) banha, gordura; **to live off the ~ of the land** viver na abundância
fatal ['feɪtl] ADJ fatal; (injury) mortal; (consequence) funesto
fatalism ['feɪtəlɪzəm] N fatalismo
fatality [fə'tælɪtɪ] N (road death etc) vítima m/f
fatally ['feɪtəlɪ] ADV: **~ injured** mortalmente ferido
fate [feɪt] N destino; (of person) sorte f
fated ['feɪtɪd] ADJ (person) condenado; (project) fadado ao fracasso
fateful ['feɪtful] ADJ fatídico
father ['fɑ:ðər] N pai m
Father Christmas N Papai m Noel
fatherhood ['fɑ:ðəhud] N paternidade f
father-in-law (pl **fathers-in-law**) N sogro
fatherland ['fɑ:ðəlænd] N pátria
fatherly ['fɑ:ðəlɪ] ADJ paternal
fathom ['fæðəm] N braça ▶ VT (Naut) sondar; (unravel) penetrar, deslindar; (understand) compreender
fatigue [fə'ti:g] N fadiga, cansaço; (Mil) faxina; **metal ~** fadiga do metal
fatness ['fætnɪs] N gordura
fatten ['fætn] VT, VI engordar; **chocolate is ~ing** o chocolate engorda
fatty ['fætɪ] ADJ (food) gorduroso ▶ N (inf) gorducho(-a)
fatuous ['fætjuəs] ADJ fátuo
faucet ['fɔ:sɪt] (US) N torneira
fault [fɔ:lt] N (error) defeito, falta; (blame) culpa; (defect) defeito; (Geo) falha; (Tennis) falta, bola fora ▶ VT criticar; **it's my ~** é minha culpa; **to find ~ with** criticar, queixar-se de; **at ~** culpado; **to a ~** em demasia
faultless ['fɔ:ltlɪs] ADJ (action) impecável; (person) irrepreensível
faulty ['fɔ:ltɪ] ADJ defeituoso
fauna ['fɔ:nə] N fauna
faux pas ['fəu'pɑ:] N INV gafe f
favour, (US) **favor** ['feɪvər] N favor m ▶ VT (proposition) favorecer, aprovar; (person etc) favorecer; (assist) auxiliar; **to ask a ~ of** pedir um favor a; **to do sb a ~** fazer favor a alguém; **to be in ~ of sth/of doing sth** estar a favor de algo/de fazer algo; **to find ~ with** cair nas boas graças de; **in ~ of** em favor de
favourable, (US) **favorable** ['feɪuərəbl] ADJ favorável
favourably, (US) **favorably** ['feɪvərəblɪ] ADV favoravelmente
favourite, (US) **favorite** ['feɪvərɪt] ADJ predileto ▶ N favorito(-a)

favouritism, (US) **favoritism** ['feɪvərɪtɪzəm] N favoritismo
fawn [fɔ:n] N cervo novo, cervato ▶ ADJ (also: **fawn-coloured**) castanho-claro inv ▶ VI: **to ~ (up)on** bajular
fax [fæks] N (document, machine) fax m, fac-símile m ▶ VT enviar por fax or fac-símile
FBI (US) N ABBR (= Federal Bureau of Investigation) FBI m
FCC (US) N ABBR = **Federal Communications Commission**
FCO (BRIT) N ABBR (= Foreign and Commonwealth Office) ministério das Relações Exteriores
FD (US) N ABBR = **fire department**
FDA (US) N ABBR (= Food and Drug Administration) órgão controlador de medicamentos e gêneros alimentícios
fear [fɪər] N medo; (misgiving) temor m ▶ VT ter medo de, temer ▶ VI: **to ~ for** recear or temer por; **to ~ that** temer que; **~ of heights** medo das alturas, vertigem f; **for ~ of** com medo de
fearful ['fɪəful] ADJ medonho, temível; (cowardly) medroso; (awful) terrível; **to be ~ of** temer, ter medo de
fearfully ['fɪəfəlɪ] ADV (timidly) timidamente; (inf: very) muito, terrivelmente
fearless ['fɪəlɪs] ADJ sem medo, intrépido; (bold) audaz
fearsome ['fɪəsəm] ADJ (opponent) medonho, temível; (sight) espantoso
feasibility [fi:zə'bɪlɪtɪ] N viabilidade f
feasibility study N estudo de viabilidade
feasible ['fi:zəbl] ADJ viável
feast [fi:st] N banquete m; (Rel: also: **feast day**) festa ▶ VI banquetear-se
feat [fi:t] N façanha, feito
feather ['fɛðər] N pena, pluma ▶ VT: **to ~ one's nest** (fig) acumular riquezas ▶ CPD (bed etc) de penas
feather-weight N (Boxing) peso-pena m
feature ['fi:tʃər] N característica; (Anat) feição f, traço; (article) reportagem f ▶ VT (subj: film) apresentar ▶ VI figurar; **features** NPL (of face) feições fpl; **it ~d prominently in ...** ocupou um lugar de destaque em ...
feature film N longa-metragem f
featureless ['fi:tʃəlɪs] ADJ anônimo
Feb. ABBR (= February) fev.
February ['fɛbruərɪ] N fevereiro; see also **July**
feces ['fi:si:z] (US) NPL = **faeces**
feckless ['fɛklɪs] ADJ displicente
Fed (US) ABBR = **federal**; **federation**
fed [fɛd] PT, PP of **feed**
Fed. [fɛd] (US inf) N ABBR = **Federal Reserve Board**
federal ['fɛdərəl] ADJ federal
Federal Reserve Board (US) N órgão controlador do banco central dos EUA
Federal Trade Commission (US) N órgão regulador de práticas comerciais
federation [fɛdə'reɪʃən] N federação f

fed up ADJ: **to be ~** estar (de saco) cheio (BR), estar farto (PT)
fee [fi:] N taxa (BR), propina (PT); (of school) matrícula; (of doctor, lawyer) honorários mpl; **entrance ~** (to club) joia; (to museum etc) entrada; **membership ~** (to join) joia; (annual etc) quota; **for a small ~** em troca de uma pequena taxa
feeble ['fi:bl] ADJ fraco, débil; (attempt) ineficaz
feeble-minded ADJ imbecil
feed [fi:d] (pt, pp **fed**) N comida; (of baby) alimento infantil; (of animal) ração f; (on printer) mecanismo alimentador ▶ VT (gen, machine) alimentar; (baby: breastfeed) amamentar; (animal) dar de comer a; (data, information): **to ~ into** introduzir em
▶ **feed on** VT FUS alimentar-se de
feedback ['fi:dbæk] N (Elec) feedback m; (from person) reação f
feeder ['fi:də'] N (bib) babador m
feeding bottle ['fi:dɪŋ-] (BRIT) N mamadeira
feel [fi:l] (pt, pp **felt**) VT (touch) tocar, apalpar; (anger, pain etc) sentir; (think, believe) achar, acreditar ▶ N (sensation) sensação f; (sense of touch) tato; (impression) impressão f; **to ~ (that)** achar (que); **I ~ that you ought to do it** eu acho que você deveria fazê-lo; **to ~ hungry/cold** estar com fome/frio (BR), ter fome/frio (PT); **to ~ lonely/better** sentir-se só/melhor; **to ~ sorry for** ter pena de; **I don't ~ well** não estou me sentindo bem; **it ~s soft** é macio; **it ~s colder here** sente-se mais frio aqui; **it ~s like velvet** parece veludo; **to ~ like** (want) querer; **to ~ about** or **around** apalpar, tatear; **I'm still ~ing my way** (fig) ainda estou me ambientando; **to get the ~ of sth** (fig) acostumar-se a algo
feeler ['fi:lə'] N (of insect) antena; **to put out ~s** or **a ~** (fig) sondar opiniões, lançar um balão-de-ensaio
feeling ['fi:lɪŋ] N sensação f; (foreboding) pressentimento; (opinion) opinião f; (emotion) sentimento; (impression) impressão f; **to hurt sb's ~s** magoar alguém; **~s ran high about it** os sentimentos se esquentaram a respeito disso; **what are your ~s about the matter?** qual é a sua opinião sobre o assunto?; **my ~ is that ...** eu acho que ...; **I have a ~ that ...** tenho a impressão de que ...
feet [fi:t] NPL of **foot**
feign [feɪn] VT fingir
felicitous [fɪ'lɪsɪtəs] ADJ feliz
feline ['fi:laɪn] ADJ felino
fell [fɛl] PT of **fall** ▶ VT (tree) lançar por terra, derrubar ▶ N (BRIT: mountain) montanha; (: moorland): **the ~s** a charneca ▶ ADJ: **with one ~ blow** de um só golpe
fellow ['fɛləu] N (gen) camarada m/f; (inf: man) cara m (BR), tipo (PT); (of learned society) membro; (of university) membro do conselho

universitário ▶ CPD: **~ students** colegas mpl/ fpl de curso; **his ~ workers** seus colegas de trabalho
fellow citizen N concidadão(-dã) m/f
fellow countryman (irreg: like **man**) N compatriota m
fellow feeling N simpatia
fellow men NPL semelhantes mpl
fellowship ['fɛləuʃɪp] N (comradeship) amizade f; (grant) bolsa de estudo; (society) associação f
fellow traveller, (US) **fellow traveler** N companheiro(-a) de viagem; (Pol) simpatizante m/f
fell-walking (BRIT) N caminhadas fpl nas montanhas
felon ['fɛlən] N (Law) criminoso(-a)
felony ['fɛlənɪ] N (Law) crime m
felt [fɛlt] PT, PP of **feel** ▶ N feltro
felt-tip pen N caneta pilot® (BR) or de feltro (PT)
female ['fi:meɪl] N (pej: woman) mulher f; (Zool) fêmea ▶ ADJ (Bio, Elec) fêmeo(-a); (sex, character) feminino; (vote etc) das mulheres; (child etc) do sexo feminino; **male and ~ teachers** professores e professoras
female impersonator N (Theatre) travesti m
feminine ['fɛmɪnɪn] ADJ feminino; (womanly) feminil ▶ N feminino
femininity [fɛmɪ'nɪnɪtɪ] N feminilidade f
feminism ['fɛmɪnɪzəm] N feminismo
feminist ['fɛmɪnɪst] N feminista m/f
fen [fɛn] (BRIT) N: **the F~s** os pântanos de Norfolk
fence [fɛns] N cerca; (Sport) obstáculo; (inf: person) receptor(a) m/f ▶ VT (also: **fence in**) cercar ▶ VI esgrimir; **to sit on the ~** (fig) ficar no muro
fencing ['fɛnsɪŋ] N (sport) esgrima
fend [fɛnd] VI: **to ~ for o.s.** defender-se, virar-se
▶ **fend off** VT (attack, attacker) defender-se de
fender ['fɛndə'] N (of fireplace) guarda-fogo m; (on boat) defesa de embarcação; (US: Aut) para-lama m; (: Rail) limpa-trilhos m inv
fennel ['fɛnl] N erva-doce f, funcho
ferment [vi fə'mɛnt, n 'fə:mɛnt] VI fermentar ▶ N (fig) agitação f
fermentation [fə:mən'teɪʃən] N fermentação f
fern [fə:n] N samambaia (BR), feto (PT)
ferocious [fə'rəuʃəs] ADJ feroz
ferocity [fə'rɒsɪtɪ] N ferocidade f
ferret ['fɛrɪt] N furão m
▶ **ferret about** (BRIT) VI = **ferret around**
▶ **ferret around** VI: **to ~ around in sth** vasculhar algo
▶ **ferret out** VT (information) desenterrar, descobrir
ferry ['fɛrɪ] N (small) barco (de travessia); (large: also: **ferryboat**) balsa ▶ VT transportar; **to ~ sth/sb across** or **over** transportar algo/ alguém para o outro lado
ferryman ['fɛrɪmən] (irreg: like **man**) N barqueiro, balseiro
fertile ['fə:taɪl] ADJ fértil; (Bio) fecundo

fertility [fə'tɪlɪtɪ] N fertilidade f; (Bio) fecundidade f

fertility drug N droga que propicia a fecundação

fertilize ['fə:tɪlaɪz] VT fertilizar; (Bio) fecundar

fertilizer ['fə:tɪlaɪzəʳ] N adubo, fertilizante m

fervent ['fə:vənt] ADJ ardente, apaixonado

fervour, (US) **fervor** ['fə:vəʳ] N fervor m

fester ['fɛstəʳ] VI inflamar-se

festival ['fɛstɪvəl] N (Rel) festa; (Art, Mus) festival m

festive ['fɛstɪv] ADJ festivo; **the ~ season** (BRIT: Christmas) a época do Natal

festivities [fɛs'tɪvɪtɪz] NPL festas fpl, festividades fpl

festoon [fɛs'tu:n] VT: **to ~ with** engrinaldar de or com

fetch [fɛtʃ] VT ir buscar, trazer; (BRIT: sell for) alcançar; **how much did it ~?** quanto rendeu?, por quanto foi vendido?
 ▶ **fetch up** (US) VI ir parar

fetching ['fɛtʃɪŋ] ADJ atraente

fête [feɪt] N festa

fetid ['fɛtɪd] ADJ fétido

fetish ['fɛtɪʃ] N fetiche m

fetter ['fɛtəʳ] VT restringir, refrear

fetters ['fɛtəz] NPL grilhões mpl

fettle ['fɛtl] (BRIT) N: **in fine ~** (car etc) em bom estado; (person) em forma

fetus ['fi:təs] (US) N = **foetus**

feud [fju:d] N (hostility) inimizade f; (quarrel) disputa, rixa ▶ VI brigar; **a family ~** uma briga de família

feudal ['fju:dl] ADJ feudal

feudalism ['fju:dəlɪzəm] N feudalismo

fever ['fi:vəʳ] N febre f; **he has a ~** ele está com febre

feverish ['fi:vərɪʃ] ADJ febril; (activity) febril

few [fju:] ADJ, PRON poucos(-as); **a ~ ...** alguns/algumas ...; **I know a ~** conheço alguns; **quite a ~ ...** vários(-as) ...; **in the next ~ days** nos próximos dias; **in the past ~ days** nos últimos dias; **every ~ days/ months** cada dois ou três dias/meses; **a ~ more ...** mais alguns/algumas ...

fewer ['fju:əʳ] ADJ, PRON menos

fewest ['fju:ɪst] ADJ o menor número de

FFA N ABBR = **Future Farmers of America**

FH (BRIT) ABBR = **fire hydrant**

FHA (US) N ABBR (= Federal Housing Administration) secretaria federal da habitação

fiancé [fɪ'ã:ŋseɪ] N noivo

fiancée [fɪ'ã:ŋseɪ] N noiva

fiasco [fɪ'æskəu] N fiasco

fib [fɪb] N lorota

fibre, (US) **fiber** ['faɪbəʳ] N fibra

fibreboard, (US) **fiberboard** ['faɪbəbɔ:d] N madeira compensada, compensado

fibre-glass, (US) **fiber-glass** N fibra de vidro

fibrositis [faɪbrə'saɪtɪs] N aponeurosite f

FICA (US) N ABBR = **Federal Insurance Contributions Act**

fickle ['fɪkl] ADJ inconstante; (weather) instável

fiction ['fɪkʃən] N ficção f; (invention) invenção f

fictional ['fɪkʃənl] ADJ de ficção

fictionalize ['fɪkʃnəlaɪz] VT romancear

fictitious [fɪk'tɪʃəs] ADJ fictício

fiddle ['fɪdl] N (Mus) violino; (cheating) fraude f, embuste m; (swindle) trapaça ▶ VT (BRIT: accounts) falsificar
 ▶ **fiddle with** VT FUS brincar com

fiddler ['fɪdləʳ] N violinista m/f

fiddly ['fɪdlɪ] ADJ (task) espinhoso

fidelity [fɪ'dɛlɪtɪ] N fidelidade f

fidget ['fɪdʒɪt] VI estar irrequieto, mexer-se

fidgety ['fɪdʒɪtɪ] ADJ inquieto, nervoso

fiduciary [fɪ'dju:ʃɪərɪ] N fiduciário(-a)

field [fi:ld] N campo; (fig) área, esfera, especialidade f; **to lead the ~** (Sport) tomar a dianteira; (Comm) liderar; **to have a ~ day** (fig) fazer a festa

field glasses NPL binóculo

field marshal N marechal-de-campo

fieldwork ['fi:ldwə:k] N trabalho de campo

fiend [fi:nd] N demônio

fiendish ['fi:ndɪʃ] ADJ diabólico

fierce [fɪəs] ADJ feroz; (wind, attack) violento; (heat) intenso; (fighting, enemy) feroz, violento

fiery ['faɪərɪ] ADJ (burning) ardente; (temperament) fogoso

FIFA ['fi:fə] N ABBR (= Fédération Internationale de Football Association) FIFA

fifteen [fɪf'ti:n] NUM quinze; see also **five**

fifth [fɪfθ] NUM quinto; **I was (the) ~ to arrive** eu fui o quinto a chegar; **he came ~ in the competition** ele tirou o quinto lugar; (in race) ele chegou em quinto lugar; **Henry the F~** Henrique Quinto; **the ~ of July, July the ~** dia cinco de julho; **I wrote to him on the ~** eu lhe escrevi no dia cinco

fiftieth ['fɪftɪɪθ] NUM quinquagésimo; see also **fifth**

fifty ['fɪftɪ] NUM cinquenta; **about ~ people** umas cinquenta pessoas; **he'll be ~ (years old) next birthday** ele fará cinquenta anos no seu próximo aniversário; **he's about ~** ele tem uns cinquenta anos; **the fifties** os anos 50; **to be in one's fifties** estar na casa dos cinquenta anos; **the temperature was in the fifties** a temperatura estava na faixa dos cinquenta graus; **to do ~** (Aut) ir a 50 (quilômetros por hora)

fifty-fifty ['fɪftɪ'fɪftɪ] ADV: **to share** or **go ~ with sb** dividir meio a meio com alguém, rachar com alguém ▶ ADJ: **to have a ~ chance** ter 50% de chance

fig [fɪg] N figo

fight [faɪt] (pt, pp **fought**) N briga; (Mil) combate m; (struggle: against illness etc) luta ▶ VT lutar contra; (cancer, alcoholism) combater; (election) competir; (Law: case) defender ▶ VI brigar, bater-se; (fig): **to ~ (for/ against)** lutar (por/contra)

▶ **fight back** vɪ revidar; *(Sport, from illness etc)* reagir ▶ vᴛ *(tears)* tentar reter

▶ **fight off** vᴛ *(attack, attacker)* repelir; *(illness, sleep, urge)* lutar contra

▶ **fight out** vᴛ: **to ~ it out** resolver a questão pela briga

fighter ['faɪtə^r] ɴ combatente *m/f*; *(fig)* lutador(a) *m/f*; *(plane)* caça *m*

fighter pilot ɴ piloto de caça

fighting ['faɪtɪŋ] ɴ *(battle)* batalha; *(brawl)* briga

figment ['fɪgmənt] ɴ: **a ~ of the imagination** um produto da imaginação

figurative ['fɪgjuratɪv] ᴀᴅJ *(expression)* figurado; *(style)* figurativo

figure ['fɪgə^r] ɴ *(Drawing, Math)* figura, desenho; *(numeral)* algarismo; *(number, cipher)* número, cifra; *(outline)* forma; *(of woman)* corpo; *(person)* personagem *m* ▶ vᴛ *(esp US)* imaginar ▶ vɪ *(appear)* figurar; *(US: make sense)* fazer sentido; **public ~** personalidade *f*

▶ **figure on** (US) vᴛ ꜰᴜꜱ: **to ~ on doing** contar em fazer

▶ **figure out** vᴛ compreender

figurehead ['fɪgəhɛd] ɴ *(Naut)* carranca de proa; *(pej: leader)* chefe *m* nominal

figure of speech ɴ figura de linguagem

figure skating ɴ movimentos *mpl* de patinação

Fiji ['fiːdʒiː] ɴ Fiji

Fiji Islands ɴᴘʟ *(ilhas fpl)* Fiji *(no article)*

filament ['fɪləmənt] ɴ filamento

filch [fɪltʃ] *(inf)* vᴛ surripiar, afanar

file [faɪl] ɴ *(tool)* lixa; *(dossier)* dossiê *m*, pasta; *(folder)* pasta; *(: binder)* fichário; *(Comput)* arquivo; *(row)* fila, coluna ▶ vᴛ *(wood, nails)* lixar; *(papers)* arquivar; *(Law: claim)* apresentar, dar entrada em; *(store)* arquivar ▶ vɪ: **to ~ in/out** entrar/sair em fila; **to ~ past** desfilar em frente de; **to ~ a suit against sb** *(Law)* abrir processo contra alguém

file name ɴ *(Comput)* nome *m* do arquivo

file sharing [-ʃɛərɪŋ] ɴ *(Comput)* compartilhamento de arquivos

filibuster ['fɪlɪbʌstə^r] ɴ *(Pol)* obstrucionista *m/f* ▶ vɪ obstruir

filing ['faɪlɪŋ] ɴ arquivamento; **filings** ɴᴘʟ *(of iron etc)* limalha

filing cabinet ɴ fichário, arquivo

filing clerk ɴ arquivista *m/f*

Filipino [fɪlɪ'piːnəu] ɴ *(person)* filipino(-a); *(Ling)* filipino

fill [fɪl] vᴛ encher; *(vacancy)* preencher; *(order)* atender; *(need)* satisfazer ▶ ɴ: **to eat one's ~** encher-se *or* fartar-se de comer; **~ed with admiration** cheio de admiração

▶ **fill in** vᴛ *(form)* preencher; *(hole)* tapar; *(time)* encher

▶ **fill up** vᴛ encher ▶ vɪ *(Aut)* abastecer o carro; **~ it up, please** *(Aut)* pode encher (o tanque), por favor

fillet ['fɪlɪt] ɴ filete *m*, filé *m* ▶ vᴛ preparar em filés

fillet steak ɴ filé *m*

filling ['fɪlɪŋ] ɴ *(Culin)* recheio; *(for tooth)* obturação *f* (ʙʀ), chumbo (ᴘᴛ)

filling station ɴ posto de gasolina

fillip ['fɪlɪp] ɴ estímulo, incentivo

filly ['fɪlɪ] ɴ potranca

film [fɪlm] ɴ filme *m*; *(of liquid etc)* camada fina, veu *m* ▶ vᴛ *(scene)* rodar, filmar ▶ vɪ filmar

film star ɴ astro/estrela do cinema

film strip ɴ diafilme *m*

film studio ɴ estúdio (de cinema)

filter ['fɪltə^r] ɴ filtro ▶ vᴛ filtrar

filter coffee ɴ café *m* filtro

filter lane (ʙʀɪᴛ) ɴ *(Aut)* pista para se dobrar à esquerda *(or* à direita)

filter tip ɴ filtro

filter-tipped ᴀᴅJ filtrado

filth [fɪlθ] ɴ sujeira (ʙʀ), sujidade *f* (ᴘᴛ)

filthy ['fɪlθɪ] ᴀᴅJ sujo; *(language)* indecente, obsceno

fin [fɪn] ɴ barbatana

final ['faɪnl] ᴀᴅJ final, último; *(definitive)* definitivo ▶ ɴ *(Sport)* final *f*; **finals** ɴᴘʟ *(Sch)* exames *mpl* finais

final demand ɴ *(on invoice etc)* demanda final

finale [fɪ'nɑːlɪ] ɴ final *m*

finalist ['faɪnəlɪst] ɴ *(Sport)* finalista *m/f*

finalize ['faɪnəlaɪz] vᴛ concluir, completar

finally ['faɪnəlɪ] ᴀᴅv *(lastly)* finalmente, por fim; *(eventually)* por fim; *(irrevocably)* definitivamente

finance [faɪ'næns] ɴ *(money)* fundos *mpl*; *(money management)* finanças *fpl* ▶ vᴛ financiar; **finances** ɴᴘʟ *(personal finances)* finanças

financial [faɪ'nænʃəl] ᴀᴅJ financeiro; **~ statement** demonstração financeira

financially [faɪ'nænʃəlɪ] ᴀᴅv financeiramente

financial year ɴ ano fiscal, exercício

financier [fɪ'nænsɪə^r] ɴ financista *m/f*; *(backer)* financiador(a) *m/f*

find [faɪnd] *(pt, pp found)* vᴛ encontrar, achar; *(discover)* descobrir ▶ ɴ achado, descoberta; **to ~ sb guilty** *(Law)* declarar alguém culpado

▶ **find out** vᴛ descobrir; *(person)* desmascarar ▶ vɪ: **to ~ out about** informar-se sobre; *(by chance)* saber de

findings ['faɪndɪŋz] ɴᴘʟ *(Law)* veredito, decisão *f*; *(of report)* constatações *fpl*

fine [faɪn] ᴀᴅJ fino; *(excellent)* excelente; *(good)* bom/boa; *(beautiful)* bonito ▶ ᴀᴅv *(well)* muito bem ▶ ɴ *(Law)* multa ▶ vᴛ *(Law)* multar; **to be ~** *(person)* estar bem; *(weather)* estar bom; **you're doing ~** você se dá bem; **to cut it ~** deixar pouca margem; *(arrive just in time)* chegar em cima da hora

fine arts ɴᴘʟ belas artes *fpl*

finely ['faɪnlɪ] ᴀᴅv *(tune)* finamente; **~ chopped** picado

finery ['faɪnərɪ] N enfeites mpl
finesse [fɪ'nɛs] N sutileza
fine-tooth comb N: **to go through sth with a ~** (fig) passar o pente fino em algo
finger ['fɪŋgəʳ] N dedo ▶ VT (touch) manusear; (Mus) dedilhar; **little/index ~** dedo mínimo/indicador
fingermark ['fɪŋgəmɑːk] N dedada
fingernail ['fɪŋgəneɪl] N unha
fingerprint ['fɪŋgəprɪnt] N impressão f digital ▶ VT (person) tirar as impressões digitais de
fingerstall ['fɪŋgəstɔːl] N dedeira
fingertip ['fɪŋgətɪp] N ponta do dedo; **to have sth at one's ~s** ter algo à sua disposição, dispor de algo; (knowledge) saber algo na ponta da língua
finicky ['fɪnɪkɪ] ADJ (fussy) fresco, cheio de coisas
finish ['fɪnɪʃ] N (end) fim m; (Sport) chegada; (on wood etc) acabamento ▶ VT, VI terminar, acabar; **to ~ doing sth** terminar de fazer algo; **to ~ with sb** (end relationship) acabar com alguém; **to ~ third** chegar no terceiro lugar
▶ **finish off** VT terminar; (kill) liquidar
▶ **finish up** VT acabar ▶ VI acabar; (in place) ir parar
finished product ['fɪnɪʃt-] N produto acabado
finishing line ['fɪnɪʃɪŋ-] N linha de chegada, meta
finishing school ['fɪnɪʃɪŋ-] N escola de aperfeiçoamento (para moças)
finishing touches ['fɪnɪʃɪŋ-] NPL últimos retoques mpl
finite ['faɪnaɪt] ADJ finito
Finland ['fɪnlənd] N Finlândia
Finn [fɪn] N finlandês(-esa) m/f
Finnish ['fɪnɪʃ] ADJ finlandês(-esa) ▶ N (Ling) finlandês m
fiord [fjɔːd] N = **fjord**
fir [fəːʳ] N abeto
fire ['faɪəʳ] N fogo; (accidental) incêndio; (gas fire, electric fire) aquecedor m ▶ VT (gun) disparar; (arrow) atirar; (interest) estimular; (dismiss) despedir; (excite): **to ~ sb with enthusiasm** encher alguém de entusiasmo ▶ VI disparar ▶ CPD: **~ hazard, ~ risk** perigo or risco de incêndio; **on ~** em chamas; **to set ~ to sth, set sth on ~** incendiar algo; **insured against ~** segurado contra fogo; **to come under ~ (from)** (fig) ser atacado (por)
fire alarm N alarme m de incêndio
firearm ['faɪərɑːm] N arma de fogo
fire brigade N (corpo de) bombeiros mpl
fire chief (US) N = **fire master**
fire department (US) N = **fire brigade**
fire drill N treinamento de incêndio
fire engine N carro de bombeiro
fire escape N escada de incêndio
fire exit N saída de emergência
fire extinguisher N extintor m de incêndio
fireguard ['faɪəgɑːd] (BRIT) N guarda-fogo m

fire insurance N seguro contra fogo
fireman ['faɪəmɛn] (irreg: like **man**) N bombeiro
fire master (BRIT) N capitão m dos bombeiros
firemen ['faɪəmɛn] NPL of **fireman**
fireplace ['faɪəpleɪs] N lareira
fireproof ['faɪəpruːf] ADJ à prova de fogo
fire regulations NPL normas fpl preventivas contra incêndio
fire screen N guarda-fogo m
fireside ['faɪəsaɪd] N lugar m junto à lareira
fire station N posto de bombeiros
firewall ['faɪəwɔːl] N (Comput) firewall m
firewood ['faɪəwud] N lenha
fireworks ['faɪəwəːks] NPL fogos mpl de artifício; (display) queima de fogos
firing ['faɪərɪŋ] N (Mil) tiros mpl, tiroteio
firing line N (Mil) linha de fogo; **to be in the ~** (fig) estar na linha de frente
firing squad N pelotão m de fuzilamento
firm [fəːm] ADJ firme ▶ N firma; **to be a ~ believer in sth** ser partidário perseverante de algo; **to stand ~** or **take a ~ stand on sth** (fig) manter-se firme em algo
firmly ['fəːmlɪ] ADV firmemente
firmness ['fəːmnɪs] N firmeza
first [fəːst] ADJ primeiro ▶ ADV (before others) primeiro; (when listing reasons etc) em primeiro lugar ▶ N (person: in race) primeiro(-a); (Aut) primeira; (BRIT Sch) menção f honrosa; **the ~ of January** primeiro de janeiro (BR), dia um de Janeiro (PT); **at ~** no início; **~ of all** antes de tudo, antes de mais nada; **in the ~ place** em primeiro lugar; **I'll do it ~ thing tomorrow** vou fazê-lo amanhã cedo; **head ~** com a cabeça para a frente; **for the ~ time** pela primeira vez; **from the (very) ~** desde o início; see also **fifth**
first aid N primeiros socorros mpl
first-aid kit N estojo de primeiros socorros
first-aid post N pronto-socorro
first-class ADJ de primeira classe
first-class mail N correspondência prioritária
first-hand ADJ de primeira mão
first lady (US) N primeira dama
firstly ['fəːstlɪ] ADV primeiramente, em primeiro lugar
first name N primeiro nome m
first night N (Theatre) estreia
first-rate ADJ de primeira categoria
fir tree N abeto
FIS (BRIT) N ABBR (= Family Income Supplement) abono-família m
fiscal ['fɪskəl] ADJ fiscal; **~ year** ano-fiscal
fish [fɪʃ] N INV peixe m ▶ VT, VI pescar; **to go ~ing** ir pescar
▶ **fish out** VT (from water) pescar; (from box etc) tirar
fish bone N espinha de peixe
fisherman ['fɪʃəmən] (irreg: like **man**) N pescador m
fishery ['fɪʃərɪ] N pescaria

fish factory (BRIT) N fábrica de processamento de pescados
fish farm N viveiro (de piscicultura)
fish fingers (BRIT) NPL filezinhos mpl de peixe
fish hook N anzol m
fishing boat ['fɪʃɪŋ-] N barco de pesca
fishing industry ['fɪʃɪŋ-] N indústria da pesca
fishing line ['fɪʃɪŋ-] N linha de pesca
fishing net ['fɪʃɪŋ-] N rede f de pesca
fishing rod ['fɪʃɪŋ-] N vara (de pesca)
fishing tackle ['fɪʃɪŋ-] N apetrechos mpl (de pesca)
fish market N mercado de peixe
fishmonger ['fɪʃmʌŋgəʳ] N peixeiro(-a); **~'s (shop)** peixaria
fish sticks (US) NPL = **fish fingers**
fishy ['fɪʃɪ] (inf) ADJ (tale) suspeito
fission ['fɪʃən] N fissão f; **nuclear ~** fissão nuclear
fissure ['fɪʃəʳ] N fenda, fissura
fist [fɪst] N punho
fistfight ['fɪstfaɪt] N briga de socos
fit [fɪt] ADJ (healthy) em (boa) forma; (suitable) adequado, apropriado ▶ VT (subj: clothes) caber em; (try on: clothes) experimentar, provar; (facts) enquadrar-se or condizer com; (accommodate) ajustar, adaptar; (correspond exactly) encaixar em; (put in, attach) colocar; (equip) equipar ▶ VI (clothes) servir; (parts) ajustar-se; (in space, gap) caber; (correspond) encaixar-se ▶ N (Med) ataque m; **~ to** bom para; **~ for** adequado para; **a ~ of anger/pride** um acesso de raiva/orgulho; **to have a ~** (Med) sofrer or ter um ataque; (fig: inf) fazer escândalo; **this dress is a good/tight ~** este vestido tem um bom corte/está um pouco justo; **do as you think** or **see ~** faça como você achar melhor; **by ~s and starts** espasmodicamente
▶ **fit in** VI encaixar-se; (fig: person) dar-se bem (com todos)
▶ **fit out** (BRIT) VT (also: **fit up**) equipar
fitful ['fɪtful] ADJ espasmódico, intermitente
fitment ['fɪtmənt] N móvel m
fitness ['fɪtnɪs] N (Med) saúde f, boa forma; (of remark) conveniência
fitness instructor N instrutor(a) m/f de academia, instrutor(a) m/f de fitness
fitted ['fɪtɪd] ADJ (cupboards) embutido; (BRIT: kitchen) com armários embutidos; **~ carpet** carpete m
fitted kitchen ['fɪtɪd-] (BRIT) N cozinha planejada
fitter ['fɪtəʳ] N ajustador(a) m/f, montador(a) m/f; (also: **gas fitter**) gasista m/f
fitting ['fɪtɪŋ] ADJ apropriado ▶ N (of dress) prova; **fittings** NPL (in building) instalações fpl, acessórios mpl
fitting room N (in shop) cabine f (para experimentar roupa)
five [faɪv] NUM cinco; **she is ~ (years old)** ela tem cinco anos; **they live at number ~/ at ~ Green Street** eles moram no número cinco/na Green Street número cinco; **there are ~ of us** somos cinco; **all ~ of them came** todos os cinco vieram; **it costs ~ pounds** custa cinco libras; **~ and a quarter/half** cinco e um quarto/e meio; **it's ~ (o'clock)** são cinco horas; **to divide sth into ~** dividir algo em cinco partes; **they are sold in ~s** eles são vendidos em pacotes de cinco
five-day week N semana de cinco dias
fiver ['faɪvəʳ] (inf) N (BRIT) nota de cinco libras; (US) nota de cinco dólares
fix [fɪks] VT (secure) fixar, colocar; (arrange) arranjar; (mend) consertar; (meal, drink) preparar; (inf: game etc) arranjar ▶ N: **to be in a ~** estar em apuros; **the fight was a ~** a luta foi uma marmelada; **to ~ sth in one's mind** gravar algo
▶ **fix up** VT (meeting) marcar; **to ~ sb up with sth** arranjar algo para alguém
fixation [fɪk'seɪʃən] N fixação f
fixative ['fɪksətɪv] N fixador m
fixed [fɪkst] ADJ (prices, smile) fixo; **how are you ~ for money?** (inf) a quantas anda você em matéria de dinheiro?
fixed assets NPL ativo fixo
fixture ['fɪkstʃəʳ] N coisa fixa; (furniture) móvel m fixo; (Sport) desafio, encontro
fizz [fɪz] VI efervescer
fizzle ['fɪzl] VI chiar
▶ **fizzle out** VI fracassar; (interest) diminuir
fizzy ['fɪzɪ] ADJ (drink) com gás, gasoso; (gen) efervescente
fjord [fjɔːd] N fiorde m
FL (US) ABBR (Post) = **Florida**
flabbergasted ['flæbəgɑːstɪd] ADJ pasmado
flabby ['flæbɪ] ADJ flácido
flag [flæg] N bandeira; (for signalling) bandeirola; (flagstone) laje f ▶ VI acabar-se, descair; **~ of convenience** bandeira de conveniência
▶ **flag down** VT: **to ~ sb down** fazer sinais a alguém para que pare
flagon ['flægən] N garrafão m
flagpole ['flægpəul] N mastro de bandeira
flagrant ['fleɪgrənt] ADJ flagrante
flagship ['flægʃɪp] N nau f capitânia; (fig) carro-chefe m
flag stop (US) N (for bus) parada facultativa
flair [fleəʳ] N (talent) talento; (style) habilidade f
flak [flæk] N (Mil) fogo antiaéreo; (inf: criticism) críticas fpl
flake [fleɪk] N (of rust, paint) lasca; (of snow, soap powder) floco ▶ VI (also: **flake off**) lascar, descamar-se
flaky ['fleɪkɪ] ADJ (paintwork) laminoso; (skin) escamoso; (pastry) folhado
flamboyant [flæm'bɔɪənt] ADJ (dress) espalhafatoso; (person) extravagante
flame [fleɪm] N chama; **to burst into ~s** irromper em chamas; **old ~** (inf) velha paixão f

flamingo [flə'mɪŋgəu] (pl **flamingoes**) N
flamingo
flammable ['flæməbl] ADJ inflamável
flan [flæn] (BRIT) N torta
flange [flændʒ] N flange m
flank [flæŋk] N flanco; (of person) lado ▶ VT
ladear
flannel ['flænl] N (BRIT: also: **face flannel**)
pano de rosto; (fabric) flanela; (BRIT inf)
conversa fiada; **flannels** NPL calça (BR) or
calças fpl (PT) de flanela
flannelette [flænə'lɛt] N baetilha
flap [flæp] N (of pocket, table) aba; (of envelope)
dobra; (wing movement) bater m; (Aviat) flap m
▶ VT (arms) oscilar; (wings) bater ▶ VI (sail, flag)
ondular; (inf: also: **be in a flap**) estar
atarantado
flapjack ['flæpdʒæk] N (US: pancake) panqueca;
(BRIT: biscuit) biscoito de aveia
flare [flɛəʳ] N fogacho, chama; (Mil) foguete m
sinalizador; (in skirt etc) folga
▶ **flare up** VI chamejar; (fig: person)
encolerizar-se; (: violence) irromper
flared ['flɛəd] ADJ (trousers) com roda; (skirt)
rodado
flash [flæʃ] N (of lightning) clarão m; (also: **news
flash**) notícias fpl de última hora; (Phot)
flash m; (of inspiration) lampejo ▶ VT (light,
headlights) piscar; (torch) acender; (news,
message) transmitir; (look, smile) brilhar ▶ VI
brilhar; (light on ambulance, eyes etc) piscar;
in a ~ num instante; **to ~ by** or **past** passar
como um raio; **to ~ sth about** (fig: inf)
ostentar or exibir algo
flashback ['flæʃbæk] N flashback m
flashbulb ['flæʃbʌlb] N lâmpada de flash
flash card N (Sch) cartão m
flashcube ['flæʃkjuːb] N cubo de flash
flash drive N (Comput) pen drive m
flasher ['flæʃəʳ] N (Aut) pisca-pisca m
flashlight ['flæʃlaɪt] N lanterna de bolso
flash point N ponto de centelha
flashy ['flæʃɪ] (pej) ADJ espalhafatoso
flask [flɑːsk] N frasco; (also: **vacuum flask**)
garrafa térmica (BR), termo (PT)
flat [flæt] ADJ plano; (smooth) liso; (battery)
descarregado; (tyre) vazio; (beer) choco;
(denial) categórico; (Mus) abemolado; (: voice)
desafinado; (rate) único; (fee) fixo ▶ N (BRIT:
apartment) apartamento; (Mus) bemol m;
(Aut) pneu m furado; **~ out** (work) a toque de
caixa; (race) a toda; **~ rate of pay** (Comm)
salário fixo
flat-footed [-'futɪd] ADJ de pés chatos
flatly ['flætlɪ] ADV terminantemente
flatmate ['flætmeɪt] (BRIT) N companheiro(-a)
de apartamento
flatness ['flætnɪs] N (of land) planura, lisura
flatten ['flætən] VT (also: **flatten out**) aplanar;
(smooth out) alisar; (demolish) arrasar; (defeat)
derrubar
flatter ['flætəʳ] VT lisonjear; (show to advantage)
favorecer

flatterer ['flætərəʳ] N lisonjeador(a) m/f
flattering ['flætərɪŋ] ADJ lisonjeiro; (clothes
etc) favorecedor(a)
flattery ['flætərɪ] N bajulação f
flatulence ['flætjuləns] N flatulência
flaunt [flɔːnt] VT ostentar, pavonear
flavour, (US) **flavor** ['fleɪvəʳ] N sabor m ▶ VT
condimentar, aromatizar; **strawberry-~ed**
com sabor de morango
flavouring, (US) **flavoring** ['fleɪvərɪŋ] N
condimento; (synthetic) aromatizante m
flaw [flɔː] N (in cloth, glass) defeito; (in character)
falha; (in argument) erro
flawless ['flɔːlɪs] ADJ impecável
flax [flæks] N linho
flaxen ['flæksən] ADJ da cor de linho
flea [fliː] N pulga
flea market N feira de quinquilharias
fleck [flɛk] N (mark) mancha, sinal m; (of dust)
partícula; (of mud) salpico; (of paint)
pontinho ▶ VT salpicar; **brown ~ed with
white** marrom salpicado de branco
fled [flɛd] PT, PP of **flee**
fledgeling, fledgling ['flɛdʒlɪŋ] N ave f
recém-emplumada
flee [fliː] (pt, pp **fled**) VT fugir de ▶ VI fugir
fleece [fliːs] N tosão m; (coat) velo; (wool) lã f
▶ VT (inf) espoliar
fleecy ['fliːsɪ] ADJ (blanket) felpudo; (cloud) fofo
fleet [fliːt] N (gen, of lorries etc) frota; (of ships)
esquadra
fleeting ['fliːtɪŋ] ADJ fugaz
Flemish ['flɛmɪʃ] ADJ flamengo ▶ N (Ling)
flamengo; **the Flemish** NPL os flamengos
flesh [flɛʃ] N carne f; (of fruit) polpa; **of ~ and
blood** de carne e osso
flesh wound N ferimento de superfície
flew [fluː] PT of **fly**
flex [flɛks] N fio ▶ VT (muscles) flexionar
flexibility [flɛksɪ'bɪlɪtɪ] N flexibilidade f
flexible ['flɛksɪbl] ADJ flexível
flick [flɪk] N pancada leve; (with finger)
peteleco, piparote m; (with whip) chicotada
▶ VT dar um peteleco; (switch) apertar; **flicks**
NPL (BRIT inf) cinema m
▶ **flick through** VT FUS folhear
flicker ['flɪkəʳ] VI (light, flame) tremular;
(eyelids) tremer ▶ N tremulação f; **a ~ of light**
um fio de luz
flick knife (BRIT) (irreg: like **knife**) N canivete m
de mola
flier ['flaɪəʳ] N aviador(a) m/f
flight [flaɪt] N voo m; (escape) fuga; (of steps)
lance m; **to take ~** fugir, pôr-se em fuga;
to put to ~ pôr em fuga
flight attendant (US) N comissário(-a) de
bordo
flight crew N tripulação f
flight deck N (Aviat) cabine f do piloto; (Naut)
pista de aterrissagem (BR) or aterragem (PT)
flight recorder N gravador m de voo
flimsy ['flɪmzɪ] ADJ (thin) delgado, franzino;
(weak) débil; (excuse) fraco

flinch [flɪntʃ] vɪ encolher-se; **to ~ from sth/ from doing sth** vacilar diante de algo/em fazer algo

fling [flɪŋ] vᴛ (*pt, pp* **flung**) lançar ▸ N (*love affair*) caso

flint [flɪnt] N pederneira; (*in lighter*) pedra

flip [flɪp] vᴛ (*turn over*) dar a volta em; (*throw*) jogar; **to ~ a coin** tirar cara ou coroa ▸ **flip through** vᴛ Fᴜs folhear

flip-flops ['flɪpflɔps] (*esp* BRɪᴛ) NPL chinelo (de dedo)

flippant ['flɪpənt] ADJ petulante, irreverente

flipper ['flɪpəʳ] N (*of animal*) nadadeira; (*for swimmer*) pé de pato, nadadeira

flip side N (*of record*) outro lado

flirt [fləːt] vɪ flertar ▸ N namorador(a) *m/f*, paquerador(a) *m/f*

flirtation [fləː'teɪʃən] N flerte *m*, paquera

flit [flɪt] vɪ esvoaçar

float [fləʊt] N boia; (*in procession*) carro alegórico; (*sum of money*) caixa ▸ vɪ flutuar; (*swimmer*) boiar ▸ vᴛ fazer flutuar; (*company*) lançar (na Bolsa)

floating ['fləʊtɪŋ] ADJ flutuante; **~ vote** voto oscilante; **~ voter** indeciso(-a)

flock [flɔk] N (*of sheep, Rel*) rebanho; (*of birds*) bando; (*of people*) multidão *f* ▸ vɪ: **to ~ to** afluir a

floe [fləʊ] N (*also:* **ice floe**) banquisa

flog [flɔg] vᴛ açoitar; (*inf*) vender

flood [flʌd] N enchente *f*, inundação *f*; (*of words, tears etc*) torrente *m* ▸ vᴛ inundar, alagar; (*Aut: carburettor*) afogar ▸ vɪ (*place*) alagar; (*people, goods*): **to ~ into** inundar; **to ~ the market** (*Comm*) inundar o mercado; **in ~** transbordante

flooding ['flʌdɪŋ] N inundação *f*

floodlight ['flʌdlaɪt] (*irreg: like* **light**) N refletor *m*, holofote *m* ▸ vᴛ iluminar com holofotes

floodlit ['flʌdlɪt] Pᴛ, PP *of* **floodlight** ▸ ADJ iluminado (por holofotes)

flood tide N maré *f* enchente

floor [flɔːʳ] N chão *m*; (*in house*) soalho; (*storey*) andar *m*; (*of sea*) fundo; (*dance floor*) pista de dança ▸ vᴛ (*fig: confuse*) confundir, pasmar; **ground ~** (BRɪᴛ) *or* **first ~** (ᴜs) andar térreo (BR), rés-do-chão (Pᴛ); **first ~** (BRɪᴛ) *or* **second ~** (ᴜs) primeiro andar; **top ~** último andar; **to have the ~** (*speaker*) ter a palavra

floorboard ['flɔːbɔːd] N tábua de assoalho

flooring ['flɔːrɪŋ] N piso

floor lamp (ᴜs) N abajur *m* de pé

floor show N show *m*

floorwalker ['flɔːwɔːkəʳ] (*esp* ᴜs) N supervisor(a) *m/f* (numa loja de departamentos)

flop [flɔp] N fracasso ▸ vɪ (*fail*) fracassar; (*into chair etc*) cair pesadamente

floppy ['flɔpɪ] ADJ frouxo, mole

floppy disk N disquete *m*

flora ['flɔːrə] N flora

floral ['flɔːrl] ADJ floral

Florence ['flɔrəns] N Florença

florid ['flɔrɪd] ADJ (*style*) florido; (*complexion*) corado

florist ['flɔrɪst] N florista *m/f*

florist's, florist's shop N floricultura

flotation [fləʊ'teɪʃən] N (*of shares*) emissão *f*; (*of company*) lançamento (na Bolsa)

flounce [flaʊns] N babado, debrum *m* ▸ **flounce out** vɪ sair indignado

flounder ['flaʊndəʳ] N (*pl* **flounder** *or* **flounders**) (*Zool*) linguado ▸ vɪ (*swimmer*) debater-se; (*fig*) atrapalhar-se

flour ['flaʊəʳ] N farinha

flourish ['flʌrɪʃ] vɪ florescer ▸ vᴛ brandir, menear ▸ N floreio; (*bold gesture*): **with a ~** con gestos floreados; (*of trumpets*) fanfarra

flourishing ['flʌrɪʃɪŋ] ADJ próspero

flout [flaʊt] vᴛ (*law*) desrespeitar; (*offer*) desprezar

flow [fləʊ] N (*of tide, traffic*) fluxo; (*direction*) curso; (*of river, Elec*) corrente *f*; (*of blood*) circulação *f* ▸ vɪ correr; (*traffic*) fluir; (*blood, Elec*) circular; (*clothes, hair*) ondular

flow chart N fluxograma *m*

flow diagram N fluxograma *m*

flower ['flaʊəʳ] N flor *f* ▸ vɪ florescer, florir; **in ~** em flor

flower bed N canteiro

flowerpot ['flaʊəpɔt] N vaso

flowery ['flaʊərɪ] ADJ (*perfume*) a base de flor; (*pattern*) florido; (*speech*) floreado

flown [fləʊn] PP *of* **fly**

flu [fluː] N gripe *f*

fluctuate ['flʌktjueɪt] vɪ flutuar; (*temperature*) variar

fluctuation [flʌktju'eɪʃən] N flutuação *f*, oscilação *f*

flue [fluː] N fumeiro

fluency ['fluːənsɪ] N fluência

fluent ['fluːənt] ADJ (*speech*) fluente; **he speaks ~ French, he's ~ in French** ele fala francês fluentemente

fluently ['fluːəntlɪ] ADV fluentemente

fluff [flʌf] N felpa, penugem *f*

fluffy ['flʌfɪ] ADJ macio, fofo; **~ toy** brinquedo de pelúcia

fluid ['fluːɪd] ADJ fluido ▸ N fluido; (*in diet*) líquido

fluid ounce (BRɪᴛ) N (= 0.028 l) 0.05 *pints*

fluke [fluːk] (*inf*) N sorte *f*

flummox ['flʌməks] vᴛ desconcertar

flung [flʌŋ] Pᴛ, PP *of* **fling**

flunky ['flʌŋkɪ] N lacaio

fluorescent [fluə'rɛsnt] ADJ fluorescente

fluoride ['fluəraɪd] N fluoreto ▸ CPD: **~ toothpaste** pasta de dentes com flúor

fluorine ['fluəriːn] N flúor *m*

flurry ['flʌrɪ] N (*of snow*) lufada; (*haste*) agitação *f*; **~ of activity/excitement** muita atividade/animação

flush [flʌʃ] N (*on face*) rubor *m*; (*plenty*) abundância ▸ vᴛ lavar com água ▸ vɪ ruborizar-se ▸ ADJ: **~ with** rente com;

to ~ the toilet dar descarga; **hot ~es** (*Med*) calores
▶ **flush out** vt levantar
flushed [flʌʃt] ADJ ruborizado, corado
fluster ['flʌstər] N agitação f ▶ vt atrapalhar, desconcertar
flustered ['flʌstəd] ADJ atrapalhado
flute [flu:t] N flauta
fluted ['flu:tɪd] ADJ acanelado
flutter ['flʌtər] N agitação f; (*of wings*) bater m; (*inf: bet*) aposta ▶ vi esvoaçar
flux [flʌks] N fluxo; **in a state of ~** mudando continuamente
fly [flaɪ] (*pt* **flew**, *pp* **flown**) N (*insect*) mosca; (*on trousers: also:* **flies**) braguilha ▶ vt (*plane*) pilotar; (*passengers, cargo*) transportar (de avião); (*flag*) hastear; (*distances*) percorrer; (*kite*) soltar, empinar ▶ vi voar; (*passengers*) ir de avião; (*escape*) fugir; (*flag*) hastear-se; **to ~ open** abrir-se bruscamente; **to ~ off the handle** perder as estribeiras
▶ **fly away** vi voar
▶ **fly in** vi chegar
▶ **fly off** vi = **fly away**
▶ **fly out** vi sair (de avião)
fly-fishing N pesca com iscas artificiais
flying ['flaɪɪŋ] N (*activity*) aviação f ▶ ADJ: **~ visit** visita de médico; **with ~ colours** brilhantemente; **he doesn't like ~** ele não gosta de andar de avião
flying buttress N arcobotante m
flying saucer N disco voador
flying start N: **to get off to a ~** (*in race*) disparar; (*fig*) começar muito bem
fly leaf ['flaɪliːf] (*irreg: like* **leaf**) N guarda (*num livro*)
flyover ['flaɪəuvər] (*BRIT*) N (*bridge*) viaduto
flypast ['flaɪpɑːst] N desfile m aéreo
fly sheet N (*for tent*) duplo teto
flywheel ['flaɪwiːl] N volante m
FM ABBR (*BRIT Mil*) = **field marshal**; (*Radio*: = *frequency modulation*) FM
FMB (*US*) N ABBR = **Federal Maritime Board**
FMCS (*US*) N ABBR (= *Federal Mediation and Conciliation Service*) ≈ Justiça do Trabalho
FO (*BRIT*) N ABBR = **Foreign Office**
foal [fəul] N potro
foam [fəum] N espuma ▶ vi espumar
foam rubber N espuma de borracha
FOB ABBR (= *free on board*) FOB
fob [fɔb] vt: **to ~ sb off with sth** despachar alguém com algo; **to ~ sth off on sb** impingir algo a alguém
foc (*BRIT*) ABBR = **free of charge**
focal ['fəukəl] ADJ focal
focal point N foco
focus ['fəukəs] N (*pl* **focuses**) foco ▶ vt (*field glasses etc*) enfocar ▶ vi: **to ~ on** enfocar, focalizar; **in/out of ~** em foco/fora de foco
fodder ['fɔdər] N forragem f
FOE N ABBR (= *Friends of the Earth*) organização ecologista; (*US*: = *Fraternal Order of Eagles*) associação beneficente

foe [fəu] N inimigo
foetus, (*US*) **fetus** ['fiːtəs] N feto
fog [fɔg] N nevoeiro
fogbound ['fɔgbaund] ADJ imobilizado pelo nevoeiro
foggy ['fɔgɪ] ADJ nevoento
fog lamp, (*US*) **fog light** N farol m de neblina
foible ['fɔɪbl] N fraqueza, ponto fraco
foil [fɔɪl] vt frustrar ▶ N folha metálica; (*also*: **kitchen foil**) folha *or* papel m de alumínio; (*complement*) contraste m, complemento; (*Fencing*) florete m; **to act as a ~ to** (*fig*) dar realce a
foist [fɔɪst] vt: **to ~ sth on sb** impingir algo a alguém
fold [fəuld] N (*bend, crease*) dobra, vinco, prega; (*of skin*) ruga; (*Agr*) redil m, curral m ▶ vt dobrar; **to ~ one's arms** cruzar os braços
▶ **fold up** vi (*map etc*) dobrar; (*business*) abrir falência ▶ vt (*map etc*) dobrar
folder ['fəuldər] N (*for papers*) pasta; (: *binder*) fichário; (*brochure*) folheto
folding ['fəuldɪŋ] ADJ (*chair, bed*) dobrável
foliage ['fəulɪɪdʒ] N folhagem f
folk [fəuk] NPL gente f ▶ CPD popular, folclórico; **folks** NPL (*family*) família, parentes *mpl*; (*people*) gente f
folklore ['fəuklɔːr] N folclore m
folk song N canção f popular *or* folclórica
follow ['fɔləu] vt seguir ▶ vi seguir; (*result*) resultar; **to ~ sb's advice** seguir o conselho de alguém; **I don't quite ~ you** não consigo acompanhar o seu raciocínio; **to ~ in sb's footsteps** seguir os passos de alguém; **it doesn't ~ that ...** (isso) não quer dizer que ...; **to ~ suit** fazer o mesmo
▶ **follow out** vt (*idea, plan*) levar a cabo, executar
▶ **follow through** vt levar a cabo, executar
▶ **follow up** vt (*letter*) responder a; (*offer*) levar adiante; (*case*) acompanhar
follower ['fɔləuər] N seguidor(a) *m/f*; (*Pol*) partidário(-a)
following ['fɔləuɪŋ] ADJ seguinte ▶ N adeptos *mpl*
follow-up N continuação f ▶ CPD: **~ letter** carta suplementar de reforço
folly ['fɔlɪ] N loucura
fond [fɔnd] ADJ (*memory, look*) carinhoso; (*hopes*) absurdo, descabido; **to be ~ of** gostar de
fondle ['fɔndl] vt acariciar
fondly ['fɔndlɪ] ADV (*lovingly*) afetuosamente; (*naïvely*): **he ~ believed that ...** ele acreditava piamente que ...
fondness ['fɔndnɪs] N (*for things*) gosto, afeição f; (*for people*) carinho
font [fɔnt] N (*Rel*) pia batismal; (*Typ*) fonte f, família
food [fuːd] N comida
food mixer N batedeira
food poisoning N intoxicação f alimentar

food processor N multiprocessador *m* de cozinha

foodstuffs ['fu:dstʌfs] NPL gêneros *mpl* alimentícios

fool [fu:l] N tolo(-a); (*History: of king*) bobo; (*Culin*) purê *m* de frutas com creme ▶ VT enganar ▶ VI (*gen: fool around*) brincar; (*waste time*) fazer bagunça; **to make a ~ of sb** (*ridicule*) ridicularizar alguém; (*trick*) fazer alguém de bobo; **to make a ~ of o.s.** fazer papel de bobo, fazer-se de bobo; **you can't ~ me** você não pode me fazer de bobo
▶ **fool about** (*pej*) VI (*waste time*) fazer bagunça; (*behave foolishly*) fazer-se de bobo
▶ **fool around** (*pej*) VI (*waste time*) fazer bagunça; (*behave foolishly*) fazer-se de bobo

foolhardy ['fu:lhɑ:dɪ] ADJ temerário

foolish ['fu:lɪʃ] ADJ bobo; (*stupid*) burro; (*careless*) imprudente

foolishly ['fu:lɪʃlɪ] ADV imprudentemente

foolishness ['fu:lɪʃnɪs] N tolice *f*

foolproof ['fu:lpru:f] ADJ (*plan etc*) infalível

foolscap ['fu:lskæp] N papel *m* ofício

foot [fut] N (*pl* **feet**) pé *m*; (*of animal*) pata; (*measure*) pé (304 *mm*; 12 *inches*) ▶ VT (*bill*) pagar; **on ~** a pé; **to find one's feet** (*fig*) ambientar-se; **to put one's ~ down** (*Aut*) acelerar; (*say no*) bater o pé

footage ['futɪdʒ] N (*Cinema: length*) ≈ metragem *f*; (*: material*) sequências *fpl*

foot and mouth, foot and mouth disease N febre *f* aftosa

football ['futbɔ:l] N bola; (*game: BRIT*) futebol *m*; (*: US*) futebol norte-americano

footballer ['futbɔ:ləʳ], **football player** N futebolista *m*, jogador *m* de futebol

football ground N campo de futebol

football match (*BRIT*) N partida de futebol

foot brake N freio (*BR*) or travão *m* (*PT*) de pé

footbridge ['futbrɪdʒ] N passarela

foothills ['futhɪlz] NPL contraforte *m*

foothold ['futhəuld] N apoio para o pé

footing ['futɪŋ] N (*fig*) posição *f*; **to lose one's ~** escorregar; **on an equal ~** em pé de igualdade

footlights ['futlaɪts] NPL ribalta

footman ['futmən] (*irreg: like* **man**) N lacaio

footnote ['futnəut] N nota ao pé da página, nota de rodapé

footpath ['futpɑ:θ] N caminho, atalho; (*pavement*) calçada

footprint ['futprɪnt] N pegada

footrest ['futrest] N suporte *m* para os pés

footsore ['futsɔ:ʳ] ADJ com os pés doloridos

footstep ['futstɛp] N passo

footwear ['futwɛəʳ] N calçados *mpl*

FOR ABBR (= *free on rail*) franco sobre vagão

(KEYWORD)

for [fɔ:ʳ] PREP **1** (*indicating destination, direction*) para; **the train for London** o trem para Londres; **he went for the paper** foi pegar o jornal; **is this for me?** é para mim?; **it's time for lunch** é hora de almoçar
2 (*indicating purpose*) para; **what's it for?** para quê serve?; **to pray for peace** orar pela paz
3 (*on behalf of, representing*) por; **the MP for Hove** o MP por Hove; **he works for the government/a local firm** ele trabalha para o governo/uma firma local; **I'll ask him for you** vou pedir a ele por você; **G for George** G de George
4 (*because of*) por; **for this reason** por esta razão; **for fear of being criticized** com medo de ser criticado
5 (*with regard to*) para; **it's cold for July** está frio para julho; **for everyone who voted yes, 50 voted no** para cada um que votou sim, cinquenta votaram não
6 (*in exchange for*) por; **it was sold for £5** foi vendido por £5
7 (*in favour of*) a favor de; **are you for or against us?** você está a favor de ou contra nós?; **I'm all for it** concordo plenamente, tem todo o meu apoio; **vote for X** vote em X
8 (*referring to distance*): **there are road works for 5 km** há obras na estrada por 5 quilômetros; **we walked for miles** andamos quilômetros
9 (*referring to time*): **he was away for 2 years** esteve fora 2 anos; **she will be away for a month** ela ficará fora um mês; **I have known her for years** eu a conheço há anos; **can you do it for tomorrow?** você pode fazer isso para amanhã?
10 (*with infinite clause*): **it is not for me to decide** não cabe a mim decidir; **it would be best for you to leave** seria melhor que você fosse embora; **there is still time for you to do it** ainda há tempo para você fazer isso; **for this to be possible …** para que isso seja possível …
11 (*in spite of*) apesar de; **for all his complaints …** apesar de suas reclamações, …
▶ CONJ (*since, as: rather formal*) pois, porque; **she was very angry, for he was late again** ela estava muito zangada pois ele se atrasou novamente

forage ['fɔrɪdʒ] N forragem *f* ▶ VI ir à procura de alimentos

forage cap N casquete *m*

foray ['fɔreɪ] N incursão *f*

forbad(e), forbade [fə'bæd] PT *of* **forbid**

forbearing [fɔ:'bɛərɪŋ] ADJ indulgente

forbid [fə'bɪd] (*pt* **forbad(e)**, *pp* **forbidden**) VT proibir; **to ~ sb to do sth** proibir alguém de fazer algo

forbidden [fə'bɪdn] PP *of* **forbid** ▶ ADJ proibido

forbidding [fə'bɪdɪŋ] ADJ (*look, prospect*) sombrio; (*severe*) severo

force [fɔ:s] N força ▶ VT (*gen, smile*) forçar; (*confession*) arrancar à força; **the Forces** (*BRIT*) NPL as Forças Armadas; **to ~ sb to do** forçar

alguém a fazer; **in** ~ em vigor; **to come into** ~ entrar em vigor; **a ~ 5 wind** um vento força 5; **the sales** ~ (*Comm*) a equipe de vendas; **to join** ~**s** unir forças; **by** ~ à força
▶ **force back** VT (*crowd, enemy*) fazer recuar; (*tears*) reprimir
▶ **force down** VT (*food*) forçar-se a comer

forced [fɔːst] ADJ forçado

force-feed ['fɔːsfiːd] (*irreg: like* **feed**) VT alimentar à força

forceful ['fɔːsful] ADJ enérgico, vigoroso

forcemeat ['fɔːsmiːt] (BRIT) N (*Culin*) recheio

forceps ['fɔːsɛps] NPL fórceps *m inv*

forcibly ['fɔːsəblɪ] ADV à força

ford [fɔːd] N vau *m* ▶ VT vadear

fore [fɔːʳ] N: **to bring to the** ~ pôr em evidência; **to come to the** ~ (*person*) salientar-se

forearm ['fɔːrɑːm] N antebraço

forebear ['fɔːbɛəʳ] N antepassado

foreboding [fɔː'bəudɪŋ] N mau presságio

forecast ['fɔːkɑːst] (*irreg: like* **cast**) N prognóstico, previsão *f*; (*also:* **weather forecast**) previsão do tempo ▶ VT prognosticar, prever

foreclose [fɔː'kləuz] VT (*Law: also:* **foreclose on**) executar

foreclosure [fɔː'kləuʒəʳ] N execução *f* de uma hipoteca

forecourt ['fɔːkɔːt] N (*of garage*) área de estacionamento

forefathers ['fɔːfɑːðəz] NPL antepassados *mpl*

forefinger ['fɔːfɪŋɡəʳ] N (*dedo*) indicador *m*

forefront ['fɔːfrʌnt] N: **in the ~ of** em primeiro plano em

forego [fɔː'ɡəu] (*irreg: like* **go**) VT (*give up*) renunciar a; (*go without*) abster-se de

foregoing ['fɔːɡəuɪŋ] ADJ acima mencionado ▶ N: **the** ~ o supracitado

foregone ['fɔːɡɔn] PP *of* **forego** ▶ ADJ: **it's a ~ conclusion** é uma conclusão inevitável

foreground ['fɔːɡraund] N primeiro plano ▶ CPD (*Comput*) de primeiro plano

forehand ['fɔːhænd] N (*Tennis*) golpe *m* de frente

forehead ['fɔrɪd] N testa

foreign ['fɔrɪn] ADJ estrangeiro; (*trade*) exterior

foreign body N corpo estranho

foreign currency N câmbio, divisas *fpl*

foreigner ['fɔrɪnəʳ] N estrangeiro(-a)

foreign exchange N (*system*) câmbio; (*money*) divisas *fpl*

foreign exchange market N mercado de câmbio

foreign exchange rate N taxa de câmbio

foreign investment N investimento estrangeiro

Foreign Office (BRIT) N Ministério das Relações Exteriores

foreign secretary (BRIT) N ministro das Relações Exteriores

foreleg ['fɔːlɛɡ] N perna dianteira

foreman ['fɔːmən] (*irreg: like* **man**) N capataz *m*; (*in construction*) contramestre *m*; (*Law: of jury*) primeiro jurado

foremost ['fɔːməust] ADJ principal ▶ ADV: **first and** ~ antes de mais nada

forename ['fɔːneɪm] N prenome *m*

forensic [fə'rɛnsɪk] ADJ forense; ~ **medicine** medicina legal; ~ **expert** perito(-a) criminal

foreplay ['fɔːpleɪ] N preliminares *fpl*

forerunner ['fɔːrʌnəʳ] N precursor(a) *m/f*

foresee [fɔː'siː] (*irreg: like* **see**) VT prever

foreseeable [fɔː'siːəbl] ADJ previsível

foreshadow [fɔː'fædəu] VT prefigurar

foreshorten [fɔː'fɔːtn] VT escorçar

foresight ['fɔːsaɪt] N previdência

foreskin ['fɔːskɪn] N (*Anat*) prepúcio

forest ['fɔrɪst] N floresta

forestall [fɔː'stɔːl] VT prevenir

forestry ['fɔrɪstrɪ] N silvicultura

foretaste ['fɔːteɪst] N antegosto, antegozo; (*sample*) amostra

foretell [fɔː'tɛl] (*irreg: like* **tell**) VT predizer, profetizar

forethought ['fɔːθɔːt] N previdência

foretold [fɔː'təuld] PT, PP *of* **foretell**

forever [fə'rɛvəʳ] ADV para sempre; (*a long time*) muito tempo, um tempão (*inf*); **he's** ~ **forgetting my name** ele vive esquecendo o meu nome

forewarn [fɔː'wɔːn] VT prevenir

forewent [fɔː'wɛnt] PT *of* **forego**

foreword ['fɔːwəːd] N prefácio

forfeit ['fɔːfɪt] N prenda, perda; (*fine*) multa ▶ VT perder (direito a); (*one's life, health*) pagar com

forgave [fə'ɡeɪv] PT *of* **forgive**

forge [fɔːdʒ] N forja; (*smithy*) ferraria ▶ VT (*signature, money*) falsificar; (*metal*) forjar ▶ **forge ahead** VI avançar constantemente

forger ['fɔːdʒəʳ] N falsificador(a) *m/f*

forgery ['fɔːdʒərɪ] N falsificação *f*

forget [fə'ɡɛt] (*pt* **forgot**, *pp* **forgotten**) VT, VI esquecer

forgetful [fə'ɡɛtful] ADJ esquecido

forgetfulness [fə'ɡɛtfulnɪs] N esquecimento

forget-me-not N miosótis *m*

forgive [fə'ɡɪv] (*pt* **forgave**, *pp* **forgiven**) VT perdoar; **to ~ sb for sth** perdoar algo a alguém, perdoar alguém de algo

forgiveness [fə'ɡɪvnɪs] N perdão *m*

forgiving [fə'ɡɪvɪŋ] ADJ clemente

forgo [fɔː'ɡəu] (*irreg: like* **go**) VT = **forego**

forgot [fə'ɡɔt] PT *of* **forget**

forgotten [fə'ɡɔtn] PP *of* **forget**

fork [fɔːk] N (*for eating*) garfo; (*for gardening*) forquilha; (*of roads etc*) bifurcação *f* ▶ VI (*road*) bifurcar-se
▶ **fork out** (*inf*) VT (*pay*) desembolsar, morrer em ▶ VI (*pay*) descolar uma grana

forked [fɔːkt] ADJ (*lightning*) em ziguezague

fork-lift truck N empilhadeira

forlorn [fə'lɔːn] ADJ (*person, place*) desolado; (*attempt*) desesperado; (*hope*) último

form [fɔːm] N forma; (*type*) tipo; (*Sch*) série *f*; (*questionnaire*) formulário ▶ VT formar; (*organization*) criar; **in the ~ of** na forma de; **to ~ part of sth** fazer parte de algo; **to ~ a queue** (BRIT) fazer fila; **to be in good ~** (*Sport*, *fig*) estar em forma; **in top ~** em plena forma

formal ['fɔːməl] ADJ (*offer, receipt*) oficial; (*person etc*) cerimonioso; (*occasion, education*) formal; (*dress*) a rigor (BR), de cerimônia (PT); (*garden*) simétrico

formalities [fɔː'mælɪtɪz] NPL (*procedures*) formalidades *fpl*

formality [fɔː'mælɪtɪ] N (*of person*) formalismo; (*formal requirement*) formalidade *f*; (*ceremony*) cerimônia

formalize ['fɔːməlaɪz] VT formalizar

formally ['fɔːməlɪ] ADV oficialmente, formalmente; (*in a formal way*) formalmente

format ['fɔːmæt] N formato ▶ VT (*Comput*) formatar

formation [fɔː'meɪʃən] N formação *f*

formative ['fɔːmətɪv] ADJ (*years*) formativo

former ['fɔːmə^r] ADJ anterior; (*earlier*) antigo; (*ex*) ex-; **the ~ ... the latter ...** aquele ... este ...; **the ~ president** o ex-presidente

formerly ['fɔːməlɪ] ADV anteriormente

form feed N (*on printer*) alimentar formulário

formidable ['fɔːmɪdəbl] ADJ terrível, temível

formula ['fɔːmjulə] (*pl* **formulas** *or* **formulae**) N fórmula; **F~ One** (*Aut*) Fórmula Um

formulate ['fɔːmjuleɪt] VT formular

fornicate ['fɔːnɪkeɪt] VI fornicar

forsake [fə'seɪk] (*pt* **forsook**, *pp* **forsaken**) VT abandonar; (*plan*) renunciar a

forsaken [fə'seɪkən] PP *of* **forsake**

forsook [fə'suk] PT *of* **forsake**

fort [fɔːt] N forte *m*; **to hold the ~** (*fig*) aguentar a mão

forte ['fɔːtɪ] N forte *m*

forth [fɔːθ] ADV para adiante; **back and ~** de cá para lá; **and so ~** e assim por diante

forthcoming ['fɔːθ'kʌmɪŋ] ADJ próximo, que está para aparecer; (*help*) disponível; (*person*) comunicativo; (*book*) a ser publicado

forthright ['fɔːθraɪt] ADJ franco

forthwith ['fɔːθ'wɪθ] ADV em seguida

fortieth ['fɔːtɪɪθ] NUM quadragésimo; *see also* **fifth**

fortification [fɔːtɪfɪ'keɪʃən] N fortificação *f*

fortified wine ['fɔːtɪfaɪd-] N vinho generoso

fortify ['fɔːtɪfaɪ] VT (*city*) fortificar; (*person*) fortalecer

fortitude ['fɔːtɪtjuːd] N fortaleza

fortnight ['fɔːtnaɪt] (BRIT) N quinzena, quinze dias *mpl*

fortnightly ['fɔːtnaɪtlɪ] ADJ quinzenal ▶ ADV quinzenalmente

FORTRAN ['fɔːtræn] N FORTRAN *m*

fortress ['fɔːtrɪs] N fortaleza

fortuitous [fɔː'tjuːɪtəs] ADJ fortuito

fortunate ['fɔːtʃənɪt] ADJ (*event*) feliz; (*person*): **to be ~** ter sorte; **it is ~ that ...** é uma sorte que ...

fortunately ['fɔːtʃənɪtlɪ] ADV felizmente

fortune ['fɔːtʃən] N sorte *f*; (*wealth*) fortuna; **to make a ~** fazer fortuna

fortune-teller N adivinho(-a)

forty ['fɔːtɪ] NUM quarenta; *see also* **fifty**

forum ['fɔːrəm] N foro

forward ['fɔːwəd] ADJ (*movement*) para a frente; (*position*) avançado; (*front*) dianteiro; (*not shy*) imodesto, presunçoso; (*Comm: delivery*) futuro; (: *sales, exchange*) a termo ▶ N (*Sport*) atacante *m* ▶ ADV para a frente ▶ VT (*letter*) remeter; (*goods, parcel*) expedir; (*career*) promover; (*plans*) ativar; **to move ~** avançar; **"please ~"** "por favor remeta a novo endereço"; **~ planning** planejamento para o futuro

forwards ['fɔːwədz] ADV para a frente

forward slash N barra

forwent [fɔː'wɛnt] PT *of* **forgo**

fossil ['fɔsl] N fóssil *m*

fossil fuel N combustível *m* fóssil

foster ['fɔstə^r] VT tutelar; (*activity*) promover

foster brother N irmão *m* de criação

foster child (*irreg: like* **child**) N tutelado(-a)

foster mother N tutora

foster sister N irmã *f* de criação

fought [fɔːt] PT, PP *of* **fight**

foul [faul] ADJ sujo, porco; (*food*) podre; (*weather*) horrível; (*language*) obsceno; (*deed*) infame ▶ N (*Sport*) falta ▶ VT (*dirty*) sujar; (*block*) entupir; (*football player*) cometer uma falta contra; (*entangle: anchor, propeller*) enredar

foul play N (*Sport*) jogada suja; (*Law*) crime *m*

found [faund] PT, PP *of* **find** ▶ VT (*establish*) fundar

foundation [faun'deɪʃən] N (*act*) fundação *f*; (*base*) base *f*; (*also:* **foundation cream**) creme *m* base; **foundations** NPL (*of building*) alicerces *mpl*; **to lay the ~s** (*fig*) lançar os alicerces

foundation stone N pedra fundamental

founder ['faundə^r] N fundador(a) *m/f* ▶ VI naufragar

founding ['faundɪŋ] N fundação *f* ▶ ADJ fundador(a)

foundry ['faundrɪ] N fundição *f*

fount [faunt] N fonte *f*

fountain ['fauntɪn] N chafariz *m*

fountain pen N caneta-tinteiro *f*

four [fɔː^r] NUM quatro; **on all ~s** de quatro; *see also* **five**

four-by-four [fɔːbaɪ'fɔː^r] N 4x4 *m* (*quatro por quatro*)

four-letter word ['fɔːlɛtə-] N palavrão *m*

four-poster N (*also:* **four-poster bed**) cama com colunas

foursome ['fɔːsəm] N grupo de quatro pessoas

fourteen ['fɔː'tiːn] NUM catorze; *see also* **five**

fourteenth ['fɔː'tiːnθ] NUM décimo-quarto; *see also* **fifth**

fourth [fɔːθ] NUM quarto ▶ N (*Aut: also:* **fourth gear**) quarta; *see also* **fifth**

four-wheel drive N (*Aut*): **with ~** com tração nas quatro rodas
fowl [faul] N ave *f* (doméstica)
fox [fɔks] N raposa ▶ VT deixar perplexo
fox fur N raposa
foxglove ['fɔksglʌv] N (*Bot*) dedaleira
fox-hunting N caça à raposa
foxtrot ['fɔkstrɔt] N foxtrote *m*
foyer ['fɔɪeɪ] N saguão *m*
FP N ABBR (*BRIT*) = **former pupil**; (*US*) = **fireplug**
FPA (*BRIT*) N ABBR = **Family Planning Association**
Fr. ABBR (*Rel*: = *father*) P.; (= *friar*) Fr.
fr. ABBR (= *franc*) fr.
fracas ['fræka:] N desordem *f*, rixa
fraction ['frækʃən] N fração *f*
fractionally ['frækʃnəlɪ] ADV ligeiramente
fractious ['frækʃəs] ADJ irascível
fracture ['fræktʃəʳ] N fratura ▶ VT fraturar
fragile ['frædʒaɪl] ADJ frágil
fragment ['frægmənt] N fragmento
fragmentary ['frægməntərɪ] ADJ fragmentário
fragrance ['freɪgrəns] N fragrância
fragrant ['freɪgrənt] ADJ fragrante, perfumado
frail [freɪl] ADJ (*person*) fraco; (*structure*) frágil; (*weak*) delicado
frame [freɪm] N (*of building*) estrutura; (*body*) corpo; (*Tech*) armação *f*; (*of picture, door*) moldura; (*of spectacles: also*: **frames**) armação *f*, aro ▶ VT enquadrar, encaixilhar; (*picture*) emoldurar; (*reply*) formular; (*inf*) incriminar
frame of mind N estado de espírito
framework ['freɪmwə:k] N armação *f*; (*fig*) sistema *m*, quadro
France [fra:ns] N França
franchise ['fræntʃaɪz] N (*Pol*) direito de voto; (*Comm*) concessão *f*
franchisee [fræntʃaɪ'zi:] N concessionário(-a)
franchiser ['fræntʃaɪzəʳ] N concedente *m/f*
frank [fræŋk] ADJ franco ▶ VT (*letter*) franquear
Frankfurt ['fræŋkfə:t] N Frankfurt (*BR*), Francoforte (*PT*)
frankfurter ['fræŋkfə:təʳ] N salsicha de cachorro quente
franking machine ['fræŋkɪŋ-] N máquina de selagem
frankly ['fræŋklɪ] ADV francamente; (*candidly*) abertamente
frankness ['fræŋknɪs] N franqueza
frantic ['fræntɪk] ADJ frenético; (*person*) fora de si
frantically ['fræntɪklɪ] ADV freneticamente
fraternal [frə'tə:nl] ADJ fraterno
fraternity [frə'tə:nɪtɪ] N (*club*) fraternidade *f*; (*US*) clube *m* de estudantes; (*guild*) confraria
fraternize ['frætənaɪz] VI confraternizar
fraud [frɔ:d] N fraude *f*; (*person*) impostor(a) *m/f*
fraudulent ['frɔ:djulənt] ADJ fraudulento

fraught [frɔ:t] ADJ tenso; **~ with** repleto de
fray [freɪ] N combate *m*, luta ▶ VT esfiapar ▶ VI esfiapar-se; **tempers were ~ed** estavam com os nervos em frangalhos
FRB (*US*) N ABBR = **Federal Reserve Board**
FRCM (*BRIT*) N ABBR = **Fellow of the Royal College of Music**
FRCO (*BRIT*) N ABBR = **Fellow of the Royal College of Organists**
FRCP (*BRIT*) N ABBR = **Fellow of the Royal College of Physicians**
FRCS (*BRIT*) N ABBR = **Fellow of the Royal College of Surgeons**
freak [fri:k] N (*person*) anormal *m/f*; (*event*) anomalia; (*thing*) aberração *f*; (*inf: enthusiast*): **health ~** maníaco(-a) com a saúde
▶ **freak out** (*inf*) VI (*on drugs*) baratinar-se; (*get angry*) ficar uma fera
freakish ['fri:kɪʃ] ADJ anormal
freckle ['frekl] N sarda
free [fri:] ADJ livre; (*seat*) desocupado; (*not fixed*) solto; (*costing nothing*) gratis, gratuito; (*liberal*) generoso ▶ VT (*prisoner etc*) pôr em liberdade; (*jammed object*) soltar; **to give sb a ~ hand** dar carta branca a alguém; **~ and easy** informal; **admission ~** entrada livre; **~ (of charge)** (*for free*) grátis, de graça
freebie ['fri:bɪ] (*inf*) N brinde *m*; (*trip etc*): **it's a ~** está tudo pago
freedom ['fri:dəm] N liberdade *f*
freedom fighter N lutador(a) *m/f* pela liberdade
free enterprise N livre iniciativa
free-for-all N quebra-quebra *m*
free gift N brinde *m*
freehold ['fri:həuld] N propriedade *f* livre e alodial
free kick N (tiro) livre *m*
freelance ['fri:la:ns] ADJ freelance
freelancer ['fri:la:nsəʳ] N freelance *m/f*
freeloader ['fri:ləudəʳ] (*pej*) N sanguessuga *m*
freely ['fri:lɪ] ADV livremente
freemason ['fri:meɪsən] N maçom *m*
freemasonry ['fri:meɪsnrɪ] N maçonaria
Freepost® ['fri:pəust] N porte *m* pago
free-range N (*egg*) caseiro
free sample N amostra grátis
free speech N liberdade *f* de expressão
free trade N livre comércio
freeway ['fri:weɪ] (*US*) N via expressa
freewheel [fri:'wi:l] VI ir em ponto morto
freewheeling [fri:'wi:lɪŋ] ADJ independente, livre
free will N livre arbítrio; **of one's own ~** por sua própria vontade
freeze [fri:z] (*pt* **froze**, *pp* **frozen**) VI gelar(-se), congelar-se ▶ VT gelar; (*prices, food, salaries*) congelar ▶ N geada; (*on arms, wages*) congelamento
▶ **freeze over** VI (*lake, river*) gelar; (*windscreen*) cobrir-se de gelo
▶ **freeze up** VI gelar

freeze-dried ADJ liofilizado

freezer ['fri:zə^r] N congelador *m*, freezer *m* (BR)

freezing ['fri:zɪŋ] ADJ: **~ (cold)** (*weather*) glacial; (*water*) gelado; **3 degrees below ~** 3 graus abaixo de zero

freezing point N ponto de congelamento

freight [freɪt] N (*goods*) carga; (*money charged*) frete *m*; **~ forward** frete pago na chegada; **~ inward** frete incluído no preço

freight car (US) N vagão *m* de carga

freighter ['freɪtə^r] N cargueiro

freight forwarder [-'fɔ:wədə^r] N despachante *m/f*

freight train (US) N trem *m* de carga

French [frɛntʃ] ADJ francês(-esa) ▶ N (*Ling*) francês *m*; **the French** NPL os franceses

French bean (BRIT) N feijão *m* comum

French-Canadian ADJ franco-canadense ▶ N canadense *m/f* francês(-esa) *or* da parte francesa; (*Ling*) francês *m* do Canadá

French dressing N (*Culin*) molho francês (de salada)

French fried potatoes, French fries (*esp US*) NPL batatas *fpl* fritas

French Guiana [-gaɪˈænə] N Guiana Francesa

French kiss N beijo de língua

Frenchman ['frɛntʃmən] (*irreg: like* **man**) N francês *m*

French Riviera N: **the ~** a Costa Azul

French window N porta-janela, janela de batente

Frenchwoman ['frɛntʃwumən] (*irreg: like* **woman**) N francesa

frenetic [frəˈnɛtɪk] ADJ frenético

frenzy ['frɛnzɪ] N frenesi *m*

frequency ['fri:kwənsɪ] N frequência

frequency modulation N frequência modulada

frequent [*adj* 'fri:kwənt, *vt* frɪ'kwɛnt] ADJ frequente ▶ VT frequentar

frequently ['fri:kwəntlɪ] ADV frequentemente, a miúdo

fresco ['frɛskəu] N fresco

fresh [frɛʃ] ADJ fresco; (*new*) novo; (*cheeky*) atrevido; **to make a ~ start** começar de novo

freshen ['frɛʃən] VI (*wind, air*) tornar-se mais forte

▶ **freshen up** VI (*person*) lavar-se, refrescar-se

freshener ['frɛʃnə^r] N: **skin ~** refrescante *m* da pele; **air ~** purificador *m* de ar

fresher ['frɛʃə^r] (BRIT *inf*) N (*Sch*) calouro(-a)

freshly ['frɛʃlɪ] ADV (*newly*) novamente; (*recently*) recentemente, há pouco

freshman ['frɛʃmən] (US) (*irreg: like* **man**) N = **fresher**

freshness ['frɛʃnɪs] N frescor *m*

freshwater ['frɛʃwɔ:tə^r] ADJ de água doce

fret [frɛt] VI afligir-se

fretful ['frɛtful] ADJ irritável

Freudian ['frɔɪdɪən] ADJ freudiano; **~ slip** ato falho

FRG N ABBR (= *Federal Republic of Germany*) RFA *f*

Fri. ABBR (= *Friday*) sex.

friar ['fraɪə^r] N frade *m*; (*before name*) frei *m*

friction ['frɪkʃən] N fricção *f*; (*between people*) atrito

friction feed N (*on printer*) alimentação *f* por fricção

Friday ['fraɪdɪ] N sexta-feira *f*; *see also* **Tuesday**

fridge [frɪdʒ] N geladeira (BR), frigorífico (PT)

fried [fraɪd] PT, PP *of* **fry** ▶ ADJ frito; **~ egg** ovo estrelado *or* frito

friend [frɛnd] N amigo(-a) ▶ VT (*on social network*) adicionar como amigo; **to make ~s with sb** fazer amizade com alguém

friendliness ['frɛndlɪnɪs] N simpatia

friendly ['frɛndlɪ] ADJ (*kind*) simpático; (*relations, behaviour*) amigável ▶ N (*also:* **friendly match**) amistoso; **to be ~ with** ser amigo de; **to be ~ to** ser simpático com

friendly society N sociedade *f* mutuante, mútua

friendship ['frɛndʃɪp] N amizade *f*

fries [fraɪz] (*esp US*) NPL = **French fried potatoes**

frieze [fri:z] N friso

frigate ['frɪgɪt] N fragata

fright [fraɪt] N (*terror*) terror *m*; (*scare*) pavor *m*; **to take ~** assustar-se

frighten ['fraɪtən] VT assustar

▶ **frighten away** VT espantar

▶ **frighten off** VT espantar

frightened ['fraɪtnd] ADJ: **to be ~ of** ter medo de

frightening ['fraɪtnɪŋ] ADJ assustador(a)

frightful ['fraɪtful] ADJ terrível, horrível

frightfully ['fraɪtfulɪ] ADV terrivelmente

frigid ['frɪdʒɪd] ADJ (*Med*) frígido, frio

frigidity [frɪˈdʒɪdɪtɪ] N (*Med*) frigidez *f*

frill [frɪl] N babado; **without ~s** (*fig: car*) sem nenhum luxo; (: *dinner*) simples; (: *service*) sem mordomias; (: *holiday*) sem extras

fringe [frɪndʒ] N franja; (*on shawl etc*) beira, orla; (*edge: of forest etc*) margem *f*; (*fig*): **on the ~ of** à margem de

fringe benefits NPL benefícios *mpl* adicionais

fringe theatre N teatro de vanguarda

frisk [frɪsk] VT revistar

frisky ['frɪskɪ] ADJ alegre, animado

fritter ['frɪtə^r] N bolinho frito

▶ **fritter away** VT desperdiçar

frivolity [frɪˈvɔlɪtɪ] N frivolidade *f*

frivolous ['frɪvələs] ADJ frívolo; (*activity*) fútil

frizzy ['frɪzɪ] ADJ frisado

fro [frəu] ADJ *see* **to**

frock [frɔk] N vestido

frog [frɔg] N rã *f*; **to have a ~ in one's throat** ter pigarro

frogman ['frɔgmən] (*irreg: like* **man**) N homem-rã *m*

frogmarch ['frɔgmɑ:tʃ] (BRIT) VT: **to ~ sb in/ out** arrastar alguém para dentro/para fora

frolic ['frɔlɪk] VI brincar

KEYWORD

from [frɔm] PREP **1** (*indicating starting place*) de; **where do you come from?** de onde você é?; **we flew from London to Glasgow** fomos de avião de Londres para Glasgow; **to escape from sth/sb** escapar de algo/ alguém

2 (*indicating origin etc*) de; **a letter/telephone call from my sister** uma carta/um telefonema da minha irmã; **tell him from me that ...** diga a ele que da minha parte ...; **to drink from the bottle** beber na garrafa

3 (*indicating time*): **from one o'clock to** *or* **until** *or* **till two** da uma hora até às duas; **from January (on)** a partir de janeiro

4 (*indicating distance*) de; **we're still a long way from home** ainda estamos muito longe de casa

5 (*indicating price, number etc*) de; **prices range from £10 to £50** os preços vão de £10 a £50; **the interest rate was increased from 9% to 10%** a taxa de juros foi aumentada de 9% para 10%

6 (*indicating difference*) de; **he can't tell red from green** ele não pode diferenciar vermelho do verde; **to be different from sb/sth** ser diferente de alguém/algo

7 (*because of/on the basis of*): **from what he says** pelo que ele diz; **from what I understand** pelo que eu entendo; **to act from conviction** agir por convicção; **weak from hunger** fraco de fome

frond [frɔnd] N fronde *f*

front [frʌnt] N (*of dress*) frente *f*; (*of vehicle*) parte *f* dianteira; (*of house*) fachada; (*of book*) capa; (*promenade: also:* **sea front**) orla marítima; (*Mil, Pol, Meteorology, of dress*) frente *f*; (*fig: appearances*) fachada ▶ ADJ dianteiro, da frente ▶ VI: **to ~ onto sth** dar para algo; **in ~ (of)** em frente de

frontage ['frʌntɪdʒ] N fachada

frontal ['frʌntəl] ADJ frontal

front bench (BRIT) N (*Pol*) *os dirigentes do partido no poder ou da oposição*

front desk (US) N (*in hotel, at doctor's*) recepção *f*

front door N porta principal; (*of car*) porta dianteira

frontier ['frʌntɪə'] N fronteira

frontispiece ['frʌntɪspiːs] N frontispício

front page N primeira página

front room (BRIT) N salão *m*, sala de estar

front runner N (*fig*) favorito(-a)

front-wheel drive N tração *f* dianteira

frost [frɔst] N geada; (*also:* **hoarfrost**) gelo

frostbite ['frɔstbaɪt] N ulceração *f* produzida pelo frio

frosted ['frɔstɪd] ADJ (*glass*) fosco; (*esp US: cake*) com cobertura

frosting ['frɔstɪŋ] (*esp US*) N (*on cake*) glacê *f*

frosty ['frɔstɪ] ADJ (*window*) coberto de geada; (*welcome*) glacial

froth [frɔθ] N espuma

frown [fraun] N olhar *m* carrancudo, cara amarrada ▶ VI franzir as sobrancelhas, amarrar a cara
▶ **frown on** VT FUS (*fig*) desaprovar, não ver com bons olhos

froze [frəuz] PT *of* **freeze**

frozen ['frəuzn] PP *of* **freeze** ▶ ADJ congelado; **~ foods** congelados *mpl*

FRS N ABBR (BRIT: = *Fellow of the Royal Society*) *membro de associação promovedora de pesquisa científica*; (US: = *Federal Reserve System*) *banco central dos EUA*

frugal ['fruːgəl] ADJ frugal

fruit [fruːt] N INV fruta; (*fig: results*) fruto

fruiterer ['fruːtərə'] N fruteiro(-a); **~'s (shop)** fruteiro (BR), frutaria (PT)

fruitful ['fruːtful] ADJ proveitoso

fruition [fruː'ɪʃən] N: **to come to ~** realizar-se

fruit juice N suco (BR) *or* sumo (PT) de frutas

fruitless ['fruːtlɪs] ADJ inútil, vão(-vã)

fruit machine (BRIT) N caça-níqueis *m inv* (BR), máquina de jogo (PT)

fruit salad N salada de frutas

frump [frʌmp] N careta (*mulher antiquada*)

frustrate [frʌs'treɪt] VT frustrar

frustrated [frʌs'treɪtɪd] ADJ frustrado

frustrating [frʌs'treɪtɪŋ] ADJ frustrante

frustration [frʌs'treɪʃən] N frustração *f*; (*disappointment*) decepção *f*

fry [fraɪ] (*pt, pp* **fried**) VT fritar; *see also* **small fry**

frying pan ['fraɪɪŋ-] N frigideira

FT (BRIT) N ABBR (= *Financial Times*) *jornal financeiro*; **the FT index** o índice da Bolsa de Valores de Londres

ft. ABBR = **foot**; **feet**

FTC (US) N ABBR = **Federal Trade Commission**

fuchsia ['fjuːʃə] N fúcsia

fuck [fʌk] (!) VI trepar (!) ▶ VT trepar com (!); **~ off** vai tomar no cu! (!)

fuddled ['fʌdld] ADJ (*muddled*) confuso, enrolado

fuddy-duddy ['fʌdɪdʌdɪ] (*pej*) ADJ, N careta *m/f*

fudge [fʌdʒ] N (*Culin*) ≈ doce *m* de leite ▶ VT (*issue, problem*) evadir

fuel [fjuəl] N (*gen, for heating*) combustível *m*; (*for propelling*) carburante *m*

fuel oil N óleo combustível

fuel pump N (*Aut*) bomba de gasolina

fuel tank N depósito de combustível

fug [fʌg] (BRIT) N bafio

fugitive ['fjuːdʒɪtɪv] N fugitivo(-a)

fulfil, (US) **fulfill** [ful'fɪl] VT (*function*) cumprir; (*condition*) satisfazer; (*wish, desire*) realizar

fulfilled [ful'fɪld] ADJ (*person*) realizado

fulfilment, (US) **fulfillment** [ful'fɪlmənt] N satisfação *f*; (*of wish, desire*) realização *f*

full [ful] ADJ cheio; (*fig*) pleno; (*use, volume*) máximo; (*complete*) completo; (*information*) detalhado; (*price*) integral; (*skirt*) folgado ▶ ADV: **~ well** perfeitamente; **I'm ~ (up)** estou satisfeito; **~ (up)** (*hotel etc*) lotado; **~ employment** pleno emprego; **~ fare**

passagem completa; **a ~ two hours** duas horas completas; **at ~ speed** a toda a velocidade; **in ~** (*reproduce, quote*) integralmente; (*name*) por completo; **~ employment** pleno emprego

fullback ['fulbæk] N zagueiro (BR), defesa *m* (PT)

full-blooded [-'blʌdɪd] ADJ (*vigorous*) vigoroso

full-cream (BRIT) ADJ: **~ milk** leite *m* integral

full-grown ADJ crescido, adulto

full-length ADJ (*portrait*) de corpo inteiro; (*coat*) longo; **~ (feature) film** longa-metragem *m*

full moon N lua cheia

full-scale ADJ (*model*) em tamanho natural; (*war*) em grande escala

full-sized [-saɪzd] ADJ (*portrait etc*) em tamanho natural

full stop N ponto (final)

full-time ADJ (*work*) de tempo completo *or* integral ▶ N: **full time** (*Sport*) final *m*

fully ['fulɪ] ADV completamente; (*at least*) pelo menos

fully-fledged [-flɛdʒd] ADJ (*teacher, barrister*) diplomado; (*citizen, member*) verdadeiro

fulsome ['fulsəm] (*pej*) ADJ extravagante

fumble ['fʌmbl] VI atrapalhar-se ▶ VT (*ball*) atrapalhar-se com, apanhar de (*inf*)
▶ **fumble with** VT FUS atrapalhar-se com, apanhar de (*inf*)

fume [fju:m] VI fumegar; (*be angry*) estar com raiva; **fumes** NPL gases *mpl*

fumigate ['fju:mɪgeɪt] VT fumigar; (*against pests etc*) pulverizar

fun [fʌn] N (*amusement*) divertimento; (*joy*) alegria; **to have ~** divertir-se; **for ~** de brincadeira; **it's not much ~** não tem graça; **to make ~ of** fazer troça de, zombar de

function ['fʌŋkʃən] N função *f*; (*reception, dinner*) recepção *f* ▶ VI funcionar; **to ~ as** funcionar como

functional ['fʌŋkʃənəl] ADJ funcional; (*practical*) prático

function key N (*Comput*) tecla de função

fund [fʌnd] N fundo; (*source, store*) fonte *f*; **funds** NPL (*money*) fundos *mpl*

fundamental [fʌndə'mɛntl] ADJ fundamental

fundamentalist [fʌndə'mɛntəlɪst] N fundamentalista *m/f*

fundamentally [fʌndə'mɛntəlɪ] ADV fundamentalmente

fundamentals [fʌndə'mɛntlz] NPL fundamentos *mpl*

fund-raising [-'reɪzɪŋ] N angariação *f* de fundos

funeral ['fju:nərəl] N (*burial*) enterro; (*ceremony*) exéquias *fpl*

funeral director N agente *m/f* funerário(-a)

funeral parlour N casa funerária

funeral service N missa fúnebre

funereal [fju:'nɪərɪəl] ADJ fúnebre, funéreo

funfair ['fʌnfeə^r] (BRIT) N parque *m* de diversões

fungi ['fʌŋgaɪ] NPL of **fungus**

fungus ['fʌŋgəs] (*pl* **fungi**) N fungo; (*mould*) bolor *m*, mofo

funicular [fju:'nɪkjulə^r] N (*also*: **funicular railway**) funicular *m*

funky ['fʌŋkɪ] ADJ (*music*) funkado; (*esp US inf: unusual*) superdiferente

funnel ['fʌnl] N funil *m*; (*of ship*) chaminé *f*

funnily ['fʌnɪlɪ] ADV: **~ enough** por incrível que pareça

funny ['fʌnɪ] ADJ engraçado, divertido; (*strange*) esquisito, estranho

funny bone N *parte sensível do cotovelo*

fur [fə:^r] N pele *f*; (BRIT: *in kettle etc*) depósito, crosta

fur coat N casaco de peles

furious ['fjuərɪəs] ADJ furioso; (*effort*) incrível

furiously ['fjuərɪəslɪ] ADV com fúria; (*argue*) com violência

furl [fə:l] VT enrolar; (*Naut*) colher

furlong ['fə:lɔŋ] N 201.17m

furlough ['fə:ləu] N licença

furnace ['fə:nɪs] N forno

furnish ['fə:nɪʃ] VT mobiliar (BR), mobilar (PT); (*supply*): **to ~ sb with sth** fornecer algo a alguém; **~ed flat** (BRIT) *or* **apartment** (US) apartamento mobiliado (BR) *or* mobilado (PT)

furnishings ['fə:nɪʃɪŋz] NPL mobília

furniture ['fə:nɪtʃə^r] N mobília, móveis *mpl*; **piece of ~** móvel *m*

furniture polish N cera de lustrar móveis

furore [fjuə'rɔ:rɪ] N furor *m*

furrier ['fʌrɪə^r] N peleiro(-a)

furrow ['fʌrəu] N (*in field*) rego; (*in skin*) sulco

furry ['fə:rɪ] ADJ peludo; (*toy*) de pelúcia

further ['fə:ðə^r] ADJ (*new*) novo, adicional ▶ ADV mais longe; (*more*) mais; (*moreover*) além disso ▶ VT promover; **how much ~ is it?** quanto mais tem que se ir?; **until ~ notice** até novo aviso; **~ to your letter of …** (*Comm*) em resposta à sua carta do …

further education (BRIT) N educação *f* superior

furthermore [fə:ðə'mɔ:^r] ADV além disso

furthermost ['fə:ðəməust] ADJ mais distante

furthest ['fə:ðɪst] SUPERL of **far**

furtive ['fə:tɪv] ADJ furtivo

furtively ['fə:tɪvlɪ] ADV furtivamente

fury ['fjuərɪ] N fúria

fuse, (US) **fuze** [fju:z] N fusível *m*; (*for bomb etc*) espoleta, mecha ▶ VT fundir; (*fig*) unir ▶ VI (*metal*) fundir-se; unir-se; **to ~ the lights** (BRIT *Elec*) queimar as luzes; **a ~ has blown** queimou um fusível

fuse box N caixa de fusíveis

fuselage ['fju:zəlɑ:ʒ] N fuselagem *f*

fuse wire N fio fusível

fusillade [fju:zɪ'leɪd] N fuzilada; (*fig*) saraivada

fusion ['fju:ʒən] N fusão *f*

fuss [fʌs] N (*uproar*) rebuliço; (*excitement*) estardalhaço; (*complaining*) escândalo ▶ VI criar caso; **to make a ~** criar caso; **to make**

a ~ **of sb** paparicar alguém
▶ **fuss over** VT FUS (*person*) paparicar
fussy ['fʌsɪ] ADJ (*person*) exigente, complicado, cheio de coisas (*inf*); (*dress, style*) espalhafatoso; **I'm not ~** (*inf*) para mim, tanto faz
futile ['fju:taɪl] ADJ (*existence*) fútil; (*attempt*) inútil, fútil
futility [fju:'tɪlɪtɪ] N inutilidade f
future ['fju:tʃəʳ] ADJ futuro ▶ N futuro; (*prospects*) perspectiva; **futures** NPL (*Comm*) operações *fpl* a termo; **in (the) ~** no futuro;

in the near/immediate ~ em futuro próximo/imediato
futuristic [fju:tʃə'rɪstɪk] ADJ futurístico
fuze [fju:z] (*US*) N, VT, VI = **fuse**
fuzzy ['fʌzɪ] ADJ (*Phot*) indistinto; (*hair*) frisado, encrespado
fwd. ABBR = **forward**
fwy (*US*) ABBR = **freeway**
FY ABBR = **fiscal year**
FYI ABBR (= *for your information*) para seu conhecimento

Gg

G¹, g [dʒiː] N (*letter*) G, g *m*; (*Mus*): **G** sol *m*;
G for George G de Gomes

G² N ABBR (*BRIT Sch*) = **good**; (*US Cinema*:
= *general (audience)*) livre

g ABBR (= *gram*) g; (= *gravity*) g

GA (*US*) ABBR (*Post*) = **Georgia**

gab [gæb] (*inf*) N: **to have the gift of the ~**
lábia, ser bom de bico

gabble ['gæbl] VI tagarelar

gaberdine [gæbə'diːn] N gabardina,
gabardine *f*

gable ['geɪbl] N cumeeira

Gabon [gə'bɔn] N Gabão *m*

gad about [gæd-] (*inf*) VI badalar

gadget ['gædʒɪt] N aparelho, engenhoca;
(*in kitchen*) pequeno utensílio

Gaelic ['geɪlɪk] ADJ gaélico(-a) ▶ N (*Ling*) gaélico

gaffe [gæf] N gafe *f*

gag [gæg] N (*on mouth*) mordaça; (*joke*) piada
▶ VT amordaçar

gaga ['gɑːgɑː] ADJ: **to go ~** ficar gagá

gaiety ['geɪɪtɪ] N alegria

gaily ['geɪlɪ] ADV alegremente; (*coloured*)
vivamente

gain [geɪn] N ganho; (*profit*) lucro ▶ VT ganhar
▶ VI (*watch*) adiantar-se; (*benefit*): **to ~ from**
sth tirar proveito de algo; **to ~ on sb**
aproximar-se de alguém; **to ~ 3lbs (in**
weight) engordar 3 libras; **to ~ ground**
ganhar terreno

gainful ['geɪnful] ADJ lucrativo, proveitoso

gainsay [geɪn'seɪ] (*irreg: like* **say**) VT (*contradict*)
contradizer; (*deny*) negar

gait [geɪt] N modo de andar

gal. ABBR = **gallon**

gala ['gɑːlə] N festa, gala; **swimming ~**
festival de natação

Galapagos [gə'læpəgəs], **Galapagos Islands**
NPL: **the ~ (Islands)** as ilhas Galápagos

galaxy ['gæləksɪ] N galáxia

gale [geɪl] N (*wind*) ventania; **~ force 10** vento
de força 10

gall [gɔːl] N (*Anat*) fel *m*, bílis *f*; (*fig*)
descaramento ▶ VT irritar

gall. ABBR = **gallon**

gallant ['gælənt] ADJ valente; (*polite*) galante

gallantry ['gæləntrɪ] N valentia; (*courtesy*)
galanteria

gall bladder [gɔːl-] N vesícula biliar

galleon ['gælɪən] N galeão *m*

gallery ['gælərɪ] N (*in theatre etc*) galeria; (*also*:
art gallery: *public*) museu *m*; (: *private*) galeria
(de arte)

galley ['gælɪ] N (*ship's kitchen*) cozinha; (*ship*)
galé *f*; (*also*: **galley proof**) paquê *m*

Gallic ['gælɪk] ADJ francês(-esa)

galling ['gɔːlɪŋ] ADJ irritante

gallon ['gæln] N galão *m* (*Brit* = 4.5 *litros*, *US* =
3.8 *litros*)

gallop ['gæləp] N galope *m* ▶ VI galopar; **~ing**
inflation inflação galopante

gallows ['gæləuz] N forca

gallstone ['gɔːlstəun] N cálculo biliar

galore [gə'lɔːʳ] ADV à beça

galvanize ['gælvənaɪz] VT galvanizar; (*person*,
support) arrebatar; **to ~ sb into action**
galvanizar *or* eletrizar alguém

Gambia ['gæmbɪə] N Câmbia (*no article*)

gambit ['gæmbɪt] N (*fig*): (**opening**) **~** início
(de conversa)

gamble ['gæmbl] N (*risk*) risco; (*bet*) aposta
▶ VT, VI jogar, arriscar; (*Comm*) especular;
to ~ on apostar em

gambler ['gæmbləʳ] N jogador(a) *m/f*

gambling ['gæmblɪŋ] N jogo

gambol ['gæmbl] VI cabriolar

game [geɪm] N jogo; (*match*) partida; (*Tennis*)
jogada; (*strategy*) plano, esquema *m*;
(*Hunting*) caça ▶ ADJ valente; (*willing*): **to be ~**
for anything topar qualquer parada;
games NPL (*Sch*) esporte *m* (*BR*), desporto (*PT*);
I'm ~ eu topo; **big ~** caça grossa

game bird N ave *f* de caça

gamekeeper ['geɪmkiːpəʳ] N guarda-caça *m*

gamely ['geɪmlɪ] ADV valentemente

game reserve N reserva de caça

games console [geɪmz-] N console *m* de
videogames (*BR*), consola de videojogos (*PT*)

game show ['geɪmʃəu] N game show *m*

gamesmanship ['geɪmzmənʃɪp] N tática

gaming ['geɪmɪŋ] N (*with video games*) jogos *mpl*
de computador; (*gambling*) jogo

gammon ['gæmən] N (*bacon*) toucinho
(defumado); (*ham*) presunto

gamut ['gæmət] N gama

gang [gæŋ] N bando, grupo; (*of criminals*)
gangue *f*; (*of workmen*) turma ▶ VI: **to ~ up on**
sb conspirar contra alguém

Ganges ['gændʒiːz] N: **the ~** o Ganges
gangling ['gæŋglɪŋ] ADJ desengonçado
gangplank ['gæŋplæŋk] N prancha (de desembarque)
gangrene ['gæŋgriːn] N gangrena
gangster ['gæŋstə'] N gângster m, bandido
gangway ['gæŋweɪ] N (BRIT: in cinema, bus) corredor m; (on ship) passadiço; (on dock) portaló m
gantry ['gæntrɪ] N pórtico; (for rocket) guindaste m
GAO (US) N ABBR (= General Accounting Office) ≈ Tribunal m de Contas da União
gaol [dʒeɪl] (BRIT) N, VT = **jail**
gap [gæp] N brecha, fenda; (in trees, traffic) abertura; (in time) intervalo; (fig) lacuna; (difference): ~ **(between)** diferença (entre)
gape [geɪp] VI (person) estar or ficar boquiaberto; (hole) abrir-se
gaping ['geɪpɪŋ] ADJ (hole) muito aberto
garage ['gærɑːʒ] N garagem f; (for car repairs) oficina (mecânica)
garb [gɑːb] N traje m
garbage ['gɑːbɪdʒ] N (US) lixo; (inf: nonsense) disparates mpl; **the book/film is ~** o livro/filme é uma droga
garbage can (US) N lata de lixo
garbage collector (US) N lixeiro(-a)
garbage disposal, garbage disposal unit N triturador m de lixo
garbage truck N (US) caminhão m do lixo
garbled ['gɑːbld] ADJ (account) deturpado, destorcido
garden ['gɑːdn] N jardim m ▶ VI jardinar; **gardens** NPL (public park) jardim público, parque m
garden centre N loja de jardinagem
gardener ['gɑːdnə'] N jardineiro(-a)
gardening ['gɑːdnɪŋ] N jardinagem f
gargle ['gɑːgl] VI gargarejar ▶ N gargarejo
gargoyle ['gɑːgɔɪl] N gárgula
garish ['gɛərɪʃ] ADJ vistoso, chamativo; (colour) berrante; (light) brilhante
garland ['gɑːlənd] N guirlanda
garlic ['gɑːlɪk] N alho
garment ['gɑːmənt] N peça de roupa
garner ['gɑːnə'] VT acumular, amontoar
garnish ['gɑːnɪʃ] VT adornar; (food) enfeitar
garret ['gærət] N mansarda
garrison ['gærɪsn] N guarnição f ▶ VT guarnecer
garrulous ['gærjuləs] ADJ tagarela
garter ['gɑːtə'] N liga
garter belt (US) N cinta-liga
gas [gæs] N gás m; (US: gasoline) gasolina ▶ VT asfixiar com gás; (Mil) gasear
gas cooker (BRIT) N fogão m a gás
gas cylinder N bujão m de gás
gaseous ['gæsɪəs] ADJ gasoso
gas fire (BRIT) N aquecedor m a gás
gash [gæʃ] N talho; (tear) corte m ▶ VT talhar; cortar
gasket ['gæskɪt] N (Aut) junta, gaxeta

gas mask N máscara antigás
gas meter N medidor m de gás
gasoline ['gæsəliːn] (US) N gasolina
gasp [gɑːsp] N arfada ▶ VI arfar
▶ **gasp out** VT (say) dizer com voz entrecortada
gas ring N boca de gás
gas station (US) N posto de gasolina
gas stove N (cooker) fogão m a gás; (heater) aquecedor m a gás
gassy ['gæsɪ] ADJ gasoso
gas tank (US) N (Aut) tanque m de gasolina
gas tap N torneira do gás
gastric ['gæstrɪk] ADJ gástrico
gastric band N (Med) banda gástrica
gastric ulcer N úlcera gástrica
gastroenteritis ['gæstrəuɛntə'raɪtɪs] N gastrenterite f
gastronomy [gæs'trɔnəmɪ] N gastronomia
gasworks ['gæswəːks] N, NPL usina de gás, gasômetro
gate [geɪt] N portão m; (Rail) barreira; (of town, castle) porta; (at airport) portão m; (of lock) comporta
gateau ['gætəu] (pl **-x**) N bolo com creme e frutas
gateaux ['gætəuz] NPL of **gateau**
gate-crash ['geɪtkræʃ] (BRIT) VT entrar de penetra em
gated community ['geɪtɪd-] N condomínio fechado
gateway ['geɪtweɪ] N portão m, passagem f
gather ['gæðə'] VT (flowers, fruit) colher; (assemble) reunir; (pick up) colher; (Sewing) franzir; (understand) compreender ▶ VI (assemble) reunir-se; (dust, clouds) acumular-se; **to ~ (from/that)** concluir or depreender (de/que); **as far as I can ~** ao que eu entendo; **to ~ speed** acelerar(-se)
gathering ['gæðərɪŋ] N reunião f, assembleia
GATT [gæt] N (= General Agreement on Tariffs and Trade) GATT m
gauche [gəuʃ] ADJ desajeitado
gaudy ['gɔːdɪ] ADJ chamativo; (pej) cafona
gauge [geɪdʒ] N (instrument) medidor m; (measure, also fig) medida; (Rail) bitola ▶ VT medir; (fig: sb's capabilities, character) avaliar; **to ~ the right moment** calcular o momento azado; **petrol** (BRIT) or **gas** (US) **~** medidor de gasolina
gaunt [gɔːnt] ADJ descarnado; (bare, stark) desolado
gauntlet ['gɔːntlɪt] N luva; (fig): **to run the ~** expôr-se (à crítica); **to throw down the ~** lançar um desafio
gauze [gɔːz] N gaze f
gave [geɪv] PT of **give**
gawky ['gɔːkɪ] ADJ desengonçado
gawp [gɔːp] VI: **to ~ at** olhar boquiaberto para
gay [geɪ] ADJ (homosexual) gay; (old-fashioned: cheerful) alegre; (colour) vistoso; (music) vivo

gaze [geɪz] N olhar *m* fixo ▶ VI: **to ~ at sth** fitar algo
gazelle [gə'zɛl] N gazela
gazette [gə'zɛt] N (*newspaper*) jornal *m*; (*official publication*) boletim *m* oficial
gazetteer [gæzə'tɪər] N dicionário geográfico
GB ABBR = **Great Britain**
GBH (*BRIT inf*) N ABBR (*Law*) = **grievous bodily harm**
GC (*BRIT*) N ABBR (= *George Cross*) distinção militar
GCE (*BRIT*) N ABBR = **General Certificate of Education**
GCHQ (*BRIT*) N ABBR (= *Government Communications Headquarters*) centro de intercepção de radiotransmissões estrangeiras
GCSE (*BRIT*) N ABBR = **General Certificate of Secondary Education**
GDP N ABBR = **gross domestic product**
GDR N ABBR (= *German Democratic Republic*) RDA *f*
gear [gɪər] N equipamento; (*Tech*) engrenagem *f*; (*Aut*) velocidade *f*, marcha (*BR*), mudança (*PT*) ▶ VT (*fig: adapt*): **to ~ sth to** preparar algo para; **our service is ~ed to meet the needs of the disabled** o nosso serviço está adequado às necessidades dos deficientes físicos; **top** (*BRIT*) or **high** (*US*)/**low** ~ quinta/primeira (marcha); **in** ~ engrenado; **out of** ~ desengrenado
▶ **gear up** VI: **to ~ up to do** preparar-se para fazer
gearbox ['gɪəbɔks] N caixa de mudança (*BR*) or velocidades (*PT*)
gear lever, (*US*) **gear shift** N alavanca de mudança (*BR*) or mudanças (*PT*)
GED (*US*) N ABBR (*Sch*) = **general educational development**
geese [giːs] NPL of **goose**
Geiger counter ['gaɪgə-] N contador *m* Geiger
gel [dʒɛl] N gel *m*
gelatin, gelatine ['dʒɛləti:n] N gelatina
gelignite ['dʒɛlɪgnaɪt] N gelignite *f*
gem [dʒɛm] N joia, gema
Gemini ['dʒɛmɪnaɪ] N Gêminis *m*, Gêmeos *mpl*
gen [dʒɛn] (*BRIT inf*) N: **to give sb the ~ on sth** pôr alguém a par de algo
Gen. ABBR (*Mil: = general*) Gal.
gen. ABBR (= *general, generally*) ger.
gender ['dʒɛndər] N gênero
gene [dʒi:n] N (*Bio*) gene *m*
genealogy [dʒi:nɪ'ælədʒɪ] N genealogia
general ['dʒɛnərl] N general *m* ▶ ADJ geral; **in** ~ em geral; **the ~ public** o grande público; ~ **audit** (*Comm*) exame *m* geral de auditoria
general anaesthetic, (*US*) **general anesthetic** N anestesia geral
general delivery (*US*) N posta-restante
general election N eleições *fpl* gerais
generalization [dʒɛnrəlaɪ'zeɪʃən] N generalização *f*
generalize ['dʒɛnrəlaɪz] VI generalizar
generally ['dʒɛnrəlɪ] ADV geralmente

general manager N diretor(a) *m/f* geral
general practitioner N clínico(-a) geral
general strike N greve *f* geral
generate ['dʒɛnəreɪt] VT gerar; (*fig*) produzir
generation [dʒɛnə'reɪʃən] N geração *f*
generator ['dʒɛnəreɪtər] N gerador *m*
generic [dʒə'nɛrɪk] ADJ genérico
generosity [dʒɛnə'rɔsɪtɪ] N generosidade *f*
generous ['dʒɛnərəs] ADJ generoso; (*measure etc*) abundante
genesis ['dʒɛnəsɪs] N gênese *f*
genetic [dʒə'nɛtɪk] ADJ genético; ~ **engineering** engenharia genética
genetically [dʒɪ'nɛtɪklɪ] ADV: ~ **modified** (*food etc*) transgênico
genetics [dʒɪ'nɛtɪks] N genética
Geneva [dʒɪ'ni:və] N Genebra
genial ['dʒi:nɪəl] ADJ cordial, simpático
genitals ['dʒɛnɪtlz] NPL órgãos *mpl* genitais
genitive ['dʒɛnətɪv] N genitivo
genius ['dʒi:nɪəs] N gênio
genocide ['dʒɛnəusaɪd] N genocídio
genome ['dʒi:nəum] N genoma *m*
gent [dʒɛnt] N ABBR = **gentleman**
genteel [dʒɛn'ti:l] ADJ fino
gentle ['dʒɛntl] ADJ (*sweet*) amável, doce; (*touch, breeze*) leve, suave; (*landscape*) suave; (*animal*) manso
gentleman ['dʒɛntlmən] (*irreg: like* **man**) N senhor *m*; (*referring to social position*) fidalgo; (*well-bred man*) cavalheiro; ~'s **agreement** acordo de cavalheiros
gentlemanly ['dʒɛntlmənlɪ] ADJ cavalheiresco
gentlemen ['dʒɛntlmen] NPL of **gentleman**
gentleness ['dʒɛntlnɪs] N doçura, meiguice *f*; (*of touch*) suavidade *f*; (*of animal*) mansidão *f*
gently ['dʒɛntlɪ] ADV suavemente
gentry ['dʒɛntrɪ] N pequena nobreza
gents [dʒɛnts] N banheiro de homens (*BR*), casa de banho dos homens (*PT*)
genuine ['dʒɛnjuɪn] ADJ autêntico; (*person*) sincero
genuinely ['dʒɛnjuɪnlɪ] ADJ sinceramente, realmente
geographer [dʒɪ'ɔgrəfər] N geógrafo(-a)
geographic [dʒɪə'græfɪk], **geographical** [dʒɪə'græfɪkl] ADJ geográfico
geography [dʒɪ'ɔgrəfɪ] N geografia
geological [dʒɪə'lɔdʒɪkl] ADJ geológico
geologist [dʒɪ'ɔlədʒɪst] N geólogo(-a)
geology [dʒɪ'ɔlədʒɪ] N geologia
geometric [dʒɪə'mɛtrɪk], **geometrical** [dʒɪə'mɛtrɪkl] ADJ geométrico
geometry [dʒɪ'ɔmətrɪ] N geometria
Geordie ['dʒɔ:dɪ] (*BRIT inf*) N natural *m/f* da cidade de Newcastle-upon-Tyne
geranium [dʒɪ'reɪnjəm] N gerânio
geriatric [dʒɛrɪ'ætrɪk] ADJ geriátrico
germ [dʒə:m] N micróbio, bacilo; (*Bio: fig*) germe *m*
German ['dʒə:mən] ADJ alemão(-mã) ▶ N alemão(-mã) *m/f*; (*Ling*) alemão *m*

German measles N rubéola
Germany [ˈdʒɜːmənɪ] N Alemanha
germination [dʒɜːmɪˈneɪʃən] N germinação f
germ warfare N guerra bacteriológica
gerrymandering [ˈdʒɛrɪmændərɪŋ] N
reorganização dos distritos eleitorais para garantir a vitória do próprio partido
gestation [dʒɛsˈteɪʃən] N gestação f
gesticulate [dʒɛsˈtɪkjuleɪt] vi gesticular
gesture [ˈdʒɛstjəʳ] N gesto; **as a ~ of friendship** em sinal de amizade

(KEYWORD)

get [gɛt] (*pt, pp* **got** *or* US *pp* **gotten**) vi **1** (*become, be*) ficar, tornar-se; **to get old/tired/cold** envelhecer/cansar-se/resfriar-se; **to get annoyed/bored** aborrecer-se/amuar-se; **to get drunk** embebedar-se; **to get dirty** sujar-se; **to get killed/married** ser morto/casar-se; **when do I get paid?** quando eu recebo?, quando eu vou ser pago?; **it's getting late** está ficando tarde
2 (*go*): **to get to/from** ir para/de; **to get home** chegar em casa
3 (*begin*) começar a; **to get to know sb** começar a conhecer alguém; **let's get going** *or* **started** vamos lá!
▶ MODAL AUX VB: **you've got to do it** você tem que fazê-lo
▶ VT **1**: **to get sth done** (*do*) fazer algo; (*have done*) mandar fazer algo; **to get the washing/dishes done** lavar roupa/a louça; **to get one's hair cut** cortar o cabelo; **to get the car going** *or* **to go** fazer o carro andar; **to get sb to do sth** convencer alguém a fazer algo; **to get sth/sb ready** preparar algo/arrumar alguém; **to get sb drunk/into trouble** embebedar alguém/meter alguém em confusão
2 (*obtain: money, permission, results*) ter; (*find: job, flat*) achar; (*fetch: person, doctor, object*) buscar; **to get sth for sb** arranjar algo para alguém; (*fetch*) ir buscar algo para alguém; **he got a job in London** ele arrumou um emprego em Londres; **get me Mr Harris, please** (*Tel*) pode chamar o Sr Harris, por favor; **can I get you a drink?** você está servido?
3 (*receive: present, letter*) receber; (*acquire: reputation, prize*) ganhar; **how much did you get for the painting?** quanto você recebeu pela pintura?
4 (*catch*) agarrar; (*hit: target etc*) pegar; **to get sb by the arm/throat** agarrar alguém pelo braço/pela garganta; **get him!** pega ele!; **the bullet got him in the leg** a bala pegou na perna dele
5 (*take, move*) levar; **to get sth to sb** levar algo para alguém; **I can't get it in/out/through** não consigo enfiá-lo/tirá-lo/passá-lo; **do you think we'll get it through the door?** você acha que conseguiremos passar isto na porta?; **we must get him to**

a hospital temos que levá-lo para um hospital
6 (*plane, bus etc*) pegar, tomar; **where do I get the train to Birmingham?** onde eu pego o trem para Birmingham?
7 (*understand*) entender; (*hear*) ouvir; **I've got it** entendi; **I don't get your meaning** não entendo o que você quer dizer
8 (*have, possess*): **to have got** ter; **how many have you got?** quantos você tem?
▶ **get about** vi (*news*) espalhar-se
▶ **get along** vi (*agree*) entender-se; (*depart*) ir embora; (*manage*) = **get by**
▶ **get around** = **get round**
▶ **get at** vt fus (*attack, criticize*) atacar; (*reach*) alcançar; **what are you getting at?** o que você está querendo dizer?
▶ **get away** vi (*leave*) partir; (*escape*) escapar
▶ **get away with** vt fus conseguir fazer impunemente
▶ **get back** vi (*return*) regressar, voltar ▶ vt receber de volta, recobrar
▶ **get by** vi (*pass*) passar; (*manage*) virar-se
▶ **get down** vi descer ▶ vt fus abaixar ▶ vt (*object*) abaixar, descer; (*depress: person*) deprimir
▶ **get down to** vt fus (*work*) pôr-se a (fazer)
▶ **get in** vi entrar; (*train*) chegar; (*arrive home*) voltar para casa
▶ **get into** vt fus entrar em; (*vehicle*) subir em; (*clothes*) pôr, vestir, enfiar; **to get into bed/a rage** meter-se na cama/ficar com raiva
▶ **get off** vi (*from train etc*) saltar (BR), descer (PT); (*depart: person, car*) sair; (*escape*) escapar ▶ vt (*remove: clothes, stain*) tirar; (*send off*) mandar ▶ vt fus (*train, bus*) saltar de (BR), sair de (PT)
▶ **get on** vi (*at exam etc*): **how are you getting on?** como vai?; (*agree*): **to get on (with)** entender-se (com) ▶ vt fus (*train etc*) subir em (BR), subir para (PT); (*horse*) montar em
▶ **get out** vi (*of place, vehicle*) sair ▶ vt (*take out*) tirar
▶ **get out of** vt fus (*duty etc*) escapar de
▶ **get over** vt fus (*illness*) restabelecer-se de
▶ **get round** vt fus rodear; (*fig: person*) convencer
▶ **get through** vi (*Tel*) completar a ligação
▶ **get through to** vt fus (*Tel*) comunicar-se com
▶ **get together** vi (*people*) reunir-se ▶ vt reunir
▶ **get up** vi levantar-se ▶ vt fus levantar
▶ **get up to** vt fus (*reach*) chegar a; (BRIT: *prank etc*) fazer

getaway [ˈgɛtəweɪ] N fuga, escape m
getaway car N carro de fuga
get-together N reunião f
get-up (*inf*) N (*outfit*) roupa
get-well card N cartão m com votos de melhoras

geyser ['giːzəʳ] N (Geo) gêiser m; (BRIT) aquecedor m de água

Ghana ['gɑːnə] N Gana (no article)

Ghanaian [gɑːˈneɪən] ADJ, N ganense m/f

ghastly ['gɑːstlɪ] ADJ horrível; (building) medonho; (appearance) horripilante; (pale) pálido

gherkin ['gəːkɪn] N pepino em vinagre

ghetto ['gɛtəu] N gueto

ghost [gəust] N fantasma m ▶ VT (sb else's book) escrever

ghostly ['gəustlɪ] ADJ fantasmal

ghostwriter ['gəustraɪtəʳ] N escritor(a) m/f cujos trabalhos são assinados por outrem

ghoul [guːl] N assombração f

ghoulish ['guːlɪʃ] ADJ (tastes etc) macabro

GHQ N ABBR (Mil) = **general headquarters**

GI (US inf) N ABBR (= government issue) soldado do exército americano

giant ['dʒaɪənt] N gigante m ▶ ADJ gigantesco, gigante; **~ (size) packet** pacote tamanho gigante

gibber ['dʒɪbəʳ] VI algaraviar

gibberish ['dʒɪbərɪʃ] N algaravia

gibe [dʒaɪb] N deboche m ▶ VI: **to ~ at** debochar de

giblets ['dʒɪblɪts] NPL miúdos mpl

Gibraltar [dʒɪˈbrɔːltəʳ] N Gibraltar m (no article)

giddiness ['gɪdɪnɪs] N vertigem f

giddy ['gɪdɪ] ADJ (dizzy) tonto; (speed) vertiginoso; (frivolous) frívolo; **it makes me ~** me dá vertigem; **to be** or **feel ~** estar com vertigem

gift [gɪft] N presente m, dádiva; (offering) oferta; (ability) dom m, talento; (Comm: also: **free gift**) brinde m; **to have a ~ for sth** ter o dom de algo, ter facilidade para algo

gifted ['gɪftɪd] ADJ bem-dotado

gift shop, (US) **gift store** N loja de presentes

gift token N vale m para presente

gift voucher N = **gift token**

gig [gɪg] (inf) N (of musician) show m

gigabyte ['gɪgəbaɪt] N gigabyte m

gigantic [dʒaɪˈgæntɪk] ADJ gigantesco

giggle ['gɪgl] VI dar risadinha boba ▶ N risadinha boba

gild [gɪld] VT dourar

gill [dʒɪl] N (measure) = 0.25 pints (Brit = 0.148l, US = 0.118l)

gills [gɪlz] NPL (of fish) guelras fpl, brânquias fpl

gilt [gɪlt] ADJ dourado ▶ N dourado

gilt-edged [-ˈɛdʒd] ADJ (stocks, securities) do Estado, de toda confiança

gimlet ['gɪmlɪt] N verruma

gimmick ['gɪmɪk] N truque m or macete m (publicitário)

gin [dʒɪn] N gim m, genebra

ginger ['dʒɪndʒəʳ] N gengibre m
  ▶ **ginger up** VT animar

ginger ale N cerveja de gengibre

ginger beer N cerveja de gengibre

gingerbread ['dʒɪndʒəbrɛd] N (cake) pão m de gengibre; (biscuit) biscoito de gengibre

ginger-haired ADJ ruivo

gingerly ['dʒɪndʒəlɪ] ADV cuidadosamente

gingham ['gɪŋəm] N riscadinho

gipsy ['dʒɪpsɪ] N cigano ▶ CPD (caravan, camp) de ciganos

giraffe [dʒɪˈrɑːf] N girafa

girder ['gəːdəʳ] N viga, trave f

girdle ['gəːdl] N (corset) cinta ▶ VT cintar

girl [gəːl] N (small) menina (BR), rapariga (PT); (young woman) jovem f, moça; (daughter) filha; **an English ~** uma moça inglesa

girlfriend ['gəːlfrɛnd] N (of girl) amiga; (of boy) namorada

Girl Guide (BRIT) N bandeirante f

girlish ['gəːlɪʃ] ADJ ameninado, de menina

Girl Scout (US) N escoteira

Giro ['dʒaɪrəu] N: **the National ~** (BRIT) serviço bancário do correio

giro ['dʒaɪrəu] N (bank giro) transferência bancária; (post office giro) transferência postal; (BRIT: welfare cheque) cheque do governo destinado a desempregados

girth [gəːθ] N circunferência; (stoutness) gordura; (of horse) cilha

gist [dʒɪst] N essencial m

(KEYWORD)

give [gɪv] (pt **gave**, pp **given**) VT **1** (hand over) dar; **to give sb sth, give sth to sb** dar algo a alguém; **give it to him, give him it** dê isso a ele/dê-lhe isso; **I'll give you £5 for it** eu te dou £5 por isso

2 (used with n to replace a vb): **to give a cry/sigh/ push** etc dar um grito/suspiro/empurrão etc; **to give a groan/shrug/shout** dar um gemido de ombros/um grito; **to give a speech/a lecture** fazer um discurso/uma palestra; **to give three cheers** dar três vivas

3 (tell, deliver: news, advice, message etc) dar; **did you give him the message/the news?** você deu a mensagem/notícia a ele?; **to give the right/wrong answer** dar a resposta certa/ errada

4 (supply, provide: opportunity, surprise, job etc) dar; (bestow: title, honour, right) conceder; **the sun gives warmth and light** o sol fornece calor e luz; **that's given me an idea** isso me deu uma ideia

5 (dedicate: time, one's life/attention) dedicar; **she gave it all her attention** ela dedicou toda sua atenção a isto

6 (organize): **to give a party/dinner** etc dar uma festa/jantar etc
  ▶ VI **1** (also: **give way**: break, collapse) dar folga; **his legs gave beneath him** suas pernas bambearam; **the roof/floor gave as I stepped on it** o telhado/chão desabou quando eu pisei nele

2 (stretch: fabric) dar de si
  ▶ **give away** VT (money, opportunity) dar; (secret, information) revelar
  ▶ **give back** VT devolver

▶ **give in** VI (*yield*) ceder ▶ VT (*essay etc*) entregar

▶ **give off** VT (*heat, smoke*) soltar

▶ **give out** VT (*distribute*) distribuir; (*make known*) divulgar

▶ **give up** VI (*surrender*) desistir, dar-se por vencido ▶ VT (*job, boyfriend, habit*) renunciar a; (*idea, hope*) abandonar; **to give up smoking** deixar de fumar; **to give o.s. up** entregar-se

▶ **give way** VI (*yield*) ceder; (*break, collapse: rope*) arrebentar; (: *ladder*) quebrar; (BRIT *Aut*) dar a preferência (BR), dar prioridade (PT)

give-and-take N toma-lá-dá-cá *m*

giveaway ['gɪvəweɪ] CPD: ~ **prices** preços de liquidação ▶ N (*inf*): **her expression was a ~** a expressão dela a atraiçoava; **the exam was a ~!** o exame foi sopa!

given ['gɪvn] PP *of* **give** ▶ ADJ (*fixed: time, amount*) dado, determinado ▶ CONJ: ~ **the circumstances** ... dadas as circunstâncias ...; ~ **that** ... dado que ..., já que ...

glacial ['gleɪsɪəl] ADJ (*Geo*) glaciário; (*wind, weather*) glacial

glacier ['glæsɪə^r] N glaciar *m*, geleira

glad [glæd] ADJ contente; **to be ~ about sth/ that** estar contente com algo/contente que; **I was ~ of his help** eu lhe agradeci (por) sua ajuda

gladden ['glædən] VT alegrar

glade [gleɪd] N clareira

gladioli [glædɪ'əʊlaɪ] NPL gladíolos *mpl*

gladly ['glædlɪ] ADV com muito prazer

glamorous ['glæmərəs] ADJ encantador(a), glamouroso

glamour ['glæmə^r] N encanto, glamour *m*

glance [glɑːns] N relance *m*, vista de olhos ▶ VI: **to ~ at** olhar (de relance)

▶ **glance off** VT FUS (*bullet*) ricochetear de

glancing ['glɑːnsɪŋ] ADJ (*blow*) oblíquo

gland [glænd] N glândula

glandular fever ['glændjulə^r-] (BRIT) ADJ mononucleose *f* infecciosa

glare [glɛə^r] N (*of anger*) olhar *m* furioso; (*of light*) luminosidade *f*; (*of publicity*) foco ▶ VI brilhar; **to ~ at** olhar furiosamente para

glaring ['glɛərɪŋ] ADJ (*mistake*) notório

glass [glɑːs] N vidro, cristal *m*; (*for drinking*) copo; (: *with stem*) cálice *m*; (*also:* **looking glass**) espelho; **glasses** NPL (*spectacles*) óculos *mpl*

glass-blowing [-bləʊɪŋ] N modelagem *f* de vidro a quente

glass fibre N fibra de vidro

glasshouse ['glɑːshaus] N estufa

glassware ['glɑːswɛə^r] N objetos *mpl* de cristal

glassy ['glɑːsɪ] ADJ (*eyes*) vidrado

Glaswegian [glæs'wiːdʒən] ADJ de Glasgow ▶ N natural *m/f* de Glasgow

glaze [gleɪz] VT (*door*) envidraçar; (*pottery*) vitrificar; (*Culin*) glaçar ▶ N verniz *m*; (*Culin*) glacê *m*

glazed [gleɪzd] ADJ (*eye*) vidrado; (*pottery*) vitrificado

glazier ['gleɪzɪə^r] N vidraceiro(-a)

gleam [gliːm] N brilho ▶ VI brilhar; **a ~ of hope** um fio de esperança

gleaming ['gliːmɪŋ] ADJ brilhante

glean [gliːn] VT (*information*) colher

glee [gliː] N alegria, regozijo

gleeful ['gliːful] ADJ alegre

glen [glɛn] N vale *m*

glib [glɪb] ADJ (*answer*) pronto; (*person*) labioso

glide [glaɪd] VI deslizar; (*Aviat: birds*) planar ▶ N deslizamento; (*Aviat*) voo planado

glider ['glaɪdə^r] N (*Aviat*) planador *m*

gliding ['glaɪdɪŋ] N (*Aviat*) voo sem motor

glimmer ['glɪmə^r] N luz *f* trêmula; (*of interest, hope*) lampejo ▶ VI tremeluzir

glimpse [glɪmps] N vista rápida, vislumbre *m* ▶ VT vislumbrar, ver de relance; **to catch a ~ of** vislumbrar

glint [glɪnt] N brilho; (*in the eye*) cintilação *f* ▶ VI cintilar

glisten ['glɪsn] VI brilhar

glitter ['glɪtə^r] VI reluzir, brilhar ▶ N brilho

glitz [glɪts] (*inf*) N cafonice *f*

gloat [gləut] VI: **to ~ (over)** exultar (com)

global ['gləubl] ADJ (*worldwide*) mundial; (*overall*) global

globalization [gləubəlaɪ'zeɪʃən] N globalização *f*

global warming N aquecimento global

globe [gləub] N globo, esfera

globetrotter ['gləubtrɔtə^r] N pessoa que corre mundo

globule ['glɔbjuːl] N glóbulo

gloom [gluːm] N escuridão *f*; (*sadness*) tristeza

gloomy ['gluːmɪ] ADJ (*dark*) escuro; (*sad*) triste; (*pessimistic*) pessimista; **to feel ~** estar abatido

glorification [glɔːrɪfɪ'keɪʃən] N glorificação *f*

glorify ['glɔːrɪfaɪ] VT glorificar; (*praise*) adorar

glorious ['glɔːrɪəs] ADJ (*weather*) magnífico; (*future*) glorioso; (*splendid*) excelente

glory ['glɔːrɪ] N glória ▶ VI: **to ~ in** gloriar-se de

glory hole (*inf*) N zona

Glos (BRIT) ABBR = **Gloucestershire**

gloss [glɔs] N (*shine*) brilho; (*also:* **gloss paint**) pintura brilhante, esmalte *m* ▶ **gloss over** VT FUS encobrir

glossary ['glɔsərɪ] N glossário

glossy ['glɔsɪ] ADJ lustroso ▶ N (*also:* **glossy magazine**) revista de luxo

glove [glʌv] N luva

glove compartment N (*Aut*) porta-luvas *m inv*

glow [gləu] VI (*shine*) brilhar; (*fire*) arder ▶ N brilho

glower ['glauə^r] VI: **to ~ at (sb)** olhar (alguém) de modo ameaçador

glowing ['gləuɪŋ] ADJ (*fire*) ardente; (*complexion*) afogueado; (*report, description etc*) entusiástico

glow-worm N pirilampo, vaga-lume *m*

glucose ['glu:kəus] N glicose f
glue [glu:] N cola ▶ VT colar
glue-sniffing [-'snɪfɪŋ] N cheira-cola m
glum [glʌm] ADJ (mood) abatido; (person, tone) triste
glut [glʌt] N abundância, fartura ▶ VT (market) saturar
glutinous ['glu:tɪnəs] ADJ glutinoso
glutton ['glʌtn] N glutão(-ona) m/f; **a ~ for work/punishment** um(a) trabalhador(a) incansável/um(a) masoquista
gluttonous ['glʌtənəs] ADJ glutão(-ona)
gluttony ['glʌtənɪ] N gula
glycerin, glycerine ['glɪsəri:n] N glicerina
GM ADJ ABBR (= genetically modified) geneticamente modificado
gm ABBR (= gram) g
GMAT (US) N ABBR (= Graduate Management Admissions Test) exame de admissão aos cursos de pós-graduação
GMB (BRIT) N ABBR (= General Municipal Boilermakers and Allied Trade Union) sindicato dos empregados dos municípios
GM crop N plantação f geneticamente modificada
GM foods NPL alimentos mpl geneticamente modificados
GMT ABBR (= Greenwich Mean Time) GMT m
gnarled [nɑ:ld] ADJ (tree) nodoso; (tree) retorcido
gnash [næʃ] VT: **to ~ one's teeth** ranger os dentes
gnat [næt] N mosquito
gnaw [nɔ:] VT roer
gnome [nəum] N gnomo
GNP N ABBR = **gross national product**

(KEYWORD)

go [gəu] (pt **went**, pp **gone**) VI **1** ir; (travel, move) viajar; **a car went by** um carro passou; **he has gone to Aberdeen** ele foi para Aberdeen
2 (depart) sair, ir embora; **"I must go,"** she said "preciso ir" ela disse; **our plane went at 6pm** nosso avião saiu às 6 da tarde; **they came at 8 and went at 9** eles chegaram às 8 e foram embora às 9
3 (attend) ir; **she went to university in Rio** ela fez universidade no Rio; **she goes to her dancing class on Tuesdays** ela vai a aula de dança às terças-feiras; **he goes to the local church** ele frequenta a igreja local
4 (take part in an activity) ir; **to go for a walk** ir passear
5 (work) funcionar; **the clock stopped going** o relógio parou de funcionar; **the bell went just then** a campainha acabou de tocar
6 (become): **to go pale/mouldy** ficar pálido/mofado
7 (be sold): **to go for £10** ser vendido por £10
8 (fit, suit): **to go with** acompanhar, combinar com
9 (be about to, intend to): **he's going to do it** ele

vai fazê-lo; **we're going to leave in an hour** vamos partir dentro de uma hora; **are you going to come?** você vem?
10 (time) passar
11 (event, activity) ser; **how did it go?** como foi?
12 (be given) ir (ser dado); **the job is to go to someone else** o emprego vai ser dado para outra pessoa
13 (break) romper-se; **the fuse went** o fusível queimou; **the leg of the chair went** a perna da cadeira quebrou
14 (be placed): **where does this cup go?** onde é que põe esta xícara?; **the milk goes in the fridge** pode guardar o leite na geladeira
▶ N (pl **goes**) **1** (try): **to have a go (at)** tentar
2 (turn) vez f; **whose go is it?** de quem é a vez?
3 (move): **to be on the go** ter muito para fazer
▶ **go about** VI (also: **go around**: rumour) espalhar-se ▶ VT FUS: **how do I go about this?** como é que eu faço isto?
▶ **go ahead** VI (make progress) progredir; (get going) ir em frente
▶ **go along** VI ir ▶ VT FUS ladear; **to go along with** (agree with: plan, idea, policy) concordar com
▶ **go away** VI (leave) ir-se, ir embora
▶ **go back** VI (return) voltar; (go again) ir de novo
▶ **go back on** VT FUS (promise) faltar com
▶ **go by** VI (years, time) passar ▶ VT FUS (book, rule) guiar-se por
▶ **go down** VI (descend) descer, baixar; (ship) afundar; (sun) pôr-se ▶ VT FUS (stairs, ladder) descer
▶ **go for** VT FUS (fetch) ir buscar; (like) gostar de; (attack) atacar
▶ **go in** VI (enter) entrar
▶ **go in for** VT FUS (competition) inscrever-se em; (like) gostar de
▶ **go into** VT FUS (enter) entrar em; (investigate) investigar; (embark on) embarcar em
▶ **go off** VI (leave) ir-se; (food) estragar, apodrecer; (bomb, gun) explodir; (event) realizar-se ▶ VT FUS (person, place, food etc) deixar de gostar de
▶ **go on** VI (continue) seguir, continuar; (happen) acontecer, ocorrer; **to go on doing sth** continuar fazendo a fazer algo
▶ **go out** VI (leave: room, building) sair; (for entertainment): **are you going out tonight?** você vai sair hoje à noite?; (couple): **they went out for 3 years** eles namoraram durante 3 anos; (fire, light) apagar-se
▶ **go over** VI (ship) soçobrar ▶ VT FUS (check) revisar
▶ **go round** VI (news, rumour) circular
▶ **go through** VT FUS (town etc) atravessar; (search through: files, papers) vasculhar; (examine: list, book, story) percorrer de cabo a rabo

g

▶ **go up** VI (*ascend*) subir; (*price, level*) aumentar

▶ **go without** VT FUS (*food, treats*) passar sem

goad [gəud] VT aguilhoar

go-ahead ADJ empreendedor(a) ▶ N luz *f* verde

goal [gəul] N meta, alvo; (*Sport*) gol *m* (BR), golo (PT)

goal difference N diferença de gols

goalie ['gəulı] N (*inf*) goleiro(-a)

goalkeeper ['gəulki:pər] N goleiro(-a) (BR), guarda-redes *m/f inv* (PT)

goalpost ['gəulpəust] N trave *f*

goat [gəut] N cabra; (*also:* **billy goat**) bode *m*

gobble ['gɔbl] VT (*also:* **gobble down, gobble up**) engolir rapidamente, devorar

go-between N intermediário(-a)

Gobi Desert ['gəubı-] N Deserto de Gobi

goblet ['gɔblıt] N cálice *m*

goblin ['gɔblın] N duende *m*

go-cart N kart *m* ▶ CPD: ~ **racing** kartismo

god [gɔd] N deus *m*; **G~** Deus

godchild ['gɔdtʃaıld] (*irreg: like* **child**) N afilhado(-a)

goddamn ['gɔddæm], **goddamned** ['gɔddæmd] EXCL (*esp US inf*): ~ **(it)!** cacete! ▶ ADJ maldito ▶ ADV pra cacete

goddaughter ['gɔddɔ:tər] N afilhada

goddess ['gɔdıs] N deusa

godfather ['gɔdfɑ:ðər] N padrinho

god-forsaken [-fə'seıkən] ADJ miserável, abandonado

godmother ['gɔdmʌðər] N madrinha

godparents ['gɔdpɛərənts] NPL padrinhos *mpl*

godsend ['gɔdsend] N dádiva do céu

godson ['gɔdsʌn] N afilhado

goes [gəuz] VB *see* **go**

go-getter [-'gɛtər] N pessoa dinâmica, pessoa furona (*inf*)

goggle ['gɔgl] VI: **to ~ at** olhar de olhos esbugalhados

goggles ['gɔglz] NPL óculos *mpl* de proteção

going ['gəuıŋ] N (*conditions*) estado do terreno ▶ ADJ: **the ~ rate** tarifa corrente *or* em vigor; **~ concern** empresa em funcionamento, empresa com fundo de comérico; **it was slow ~** ia devagar

goings-on (*inf*) NPL maquinações *fpl*

go-kart [-kɑ:t] N = **go-cart**

gold [gəuld] N ouro ▶ ADJ de ouro

golden ['gəuldən] ADJ (*made of gold*) de ouro; (*gold in colour*) dourado

golden age N idade *f* de ouro

golden handshake (BRIT) N bolada

golden rule N regra de ouro

goldfish ['gəuldfıʃ] N INV peixe-dourado *m*

gold leaf N ouro em folha

gold medal N (*Sport*) medalha de ouro

gold mine N mina de ouro

gold-plated [-'pleıtıd] ADJ plaquê *inv*

gold-rush N corrida do ouro

goldsmith ['gəuldsmıθ] N ourives *m/f inv*

gold standard N padrão-ouro *m*

golf [gɔlf] N golfe *m*

golf ball N bola de golfe; (*on typewriter*) esfera

golf club N clube *m* de golfe; (*stick*) taco

golf course N campo de golfe

golfer ['gɔlfər] N jogador(a) *m/f* de golfe, golfista *m/f*

gondola ['gɔndələ] N gôndola

gondolier [gɔndə'lıər] N gondoleiro

gone [gɔn] PP *of* **go**

gong [gɔŋ] N gongo

good [gud] ADJ bom/boa; (*kind*) bom, bondoso; (*well-behaved*) educado; (*useful*) útil ▶ N bem *m*; **goods** NPL (*possessions*) bens *mpl*; (*Comm*) mercadorias *fpl*; **~s and chattels** bens móveis; **~!** bom!; **to be ~ at** ser bom em; **to be ~ for** servir para; **it's ~ for you** faz-lhe bem; **would you be ~ enough to ...?** podia fazer-me o favor de ...?, poderia me fazer a gentileza de ...?; **it's a ~ thing you were there** ainda bem que você estava lá; **she is ~ with children/her hands** ela tem habilidade com crianças/com as mãos; **to feel ~** sentir-se bem, estar bom; **it's ~ to see you** é bom ver você; (*formal*) prazer em vê-lo; **he's up to no ~** ele tem más intenções; **for the common ~** para o bem comum; **that's very ~ of you** é muita bondade sua; **is this any ~?** (*will it do?*) será que isso serve?; (*what's it like?*) será que vale a pena?; **a ~ deal (of)** muito; **a ~ many** muitos; **to make ~** reparar; **it's no ~ complaining** não adianta se queixar; **for ~** (*forever*) para sempre, definitivamente; (*once and for all*) de uma vez por todas; **~ morning/afternoon!** bom dia/boa tarde!; **~ evening!** boa noite!; **~ night!** boa noite!

goodbye [gud'baı] EXCL até logo (BR), adeus (PT); **to say ~** despedir-se

good faith N boa fé

good-for-nothing ADJ imprestável

Good Friday N Sexta-Feira Santa

good-humoured [-'hju:məd] ADJ (*person*) alegre; (*remark, joke*) sem malícia

good-looking [-'lukıŋ] ADJ bonito

good-natured ADJ (*person*) de bom gênio; (*pet*) de boa índole; (*discussion*) cordial

goodness ['gudnıs] N (*of person*) bondade *f*; **for ~ sake!** pelo amor de Deus!; **~ gracious!** meu Deus do céu!, nossa (senhora)!

goods train (BRIT) N trem *m* de carga

goodwill [gud'wıl] N boa vontade *f*; (*Comm*) fundo de comércio, aviamento

goody-goody ['gudıgudı] (*pej*) N puxa-saco *m*

Google® ['gu:gəl] VT, VI pesquisar no Google®

goose [gu:s] (*pl* **geese**) N ganso

gooseberry ['guzbərı] N groselha; **to play ~** (BRIT) ficar de vela, segurar a vela

gooseflesh ['gu:sfleʃ] N = **goose pimples**

goose pimples NPL pele *f* arrepiada

goose step N (*Mil*) passo de ganso

GOP (*US inf*) N ABBR (*Pol*: = *Grand Old Party*) partido republicano

gore [gɔ:r] VT escornar ▶ N sangue *m*

gorge [gɔːdʒ] N desfiladeiro ▶ VT: **to ~ o.s. (on)** empanturrar-se (de)

gorgeous ['gɔːdʒəs] ADJ magnífico, maravilhoso; (person) lindo

gorilla [gə'rɪlə] N gorila m

gormless ['gɔːmlɪs] (BRIT inf) ADJ burro

gorse [gɔːs] N tojo

gory ['gɔːrɪ] ADJ sangrento

gosh [gɔʃ] (inf) EXCL puxa

go-slow (BRIT) N greve f de trabalho lento, operação f tartaruga

gospel ['gɔspl] N evangelho

gossamer ['gɔsəməʳ] N (cobweb) teia de aranha; (cloth) tecido diáfano, gaze f fina

gossip ['gɔsɪp] N (scandal) fofocas fpl (BR), mexericos mpl (PT); (chat) conversa; (scandalmonger) fofoqueiro(-a) (BR), mexeriqueiro(-a) (PT) ▶ VI (spread scandal) fofocar (BR), mexericar (PT); (chat) bater (um) papo (BR), cavaquear (PT); **a piece of ~** uma fofoca (BR), um mexerico (PT)

gossip column N (Press) coluna social

got [gɔt] PT, PP of **get**

Gothic ['gɔθɪk] ADJ gótico

gotten ['gɔtn] (US) PP of **get**

gouge [gaudʒ] VT (also: **gouge out**: hole etc) abrir; (: initials) talhar; **to ~ sb's eyes out** arrancar os olhos de alguém

gourd [guəd] N cabaça, cucúrbita

gourmet ['guəmeɪ] N gourmet m, gastrônomo(-a)

gout [gaut] N gota

govern ['gʌvən] VT governar; (event) controlar

governess ['gʌvənɪs] N governanta

governing ['gʌvənɪŋ] ADJ (Pol) no governo, ao poder; **~ body** conselho de administração

government ['gʌvnmənt] N governo ▶ CPD (of administration) governamental; (of state) do Estado; **local ~** governo municipal

governmental [gʌvn'mɛntl] ADJ governamental

government housing (US) N casas fpl populares

government stock N títulos mpl do governo

governor ['gʌvənəʳ] N governador(a) m/f; (of school, hospital, jail) diretor(a) m/f

Govt ABBR = **government**

gown [gaun] N vestido; (of teacher, judge) toga

GP N ABBR (Med) = **general practitioner**

GPO N ABBR (BRIT: old) = **General Post Office**; (US) = **Government Printing Office**

GPS N ABBR (= global positioning system) GPS m

gr. ABBR (Comm) = **gross**

grab [græb] VT agarrar ▶ VI: **to ~ at** tentar agarrar

grace [greɪs] N (Rel) graça; (gracefulness) elegância, fineza ▶ VT (honour) honrar; (adorn) adornar; **5 days' ~** um prazo de 5 dias; **to say ~** dar graças (antes de comer); **with a good/bad ~** de bom/mau grado; **his sense of humour is his saving ~** seu único mérito é seu senso de humor

graceful ['greɪsful] ADJ elegante, gracioso

gracious ['greɪʃəs] ADJ gracioso, afável; (benevolent) bondoso, complacente; (formal: God) misericordioso ▶ EXCL: **(good) ~!** meu Deus do céu!, nossa (senhora)!

gradation [grə'deɪʃn] N gradação f

grade [greɪd] N (quality) classe f, qualidade f; (degree) grau m; (US: Sch) série f, classe; (: gradient) declive m ▶ VT classificar; **to make the ~** (fig) ter sucesso

grade crossing (US) N passagem f de nível

grade school (US) N escola primária

gradient ['greɪdɪənt] N declive m; (Geom) gradiente m

gradual ['grædjuəl] ADJ gradual, gradativo

gradually ['grædjuəlɪ] ADV gradualmente, gradativamente, pouco a pouco

graduate [n 'grædjuɪt, vi 'grædjueɪt] N graduado, licenciado; (US) diplomado do colégio ▶ VI formar-se, licenciar-se

graduated pension ['grædjueɪtɪd-] N aposentadoria calculada em função dos últimos salários

graduation [grædju'eɪʃən] N formatura

graffiti [grə'fiːtɪ] N, NPL pichações fpl

graft [grɑːft] N (Agr, Med) enxerto; (BRIT inf) trabalho pesado; (bribery) suborno ▶ VT enxertar; **hard ~** (inf) labuta

grain [greɪn] N grão m; (no pl: cereals) cereais mpl; (US: corn) trigo; (in wood) veio, fibra; **it goes against the ~** é contra a sua (or minha etc) natureza

gram [græm] N grama m

grammar ['græməʳ] N gramática

grammar school N (BRIT) ≈ liceo

grammatical [grə'mætɪkl] ADJ gramatical

gramme [græm] N = **gram**

gramophone ['græməfəun] (BRIT) N (old) gramofone m

gran [græn] (BRIT inf) N vó f

granary ['grænərɪ] N celeiro

grand [grænd] ADJ grandioso; (inf: wonderful) ótimo ▶ N (inf: thousand) mil libras fpl (or dólares mpl)

grandchild ['græntʃaɪld] (irreg: like **child**) N neto(-a)

granddad ['grændæd] N vovô m

granddaughter ['grændɔːtəʳ] N neta

grandeur ['grændjəʳ] N grandeza, magnificência; (of event) grandiosidade f; (of house, style) imponência

grandfather ['grænfɑːðəʳ] N avô m

grandiose ['grændɪəuz] ADJ grandioso; (pej) pomposo; (house, style) imponente

grand jury (US) N júri m de instrução

grandma ['grænmɑː] N avó f, vovó f

grandmother ['grænmʌðəʳ] N avó f

grandpa ['grænpɑː] N = **grandma**

grandparents ['grændpɛərənts] NPL avós mpl

grand piano N piano de cauda

Grand Prix ['grɑː'priː] N (Aut) Grande Prêmio

grandson ['grænsʌn] N neto

grandstand ['grænstænd] N (Sport) tribuna principal

grand total N total m geral or global
granite ['grænɪt] N granito
granny ['grænɪ] (inf) N avó f, vovó f
grant [grɑːnt] VT (concede) conceder; (a request etc) anuir a; (admit) admitir ▶ N (Sch) bolsa; (Admin) subvenção f, subsídio; **to take sth for ~ed** dar algo por certo; **to ~ that** admitir que
granulated sugar ['grænjuleɪtɪd-] N açúcar m granulado
granule ['grænjuːl] N grânulo
grape [greɪp] N uva; **sour ~s** (fig) inveja; **a bunch of ~s** um cacho de uvas
grapefruit ['greɪpfruːt] N toranja, grapefruit m (BR)
grapevine ['greɪpvaɪn] N parreira; **I heard it on** or **through the ~** (fig) um passarinho me contou
graph [grɑːf] N gráfico
graphic ['græfɪk] ADJ gráfico
graphic designer N desenhista m/f industrial
graphics ['græfɪks] N (art) artes fpl gráficas ▶ NPL (drawings) desenhos mpl; (: Comput) gráficos mpl
graphite ['græfaɪt] N grafita
graph paper N papel m quadriculado
grapple ['græpl] VI: **to ~ with sth** estar às voltas com algo
grappling iron ['græplɪŋ-] N (Naut) arpéu m
grasp [grɑːsp] VT agarrar, segurar; (understand) compreender, entender ▶ N (grip) mão f; (reach) alcance m; (understanding) compreensão f; **to have sth within one's ~** ter algo ao seu alcance; **to have a good ~ of sth** (fig) ter um bom domínio de algo, dominar algo
▶ **grasp at** VT FUS (rope etc) tentar agarrar; (opportunity) agarrar
grasping ['grɑːspɪŋ] ADJ avaro
grass [grɑːs] N grama (BR), relva (PT); (uncultivated) cupim m; (lawn) gramado (BR), relvado (PT); (BRIT inf: informer) dedo-duro m
grasshopper ['grɑːshɔpəʳ] N gafanhoto
grassland ['grɑːslænd] N pradaria
grass roots NPL (fig) raízes fpl, base f ▶ ADJ: **grass-roots** popular
grass snake N serpente f
grassy ['grɑːsɪ] ADJ coberto de grama (BR) or de relva (PT)
grate [greɪt] N (fireplace) lareira; (of iron) grelha ▶ VI ranger ▶ VT (Culin) ralar
grateful ['greɪtful] ADJ agradecido, grato
gratefully ['greɪtfəlɪ] ADV agradecidamente
grater ['greɪtəʳ] N ralador m
gratification [grætɪfɪ'keɪʃən] N satisfação f
gratify ['grætɪfaɪ] VT gratificar; (whim) satisfazer
gratifying ['grætɪfaɪɪŋ] ADJ gratificante
grating ['greɪtɪŋ] N (iron bars) grade f ▶ ADJ (noise) áspero
gratitude ['grætɪtjuːd] N agradecimento
gratuitous [grə'tjuːɪtəs] ADJ gratuito
gratuity [grə'tjuːɪtɪ] N gratificação f, gorjeta

grave [greɪv] N cova, sepultura ▶ ADJ sério; (mistake) grave
grave digger N coveiro
gravel ['grævl] N cascalho
gravely ['greɪvlɪ] ADV gravemente; **~ ill** gravemente doente
gravestone ['greɪvstəun] N lápide f
graveyard ['greɪvjɑːd] N cemitério
gravitate ['grævɪteɪt] VI: **to ~ towards** ser atraído por
gravity ['grævɪtɪ] N (Phys) gravidade f; (seriousness) seriedade f, gravidade f
gravy ['greɪvɪ] N molho (de carne)
gravy boat N molheira
gravy train (inf) N: **to be on** or **ride the ~** ter achado uma mina
gray [greɪ] (US) ADJ = **grey**
graze [greɪz] VI pastar ▶ VT (touch lightly) roçar; (scrape) raspar; (Med) esfolar ▶ N (Med) esfoladura, arranhadura
grazing ['greɪzɪŋ] N (pasture) pasto, pastagem f
grease [griːs] N (fat) gordura; (lubricant) graxa, lubrificante m ▶ VT (Culin: dish) untar; (Tech: brakes etc) lubrificar, engraxar
grease gun N bomba de graxa
greasepaint [griːspeɪnt] N maquilagem f (para o teatro)
greaseproof paper ['griːspruːf-] (BRIT) N papel m de cera (vegetal)
greasy ['griːzɪ] ADJ gordurento, gorduroso; (skin, hair) oleoso; (hands, clothes) engordurado; (BRIT: road, surface) escorregadio
great [greɪt] ADJ grande; (inf) genial; (pain, heat) forte; (important) importante; **they're ~ friends** eles são grandes amigos; **we had a ~ time** nos divertimos à beça; **it was ~!** foi ótimo, foi um barato (inf); **the ~ thing is that ...** o melhor é que ...
Great Barrier Reef N: **the ~** a Grande Barreira
Great Britain N Grã-Bretanha

> A Grã-Bretanha, **Great Britain** em inglês, designa a maior das ilhas britânicas e, portanto, engloba a Escócia e o País de Gales. Junto com a Irlanda, a ilha de Man e as ilhas Anglo-normandas, a Grã-Bretanha forma as ilhas Britânicas, ou British Isles. Reino Unido, em inglês United Kingdom ou UK, é o nome oficial da entidade política que compreende a Grã-Bretanha e a Irlanda do Norte.

great-grandchild (irreg: like child) N bisneto(-a)
great-grandfather N bisavô m
great-grandmother N bisavó f
Great Lakes NPL: **the ~** os Grandes Lagos
greatly ['greɪtlɪ] ADV imensamente, muito
greatness ['greɪtnɪs] N grandeza
Grecian ['griːʃən] ADJ grego
Greece [griːs] N Grécia
greed [griːd] N (also: **greediness**) avidez f, cobiça; (for food) gula

greedily ['gri:dɪlɪ] ADV com avidez; (*eat*) gulosamente

greedy ['gri:dɪ] ADJ avarento; (*for food*) guloso

Greek [gri:k] ADJ grego ▶ N grego(-a); (*Ling*) grego; **ancient/modern ~** grego clássico/moderno

green [gri:n] ADJ verde; (*inexperienced*) inexperiente, ingênuo ▶ N verde *m*; (*stretch of grass*) gramado (BR), relvado (PT); (*on golf course*) green *m*; (*also*: **village green**) ≈ praça; **greens** NPL (*vegetables*) verduras *fpl*; **to have ~ fingers** (BRIT) *or* **a ~ thumb** (US) ter mão boa (para plantar)

green belt N (*round town*) cinturão *m* verde

green card N (BRIT *Aut*) carta verde; (US) autorização *f* de residência

greenery ['gri:nərɪ] N verdura

greenfly ['gri:nflaɪ] (BRIT) N pulgão *m*

greengage ['gri:ngeɪdʒ] N rainha-cláudia

greengrocer ['gri:nɡrəʊsəʳ] (BRIT) N verdureiro(-a)

greenhouse ['gri:nhaʊs] N estufa

greenhouse effect N: **the ~** o efeito estufa

greenhouse gas N gás *m* de efeito estufa

greenish ['gri:nɪʃ] ADJ esverdeado

Greenland ['gri:nlənd] N Groenlândia

Greenlander ['gri:nləndəʳ] N groenlandês(-esa) *m/f*

green pepper N pimentão *m* verde

green tax N imposto ecológico

greet [gri:t] VT saudar; (*welcome*) acolher; (*news*) receber

greeting ['gri:tɪŋ] N cumprimento; (*welcome*) acolhimento; **Christmas/birthday ~s** votos de boas festas/feliz aniversário

greeting card, greetings card N cartão *m* comemorativo

gregarious [grə'ɡɛərɪəs] ADJ gregário

grenade [grə'neɪd] N (*also*: **hand grenade**) granada

grew [gru:] PT *of* **grow**

grey, (US) **gray** [greɪ] ADJ cinzento; (*dismal*) sombrio; **to go ~** (*hair, person*) ficar grisalho

grey-haired ADJ grisalho

greyhound ['greɪhaʊnd] N galgo

grey vote N voto dos idosos

grid [grɪd] N grade *f*; (*Elec*) rede *f*; (US *Aut*) cruzamento

griddle [grɪdl] N (*on cooker*) chapa de assar

gridiron ['ɡrɪdaɪən] N grelha; (US *Football*) campo

gridlock ['ɡrɪdlɔk] N (*traffic jam*) paralisia do trânsito

grief [gri:f] N dor *f*, pesar *m*; **to come to ~** fracassar

grievance ['gri:vəns] N motivo de queixa, agravo

grieve [gri:v] VI sofrer ▶ VT dar pena a, afligir; **to ~ for** chorar por

grievous ['gri:vəs] ADJ penoso; **~ bodily harm** (*Law*) lesão *f* corporal (grave)

grill [grɪl] N (*on cooker*) grelha; (*also*: **grillroom**) grill) prato de grelhados; (*also*: **grillroom**)

grill-room *m*, ≈ churrascaria ▶ VT (BRIT) grelhar; (*question*) interrogar cerradamente

grille [grɪl] N grade *f*; (*Aut*) grelha

grillroom ['ɡrɪlrum] N grill-room *m*, ≈ churrascaria

grim [grɪm] ADJ sinistro, lúgubre; (*unpleasant*) desagradável; (*unattractive*) feio; (*stern*) severo; (*inf: dreadful*) horrível

grimace [grɪ'meɪs] N careta ▶ VI fazer caretas

grime [graɪm] N sujeira (BR), sujidade *f* (PT)

grimy ['graɪmɪ] ADJ sujo, encardido

grin [grɪn] N sorriso largo ▶ VI sorrir abertamente; **to ~ (at)** dar um sorriso largo (para)

grind [graɪnd] (*pt, pp* **ground**) VT (*crush*) triturar; (*coffee, pepper etc*) moer; (*make sharp*) afiar; (US: *meat*) picar; (*polish: gem*) lapidar; (: *lens*) polir ▶ VI (*car gears*) ranger ▶ N (*work*) trabalho (repetitivo e maçante); **to ~ one's teeth** ranger os dentes; **to ~ to a halt** (*vehicle*) parar com um ranger de freios; (*fig: work, production*) paralisar-se; (: *talks, process*) empacar; **the daily ~** (*inf*) a labuta diária

grinder ['graɪndəʳ] N (*machine: for coffee*) moinho; (: *for waste disposal*) triturador *m*

grindstone ['graɪndstəʊn] N: **to keep one's nose to the ~** trabalhar sem descanso

grip [grɪp] N (*of hands*) aperto; (*handle*) punho; (*of racquet etc*) cabo; (*of tyre, shoe*) aderência; (*holdall*) valise *f* ▶ VT agarrar; (*attention*) prender; **to come** *or* **get to ~s with** arcar com; **to ~ the road** (*Aut*) aderir à estrada; **to lose one's ~** perder a pega; (*fig*) perder a eficiência

gripe [graɪp] N (*Med*) cólicas *fpl*; (*inf: complaint*) queixa ▶ VI (*inf*) bufar

gripping ['ɡrɪpɪŋ] ADJ absorvente, emocionante

grisly ['ɡrɪzlɪ] ADJ horrendo, medonho

grist [grɪst] N (*fig*): **it's (all) ~ to his mill** ele se vale de tudo

gristle ['ɡrɪsl] N cartilagem *f*; (*on meat*) nervo

grit [grɪt] N areia, grão *m* de areia; (*courage*) coragem *f* ▶ VT (*road*) pôr areia em; **grits** NPL (US) canjica; **to ~ one's teeth** cerrar os dentes; **to have a piece of ~ in one's eye** ter uma pedrinha no olho

grizzle ['ɡrɪzl] (BRIT) VI choramingar

grizzly ['ɡrɪzlɪ] N (*also*: **grizzly bear**) urso pardo

groan [grəʊn] N gemido ▶ VI gemer

grocer ['ɡrəʊsəʳ] N dono(-a) de mercearia

grocer's, grocer's shop N mercearia

grocery ['ɡrəʊsərɪ] N mercearia; **groceries** NPL comestíveis *mpl*

grog [ɡrɔg] N grogue *m*

groggy ['ɡrɔgɪ] ADJ grogue

groin [ɡrɔɪn] N virilha

groom [gru:m] N cavalariço; (*also*: **bridegroom**) noivo ▶ VT (*horse*) tratar; (*fig*): **to ~ sb for sth** preparar alguém para algo; **well-~ed** bem-posto

groove [gru:v] N ranhura, entalhe *m*

grope [grəup] vi tatear; **to ~ for** procurar às cegas

gross [grəus] ADJ grosso; (*flagrant*) grave; (*vulgar*) vulgar; (: *building*) de mau-gosto; (*Comm*) bruto ▶ N INV (*twelve dozen*) grosa ▶ VT (*Comm*): **to ~ £500,000** dar uma receita bruta de £500,000

gross domestic product N produto interno bruto

grossly ['grəuslı] ADV (*greatly*) enormemente, gritantemente

gross national product N produto nacional bruto

grotesque [grə'tɛsk] ADJ grotesco

grotto ['grɔtəu] N gruta

grotty ['grɔtı] (BRIT *inf*) ADJ vagabundo; (*room etc*) mixa; **I'm feeling ~** estou me sentindo podre

grouch [grautʃ] (*inf*) vi ralhar ▶ N (*person*) pessoa geniosa, rabugento(-a)

ground [graund] PT, PP *of* **grind** ▶ N terra, chão m; (*Sport*) campo; (*land*) terreno; (*reason: gen pl*) motivo, razão f; (*US: also*: **ground wire**) (ligação f à) terra, fio-terra m ▶ VT (*plane*) manter em terra; (*US Elec*) ligar à terra ▶ vi (*ship*) encalhar ▶ ADJ (*coffee etc*) moído; (*US: meat*) picado; **grounds** NPL (*of coffee etc*) borra; (*gardens etc*) jardins mpl, parque m; **on the ~** no chão; **to the ~** por terra; **below ~** embaixo da terra; **to gain/lose ~** ganhar/perder terreno; **common ~** consenso; **he covered a lot of ~ in his lecture** sua palestra cobriu uma área considerável

ground cloth (US) N = **groundsheet**

ground control N (*Aviat, Space*) controle m de solo *or* terra

ground floor N andar m térreo (BRIT), rés do chão m (PT)

grounding ['graundıŋ] N (*Sch*) conhecimentos mpl básicos

groundless ['graundlıs] ADJ infundado

groundnut ['graundnʌt] N amendoim m

ground rent (BRIT) N foro

groundsheet ['graundʃi:t] (BRIT) N capa impermeável

grounds keeper (US) N (*Sport*) zelador m de um campo esportivo

groundsman ['graundzmən] (*irreg: like* **man**) N (*Sport*) zelador m de um campo esportivo

ground staff N pessoal m de terra

ground swell N (*of opinion*) onda

ground-to-ground missile N míssil m terra-terra

groundwork ['graundwə:k] N base f, preparação f

group [gru:p] N grupo; (*also*: **pop group**) conjunto ▶ VT (*also*: **group together**) agrupar ▶ vi (*also*: **group together**) agrupar-se

grouse [graus] N INV (*bird*) tetraz m, galo-silvestre m ▶ vi (*complain*) queixar-se, resmungar

grove [grəuv] N arvoredo

grovel ['grɔvl] vi (*fig*) humilhar-se; **to ~ (before)** abaixar-se (diante de)

grow [grəu] (PT **grew**, PP **grown**) vi crescer; (*increase*) aumentar; (*develop*): **to ~ (out of/ from)** originar-se (de) ▶ VT plantar, cultivar; (*beard*) deixar crescer; **to ~ rich/weak** enriquecer(-se)/enfraquecer-se
  ▶ **grow apart** vi (*fig*) afastar-se (um do outro)
  ▶ **grow away from** VT FUS (*fig*) afastar-se de
  ▶ **grow on** VT FUS: **that painting is ~ing on me** estou gostando cada vez mais daquele quadro
  ▶ **grow out of** VT FUS (*clothes*) ficar muito grande para; (*habit*) superar com *or* perder o tempo
  ▶ **grow up** vi crescer, fazer-se homem/mulher

grower ['grəuər] N cultivador(a) m/f, produtor(a) m/f

growing ['grəuıŋ] ADJ crescente; **~ pains** (*Med*) dores fpl do crescimento; (*fig*) dificuldades fpl iniciais

growl [graul] vi rosnar

grown [grəun] PP *of* **grow** ▶ ADJ crescido, adulto

grown-up N adulto(-a), pessoa mais velha

growth [grəuθ] N crescimento; (*what has grown*) crescimento; (*increase*) aumento; (*Med*) abcesso, tumor m

growth rate N taxa de crescimento

GRSM (BRIT) N ABBR = **Graduate of the Royal Schools of Music**

grub [grʌb] N larva, lagarta; (*inf: food*) comida, rango (BR)

grubby ['grʌbı] ADJ encardido

grudge [grʌdʒ] N motivo de rancor ▶ VT: **to ~ sb sth** dar algo a alguém de má vontade, invejar algo a alguém; **to bear sb a ~ for sth** guardar rancor de alguém por algo; **he ~s (giving) the money** ele dá dinheiro de má vontade

grudgingly ['grʌdʒıŋlı] ADV de má vontade

gruelling, (US) **grueling** ['gruəlıŋ] ADJ duro, árduo

gruesome ['gru:səm] ADJ horrível

gruff [grʌf] ADJ (*voice*) rouco; (*manner*) brusco

grumble ['grʌmbl] vi resmungar, bufar

grumpy ['grʌmpı] ADJ rabugento

grunt [grʌnt] vi grunhir ▶ N grunhido

G-string N (*garment*) tapa-sexo m

GSUSA N ABBR = **Girl Scouts of the United States of America**

GU (US) ABBR (*Post*) = **Guam**

guarantee [gærən'ti:] N garantia ▶ VT garantir

guarantor [gærən'tɔ:r] N fiador(a) m/f

guard [gɑ:d] N guarda; (*one person*) guarda m; (BRIT *Rail*) guarda-freio; (*on machine*) dispositivo de segurança; (*also*: **fireguard**) guarda-fogo ▶ VT guardar; (*protect*): **to ~ (against)** proteger (contra); (*prisoner*) vigiar; **to be on one's ~** estar prevenido
  ▶ **guard against** VT FUS prevenir-se contra;

to ~ against doing sth guardar-se de fazer algo

guard dog N cão m de guarda

guarded ['gɑːdɪd] ADJ (*statement*) cauteloso

guardian ['gɑːdɪən] N protetor(a) m/f; (*of minor*) tutor(a) m/f

guard's van (BRIT) N (*Rail*) vagão m de freio

Guatemala [gwɔtə'mɑːlə] N Guatemala

Guernsey ['gɜːnzɪ] N Guernsey f (*no article*)

guerrilla [gə'rɪlə] N guerrilheiro(-a)

guerrilla warfare N guerrilha

guess [gɛs] VT, VI (*estimate*) avaliar, conjeturar; (*correct answer*) adivinhar; (US: *suppose*) achar, supor ▶ N suposição f, conjetura; **to take** or **have a ~** adivinhar, chutar (*inf*); **to keep sb ~ing** não contar a alguém; **my ~ is that ...** meu palpite é que ...; **to ~ right/wrong** acertar/errar

guesstimate ['gɛstɪmɪt] (*inf*) N estimativa aproximada

guesswork ['gɛswəːk] N conjeturas fpl; **I got the answer by ~** obtive a resposta por adivinhação

guest [gɛst] N convidado(-a); (*in hotel*) hóspede m/f; **be my ~** fique à vontade

guest-house N pensão f

guest room N quarto de hóspedes

guffaw [gʌ'fɔː] N gargalhada ▶ VI dar gargalhadas

guidance ['gaɪdəns] N orientação f; (*advice*) conselhos mpl; **under the ~ of** sob a direção de, orientado por; **vocational** or **careers ~** orientação vocacional; **marriage ~** aconselhamento conjugal

guide [gaɪd] N (*person*) guia m/f; (*book, fig*) guia m; (BRIT: *also:* **girl guide**) escoteira ▶ VT guiar; **to be ~d by sb/sth** orientar-se com alguém/por algo

guidebook ['gaɪdbʊk] N guia m

guided missile ['gaɪdɪd-] N (*internally controlled*) míssil m guiado; (*remote-controlled*) míssil m teleguiado

guide dog N cão m de guia

guided tour N visita guiada

guidelines ['gaɪdlaɪnz] NPL (*advice*) orientação f; (*fig*) princípios mpl gerais, diretrizes fpl

guild [gɪld] N grêmio

guildhall ['gɪldhɔːl] (BRIT) N sede f da prefeitura

guile [gaɪl] N astúcia

guileless ['gaɪllɪs] ADJ ingênuo, cândido

guillotine ['gɪlətiːn] N guilhotina

guilt [gɪlt] N culpa

guilty ['gɪltɪ] ADJ culpado; **to plead ~/not ~** declarar-se culpado/inocente

Guinea ['gɪnɪ] N: **Republic of ~** (República da) Guiné f

guinea ['gɪnɪ] (BRIT) N guinéu m (= 21 shillings: *antiga unidade monetária equivalente a £1.05*)

guinea pig ['gɪnɪpɪg] N porquinho-da-Índia m, cobaia; (*fig*) cobaia

guise [gaɪz] N: **in** or **under the ~ of** sob a aparência de, sob o pretexto de

guitar [gɪ'tɑːʳ] N violão m

guitarist [gɪ'tɑːrɪst] N violonista m/f

gulch [gʌltʃ] (US) N ravina

gulf [gʌlf] N golfo; (*abyss: also fig*) abismo; **the (Persian) G~** o Golfo Pérsico

Gulf States NPL: **the ~** (*in Middle East*) os países do Golfo Pérsico

Gulf Stream N: **the ~** a corrente do Golfo

gull [gʌl] N gaivota

gullet ['gʌlɪt] N esôfago

gullibility [gʌlə'bɪlɪtɪ] N credulidade f

gullible ['gʌlɪbl] ADJ crédulo

gully ['gʌlɪ] N barranco

gulp [gʌlp] VI engolir em seco ▶ VT (*also:* **gulp down**) engolir ▶ N (*of drink*) gole m; **at one ~** de um gole só

gum [gʌm] N (*Anat*) gengiva; (*glue*) goma; (*also:* **gum drop**) bala de goma; (*also:* **chewing-gum**) chiclete m (BR), pastilha elástica (PT) ▶ VT colar
▶ **gum up** VT: **to ~ up the works** (*inf*) estragar tudo

gumboil ['gʌmbɔɪl] N abscesso gengival, parúlide f

gumboots ['gʌmbuːts] (BRIT) NPL botas fpl de borracha, galochas fpl

gumption ['gʌmpʃən] N juízo, bom senso

gun [gʌn] N (*gen*) arma (de fogo); (*revolver*) revólver m; (*small*) pistola; (*rifle*) espingarda; (*cannon*) canhão m ▶ VT (*also:* **gun down**) balear; **to stick to one's ~s** (*fig*) não dar o braço a torcer, ser durão (*inf*)

gunboat ['gʌnbəʊt] N canhoneira

gun dog N cão m de caça

gunfire ['gʌnfaɪəʳ] N tiroteio

gunk [gʌŋk] (*inf*) N sujeira (BR), sujidade f (PT)

gunman ['gʌnmən] (*irreg: like* **man**) N pistoleiro

gunner ['gʌnəʳ] N artilheiro

gunpoint ['gʌnpɔɪnt] N: **at ~** sob a ameaça de uma arma

gunpowder ['gʌnpaʊdəʳ] N pólvora

gunrunner ['gʌnrʌnəʳ] N contrabandista m/f de armas

gunrunning ['gʌnrʌnɪŋ] N contrabando de armas

gunshot ['gʌnʃɔt] N tiro (de arma de fogo); **within ~** ao alcance do tiro

gunsmith ['gʌnsmɪθ] N armeiro(-a)

gurgle ['gəːgl] VI (*baby*) balbuciar; (*water*) gorgolejar ▶ N gorgolejo

guru ['guːruː] N guru m

gush [gʌʃ] VI jorrar; (*fig*) alvoroçar-se ▶ N jorro

gusset ['gʌsɪt] N nesga; (*of tights, pants*) entreperna

gust [gʌst] N (*of wind*) rajada

gusto ['gʌstəʊ] N: **with ~** com garra

gut [gʌt] N intestino, tripa; (*Mus etc*) corda de tripa ▶ VT (*poultry, fish*) estripar; (*building*) destruir o interior de; **guts** NPL (*Anat*) entranhas fpl; (*inf: courage*) coragem f, raça (*inf*); **to hate sb's ~s** ter alguém atravessado na garganta, não poder ver alguém nem pintado

gut reaction N reação f instintiva

gutted ['gʌtɪd] (inf) ADJ (disappointed) arrasado

gutter ['gʌtəʳ] N (of roof) calha; (in street) sarjeta

guttural ['gʌtərl] ADJ gutural

guy [gaɪ] N (also: **guyrope**) corda; (inf: man) cara m (BR), tipo (PT)

Guyana [gaɪ'ænə] N Guiana

Guy Fawkes' Night N ver nota

A **Guy Fawkes' Night**, também chamada de bonfire night, é a ocasião em que se comemora o fracasso da conspiração (a Gunpowder Plot) contra James I e o Parlamento, em 5 de novembro de 1605. Um dos conspiradores, Guy Fawkes, foi surpreendido no porão do Parlamento quando estava prestes a atear fogo a explosivos. Todo ano, no dia 5 de novembro, as crianças preparam antecipadamente um boneco de Guy Fawkes e pedem às pessoas que passam na rua a penny for the Guy (uma moedinha para o Guy), com o qual compram fogos de artifício.

guzzle ['gʌzl] VI comer or beber com gula ▶ VT engolir com gula

gym [dʒɪm] N (also: **gymnasium**) ginásio; (also: **gymnastics**) ginástica

gymkhana [dʒɪm'kɑːnə] N gincana

gymnasium [dʒɪm'neɪzɪəm] N ginásio

gymnast ['dʒɪmnæst] N ginasta m/f

gymnastics [dʒɪm'næstɪks] N ginástica

gym shoes NPL tênis mpl

gym slip (BRIT) N uniforme m escolar

gynaecologist, (US) **gynecologist** [gaɪnɪ'kɔlədʒɪst] N ginecologista m/f

gynaecology, (US) **gynecology** [gaɪnə'kɔlədʒɪ] N ginecologia

gypsy ['dʒɪpsɪ] N, CPD = **gipsy**

gyrate [dʒaɪ'reɪt] VI girar

gyroscope ['dʒaɪərəskəup] N giroscópio

Hh

H, h [eɪtʃ] N (*letter*) H, h *m*; **H for Harry** (*BRIT*), **H for How** (*US*) H de Henrique
habeas corpus [ˈheɪbɪəsˈkɔːpəs] N (*Law*) habeas-corpus *m*
haberdashery [ˈhæbəˈdæʃərɪ] (*BRIT*) N armarinho
habit [ˈhæbɪt] N hábito, costume *m*; (*addiction*) vício; (*Rel*) hábito; **to get out of/into the ~ of doing sth** perder/criar o hábito de fazer algo
habitable [ˈhæbɪtəbl] ADJ habitável
habitat [ˈhæbɪtæt] N habitat *m*
habitation [hæbɪˈteɪʃən] N habitação *f*
habitual [həˈbɪtjuəl] ADJ habitual, costumeiro; (*drinker, liar*) inveterado
habitually [həˈbɪtjuəlɪ] ADV habitualmente
hack [hæk] VT (*cut*) cortar; (*chop*) talhar ▶ N corte *m*; (*axe blow*) talho; (*pej: writer*) escrevinhador(a) *m/f*; (*old horse*) metungo
hacker [ˈhækəʳ] N (*Comput*) hacker *m*
hackles [ˈhæklz] NPL: **to make sb's ~ rise** (*fig*) enfurecer alguém
hackney cab [ˈhæknɪ-] N fiacre *m*
hackneyed [ˈhæknɪd] ADJ corriqueiro, batido
had [hæd] PT, PP *of* **have**
haddock [ˈhædək] (*pl* **haddocks** *or* **haddock**) N hadoque *m* (*BR*), eglefim *m* (*PT*)
hadn't [ˈhædnt] = **had not**
haematology, (*US*) **hematology** [ˈhiːməˈtɔlədʒɪ] N hematologia
haemoglobin, (*US*) **hemoglobin** [ˈhiːməˈɡləubɪn] N hemoglobina
haemophilia, (*US*) **hemophilia** [ˈhiːməˈfɪlɪə] N hemofilia
haemorrhage, (*US*) **hemorrhage** [ˈhemərɪdʒ] N hemorragia
haemorrhoids, (*US*) **hemorrhoids** [ˈhemərɔɪdz] NPL hemorróidas *fpl*
hag [hæg] N (*ugly*) bruxa; (*nasty*) megera; (*witch*) bruxa
haggard [ˈhæɡəd] ADJ emaciado, macilento
haggis [ˈhæɡɪs] N *miúdos de carneiro com aveia, cozidos no estômago do animal*
haggle [ˈhæɡl] VI (*bargain*) pechinchar, regatear; **to ~ over** discutir sobre
haggling [ˈhæɡlɪŋ] N regateio
Hague [heɪɡ] N: **The ~** Haia
hail [heɪl] N (*weather*) granizo; (*of objects*) chuva; (*of criticism*) torrente *f* ▶ VT (*greet*)

cumprimentar, saudar; (*call*) chamar ▶ VI chover granizo; (*originate*): **he ~s from Scotland** ele é originário da Escócia
hailstone [ˈheɪlstəun] N pedra de granizo
hailstorm [ˈheɪlstɔːm] N tempestade *f* de granizo
hair [hɛəʳ] N (*of human*) cabelo; (*of animal, on legs*) pelo; (*one hair*) fio de cabelo, pelo; (*head of hair*) cabeleira; **grey ~** cabelo grisalho; **to do one's ~** pentear-se
hairbrush [ˈhɛəbrʌʃ] N escova de cabelo
haircut [ˈhɛəkʌt] N corte *m* de cabelo
hairdo [ˈhɛəduː] N penteado
hairdresser [ˈhɛədrɛsəʳ] N cabeleireiro(-a)
hairdresser's N cabeleireiro
hair dryer N secador *m* de cabelo
-haired [hɛəd] SUFFIX: **fair/long~** de cabelo louro/comprido
hair gel N gel *m* para o cabelo
hairgrip [ˈhɛəɡrɪp] N grampo (*BR*), gancho (*PT*)
hairline [ˈhɛəlaɪn] N contorno do couro cabeludo
hairline fracture N fratura muito fina
hairnet [ˈhɛənɛt] N rede *f* de cabelo
hair oil N óleo para o cabelo
hairpiece [ˈhɛəpiːs] N aplique *m*
hairpin [ˈhɛəpɪn] N grampo (*BR*), gancho (*PT*)
hairpin bend, (*US*) **hairpin curve** N curva fechada
hair-raising [-ˈreɪzɪŋ] ADJ horripilante, de arrepiar os cabelos
hair remover N (creme *m*) depilatório
hair spray N laquê *m* (*BR*), laca (*PT*)
hairstyle [ˈhɛəstaɪl] N penteado
hairy [ˈhɛərɪ] ADJ cabeludo, peludo; (*inf: situation*) perigoso
Haiti [ˈheɪtɪ] N Haiti *m*
haka (*AUST*) [ˈhɑːkə] N haka *m or f*, *canto entoado por jogadores de rúgbi antes de uma partida*
hake [heɪk] (*pl* **hakes** *or* **hake**) N abrótea
halcyon [ˈhælsɪən] ADJ tranquilo
hale [heɪl] ADJ: **~ and hearty** robusto, em ótima forma
half [hɑːf] N (*pl* **halves**) metade *f*; (*Sport: of match*) tempo; (*of ground*) lado ▶ ADJ meio ▶ ADV meio, pela metade; **~-an-hour** meia hora; **~ a pound** meia libra; **two and a ~** dois e meio; **~ a dozen** meia-dúzia; **a week and a ~** uma semana e meia; **~ (of it)** a

metade; ~ **(of)** a metade de; ~ **the amount of** a metade de; **to cut sth in** ~ cortar algo ao meio; ~ **past three** três e meia; ~ **asleep/empty/closed** meio adormecido/vazio/fechado; **to go halves (with sb)** rachar as despesas (com alguém)

half-back N (Sport) meio-de-campo

half-baked (inf) ADJ (idea, scheme) mal planejado

half-breed N mestiço(-a)

half-brother N meio-irmão m

half-caste N mestiço(-a)

half-hearted ADJ irresoluto, indiferente

half-hour N meia hora

half-mast N: **at** ~ (flag) a meio-pau

halfpenny ['heɪpnɪ] N meio pêni m

half-price ADJ pela metade do preço ▶ ADV (also: **at half-price**) pela metade do preço

half term (BRIT) N (Sch) dias de folga no meio do semestre

half-time N meio tempo

halfway ['hɑːfweɪ] ADV a meio caminho; (in time) no meio; **to meet sb** ~ (fig) chegar a um meio-termo com alguém

half-yearly ADV semestralmente ▶ ADJ semestral

halibut ['hælɪbət] N INV hipoglosso

halitosis [hælɪ'təʊsɪs] N halitose f, mau hálito

hall [hɔːl] N (for concerts) sala; (entrance way) hall m, entrada; (corridor) corredor m; **town** ~ prefeitura (BR), câmara municipal (PT)

hallmark ['hɔːlmɑːk] N (also fig) marca

hallo [hə'ləʊ] EXCL = **hello**

hall of residence (pl **halls of residence**) (BRIT) N residência universitária

Hallowe'en ['hæləʊ'iːn] N Dia m das Bruxas (31 de outubro)

Segundo a tradição, **Hallowe'en** é a noite dos fantasmas e dos bruxos. Na Escócia e nos Estados Unidos, sobretudo (bem menos na Inglaterra), as crianças, para festejar o **Hallowe'en**, se fantasiam e batem de porta em porta pedindo prendas (chocolates, maçãs etc).

hallucination [həluːsɪ'neɪʃən] N alucinação f

hallway ['hɔːlweɪ] N hall m, entrada; (corridor) corredor m

halo ['heɪləʊ] N (of saint etc) auréola; (of sun) halo

halt [hɔːlt] N (stop) parada (BR), paragem f (PT); (Rail) pequena parada; (Mil) alto ▶ VI parar; (Mil) fazer alto ▶ VT deter; (process) interromper; **to call a** ~ **to sth** (fig) pôr um fim a algo

halter ['hɔːltəʳ] N (for horse) cabresto

halter-neck ['hɔːltənɛk] ADJ (dress) frente-única inv

halve [hɑːv] VT (divide) dividir ao meio; (reduce by half) reduzir à metade

halves [hɑːvz] NPL of **half**

ham [hæm] N presunto, fiambre m (PT); (inf: actor, actress) canastrão(-trona) m/f;

(also: **radio ham**) radioamador(a) m/f

hamburger ['hæmbəːgəʳ] N hambúrguer m

ham-fisted [-'fɪstɪd] (BRIT) ADJ desajeitado

ham-handed [-'hændɪd] (US) ADJ desajeitado

hamlet ['hæmlɪt] N aldeola, lugarejo

hammer ['hæməʳ] N martelo ▶ VT martelar; (fig) dar uma surra em ▶ VI (on door) bater insistentemente; **to** ~ **a point home to sb** fincar uma ideia na mente de alguém
▶ **hammer out** VT (metal) malhar; (fig: solution) elaborar

hammock ['hæmək] N rede f

hamper ['hæmpəʳ] VT dificultar, atrapalhar
▶ N cesto

hamster ['hæmstəʳ] N hamster m

hamstring ['hæmstrɪŋ] N (Anat) tendão m do jarrete

hand [hænd] N mão f; (of clock) ponteiro; (writing) letra; (applause) aplauso; (of cards) cartas fpl; (worker) trabalhador m; (measurement) palmo ▶ VT (give) dar, passar; (deliver) entregar; **to give** or **lend sb a** ~ dar uma mãozinha a alguém, dar uma ajuda a alguém; **at** ~ à mão, disponível; **in** ~ livre; (situation) sob controle; (Comm) em caixa, à disposição; **to be on** ~ (person) estar disponível; (emergency services) estar num estado de prontidão; **to** ~ (information) à mão; **to force sb's** ~ forçar alguém a agir; **to have a free** ~ ter carta branca; **to have sth in one's** ~ ter algo na mão; **on the one** ~ ..., **on the other** ~ ... por um lado ..., por outro (lado) ...
▶ **hand down** VT passar; (tradition, heirloom) transmitir; (US: sentence, verdict) proferir
▶ **hand in** VT entregar
▶ **hand out** VT distribuir
▶ **hand over** VT (deliver) entregar; (surrender) ceder; (powers etc) transmitir
▶ **hand round** (BRIT) VT (information) fazer circular; (chocolates) oferecer

handbag ['hændbæg] N bolsa

handball ['hændbɔːl] N handebol m

hand basin ['hændbeɪsn] N pia (BR), lavatório (PT)

handbook ['hændbʊk] N manual m

handbrake ['hændbreɪk] N freio (BR) or travão m (PT) de mão

h & c (BRIT) ABBR = **hot and cold (water)**

hand cream N creme m para as mãos

handcuffs ['hændkʌfs] NPL algemas fpl

handful ['hændfʊl] N punhado; (of people) grupo

handicap ['hændɪkæp] N (Med) incapacidade f; (disadvantage) desvantagem f; (Sport) handicap m ▶ VT prejudicar; **mentally/physically ~ped** deficiente mental/físico

handicraft ['hændɪkrɑːft] N artesanato, trabalho manual

handiwork ['hændɪwəːk] N obra; **this looks like his** ~ (pej) isso parece coisa dele

handkerchief ['hæŋkətʃɪf] N lenço

handle ['hændl] N (*of door etc*) maçaneta; (*of bag etc*) alça; (*of cup etc*) asa; (*of knife etc*) cabo; (*for winding*) manivela; (*inf: name*) título ▶ VT manusear; (*deal with*) tratar de; (*treat: people*) lidar com; **"~ with care"** "cuidado – frágil"; **to fly off the ~** perder as estribeiras

handlebar ['hɑːndlbɑːʳ] N, **handlebars** ['hɑːndlbɑːz] NPL guidom *m* (BR), guidão *m* (PT)

handling charges ['hændlɪŋ-] NPL taxa de manuseio; (*Banking*) comissão *f*

hand-luggage N bagagem *f* de mão

handmade ['hændmeɪd] ADJ feito a mão

handout ['hændaut] N (*money, food*) doação *f*, esmola; (*leaflet*) folheto; (*at lecture*) apostila

hand-picked [-'pɪkt] ADJ (*fruit*) colhido à mão; (*staff*) escolhido a dedo

handrail ['hændreɪl] N (*on staircase*) corrimão *m*

hands-free kit ['hændzfriː-] N viva-voz *m*

handshake ['hændʃeɪk] N aperto de mão; (*Comput*) handshake *m*

handsome ['hænsəm] ADJ bonito; (*woman*) vistoso; (*gift*) generoso; (*building*) imponente, elegante; (*profit*) considerável

handstand ['hændstænd] N: **to do a ~** plantar bananeira

hand-to-mouth ADJ (*existence*) ao deus-dará

handwriting ['hændraɪtɪŋ] N letra, caligrafia

handwritten ['hændrɪtn] ADJ escrito à mão, manuscrito

handy ['hændɪ] ADJ (*close at hand*) à mão; (*useful*) útil; (*skilful*) habilidoso, hábil; **to come in ~** ser útil

handyman ['hændɪmæn] (*irreg: like* **man**) N faz-tudo *m*; (*in hotel etc*) biscateiro

hang [hæŋ] (*pt, pp* **hung**) VT pendurar; (*on wall etc*) prender; (*head*) baixar; (*criminal: pt, pp* **hanged**) enforcar ▶ VI estar pendurado; (*hair, drapery*) cair ▶ N (*inf*): **to get the ~ of (doing) sth** pegar o jeito de (fazer) algo
▶ **hang about** VI vadiar, vagabundear; **~ about!** (*inf*) 'pera aí!
▶ **hang around** VI = **hang about**
▶ **hang back** VI (*hesitate*): **to ~ back from (doing) sth** vacilar em (fazer) algo
▶ **hang on** VI (*wait*) esperar ▶ VT FUS (*depend on*) depender de; **to ~ on to** (*keep hold of*) não soltar, segurar; (*keep*) ficar com
▶ **hang out** VT (*washing*) estender ▶ VI (*be visible*) aparecer; (*inf: spend time*) fazer ponto
▶ **hang together** VI (*argument etc*) ser coerente
▶ **hang up** VT (*coat*) pendurar ▶ VI (*Tel*) desligar; **to ~ up on sb** bater o telefone na cara de alguém

hangar ['hæŋəʳ] N hangar *m*

hangdog ['hæŋdɔg] ADJ (*look, expression*) envergonhado

hanger ['hæŋəʳ] N cabide *m*

hanger-on N parasita *m/f*, filão(-lona) *m/f*

hang-glider ['hæŋglaɪdəʳ] N asa-delta

hang-gliding N voo livre

hanging ['hæŋɪŋ] N enforcamento

hangman ['hæŋmən] (*irreg: like* **man**) N carrasco

hangover ['hæŋəuvəʳ] N (*after drinking*) ressaca; **to have a ~** estar de ressaca

hang-up N grilo

hank [hæŋk] N meada

hanker ['hæŋkəʳ] VI: **to ~ after** (*miss*) sentir saudade de; (*long for*) ansiar por

hankie ['hæŋkɪ] N ABBR = **handkerchief**

hanky ['hæŋkɪ] N ABBR = **handkerchief**

Hants (BRIT) ABBR = **Hampshire**

haphazard [hæp'hæzəd] ADJ (*random*) fortuito; (*disorganized*) desorganizado

hapless ['hæplɪs] ADJ desafortunado

happen ['hæpən] VI acontecer; **what's ~ing?** o que é que está acontecendo?; **she ~ed to be in London** aconteceu que estava em Londres; **if anything ~ed to him** se lhe acontecesse alguma coisa; **as it ~s ...** acontece que ...
▶ **happen on, happen upon** VT FUS dar com

happening ['hæpənɪŋ] N acontecimento, ocorrência

happily ['hæpɪlɪ] ADV (*luckily*) felizmente; (*cheerfully*) alegremente

happiness ['hæpɪnɪs] N felicidade *f*; (*joy*) alegria

happy ['hæpɪ] ADJ feliz; (*cheerful*) contente; **to be ~ (with)** estar contente (com); **to be ~** ser feliz; **to be ~ to do** (*willing*) estar disposto a fazer; **yes, I'd be ~ to** sim, com muito prazer; **~ birthday!** feliz aniversário; (*said to somebody*) parabéns!; **~ Christmas/New Year** feliz Natal/Ano Novo

happy-go-lucky ADJ despreocupado

harangue [hə'ræŋ] VT arengar

harass ['hærəs] VT (*bother*) importunar; (*pursue*) acossar

harassed ['hærəst] ADJ chateado

harassment ['hærəsmənt] N perseguição *f*; (*worry*) preocupação *f*

harbour, (US) **harbor** ['hɑːbəʳ] N porto ▶ VT (*hope etc*) abrigar; (*hide*) esconder; **to ~ a grudge against sb** guardar rancor a alguém

harbour dues, (US) **harbor dues** NPL direitos *mpl* portuários

harbour master, (US) **harbor master** N capitão *m* do porto

hard [hɑːd] ADJ duro; (*difficult*) difícil; (*work*) árduo; (*person*) severo, cruel; (*facts*) verdadeiro ▶ ADV (*work*) muito, diligentemente; (*think, try*) seriamente; **to look ~ at** olhar firme *or* fixamente para; **~ luck!** azar!; **no ~ feelings!** sem ressentimentos!; **to be ~ of hearing** ser surdo; **to be ~ done by** ser tratado injustamente; **to be ~ on sb** ser rigoroso com alguém; **I find it ~ to believe that ...** acho difícil acreditar que ...

hard-and-fast ADJ rígido

hardback ['hɑːdbæk] N livro de capa dura

hardboard ['hɑːdbɔːd] N madeira compensada

hard-boiled egg [-'bɔɪld-] N ovo cozido

hard cash N dinheiro vivo or em espécie

hard copy N (Comput) cópia impressa

hard-core ADJ (pornography) pesado; (supporters) ferrenho

hard court N (Tennis) quadra de cimento

hard disk N (Comput) disco rígido

hard drive N (Comput) disco rígido

harden ['hɑːdən] VT endurecer; (steel) temperar; (fig) tornar insensível ▶ VI endurecer-se

hardened ['hɑːdnd] ADJ (criminal, drinker) inveterado; **to be ~ to sth** ser insensível a algo

hardening ['hɑːdnɪŋ] N endurecimento

hard-headed [-'hɛdɪd] ADJ prático

hard-hearted ADJ empedernido, insensível

hard labour N trabalhos mpl forçados

hardliner [hɑːd'laɪnəʳ] N intransigente m/f

hardly ['hɑːdlɪ] ADV (scarcely) apenas; (no sooner) mal; **that can ~ be true** dificilmente pode ser verdade; **~ ever** quase nunca; **I can ~ believe it** mal posso acreditar nisso

hardness ['hɑːdnɪs] N dureza

hard-pressed ['hɑːd'prɛst] ADJ massacrado; **be ~ to do** dificilmente poder fazer

hard sell N venda agressiva

hardship ['hɑːdʃɪp] N (difficulty) privação f

hard shoulder (BRIT) N (Aut) acostamento (BR), berma (PT)

hard up (inf) ADJ duro (BR), liso (PT)

hardware ['hɑːdwɛəʳ] N ferragens fpl; (Comput) hardware m

hardware shop N loja de ferragens

hard-wearing [-'wɛərɪŋ] ADJ resistente

hard-working ADJ trabalhador(a); (student) aplicado

hardy ['hɑːdɪ] ADJ forte; (plant) resistente

hare [hɛəʳ] N lebre f

hare-brained [-breɪnd] ADJ maluco, absurdo

harelip ['hɛəlɪp] N (Med) lábio leporino

harem [hɑː'riːm] N harém m

hark back [hɑːk-] VI: **to ~ to** (reminisce) recordar; (be reminiscent of) lembrar

harm [hɑːm] N mal m; (damage) dano ▶ VT (person) fazer mal a, prejudicar; (thing) danificar; **to mean no ~** ter boas intenções; **there's no ~ in trying** não faz mal tentar; **out of ~'s way** a salvo

harmful ['hɑːmful] ADJ prejudicial, nocivo; (plant, weed) daninho

harmless ['hɑːmlɪs] ADJ inofensivo; (activity) inofensivo

harmonic [hɑː'mɔnɪk] ADJ harmônico

harmonica [hɑː'mɔnɪkə] N gaita de boca, harmônica

harmonics [hɑː'mɔnɪks] NPL harmônicos mpl

harmonious [hɑː'məunɪəs] ADJ harmonioso

harmonium [hɑː'məunɪəm] N harmônio

harmonize [hɑː'mənaɪz] VT, VI harmonizar

harmony ['hɑːmənɪ] N harmonia

harness ['hɑːnɪs] N (for horse) arreios mpl; (for child) correia; (safety harness) correia de

segurança ▶ VT (horse) arrear, pôr arreios em; (resources) aproveitar

harp [hɑːp] N harpa ▶ VI: **to ~ on about** bater sempre na mesma tecla sobre

harpist ['hɑːpɪst] N harpista m/f

harpoon [hɑː'puːn] N arpão m ▶ VT arpoar

harpsichord ['hɑːpsɪkɔːd] N cravo, clavecino

harrow ['hærəu] N (Agr) grade f, rastelo

harrowing ['hærəuɪŋ] ADJ doloroso, pungente

harry ['hærɪ] VT (Mil, fig) assolar

harsh [hɑːʃ] ADJ (life) duro; (judge, criticism) severo; (rough: surface, taste) áspero; (: sound) desarmonioso

harshly ['hɑːʃlɪ] ADV severamente

harshness ['hɑːʃnɪs] N dureza, severidade f; (roughness) aspereza

harvest ['hɑːvɪst] N colheita; (of grapes) vindima ▶ VT, VI colher

harvester ['hɑːvɪstəʳ] N (machine) segadora; (also: **combine harvester**) ceifeira-debulhadora; (person) segador(a) m/f

has [hæz] VB see **have**

has-been (inf) N (person): **he/she's a ~** ele/ela já era

hash [hæʃ] N (Culin) picadinho; (fig: mess) confusão f; (symbol) sustenido ▶ N ABBR (inf) = **hashish**

hashish ['hæʃɪʃ] N haxixe m

hashtag ['hæʃtæg] N (on Twitter) hashtag f

hasn't ['hæznt] = **has not**

hassle ['hæsl] (inf) N (fuss, problems) complicação f ▶ VT molestar, chatear

haste [heɪst] N pressa; **in ~** às pressas

hasten ['heɪsn] VT acelerar ▶ VI: **to ~ to do sth** apressar-se em fazer algo

hastily ['heɪstɪlɪ] ADV depressa

hasty ['heɪstɪ] ADJ apressado; (rash) precipitado

hat [hæt] N chapéu m

hatbox ['hætbɔks] N chapeleira

hatch [hætʃ] N (Naut: also: **hatchway**) escotilha; (also: **service hatch**) comunicação f entre a cozinha e a sala de jantar ▶ VI sair do ovo, chocar ▶ VT chocar; (plot) tramar, arquitetar

hatchback ['hætʃbæk] N (Aut) camionete f, hatch m

hatchet ['hætʃɪt] N machadinha

hate [heɪt] VT odiar, detestar ▶ N ódio; **to ~ to do** or **doing** odiar or detestar fazer; **I ~ to trouble you, but …** desculpe incomodá-lo, mas …

hateful ['heɪtful] ADJ odioso

hatred ['heɪtrɪd] N ódio

hat trick (BRIT) N (Sport, fig) três vitórias (or gols etc) consecutivas

haughty ['hɔːtɪ] ADJ soberbo, arrogante

haul [hɔːl] VT puxar; (by lorry) carregar, fretar; (Naut) levar à orça ▶ N (of fish) redada; (of stolen goods etc) pilhagem f, presa

haulage ['hɔːlɪdʒ] N transporte m (rodoviário); (costs) gasto com transporte

haulage contractor (BRIT) N (firm)
transportadora; (person) transportador(a) m/f
hauler ['hɔːləʳ] (US) N = **haulier**
haulier ['hɔːljəʳ] (BRIT) N (firm) transportadora;
(person) transportador(a) m/f
haunch [hɔːntʃ] N anca, quadril m; (of meat)
quarto traseiro
haunt [hɔːnt] VT (subj: ghost) assombrar;
(: problem, memory) perseguir; (frequent)
frequentar; (obsess) obcecar ▶ N reduto;
(haunted house) casa mal-assombrada
haunted ['hɔːntɪd] ADJ (castle etc) mal-
assombrado
haunting ['hɔːntɪŋ] ADJ (sight, music) obcecante
Havana [hə'vænə] N Havana

(KEYWORD)

have [hæv] (pt, pp **had**) AUX VB **1** (gen) ter; **to
have arrived/gone/eaten/slept** ter
chegado/ido/comido/dormido; **he has been
kind/promoted** ele foi bondoso/
promovido; **having finished** or **when he
had finished, he left** quando ele terminou,
foi embora
2 (in tag questions): **you've done it, haven't
you?** você fez isto, não foi?; **he hasn't done
it, has he?** ele não fez isto, fez?
3 (in short questions and answers): **you've made
a mistake — no I haven't/so I have** você fez
um erro — não, eu não fiz/sim, eu fiz; **I've
been there before, have you?** eu já estive
lá, e você?
▶ MODAL AUX VB (be obliged): **to have (got) to
do sth** ter que fazer algo; **I haven't got** or
I don't have to wear glasses eu não preciso
usar óculos; **this has to be a mistake** isto
tem que ser um erro
▶ VT **1** (possess) ter; **he has (got) blue eyes/
dark hair** ele tem olhos azuis/cabelo escuro
2 (referring to meals etc): **to have breakfast**
tomar café (BR), tomar o pequeno almoço
(PT); **to have lunch/dinner** almoçar/jantar;
to have a drink/a cigarette tomar um
drinque/fumar um cigarro
3 (receive, obtain etc): **may I have your
address?** pode me dar seu endereço?; **you
can have it for 5 pounds** você pode levá-lo
por 5 libras; **I must have it by tomorrow**
preciso ter isto até amanhã; **to have a baby**
dar à luz (BR), ter um nenê or bebê (PT)
4 (maintain, allow): **he will have it that he is
right** ele vai insistir que ele está certo;
I won't have it/this nonsense! não vou
aguentar isso/este absurdo!; **we can't have
that** não podemos permitir isto
5: **to have sth done** mandar fazer algo; **to
have one's hair cut** ir cortar o cabelo; **to
have sb do sth** mandar alguém fazer algo;
he soon had them all laughing/working
logo ele tinha feito com que todos rissem/
trabalhassem
6 (experience, suffer): **to have a cold/flu** estar
resfriado (BR) or constipado (PT)/com gripe;

she had her bag stolen/her arm broken
ela teve sua bolsa roubada/ela quebrou o
braço; **to have an operation** fazer uma
operação
7 (+ n: take, hold etc): **to have a swim/walk/
bath/rest** ir nadar/passear/tomar um
banho/descansar; **let's have a look** vamos
dar uma olhada; **to have a party** fazer uma
festa; **to have a meeting** ter um encontro;
let me have a try deixe-me tentar
8 (inf: dupe): **he's been had** ele comprou gato
por lebre
▶ **have out** VT: **to have it out with sb** (settle
a problem) explicar-se com alguém

haven ['heɪvn] N porto; (fig) abrigo, refúgio
haven't ['hævnt] = **have not**
haversack ['hævəsæk] N mochila
havoc ['hævək] N destruição f; **to play ~ with**
(fig) estragar
Hawaii [hə'waɪiː] N Havaí m
Hawaiian [hə'waɪjən] ADJ, N havaiano(-a)
hawk [hɔːk] N falcão m ▶ VT (goods for sale)
mascatear
hawker ['hɔːkəʳ] N camelô m, mascate m
hawthorn ['hɔːθɔːn] N pilriteiro, estripeiro
hay [heɪ] N feno
hay fever N febre f do feno
haystack ['heɪstæk] N palheiro
haywire ['heɪwaɪəʳ] (inf) ADJ: **to go ~** (person)
ficar maluco; (plan) desorganizar-se,
degringolar
hazard ['hæzəd] N (danger) perigo, risco;
(chance) acaso ▶ VT aventurar, arriscar;
to be a health/fire ~ ser um risco para a
saúde/de incêndio; **to ~ a guess** arriscar
um palpite
hazardous ['hæzədəs] ADJ (dangerous)
perigoso; (risky) arriscado
hazard pay (US) N adicional m por
insalubridade
hazard warning lights NPL (Aut) pisca-
alerta m
haze [heɪz] N névoa
hazel [heɪzl] N (tree) aveleira ▶ ADJ (eyes)
castanho-claro inv
hazelnut ['heɪzlnʌt] N avelã f
hazy ['heɪzɪ] ADJ nublado; (idea) confuso
H-bomb N bomba de hidrogênio
HE ABBR = **high explosive**; (Rel, Diplomacy)
= **His/Her Excellency**
he [hiː] PRON ele; **he who ...** quem ..., aquele
que ...; **he-bear** etc n urso macho etc
head [hɛd] N cabeça; (of table) cabeceira;
(of queue) frente f; (of organization) chefe m/f;
(of school) diretor(a) m/f ▶ VT (list) encabeçar;
(group) liderar; **~s or tails** cara ou coroa;
~ first de cabeça; **~ over heels** de pernas
para o ar; **~ over heels in love**
apaixonadíssimo; **to ~ the ball** cabecear a
bola; **£10 a** or **per ~** £10 por pessoa or cabeça;
to sit at the ~ of the table sentar-se à
cabeceira da mesa; **to have a ~ for business**

ter tino para negócios; **to have no ~ for heights** não suportar alturas; **to come to a ~** (*fig: situation etc*) chegar a um ponto crítico; **on your ~ be it** você que arque com as consequências

▶ **head for** VT FUS dirigir-se a; (*disaster*) estar procurando

▶ **head off** VT (*danger, threat*) desviar

headache ['hɛdeɪk] N dor f de cabeça; **to have a ~** estar com dor de cabeça

head cold N resfriado (BR), constipação f (PT)

headdress ['hɛddrɛs] N (*of Indian etc*) cocar m; (*of bride*) grinalda

header ['hɛdəʳ] N (BRIT inf: Football) cabeçada; (*on page*) cabeçalho

headhunter ['hɛdhʌntəʳ] N caçador m de cabeças

heading ['hɛdɪŋ] N título, cabeçalho; (*subject title*) rubrica

headlamp ['hɛdlæmp] (BRIT) N = **headlight**

headland ['hɛdlənd] N promontório

headlight ['hɛdlaɪt] N farol m

headline ['hɛdlaɪn] N manchete f

headlong ['hɛdlɔŋ] ADV (*fall*) de cabeça; (*rush*) precipitadamente

headmaster [hɛd'mɑ:stəʳ] N diretor m (de escola)

headmistress [hɛd'mɪstrɪs] N diretora f (de escola)

head office N matriz f

head-on ADJ (*collision*) de frente; (*confrontation*) direto

headphones ['hɛdfəunz] NPL fones mpl de ouvido

headquarters [hɛd'kwɔ:təz] NPL (*of business etc*) sede f; (*Mil*) quartel m general

headrest ['hɛdrɛst] N apoio para a cabeça

headroom ['hɛdrum] N (*in car*) espaço (para a cabeça); (*under bridge*) vão m livre

headscarf ['hɛdskɑ:f] (*irreg: like* **scarf**) N lenço de cabeça

headset ['hɛdsɛt] N fones mpl de ouvido

headstone ['hɛdstəun] N lápide f de ponta cabeça

headstrong ['hɛdstrɔŋ] ADJ voluntarioso, teimoso

head waiter N maitre m (BR), chefe m de mesa (PT)

headway ['hɛdweɪ] N progresso; **to make ~** avançar

headwind ['hɛdwɪnd] N vento contrário

heady ['hɛdɪ] ADJ (*exciting*) emocionante; (*intoxicating*) estonteante

heal [hi:l] VT curar ▶ VI cicatrizar

health [hɛlθ] N saúde f; **good ~!** saúde!; **Department of H~** (US) ≈ Ministério da Saúde

health care N assistência médica

health centre (BRIT) N posto de saúde

health food N, **health foods** NPL alimentos mpl naturais

health food shop N loja de comida natural

health hazard N risco para a saúde

Health Service (BRIT) N: **the ~** o Serviço Nacional da Saúde, ≈ a Previdência Social

healthy ['hɛlθɪ] ADJ (*person*) saudável; (*air, walk*) sadio; (*economy*) próspero, forte

heap [hi:p] N pilha, montão m ▶ VT amontoar, empilhar; (*plate*) encher; **~s (of)** (*inf: lots*) um monte (de); **to ~ favours/praise/gifts** *etc* **on sb** cobrir *or* cumular alguém de favores/elogios/presentes *etc*

hear [hɪəʳ] (*pt, pp* **heard**) VT ouvir; (*listen to*) escutar; (*news*) saber; (*lecture*) assistir a ▶ VI ouvir; **to ~ about** ouvir falar de; **when did you ~ about this?** quando você soube disso?; **to ~ from sb** ter notícias de alguém; **I've never ~d of the book** eu nunca ouvi falar no livro

▶ **hear out** VT ouvir sem interromper

heard [hə:d] PT, PP *of* **hear**

hearing ['hɪərɪŋ] N (*sense*) audição f; (*Law*) audiência; **to give sb a ~** (BRIT) ouvir alguém

hearing aid N aparelho para a surdez

hearsay ['hɪəseɪ] N boato, ouvir-dizer m; **by ~** por ouvir dizer

hearse [hə:s] N carro fúnebre

heart [hɑ:t] N coração m; (*of problem, city*) centro; **hearts** NPL (*Cards*) copas fpl; **to lose/take ~** perder o ânimo/criar coragem; **at ~** no fundo; **by ~** (*learn, know*) de cor; **to set one's ~ on sth/on doing sth** decidir-se por algo/a fazer algo; **the ~ of the matter** a essência da questão

heart attack N ataque m de coração

heartbeat ['hɑ:tbi:t] N batida do coração

heartbreak ['hɑ:tbreɪk] N desgosto, dor f

heartbreaking ['hɑ:tbreɪkɪŋ] ADJ desolador(a)

heartbroken ['hɑ:tbrəukən] ADJ: **to be ~** estar inconsolável

heartburn ['hɑ:tbə:n] N azia

-hearted ['hɑ:tɪd] SUFFIX: **kind~** bondoso

heartening ['hɑ:tnɪŋ] ADJ animador(a)

heart failure N parada cardíaca

heartfelt ['hɑ:tfɛlt] ADJ (*cordial*) cordial; (*deeply felt*) sincero

hearth [hɑ:θ] N lar m; (*fireplace*) lareira

heartily ['hɑ:tɪlɪ] ADV sinceramente, cordialmente; (*laugh*) a gargalhadas, com vontade; (*eat*) apetitosamente; **I ~ agree** concordo completamente; **to be ~ sick of** (BRIT) estar farto de

heartland ['hɑ:tlænd] N coração m (do país)

heartless ['hɑ:tlɪs] ADJ cruel, sem coração

heartthrob ['hɑ:tθrɔb] N gatão m

heart-to-heart ADJ (*conversation*) franco, sincero ▶ N conversa franca

heart transplant N transplante m de coração

heartwarming ['hɑ:twɔ:mɪŋ] ADJ emocionante

hearty ['hɑ:tɪ] ADJ (*person*) energético; (*laugh*) animado; (*appetite*) bom/boa; (*welcome*) sincero; (*dislike*) absoluto

heat [hi:t] N calor m; (*excitement*) ardor m; (*Sport: also:* **qualifying heat**) (prova)

eliminatória; (Zool): **in ~, on ~** (BRIT) no cio
▶ VT esquentar; (room, house) aquecer; (fig)
acalorar
▶ **heat up** VI aquecer-se, esquentar ▶ VT
esquentar
heated ['hi:tɪd] ADJ aquecido; (fig) acalorado
heater ['hi:tə^r] N aquecedor m
heath [hi:θ] (BRIT) N charneca
heathen ['hi:ðn] ADJ, N pagão/pagã m/f
heather ['hɛðə^r] N urze f
heating ['hi:tɪŋ] N aquecimento, calefação f
heat-resistant ADJ resistente ao calor
heatstroke ['hi:tstrəuk] N insolação f
heat wave N onda de calor
heave [hi:v] VT (pull) puxar; (push) empurrar
(com esforço); (lift) levantar (com esforço)
▶ VI (water) agitar-se; (retch) ter ânsias de
vômito ▶ N puxão m; empurrão m; **to ~ a
sigh** soltar um suspiro
▶ **heave to** VI (Naut) capear
heaven ['hɛvn] N céu m, paraíso; **~ forbid!**
Deus me livre!; **thank ~!** graças a Deus!;
for ~'s sake! pelo amor de Deus!
heavenly ['hɛvnlɪ] ADJ celestial; (Rel) divino
heavily ['hɛvɪlɪ] ADV pesadamente; (drink,
smoke) excessivamente; (sleep, depend)
profundamente
heavy ['hɛvɪ] ADJ pesado; (work) duro;
(responsibility) grande; (sea) violento; (rain,
meal) forte; (drinker, smoker) inveterado; **it's ~
going** é difícil
heavy cream (US) N creme m de leite
heavy-duty ADJ de serviço pesado
heavy goods vehicle (BRIT) N caminhão m de
carga pesada
heavy-handed [-'hændɪd] ADJ (fig)
desajeitado, sem tato
heavy-set ['hɛvɪ'sɛt] ADJ (esp US) parrudo
heavyweight ['hɛvɪweɪt] N (Sport) peso-
pesado
Hebrew ['hi:bru:] ADJ hebreu/hebreia; (Ling)
hebraico ▶ N (Ling) hebraico
Hebrides ['hɛbrɪdi:z] NPL: **the ~** as (ilhas)
Hébridas
heckle ['hɛkl] VT apartear
heckler ['hɛklə^r] N pessoa que aparteia
hectare ['hɛktɛə^r] (BRIT) N hectare m
hectic ['hɛktɪk] ADJ agitado
hector ['hɛktə^r] VT importunar, implicar
com
he'd [hi:d] = **he would; he had**
hedge [hɛdʒ] N cerca viva, sebe f ▶ VI dar
evasivas ▶ VT: **to ~ one's bets** (fig)
resguardar-se; **as a ~ against inflation**
para precaver-se da inflação
▶ **hedge in** VT cercar com uma sebe
hedgehog ['hɛdʒhɔg] N ouriço
hedgerow ['hɛdʒrəu] N cercas fpl vivas,
sebes fpl
hedonism ['hi:dənɪzm] N hedonismo
heed [hi:d] VT (also: **take heed of**: attend to)
prestar atenção a; (: bear in mind) levar em
consideração

heedless ['hi:dlɪs] ADJ desatento, negligente
heel [hi:l] N (of shoe) salto; (of foot) calcanhar m
▶ VT (shoe) pôr salto em; **to take to one's ~s**
dar no pé or aos calcanhares
hefty ['hɛftɪ] ADJ (person) robusto; (parcel)
pesado; (piece) grande; (profit) alto
heifer ['hɛfə^r] N novilha, bezerra
height [haɪt] N (of person) estatura; (of building,
tree) altura; (of plane) altitude f; (high ground)
monte m; (altitude) altitude f; (fig: of power)
auge m; (: of luxury) máximo; (: of stupidity)
cúmulo; **what ~ are you?** quanto você tem
de altura?; **of average ~** de estatura
mediana; **to be afraid of ~s** ter medo de
alturas; **it's the ~ of fashion** é a última
palavra or moda
heighten ['haɪtən] VT elevar; (fig) aumentar
heinous ['hi:nəs] ADJ hediondo, abominável
heir [ɛə^r] N herdeiro
heir apparent N herdeiro presuntivo
heiress ['ɛərɪs] N herdeira
heirloom ['ɛəlu:m] N relíquia de família
heist [haɪst] (US inf) N (hold-up) assalto
held [hɛld] PT, PP of **hold**
helicopter ['hɛlɪkɔptə^r] N helicóptero
heliport ['hɛlɪpɔ:t] N (Aviat) heliporto
helium ['hi:lɪəm] N hélio
hell [hɛl] N inferno; **a ~ of a ...** (inf) um ...
danado; **~!** (inf) droga!
he'll [hi:l] = **he will; he shall**
hellish ['hɛlɪʃ] ADJ infernal; (inf) terrível
hello [hə'ləu] EXCL oi! (BR), olá! (PT); (on phone)
alô! (BR), está! (PT); (surprise) ora essa!
helm [hɛlm] N (Naut) timão m, leme m
helmet ['hɛlmɪt] N capacete m
helmsman ['hɛlmzmən] (irreg: like **man**) N
timoneiro
help [hɛlp] N ajuda; (charwoman) faxineira;
(assistant) auxiliar m/f ▶ VT ajudar; **~!**
socorro!; **~ yourself** sirva-se; **can I ~ you?**
(in shop) deseja alguma coisa?; **with the ~ of**
com a ajuda de; **to be of ~ to sb** ajudar
alguém, ser útil a alguém; **to ~ sb (to) do
sth** ajudar alguém a fazer algo; **he can't ~
it** não tem culpa
help desk N atendimento telefônico
helper ['hɛlpə^r] N ajudante m/f
helpful ['hɛlpful] ADJ (person) prestativo;
(advice) útil
helping ['hɛlpɪŋ] N porção f
helpless ['hɛlplɪs] ADJ (incapable) incapaz;
(defenceless) indefeso; (baby) desamparado
helplessly ['hɛlplɪslɪ] ADV (watch) sem poder
fazer nada
helpline ['hɛlplaɪn] N disque-ajuda m (BR),
linha de apoio (PT)
Helsinki ['hɛlsɪŋkɪ] N Helsinque
helter-skelter ['hɛltə'skɛltə^r] (BRIT) N (at
amusement park) tobogã m
hem [hɛm] N bainha ▶ VT embainhar
▶ **hem in** VT cercar, encurralar; **to feel ~med
in** sentir-se acuado
he-man (irreg: like **man**) N macho

h

hematology ['hiːmə'tɔlədʒɪ] (US) N
= **haematology**
hemisphere ['hɛmɪsfɪə^r] N hemisfério
hemlock ['hɛmlɔk] N cicuta
hemoglobin ['hiːmə'gləubɪn] (US) N
= **haemoglobin**
hemophilia ['hiːmə'fɪlɪə] (US) N
= **haemophilia**
hemorrhage ['hɛmərɪdʒ] (US) N
= **haemorrhage**
hemorrhoids ['hɛmərɔɪdz] (US) NPL
= **haemorrhoids**
hemp [hɛmp] N cânhamo
hen [hɛn] N galinha; (*female bird*) fêmea
hence [hɛns] ADV (*therefore*) daí, portanto;
2 years ~ daqui a 2 anos
henceforth ['hɛns'fɔːθ] ADV de agora em
diante, doravante
henchman ['hɛntʃmən] (*pej*) (*irreg: like* **man**) N
jagunço, capanga *m*
henna ['hɛnə] N hena
hen party (*inf*) N reunião *f* de mulheres
henpecked ['hɛnpɛkt] ADJ dominado pela
esposa
hepatitis [hɛpə'taɪtɪs] N hepatite *f*
her [həː^r] PRON (*direct*) a; (*indirect*) lhe;
(*stressed*, *after prep*) ela ▶ ADJ seu/sua, dela; **~ name** o
nome dela; **I see ~** vejo-a, vejo ela (*BR inf*);
give ~ a book dá-lhe um livro, dá um livro a
ela; *see also* **me, my**
herald ['hɛrəld] N (*forerunner*) precursor(a) *m/f*
▶ VT anunciar
heraldic [hɛ'rældɪk] ADJ heráldico
heraldry ['hɛrəldrɪ] N heráldica
herb [həːb] N erva
herbaceous [həː'beɪʃəs] ADJ herbáceo
herbal ['həːbəl] ADJ herbáceo; **~ tea** tisana
herd [həːd] N rebanho ▶ VT (*drive: animals*,
people) conduzir; (*gather*) arrebanhar
here [hɪə^r] ADV aqui; (*to this place*) para cá;
(*at this point*) nesse ponto ▶ EXCL toma!; **~!**
(*present*) presente!; **~ is/are** aqui está/estão;
~ he/she is! aqui está ele/ela!; **~ she comes**
lá vem ela; **come ~!** vem cá!; **~ and there**
aqui e ali
hereabouts ['hɪərə'bauts] ADV por aqui
hereafter [hɪər'ɑːftə^r] ADV daqui por diante
▶ N: **the ~** a vida de além-túmulo
hereby [hɪə'baɪ] ADV (*in letter*) por este meio
hereditary [hɪ'rɛdɪtrɪ] ADJ hereditário
heredity [hɪ'rɛdɪtɪ] N hereditariedade *f*
heresy ['hɛrəsɪ] N heresia
heretic ['hɛrətɪk] N herege *m/f*
heretical [hɪ'rɛtɪkl] ADJ herético
herewith [hɪə'wɪð] ADV em anexo, junto
heritage ['hɛrɪtɪdʒ] N herança; (*fig*)
patrimônio; **our national ~** nosso
patrimônio nacional
hermetically [həː'mɛtɪklɪ] ADV
hermeticamente; **~ sealed**
hermeticamente fechado
hermit ['həːmɪt] N eremita *m/f*
hernia ['həːnɪə] N hérnia

hero ['hɪərəu] (*pl* **heroes**) N herói *m*; (*of book*,
film) protagonista *m*
heroic [hɪ'rəuɪk] ADJ heroico
heroin ['hɛrəuɪn] N heroína
heroin addict N viciado(-a) em heroína
heroine ['hɛrəuɪn] N heroína; (*of book, film*)
protagonista
heroism ['hɛrəuɪzm] N heroísmo
heron ['hɛrən] N garça
hero worship N culto de heróis
herring ['hɛrɪŋ] (*pl* **herrings** *or* **herring**) N
arenque *m*
hers [həːz] PRON (o) seu/(a) sua, (o/a) dela; **a**
friend of ~ uma amiga dela; **this is ~** isto é
dela; *see also* **mine**¹
herself [həː'sɛlf] PRON (*reflexive*) se; (*emphatic*)
ela mesma; (*after prep*) si (mesma); *see also*
oneself
Herts (*BRIT*) ABBR = **Hertfordshire**
he's [hiːz] = **he is; he has**
hesitant ['hɛzɪtənt] ADJ hesitante, indeciso;
to be ~ about doing sth hesitar em fazer
algo
hesitate ['hɛzɪteɪt] VI hesitar; **to ~ to do**
hesitar em fazer; **don't ~ to phone** não
deixe de telefonar
hesitation [hɛzɪ'teɪʃən] N hesitação *f*,
indecisão *f*; **I have no ~ in saying (that)** ...
não hesito em dizer (que) ...
hessian ['hɛsɪən] N aniagem *f*
heterogeneous ['hɛtərə'dʒiːnɪəs] ADJ
heterogêneo
heterosexual ['hɛtərəu'sɛksjuəl] ADJ
heterossexual ▶ N heterossexual *m/f*
het up [hɛt-] (*inf*) ADJ excitado
HEW (*US*) N ABBR (= *Department of*
Health, Education and Welfare) ministério da saúde,
da educação e da previdência social
hew [hjuː] (*pp* **hewed** *or* **hewn**) VT cortar (com
machado)
hex [hɛks] (*US*) N feitiço ▶ VT enfeitiçar
hexagon ['hɛksəgən] N hexágono
hexagonal [hɛk'sægənl] ADJ hexagonal
hey [heɪ] EXCL eh! ei!
heyday ['heɪdeɪ] N: **the ~ of** o auge *or*
apogeu de
HF N ABBR (= *high frequency*) HF *f*
HGV (*BRIT*) N ABBR = **heavy goods vehicle**
HI (*US*) ABBR (*Post*) = **Hawaii**
hi [haɪ] EXCL oi!
hiatus [haɪ'eɪtəs] N hiato
hibernate ['haɪbəneɪt] VI hibernar
hibernation [haɪbə'neɪʃən] N hibernação *f*
hiccough ['hɪkʌp] = **hiccup**
hiccup ['hɪkʌp] VI soluçar ▶ NPL: **~s** soluço;
to have (the) ~s estar com soluço
hid [hɪd] PT *of* **hide**
hidden ['hɪdn] PP *of* **hide** ▶ ADJ (*costs*) oculto
hide [haɪd] (*pt* **hid**, *pp* **hidden**) VT esconder,
ocultar; (*view*) obscurecer ▶ VI: **to ~ (from**
sb) esconder-se *or* ocultar-se (de alguém)
▶ N (*skin*) pele *f*
hide-and-seek N esconde-esconde *m*

hideaway ['haɪdəweɪ] N esconderijo
hideous ['hɪdɪəs] ADJ horrível
hide-out N esconderijo
hiding ['haɪdɪŋ] N (*beating*) surra; **to be in ~**
(*concealed*) estar escondido
hiding place N esconderijo
hierarchy ['haɪərɑːkɪ] N hierarquia
hieroglyphic [haɪərə'glɪfɪk] ADJ hieroglífico
hieroglyphics [haɪərə'glɪfɪks] NPL
hieroglifos *mpl*
hi-fi ['haɪfaɪ] ABBR = **high fidelity** ► N
alta-fidelidade *f*; (*system*) som *m* ► ADJ de
alta-fidelidade
higgledy-piggledy ['hɪgldɪ'pɪgldɪ] ADV
desordenadamente
high [haɪ] ADJ alto; (*number*) grande; (*price*)
alto, elevado; (*wind*) forte; (*voice*) agudo;
(*opinion*) ótimo; (*principles*) nobre; (*inf: person:
on drugs*) alto, baratinado; (*BRIT: Culin: meat,
game*) faisandé *inv*; (: *spoilt*) estragado ► ADV
alto, a grande altura ► N: **exports have
reached a new ~** as exportações atingiram
um novo pico; **it is 20 m ~** tem 20 m de
altura; **~ in the air** nas alturas; **to pay a ~
price for sth** pagar caro por algo
highball ['haɪbɔːl] (US) N uísque com soda
highboy ['haɪbɔɪ] (US) N cômoda alta
highbrow ['haɪbrau] ADJ intelectual, erudito
highchair ['haɪtʃɛəʳ] N cadeira alta (para
criança)
high-class ADJ (*neighbourhood*) nobre; (*hotel*) de
primeira categoria; (*person*) da classe alta;
(*performance etc*) de alto nível
high court N (*Law*) tribunal *m* superior
higher ['haɪəʳ] ADJ (*form of life, study etc*)
superior ► ADV mais alto
higher education N ensino superior
high finance N altas finanças *fpl*
high-flier N estudante *m/f* ou empregado(-a))
talentoso(-a) e ambicioso(-a)
high-flying ADJ (*fig*) ambicioso, talentoso
high-handed [-'hændɪd] ADJ despótico
high-heeled [-'hiːld] ADJ de salto alto
highjack ['haɪdʒæk] N, VT = **hijack**
high jump N (*Sport*) salto em altura
highlands ['haɪləndz] NPL serrania, serra;
the H~ (*in Scotland*) a Alta Escócia
high-level ADJ de alto nível; **~ language**
(*Comput*) linguagem *f* de alto nível
highlight ['haɪlaɪt] N (*fig: of event*) ponto
alto; (*in hair*) mecha ► VT realçar, ressaltar;
the ~s of the match os melhores lances
do jogo
highlighter ['haɪlaɪtəʳ] N (*pen*) caneta
marca-texto
highly ['haɪlɪ] ADV altamente; (*very*) muito;
~ paid muito bem pago; **to speak ~ of** falar
elogiosamente de
highly strung ADJ tenso, irritadiço
High Mass N missa cantada
highness ['haɪnɪs] N altura; **Her** (*or* **His**) **H~**
Sua Alteza
high-pitched ADJ agudo

high-powered ADJ (*engine*) muito potente, de
alta potência; (*fig: person*) dinâmico; (: *job,
businessman*) muito importante
high-pressure ADJ de alta pressão
high-rise ADJ alto
high-rise block N edifício alto, espigão *m*
high school N (*BRIT*) escola secundária; (*US*)
científico

> Uma **high school** é um estabelecimento
> de ensino secundário. Nos Estados
> Unidos, existem a *Junior High School*, que
> equivale aproximadamente aos dois
> últimos anos do primeiro grau, e a *Senior
> High School*, que corresponde ao segundo
> grau. Na Grã-Bretanha, esse termo às
> vezes é utilizado para as escolas
> secundárias.

high season (*BRIT*) N alta estação *f*
high spirits NPL alegria; **to be in ~** estar
alegre
high street (*BRIT*) N rua principal
highway ['haɪweɪ] (*US*) N (*between states, towns*)
estrada; (*main road*) rodovia
Highway Code (*BRIT*) N Código Nacional de
Trânsito
highwayman ['haɪweɪmən] (*irreg: like* **man**) N
salteador *m* de estrada
hijack ['haɪdʒæk] VT sequestrar ► N (*also:*
hijacking) sequestro (de avião)
hijacker ['haɪdʒækəʳ] N sequestrador(a) *m/f*
(de avião)
hike [haɪk] VI (*go walking*) caminhar ► N
caminhada, excursão *f* a pé; (*inf: in prices etc*)
aumento ► VT (*inf*) aumentar
hiker ['haɪkəʳ] N caminhante *m/f*,
andarilho(-a)
hiking ['haɪkɪŋ] N excursões *fpl* a pé,
caminhar *m*
hilarious [hɪ'lɛərɪəs] ADJ (*behaviour, event*)
hilariante
hilarity [hɪ'lærɪtɪ] N hilaridade *f*
hill [hɪl] N colina; (*high*) montanha; (*slope*)
ladeira, rampa
hillbilly ['hɪlbɪlɪ] (*US*) N montanhês(-esa) *m/f*;
(*pej*) caipira *m/f*, jeca *m/f*
hillock ['hɪlək] N morro pequeno
hillside ['hɪlsaɪd] N vertente *f*
hill start N (*Aut*) partida em ladeira
hilly ['hɪlɪ] ADJ montanhoso; (*uneven*)
acidentado
hilt [hɪlt] N (*of sword*) punho, guarda; **to the ~**
(*fig: support*) plenamente
him [hɪm] PRON (*direct*) o; (*indirect*) lhe;
(*stressed, after prep*) ele; **I see ~** vejo-o, vejo ele
(*BR inf*); **give ~ a book** dá-lhe um livro, dá
um livro a ele; *see also* **me**
Himalayas [hɪmə'leɪəz] NPL: **the ~** o
Himalaia
himself [hɪm'sɛlf] PRON (*reflexive*) se; (*emphatic*)
ele mesmo; (*after prep*) si (mesmo); *see also*
oneself
hind [haɪnd] ADJ traseiro ► N corça
hinder ['hɪndəʳ] VT atrapalhar; (*delay*) retardar

hindquarters ['haɪnd'kwɔːtəz] NPL (Zool) quartos mpl traseiros

hindrance ['hɪndrəns] N (nuisance) estorvo; (interruption) impedimento

hindsight ['haɪndsaɪt] N: **with (the benefit of)** ~ em retrospecto

Hindu ['hɪnduː] ADJ hindu ▶ N hindu m/f

hinge [hɪndʒ] N dobradiça ▶ VI (fig): **to** ~ **on** depender de

hint [hɪnt] N (suggestion) indireta; (advice) dica; (sign) sinal m ▶ VT: **to** ~ **that** insinuar que ▶ VI dar indiretas; **to** ~ **at** fazer alusão a; **to drop a** ~ dar uma indireta; **give me a** ~ (clue) me dá uma pista

hip [hɪp] N quadril m

hip flask N cantil m

hippie ['hɪpɪ] N hippie m/f

hip pocket N bolso traseiro

hippopotami [hɪpə'pɒtəmaɪ] NPL of **hippopotamus**

hippopotamus [hɪpə'pɒtəməs] (pl **hippopotamuses** or **hippopotami**) N hipopótamo

hippy ['hɪpɪ] N = **hippie**

hire ['haɪəʳ] VT (BRIT: car, equipment) alugar; (worker) contratar ▶ N aluguel m; (of person) contratação f; **for** ~ aluga-se; (taxi) livre; **on** ~ alugado
▶ **hire out** VT alugar

hire car, hired car ['haɪəd-] (BRIT) N carro alugado

hire purchase (BRIT) N compra a prazo; **to buy sth on** ~ comprar algo a prazo or pelo crediário

his [hɪz] PRON (o) seu/(a) sua, (o/a) dele ▶ ADJ seu/sua, dele; ~ **name** o nome dele; **it's** ~ é dele; see also **my, mine¹**

Hispanic [hɪs'pænɪk] ADJ hispânico

hiss [hɪs] VI (snake, fat) assoviar; (gas) silvar; (boo) vaiar ▶ N silvo; vaia

histogram ['hɪstəgræm] N histograma m

historian [hɪ'stɔːrɪən] N historiador(a) m/f

historic [hɪ'stɔrɪk], **historical** [hɪ'stɔrɪkl] ADJ histórico

history ['hɪstərɪ] N história; (of illness etc) histórico; **medical** ~ (of patient) histórico médico

histrionics [hɪstrɪ'ɒnɪks] N teatro

hit [hɪt] (pt, pp **hit**) VT (strike: person, thing) bater em; (reach: target) acertar, alcançar; (collide with: car) bater em, colidir com; (fig: affect) atingir ▶ N (blow) golpe m; (success) sucesso, grande êxito; (song) sucesso; (internet visit) visita; **to** ~ **it off with sb** dar-se bem com alguém; **to** ~ **the headlines** virar or fazer manchete; **to** ~ **the road** (inf) dar o fora, mandar-se
▶ **hit back** VI: **to** ~ **back at sb** revidar ao ataque (or à crítica etc) de alguém
▶ **hit on** VT FUS (answer) descobrir
▶ **hit out at** VT FUS tentar bater em; (fig) criticar veementemente
▶ **hit upon** VT FUS = **hit on**

hit-and-miss ['hɪtænd'mɪs] ADJ (not failsafe) sem garantia de sucesso

hit-and-run driver N motorista que atropela alguém e foge da cena do acidente

hitch [hɪtʃ] VT (fasten) atar, amarrar; (also: **hitch up**) levantar ▶ N (difficulty) dificuldade f; **to** ~ **a lift** pegar carona (BR), arranjar uma boleia (PT); **technical** ~ probleminha técnico
▶ **hitch up** VT (horse, cart) atrelar; see also **hitch**

hitch-hike VI pegar carona (BR), andar à boleia (PT)

hitch-hiker N carona m/f (BR), viajante m/f à boleia (PT)

hi-tech ADJ tecnologicamente avançado ▶ N alta tecnologia

hitherto [hɪðə'tuː] ADV até agora

hit-man ['hɪtmæn] (irreg: like **man**) N sicário

hit-or-miss ['hɪtə'mɪs] ADJ (not failsafe) sem garantia de sucesso; **it's** ~ **whether ...** não há garantia de que ...

hit parade N parada de sucessos

HIV ABBR: ~**-negative/-positive** HIV negativo/positivo

hive [haɪv] N colmeia; **the shop was a** ~ **of activity** (fig) a loja fervilhava de atividade
▶ **hive off** (inf) VT transferir

hl ABBR (= hectolitre) hl

HM ABBR (= His (or Her) Majesty) SM

HMG (BRIT) ABBR = **His (or Her) Majesty's Government**

HMI (BRIT) ABBR (Sch) = **His (or Her) Majesty's Inspector**

HMO (US) N ABBR (= health maintenance organization) órgão que garante a manutenção de saúde

HMS (BRIT) ABBR = **His (or Her) Majesty's Ship**

HMSO (BRIT) N ABBR (= His (or Her) Majesty's Stationery Office) imprensa do governo

HNC (BRIT) N ABBR = **Higher National Certificate**

HND (BRIT) N ABBR = **Higher National Diploma**

hoard [hɔːd] N provisão f; (of money) tesouro ▶ VT acumular

hoarding ['hɔːdɪŋ] (BRIT) N tapume m, outdoor m

hoarfrost ['hɔːfrɒst] N geada

hoarse [hɔːs] ADJ rouco

hoax [həuks] N trote m

hob [hɒb] N parte de cima do fogão

hobble ['hɒbl] VI coxear

hobby ['hɒbɪ] N hobby m, passatempo predileto

hobby-horse N cavalinho-de-pau; (fig) tema m favorito

hobnob ['hɒbnɒb] VI: **to** ~ **with** ter intimidade com

hobo ['həubəu] (pl **hobos** or **hoboes**) (US) N vagabundo

hock [hɒk] N (BRIT: wine) vinho branco do Reno; (of animal, Culin) jarrete m; (inf): **to be in** ~ (person) estar endividado; (object) estar no prego or empenhado

hockey ['hɔkɪ] N hóquei m
hocus-pocus ['həukəs'pəukəs] N (trickery) tapeação f; (words) embromação f
hodgepodge ['hɔdʒpɔdʒ] N = **hotchpotch**
hoe [həu] N enxada ▶ VT trabalhar com enxada, capinar
hog [hɔg] N porco; (person) glutão(-ona) m/f ▶ VT (fig) monopolizar; **to go the whole ~** ir até o fim
hoist [hɔɪst] N (lift) guincho; (crane) guindaste m ▶ VT içar
hold [həuld] (pt, pp **held**) VT segurar; (contain) conter; (keep back) reter; (believe) sustentar; (have) ter; (record etc) deter; (take weight) aguentar; (meeting) realizar; (detain) deter; (consider): **to ~ sb responsible (for sth)** responsabilizar alguém (por algo) ▶ VI (withstand pressure) resistir; (be valid) ser válido ▶ N (handle) apoio (para a mão); (fig: grasp) influência, domínio; (of ship) porão m; (of plane) compartimento para cargo; **to ~ office** (Pol) exercer um cargo; **he ~s the view that ...** ele sustenta que ...; **~ the line!** (Tel) não desligue!; **to ~ one's own** (fig) virar-se, sair-se bem; **to ~ firm** or **fast** aguentar; **to catch** or **get (a) ~ of** agarrar, pegar; **to get ~ of** (fig) arranjar; **to get ~ of o.s.** controlar-se
 ▶ **hold back** VT reter; (secret) manter, guardar; (prevent): **to ~ sb back from doing sth** impedir alguém de fazer algo
 ▶ **hold down** VT (person) segurar; (job) manter
 ▶ **hold forth** VI discursar, deitar falação
 ▶ **hold off** VT (enemy) afastar, repelir ▶ VI (rain): **if the rain ~s off** se não chover
 ▶ **hold on** VI agarrar-se; (wait) esperar; **~ on!** espera aí!; (Tel) não desligue!
 ▶ **hold on to** VT FUS agarrar-se a; (keep) guardar, ficar com
 ▶ **hold out** VT estender ▶ VI (resist) resistir; **to ~ out (against)** defender-se (contra)
 ▶ **hold over** VT (meeting etc) adiar
 ▶ **hold up** VT (raise) levantar; (support) apoiar; (delay) atrasar; (traffic) reter; (rob) assaltar
holdall ['həuldɔːl] (BRIT) N bolsa de viagem
holder ['həuldər] N (of ticket) portador(a) m/f; (of record) detentor(a) m/f; (of office, title etc) titular m/f
holding ['həuldɪŋ] N (share) participação f; **holdings** NPL posses fpl
holding company N holding f
hold-up ['həuldʌp] N (robbery) assalto; (delay) demora; (BRIT: in traffic) engarrafamento
hole [həul] N buraco; (small: in sock etc) furo ▶ VT esburacar; **~ in the heart** (Med) defeito na membrana cardíaca; **to pick ~s (in)** (fig) botar defeito (em)
 ▶ **hole up** VI esconder-se
holiday ['hɔlədɪ] N (BRIT: vacation) férias fpl; (day off) dia m de folga; (public holiday) feriado; **to be on ~** estar de férias; **tomorrow is a ~** amanhã é feriado
holiday camp (BRIT) N colônia de férias

holiday-maker (BRIT) N pessoa (que está) de férias
holiday pay N salário de férias
holiday resort N local m de férias
holiday season N temporada de férias
holiness ['həulɪnɪs] N santidade f
Holland ['hɔlənd] N Holanda
holler ['hɔlər] VI (inf) berrar
hollow ['hɔləu] ADJ oco, vazio; (cheeks) côncavo; (eyes) fundo; (sound) surdo; (laugh, claim) falso ▶ N (in ground) cavidade f, depressão f ▶ VT: **to ~ out** escavar
holly ['hɔlɪ] N azevinho
hollyhock ['hɔlɪhɔk] N malva-rosa
holocaust ['hɔləkɔːst] N holocausto
hologram ['hɔləgræm] N holograma m
hols [hɔlz] NPL (inf) férias fpl
holster ['həulstər] N coldre m
holy ['həulɪ] ADJ sagrado; (person) santo; (water) bento
Holy Ghost N Espírito Santo
Holy Land N: **the ~** a Terra Santa
holy orders NPL ordens fpl sacras
Holy Spirit N = **Holy Ghost**
homage ['hɔmɪdʒ] N homenagem f; **to pay ~ to** prestar homenagem a, homenagear
home [həum] N casa, lar m; (country) pátria; (institution) asilo ▶ CPD (domestic) caseiro, doméstico; (of family) familiar; (heating, computer etc) residencial; (Econ, Pol) nacional, interno; (Sport: team) de casa; (: game) no próprio campo ▶ ADV (direction) para casa; (right in: nail etc) até o fundo; **to go/come ~** ir/vir para casa; **at ~** em casa; **make yourself at ~** fique à vontade; **near my ~** perto da minha casa
 ▶ **home in on** VT FUS (missiles) dirigir-se automaticamente para
home address N endereço residencial
home-brew N (wine) vinho feito em casa; (beer) cerveja feita em casa
homecoming ['həumkʌmɪŋ] N regresso ao lar
home computer N computador m residencial
Home Counties NPL os condados por volta de Londres
home economics N economia doméstica
home-grown ADJ (not foreign) nacional; (from garden) plantado em casa
homeland ['həumlænd] N terra (natal)
homeless ['həumlɪs] ADJ sem casa, desabrigado ▶ NPL: **the ~** os desabrigados
home loan N crédito imobiliário, financiamento habitacional
homely ['həumlɪ] ADJ (domestic) caseiro; (simple) simples imv
home-made ADJ caseiro
Home Office (BRIT) N Ministério do Interior
homeopathy [həumɪˈɔpəθɪ] (US) = **homoeopathy**
home page N (Comput) página inicial
home rule N autonomia

Home Secretary (*BRIT*) N Ministro(a) do Interior

homesick ['həʊmsɪk] ADJ: **to be ~** estar com saudades (do lar)

homestead ['həʊmstɛd] N propriedade *f*; (*farm*) fazenda

home town N cidade *f* natal

homeward ['həʊmwəd] ADJ (*journey*) para casa, para a terra natal ▶ ADV para casa

homewards ['həʊmwəd] ADV para casa

homework ['həʊmwəːk] N dever *m* de casa

homicidal [hɔmɪ'saɪdl] ADJ homicida

homicide ['hɔmɪsaɪd] (*US*) N homicídio

homily ['hɔmɪlɪ] N homilia

homing ['həʊmɪŋ] ADJ (*device, missile*) de correção de rumo; **~ pigeon** pombo-correio

homoeopath, (*US*) **homeopath** ['həʊmɪəpæθ] N homeopata *m/f*

homoeopathic, (*US*) **homeopathic** [həʊmɪə'pæθɪk] ADJ homeopático

homoeopathy, (*US*) **homeopathy** [həʊmɪ'ɔpəθɪ] N homeopatia

homogeneous [hɔməʊ'dʒiːnɪəs] ADJ homogêneo

homogenize [hə'mɔdʒənaɪz] VT homogeneizar

homosexual [hɔməʊ'sɛksjuəl] ADJ, N homossexual *m/f*

homosexuality [hɔməsɛksju'ælətɪ] N homossexualidade *f*

Hon. ABBR = **honourable; honorary**

Honduras [hɔn'djuərəs] N Honduras *m* (*no article*)

hone [həʊn] VT amolar, afiar

honest ['ɔnɪst] ADJ (*truthful*) franco; (*trustworthy*) honesto; (*sincere*) sincero, franco; **to be quite ~ with you ...** para falar a verdade ...

honestly ['ɔnɪstlɪ] ADV honestamente, francamente

honesty ['ɔnɪstɪ] N honestidade *f*, sinceridade *f*

honey ['hʌnɪ] N mel *m*; (*US inf: darling*) querido(-a)

honeycomb ['hʌnɪkəʊm] N favo de mel; (*pattern*) em forma de favo ▶ VT (*fig*): **to ~ with** crivar de

honeymoon ['hʌnɪmuːn] N lua-de-mel *f*; (*trip*) viagem *f* de lua-de-mel

honeysuckle ['hʌnɪsʌkl] N madressilva

Hong Kong ['hɔŋ'kɔŋ] N Hong Kong (*no article*)

honk [hɔŋk] N buzinada ▶ VI (*Aut*) buzinar

Honolulu [hɔnə'luːluː] N Honolulu

honor, (*US*) **honour** ['ɔnəʳ] (*US*) VT, N = **honour**

honorary ['ɔnərərɪ] ADJ (*unpaid*) não remunerado; (*duty, title*) honorário

honour, (*US*) **honor** ['ɔnəʳ] VT honrar ▶ N honra; **in ~ of** em honra de

honourable, (*US*) **honorable** ['ɔnərəbl] ADJ honrado

honour-bound, (*US*) **honor-bound** ADJ: **to be ~ to do** estar moralmente obrigado a fazer

honours degree N (*Sch*) diploma *m* com distinção

Hons. ABBR (*Sch*) = **honours degree**

hood [hud] N capuz *m*; (*of cooker*) tampa; (*BRIT Aut*) capota; (*US Aut*) capô *m*; (*inf: hoodlum*) pinta-brava *m*

hooded ['hudɪd] ADJ encapuzado, mascarado

hoodlum ['huːdləm] N pinta-brava *m*

hoodwink ['hudwɪŋk] VT tapear

hoof [huːf] (*pl* **hooves**) N casco, pata

hook [huk] N gancho; (*on dress*) colchete *m*; (*for fishing*) anzol *m* ▶ VT (*fasten*) prender com gancho (*or* colchete); (*fish*) fisgar; **~ and eye** colchete *m*; **by ~ or by crook** custe o que custar; **to be ~ed (on)** (*inf*) estar viciado (em); (*person*) estar fissurado (em) ▶ **hook up** VT ligar

hooligan ['huːlɪgən] N desordeiro(-a), bagunceiro(-a)

hooliganism ['huːlɪgənɪzm] N vandalismo

hoop [huːp] N arco

hooray [huː'reɪ] EXCL = **hurrah**

hoot [huːt] VI (*Aut*) buzinar; (*siren*) tocar; (*owl*) piar ▶ VT (*jeer at*) vaiar ▶ N buzinada; toque *m* de sirena; **to ~ with laughter** morrer de rir

hooter ['huːtəʳ] N (*BRIT Aut*) buzina; (*Naut, factory*) sirena

hoover® ['huːvəʳ] (*BRIT*) N aspirador *m* (de pó) ▶ VT passar o aspirador em

hooves [huːvz] NPL *of* **hoof**

hop [hɔp] VI saltar, pular; (*on one foot*) pular num pé só ▶ N salto, pulo

hope [həʊp] VT: **to ~ that/to do** esperar que/ fazer ▶ VI esperar ▶ N esperança; **I ~ so/not** espero que sim/não

hopeful ['həʊpful] ADJ (*person*) otimista, esperançoso; (*situation*) promissor(a); **I'm ~ that she'll manage to come** acredito que ela conseguirá vir

hopefully ['həʊpfulɪ] ADV (*with hope*) esperançosamente; (*one hopes*): **~, they'll come back** é de esperar *or* esperamos que voltem

hopeless ['həʊplɪs] ADJ desesperado, irremediável; (*useless*) inútil; (*bad*) péssimo

hopelessly ['həʊpləslɪ] ADV (*confused, involved*) irremediavelmente

hopper ['hɔpəʳ] N tremonha

hops [hɔps] NPL (*Bot*) lúpulo

horde [hɔːd] N multidão *f*

horizon [hə'raɪzn] N horizonte *m*

horizontal [hɔrɪ'zɔntl] ADJ horizontal

hormone ['hɔːməʊn] N hormônio

hormone replacement therapy N terapia de reposição hormonal

horn [hɔːn] N corno, chifre *m*; (*material*) chifre; (*Mus*) trompa; (*Aut*) buzina

horned [hɔːnd] ADJ (*animal*) com chifres, chifrudo

hornet ['hɔːnɪt] N vespão *m*

horny ['hɔːnɪ] ADJ (*material*) córneo; (*hands*) calejado; (*inf: aroused*) excitado (sexualmente), com tesão (*BR !*)

horoscope ['hɔrəskəup] N horóscopo
horrendous [hə'rɛndəs] ADJ horrendo
horrible ['hɔrɪbl] ADJ horrível; (terrifying) terrível
horrid ['hɔrɪd] ADJ horrível
horrific [hə'rɪfɪk] ADJ horroroso
horrify ['hɔrɪfaɪ] VT horrorizar
horrifying ['hɔrɪfaɪɪŋ] ADJ horripilante
horror ['hɔrəʳ] N horror m
horror film N filme m de terror
horror-stricken ADJ = **horror-struck**
horror-struck ADJ horrorizado
hors d'œuvre [ɔ:'də:vrə] N entrada
horse [hɔ:s] N cavalo
horseback ['hɔ:sbæk]: **on ~** ADJ, ADV a cavalo
horsebox ['hɔ:sbɔks] N reboque m (para transportar cavalos)
horse chestnut N castanha-da-índia
horse-drawn ADJ puxado a cavalo
horsefly ['hɔ:sflaɪ] N mutuca
horseman ['hɔ:smən] (irreg: like **man**) N cavaleiro; (skilled) ginete m
horsemanship ['hɔ:smənʃɪp] N equitação f
horsemen ['hɔ:smən] NPL of **horseman**
horseplay ['hɔ:spleɪ] N zona, bagunça (brincadeiras etc)
horsepower ['hɔ:spauəʳ] N cavalo-vapor m
horse-racing N corridas fpl de cavalo, turfe m
horseradish ['hɔ:srædɪʃ] N rábano-bastardo
horseshoe ['hɔ:sʃu:] N ferradura
horse show N concurso hípico
horse-trading N regateio
horse trials NPL = **horse show**
horsewhip ['hɔ:swɪp] VT chicotear
horsewoman ['hɔ:swumən] (irreg: like **woman**) N amazona
horsey ['hɔ:sɪ] ADJ aficionado por cavalos; (appearance) com cara de cavalo
horticulture ['hɔ:tɪkʌltʃəʳ] N horticultura
hose [həuz] N (also: **hosepipe**) mangueira
 ▶ **hose down** VT lavar com mangueira
hosiery ['həuzɪərɪ] N meias fpl e roupa de baixo
hospice ['hɔspɪs] N asilo
hospitable ['hɔspɪtəbl] ADJ hospitaleiro
hospital ['hɔspɪtl] N hospital m
hospitality [hɔspɪ'tælɪtɪ] N hospitalidade f
hospitalize ['hɔspɪtəlaɪz] VT hospitalizar
host [həust] N anfitrião m; (in hotel etc) hospedeiro; (TV, Radio) apresentador(a) m/f; (Rel) hóstia; (large number): **a ~ of** uma multidão de ▶ VT (TV programme) apresentar, animar
hostage ['hɔstɪdʒ] N refém m/f
host country N país m anfitrião
hostel ['hɔstl] N hospedaria; (for students) residência; (for the homeless) albergue m, abrigo; (also: **youth hostel**) albergue da juventude
hostelling ['hɔstlɪŋ] N: **to go (youth) ~** viajar de férias pernoitando em albergues de juventude
hostess ['həustɪs] N anfitriã f; (BRIT: air hostess) aeromoça (BR), hospedeira de bordo (PT); (TV, Radio) apresentadora; (in nightclub) taxi-girl f
hostile ['hɔstaɪl] ADJ hostil
hostility [hɔ'stɪlɪtɪ] N hostilidade f
hot [hɔt] ADJ quente; (as opposed to only warm) muito quente; (spicy) picante; (fierce) ardente; **to be ~** (person) estar com calor; (thing, weather) estar quente
 ▶ **hot up** (BRIT inf) VI (party, debate) esquentar
 ▶ VT (pace) acelerar; (engine) envenenar
hot-air balloon N balão m de ar quente
hotbed ['hɔtbɛd] N (fig) foco, ninho
hotchpotch ['hɔtʃpɔtʃ] (BRIT) N mixórdia, salada
hot dog N cachorro-quente m
hotel [həu'tɛl] N hotel m
hotelier [hɔ'teljeɪ] N hoteleiro(-a); (manager) gerente m/f
hotel industry N indústria hoteleira
hotel room N quarto de hotel
hotfoot ['hɔtfut] ADV a mil, a toda
hot-headed [-'hɛdɪd] ADJ impetuoso
hothouse ['hɔthaus] N estufa
hot line N (Pol) telefone m vermelho, linha direta
hotly ['hɔtlɪ] ADV ardentemente, apaixonadamente
hotplate ['hɔtpleɪt] N (on cooker) chapa elétrica
hotpot ['hɔtpɔt] (BRIT) N (Culin) ragu m
hot seat N (fig) posição f de responsabilidade
hotspot ['hɔtspɔt] N área de tensão; (Comput: also: **wireless hotspot**) hotspot m (local público com acesso à Internet sem fio)
hot spring N fonte f termal
hot-tempered ADJ esquentado, de pavio curto
hot-water bottle N bolsa de água quente
hound [haund] VT acossar, perseguir ▶ N cão m de caça, sabujo
hour ['auəʳ] N hora; **at 30 miles an ~** ≈ a 50 km por hora; **lunch ~** hora do almoço; **to pay sb by the ~** pagar alguém por hora
hourly ['auəlɪ] ADV de hora em hora ▶ ADJ de hora em hora; (rate) por hora
house [n haus, pl hauzɪz, vt hauz] N (gen, firm) casa; (Pol) câmara; (Theatre) assistência, lotação f ▶ VT (person) alojar; (collection) abrigar; **to/at my ~** para a/na minha casa; **the H ~ (of Commons)** (BRIT) a Câmara dos Comuns; **the H ~ (of Representatives)** (US) a Câmara de Deputados; **on the ~** (fig) por conta da casa
house arrest N prisão f domiciliar
houseboat ['hausbəut] N casa flutuante
housebound ['hausbaund] ADJ preso em casa
housebreaking ['hausbreɪkɪŋ] N arrombamento de domicílio
house-broken (US) ADJ = **house-trained**
housecoat ['hauskəut] N roupão m
household ['haushəuld] N família; (house) casa
householder ['haushəuldəʳ] N (owner) dono(-a) de casa; (head of family) chefe m/f de família

h

household name N nome *m* conhecido por todos

house-hunting ['haushʌntɪŋ] N: **to go ~** procurar casa para morar

housekeeper ['hauski:pəʳ] N governanta

housekeeping ['hauski:pɪŋ] N (*work*) trabalhos *mpl* domésticos; (*money*) economia doméstica

houseman ['hausmən] (*BRIT*) (*irreg: like* **man**) N (*Med*) interno

house-proud ADJ preocupado com a aparência da casa

house-to-house ADJ (*enquiries*) de porta em porta; (*search*) de casa em casa

house-trained (*BRIT*) ADJ (*animal*) domesticado

house-warming [-'wɔ:mɪŋ], **house-warming party** N festa de inauguração de uma casa

housewife ['həuswaɪf] (*irreg: like* **wife**) N dona de casa

housework ['hauswə:k] N trabalhos *mpl* domésticos

housing ['hauzɪŋ] N (*provision*) alojamento; (*houses*) residências *fpl*; (*as issue*) habitação *f* ▶ CPD (*problem, shortage*) habitacional

housing association N organização beneficente que vende ou alaga casas

housing conditions NPL condições *fpl* de habitação

housing development N conjunto residencial

housing estate (*BRIT*) N = **housing development**

hovel ['hɔvl] N casebre *m*

hover ['hɔvəʳ] VI pairar; (*person*) rondar

hovercraft ['hɔvəkrɑ:ft] N aerobarco

hoverport ['hɔvəpɔ:t] N porto para aerobarcos

(KEYWORD)

how [hau] ADV **1** (*in what way*) como; **how was the film?** que tal o filme?; **how are you?** como vai?

2 (*to what degree*) quanto; **how much milk/ many people?** quanto de leite/quantas pessoas?; **how long have you been here?** há quanto tempo você está aqui?; **how old are you?** quantos anos você tem?; **how tall is he?** qual é a altura dele?; **how lovely/ awful!** que ótimo/terrível!

however [hau'ɛvəʳ] ADV de qualquer modo; (+ *adj*) por mais ... que; (*in questions*) como ▶ CONJ no entanto, contudo, todavia

howitzer ['hauɪtsəʳ] N (*Mil*) morteiro, obus *m*

howl [haul] N uivo ▶ VI uivar

howler ['hauləʳ] N besteira, erro

H.P. (*BRIT*) N ABBR = **hire purchase**

h.p. ABBR (*Aut*: = *horsepower*) CV

HQ N ABBR (= *headquarters*) QG *m*

HR (*US*) N ABBR = **House of Representatives**

hr ABBR (= *hour*) h

HRH ABBR (= *His (or Her) Royal Highness*) SAR

hrs ABBR (= *hours*) hs

HRT N ABBR = **hormone replacement therapy**; TRH *f*

HS (*US*) ABBR = **high school**

HST (*US*) ABBR (= *Hawaiian Standard Time*) hora do Havaí

HTML N ABBR (= *Hypertext Mark-up Language*) HTML *f*

hub [hʌb] N (*of wheel*) cubo; (*fig*) centro

hubbub ['hʌbʌb] N algazarra, vozerio

hubcap ['hʌbkæp] N (*Aut*) calota

HUD (*US*) N ABBR (= *Department of Housing and Urban Development*) ministério do urbanismo e da habitação

huddle ['hʌdl] VI: **to ~ together** aconchegar-se

hue [hju:] N cor *f*, matiz *m*

hue and cry N clamor *m* público

huff [hʌf] N: **in a ~** com raiva; **to take the ~** ficar sem graça

hug [hʌg] VT abraçar; (*thing*) agarrar, prender ▶ N abraço; **to give sb a ~** dar um abraço em alguém, abraçar alguém

huge [hju:dʒ] ADJ enorme, imenso

hulk [hʌlk] N (*wreck*) navio velho; (*hull*) casco, carcaça; (*person*) brutamontes *m inv*; (*building*) trambolho

hulking ['hʌlkɪŋ] ADJ pesado, grandão(-ona)

hull [hʌl] N (*of ship*) casco

hullabaloo ['hʌləbə'lu:] (*inf*) N algazarra

hullo [hə'ləu] EXCL = **hello**

hum [hʌm] VT (*tune*) cantarolar ▶ VI cantarolar; (*insect, machine etc*) zumbir ▶ N zumbido

human ['hju:mən] ADJ humano ▶ N (*also:* **human being**) ser *m* humano

humane [hju:'meɪn] ADJ humano

humanism ['hju:mənɪzm] N humanismo

humanitarian [hju:mænɪ'tɛərɪən] ADJ humanitário

humanity [hju:'mænɪtɪ] N humanidade *f*

humanly ['hju:mən'lɪ] ADV humanamente

humanoid ['hju:mənɔɪd] ADJ, N humanoide *m/f*

human rights NPL direitos *mpl* humanos

humble ['hʌmbl] ADJ humilde ▶ VT humilhar

humbly ['hʌmblɪ] ADV humildemente

humbug ['hʌmbʌg] N fraude *f*, embuste *m*; (*BRIT: sweet*) bala de hortelã

humdrum ['hʌmdrʌm] ADJ (*boring*) monótono, enfadonho; (*routine*) rotineiro

humid ['hju:mɪd] ADJ úmido

humidifier [hju:'mɪdɪfaɪəʳ] N umidificador *m*

humidity [hju:'mɪdɪtɪ] N umidade *f*

humiliate [hju:'mɪlɪeɪt] VT humilhar

humiliation [hju:mɪlɪ'eɪʃən] N humilhação *f*

humility [hju:'mɪlɪtɪ] N humildade *f*

humor ['hju:məʳ] (*US*) N, VT = **humour**

humorist ['hju:mərɪst] N humorista *m/f*

humorous ['hju:mərəs] ADJ humorístico; (*person*) engraçado

humour, (*US*) **humor** ['hju:məʳ] N humorismo, senso de humor; (*mood*) humor *m* ▶ VT (*person*) fazer a vontade de; **sense of ~** senso de humor; **to be in a**

good/bad ~ estar de bom/mau humor

humourless, (US) **humorless** ['hju:mələs] ADJ sem senso de humor

hump [hʌmp] N (in ground) elevação f; (camel's) corcova, giba; (deformity) corcunda

humpback ['hʌmpbæk] N corcunda m/f

humpbacked ['hʌmpbækt] ADJ: ~ **bridge** ponte pequena e muito arqueada

humus ['hju:məs] N húmus m, humo

hunch [hʌntʃ] N (premonition) pressentimento, palpite m

hunchback ['hʌntʃbæk] N corcunda m/f

hunched [hʌntʃt] ADJ corcunda

hundred ['hʌndrəd] NUM cem; (before lower numbers) cento; (collective) centena; **~s of people** centenas de pessoas; **I'm a ~ per cent sure** tenho certeza absoluta

hundredth [-ɪdθ] NUM centésimo

hundredweight ['hʌndrədweɪt] N (BRIT) 50.8 kg; 112 lb; (US) = 45.3 kg; 100 lb

hung [hʌŋ] PT, PP of **hang**

Hungarian [hʌŋ'gɛərɪən] ADJ húngaro ▶ N húngaro(-a); (Ling) húngaro

Hungary ['hʌŋgərɪ] N Hungria

hunger ['hʌŋgə'] N fome f ▶ VI: **to ~ for** ter fome de; (desire) desejar ardentemente

hunger strike N greve f de fome

hungover [hʌŋ'əuvə'] ADJ (inf): **to be ~** estar de ressaca

hungrily ['hʌŋgrəlɪ] ADV (eat) vorazmente; (fig) avidamente

hungry ['hʌŋgrɪ] ADJ faminto, esfomeado; (keen): **~ for** (fig) ávido de, ansioso por; **to be ~** estar com fome

hung up (inf) ADJ complexado, grilado

hunk [hʌŋk] N naco; (inf: man) gatão m

hunt [hʌnt] VT (seek) buscar, perseguir; (Sport) caçar ▶ VI caçar ▶ N caça, caçada
  ▶ **hunt down** VT acossar

hunter ['hʌntə'] N caçador(a) m/f; (BRIT: horse) cavalo de caça

hunting ['hʌntɪŋ] N caça

hurdle ['hə:dl] N (Sport) barreira; (fig) obstáculo

hurl [hə:l] VT arremessar, lançar; (abuse) gritar

hurrah [hu'rɑ:] EXCL oba!, viva!

hurray [hu'reɪ] EXCL = **hurrah**

hurricane ['hʌrɪkən] N furacão m

hurried ['hʌrɪd] ADJ (fast) apressado; (rushed) feito às pressas

hurriedly ['hʌrɪdlɪ] ADV depressa, apressadamente

hurry ['hʌrɪ] N pressa ▶ VI (also: **hurry up**) apressar-se ▶ VT (also: **hurry up**: person) apressar; (: work) acelerar; **to be in a ~** estar com pressa; **to do sth in a ~** fazer algo às pressas; **to ~ in/out** entrar/sair correndo; **to ~ home** correr para casa
  ▶ **hurry along** VI andar às pressas
  ▶ **hurry away** VI sair correndo
  ▶ **hurry off** VI sair correndo
  ▶ **hurry up** VI apressar-se

hurt [hə:t] (pt, pp **hurt**) VT machucar; (injure) ferir; (damage: business etc) prejudicar; (fig) magoar ▶ VI doer ▶ ADJ machucado, ferido; **I ~ my arm** machuquei o braço; **where does it ~?** onde é que dói?

hurtful ['hə:tful] ADJ (remark) que magoa, ofensivo

hurtle ['hə:tl] VI correr; **to ~ past** passar como um raio; **to ~ down** cair com violência

husband ['hʌzbənd] N marido, esposo

hush [hʌʃ] N silêncio, quietude f ▶ VT silenciar, fazer calar; **~!** silêncio!, psiu!
  ▶ **hush up** VT (fact) abafar, encobrir

hushed [hʌʃt] ADJ (tone) baixo

hush-hush [hʌʃ] ADJ secreto

husk [hʌsk] N (of wheat) casca; (of maize) palha

husky ['hʌskɪ] ADJ rouco; (burly) robusto ▶ N cão m esquimó

hustings ['hʌstɪŋz] (BRIT) NPL (Pol) campanha (eleitoral)

hustle ['hʌsl] VT (push) empurrar; (hurry) apressar ▶ N agitação f, atividade f febril; **~ and bustle** grande movimento

hut [hʌt] N cabana, choupana; (shed) alpendre m

hutch [hʌtʃ] N coelheira

hyacinth ['haɪəsɪnθ] N jacinto

hybrid ['haɪbrɪd] ADJ, N híbrido; (mixture) combinação f

hydrant ['haɪdrənt] N: **fire ~** hidrante m

hydraulic [haɪ'drɔ:lɪk] ADJ hidráulico

hydraulics [haɪ'drɔ:lɪks] N hidráulica

hydrochloric acid ['haɪdrəu'klɒrɪk-] N ácido clorídrico

hydroelectric [haɪdrəuɪ'lɛktrɪk] ADJ hidroelétrico

hydrofoil ['haɪdrəfɔɪl] N hidrofoil m, aliscafo

hydrogen ['haɪdrədʒən] N hidrogênio

hydrogen bomb N bomba de hidrogênio

hydrophobia ['haɪdrə'fəubɪə] N hidrofobia

hydroplane ['haɪdrəpleɪn] N lancha planadora

hyena [haɪ'i:nə] N hiena

hygiene ['haɪdʒi:n] N higiene f

hygienic [haɪ'dʒi:nɪk] ADJ higiênico

hymn [hɪm] N hino

hype [haɪp] (inf) N tititi m, falatório

hyperactive ['haɪpər'æktɪv] ADJ hiperativo

hyperlink ['haɪpəlɪŋk] N hiperlink m

hypermarket ['haɪpəmɑ:kɪt] (BRIT) N hipermercado

hypertension ['haɪpə'tɛnʃən] N (Med) hipertensão f

hyphen ['haɪfn] N hífen m

hypnosis [hɪp'nəusɪs] N hipnose f

hypnotic [hɪp'nɒtɪk] ADJ hipnótico

hypnotism ['hɪpnətɪzm] N hipnotismo

hypnotist ['hɪpnətɪst] N hipnotizador(a) m/f

hypnotize ['hɪpnətaɪz] VT hipnotizar

hypoallergenic ['haɪpəuælə'dʒɛnɪk] ADJ hipoalergênico

hypochondriac [haɪpə'kɒndrɪæk] N hipocondríaco(-a)

hypocrisy [hɪˈpɔkrɪsɪ] N hipocrisia
hypocrite [ˈhɪpəkrɪt] N hipócrita *m/f*
hypocritical [hɪpəˈkrɪtɪkl] ADJ hipócrita
hypodermic [haɪpəˈdəːmɪk] ADJ hipodérmico
▶ N seringa hipodérmica
hypothermia [haɪpəˈθəːmɪa] N hipotermia
hypotheses [haɪˈpɔθɪsiːz] NPL *of* **hypothesis**
hypothesis [haɪˈpɔθɪsɪs] (*pl* **hypotheses**) N
hipótese *f*
hypothetic [haɪpəuˈθɛtɪk], **hypothetical**

[haɪpəuˈθɛtɪkl] ADJ hipotético
hysterectomy [hɪstəˈrɛktəmɪ] N
histerectomia
hysteria [hɪˈstɪərɪə] N histeria
hysterical [hɪˈstɛrɪkl] ADJ histérico; (*funny*)
hilariante
hysterics [hɪˈstɛrɪks] NPL (*nervous*) crise *f*
histérica; (*laughter*) ataque *m* de riso; **to be
in** *or* **have ~** ter uma crise histérica
Hz ABBR (= *hertz*) Hz

I¹, i [aɪ] N (*letter*) I, i *m*; **I for Isaac** (BRIT) *or* **Item** (US) I de Irene

I² [aɪ] PRON eu ▶ ABBR (= *island, isle*) I

IA (US) ABBR (*Post*) = **Iowa**

IAEA N ABBR (= *International Atomic Energy Agency*) IAEA *f*

IBA (BRIT) N (= *Independent Broadcasting Authority*) órgão que supervisiona as emissoras comerciais de TV

Iberian [aɪˈbɪərɪən] ADJ ibérico

Iberian Peninsula N: **the ~** a península Ibérica

IBEW (US) N ABBR (= *International Brotherhood of Electrical Workers*) sindicato internacional dos eletricistas

i/c (BRIT) ABBR = **in charge**

ICC N ABBR = **International Chamber of Commerce**; (US) = **Interstate Commerce Commission**

ice [aɪs] N gelo; (*ice cream*) sorvete *m* ▶ VT (*cake*) cobrir com glacê; (*drink*) gelar ▶ VI (*also*: **ice over, ice up**) gelar; **to put sth on ~** (*fig*) engavetar algo

ice age N era glacial

ice axe N picareta para o gelo

iceberg [ˈaɪsbəːg] N iceberg *m*; **this is just the tip of the ~** isso é só a ponta do iceberg

icebox [ˈaɪsbɔks] N (US) geladeira; (BRIT: *in fridge*) congelador *m*; (*insulated box*) geladeira portátil

icebreaker [ˈaɪsbreɪkəʳ] N navio quebra-gelo *m*

ice bucket N balde *m* de gelo

ice-cold ADJ gelado

ice cream N sorvete *m* (BR), gelado (PT)

ice cube N pedra de gelo

iced [aɪst] ADJ (*drink*) gelado; (*cake*) glaçado

ice hockey N hóquei *m* sobre o gelo

Iceland [ˈaɪslənd] N Islândia

Icelander [ˈaɪsləndəʳ] N islandês(-esa) *m/f*

Icelandic [aɪsˈlændɪk] ADJ islandês(-esa) ▶ N (*Ling*) islandês *m*

ice lolly (BRIT) N picolé *m*

ice pick N furador *m* de gelo

ice rink N pista de gelo, rinque *m*

ice-skate N patim *m* (para o gelo) ▶ VI patinar no gelo

ice-skating N patinação *f* no gelo

icicle [ˈaɪsɪkl] N pingente *m* de gelo

icing [ˈaɪsɪŋ] N (*Culin*) glacê *m*; (*Aviat etc*) formação *f* de gelo

icing sugar (BRIT) N açúcar *m* glacê

ICJ N ABBR = **International Court of Justice**

icon [ˈaɪkɔn] N (*gen*, *Comput*) ícone *m*

ICR (US) N ABBR = **Institute for Cancer Research**

ICT N ABBR (= *Information and Communication(s) Technology*) TIC *f*

ICU N ABBR (= *intensive care unit*) UTI *f*

icy [ˈaɪsɪ] ADJ gelado; (*fig*) glacial, indiferente

ID (US) ABBR (*Post*) = **Idaho**

I'd [aɪd] = **I would**; **I had**

ID card N = **identity card**

IDD (BRIT) N ABBR (*Tel*: = *international direct dialling*) DDI *f*

idea [aɪˈdɪə] N ideia; **good ~!** boa ideia!; **to have an ~ that ...** ter a impressão de que ...; **I haven't the least ~** não tenho a mínima ideia

ideal [aɪˈdɪəl] N ideal *m* ▶ ADJ ideal

idealist [aɪˈdɪəlɪst] N idealista *m/f*

ideally [aɪˈdɪəlɪ] ADV de preferência; **~ the book should have ...** seria ideal que o livro tivesse ...

identical [aɪˈdɛntɪkl] ADJ idêntico

identification [aɪdɛntɪfɪˈkeɪʃən] N identificação *f*; **means of ~** documentos pessoais

identify [aɪˈdɛntɪfaɪ] VT identificar ▶ VI: **to ~ with** identificar-se com

Identikit® [aɪˈdɛntɪkɪt] N: **~ picture** retrato falado

identity [aɪˈdɛntɪtɪ] N identidade *f*

identity card N carteira de identidade

identity parade (BRIT) N identificação *f*

identity theft N roubo de identidade

ideological [aɪdɪəˈlɔdʒɪkəl] ADJ ideológico

ideology [aɪdɪˈɔlədʒɪ] N ideologia

idiocy [ˈɪdɪəsɪ] N idiotice *f*; (*stupid act*) estupidez *f*

idiom [ˈɪdɪəm] N expressão *f* idiomática; (*style of speaking*) idioma *m*, linguagem *f*

idiomatic [ɪdɪəˈmætɪk] ADJ idiomático

idiosyncrasy [ɪdɪəʊˈsɪŋkrəsɪ] N idiossincrasia

idiot [ˈɪdɪət] N idiota *m/f*

idiotic [ɪdɪˈɔtɪk] ADJ idiota

idle [ˈaɪdl] ADJ ocioso; (*lazy*) preguiçoso; (*unemployed*) desempregado; (*pointless*) inútil, vão/vã ▶ VI (*machine*) funcionar com a transmissão desligada

▶ **idle away** VT: **to ~ away the time** perder or desperdiçar tempo

idleness ['aɪdlnɪs] N ociosidade f; preguiça; (*pointlessness*) inutilidade f

idler ['aɪdlə'] N preguiçoso(-a)

idle time N (*Comm*) tempo ocioso

idol ['aɪdl] N ídolo

idolize ['aɪdəlaɪz] VT idolatrar

idyllic [ɪ'dɪlɪk] ADJ idílico

i.e. ABBR (= *id est*) i.e., isto é

KEYWORD

if [ɪf] CONJ **1** (*conditional use*) se; **I'll go if you come with me** irei se você vier comigo; **if necessary** se necessário; **if I were you** se eu fôsse você
2 (*whenever*) quando
3 (*although*): **(even) if** mesmo que; **I like it, (even) if you don't** eu gosto disto, mesmo que você não goste
4 (*whether*) se
5: **if so/not** sendo assim/do contrário; **if only** se pelo menos; *see also* **as**

iffy ['ɪfɪ] ADJ (*inf: uncertain*) duvidoso; (*not good*) de qualidade duvidosa

igloo ['ɪglu:] N iglu m

ignite [ɪg'naɪt] VT acender; (*set fire to*) incendiar ▶ VI acender

ignition [ɪg'nɪʃən] N (*Aut*) ignição f; **to switch on/off the ~** ligar/desligar o motor

ignition key N (*Aut*) chave f de ignição

ignoble [ɪg'nəubl] ADJ ignóbil

ignominious [ɪgnə'mɪnɪəs] ADJ vergonhoso, humilhante

ignoramus [ɪgnə'reɪməs] N ignorante m/f

ignorance ['ɪgnərəns] N ignorância; **to keep sb in ~ of sth** deixar alguém na ignorância de algo

ignorant ['ɪgnərənt] ADJ ignorante; **to be ~ of** ignorar

ignore [ɪg'nɔ:'] VT (*person*) não fazer caso de; (*fact*) não levar em consideração, ignorar

ikon ['aɪkɔn] N = **icon**

IL (*US*) ABBR (*Post*) = **Illinois**

ILA (*US*) N ABBR (= *International Longshoremen's Association*) sindicato internacional dos portuários

ill [ɪl] ADJ doente; (*slightly ill*) indisposto; (*bad*) mau/má; (*harmful: effects*) nocivo ▶ N mal m; (*fig*) desgraça ▶ ADV: **to speak/think ~ of sb** falar/pensar mal de alguém; **to take** or **be taken ~** ficar doente

I'll [aɪl] = **I will; I shall**

ill-advised [-əd'vaɪzd] ADJ pouco recomendado; (*misled*) mal aconselhado

ill-at-ease ADJ constrangido, pouco à vontade

ill-considered [-kən'sɪdəd] ADJ (*plan*) imponderado

ill-disposed ADJ: **to be ~ towards sb/sth** ser desfavorável a alguém/algo

illegal [ɪ'li:gl] ADJ ilegal

illegally [ɪ'li:gəlɪ] ADV ilegalmente

illegible [ɪ'lɛdʒɪbl] ADJ ilegível

illegitimate [ɪlɪ'dʒɪtɪmət] ADJ ilegítimo

ill-fated ADJ malfadado

ill-favoured, (*US*) **ill-favored** [-'feɪvəd] ADJ desagradável

ill feeling N má vontade f, rancor m

ill-gotten ADJ (*gains etc*) mal adquirido

illicit [ɪ'lɪsɪt] ADJ ilícito

ill-informed ADJ mal informado

illiterate [ɪ'lɪtərət] ADJ analfabeto

ill-mannered [-'mænəd] ADJ mal-educado, grosseiro

illness ['ɪlnɪs] N doença

illogical [ɪ'lɔdʒɪkl] ADJ ilógico

ill-suited [-'su:tɪd] ADJ (*couple*) desajustado; **he is ~ to the job** ele é inadequado para o cargo

ill-timed [-taɪmd] ADJ inoportuno

ill-treat VT maltratar

ill-treatment N maus tratos mpl

illuminate [ɪ'lu:mɪneɪt] VT (*room, street*) iluminar, clarear; (*subject*) esclarecer; **~d sign** anúncio luminoso

illuminating [ɪ'lu:mɪneɪtɪŋ] ADJ esclarecedor

illumination [ɪlu:mɪ'neɪʃən] N iluminação f; **illuminations** NPL (*decorative lights*) luminárias fpl

illusion [ɪ'lu:ʒən] N ilusão f; **to be under the ~ that ...** estar com a ilusão de que ...

illusive [ɪ'lu:sɪv] ADJ ilusório

illusory [ɪ'lu:sərɪ] ADJ ilusório

illustrate ['ɪləstreɪt] VT ilustrar; (*subject*) esclarecer; (*point*) exemplificar

illustration [ɪlə'streɪʃən] N (*art*) ilustração f; (*example*) exemplo; (*explanation*) esclarecimento; (*in book*) gravura, ilustração

illustrator ['ɪləstreɪtə'] N ilustrador(a) m/f

illustrious [ɪ'lʌstrɪəs] ADJ ilustre

ill will N animosidade f

ILO N ABBR (= *International Labour Organization*) OIT f

ILWU (*US*) N ABBR (= *International Longshoremen's and Warehousemen's Union*) sindicato dos portuários

I'm [aɪm] = **I am**

image ['ɪmɪdʒ] N imagem f

imagery ['ɪmɪdʒərɪ] N imagens fpl

imaginable [ɪ'mædʒɪnəbl] ADJ imaginável, concebível

imaginary [ɪ'mædʒɪnərɪ] ADJ imaginário

imagination [ɪmædʒɪ'neɪʃən] N imaginação f; (*inventiveness*) inventividade f; (*illusion*) fantasia

imaginative [ɪ'mædʒɪnətɪv] ADJ imaginativo

imagine [ɪ'mædʒɪn] VT imaginar; (*delude o.s.*) fantasiar

imbalance [ɪm'bæləns] N desequilíbrio; (*inequality*) desigualdade f

imbecile ['ɪmbəsi:l] N imbecil m/f

imbue [ɪm'bju:] VT: **to ~ sth with** imbuir or impregnar algo de

IMF N ABBR (= *International Monetary Fund*) FMI m

imitate ['ɪmɪteɪt] VT imitar

imitation [ɪmɪ'teɪʃən] N imitação f; (*copy*) cópia; (*mimicry*) mímica

imitator ['ɪmɪteɪtə'] N imitador(a) m/f

immaculate [ɪ'mækjulət] ADJ impecável; (Rel) imaculado

immaterial [ɪmə'tɪərɪəl] ADJ irrelevante; **it is ~ whether ...** é indiferente se ...

immature [ɪmə'tjuər] ADJ (person, organism) imaturo; (fruit) verde; (of one's youth) juvenil

immaturity [ɪmə'tjuərɪtɪ] N imaturidade f

immeasurable [ɪ'mɛʒrəbl] ADJ incomensurável, imensurável

immediacy [ɪ'mi:dɪəsɪ] N (of events etc) proximidade f; (of needs) urgência

immediate [ɪ'mi:dɪət] ADJ imediato; (pressing) urgente, premente; (neighbourhood, family) próximo

immediately [ɪ'mi:dɪətlɪ] ADV (at once) imediatamente; **~ next to** bem junto a

immense [ɪ'mɛns] ADJ imenso; (importance) enorme

immensity [ɪ'mɛnsətɪ] N imensidade f

immerse [ɪ'mə:s] VT (submerge) submergir; (sink) imergir, mergulhar; **to be ~d in** (fig) estar absorto em

immersion heater [ɪ'mə:ʃn-] (BRIT) N aquecedor m de imersão

immigrant ['ɪmɪgrənt] N imigrante m/f

immigrate ['ɪmɪgreɪt] VI imigrar

immigration [ɪmɪ'greɪʃən] N imigração f

immigration authorities NPL fiscais mpl de imigração, ≈ polícia federal

immigration laws NPL leis fpl imigratórias

imminent ['ɪmɪnənt] ADJ iminente

immobile [ɪ'məubaɪl] ADJ imóvel

immobilize [ɪ'məubɪlaɪz] VT imobilizar

immoderate [ɪ'mɔdərət] ADJ imoderado

immodest [ɪ'mɔdɪst] ADJ (indecent) indecente, impudico; (person: boasting) presumido, arrogante

immoral [ɪ'mɔrl] ADJ imoral

immorality [ɪmə'rælɪtɪ] N imoralidade f

immortal [ɪ'mɔ:tl] ADJ imortal

immortalize [ɪ'mɔ:təlaɪz] VT imortalizar

immovable [ɪ'mu:vəbl] ADJ (object) imóvel, fixo; (person) inflexível

immune [ɪ'mju:n] ADJ: **~ to** imune a, imunizado contra

immune system N sistema m imunológico

immunity [ɪ'mju:nɪtɪ] N (Med) imunidade f; (Comm) isenção f; **diplomatic ~** imunidade diplomática

immunization [ɪmjunaɪ'zeɪʃən] N imunização f

immunize ['ɪmjunaɪz] VT imunizar

imp [ɪmp] N diabinho, criança levada

impact ['ɪmpækt] N impacto (BR), impacte m (PT)

impair [ɪm'pɛər] VT prejudicar

impale [ɪm'peɪl] VT perfurar, empalar

impart [ɪm'pɑ:t] VT (make known) comunicar; (bestow) dar

impartial [ɪm'pɑ:ʃl] ADJ imparcial

impartiality [ɪmpɑ:ʃɪ'ælɪtɪ] N imparcialidade f

impassable [ɪm'pɑ:səbl] ADJ (barrier, river) intransponível; (road) intransitável

impasse [æm'pɑ:s] N (fig) impasse m

impassioned [ɪm'pæʃənd] ADJ ardente, veemente

impassive [ɪm'pæsɪv] ADJ impassível

impatience [ɪm'peɪʃəns] N impaciência

impatient [ɪm'peɪʃənt] ADJ impaciente; **to get or grow ~** impacientar-se

impeach [ɪm'pi:tʃ] VT impugnar; (public official) levar a juízo

impeachment [ɪm'pi:tʃmənt] N (Law) impeachment m

impeccable [ɪm'pɛkəbl] ADJ impecável

impecunious [ɪmpə'kju:nɪəs] ADJ impecunioso, sem recursos

impede [ɪm'pi:d] VT impedir, estorvar

impediment [ɪm'pedɪmənt] N obstáculo; (also: **speech impediment**) defeito (de fala)

impel [ɪm'pɛl] VT (force): **to ~ sb (to do sth)** impelir alguém (a fazer algo)

impending [ɪm'pɛndɪŋ] ADJ (near) iminente, próximo

impenetrable [ɪm'pɛnɪtrəbl] ADJ impenetrável; (fig) incompreensível

imperative [ɪm'pɛrətɪv] ADJ (tone) imperioso, obrigatório; (necessary) indispensável; (pressing) premente ▶ N (Ling) imperativo

imperceptible [ɪmpə'sɛptɪbl] ADJ imperceptível

imperfect [ɪm'pə:fɪkt] ADJ imperfeito; (goods etc) defeituoso ▶ N (Ling: also: **imperfect tense**) imperfeito

imperfection [ɪmpə'fɛkʃən] N (blemish) defeito; (state) imperfeição f

imperial [ɪm'pɪərɪəl] ADJ imperial

imperialism [ɪm'pɪərɪəlɪzəm] N imperialismo

imperil [ɪm'pɛrɪl] VT pôr em perigo, arriscar

imperious [ɪm'pɪərɪəs] ADJ imperioso

impersonal [ɪm'pə:sənl] ADJ impessoal

impersonate [ɪm'pə:səneɪt] VT fazer-se passar por, personificar; (Theatre) imitar

impersonation [ɪmpə:sə'neɪʃən] N (Law) impostura; (Theatre) imitação f

impersonator [ɪm'pə:səneɪtər] N impostor(a) m/f; (Theatre) imitador(a) m/f

impertinence [ɪm'pə:tɪnəns] N impertinência, insolência

impertinent [ɪm'pə:tɪnənt] ADJ impertinente, insolente

imperturbable [ɪmpə'tə:bəbl] ADJ imperturbável, inabalável

impervious [ɪm'pə:vɪəs] ADJ impenetrável; (fig): **~ to** insensível a

impetuous [ɪm'pɛtjuəs] ADJ impetuoso, prec ipitado

impetus ['ɪmpətəs] N ímpeto; (fig) impulso

impinge [ɪm'pɪndʒ]: **to ~ on** VT FUS impressionar, impingir em; (affect) afetar

impish ['ɪmpɪʃ] ADJ levado, travesso

implacable [ɪm'plækəbl] ADJ implacável, impiedoso

implant [vt ɪm'plɑ:nt, n 'ɪmplɑ:nt] VT (Med) implantar; (fig) inculcar ▶ N implante m

implausible [ɪmˈplɔːzɪbl] ADJ inverossímil (BR), inverosímil (PT)

implement [n ˈɪmplɪmənt, vt ˈɪmplɪmɛnt] N instrumento, ferramenta; (for cooking) utensílio ▶ VT efetivar; (carry out) realizar, executar

implicate [ˈɪmplɪkeɪt] VT (compromise) comprometer; (involve) implicar, envolver

implication [ɪmplɪˈkeɪʃən] N implicação f, consequência; (involvement) involvimento; **by ~** por consequência

implicit [ɪmˈplɪsɪt] ADJ implícito; (complete) absoluto

implicitly [ɪmˈplɪsɪtlɪ] ADV implicitamente; (completely) completamente

implore [ɪmˈplɔːʳ] VT (person) implorar, suplicar

imply [ɪmˈplaɪ] VT (involve) implicar; (mean) significar; (hint) dar a entender que; **it is implied** se subentende

impolite [ɪmpəˈlaɪt] ADJ indelicado, mal-educado

imponderable [ɪmˈpɔndərəbl] ADJ imponderável

import [vt ɪmˈpɔːt, n, cpd ˈɪmpɔːt] VT importar ▶ N (Comm) importação f; (: article) mercadoria importada; (meaning) significado, sentido ▶ CPD (duty, licence etc) de importação

importance [ɪmˈpɔːtəns] N importância; **o be of great/little ~** ser de grande/pouca importância

important [ɪmˈpɔːtənt] ADJ importante; **it is ~ that ...** é importante or importa que ...; **it's not ~** não tem importância, não importa

importantly [ɪmˈpɔːtəntlɪ] ADV: **but, more ~ ...** mas, o que é mais importante ...

importation [ɪmpɔːˈteɪʃən] N importação f

imported [ɪmˈpɔːtɪd] ADJ importado

importer [ɪmˈpɔːtəʳ] N importador(a) m/f

impose [ɪmˈpəuz] VT impor ▶ VI: **to ~ on sb** abusar de alguém

imposing [ɪmˈpəuzɪŋ] ADJ imponente

imposition [ɪmpəˈzɪʃən] N (of tax etc) imposição f; **to be an ~ on sb** (person) abusar de alguém

impossibility [ɪmpɔsɪˈbɪlɪtɪ] N impossibilidade f

impossible [ɪmˈpɔsɪbl] ADJ impossível; (situation) inviável; (person) insuportável; **it's ~ for me to leave** é-me impossível sair, não dá para eu sair (inf)

impostor [ɪmˈpɔstəʳ] N impostor(a) m/f

impotence [ˈɪmpətəns] N impotência

impotent [ˈɪmpətənt] ADJ impotente

impound [ɪmˈpaund] VT confiscar

impoverished [ɪmˈpɔvərɪʃt] ADJ empobrecido; (land) esgotado

impracticable [ɪmˈpræktɪkəbl] ADJ impraticável, inexequível

impractical [ɪmˈpræktɪkl] ADJ pouco prático

imprecise [ɪmprɪˈsaɪs] ADJ impreciso, inexato

impregnable [ɪmˈprɛgnəbl] ADJ invulnerável; (castle) inexpugnável

impregnate [ˈɪmprɛgneɪt] VT (gen) impregnar; (soak) embeber; (fertilize) fecundar

impresario [ɪmprɪˈsɑːrɪəu] N empresário(-a)

impress [ɪmˈprɛs] VT impressionar; (mark) imprimir ▶ VI causar boa impressão; **to ~ sth on sb** inculcar algo em alguém; **it ~ed itself on me** fiquei com isso gravado (na memória)

impression [ɪmˈprɛʃən] N impressão f; (footprint etc) marca; (print run) edição f; **to make a good/bad ~ on sb** causar boa/má impressão em alguém; **to be under the ~ that** estar com a impressão de que

impressionable [ɪmˈprɛʃənəbl] ADJ impressionável; (sensitive) sensível

impressionist [ɪmˈprɛʃənɪst] N impressionista m/f

impressive [ɪmˈprɛsɪv] ADJ impressionante

imprint [ˈɪmprɪnt] N impressão f, marca; (Publishing) nome m (da coleção)

imprinted [ɪmˈprɪntɪd] ADJ: **~ on** imprimido em; (fig) gravado em

imprison [ɪmˈprɪzn] VT encarcerar

imprisonment [ɪmˈprɪznmənt] N prisão f

improbable [ɪmˈprɔbəbl] ADJ improvável; (story) inverossímil (BR), inverosímil (PT)

impromptu [ɪmˈprɔmptjuː] ADJ improvisado ▶ ADV de improviso

improper [ɪmˈprɔpəʳ] ADJ (unsuitable) impróprio; (dishonest) desonesto; (unseemly) indecoroso; (indecent) indecente

impropriety [ɪmprəˈpraɪətɪ] N falta de decoro, inconveniência; (indecency) indecência; (of language) impropriedade f

improve [ɪmˈpruːv] VT melhorar ▶ VI melhorar; (pupils) progredir ▶ **improve on, improve upon** VT FUS melhorar

improvement [ɪmˈpruːvmənt] N melhora; (of pupils) progresso; **to make ~s to** melhorar

improvisation [ɪmprəvaɪˈzeɪʃən] N improvisação f

improvise [ˈɪmprəvaɪz] VT, VI improvisar

imprudence [ɪmˈpruːdns] N imprudência

imprudent [ɪmˈpruːdnt] ADJ imprudente

impudent [ˈɪmpjudnt] ADJ insolente, impudente

impugn [ɪmˈpjuːn] VT impugnar, contestar

impulse [ˈɪmpʌls] N impulso, ímpeto; (Elec) impulso; **to act on ~** agir sem pensar or num impulso

impulse buy N compra por impulso

impulsive [ɪmˈpʌlsɪv] ADJ impulsivo

impunity [ɪmˈpjuːnɪtɪ] N: **with ~** impunemente

impure [ɪmˈpjuəʳ] ADJ (adulterated) adulterado; (not pure) impuro

impurity [ɪmˈpjuərɪtɪ] N impureza

IN (US) ABBR (Post) = **Indiana**

in [ɪn] PREP **1** (*indicating place, position*) em; **in
the house/garden** na casa/no jardim; **I have
the money in my hand** estou com o
dinheiro na mão; **in here/there** aqui
dentro/lá dentro
2 (*with place names: of town, country, region*) em;
in London em Londres; **in England/Japan/
Canada/the United States** na Inglaterra/
no Japão/no Canadá/nos Estados Unidos; **in
Rio** no Rio
3 (*indicating time: during*) em; **in spring/
autumn** na primavera/no outono; **in 1988**
em 1988; **in May** em maio; **I'll see you in
July** até julho; **in the morning** de manhã;
at 4 o'clock in the afternoon às 4 da tarde
4 (*indicating time: in the space of*) em; **I did it in 3
hours/days** fiz isto em 3 horas/dias; **in 2
weeks, in 2 weeks' time** daqui a 2 semanas
5 (*indicating manner etc*): **in a loud/soft voice**
em voz alta/numa voz suave; **written in
pencil/ink** escrito a lápis/à caneta; **in
English/Portuguese** em inglês/português;
the boy in the blue shirt o menino de
camisa azul
6 (*indicating circumstances*): **in the sun** ao *or*
sob o sol; **in the rain** na chuva; **a rise in
prices** um aumento nos preços
7 (*indicating mood, state*): **in tears** aos prantos;
in anger/despair com raiva/desesperado;
in good condition em boas condições; **to
live in luxury** viver no luxo
8 (*with ratios, numbers*): **1 in 10** 1 em 10, 1 em
cada 10; **20 pence in the pound** vinte pênis
numa libra; **they lined up in twos** eles se
alinharam dois a dois
9 (*referring to people, works*) em; **in (the works
of) Dickens** nas obras de Dickens
10 (*indicating profession etc*): **to be in teaching/
publishing** ser professor/trabalhar numa
editora
11 (*after superl*): **the best pupil in the class** o
melhor aluno da classe; **the biggest/
smallest in Europe** o maior/menor na
Europa
12 (*with present participle*): **in saying this** ao
dizer isto
▶ ADV: **to be in** (*person: at home*) estar em casa;
(: *at work*) estar no trabalho; (*fashion*) estar na
moda; (*ship, plane, train*): **it's in** chegou; **is he
in?** ele está?; **to ask sb in** convidar alguém
para entrar; **to run/limp** *etc* **in** entrar
correndo/mancando *etc*
▶ N: **the ins and outs** (*of proposal, situation etc*)
os cantos e recantos, os pormenores

in. ABBR = **inch**

inability [ɪnə'bɪlɪtɪ] N: ~ **(to do)** incapacidade
f (de fazer); ~ **to pay** impossibilidade de
pagar
inaccessible [ɪnək'sɛsɪbl] ADJ inacessível
inaccuracy [ɪn'ækjurəsɪ] N inexatidão *f*,
imprecisão *f*

inaccurate [ɪn'ækjurət] ADJ inexato,
impreciso
inaction [ɪn'ækʃən] N inação *f*
inactivity [ɪnæk'tɪvɪtɪ] N inatividade *f*
inadequacy [ɪn'ædɪkwəsɪ] ADJ (*insufficiency*)
insuficiência
inadequate [ɪn'ædɪkwət] ADJ (*insufficient*)
insuficiente; (*unsuitable*) inadequado;
(*person*) impróprio
inadmissible [ɪnəd'mɪsəbl] ADJ inadmissível
inadvertent [ɪnəd'vɜːtənt] ADJ (*mistake*)
cometido sem querer
inadvertently [ɪnəd'vɜːtntlɪ] ADV
inadvertidamente, sem querer
inadvisable [ɪnəd'vaɪzəbl] ADJ
desaconselhável, inoportuno
inane [ɪ'neɪn] ADJ tolo; (*fatuous*) vazio
inanimate [ɪn'ænɪmət] ADJ inanimado
inapplicable [ɪn'æplɪkəbl] ADJ inaplicável
inappropriate [ɪnə'prəuprɪət] ADJ
inadequado; (*word, expression*) impróprio
inapt [ɪn'æpt] ADJ inapto
inaptitude [ɪn'æptɪtjuːd] N incapacidade *f*,
inaptidão *f*
inarticulate [ɪnɑː'tɪkjulət] ADJ (*person*)
incapaz de expressar-se (bem); (*speech*)
inarticulado
inasmuch as [ɪnəz'mʌtʃ-] ADV, CONJ (*given that*)
visto que; (*since*) desde que, já que
inattention [ɪnə'tɛnʃən] N inatenção *f*
inattentive [ɪnə'tɛntɪv] ADJ desatento
inaudible [ɪn'ɔːdɪbl] ADJ inaudível
inaugural [ɪ'nɔːgjurəl] ADJ (*speech*) inaugural;
(: *of president*) de posse
inaugurate [ɪ'nɔːgjureɪt] VT inaugurar;
(*president, official*) empossar
inauguration [ɪnɔːgju'reɪʃən] N inauguração *f*;
(*of president, official*) posse *f*
inauspicious [ɪnɔːs'pɪʃəs] ADJ infausto
in-between ADJ intermediário
inborn [ɪn'bɔːn] ADJ (*feeling*) inato; (*defect*)
congênito
inbox ['ɪnbɒks] N (*Comput*) caixa de entrada;
(*US: for papers*) cesta para correspondência de
entrada
inbred [ɪn'brɛd] ADJ inato; (*family*) de
procriação consanguínea
inbreeding [ɪn'briːdɪŋ] N endogamia
Inc. ABBR = **incorporated**
Inca ['ɪŋkə] ADJ (*also:* **Incan**) inca, incaico ▶ N
inca *m/f*
incalculable [ɪn'kælkjuləbl] ADJ incalculável
incapability [ɪnkeɪpə'bɪlɪtɪ] N incapacidade *f*
incapable [ɪn'keɪpəbl] ADJ incapaz; ~ **of doing**
incapaz de fazer
incapacitate [ɪnkə'pæsɪteɪt] VT incapacitar
incapacitated [ɪnkə'pæsɪteɪtɪd] ADJ (*Law*)
incapacitado
incapacity [ɪnkə'pæsɪtɪ] N (*inability*)
incapacidade *f*
incarcerate [ɪn'kɑːsəreɪt] VT encarcerar
incarnate [*adj* ɪn'kɑːnɪt, *vt* 'ɪnkɑːneɪt] ADJ
encarnado, personificado ▶ VT encarnar

incarnation [ɪnkɑːˈneɪʃən] N encarnação f
incendiary [ɪnˈsɛndɪərɪ] ADJ incendiário ▶ N
(*bomb*) bomba incendiária
incense [*n* ˈɪnsɛns, *vt* ɪnˈsɛns] N incenso ▶ VT
(*anger*) exasperar, enraivecer
incense burner N incensório
incentive [ɪnˈsɛntɪv] N incentivo, estímulo
incentive scheme N plano de incentivos
inception [ɪnˈsɛpʃən] N começo, início
incessant [ɪnˈsɛsnt] ADJ incessante, contínuo
incessantly [ɪnˈsɛsntlɪ] ADV constantemente
incest [ˈɪnsɛst] N incesto
inch [ɪntʃ] N polegada (= 25 mm; 12 in a foot); **to
be within an ~ of** estar a um passo de; **he
didn't give an ~** ele não cedeu nem um
milímetro
▶ **inch forward** VI avançar palmo a palmo
inch tape (BRIT) N fita métrica
incidence [ˈɪnsɪdns] N (*of crime, disease*)
incidência
incident [ˈɪnsɪdnt] N incidente *m*, evento;
(*in book*) episódio
incidental [ɪnsɪˈdɛntl] ADJ acessório, não
essencial; (*unplanned*) acidental, casual;
~ expenses despesas *fpl* adicionais
incidentally [ɪnsɪˈdɛntəlɪ] ADV (*by the way*)
a propósito
incidental music N música de cena *or* de
fundo
incinerate [ɪnˈsɪnəreɪt] VT incinerar
incinerator [ɪnˈsɪnəreɪtəʳ] N incinerador *m*
incipient [ɪnˈsɪpɪənt] ADJ incipiente
incision [ɪnˈsɪʒən] N incisão f
incisive [ɪnˈsaɪsɪv] ADJ (*mind*) penetrante,
perspicaz; (*tone*) mordaz, sarcástico; (*remark
etc*) incisivo
incisor [ɪnˈsaɪzəʳ] N incisivo
incite [ɪnˈsaɪt] VT (*rioters*) incitar; (*violence*)
provocar
incl. ABBR = **including; inclusive**
inclement [ɪnˈklɛmənt] ADJ (*weather*)
inclemente
inclination [ɪnklɪˈneɪʃən] N (*tendency*)
tendência; (*disposition*) inclinação f
incline [*n* ˈɪnklaɪn, *vt, vi* ɪnˈklaɪn] N inclinação f,
ladeira ▶ VT (*slope*) inclinar; (*head*) curvar,
inclinar ▶ VI inclinar-se; **to be ~d to** (*tend*)
tender a, ser propenso a; (*be willing*) estar
disposto a
include [ɪnˈkluːd] VT incluir; **the service is/is
not ~d** o serviço está/não está incluído
including [ɪnˈkluːdɪŋ] PREP inclusive; **~ tip**
gorjeta incluída
inclusion [ɪnˈkluːʒən] N inclusão f
inclusive [ɪnˈkluːsɪv] ADJ incluído, incluso
▶ ADV inclusive; **~ of** incluindo; **£50 ~ of all
surcharges** £50, incluídas todas as
sobretaxas
inclusive terms (BRIT) NPL preço global
incognito [ɪnkɔɡˈniːtəu] ADV incógnito
incoherent [ɪnkəuˈhɪərənt] ADJ incoerente
income [ˈɪŋkʌm] N (*earnings*) renda,
rendimentos *mpl*; (*unearned*) renda; (*profit*)

lucro; **gross/net ~** renda bruta/líquida;
~ and expenditure account conta de
receitas e despesas
income bracket N faixa salarial
income tax N imposto de renda (BR), imposto
complementar (PT)
income tax inspector N fiscal *m/f* do imposto
de renda
income tax return N declaração f do imposto
de renda
incoming [ˈɪnkʌmɪŋ] ADJ (*flight, passenger*) de
chegada; (*mail*) de entrada; (*government,
tenant*) novo; **~ tide** maré enchente
incommunicado [ɪnkəmjunɪˈkɑːdəu] ADJ
incomunicável
incomparable [ɪnˈkɔmpərəbl] ADJ
incomparável
incompatible [ɪnkəmˈpætɪbl] ADJ
incompatível
incompetence [ɪnˈkɔmpɪtəns] N
incompetência
incompetent [ɪnˈkɔmpɪtənt] ADJ
incompetente
incomplete [ɪnkəmˈpliːt] ADJ incompleto;
(*unfinished*) por terminar
incomprehensible [ɪnkɔmprɪˈhɛnsɪbl] ADJ
incompreensível
inconceivable [ɪnkənˈsiːvəbl] ADJ
inconcebível
inconclusive [ɪnkənˈkluːsɪv] ADJ
inconclusivo; (*argument*) pouco convincente
incongruous [ɪnˈkɔŋɡruəs] ADJ (*foolish*)
ridículo, absurdo; (*situation, figure*)
incongruente; (*remark, act*) impróprio
inconsequential [ɪnkɔnsɪˈkwɛnʃl] ADJ sem
importância
inconsiderable [ɪnkənˈsɪdərəbl] ADJ: **not ~**
importante
inconsiderate [ɪnkənˈsɪdərət] ADJ sem
consideração; **how ~ of him!** que falta de
consideração (de sua parte)!
inconsistency [ɪnkənˈsɪstənsɪ] N
inconsistência
inconsistent [ɪnkənˈsɪstnt] ADJ
inconsistente; **~ with** (*beliefs*) incompatível
com
inconsolable [ɪnkənˈsəuləbl] ADJ inconsolável
inconspicuous [ɪnkənˈspɪkjuəs] ADJ modesto,
discreto; (*more intensely: modest*) modesto; **to
make o.s. ~** não chamar a atenção
inconstant [ɪnˈkɔnstnt] ADJ inconstante
incontinence [ɪnˈkɔntɪnəns] N incontinência
incontinent [ɪnˈkɔntɪnənt] ADJ incontinente
incontrovertible [ɪnkɔntrəˈvəːtəbl] ADJ
incontestável
inconvenience [ɪnkənˈviːnjəns] N (*quality*)
inconveniência; (*problem*) inconveniente *m*
▶ VT incomodar; **don't ~ yourself** não se
incomode
inconvenient [ɪnkənˈviːnjənt] ADJ
inconveniente, incômodo; (*time, place*)
inoportuno; **that time is very ~ for me**
esse horário me é muito inconveniente

incorporate [ɪn'kɔ:pəreɪt] VT incorporar; (*contain*) compreender; (*add*) incluir

incorporated company [ɪn'kɔ:pəreɪtɪd-] (US) N ≈ sociedade f anônima

incorrect [ɪnkə'rɛkt] ADJ incorreto

incorrigible [ɪn'kɔrɪdʒɪbl] ADJ incorrigível

incorruptible [ɪnkə'rʌptɪbl] ADJ incorruptível; (*not open to bribes*) insubornável

increase [n 'ɪnkri:s, vi, vt ɪn'kri:s] N aumento ▶ VI, VT aumentar; **an ~ of 5%** um aumento de 5%; **to be on the ~** estar em crescimento *or* alta

increasing [ɪn'kri:sɪŋ] ADJ (*number*) crescente, em aumento

increasingly [ɪn'kri:sɪŋlɪ] ADV (*more intensely*) progressivamente; (*more often*) cada vez mais

incredible [ɪn'krɛdɪbl] ADJ inacreditável; (*enormous*) incrível

incredulous [ɪn'krɛdjuləs] ADJ incrédulo

increment ['ɪnkrɪmənt] N aumento, incremento

incriminate [ɪn'krɪmɪneɪt] VT incriminar

incriminating [ɪn'krɪmɪneɪtɪŋ] ADJ incriminador(a)

incubate ['ɪnkjubeɪt] VT, VI incubar

incubation [ɪnkju'beɪʃən] N incubação f

incubation period N período de incubação

incubator ['ɪnkjubeɪtəʳ] N incubadora; (*for eggs*) chocadeira

inculcate ['ɪnkʌlkeɪt] VT: **to ~ sth in sb** inculcar algo a alguém

incumbent [ɪn'kʌmbənt] N titular m/f ▶ ADJ: **it is ~ on him to ...** cabe a ele ...

incur [ɪn'kə:ʳ] VT incorrer em; (*expenses*) contrair

incurable [ɪn'kjuərəbl] ADJ incurável; (*fig*) irremediável

incursion [ɪn'kə:ʃən] N incursão f

indebted [ɪn'dɛtɪd] ADJ: **to be ~ to sb** estar em dívida com alguém, dever obrigação a alguém

indecency [ɪn'di:snsɪ] N indecência

indecent [ɪn'di:snt] ADJ indecente

indecent assault (BRIT) N atentado contra o pudor

indecent exposure N exibição f obscena, exibicionismo

indecipherable [ɪndɪ'saɪfərəbl] ADJ indecifrável

indecision [ɪndɪ'sɪʒən] N indecisão f

indecisive [ɪndɪ'saɪsɪv] ADJ indeciso; (*discussion*) inconcludente, sem resultados

indeed [ɪn'di:d] ADV de fato; (*certainly*) certamente; (*furthermore*) aliás; **yes ~!** claro que sim!

indefatigable [ɪndɪ'fætɪgəbl] ADJ incansável

indefensible [ɪndɪ'fɛnsɪbl] ADJ indefensível

indefinable [ɪndɪ'faɪnəbl] ADJ indefinível

indefinite [ɪn'dɛfɪnɪt] ADJ indefinido; (*uncertain*) impreciso; (*period, number*) indeterminado

indefinitely [ɪn'dɛfɪnɪtlɪ] ADV (*wait*) indefinidamente

indelible [ɪn'dɛlɪbl] ADJ indelével

indelicate [ɪn'dɛlɪkɪt] ADJ (*tactless*) inábil; (*not polite*) indelicado, rude

indemnify [ɪn'dɛmnɪfaɪ] VT indenizar, compensar

indemnity [ɪn'dɛmnɪtɪ] N (*insurance*) garantia, seguro; (*compensation*) indenização f

indent [ɪn'dɛnt] VT (*text*) recolher ▶ VI: **to ~ for sth** (*Comm*) encomendar algo

indentation [ɪndɛn'teɪʃən] N entalhe m, recorte m; (*Typ*) parágrafo, recuo

indenture [ɪn'dɛntʃəʳ] N contrato de aprendizagem

independence [ɪndɪ'pɛndns] N independência

Independence Day N *ver nota*

> O dia da Independência (**Independence Day**) é a festa nacional dos Estados Unidos. Todo dia 4 de julho os americanos comemoram a adoção, em 1776, da declaração de Independência escrita por Thomas Jefferson que proclamava a separação das 13 colônias americanas da Grã-Bretanha.

independent [ɪndɪ'pɛndnt] ADJ independente; (*business, school*) privado; (*inquiry*) imparcial; **to become ~** tornar-se independente

independently [ɪndɪ'pɛndntlɪ] ADV independentemente

in-depth ['ɪndɛpθ] ADJ aprofundado

indescribable [ɪndɪ'skraɪbəbl] ADJ indescritível

indestructible [ɪndɪ'strʌktəbl] ADJ indestrutível

indeterminate [ɪndɪ'tə:mɪnɪt] ADJ indeterminado

index ['ɪndɛks] N (*pl* **indexes**) (*in book*) índice m; (*in library etc*) catálogo; (*pl* **indices** ['ɪndɪsi:z]) (*ratio, sign*) índice m, expoente m

index card N ficha de arquivo

indexed ['ɪndɛkst] (US) ADJ = **index-linked**

index finger N dedo indicador

index-linked [-lɪŋkt] (BRIT) ADJ vinculado ao índice (do custo de vida)

India ['ɪndɪə] N Índia

Indian ['ɪndɪən] ADJ, N (*from India*) indiano(-a); (*American, Brazilian*) índio(-a); **Red ~** índio(-a) pele vermelha

Indian ink N tinta nanquim

Indian Ocean N: **the ~** o oceano Índico

Indian summer N (*fig*) veranico

India paper N papel m da China

India rubber N borracha

indicate ['ɪndɪkeɪt] VT (*show*) sugerir; (*point to*) indicar; (*mention*) mencionar ▶ VI (BRIT Aut): **to ~ left/right** indicar para a esquerda/direita

indication [ɪndɪ'keɪʃən] N indício, sinal m

indicative [ɪn'dɪkətɪv] ADJ indicativo ▶ N (*Ling*) indicativo; **to be ~ of sth** ser sintomático de algo

indicator ['ɪndɪkeɪtəʳ] N indicador m; (Aut) pisca-pisca m

indices ['ɪndɪsiːz] NPL of **index**

indict [ɪn'daɪt] VT acusar

indictable [ɪn'daɪtəbl] ADJ (person) culpado; ~ **offence** crime sujeito às penas da lei

indictment [ɪn'daɪtmənt] N acusação f, denúncia

indifference [ɪn'dɪfrəns] N indiferença

indifferent [ɪn'dɪfrənt] ADJ indiferente; (quality) medíocre

indigenous [ɪn'dɪdʒɪnəs] ADJ indígena, nativo

indigestible [ɪndɪ'dʒɛstɪbl] ADJ indigesto

indigestion [ɪndɪ'dʒɛstʃən] N indigestão f

indignant [ɪn'dɪgnənt] ADJ: **to be ~ about sth/with sb** estar indignado com algo/alguém, indignar-se de algo/alguém

indignation [ɪndɪg'neɪʃən] N indignação f

indignity [ɪn'dɪgnɪtɪ] N indignidade f; (insult) ultraje m, afronta

indigo ['ɪndɪgəu] ADJ cor de anil inv ▶ N anil m

indirect [ɪndɪ'rɛkt] ADJ indireto

indirectly [ɪndɪ'rɛktlɪ] ADV indiretamente

indiscreet [ɪndɪ'skriːt] ADJ indiscreto; (rash) imprudente

indiscretion [ɪndɪ'skrɛʃən] N indiscrição f; imprudência

indiscriminate [ɪndɪ'skrɪmɪnət] ADJ indiscriminado

indispensable [ɪndɪ'spɛnsəbl] ADJ indispensável, imprescindível

indisposed [ɪndɪ'spəuzd] ADJ (unwell) indisposto

indisposition [ɪndɪspə'zɪʃən] N (illness) mal-estar m, indisposição f

indisputable [ɪndɪ'spjuːtəbl] ADJ incontestável

indistinct [ɪndɪ'stɪŋkt] ADJ indistinto; (memory, noise) confuso, vago

indistinguishable [ɪndɪ'stɪŋwɪʃəbl] ADJ indistinguível

individual [ɪndɪ'vɪdjuəl] N indivíduo ▶ ADJ individual; (personal) pessoal; (characteristic) particular

individualist [ɪndɪ'vɪdjuəlɪst] N individualista m/f

individuality [ɪndɪvɪdju'ælɪtɪ] N individualidade f

individually [ɪndɪ'vɪdjuəlɪ] ADV individualmente, particularmente

indivisible [ɪndɪ'vɪzɪbl] ADJ indivisível

Indo-China ['ɪndəu-] N Indochina

indoctrinate [ɪn'dɔktrɪneɪt] VT doutrinar

indoctrination [ɪndɔktrɪ'neɪʃən] N doutrinação f

indolent ['ɪndələnt] ADJ indolente, preguiçoso

Indonesia [ɪndə'niːzɪə] N Indonésia

Indonesian [ɪndə'niːzɪən] ADJ indonésio ▶ N indonésio(-a); (Ling) indonésio

indoor ['ɪndɔːʳ] ADJ (inner) interno, interior; (inside) dentro de casa; (swimming pool) coberto; (games, sport) de salão

indoors [ɪn'dɔːz] ADV em lugar fechado; (at home) em casa

indubitable [ɪn'djuːbɪtəbl] ADJ indubitável

induce [ɪn'djuːs] VT (Med) induzir; (bring about) causar, produzir; (provoke) provocar; **to ~ sb to do sth** induzir alguém a fazer algo

inducement [ɪn'djuːsmənt] N (incentive) incentivo

induct [ɪn'dʌkt] VT instalar

induction [ɪn'dʌkʃən] N (Med: of birth) indução f

induction course (BRIT) N curso de indução

indulge [ɪn'dʌldʒ] VT (desire) satisfazer; (whim) condescender com; (person) comprazer; (child) fazer a vontade de ▶ VI: **to ~ in** entregar-se a, satisfazer-se com

indulgence [ɪn'dʌldʒəns] N (of desire) satisfação f; (leniency) indulgência, tolerância

indulgent [ɪn'dʌldʒənt] ADJ indulgente

industrial [ɪn'dʌstrɪəl] ADJ industrial; (injury) de trabalho; (dispute) trabalhista

industrial action N greve f

industrial design N desenho industrial

industrial estate (BRIT) N zona industrial

industrialist [ɪn'dʌstrɪəlɪst] N industrial m/f

industrialize [ɪn'dʌstrɪəlaɪz] VT industrializar

industrial park (US) N = **industrial estate**

industrial relations NPL relações fpl industriais

industrial tribunal (BRIT) N ≈ tribunal m do trabalho

industrial unrest (BRIT) N agitação f operária

industrious [ɪn'dʌstrɪəs] ADJ trabalhador(a); (student) aplicado

industry ['ɪndəstrɪ] N indústria; (diligence) aplicação f, diligência

inebriated [ɪ'niːbrɪeɪtɪd] ADJ embriagado, bêbado

inedible [ɪn'ɛdɪbl] ADJ não-comestível

ineffective [ɪnɪ'fɛktɪv] ADJ ineficaz

ineffectual [ɪnɪ'fɛktʃuəl] ADJ = **ineffective**

inefficiency [ɪnɪ'fɪʃənsɪ] N ineficiência

inefficient [ɪnɪ'fɪʃənt] ADJ ineficiente

inelegant [ɪn'ɛlɪgənt] ADJ deselegante

ineligible [ɪn'ɛlɪdʒɪbl] ADJ (candidate) inelegível; **to be ~ for sth** não estar qualificado para algo

inept [ɪ'nɛpt] ADJ inepto

ineptitude [ɪ'nɛptɪtjuːd] N inépcia, incompetência

inequality [ɪnɪ'kwɔlɪtɪ] N desigualdade f

inequitable [ɪn'ɛkwɪtəbl] ADJ injusto, iníquo

ineradicable [ɪnɪ'rædɪkəbl] ADJ inerradicável

inert [ɪ'nəːt] ADJ inerte; (immobile) imóvel

inertia [ɪ'nəːʃə] N inércia; (laziness) lerdeza

inertia-reel seat belt N cinto de segurança retrátil

inescapable [ɪnɪ'skeɪpəbl] ADJ inevitável

inessential [ɪnɪ'sɛnʃl] ADJ desnecessário

inestimable [ɪn'ɛstɪməbl] ADJ inestimável, incalculável

inevitable [ɪn'ɛvɪtəbl] ADJ inevitável; (necessary) forçoso, necessário

inevitably [ɪn'ɛvɪtəblɪ] ADV inevitavelmente

inexact [ɪnɪg'zækt] ADJ inexato

inexcusable [ɪnɪks'kjuːzəbl] ADJ imperdoável, indesculpável

inexhaustible [ɪnɪg'zɔːstɪbl] ADJ inesgotável, inexaurível

inexorable [ɪn'ɛksərəbl] ADJ inexorável

inexpensive [ɪnɪk'spɛnsɪv] ADJ barato, econômico

inexperience [ɪnɪk'spɪərɪəns] N inexperiência, falta de experiência

inexperienced [ɪnɪk'spɪərɪənst] ADJ inexperiente

inexplicable [ɪnɪk'splɪkəbl] ADJ inexplicável

inexpressible [ɪnɪk'sprɛsɪbl] ADJ inexprimível

inextricable [ɪnɪk'strɪkəbl] ADJ inextricável

infallibility [ɪnfælə'bɪlɪtɪ] N infalibilidade f

infallible [ɪn'fælɪbl] ADJ infalível

infamous ['ɪnfəməs] ADJ infame, abominável

infamy ['ɪnfəmɪ] N infâmia

infancy ['ɪnfənsɪ] N infância

infant ['ɪnfənt] N (baby) bebê m; (young child) criança

infantile ['ɪnfəntaɪl] ADJ infantil; (pej) acriançado

infant mortality N mortalidade f infantil

infantry ['ɪnfəntrɪ] N infantaria

infantryman ['ɪnfəntrɪmən] (irreg: like **man**) N soldado de infantaria

infant school (BRIT) N pré-escola

infatuated [ɪn'fætjueɪtɪd] ADJ: ~ **with** apaixonado por

infatuation [ɪnfætju'eɪʃən] N gamação f, paixão f louca

infect [ɪn'fɛkt] VT (wound) infeccionar, infetar; (person) contagiar; (food) contaminar; (fig: pej) corromper, contaminar; **~ed with** (illness) contagiado por; **to become ~ed** (wound) infeccionar(-se), infetar(-se)

infection [ɪn'fɛkʃən] N infecção f; (fig) contágio

infectious [ɪn'fɛkʃəs] ADJ contagioso; (fig) infeccioso

infer [ɪn'fəːʳ] VT deduzir, inferir

inference ['ɪnfərəns] N dedução f, inferência

inferior [ɪn'fɪərɪəʳ] ADJ inferior; (goods) de qualidade inferior ▶ N inferior m/f; (in rank) subalterno(-a); **to feel ~** sentir-se inferior

inferiority [ɪnfɪərɪ'ɔrətɪ] N inferioridade f

inferiority complex N complexo de inferioridade

infernal [ɪn'fəːnl] ADJ infernal

infernally [ɪn'fəːnəlɪ] ADV (very) muito

inferno [ɪn'fəːnəu] N inferno; (fig) inferno de chamas

infertile [ɪn'fəːtaɪl] ADJ infértil; (person, animal) estéril

infertility [ɪnfə'tɪlɪtɪ] N infertilidade f; (of person, animal) esterilidade f

infested [ɪn'fɛstɪd] ADJ: ~ **(with)** infestado (de), assolado (por)

infidelity [ɪnfɪ'dɛlɪtɪ] N infidelidade f

in-fighting N lutas fpl internas, conflitos mpl internos

infiltrate ['ɪnfɪltreɪt] VT (troops etc) infiltrar-se em ▶ VI infiltrar-se

infinite ['ɪnfɪnɪt] ADJ infinito; (time, money) ilimitado

infinitely ['ɪnfɪnɪtlɪ] ADV infinitamente

infinitesimal [ɪnfɪnɪ'tɛsɪməl] ADJ infinitésimo

infinitive [ɪn'fɪnɪtɪv] N infinitivo

infinity [ɪn'fɪnɪtɪ] N (also Math) infinito; (an infinity) infinidade f

infirm [ɪn'fəːm] ADJ enfermo, fraco

infirmary [ɪn'fəːmərɪ] N enfermaria, hospital m

infirmity [ɪn'fəːmɪtɪ] N fraqueza; (illness) enfermidade f, achaque m

inflame [ɪn'fleɪm] VT inflamar

inflamed [ɪn'fleɪmd] ADJ inflamado

inflammable [ɪn'flæməbl] (BRIT) ADJ inflamável

inflammation [ɪnflə'meɪʃən] N inflamação f

inflammatory [ɪn'flæmətərɪ] ADJ (speech) incendiário

inflatable [ɪn'fleɪtəbl] ADJ inflável

inflate [ɪn'fleɪt] VT (tyre, balloon) inflar, encher; (price) inflar

inflated [ɪn'fleɪtɪd] ADJ (style) empolado, pomposo; (value) excessivo

inflation [ɪn'fleɪʃən] N (Econ) inflação f

inflationary [ɪn'fleɪʃənərɪ] ADJ inflacionário

inflexible [ɪn'flɛksɪbl] ADJ inflexível

inflict [ɪn'flɪkt] VT: **to ~ sth on sb** infligir algo em alguém; (tax etc) impor algo a alguém

infliction [ɪn'flɪkʃən] N imposição f, inflição f

in-flight ADJ (refuelling) em voo; (movie) exibido durante o voo; (service) de bordo

inflow ['ɪnfləu] N afluência

influence ['ɪnfluəns] N influência ▶ VT influir em, influenciar; (persuade) persuadir; **under the ~ of alcohol** sob o efeito do álcool

influential [ɪnflu'ɛnʃl] ADJ influente

influenza [ɪnflu'ɛnzə] N gripe f

influx ['ɪnflʌks] N (of refugees) afluxo; (of funds) influxo

infomercial ['ɪnfəuməːʃl] (US) N (for product) infomercial m

inform [ɪn'fɔːm] VT: **to ~ sb of sth** informar alguém de algo; (warn) avisar alguém de algo; (communicate) comunicar algo a alguém ▶ VI: **to ~ on sb** delatar alguém; **to ~ sb about** informar alguém sobre

informal [ɪn'fɔːml] ADJ informal; (visit, discussion) extraoficial; (intimate) familiar; **"dress ~"** "traje de passeio"

informality [ɪnfɔː'mælɪtɪ] N falta de cerimônia; (intimacy) intimidade f; (familiarity) familiaridade f; (ease) informalidade f

informally [ɪn'fɔːməlɪ] ADV sem formalidade; (unofficially) não oficialmente

informant [ɪn'fɔːmənt] N informante m/f; (to police) delator(a) m/f

information [ɪnfə'meɪʃən] N informação f, informações fpl; (news) notícias fpl; (knowledge) conhecimento; **a piece of ~**

uma informação; **for your ~** para a sua informação, para o seu governo

information bureau N balcão *m* de informações

information office N escritório de informações

information processing N processamento de informações

information retrieval N recuperação *f* de informações

information technology N informática

informative [ɪnˈfɔːmətɪv] ADJ informativo

informed [ɪnˈfɔːmd] ADJ informado; **an ~ guess** um palpite baseado em conhecimento dos fatos

informer [ɪnˈfɔːməʳ] N delator(a) *m/f*

infra dig [ˈɪnfrə-] (*inf*) ADJ ABBR (= *infra dignitatem*) abaixo da minha (*or* sua *etc*) dignidade

infra-red [ˈɪnfrə-] ADJ infravermelho

infrastructure [ˈɪnfrəstrʌktʃəʳ] N infraestrutura

infrequent [ɪnˈfriːkwənt] ADJ infrequente

infringe [ɪnˈfrɪndʒ] VT infringir, transgredir ▶ VI: **to ~ on** violar

infringement [ɪnˈfrɪndʒmənt] N transgressão *f*; (*of rights*) violação *f*; (*Sport*) infração *f*

infuriate [ɪnˈfjuərɪeɪt] VT enfurecer, enraivecer

infuriating [ɪnˈfjuərɪeɪtɪŋ] ADJ de dar raiva, enfurecedor(a)

infuse [ɪnˈfjuːz] VT: **to ~ sb with sth** (*fig*) inspirar *or* infundir algo em alguém

infusion [ɪnˈfjuːʒən] N (*tea etc*) infusão *f*

ingenious [ɪnˈdʒiːnjəs] ADJ engenhoso

ingenuity [ɪndʒɪˈnjuːɪtɪ] N engenho, habilidade *f*

ingenuous [ɪnˈdʒɛnjuəs] ADJ ingênuo

ingot [ˈɪŋɡət] N lingote *m*

ingrained [ɪnˈɡreɪnd] ADJ arraigado, enraizado

ingratiate [ɪnˈɡreɪʃɪeɪt] VT: **to ~ o.s. with** cair nas (boas) graças de

ingratiating [ɪnˈɡreɪʃɪeɪtɪŋ] ADJ insinuante

ingratitude [ɪnˈɡrætɪtjuːd] N ingratidão *f*

ingredient [ɪnˈɡriːdɪənt] N ingrediente *m*; (*of situation*) fator *m*

ingrowing toenail [ˈɪnɡrəʊɪŋ-], **ingrown toenail** [ˈɪnɡrəʊn-] N unha encravada

inhabit [ɪnˈhæbɪt] VT habitar; (*occupy*) ocupar

inhabitable [ɪnˈhæbɪtəbl] ADJ habitável

inhabitant [ɪnˈhæbɪtənt] N habitante *m/f*

inhale [ɪnˈheɪl] VT inalar ▶ VI (*in smoking*) tragar

inhaler [ɪnˈheɪləʳ] N inalador *m*

inherent [ɪnˈhɪərənt] ADJ: **~ in** *or* **to** inerente a

inherently [ɪnˈhɪərəntlɪ] ADV inerentemente, em si

inherit [ɪnˈhɛrɪt] VT herdar

inheritance [ɪnˈhɛrɪtəns] N herança; (*fig*) patrimônio

inhibit [ɪnˈhɪbɪt] VT inibir; **to ~ sb from doing sth** impedir alguém de fazer algo

inhibited [ɪnˈhɪbɪtɪd] ADJ inibido

inhibiting [ɪnˈhɪbɪtɪŋ] ADJ constrangedor(a)

inhibition [ɪnhɪˈbɪʃən] N inibição *f*

inhospitable [ɪnhɔsˈpɪtəbl] ADJ (*person*) inospitaleiro; (*place*) inóspito

inhuman [ɪnˈhjuːmən] ADJ inumano, desumano

inhumane [ɪnhjuːˈmeɪn] ADJ desumano

inimitable [ɪˈnɪmɪtəbl] ADJ inimitável

iniquity [ɪˈnɪkwɪtɪ] N iniquidade *f*; (*injustice*) injustiça

initial [ɪˈnɪʃl] ADJ inicial; (*first*) primeiro ▶ N inicial *f* ▶ VT marcar com iniciais; **initials** NPL (*of name*) iniciais *fpl*; (*abbreviation*) abreviatura, sigla

initialize [ɪˈnɪʃəlaɪz] VT (*Comput*) inicializar

initially [ɪˈnɪʃəlɪ] ADV inicialmente, no início; (*first*) primeiramente

initiate [ɪˈnɪʃɪeɪt] VT (*start*) iniciar, começar; (*person*) iniciar; **to ~ sb into a secret** revelar um segredo a alguém; **to ~ proceedings against sb** (*Law*) abrir um processo contra alguém

initiation [ɪnɪʃɪˈeɪʃən] N (*into secret etc*) iniciação *f*; (*beginning*) começo, início

initiative [ɪˈnɪʃətɪv] N iniciativa; **to take the ~** tomar a iniciativa

inject [ɪnˈdʒɛkt] VT (*liquid, fig: money*) injetar; (*person*) dar uma injeção em; (*fig: put in*) introduzir

injection [ɪnˈdʒɛkʃən] N injeção *f*; **to have an ~** tomar uma injeção

injudicious [ɪndʒuˈdɪʃəs] ADJ imprudente

injunction [ɪnˈdʒʌŋkʃən] N injunção *f*, ordem *f*

injure [ˈɪndʒəʳ] VT ferir; (*damage: reputation etc*) prejudicar; (*offend*) ofender, magoar; **to ~ o.s.** ferir-se

injured [ˈɪndʒəd] ADJ (*person, leg*) ferido; (*feelings*) ofendido, magoado; **~ party** (*Law*) parte *f* lesada

injurious [ɪnˈdʒuərɪəs] ADJ: **~ (to)** prejudicial (a)

injury [ˈɪndʒərɪ] N ferida; (*wrong*) dano, prejuízo; **to escape without ~** escapar ileso

injury time N (*Sport*) desconto

injustice [ɪnˈdʒʌstɪs] N injustiça; **to do sb an ~** fazer mau juízo de alguém

ink [ɪŋk] N tinta

ink-jet printer N impressora a tinta

inkling [ˈɪŋklɪŋ] N suspeita; (*idea*): **to have an ~ of** ter uma vaga ideia de

ink pad N almofada de tinta

inky [ˈɪŋkɪ] ADJ manchado de tinta

inlaid [ˈɪnleɪd] ADJ (*with gems*) incrustado; (*table etc*) marchetado

inland [*adj* ˈɪnlənd, *adv* ɪnˈlænd] ADJ interior, interno ▶ ADV para o interior; **~ waterways** hidrovias *fpl*

Inland Revenue (BRIT) N ≈ fisco, ≈ receita federal (BR)

in-laws NPL sogros *mpl*

inlet [ˈɪnlɛt] N (*Geo*) enseada, angra; (*Tech*) entrada

inlet pipe N tubo de admissão
inmate ['ɪnmeɪt] N (*in prison*) presidiário(-a); (*in asylum*) internado(-a)
inmost ['ɪnməʊst] ADJ mais íntimo
inn [ɪn] N hospedaria, taberna
innards ['ɪnədʒ] (*inf*) NPL entranhas *fpl*
innate [ɪ'neɪt] ADJ inato
inner ['ɪnə^r] ADJ (*place*) interno; (*feeling*) interior
inner city N aglomeração *f* urbana, metrópole *f*
innermost ['ɪnəməʊst] ADJ mais íntimo
inner tube N (*of tyre*) câmara de ar
innings ['ɪnɪŋz] N (*Sport*) turno; (BRIT *fig*): **he's had a good ~** ele aproveitou bem a vida
innocence ['ɪnəsns] N inocência
innocent ['ɪnəsnt] ADJ inocente
innocuous [ɪ'nɔkjuəs] ADJ inócuo
innovation [ɪnəu'veɪʃən] N inovação *f*, novidade *f*
innuendo [ɪnju'ɛndəu] (*pl* **innuendoes**) N insinuação *f*, indireta
innumerable [ɪ'njuːmrəbl] ADJ incontável
inoculate [ɪ'nɔkjuleɪt] VT: **to ~ sb with sth** inocular algo em alguém; **to ~ sb against sth** vacinar alguém contra algo
inoculation [ɪnɔkju'leɪʃən] N inoculação *f*, vacinação *f*
inoffensive [ɪnə'fɛnsɪv] ADJ inofensivo
inopportune [ɪn'ɔpətjuːn] ADJ inoportuno
inordinate [ɪn'ɔːdɪnət] ADJ desmesurado, excessivo
inordinately [ɪ'nɔːdɪnətlɪ] ADV desmedidamente, excessivamente
inorganic [ɪnɔː'gænɪk] ADJ inorgânico
in-patient N paciente *m/f* interno(-a)
input ['ɪnput] N (*information, Comput*) entrada; (*resources*) investimento ▶ VT (*Comput*) entrar com
inquest ['ɪnkwɛst] N inquérito policial; (*coroner's*) inquérito judicial
inquire [ɪn'kwaɪə^r] VI pedir informação ▶ VT (*ask*) perguntar; **to ~ about** pedir informações sobre; **to ~ when/where/whether** perguntar quando/onde/se ▶ **inquire after** VT FUS (*person*) perguntar por ▶ **inquire into** VT FUS investigar, indagar
inquiring [ɪn'kwaɪərɪŋ] ADJ (*mind*) inquiridor(a); (*look*) interrogativo
inquiry [ɪn'kwaɪərɪ] N pergunta; (*Law*) investigação *f*, inquérito; (*commission*) comissão *f* de inquérito; **to hold an ~ into sth** realizar uma investigação sobre algo
inquiry desk (BRIT) N balcão *m* de informações
inquiry office (BRIT) N seção *f* de informações
inquisition [ɪnkwɪ'zɪʃən] N inquérito; (*Rel*): **the I~** a Inquisição
inquisitive [ɪn'kwɪzɪtɪv] ADJ (*curious*) curioso, perguntador(a); (*prying*) indiscreto, intrometido
inroads ['ɪnrəudz] NPL: **to make ~ into** (*savings, supplies*) consumir parte de
ins. ABBR = **inches**

insane [ɪn'seɪn] ADJ louco, doido; (*Med*) demente, insano
insanitary [ɪn'sænɪtərɪ] ADJ insalubre
insanity [ɪn'sænɪtɪ] N loucura; (*Med*) insanidade *f*, demência
insatiable [ɪn'seɪʃəbl] ADJ insaciável
inscribe [ɪn'skraɪb] VT inscrever; (*book etc*): **to ~ (to sb)** dedicar (a alguém)
inscription [ɪn'skrɪpʃən] N inscrição *f*; (*in book*) dedicatória
inscrutable [ɪn'skruːtəbl] ADJ inescrutável, impenetrável
inseam measurement ['ɪnsiːm-] (US) N altura de entrepernas
insect ['ɪnsɛkt] N inseto
insect bite N picada de inseto
insecticide [ɪn'sɛktɪsaɪd] N inseticida *m*
insect repellent N repelente *m* contra insetos, insetífugo
insecure [ɪnsɪ'kjuə^r] ADJ inseguro
insecurity [ɪnsɪ'kjuərətɪ] N insegurança
insemination [ɪnsɛmɪ'neɪʃən] N: **artificial ~** inseminação *f* artificial
insensible [ɪn'sɛnsɪbl] ADJ impassível, insensível; (*unconscious*) inconsciente
insensitive [ɪn'sɛnsɪtɪv] ADJ insensível
insensitivity [ɪnsɛnsɪ'tɪvɪtɪ] N insensibilidade *f*
inseparable [ɪn'sɛprəbl] ADJ inseparável
insert [*vt* ɪn'səːt, *n* 'ɪnsəːt] VT (*between things*) intercalar; (*into sth*) introduzir, inserir; (*in paper*) publicar; (: *advert*) pôr ▶ N folha solta
insertion [ɪn'səːʃən] N inserção *f*; (*publication*) publicação *f*; (*of pages*) matéria inserida
in-service ADJ (*training*) contínuo; (*course*) de aperfeiçoamento, de reciclagem
inshore [ɪn'ʃɔː^r] ADJ perto da costa, costeiro ▶ ADV (*be*) perto da costa; (*move*) em direção à costa
inside ['ɪn'saɪd] N interior *m*; (*lining*) forro; (*of road: in Britain*) lado esquerdo (da estrada); (: *in US, Europe etc*) lado direito (da estrada) ▶ ADJ interior, interno; (*secret*) secreto ▶ ADV (*be*) dentro; (*go*) para dentro; (*inf: in prison*) na prisão ▶ PREP dentro de; (*of time*): **~ 10 minutes** em menos de 10 minutos; **insides** NPL (*inf*) entranhas *fpl*; **the ~ story** a verdade sobre os fatos
inside forward N (*Sport*) centro avante
inside information N informação *f* privilegiada
inside lane N (*Aut: in Britain*) pista da esquerda; (: *in US, Europe etc*) pista da direita
inside leg measurement (BRIT) N altura de entrepernas
inside out ADV às avessas; (*know*) muito bem; **to turn sth ~** virar algo pelo avesso
insider [ɪn'saɪdə^r] N iniciado(-a)
insider dealing N (*Stock Exchange*) uso de informações privilegiadas
insidious [ɪn'sɪdɪəs] ADJ insidioso; (*underground*) clandestino

insight ['ɪnsaɪt] N (into situation) insight m; (quality) discernimento; **an ~ into sth** uma ideia de algo

insignia [ɪn'sɪɡnɪə] N INV insígnias fpl

insignificant [ɪnsɪɡ'nɪfɪknt] ADJ insignificante

insincere [ɪnsɪn'sɪəʳ] ADJ insincero

insincerity [ɪnsɪn'sɛrɪtɪ] N insinceridade f

insinuate [ɪn'sɪnjueɪt] VT insinuar

insinuation [ɪnsɪnju'eɪʃən] N insinuação f; (hint) indireta

insipid [ɪn'sɪpɪd] ADJ insípido, insosso; (person) sem graça

insist [ɪn'sɪst] VI insistir; **to ~ on doing** insistir em fazer; (stubbornly) teimar em fazer; **to ~ that** insistir que; (claim) cismar que

insistence [ɪn'sɪstəns] N insistência; (stubbornness) teimosia

insistent [ɪn'sɪstənt] ADJ insistente, pertinaz; (continual) persistente

insole ['ɪnsəul] N palmilha

insolence ['ɪnsələns] N insolência, atrevimento

insolent ['ɪnsələnt] ADJ insolente, atrevido

insoluble [ɪn'sɔljubl] ADJ insolúvel

insolvency [ɪn'sɔlvənsɪ] N insolvência

insolvent [ɪn'sɔlvənt] ADJ insolvente

insomnia [ɪn'sɔmnɪə] N insônia

insomniac [ɪn'sɔmnɪæk] N insone m/f

inspect [ɪn'spɛkt] VT inspecionar; (building) vistoriar; (BRIT: tickets) fiscalizar; (troops) passar revista em

inspection [ɪn'spɛkʃən] N inspeção f; (of building) vistoria; (BRIT: of tickets) fiscalização f

inspector [ɪn'spɛktəʳ] N inspetor(a) m/f; (BRIT: on buses, trains) fiscal m

inspiration [ɪnspə'reɪʃən] N inspiração f

inspire [ɪn'spaɪəʳ] VT inspirar

inspired [ɪn'spaɪəd] ADJ (writer, book etc) inspirado; **in an ~ moment** num momento de inspiração

inspiring [ɪn'spaɪərɪŋ] ADJ inspirador(a)

inst. (BRIT) ABBR (Comm) = **instant**

instability [ɪnstə'bɪlɪtɪ] N instabilidade f

install [ɪn'stɔ:l] VT instalar; (official) nomear

installation [ɪnstə'leɪʃən] N instalação f

installment [ɪn'stɔ:lmənt] (US) N = **instalment**

installment plan (US) N crediário

instalment [ɪn'stɔ:lmənt] (BRIT) N (of money) prestação f; (of story) fascículo; (of TV serial etc) capítulo; **in ~s** (pay) a prestações; (receive) em várias vezes

instance ['ɪnstəns] N (example) exemplo; (case) caso; **for ~** por exemplo; **in many ~s** em muitos casos; **in that ~** naquele caso; **in the first ~** em primeiro lugar

instant ['ɪnstənt] N instante m, momento ▶ ADJ imediato; (coffee) instantâneo; **of the 10th ~** (BRIT Comm) de 10 do corrente

instantaneous [ɪnstən'teɪnɪəs] ADJ instantâneo

instantly ['ɪnstəntlɪ] ADV imediatamente

instant message N mensagem f instantânea

instant messaging N sistema m de mensagens instantâneas

instant replay (US) N (TV) replay m

instead [ɪn'stɛd] ADV em vez disso; **~ of** em vez de, em lugar de

instep ['ɪnstɛp] N peito do pé; (of shoe) parte f de dentro

instigate ['ɪnstɪɡeɪt] VT (rebellion, strike) fomentar; (new ideas) suscitar

instigation [ɪnstɪ'ɡeɪʃən] N instigação f; **at sb's ~** por incitação de alguém

instil [ɪn'stɪl] VT: **to ~ sth (into)** infundir or incutir algo (em)

instinct ['ɪnstɪŋkt] N instinto

instinctive [ɪn'stɪŋktɪv] ADJ instintivo

instinctively [ɪn'stɪŋktɪvlɪ] ADV por instinto, instintivamente

institute ['ɪnstɪtju:t] N instituto; (professional body) associação f ▶ VT (inquiry) começar, iniciar; (proceedings) instituir, estabelecer

institution [ɪnstɪ'tju:ʃən] N instituição f; (beginning) início; (organization) instituto; (Med: home) asilo; (asylum) manicômio; (custom) costume m

institutional [ɪnstɪ'tju:ʃənəl] ADJ institucional

instruct [ɪn'strʌkt] VT: **to ~ sb in sth** instruir alguém em or sobre algo; **to ~ sb to do sth** dar instruções a alguém para fazer algo

instruction [ɪn'strʌkʃən] N (teaching) instrução f; **instructions** NPL ordens fpl; **~s (for use)** modo de usar

instruction book N livro de instruções

instructive [ɪn'strʌktɪv] ADJ instrutivo

instructor [ɪn'strʌktəʳ] N instrutor(a) m/f

instrument ['ɪnstrumənt] N instrumento

instrumental [ɪnstru'mɛntl] ADJ (Mus) instrumental; **to be ~ in** contribuir para

instrumentalist [ɪnstru'mɛntəlɪst] N instrumentalista m/f

instrument panel N painel m de instrumentos

insubordinate [ɪnsə'bɔ:dənɪt] ADJ insubordinado

insubordination [ɪnsəbɔ:də'neɪʃən] N insubordinação f

insufferable [ɪn'sʌfrəbl] ADJ insuportável

insufficient [ɪnsə'fɪʃnt] ADJ insuficiente

insufficiently [ɪnsə'fɪʃəntlɪ] ADV insuficientemente

insular ['ɪnsjuləʳ] ADJ insular; (outlook) estreito; (person) de mente limitada

insulate ['ɪnsjuleɪt] VT isolar; (protect: person, group) segregar

insulating tape ['ɪnsjuleɪtɪŋ-] N fita isolante

insulation [ɪnsju'leɪʃən] N isolamento

insulin ['ɪnsjulɪn] N insulina

insult [n 'ɪnsʌlt, vt ɪn'sʌlt] N insulto; (offence) ofensa ▶ VT insultar, ofender

insulting [ɪn'sʌltɪŋ] ADJ insultante, ofensivo

insuperable [ɪn'sju:prəbl] ADJ insuperável

insurance [ɪnˈʃʊərəns] N seguro; **fire/life ~** seguro contra incêndio/de vida; **to take out ~ (against)** segurar-se or fazer seguro (contra)
insurance agent N agente m/f de seguros
insurance broker N corretor(a) m/f de seguros
insurance company N seguradora
insurance policy N apólice f de seguro
insurance premium N prêmio de seguro
insure [ɪnˈʃʊəʳ] VT segurar; **to ~ sb/sb's life** segurar alguém/a vida de alguém; **to be ~d for £5000** estar segurado em £5000
insured [ɪnˈʃʊad] N: **the ~** o(-a) segurado/a
insurer [ɪnˈʃʊərəʳ] N (person) segurador(a) m/f; (company) seguradora
insurgent [ɪnˈsəːdʒənt] ADJ, N insurgente m/f
insurmountable [ɪnsəˈmauntəbl] ADJ insuperável
insurrection [ɪnsəˈrɛkʃən] N insurreição f
intact [ɪnˈtækt] ADJ intacto, íntegro; (unharmed) ileso, são e salvo
intake [ˈɪnteɪk] N (Tech) entrada, tomada; (: pipe) tubo de entrada; (of food) quantidade f ingerida; (BRIT Sch): **an ~ of 200 a year** 200 matriculados por ano
intangible [ɪnˈtændʒɪbl] ADJ intangível
integral [ˈɪntɪɡrəl] ADJ (whole) integral, total; (part) integrante, essencial
integrate [ˈɪntɪɡreɪt] VT integrar ▶ VI integrar-se
integrated circuit [ˈɪntɪɡreɪtɪd-] N (Comput) circuito integrado
integration [ɪntɪˈɡreɪʃən] N integração f; **racial ~** integração racial
integrity [ɪnˈtɛɡrɪtɪ] N integridade f, honestidade f, retidão f
intellect [ˈɪntəlɛkt] N intelecto; (cleverness) inteligência
intellectual [ɪntəˈlɛktjuəl] ADJ, N intelectual m/f
intelligence [ɪnˈtɛlɪdʒəns] N inteligência; (Mil etc) informações fpl
intelligence quotient N quociente m de inteligência
intelligence service N serviço de informações
intelligence test N teste m de inteligência
intelligent [ɪnˈtɛlɪdʒənt] ADJ inteligente
intelligently [ɪnˈtɛlɪdʒəntlɪ] ADV inteligentemente
intelligentsia [ɪntɛlɪˈdʒəntsɪə] N: **the ~** a intelligentsia
intelligible [ɪnˈtɛlɪdʒɪbl] ADJ inteligível, compreensível
intemperate [ɪnˈtɛmpərət] ADJ imoderado; (with alcohol) intemperado
intend [ɪnˈtɛnd] VT (gift etc): **to ~ sth for** destinar algo a; **to ~ to do sth** tencionar or pretender fazer algo; (plan) planejar fazer algo
intended [ɪnˈtɛndɪd] ADJ (effect) desejado; (insult) intencional ▶ N noivo(-a)
intense [ɪnˈtɛns] ADJ intenso; (person) muito emotivo

intensely [ɪnˈtɛnslɪ] ADV intensamente; (very) extremamente
intensify [ɪnˈtɛnsɪfaɪ] VT intensificar; (increase) aumentar
intensity [ɪnˈtɛnsɪtɪ] N intensidade f; (of emotion) força, veemência
intensive [ɪnˈtɛnsɪv] ADJ intensivo
intensive care N: **to be in ~** estar na UTI
intensive care unit N unidade f de tratamento intensivo
intent [ɪnˈtɛnt] N intenção f ▶ ADJ (absorbed) absorto; (attentive) atento; **to be ~ on doing sth** estar resolvido a fazer algo; **to all ~s and purposes** para todos os efeitos
intention [ɪnˈtɛnʃən] N intenção f, propósito
intentional [ɪnˈtɛnʃənl] ADJ intencional, propositado
intentionally [ɪnˈtɛnʃənəlɪ] ADV de propósito
intently [ɪnˈtɛntlɪ] ADV atentamente
inter [ɪnˈtəːʳ] VT enterrar
interact [ɪntərˈækt] VI interagir
interaction [ɪntərˈækʃən] N interação f, ação f recíproca
interactive [ɪntərˈæktɪv] ADJ interativo
intercede [ɪntəˈsiːd] VI: **to ~ (with sb/on behalf of sb)** interceder (junto a alguém/ em favor de alguém)
intercept [ɪntəˈsɛpt] VT interceptar; (person) deter
interception [ɪntəˈsɛpʃən] N interceptação f; (of person) detenção f
interchange [n ˈɪntətʃeɪndʒ, vt ɪntəˈtʃeɪndʒ] N intercâmbio; (exchange) troca, permuta; (on motorway) trevo ▶ VT intercambiar, trocar
interchangeable [ɪntəˈtʃeɪndʒəbl] ADJ permutável
intercity [ɪntəˈsɪtɪ], **intercity train** N expresso
intercom [ˈɪntəkɔm] N interfone m
interconnect [ɪntəkəˈnɛkt] VI interligar
intercontinental [ɪntəkɔntɪˈnɛntl] ADJ intercontinental
intercourse [ˈɪntəkɔːs] N (social) relacionamento; **sexual ~** relações fpl sexuais
interdependent [ɪntədɪˈpɛndənt] ADJ interdependente
interest [ˈɪntrɪst] N interesse m; (Comm: sum of money) juros mpl; (: in company) participação f ▶ VT interessar; **to be ~ed in** interessar-se por, estar interessado em; **compound/ simple ~** juros compostos/simples; **British ~s in the Middle East** os interesses britânicos no Oriente Médio
interested [ˈɪntrɛstɪd] ADJ interessado; **to be ~ in** interessar-se por, estar interessado em
interest-free ADJ sem juros
interesting [ˈɪntrɪstɪŋ] ADJ interessante
interest rate N taxa de juros
interface [ˈɪntəfeɪs] N (Comput) interface f
interfere [ɪntəˈfɪəʳ] VI: **to ~ in** (quarrel, other people's business) interferir or intrometer-se em; **to ~ with** (objects) mexer em; (hinder)

impedir; (*plans*) interferir em; **don't ~** não se meta

interference [ɪntəˈfɪərəns] N intromissão *f*; (*Radio, TV*) interferência

interfering [ɪntəˈfɪərɪŋ] ADJ intrometido

interim [ˈɪntərɪm] ADJ interino, provisório ▶ N: **in the ~** neste ínterim, nesse meio tempo

interior [ɪnˈtɪərɪəʳ] N interior *m* ▶ ADJ interno; (*ministry*) do interior

interior decorator N decorador(a) *m/f*, arquiteto(-a) de interiores

interior designer N arquiteto(-a) de interiores

interject [ɪntəˈdʒɛkt] VT inserir, interpor

interjection [ɪntəˈdʒɛkʃən] N interrupção *f*; (*Ling*) interjeição *f*, exclamação *f*

interlock [ɪntəˈlɔk] VI entrelaçar-se; (*wheels etc*) engatar-se, engrenar-se ▶ VT engrenar

interloper [ˈɪntələupəʳ] N intruso(-a)

interlude [ˈɪntəluːd] N interlúdio; (*rest*) descanso; (*Theatre*) intervalo

intermarry [ɪntəˈmærɪ] VI ligar-se por casamento

intermediary [ɪntəˈmiːdɪərɪ] N intermediário(-a)

intermediate [ɪntəˈmiːdɪət] ADJ intermediário

interminable [ɪnˈtəːmɪnəbl] ADJ interminável

intermission [ɪntəˈmɪʃən] N intervalo

intermittent [ɪntəˈmɪtnt] ADJ intermitente; (*publication*) periódico

intermittently [ɪntəˈmɪtntlɪ] ADV intermitentemente, a intervalos

intern [*vt* ɪnˈtəːn, *n* ˈɪntəːn] VT internar; (*enclose*) encerrar ▶ N (*US: in hospital*) médico interno/médica interna; (*on work placement*) estagiário(-a)

internal [ɪnˈtəːnl] ADJ interno; **~ injuries** ferimentos *mpl* internos

internally [ɪnˈtəːnəlɪ] ADV interiormente, **"not to be taken ~"** "uso externo"

Internal Revenue, (*US*) **Internal Revenue Service** N ≈ fisco, ≈ receita federal (*BR*)

international [ɪntəˈnæʃənl] ADJ internacional ▶ N (*BRIT Sport: game*) jogo internacional; (: *player*) jogador(a) *m/f* internacional

International Atomic Energy Agency N Agência Internacional de Energia Atômica

International Court of Justice N Corte *f* Internacional de Justiça

international date line N linha internacional de mudança de data

internationally [ɪntəˈnæʃnəlɪ] ADV internacionalmente

International Monetary Fund N Fundo Monetário Internacional

internecine [ɪntəˈniːsaɪn] ADJ mutuamente destrutivo

internee [ɪntəːˈniː] N internado(-a)

Internet [ˈɪntənɛt] N: **the ~** a Internet

Internet café N cibercafé *m*

Internet Service Provider N provedor de acesso à Internet

Internet user N internauta *m/f*

internment [ɪnˈtəːnmənt] N internamento

interplay [ˈɪntəpleɪ] N interação *f*

Interpol [ˈɪntəpɔl] N Interpol *m*

interpret [ɪnˈtəːprɪt] VT interpretar; (*translate*) traduzir ▶ VI interpretar

interpretation [ɪntəːprɪˈteɪʃən] N interpretação *f*; (*translation*) tradução *f*

interpreter [ɪnˈtəːprɪtəʳ] N intérprete *m/f*

interpreting [ɪnˈtəːprɪtɪŋ] N (*profession*) interpretação *f*

interrelated [ɪntərɪˈleɪtɪd] ADJ inter-relacionado

interrogate [ɪnˈtɛrəugeɪt] VT interrogar

interrogation [ɪntɛrəˈgeɪʃən] N interrogatório

interrogative [ɪntəˈrɔgətɪv] ADJ interrogativo ▶ N (*Ling*) interrogativo

interrogator [ɪnˈtɛrəgeɪtəʳ] N interrogador(a) *m/f*

interrupt [ɪntəˈrʌpt] VT, VI interromper

interruption [ɪntəˈrʌpʃən] N interrupção *f*

intersect [ɪntəˈsɛkt] VT cruzar ▶ VI (*roads*) cruzar-se

intersection [ɪntəˈsɛkʃən] N intersecção *f*; (*of roads*) cruzamento

intersperse [ɪntəˈspəːs] VT entremear; **to ~ with** entremear com *or* de

intertwine [ɪntəˈtwaɪn] VT entrelaçar ▶ VI entrelaçar-se

interval [ˈɪntəvl] N intervalo; (*BRIT: Sch*) recreio; (: *Theatre, Sport*) intervalo; **sunny ~s** (*in weather*) períodos de melhoria; **at ~s** a intervalos

intervene [ɪntəˈviːn] VI intervir; (*event*) ocorrer; (*time*) decorrer

intervention [ɪntəˈvɛnʃən] N intervenção *f*

interview [ˈɪntəvjuː] N entrevista ▶ VT entrevistar

interviewee [ɪntəvjuːˈiː] N entrevistado(-a)

interviewer [ˈɪntəvjuːəʳ] N entrevistador(a) *m/f*

intestate [ɪnˈtɛsteɪt] ADJ intestado

intestinal [ɪnˈtɛstɪnl] ADJ intestinal

intestine [ɪnˈtɛstɪn] N intestino; **large/small ~** intestino grosso/delgado

intimacy [ˈɪntɪməsɪ] N intimidade *f*

intimate [*adj* ˈɪntɪmət, *vt* ˈɪntɪmeɪt] ADJ íntimo; (*knowledge*) profundo ▶ VT insinuar, sugerir

intimately [ˈɪntɪmətlɪ] ADV intimamente

intimation [ɪntɪˈmeɪʃən] N insinuação *f*, sugestão *f*

intimidate [ɪnˈtɪmɪdeɪt] VT amedrontar

intimidation [ɪntɪmɪˈdeɪʃən] N intimidação *f*

⌐KEYWORD¬

into [ˈɪntu] PREP em **1** (*indicating motion or direction*) em; **come into the house/garden** venha para dentro/o jardim; **go into town** ir para a cidade; **he got into the car** ele entrou no carro; **throw it into the fire** jogue isto na fogueira; **research into cancer** pesquisa sobre o câncer; **he worked late into the night** ele trabalhou até altas horas; **the car bumped into the wall** o carro bateu no muro; **she poured tea into the cup** ela botou o chá na xícara **2** (*indicating change of condition, result*): **she burst into tears** ela desatou a chorar; **he was shocked into silence** ele ficou mudo de choque; **into 3 pieces/French** em 3 pedaços/para o francês; **they got into trouble** eles se deram mal

intolerable [ɪn'tɔlərəbl] ADJ intolerável, insuportável

intolerance [ɪn'tɔlərəns] N intolerância

intolerant [ɪn'tɔlərənt] ADJ: **~ (of)** intolerante (com or para com)

intonation [ɪntəu'neɪʃən] N entonação f, inflexão f

intoxicate [ɪn'tɔksɪkeɪt] VT embriagar

intoxicated [ɪn'tɔksɪkeɪtɪd] ADJ embriagado

intoxication [ɪntɔksɪ'keɪʃən] N intoxicação f, embriaguez f

intractable [ɪn'træktəbl] ADJ (*child, illness*) intratável; (*material*) difícil de trabalhar; (*problem*) espinhoso

intranet ['ɪntrənet] N intranet f

intransigent [ɪn'trænsɪdʒənt] ADJ intransigente

intransitive [ɪn'trænsɪtɪv] ADJ intransitivo

intra-uterine device ['ɪntrə'juːtəraɪn-] N dispositivo intrauterino

intravenous [ɪntrə'viːnəs] ADJ intravenoso

in-tray N cesta para correspondência de entrada

intrepid [ɪn'trepɪd] ADJ intrépido

intricacy ['ɪntrɪkəsɪ] N complexidade f

intricate ['ɪntrɪkət] ADJ complexo, complicado

intrigue [ɪn'triːg] N intriga ▶ VT intrigar ▶ VI fazer intriga

intriguing [ɪn'triːgɪŋ] ADJ intrigante

intrinsic [ɪn'trɪnsɪk] ADJ intrínseco

introduce [ɪntrə'djuːs] VT introduzir; **to ~ sb (to sb)** apresentar alguém (a alguém); **to ~ sb to** (*pastime, technique*) iniciar alguém em; **may I ~ …?** permita-me apresentar …

introduction [ɪntrə'dʌkʃən] N introdução f; (*of person*) apresentação f; **a letter of ~** uma carta de recomendação

introductory [ɪntrə'dʌktərɪ] ADJ introdutório; **~ remarks** observações preliminares; **~ offer** oferta de lançamento

introspection [ɪntrəu'spekʃən] N introspecção f

introspective [ɪntrəu'spektɪv] ADJ introspectivo

introvert ['ɪntrəuvəːt] N introvertido(-a) ▶ ADJ (*also:* **introverted**) introvertido

intrude [ɪn'truːd] VI: **to ~ (on** or **into)** intrometer-se (em)

intruder [ɪn'truːdər] N intruso(-a)

intrusion [ɪn'truːʒən] N intromissão f

intrusive [ɪn'truːsɪv] ADJ intruso

intuition [ɪntjuː'ɪʃən] N intuição f

intuitive [ɪn'tjuːɪtɪv] ADJ intuitivo

inundate ['ɪnʌndeɪt] VT: **to ~ with** inundar de

inure [ɪn'juər] VT: **to ~ (to)** habituar (a)

invade [ɪn'veɪd] VT invadir

invader [ɪn'veɪdər] N invasor(a) m/f

invalid [n 'ɪnvəlɪd, adj ɪn'vælɪd] N inválido(-a) ▶ ADJ (*not valid*) inválido, nulo

invalidate [ɪn'vælɪdeɪt] VT invalidar, anular

invalid chair ['ɪnvəlɪd-] (*BRIT*) N cadeira de rodas

invaluable [ɪn'væljuəbl] ADJ valioso, inestimável

invariable [ɪn'vɛərɪəbl] ADJ invariável

invariably [ɪn'vɛərɪəblɪ] ADV invariavelmente; **she is ~ late** ela sempre chega atrasada

invasion [ɪn'veɪʒən] N invasão f

invective [ɪn'vektɪv] N invectiva

inveigle [ɪn'viːgl] VT: **to ~ sb into (doing) sth** aliciar alguém para (fazer) algo

invent [ɪn'vent] VT inventar

invention [ɪn'venʃən] N invenção f; (*inventiveness*) engenho; (*lie*) ficção f, mentira

inventive [ɪn'ventɪv] ADJ engenhoso

inventiveness [ɪn'ventɪvnɪs] N engenhosidade f, inventiva

inventor [ɪn'ventər] N inventor(a) m/f

inventory ['ɪnvəntrɪ] N inventário, relação f

inventory control N (*Comm*) controle m de estoques

inverse [ɪn'vəːs] ADJ, N inverso; **in ~ proportion to** em proporção inversa a

inversely [ɪn'vəːslɪ] ADV inversamente

invert [ɪn'vəːt] VT inverter

invertebrate [ɪn'vəːtɪbrət] N invertebrado

inverted commas [ɪn'vəːtɪd-] (*BRIT*) NPL aspas fpl

invest [ɪn'vest] VT investir; (*endow*): **to ~ sb with sth** conferir algo a alguém, investir alguém de algo ▶ VI investir; **to ~ in** investir em; (*acquire*) comprar

investigate [ɪn'vestɪgeɪt] VT investigar; (*study*) estudar, examinar

investigation [ɪnvestɪ'geɪʃən] N investigação f

investigative journalism [ɪn'vestɪgətɪv-] N jornalismo de investigação

investigator [ɪn'vestɪgeɪtər] N investigador(a) m/f; **private ~** detetive particular

investiture [ɪn'vestɪtʃər] N investidura

investment [ɪn'vestmənt] N investimento

investment income N rendimento de investimentos

investment trust N fundo mútuo

investor [ɪn'vestər] N investidor(a) m/f

inveterate [ɪn'vetərət] ADJ inveterado

invidious [ɪn'vɪdɪəs] ADJ injusto; (*task*) desagradável

invigilate [ɪn'vɪdʒɪleɪt] (*BRIT*) VT fiscalizar ▶ VI fiscalizar o exame

invigilator [ɪn'vɪdʒɪleɪtər] N fiscal m/f (de exame)

invigorating [ɪn'vɪgəreɪtɪŋ] ADJ revigorante

invincible [ɪn'vɪnsɪbl] ADJ invencível

inviolate [ɪn'vaɪələt] ADJ inviolado

invisible [ɪn'vɪzɪbl] ADJ invisível

invisible assets (BRIT) NPL ativo intangível

invisible ink N tinta invisível

invisible mending N cerzidura

invitation [ɪnvɪˈteɪʃən] N convite *m*; **by ~ only** estritamente mediante convite; **at sb's ~** a convite de alguém

invite [ɪnˈvaɪt] VT convidar; (*opinions etc*) solicitar, pedir; (*trouble*) pedir; **to ~ sb to do** convidar alguém para fazer; **to ~ sb to dinner** convidar alguém para jantar
  ▸ **invite out** VT convidar *or* chamar para sair
  ▸ **invite over** VT chamar

inviting [ɪnˈvaɪtɪŋ] ADJ convidativo

invoice [ˈɪnvɔɪs] N fatura ▸ VT faturar; **to ~ sb for goods** faturar mercadorias em nome de alguém

invoke [ɪnˈvəuk] VT invocar; (*aid*) implorar; (*law*) apelar para

involuntary [ɪnˈvɔləntrɪ] ADJ involuntário

involve [ɪnˈvɔlv] VT (*entail*) implicar; (*require*) exigir; **to ~ sb (in)** envolver alguém (em)

involved [ɪnˈvɔlvd] ADJ envolvido; (*emotionally*) comprometido; (*complex*) complexo; **to be/ get ~ in sth** estar/ficar envolvido em algo

involvement [ɪnˈvɔlvmənt] N envolvimento; (*obligation*) compromisso

invulnerable [ɪnˈvʌlnərəbl] ADJ invulnerável

inward [ˈɪnwəd] ADJ (*movement*) interior, interno; (*thought, feeling*) íntimo ▸ ADV para dentro

inwardly [ˈɪnwədlɪ] ADV (*feel, think etc*) para si, para dentro

inwards [ˈɪnwədz] ADV para dentro

I/O ABBR (*Comput: = input/output*) E/S, I/O

IOC N ABBR (= *International Olympic Committee*) COI *m*

iodine [ˈaɪəudiːn] N iodo

ion [ˈaɪən] N íon *m*, ião *m* (PT)

Ionian Sea [aɪˈəunɪən-] N: **the ~** o mar Iônico

iota [aɪˈəutə] N (*fig*) pouquinho, tiquinho

IOU N ABBR (= *I owe you*) vale *m*

IOW (BRIT) ABBR = **Isle of Wight**

IPA N ABBR (= *International Phonetic Alphabet*) AFI *m*

iPod® [ˈaɪpɔd] N iPod® *m*

IQ N ABBR (= *intelligence quotient*) QI *m*

IRA N ABBR (= *Irish Republican Army*) IRA *m*; (US) = **individual retirement account**

Iran [ɪˈrɑːn] N Irã *m* (BR), Irão *m* (PT)

Iranian [ɪˈreɪnɪən] ADJ iraniano ▸ N iraniano(-a); (*Ling*) iraniano

Iraq [ɪˈrɑːk] N Iraque *m*

Iraqi [ɪˈrɑːkɪ] ADJ, N iraquiano(-a)

irascible [ɪˈræsɪbl] ADJ irascível

irate [aɪˈreɪt] ADJ irado, enfurecido

Ireland [ˈaɪələnd] N Irlanda; **Republic of ~** República da Irlanda

iris [ˈaɪrɪs] (*pl* **irises**) N íris *f*

Irish [ˈaɪrɪʃ] ADJ irlandês(-esa) ▸ N (*Ling*) irlandês *m*; **the Irish** NPL os irlandeses

Irishman [ˈaɪrɪʃmən] (*irreg: like* **man**) N irlandês *m*

Irish Sea N: **the ~** o mar da Irlanda

Irishwoman [ˈaɪrɪʃwumən] (*irreg: like* **woman**) N irlandesa

irk [əːk] VT aborrecer

irksome [ˈəːksəm] ADJ aborrecido

IRN (BRIT) N ABBR (= *Independent Radio News*) agência de notícias radiofônicas

IRO (US) N ABBR = **International Refugee Organization**

iron [ˈaɪən] N ferro; (*for clothes*) ferro de passar roupa ▸ ADJ de ferro ▸ VT (*clothes*) passar; **irons** NPL (*chains*) grilhões *mpl*
  ▸ **iron out** VT (*crease*) tirar; (*fig: problem*) resolver

Iron Curtain N: **the ~** a cortina de ferro

iron foundry N fundição *f*

ironic [aɪˈrɔnɪk], **ironical** [aɪˈrɔnɪkl] ADJ irônico

ironically [aɪˈrɔnɪklɪ] ADV ironicamente

ironing [ˈaɪənɪŋ] N (*activity*) passar roupa; (*clothes*) roupa passada; (*to be ironed*) roupa a ser passada

ironing board N tábua de passar roupa

ironmonger [ˈaɪənmʌŋgəʳ] (BRIT) N ferreiro(-a)

ironmonger's, (BRIT) **ironmonger's shop** N loja de ferragens

iron ore N minério de ferro

ironworks [ˈaɪənwəːks] N siderúrgica

irony [ˈaɪrənɪ] N ironia; **the ~ of it is that ...** o irônico é que ...

irrational [ɪˈræʃənl] ADJ irracional

irreconcilable [ɪrɛkənˈsaɪləbl] ADJ (*disagreement*) irreconciliável; (*ideas*) incompatível

irredeemable [ɪrɪˈdiːməbl] ADJ (*Comm*) irresgatável

irrefutable [ɪrɪˈfjuːtəbl] ADJ irrefutável

irregular [ɪˈregjuləʳ] ADJ irregular; (*surface*) desigual; (*illegal*) ilegal

irregularity [ɪregjuˈlærɪtɪ] N irregularidade *f*; (*of surface*) desigualdade *f*

irrelevance [ɪˈreləvəns] N irrelevância

irrelevant [ɪˈreləvənt] ADJ irrelevante

irreligious [ɪrɪˈlɪdʒəs] ADJ irreligioso

irreparable [ɪˈrɛprəbl] ADJ irreparável

irreplaceable [ɪrɪˈpleɪsəbl] ADJ insubstituível

irrepressible [ɪrɪˈpresəbl] ADJ irreprimível, irrefreável

irreproachable [ɪrɪˈprəutʃəbl] ADJ irrepreensível

irresistible [ɪrɪˈzɪstɪbl] ADJ irresistível

irresolute [ɪˈrezəluːt] ADJ irresoluto

irrespective [ɪrɪˈspɛktɪv]: **~ of** PREP independente de, sem considerar

irresponsible [ɪrɪˈspɔnsɪbl] ADJ (*act, person*) irresponsável

irretrievable [ɪrɪˈtriːvəbl] ADJ (*object*) irrecuperável; (*loss, damage*) irreparável

irreverent [ɪˈrevərnt] ADJ irreverente, desrespeitoso

irrevocable [ɪˈrevəkəbl] ADJ irrevogável

irrigate [ˈɪrɪgeɪt] VT irrigar

irrigation [ɪrɪˈgeɪʃən] N irrigação *f*

irritable ['ɪrɪtəbl] ADJ irritável; *(mood)* de mal humor, nervoso
irritate ['ɪrɪteɪt] VT irritar
irritating ['ɪrɪteɪtɪŋ] ADJ irritante
irritation [ɪrɪ'teɪʃən] N irritação f
IRS (US) N ABBR = **Internal Revenue Service**; *see* **Internal Revenue**
is [ɪz] VB *see* **be**
ISBN N ABBR (= *International Standard Book Number*) ISBN m
ISDN N ABBR (= *Integrated Services Digital Network*) RDSI f, ISDN f
Islam ['ɪzlɑːm] N islamismo
Islamic [ɪz'læmɪk] ADJ islâmico(-a)
island ['aɪlənd] N ilha; (*also:* **traffic island**) abrigo
islander ['aɪləndəʳ] N ilhéu/ilhoa m/f
isle [aɪl] N ilhota, ilha
isn't ['ɪznt] = **is not**
isolate ['aɪsəleɪt] VT isolar
isolated ['aɪsəleɪtɪd] ADJ isolado
isolation [aɪsə'leɪʃən] N isolamento
isolationism [aɪsə'leɪʃənɪzm] N isolacionismo
isotope ['aɪsəutəup] N isótopo
ISP N ABBR (= *Internet Service Provider*) ISP m
Israel ['ɪzreɪl] N Israel
Israeli [ɪz'reɪlɪ] ADJ, N israelense m/f
issue ['ɪsjuː] N questão f, tema m; *(outcome)* resultado; *(of book)* edição f; *(of stamps)* emissão f; *(of newspaper etc)* número; *(offspring)* sucessão f, descendência ▶ VT *(rations, equipment)* distribuir; *(orders)* dar; *(certificate)* emitir; *(decree)* promulgar; *(book)* publicar; *(cheques, banknotes, stamps)* emitir ▶ VI: **to ~ from** *(smell, liquid)* emanar de; **at ~** em debate; **to avoid the ~** contornar o problema; **to take ~ with sb (over sth)** discordar de alguém (sobre algo); **to make an ~ of sth** criar caso com algo; **to confuse** *or* **obscure the ~** complicar as coisas
Istanbul [ɪstæn'buːl] N Istambul
isthmus ['ɪsməs] N istmo
IT N ABBR = **information technology**

(KEYWORD)

it [ɪt] PRON **1** *(specific: subject)* ele/ela; (: *direct object*) o/a; (: *indirect object*) lhe; **it's on the table** está em cima da mesa; **I can't find it** não consigo achá-lo; **give it to me** dê-mo; **about/from it** sobre/de isto; **did you go to it?** *(party, concert etc)* você foi?
2 *(impers)* isto, isso; *(after prep)* ele, ela; **it's raining** está chovendo (BR) *or* a chover (PT); **it's cold today** está frio hoje; **it's Friday tomorrow** amanhã é sexta-feira; **it's six o'clock/the 10th of August** são seis horas/ hoje é (dia) 10 de agosto; **who is it? — it's me** quem é? — sou eu

ITA (BRIT) N ABBR (= *initial teaching alphabet*) alfabeto modificado utilizado na alfabetização
Italian [ɪ'tæljən] ADJ italiano ▶ N italiano(-a); *(Ling)* italiano
italic [ɪ'tælɪk] ADJ itálico
italics [ɪ'tælɪks] NPL itálico
Italy ['ɪtəlɪ] N Itália
itch [ɪtʃ] N comichão f, coceira ▶ VI *(person)* estar com *or* sentir comichão *or* coceira; *(part of body)* comichar, coçar; **I'm ~ing to do something** estou louco para fazer algo
itching ['ɪtʃɪŋ] N comichão f, coceira
itchy ['ɪtʃɪ] ADJ que coça; **to be ~** *(person)* estar com *or* sentir comichão *or* coceira; *(part of body)* comichar, coçar
it'd ['ɪtd] = **it would; it had**
item ['aɪtəm] N item m; *(on agenda)* assunto; *(in programme)* número; (*also:* **news item**) notícia; **~s of clothing** artigos de vestuário
itemize ['aɪtəmaɪz] VT detalhar, especificar
itinerant [ɪ'tɪnərənt] ADJ itinerante
itinerary [aɪ'tɪnərərɪ] N itinerário
it'll ['ɪtl] = **it will; it shall**
ITN (BRIT) N ABBR (= *Independent Television News*) agência de notícias televisivas
its [ɪts] ADJ seu/sua, dele/dela ▶ PRON o seu/a sua, o dele/a dela
it's [ɪts] = **it is; it has**
itself [ɪt'self] PRON *(reflexive)* si mesmo(-a); *(emphatic)* ele mesmo/ela mesma
ITV (BRIT) N ABBR (= *Independent Television*) canal de televisão comercial
IUD N ABBR (= *intra-uterine device*) DIU m
I've [aɪv] = **I have**
ivory ['aɪvərɪ] N marfim m; *(colour)* cor f de marfim
Ivory Coast N Costa do Marfim
ivory tower N *(fig)* torre f de marfim
ivy ['aɪvɪ] N hera
Ivy League (US) N *as grandes faculdades (Harvard, Yale, Princeton etc) do nordeste dos EUA*

Jj

J, j [dʒeɪ] N (letter) J, j m; **J for Jack** (BRIT) or **Jig** (US) J de José

JA N ABBR = **judge advocate**

J/A ABBR = **joint account**

jab [dʒæb] VT (elbow) cutucar; (punch) esmurrar, socar ▶ N cotovelada, murro; (Med: inf) injeção f; **to ~ sth into sth** cravar algo em algo

jabber ['dʒæbə'] VT, VI tagarelar

jack [dʒæk] N (Aut) macaco; (Bowling) bola branca; (Cards) valete m
  ▶ **jack in** (inf) VT largar
  ▶ **jack up** VT (Aut) levantar com macaco; (raise: prices) aumentar

jackal ['dʒækl] N chacal m

jackass ['dʒækæs] N (fig) burro

jackdaw ['dʒækdɔ:] N gralha

jacket ['dʒækɪt] N jaqueta, casaco curto; (of boiler etc) capa, forro; (of book) sobrecapa; **potatoes in their ~s** (BRIT) batatas com casca

jack-in-the-box N caixa de surpresas

jack-knife (irreg: like **knife**) N canivete m ▶ VI: **the lorry ~d** o reboque do caminhão deu uma guinada

jack-of-all-trades N pau m para toda obra, homem m dos sete instrumentos

jack plug N pino

jackpot ['dʒækpɔt] N bolada, sorte f grande

jacuzzi® [dʒə'ku:zı] N jacuzzi® m, banheira de hidromassagem

jade [dʒeɪd] N (stone) jade m

jaded ['dʒeɪdɪd] ADJ (tired) cansado; (fed-up) aborrecido, amolado

jagged ['dʒægɪd] ADJ dentado, denteado

jaguar ['dʒægjuə'] N jaguar m

jail [dʒeɪl] N prisão f, cadeia ▶ VT encarcerar

jailbird ['dʒeɪlbə:d] N criminoso inveterado

jailbreak ['dʒeɪlbreɪk] N fuga da prisão

jailer ['dʒeɪlə'] N carcereiro

jalopy [dʒə'lɔpɪ] (inf) N calhambeque m

jam [dʒæm] N geleia; (also: **traffic jam**) engarrafamento; (inf: difficulty) apuro ▶ VT (passage etc) obstruir, atravancar; (mechanism) emperrar; (Radio) bloquear, interferir ▶ VI (mechanism, drawer etc) emperrar; **to get sb out of a ~** (inf) tirar alguém de uma enrascada; **to ~ sth into sth** forçar algo dentro de algo; **the telephone lines are ~med** as linhas telefônicas estão congestionadas

Jamaica [dʒə'meɪkə] N Jamaica

Jamaican [dʒə'meɪkən] ADJ, N jamaicano(-a) m/f

jamb ['dʒæm] N umbral m

jam-packed ADJ: **~ (with)** abarrotado (de)

jam session N jam session m

Jan. ABBR (= January) jan.

jangle ['dʒæŋgl] VI soar estridentemente

janitor ['dʒænɪtə'] N (caretaker) zelador m; (doorman) porteiro

January ['dʒænjuərɪ] N janeiro; see also **July**

Japan [dʒə'pæn] N Japão m

Japanese [dʒæpə'ni:z] ADJ japonês(-esa) ▶ N INV japonês(-esa) m/f; (Ling) japonês m

jar [dʒɑ:'] N (glass container: large) jarro; (: small) pote m ▶ VI (sound) ranger, chiar; (colours) destoar ▶ VT (shake) abalar

jargon ['dʒɑ:gən] N jargão m

jarring ['dʒɑ:rɪŋ] ADJ (sound, colour) destoante

Jas. ABBR = **James**

jasmine, jasmin ['dʒæzmɪn] N jasmim m

jaundice ['dʒɔ:ndɪs] N icterícia

jaundiced ['dʒɔ:ndɪst] ADJ (fig: unenthusiastic) desanimado; (: embittered) amargurado, despeitado; (: disillusioned) desiludido

jaunt [dʒɔ:nt] N excursão f

jaunty ['dʒɔ:ntɪ] ADJ alegre, jovial; (step) enérgico

Java ['dʒɑ:və] N Java (no article)

javelin ['dʒævlɪn] N dardo de arremesso

jaw [dʒɔ:] N mandíbula, maxilar m

jawbone ['dʒɔ:bəun] N osso maxilar, maxila

jay [dʒeɪ] N gaio

jaywalker ['dʒeɪwɔ:kə'] N pedestre m/f imprudente (BR), peão m imprudente (PT)

jazz [dʒæz] N jazz m
  ▶ **jazz up** VT (liven up) animar, avivar

jazz band N banda de jazz

jazzy ['dʒæzɪ] ADJ (of jazz) jazzístico; (bright) de cor berrante

JCB® N escavadeira

JCS (US) N ABBR = **Joint Chiefs of Staff**

JD (US) N ABBR (= Doctor of Laws) título universitário; (= Justice Department) ministério da Justiça

jealous ['dʒɛləs] ADJ ciumento; (envious) invejoso; **to be ~** estar com ciúmes

jealously ['dʒɛləslɪ] ADV (*enviously*) invejosamente; (*guard*) zelosamente
jealousy ['dʒɛləsɪ] N ciúmes *mpl*; (*envy*) inveja
jeans [dʒiːnz] NPL jeans *m* (BR), jeans *mpl* (PT)
jeep® [dʒiːp] N jipe® *m*
jeer [dʒɪəʳ] VI: **to ~ (at)** (*boo*) vaiar; (*mock*) zombar (de)
jeering ['dʒɪərɪŋ] ADJ vaiador(a) ▶ N vaias *fpl*
jeers ['dʒɪəz] NPL (*boos*) vaias *fpl*; (*mocking*) zombarias *fpl*
jelly ['dʒɛlɪ] N (*jam*) geleia
jellyfish ['dʒɛlɪfɪʃ] N INV água-viva
jeopardize ['dʒɛpədaɪz] VT arriscar, pôr em perigo
jeopardy ['dʒɛpədɪ] N: **to be in ~** estar em perigo, estar correndo risco
jerk [dʒəːk] N (*jolt*) solavanco, sacudida; (*wrench*) puxão *m*; (*inf: idiot*) babaca *m* ▶ VT sacudir ▶ VI (*vehicle*) dar um solavanco
jerkin ['dʒəːkɪn] N jaqueta
jerky ['dʒəːkɪ] ADJ espasmódico, aos arrancos
jerry-built ['dʒɛrɪ-] ADJ mal construído
jerry can ['dʒɛrɪ-] N lata
Jersey ['dʒəːzɪ] N Jersey (*no article*)
jersey ['dʒəːzɪ] N suéter *m* (BR), camisola (PT); (*fabric*) jérsei *m*, malha
Jerusalem [dʒəˈruːsələm] N Jerusalém
Jerusalem artichoke N topinambo
jest [dʒɛst] N gracejo, brincadeira; **in ~** de brincadeira
jester ['dʒɛstəʳ] N (*History*) bobo
Jesus ['dʒiːzəs], **Jesus Christ** N Jesus *m* (Cristo)
jet [dʒɛt] N (*of gas, liquid*) jato; (*Aviat*) (avião *m* a) jato; (*stone*) azeviche *m*
jet-black ADJ da cor do azeviche
jet engine N motor *m* a jato
jet lag N cansaço devido à diferença de fuso horário
jetsam ['dʒɛtsəm] N objetos *mpl* alijados ao mar
jettison ['dʒɛtɪsn] VT alijar
jetty ['dʒɛtɪ] N quebra-mar *m*, cais *m*
Jew [dʒuː] N judeu(-dia) *m/f*
jewel ['dʒuːəl] N joia; (*in watch*) rubi *m*
jeweller, (US) **jeweler** ['dʒuːələʳ] N joalheiro(-a)
jeweller's, jeweller's shop N joalheria
jewellery, (US) **jewelry** ['dʒuːəlrɪ] N joias *fpl*, pedrarias *fpl*
Jewess ['dʒuːɪs] N (*offensive*) judia
Jewish ['dʒuːɪʃ] ADJ judeu/judia
JFK (US) N ABBR = **John Fitzgerald Kennedy International Airport**
jib [dʒɪb] N (*Naut*) bujarrona; (*of crane*) lança ▶ VI (*horse*) empacar; **to ~ at doing sth** relutar em fazer algo
jibe [dʒaɪb] N = **gibe**
jiffy ['dʒɪfɪ] (*inf*) N: **in a ~** num instante
jig [dʒɪg] N jiga
jigsaw ['dʒɪgsɔː] N (*also:* **jigsaw puzzle**) quebra-cabeça *m*; (*tool*) serra de vaivém
jilt [dʒɪlt] VT dar o fora em
jingle ['dʒɪŋgl] N (*for advert*) música de

propaganda ▶ VI tilintar, retinir
jingoism ['dʒɪŋgəuɪzm] N jingoísmo
jinx [dʒɪŋks] (*inf*) N caipora, pé *m* frio
jitters ['dʒɪtəz] (*inf*) NPL: **to get the ~** ficar muito nervoso
jittery ['dʒɪtərɪ] (*inf*) ADJ nervoso
jiu-jitsu [dʒuːˈdʒɪtsuː] N jiu-jítsu *m*
job [dʒɔb] N trabalho; (*task*) tarefa; (*duty*) dever *m*; (*post*) emprego; (*inf: difficulty*): **you'll have a ~ to do that** não vai ser fácil você fazer isso; **it's not my ~** não faz parte das minhas funções; **a part-time/full-time ~** um trabalho de meio-expediente/de tempo integral; **it's a good ~ that ...** ainda bem que ...; **just the ~!** justo o que queria!
jobber ['dʒɔbəʳ] (BRIT) N (*Stock Exchange*) operador(a) *m/f* intermediário(-a)
jobbing ['dʒɔbɪŋ] (BRIT) ADJ (*workman*) tarefeiro, pago por tarefa
job centre ['dʒɔbsɛntəʳ] N agência de emprego
job creation scheme N plano para a criação de empregos
job description N descrição *f* do cargo
jobless ['dʒɔblɪs] ADJ desempregado
job lot N lote *m* (de mercadorias variadas)
job satisfaction N satisfação *f* profissional
job security N estabilidade *f* de emprego
job specification N especificação *f* do cargo
jockey ['dʒɔkɪ] N jóquei *m* ▶ VI: **to ~ for position** manobrar para conseguir uma posição
jockey box (US) N (*Aut*) porta-luvas *m inv*
jockstrap ['dʒɔkstræp] N suporte *m* atlético
jocular ['dʒɔkjuləʳ] ADJ (*remark*) jocoso, divertido; (*person*) alegre
jog [dʒɔg] VT empurrar, sacudir ▶ VI (*run*) fazer jogging *or* cooper; **to ~ sb's memory** refrescar a memória de alguém
▶ **jog along** VI ir levando
jogger ['dʒɔgəʳ] N corredor(a) *m/f*, praticante *m/f* de jogging
jogging ['dʒɔgɪŋ] N jogging *m*
john [dʒɔn] (US inf) N trono *m* (inf: *no banheiro*)
join [dʒɔɪn] VT (*things*) juntar, unir; (*queue*) entrar em; (*become member of*) associar-se a; (*meet*) encontrar-se com; (*accompany*) juntar-se a ▶ VI (*roads, rivers*) confluir ▶ N junção *f*; **will you ~ us for dinner?** você janta conosco?; **I'll ~ you later** vou me encontrar com você mais tarde; **to ~ forces (with)** associar-se (com)
▶ **join in** VI participar ▶ VT FUS participar em
▶ **join up** VI unir-se; (*Mil*) alistar-se
joiner ['dʒɔɪnəʳ] N marceneiro
joinery ['dʒɔɪnərɪ] N marcenaria
joint [dʒɔɪnt] N (*Tech*) junta, união *f*; (*wood*) encaixe *m*; (*Anat*) articulação *f*; (*BRIT Culin*) quarto; (*inf: place*) espelunca; (: *marijuana cigarette*) baseado ▶ ADJ (*common*) comum; (*combined*) conjunto; (*committee*) misto; **by ~ agreement** por comum acordo; **~ responsibility** corresponsabilidade *f*

joint account N conta conjunta
jointly ['dʒɔɪntlɪ] ADV em comum; (collectively) coletivamente; (together) conjuntamente
joint ownership N co-propriedade f, condomínio
joint-stock company N sociedade f anônima por ações
joint venture N joint venture m
joist [dʒɔɪst] N barrote m
joke [dʒəuk] N piada; (also: **practical joke**) brincadeira, peça ▶ vi brincar; **to play a ~ on** pregar uma peça em
joker ['dʒəukər] N piadista m/f, brincalhão(-lhona) m/f; (Cards) curingão m
joking ['dʒəukɪŋ] N brincadeira
jollity ['dʒɔlɪtɪ] N alegria
jolly ['dʒɔlɪ] ADJ (merry) alegre; (enjoyable) divertido ▶ ADV (BRIT inf) muito, extremamente ▶ VT (BRIT): **to ~ sb along** animar alguém; **~ good!** (BRIT) excelente!
jolt [dʒəult] N (shake) sacudida, solavanco; (shock) susto ▶ VT sacudir; (emotionally) abalar
Jordan ['dʒɔːdən] N Jordânia; (river) Jordão m
Jordanian [dʒɔːˈdeɪnɪən] ADJ, N jordaniano(-a)
joss stick [dʒɔs-] N palito perfumado
jostle ['dʒɔsl] VT acotovelar, empurrar
jot [dʒɔt] N: **not one ~** nem um pouquinho ▶ **jot down** VT anotar
jotter ['dʒɔtər] (BRIT) N bloco (de anotações)
journal ['dʒəːnl] N (paper) jornal m; (magazine) revista; (diary) diário
journalese [dʒəːnəˈliːz] (pej) N linguagem f jornalística
journalism ['dʒəːnəlɪzəm] N jornalismo
journalist ['dʒəːnəlɪst] N jornalista m/f
journey ['dʒəːnɪ] N viagem f; (distance covered) trajeto ▶ vi viajar; **return ~** volta; **a 5-hour ~** 5 horas de viagem
jovial ['dʒəuvɪəl] ADJ jovial, alegre
jowl [dʒaul] N papada
joy [dʒɔɪ] N alegria
joyful ['dʒɔɪful] ADJ alegre
joyous ['dʒɔɪəs] ADJ alegre
joyride ['dʒɔɪraɪd] N passeio de carro; (illegal) passeio (com veículo roubado)
joystick ['dʒɔɪstɪk] N (Aviat) manche m, alavanca de controle; (Comput) joystick m
JP N ABBR = **Justice of the Peace**
Jr ABBR = **junior**
jubilant ['dʒuːbɪlnt] ADJ jubilante
jubilation [dʒuːbɪˈleɪʃən] N júbilo, regozijo
jubilee ['dʒuːbɪliː] N jubileu m; **silver ~** jubileu de prata
judge [dʒʌdʒ] N juiz/juíza m/f; (in competition) árbitro; (fig: expert) especialista m/f, conhecedor(a) m/f ▶ VT julgar; (competition) arbitrar; (estimate: weight, size etc) avaliar; (consider) considerar ▶ vi: **judging or to ~ by ...** a julgar por ...; **as far as I can ~** ao que me parece, no meu entender; **I ~d it necessary to inform him** julguei necessário informá-lo
judge advocate N (Mil) auditor m de guerra

Judge Advocate General N (Mil) procurador m geral da Justiça Militar
judgement, judgment ['dʒʌdʒmənt] N juízo; (punishment) decisão f, sentença; (opinion) opinião f; (discernment) discernimento; **in my judg(e)ment** na minha opinião; **to pass judg(e)ment on** (Law) julgar, dar sentença sobre
judicial [dʒuːˈdɪʃl] ADJ judicial; (fair) imparcial
judiciary [dʒuːˈdɪʃɪərɪ] N poder m judiciário
judicious [dʒuːˈdɪʃəs] ADJ judicioso
judo ['dʒuːdəu] N judô m
jug [dʒʌg] N jarro
jugged hare [dʒʌgd-] (BRIT) N guisado de lebre
juggernaut ['dʒʌgənɔːt] (BRIT) N (huge truck) jamanta
juggle ['dʒʌgl] vi fazer malabarismos
juggler ['dʒʌglər] N malabarista m/f
Jugoslav ['juːgəuslɑːv] ADJ, N = **Yugoslav**
jugular ['dʒʌgjulər], **jugular vein** N veia jugular
juice [dʒuːs] N suco (BR), sumo (PT); (inf: petrol): **we've run out of ~** estamos sem gasolina
juicy ['dʒuːsɪ] ADJ suculento
jukebox ['dʒuːkbɔks] N juke-box m
Jul. ABBR (= July) jul.
July [dʒuːˈlaɪ] N julho; **the first of ~** dia primeiro de julho; **(on) the eleventh of ~** (no) dia onze de julho; **in the month of ~** no mês de julho; **at the beginning/end of ~** no começo/fim de julho; **in the middle of ~** em meados de julho; **during ~** durante o mês de julho; **in ~ of next year** em julho do ano que vem; **each or every ~** todo ano em julho; **~ was wet this year** choveu muito em julho deste ano
jumble ['dʒʌmbl] N confusão f, mixórdia ▶ VT (also: **jumble up**: mix up) misturar; (: disarrange) desorganizar
jumble sale (BRIT) N bazar m

> As **jumble sales** têm lugar dentro de igrejas, salões de festa e escolas, onde são vendidos diversos tipos de mercadorias, em geral baratas e sobretudo de segunda mão, a fim de coletar dinheiro para uma obra de caridade, uma escola ou uma igreja.

jumbo ['dʒʌmbəu], **jumbo jet** N avião m jumbo
jump [dʒʌmp] vi saltar, pular; (start) sobressaltar-se; (increase) disparar ▶ VT pular, saltar ▶ N pulo, salto; (increase) alta; (fence) obstáculo; **to ~ the queue** (BRIT) furar a fila (BR), pôr-se à frente (PT); **to ~ for joy** pular de alegria
▶ **jump about** vi saltitar
▶ **jump at** VT FUS (accept) aceitar imediatamente; (chance) agarrar
▶ **jump down** vi pular para baixo
▶ **jump up** vi levantar-se num ímpeto
jumped-up [dʒʌmpt-] (BRIT pej) ADJ arrivista
jumper ['dʒʌmpər] N (BRIT: pullover) suéter m (BR), camisola (PT); (US: pinafore dress) avental m; (Sport) saltador(a) m/f

jumper cables (*us*), (*BRIT*) **jump leads** NPL cabos *mpl* para ligar a bateria

jump-start ['dʒʌmpstɑ:t] VT (*car: push*) fazer pegar no tranco; (: *with jump leads*) fazer chupeta em; (*fig: project, situation*) alavancar

jumpy ['dʒʌmpɪ] ADJ nervoso

Jun. ABBR = **June; junior**

junction ['dʒʌŋkʃən] (*BRIT*) N (*of roads*) cruzamento; (: *on motorway*) trevo; (*Rail*) entroncamento

juncture ['dʒʌŋktʃər] N: **at this ~** neste momento, nesta conjuntura

June [dʒu:n] N junho; *see also* **July**

jungle ['dʒʌŋgl] N selva, mato

junior ['dʒu:nɪər] ADJ (*in age*) mais novo *or* moço; (*competition*) juvenil; (*position*) subalterno ▶ N jovem *m/f*; (*Sport*) júnior *m*; **he's ~ to me (by 2 years), he's (2 years) my ~** ele é (dois anos) mais novo do que eu; **he's ~ to me** (*seniority*) tenho mais antiguidade do que ele

junior executive N executivo(-a) júnior

junior high school (*us*) N ≈ colégio (2° e 3° ginasial)

junior minister (*BRIT*) N ministro(-a) subalterno(-a)

junior partner N sócio(-a) minoritário(-a)

junior school (*BRIT*) N escola primária

junior sizes NPL (*Comm*) tamanhos *mpl* para crianças

juniper ['dʒu:nɪpər] N junípero

junk [dʒʌŋk] N (*cheap goods*) tranqueira, velharias *fpl*; (*lumber*) trastes *mpl*; (*rubbish*) lixo; (*ship*) junco ▶ VT (*inf*) jogar no lixo

junk dealer N belchior *m*

junket ['dʒʌŋkɪt] N (*Culin*) coalhada; (*BRIT inf*): **to go on a ~** viajar à custa do governo ▶ VI (*BRIT inf*): **to go ~ing** = **to go on a junket**

junk food N comida pronta de baixo valor nutritivo

junkie ['dʒʌŋkɪ] (*inf*) N drogado(-a)

junk mail N correspondência não-solicitada

junk room (*us*) N quarto de despejo

junk shop N loja de objetos usados

Junr ABBR = **junior**

junta ['dʒʌntə] N junta

Jupiter ['dʒu:pɪtər] N Júpiter *m*

jurisdiction [dʒuərɪs'dɪkʃən] N jurisdição *f*; **it falls** *or* **comes within/outside our ~** é/não é da nossa competência

jurisprudence [dʒuərɪs'pru:dəns] N jurisprudência

juror ['dʒuərər] N jurado(-a)

jury ['dʒuərɪ] N júri *m*

jury box N banca dos jurados

juryman ['dʒuərɪmən] (*irreg: like* **man**) N = **juror**

just [dʒʌst] ADJ justo ▶ ADV (*exactly*) justamente, exatamente; (*only*) apenas, somente; **he's ~ done it/left** ele acabou (*BR*) *or* acaba (*PT*) de fazê-lo/ir; **~ as I expected** exatamente como eu esperava; **~ right** perfeito; **~ two o'clock** duas (horas) em ponto; **she's ~ as clever as you** ela é tão inteligente como você; **it's ~ as good** é igualmente bom; **~ as well that ...** ainda bem que ...; **I was ~ about to phone** eu já ia telefonar; **we were ~ leaving** estávamos de saída; **~ as he was leaving** no momento em que ele saía; **~ before/enough** justo antes/o suficiente; **~ here** bem aqui; **it's ~ a mistake** não passa de um erro; **he ~ missed** falhou por pouco; **~ listen** escute aqui!; **~ ask someone the way** é só pedir uma indicação; **not ~ now** não neste momento; **~ a minute!, ~ one moment!** só um minuto!, espera aí!, peraí! (*inf*)

justice ['dʒʌstɪs] N justiça; (*us: judge*) juiz/ juíza *m/f*; **Lord Chief J~** (*BRIT*) presidente do tribunal de recursos; **to do ~ to** (*fig*) apreciar devidamente; **this photo doesn't do you ~** esta foto não te faz justiça

Justice of the Peace N juiz/juíza *m/f* de paz

justifiable [dʒʌstɪ'faɪəbl] ADJ justificável

justifiably [dʒʌstɪ'faɪəblɪ] ADV justificadamente

justification [dʒʌstɪfɪ'keɪʃən] N (*reason*) justificativa; (*action*) justificação *f*

justify ['dʒʌstɪfaɪ] VT justificar; **to be justified in doing sth** ter razão de fazer algo

justly ['dʒʌstlɪ] ADV justamente; (*with reason*) com razão

justness ['dʒʌstnɪs] N justiça

jut [dʒʌt] VI (*also:* **jut out**) sobressair

jute [dʒu:t] N juta

juvenile ['dʒu:vənaɪl] ADJ juvenil; (*court*) de menores; (*books*) para adolescentes ▶ N jovem *m/f*; (*Law*) menor *m/f* de idade

juvenile delinquency N delinquência juvenil

juvenile delinquent N delinquente *m/f* juvenil

juxtapose [dʒʌkstəpəuz] VT justapor

juxtaposition [dʒʌkstəpə'zɪʃən] N justaposição *f*

Kk

K¹, k [keɪ] N (*letter*) K, k *m*; **K for King** K de Kátia

K² ABBR (= *kilobyte*) K; (BRIT: = *Knight*) título honorífico ▶ N ABBR (= *one thousand*) mil

kaftan ['kæftæn] N cafetã *m*

Kalahari Desert [kælə'hɑːrɪ-] N deserto de Kalahari

kale [keɪl] N couve *f*

kaleidoscope [kə'laɪdəskəup] N calidoscópio, caleidoscópio

Kampala [kæm'pɑːlə] N Campala

Kampuchea [kæmpu'tʃɪə] N Kampuchea *m*, Camboja *m*

kangaroo [kæŋgə'ruː] N canguru *m*

kaput [kə'put] (*inf*) ADJ pifado

karate [kə'rɑːtɪ] N karatê *m*

Kashmir [kæʃ'mɪəʳ] N Cachemira

KC (BRIT) N ABBR (*Law*: = *King's Counsel*) título dado a certos advogados

kd ABBR (= *knocked down*) em pedaços

kebab [kə'bæb] N churrasquinho, espetinho

keel [kiːl] N quilha; **on an even ~** (*fig*) em equilíbrio
   ▶ **keel over** VI (*Naut*) emborcar; (*person*) desmaiar

keen [kiːn] ADJ (*interest, desire*) grande, vivo; (*eye, intelligence*) penetrante; (*competition*) acirrado, intenso; (*edge*) afiado; (*eager*) entusiasmado; **to be ~ to do** or **on doing sth** sentir muita vontade de fazer algo; **to be ~ on sth/sb** gostar de algo/alguém; **I'm not ~ on going** não estou a fim de ir

keenly ['kiːnlɪ] ADV (*enthusiastically*) com entusiasmo; (*feel*) profundamente, agudamente

keenness ['kiːnnɪs] N (*eagerness*) entusiasmo, interesse *m*; **~ to do** vontade de fazer

keep [kiːp] (*pt, pp* **kept**) VT (*retain*) ficar com; (*maintain: house etc*) cuidar; (*detain*) deter; (*look after: shop etc*) tomar conta de; (*preserve*) conservar; (*hold back*) reter; (*accounts, diary*) manter; (*support: family etc*) manter; (*promise*) cumprir; (*chickens, bees etc*) criar; (*prevent*): **to ~ sb from doing sth** impedir alguém de fazer algo ▶ VI (*food*) conservar-se; (*remain*) ficar ▶ N (*of castle*) torre *f* de menagem; (*food etc*): **to earn one's ~** ganhar a vida; (*inf*): **for ~s** para sempre; **to ~ doing sth** continuar fazendo algo; **to ~ sth from happening** impedir que algo aconteça; **to ~ sb happy** manter alguém satisfeito; **to ~ a place tidy** manter um lugar limpo; **to ~ sb waiting** deixar alguém esperando; **to ~ an appointment** manter um compromisso; **to ~ a record of sth** anotar algo; **to ~ sth to o.s.** guardar algo para si mesmo; **to ~ sth (back) from sb** ocultar algo de alguém; **to ~ time** (*clock*) marcar a hora exata
   ▶ **keep away** VT: **to ~ sth/sb away from sb** manter algo/alguém afastado de alguém
   ▶ VI: **to ~ away (from)** manter-se afastado (de)
   ▶ **keep back** VT (*crowd, tears*) conter; (*money*) reter ▶ VI manter-se afastado
   ▶ **keep down** VT (*control: prices, spending*) limitar, controlar ▶ VI não se levantar; **I can't ~ my food down** o que como não para no estômago
   ▶ **keep in** VT (*invalid, child*) não deixar sair; (*Sch*) reter ▶ VI: **to ~ in with sb** manter boas relações com alguém
   ▶ **keep off** VI não se aproximar ▶ VT afastar; **"~ off the grass"** "não pise na grama"; **~ your hands off!** tira a mão!
   ▶ **keep on** VI: **to ~ on doing** continuar fazendo
   ▶ **keep out** VT impedir de entrar ▶ VI (*stay out*) permanecer fora; **"~ out"** "entrada proibida"
   ▶ **keep up** VT manter ▶ VI não atrasar-se, acompanhar; **to ~ up with** (*pace*) acompanhar; (*level*) manter-se ao nível de

keeper ['kiːpəʳ] N guarda *m*, guardião(-diã) *m/f*

keep fit N ginástica

keeping ['kiːpɪŋ] N (*care*) cuidado; **in ~ with** de acordo com

keepsake ['kiːpseɪk] N lembrança

keg [kɛg] N barrilete *m*, barril *m* pequeno

kennel ['kɛnl] N casa de cachorro; **kennels** N (*establishment*) canil *m*

Kenya ['kɛnjə] N Quênia *m*

Kenyan ['kɛnjən] ADJ, N queniano(-a) *m/f*

kept [kɛpt] PT, PP *of* **keep**

kerb [kə:b] (BRIT) N meio-fio (BR), borda do passeio (PT)

kernel ['kə:nl] N amêndoa; (*fig*) cerne *m*

kerosene ['kɛrəsiːn] N querosene *m*

ketchup ['kɛtʃəp] N molho de tomate, catsup m
kettle ['kɛtl] N chaleira
kettle drums NPL tímpanos mpl
key [ki:] N chave f; (Mus) clave f; (of piano, typewriter) tecla; (on map) legenda ▶ CPD (issue etc) chave ▶ VT (also: **key in**) digitar
keyboard ['ki:bɔ:d] N teclado ▶ VT (text) teclar, digitar
keyed up [ki:d-] ADJ: **to be (all)** ~ estar excitado or ligado (inf)
keyhole ['ki:həul] N buraco da fechadura
keyhole surgery N laparoscopia
keynote ['ki:nəut] N (Mus) tônica; (fig) ideia fundamental ▶ CPD: ~ **speech** discurso programático
keypad ['ki:pæd] N teclado complementar
keyring ['ki:rɪŋ] N chaveiro
keystone ['ki:stəun] N pedra angular
keystroke ['ki:strəuk] N batida de tecla
kg ABBR (= kilogram) kg
KGB N ABBR KGB f
khaki ['ka:kɪ] ADJ cáqui
kibbutz [kɪ'buts] (pl **kibbutzim**) N kibutz m
kick [kɪk] VT (person) dar um pontapé em; (ball) chutar; (inf: habit) conseguir superar ▶ VI (horse) dar coices ▶ N (from person) pontapé m; (from animal) coice m, patada; (to ball) chute m; (of rifle) recuo; (inf: thrill): **he does it for ~s** faz isso para curtir
 ▶ **kick around** (inf) VI ficar por aí
 ▶ **kick off** VI (Sport) dar o chute inicial
kick-off N (Sport) chute m inicial
kick-start N (also: **kick-starter**) arranque m
 ▶ VT dar partida em
kid [kɪd] N (inf: child) criança; (animal) cabrito; (leather) pelica ▶ VI (inf) brincar
kidnap ['kɪdnæp] VT sequestrar
kidnapper ['kɪdnæpəʳ] N sequestrador(a) m/f
kidnapping ['kɪdnæpɪŋ] N sequestro
kidney ['kɪdnɪ] N rim m
kidney bean N feijão m roxo
kidney machine N (Med) aparelho de hemodiálise
Kilimanjaro [kɪlɪmən'dʒɑ:rəu] N: **Mount ~** Kilimanjaro
kill [kɪl] VT matar; (murder) assassinar; (destroy) destruir; (finish off) acabar com, aniquilar ▶ N ato de matar; **to ~ time** matar o tempo
 ▶ **kill off** VT aniquilar; (fig) eliminar
killer ['kɪləʳ] N assassino(-a)
killing ['kɪlɪŋ] N (one) assassinato; (several) matança; (instance) morte f ▶ ADJ (funny) divertido, engraçado; **to make a ~** (inf) faturar uma boa nota
killjoy ['kɪldʒɔɪ] N desmancha-prazeres m inv
kiln [kɪln] N forno
kilo ['ki:ləu] N quilo
kilobyte ['ki:ləubaɪt] N kilobyte m
kilogram, kilogramme ['kɪləugræm] N quilograma m
kilometre, (US) **kilometer** ['kɪləmi:təʳ] N quilômetro

kilowatt ['kɪləuwɔt] N quilowatt m
kilt [kɪlt] N saiote m escocês
kimono [kɪ'məunəu] N quimono
kin [kɪn] N parentela; see **kith, next-of-kin**
kind [kaɪnd] ADJ (friendly) gentil; (generous) generoso; (good) bom/boa, bondoso, amável
 ▶ N espécie f, classe f; (species) gênero; **in ~** (Comm) em espécie; **a ~ of** uma espécie de; **two of a ~** dois da mesma espécie; **would you be ~ enough to ...?, would you be so ~ as to ...?** pode me fazer a gentileza de ...?; **it's very ~ of you (to do)** é muito gentil da sua parte (fazer); **to repay sb in ~** (fig) pagar alguém na mesma moeda
kindergarten ['kɪndəgɑ:tn] N jardim m de infância
kind-hearted ADJ de bom coração, bondoso
kindle ['kɪndl] VT acender; (emotion) despertar
kindling ['kɪndlɪŋ] N gravetos mpl
kindly ['kaɪndlɪ] ADJ (good) bom/boa, bondoso; (gentle) gentil, carinhoso ▶ ADV bondosamente, amavelmente; **will you ~ ...** você pode fazer o favor de ...; **he didn't take it ~** não gostou
kindness ['kaɪndnɪs] N bondade f, gentileza
kindred ['kɪndrɪd] ADJ aparentado; **~ spirit** pessoa com os mesmos gostos
kinetic [kɪ'nɛtɪk] ADJ cinético
king [kɪŋ] N rei m
kingdom ['kɪŋdəm] N reino
kingfisher ['kɪŋfɪʃəʳ] N martim-pescador m
kingpin ['kɪŋpɪn] N (Tech) pino mestre; (fig) mandachuva m
king-size [-saɪz], **king-sized** [-saɪzd] ADJ tamanho grande; (cigarettes) king-size
kink [kɪŋk] N (of rope) dobra, coca; (inf: fig) mania
kinky ['kɪŋkɪ] (pej) ADJ (odd) excêntrico, esquisito; (sexually) pervertido
kinship ['kɪnʃɪp] N parentesco
kinsman ['kɪnzmən] (irreg: like **man**) N parente m
kinswoman ['kɪnzwumən] (irreg: like **woman**) N parenta
kiosk ['ki:ɔsk] N banca (BR), quiosque m (PT); (BRIT: also: **telephone kiosk**) cabine f
kipper ['kɪpəʳ] N tipo de arenque defumado
kiss [kɪs] N beijo ▶ VT beijar; **to ~ (each other)** beijar-se; **to ~ sb goodbye** despedir-se de alguém com beijos
kiss of life (BRIT) N respiração f boca-a-boca
kit [kɪt] N apetrechos mpl; (clothes: for sport etc) kit m; (equipment) equipamento; (set of tools etc) caixa de ferramentas; (for assembly) kit m para montar
 ▶ **kit out** (BRIT) VT equipar
kitbag ['kɪtbæg] N saco de viagem
kitchen ['kɪtʃɪn] N cozinha
kitchen garden N horta
kitchen sink N pia (de cozinha)
kitchen unit (BRIT) N módulo de cozinha
kitchenware ['kɪtʃɪnwɛəʳ] N bateria de cozinha

k

kite [kaɪt] N (*toy*) papagaio, pipa; (*Zool*) milhafre *m*
kith [kɪθ] N: ~ **and kin** amigos e parentes *mpl*
kitten ['kɪtn] N gatinho
kitty ['kɪtɪ] N (*pool of money*) fundo comum, vaquinha; (*Cards*) bolo
KKK (*US*) N ABBR = **Ku Klux Klan**
Kleenex® ['kli:nɛks] N lenço de papel
kleptomaniac [klɛptəu'meɪnɪæk] N cleptomaníaco(-a)
km ABBR (= *kilometre*) km
km/h ABBR (= *kilometres per hour*) km/h
knack [næk] N: **to have the ~ of doing sth** ter um jeito *or* queda para fazer algo; **there's a ~ (to it)** tem um jeito
knackered ['nækəd] ADJ (*inf*) exausto, podre
knapsack ['næpsæk] N mochila
knave [neɪv] N (*Cards*) valete *m*
knead [ni:d] VT amassar
knee [ni:] N joelho
kneecap ['ni:kæp] N rótula
knee-deep ADJ: **the water was ~** a água batia no joelho
kneel [ni:l] (*pt, pp* **knelt**) VI (*also:* **kneel down**) ajoelhar-se
kneepad ['ni:pæd] N joelheira
knell [nɛl] N dobre *m* de finados
knelt [nɛlt] PT, PP *of* **kneel**
knew [nju:] PT *of* **know**
knickers ['nɪkəz] (*BRIT*) NPL calcinha (*BR*), cuecas *fpl* (*PT*)
knick-knack ['nɪk-] N bibelô *m*
knife [naɪf] N (*pl* **knives**) faca ▶ VT esfaquear; **~, fork and spoon** talher *m*
knight [naɪt] N cavaleiro; (*Chess*) cavalo
knighthood ['naɪthud] (*BRIT*) N cavalaria; (*title*): **to get a ~** receber o título de Sir
knit [nɪt] VT tricotar; (*brows*) franzir ▶ VI tricotar (*BR*), fazer malha (*PT*); (*bones*) consolidar-se; **to ~ together** (*fig*) unir, juntar
knitted ['nɪtɪd] ADJ de malha
knitting ['nɪtɪŋ] N ato de tricotar, tricô (*BR*), malha (*PT*)
knitting machine N máquina de tricotar
knitting needle N agulha de tricô (*BR*) *or* de malha (*PT*)
knitting pattern N molde *m* para tricotar
knitwear ['nɪtwɛər] N roupa de malha
knives [naɪvz] NPL *of* **knife**
knob [nɔb] N (*of door*) maçaneta; (*of drawer*) puxador *m*; (*of stick*) castão *m*; (*on radio, TV etc*) botão *m*; (*lump*) calombo; **a ~ of butter** (*BRIT*) uma porção de manteiga
knobbly ['nɔblɪ] (*BRIT*) ADJ (*wood, surface*) nodoso; (*knees*) ossudo
knobby ['nɔbɪ] (*US*) ADJ = **knobbly**
knock [nɔk] VT (*strike*) bater em; (*bump into*) colidir com; (*inf: criticize*) criticar, malhar ▶ N pancada, golpe *m*; (*on door*) batida ▶ VI: **to ~ at** *or* **on the door** bater à porta; **to ~ a hole in sth** abrir um buraco em algo; **to ~ a nail into** pregar um prego em

▶ **knock down** VT derrubar; (*price*) abater; (*pedestrian*) atropelar
▶ **knock off** VI (*inf: finish*) terminar ▶ VT (*inf: steal*) abafar; (*vase*) derrubar; (*from price*): **to ~ off £10** dar um desconto de £10
▶ **knock out** VT pôr nocaute, nocautear; (*defeat*) eliminar
▶ **knock over** VT (*object*) derrubar; (*pedestrian*) atropelar
knockdown ['nɔkdaun] ADJ (*price*) de liquidação, de queima (*inf*)
knocker ['nɔkər] N (*on door*) aldrava
knocking ['nɔkɪŋ] N pancadas *fpl*
knock-kneed [-ni:d] ADJ cambaio
knockout ['nɔkaut] N (*Boxing*) nocaute *m* ▶ CPD (*competition*) com eliminatórias
knock-up N (*Tennis*) bate-bola *m*
knot [nɔt] N nó *m* ▶ VT dar nó em; **to tie a ~** dar *or* fazer um nó
knotty ['nɔtɪ] ADJ (*fig*) cabeludo, espinhoso
know [nəu] (*pt* **knew**, *pp* **known**) VT saber; (*person, author, place*) conhecer; (*recognize*) reconhecer ▶ VI: **to ~ about** *or* **of sth** saber de algo; **to ~ that ...** saber que ...; **to ~ how to swim** saber nadar; **to get to ~ sth** (*fact*) saber, descobrir; (*place*) conhecer; **I don't ~ him** não o conheço; **to ~ right from wrong** saber distinguir o bem e o mal; **as far as I ~ ...** que eu saiba ...
know-all (*BRIT pej*) N sabichão(-chona) *m/f*
know-how N know-how *m*, experiência
knowing ['nəuɪŋ] ADJ (*look: of complicity*) de cumplicidade
knowingly ['nəuɪŋlɪ] ADV (*purposely*) de propósito; (*spitefully*) maliciosamente
know-it-all (*US*) N = **know-all**
knowledge ['nɔlɪdʒ] N conhecimento; (*range of learning*) saber *m*, conhecimentos *mpl*; **to have no ~ of** não ter conhecimento de; **not to my ~** que eu saiba, não; **without my ~** sem eu saber; **to have a working ~ of Portuguese** ter um conhecimento básico do português; **it's common ~ that ...** todos sabem que ...; **it has come to my ~ that ...** chegou ao meu conhecimento que ...
knowledgeable ['nɔlɪdʒəbl] ADJ entendido, versado
known [nəun] PP *of* **know** ▶ ADJ (*thief*) famigerado; (*fact*) conhecido
knuckle ['nʌkl] N nó *m*
▶ **knuckle under** VI ceder
knuckleduster ['nʌkldʌstər] N soco inglês
K.O. N ABBR = **knockout** ▶ VT nocautear, pôr nocaute
koala [kəu'ɑ:lə] N (*also:* **koala bear**) coala *m*
kook [ku:k] (*US inf*) N maluco(-a), biruta (*inf*)
Koran [kɔ'rɑ:n] N: **the ~** o Alcorão
Korea [kə'rɪə] N Coreia; **North/South ~** Coreia do Norte/Sul
Korean [kə'rɪən] ADJ coreano ▶ N coreano(-a); (*Ling*) coreano
kosher ['kəuʃər] ADJ kosher *inv*
Kosovo ['kɔsɔvəu] N Kosovo *m*

kowtow ['kau'tau] VI: **to ~ to sb** bajular
   alguém
Kremlin ['krɛmlɪn] N: **the ~** o Kremlin
KS (US) ABBR (Post) = **Kansas**
Kt (BRIT) ABBR (= Knight) título honorífico
Kuala Lumpur ['kwɑːlə'lumpuəʳ] N

Cuala Lumpur
kudos ['kjuːdɔs] N glória, fama
Kuwait [ku'weɪt] N Kuweit m
Kuwaiti [ku'weɪtɪ] ADJ, N kuweitiano(-a)
kW ABBR (= kilowatt) kW
KY (US) ABBR (Post) = **Kentucky**

L¹, l [ɛl] N (*letter*) L, l *m*; **L for Lucy** (BRIT) *or* **Love** (US) L de Lúcia

L² ABBR (= *lake*) L; (= *large*) G; (= *left*) esq; (BRIT *Aut*: = *learner*) (condutor(a) *m/f*) aprendiz *m/f*

l ABBR (= *litre*) l

LA (US) N ABBR = **Los Angeles** ▶ ABBR (*Post*) = **Louisiana**

lab [læb] N ABBR = **laboratory**

label ['leɪbl] N etiqueta, rótulo; (*brand: of record*) selo ▶ VT etiquetar, rotular; **to ~ sb a ...** rotular alguém de ...

labor ['leɪbə'] (US) = **labour**

laboratory [lə'bɔrətərɪ] N laboratório

Labor Day (US) N Dia *m* do Trabalho

laborious [lə'bɔːrɪəs] ADJ laborioso

labor union (US) N sindicato

labour, (US) **labor** ['leɪbə'] N (*task*) trabalho; (*work force*) mão-de-obra *f*; (*workers*) trabalhadores *mpl*; (*Med*): **to be in ~** estar em trabalho de parto ▶ VI: **to ~ (at)** trabalhar (em) ▶ VT insistir em; **L~, the L~ Party** (BRIT) o Partido Trabalhista

labour camp, (US) **labor camp** N campo de trabalhos forçados

labour cost, (US) **labor cost** N custo de mão-de-obra

laboured, (US) **labored** ['leɪbəd] ADJ (*movement*) forçado; (*style*) elaborado

labourer, (US) **laborer** ['leɪbərə'] N operário; **farm ~** trabalhador *m* rural, peão *m*; **day ~** diarista *m*

labour force, (US) **labor force** N mão-de-obra *f*

labour-intensive, (US) **labor-intensive** ADJ intensivo de mão-de-obra

labour market, (US) **labor market** N mercado de trabalho

labour pains, (US) **labor pains** NPL dores *fpl* do parto

labour relations, (US) **labor relations** NPL relações *fpl* trabalhistas

labour-saving, (US) **labor-saving** ADJ que poupa trabalho

labour unrest, (US) **labor unrest** N agitação *f* operária

labyrinth ['læbɪrɪnθ] N labirinto

lace [leɪs] N renda; (*of shoe etc*) cadarço ▶ VT (*shoe*) amarrar; (*drink*) misturar aguardente a

lace-making ['leɪsmeɪkɪŋ] N feitura de renda

laceration [læsə'reɪʃən] N laceração *f*

lace-up ADJ (*shoes etc*) de cordões

lack [læk] N falta ▶ VT (*money, confidence*) faltar; (*intelligence*) carecer de; **through** *or* **for ~ of** por falta de; **to be ~ing** faltar; **to be ~ing in** carecer de

lackadaisical [lækə'deɪzɪkl] ADJ (*careless*) descuidado; (*indifferent*) apático, indiferente

lackey ['lækɪ] N (*fig*) lacaio

lacklustre ['læklʌstə'] ADJ sem brilho, insosso

laconic [lə'kɔnɪk] ADJ lacônico

lacquer ['lækə'] N laca; (*hair*) fixador *m*

lacy ['leɪsɪ] ADJ rendado

lad [læd] N menino, rapaz *m*, moço; (BRIT: *in stable etc*) empregado

ladder ['lædə'] N escada *f* de mão; (BRIT: *in tights*) defeito (em forma de escada) ▶ VT (BRIT: *tights*) desfiar ▶ VI (BRIT: *tights*) desfiar

laden ['leɪdn] ADJ: **~ (with)** carregado (de); **fully ~** (*truck, ship*) completamente carregado, com a carga máxima

ladle ['leɪdl] N concha (de sopa)

lady ['leɪdɪ] N senhora; (*distinguished, noble*) dama; (*in address*): **ladies and gentlemen, ...** senhoras e senhores, ...; **young ~** senhorita; **L~ Smith** a lady Smith; **"ladies' (toilets)"** "senhoras"; **a ~ doctor** uma médica

ladybird ['leɪdɪbəːd], (US) **ladybug** ['leɪdɪbʌg] N joaninha

lady-in-waiting N dama de companhia

lady-killer ['leɪdɪkɪlə'] N mulherengo

ladylike ['leɪdɪlaɪk] ADJ elegante, refinado

ladyship ['leɪdɪʃɪp] N: **your ~** Sua Senhoria

lag [læg] N (*period of time*) atraso, retardamento ▶ VI (*also:* **lag behind**) ficar para trás ▶ VT (*pipes*) revestir com isolante térmico

lager ['lɑːgə'] N cerveja leve e clara

lagging ['lægɪŋ] N revestimento

lagoon [lə'guːn] N lagoa

Lagos ['leɪgɔs] N Lagos

laid [leɪd] PT, PP *of* **lay**

laid-back (*inf*) ADJ descontraído

laid up ADJ: **to be ~ with flu** ficar de cama com gripe

lain [leɪn] PP *of* **lie**

lair [lɛə'] N covil *m*, toca

laissez-faire [lɛseɪ'fɛə'] N laissez-faire *m*

laity ['leɪətɪ] N leigos *mpl*

lake [leɪk] N lago

Lake District (BRIT) N: **the ~** a região dos Lagos

lamb [læm] N cordeiro
lamb chop N costeleta de cordeiro
lambskin ['læmskɪn] N pele f de cordeiro
lambswool ['læmzwʊl] N lã f de cordeiro
lame [leɪm] ADJ coxo, manco; *(excuse, argument)* pouco convincente, fraco; **~ duck** *(fig)* pessoa incapaz
lamely ['leɪmlɪ] ADV *(fig)* sem convicção
lament [lə'mɛnt] N lamento, queixa ▶ VT lamentar-se de
lamentable ['læməntəbl] ADJ lamentável
laminated ['læmɪneɪtɪd] ADJ laminado
lamp [læmp] N lâmpada
lamplight ['læmplaɪt] N: **by ~** à luz da lâmpada
lampoon [læm'puːn] VT satirizar
lamppost ['læmppəʊst] *(BRIT)* N poste m
lampshade ['læmpʃeɪd] N abajur m, quebra-luz m
lance [lɑːns] N lança ▶ VT *(Med)* lancetar
lance corporal *(BRIT)* N cabo
lancet ['lɑːnsɪt] N *(Med)* bisturi, lanceta
Lancs [læŋks] *(BRIT)* ABBR = **Lancashire**
land [lænd] N terra; *(country)* país m; *(piece of land)* terreno; *(estate)* terras fpl, propriedades fpl; *(Agr)* solo ▶ VI *(from ship)* desembarcar; *(Aviat)* pousar, aterrissar *(BR)*, aterrar *(PT)*; *(fig: arrive unexpectedly)* cair, terminar ▶ VT *(obtain)* conseguir; *(passengers, goods)* desembarcar; **to go/travel by ~** ir/viajar por terra; **to own ~** ter propriedades; **to ~ on one's feet** *(fig)* dar-se bem, cair de pé; **to ~ sb with sth** *(inf)* sobrecarregar alguém com algo
▶ **land up** VI: **to ~ up in/at** ir parar em
landed gentry ['lændɪd-] N proprietários mpl de terras
landfill site ['lændfɪl-] N aterro sanitário
landing ['lændɪŋ] N *(from ship)* desembarque m; *(Aviat)* pouso, aterrissagem f *(BR)*, aterragem f *(PT)*; *(of staircase)* patamar m
landing card N cartão m de desembarque
landing craft N navio para desembarque
landing gear N trem m de aterrissagem *(BR)* or de aterragem *(PT)*
landing stage *(BRIT)* N cais m de desembarque
landing strip N pista de aterrissagem *(BR)* or de aterragem *(PT)*
landlady ['lændleɪdɪ] N *(of rented property)* senhoria; *(of pub)* dona, proprietária
landline ['lændlaɪn] N telefone m fixo
landlocked ['lændlɔkt] ADJ cercado de terra
landlord ['lændlɔːd] N senhorio, locador m; *(of pub etc)* dono, proprietário
landlubber ['lændlʌbə'] N *pessoa desacostumada ao mar*
landmark ['lændmɑːk] N lugar m conhecido; *(fig)* marco
landowner ['lændəʊnə'] N latifundiário(-a)
landscape ['lændskeɪp] N paisagem f
landscape architect N paisagista m/f
landscaped ['lændskeɪpt] ADJ projetado paisagisticamente

landscape gardener N paisagista m/f
landscape painting N *(Art: genre)* paisagismo; *(: picture)* paisagem f
landslide ['lændslaɪd] N *(Geo)* desmoronamento, desabamento; *(fig: Pol)* vitória esmagadora
lane [leɪn] N *(in country)* caminho, estrada estreita; *(in town)* ruela; *(Aut)* pista; *(in race)* raia; *(for air or sea traffic)* rota
language ['læŋgwɪdʒ] N língua; *(way one speaks, Comput, style)* linguagem f; **bad ~** palavrões mpl
language laboratory N laboratório de línguas
language school N escola de línguas
languid ['læŋgwɪd] ADJ lânguido
languish ['læŋgwɪʃ] VI elanguescer, debilitar-se
lank [læŋk] ADJ *(hair)* liso
lanky ['læŋkɪ] ADJ magricela
lanolin, lanoline ['lænəlɪn] N lanolina
lantern ['læntn] N lanterna
Laos [laʊs] N Laos m
lap [læp] N *(of track)* volta; *(of person)* colo ▶ VT *(also: **lap up**)* lamber ▶ VI *(waves)* marulhar
▶ **lap up** VT *(fig: food)* comer sofregamente; *(: compliments)* receber com sofreguidão
La Paz [læ'pæz] N La Paz
lapdog ['læpdɔg] N cãozinho de estimação
lapel [lə'pɛl] N lapela
Lapland ['læplænd] N Lapônia
Lapp [læp] ADJ, N lapão(-ona) m/f
lapse [læps] N lapso; *(bad behaviour)* deslize m ▶ VI *(expire)* caducar; *(law)* prescrever; *(morally)* decair; **to ~ into bad habits** adquirir maus hábitos; **~ of time** lapso, intervalo; **a ~ of memory** um lapso de memória
laptop ['læptɔp], **laptop computer** N laptop m
larceny ['lɑːsənɪ] N furto; **petty ~** delito leve
larch [lɑːtʃ] N lariço
lard [lɑːd] N banha de porco
larder ['lɑːdə'] N despensa
large [lɑːdʒ] ADJ grande; *(fat)* gordo; **at ~** *(free)* em liberdade; *(generally)* em geral; **to make ~r** ampliar; **a ~ number of people** um grande número de pessoas; **by and ~** de modo geral; **on a ~ scale** em grande escala
largely ['lɑːdʒlɪ] ADV em grande parte; *(introducing reason)* principalmente
large-scale ADJ *(map)* em grande escala; *(fig)* importante, de grande alcance
largesse [lɑː'dʒɛs] N generosidade f
lark [lɑːk] N *(bird)* cotovia; *(joke)* brincadeira, peça
▶ **lark about** VI divertir-se, brincar
larva ['lɑːvə] *(pl **larvae**)* N larva
larvae ['lɑːviː] NPL *of* **larva**
laryngitis [lærɪn'dʒaɪtɪs] N laringite f
larynx ['lærɪŋks] N laringe f
lascivious [lə'sɪvɪəs] ADJ lascivo
laser ['leɪzə'] N laser m
laser beam N raio laser

laser printer N impressora a laser
lash [læʃ] N chicote m, açoite m; (blow)
chicotada; (also: **eyelash**) pestana, cílio ▶ VT
chicotear, açoitar; (subj: rain, wind) castigar;
(tie) atar
▶ **lash down** VT atar, amarrar ▶ VI (rain) cair
em bátegas
▶ **lash out** VI: **to ~ out (at sb)** atacar
(alguém) violentamente; **to ~ out at** or
against sb (criticize) atacar alguém
verbalmente; **to ~ out (on sth)** (inf: spend)
esbanjar dinheiro (em algo)
lashings ['læʃɪŋz] (BRIT inf) NPL: ~ **of** (cream etc)
montes mpl de, um montão de
lass [læs] (BRIT) N moça
lasso [læ'su:] N laço ▶ VT laçar
last [lɑ:st] ADJ último; (final) derradeiro ▶ ADV
em último lugar ▶ VI (endure) durar; (continue)
continuar; ~ **week** na semana passada;
~ **night** ontem à noite; **at ~** finalmente;
at ~! até que enfim!; ~ **but one** penúltimo;
the ~ time a última vez; **it ~s (for) 2 hours**
dura 2 horas
last-ditch ADJ desesperado, derradeiro
lasting ['lɑ:stɪŋ] ADJ duradouro
lastly ['lɑ:stlɪ] ADV (last of all) por fim, por
último; (finally) finalmente
last-minute ADJ de última hora
latch [lætʃ] N trinco, fecho, tranca
▶ **latch on to** VT FUS (cling to: person) grudar
em; (: idea) agarrar-se a
latchkey ['lætʃki:] N chave f de trinco
late [leɪt] ADJ (not on time) atrasado; (far on in day
etc) tardio; (hour) avançado; (recent) recente;
(former) antigo, ex-, anterior; (dead) falecido
▶ ADV tarde; (behind time, schedule) atrasado;
to be ~ estar atrasado, atrasar; **to be**
10 minutes ~ estar atrasado dez minutos;
to work ~ trabalhar até tarde; ~ **in life** com
idade avançada; **it was too ~** já era tarde;
of ~ recentemente; **in ~ May** no final de
maio; **the ~ Mr X** o falecido Sr X
latecomer ['leɪtkʌmər] N retardatário(-a)
lately ['leɪtlɪ] ADV ultimamente
lateness ['leɪtnɪs] N (of person) atraso; (of event)
hora avançada
latent ['leɪtnt] ADJ latente
later ['leɪtər] ADJ (date etc) posterior; (version etc)
mais recente ▶ ADV mais tarde, depois; ~ **on**
mais tarde
lateral ['lætərl] ADJ lateral
latest ['leɪtɪst] ADJ último; **the ~ news** as
últimas novidades; **at the ~** no mais tardar
latex ['leɪteks] N látex m
lath [læθ] (pl **laths** [læðz]) N ripa
lathe [leɪð] N torno
lather ['lɑ:ðər] N espuma (de sabão) ▶ VT
ensaboar ▶ VI fazer espuma
Latin ['lætɪn] N (Ling) latim m ▶ ADJ latino
Latin America N América Latina
Latin American ADJ, N latino-americano(-a)
latitude ['lætɪtju:d] N (also fig) latitude f
latrine [lə'tri:n] N latrina

latter ['lætər] ADJ último; (of two) segundo
▶ N: **the ~** o último, este
latterly ['lætəlɪ] ADV ultimamente
lattice ['lætɪs] N treliça
lattice window N janela com treliça de
chumbo
Latvia ['lætvɪə] N Letônia
laudable ['lɔ:dəbl] ADJ louvável
laudatory ['lɔ:dətrɪ] ADJ laudatório, elogioso
laugh [lɑ:f] N riso, risada; (loud) gargalhada
▶ VI rir, dar risada (or gargalhada); **(to do**
sth) for a ~ (fazer algo) só de curtição
▶ **laugh at** VT FUS rir de
▶ **laugh off** VT disfarçar sorrindo
laughable ['lɑ:fəbl] ADJ ridículo, absurdo
laughing ['lɑ:fɪŋ] ADJ risonho; **this is no ~**
matter isto não é para rir
laughing gas N gás m hilariante
laughing stock N alvo de riso
laughter ['lɑ:ftər] N riso, risada; (people
laughing) risos mpl
launch [lɔ:ntʃ] N (boat) lancha; (Comm, of rocket
etc) lançamento ▶ VT (ship, rocket, plan) lançar
▶ **launch into** VT FUS lançar-se a
▶ **launch out** VI: **to ~ out (into)** lançar-se (a)
launching ['lɔ:ntʃɪŋ] N (of rocket etc)
lançamento
launching pad, launch pad N plataforma de
lançamento
launder ['lɔ:ndər] VT lavar e passar; (money)
lavar
Launderette® [lɔ:n'dret] (BRIT) N lavanderia
automática
Laundromat® ['lɔ:ndrəmæt] (US) N
lavanderia automática
laundry ['lɔ:ndrɪ] N lavanderia; (clothes) roupa
para lavar; **to do the ~** lavar a roupa
laureate ['lɔ:rɪət] ADJ see **poet**
laurel ['lɔrl] N louro; (Bot) loureiro; **to rest on**
one's ~s dormir sobre os louros
lava ['lɑ:və] N lava
lavatory ['lævətərɪ] N privada (BR), casa de
banho (PT); **lavatories** NPL (public) sanitários
mpl (BR), lavabos mpl (PT)
lavatory paper N papel m higiênico
lavender ['lævəndər] N lavanda
lavish ['lævɪʃ] ADJ (amount) generoso; (person):
~ **with** pródigo em, generoso com ▶ VT: **to ~**
sth on sb encher ou cobrir alguém de algo
lavishly ['lævɪʃlɪ] ADV (give, spend)
prodigamente; (furnished) luxuosamente
law [lɔ:] N lei f; (rule) regra; (Sch) direito;
against the ~ contra a lei; **to study ~**
estudar direito; **to go to ~** (BRIT) recorrer à
justiça
law-abiding [-ə'baɪdɪŋ] ADJ obediente à lei
law and order N a ordem pública
lawbreaker ['lɔ:breɪkər] N infrator(a) m/f (da lei)
law court N tribunal m de justiça
lawful ['lɔ:ful] ADJ legal, lícito
lawfully ['lɔ:fulɪ] ADV legalmente
lawless ['lɔ:lɪs] ADJ (act) ilegal; (person)
rebelde; (country) sem lei, desordenado

lawmaker ['lɔːmeɪkəʳ] N legislador(a) m/f
lawn [lɔːn] N gramado (BR), relvado (PT)
lawnmower ['lɔːnməuəʳ] N cortador m de grama (BR) or de relva (PT)
lawn tennis N tênis m de gramado (BR) or de relvado (PT)
law school (US) N faculdade f de direito
law student N estudante m/f de direito
lawsuit ['lɔːsuːt] N ação f judicial, processo; **to bring a ~ against** mover processo contra
lawyer ['lɔːjəʳ] N advogado(-a); (for sales, wills etc) notário(-a), tabelião(-liã) m/f
lax [læks] ADJ (discipline) relaxado; (person) negligente
laxative ['læksətɪv] N laxante m
laxity ['læksɪtɪ] N: **moral ~** falta de escrúpulo or caráter
lay [leɪ] (pt, pp laid) VT (place) colocar; (eggs, table) pôr; (trap) armar; (plan) traçar ▶ PT of **lie** ▶ ADJ leigo; **to ~ the table** pôr a mesa; **to ~ the facts/one's proposals before sb** apresentar os fatos/suas propostas a alguém; **to get laid** (!) trepar (!)
▶ **lay aside** VT pôr de lado
▶ **lay by** VT = **lay aside**
▶ **lay down** VT (object) depositar; (flat) deitar; (arms) depor; (rules etc) impor, estabelecer; **to ~ down the law** (pej) impor regras; **to ~ down one's life** sacrificar voluntariamente a vida
▶ **lay in** VT armazenar, abastecer-se de
▶ **lay into** (inf) VT FUS (attack) surrar, espancar; (scold) dar uma bronca em
▶ **lay off** VT (workers) demitir
▶ **lay on** VT (water, gas) instalar; (meal, entertainment) prover; (paint) aplicar
▶ **lay out** VT (spread out) dispor em ordem; (design) planejar; (display) expor; (spend) esbanjar
▶ **lay up** VT (store) estocar; (ship) pôr fora de serviço; (subj: illness) acometer
layabout ['leɪəbaut] (inf) N vadio(-a), preguiçoso(-a)
lay-by (BRIT) N acostamento
lay days NPL (Naut) dias mpl de estadia
layer ['leɪəʳ] N camada
layette [leɪ'ɛt] N enxoval m de bebê
layman ['leɪmən] (irreg: like man) N leigo
lay-off N demissão f
layout ['leɪaut] N (of garden, building) desenho; (of piece of writing) leiaute m; (disposition) disposição f; (Press) composição f
laze [leɪz] VI descansar; (also: **laze about**) vadiar
laziness ['leɪzɪnɪs] N preguiça
lazy ['leɪzɪ] ADJ preguiçoso; (movement) lento
lb. ABBR (weight) = **pound**
lbw ABBR (Cricket: = leg before wicket) falta em que o batedor está com a perna em frente da meta
LC (US) N ABBR = **Library of Congress**
L/C ABBR = **letter of credit**
LCD N ABBR = **liquid crystal display**
Ld (BRIT) ABBR (= lord) título honorífico

LDS N ABBR (= Licentiate in Dental Surgery) diploma universitário; (= Latter-day Saints) os Santos dos Últimos Dias
LEA (BRIT) N ABBR (= local education authority) departamento de ensino do município
lead¹ [liːd] (pt, pp led) N (front position) dianteira; (Sport) liderança; (fig) vantagem f; (clue) pista; (Elec) fio; (for dog) correia; (in play, film) papel m principal ▶ VT conduzir; (guide) levar; (induce) levar, induzir; (be leader of) chefiar; (start, guide: activity) encabeçar; (Sport) liderar; (orchestra: BRIT) ser a primeira figura de; (: US) reger ▶ VI encabeçar; **to ~ sb astray** desencaminhar alguém; **to be in the ~** (Sport: in race) estar na frente; (: in match) estar ganhando; **to take the ~** (Sport) disparar na frente; (fig) tomar a dianteira; **to ~ the way** assumir a direcão; **to ~ sb to believe that …** levar alguém a acreditar que …; **to ~ sb to do sth** levar alguém a fazer algo
▶ **lead away** VT levar
▶ **lead back** VT levar de volta
▶ **lead off** VI (in game etc) começar
▶ **lead on** VT (tease) provocar; **to ~ sb on to** induzir alguém a
▶ **lead to** VT FUS levar a, conduzir a
▶ **lead up to** VT FUS conduzir a
lead² [lɛd] N chumbo; (in pencil) grafite f
leaded ['lɛdɪd] ADJ (petrol) com chumbo; **~ window** janela com pequenas lâminas de vidro presas por tiras de chumbo
leaden ['lɛdən] ADJ (sky, sea) cor de chumbo, cinzento
leader ['liːdəʳ] N líder m/f, chefe m/f; (of party, union etc) líder m/f; (of gang) cabeça m/f; (of newspaper) artigo de fundo; **they are ~s in their field** são os líderes na área em que atuam; **the L~ of the House** (BRIT) o chefe dos ministros na Câmara
leadership ['liːdəʃɪp] N liderança; (quality) poder m de liderança; **under the ~ of …** sob a liderança de …; (army) sob o comando de …; **qualities of ~** qualidades de liderança
lead-free [lɛd-] ADJ sem chumbo
leading ['liːdɪŋ] ADJ (main) principal; (role) de destaque; (first, front) primeiro, dianteiro; **a ~ question** uma pergunta capciosa; **~ role** papel de destaque
leading lady N (Theatre) primeira atriz f
leading light N (person) figura principal, destaque m
leading man (irreg: like man) N (Theatre) ator m principal
lead pencil [lɛd-] N lápis f de grafite
lead poisoning [lɛd-] N saturnismo
lead singer [liːd-] N (in pop group) cantor(a) m/f
lead time [liːd-] N (Comm) prazo de entrega
lead weight [lɛd-] N peso de chumbo
leaf [liːf] N (pl leaves) folha; (of table) aba ▶ VI: **to ~ through** (book) folhear; **to turn over a new ~** mudar de vida, partir para outra (inf); **to take a ~ out of sb's book** (fig) seguir o exemplo de alguém

leaflet ['li:flɪt] N folheto
leafy ['li:fɪ] ADJ folhoso, folhudo
league [li:g] N liga; *(Football: championship)*
campeonato; *(: table)* classificação *f*; **to be in**
~ with estar de comum acordo com
leak [li:k] N *(of liquid, gas)* escape *m*,
vazamento; *(hole)* buraco, rombo; *(in roof)*
goteira; *(fig: of information)* vazamento ▶ VI
(ship) fazer água; *(shoe)* deixar entrar água;
(roof) gotejar; *(pipe, container, liquid)* vazar; *(gas)*
escapar; *(fig: news)* vazar ▶ VT *(news)* vazar;
the information was ~ed to the enemy as
informações foram passadas para o inimigo
▶ **leak out** VI vazar
leakage ['li:kɪdʒ] N *(fig)* vazamento
leaky ['li:kɪ] ADJ *(pipe, shoe, boat)* furado; *(roof)*
com goteira
lean [li:n] *(pt, pp leaned or leant)* ADJ magro
▶ N *(of meat)* carne *f* magra ▶ VT: **to ~ sth on**
encostar or apoiar algo em ▶ VI *(slope)*
inclinar-se; **to ~ against** encostar-se or
apoiar-se contra; **to ~ on** encostar-se or
apoiar-se em
▶ **lean back** VI *(move body)* inclinar-se para
trás; *(against wall, in chair)* recostar-se
▶ **lean forward** VI inclinar-se para frente
▶ **lean out** VI: **to ~ out (of)** inclinar-se para
fora (de)
▶ **lean over** VI debruçar-se ▶ VT FUS
debruçar-se sobre
leaning ['li:nɪŋ] ADJ inclinado ▶ N:
~ (towards) inclinação *f* (para); **the L~**
Tower of Pisa a torre inclinada de Pisa
leant [lɛnt] PT, PP *of* **lean**
lean-to N alpendre *m*
leap [li:p] *(pt, pp leaped or leapt)* N salto, pulo
▶ VI saltar
▶ **leap at** VT FUS: **to ~ at an offer** agarrar
uma oferta
▶ **leap up** VI *(person)* levantar-se num ímpeto
leapfrog ['li:pfrɔg] N jogo de pular carniça
leapt [lɛpt] PT, PP *of* **leap**
leap year N ano bissexto
learn [lə:n] *(pt, pp learned or learnt)* VT
aprender; *(by heart)* decorar ▶ VI aprender;
to ~ about sth *(Sch)* instruir-se sobre algo;
(hear, read) saber de algo; **we were sorry to ~**
that ... sentimos tomar conhecimento de
que ...; **to ~ to do sth** aprender a fazer algo
learned ['lə:nɪd] ADJ erudito
learner ['lə:nə'] N principiante *m/f*; *(BRIT: also:*
learner driver) aprendiz *m/f* de motorista
learning ['lə:nɪŋ] N *(process)* aprendizagem *f*;
(quality) erudição *f*; *(knowledge)* saber *m*
learnt [lə:nt] PT, PP *of* **learn**
lease [li:s] N arrendamento ▶ VT arrendar;
on ~ em arrendamento
▶ **lease back** VT vender e alugar do
comprador
leaseback ['li:sbæk] N *venda de uma propriedade*
com a condição do comprador alugá-la ao vendedor
leasehold ['li:shəuld] N *(contract)*
arrendamento ▶ ADJ arrendado

leash [li:ʃ] N correia
least [li:st] ADJ: **the ~** *(+ n)* o/a menor; *(smallest*
amount of) a menor quantidade de ▶ ADV:
the ~ *(+ adj)* o/a menos; **the ~ money** o
menos dinheiro de todos; **the ~ expensive**
o menos caro/a menos cara; **the ~ possible**
effort o menor esforço possível; **at ~** pelo
menos; **you could at ~ have written** você
poderia pelo menos ter escrito; **not in the ~**
de maneira nenhuma
leather ['lɛðə'] N couro ▶ CPD de couro;
~ goods artigos *mpl* de couro
leave [li:v] *(pt, pp left)* VT deixar; *(go away from)*
abandonar ▶ VI ir-se, sair; *(train)* sair ▶ N
(consent) permissão *f*, licença; *(time off, Mil)*
licença; **to ~ sth to sb** *(money etc)* deixar algo
para alguém; **to be left** sobrar; **there's**
some milk left over sobrou um pouco de
leite; **to ~ school** sair da escola; **~ it to me!**
deixe comigo!; **on ~** de licença; **to take**
one's ~ despedir-se de
▶ **leave behind** VT *(also fig)* deixar para trás;
(forget) esquecer
▶ **leave off** VT *(lid, cover)* não colocar; *(heating)*
não ligar; *(light)* deixar apagado; *(BRIT inf:*
stop): **to ~ off (doing sth)** parar (de fazer algo)
▶ **leave on** VT *(coat etc)* ficar com, não tirar;
(lid) não tirar; *(light, fire)* deixar aceso; *(radio)*
deixar ligado
▶ **leave out** VT omitir
leave of absence N licença excepcional
leaves [li:vz] NPL *of* **leaf**
Lebanese [lɛbə'ni:z] ADJ, N INV libanês(-esa) *m/f*
Lebanon ['lɛbənən] N Líbano
lecherous ['lɛtʃərəs] ADJ lascivo
lectern ['lɛktə:n] N atril *m*
lecture ['lɛktʃə'] N conferência, palestra; *(Sch)*
aula ▶ VI dar aulas, lecionar ▶ VT *(scold)*
passar um sermão em; **to give a ~ on** dar
uma conferência sobre
lecture hall N salão *m* de conferências,
anfiteatro
lecturer ['lɛktʃərə'] N conferencista *m/f* (BR),
conferente *m/f* (PT); *(BRIT: at university)*
professor(a) *m/f*; **assistant ~** (BRIT)
assistente *m/f*; **senior ~** (BRIT) lente *m/f*
lecture theatre N = **lecture hall**
LED N ABBR (= *light-emitting diode*) LED *m*
led [lɛd] PT, PP *of* **lead**[1]
ledge [lɛdʒ] N *(of window)* peitoril *m*; *(of*
mountain) saliência, proeminência
ledger ['lɛdʒə'] N livro-razão *m*, razão *m*
lee [li:] N sotavento; **in the ~ of** ao abrigo de
leech [li:tʃ] N sanguessuga
leek [li:k] N alho-poró *m*
leer [lɪə'] VI: **to ~ at sb** olhar maliciosamente
para alguém
leeward ['li:wəd] ADJ de sotavento ▶ ADV a
sotavento ▶ N sotavento; **to ~** para
sotavento
leeway ['li:weɪ] N *(fig)*: **to make up ~** reduzir
o atraso; **to have some ~** ter certa liberdade
de ação

left [lɛft] PT, PP of **leave** ▶ ADJ esquerdo ▶ N esquerda ▶ ADV à esquerda; **on the ~** à esquerda; **to the ~** para a esquerda; **the L~** (Pol) a Esquerda

left-hand drive (BRIT) N direção f do lado esquerdo

left-handed [-'hændɪd] ADJ canhoto; (scissors etc) para canhotos

left-hand side N lado esquerdo

leftie ['lɛftɪ] N (inf) esquerdista m/f

leftist ['lɛftɪst] ADJ (Pol) esquerdista

left-luggage, (BRIT) **left-luggage office** N depósito de bagagem

leftovers ['lɛftəʊvəz] NPL sobras fpl

left wing N (Mil, Sport) ala esquerda; (Pol) esquerda

left-wing ADJ (Pol) de esquerda, esquerdista

left-winger N (Pol) esquerdista m/f; (Sport) ponta-esquerda m/f

leg [lɛg] N perna; (of animal) pata; (of chair) pé m; (Culin: of meat) perna; (of journey) etapa; **1st/2nd ~** (Sport) primeiro/segundo turno; **to pull sb's ~** brincar or mexer com alguém; **to stretch one's ~s** esticar as pernas

legacy ['lɛgəsɪ] N legado; (fig) herança

legal ['li:gl] ADJ (lawful, of law) legal; (terminology, enquiry etc) jurídico; **to take ~ proceedings** or **action against sb** instaurar processo contra alguém

legal adviser N consultor(a) m/f jurídico(-a)

legal holiday (US) N feriado

legality [lɪ'gælɪtɪ] N legalidade f

legalize ['li:gəlaɪz] VT legalizar

legally ['li:gəlɪ] ADV legalmente; (in terms of law) de acordo com a lei

legal tender N moeda corrente

legation [lə'geɪʃən] N legação f

legend ['lɛdʒənd] N lenda; (person) mito

legendary ['lɛdʒəndərɪ] ADJ legendário

-legged ['lɛgɪd] SUFFIX: **two~** de duas patas (or pernas)

leggings ['lɛgɪŋz] NPL (over-trousers) perneiras fpl; (women's) legging f

legibility [lɛdʒɪ'bɪlɪtɪ] N legibilidade f

legible ['lɛdʒəbl] ADJ legível

legibly ['lɛdʒəblɪ] ADV legivelmente

legion ['li:dʒən] N legião f

legionnaire [li:dʒə'nɛəʳ] N legionário; **~'s disease** doença rara parecida à pneumonia

legislate ['lɛdʒɪsleɪt] VI legislar

legislation [lɛdʒɪs'leɪʃən] N legislação f; **a piece of ~** uma lei

legislative ['lɛdʒɪslətɪv] ADJ legislativo

legislator ['lɛdʒɪsleɪtəʳ] N legislador(a) m/f

legislature ['lɛdʒɪslətʃəʳ] N legislatura

legitimacy [lɪ'dʒɪtɪməsɪ] N legitimidade f

legitimate [lɪ'dʒɪtɪmət] ADJ legítimo

legitimize [lɪ'dʒɪtɪmaɪz] VT legitimar

legless ['lɛglɪs] ADJ (BRIT inf) bêbum

leg-room N espaço para as pernas

Leics (BRIT) ABBR = **Leicestershire**

leisure ['lɛʒəʳ] N lazer m; **at ~** desocupado, livre

leisure centre N centro de lazer

leisurely ['lɛʒəlɪ] ADJ calmo, vagaroso

leisure suit (BRIT) N jogging m

lemon ['lɛmən] N limão(-galego) m

lemonade [lɛmə'neɪd] N limonada

lemon cheese N coalho or pasta de limão

lemon curd N coalho or pasta de limão

lemon juice N suco (BR) or sumo (PT) de limão

lemon squeezer [-'skwi:zəʳ] N espremedor m de limão

lemon tea N chá m de limão

lend [lɛnd] (pt, pp lent) VT: **to ~ sth to sb** emprestar algo a alguém; **to ~ a hand** dar uma ajuda

lender ['lɛndəʳ] N emprestador(a) m/f

lending library ['lɛndɪŋ] N biblioteca circulante

length [lɛŋθ] N comprimento, extensão f; (of swimming pool) extensão f; (piece: of wood, string etc) comprimento; (section: of road, pipe etc) trecho; (amount of time) duração f; **what ~ is it?** de que comprimento é?; **it is 2 metres in ~** tem dois metros de comprimento; **to fall full ~** cair estirado; **at ~** (at last) finalmente, afinal; (lengthily) por extenso; **to go to any ~(s) to do sth** fazer qualquer coisa para fazer algo

lengthen ['lɛŋθən] VT encompridar, alongar ▶ VI encompridar-se

lengthways ['lɛŋθweɪz] ADV longitudinalmente, ao comprido

lengthy ['lɛŋθɪ] ADJ comprido, longo; (meeting) prolongado

leniency ['li:nɪənsɪ] N indulgência

lenient ['li:nɪənt] ADJ indulgente

leniently ['li:nɪəntlɪ] ADV com indulgência

lens [lɛnz] N (of spectacles) lente f; (of camera) objetiva

Lent [lɛnt] N Quaresma

lent [lɛnt] PT, PP of **lend**

lentil ['lɛntl] N lentilha

Leo ['li:əu] N Leão m

leopard ['lɛpəd] N leopardo

leotard ['li:əta:d] N collant m

leper ['lɛpəʳ] N leproso(-a)

leper colony N leprosário

leprosy ['lɛprəsɪ] N lepra

lesbian ['lɛzbɪən] ADJ lésbico ▶ N lésbica

lesion ['li:ʒən] N (Med) lesão f

Lesotho [lɪ'su:tu:] N Lesoto

less [lɛs] ADJ, PRON, ADV menos ▶ PREP: **~ tax/10% discount** menos imposto/10% de desconto; **~ than that/you** menos que isso/você; **~ than half** menos da metade; **~ than ever** menos do que nunca; **~ than 1/a kilo/3 metres** menos de um/um quilo/3 metros; **~ and ~** cada vez menos; **the ~ he works ...** quanto menos trabalha ...; **income ~ expenses** renda menos despesas

lessee [lɛ'si:] N arrendatário(-a), locatário(-a)

lessen ['lɛsn] VI diminuir, minguar ▶ VT diminuir, reduzir

lesser ['lɛsəʳ] ADJ menor; **to a ~ extent** or **degree** nem tanto

lesson ['lɛsn] N aula; (example, warning) lição f; **a maths ~** uma aula or uma lição de matemática; **to give ~s in** dar aulas de; **to teach sb a ~** (fig) dar uma lição em alguém

lessor ['lɛsəʳ] N arrendador(a) m/f, locador(a) m/f

lest [lɛst] CONJ: **~ it happen** para que não aconteça; **I was afraid ~ he forget** temi que ele esquecesse

let [lɛt] (pt, pp **let**) VT (allow) deixar; (BRIT: lease) alugar; **to ~ sb do sth** deixar alguém fazer algo; **to ~ sb know sth** avisar alguém de algo; **he ~ me go** ele me deixou ir; **~ the water boil and …** deixe ferver a água e …; **~'s go!** vamos!; **~ him come!** deixa ele vir!; **"to ~"** "aluga-se"

▶ **let down** VT (lower) abaixar; (dress) encompridar; (BRIT: tyre) esvaziar; (hair) soltar; (disappoint) desapontar

▶ **let go** VT, VI soltar

▶ **let in** VT deixar entrar; (visitor etc) fazer entrar; **what have you ~ yourself in for?** onde você foi se meter?

▶ **let off** VT (allow to leave) deixar ir; (culprit) perdoar; (subj: bus driver) deixar (saltar); (firework etc) soltar; **to ~ off steam** (fig) desabafar

▶ **let on** VI revelar ▶ VT (inf): **to ~ on that …** dizer por aí que …, contar que …

▶ **let out** VT deixar sair; (dress) alargar; (scream) soltar; (rent out) alugar

▶ **let up** VI cessar, afrouxar

let-down N (disappointment) decepção f

lethal ['li:θl] ADJ letal; (wound) mortal

lethargic [lɛ'θɑːdʒɪk] ADJ letárgico

lethargy ['lɛθədʒɪ] N letargia

letter ['lɛtəʳ] N (of alphabet) letra; (correspondence) carta; **small/capital ~** minúscula/maiúscula

letter bomb N carta-bomba

letterbox ['lɛtəbɒks] (BRIT) N caixa do correio

letterhead ['lɛtəhɛd] N cabeçalho

lettering ['lɛtərɪŋ] N letras fpl

letter opener N corta-papel m

letterpress ['lɛtəprɛs] N (method) impressão f tipográfica

letter quality N qualidade f carta

letters patent N carta patente

lettuce ['lɛtɪs] N alface f

let-up N diminuição f, afrouxamento

leukaemia, (US) **leukemia** [lu:'ki:mɪə] N leucemia

level ['lɛvl] ADJ (flat) plano; (flattened) nivelado; (uniform) uniforme ▶ ADV no mesmo nível ▶ N nível m; (height) altura; (flat place) plano; (also: **spirit level**) nível de bolha ▶ VT alinhar; (gun) apontar; (accusation): **to ~ (against)** dirigir or lançar (contra) ▶ VI (inf): **to ~ with sb** ser franco com alguém; **"A" ~s** (npl: BRIT) ≈ vestibular m; **"O" ~s** (npl: BRIT) provas prestadas no final do

ensino fundamental; **a ~ spoonful** (Culin) uma colherada rasa; **to be ~ with** estar no mesmo nível que; **to draw ~ with** (team) empatar com; (runner, car) alcançar; **on the ~** em nível; (fig: honest) sincero

▶ **level off** VI (prices etc) estabilizar-se ▶ VT (ground) nivelar, aplanar

▶ **level out** VI, VT = **level off**

level crossing (BRIT) N passagem f de nível

level-headed [-'hɛdɪd] ADJ sensato

levelling, (US) **leveling** ['lɛvlɪŋ] ADJ (process) de nivelamento; (effect) nivelador(a)

lever ['li:vəʳ] N alavanca; (fig) estratagema m ▶ VT: **to ~ up** levantar com alavanca

leverage ['li:vərɪdʒ] N força de uma alavanca; (fig: influence) influência

levity ['lɛvɪtɪ] N leviandade f, frivolidade f

levy ['lɛvɪ] N imposto, tributo ▶ VT arrecadar, cobrar

lewd [lu:d] ADJ obsceno, lascivo

LI (US) ABBR = **Long Island**

liability [laɪə'bɪlətɪ] N responsabilidade f; (handicap) desvantagem f; **liabilities** NPL (Comm) exigibilidades fpl, obrigações fpl; (on balance sheet) passivo

liable ['laɪəbl] ADJ (subject): **~ to** sujeito a; (responsible): **~ for** responsável por; (likely): **~ to do** capaz de fazer; **to be ~ to a fine** ser passível de or sujeito a uma multa

liaise [li:'eɪz] VI: **to ~ (with)** cooperar (com)

liaison [li:'eɪzɔn] N (coordination) ligação f; (affair) relação f amorosa

liar ['laɪəʳ] N mentiroso(-a)

libel ['laɪbl] N difamação f ▶ VT caluniar, difamar

libellous, (US) **libelous** ['laɪbləs] ADJ difamatório

liberal ['lɪbərl] ADJ liberal; (generous) generoso ▶ N: **L~** (Pol) Liberal m/f

liberality [lɪbə'rælɪtɪ] N (generosity) generosidade f

liberalize ['lɪbərəlaɪz] VT liberalizar

liberal-minded ADJ liberal

liberate ['lɪbəreɪt] VT libertar

liberation [lɪbə'reɪʃən] N liberação f, libertação f

Liberia [laɪ'bɪərɪə] N Libéria

Liberian [laɪ'bɪərɪən] ADJ, N liberiano(-a)

liberty ['lɪbətɪ] N liberdade f; (criminal): **to be at ~** estar livre; **to be at ~ to do** ser livre de fazer; **to take the ~ of doing sth** tomar a liberdade de fazer algo

libido [lɪ'bi:dəu] N libido f

Libra ['li:brə] N Libra, Balança

librarian [laɪ'brɛərɪən] N bibliotecário(-a)

library ['laɪbrərɪ] N biblioteca

library book N livro de biblioteca

libretto [lɪ'brɛtəu] N libreto

Libya ['lɪbɪə] N Líbia

Libyan ['lɪbɪən] ADJ, N líbio(-a)

lice [laɪs] NPL of **louse**

licence, (US) **license** ['laɪsns] N (gen, Comm) licença; (Aut) carta de motorista (BR), carta de condução (PT); (*excessive freedom*) libertinagem f; **produced under ~** fabricado sob licença

licence number (BRIT) N (*Aut*) número da placa

license ['laɪsns] N (US) = **licence** ▶ VT autorizar, dar licença a; (*car*) licenciar

licensed ['laɪsnst] ADJ (*car*) autorizado oficialmente; (*for alcohol*) autorizado para vender bebidas alcoólicas

licensee [laɪsən'siː] N (*in a pub*) dono(-a)

license plate (US) N (*Aut*) placa (de identificação) (*do carro*)

licentious [laɪ'sɛnʃəs] ADJ licencioso

lichen ['laɪkən] N líquen m

lick [lɪk] VT lamber; (*inf: defeat*) arrasar, surrar ▶ N lambida; **to ~ one's lips** (*also fig*) lamber os beiços; **a ~ of paint** uma mão de pintura

licorice ['lɪkərɪs] (US) N = **liquorice**

lid [lɪd] N (*of box, case, pan*) tampa; (*eyelid*) pálpebra; **to take the ~ off sth** (*fig*) desvendar algo

lido ['laɪdəu] N *piscina pública ao ar livre*

lie [laɪ] VI (*pt* **lay**, *pp* **lain**) (*act*) deitar-se; (*state*) estar deitado; (*object: be situated*) estar, encontrar-se; (*fig: problem, cause*) residir; (*in race, league*) ocupar; (*pt, pp* **lied**) (: *tell lies*) mentir ▶ N mentira; **to ~ low** (*fig*) esconder-se; **to tell ~s** dizer mentiras, mentir
    ▶ **lie about** VI (*things*) estar espalhado; (*people*) vadiar
    ▶ **lie around** VI = **lie about**
    ▶ **lie back** VI recostar-se
    ▶ **lie down** VI deitar-se

Liechtenstein ['lɪktənstaɪn] N Liechtenstein m

lie detector N detector m de mentiras

lie-down (BRIT) N: **to have a ~** descansar

lie-in (BRIT) N: **to have a ~** dormir até tarde

lieu [luː]: **in ~ of** PREP em vez de

Lieut. ABBR (= *lieutenant*) Ten.

lieutenant [lɛf'tɛnənt, (US) luː'tɛnənt] N (*Mil*) tenente m

lieutenant-colonel N tenente-coronel m

life [laɪf] N (*pl* **lives**) vida ▶ CPD (*imprisonment*) perpétuo; (*style*) de vida; **true to ~** fiel à realidade; **to come to ~** (*fig*) animar-se; **to paint from ~** pintar copiando a natureza; **to be sent to prison for ~** ser condenado a prisão perpétua; **country/city ~** vida campestre/urbana

life annuity N renda vitalícia

life assurance (BRIT) N = **life insurance**

lifebelt ['laɪfbɛlt] (BRIT) N cinto salva-vidas

lifeblood ['laɪfblʌd] N (*fig*) força vital

lifeboat ['laɪfbəut] N barco salva-vidas

lifebuoy ['laɪfbɔɪ] N boia salva-vidas

life expectancy N expectativa de vida

lifeguard ['laɪfgɑːd] N salva-vidas m/f

life imprisonment N prisão f perpétua

life insurance N seguro de vida

life jacket N colete m salva-vidas

lifeless ['laɪflɪs] ADJ sem vida; (*fig*) sem graça

lifelike ['laɪflaɪk] ADJ natural; (*realistic*) realista

lifeline ['laɪflaɪn] N corda salva-vidas

lifelong ['laɪflɔŋ] ADJ que dura todo a vida

life preserver [-prɪ'zəːvəʳ] (US) N = **lifebelt**; **life jacket**

life-raft N balsa salva-vidas

life-saver [-'seɪvəʳ] N (guarda m) salva-vidas m/f

life sentence N pena de prisão perpétua

life-size [-saɪz], **life-sized** [-saɪzd] ADJ de tamanho natural

life-span N vida, duração f

life style N estilo de vida

life support system N (*Med*) sistema m de respiração artificial

lifetime ['laɪftaɪm] N vida; **in his ~** durante a sua vida; **once in a ~** uma vez na vida; **the chance of a ~** uma oportunidade única

lift [lɪft] VT levantar; (*steal*) roubar ▶ VI (*fog*) dispersar-se, dissipar-se ▶ N (BRIT: *elevator*) elevador m; **to give sb a ~** (BRIT) dar uma carona para alguém (BR), dar uma boleia a alguém (PT)
    ▶ **lift off** VI (*rocket, helicopter*) decolar
    ▶ **lift out** VT tirar; (*troops etc*) evacuar de avião or helicóptero
    ▶ **lift up** VT levantar

lift-off ['lɪftɔf] N decolagem f

ligament ['lɪgəmənt] N ligamento

light [laɪt] (*pt, pp* **lit**) N luz f; (*lamp*) luz, lâmpada; (*daylight*) (luz do) dia m; (*Aut: headlight*) farol m; (: *rear light*) luz traseira; (*for cigarette etc*): **have you got a ~?** tem fogo? ▶ VT (*candle, cigarette, fire*) acender; (*room*) iluminar ▶ ADJ (*colour, room*) claro; (*not heavy: also fig*) leve; (*rain, traffic*) fraco; (*movement, action*) delicado ▶ ADV (*travel*) com pouca bagagem; **lights** NPL (*Aut*) sinal m de trânsito; **to turn the ~ on/off** acender/ apagar a luz; **to cast** or **shed** or **throw ~ on** esclarecer; **to come to ~** vir à tona; **in the ~ of** à luz de; **to make ~ of sth** (*fig*) não levar algo a sério, fazer pouco caso de algo
    ▶ **light up** VI (*smoke*) acender um cigarro; (*face*) iluminar-se ▶ VT (*illuminate*) iluminar; (*cigarette etc*) acender

light bulb N lâmpada

lighten ['laɪtən] VI (*grow light*) clarear ▶ VT (*give light to*) iluminar; (*make lighter*) clarear; (*make less heavy*) tornar mais leve

lighter ['laɪtəʳ] N (*also*: **cigarette lighter**) isqueiro, acendedor m; (*boat*) chata

light-fingered [-'fɪŋgəd] ADJ gatuno; **to be ~** ter mão leve

light-headed [-'hɛdɪd] ADJ (*dizzy*) aturdido, tonto; (*excited*) exaltado; (*by nature*) estouvado

light-hearted ADJ alegre, despreocupado

lighthouse ['laɪthaus] N farol m

lighting ['laɪtɪŋ] N (*act, system*) iluminação f

lighting-up time (BRIT) N *hora oficial hora oficialdo anoitecer*

lightly ['laɪtlɪ] ADV (touch) ligeiramente; (thoughtlessly) despreocupadamente; (slightly) levemente; (not seriously) levianamente; **to get off ~** conseguir se safar, livrar a cara (inf)

light meter N (Phot) fotômetro

lightness ['laɪtnɪs] N claridade f; (in weight) leveza

lightning ['laɪtnɪŋ] N relâmpago, raio

lightning conductor N para-raios m inv

lightning rod (US) N = **lightning conductor**

lightning strike (BRIT) N greve f relâmpago

light pen N caneta leitora

lightship ['laɪtʃɪp] N navio-farol m

lightweight ['laɪtweɪt] ADJ (suit) leve; (Boxing) peso-leve

light year N ano-luz m

like [laɪk] VT gostar de ▶ PREP como; (such as) tal qual ▶ ADJ parecido, semelhante ▶ N: **the ~** coisas fpl parecidas; **his ~s and dislikes** seus gostos e aversões; **I would ~**, **I'd ~** (eu) gostaria de; **would you ~ a coffee?** você quer um café?; **to be** or **look ~ sb/sth** parecer-se com alguém/algo, parecer alguém/algo; **what does it look/taste/sound ~?** como é que é?/tem gosto de quê?/como é que soa?; **what's the weather ~?** como está o tempo?; **that's just ~ him** é típico dele; **something ~ that** uma coisa dessas; **do it ~ this** faça isso assim; **I feel ~ a drink** estou com vontade de tomar um drinque; **it is nothing ~ ...** não se parece nada com ...

likeable ['laɪkəbl] ADJ simpático, agradável

likelihood ['laɪklɪhud] N probabilidade f

likely ['laɪklɪ] ADJ provável; (excuse) plausível; **he's ~ to leave** é provável que ele se vá; **not ~!** (inf) nem morto!

like-minded ADJ da mesma opinião

liken ['laɪkən] VT: **to ~ sth to sth** comparar algo com algo

likeness ['laɪknɪs] N semelhança; **that's a good ~** tem uma grande semelhança

likewise ['laɪkwaɪz] ADV igualmente; **to do ~** fazer o mesmo

liking ['laɪkɪŋ] N afeição f, simpatia; **to take a ~ to sb** simpatizar com alguém; **to be to sb's ~** ser ao gosto de alguém

lilac ['laɪlək] N lilás m ▶ ADJ (colour) de cor lilás

lilt [lɪlt] N cadência

lilting ['lɪltɪŋ] N cadenciado

lily ['lɪlɪ] N lírio, açucena

lily of the valley N lírio-do-vale m

Lima ['liːmə] N Lima

limb [lɪm] N membro; **to be out on a ~** (fig) estar isolado

limber up ['lɪmbər-] VI (Sport) fazer aquecimento

limbo ['lɪmbəu] N: **to be in ~** (fig) viver na expectativa

lime [laɪm] N (tree) limeira; (fruit) limão m; (also: **lime juice**) suco (BR) or sumo (PT) de limão; (Geo) cal f

limelight ['laɪmlaɪt] N: **to be in the ~** (fig) ser o centro das atenções

limerick ['lɪmərɪk] N quintilha humorística

limestone ['laɪmstəun] N pedra calcária

limit ['lɪmɪt] N limite m ▶ VT limitar; **weight/speed ~** limite de peso/de velocidade

limitation [lɪmɪ'teɪʃən] N limitação f

limited ['lɪmɪtɪd] ADJ limitado; **to be ~ to** limitar-se a; **~ edition** edição f limitada

limited company, (BRIT) **limited liability company** N ≈ sociedade f anônima

limitless ['lɪmɪtlɪs] ADJ ilimitado

limousine ['lɪməziːn] N limusine f

limp [lɪmp] N: **to have a ~** mancar, ser coxo ▶ VI mancar ▶ ADJ frouxo

limpet ['lɪmpɪt] N lapa

limpid ['lɪmpɪd] ADJ límpido, cristalino

linchpin ['lɪntʃpɪn] N cavilha; (fig) pivô m

Lincs [lɪŋks] (BRIT) ABBR = **Lincolnshire**

line [laɪn] N linha; (straight line) reta; (rope) corda; (for fishing) linha; (US: queue) fila (BR), bicha (PT); (wire) fio; (row) fila, fileira; (of writing) linha; (on face) ruga; (speciality) ramo (de negócio); (Comm: type of goods) linha ▶ VT (road, room) encarreirar; (container, clothing): **to ~ sth (with)** forrar algo (de); **to ~ the streets** ladear as ruas; **in ~** em fila; **to cut in ~** (US) furar a fila (BR), pôr-se à frente (PT); **in his ~ of business** no ramo dele; **on the right ~s** no caminho certo; **a new ~ in cosmetics** uma nova linha de cosméticos; **hold the ~ please** (BRIT Tel) não desligue; **to be in ~ for sth** estar na bica para algo; **in ~ with** de acordo com; **to bring sth into ~ with sth** alinhar algo com algo; **to draw the ~ at doing sth** (fig) recusar-se a fazer algo; **to take the ~ that ...** ser de opinião que ...

▶ **line up** VI enfileirar-se ▶ VT enfileirar; (set up, have ready) preparar, arranjar; **to have sth/sb ~d up** ter algo programado/alguém em vista

linear ['lɪnɪər] ADJ linear

lined [laɪnd] ADJ (face) enrugado; (paper) pautado; (clothes) forrado

line feed N (Comput) entrelinha

linen ['lɪnɪn] N artigos de cama e mesa; (cloth) linho

line printer N impressora de linha

liner ['laɪnər] N navio de linha regular; (also: **bin liner**) saco para lata de lixo

linesman ['laɪnzmən] (irreg: like **man**) N (Sport) juiz m de linha

line-up N formação f em linha, alinhamento; (Sport) escalação f

linger ['lɪŋgər] VI demorar-se, retardar-se; (smell, tradition) persistir

lingerie ['lænʒəriː] N lingerie f, roupa de baixo (de mulher)

lingering ['lɪŋgərɪŋ] ADJ persistente; (death) lento, vagaroso

lingo ['lɪŋgəu] (pl **lingoes**: inf) N língua

linguist ['lɪŋgwɪst] N linguista m/f

linguistic [lɪŋ'gwɪstɪk] ADJ linguístico
linguistics [lɪŋ'gwɪstɪks] N linguística
lining ['laɪnɪŋ] N forro; (Anat) parede f; (Tech) revestimento; (: of brakes) lona
link [lɪŋk] N (of a chain) elo; (connection) conexão f; (bond) vínculo, laço ▶ VT vincular, unir; (associate): **to ~ with** or **to** unir a; **links** NPL (Golf) campo de golfe; **rail ~** ligação ferroviária
▶ **link up** VT acoplar ▶ VI unir-se
link-up N ligação f; (in space) acoplamento; (of roads) junção f, confluência; (Radio, TV) transmissão f em rede
lino ['laɪnəu] N = **linoleum**
linoleum [lɪ'nəulɪəm] N linóleo
linseed oil ['lɪnsi:d-] N óleo de linhaça
lint [lɪnt] N fibra de algodão; (thread) fio
lintel ['lɪntl] N verga
lion ['laɪən] N leão m
lion cub N filhote m de leão
lioness ['laɪənɪs] N leoa
lip [lɪp] N lábio; (of jug) bico; (of cup etc) borda; (insolence) insolência
liposuction ['lɪpəusʌkʃən] N lipoaspiração f
lipread ['lɪpri:d] (irreg: like **read**) VI ler os lábios
lip salve N pomada para os lábios
lip service N: **to pay ~ to sth** devotar-se a or elogiar algo falsamente
lipstick ['lɪpstɪk] N batom m
liquefy ['lɪkwɪfaɪ] VT liquefazer ▶ VI liquefazer-se
liqueur [lɪ'kjuəʳ] N licor m
liquid ['lɪkwɪd] ADJ líquido ▶ N líquido
liquid assets NPL ativo disponível, disponibilidades fpl
liquidate ['lɪkwɪdeɪt] VT liquidar
liquidation [lɪkwɪ'deɪʃən] N: **to go into ~** entrar em liquidação
liquidator ['lɪkwɪdeɪtəʳ] N liquidador(a) m/f
liquid crystal display N display m digital em cristal líquido
liquidity [lɪ'kwɪdətɪ] N (Comm) liquidez f
liquidize ['lɪkwɪdaɪz] (BRIT) VT (Culin) liquidificar, passar no liquidificador
liquidizer ['lɪkwɪdaɪzəʳ] (BRIT) N (Culin) liquidificador m
liquor ['lɪkəʳ] N licor m, bebida alcoólica
liquorice ['lɪkərɪs] (BRIT) N alcaçuz m
liquor store (US) N loja que vende bebidas alcoólicas
Lisbon ['lɪzbən] N Lisboa
lisp [lɪsp] N ceceio ▶ VI cecear, falar com a língua presa
lissom ['lɪsəm] ADJ gracioso, ágil
list [lɪst] N lista; (of ship) inclinação f ▶ VT (write down) fazer uma lista or relação de; (enumerate) enumerar; (Comput) listar ▶ VI (ship) inclinar-se, adernar; **shopping ~** lista de compras
listed building ['lɪstɪd-] (BRIT) N prédio tombado
listed company ['lɪstɪd-] N ≈ sociedade f de capital aberto, sociedade cotada na Bolsa

listen ['lɪsn] VI escutar, ouvir; (pay attention) prestar atenção; **to ~ to** escutar
listener ['lɪsnəʳ] N ouvinte m/f
listing ['lɪstɪŋ] N (Comput) listagem f
listless ['lɪstlɪs] ADJ apático, indiferente
listlessly ['lɪstlɪslɪ] ADV apaticamente
list price N preço de tabela
lit [lɪt] PT, PP of **light**
litany ['lɪtənɪ] N ladainha, litania
liter ['li:təʳ] (US) N = **litre**
literacy ['lɪtərəsɪ] N capacidade f de ler e escrever, alfabetização f
literacy campaign N campanha de alfabetização
literal ['lɪtərl] ADJ literal
literally ['lɪtərəlɪ] ADV literalmente
literary ['lɪtərərɪ] ADJ literário
literate ['lɪtərət] ADJ alfabetizado, instruído; (educated) culto, letrado
literature ['lɪtərɪtʃəʳ] N literatura; (brochures etc) folhetos mpl
lithe [laɪð] ADJ ágil
lithography [lɪ'θɔgrəfɪ] N litografia
Lithuania [lɪθju'eɪnɪə] N Lituânia
litigate ['lɪtɪgeɪt] VT, VI litigar
litigation [lɪtɪ'geɪʃən] N litígio
litmus paper ['lɪtməs-] N papel m de tornassol
litre, (US) **liter** ['li:təʳ] N litro
litter ['lɪtəʳ] N (rubbish) lixo; (paper) papéis mpl; (young animals) ninhada; (stretcher) maca, padiola ▶ VT (subj: person) jogar lixo em; (: papers etc) estar espalhado por; **~ed with** (scattered) semeado de; (covered) coberto de
litter bin (BRIT) N lata de lixo
litterbug ['lɪtəbʌg] N sujismundo
litter lout (BRIT) N = **litterbug**
little ['lɪtl] ADJ (small) pequeno; (not much) pouco ▶ ADV pouco; **a ~** um pouco (de); **~ milk** pouco leite; **a ~ milk** um pouco de leite; **~ house** casinha; **for a ~ while** por um instante; **with ~ difficulty** com pouca dificuldade; **as ~ as possible** o menos possível; **~ by ~** pouco a pouco; **to make ~ of** fazer pouco de
little finger N dedo mindinho
liturgy ['lɪtədʒɪ] N liturgia
live [vi, vt lɪv, adj laɪv] VI viver; (reside) morar ▶ VT (a life) levar; (experience) viver ▶ ADJ (animal) vivo; (wire) eletrizado; (broadcast) ao vivo; (shell) carregado; **to ~ in London** morar em Londres; **to ~ with sb** morar com alguém; **~ ammunition** munição de guerra
▶ **live down** VT redimir
▶ **live in** VI (maid) dormir no emprego; (student, nurse) ser interno(-a)
▶ **live off** VT FUS (land, fish etc) viver de; (pej: parents etc) viver às custas de
▶ **live on** VT FUS (food) viver de, alimentar-se de ▶ VI continuar vivo; **to ~ on £50 a week** viver com £50 por semana
▶ **live out** VI (BRIT: student) ser externo ▶ VT: **to ~ out one's days** or **life** viver o resto de seus dias

▶ **live together** vɪ viver juntos

▶ **live up** (inf) vᴛ: **to ~ it up** cair na farra

▶ **live up to** vᴛ Fᴜs (fulfil) cumprir; (justify) justificar

livelihood ['laɪvlɪhud] ɴ meio de vida, subsistência

liveliness ['laɪvlɪnɛs] ɴ vivacidade f

lively ['laɪvlɪ] ᴀᴅᴊ vivo; (talk) animado; (pace) rápido; (party, tune) alegre

liven up ['laɪvn-] vᴛ (room) dar nova vida a; (discussion, evening) animar ▶ vɪ animar-se

liver ['lɪvəʳ] ɴ fígado

liverish ['lɪvərɪʃ] ᴀᴅᴊ (fig) rabugento, mal-humorado

Liverpudlian [lɪvə'pʌdlɪən] ᴀᴅᴊ de Liverpool ▶ ɴ natural m/f de Liverpool

livery ['lɪvərɪ] ɴ libré f

lives [laɪvz] ɴᴘʟ of **life**

livestock ['laɪvstɔk] ɴ gado

livid ['lɪvɪd] ᴀᴅᴊ lívido; (inf: furious) furioso

living ['lɪvɪŋ] ᴀᴅᴊ (alive) vivo ▶ ɴ: **to earn** or **make a ~** ganhar a vida; **cost of ~** custo de vida; **within ~ memory** na memória de pessoas ainda vivas

living conditions ɴᴘʟ condições fpl de vida

living expenses ɴᴘʟ despesas fpl para sobrevivência quotidiana

living room ɴ sala de estar

living standards ɴᴘʟ padrão m or nível m de vida

living wage ɴ salário de subsistência

living will ɴ testamento em vida

lizard ['lɪzəd] ɴ lagarto

llama ['lɑ:mə] ɴ lhama

LLB ɴ ᴀʙʙʀ (= Bachelor of Laws) título universitário

LLD ɴ ᴀʙʙʀ (= Doctor of Laws) título universitário

LMT (ᴜs) ᴀʙʙʀ (= Local Mean Time) hora local

load [ləud] ɴ carga; (weight) peso ▶ vᴛ (gen, Comput) carregar; (fig) cumular, encher; **a ~ of rubbish** um monte de besteira; **a ~ of**, **~s of** (fig) um monte de, uma porção de

loaded ['ləudɪd] ᴀᴅᴊ (dice) viciado; (question, word) intencionado; (inf: rich) cheio da nota; (: drunk) de porre; (vehicle): **to be ~ with** estar carregado de

loading bay ['ləudɪŋ-] ɴ vão m de carregamento

loaf [ləuf] ɴ (pl **loaves**) pão-de-forma m ▶ vɪ (also: **loaf about**, **loaf around**) vadiar, vagabundar

loam [ləum] ɴ marga

loan [ləun] ɴ empréstimo ▶ vᴛ emprestar; **on ~** emprestado; **to raise a ~** levantar um empréstimo

loan account ɴ conta de empréstimo

loan capital ɴ capital-obrigações m

loath [ləuθ] ᴀᴅᴊ: **to be ~ to do sth** estar pouco inclinado a fazer also, relutar em fazer algo

loathe [ləuð] vᴛ detestar, odiar

loathing ['ləuðɪŋ] ɴ ódio; **it fills me with ~** me dá (um) ódio

loathsome ['ləuðsəm] ᴀᴅᴊ repugnante, asqueroso

loaves [ləuvz] ɴᴘʟ of **loaf**

lob [lɔb] ɴ (Tennis) lobe m ▶ vᴛ: **to ~ the ball** dar um lobe

lobby ['lɔbɪ] ɴ vestíbulo, saguão m; (Pol: pressure group) grupo de pressão, lobby m ▶ vᴛ pressionar

lobbyist ['lɔbɪɪst] ɴ membro de um grupo de pressão

lobe [ləub] ɴ lóbulo

lobster ['lɔbstəʳ] ɴ lagostim m; (large) lagosta

lobster pot ɴ armadilha para pegar lagosta

local ['ləukl] ᴀᴅᴊ local ▶ ɴ (pub) bar m (local); **the locals** ɴᴘʟ (local inhabitants) os moradores locais

local anaesthetic, (ᴜs) **local anesthetic** ɴ anestesia local

local authority ɴ município

local call ɴ (Tel) ligação f local

local government ɴ administração f municipal

locality [ləu'kælɪtɪ] ɴ localidade f

localize ['ləukəlaɪz] vᴛ localizar

locally ['ləukəlɪ] ᴀᴅᴠ nos arredores, na vizinhança

locate [ləu'keɪt] vᴛ (find) localizar, situar; (situate): **to be ~d in** estar localizado em

location [ləu'keɪʃən] ɴ local m, posição f; **on ~** (Cinema) em externas

loch [lɔx] ɴ lago

lock [lɔk] ɴ (of door, box) fechadura; (of canal) eclusa; (of hair) anel m, mecha ▶ vᴛ (with key) trancar; (immobilize) travar ▶ vɪ (door etc) fechar-se à chave; (wheels) travar-se; **~, stock and barrel** (fig) com tudo; **on full ~** (ʙʀɪᴛ Aut) com o volante virado ao máximo

▶ **lock away** vᴛ (valuables) guardar a sete chaves; (person) encarcerar

▶ **lock in** vᴛ trancar dentro

▶ **lock out** vᴛ trancar do lado de fora; (on purpose) deixar na rua; (: workers) recusar trabalho a

▶ **lock up** vᴛ (criminal, mental patient) prender; (house) trancar ▶ vɪ fechar tudo

locker ['lɔkəʳ] ɴ compartimento com chave

locker-room ['lɔkəʳru:m] (ᴜs) ɴ (Sport) vestiário

locket ['lɔkɪt] ɴ medalhão m

lockjaw ['lɔkdʒɔ:] ɴ trismo

lockout ['lɔkaut] ɴ greve f de patrões, lockout m

locksmith ['lɔksmɪθ] ɴ serralheiro(-a)

lockup ['lɔkʌp] ɴ (prison) prisão f; (cell) cela; (also: **lockup garage**) compartimento seguro

locomotive [ləukə'məutɪv] ɴ locomotiva

locum ['ləukəm] ɴ (Med) (médico(-a)) interino(-a)

locust ['ləukəst] ɴ gafanhoto

lodge [lɔdʒ] ɴ casa do guarda, guarita; (hunting lodge) pavilhão m de caça; (porter's) portaria; (Freemasonry) loja ▶ vɪ (person): **to ~ (with)** alojar-se (na casa de) ▶ vᴛ (complaint)

apresentar; **to ~ (itself) in/between**
cravar-se em/entre
lodger ['lɔdʒəʳ] N inquilino(-a), hóspede m/f
lodging ['lɔdʒɪŋ] N alojamento; **lodgings** NPL
quarto (mobiliado); *see also* **board**
lodging house (BRIT) N casa de hóspedes
loft [lɔft] N sótão m
lofty ['lɔftɪ] ADJ alto, elevado; (*haughty*) altivo,
arrogante; (*sentiments, aims*) nobre
log [lɔg] N (*of wood*) tora; (*book*) = **logbook** ▶ N
ABBR (= *logarithm*) log m ▶ VT registrar
 ▶ **log in** VI (*Comput*) fazer o login
 ▶ **log off** VI (*Comput*) fazer logoff
 ▶ **log on** VI (*Comput*) fazer o login
 ▶ **log out** VI (*Comput*) fazer logoff
logarithm ['lɔgərɪðəm] N logaritmo
logbook ['lɔgbuk] N (*Naut*) diário de bordo;
(*Aviat*) diário de voo; (*of car*) documentação f
(do carro)
log cabin N cabana de madeira
log fire N fogueira
loggerheads ['lɔgəhɛdz] NPL: **at ~ (with)** às
turras (com)
logic ['lɔdʒɪk] N lógica
logical ['lɔdʒɪkl] ADJ lógico
logically ['lɔdʒɪkəlɪ] ADV logicamente
login ['lɔgɪn] N (*Comput*) login m
logistics [lɔ'dʒɪstɪks] N logística
logo ['ləugəu] N logotipo
loin [lɔɪn] N (*Culin*) (carne f de) lombo; **loins**
NPL lombos mpl
loin cloth N tanga
loiter ['lɔɪtəʳ] VI perder tempo; (*pej*) vadiar,
vagabundar
LOL (*inf*) ABBR (= *laugh out loud*) rs, LOL
loll [lɔl] VI (*also*: **loll about**) refestelar-se,
reclinar-se
lollipop ['lɔlɪpɔp] N pirulito (BR), chupa-
chupa m (PT); (*iced*) picolé m
lollipop lady (BRIT) N *mulher que ajuda as crianças
a atravessarem a rua*
lollipop man (BRIT) N *homem que ajuda as crianças
a atravessarem a rua*

> **Lollipop men/ladies** são as pessoas que
> ajudam as crianças a atravessar a rua nas
> proximidades das escolas na hora da
> entrada e da saída. São facilmente
> localizados graças a suas longas capas
> brancas e à placa redonda com a qual
> pedem aos motoristas que parem. São
> chamados assim por causa da forma
> circular da placa, que lembra um pirulito
> (*lollipop*).

lollop ['lɔləp] (BRIT) VI andar com pachorra
lolly ['lɔlɪ] (*inf*) N (*ice*) picolé m; (*lollipop*)
pirulito; (*money*) dindim m
London ['lʌndən] N Londres
Londoner ['lʌndənəʳ] N londrino(-a)
lone [ləun] ADJ (*person*) solitário; (*thing*) único
loneliness ['ləunlɪnɪs] N solidão f,
isolamento
lonely ['ləunlɪ] ADJ (*person*) só; (*place, childhood*)
solitário, isolado; **to feel ~** sentir-se só

loner ['ləunəʳ] N solitário(-a)
lonesome ['ləunsəm] ADJ (*person*) só; (*place,
childhood*) solitário
long [lɔŋ] ADJ longo; (*road, hair, table*) comprido
 ▶ ADV muito tempo ▶ N: **the ~ and the short
of it is that ...** (*fig*) em poucas palavras ...
 ▶ VI: **to ~ for sth** ansiar *or* suspirar por algo;
he had ~ understood that ... fazia muito
tempo que ele entendia ...; **how ~ is the
street?** qual é a extensão da rua?; **how ~ is
the lesson?** quanto dura a lição?; **6 metres
~** de 6 metros de comprimento; **6 months ~**
de 6 meses de duração; **all night ~** a noite
inteira; **he no ~er comes** ele não vem
mais; **~ before/after** muito antes/depois;
before ~ (+*future*) dentro de pouco; (+*past*)
pouco tempo depois; **~ ago** há muito tempo
atrás; **don't be ~!** não demore!; **I shan't
be ~** não vou demorar; **at ~ last** por fim, no
final; **in the ~ run** no final de contas; **so** *or*
as ~ as contanto que
long-distance ADJ (*travel*) de longa distância;
(*call*) interurbano
longevity [lɔn'dʒɛvɪtɪ] N longevidade f
long-haired ADJ (*person*) cabeludo; (*animal*)
peludo
longhand ['lɔŋhænd] N escrita usual
longing ['lɔŋɪŋ] N desejo, anseio; (*nostalgia*)
saudade f ▶ ADJ saudoso
longingly ['lɔŋɪŋlɪ] ADV ansiosamente;
(*nostalgically*) saudosamente
longitude ['lɔŋgɪtjuːd] N longitude f
long johns [-dʒɔnz] NPL ceroulas fpl
long jump N salto em distância
long-life ADJ (*milk, batteries*) longa vida
long-lost ADJ perdido há muito (tempo)
long-playing record [-'pleɪɪŋ-] N elepê m (BR),
LP m (PT)
long-range ADJ de longo alcance; (*forecast*) a
longo prazo
longshoreman ['lɔŋʃɔːmən] (US) (*irreg: like
man*) N estivador m, portuário
long-sighted ADJ presbita; (*fig*) previdente
long-standing ADJ de muito tempo
long-suffering ADJ paciente, resignado
long-term ADJ a longo prazo
long wave N (*Radio*) onda longa
long-winded [-'wɪndɪd] ADJ prolixo, cansativo
loo [luː] (BRIT *inf*) N banheiro (BR), casa de
banho (PT)
loofah ['luːfə] N tipo de esponja
look [luk] VI olhar; (*seem*) parecer; (*building
etc*): **to ~ south/(out) onto the sea** dar para
o sul/o mar ▶ N olhar m; (*glance*) olhada, vista
de olhos; (*appearance*) aparência, aspecto;
(*style*) visual m; **looks** NPL (*good looks*) físico,
aparência; **~ (here)!** (*annoyance*) escuta aqui!;
~! (*surprise*) olha!; **to ~ like sb** parecer-se com
alguém; **it ~s like him** parece ele; **it ~s
about 4 metres long** deve ter uns 4 metros
de comprimento; **it ~s all right to me** para
mim está bem; **to have a ~ at sth** dar uma
olhada em algo; **to have a ~ for sth**

procurar algo; **to ~ ahead** olhar para a frente; *(fig)* pensar no futuro

▶ **look after** vt fus cuidar de; *(deal with)* lidar com; *(luggage etc: watch over)* ficar de olho em

▶ **look around** vi olhar em torno; *(in shop)* dar uma olhada

▶ **look at** vt fus olhar (para); *(read quickly)* ler rapidamente; *(consider)* considerar

▶ **look back** vi: **to ~ back at sth/sb** voltar-se para ver algo/alguém; **to ~ back on** *(remember)* recordar, rever

▶ **look down on** vt fus *(fig)* desdenhar, desprezar

▶ **look for** vt fus procurar

▶ **look forward to** vt fus aguardar com prazer, ansiar por; *(in letter)*: **we ~ forward to hearing from you** no aguardo de suas notícias; **to ~ forward to doing sth** não ver a hora de fazer algo; **I'm not ~ing forward to it** não estou nada animado com isso

▶ **look in** vi: **to ~ in on sb** dar uma passada na casa de alguém

▶ **look into** vt fus investigar

▶ **look on** vi assistir

▶ **look out** vi *(beware)*: **to ~ out (for)** tomar cuidado (com)

▶ **look out for** vt fus *(seek)* procurar; *(await)* esperar

▶ **look over** vt *(essay)* dar uma olhada em; *(town, building)* visitar; *(person)* olhar da cabeça aos pés

▶ **look round** vi virar a cabeça, voltar-se; **to ~ round for sth** procurar algo

▶ **look through** vt fus *(papers, book)* examinar; *(: briefly)* folhear; *(telescope)* olhar através de

▶ **look to** vt fus cuidar de; *(rely on)* contar com

▶ **look up** vi levantar os olhos; *(improve)* melhorar ▶ vt *(word)* procurar; *(friend)* visitar

▶ **look up to** vt fus admirar, respeitar

lookout ['lukaut] n *(tower etc)* posto de observação, guarita; *(person)* vigia *m*; **to be on the ~ for sth** estar na expectativa de algo

look-up table n *(Comput)* tabela de pesquisa

loom [lu:m] n tear *m* ▶ vi *(also: **loom up**)* agigantar-se; *(event)* aproximar-se; *(threaten)* ameaçar

loony ['lu:nɪ] *(inf)* adj meio doido ▶ n debil *m/f* mental

loop [lu:p] n laço; *(bend)* volta, curva; *(contraceptive)* DIU *m* ▶ vt: **to ~ sth round sth** prender algo em torno de algo

loophole ['lu:phəul] n escapatória

loose [lu:s] adj *(not fixed)* solto; *(not tight)* frouxo; *(animal, hair)* solto; *(clothes)* folgado; *(morals, discipline)* relaxado; *(sense)* impreciso

▶ n: **to be on the ~** estar solto ▶ vt *(free)* soltar; *(slacken)* afrouxar; **~ connection** *(Elec)* conexão solta; **to tie up ~ ends (of sth)** *(fig)* amarrar (algo)

loose change n trocado

loose chippings [-'tʃɪpɪŋz] npl *(on road)* pedrinhas *fpl* soltas

loose end n: **to be at a ~** *(BRIT)* or **at ~s** *(US fig)* não ter o que fazer

loose-fitting adj *(clothes)* folgado, largo

loose-leaf adj: **~ binder** or **folder** pasta de folhas soltas

loose-limbed [-'lɪmd] adj ágil

loosely ['lu:slɪ] adv frouxamente, folgadamente; *(not closely)* aproximativamente

loosen ['lu:sən] vt *(free)* soltar; *(untie)* desatar; *(slacken)* afrouxar

▶ **loosen up** vi *(before game)* aquecer; *(inf: relax)* descontrair-se

loot [lu:t] n saque *m*, despojo ▶ vt saquear, pilhar

looter ['lu:tə**r**] n saqueador(a) *m/f*

looting ['lu:tɪŋ] n saque *m*, pilhagem *f*

lop off [lɔp-] vt cortar; *(branches)* podar

lop-sided [lɔp'saɪdɪd] adj torto

lord [lɔ:d] n senhor *m*; **L~ Smith** Lord Smith; **the L~** *(Rel)* o Senhor; **good L~!** Deus meu!; **the (House of) L~s** *(BRIT)* a Câmara dos Lordes

lordly ['lɔ:dlɪ] adj senhorial; *(arrogant)* arrogante

lordship ['lɔ:dʃɪp] *(BRIT)* n: **Your L~** Vossa senhoria

lore [lɔ:**r**] n sabedoria popular, tradições *fpl*

lorry ['lɔrɪ] *(BRIT)* n caminhão *m* (BR), camião *m* (PT)

lorry driver *(BRIT)* n caminhoneiro (BR), camionista *m/f* (PT)

lose [lu:z] *(pt, pp lost)* vt, vi perder; **to ~ (time)** *(clock)* atrasar-se; **to ~ no time (in doing sth)** não demorar (a fazer algo); **to get lost** *(person)* perder-se; *(thing)* extraviar-se

loser ['lu:zə**r**] n perdedor(a) *m/f*; *(inf: failure)* derrotado(-a), fracassado(-a); **to be a good/bad ~** ser bom/mau perdedor

loss [lɔs] n perda; *(Comm)*: **to make a ~** sair com prejuízo; **to cut one's ~es** reduzir os prejuízos; **to sell sth at a ~** vender algo com prejuízo; **heavy ~es** *(Mil)* grandes perdas; **to be at a ~** estar perplexo; **to be at a ~ to do** ser incapaz de fazer; **to be a dead ~** ser totalmente inútil

loss adjuster n *(Insurance)* árbitro regulador de avarias

loss leader n *(Comm)* chamariz *m*

lost [lɔst] pt, pp of **lose** ▶ adj perdido; **~ in thought** perdido em seus pensamentos; **~ and found property** *(US)* (objetos *mpl*) perdidos e achados *mpl*; **~ and found** *(US)* (seção *f* de) perdidos e achados *mpl*

lost property *(BRIT)* n (objetos *mpl*) perdidos e achados *mpl*; **~ office** or **department** (seção *f* de) perdidos e achados *mpl*

lot [lɔt] n *(set of things)* porção *f*; *(at auctions)* lote *m*; *(destiny)* destino, sorte *f*; **the ~** tudo, todos(-as); **a ~** muito, bastante; **a ~ of, ~s of** muito(s); **I read a ~** leio bastante; **to draw ~s** tirar à sorte; **parking ~** *(US)* estacionamento

lotion ['ləuʃən] N loção f
lottery ['lɔtərɪ] N loteria
loud [laud] ADJ (voice) alto; (shout) forte; (noise) barulhento; (support, condemnation) veemente; (gaudy) berrante ▶ ADV alto; **out ~** em voz alta
loud-hailer [-'heɪlər] (BRIT) N megafone m
loudly ['laudlɪ] ADV (noisily) ruidosamente; (aloud) em voz alta
loudspeaker [laud'spi:kər] N alto-falante m
lounge [laundʒ] N sala de estar f; (of airport) salão m; (BRIT: also: **lounge bar**) bar m social ▶ VI recostar-se, espreguiçar-se
  ▶ **lounge about, lounge around** VI ficar à-toa
lounge suit (BRIT) N terno (BR), fato (PT)
louse [laus] N (pl **lice**) piolho
  ▶ **louse up** (inf) VT estragar
lousy ['lauzɪ] (inf) ADJ ruim, péssimo; (ill): **to feel ~** sentir-se mal
lout [laut] N rústico, grosseiro
louvre, (US) **louver** ['lu:vər] ADJ: **~ door** porta de veneziana; **~ window** veneziana
lovable ['lʌvəbl] ADJ adorável, simpático
love [lʌv] N amor m ▶ VT amar; (like a lot) adorar; **to ~ to do** adorar fazer; **~ (from) Anne** (on letter) um abraço or um beijo, Anne; **I ~ you** eu te amo; **I ~ coffee** adoro o café; **I'd ~ to come** gostaria muito de ir; **"15 ~"** (Tennis) "15 a zero"; **to be in ~ with** estar apaixonado por; **to fall in ~ with** apaixonar-se por; **to make ~** fazer amor; **~ at first sight** amor à primeira vista; **for the ~ of** pelo amor de; **to send one's ~ to sb** mandar um abraço para alguém
love affair N aventura (amorosa), caso (de amor)
loved ones ['lʌvdwʌnz] NPL entes mpl queridos
love letter N carta de amor
love life N vida sentimental
lovely ['lʌvlɪ] ADJ (delightful) encantador(a), delicioso; (beautiful) lindo, belo; (holiday, surprise) muito agradável, maravilhoso; **we had a ~ time** foi maravilhoso, nós nos divertimos muito
lover ['lʌvər] N amante m/f; **a ~ of art/music** um(a) apreciador(a) de or um(a) amante de arte/música
lovesick ['lʌvsɪk] ADJ perdido de amor
love song N canção f de amor
loving ['lʌvɪŋ] ADJ carinhoso, afetuoso; (actions) dedicado
low [ləu] ADJ baixo; (depressed) deprimido; (ill) doente ▶ ADV baixo ▶ N (Meteorology) área de baixa pressão ▶ VI (cow) mugir; **to turn (down) ~** baixar, diminuir; **to be ~ on** (supplies) ter pouco; **to reach a new or an all-time ~** cair para o seu nível mais baixo
low-alcohol ADJ de baixo teor alcoólico
lowbrow ['ləubrau] ADJ sem pretensões intelectuais
low-calorie ADJ baixo em calorias, de baixo teor calórico

low-carb (inf) ADJ (diet, meal) com baixo carboidrato
low-cut ADJ (dress) decotado
low-down N (inf): **he gave me the ~ on it** me deu a dica sobre isso ▶ ADJ (mean) vil, desprezível
lower¹ ['ləuər] ADJ mais baixo; (less important) inferior ▶ VT abaixar; (reduce) reduzir, diminuir; **to ~ o.s. to** (fig) rebaixar-se a
lower² ['lauər] VI (sky, clouds) escurecer; (person): **to ~ at sb** olhar para alguém com raiva
low-fat ADJ magro
low-grade ADJ de baixa qualidade
low-key ADJ discreto
lowlands ['ləuləndz] NPL planície f
low-level ADJ de baixo nível, baixo; (flying) a baixa altura
lowly ['ləulɪ] ADJ humilde
low-lying ADJ de baixo nível
low-paid ADJ (person) de renda baixa; (work) mal pago
loyal ['lɔɪəl] ADJ leal
loyalist ['lɔɪəlɪst] N legalista m/f
loyalty ['lɔɪəltɪ] N lealdade f
loyalty card (BRIT) N cartão m de fidelidade
lozenge ['lɔzɪndʒ] N (Med) pastilha; (Geom) losango, rombo
LP N ABBR = **long-playing record**
L-plates ['ɛlpleɪts] (BRIT) NPL placas fpl de aprendiz de motorista

As **L-plates** são placas quadradas com um "L" vermelho que são colocadas na parte de trás do carro para mostrar que a pessoa ao volante ainda não tem carteira de motorista. Até a obtenção da carteira, o motorista aprendiz possui uma permissão provisória e não tem direito de dirigir sem um motorista qualificado ao lado. Os motoristas aprendizes não podem dirigir em estradas mesmo que estejam acompanhados.

LPN (US) N ABBR (= Licensed Practical Nurse) enfermeiro(-a) diplomado(-a)
LRAM (BRIT) N ABBR = **Licentiate of the Royal Academy of Music**
LSAT (US) N ABBR = **Law Schools Admissions Test**
LSD N ABBR (= lysergic acid diethylamide) LSD m; (BRIT: = pounds, shillings and pence) sistema monetário usado na Grã-Bretanha até 1971
LSE N ABBR = **London School of Economics**
LT ABBR (Elec: = low tension) BT
Lt. ABBR (= lieutenant) Ten.
Ltd (BRIT) ABBR (= limited (liability) company) SA
lubricant ['lu:brɪkənt] N lubrificante m
lubricate ['lu:brɪkeɪt] VT lubrificar
lucid ['lu:sɪd] ADJ lúcido
lucidity [lu:'sɪdɪtɪ] N lucidez f
luck [lʌk] N sorte f; **bad ~** azar m; **good ~!** boa sorte!; **to be in ~** ter or dar sorte; **to be out of ~** ter azar; **bad** or **hard** or **tough ~!** que azar!
luckily ['lʌkɪlɪ] ADV por sorte, felizmente

lucky ['lʌkɪ] ADJ (person) sortudo; (coincidence) feliz; (situation) afortunado; (object) de sorte
lucrative ['lu:krətɪv] ADJ lucrativo
ludicrous ['lu:dɪkrəs] ADJ ridículo
ludo ['lu:dəu] N ludo
lug [lʌg] (inf) VT (drag) arrastar; (pull) puxar
luggage ['lʌgɪdʒ] N bagagem f
luggage car (US) N (Rail) vagão m de bagagens
luggage rack N (in train) rede f para bagagem; (on car) porta-bagagem m, bagageiro
luggage van (BRIT) N (Rail) vagão m de bagagens
lugubrious [lu'gu:brɪəs] ADJ lúgubre
lukewarm ['lu:kwɔ:m] ADJ morno, tépido; (fig) indiferente
lull [lʌl] N pausa, interrupção f ▶ VT: **to ~ sb to sleep** acalentar alguém; **to be ~ed into a false sense of security** ser acalmado com uma falsa sensação de segurança
lullaby ['lʌləbaɪ] N canção f de ninar
lumbago [lʌm'beɪgəu] N lumbago
lumber ['lʌmbə'] N (junk) trastes mpl velhos; (wood) madeira serrada, tábua ▶ VT: **to ~ sb with sth/sb** empurrar algo/alguém para cima de alguém ▶ VI (also: **lumber about, lumber along**) mover-se pesadamente
lumberjack ['lʌmbədʒæk] N madeireiro, lenhador m
lumber room (BRIT) N quarto de despejo
lumber yard N depósito de madeira
luminous ['lu:mɪnəs] ADJ luminoso
lump [lʌmp] N torrão m; (fragment) pedaço; (in sauce) caroço; (in throat) nó m; (on body) galo, caroço; (also: **sugar lump**) cubo de açúcar ▶ VT: **to ~ together** amontoar
lump sum N montante m único
lumpy ['lʌmpɪ] ADJ (sauce, bed) encaroçado
lunacy ['lu:nəsɪ] N loucura
lunar ['lu:nə'] ADJ lunar
lunatic ['lu:nətɪk] ADJ, N louco(-a)
lunatic asylum N manicômio, hospício
lunch [lʌntʃ] N almoço ▶ VI almoçar; **to invite sb for ~** convidar alguém para almoçar
lunch break, lunch hour N hora do almoço
luncheon ['lʌntʃən] N almoço formal
luncheon meat N bolo de carne

luncheon voucher (BRIT) N vale m para refeição, ticket m restaurante
lunch hour N hora do almoço
lunch time N hora do almoço
lung [lʌŋ] N pulmão m
lung cancer N câncer m (BR) or cancro (PT) de pulmão
lunge [lʌndʒ] VI (also: **lunge forward**) dar estocada or bote; **to ~ at** arremeter-se contra
lupin ['lu:pɪn] N tremoço
lurch [lə:tʃ] VI balançar ▶ N solavanco; **to leave sb in the ~** deixar alguém em apuros, deixar alguém na mão (inf)
lure [luə'] N (bait) isca; (decoy) chamariz m, engodo ▶ VT atrair, seduzir
lurid ['luərɪd] ADJ (account) sensacional; (detail) horrível
lurk [lə:k] VI (hide) esconder-se; (wait) estar à espreita
luscious ['lʌʃəs] ADJ (person, thing) atraente; (food) delicioso
lush [lʌʃ] ADJ exuberante
lust [lʌst] N luxúria; (greed) cobiça
  ▶ **lust after** VT FUS cobiçar
  ▶ **lust for** VT FUS = **lust after**
luster ['lʌstə'] (US) N = **lustre**
lustful ['lʌstful] ADJ lascivo, sensual
lustre, (US) **luster** ['lʌstə'] N lustre m, brilho
lusty ['lʌstɪ] ADJ robusto, forte
lute [lu:t] N alaúde m
Luxembourg ['lʌksəmbə:g] N Luxemburgo
luxuriant [lʌg'zjuərɪənt] ADJ luxuriante, exuberante
luxurious [lʌg'zjuərɪəs] ADJ luxuoso
luxury ['lʌkʃərɪ] N luxo ▶ CPD de luxo
LV (BRIT) N ABBR = **luncheon voucher**
LW ABBR (Radio: = long wave) OL
lying ['laɪɪŋ] N mentira(s) f(pl) ▶ ADJ mentiroso, falso
lynch [lɪntʃ] VT linchar
lynching ['lɪntʃɪŋ] N linchamento
lynx [lɪŋks] N lince m
lyre ['laɪə'] N lira
lyric ['lɪrɪk] ADJ lírico
lyrical ['lɪrɪkəl] ADJ lírico
lyricism ['lɪrɪsɪzəm] N lirismo
lyrics ['lɪrɪks] NPL (of song) letra

Mm

M¹, m [ɛm] N (letter) M, m m; **M for Mary**
(BRIT) or **Mike** (US) M de Maria

M² N ABBR (BRIT) = **motorway; the M8** ≈ BR 8 f;
(= medium) M

m ABBR (= metre) m; (= mile) mil.; = **million**

M.A. ABBR (Sch) = **Master of Arts**; (US)
= **military academy**; (: Post)
= **Massachusetts**

mac [mæk] (BRIT) N capa impermeável

macabre [mə'kɑːbrə] ADJ macabro

Macao [mə'kau] N Macau

macaroni [mækə'rəunɪ] N macarrão m

macaroon [mækə'ruːn] N biscoitinho de
amêndoas

mace [meɪs] N (Bot) macis m; (sceptre) bastão m

machinations [mækɪ'neɪʃənz] NPL
maquinações fpl, intrigas fpl

machine [mə'ʃiːn] N máquina ▶ VT (dress etc)
costurar à máquina; (Tech) usinar

machine code N (Comput) código de máquina

machine gun N metralhadora

machine language N (Comput) linguagem f de
máquina

machine readable ADJ (Comput) legível por
máquina

machinery [mə'ʃiːnərɪ] N maquinaria; (fig)
máquina

machine shop N oficina mecânica

machine tool N máquina-ferramenta f

machine washable ADJ (garment) lavável à
máquina

machinist [mə'ʃiːnɪst] N operário(-a) (de
máquina); (Rail) maquinista m/f

macho ['mætʃəu] ADJ machista

mackerel ['mækrl] N INV cavala

mackintosh ['mækɪntɔʃ] (BRIT) N capa
impermeável

macro... ['mækrəu] PREFIX macro...

macro-economics N macroeconomia

mad [mæd] ADJ louco; (foolish) tolo; (angry)
furioso, brabo; (keen) **to be ~ about** ser
louco por; **to go ~** enlouquecer

madam ['mædəm] N senhora, madame f;
yes, ~ sim, senhora; **M~ Chairman**
Senhora Presidente; **can I help you, ~?**
a senhora já foi atendida?

madden ['mædn] VT exasperar

maddening ['mædnɪŋ] ADJ exasperante

made [meɪd] PT, PP of **make**

Madeira [mə'dɪərə] N (Geo) Madeira; (wine)
(vinho) Madeira m

Madeiran [mə'dɪərən] ADJ, N madeirense m/f

made-to-measure (BRIT) ADJ feito sob medida

made-up ['meɪdʌp] ADJ (story) inventado

madly ['mædlɪ] ADV loucamente; **~ in love**
louco de amor

madman ['mædmən] (irreg: like **man**) N louco

madness ['mædnɪs] N loucura; (foolishness)
tolice f

Madrid [mə'drɪd] N Madri (BR), Madrid (PT)

Mafia ['mæfɪə] N máfia

mag. [mæg] (BRIT inf) N ABBR = **magazine**

magazine [mægə'ziːn] N (Press) revista; (Radio,
TV) programa m de atualidades; (Mil: store)
depósito; (of firearm) câmara

magazine rack N porta-revistas m inv

maggot ['mægət] N larva de inseto

magic ['mædʒɪk] N magia, mágica ▶ ADJ
mágico

magical ['mædʒɪkl] ADJ mágico

magician [mə'dʒɪʃən] N mago(-a); (entertainer)
mágico(-a)

magistrate ['mædʒɪstreɪt] N magistrado(-a),
juiz/juíza m/f

magnanimous [mæg'nænɪməs] ADJ
magnânimo

magnate ['mægneɪt] N magnata m

magnesium [mæg'niːzɪəm] N magnésio

magnet ['mægnɪt] N ímã m, iman m (PT)

magnetic [mæg'nɛtɪk] ADJ magnético

magnetic tape N fita magnética

magnetism ['mægnɪtɪzəm] N magnetismo

magnification [mægnɪfɪ'keɪʃən] N aumento

magnificence [mæg'nɪfɪsns] N
magnificência

magnificent [mæg'nɪfɪsnt] ADJ magnífico

magnify ['mægnɪfaɪ] VT aumentar

magnifying glass ['mægnɪfaɪɪŋ-] N lupa,
lente f de aumento

magnitude ['mægnɪtjuːd] N magnitude f

magnolia [mæg'nəulɪə] N magnólia

magpie ['mægpaɪ] N pega

mahogany [mə'hɔgənɪ] N mogno, acaju m
▶ CPD de mogno or acaju

maid [meɪd] N empregada; **old ~** (pej)
solteirona

maiden ['meɪdn] N moça, donzela ▶ ADJ (aunt
etc) solteirona; (speech, voyage) inaugural

maiden name ['meɪdn-] N nome *m* de solteira
mail [meɪl] N correio; (*letters*) cartas *fpl* ▶ VT (*post*) pôr no correio; (*send*) mandar pelo correio; **by ~** pelo correio
mailbox ['meɪlbɔks] N (*US: for letters*) caixa do correio; (*Comput*) caixa de entrada
mailing list ['meɪlɪŋ-] N lista de clientes, mailing list *m*
mailman ['meɪlmæn] (*US*) (*irreg: like* **man**) N carteiro
mail order N pedido por reembolso postal; (*business*) venda por correspondência ▶ CPD: **mail-order firm** *or* **house** firma de vendas por correspondência
mailshot ['meɪlʃɔt] (*BRIT*) N mailing *m*
mail train N trem-correio, trem *m* postal
mail truck (*US*) (*Aut*) = **mail van**
mail van (*BRIT*) N (*Aut*) furgão *m* do correio; (*Rail*) vagão *m* postal
maim [meɪm] VT mutilar, aleijar
main [meɪn] ADJ principal ▶ N (*pipe*) cano *or* esgoto principal; **the mains** NPL (*Elec, gas, water*) a rede; **in the ~** na maior parte
main course N (*Culin*) prato principal
mainframe ['meɪnfreɪm] N (*Comput*) mainframe *m*
mainland ['meɪnlənd] N: **the ~** o continente
mainline ['meɪnlaɪn] (*inf*) VT (*heroin*) picar-se com ▶ VI picar-se, aplicar-se
main line N (*Rail*) linha-tronco *f* ▶ ADJ: **main-line** de linha-tronco
mainly ['meɪnlɪ] ADV principalmente
main road N estrada principal
mainstay ['meɪnsteɪ] N (*fig*) esteio
mainstream ['meɪnstriːm] N corrente *f* principal
maintain [meɪn'teɪn] VT manter; (*keep up*) conservar (em bom estado); (*affirm*) sustentar, afirmar; **to ~ that ...** afirmar que ...
maintenance ['meɪntənəns] N manutenção *f*; (*Law: alimony*) alimentos *mpl*, pensão *f* alimentícia
maintenance contract N contrato de assistência técnica
maintenance order N (*Law*) ordem *f* de pensão
maisonette [meɪzə'nɛt] (*BRIT*) N duplex *m*
maize [meɪz] N milho
Maj. ABBR (*Mil*) = **major**
majestic [mə'dʒɛstɪk] ADJ majestoso
majesty ['mædʒɪstɪ] N majestade *f*; (*title*): **Your M~** Sua Majestade
major ['meɪdʒəʳ] N (*Mil*) major *m* ▶ ADJ (*main*) principal; (*considerable*) importante; (*great*) grande; (*Mus*) maior ▶ VI (*US Sch*): **to ~ (in)** especializar-se (em); **a ~ operation** (*Med*) uma operação séria
Majorca [mə'jɔːkə] N Maiorca
major general N (*Mil*) general-de-divisão *m*
majority [mə'dʒɔrɪtɪ] N maioria ▶ CPD (*verdict, holding*) majoritário
make [meɪk] (*pt, pp* **made**) VT fazer; (*manufacture*) fabricar, produzir; (*cause to be*):

to ~ sb sad entristecer alguém, fazer alguém ficar triste; (*force*): **to ~ sb do sth** fazer com que alguém faça algo; (*equal*): **2 and 2 ~ 4** dois e dois são quatro ▶ N marca; **to ~ the bed** fazer a cama; **to ~ a fool of sb** fazer alguém de bobo; **to ~ a profit/loss** ter um lucro/uma perda; **to ~ it** (*arrive*) chegar; (*succeed*) ter sucesso; **what time do you ~ it?** que horas você tem?; **to ~ good** (*succeed*) dar-se bem; (*losses*) indenizar; **to ~ do with** contentar-se com
▶ **make for** VT FUS (*place*) dirigir-se a
▶ **make off** VI fugir
▶ **make out** VT (*decipher*) decifrar; (*understand*) compreender; (*see*) divisar, avistar; (*write out: prescription*) escrever; (*: form, cheque*) preencher; (*claim, imply*) afirmar; (*pretend*) fazer de conta; **to ~ out a case for sth** argumentar em favor de algo, defender algo
▶ **make over** VT (*assign*): **to ~ over (to)** transferir (para)
▶ **make up** VT (*constitute*) constituir; (*invent*) inventar; (*parcel*) embrulhar ▶ VI reconciliar-se; (*with cosmetics*) maquilar-se (*BR*), maquilhar-se (*PT*); **to be made up of** compor-se de, ser composto de; **to ~ up one's mind** decidir-se
▶ **make up for** VT FUS compensar
make-believe N fingido, simulado ▶ N: **a world of ~** um mundo de faz-de-conta; **it's just ~** é pura ilusão
maker ['meɪkəʳ] N (*of film, programme*) criador *m*; (*manufacturer*) fabricante *m/f*
makeshift ['meɪkʃɪft] ADJ provisório
make-up ['meɪkʌp] N maquilagem *f* (*BR*), maquilhagem *f* (*PT*)
make-up bag N bolsa de maquilagem (*BR*), bolsa de maquilhagem (*PT*)
make-up remover N removidor *m* de maquilagem
making ['meɪkɪŋ] N (*fig*): **in the ~** em vias de formação; **he has the ~s of an actor** ele tem tudo para ser ator
maladjusted [mælə'dʒʌstɪd] ADJ inadaptado, desajustado
malaise [mæ'leɪz] N mal-estar *m*, indisposição *f*
malaria [mə'lɛərɪə] N malária
Malawi [mə'lɑːwɪ] N Malavi *m*
Malay [mə'leɪ] ADJ malaio ▶ N malaio(-a); (*Ling*) malaio
Malaya [mə'leɪə] N Malaia
Malayan [mə'leɪən] ADJ, N = **Malay**
Malaysia [mə'leɪzɪə] N Malaísia (*BR*), Malásia (*PT*)
Malaysian [mə'leɪzɪən] ADJ, N malaísio(-a)
Maldives ['mɔːldaɪvz] NPL: **the ~** as ilhas Maldivas
male [meɪl] N (*Bio, Elec*) macho ▶ ADJ (*sex, attitude*) masculino; (*animal*) macho; (*child etc*) do sexo masculino
male chauvinist N machista *m*
male nurse N enfermeiro

malevolence [mə'lεvələns] N malevolência
malevolent [mə'lεvələnt] ADJ malévolo
malfunction [mæl'fʌŋkʃən] N
funcionamento defeituoso
malice ['mælɪs] N (ill will) malícia; (rancour)
rancor m
malicious [mə'lɪʃəs] ADJ malevolente; (Law)
com intenção criminosa
malign [mə'laɪn] VT caluniar, difamar
malignant [mə'lɪgnənt] ADJ (Med) maligno
malingerer [mə'lɪŋgərəʳ] N doente m/f
fingido(-a)
mall [mɔ:l] N (also: **shopping mall**) shopping m
malleable ['mælɪəbl] ADJ maleável
mallet ['mælɪt] N maço, marreta
malnutrition [mælnju:'trɪʃən] N desnutrição f
malpractice [mæl'præktɪs] N falta
profissional
malt [mɔ:lt] N malte m; (malt whisky) uísque m
de malte
Malta ['mɔ:ltə] N Malta
Maltese [mɔ:l'ti:z] ADJ maltês(-esa) ▶ N INV
maltês(-esa) m/f; (Ling) maltês m
maltreat [mæl'tri:t] VT maltratar
malware ['mælwεəʳ] N (Comput) software m
malicioso
mammal ['mæml] N mamífero
mammoth ['mæməθ] N mamute m ▶ ADJ
gigantesco, imenso
man [mæn] N (pl **men**) homem m; (Chess) peça
▶ VT (Naut) tripular; (Mil) guarnecer; (operate:
machine) operar; **an old ~** um velho; **a
young ~** um jovem; **~ and wife** marido e
mulher
manacles ['mænəklz] NPL grilhões mpl
manage ['mænɪdʒ] VI arranjar-se, virar-se
▶ VT (be in charge of) dirigir, administrar;
(business) gerenciar; (ship, person) controlar;
(device) manusear; (carry) carregar; **to ~ to do
sth** conseguir fazer algo; **to ~ without sb/
sth** passar sem alguém/algo; **can you ~?**
você consegue?
manageable ['mænɪdʒəbl] ADJ manejável;
(task etc) viável
management ['mænɪdʒmənt] N
administração f, direção f, gerência; "**under
new ~**" "sob nova direção"
management accounting N contabilidade f
administrativa or gerencial
management consultant N consultor(a) m/f
em administração
manager ['mænɪdʒəʳ] N gerente m/f; (Sport)
técnico(-a); (of project) superintendente m/f;
(of department, unit) chefe m/f, diretor(a) m/f;
(of artist) empresário(-a); **sales ~** gerente de
vendas
manageress [mænɪdʒə'rεs] N gerente f
managerial [mænə'dʒɪərɪəl] ADJ
administrativo, gerencial
managing director ['mænɪdʒɪŋ-] N diretor(a)
m/f, diretor-gerente/diretora-gerente m/f
Mancunian [mæŋ'kju:nɪən] ADJ de
Manchester ▶ N natural m/f de Manchester

mandarin ['mændərɪn] N (also: **mandarin
orange**) tangerina; (person) mandarim m
mandate ['mændeɪt] N mandato
mandatory ['mændətərɪ] ADJ obrigatório;
(powers etc) mandatário
mandolin, mandoline ['mændəlɪn] N
bandolim m
mane [meɪn] N (of horse) crina; (of lion) juba
maneuver [mə'nu:vəʳ] (US) VB, N
= **manoeuvre**
manfully ['mænfəlɪ] ADV valentemente
manganese ['mæŋgəni:z] N manganês m
mangle ['mæŋgl] VT mutilar, estropiar ▶ N
calandra
mango ['mæŋgəu] (pl **mangoes**) N manga
mangrove ['mæŋgrəuv] N mangue m
mangy ['meɪndʒɪ] ADJ sarnento, esfarrapado
manhandle ['mænhændl] VT (mistreat)
maltratar; (move by hand) manipular
manhole ['mænhəul] N poço de inspeção
manhood ['mænhud] N (age) idade f adulta;
(masculinity) virilidade f
man-hour N hora-homem f
manhunt ['mænhʌnt] N caça ao homem
mania ['meɪnɪə] N mania
maniac ['meɪnɪæk] N maníaco(-a); (fig)
louco(-a)
manic ['mænɪk] ADJ maníaco
manic-depressive ADJ, N maníaco-
depressivo(-a)
manicure ['mænɪkjuəʳ] N manicure f (BR),
manicura (PT)
manicure set N estojo de manicure (BR) or
manicura (PT)
manifest ['mænɪfεst] VT manifestar, mostrar
▶ ADJ manifesto, evidente ▶ N (Aviat, Naut)
manifesto
manifestation [mænɪfεs'teɪʃən] N
manifestação f
manifesto [mænɪ'fεstəu] (pl **manifestos** or
manifestoes) N manifesto
manifold ['mænɪfəuld] ADJ múltiplo ▶ N (Aut
etc) see **exhaust**
Manila [mə'nɪlə] N Manilha
manila [mə'nɪlə] ADJ: **~ paper** papel-manilha m
manipulate [mə'nɪpjuleɪt] VT manipular
manipulation [mənɪpju'leɪʃən] N
manipulação f
mankind [mæn'kaɪnd] N humanidade f, raça
humana
manliness ['mænlɪnɪs] N virilidade f
manly ['mænlɪ] ADJ másculo, viril
man-made ADJ sintético, artificial
manna ['mænə] N maná m
mannequin ['mænɪkɪn] N manequim m
manner ['mænəʳ] N modo, maneira;
(behaviour) conduta, comportamento;
manners NPL (conduct) boas maneiras fpl,
educação f; **bad ~s** falta de educação; **all ~
of** todo tipo de; **all ~ of things** todos os
tipos de coisa
mannerism ['mænərɪzəm] N maneirismo,
hábito

m

mannerly ['mænəlɪ] ADJ polido, educado
manoeuvrable, (US) **maneuverable** [mə'nu:vrəbl] ADJ manobrável
manoeuvre, (US) **maneuver** [mə'nu:və^r] VT manobrar; (manipulate) manipular ▶ VI manobrar ▶ N manobra; **to ~ sb into doing sth** induzir alguém a fazer algo
manor ['mænə^r] N (also: **manor house**) casa senhorial, solar m
manpower ['mænpauə^r] N potencial m humano, mão-de-obra f
manservant ['mænsə:vənt] (pl **menservants**) N criado
mansion ['mænʃən] N mansão f, palacete m
manslaughter ['mænslɔ:tə^r] N homicídio involuntário
mantelpiece ['mæntlpi:s] N consolo da lareira
mantle ['mæntl] N manto; (fig) camada
man-to-man ADJ, ADV de homem para homem
manual ['mænjuəl] ADJ manual ▶ N manual m; (Mus) teclado
manual worker N trabalhador(a) m/f braçal
manufacture [mænju'fæktʃə^r] VT manufaturar, fabricar ▶ N fabricação f
manufactured goods [mænju'fæktʃəd-] NPL produtos mpl industrializados
manufacturer [mænju'fæktʃərə^r] N fabricante m/f
manufacturing industries [mænju'fæktʃərɪŋ] NPL indústrias fpl de transformação
manure [mə'njuə^r] N estrume m, adubo
manuscript ['mænjuskrɪpt] N manuscrito
many ['mɛnɪ] ADJ, PRON muitos(-as); **how ~?** quantos(-as)?; **a great ~** muitíssimos; **twice as ~** adj duas vezes mais; pron o dobro; **~ a time** muitas vezes
map [mæp] N mapa m ▶ VT fazer o mapa de ▶ **map out** VT traçar; (fig: career, holiday) planejar
maple ['meɪpl] N bordo
mar [mɑ:^r] VT estragar
Mar. ABBR = **March**
marathon ['mærəθən] N maratona ▶ ADJ: **a ~ session** uma sessão exaustiva
marathon runner N corredor(a) m/f de maratona, maratonista m/f
marauder [mə'rɔ:də^r] N saqueador(a) m/f
marble ['mɑ:bl] N mármore m; (toy) bola de gude; **marbles** N (game) jogo de gude
March [mɑ:tʃ] N março; see also **July**
march [mɑ:tʃ] VI (Mil) marchar; (demonstrators) desfilar ▶ N marcha; (demonstration) passeata; **to ~ out of/into** etc sair de/entrar em marchando etc
marcher ['mɑ:tʃə^r] N (demonstrator) manifestante m/f
marching ['mɑ:tʃɪŋ] N: **to give sb his ~ orders** (fig) dar um bilhete azul a alguém, mandar passear alguém
march-past N desfile m
mare [mɛə^r] N égua

marg. [mɑ:dʒ] (inf) N ABBR = **margarine**
margarine [mɑ:dʒə'ri:n] N margarina
margin ['mɑ:dʒɪn] N margem f
marginal ['mɑ:dʒɪnl] ADJ marginal; **~ seat** (Pol) cadeira ganha por pequena maioria
marginally ['mɑ:dʒɪnəlɪ] ADV ligeiramente
marigold ['mærɪgəuld] N malmequer m
marijuana [mærɪ'wɑ:nə] N maconha
marina [mə'ri:nə] N marina
marinade [n mærɪ'neɪd, vt 'mærɪneɪd] N escabeche m ▶ VT = **marinate**
marinate ['mærɪneɪt] VT marinar, pôr em escabeche
marine [mə'ri:n] ADJ (in the sea) marinho; (engineer) naval; (of seafaring) marítimo ▶ N fuzileiro naval
marine insurance N seguro marítimo
marital ['mærɪtl] ADJ matrimonial, marital; **~ status** estado civil
maritime ['mærɪtaɪm] ADJ marítimo
maritime law N direito marítimo
marjoram ['mɑ:dʒərəm] N manjerona
mark [mɑ:k] N marca, sinal m; (imprint) impressão f; (stain) mancha; (BRIT Sch) nota; (currency) marco; (BRIT Tech): **M~ 2** 2ª versão ▶ VT (also Sport: player) marcar; (stain) manchar; (indicate) indicar; (commemorate) comemorar; (BRIT Sch: grade) dar nota em; (: correct) corrigir; **to ~ time** marcar passo; **to be quick off the ~ (in doing)** (fig) não perder tempo (para fazer); **up to the ~ (in efficiency)** à altura das exigências
▶ **mark down** VT (prices, goods) rebaixar, remarcar para baixo
▶ **mark off** VT (tick off) ticar
▶ **mark out** VT (trace) traçar; (designate) destinar
▶ **mark up** VT (price) aumentar, remarcar
marked [mɑ:kt] ADJ acentuado
markedly ['mɑ:kɪdlɪ] ADV marcadamente
marker ['mɑ:kə^r] N (sign) marcador m, marca; (bookmark) marcador
market ['mɑ:kɪt] N mercado ▶ VT (Comm) comercializar; **to be on the ~** estar à venda; **on the open ~** no mercado livre; **to play the ~** especular na bolsa de valores
marketable ['mɑ:kɪtəbl] ADJ comercializável
market analysis N análise f de mercado
market day N dia m de mercado
market demand N procura de mercado
market forces NPL forças fpl do mercado
market garden (BRIT) N horta
marketing ['mɑ:kɪtɪŋ] N marketing m
market leader N líder m do mercado
marketplace ['mɑ:kɪtpleɪs] N mercado
market price N preço de mercado
market research N pesquisa de mercado
market value N valor m de mercado
marking ['mɑ:kɪŋ] N (on animal) marcação f; (on road) marca
marksman ['mɑ:ksmən] N (irreg: like **man**) N bom atirador m
marksmanship ['mɑ:ksmənʃɪp] N boa pontaria

marksmen ['mɑːksmɛn] NPL *of* **marksman**

mark-up ['mɑːkʌp] N (*Comm: margin*) margem *f* (de lucro), markup *m*; (: *increase*) remarcação *f*, aumento

marmalade ['mɑːməleɪd] N geleia de laranja

maroon [mə'ruːn] VT: **to be ~ed** ficar abandonado (numa ilha) ▶ ADJ vinho *inv*

marquee [mɑː'kiː] N toldo, tenda

marquess ['mɑːkwɪs] N marquês *m*

marquis ['mɑːkwɪs] N = **marquess**

marriage ['mærɪdʒ] N casamento

marriage bureau (*irreg: like* **bureau**) N agência matrimonial

marriage certificate N certidão *f* de casamento

marriage counselling (US) N = **marriage guidance**

marriage guidance (BRIT) N orientação *f* matrimonial

married ['mærɪd] ADJ casado; (*life, love*) conjugal; **to get ~** casar(-se)

marrow ['mærəu] N medula; (*vegetable*) abóbora

marry ['mærɪ] VT casar(-se) com; (*subj: father, priest etc*) casar, unir ▶ VI (*also:* **get married**) casar(-se)

Mars [mɑːz] N (*planet*) Marte *m*

marsh [mɑːʃ] N pântano; (*salt marsh*) marisma

marshal ['mɑːʃl] N (*Mil: also:* **field marshal**) marechal *m*; (*at sports meeting etc*) oficial *m* ▶ VT (*thoughts, support*) organizar; (*soldiers*) formar

marshalling yard ['mɑːʃlɪŋ-] N (*Rail*) local *m* de manobras

marshmallow [mɑːʃ'mæləu] N *espécie de doce de malvavisco*

marshy ['mɑːʃɪ] ADJ pantanoso

marsupial [mɑː'suːpɪəl] ADJ marsupial ▶ N marsupial *m*

martial ['mɑːʃl] ADJ marcial

martial arts NPL artes *fpl* marciais

martial law N lei *f* marcial

Martian ['mɑːʃən] N marciano(-a)

martin ['mɑːtɪn] N (*also:* **house martin**) andorinha-de-casa

martyr ['mɑːtəʳ] N mártir *m/f* ▶ VT martirizar

martyrdom ['mɑːtədəm] N martírio

marvel ['mɑːvl] N maravilha ▶ VI: **to ~ (at)** maravilhar-se (de *or* com)

marvellous, (US) **marvelous** ['mɑːvələs] ADJ maravilhoso

Marxism ['mɑːksɪzəm] N marxismo

Marxist ['mɑːksɪst] ADJ, N marxista *m/f*

marzipan ['mɑːzɪpæn] N maçapão *m*

mascara [mæs'kɑːrə] N rímel *m*

mascot ['mæskət] N mascote *f*

masculine ['mæskjulɪn] ADJ, N masculino

masculinity [mæskju'lɪnɪtɪ] N masculinidade *f*

MASH [mæʃ] (US) N ABBR (*Mil*) = **mobile army surgical hospital**

mash [mæʃ] VT (*Culin*) fazer um purê de; (*crush*) amassar

mashed potatoes [mæʃt-] N purê *m* de batatas

mask [mɑːsk] N máscara ▶ VT (*face*) encobrir; (*feelings*) esconder, ocultar

masochism ['mæsəkɪzəm] N masoquismo

masochist ['mæsəkɪst] N masoquista *m/f*

mason ['meɪsn] N (*also:* **stone mason**) pedreiro(-a); (*also:* **freemason**) maçom *m*

masonic [mə'sɔnɪk] ADJ maçônico

masonry ['meɪsənrɪ] N (*also:* **freemasonry**) maçonaria; (*building*) alvenaria

masquerade [mæskə'reɪd] N baile *m* de máscaras; (*fig*) farsa, embuste *m* ▶ VI: **to ~ as** disfarçar-se de, fazer-se passar por

mass [mæs] N (*of papers etc*) quantidade *f*; (*people*) multidão *f*; (*Phys*) massa; (*Rel*) missa; (*great quantity*) montão *m* ▶ CPD de massa ▶ VI reunir-se; (*Mil*) concentrar-se; **the masses** NPL (*ordinary people*) as massas; **~es of** (*inf*) montes de; **to go to ~** ir à missa

massacre ['mæsəkəʳ] N massacre *m*, carnificina ▶ VT massacrar

massage ['mæsɑːʒ] N massagem *f* ▶ VT fazer massagem em, massagear

masseur [mæ'səːʳ] N massagista *m*

masseuse [mæ'səːz] N massagista

massive ['mæsɪv] ADJ (*large*) enorme; (*support*) massivo

mass market N mercado de consumo em massa

mass media NPL meios *mpl* de comunicação de massa, mídia

mass meeting N concentração *f* de massa

mass-produce VT produzir em massa, fabricar em série

mass-production N produção *f* em massa, fabricação *f* em série

mast [mɑːst] N (*Naut*) mastro; (*Radio etc*) antena

master ['mɑːstəʳ] N mestre *m*; (*landowner*) senhor *m*, dono; (*fig: of situation*) dono; (*in secondary school*) professor *m*; (*title for boys*): **M~ X** o menino X ▶ VT controlar; (*learn*) conhecer a fundo; **~ of ceremonies** mestre de cerimônias; **M~'s degree** mestrado

masterful ['mɑːstəful] ADJ autoritário, imperioso

master key N chave *f* mestra

masterly ['mɑːstəlɪ] ADJ magistral

mastermind ['mɑːstəmaɪnd] N (*fig*) cabeça ▶ VT dirigir, planejar

Master of Arts/Science N detentor(a) *m/f* de mestrado em letras/ciências; (*degree*) mestrado

masterpiece ['mɑːstəpiːs] N obra-prima

master plan N plano piloto

master stroke N golpe *m* de mestre

mastery ['mɑːstərɪ] N domínio

mastiff ['mæstɪf] N mastim *m*

masturbate ['mæstəbeɪt] VI masturbar-se

masturbation [mæstə'beɪʃən] N masturbação *f*

mat [mæt] N esteira; (*also:* **doormat**) capacho; (*also:* **table mat**) descanso ▶ ADJ = **matt**

match [mætʃ] N fósforo; (*game*) jogo, partida; (*equal*) igual *m/f* ▶ VT (*also:* **match up**) casar, emparelhar; (*go well with*) combinar com; (*equal*) igualar; (*correspond to*) corresponder a ▶ VI combinar; **to be a good ~** (*couple*) formar um bom casal
▶ **match up** VT casar, emparelhar
matchbox ['mætʃbɒks] N caixa de fósforos
matching ['mætʃɪŋ] ADJ que combina (com)
matchless ['mætʃlɪs] ADJ sem igual, incomparável
mate [meɪt] N (*inf*) colega *m/f*; (*assistant*) ajudante *m/f*; (*Chess*) mate *m*; (*animal*) macho/fêmea; (*in merchant navy*) imediato ▶ VI acasalar-se ▶ VT acasalar
material [mə'tɪərɪəl] N (*substance*) matéria; (*equipment*) material *m*; (*cloth*) pano, tecido; (*data*) dados *mpl* ▶ ADJ material; (*important*) importante; **materials** NPL (*equipment*) material; **reading ~** (material de) leitura
materialistic [mətɪərɪə'lɪstɪk] ADJ materialista
materialize [mə'tɪərɪəlaɪz] VI materializar-se, concretizar-se
materially [mə'tɪərɪəlɪ] ADV materialmente
maternal [mə'tə:nl] ADJ maternal
maternity [mə'tə:nɪtɪ] N maternidade *f* ▶ CPD de maternidade, de gravidez
maternity benefit N auxílio-maternidade *m*
maternity dress N vestido de gestante
maternity hospital N maternidade *f*
matey ['meɪtɪ] (BRIT *inf*) ADJ chapinha
math [mæθ] (US) N = **maths**
mathematical [mæθə'mætɪkl] ADJ matemático
mathematician [mæθəmə'tɪʃən] N matemático(-a)
mathematics [mæθə'mætɪks] N matemática
maths, (US) **math** [mæθs] N matemática
matinée ['mætɪneɪ] N matinê *f*
mating ['meɪtɪŋ] N acasalamento
mating call N chamado do macho
mating season N época de cio
matriarchal [meɪtrɪ'ɑ:kl] ADJ matriarcal
matrices ['meɪtrɪsi:z] NPL *of* **matrix**
matriculation [mətrɪkju'leɪʃən] N matrícula
matrimonial [mætrɪ'məunɪəl] ADJ matrimonial
matrimony ['mætrɪmənɪ] N matrimônio, casamento
matrix ['meɪtrɪks] (*pl* **matrices**) N matriz *f*
matron ['meɪtrən] N (*in hospital*) enfermeira-chefe *f*; (*in school*) inspetora
matronly ['meɪtrənlɪ] ADJ matronal; (*fig: figure*) corpulento
matt [mæt] ADJ fosco, sem brilho
matted ['mætɪd] ADJ embaraçado
matter ['mætə^r] N questão *f*, assunto; (*Phys*) matéria; (*substance*) substância; (*content*) conteúdo; (*reading matter etc*) material *m*; (*Med: pus*) pus *m* ▶ VI importar; **matters** NPL (*affairs*) questões *fpl*; **it doesn't ~** não importa; (*I don't mind*) tanto faz; **what's**

the ~? o que (é que) há?, qual é o problema?; **no ~ what** aconteça o que acontecer; **as a ~ of course** o que é de se esperar; (*routine*) por rotina; **as a ~ of fact** na realidade, de fato; **it's a ~ of habit** é uma questão de hábito; **printed ~** impressos; **reading ~** (BRIT) (material de) leitura
matter-of-fact [mætərə'fækt] ADJ prosaico, prático
matting ['mætɪŋ] N esteira
mattress ['mætrɪs] N colchão *m*
mature [mə'tjuə^r] ADJ maduro; (*cheese, wine*) amadurecido ▶ VI amadurecer
maturity [mə'tjuərɪtɪ] N maturidade *f*
maudlin ['mɔ:dlɪn] ADJ (*film, book*) piegas *inv*; (*person*) chorão(-rona)
maul [mɔ:l] VT machucar, maltratar
Mauritania [mɔ:rɪ'teɪnɪə] N Mauritânia
Mauritius [mə'rɪʃəs] N Maurício *f* (*no article*)
mausoleum [mɔ:sə'lɪəm] N mausoléu *m*
mauve [məuv] ADJ cor de malva *inv*
maverick ['mævrɪk] N (*fig*) dissidente *m/f*
mawkish ['mɔ:kɪʃ] ADJ piegas *inv*
max. ABBR = **maximum**
maxim ['mæksɪm] N máxima
maxima ['mæksɪmə] NPL *of* **maximum**
maximize ['mæksɪmaɪz] VT maximizar
maximum ['mæksɪməm] N (*pl* **maxima** *or* **maximums**) máximo ▶ ADJ máximo
May [meɪ] N maio; *see also* **July**
may [meɪ] (*conditional* **might**) AUX VB (*indicating possibility*): **he ~ come** pode ser que ele venha, é capaz de vir; (*be allowed to*): **~ I smoke?** posso fumar?; (*wishes*): **~ God bless you!** que Deus lhe abençoe; **he might be there** ele poderia estar lá, ele é capaz de estar lá; **I might as well go** mais vale que eu vá; **you might like to try** talvez você queira tentar
maybe ['meɪbi:] ADV talvez; **~ he'll come** talvez ele venha; **~ not** talvez não
mayday ['meɪdeɪ] N S.O.S. *m* (*chamada de socorro internacional*)
May Day N dia *m* primeiro de maio
mayhem ['meɪhɛm] N caos *m*
mayonnaise [meɪə'neɪz] N maionese *f*
mayor [mɛə^r] N prefeito (BR), presidente *m* do município (PT)
mayoress ['mɛərɪs] N prefeita (BR), presidenta do município (PT)
maypole ['meɪpəul] N *mastro erguido no dia primeiro de maio*
maze [meɪz] N labirinto
MB ABBR (*Comput*) = **megabyte**; (CANADA) = **Manitoba**
MBA N ABBR (= *Master of Business Administration*) *grau universitário*
MBBS (BRIT) N ABBR (= *Bachelor of Medicine and Surgery*) *grau universitário*
MBChB (BRIT) N ABBR (= *Bachelor of Medicine and Surgery*) *grau universitário*
MBE (BRIT) N ABBR (= *Member of the Order of the British Empire*) *título honorífico*
MC N ABBR = **master of ceremonies**

MCAT (US) N ABBR = **Medical College Admissions Test**

MCP (BRIT inf) N ABBR (= *male chauvinist pig*) machista *m*

MD N ABBR = **Doctor of Medicine**; (*Comm*) = **managing director** ▶ ABBR (US *Post*) = **Maryland**

MDT (US) ABBR (= *Mountain Daylight Time*) hora de verão nas montanhas Rochosas

ME (US) ABBR (*Post*) = **Maine** ▶ N ABBR (*Med*) = **medical examiner**

(KEYWORD)

me [mi:] PRON **1** (*direct*) me; **can you hear me?** você pode me ouvir?; **he heard me** ele me ouviu; **he heard ME!** (*not anyone else*) ele me ouviu; **it's me** sou eu
2 (*indirect*) me; **he gave me the money** ele me deu o dinheiro; **he gave the money to me** ele deu o dinheiro para mim; **give it to me** dá isso para mim
3 (*stressed, after prep*) mim; **it's for me** é para mim; **with me** comigo; **without me** sem mim

meadow ['mɛdəu] N prado, campina
meagre, (US) **meager** ['mi:gəʳ] ADJ escasso
meal [mi:l] N refeição *f*; (*flour*) farinha; **to go out for a ~** jantar fora
mealtime ['mi:ltaɪm] N hora da refeição
mealy-mouthed ['mi:lɪmauðd] ADJ insincero
mean [mi:n] VT (*pt, pp* **meant**) (*signify*) significar, querer dizer; (*refer to*): **I thought you ~t her** eu pensei que você estivesse se referindo a ela; (*intend*): **to ~ to do sth** pretender *or* tencionar fazer algo ▶ ADJ (*with money*) sovina, avarento, pão-duro *inv* (BR); (*unkind*) mesquinho; (*shabby*) malcuidado, dilapidado; (*of poor quality*) inferior; (*average*) médio ▶ N meio, meio termo; **means** NPL (*way, money*) meio; **do you ~ it?** você está falando sério?; **what do you ~?** o que você quer dizer?; **to be ~t for** estar destinado a; **by ~s of** por meio de, mediante; **by all ~s!** claro que sim!, pois não
meander [mɪ'ændəʳ] VI (*river*) serpentear; (*person*) vadiar, perambular
meaning ['mi:nɪŋ] N sentido, significado
meaningful ['mi:nɪŋful] ADJ significativo; (*relationship*) sério
meaningless ['mi:nɪŋlɪs] ADJ sem sentido
meanness ['mi:nnɪs] N (*with money*) avareza, sovinice *f*; (*shabbiness*) pobreza, miséria; (*unkindness*) maldade *f*, mesquinharia
means test N (*Admin*) avaliação *f* de rendimento
meant [mɛnt] PT, PP *of* **mean**
meantime ['mi:ntaɪm] ADV (*also*: **in the meantime**) entretanto, enquanto isso
meanwhile ['mi:nwaɪl] ADV = **meantime**
measles ['mi:zlz] N sarampo
measly ['mi:zlɪ] (*inf*) ADJ miserável

measure ['mɛʒəʳ] VT medir; (*for clothes etc*) tirar as medidas de; (*consider*) avaliar, ponderar ▶ VI medir ▶ N medida; (*also*: **tape measure**) fita métrica; **a litre ~** um litro; **some ~ of success** certo grau de sucesso; **to take ~s to do sth** tomar medidas *or* providências para fazer algo
▶ **measure up** VI: **to ~ up (to)** corresponder (a)
measured ['mɛʒəd] ADJ medido, calculado; (*tone*) ponderado
measurement ['mɛʒəmənt] N (*act*) medição *f*; (*dimension*) medida; **measurements** NPL (*size*) medidas *fpl*; **to take sb's ~s** tirar as medidas de alguém; **chest/hip ~** medida de peito/quadris
meat [mi:t] N carne *f*; **cold ~s** (BRIT) frios; **crab ~** caranguejo
meatball ['mi:tbɔ:l] N almôndega
meat pie N bolo de carne
meaty ['mi:tɪ] ADJ carnudo; (*fig*) substancial
Mecca ['mɛkə] N Meca; (*fig*): **a ~ (for)** a meca (de)
mechanic [mɪ'kænɪk] N mecânico
mechanical [mɪ'kænɪkl] ADJ mecânico
mechanical engineer N engenheiro(-a) mecânico(-a)
mechanical engineering N (*science*) mecânica; (*industry*) engenharia mecânica
mechanics [mɪ'kænɪks] N mecânica ▶ NPL mecanismo
mechanism ['mɛkənɪzəm] N mecanismo
mechanization [mɛkənaɪ'zeɪʃən] N mecanização *f*
MEd N ABBR (= *Master of Education*) grau universitário
medal ['mɛdl] N medalha
medalist ['mɛdəlɪst] (US) N = **medallist**
medallion [mɪ'dælɪən] N medalhão *m*
medallist, (US) **medalist** ['mɛdəlɪst] N (*Sport*) ganhador(a) *m/f* de medalha
meddle ['mɛdl] VI: **to ~ in** meter-se em, intrometer-se em; **to ~ with sth** mexer em algo
meddlesome ['mɛdlsəm] ADJ intrometido
meddling ['mɛdlɪŋ] ADJ intrometido
media ['mi:dɪə] NPL meios *mpl* de comunicação, mídia
mediaeval [mɛdɪ'i:vl] ADJ = **medieval**
median ['mi:dɪən] (US) N (*also*: **median strip**) canteiro divisor
media research N pesquisa de audiência
mediate ['mi:dɪeɪt] VI mediar
mediation [mi:dɪ'eɪʃən] N mediação *f*
mediator ['mi:dɪeɪtəʳ] N mediador(a) *m/f*
Medicaid ['mɛdɪkeɪd] (US) N programa de ajuda médica.
medical ['mɛdɪkl] ADJ médico ▶ N (*examination*) exame *m* médico
medical certificate N atestado médico
medical student N estudante *m/f* de medicina
Medicare ['mɛdɪkeəʳ] (US) N sistema federal de seguro saúde

medicated ['mɛdɪkeɪtɪd] ADJ medicinal, higienizado

medication [mɛdɪ'keɪʃən] N (drugs etc) medicação f

medicinal [mɛ'dɪsɪnl] ADJ medicinal

medicine ['mɛdsɪn] N medicina; (drug) remédio, medicamento

medicine chest N armário de remédios

medicine man (irreg: like **man**) N curandeiro m, pajé m

medieval [mɛdɪ'i:vl] ADJ medieval

mediocre [mi:dɪ'əukə˞] ADJ medíocre

mediocrity [mi:dɪ'ɔkrɪtɪ] N mediocridade f

meditate ['mɛdɪteɪt] VI meditar

meditation [mɛdɪ'teɪʃən] N meditação f

Mediterranean [mɛdɪtə'reɪnɪən] ADJ mediterrâneo; **the ~ (Sea)** o (mar) Mediterrâneo

medium ['mi:dɪəm] ADJ médio ▶ N (pl **media** or **mediums**) (means) meio; (pl **mediums**) (person) médium m/f; **the happy ~** o justo meio

medium-sized [-saɪzd] ADJ de tamanho médio

medium wave N (Radio) onda média

medley ['mɛdlɪ] N mistura; (Mus) pot-pourri m

meek [mi:k] ADJ manso, dócil

meet [mi:t] (pt, pp **met**) VT (gen) encontrar; (accidentally) topar com, dar de cara com; (by arrangement) encontrar-se com, ir ao encontro de; (for the first time) conhecer; (go and fetch) ir buscar; (opponent, problem) enfrentar; (obligations) cumprir; (need) satisfazer ▶ VI encontrar-se; (for talks) reunir-se; (join: objects) unir-se; (get to know) conhecer-se ▶ N (BRIT Hunting) reunião f de caçadores; (US Sport) promoção f, competição f; **pleased to ~ you!** prazer em conhecê-lo/-la

▶ **meet up** VI: **to ~ up with sb** encontrar-se com alguém

▶ **meet with** VT FUS reunir-se com; (face: difficulty) encontrar

meeting ['mi:tɪŋ] N encontro; (session: of club, Comm) reunião f; (assembly: of people, Pol) assembleia; (interview) entrevista; (Sport) corrida; **she's in** or **at a ~** ela está em conferência; **to call a ~** convocar uma reunião

meeting place N ponto de encontro

megabyte ['mɛɡəbaɪt] N (Comput) megabyte m

megalomaniac [mɛɡələu'meɪnɪæk] ADJ, N megalomaníaco(-a)

megaphone ['mɛɡəfəun] N megafone m

megapixel ['mɛɡəpɪksl] N megapixel m

melancholy ['mɛlənkəlɪ] N melancolia ▶ ADJ melancólico

melee ['mɛleɪ] N briga, refrega

mellow ['mɛləu] ADJ (sound) melodioso, suave; (colour, wine) suave; (fruit) maduro ▶ VI (person) amadurecer

melodious [mɪ'ləudɪəs] ADJ melodioso

melodrama ['mɛləudrɑːmə] ADJ melodrama m

melodramatic [mɛlədrə'mætɪk] ADJ melodramático

melody ['mɛlədɪ] N melodia

melon ['mɛlən] N melão m

melt [mɛlt] VI (metal) fundir-se; (snow) derreter; (fig) desvanecer-se ▶ VT derreter

▶ **melt away** VI desaparecer

▶ **melt down** VT fundir

meltdown ['mɛltdaun] N fusão f

melting point ['mɛltɪŋ-] N ponto de fusão

melting pot ['mɛltɪŋ-] N (fig) mistura

member ['mɛmbə˞] N membro(-a); (of club) sócio(-a); (Anat) membro ▶ CPD: **~ state** estado membro; **M~ of Parliament** (BRIT) deputado(-a); **M~ of the European Parliament** (BRIT) Membro(-a) do Parlamento Europeu; **M~ of the House of Representatives** (US) membro(-a) da Câmara dos representantes

membership ['mɛmbəʃɪp] N (state) adesão f; (of club) associação f; (members) número de sócios; **to seek ~ of** candidatar-se a sócio de

membership card N carteira de sócio

membrane ['mɛmbreɪn] N membrana

memento [mə'mɛntəu] (pl **mementos** or **mementoes**) N lembrança

memo ['mɛməu] N memorando, nota

memoirs ['mɛmwɑːz] NPL memórias fpl

memo pad N bloco de memorando

memorable ['mɛmərəbl] ADJ memorável

memoranda [mɛmə'rændə] NPL of **memorandum**

memorandum [mɛmə'rændəm] (pl **memoranda**) N memorando

memorial [mɪ'mɔːrɪəl] N monumento comemorativo ▶ ADJ comemorativo

Memorial Day (US) N ver nota

> **Memorial Day** é um feriado nos Estados Unidos, a última segunda-feira de maio na maior parte dos estados, em memória aos soldados americanos mortos em combate.

memorize ['mɛməraɪz] VT decorar, aprender de cor

memory ['mɛmərɪ] N memória; (recollection) lembrança; (of dead person): **in ~ of** em memória de; **to have a good/bad ~** ter memória boa/ruim; **loss of ~** perda de memória

memory stick N (Comput: flash pen) pen drive m; (card) cartão m de memória

men [mɛn] NPL of **man**

menace ['mɛnəs] N ameaça; (nuisance) droga ▶ VT ameaçar

menacing ['mɛnəsɪŋ] ADJ ameaçador(a)

menagerie [mə'nædʒərɪ] N coleção f de animais

mend [mɛnd] VT consertar, reparar; (darn) remendar ▶ N remendo; **to be on the ~** estar melhorando

mending ['mɛndɪŋ] N conserto, reparo; (clothes) roupas fpl por consertar

menial ['mi:nɪəl] ADJ (often pej) humilde, subalterno

meningitis [mɛnɪn'dʒaɪtɪs] N meningite f

menopause ['mɛnəupɔːz] N menopausa
menservants ['mɛnsəːvənts] NPL *of*
  manservant
menstruate ['mɛnstrueɪt] VI menstruar
menstruation [mɛnstru'eɪʃən] N
  menstruação *f*
mental ['mɛntl] ADJ mental; ~ **illness** doença
  mental
mentality [mɛn'tælɪtɪ] N mentalidade *f*
mentally ['mɛntlɪ] ADV: **to be ~ handicapped**
  ser deficiente mental
menthol ['mɛnθɒl] N mentol *m*
mention ['mɛnʃən] N menção *f* ▶ VT
  mencionar; (*speak of*) falar de; **don't ~ it!**
  não tem de quê!, de nada!; **I need hardly ~**
  that ... não preciso dizer que ...; **not to ~ ...,**
  without ~ing ... para não falar de ..., sem
  falar de ...
mentor ['mɛntɔːʳ] N mentor *m*
menu ['mɛnjuː] N (*set menu, Comput*) menu *m*;
  (*printed*) cardápio (BR), ementa (PT)
menu-driven ADJ (*Comput*) que se navega
  através de menus
MEP N ABBR (= *Member of the European Parliament*)
  deputado(-a)
mercantile ['məːkəntaɪl] ADJ mercantil; (*law*)
  comercial
mercenary ['məːsɪnərɪ] ADJ mercenário ▶ N
  mercenário
merchandise ['məːtʃəndaɪz] N mercadorias *fpl*
  ▶ VT comercializar
merchandiser ['məːtʃəndaɪzəʳ] N
  comerciante *m/f*
merchant ['məːtʃənt] N comerciante *m/f*;
  timber/wine ~ negociante de madeira/
  vinhos
merchant bank (BRIT) N banco mercantil
merchantman ['məːtʃəntmən] (*irreg: like* **man**)
  N navio mercante
merchant navy, (US) **merchant marine** N
  marinha mercante
merciful ['məːsɪful] ADJ (*person*)
  misericordioso, humano; (*release*)
  afortunado
mercifully ['məːsɪflɪ] ADV
  misericordiosamente, generosamente;
  (*fortunately*) graças a Deus, felizmente
merciless ['məːsɪlɪs] ADJ desumano,
  inclemente
mercurial [məː'kjuərɪəl] ADJ volúvel; (*lively*)
  vivo
mercury ['məːkjurɪ] N mercúrio
mercy ['məːsɪ] N piedade *f*; (*Rel*) misericórdia;
  to have ~ on sb apiedar-se de alguém; **at**
  the ~ of à mercê de
mercy killing N eutanásia
mere [mɪəʳ] ADJ mero, simples *inv*
merely ['mɪəlɪ] ADV simplesmente, somente,
  apenas
merge [məːdʒ] VT (*join*) unir; (*mix*) misturar;
  (*Comm*) fundir; (*Comput*) intercalar ▶ VI
  unir-se; (*Comm*) fundir-se
merger ['məːdʒəʳ] N (*Comm*) fusão *f*

meridian [mə'rɪdɪən] N meridiano
meringue [mə'ræŋ] N suspiro, merengue *m*
merit ['mɛrɪt] N mérito; (*advantage*)
  vantagem *f* ▶ VT merecer
meritocracy [mɛrɪ'tɔkrəsɪ] N sistema *m* social
  baseado no mérito
mermaid ['məːmeɪd] N sereia
merrily ['mɛrɪlɪ] ADV alegremente, com
  alegria
merriment ['mɛrɪmənt] N alegria
merry ['mɛrɪ] ADJ alegre; **M~ Christmas!**
  Feliz Natal!
merry-go-round N carrossel *m*
mesh [mɛʃ] N malha; (*Tech*) engrenagem *f*
  ▶ VI (*gears*) engrenar
mesmerize ['mɛzməraɪz] VT hipnotizar
mess [mɛs] N (*situation*) confusão *f*; (*of objects*)
  desordem *f*; (*in room*) bagunça; (*Mil*) rancho;
  to be in a ~ (*untidy*) ser uma bagunça, estar
  numa bagunça; (*fig: marriage, life*) estar
  bagunçado; **to be/get o.s. in a ~** (*fig*)
  meter-se numa encrenca
  ▶ **mess about** (*inf*) VI perder tempo; (*pass the*
  time) vadiar
  ▶ **mess about with** (*inf*) VT FUS mexer com
  ▶ **mess around** (*inf*) VI = **mess about**
  ▶ **mess around with** (*inf*) VT FUS = **mess**
  about with
  ▶ **mess up** VT (*disarrange*) desarrumar; (*spoil*)
  estragar; (*dirty*) sujar
message ['mɛsɪdʒ] N recado, mensagem *f*
  ▶ VT (*contact*) enviar uma mensagem para;
  to get the ~ (*fig: inf*) sacar, pescar
message board N (*on Internet*) fórum *m* de
  discussão
messenger ['mɛsɪndʒəʳ] N mensageiro(-a)
Messiah [mɪ'saɪə] N Messias *m*
Messrs ['mɛsəz] ABBR (*on letters*: = *messieurs*) Srs
messy ['mɛsɪ] ADJ (*dirty*) sujo; (*untidy*)
  desarrumado; (*confused*) bagunçado
Met [mɛt] (US) N ABBR = **Metropolitan Opera**
met [mɛt] PT, PP *of* **meet** ▶ ADJ ABBR
  = **meteorological**
metabolism [mɛ'tæbəlɪzəm] N metabolismo
metal ['mɛtl] N metal *m* ▶ VT (*road*) empedrar
metallic [mɛ'tælɪk] ADJ metálico
metallurgy [mɛ'tælədʒɪ] N metalurgia
metalwork ['mɛtlwəːk] N (*craft*) trabalho em
  metal
metamorphosis [mɛtə'mɔːfəsɪs] (*pl*
  metamorphoses) N metamorfose *f*
metaphor ['mɛtəfəʳ] N metáfora
metaphysics [mɛtə'fɪzɪks] N metafísica
meteor ['miːtɪəʳ] N meteoro
meteoric [miːtɪ'ɔrɪk] ADJ (*fig*) meteórico
meteorite ['miːtɪəraɪt] N meteorito
meteorological [miːtɪərə'lɔdʒɪkl] ADJ
  meteorológico
meteorology [miːtɪə'rɔlədʒɪ] N meteorologia
mete out [miːt-] VT infligir
meter ['miːtəʳ] N (*instrument*) medidor *m*; (*also*:
  parking meter) parcômetro; (US: *unit*)
  = **metre**

m

methane ['mi:θeɪn] N metano
method ['mεθəd] N método; **~ of payment**
modalidade de pagamento
methodical [mɪ'θɒdɪkl] ADJ metódico
Methodist ['mεθədɪst] ADJ, N metodista m/f
methodology [mεθəd'ɒlədʒɪ] N metodologia
meths [mεθs] (BRIT) N = **methylated spirit**
methylated spirit ['mεθɪleɪtɪd-] (BRIT) N
álcool m metílico or desnaturado
meticulous [mε'tɪkjuləs] ADJ meticuloso
metre, (US) **meter** ['mi:tər] N metro
metric ['mεtrɪk] ADJ métrico; **to go ~** adotar o
sistema métrico decimal
metrical ['mεtrɪkl] ADJ métrico
metrication [mεtrɪ'keɪʃən] N conversão f ao
sistema métrico decimal
metric system N sistema m métrico decimal
metric ton N tonelada (métrica)
metronome ['mεtrənəum] N metrônomo
metropolis [mɪ'trɒpəlɪs] N metrópole f
metropolitan [mεtrə'pɒlɪtən] ADJ
metropolitano
Metropolitan Police (BRIT) N: **the ~** a polícia
de Londres
mettle ['mεtl] N (spirit) caráter m, têmpera;
(courage) coragem f
mew [mju:] VI (cat) miar
mews [mju:z] (BRIT) N: **~ cottage** pequena casa
resultante de reforma de antigos estábulos
Mexican ['mεksɪkən] ADJ, N mexicano(-a)
Mexico ['mεksɪkəu] N México
Mexico City N Cidade f do México
mezzanine ['mεtsəni:n] N sobreloja,
mezanino
MFA (US) N ABBR (= Master of Fine Arts) grau
universitário
mfr ABBR = **manufacture**; **manufacturer**
mg ABBR (= milligram) mg
Mgr ABBR = **Monseigneur**; **Monsignor**;
(= manager) dir
MHR (US) N ABBR = **Member of the House of
Representatives**
MHz ABBR (= megahertz) MHz
MI (US) ABBR (Post) = **Michigan**
MI5 (BRIT) N ABBR (= Military Intelligence 5) ≈ SNI m
MI6 (BRIT) N ABBR (= Military Intelligence 6) ≈ SNI m
MIA ABBR = **missing in action**
miaow [mi:'au] VI miar
mice [maɪs] NPL of **mouse**
micro ['maɪkrəu] N (also: **microcomputer**)
micro(computador) m
micro... [maɪkrəu] PREFIX micro
microbe ['maɪkrəub] N micróbio
microbiology [maɪkrəubaɪ'ɒlədʒɪ] N
microbiologia
microblog ['maɪkrəublɒg] N microblog(ue) m
microchip ['maɪkrəutʃɪp] N microchip m
microcomputer ['maɪkrəukəm'pju:tər] N
microcomputador m
microcosm ['maɪkrəukɒzəm] N microcosmo
microeconomics [maɪkrəui:kə'nɒmɪks] N
microeconomia
microfiche ['maɪkrəufi:ʃ] N microficha

microfilm ['maɪkrəufɪlm] N microfilme m
▶ VT microfilmar
microlight ['maɪkrəulaɪt] N ultraleve m
micrometer [maɪ'krɒmɪtər] N micrômetro
microphone ['maɪkrəfəun] N microfone m
microprocessor [maɪkrəu'prəusεsər] N
microprocessador m
microscope ['maɪkrəskəup] N microscópio;
under the ~ com microscópio
microscopic [maɪkrə'skɒpɪk] ADJ
microscópico
microwave ['maɪkrəuweɪv] N (also:
microwave oven) micro-ondas m inv
mid [mɪd] ADJ: **in ~ May** em meados de maio;
in ~ afternoon no meio da tarde; **in ~ air**
em pleno ar; **he's in his ~ thirties** ele tem
trinta e poucos anos
midday ['mɪddeɪ] N meio-dia m
middle ['mɪdl] N meio; (waist) cintura ▶ ADJ
meio; (quantity, size) médio, mediano; **in
the ~ of the night** no meio da noite; **I'm
in the ~ of reading it** estou no meio da
leitura
middle age N meia-idade f ▶ CPD: **middle-
age spread** barriga de meia-idade
middle-aged ADJ de meia-idade
Middle Ages NPL: **the ~** a Idade Média
middle class N: **the ~(es)** a classe média ▶ ADJ
(also: **middle-class**) de classe média
Middle East N: **the ~** o Oriente Médio
middleman ['mɪdlmæn] (irreg: like **man**) N
intermediário; (Comm) atravessador m
middle management N escalão gerencial
intermediário
middlemen ['mɪdlmεn] NPL of **middleman**
middle name N segundo nome m
middle-of-the-road ADJ (policy) de meio-
termo; (music) romântico
middleweight ['mɪdlweɪt] N (Boxing) peso
médio
middling ['mɪdlɪŋ] ADJ mediano
midge [mɪdʒ] N mosquito
midget ['mɪdʒɪt] N anão(-anã) m/f ▶ ADJ
minúsculo
Midlands ['mɪdləndz] NPL região central da
Inglaterra
midnight ['mɪdnaɪt] N meia-noite f; **at ~**
à meia-noite
midriff ['mɪdrɪf] N barriga
midst [mɪdst] N: **in the ~ of** no meio de,
entre
midsummer [mɪd'sʌmər] N: **a ~ day** um dia
em pleno verão
midway [mɪd'weɪ] ADJ, ADV: **~ (between)** no
meio do caminho (entre)
midweek [mɪd'wi:k] ADV no meio da semana
midwife ['mɪdwaɪf] (pl **midwives**) N parteira
midwifery ['mɪdwɪfərɪ] N trabalho de
parteira, obstetrícia
midwinter [mɪd'wɪntər] N: **in ~** em pleno
inverno
midwives ['mɪdwaɪvz] NPL of **midwife**
might [maɪt] VB see **may** ▶ N poder m, força

mighty ['maɪtɪ] ADJ poderoso, forte ▶ ADV (inf):
~ ... ... pra burro

migraine ['miːɡreɪn] N enxaqueca

migrant ['maɪɡrənt] N (bird) ave f de arribação;
(person) emigrante m/f; (fig) nômade m/f ▶ ADJ
migratório; (worker) emigrante

migrate [maɪˈɡreɪt] VI emigrar; (birds) arribar

migration [maɪˈɡreɪʃən] N emigração f; (of
birds) arribação f

mike [maɪk] N ABBR = **microphone**

mild [maɪld] ADJ (character) pacífico; (climate)
temperado; (slight) ligeiro; (taste) suave;
(illness) leve, benigno; (interest) pequeno ▶ N
cerveja ligeira

mildew ['mɪldjuː] N mofo; (Bot) míldio

mildly ['maɪldlɪ] ADV brandamente; (slightly)
ligeiramente, um tanto; **to put it ~** (inf) para
não dizer coisa pior

mildness ['maɪldnɪs] N (softness) suavidade f;
(gentleness) doçura; (quiet character) brandura

mile [maɪl] N milha (1609 m); **to do 30 ~s per
gallon** ≈ fazer 10.64 quilômetros por litro

mileage ['maɪlɪdʒ] N número de milhas; (Aut)
≈ quilometragem f

mileage allowance N ≈ ajuda de custo com
base na quilometragem rodada

mileometer [maɪˈlɒmɪtəʳ] (BRIT) N ≈ conta-
quilômetros m inv

milestone ['maɪlstəun] N marco miliário;
(event) marco

milieu ['miːljəː] (pl **milieus** or **milieux**) N meio,
meio social

milieux ['miːljəːz] NPL of **milieu**

militant ['mɪlɪtnt] ADJ, N militante m/f

militarism ['mɪlɪtərɪzəm] N militarismo

militaristic [mɪlɪtəˈrɪstɪk] ADJ militarista

military ['mɪlɪtərɪ] ADJ militar ▶ N: **the ~** as
forças armadas, os militares

militate ['mɪlɪteɪt] VI: **to ~ against** militar
contra

militia [mɪˈlɪʃə] N milícia

milk [mɪlk] N leite m ▶ VT (cow) ordenhar; (fig)
explorar, chupar

milk chocolate N chocolate m de leite

milk float (BRIT) N furgão m de leiteiro

milking ['mɪlkɪŋ] N ordenhação f, ordenha

milkman ['mɪlkmən] (irreg: like **man**) N leiteiro

milk shake N milk-shake m, leite m batido
com sorvete

milk tooth (irreg: like **tooth**) N dente m de leite

milk truck (US) N = **milk float**

milky ['mɪlkɪ] ADJ leitoso

Milky Way N Via Láctea

mill [mɪl] N (windmill etc) moinho; (coffee mill)
moedor m de café; (factory) moinho,
engenho; (spinning mill) fábrica de tecelagem,
fiação f ▶ VT moer ▶ VI (also: **mill about**)
aglomerar-se, remoinhar

millennia [mɪˈlɛnɪə] NPL of **millennium**

millennium [mɪˈlɛnɪəm] (pl **millenniums** or
millennia) N milênio, milenário

miller ['mɪləʳ] N moleiro(-a)

millet ['mɪlɪt] N milhete m

milli... ['mɪlɪ] PREFIX mili...

milligram, milligramme ['mɪlɪɡræm] N
miligrama m

millilitre, (US) milliliter ['mɪlɪliːtəʳ] N mililitro

millimetre, (US) millimeter ['mɪlɪmiːtəʳ] N
milímetro

milliner ['mɪlɪnəʳ] N chapeleiro(-a) de
senhoras

millinery ['mɪlɪnərɪ] N chapelaria de
senhoras

million ['mɪljən] N milhão m; **a ~ times** um
milhão de vezes

millionaire [mɪljəˈnɛəʳ] N milionário(-a)

millionth [-θ] NUM milionésimo

millipede ['mɪlɪpiːd] N embuá m

millstone ['mɪlstəun] N mó f, pedra (de
moinho)

millwheel ['mɪlwiːl] N roda de azenha

milometer [maɪˈlɒmɪtəʳ] N = **mileometer**

mime [maɪm] N mimo; (actor) mímico(-a),
comediante m/f ▶ VT imitar ▶ VI fazer
mímica

mimic ['mɪmɪk] N mímico(-a), imitador(a) m/f
▶ VT imitar, parodiar

mimicry ['mɪmɪkrɪ] N imitação f; (Zool)
mimetismo

Min. (BRIT) ABBR (Pol) = **ministry**

min. ABBR (= minute, minimum) min.

minaret [mɪnəˈrɛt] N minarete m

mince [mɪns] VT moer ▶ VI (in walking) andar
com afetação ▶ N (BRIT Culin) carne f moída;
he does not ~ (his) words ele não tem
papas na língua

mincemeat ['mɪnsmiːt] N recheio de sebo e frutas
picadas; (US: meat) carne f moída

mince pie N pastel com recheio de sebo e frutas
picadas

mincer ['mɪnsəʳ] N moedor m de carne

mincing ['mɪnsɪŋ] ADJ afetado

mind [maɪnd] N mente f; (intellect) intelecto;
(opinion): **to my ~** a meu ver; (sanity): **to be
out of one's ~** estar fora de si ▶ VT (attend to,
look after) tomar conta de, cuidar de; (be careful
of) ter cuidado com; (object to): **I don't ~ the
noise** o barulho não me incomoda; **do you ~
if ...?** você se incomoda se ...?; **it is on my ~**
não me sai da cabeça; **to keep** or **bear sth in
~** levar algo em consideração, não
esquecer-se de algo; **to make up one's ~**
decidir-se; **I don't ~** (it doesn't worry me) eu
nem ligo; (it's all the same to me) para mim
tanto faz; **~ you, ...** se bem que ...; **never ~!**
não faz mal, não importa!; (don't worry) não se
preocupe!; **to change one's ~** mudar de
ideia; **to be in two ~s about sth** (BRIT) estar
dividido em relação a algo; **to have sb/sth
in ~** ter alguém/algo em mente; **to have in
~ to do** pretender fazer; **it went right out
of my ~** saiu-me totalmente da cabeça; **to
bring** or **call sth to ~** lembrar algo; **"~ the
step"** "cuidado com o degrau"

mind-boggling ['maɪndbɒɡlɪŋ] ADJ (inf)
alucinante

-minded ['maɪndɪd] SUFFIX: **fair~** imparcial, justo; **an industrially~ nation** uma nação de vocação industrial

minder ['maɪndə^r] N (*childminder*) pessoa que toma conta de crianças; (*bodyguard*) guarda-costas *m/f inv*

mindful ['maɪndful] ADJ: **~ of** consciente de, atento a

mindless ['maɪndlɪs] ADJ estúpido; (*violence, crime*) insensato; (*job*) monótono

mine¹ [maɪn] PRON o meu/a minha; **that book is ~** esso livro é meu; **these cases are ~** estas caixas são minhas; **this is ~** este é meu; **yours is red, ~ is green** o seu é vermelho, o meu é verde; **a friend of ~** um amigo meu

mine² [maɪn] N mina ▶ VT (*coal*) extrair, explorar; (*ship, beach*) minar

mine detector N detector *m* de minas

minefield ['maɪnfi:ld] N campo minado; (*fig*) área delicada

miner ['maɪnə^r] N mineiro

mineral ['mɪnərəl] ADJ mineral ▶ N mineral *m*; **minerals** NPL (*BRIT: soft drinks*) refrigerantes *mpl*

mineralogy [mɪnə'rælədʒɪ] N mineralogia

mineral water N água mineral

minesweeper ['maɪnswi:pə^r] N caça-minas *m inv*

mingle ['mɪŋgl] VT misturar ▶ VI: **to ~ with** misturar-se com

mingy ['mɪndʒɪ] (*inf*) ADJ sovina, pão-duro *inv* (*BR*)

miniature ['mɪnətʃə^r] ADJ em miniatura ▶ N miniatura

minibus ['mɪnɪbʌs] N micro-ônibus *m*

minicab ['mɪnɪkæb] (*BRIT*) N ≈ (táxi *m*) cooperativado

minicomputer ['mɪnɪkəm'pju:tə^r] N minicomputador *m*, míni *m*

MiniDisc® ['mɪnɪdɪsk] N MiniDisc® *m*

minim ['mɪnɪm] N (*Mus*) mínima

minima ['mɪnɪmə] NPL *of* **minimum**

minimal ['mɪnɪml] ADJ mínimo

minimize ['mɪnɪmaɪz] VT minimizar

minimum ['mɪnɪməm] ADJ mínimo ▶ N (*pl* **minima**) mínimo; **to reduce to a ~** reduzir ao mínimo

minimum lending rate N (*Econ*) taxa mínima de empréstimos

minimum wage N salário mínimo

mining ['maɪnɪŋ] N exploração *f* de minas ▶ ADJ mineiro

minion ['mɪnjən] (*pej*) N lacaio

miniscule ['mɪnəskju:l] ADJ minúsculo

miniskirt ['mɪnɪskə:t] N minissaia

minister ['mɪnɪstə^r] N (*BRIT Pol*) ministro(-a); (*Rel*) pastor *m* ▶ VI: **to ~ to sb** prestar assistência a alguém; **to ~ to sb's needs** atender às necessidades de alguém

ministerial [mɪnɪs'tɪərɪəl] (*BRIT*) ADJ (*Pol*) ministerial

ministry ['mɪnɪstrɪ] N (*BRIT Pol*) ministério;

(*Rel*): **to go into the ~** ingressar no sacerdócio

mink [mɪŋk] N marta

mink coat N casaco de marta

minnow ['mɪnəu] N peixinho (de água doce)

minor ['maɪnə^r] ADJ menor; (*unimportant*) de pouca importância; (*inferior*) inferior; (*Mus*) menor ▶ N (*Law*) menor *m/f* de idade

Minorca [mɪ'nɔ:kə] N Minorca

minority [maɪ'nɔrɪtɪ] N minoria; (*age*) menoridade *f*; **to be in a ~** estar em minoria

minster ['mɪnstə^r] N catedral *f*

minstrel ['mɪnstrəl] N menestrel *m*

mint [mɪnt] N (*plant*) hortelã *f*; (*sweet*) bala de hortelã ▶ VT (*coins*) cunhar; **the (Royal) M~** (*BRIT*) *or* **the (US) M~** (*US*) ≈ a Casa da Moeda; **in ~ condition** em perfeito estado

mint sauce N molho de hortelã

minuet [mɪnju'ɛt] N minueto

minus ['maɪnəs] N (*also*: **minus sign**) sinal *m* de subtração ▶ PREP menos; (*without*) sem

minute¹ ['mɪnɪt] N minuto; (*official record*) ata; **minutes** NPL (*of meeting*) atas *fpl*; **it is 5 ~s past 3** são 3 e 5; **wait a ~!** (espere) um minuto *or* minutinho!; **at the last ~** no último momento; **to leave sth till the last ~** deixar algo até em cima da hora; **up to the ~** (*fashion*) último; (*news*) de última hora; **up to the ~ technology** a última tecnologia

minute² [maɪ'nju:t] ADJ miúdo, diminuto; (*search*) minucioso; **in ~ detail** por miúdo, em miúdos

minute book N livro de atas

minute hand N ponteiro dos minutos

minutely [maɪ'nju:tlɪ] ADV (*by a small amount*) ligeiramente; (*in detail*) minuciosamente

miracle ['mɪrəkl] N milagre *m*

miraculous [mɪ'rækjuləs] ADJ milagroso

mirage ['mɪrɑ:ʒ] N miragem *f*

mire ['maɪə^r] N lamaçal *m*

mirror ['mɪrə^r] N espelho; (*in car*) retrovisor *m* ▶ VT refletir

mirror image N imagem *f* de espelho

mirth [mə:θ] N alegria; (*laughter*) risada

misadventure [mɪsəd'ventʃə^r] N desgraça, infortúnio; **death by ~** (*BRIT*) morte acidental

misanthropist [mɪ'zænθrəpɪst] N misantropo(-a)

misapply [mɪsə'plaɪ] VT empregar mal

misapprehension [mɪsæprɪ'hɛnʃən] N mal-entendido, equívoco

misappropriate [mɪsə'prəuprɪeɪt] VT desviar

misappropriation [mɪsəprəuprɪ'eɪʃən] N desvio

misbehave [mɪsbɪ'heɪv] VI comportar-se mal

misbehaviour, (*US*) **misbehavior** [mɪsbɪ'heɪvjə^r] N mau comportamento

misc. ABBR = **miscellaneous**

miscalculate [mɪs'kælkjuleɪt] VT calcular mal

miscalculation [mɪskælkju'leɪʃən] N erro de cálculo

miscarriage ['mɪskærɪdʒ] N (Med) aborto (espontâneo); (failure): **~ of justice** erro judicial

miscarry [mɪs'kærɪ] VI (Med) abortar espontaneamente; (fail: plans) fracassar

miscellaneous [mɪsɪ'leɪnɪəs] ADJ (items, expenses) diverso; (selection) variado

miscellany [mɪ'selənɪ] N coletânea

mischance [mɪs'tʃɑːns] N infelicidade f, azar m

mischief ['mɪstʃɪf] N (naughtiness) travessura; (fun) diabrura; (harm) dano, prejuízo; (maliciousness) malícia

mischievous ['mɪstʃɪvəs] ADJ malicioso; (naughty) travesso; (playful) traquino

misconception [mɪskən'sɛpʃən] N concepção f errada, conceito errado

misconduct [mɪs'kɔndʌkt] N comportamento impróprio; **professional ~** má conduta profissional

misconstrue [mɪskən'struː] VT interpretar mal

miscount [mɪs'kaunt] VT, VI contar mal

misdeed [mɪs'diːd] N delito, ofensa

misdemeanour, (US) **misdemeanor** [mɪsdɪ'miːnəʳ] N má ação, contravenção f

misdirect [mɪsdɪ'rɛkt] VT (person) orientar or informar mal; (letter) endereçar mal

miser ['maɪzəʳ] N avaro(-a), sovina m/f

miserable ['mɪzərəbl] ADJ (unhappy) triste; (wretched) miserável; (unpleasant: weather, person) deprimente; (contemptible: offer) desprezível; (: failure) humilhante; **to feel ~** estar na fossa, estar de baixo astral

miserably ['mɪzərəblɪ] ADV (smile, answer) tristemente; (fail, live, pay) miseravelmente

miserly ['maɪzəlɪ] ADJ avarento, mesquinho

misery ['mɪzərɪ] N (unhappiness) tristeza; (wretchedness) miséria

misfire [mɪs'faɪəʳ] VI falhar

misfit ['mɪsfɪt] N (person) inadaptado(-a), deslocado(-a)

misfortune [mɪs'fɔːtʃən] N desgraça, infortúnio

misgiving [mɪs'gɪvɪŋ] N, **misgivings** NPL (mistrust) desconfiança, receio; (apprehension) mau pressentimento; **to have ~s about sth** ter desconfianças em relação a algo

misguided [mɪs'gaɪdɪd] ADJ enganado

mishandle [mɪs'hændl] VT (treat roughly) maltratar; (mismanage) manejar mal

mishap ['mɪshæp] N desgraça, contratempo

mishear [mɪs'hɪəʳ] (irreg: like **hear**) VT ouvir mal

mishmash ['mɪʃmæʃ] (inf) N mixórdia, salada

misinform [mɪsɪn'fɔːm] VT informar mal

misinterpret [mɪsɪn'təːprɪt] VT interpretar mal

misinterpretation [mɪsɪntəːprɪ'teɪʃən] N interpretação f errônea

misjudge [mɪs'dʒʌdʒ] VT fazer um juízo errado de, julgar mal

mislay [mɪs'leɪ] (irreg: like **lay**) VT extraviar, perder

mislead [mɪs'liːd] (irreg: like **lead**) VT induzir em erro, enganar

misleading [mɪs'liːdɪŋ] ADJ enganoso, errôneo

misled [mɪs'lɛd] PT, PP of **mislead**

mismanage [mɪs'mænɪdʒ] VT administrar mal; (situation) tratar de modo ineficiente

mismanagement [mɪs'mænɪdʒmənt] N má administração f

misnomer [mɪs'nəuməʳ] N termo impróprio or errado

misogynist [mɪ'sɔdʒɪnɪst] N misógino

misplace [mɪs'pleɪs] VT (lose) extraviar, perder; (wrongly) colocar em lugar errado; **to be ~d** (trust etc) ser imerecido

misprint ['mɪsprɪnt] N erro tipográfico

mispronounce [mɪsprə'nauns] VT pronunciar mal

misquote [mɪs'kwəut] VT citar incorretamente

misread [mɪs'riːd] (irreg: like **read**) VT interpretar or ler mal

misrepresent [mɪsrɛprɪ'zɛnt] VT desvirtuar, deturpar

Miss [mɪs] N Senhorita (BR), a menina (PT); **Dear ~ Smith** Ilma. Srta. Smith (BR), Exma. Sra. Smith (PT)

miss [mɪs] VT (train, class, opportunity) perder; (fail to hit) errar, não acertar em; (fail to see): **you can't ~ it** e impossível não ver; (notice loss of: money etc) dar por falta de; (regret the absence of): **I ~ him** sinto a falta dele ▶ VI falhar ▶ N (shot) tiro perdido or errado; (fig): **that was a near ~** (near accident) essa foi por pouco; **the bus just ~ed the wall** o ônibus por pouco não bateu no muro; **you're ~ing the point** você não está entendendo
  ▶ **miss out** (BRIT) VT omitir
  ▶ **miss out on** VT FUS perder, ficar por fora de

missal ['mɪsl] N missal m

misshapen [mɪs'ʃeɪpən] ADJ disforme

missile ['mɪsaɪl] N (Mil) míssil m; (object thrown) projétil m

missile base N base f de mísseis

missile launcher [-'lɔːntʃəʳ] N plataforma para lançamento de mísseis

missing ['mɪsɪŋ] ADJ (pupil) ausente; (thing) perdido; (removed) que está faltando; (Mil) desaparecido; **to be ~** estar desaparecido; **to go ~** desaparecer; **~ person** pessoa desaparecida

mission ['mɪʃən] N missão f; (official representatives) delegação f; **on a ~ to sb** em missão a alguém

missionary ['mɪʃənərɪ] N missionário(-a)

missive ['mɪsɪv] N missiva

misspell [mɪs'spɛl] (irreg: like **spell**) VT escrever errado, errar na ortografia de

misspent [mɪs'spɛnt] ADJ: **his ~ youth** sua juventude desperdiçada

mist [mɪst] N (light) neblina; (heavy) névoa; (at sea) bruma ▶ VI (eyes: also: **mist over**) enevoar-se; (BRIT: also: **mist over**, **mist up**: windows) embaçar

mistake [mɪs'teɪk] (irreg: like **take**) N erro, engano ▶ VT entender or interpretar mal; **by ~** por engano; **to make a ~** fazer um erro; **to make a ~ about sb/sth** enganar-se a respeito de alguém/algo; **to ~ A for B** confundir A com B

mistaken [mɪs'teɪkən] PP of **mistake** ▶ ADJ (idea etc) errado; (person) enganado; **to be ~** enganar-se, equivocar-se

mistaken identity N identidade f errada

mistakenly [mɪs'teɪkənlɪ] ADV por engano

mister ['mɪstər] (inf) N senhor m; see **Mr**

mistletoe ['mɪsltəu] N visco

mistook [mɪs'tuk] PT of **mistake**

mistranslation [mɪstræns'leɪʃən] N erro de tradução, tradução f incorreta

mistreat [mɪs'triːt] VT maltratar

mistreatment [mɪs'triːtmənt] N maus tratos mpl

mistress ['mɪstrɪs] N (lover) amante f; (of house) dona (da casa); (BRIT: in school) professora, mestra; (of situation) dona; see **Mrs**

mistrust [mɪs'trʌst] VT desconfiar de ▶ N: **~ (of)** desconfiança (em relação a)

mistrustful [mɪs'trʌstful] ADJ: **~ (of)** desconfiado (em relação a)

misty ['mɪstɪ] ADJ enevoado, nebuloso; (day) nublado; (glasses etc) embaçado

misty-eyed [-aɪd] ADJ (fig) sentimental

misunderstand [mɪsʌndə'stænd] (irreg: like **stand**) VT, VI entender or interpretar mal

misunderstanding [mɪsʌndə'stændɪŋ] N mal-entendido; (disagreement) desentendimento

misunderstood [mɪsʌndə'stud] PT, PP of **misunderstand**

misuse [n mɪs'juːs, vt mɪs'juːz] N uso impróprio; (of power) abuso; (of funds) desvio ▶ VT (use wrongly) empregar mal; abusar de; desviar

MIT (US) N ABBR = **Massachusetts Institute of Technology**

mite [maɪt] N (small quantity) pingo; (BRIT: small child) criancinha

miter ['maɪtər] (US) N = **mitre**

mitigate ['mɪtɪgeɪt] VT mitigar, atenuar; **mitigating circumstances** circunstâncias fpl atenuantes

mitigation [mɪtɪ'geɪʃən] N abrandamento, mitigação f

mitre, (US) **miter** ['maɪtər] N mitra; (Carpentry) meia-esquadria

mitt ['mɪt], **mitten** ['mɪtn] N mitene f

mix [mɪks] VT (gen) misturar; (combine) combinar ▶ VI misturar-se; (people) entrosar-se ▶ N mistura; (combination) combinação f; **to ~ sth with sth** misturar algo com algo; **to ~ business with pleasure** misturar trabalho com divertimento
▶ **mix in** VT misturar
▶ **mix up** VT (confuse: things) misturar; (: people) confundir; **to be ~ed up in sth** estar envolvido or metido em algo

mixed [mɪkst] ADJ misto; (assorted) sortido, variado

mixed blessing N: **it's a ~** é uma faca de dois gumes

mixed doubles NPL (Sport) duplas fpl mistas

mixed economy N economia mista

mixed grill (BRIT) N carnes fpl grelhadas

mixed-up ADJ (confused) confuso

mixer ['mɪksər] N (for food) batedeira; (person) pessoa sociável

mixture ['mɪkstʃər] N mistura; (Med) preparado

mix-up N trapalhada, confusão f

Mk (BRIT) ABBR (Tech) = **mark**

mk ABBR (currency) = **mark**

mkt ABBR = **market**

MLitt N ABBR (= Master of Literature, Master of Letters) grau universitário

MLR (BRIT) N ABBR = **minimum lending rate**

mm ABBR (= millimetre) mm

MN ABBR (BRIT) = **merchant navy**; (US Post) = **Minnesota**

MO N ABBR (Med) = **medical officer**; (US inf: = modus operandi) método ▶ ABBR (US Post) = **Missouri**

M.O. ABBR = **money order**

moan [məun] N gemido ▶ VI gemer; (inf: complain): **to ~ (about)** queixar-se (de), bufar (sobre) (inf)

moaning ['məunɪŋ] N gemidos mpl; (inf: complaining) queixas fpl

moat [məut] N fosso

mob [mɔb] N multidão f; (pej): **the ~** (masses) o povinho; (mafia) a máfia ▶ VT cercar

mob. ABBR (= mobile phone) cel.

mobile ['məubaɪl] ADJ móvel ▶ N móvel m; **applicants must be ~** (BRIT) os candidatos devem estar dispostos a aceitar qualquer deslocamento

mobile home N trailer m, casa móvel

mobile phone N telefone m celular (BR), telemóvel m (PT)

mobile shop (BRIT) N loja circulante

mobility [məu'bɪlɪtɪ] N mobilidade f

mobilize ['məubɪlaɪz] VT mobilizar ▶ VI mobilizar-se; (Mil) ser mobilizado

moccasin ['mɔkəsɪn] N mocassim m

mock [mɔk] VT (make ridiculous) ridicularizar; (laugh at) zombar de, gozar de ▶ ADJ falso, fingido; (exam, battle) simulado

mockery ['mɔkərɪ] N zombaria; **to make a ~ of sth** ridicularizar algo

mocking ['mɔkɪŋ] ADJ zombeteiro

mockingbird ['mɔkɪŋbəːd] N tordo-dos-remédios m

mock-up N maqueta, modelo

MOD (BRIT) N ABBR = **Ministry of Defence**

mod cons [mɔd-] (BRIT) NPL ABBR = **modern conveniences**; see **convenience**

mode [məud] N modo; (of transport) meio

model ['mɔdl] N modelo; (Arch) maqueta; (person: for fashion, Art) modelo m/f ▶ ADJ (car, toy) de brinquedo; (child, factory etc) exemplar

▶ VT modelar; (*copy*): **to ~ o.s. on** mirar-se em ▶ VI servir de modelo; (*in fashion*) trabalhar como modelo; **to ~ clothes** desfilar apresentando modelos; **to ~ sb/sth on** modelar alguém/algo a *or* por

modeller, (US) **modeler** ['mɔdlər] N modelador(a) *m/f*; (*model maker*) maquetista *m/f*

model railway N trenzinho de brinquedo

modem ['məudɛm] N modem *m*

moderate [*adj, n* 'mɔdərət, *vi, vt* 'mɔdəreit] ADJ, N moderado(-a) ▶ VI moderar-se, acalmar-se ▶ VT moderar

moderately ['mɔdərətlɪ] ADV (*act*) com moderação, moderadamente; (*pleased, happy*) razoavelmente; **~ priced** de preço médio *or* razoável

moderation [mɔdə'reɪʃən] N moderação *f*; **in ~** com moderação

modern ['mɔdən] ADJ moderno; **~ languages** línguas *fpl* vivas

modernization [mɔdənaɪ'zeɪʃən] N modernização *f*

modernize ['mɔdənaɪz] VT modernizar, atualizar

modest ['mɔdɪst] ADJ modesto

modesty ['mɔdɪstɪ] N modéstia

modicum ['mɔdɪkəm] N: **a ~ of** um mínimo de

modification [mɔdɪfɪ'keɪʃən] N modificação *f*

modify ['mɔdɪfaɪ] VT modificar

Mods [mɔdz] (BRIT) N ABBR (= (*Honour*) *Moderations*) *primeiro exame universitário (em Oxford)*

modular ['mɔdjulər] ADJ (*filing, unit*) modular

modulate ['mɔdjuleɪt] VT modular

modulation [mɔdju'leɪʃən] N modulação *f*

module ['mɔdju:l] N módulo

mogul ['məugl] N (*fig*) magnata *m*

MOH (BRIT) N ABBR = **Medical Officer of Health**

mohair ['məuhɛər] N mohair *m*, angorá *m*

Mohammed [mə'hæmɪd] N Maomé *m*

moist [mɔɪst] ADJ úmido (BR), húmido (PT), molhado

moisten ['mɔɪsn] VT umedecer (BR), humedecer (PT)

moisture ['mɔɪstʃər] N umidade *f* (BR), humidade *f* (PT)

moisturize ['mɔɪstʃəraɪz] VT (*skin*) hidratar

moisturizer ['mɔɪstʃəraɪzər] N creme *m* hidratante

mojo ['məudʒəu] (*pl* **mojos** *or* **mojoes**) (*inf*) N (*fig: power*) magia *f*

molar ['məulər] N molar *m*

molasses [məu'læsɪz] N melaço, melado

mold [məuld] (US) N, VT = **mould**

mole [məul] N (*animal*) toupeira; (*spot*) sinal *m*, lunar *m*; (*fig*) espião(-piã) *m/f*

molecule ['mɔlɪkju:l] N molécula

molehill ['məulhɪl] N montículo (feito por uma toupeira)

molest [məu'lɛst] VT molestar; (*attack sexually*) atacar sexualmente

mollusc ['mɔləsk] N molusco

mollycoddle ['mɔlɪkɔdl] VT mimar

molt [məult] (US) VI = **moult**

molten ['məultən] ADJ fundido; (*lava*) liquefeito

mom [mɔm] (US) N = **mum**

moment ['məumənt] N momento; (*importance*) importância; **at the ~** neste momento; **for the ~** por enquanto; **in a ~** num instante; **"one ~ please"** (*Tel*) "não desligue"

momentarily ['məuməntrɪlɪ] ADV momentaneamente; (US: *soon*) daqui a pouco

momentary ['məuməntərɪ] ADJ momentâneo

momentous [məu'mɛntəs] ADJ importantíssimo

momentum [məu'mɛntəm] N momento; (*fig*) ímpeto; **to gather ~** ganhar ímpeto

mommy ['mɔmɪ] (US) N = **mummy**

Mon. ABBR (= *Monday*) seg., 2ª

Monaco ['mɔnəkəu] N Mônaco (*no article*)

monarch ['mɔnək] N monarca *m/f*

monarchist ['mɔnəkɪst] N monarquista *m/f*

monarchy ['mɔnəkɪ] N monarquia

monastery ['mɔnəstərɪ] N mosteiro, convento

monastic [mə'næstɪk] ADJ monástico

Monday ['mʌndɪ] N segunda-feira; *see also* **Tuesday**

monetarist ['mʌnɪtərɪst] N monetarista *m/f*

monetary ['mʌnɪtərɪ] ADJ monetário

money ['mʌnɪ] N dinheiro; (*currency*) moeda; **to make ~** ganhar dinheiro; **I've got no ~ left** não tenho mais dinheiro

moneyed ['mʌnɪd] ADJ rico, endinheirado

moneylender ['mʌnɪlɛndər] N agiota *m/f*

moneymaking ['mʌnɪmeɪkɪŋ] ADJ lucrativo, rendoso

money market N mercado financeiro

money order N vale *m* (postal)

money-spinner (*inf*) N mina

money supply N meios *mpl* de pagamento, suprimento monetário

Mongol ['mɔŋgəl] N mongol *m/f*; (*Ling*) mongol *m*

mongol ['mɔŋgəl] ADJ, N (*offensive*) mongoloide *m/f*

Mongolia [mɔŋ'gəulɪə] N Mongólia

Mongolian [mɔŋ'gəulɪən] ADJ mongol ▶ N mongol *m/f*; (*Ling*) mongol *m*

mongoose ['mɔŋgu:s] N mangusto

mongrel ['mʌŋgrəl] N (*dog*) vira-lata *m*

monitor ['mɔnɪtər] N (*Sch*) monitor(a) *m/f*; (*Comput*) monitor *m* ▶ VT (*heartbeat, pulse*) controlar; (*broadcasts, progress*) monitorar

monk [mʌŋk] N monge *m*

monkey ['mʌŋkɪ] N macaco

monkey business N trapaça, travessura

monkey nut (BRIT) N amendoim *m*

monkey wrench N chave *f* inglesa

mono ['mɔnəu] ADJ mono *inv*

mono... ['mɔnəu] PREFIX mono...

monochrome ['mɔnəkrəum] ADJ monocromático

m

monocle ['mɔnəkl] N monóculo
monogamous [mɔ'nɔgəməs] ADJ monogâmico
monogram ['mɔnəgræm] N monograma m
monolith ['mɔnəlɪθ] N monólito
monologue ['mɔnəlɔg] N monólogo
monoplane ['mɔnəpleɪn] N monoplano
monopolize [mə'nɔpəlaɪz] VT monopolizar
monopoly [mə'nɔpəlɪ] N monopólio; **Monopolies and Mergers Commission** (BRIT) comissão de inquérito sobre os monopólios
monorail ['mɔnəureɪl] N monotrilho
monosodium glutamate [mɔnə'səudɪəm 'glu:təmeɪt] N glutamato de monossódio
monosyllabic [mɔnəusɪ'læbɪk] ADJ monossilábico; (person) lacônico
monosyllable ['mɔnəsɪləbl] N monossílabo
monotone ['mɔnətəun] N monotonia; **to speak in a ~** falar num tom monótono
monotonous [mə'nɔtənəs] ADJ monótono
monotony [mə'nɔtənɪ] N monotonia
monoxide [mɔ'nɔksaɪd] N see **carbon monoxide**
monsoon [mɔn'su:n] N monção f
monster ['mɔnstəʳ] N monstro
monstrosity [mɔns'trɔsɪtɪ] N monstruosidade f
monstrous ['mɔnstrəs] ADJ (huge) descomunal; (atrocious) monstruoso
montage [mɔn'tɑ:ʒ] N montagem f
Mont Blanc [mɔ̃blɑ̃] N Monte m Branco
Montevideo ['mɔnteɪvɪ'deɪəu] N Montevidéu
month [mʌnθ] N mês m; **every ~** todo mês; **300 dollars a ~** 300 dólares mensais or por mês
monthly ['mʌnθlɪ] ADJ mensal ▶ ADV mensalmente ▶ N (magazine) revista mensal; **twice ~** duas vezes por mês
monument ['mɔnjumənt] N monumento
monumental [mɔnju'mɛntl] ADJ monumental; (terrific) terrível
monumental mason N marmorista m/f
moo [mu:] VI mugir
mood [mu:d] N humor m; (of crowd) atmosfera; **to be in a good/bad ~** estar de bom/mau humor; **to be in the ~ for** estar a fim or com vontade de
moody ['mu:dɪ] ADJ (variable) caprichoso, de veneta; (sullen) rabugento
moon [mu:n] N lua
moonbeam ['mu:nbi:m] N raio de lua
moon landing N alunissagem f
moonlight ['mu:nlaɪt] N luar m ▶ VI ter dois empregos, ter um bico
moonlighting ['mu:nlaɪtɪŋ] N trabalho adicional, bico
moonlit ['mu:nlɪt] ADJ enluarado; **a ~ night** uma noite de lua
moonshot ['mu:nʃɔt] N (Space) lançamento de nave para a lua
moonstruck ['mu:nstrʌk] ADJ lunático, aluado
Moor [muəʳ] N mouro(-a)

moor [muəʳ] N charneca ▶ VT (ship) amarrar ▶ VI fundear, atracar
mooring ['muərɪŋ] N (place) ancoradouro; **moorings** NPL (chains) amarras fpl
Moorish ['muərɪʃ] ADJ mouro; (architecture) mourisco
moorland ['muələnd] N charneca
moose [mu:s] N INV alce m
moot [mu:t] VT levantar ▶ ADJ: **~ point** ponto discutível
mop [mɔp] N esfregão m; (for dishes) esponja com cabeça; (of hair) grenha ▶ VT esfregar ▶ **mop up** VT limpar
mope [məup] VI estar or andar deprimido or desanimado
▶ **mope about** VI andar por aí desanimado
▶ **mope around** VI = **mope about**
moped ['məupɛd] N moto f pequena (BR), motorizada (PT)
moral ['mɔrl] ADJ moral ▶ N moral f; **morals** NPL (principles) moralidade f, costumes mpl
morale [mɔ'rɑ:l] N moral f, estado de espírito
morality [mə'rælɪtɪ] N moralidade f; (correctness) retidão f, probidade f
moralize ['mɔrəlaɪz] VI: **to ~ (about)** dar lições de moral (sobre)
morally ['mɔrəlɪ] ADV moralmente
morass [mə'ræs] N pântano, brejo
moratorium [mɔrə'tɔ:rɪəm] (pl **moratoriums** or **moratoria**) N moratória
morbid ['mɔ:bɪd] ADJ mórbido

(KEYWORD)

more [mɔ:ʳ] ADJ **1** (greater in number etc) mais; **more people/work/letters than we expected** mais pessoas/trabalho/cartas do que esperávamos; **I have more wine/money than you** tenho mais vinho/dinheiro do que você
2 (additional) mais; **do you want (some) more tea?** você quer mais chá?; **I have no** or **I don't have any more money** não tenho mais dinheiro; **it'll take a few more weeks** levará mais algumas semanas
▶ PRON **1** (greater amount) mais; **more than 10** mais de 10; **it cost more than we expected** custou mais do que esperávamos
2 (further or additional amount) mais; **is there any more?** tem ainda mais?; **there's no more** não tem mais; **many/much more** muitos/muito mais
▶ ADV mais; **more dangerous/difficult** etc **than** mais perigoso/difícil etc do que; **more easily/economically/quickly (than)** mais fácil/econômico/rápido (do que); **more and more** cada vez mais; **more or less** mais ou menos; **more than ever** mais do que nunca; **more beautiful than ever** mais bonito do que nunca

moreover [mɔ:'rəuvəʳ] ADV além do mais, além disso
morgue [mɔ:g] N necrotério

MORI ['mɔrɪ] (BRIT) N ABBR (= *Market and Opinion Research Institute*) = IBOPE *m*
moribund ['mɔrɪbʌnd] ADJ agonizante
Mormon ['mɔːmən] N mórmon *m/f*
morning ['mɔːnɪŋ] N manhã *f*; (*early morning*) madrugada ▶ CPD da manhã; **good ~** bom dia; **in the ~** de manhã; **7 o'clock in the ~** (as) 7 da manhã; **3 o'clock in the ~** (as) 3 da madrugada; **tomorrow ~** amanhã de manhã; **this ~** hoje de manhã
morning sickness N náusea matinal
Moroccan [mə'rɔkən] ADJ, N marroquino(-a)
Morocco [mə'rɔkəu] N Marrocos *m*
moron ['mɔːrɔn] (*inf*) N débil mental *m/f*, idiota *m/f*
moronic [mə'rɔnɪk] ADJ imbecil, idiota
morose [mə'rəus] ADJ taciturno, rabugento
morphine ['mɔːfiːn] N morfina
Morse [mɔːs] N (*also*: **Morse code**) código Morse
morsel ['mɔːsl] N (*of food*) bocado
mortal ['mɔːtl] ADJ, N mortal *m/f*
mortality [mɔː'tælɪtɪ] N mortalidade *f*
mortality rate N (taxa de) mortalidade *f*
mortar ['mɔːtə'] N (*cannon*) morteiro; (*Constr*) argamassa; (*dish*) pilão *m*, almofariz *m*
mortgage ['mɔːgɪdʒ] N hipoteca; (*for house*) financiamento ▶ VT hipotecar; **to take out a ~** fazer um crédito imobiliário
mortgage company (US) N sociedade *f* de crédito imobiliário
mortgagee [mɔːgə'dʒiː] N credor(a) *m/f* hipotecário(-a)
mortgagor ['mɔːgədʒə'] N devedor(a) *m/f* hipotecário(-a)
mortician [mɔː'tɪʃən] (US) N agente *m/f* funerário(-a)
mortified ['mɔːtɪfaɪd] ADJ morto de vergonha
mortify ['mɔːtɪfaɪ] VT mortificar
mortise lock ['mɔːtɪs-] N fechadura embutida
mortuary ['mɔːtjuərɪ] N necrotério
mosaic [məu'zeɪɪk] N mosaico
Moscow ['mɔskəu] N Moscou (BR), Moscovo (PT)
Moslem ['mɔzləm] ADJ, N = **Muslim**
mosque [mɔsk] N mesquita
mosquito [mɔs'kiːtəu] (*pl* **mosquitoes**) N mosquito
mosquito net N mosquiteiro
moss [mɔs] N musgo
mossy ['mɔsɪ] ADJ musgoso, musguento

(KEYWORD)

most [məust] ADJ **1** (*almost all: people, things etc*) a maior parte de, a maioria de; **most people** a maioria das pessoas
2 (*largest, greatest: interest*) máximo; (*money*): **who has (the) most money?** quem é que tem mais dinheiro?; **he derived the most pleasure from her visit** ele teve o maior prazer em recebê-la
▶ PRON (*greatest quantity, number*) a maior parte, a maioria; **most of it/them** a maioria dele/deles; **most of the money** a

maior parte do dinheiro; **most of her friends** a maioria dos seus amigos; **do the most you can** faça o máximo que você puder; **I saw the most** vi mais; **to make the most of sth** aproveitar algo ao máximo; **at the (very) most** quando muito, no máximo
▶ ADV (+ *vb, adj, adv*) o mais; **the most intelligent/expensive** *etc* o mais inteligente/caro *etc*; (*very: polite, interesting etc*) muito; **a most interesting book** um livro interessantíssimo

mostly ['məustlɪ] ADV principalmente, na maior parte
MOT (BRIT) N ABBR = **Ministry of Transport**; **the ~ (test)** vistoria anual dos veículos automotores
motel [məu'tɛl] N motel *m*
moth [mɔθ] N mariposa; (*clothes moth*) traça
mothball ['mɔθbɔːl] N bola de naftalina
moth-eaten ADJ roído pelas traças
mother ['mʌðə'] N mãe *f* ▶ ADJ materno ▶ VT (*care for*) cuidar de (como uma mãe)
mother board N (*Comput*) placa-mãe *f*
motherhood ['mʌðəhud] N maternidade *f*
mother-in-law (*pl* **mothers-in-law**) N sogra
motherly ['mʌðəlɪ] ADJ maternal
mother-of-pearl N madrepérola
mother-to-be (*pl* **mothers-to-be**) N futura mamãe *f*
mother tongue N língua materna
mothproof ['mɔθpruːf] ADJ à prova de traças
motif [məu'tiːf] N motivo
motion ['məuʃən] N movimento; (*gesture*) gesto, sinal *m*; (*at meeting*) moção *f*; (BRIT: *of bowels*) fezes *fpl* ▶ VT, VI: **to ~ (to) sb to do sth** fazer sinal a alguém para que faça algo; **to be in ~** (*vehicle*) estar em movimento; **to set in ~** pôr em movimento; **to go through the ~s of doing sth** (*fig*) fazer algo automaticamente ou sem convicção
motionless ['məuʃənlɪs] ADJ imóvel
motion picture N filme *m* (cinematográfico)
motivate ['məutɪveɪt] VT motivar
motivated ['məutɪveɪtɪd] ADJ: **~ (by)** motivado (por)
motivation [məutɪ'veɪʃən] N motivação *f*
motive ['məutɪv] N motivo ▶ ADJ motor/ motriz; **from the best (of) ~s** com as melhores intenções
motley ['mɔtlɪ] ADJ variado, heterogêneo
motor ['məutə'] N motor *m*; (BRIT inf: *vehicle*) carro, automóvel *m* ▶ CPD (*industry*) de automóvel ▶ ADJ motor/motriz
motorbike ['məutəbaɪk] N moto(cicleta) *f*, motoca (*inf*)
motorboat ['məutəbəut] N barco a motor
motorcar ['məutəkaː] (BRIT) N carro, automóvel *m*
motorcoach ['məutəkəutʃ] N ônibus *m* turístico
motorcycle ['məutəsaɪkl] N motocicleta

motorcycle racing N corrida de motocicleta
motorcyclist ['məʊtəsaɪklɪst] N
motociclista m/f
motoring ['məʊtərɪŋ] (BRIT) N automobilismo
▶ ADJ (accident, offence) de trânsito; ~ **holiday**
passeio de carro
motorist ['məʊtərɪst] N motorista m/f
motorize ['məʊtəraɪz] VT motorizar
motor oil N óleo de motor
motor racing (BRIT) N corrida de carros,
automobilismo
motor scooter N lambreta (BR), motoreta (PT)
motor vehicle N automóvel m, veículo
automotor
motorway ['məʊtəweɪ] (BRIT) N rodovia (BR),
autoestrada (PT)
mottled ['mɔtld] ADJ mosqueado, em
furta-cores
motto ['mɔtəʊ] (pl **mottoes**) N lema m
mould, (US) **mold** [məʊld] N molde m;
(mildew) mofo, bolor m ▶ VT moldar; (fig)
moldar
moulder, (US) **molder** ['məʊldəᴿ] VI (decay)
desfazer-se
moulding, (US) **molding** ['məʊldɪŋ] N
moldura
mouldy, (US) **moldy** ['məʊldɪ] ADJ mofado
moult, (US) **molt** [məʊlt] VI mudar (de
penas etc)
mound [maʊnd] N (of earth) monte m; (of
blankets, leaves etc) pilha, montanha
mount [maʊnt] N monte m; (horse) montaria;
(for jewel etc) engaste m; (for picture) moldura
▶ VT (horse etc) montar em, subir a; (stairs)
subir; (exhibition) montar; (attack) montar,
desfechar; (picture) emoldurar ▶ VI (increase)
aumentar
▶ **mount up** VI aumentar
mountain ['maʊntɪn] N montanha ▶ CPD de
montanha; **to make a ~ out of a molehill**
(fig) fazer um bicho de sete cabeças or um
cavalo de batalha (de algo)
mountain bike N mountain bike f
mountaineer [maʊntɪˈnɪəᴿ] N alpinista m/f,
montanhista m/f
mountaineering [maʊntɪˈnɪərɪŋ] N
alpinismo; **to go ~** praticar o alpinismo
mountainous ['maʊntɪnəs] ADJ montanhoso
mountain rescue team N equipe m de socorro
para alpinistas
mountainside ['maʊntɪnsaɪd] N lado da
montanha
mounted ['maʊntɪd] ADJ montado
Mount Everest N monte m Everest
mourn [mɔ:n] VT chorar, lamentar ▶ VI: **to ~
for** chorar or lamentar a morte de
mourner ['mɔ:nəᴿ] N parente(-a) m/f or
amigo(-a) do defunto
mournful ['mɔ:nful] ADJ desolado, triste
mourning ['mɔ:nɪŋ] N luto ▶ CPD (dress) de
luto; **(to be) in ~** (estar) de luto
mouse [maʊs] (pl **mice**) N camundongo (BR),
rato (PT); (Comput) mouse m

mouse mat, mouse pad N (Comput) mouse
pad m
mousetrap ['maʊstræp] N ratoeira
mousse [mu:s] N musse f; (for hair) mousse f
moustache, (US) **mustache** [məsˈtɑ:ʃ] N
bigode m
mousy ['maʊsɪ] ADJ (person) tímido; (hair)
pardacento
mouth [maʊθ] (pl **mouths** [maʊðz]) N boca;
(of cave, hole) entrada; (of river)
desembocadura
mouthful ['maʊθful] N bocado
mouth organ N gaita
mouthpiece ['maʊθpi:s] N (of musical
instrument) bocal m; (representative) porta-voz
m/f
mouth-to-mouth ADJ: ~ **resuscitation**
respiração f boca-a-boca
mouthwash ['maʊθwɔʃ] N colutório
mouth-watering ADJ de dar água na boca
movable ['mu:vəbl] ADJ móvel
move [mu:v] N (movement) movimento;
(in game) lance m, jogada; (: turn to play) turno,
vez f; (change: of house, job) mudança ▶ VT
(change position of) mudar; (in game) jogar;
(hand etc) mexer, mover; (from one place to
another) deslocar; (emotionally) comover;
(Pol: resolution etc) propor ▶ VI mexer-se,
mover-se; (traffic) circular; (also: **move
house**) mudar-se; (develop: situation)
desenvolver; **to ~ sb to do sth** convencer
alguém a fazer algo; **to get a ~ on**
apressar-se; **to be ~d** (emotionally) ficar
comovido
▶ **move about** VI (fidget) mexer-se; (travel)
deslocar-se
▶ **move along** VI avançar
▶ **move around** VI = **move about**
▶ **move away** VI afastar-se
▶ **move back** VI (step back) recuar; (return)
voltar
▶ **move down** VT abaixar; (demote) rebaixar
▶ **move forward** VI avançar ▶ VT adiantar
▶ **move in** VI (to a house) instalar-se (numa
casa)
▶ **move off** VI partir
▶ **move on** VI ir andando ▶ VT (onlookers)
afastar
▶ **move out** VI (of house) sair (de uma casa)
▶ **move over** VI afastar-se; ~ **over!** (towards
speaker) chega mais para cá!; (away from
speaker) chega mais para lá!
▶ **move up** VI subir; (employee) ser
promovido; (move aside) chegar mais para
lá or cá
moveable ['mu:vəbl] ADJ = **movable**
movement ['mu:vmənt] N movimento;
(gesture) gesto; (of goods) transporte m; (in
attitude, policy) mudança; (Tech) mecanismo;
(Med: also: **bowel movement**) defecação f
mover ['mu:vəᴿ] N autor(a) m/f de proposta
movie ['mu:vɪ] N filme m; **to go to the ~s** ir
ao cinema

movie camera N câmara cinematográfica
moviegoer ['mu:vɪgəuəʳ] (US) N
frequentador(a) m/f de cinema
moving ['mu:vɪŋ] ADJ (emotional) comovente;
(that moves) móvel; (in motion) em movimento
▶ N (US) mudança
mow [məu] (pt **mowed**, pp **mowed** or **mown**)
VT (grass) cortar; (corn) ceifar
▶ **mow down** VT ceifar; (massacre) chacinar
mower ['məuəʳ] N ceifeira; (also:
lawnmower) cortador m de grama (BR) or
de relva (PT)
mown [məun] PP of **mow**
Mozambique [məuzəm'bi:k] N Moçambique
m (no article)
MP N ABBR (= Military Police) PM f; (BRIT)
= **Member of Parliament**; (CANADA)
= **Mounted Police**
MP3 player N tocador m de MP3
mpg N ABBR = **miles per gallon**
mph ABBR = **miles per hour**
MPhil N ABBR (= Master of Philosophy) grau
universitário
MPS (BRIT) N ABBR = **Member of the
Pharmaceutical Society**
Mr, (US) **Mr.** ['mɪstəʳ] N: **Mr Smith** (o) Sr.
Smith
MRC (BRIT) N ABBR = **Medical Research
Council**
MRCP (BRIT) N ABBR = **Member of the Royal
College of Physicians**
MRCS (BRIT) N ABBR = **Member of the Royal
College of Surgeons**
MRCVS (BRIT) N ABBR = **Member of the Royal
College of Veterinary Surgeons**
Mrs, (US) **Mrs.** ['mɪsɪz] N: **~ Smith** (a) Sra.
Smith
MS N ABBR (= manuscript) ms; = **multiple
sclerosis**; (US: = Master of Science) grau
universitário ▶ ABBR (US Post) = **Mississippi**
Ms, (US) **Ms.** [mɪz] N (= Miss or Mrs): **Ms X** (a)
Sra. X

> **Ms** é um título utilizado em lugar de Mrs
> (senhora) ou de Miss (senhorita) para
> evitar a distinção tradicional entre
> mulheres casadas e solteiras. É aceito,
> portanto, como o equivalente de Mr
> (senhor) para os homens. Muitas vezes
> reprovado por ter surgido como
> manifestação do feminismo
> exacerbado, é uma forma de tratamento
> muito comum hoje em dia.

MSA (US) N ABBR (= Master of Science in
Agriculture) grau universitário
MSc N ABBR = **Master of Science**
MSG N ABBR = **monosodium glutamate**
MST (US) ABBR (= Mountain Standard Time) hora de
inverno das montanhas Rochosas
MSW (US) N ABBR (= Master of Social Work) grau
universitário
MT N ABBR = **machine translation** ▶ ABBR (US
Post) = **Montana**
Mt ABBR (Geo: = mount) Mt

much [mʌtʃ] ADJ (time, money, effort) muito;
how much money/time do you need?
quanto dinheiro/tempo você precisa?; **he's
done so much work for the charity** ele
trabalhou muito para a obra de caridade;
as much as tanto como
▶ PRON muito; **there isn't much to do** não
há muito o que fazer; **much has been
gained from our discussions** nossas
discussões foram muito proveitosas; **how
much does it cost? — too much** quanto
custa isso? — caro demais; **how much is it?**
quanto é?, quanto custa?
▶ ADV **1** (greatly, a great deal) muito; **thank you
very much** muito obrigado(-a); **we are
very much looking forward to your visit**
estamos aguardando a sua visita com muito
ansiedade; **he is very much the
gentleman/politician** ele é muito
cavalheiro/político; **as much as** tanto
como; **as much as you** tanto quanto você;
I read as much as possible/as I can/as ever
leio o máximo possível/que eu posso/como
nunca; **he is as much part of the
community as you** ele faz parte da
comunidade tanto quanto você
2 (by far) de longe; **I'm much better now**
estou bem melhor agora
3 (almost) quase; **the view is much as it was
10 years ago** a vista é quase a mesma que há
dez anos; **how are you feeling? — much
the same** como você está (se sentindo)? —
do mesmo jeito

muck [mʌk] N (dirt) sujeira (BR), sujidade f
(PT); (manure) estrume m; (fig) porcaria
▶ **muck about** (inf) VI (fool about) fazer
besteiras; (waste time) fazer cera; (tinker)
mexer
▶ **muck around** VI = **muck about**
▶ **muck in** (BRIT inf) VI dar uma ajuda
▶ **muck out** VT (stable) limpar
▶ **muck up** (inf) VT (ruin) estragar; (dirty) sujar
muckraking ['mʌkreɪkɪŋ] (inf) N (Press)
sensacionalismo
mucky ['mʌkɪ] ADJ (dirty) sujo
mucus ['mju:kəs] N muco
mud [mʌd] N lama
muddle ['mʌdl] N confusão f, bagunça;
(mix-up) trapalhada ▶ VT (also: **muddle up**:
person, story) confundir; (: things) misturar;
to be in a ~ (person) estar confuso; **to get in
a ~** (while explaining etc) enrolar-se
▶ **muddle along** VI viver sem rumo
▶ **muddle through** VI virar-se
muddle-headed [-'hedɪd] ADJ (person) confuso
muddy ['mʌdɪ] ADJ (road) lamacento; (person,
clothes) enlameado
mud flats NPL extensão f de terra lamacenta
mudguard ['mʌdgɑ:d] N para-lama m
mudpack ['mʌdpæk] N máscara (de beleza)
mud-slinging [-slɪŋɪŋ] N difamação f, injúria

m

muesli ['mjuːzlɪ] N muesli *m*

muff [mʌf] N regalo ▸ VT (*chance*) desperdiçar, perder; (*lines*) estropiar

muffin ['mʌfɪn] N bolinho redondo e chato

muffle ['mʌfl] VT (*sound*) abafar; (*against cold*) agasalhar

muffled ['mʌfld] ADJ abafado, surdo

muffler ['mʌflə'] N (*scarf*) cachecol *m*; (*US Aut*) silencioso (BR), panela de escape (PT)

mufti ['mʌftɪ] N: **in ~** vestido à paisana

mug [mʌg] N (*cup*) caneca; (*for beer*) caneco, canecão; (*inf: face*) careta; (: *fool*) bobo(-a) ▸ VT (*assault*) assaltar
▸ **mug up** (BRIT *inf*) VT (*also*: **mug up on**) decorar

mugger ['mʌgə'] N assaltante *m/f*

mugging ['mʌgɪŋ] N assalto

muggy ['mʌgɪ] ADJ abafado

mulatto [mjuː'lætəu] (*pl* **mulattoes**) N mulato(-a)

mulberry ['mʌlbrɪ] N (*fruit*) amora; (*tree*) amoreira

mule [mjuːl] N mula

mulled [mʌld] ADJ: **~ wine** quentão *m*

mull over [mʌl-] VT meditar sobre

multi... [mʌltɪ] PREFIX multi...

multi-access ADJ (*Comput*) de múltiplo acesso

multicoloured, (US) **multicolored** ['mʌltɪkʌləd] ADJ multicolor

multifarious [mʌltɪ'fɛərɪəs] ADJ diverso, variado

multilateral [mʌltɪ'lætrəl] ADJ (*Pol*) multilateral

multi-level (US) ADJ = **multistorey**

multimedia [mʌltɪ'miːdɪə] ADJ multimídia

multimillionaire [mʌltɪmɪljə'nɛə'] N multimilionário(-a)

multinational [mʌltɪ'næʃənl] N multinacional *f* ▸ ADJ multinacional

multiple ['mʌltɪpl] ADJ múltiplo ▸ N múltiplo

multiple choice N múltipla escolha

multiple crash N engavetamento

multiple sclerosis [-sklɪ'rəusɪs] N esclerose *f* múltipla

multiplication [mʌltɪplɪ'keɪʃən] N multiplicação *f*

multiplication table N tabela de multiplicação

multiplicity [mʌltɪ'plɪsɪtɪ] N multiplicidade *f*

multiply ['mʌltɪplaɪ] VT multiplicar ▸ VI multiplicar-se

multiracial [mʌltɪ'reɪʃl] ADJ multirracial

multistorey ['mʌltɪ'stɔːrɪ] (BRIT) ADJ de vários andares

multitude ['mʌltɪtjuːd] N multidão *f*; (*large number*): **a ~ of** um grande número de

mum [mʌm] N (BRIT *inf*) mamãe *f* ▸ ADJ: **to keep ~** ficar calado; **~'s the word!** bico calado!

mumble ['mʌmbl] VT, VI resmungar, murmurar

mummify ['mʌmɪfaɪ] VT mumificar

mummy ['mʌmɪ] N (BRIT: *mother*) mamãe *f*; (*embalmed*) múmia

mumps [mʌmps] N caxumba

munch [mʌntʃ] VT, VI mascar

mundane [mʌn'deɪn] ADJ banal, mundano

municipal [mjuː'nɪsɪpl] ADJ municipal

municipality [mjuːnɪsɪ'pælɪtɪ] N municipalidade *f*; (*area*) município

munitions [mjuː'nɪʃənz] NPL munições *fpl*

mural ['mjuərl] N mural *m*

murder ['məːdə'] N assassinato; (*Law*) homicídio ▸ VT assassinar; (*spoil*) estragar; **to commit ~** cometer um assassinato

murderer ['məːdərə'] N assassino

murderess ['məːdərɪs] N assassina

murderous ['məːdərəs] ADJ homicida

murk [məːk] N escuridão *f*

murky ['məːkɪ] ADJ escuro; (*water*) turvo; (*fig*) sombrio

murmur ['məːmə'] N murmúrio ▸ VT, VI murmurar; **heart ~** (*Med*) sopro cardíaco *or* no coração

MusB, MusBac N ABBR (= *Bachelor of Music*) grau universitário

muscle ['mʌsl] N músculo; (*fig: strength*) força (muscular)
▸ **muscle in** VI imiscuir-se, impor-se

muscular ['mʌskjulə'] ADJ muscular; (*person*) musculoso

muscular dystrophy N distrofia muscular

MusD, MusDoc N ABBR (= *Doctor of Music*) grau universitário

muse [mjuːz] VI meditar ▸ N musa

museum [mjuː'zɪəm] N museu *m*

mush [mʌʃ] N pasta, papa; (*fig*) pieguice *f*

mushroom ['mʌʃrum] N cogumelo ▸ VI (*fig*) crescer da noite para o dia, pipocar

mushy ['mʌʃɪ] ADJ mole; (*pej*) piegas *inv*

music ['mjuːzɪk] N música

musical ['mjuːzɪkl] ADJ (*of music, person*) musical; (*harmonious*) melodioso ▸ N (*show*) musical *m*

musical instrument N instrumento musical

music box N caixinha de música

music hall N teatro de variedades

musician [mjuː'zɪʃən] N músico(-a)

music stand N atril *m*, estante *f* de música

musk [mʌsk] N almíscar *m*

musket ['mʌskɪt] N mosquete *m*

muskrat ['mʌskræt] N rato almiscarado

musk rose N (*Bot*) rosa-moscada

Muslim ['mʌzlɪm] ADJ, N muçulmano(-a)

muslin ['mʌzlɪn] N musselina

musquash ['mʌskwɔʃ] N rato almiscarado; (*fur*) pele *f* de rato almiscarado

mussel ['mʌsl] N mexilhão *m*

must [mʌst] AUX VB (*obligation*): **I ~ do it** tenho que *or* devo fazer isso; (*probability*): **he ~ be there by now** ele já deve estar lá; (*suggestion, invitation*): **you ~ come and see me soon** você tem que vir me ver em breve; (*indicating sth unwelcome*): **why ~ he behave so badly?**

por que ele tem que se comportar tão mal?
▶ N (*necessity*) necessidade *f*; **it's a ~** é
imprescindível; **I ~ have made a mistake**
eu devo ter feito um erro
mustache ['mʌstæʃ] (*US*) N = **moustache**
mustard ['mʌstəd] N mostarda
mustard gas N gás *m* de mostarda
muster ['mʌstər] VT (*support*) reunir; (*energy*)
juntar; (*Mil*) formar; (*also:* **muster up**:
strength, courage) criar, juntar
mustiness ['mʌstɪnɪs] N mofo
mustn't ['mʌsnt] = **must not**
musty ['mʌstɪ] ADJ mofado, com cheiro de
bolor
mutant ['mju:tənt] ADJ, N mutante *m/f*
mutate [mju:'teɪt] VI sofrer mutação genética
mutation [mju:'teɪʃən] N mutação *f*
mute [mju:t] ADJ, N mudo(-a)
muted ['mju:tɪd] ADJ (*colour*) suave; (*reaction*)
moderado; (*noise, Mus*) abafado; (*criticism*)
velado
mutilate ['mju:tɪleɪt] VT mutilar
mutilation [mju:tɪ'leɪʃən] N mutilação *f*
mutinous ['mju:tɪnəs] ADJ (*troops*) amotinado;
(*attitude*) rebelde
mutiny ['mju:tɪnɪ] N motim *m*, rebelião *f* ▶ VI
amotinar-se
mutter ['mʌtər] VT, VI resmungar, murmurar
mutton ['mʌtn] N carne *f* de carneiro
mutual ['mju:tʃuəl] ADJ mútuo; (*shared*)
comum

mutually ['mju:tʃuəlɪ] ADV mutuamente,
reciprocamente
muzzle ['mʌzl] N (*of animal*) focinho; (*guard: for
dog*) focinheira; (*of gun*) boca ▶ VT (*press etc*)
amordaçar; (*dog*) pôr focinheira em
MVP (*US*) N ABBR (*Sport*) = **most valuable
player**
MW ABBR (= *medium wave*) OM
my [maɪ] ADJ meu/minha; **this is my house/
car/brother** esta é a minha casa/meu carro/
meu irmão; **I've washed my hair/cut my
finger** lavei meu cabelo/cortei meu dedo;
is this my pen or yours? esta caneta é
minha ou sua?
myopic [maɪ'ɔpɪk] ADJ míope
myriad ['mɪrɪəd] N miríade *f*
myself [maɪ'sɛlf] PRON (*reflexive*) me; (*emphatic*)
eu mesmo; (*after prep*) mim mesmo; *see also*
oneself
mysterious [mɪs'tɪərɪəs] ADJ misterioso
mystery ['mɪstərɪ] N mistério
mystery story N romance *m* policial
mystic ['mɪstɪk] ADJ, N místico(-a)
mystical ['mɪstɪkl] ADJ místico
mystify ['mɪstɪfaɪ] VT (*perplex*) mistificar,
confundir; (*disconcert*) desconcertar
mystique [mɪs'ti:k] N místico
myth [mɪθ] N mito
mythical ['mɪθɪkəl] ADJ mítico
mythological [mɪθə'lɔdʒɪkl] ADJ mitológico
mythology [mɪ'θɔlədʒɪ] N mitologia

m

Nn

N¹, n [ɛn] N (letter) N, n m; **N for Nellie** (BRIT) or **Nan** (US) N de Nair

N² ABBR (= north) N

NA (US) N ABBR (= Narcotics Anonymous) associação de assistência aos toxicômanos; = **National Academy**

n/a ABBR = **not applicable**; (Comm etc) = **no account**

NAACP (US) N ABBR = **National Association for the Advancement of Colored People**

NAAFI ['næfɪ] (BRIT) N ABBR (= Navy, Army & Air Force Institute) órgão responsável pelas lojas e cantinas do exército

nab [næb] (inf) VT pegar, prender

NACU (US) N ABBR = **National Association of Colleges and Universities**

nadir ['neɪdɪəʳ] N (Astronomy, fig) nadir m

naff [næf] (BRIT inf) ADJ brega

nag [næg] N (pej: horse) rocim m ▶ VT ralhar, apoquentar

nagging ['nægɪŋ] ADJ (doubt) persistente; (pain) contínuo ▶ N queixas fpl, censuras fpl, apoquentação f

nail [neɪl] N (human) unha; (metal) prego ▶ VT pregar; **to ~ sb down to a date/price** conseguir que alguém se defina sobre a data/o preço; **to pay cash on the ~** (BRIT) pagar na bucha

nailbrush ['neɪlbrʌʃ] N escova de unhas

nailfile ['neɪlfaɪl] N lixa de unhas

nail polish N esmalte m (BR) or verniz m (PT) de unhas

nail polish remover N removedor m de esmalte (BR) or verniz (PT)

nail scissors NPL tesourinha de unhas

nail varnish (BRIT) N = **nail polish**

Nairobi [naɪ'rəubɪ] N Nairóbi

naïve [naɪ'iːv] ADJ ingênuo

naïveté [naɪ'iːvteɪ] N = **naïvety**

naïvety [naɪ'iːvətɪ], **naïveté** N ingenuidade f

naked ['neɪkɪd] ADJ nu(a); **with the ~ eye** a olho nu

nakedness ['neɪkɪdnɪs] N nudez f

NAM (US) N ABBR = **National Association of Manufacturers**

name [neɪm] N nome m; (surname) sobrenome m; (reputation) reputação f, fama ▶ VT (child) pôr nome em; (criminal) apontar; (appoint) nomear; (price) fixar; (date) marcar; **what's**

your **~?** qual é o seu nome?, como (você) se chama?; **my ~ is Peter** eu me chamo Peter; **by ~** de nome; **in the ~ of** em nome de; **to give one's ~ and address** (to police etc) dar o seu nome e endereço; **to make a ~ for o.s.** fazer nome; **to get (o.s.) a bad ~** fazer má reputação; **to call sb ~s** xingar alguém

name-dropping [-'drɔpɪŋ] N: **she loves ~** ela adora esnobar conhecimento de gente importante

nameless ['neɪmlɪs] ADJ (unknown) sem nome; (anonymous) anônimo

namely ['neɪmlɪ] ADV a saber, isto é

nameplate ['neɪmpleɪt] N (on door etc) placa

namesake ['neɪmseɪk] N xará m/f (BR), homônimo(-a) (PT)

nanny ['nænɪ] N babá f

nanny goat N cabra

nap [næp] N (sleep) soneca; (of cloth) felpa ▶ VI: **to be caught ~ping** ser pego de surpresa

NAPA (US) N ABBR (= National Association of Performing Artists) sindicato dos artistas de teatro e de cinema

napalm ['neɪpɑːm] N napalm m

nape [neɪp] N: **~ of the neck** nuca

napkin ['næpkɪn] N (also: **table napkin**) guardanapo

nappy ['næpɪ] (BRIT) N fralda

nappy liner (BRIT) N gaze f

nappy rash (BRIT) N assadura

narcissi [nɑː'sɪsaɪ] NPL of **narcissus**

narcissistic [nɑːsɪ'sɪstɪk] ADJ narcisista

narcissus [nɑː'sɪsəs] (pl **narcissi**) N narciso

narcotic [nɑː'kɔtɪk] ADJ narcótico ▶ N narcótico; **narcotics** NPL (drugs) entorpecentes mpl

nark [nɑːk] (BRIT inf) VT encher o saco de

narrate [nə'reɪt] VT narrar, contar

narration [nə'reɪʃən] N narração f

narrative ['nærətɪv] N narrativa ▶ ADJ narrativo

narrator [nə'reɪtəʳ] N narrador(a) m/f

narrow ['nærəu] ADJ estreito; (shoe) apertado; (fig: majority) pequeno; (: ideas) tacanho ▶ VI (road) estreitar-se; (difference) diminuir; **to have a ~ escape** escapar por um triz; **to ~ sth down to** restringir or reduzir algo a

narrow gauge ADJ (Rail) de bitola estreita

narrowly ['nærəuli] ADV *(miss)* por pouco;
he ~ missed injury/the tree por pouco não
se machucou/não bateu na árvore
narrow-minded [-'maindid] ADJ de visão
limitada, bitolado
NAS *(US)* N ABBR = **National Academy of
Sciences**
NASA ['næsə] *(US)* N ABBR (= *National
Aeronautics and Space Administration*) NASA *f*
nasal ['neizl] ADJ nasal
Nassau ['næsɔː] N *(in Bahamas)* Nassau
nastily ['nɑːstili] ADV *(say, act)* maldosamente
nastiness ['nɑːstinis] N *(malice)* maldade *f*;
(rudeness) grosseria
nasturtium [nəs'təːʃəm] N chagas *fpl*,
capuchinha
nasty ['nɑːsti] ADJ *(unpleasant: remark)*
desagradável; (: *person*) mau, ruim; *(malicious)*
maldoso; *(rude)* grosseiro, obsceno; *(revolting:
taste, smell)* repugnante, asqueroso; *(wound,
disease etc)* grave, sério; **to turn ~** *(situation,
weather)* ficar feio; *(person)* engrossar
NAS/UWT *(BRIT)* N ABBR (= *National Association
of Schoolmasters/Union of Women Teachers*)
sindicato dos professores
nation ['neiʃən] N nação *f*
national ['næʃənl] ADJ, N nacional *m/f*
national anthem N hino nacional
national debt N dívida pública
national dress N traje *m* nacional
National Guard *(US)* N guarda nacional
National Health Service *(BRIT)* N *serviço
nacional de saúde*
National Insurance *(BRIT)* N previdência
social
nationalism ['næʃənəlizəm] N nacionalismo
nationalist ['næʃənəlist] ADJ, N nacionalista *m/f*
nationality [næʃə'næliti] N nacionalidade *f*
nationalization [næʃənəlai'zeiʃən] N
nacionalização *f*
nationalize ['næʃənəlaiz] VT nacionalizar
nationally ['næʃənəli] ADV *(nationwide)* de
âmbito nacional; *(as a nation)*
nacionalmente, como nação
national park N parque *m* nacional
national press N imprensa nacional
National Security Council *(US)* N conselho
nacional de segurança
national service N *(Mil)* serviço militar
National Trust *(BRIT)* N *ver nota*

> O **National Trust** é uma instituição
> independente, sem fins lucrativos, cuja
> missão é proteger e valorizar os
> monumentos e a paisagem da Grã-
> Bretanha devido a seu interesse histórico
> ou beleza natural.

nationwide ['neiʃənwaid] ADJ de âmbito *or* a
nível nacional ▶ ADV em todo o país
native ['neitiv] N *(local inhabitant)* natural *m/f*,
nativo(-a); *(in colonies)* indígena *m/f*,
nativo(-a) ▶ ADJ *(indigenous)* indígena; *(of
one's birth)* natal; *(language)* materno; *(innate)*
inato, natural; **a ~ of Russia** um natural da

Rússia; **a ~ speaker of Portuguese** uma
pessoa de língua (materna) portuguesa
Nativity [nə'tiviti] N *(Rel)*: **the ~** a Natividade
NATO ['neitəu] N ABBR (= *North Atlantic Treaty
Organization*) OTAN *f*
natter ['nætəʳ] *(BRIT)* VI conversar fiado
natural ['nætʃrəl] ADJ natural; **death from ~
causes** morte *f* natural
natural childbirth N parto natural
natural gas N gás *m* natural
naturalist ['nætʃrəlist] N naturalista *m/f*
naturalization [nætʃrəlai'zeiʃən] N
naturalização *f*
naturalize ['nætʃrəlaiz] VT: **to become ~d**
(person) naturalizar-se
naturally ['nætʃrəli] ADV naturalmente; *(of
course)* claro, evidentemente; *(instinctively)* por
instinto, espontaneamente
naturalness ['nætʃrəlnis] N naturalidade *f*
natural resources NPL recursos *mpl* naturais
natural wastage N *(Industry)* afastamentos
mpl naturais e voluntários
nature ['neitʃəʳ] N natureza; *(character)* caráter
m, índole *f*; **by ~** por natureza; **documents
of a confidential ~** documentos de caráter
confidencial
-natured ['neitʃəd] SUFFIX: **ill~** de mau
caráter
nature reserve *(BRIT)* N reserva natural
nature trail N *trilha de descoberta da natureza*
naturist ['neitʃərist] N naturista *m/f*
naught [nɔːt] N = **nought**
naughtiness ['nɔːtinis] N *(of child)* travessura,
mau comportamento; *(of story etc)* picante *m*
naughty ['nɔːti] ADJ *(child)* travesso, levado;
(story, film) picante
nausea ['nɔːsiə] N náusea
nauseate ['nɔːsieit] VT dar náuseas a; *(fig)*
repugnar
nauseating ['nɔːsieitiŋ] ADJ nauseabundo,
enjoativo; *(fig)* nojento, repugnante
nauseous ['nɔːsiəs] ADJ *(nauseating)*
nauseabundo, enjoativo; *(feeling sick)*: **to be ~**
estar enjoado
nautical ['nɔːtikl] ADJ náutico
nautical mile N milha marítima *(1853 m)*
naval ['neivl] ADJ naval
naval officer N oficial *m* de marinha
nave [neiv] N nave *f*
navel ['neivl] N umbigo
navigable ['nævigəbl] ADJ navegável
navigate ['nævigeit] VT *(ship)* pilotar; *(sea)*
navegar ▶ VI navegar; *(Aut)* ler o mapa
navigation [nævi'geiʃən] N *(action)*
navegação *f*; *(science)* náutica
navigator ['nævigeitəʳ] N navegador(a) *m/f*
navvy ['nævi] *(BRIT)* N trabalhador *m* braçal,
cavouqueiro
navy ['neivi] N marinha (de guerra); *(ships)*
armada, frota ▶ ADJ *(also:* **navy-blue**)
azul-marinho *inv*; **Department of the N~**
(US) ministério da Marinha
navy-blue ADJ azul-marinho *inv*

n

Nazareth ['næzərəθ] N Nazaré

Nazi ['nɑ:tsɪ] ADJ, N nazista *m/f* (*BR*), nazi *m/f* (*PT*)

Nazism ['nɑ:tsɪzəm] N nazismo

NB ABBR (= *nota bene*) NB; (*CANADA*) = **New Brunswick**

NBA (*US*) N ABBR = **National Basketball Association; National Boxing Association**

NBC (*US*) N ABBR (= *National Broadcasting Company*) *rede de televisão*

NBS (*US*) N ABBR (= *National Bureau of Standards*) *órgão de padronização*

NC ABBR (*Comm etc*) = **no charge**; (*US Post*) = **North Carolina**

NCC N ABBR (*BRIT*: = *Nature Conservancy Council*) *órgão de proteção à natureza*; (*US*) = **National Council of Churches**

NCCL (*BRIT*) N ABBR (= *National Council for Civil Liberties*) *associação de defesa das liberdades civis*

NCO N ABBR = **non-commissioned officer**

ND (*US*) ABBR (*Post*) = **North Dakota**

NE (*US*) ABBR (*Post*) = **Nebraska; New England**

NEA (*US*) N ABBR = **National Education Association**

neap tide [ni:p-] N maré *f* morta

near [nɪər] ADJ (*place*) vizinho; (*time*) próximo; (*relation*) íntimo ▶ ADV perto ▶ PREP (*also*: **near to**: *space*) perto de; (: *time*) perto de, quase ▶ VT aproximar-se de; **~ here/there** aqui/ali perto; **£25,000 or ~est offer** (*BRIT*) £25,000 ou melhor oferta; **in the ~ future** no próximo futuro; **the building is ~ing completion** o edifício está quase pronto; **to come ~** aproximar-se

nearby [nɪə'baɪ] ADJ próximo, vizinho ▶ ADV à mão, perto

Near East N: **the ~** o Oriente Próximo

nearer ['nɪərər] ADJ que fica mais perto ▶ ADV mais perto

nearly ['nɪəlɪ] ADV quase; **I ~ fell** quase que caí; **it's not ~ big enough** é pequeno demais

near miss N (*of planes*) quase-colisão *f*; (*shot*) tiro que passou de raspão

nearness ['nɪənɪs] N proximidade *f*; (*relationship*) intimidade *f*

nearside ['nɪəsaɪd] N (*Aut: right-hand drive*) lado esquerdo; (: *left-hand drive*) lado direito ▶ ADJ esquerdo; direito

near-sighted [-'saɪtɪd] ADJ míope

neat [ni:t] ADJ (*place*) arrumado, em ordem; (*person*) asseado, arrumado; (*work*) caprichado; (*plan*) engenhoso, bem bolado; (*spirits*) puro

neatly ['ni:tlɪ] ADV caprichosamente, com capricho; (*skilfully*) habilmente

neatness ['ni:tnɪs] N (*tidiness*) asseio; (*skilfulness*) habilidade *f*

nebulous ['nɛbjuləs] ADJ nebuloso; (*fig*) vago, confuso

necessarily ['nɛsɪsrɪlɪ] ADV necessariamente; **not ~** não necessariamente

necessary ['nɛsɪsrɪ] ADJ necessário; **he did all that was ~** fez tudo o que foi necessário; **if ~** se necessário for

necessitate [nɪ'sɛsɪteɪt] VT exigir, tornar necessário

necessity [nɪ'sɛsɪtɪ] N (*thing needed*) necessidade *f*, requisito; (*compelling circumstances*) necessidade; **necessities** NPL (*essentials*) artigos *mpl* de primeira necessidade; **in case of ~** em caso de necessidade

neck [nɛk] N (*Anat*) pescoço; (*of garment*) gola; (*of bottle*) gargalo ▶ VI (*inf*) ficar de agarramento; **~ and ~** emparelhados; **to stick one's ~ out** (*inf*) arriscar-se

necklace ['nɛklɪs] N colar *m*

neckline ['nɛklaɪn] N decote *m*

necktie ['nɛktaɪ] (*esp US*) N gravata

nectar ['nɛktər] N néctar *m*

nectarine ['nɛktərɪn] N nectarina

NEDC (*BRIT*) N ABBR = **National Economic Development Council**

née [neɪ] ADJ: **~ Scott** em solteira Scott

need [ni:d] N (*lack*) falta, carência; (*necessity*) necessidade *f*; (*thing needed*) requisito, necessidade ▶ VT (*require*) precisar de; **I ~ to do it** preciso fazê-lo; **you don't ~ to go** você não precisa ir; **a signature is ~ed** é necessária uma assinatura; **to be in ~ of** *or* **have ~ of** estar precisando de; **to meet sb's ~s** atender às necessidades de alguém; **in case of ~** em caso de necessidade; **there's no ~ to do ...** não é preciso fazer ...; **there's no ~ for that** isso não é necessário

needle ['ni:dl] N agulha ▶ VT (*inf*) provocar, alfinetar

needlecord ['ni:dlkɔ:d] (*BRIT*) N veludo cotelê

needless ['ni:dlɪs] ADJ inútil, desnecessário; **~ to say ...** desnecessário dizer que ...

needlessly ['ni:dlɪslɪ] ADV desnecessariamente, à toa

needlework ['ni:dlwɜ:k] N costura

needn't ['ni:dnt] = **need not**

needy ['ni:dɪ] ADJ necessitado, carente

negation [nɪ'geɪʃən] N negação *f*

negative ['nɛgətɪv] ADJ negativo ▶ N (*Phot*) negativo; (*Ling*) negativa; **to answer in the ~** responder negativamente

neglect [nɪ'glɛkt] VT (*one's duty*) negligenciar, não cumprir com; (*child*) descuidar, esquecer-se de ▶ N (*of child*) descuido, desatenção *f*; (*personal*) desleixo; (*of house etc*) abandono; (*of duty*) negligência; **to ~ to do sth** omitir de fazer algo

neglected [nɪ'glɛktɪd] ADJ abandonado

neglectful [nɪ'glɛktful] ADJ negligente; **to be ~ of sb/sth** descuidar de alguém/algo

negligee ['nɛglɪʒeɪ] N négligé *m*

negligence ['nɛglɪdʒəns] N negligência, descuido

negligent ['nɛglɪdʒənt] ADJ negligente

negligently ['nɛglɪdʒəntlɪ] ADV por negligência; (*offhandedly*) negligentemente

negligible ['nɛglɪdʒɪbl] ADJ insignificante, desprezível, ínfimo

negotiable [nɪ'gəʊʃɪəbl] ADJ (*cheque*) negociável; (*road*) transitável

negotiate [nɪ'gəʊʃɪeɪt] VI negociar ▶ VT (*treaty, transaction*) negociar; (*obstacle*) contornar; (*bend in road*) fazer; **to ~ with sb for sth** negociar com alguém para obter algo

negotiation [nɪgəʊʃɪ'eɪʃən] N negociação f; **to enter into ~s with sb** entrar em negociações com alguém

negotiator [nɪ'gəʊʃɪeɪtə^r] N negociador(a) m/f

Negress ['niːgrɪs] N negra

Negro ['niːgrəʊ] (*pl* **Negroes**) ADJ, N negro(-a)

neigh [neɪ] N relincho ▶ VI relinchar

neighbour, (*US*) **neighbor** ['neɪbə^r] N vizinho(-a)

neighbourhood, (*US*) **neighborhood** ['neɪbəhud] N (*place*) vizinhança, bairro; (*people*) vizinhos mpl

neighbouring, (*US*) **neighboring** ['neɪbərɪŋ] ADJ vizinho

neighbourly, (*US*) **neighborly** ['neɪbəlɪ] ADJ amistoso, prestativo

neither ['naɪðə^r] CONJ: **I didn't move and ~ did he** não me movi nem ele ▶ ADJ, PRON nenhum (dos dois), nem um nem outro ▶ ADV: **~ good nor bad** nem bom nem mau; **~ story is true** nenhuma das estórias é verdade

neo... [niːəʊ] PREFIX neo-

neolithic [niːəʊ'lɪθɪk] ADJ neolítico

neologism [nɪ'ɔlədʒɪzəm] N neologismo

neon ['niːɔn] N neônio, néon m

neon light N luz f de neônio

neon sign N anúncio luminoso a neônio

Nepal [nɪ'pɔːl] N Nepal m

nephew ['nɛvjuː] N sobrinho

nepotism ['nɛpətɪzm] N nepotismo

nerve [nəːv] N (*Anat*) nervo; (*courage*) coragem f; (*impudence*) descaramento, atrevimento; **he gets on my ~s** ele me irrita, ele me dá nos nervos; **to have a fit of ~s** ter uma crise nervosa; **to lose one's ~** (*self-confidence*) perder o sangue frio

nerve centre, (*US*) **nerve center** N (*Anat*) centro nervoso; (*fig*) centro de operações

nerve gas N gás m tóxico

nerve-racking [-'rækɪŋ] ADJ angustiante

nervous ['nəːvəs] ADJ (*Anat*) nervoso; (*anxious*) apreensivo; (*timid*) tímido, acanhado; **~ exhaustion** esgotamento nervoso

nervous breakdown N esgotamento nervoso

nervously ['nəːvəslɪ] ADV nervosamente; (*timidly*) timidamente

nervousness ['nəːvəsnɪs] N nervosismo; (*timidity*) timidez f

nervous wreck N: **to be a ~** estar uma pilha de nervos

nest [nɛst] VI aninhar-se ▶ N (*of bird*) ninho; (*of wasp*) vespeiro

nest egg N (*fig*) pé-de-meia m

nestle ['nɛsl] VI: **to ~ up to sb** aconchegar-se a alguém

nestling ['nɛstlɪŋ] N filhote m (de passarinho)

net [nɛt] N rede f; (*fabric*) filó m ▶ ADJ (*Comm*) líquido ▶ VT pegar na rede; (*money: subj: person*) faturar; (: *deal, sale*) render; **~ of tax** isento de impostos; **he earns £10,000 ~ per year** ele ganha £10,000 líquidas por ano; **the Net** (*Internet*) a Rede

netball ['nɛtbɔːl] N *espécie de basquetebol*

net curtains NPL cortinas fpl de voile

Netherlands ['nɛðələndz] NPL: **the ~** os Países Baixos

net profit N lucro líquido

nett [nɛt] ADJ = **net**

netting ['nɛtɪŋ] N rede f, redes fpl; (*fabric*) voile m

nettle ['nɛtl] N urtiga

network ['nɛtwəːk] N rede f ▶ VT (*Radio, TV*) transmitir em rede; (*computers*) interligar; **there's no ~ coverage here** (*Tel*) aqui não tem cobertura

neuralgia [njuə'rældʒə] N neuralgia

neuroses [njuə'rəusiːz] NPL *of* **neurosis**

neurosis [njuə'rəusɪs] (*pl* **neuroses**) N neurose f

neurotic [njuə'rɔtɪk] ADJ, N neurótico(-a)

neuter ['njuːtə^r] ADJ neutro ▶ N neutro ▶ VT (*cat etc*) castrar, capar

neutral ['njuːtrəl] ADJ neutro ▶ N (*Aut*) ponto morto

neutrality [njuː'trælɪtɪ] N neutralidade f

neutralize ['njuːtrəlaɪz] VT neutralizar

neutron bomb N bomba de nêutrons (*BR*) or neutrões (*PT*)

never ['nɛvə^r] ADV nunca; **I ~ went** nunca fui; **~ again** nunca mais; **~ in my life** nunca na minha vida; *see also* **mind**

never-ending [-'ɛndɪŋ] ADJ sem fim, interminável

nevertheless [nɛvəðə'lɛs] ADV todavia, contudo

new [njuː] ADJ novo; **as good as ~** como novo

New Age N esoterismo

newborn ['njuːbɔːn] ADJ recém-nascido

newcomer ['njuːkʌmə^r] N recém-chegado(-a), novato(-a)

new-fangled [-'fæŋgld] (*pej*) ADJ ultramoderno

new-found ADJ (*friend*) novo; (*enthusiasm*) recente

Newfoundland ['njuːfənlənd] N Terra Nova

New Guinea N Nova Guiné f

newly ['njuːlɪ] ADV recém, novamente

newly-weds NPL recém-casados mpl

new moon N lua nova

newness ['njuːnɪs] N novidade f

news [njuːz] N notícias fpl; (*Radio, TV*) noticiário; **a piece of ~** uma notícia; **good/ bad ~** boa/má notícia; **financial ~** noticiário financeiro

news agency N agência de notícias

newsagent ['njuːzeɪdʒənt] (*BRIT*) N jornaleiro(-a)

news bulletin N (*Radio, TV*) noticiário

newscaster ['njuːzkɑːstə^r] N locutor(a) m/f

newsdealer ['nju:zdi:lə'] (US) N = **newsagent**
news flash N notícia de última hora
newsletter ['nju:zlɛtə'] N boletim *m*
informativo
newspaper ['nju:zpeɪpə'] N jornal *m*;
(*material*) papel *m* de jornal; **daily** ~ diário;
weekly ~ semanário
newsprint ['nju:zprɪnt] N papel *m* de jornal
newsreader ['nju:zri:də'] N = **newscaster**
newsreel ['nju:zri:l] N jornal *m*
cinematográfico, atualidades *fpl*
newsroom ['nju:zru:m] N (*Press*) sala da
redação, (TV) estúdio
news stand N banca de jornais
newt [nju:t] N tritão *m*
New Year N ano novo; **Happy** ~! Feliz Ano
Novo!; **to wish sb a happy** ~ desejar feliz
ano novo a alguém
New Year's Day N dia *m* de ano novo
New Year's Eve N véspera de ano novo
New York [-jɔ:k] N Nova Iorque
New Zealand [-'zi:lənd] N Nova Zelândia
▶ CPD neozelandês(-esa)
New Zealander [-'zi:ləndə'] N
neozelandês(-esa) *m/f*
next [nɛkst] ADJ (*in space*) próximo, vizinho;
(*in time*) seguinte, próximo ▶ ADV depois;
the ~ **day** o dia seguinte; ~ **time** na próxima
vez; ~ **year** o ano que vem; **"turn to the** ~
page" "vire para a página seguinte"; **the**
week after ~ sem ser a semana que vem, a
outra; ~ **to** ao lado de; ~ **to nothing** quase
nada; **who's** ~? quem é o próximo?; ~ **please!**
próximo, por favor!; **when do we meet** ~?
quando é que nós nos reencontramos?
next door ADV na casa do lado ▶ ADJ vizinho
next-of-kin N parentes *mpl* mais próximos
NF N ABBR (*BRIT Pol:* = *National Front*) *partido*
político da extrema direita ▶ ABBR (*CANADA*)
= **Newfoundland**
NFL (US) N ABBR = **National Football League**
NG (US) ABBR = **National Guard**
NGO N ABBR (= *non-governmental organization*)
ONG *f*
NH (US) ABBR (*Post*) = **New Hampshire**
NHL (US) N ABBR = **National Hockey League**
NHS (*BRIT*) N ABBR = **National Health Service**
NI ABBR = **Northern Ireland**; (*BRIT*) = **National**
Insurance
Niagara Falls [naɪ'ægrə-] NPL: **the** ~ as
cataratas do Niagara
nib [nɪb] N ponta *or* bico da pena
nibble ['nɪbl] VT mordiscar, beliscar; (*animal*)
roer
Nicaragua [nɪkə'rægjuə] N Nicarágua
Nicaraguan [nɪkə'rægjuən] ADJ, N
nicaraguense *m/f*
nice [naɪs] ADJ (*likeable*) simpático; (*kind*)
amável, atencioso; (*pleasant*) agradável;
(*attractive*) bonito; (*subtle*) sutil, fino
nice-looking [-'lukɪŋ] ADJ bonito
nicely ['naɪslɪ] ADV agradavelmente, bem;
that will do ~ isso será perfeito

niceties ['naɪsɪtɪz] NPL sutilezas *fpl*
niche [ni:ʃ] N nicho
nick [nɪk] N (*wound*) corte *m*; (*cut, indentation*)
entalhe *m*, incisão *f*; (*BRIT inf*): **in good** ~ em
bom estado ▶ VT (*cut*) entalhar; (*inf: steal*)
furtar; (: *BRIT: arrest*) prender; **in the** ~ **of**
time na hora H, em cima da hora; **to** ~ **o.s.**
cortar-se
nickel ['nɪkl] N níquel *m*; (US) moeda de 5
centavos
nickname ['nɪkneɪm] N apelido (*BR*), alcunha
(*PT*) ▶ VT apelidar de (*BR*), alcunhar de (*PT*)
Nicosia [nɪkə'si:ə] N Nicósia
nicotine ['nɪkəti:n] N nicotina
niece [ni:s] N sobrinha
nifty ['nɪftɪ] (*inf*) ADJ (*car, jacket*) chique; (*gadget,*
tool) jeitoso
Niger ['naɪdʒə'] N (*country, river*) Níger *m*
Nigeria [naɪ'dʒɪərɪə] N Nigéria
Nigerian [naɪ'dʒɪərɪən] ADJ, N nigeriano(-a)
niggardly ['nɪgədlɪ] ADJ (*person*) avarento,
sovina; (*amount*) miserável
nigger ['nɪgə'] (!) N (*highly offensive*)
crioulo(-a)
niggle ['nɪgl] VI (*find fault*) botar defeito; (*fuss*)
fazer histórias ▶ VT irritar
niggling ['nɪglɪŋ] ADJ (*trifling*) insignificante,
mesquinho; (*annoying*) irritante; (*pain, doubt*)
persistente
night [naɪt] N noite *f*; **at** *or* **by** ~ à *or* de noite;
in *or* **during the** ~ durante a noite; **last** ~
ontem à noite; **the** ~ **before last** anteontem
à noite; **good** ~! boa noite!
night-bird N (*Zool*) ave *f* noturna; (*fig*)
noctívago(-a)
nightcap ['naɪtkæp] N *bebida tomada antes de*
dormir
nightclub ['naɪtklʌb] N boate *f*
nightdress ['naɪtdrɛs] N camisola (*BR*),
camisa de noite (*PT*)
nightfall ['naɪtfɔ:l] N anoitecer *m*
nightgown ['naɪtgaun] N = **nightdress**
nightie ['naɪtɪ] N = **nightdress**
nightingale ['naɪtɪŋgeɪl] N rouxinol *m*
nightlife ['naɪtlaɪf] N vida noturna
nightly ['naɪtlɪ] ADJ noturno, de noite ▶ ADV
todas as noites, cada noite
nightmare ['naɪtmɛə'] N pesadelo
night porter N porteiro da noite
night safe N cofre *m* noturno
night school N escola noturna
nightshade ['naɪtʃeɪd] N: **deadly** ~ (*Bot*)
beladona
night shift N turno da noite
night-time N noite *f*
night watchman (*irreg: like* **man**) N vigia *m*,
guarda-noturno *m*
nihilism ['naɪɪlɪzm] N niilismo
nil [nɪl] N nada; (*BRIT Sport*) zero
Nile [naɪl] N: **the** ~ o Nilo
nimble ['nɪmbl] ADJ (*agile*) ágil, ligeiro; (*skilful*)
hábil, esperto
nine [naɪn] NUM nove; *see also* **five**

nineteen [naɪn'tiːn] NUM dezenove (BR), dezanove (PT); *see also* **five**
nineteenth [naɪn'tiːnθ] NUM décimo nono
ninetieth ['naɪntɪɪθ] NUM nonagésimo
ninety ['naɪntɪ] NUM noventa; *see also* **fifty**
ninth [naɪnθ] NUM nono; *see also* **fifth**
nip [nɪp] VT *(pinch)* beliscar; *(bite)* morder ▶ VI *(BRIT inf)*: **to ~ out/down/up** dar uma saidinha/descida/subida ▶ N *(drink)* gole *m*, trago; **to ~ into a shop** dar um pulo numa loja
nipple ['nɪpl] N *(Anat)* bico do seio, mamilo; *(of bottle)* bocal *m*, bico; *(Tech)* bocal (roscado)
nippy ['nɪpɪ] *(BRIT)* ADJ *(person)* rápido, ágil; *(cold)* friozinho
nit [nɪt] N *(in hair)* lêndea, ovo de piolho; *(inf: idiot)* imbecil *m/f*, idiota *m/f*
nit-pick *(inf)* VI ser implicante
nitrate ['naɪtreɪt] N nitrato
nitrogen ['naɪtrədʒən] N nitrogênio
nitroglycerin, nitroglycerine [naɪtrəʊ'glɪsəriːn] N nitroglicerina
nitty-gritty ['nɪtɪ'grɪtɪ] *(inf)* N: **to get down to the ~** chegar ao âmago
nitwit ['nɪtwɪt] *(inf)* N pateta *m/f*, bobalhão(-ona) *m/f*
NJ *(US)* ABBR *(Post)* = **New Jersey**
NLF N ABBR = **National Liberation Front**
NLQ ABBR (= *near letter quality*) qualidade *f* carta
NLRB *(US)* N ABBR (= *National Labor Relations Board*) órgão de proteção aos trabalhadores
NM *(US)* ABBR *(Post)* = **New Mexico**

(KEYWORD)

no [nəʊ] ADV *(opposite of "yes")* não; **are you coming? — no (I'm not)** você vem? — não (não vou); **no thank you** não obrigado ▶ ADJ *(not any)* nenhum(a), não ... algum(a); **I have no more money/time/books** não tenho mais dinheiro/tempo/livros; **no other man would have done it** nenhum outro homem teria feito isto; **"no entry"** "entrada proibida"; **"no smoking"** "é proibido fumar" ▶ N *(pl* **noes**) não *m*, negativa; **there were 20 noes and one "don't know"** houve 20 nãos e um "não sei"

no. ABBR (= *number*) n°
nobble ['nɔbl] *(BRIT inf)* VT *(bribe)* subornar; *(person: speak to)* agarrar; *(Racing: horse)* incapacitar *(com drogas)*
Nobel prize [nəʊ'bɛl-] N prêmio Nobel
nobility [nəʊ'bɪlɪtɪ] N nobreza
noble ['nəʊbl] ADJ *(person)* nobre; *(title)* de nobreza
nobleman ['nəʊblmən] *(irreg: like* **man**) N nobre *m*, fidalgo
nobly ['nəʊblɪ] ADV nobremente
nobody ['nəʊbədɪ] PRON ninguém
no-brainer [nəʊ'breɪnəʳ] *(inf)* N: **it's a ~** isso é meio óbvio
no-claims bonus N bonificação *f (por não ter reclamado indenização)*

nocturnal [nɔk'tə:nəl] ADJ noturno
nod [nɔd] VI *(greeting)* cumprimentar com a cabeça; *(in agreement)* acenar (que sim) com a cabeça; *(doze)* cochilar, dormitar ▶ VT: **to ~ one's head** inclinar a cabeça ▶ N inclinação *f* da cabeça; **they ~ded their agreement** inclinaram a cabeça afirmando seu acordo
  ▶ **nod off** VI cochilar
noise [nɔɪz] N barulho
noise abatement N luta contra a poluição sonora
noiseless ['nɔɪzlɪs] ADJ silencioso
noisily ['nɔɪzɪlɪ] ADV ruidosamente, com muito barulho
noisy ['nɔɪzɪ] ADJ barulhento
nomad ['nəʊmæd] N nômade *m/f*
nomadic [nəʊ'mædɪk] ADJ nômade
no man's land N terra de ninguém
nominal ['nɔmɪnl] ADJ nominal
nominate ['nɔmɪneɪt] VT *(propose)* propor; *(appoint)* nomear
nomination [nɔmɪ'neɪʃən] N *(proposal)* proposta; *(appointment)* nomeação *f*
nominee [nɔmɪ'niː] N pessoa nomeada, candidato(-a)
non... [nɔn] PREFIX não-, des..., in..., anti-...
non-alcoholic ADJ não-alcoólico
non-breakable ADJ inquebrável
nonce word ['nɔns-] N palavra criada para a ocasião
nonchalant ['nɔnʃələnt] ADJ despreocupado
non-commissioned [-kə'mɪʃənd] ADJ: **~ officer** oficial *m* subalterno
non-committal [-kə'mɪtl] ADJ evasivo
nonconformist [nɔnkən'fɔːmɪst] ADJ não-conformista, dissidente ▶ N não-conformista *m/f*
non-contributory ADJ: **~ pension scheme** *(BRIT)* or **plan** *(US)* caixa de aposentadoria não-contributária
non-cooperation N não-cooperação *f*
nondescript ['nɔndɪskrɪpt] ADJ qualquer; *(pej)* medíocre
none [nʌn] PRON *(person)* ninguém; *(thing)* nenhum(a), nada; **~ of you** nenhum de vocês; **I have ~** não tenho; **I've ~ left** não tenho mais; **~ at all** *(not one)* nenhum; **how much milk? — ~ at all** quanto leite? — nada; **he's ~ the worse for it** isso não o afetou
nonentity [nɔ'nɛntɪtɪ] N nulidade *f*, zero à esquerda *m*
non-essential ADJ não essencial, dispensável ▶ NPL: **~s** desnecessários *mpl*
nonetheless [nʌnðə'lɛs] ADV no entanto, apesar disso, contudo
non-executive ADJ: **~ director** administrador(a) *m/f*, conselheiro(-a)
non-existent [-ɪg'zɪstənt] ADJ inexistente
non-fiction [nɔn-] N literatura de não-ficção
non-flammable ADJ não inflamável
non-intervention N não-intervenção *f*

n

non obst. ABBR (= *non obstante, notwithstanding*) não obstante

non-payment N falta de pagamento

nonplussed [nɔnˈplʌst] ADJ perplexo, pasmado

non-profit-making ADJ sem fins lucrativos

nonsense [ˈnɔnsəns] N disparate *m*, besteira, absurdo; ~! bobagem!, que nada!; **it's ~ to say ...** é um absurdo dizer que ...

non-shrink (BRIT) ADJ que não encolhe

non-skid ADJ antiderrapante

non-smoker N não-fumante *m/f*

nonstarter [nɔnˈstaːtə'] N: **it's a ~** está fadado ao fracasso

non-stick ADJ tefal®, não-aderente

non-stop ADJ ininterrupto; (*Rail*) direto; (*Aviat*) sem escala ▶ ADV sem parar

non-taxable income N renda não-tributável

non-U (BRIT *inf*) ADJ ABBR (= *non-upper class*) que não se diz (*or* se faz)

non-voting shares NPL ações *fpl* sem direito de voto

non-white ADJ, N não-branco(-a)

noodles [ˈnuːdlz] NPL talharim *m*

nook [nuk] N canto, recanto; **~s and crannies** esconderijos *mpl*

noon [nuːn] N meio-dia *m*

no-one PRON = **nobody**

noose [nuːs] N laço corrediço; (*hangman's*) corda da forca

nor [nɔːʳ] CONJ = **neither** ▶ ADV *see* **neither**

norm [nɔːm] N (*convention*) norma; (*requirement*) regra

normal [ˈnɔːml] ADJ normal ▶ N: **to return to ~** normalizar-se

normality [nɔːˈmælɪtɪ] N normalidade *f*

normally [ˈnɔːməlɪ] ADV normalmente

Normandy [ˈnɔːməndɪ] N Normandia

north [nɔːθ] N norte *m* ▶ ADJ do norte, setentrional ▶ ADV ao *or* para o norte

North Africa N África do Norte

North African ADJ, N norte-africano(-a)

North America N América do Norte

North American ADJ, N norte-americano(-a)

Northants [nɔːˈθænts] (BRIT) ABBR = **Northamptonshire**

northbound [ˈnɔːθbaund] ADJ em direção norte

north-east N nordeste *m*

northerly [ˈnɔːðəlɪ] ADJ (*wind, course*) norte

northern [ˈnɔːðən] ADJ do norte, setentrional

Northern Ireland N Irlanda do Norte

North Pole N: **the ~** o Pólo Norte

North Sea N: **the ~** o Mar do Norte

North Sea oil N petróleo do Mar do Norte

northward [ˈnɔːθwəd], **northwards** [ˈnɔːθwədz] ADV em direção norte

north-west N noroeste *m*

Norway [ˈnɔːweɪ] N Noruega

Norwegian [nɔːˈwiːdʒən] ADJ norueguês(-esa) ▶ N norueguês(-esa) *m/f*; (*Ling*) norueguês *m*

nos. ABBR (= *numbers*) n°

nose [nəuz] N (*Anat*) nariz *m*; (*Zool*) focinho; (*sense of smell: of person*) olfato; (: *of animal*) faro

▶ VI (*also*: **nose one's way**) avançar cautelosamente; **to turn up one's ~ at** desdenhar; **to pay through the ~ (for sth)** (*inf*) pagar os olhos da cara por algo

▶ **nose about** VI bisbilhotar

▶ **nose around** VI = **nose about**

nosebleed [ˈnəuzbliːd] N hemorragia nasal

nose-dive N (*deliberate*) voo picado; (*involuntary*) parafuso

nose drops NPL gotas *fpl* para o nariz

nosey [ˈnəuzɪ] (*inf*) ADJ = **nosy**

nostalgia [nɔsˈtældʒɪə] N nostalgia

nostalgic [nɔsˈtældʒɪk] ADJ nostálgico

nostril [ˈnɔstrɪl] N narina

nosy [ˈnəuzɪ] (*inf*) ADJ intrometido, abelhudo

not [nɔt] ADV não; **he is ~** *or* **isn't here** ele não está aqui; **you must ~** *or* **mustn't do that** você não deve fazer isso; **it's too late, isn't it?** é muito tarde, não?; **he asked me ~ to do it** ele me pediu para não fazer isto; **~ that (I don't like him/he isn't interesting)** não é que (eu não goste dele/ ele não seja interessante); **~ yet/now** ainda/ agora não; *see also* **all, only**

notable [ˈnəutəbl] ADJ notável

notably [ˈnəutəblɪ] ADV (*particularly*) particularmente; (*markedly*) notavelmente

notary [ˈnəutərɪ] N (*also*: **notary public**) tabelião/tabelioa *m/f*, notário(-a)

notation [nəuˈteɪʃən] N notação *f*

notch [nɔtʃ] N (*in wood*) entalhe *m*; (*in blade*) corte *m*

▶ **notch up** VT (*score*) marcar; (*victory*) registrar

note [nəut] N (*Mus, banknote*) nota; (*letter*) nota, bilhete *m*; (*record*) nota, anotação *f*; (*tone*) tom *m* ▶ VT (*observe*) observar, reparar em; (*also*: **note down**) anotar, tomar nota de; **just a quick ~ to let you know ...** apenas um bilhete rápido para avisá-lo ...; **to take ~s** tomar notas; **to compare ~s** (*fig*) trocar impressões; **to take ~ of** fazer caso de; **a person of ~** uma pessoa eminente

notebook [ˈnəutbuk] N caderno

note-case (BRIT) N carteira

noted [ˈnəutɪd] ADJ célebre, conhecido

notepad [ˈnəutpæd] N bloco de anotações

notepaper [ˈnəutpeɪpə'] N papel *m* de carta

noteworthy [ˈnəutwəːθɪ] ADJ notável

nothing [ˈnʌθɪŋ] N nada; (*zero*) zero; **he does ~** ele não faz nada; **~ new/much** nada de novo/de mais; **for ~** (*free*) de graça, grátis; (*in vain*) à toa, por nada; **~ at all** absolutamente nada, coisa nenhuma

notice [ˈnəutɪs] N (*sign*) aviso, anúncio; (*warning*) aviso; (*of leaving or losing job*) aviso prévio; (BRIT: *review: of play etc*) resenha ▶ VT (*observe*) reparar em, notar; **without ~** sem aviso prévio; **advance ~** aviso prévio, preaviso; **to give sb ~ of sth** dar aviso a alguém de algo; **at short ~** de repente, em cima da hora; **until further ~** até nova ordem; **to hand in** *or* **give one's ~** (*subj*:

employee) demitir, pedir a demissão; **to take ~ of** prestar atenção a, fazer caso de; **to bring sth to sb's ~** levar algo ao conhecimento de alguém; **it has come to my ~ that ...** tornei-me ciente que ...; **to escape** *or* **avoid ~** passar desapercebido

noticeable ['nəutɪsəbl] ADJ evidente, visível

notice board (BRIT) N quadro de avisos

notification [nəutɪfɪ'keɪʃən] N aviso, notificação *f*

notify ['nəutɪfaɪ] VT avisar, notificar; **to ~ sth to sb** notificar algo a alguém; **to ~ sb of sth** avisar alguém de algo

notion ['nəuʃən] N noção *f*, ideia; **notions** NPL (US) miudezas *fpl*

notoriety [nəutə'raɪətɪ] N notoriedade *f*, má fama

notorious [nəu'tɔːrɪəs] ADJ notório

notoriously [nəu'tɔːrɪəslɪ] ADV notoriamente

Notts [nɔts] (BRIT) ABBR = **Nottinghamshire**

notwithstanding [nɔtwɪθ'stændɪŋ] ADV no entanto, não obstante ▸ PREP: **~ this** apesar disto

nougat ['nuːgɑː] N torrone *m*, nugá *m*

nought [nɔːt] N zero

noun [naun] N substantivo

nourish ['nʌrɪʃ] VT nutrir, alimentar; (*fig*) fomentar, alentar

nourishing ['nʌrɪʃɪŋ] ADJ nutritivo, alimentício

nourishment ['nʌrɪʃmənt] N alimento, nutrimento

Nov. ABBR (= *November*) nov.

Nova Scotia ['nəuvə'skəuʃə] N Nova Escócia

novel ['nɔvl] N romance *m*; (*short*) novela ▸ ADJ (*new*) novo, recente; (*unexpected*) insólito

novelist ['nɔvəlɪst] N romancista *m/f*

novelty ['nɔvəltɪ] N novidade *f*

November [nəu'vɛmbə^r] N novembro; *see also* **July**

novice ['nɔvɪs] N principiante *m/f*, novato(-a); (*Rel*) noviço(-a)

NOW [nau] (US) N ABBR = **National Organization for Women**

now [nau] ADV (*at the present time*) agora; (*these days*) atualmente, hoje em dia ▸ CONJ: **~ (that)** agora que; **right ~** agora mesmo; **by ~** já; **just ~** agora; **that's the fashion just ~** é a moda atualmente; **I saw her just ~** eu a vi agora, acabei de vê-la; **~ and then, ~ and again** de vez em quando; **from ~ on** de agora em diante; **in 3 days from ~** daqui a 3 dias; **between ~ and Monday** até segunda-feira; **that's all for ~** por agora é tudo

nowadays ['nauədeɪz] ADV hoje em dia

nowhere ['nəuwɛə^r] ADV (*go*) a lugar nenhum; (*be*) em nenhum lugar; **~ else** em nenhum outro lugar

no-win situation [nəu'wɪn-] N beco sem saída; **we're in a ~** se correr o bicho pega, se ficar o bicho come

noxious ['nɔkʃəs] ADJ nocivo

nozzle ['nɔzl] N bico, bocal *m*; (*Tech*) tubeira; (: *hose*) agulheta

NP N ABBR = **notary public**

NS (CANADA) ABBR = **Nova Scotia**

NSC (US) N ABBR = **National Security Council**

NSF (US) N ABBR = **National Science Foundation**

NSPCC (BRIT) N ABBR = **National Society for the Prevention of Cruelty to Children**

NSW (AUST) ABBR = **New South Wales**

NT N ABBR (= *New Testament*) NT

nth [ɛnθ] ADJ: **for the ~ time** pela enésima vez

NUAAW (BRIT) N ABBR (= *National Union of Agricultural and Allied Workers*) sindicato da agropecuária

nuance ['njuːɑːns] N nuança, matiz *m*

NUBE (BRIT) N ABBR (= *National Union of Bank Employees*) sindicato dos bancários

nubile ['njuːbaɪl] ADJ (*woman*) jovem e bela

nuclear ['njuːklɪə^r] ADJ nuclear

nuclear disarmament N desarmamento nuclear

nuclei ['njuːklɪaɪ] NPL *of* **nucleus**

nucleus ['njuːklɪəs] (*pl* **nuclei**) N núcleo

nude [njuːd] ADJ nu(a) ▸ N (*Art*) nu *m*; **in the ~** nu, pelado

nudge [nʌdʒ] VT acotovelar, cutucar (BR)

nudist ['njuːdɪst] N nudista *m/f*

nudist colony N colonia nudista

nudity ['njuːdɪtɪ] N nudez *f*

nugget ['nʌgɪt] N pepita

nuisance ['njuːsns] N amolação *f*, aborrecimento; (*person*) chato; **what a ~!** que saco! (BR), que chatice! (PT)

NUJ (BRIT) N ABBR (= *National Union of Journalists*) sindicato dos jornalistas

nuke [njuːk] (*inf*) N usina nuclear

null [nʌl] ADJ: **~ and void** írrito e nulo

nullify ['nʌlɪfaɪ] VT anular, invalidar

NUM (BRIT) N ABBR (= *National Union of Mineworkers*) sindicato dos mineiros

numb [nʌm] ADJ dormente, entorpecido; (*fig*) estupefato ▸ VT adormecer, entorpecer; **~ with cold** duro de frio; **~ with fear** paralisado de medo

number ['nʌmbə^r] N número; (*numeral*) algarismo ▸ VT (*pages etc*) numerar; (*amount to*) montar a; **a ~ of** vários, muitos; **to be ~ed among** figurar entre; **they were ten in ~** eram em número de dez; **wrong ~** (*Tel*) engano

numbered account ['nʌmbəd-] N (*in bank*) conta numerada

number plate (BRIT) N placa (do carro)

Number Ten (BRIT) N (= *10 Downing Street*) residência do primeiro-ministro

numbness ['nʌmnɪs] N torpor *m*, dormência; (*fig*) insensibilidade *f*

numeral ['njuːmərəl] N algarismo

numerate ['njuːmərɪt] (BRIT) ADJ: **to be ~** ter uma noção básica da aritmética

numerical [njuː'mɛrɪkl] ADJ numérico

numerous ['nju:mərəs] ADJ numeroso
nun [nʌn] N freira
nuptial ['nʌpʃəl] ADJ nupcial
nurse [nəːs] N enfermeiro(-a); (also:
  nursemaid) ama-seca, babá f ▶ VT (patient)
  cuidar de, tratar de; (baby: feed) criar,
  amamentar; (: BRIT: rock) embalar; (fig)
  alimentar; **wet ~** ama de leite
nursery ['nəːsərɪ] N (institution) creche f; (room)
  quarto das crianças; (for plants) viveiro
nursery rhyme N poesia infantil
nursery school N escola maternal
nursery slope (BRIT) N (Ski) rampa para
  principiantes
nursing ['nəːsɪŋ] N (profession) enfermagem f;
  (care) cuidado, assistência
nursing home N sanatório, clínica de repouso
nursing mother N lactante f
nurture ['nəːtʃər] VT alimentar
NUS (BRIT) N ABBR (= National Union of Seamen)
  sindicato dos marinheiros; (= National Union of
  Students) sindicato dos estudantes
NUT (BRIT) N ABBR (= National Union of Teachers)
  sindicato dos professores
nut [nʌt] N (Tech) porca; (Bot) noz f ▶ CPD
  (chocolate etc) de nozes
nutcase ['nʌtkeɪs] (inf) N doido(-a), biruta m/f

nutcrackers ['nʌtkrækəz] NPL quebra-nozes
  m inv
nutmeg ['nʌtmɛg] N noz-moscada
nutrient ['nju:trɪənt] N nutrimento ▶ ADJ
  nutritivo
nutrition [nju:'trɪʃən] N (diet) alimentação f;
  (nourishment) nutrição f
nutritionist [nju:'trɪʃənɪst] N nutricionista
  m/f
nutritious [nju:'trɪʃəs] ADJ nutritivo
nuts [nʌts] (inf) ADJ: **he's ~** ele é doido
nutshell ['nʌtʃɛl] N casca de noz; **in a ~** (fig)
  em poucas palavras
nuzzle ['nʌzl] VI: **to ~ up to** aconchegar-se
  com
NV (US) ABBR (Post) = **Nevada**
NWT (CANADA) ABBR = **Northwest Territories**
NY (US) ABBR (Post) = **New York**
NYC (US) ABBR (Post) = **New York City**
nylon ['naɪlɔn] N náilon m (BR), nylon m (PT)
  ▶ ADJ de náilon or nylon; **nylons** NPL
  (stockings) meias fpl (de náilon)
nymph [nɪmf] N ninfa
nymphomaniac [nɪmfəu'meɪnɪæk] N
  ninfômana
NYSE (US) N ABBR = **New York Stock Exchange**
NZ ABBR = **New Zealand**

Oo

O, o [əu] N (*letter*) O, o *m*; (*US Sch*)
= **outstanding**; **O for Olive** (BRIT) *or* **Oboe**
(US) O de Osvaldo
oaf [əuf] N imbecil *m/f*
oak [əuk] N carvalho ▶ ADJ de carvalho
OAP (BRIT) N ABBR = **old-age pensioner**
oar [ɔːʳ] N remo; **to put** *or* **shove one's ~ in**
(*fig: inf*) meter o bedelho *or* a colher
oarsman ['ɔːzmən] (*irreg: like* **man**) N
remador *m*
oarswoman ['ɔːzwumən] (*irreg: like* **woman**) N
remadora
OAS N ABBR (= *Organization of American States*)
OEA *f*
oases [əu'eɪsiːz] NPL *of* **oasis**
oasis [əu'eɪsɪs] (*pl* **oases**) N oásis *m inv*
oath [əuθ] N juramento; (*swear word*) palavrão *m*;
(*curse*) praga; **on** (BRIT) *or* **under ~** sob
juramento; **to take an ~** prestar juramento
oatmeal ['əutmiːl] N farinha *or* mingau *m* de
aveia
oats [əuts] N aveia
OAU N ABBR (= *Organization of African Unity*)
OUA *f*
obdurate ['ɔbdjurɪt] ADJ (*obstinate*) teimoso;
(*sinner*) empedernido; (*unyielding*) inflexível
obedience [ə'biːdɪəns] N obediência; **in ~ to**
em conformidade com
obedient [ə'biːdɪənt] ADJ obediente; **to be ~
to sb/sth** obedecer a alguém/algo
obelisk ['ɔbɪlɪsk] N obelisco
obese [əu'biːs] ADJ obeso
obesity [əu'biːsɪtɪ] N obesidade *f*
obey [ə'beɪ] VT obedecer a; (*instructions,
regulations*) cumprir ▶ VI obedecer
obituary [ə'bɪtjuərɪ] N necrológio
object [*n* 'ɔbdʒɪkt, *vi* əb'dʒɛkt] N (*gen, Ling*)
objeto; (*purpose*) objetivo ▶ VI: **to ~ to**
(*attitude*) desaprovar, objetar a; (*proposal*)
opor-se a; **I ~!** protesto!; **he ~ed that ...** ele
objetou que ...; **do you ~ to my smoking?**
você se incomoda que eu fume?; **what's the
~ of doing that?** qual o objetivo de fazer
isso?; **expense is no ~** o preço não é
problema
objection [əb'dʒɛkʃən] N objeção *f*; (*drawback*)
inconveniente *m*; **I have no ~ to ...** não
tenho nada contra ...; **to make** *or* **raise an ~**
fazer *or* levantar uma objeção

objectionable [əb'dʒɛkʃənəbl] ADJ
desagradável; (*conduct*) censurável
objective [əb'dʒɛktɪv] ADJ objetivo ▶ N
objetivo
objectivity [ɔbdʒɪk'tɪvɪtɪ] N objetividade *f*
object lesson N (*fig*): ~ **(in)** demonstração *f*
(de)
objector [əb'dʒɛktəʳ] N opositor(a) *m/f*
obligation [ɔblɪ'geɪʃən] N obrigação *f*; (*debt*)
dívida (de gratidão); **without ~** sem
compromisso; **to be under an ~ to do sth**
ser obrigado a fazer algo
obligatory [ə'blɪgətərɪ] ADJ obrigatório
oblige [ə'blaɪdʒ] VT (*do a favour for*) obsequiar,
fazer um favor a; (*force*) obrigar, forçar; **to ~
sb to do sth** obrigar *or* forçar alguém a fazer
algo; **to be ~d to sb for doing sth** ficar
agradecido por alguém fazer algo; **anything
to ~!** (*inf*) estou à sua disposição!
obliging [ə'blaɪdʒɪŋ] ADJ prestativo
oblique [ə'bliːk] ADJ oblíquo; (*allusion*)
indireto
obliterate [ə'blɪtəreɪt] VT (*erase*) apagar;
(*destroy*) destruir
oblivion [ə'blɪvɪən] N esquecimento
oblivious [ə'blɪvɪəs] ADJ: **~ of** inconsciente de,
esquecido de
oblong ['ɔblɔŋ] ADJ oblongo, retangular ▶ N
retângulo
obnoxious [əb'nɔkʃəs] ADJ odioso, detestável;
(*smell*) enjoativo
o.b.o (US) ABBR (= *or best offer*) ou melhor oferta
oboe ['əubəu] N oboé *m*
obscene [əb'siːn] ADJ obsceno
obscenity [əb'sɛnɪtɪ] N obscenidade *f*
obscure [əb'skjuəʳ] ADJ obscuro,
desconhecido; (*difficult to understand*) pouco
claro ▶ VT ocultar, escurecer; (*hide: sun etc*)
esconder
obscurity [əb'skjuərɪtɪ] N obscuridade *f*;
(*darkness*) escuridão *f*
obsequious [əb'siːkwɪəs] ADJ obsequioso,
servil
observable [əb'zəːvəbl] ADJ observável;
(*appreciable*) perceptível
observance [əb'zəːvns] N observância,
cumprimento; (*ritual*) prática, hábito;
religious ~s observância religiosa
observant [əb'zəːvnt] ADJ observador(a)

observation [ɔbzə'veɪʃən] N observação f; (by police etc) vigilância; (Med) exame m

observation post N (Mil) posto de observação

observatory [əb'zə:vətrɪ] N observatório

observe [əb'zə:v] VT observar; (rule) cumprir

observer [əb'zə:və'] N observador(a) m/f

obsess [əb'sɛs] VT obsedar, obcecar; **to be ~ed by** or **with sb/sth** estar obcecado por or com alguém/algo

obsession [əb'sɛʃən] N obsessão f, ideia fixa

obsessive [əb'sɛsɪv] ADJ obsessivo

obsolescence [ɔbsə'lɛsns] N obsolescência; **built-in** or **planned ~** (Comm) obsolescência pré-incorporada

obsolescent [ɔbsə'lɛsnt] ADJ obsolescente, antiquado

obsolete ['ɔbsəli:t] ADJ obsoleto; **to become ~** cair em desuso

obstacle ['ɔbstəkl] N obstáculo; (hindrance) estorvo, impedimento

obstacle race N corrida de obstáculos

obstetrician [ɔbstə'trɪʃən] N obstetra m/f

obstetrics [ɔb'stɛtrɪks] N obstetrícia

obstinacy ['ɔbstɪnəsɪ] N teimosia, obstinação f

obstinate ['ɔbstɪnɪt] ADJ obstinado

obstreperous [əb'strɛpərəs] ADJ turbulento

obstruct [əb'strʌkt] VT obstruir; (block: pipe) entupir; (hinder) estorvar

obstruction [əb'strʌkʃən] N obstrução f; (object) obstáculo

obstructive [əb'strʌktɪv] ADJ obstrutor(a)

obtain [əb'teɪn] VT (get) obter; (achieve) conseguir ▶ VI prevalecer

obtainable [əb'teɪnəbl] ADJ disponível

obtrusive [əb'tru:sɪv] ADJ (person) intrometido, intruso; (building etc) que dá muito na vista

obtuse [əb'tju:s] ADJ obtuso

obverse ['ɔbvə:s] N (of medal, coin) obverso; (fig) contrapartida

obviate ['ɔbvɪeɪt] VT obviar a, prevenir

obvious ['ɔbvɪəs] ADJ (clear) óbvio, evidente; (unsubtle) nada sutil

obviously ['ɔbvɪəslɪ] ADV evidentemente; **~, he was not drunk** or **he was ~ not drunk** certamente ele não estava bêbado; **he was not ~ drunk** ele não aparentava estar bêbado; **~!** claro!, lógico!; **~ not!** (é)claro que não!

OCAS N ABBR (= Organization of Central American States) ODECA f

occasion [ə'keɪʒən] N ocasião f; (event) acontecimento ▶ VT ocasionar, causar; **on that ~** naquela ocasião; **to rise to the ~** mostrar-se à altura da situação

occasional [ə'keɪʒənl] ADJ de vez em quando

occasionally [ə'keɪʒənəlɪ] ADV de vez em quando; **very ~** raramente

occasional table N mesinha

occult [ɔ'kʌlt] ADJ oculto ▶ N: **the ~** as ciências ocultas

occupancy ['ɔkjupənsɪ] N ocupação f, posse f

occupant ['ɔkjupənt] N (of house)

inquilino(-a); (of car) ocupante m/f

occupation [ɔkju'peɪʃən] N ocupação f; (job) profissão f; **unfit for ~** (house) inabitável

occupational [ɔkju'peɪʃənl] ADJ (accident) de trabalho; (disease) profissional

occupational guidance (BRIT) N orientação f vocacional

occupational hazard N risco profissional

occupational pension N pensão f profissional

occupational therapy N terapia ocupacional

occupier ['ɔkjupaɪə'] N inquilino(-a)

occupy ['ɔkjupaɪ] VT ocupar; (house) morar em; **to ~ o.s. in doing** (as job) dedicar-se a fazer; (be busy with) ocupar-se de fazer; **to be occupied with sth** ocupar-se de algo

occur [ə'kə:'] VI (event) ocorrer; (phenomenon) acontecer; (difficulty, opportunity) surgir; **to ~ to sb** ocorrer a alguém; **it ~s to me that ...** ocorre-me que ...

occurrence [ə'kʌrəns] N (event) ocorrência, acontecimento; (existence) existência

ocean ['əuʃən] N oceano; **~s of** (inf) um monte de

ocean bed N fundo do oceano

ocean-going [-'gəuɪŋ] ADJ de longo curso

Oceania [əuʃɪ'eɪnɪə] N Oceania

ocean liner N transatlântico

ochre, (US) **ocher** ['əukə'] N cor de ocre inv

o'clock [ə'klɔk] ADV: **it is 5 ~** são cinco horas

OCR N ABBR = **optical character reader**; **optical character recognition**

Oct. ABBR (= October) out.

octagonal [ɔk'tægənl] ADJ octogonal

octane ['ɔkteɪn] N octano; **high-~ petrol** (BRIT) or **gas** (US) gasolina de alto índice de octana

octave ['ɔktɪv] N oitava

October [ɔk'təubə'] N outubro; see also **July**

octogenarian [ɔktəudʒɪ'nɛərɪən] N octogenário(-a)

octopus ['ɔktəpəs] N polvo

odd [ɔd] ADJ (strange) estranho, esquisito; (number) ímpar; (sock etc) desemparelhado; (left over) avulso, de sobra; **60-~** 60 e tantos; **at ~ times** às vezes, de vez em quando; **to be the ~ one out** ficar sobrando, ser a exceção

oddball ['ɔdbɔ:l] (inf) N excêntrico(-a), esquisitão(-ona) m/f

oddity ['ɔdɪtɪ] N coisa estranha, esquisitice f; (person) excêntrico(-a)

odd-job man (irreg: like **man**) N faz-tudo m

odd jobs NPL biscates mpl, bicos mpl

oddly ['ɔdlɪ] ADV curiosamente; see also **enough**

oddments ['ɔdmənts] (BRIT) NPL (Comm) retalhos mpl

odds [ɔdz] NPL (in betting) pontos mpl de vantagem; **the ~ are against his coming** é pouco provável que ele venha; **it makes no ~** dá no mesmo; **to succeed against all the ~** conseguir contra todas as expectativas; **at ~** brigados(-as), de mal

odds and ends NPL miudezas *fpl*
ode [əud] N ode *f*
odious ['əudɪəs] ADJ odioso
odometer [əu'dɔmɪtəʳ] N conta-quilômetros *m inv*
odour, (US) **odor** ['əudəʳ] N odor *m*, cheiro; (*unpleasant*) fedor *m*
odourless, (US) **odorless** ['əudəlɪs] ADJ inodoro
OECD N ABBR (= *Organization for Economic Cooperation and Development*) OCDE *f*
oesophagus, (US) **esophagus** [i:'sɔfəgəs] N esôfago
oestrogen, (US) **estrogen** ['i:strəudʒən] N estrogênio

(KEYWORD)

of [ɔv, əv] PREP **1** (*gen*) de; **the history of France** a história da França; **a friend of ours** um amigo nosso; **a boy of 10** um menino de 10 anos; **that was very kind of you** foi muito gentil da sua parte; **the city of New York** a cidade de Nova Iorque
2 (*expressing quantity, amount, dates etc*) de; **a kilo of flour** um quilo de farinha; **how much of this do you need?** de quanto você precisa?; **3 of them** 3 deles; **3 of us went** 3 de nós foram; **a cup of tea/vase of flowers** uma xícara de chá/um vaso de flores; **the 5th of July** dia 5 de julho
3 (*from, out of*) de; **a statue of marble** uma estátua de mármore; **made of wood** feito de madeira

(KEYWORD)

off [ɔf] ADV **1** (*distance, time*): **it's a long way off** fica bem longe; **the game is 3 days off** o jogo é daqui a 3 dias
2 (*departure*): **I'm off** estou de partida; **to go off to Paris/Italy** ir para Paris/a Itália; **I must be off** devo ir-me
3 (*removal*): **to take off one's hat/coat/clothes** tirar o chapéu/o casaco/a roupa; **the button came off** o botão caiu; **10% off** (*Comm*) 10% de abatimento *or* desconto
4 (*not at work: on holiday*) **to have a day off** tirar um dia de folga; (: *sick*): **to be off sick** estar ausente por motivo de saúde; **I'm off on Fridays** estou de folga às sextas-feiras
▶ ADJ **1** (*not turned on: machine, water, gas*) desligado; (: *light*) apagado; (: *tap*) fechado
2 (*cancelled: meeting, match, agreement*) cancelado
3 (*BRIT: not fresh: food*) passado; (: *milk*) talhado, anulado
4: **on the off chance** (*just in case*) ao acaso; **today I had an off day** (*not as good as usual*) hoje não foi o meu dia
▶ PREP **1** (*indicating motion, removal, etc*) de; **the button came off my coat** o botão do meu casaco caiu
2 (*distant from*) de; **5 km off (the road)** a 5 km (da estrada); **off the coast** em frente à costa

3: **to be off meat** (*no longer eat it*) não comer mais carne; (*no longer like it*) enjoar de carne

offal ['ɔfl] N (*Culin*) sobras *fpl*, restos *mpl*
offbeat ['ɔfbi:t] ADJ excêntrico
off-centre, (US) **off-center** ADJ descentrado, excêntrico
off-colour (BRIT) ADJ (*ill*) indisposto
offence, (US) **offense** [ə'fɛns] N (*crime*) delito; (*insult*) insulto, ofensa; **to give ~ to** ofender; **to take ~ at** ofender-se com, melindrar-se com; **to commit an ~** cometer uma infração
offend [ə'fɛnd] VT (*person*) ofender ▶ VI: **to ~ against** (*law, rule*) pecar contra, transgredir
offender [ə'fɛndəʳ] N delinquente *m/f*; (*against regulations*) infrator(a) *m/f*
offending [ə'fɛndɪŋ] ADJ polêmico
offense [ə'fɛns] (US) N = **offence**
offensive [ə'fɛnsɪv] ADJ (*weapon, remark*) ofensivo; (*smell etc*) repugnante ▶ N (*Mil*) ofensiva
offer ['ɔfəʳ] N oferta; (*proposal*) proposta ▶ VT oferecer; (*opportunity*) proporcionar; **to make an ~ for sth** fazer uma oferta por algo; **to ~ sth to sb, ~ sb sth** oferecer algo a alguém; **to ~ to do sth** oferecer-se para fazer algo; **"on ~"** (*Comm*) "em oferta"
offering ['ɔfərɪŋ] N oferenda
offertory ['ɔfətərɪ] N (*Rel*) ofertório
off-hand [ɔf'hænd] ADJ informal ▶ ADV de improviso; **I can't tell you ~** não posso te dizer assim de improviso
office ['ɔfɪs] N (*place*) escritório; (*room*) gabinete *m*; (*position*) cargo, função *f*; **to take ~** tomar posse; **doctor's ~** (US) consultório; **through his good ~s** (*fig*) graças aos grandes préstimos dele; **O~ of Fair Trading** (BRIT) *órgão de proteção ao consumidor*
office automation N automação *f* de escritórios
office bearer N (*of club etc*) detentor(a) *m/f* de um cargo
office block, (US) **office building** N conjunto de escritórios
office boy N contínuo, bói *m*
office building (US) N conjunto de escritórios
office hours NPL (horas *fpl* de) expediente *m*; (US Med) horas *fpl* de consulta
office manager N gerente *m/f* de escritório
officer ['ɔfɪsəʳ] N (Mil etc) oficial *m/f*; (*of organization*) diretor(a) *m/f*; (*also*: **police officer**) agente *m/f* policial *or* de polícia
office work N trabalho de escritório
office worker N empregado(-a) *or* funcionário(-a) de escritório
official [ə'fɪʃl] ADJ oficial ▶ N oficial *m/f*; (*civil servant*) funcionário(-a) público(-a)
officialdom [ə'fɪʃldəm] (*pej*) N burocracia
officially [ə'fɪʃəlɪ] ADV oficialmente
official receiver N síndico(-a) de massa falida

O

officiate [ə'fɪʃɪeɪt] vi (Rel) oficiar; **to ~ as Mayor** exercer as funções de prefeito; **to ~ at a marriage** celebrar um casamento

officious [ə'fɪʃəs] ADJ intrometido

offing ['ɔfɪŋ] N: **in the ~** (fig) em perspectiva

off-key ADJ, ADV desafinado

off-licence (BRIT) N (shop) loja de bebidas alcoólicas

> Uma loja **off-licence** vende bebidas alcoólicas (para viagem) nos horários em que os pubs estão fechados. Nesses estabelecimentos também se pode comprar bebidas não-alcoólicas, cigarros, batatas fritas, balas, chocolates etc.

off-limits (esp US) ADJ proibido

offline ['ɔf'laɪn] ADJ, ADV (Comput) off-line; (switched off) desligado

off-load vT: **to ~ sth (onto)** (goods) descarregar algo (sobre); (job) descarregar algo (em)

off-peak ADJ (heating etc) de período de pouco consumo; (ticket, train) de período de pouco movimento

off-putting [-'putɪŋ] (BRIT) ADJ desconcertante

off-season ADJ, ADV fora de estação or temporada

offset ['ɔfsɛt] (irreg: like **set**) vT (counteract) compensar, contrabalançar ▶ N (also: **offset printing**) ofsete m

offshoot ['ɔfʃuːt] (fig) N desdobramento

offshore [ɔf'ʃɔːʳ] ADV a pouca distância da costa, ao largo ▶ ADJ (breeze) de terra; (island) perto do litoral; (fishing) costeiro; **~ oilfield** campo petrolífero ao largo

offside ['ɔf'saɪd] N (Aut) lado do motorista ▶ ADJ (Sport) impedido; (Aut) do lado do motorista

offspring ['ɔfsprɪŋ] N descendência, prole f

offstage ['ɔf'steɪdʒ] ADV nos bastidores

off-the-cuff ADJ improvisado ▶ ADV de improviso

off-the-job training N treinamento fora do local de trabalho

off-the-peg, (US) **off-the-rack** ADJ pronto

off-white ADJ quase branco

often ['ɔfn] ADV muitas vezes, frequentemente; **how ~ do you go?** com que frequência você vai?; **as ~ as not** quase sempre; **very ~** com muita frequência

ogle ['əugl] vT comer com os olhos

ogre ['əugəʳ] N ogre m

OH (US) ABBR (Post) = **Ohio**

oh [əu] EXCL oh!, ô!, ah!

OHMS (BRIT) ABBR = **On His (or Her) Majesty's Service**

oil [ɔɪl] N (Culin) azeite m; (petroleum) petróleo; (for heating) óleo ▶ vT (machine) lubrificar

oilcan ['ɔɪlkæn] N almotolia; (for storing) lata

oil change N mudança de óleo

oilfield ['ɔɪlfiːld] N campo petrolífero

oil filter N (Aut) filtro de óleo

oil-fired [-'faɪəd] ADJ que usa óleo combustível

oil gauge N indicador m do nível de óleo

oil industry N indústria petroleira

oil level N nível m de óleo

oil painting N pintura a óleo

oil refinery N refinaria de petróleo

oil rig N torre f de perfuração

oilskins ['ɔɪlskɪnz] NPL capa de oleado

oil slick N mancha de óleo

oil tanker N (ship) petroleiro; (truck) carro-tanque m de petróleo

oil well N poço petrolífero

oily ['ɔɪlɪ] ADJ oleoso; (food) gorduroso

ointment ['ɔɪntmənt] N pomada

OK (US) ABBR (Post) = **Oklahoma**

O.K. ['əu'keɪ] EXCL está bem, está bom, tá (bem or bom) (inf) ▶ ADJ bom; (correct) certo ▶ vT aprovar ▶ N: **to give sth the ~** dar luz verde a algo; **is it ~?** tá bom?; **are you ~?** você está bem?; **are you ~ for money?** você está bem de dinheiro?; **it's ~ with** or **by me** para mim tudo bem

okay ['əu'keɪ] = **O.K.**

old [əuld] ADJ velho; (former) antigo, anterior; **how ~ are you?** quantos anos você tem?; **he's 10 years ~** ele tem 10 anos; **~er brother** irmão mais velho; **any ~ thing will do** qualquer coisa serve

old age N velhice f

old-age pensioner (BRIT) N aposentado(-a) (BR), reformado(-a) (PT)

old-fashioned [-'fæʃnd] ADJ fora de moda; (person) antiquado; (values) obsoleto, retrógrado

old maid N solteirona

old people's home N asilo de velhos

old-time ADJ antigo, do tempo antigo

old-timer N veterano

old wives' tale N conto da carochinha

olive ['ɔlɪv] N (fruit) azeitona; (tree) oliveira ▶ ADJ (also: **olive-green**) verde-oliva inv

olive oil N azeite m de oliva

Olympic [əu'lɪmpɪk] ADJ olímpico; **the ~ Games**, **the ~s** os Jogos Olímpicos, as Olimpíadas

OM (BRIT) N ABBR (= Order of Merit) título honorífico

Oman [əu'maːn] N Omã m (BR), Oman m (PT)

OMB (US) N ABBR (= Office of Management and Budget) serviço que assessora o presidente em assuntos orçamentários

omelette, (US) **omelet** ['ɔmlɪt] N omelete f

omen ['əumən] N presságio, agouro

OMG (inf) ABBR (= Oh my God!) OMG

ominous ['ɔmɪnəs] ADJ (menacing) preocupante; (event) de mau agouro

omission [əu'mɪʃən] N omissão f; (error) descuido, negligência

omit [əu'mɪt] vT omitir; (by mistake) esquecer; **to ~ to do sth** deixar de fazer algo

omnivorous [ɔm'nɪvərəs] ADJ onívoro

ON (CANADA) ABBR = **Ontario**

[KEYWORD]

on [ɔn] PREP **1** (indicating position) sobre, em (cima de); **on the wall** na parede; **on the left** à esquerda; **the house is on the main**

road a casa fica na rua principal
2 (*indicating means, method, condition etc*): **on foot** a pé; **on the train/plane** no trem/avião; **on the telephone/radio** no telefone/rádio; **on television** na televisão; **to be on drugs** (*addicted*) ser viciado em drogas; (*Med*) estar sob medicação; **to be on holiday/business** estar de férias/a negócio
3 (*referring to time*): **on Friday** na sexta-feira; **a week on Friday** sem ser esta sexta-feira, a outra; **on arrival** ao chegar; **on seeing this** ao ver isto
4 (*about, concerning*) sobre
▶ ADV **1** (*referring to dress*): **to have one's coat on** estar de casaco; **what's she got on?** o que ela está usando?; **she put her boots on** ela calçou as botas; **he put his gloves/hat on** ele colocou as luvas/o chapéu
2 (*referring to covering*): **screw the lid on tightly** atarraxar bem a tampa
3 (*further, continuously*): **to walk/drive on** continuar andando/dirigindo; **to go on** continuar (em frente); **to read on** continuar a ler
▶ ADJ **1** (*functioning, in operation: machine*) em funcionamento; (: *light*) aceso; (: *radio*) ligado; (: *tap*) aberto; (: *brakes: of car etc*): **to be on** estar freado; (*event*): **is the meeting still on?** (*in progress*) a reunião ainda está sendo realizada?; (*not cancelled*) ainda vai haver reunião?; **there's a good film on at the cinema** tem um bom filme passando no cinema
2: **that's not on!** (*inf: of behaviour*) isso não se faz!

ONC (*BRIT*) N ABBR = **Ordinary National Certificate**
once [wʌns] ADV uma vez; (*formerly*) outrora
▶ CONJ depois que; **~ he had left/it was done** depois que ele saiu/foi feito; **at ~** imediatamente; (*simultaneously*) de uma vez, ao mesmo tempo; **all at ~** de repente; **~ a week** uma vez por semana; **~ more** mais uma vez; **I knew him ~** eu o conheci antigamente; **~ and for all** uma vez por todas, definitivamente; **~ upon a time** era uma vez
oncoming [ˈɔnkʌmɪŋ] ADJ (*traffic*) que vem de frente
OND (*BRIT*) N ABBR = **Ordinary National Diploma**

(KEYWORD)

one [wʌn] NUM um(a); **one hundred and fifty** cento e cinquenta; **one by one** um por um
▶ ADJ **1** (*sole*) único; **the one book which ...** o único livro que ...
2 (*same*) mesmo; **they came in the one car** eles vieram no mesmo carro
▶ PRON **1** um(a); **this one** este/esta; **that one** esse/essa, aquele/aquela; **I've already got one/a red one** eu já tenho um/um vermelho
2: **one another** um ao outro; **do you two ever see one another?** vocês dois se veem de vez em quando?; **the boys didn't dare look at one another** os meninos não ousaram olhar um para o outro
3 (*impers*): **one never knows** nunca se sabe; **to cut one's finger** cortar o dedo; **one needs to eat** é preciso comer

one-armed bandit N caça-níqueis *m inv*
one-day excursion (*US*) N bilhete *m* de ida e volta
one-man ADJ (*business*) individual
one-man band N homem-orquestra *m*
one-off (*BRIT inf*) N exemplar *m* único ▶ ADJ único
one-piece ADJ: **~ bathing suit** maiô inteiro
onerous [ˈəunərəs] ADJ (*task, duty*) incômodo; (*responsibility*) pesado
oneself [wʌnˈsɛlf] PRON (*reflexive*) se; (*after prep, emphatic*) si (mesmo(-a)); **by ~** sozinho(-a); **to hurt ~** ferir-se; **to keep sth for ~** guardar algo para si mesmo; **to talk to ~** falar consigo mesmo
one-sided [-ˈsaɪdɪd] ADJ (*decision*) unilateral; (*judgement, account*) parcial; (*contest*) desigual
one-time ADJ antigo
one-to-one ADJ (*relationship*) individual
one-upmanship [-ˈʌpmənʃɪp] N: **the art of ~** a arte de aparentar ser melhor do que os outros
one-way ADJ (*street, traffic*) de mão única (*BR*), de sentido único (*PT*)
ongoing [ˈɔngəuɪŋ] ADJ (*project*) em andamento; (*situation*) existente
onion [ˈʌnjən] N cebola
online [ˈɔnˈlaɪn] ADJ, ADV (*Comput*) on-line, online; (*switched on*) ligado
onlooker [ˈɔnlukəʳ] N espectador(a) *m/f*
only [ˈəunlɪ] ADV somente, apenas ▶ ADJ único, só ▶ CONJ só que, porém; **an ~ child** um filho único; **not ~ ... but also ...** não só ... mas também ...; **I ~ ate one** eu comi só um; **I saw her ~ yesterday** apenas ontem eu a vi; **I'd be ~ too pleased to help** eu teria muitíssimo prazer em ajudar; **I would come, ~ I'm very busy** eu iria, porém estou muito ocupado
ono ABBR (= *or nearest offer*) ou melhor oferta
onset [ˈɔnsɛt] N (*beginning*) começo; (*attack*) ataque *m*
onshore [ˈɔnʃɔːʳ] ADJ (*wind*) do mar
onslaught [ˈɔnslɔːt] N investida, arremetida
on-the-job training N treinamento no serviço
onto [ˈɔntu] PREP = **on to**
onus [ˈəunəs] N responsabilidade *f*; **the ~ is upon him to prove it** cabe a ele comprová-lo
onward [ˈɔnwəd], **onwards** [ˈɔnwədz] ADV (*move*) para diante, para a frente; **from this time ~(s)** de (ag)ora em diante

O

onyx ['ɒnɪks] N ônix m

ooze [uːz] VI ressumar, filtrar-se; **to ~ a feeling** mostrar um sentimento exagerado

opacity [əu'pæsɪtɪ] N opacidade f

opal ['əupl] N opala

opaque [əu'peɪk] ADJ opaco, fosco

OPEC ['əupɛk] N ABBR (= Organization of Petroleum-Exporting Countries) OPEP f

open ['əupn] ADJ aberto; (car) descoberto; (road) livre; (fig: frank) aberto, franco; (meeting) aberto, sem restrições; (admiration) declarado; (question) discutível; (enemy) assumido ▶ VT abrir ▶ VI (gen) abrir(-se); (shop) abrir; (book etc: commence) começar; **in the ~ (air)** ao ar livre; **the ~ sea** o largo; **~ ground** (among trees) clareira, abertura; (waste ground) terreno baldio; **to have an ~ mind (on sth)** estar imparcial (quanto a algo)
▶ **open on to** VT FUS (subj: room, door) dar para
▶ **open out** VT abrir ▶ VI abrir-se
▶ **open up** VT abrir; (blocked road) desobstruir ▶ VI (Comm) abrir

open-air ADJ a céu aberto

open-and-shut ADJ: **~ case** caso evidente

open day (BRIT) N dia m de visita

open-ended [-'ɛndɪd] ADJ (fig) não limitado

opener ['əupnə^r] N (also: **can opener, tin opener**) abridor m de latas (BR), abre-latas m inv (PT)

open-heart surgery N cirurgia de coração aberto

opening ['əupnɪŋ] ADJ de abertura ▶ N abertura; (start) início; (opportunity) oportunidade f; (job) vaga

opening night N (Theatre) estreia

openly ['əupnlɪ] ADV abertamente

open-minded [-'maɪndɪd] ADJ aberto, imparcial

open-necked [-nɛkt] ADJ aberto no colo

openness ['əupnnɪs] N abertura, sinceridade f

open-plan ADJ sem paredes divisórias

open sandwich N canapê m

open shop N empresa que admite trabalhadores não sindicalizados

Open University (BRIT) N ver nota

> Fundada em 1969, a **Open University** oferece um tipo de ensino que compreende cursos (alguns blocos da programação da TV e do rádio são reservados para esse fim), deveres que são enviados pelo aluno ao diretor ou diretora de estudos e uma estada obrigatória em uma universidade de verão. É preciso cumprir um certo número de unidades ao longo de um período determinado e obter a média em um certo número delas para receber o diploma almejado.

opera ['ɒpərə] N ópera

opera glasses NPL binóculo de teatro

opera house N teatro lírico or de ópera

opera singer N cantor(a) m/f de ópera

operate ['ɒpəreɪt] VT (machine) fazer funcionar, pôr em funcionamento; (company) dirigir ▶ VI funcionar; (drug) fazer efeito; (Med): **to ~ on sb** operar alguém

operatic [ɒpə'rætɪk] ADJ lírico, operístico

operating ['ɒpəreɪtɪŋ] ADJ (Comm: costs, profit) operacional

operating system N (Comput) sistema m operacional

operating table N mesa de operações

operating theatre N sala de operações

operation [ɒpə'reɪʃən] N operação f; (of machine) funcionamento; **to have an ~** fazer uma operação; **to be in ~** (system) estar em vigor; (machine) estar funcionando

operational [ɒpə'reɪʃənl] ADJ operacional; **when the service is fully ~** quando o serviço estiver com toda a sua eficácia

operative ['ɒpərətɪv] ADJ (measure) em vigor ▶ N (in factory) operário(-a); **the ~ word** a palavra mais importante or atuante

operator ['ɒpəreɪtə^r] N (of machine) operador(a) m/f, manipulador(a) m/f; (Tel) telefonista m/f

operetta [ɒpə'rɛtə] N opereta

ophthalmic [ɒf'θælmɪk] ADJ oftálmico

ophthalmologist [ɒfθæl'mɔlədʒɪst] N oftalmologista m/f, oftalmólogo(-a)

opinion [ə'pɪnɪən] N opinião f; **in my ~** na minha opinião, a meu ver; **to seek a second ~** procurar uma segunda opinião

opinionated [ə'pɪnɪəneɪtɪd] ADJ opinioso

opinion poll N pesquisa, levantamento

opium ['əupɪəm] N ópio

opponent [ə'pəunənt] N oponente m/f; (Mil, Sport) adversário(-a)

opportune ['ɒpətjuːn] ADJ oportuno

opportunism [ɒpə'tjuːnɪzəm] N oportunismo

opportunist [ɒpə'tjuːnɪst] N (pej) oportunista m/f

opportunity [ɒpə'tjuːnɪtɪ] N oportunidade f; **to take the ~ of doing** aproveitar a oportunidade para fazer

oppose [ə'pəuz] VT opor-se a; **to be ~d to sth** opor-se a algo, estar contra algo; **as ~d to** em oposição a

opposing [ə'pəuzɪŋ] ADJ (side) oposto, contrário

opposite ['ɒpəzɪt] ADJ oposto; (house etc) em frente ▶ ADV (lá) em frente ▶ PREP em frente de, defronte de ▶ N oposto, contrário; **the ~ sex** o sexo oposto

opposite number (BRIT) N homólogo(-a)

opposition [ɒpə'zɪʃən] N oposição f

oppress [ə'prɛs] VT oprimir

oppression [ə'prɛʃən] N opressão f

oppressive [ə'prɛsɪv] ADJ opressivo

opprobrium [ə'prəubrɪəm] N (formal) opróbrio

opt [ɒpt] VI: **to ~ for** optar por; **to ~ to do** optar por fazer
▶ **opt out** VI: **to ~ out of doing sth** optar por não fazer algo

optical ['ɔptɪkl] ADJ ótico
optical character reader N leitora de caracteres óticos
optical character recognition N reconhecimento de caracteres óticos
optical fibre N fibra ótica
optical illusion N ilusão f ótica
optician [ɔp'tɪʃən] N oculista m/f
optics ['ɔptɪks] N ótica
optimism ['ɔptɪmɪzəm] N otimismo
optimist ['ɔptɪmɪst] N otimista m/f
optimistic [ɔptɪ'mɪstɪk] ADJ otimista
optimum ['ɔptɪməm] ADJ ótimo
option ['ɔpʃən] N opção f; **to keep one's ~s open** (fig) manter as opções em aberto;
I have no ~ não tenho opção or escolha
optional ['ɔpʃənəl] ADJ opcional, facultativo;
~ extras acessórios mpl opcionais
opulence ['ɔpjuləns] N opulência
opulent ['ɔpjulənt] ADJ opulento
OR (US) ABBR (Post) = **Oregon**
or [ɔːʳ] CONJ ou; (with negative): **he hasn't seen or heard anything** ele não viu nem ouviu nada; **or else** senão; **either …, or else** ou …, ou (então)
oracle ['ɔrəkl] N oráculo
oral ['ɔːrəl] ADJ oral ▶ N prova f oral
orange ['ɔrɪndʒ] N (fruit) laranja ▶ ADJ cor de laranja inv, alaranjado
orangeade [ɔrɪndʒ'eɪd] N laranjada
oration [ɔː'reɪʃən] N oração f
orator ['ɔrətəʳ] N orador(a) m/f
oratorio [ɔrə'tɔːrɪəu] N oratório
orb [ɔːb] N orbe m
orbit ['ɔːbɪt] N órbita ▶ VT, VI orbitar; **to be/go into ~ (around)** estar/entrar em órbita (em torno de)
orchard ['ɔːtʃəd] N pomar m; **apple ~** pomar de macieiras
orchestra ['ɔːkɪstrə] N orquestra; (US: seating) plateia
orchestral [ɔː'kɛstrəl] ADJ orquestral; (concert) sinfônico
orchestrate ['ɔːkɪstreɪt] VT (Mus, fig) orquestrar
orchid ['ɔːkɪd] N orquídea
ordain [ɔː'deɪn] VT ordenar, decretar; (decide) decidir, mandar
ordeal [ɔː'diːl] N experiência penosa, provação f
order ['ɔːdəʳ] N (gen) ordem f; (Comm) encomenda ▶ VT (also: **put in order**) pôr em ordem, arrumar; (in restaurant) pedir; (Comm) encomendar; (command) mandar, ordenar;
in ~ em ordem; **in (working) ~** em bom estado; **in ~ of preference** por ordem de preferência; **in ~ to do/that** para fazer/que (+ sub); **good ~** bom estado; **on ~** (Comm) encomendado; **out of ~** com defeito, enguiçado; **to ~ sb to do sth** mandar alguém fazer algo; **to place an ~ for sth with sb** fazer uma encomenda a alguém para algo, encomendar algo a alguém;

made to ~ feito sob encomenda; **to be under ~s to do sth** ter ordens para fazer algo; **a point of ~** uma questão de ordem; **to the ~ of** (Banking) à ordem de
order book N livro de encomendas
order form N impresso para encomendas
orderly ['ɔːdəlɪ] N (Mil) ordenança m; (Med) servente m/f ▶ ADJ (room) arrumado, ordenado; (person) metódico
order number N número de encomenda
ordinal ['ɔːdɪnl] ADJ (number) ordinal
ordinary ['ɔːdnrɪ] ADJ comum, usual; (pej) ordinário, medíocre; **out of the ~** fora do comum, extraordinário
ordinary seaman (BRIT) (irreg: like **man**) N marinheiro de segunda classe
ordinary shares NPL ações fpl ordinárias
ordination [ɔːdɪ'neɪʃən] N ordenação f
ordnance ['ɔːdnəns] N (Mil: unit) artilharia
Ordnance Survey (BRIT) N serviço oficial de topografia e cartografia
ore [ɔːʳ] N minério
organ ['ɔːɡən] N (gen) órgão m
organic [ɔː'ɡænɪk] ADJ orgânico
organism ['ɔːɡənɪzəm] N organismo
organist ['ɔːɡənɪst] N organista m/f
organization [ɔːɡənaɪ'zeɪʃən] N organização f
organization chart N organograma m
organize ['ɔːɡənaɪz] VT organizar; **to get ~d** organizar-se
organized crime ['ɔːɡənaɪzd-] N crime m organizado
organized labour ['ɔːɡənaɪzd-] N mão-de-obra f sindicalizada
organizer ['ɔːɡənaɪzəʳ] N organizador(a) m/f
orgasm ['ɔːɡæzəm] N orgasmo
orgy ['ɔːdʒɪ] N orgia
Orient ['ɔːrɪənt] N: **the ~** o Oriente
oriental [ɔːrɪ'entl] ADJ, N oriental m/f
orientate ['ɔːrɪənteɪt] VT: **to ~ o.s.** orientar-se
orifice ['ɔrɪfɪs] N orifício
origin ['ɔrɪdʒɪn] N origem f; (point of departure) procedência; **country of ~** país de origem
original [ə'rɪdʒɪnl] ADJ original ▶ N original m
originality [ərɪdʒɪ'nælɪtɪ] N originalidade f
originally [ə'rɪdʒɪnəlɪ] ADV (at first) originalmente; (with originality) com originalidade
originate [ə'rɪdʒɪneɪt] VI: **to ~ from** originar-se de, surgir de; **to ~ in** ter origem em
originator [ə'rɪdʒɪneɪtəʳ] N iniciador(a) m/f
Orkney ['ɔːknɪ] N (also: **the Orkney Islands, the Orkneys**) as ilhas Órcadas
ornament ['ɔːnəmənt] N ornamento; (trinket) quinquilharia; (on dress) enfeite m
ornamental [ɔːnə'mentl] ADJ decorativo, ornamental
ornamentation [ɔːnəmɛn'teɪʃən] N ornamentação f

O

ornate [ɔː'neɪt] ADJ enfeitado, requintado
ornithologist [ɔːnɪ'θɔlədʒɪst] N ornitólogo(-a)
ornithology [ɔːnɪ'θɔlədʒɪ] N ornitologia
orphan ['ɔːfn] N órfão/órfã *m/f* ▶ VT: **to be ~ed**
ficar órfão
orphanage ['ɔːfənɪdʒ] N orfanato
orthodox ['ɔːθədɔks] ADJ ortodoxo
orthopaedic, (*US*) **orthopedic** [ɔːθə'piːdɪk]
ADJ ortopédico
OS (*BRIT*) ABBR = **Ordnance Survey**; (*Naut*)
= **ordinary seaman**; (*Dress*) = **outsize**
O/S ABBR = **out of stock**
oscillate ['ɔsɪleɪt] VI oscilar; (*person*) vacilar,
hesitar
OSHA (*US*) N ABBR (= *Occupational Safety and
Health Administration*) *órgão que supervisiona a
higiene e a segurança do trabalho*
Oslo ['ɔzləu] N Oslo
ostensible [ɔs'tɛnsɪbl] ADJ aparente
ostensibly [ɔs'tɛnsɪblɪ] ADV aparentemente
ostentation [ɔstɛn'teɪʃən] N ostentação *f*
ostentatious [ɔstɛn'teɪʃəs] ADJ pomposo,
espalhafatoso; (*person*) ostentoso
osteopath ['ɔstɪəpæθ] N osteopata *m/f*
ostracize ['ɔstrəsaɪz] VT condenar ao
ostracismo
ostrich ['ɔstrɪtʃ] N avestruz *m/f*
OT N ABBR (= *Old Testament*) AT *m*
OTB (*US*) N ABBR (= *off-track betting*) *apostas
tomadas fora da pista de corridas*
other ['ʌðəʳ] ADJ outro ▶ PRON: **the ~ (one)**
o outro/a outra ▶ ADV (*usually in negatives*):
~ than (*apart from*) além de; (*anything but*)
exceto; **~s** (*other people*) outros; **some ~
people have still to arrive** outras pessoas
ainda não chegaram; **the ~ day** outro dia;
some actor or ~ um certo ator; **somebody
or ~** não sei quem, alguém; **the car was
none ~ than John's** o carro não era nenhum
outro senão o de João
otherwise ['ʌðəwaɪz] ADV (*in a different way*) de
outra maneira; (*apart from that*) além disso
▶ CONJ (*if not*) senão; **an ~ good piece of
work** sob outros aspectos um trabalho bem
feito
OTT (*inf*) ABBR = **over the top**; *see* **top**
otter ['ɔtəʳ] N lontra
OU (*BRIT*) N ABBR = **Open University**
ouch [autʃ] EXCL ai!
ought [ɔːt] (*pt* **ought**) AUX VB: **I ~ to do it** eu
deveria fazê-lo; **this ~ to have been
corrected** isto deveria ter sido corrigido;
he ~ to win (*probability*) ele deve ganhar;
you ~ to go and see it você deveria ir vê-lo
ounce [auns] N onça (= *28.35g*)
our ['auəʳ] ADJ nosso; *see also* **my**
ours ['auəz] PRON (o) nosso/(a) nossa *etc*; *see
also* **mine¹**
ourselves [auə'sɛlvz] PRON PL (*reflexive, after
prep*) nós; (*emphatic*) nós mesmos(-as); **we did
it (all) by ~** nós fizemos isso sozinhos; *see
also* **oneself**
oust [aust] VT expulsar

out [aut] ADV **1** (*not in*) fora; (**to stand**) **out
in the rain/snow** (estar em pé) na chuva/
neve; **it's cold out here/out in the desert**
está frio aqui fora/faz frio lá no deserto;
out here/there aqui/lá fora; **to go/come etc
out** sair/vir *etc* para fora; **out loud** em voz
alta
2 (*not at home, absent*) fora (de casa); **Mr Green
is out at the moment** Sr. Green não está no
momento; **to have a day/night out** passar
o dia fora/sair à noite
3 (*indicating distance*): **the boat was 10 km
out** o barco estava a 10 km da costa; **3 days
out from Plymouth** a 3 dias de Plymouth
4 (*Sport*): **the ball is/has gone out** a bola
caiu fora; **out!** (*Tennis etc*) fora!
▶ ADJ **1**: **to be out** (*unconscious*) estar
inconsciente; (*out of game*) estar fora; (*out of
fashion*) estar fora de moda
2 (*have appeared: news, secret*) do conhecimento
público; **the flowers are out** as flores
desabrocharam
3 (*extinguished: light, fire*) apagado; **before the
week was out** (*finished*) antes da semana
acabar
4: **to be out to do sth** (*intend*) pretender
fazer algo; **to be out in one's calculations**
(*wrong*) enganar-se nos cálculos
▶ **out of** PREP **1** (*outside, beyond*) fora de; **to go
out of the house** sair da casa; **to look out
of the window** olhar pela janela
2 (*cause, motive*) por; **out of curiosity/fear/
greed** por curiosidade/medo/ganância
3 (*origin*): **to drink sth out of a cup** beber
algo na xícara; **to copy sth out of a book**
copiar algo de um livro
4 (*from among*): **1 out of every 3 smokers** 1
entre 3 fumantes; **out of 100 cars sold,
only one had any faults** dos 100 carros
vendidos, só um tinha defeito
5 (*without*) sem; **to be out of milk/sugar/
petrol** *etc* não ter leite/açúcar/gasolina *etc*

outage ['autɪdʒ] (*esp US*) N (*power failure*)
blecaute *m*
out-and-out ADJ (*liar etc*) completo, rematado
outback ['autbæk] N (*in Australia*): **the ~** o
interior
outbid [aut'bɪd] (*pt, pp* **outbid**) VT sobrepujar
outboard ['autbɔːd] N (*also*: **outboard motor**)
motor *m* de popa
outbox ['autbɔks] N (*Comput*) caixa de saída;
(*US: for papers*) cesta de saída
outbreak ['autbreɪk] N (*of war*) deflagração *f*;
(*of disease*) surto; (*of violence etc*) explosão *f*
outbuilding ['autbɪldɪŋ] N dependência
outburst ['autbəːst] N explosão *f*
outcast ['autkɑːst] N pária *m/f*
outclass [aut'klɑːs] VT ultrapassar, superar
outcome ['autkʌm] N resultado
outcrop ['autkrɔp] N afloramento
outcry ['autkraɪ] N clamor *m* (de protesto)

outdated [aut'deɪtɪd] ADJ antiquado, fora de moda

outdistance [aut'dɪstəns] VT deixar para trás

outdo [aut'duː] (*irreg: like* **do**) VT ultrapassar, exceder

outdoor [aut'dɔːʳ] ADJ ao ar livre; (*clothes*) de sair

outdoors [aut'dɔːz] ADV ao ar livre

outer ['autəʳ] ADJ exterior, externo

outer space N espaço (exterior)

outfit ['autfɪt] N roupa, traje *m*; (*inf: Comm*) firma

outfitter's ['autfɪtəz] (BRIT) N fornecedor *m* de roupas

outgoing ['autgəuɪŋ] ADJ (*president, tenant*) de saída; (*character*) extrovertido, sociável

outgoings ['autgəuɪŋz] (BRIT) NPL despesas *fpl*

outgrow [aut'grəu] (*irreg: like* **grow**) VT: **he has ~n his clothes** a roupa ficou pequena para ele

outhouse ['authaus] N anexo

outing ['autɪŋ] N (*going out*) saída; (*excursion*) excursão *f*

outlandish [aut'lændɪʃ] ADJ estranho, bizarro

outlast [aut'lɑːst] VT sobreviver a

outlaw ['autlɔː] N fora-da-lei *m/f* ▶ VT (*person*) declarar fora da lei; (*practice*) declarar ilegal

outlay ['autleɪ] N despesas *fpl*

outlet ['autlɛt] N saída, escape *m*; (*of pipe*) desague *m*, escoadouro; (*US Elec*) tomada; (*also:* **retail outlet**) posto de venda

outline ['autlaɪn] N (*shape*) contorno, perfil *m*; (*of plan*) traçado; (*sketch*) esboço, linhas *fpl* gerais ▶ VT (*theory, plan*) traçar, delinear

outlive [aut'lɪv] VT sobreviver a

outlook ['autluk] N (*attitude*) ponto de vista; (*fig: prospects*) perspectiva; (*: for weather*) previsão *f*

outlying ['autlaɪɪŋ] ADJ afastado, remoto

outmanoeuvre, (US) **outmaneuver** [autmə'nuːvəʳ] VT (*rival etc*) passar a perna em

outmoded [aut'məudɪd] ADJ antiquado, fora de moda, obsoleto

outnumber [aut'nʌmbəʳ] VT exceder em número

out-of-court [autəv'kɔːt] ADJ extrajudicial ▶ ADV extrajudicialmente

out-of-date ADJ (*passport, ticket*) sem validade; (*theory, idea*) antiquado, superado; (*custom*) antiquado; (*clothes*) fora de moda

out-of-the-way ADJ remoto, afastado; (*fig*) insólito

outpatient ['autpeɪʃənt] N paciente *m/f* externo(-a) *or* de ambulatório

outpost ['autpəust] N posto avançado

output ['autput] N (*volume m de*) produção *f*; (*Tech*) rendimento; (*Comput*) saída ▶ VT (*Comput*) dar saída em

outrage ['autreɪdʒ] N (*scandal*) escândalo; (*atrocity*) atrocidade *f* ▶ VT ultrajar

outrageous [aut'reɪdʒəs] ADJ ultrajante, escandaloso

outrider ['autraɪdəʳ] N (*on motorcycle*) batedor(a) *m/f*

outright [*adv* aut'raɪt, *adj* 'autraɪt] ADV (*kill, win*) completamente; (*ask, refuse*) abertamente ▶ ADJ completo; franco

outrun [aut'rʌn] (*irreg: like* **run**) VT ultrapassar

outset ['autsɛt] N início, princípio

outshine [aut'ʃaɪn] (*irreg: like* **shine**) VT (*fig*) eclipsar

outside [aut'saɪd] N exterior *m* ▶ ADJ exterior, externo; (*contractor etc*) de fora ▶ ADV (lá) fora ▶ PREP fora de; (*beyond*) além (dos limites) de; **at the ~** (*fig*) no máximo; **an ~ chance** uma possibilidade remota

outside broadcast N (*Radio, TV*) transmissão *f* de exteriores

outside lane N (*Aut: in Britain*) pista da direita; (*: in US, Europe*) pista da esquerda

outside left N (*Football*) extremo-esquerdo

outside line N (*Tel*) linha de saída

outsider [aut'saɪdəʳ] N (*stranger*) estranho(-a), forasteiro(-a); (*in race etc*) outsider *m*

outsize ['autsaɪz] ADJ (*clothes*) de tamanho extra-grande *or* especial

outskirts ['autskəːts] NPL arredores *mpl*, subúrbios *mpl*

outsmart [aut'smɑːt] VT passar a perna em

outspoken [aut'spəukən] ADJ franco, sem rodeios

outspread [aut'sprɛd] ADJ estendido

outstanding [aut'stændɪŋ] ADJ excepcional; (*work, debt*) pendente; **your account is still ~** a sua conta ainda não está liquidada

outstay [aut'steɪ] VT: **to ~ one's welcome** abusar da hospitalidade (demorando mais tempo)

outstretched [aut'strɛtʃt] ADJ (*hand*) estendido; (*body*) esticado

outstrip [aut'strɪp] VT (*competitors, demand*) ultrapassar

out tray N cesta de saída

outvote [aut'vəut] VT: **to ~ sb (by ...)** vencer alguém (por ... votos); **to ~ sth (by ...)** rejeitar algo (por ... votos)

outward ['autwəd] ADJ (*sign, appearances*) externo; (*journey*) de ida

outwardly ['autwədlɪ] ADV para fora

outwards ['autwədz] (*esp* BRIT) ADV para fora

outweigh [aut'weɪ] VT ter mais valor do que

outwit [aut'wɪt] VT passar a perna em

oval ['əuvl] ADJ ovalado ▶ N oval *m*

Oval Office N *ver nota*

O Salão Oval (**Oval Office**) é o escritório particular do presidente dos Estados Unidos na Casa Branca, assim chamado devido a sua forma oval. Por extensão, o termo se refere à presidência em si.

ovary ['əuvərɪ] N ovário

ovation [əu'veɪʃən] N ovação *f*

oven ['ʌvn] N forno

ovenproof ['ʌvnpruːf] ADJ refratário

oven-ready ADJ pronto para o forno

ovenware ['ʌvnwɛəʳ] N louça refratária

(KEYWORD)

over ['əʊvə'] ADV **1** (*across: walk, jump, fly etc*) por cima; **to cross over to the other side of the road** atravessar para o outro lado da rua; **over here** por aqui, cá; **over there** por ali, lá; **to ask sb over** (*to one's home*) convidar alguém
2: **to fall over** cair; **to knock over** derrubar; **to turn over** virar; **to bend over** curvar-se, debruçar-se
3 (*finished*): **to be over** estar acabado
4 (*excessively: clever, rich, fat etc*) muito, demais; **she's not over intelligent** ela não é superdotada
5 (*remaining: money, food etc*): **there are 3 over** tem 3 sobrando/sobraram 3; **is there any cake left over?** sobrou bolo?
6: **all over** (*everywhere*) por todos os lados; **over and over** (*again*) repetidamente
▶ PREP **1** (*on top of*) sobre; (*above*) acima de
2 (*on the other side of*) no outro lado de; **he jumped over the wall** ele pulou o muro
3 (*more than*) mais de; **over and above** além de; **this order is over and above what we have already ordered** esta encomenda está acima do que já havíamos pedido
4 (*during*) durante; **let's discuss it over dinner** vamos discutir isto durante o jantar

over... ['əʊvə'] PREFIX sobre..., super...
overabundant [əʊvərə'bʌndənt] ADJ superabundante
overact [əʊvər'ækt] VI (*Theatre*) exagerar
overall [*n, adj* 'əʊvərɔːl, *adv* əʊvər'ɔːl] ADJ (*length*) total; (*study*) global ▶ ADV (*view*) globalmente; (*measure, paint*) totalmente; **overalls** NPL macacão *m* (BR), (fato) macaco (PT)
overanxious [əʊvər'æŋkʃəs] ADJ muito ansioso
overawe [əʊvər'ɔː] VT intimidar
overbalance [əʊvə'bæləns] VI perder o equilíbrio, desequilibrar-se
overbearing [əʊvə'bɛərɪŋ] ADJ autoritário, dominador(a); (*arrogant*) arrogante
overboard ['əʊvəbɔːd] ADV (*Naut*) ao mar; **man ~!** homem ao mar!; **to go ~ for sth** (*fig*) empolgar-se com algo
overbook [əʊvə'bʊk] VI reservar em excesso
overcapitalize [əʊvə'kæpɪtəlaɪz] VT sobrecapitalizar
overcast ['əʊvəkɑːst] ADJ nublado, fechado
overcharge [əʊvə'tʃɑːdʒ] VT: **to ~ sb** cobrar em excesso a alguém
overcoat ['əʊvəkəʊt] N sobretudo
overcome [əʊvə'kʌm] (*irreg: like* **come**) VT vencer, dominar; (*difficulty*) superar ▶ ADJ (*emotionally*) assolado; **~ with grief** tomado pela dor
overconfident [əʊvə'kɒnfɪdənt] ADJ confiante em excesso
overcrowded [əʊvə'kraʊdɪd] ADJ superlotado; (*country*) superpovoado

overcrowding [əʊvə'kraʊdɪŋ] N superlotação *f*; (*in country*) superpovoamento
overdo [əʊvə'duː] (*irreg: like* **do**) VT exagerar; (*overcook*) cozinhar demais; **to ~ it, to ~ things** (*work too hard*) exceder-se; (*go too far*) exagerar
overdose ['əʊvədəʊs] N overdose *f*, dose *f* excessiva
overdraft ['əʊvədrɑːft] N saldo negativo
overdrawn [əʊvə'drɔːn] ADJ (*account*) sem fundos, a descoberto
overdue [əʊvə'djuː] ADJ atrasado; (*Comm*) vencido; (*change*) tardio; **that change was long ~** essa mudança foi muito protelada
overestimate [əʊvər'ɛstɪmeɪt] VT sobrestimar
overexcited [əʊvərɪk'saɪtɪd] ADJ superexcitado
over-exertion [əʊvərɪg'zəːʃən] N estafa
overexpose [əʊvərɪk'spəʊz] VT (*Phot*) expor demais (à luz)
overflow [*vi* əʊvə'fləʊ, *n* 'əʊvəfləʊ] VI transbordar ▶ N (*excess*) excesso; (*also:* **overflow pipe**) tubo de descarga, ladrão *m*
overfly [əʊvə'flaɪ] (*irreg: like* **fly**) VT sobrevoar
overgenerous [əʊvə'dʒɛnərəs] ADJ pródigo; (*offer*) excessivo
overgrown [əʊvə'grəʊn] ADJ (*garden*) coberto de vegetação; **he's just an ~ schoolboy** (*fig*) ele é apenas um garotão de escola
overhang [*vt, vi* əʊvə'hæŋ, *n* 'əʊvəhæŋ] (*irreg: like* **hang**) VT sobrepairar ▶ VI sobressair ▶ N saliência, ressalto
overhaul [*vt* əʊvə'hɔːl, *n* 'əʊvəhɔːl] VT revisar ▶ N revisão *f*
overhead [*adv* əʊvə'hɛd, *adj, n* 'əʊvəhɛd] ADV por cima, em cima; (*in the sky*) no céu ▶ ADJ (*lighting*) superior; (*railway*) suspenso ▶ N (US) = **overheads**
overheads ['əʊvəhɛdz] NPL (*expenses*) despesas *fpl* gerais
overhear [əʊvə'hɪə'] (*irreg: like* **hear**) VT ouvir por acaso
overheat [əʊvə'hiːt] VI ficar superaquecido; (*engine*) aquecer demais
overjoyed [əʊvə'dʒɔɪd] ADJ: **to be ~ (at)** estar muito alegre (com)
overkill ['əʊvəkɪl] N (*fig*): **it would be ~** seria exagero, seria matar mosquito com tiro de canhão
overland ['əʊvəlænd] ADJ, ADV por terra
overlap [*vi* əʊvə'læp, *n* 'əʊvəlæp] VI (*edges*) sobrepor-se em parte; (*fig*) coincidir ▶ N sobreposição *f*
overleaf [əʊvə'liːf] ADV no verso
overload [əʊvə'ləʊd] VT sobrecarregar
overlook [əʊvə'lʊk] VT (*have view on*) dar para; (*miss*) omitir; (*forgive*) fazer vista grossa a
overlord ['əʊvəlɔːd] N suserano
overmanning [əʊvə'mænɪŋ] N excesso de pessoal
overnight [*adv* əʊvə'naɪt, *adj* 'əʊvənaɪt] ADV durante a noite; (*fig: suddenly*) da noite para

o dia ▸ ADJ de uma (or de) noite; (decision) tomada da noite para o dia; **to stay ~** passar a noite, pernoitar; **if you travel ~ ...** se você viajar de noite ...; **he'll be away ~** ele não voltará hoje

overpaid [əuvə'peɪd] PT, PP of **overpay**

overpass ['əuvəpɑːs] (esp US) N viaduto

overpay [əuvə'peɪ] (irreg: like **pay**) VT: **to ~ sb by £50** pagar £50 em excesso a alguém

overpower [əuvə'pauəʳ] VT dominar, subjugar; (fig) assolar

overpowering [əuvə'pauərɪŋ] ADJ (heat, stench) sufocante

overproduction [əuvəprə'dʌkʃən] N super-produção f

overrate [əuvə'reɪt] VT sobrestimar, supervalorizar

overreach [əuvə'riːtʃ] VT: **to ~ o.s.** exceder-se

overreact [əuvəriː'ækt] VI reagir com exagero

override [əuvə'raɪd] (irreg: like **ride**) VT (order, objection) não fazer caso de, ignorar; (decision) anular

overriding [əuvə'raɪdɪŋ] ADJ primordial

overrule [əuvə'ruːl] VT (decision) anular; (claim) indeferir

overrun [əuvə'rʌn] (irreg: like **run**) VT (country etc) invadir; (time limit) ultrapassar, exceder ▸ VI ultrapassar o devido tempo; **the town is ~ with tourists** a cidade está infestada de turistas

overseas [əuvə'siːz] ADV (abroad) no estrangeiro, no exterior ▸ ADJ (trade) exterior; (visitor) estrangeiro

overseer ['əuvəsɪəʳ] N (in factory) superintendente m/f; (foreman) capataz m

overshadow [əuvə'ʃædəu] VT ofuscar

overshoot [əuvə'ʃuːt] (irreg: like **shoot**) VT passar

oversight ['əuvəsaɪt] N descuido; **due to an ~** devido a um descuido or uma inadvertência

oversimplify [əuvə'sɪmplɪfaɪ] VT simplificar demais

oversleep [əuvə'sliːp] (irreg: like **sleep**) VI dormir além da hora

overspend [əuvə'spɛnd] (irreg: like **spend**) VI gastar demais; **we have overspent by $5000** gastamos $5000 além dos nossos recursos

overspill ['əuvəspɪl] N excesso (de população)

overstaffed [əuvə'stɑːft] ADJ: **to be ~** ter um excesso de pessoal

overstate [əuvə'steɪt] VT exagerar

overstatement [əuvə'steɪtmənt] N exagero

overstep [əuvə'stɛp] VT: **to ~ the mark** ultrapassar o limite

overstock [əuvə'stɔk] VT estocar em excesso

overstrike [n 'əuvəstraɪk, vt əuvə'straɪk] (irreg: like **strike**) N (on printer) batida múltipla ▸ VT sobreimprimir

overt [əu'vəːt] ADJ aberto, indissimulado

overtake [əuvə'teɪk] (irreg: like **take**) VT ultrapassar

overtaking [əuvə'teɪkɪŋ] N (Aut) ultrapassagem f

overtax [əuvə'tæks] VT (Econ) sobrecarregar de impostos; (fig: strength, patience) abusar de; (: person) exigir demais de; **to ~ o.s.** exceder-se

overthrow [əuvə'θrəu] (irreg: like **throw**) VT (government) derrubar

overtime ['əuvətaɪm] N horas fpl extras; **to do** or **work ~** fazer horas extras

overtime ban N recusa de fazer horas extras

overtone ['əuvətəun] N (fig: also: **overtones**) implicação f, tom m

overture ['əuvətʃuəʳ] N (Mus) abertura; (fig) proposta, oferta

overturn [əuvə'təːn] VT virar; (system) derrubar; (decision) anular ▸ VI virar; (car) capotar

overweight [əuvə'weɪt] ADJ acima do peso; (luggage) com excesso de peso

overwhelm [əuvə'wɛlm] VT (defeat) esmagar, assolar; (affect deeply) esmagar, sufocar

overwhelming [əuvə'wɛlmɪŋ] ADJ (victory, defeat) esmagador(a); (heat) sufocante; (desire) irresistível; **one's ~ impression is of heat** a impressão mais forte é de calor

overwhelmingly [əuvə'wɛlmɪŋlɪ] ADV (vote) em massa; (win) esmagadoramente

overwork [əuvə'wəːk] N excesso de trabalho ▸ VT sobrecarregar de trabalho ▸ VI trabalhar demais

overwrite [əuvə'raɪt] (irreg: like **write**) VT (Comput) gravar em cima de

overwrought [əuvə'rɔːt] ADJ extenuado, superexcitado

ovulation [ɔvju'leɪʃən] N ovulação f

owe [əu] VT dever; **to ~ sb sth, to ~ sth to sb** dever algo a alguém

owing to ['əuɪŋ-] PREP devido a, por causa de

owl [aul] N coruja

own [əun] ADJ próprio ▸ VI (BRIT): **to ~ to (having done) sth** confessar (ter feito) algo ▸ VT possuir, ter; **a room of my ~** meu próprio quarto; **can I have it for my (very) ~?** posso ficar com isso para mim?; **to get one's ~ back** ir à forra; **on one's ~** sozinho; **to come into one's ~** revelar-se ▸ **own up** VI: **to ~ up to sth** confessar algo; **to ~ up to having done sth** confessar ter feito algo

own brand N (Comm) marca de distribuidora

owner ['əunəʳ] N dono(-a), proprietário(-a)

owner-occupier N proprietário(-a) com posse e uso

ownership ['əunəʃɪp] N posse f; **it's under new ~** (shop etc) está sob novo proprietário

ox [ɔks] (pl **oxen**) N boi m

oxen ['ɔksn] NPL of **ox**

Oxfam ['ɔksfæm] (BRIT) N ABBR (= Oxford Committee for Famine Relief) associação de assistência

oxide ['ɔksaɪd] N óxido
Oxon. ['ɔksn] (BRIT) ABBR = **Oxoniensis, of Oxford**
oxtail ['ɔksteɪl] N: ~ **soup** sopa de rabada
oxyacetylene [ɔksɪə'sɛtɪliːn] N oxiacetileno
 ▶ CPD: ~ **burner,** ~ **torch** maçarico oxiacetilênico

oxygen ['ɔksɪdʒən] N oxigênio
oxygen mask N máscara de oxigênio
oxygen tent N tenda de oxigênio
oyster ['ɔɪstəʳ] N ostra
oz. ABBR = **ounce**
ozone ['əuzəun] N ozônio
ozone layer N camada de ozônio

Pp

P¹, p [pi:] N (*letter*) P, p *m*; **P for Peter** P de Pedro

P² ABBR = **president; prince**

p [pi:] ABBR (= *page*) p; (*BRIT*) = **penny; pence**

PA N ABBR = **personal assistant; public address system** ▶ ABBR (*US Post*) = **Pennsylvania**

pa [pɑː] (*inf*) N papai *m*

p.a. ABBR (= *per annum*) por ano

PAC (*US*) N ABBR = **political action committee**

pace [peɪs] N (*step*) passo; (*speed*) velocidade *f*; (*rhythm*) ritmo ▶ VI: **to ~ up and down** andar de um lado para o outro; **to keep ~ with** acompanhar o passo de; (*events*) manter-se inteirado de *or* atualizado com; **to set the ~** (*running*) regular a marcha; (*fig*) dar o tom; **to put sb through his ~s** (*fig*) pôr alguém à prova

pacemaker ['peɪsmeɪkə'] N (*Med*) marcapasso *m*

Pacific [pə'sɪfɪk] ADJ pacífico ▶ N: **the ~ (Ocean)** o (Oceano) Pacífico

pacification [pæsɪfɪ'keɪʃən] N pacificação *f*

pacifier ['pæsɪfaɪə'] (*US*) N chupeta

pacifist ['pæsɪfɪst] N pacifista *m/f*

pacify ['pæsɪfaɪ] VT (*soothe*) acalmar, serenar; (*country*) pacificar

pack [pæk] N pacote *m*, embrulho; (*US: packet*) pacote *m*; (*: of cigarettes*) maço; (*of hounds*) matilha; (*of thieves etc*) bando, quadrilha; (*of cards*) baralho; (*bundle*) trouxa; (*backpack*) mochila ▶ VT (*wrap*) empacotar, embrulhar; (*fill*) encher; (*in suitcase etc*) arrumar (na mala); (*cram*): **to ~ into** entupir de, entulhar com; (*fig: room etc*) lotar ▶ VI: **to ~ (one's bags)** fazer as malas; **to ~ into** (*room, stadium*) apinhar-se em; **to send sb ~ing** (*inf*) dar o fora em alguém
▶ **pack in** (*BRIT inf*) VI (*machine*) pifar ▶ VT (*boyfriend*) dar o fora em; **~ it in!** para com isso!
▶ **pack off** VT (*person*) despedir
▶ **pack up** VI (*BRIT inf: machine*) pifar; (*: person*) desistir, parar ▶ VT (*belongings*) arrumar; (*goods, presents*) empacotar, embrulhar

package ['pækɪdʒ] N pacote *m*; (*bulky*) embrulho, fardo; (*also*: **package deal**) pacote; (*Comput*) pacote ▶ VT (*goods*) empacotar, acondicionar

package holiday (*BRIT*) N pacote *m* (de férias)

package tour (*BRIT*) N excursão *f* organizada

packaging ['pækɪdʒɪŋ] N embalagem *f*

packed [pækt] ADJ (*crowded*) lotado, apinhado

packed lunch [pækt-] (*BRIT*) N merenda

packer ['pækə'] N (*person*) empacotador(a) *m/f*

packet ['pækɪt] N pacote *m*; (*of cigarettes*) maço; (*of washing powder etc*) caixa; (*Naut*) paquete *m*

pack ice N gelo flutuante

packing ['pækɪŋ] N embalagem *f*; (*internal*) enchimento; (*act*) empacotamento

packing case N caixa de embalagem

pact [pækt] N pacto; (*Comm*) convênio

pad [pæd] N (*of paper*) bloco; (*for inking*) almofada; (*launch pad*) plataforma (de lançamento); (*to prevent friction*) acolchoado; (*inf: home*) casa ▶ VT acolchoar, enchumaçar ▶ VI: **to ~ in/about** *etc* entrar/andar *etc* sem ruído

padding ['pædɪŋ] N enchimento; (*fig*) palavreado inútil

paddle ['pædl] N (*oar*) remo curto; (*US: for table tennis*) raquete *f* ▶ VT remar ▶ VI (*with feet*) patinhar

paddle steamer N vapor *m* movido a rodas

paddling pool ['pædlɪŋ-] (*BRIT*) N lago de recreação

paddock ['pædək] N cercado; (*at race course*) paddock *m*

paddy field ['pædɪ-] N arrozal *m*

padlock ['pædlɔk] N cadeado ▶ VT fechar com cadeado

padre ['pɑːdrɪ] N capelão *m*, padre *m*

paediatrics, (*US*) **pediatrics** [piːdɪ'ætrɪks] N pediatria

paedophile, (*US*) **pedophile** ['piːdəufaɪl] N pedófilo(-a)

pagan ['peɪgən] ADJ, N pagão/pagã *m/f*

page [peɪdʒ] N página; (*also*: **page boy**) mensageiro; (*at wedding*) pajem *m* ▶ VT (*in hotel etc*) mandar chamar

pageant ['pædʒənt] N (*procession*) cortejo suntuoso; (*show*) desfile *m* alegórico

pageantry ['pædʒəntrɪ] N pompa, fausto

page break N quebra de página

pager ['peɪdʒə'] N bip *m*

paginate ['pædʒɪneɪt] VT paginar

pagination [pædʒɪ'neɪʃən] N paginação *f*

pagoda [pə'gəudə] N pagode m

paid [peɪd] PT, PP of **pay** ▶ ADJ (work) remunerado; (holiday) pago; (official) assalariado; **to put ~ to** (BRIT) acabar com

paid-up, (US) **paid-in** ADJ (member) efetivo; (shares) integralizado; **~ capital** capital m realizado

pail [peɪl] N balde m

pain [peɪn] N dor f; **to be in ~** sofrer or sentir dor; **to have a ~ in** estar com uma dor em; **on ~ of death** sob pena de morte; **to take ~s to do sth** dar-se ao trabalho de fazer algo

pained [peɪnd] ADJ (expression) magoado, aflito

painful ['peɪnful] ADJ doloroso; (laborious) penoso; (unpleasant) desagradável

painfully ['peɪnfulɪ] ADV (fig: very) terrivelmente

painkiller ['peɪnkɪlə'] N analgésico

painless ['peɪnlɪs] ADJ sem dor, indolor

painstaking ['peɪnzteɪkɪŋ] ADJ (work) esmerado; (person) meticuloso

paint [peɪnt] N pintura ▶ VT pintar; **to ~ the door blue** pintar a porta de azul; **to ~ the town red** (fig) cair na farra

paintbox ['peɪntbɔks] N estojo de tintas

paintbrush ['peɪntbrʌʃ] N (artist's) pincel m; (decorator's) broxa

painter ['peɪntə'] N pintor(a) m/f

painting ['peɪntɪŋ] N pintura; (picture) tela, quadro

paint-stripper N removedor m de tinta

paintwork ['peɪntwə:k] N pintura

pair [peə'] N (of shoes, gloves etc) par m; (of people) casal m; (twosome) dupla; **a ~ of scissors** uma tesoura; **a ~ of trousers** uma calça (BR), umas calças (PT)
▶ **pair off** VI formar pares

pajamas [pɪ'dʒɑːməz] (US) NPL pijama m

Pakistan [pɑːkɪ'stɑːn] N Paquistão m

Pakistani [pɑːkɪ'stɑːnɪ] ADJ, N paquistanês(-esa) m/f

PAL [pæl] N ABBR (TV: phase alternation line) PAL m

pal [pæl] (inf) N camarada m/f, colega m/f

palace ['pæləs] N palácio

palatable ['pælɪtəbl] ADJ saboroso, apetitoso; (acceptable) aceitável

palate ['pælɪt] N paladar m

palatial [pə'leɪʃəl] ADJ suntuoso, magnífico

palaver [pə'lɑːvə'] (inf) N (fuss) confusão f; (hindrances) complicação f

pale [peɪl] ADJ (face) pálido; (colour) claro; (light) fraco ▶ VI empalidecer ▶ N: **to be beyond the ~** passar dos limites; **to grow or turn ~** empalidecer; **~ blue** azul claro inv; **to ~ into insignificance (beside)** perder a importância (diante de)

paleness ['peɪlnɪs] N palidez f

Palestine ['pælɪstaɪn] N Palestina

Palestinian [pælɪs'tɪnɪən] ADJ, N palestino(-a)

palette ['pælɪt] N palheta

paling ['peɪlɪŋ] N (stake) estaca; **palings** NPL (fence) cerca

palisade [pælɪ'seɪd] N paliçada

pall [pɔːl] N (of smoke) manto ▶ VI perder a graça

pallet ['pælɪt] N (for goods) paleta

pallid ['pælɪd] ADJ pálido, descorado

pallor ['pælə'] N palidez f

pally ['pælɪ] (inf) ADJ chapinha

palm [pɑːm] N (hand, leaf) palma; (also: **palm tree**) palmeira ▶ VT: **to ~ sth off on sb** (inf) impingir algo a alguém

palmist ['pɑːmɪst] N quiromante m/f

Palm Sunday N Domingo de Ramos

palpable ['pælpəbl] ADJ palpável

palpitations [pælpɪ'teɪʃənz] NPL palpitações fpl; **to have ~** sentir palpitações

paltry ['pɔːltrɪ] ADJ irrisório

pamper ['pæmpə'] VT paparicar, mimar

pamphlet ['pæmflət] N panfleto

pan [pæn] N (also: **saucepan**) panela (BR), caçarola (PT); (also: **frying pan**) frigideira; (of lavatory) vaso ▶ VI (Cinema) tomar uma panorâmica ▶ VT (inf: book, film) arrasar com; **to ~ for gold** batear à procura de ouro

panacea [pænə'sɪə] N panaceia

panache [pə'næʃ] N desenvoltura

Panama ['pænəmɑː] N Panamá m

Panama Canal N canal m do Panamá

pancake ['pænkeɪk] N panqueca

Pancake Day (BRIT) N terça-feira de Carnaval

pancreas ['pæŋkrɪəs] N pâncreas m inv

panda ['pændə] N panda m/f

panda car (BRIT) N patrulhinha, carro policial

pandemic [pæn'dɛmɪk] N pandemia

pandemonium [pændɪ'məunɪəm] N (noise) pandemônio; (mess) caos m

pander ['pændə'] VI: **to ~ to** favorecer

p & h (US) ABBR = **postage and handling**

P&L ABBR = **profit and loss**

p&p (BRIT) ABBR (= postage and packing) porte e embalagem

pane [peɪn] N vidraça, vidro

panel ['pænl] N (of wood, Radio, TV) painel m; (of cloth) pano

panel game (BRIT) N jogo em painel

panelling, (US) **paneling** ['pænəlɪŋ] N painéis mpl

panellist, (US) **panelist** ['pænəlɪst] N convidado(-a), integrante m/f do painel

pang [pæŋ] N: **a ~ of regret** uma sensação de pesar; **~s of hunger** fome aguda

panic ['pænɪk] N pânico ▶ VI entrar em pânico

panicky ['pænɪkɪ] ADJ (person) assustadiço, apavorado

panic-stricken [-'strɪkən] ADJ tomado de pânico

pannier ['pænɪə'] N (on bicycle) cesta; (on mule etc) cesto, alcofa

panorama [pænə'rɑːmə] N panorama m

panoramic [pænə'ræmɪk] ADJ panorâmico

pansy ['pænzɪ] N (Bot) amor-perfeito; (inf, pej) bicha (BR), maricas m (PT)

pant [pænt] VI arquejar, ofegar

pantechnicon [pæn'tɛknɪkən] (BRIT) N caminhão m de mudanças

panther ['pænθəʳ] N pantera

panties ['pæntɪz] NPL calcinha (BR), cuecas fpl (PT)

pantihose ['pæntɪhəuz] (US) N meia-calça (BR), collants mpl (PT)

pantomime ['pæntəmaɪm] (BRIT) N pantomima

Uma **pantomime**, também chamada simplesmente de *panto*, é um gênero de comédia em que o personagem principal em geral é um rapaz e na qual há sempre uma **dame**, isto é, uma mulher idosa representada por um homem, e um vilão. Na maior parte das vezes, a história é baseada em um conto de fadas, como "A gata borralheira" ou "O gato de botas", e a plateia é encorajada a participar prevenindo os heróis dos perigos que estão por vir. Esse tipo de espetáculo, voltado sobretudo para as crianças, visa também ao público adulto por meio de diversas brincadeiras que fazem alusão aos fatos atuais.

pantry ['pæntrɪ] N despensa

pants [pænts] NPL (BRIT: underwear: woman's) calcinha (BR), cuecas fpl (PT); (: man's) cueca (BR), cuecas (PT); (US: trousers) calça (BR), calças fpl (PT)

pantsuit ['pæntsu:t] (US) N terninho (de mulher)

papacy ['peɪpəsɪ] N papado

papal ['peɪpəl] ADJ papal

paper ['peɪpəʳ] N papel m; (also: **newspaper**) jornal m; (also: **wallpaper**) papel de parede; (study, article) artigo, dissertação f; (exam) exame m, prova ▶ ADJ de papel ▶ VT (room) revestir (com papel de parede); **papers** NPL (also: **identity papers**) documentos mpl; **a piece of** ~ um papel; **to put sth down on** ~ pôr algo por escrito

paper advance N (on printer) avançar formulário

paperback ['peɪpəbæk] N livro de capa mole ▶ ADJ: ~ **edition** edição f brochada

paper bag N saco de papel

paperboy ['peɪpəbɔɪ] N jornaleiro

paper clip N clipe m

paper hankie N lenço de papel

paper mill N fábrica de papel

paper money N papel-moeda m

paper profit N lucro fictício

paperweight ['peɪpəweɪt] N pesa-papéis m inv

paperwork ['peɪpəwə:k] N trabalho burocrático; (pej) papelada

papier-mâché ['pæpɪeɪ'mæʃeɪ] N papel m machê

paprika ['pæprɪkə] N páprica, pimentão-doce m

Pap smear [pæp-] N (Med) esfregaço

Pap test [pæp-] N (Med) esfregaço

par [pɑːʳ] N (equality of value) paridade f, igualdade f; (Golf) média f; **on a** ~ **with** em

pé de igualdade com; **at** ~ ao par; **above/below** ~ acima/abaixo do par; **to feel below** or **under** ~ or **not up to** ~ não se sentir bem

parable ['pærəbl] N parábola

parabola [pə'ræbələ] N parábola

parachute ['pærəʃu:t] N para-quedas m inv ▶ VI saltar de para-quedas

parachute jump N salto de para-quedas

parachutist ['pærəʃu:tɪst] N para-quedista m/f

parade [pə'reɪd] N desfile m ▶ VT desfilar; (show off) exibir ▶ VI desfilar; (Mil) passar revista

parade ground N praça de armas

paradise ['pærədaɪs] N paraíso

paradox ['pærədɔks] N paradoxo

paradoxical [pærə'dɔksɪkl] ADJ paradoxal

paradoxically [pærə'dɔksɪklɪ] ADV paradoxalmente

paraffin ['pærəfɪn] (BRIT) N: ~ (**oil**) querosene m; **liquid** ~ óleo de parafina

paraffin heater (BRIT) N aquecedor m a parafina

paraffin lamp (BRIT) N lâmpada de parafina

paragon ['pærəgən] N modelo

paragraph ['pærəgrɑ:f] N parágrafo

Paraguay ['pærəgwaɪ] N Paraguai m

Paraguayan [pærə'gwaɪən] ADJ, N paraguaio(-a)

parallel ['pærəlɛl] ADJ (lines etc) paralelo; (fig) correspondente ▶ N paralela; correspondência

paralyse ['pærəlaɪz] (BRIT) VT paralisar

paralyses [pə'rælisi:z] NPL of **paralysis**

paralysis [pə'rælɪsɪs] (pl **paralyses**) N paralisia

paralytic [pærə'lɪtɪk] ADJ paralítico; (BRIT inf: drunk) de cara cheia

paralyze ['pærəlaɪz] (US) VT = **paralyse**

parameter [pə'ræmɪtəʳ] N parâmetro

paramilitary [pærə'mɪlɪtərɪ] ADJ paramilitar

paramount ['pærəmaunt] ADJ primordial; **of** ~ **importance** de suma importância

paranoia [pærə'nɔɪə] N paranoia

paranoid ['pærənɔɪd] ADJ paranoico

paranormal [pærə'nɔ:məl] ADJ paranormal

parapet ['pærəpɪt] N parapeito, balaustrada

paraphernalia [pærəfə'neɪlɪə] N (gear) acessórios mpl, parafernália, equipamento

paraphrase ['pærəfreɪz] VT parafrasear

paraplegic [pærə'pli:dʒɪk] N paraplégico(-a)

parapsychology [pærəsaɪ'kɔlədʒɪ] N parapsicologia

parasite ['pærəsaɪt] N parasito(-a)

parasol ['pærəsɔl] N guarda-sol m, sombrinha

paratrooper ['pærətru:pəʳ] N para-quedista m/f

parcel ['pɑːsl] N pacote m ▶ VT (also: **parcel up**) embrulhar, empacotar
▶ **parcel out** VT repartir, distribuir

parcel bomb (BRIT) N pacote-bomba m

parcel post N serviço de encomenda postal

parch [pɑːtʃ] VT secar, ressecar

parched [pɑːtʃt] ADJ (person) morto de sede

parchment ['pɑːtʃmənt] N pergaminho

P

pardon ['pɑːdn] N perdão m; (Law) indulto
▶ VT perdoar; (Law) indultar; ~! desculpe!;
~ **me!, I beg your** ~ (apologizing) desculpe(-
me); **(I beg your)** ~? (BRIT), ~ **me?** (US: not
hearing) como?, como disse?

pare [pɛəʳ] VT (BRIT: nails) aparar; (fruit etc)
descascar; (fig: costs etc) reduzir, cortar

parent ['pɛərənt] N (father) pai m; (mother)
mãe f; **parents** NPL (mother and father) pais mpl

parentage ['pɛərəntɪdʒ] N ascendência; **of
unknown** ~ de pais desconhecidos

parental [pə'rɛntl] ADJ paternal (or maternal),
dos pais

parent company N (empresa) matriz f

parentheses [pə'rɛnθɪsiːz] NPL of **parenthesis**

parenthesis [pə'rɛnθɪsɪs] (pl **parentheses**) N
parêntese m; **in parentheses** entre
parênteses

parenthood ['pɛərənthud] N paternidade f
(or maternidade f)

parenting ['pɛərəntɪŋ] N trabalho de ser pai
(or mãe)

Paris ['pærɪs] N Paris

parish ['pærɪʃ] N paróquia, freguesia ▶ ADJ
paroquial

parish council (BRIT) N ≈ junta da freguesia

parishioner [pə'rɪʃənəʳ] N paroquiano(-a)

Parisian [pə'rɪzɪən] ADJ, N parisiense m/f

parity ['pærɪtɪ] N paridade f, igualdade f

park [pɑːk] N parque m ▶ VT, VI estacionar

parka ['pɑːkə] N parka m

park and ride N esquema de transporte feito
parcialmente com carro, que em seguida é estacionado
para o uso de transporte público

parking ['pɑːkɪŋ] N estacionamento; **"no** ~**"**
"estacionamento proibido"

parking lights NPL luzes fpl de estacionamento

parking lot (US) N (parque m de)
estacionamento

parking meter N parquímetro

parking offence (BRIT) N = **parking offence**

parking place N vaga

parking ticket N multa por estacionamento
proibido

parking violation (US) N infração f por
estacionamento não permitido

Parkinson's ['pɑːkɪnsənz] N (also: **Parkinson's
disease**) mal m de Parkinson

parkway ['pɑːkweɪ] (US) N rodovia arborizada

parlance ['pɑːləns] N: **in common/modern** ~
na linguagem cotidiana or corrente/
moderna

parliament ['pɑːləmənt] (BRIT) N parlamento

parliamentary [pɑːlə'mɛntərɪ] ADJ
parlamentar

parlour, (US) **parlor** ['pɑːləʳ] N sala de visitas,
salão m, saleta

parlous ['pɑːləs] ADJ (formal) precário

Parmesan [pɑːmɪ'zæn] N (also: **Parmesan
cheese**) parmesão m

parochial [pə'rəukɪəl] ADJ paroquial; (pej)
provinciano

parody ['pærədɪ] N paródia ▶ VT parodiar

parole [pə'rəul] N: **on** ~ em liberdade
condicional, sob promessa

paroxysm ['pærəksɪzəm] N paroxismo;
(of anger, coughing) acesso

parquet ['pɑːkeɪ] N: ~ **floor(ing)** parquete m,
assoalho de tacos

parrot ['pærət] N papagaio

parrot fashion ADV mecanicamente, feito
papagaio

parry ['pærɪ] VT aparar, desviar

parsimonious [pɑːsɪ'məunɪəs] ADJ sovina,
parsimonioso

parsley ['pɑːslɪ] N salsa

parsnip ['pɑːsnɪp] N cherivia, pastinaga

parson ['pɑːsn] N padre m, clérigo; (in Church of
England) pastor m

parsonage ['pɑːsnɪdʒ] N presbitério

part [pɑːt] N (gen, Mus) parte f; (of machine)
peça; (Theatre etc) papel m; (of serial) capítulo;
(US: in hair) risca, repartido ▶ ADJ parcial
▶ ADV = **partly** ▶ VT dividir; (break) partir;
(hair) repartir ▶ VI (people) separar-se; (roads)
bifurcar-se; (crowd) dispersar-se; (break)
partir-se; **to take** ~ **in** participar de, tomar
parte em; **to take sb's** ~ defender alguém;
on his ~ da sua parte; **for my** ~ pela minha
parte; **for the most** ~ na maior parte; **for
the better** ~ **of the day** durante a maior
parte do dia; **to be** ~ **and parcel of** fazer
parte de; **to take sth in good** ~ não se
ofender com algo; ~ **of speech** (Ling)
categoria gramatical
▶ **part with** VT FUS ceder, entregar; (money)
pagar

partake [pɑː'teɪk] (irreg: like **take**) VI (formal): **to
** ~ **of sth** participar de algo

part exchange (BRIT) N: **in** ~ como parte do
pagamento

partial ['pɑːʃl] ADJ parcial; **to be** ~ **to** gostar
de, ser apreciador(a) de

partially ['pɑːʃəlɪ] ADV parcialmente

participant [pɑː'tɪsɪpənt] N participante m/f

participate [pɑː'tɪsɪpeɪt] VI: **to** ~ **in**
participar de

participation [pɑːtɪsɪ'peɪʃən] N participação f

participle ['pɑːtɪsɪpl] N particípio

particle ['pɑːtɪkl] N partícula; (of dust) grão m

particular [pə'tɪkjuləʳ] ADJ (special) especial;
(specific) específico; (given) determinado;
(fussy) exigente, minucioso; **in** ~ em
particular; **I'm not** ~ para mim tanto faz

particularly [pə'tɪkjuləlɪ] ADV em particular,
especialmente

particulars [pə'tɪkjuləz] NPL detalhes mpl;
(personal details) dados mpl pessoais

parting ['pɑːtɪŋ] N (act) separação f; (farewell)
despedida; (BRIT: in hair) risca, repartido ▶ ADJ
de despedida; ~ **shot** (fig) flecha de parte

partisan [pɑːtɪ'zæn] ADJ partidário ▶ N
partidário(-a); (in war) guerrilheiro(-a)

partition [pɑː'tɪʃən] N (Pol) divisão f; (wall)
tabique m, divisória ▶ VT separar com
tabique; (fig) dividir

partly ['pɑːtlɪ] ADV em parte
partner ['pɑːtnəʳ] N (*Comm*) sócio(-a); (*Sport*) parceiro(-a); (*at dance*) par *m*; (*spouse*) cônjuge *m/f*; (*friend etc*) companheiro(-a) ▶ VT acompanhar
partnership ['pɑːtnəʃɪp] N associação *f*, parceria; (*Comm*) sociedade *f*; **to go into** *or* **form a ~ (with)** associar-se (com), formar sociedade (com)
part payment N parcela, prestação *f*
partridge ['pɑːtrɪdʒ] N perdiz *f*
part-time ADJ, ADV de meio expediente
part-timer N (*also*: **part-time worker**) trabalhador(a) *m/f* de meio expediente
party ['pɑːtɪ] N (*Pol*) partido; (*celebration*) festa; (*group*) grupo; (*Law*) parte *f* interessada, litigante *m/f* ▶ CPD (*Pol*) do partido, partidário; **dinner ~** jantar *m*; **to give** *or* **have** *or* **throw a ~** dar uma festa; **to be a ~ to a crime** ser cúmplice num crime
party dress N vestido de gala
party line N (*Pol*) linha partidária; (*Tel*) linha compartilhada
par value N (*of share, bond*) valor *m* nominal
pass [pɑːs] VT (*time, object*) passar; (*exam*) passar em; (*place*) passar por; (*overtake, surpass*) ultrapassar; (*approve*) aprovar; (*candidate*) aprovar ▶ VI passar; (*Sch*) ser aprovado, passar ▶ N (*permit*) passe *m*; (*membership card*) carteira; (*in mountains*) desfiladeiro; (*Sport*) passe *m*; (*Sch*: *also*: **pass mark**): **to get a ~ in** ser aprovado em; **to ~ sth through sth** passar algo por algo; **things have come to a pretty ~** (*BRIT*) as coisas ficaram pretas; **to make a ~ at sb** tomar liberdade com alguém
▶ **pass away** VI falecer
▶ **pass by** VI passar ▶ VT (*ignore*) passar por cima de
▶ **pass down** VT (*customs, inheritance*) passar
▶ **pass for** VT FUS passar por
▶ **pass on** VI (*die*) falecer ▶ VT (*hand on: news, illness*) transmitir; (*object*) passar para; (*price rises*) repassar
▶ **pass out** VI desmaiar; (*BRIT Mil*) sair (*de uma escola militar*)
▶ **pass over** VT (*ignore*) passar por cima de
▶ **pass up** VT deixar passar
passable ['pɑːsəbl] ADJ (*road*) transitável; (*work*) aceitável
passage ['pæsɪdʒ] N (*also*: **passageway**: *indoors*) corredor *m*; (: *outdoors*) passagem *f*; (*Anat*) via; (*act of passing*) trânsito; (*in book*) trecho; (*fare*) passagem (*BR*), bilhete *m* (*PT*); (*by boat*) travessia; (*Mechanics, Med*) conduto
passbook ['pɑːsbuk] N caderneta
passenger ['pæsɪndʒəʳ] N passageiro(-a)
passer-by ['pɑːsəʳ-] (*pl* **passers-by**) N transeunte *m/f*
passing ['pɑːsɪŋ] ADJ (*fleeting*) passageiro, fugaz; **in ~** de passagem
passing place N trecho de ultrapassagem

passion ['pæʃən] N paixão *f*; **to have a ~ for sth** ser aficionado(-a) de algo
passionate ['pæʃənɪt] ADJ apaixonado
passion fruit N maracujá *m*
passive ['pæsɪv] ADJ (*also Ling*) passivo
passkey ['pɑːskiː] N chave *f* mestra
Passover ['pɑːsəuvəʳ] N Páscoa (*dos judeus*)
passport ['pɑːspɔːt] N passaporte *m*
passport control N controle *m* dos passaportes
password ['pɑːswɜːd] N senha
past [pɑːst] PREP (*drive, walk etc: in front of*) por; (: *beyond, further than*) mais além de; (*later than*) depois de ▶ ADJ passado; (*president etc*) ex-, anterior ▶ N passado; **he's ~ forty** ele tem mais de quarenta anos; **ten/quarter ~ four** quatro e dez/quinze; **for the ~ few/3 days** nos últimos/3 dias; **to run ~** passar correndo (por); **it's ~ midnight** é mais de meia-noite; **in the ~** no passado; **I'm ~ caring** já não ligo mais; **he's ~ it** (*BRIT inf*: *person*) ele já passou da idade
pasta ['pæstə] N massa
paste [peɪst] N pasta; (*glue*) grude *m*, cola; (*jewellery*) vidro ▶ VT (*stick*) grudar; (*glue*) colar; **tomato ~** massa de tomate
pastel ['pæstl] ADJ pastel; (*painting*) a pastel
pasteurized ['pæstəraɪzd] ADJ pasteurizado
pastille ['pæstl] N pastilha
pastime ['pɑːstaɪm] N passatempo
past master (*BRIT*) N: **to be a ~ at** ser perito em
pastor ['pɑːstəʳ] N pastor(a) *m/f*
pastoral ['pɑːstərl] ADJ pastoral
pastry ['peɪstrɪ] N massa; (*cake*) bolo
pasture ['pɑːstʃəʳ] N (*grass*) pasto; (*land*) pastagem *f*, pasto
pasty [*n* 'pæstɪ, *adj* 'peɪstɪ] N empadão *m* de carne ▶ ADJ pastoso; (*complexion*) pálido
pat [pæt] VT dar palmadinhas em; (*dog etc*) fazer festa em ▶ N (*of butter*) porção *f* ▶ ADV: **he knows it off ~** (*BRIT*), **he has it down ~** (*US*) ele sabe isso de cor; **to give sb a ~ on the back** (*fig*) animar alguém
patch [pætʃ] N (*of material*) retalho; (*eye patch*) tapa-olho *m*; (*area*) área pequena; (*spot*) mancha; (*mend*) remendo; (*of land*) lote *m*, terreno ▶ VT (*clothes*) remendar; (**to go through**) **a bad ~** (passar por) um mau pedaço
▶ **patch up** VT (*mend temporarily*) consertar provisoriamente; (*quarrel*) resolver
patchwork ['pætʃwɜːk] N colcha de retalhos ▶ ADJ (*feito*) de retalhos
patchy ['pætʃɪ] ADJ (*colour*) desigual; (*information*) incompleto
pate [peɪt] N: **a bald ~** uma calva, uma careca
pâté ['pæteɪ] N patê *m*
patent ['peɪtnt] N patente *f* ▶ VT patentear ▶ ADJ patente, evidente
patent leather N verniz *m*
patently ['peɪtntlɪ] ADV claramente
patent medicine N medicamento registrado

patent office N escritório de registro de patentes

paternal [pə'tə:nl] ADJ paternal; (*relation*) paterno

paternity [pə'tə:nɪtɪ] N paternidade *f*

paternity suit N (*Law*) processo de paternidade

path [pɑ:θ] N caminho; (*trail, track*) trilha, senda; (*trajectory*) trajetória; (*of planet*) órbita

pathetic [pə'θɛtɪk] ADJ (*pitiful*) patético, digno de pena; (*very bad*) péssimo; (*moving*) comovente

pathological [pæθə'lɔdʒɪkl] ADJ patológico

pathologist [pə'θɔlədʒɪst] N patologista *m/f*

pathology [pə'θɔlədʒɪ] N patologia

pathos ['peɪθɔs] N patos *m*, patético

pathway ['pɑ:θweɪ] N caminho, trilha

patience ['peɪʃns] N paciência; **to lose one's ~** perder a paciência

patient ['peɪʃnt] ADJ, N paciente *m/f*

patiently ['peɪʃntlɪ] ADV pacientemente

patio ['pætɪəu] N pátio

patriot ['peɪtrɪət] N patriota *m/f*

patriotic [pætrɪ'ɔtɪk] ADJ patriótico

patriotism ['pætrɪətɪzəm] N patriotismo

patrol [pə'trəul] N patrulha ▶ VT patrulhar; **to be on ~** fazer ronda, patrulhar

patrol boat N barco de patrulha

patrol car N carro de patrulha

patrolman [pə'trəulmən] (*US*) (*irreg: like* **man**) N guarda *m*, policial *m* (*BR*), polícia *m* (*PT*)

patron ['peɪtrən] N (*customer*) cliente *m/f*, freguês(-esa) *m/f*; (*of charity*) benfeitor(a) *m/f*; **~ of the arts** mecenas *m*

patronage ['pætrənɪdʒ] N patrocínio *m*

patronize ['pætrənaɪz] VT (*pej: look down on*) tratar com ar de superioridade; (*shop*) ser cliente de; (*business, artist*) patrocinar

patronizing ['pætrənaɪzɪŋ] ADJ condescendente

patron saint N (*santo*(-a)) padroeiro(-a)

patter ['pætər] N (*of rain*) tamborilada; (*of feet*) passos miúdos *mpl*; (*sales talk*) jargão *m* profissional ▶ VI correr dando passinhos; (*rain*) tamborilar

pattern ['pætən] N modelo, padrão *m*; (*Sewing*) molde *m*; (*design*) desenho; (*sample*) amostra; **behaviour ~** modo de comportamento

patterned ['pætənd] ADJ padronizado

paucity ['pɔ:sɪtɪ] N penúria, escassez *f*

paunch [pɔ:ntʃ] N pança, barriga

pauper ['pɔ:pər] N pobre *m/f*; **~'s grave** vala comum

pause [pɔ:z] N pausa; (*interval*) intervalo ▶ VI fazer uma pausa; **to ~ for breath** tomar fôlego; (*fig*) fazer uma pausa

pave [peɪv] VT pavimentar; **to ~ the way for** preparar o terreno para

pavement ['peɪvmənt] N (*BRIT*) calçada (*BR*), passeio (*PT*); (*US*) pavimento

pavilion [pə'vɪlɪən] N pavilhão *m*; (*for band etc*) coreto; (*Sport*) barraca

paving ['peɪvɪŋ] N pavimento, calçamento

paving stone N laje *f*, paralelepípedo

paw [pɔ:] N pata; (*of cat*) garra ▶ VT passar a pata em; (*touch*) manusear; (*amorously*) apalpar

pawn [pɔ:n] N (*Chess*) peão *m*; (*fig*) títere *m* ▶ VT empenhar

pawnbroker ['pɔ:nbrəukər] N agiota *m/f*

pawnshop ['pɔ:nʃɔp] N loja de penhores

pay [peɪ] (*pt, pp* **paid**) N salário; (*of manual worker*) paga ▶ VT pagar; (*debt*) liquidar, saldar; (*visit*) fazer ▶ VI pagar; (*be profitable*) valer a pena, render; **how much did you ~ for it?** quanto você pagou por isso?; **I paid £5 for that record** paguei *or* dei £5 por esse disco; **to ~ one's way** pagar sua parte; (*company*) render; **to ~ dividends** (*fig*) trazer vantagens *or* benefícios; **it won't ~ you to do that** não vale a pena você fazer isso; **to ~ attention (to)** prestar atenção (a); **to ~ one's respects to sb** fazer uma visita de cortesia a alguém

▶ **pay back** VT (*money*) devolver; (*person*) pagar; (*debt*) saldar

▶ **pay for** VT FUS pagar a; (*fig*) recompensar

▶ **pay in** VT depositar

▶ **pay off** VT (*debts*) saldar, liquidar; (*mortgage*) resgatar; (*creditor*) pagar, reembolsar; (*worker*) despedir ▶ VI (*plan, patience*) valer a pena; **to ~ sth off in instalments** pagar algo a prazo

▶ **pay out** VT (*money*) pagar, desembolsar; (*rope*) dar

▶ **pay up** VT (*debts*) pagar, liquidar; (*amount*) pagar

payable ['peɪəbl] ADJ pagável; (*cheque*): **~ to** nominal em favor de

pay day N dia *m* do pagamento

PAYE (*BRIT*) N ABBR (= *pay as you earn*) tributação na fonte

payee [peɪ'i:] N beneficiário(-a)

pay envelope (*US*) N = **pay packet**

paying ['peɪɪŋ] ADJ pagador(a); (*business*) rendoso; **~ guest** pensionista *m/f*

payload ['peɪləud] N carga paga

payment ['peɪmənt] N pagamento; **advance ~** (*part sum*) entrada; (*total sum*) pagamento adiantado; **deferred ~, ~ by instalments** pagamento a prazo; **monthly ~** pagamento mensal; **in ~ for or of** em pagamento por; **on ~ of £5** contra pagamento de £5

pay packet (*BRIT*) N envelope *m* de pagamento

pay phone ['peɪfəun] N telefone *m* público

payroll ['peɪrəul] N folha de pagamento; **to be on a firm's ~** receber salário de uma firma

pay slip (*BRIT*) N contracheque *m*

pay station (*US*) N cabine *f* telefônica, orelhão *m* (*BR*)

pay television N televisão *f* por assinatura

paywall ['peɪwɔ:l] N (*Comput*) muro de cobrança

PBS (US) N ABBR = **Public Broadcasting Service**
PC N ABBR (= *personal computer*) PC *m*; (BRIT)
= **police constable** ▶ ABBR (BRIT) = **Privy**
Councillor
pc ABBR = **per cent; postcard**
p/c ABBR = **petty cash**
PCB N ABBR = printed circuit board
PD (US) N ABBR = **police department**
pd ABBR = **paid**
PDA N ABBR (= *personal digital assistant*) PDA *m*
(*assistente digital pessoal*)
PDSA (BRIT) N ABBR = **People's Dispensary for**
Sick Animals
PDT (US) ABBR (= *Pacific Daylight Time*) hora de
verão do Pacífico
PE N ABBR = **physical education** ▶ ABBR
(CANADA) = **Prince Edward Island**
pea [pi:] N ervilha
peace [pi:s] N paz *f*; (*calm*) tranquilidade *f*,
quietude *f*; **to be at ~ with sb/sth** estar em
paz com alguém/algo; **to keep the ~** (*subj:*
policeman) manter a ordem; (: *citizen*) não
perturbar a ordem pública
peaceable ['pi:səbl] ADJ pacato
peaceful ['pi:sful] ADJ (*person*) tranquilo,
pacífico; (*place, time*) tranquilo, sossegado
peace-keeping [-'ki:pɪŋ] N pacificação *f*
peace offering N proposta de paz
peach [pi:tʃ] N pêssego
peacock ['pi:kɔk] N pavão *m*
peak [pi:k] N (*of mountain: top*) cume *m*; (: *point*)
pico; (*of cap*) pala, viseira; (*fig: of career, fame*)
apogeu *m*; (: *highest level*) máximo
peak-hour ADJ (*traffic etc*) no horário de maior
movimento, na hora de pique
peak hours NPL horário de maior
movimento
peak period N período de pique
peaky ['pi:kɪ] (BRIT *inf*) ADJ adoentado
peal [pi:l] N (*of bells*) repique *m*, toque *m*; **~ of**
laughter gargalhada
peanut ['pi:nʌt] N amendoim *m*
peanut butter N manteiga de amendoim
pear [pɛər] N pera
pearl [pə:l] N pérola
pear tree N pereira
peasant ['pɛznt] N camponês(-esa) *m/f*
peat [pi:t] N turfa
pebble ['pɛbl] N seixo, calhau *m*
peck [pɛk] VT (*also:* **peck at**) bicar, dar bicadas
em; (*food*) beliscar ▶ N bicada; (*kiss*) beijoca
pecking order ['pɛkɪŋ-] N ordem *f* de
hierarquia
peckish ['pɛkɪʃ] (BRIT *inf*) ADJ: **I feel ~** estou a
fim de comer alguma coisa
peculiar [pɪ'kju:lɪər] ADJ (*strange*) estranho,
esquisito; (*marked*) especial; **~ to** (*belonging to*)
próprio de
peculiarity [pɪkju:lɪ'ærɪtɪ] N (*distinctive feature*)
peculiaridade *f*; (*oddity*) excentricidade *f*
pecuniary [pɪ'kju:nɪərɪ] ADJ pecuniário
pedal ['pɛdl] N pedal *m* ▶ VI pedalar
pedal bin (BRIT) N lata de lixo com pedal

pedantic [pɪ'dæntɪk] ADJ pedante
peddle ['pɛdl] VT vender nas ruas, mascatear;
(*drugs*) traficar, fazer tráfico de
peddler ['pɛdlər] N (*also:* **drugs peddler**)
mascate *m/f*, camelô *m*
pedestal ['pɛdəstl] N pedestal *m*
pedestrian [pɪ'dɛstrɪən] N pedestre *m/f* (BR),
peão *m* (PT) ▶ ADJ pedestre (BR), para peões
(PT); (*fig*) prosaico
pedestrian crossing (BRIT) N passagem *f* para
pedestres (BR), passadeira (PT)
pediatrics [pi:dɪ'ætrɪks] (US) N
= **paediatrics**
pedigree ['pɛdɪgri:] N (*of animal*) raça; (*fig*)
genealogia ▶ CPD (*animal*) de raça
pedlar ['pɛdlər] N = **peddler**
pedophile ['pi:dəufaɪl] (US) N = **paedophile**
pee [pi:] (*inf*) VI fazer xixi, mijar
peek [pi:k] VI: **to ~ at** espiar, espreitar; **to ~**
over/into espiar por cima de/dentro,
espreitar por cima de/dentro
peel [pi:l] N casca ▶ VT descascar ▶ VI (*paint,*
skin) descascar; (*wallpaper*) desprender-se
▶ **peel back** VT descascar
peeler ['pi:lər] N (*potato etc peeler*)
descascador *m*
peelings ['pi:lɪŋz] NPL cascas *fpl*
peep [pi:p] N (BRIT: *look*) espiadela; (*sound*) pio
▶ VI (BRIT: *look*) espreitar; (*sound*) piar
▶ **peep out** (BRIT) VI mostrar-se, surgir
peephole ['pi:phəul] N vigia, olho mágico
peer [pɪər] VI: **to ~ at** perscrutar, fitar ▶ N
(*noble*) par *m/f*; (*equal*) igual *m/f*; (*contemporary*)
contemporâneo(-a)
peerage ['pɪərɪdʒ] N pariato
peerless ['pɪəlɪs] ADJ sem igual
peeved [pi:vd] ADJ irritado
peevish ['pi:vɪʃ] ADJ rabugento
peg [pɛg] N cavilha; (*for coat etc*) cabide *m*;
(BRIT: *also:* **clothes peg**) pregador *m*; (*tent peg*)
estaca ▶ VT (*clothes*) prender; (BRIT:
groundsheet) segurar com estacas; (*fig: prices,*
wages) fixar, tabelar
pejorative [pɪ'dʒɔrətɪv] ADJ pejorativo
Pekin [pi:'kɪn] N Pequim
Pekinese, Pekingese [pi:kɪ'ni:z] N
pequinês *m*
Peking [pi:'kɪŋ] N = **Pekin**
pelican ['pɛlɪkən] N pelicano
pelican crossing (BRIT) N (*Aut*) passagem *f*
sinalizada para pedestres (BR), passadeira
para peões (PT)
pellet ['pɛlɪt] N bolinha; (*for shotgun*) pelota de
chumbo
pell-mell ['pɛl'mɛl] ADV a esmo
pelmet ['pɛlmɪt] N sanefa
pelt [pɛlt] VT: **to ~ sb with sth** atirar algo em
alguém ▶ VI (*rain: also:* **pelt down**) chover a
cântaros; (*inf: run*) correr ▶ N pele *f* (não
curtida)
pelvis ['pɛlvɪs] N pelvis *f*, bacia
pen [pɛn] N caneta; (*for sheep etc*) redil *m*,
cercado; (US *inf: prison*) cadeia; **to put ~ to**

paper escrever
▶ **pen in** VT encurralar
penal ['pi:nl] ADJ penal
penalize ['pi:nəlaɪz] VT impor penalidade a; (*Sport*) penalizar; (*fig*) prejudicar
penal servitude [-'sə:vɪtju:d] N pena de trabalhos forçados
penalty ['pɛnltɪ] N pena, penalidade *f*; (*fine*) multa; (*Sport*) punição *f*; (*Football*) pênalti *m*; **to take a ~** cobrar um pênalti
penalty area (BRIT) N área de pênalti
penalty clause N cláusula penal
penalty kick N (*Rugby*) chute *m* de pênalti; (*Football*) cobrança de pênalti
penalty shoot-out [-'ʃu:taut] N (*Football*) decisão *f* por pênaltis
penance ['pɛnəns] N penitência
pence [pɛns] (BRIT) NPL *of* **penny**
penchant ['pɑ̃:ʃɑ̃:ŋ] N pendor *m*, queda
pencil ['pɛnsl] N lápis *m* ▶ VT: **to ~ sth in** anotar algo a lápis
pencil case N lapiseira, porta-lápis *m inv*
pencil sharpener N apontador *m* (de lápis) (BR), apara-lápis *m inv* (PT)
pendant ['pɛndnt] N pingente *m*
pending ['pɛndɪŋ] PREP (*during*) durante; (*until*) até ▶ ADJ pendente
pendulum ['pɛndjuləm] N pêndulo
penetrate ['pɛnɪtreɪt] VT penetrar
penetrating ['pɛnɪtreɪtɪŋ] ADJ penetrante
penetration [pɛnɪ'treɪʃən] N penetração *f*
penfriend ['pɛnfrɛnd] (BRIT) N amigo(-a) por correspondência
penguin ['pɛŋgwɪn] N pinguim *m*
penicillin [pɛnɪ'sɪlɪn] N penicilina
peninsula [pə'nɪnsjulə] N península
penis ['pi:nɪs] N pênis *m*
penitence ['pɛnɪtns] N penitência
penitent ['pɛnɪtnt] ADJ arrependido; (*Rel*) penitente
penitentiary [pɛnɪ'tɛnʃərɪ] (US) N penitenciária, presídio
penknife ['pɛnnaɪf] (*irreg: like* **knife**) N canivete *m*
pen name N pseudônimo
pennant ['pɛnənt] N flâmula
penniless ['pɛnɪlɪs] ADJ sem dinheiro, sem um tostão
Pennines ['pɛnaɪnz] NPL: **the ~** as Pennines
penny ['pɛnɪ] (*pl* **pennies** *or* BRIT **pence**) N pêni *m*; (US) cêntimo
penpal ['pɛnpæl] N amigo(-a) por correspondência
pension ['pɛnʃən] N pensão *f*; (*old-age pension*) aposentadoria; (*Mil*) reserva
▶ **pension off** VT aposentar
pensionable ['pɛnʃnəbl] ADJ (*person*) com direito a uma pensão; (*age*) de aposentadoria
pensioner ['pɛnʃənər] (BRIT) N aposentado(-a) (BR), reformado(-a) (PT)
pension fund N fundo da aposentadoria
pensive ['pɛnsɪv] ADJ pensativo; (*withdrawn*) absorto

Pentagon ['pɛntəgən] N: **the ~** o Pentágono

> O Pentágono (**Pentagon**) é o nome dado aos escritórios do Ministério da Defesa americano, localizados em Arlington, no estado da Virgínia, por causa da forma pentagonal do edifício onde se encontram. Por extensão, o termo é utilizado também para se referir ao ministério.

pentathlon [pɛn'tæθlən] N pentatlo
Pentecost ['pɛntɪkɔst] N Pentecostes *m*
penthouse ['pɛnthaus] N cobertura
pent-up [pɛnt-] ADJ (*feelings*) reprimido
penultimate [pɛ'nʌltɪmət] ADJ penúltimo
penury ['pɛnjurɪ] N pobreza, miséria
people ['pi:pl] NPL gente *f*, pessoas *fpl*; (*inhabitants*) habitantes *mpl/fpl*; (*citizens*) povo; (*Pol*): **the ~** o povo ▶ N (*nation, race*) povo ▶ VT povoar; **several ~ came** vieram várias pessoas; **I know ~ who ...** conheço gente que ...; **~ say that ...** dizem que ...; **old ~** os idosos; **young ~** os jovens; **a man of the ~** um homem do povo
pep [pɛp] (*inf*) N pique *m*, energia, dinamismo
▶ **pep up** VT animar
pepper ['pɛpər] N pimenta; (*vegetable*) pimentão *m* ▶ VT apimentar; (*fig*): **to ~ with** salpicar de
peppermint ['pɛpəmɪnt] N hortelã-pimenta; (*sweet*) bala de hortelã
pepper pot N pimenteiro
pep talk ['pɛptɔ:k] (*inf*) N conversa para levantar o espírito
per [pə:r] PREP por; **~ day/person** por dia/pessoa; **~ annum** por ano; **as ~ your instructions** conforme suas instruções
per capita ADJ, ADV per capita, por pessoa
perceive [pə'si:v] VT perceber; (*notice*) notar; (*realize*) compreender
per cent N por cento; **a 20 ~ discount** um desconto de 20 por cento
percentage [pə'sɛntɪdʒ] N porcentagem *f*, percentagem *f*; **on a ~ basis** na base de percentagem
perceptible [pə'sɛptɪbl] ADJ perceptível, sensível
perception [pə'sɛpʃən] N percepção *f*; (*insight*) perspicácia
perceptive [pə'sɛptɪv] ADJ perceptivo
perch [pə:tʃ] N (*pl* **perches**) (*for bird*) poleiro; (*fish*) perca ▶ VI: **to ~ (on)** (*bird*) empoleirar-se (em); (*person*) encarapitar-se (em)
percolate ['pə:kəleɪt] VT, VI passar
percolator ['pə:kəleɪtər] N (*also*: **coffee percolator**) cafeteira de filtro
percussion [pə'kʌʃən] N percussão *f*
peremptory [pə'rɛmptərɪ] ADJ peremptório; (*person: imperious*) autoritário
perennial [pə'rɛnɪəl] ADJ perene; (*fig*) constante ▶ N planta perene
perfect [*adj, n* 'pə:fɪkt, *vt* pə'fɛkt] ADJ perfeito; (*utter*) completo ▶ N (*also*: **perfect tense**) perfeito ▶ VT aperfeiçoar; **a ~ stranger** uma pessoa completamente desconhecida

perfection [pə'fɛkʃən] N perfeição f
perfectionist [pə'fɛkʃənɪst] N
perfeccionista m/f
perfectly ['pə:fɪktlɪ] ADV perfeitamente;
I'm ~ happy with the situation estou
completamente satisfeito com a situação;
you know ~ well você sabe muito bem
perforate ['pə:fəreɪt] VT perfurar
perforated ['pə:fəreɪtɪd] ADJ (stamp) picotado
perforated ulcer N (Med) úlcera perfurada
perforation [pə:fə'reɪʃən] N perfuração f; (line
of holes) picote m
perform [pə'fɔ:m] VT (carry out) realizar, fazer;
(concert etc) executar; (piece of music)
interpretar ▶ VI (well, badly) interpretar;
(animal) fazer truques de amestramento;
(Theatre) representar; (Tech) funcionar
performance [pə'fɔ:məns] N (of engine, athlete,
economy) desempenho; (of play, by artist)
atuação f; (of car) performance f
performer [pə'fɔ:mə'] N (actor) artista m/f,
ator/atriz m/f; (Mus) intérprete m/f
performing [pə'fɔ:mɪŋ] ADJ (animal)
amestrado, adestrado
performing arts NPL: **the ~** as artes cênicas
perfume ['pə:fju:m] N perfume m ▶ VT
perfumar
perfunctory [pə'fʌŋktərɪ] ADJ superficial,
negligente
perhaps [pə'hæps] ADV talvez; **~ he'll come**
talvez ele venha; **~ so/not** talvez seja assim/
talvez não
peril ['pɛrɪl] N perigo, risco
perilous ['pɛrɪləs] ADJ perigoso
perilously ['pɛrɪləslɪ] ADV: **they came ~ close
to being caught** não foram presos por um
triz
perimeter [pə'rɪmɪtə'] N perímetro
perimeter wall N muro periférico
period ['pɪərɪəd] N período; (History) época;
(time limit) prazo; (Sch) aula; (US: full stop)
ponto final; (Med) menstruação f, regra
▶ ADJ (costume, furniture) da época; **for a ~ of
three weeks** por um período de três
semanas; **the holiday ~** (BRIT) o período de
férias
periodic [pɪərɪ'ɔdɪk] ADJ periódico
periodical [pɪərɪ'ɔdɪkl] N periódico ▶ ADJ
periódico
periodically [pɪərɪ'ɔdɪklɪ] ADV
periodicamente, de vez em quando
period pains (BRIT) NPL cólicas fpl menstruais
peripatetic [pɛrɪpə'tɛtɪk] ADJ (salesman)
viajante; (teacher) que trabalha em vários
lugares
peripheral [pə'rɪfərəl] ADJ periférico ▶ N
(Comput) periférico
periphery [pə'rɪfərɪ] N periferia
periscope ['pɛrɪskəup] N periscópio
perish ['pɛrɪʃ] VI perecer; (decay) deteriorar-se
perishable ['pɛrɪʃəbl] ADJ perecível,
deteriorável
perishables ['pɛrɪʃəblz] NPL perecíveis mpl

perishing ['pɛrɪʃɪŋ] (BRIT inf) ADJ (cold) gelado,
glacial
peritonitis [pɛrɪtə'naɪtɪs] N peritonite f
perjure ['pə:dʒə'] VT: **to ~ o.s.** prestar falso
testemunho
perjury ['pə:dʒərɪ] N (Law) perjúrio, falso
testemunho
perk [pə:k] (inf) N mordomia, regalia
▶ **perk up** VI (cheer up) animar-se; (in health)
recuperar-se
perky ['pə:kɪ] ADJ (cheerful) animado, alegre
perm [pə:m] N permanente f ▶ VT: **to have
one's hair ~ed** fazer permanente (no
cabelo)
permanence ['pə:mənəns] N permanência,
continuidade f
permanent ['pə:mənənt] ADJ permanente;
I'm not ~ here não estou aqui em caráter
permanente
permanently ['pə:mənəntlɪ] ADV
permanentemente
permeable ['pə:mɪəbl] ADJ permeável
permeate ['pə:mɪeɪt] VI difundir-se ▶ VT
penetrar; (subj: idea) difundir
permissible [pə'mɪsɪbl] ADJ permissível, lícito
permission [pə'mɪʃən] N permissão f;
(authorization) autorização f; **to give sb ~ to
do sth** dar permissão a alguém para fazer
algo
permissive [pə'mɪsɪv] ADJ permissivo
permit [n 'pə:mɪt, vt pə'mɪt] N permissão f;
(for fishing, export etc) licença; (to enter) passe m
▶ VT permitir; (authorize) autorizar; **to ~ sb to
do sth** permitir a alguém fazer or que faça
algo; **weather ~ting** se o tempo permitir
permutation [pə:mju'teɪʃən] N permutação f
pernicious [pə:'nɪʃəs] ADJ nocivo; (Med)
pernicioso, maligno
pernickety [pə'nɪkɪtɪ] (inf) ADJ cheio de
nove-horas or luxo; (task) minucioso
perpendicular [pə:pən'dɪkjulə'] ADJ
perpendicular ▶ N perpendicular f
perpetrate ['pə:pɪtreɪt] VT cometer
perpetual [pə'pɛtjuəl] ADJ perpétuo
perpetuate [pə'pɛtjueɪt] VT perpetuar
perpetuity [pə:pɪ'tju:ɪtɪ] N: **in ~** para sempre
perplex [pə'plɛks] VT deixar perplexo
perplexing [pə:'plɛksɪŋ] ADJ desconcertante
perquisites ['pə:kwɪzɪts] NPL (also: **perks**)
mordomias fpl, regalias fpl
persecute ['pə:sɪkju:t] VT perseguir
persecution [pə:sɪ'kju:ʃən] N perseguição f
perseverance [pə:sɪ'vɪərəns] N perseverança
persevere [pə:sɪ'vɪə'] VI perseverar
Persia ['pə:ʃə] N Pérsia
Persian ['pə:ʃən] ADJ persa ▶ N (Ling) persa m;
the (~) Gulf o golfo Pérsico
persist [pə'sɪst] VI: **to ~ (in doing sth)**
persistir (em fazer algo)
persistence [pə'sɪstəns] N persistência; (of
disease) insistência; (obstinacy) teimosia
persistent [pə'sɪstənt] ADJ persistente;
(determined) teimoso; (disease) insistente,

persistente; **~ offender** (*Law*) infrator(a) *m/f* contumaz

persnickety [pə'snɪkɪtɪ] (*US inf*) ADJ = **pernickety**

person ['pɜːsn] N pessoa; **in ~** em pessoa; **on** *or* **about one's ~** consigo; **~ to ~ call** (*Tel*) chamada pessoal

personable ['pɜːsənəbl] ADJ atraente, bem apessoado

personal ['pɜːsənl] ADJ pessoal; (*private*) particular; (*visit*) em pessoa, pessoal; **~ belongings** *or* **effects** pertences *mpl* particulares; **~ hygiene** higiene *f* íntima; **a ~ interview** uma entrevista particular

personal allowance N (*Tax*) abatimento da renda de pessoa física

personal assistant N secretário(-a) particular

personal call N (*Tel*) chamada pessoal

personal column N anúncios *mpl* pessoais

personal computer N computador *m* pessoal

personal details NPL (*on form etc*) dados *mpl* pessoais

personal identification number N (*Comput, Banking*) senha

personality [pɜːsə'nælɪtɪ] N personalidade *f*

personally ['pɜːsənəlɪ] ADV pessoalmente; **to take sth ~** ofender-se

personal organizer N agenda

personal property N bens *mpl* móveis

personal stereo N Walkman® *m*

personify [pɜː'sɔnɪfaɪ] VT personificar

personnel [pɜːsə'nɛl] N pessoal *m*

personnel department N departamento de pessoal

personnel manager N gerente *m/f* de pessoal

perspective [pə'spɛktɪv] N perspectiva; **to get sth into ~** colocar algo em perspectiva

Perspex® ['pɜːspɛks] (*BRIT*) N acrílico

perspicacity [pɜːspɪ'kæsɪtɪ] N perspicácia

perspiration [pɜːspɪ'reɪʃən] N transpiração *f*

perspire [pə'spaɪəʳ] VI transpirar

persuade [pə'sweɪd] VT persuadir; **to ~ sb to do sth** persuadir alguém a fazer algo; **to ~ sb that/of sth** persuadir alguém que/de algo

persuasion [pə'sweɪʒən] N persuasão *f*; (*persuasiveness*) poder *m* de persuasão; (*creed*) convicção *f*, crença

persuasive [pə'sweɪsɪv] ADJ persuasivo

pert [pɜːt] ADJ atrevido, descarado

pertaining [pə'teɪnɪŋ] PREP: **~ to** relativo a

pertinent ['pɜːtɪnənt] ADJ pertinente, a propósito

perturb [pə'tɜːb] VT inquietar

perturbing [pə'tɜːbɪŋ] ADJ inquietante

Peru [pə'ruː] N Peru *m*

perusal [pə'ruːzl] N leitura

peruse [pə'ruːz] VT ler com atenção, examinar

Peruvian [pə'ruːvjən] ADJ, N peruano(-a)

pervade [pə'veɪd] VT impregnar, penetrar em

pervasive [pə'veɪsɪv] ADJ (*smell*) penetrante; (*influence, ideas, gloom*) difundido

perverse [pə'vɜːs] ADJ perverso; (*stubborn*) teimoso; (*wayward*) caprichoso

perversion [pə'vɜːʃən] N perversão *f*; (*of truth*) currupção *f*

perversity [pə'vɜːsɪtɪ] N perversidade *f*

pervert [*n* 'pɜːvɜːt, *vt* pə'vɜːt] N pervertido(-a) ▶ VT perverter, corromper; (*truth*) distorcer

pessary ['pɛsərɪ] N pessário

pessimism ['pɛsɪmɪzəm] N pessimismo

pessimist ['pɛsɪmɪst] N pessimista *m/f*

pessimistic [pɛsɪ'mɪstɪk] ADJ pessimista

pest [pɛst] N (*animal*) praga; (*fig*) peste *f*

pest control N dedetização *f*; (*for mice*) desratização *f*

pester ['pɛstəʳ] VT incomodar

pesticide ['pɛstɪsaɪd] N pesticida *m*

pestilent ['pɛstɪlənt] (*inf*) ADJ (*exasperating*) chato

pestle ['pɛsl] N mão *f* (de almofariz)

pet [pɛt] N animal *m* de estimação ▶ CPD predileto ▶ VT acariciar ▶ VI (*inf*) acariciar-se; **teacher's ~** (*favourite*) preferido(-a) do professor; **~ lion** *etc* leão *etc* de estimação; **my ~ hate** a coisa que eu mais odeio

petal ['pɛtl] N pétala

peter out ['piːtər-] VI (*conversation*) esgotar-se; (*road etc*) acabar-se

petite [pə'tiːt] ADJ delicado, mignon

petition [pə'tɪʃən] N petição *f*; (*list of signatures*) abaixo-assinado ▶ VT apresentar uma petição a ▶ VI: **to ~ for divorce** requerer divórcio

pet name (*BRIT*) N apelido carinhoso

petrified ['pɛtrɪfaɪd] ADJ (*fig*) petrificado, paralisado

petrify ['pɛtrɪfaɪ] VT paralisar; (*frighten*) petrificar

petrochemical [pɛtrə'kɛmɪkl] ADJ petroquímico

petrodollars ['pɛtrəudɔləz] NPL petrodólares *mpl*

petrol ['pɛtrəl] (*BRIT*) N gasolina; **two/four-star ~** gasolina comum/premium

petrol can (*BRIT*) N lata de gasolina

petrol engine (*BRIT*) N motor *m* a gasolina

petroleum [pə'trəulɪəm] N petróleo

petroleum jelly N vaselina®

petrol pump (*BRIT*) N (*in car, at garage*) bomba de gasolina

petrol station (*BRIT*) N posto (*BR*) *or* bomba (*PT*) de gasolina

petrol tank (*BRIT*) N tanque *m* de gasolina

petticoat ['pɛtɪkəut] N anágua; (*slip*) combinação *f*

pettifogging ['pɛtɪfɔgɪŋ] ADJ chicaneiro

pettiness ['pɛtɪnɪs] N mesquinharia *f*

petty ['pɛtɪ] ADJ (*mean*) mesquinho; (*unimportant*) insignificante

petty cash N fundo para despesas miúdas, caixa pequena, fundo de caixa

petty officer N suboficial *m* da marinha

petulant ['pɛtjulənt] ADJ irascível

pew [pjuː] N banco (de igreja)

pewter ['pju:tər] N peltre m
Pfc (US) ABBR (Mil) = **private first class**
PG N ABBR (Cinema: = parental guidance) aviso dos pais recomendado
PGA N ABBR = **Professional Golfers' Association**
PH (US) N ABBR (Mil: = Purple Heart) condecoração para feridos em combate
PHA (US) N ABBR (= Public Housing Administration) órgão que supervisiona a construção
phallic ['fælɪk] ADJ fálico
phantom ['fæntəm] N fantasma m
Pharaoh ['fɛərəu] N faraó m
pharmaceutical [fɑ:mə'sju:tɪkl] ADJ farmacêutico
pharmaceuticals [fɑ:mə'sju:tɪklz] NPL farmacêuticos mpl
pharmacist ['fɑ:məsɪst] N farmacêutico(-a)
pharmacy ['fɑ:məsɪ] N farmácia
phase [feɪz] N fase f ▶ VT: **to ~ in/out** introduzir/retirar por etapas
PhD N ABBR (= Doctor of Philosophy) = doutorado
pheasant ['fɛznt] N faisão m
phenomena [fə'nɔmɪnə] NPL of **phenomenon**
phenomenal [fə'nɔmɪnəl] ADJ fenomenal
phenomenon [fə'nɔmɪnən] (pl **phenomena**) N fenômeno
phew [fju:] EXCL ufa!
phial ['faɪəl] N frasco
philanderer [fɪ'lændərər] N mulherengo
philanthropic [fɪlən'θrɔpɪk] ADJ filantrópico
philanthropist [fɪ'lænθrəpɪst] N filantropo(-a)
philatelist [fɪ'lætəlɪst] N filatelista m/f
philately [fɪ'lætəlɪ] N filatelia
Philippines ['fɪlɪpi:nz] NPL (also: **Philippine Islands**): **the ~** as Filipinas
philosopher [fɪ'lɔsəfər] N filósofo(-a)
philosophical [fɪlə'sɔfɪkl] ADJ filosófico; (fig) calmo, sereno
philosophy [fɪ'lɔsəfɪ] N filosofia
phishing [fɪʃɪŋ] N phishing m; **~ attack** golpe m de phishing
phlegm [flɛm] N fleuma
phlegmatic [flɛg'mætɪk] ADJ fleumático
phobia ['fəubjə] N fobia
phone [fəun] N telefone m ▶ VT telefonar para, ligar para ▶ VI telefonar, ligar; **to be on the ~** ter telefone; (be calling) estar no telefone
  ▶ **phone back** VT, VI ligar de volta
  ▶ **phone up** VT telefonar para ▶ VI telefonar
phone book N lista telefônica
phone booth N cabine f telefônica
phone box (BRIT) N cabine f telefônica
phone call N telefonema m, ligação f
phone card N cartão m telefônico
phone-in (BRIT) N (Radio) programa com participação dos ouvintes; (TV) programa com participação dos espectadores
phone number N número de telefone
phonetics [fə'nɛtɪks] N fonética

phoney ['fəunɪ] ADJ falso; (person) fingido ▶ N (person) impostor(a) m/f
phonograph ['fəunəgrɑ:f] (US) N vitrola
phony ['fəunɪ] ADJ, N = **phoney**
phosphate ['fɔsfeɪt] N fosfato
phosphorus ['fɔsfərəs] N fósforo
photo ['fəutəu] N foto f
photo... ['fəutəu] PREFIX foto...
photocopier ['fəutəukɔpɪər] N fotocopiadora f
photocopy ['fəutəukɔpɪ] N fotocópia, xerox® m ▶ VT fotocopiar, xerocar
photoelectric [fəutəuɪ'lɛktrɪk] ADJ fotoelétrico; **~ cell** célula fotoelétrica
photogenic [fəutəu'dʒɛnɪk] ADJ fotogênico
photograph ['fəutəgrɑ:f] N fotografia ▶ VT fotografar; **to take a ~ of sb** bater or tirar uma foto de alguém
photographer [fə'tɔgrəfər] N fotógrafo(-a)
photographic [fəutə'græfɪk] ADJ fotográfico
photography [fə'tɔgrəfɪ] N fotografia
photostat ['fəutəustæt] N cópia fotostática
photosynthesis [fəutəu'sɪnθəsɪs] N fotossíntese f
phrase [freɪz] N frase f ▶ VT expressar; (letter) redigir
phrase book N livro de expressões idiomáticas (para turistas)
physical ['fɪzɪkl] ADJ físico; **~ examination** exame m físico; **~ exercise** exercício físico, movimento
physical education N educação f física
physically ['fɪzɪklɪ] ADV fisicamente
physician [fɪ'zɪʃən] N médico(-a)
physicist ['fɪzɪsɪst] N físico(-a)
physics ['fɪzɪks] N física
physiological [fɪzɪə'lɔdʒɪkl] ADJ fisiológico
physiology [fɪzɪ'ɔlədʒɪ] N fisiologia
physiotherapist [fɪzɪəu'θɛrəpɪst] N fisioterapeuta m/f
physiotherapy [fɪzɪəu'θɛrəpɪ] N fisioterapia
physique [fɪ'zi:k] N físico
pianist ['pi:ənɪst] N pianista m/f
piano [pɪ'ænəu] N piano
piano accordion (BRIT) N acordeão m, sanfona
piccolo ['pɪkələu] N flautim m
pick [pɪk] N (also: **pickaxe**) picareta ▶ VT (select) escolher, selecionar; (gather) colher; (remove) tirar; (lock) forçar; **take your ~** escolha o que quiser; **the ~ of** o melhor de; **to ~ a bone** roer um osso; **to ~ one's nose** colocar o dedo no nariz; **to ~ one's teeth** palitar os dentes; **to ~ sb's brains** aproveitar os conhecimentos de alguém; **to ~ pockets** roubar or bater carteira; **to ~ a quarrel or a fight with sb** comprar uma briga com alguém; **to ~ and choose** ser exigente
  ▶ **pick at** VT FUS (food) beliscar
  ▶ **pick off** VT (kill) matar de um tiro
  ▶ **pick on** VT FUS (person: criticize) criticar; (: treat badly) azucrinar, aporrinhar
  ▶ **pick out** VT escolher; (distinguish) distinguir
  ▶ **pick up** VI (improve) melhorar ▶ VT (from floor, Aut) apanhar; (Police) prender; (telephone)

p

atender, tirar do gancho; *(collect)* buscar; *(for sexual encounter)* paquerar; *(learn)* aprender; *(Radio, TV, Tel)* pegar; **to ~ up speed** acelerar; **to ~ o.s. up** levantar-se; **to ~ up where one left off** continuar do ponto onde se parou

pickaxe, (US) **pickax** ['pɪkæks] N picareta

picket ['pɪkɪt] N *(in strike)* piquete *m*; *(person)* piqueteiro(-a) ▶ VT formar piquete em frente de

picket line N piquete *m*

pickings ['pɪkɪŋz] NPL: **there are rich ~ to be had for investors in gold** os investidores em ouro vão se dar bem

pickle ['pɪkl] N *(also:* **pickles:** *as condiment)* picles *mpl*; *(fig: mess)* apuro ▶ VT *(in vinegar)* conservar em vinagre; *(in salt)* conservar em sal e água

pick-me-up N estimulante *m*

pickpocket ['pɪkpɔkɪt] N batedor(a) *m/f* de carteira (BR), carteirista *m/f* (PT)

pickup ['pɪkʌp] N *(on record player)* pick-up *m*; *(small truck: also:* **pickup truck, pickup van)** camioneta, pick-up *m*

picnic ['pɪknɪk] N piquenique *m* ▶ VI fazer um piquenique

picnicker ['pɪknɪkə^r] N pessoa que faz piquenique

pictorial [pɪk'tɔ:rɪəl] ADJ pictórico; *(magazine etc)* ilustrado

picture ['pɪktʃə^r] N quadro; *(painting)* pintura; *(drawing)* desenho; *(etching)* água-forte *f*; *(photograph)* foto(grafia) *f*; *(TV)* imagem *f*; *(film)* filme *m*; *(fig: description)* descrição *f*; *(: situation)* conjuntura ▶ VT imaginar-se; *(describe)* retratar; **the pictures** NPL (BRIT inf) o cinema; **to take a ~ of sb/sth** tirar uma foto de alguém/algo; **the overall ~** o quadro geral; **to put sb in the ~** pôr alguém a par da situação

picture book N livro de figuras

picture messaging N serviço de mensagens multimídia

picturesque [pɪktʃə'rɛsk] ADJ pitoresco

picture window N janela panorâmica

piddling ['pɪdlɪŋ] *(inf)* ADJ irrisório

pidgin ['pɪdʒɪn] ADJ: **~ English** *forma achinesada do inglês usada entre comerciantes*

pie [paɪ] N *(vegetable)* pastelão *m*; *(fruit)* torta; *(meat)* empadão *m*

piebald ['paɪbɔ:ld] ADJ malhado

piece [pi:s] N pedaço; *(portion)* fatia; *(of land)* lote *m*, parcela; *(Chess etc)* peça; *(item)*: **a ~ of clothing/furniture/advice** uma roupa/um móvel/um conselho ▶ VT: **to ~ together** juntar; *(Tech)* montar; **in ~s** *(broken)* em pedaços; *(not yet assembled)* desmontado; **to fall to ~s** cair aos pedaços; **to take to ~s** desmontar; **in one ~** *(object)* inteiro; *(person)* ileso; **a 10p ~** (BRIT) uma moeda de 10p; **~ by ~** pedaço por pedaço; **a six-~ band** um sexteto; **to say one's ~** vender o seu peixe

piecemeal ['pi:smi:l] ADV pouco a pouco

piece rate N salário por peça

piecework ['pi:swə:k] N trabalho por empreitada *or* peça

pie chart N gráfico de setores

pier [pɪə^r] N cais *m*; *(jetty)* embarcadouro, molhe *m*; *(of bridge etc)* pilar *m*, pilastra

pierce [pɪəs] VT furar, perfurar; **to have one's ears ~d** furar as orelhas

piercing ['pɪəsɪŋ] ADJ *(cry)* penetrante, agudo; *(stare)* penetrante; *(wind)* cortante

piety ['paɪətɪ] N piedade *f*

piffling ['pɪflɪŋ] ADJ irrisório

pig [pɪg] N porco; *(fig)* porcalhão(-lhona) *m/f*; *(pej: unkind person)* grosseiro(-a); *(: greedy person)* ganancioso(-a)

pigeon ['pɪdʒən] N pombo

pigeonhole ['pɪdʒənhəul] N escaninho

pigeon-toed [-təud] ADJ com pé de pombo

piggy bank ['pɪgɪ-] N *cofre em forma de porquinho*

pig-headed [-'hɛdɪd] *(pej)* ADJ teimoso, cabeçudo

piglet ['pɪglɪt] N porquinho, leitão *m*

pigment ['pɪgmənt] N pigmento

pigmentation [pɪgmən'teɪʃən] N pigmentação *f*

pigmy ['pɪgmɪ] N = **pygmy**

pigskin ['pɪgskɪn] N couro de porco

pigsty ['pɪgstaɪ] N chiqueiro

pigtail ['pɪgteɪl] N *(girl's)* rabo-de-cavalo, trança; *(Chinese)* rabicho

pike [paɪk] N *(pl* **pike** *or* **pikes)** *(spear)* lança, pique *m*; *(fish)* lúcio

pilchard ['pɪltʃəd] N sardinha

pile [paɪl] N *(of books)* pilha; *(heap)* monte *m*; *(of carpet)* pelo; *(of cloth)* lado felpudo; *(support: in building)* estaca ▶ VT *(also:* **pile up)** empilhar; *(heap)* amontoar; *(fig)* acumular ▶ VI *(also:* **pile up:** *objects)* empilhar-se; *(: problems, work)* acumular-se; **in a ~** numa pilha
 ▶ **pile into** VT FUS *(car)* apinhar-se
 ▶ **pile on** VT: **to ~ it on** *(inf)* exagerar

piles [paɪlz] NPL *(Med)* hemorróidas *fpl*

pile-up N *(Aut)* engavetamento

pilfer ['pɪlfə^r] VT, VI furtar, afanar, surripiar

pilfering ['pɪlfərɪŋ] N furto

pilgrim ['pɪlgrɪm] N peregrino(-a)

pilgrimage ['pɪlgrɪmɪdʒ] N peregrinação *f*, romaria

pill [pɪl] N pílula; **the ~** a pílula; **to be on the ~** usar *or* tomar a pílula

pillage ['pɪlɪdʒ] N pilhagem *f* ▶ VT saquear, pilhar

pillar ['pɪlə^r] N pilar *m*; *(concrete)* coluna

pillar box (BRIT) N caixa coletora (do correio) (BR), marco do correio (PT)

pillion ['pɪljən] N *(of motor cycle)* garupa; **to ride ~** andar na garupa

pillory ['pɪlərɪ] N pelourinho ▶ VT expor ao ridículo

pillow ['pɪləu] N travesseiro (BR), almofada (PT)

pillowcase ['pɪləukeɪs] N fronha

pillowslip ['pɪləuslɪp] N fronha

pilot ['paɪlət] N piloto(-a) ▶ CPD *(scheme etc)* piloto *inv* ▶ VT pilotar; *(fig)* guiar

pilot boat N barco-piloto
pilot light N piloto
pimento [pɪ'mɛntəu] N pimentão-doce *m*
pimp [pɪmp] N cafetão *m* (BR), cáften *m* (PT)
pimple ['pɪmpl] N espinha
pimply ['pɪmplɪ] ADJ espinhento
PIN N ABBR (= *personal identification number*) senha
pin [pɪn] N alfinete *m*; (*Tech*) cavilha; (*wooden, BRIT Elec: of plug*) pino ▶ VT alfinetar; **~s and needles** comichão *f*, sensação *f* de formigamento; **to ~ sb against** *or* **to** apertar alguém contra; **to ~ sth on sb** (*fig*) culpar alguém de algo
▶ **pin down** VT (*fig*): **to ~ sb down** conseguir que alguém se defina *or* tome atitude; **there's something strange here but I can't quite ~ it down** há alguma coisa estranha aqui mas não consigo precisar o quê
pinafore ['pɪnəfɔːʳ] N (*also*: **pinafore dress**) avental *m*
pinball ['pɪnbɔːl] N fliper *m*, fliperama *m*
pincers ['pɪnsəz] NPL pinça, tenaz *f*
pinch [pɪntʃ] N beliscão *m*; (*of salt etc*) pitada ▶ VT beliscar; **at a ~** em último caso; **to feel the ~** (*fig*) apertar o cinto, passar por um aperto
pinched [pɪntʃt] ADJ (*drawn*) abatido; **~ with cold** transido de frio; **~ for money** desprovido de dinheiro; **to be ~ for space** não dispor de muito espaço
pincushion ['pɪnkuʃən] N alfineteira
pine [paɪn] N (*also*: **pine tree**) pinho; (*wood*) madeira de pinho ▶ VI: **to ~ for** ansiar por
▶ **pine away** VI consumir-se, definhar
pineapple ['paɪnæpl] N abacaxi *m* (BR), ananás *m* (PT)
ping [pɪŋ] N (*noise*) silvo, sibilo
ping-pong® N pingue-pongue *m*
pink [pɪŋk] ADJ cor de rosa *inv* ▶ N (*colour*) cor *f* de rosa; (*Bot*) cravo, cravina
pinking scissors ['pɪŋkɪŋ-] NPL tesoura para picotar
pinking shears ['pɪŋkɪŋ-] NPL tesoura para picotar
pin money (BRIT) N dinheiro extra
pinnacle ['pɪnəkl] N cume *m*; (*fig*) auge *m*
pinpoint ['pɪnpɔɪnt] VT (*discover*) descobrir; (*explain*) identificar; (*locate*) localizar com precisão
pinstripe ['pɪnstraɪp] N tecido listrado ▶ ADJ listrado
pint [paɪnt] N quartilho (*Brit* = 568cc, *US* = 473cc); **to go for a ~** (BRIT *inf*) ir tomar uma cerveja
pin-up N pin-up *f*, retrato de mulher atraente
pioneer [paɪə'nɪəʳ] N pioneiro(-a) ▶ VT ser pioneiro de
pious ['paɪəs] ADJ pio, devoto
pip [pɪp] N (*seed*) caroço, semente *f*; **the pips** NPL (BRIT: *time signal on radio*) ≈ o toque de seis segundos
pipe [paɪp] N cano; (*for smoking*) cachimbo; (*Mus*) flauta ▶ VT canalizar, encanar;

pipes NPL (*also*: **bagpipes**) gaita de foles
▶ **pipe down** (*inf*) VI calar o bico, meter a viola no saco
pipe cleaner N limpa-cachimbo
piped music [paɪpt-] N música enlatada
pipe dream N sonho impossível, castelo no ar
pipeline ['paɪplaɪn] N (*for oil*) oleoduto; (*for gas*) gaseoduto; **it's in the ~** (*fig*) está na bica (*inf*)
piper ['paɪpəʳ] N (*gen*) flautista *m/f*; (*of bagpipes*) gaiteiro(-a)
pipe tobacco N fumo (BR) *or* tabaco (PT) para cachimbo
piping ['paɪpɪŋ] ADV: **~ hot** chiando de quente
piquant ['piːkənt] ADJ picante
pique [piːk] N ressentimento, melindre *m*
piracy ['paɪərəsɪ] N pirataria
pirate ['paɪərət] N pirata *m* ▶ VT (*record, video, book*) piratear
pirate radio (BRIT) N rádio pirata
pirouette [pɪru'ɛt] N pirueta ▶ VI fazer pirueta(s)
Pisces ['paɪsiːz] N Pisces *m*, Peixes *mpl*
piss [pɪs] (!) VI mijar; **~ off!** vai à merda (!)
pissed [pɪst] (!) ADJ (*drunk*) bêbado, de porre
pistol ['pɪstl] N pistola
piston ['pɪstən] N pistão *m*, êmbolo
pit [pɪt] N cova, fossa; (*quarry, hole in surface of sth*) buraco; (*also*: **coal pit**) mina de carvão; (*also*: **orchestra pit**) fosso ▶ VT: **to ~ one's wits against sb** competir em conhecimento *or* inteligência contra alguém; **pits** NPL (*Aut*) box *m*; **to ~ A against B** opor A a B; **to ~ o.s. against** opor-se a
pitapat ['pɪtə'pæt] (BRIT) ADV: **to go ~** (*heart*) disparar; (*rain*) tiquetaquear
pitch [pɪtʃ] N (*throw*) arremesso, lance *m*; (*Mus*) tom *m*; (*of voice*) altura; (*fig: degree*) intensidade *f*; (*also*: **sales pitch**) papo (de vendedor); (BRIT *Sport*) campo; (*tar*) piche *m*, breu *m*; (*Naut*) arfada; (*in market etc*) barraca ▶ VT (*throw*) arremessar, lançar; (*tent*) armar; (*set: price, message*) adaptar ▶ VI (*fall forwards*) cair (para frente); (*Naut*) jogar, arfar; **to be ~ed forward** ser jogado para frente; **at this ~** neste pique *or* ritmo; **to ~ one's aspirations too high** colocar as aspirações alto demais
▶ **pitch in** VI contribuir
pitch-black ADJ escuro como o breu
pitched battle [pɪtʃt-] N batalha campal
pitcher ['pɪtʃəʳ] N jarro, cântaro; (*US Baseball*) arremessador *m*
pitchfork ['pɪtʃfɔːk] N forcado
piteous ['pɪtɪəs] ADJ lastimável
pitfall ['pɪtfɔːl] N perigo (imprevisto), armadilha
pith [pɪθ] N (*of orange*) casca interna e branca; (*fig*) essência, parte *f* essencial
pithead ['pɪthɛd] (BRIT) N boca do poço
pithy ['pɪθɪ] ADJ substancial
pitiable ['pɪtɪəbl] ADJ deplorável
pitiful ['pɪtɪful] ADJ (*touching*) comovente, tocante; (*contemptible*) desprezível, lamentável

P

pitifully ['pɪtɪfəlɪ] ADV lamentavelmente, deploravelmente

pitiless ['pɪtɪlɪs] ADJ impiedoso

pittance ['pɪtns] N ninharia, miséria

pitted ['pɪtɪd] ADJ: ~ **with** (chickenpox) marcado com; (rust) picado de; ~ **with potholes** esburacado

pity ['pɪtɪ] N (compassion) compaixão f, piedade f; (shame) pena ▶ VT ter pena de, compadecer-se de; **what a ~!** que pena!; **it's a ~ (that) you can't come** é uma pena que você não possa vir; **to have** or **take ~ on sb** ter pena de alguém

pitying ['pɪtɪɪŋ] ADJ compassivo, compadecido

pivot ['pɪvət] N pino, eixo; (fig) pivô m ▶ VI: **to ~ on** girar sobre; (fig) depender de

pixel ['pɪksl] N (Comput) pixel m

pixie ['pɪksɪ] N duende m

pizza ['pi:tsə] N pizza

placard ['plæka:d] N placar m; (in march etc) cartaz m

placate [plə'keɪt] VT apaziguar, aplacar

placatory [plə'keɪtərɪ] ADJ apaziguador(a), aplacador(a)

place [pleɪs] N lugar m; (rank, position) posição f; (post) posto; (role) papel m; (home): **at/to his ~** na/para a casa dele ▶ VT (object) pôr, colocar; (identify) identificar, situar; (find a post for) colocar; **to take ~** realizar-se; (occur) ocorrer; **from ~ to ~** de lugar em lugar; **all over the ~** em tudo quanto é lugar; **out of ~** (not suitable) fora de lugar, deslocado; **I feel out of ~ here** eu me sinto deslocado aqui; **in the first ~** em primeiro lugar; **to change ~s with sb** trocar de lugar com alguém; **to put sb in his ~** (fig) pôr alguém no seu lugar; **he's going ~s** (fig) ele vai se dar bem; **it's not my ~ to do it** não me compete fazê-lo; **to ~ an order with sb for sth** (Comm) encomendar algo a alguém; **to be ~d** (in race, exam) classificar-se; **how are you ~d next week?** você tem tempo na semana que vem?

placebo [plə'si:bəu] N placebo

place mat N descanso

placement ['pleɪsmənt] N (placing) colocação f; (job) cargo

place name N topônimo

placenta [plə'sentə] N placenta

place of birth N local m de nascimento

placid ['plæsɪd] ADJ plácido, sereno

placidity [plə'sɪdɪtɪ] N placidez f

plagiarism ['pleɪdʒjərɪzm] N plágio

plagiarist ['pleɪdʒjərɪst] N plagiário(-a)

plagiarize ['pleɪdʒjəraɪz] VT plagiar

plague [pleɪg] N (Med) peste f; (fig) praga ▶ VT (fig) atormentar, importunar; **to ~ sb with questions** importunar alguém com perguntas

plaice [pleɪs] N INV solha

plaid [plæd] N (material) tecido de xadrez; (pattern) xadrez m escocês

plain [pleɪn] ADJ (unpatterned) liso; (clear) claro, evidente; (simple) simples inv, despretensioso; (frank) franco, sem rodeios; (not handsome) sem atrativos; (pure) puro, natural ▶ ADV claramente, com franqueza ▶ N planície f, campina; **to make sth ~ to sb** dar claramente a entender algo a alguém

plain chocolate N chocolate m amargo

plain-clothes ADJ (police officer) à paisana

plainly ['pleɪnlɪ] ADV claramente, obviamente; (hear, see) facilmente; (state) francamente

plainness ['pleɪnnɪs] N clareza; (simplicity) simplicidade f; (frankness) franqueza

plaintiff ['pleɪntɪf] N querelante m/f, queixoso(-a)

plaintive ['pleɪntɪv] ADJ (voice, tone) queixoso; (song) lamentoso; (look) tristonho

plait [plæt] N trança, dobra ▶ VT trançar

plan [plæn] N plano; (scheme) projeto; (schedule) programa m ▶ VT planejar (BR), planear (PT) ▶ VI fazer planos; **to ~ to do** pretender fazer; **how long do you ~ to stay?** quanto tempo você pretende ficar?

plane [pleɪn] N (Aviat) avião m; (also: **plane tree**) plátano; (fig: level) nivel m; (tool) plaina; (Math) plano ▶ ADJ plano ▶ VT (with tool) aplainar

planet ['plænɪt] N planeta m

planetarium [plænɪ'tɛərɪəm] N planetário

plank [plæŋk] N tábua; (Pol) item m da plataforma política

plankton ['plæŋktən] N plâncton m

planner ['plænər] N (town planejador(a) m/f (BR), planeador(a) m/f (PT); (chart) agenda (quadro); (town planner) urbanista m/f; (of TV programme, project) programador(a) m/f

planning ['plænɪŋ] N planejamento (BR), planeamento (PT); **family ~** planejamento or planeamento familiar

planning permission (BRIT) N autorização f para construir

plant [pla:nt] N planta; (machinery) maquinaria; (factory) usina, fábrica ▶ VT plantar; (field) semear; (bomb) colocar, pôr; (inf) pôr às escondidas; (incriminating evidence) incriminar

plantation [plæn'teɪʃən] N plantação f; (estate) fazenda; (area of trees) bosque m

plant hire N locação f de equipamentos

plant pot (BRIT) N vaso para planta

plaque [plæk] N placa, insígnia; (also: **dental plaque**) placa dental

plasma ['plæzmə] N plasma m

plaster ['pla:stər] N (for walls) reboco; (also: **plaster of Paris**) gesso; (BRIT: also: **sticking plaster**) esparadrapo, band-aid m ▶ VT rebocar; (cover): **to ~ with** encher or cobrir de; **in ~** (BRIT: leg etc) engessado; ~ **of Paris** gesso

plaster cast N (Med) aparelho de gesso; (Art) molde m de gesso

plastered ['pla:stəd] (inf) ADJ bêbado, de porre

plasterer ['plɑːstərəʳ] N rebocador(a) m/f, caiador(a) m/f
plastic ['plæstɪk] N plástico ▸ ADJ de plástico; (flexible) plástico; (art) plástico
plastic bag N sacola de plástico
Plasticine® ['plæstɪsiːn] N plasticina®
plastic surgery N cirurgia plástica
plate [pleɪt] N prato; (on door, dental, Phot) chapa; (Typ) clichê m; (in book) gravura; (Aut: number plate) placa; **gold/silver ~** placa de ouro/prata
plateau ['plætəu] (pl **plateaus** or **plateaux**) N planalto
plateaux ['plætəuz] NPL of **plateau**
plateful ['pleɪtful] N pratada
plate glass N vidro laminado
platen ['plætən] N (on typewriter, printer) rolo
plate rack N escorredor m de pratos
platform ['plætfɔːm] N (Rail) plataforma (BR), cais m (PT); (stage) estrado; (at meeting) tribuna; (raised structure: for landing etc) plataforma; (BRIT: of bus) plataforma; (Pol) programa m partidário
platform ticket (BRIT) N bilhete m de plataforma (BR) or cais (PT)
platinum ['plætɪnəm] N platina
platitude ['plætɪtjuːd] N lugar m comum, chavão m
platonic [plə'tɔnɪk] ADJ platônico
platoon [plə'tuːn] N pelotão m
platter ['plætəʳ] N travessa
plaudits ['plɔːdɪts] NPL aclamações fpl, aplausos mpl
plausible ['plɔːzɪbl] ADJ plausível; (person) convincente
play [pleɪ] N jogo; (Theatre) obra, peça ▸ VT jogar; (team, opponent) jogar contra; (instrument, music, record) tocar; (Theatre) representar; (: role) fazer o papel de; (fig) desempenhar ▸ VI (sport, game) jogar; (music) tocar; (frolic) brincar; **to bring** or **call into ~** (plan) acionar; (emotions) detonar; **~ on words** jogo de palavras, trocadilho; **to ~ a trick on sb** pregar uma peça em alguém; **they're ~ing at soldiers** eles estão brincando de soldados; **to ~ for time** (fig) tentar ganhar tempo, protelar; **to ~ into sb's hands** (fig) fazer o jogo de alguém; **to ~ the fool/innocent** bancar o tolo/inocente; **to ~ safe** não se arriscar, não correr riscos
▸ **play about** VI brincar
▸ **play along** VI (fig): **to ~ along with sb** fazer o jogo de alguém ▸ VT (fig): **to ~ sb along** fazer alguém de criança
▸ **play around** VI brincar
▸ **play back** VT repetir
▸ **play down** VT minimizar
▸ **play on** VT FUS (sb's feelings, credulity) tirar proveito de, usar
▸ **play up** VI (person) dar trabalho; (TV, car) estar com defeito
playact ['pleɪækt] VI fazer fita
playboy ['pleɪbɔɪ] N playboy m

played-out [pleɪd-] ADJ gasto
player ['pleɪəʳ] N jogador(a) m/f; (Theatre) ator/atriz m/f; (Mus) músico(-a)
playful ['pleɪful] ADJ brincalhão(-lhona)
playgoer ['pleɪgəuəʳ] N frequentador(a) m/f de teatro
playground ['pleɪgraund] N (in park) playground m; (in school) pátio de recreio
playgroup ['pleɪgruːp] N espécie de jardim de infância
playing card ['pleɪɪŋ-] N carta de baralho
playing field ['pleɪɪŋ-] N campo de esportes (BR) or jogos (PT)
playmate ['pleɪmeɪt] N colega m/f, camarada m/f
play-off N (Sport) partida de desempate
playpen ['pleɪpɛn] N cercado para crianças
playroom ['pleɪruːm] N sala de jogos
plaything ['pleɪθɪŋ] N brinquedo; (fig) joguete m
playtime ['pleɪtaɪm] N (Sch) recreio
playwright ['pleɪraɪt] N dramaturgo(-a)
plc ABBR = **public limited company**
plea [pliː] N (request) apelo, petição f; (excuse) justificativa; (Law: defence) defesa
plead [pliːd] VT (Law) defender, advogar; (give as excuse) alegar ▸ VI (Law) declarar-se; (beg): **to ~ with sb** suplicar or rogar a alguém; **to ~ guilty/not guilty** declarar-se culpado/inocente
pleasant ['plɛznt] ADJ agradável; (person) simpático
pleasantly ['plɛzntlɪ] ADV agradavelmente
pleasantness ['plɛzntnɪs] N (of person) amabilidade f, simpatia; (of place) encanto
pleasantry ['plɛzntrɪ] N (joke) brincadeira; **pleasantries** NPL (polite remarks) amenidades fpl (na conversa)
please [pliːz] EXCL por favor ▸ VT (give pleasure to) agradar a, dar prazer a ▸ VI agradar, dar prazer; (think fit): **do as you ~** faça o que or como quiser; **~ yourself!** (inf) como você quiser!, você que sabe!
pleased [pliːzd] ADJ (happy) satisfeito, contente; **~ (with)** satisfeito (com); **~ to meet you** prazer (em conhecê-lo); **we are ~ to inform you that ...** temos a satisfação de informá-lo de que ...
pleasing ['pliːzɪŋ] ADJ agradável
pleasurable ['plɛʒərəbl] ADJ agradável
pleasure ['plɛʒəʳ] N prazer m; **"it's a ~"** "não tem de quê"; **with ~** com muito prazer; **is this trip for business or ~?** esta viagem é de negócios ou de recreio?
pleasure boat N barco de recreio
pleasure steamer N vapor m de recreio
pleat [pliːt] N prega
plebiscite ['plɛbɪsɪt] N plebiscito
plebs [plɛbz] (pej) NPL plebe f
plectrum ['plɛktrəm] N plectro
pledge [plɛdʒ] N (object) penhor m; (promise) promessa ▸ VT (invest) empenhar; (promise) prometer; **to ~ support for sb** empenhar-

se a apoiar alguém; **to ~ sb to secrecy**
comprometer alguém a guardar sigilo
plenary ['pli:nərɪ] ADJ: **in ~ session** no
plenário
plentiful ['plɛntɪful] ADJ abundante
plenty ['plɛntɪ] N abundância; **~ of** (food,
money) bastante; (jobs, people) muitos(-as);
we've got ~ of time temos tempo de sobra
pleurisy ['pluərɪsɪ] N pleurisia
Plexiglas® ['plɛksɪglɑːs] (US) N Blindex® m
pliable ['plaɪəbl] ADJ flexível; (fig: person)
adaptável, moldável
pliant ['plaɪənt] ADJ = **pliable**
pliers ['plaɪəz] NPL alicate m
plight [plaɪt] N situação f difícil, apuro
plimsolls ['plɪmsəlz] (BRIT) NPL tênis mpl
plinth [plɪnθ] N peinto
PLO N ABBR (= Palestine Liberation Organization)
OLP f
plod [plɔd] VI caminhar pesadamente; (fig)
trabalhar laboriosamente
plodder ['plɔdə*r*] N burro-de-carga m
plodding ['plɔdɪŋ] ADJ mourejador(a)
plonk [plɔŋk] (inf) N (BRIT: wine) zurrapa ▶ VT:
to ~ sth down deixar cair algo
(pesadamente)
plot [plɔt] N (scheme) conspiração f, complô m;
(of story, play) enredo, trama; (of land) lote m
▶ VT (mark out) traçar; (conspire) tramar,
planejar (BR), planear (PT); (Aviat, Naut, Math)
plotar ▶ VI conspirar; **a vegetable ~** (BRIT)
uma horta
plotter ['plɔtə*r*] N conspirador(a) m/f;
(instrument) plotadora; (Comput) plotter m,
plotadora
plough, (US) **plow** [plau] N arado ▶ VT (earth)
arar; **to ~ money into** investir dinheiro em
▶ **plough back** VT (Comm) reinvestir
▶ **plough through** VT FUS (crowd) abrir
caminho por; (snow) avançar penosamente
por
ploughing, (US) **plowing** ['plauɪŋ] N aradura
ploughman, (US) **plowman** (irreg: like **man**)
['plaumən] N lavrador m
ploughman's lunch (BRIT) N lanche de
pão, queijo e picles
plow [plau] (US) N = **plough**
ploy [plɔɪ] N estratagema m
pls ABBR (= please) por favor
pluck [plʌk] VT (fruit) colher; (musical
instrument) dedilhar; (bird) depenar ▶ N
coragem f, puxão m; **to ~ one's eyebrows**
fazer as sobrancelhas; **to ~ up courage** criar
coragem
plucky ['plʌkɪ] ADJ corajoso, valente
plug [plʌg] N tampão m; (Elec) tomada (BR),
ficha (PT); (in sink) tampa; (Aut: also:
spark(ing) plug) vela (de ignição) ▶ VT (hole)
tapar; (inf: advertise) fazer propaganda de; **to
give sb/sth a ~** (inf) fazer propaganda de
alguém/algo
▶ **plug in** VT (Elec) ligar
plughole ['plʌghəul] (BRIT) N (in sink) escoadouro

plug-in N ['plʌgɪn] (Comput) plug-in m
plum [plʌm] N (fruit) ameixa ▶ CPD (inf): **a ~
job** um emprego joia
plumage ['pluːmɪdʒ] N plumagem f
plumb [plʌm] ADJ vertical ▶ N prumo ▶ ADV
(exactly) exatamente ▶ VT sondar; **to ~ the
depths** (fig) chegar ao extremo
▶ **plumb in** VT (washing machine) instalar
plumber ['plʌmə*r*] N bombeiro(-a) (BR),
encanador(a) m/f (BR), canalizador(a) m/f (PT)
plumbing ['plʌmɪŋ] N (trade) ofício de
encanador; (piping) encanamento
plumb line ['plʌmlaɪn] N fio de prumo
plume [pluːm] N pluma; (on helmet) penacho
plummet ['plʌmɪt] VI: **to ~ (down)** (bird,
aircraft) cair rapidamente; (price) baixar
rapidamente
plump [plʌmp] ADJ roliço, rechonchudo ▶ VT:
to ~ sth (down) on deixar cair algo em ▶ VI:
to ~ for (inf: choose) escolher, optar por
▶ **plump up** VT (cushion) afofar
plunder ['plʌndə*r*] N pilhagem f; (loot) despojo
▶ VT pilhar, espoliar
plunge [plʌndʒ] N (dive) salto; (submersion)
mergulho; (fig) queda ▶ VT (hand, knife)
enfiar, meter ▶ VI (fall, fig) cair; (dive)
mergulhar; **to take the ~** topar a parada;
to ~ a room into darkness mergulhar um
aposento na escuridão
plunger ['plʌndʒə*r*] N êmbolo; (for blocked sink)
desentupidor m
plunging ['plʌndʒɪŋ] ADJ (neckline) decotado
pluperfect [pluː'pəːfɪkt] N mais-que-perfeito
plural ['pluərl] ADJ plural ▶ N plural m
plus [plʌs] N (also: **plus sign**) sinal m de adição
▶ PREP mais; **ten/twenty ~** dez/vinte e
tantos; **it's a ~** é uma vantagem
plus fours NPL calça (BR) or calças fpl (PT) de
golfe
plush [plʌʃ] ADJ de pelúcia; (car, hotel etc)
suntuoso ▶ N pelúcia
plus-one ['plʌs'wʌn] (inf) N acompanhante
m/f
plutonium [pluː'təunɪəm] N plutônio
ply [plaɪ] N (of wool) fio; (of wood) espessura
▶ VT (a trade) exercer ▶ VI (ship) ir e vir; **three ~**
(wool) de três fios; **to ~ sb with drink/
questions** bombardear alguém com
bebidas/perguntas
plywood ['plaɪwud] N madeira compensada
PM (BRIT) N ABBR = **Prime Minister**
p.m. ADV ABBR (= post meridiem) da tarde, da
noite
PMT N ABBR (= premenstrual tension) TPM f,
tensão f pré-menstrual
pneumatic [njuː'mætɪk] ADJ pneumático
pneumatic drill [njuː'mætɪk drɪl] N
perfuratriz f
pneumonia [njuː'məunɪə] N pneumonia
PO N ABBR = **Post Office**; (Mil) = **petty officer**
po ABBR = **postal order**
POA (BRIT) N ABBR = **Prison Officers'
Association**

poach [pəutʃ] VT (cook: fish) escaldar; (: eggs) fazer pochê (BR), escalfar (PT); (steal) furtar ▶ VI caçar (or pescar) em propriedade alheia

poached [pəutʃt] ADJ (egg) pochê (BR), escalfado (PT)

poacher ['pəutʃər] N caçador m (or pescador m) furtivo

poaching ['pəutʃɪŋ] N caça (or pesca) furtiva

PO Box N ABBR = **post office box**

pocket ['pɔkɪt] N bolso; (fig: small area) pedaço; (Billiards) caçapa, ventanilha ▶ VT meter no bolso; (steal) embolsar; (Billiards) encaçapar; **to be out of ~** (BRIT) ter prejuízo; **~ of resistance** foco de resistência

pocketbook ['pɔkɪtbuk] (US) N carteira

pocket calculator N calculadora de bolsa

pocket knife (irreg: like knife) N canivete m

pocket money N dinheiro para despesas miúdas; (for child) mesada

pockmarked ['pɔkmɑːkt] ADJ (face) com marcas de varíola

pod [pɔd] N vagem f ▶ VT descascar

podcast [pɔdkɑːst] N podcast m

podcasting ['pɔdkɑːstɪŋ] N podcasting m

podgy ['pɔdʒɪ] (inf) ADJ gorducho, rechanchudo

podiatrist [pɔ'diːətrɪst] (US) N pedicuro(-a)

podiatry [pɔ'diːətrɪ] (US) N podiatria

podium ['pəudɪəm] N pódio

POE N ABBR = **port of embarkation**; **port of entry**

poem ['pəuɪm] N poema m

poet ['pəuɪt] N poeta/poetisa m/f

poetess ['pəuɪtɪs] N poetisa

poetic [pəu'ɛtɪk] ADJ poético

poet laureate [-'lɔːrɪət] N poeta m laureado

poetry ['pəuɪtrɪ] N poesia

poignant ['pɔɪnjənt] ADJ comovente; (sharp) agudo

point [pɔɪnt] N (gen) ponto; (of needle, knife etc) ponta; (purpose) finalidade f; (significant part) ponto principal; (position, place) lugar m, posição f; (moment) momento; (stage) estágio; (BRIT Elec: also: **power point**) tomada; (also: **decimal point**): **2 ~ 3 (2.3)** dois vírgula três ▶ VT (show, mark) mostrar; (window, wall) tomar com argamassa; (gun etc): **to ~ sth at sb** apontar algo para alguém ▶ VI apontar; **points** NPL (Aut) platinado, contato; (Rail) agulhas fpl; **to ~ at** apontar para; **good ~s** qualidades; **to be on the ~ of doing sth** estar prestes a or a ponto de fazer algo; **to make a ~** fazer uma observação; **to make a ~ of** fazer questão de, insistir em; **to make one's ~** dar sua opinião; **you've made your ~** você já disse o que queria, você já falou (inf); **to get the ~** perceber; **to miss the ~** compreender mal; **to come to the ~** ir ao assunto; **when it comes to the ~** na hora; **there's no ~ (in doing)** não há razão (para fazer); **that's the whole ~!** aí é que está a questão!, aí é que 'tá! (inf); **to be beside the ~** estar fora do assunto; **you've got a ~ there!** você tem razão!; **in ~ of fact** na verdade, na realidade; **~ of departure** ponto de partida; **~ of sale** (Comm) ponto de venda; **~ of view** ponto de vista ▶ **point out** VT (indicate) indicar; (in debate etc) ressaltar ▶ **point to** VT FUS apontar para; (fig) indicar

point-blank ADV categoricamente; (also: **at point-blank range**) à queima-roupa ▶ ADJ (fig) categórico

point duty (BRIT) N: **to be on ~** estar de serviço no controle do trânsito

pointed ['pɔɪntɪd] ADJ (stick etc) pontudo; (remark) mordaz

pointedly ['pɔɪntɪdlɪ] ADV sugestivamente

pointer ['pɔɪntər] N (on chart) indicador m; (on machine) ponteiro; (needle) agulha; (dog) pointer m; (fig) dica

pointless ['pɔɪntlɪs] ADJ (useless) inútil; (senseless) sem sentido; (motiveless) sem razão

poise [pɔɪz] N (composure) elegância; (balance) equilíbrio; (of head, body) porte m; (calmness) serenidade f ▶ VT pôr em equilíbrio; **to be ~d for** (fig) estar pronto para

poison ['pɔɪzn] N veneno ▶ VT envenenar

poisoning ['pɔɪznɪŋ] N envenenamento

poisonous ['pɔɪzənəs] ADJ venenoso; (fumes etc) tóxico; (fig) pernicioso

poke [pəuk] VT (fire) atiçar; (jab with finger, stick etc) cutucar; (put): **to ~ sth in(to)** enfiar or meter algo em ▶ N (to fire) remexida; (jab) cutucada; (with elbow) cotovelada; **to ~ one's nose into** meter o nariz em; **to ~ one's head out of the window** meter a cabeça para fora da janela; **to ~ fun at sb** ridicularizar or fazer troça de alguém ▶ **poke about** VI escarafunchar, espionar

poker ['pəukər] N atiçador m (de brasas); (Cards) pôquer m

poker-faced [-feɪst] ADJ com rosto impassível

poky ['pəukɪ] (pej) ADJ apertado

Poland ['pəulənd] N Polônia

polar ['pəulər] ADJ polar

polar bear N urso polar

polarize ['pəuləraɪz] VT polarizar

Pole [pəul] N polonês(-esa) m/f

pole [pəul] N vara; (Geo) polo; (telegraph pole) poste m; (flagpole) mastro; (tent pole) estaca

pole bean (US) N feijão-trepador m

polecat ['pəulkæt] N furão-bravo

Pol. Econ. ['pɔlɪkɔn] N ABBR = **political economy**

polemic [pɔ'lɛmɪk] N polêmica

pole star N estrela Polar

pole vault N salto com vara

police [pə'liːs] N polícia ▶ VT policiar

police car N rádio-patrulha f

police constable (BRIT) N policial m/f (BR), polícia m/f (PT)

police department (US) N polícia

police force N polícia

policeman [pə'liːsmən] (irreg: like **man**) N policial m (BR), polícia m (PT)

police officer N policial *m/f* (BR), polícia *m/f* (PT)
police record N ficha na polícia
police state N estado policial
police station N delegacia (de polícia) (BR), esquadra (PT)
policewoman [pə'li:swumən] (*irreg: like* **woman**) N policial *f* (feminina) (BR), mulher *f* polícia (PT)
policy ['pɔlısı] N política; (*also:* **insurance policy**) apólice *f*; (*of newspaper, company*) orientação *f*; **to take out a ~** (*Insurance*) fazer uma apólice *or* um contrato de seguro
policy holder N segurado(-a)
polio ['pəuliəu] N polio(mielite) *f*
Polish ['pəulıʃ] ADJ polonês(-esa) ► N (*Ling*) polonês *m*
polish ['pɔlıʃ] N (*for shoes*) graxa; (*for floor*) cera (para encerar); (*for nails*) esmalte *m*; (*shine*) brilho; (*fig: refinement*) refinamento, requinte *m* ► VT (*shoes*) engraxar; (*make shiny*) lustrar, dar brilho a; (*fig: improve*) refinar, polir
► **polish off** VT (*work*) dar os arremates a; (*food*) raspar
polished ['pɔlıʃt] ADJ (*fig: person*) culto; (*: manners*) refinado
polite [pə'laıt] ADJ educado; (*formal*) cortês; (*company, society*) refinado; **it's not ~ to do that** é falta de educação fazer isso
politely [pə'laıtlı] ADV educadamente
politeness [pə'laıtnıs] N gentileza, cortesia
politic ['pɔlıtık] ADJ prudente
political [pə'lıtıkl] ADJ político
political asylum N asilo político; **to seek ~** pedir asilo político
politically [pə'lıtıklı] ADV politicamente
politician [pɔlı'tıʃən] N político(-a)
politics ['pɔlıtıks] N, NPL política
polka ['pɔlkə] N polca
polka dot N bolinha
poll [pəul] N (*votes*) votação *f*; (*also:* **opinion poll**) pesquisa, sondagem *f* ► VT (*votes*) receber, obter; **to go to the ~s** (*voters*) ir às urnas; (*government*) convocar eleições
pollen ['pɔlən] N pólen *m*
pollen count N contagem *f* de pólen
pollination [pɔlı'neıʃən] N polinização *f*
polling ['pəulıŋ] N (*BRIT Pol*) votação *f*; (*Tel*) apuração *f*
polling booth (*BRIT*) N cabine *f* de votar
polling day (*BRIT*) N dia *m* de eleição
polling station (*BRIT*) N centro eleitoral
pollute [pə'lu:t] VT poluir
pollution [pə'lu:ʃən] N poluição *f*
polo ['pəuləu] N (*sport*) polo
polo neck N gola rulê ► ADJ: **polo-neck** de gola rulê
polo-necked [-nɛkt] ADJ de gola rulê
poltergeist ['pɔltegaıst] N espírito pertubador (*espécie de fantasma*)
poly ['pɔlı] (*BRIT*) N ABBR = **polytechnic**
polyester [pɔlı'ɛstəʳ] N poliéster *m*
polyethylene [pɔlı'ɛθıli:n] (*US*) N polietileno

polygamy [pə'lıgəmı] N poligamia
Polynesia [pɔlı'ni:zıə] N Polinésia
Polynesian [pɔlı'ni:zıən] ADJ, N polinésio(-a)
polyp ['pɔlıp] N (*Med*) pólipo
polystyrene [pɔlı'staıri:n] N isopor® *m*
polytechnic [pɔlı'tɛknık] N politécnico, escola politécnica
polythene ['pɔlıθi:n] N politeno
polythene bag N bolsa de plástico
polyurethane [pɔlı'juːrəθeın] N poliuretano
pomegranate ['pɔmıgrænıt] N romã *f*
pommel ['pɔml] N botão *m*; (*saddle*) maçaneta ► VT = **pummel**
pomp [pɔmp] N pompa, fausto
pompom ['pɔmpɔm] N pompom *m*
pompon ['pɔmpɔn] N = **pompom**
pompous ['pɔmpəs] (*pej*) ADJ pomposo
pond [pɔnd] N (*natural*) lago pequeno; (*artificial*) tanque *m*
ponder ['pɔndəʳ] VT, VI ponderar, meditar (sobre)
ponderous ['pɔndərəs] ADJ pesado
pong [pɔŋ] (*BRIT inf*) N fedor *m*, fartum *m* (*inf*), catinga (*inf*) ► VI feder
pontiff ['pɔntıf] N pontífice *m*
pontificate [pɔn'tıfıkeıt] VI (*fig*): **to ~ (about)** pontificar (sobre)
pontoon [pɔn'tu:n] N pontão *m*; (*BRIT: card game*) vinte-e-um *m*
pony ['pəunı] N pônei *m*
ponytail ['pəunıteıl] N rabo-de-cavalo
pony trekking [-'trɛkıŋ] (*BRIT*) N excursão *f* em pônei
poodle ['pu:dl] N cão-d'água *m*
pooh-pooh [pu:'pu:] VT desprezar
pool [pu:l] N (*puddle*) poça, charco; (*pond*) lago; (*also:* **swimming pool**) piscina; (*fig: of light*) feixe *m*; (*: of liquid*) poça; (*Sport*) sinuca; (*sth shared*) fundo comum; (*money at cards*) bolo; (*Comm: consortium*) consórcio, pool *m*; (*US: monopoly trust*) truste *m* ► VT juntar; **pools** NPL (*football pools*) loteria esportiva (BR), totobola (PT); **typing** (*BRIT*) *or* **secretary** (*US*) ~ seção *f* de datilografia
poor [puəʳ] ADJ pobre; (*bad*) inferior, mau ► NPL: **the ~** os pobres; **~ in** (*resources etc*) deficiente em
poorly ['puəlı] ADJ adoentado, indisposto ► ADV mal
pop [pɔp] N (*sound*) estalo, estouro; (*Mus*) pop *m*; (*US inf: father*) papai *m*; (*inf: fizzy drink*) bebida gasosa ► VT: **to ~ sth into/onto** *etc* (*put*) pôr algo em/sobre *etc* ► VI estourar; (*cork*) saltar; **she ~ped her head out of the window** ela meteu a cabeça fora da janela
► **pop in** VI dar um pulo
► **pop out** VI dar uma saída
► **pop up** VI surgir, aparecer inesperadamente
pop concert N concerto pop
popcorn ['pɔpkɔ:n] N pipoca
pope [pəup] N papa *m*
poplar ['pɔpləʳ] N álamo, choupo

poplin ['pɔplɪn] N popeline f
popper ['pɔpər] (BRIT) N presilha
poppy ['pɔpɪ] N papoula
poppycock ['pɔpɪkɔk] (inf) N conversa fiada, papo furado
popsicle® ['pɔpsɪkl] (US) N picolé m
pop star N pop star m/f
populace ['pɔpjuləs] N povo
popular ['pɔpjulər] ADJ popular; (person) querido; (fashionable) badalado; **to be ~ (with)** (person) fazer sucesso (com); (decision) ser aplaudido (por)
popularity [pɔpju'lærɪtɪ] N popularidade f
popularize ['pɔpjuləraɪz] VT popularizar; (science) vulgarizar
populate ['pɔpjuleɪt] VT povoar
population [pɔpju'leɪʃən] N população f
population explosion N explosão f demográfica
populous ['pɔpjuləs] ADJ populoso
pop-up ['pɔpʌp] ADJ (Comput) (de) pop-up ▶ N pop-up m
porcelain ['pɔːslɪn] N porcelana
porch [pɔːtʃ] N pórtico; (US: verandah) varanda
porcupine ['pɔːkjupaɪn] N porco-espinho
pore [pɔːr] N poro ▶ VI: **to ~ over** examinar minuciosamente
pork [pɔːk] N carne f de porco
pork chop N costeleta de porco
pornographic [pɔːnə'græfɪk] ADJ pornográfico
pornography [pɔː'nɔgrəfɪ] N pornografia
porous ['pɔːrəs] ADJ poroso
porpoise ['pɔːpəs] N golfinho, boto
porridge ['pɔrɪdʒ] N mingau m (de aveia)
port [pɔːt] N (harbour) porto; (Naut: left side) bombordo; (wine) vinho do Porto; (Comput) porta ▶ CPD portuário; **to ~** (Naut) a bombordo; **~ of call** porto de escala
portable ['pɔːtəbl] ADJ portátil
portal ['pɔːtl] N portal m
portcullis [pɔːt'kʌlɪs] N grade f levadiça
portend [pɔː'tɛnd] VT pressagiar
portent ['pɔːtɛnt] N presságio, portento
porter ['pɔːtər] N (for luggage) carregador m; (doorkeeper) porteiro
portfolio [pɔːt'fəulɪəu] N (case) pasta; (Pol) pasta ministerial; (Finance) carteira de ações ou títulos; (of artist) pasta, portfolió
porthole ['pɔːthəul] N vigia
portico ['pɔːtɪkəu] N pórtico
portion ['pɔːʃən] N porção f, quinhão m; (of food) ração f
portly ['pɔːtlɪ] ADJ corpulento
portrait ['pɔːtreɪt] N retrato
portray [pɔː'treɪ] VT retratar; (act) interpretar
portrayal [pɔː'treɪəl] N retrato; (actor's) interpretação f; (in book, film) representação f
Portugal ['pɔːtjugl] N Portugal m (no article)
Portuguese [pɔːtju'giːz] ADJ português(-esa) ▶ N INV português(-esa) m/f; (Ling) português m
Portuguese man-of-war (irreg: like **man**) N (jellyfish) urtiga-do-mar f, caravela

pose [pəuz] N postura, pose f; (pej) pose, afetação f ▶ VI posar; (pretend): **to ~ as** fazer-se passar por ▶ VT (question) fazer; (problem) causar; **to strike a ~** fazer pose; **to ~ for** (painting) posar para
poser ['pəuzər] N problema m, abacaxi m (BR inf); (person) = **poseur**
poseur [pəu'zəːr] (pej) N posudo(-a), pessoa afetada
posh [pɔʃ] (inf) ADJ fino, chique; (upper-class) de classe alta; **to talk ~** falar com sotaque fino
position [pə'zɪʃən] N posição f; (situation) situação f ▶ VT colocar, situar; **to be in a ~ to do sth** estar em posição de fazer algo
positive ['pɔzɪtɪv] ADJ positivo; (certain) certo; (definite) definitivo; **I'm ~** tenho certeza absoluta
posse ['pɔsɪ] (US) N pelotão m de civis armados
possess [pə'zɛs] VT possuir; **like one ~ed** como um possuído do demônio; **whatever can have ~ed you?** o que é que te deu?
possession [pə'zɛʃən] N posse f, possessão f; (object) bem m, posse; **possessions** NPL (belongings) pertences mpl; **to take ~ of sth** tomar posse de algo
possessive [pə'zɛsɪv] ADJ possessivo
possessively [pə'zɛsɪvlɪ] ADV possessivamente
possessor [pə'zɛsər] N possuidor(a) m/f
possibility [pɔsɪ'bɪlɪtɪ] N possibilidade f; (of sth happening) probabilidade f
possible ['pɔsɪbl] ADJ possível; **it is ~ to do it** é possível fazê-lo; **as far as ~** tanto quanto possível, na medida do possível; **if ~** se for possível; **as big as ~** o maior possível
possibly ['pɔsɪblɪ] ADV (perhaps) pode ser, talvez; (surprise): **what could they ~ want with me?** o que eles podem querer comigo?; (emphasizing effort): **they did everything they ~ could** eles fizeram tudo o que podiam; **if you ~ can** se lhe for possível; **could you ~ come over?** será qué você podia vir para ca?; **I cannot ~ go** não posso ir de jeito nenhum
post [pəust] N (BRIT: mail) correio; (job) cargo, posto; (pole) poste m; (on internet) post m; (Mil) nomeação f; (trading post) entreposto comercial ▶ VT (BRIT: send by post) pôr no correio; (Mil) nomear; (bills) afixar, pregar; (on internet) postar; (BRIT: appoint): **to ~ to** destinar a; **by ~** (BRIT) pelo correio; **by return of ~** (BRIT) na volta do correio; **to keep sb ~ed** manter alguém informado
post- [pəust] PREFIX pós...; **~1990** depois de 1990
postage ['pəustɪdʒ] N porte m, franquia; **~ paid** porte pago; **~ prepaid** (US) franquia de porte
postage stamp N selo postal
postal ['pəustəl] ADJ postal
postal order N vale m postal
postbag ['pəustbæg] (BRIT) N mala de correio; (postman's) sacola

P

postbox ['pəustbɔks] (BRIT) N caixa de correio
postcard ['pəustka:d] N cartão m postal
postcode ['pəustkəud] (BRIT) N código postal, ≈ CEP m (BR)
postdate [pəust'deit] VT (cheque) pós-datar
poster ['pəustər] N cartaz m; (as decoration) pôster m
poste restante [pəust'rɛstã:nt] (BRIT) N posta-restante f
posterior [pɔs'tiəriər] (inf) N traseiro, nádegas fpl
posterity [pɔs'tɛriti] N posteridade f
poster paint N guache m
post exchange (US) N (Mil) loja do exército
post-free (BRIT) ADJ franco de porte
postgraduate [pəust'grædjuət] N pós-graduado(-a)
posthumous ['pɔstjuməs] ADJ póstumo
posthumously ['pɔstjuməsli] ADV postumamente
posting ['pəustiŋ] (BRIT) N nomeação f
postman ['pəustmən] (irreg: like **man**) N carteiro
postmark ['pəustma:k] N carimbo do correio
postmaster ['pəustma:stər] N agente m (BR) or chefe m (PT) do correio
Postmaster General N ≈ Superintendente m Geral dos Correios
postmen ['pəustmɛn] NPL of **postman**
postmistress ['pəustmistris] N agente f (BR) or chefe f (PT) do correio
postmortem [pəust'mɔ:təm] N autópsia
postnatal [pəust'neitl] ADJ pós-natal
post office N (building) agência do correio, correio; (organization) ≈ Empresa Nacional dos Correios e Telégrafos (BR), ≈ Correios, Telégrafos e Telefones (PT)
post office box N caixa postal
post-paid (BRIT) ADJ porte pago
postpone [pəs'pəun] VT adiar
postponement [pəs'pəunmənt] N adiamento
postscript ['pəustskript] N pós-escrito
postulate ['pɔstjuleit] VT postular
posture ['pɔstʃər] N postura; (fig) atitude f ▸ VI posar
postwar [pəust'wɔ:r] ADJ de após-guerra
posy ['pəuzi] N ramalhete m
pot [pɔt] N (for cooking) panela; (for flowers) vaso; (container) pote m; (teapot) bule m; (inf: marijuana) maconha ▸ VT (plant) plantar em vaso; (conserve) pôr em conserva; **to go to ~** (inf: country, economy) arruinar-se, degringolar; **the town has gone to ~** a cidade mixou; **~s of ...** (BRIT inf) ... aos potes
potash ['pɔtæʃ] N potassa
potassium [pə'tæsiəm] N potássio
potato [pə'teitəu] (pl **potatoes**) N batata
potato crisps, (US) **potato chips** NPL batatinhas fpl fritas
potato flour N fécula (de batata)
potato peeler N descascador m de batatas
potbellied ['pɔtbɛlid] ADJ barrigudo

potency ['pəutənsi] N potência; (of drink) teor m alcoólico
potent ['pəutnt] ADJ (weapon, argument) poderoso; (drink) forte; (man) potente
potentate ['pəutnteit] N potentado
potential [pə'tɛnʃl] ADJ potencial ▸ N potencial m; **to have ~** ser promissor
potentially [pə'tɛnʃəli] ADV potencialmente
pothole ['pɔthəul] N (in road) buraco; (BRIT: underground) caldeirão m, cova
potholer ['pɔthəulər] (BRIT) N espeleologista m/f
potholing ['pɔthəuliŋ] (BRIT) N: **to go ~** dedicar-se à espeleologia
potion ['pəuʃən] N poção f
potluck [pɔt'lʌk] N: **to take ~** contentar-se com o que houver
potpourri [pəu'puri:] N potpourri m (de pétalas e folhas secas para perfumar o ambiente)
pot roast N carne f assada
potshot ['pɔtʃɔt] N: **to take a ~ at sth** atirar em algo a esmo
potted ['pɔtid] ADJ (food) em conserva; (plant) de vaso; (fig: shortened) resumido
potter ['pɔtər] N (artistic) ceramista m/f; (artisan) oleiro(-a) ▸ VI (BRIT): **to ~ around, ~ about** ocupar-se com pequenos trabalhos; **~'s wheel** roda or torno de oleiro
pottery ['pɔtəri] N cerâmica; (factory) olaria; **a piece of ~** uma cerâmica
potty ['pɔti] ADJ (inf: mad) maluco, doido ▸ N penico
potty-training N treino (da criança) para o uso do urinol
pouch [pautʃ] N (Zool) bolsa; (for tobacco) tabaqueira
pouf, pouffe [pu:f] N pufe m
poultice ['pəultis] N cataplasma
poultry ['pəultri] N aves fpl domésticas; (meat) carne f de aves domésticas
poultry farm N granja avícola
poultry farmer N avicultor(a) m/f
pounce [pauns] VI: **to ~ on** lançar-se sobre; (person) agarrar em; (fig: mistake etc) apontar ▸ N salto, arremetida
pound [paund] N libra (weight = 453g, 16 ounces; money = 100 pence); (for dogs) canil m; (for cars) depósito ▸ VT (beat) socar, esmurrar; (crush) triturar ▸ VI (heart) bater; **half a ~ (of)** meia libra (de); **a five-~ note** uma nota de cinco libras
pounding ['paundiŋ] N: **to take a ~** (fig) levar uma surra
pound sterling N libra esterlina
pour [pɔ:r] VT despejar; (drink) servir ▸ VI correr, jorrar; (rain) chover a cântaros; **to ~ sb a drink** servir uma bebida a alguém
  ▸ **pour away** VT esvaziar, decantar
  ▸ **pour in** VI (people) entrar numa enxurrada; (information) chegar numa enxurrada
  ▸ **pour off** VT esvaziar, decantar
  ▸ **pour out** VI (people) sair aos borbotões ▸ VT (drink) servir; (water etc) esvaziar; (fig) extravasar

pouring ['pɔ:rɪŋ] ADJ: ~ **rain** chuva
torrencial

pout [paut] VI fazer beicinho or biquinho

poverty ['pɔvətɪ] N pobreza, miséria

poverty-stricken ADJ muito pobre, carente

poverty trap (BRIT) N armadilha da pobreza

POW N ABBR = **prisoner of war**

powder ['paudəʳ] N pó m; (face powder)
pó-de-arroz m; (gunpowder) pólvora ▶ VT
pulverizar; (face) empoar, passar pó em; **to ~
one's nose** empoar-se; (euphemism) ir ao
banheiro

powder compact N estojo (de pó-de-arroz)

powdered milk ['paudəd-] N leite m em pó

powder puff N esponja de pó-de-arroz

powder room N toucador m, banheiro de
senhoras

powdery ['paudərɪ] ADJ poeirento

power ['pauəʳ] N poder m; (of explosion, engine)
força, potência; (nation) potência; (ability, Pol:
of party, leader) poder; (of speech, thought)
faculdade f; (Math, Tech) potência; (electricity)
força ▶ VT (Elec) alimentar; (engine, machine)
acionar; (car, plane) propulsionar; **to do all
in one's ~ to help sb** fazer tudo que tiver ao
seu alcance para ajudar alguém; **the world
~s** as grandes potências; **to be in ~** estar no
poder; ~ **of attorney** procuração f

powerboat ['pauəbəut] (BRIT) N barco a
motor

power cut (BRIT) N corte m de energia,
blecaute m (BR)

power-driven ADJ movido a motor; (Elec)
elétrico

powered ['pauəd] ADJ: ~ **by** movido a;
nuclear-~ submarine submarino nuclear

power failure N corte m de energia

powerful ['pauəful] ADJ poderoso; (engine)
potente; (body) vigoroso; (blow) violento;
(argument) convincente; (emotion) intenso

powerhouse ['pauəhaus] N (fig: person) poço de
energia; **a ~ of ideas** um poço de ideias

powerless ['pauəlɪs] ADJ impotente

power line N fio de alta tensão

power point (BRIT) N tomada

power station N central f elétrica

power steering N direção f hidráulica

powwow ['pauwau] N reunião f

pox [pɔks] (inf) N sífilis f; see also **chickenpox,
smallpox**

pp ABBR (= per procurationem) p.p.; = **pages**

PPE (BRIT) N ABBR (Sch) = **philosophy, politics
and economics**

PPS N ABBR (= post postscriptum) PPS; (BRIT:
= parliamentary private secretary) parlamentário no
serviço de um ministro

PQ (CANADA) ABBR = **Province of Quebec**

PR N ABBR = **proportional representation**;
public relations ▶ ABBR (US Post) = **Puerto
Rico**

Pr. ABBR (= prince) P.R.

practicability [præktɪkə'bɪlɪtɪ] N viabilidade f

practicable ['præktɪkəbl] ADJ (scheme) viável

practical ['præktɪkl] ADJ prático

practicality [præktɪ'kælɪtɪ] N (of plan)
viabilidade f; (of person) índole f prática;
practicalities NPL (of situation) aspectos mpl
práticos

practical joke N brincadeira, peça

practically ['præktɪkəlɪ] ADV (almost)
praticamente

practice ['præktɪs] N (habit, Rel) costume m,
hábito; (exercise) prática; (of profession)
exercício; (training) treinamento; (Med)
consultório; (Law) escritório ▶ VT, VI (US)
= **practise**; **in ~** (in reality) na prática; **out of ~**
destreinado; **it's common ~** é comum; **to
put sth into ~** pôr algo em prática; **to set
up in ~** abrir consultório

practice match N jogo de treinamento

practise, (US) **practice** ['præktɪs] VT praticar;
(profession) exercer; (sport) treinar ▶ VI (doctor)
ter consultório; (lawyer) ter escritório; (train)
treinar, praticar

practised ['præktɪst] (BRIT) ADJ (person)
experiente, experimentado; (performance)
competente; (liar) contumaz; **with a ~ eye**
com olhar de entendedor

practising ['præktɪsɪŋ] ADJ (Christian etc)
praticante; (lawyer) que exerce; (homosexual)
assumido

practitioner [præk'tɪʃənəʳ] N praticante m/f;
(Med) médico(-a)

pragmatic [præg'mætɪk] ADJ pragmático

Prague [prɑ:g] N Praga

prairie ['prɛərɪ] N campina, pradaria

praise [preɪz] N (approval) louvor m; (admiration)
elogio ▶ VT elogiar, louvar

praiseworthy ['preɪzwə:ðɪ] ADJ louvável,
digno de elogio

pram [præm] (BRIT) N carrinho de bebê

prance [prɑ:ns] VI: **to ~ about/up and down**
etc (horse) curvetear, fazer cabriolas; (person)
andar espalhafatosamente

prank [præŋk] N travessura, peça

prattle ['prætl] VI tagarelar; (child) balbuciar

prawn [prɔ:n] N pitu m; (small) camarão m

pray [preɪ] VI: **to ~ for/that** rezar por/para
que

prayer [prɛəʳ] N (activity) reza; (words) oração f,
prece f; (entreaty) súplica, rogo

prayer book N missal m, livro de orações

pre- ['pri:] PREFIX pré-; **~1970** antes de 1970

preach [pri:tʃ] VT, VI pregar ▶ VI pregar; (pej:
moralize) catequizar; **to ~ at sb** fazer sermões
a alguém

preacher ['pri:tʃəʳ] N pregador(a) m/f; (US:
clergyman) pastor m

preamble [prɪ'æmbl] N preâmbulo

prearranged [pri:ə'reɪndʒd] ADJ combinado
de antemão

precarious [prɪ'kɛərɪəs] ADJ precário

precaution [prɪ'kɔ:ʃən] N precaução f

precautionary [prɪ'kɔ:ʃənrɪ] ADJ (measure) de
precaução

precede [prɪ'si:d] VT, VI preceder

precedence ['prɛsɪdəns] N precedência; (*priority*) prioridade *f*

precedent ['prɛsɪdənt] N precedente *m*; **to establish** *or* **set a ~** estabelecer *or* abrir precedente

preceding [prɪ'siːdɪŋ] ADJ anterior

precept ['priːsɛpt] N preceito

precinct ['priːsɪŋkt] N (*round church*) recinto; (*US: district*) distrito policial; **precincts** NPL (*of large building*) arredores *mpl*; **pedestrian ~** (*BRIT*) zona para pedestres (*BR*) *or* peões (*PT*); **shopping ~** (*BRIT*) zona comercial

precious ['prɛʃəs] ADJ precioso; (*stylized*) afetado ▶ ADV (*inf*): **~ little** muito pouco, pouquíssimo; **your ~ dog** (*ironic*) seu adorado cãozinho

precipice ['prɛsɪpɪs] N precipício

precipitate [*adj* prɪ'sɪpɪtɪt, *vt* prɪ'sɪpɪteɪt] ADJ (*hasty*) precipitado, apressado ▶ VT (*hasten*) precipitar, acelerar; (*bring about*) causar

precipitation [prɪsɪpɪ'teɪʃən] N precipitação *f*

precipitous [prɪ'sɪpɪtəs] ADJ (*steep*) íngreme, escarpado

précis ['preɪsiː] N INV resumo, sumário

precise [prɪ'saɪs] ADJ exato, preciso; (*plans*) detalhado; (*person*) escrupuloso, meticuloso

precisely [prɪ'saɪslɪ] ADV precisamente; (*exactly*) exatamente

precision [prɪ'sɪʒən] N precisão *f*

preclude [prɪ'kluːd] VT excluir; **to ~ sb from doing** impedir que alguém faça

precocious [prɪ'kəʊʃəs] ADJ precoce

preconceived [priːkən'siːvd] ADJ (*idea*) preconcebido

preconception [priːkən'sɛpʃən] N preconceito

precondition [priːkən'dɪʃən] N condição *f* prévia

precursor [priː'kəːsə^r] N precursor(a) *m/f*

predate ['priː'deɪt] VT (*precede*) preceder

predator ['prɛdətə^r] N predador *m*

predatory ['prɛdətərɪ] ADJ predatório, rapace

predecessor ['priːdɪsɛsə^r] N predecessor(a) *m/f*, antepassado(-a)

predestination [priːdɛstɪ'neɪʃən] N predestinação *f*, destino

predetermine [priːdɪ'təːmɪn] VT predeterminar, predispor

predicament [prɪ'dɪkəmənt] N situação *f* difícil, apuro

predicate ['prɛdɪkɪt] N (*Ling*) predicado

predict [prɪ'dɪkt] VT prever, predizer, prognosticar

predictable [prɪ'dɪktəbl] ADJ previsível

predictably [prɪ'dɪktəblɪ] ADV (*behave, react*) de maneira previsível; **~ she didn't come** como era de se esperar, ela não veio

prediction [prɪ'dɪkʃən] N previsão *f*, prognóstico

predispose [priːdɪs'pəʊz] VT predispor

predominance [prɪ'dɔmɪnəns] N predominância, preponderância

predominant [prɪ'dɔmɪnənt] ADJ predominante, preponderante

predominantly [prɪ'dɔmɪnəntlɪ] ADV predominantemente; (*for the most part*) na maioria; (*above all*) sobretudo

predominate [prɪ'dɔmɪneɪt] VI predominar

pre-eminent ADJ preeminente

pre-empt [-ɛmt] (*BRIT*) VT (*obtain*) adquirir por preempção *or* de antemão; (*fig*): **to ~ sb/sth** antecipar-se a alguém/antecipar algo

pre-emptive [-ɛmtɪv] ADJ: **~ strike** ataque *m* preventivo

preen [priːn] VT: **to ~ itself** (*bird*) limpar e alisar as penas (com o bico); **to ~ o.s.** enfeitar-se, envaidecer-se

prefab ['priːfæb] N casa pré-fabricada

prefabricated [priː'fæbrɪkeɪtɪd] ADJ pré-fabricado

preface ['prɛfəs] N prefácio

prefect ['priːfɛkt] N (*BRIT Sch*) monitor(a) *m/f*, tutor(a) *m/f*; (*in Brazil*) prefeito(-a)

prefer [prɪ'fəː^r] VT preferir; (*Law*): **to ~ charges** intentar uma ação judicial; **to ~ coffee to tea** preferir café a chá

preferable ['prɛfrəbl] ADJ preferível

preferably ['prɛfrəblɪ] ADV de preferência

preference ['prɛfrəns] N preferência; **in ~ to sth** de preferência a algo

preference shares (*BRIT*) NPL ações *fpl* preferenciais

preferential [prɛfə'rɛnʃəl] ADJ preferencial; **~ treatment** preferência

preferred stock [prɪ'fəːd-] (*US*) NPL ações *fpl* preferenciais

prefix ['priːfɪks] N prefixo

pregnancy ['prɛgnənsɪ] N gravidez *f*; (*animal*) prenhez *f*

pregnant ['prɛgnənt] ADJ grávida; (*animal*) prenha; **3 months ~** grávida de 3 meses; **~ with** rico de, cheio de

prehistoric [priːhɪs'tɔrɪk] ADJ pré-histórico

prehistory [priː'hɪstərɪ] N pré-história

prejudge [priː'dʒʌdʒ] VT fazer um juízo antecipado de, prejulgar

prejudice ['prɛdʒudɪs] N (*bias*) preconceito; (*harm*) prejuízo ▶ VT (*predispose*) predispor; (*harm*) prejudicar; **to ~ sb in favour of/ against** predispor alguém a favor de/ contra

prejudiced ['prɛdʒudɪst] ADJ (*person*) preconceituoso; (*view*) parcial, preconcebido; **to be ~ against sb/sth** estar com prevenção contra alguém/algo

prelate ['prɛlət] N prelado

preliminaries [prɪ'lɪmɪnərɪz] NPL preliminares *fpl*

preliminary [prɪ'lɪmɪnərɪ] ADJ preliminar, prévio

prelude ['prɛljuːd] N prelúdio

premarital [priː'mærɪtl] ADJ pré-nupcial

premature ['prɛmətʃʊə^r] ADJ prematuro; **to be ~ (in doing sth)** precipitar-se (em fazer algo)

premeditated [priː'mɛdɪteɪtɪd] ADJ premeditado

premeditation [pri:ˈmɛdɪˈteɪʃən] N premeditação f

premenstrual [pri:ˈmɛnstruəl] ADJ pré-menstrual

premenstrual tension N tensão f pré-menstrual

premier [ˈprɛmɪəʳ] ADJ primeiro, principal ▶ N (*Pol*) primeiro-ministro/primeira-ministra

première [ˈprɛmɪɛəʳ] N estreia

premise [ˈprɛmɪs] N premissa; **premises** NPL (*of business, institution*) local m; (*house*) casa; (*shop*) loja; **on the ~s** no local; **business ~s** local utilizado para fins comerciais

premium [ˈpri:mɪəm] N prêmio; **to be at a ~** ser caro; **to sell at a ~** (*shares*) vender acima do par

premium bond (BRIT) N *obrigação qué dá direito a prêmio mediante sorteio*

premium deal N (*Comm*) oferta especial

premium gasoline (US) N gasolina azul *or* super

premonition [prɛməˈnɪʃən] N presságio, pressentimento

preoccupation [pri:ɔkjuˈpeɪʃən] N preocupação f

preoccupied [pri:ˈɔkjupaɪd] ADJ (*worried*) preocupado, apreensivo; (*absorbed*) absorto

prep [prɛp] ADJ ABBR: **~ school = preparatory school** ▶ N (*Sch*: = *study*) deveres mpl

prepackaged [pri:ˈpækɪdʒd] ADJ embalado para venda ao consumidor

prepaid [pri:ˈpeɪd] ADJ com porte pago

preparation [prɛpəˈreɪʃən] N preparação f; **preparations** NPL (*arrangements*) preparativos mpl; **in ~ for** em preparação para

preparatory [prɪˈpærətərɪ] ADJ preparatório; **~ to** antes de

preparatory school N *escola particular para crianças até 11 ou 13 anod de idade*

prepare [prɪˈpɛəʳ] VT preparar ▶ VI: **to ~ for** preparar-se *or* aprontar-se para; (*make preparations*) fazer preparativos para; **~d to** disposto a; **~d for** pronto para

preponderance [prɪˈpɔndərns] N predomínio

preposition [prɛpəˈzɪʃən] N preposição f

prepossessing [pri:pəˈzɛsɪŋ] ADJ atraente

preposterous [prɪˈpɔstərəs] ADJ absurdo, disparatado

prep school N = **preparatory school**

prerecorded [ˈpri:rɪˈkɔ:dɪd] ADJ pré-gravado

prerequisite [pri:ˈrɛkwɪzɪt] N pré-requisito, condição f prévia

prerogative [prɪˈrɔgətɪv] N prerrogativa

presbyterian [prɛzbɪˈtɪərɪən] ADJ, N presbiteriano(-a)

presbytery [ˈprɛzbɪtərɪ] N presbitério

preschool [ˈpri:ˈsku:l] ADJ (*education, age*) pré-escolar; (*child*) de idade pré-escolar

prescribe [prɪˈskraɪb] VT prescrever; (*Med*) receitar; **~d books** (BRIT *Sch*) livros mpl requisitados

prescription [prɪˈskrɪpʃən] N prescrição f, ordem f; (*Med*) receita; **to make up** (BRIT) *or*

fill (US) **a ~** aviar uma receita; **"only available on ~"** "venda exclusivamente mediante receita médica"

prescription charges (BRIT) NPL participação f no preço das receitas médicas

prescriptive [prɪˈskrɪptɪv] ADJ prescritivo

presence [ˈprɛzns] N presença; (*spirit*) espectro

presence of mind N presença de espírito

present [*adj, n* ˈprɛznt, *vt* prɪˈzɛnt] ADJ (*in attendance*) presente; (*current*) atual ▶ N (*gift*) presente m; (*actuality*): **the ~** o presente ▶ VT (*give*): **to ~ sth to sb, to ~ sb with sth** (*as gift*) presentear alguém com algo; (*as prize*) entregar algo a alguém; (*expound*) expor; (*information, programme, person, difficulty, threat*) apresentar; (*describe*) descrever; (*Theatre*) representar; **at ~** no momento, agora; **for the ~** por enquanto; **to be ~ at** estar presente a, presenciar; **to give sb a ~** presentear alguém

presentable [prɪˈzɛntəbl] ADJ apresentável

presentation [prɛznˈteɪʃən] N apresentação f; (*gift*) presente m; (*ceremony*) entrega; (*of plan etc*) exposição f; (*Theatre*) representação f; **on ~ of** mediante apresentação de

present-day ADJ atual, de hoje

presenter [prɪˈzɛntəʳ] N (*Radio, TV*) apresentador(a) m/f

presently [ˈprɛzntlɪ] ADV (*soon after*) logo depois; (*soon*) logo, em breve; (*now*) atualmente

preservation [prɛzəˈveɪʃən] N conservação f, preservação f

preservative [prɪˈzə:vətɪv] N conservante m

preserve [prɪˈzə:v] VT (*situation*) conservar, manter; (*building, manuscript*) preservar; (*food*) pôr em conserva; (*in salt*) conservar em sal, salgar ▶ N (*for game*) reserva de caça; (*often pl: jam*) geleia; (: *fruit*) compota, conserva

preshrunk [ˈpri:ˈʃrʌŋk] ADJ pré-encolhido

preside [prɪˈzaɪd] VI: **to ~ (over)** presidir

presidency [ˈprɛzɪdənsɪ] N presidência

president [ˈprɛzɪdənt] N presidente(-a) m/f

presidential [prɛzɪˈdɛnʃl] ADJ presidencial

press [prɛs] N (*tool, machine*) prensa; (*printer's*) imprensa, prelo; (*newspapers*) imprensa; (*of switch*) pressão f; (*crowd*) turba, apinhamento; (*of hand*) apertão m ▶ VT apertar; (*squeeze: fruit etc*) espremer; (*clothes: iron*) passar; (*put pressure on: person*) pressionar; (*Tech*) prensar; (*harry*) assediar; (*insist*): **to ~ sth on sb** insistir para que alguém aceite algo; (*urge*): **to ~ sb to do** *or* **into doing sth** impelir *or* pressionar alguém a fazer algo ▶ VI (*squeeze*) apertar; (*pressurize*): **to ~ for** pressionar por; **we are ~ed for time/money** estamos com pouco tempo/dinheiro; **to ~ for sth** pressionar por algo; **to ~ sb for an answer** pressionar alguém por uma resposta; **to ~ charges against sb** (*Law*) intentar ação judicial contra alguém; **to go to ~** (*newspaper*) ir para o prelo; **to be in the ~**

P

estar no prelo; **to appear in the ~** sair no jornal
▶ **press on** VI continuar
press agency N agência de informações
press clipping N recorte m de jornal
press conference N entrevista coletiva (para a imprensa)
press cutting N recorte m de jornal
press-gang N *pelotão de recrutamento da marinha*
▶ VT: **to be ~ed into doing** ser impelido a fazer
pressing ['prɛsɪŋ] ADJ urgente ▶ N ação f (*or* serviço m) de passar roupa *etc*
pressman ['prɛsmæn] (*irreg: like* **man**) N jornalista m
press release N release m *or* comunicado à imprensa
press stud (*BRIT*) N botão m de pressão
press-up (*BRIT*) N flexão f
pressure ['prɛʃəʳ] N pressão f ▶ VT = **to put pressure on**; **to put ~ on sb (to do sth)** pressionar alguém (a fazer algo)
pressure cooker N panela de pressão
pressure gauge N manômetro
pressure group N grupo de pressão
pressurize ['prɛʃəraɪz] VT pressurizar; (*BRIT fig*): **to ~ sb (into doing sth)** pressionar alguém (a fazer algo)
pressurized ['prɛʃəraɪzd] ADJ pressurizado
prestige [prɛs'tiːʒ] N prestígio
prestigious [prɛs'tɪdʒəs] ADJ prestigioso
presumably [prɪ'zjuːməblɪ] ADV presumivelmente, provavelmente; **~ he did it** é de se presumir que ele o fez
presume [prɪ'zjuːm] VT supor; **to ~ to do** (*dare*) ousar fazer, atrever-se a fazer; (*set out to*) pretender fazer
presumption [prɪ'zʌmpʃən] N suposição f; (*pretension*) presunção f; (*boldness*) atrevimento, audácia
presumptuous [prɪ'zʌmpʃəs] ADJ presunçoso
presuppose [priːsə'pəuz] VT pressupor
pre-tax ADJ antes de impostos
pretence, (*US*) **pretense** [prɪ'tɛns] N (*claim*) pretensão f; (*display*) ostentação f; (*pretext*) pretexto; (*make-believe*) fingimento; **under false ~s** por meios fraudulentos; **on the ~ of** sob o máscara de; **to make a ~ of doing** fingir fazer
pretend [prɪ'tɛnd] VT fingir ▶ VI (*feign*) fingir; (*claim*): **to ~ to sth** aspirar a *or* pretender a algo; **to ~ to do** fingir fazer
pretense [prɪ'tɛns] (*US*) N = **pretence**
pretension [prɪ'tɛnʃən] N (*presumption*) presunção f; (*claim*) pretensão f; **to have no ~s to sth/to being sth** não ter pretensão a algo/a ser algo
pretentious [prɪ'tɛnʃəs] ADJ pretensioso, presunçoso
preterite ['prɛtərɪt] N pretérito
pretext ['priːtɛkst] N pretexto; **on** *or* **under the ~ of doing sth** sob o *or* a pretexto de fazer algo

pretty ['prɪtɪ] ADJ bonito ▶ ADV (*quite*) bastante
prevail [prɪ'veɪl] VI (*gain acceptance*) triunfar; (*be current*) imperar; (*be usual*) prevalecer, vigorar; (*persuade*): **to ~ (up)on sb to do sth** persuadir alguém a fazer algo
prevailing [prɪ'veɪlɪŋ] ADJ (*wind*) dominante; (*fashion, attitude*) predominante; (*usual*) corrente
prevalent ['prɛvələnt] ADJ (*common*) predominante; (*usual*) corrente; (*fashionable*) da moda
prevarication [prɪværɪ'keɪʃən] N embromação f
prevent [prɪ'vɛnt] VT impedir; **to ~ sb from doing sth** impedir alguém de fazer algo; **to ~ sth from happening** impedir que algo aconteça
preventable [prɪ'vɛntəbl] ADJ evitável
preventative [prɪ'vɛntətɪv] ADJ = **preventive**
prevention [prɪ'vɛnʃən] N prevenção f
preventive [prɪ'vɛntɪv] ADJ preventivo
preview ['priːvjuː] N (*of film etc*) pré-estreia; (*fig*) antecipação f
previous ['priːvɪəs] ADJ (*experience, notice*) prévio; (*earlier*) anterior; **I have a ~ engagement** já tenho compromisso; **~ to doing** antes de fazer
previously ['priːvɪəslɪ] ADV (*before*) previamente; (*in the past*) anteriormente
prewar [priː'wɔːʳ] ADJ anterior à guerra
prey [preɪ] N presa ▶ VI: **to ~ on** viver às custas de; (*feed on*) alimentar-se de; (*plunder*) saquear, pilhar; **it was ~ing on his mind** preocupava-o, atormentava-o
price [praɪs] N preço; (*of shares*) cotação f ▶ VT fixar o preço de; **what is the ~ of ...?** qual é o preço de ...?, quanto é ...?; **to go up** *or* **rise in ~** subir de preço; **to put a ~ on sth** determinar o preço de algo; **to be ~d out of the market** (*article*) não ser competitivo; (*producer, country*) perder freguesia por causa de preços muito altos; **what ~ his promises now?** que valem suas promessas agora?; **he regained his freedom, but at a ~** ele recobrou a liberdade, mas pagou caro; **at any ~** por qualquer preço
price control N controle m de preços
price-cutting N corte m de preços
priceless ['praɪslɪs] ADJ inestimável; (*inf: amusing*) impagável
price list N lista *or* tabela de preços
price range N gama de preços; **it's within my ~** está dentro do meu preço
price tag N etiqueta de preço
price war N guerra de preços
pricey ['praɪsɪ] (*inf*) ADJ salgado
prick [prɪk] N picada; (*with pin*) alfinetada; (*!: penis*) pau m (!); (*!: person*) filho-da-puta m (!) ▶ VT picar; (*make hole in*) furar; **to ~ up one's ears** aguçar os ouvidos
prickle ['prɪkl] N (*sensation*) comichão f, ardência; (*Bot*) espinho
prickly ['prɪklɪ] ADJ espinhoso; (*fig: person*) irritadiço

prickly heat N brotoeja
prickly pear N opúncia
pride [praɪd] N orgulho; (pej) soberba ▶ VT: **to ~ o.s. on** orgulhar-se de; **to take (a) ~ in** orgulhar-se de, sentir orgulho em; **to have ~ of place** (BRIT) ocupar o lugar de destaque, ter destaque; **her ~ and joy** seu tesouro
priest [priːst] N (Christian) padre m; (non-Christian) sacerdote m
priestess ['priːstɪs] N sacerdotisa
priesthood ['priːsthud] N (practice) sacerdócio; (priests) clero
prig [prɪg] N esnobe m/f
prim [prɪm] (pej) ADJ (formal) empertigado; (affected) afetado; (easily shocked) pudico
prima facie ['praɪmə'feɪʃi] ADJ: **to have a ~ case** (Law) ter uma causa convincente
primarily ['praɪmərɪlɪ] ADV (above all) principalmente; (firstly) em primeiro lugar
primary ['praɪmərɪ] ADJ primário; (first in importance) principal ▶ N (US: election) eleição f primária
primary colour N cor f primária
primary products NPL produtos mpl básicos
primary school (BRIT) N escola primária

> As **primary schools** da Grã-Bretanha acolhem crianças de 5 a 11 anos. Assinalam o início do ciclo escolar obrigatório e normalmente são compostas de duas partes: a pré-escola (infant school) e o primário (junior school).

primate¹ ['praɪmɪt] N (Rel) primaz m
primate² ['praɪmeɪt] N (Zool) primata m
prime [praɪm] ADJ primeiro, principal; (basic) fundamental, primário; (excellent) de primeira ▶ VT (wood) imprimir; (gun, pump) escorvar; (fig) preparar ▶ N: **in the ~ of life** na primavera da vida; **~ example** exemplo típico
prime minister N primeiro-ministro/primeira-ministra
primer ['praɪmə'] N (book) livro de leitura; (paint) pintura de base; (of gun) escorva
prime time N (Radio, TV) horário nobre
primeval [praɪ'miːvl] ADJ primitivo
primitive ['prɪmɪtɪv] ADJ primitivo; (crude) rudimentar; (uncivilized) grosseiro, inculto
primrose ['prɪmrəʊz] N prímula, primavera
primus® ['praɪməs], (BRIT) **primus stove** N fogão m portátil movido à parafina
prince [prɪns] N príncipe m
princess [prɪn'sɛs] N princesa
principal ['prɪnsɪpl] ADJ principal ▶ N (of school, college) diretor(a) m/f; (in play) papel m principal; (money) principal m
principality [prɪnsɪ'pælɪtɪ] N principado
principally ['prɪnsɪplɪ] ADV principalmente
principle ['prɪnsɪpl] N princípio; **in ~** em princípio; **on ~** por princípio
print [prɪnt] N (impression) impressão f, marca; (letters) letra de forma; (fabric) estampado; (Art) estampa, gravura; (Phot) cópia; (footprint) pegada; (fingerprint) impressão f

digital ▶ VT imprimir; (write in capitals) escrever em letra de imprensa; **out of ~** esgotado
▶ **print out** VT (Comput) imprimir
printed circuit board ['prɪntɪd-] N placa de circuito impresso
printed matter ['prɪntɪd-] N impressos mpl
printer ['prɪntə'] N (person) impressor(a) m/f; (firm) gráfica; (machine) impressora
printhead ['prɪnthɛd] N cabeçote m de impressão
printing ['prɪntɪŋ] N (art) imprensa; (act) impressão f; (quantity) tiragem f
printing press N prelo, máquina impressora
printout ['prɪntaʊt] N (Comput) cópia impressa
print wheel N margarida
prior ['praɪə'] ADJ anterior, prévio; (more important) prioritário ▶ N (Rel) prior m; **~ to doing** antes de fazer; **without ~ notice** sem aviso prévio; **to have a ~ claim to sth** ter prioridade na reivindicação de algo
priority [praɪ'ɔrɪtɪ] N prioridade f; **to have ~ (over)** ter prioridade (sobre)
priory ['praɪərɪ] N priorado
prise [praɪz] VT: **to ~ open** arrombar
prism ['prɪzəm] N prisma m
prison ['prɪzn] N prisão f ▶ CPD carcerário
prison camp N campo de prisioneiros
prisoner ['prɪznə'] N (in prison) preso(-a), presidiário(-a); (under arrest) detido(-a); (in dock) acusado(-a), réu(-ré) m/f; **to take sb ~** aprisionar alguém, prender alguém
prisoner of war N prisioneiro de guerra
prissy ['prɪsɪ] ADJ fresco, cheio de luxo
pristine ['prɪstiːn] ADJ imaculado
privacy ['prɪvəsɪ] N (seclusion) isolamento, solidão f; (intimacy) intimidade f, privacidade f
private ['praɪvɪt] ADJ privado; (personal) particular; (confidential) confidencial, reservado; (lesson, car) particular; (personal: belongings) pessoal; (: thoughts, plans) secreto, íntimo; (place) isolado; (quiet: person) reservado; (intimate) privado, íntimo; (sitting etc) a portas fechadas ▶ N soldado raso; **"~"** (on envelope) "confidencial"; (on door) "privativo"; **in ~** em particular; **in (his) ~ life** em (sua) vida particular; **he is a very ~ person** ele é uma pessoa muito reservada; **to be in ~ practice** ter clínica particular
private enterprise N iniciativa privada
private eye N detetive m/f particular
private hearing N (Law) audiência em segredo da justiça
private limited company (BRIT) N sociedade f anônima fechada
privately ['praɪvɪtlɪ] ADV em particular; (in oneself) no fundo
private parts NPL partes fpl (pudendas)
private property N propriedade f privada
private school N escola particular
privation [praɪ'veɪʃən] N privação f

P

privatize ['praɪvɪtaɪz] VT privatizar
privet ['prɪvɪt] N alfena
privilege ['prɪvɪlɪdʒ] N privilégio
privileged ['prɪvɪlɪdʒd] ADJ privilegiado
privy ['prɪvɪ] ADJ: **to be ~ to** estar inteirado de
Privy Council (BRIT) N Conselho Privado
prize [praɪz] N prêmio ▶ ADJ (bull, novel) premiado; (first class) de primeira classe; (example) perfeito ▶ VT valorizar
prize fight N luta de boxe profissional
prize-giving [-'gɪvɪŋ] N distribuição f dos prêmios
prize money N dinheiro do prêmio
prizewinner ['praɪzwɪnəʳ] N premiado(-a)
prizewinning ['praɪzwɪnɪŋ] ADJ premiado
PRO N ABBR (= public relations officer) RP m/f inv
pro [prəu] N (Sport) profissional m/f ▶ PREP a favor de; **the ~s and cons** os prós e os contras
pro- [prəu] PREFIX (in favour of) pró-
pro-active [prəu'æktɪv] ADJ proativo
probability [prɔbə'bɪlɪtɪ] N probabilidade f; **in all ~** com toda a probabilidade
probable ['prɔbəbl] ADJ provável; (plausible) verossímil; **it is ~/hardly ~ that ...** é provável/pouco provável que ...
probably ['prɔbəblɪ] ADV provavelmente
probate ['prəubɪt] N (Law) homologação f, legitimação f
probation [prə'beɪʃən] N (in employment) estágio probatório; (Law) liberdade f condicional; (Rel) noviciado; **on ~** (employee) em estágio probatório; (Law) em liberdade condicional
probationary [prə'beɪʃənrɪ] ADJ (period) probatório
probe [prəub] N (Med, Space) sonda; (enquiry) pesquisa ▶ VT investigar, esquadrinhar
probity ['prəubɪtɪ] N probidade f
problem ['prɔbləm] N problema m; **what's the ~?** qual é o problema?; **I had no ~ in finding her** não foi difícil encontrá-la; **no ~!** não tem problema!
problematic [prɔblə'mætɪk], **problematical** [prɔblə'mætɪkəl] ADJ problemático
procedure [prə'si:dʒəʳ] N (Admin, Law) procedimento; (method) método, processo; **cashing a cheque is a simple ~** descontar um cheque é uma operação simples
proceed [prə'si:d] VI (do afterwards): **to ~ to do sth** passar a fazer algo; (continue): **to ~ (with)** continuar or prosseguir (com); (activity, event: carry on) continuar; (act) proceder; **I am not sure how to ~** não sei como proceder; **to ~ against sb** (Law) processar alguém, instaurar processo contra alguém
proceedings [prə'si:dɪŋz] NPL (organized events) evento, acontecimento; (Law) processo
proceeds ['prəusi:dz] NPL produto, proventos mpl
process [n, vt 'prəuses, vi prə'ses] N processo ▶ VT processar ▶ VI (BRIT: formal: go in procession) desfilar; **in ~** em andamento; **we are in the**

~ of moving to Rio estamos de mudança para o Rio
processed cheese ['prəuses-] N ≈ requeijão m
processing ['prəusesɪŋ] N processamento
procession [prə'seʃən] N desfile m, procissão f; **funeral ~** cortejo fúnebre
proclaim [prə'kleɪm] VT proclamar; (announce) anunciar
proclamation [prɔklə'meɪʃən] N proclamação f; (written) promulgação f
proclivity [prə'klɪvɪtɪ] N inclinação f
procrastinate [prəu'kræstɪneɪt] VI protelar
procrastination [prəukræstɪ'neɪʃən] N protelação f
procreation [prəukrɪ'eɪʃən] N procriação f
procure [prə'kjuəʳ] VT obter
procurement [prə'kjuəmənt] N obtenção f; (purchase) compra
prod [prɔd] VT (push) empurrar; (with elbow) acotovelar; (with finger, stick) cutucar; (jab) espetar ▶ N empurrão m; cotovelada; espetada
prodigal ['prɔdɪgl] ADJ pródigo
prodigious [prə'dɪdʒəs] ADJ colossal, extraordinário
prodigy ['prɔdɪdʒɪ] N prodígio
produce [n 'prɔdju:s, vt prə'dju:s] N (Agr) produtos mpl agrícolas ▶ VT produzir; (profit) render; (cause) provocar; (evidence, argument) apresentar, mostrar; (show) apresentar, exibir; (Theatre) pôr em cena or em cartaz; (offspring) dar à luz
producer [prə'dju:səʳ] N (Theatre) diretor(a) m/f; (Agr, Cinema, of record) produtor(a) m/f; (country) produtor m
product ['prɔdʌkt] N produto
production [prə'dʌkʃən] N produção f; (of electricity) geração f; (thing) produto; (Theatre) encenação f; **to put into ~** (goods) passar a fabricar
production agreement (US) N acordo sobre produtividade
production control N controle m de produção
production line N linha de produção or de montagem
production manager N gerente m/f de produção
productive [prə'dʌktɪv] ADJ produtivo
productivity [prɔdʌk'tɪvɪtɪ] N produtividade f
productivity agreement (BRIT) N acordo sobre produtividade
productivity bonus N prêmio de produção
Prof. [prɔf] ABBR (= professor) Prof.
profane [prə'feɪn] ADJ profano; (language etc) irreverente, sacrílego
profess [prə'fes] VT professar; (feeling, opinion) manifestar; **I do not ~ to be an expert** não me tenho na conta de entendido
professed [prə'fest] ADJ (self-declared) assumido
profession [prə'feʃən] N profissão f; (people) classe f; **the professions** NPL as profissões liberais

professional [prə'fɛʃənl] N profissional m/f
▶ ADJ profissional; (work) de profissional;
he's a ~ man ele exerce uma profissão
liberal; **to take ~ advice** consultar um
profissional
professionalism [prə'fɛʃnəlɪzm] N
profissionalismo
professionally [prə'fɛʃnəlɪ] ADV
profissionalmente; (as a job) de profissão;
I only know him ~ eu só conheço ele pelo
trabalho
professor [prə'fɛsəʳ] N (BRIT) catedrático(-a);
(US, CANADA) professor(a) m/f
professorship [prə'fɛsəʃɪp] N cátedra
proffer ['prɔfəʳ] VT (hand) estender; (remark)
fazer; (apologies) apresentar
proficiency [prə'fɪʃənsɪ] N competência,
proficiência
proficient [prə'fɪʃənt] ADJ competente,
proficiente
profile ['prəufaɪl] N perfil m; **to keep a high ~**
destacar-se; **to keep a low ~** sair de
circulação
profit ['prɔfɪt] N (Comm) lucro; (fig) proveito,
vantagem f ▶ VI: **to ~ by** or **from** (financially)
lucrar com; (benefit) aproveitar-se de, tirar
proveito de; **~ and loss account** conta de
lucros e perdas; **to make a ~** lucrar; **to sell**
sth at a ~ vender algo com lucro
profitability [prɔfɪtə'bɪlɪtɪ] N rentabilidade f
profitable ['prɔfɪtəbl] ADJ (Econ) lucrativo,
rendoso; (useful) proveitoso
profit centre N centro de lucro
profiteering [prɔfɪ'tɪərɪŋ] N mercantilismo,
exploração f
profit-making ADJ com fins lucrativos
profit margin N margem f de lucro
profit-sharing [-'ʃɛərɪŋ] N participação f nos
lucros
profits tax (BRIT) N imposto sobre os lucros
profligate ['prɔflɪgɪt] ADJ (behaviour, person)
devasso; (extravagant): **~ (with)** pródigo (de)
pro forma [-'fɔ:mə] ADJ: **~ invoice** fatura
pro-forma or simulada
profound [prə'faund] ADJ profundo
profuse [prə'fju:s] ADJ abundante
profusely [prə'fju:slɪ] ADV profusamente
profusion [prə'fju:ʒən] N profusão f,
abundância
progeny ['prɔdʒɪnɪ] N prole f, progênie f
prognoses [prɔg'nəusi:z] NPL of **prognosis**
prognosis [prɔg'nəusɪs] (pl **prognoses**) N
prognóstico
programme, (US or Comput) **program**
['prəugræm] N programa m ▶ VT programar
programmer, (US) **programer** ['prəugræməʳ]
N programador(a) m/f
programming, (US) **programing**
['prəugræmɪŋ] N programação f
programming language, (US) **programing**
language N linguagem f de programação
progress [n 'prəugrɛs, vi prə'grɛs] N progresso
▶ VI progredir, avançar; **in ~** em andamento;

to make ~ fazer progressos; **as the match**
~ed à medida que o jogo se desenvolvia
progression [prə'grɛʃən] N progressão f
progressive [prə'grɛsɪv] ADJ progressivo;
(person) progressista
progressively [prə'grɛsɪvlɪ] ADV
progressivamente
progress report N (Med) boletim m médico;
(Admin) relatório sobre o andamento dos
trabalhos
prohibit [prə'hɪbɪt] VT proibir; **to ~ sb from**
doing sth proibir alguém de fazer algo;
"smoking ~ed" "proibido fumar"
prohibition [prəuɪ'bɪʃən] N proibição f; (US):
P~ lei f seca
prohibitive [prə'hɪbɪtɪv] ADJ (price etc)
proibitivo
project [n 'prɔdʒɛkt, vt, vi prə'dʒɛkt] N projeto;
(Sch: research) pesquisa ▶ VT projetar; (figure)
estimar ▶ VI (stick out) ressaltar, sobressair
projectile [prə'dʒɛktaɪl] N projétil m
projection [prə'dʒɛkʃən] N projeção f;
(overhang) saliência
projectionist [prə'dʒɛkʃənɪst] N operador(a)
m/f de projetor
projection room N (Cinema) sala de projeção
projector [prə'dʒɛktəʳ] N projetor m
proletarian [prəulɪ'tɛərɪən] ADJ, N
proletário(-a)
proletariat [prəulɪ'tɛərɪət] N proletariado
proliferate [prə'lɪfəreɪt] VI proliferar
proliferation [prəlɪfə'reɪʃən] N proliferação f
prolific [prə'lɪfɪk] ADJ prolífico
prologue, (US) **prolog** ['prəulɔg] N prólogo
prolong [prə'lɔŋ] VT prolongar
prom [prɔm] N ABBR = **promenade**;
promenade concert; (US: ball) baile m de
estudantes
promenade [prɔmə'nɑ:d] N (by sea) passeio
(à orla marítima)
promenade concert (BRIT) N concerto (de
música clássica)

> Na Grã-Bretanha, um **promenade**
> **concert** (ou **prom**) é um concerto de
> música clássica, assim chamado porque
> originalmente o público não ficava
> sentado, mas de pé ou caminhando. Hoje
> em dia, uma parte do público permanece
> de pé, mas há também lugares sentados
> (mais caros). Os **Proms** mais conhecidos
> são os londrinos. A última sessão (the Last
> Night of the Proms) é um acontecimento
> carregado de emoção, quando são
> executadas árias tradicionais e
> patrióticas. Nos Estados Unidos e no
> Canadá, o **prom**, ou **promenade**, é um
> baile organizado pelas escolas
> secundárias.

promenade deck N (Naut) convés m superior
prominence ['prɔmɪnəns] N eminência,
importância
prominent ['prɔmɪnənt] ADJ (standing out)
proeminente; (important) eminente, notório;

he is ~ **in the field of ...** ele é muito conhecido no campo de ...

prominently ['prɒmɪnəntlɪ] ADV (display, set) bem à vista; **he figured ~ in the case** ele teve um papel importante no caso

promiscuity [prɒmɪ'skju:ɪtɪ] N promiscuidade f

promiscuous [prə'mɪskjuəs] ADJ promíscuo

promise ['prɒmɪs] N promessa; (hope) esperança ▶ VT, VI prometer; **to make sb a ~** fazer uma promessa a alguém; **to ~ sb sth, ~ sth to sb** prometer a alguém algo, prometer algo a alguém; **to ~ (sb) to do sth/that** prometer (a alguém) fazer algo/que; **a young man of ~** um jovem que promete; **to ~ well** prometer

promising ['prɒmɪsɪŋ] ADJ promissor(a), prometedor(a)

promissory note ['prɒmɪsərɪ-] N (nota) promissória

promontory ['prɒməntrɪ] N promontório

promote [prə'məut] VT promover; (product) promover, fazer propaganda de; (event) patrocinar

promoter [prə'məutər] N (of sporting event etc) patrocinador(a) m/f; (of cause etc) partidário(-a)

promotion [prə'məuʃən] N promoção f

prompt [prɒmpt] ADJ pronto, rápido ▶ ADV (exactly) em ponto, pontualmente ▶ N (Comput) sinal m de orientação, prompt m ▶ VT (urge) incitar, impelir; (cause) provocar, ocasionar; (Theatre) servir de ponto a; **to ~ sb to do sth** induzir alguém a fazer algo; **he's very ~** (punctual) ele é pontual; **at 8 o'clock ~** às 8 horas em ponto; **he was ~ to accept** ele não hesitou em aceitar

prompter ['prɒmptər] N (Theatre) ponto

promptly ['prɒmptlɪ] ADV (immediately) imediatamente; (exactly) pontualmente; (rapidly) rapidamente

promptness ['prɒmptnɪs] N (punctuality) pontualidade f; (rapidity) rapidez f

promulgate ['prɒməlgeɪt] VT promulgar

prone [prəun] ADJ (lying) de bruços; **~ to** propenso a, predisposto a; **she is ~ to burst into tears if ...** ela tende a desatar a chorar se ...

prong [prɒŋ] N ponta; (of fork) dente m

pronoun ['prəunaun] N pronome m

pronounce [prə'nauns] VT pronunciar; (verdict, opinion) declarar ▶ VI: **to ~ (up)on** pronunciar-se sobre

pronounced [prə'naunst] ADJ (marked) pronunciado, marcado

pronouncement [prə'naunsmənt] N pronunciamento

pronunciation [prənʌnsɪ'eɪʃən] N pronúncia

proof [pru:f] N prova; (of alcohol) teor m alcoólico ▶ ADJ: **~ against** à prova de ▶ VT (BRIT: tent, anorak) impermeabilizar; **to be 70°** ~ ter 70° de gradação

proofreader ['pru:fri:dər] N revisor(a) m/f de provas

prop [prɒp] N suporte m, escora; (fig) amparo, apoio ▶ VT (also: **prop up**) apoiar, escorar; (lean): **to ~ sth against** apoiar algo contra

Prop. ABBR (Comm) = **proprietor**

propaganda [prɒpə'gændə] N propaganda

propagate ['prɒpəgeɪt] VT propagar

propel [prə'pɛl] VT propelir, propulsionar; (fig) impelir

propeller [prə'pɛlər] N hélice f

propelling pencil [prə'pɛlɪŋ-] (BRIT) N lapiseira

propensity [prə'pɛnsɪtɪ] N: **a ~ for/to/to do** uma propensão para/a/para fazer

proper ['prɒpər] ADJ (correct) correto; (socially acceptable) respeitável, digno; (authentic) genuíno, autêntico; (referring to place): **the village ~** a cidadezinha propriamente dita; **physics ~** a física propriamente dita; **to go through the ~ channels** (Admin) seguir os trâmites oficiais

properly ['prɒpəlɪ] ADV (eat, study) bem; (behave) decentemente

proper noun N nome m próprio

property ['prɒpətɪ] N (possessions, quality) propriedade f; (goods) posses fpl, bens mpl; (buildings) imóveis mpl; (estate) propriedade f, fazenda; **it's their ~** é deles, pertence a eles

property developer (BRIT) N empresário(-a) de imóveis

property owner N proprietário(-a)

property tax N imposto predial e territorial

prophecy ['prɒfɪsɪ] N profecia

prophesy ['prɒfɪsaɪ] VT profetizar; (fig) predizer ▶ VI profetizar

prophet ['prɒfɪt] N profeta m/f

prophetic [prə'fɛtɪk] ADJ profético

proportion [prə'pɔ:ʃən] N proporção f; (share) parte f, porção f ▶ VT proporcionar; **in ~ to or with sth** em proporção or proporcional a algo; **out of ~** desproporcionado; **to see sth in ~** (fig) ter a visão adequada de algo

proportional [prə'pɔ:ʃənl] ADJ proporcional

proportional representation N (Pol) representação f proporcional

proportionate [prə'pɔ:ʃənɪt] ADJ: **~ (to)** proporcionado(a)

proposal [prə'pəuzl] N proposta; (of marriage) pedido

propose [prə'pəuz] VT propor; (toast) erguer ▶ VI propor casamento; **to ~ to do** propor-se fazer

proposer [prə'pəuzər] (BRIT) N (of motion etc) apresentador(a) m/f

proposition [prɒpə'zɪʃən] N proposta, proposição f; (offer) oferta; **to make sb a ~** fazer uma proposta a alguém

propound [prə'paund] VT propor

proprietary [prə'praɪətrɪ] ADJ: **~ brand** marca registrada; **~ product** produto patenteado

proprietor [prə'praɪətər] N proprietário(-a), dono(-a)

propriety [prə'praɪətɪ] N propriedade f

propulsion [prə'pʌlʃən] N propulsão f

pro rata [-'rɑ:tə] ADV pro rata, proporcionalmente

prosaic [prəu'zeɪɪk] ADJ prosaico

Pros. Atty. (US) ABBR = **prosecuting attorney**

proscribe [prə'skraɪb] VT proscrever

prose [prəuz] N prosa

prosecute ['prɔsɪkju:t] VT (Law) processar

prosecuting attorney ['prɔsɪkju:tɪŋ-] (US) N promotor(a) m/f público(-a)

prosecution [prɔsɪ'kju:ʃən] N acusação f; (accusing side) autor m da demanda

prosecutor ['prɔsɪkju:tə'] N promotor(a) m/f; (also: **public prosecutor**) promotor(a) m/f público(-a)

prospect [n 'prɔspɛkt, vt, vi prə'spɛkt] N (chance) probabilidade f; (outlook, potential) perspectiva ▶ VT explorar ▶ VI: **to ~ (for)** prospectar (por); **prospects** NPL (for work etc) perspectivas fpl; **we are faced with the ~ of ...** nós estamos diante da perspectiva de ...; **there is every ~ of an early victory** há toda probabilidade de uma vitória rápida

prospecting [prə'spɛktɪŋ] N prospecção f

prospective [prə'spɛktɪv] ADJ (possible) provável; (future) futuro

prospector [prə'spɛktə'] N garimpeiro(-a)

prospectus [prə'spɛktəs] N prospecto, programa m

prosper ['prɔspə'] VI prosperar

prosperity [prɔ'spɛrɪtɪ] N prosperidade f

prosperous ['prɔspərəs] ADJ próspero

prostate ['prɔsteɪt] N (also: **prostate gland**) próstata

prostitute ['prɔstɪtju:t] N prostituta; **male ~** prostituto

prostitution [prɔstɪ'tju:ʃən] N prostituição f

prostrate [adj 'prɔstreɪt, vt prɔ'streɪt] ADJ prostrado; (fig) abatido, aniquilado ▶ VT: **to ~ o.s. (before sb)** prostrar-se (diante de alguém)

protagonist [prə'tægənɪst] N protagonista m/f; (leading participant) líder m/f

protect [prə'tɛkt] VT proteger

protection [prə'tɛkʃən] N proteção f; **to be under sb's ~** estar sob a proteção de alguém

protectionism [prə'tɛkʃənɪzm] N protecionismo

protection racket N extorsão f

protective [prə'tɛktɪv] ADJ protetor(a); **~ custody** (Law) prisão f preventiva

protector [prə'tɛktə'] N protetor(a) m/f

protégé ['prəutɛʒeɪ] N protegido

protégée ['prəutɛʒeɪ] N protegida

protein ['prəuti:n] N proteína

pro tem [-tɛm] ADV ABBR (= pro tempore) provisoriamente

protest [n 'prəutɛst, vi, vt prə'tɛst] N protesto ▶ VI protestar ▶ VT (insist) insistir; **to ~ about** or **against** or **at** protestar contra

Protestant ['prɔtɪstənt] ADJ, N protestante m/f

protester [prə'tɛstə'] N manifestante m/f

protest march N passeata

protestor [prə'tɛstə'] N = **protester**

protocol ['prəutəkɔl] N protocolo

prototype ['prəutətaɪp] N protótipo

protracted [prə'træktɪd] ADJ prolongado, demorado

protractor [prə'træktə'] N (Geom) transferidor m

protrude [prə'tru:d] VI projetar-se

protuberance [prə'tju:bərəns] N protuberância

proud [praud] ADJ orgulhoso; (pej) vaidoso, soberbo; **to be ~ to do sth** sentir-se orgulhoso de fazer algo; **to do sb ~** (inf) fazer muita festa a alguém

proudly ['praudlɪ] ADV orgulhosamente

prove [pru:v] VT comprovar ▶ VI: **to ~ (to be) correct** etc vir a ser correto etc; **to ~ o.s.** mostrar seu valor; **to ~ itself (to be) useful** etc revelar-se or mostrar-se útil etc; **he was ~d right in the end** no final deram-lhe razão

proverb ['prɔvə:b] N provérbio

proverbial [prə'və:bɪəl] ADJ proverbial

provide [prə'vaɪd] VT fornecer, proporcionar; **to ~ sb with sth** fornecer alguém de algo, fornecer algo a alguém; **to be ~d with** estar munido de
▶ **provide for** VT FUS (person) prover à subsistência de; (emergency) prevenir

provided [prə'vaɪdɪd], **provided that** CONJ contanto que (+ sub), sob condição de (que) (+ sub)

Providence ['prɔvɪdəns] N a Divina Providência

providing [prə'vaɪdɪŋ] CONJ: **~ (that)** contanto que (+ sub)

province ['prɔvɪns] N província; (fig) esfera

provincial [prə'vɪnʃəl] ADJ provincial; (pej) provinciano

provision [prə'vɪʒən] N provisão f; (supply) fornecimento; (supplying) abastecimento; (in contract) cláusula, condição f; **provisions** NPL (food) mantimentos mpl; **to make ~ for** fazer provisão para; **there's no ~ for this in the contract** não há cláusula nesse sentido no contrato

provisional [prə'vɪʒənəl] ADJ provisório, interino; (agreement, licence) provisório ▶ N: **P~** (IRELAND Pol) militante do braço armado do IRA

provisional licence (BRIT) N (Aut) licença prévia para aprendizagem

provisionally [prə'vɪʒnəlɪ] ADV provisoriamente

proviso [prə'vaɪzəu] N condição f; (reservation) ressalva; (Law) cláusula; **with the ~ that** com a ressalva que

Provo ['prɔvəu] (inf) N ABBR = **Provisional**

provocation [prɔvə'keɪʃən] N provocação f

provocative [prə'vɔkətɪv] ADJ provocante; (sexually) excitante

provoke [prə'vəuk] VT provocar; (cause) causar; **to ~ sb to sth/to do** or **into doing sth** provocar alguém a algo/a fazer algo

provoking [prə'vəukɪŋ] ADJ provocante

P

provost ['prɔvəst] N (BRIT: of university) reitor(a) m/f; (SCOTLAND) prefeito(-a)
prow [prau] N proa
prowess ['prauis] N destreza, perícia
prowl [praul] VI (also: **prowl about, prowl around**) rondar, andar à espreita ► N: **on the ~** de ronda, rondando
prowler ['praulə'] N rondador(a)
proximity [prɔk'sɪmɪtɪ] N proximidade f
proxy ['prɔksɪ] N procuração f; (person) procurador(a) m/f; **by ~** por procuração
prude [pru:d] N pudico(-a)
prudence ['pru:dns] N prudência
prudent ['pru:dənt] ADJ prudente
prudish ['pru:dɪʃ] ADJ pudico(-a)
prune [pru:n] N ameixa seca ► VT podar
pry [praɪ] VI: **to ~ (into)** intrometer-se (em)
PS N ABBR (= postscript) PS m
psalm [sɑ:m] N salmo
PSAT (US) N ABBR = **Preliminary Scholastic Aptitude Test**
PSBR (BRIT) N ABBR (= public sector borrowing requirement) necessidade f de empréstimos no setor público
pseud [sju:d] (BRIT inf) N posudo(-a)
pseudo- [sju:dəu] PREFIX pseudo-
pseudonym ['sju:dənɪm] N pseudônimo
PST (US) ABBR (= Pacific Standard Time) hora de inverno do Pacífico
PSV (BRIT) N ABBR = **public service vehicle**
psyche ['saɪkɪ] N psiquismo
psychiatric [saɪkɪ'ætrɪk] ADJ psiquiátrico
psychiatrist [saɪ'kaɪətrɪst] N psiquiatra m/f
psychiatry [saɪ'kaɪətrɪ] N psiquiatria
psychic ['saɪkɪk] ADJ psíquico; (also: **psychical**: person) sensível a forças psíquicas ► N médium m/f
psychoanalyse [saɪkəu'ænəlaɪz] VT psicanalisar
psychoanalysis [saɪkəuə'nælɪsɪs] N psicanálise f
psychoanalyst [saɪkəu'ænəlɪst] N psicanalista m/f
psychological [saɪkə'lɔdʒɪkl] ADJ psicológico
psychologist [saɪ'kɔlədʒɪst] N psicólogo(-a)
psychology [saɪ'kɔlədʒɪ] N psicologia
psychopath ['saɪkəupæθ] N psicopata m/f
psychoses [saɪ'kəusi:z] NPL of psychosis
psychosis [saɪ'kəusɪs] (pl **psychoses**) N psicose f
psychosomatic [saɪkəusə'mætɪk] ADJ psicossomático
psychotherapy [saɪkəu'θɛrəpɪ] N psicoterapia
psychotic [saɪ'kɔtɪk] ADJ, N psicótico(-a)
PT (BRIT) N ABBR = **physical training**
pt ABBR = **pint**; **point**
Pt. ABBR (in place name: = Point) pt
PTA N ABBR = **Parent-Teacher Association**
Pte. (BRIT) ABBR (Mil) = **private**
PTO ABBR (= please turn over) v.v., vire
PTV (US) N ABBR = **public television**; **pay television**

pub [pʌb] N ABBR (= public house) pub m, bar m, botequim m

> Um **pub** geralmente consiste em duas salas: uma (the lounge) é bastante confortável, com poltronas e bancos estofados, enquanto a outra (the public bar) é simplesmente um bar onde a consumação é em geral mais barata. O (public bar) é muitas vezes também um salão de jogos, dos quais os mais comuns são os dardos, dominó e bilhar. Atualmente muitos pubs servem refeições, sobretudo na hora do almoço, e essa é a única hora em que a entrada de crianças é permitida, desde que estejam acompanhadas por adultos. Em geral os pubs funcionam das 11 às 23 horas, mas isso pode variar de acordo com sua permissão de funcionamento; alguns pubs fecham à tarde.

puberty ['pju:bətɪ] N puberdade f
pubic ['pju:bɪk] ADJ púbico, pubiano
public ['pʌblɪk] ADJ público ► N público; **in ~** em público; **to make ~** tornar público; **the general ~** o grande público; **to be ~ knowledge** ser de conhecimento público; **to go ~** (Comm) tornar-se uma companhia de capital aberto, passar a ser cotado na Bolsa de Valores
public address system N sistema m (de reforço) de som
publican ['pʌblɪkən] N dono(-a) de pub
publication [pʌblɪ'keɪʃən] N publicação f
public company N sociedade f anônima aberta
public convenience (BRIT) N banheiro público
public holiday N feriado
public house (BRIT) N pub m, bar m, taberna
publicity [pʌb'lɪsɪtɪ] N publicidade f
publicize ['pʌblɪsaɪz] VT divulgar; (product) promover
public limited company N sociedade f anônima aberta
publicly ['pʌblɪklɪ] ADV publicamente
public opinion N opinião f pública
public ownership N: **to be taken into ~** ser estatizado
public relations N relações fpl públicas
public relations officer N relações-públicas m/f inv
public school N (BRIT) escola particular; (US) escola pública
public sector N setor m público
public service vehicle (BRIT) N veículo para o transporte público
public-spirited [-'spɪrɪtɪd] ADJ zeloso pelo bem-estar público
public transport, (US) **public transportation** N transporte m coletivo
public utility N (serviço de) utilidade f pública
public works NPL obras fpl públicas
publish ['pʌblɪʃ] VT publicar
publisher ['pʌblɪʃə'] N editor(a) m/f; (company) editora

publishing ['pʌblɪʃɪŋ] N (*industry*) a indústria editorial
publishing company N editora
puce [pjuːs] ADJ roxo
puck [pʌk] N (*elf*) duende *m*; (*Ice Hockey*) disco
pucker ['pʌkər] VT (*fabric*) amarrotar; (*brow etc*) franzir
pudding ['pʊdɪŋ] N (*BRIT: dessert*) sobremesa; (*cake*) pudim *m*, doce *m*; **black** (*BRIT*) *or* **blood** (*US*) ~ morcela; **rice** ~ arroz doce
puddle ['pʌdl] N poça
puerile ['pjʊəraɪl] ADJ infantil
Puerto Rican ['pwɜːtəˈriːkən] ADJ, N porto-riquenho(-a)
Puerto Rico ['pwɜːtəʊˈriːkəʊ] N Porto Rico (*no article*)
puff [pʌf] N sopro; (*of cigarette*) baforada; (*of air, smoke*) lufada; (*gust*) rajada, lufada; (*sound*) sopro; (*also:* **powder puff**) pompom *m* ▶ VT: **to ~ one's pipe** tirar baforadas do cachimbo ▶ VI soprar; (*pant*) arquejar
▶ **puff out** VT (*sails*) enfunar; (*cheeks*) encher; **to ~ out smoke** lançar baforadas
▶ **puff up** VT inflar
puffed [pʌft] (*inf*) ADJ (*out of breath*) sem fôlego
puffin ['pʌfɪn] N papagaio-do-mar *m*
puff pastry, (*US*) **puff paste** N massa folhada
puffy ['pʌfɪ] ADJ inchado, entumecido
pugnacious [pʌgˈneɪʃəs] ADJ pugnaz, brigão(-ona)
pull [pʊl] N (*of magnet, sea etc*) atração *f*; (*influence*) influência; (*tug*): **to give sth a ~** dar um puxão em algo ▶ VT puxar; (*trigger*) apertar; (*curtain, blind*) fechar; (*muscle*) distender ▶ VI puxar, dar um puxão; **to ~ a face** fazer careta; **to ~ to pieces** picar em pedacinhos; **to ~ one's punches** não usar toda a força; **to ~ one's weight** fazer a sua parte; **to ~ o.s. together** recompor-se; **to ~ sb's leg** (*fig*) brincar com alguém, sacanear alguém (*inf*); **to ~ strings for sb** mexer os pauzinhos para alguém
▶ **pull about** (*BRIT*) VT (*handle roughly*) maltratar
▶ **pull apart** VT separar; (*break*) romper
▶ **pull down** VT abaixar; (*building*) demolir, derrubar; (*tree*) abater, derrubar
▶ **pull in** VI (*Aut: at the kerb*) encostar; (*Rail*) chegar (na plataforma)
▶ **pull off** VT tirar; (*fig: deal etc*) acertar
▶ **pull out** VI arrancar, partir; (*withdraw*) retirar-se; (*Aut: from kerb*) sair; (*Rail*) partir ▶ VT tirar, arrancar; **to ~ out in front of sb** (*Aut*) dar uma fechada em alguém
▶ **pull over** VI (*Aut*) encostar
▶ **pull round** VI (*unconscious person*) voltar a si; (*sick person*) recuperar-se
▶ **pull through** VI sair-se bem (de um aperto); (*Med*) sobreviver
▶ **pull up** VI (*stop*) deter-se, parar ▶ VT levantar; (*uproot*) desarraigar, arrancar; (*stop*) parar
pulley ['pʊlɪ] N roldana
pull-out N (*withdrawal*) retirada; (*section: in*

magazine, newspaper) encarte *m* ▶ CPD (*magazine, pages*) destacável
pullover ['pʊləʊvər] N pulôver *m*
pulp [pʌlp] N (*of fruit*) polpa; (*for paper*) pasta, massa; **to reduce sth to a ~** amassar algo
pulpit ['pʊlpɪt] N púlpito
pulsate [pʌlˈseɪt] VI pulsar, palpitar; (*music*) vibrar
pulse [pʌls] N (*Anat*) pulso; (*of music, engine*) cadência; (*Bot*) legume *m*; **to feel** *or* **take sb's ~** tomar o pulso de alguém
pulse rate N frequência de pulsos
pulverize ['pʌlvəraɪz] VT pulverizar; (*fig*) esmagar, aniquilar
puma ['pjuːmə] N puma, onça-parda
pumice ['pʌmɪs] N (*also:* **pumice stone**) pedra-pomes *f*
pummel ['pʌml] VT esmurrar, socar
pump [pʌmp] N bomba; (*shoe*) sapatilha (de dança) ▶ VT bombear; (*fig: inf*) sondar; **to ~ sb for information** tentar extrair informações de alguém
▶ **pump up** VT encher
pumpkin ['pʌmpkɪn] N abóbora
pun [pʌn] N jogo de palavras, trocadilho
punch [pʌntʃ] N (*blow*) soco, murro; (*tool*) punção *m*; (*for tickets*) furador *m*; (*drink*) ponche *m*; (*fig: force*) vigor *m*, força ▶ VT (*make a hole in*) perfurar, picotar; (*hit*): **to ~ sb/sth** esmurrar *or* socar alguém/algo
▶ **punch in** (*US*) VI assinar o ponto na entrada
▶ **punch out** (*US*) VI assinar o ponto na saída
punch card N cartão *m* perfurado
punch-drunk (*BRIT*) ADJ estupidificado
punched card [pʌntʃt-] N = **punch card**
punch line N (*of joke*) remate *m*
punch-up (*BRIT inf*) N briga
punctual ['pʌŋktjʊəl] ADJ pontual
punctuality [pʌŋktjuˈælɪtɪ] N pontualidade *f*
punctually ['pʌŋktjʊəlɪ] ADV pontualmente; **it will start ~ at 6** começará às 6 horas em ponto
punctuate ['pʌŋktjʊeɪt] VT pontuar
punctuation [pʌŋktjuˈeɪʃən] N pontuação *f*
punctuation marks NPL sinais *mpl* de pontuação
puncture ['pʌŋktʃər] N picada; (*flat tyre*) furo ▶ VT picar, furar; (*tyre*) furar; **I have a ~** (*Aut*) estou com um pneu furado
pundit ['pʌndɪt] N entendedor(a) *m/f*
pungent ['pʌndʒənt] ADJ (*smell, taste*) acre; (*fig*) mordaz
punish ['pʌnɪʃ] VT punir, castigar; **to ~ sb for sth/for doing sth** punir alguém por algo/ por ter feito algo
punishable ['pʌnɪʃəbl] ADJ punível, castigável
punishing ['pʌnɪʃɪŋ] ADJ (*fig: exhausting*) desgastante ▶ N punição *f*
punishment ['pʌnɪʃmənt] N castigo, punição *f*; (*fig: wear*) desgaste *m*
punk [pʌŋk] N (*also:* **punk rocker**) punk *m/f*; (*also:* **punk rock**) punk *m*; (*US inf: hoodlum*) pinta-brava *m*

P

punt [pʌnt] N (boat) chalana

punter ['pʌntəʳ] N (BRIT: gambler) jogador(a) m/f; (inf: client) cliente m/f

puny ['pju:nɪ] ADJ débil, fraco

pup [pʌp] N (dog) cachorrinho (BR), cachorro (PT); (seal etc) filhote m

pupil ['pju:pl] N aluno(-a); (of eye) pupila

puppet ['pʌpɪt] N marionete f, títere m; (fig) fantoche m

puppet government N governo fantoche or títere

puppy ['pʌpɪ] N cachorrinho (BR), cachorro (PT)

purchase ['pə:tʃɪs] N compra; (grip) ponto de apoio ▶ VT comprar; **to get a ~ on** apoiar-se em

purchase order N ordem f de compra

purchase price N preço de compra

purchaser ['pə:tʃɪsəʳ] N comprador(a) m/f

purchase tax (BRIT) N ≈ imposto de circulação de mercadorias

purchasing power ['pə:tʃɪsɪŋ-] N poder m aquisitivo

pure [pjuəʳ] ADJ puro; **a ~ wool jumper** um pulôver de pura lã; **~ and simple** puro e simples

purebred ['pjuəbred] ADJ de sangue puro

purée ['pjuəreɪ] N purê m

purely ['pjuəlɪ] ADV puramente; (only) meramente

purgatory ['pə:gətərɪ] N purgatório; (fig) inferno

purge [pə:dʒ] N (Med) purgante m; (Pol) expurgo ▶ VT purgar; (Pol) expurgar

purification [pjuərɪfɪ'keɪʃən] N purificação f, depuração f

purify ['pjuərɪfaɪ] VT purificar, depurar

purist ['pjuərɪst] N purista m/f

puritan ['pjuərɪtən] N puritano(-a)

puritanical [pjuərɪ'tænɪkl] ADJ puritano

purity ['pjuərɪtɪ] N pureza

purl [pə:l] N ponto reverso ▶ VT fazer ponto de tricô

purloin [pə:'lɔɪn] VT surripiar

purple ['pə:pl] ADJ roxo, purpúreo

purport [pə:'pɔ:t] VI: **to ~ to be/do** dar a entender que é/faz

purpose ['pə:pəs] N propósito, objetivo; **on ~** de propósito; **for teaching ~s** para fins pedagógicos; **for the ~s of this meeting** para esta reunião; **to no ~** em vão

purpose-built (BRIT) ADJ feito sob medida

purposeful ['pə:pəsful] ADJ decidido, resoluto

purposely ['pə:pəslɪ] ADV de propósito

purr [pə:ʳ] N ronrom m ▶ VI ronronar

purse [pə:s] N (BRIT: for money) carteira; (US: bag) bolsa ▶ VT enrugar, franzir

purser ['pə:səʳ] N (Naut) comissário de bordo

purse snatcher ['-snætʃəʳ] N trombadinha m/f

pursue [pə'sju:] VT perseguir; (fig: activity) exercer; (: interest, plan) dedicar-se a; (: result) lutar por

pursuer [pə'sju:əʳ] N perseguidor(a) m/f

pursuit [pə'sju:t] N (chase) perseguição f; (fig) busca; (occupation) ocupação f, atividade f; (pastime) passatempo; **in (the) ~ of sth** em busca de algo

purveyor [pə'veɪəʳ] N fornecedor(a) m/f

pus [pʌs] N pus m

push [puʃ] N empurrão m; (of button) aperto; (attack) ataque m, arremetida; (advance) avanço ▶ VT empurrar; (button) apertar; (promote) promover; (thrust): **to ~ sth (into)** enfiar algo (em) ▶ VI empurrar; (press) apertar; (fig): **to ~ for** reivindicar; **to ~ a door open/shut** abrir/fechar uma porta empurrando-a; **"~"** (on door) "empurre"; (on bell) "aperte"; **to be ~ed for time/money** estar com pouco tempo/dinheiro; **she is ~ing fifty** (inf) ela está beirando os 50; **at a ~** (BRIT inf) em último caso
  ▶ **push aside** VT afastar com a mão
  ▶ **push in** VI furar a fila
  ▶ **push off** (inf) VI dar o fora
  ▶ **push on** VI (continue) prosseguir
  ▶ **push over** VT derrubar
  ▶ **push through** VI abrir caminho ▶ VT (measure) forçar a aceitação de
  ▶ **push up** VT (total, prices) forçar a alta de

push-bike (BRIT) N bicicleta

push-button ADJ por botões de pressão

pushchair ['puʃtʃɛəʳ] (BRIT) N carrinho

pusher ['puʃəʳ] N (also: drug pusher) traficante m/f

pushing ['puʃɪŋ] ADJ empreendedor(a)

pushover ['puʃəuvəʳ] (inf) N: **it's a ~** é sopa

push-up (US) N flexão f

pushy ['puʃɪ] (pej) ADJ intrometido, agressivo

puss [pus] (inf) N gatinho

pussy ['pusɪ], **pussycat** ['pusɪkæt] (inf) N gatinho

put [put] (pt, pp **put**) VT (place) pôr, colocar; (put into) meter; (person: in institution etc) internar; (say) dizer, expressar; (case) expor; (question) fazer; (person: in situation) colocar; (estimate) avaliar, calcular; (write, type etc) colocar; **to ~ sb in a good/bad mood** deixar alguém de bom/mau humor; **to ~ sb to bed** pôr alguém para dormir; **to ~ sb to a lot of trouble** incomodar alguém; **how shall I ~ it?** como dizer?; **to ~ a lot of time into sth** investir muito tempo em algo; **to ~ money on a horse** apostar num cavalo; **I ~ it to you that ...** (BRIT) eu gostaria de colocar que ...; **to stay ~** não se mexer
  ▶ **put about** VI (Naut) mudar de rumo ▶ VT (rumour) espalhar
  ▶ **put across** VT (ideas) comunicar
  ▶ **put aside** VT deixar de lado
  ▶ **put away** VT (store) guardar
  ▶ **put back** VT (replace) repor; (postpone) adiar; (delay) atrasar
  ▶ **put by** VT (money etc) poupar, pôr de lado
  ▶ **put down** VT pôr em; (pay) pagar; (animal) sacrificar; (in writing) anotar, inscrever;

(*revolt etc*) sufocar; (*attribute*): **to ~ sth down to** atribuir algo a

▶ **put forward** VT (*ideas*) apresentar, propor; (*date, clock*) adiantar

▶ **put in** VT (*application, complaint*) apresentar; (*time, effort*) investir, gastar; (*gas, electricity*) instalar

▶ **put in for** VT FUS (*job*) candidatar-se a; (*promotion, pay rise*) solicitar

▶ **put off** VT (*light*) apagar; (*postpone*) adiar, protelar; (*discourage*) desanimar

▶ **put on** VT (*clothes, make-up, dinner*) pôr; (*light*) acender; (*play*) encenar; (*food, meal*) preparar; (*weight*) ganhar; (*brake*) aplicar; (*record, video, kettle*) ligar; (*attitude*) fingir, simular; (*accent, manner*) assumir; (*inf: tease*) fazer de criança; (*inform*): **to ~ sb on to sth** indicar algo a alguém

▶ **put out** VT (*take out*) colocar fora; (*fire, cigarette, light*) apagar; (*one's hand*) estender; (*news*) anunciar; (*rumour*) espalhar; (*tongue etc*) mostrar; (*person: inconvenience*) incomodar; (BRIT: *dislocate*) deslocar; (*inf: person*): **to be ~ out** estar aborrecido ▶ VI (*Naut*): **to ~ out to sea** fazer-se ao mar; **to ~ out from Plymouth** zarpar de Plymouth

▶ **put through** VT (*call*) transferir; (*plan*) aprovar; **I'd like to ~ a call through to Brazil** eu gostaria de fazer uma ligação para o Brasil

▶ **put together** VT colocar junto(s); (*assemble*) montar; (*meal*) preparar

▶ **put up** VT (*raise*) levantar, erguer; (*hang*) prender; (*build*) construir, edificar; (*tent*) armar; (*increase*) aumentar; (*accommodate*) hospedar; **to ~ sb up to doing sth** incitar alguém a fazer algo; **to ~ sth up for sale** pôr algo à venda

▶ **put upon** VT FUS: **to be ~ upon** sofrer abusos

▶ **put up with** VT FUS suportar, aguentar

putrid ['pjuːtrɪd] ADJ pútrido, podre

putt [pʌt] VT (*Golf*) fazer um putt ▶ N putt *m*, tacada leve

putter ['pʌtə'] N (*Golf*) putter *m*

putting green ['pʌtɪŋ-] N campo de golfe em miniatura

putty ['pʌtɪ] N massa de vidraceiro, betume *m*

put-up ADJ: **~ job** (BRIT) embuste *m*

puzzle ['pʌzl] N (*riddle*) charada; (*jigsaw*) quebra-cabeça *m*; (*also:* **crossword puzzle**) palavras cruzadas *fpl*; (*mystery*) mistério ▶ VT desconcertar, confundir ▶ VI: **to ~ over sth** tentar entender algo; **to be ~d about sth** estar perplexo com algo

puzzling ['pʌzlɪŋ] ADJ (*thing, action*) intrigante, confuso; (*mysterious*) enigmático, misterioso; (*unnerving*) desconcertante; (*incomprehensible*) incompreensível

PVC N ABBR (= *polyvinyl chloride*) PVC *m*

Pvt. (US) ABBR (*Mil*) = **private**

pw ABBR (= *per week*) por semana

PX (US) N ABBR (*Mil*) = **post exchange**

pygmy ['pɪgmɪ] N pigmeu(-meia) *m/f*

pyjamas, (US) **pajamas** [pɪ'dʒɑːməz] NPL pijama *m or f*

pylon ['paɪlən] N pilono, poste *m*, torre *f*

pyramid ['pɪrəmɪd] N pirâmide *f*

Pyrenees [pɪrə'niːz] NPL: **the ~** os Pirineus

Pyrex® ['paɪrɛks] N Pirex® *m* ▶ CPD: **a ~ dish** um pirex

python ['paɪθən] N pitão *m*

Qq

Q, q [kju:] N (letter) Q, q m; **Q for Queen** Q de Quinteta
Qatar [kæ'tɑ:ʳ] N Catar m
QC (BRIT) N ABBR (= Queen's Counsel) título dado a certos advogados
QED ABBR (= quod erat demonstrandum) QED
QM N ABBR = **quartermaster**
q.t. (inf) N ABBR = **quiet; on the ~** de fininho
qty ABBR (= quantity) quant
quack [kwæk] N (of duck) grasnido; (pej: doctor) curandeiro(-a), charlatão(-tã) m/f ▶ VI grasnar
quad [kwɔd] ABBR = **quadrangle; quadruplet**
quadrangle ['kwɔdræŋgl] N (courtyard) pátio quadrangular
quadruped ['kwɔdrupɛd] N quadrúpede m
quadruple [kwɔ'drupl] ADJ quádruplo ▶ N quádruplo ▶ VT, VI quadruplicar
quadruplet [kwɔ:'dru:plɪt] N quadrigêmeo m, quádruplo m
quagmire ['kwægmaɪəʳ] N lamaçal m, atoleiro
quail [kweɪl] N (bird) codorniz f, codorna (BR) ▶ VI acovardar-se
quaint [kweɪnt] ADJ (ideas) curioso, esquisito; (village etc) pitoresco
quake [kweɪk] VI (with fear) tremer ▶ N ABBR = **earthquake**
Quaker ['kweɪkəʳ] N quacre m/f
qualification [kwɔlɪfɪ'keɪʃən] N (skill, quality) qualificação f; (reservation) restrição f, ressalva; (modification) modificação f; (often pl: degree, training) título, qualificação; **what are your ~s?** quais são as suas qualificações?
qualified ['kwɔlɪfaɪd] ADJ (trained) habilitado, qualificado; (professionally) diplomado; (fit): **~ to** apto para, capaz de; (limited) limitado; **~ for/to do** credenciado or qualificado para/para fazer
qualify ['kwɔlɪfaɪ] VT qualificar; (modify) modificar; (limit) restringir, limitar ▶ VI (Sport) classificar-se; **to ~ (as)** classificar (como); (pass examination(s)) formar-se or diplomar-se (em); **to ~ (for)** reunir os requisitos (para)
qualifying ['kwɔlɪfaɪɪŋ] ADJ: **~ exam** exame m de habilitação; **~ round** eliminatórias fpl
qualitative ['kwɔlɪteɪtɪv] ADJ qualitativo

quality ['kwɔlɪtɪ] N qualidade f ▶ CPD de qualidade; **of good/poor ~** de boa/má qualidade
quality control N controle m de qualidade
quality (news)papers (BRIT) NPL ver nota
> Os **quality (news)papers** (ou **quality press**) englobam os jornais "sérios", diários ou semanais, em oposição aos jornais populares (**tabloid press**). Esses jornais visam a um público que procura informações detalhadas sobre uma grande variedade de assuntos e que está disposto a dedicar um bom tempo à leitura.

qualm [kwɑ:m] N (doubt) dúvida; (scruple) escrúpulo; **to have ~s about sth** ter dúvidas sobre a retidão de algo
quandary ['kwɔndrɪ] N: **to be in a ~** estar num dilema
quango ['kwæŋgəu] (BRIT) N ABBR (= quasi-autonomous non-governmental organization) comissão nomeada pelo governo
quantify ['kwɔntɪfaɪ] VT quantificar
quantitative ['kwɔntɪtətɪv] ADJ quantitativo
quantity ['kwɔntɪtɪ] N quantidade f; **in ~** em quantidade
quantity surveyor N calculista m/f de obra
quantum leap ['kwɔntəm-] N (fig) salto quântico
quarantine ['kwɔrnti:n] N quarentena
quarrel ['kwɔrl] N (argument) discussão f; (fight) briga ▶ VI: **to ~ (with)** brigar (com); **to have a ~ with sb** ter uma briga or brigar com alguém; **I have no ~ with him** não tenho nada contra ele; **I can't ~ with that** não posso discordar disso
quarrelsome ['kwɔrlsəm] ADJ brigão(-gona)
quarry ['kwɔrɪ] N (for stone) pedreira; (animal) presa, caça ▶ VT (marble etc) extrair
quart [kwɔ:t] N quarto de galão (1.136 l)
quarter ['kwɔ:təʳ] N quarto, quarta parte f; (of year) trimestre m; (district) bairro; (US: 25 cents) (moeda de) 25 centavos mpl de dólar ▶ VT dividir em quatro; (Mil: lodge) aquartelar; **quarters** NPL (Mil) quartel m; (living quarters) alojamento; **a ~ of an hour** um quarto de hora; **it's a ~ to** (BRIT) or **of** (US) **3** são quinze para as três (BR), são três menos um quarto (PT); **it's a ~ past** (BRIT) or **after**

(*US*) **3** são três e quinze (*BR*), são três e um quarto (*PT*); **from all ~s** de toda parte; **at close ~s** de perto

quarter-deck N (*Naut*) tombadilho superior

quarter final N quarta de final

quarterly ['kwɔːtəlɪ] ADJ trimestral ▶ ADV trimestralmente ▶ N (*Press*) revista trimestral

quartermaster ['kwɔːtəmɑːstəʳ] N (*Mil*) quartel-mestre *m*; (*Naut*) contramestre *m*

quartet, quartette [kwɔːˈtɛt] N quarteto

quarto ['kwɔːtəu] ADJ, N in-quarto *inv*

quartz [kwɔːts] N quartzo ▶ CPD de quartzo

quash [kwɔʃ] VT (*verdict*) anular

quasi- ['kweɪzaɪ] PREFIX quase-

quaver ['kweɪvəʳ] N (*BRIT Mus*) colcheia ▶ VI tremer

quay [kiː] N (*also:* **quayside**) cais *m*

queasy ['kwiːzɪ] ADJ (*sickly*) enjoado

Quebec [kwɪˈbɛk] N Quebec

queen [kwiːn] N rainha; (*also:* **queen bee**) abelha-mestra, rainha; (*Cards etc*) dama

queen mother N rainha-mãe *f*

queer [kwɪəʳ] ADJ (*odd*) esquisito, estranho; (*suspect*) suspeito, duvidoso; (*BRIT: sick*): **I feel ~** não estou bem ▶ N (*inf: homosexual*) bicha *m* (*BR*), maricas *m inv* (*PT*)

quell [kwɛl] VT (*opposition*) sufocar; (*fears*) abrandar, sufocar

quench [kwɛntʃ] VT apagar; **to ~ one's thirst** matar a sede

querulous ['kwɛruləs] ADJ lamuriante

query ['kwɪərɪ] N (*question*) pergunta; (*doubt*) dúvida; (*question mark*) ponto de interrogação ▶ VT questionar

quest [kwɛst] N busca; (*journey*) expedição *f*

question ['kwɛstʃən] N pergunta; (*doubt*) dúvida; (*issue, in test*) questão *f* ▶ VT (*doubt*) duvidar; (*interrogate*) interrogar, inquirir; **to ask sb a ~, to put a ~ to sb** fazer uma pergunta a alguém; **to bring** or **call sth into ~** colocar algo em questão, pôr algo em dúvida; **the ~ is ...** a questão é ...; **it is a ~ of** é questão de; **beyond ~** sem dúvida; **out of the ~** fora de cogitação, impossível

questionable ['kwɛstʃənəbl] ADJ discutível; (*doubtful*) duvidoso

questioner ['kwɛstʃənəʳ] N pessoa que faz uma pergunta (*or que fez a pergunta etc*)

questioning ['kwɛstʃənɪŋ] ADJ interrogador(a) ▶ N interrogatório

question mark N ponto de interrogação

questionnaire [kwɛstʃəˈnɛəʳ] N questionário

queue [kjuː] (*BRIT*) N fila (*BR*), bicha (*PT*) ▶ VI (*also:* **queue up**) fazer fila (*BR*) or bicha (*PT*); **to jump the ~** furar a fila (*BR*), pôr-se à frente (*PT*)

quibble ['kwɪbl] VI: **to ~ about** or **over/with** tergiversar sobre/com

quiche [kiːʃ] N quiche *m*

quick [kwɪk] ADJ rápido; (*temper*) vivo; (*agile*) ágil; (*mind*) sagaz, despachado ▶ ADV rápido ▶ N: **to cut sb to the ~** ferir alguém; **be ~!** ande depressa!, vai rápido!; **to be ~ to act**

agir com rapidez; **she was ~ to see that ...** ela não tardou a ver que ...

quicken ['kwɪkən] VT apressar ▶ VI apressar-se

quicklime ['kwɪklaɪm] N cal *f* viva

quickly ['kwɪklɪ] ADV rapidamente, depressa

quickness ['kwɪknɪs] N rapidez *f*; (*agility*) agilidade *f*; (*liveliness*) vivacidade *f*

quicksand ['kwɪksænd] N areia movediça

quickstep ['kwɪkstɛp] N dança de ritmo rápido

quick-tempered ADJ irritadiço, de pavio curto

quick-witted [-'wɪtɪd] ADJ perspicaz, vivo

quid [kwɪd] (*BRIT inf*) N INV libra

quid pro quo [-kwəu] N contrapartida

quiet ['kwaɪət] ADJ (*voice, music*) baixo; (*peaceful: place*) tranquilo; (*calm: person*) calmo; (*not noisy: place*) silencioso; (*not talkative: person*) calado; (*silent*) silencioso; (*not busy: day, business*) calmo; (*ceremony*) discreto ▶ N (*peacefulness*) sossego; (*silence*) quietude *f* ▶ VT, VI (*US*) = **quieten**; **keep ~!** cale-se!, fique quieto!; **on the ~** de fininho

quieten ['kwaɪətən], **quieten down** VI (*grow calm*) acalmar-se; (*grow silent*) calar-se ▶ VT tranquilizar; fazer calar

quietly ['kwaɪətlɪ] ADV tranquilamente; (*silently*) silenciosamente; (*talk*) baixo

quietness ['kwaɪətnɪs] N (*silence*) quietude *f*; (*calm*) tranquilidade *f*

quill [kwɪl] N pena (*de escrever*)

quilt [kwɪlt] N acolchoado, colcha; (*BRIT: also:* **continental quilt**) edredom *m* (*BR*), edredão *m* (*PT*)

quin [kwɪn] N ABBR = **quintuplet**

quince [kwɪns] N (*fruit*) marmelo; (*tree*) marmeleiro

quinine [kwɪˈniːn] N quinina

quintet, quintette [kwɪnˈtɛt] N quinteto

quintuplet [kwɪnˈtjuːplɪt] N quíntuplo *m*

quip [kwɪp] N escárnio, dito espirituoso ▶ VT: **... he ~ped ...** soltou

quire ['kwaɪəʳ] N mão *f* (*de papel*)

quirk [kwəːk] N peculiaridade *f*; **by some ~ of fate** por uma singularidade do destino, por uma dessas coisas que acontecem

quit [kwɪt] (*pt, pp* **quit** *or* **quitted**) VT (*smoking etc*) parar; (*job*) deixar; (*premises*) desocupar ▶ VI parar; (*give up*) desistir; (*resign*) pedir demissão; **to ~ doing** parar or deixar de fazer; **~ stalling!** (*US inf*) chega de evasivas!; **notice to ~** (*BRIT*) aviso para desocupar (um imóvel)

quite [kwaɪt] ADV (*rather*) bastante; (*entirely*) completamente, totalmente; (*following a negative: almost*): **that's not ~ big enough** não é suficientemente grande; **~ new** novinho; **she's ~ pretty** ela é bem bonita; **I ~ understand** eu entendo completamente; **~ a few of them** um bom número deles; **that's not ~ right** não é bem assim; **not ~ as many as last time** um pouco menos do que da vez passada; **~ (so)!** exatamente!, isso mesmo!

Quito ['kiːtəu] N Quito

quits [kwɪts] ADJ: ~ **(with)** quite (com); **let's call it** ~ ficamos quites

quiver ['kwɪvəʳ] VI estremecer ▶ N (for arrows) carcás m, aljava

quiz [kwɪz] N (game) concurso (de cultura geral); (in magazine etc) questionário, teste m ▶ VT interrogar

quizzical ['kwɪzɪkəl] ADJ zombeteiro

quoits [kwɔɪts] NPL jogo de malha

quorum ['kwɔːrəm] N quorum m

quota ['kwəutə] N cota, quota

quotation [kwəu'teɪʃən] N citação f; (estimate) orçamento; (of shares) cotação f

quotation marks NPL aspas fpl

quote [kwəut] N citação f; (estimate) orçamento ▶ VT (sentence) citar; (price) propor; (figure, example) citar, dar; (shares) cotar ▶ VI: **to ~ from** citar; **quotes** NPL (quotation marks) aspas fpl; **to ~ for a job** propor um preço para um trabalho; **in ~s** entre aspas; ~ ... **un~** (in dictation) abre aspas ... fecha aspas

quotient ['kwəuʃənt] N quociente m

qv ABBR (= quod vide) vide

qwerty keyboard ['kwəːtɪ-] N teclado qwerty

Rr

R¹, r [ɑːʳ] N (letter) R, r m; **R for Robert** (BRIT) or **Roger** (US) R de Roberto

R² ABBR (= right) dir.; (= river) R.; (= Réaumur (scale)) R; (US Cinema: = restricted) proibido para menores de 17 anos; (US Pol) = **republican**; (BRIT) = **Rex; Regina**

RA ABBR = **rear admiral** ▶ N ABBR (BRIT) = **Royal Academician; Royal Academy**

RAAF N ABBR = **Royal Australian Air Force**

Rabat [rə'bɑːt] N Rabat

rabbi ['ræbaɪ] N rabino(-a)

rabbit ['ræbɪt] N coelho ▶ VI: **to ~ (on)** (BRIT) tagarelar

rabbit hole N toca, lura

rabbit hutch N coelheira

rabble ['ræbl] (pej) N povinho, ralé f

rabid ['ræbɪd] ADJ raivoso

rabies ['reɪbiːz] N raiva

RAC (BRIT) N ABBR (= Royal Automobile Club) ≈ TCB m (BR), ≈ ACP m (PT)

raccoon [rə'kuːn] N mão-pelada m, guaxinim m

race [reɪs] N (competition, rush) corrida; (species) raça ▶ VT (person) apostar corrida com; (horse) fazer correr; (engine) acelerar ▶ VI (compete) competir; (run) correr; (pulse) bater rapidamente; **the human ~** a raça humana; **to ~ in/out** etc entrar/sair correndo etc

race car (US) N = **racing car**

race car driver (US) N = **racing driver**

racecourse ['reɪskɔːs] N hipódromo

racehorse ['reɪshɔːs] N cavalo de corridas

race relations NPL relações fpl entre as raças

racetrack ['reɪstræk] N pista de corridas; (for cars) autódromo

racial ['reɪʃl] ADJ racial

racialism ['reɪʃəlɪzəm] N racismo

racialist ['reɪʃəlɪst] ADJ, N racista m/f

racing ['reɪsɪŋ] N corrida

racing car (BRIT) N carro de corrida

racing driver (BRIT) N piloto(-a) de corrida

racism ['reɪsɪzəm] N racismo

racist ['reɪsɪst] (pej) ADJ, N racista m/f

rack [ræk] N (also: **luggage rack**) bagageiro; (shelf) estante f; (also: **roof rack**) xalmas fpl, porta-bagagem m; (also: **dish rack**) secador m de prato; (also: **clothes rack**) cabide m ▶ VT (cause pain to) atormentar; **~ed by** (pain, anxiety) tomado por; **to ~ one's brains** quebrar a cabeça; **to go to ~ and ruin** (building) cair aos pedaços; (business) falir ▶ **rack up** VT acumular

racket ['rækɪt] N (for tennis) raquete f (BR), raqueta (PT); (noise) barulheira, zoeira; (swindle) negócio ilegal, fraude f

racketeer [rækɪ'tɪəʳ] (esp US) N chantagista m/f

racoon [rə'kuːn] N = **raccoon**

racquet ['rækɪt] N raquete f (BR), raqueta (PT)

racy ['reɪsɪ] ADJ ousado, picante

RADA ['rɑːdə] (BRIT) N ABBR = **Royal Academy of Dramatic Art**

radar ['reɪdɑːʳ] N radar m ▶ CPD de radar

radar trap N radar m rodoviário

radial ['reɪdɪəl] ADJ (also: **radial-ply**) radial

radiance ['reɪdɪəns] N brilho, esplendor m

radiant ['reɪdɪənt] ADJ radiante, brilhante; (Phys) radiante

radiate ['reɪdɪeɪt] VT (heat, emotion) irradiar; (emit) emitir ▶ VI (lines) difundir-se, estender-se

radiation [reɪdɪ'eɪʃən] N radiação f

radiation sickness N radiointoxicação f, intoxicação f radioativa

radiator ['reɪdɪeɪtəʳ] N radiador m

radiator cap N tampa do radiador

radiator grill N (Aut) grade f do radiador

radical ['rædɪkl] ADJ radical

radii ['reɪdɪaɪ] NPL of **radius**

radio ['reɪdɪəu] N rádio ▶ VI: **to ~ to sb** comunicar com alguém por rádio ▶ VT: **to ~ sb** comunicar-se por rádio com alguém; (information) transmitir por rádio; (position) comunicar por rádio; **on the ~** no rádio

radio... [reɪdɪəu] PREFIX radio...

radioactive ['reɪdɪəu'æktɪv] ADJ radioativo

radioactivity [reɪdɪəuæk'tɪvɪtɪ] N radioatividade f

radio announcer N locutor(a) m/f de rádio

radio-controlled [-kən'trəuld] ADJ controlado por rádio

radiographer [reɪdɪ'ɔgrəfəʳ] N radiógrafo(-a)

radiography [reɪdɪ'ɔgrəfɪ] N radiografia

radiologist [reɪdɪ'ɔlədʒɪst] N radiologista m/f

radiology [reɪdɪ'ɔlədʒɪ] N radiologia

radio station N emissora, estação f de rádio

radio taxi N rádio-táxi m

radiotelephone [reɪdɪəu'tɛlɪfəun] N radiotelefone m

radiotherapist [reɪdɪəu'θɛrəpɪst] N
radioterapeuta *m/f*

radiotherapy [reɪdɪəu'θɛrəpɪ] N radioterapia *m*

radish ['rædɪʃ] N rabanete *m*

radium ['reɪdɪəm] N rádio

radius ['reɪdɪəs] (*pl* **radii**) N raio; (*Anat*) rádio;
within a 50-mile ~ dentro de um raio de 50
milhas

RAF (*BRIT*) N ABBR = **Royal Air Force**

raffia ['ræfɪə] N ráfia

raffish ['ræfɪʃ] ADJ reles *inv*, ordinário

raffle ['ræfl] N rifa ▶ VT rifar

raft [rɑ:ft] N (*craft: also* **life raft**) balsa; (*logs*)
flutuante *m* de árvores

rafter ['rɑ:ftər] N viga, caibro

rag [ræg] N (*piece of cloth*) trapo; (*torn cloth*)
farrapo; (*pej: newspaper*) jornaleco; (*University:
for charity*) atividades estudantis beneficentes ▶ VT
(*BRIT*) encarnar em, zombar de; **rags** NPL (*torn
clothes*) trapos *mpl*, farrapos *mpl*; **in ~s** em
farrapos

rag-and-bone man (*BRIT*) (*irreg: like* **man**) N
= **ragman**

ragbag ['rægbæg] N (*fig*) salada

rag doll N boneca de trapo

rage [reɪdʒ] N (*fury*) raiva, furor *m* ▶ VI (*person*)
estar furioso; (*storm*) assolar; (*debate*)
continuar calorosamente; **to fly into a ~**
enfurecer-se; **it's all the ~** é a última
moda

ragged ['rægɪd] ADJ (*edge*) irregular, desigual;
(*clothes*) puído, gasto; (*appearance*)
esfarrapado, andrajoso; (*coastline*)
acidentado

raging ['reɪdʒɪŋ] ADJ furioso; (*fever, pain*)
violento; **~ toothache** dor de dente
alucinante; **in a ~ temper** enfurecido

ragman ['rægmæn] (*irreg: like* **man**) N
negociante *m* de trastes

rag trade (*inf*) N: **the ~** a confecção e venda de
roupa

raid [reɪd] N (*Mil*) incursão *f*; (*criminal*) assalto;
(*attack*) ataque *m*; (*by police*) batida ▶ VT
invadir, atacar; assaltar; atacar; fazer uma
batida em

raider ['reɪdər] N atacante *m/f*; (*criminal*)
assaltante *m/f*

rail [reɪl] N (*on stair*) corrimão *m*; (*on bridge,
balcony*) parapeito, anteparo; (*of ship*)
amurada; **rails** (*for train*) trilhos *mpl*; **by ~**
de trem (*BR*), por caminho de ferro (*PT*)

railing ['reɪlɪŋ] N, **railings** ['reɪlɪŋz] NPL
grade *f*

railroad ['reɪlrəud] (*US*) N = **railway**

railway ['reɪlweɪ] N estrada (*BR*) *or* caminho
(*PT*) de ferro

railway engine N locomotiva

railway line (*BRIT*) N linha de trem (*BR*) *or* de
comboio (*PT*)

railwayman ['reɪlweɪmən] (*BRIT*) (*irreg: like*
man) N ferroviário

railway station (*BRIT*) N estação *f* ferroviária
(*BR*) *or* de caminho de ferro (*PT*)

rain [reɪn] N chuva ▶ VI chover; **in the ~** na
chuva; **it's ~ing** está chovendo (*BR*), está a
chover (*PT*); **it's ~ing cats and dogs** chove a
cântaros

rainbow ['reɪnbəu] N arco-íris *m inv*

raincoat ['reɪnkəut] N impermeável *m*, capa
de chuva

raindrop ['reɪndrɔp] N gota de chuva

rainfall ['reɪnfɔ:l] N chuva; (*measurement*)
pluviosidade *f*

rainforest ['reɪnfɔrɪst] N floresta tropical

rainproof ['reɪnpru:f] ADJ impermeável

rainstorm ['reɪnstɔ:m] N chuvada torrencial

rainwater ['reɪnwɔ:tər] N água pluvial

rainy ['reɪnɪ] ADJ chuvoso; **a ~ day** um dia de
chuva

raise [reɪz] N aumento ▶ VT (*lift*) levantar;
(*end: siege, embargo*) levantar, terminar; (*build*)
erguer, edificar; (*salary, production*) aumentar;
(*morale, standards*) melhorar; (*doubts*) suscitar,
despertar; (*a question*) fazer, expor; (*cattle,
family*) criar; (*crop*) cultivar, plantar; (*army*)
recrutar, alistar; (*funds*) angariar; (*loan*)
levantar, obter; **to ~ one's voice** levantar a
voz; **to ~ one's glass to sb/sth** brindar à
saúde de alguém/brindar algo; **to ~ sb's
hopes** dar esperanças a alguém; **to ~ a
laugh/smile** provocar risada/sorrisos

raisin ['reɪzn] N passa, uva seca

Raj [rɑ:dʒ] N: **the ~** o império (na Índia)

rajah ['rɑ:dʒə] N rajá *m*

rake [reɪk] N (*tool*) ancinho; (*person*) libertino
▶ VT (*garden*) revolver *or* limpar com o
ancinho; (*fire*) remover as cinzas de; (*with
machine gun*) varrer ▶ VI: **to ~ through** (*fig:
search*) vascular

rake-off (*inf*) N comissão *f*

rakish ['reɪkɪʃ] ADJ (*dissolute*) devasso,
dissoluto; **at a ~ angle** de banda, inclinado

rally ['rælɪ] N (*Pol etc*) comício; (*Aut*) rally *m*,
rali *m*; (*Tennis*) rebatida ▶ VT reunir ▶ VI
reorganizar-se; (*sick person, stock exchange*)
recuperar-se

▶ **rally round** VI dar apoio ▶ VT FUS dar
apoio a

rallying point ['rælɪɪŋ-] N (*Pol, Mil*) ponto de
encontro

RAM [ræm] N ABBR (*Comput:* = *random access
memory*) RAM *f*

ram [ræm] N carneiro; (*Tech*) êmbolo, aríete *m*
▶ VT (*push*) cravar; (*crash into*) colidir com;
(*tread down*) pisar, calcar

ramble ['ræmbl] N caminhada, excursão *f* a
pé ▶ VI caminhar; (*talk: also:* **ramble on**)
divagar

rambler ['ræmblər] N caminhante *m/f*; (*Bot*)
roseira trepadeira

rambling ['ræmblɪŋ] ADJ (*speech*) desconexo,
incoerente; (*house*) cheio de recantos; (*plant*)
rastejante ▶ N excursionismo

RAMC (*BRIT*) N ABBR = **Royal Army Medical
Corps**

ramification [ræmɪfɪ'keɪʃən] N ramificação *f*

ramp [ræmp] N (*incline*) rampa; (*in road*) lombada; **on/off ~** (*US Aut*) entrada (para a rodovia)/saída da rodovia

rampage [ræm'peɪdʒ] N: **to be on the ~** alvoroçar-se ▶ VI: **they went rampaging through the town** correram feito loucos pela cidade

rampant ['ræmpənt] ADJ (*disease etc*) violento, implacável

rampart ['ræmpɑːt] N baluarte m; (*wall*) muralha

ramshackle ['ræmʃækl] ADJ caindo aos pedaços

RAN N ABBR = **Royal Australian Navy**

ran [ræn] PT of **run**

ranch [rɑːntʃ] N rancho, fazenda, estância

rancher ['rɑːntʃəʳ] N rancheiro(-a), fazendeiro(-a)

rancid ['rænsɪd] ADJ rançoso, râncio

rancour, (*US*) **rancor** ['ræŋkəʳ] N rancor m

R&B N ABBR = **rhythm and blues**

R&D N ABBR = **research and development**

random ['rændəm] ADJ ao acaso, casual, fortuito; (*Comput, Math*) aleatório ▶ N: **at ~** a esmo, aleatoriamente

random access N (*Comput*) acesso randômico *or* aleatório

random access memory N (*Comput*) memória de acesso randômico *or* aleatório

R&R (*US*) N ABBR (*Mil*) = **rest and recreation**

randy ['rændɪ] (*BRIT inf*) ADJ de fogo

rang [ræŋ] PT of **ring**

range [reɪndʒ] N (*of mountains*) cadeia, cordilheira; (*of missile*) alcance m; (*of voice*) extensão f; (*series*) série f; (*of products*) gama, sortimento; (*Mil: also:* **shooting range**) estande m; (*also:* **kitchen range**) fogão m ▶ VT (*place*) colocar; (*arrange*) arrumar, ordenar ▶ VI: **to ~ over** (*wander*) percorrer; (*extend*) estender-se por; **to ~ from ... to ...** variar de ... a ..., oscilar entre ... e ...; **do you have anything else in this price ~?** você tem outras coisas dentro desta faixa de preço?; **within (firing) ~** ao alcance de tiro; **~d left/right** (*text*) alinhado à esquerda/direita

ranger ['reɪndʒəʳ] N guarda-florestal m/f

Rangoon [ræŋ'guːn] N Rangum

rank [ræŋk] N (*row*) fila, fileira; (*Mil*) posto; (*status*) categoria, posição f; (*BRIT: also:* **taxi rank**) ponto de táxi ▶ VI: **to ~ among** figurar entre ▶ VT: **I ~ him sixth** eu o coloco em sexto lugar ▶ ADJ (*stinking*) fétido, malcheiroso; (*hypocrisy, injustice*) total; **the ranks** NPL (*Mil*) a tropa; **the ~ and file** (*fig*) a gente comum; **to close ~s** (*Mil, fig*) cerrar fileiras

rankle ['ræŋkl] VI (*insult*) doer, magoar

ransack ['rænsæk] VT (*search*) revistar; (*plunder*) saquear, pilhar

ransom ['rænsəm] N resgate m; **to hold sb to ~** (*fig*) encostar alguém contra a parede

rant [rænt] VI arengar

ranting ['ræntɪŋ] N palavreado oco

rap [ræp] N batida breve e seca, tapa; (*also:* **rap music**) rap m ▶ VT bater de leve

rape [reɪp] N estupro; (*Bot*) colza ▶ VT violentar, estuprar

rape oil, rapeseed oil ['reɪpsiːd-] N óleo de colza

rapid ['ræpɪd] ADJ rápido

rapidity [rə'pɪdɪtɪ] N rapidez f

rapidly ['ræpɪdlɪ] ADV rapidamente

rapids ['ræpɪdz] NPL (*Geo*) cachoeira

rapist ['reɪpɪst] N estuprador m

rapport [ræ'pɔːʳ] N harmonia, afinidade f

rapt [ræpt] ADJ absorvido; **to be ~ in contemplation** estar contemplando embevecido

rapture ['ræptʃəʳ] N êxtase m, arrebatamento; **to go into ~s over** extasiar-se com

rapturous ['ræptʃərəs] ADJ extático; (*applause*) entusiasta

rare [rɛəʳ] ADJ raro; (*Culin: steak*) mal passado

rarebit ['rɛəbɪt] N *see* **Welsh rarebit**

rarefied ['rɛərɪfaɪd] ADJ (*air, atmosphere*) rarefeito

rarely ['rɛəlɪ] ADV raramente

raring ['rɛərɪŋ] ADJ: **to be ~ to go** (*inf*) estar louco para começar

rarity ['rɛərɪtɪ] N raridade f

rascal ['rɑːskl] N maroto, malandro

rash [ræʃ] ADJ impetuoso, precipitado ▶ N (*Med*) exantema m, erupção f cutânea; (*of events*) série f, torrente f; **he came out in a ~** apareceu-lhe uma irritação na pele

rasher ['ræʃəʳ] N fatia fina

rashness ['ræʃnɪs] N impetuosidade f

rasp [rɑːsp] N (*tool*) lima, raspadeira ▶ VT (*speak: also:* **rasp out**) falar em voz áspera

raspberry ['rɑːzbərɪ] N framboesa

raspberry bush N framboeseira

rasping ['rɑːspɪŋ] ADJ: **a ~ noise** um ruído áspero *or* irritante

rat [ræt] N rato (*BR*), ratazana (*PT*)

ratable ['reɪtəbl] ADJ = **rateable**

ratchet ['rætʃɪt] N (*Tech*) roquete m, catraca

rate [reɪt] N (*ratio*) razão f; (*percentage*) percentagem f, proporção f; (*price*) preço, taxa; (: *of hotel*) diária; (*of interest, change*) taxa; (*speed*) velocidade f ▶ VT (*value*) taxar; (*estimate*) avaliar; **rates** NPL (*BRIT*) imposto predial e territorial; (*fees*) pagamento; **to ~ as** ser considerado como; **to ~ sb/sth as** considerar alguém/algo como; **to ~ sth among** considerar algo como um(a) dos/das; **to ~ sb/sth highly** valorizar alguém/algo; **at a ~ of 60 km/h** à velocidade de 60 km/h; **at any ~** de qualquer modo; **~ of exchange** taxa de câmbio; **~ of growth** taxa de crescimento; **~ of return** taxa de retorno

rateable value ['reɪtəbl-] (*BRIT*) N valor m tributável (*de um imóvel*)

ratepayer ['reɪtpeɪəʳ] (*BRIT*) N contribuinte m/f de imposto predial

r

rather ['rɑːðəʳ] ADV (*somewhat*) um tanto, meio; (*to some extent*) até certo ponto; (*more accurately*): **or ~** ou melhor; **it's ~ expensive** (*quite*) é meio caro; (*too*) é caro demais; **there's ~ a lot** há bastante *or* muito; **~ than** em vez de; **I would** *or* **I'd ~ go** preferiria *or* preferia ir; **I'd ~ not leave** eu preferiria *or* preferia não sair; **or ~** (*more accurately*) ou melhor; **I ~ think he won't come** eu estou achando que ele não vem

ratification [rætɪfɪ'keɪʃən] N ratificação *f*

ratify ['rætɪfaɪ] VT ratificar

rating ['reɪtɪŋ] N (*assessment*) avaliação *f*; (*score*) classificação *f*; (*value*) valor *m*; (*standing*) posição *f*; (: BRIT: *sailor*) marinheiro; **ratings** NPL (*Radio, TV*) índice(s) *m(pl)* de audiência

ratio ['reɪʃɪəu] N razão *f*, proporção *f*; **in the ~ of 100 to 1** na proporção *or* razão de 100 para 1

ration ['ræʃən] N ração *f* ▶ VT racionar; **rations** NPL (*Mil*) mantimentos *mpl*, víveres *mpl*

rational ['ræʃənl] ADJ racional; (*solution, reasoning*) lógico; (*person*) sensato, razoável

rationale [ræʃə'nɑːl] N razão *f* fundamental

rationalization [ræʃnəlaɪ'zeɪʃən] N racionalização *f*

rationalize ['ræʃənəlaɪz] VT racionalizar

rationally ['ræʃənəlɪ] ADV racionalmente; (*logically*) logicamente

rationing ['ræʃnɪŋ] N racionamento

rat poison N raticida *m*

rat race N: **the ~** a competição acirrada na vida moderna

rattan [ræ'tæn] N rotim *m*

rattle ['rætl] N (*of door*) batida; (*of train etc*) chocalhada; (*of coins*) chocalhar *m*; (*of hail*) saraivada; (*object: for baby*) chocalho; (: *of sports fan*) matraca; (*of snake*) guizo ▶ VI chocalhar; (*small objects*) tamborilar; (*vehicle*): **to ~ along** mover-se ruidosamente ▶ VT sacudir, fazer bater; (*unnerve*) perturbar; (*disconcert*) desconcertar; (*annoy*) encher

rattlesnake ['rætlsneɪk] N cascavel *f*

ratty ['rætɪ] (*inf*) ADJ rabugento

raucous ['rɔːkəs] ADJ espalhafatoso, banelhento

raucously ['rɔːkəslɪ] ADV em voz rouca

raunchy ['rɔːntʃɪ] ADJ (*inf: voice, image, act*) sensual; (: *scenes, film*) picante

ravage ['rævɪdʒ] VT devastar, estragar

ravages ['rævɪdʒɪz] NPL estragos *mpl*

rave [reɪv] VI (*in anger*) encolerizar-se; (*Med*) delirar; (*with enthusiasm*): **to ~ about** vibrar com ▶ CPD: **~ review** (*inf*) crítica estrondosa

raven ['reɪvən] N corvo

ravenous ['rævənəs] ADJ morto de fome, esfomeado

ravine [rə'viːn] N ravina, barranco

raving ['reɪvɪŋ] ADJ: **~ lunatic** doido(-a) varrido(-a)

ravings ['reɪvɪŋz] NPL delírios *mpl*

ravioli [rævɪ'əulɪ] N ravióli *m*

ravish ['rævɪʃ] VT arrebatar; (*delight*) encantar

ravishing ['rævɪʃɪŋ] ADJ encantador(a)

raw [rɔː] ADJ (*uncooked*) cru(a); (*not processed*) bruto; (*sore*) vivo; (*inexperienced*) inexperiente, novato; (*weather*) muito frio

raw deal (*inf*) N: **to get a ~** levar a pior

raw material N matéria-prima

ray [reɪ] N raio; **~ of hope** fio de esperança

rayon ['reɪɔn] N raiom *m*

raze [reɪz] VT (*also*: **raze to the ground**) arrasar, aniquilar

razor ['reɪzəʳ] N (*open*) navalha; (*safety razor*) aparelho de barbear; (*electric*) aparelho de barbear elétrico

razor blade N gilete *m* (BR), lâmina de barbear (PT)

razzle ['ræzl], (BRIT) **razzle-dazzle** (*inf*) N: **to go on the ~(-dazzle)** cair na farra

razzmatazz ['ræzmə'tæz] (*inf*) N alvoroço

RC N ABBR = **Roman Catholic**

RCAF N ABBR = **Royal Canadian Air Force**

RCMP N ABBR = **Royal Canadian Mounted Police**

RCN N ABBR = **Royal Canadian Navy**

RD (US) ABBR (*Post*) = **rural delivery**

Rd ABBR = **road**

RDC (BRIT) N ABBR = **rural district council**

RE (BRIT) N ABBR = **religious education**; (*Mil*) = **Royal Engineers**

re [riː] PREP referente a

reach [riːtʃ] N alcance *m*; (*Boxing*) campo de ação; (*of river etc*) extensão *f* ▶ VT (*be able to touch*) alcançar; (*arrive at: place*) chegar em; (: *agreement, conclusion*) chegar a; (*achieve*) conseguir; (*stretch out*) estender, esticar; (*by telephone*) conseguir falar com ▶ VI alcançar; (*stretch out*) esticar-se; **within ~** (*object*) ao alcance (da mão); **out of** *or* **beyond ~** fora de alcance; **within easy ~ of the shops/ station** perto das lojas/da estação; **"keep out of the ~ of children"** "manter fora do alcance de crianças"; **to ~ out for sth** estender *or* esticar a mão para pegar (em) algo; **to ~ sb by phone** comunicar-se com alguém por telefone; **can I ~ you at your hotel?** posso entrar em contato com você no seu hotel?

▶ **reach out** VT (*hand*) esticar ▶ VI: **to ~ out for sth** estender *or* esticar a mão para pegar (em) algo

react [riː'ækt] VI reagir

reaction [riː'ækʃən] N reação *f*; **reactions** NPL (*reflexes*) reflexos *mpl*

reactionary [riː'ækʃənrɪ] ADJ, N reacionário(-a)

reactor [riː'æktəʳ] N (*also*: **nuclear reactor**) reator *m* nuclear

read [riːd] (*pt, pp* **read** [rɛd]) VI ler ▶ VT ler; (*understand*) compreender; (*study*) estudar; **to take sth as ~** (*fig*) considerar algo como

garantido; **do you ~ me?** (*Tel*) está me
ouvindo?; **to ~ between the lines** ler nas
entrelinhas
▶ **read out** VT ler em voz alta
▶ **read over** VT reler
▶ **read through** VT (*quickly*) dar uma lida em;
(*thoroughly*) ler até o fim
▶ **read up, read up on** VT FUS estudar

readable ['riːdəbl] ADJ (*writing*) legível; (*book*)
que merece ser lido

reader ['riːdəʳ] N leitor(a) *m/f*; (*book*) livro de
leituras; (*BRIT: at university*) professor(a) *m/f*
adjunto(-a)

readership ['riːdəʃɪp] N (*of paper: readers*)
leitores *mpl*; (: *number of readers*) número de
leitores

readily ['rɛdɪlɪ] ADV (*willingly*) de boa vontade;
(*easily*) facilmente; (*quickly*) sem demora,
prontamente

readiness ['rɛdɪnɪs] N (*willingness*) boa vontade
f; (*preparedness*) prontidão *f*; **in ~** (*prepared*)
preparado, pronto

reading ['riːdɪŋ] N leitura; (*understanding*)
compreensão *f*; (*on instrument*) indicação *f*,
registro (BR), registo (PT)

reading lamp N lâmpada de leitura

reading room N sala de leitura

readjust [riːə'dʒʌst] VT reajustar ▶ VI (*adapt*):
to ~ to reorientar-se para

ready ['rɛdɪ] ADJ pronto, preparado; (*willing*)
disposto; (*available*) disponível ▶ ADV:
~-cooked pronto para comer ▶ N: **at the ~**
(*Mil*) pronto para atirar; (*fig*) pronto; **~ for
use** pronto para o uso; **to be ~ to do sth**
estar pronto *or* preparado para fazer algo;
to get ~ vi preparar-se; vt preparar

ready cash N dinheiro vivo

ready-made ADJ (*já*) feito; (*clothes*) pronto

ready-mix N (*for cakes etc*) massa pronta

ready money N dinheiro vivo *or* disponível

ready reckoner [-'rɛkənəʳ] (BRIT) N tabela de
cálculos feitos

ready-to-wear ADJ pronto, prêt à porter *inv*

reaffirm [riːə'fəːm] VT reafirmar

reagent [riːˈeɪdʒənt] N reagente *m*, reativo

real [rɪəl] ADJ real; (*genuine*) verdadeiro,
autêntico; (*proper*) de verdade; (*for emphasis*):
a ~ idiot/miracle um verdadeiro idiota/
milagre ▶ ADV (*US inf: very*) bem; **in ~ life** na
vida real; **in ~ terms** em termos reais

real estate N bens *mpl* imobiliários *or* de raiz

realism ['rɪəlɪzəm] N realismo

realist ['rɪəlɪst] N realista *m/f*

realistic [rɪə'lɪstɪk] ADJ realista

reality [riːˈælɪtɪ] N realidade *f*; **in ~** na
verdade, na realidade

reality TV N reality TV *f*

realization [rɪəlaɪˈzeɪʃən] N (*fulfilment*)
realização *f*; (*understanding*) compreensão *f*;
(*Comm*) conversão *f* em dinheiro, realização

realize ['rɪəlaɪz] VT (*understand*) perceber;
(*fulfil, Comm*) realizar; **I ~ that ...** eu concordo
que ...

really ['rɪəlɪ] ADV (*for emphasis*) realmente;
(*actually*): **what ~ happened?** o que
aconteceu na verdade?; **~?** (*interest*) é
mesmo?; (*surprise*) verdade!; **~!** (*annoyance*)
realmente!

realm [rɛlm] N reino; (*fig*) esfera, domínio

real-time ADJ (*Comput*) em tempo real

realtor ['rɪəltəʳ] (US) N corretor(a) *m/f* de
imóveis (BR), agente *m/f* imobiliário(-a) (PT)

ream [riːm] N resma; **reams** NPL (*fig: inf*)
páginas *fpl* e páginas

reap [riːp] VT segar, ceifar; (*fig*) colher

reaper ['riːpəʳ] N segador(a) *m/f*, ceifeiro(-a);
(*machine*) segadora

reappear [riːə'pɪəʳ] VI reaparecer

reappearance [riːə'pɪərəns] N reaparição *f*

reapply [riːə'plaɪ] VI: **to ~ for** requerer de
novo; (*job*) candidatar-se de novo a

reappraisal [riːə'preɪzl] N reavaliação *f*

rear [rɪəʳ] ADJ traseiro, de trás ▶ N traseira;
(*inf: bottom*) traseiro ▶ VT (*cattle, family*) criar
▶ VI (*also*: **rear up**) empinar-se

rear-engined [-'ɛndʒɪnd] ADJ (*Aut*) com motor
traseiro

rearguard ['rɪəgɑːd] N retaguarda

rearm [riːˈɑːm] VT, VI rearmar

rearmament [riːˈɑːməmənt] N
rearmamento *m*

rearrange [riːə'reɪndʒ] VT arrumar de novo,
reorganizar

rear-view mirror N (*Aut*) espelho retrovisor

reason ['riːzn] N (*cause*) razão *f*; (*ability to think*)
raciocínio; (*sense*) bom-senso ▶ VI: **to ~ with
sb** argumentar com alguém, persuadir
alguém; **the ~ for/why** a razão de/pela qual;
to have ~ to think ter motivo para pensar;
it stands to ~ that é razoável *or* lógico que;
she claims with good ~ that ... ela afirma
com toda a razão que ...; **all the more ~ why
you should not sell it** mais uma razão para
você não vendê-lo

reasonable ['riːzənəbl] ADJ (*fair*) razoável;
(*sensible*) sensato

reasonably ['riːzənəblɪ] ADV (*fairly*)
razoavelmente; (*sensibly*) sensatamente;
one can ~ assume that ... tudo indica
que ...

reasoned ['riːzənd] ADJ (*argument*)
fundamentado

reasoning ['riːzənɪŋ] N raciocínio

reassemble [riːə'sɛmbl] VT (*people*) reunir;
(*machine*) montar de novo ▶ VI reunir-se de
novo

reassert [riːə'səːt] VT reafirmar

reassurance [riːə'ʃuərəns] N garantia;
(*comfort*) reconforto

reassure [riːə'ʃuəʳ] VT tranquilizar; **to ~ sb of**
reafirmar a confiança de alguém acerca de

reassuring [riːə'ʃuərɪŋ] ADJ animador(a),
tranquilizador(a)

reawakening [riːə'weɪknɪŋ] N despertar *m*

rebate ['riːbeɪt] N (*on product*) abatimento;
(*on tax etc*) devolução *f*; (*refund*) reembolso

rebel [*n* 'rɛbl, *vi* rɪ'bɛl] N rebelde *m/f* ▶ vi rebelar-se

rebellion [rɪ'bɛljən] N rebelião *f*, revolta

rebellious [rɪ'bɛljəs] ADJ insurreto; (*behaviour*) rebelde

rebirth [riː'bəːθ] N renascimento

rebound [*vi* rɪ'baund, *n* 'riːbaund] vi (*ball*) ressaltar ▶ N: **on the ~** ressalto; (*person*): **she married him on the ~** ela casou com ele logo após o rompimento do casamento (*or* relacionamento) anterior

rebuff [rɪ'bʌf] N repulsa, recusa ▶ vT repelir

rebuild [riː'bɪld] (*irreg: like* **build**) vT reconstruir; (*economy, confidence*) recuperar

rebuke [rɪ'bjuːk] N reprimenda, censura ▶ vT repreender

rebut [rɪ'bʌt] vT refutar

rebuttal [rɪ'bʌtl] N refutação *f*

recalcitrant [rɪ'kælsɪtrənt] ADJ recalcitrante, teimoso

recall [rɪ'kɔːl] vT (*remember*) recordar, lembrar; (*parliament*) reunir de volta; (*ambassador etc*) chamar de volta ▶ N (*memory*) recordação *f*, lembrança; (*of ambassador etc*) chamada (de volta); **it is beyond ~** caiu no esquecimento

recant [rɪ'kænt] vi retratar-se

recap ['riːkæp] vT sintetizar ▶ vi recapitular ▶ N recapitulação *f*

recapitulate [riːkə'pɪtjuleɪt] vT, vi = **recap**

recapture [riː'kæptʃə^r] vT (*town*) retomar, recobrar; (*atmosphere*) recriar

recd. ABBR = **received**

recede [rɪ'siːd] vi (*tide*) baixar; (*lights*) diminuir; (*memory*) enfraquecer; (*hair*) escassear

receding [rɪ'siːdɪŋ] ADJ (*forehead, chin*) metido *or* puxado para dentro; (*hair*) que está escasseando nas têmporas; **~ hairline** entradas *fpl* (no cabelo)

receipt [rɪ'siːt] N (*document*) recibo; (*act of receiving*) recebimento (BR), recepção *f* (PT); **receipts** NPL (*Comm*) receitas *fpl*; **on ~ of** ao receber; **to acknowledge ~ of** acusar o recebimento (BR) *or* a recepção (PT) de; **we are in ~ of ...** recebimos ...

receivable [rɪ'siːvəbl] ADJ (*Comm*) a receber

receive [rɪ'siːv] vT receber; (*guest*) acolher; (*wound, criticism*) sofrer; **"~d with thanks"** (*Comm*) "recebido"

receiver [rɪ'siːvə^r] N (*Tel*) fone *m* (BR), auscultador *m* (PT); (*Radio, TV*) receptor *m*; (*of stolen goods*) receptador(a) *m/f*; (*Comm*) curador(a) *m/f* síndico(-a) de massa falida

recent ['riːsnt] ADJ recente; **in ~ years** nos últimos anos

recently ['riːsntlɪ] ADV (*a short while ago*) recentemente; (*in recent times*) ultimamente; **as ~ as yesterday** ainda ontem; **until ~** até recentemente

receptacle [rɪ'sɛptɪkl] N receptáculo, recipiente *m*

reception [rɪ'sɛpʃən] N recepção *f*; (*welcome*) acolhida

reception centre (BRIT) N centro de recepção

reception desk N (mesa de) recepção *f*

receptionist [rɪ'sɛpʃənɪst] N recepcionista *m/f*

receptive [rɪ'sɛptɪv] ADJ receptivo

recess [rɪ'sɛs] N (*in room*) recesso, vão *m*; (*for bed*) nicho; (*secret place*) esconderijo; (*Pol: etc holiday*) férias *fpl*; (*US Law: short break*) recesso; (*Sch: esp US*) recreio

recession [rɪ'sɛʃən] N recessão *f*

recharge [riː'tʃaːdʒ] vT (*battery*) recarregar

rechargeable [riː'tʃaːdʒəbl] ADJ recarregável

recipe ['rɛsɪpɪ] N receita

recipient [rɪ'sɪpɪənt] N recipiente *m/f*, recebedor(a) *m/f*; (*of letter*) destinatário(-a)

reciprocal [rɪ'sɪprəkl] ADJ recíproco

reciprocate [rɪ'sɪprəkeɪt] vT retribuir ▶ vi (*in hospitality etc*) retribuir; (*in aggression etc*) revidar

recital [rɪ'saɪtl] N recital *m*

recite [rɪ'saɪt] vT (*poem*) recitar; (*complaints etc*) enumerar

reckless ['rɛkləs] ADJ (*driver*) imprudente; (*speed*) imprudente, excessivo; (*spending*) irresponsável

recklessly ['rɛkləslɪ] ADV temerariamente, sem prudência; (*speed*) irresponsavelmente

reckon ['rɛkən] vT (*calculate*) calcular, contar; (*consider*) considerar; (*think*): **I ~ that ...** acho que ... ▶ vi: **he is somebody to be ~ed with** ele é alguém que não pode ser esquecido; **to ~ without sb/sth** não levar alguém/algo em conta, não contar com alguém/algo
  ▶ **reckon on** vT FUS contar com

reckoning ['rɛkənɪŋ] N (*calculation*) cálculo; **the day of ~** o dia do Juízo Final

reclaim [rɪ'kleɪm] vT (*get back*) recuperar; (*demand back*) reivindicar; (*land*) desbravar; (*: from sea*) aterrar; (*waste materials*) reaproveitar

reclamation [rɛklə'meɪʃən] N recuperação *f*; (*of land from sea*) aterro

recline [rɪ'klaɪn] vi reclinar-se; (*lean*) apoiar-se, recostar-se

reclining [rɪ'klaɪnɪŋ] ADJ (*seat*) reclinável

recluse [rɪ'kluːs] N recluso(-a)

recognition [rɛkəg'nɪʃən] N reconhecimento; **transformed beyond ~** tão transformado que está irreconhecível; **in ~ of** em reconhecimento de; **to gain ~** ser reconhecido

recognizable ['rɛkəgnaɪzəbl] ADJ: **~ (by)** reconhecível (por)

recognize ['rɛkəgnaɪz] vT reconhecer; (*accept*) aceitar; **to ~ by/as** reconhecer por/como

recoil [*vi* rɪ'kɔɪl, *n* 'riːkɔɪl] vi recuar; (*person*): **to ~ from doing sth** recusar-se a fazer algo ▶ N (*of gun*) coice *m*

recollect [rɛkə'lɛkt] vT lembrar, recordar

recollection [rɛkə'lɛkʃən] N (*memory*) recordação *f*; (*remembering*) lembrança; **to the best of my ~** se não me falha a memória

recommend [rɛkə'mɛnd] vt recomendar; **she has a lot to ~ her** ela tem muito a seu favor

recommendation [rɛkəmɛn'deɪʃən] N recomendação f

recommended retail price [rɛkə'mɛndɪd-] (BRIT) N preço máximo consumidor

recompense ['rɛkəmpɛns] vt recompensar ▶ N recompensa

reconcilable [rɛkən'saɪləbl] ADJ (ideas) conciliável

reconcile ['rɛkənsaɪl] vt (two people) reconciliar; (two facts) conciliar, harmonizar; **to ~ o.s. to sth** resignar-se a or conformar-se com algo

reconciliation [rɛkənsɪlɪ'eɪʃən] N reconciliação f

recondite [rɪ'kɔndaɪt] ADJ obscuro

recondition [riːkən'dɪʃən] vt recondicionar

reconnaissance [rɪ'kɔnɪsns] N (Mil) reconhecimento

reconnoitre, (US) **reconnoiter** [rɛkə'nɔɪtəʳ] vt (Mil) reconhecer ▶ vi fazer um reconhecimento

reconsider [riːkən'sɪdəʳ] vt reconsiderar

reconstitute [riː'kɔnstɪtjuːt] vt reconstituir

reconstruct [riːkən'strʌkt] vt reconstruir; (event) reconstituir

reconstruction [riːkən'strʌkʃən] N reconstrução f

record [n, adj 'rɛkɔːd, vt rɪ'kɔːd] N (Mus) disco; (of meeting etc) ata, minuta; (Comput, of attendance) registro (BR), registo (PT); (file) arquivo; (written) história; (also: **criminal record**) antecedentes mpl; (Sport) recorde m ▶ vt (write down) anotar; (temperature, speed) registrar (BR), registar (PT); (relate) relatar, referir; (Mus: song etc) gravar ▶ ADJ: **in ~ time** num tempo recorde; **public ~s** arquivo público; **to keep a ~ of** anotar; **to put the ~ straight** (fig) corrigir um equívoco; **he is on ~ as saying that ...** ele declarou publicamente que ...; **Italy's excellent ~** o excelente desempenho da Itália; **off the ~** adj confidencial; adv confidencialmente

record card N (in file) ficha

recorded delivery letter [rɪ'kɔːdɪd-] (BRIT) N (Post) ≈ carta registrada (BR) or registada (PT)

recorder [rɪ'kɔːdəʳ] N (Mus) flauta; (Tech) indicador m mecânico; (official) escrivão(-vã) m/f

record holder N (Sport) detentor(a) m/f do recorde

recording [rɪ'kɔːdɪŋ] N (Mus) gravação f

recording studio N estúdio de gravação

record library N discoteca

record player N toca-discos m inv (BR), gira-discos m inv (PT)

recount [rɪ'kaunt] vt relatar

re-count [n 'riːkaunt, vt riː'kaunt] N (Pol: of votes) nova contagem f, recontagem f ▶ vt recontar

recoup [rɪ'kuːp] vt: **to ~ one's losses** recuperar-se dos prejuízos

recourse [rɪ'kɔːs] N recurso; **to have ~ to** recorrer a

recover [rɪ'kʌvəʳ] vt recuperar; (rescue) resgatar ▶ vi (from illness) recuperar-se; (from shock) refazer-se

re-cover vt (chair etc) revestir

recovery [rɪ'kʌvərɪ] N recuperação f; (Med) recuperação, melhora

recreate [riːkrɪ'eɪt] vt recriar

recreation [rɛkrɪ'eɪʃən] N recreação f; (play) recreio

recreational [rɛkrɪ'eɪʃənl] ADJ recreativo

recreational drug N droga recreacional

recreational vehicle (US) N kombi m

recrimination [rɪkrɪmɪ'neɪʃən] N recriminação f

recruit [rɪ'kruːt] N recruta m/f; (in company) novato(-a) ▶ vt recrutar

recruiting office [rɪ'kruːtɪŋ-] N centro de recrutamento

recruitment [rɪ'kruːtmənt] N recrutamento

rectangle ['rɛktæŋgl] N retângulo

rectangular [rɛk'tæŋgjuləʳ] ADJ retangular

rectify ['rɛktɪfaɪ] vt retificar

rector ['rɛktəʳ] N (Rel) pároco; (Sch) reitor(a) m/f

rectory ['rɛktərɪ] N residência paroquial

rectum ['rɛktəm] N (Anat) reto

recuperate [rɪ'kuːpəreɪt] vi recuperar-se

recur [rɪ'kəːʳ] vi repetir-se, ocorrer outra vez; (opportunity) surgir de novo; (symptoms) reaparecer

recurrence [rɪ'kʌrəns] N repetição f; (of symptoms) reaparição f

recurrent [rɪ'kʌrənt] ADJ repetido, periódico

recurring [rɪ'kəːrɪŋ] ADJ (Math) periódico

recyclable [riː'saɪkləbl] ADJ reciclável

recycle [riː'saɪkl] vt reciclar

recycling [riː'saɪklɪŋ] N reciclagem f

red [rɛd] N vermelho; (Pol: pej) vermelho(-a) ▶ ADJ vermelho; (hair) ruivo; (wine) tinto; **to be in the ~** (person) estar no vermelho; (account) não ter fundos

red carpet treatment N: **she was given the ~** ela foi recebida com todas as honras

Red Cross N Cruz f Vermelha

redcurrant ['rɛd'kʌrənt] N groselha

redden ['rɛdən] vt avermelhar ▶ vi corar, ruborizar-se

reddish ['rɛdɪʃ] ADJ avermelhado; (hair) arruivado

redecorate [riː'dɛkəreɪt] vt decorar de novo, redecorar

redecoration [riːdɛkə'reɪʃən] N remodelação f

redeem [rɪ'diːm] vt (Rel) redimir; (sth in pawn) tirar do prego; (loan, fig: situation) salvar

redeemable [rɪ'diːməbl] ADJ resgatável

redeeming [rɪ'diːmɪŋ] ADJ: **~ feature** lado bom or que salva

redeploy [riːdɪ'plɔɪ] vt (resources, troops) redistribuir

redeployment [riːdɪˈplɔɪmənt] N redistribuição f

redevelop [riːdɪˈvɛləp] VT renovar

redevelopment [riːdɪˈvɛləpmənt] N renovação f

red-haired ADJ ruivo

red-handed [-ˈhændɪd] ADJ: **to be caught ~** ser apanhado em flagrante, ser flagrado

redhead [ˈrɛdhɛd] N ruivo(-a)

red herring N (fig) pista falsa

red-hot ADJ incandescente

redid [riːˈdɪd] PT of **redo**

redirect [riːdaɪˈrɛkt] VT (mail) endereçar de novo

redistribute [riːdɪˈstrɪbjuːt] VT redistribuir

red-letter day N dia m memorável

red light N: **to go through a ~** (Aut) avançar o sinal

red-light district N zona (de meretrício)

redness [ˈrɛdnɪs] N vermelhidão f

redo [riːˈduː] (irreg: like **do**) VT refazer

redolent [ˈrɛdələnt] ADJ: **~ of** que cheira a; (fig) que evoca

redone [riːˈdʌn] PP of **redo**

redouble [riːˈdʌbl] VT: **to ~ one's efforts** redobrar os esforços

redraft [riːˈdrɑːft] VT redigir de novo

redress [rɪˈdrɛs] N compensação f ▶ VT retificar; **to ~ the balance** restituir o equilíbrio

Red Sea N: **the ~** o mar Vermelho

redskin [ˈrɛdskɪn] N pele-vermelha m/f

red tape N (fig) papelada, burocracia

reduce [rɪˈdjuːs] VT reduzir; (lower) rebaixar; **"~ speed now"** (Aut) "diminua a velocidade"; **to ~ sth by/to** diminuir algo em/reduzir algo a; **to ~ sb to** (silence, begging) levar alguém a; (tears) reduzir alguém a; **"greatly ~d prices"** "preços altamente reduzidos"; **at a ~d price** a preço reduzido

reduction [rɪˈdʌkʃən] N redução f; (of price) abatimento, (discount) desconto

redundancy [rɪˈdʌndənsɪ] N redundância; (BRIT: dismissal) demissão f; (unemployment) desemprego; **compulsory ~** demissão; **voluntary ~** demissão voluntária

redundancy payment (BRIT) N indenização paga aos empregados dispensados sem justa causa

redundant [rɪˈdʌndnt] ADJ (BRIT: worker) desempregado; (detail, object) redundante, supérfluo; **to be made ~** ficar desempregado or sem trabalho

reed [riːd] N (Bot) junco; (Mus: of clarinet etc) palheta

reedy [ˈriːdɪ] ADJ (voice, instrument) agudo

reef [riːf] N (at sea) recife m

reek [riːk] VI: **to ~ (of)** cheirar (a), feder (a)

reel [riːl] N carretel m, bobina; (of film) rolo, filme m; (on fishing rod) carretilha; (dance) dança típica da Escócia ▶ VT (Tech) bobinar; (also: **reel up**) enrolar ▶ VI (sway) cambalear, oscilar; **my head is ~ing** estou completamente confuso

▶ **reel in** VT puxar enrolando a linha

▶ **reel off** VT (say) enumerar, recitar

re-election N reeleição f

re-enter VT reentrar em

re-entry N reentrada

re-export [vt riːɪksˈpɔːt, n riːˈɛkspɔːt] VT reexportar ▶ N reexportação f

ref [rɛf] (inf) N ABBR = **referee**

ref. ABBR (Comm: = reference) ref.

refectory [rɪˈfɛktərɪ] N refeitório

refer [rɪˈfəːʳ] VT (matter, problem): **to ~ sth to** submeter algo à apreciação de; (person, patient): **to ~ sb to** encaminhar alguém a; (reader: to text): **to ~ sb to** remeter alguém a ▶ VI: **to ~ to** (allude to) referir-se or aludir a; (apply to) aplicar-se a; (consult) recorrer a; **~ring to your letter** (Comm) com referência à sua carta

referee [rɛfəˈriː] N árbitro(-a); (BRIT: for job application) referência ▶ VT arbitrar; (football match) apitar

reference [ˈrɛfrəns] N referência; (mention) menção f; **with ~ to** com relação a; (Comm: in letter) com referência a; **"please quote this ~"** (Comm) "queira citar esta referência"

reference book N livro de consulta

reference number N número de referência

referenda [rɛfəˈrɛndə] NPL of **referendum**

referendum [rɛfəˈrɛndəm] (pl **referenda**) N referendum m, plebiscito

refill [vt riːˈfɪl, n riːfɪl] VT reencher; (lighter etc) reabastecer ▶ N (for pen) carga nova; (Comm) refill m

refine [rɪˈfaɪn] VT refinar

refined [rɪˈfaɪnd] ADJ (person, taste) refinado, culto

refinement [rɪˈfaɪnmənt] N (of person) cultura, refinamento, requinte m; (of system) refinamento

refinery [rɪˈfaɪnərɪ] N refinaria

refit [n riːfɪt, vt riːˈfɪt] N (Naut) reequipamento ▶ VT reequipar

reflate [riːˈfleɪt] VT (economy) reflacionar

reflation [riːˈfleɪʃən] N reflação f

reflationary [riːˈfleɪʃənrɪ] ADJ reflacionário

reflect [rɪˈflɛkt] VT refletir ▶ VI (think) refletir, meditar; **it ~s badly/well on him** isso repercute mal/bem para ele

reflection [rɪˈflɛkʃən] N reflexo; (thought, act) reflexão f; (criticism): **~ on** crítica de; **on ~** pensando bem

reflector [rɪˈflɛktəʳ] N (Aut, on bicycle, for light) refletor m

reflex [ˈriːflɛks] ADJ, N reflexo

reflexive [rɪˈflɛksɪv] ADJ (Ling) reflexivo

reform [rɪˈfɔːm] N reforma ▶ VT reformar

reformat [riːˈfɔːmæt] VT (Comput) reformatar

Reformation [rɛfəˈmeɪʃən] N: **the ~** a Reforma

reformatory [rɪˈfɔːmətərɪ] (US) N reformatório

reformed [rɪˈfɔːmd] ADJ emendado, reformado

reformer [rɪ'fɔ:mə^r] N reformador(a) m/f
reformist [rɪ'fɔ:mɪst] N reformista m/f
refrain [rɪ'freɪn] VI: **to ~ from doing**
abster-se de fazer ▶ N estribilho, refrão m
refresh [rɪ'frɛʃ] VT refrescar
refresher course [rɪ'frɛʃə^r-] (BRIT) N curso de
reciclagem
refreshing [rɪ'frɛʃɪŋ] ADJ refrescante; (sleep)
repousante; (change) agradável; (idea, thought)
original
refreshment [rɪ'frɛʃmənt] N (eating): **for
some ~** para comer alguma coisa; (resting
etc): **in need of ~** precisando se refazer,
precisando refazer as suas forças;
refreshments NPL (food and drink) comes e
bebes mpl
refrigeration [rɪfrɪdʒə'reɪʃən] N refrigeração f
refrigerator [rɪ'frɪdʒəreɪtə^r] N refrigerador m,
geladeira (BR), frigorífico (PT)
refuel [ri:'fjuəl] VT, VI reabastecer
refuge ['rɛfju:dʒ] N refúgio; **to take ~ in**
refugiar-se em
refugee [rɛfju'dʒi:] N refugiado(-a)
refugee camp N campo de refugiados
refund [n 'ri:fʌnd, vt rɪ'fʌnd] N reembolso ▶ VT
devolver, reembolsar
refurbish [ri:'fə:bɪʃ] VT renovar
refurnish [ri:'fə:nɪʃ] VT colocar móveis novos
em
refusal [rɪ'fju:zəl] N recusa, negativa; **first ~**
primeira opção
refuse¹ [rɪ'fju:z] VT recusar; (order) recusar-se
a ▶ VI recusar-se, negar-se; (horse) recusar-se
a pular a cerca; **to ~ to do sth** recusar-se a
fazer algo
refuse² ['rɛfju:s] N refugo, lixo
refuse bin N lata de lixo
refuse collection N remoção f de lixo
refuse collector N lixeiro(-a), gari m/f (BR)
refuse disposal N destruição f de lixo
refuse tip N depósito de lixo
refute [rɪ'fju:t] VT refutar
regain [rɪ'geɪn] VT recuperar, recobrar
regal ['ri:gl] ADJ real, régio
regale [rɪ'geɪl] VT: **to ~ sb with sth** regalar
alguém com algo
regalia [rɪ'geɪlɪə] N, NPL insígnias fpl reais
regard [rɪ'gɑ:d] N (gaze) olhar m firme; (aspect)
respeito; (attention) atenção f; (esteem)
estima, consideração f ▶ VT (consider)
considerar; **to give one's ~s to** dar
lembranças a; **"with kindest ~s"**
"cordialmente"; **as ~s, with ~ to** com
relação a, com respeito a, quanto a
regarding [rɪ'gɑ:dɪŋ] PREP com relação a
regardless [rɪ'gɑ:dlɪs] ADV apesar de tudo;
~ of apesar de
regatta [rɪ'gætə] N regata
regency ['ri:dʒənsɪ] N regência
regenerate [rɪ'dʒɛnəreɪt] VT regenerar ▶ VI
regenerar-se
regent ['ri:dʒənt] N regente m/f
régime [reɪ'ʒi:m] N regime m

regiment [n 'rɛdʒɪmənt, vt 'rɛdʒɪmɛnt] N
regimento ▶ VT regulamentar; (children etc)
subordinar a disciplina rígida
regimental [rɛdʒɪ'mɛntl] ADJ regimental
regimentation [rɛdʒɪmɛn'teɪʃən] N
organização f
region ['ri:dʒən] N região f; **in the ~ of** (fig) por
volta de, ao redor de
regional ['ri:dʒənl] ADJ regional
regional development N desenvolvimento
regional
register ['rɛdʒɪstə^r] N registro (BR), registo
(PT); (Sch) chamada; (list) lista ▶ VT registrar
(BR), registar (PT); (subj: instrument) marcar,
indicar ▶ VI (at hotel) registrar-se (BR),
registar-se (PT); (for work) candidatar-se; (as
student) inscrever-se; (make impression) causar
impressão; **to ~ for a course** matricular-se
num curso; **to ~ a protest** registrar (BR) or
registar (PT) uma queixa
registered ['rɛdʒɪstəd] ADJ (letter, parcel)
registrado (BR), registado (PT); (student)
matriculado; (voter) inscrito
registered company N sociedade f registrada
(BR) or registada (PT)
registered nurse (US) N enfermeiro(-a)
formado(-a)
registered office N sede f social
registered trademark N marca registrada (BR)
or registada (PT)
registrar ['rɛdʒɪstrɑ:^r] N oficial m/f de registro
(BR) or registo (PT), escrivão(-vã) m/f; (in
college) funcionário(-a) administrativo(-a)
sênior; (in hospital) médico(-a) sênior
registration [rɛdʒɪs'treɪʃən] N (act) registro
(BR), registo (PT); (Aut: also: **registration
number**) número da placa
registry ['rɛdʒɪstrɪ] N registro (BR), registo (PT),
cartório
registry office (BRIT) N registro (BR) or registo
(PT) civil, cartório; **to get married in a ~**
casar-se no civil
regret [rɪ'grɛt] N desgosto, pesar m; (remorse)
remorso ▶ VT (deplore) lamentar; (repent of)
arrepender-se de; **to ~ that ...** lamentar
que ... (+sub); **we ~ to inform you that ...**
lamentamos informá-lo de que ...
regretfully [rɪ'grɛtfulɪ] ADV com pesar,
pesarosamente
regrettable [rɪ'grɛtəbl] ADJ deplorável; (loss)
lamentável
regrettably [rɪ'grɛtəblɪ] ADV
lamentavelmente; **~, he was unable ...**
infelizmente, ele não pôde ...
regroup [ri:'gru:p] VT reagrupar ▶ VI
reagrupar-se
regt ABBR = **regiment**
regular ['rɛgjulə^r] ADJ (verb, service, shape)
regular; (frequent) frequente; (usual)
habitual; (soldier) de linha; (listener, reader)
assíduo; (Comm: size) médio ▶ N (client etc)
habitual m/f
regularity [rɛgju'lærɪtɪ] N regularidade f

regularly ['rɛgjʊləlɪ] ADV regularmente; (shaped) simetricamente; (often) frequentemente

regulate ['rɛgjuleɪt] VT (speed) regular; (spending) controlar; (Tech) regular, ajustar

regulation [rɛgju'leɪʃən] N (rule) regra, regulamento; (adjustment) ajuste m ▸ CPD regulamentar

rehabilitation [riːhəbɪlɪ'teɪʃən] N reabilitação f

rehash [riː'hæʃ] (inf) VT retocar

rehearsal [rɪ'həːsəl] N ensaio; see also **dress**

rehearse [rɪ'həːs] VT, VI ensaiar

rehouse [riː'hauz] VT realojar

reign [reɪn] N reinado; (fig) domínio ▸ VI reinar; imperar

reigning ['reɪnɪŋ] ADJ (monarch) reinante; (champion) atual

reimburse [riːɪm'bəːs] VT reembolsar

reimbursement [riːɪm'bəːsmənt] N reembolso

rein [reɪn] N (for horse) rédea; **to give ~ to** dar rédeas a, dar rédea larga a; **to give sb free ~** (fig) dar carta branca a alguém

reincarnation [riːɪnkɑː'neɪʃən] N reencarnação f

reindeer ['reɪndɪəʳ] N INV rena

reinforce [riːɪn'fɔːs] VT reforçar

reinforced [riːɪn'fɔːst] ADJ (concrete) armado

reinforcement [riːɪn'fɔːsmənt] N reforço; **reinforcements** NPL (Mil) reforços mpl

reinstate [riːɪn'steɪt] VT (worker) readmitir; (official) reempossar; (tax, law) reintroduzir

reinstatement [riːɪn'steɪtmənt] N readmissão f

reissue [riː'ɪʃuː] VT (book) reeditar; (film) relançar

reiterate [riː'ɪtəreɪt] VT reiterar, repetir

reject [n 'riːdʒɛkt, vt rɪ'dʒɛkt] N (Comm) artigo defeituoso ▸ VT rejeitar; (offer of help) recusar; (goods) refugar

rejection [rɪ'dʒɛkʃən] N rejeição f; (of offer of help) recusa

rejoice [rɪ'dʒɔɪs] VI: **to ~ at** or **over** regozijar-se or alegrar-se de

rejoinder [rɪ'dʒɔɪndəʳ] N (retort) réplica

rejuvenate [rɪ'dʒuːvəneɪt] VT rejuvenescer

rekindle [riː'kɪndl] VT reacender; (fig) despertar, reanimar

relapse [rɪ'læps] N (Med) recaída; (into crime) reincidência

relate [rɪ'leɪt] VT (tell) contar, relatar; (connect): **to ~ sth to** relacionar algo com ▸ VI: **to ~ to** relacionar-se com; **~d to** ligado a, relacionado a

relating [rɪ'leɪtɪŋ]: **~ to** PREP relativo a, acerca de

relation [rɪ'leɪʃən] N (person) parente m/f; (link) relação f; **relations** NPL (dealings) relações fpl; (relatives) parentes mpl; **diplomatic/international ~s** relações diplomáticas/internacionais; **in ~ to** em relação a; **to bear no ~ to** não ter relação com

relationship [rɪ'leɪʃənʃɪp] N relacionamento; (between two things) relação f; (also: **family relationship**) parentesco; (affair) caso

relative ['rɛlətɪv] N parente m/f ▸ ADJ relativo; (respective) respectivo

relatively ['rɛlətɪvlɪ] ADV relativamente

relax [rɪ'læks] VI (rest) descansar; (unwind) descontrair-se; (muscle) relaxar-se; (calm down) acalmar-se ▸ VT (grip) afrouxar; (control) relaxar; (mind, person) descansar; **~!** (calm down) calma!; **to ~ one's grip** or **hold** afrouxar um pouco

relaxation [riːlæk'seɪʃən] N (rest) descanso; (of muscle, control) relaxamento; (of grip) afrouxamento; (recreation) lazer m

relaxed [rɪ'lækst] ADJ relaxado; (tranquil) descontraído

relaxing [rɪ'læksɪŋ] ADJ relaxante

relay ['riːleɪ] N (race) (corrida de) revezamento ▸ VT (message) retransmitir

release [rɪ'liːs] N (from prison) libertação f; (from obligation) liberação f; (of shot) disparo; (of gas) escape m; (of water) despejo; (of film, book etc) lançamento; (device) desengate m ▸ VT (prisoner) pôr em liberdade; (book, film) lançar; (report, news) publicar; (gas etc) soltar; (free: from wreckage etc) soltar; (Tech: catch, spring etc) desengatar, desapertar; (let go) soltar; **to ~ one's grip** or **hold** afrouxar; **to ~ the clutch** (Aut) desembrear

relegate ['rɛləgeɪt] VT relegar; (Sport): **to be ~d** ser rebaixado

relent [rɪ'lɛnt] VI abrandar-se; (yield) ceder

relentless [rɪ'lɛntlɪs] ADJ (unceasing) contínuo; (determined) implacável

relevance ['rɛləvəns] N pertinência; (of question etc) importância; **~ of sth to sth** relação de algo com algo

relevant ['rɛləvənt] ADJ (fact, information) pertinente; (apt) apropriado; (important) relevante; **~ to** relacionado com

reliability [rɪlaɪə'bɪlɪtɪ] N (of person, firm) confiabilidade f, seriedade f; (of method, machine) segurança; (of news) fidedignidade f

reliable [rɪ'laɪəbl] ADJ (person, firm) de confiança, confiável, sério; (method, machine) seguro; (news) fidedigno

reliably [rɪ'laɪəblɪ] ADV: **to be ~ informed that ...** saber através de fonte segura que ...

reliance [rɪ'laɪəns] N: **~ (on)** (trust) confiança (em), esperança (em); (dependence) dependência (de)

reliant [rɪ'laɪənt] ADJ: **to be ~ on sth/sb** depender de algo/alguém

relic ['rɛlɪk] N (Rel) relíquia; (of the past) vestígio

relief [rɪ'liːf] N (from pain, anxiety) alívio; (help, supplies) ajuda, socorro; (of guard) rendição f; (Art, Geo) relevo; **by way of light ~** como forma de diversão

relief map N mapa m em relevo

relief road (BRIT) N estrada alternativa

relieve [rɪ'li:v] vt (*pain, fear*) aliviar; (*bring help to*) ajudar, socorrer; (*burden*) abrandar, mitigar; (*take over from: gen*) substituir, revezar; (: *guard*) render; **to ~ sb of sth** (*load*) tirar algo de alguém; (*duties*) destituir alguém de algo; **to ~ sb of his command** exonerar alguém, destituir alguém de sua função; **to ~ o.s.** fazer as necessidades
religion [rɪ'lɪdʒən] N religião f
religious [rɪ'lɪdʒəs] ADJ religioso
reline [ri:'laɪn] vt (*brakes*) trocar o forro de
relinquish [rɪ'lɪŋkwɪʃ] vt abandonar; (*plan, habit*) renunciar a
relish ['rɛlɪʃ] N (*Culin*) condimento, tempero; (*enjoyment*) entusiasmo ▶ vt (*food etc*) saborear; (*thought*) ver com satisfação; **to ~ doing** gostar de fazer
relive [ri:'lɪv] vt reviver
reload [ri:'ləud] vt recarregar
relocate [ri:ləu'keɪt] vt deslocar ▶ vi deslocar-se; **to ~ in** instalar-se em
reluctance [rɪ'lʌktəns] N relutância
reluctant [rɪ'lʌktənt] ADJ relutante; **to be ~ to do sth** relutar em fazer algo
reluctantly [rɪ'lʌktəntlɪ] ADV relutantemente, de má vontade
rely on [rɪ'laɪ-] vt FUS confiar em, contar com; (*be dependent on*) depender de
remain [rɪ'meɪn] vi (*survive*) sobreviver; (*stay*) ficar, permanecer; (*be left*) sobrar; (*continue*) continuar; **to ~ silent** ficar calado; **I ~, yours faithfully** (BRIT: *in letters*) subscrevo-me atenciosamente
remainder [rɪ'meɪndər] N resto, restante m
remaining [rɪ'meɪnɪŋ] ADJ restante
remains [rɪ'meɪnz] NPL (*of body*) restos mpl; (*of meal*) sobras fpl; (*of building*) ruínas fpl
remake ['ri:meɪk] N (*Cinema*) refilmagem f
remand [rɪ'mɑ:nd] N: **on ~** sob prisão preventiva ▶ vt: **to be ~ed in custody** continuar sob prisão preventiva, manter sob custódia
remand home (BRIT) N instituição f do juizado de menores, reformatório
remark [rɪ'mɑ:k] N observação f, comentário ▶ vt comentar ▶ vi: **to ~ on sth** comentar algo, fazer um comentário sobre algo
remarkable [rɪ'mɑ:kəbl] ADJ notável; (*outstanding*) extraordinário
remarry [ri:'mærɪ] vi casar-se de novo
remedial [rɪ'mi:dɪəl] ADJ (*tuition, classes*) de reforço; (*exercise*) terapêutico
remedy ['rɛmədɪ] N: **~ (for)** remédio (contra or a) ▶ vt remediar
remember [rɪ'mɛmbər] vt lembrar-se de, lembrar; (*memorize*) guardar; (*bear in mind*) ter em mente; (*send greetings*): **~ me to her** dê lembranças a ela; **I ~ seeing it, I ~ having seen it** eu me lembro de ter visto aquilo; **she ~ed to do it** ela se lembrou de fazer aquilo
remembrance [rɪ'mɛmbrəns] N (*memory*) memória; (*souvenir*) lembrança, recordação f

Remembrance Sunday N *ver nota*

| **Remembrance Sunday** ou **Remembrance Day** é o domingo mais próximo do dia 11 de novembro, dia em que a Primeira Guerra Mundial terminou oficialmente e no qual se homenageia as vítimas das duas guerras mundiais. Nessa ocasião são observados dois minutos de silêncio às 11 horas, horário da assinatura do armistício com a Alemanha em 1918. Nos dias anteriores, papoulas de papel são vendidas por associações de caridade e a renda é revertida aos ex-combatentes e suas famílias.

remind [rɪ'maɪnd] vt: **to ~ sb to do sth** lembrar a alguém que tem de fazer algo; **to ~ sb of sth** lembrar algo a alguém, lembrar alguém de algo; **she ~s me of her mother** ela me lembra a mãe dela; **that ~s me, ...** falando nisso, ...
reminder [rɪ'maɪndər] N lembrete m; (*souvenir*) lembrança; (*letter*) carta de advertência
reminisce [rɛmɪ'nɪs] vi relembrar velhas histórias; **to ~ about sth** relembrar algo
reminiscences [rɛmɪ'nɪsnsɪz] NPL recordações fpl, lembranças fpl
reminiscent [rɛmɪ'nɪsənt] ADJ: **to be ~ of sth** lembrar algo
remiss [rɪ'mɪs] ADJ negligente, desleixado; **it was ~ of him** foi um descuido dele
remission [rɪ'mɪʃən] N remissão f; (*of sentence*) diminuição f
remit [rɪ'mɪt] vt (*send: money*) remeter, enviar, mandar
remittance [rɪ'mɪtəns] N remessa
remnant ['rɛmnənt] N resto; (*of cloth*) retalho; **remnants** NPL (*Comm*) retalhos mpl
remonstrate ['rɛmənstreɪt] vi: **to ~ (with sb about sth)** reclamar (a alguém de algo)
remorse [rɪ'mɔ:s] N remorso
remorseful [rɪ'mɔ:sful] ADJ arrependido
remorseless [rɪ'mɔ:slɪs] ADJ (*fig*) implacável
remote [rɪ'məut] ADJ (*distant*) remoto, distante; (*person*) reservado, afastado; (*slight*): **there is a ~ possibility that ...** existe uma possibilidade remota de que ...
remote control N controle m remoto
remote-controlled [-kən'trəuld] ADJ (*plane*) telecomandado; (*missile*) teleguiado
remotely [rɪ'məutlɪ] ADV remotamente; (*slightly*) levemente
remoteness [rɪ'məutnɪs] N afastamento, isolamento
remould ['ri:məuld] (BRIT) N (*tyre*) pneu m recauchutado
removable [rɪ'mu:vəbl] ADJ (*detachable*) removível
removal [rɪ'mu:vəl] N (*taking away*) remoção f; (BRIT: *from house*) mudança; (*from office: sacking*) afastamento, demissão f; (*Med*) extração f
removal man (*irreg: like* **man**) N homem m da companhia de mudanças

r

removal van (BRIT) N caminhão m (BR) or camião m (PT) de mudanças

remove [rɪˈmuːv] VT tirar, retirar; (clothing) tirar; (stain) remover; (employee) afastar, demitir; (name from list, obstacle) eliminar, remover; (doubt, abuse) afastar; (Tech) retirar, separar; (Med) extrair, extirpar; **first cousin once ~d** primo(-a) em segundo grau

remover [rɪˈmuːvəʳ] N (substance) removedor m; **removers** NPL (BRIT: company) companhia de mudanças

remunerate [rɪˈmjuːnəreɪt] VT remunerar

remuneration [rɪmjuːnəˈreɪʃən] N remuneração f

Renaissance [rɪˈneɪsɔns] N: **the ~** a Renascença

rename [riːˈneɪm] VT dar novo nome a

rend [rɛnd] (pt, pp rent) VT rasgar, despedaçar

render [ˈrɛndəʳ] VT (thanks) trazer; (service) prestar; (account) entregar; (make) fazer, tornar; (translate) traduzir; (fat: also: **render down**) clarificar; (wall) rebocar

rendering [ˈrɛndərɪŋ] N (Mus etc) interpretação f

rendezvous [ˈrɔndɪvuː] N encontro; (place) ponto de encontro ▸ VI encontrar-se; **to ~ with sb** encontrar-se com alguém

renegade [ˈrɛnɪgeɪd] N renegado(-a)

renew [rɪˈnjuː] VT renovar; (resume) retomar, recomeçar; (loan etc) prorrogar; (negotiations, acquaintance) reatar

renewable [rɪˈnjuːəbl] ADJ renovável

renewal [rɪˈnjuːəl] N (of contract) renovação f; (resumption) retomada; (of loan) prorrogação f

renounce [rɪˈnauns] VT renunciar a; (disown) repudiar, rejeitar

renovate [ˈrɛnəveɪt] VT renovar; (house, room) reformar

renovation [rɛnəˈveɪʃən] N renovação f; (of house etc) reforma

renown [rɪˈnaun] N renome m

renowned [rɪˈnaund] ADJ renomado, famoso

rent [rɛnt] PT, PP of **rend** ▸ N aluguel m (BR), aluguer m (PT) ▸ VT (also: **rent out**) alugar

rental [ˈrɛntəl] N (for television, car) aluguel m (BR), aluguer m (PT)

rent boy N (BRIT inf) michê m

renunciation [rɪnʌnsɪˈeɪʃən] N renúncia

reopen [riːˈəupən] VT reabrir

reopening [riːˈəupənɪŋ] N reabertura

reorder [riːˈɔːdəʳ] VT encomendar novamente; (rearrange) reorganizar

reorganize [riːˈɔːgənaɪz] VT reorganizar

rep [rɛp] N ABBR (Comm) = **representative**; (Theatre) = **repertory**

Rep. (US) ABBR (Pol) = **representative**; **republican**

repaid [riːˈpeɪd] PT, PP of **repay**

repair [rɪˈpɛəʳ] N reparação f, conserto; (patch) remendo ▸ VT consertar; **beyond ~** irreparável; **in good/bad ~** em bom/mau estado; **under ~** no conserto

repair kit N caixa de ferramentas

repair man (irreg: like **man**) N consertador m

repair shop N oficina de reparos

repartee [rɛpɑːˈtiː] N resposta arguta e engenhosa; (skill) presteza em replicar

repast [rɪˈpɑːst] N (formal) repasto

repatriate [riːˈpætrɪeɪt] VT repatriar

repay [riːˈpeɪ] (irreg: like **pay**) VT (money) reembolsar, restituir; (person) pagar de volta; (debt) saldar, liquidar; (sb's efforts) corresponder, retribuir; (favour) retribuir

repayment [riːˈpeɪmənt] N reembolso; (of debt) pagamento; (of mortgage etc) prestação f

repeal [rɪˈpiːl] N (of law) revogação f; (of sentence) anulação f ▸ VT revogar; anular

repeat [rɪˈpiːt] N (Radio, TV) repetição f ▸ VT repetir; (Comm: order) renovar ▸ VI repetir-se

repeatedly [rɪˈpiːtɪdlɪ] ADV repetidamente

repel [rɪˈpɛl] VT repelir; (disgust) repugnar

repellent [rɪˈpɛlənt] ADJ repugnante ▸ N: **insect ~** repelente m de insetos

repent [rɪˈpɛnt] VI: **to ~ (of)** arrepender-se (de)

repentance [rɪˈpɛntəns] N arrependimento

repercussions [riːpəˈkʌʃənz] NPL repercussões fpl; **to have ~** repercutir

repertoire [ˈrɛpətwɑːʳ] N repertório

repertory [ˈrɛpətərɪ] N (also: **repertory theatre**) teatro de repertório

repertory company N companhia teatral

repetition [rɛpɪˈtɪʃən] N repetição f

repetitious [rɛpɪˈtɪʃəs] ADJ (speech) repetitivo

repetitive [rɪˈpɛtɪtɪv] ADJ repetitivo

replace [rɪˈpleɪs] VT (put back) repor, devolver; (take the place of) substituir; (Tel): **"~ the receiver"** "desligue"

replacement [rɪˈpleɪsmənt] N (substitution) substituição f; (putting back) reposição f; (substitute) substituto(-a)

replacement part N peça sobressalente

replay [ˈriːpleɪ] N (of match) partida decisiva; (TV: also: **action replay**) replay m

replenish [rɪˈplɛnɪʃ] VT (glass) reencher; (stock etc) completar, prover; (with fuel) reabastecer

replete [rɪˈpliːt] ADJ repleto; (well-fed) cheio, empanturrado

replica [ˈrɛplɪkə] N réplica, cópia, reprodução f

reply [rɪˈplaɪ] N resposta ▸ VI responder; **in ~ (to)** em resposta (a); **there's no ~** (Tel) ninguém atende

reply coupon N cartão-resposta m

report [rɪˈpɔːt] N relatório m; (Press etc) reportagem f; (BRIT: also: **school report**) boletim m escolar; (of gun) estampido, detonação f ▸ VT informar sobre; (Press etc) fazer uma reportagem sobre; (bring to notice: occurrence) comunicar, anunciar; (: person) denunciar ▸ VI (make a report): **to ~ (on)** apresentar um relatório (sobre); (for newspaper) fazer uma reportagem (sobre); (present o.s.): **to ~ (to sb)** apresentar-se (a alguém); (be responsible to): **to ~ to sb** obedecer as ordens de alguém; **it is ~ed that** dizem que; **it is ~ed from Berlin that** há notícias de Berlim de que

report card (*US*, *SCOTLAND*) N boletim *m* escolar
reportedly [rɪ'pɔːtɪdlɪ] ADV: **she is ~ living in Spain** dizem que ela mora na Espanha
reported speech [rɪ'pɔːtɪd-] N (*Ling*) discurso indireto
reporter [rɪ'pɔːtəʳ] N (*Press*) jornalista *m/f*, repórter *m/f*; (*Radio, TV*) repórter
repose [rɪ'pəuz] N: **in ~** em repouso
repossess [riːpə'zɛs] VT retomar
reprehensible [rɛprɪ'hɛnsɪbl] ADJ repreensível, censurável, condenável
represent [rɛprɪ'zɛnt] VT representar; (*constitute*) constituir; (*Comm*) ser representante de; (*describe*): **to ~ sth as** representar algo como; (*explain*): **to ~ to sb that** explicar a alguém que
representation [rɛprɪzɛn'teɪʃən] N representação *f*; (*picture, statue*) representação, retrato; (*petition*) petição *f*; **representations** NPL (*protest*) reclamação *f*, protesto
representative [rɛprɪ'zɛntətɪv] N representante *m/f*; (*US Pol*) deputado(-a) ▶ ADJ: **~ (of)** representativo (de)
repress [rɪ'prɛs] VT reprimir
repression [rɪ'prɛʃən] N repressão *f*
repressive [rɪ'prɛsɪv] ADJ repressivo
reprieve [rɪ'priːv] N (*Law*) suspensão *f* temporária; (*fig*) adiamento ▶ VT suspender temporariamente; aliviar
reprimand ['rɛprɪmɑːnd] N reprimenda ▶ VT repreender, censurar
reprint [*n* 'riːprɪnt, *vt* riː'prɪnt] N reimpressão *f* ▶ VT reimprimir
reprisal [rɪ'praɪzl] N represália; **reprisals** NPL (*acts of revenge*) represálias *fpl*; **to take ~s** fazer *or* exercer represálias
reproach [rɪ'prəutʃ] N repreensão *f*, censura ▶ VT: **to ~ sb with sth** repreender alguém por algo; **beyond ~** irrepreensível, impecável
reproachful [rɪ'prəutʃful] ADJ repreensivo, acusatório
reproduce [riːprə'djuːs] VT reproduzir ▶ VI reproduzir-se
reproduction [riːprə'dʌkʃən] N reprodução *f*
reproductive [riːprə'dʌktɪv] ADJ reprodutivo
reproof [rɪ'pruːf] N reprovação *f*, repreensão *f*
reprove [rɪ'pruːv] VT (*action*) reprovar; **to ~ sb for sth** repreender alguém por algo
reproving [rɪ'pruːvɪŋ] ADJ (*look*) de reprovação; (*tone*) de censura
reptile ['rɛptaɪl] N réptil *m*
Repub. (*US*) ABBR (*Pol*) = **republican**
republic [rɪ'pʌblɪk] N república
republican [rɪ'pʌblɪkən] ADJ, N republicano(-a); (*US Pol*): **R~** membro(-a) do Partido Republicano
repudiate [rɪ'pjuːdɪeɪt] VT (*accusation*) rejeitar, negar; (*violence*) repudiar; (*obligation*) desconhecer
repugnant [rɪ'pʌgnənt] ADJ repugnante, repulsivo

repulse [rɪ'pʌls] VT repelir
repulsion [rɪ'pʌlʃən] N repulsa; (*Phys*) repulsão *f*
repulsive [rɪ'pʌlsɪv] ADJ repulsivo
reputable ['rɛpjutəbl] ADJ (*make etc*) bem conceituado, de confiança; (*person*) honrado, respeitável
reputation [rɛpju'teɪʃən] N reputação *f*; **to have a ~ for** ter fama por; **he has a ~ for being cruel** ele tem fama de ser cruel
repute [rɪ'pjuːt] N reputação *f*, renome *m*
reputed [rɪ'pjuːtɪd] ADJ suposto, pretenso; **he is ~ to be rich** dizem que ele é rico
reputedly [rɪ'pjuːtɪdlɪ] ADV segundo se diz, supostamente
request [rɪ'kwɛst] N pedido; (*formal*) petição *f* ▶ VT: **to ~ sth of** *or* **from sb** pedir algo a alguém; (*formally*) solicitar algo a alguém; **on ~** a pedido; **at the ~ of** a pedido de; **"you are ~ed not to smoke"** "pede-se *or* favor não fumar"
request stop (*BRIT*) N (*for bus*) parada não obrigatória
requiem ['rɛkwɪəm] N réquiem *m*
require [rɪ'kwaɪəʳ] VT (*need: subj: person*) precisar de, necessitar; (: *thing, situation*) requerer, exigir; (*want*) pedir; (*order*): **to ~ sb to do sth/sth of sb** exigir que alguém faça algo/algo de alguém; **if ~d** se for necessário; **what qualifications are ~d?** quais são as qualificações necessárias?; **~d by law** exigido por lei
required [rɪ'kwaɪəd] ADJ (*necessary*) necessário; (*desired*) desejado
requirement [rɪ'kwaɪəmənt] N requisito; (*need*) necessidade *f*; (*want*) pedido
requisite ['rɛkwɪzɪt] N requisito ▶ ADJ necessário, indispensável; **toilet ~s** artigos de toalete pessoal
requisition [rɛkwɪ'zɪʃən] N: **~ (for)** requerimento (para) ▶ VT (*Mil*) requisitar, confiscar
reroute [riː'ruːt] VT (*train etc*) desviar
resale ['riːseɪl] N revenda
resale price maintenance N manutenção *f* de preços de revenda
rescind [rɪ'sɪnd] VT (*contract*) rescindir; (*law*) revogar; (*verdict*) anular
rescue ['rɛskjuː] N salvamento, resgate *m* ▶ VT: **to ~ (from)** (*survivors, wounded etc*) resgatar (de); (*save, fig*) salvar (de); **to come to sb's ~** ir ao socorro de alguém
rescue party N grupo *or* expedição *f* de resgate
rescuer ['rɛskjuəʳ] N (*in disaster etc*) resgatador(a) *m/f*; (*fig*) salvador(a) *m/f*
research [rɪ'səːtʃ] N pesquisa ▶ VT pesquisar ▶ VI: **to ~ (into sth)** pesquisar (algo), fazer pesquisas (sobre algo); **a piece of ~** uma pesquisa; **~ and development** pesquisa e desenvolvimento
researcher [rɪ'səːtʃəʳ] N pesquisador(a) *m/f*
research work N trabalho de pesquisa
resell [riː'sɛl] (*irreg: like* **sell**) VT revender

resemblance [rɪ'zɛmbləns] N semelhança; **to bear a strong ~ to** ser muito parecido com

resemble [rɪ'zɛmbl] VT parecer-se com

resent [rɪ'zɛnt] VT (attitude) ressentir-se de; (person) estar ressentido com

resentful [rɪ'zɛntful] ADJ ressentido

resentment [rɪ'zɛntmənt] N ressentimento

reservation [rɛzə'veɪʃən] N (booking, doubt, protected area) reserva; (BRIT Aut: also: **central reservation**) canteiro divisor; **to make a ~** fazer reserva; **with ~s** (doubts) com reservas

reservation desk (US) N (in hotel) recepção f

reserve [rɪ'zə:v] N reserva; (Sport) suplente m/f, reserva m/f (BR) ► VT reservar; **reserves** NPL (Mil) (tropas fpl da) reserva; (Comm) reserva; **in ~** de reserva

reserve currency N moeda de reserva

reserved [rɪ'zə:vd] ADJ reservado

reserve price (BRIT) N preço mínimo de venda

reserve team (BRIT) N time m reserva

reservist [rɪ'zə:vɪst] N reservista m

reservoir ['rɛzəvwɑ:ʳ] N (large) represa; (small) depósito

reset [ri:'sɛt] (irreg: like **set**) VT reajustar; (Comput) dar reset em

reshape [ri:'ʃeɪp] VT (policy) reformar, remodelar

reshuffle [ri:'ʃʌfl] N: **Cabinet ~** reforma ministerial

reside [rɪ'zaɪd] VI residir

residence ['rɛzɪdəns] N residência; (formal: home) domicílio; **to take up ~** instalar-se; **in ~** (monarch) em residência; (doctor) residente

residence permit (BRIT) N autorização f de residência

resident ['rɛzɪdənt] N (of country, town) habitante m/f; (of house, area) morador(a) m/f; (in hotel) hóspede m/f ► ADJ (population) permanente; (doctor) interno, residente

residential [rɛzɪ'dɛnʃəl] ADJ residencial

residue ['rɛzɪdju:] N resto; (Comm) montante m líquido; (Chem, Phys) resíduo

resign [rɪ'zaɪn] VT (one's post) renunciar a, demitir-se de ► VI: **to ~ (from)** demitir-se (de); **to ~ o.s.** (endure) resignar-se a

resignation [rɛzɪg'neɪʃən] N demissão f; (state of mind) resignação f; **to tender one's ~** pedir demissão

resigned [rɪ'zaɪnd] ADJ resignado

resilience [rɪ'zɪlɪəns] N (of material) elasticidade f; (of person) resistência

resilient [rɪ'zɪlɪənt] ADJ (person) forte; (material) resistente

resin ['rɛzɪn] N resina

resist [rɪ'zɪst] VT resistir a

resistance [rɪ'zɪstəns] N resistência

resistant [rɪ'zɪstənt] ADJ: **~ (to)** resistente (a)

resold [ri:'səuld] PT, PP of **resell**

resolute ['rɛzəlu:t] ADJ resoluto, firme; (refusal) firme

resolution [rɛzə'lu:ʃən] N resolução f; (of problem) solução f; **to make a ~** tomar uma resolução

resolve [rɪ'zɔlv] N resolução f; (purpose) intenção f ► VT resolver ► VI: **to ~ to do** resolver-se a fazer

resolved [rɪ'zɔlvd] ADJ decidido

resonance ['rɛzənəns] N ressonância

resonant ['rɛzənənt] ADJ ressonante

resort [rɪ'zɔ:t] N (town) local m turístico, estação f de veraneio; (recourse) recurso ► VI: **to ~ to** recorrer a; **seaside/winter sports ~** balneário/estação de inverno; **in the last ~** em último caso, em última instância

resound [rɪ'zaund] VI ressoar; **the room ~ed with shouts** os gritos ressoaram no quarto

resounding [rɪ'zaundɪŋ] ADJ retumbante

resource [rɪ'sɔ:s] N (raw material) recurso natural; **resources** NPL (coal, money, energy) recursos mpl; **natural ~s** recursos naturais

resourceful [rɪ'sɔ:sful] ADJ engenhoso, habilidoso

resourcefulness [rɪ'sɔ:sfəlnɪs] N desembaraço, engenho

respect [rɪ'spɛkt] N respeito ► VT respeitar; **respects** NPL (greetings) cumprimentos mpl; **to pay one's ~s to sb** fazer visita de cortesia a alguém; **to pay one's last ~s to sb** prestar a última homenagem a alguém; **to have** or **show ~ for sb/sth** ter or mostrar respeito por alguém/algo; **out of ~ for** por respeito a; **with ~ to** com respeito a; **in ~ of** a respeito de; **in this ~** neste respeito; **in some ~s** em alguns pontos; **with all due ~, I ...** com todo respeito, eu ...

respectability [rɪspɛktə'bɪlɪtɪ] N respeitabilidade f

respectable [rɪ'spɛktəbl] ADJ respeitável; (large) considerável; (quite good: result, player) razoável

respectful [rɪ'spɛktful] ADJ respeitoso

respective [rɪ'spɛktɪv] ADJ respectivo

respectively [rɪ'spɛktɪvlɪ] ADV respectivamente

respiration [rɛspɪ'reɪʃən] N respiração f

respiratory [rɛ'spɪrətərɪ] ADJ respiratório

respite ['rɛspaɪt] N pausa, folga; (Law) adiamento, suspensão f

resplendent [rɪ'splɛndənt] ADJ resplandecente

respond [rɪ'spɔnd] VI (answer) responder; (react) reagir

respondent [rɪ'spɔndənt] N (in survey) respondedor(a) m/f; (Law) réu/ré m/f

response [rɪ'spɔns] N (answer) resposta f; (reaction) reação f; **in ~ to** em resposta a

responsibility [rɪspɔnsɪ'bɪlɪtɪ] N responsabilidade f; (duty) dever m; **to take ~ for sth/sb** assumir a responsabilidade por algo/alguém

responsible [rɪ'spɔnsɪbl] ADJ (character) sério, responsável; (job) de responsabilidade; (liable): **~ (for)** responsável (por); **to be ~ to**

sb (for sth) ser responsável diante de alguém (por algo); **to hold sb ~ (for sth)** responsabilizar alguém (por algo)

responsibly [rɪ'spɔnsɪblɪ] ADV com responsabilidade

responsive [rɪ'spɔnsɪv] ADJ receptivo

rest [rɛst] N descanso, repouso; (*pause*) pausa, intervalo; (*support*) apoio; (*remainder*) resto; (*Mus*) pausa ▶ vi descansar; (*stop*) parar; (*be supported*): **to ~ on** apoiar-se em ▶ vt descansar; (*lean*): **to ~ sth on/against** apoiar algo em or sobre/contra; **the ~ of them** os outros; **to set sb's mind at ~** tranquilizar alguém; **it ~s with him to do it** cabe a ele fazê-lo; **~ assured that ...** tenha certeza de que ...

restart [riː'stɑːt] vt (*engine*) arrancar de novo; (*work*) reiniciar, recomeçar

restaurant ['rɛstərɔŋ] N restaurante *m*

restaurant car (BRIT) N vagão-restaurante *m*

rest cure N repouso forçado (*para tratamento de saúde*)

restful ['rɛstful] ADJ tranquilo, repousante

rest home N asilo, casa de repouso

restitution [rɛstɪ'tjuːʃən] N: **to make ~ to sb for sth** indenizar alguém por algo

restive ['rɛstɪv] ADJ inquieto, impaciente; (*horse*) rebelão(-ona), teimoso

restless ['rɛstlɪs] ADJ desassossegado, irrequieto; **to get ~** impacientar-se

restlessly ['rɛstlɪslɪ] ADV inquietamente

restock [riː'stɔk] vt reabastecer

restoration [rɛstə'reɪʃən] N restauração *f*

restorative [rɪ'stɔrətɪv] ADJ reconstituinte ▶ N reconstituinte *m*

restore [rɪ'stɔːʳ] vt (*building, order*) restaurar; (*sth stolen*) restituir; (*peace, health*) restabelecer

restorer [rɪ'stɔːrəʳ] N (*Art etc*) restaurador(a) *m/f*

restrain [rɪ'streɪn] vt (*feeling*) reprimir; (*growth, inflation*) refrear; (*person*): **to ~ (from doing)** impedir (de fazer)

restrained [rɪ'streɪnd] ADJ (*style*) moderado, comedido; (*person*) comedido

restraint [rɪ'streɪnt] N (*restriction*) restrição *f*; (*moderation*) moderação *f*, comedimento; (*of style*) sobriedade *f*; **wage ~** restrição salarial

restrict [rɪ'strɪkt] vt restringir, limitar; (*people, animals*) confinar; (*activities*) limitar

restricted area [rɪ'strɪktɪd-] N (*Aut*) zona com limite de velocidade

restriction [rɪ'strɪkʃən] N restrição *f*, limitação *f*; **~ (on)** restrição (em)

restrictive [rɪ'strɪktɪv] ADJ restritivo

restrictive practices NPL (*Industry*) práticas *fpl* restritivas

rest room (US) N banheiro (BR), lavabo (PT)

restructure [riː'strʌktʃəʳ] vt reestruturar

result [rɪ'zʌlt] N resultado ▶ vi: **to ~ (from)** resultar (de); **to ~ in** resultar em; **as a ~ of** como resultado or consequência de

resultant [rɪ'zʌltənt] ADJ resultante

resume [rɪ'zjuːm] vt (*work, journey*) retomar, recomeçar; (*sum up*) resumir ▶ vi recomeçar

résumé ['reɪzjuːmeɪ] N (*summary*) resumo; (*US: curriculum vitae*) curriculum vitae *m*, currículo

resumption [rɪ'zʌmpʃən] N retomada

resurgence [rɪ'səːdʒəns] N ressurgimento

resurrection [rɛzə'rɛkʃən] N ressurreição *f*

resuscitate [rɪ'sʌsɪteɪt] vt (*Med*) ressuscitar, reanimar

resuscitation [rɪsʌsɪ'teɪʃən] N ressuscitação *f*

retail ['riːteɪl] N varejo (BR), venda a retalho (PT) ▶ ADJ a varejo (BR), a retalho (PT) ▶ ADV a varejo (BR), a retalho (PT) ▶ vt vender no varejo (BR) or a retalho (PT) ▶ vi: **to ~ at $10** ser vendido no varejo (BR) or a retalho (PT) por $10

retailer ['riːteɪləʳ] N varejista *m/f* (BR), retalhista *m/f* (PT)

retail outlet N ponto de venda

retail price N preço no varejo (BR) or de venda a retalho (PT)

retail price index N ≈ índice *m* de preços ao consumidor

retain [rɪ'teɪn] vt (*keep*) reter, conservar; (*employ*) contratar

retainer [rɪ'teɪnəʳ] N (*servant*) empregado; (*fee*) adiantamento

retaliate [rɪ'tælɪeɪt] vi: **to ~ (against)** revidar (contra)

retaliation [rɪtælɪ'eɪʃən] N represálias *fpl*, vingança; **in ~ for** em retaliação por

retaliatory [rɪ'tælɪətərɪ] ADJ retaliativo, retaliatório

retarded [rɪ'tɑːdɪd] ADJ retardado

retch [rɛtʃ] vi fazer esforço para vomitar

retentive [rɪ'tɛntɪv] ADJ (*memory*) tenaz, de anjo

rethink ['riː'θɪŋk] (*irreg: like* **think**) vt reconsiderar, repensar

reticence ['rɛtɪsns] N reserva

reticent ['rɛtɪsnt] ADJ reservado

retina ['rɛtɪnə] N retina

retinue ['rɛtɪnjuː] N séquito, comitiva

retire [rɪ'taɪəʳ] vi (*give up work*) aposentar-se; (*withdraw*) retirar-se; (*go to bed*) deitar-se

retired [rɪ'taɪəd] ADJ (*person*) aposentado (BR), reformado (PT)

retirement [rɪ'taɪəmənt] N (*state, act*) aposentadoria (BR), reforma (PT)

retirement age N idade *f* de aposentadoria (BR) or de reforma (PT)

retiring [rɪ'taɪərɪŋ] ADJ (*leaving*) de saída; (*shy*) acanhado, retraído

retort [rɪ'tɔːt] N (*reply*) réplica; (*container*) retorta ▶ vi replicar, retrucar

retrace [riː'treɪs] vt: **to ~ one's steps** voltar sobre (os) seus passos, refazer o mesmo caminho

retract [rɪ'trækt] vt (*statement, offer*) retirar, retratar; (*claws*) encolher; (*undercarriage, aerial*) recolher ▶ vi retratar-se

retractable [rɪ'træktəbl] ADJ retrátil

retrain [riː'treɪn] vt reciclar ▶ vi ser reciclado

r

retraining [riː'treɪnɪŋ] N readaptação f
profissional, reciclagem f

retread [n 'riː'trɛd, vt riː'trɛd] N (tyre) pneu m
recauchutado ▶ vt recauchutar

retreat [rɪ'triːt] N (place) retiro; (act) retirada
▶ vi retirar-se; (flood) retroceder; **to beat a
hasty ~** bater em retirada

retrial [riː'traɪəl] N revisão f do processo

retribution [rɛtrɪ'bjuːʃən] N desforra, revide m,
vingança

retrieval [rɪ'triːvəl] N recuperação f

retrieve [rɪ'triːv] vt (sth lost) reaver, recuperar;
(situation, honour) salvar; (error, loss) reparar;
(Comput) recuperar

retriever [rɪ'triːvəʳ] N cão m de busca,
perdigueiro

retroactive [rɛtrəʊ'æktɪv] ADJ retroativo

retrograde ['rɛtrəgreɪd] ADJ retrógrado

retrospect ['rɛtrəspɛkt] N: **in ~**
retrospectivamente, em retrospecto

retrospective [rɛtrə'spɛktɪv] ADJ
retrospectivo; (law) retroativo ▶ N (Art)
retrospectiva

return [rɪ'təːn] N (going or coming back) regresso,
volta; (of sth stolen etc) devolução f;
(recompense) recompensa; (Finance: from land,
shares) rendimento; (report) relatório ▶ CPD
(journey) de volta; (BRIT: ticket) de ida e volta;
(match) de revanche ▶ vi (person etc: come or go
back) voltar, regressar; (symptoms etc) voltar;
(regain): **to ~ to** (consciousness) recobrar; (power)
retornar a ▶ vt devolver; (favour, love etc)
retribuir; (verdict) proferir, anunciar; (Pol:
candidate) eleger; **returns** NPL (Comm) receita;
(: returned goods) mercadorias fpl devolvidas;
in ~ (for) em troca (de); **many happy ~s
(of the day)!** parabéns!; **by ~ (of post)** por
volta do correio

returnable [rɪ'təːnəbl] ADJ (bottle etc)
restituível

return key N (Comput) tecla de retorno

retweet [riː'twiːt] N (on Twitter) retweet m

reunion [riː'juːnɪən] N (family) reunião f; (two
people, class) reencontro

reunite [riːjuː'naɪt] vt reunir; (reconcile)
reconciliar

rev [rɛv] N ABBR (Aut: = revolution) revolução f
▶ vt (also: **rev up**) aumentar a velocidade de
▶ vi acelerar

Rev. ABBR = **reverend**

revaluation [riːvæljuː'eɪʃən] N reavaliação f

revamp ['riː'væmp] vt dar um jeito em

rev counter (BRIT) N tacômetro

Revd. ABBR = **reverend**

reveal [rɪ'viːl] vt revelar; (make visible)
mostrar

revealing [rɪ'viːlɪŋ] ADJ revelador(a)

reveille [rɪ'vælɪ] N (Mil) toque m de alvorada

revel ['rɛvl] vi: **to ~ in sth/in doing sth**
deleitar-se com algo/em fazer algo

revelation [rɛvə'leɪʃən] N revelação f

reveller ['rɛvləʳ] N farrista m/f, folião(-liã) m/f

revelry ['rɛvəlrɪ] N festança, folia

revenge [rɪ'vɛndʒ] N vingança, desforra; (in
sport) revanche f ▶ vt vingar; **to take ~ on**
vingar-se de

revengeful [rɪ'vɛndʒful] ADJ vingativo

revenue ['rɛvənjuː] N receita, renda; (on
investment) rendimento

reverberate [rɪ'vəːbəreɪt] vi (sound) ressoar,
repercutir, ecoar; (light) reverberar; (fig)
repercutir

reverberation [rɪvəːbə'reɪʃən] N
repercussão f

revere [rɪ'vɪəʳ] vt reverenciar, venerar

reverence ['rɛvərəns] N reverência

reverend ['rɛvrənd] ADJ reverendo; (in titles):
the R~ John Smith o reverendo John Smith

reverent ['rɛvərənt] ADJ reverente

reverie ['rɛvərɪ] N devaneio, sonho

reversal [rɪ'vəːsl] N (of order) reversão f; (of
direction) mudança em sentido contrário;
(of decision) revogação f; (of opinion)
reviravolta; (of roles) inversão f

reverse [rɪ'vəːs] N (opposite) contrário; (back: of
cloth) avesso; (: of coin) reverso; (: of paper)
dorso; (Aut: also: **reverse gear**) marcha à ré
(BR), marcha atrás (PT); (setback) revés m,
derrota ▶ ADJ (order) inverso, oposto;
(direction) contrário; (process) inverso ▶ vt
(turn over) virar do lado do avesso; (direction,
roles) inverter; (position) mudar; (process,
decision) revogar; (car) dar ré com ▶ vi (BRIT
Aut) dar (marcha à) ré (BR), fazer marcha
atrás (PT); **to go into ~** dar ré (BR), fazer
marcha atrás (PT); **in ~ order** na ordem
inversa

reverse-charge call (BRIT) N (Tel) ligação f a
cobrar

reverse video N vídeo reverso

reversible [rɪ'vəːsəbl] ADJ reversível

reversing lights [rɪ'vəːsɪŋ-] (BRIT) NPL luzes fpl
de ré (BR), luzes fpl de marcha atrás (PT)

reversion [rɪ'vəːʃən] N volta

revert [rɪ'vəːt] vi: **to ~ to** voltar a; (Law)
reverter a

review [rɪ'vjuː] N (magazine, Mil) revista; (of
book, film) crítica, resenha; (examination)
recapitulação f, exame m ▶ vt (situation)
rever, examinar; (Mil) passar em revista;
(book, film) fazer a crítica or resenha de; **to
come under ~** ser estudado

reviewer [rɪ'vjuːəʳ] N crítico(-a)

revile [rɪ'vaɪl] vt insultar

revise [rɪ'vaɪz] vt (manuscript) corrigir; (opinion,
procedure) alterar; (price) revisar; (study: subject)
recapitular; (look over) revisar, rever; **~d
edition** edição f revista

revision [rɪ'vɪʒən] N correção f; (for exam)
revisão f; (revised version) revisão f

revitalize [riː'vaɪtəlaɪz] vt revitalizar,
revivificar

revival [rɪ'vaɪvəl] N (recovery)
restabelecimento; (of interest) renascença,
renascimento; (Theatre) reestreia; (of faith)
despertar m

revive [rɪ'vaɪv] VT (*person*) reanimar, ressuscitar; (*economy*) recuperar; (*custom*) restabelecer, restaurar; (*hope, courage*) despertar; (*play*) reapresentar ▶ VI (*person: from faint*) voltar a si, recuperar os sentidos; (*: from ill-health*) recuperar-se; (*activity, economy*) reativar-se; (*hope, interest*) renascer

revoke [rɪ'vəuk] VT revogar; (*decision, promise*) voltar atrás com

revolt [rɪ'vəult] N revolta, rebelião f, insurreição f ▶ VI revoltar-se ▶ VT causar aversão a, repugnar

revolting [rɪ'vəultɪŋ] ADJ revoltante, repulsivo

revolution [rɛvə'luːʃən] N revolução f; (*of wheel, earth*) rotação f

revolutionary [rɛvə'luːʃənərɪ] ADJ, N revolucionário(-a)

revolutionize [rɛvə'luːʃənaɪz] VT revolucionar

revolve [rɪ'vɔlv] VI girar; (*life*): **to ~ (a)round** girar em torno de

revolver [rɪ'vɔlvə^r] N revólver m

revolving [rɪ'vɔlvɪŋ] ADJ (*chair etc*) giratório

revolving credit N crédito rotativo

revolving door N porta giratória

revue [rɪ'vjuː] N (*Theatre*) revista

revulsion [rɪ'vʌlʃən] N aversão f, repugnância

reward [rɪ'wɔːd] N recompensa ▶ VT: **to ~ (for)** recompensar or premiar (por)

rewarding [rɪ'wɔːdɪŋ] ADJ (*fig*) gratificante, compensador(a)

rewind [riː'waɪnd] (*irreg: like* **wind**) VT (*watch*) dar corda em; (*tape*) voltar para trás

rewire [riː'waɪə^r] VT (*house*) renovar a instalação elétrica de

reword [riː'wəːd] VT reformular, exprimir em outras palavras

rewound [riː'waund] PT, PP *of* **rewind**

rewritable [riː'raɪtəbl] ADJ regravável

rewrite [riː'raɪt] (*irreg: like* **write**) VT reescrever, escrever de novo

Reykjavik ['reɪkjəviːk] N Reikjavik

RFD (*US*) ABBR (*Post*) = **rural free delivery**

Rh ABBR (= *rhesus*) Rh

rhapsody ['ræpsədɪ] N (*Mus*) rapsódia; (*fig*) elocução f exagerada or empolada

rhesus factor ['riːsəs-] N (*Med*) fator m Rh

rhetoric ['rɛtərɪk] N retórica

rhetorical [rɪ'tɔrɪkl] ADJ retórico

rheumatic [ruː'mætɪk] ADJ reumático

rheumatism ['ruːmətɪzəm] N reumatismo

rheumatoid arthritis ['ruːmətɔɪd-] N artrite f reumatoide

Rhine [raɪn] N: **the ~** o (rio) Reno

rhinestone ['raɪnstəun] N diamante m postiço

rhinoceros [raɪ'nɔsərəs] N rinoceronte m

Rhodes [rəudz] N (ilha de) Rodes

Rhodesia [rəu'diːʒə] N Rodésia

Rhodesian [rəu'diːʒən] ADJ, N rodésio(-a)

rhododendron [rəudə'dɛndrən] N rododendro

Rhone [rəun] N: **the ~** o (rio) Ródano

rhubarb ['ruːbɑːb] N ruibarbo

rhyme [raɪm] N rima; (*verse*) verso(s) m(pl) rimado(s), poesia ▶ VI: **to ~ (with)** rimar (com); **without ~ or reason** sem pé nem cabeça

rhythm ['rɪðm] N ritmo

rhythmic ['rɪðmɪk], **rhythmical** ['rɪðmɪkl] ADJ rítmico, com passado

rhythmically ['rɪðmɪklɪ] ADV ritmicamente

RI N ABBR (*BRIT*) = **religious instruction** ▶ ABBR (*US Post*) = **Rhode Island**

rib [rɪb] N (*Anat*) costela ▶ VT (*mock*) zombar de, encarnar em

ribald ['rɪbəld] ADJ vulgarmente engraçado, irreverente

ribbed [rɪbd] ADJ (*knitting*) em ponto de meia

ribbon ['rɪbən] N fita; (*strip*) faixa, tira; **in ~s** (*torn*) em tirinhas, esfarrapado

rice [raɪs] N arroz m

rice field N arrozal m

rice pudding N arroz m doce

rich [rɪtʃ] ADJ rico; (*clothes*) valioso; (*banquet*) suntuoso, opulento; (*soil*) fértil; (*food*) suculento, forte; (*: sweet*) rico; (*colour*) intenso; (*voice*) suave, cheio ▶ NPL: **the ~** os ricos; **riches** NPL (*wealth*) riquezas fpl; **to be ~ in sth** ser rico em algo

richly ['rɪtʃlɪ] ADV (*decorated*) ricamente; (*rewarded*) generosamente; (*deserved*) bem

richness ['rɪtʃnɪs] N riqueza, opulência; (*of soil etc*) fertilidade f

rickets ['rɪkɪts] N raquitismo

rickety ['rɪkɪtɪ] ADJ fraco, sem firmeza

rickshaw ['rɪkʃɔː] N jinriquixá m

ricochet ['rɪkəʃeɪ] N ricochete m ▶ VI ricochetear

rid [rɪd] (*pt, pp* **rid**) VT: **to ~ sb of sth** livrar alguém de algo; **to get ~ of** livrar-se de; (*sth no longer required*) desfazer-se de

riddance ['rɪdns] N: **good ~!** bons ventos o levem!

ridden ['rɪdn] PP *of* **ride**

riddle ['rɪdl] N (*conundrum*) adivinhação f; (*mystery*) enigma m, charada ▶ VT: **to be ~d with** estar cheio de

ride [raɪd] (*pt* **rode**, *pp* **ridden**) N (*gen*) passeio; (*on horse*) passeio a cavalo; (*distance covered*) percurso, trajeto ▶ VI (*as sport*) montar; (*go somewhere: on horse, bicycle*) ir (a cavalo, de bicicleta); (*journey: on bicycle, motorcycle, bus*) viajar ▶ VT (*a horse*) montar a; (*bicycle, motorcycle*) andar de; (*distance*) percorrer; **to ~ a bicycle** andar de bicicleta; **can you ~ a bike?** você sabe andar de bicicleta?; **to ~ at anchor** (*Naut*) estar ancorado; **horse/car ~** passeio a cavalo/de carro; **to go for a ~** dar um passeio or uma volta (de carro or de bicicleta *etc*); **to take sb for a ~** (*fig*) enganar alguém

▶ **ride out** VT: **to ~ out the storm** (*fig*) superar as dificuldades

rider ['raɪdə^r] N (*on horse: male*) cavaleiro; (*: female*) amazona; (*on bicycle*) ciclista m/f; (*on* *motorcycle*) motociclista *m/f*; (*in document*) cláusula adicional

ridge [rɪdʒ] N (*of hill*) cume *m*, topo; (*of roof*) cumeeira; (*wrinkle*) ruga

ridicule ['rɪdɪkjuːl] N escárnio, zombaria, mofa ▸ VT ridicularizar, zombar de; **to hold sb/sth up to ~** ridicularizar alguém/algo

ridiculous [rɪ'dɪkjuləs] ADJ ridículo

riding ['raɪdɪŋ] N equitação *f*

riding school N escola de equitação

rife [raɪf] ADJ: **to be ~** ser comum; **to be ~ with** estar repleto de, abundar em

riffraff ['rɪfræf] N plebe *f*, ralé *f*, povinho

rifle ['raɪfl] N rifle *m*, fuzil *m* ▸ VT saquear
▸ **rifle through** VT FUS vasculhar

rifle range N campo de tiro; (*at fair*) tiro ao alvo

rift [rɪft] N (*in ground*) fenda, fratura; (*in clouds*) brecha; (*fig: disagreement: between friends*) desentendimento; (: *in party*) rompimento, divergência

rig [rɪg] N (*also*: **oil rig**) torre *f* de perfuração
▸ VT (*election etc*) adulterar *or* falsificar os resultados de
▸ **rig out** (*BRIT*) VT: **to ~ out as/in** ataviar *or* vestir como/com
▸ **rig up** VT instalar, montar, improvisar

rigging ['rɪgɪŋ] N (*Naut*) cordame *m*

right [raɪt] ADJ (*true, correct*) certo, correto; (*suitable*) adequado, conveniente; (: *decision*) certo; (*just*) justo; (*morally good*) bom; (*not left*) direito ▸ N direito; (*not left*) direita ▸ ADV (*correctly*) bem, corretamente; (*fairly*) adequadamente, justamente; (*not on the left*) à direita; (*to the right*) para a direita; (*exactly*): **~ now** agora mesmo ▸ VT colocar em pé; (*correct*) corrigir, indireitar ▸ EXCL bom!; **all ~!** tudo bem!, está bem!; (*enough*) chega!, basta!; **the ~ time** (*precise*) a hora exata; (*not wrong*) a hora certa; **to be ~** (*person*) ter razão (: *in guess etc*) acertar; (*answer, clock*) estar certo; **to get sth ~** acertar em algo; **let's get it ~ this time!** vamos acertar desta vez; **you did the ~ thing** você fez a coisa certa; **to put a mistake ~** (*BRIT*) consertar um erro; **~ before/after** logo antes/depois; **~ against the wall** rente à parede; **to go ~ to the end of sth** ir até o finalzinho de algo; **by ~s** por direito; **on the ~** à direita; **to be in the ~** ter razão; **~ away** imediatamente, logo, já; **~ in the middle** bem no meio; **film ~s** direitos de adaptação para o cinema

right angle N ângulo reto

righteous ['raɪtʃəs] ADJ justo, honrado; (*anger*) justificado

righteousness ['raɪtʃəsnɪs] N justiça

rightful ['raɪtful] ADJ (*heir*) legítimo; (*place*) justo, legítimo

rightfully ['raɪtfəlɪ] ADV legitimamente

right-hand ADJ à direita

right-handed [-'hændɪd] ADJ (*person*) destro

right-hand man N braço direito

right-hand side N lado direito

rightly ['raɪtlɪ] ADV corretamente, devidamente; (*with reason*) com razão; **if I remember ~** (*BRIT*) se me lembro bem, se não me engano

right-minded ADJ sensato, ajuizado

right of way N prioridade *f* de passagem; (*Aut*) preferência

rights issue N (*Stock Exchange*) emissão *f* de bônus de subscrição

right wing N (*Pol*) direita; (*Sport*) ponta direita; (*Mil*) ala direita ▸ ADJ: **right-wing** de direita

right-wing ADJ de direita

right-winger N (*Pol*) direitista *m/f*; (*Sport*) ponta-direita *m*

rigid ['rɪdʒɪd] ADJ rígido; (*principle*) inflexível

rigidity [rɪ'dʒɪdɪtɪ] N rigidez *f*, inflexibilidade *f*

rigidly ['rɪdʒɪdlɪ] ADV rigidamente; (*behave*) inflexivelmente

rigmarole ['rɪgmərəul] N (*process*) processo; (*story*) ladainha

rigor ['rɪgə'] (*US*) N = **rigour**

rigor mortis [-'mɔːtɪs] N rigidez *f* cadavérica

rigorous ['rɪgərəs] ADJ rigoroso

rigorously ['rɪgərəslɪ] ADV rigorosamente

rigour, (*US*) **rigor** ['rɪgə'] N rigor *m*

rig-out (*BRIT inf*) N roupa, traje *m*

rile [raɪl] VT irritar, aborrecer

rim [rɪm] N borda, beira; (*of spectacles, wheel*) aro

rimless ['rɪmlɪs] ADJ (*spectacles*) sem aro

rind [raɪnd] N (*of bacon*) pele *f*; (*of lemon etc*) casca; (*of cheese*) crosta, casca

ring [rɪŋ] (*pt* **rang**, *pp* **rung**) N (*of metal*) aro; (*on finger*) anel *m*; (*also*: **wedding ring**) aliança; (*of people, objects*) círculo, grupo; (*of spies etc*) grupo; (*for boxing*) ringue *m*; (*of circus*) pista, picadeiro; (*bullring*) picadeiro, arena; (*of light, smoke*) círculo; (*sound: of small bell*) toque *m*; (: *of large bell*) badalada, repique *m*; (*telephone call*) chamada (telefônica), ligada ▸ VI (*on telephone*) telefonar; (*bell*) tocar; (*also*: **ring out**: *voice, words*) soar; (*ears*) zumbir ▸ VT (*BRIT Tel*) telefonar a, ligar para; (*bell etc*) badalar; (*doorbell*) tocar; **to give sb a ~** (*BRIT Tel*) dar uma ligada *or* ligar para alguém; **that has the ~ of truth about it** isso tem jeito de ser verdade; **the name doesn't ~ a bell (with me)** o nome não me diz nada
▸ **ring back** (*BRIT*) VI (*Tel*) telefonar *or* ligar de volta ▸ VT telefonar *or* ligar de volta para
▸ **ring off** (*BRIT*) VI (*Tel*) desligar
▸ **ring up** (*BRIT*) VT (*Tel*) telefonar a, ligar para

ring binder N fichário (*pasta*)

ring-fence VT (*money, tax*) restringir (o uso de alguma verba)

ring finger N dedo anelar

ringing ['rɪŋɪŋ] N (*of telephone*) toque *m*; (*of large bell*) repicar *m*; (*of doorbell*) tocar *m*; (*in ears*) zumbido

ringing tone (*BRIT*) N (*Tel*) sinal *m* de chamada

ringleader ['rɪŋliːdə'] N (*of gang*) cabeça *m/f*, cérebro

ringlets ['rɪŋlɪts] NPL caracóis *mpl*, anéis *mpl*
ring road ['rɪŋtəun] (BRIT) N estrada
periférica *or* perimetral
ringtone ['rɪŋtəun] (BRIT) N (*on cellphone*)
toque *m*
rink [rɪŋk] N (*also*: **ice rink**) pista de patinação,
rinque *m*; (*for roller skating*) rinque
rinse [rɪns] N enxaguada ▶ VT enxaguar; (*also*:
rinse out: *mouth*) bochechar
Rio ['ri:əu], **Rio de Janeiro**
['ri:əudədʒə'nɪərəu] N o Rio (de Janeiro)
riot ['raɪət] N distúrbio, motim *m*, desordem *f*;
(*of colour*) festival *m*, profusão *f* ▶ VI provocar
distúrbios, amotinar-se; **to run ~**
desenfrear-se
rioter ['raɪətə^r] N desordeiro(-a),
amotinador(a) *m/f*
riotous ['raɪətəs] ADJ (*crowd*) desordeiro;
(*behaviour*) turbulento; (*party*) tumultuado,
barulhento; (*uncontrolled*) desenfreado
riotously ['raɪətəslɪ] ADV: **~ funny** hilariante
riot police N polícia anti-motim
RIP ABBR (= *rest in peace*) RIP
rip [rɪp] N rasgão *m*; (*opening*) abertura ▶ VT
rasgar ▶ VI rasgar-se
▶ **rip up** VT rasgar
ripcord ['rɪpkɔːd] N corda de abertura (de
para-quedas)
ripe [raɪp] ADJ maduro; (*ready*) pronto
ripen ['raɪpən] VT, VI amadurecer
ripeness ['raɪpnɪs] N maturidade *f*,
amadurecimento
rip-off (*inf*) N: **this is a ~** isso é roubo
riposte [rɪ'pɔst] N riposta
ripple ['rɪpl] N ondulação *f*, encrespação *f*; (*of
laughter etc*) onda; (*sound*) murmúrio ▶ VI
encrespar-se ▶ VT ondular
rise [raɪz] VI (*pt* **rose**, *pp* **risen**) (*gen*) levantar-
se, erguer-se; (*prices, waters*) subir; (*river*)
encher; (*sun*) nascer; (*wind, person: from bed etc*)
levantar(-se); (*sound, voice*) aumentar, erguer-
se; (*also*: **rise up**: *building*) erguer-se; (: *rebel*)
sublevar-se; (*in rank*) ascender, subir ▶ N
(*slope*) elevação *f*, ladeira; (*hill*) colina, rampa;
(*increase*: BRIT: *in wages*) aumento; (: *in prices,
temperature*) subida; (*fig: to power etc*) ascensão *f*;
to ~ to the occasion mostrar-se à altura
da situação; **to give ~ to** ocasionar, dar
origem a
risen ['rɪzn] PP *of* **rise**
rising ['raɪzɪŋ] ADJ (*increasing: prices*) em alta;
(: *number*) crescente, cada vez maior;
(: *unemployment*) crescente; (*tide*) montante;
(*sun, moon*) nascente ▶ N (*uprising*) insurreição *f*
rising damp N umidade *f* que sobe
risk [rɪsk] N risco, perigo; (*Insurance*) risco ▶ VT
(*endanger*) pôr em risco; (*chance*) arriscar,
aventurar; (*dare*) atrever-se a; **to take** *or* **run
the ~ of doing** correr o risco de fazer; **at ~**
em perigo; **at one's own ~** por sua própria
conta e risco; **a fire/health/security ~** um
risco de incêndio/à saúde/à segurança;
I'll ~ it eu vou me arriscar

risk capital N capital *m* de risco
risky ['rɪskɪ] ADJ perigoso
risqué ['ri:skeɪ] ADJ (*joke*) picante
rissole ['rɪsəul] N rissole *m*
rite [raɪt] N rito; **funeral ~s** exéquias,
cerimônia fúnebre; **last ~s** últimos
sacramentos
ritual ['rɪtjuəl] ADJ ritual ▶ N ritual *m*; (*of
initiation*) rito
rival ['raɪvl] ADJ, N rival *m/f*; (*in business*)
concorrente *m/f* ▶ VT competir com; **to ~ sb/
sth in** rivalizar com alguém/algo em
rivalry ['raɪvlrɪ] N rivalidade *f*; (*between
companies*) concorrência
river ['rɪvə^r] N rio ▶ CPD (*port, traffic*) fluvial;
up/down ~ rio acima/abaixo
riverbank ['rɪvəbæŋk] N margem *f* (do rio)
riverbed ['rɪvəbɛd] N leito (do rio)
riverside ['rɪvəsaɪd] N beira, orla (do rio)
rivet ['rɪvɪt] N rebite *m*, cravo ▶ VT rebitar; (*fig*)
fixar
riveting ['rɪvɪtɪŋ] ADJ (*fig*) fascinante
Riviera [rɪvɪ'ɛərə] N: **the (French) ~** a Costa
Azul (francesa), a Riviera francesa; **the
Italian ~** a Riviera italiana
Riyadh [rɪ'jɑːd] N Riad
RN N ABBR (BRIT) = **Royal Navy**; (US)
= **registered nurse**
RNA N ABBR (= *ribonucleic acid*) ARN *m*
RNLI (BRIT) N ABBR (= *Royal National Lifeboat
Institution*) ≈ Salvamar
RNZAF N ABBR = **Royal New Zealand Air Force**
RNZN N ABBR = **Royal New Zealand Navy**
road [rəud] N via; (*motorway etc*) estrada (de
rodagem); (*in town*) rua; (*fig*) caminho ▶ CPD
rodoviário; **main ~** estrada principal;
major/minor ~ via preferencial/
secundária; **it takes four hours by ~**
leva quatro horas de carro; **"~ up"** (BRIT)
"obras"
road accident N acidente *m* de trânsito
roadblock ['rəudblɔk] N barricada
road haulage N transportes *mpl* rodoviários
road hog N dono da estrada
road map N mapa *m* rodoviário
road rage N *conduta agressiva dos motoristas no
trânsito*
road safety N segurança do trânsito
roadside ['rəudsaɪd] N beira da estrada ▶ CPD
à beira da estrada; **by the ~** à beira da
estrada
road sign N placa de sinalização
road sweeper (BRIT) N (*person*) gari *m/f* (BR),
varredor(a) *m/f* (PT)
road transport N transportes *mpl* rodoviários
road user N usuário(-a) da via pública
roadway ['rəudweɪ] N pista, estrada
road works ['rəudwəːks] NPL obras *fpl* (na
estrada)
roadworthy ['rəudwəːðɪ] ADJ (*car*) em bom
estado de conservação e segurança
roam [rəum] VI vagar, perambular, errar ▶ VT
vagar *or* vadiar por

r

roar [rɔ:ʳ] N (of animal) rugido, urro; (of crowd) bramido; (of vehicle, storm) estrondo; (of laughter) barulho ▶ VI (animal, engine) rugir; (person, crowd) bradar; **to ~ with laughter** dar gargalhadas

roaring ['rɔ:rɪŋ] ADJ: **a ~ fire** labaredas; **a ~ success** um sucesso estrondoso; **to do a ~ trade** fazer um bom negócio

roast [rəust] N carne f assada, assado ▶ VT assar; (coffee) torrar

roast beef N rosbife m

rob [rɔb] VT roubar; (bank) assaltar; **to ~ sb of sth** roubar algo de alguém; (fig: deprive) despojar alguém de algo

robber ['rɔbəʳ] N ladrão/ladra m/f

robbery ['rɔbərɪ] N roubo

robe [rəub] N (for ceremony etc) toga, beca; (also: **bath robe**) roupão m (de banho) ▶ VT revestir

robin ['rɔbɪn] N pisco-de-peito-ruivo (BR), pintarroxo (PT)

robot ['rəubɔt] N robô m

robotics [rə'bɔtɪks] N robótica

robust [rəu'bʌst] ADJ robusto, forte; (appetite) sadio; (economy) forte

rock [rɔk] N rocha; (boulder) penhasco, rochedo; (US: small stone) cascalho; (BRIT: sweet) pirulito ▶ VT (swing gently: cradle) balançar, oscilar; (: child) embalar, acalentar; (shake) sacudir ▶ VI (object) balançar-se; (person) embalar-se; (shake) sacudir-se; **on the ~s** (drink) com gelo; (marriage etc) arruinado, em dificuldades; **to ~ the boat** (fig) criar confusão

rock and roll N rock-and-roll m

rock-bottom ADJ (fig) mínimo, ínfimo ▶ N: **to hit** or **reach ~** (prices) chegar ao nível mais baixo; (person) chegar ao fundo do poço

rock climber N alpinista m/f

rock climbing N alpinismo

rockery ['rɔkərɪ] N jardim de plantas rasteiras entre pedras

rocket ['rɔkɪt] N foguete m ▶ VI (prices) disparar

rocket launcher [-'lɔ:ntʃəʳ] N dispositivo lança-foguetes

rock face N rochedo a pique

rock fall N queda de pedras

rocking chair ['rɔkɪŋ-] N cadeira de balanço

rocking horse ['rɔkɪŋ-] N cavalo de balanço

rocky ['rɔkɪ] ADJ rochoso; (unsteady: table) bambo, instável; (marriage etc) instável

Rocky Mountains NPL: **the ~** as Montanhas Rochosas

rod [rɔd] N vara, varinha; (Tech) haste f; (also: **fishing rod**) vara de pescar

rode [rəud] PT of **ride**

rodent ['rəudnt] N roedor m

rodeo ['rəudɪəu] (US) N rodeio

roe [rəu] N (also: **roe deer**) corça, cerva; (of fish): **hard/soft ~** ova/esperma m de peixe

rogue [rəug] N velhaco, maroto

roguish ['rəugɪʃ] ADJ travesso, brincalhão(-lhona)

role [rəul] N papel m

role model ['rəulmɔdl] N modelo

roll [rəul] N rolo; (of banknotes) maço; (also: **bread roll**) pãozinho; (register) rol m, lista; (sound: of drums etc) rufar m; (movement: of ship) jogo ▶ VT rolar; (also: **roll up**: string) enrolar; (: sleeves) arregaçar; (cigarette) enrolar; (eyes) virar; (also: **roll out**: pastry) esticar; (lawn, road etc) aplanar ▶ VI rolar; (drum) rufar; (in walking) gingar; (vehicle: also: **roll along**) rodar; (ship) balançar, jogar; **cheese ~** sanduíche de queijo (num pãozinho)
  ▶ **roll about** VI ficar rolando
  ▶ **roll around** VI = **roll about**
  ▶ **roll by** VI (time) passar
  ▶ **roll in** VI (mail, cash) chegar em grande quantidade
  ▶ **roll over** VI dar uma volta
  ▶ **roll up** VI (inf: arrive) pintar, chegar, aparecer
  ▶ VT (carpet etc) enrolar; (sleeves) arregaçar;
  to ~ o.s. up into a ball enrolar-se

roll call N chamada, toque m de chamada

rolled gold [rəuld-] N plaquê m

roller ['rəuləʳ] N (in machine) rolo, cilindro; (wheel) roda, roldana; (for lawn, road) rolo compressor; (for hair) rolo

Rollerblades® ['rəubleidz] N patins mpl em linha

roller blind (BRIT) N estore m

roller coaster N montanha-russa

roller skates NPL patins mpl de roda

rollicking ['rɔlɪkɪŋ] ADJ alegre, brincalhão(-lhona), divertido

rolling ['rəulɪŋ] ADJ (landscape) ondulado

rolling mill N laminador m

rolling pin N rolo de pastel

rolling stock N (Rail) material m rodante

roll-on-roll-off (BRIT) ADJ (ferry) para veículos

roly-poly ['rəulɪ'pəulɪ] (BRIT) N (Culin) bolo de rolo

ROM [rɔm] N ABBR (Comput: = read-only memory) ROM f

Roman ['rəumən] ADJ, N romano(-a)

Roman Catholic ADJ, N católico(-a) (romano(-a))

romance [rə'mæns] N (love affair) aventura amorosa, romance m; (book etc) história de amor; (charm) romantismo

Romania [ru:'meɪnɪə] N Romênia

Romanian [ru:'meɪnɪən] ADJ romeno ▶ N romeno(-a); (Ling) romeno

Roman numeral N número romano

romantic [rə'mæntɪk] ADJ romântico

romanticism [rə'mæntɪsɪzəm] N romantismo

Romany ['rəumənɪ] ADJ cigano ▶ N cigano(-a); (Ling) romani m

Rome [rəum] N Roma

romp [rɔmp] N brincadeira, travessura ▶ VI (also: **romp about**) brincar ruidosamente; **to ~ home** (horse) ganhar fácil

rompers ['rɔmpəz] NPL macacão m de bebê

rondo ['rɔndəu] N (Mus) rondó

roof [ruːf] N (*of house*) telhado; (*of car*) capota, teto; (*of tunnel, cave*) teto ▶ VT telhar, cobrir com telhas; **the ~ of the mouth** o céu da boca

roof garden N jardim *m* em terraço

roofing ['ruːfɪŋ] N cobertura

roof rack N (*Aut*) bagageiro

rook [ruk] N (*bird*) gralha; (*Chess*) torre *f*

room [ruːm] N (*in house*) quarto, aposento; (*also*: **bedroom**) quarto, dormitório; (*in school etc*) sala; (*space*) espaço, lugar *m*; (*scope: for improvement etc*) espaço; **rooms** NPL (*lodging*) alojamento; **"~s to let"** (BRIT), **"~s for rent"** (US) "alugam-se quartos *or* apartamentos"; **single ~** quarto individual; **double ~** quarto duplo *or* de casal *or* para duas pessoas; **is there ~ for this?** tem lugar para isto aqui?; **to make ~ for sb** dar lugar a alguém; **there is ~ for improvement** isso podia estar melhor

rooming house ['ruːmɪŋ-] (US) N casa de cômodos

roommate ['ruːmmeɪt] N companheiro(-a) de quarto

room service N serviço de quarto

room temperature N temperatura ambiente

roomy ['ruːmɪ] ADJ espaçoso; (*garment*) folgado

roost [ruːst] N poleiro ▶ VI empoleirar-se, pernoitar

rooster ['ruːstəʳ] N galo

root [ruːt] N raiz *f*; (*fig: of problem, belief*) origem *f* ▶ VI (*plant, belief*) enraizar, arraigar; **roots** NPL (*family origins*) raízes *fpl*; **to take ~** (*plant*) enraizar; (*idea*) criar raízes
  ▶ **root about** VI (*fig*): **to ~ about in** (*drawer*) vasculhar; (*house*) esquadrinhar
  ▶ **root for** VT FUS torcer por
  ▶ **root out** VT extirpar

rope [rəup] N corda; (*Naut*) cabo ▶ VT (*tie*) amarrar; (*horse, cow*) laçar; (*climbers: also*: **rope together**) amarrar *or* atar com uma corda; (*area: also*: **rope off**) isolar; **to know the ~s** (*fig*) estar por dentro (do assunto)
  ▶ **rope in** VT (*fig*): **to ~ sb in** persuadir alguém a tomar parte

rope ladder N escada de corda

rose [rəuz] PT *of* **rise** ▶ N rosa; (*also*: **rosebush**) roseira; (*on watering can*) crivo ▶ ADJ rosado, cor de rosa *inv*

rosé ['rəuzeɪ] N rosado, rosé *m*

rose bed N roseiral *m*

rosebud ['rəuzbʌd] N botão *m* de rosa

rosebush ['rəuzbuʃ] N roseira

rosemary ['rəuzmərɪ] N alecrim *m*

rosette [rəu'zɛt] N roseta

ROSPA ['rɔspə] (BRIT) N ABBR = **Royal Society for the Prevention of Accidents**

roster ['rɔstəʳ] N: **duty ~** lista de tarefas, escala de serviço

rostrum ['rɔstrəm] N tribuna

rosy ['rəuzɪ] ADJ rosado, rosáceo; (*cheeks*) rosado; (*situation*) cor-de-rosa *inv*; **a ~ future**

um futuro promissor

rot [rɔt] N (*decay*) putrefação *f*, podridão *f*; (*fig: pej*) besteira ▶ VT, VI apodrecer; **to stop the ~** (BRIT fig) acabar com a onda de fracassos; **dry ~** apodrecimento seco (*de madeira*); **wet ~** putrefação fungosa

rota ['rəutə] N lista de tarefas, escala de serviço; **on a ~ basis** em rodízio

rotary ['rəutərɪ] ADJ rotativo

rotate [rəu'teɪt] VT (*revolve*) fazer girar, dar voltas em; (*change round: crops*) alternar; (*: jobs*) alternar, revezar ▶ VI (*revolve*) girar, dar voltas

rotating [rəu'teɪtɪŋ] ADJ (*movement*) rotativo

rotation [rəu'teɪʃən] N rotação *f*; **in ~** por turnos

rote [rəut] N: **by ~** de cor

rotor ['rəutəʳ] N (*also*: **rotor blade**) rotor *m*

rotten ['rɔtn] ADJ (*decayed*) podre; (*wood*) carcomido; (*fig*) corrupto; (*inf: bad*) péssimo; **to feel ~** (*ill*) sentir-se podre

rotting ['rɔtɪŋ] ADJ podre

rotund [rəu'tʌnd] ADJ rotundo; (*person*) rechonchudo

rouble, (US) **ruble** ['ruːbl] N rublo

rouge [ruːʒ] N rouge *m*, blush *m*, carmim *m*

rough [rʌf] ADJ (*skin, surface*) áspero; (*terrain*) acidentado; (*road*) desigual; (*voice*) áspero, rouco; (*person, manner: coarse*) grosseiro, grosso; (*: violent*) violento; (*: brusque*) ríspido; (*weather*) tempestuoso; (*treatment*) brutal, mau/má; (*sea*) agitado; (*district*) violento; (*plan*) preliminar; (*work, cloth*) grosseiro; (*guess*) aproximado ▶ N (*person*) grosseirão *m*; (*Golf*): **in the ~** na grama crescida; **to have a ~ time** (*of it*) passar maus bocados; **~ estimate** estimativa aproximada; **to ~ it** passar aperto; **to play ~** jogar bruto; **to sleep ~** (BRIT) dormir na rua; **to feel ~** (BRIT) passar mal
  ▶ **rough out** VT (*draft*) rascunhar

roughage ['rʌfɪdʒ] N fibras *fpl*

rough-and-ready ADJ improvisado, feito às pressas

rough-and-tumble N luta, confusão *f*

roughcast ['rʌfkaːst] N reboco

rough copy N rascunho

rough draft N rascunho

roughen ['rʌfən] VT (*surface*) tornar áspero

rough justice N justiça sumária

roughly ['rʌflɪ] ADV (*handle*) bruscamente; (*make*) toscamente; (*speak*) bruscamente; (*approximately*) aproximadamente

roughness ['rʌfnɪs] N aspereza; (*rudeness*) grosseria

roughshod ['rʌfʃɔd] ADV: **to ride ~ over** (*person*) tratar a pontapés; (*objection*) passar por cima de

rough work N (*at school etc*) rascunho

roulette [ruː'lɛt] N roleta

Roumania [ruː'meɪnɪə] N = **Romania**

round [raund] ADJ redondo ▶ N círculo; (BRIT: *of toast*) rodela; (*of drinks*) rodada; (*of*

policeman) ronda; (*of milkman*) trajeto; (*of doctor*) visitas *fpl*; (*game: of cards, golf, in competition*) partida; (*stage of competition*) rodada, turno; (*of ammunition*) cartucho; (*Boxing*) rounde *m*, assalto; (*of talks*) ciclo ▶ VT (*corner*) virar, dobrar; (*bend*) fazer; (*cape*) dobrar ▶ PREP (*surrounding*): ~ **his neck/the table** em volta de seu pescoço/ao redor da mesa; (*in a circular movement*): **to go ~ the world** dar a volta ao mundo; (*in various directions*): **to move ~ a house** mover-se por uma casa; (*approximately*): ~ **about** aproximadamente ▶ ADV: **all ~, right ~** por todos os lados; **the long way ~** o caminho mais comprido; **all the year ~** durante todo o ano; **in ~ figures** em números redondos; **it's just ~ the corner** está logo depois de virar a esquina; (*fig*) está pertinho; ~ **the clock** ininterrupto; **to ask sb ~** convidar alguém (para sua casa); **I'll be ~ at 6 o'clock** passo aí às 6 horas; **to go ~** dar a volta; **to go ~ to sb's (house)** dar um pulinho na casa de alguém; **to go ~ an obstacle** contornar um obstáculo; **to go ~ the back** passar por detrás; **to go ~ a house** visitar uma casa; **enough to go ~** suficiente para todos; **she arrived ~ (about) noon** (*BRIT*) ela chegou por volta do meio-dia; **to go the ~s** (*story*) divulgar-se; **the daily ~** (*fig*) o cotidiano; **a ~ of applause** uma salva de palmas; **a ~ of drinks** uma rodada de bebidas; ~ **of sandwiches** sanduíche *m* (*BR*), sandes *f inv* (*PT*)
▶ **round off** VT (*speech etc*) terminar, completar
▶ **round up** VT (*cattle*) encurralar; (*people*) reunir; (*price, figure*) arredondar

roundabout ['raundəbaut] N (*BRIT: Aut*) rotatória; (: *at fair*) carrossel *m* ▶ ADJ (*route, means*) indireto

rounded ['raundɪd] ADJ arredondado; (*style*) expressivo

rounders ['raundəz] NPL (*game*) jogo semelhante ao beisebol

roundly ['raundlɪ] ADV (*fig*) energicamente, totalmente

round-shouldered [-'ʃəuldəd] ADJ encurvado

roundsman ['raundzmən] (*BRIT*) (*irreg: like* **man**) N entregador *m* a domicílio

round trip N viagem *f* de ida e volta

roundup ['raundʌp] N (*of news*) resumo; (*of animals*) rodeio; (*of criminals*) batida

rouse [rauz] VT (*wake up*) despertar, acordar; (*stir up*) suscitar

rousing ['rauzɪŋ] ADJ emocionante, vibrante

rout [raut] N (*Mil*) derrota; (*flight*) fuga, debandada ▶ VT derrotar

route [ruːt] N caminho, rota; (*of bus*) trajeto; (*of shipping*) rumo, rota; (*of procession*) rota; **"all ~s"** (*Aut*) "todas as direções"; **the best ~ to London** o melhor caminho para Londres; **en ~ for** a caminho de; **en ~ from ... to** a caminho de ... para

route map (*BRIT*) N (*for journey*) mapa *m* rodoviário; (*for trains etc*) mapa da rede

routine [ruː'tiːn] ADJ (*work*) rotineiro; (*procedure*) de rotina ▶ N rotina; (*Theatre*) número; **daily ~** cotidiano

rove [rəuv] VT vagar por, perambular por

roving ['rəuvɪŋ] ADJ (*wandering*) errante

roving reporter N correspondente *m/f*

row¹ [rəu] N (*line*) fila, fileira; (*in theatre, boat*) fileira; (*Knitting*) carreira, fileira ▶ VI, VT remar; **in a ~** (*fig*) a fio, seguido

row² [rau] N (*racket*) barulho, balbúrdia; (*dispute*) discussão *f*, briga; (*fuss*) confusão *f*, bagunça; (*scolding*) repreensão *f* ▶ VI brigar; **to have a ~** ter uma briga

rowboat ['rəubəut] (*US*) N barco a remo

rowdiness ['raudɪnɪs] N barulheira; (*fighting*) brigas *fpl*

rowdy ['raudɪ] ADJ (*person: noisy*) barulhento; (: *quarrelsome*) brigão(-ona); (*occasion*) tumultuado ▶ N encrenqueiro, criador *m* de caso

rowdyism ['raudɪɪzəm] N violência

rowing ['rəuɪŋ] N remo

rowing boat (*BRIT*) N barco a remo

rowlock ['rɔlək] (*BRIT*) N toleteira, forqueta

royal ['rɔɪəl] ADJ real

Royal Academy (*BRIT*) N *ver nota*

> A **Royal Academy**, ou **Royal Academy of Arts**, fundada em 1768 por George III para desenvolver a pintura, a escultura e a arquitetura, situa-se em Burlington House, Piccadilly. A cada verão há uma exposição de obras de artistas contemporâneos. A **Royal Academy** também oferece cursos de pintura, escultura e arquitetura.

Royal Air Force (*BRIT*) N força aérea britânica

royal blue ADJ azul vivo *inv*

royalist ['rɔɪəlɪst] ADJ, N monarquista *m/f* (*BR*), monárquico(-a) (*PT*)

Royal Navy (*BRIT*) N marinha de guerra britânica

royalty ['rɔɪəltɪ] N (*persons*) família real, realeza; (*payment: to author*) direitos *mpl* autorais; (: *to inventor*) direitos *mpl* de exploração de patente

RP (*BRIT*) N ABBR (= *received pronunciation*) norma de pronúncia

rpm ABBR (= *revolutions per minute*) rpm

RR (*US*) ABBR = **railroad**

RSA (*BRIT*) N ABBR = **Royal Society of Arts**; **Royal Scottish Academy**

RSI N ABBR (*Med*: = *repetitive strain injury*) lesão *f* por esforço repetitivo, LER *f*

RSPB (*BRIT*) N ABBR = **Royal Society for the Protection of Birds**

RSPCA (*BRIT*) N ABBR = **Royal Society for the Prevention of Cruelty to Animals**

RSVP ABBR (= *répondez s'il vous plaît*) ER

Rt Hon. (*BRIT*) ABBR (= *Right Honourable*) título honorífico de conselheiro do estado ou juiz

Rt Rev. ABBR (= *Right Reverend*) reverendíssimo

rub [rʌb] VT (*part of body*) esfregar; (*object: with*

cloth, substance) friccionar ▸ N esfregadela; (*hard*) fricção *f*; (*touch*) roçar *m*; **to give sth a ~** dar uma esfregada em algo; **to ~ sb up** (*BRIT*) *or* ~ **sb** (*US*) **the wrong way** irritar alguém
▸ **rub down** VT (*person*) esfregar; (*horse*) almofaçar
▸ **rub in** VT (*ointment*) esfregar
▸ **rub off** VI sair esfregando
▸ **rub off on** VT FUS transmitir-se para, influir sobre
▸ **rub out** VT apagar ▸ VI apagar-se

rubber ['rʌbəʳ] N borracha; (*BRIT: eraser*) borracha
rubber band N elástico, tira elástica
rubber plant N (*tree*) seringueira; (*plant*) figueira
rubber ring N (*for swimming*) boia
rubber stamp N carimbo ▸ VT: **to rubber-stamp** (*fig*) aprovar sem questionar
rubbery ['rʌbərɪ] ADJ elástico; (*food*) sem gosto
rubbish ['rʌbɪʃ] N (*waste*) refugo; (*from household, in street*) lixo; (*junk*) coisas *fpl* sem valor; (*fig: pej: nonsense*) disparates *mpl*, asneiras *fpl* ▸ VT (*BRIT inf*) desprezar; **what you've just said is ~** você acabou de dizer uma besteira; **~!** que nada!, nado disso!
rubbish bin (*BRIT*) N lata de lixo
rubbish dump N (*in town*) depósito (de lixo)
rubbishy ['rʌbɪʃɪ] (*BRIT inf*) ADJ micha, chinfrim
rubble ['rʌbl] N (*debris*) entulho; (*Constr*) escombros *mpl*
ruble ['ruːbl] (*US*) N = **rouble**
ruby ['ruːbɪ] N rubi *m*
RUC (*BRIT*) N ABBR = **Royal Ulster Constabulary**
rucksack ['rʌksæk] N mochila
ructions ['rʌkʃənz] NPL confusão *f*, tumulto
rudder ['rʌdəʳ] N leme *m*; (*of plane*) leme de direção
ruddy ['rʌdɪ] ADJ (*face*) corado, avermelhado; (*inf: damned*) maldito, desgraçado
rude [ruːd] ADJ (*impolite: person*) grosso, mal-educado; (: *word, manners*) grosseiro; (*sudden*) brusco; (*shocking*) obsceno, chocante; **to be ~ to sb** ser grosso com alguém
rudely ['ruːdlɪ] ADV grosseiramente
rudeness ['ruːdnɪs] N falta de educação
rudiment ['ruːdɪmənt] N rudimento; **rudiments** NPL (*basics*) primeiras noções *fpl*
rudimentary [ruːdɪ'mɛntərɪ] ADJ rudimentar
rue [ruː] VT arrepender-se de
rueful ['ruːful] ADJ arrependido
ruff [rʌf] N rufo
ruffian ['rʌfɪən] N brigão *m*, desordeiro
ruffle ['rʌfl] VT (*hair*) despentear, desmanchar; (*clothes*) enrugar, amarrotar; (*fig: person*) perturbar, irritar
rug [rʌg] N tapete *m*; (*BRIT: for knees*) manta (de viagem)
rugby ['rʌgbɪ] N (*also:* **rugby football**) rúgbi *m* (*BR*), râguebi *m* (*PT*)

rugged ['rʌgɪd] ADJ (*landscape*) acidentado, irregular; (*features*) marcado; (*character*) severo, austero; (*determination*) teimoso
rugger ['rʌgəʳ] (*BRIT inf*) N rúgbi *m* (*BR*), râguebi *m* (*PT*)
ruin ['ruːɪn] N (*of building*) ruína; (*destruction: of plans*) destruição *f*; (*downfall*) queda; (*bankruptcy*) bancarrota ▸ VT destruir; (*future, person*) arruinar; (*spoil*) estragar; **ruins** NPL (*of building*) ruínas *fpl*; **in ~s** em ruínas
ruination [ruːɪ'neɪʃən] N ruína
ruinous ['ruːɪnəs] ADJ desastroso
rule [ruːl] N (*norm*) regra; (*regulation*) regulamento; (*government*) governo, domínio; (*ruler*) régua ▸ VT (*country, person*) governar; (*decide*) decidir; (*draw: lines*) traçar ▸ VI (*leader*) governar; (*monarch*) reger; (*Law*): **to ~ in favour of/against** decidir oficialmente a favor de/contra; **to ~ that** (*umpire, judge*) decidir que; **under British ~** sob domínio britânico; **it's against the ~s** não é permitido; **by ~ of thumb** empiricamente; **as a ~** por via de regra, geralmente
▸ **rule out** VT excluir
ruled [ruːld] ADJ (*paper*) pautado
ruler ['ruːləʳ] N (*sovereign*) soberano(-a); (*for measuring*) régua
ruling ['ruːlɪŋ] ADJ (*party*) dominante; (*class*) dirigente ▸ N (*Law*) parecer *m*, decisão *f*
rum [rʌm] N rum *m* ▸ ADJ (*BRIT inf*) esquisito
Rumania [ruː'meɪnɪə] N = **Romania**
rumble ['rʌmbl] N ruído surdo, barulho; (*of thunder*) estrondo, ribombo ▸ VI ribombar, ressoar; (*stomach*) roncar; (*pipe*) fazer barulho; (*thunder*) ribombar
rumbustious [rʌm'bʌstʃəs] (*BRIT*) ADJ (*person*) enérgico
rummage ['rʌmɪdʒ] VI vasculhar; **to ~ in** (*drawer*) vasculhar
rumour, (*US*) **rumor** ['ruːməʳ] N rumor *m*, boato ▸ VT: **it is ~ed that …** corre o boato de que …
rump [rʌmp] N (*of animal*) anca, garupa
rumple ['rʌmpl] VT (*hair*) despentear; (*clothes*) amarrotar
rump steak N alcatra
rumpus ['rʌmpəs] N barulho, confusão *f*, zorra; (*quarrel*) bate-boca *m*; **to kick up a ~** fazer um escândalo
run [rʌn] (*pt* **ran**, *pp* **run**) N corrida; (*in car*) passeio (de carro); (*distance travelled*) trajeto, percurso; (*journey*) viagem *f*; (*series*) série *f*; (*Theatre*) temporada; (*Ski*) pista; (*in stockings*) fio puxado ▸ VT (*race*) correr; (*operate: business*) dirigir; (: *competition, course*) organizar; (: *hotel, house*) administrar; (*water*) deixar correr; (*bath*) encher; (*Press: feature*) publicar; (*Comput: program*) rodar; (*pass: hand, finger*) passar ▸ VI correr; (*pass: road etc*) passar; (*work: machine*) funcionar; (*bus, train: operate*) circular; (: *travel*) ir; (*continue: play*) continuar em cartaz; (: *contract*) ser válido; (*slide: drawer*)

r

deslizar; *(flow: river, bath)* fluir, correr; *(colours, washing)* desbotar; *(in election)* candidatar-se; *(nose)* escorrer; **to go for a ~** fazer cooper; *(in car)* dar uma volta (de carro); **to break into a ~** pôr-se a correr; **a ~ of luck** um período de sorte; **to have the ~ of sb's house** ter a casa de alguém à sua disposição; **there was a ~ on** *(meat, tickets)* houve muita procura de; **in the long ~** no final das contas, mais cedo ou mais tarde; **on the ~** em fuga, foragido; **to ~ for the bus** correr até o ônibus; **we'll have to ~ for it** vamos ter que correr atrás; **I'll ~ you to the station** vou te levar à estação; **to ~ a risk** correr um risco; **to ~ errands** fazer recados; **to make a ~ for it** fugir, dar no pé; **the train ~s between Gatwick and Victoria** o trem faz o percurso entre Gatwick e Victoria; **the bus ~s every 20 minutes** o ônibus passa a cada 20 minutos; **it's very cheap to ~** *(car, machine)* é muito econômico; **to ~ on petrol** (BRIT) *or* **gas** (US)/**on diesel/off batteries** funcionar a gasolina/a óleo diesel/a pilhas; **I'll ~ for president** candidatar-se à presidência, ser presidenciável; **their losses ran into millions** suas perdas se elevaram a milhões; **to be ~ off one's feet** (BRIT) não ter descanso, não parar um minuto; **my salary won't ~ to a car** meu salário não é suficiente para comprar um carro
▶ **run about** VI *(children)* correr por todos os lados
▶ **run across** VT FUS *(find)* encontrar por acaso, topar com, dar com
▶ **run around** VI = **run about**
▶ **run away** VI fugir
▶ **run down** VI *(clock)* parar ▶ VT *(Aut)* atropelar; *(production)* reduzir; *(factory)* reduzir a produção de; *(criticize)* criticar; **to be ~ down** *(tired)* estar enfraquecido *or* exausto
▶ **run in** (BRIT) VT *(car)* rodar
▶ **run into** VT FUS *(meet: person)* dar com, topar com; *(: trouble)* esbarrar em; *(collide with)* bater em; **to ~ into debt** endividar-se
▶ **run off** VT *(water)* deixar correr; *(copies)* fotocopiar ▶ VI fugir
▶ **run out** VI *(person)* sair correndo; *(liquid)* escorrer, esgotar-se; *(lease, passport)* caducar, vencer; *(money)* acabar
▶ **run out of** VT FUS ficar sem; **I've ~ out of petrol** (BRIT) *or* **gas** (US) estou sem gasolina
▶ **run over** VT *(Aut)* atropelar ▶ VT FUS *(revise)* recapitular
▶ **run through** VT FUS *(instructions)* examinar, recapitular; *(rehearse)* recapitular
▶ **run up** VT *(debt)* acumular ▶ VI: **to ~ up against** *(difficulties)* esbarrar em
runaway ['rʌnəweɪ] ADJ *(horse)* desembestado; *(truck)* desgovernado; *(person)* fugitivo; *(inflation)* galopante
rundown ['rʌndaun] (BRIT) N *(of industry etc)* redução *f* progressiva

rung [rʌŋ] PP *of* **ring** ▶ N *(of ladder)* degrau *m*
run-in *(inf)* N briga, bate-boca *m*
runner ['rʌnəʳ] N *(in race: person)* corredor(a) *m/f*; *(: horse)* corredor *m*; *(on sledge)* patim *m*, lâmina; *(on curtain)* anel *m*; *(wheel)* roldana, roda; *(for drawer)* corrediça; *(carpet: in hall etc)* passadeira
runner bean (BRIT) N *(Bot)* vagem *f* (BR), feijão *m* verde (PT)
runner-up N segundo(-a) colocado(-a)
running ['rʌnɪŋ] N *(sport, race)* corrida; *(of business)* direção *f*; *(of event)* organização *f*; *(of machine etc)* funcionamento ▶ ADJ *(water)* corrente; *(commentary)* contínuo, seguido; **6 days ~** 6 dias seguidos *or* consecutivos; **to be in/out of the ~ for sth** disputar algo/estar fora da disputa por algo
running costs NPL *(of business)* despesas *fpl* operacionais; *(of car)* custos *mpl* de manutenção
running head N *(Typ)* título corrido
running mate (US) N *(Pol)* companheiro(-a) de chapa
runny ['rʌnɪ] ADJ *(sauce, paint)* aguado; *(egg)* mole; **to have a ~ nose** estar com coriza, estar com o nariz escorrendo
run-off N *(in contest, election)* segundo turno; *(extra race etc)* corrida decisiva
run-of-the-mill ADJ mediocre, ordinário
runt [rʌnt] N *(animal)* nanico; *(pej: person)* anão(-anã) *m/f*
run-through N ensaio
run-up N: **~ to sth** *(election etc)* período que antecede algo; **during** *or* **in the ~ to** nas vésperas de
runway ['rʌnweɪ] N *(Aviat)* pista (de decolagem *or* de pouso)
rupee [ruːˈpiː] N rupia
rupture ['rʌptʃəʳ] N *(Med)* hérnia ▶ VT: **to ~ o.s.** provocar-se uma hérnia
rural ['ruərl] ADJ rural
ruse [ruːz] N ardil *m*, manha
rush [rʌʃ] N *(hurry)* pressa; *(Comm)* grande procura *or* demanda; *(Bot)* junco; *(current)* torrente *f*; *(of emotion)* ímpeto ▶ VT apressar; *(work)* fazer depressa; *(attack: town etc)* assaltar; *(BRIT inf: charge)* cobrar ▶ VI apressar-se, precipitar-se; *(air)* suprar impetuosamente; *(water)* afluir impetuosamente; **don't ~ me!** não me apresse!; **is there any ~ for this?** isso é urgente?; **to ~ sth off** *(do quickly)* fazer algo às pressas; *(send)* enviar depressa; **we've had a ~ of orders** recebimos uma enxurrada de pedidos; **to be in a ~** estar com pressa; **to do sth in a ~** fazer algo às pressas; **to be in a ~ to do sth** ter urgência em fazer algo
▶ **rush through** VT FUS *(work)* fazer às pressas ▶ VT *(Comm: order)* executar com toda a urgência
rush hour N rush *m* (BR), hora de ponta (PT)
rush job N trabalho urgente

rush matting [-'mætɪŋ] N tapete *m* de palha
rusk [rʌsk] N rosca
Russia ['rʌʃə] N Rússia
Russian ['rʌʃən] ADJ russo ▶ N russo(-a); (*Ling*) russo
rust [rʌst] N ferrugem *f* ▶ VI enferrujar
rustic ['rʌstɪk] ADJ rústico ▶ N (*pej*) caipira *m/f*
rustle ['rʌsl] VI sussurrar ▶ VT (*paper*) farfalhar; (*US: cattle*) roubar, afanar
rustproof ['rʌstpruːf] ADJ inoxidável, à prova de ferrugem
rustproofing ['rʌstpruːfɪŋ] N tratamento contra ferrugem

rusty ['rʌstɪ] ADJ enferrujado
rut [rʌt] N sulco; (*Zool*) cio; **to be in a ~** ser escravo da rotina
rutabaga [ruːtə'beɪgə] (*US*) N rutabaga
ruthless ['ruːθlɪs] ADJ implacável, sem piedade
ruthlessness ['ruːθlɪsnɪs] N crueldade *f*, desumanidade *f*, insensibilidade *f*
RV ABBR (= *revised version*) tradução inglesa da *Bíblia de 1885* ▶ N ABBR (*US*) = **recreational vehicle**
rye [raɪ] N centeio
rye bread N pão *m* de centeio

r

Ss

S¹, s [ɛs] N (*letter*) S, s *m*; (*US Sch*: = *satisfactory*) satisfatório; **S for Sugar** S de Sandra

S² ABBR (= *south*) S; (= *saint*) S, Sᵗᵒ, Sᵗᵃ

SA N ABBR = **South Africa; South America**

Sabbath ['sæbəθ] N (*Christian*) domingo; (*Jewish*) sábado

sabbatical [sə'bætɪkl] N (*also*: **sabbatical year**) ano sabático *or* de licença

sabotage ['sæbətɑːʒ] N sabotagem *f* ▶ VT sabotar

saccharin, saccharine ['sækərɪn] N sacarina

sachet ['sæʃeɪ] N sachê *m*

sack [sæk] N (*bag*) saco, saca ▶ VT (*dismiss*) despedir; (*plunder*) saquear; **to get the ~** ser demitido; **to give sb the ~** pôr alguém no olho da rua, despedir alguém

sackful ['sækful] N: **a ~ of** um saco de

sacking ['sækɪŋ] N (*dismissal*) demissão *f*; (*material*) aniagem *f*

sacrament ['sækrəmənt] N sacramento

sacred ['seɪkrɪd] ADJ sagrado

sacrifice ['sækrɪfaɪs] N sacrifício ▶ VT sacrificar; **to make ~s (for sb)** fazer um sacrifício (por alguém)

sacrilege ['sækrɪlɪdʒ] N sacrilégio

sacrosanct ['sækrəusæŋkt] ADJ sacrossanto

sad [sæd] ADJ triste; (*deplorable*) deplorável, triste

sadden ['sædn] VT entristecer

saddle ['sædl] N sela; (*of cycle*) selim *m* ▶ VT (*horse*) selar; **to ~ sb with sth** (*inf: task, bill*) pôr algo nas costas de alguém; (: *responsibility*) sobrecarregar alguém com algo

saddlebag ['sædlbæg] N alforje *m*

sadism ['seɪdɪzm] N sadismo

sadist ['seɪdɪst] N sádico(-a)

sadistic [sə'dɪstɪk] ADJ sádico

sadly ['sædlɪ] ADV tristemente; (*regrettably*) infelizmente; (*mistaken, neglected*) gravemente; **~ lacking (in)** muito carente (de)

sadness ['sædnɪs] N tristeza

sae ABBR (= *stamped addressed envelope*) envelope *selado e sobrescritado*

safari [sə'fɑːrɪ] N safári *m*

safari park N *parque com animais selvagens*

safe [seɪf] ADJ seguro; (*out of danger*) fora de perigo; (*unharmed*) ileso, incólume; (*trustworthy*) digno de confiança ▶ N cofre *m*,

caixa-forte *f*; **~ from** protegido de; **~ and sound** são e salvo; **(just) to be on the ~ side** por via das dúvidas; **to play ~** não correr riscos; **it is ~ to say that ...** posso afirmar que ...; **~ journey!** boa viagem!

safe-breaker (*BRIT*) N arrombador *m* de cofres

safe-conduct N salvo-conduto

safe-cracker N arrombador *m* de cofres

safe-deposit N (*vault*) cofre *m* de segurança; (*box*) caixa-forte *f*

safeguard ['seɪfgɑːd] N salvaguarda, proteção *f* ▶ VT proteger, defender

safekeeping [seɪf'kiːpɪŋ] N custódia, proteção *f*

safely ['seɪflɪ] ADV com segurança, a salvo; (*without mishap*) sem perigo; **I can ~ say ...** posso seguramente dizer ...

safety ['seɪftɪ] N segurança

safety belt N cinto de segurança

safety curtain N cortina de ferro

safety net N rede *f* de segurança

safety pin N alfinete *m* de segurança

safety valve N válvula de segurança

saffron ['sæfrən] N açafrão *m*

sag [sæg] VI (*breasts*) cair; (*roof*) afundar; (*hem*) desmanchar

saga ['sɑːgə] N saga; (*fig*) novela

sage [seɪdʒ] N (*herb*) salva; (*man*) sábio

Sagittarius [sædʒɪ'tɛərɪəs] N Sagitário

sago ['seɪgəu] N sagu *m*

Sahara [sə'hɑːrə] N: **the ~ (Desert)** o Saara

said [sɛd] PT, PP *of* **say**

sail [seɪl] N (*on boat*) vela; (*trip*): **to go for a ~** dar um passeio de barco a vela ▶ VT (*boat*) governar ▶ VI (*travel: ship*) navegar, velejar; (: *passenger*) ir de barco; (*Sport*) velejar; (*set off*) zarpar; **to set ~** zarpar; **they ~ed into Rio de Janeiro** entraram no porto do Rio de Janeiro

▶ **sail through** VT FUS (*fig*) fazer com facilidade ▶ VI fazer de letra, fazer com um pé nas costas

sailboat ['seɪlbəut] (*US*) N barco a vela

sailing ['seɪlɪŋ] N (*Sport*) navegação *f* a vela, vela; **to go ~** ir velejar

sailing boat N barco a vela

sailing ship N veleiro

sailor ['seɪləʳ] N marinheiro, marujo

saint [seɪnt] N santo(-a); **S~ John** São João

saintly ['seɪntlɪ] ADJ santo; *(life, expression)* de santo

sake [seɪk] N: **for the ~ of** por (causa de), em consideração a; **for sb's/sth's ~** pelo bem de alguém/algo; **for my ~** por mim; **arguing for arguing's ~** brigar por brigar; **for the ~ of argument** por exemplo; **for heaven's ~!** pelo amor de Deus!

salad ['sæləd] N salada

salad bowl N saladeira

salad cream (BRIT) N maionese *f*

salad dressing N tempero *or* molho da salada

salad oil N azeite *m* de mesa

salami [sə'lɑːmɪ] N salame *m*

salaried ['sælərɪd] ADJ *(staff)* assalariado

salary ['sælərɪ] N salário

salary scale N escala salarial

sale [seɪl] N venda; *(at reduced prices)* liquidação *f*, saldo; *(auction)* leilão *m*; **sales** NPL *(total amount sold)* vendas *fpl*; **"for ~"** "vende-se"; **on ~** à venda; **on ~ or return** em consignação; **~ and lease back** *venda com cláusula de aluguel ao vendedor do item vendido*

saleroom ['seɪlrum] N sala de vendas

sales assistant, (US) **sales clerk** N vendedor(a) *m/f*

sales conference N conferência de vendas

sales drive N campanha de vendas

sales force N equipe *m* de vendas

salesman ['seɪlzmən] *(irreg: like* **man***)* N vendedor *m*; *(representative)* vendedor *m* viajante

sales manager N gerente *m/f* de vendas

salesmanship ['seɪlzmənʃɪp] N arte *f* de vender

salesmen ['seɪlzmɛn] NPL *of* **salesman**

sales tax (US) N ≈ ICM *m* (BR), ≈ IVA *m* (PT)

saleswoman ['seɪlzwumən] *(irreg: like* **woman***)* N vendedora; *(representative)* vendedora viajante

salient ['seɪlɪənt] ADJ saliente

saline ['seɪlaɪn] ADJ salino

saliva [sə'laɪvə] N saliva

sallow ['sæləu] ADJ amarelado

sally forth ['sælɪ-] VI partir, pôr-se em marcha

sally out ['sælɪ-] VI partir, pôr-se em marcha

salmon ['sæmən] N INV salmão *m*

salon ['sælɒn] N *(hairdressing salon)* salão *m* (de cabeleireiro); *(beauty salon)* salão (de beleza)

saloon [sə'luːn] N *(US)* bar *m*, botequim *m*; (BRIT *Aut)* sedã *m*; *(ship's lounge)* salão *m*

SALT [sɔːlt] N ABBR (= *Strategic Arms Limitation Talks/Treaty*) SALT *m*

salt [sɔːlt] N sal *m* ▶ VT salgar ▶ CPD de sal; *(Culin)* salgado; **an old ~** um lobo-do-mar ▶ **salt away** VT pôr de lado

salt cellar N saleiro

salt-free ADJ sem sal

saltwater ['sɔːltwɔːtəʳ] ADJ de água salgada

salty ['sɔːltɪ] ADJ salgado

salubrious [sə'luːbrɪəs] ADJ salubre, sadio

salutary ['sæljutərɪ] ADJ salutar

salute [sə'luːt] N *(greeting)* saudação *f*; *(of guns)*

salva; *(Mil)* continência ▶ VT saudar; *(guns)* receber com salvas; *(Mil)* fazer continência a

salvage ['sælvɪdʒ] N *(saving)* salvamento, recuperação *f*; *(things saved)* salvados *mpl* ▶ VT salvar

salvage vessel N navio de salvamento

salvation [sæl'veɪʃən] N salvação *f*

Salvation Army N Exército da Salvação

salve [sælv] N *(cream etc)* unguento, pomada

salver ['sælvəʳ] N bandeja, salva

salvo ['sælvəu] *(pl* **salvoes***)* N salva

Samaritan [sə'mærɪtən] N: **the ~s** *(or* **ganization***)* os Samaritanos

same [seɪm] ADJ mesmo ▶ PRON: **the ~** o mesmo/a mesma; **the ~ book as** o mesmo livro que; **at the ~ time** ao mesmo tempo; **on the ~ day** no mesmo dia; **all** *or* **just the ~** apesar de tudo, mesmo assim; **it's all the ~** dá no mesmo, tanto faz; **they're one and the ~** *(people)* são os mesmos; *(things)* são idênticos; **to do the ~ (as sb)** fazer o mesmo (que alguém); **the ~ to you!** igualmente!; **~ here!** eu também!; **the ~ again!** *(in bar etc)* mais um … por favor!

sample ['sɑːmpl] N amostra ▶ VT *(food, wine)* provar, experimentar; **to take a ~** tirar uma amostra; **free ~** amostra grátis

sanatoria [sænə'tɔːrɪə] NPL *of* **sanatorium**

sanatorium [sænə'tɔːrɪəm] *(pl* **sanatoria***)* N sanatório

sanctify ['sæŋktɪfaɪ] VT santificar

sanctimonious [sæŋktɪ'məunɪəs] ADJ carola, beato

sanction ['sæŋkʃən] N sanção *f* ▶ VT sancionar; **sanctions** NPL *(severe measures)* sanções *fpl*; **to impose economic ~s on** *or* **against** impor sanções econômicas a

sanctity ['sæŋktɪtɪ] N santidade *f*, divindade *f*; *(inviolability)* inviolabilidade *f*

sanctuary ['sæŋktjuərɪ] N *(holy place)* santuário; *(refuge)* refúgio, asilo; *(for animals)* reserva

sand [sænd] N areia; *(beach: also:* **sands***)* praia ▶ VT arear, jogar areia em; *(also:* **sand down***: wood etc)* lixar

sandal ['sændl] N sandália; *(wood)* sândalo

sandbag ['sændbæg] N saco de areia

sandbank ['sændbæŋk] N banco de areia

sandblast ['sændblɑːst] VT limpar com jato de areia

sandbox ['sændbɒks] (US) N *(for children)* caixa de areia

sand castle N castelo de areia

sand dune N duna (de areia)

sandpaper ['sændpeɪpəʳ] N lixa

sandpit ['sændpɪt] (BRIT) N *(for children)* caixa de areia

sandstone ['sændstəun] N arenito, grés *m*

sandstorm ['sændstɔːm] N tempestade *f* de areia

sandwich ['sændwɪtʃ] N sanduíche *m* (BR), sandes *f inv* (PT) ▶ VT *(also:* **sandwich in***)* intercalar; **~ed between** encaixado entre;

cheese/ham ~ sanduíche (BR) or sandes (PT) de queijo/presunto
sandwich board N cartaz m ambulante
sandwich course (BRIT) N curso profissionalizante de teoria e prática alternadas
sandy ['sændɪ] ADJ arenoso; (colour) vermelho amarelado
sane [seɪn] ADJ são/sã do juízo; (sensible) ajuizado, sensato
sang [sæŋ] PT of **sing**
sanguine ['sæŋgwɪn] ADJ otimista
sanitaria [sænɪ'tɛərɪə] (US) NPL of **sanitarium**
sanitarium [sænɪ'tɛərɪəm] (US pl **sanitaria**) N = **sanatorium**
sanitary ['sænɪtərɪ] ADJ (system, arrangements) sanitário; (clean) higiênico
sanitary towel, (US) **sanitary napkin** N toalha higiênica or absorvente
sanitation [sænɪ'teɪʃən] N (in house) instalações fpl sanitárias; (in town) saneamento
sanitation department (US) N comissão f de limpeza urbana
sanity ['sænɪtɪ] N sanidade f, equilíbrio mental; (common sense) juízo, sensatez f
sank [sæŋk] PT of **sink**
San Marino ['sænmə'riːnəu] N San Marino (no article)
Santa Claus [sæntə'klɔːz] N Papai Noel m
Santiago [sæntɪ'ɑːgəu] N (also: **Santiago de Chile**) Santiago (do Chile)
sap [sæp] N (of plants) seiva ▶ VT (strength) esgotar, minar
sapling ['sæplɪŋ] N árvore f nova
sapphire ['sæfaɪə'] N safira
sarcasm ['sɑːkæzm] N sarcasmo
sarcastic [sɑː'kæstɪk] ADJ sarcástico
sarcophagi [sɑː'kɔfəgaɪ] NPL of **sarcophagus**
sarcophagus [sɑː'kɔfəgəs] (pl **sarcophagi**) N sarcófago
sardine [sɑː'diːn] N sardinha
Sardinia [sɑː'dɪnɪə] N Sardenha
Sardinian [sɑː'dɪnɪən] ADJ sardo ▶ N sardo(-a); (Ling) sardo
sardonic [sɑː'dɔnɪk] ADJ sardônico
sari ['sɑːrɪ] N sári m
sartorial [sɑː'tɔːrɪəl] ADJ indumentário
SAS (BRIT) N ABBR (Mil) = **Special Air Service**
SASE (US) N ABBR (= self-addressed stamped envelope) envelope selado e sobrescritado
sash [sæʃ] N faixa, banda; (belt) cinto
sash window N janela de guilhotina
SAT (US) N ABBR = **Scholastic Aptitude Test**
sat [sæt] PT, PP of **sit**
Sat. ABBR (= Saturday) sáb.
Satan ['seɪtn] N Satanás m, Satã m
satanic [sə'tænɪk] ADJ satânico, diabólico
satchel ['sætʃl] N sacola
sated ['seɪtɪd] ADJ saciado, farto
satellite ['sætəlaɪt] N satélite m
satellite dish N antena parabólica
satellite television N televisão f via satélite
satiate ['seɪʃɪeɪt] VT saciar

satin ['sætɪn] N cetim m ▶ ADJ acetinado; **with a ~ finish** acetinado
satire ['sætaɪə'] N sátira
satirical [sə'tɪrɪkl] ADJ satírico
satirist ['sætɪrɪst] N (writer) satirista m/f; (cartoonist) chargista m/f
satirize ['sætɪraɪz] VT satirizar
satisfaction [sætɪs'fækʃən] N satisfação f; (refund, apology etc) compensação f; **has it been done to your ~?** você está satisfeito?
satisfactory [sætɪs'fæktərɪ] ADJ satisfatório
satisfy ['sætɪsfaɪ] VT satisfazer; (convince) convencer, persuadir; **to ~ the requirements** satisfazer as exigências; **to ~ sb (that)** convencer alguém (de que); **to ~ o.s. of sth** convencer-se de algo
satisfying ['sætɪsfaɪɪŋ] ADJ satisfatório
satsuma [sæt'suːmə] N mexerica, tangerina
saturate ['sætʃəreɪt] VT: **to ~ (with)** saturar or embeber (de)
saturation [sætʃə'reɪʃən] N saturação f
Saturday ['sætədɪ] N sábado; see also **Tuesday**
sauce [sɔːs] N molho; (sweet) calda; (fig: cheek) atrevimento
saucepan ['sɔːspən] N panela (BR), caçarola (PT)
saucer ['sɔːsə'] N pires m inv
saucy ['sɔːsɪ] ADJ atrevido, descarado; (flirtatious) flertivo, provocante
Saudi ['saudɪ] ADJ, N (also: **Saudi Arabia**) Arábia Saudita; (also: **Saudi Arabian**) saudita m/f
Saudi Arabian ADJ, N saudita m/f
sauna ['sɔːnə] N sauna
saunter ['sɔːntə'] VI: **to ~ over/along/into** andar devagar para/por/entrar devagar em
sausage ['sɔsɪdʒ] N salsicha, linguiça; (cold meat) frios mpl
sausage roll N folheado de salsicha
sauté ['səuteɪ] ADJ (Culin: potatoes) sauté; (: onions) frito rapidamente ▶ VT fritar levemente
savage ['sævɪdʒ] ADJ (cruel, fierce) cruel, feroz; (primitive) selvagem ▶ N selvagem m/f ▶ VT (attack) atacar ferozmente
savagery ['sævɪdʒrɪ] N selvageria, ferocidade f
save [seɪv] VT (rescue, Comput) salvar; (money) poupar, economizar; (time) ganhar; (put by: food) guardar; (Sport) impedir; (avoid: trouble) evitar; (keep: seat) guardar ▶ VI (also: **save up**) poupar ▶ N (Sport) salvamento ▶ PREP salvo, exceto; **it will ~ me an hour** vou ganhar uma hora; **to ~ face** salvar as aparências; **God ~ the Queen!** Deus salve a Rainha!
saving ['seɪvɪŋ] N (on price etc) economia ▶ ADJ: **the ~ grace of** o único mérito de; **savings** NPL (money) economias fpl; **to make ~s** economizar
savings account N (caderneta de) poupança
savings bank N caixa econômica, caderneta de poupança
saviour, (US) **savior** ['seɪvjə'] N salvador(a) m/f
savour, (US) **savor** ['seɪvə'] N sabor m ▶ VT saborear; (experience) apreciar

savoury, (US) **savory** ['seɪvərɪ] ADJ saboroso; (dish: not sweet) salgado
savvy ['sævɪ] (inf) N juízo
saw [sɔ:] PT of **see** ▶ VT (pt **sawed**, pp **sawed** or **sawn**) serrar ▶ N (tool) serra; **to ~ sth up** serrar algo em pedaços
sawdust ['sɔ:dʌst] N serragem f, pó m de serra
sawed-off shotgun [sɔ:d-] (US) N = **sawn-off shotgun**
sawmill ['sɔ:mɪl] N serraria
sawn [sɔ:n] PP of **saw**
sawn-off shotgun (BRIT) N espingarda de cano serrado
sax [sæks] (inf) N saxofone m
saxophone ['sæksəfəʊn] N saxofone m
say [seɪ] VT (pt, pp **said**) dizer, falar ▶ N: **to have one's ~** exprimir sua opinião, vender seu peixe (inf); **to have a** or **some ~ in sth** opinar sobre algo, ter que ver com algo; **~ after me ...** repita comigo ...; **to ~ yes/no** dizer (que) sim/não; **could you ~ that again?** poderia repetir?; **she said (that) I was to give you this** ela disse que eu deveria te dar isso; **my watch ~s 3 o'clock** meu relógio marca 3 horas; **shall we ~ Tuesday?** marcamos para terça?; **I should ~ it's worth about £100** eu diria que vale mais ou menos £100; **that doesn't ~ much for him** aquilo não o favorece; **when all is said and done** afinal das contas; **there is something** or **a lot to be said for it** isto tem muitas vantagens; **that is to ~** ou seja; **to ~ nothing of ...** por não falar em ...; **~ that ...** vamos supor que ...; **that goes without ~ing** é óbvio, nem é preciso dizer
saying ['seɪɪŋ] N ditado, provérbio
SBA (US) N ABBR (= Small Business Administration) órgão de auxílio às pequenas empresas
SC N ABBR = **Supreme Court** ▶ ABBR (Post) = **South Carolina**
s/c ABBR = **self-contained**
scab [skæb] N casca, crosta (de ferida); (pej) fura-greve m/f inv
scabby ['skæbɪ] ADJ cheio de casca or cicatrizes
scaffold ['skæfəʊld] N (for execution) cadafalso, patíbulo
scaffolding ['skæfəʊldɪŋ] N andaime m
scald [skɔ:ld] N escaldadura ▶ VT escaldar, queimar
scalding ['skɔ:ldɪŋ] ADJ (also: **scalding hot**) escaldante
scale [skeɪl] N (gen, Mus) escala; (of fish) escama; (of salaries, fees etc) tabela; (of map, also size, extent) escala ▶ VT (mountain) escalar; (fish) escamar; **scales** NPL (for weighing) balança; **pay ~** tabela de salários; **on a large ~** em grande escala; **~ of charges** tarifa, lista de preços; **to draw sth to ~** desenhar algo em escala; **small-~ model** modelo reduzido
▶ **scale down** VT reduzir
scale drawing N desenho em escala
scale model N maquete f em escala

scallion ['skæljən] N cebola
scallop ['skɔləp] N (Zool) vieira, venera; (Sewing) barra, arremate m
scalp [skælp] N couro cabeludo ▶ VT escalpar
scalpel ['skælpl] N bisturi m
scalper ['skælpər] (US inf) N (of tickets) cambista m/f
scam [skæm] (inf) N maracutaia, falcatrua
scamp [skæmp] N moleque m
scamper ['skæmpər] VI: **to ~ away** or **off** sair correndo
scampi ['skæmpɪ] NPL camarões mpl fritos
scan [skæn] VT (examine) esquadrinhar, perscrutar; (glance at quickly) passar uma vista de olhos por; (TV, Radar) explorar ▶ N (Med) exame m
scandal ['skændl] N escândalo; (gossip) fofocas fpl; (fig: disgrace) vergonha
scandalize ['skændəlaɪz] VT escandalizar
scandalous ['skændələs] ADJ escandaloso; (disgraceful) vergonhoso; (libellous) difamatório, calunioso
Scandinavia [skændɪ'neɪvɪə] N Escandinávia
Scandinavian [skændɪ'neɪvɪən] ADJ, N escandinavo(-a)
scanner ['skænər] N (Radar) antena; (Med, Comput) scanner m
scant [skænt] ADJ escasso, insuficiente
scantily ['skæntɪlɪ] ADV: **~ clad** or **dressed** precariamente vestido
scanty ['skæntɪ] ADJ (meal) insuficiente, pobre; (underwear) sumário
scapegoat ['skeɪpgəʊt] N bode m expiatório
scar [skɑ:] N cicatriz f ▶ VT marcar (com uma cicatriz)
scarce [skɛəs] ADJ escasso, raro; **to make o.s. ~** (inf) dar o fora, cair fora
scarcely ['skɛəslɪ] ADV mal, quase não; (with numbers: barely) apenas; **~ anybody** quase ninguém; **I can ~ believe it** mal posso acreditar
scarcity ['skɛəsɪtɪ] N escassez f
scarcity value N valor m de escassez
scare [skɛər] N susto; (panic) pânico ▶ VT assustar; **to ~ sb stiff** deixar alguém morrendo de medo; **bomb ~** alarme de bomba
▶ **scare away** VT espantar
▶ **scare off** VT = **scare away**
scarecrow ['skɛəkrəʊ] N espantalho
scared [skɛəd] ADJ: **to be ~** estar assustado or com medo
scaremonger ['skɛəmʌŋgər] N alarmista m/f
scarf [skɑ:f] (pl **scarfs** or **scarves**) N (long) cachecol m; (square) lenço (de cabeça)
scarlet ['skɑ:lɪt] ADJ escarlate
scarlet fever N escarlatina
scarves [skɑ:vz] NPL of **scarf**
scary ['skɛərɪ] (inf) ADJ assustador(a)
scathing ['skeɪðɪŋ] ADJ mordaz; **to be ~ about sth** fazer uma crítica mordaz sobre algo
scatter ['skætər] VT (spread) espalhar; (put to flight) dispersar ▶ VI espalhar-se

scatterbrained ['skætəbreɪnd] (*inf*) ADJ desmiolado, avoado; (*forgetful*) esquecido

scattered ['skætəd] ADJ espalhado

scatty ['skætɪ] (*BRIT inf*) ADJ maluquinho

scavenge ['skævəndʒ] VI (*person*): **to ~ (for)** filar; **to ~ for food** (*hyenas etc*) procurar comida

scavenger ['skævəndʒəʳ] N (*person*) pessoa que procura comida no lixo; (*Zool*) animal *m* (*or* ave *f*) que se alimenta de carniça

SCE N ABBR = **Scottish Certificate of Education**

scenario [sɪ'nɑːrɪəu] N (*Theatre, Cinema*) sinopse *f*; (*fig*) quadro

scene [siːn] N (*Theatre, fig*) cena; (*of crime, accident*) cenário; (*sight*) vista, panorama *m*; (*fuss*) escândalo; **behind the ~s** nos bastidores; **to make a ~** (*inf: fuss*) fazer um escândalo; **to appear on the ~** entrar em cena; **the political ~** o panorama político

scenery ['siːnərɪ] N (*Theatre*) cenário; (*landscape*) paisagem *f*

scenic ['siːnɪk] ADJ pitoresco

scent [sɛnt] N perfume *m*; (*smell*) aroma; (*track, fig*) pista, rastro; (*sense of smell*) olfato ▶ VT perfumar; **to put** *or* **throw sb off the ~** despistar alguém

scepter ['sɛptəʳ] (*US*) N = **sceptre**

sceptic, (*US*) **skeptic** ['skɛptɪk] N cético(-a)

sceptical, (*US*) **skeptical** ['skɛptɪkl] ADJ cético

scepticism, (*US*) **skepticism** ['skɛptɪsɪzm] N ceticismo

sceptre, (*US*) **scepter** ['sɛptəʳ] N cetro

schedule [(*BRIT*) 'ʃɛdjuːl, (*US*) 'skɛdjuːl] N (*of trains*) horário; (*of events*) programa *m*; (*plan*) plano; (*list*) lista ▶ VT (*timetable*) planejar; (*visit*) marcar (a hora de); **as ~d** como previsto; **the meeting is ~d for 7.00** a reunião está programada para as 7.00h; **on ~** na hora, sem atraso; **to be ahead of/behind ~** estar adiantado/atrasado; **we are working to a very tight ~** nosso horário está muito apertado; **everything went according to ~** tudo correu como planejado

scheduled ['ʃɛdjuːld, (*US*) 'skɛdjuːld] ADJ (*date, time*) marcado; (*visit, event*) programado; (*train, bus, flight*) de linha

schematic [skɪ'mætɪk] ADJ esquemático

scheme [skiːm] N (*plan, plot*) maquinação *f*; (*method*) método; (*pension scheme etc*) projeto; (*trick*) ardil *m*; (*arrangement*) arranjo ▶ VI conspirar

scheming ['skiːmɪŋ] ADJ intrigante ▶ N intrigas *fpl*

schism ['skɪzəm] N cisma *m*

schizophrenia [skɪtsəu'friːnɪə] N esquizofrenia

schizophrenic [skɪtsə'frɛnɪk] ADJ esquizofrênico

scholar ['skɔləʳ] N (*pupil*) aluno(-a), estudante *m/f*; (*learned person*) sábio(-a), erudito(-a)

scholarly ['skɔlǝlɪ] ADJ erudito

scholarship ['skɔləʃɪp] N erudição *f*; (*grant*) bolsa de estudos

school [skuːl] N escola; (*in university*) faculdade *f*; (*secondary school*) colégio; (*US: university*) universidade *f*; (*of fish*) cardume *m* ▶ CPD escolar ▶ VT (*animal*) adestrar, treinar

school age N idade *f* escolar

schoolbook ['skuːlbuk] N livro escolar

schoolboy ['skuːlbɔɪ] N aluno

schoolchildren ['skuːltʃɪldrən] NPL alunos *mpl*

schooldays ['skuːldeɪz] NPL anos *mpl* escolares

schoolgirl ['skuːlgɜːl] N aluna

schooling ['skuːlɪŋ] N educação *f*, ensino

school-leaving age [-'liːvɪŋ-] N idade *f* em que se termina a escola

schoolmaster ['skuːlmɑːstəʳ] N professor *m*

schoolmistress ['skuːlmɪstrɪs] N professora

school report (*BRIT*) N boletim *m* escolar

schoolroom ['skuːlrum] N sala de aula

schoolteacher ['skuːltiːtʃəʳ] N professor(a) *m/f*

schooner ['skuːnəʳ] N (*ship*) escuna; (*glass*) caneca, canecão *m*

sciatica [saɪ'ætɪkə] N ciática

science ['saɪəns] N ciência

science fiction N ficção *f* científica

scientific [saɪən'tɪfɪk] ADJ científico

scientist ['saɪəntɪst] N cientista *m/f*

sci-fi ['saɪfaɪ] (*inf*) N ABBR = **science fiction**

Scillies ['sɪlɪz] NPL: **the ~** as ilhas Scilly

Scilly Isles ['sɪlɪ'aɪlz] NPL: **the ~** as ilhas Scilly

scintillating ['sɪntɪleɪtɪŋ] ADJ (*wit etc*) brilhante

scissors ['sɪzəz] NPL tesoura; **a pair of ~** uma tesoura

sclerosis [sklɪ'rəusɪs] N esclerose *f*

scoff [skɔf] VT (*BRIT inf: eat*) engolir ▶ VI: **to ~ (at)** (*mock*) zombar (de)

scold [skəuld] VT ralhar

scolding ['skəuldɪŋ] N repreensão *f*

scone [skɔn] N bolinho de trigo

scoop [skuːp] N colherona; (*for flour etc*) pá *f*; (*Press*) furo (jornalístico)
▶ **scoop out** VT escavar
▶ **scoop up** VT recolher

scooter ['skuːtəʳ] N (*also:* **motor scooter**) lambreta; (*toy*) patinete *m*

scope [skəup] N liberdade *f* de ação; (*of plan, undertaking*) âmbito; (*reach*) alcance *m*; (*of person*) competência; (*opportunity*) oportunidade *f*; **within the ~ of** dentro dos limites de; **there is plenty of ~ for improvement** (*BRIT*) poderia ser muito melhor

scorch [skɔːtʃ] VT (*clothes*) chamuscar; (*earth, grass*) secar, queimar

scorched earth policy [skɔːtʃt-] N tática da terra arrasada

scorcher ['skɔːtʃəʳ] (*inf*) N (*hot day*) dia *m* muito quente

scorching ['skɔːtʃɪŋ] ADJ ardente

score [skɔːʳ] N (*points etc*) escore *m*, contagem *f*; (*Mus*) partitura; (*reckoning*) conta; (*twenty*) vintena ▸ VT (goal, point) fazer; (mark) marcar, entalhar; (success) alcançar ▸ VI (in game) marcar; (Football) marcar or fazer um gol; (keep score) marcar o escore; **on that ~** a esse respeito, por esse motivo; **to have an old ~ to settle with sb** (fig) ter umas contas a ajustar com alguém; **~s of** (fig) um monte de; **to keep (the) ~** marcar os pontos; **to ~ 6 out of 10** tirar nota 6 num total de 10 ▸ **score out** VT riscar

scoreboard ['skɔːbɔːd] N marcador m, placar m

scorecard ['skɔːkɑːd] N (Sport) cartão m de marcação

scorer ['skɔːrəʳ] N marcador(a) m/f

scorn [skɔːn] N desprezo ▸ VT desprezar, rejeitar

scornful ['skɔːnful] ADJ desdenhoso, zombador(a)

Scorpio ['skɔːpɪəu] N Escorpião m

scorpion ['skɔːpɪən] N escorpião m

Scot [skɔt] N escocês(-esa) m/f

Scotch [skɔtʃ] N uísque m (BR) or whisky m (PT) escocês

scotch [skɔtʃ] VT (rumour) desmentir; (plan) estragar

Scotch tape® N fita adesiva, durex® m (BR)

scot-free ADJ: **to get off ~** (unpunished) sair impune; (unhurt) sair ileso

Scotland ['skɔtlənd] N Escócia

Scots [skɔts] ADJ escocês(-esa)

Scotsman ['skɔtsmən] (irreg: like **man**) N escocês m

Scotswoman ['skɔtswumən] (irreg: like **woman**) N escocesa

Scottish ['skɔtɪʃ] ADJ escocês(-esa)

scoundrel ['skaundrəl] N canalha m/f, patife m

scour ['skauəʳ] VT (clean) limpar, esfregar; (search) esquadrinhar, procurar em

scourer ['skaurəʳ] N esponja de aço, bombril® m (BR)

scourge [skəːdʒ] N flagelo, tormento

scout [skaut] N (Mil) explorador m, batedor m; (also: **boy scout**) escoteiro; **girl ~** (US) escoteira ▸ **scout around** VI explorar

scowl [skaul] VI franzir a testa; **to ~ at sb** olhar de cara feia para alguém

scrabble ['skræbl] VI (claw): **to ~ at** arranhar ▸ N: **S~**® mexe-mexe m; **to ~ (around) for sth** (search) tatear procurando algo

scraggy ['skrægɪ] ADJ magricela, descarnado

scram [skræm] (inf) VI dar o fora, safar-se

scramble ['skræmbl] N (climb) escalada (difícil); (struggle) luta ▸ VI: **to ~ out/ through** conseguir sair com dificuldade; **to ~ for** lutar por

scrambled eggs ['skræmbld-] NPL ovos mpl mexidos

scrap [skræp] N (of paper) pedacinho; (of material) fragmento; (fig: of truth) mínimo; (fight) rixa, luta; (also: **scrap iron**) ferro velho, sucata ▸ VT sucatar, jogar no ferro velho; (fig) descartar, abolir ▸ VI brigar; **scraps** NPL (leftovers) sobras fpl, restos mpl; **to sell sth for ~** vender algo como sucata

scrapbook ['skræpbuk] N álbum m de recortes

scrap dealer N ferro-velho m, sucateiro(-a)

scrape [skreɪp] N (fig): **to get into a ~** meter-se numa enrascada ▸ VT raspar; (also: **scrape against**: hand, car) arranhar, roçar ▸ VI: **to ~ through** (in exam) passar raspando ▸ **scrape together** VT (money) juntar com dificuldade

scraper ['skreɪpəʳ] N raspador m

scrap heap N (fig): **on the ~** rejeitado, jogado fora

scrap merchant (BRIT) N sucateiro(-a)

scrap metal N sucata, ferro-velho

scrap paper N papel m de rascunho

scrappy ['skræpɪ] ADJ (piece of work) desconexo; (speech) incoerente, desconexo; (bitty) fragmentário

scrap yard N ferro-velho

scratch [skrætʃ] N arranhão m; (from claw) arranhadura ▸ CPD: **~ team** time m improvisado, escrete m ▸ VT (rub: one's nose etc) coçar; (with claw, nail) arranhar, unhar; (damage: paint, car) arranhar ▸ VI coçar(-se); **to start from ~** partir do zero; **to be up to ~** estar à altura (das circunstâncias)

scratch pad (US) N bloco de rascunho

scrawl [skrɔːl] N garrancho, garatujas fpl ▸ VI garatujar, rabiscar

scrawny ['skrɔːnɪ] ADJ magricela

scream [skriːm] N grito ▸ VI gritar; **it was a ~** (inf) foi engraçadíssimo; **to ~ at sb** gritar com alguém

scree [skriː] N seixos mpl

screech [skriːtʃ] VI guinchar ▸ N guincho

screen [skriːn] N (Cinema, TV, Comput) tela (BR), ecrã m (PT); (movable) biombo; (wall) tapume m; (also: **windscreen**) para-brisa m; (fig) cortina ▸ VT (conceal) esconder, tapar; (from the wind etc) proteger; (film) projetar; (candidates etc, Med) examinar

screen editing [-'ɛdɪtɪŋ] N (Comput) edição f na tela

screening ['skriːnɪŋ] N (Med) exame m médico; (of film) exibição f; (for security) controle m

screen memory N (Comput) memória da tela

screenplay ['skriːnpleɪ] N roteiro

screensaver ['skriːnseɪvəʳ] N protetor m de tela

screenshot ['skriːnʃɔt] N (Comput) captura de tela

screen test N teste m de cinema

screw [skruː] N parafuso; (propeller) hélice f ▸ VT aparafusar; (also: **screw in**) apertar, atarraxar; (!: have sex with) comer (!), trepar com (!); **to ~ sth to the wall** pregar algo na parede; **to have one's head ~ed on** (fig) ter juízo ▸ **screw up** VT (paper etc) amassar; (inf: ruin) estragar; **to ~ up one's eyes** franzir os olhos; **to ~ up one's face** contrair as feições

screwdriver ['skru:draɪvəʳ] N chave f de fenda or de parafuso

screwy ['skru:ɪ] (inf) ADJ maluco, estranho

scribble ['skrɪbl] N garrancho ▶ VT escrevinhar ▶ VI rabiscar; **to ~ sth down** anotar algo apressadamente

scribe [skraɪb] N escriba m/f

script [skrɪpt] N (Cinema etc) roteiro, script m; (writing) escrita, caligrafia

scripted ['skrɪptɪd] ADJ (Radio, TV) com script

Scripture ['skrɪptʃəʳ] N, **Scriptures** ['skrɪptʃəz] NPL Sagrada Escritura

scriptwriter ['skrɪptraɪtəʳ] N roteirista m/f

scroll [skrəul] N rolo de pergaminho ▶ VT (Comput) rolar
▶ **scroll up/down** VI rolar o texto para cima/para baixo

scrotum ['skrəutəm] N escroto

scrounge [skraundʒ] (inf) VT: **to ~ sth off** or **from sb** filar algo de alguém ▶ VI: **to ~ on sb** viver às custas de alguém ▶ N: **on the ~** viver às custas de alguém (or dos outros etc)

scrounger ['skraundʒəʳ] (inf) N filão(-lona) m/f

scrub [skrʌb] N (clean) esfregação f, limpeza; (land) mato, cerrado ▶ VT esfregar; (inf: reject) cancelar, eliminar

scrubbing brush ['skrʌbɪŋ-] N escova de esfrega

scruff [skrʌf] N: **by the ~ of the neck** pelo cangote

scruffy ['skrʌfɪ] ADJ desmazelado

scrum ['skrʌm], **scrummage** ['skrʌmɪdʒ] N rolo

scruple ['skru:pl] N escrúpulo; **to have no ~s about doing sth** não ter escrúpulos em fazer algo

scrupulous ['skru:pjuləs] ADJ escrupuloso

scrupulously ['skru:pjələslɪ] ADV escrupulosamente

scrutinize ['skru:tɪnaɪz] VT examinar minuciosamente; (votes) escrutinar

scrutiny ['skru:tɪnɪ] N escrutínio, exame m cuidadoso; **under the ~ of** vigiado por

scuba ['sku:bə] N equipamento de mergulho

scuba diving N mergulho

scuff [skʌf] VT desgastar

scuffle ['skʌfl] N tumulto

scull [skʌl] N ginga

scullery ['skʌlərɪ] N copa

sculptor ['skʌlptəʳ] N escultor(a) m/f

sculpture ['skʌlptʃəʳ] N escultura

scum [skʌm] N (on liquid) espuma; (pej: people) ralé f, gentinha; (fig) escória

scupper ['skʌpəʳ] (BRIT) VT (ship) afundar; (inf: plans) estragar

scurrilous ['skʌrɪləs] ADJ calunioso

scurry ['skʌrɪ] VI sair correndo
▶ **scurry off** VI sair correndo, dar no pé

scurvy ['skə:vɪ] N escorbuto

scuttle ['skʌtl] N (also: **coal scuttle**) balde m para carvão ▶ VT (ship) afundar voluntariamente, fazer ir a pique ▶ VI (scamper): **to ~ away** or **off** sair em disparada

scythe [saɪð] N segadeira, foice f grande

SD (US) ABBR (Post) = **South Dakota**

SDI N ABBR (= Strategic Defense Initiative) IDE f

SDLP (BRIT) N ABBR (Pol) = **Social Democratic and Labour Party**

SDP (BRIT) N ABBR = **Social Democratic Party**

sea [si:] N mar m ▶ CPD do mar, marino; **on the ~** (boat) no mar; (town) junto ao mar; **by** or **beside the ~** (holiday) na praia; (village) à beira-mar; **to go by ~** viajar por mar; **out to** or **at ~** em alto mar; **heavy** or **rough ~(s)** mar agitado; **a ~ of faces** (fig) uma grande quantidade de pessoas; **to be all at ~** (fig) estar confuso or desorientado

sea anemone N anêmona-do-mar f

sea bed N fundo do mar

sea bird N ave f marinha

seaboard ['si:bɔ:d] N costa, litoral m

sea breeze N brisa marítima, viração f

seafarer ['si:fɛərəʳ] N marinheiro, homem m do mar

seafaring ['si:fɛərɪŋ] ADJ (life) de marinheiro; **~ people** povo navegante

seafood ['si:fu:d] N mariscos mpl

sea front N orla marítima

seagoing ['si:gəuɪŋ] ADJ (ship) de longo curso

seagull ['si:gʌl] N gaivota

seal [si:l] N (animal) foca; (stamp) selo ▶ VT (close) fechar; (: with seal) selar; (decide: sb's fate) decidir; (: bargain) fechar; **~ of approval** aprovação f
▶ **seal off** VT (close) fechar; (cordon off) isolar

sea level N nível m do mar

sealing wax ['si:lɪŋ-] N lacre m

sea lion N leão-marinho m

sealskin ['si:lskɪn] N pele f de foca

seam [si:m] N costura; (where edges meet) junta; (of coal) veio, filão m; **the hall was bursting at the ~s** a sala estava apinhada de gente

seaman ['si:mən] N (irreg: like **man**) N marinheiro

seamanship ['si:mənʃɪp] N náutica

seamen ['si:men] NPL of **seaman**

seamless ['si:mlɪs] ADJ sem costura

seamstress ['sɛmstrɪs] N costureira

seamy ['si:mɪ] ADJ sórdido

seance ['seɪɔns] N sessão f espírita

seaplane ['si:pleɪn] N hidroavião m

seaport ['si:pɔ:t] N porto de mar

search [sə:tʃ] N (for person, thing) busca, procura; (Comput) busca; (of drawer, pockets) revista; (inspection) exame m, investigação f
▶ VT (look in) procurar em; (examine) examinar; (person, place) revistar ▶ VI: **to ~ for** procurar; **in ~ of** à procura de; **"~ and replace"** (Comput) "procurar e substituir"
▶ **search through** VT FUS dar busca em

search engine N (on Internet) site m de busca

searching ['sə:tʃɪŋ] ADJ penetrante, perscrutador(a); (study) minucioso

searchlight ['sə:tʃlaɪt] N holofote m

search party N equipe f de salvamento

search warrant N mandado de busca
searing ['sɪərɪŋ] ADJ (heat) ardente; (pain) agudo
seashore ['siːʃɔːʳ] N praia, beira-mar f, litoral m; **on the ~** na praia
seasick ['siːsɪk] ADJ enjoado, mareado; **to be** or **get ~** enjoar
seaside ['siːsaɪd] N praia
seaside resort N balneário
season [siːzn] N (of year) estação f; (sporting etc) temporada; (of films etc) série f ▶ VT (food) temperar; **to be in/out of ~** (fruit) estar na época/fora de época; **the busy ~** (shops) a época de muito movimento; (hotels) a temporada de férias; **the open ~** (Hunting) a temporada de caça
seasonal ['siːzənəl] ADJ sazonal
seasoned ['siːznd] ADJ (wood) tratado; (fig: traveller) experiente; (: worker, troops) calejado; **a ~ campaigner** um combatente experiente
seasoning ['siːzənɪŋ] N tempero
season ticket N bilhete m de temporada
seat [siːt] N (in bus, train: place) assento; (chair) cadeira; (Pol) lugar m, cadeira; (of bicycle) selim m; (buttocks) traseiro, nádegas fpl; (of government) sede f; (of trousers) fundilhos mpl ▶ VT sentar; (have room for) ter capacidade para; **to be ~ed** estar sentado; **are there any ~s left?** há algum lugar vago?; **to take one's ~** sentar-se; **please be ~ed** sentem-se
seat belt N cinto de segurança
seating ['siːtɪŋ] N lugares mpl sentados ▶ CPD: **~ arrangements** distribuição f dos lugares sentados
seating capacity N lotação f
SEATO ['siːtəu] N ABBR (= Southeast Asia Treaty Organization) OTSA f
sea urchin N ouriço-do-mar m
sea water N água do mar
seaweed ['siːwiːd] N alga marinha
seaworthy ['siːwəːðɪ] ADJ em condições de navegar, resistente
SEC (US) N ABBR (= Securities and Exchange Commission) órgão que supervisiona o funcionamento da Bolsa de Valores
sec. ABBR (= second) seg.
secateurs [sɛkə'təːz] NPL tesoura para podar plantas
secede [sɪ'siːd] VI separar-se
secluded [sɪ'kluːdɪd] ADJ (place) afastado; (life) solitário
seclusion [sɪ'kluːʒən] N reclusão f, isolamento
second¹ [sɪ'kɔnd] (BRIT) VT (employee) transferir temporariamente
second² ['sɛkənd] ADJ segundo ▶ ADV (in race etc) em segundo lugar ▶ N segundo; (Aut: also: **second gear**) segunda; (Comm) artigo defeituoso; (BRIT Sch: degree) uma qualificação boa mas sem distinção ▶ VT (motion) apoiar, secundar; **Charles the S~** Carlos II; **just a ~!** um minuto or minutinho!; **~ floor** (BRIT) segundo andar; (US) primeiro andar; **to ask**

for a ~ opinion (Med) querer uma segunda opinião
secondary ['sɛkəndərɪ] ADJ secundário
secondary school N escola secundária, colégio

> Na Grã-Bretanha, uma **secondary school** é um estabelecimento de ensino para alunos de 11 a 18 anos, alguns dos quais interrompem os estudos aos 16 anos.

second-best N segunda opção f
second-class ADJ de segunda classe ▶ ADV em segunda classe; **to send sth ~** remeter algo em segunda classe; **to travel ~** viajar em segunda classe; **~ citizen** cidadão(-dã) da segunda classe
second cousin N primo(-a) em segundo grau
seconder ['sɛkəndəʳ] N pessoa que secunda uma moção
secondhand [sɛkənd'hænd] ADJ de (BR) or em (PT) segunda mão, usado ▶ ADV (buy) de (BR) or em (PT) segunda mão; **to hear sth ~** ouvir algo de fonte indireta
second hand N (on clock) ponteiro de segundos
second-in-command N suplente m/f
secondly ['sɛkəndlɪ] ADV em segundo lugar
secondment [sɪ'kɔndmənt] (BRIT) N substituição f temporária
second-rate ADJ de segunda categoria
second thoughts NPL, (US) **second thought** N: **to have ~ (about doing sth)** pensar duas vezes (antes de fazer algo); **on ~** pensando bem
secrecy ['siːkrəsɪ] N sigilo; **in ~** sob sigilo, sigilosamente
secret ['siːkrɪt] ADJ secreto ▶ N segredo; **in ~** em segredo; **to keep sth ~ from sb** esconder algo de alguém; **keep it ~** não diz nada a ninguém; **to make no ~ of sth** não esconder algo de ninguém
secret agent N agente m/f secreto(-a)
secretarial [sɛkrɪ'tɛərɪəl] ADJ de secretário(-a), secretarial
secretariat [sɛkrɪ'tɛərɪət] N secretaria, secretariado
secretary ['sɛkrətərɪ] N secretário(-a); (BRIT Pol): **S~ of State** Ministro(-a) de Estado; **Foreign S~** (US Pol) Ministro(-a) das Relações Exteriores
secrete [sɪ'kriːt] VT (Anat, Bio, Med) secretar; (hide) esconder
secretion [sɪ'kriːʃən] N secreção f
secretive ['siːkrətɪv] ADJ sigiloso, reservado
secretly ['siːkrətlɪ] ADV secretamente
sect [sɛkt] N seita
sectarian [sɛk'tɛərɪən] ADJ sectário
section ['sɛkʃən] N seção f; (part) parte f, porção f; (of document) parágrafo, artigo; (of opinion) setor m ▶ VT secionar; **the business** etc **~** (Press) a seção de negócios etc; **cross-~** corte m transversal
sector ['sɛktəʳ] N setor m
secular ['sɛkjuləʳ] ADJ (priest) secular; (music, society) leigo

S

secure [sɪ'kjuəʳ] ADJ (*safe*) seguro; (*firmly fixed*) firme, rígido; (*in safe place*) a salvo, em segurança ▸ VT (*fix*) prender; (*get*) conseguir, obter; (*Comm: loan*) garantir; **to make sth ~** firmar algo, segurar algo; **to ~ sth for sb** arranjar algo para alguém

secured creditor [sɪ'kjuəd-] N credor *m* com garantia

security [sɪ'kjurɪtɪ] N segurança; (*for loan*) fiança, garantia; (: *object*) penhor *m*; **securities** NPL (*Stock Exchange*) títulos *mpl*, valores *mpl*; **to increase** *or* **tighten ~** aumentar a segurança

Security Council N: **the ~** o Conselho de Segurança

security forces NPL forças *fpl* de segurança

security guard N segurança *m/f*

security risk N risco à segurança

sedan [sɪ'dæn] N (*Aut*) sedã *m*

sedate [sɪ'deɪt] ADJ calmo; (*calm*) sossegado, tranquilo; (*formal*) sério, ponderado ▸ VT sedar, tratar com calmantes

sedation [sɪ'deɪʃən] N (*Med*) sedação *f*; **to be under ~** estar sob o efeito de sedativos

sedative ['sɛdɪtɪv] N calmante *m*, sedativo

sedentary ['sɛdntrɪ] ADJ sedentário

sediment ['sɛdɪmənt] N sedimento

sedition [sɪ'dɪʃən] N sedição *f*

seduce [sɪ'djuːs] VT seduzir

seduction [sɪ'dʌkʃən] N sedução *f*

seductive [sɪ'dʌktɪv] ADJ sedutor(a)

see [siː] (*pt* **saw**, *pp* **seen**) VT ver; (*make out*) enxergar; (*understand*) entender; (*accompany*): **to ~ sb to the door** acompanhar *or* levar alguém até a porta ▸ VI ver; (*find out*) achar ▸ N sé *f*, sede *f*; **to ~ that** (*ensure*) assegurar que; **there was nobody to be ~n** não havia ninguém; **let me ~** deixa eu ver; **to go and ~ sb** ir visitar alguém; **~ for yourself** veja você mesmo, confira; **I don't know what she ~s in him** não sei o que ela vê nele; **as far as I can ~** que eu saiba; **~ you!** até logo! (BR), adeus! (PT); **~ you soon/later/ tomorrow!** até logo/mais tarde/amanhã!
▸ **see about** VT FUS tratar de
▸ **see off** VT despedir-se de
▸ **see through** VT FUS enxergar através de ▸ VT levar a cabo
▸ **see to** VT FUS providenciar

seed [siːd] N semente *f*; (*sperm*) esperma *m*; (*fig: gen pl*) germe *m*; (*Tennis*) pré-selecionado(-a); **to go to ~** produzir sementes; (*fig*) deteriorar-se

seedless ['siːdlɪs] ADJ sem caroços

seedling ['siːdlɪŋ] N planta brotada da semente, muda

seedy ['siːdɪ] ADJ (*shabby: place*) mal-cuidado; (: *person*) maltrapilho

seeing ['siːɪŋ] CONJ: **~ (that)** visto (que), considerando (que)

seek [siːk] (*pt, pp* **sought**) VT procurar; (*post*) solicitar; **to ~ advice/help from sb** pedir um conselho a alguém/procurar ajuda de alguém

▸ **seek out** VT (*person*) procurar

seem [siːm] VI parecer; **there ~s to be ...** parece que há ...; **what ~s to be the trouble?** qual é o problema?; **I did what ~ed best** fiz o que me pareceu melhor

seemingly ['siːmɪŋlɪ] ADV aparentemente, pelo que aparenta

seen [siːn] PP *of* **see**

seep [siːp] VI filtrar-se, penetrar

seer [sɪəʳ] N vidente *m/f*, profeta *m/f*

seersucker ['sɪəsʌkəʳ] N tecido listrado de algodão

seesaw ['siːsɔː] N gangorra, balanço

seethe [siːð] VI ferver; **to ~ with anger** estar danado (da vida)

see-through ADJ transparente

segment ['sɛgmənt] N segmento; (*of orange*) gomo

segregate ['sɛgrɪgeɪt] VT segregar

segregation [sɛgrɪ'geɪʃən] N segregação *f*

Seine [seɪn] N: **the ~** o Sena

seismic ['saɪzmɪk] ADJ sísmico

seize [siːz] VT (*grasp*) agarrar, pegar; (*take possession of: power, hostage*) apoderar-se de, confiscar; (: *territory*) tomar posse de; (*opportunity*) aproveitar
▸ **seize on** VT FUS valer-se de
▸ **seize up** VI (*Tech*) gripar
▸ **seize upon** VT FUS = **seize on**

seizure ['siːʒəʳ] N (*Med*) ataque *m*, acesso; (*Law, of power*) confisco, embargo

seldom ['sɛldəm] ADV raramente

select [sɪ'lɛkt] ADJ seleto, fino ▸ VT escolher, selecionar; (*Sport*) selecionar, escalar; **a ~ few** uns poucos escolhidos

selection [sɪ'lɛkʃən] N seleção *f*, escolha; (*Comm*) sortimento

selection committee N comissão *f* de seleção

selective [sɪ'lɛktɪv] ADJ seletivo

selector [sɪ'lɛktəʳ] N (*person*) selecionador(a) *m/f*, seletor(a) *m/f*; (*Tech*) selecionador *m*

self [sɛlf] PRON *see* **herself, himself, itself, myself, oneself, ourselves, themselves, yourself** ▸ N (*pl* **selves**) **the ~** o eu

self... [sɛlf] PREFIX auto...

self-addressed [-ə'drɛst] ADJ: **~ envelope** envelope *m* endereçado ao remetente

self-adhesive ADJ autoadesivo

self-appointed [-ə'pɔɪntɪd] ADJ autonomeado

self-assertive ADJ autoritário

self-assurance N autoconfiança

self-assured [-ə'ʃuəd] ADJ seguro de si

self-catering (BRIT) ADJ (*flat*) com cozinha; (*holiday*) em casa alugada

self-centred, (US) **self-centered** [-'sɛntəd] ADJ egocêntrico

self-cleaning ADJ de limpeza automática

self-coloured, (US) **self-colored** ADJ de cor natural; (*of one colour*) de uma só cor

self-confessed [-kən'fɛst] ADJ assumido

self-confidence N autoconfiança, confiança em si

self-conscious ADJ inibido, constrangido

self-contained [-kən'teɪnd] (BRIT) ADJ (gen)
independente; (flat) completo, autônomo
self-control N autocontrole m, autodomínio
self-defeating [-dɪ'fiːtɪŋ] ADJ
contraproducente
self-defence, (US) **self-defense** N legítima
defesa, autodefesa; **in ~** em legítima defesa
self-discipline N autodisciplina
self-employed [-ɪm'plɔɪd] ADJ autônomo
self-esteem N amor m próprio
self-evident ADJ patente
self-explanatory ADJ que se explica por si
mesmo
self-governing [-'gʌvənɪŋ] ADJ autônomo
self-harm N autoimolação f ▶ VI
autoimolar(-se)
self-help N iniciativa própria, esforço pessoal
self-importance N presunção f
self-important ADJ presunçoso, que se dá
muita importância
self-indulgent ADJ que se permite excessos
self-inflicted [-ɪn'flɪktɪd] ADJ infligido a si
mesmo
self-interest N egoísmo
selfish ['sɛlfɪʃ] ADJ egoísta
selfishness ['sɛlfɪʃnɪs] N egoísmo
selfless ['sɛlflɪs] ADJ desinteressado
selflessly ['sɛlflɪslɪ] ADV desinteressadamente
self-made N: **~ man** homem m que se fez por
conta própria
self-pity N pena de si mesmo
self-portrait N autorretrato
self-possessed [-pə'zɛst] ADJ calmo, senhor(a)
de si
self-preservation N autopreservação f
self-raising [-'reɪzɪŋ] (BRIT) ADJ: **~ flour**
farinha de trigo com fermento acrescentado
self-reliant ADJ seguro de si, independente
self-respect N amor m próprio
self-respecting [-rɪs'pɛktɪŋ] ADJ que se preza
self-righteous ADJ farisaico, santarrão(-rona)
self-rising (US) ADJ: **~ flour** farinha de trigo
com fermento acrescentado
self-sacrifice N abnegação f, altruísmo
self-same ADJ mesmo
self-satisfied [-'sætɪsfaɪd] ADJ satisfeito
consigo mesmo
self-sealing ADJ (envelope) autoadesivo
self-service ADJ de autosserviço ▶ N
autosserviço
self-styled [-staɪld] ADJ pretenso
self-sufficient ADJ autossuficiente
self-supporting [-sə'pɔːtɪŋ] ADJ
financeiramente independente
self-tanning ADJ autobronzeador
self-taught ADJ autodidata
self-test N (Comput) auto-teste m
sell [sɛl] (pt, pp **sold**) VT vender; (fig): **to ~ sb an
idea** convencer alguém de uma ideia ▶ VI
vender-se; **to ~ at** or **for £10** vender a or por
£10
▶ **sell off** VT liquidar
▶ **sell out** VI vender todo o estoque ▶ VT: **the**

tickets are all sold out todos os ingressos
já foram vendidos; **to ~ out (to)** (Comm)
vender o negócio (a); (fig) vender-se (a)
▶ **sell up** VI vender o negócio
sell-by date N vencimento
seller ['sɛlə'] N vendedor(a) m/f; **~'s market**
mercado de vendedor
selling price ['sɛlɪŋ-] N preço de venda
sellotape® ['sɛləuteɪp] (BRIT) N fita adesiva,
durex® m (BR)
sellout ['sɛlaut] N traição f; (of tickets): **it was a
~** foi um sucesso de bilheteria
selves [sɛlvz] PL of **self**
semantic [sə'mæntɪk] ADJ semântico
semantics [sə'mæntɪks] N semântica
semaphore ['sɛməfɔː'] N semáforo
semblance ['sɛmbləns] N aparência
semen ['siːmən] N sêmen m
semester [sə'mɛstə'] (esp US) N semestre m
semi ['sɛmɪ] (BRIT inf) N (casa) geminada
semi... [sɛmɪ] PREFIX semi..., meio...
semibreve ['sɛmɪbriːv] (BRIT) N semibreve f
semicircle ['sɛmɪsəːkl] N semicírculo
semicircular [sɛmɪ'səːkjulə'] ADJ semicircular
semicolon [sɛmɪ'kəulən] N ponto e vírgula
semiconductor [sɛmɪkən'dʌktə'] N
semicondutor m
semi-conscious ADJ semiconsciente
semidetached [sɛmɪdɪtætʃt], **semidetached
house** (BRIT) N (casa) geminada
semifinal [sɛmɪfaɪnl] N semifinal f
seminar ['sɛmɪnɑː'] N seminário
seminary ['sɛmɪnərɪ] N (for priests) seminário
semiprecious [sɛmɪ'prɛʃəs] ADJ semiprecioso
semiquaver ['sɛmɪkweɪvə'] (BRIT) N
semicolcheia
semiskilled [sɛmɪ'skɪld] ADJ (work, worker)
semiespecializado
semi-skimmed milk [sɛmɪ'skɪmd-] N leite m
semidesnatado
semitone ['sɛmɪtəun] N (Mus) semitom m
semolina [sɛmə'liːnə] N sêmola, semolina
SEN (BRIT) N ABBR = **State Enrolled Nurse**
Sen., sen. ABBR = **senator; senior**
senate ['sɛnɪt] N senado
senator ['sɛnətə'] N senador(a) m/f
send [sɛnd] (pt, pp **sent**) VT mandar, enviar;
(dispatch) expedir, remeter; (transmit)
transmitir; (telegram) passar; **to ~ by post**
(BRIT) or **mail** (US) mandar pelo correio; **to ~
sb for sth** mandar alguém buscar algo; **to ~
word that ...** mandar dizer que ...; **she ~s
(you) her love** ela lhe envia lembranças; **to
~ sb to Coventry** (BRIT) colocar alguém em
ostracismo; **to ~ sb to sleep** dar sono a
alguém; **to ~ sb into fits of laughter** dar
um ataque de riso a alguém; **to ~ sth flying**
derrubar algo
▶ **send away** VT (letter, goods) expedir,
mandar; (unwelcome visitor) mandar embora
▶ **send away for** VT FUS encomendar, pedir
pelo correio
▶ **send back** VT devolver, mandar de volta

▶ **send for** VT FUS mandar buscar; *(by post)* pedir pelo correio, encomendar

▶ **send in** VT *(report, application)* entregar

▶ **send off** VT *(goods)* despachar, expedir; *(BRIT Sport: player)* expulsar

▶ **send on** VT *(BRIT: letter)* remeter; *(luggage etc: in advance)* mandar com antecedência

▶ **send out** VT *(invitation)* distribuir; *(signal)* emitir

▶ **send round** VT *(letter, document)* circular

▶ **send up** VT *(person, price)* fazer subir; *(BRIT: parody)* parodiar

sender ['sɛndər] N remetente *m/f*

send-off N: **a good ~** uma boa despedida

Senegal [sɛnɪ'gɔːl] N Senegal *m*

Senegalese [sɛnɪgə'liːz] ADJ, N INV senegalês(-esa) *m/f*

senile ['siːnaɪl] ADJ senil

senility [sɪ'nɪlɪtɪ] N senilidade *f*

senior ['siːnɪər] ADJ *(older)* mais velho *or* idoso; *(on staff)* mais antigo; *(of higher rank)* superior ▶ N o mais velho/a mais velha; *(on staff)* o mais antigo/a mais antiga; **P. Jones ~** P. Jones Sênior

senior citizen N idoso(-a)

senior high school *(US)* N ≈ colégio

seniority [siːnɪ'ɔrɪtɪ] N antiguidade *f*; *(in service)* status *m*

sensation [sɛn'seɪʃən] N sensação *f*; **to cause a ~** causar sensação

sensational [sɛn'seɪʃənəl] ADJ sensacional; *(headlines, result)* sensacionalista

sensationalism [sɛn'seɪʃənəlɪzəm] N sensacionalismo

sense [sɛns] N sentido; *(feeling)* sensação *f*; *(good sense)* bom senso ▶ VT sentir, perceber; **senses** NPL juízo; **it makes ~** faz sentido; **there is no ~ in (doing) that** não há sentido em (fazer) isso; **to come to one's ~s** *(regain consciousness)* recobrar os sentidos; *(become reasonable)* recobrar o juízo; **to take leave of one's ~s** enlouquecer

senseless ['sɛnslɪs] ADJ insensato, estúpido; *(unconscious)* sem sentidos, inconsciente

sense of humour N senso de humor

sensibility [sɛnsɪ'bɪlɪtɪ] N sensibilidade *f*; **sensibilities** NPL suscetibilidade *f*

sensible ['sɛnsɪbl] ADJ sensato, de bom senso; *(reasonable: price)* razoável; *(: advice, decision)* sensato; *(shoes etc)* prático

sensitive ['sɛnsɪtɪv] ADJ sensível; *(fig: touchy)* suscetível

sensitivity [sɛnsɪ'tɪvɪtɪ] N sensibilidade *f*; *(touchiness)* suscetibilidade *f*

sensual ['sɛnsjuəl] ADJ sensual

sensuous ['sɛnsjuəs] ADJ sensual

sent [sɛnt] PT, PP of **send**

sentence ['sɛntəns] N *(Ling)* frase *f*, oração *f*; *(Law: verdict)* sentença; *(: punishment)* pena ▶ VT: **to ~ sb to death/to 5 years** condenar alguém à morte/a 5 anos de prisão; **to pass ~ on sb** sentenciar alguém

sentiment ['sɛntɪmənt] N sentimento; *(opinion: also pl)* opinião *f*

sentimental [sɛntɪ'mɛntl] ADJ sentimental

sentimentality [sɛntɪmɛn'tælɪtɪ] N sentimentalismo

sentry ['sɛntrɪ] N sentinela *f*

sentry duty N: **to be on ~** estar de guarda

Seoul [səul] N Seul

separable ['sɛprəbl] ADJ separável

separate [adj 'sɛprɪt, vt, vi 'sɛpəreɪt] ADJ separado; *(distinct)* diferente ▶ VT separar; *(part)* dividir ▶ VI separar-se; **~ from** separado de; **under ~ cover** *(Comm)* em separado; **to ~ into** dividir em

separated ['sɛpəreɪtd] ADJ *(from spouse)* separado

separately ['sɛprɪtlɪ] ADV separadamente

separates ['sɛprɪts] NPL *(clothes)* roupas *fpl* que fazem jogo

separation [sɛpə'reɪʃən] N separação *f*

Sept. ABBR (= *September*) set

September [sɛp'tɛmbər] N setembro; *see also* **July**

septic ['sɛptɪk] ADJ sético; *(wound)* infeccionado

septicaemia, *(US)* **septicemia** [sɛptɪ'siːmɪə] N septicemia

septic tank N fossa sética

sequel ['siːkwl] N consequência, resultado; *(of film, story)* continuação *f*

sequence ['siːkwəns] N série *f*, sequência; *(Cinema)* série; **in ~** em sequência

sequin ['siːkwɪn] N lantejoula, paetê *m*

Serbo-Croat ['səːbəu'krəuæt] N *(Ling)* serbo-croata *m*

serenade [sɛrə'neɪd] N serenata ▶ VT fazer serenata para

serene [sɪ'riːn] ADJ sereno, tranquilo

serenity [sə'rɛnɪtɪ] N serenidade *f*, tranquilidade *f*

sergeant ['sɑːdʒənt] N sargento

sergeant major N sargento-ajudante *m*

serial ['sɪərɪəl] N *(TV, Radio, magazine)* seriado; *(in newspaper)* história em folhetim ▶ ADJ *(Comput: interface, printer)* serial; *(: access)* sequencial

serialize ['sɪərɪəlaɪz] VT *(book)* publicar em folhetim; *(TV)* seriar

serial killer N assassino(-a) em série, serial killer *m/f*

serial number N número de série

series ['sɪəriːz] N INV série *f*

serious ['sɪərɪəs] ADJ sério; *(matter)* importante; *(illness)* grave; **are you ~ (about it)?** você está falando sério?

seriously ['sɪərɪəslɪ] ADV a sério, com seriedade; *(hurt)* gravemente; **to take sth/sb ~** levar algo/alguém a sério

seriousness ['sɪərɪəsnɪs] N *(of manner)* seriedade *f*; *(importance)* importância; *(gravity)* gravidade *f*

sermon ['səːmən] N sermão *m*

serrated [sɪ'reɪtɪd] ADJ serrado, dentado

serum ['sɪərəm] N soro
servant ['sə:vənt] N empregado(-a); (*fig*) servidor(a) *m/f*
serve [sə:v] VT servir; (*customer*) atender; (*subj: train*) passar por; (*treat*) tratar; (*apprenticeship*) fazer; (*prison term*) cumprir ▶ VI (*at table*) servir-se; (*Tennis*) sacar; (*be useful*): **to ~ as/for/to do** servir como/para/para fazer ▶ N (*Tennis*) saque *m*; **are you being ~d?** você já foi atendido?; **to ~ on a committee/jury** fazer parte de um comitê/júri; **it ~s him right** é bem feito para ele; **it ~s my purpose** isso me serve
▶ **serve out** VT (*food*) servir
▶ **serve up** VT = **serve out**
server ['sə:və'] N (*Comput*) servidor *m*
service ['sə:vɪs] N serviço; (*Rel*) culto; (*Aut*) revisão *f*; (*Tennis*) saque *m*; (*also:* **dinner service**) aparelho de jantar ▶ VT (*car, washing machine*) fazer a revisão de, revisar; (: *repair*) consertar; **the Services** NPL (*army, navy etc*) as Forças Armadas; **to be of ~ to sb, to do sb a ~** ser útil a alguém
serviceable ['sə:vɪsəbl] ADJ aproveitável, prático, durável
service area N (*on motorway*) posto de gasolina com bar, restaurante etc
service charge (BRIT) N serviço
service industries NPL setor *m* de serviços
serviceman ['sə:vɪsmæn] (*irreg: like* **man**) N militar *m*
service station N posto de gasolina (BR), estação *f* de serviço (PT)
serviette [sə:vɪ'ɛt] (BRIT) N guardanapo
servile ['sə:vaɪl] ADJ servil
session ['sɛʃən] N (*period of activity*) sessão *f*; (*Sch*) ano letivo; **to be in ~** estar reunido em sessão
set [sɛt] (*pt, pp* **set**) N (*collection of things*) jogo; (*radio set, TV set*) aparelho; (*of utensils*) bateria de cozinha; (*of cutlery*) talher *m*; (*of books*) coleção *f*; (*group of people*) grupo; (*Tennis*) set *m*; (*Theatre, Cinema*) cenário; (*Hairdressing*) penteado; (*Math*) conjunto ▶ ADJ (*fixed*) fixo; (*ready*) pronto; (*resolved*) decidido, estabelecido ▶ VT (*place*) pôr, colocar; (*table*) pôr; (*price*) fixar; (*rules etc*) estabelecer, decidir; (*record*) estabelecer; (*time*) marcar; (*adjust*) ajustar; (*task, exam*) passar; (*Typ*) compor ▶ VI (*sun*) pôr-se; (*jam, jelly, concrete*) endurecer, solidificar-se; **to be ~ on doing sth** estar decidido a fazer algo; **to be all ~ to do** estar todo pronto para fazer; **to be (dead) ~ against** estar (completamente) contra; **he's ~ in his ways** ele tem opiniões fixas; **to ~ to music** musicar, pôr música em; **to ~ on fire** botar fogo em, incendiar; **to ~ free** libertar; **to ~ sth going** pôr algo em movimento; **to ~ sail** zarpar, alçar velas; **~ phrase** frase *f* feita; **a ~ of false teeth** uma dentadura; **a ~ of dining-room furniture** um conjunto de salade jantar; **a film ~ in Rome** um filme ambientado em Roma

▶ **set about** VT FUS (*task*) começar com; **to ~ about doing sth** começar a fazer algo
▶ **set aside** VT deixar de lado
▶ **set back** VT (*cost*): **it ~ me back £50** custou £50; (*in time*): **to ~ sb back (by)** atrasar alguém (em); (*place*): **a house ~ back from the road** uma casa afastada da estrada
▶ **set in** VI (*infection*) manifestar-se; (*complications*) surgir; **the rain has ~ in for the day** vai chover o dia inteiro
▶ **set off** VI partir, ir indo ▶ VT (*bomb*) fazer explodir; (*alarm*) disparar; (*chain of events*) iniciar; (*show up well*) ressaltar
▶ **set out** VI partir ▶ VT (*arrange*) colocar, dispor; (*state*) expor, explicar; **to ~ out to do sth** pretender fazer algo; **to ~ out (from)** sair (de)
▶ **set up** VT (*organization*) fundar, estabelecer; **to ~ up shop** (*fig*) estabelecer-se
setback ['sɛtbæk] N (*hitch*) revés *m*, contratempo; (*in health*) piora
set menu N refeição *f* a preço fixo
set square N esquadro
settee [sɛ'ti:] N sofá *m*
setting ['sɛtɪŋ] N (*background*) cenário; (*position*) posição *f*; (*frame*) moldura; (*placing*) colocação *f*; (*of sun*) pôr (do sol) *m*; (*of jewel*) engaste *m*
setting lotion N loção *f* fixadora
settle ['sɛtl] VT (*argument, matter*) resolver, esclarecer; (*accounts*) ajustar, liquidar; (*land*) colonizar; (*Med: calm*) acalmar, tranquilizar ▶ VI (*dust etc*) assentar; (*calm down: children*) acalmar-se; (*weather*) firmar, melhorar; (*also:* **settle down**) instalar-se, estabilizar-se; **to ~ to sth** concentrar-se em algo; **to ~ for sth** concordar em aceitar algo; **to ~ on sth** optar por algo; **that's ~d then** está resolvido então; **to ~ one's stomach** acomodar o estômago
▶ **settle in** VI instalar-se
▶ **settle up** VI: **to ~ up with sb** ajustar as contas com alguém
settlement ['sɛtlmənt] N (*payment*) liquidação *f*; (*agreement*) acordo, convênio; (*village etc*) povoado, povoação *f*; **in ~ of our account** (*Comm*) em liquidação da nossa conta
settler ['sɛtlə'] N colono(-a), colonizador(a) *m/f*
setup ['sɛtʌp] N (*organization*) organização *f*; (*situation*) situação *f*
seven ['sɛvn] NUM sete; *see also* **five**
seventeen [sɛvn'ti:n] NUM dezessete; *see also* **five**
seventeenth [sɛvn'ti:nθ] NUM décimo sétimo
seventh ['sɛvnθ] NUM sétimo; *see also* **fifth**
seventieth ['sɛvntɪɪθ] NUM septuagésimo
seventy ['sɛvntɪ] NUM setenta; *see also* **fifty**
sever ['sɛvə'] VT cortar; (*relations*) romper
several ['sɛvərl] ADJ, PRON vários(-as); **~ of us** vários de nós; **~ times** várias vezes
severance ['sɛvərəns] N (*of relations*) rompimento

severance pay N indenização f pela demissão
severe [sɪ'vɪəʳ] ADJ severo; (serious) grave; (hard) duro; (pain) intenso; (dress) austero
severely [sɪ'vɪəlɪ] ADV severamente; (wounded, ill) gravemente
severity [sɪ'vɛrɪtɪ] N severidade f; (of pain) intensidade f; (of dress) austeridade f
sew [səu] (pt **sewed**, pp **sewn**) VT, VI coser, costurar
   ▶ **sew up** VT coser, costurar; **it's all ~n up** (fig) está no papo
sewage ['su:ɪdʒ] N detritos mpl
sewer ['su:əʳ] N (cano do) esgoto, bueiro
sewing ['səuɪŋ] N costura
sewing machine N máquina de costura
sewn [səun] PP of **sew**
sex [sɛks] N sexo; **to have ~ with sb** fazer sexo com alguém
sex act N ato sexual
sexism ['sɛksɪzm] N sexismo
sexist ['sɛksɪst] ADJ sexista
sextet [sɛks'tɛt] N sexteto
sexual ['sɛksjuəl] ADJ sexual; **~ assault** atentado ao pudor; **~ intercourse** relações fpl sexuais
sexuality [sɛksju'ælɪtɪ] N sexualidade f
sexy ['sɛksɪ] ADJ sexy
Seychelles [seɪ'ʃɛl(z)] NPL: **the ~** Seychelles (no article)
SF N ABBR = **science fiction**
SG (US) N ABBR = **Surgeon General**
Sgt ABBR (= sergeant) sarg
shabbiness ['ʃæbɪnɪs] N (of clothes) pobreza; (of building) mau estado de conservação
shabby ['ʃæbɪ] ADJ (person) esfarrapado, maltrapilho; (clothes) usado, surrado; (behaviour) indigno
shack [ʃæk] N choupana, barraca
shackles ['ʃæklz] NPL algemas fpl, grilhões mpl
shade [ʃeɪd] N sombra; (for lamp) quebra-luz m; (for eyes) viseira; (of colour) tom m, tonalidade f; (US: window shade) estore m; (small quantity): **a ~ (more/too big)** um pouquinho (mais/grande) ▶ VT dar sombra a; (eyes) sombrear; **shades** NPL (US: sunglasses) óculos mpl escuros; **in the ~** à sombra
shadow ['ʃædəu] N sombra ▶ VT (follow) seguir de perto (sem ser visto); **without or beyond a ~ of doubt** sem sombra de dúvida
shadow cabinet (BRIT) N (Pol) gabinete paralelo formado pelo partido da oposição
shadowy ['ʃædəuɪ] ADJ escuro; (dim) vago, indistinto
shady ['ʃeɪdɪ] ADJ à sombra; (fig: dishonest: person) suspeito, duvidoso; (: deal) desonesto
shaft [ʃɑ:ft] N (of arrow, spear) haste f; (column) fuste m; (Aut, Tech) eixo, manivela; (of mine, of lift) poço; (of light) raio
shaggy ['ʃægɪ] ADJ desgrenhado
shake [ʃeɪk] (pt **shook**, pp **shaken**) VT sacudir; (building, confidence) abalar; (surprise) surpreender ▶ VI tremer ▶ N (movement) sacudidela; (violent) safanão m; **to ~ hands**

with sb apertar a mão de alguém; **to ~ one's head** (in refusal etc) dizer não com a cabeça; (in dismay) sacudir a cabeça
   ▶ **shake off** VT sacudir; (fig) livrar-se de
   ▶ **shake up** VT sacudir; (fig) reorganizar
shake-up N reorganização f
shakily ['ʃeɪkɪlɪ] ADV (reply) de voz trêmula; (walk) vacilante; (write) de mão trêmula
shaky ['ʃeɪkɪ] ADJ (hand, voice) trêmulo; (table) instável; (building) abalado; (person: in shock) abalado; (: old) frágil; (knowledge) duvidoso
shale [ʃeɪl] N argila xistosa
shall [ʃæl] AUX VB: **I ~ go** irei; **~ I open the door?** posso abrir a porta?; **I'll get some, ~ I?** eu vou pegar algum, está bem?
shallot [ʃə'lɔt] (BRIT) N cebolinha
shallow ['ʃæləu] ADJ raso; (breathing) fraco; (fig) superficial
sham [ʃæm] N fraude f, fingimento ▶ ADJ falso, simulado ▶ VT fingir, simular
shambles ['ʃæmblz] N confusão f; **the economy is (in) a complete ~** a economia está completamente desorganizada
shambolic [ʃæm'bɔlɪk] ADJ (inf) bagunçado, esculhambado
shame [ʃeɪm] N vergonha; (pity) pena ▶ VT envergonhar; **it is a ~ (that/to do)** é (uma) pena (que/fazer); **what a ~!** que pena!; **to put sb/sth to ~** deixar alguém/algo envergonhado
shamefaced ['ʃeɪmfeɪst] ADJ envergonhado
shameful ['ʃeɪmful] ADJ vergonhoso
shameless ['ʃeɪmlɪs] ADJ sem vergonha, descarado; (immodest) cínico, impudico
shampoo [ʃæm'pu:] N xampu m (BR), champô m (PT) ▶ VT lavar o cabelo (com xampu or champô)
shampoo and set N lavagem f e penteado
shamrock ['ʃæmrɔk] N trevo
shandy ['ʃændɪ] N mistura de cerveja com refresco gaseificado
shan't [ʃɑ:nt] = **shall not**
shanty town ['ʃæntɪ-] N favela
SHAPE [ʃeɪp] N ABBR (= Supreme Headquarters Allied Powers, Europe) QG das forças aliadas na Europa
shape [ʃeɪp] N forma ▶ VT (form) moldar; (clay, stone) dar forma a; (sb's ideas) formar; (sb's life) definir, determinar; **to take ~** tomar forma; **in the ~ of a heart** em forma de coração; **I can't bear gardening in any ~ or form** não suporto jardinagem de forma alguma; **to get o.s. into ~** ficar em forma
   ▶ **shape up** VI (events) desenrolar-se; (person) tomar jeito
-shaped [ʃeɪpt] SUFFIX: **heart~** em forma de coração
shapeless ['ʃeɪplɪs] ADJ informe, sem forma definida
shapely ['ʃeɪplɪ] ADJ escultural
share [ʃɛəʳ] N (part) parte f; (contribution) cota; (Comm) ação f ▶ VT dividir; (have in common) compartilhar; **to ~ in** participar de; **to have**

a ~ in the profits ter uma participação nos lucros

▶ **share out** vi distribuir; **to ~ out (among** or **between)** distribuir (entre)

share capital N capital m em ações

share certificate N cautela de ação

shareholder ['ʃɛəhəuldə'] N acionista m/f

share index N índice m da Bolsa de Valores

share issue N emissão f de ações

shark [ʃɑːk] N tubarão m

sharp [ʃɑːp] ADJ (razor, knife) afiado; (point, features) pontiagudo; (outline) definido, bem marcado; (pain, voice) agudo; (taste) acre; (curve, bend) fechado; (Mus) desafinado; (contrast) marcado; (person: quick-witted) perspicaz; (dishonest) desonesto ▶ N (Mus) sustenido ▶ ADV: **at 2 o'clock ~** às 2 (horas) em ponto; **turn ~ left** vira logo à esquerda; **to be ~ with sb** ser brusco com alguém; **look ~!** rápido!

sharpen ['ʃɑːpən] VT afiar; (pencil) apontar, fazer a ponta de; (fig) aguçar

sharpener ['ʃɑːpnə'] N (also: **pencil sharpener**) apontador m (BR), apara-lápis m inv (PT)

sharp-eyed [-aɪd] ADJ de vista aguda

sharply ['ʃɑːplɪ] ADV (abruptly) bruscamente; (clearly) claramente; (harshly) severamente

sharp-tempered ADJ irascível

sharp-witted [-'wɪtɪd] ADJ perspicaz, observador(a)

shatter ['ʃætə'] VT despedaçar, estilhaçar; (fig: ruin) destruir, acabar com; (: upset) arrasar ▶ vi despedaçar-se, estilhaçar-se

shattered ['ʃætəd] ADJ (overwhelmed) arrasado; (exhausted) exausto

shatterproof ['ʃætəpruːf] ADJ inestilhaçável

shave [ʃeɪv] VT barbear, fazer a barba de ▶ vi fazer a barba, barbear-se ▶ N: **to have a ~** fazer a barba

shaven ['ʃeɪvn] ADJ (head) raspado

shaver ['ʃeɪvə'] N barbeador m; **electric ~** barbeador elétrico

shaving ['ʃeɪvɪŋ] N (action) barbeação f; **shavings** NPL (of wood) aparas fpl

shaving brush N pincel m de barba

shaving cream N creme m de barbear

shaving foam N espuma de barbear

shaving soap N sabão m de barba

shawl [ʃɔːl] N xale m

she [ʃiː] PRON ela ▶ PREFIX: **~-elephant** etc elefante etc fêmea; **there ~ is** lá está ela

sheaf [ʃiːf] (pl **sheaves**) N (of corn) gavela; (of arrows) feixe m; (of papers) maço

shear [ʃɪə'] (pt **sheared**, pp **shorn**) VT (sheep) tosquiar, tosar

▶ **shear off** VT cercear ▶ vi cisalhar

shears [ʃɪəz] NPL (for hedge) tesoura de jardim

sheath [ʃiːθ] N bainha; (contraceptive) camisa-de-vênus f, camisinha

sheathe [ʃiːð] VT embainhar

sheath knife (irreg: like **knife**) N faca com bainha

sheaves [ʃiːvz] NPL of **sheaf**

shed [ʃɛd] N alpendre m, galpão m; (Industry, Rail) galpão m ▶ VT (pt, pp **shed**) (skin) mudar; (load, leaves, fur) perder; (tears, blood) derramar; (workers) despedir; **to ~ light on** (problem, mystery) esclarecer

she'd [ʃiːd] = **she had; she would**

sheen [ʃiːn] N brilho

sheep [ʃiːp] N INV ovelha

sheepdog ['ʃiːpdɔg] N cão m pastor

sheep farmer N criador(a) m/f de ovelhas

sheepish ['ʃiːpɪʃ] ADJ tímido, acanhado

sheepskin [ʃiːpskɪn] N pele f de carneiro, pelego

sheepskin jacket N casaco de pele de carneiro

sheer [ʃɪə'] ADJ (utter) puro, completo; (steep) íngreme, empinado; (almost transparent) fino, translúcido ▶ ADV a pique; **by ~ chance** totalmente por acaso

sheet [ʃiːt] N (on bed) lençol m; (of paper) folha; (of glass, metal) lâmina, chapa; (of ice) camada

sheet feed N (on printer) alimentação f de papel (em folhas soltas)

sheet lightning N relâmpago difuso

sheet metal N metal m em chapa

sheet music N música

sheik, sheikh [ʃeɪk] N xeque m

shelf [ʃɛlf] (pl **shelves**) N prateleira; **set of shelves** estante f

shelf life N (Comm) validade f (de produtos perecíveis)

shell [ʃɛl] N (on beach) concha; (of egg, nut etc) casca; (explosive) obus m; (of building) armação f, esqueleto ▶ VT (peas) descascar; (Mil) bombardear

▶ **shell out** (inf) vi: **to ~ out (for)** pagar

she'll [ʃiːl] = **she will; she shall**

shellfish ['ʃɛlfɪʃ] N INV crustáceo; (as food) frutos mpl do mar, mariscos mpl

shelter ['ʃɛltə'] N (building) abrigo; (protection) refúgio ▶ VT (protect) proteger; (give lodging to) abrigar; (hide) esconder ▶ vi abrigar-se, refugiar-se; **to take ~ from** abrigar-se de

sheltered ['ʃɛltəd] ADJ (life) protegido; (spot) abrigado, protegido; **~ housing** acomodação para idosos e defeituosos

shelve [ʃɛlv] VT (fig) pôr de lado, engavetar

shelves [ʃɛlvz] NPL of **shelf**

shelving ['ʃɛlvɪŋ] N (shelves) prateleiras fpl

shepherd ['ʃɛpəd] N pastor m ▶ VT (guide) guiar, conduzir

shepherdess ['ʃɛpədɪs] N pastora

shepherd's pie (BRIT) N empadão m de carne e batata

sherbet ['ʃəːbət] N (BRIT: powder) pó doce e efervescente; (US: water ice) sorvete de frutas à base de água

sheriff ['ʃɛrɪf] (US) N xerife m

sherry ['ʃɛrɪ] N (vinho de) Xerez m

she's [ʃiːz] = **she is; she has**

Shetland ['ʃɛtlənd] N (also: **the Shetlands, the Shetland Isles**) as ilhas Shetland

shield [ʃiːld] N escudo; (Sport) escudo, brasão m; (protection) proteção f; (Tech) blindagem f

▶ VT: **to ~ (from)** proteger (contra)

shift [ʃɪft] N (*change*) mudança; (*of place*) transferência; (*of work*) turno; (*of workers*) turma ▶ VT transferir; (*remove*) tirar ▶ VI mudar; (*change place*) mudar de lugar; **the wind has ~ed to the south** o vento virou para o sul; **a ~ in demand** (*Comm*) um deslocamento de demanda

shift key N (*on typewriter*) tecla para maiúsculas

shiftless [ˈʃɪftlɪs] ADJ indolente

shift work N trabalho em turnos; **to do ~** trabalhar em turnos

shifty [ˈʃɪftɪ] ADJ esperto, trapaceiro; (*eyes*) velhaco, maroto

Shiite [ˈʃiːaɪt] ADJ, N xiita

shilling [ˈʃɪlɪŋ] (*BRIT*) N xelim *m* (= 12 *old pence; 20 in a pound*)

shilly-shally [ˈʃɪlɪʃælɪ] VI vacilar

shimmer [ˈʃɪməʳ] N reflexo trêmulo ▶ VI cintilar, tremeluzir

shin [ʃɪn] N canela (da perna) ▶ VI: **to ~ up/ down a tree** subir em/descer de uma árvore com mãos e pernas

shindig [ˈʃɪndɪg] (*inf*) N arrasta-pé *m*

shine [ʃaɪn] VI (*pt, pp* shone) brilhar ▶ VT (*shoes: pt, pp* shined) lustrar ▶ N brilho, lustre *m*; **to ~ a torch on sth** apontar uma lanterna para algo

shingle [ˈʃɪŋgl] N (*on beach*) pedrinhas *fpl*, seixinhos *mpl*; (*on roof*) telha

shingles [ˈʃɪŋglz] N (*Med*) herpes-zoster *m*

shining [ˈʃaɪnɪŋ] ADJ brilhante

shiny [ˈʃaɪnɪ] ADJ brilhante, lustroso

ship [ʃɪp] N barco; (*large*) navio ▶ VT (*goods*) embarcar; (*send*) transportar or mandar (por via marítima); **on board ~** a bordo

shipbuilder [ˈʃɪpbɪldəʳ] N construtor *m* naval

shipbuilding [ˈʃɪpbɪldɪŋ] N construção *f* naval

ship chandler [-ˈtʃændləʳ] N fornecedor *m* de provisões para navios

shipment [ˈʃɪpmənt] N (*act*) embarque *m*; (*goods*) carregamento

shipowner [ˈʃɪpəunəʳ] N armador(a) *m/f*

shipper [ˈʃɪpəʳ] N exportador(a) *m/f*, expedidor(a) *m/f*

shipping [ˈʃɪpɪŋ] N (*ships*) navios *mpl*; (*cargo*) transporte *m* de mercadorias (por via marítima); (*traffic*) navegação *f*

shipping agent N agente *m/f* marítimo(-a)

shipping company N companhia de navegação

shipping lane N rota de navegação

shipping line N companhia de navegação

shipshape [ˈʃɪpʃeɪp] ADJ em ordem

shipwreck [ˈʃɪprɛk] N (*event*) malogro; (*ship*) naufrágio ▶ VT: **to be ~ed** naufragar

shipyard [ˈʃɪpjɑːd] N estaleiro

shire [ˈʃaɪəʳ] (*BRIT*) N condado

shirk [ʃəːk] VT (*work*) esquivar-se de; (*obligations*) não cumprir, faltar a

shirt [ʃəːt] N (*man's*) camisa; (*woman's*) blusa; **in ~ sleeves** em manga de camisa

shirty [ˈʃəːtɪ] (*BRIT inf*) ADJ chateado, sem graça

shit [ʃɪt] (!) EXCL merda (!)

shiver [ˈʃɪvəʳ] N tremor *m*, arrepio ▶ VI tremer, estremecer, tiritar

shoal [ʃəul] N (*of fish*) cardume *m*; (*fig: also:* **shoals**) bando, multidão *f*

shock [ʃɔk] N (*impact*) choque *m*; (*Elec*) descarga; (*emotional*) comoção *f*, abalo; (*start*) susto, sobressalto; (*Med*) trauma *m* ▶ VT dar um susto em, chocar; (*offend*) escandalizar; **suffering from ~** (*Med*) traumatizado; **it gave us a ~** ficamos chocados; **it came as a ~ to hear that ...** ficamos atônitos ao saber que ...

shock absorber [-əbˈzɔːbəʳ] N amortecedor *m*

shocking [ˈʃɔkɪŋ] ADJ (*awful*) chocante, lamentável; (*outrageous*) revoltante, chocante; (*improper*) escandaloso; (*very bad*) péssimo

shockproof [ˈʃɔkpruːf] ADJ à prova de choque

shock therapy N terapia de choque

shock treatment N terapia de choque

shod [ʃɔd] PT, PP *of* shoe ▶ ADJ calçado

shoddy [ˈʃɔdɪ] ADJ de má qualidade

shoe [ʃuː] N sapato; (*for horse*) ferradura; (*also:* **brake shoe**) sapata ▶ VT (*pt, pp* shod) (*horse*) ferrar

shoe brush N escova de sapato

shoehorn [ˈʃuːhɔːn] N calçadeira

shoelace [ˈʃuːleɪs] N cadarço, cordão *m* (de sapato)

shoemaker [ˈʃuːmeɪkəʳ] N sapateiro(-a)

shoe polish N graxa de sapato

shoe rack N porta-sapatos *m inv*

shoeshop [ˈʃuːʃɔp] N sapataria

shoestring [ˈʃuːstrɪŋ] N (*fig*): **on a ~** com muito pouco dinheiro

shoetree [ˈʃuːtriː] N fôrma de sapato

shone [ʃɔn] PT, PP *of* shine

shoo [ʃuː] EXCL xô! ▶ VT (*also:* **shoo away, shoo off**) enxotar

shook [ʃuk] PT *of* shake

shoot [ʃuːt] N (*on branch, seedling*) broto ▶ VT disparar; (*kill*) matar à bala, balear; (*wound*) ferir à bala, balear; (*execute*) fuzilar; (*film*) filmar, rodar ▶ VI (*with gun, bow*): **to ~ (at)** atirar (em); (*Football*) chutar; **to ~ past sb** passar disparado por alguém
▶ **shoot down** VT (*plane*) derrubar, abater
▶ **shoot in** VI entrar correndo
▶ **shoot out** VI sair correndo
▶ **shoot up** VI (*fig*) subir vertiginosamente

shooting [ˈʃuːtɪŋ] N (*shots*) tiros *mpl*, tiroteio; (*Hunting*) caçada (com espingarda); (*attack*) tiroteio; (*: murder*) assassinato; (*Cinema*) filmagens *fpl*

shooting range N estande *m*

shooting star N estrela cadente

shop [ʃɔp] N loja; (*workshop*) oficina ▶ VI (*also:* **go shopping**) ir fazer compras; **to talk ~** (*fig*) falar de negócios
▶ **shop around** VI comparar preços; (*fig*) estudar todas as possibilidades

shop assistant (*BRIT*) N vendedor(a) *m/f*

shop floor (BRIT) N operários mpl
shopkeeper ['ʃɔpkiːpəʳ] N lojista m/f
shoplift ['ʃɔplɪft] VI furtar (em lojas)
shoplifter ['ʃɔplɪftəʳ] N larápio(-a) de loja
shoplifting ['ʃɔplɪftɪŋ] N furto (em lojas)
shopper ['ʃɔpəʳ] N comprador(a) f
shopping ['ʃɔpɪŋ] N (goods) compras fpl
shopping bag N bolsa (de compras)
shopping cart (US) N carrinho de compras
shopping centre, (US) **shopping center** N shopping (center) m
shopping mall N shopping m
shopping trolley (BRIT) N carrinho de compras
shop-soiled ADJ danificado (pelo tempo ou manuseio)
shop steward (BRIT) N (Industry) representante m/f sindical
shop window N vitrine f (BR), montra (PT)
shore [ʃɔːʳ] N (of sea) costa, praia; (of lake) margem f ▶ VT: **to ~ (up)** reforçar, escorar; **on ~** em terra
shore leave N (Naut) licença para desembarcar
shorn [ʃɔːn] PP of **shear**
short [ʃɔːt] ADJ (not long) curto; (in time) breve, de curta duração; (person) baixo; (curt) seco, brusco; (insufficient) insuficiente, em falta ▶ N (also: **short film**) curta-metragem m; **to be ~ of sth** estar em falta de algo; **to be in ~ supply** estar em falta; **I'm 3 ~** estão me faltando três; **in ~** em resumo; **~ of doing ...** a não ser fazer ...; **everything ~ of ...** tudo a não ser ...; **a ~ time ago** pouco tempo atrás; **in the ~ term** a curto prazo; **I'm ~ of time** tenho pouco tempo; **it is ~ for** é a abreviatura de; **to cut ~** (speech, visit) encurtar; (person) interromper; **to fall ~** ser deficiente; **to fall ~ of** não ser à altura de; **to run ~ of sth** ficar sem algo; **to stop ~** parar de repente; **to stop ~ of** chegar quase a
shortage ['ʃɔːtɪdʒ] N escassez f, falta
shortbread ['ʃɔːtbred] N biscoito amanteigado
short-change VT: **to ~ sb** roubar alguém no troco
short circuit N curto-circuito ▶ VT provocar um curto-circuito ▶ VI entrar em curto-circuito
shortcoming ['ʃɔːtkʌmɪŋ] N defeito, imperfeição f, falha
shortcrust pastry (BRIT) ['ʃɔːtkrʌst-], **short pastry** N massa amanteigada
shortcut ['ʃɔːtkʌt] N atalho
shorten ['ʃɔːtən] VT encurtar; (visit) abreviar
shortening ['ʃɔːtnɪŋ] N (Culin) gordura
shortfall ['ʃɔːtfɔːl] N déficit m
shorthand ['ʃɔːthænd] (BRIT) N estenografia
shorthand notebook (BRIT) N bloco para estenografia
shorthand typist (BRIT) N estenodatilógrafo(-a)

short list (BRIT) N (for job) lista dos candidatos escolhidos
short-lived [-lɪvd] ADJ de curta duração
shortly ['ʃɔːtlɪ] ADV em breve, dentro em pouco
shortness ['ʃɔːtnɪs] N (of distance) curteza; (of time) brevidade f; (manner) maneira brusca, secura
short pastry N = **shortcrust pastry**
shorts NPL: **(a pair of)** ~ um calção (BR), um short (BR), uns calções (PT)
short-sighted (BRIT) ADJ míope; (fig) imprevidente
short-staffed [-stɑːft] ADJ com falta de pessoal
short story N conto
short-tempered ADJ irritadiço
short-term ADJ (effect) a curto prazo
short time N: **to work ~, to be on ~** trabalhar em regime de semana reduzida
short wave N (Radio) onda curta
shot [ʃɔt] PT, PP of **shoot** ▶ N (of gun) tiro; (pellets) chumbo; (person) atirador(a) m/f; (try, Football) tentativa; (injection) injeção f; (Phot) fotografia; **to be a good/bad ~** (person) ter boa/má pontaria; **to fire a ~ at sb/sth** atirar em alguém/algo; **to have a ~ at (doing) sth** tentar fazer algo; **like a ~** como um relâmpago, de repente; **to get ~ of sb/sth** (inf) livrar-se de alguém/algo; **a big ~** (inf) um mandachuva, um figurão
shotgun ['ʃɔtgʌn] N espingarda
should [ʃud] AUX VB: **I ~ go now** devo ir embora agora; **he ~ be there now** ele já deve ter chegado; **I ~ go if I were you** se eu fosse você eu iria; **I ~ like to** eu gostaria de; **~ he phone ...** caso ele telefone ...
shoulder ['ʃəuldəʳ] N ombro; (BRIT: of road): **hard ~** acostamento (BR), berma (PT) ▶ VT (fig) arcar com; **to look over one's ~** olhar para trás; **to rub ~s with sb** (fig) andar com alguém; **to give sb the cold ~** (fig) desprezar alguém, dar uma fria em alguém (inf)
shoulder bag N sacola a tiracolo
shoulder blade N omoplata m
shoulder strap N alça
shouldn't ['ʃudnt] = **should not**
shout [ʃaut] N grito ▶ VT gritar ▶ VI (also: **shout out**) gritar, berrar; **to give sb a ~** chamar alguém
▶ **shout down** VT fazer calar com gritos
shouting N gritaria, berreiro
shove [ʃʌv] N empurrão m ▶ VT empurrar; (inf: put): **to ~ sth in** botar algo em; **he ~d me out of the way** ele me empurrou para o lado ▶ **shove off** VI (Naut) zarpar, partir; (inf) dar o fora
shovel ['ʃʌvl] N pá f; (mechanical) escavadeira ▶ VT cavar com pá
show [ʃəu] (pt **showed**, pp **shown**) N (of emotion) demonstração f; (semblance) aparência; (exhibition) exibição f; (Theatre) espetáculo, representação f; (Cinema) sessão f ▶ VT

S

mostrar; (*courage etc*) demonstrar, dar prova de; (*exhibit*) exibir, expor; (*depict*) ilustrar; (*film*) exibir ▶ VI mostrar-se; (*appear*) aparecer; **it doesn't ~** não parece; **I've nothing to ~ for it** não consegui nada; **to ~ sb to his seat/to the door** levar alguém ao seu lugar/até a porta; **to ~ a profit/loss** (Comm) apresentar lucros/prejuízo; **it just goes to ~ (that)** ... isso só mostra (que) ...; **to ask for a ~ of hands** pedir uma votação pelo levantamento das mãos; **it's just for ~** isso é só para mostrar; **to be on ~** estar em exposição; **who's running the ~ here?** (inf) quem é que manda aqui?

▶ **show in** VT mandar entrar

▶ **show off** VI (pej) mostrar-se, exibir-se ▶ VT (display) exibir, mostrar; (pej) fazer ostentação de

▶ **show out** VT levar até a porta

▶ **show up** VI (stand out) destacar-se; (inf: turn up) aparecer, pintar ▶ VT descobrir; (unmask) desmascarar

showbiz ['ʃəʊbɪz] N (inf) o mundo do espetáculo

show business N o mundo do espetáculo

showcase ['ʃəʊkeɪs] N vitrina

showdown ['ʃəʊdaʊn] N confrontação f

shower ['ʃaʊəʳ] N (rain) pancada de chuva; (of stones etc) chuva, enxurrada; (also: **shower bath**) chuveiro ▶ VI tomar banho (de chuveiro) ▶ VT: **to ~ sb with** (gifts etc) cumular alguém de; **to have** or **take a ~** tomar banho (de chuveiro)

shower cap N touca de banho

showerproof ['ʃaʊəpruːf] ADJ impermeável

showery ['ʃaʊərɪ] ADJ (weather) chuvoso

showground ['ʃəʊgraʊnd] N recinto da feira

showing ['ʃəʊɪŋ] N (of film) projeção f, exibição f

show jumping [-'dʒʌmpɪŋ] N hipismo

showman ['ʃəʊmən] (irreg: like **man**) N artista m/f; (fig) pessoa expansiva

showmanship ['ʃəʊmənʃɪp] N senso teatral

showmen ['ʃəʊmɛn] NPL of **showman**

shown [ʃəʊn] PP of **show**

show-off (inf) N (person) exibicionista m/f, faroleiro(-a)

showpiece ['ʃəʊpiːs] N (of exhibition etc) obra mais importante; **that hospital is a ~** aquele é um hospital modelo

showroom ['ʃəʊrʊm] N sala de exposição

showy ['ʃəʊɪ] ADJ vistoso, chamativo

shrank [ʃræŋk] PT of **shrink**

shrapnel ['ʃræpnl] N estilhaços mpl

shred [ʃrɛd] N (gen pl) tira, pedaço ▶ VT rasgar em tiras, retalhar; (Culin) desfiar, picar; (documents) fragmentar; **not a ~ of evidence** prova alguma

shredder ['ʃrɛdəʳ] N (for vegetables) ralador m; (for documents) fragmentadora

shrew [ʃruː] N (Zool) musaranho; (pej: woman) megera

shrewd [ʃruːd] ADJ perspicaz

shrewdness ['ʃruːdnɪs] N astúcia

shriek [ʃriːk] N grito ▶ VT, VI gritar, berrar

shrift [ʃrɪft] N: **to give sb short ~** dar uma resposta a alguém sem maiores explicações

shrill [ʃrɪl] ADJ agudo, estridente

shrimp [ʃrɪmp] N camarão m

shrine [ʃraɪn] N santuário

shrink [ʃrɪŋk] (pt **shrank**, pp **shrunk**) VI encolher; (be reduced) reduzir-se; (also: **shrink away**) encolher-se ▶ VT (cloth) fazer encolher ▶ N (inf, pej) psicanalista m/f; **to ~ from doing sth** não se atrever a fazer algo

shrinkage ['ʃrɪŋkɪdʒ] N encolhimento, redução f

shrink-wrap VT embalar a vácuo

shrivel ['ʃrɪvl] VT (also: **shrivel up**: dry) secar; (: crease) enrugar ▶ VI secar-se; enrugar-se, murchar

shroud [ʃraʊd] N mortalha ▶ VT: **~ed in mystery** envolto em mistério

Shrove Tuesday [ʃrəʊv-] N terça-feira gorda

shrub [ʃrʌb] N arbusto

shrubbery ['ʃrʌbərɪ] N arbustos mpl

shrug [ʃrʌg] N encolhimento dos ombros ▶ VT, VI: **to ~ (one's shoulders)** encolher os ombros, dar de ombros (BR)

▶ **shrug off** VT negar a importância de

shrunk [ʃrʌŋk] PP of **shrink**

shrunken ['ʃrʌŋkn] ADJ encolhido

shudder ['ʃʌdəʳ] N estremecimento, tremor m ▶ VI estremecer, tremer de medo

shuffle ['ʃʌfl] VT (cards) embaralhar ▶ VI: **to ~ (one's feet)** arrastar os pés

shun [ʃʌn] VT evitar, afastar-se de

shunt [ʃʌnt] VT (Rail) manobrar, desviar; (object) desviar ▶ VI: **to ~ (to and fro)** ir e vir

shunting ['ʃʌntɪŋ] N (Rail) manobras fpl

shunting yard N pátio de manobras

shush [ʃuʃ] EXCL psiu!

shut [ʃʌt] (pt, pp **shut**) VT fechar ▶ VI fechar(-se)

▶ **shut down** VT fechar; (machine) parar ▶ VI fechar

▶ **shut off** VT (supply etc) cortar, interromper

▶ **shut out** VT (person, cold) impedir que entre; (noise) abafar; (memory) reprimir

▶ **shut up** VI (inf: keep quiet) calar-se, calar a boca ▶ VT (close) fechar; (silence) calar

shutdown ['ʃʌtdaʊn] N paralização f

shutter ['ʃʌtəʳ] N veneziana; (Phot) obturador m

shuttle ['ʃʌtl] N (in weaving) lançadeira; (plane: also: **shuttle service**) ponte f aérea; (space shuttle) ônibus m espacial ▶ VI (vehicle, person) ir e vir ▶ VT (passengers) transportar de ida e volta

shuttlecock ['ʃʌtlkɔk] N peteca

shy [ʃaɪ] ADJ tímido; (reserved) reservado ▶ VI: **to ~ away from doing sth** (fig) não se atrever a fazer algo

shyness ['ʃaɪnɪs] N timidez f

Siam [saɪ'æm] N Sião m

Siamese [saɪə'miːz] ADJ: **~ cat** gato siamês; **~ twins** irmãos mpl siameses/irmãs fpl siamesas

Siberia [saɪˈbɪərɪə] N Sibéria f
sibling [ˈsɪblɪŋ] N irmão/irmã m/f
Sicilian [sɪˈsɪlɪən] ADJ, N siciliano(-a)
Sicily [ˈsɪsɪlɪ] N Sicília
sick [sɪk] ADJ (ill) doente; (nauseated) enjoado; (humour) negro; (vomiting): **to be ~** vomitar; **to feel ~** estar enjoado; **to fall ~** ficar doente; **to be (off)** ~ estar ausente por motivo de doença; **to be ~ of** (fig) estar cheio or farto de; **he makes me ~** (fig: inf) ele me enche o saco
sickbay [ˈsɪkbeɪ] N enfermaria
sicken [ˈsɪkən] VT dar náuseas a; (disgust) enojar, repugnar ▶ VI: **to be ~ing for sth** (cold, flu etc) estar no começo de algo
sickening [ˈsɪkənɪŋ] ADJ (fig) repugnante
sickle [ˈsɪkl] N foice f
sick leave N licença por doença
sickly [ˈsɪklɪ] ADJ doentio; (causing nausea) nauseante
sickness [ˈsɪknɪs] N doença, indisposição f; (vomiting) náusea, enjoo
sickness benefit N auxílio-enfermidade m, auxílio-doença m
sick note N (from parents) bilhete m dos pais; (from doctor) atestado médico
sick pay N salário pago em período de doença
sickroom [ˈsɪkruːm] N enfermaria
side [saɪd] N (gen) lado; (of body) flanco; (of lake) margem f; (aspect) aspecto; (team) time m (BR), equipa (PT); (of hill) declive m; (page) página; (of meat) costela ▶ CPD (door, entrance) lateral ▶ VI: **to ~ with sb** tomar o partido de alguém; **by the ~ of** ao lado de; **~ by ~** lado a lado, juntos; **on this/that** or **the other ~** do lado de cá/do lado de lá; **they are on our ~** (in game) fazem parte do nosso time; (in discussion) concordam com nós; **from ~ to ~** para lá e para cá; **from all ~s** de todos os lados; **to take ~s with** pôr-se ao lado de
sideboard [ˈsaɪdbɔːd] N aparador m; **sideboards** NPL (BRIT) = **sideburns**
sideburns [ˈsaɪdbəːnz] NPL suíças fpl, costeletas fpl
sidecar [ˈsaɪdkɑːʳ] N sidecar m
side dish N guarnição f
side drum N (Mus) caixa clara
side effect N efeito colateral
sidekick [ˈsaɪdkɪk] (inf) N camarada m/f
sidelight [ˈsaɪdlaɪt] N (Aut) luz f lateral
sideline [ˈsaɪdlaɪn] N (Sport) linha lateral; (fig) linha adicional de produtos; (: job) emprego suplementar
sidelong [ˈsaɪdlɔŋ] ADJ de soslaio
side order N acompanhamento
side plate N pequeno prato
side road N rua lateral
side-saddle ADV de silhão
sideshow [ˈsaɪdʃəu] N (stall) barraca
sidestep [ˈsaɪdstɛp] VT evitar ▶ VI (Boxing etc) dar um passo ao lado
sidetrack [ˈsaɪdtræk] VT (fig) desviar (do seu propósito)

sidewalk [ˈsaɪdwɔːk] (US) N calçada
sideways [ˈsaɪdweɪz] ADV de lado
siding [ˈsaɪdɪŋ] N (Rail) desvio, ramal m
sidle [ˈsaɪdl] VI: **to ~ up (to)** aproximar-se furtivamente (de)
siege [siːdʒ] N sítio, assédio; **to lay ~ to** assediar
siege economy N economia de guerra
Sierra Leone [sɪˈɛrəlɪˈəun] N Serra Leoa (no article)
siesta [sɪˈɛstə] N sesta
sieve [sɪv] N peneira ▶ VT peneirar
sift [sɪft] VT peneirar; (fig: information) esquadrinhar, analisar minuciosamente ▶ VI (fig): **to ~ through** examinar minuciosamente
sigh [saɪ] N suspiro ▶ VI suspirar
sight [saɪt] N (faculty) vista, visão f; (spectacle) espetáculo; (on gun) mira ▶ VT avistar; **in ~** à vista; **on ~** (shoot) no local; **out of ~** longe dos olhos; **at ~** (Comm) à vista; **at first ~** à primeira vista; **I know her by ~** conheço-a de vista; **to catch ~ of sb/sth** avistar alguém/algo; **to lose ~ of sb/sth** perder alguém/algo de vista; **to set one's ~s on sth** visar algo
sighted [ˈsaɪtɪd] ADJ que enxerga; **partially ~** com vista parcial
sightseeing [ˈsaɪtsiːɪŋ] N turismo; **to go ~** fazer turismo, passear
sightseer [ˈsaɪtsiːəʳ] N turista m/f
sign [saɪn] N (with hand) sinal m, aceno; (indication) indício; (trace) vestígio; (notice) letreiro, tabuleta; (also: **road sign**) placa; (written, of zodiac) signo ▶ VT assinar; **as a ~ of** como sinal de; **it's a good/bad ~** é um bom/mau sinal; **plus/minus ~** sinal de mais/menos; **there's no ~ of a change of mind** não há sinal or indícios de uma mudança de atitude; **he was showing ~s of improvement** ele estava começando a melhorar; **to ~ one's name** assinar; **to ~ sth over to sb** assinar a transferência de algo para alguém
▶ **sign away** VT (rights etc) abrir mão de
▶ **sign off** VI (Radio, TV) terminar a transmissão
▶ **sign on** VI (Mil) alistar-se; (BRIT: as unemployed) cadastrar-se para receber auxílio-desemprego; (for course) inscrever-se ▶ VT (Mil) alistar; (employee) efetivar
▶ **sign out** VI assinar o registro na partida
▶ **sign up** VI (Mil) alistar-se; (for course) inscrever-se ▶ VT recrutar
signal [ˈsɪgnl] N sinal m, aviso; (US Tel) ruído discal ▶ VI (also Aut) sinalizar, dar sinal ▶ VT (person) fazer sinais para; (message) transmitir; **to ~ a left/right turn** (Aut) dar sinal para esquerda/direita; **to ~ to sb (to do sth)** fazer sinais para alguém (fazer algo)
signal box N (Rail) cabine f de sinaleiro
signalman [ˈsɪgnlmən] (irreg: like **man**) N sinaleiro

S

signatory ['sɪgnətərɪ] N signatário(-a)
signature ['sɪgnətʃəʳ] N assinatura
signature tune N tema m (de abertura)
signet ring ['sɪgnət-] N anel m com o sinete or a chancela
significance [sɪg'nɪfɪkəns] N significado; (importance) importância; **that is of no ~** isto não tem importância alguma
significant [sɪg'nɪfɪkənt] ADJ significativo; (important) importante
significantly [sɪg'nɪfɪkəntlɪ] ADV (improve, increase) significativamente; (smile) sugestivamente; **and, ~, ...** e, significativamente, ...
signify ['sɪgnɪfaɪ] VT significar
sign language N mímica, linguagem f através de sinais
sign post N indicador m; (traffic) placa de sinalização
silage ['saɪlɪdʒ] N (fodder) silagem f; (method) ensilagem f
silence ['saɪləns] N silêncio ▶ VT silenciar, impor silêncio a; (guns) silenciar
silencer ['saɪlənsəʳ] N (on gun) silenciador m; (BRIT Aut) silencioso
silent ['saɪlənt] ADJ silencioso; (not speaking) calado; (film) mudo; **to keep** or **remain ~** manter-se em silêncio
silently ['saɪləntlɪ] ADV silenciosamente
silent partner N (Comm) sócio(-a) comanditário(-a)
silhouette [sɪluː'ɛt] N silhueta ▶ VT: **~d against** em silhueta contra
silicon ['sɪlɪkən] N silício
silicon chip ['sɪlɪkən-] N placa or chip m de silício
silicone ['sɪlɪkəun] N silicone m
silk [sɪlk] N seda ▶ ADJ de seda
silky ['sɪlkɪ] ADJ sedoso
sill [sɪl] N (also: **window sill**) parapeito, peitoril m; (Aut) soleira
silly ['sɪlɪ] ADJ (person) bobo, idiota, imbecil; (idea) absurdo, ridículo; **to do something ~** fazer uma besteira
silo ['saɪləu] N silo
silt [sɪlt] N sedimento, aluvião m
silver ['sɪlvəʳ] N prata; (money) moedas fpl; (also: **silverware**) prataria ▶ ADJ de prata
silver foil N papel m de prata
silver paper (BRIT) N papel m de prata
silver-plated [-'pleɪtɪd] ADJ prateado, banhado a prata
silversmith ['sɪlvəsmɪθ] N prateiro(-a)
silverware ['sɪlvəwɛəʳ] N prataria
silver wedding N (anniversary) bodas fpl de prata
silvery ['sɪlvərɪ] ADJ prateado
SIM card ['sɪm-] N (Tel) cartão m SIM, chip m
similar ['sɪmɪləʳ] ADJ: **~ to** parecido com, semelhante a
similarity [sɪmɪ'lærɪtɪ] N semelhança
similarly ['sɪmɪləlɪ] ADV da mesma maneira
simile ['sɪmɪlɪ] N símile f

simmer ['sɪməʳ] VI cozer em fogo lento, ferver lentamente
▶ **simmer down** (inf) VI (fig) acalmar-se
simper ['sɪmpəʳ] VI sorrir afetadamente
simpering ['sɪmpərɪŋ] ADJ idiota
simple ['sɪmpl] ADJ simples inv; (foolish) ingênuo; **the ~ truth** a pura verdade
simple interest N juros mpl simples
simple-minded ADJ simplório
simpleton ['sɪmpltən] N simplório(-a), pateta m/f
simplicity [sɪm'plɪsɪtɪ] N simplicidade f
simplification [sɪmplɪfɪ'keɪʃən] N simplificação f
simplify ['sɪmplɪfaɪ] VT simplificar
simply ['sɪmplɪ] ADV de maneira simples; (merely) simplesmente
simulate ['sɪmjuleɪt] VT simular
simulated ['sɪmjuleɪtɪd] ADJ simulado
simulation [sɪmju'leɪʃən] N simulação f
simultaneous [sɪməl'teɪnɪəs] ADJ simultâneo
simultaneously [sɪməl'teɪnɪəslɪ] ADV simultaneamente
sin [sɪn] N pecado ▶ VI pecar
Sinai ['saɪneɪaɪ] N Sinai m
since [sɪns] ADV desde então, depois ▶ PREP desde ▶ CONJ (time) desde que; (because) porque, visto que, já que; **~ then** desde então; **~ Monday** desde segunda-feira; **(ever) ~ I arrived** desde que eu cheguei
sincere [sɪn'sɪəʳ] ADJ sincero
sincerely [sɪn'sɪəlɪ] ADV sinceramente; **yours ~** (BRIT), **~ yours** (US) (at end of letter) atenciosamente
sincerity [sɪn'sɛrɪtɪ] N sinceridade f
sine [saɪn] N (Math) seno
sinew ['sɪnjuː] N tendão m
sinful ['sɪnful] ADJ (thought) pecaminoso; (person) pecador(a)
sing [sɪŋ] (pt **sang**, pp **sung**) VT, VI cantar
Singapore [sɪŋgə'pɔːʳ] N Cingapura (no article)
singe [sɪndʒ] VT chamuscar
singer ['sɪŋəʳ] N cantor(a) m/f
Singhalese [sɪŋə'liːz] ADJ = **Sinhalese**
singing ['sɪŋɪŋ] N (gen) canto; (songs) canções fpl; (in the ears) zumbido
single ['sɪŋgl] ADJ único, só; (unmarried) solteiro; (not double) simples inv ▶ N (BRIT: also: **single ticket**) passagem f de ida; (record) compacto; **not a ~ one was left** não sobrou nenhum; **every ~ day** todo santo dia
▶ **single out** VT (choose) escolher; (distinguish) distinguir
single bed N cama de solteiro
single-breasted [-'brɛstɪd] ADJ não trespassado
single file N: **in ~** em fila indiana
single-handed [-'hændɪd] ADV sem ajuda, sozinho
single-minded ADJ determinado
single parent N pai m solteiro/mãe f solteira
single room N quarto individual
singles ['sɪŋglz] N (Tennis) partida simples
▶ NPL (US: people) solteiros mpl

singlet ['sɪŋglɪt] N camiseta

singly ['sɪŋglɪ] ADV separadamente

singsong ['sɪŋsɔŋ] ADJ (tone) cantado ▶ N (songs): **to have a ~** cantar

singular ['sɪŋgjulə^r] ADJ (odd) esquisito; (outstanding) extraordinário, excepcional; (Ling) singular ▶ N (Ling) singular m; **in the feminine ~** no feminino singular

singularly ['sɪŋgjulǝlɪ] ADV particularmente

Sinhalese [sɪnhǝ'liːz] ADJ cingalês(-esa)

sinister ['sɪnɪstǝ^r] ADJ sinistro

sink [sɪŋk] (pt **sank**, pp **sunk**) N pia ▶ VT (ship) afundar; (foundations) escavar ▶ VI (ship, ground) afundar-se; (heart) partir; (spirits) ficar deprimido; (also: **sink back, sink down**) cair or mergulhar gradativamente; (share prices) cair; **to ~ sth into** (teeth etc) enterrar algo em; **he sank into a chair/the mud** ele afundou na cadeira/na lama; **a ~ing feeling** um vazio no estômago
▶ **sink in** VI (fig) penetrar; **it took a long time to ~ in** demorou muito para ser entendido

sinking fund ['sɪŋkɪŋ-] N fundo de amortização

sink unit N pia

sinner ['sɪnǝ^r] N pecador(a) m/f

sinuous ['sɪnjuǝs] ADJ sinuoso

sinus ['saɪnǝs] N (Anat) seio (paranasal)

sinusitis [saɪnǝ'saɪtǝs] N sinusite f

sip [sɪp] N gole m ▶ VT sorver, bebericar

siphon ['saɪfǝn] N sifão m
▶ **siphon off** VT extrair com sifão; (funds) desviar

sir [sǝ^r] N senhor m; **S~ John Smith** Sir John Smith; **yes, ~** sim, senhor; **Dear S~** (in letter) (Prezado) Senhor

siren ['saɪǝrn] N sirena

sirloin ['sǝːlɔɪn] N lombo de vaca

sirloin steak N filé m de alcatra

sisal ['saɪsǝl] N sisal m

sissy ['sɪsɪ] (inf) N fresco

sister ['sɪstǝ^r] N irmã f; (BRIT: nurse) enfermeira-chefe f; (nun) freira ▶ CPD: **~ organization** organização f congênere; **~ ship** navio gêmeo

sister-in-law (pl **sisters-in-law**) N cunhada

sit [sɪt] (pt, pp **sat**) VI sentar-se; (be sitting) estar sentado; (assembly) reunir-se; (for painter) posar; (dress) cair ▶ VT (exam) prestar; **to ~ on a committee** ser membro de um comitê; **to ~ tight** não se mexer; (fig) esperar
▶ **sit about** VI ficar sentado não fazendo nada
▶ **sit around** VI ficar sentado não fazendo nada
▶ **sit back** VI acomodar-se num assento
▶ **sit down** VI sentar-se; **to be ~ting down** estar sentado
▶ **sit in on** VT FUS assistir a
▶ **sit up** VI (after lying) levantar-se; (straight) endireitar-se; (not go to bed) aguardar acordado, velar

sitcom ['sɪtkɔm] N ABBR (= situation comedy) comédia de costumes

sit-down ADJ: **~ strike** greve f de braços cruzados; **a ~ meal** uma refeição servida à mesa

site [saɪt] N local m, sítio; (also: **building site**) lote m (de terreno) ▶ VT situar, localizar

sit-in N (demonstration) ocupação de um local como forma de protesto, manifestação f pacífica

siting ['saɪtɪŋ] N (location) localização f

sitter ['sɪtǝ^r] N (for painter) modelo; (also: **babysitter**) baby-sitter m/f

sitting ['sɪtɪŋ] N (of assembly etc) sessão f; (in canteen) turno

sitting member N (Pol) parlamentar m/f

sitting room N sala de estar

sitting tenant (BRIT) N inquilino(-a)

situate ['sɪtjueɪt] VT situar

situated ['sɪtjueɪtɪd] ADJ situado

situation [sɪtju'eɪʃǝn] N situação f; (job) posição f; (location) local m; **"~s vacant/wanted"** (BRIT) "empregos oferecem-se/procurados"

situation comedy N (Theatre, TV) comédia de costumes

six [sɪks] NUM seis; see also **five**

six-pack ['sɪkspæk] N (of beer) seis latas; (stomach) tanquinho

sixteen ['sɪks'tiːn] NUM dezesseis; see also **five**

sixteenth [sɪks'tiːnθ] NUM décimo sexto

sixth [sɪksθ] NUM sexto; **the upper/lower ~** (BRIT Sch) os dois últimos anos do colégio; see also **fifth**

sixtieth ['sɪkstɪɪθ] NUM sexagésimo

sixty ['sɪkstɪ] NUM sessenta; see also **fifty**

size [saɪz] N (gen) tamanho; (extent) extensão f; (of clothing) tamanho, medida; (of shoes) número; (glue) goma; **I take ~ 14** (of dress) = meu tamanho é 44; **the small/large ~** (of soap powder etc) o tamanho pequeno/grande; **what ~ do you take in shoes?** que número você calça?; **it's the ~ of ...** é do tamanho de ...
▶ **size up** VT avaliar, formar uma opinião sobre

sizeable ['saɪzǝbl] ADJ considerável, importante

sizzle ['sɪzl] VI chiar

SK (CANADA) ABBR = **Saskatchewan**

skate [skeɪt] N patim m; (fish: pl inv) arraia
▶ VI patinar
▶ **skate around** VT FUS (problem) evitar
▶ **skate over** VT FUS = **skate around**

skateboard ['skeɪtbɔːd] N skate m, patim-tábua m

skater ['skeɪtǝ^r] N patinador(a) m/f

skating ['skeɪtɪŋ] N patinação f

skating rink N rinque m de patinação

skeleton ['skelɪtn] N esqueleto; (Tech) armação f; (outline) esquema m, esboço

skeleton key N chave f mestra

skeleton staff N pessoal m reduzido (ao mínimo)

S

skeptic ['skɛptɪk] (US) N = **sceptic**
sketch [skɛtʃ] N (drawing) desenho; (outline) esboço, croqui m; (Theatre) quadro, esquete m ▶ VT desenhar, esboçar; (ideas: also: **sketch out**) esboçar
sketchbook ['skɛtʃbuk] N caderno de rascunho
sketch pad N bloco de desenho
sketchy ['skɛtʃɪ] ADJ incompleto, superficial
skew [skju:] (BRIT) N: **on the ~** fora de esquadria
skewer ['skju:əʳ] N espetinho
ski [ski:] N esqui m ▶ VI esquiar
ski boot N bota de esquiar
skid [skɪd] N derrapagem f ▶ VI deslizar; (Aut) derrapar
skid mark N marca de derrapagem
skier ['ski:əʳ] N esquiador(a) m/f
skiing ['ski:ɪŋ] N esqui m; **to go ~** ir esquiar
ski instructor N instrutor(a) m/f de esqui
ski jump N pista para saltos de esqui; (event) salto de esqui
skilful, (US) **skillful** ['skɪlful] ADJ habilidoso, jeitoso
skilfully, (US) **skillfully** ['skɪlfəlɪ] ADV habilmente
ski lift N ski lift m
skill [skɪl] N habilidade f, perícia; (for work) técnica
skilled [skɪld] ADJ hábil, perito; (worker) especializado, qualificado
skillet ['skɪlɪt] N frigideira
skillful ['skɪlful] (US) ADJ = **skilful**
skim [skɪm] VT (milk) desnatar; (glide over) roçar ▶ VI: **to ~ through** (book) folhear
skimmed milk [skɪmd-] N leite m desnatado
skimp [skɪmp] VT (work: also: **skimp on**) atamancar; (cloth etc) economizar, regatear
skimpy ['skɪmpɪ] ADJ (meagre) escasso, insuficiente; (skirt) sumário
skin [skɪn] N (gen) pele f; (of fruit, vegetable) casca; (on pudding, paint) película ▶ VT (fruit etc) descascar; (animal) tirar a pele de; **wet or soaked to the ~** encharcado, molhado como um pinto
skin-deep ADJ superficial
skin diver N mergulhador(a) m/f
skin diving N caça-submarina
skinflint ['skɪnflɪnt] N pão-duro m
skin graft N enxerto de pele
skinny ['skɪnɪ] ADJ magro, descarnado
skin test N cutirreação f
skintight ['skɪntaɪt] ADJ (dress etc) justo, grudado (no corpo)
skip [skɪp] N salto, pulo; (BRIT: container) balde m ▶ VI saltar; (with rope) pular corda ▶ VT (pass over) omitir, saltar; (miss) deixar de; **to ~ school** (esp US) matar aula
ski pants NPL calça (BR) or calças fpl (PT) de esquiar
ski pole N vara de esqui
skipper ['skɪpəʳ] N (Naut, Sport) capitão m ▶ VT capitanear

skipping rope ['skɪpɪŋ-] (BRIT) N corda (de pular)
ski resort N estação f de esqui
skirmish ['skə:mɪʃ] N escaramuça
skirt [skə:t] N saia ▶ VT (surround) rodear; (go round) orlar, circundar
skirting board ['skə:tɪŋ-] (BRIT) N rodapé m
ski run N pista de esqui
ski slope N pista de esqui
ski suit N traje m de esqui
skit [skɪt] N paródia, sátira
ski tow N ski lift m
skittle ['skɪtl] N pau m; **skittles** N (game) (jogo de) boliche m (BR), jogo da bola (PT)
skive [skaɪv] (BRIT inf) VI evitar trabalhar
skulk [skʌlk] VI esconder-se
skull [skʌl] N caveira; (Anat) crânio
skullcap ['skʌlkæp] N solidéu m; (worn by Pope) barrete m
skunk [skʌŋk] N gambá m; (fig: person) cafajeste m/f, pessoa vil
sky [skaɪ] N céu m; **to praise sb to the skies** pôr alguém nas nuvens
sky-blue ADJ azul-celeste inv
sky-high ADV muito alto ▶ ADJ: **prices are ~** os preços dispararam
skylark ['skaɪlɑ:k] N (bird) cotovia
skylight ['skaɪlaɪt] N claraboia, escotilha
skyline ['skaɪlaɪn] N (horizon) linha do horizonte; (of city) silhueta
skyscraper ['skaɪskreɪpəʳ] N arranha-céu m
slab [slæb] N (stone) bloco; (flat) laje f; (of cake) fatia grossa
slack [slæk] ADJ (loose) frouxo; (slow) lerdo; (careless) descuidado, desmazelado; (Comm: market) inativo, frouxo; (: demand) fraco ▶ N (in rope) brando; **slacks** NPL (trousers) calça (BR), calças fpl (PT); **business is ~** os negócios vão mal
slacken ['slækən] VI (also: **slacken off**) afrouxar-se ▶ VT afrouxar; (speed) diminuir
slag [slæg] N escória, escombros mpl
slag heap N monte m de escória or de escombros
slag off (BRIT inf) VT malhar
slain [sleɪn] PP of **slay**
slake [sleɪk] VT (one's thirst) matar
slalom ['slɑ:ləm] N slalom m
slam [slæm] VT (door) bater or fechar (com violência); (throw) atirar violentamente; (criticize) malhar, criticar ▶ VI fechar-se (com violência)
slander ['slɑ:ndəʳ] N calúnia, difamação f ▶ VT caluniar, difamar
slanderous ['slɑ:ndərəs] ADJ calunioso, difamatório
slang [slæŋ] N gíria; (jargon) jargão m
slant [slɑ:nt] N declive m, inclinação f; (fig) ponto de vista
slanted ['slɑ:ntɪd] ADJ (roof) inclinado; (eyes) puxado
slanting ['slɑ:ntɪŋ] ADJ = **slanted**
slap [slæp] N tapa m or f ▶ VT dar um(a) tapa em; (paint etc): **to ~ sth on sth** passar algo

em algo descuidadamente ▸ ADV (*directly*)
diretamente, exatamente

slapdash ['slæpdæʃ] ADJ impetuoso; (*work*)
descuidado

slapstick ['slæpstɪk] N (*comedy*) (comédia-)
pastelão *m*

slap-up (BRIT) ADJ: **a ~ meal** uma refeição
suntuosa

slash [slæʃ] VT cortar, talhar; (*fig: prices*) cortar

slat [slæt] N (*of wood*) ripa; (*of plastic*) tira

slate [sleɪt] N ardósia ▸ VT (*fig: criticize*) criticar
duramente, arrasar

slaughter ['slɔːtər] N (*of animals*) matança; (*of
people*) carnificina ▸ VT abater; matar,
massacrar

slaughterhouse ['slɔːtəhaus] N matadouro

Slav [slɑːv] ADJ, N eslavo(-a)

slave [sleɪv] N escravo(-a) ▸ VI (*also:* **slave
away**) trabalhar como escravo; **to ~ (away)
at sth/at doing sth** trabalhar feito
condenado em algo/fazendo algo

slave labour N trabalho escravo

slaver ['slævər] VI (*dribble*) babar

slavery ['sleɪvərɪ] N escravidão *f*

Slavic ['slɑːvɪk] ADJ eslavo

slavish ['sleɪvɪʃ] ADJ servil; (*copy*) descarado

Slavonic [sləˈvɔnɪk] ADJ eslavo

slay [sleɪ] (*pt* **slew**, *pp* **slain**) VT (*literary*) matar

SLD (BRIT) N ABBR (*Pol*) = **Social and Liberal
Democratic Party**

sleazy ['sliːzɪ] ADJ (*place*) sórdido

sled [slɛd] (US) N trenó *m*

sledge [slɛdʒ] (BRIT) N trenó *m*

sledgehammer ['slɛdʒhæmər] N marreta,
malho

sleek [sliːk] ADJ (*hair, fur*) macio, lustroso; (*car,
boat*) aerodinâmico

sleep [sliːp] (*pt, pp* **slept**) N sono ▸ VI dormir
▸ VT: **we can ~ 4** podemos acomodar 4
pessoas; **to go to ~** dormir, adormecer; **to
have a good night's ~** ter uma boa noite de
sono; **to put to ~** (*patient*) fazer dormir;
(*animal: euphemism: kill*) sacrificar; **to ~ lightly**
ter sono leve; **to ~ with sb** (*euphemism*)
dormir com alguém
▸ **sleep around** VI ser promíscuo
sexualmente
▸ **sleep in** VI (*oversleep*) dormir demais; (*lie in*)
dormir até tarde

sleeper ['sliːpər] N (*person*) dorminhoco(-a);
(*Rail: on track*) dormente *m*; (: *train*) vagão-
leitos *m* (BR), carruagem-camas *f* (PT)

sleepily ['sliːpɪlɪ] ADV sonolentamente

sleeping ['sliːpɪŋ] ADJ adormecido, que dorme

sleeping bag N saco de dormir

sleeping car N vagão-leitos *m* (BR),
carruagem-camas *f* (PT)

sleeping partner (BRIT) N (*Comm*) sócio
comanditário

sleeping pill N pílula para dormir

sleepless ['sliːplɪs] ADJ: **a ~ night** uma noite
em claro

sleeplessness ['sliːplɪsnɪs] N insônia

sleepwalker ['sliːpwɔːkər] N sonâmbulo

sleepy ['sliːpɪ] ADJ sonolento; (*fig*) morto; **to
be** or **feel ~** estar com sono

sleet [sliːt] N chuva com neve or granizo

sleeve [sliːv] N manga; (*of record*) capa

sleeveless ['sliːvlɪs] ADJ (*garment*) sem manga

sleigh [sleɪ] N trenó *m*

sleight [slaɪt] N: **~ of hand** prestidigitação *f*

slender ['slɛndər] ADJ esbelto, delgado; (*means*)
escasso, insuficiente

slept [slɛpt] PT, PP of **sleep**

sleuth [sluːθ] (*inf*) N detetive *m*

slew [sluː] PT of **slay** ▸ VI (BRIT: *also:* **slew
round**) virar

slice [slaɪs] N (*of meat, bread*) fatia; (*of lemon*)
rodela; (*of fish*) posta; (*utensil*) pá *f* or espátula
de bolo ▸ VT cortar em fatias; **~d bread**
pão *m* em fatias

slick [slɪk] ADJ (*skilful*) jeitoso, ágil, engenhoso;
(*quick*) rápido; (*clever*) esperto, astuto ▸ N
(*also:* **oil slick**) mancha de óleo

slid [slɪd] PT, PP of **slide**

slide [slaɪd] (*pt, pp* **slid**) VT deslizar ▸ VI (*slip*)
escorregar; (*glide*) deslizar ▸ N (*downward
movement*) deslizamento, escorregão *m*; (*in
playground*) escorregador *m*; (*Phot*) slide *m*;
(BRIT: *also:* **hair slide**) passador *m*; (*microscope
slide*) lâmina; (*in prices*) queda, baixa; **to let
things ~** (*fig*) deixar tudo ir por água abaixo

slide projector N (*Phot*) projetor *m* deslides

slide rule N régua de cálculo

slide show N apresentação *f* de slides

sliding ['slaɪdɪŋ] ADJ (*door*) corrediço; **~ roof**
(*Aut*) teto deslizante

sliding scale N escala móvel

slight [slaɪt] ADJ (*slim*) fraco, franzino; (*frail*)
delicado; (*error, pain, increase*) pequeno; (*trivial*)
insignificante ▸ N desfeita, desconsideração *f*
▸ VT (*offend*) desdenhar, menosprezar; **not in
the ~est** em absoluto, de maneira alguma;
the ~est o(-a) menor; **a ~ improvement**
uma pequena melhora

slightly ['slaɪtlɪ] ADV ligeiramente, um pouco;
~ built magrinho

slim [slɪm] ADJ esbelto, delgado; (*chance*)
pequeno ▸ VI emagrecer

slime [slaɪm] N lodo, limo, lama

slimming ['slɪmɪŋ] N emagrecimento ▸ ADJ
(*diet, pills*) para emagrecer

slimy ['slaɪmɪ] ADJ pegajoso; (*pond*) lodoso;
(*fig*) falso

sling [slɪŋ] VT (*pt, pp* **slung**) atirar, arremessar,
lançar ▸ N (*Med*) tipoia; (*for baby*) bebêbag *m*;
(*weapon*) estilingue *m*, funda; **to have one's
arm in a ~** estar com o braço na tipoia

slink [slɪŋk] (*pt, pp* **slunk**) VI: **to ~ away** or **off**
escapulir

slip [slɪp] N (*slide*) tropeção *m*; (*fall*) escorregão
m; (*mistake*) erro, lapso; (*underskirt*)
combinação *f*; (*of paper*) tira ▸ VT deslizar ▸ VI
(*slide*) deslizar; (*lose balance*) escorregar;
(*decline*) decair; (*move smoothly*): **to ~ into/out
of** entrar furtivamente em/sair

S

furtivamente de; **to let a chance ~ by**
deixar passar uma oportunidade; **to ~ sth
on/off** enfiar/tirar algo; **it ~ped from her
hand** escorregou da mão dela; **to give sb
the ~** esgueirar-se de alguém; **a ~ of the
tongue** um lapso da língua; *see also*
Freudian
▸ **slip away** vi escapulir
▸ **slip in** vt meter ▸ vi *(errors)* surgir
▸ **slip out** vi *(go out)* sair (um momento)
▸ **slip up** vi cometer um erro
slip-on ADJ sem fecho ou botões; **~ shoes**
mocassins *mpl*
slipped disc [slɪpt-] N disco deslocado
slipper ['slɪpə^r] N chinelo
slippery ['slɪpərɪ] ADJ escorregadio
slip road *(BRIT)* N *(to motorway)* entrada para a
rodovia
slipshod ['slɪpʃɔd] ADJ descuidoso,
desmazelado
slip-up N *(error)* equívoco, mancada; *(by neglect)*
descuido
slipway ['slɪpweɪ] N carreira
slit [slɪt] VT *(pt, pp* **slit***) (cut)* rachar, cortar;
(open) abrir ▸ N fenda; *(cut)* corte *m*; **to ~ sb's
throat** cortar o pescoço de alguém
slither ['slɪðə^r] vi escorregar, deslizar
sliver ['slɪvə^r] N *(of glass, wood)* lasca; *(of cheese
etc)* fatia fina
slob [slɔb] *(inf)* N *(in manners)* porco(-a); *(in
appearance)* maltrapilho(-a)
slog [slɔg] *(BRIT)* vi mourejar ▸ N: **it was a ~**
deu um trabalho louco
slogan ['sləugən] N lema *m*, slogan *m*
slop [slɔp] vi *(also:* **slop over***)* transbordar,
derramar ▸ vt transbordar, entornar
slope [sləup] N ladeira; *(side of mountain)*
encosta, vertente *f*; *(ski slope)* pista; *(slant)*
inclinação *f*, declive *m* ▸ vi: **to ~ down** estar
em declive; **to ~ up** inclinar-se
sloping ['sləupɪŋ] ADJ inclinado, em declive;
(handwriting) torto
sloppy ['slɔpɪ] ADJ *(work)* descuidado;
(appearance) relaxado; *(film etc)* piegas *inv*
slosh [slɔʃ] *(inf)* vi: **to ~ about** *or* **around**
(children) patinhar; *(liquid)* esparrinhar
sloshed [slɔʃt] *(inf)* ADJ *(drunk)* com a cara
cheia
slot [slɔt] N *(in machine)* fenda; *(opening)*
abertura; *(fig: in timetable, Radio, TV)* horário
▸ vt: **to ~ into** encaixar em ▸ vi encaixar-se
em
sloth [sləuθ] N *(vice, Zool)* preguiça
slot machine N *(for gambling)* caça-níqueis *m
inv*; *(BRIT: vending machine)* distribuidora
automática
slot meter *(BRIT)* N contador *m* *(de eletricidade ou
gás)* operado por moedas
slouch [slautʃ] vi ter má postura
▸ **slouch about** vi vadiar
▸ **slouch around** vi = **slouch about**
slovenly ['slʌvənlɪ] ADJ *(dirty)* desalinhado,
sujo; *(careless)* desmazelado

slow [sləu] ADJ lento; *(not clever)* bronco, de
raciocínio lento; *(watch)*: **to be ~** atrasar
▸ ADV lentamente, devagar ▸ vt *(also:* **slow
down, slow up***: vehicle)* ir (mais) devagar;
(business) estar devagar ▸ vi ir (mais) devagar;
"~" *(road sign)* "devagar"; **at a ~ speed** devagar;
to be ~ to act/decide ser lento nas ações/
decisões, vacilar; **my watch is 20 minutes ~**
meu relógio está atrasado vinte minutos;
business is ~ os negócios vão mal; **to go ~**
(driver) dirigir devagar; *(in industrial dispute)*
fazer uma greve tartaruga; **the ~ lane** a
faixa da direita; **bake for 2 hours in a ~
oven** asse durante 2 horas em fogo brando
slow-acting ADJ de ação lenta
slowcoach ['sləukəutʃ] N *(BRIT inf)* lesma
slowdown ['sləudaun] *(US)* N greve *f* de
trabalho lento, operação *f* tartaruga
slowly ['sləulɪ] ADV lentamente, devagar
slow motion N: **in ~** em câmara lenta
slowness ['sləunɪs] N lentidão *f*
slowpoke ['sləupəuk] N *(US inf)* = **slowcoach**
sludge [slʌdʒ] N lama, lodo
slue [slu:] *(US)* vi = **slew**
slug [slʌg] N lesma; *(bullet)* bala
sluggish ['slʌgɪʃ] ADJ vagaroso; *(business)* lento
sluice [slu:s] N *(gate)* comporta, eclusa;
(channel) canal *m* ▸ vt: **to ~ down** *or* **out**
lavar com jorro d'água
slum [slʌm] N *(area)* favela; *(house)* cortiço,
barraco
slumber ['slʌmbə^r] N sono
slump [slʌmp] N *(economic)* depressão *f*;
(Comm) baixa, queda ▸ vi *(person)* cair; *(prices)*
baixar repentinamente; **he was ~ed over
the wheel** estava caído sobre a direção
slung [slʌŋ] PT, PP *of* **sling**
slunk [slʌŋk] PT, PP *of* **slink**
slur [slə:^r] N calúnia ▸ vt difamar, caluniar;
(word) pronunciar indistintamente; **to cast
a ~ on sb** manchar a reputação de alguém
slurred [slə:d] ADJ *(pronunciation)* indistinto,
ininteligível
slush [slʌʃ] N neve *f* meio derretida
slush fund N verba para suborno
slushy ['slʌʃɪ] ADJ *(snow)* meio derretido;
(street) lamacento; *(BRIT fig)* piegas *inv*
slut [slʌt] *(pej)* N mulher *f* desmazelada;
(whore) prostituta
sly [slaɪ] ADJ *(person)* astuto; *(smile, remark)*
malicioso, velhaco; **on the ~** às escondidas
smack [smæk] N *(slap)* palmada; *(blow)* tabefe
m ▸ vt bater; *(child)* dar uma palmada em;
(on face) dar um tabefe em ▸ vi: **to ~ of**
cheirar a, saber a ▸ ADV *(inf)*: **it fell ~ in the
middle** caiu exatamente no meio
smacker ['smækə^r] *(inf)* N *(kiss)* beijoca;
(BRIT: pound note) libra; *(US: dollar bill)* dólar *m*
small [smɔ:l] ADJ pequeno; *(short)* baixo;
(letter) minúsculo ▸ N: **the ~ of the back** os
rins; **to get** *or* **grow ~er** diminuir; **to make
~er** diminuir; **a ~ shopkeeper** um pequeno
comerciante

small ads (BRIT) NPL classificados *mpl*
small arms NPL armas *fpl* leves
small change N trocado
small fry NPL gente *f* sem importância
smallholder ['smɔ:lhəuldəʳ] (BRIT) N pequeno(-a) proprietário(-a)
smallholding ['smɔ:lhəuldɪŋ] (BRIT) N minifúndio
small hours NPL: **in the ~** na madrugada, lá pelas tantas (*inf*)
smallish ['smɔ:lɪʃ] ADJ de pequeno porte
small-minded ADJ mesquinho
smallpox ['smɔ:lpɔks] N varíola
small print N tipo miúdo
small-scale ADJ (*model, map*) reduzido; (*business, farming*) de pequeno porte
small talk N conversa fiada
small-time ADJ (*farmer etc*) pequeno; **a ~ thief** um ladrão de galinha
smart [smɑ:t] ADJ elegante; (*clever*) inteligente, astuto; (*quick*) vivo, esperto ▶ VI sofrer; **the ~ set** a alta sociedade; **to look ~** estar elegante; **my eyes are ~ing** meus olhos estão ardendo
SMART Board® N quadro interativo
smart card N smart card *m*, cartão *m* inteligente
smarten up ['smɑ:tən-] VI arrumar-se ▶ VT arrumar
smart phone N smartphone *m*
smash [smæʃ] N (*also*: **smash-up**) colisão *f*, choque *m*; (*smash hit*) sucesso de bilheteira; (*sound*) estrondo ▶ VT (*break*) escangalhar, despedaçar; (*car etc*) bater com; (*Sport: record*) quebrar ▶ VI despedaçar-se; (*against wall etc*) espatifar-se
▶ **smash up** VT destruir
smash hit N sucesso absoluto
smashing ['smæʃɪŋ] (*inf*) ADJ excelente
smattering ['smætərɪŋ] N: **a ~ of** um conhecimento superficial de
smear [smɪəʳ] N mancha, nódoa; (*Med*) esfregaço; (*insult*) difamação *f* ▶ VT untar; (*to make dirty*) lambuzar; (*fig*) caluniar, difamar; **his hands were ~ed with oil/ink** as mãos dele estavam manchadas de óleo/tinta
smear campaign N campanha de desmoralização
smear test (BRIT) N (*Med*) esfregaço
smell [smɛl] (*pt, pp* **smelt** *or* **smelled**) VT cheirar ▶ VI (*food etc*) cheirar; (*pej*) cheirar mal ▶ N cheiro; (*sense*) olfato; **to ~ of** cheirar a; **it ~s good** cheira bem, tem um bom cheiro
smelly ['smɛlɪ] (*pej*) ADJ fedorento, malcheiroso
smelt [smɛlt] PT, PP *of* **smell** ▶ VT (*ore*) fundir
smile [smaɪl] N sorriso ▶ VI sorrir
smiling ['smaɪlɪŋ] ADJ sorridente, risonho
smirk [smə:k] (*pej*) N sorriso falso *or* afetado
smith [smɪθ] N ferreiro
smithy ['smɪðɪ] N forja, oficina de ferreiro
smitten ['smɪtn] ADJ: **~ with** (*charmed by*) encantado por; (*grief etc*) tomado por

smock [smɔk] N guarda-pó *m*; (*children's*) avental *m*
smog [smɔg] N nevoeiro com fumaça (BR) *or* fumo (PT)
smoke [sməuk] N fumaça (BR), fumo (PT) ▶ VI fumar; (*chimney*) fumegar ▶ VT (*cigarettes*) fumar; **to have a ~** fumar; **do you ~?** você fuma?; **to go up in ~** (*house etc*) queimar num incêndio; (*fig*) não dar em nada
smoke alarm N detector *m* de fumaça
smoked [sməukt] ADJ (*bacon*) defumado; (*glass*) fumée
smokeless fuel ['sməuklɪs-] N combustível *m* não poluente
smokeless zone ['sməuklɪs-] (BRIT) N *zona onde não é permitido o uso de combustíveis poluentes*
smoker ['sməukəʳ] N (*person*) fumante *m/f*; (*Rail*) vagão *m* para fumantes
smokescreen ['sməukskri:n] N cortina de fumaça
smoke shop (US) N tabacaria, charutaria (BR)
smoking ['sməukɪŋ] N: **"no ~"** (*sign*) "proibido fumar"; **he's given up ~** ele deixou de fumar
smoking compartment, (US) **smoking car** N vagão *m* para fumantes
smoky ['sməukɪ] ADJ (*room*) enfumaçado; (*taste*) defumado
smolder ['sməuldəʳ] (US) VI = **smoulder**
smooth [smu:ð] ADJ liso, macio; (*sauce*) cremoso; (*sea*) tranquilo, calmo; (*flat*) plano; (*flavour, movement*) suave; (*person*) culto, refinado; (*: pej*) meloso; (*flight, landing*) tranquilo; (*cigarette*) suave ▶ VT (*also*: **smooth out**) alisar; (*: difficulties*) aplainar
▶ **smooth over** VT: **to ~ things over** (*fig*) arranjar as coisas
smoothly ['smu:ðlɪ] ADV (*easily*) facilmente, sem problemas; **everything went ~** tudo correu muito bem
smother ['smʌðəʳ] VT (*fire*) abafar; (*person*) sufocar; (*emotions*) reprimir
smoulder, (US) **smolder** ['sməuldəʳ] VI arder sem chamas; (*fig*) estar latente
SMS N ABBR (= *short message service*) SMS *m*
smudge [smʌdʒ] N mancha ▶ VT manchar, sujar
smug [smʌg] (*pej*) ADJ convencido
smuggle ['smʌgl] VT contrabandear; **to ~ in/out** (*goods etc*) fazer entrar/sair de contrabando
smuggler ['smʌgləʳ] N contrabandista *m/f*
smuggling ['smʌglɪŋ] N contrabando
smut [smʌt] N (*of soot*) marca de fuligem; (*mark*) mancha; (*in conversation etc*) obscenidades *fpl*
smutty ['smʌtɪ] ADJ (*fig*) obsceno, indecente
snack [snæk] N lanche *m* (BR), merenda (PT); **to have a ~** fazer um lanche
snack bar N lanchonete *f* (BR), snackbar *m* (PT)
snag [snæg] N dificuldade *f*, obstáculo
snail [sneɪl] N caracol *m*; (*water snail*) caramujo
snake [sneɪk] N cobra

S

snap [snæp] N (*sound*) estalo; (*of whip*) estalido; (*click*) clique *m*; (*photograph*) foto *f* ▶ ADJ repentino ▶ VT (*break*) quebrar; (*fingers, whip*) estalar; (*photograph*) tirar uma foto de ▶ VI quebrar; (*fig: person*) retrucar asperamente; (*sound*) estalar; **to ~ shut** fechar com um estalo; **to ~ one's fingers** estalar os dedos; **a cold ~** uma onda de frio
▶ **snap at** VT FUS (*subj: person*) retrucar bruscamente a; (: *dog*) tentar morder
▶ **snap off** VT (*break*) partir
▶ **snap up** VT arrebatar, comprar rapidamente

snap fastener N colchete *m* de mola

snappy ['snæpɪ] (*inf*) ADJ rápido; (*slogan*) vigoroso; **he's a ~ dresser** ele está sempre chique; **make it ~!** faça rápido!

snapshot ['snæpʃɒt] N foto *f* (instantânea)

snare [snɛəʳ] N armadilha, laço ▶ VT apanhar no laço or na armadilha

snarl [snɑːl] N grunhido ▶ VI grunhir ▶ VT: **to get ~ed up** (*wool, plans*) ficar embaralhado; (*traffic*) ficar engarrafado

snatch [snætʃ] N (*fig*) roubo; (*small piece*) trecho ▶ VT agarrar; (*fig: look*) roubar ▶ VI: **don't ~!** não tome as coisas dos outros!; **to ~ a sandwich** fazer um lanche rapidinho; **to ~ some sleep** dormir um pouco
▶ **snatch up** VT agarrar

sneak [sniːk] (*pt, pp* **sneaked** *or* US **snuck**) VI: **to ~ in/out** entrar/sair furtivamente ▶ VT: **to ~ a look at sth** olhar disfarçadamente para algo ▶ N (*inf*) dedo-duro; **to ~ up on sb** chegar de mansinho perto de alguém

sneakers ['sniːkəz] NPL tênis *m* (BR), sapatos *mpl* de treino (PT)

sneaking ['sniːkɪŋ] ADJ: **to have a ~ suspicion that …** ter uma vaga suspeita de que …

sneaky ['sniːkɪ] ADJ sorrateiro

sneer [snɪəʳ] N sorriso de desprezo ▶ VI rir-se com desdém; (*mock*): **to ~ at** zombar de, desprezar

sneeze [sniːz] N espirro ▶ VI espirrar

snide [snaɪd] ADJ sarcástico

sniff [snɪf] N fungada; (*of dog*) farejada; (*of person*) fungadela ▶ VI fungar ▶ VT fungar, farejar; (*glue, drug*) cheirar
▶ **sniff at** VT FUS: **it's not to be ~ed at** isso não deve ser desprezado

snigger ['snɪɡəʳ] N riso dissimulado ▶ VI rir-se com dissimulação

snip [snɪp] N tesourada; (*piece*) pedaço, retalho; (BRIT *inf: bargain*) pechincha ▶ VT cortar com tesoura

sniper ['snaɪpəʳ] N franco-atirador(a) *m/f*

snippet ['snɪpɪt] N fragmento, trecho

snivelling ['snɪvlɪŋ] ADJ (*whimpering*) chorão(-rona), lamuriento

snob [snɔb] N esnobe *m/f*

snobbery ['snɔbərɪ] N esnobismo

snobbish ['snɔbɪʃ] ADJ esnobe

snooker ['snuːkəʳ] N sinuca

snoop [snuːp] VI: **to ~ about** bisbilhotar

snooper ['snuːpəʳ] N bisbilhoteiro(-a), xereta *m/f*

snooty ['snuːtɪ] ADJ arrogante

snooze [snuːz] N soneca ▶ VI tirar uma soneca, dormitar

snore [snɔːʳ] VI roncar ▶ N ronco

snoring ['snɔːrɪŋ] N roncadura, roncaria

snorkel ['snɔːkl] N tubo snorkel

snort [snɔːt] N bufo, bufido ▶ VI bufar ▶ VT (*drugs*) cheirar

snotty ['snɔtɪ] ADJ ranhoso; (*fig*) altivo, arrogante

snout [snaut] N focinho

snow [snəu] N neve *f* ▶ VI nevar ▶ VT: **to be ~ed under with work** estar atolado or sobrecarregado de trabalho

snowball ['snəubɔːl] N bola de neve ▶ VI acumular-se; (*fig*) aumentar (como bola de neve)

snowboarding ['snəubɔːdɪŋ] N snowboard *m*

snowbound ['snəubaund] ADJ bloqueado pela neve

snow-capped [-kæpt] ADJ coberto de neve

snowdrift ['snəudrɪft] N monte *m* de neve (formado pelo vento)

snowdrop ['snəudrɒp] N campainha branca

snowfall ['snəufɔːl] N nevada

snowflake ['snəufleɪk] N floco de neve

snowman ['snəumæn] (*irreg: like* **man**) N boneco de neve

snowplough, (US) **snowplow** ['snəuplau] N máquina limpa-neve, removedor *m* de neve

snowshoe ['snəuʃuː] N raquete *f* de neve

snowstorm ['snəustɔːm] N nevasca, tempestade *f* de neve

snowy ['snəuɪ] ADJ nevoso

SNP (BRIT) N ABBR (*Pol*) = **Scottish National Party**

snub [snʌb] VT desdenhar, menosprezar ▶ N repulsa

snub-nosed [-'nəuzd] ADJ de nariz arrebitado

snuck [snʌk] (US) PT, PP *of* **sneak**

snuff [snʌf] N rapé *m* ▶ VT (*also*: **snuff out**: *candle*) apagar

snug [snʌg] ADJ (*sheltered*) abrigado, protegido; (*fitted*) justo, cômodo

snuggle ['snʌgl] VI: **to ~ up to sb** aconchegar-se or aninhar-se a alguém

snugly ['snʌglɪ] ADV (*fit*) perfeitamente

SO ABBR (*Banking*) = **standing order**

(KEYWORD)

so [səu] ADV **1** (*thus, likewise*) assim, deste modo; **so saying he walked away** falou isto e foi embora; **if so** se for assim, se assim é; **I didn't do it — you did so** não fiz isso — você fez!; **so do I, so am I** *etc* eu também; **so it is!** é verdade!; **I hope/think so** espero/acho que sim; **so far** até aqui; **so far I haven't had any problems** até agora não tive nenhum problema

2 (*in comparisons etc: to such a degree*) tão; **so big/**

quickly **(that)** tão grande/rápido (que); **she's not so clever as her brother** ela não é tão inteligente quanto o irmão
3: **so much** *adj, adv* tanto; **I've got so much work** tenho tanto trabalho; **so many** tantos(-as); **there are so many people to see** tem tanta gente para ver
4 *(phrases)*: **10 or so** uns 10; **so long!** *(inf: goodbye)* tchau!
▶ CONJ **1** *(expressing purpose)*: **so as to do** para fazer; **we hurried so as not to be late** nós nos apressamos para não chegarmos atrasados; **so (that)** para que, a fim de que **2** *(result)* de modo que; **he didn't arrive so I left** como ele não chegou, eu fui embora; **so I was right after all** então eu estava certo no final das contas

soak [səuk] VT *(drench)* embeber, ensopar; *(put in water)* pôr de molho ▶ VI estar de molho, impregnar-se
▶ **soak in** VI infiltrar
▶ **soak up** VT absorver
soaking ['səukɪŋ] ADJ *(also:* **soaking wet)** encharcado
so and so N fulano(-a)
soap [səup] N sabão *m*
soap flakes NPL flocos *mpl* de sabão
soap opera N novela
soap powder N sabão *m* em pó
soapsuds ['səupsʌdz] N água de sabão
soapy ['səupɪ] ADJ ensaboado
soar [sɔːʳ] VI *(on wings)* elevar-se em voo; *(rocket, temperature)* subir; *(building etc)* levantar-se; *(price, production)* disparar; *(morale, spirits)* renascer
soaring ['sɔːrɪŋ] ADJ *(flight)* a grande altura; *(prices, inflation)* disparado
sob [sɔb] N soluço ▶ VI soluçar
s.o.b. *(US !)* N ABBR *(= son of a bitch)* filho da puta (!)
sober ['səubəʳ] ADJ *(serious)* sério; *(sensible)* sensato; *(moderate)* moderado; *(not drunk)* sóbrio; *(colour, style)* discreto
▶ **sober up** VI ficar sóbrio
sobriety [sə'braɪətɪ] N sobriedade *f*
sob story N *(inf, pej)* lamúria
Soc. ABBR = **society**
so-called [-kɔːld] ADJ chamado
soccer ['sɔkəʳ] N futebol *m*
soccer pitch N campo de futebol
soccer player N jogador *m* de futebol
sociable ['səuʃəbl] ADJ sociável
social ['səuʃl] ADJ social; *(sociable)* sociável ▶ N reunião *f* social
social climber N arrivista *m/f*
social club N clube *m*
Social Democrat N democrata-social *m/f*
social insurance *(US)* N seguro social
socialism ['səuʃəlɪzəm] N socialismo
socialist ['səuʃəlɪst] ADJ, N socialista *m/f*
socialite ['səuʃəlaɪt] N socialite *m/f*, colunável *m/f*

socialize ['səuʃəlaɪz] VI: **to ~ (with)** socializar (com)
socially ['səuʃəlɪ] ADV socialmente
social media NPL mídias *fpl* sociais *(BR)*, meios *mpl* de comunicação social *(PT)*
social networking [-'nɛtwə:kɪŋ] N redes *fpl* sociais
social networking site [-'nɛtwə:kɪŋ-] N rede *f* social
social science N ciências *fpl* sociais
social security *(BRIT)* N previdência social; **Department of Social Security** ≈ Instituto Nacional de Assistência Médica e Previdência Social *(BR)*
social welfare N bem-estar *m* social
social work N assistência social, serviço social
social worker N assistente *m/f* social
society [sə'saɪətɪ] N sociedade *f*; *(club)* associação *f*; *(also:* **high society)** alta sociedade ▶ CPD *(party, column)* da alta sociedade
socio-economic ['səusɪəu-] ADJ socioeconômico
sociological [səusɪə'lɔdʒɪkl] ADJ sociológico
sociologist [səusɪ'ɔlədʒɪst] N sociólogo(-a)
sociology [səusɪ'ɔlədʒɪ] N sociologia
sock [sɔk] N meia *(BR)*, peúga *(PT)* ▶ VT *(inf: hit)* socar, dar um soco em; **to pull one's ~s up** *(fig)* tomar jeito
socket ['sɔkɪt] N bocal *m*, encaixe *m*; *(BRIT Elec)* tomada
sod [sɔd] N *(of earth)* gramado, torrão *m*; *(BRIT !)* imbecil *m/f* ▶ VT: **~ it!** *(!)* droga!
soda ['səudə] N *(Chem)* soda; *(also:* **soda water)** água com gás; *(US: also:* **soda pop)** soda
sodden ['sɔdn] ADJ encharcado
sodium ['səudɪəm] N sódio
sodium chloride N cloreto de sódio
sofa ['səufə] N sofá *m*
Sofia ['səufɪə] N Sófia
soft [sɔft] ADJ *(gen)* macio; *(not hard)* mole; *(voice, music, light)* suave; *(kind)* meigo, bondoso; *(weak)* fraco; *(stupid)* idiota
soft-boiled egg [-bɔɪld-] N ovo quente
soft currency N moeda fraca
soft drink N refrigerante *m*
soft drugs N drogas *fpl* leves
soften ['sɔfn] VT amolecer, amaciar; *(effect)* abrandar; *(expression)* suavizar ▶ VI amolecer-se; *(voice, expression)* suavizar-se
softener ['sɔfnər] N amaciante *m*
soft fruit *(BRIT)* N bagas *fpl*
soft furnishings NPL cortinas *fpl* e estofados *mpl*
soft-hearted ADJ bondoso, caridoso
softly ['sɔftlɪ] ADV suavemente; *(gently)* delicadamente
softness ['sɔftnɪs] N maciez *f*; *(gentleness)* suavidade *f*
soft sell N venda de forma não agressiva
soft spot N: **to have a ~ for sb** ter xodó por alguém
soft toy N brinquedo de pelúcia

S

software ['softwɛəʳ] N software *m*
software package N soft *m*, pacote *m*
soggy ['sɔgɪ] ADJ ensopado, encharcado
soil [sɔɪl] N (*earth*) terra, solo; (*territory*)
território ▶ VT sujar, manchar
soiled [sɔɪld] ADJ sujo
sojourn ['sɔdʒəːn] N (*formal*) estada *f*
solace ['sɔlɪs] N consolo
solar ['səuləʳ] ADJ solar
solaria [sə'lɛərɪə] NPL *of* **solarium**
solarium [sə'lɛərɪəm] (*pl* **solaria**) N solário
solar panel N painel *m* solar
solar plexus [-'plɛksəs] N plexo solar
solar power N energia solar
sold [səuld] PT, PP *of* **sell** ▶ ADJ: ~ **out** (*Comm*)
esgotado
solder ['səuldəʳ] VT soldar ▶ N solda
soldier ['səuldʒəʳ] N soldado; (*army man*)
militar *m*; **toy** ~ soldado de chumbo
▶ **soldier on** VI aguentar firme (*inf*),
perseverar
sole [səul] N (*of foot, shoe*) sola; (*fish: pl inv*)
solha, linguado ▶ ADJ único; **the** ~ **reason**
a única razão
solely ['səullɪ] ADV somente, unicamente;
I will hold you ~ **responsible** vou
apontar-lhe como o único responsável
solemn ['sɔləm] ADJ solene
sole trader N (*Comm*) comerciante *m/f*
independente
solicit [sə'lɪsɪt] VT (*request*) solicitar ▶ VI
(*prostitute*) aliciar fregueses
solicitor [sə'lɪsɪtəʳ] (*BRIT*) N (*for wills etc*)
tabelião(-lioa) *m/f*; (*in court*) ≈ advogado(-a)
solid ['sɔlɪd] ADJ sólido; (*gold etc*) maciço;
(*person*) sério; (*line*) contínuo; (*vote*) unânime
▶ N sólido; **solids** NPL (*food*) comida sólida;
we waited 2 ~ **hours** esperamos durante
2 horas a fio; **to be on** ~ **ground** estar em
terra firme; (*fig*) ter base
solidarity [sɔlɪ'dærɪtɪ] N solidariedade *f*
solidify [sə'lɪdɪfaɪ] VI solidificar-se
solidity [sə'lɪdɪtɪ] N solidez *f*
solid-state ADJ de estado sólido
soliloquy [sə'lɪləkwɪ] N monólogo
solitaire [sɔlɪ'tɛəʳ] N (*gem*) solitário; (*game*)
solitário, jogo de paciência
solitary ['sɔlɪtərɪ] ADJ solitário, só; (*walk*) só;
(*isolated*) isolado, retirado; (*single*) único
solitary confinement N prisão *f* celular,
solitária
solitude ['sɔlɪtjuːd] N solidão *f*
solo ['səuləu] N, ADV solo
soloist ['səuləuɪst] N solista *m/f*
Solomon Islands ['sɔləmən-] NPL: **the** ~ as
ilhas Salomão
solstice ['sɔlstɪs] N solstício
soluble ['sɔljubl] ADJ solúvel
solution [sə'luːʃən] N solução *f*
solve [sɔlv] VT resolver, solucionar
solvency ['sɔlvənsɪ] N (*Comm*) solvência
solvent ['sɔlvənt] ADJ (*Comm*) solvente ▶ N
(*Chem*) solvente *m*

solvent abuse N abuso de solventes
alucinógenos
Somali [sə'mɑːlɪ] ADJ, N somaliano(-a)
Somalia [sə'mɑːlɪə] N Somália
sombre, (*US*) **somber** ['sɔmbəʳ] ADJ sombrio,
lúgubre

(KEYWORD)

some [sʌm] ADJ **1** (*a certain number or amount*):
some tea/water/biscuits um pouco de chá/
água/uns biscoitos; **some children came**
algumas crianças vieram; **there's some**
milk in the fridge há leite na geladeira;
I've got some money, but not much
tenho algum dinheiro, mas não muito
2 (*certain: in contrasts*) algum(a); **some people**
say that … algumas pessoas dizem que …
3 (*unspecified*) um pouco de; **some woman**
was asking for you uma mulher estava
perguntando por você; **some day** um dia
▶ PRON **1** (*a certain number*) alguns/algumas;
I've got some (*books etc*) tenho alguns; **some**
went for a taxi and some walked alguns
foram pegar um táxi e outros foram
andando
2 (*a certain amount*) um pouco; **I've got some**
(*milk, money etc*) tenho um pouco
▶ ADV: **some 10 people** umas 10 pessoas

somebody ['sʌmbədɪ] PRON = **someone**
someday ['sʌmdeɪ] ADV algum dia
somehow ['sʌmhau] ADV de alguma maneira;
(*for some reason*) por uma razão ou outra
someone ['sʌmwʌn] PRON alguém; **there's** ~
coming tem alguém vindo/chegando
someplace ['sʌmpleɪs] (*US*) ADV = **somewhere**
somersault ['sʌməsɔːlt] N (*deliberate*) salto
mortal; (*accidental*) cambalhota ▶ VI dar um
salto mortal *or* uma cambalhota
something ['sʌmθɪŋ] PRON alguma coisa,
algo (*BR*); ~ **nice** alguma coisa boa; ~ **to do**
alguma coisa para fazer; **there's** ~ **wrong**
tem alguma coisa errada; **would you like** ~
to eat/drink? você gostaria de comer/beber
alguma coisa?
sometime ['sʌmtaɪm] ADV (*in future*) algum
dia, em outra oportunidade; (*in past*): ~ **last**
month durante o mês passado; **I'll finish**
it ~ vou terminar uma hora dessas
sometimes ['sʌmtaɪmz] ADV às vezes, de vez
em quando
somewhat ['sʌmwɔt] ADV um tanto
somewhere ['sʌmwɛəʳ] ADV (*be*) em algum
lugar; (*go*) para algum lugar; **I must have**
lost it ~ devo ter perdido (isso) em algum
lugar; **it's** ~ **or other in Scotland** é em
algum lugar na Escócia; ~ **else** (*be*) em outro
lugar; (*go*) para outro lugar
son [sʌn] N filho
sonar ['səunɑːʳ] N sonar *m*
sonata [sə'nɑːtə] N sonata
song [sɔŋ] N canção *f*; (*of bird*) canto
songbook ['sɔŋbuk] N cancioneiro

songwriter ['sɒŋraɪtə^r] N compositor(a) m/f de canções

sonic ['sɒnɪk] ADJ (boom) sônico

son-in-law (pl **sons-in-law**) N genro

sonnet ['sɒnɪt] N soneto

sonny ['sʌnɪ] (inf) N meu filho

soon [su:n] ADV logo, brevemente; (a short time after) logo após; (early) cedo; **~ afterwards** pouco depois; **very/quite ~** logo/daqui a pouco; **how ~ can you be ready?** quando você estará pronto?; **it's too ~ to tell** é muito cedo para dizer; **see you ~!** até logo!; see also **as**

sooner ['su:nə^r] ADV (time) antes, mais cedo; (preference): **I would ~ do that** preferia fazer isso; **~ or later** mais cedo ou mais tarde; **no ~ said than done** dito e feito; **the ~ the better** quanto mais cedo melhor; **no ~ had we left than he ...** mal partimos, ele ...

soot [sut] N fuligem f

soothe [su:ð] VT acalmar, sossegar; (pain) aliviar, suavizar

soothing ['su:ðɪŋ] ADJ calmante

SOP N ABBR = **standard operating procedure**

sop [sɒp] N paliativo

sophisticated [sə'fɪstɪkeɪtɪd] ADJ sofisticado

sophistication [səfɪstɪ'keɪʃən] N sofisticação f

sophomore ['sɒfəmɔ:^r] (US) N segundanista m/f

soporific [sɒpə'rɪfɪk] ADJ soporífico

sopping ['sɒpɪŋ] ADJ: **~ (wet)** encharcado

soppy ['sɒpɪ] (pej) ADJ piegas inv

soprano [sə'prɑ:nəu] N soprano m/f

sorbet ['sɔ:beɪ] N sorvete de frutas à base de água

sorcerer ['sɔ:sərə^r] N feiticeiro

sordid ['sɔ:dɪd] ADJ (dirty) imundo, sórdido; (wretched) miserável

sore [sɔ:^r] ADJ (painful) dolorido; (offended) magoado, ofendido ▶ N chaga, ferida; **it's a ~ point** é um ponto delicado; **my eyes are ~, I've got ~ eyes** meus olhos estão doloridos

sorely ['sɔ:lɪ] ADV: **I am ~ tempted (to)** estou muito tentado (a)

sore throat N dor f de garganta

sorrel ['sɒrəl] N azeda

sorrow ['sɒrəu] N tristeza, mágoa, dor f; **sorrows** NPL (causes of grief) tristezas fpl

sorrowful ['sɒrəuful] ADJ (day) triste; (smile) aflito, magoado

sorry ['sɒrɪ] ADJ (regretful) arrependido; (condition, excuse) lamentável; **~!** desculpe!, perdão!, sinto muito!; **to feel ~ for sb** sentir pena de alguém; **I feel ~ for him** estou com pena dele; **I'm ~ to hear that ...** lamento saber que ...; **to be ~ about sth** arrepender-se de algo

sort [sɔ:t] N tipo; (brand: of coffee etc) marca ▶ VT (also: **sort out**: papers) classificar; (: problems) solucionar, resolver; **what ~ do you want?** que tipo você quer?; **what ~ of car?** que tipo de carro?; **I'll do nothing of the ~!** não farei nada do gênero!; **it's ~ of awkward** (inf) é meio difícil

sortie ['sɔ:tɪ] N surtida

sorting office ['sɔ:tɪŋ-] N departamento de distribuição

SOS N S.O.S. m

so-so ADV mais ou menos, regular

soufflé ['su:fleɪ] N suflê m

sought [sɔ:t] PT, PP of **seek**

sought-after ADJ desejado

soul [səul] N alma; (person) criatura; **I didn't see a ~** não vi uma alma; **God rest his ~** que a sua alma descanse em paz; **the poor ~ had nowhere to sleep** o pobre coitado não tinha onde dormir

soul-destroying [-dɪs'trɔɪɪŋ] ADJ desalentador(a)

soulful ['səulful] ADJ emocional, sentimental

soulless ['səullɪs] ADJ desalmado

soul mate N companheiro(-a) ideal

soul-searching N: **after much ~** depois de muita ponderação

sound [saund] ADJ (healthy) saudável, sadio; (safe, not damaged) sólido, completo; (secure) seguro; (reliable) confiável; (sensible) sensato; (argument, policy) válido; (move) acertado ▶ ADV: **~ asleep** dormindo profundamente ▶ N (noise) som m, ruído, barulho; (volume: on TV etc) volume m; (Geo) estreito, braço (de mar) ▶ VT (alarm) soar ▶ VI soar, tocar; (fig: seem) parecer; **to be of ~ mind** estar em juízo perfeito; **I don't like the ~ of it** eu não estou gostando disso; **to ~ like** parecer; **it ~s as if ...** parece que ... ▶ **sound off** (inf) VI: **to ~ off (about)** pontificar (sobre) ▶ **sound out** VI sondar

sound barrier N barreira do som

sound effects NPL efeitos mpl sonoros

sound engineer N engenheiro(-a) de som

sounding ['saundɪŋ] N (Naut etc) sondagem f

sounding board N (Mus) caixa de ressonância; (fig): **to use sb as a ~ for one's ideas** testar suas ideias em alguém

soundly ['saundlɪ] ADV (sleep) profundamente; (beat) completamente

soundproof ['saundpru:f] ADJ à prova de som ▶ VT insonorizar

soundtrack ['saundtræk] N (of film) trilha sonora

sound wave N onda sonora

soup [su:p] N (thick) sopa; (thin) caldo; **in the ~** (fig) numa encrenca

soup kitchen N local onde se distribui comida aos pobres

soup plate N prato fundo (para sopa)

soupspoon ['su:pspu:n] N colher f de sopa

sour ['sauə^r] ADJ azedo, ácido; (milk) talhado; (fig) mal-humorado, rabugento; **it's ~ grapes!** (fig) é despeito!; **to go** or **turn ~** (milk, wine) azedar; (fig: relationship, plan) azedar, dar errado

source [sɔ:s] N fonte f; **I have it from a reliable ~ that ...** uma fonte confiável me assegura que ...

S

south [sauθ] N sul *m* ▶ ADJ do sul, meridional
▶ ADV ao *or* para o sul; **(to the) ~ of** ao sul de;
the S~ of France o Sul da França; **to travel
~** viajar para o sul
South Africa N África do Sul
South African ADJ, N sul-africano(-a)
South America N América do Sul
South American ADJ, N sul-americano(-a)
southbound ['sauθbaund] ADJ em direção
ao sul
south-east N sudeste *m* ▶ ADJ do sudeste
South-East Asia N o Sudeste da Ásia
southerly ['sʌðəlɪ] ADJ para o sul; *(from the
south)* do sul
southern ['sʌðən] ADJ *(to the south)* para o sul,
em direção do sul; *(from the south)* do sul,
sulista; **the ~ hemisphere** o Hemisfério Sul
South Pole N Pólo Sul
South Sea Islands NPL: **the ~** as ilhas dos
Mares do Sul
South Seas NPL: **the ~** os Mares do Sul
southward ['sauθwəd], **southwards**
['sauθwədz] ADV para o sul
south-west N sudoeste *m*
souvenir [su:və'nɪəʳ] N lembrança
sovereign ['sɔvrɪn] ADJ, N soberano(-a)
sovereignty ['sɔvrɪntɪ] N soberania
soviet ['səuvɪət] ADJ soviético; **the S~ Union**
a União Soviética
sow¹ [sau] N porca
sow² [səu] *(pt* **sowed,** *pp* **sown)** VT semear;
(fig: spread) disseminar, espalhar
sown [səun] PP *of* **sow²**
soya ['sɔɪə], *(US)* **soy** [sɔɪ] N soja
soya bean, *(US)* **soybean** N semente *f* de soja
soya sauce, soy sauce N molho de soja
spa [spɑ:] N *(town)* estância hidro-mineral;
(US: also: **health spa)** estância balnear
space [speɪs] N *(gen)* espaço; *(room)* lugar *m*
▶ CPD espacial ▶ VT *(also:* **space out)** espaçar;
in a confined ~ num espaço confinado; **in
a short ~ of time** num curto espaço de
tempo; **(with)in the ~ of an hour** dentro do
espaço de uma hora; **to clear a ~ for sth**
abrir espaço para algo
space bar N tecla de espacejamento
spacecraft ['speɪskrɑ:ft] N nave *f* espacial
spaceman ['speɪsmæn] *(irreg: like* **man)** N
astronauta *m*, cosmonauta *m*
spaceship ['speɪsʃɪp] N = **spacecraft**
space shuttle N ônibus *m* espacial
spacesuit ['speɪssu:t] N traje *m* espacial
spacewoman ['speɪswumən] *(irreg: like*
woman) N astronauta, cosmonauta
spacing ['speɪsɪŋ] N espacejamento,
espaçamento; **single/double ~**
espacejamento simples/duplo
spacious ['speɪʃəs] ADJ espaçoso
spade [speɪd] N pá *f*; **spades** NPL *(Cards)*
espadas *fpl*
spadework ['speɪdwə:k] N *(fig)* trabalho
preliminar
spaghetti [spə'gɛtɪ] N espaguete *m*

Spain [speɪn] N Espanha
spam ['spæm] N *(junk email)* spam *m*
span [spæn] N *(also:* **wingspan)** envergadura;
(of hand) palma; *(of arch)* vão *m*; *(in time)* lapso,
espaço ▶ VT estender-se sobre, atravessar;
(fig) abarcar
Spaniard ['spænjəd] N espanhol(a) *m/f*
spaniel ['spænjəl] N spaniel *m*
Spanish ['spænɪʃ] ADJ espanhol(a) ▶ N *(Ling)*
espanhol *m*, castelhano; **the Spanish** NPL os
espanhóis
Spanish omelette N omelete *m* à espanhola
spank [spæŋk] VT bater, dar palmadas em
spanner ['spænəʳ] *(BRIT)* N chave *f* inglesa
spar [spɑ:ʳ] N mastro, verga ▶ VI *(Boxing)*
treinar
spare [spɛəʳ] ADJ *(free)* vago, desocupado;
(surplus) de sobra, a mais; *(available)*
disponível, de reserva ▶ N = **spare part** ▶ VT
(do without) dispensar, passar sem; *(make
available)* dispor de; *(afford to give)* dispor de,
ter de sobra; *(refrain from hurting)* perdoar,
poupar; *(be grudging with)* dar frugalmente;
to ~ *(surplus)* de sobra; **there are 2 going ~**
(BRIT) há 2 sobrando; **to ~ no expense** não
poupar despesas; **can you ~ (me) £10?** pode
me ceder £10?; **can you ~ the time?** você
tem tempo?; **there is no time to ~** não há
tempo a perder; **I've a few minutes to ~**
tenho alguns minutos de sobra
spare part N peça sobressalente
spare room N quarto de hóspedes
spare time N tempo livre
spare tyre N estepe *m*
spare wheel N estepe *m*
sparing ['spɛərɪŋ] ADJ: **to be ~ with** ser
econômico com
sparingly ['spɛərɪŋlɪ] ADV frugalmente, com
moderação
spark [spɑ:k] N chispa, faísca; *(fig)* centelha
sparking plug ['spɑ:kɪŋ-] N vela (de ignição)
sparkle ['spɑ:kl] N cintilação *f*, brilho ▶ VI
cintilar; *(shine)* brilhar, faiscar
sparkling ['spɑ:klɪŋ] ADJ *(mineral water)* gasoso;
(wine) espumante; *(conversation)* animado;
(performance) brilhante
spark plug N vela (de ignição)
sparrow ['spærəu] N pardal *m*
sparse [spɑ:s] ADJ escasso; *(hair)* ralo
spartan ['spɑ:tən] ADJ *(fig)* espartano
spasm ['spæzəm] N *(Med)* espasmo; *(fig)*
acesso, ataque *m*
spasmodic [spæz'mɔdɪk] ADJ espasmódico
spastic ['spæstɪk] N espástico(-a)
spat [spæt] PT, PP *of* **spit** ▶ N *(US)* bate-boca *m*
spate [speɪt] N série *f*; *(fig):* **a ~ of** uma
enxurrada de; **in ~** *(river)* em cheia
spatial ['speɪʃəl] ADJ espacial
spatter ['spætəʳ] N borrifo ▶ VT borrifar,
salpicar ▶ VI borrifar
spatula ['spætjulə] N espátula
spawn [spɔ:n] VI desovar, procriar ▶ VT gerar;
(pej: create) gerar, criar ▶ N ovas *fpl*

SPCA (US) N ABBR = **Society for the Prevention of Cruelty to Animals**

SPCC (US) N ABBR = **Society for the Prevention of Cruelty to Children**

speak [spi:k] (pt **spoke**, pp **spoken**) VT (language) falar; (truth) dizer ▶ VI falar; (make a speech) discursar; **to ~ to sb/of** or **about sth** falar com alguém/de or sobre algo; **~ up!** fale alto!; **~ing!** (on phone) é ele/ela mesmo!; **to ~ one's mind** desabafar; **he has no money to ~ of** ele quase não tem dinheiro ▶ **speak for** VT FUS: **to ~ for sb** falar por alguém; **that picture is already spoken for** aquele quadro já está vendido

speaker ['spi:kər] N (in public) orador(a) m/f; (also: **loudspeaker**) alto-falante m; (Pol): **the S~** o Presidente da Câmara; **are you a Welsh ~?** você fala galês?

speaking ['spi:kɪŋ] ADJ falante; **Italian-~ people** pessoas de língua italiana

spear [spɪər] N lança; (for fishing) arpão m ▶ VT lancear, arpoar

spearhead ['spɪəhɛd] N ponta-de-lança ▶ VT (attack) encabeçar

spearmint ['spɪəmɪnt] N hortelã f

spec [spɛk] (inf) N: **on ~** por acaso

special ['spɛʃl] ADJ especial; (edition etc) extra; (delivery) rápido ▶ N (train) trem m especial; **take ~ care** tome muito cuidado; **nothing ~** nada especial; **today's ~** (at restaurant) especialidade do dia, prato do dia

special delivery N: **by ~** por entrega rápida

specialist ['spɛʃəlɪst] N especialista m/f; **heart ~** especialista em doenças do coração

speciality [spɛʃɪ'ælɪtɪ] N especialidade f

specialize ['spɛʃəlaɪz] VI: **to ~ (in)** especializar-se (em)

specially ['spɛʃəlɪ] ADV especialmente

special offer N oferta especial

specialty ['spɛʃəltɪ] (esp US) N = **speciality**

species ['spi:ʃi:z] N INV espécie f

specific [spə'sɪfɪk] ADJ específico

specifically [spə'sɪfɪklɪ] ADV especificamente

specification [spɛsɪfɪ'keɪʃən] N especificação f; (requirement) requinto; **specifications** NPL (Tech) ficha técnica; (of building) especificações fpl

specify ['spɛsɪfaɪ] VT, VI especificar; **unless otherwise specified** salvo indicação em contrário

specimen ['spɛsɪmən] N espécime m, amostra; (for testing, Med) espécime; (fig) exemplar m

specimen copy N exemplar m de amostra

specimen signature N modelo de assinatura

speck [spɛk] N mancha, pinta; (particle) grão m

speckled ['spɛkld] ADJ pintado

specs [spɛks] (inf) NPL óculos mpl

spectacle ['spɛktəkl] N espetáculo; **spectacles** NPL (glasses) óculos mpl

spectacle case N estojo de óculos

spectacular [spɛk'tækjulər] ADJ espetacular ▶ N (Cinema etc) superprodução f

spectator [spɛk'teɪtər] N espectador(a) m/f

specter ['spɛktər] (US) N = **spectre**

spectra ['spɛktrə] NPL of **spectrum**

spectre, (US) **specter** ['spɛktər] N espectro, aparição f

spectrum ['spɛktrəm] (pl **spectra**) N espectro

speculate ['spɛkjuleɪt] VI especular; (try to guess): **to ~ about** especular sobre

speculation [spɛkju'leɪʃən] N especulação f

speculative ['spɛkjulətɪv] ADJ especulativo

speculator ['spɛkjuleɪtər] N especulador(a) m/f

sped [spɛd] PT, PP of **speed**

speech [spi:tʃ] N (faculty, Theatre) fala; (formal talk) discurso

speech day (BRIT) N (Sch) dia m de distribuição de prêmios

speech impediment N defeito m de articulação

speechless ['spi:tʃlɪs] ADJ estupefato, emudecido

speech therapy N ortofonia

speed [spi:d] (pt, pp **sped**) N (fast travel) velocidade f; (rate) rapidez f; (haste) pressa; (promptness) prontidão f; (gear) marcha ▶ VI (in car) correr; **the years speed by** os anos voaram; **at full** or **top ~** a toda a velocidade; **at a ~ of 70 km/h** a uma velocidade de 70 km/h; **shorthand/typing ~** velocidade de estenografia/datilografia; **at ~** em alta velocidade; **a five-~ gearbox** uma caixa de mudanças com cinco marchas ▶ **speed up** (pt, pp **speeded up**) VT, VI acelerar

speedboat ['spi:dbəʊt] N lancha

speed camera N radar m de velocidade

speedily ['spi:dɪlɪ] ADV depressa, rapidamente

speeding ['spi:dɪŋ] N (Aut) excesso de velocidade

speed limit N limite m de velocidade, velocidade f máxima

speedometer [spɪ'dɔmɪtər] N velocímetro

speed trap N área de fiscalização contra motoristas que dirigem em alta velocidade

speedway ['spi:dweɪ] N (Sport) pista de corrida, rodovia de alta velocidade; (also: **speedway racing**) corrida de motocicleta

speedy ['spi:dɪ] ADJ (fast) veloz, rápido; (prompt) pronto, imediato

speleologist [spi:lɪ'ɔlədʒɪst] N espeleologista m/f

spell [spɛl] (pt, pp **spelled** or **spelt**) VT (also: **spell out**) soletrar; (fig) pressagiar, ser sinal de ▶ N (also: **magic spell**) encanto, feitiço; (period of time) período, temporada; **he can't ~** não sabe escrever bem, comete erros de ortografia; **how do you ~ your name?** como você escreve o seu nome?; **can you ~ it for me?** pode soletrar isso para mim?; **to cast a ~ on sb** enfeitiçar alguém

spellbound ['spɛlbaʊnd] ADJ enfeitiçado, fascinado

spellchecker ['speltʃekər] N (Comput) corretor m ortográfico

spelling ['spɛlɪŋ] N ortografia

S

spelling mistake N erro ortográfico
spelt [spɛlt] PT, PP *of* **spell**
spend [spɛnd] (*pt, pp* **spent**) VT (*money*) gastar;
(*time*) passar; **to ~ time/money on sth**
gastar tempo/dinheiro em algo
spending ['spɛndɪŋ] N gastos *mpl*;
government ~ gastos públicos
spending money N dinheiro para pequenas
despesas
spending power N poder *m* aquisitivo
spendthrift ['spɛndθrɪft] N esbanjador(a) *m/f*,
perdulário(-a)
spent [spɛnt] PT, PP *of* **spend** ▶ ADJ gasto
sperm [spə:m] N esperma
sperm whale N cachalote *m*
spew [spju:] VT vomitar, lançar
sphere [sfɪəʳ] N esfera
spherical ['sfɛrɪkl] ADJ esférico
sphinx [sfɪŋks] N esfinge *f*
spice [spaɪs] N especiaria ▶ VT condimentar
spick-and-span [spɪk-] ADJ tudo arrumado
spicy ['spaɪsɪ] ADJ condimentado, (*fig*) picante
spider ['spaɪdəʳ] N aranha; **~'s web** teia de
aranha
spiel [spi:l] N lengalenga
spike [spaɪk] N (*point*) ponta, espigão *m*; (*Bot*)
espiga; **spikes** NPL (*Sport*) ferrões *mpl*
spike heel (*US*) N salto alto e fino
spiky ['spaɪkɪ] ADJ espinhoso
spill [spɪl] (*pt, pp* **spilt** *or* **spilled**) VT entornar,
derramar; (*blood*) derramar ▶ VI derramar-se;
to ~ the beans (*inf*) dar com a língua nos
dentes
 ▶ **spill out** VI (*come out*) sair; (*fall out*) cair
 ▶ **spill over** VI transbordar
spin [spɪn] (*pt, pp* **spun**) N (*revolution of wheel*)
volta, rotação *f*; (*Aviat*) parafuso; (*trip in car*)
volta *or* passeio de carro; (*ball*): **to put ~ on**
fazer rolar ▶ VT (*wool etc*) fiar, tecer; (*wheel*)
girar; (*clothes*) torcer ▶ VI girar, rodar; (*make
thread*) tecer; **the car spun out of control** o
carro se desgovernou
 ▶ **spin out** VT prolongar; (*money*) fazer render
spinach ['spɪnɪtʃ] N espinafre *m*
spinal ['spaɪnl] ADJ espinhal
spinal column N coluna vertebral
spinal cord N espinha dorsal
spindly ['spɪndlɪ] ADJ longo e espigado
spin doctor (*inf*) N marqueteiro(-a)
spin-dry VT torcer (na máquina)
spin-dryer (*BRIT*) N secadora
spine [spaɪn] N espinha dorsal; (*thorn*) espinho
spine-chilling [-'tʃɪlɪŋ] ADJ arrepiante
spineless ['spaɪnlɪs] ADJ (*fig*) fraco, covarde
spinner ['spɪnəʳ] N (*of thread*) fiandeiro(-a)
spinning ['spɪnɪŋ] N fiação *f*
spinning top N pião *m*
spinning wheel N roca de fiar
spin-off N subproduto
spinster ['spɪnstəʳ] N solteira; (*pej*) solteirona
spiral ['spaɪərl] N espiral *f* ▶ ADJ em espiral,
helicoidal ▶ VI (*prices*) disparar; **the
inflationary ~** a espiral inflacionária

spiral staircase N escada em caracol
spire ['spaɪəʳ] N flecha, agulha
spirit ['spɪrɪt] N espírito; (*soul*) alma; (*ghost*)
fantasma *m*; (*humour*) humor *m*; (*courage*)
coragem *f*, ânimo; (*frame of mind*) estado de
espírito; (*sense*) sentido; **spirits** NPL (*drink*)
álcool *m*; **in good ~s** alegre, de bom humor;
Holy S~ Espírito Santo; **community/
public ~** espírito comunitário/público
spirit duplicator N duplicador *m* a álcool
spirited ['spɪrɪtɪd] ADJ animado, espirituoso
spirit level N nível *m* de bolha
spiritual ['spɪrɪtjuəl] ADJ espiritual ▶ N (*also:*
Negro spiritual) canto religioso dos negros
spiritualism ['spɪrɪtjuəlɪzəm] N
espiritualismo
spit [spɪt] (*pt, pp* **spat**) VI cuspir; (*sound*)
escarrar; (*rain*) chuviscar ▶ N (*for roasting*)
espeto; (*Geo*) restinga; (*spittle*) cuspe *m*,
cusparada; (*saliva*) saliva
spite [spaɪt] N rancor *m*, ressentimento ▶ VT
contrariar; **in ~ of** apesar de, a despeito de
spiteful ['spaɪtful] ADJ maldoso, malévolo
spitting ['spɪtɪŋ] N: **"~ prohibited"**
"proibido cuspir" ▶ ADJ: **to be the ~ image
of sb** ser a imagem escarrada de alguém
spittle ['spɪtl] N cuspe *m*
spiv [spɪv] (*BRIT inf*) N negocista *m*
splash [splæʃ] N (*sound*) borrifo, respingo; (*of
colour*) mancha ▶ VT: **to ~ (with)** salpicar
(de) ▶ VI (*also:* **splash about**) borrifar,
respingar ▶ EXCL pluft
splashdown ['splæʃdaun] N amerissagem *f*
spleen [spli:n] N (*Anat*) baço
splendid ['splɛndɪd] ADJ esplêndido;
(*impressive*) impressionante
splendour, (*US*) **splendor** ['splɛndəʳ] N
esplendor *m*; (*of achievement*) pompa, glória;
splendours NPL (*features*) esplendores *mpl*
splice [splaɪs] VT juntar
splint [splɪnt] N tala
splinter ['splɪntəʳ] N (*of wood, glass*) lasca;
(*in finger*) farpa ▶ VI lascar-se, estilhaçar-se,
despedaçar-se
splinter group N grupo dissidente
split [splɪt] (*pt, pp* **split**) N fenda, brecha; (*fig:
division*) rompimento; (: *difference*) diferença;
(*Pol*) divisão *f* ▶ VT partir, fender; (*party, work*)
dividir; (*profits*) repartir ▶ VI (*divide*)
dividir-se, repartir-se; **the splits** NPL
(*Gymnastics*): **to do the ~s** abrir *or* fazer
espaguete; **to ~ sth down the middle**
partir algo ao meio; (*fig*) dividir algo (pela
metade)
 ▶ **split up** VI (*couple*) separar-se, acabar;
(*meeting*) terminar
split-level ADJ em vários níveis
split peas NPL ervilhas secas *fpl*
split personality N dupla personalidade *f*
split second N fração *f* de segundo
splitting ['splɪtɪŋ] ADJ (*headache*) lancinante
splutter ['splʌtəʳ] VI crepitar; (*person*)
balbuciar, gaguejar

spoil [spɔɪl] (pt, pp **spoilt** or **spoiled**) VT (damage) danificar; (mar) estragar, arruinar; (child) mimar; (ballot paper) violar ▶ VI: **to be ~ing for a fight** estar querendo comprar uma briga

spoils [spɔɪlz] NPL desojo, saque m

spoilsport ['spɔɪlspɔ:t] (pej) N desmancha-prazeres m/f inv

spoilt [spɔɪlt] PT, PP of **spoil** ▶ ADJ (child) mimado; (ballot paper) violado

spoke [spəuk] PT of **speak** ▶ N (of wheel) raio

spoken ['spəukn] PP of **speak**

spokesman ['spəuksmən] (irreg: like **man**) N porta-voz m

spokeswoman ['spəukswumən] (irreg: like **woman**) N porta-voz f

sponge [spʌndʒ] N esponja; (cake) pão de ló m ▶ VT lavar com esponja ▶ VI: **to ~ on sb** viver às custas de alguém

sponge bag (BRIT) N bolsa de toalete

sponge cake N pão-de-ló m

sponger ['spʌndʒəʳ] (pej) N parasito(-a)

spongy ['spʌndʒɪ] ADJ esponjoso

sponsor ['spɒnsəʳ] N patrocinador(a) m/f; (for membership) padrinho/madrinha; (Comm) fiador(a) m/f, financiador(a) m/f; (bill in parliament etc) responsável m/f ▶ VT patrocinar; apadrinhar; fiar; (applicant, proposal) apoiar, defender; **I ~ed him at 3p a mile** eu o patrocinei à razão de 3p por milha

sponsorship ['spɒnsəʃɪp] N patrocínio

spontaneity [spɒntə'neɪɪtɪ] N espontaneidade f

spontaneous [spɒn'teɪnɪəs] ADJ espontâneo

spoof [spu:f] N (parody) paródia; (trick) trote m

spooky ['spu:kɪ] (inf) ADJ arrepiante

spool [spu:l] N carretel m; (of film) rolo; (for tape) bobina; (of sewing machine) bobina, novelo

spoon [spu:n] N colher f

spoon-feed (irreg: like **feed**) VT dar de comer com colher; (fig) dar tudo mastigado a

spoonful ['spu:nful] N colherada

sporadic [spə'rædɪk] ADJ esporádico

sport [spɔ:t] N esporte m (BR), desporto (PT); (person) bom perdedor/boa perdedora m/f ▶ VT (wear) exibir; **indoor/outdoor ~s** esportes de salão/ao ar livre; **to say sth in ~** dizer algo de brincadeira

sporting ['spɔ:tɪŋ] ADJ esportivo (BR), desportivo (PT); (generous) nobre; **to give sb a ~ chance** dar uma grande chance a alguém

sport jacket (US) N = **sports jacket**

sports car N carro esporte (BR), carro de sport (PT)

sports drink N isotônico

sports ground N campo de esportes (BR) or de desportos (PT)

sports jacket (BRIT) N casaco esportivo (BR) or desportivo (PT)

sportsman ['spɔ:tsmən] (irreg: like **man**) N esportista m (BR), desportista m (PT)

sportsmanship ['spɔ:tsmənʃɪp] N espírito esportivo (BR) or desportivo (PT)

sportsmen ['spɔ:tsmen] NPL of **sportsman**

sports page N página de esportes

sports utility vehicle N veículo com tração nas quatro rodas, veículo 4x4

sportswear ['spɔ:tsweəʳ] N roupa esportiva (BR) or desportiva (PT) or esporte

sportswoman ['spɔ:tswumən] (irreg: like **woman**) N esportista (BR), desportista (PT)

sporty ['spɔ:tɪ] ADJ esportivo (BR), desportivo (PT)

spot [spɒt] N (mark) marca; (place) lugar m, local m; (dot: on pattern) mancha, ponto; (on skin) espinha; (Radio, TV) hora; (small amount): **a ~ of** um pouquinho de ▶ VT (notice) notar; **on the ~** (at once) na hora; (there) ali mesmo; (in difficulty) em apuros

spot check N fiscalização f de surpresa

spotless ['spɒtlɪs] ADJ sem mancha, imaculado

spotlight ['spɒtlaɪt] N holofote m, refletor m

spot-on (BRIT inf) ADJ acertado em cheio

spot price N preço à vista

spotted ['spɒtɪd] (pattern) com bolinhas

spotty ['spɒtɪ] ADJ (face) cheio de espinhas

spouse [spauz] N cônjuge m/f

spout [spaut] N (of jug) bico; (of pipe) cano ▶ VI jorrar

sprain [spreɪn] N distensão f, torcedura ▶ VT torcer; **to ~ one's ankle/wrist** torcer o tornozelo/a pulseira

sprang [spræŋ] PT of **spring**

sprawl [sprɔ:l] VI esparramar-se ▶ N: **urban ~** crescimento urbano; **to send sb ~ing** jogar alguém no chão

spray [spreɪ] N borrifo; (container) spray m, atomizador m; (garden spray) vaporizador m; (of paint) pistola borrifadora; (of flowers) ramalhete m ▶ VT pulverizar; (crops) borrifar, regar ▶ CPD (deodorant etc) spray

spread [spred] (pt, pp **spread**) N extensão f; (distribution) expansão f, difusão f; (Press, Typ: two pages) chapada; (Culin) pasta; (inf: food) banquete m ▶ VT espalhar; (butter) untar, passar; (wings, sails) abrir, desdobrar; (workload, wealth) distribuir; (scatter) disseminar; (payments) espaçar ▶ VI (news, stain) espalhar-se; (disease) alastrar-se ▶ **spread out** VI dispersar-se

spread-eagled [-'i:gld] ADJ: **to be** or **lie ~** estar estirado

spreadsheet ['spredʃi:t] N (Comput) planilha

spree [spri:] N: **to go on a ~** cair na farra

sprig [sprɪg] N raminho

sprightly ['spraɪtlɪ] ADJ ativo, ágil

spring [sprɪŋ] (pt **sprang**, pp **sprung**) N (leap) salto, pulo; (coiled metal) mola; (bounciness) elasticidade f; (season) primavera; (of water) fonte f ▶ VI pular, saltar ▶ VT: **to ~ a leak** (pipe etc) furar; **he sprang the news on me** ele me pegou de surpresa com a notícia; **in ~, in the ~** na primavera; **to ~ from** provir de; **to ~ into action** partir para ação; **to walk**

with a ~ in one's step andar espevitado
▶ **spring up** vi aparecer de repente
springboard ['sprɪŋbɔːd] N trampolim *m*
spring-cleaning N limpeza total, faxina (geral)
spring onion (BRIT) N cebolinha
springtime ['sprɪŋtaɪm] N primavera
springy ['sprɪŋɪ] ADJ elástico, flexível
sprinkle ['sprɪŋkl] vT (*liquid*) salpicar; (*salt,
sugar*) borrifar; **to ~ water on, ~ with water**
salpicar de água; **~d with** (*fig*) salpicado *or*
polvilhado de
sprinkler ['sprɪŋklər] N (*for lawn etc*) regador *m*;
(*to put out fire*) sprinkler *m*
sprinkling ['sprɪŋklɪŋ] N (*of water*) borrifo; (*of
salt*) pitada; (*of sugar*) bocado
sprint [sprɪnt] N corrida de pequena distância
▶ vi correr a toda velocidade
sprinter ['sprɪntər] N corredor(a) *m/f*
sprite [spraɪt] N duende *m*, elfo
sprocket ['sprɔkɪt] N (*on printer etc*) dente *m*
(de roda)
sprout [spraut] vi brotar, germinar
sprouts [sprauts] NPL (*also:* **Brussels sprouts**)
couves-de-Bruxelas *fpl*
spruce [spruːs] N INV (*Bot*) abeto ▶ ADJ
arrumado, limpo, elegante
▶ **spruce up** vT arrumar; **to ~ o.s. up**
arrumar-se
sprung [sprʌŋ] PP *of* **spring**
spry [spraɪ] ADJ ativo, ágil
SPUC N ABBR = **Society for the Protection of
Unborn Children**
spud [spʌd] (*inf*) N batata
spun [spʌn] PT, PP *of* **spin**
spur [spəːr] N espora; (*fig*) estímulo ▶ vT (*also:*
spur on) incitar, estimular; **on the ~ of the
moment** de improviso, de repente
spurious ['spjʊərɪəs] ADJ espúrio, falso
spurn [spəːn] vT desdenhar, desprezar
spurt [spəːt] N (*of energy*) acesso; (*of blood etc*)
jorro ▶ vi jorrar; **to put in** *or* **on a ~** (*runner*)
dar uma arrancada; (*fig: in work etc*) dar uma
virada
sputter ['spʌtər] vi crepitar; (*person*) balbuciar,
gaguejar
spy [spaɪ] N espião/espiã *m/f* ▶ vi: **to ~ on**
espiar, espionar ▶ vT (*see*) enxergar, avistar
▶ CPD (*film, story*) de espionagem
spying ['spaɪɪŋ] N espionagem *f*
spyware ['spaɪwɛər] N (*Comput*) spyware *m*,
software *m* espião
Sq. ABBR (*in address*) = **square**
sq. ABBR (*Math etc*) = **square**
squabble ['skwɔbl] N briga, bate-boca *m* ▶ vi
brigar, discutir
squad [skwɔd] N (*Mil, Police*) pelotão *m*,
esquadra; (*Football*) seleção *f*; **flying ~** (*Police*)
polícia de prontidão
squad car (BRIT) N (*Police*) radiopatrulha
squadron ['skwɔdrən] N (*Mil*) esquadrão *m*;
(*Aviat*) esquadrilha; (*Naut*) esquadra
squalid ['skwɔlɪd] ADJ (*conditions*) esquálido;
(*story etc*) sórdido

squall [skwɔːl] N (*storm*) tempestade *f*; (*wind*)
pé *m* (de vento), rajada
squalor ['skwɔlər] N sordidez *f*
squander ['skwɔndər] vT (*money*) esbanjar,
dissipar; (*chances*) desperdiçar
square [skwɛər] N quadrado; (*in town*) praça;
(*Math: instrument*) esquadro; (*inf: person*)
quadrado(-a), careta *m/f* ▶ ADJ quadrado; (*inf:
ideas, tastes*) careta, antiquado ▶ vT (*arrange*)
ajustar, acertar; (*Math*) elevar ao quadrado;
(*reconcile*) conciliar ▶ vi (*agree*) ajustar-se; **all
~ igual, quite; a ~ meal** uma refeição
substancial; **2 metres ~** um quadrado de
dois metros de lado; **2 ~ metres** 2 metros
quadrados; **we're back to ~ one** voltamos à
estaca zero
▶ **square up** (BRIT) vi (*settle*) ajustar; **to ~ up
with sb** acertar as contas com alguém
square bracket N (*Typ*) colchete *m*
squarely ['skwɛəlɪ] ADV em forma quadrada;
(*directly*) diretamente; (*fully*) em cheio
square root N raiz *f* quadrada
squash [skwɔʃ] N (BRIT: *drink*): **lemon/orange
~** limonada/laranjada concentrada; (*Sport*)
squash *m*; (US: *vegetable*) abóbora ▶ vT
esmagar; **to ~ together** apinhar
squat [skwɔt] ADJ atarracado ▶ vi (*also:* **squat
down**) agachar-se, acocorar-se; (*on property*)
ocupar ilegalmente
squatter ['skwɔtər] N posseiro(-a)
squawk [skwɔːk] vi grasnar
squeak [skwiːk] vi grunhir, chiar; (*door*)
ranger; (*mouse*) guinchar ▶ N grunhido,
chiado; rangido; guincho
squeal [skwiːl] vi guinchar, gritar
agudamente; (*inf: inform*) delatar
squeamish ['skwiːmɪʃ] ADJ melindroso,
delicado
squeeze [skwiːz] N (*gen, of hand*) aperto; (*in bus
etc*) apinhamento; (*Econ*) arrocho ▶ vT
comprimir, socar; (*hand, arm*) apertar ▶ vi:
to ~ past/under sth espremer-se para
passar algo/para passar por baixo de algo;
a ~ of lemon umas gotas de limão
▶ **squeeze out** vT espremer; (*fig*) extorquir
squelch [skwɛltʃ] vi fazer ruído de passos na
lama
squib [skwɪb] N busca-pé *m*
squid [skwɪd] (*pl* **squids** *or* **squid**) N lula
squiggle ['skwɪgl] N garatuja
squint [skwɪnt] vi olhar *or* ser vesgo ▶ N (*Med*)
estrabismo; **to ~ at sth** olhar algo de soslaio
or de esguelha
squire ['skwaɪər] (BRIT) N proprietário rural
squirm [skwəːm] vi retorcer-se
squirrel ['skwɪrəl] N esquilo
squirt [skwəːt] vi, vT jorrar, esguichar
Sr ABBR = **senior**; (*Rel*) = **sister**
SRC (BRIT) N ABBR = **Students' Representative
Council**
Sri Lanka [srɪ'læŋkə] N Sri Lanka *m*
SRN (BRIT) N ABBR = **State Registered Nurse**
SRO (US) ABBR = **standing room only**

SS ABBR = **steamship**
SSA (US) ABBR = **Social Security Administration**
SST (US) ABBR = **supersonic transport**
ST (US) ABBR = **Standard Time**
St ABBR (= *saint*) S.; = **street**
stab [stæb] N (*with knife etc*) punhalada; (*of pain*) pontada; (*inf: try*): **to have a ~ at (doing) sth** tentar (fazer) algo ▶ VT apunhalar; **to ~ sb to death** matar alguém a facadas, esfaquear alguém
stabbing ['stæbɪŋ] N: **there's been a ~** houve um esfaqueamento ▶ ADJ (*pain*) cortante
stability [stə'bɪlɪtɪ] N estabilidade *f*
stabilization [steɪbəlaɪ'zeɪʃən] N estabilização *f*
stabilize ['steɪbəlaɪz] VT estabilizar ▶ VI estabilizar-se
stabilizer ['steɪbəlaɪzəʳ] N estabilizador *m*
stable ['steɪbl] ADJ estável ▶ N estábulo, cavalariça; **riding ~s** clube *m* de equitação
staccato [stə'kɑːtəu] ADV destacado, staccato ▶ ADJ (*Mus*) destacado, staccato; (*noise*) interrupto; (*voice*) quebrado
stack [stæk] N montão *m*, pilha ▶ VT amontoar, empilhar; **there's ~s of time** (BRIT *inf*) tem tempo de sobra
stadium ['steɪdɪəm] (*pl* **stadia** *or* **stadiums**) N estádio
staff [stɑːf] N (*work force*) pessoal *m*, quadro; (BRIT *Sch*: *also*: **teaching staff**) corpo docente; (*stick*) cajado, bastão *m* ▶ VT prover de pessoal; **the office is ~ed by women** o escritório está composto de mulheres
staffroom ['stɑːfruːm] N sala dos professores
Staffs (BRIT) ABBR = **Staffordshire**
stag [stæg] N veado, cervo
stage [steɪdʒ] N (*in theatre*) palco, cena; (*point*) etapa, fase *f*; (*platform*) plataforma, estrado; (*profession*): **the ~** o palco, o teatro ▶ VT (*play*) pôr em cena, representar; (*demonstration*) montar, organizar; (*fig: perform: recovery etc*) realizar; **in ~s** por etapas; **to go through a difficult ~** passar por uma fase difícil; **in the early/final ~s** na fase inicial/final
stagecoach ['steɪdʒkəutʃ] N diligência
stage door N entrada dos artistas
stage fright N medo da plateia
stagehand ['steɪdʒhænd] N ajudante *m/f* de teatro
stage-manage VT (*fig*) orquestrar
stage manager N diretor(a) *m/f* de cena
stagger ['stægəʳ] VI cambalear ▶ VT (*amaze*) surpreender, chocar; (*hours, holidays*) escalonar
staggering ['stægərɪŋ] ADJ (*amazing*) surpreendente, chocante
stagnant ['stægnənt] ADJ estagnado
stagnate [stæg'neɪt] VI estagnar
stagnation [stæg'neɪʃən] N estagnação *f*
stag party N despedida de solteiro
staid [steɪd] ADJ sério, sóbrio
stain [steɪn] N mancha; (*colouring*) tinta, tintura ▶ VT manchar; (*wood*) tingir

stained glass window [steɪnd-] N janela com vitral
stainless ['steɪnlɪs] ADJ (*steel*) inoxidável
stain remover N tira-manchas *m*
stair [stɛəʳ] N (*step*) degrau *m*; **stairs** NPL (*flight of steps*) escada
staircase ['stɛəkeɪs] N escadaria, escada
stairway ['stɛəweɪ] N = **staircase**
stairwell ['stɛəwɛl] N caixa de escada
stake [steɪk] N estaca, poste *m*; (*Comm: interest*) interesse *m*, participação *f*; (*Betting: gen pl*) aposta ▶ VT apostar; (*claim*) reivindicar; **to be at ~** estar em jogo; **to have a ~ in sth** ter interesse em algo; **to ~ a claim to sth** reivindicar algo
stalactite ['stæləktaɪt] N estalactite *f*
stalagmite ['stæləgmaɪt] N estalagmite *f*
stale [steɪl] ADJ (*bread*) dormido; (*food*) estragado; (*air*) viciado; (*smell*) mofado; (*beer*) velho
stalemate ['steɪlmeɪt] N empate *m*; (*fig*) impasse *m*, beco sem saída
stalk [stɔːk] N talo, haste *f* ▶ VT caçar de tocaia; **to ~ in/out** entrar/sair silenciosamente; **to ~ off** andar com arrogância
stall [stɔːl] N (BRIT: *in market*) barraca; (*in stable*) baia ▶ VT (*Aut*) fazer morrer; (*fig: delay*) impedir, atrasar ▶ VI morrer; esquivar-se, ganhar tempo; **stalls** NPL (BRIT: *in cinema, theatre*) plateia; **a newspaper/flower ~** uma banca de jornais/uma barraca de flores
stallholder ['stɔːlhəuldəʳ] N feirante *m/f*
stallion ['stælɪən] N garanhão *m*
stalwart ['stɔːlwət] ADJ (*in build*) robusto; (*in spirit*) leal ▶ N partidário leal
stamen ['steɪmən] N estame *m*
stamina ['stæmɪnə] N resistência
stammer ['stæməʳ] N gagueira ▶ VI gaguejar, balbuciar
stamp [stæmp] N selo; (*rubber stamp*) carimbo, timbre *m*; (*mark: also fig*) marca, impressão *f* ▶ VI (*also*: **stamp one's foot**) bater com o pé ▶ VT (*letter*) selar; (*mark*) marcar; (*with rubber stamp*) carimbar; **~ed addressed envelope** envelope *m* selado e sobrescritado
▶ **stamp out** VT (*fire*) apagar com os pés; (*crime*) eliminar; (*opposition*) esmagar
stamp album N álbum *m* de selos
stamp collecting [-kə'lɛktɪŋ] N filatelia
stamp duty (BRIT) N imposto de selo
stampede [stæm'piːd] N debandada, estouro (da boiada)
stamp machine N máquina de selos
stance [stæns] N postura, posição *f*
stand [stænd] (*pt, pp* **stood**) N (*position*) posição *f*, postura; (*for taxis*) ponto; (*also*: **hall stand**) pedestal *m*; (*also*: **music stand**) estante *f*; (*Sport*) tribuna, palanque *m*; (*stall*) barraca; (*also*: **news stand**) banca de jornais ▶ VI (*be*) estar, encontrar-se; (*be on foot*) estar em pé; (*rise*) levantar-se; (*remain: decision, offer*) estar de pé; (*in election*) candidatar-se ▶ VT

(place) pôr, colocar; *(tolerate, withstand)* aguentar, suportar; *(cost)* pagar; **to make a ~** resistir; *(fig)* ater-se a um princípio; **to take a ~ on an issue** tomar posição definida sobre um assunto; **to ~ for parliament** (BRIT) apresentar-se como candidato ao parlamento; **to ~ guard** *or* **watch** *(Mil)* montar guarda; **it ~s to reason** é lógico; **as things ~** como as coisas estão; **to ~ sb a drink/meal** pagar uma bebida/refeição para alguém; **I can't ~ him** não o aguento; **to ~ still** ficar parado

▶ **stand aside** VI pôr-se de lado

▶ **stand by** VI *(be ready)* estar a postos ▶ VT FUS *(opinion)* aferrar-se a; *(person)* ficar ao lado de

▶ **stand down** VI *(withdraw)* retirar-se; *(Mil)* deixar o serviço

▶ **stand for** VT FUS *(defend)* apoiar; *(signify)* significar; *(represent)* representar; *(tolerate)* tolerar, permitir

▶ **stand in for** VT FUS substituir

▶ **stand out** VI *(be prominent)* destacar-se

▶ **stand up** VI *(rise)* levantar-se

▶ **stand up for** VT FUS defender

▶ **stand up to** VT FUS enfrentar

stand-alone ADJ *(Comput)* autônomo, stand-alone

standard ['stændəd] N padrão *m*, critério; *(flag)* estandarte *m*; *(level)* nível *m* ▶ ADJ *(size etc)* padronizado, regular, normal; **standards** NPL *(morals)* valores *mpl* morais; **to be** *or* **come up to ~** alcançar os padrões exigidos; **to apply a double ~** ter dois pesos e duas medidas; **the gold ~** *(Comm)* o padrão ouro

standardization [stændədaɪ'zeɪʃən] N padronização *f*

standardize ['stændədaɪz] VT padronizar

standard lamp (BRIT) N abajur *m* de pé

standard of living N padrão *m* de vida (BR), nível *m* de vida (PT)

standard time N hora legal *or* oficial

stand-by ADJ de reserva ▶ N: **to be on ~** estar de sobreaviso or de prontidão

stand-by ticket N bilhete *m* de stand-by

stand-in N suplente *m/f*; *(Cinema)* dublê *m/f*

standing ['stændɪŋ] ADJ *(upright)* ereto vertical; *(on foot)* em pé; *(permanent)* permanente ▶ N posição *f*, reputação *f*; **of 6 months' ~** de 6 meses de duração; **of many years' ~** de muitos anos; **he was given a ~ ovation** ele foi ovacionado; **a man of some ~** um homem de posição

standing joke N piada conhecida

standing order (BRIT) N *(at bank)* instrução *f* permanente; **standing orders** NPL *(Mil)* regulamento geral

standing room N lugar *m* em pé

stand-off N *(esp US: stalemate)* queda de braço

stand-offish [-'ɔfɪʃ] ADJ incomunicativo, reservado

standpat ['stændpæt] (US) ADJ inflexível, conservador(a)

standpipe ['stændpaɪp] N tubo de subida

standpoint ['stændpɔɪnt] N ponto de vista

standstill ['stændstɪl] N: **at a ~** paralisado, parado; **to come to a ~** *(car)* parar; *(factory, traffic)* ficar paralisado

stank [stæŋk] PT *of* **stink**

stanza ['stænzə] N estância, estrofe *f*

staple ['steɪpl] N *(for papers)* grampo; *(chief product)* produto básico ▶ ADJ *(food etc)* básico ▶ VT grampear

stapler ['steɪplə^r] N grampeador *m*

star [stɑː^r] N estrela; *(celebrity)* astro/estrela ▶ VI: **to ~ in** ser a estrela em, estrelar ▶ VT *(Cinema)* ser estrelado por; **the stars** NPL *(horoscope)* o horóscopo; **4-~ hotel** hotel 4 estrelas; **2-~ petrol** gasolina comum (BR) or normal (PT); **4-~ petrol** (BRIT) gasolina premium (BR) or súper (PT)

star attraction N atração *f* principal

starboard ['stɑːbəd] N estibordo; **to ~** a estibordo

starch [stɑːtʃ] N *(in food)* amido, fécula; *(for clothes)* goma

starched ['stɑːtʃt] ADJ *(collar)* engomado

starchy ['stɑːtʃɪ] ADJ amiláceo

stardom ['stɑːdəm] N estrelato

stare [stɛə^r] N olhar *m* fixo ▶ VI: **to ~ at** olhar fixamente, fitar

starfish ['stɑːfɪʃ] N INV estrela-do-mar *f*

stark [stɑːk] ADJ *(bleak)* severo, áspero; *(colour)* sóbrio; *(reality, truth, simplicity)* cru; *(contrast)* gritante ▶ ADV: **~ naked** completamente nu, em pelo

starlet ['stɑːlɪt] N *(Cinema)* vedete *f*

starlight ['stɑːlaɪt] N: **by ~** à luz das estrelas

starling ['stɑːlɪŋ] N estorninho

starlit ['stɑːlɪt] ADJ iluminado pelas estrelas

starry ['stɑːrɪ] ADJ estrelado

starry-eyed [-'aɪd] ADJ *(innocent)* deslumbrado

star sign N signo

star-studded [-'stʌdɪd] ADJ: **a ~ cast** um elenco cheio de estrelas

start [stɑːt] N *(beginning)* princípio, começo; *(departure)* partida; *(sudden movement)* sobressalto, susto; *(advantage)* vantagem *f* ▶ VT começar, iniciar; *(cause)* causar; *(found)* fundar; *(engine)* ligar; *(fire)* provocar ▶ VI começar, iniciar; *(with fright)* sobressaltar-se, assustar-se; *(train etc)* sair; **to ~ doing** *or* **to do sth** começar a fazer algo; **at the ~** no início; **for a ~** para início de conversa; **to make an early ~** sair *or* começar cedo; **to ~ (off) with …** *(firstly)* para começar …; *(at the beginning)* no início …; **to give sb a ~** dar um susto em alguém

▶ **start off** VI começar, principiar; *(leave)* sair, pôr-se a caminho

▶ **start over** (US) VI começar de novo

▶ **start up** VI começar; *(car)* pegar, pôr-se em marcha ▶ VT começar; *(car)* ligar

starter ['stɑːtə^r] N *(Aut)* arranque *m*; *(Sport: official)* juiz/juíza *m/f* da partida; *(: runner)* corredor(a) *m/f*; (BRIT Culin) entrada

starting handle ['stɑːtɪŋ-] (BRIT) N manivela de arranque
starting point ['stɑːtɪŋ-] N ponto de partida
starting price ['stɑːtɪŋ-] N preço inicial
startle ['stɑːtl] VT assustar, aterrar
startling ['stɑːtlɪŋ] ADJ surpreendente
star turn (BRIT) N rei m /rainha f do show
starvation [stɑː'veɪʃən] N fome f; (Med) inanição f
starve ['stɑːv] VI passar fome; (to death) morrer de fome ▶ VT fazer passar fome; (fig): **to ~ (of)** privar (de); **I'm starving** estou morrendo de fome
starving ['stɑːvɪŋ] ADJ faminto, esfomeado
state [steɪt] N estado; (pomp): **in ~** com grande pompa ▶ VT (say, declare) afirmar, declarar; (a case) expor, apresentar; **the States** NPL (Geo) os Estados Unidos; **to be in a ~** estar agitado; **~ of emergency** estado de emergência; **~ of mind** estado de espírito; **the ~ of the art** a última palavra; **to lie in ~** estar exposto em câmara ardente
State Department (US) N Departamento de Estado, ≈ Ministério das Relações Exteriores
state education (BRIT) N educação f pública
stateless ['steɪtlɪs] ADJ desnacionalizado
stately ['steɪtlɪ] ADJ majestoso, imponente
statement ['steɪtmənt] N declaração f; (Law) depoimento; (Econ) balanço; **official ~** comunicado oficial; **~ of account** extrato de conta, extrato bancário
state-owned [-əund] ADJ estatal
state secret N segredo de estado
statesman ['steɪtsmən] (irreg: like **man**) N estadista m
statesmanship ['steɪtsmənʃɪp] N arte f de governar
statesmen ['steɪtsmɛn] NPL of **statesman**
static ['stætɪk] N (Radio, TV) interferência ▶ ADJ estático
static electricity N (eletricidade f) estática
station ['steɪʃən] N estação f; (place) posto, lugar m; (Police) delegacia; (Radio) emissora; (rank) posição f social ▶ VT colocar; **to be ~ed in** (Mil) estar estacionado em
stationary ['steɪʃnərɪ] ADJ estacionário
stationer ['steɪʃənəʳ] N dono de papelaria
stationer's, stationer's shop N papelaria
stationery ['steɪʃnərɪ] N artigos mpl de papelaria; (writing paper) papel m de carta
station master N (Rail) chefe m da estação
station wagon (US) N perua (BR), canadiana (PT)
statistic [stə'tɪstɪk] N estatística
statistical [stə'tɪstɪkl] ADJ estatístico
statistics [stə'tɪstɪks] N (science) estatística
statue ['stætjuː] N estátua
statuesque [stætju'ɛsk] ADJ escultural
statuette [stætju'ɛt] N estatueta
stature ['stætʃəʳ] N estatura, altura; (fig) estatura, envergadura
status ['steɪtəs] N posição f; (official classification) categoria; (importance) status m; (Admin: also: **marital status**) estado civil

status quo [-kwəu] N: **the ~** o status quo
status symbol N símbolo de prestígio
statute ['stætjuːt] N estatuto, lei f; **statutes** NPL (of club etc) estatuto
statute book N ≈ Código
statutory ['stætjutərɪ] ADJ (according to statutes) estatutário; (holiday etc) regulamentar
staunch [stɔːntʃ] ADJ fiel ▶ VT estancar
stave [steɪv] N (Mus) pauta ▶ **stave off** VT (attack) repelir; (threat) evitar, protelar
stay [steɪ] N (period of time) estadia, estada; (Law): **~ of execution** adiamento de execução ▶ VI (remain) ficar; (as guest) hospedar-se; (spend some time) demorar-se; **to ~ put** não se mexer; **to ~ the night** pernoitar
▶ **stay behind** VI ficar atrás
▶ **stay in** VI (at home) ficar em casa
▶ **stay on** VI ficar
▶ **stay out** VI (of house) ficar fora de casa; (strikers) continuar em greve
▶ **stay up** VI (at night) velar, ficar acordado
staying power ['steɪɪŋ-] N resistência, raça
STD N ABBR (BRIT: = subscriber trunk dialling) DDD f; (= sexually transmitted disease) DST f
stead [stɛd] N: **in sb's ~** em lugar de alguém; **to stand sb in good ~** prestar bons serviços a alguém
steadfast ['stɛdfɑːst] ADJ firme, estável, resoluto
steadily ['stɛdɪlɪ] ADV (firmly) firmemente; (unceasingly) sem parar, constantemente; (walk) regularmente; (drive) a uma velocidade constante
steady ['stɛdɪ] ADJ (job, boyfriend) constante; (speed) fixo; (unswerving) firme; (regular) regular; (person, character) sensato, equilibrado; (diligent) diligente; (calm) calmo, sereno ▶ VT (hold) manter firme; (stabilize) estabilizar; (nerves) acalmar; **to ~ o.s. on** or **against sth** firmar-se em algo
steak [steɪk] N filé m; (beef) bife m
steakhouse ['steɪkhaus] N ≈ churrascaria
steal [stiːl] (pt **stole**, pp **stolen**) VT roubar ▶ VI (move secretly) mover-se furtivamente
▶ **steal away** VI sair às escondidas
▶ **steal off** VI = **steal away**
stealth [stɛlθ] N: **by ~** furtivamente, às escondidas
stealthy ['stɛlθɪ] ADJ furtivo
steam [stiːm] N vapor m ▶ VT (Culin) cozinhar no vapor ▶ VI fumegar; (ship): **to ~ along** avançar or mover-se (a vapor); **under one's own ~** (fig) por esforço próprio; **to run out of ~** (fig: person) perder o pique; **to let off ~** (fig: inf) desabafar
▶ **steam up** VI (window) embaçar; **to get ~ed up about sth** irritar-se com algo
steam engine N máquina a vapor
steamer ['stiːməʳ] N vapor m, navio (a vapor)
steam iron N ferro a vapor
steamroller ['stiːmrəuləʳ] N rolo compressor (a vapor)

S

steamy ['stiːmɪ] ADJ vaporoso; (room) cheio de vapor, úmido (BR), húmido (PT); (heat, atmosphere) vaporoso

steed [stiːd] N (literary) corcel m

steel [stiːl] N aço ▶ ADJ de aço

steel band N banda de percussão do Caribe

steel industry N indústria siderúrgica

steel mill N (usina) siderúrgica

steelworks ['stiːlwɜːks] N (usina) siderúrgica

steely ['stiːlɪ] ADJ (determination) inflexível; (gaze, eyes) duro, frio; **~-grey** cor de aço inv

steep [stiːp] ADJ íngreme; (increase) acentuado; (price) exorbitante ▶ VT (food) colocar de molho; (cloth) ensopar, encharcar

steeple ['stiːpl] N campanário, torre f

steeplechase ['stiːpltʃeɪs] N corrida de obstáculos

steeplejack ['stiːpldʒæk] N consertador m de torres or de chaminés altas

steeply ['stiːplɪ] ADV escarpadamente, a pique

steer [stɪə^r] N boi m ▶ VT (person) guiar; (vehicle) dirigir ▶ VI conduzir; **to ~ clear of sb/sth** (fig) evitar alguém/algo

steering ['stɪərɪŋ] N (Aut) direção f

steering column N (Aut) coluna da direção

steering committee N comitê m dirigente

steering wheel N volante m

stellar ['stɛlə^r] ADJ estelar

stem [stɛm] N (of plant) caule m, haste f; (of glass) pé m; (of pipe) tubo ▶ VT deter, reter; (blood) estancar
▶ **stem from** VT FUS originar-se de

stem cell N célula-tronco m

stench [stɛntʃ] (pej) N fedor m

stencil ['stɛnsl] N (pattern, design) estêncil m; (lettering) gabarito de letra ▶ VT imprimir com estêncil

stenographer [stɛ'nɔɡrəfə^r] (US) N estenógrafo(-a)

stenography [stɛ'nɔɡrəfɪ] (US) N estenografia

step [stɛp] N passo; (stair) degrau m; (action) medida, providência ▶ VI **to ~ forward** dar um passo a frente/atrás; **steps** NPL (BRIT) = **stepladder**; **~ by ~** passo a passo; **to be in ~ (with)** (fig) manter a paridade (com); **to be out of ~ (with)** (fig) estar em disparidade (com); **to take ~s** tomar providências
▶ **step down** VI (fig) renunciar
▶ **step in** VI (fig) intervir
▶ **step off** VT FUS descer de
▶ **step on** VT FUS pisar
▶ **step over** VT FUS passar por cima de
▶ **step up** VT (increase) aumentar; (intensify) intensificar

stepbrother ['stɛpbrʌðə^r] N meio-irmão m

stepchild ['stɛptʃaɪld] (irreg: like **child**) N enteado(-a)

stepdaughter ['stɛpdɔːtə^r] N enteada

stepfather ['stɛpfɑːðə^r] N padrasto

stepladder ['stɛplædə^r] (BRIT) N escada portátil or de abrir

stepmother ['stɛpmʌðə^r] N madrasta

stepping stone ['stɛpɪŋ-] N pedra utilizada em passarelas; (fig) trampolim m

stepsister ['stɛpsɪstə^r] N meia-irmã f

stepson ['stɛpsʌn] N enteado

stereo ['stɛrɪəu] N estéreo; (record player) (aparelho de) som m ▶ ADJ (also: **stereophonic**) estereofônico; **in ~** em estéreo

stereotype ['stɛrɪətaɪp] N estereótipo ▶ VT estereotipar

sterile ['stɛraɪl] ADJ (free from germs) esterelizado; (barren) estéril

sterility [stɛ'rɪlɪtɪ] N esterilidade f

sterilization [stɛrɪlaɪ'zeɪʃən] N esterilização f

sterilize ['stɛrɪlaɪz] VT esterilizar

sterling ['stɜːlɪŋ] ADJ esterlino; (silver) de lei; (fig) genuíno, puro ▶ N (currency) libra esterlina; **one pound ~** uma libra esterlina

sterling area N zona esterlina

stern [stɜːn] ADJ severo, austero ▶ N (Naut) popa, ré f

sternum ['stɜːnəm] N esterno

steroid ['stɪərɔɪd] N esteroide m

stethoscope ['stɛθəskəup] N estetoscópio

stevedore ['stiːvədɔː^r] N estivador m

stew [stjuː] N guisado, ensopado ▶ VT, VI guisar, ensopar; (fruit) cozinhar; **~ed tea** chá muito forte; **~ed fruit** compota de frutas

steward ['stjuːəd] N (Aviat) comissário de bordo; (also: **shop steward**) delegado(-a) sindical

stewardess ['stjuːədɪs] N aeromoça (BR), hospedeira de bordo (PT)

stewing steak ['stjuːɪŋ-], (US) **stew meat** N carne f para ensopado

St. Ex. ABBR = **stock exchange**

stg ABBR = **sterling**

stick [stɪk] (pt, pp **stuck**) N pau m; (as weapon) cacete m; (walking stick) bengala, cajado ▶ VT (glue) colar; (inf: put) meter; (: tolerate) aguentar, suportar; (: thrust): **to ~ sth into** cravar or enfiar algo em ▶ VI (become attached) colar-se, aderir-se; (be unmoveable) emperrar; (in mind etc) gravar-se; **to get hold of the wrong end of the ~** (BRIT fig) confundir-se; **to ~ to** (promise, principles) manter
▶ **stick around** (inf) VI ficar
▶ **stick out** VI estar saliente, projetar-se ▶ VT: **to ~ it out** (inf) aguentar firme
▶ **stick up** VI estar saliente, projetar-se
▶ **stick up for** VT FUS defender

sticker ['stɪkə^r] N adesivo

sticking plaster ['stɪkɪŋ-] N esparadrapo

stickleback ['stɪklbæk] N espinhela

stickler ['stɪklə^r] N: **to be a ~ for** insistir em, exigir

stick-on ADJ adesivo

stick-up (inf) N assalto a mão armada

sticky ['stɪkɪ] ADJ pegajoso; (label) adesivo; (fig) delicado

stiff [stɪf] ADJ (strong) forte; (hard) duro; (difficult) difícil; (moving with difficulty: person)

teso; (: *door, zip*) empenado; (*formal*) formal
▶ ADV (*bored, worried*) extremamente; **to be or
feel ~** (*person*) ter dores musculares; **~ upper
lip** (BRIT *fig*) fleuma britânica

stiffen ['stɪfən] VT endurecer; (*limb*)
entumecer ▶ VI enrijecer-se; (*grow stronger*)
fortalecer-se

stiff neck N torcicolo

stiffness ['stɪfnɪs] N rigidez *f*

stifle ['staɪfl] VT sufocar, abafar; (*opposition*)
sufocar

stifling ['staɪflɪŋ] ADJ (*heat*) sufocante,
abafado

stigma ['stɪgmə] (*pl* **stigmata**) N (*Bot, Med, Rel*)
estigma *m*; (*pl* **stigmas**): *fig* estigma *m*

stigmata [stɪg'mɑːtə] NPL *of* **stigma**

stile [staɪl] N *degraus para passar por uma cerca ou
muro*

stiletto [stɪ'lɛtəu] (BRIT) N (*also:* **stiletto heel**)
salto alto e fino

still [stɪl] ADJ parado; (*motionless*) imóvel;
(*calm*) quieto; (BRIT: *orange drink etc*) sem gás
▶ ADV (*up to this time*) ainda; (*even, yet*) ainda;
(*nonetheless*) entretanto, contudo ▶ N (*Cinema*)
still *m*; **to stand ~** ficar parado; **keep ~!** não
se mexa!; **he ~ hasn't arrived** ele ainda não
chegou

stillborn ['stɪlbɔːn] ADJ nascido morto,
natimorto

still life N natureza morta

stilt [stɪlt] N perna de pau; (*pile*) estaca,
suporte *m*

stilted ['stɪltɪd] ADJ afetado

stimulant ['stɪmjulənt] N estimulante *m*

stimulate ['stɪmjuleɪt] VT estimular

stimulating ['stɪmjuleɪtɪŋ] ADJ estimulante

stimulation [stɪmju'leɪʃən] N estimulação *f*

stimuli ['stɪmjulaɪ] NPL *of* **stimulus**

stimulus ['stɪmjuləs] (*pl* **stimuli**) N estímulo,
incentivo

sting [stɪŋ] (*pt, pp* **stung**) VT arguilhar ▶ VI
(*insect, animal*) picar; (*eyes, ointment*) queimar
▶ N (*wound*) picada; (*pain*) ardência; (*of insect*)
ferrão *m*; (*inf: confidence trick*) conto-do-
vigário

stingy ['stɪndʒɪ] (*pej*) ADJ pão-duro, sovina

stink [stɪŋk] VI (*pt* **stank**, *pp* **stunk**) feder,
cheirar mal ▶ N fedor *m*, catinga

stinker ['stɪŋkər] (*inf*) N (*problem, person*) osso
duro de roer

stinking ['stɪŋkɪŋ] ADJ fedorento, fétido; (*inf:
fig*) maldito; **~ rich** ricaço

stint [stɪnt] N tarefa, parte *f* ▶ VI: **to ~ on** ser
parco com; **to do one's ~** fazer a sua parte

stipend ['staɪpend] N (*of vicar etc*) estipêndio,
remuneração *f*

stipendiary [staɪ'pendɪərɪ] ADJ: **~ magistrate**
juiz *m* estipendiário, juíza *f* estipendiário

stipulate ['stɪpjuleɪt] VT estipular

stipulation [stɪpju'leɪʃən] N estipulação *f*,
cláusula

stir [stəːr] N (*fig: agitation*) comoção *f*, rebuliço
▶ VT (*tea etc*) mexer; (*fig: emotions*) comover

▶ VI mover-se, remexer-se; **to give sth a ~**
mexer algo; **to cause a ~** causar sensação *or*
um rebuliço

▶ **stir up** VT excitar; (*trouble*) provocar

stirring ['stəːrɪŋ] ADJ comovedor(a)

stirrup ['stɪrəp] N estribo

stitch [stɪtʃ] N (*Sewing, Knitting, Med*) ponto;
(*pain*) pontada ▶ VT costurar; (*Med*) dar
pontos em, suturar

stoat [stəut] N arminho

stock [stɔk] N (*supply*) suprimento; (*Comm:
reserves*) estoque *m*, provisão *f*; (: *selection*)
sortimento; (*Agr*) gado; (*Culin*) caldo;
(*lineage*) estirpe *f*, linhagem *f*; (*Finance*)
valores *mpl*, títulos *mpl*; (: *shares*) ações *fpl*;
(*Rail: also:* **rolling stock**) material *m*
circulante ▶ ADJ (*reply etc*) de sempre,
costumeiro; (*greeting*) habitual ▶ VT (*have in
stock*) ter em estoque, estocar; (*sell*) vender;
well-~ed bem sortido; **in ~** em estoque; **out
of ~** esgotado; **to take ~ of** (*fig*) fazer um
balanço de; **~s and shares** valores e títulos
mobiliários; **government ~** títulos do
governo, fundos públicos

▶ **stock up** VI: **to ~ up (with)** abastecer-se (de)

stockade [stɔ'keɪd] N estacada

stockbroker ['stɔkbrəukər] N corretor(a) *m/f*
de valores

stock control N (*Comm*) controle *m* de estoque

stock cube (BRIT) N (*Culin*) cubo de caldo

stock exchange N Bolsa de Valores

stockholder ['stɔkhəuldər] (US) N acionista *m/f*

Stockholm ['stɔkhəum] N Estocolmo

stocking ['stɔkɪŋ] N meia

stock-in-trade N (*tool*) instrumento de
trabalho; (*fig*) arma

stockist ['stɔkɪst] (BRIT) N estoquista *m/f*

stock market (BRIT) N Bolsa, mercado de
valores

stock phrase N frase *f* feita

stockpile ['stɔkpaɪl] N reservas *fpl*,
estocagem *f* ▶ VT acumular reservas de,
estocar

stockroom ['stɔkruːm] N almoxarifado

stocktaking ['stɔkteɪkɪŋ] (BRIT) N (*Comm*)
inventário

stocky ['stɔkɪ] ADJ (*strong*) robusto; (*short*)
atarracado

stodgy ['stɔdʒɪ] ADJ pesado

stoic ['stəuɪk] N estoico(-a)

stoical ['stəuɪkəl] ADJ estoico

stoke [stəuk] VT atiçar, alimentar

stoker ['stəukər] N (*Rail, Naut etc*) foguista *m*

stole [stəul] PT *of* **steal** ▶ N estola

stolen ['stəuln] PP *of* **steal**

stolid ['stɔlɪd] ADJ fleumático

stomach ['stʌmək] N (*Anat*) estômago; (*belly*)
barriga, ventre *m* ▶ VT suportar, tolerar

stomach ache N dor *f* de estômago

stomach pump N bomba gástrica

stomach ulcer N úlcera gástrica

stomp [stɔmp] VI: **to ~ in/out** entrar/sair
como um furacão

stone [stəun] N pedra; *(pebble)* pedrinha; *(in fruit)* caroço; *(Med)* pedra, cálculo; *(BRIT: weight)* = *6.348kg; 14 pounds* ▶ ADJ de pedra ▶ VT apedrejar; *(fruit)* tirar o(s) caroço(s) de; **within a ~'s throw of the station** pertinho da estação

Stone Age N: **the ~** a Idade da Pedra

stone-cold ADJ gelado

stoned [stəund] *(inf)* ADJ *(on drugs)* doidão(-dona), baratinado

stone-deaf ADJ surdo como uma porta

stonemason ['stəunmeɪsn] N pedreiro(-a)

stonework ['stəunwə:k] N cantaria

stony ['stəunɪ] ADJ pedregoso; *(fig)* glacial

stood [stud] PT, PP of **stand**

stool [stu:l] N tamborete m, banco

stoop [stu:p] VI *(also:* **have a stoop)** ser corcunda; *(also:* **stoop down)** debruçar-se, curvar-se; *(fig):* **to ~ to sth/doing sth** rebaixar-se para algo/fazer algo

stop [stɔp] N parada, interrupção f; *(for bus etc)* parada (BR), ponto (BR), paragem f (PT); *(also:* **full stop)** ponto ▶ VT parar, deter; *(break off)* interromper; *(pay, cheque)* sustar, suspender; *(also:* **put a stop to)** impedir ▶ VI parar, deter-se; *(watch, noise)* parar; *(end)* acabar; **to ~ doing sth** deixar de fazer algo; **to ~ sb (from) doing sth** impedir alguém de fazer algo; **to ~ dead** parar de repente; **~ it!** para com isso!
  ▶ **stop by** VI dar uma passada
  ▶ **stop off** VI dar uma parada
  ▶ **stop up** VT *(hole)* tapar

stopcock ['stɔpkɔk] N torneira de passagem

stopgap ['stɔpgæp] N *(person)* tapa-buraco m/f; *(measure)* paliativo

stoplights ['stɔplaɪts] NPL *(Aut)* luzes fpl do freio (BR), faróis mpl de stop (PT)

stopover ['stɔpəuvə'] N parada rápida; *(Aviat)* escala

stoppage ['stɔpɪdʒ] N *(strike)* greve f; *(temporary stop)* paralisação f; *(of pay)* suspensão f; *(blockage)* obstrução f

stopper ['stɔpə'] N tampa, rolha

stop press N notícia de última hora

stopwatch ['stɔpwɔtʃ] N cronômetro

storage ['stɔ:rɪdʒ] N armazenagem f

storage heater (BRIT) N tipo de aquecimento que armazena calor durante a noite emitindo-o durante o dia

store [stɔ:'] N *(stock)* suprimento; *(depot)* armazém m; *(reserve)* estoque m; *(BRIT: large shop)* loja de departamentos; *(US: shop)* loja ▶ VT armazenar; *(keep)* guardar; **stores** NPL *(provisions)* víveres mpl, provisões fpl; **who knows what is in ~ for us?** quem sabe o que nos espera?; **to set great/little ~ by sth** dar grande/pouca importância a algo
  ▶ **store up** VT acumular

storehouse ['stɔ:haus] N depósito, armazém m

storekeeper ['stɔ:ki:pə'] (US) N lojista m/f

storeroom ['stɔ:ru:m] N depósito, almoxarifado

storey, (US) **story** ['stɔ:rɪ] N andar m

stork [stɔ:k] N cegonha

storm [stɔ:m] N tempestade f; *(wind)* borrasca, vendaval m; *(fig)* tumulto ▶ VI *(fig)* enfurecer-se ▶ VT tomar de assalto, assaltar

storm cloud N nuvem f de tempestade

storm door N porta adicional

stormy ['stɔ:mɪ] ADJ tempestuoso

story ['stɔ:rɪ] N história, estória; *(Press)* matéria; *(plot)* enredo; *(lie)* mentira; *(US)* = **storey**

storybook ['stɔ:rɪbuk] N livro de contos

storyteller ['stɔ:rɪtelə'] N contador(a) m/f de estórias

stout [staut] ADJ *(strong)* sólido, forte; *(fat)* gordo, corpulento; *(resolute)* decidido, resoluto ▶ N cerveja preta

stove [stəuv] N *(for cooking)* fogão m; *(for heating)* estufa, fogareiro; **gas/electric ~** *(cooker)* fogão a gás/elétrico

stow [stəu] VT guardar; *(Naut)* estivar

stowaway ['stəuəweɪ] N passageiro(-a) clandestino(-a)

straddle ['strædl] VT cavalgar

strafe [stra:f] VT metralhar

straggle ['strægl] VI *(houses)* espalhar-se desordenadamente; *(people)* vagar, perambular; *(lag behind)* ficar para trás

straggler ['stræglə'] N pessoa que fica para trás

straggling ['stræglɪŋ] ADJ *(hair)* rebelde, emaranhado

straggly ['stræglɪ] ADJ *(hair)* rebelde, emaranhado

straight [streɪt] ADJ reto; *(back)* esticado; *(hair)* liso; *(honest)* honesto; *(frank)* franco, direto; *(simple)* simples inv; *(Theatre: part, play)* sério; *(inf: conventional)* quadrado, careta (inf); *(: heterosexual)* heterossexual ▶ ADV reto; *(drink)* puro ▶ N: **the ~** *(Sport)* a reta; **to put** or **get sth ~** esclarecer algo; **let's get this ~** *(explaining)* então, vamos fazer assim; *(warning)* ou quero que isso fique bem claro; **10 ~ wins** 10 vitórias consecutivas; **to go ~ home** ir direto para casa; **~ away, ~ off** *(at once)* imediatamente; **~ off, ~ out** sem mais nem menos

straighten ['streɪtən] VT *(skirt, bed)* arrumar; **to ~ things out** arrumar as coisas
  ▶ **straighten out** VT endireitar; *(fig)* esclarecer

straight-faced [-feɪst] ADJ impassível ▶ ADV com cara séria

straightforward [streɪt'fɔ:wəd] ADJ *(simple)* simples inv, direto; *(honest)* honesto, franco

strain [streɪn] N tensão f; *(Tech)* esforço; *(Med: back strain)* distensão f; *(: tension)* luxação f; *(breed)* raça, estirpe f; *(of virus)* classe f ▶ VT *(back etc)* forçar, torcer, distender; *(tire)* extenuar; *(stretch)* puxar, estirar; *(Culin)* coar; *(filter)* filtrar ▶ VI esforçar-se; **strains** NPL *(Mus)* acordes mpl; **he's been under a lot of ~** ele tem estado sob muita tensão

strained [streɪnd] ADJ (*muscle*) distendido; (*laugh*) forçado; (*relations*) tenso

strainer ['streɪnə^r] N (*for tea, coffee*) coador m; (*sieve*) peneira

strait [streɪt] N (*Geo*) estreito; **straits** NPL (*fig*): **to be in dire ~s** estar em apuros

straitjacket ['streɪtdʒækɪt] N camisa-de-força

strait-laced [-leɪst] ADJ puritano, austero

strand [strænd] N (*of thread, hair*) fio; (*of rope*) tira ▶ VT (*boat*) encalhar

stranded ['strændɪd] ADJ desamparado; (*holidaymakers*) preso

strange [streɪndʒ] ADJ (*not known*) desconhecido; (*odd*) estranho, esquisito

strangely ['streɪndʒlɪ] ADV estranhamente

stranger ['streɪndʒə^r] N desconhecido(-a); (*from another area*) forasteiro(-a)

strangle ['stræŋgl] VT estrangular; (*fig: economy*) sufocar

stranglehold ['stræŋglhəʊld] N (*fig*) domínio total

strangulation [stræŋgjʊ'leɪʃən] N estrangulação f

strap [stræp] N correia; (*of slip, dress*) alça ▶ VT prender com correia

straphanging ['stræphæŋɪŋ] N viajar etc em pé (no metrô m)

strapless ['stræplɪs] ADJ (*bra, dress*) sem alças

strapped [stræpt] ADJ: **to be ~ for cash** (*inf*) estar na pindaíba

strapping ['stræpɪŋ] ADJ corpulento, robusto, forte

Strasbourg ['stræzbə:g] N Estrasburgo

strata ['strɑ:tə] NPL *of* **stratum**

stratagem ['strætɪdʒəm] N estratagema m

strategic [strə'ti:dʒɪk] ADJ estratégico

strategist ['strætɪdʒɪst] N estrategista m/f

strategy ['strætɪdʒɪ] N estratégia

stratosphere ['strætəsfɪə^r] N estratosfera

stratum ['strɑ:təm] (*pl* **strata**) N camada

straw [strɔ:] N palha; (*drinking straw*) canudo; **that's the last ~!** essa foi a última gota!

strawberry ['strɔ:bərɪ] N morango; (*plant*) morangueiro

stray [streɪ] ADJ (*animal*) extraviado; (*bullet*) perdido; (*scattered*) espalhado ▶ VI perder-se

streak [stri:k] N listra, traço; (*in hair*) mecha; (*fig: of madness etc*) sinal m ▶ VT listrar ▶ VI: **to ~ past** passar como um raio; **to have ~s in one's hair** fazer mechas no cabelo; **a winning/losing ~** uma fase de sorte/azar

streaky ['stri:kɪ] ADJ listrado

streaky bacon (BRIT) N toicinho or bacon m em fatias (*entremeado com gordura*)

stream [stri:m] N riacho, córrego; (*current*) fluxo, corrente f; (*of people, vehicles*) fluxo; (*of smoke*) rastro; (*of questions etc*) torrente f ▶ VT (*Sch*) classificar ▶ VI correr, fluir; **to ~ in/out** (*people*) entrar/sair em massa; **against the ~** contra a corrente; **on ~** (*power plant etc*) em funcionamento

streamer ['stri:mə^r] N serpentina; (*pennant*) flâmula

stream feed N (*on photocopier etc*) alimentação f contínua

streamline ['stri:mlaɪn] VT aerodinamizar; (*fig*) agilizar

streamlined ['stri:mlaɪnd] ADJ aerodinâmico

street [stri:t] N rua; **the back ~s** as ruelas; **to be on the ~s** (*homeless*) estar desabrigado; (*as prostitute*) fazer a vida

streetcar ['stri:tkɑ:^r] (US) N bonde m (BR), eléctrico (PT)

street lamp N poste m de iluminação

street lighting N iluminação f pública

street map N mapa m

street market N feira

street plan N mapa m

streetwise ['stri:twaɪz] (*inf*) ADJ malandro

strength [streŋθ] N força; (*of girder, knot etc*) firmeza, resistência; (*of chemical solution*) concentração f; (*of wine*) teor m alcoólico; (*fig*) poder m; **on the ~ of** com base em; **at full ~** completo; **below ~** desfalcado

strengthen ['streŋθən] VT fortificar; (*fig*) fortalecer

strenuous ['strenjʊəs] ADJ (*tough*) árduo, estrênuo; (*energetic*) enérgico; (*determined*) tenaz

stress [stres] N (*force, pressure*) pressão f; (*mental strain*) tensão f, stress m; (*accent*) acento; (*emphasis*) ênfase f; (*Tech*) tensão ▶ VT realçar, dar ênfase a; (*syllable*) acentuar; **to lay great ~ on sth** dar muita ênfase a algo; **to be under ~** estar com estresse

stressed [strest] ADJ (*tense*) estressado; (*syllable*) tônico

stressful ['stresful] ADJ (*job*) desgastante

stretch [stretʃ] N (*of sand etc*) trecho, extensão f; (*of time*) período ▶ VI espreguiçar-se; (*extend*): **to ~ to** or **as far as** estender-se até; (*be enough: money, food*): **to ~ to** dar para ▶ VT estirar, esticar; (*fig: subj: job, task*) exigir o máximo de; **at a ~** sem parar; **to ~ one's legs** esticar as pernas ▶ **stretch out** VI esticar-se ▶ VT (*arm etc*) esticar; (*spread*) estirar

stretcher ['stretʃə^r] N maca, padiola

stretcher-bearer N padioleiro

stretch marks NPL estrias fpl

strewn [stru:n] ADJ: **~ with** coberto or cheio de

stricken ['strɪkən] ADJ (*wounded*) ferido; (*devastated*) arrasado; (*ill*) acometido; **~ with** tomado por

strict [strɪkt] ADJ (*person*) severo, rigoroso; (*meaning*) exato, estrito; **in ~ confidence** muito confidencialmente

strictly ['strɪktlɪ] ADV (*severely*) severamente; (*exactly*) estritamente; (*definitively*) rigorosamente; **~ confidential** estritamente confidencial; **~ speaking** a rigor; **~ between ourselves ...** cá entre nós ...

strictness ['strɪktnɪs] N rigor m, severidade f

stridden ['strɪdn] PP *of* **stride**

stride [straɪd] vi (pt **strode**, pp **stridden**) andar a passos largos ▸ N passo largo; **to take in one's ~** (fig: changes etc) não se perturbar com

strident ['straɪdnt] ADJ estridente; (colour) berrante

strife [straɪf] N conflito

strike [straɪk] (pt, pp **struck**) N greve f; (of oil etc) descoberta; (attack) ataque m ▸ vt bater em; (oil etc) descobrir; (obstacle) esbarrar em; (deal) fechar, acertar; (fig): **the thought** or **it ~s me that …** me ocorre que … ▸ vi estar em greve; (attack: soldiers, illness) atacar; (: disaster) assolar; (clock) bater; **on ~** em greve; **to call a ~** convocar uma greve; **to ~ a match** acender um fósforo; **to ~ a balance** (fig) encontrar um equilíbrio; **the clock struck nine** o relógio bateu nove horas
▸ **strike back** vi (Mil) contra-atacar; (fig) revidar
▸ **strike down** vt derrubar
▸ **strike off** vt (from list) tirar, cortar; (doctor) suspender
▸ **strike out** vt cancelar, rasurar
▸ **strike up** vt (Mus) começar a tocar; (conversation, friendship) travar

strikebreaker ['straɪkbreɪkər] N fura-greve m/f inv

striker ['straɪkər] N grevista m/f; (Sport) atacante m/f

striking ['straɪkɪŋ] ADJ impressionante; (colour) chamativo

string [strɪŋ] (pt, pp **strung**) N (cord) barbante m (BR), cordel m (PT); (of beads) cordão m; (of onions) réstia; (Mus) corda; (series) série f; (of people, cars) fila (BR), bicha (PT); (Comput) string m ▸ vt: **to ~ out** esticar; **the strings** NPL (Mus) os instrumentos de corda; **to ~ together** (words) unir; (ideas) concatenar; **to get a job by pulling ~s** (fig) usar pistolão; **with no ~s attached** (fig) sem condições

string bean N vagem f

stringed instrument [strɪŋd-] N (Mus) instrumento de corda

stringent ['strɪndʒənt] ADJ rigoroso

string instrument N (Mus) instrumento de corda

string quartet N quarteto de cordas

strip [strɪp] N tira; (of land) faixa; (of metal) lâmina, tira; (Sport) cores fpl ▸ vt despir; (fig): **to ~ sb of sth** despojar alguém de algo; (also: **strip down**: machine) desmontar ▸ vi despir-se

strip cartoon N história em quadrinhos (BR), banda desenhada (PT)

stripe [straɪp] N listra; (Mil) galão m

striped [straɪpt] ADJ listrado, com listras

strip light (BRIT) N lâmpada fluorescente

strip lighting (BRIT) N iluminação f fluorescente

stripper ['strɪpər] N artista m/f de striptease

striptease ['strɪptiːz] N striptease m

strive [straɪv] (pt **strove**, pp **striven**) vi: **to ~ for sth/to do sth** esforçar-se por or batalhar para algo/para fazer algo

striven ['strɪvn] PP of **strive**

strode [strəʊd] PT of **stride**

stroke [strəʊk] N (blow) golpe m; (Med) derrame m cerebral; (caress) carícia; (of pen) traço; (of paintbrush) pincelada; (Swimming: style) nado; (: movement) braçada; (of piston) curso ▸ vt acariciar, afagar; **at a ~** de repente, de golpe; **on the ~ of five** às cinco em ponto; **a ~ of luck** um golpe de sorte; **a two-~ engine** um motor de dois tempos

stroll [strəʊl] N volta, passeio ▸ vi passear, dar uma volta; **to go for a ~** dar uma volta

stroller ['strəʊlər] (US) N carrinho (de criança)

strong [strɒŋ] ADJ forte; (imagination) fértil; (personality) forte, dominante; (nerves) de aço; (object, material) sólido; (chemical) concentrado ▸ ADV: **to be going ~** (company) estar prosperando; (person) estar com boa saúde; **they are 50 ~** são em 50 pessoas

strong-arm ADJ (tactics, methods) repressivo, violento

strongbox ['strɒŋbɒks] N cofre-forte m

strong drink N bebida alcoólica

stronghold ['strɒŋhəʊld] N fortaleza; (fig) baluarte m

strong language N palavrões mpl

strongly ['strɒŋlɪ] ADV (construct) firmemente; (push, defend) vigorosamente; (believe) profundamente; **I feel ~ about it** tenho uma opinião firme sobre isso

strongman ['strɒŋmæn] (irreg: like **man**) N homem m forte

strongroom ['strɒŋruːm] N casa-forte f

stroppy ['strɒpɪ] ADJ (BRIT inf) nervoso, barraqueiro

strove [strəʊv] PT of **strive**

struck [strʌk] PT, PP of **strike**

structural ['strʌktʃərəl] ADJ estrutural

structurally ['strʌktʃrəlɪ] ADV estruturalmente

structure ['strʌktʃər] N estrutura; (building) construção f

struggle ['strʌgl] N luta, contenda ▸ vi (fight) lutar; (try hard) batalhar; **to have a ~ to do sth** ter que batalhar para fazer algo

strum [strʌm] vt (guitar) dedilhar

strung [strʌŋ] PT, PP of **string**

strut [strʌt] N escora, suporte m ▸ vi pavonear-se, empertigar-se

strychnine ['strɪkniːn] N estricnina

stub [stʌb] N (of ticket etc) canhoto; (of cigarette) toco, ponta; **to ~ one's toe** dar uma topada ▸ **stub out** vt apagar

stubble ['stʌbl] N restolho; (on chin) barba por fazer

stubborn ['stʌbən] ADJ teimoso, cabeçudo, obstinado

stubby ['stʌbɪ] ADJ atarracado

stucco ['stʌkəʊ] N estuque

stuck [stʌk] PT, PP of **stick** ▸ ADJ (jammed) emperrado; **to get ~** emperrar

stuck-up ADJ convencido, metido, esnobe

stud [stʌd] N (*shirt stud*) botão *m*; (*earring*) tarraxa, rosca; (*of boot*) cravo; (*also*: **stud farm**) fazenda de cavalos; (*also*: **stud horse**) garanhão *m* ▶ VT (*fig*): **~ded with** salpicado de

student ['stju:dənt] N estudante *m/f* ▶ ADJ estudantil; **law/medical ~** estudante de direito/medicina

student driver (US) N aprendiz *m/f*

students' union (BRIT) N (*association*) união *f* dos estudantes; (*building*) centro estudantil

studied ['stʌdɪd] ADJ estudado, calculado

studio ['stju:dɪəu] N estúdio; (*sculptor's*) ateliê *m*

studio flat, (US) **studio apartment** N (apartamento) conjugado

studious ['stju:dɪəs] ADJ estudioso, aplicado; (*careful*) cuidadoso; (*studied*) calculado

studiously ['stju:dɪəslɪ] ADV (*carefully*) com esmero

study ['stʌdɪ] N estudo; (*room*) sala de leitura *or* estudo ▶ VT estudar; (*examine*) examinar, investigar ▶ VI estudar; **studies** NPL (*subjects*) estudos *mpl*, matérias *fpl*; **to make a ~ of sth** estudar algo; **to ~ for an exam** estudar para um exame

stuff [stʌf] N (*substance*) troço; (*things*) troços *mpl*, coisas *fpl* ▶ VT encher; (*Culin*) rechear; (*animals*) empalhar; (*inf: push*) enfiar; **my nose is ~ed up** meu nariz está entupido; **get ~ed!** (!) vai tomar banho!; **~ed toy** brinquedo de pelúcia

stuffing ['stʌfɪŋ] N recheio

stuffy ['stʌfɪ] ADJ (*room*) abafado, mal ventilado; (*person*) rabujento, melindroso

stumble ['stʌmbl] VI tropeçar; **to ~ across** *or* **on** (*fig*) topar com

stumbling block ['stʌmblɪŋ-] N pedra no caminho

stump [stʌmp] N (*of tree*) toco; (*of limb*) coto ▶ VT: **to be ~ed** ficar perplexo

stun [stʌn] VT (*subj: blow*) aturdir; (: *news*) pasmar

stung [stʌŋ] PT, PP *of* **sting**

stunk [stʌŋk] PP *of* **stink**

stunning ['stʌnɪŋ] ADJ (*news*) atordoante; (*appearance*) maravilhoso

stunt [stʌnt] N façanha sensacional; (*Aviat*) voo acrobático; (*publicity stunt*) truque *m* publicitário ▶ VT tolher

stunted ['stʌntɪd] ADJ atrofiado, retardado

stuntman ['stʌntmæn] (*irreg: like* **man**) N dublê *m*

stupefaction [stju:pɪ'fækʃən] N estupefação *f*, assombro

stupefy ['stju:pɪfaɪ] VT deixar estupefato

stupendous [stju:'pɛndəs] ADJ monumental

stupid ['stju:pɪd] ADJ estúpido, idiota

stupidity [stju:'pɪdɪtɪ] N estupidez *f*

stupidly ['stju:pɪdlɪ] ADV estupidamente

stupor ['stju:pə'] N estupor *m*

sturdy ['stə:dɪ] ADJ (*person*) robusto, firme; (*thing*) sólido

sturgeon ['stə:dʒən] N INV esturjão *m*

stutter ['stʌtə'] N gagueira, gaguez *f* ▶ VI gaguejar

sty [staɪ] N (*for pigs*) chiqueiro

stye [staɪ] N (*Med*) terçol *m*

style [staɪl] N estilo; (*elegance*) elegância; (*allure*) charme *m*; **in the latest ~** na última moda; **hair ~** penteado

styli ['staɪlaɪ] NPL *of* **stylus**

stylish ['staɪlɪʃ] ADJ elegante, chique

stylist ['staɪlɪst] N (*hair stylist*) cabeleireiro(-a); (*literary*) estilista *m/f*

stylized ['staɪlaɪzd] ADJ estilizado

stylus ['staɪləs] (*pl* **styli** *or* **styluses**) N (*of record player*) agulha

Styrofoam® ['staɪrəfəum] N (US) isopor *m* ▶ ADJ de isopor

suave [swɑːv] ADJ suave, melífluo

sub [sʌb] N ABBR = **submarine**; **subscription**

sub... [sʌb] PREFIX sub...

subcommittee ['sʌbkəmɪtɪ] N subcomissão *f*

subconscious [sʌb'kɒnʃəs] ADJ do subconsciente ▶ N subconsciente *m*

subcontinent [sʌb'kɒntɪnənt] N: **the (Indian) ~** o subcontinente (da Índia)

subcontract [*n* sʌb'kɒntrækt, *vt* sʌbkən'trækt] N subcontrato ▶ VT subcontratar

subcontractor [sʌbkən'træktə'] N subempreiteiro(-a)

subdivide [sʌbdɪ'vaɪd] VT subdividir

subdivision [sʌbdɪ'vɪʒən] N subdivisão *f*

subdue [səb'dju:] VT subjugar; (*passions*) dominar

subdued [səb'dju:d] ADJ (*light*) tênue; (*person*) desanimado

subject [*n* 'sʌbdʒɪkt, *vt* səb'dʒɛkt] N (*of king*) súdito(-a); (*theme*) assunto; (*Sch*) matéria; (*Ling*) sujeito ▶ VT: **to ~ sb to sth** submeter alguém a algo; **to be ~ to** estar sujeito a; **~ to confirmation in writing** sujeito a confirmação por escrito; **to change the ~** mudar de assunto

subjection [səb'dʒɛkʃən] N submissão *f*, dependência

subjective [səb'dʒɛktɪv] ADJ subjetivo

subject matter N assunto; (*content*) conteúdo

sub judice [-'dju:dɪsɪ] ADJ (*Law*) sob apreciação judicial, sub judice

subjugate ['sʌbdʒugeɪt] VT subjugar, submeter

subjunctive [səb'dʒʌŋktɪv] ADJ, N subjuntivo

sublet [sʌb'lɛt] VT sublocar

sublime [sə'blaɪm] ADJ sublime

subliminal [sʌb'lɪmɪnl] ADJ subliminar

submachine gun ['sʌbmə'ʃi:n-] N metralhadora de mão

submarine ['sʌbməri:n] N submarino

submerge [səb'mə:dʒ] VT submergir; (*flood*) inundar ▶ VI submergir-se

submersion [səb'mə:ʃən] N submersão *f*, imersão *f*

submission [səb'mɪʃən] N submissão *f*; (*to committee*) petição *f*; (*of plan*) apresentação *f*, exposição *f*

S

submissive [səb'mɪsɪv] ADJ submisso
submit [səb'mɪt] VT submeter ▶ VI submeter-se
subnormal [sʌb'nɔːməl] ADJ anormal, subnormal; (*temperature*) abaixo do normal; (*backward*) atrasado
subordinate [sə'bɔːdɪnət] ADJ, N subordinado(-a)
subpoena [sə'piːnə] N (*Law*) intimação f, citação f judicial ▶ VT intimar a comparecer judicialmente, citar
subprime ['sʌbpraɪm] ADJ (*Finance*): ~ **mortgage** títulomhipotecário de risco
subroutine [sʌbruː'tiːn] N (*Comput*) sub-rotina
subscribe [səb'skraɪb] VI subscrever; **to ~ to** (*opinion*) concordar com; (*fund*) contribuir para; (*newspaper*) assinar
subscriber [səb'skraɪbəʳ] N (*to periodical, telephone*) assinante m/f
subscript ['sʌbskrɪpt] N (*Typ*) subscrito
subscription [səb'skrɪpʃən] N subscrição f; (*to magazine etc*) assinatura; (*to club*) cota, mensalidade f; **to take out a ~ to** fazer uma assinatura de
subsequent ['sʌbsɪkwənt] ADJ subsequente, posterior; **~ to** posterior a
subsequently ['sʌbsɪkwəntlɪ] ADV posteriormente, depois
subside [səb'saɪd] VI (*feeling, wind*) acalmar-se; (*flood*) baixar
subsidence [səb'saɪdns] N baixa; (*in road etc*) afundamento da superfície
subsidiary [səb'sɪdɪərɪ] ADJ secundário; (*BRIT Sch: subject*) suplementar ▶ N (*also*: **subsidiary company**) subsidiária
subsidize ['sʌbsɪdaɪz] VT subsidiar
subsidy ['sʌbsɪdɪ] N subsídio
subsist [səb'sɪst] VI: **to ~ on sth** subsistir de algo
subsistence [səb'sɪstəns] N subsistência; (*allowance*) subsídio, ajuda de custo
subsistence allowance N diária
subsistence level N nível m de subsistência
subsistence wage N salário de fome
substance ['sʌbstəns] N substância; (*fig*) essência; **a man of ~** um homem de recursos; **to lack ~** não ter substância
substandard [sʌb'stændəd] ADJ (*goods*) de qualidade inferior; (*housing*) inferior ao padrão
substantial [səb'stænʃl] ADJ (*solid*) sólido; (*reward, meal*) substancial
substantially [səb'stænʃəlɪ] ADV consideravelmente; (*in essence*) substancialmente
substantiate [səb'stænʃɪeɪt] VT comprovar, justificar
substitute ['sʌbstɪtjuːt] N substituto(-a); (*person*) suplente m/f ▶ VT: **to ~ A for B** substituir B por A
substitute teacher (*US*) N professor(a) m/f suplente
substitution [sʌbstɪ'tjuːʃən] N substituição f
subterfuge ['sʌbtəfjuːdʒ] N subterfúgio

subterranean [sʌbtə'reɪnɪən] ADJ subterrâneo
subtitle ['sʌbtaɪtl] N (*Cinema*) legenda
subtitled ['sʌbtaɪtld] ADJ (*film*) legendado
subtle ['sʌtl] ADJ sutil
subtlety ['sʌtltɪ] N sutileza
subtly ['sʌtlɪ] ADV sutilmente
subtotal [sʌb'təutl] N total m parcial, subtotal m
subtract [səb'trækt] VT subtrair, deduzir
subtraction [səb'trækʃən] N subtração f
subtropical [sʌb'trɔpɪkl] ADJ subtropical
suburb ['sʌbəːb] N subúrbio
suburban [sə'bəːbən] ADJ suburbano; (*train etc*) de subúrbio
suburbia [sə'bəːbɪə] N os subúrbios
subvention [səb'vɛnʃən] N subvenção f, subsídio
subversion [səb'vəːʃən] N subversão f
subversive [səb'vəːsɪv] ADJ subversivo
subway ['sʌbweɪ] N (*BRIT*) passagem f subterrânea; (*US*) metrô m (*BR*), metro(-politano) (*PT*)
sub-zero ADJ abaixo de zero
succeed [sək'siːd] VI (*person*) ser bem sucedido, ter êxito; (*plan*) sair bem ▶ VT suceder a; **to ~ in doing** conseguir fazer
succeeding [sək'siːdɪŋ] ADJ (*following*) sucessivo, posterior
success [sək'sɛs] N êxito; (*hit, person*) sucesso; (*gain*) triunfo
successful [sək'sɛsful] ADJ (*venture*) bem sucedido; (*writer*) de sucesso, bem sucedido; **to be ~ (in doing)** conseguir (fazer)
successfully [sək'sɛsfulɪ] ADV com sucesso, com êxito
succession [sək'sɛʃən] N (*series*) sucessão f, série f; (*to throne*) suceˈssão; (*descendants*) descendência; **in ~** em sucessão; **3 years in ~** três anos consecutivos
successive [sək'sɛsɪv] ADJ sucessivo; **on 3 ~ days** em 3 dias consecutivos
successor [sək'sɛsəʳ] N sucessor(a) m/f
succinct [sək'sɪŋkt] ADJ sucinto
succulent ['sʌkjulənt] ADJ suculento ▶ N (*Bot*): **~s** suculentos mpl
succumb [sə'kʌm] VI sucumbir
such [sʌtʃ] ADJ tal, semelhante; (*of that kind: singular*) ~ **a book** um livro parecido, tal livro; (: *plural*): ~ **books** tais livros; (*so much*): ~ **courage** tanta coragem ▶ ADV tão; ~ **a long trip** uma viagem tão longa; ~ **good books** livros tão bons; ~ **a lot of** tanto; **making** ~ **a noise that** fazendo tanto barulho que; ~ **a long time ago** há tanto tempo atrás; ~ **as** (*like*) tal como; **a noise** ~ **as to** um ruído tal que; ~ **books as I have** os poucos livros que eu tenho; **I said no** ~ **thing** eu não disse tal coisa; **as** ~ como tal; **until** ~ **time as** até que
such-and-such ADJ tal e qual
suchlike ['sʌtʃlaɪk] (*inf*) PRON: **and** ~ e coisas assim

suck [sʌk] vт chupar; (breast) mamar; (subj: pump, machine) sugar
sucker ['sʌkə^r] N (Bot) rebento; (Zool) ventosa; (inf) trouxa m/f, otário(-a)
suckle ['sʌkl] vт amamentar
sucrose ['su:krəuz] N sucrose f
suction ['sʌkʃən] N sucção f
suction pump N bomba de sucção
Sudan [su'dɑ:n] N Sudão m
Sudanese [su:də'ni:z] ADJ, N INV sudanês(-esa) m/f
sudden ['sʌdn] ADJ (rapid) repentino, súbito; (unexpected) imprevisto; **all of a ~** de repente; (unexpectedly) inesperadamente
suddenly ['sʌdnlı] ADV de repente; (unexpectedly) inesperadamente
sudoku [su'dəuku:] N sudoku m
suds [sʌdz] NPL água de sabão
sue [su:] vт processar ▶ vı: **to ~ (for)** processar (por), promover ação (por); **to ~ for divorce** requerer divórcio; **to ~ sb for damages** intentar uma ação de perdas e danos contra alguém
suede [sweıd] N camurça ▶ cPD de camurça
suet ['suıt] N sebo
Suez ['su:ız] N: **the ~ Canal** o Canal de Suez
suffer ['sʌfə^r] vт sofrer; (bear) aguentar, suportar ▶ vı sofrer, padecer; **to ~ from** (illness) sofrer de, estar com; **to ~ from the effects of alcohol** sofrer os efeitos do álcool
sufferance ['sʌfrəns] N: **he was only there on ~** ele estava lá por tolerância
sufferer ['sʌfərə^r] N sofredor(a) m/f; **a ~ from** (Med) uma pessoa que sofre de
suffering ['sʌfərıŋ] N sofrimento; (pain) dor f
suffice [sə'faıs] vı bastar, ser suficiente
sufficient [sə'fıʃənt] ADJ suficiente, bastante
sufficiently [sə'fıʃəntlı] ADV suficientemente
suffix ['sʌfıks] N sufixo
suffocate ['sʌfəkeıt] vт sufocar, asfixiar ▶ vı sufocar(-se), asfixiar(-se)
suffocation [sʌfə'keıʃən] N sufocação f; (Med) asfixia
suffrage ['sʌfrıdʒ] N sufrágio; (vote) direito de voto
suffused [sə'fju:zd] ADJ: **~ with** (light etc) banhado de
sugar ['ʃugə^r] N açúcar m ▶ vт pôr açúcar em, açucarar
sugar beet N beterraba (sacarina)
sugar bowl N açucareiro
sugar cane N cana-de-açúcar f
sugar-coated [-'kəutıd] ADJ cristalizado
sugar lump N torrão m de açúcar
sugar refinery N refinaria de açúcar
sugary ['ʃugərı] ADJ açucarado
suggest [sə'dʒest] vт sugerir; (indicate) indicar; (advise) aconselhar; **what do you ~ I do?** o que você sugere que eu faça?
suggestion [sə'dʒestʃən] N sugestão f; (indication) indicação f
suggestive [sə'dʒestıv] ADJ sugestivo; (pej) indecente

suicidal [suı'saıdl] ADJ suicida
suicide ['suısaıd] N suicídio; (person) suicida m/f; see also **commit**
suicide attack N ataque m suicida, atentado suicida
suicide attempt N tentativa de suicídio
suicide bid N tentativa de suicídio
suicide bomber N homem-bomba m, mulher-bomba f
suicide bombing N ataque m suicida
suit [su:t] N (man's) terno m, fato (PT); (woman's) conjunto; (Law) processo; (Cards) naipe m ▶ vт (gen) convir a; (clothes) ficar bem a; (adapt): **to ~ sth to** adaptar or acomodar algo a; **to be ~ed to sth** ser apto para algo; **they are well ~ed** fazem um bom par; **to bring a ~ against sb** mover um processo contra alguém; **to follow ~** (fig) seguir o exemplo
suitable ['su:təbl] ADJ conveniente; (appropriate) apropriado; **would tomorrow be ~?** amanhã lhe convém?
suitably ['su:təblı] ADV apropriadamente; (impressed) bem
suitcase ['su:tkeıs] N mala
suite [swi:t] N (of rooms) conjunto de salas; (Mus) suite f; (furniture): **bedroom/dining room ~** conjunto de quarto/de sala de jantar; **a three-piece ~** um conjunto estofado (sofá e duas poltronas)
suitor ['su:tə^r] N pretendente m
sulfate ['sʌlfeıt] (US) N = **sulphate**
sulfur ['sʌlfə^r] (US) N = **sulphur**
sulk [sʌlk] vı ficar emburrado, fazer beicinho or biquinho (inf)
sulky ['sʌlkı] ADJ emburrado
sullen ['sʌlən] ADJ rabugento; (silence) pesado
sulphate, (US) **sulfate** ['sʌlfeıt] N sulfato
sulphur, (US) **sulfur** ['sʌlfə^r] N enxofre m
sulphuric, (US) **sulfuric** [sʌl'fjuərık] ADJ: **~ acid** ácido sulfúrico
sultan ['sʌltən] N sultão m
sultana [sʌl'tɑ:nə] N (Culin) passa branca
sultry ['sʌltrı] ADJ (weather) abafado, mormacento; (seductive) sedutor(a)
sum [sʌm] N soma; (calculation) cálculo ▶ **sum up** vт sumariar, fazer um resumo de; (describe) resumir; (evaluate) avaliar ▶ vı resumir
Sumatra [su'mɑ:trə] N Sumatra
summarize ['sʌməraız] vт resumir
summary ['sʌmərı] N resumo ▶ ADJ (justice) sumário
summer ['sʌmə^r] N verão m ▶ ADJ de verão; **in (the) ~** no verão
summer camp (US) N colônia de férias
summerhouse ['sʌməhaus] N (in garden) pavilhão m
summertime ['sʌmətaım] N (season) verão m
summer time N (by clock) horário de verão
summery ['sʌmərı] ADJ estival, de verão
summing-up ['sʌmıŋ-] N resumo, recapitulação f

S

summit ['sʌmɪt] N topo, cume m; (also: **summit conference**) (conferência de) cúpula

summon ['sʌmən] VT (person) mandar chamar; (meeting) convocar; (Law: witness) convocar
▶ **summon up** VT concentrar

summons ['sʌmənz] N (Law) citação f, intimação f; (fig) chamada ▶ VT citar, intimar; **to serve a ~ on sb** entregar uma citação a alguém

sump [sʌmp] N (Aut) cárter m

sumptuous ['sʌmptjuəs] ADJ suntuoso

sun [sʌn] N sol m; **in the ~** ao sol; **everything under the ~** cada coisa

Sun. ABBR (= Sunday) dom

sunbathe ['sʌnbeɪð] VI tomar sol

sunbeam ['sʌnbiːm] N raio de sol

sunbed ['sʌnbɛd] N espreguiçadeira; (with sunlamp) cama para bronzeamento artificial

sunblock ['sʌnblɔk] N bloqueador m solar

sunburn ['sʌnbəːn] N queimadura do sol

sunburned ['sʌnbəːnd] ADJ = **sunburnt**

sunburnt ['sʌnbəːnt] ADJ bronzeado; (painfully) queimado

sun cream N creme m solar

sundae ['sʌndeɪ] N sorvete m (BR) or gelado (PT) com frutas e nozes

Sunday ['sʌndɪ] N domingo; see also **Tuesday**

Sunday school N escola dominical

sundial ['sʌndaɪəl] N relógio de sol

sundown ['sʌndaun] N pôr m do sol

sundries ['sʌndrɪz] NPL gêneros mpl diversos

sundry ['sʌndrɪ] ADJ vários, diversos; **all and ~** todos

sunflower ['sʌnflauə'] N girassol m

sung [sʌŋ] PP of **sing**

sunglasses ['sʌnɡlɑːsɪz] NPL óculos mpl de sol

sunk [sʌŋk] PP of **sink**

sunken ['sʌŋkn] ADJ (ship) afundado; (eyes, cheeks) cavado; (bath) enterrado

sunlamp ['sʌnlæmp] N lâmpada ultravioleta

sunlight ['sʌnlaɪt] N (luz f do) sol m

sunlit ['sʌnlɪt] ADJ ensolarado, iluminado pelo sol

sunny ['sʌnɪ] ADJ cheio de sol; (day) ensolarado, de sol; (fig) alegre; **it's ~** faz sol

sunrise ['sʌnraɪz] N nascer m do sol

sun roof N (Aut) teto solar

sunscreen ['sʌnskriːn] N protetor m solar

sunset ['sʌnsɛt] N pôr m do sol

sunshade ['sʌnʃeɪd] N (over table) para-sol m; (on beach) barraca

sunshine ['sʌnʃaɪn] N (luz f do) sol m

sunspot ['sʌnspɔt] N mancha solar

sunstroke ['sʌnstrəuk] N insolação f

suntan ['sʌntæn] N bronzeado

suntan lotion N loção f de bronzear

suntanned ['sʌntænd] ADJ bronzeado, moreno

suntan oil N óleo de bronzear, bronzeador m

suntrap ['sʌntræp] N lugar m muito ensolarado

super ['suːpə'] (inf) ADJ bacana (BR), muito giro (PT)

superannuation [suːpərænjuˈeɪʃən] N pensão f de aposentadoria

superb [suːˈpəːb] ADJ excelente

supercilious [suːpəˈsɪlɪəs] ADJ (disdainful) arrogante, desdenhoso; (haughty) altivo

superficial [suːpəˈfɪʃəl] ADJ superficial

superficially [suːpəˈfɪʃəlɪ] ADV superficialmente

superfluous [suˈpəːfluəs] ADJ supérfluo, desnecessário

superhuman [suːpəˈhjuːmən] ADJ sobre-humano

superimpose [suːpərɪmˈpəuz] VT: **to ~ (on/with)** sobrepor (a)

superintend [suːpərɪnˈtɛnd] VT superintender, dirigir

superintendent [suːpərɪnˈtɛndənt] N superintendente m/f; (Police) chefe m/f de polícia

superior [suˈpɪərɪə'] ADJ superior; (smug) desdenhoso ▶ N superior m; **Mother S~** (Rel) Madre Superiora

superiority [supɪərɪˈɔrɪtɪ] N superioridade f

superlative [suˈpəːlətɪv] ADJ superlativo ▶ N superlativo

superman ['suːpəmæn] (irreg: like **man**) N super-homem m

supermarket ['suːpəmɑːkɪt] N supermercado

supernatural [suːpəˈnætʃərəl] ADJ sobrenatural ▶ N: **the ~** o sobrenatural

superpower ['suːpəpauə'] N (Pol) superpotência

supersede [suːpəˈsiːd] VT suplantar

supersonic [suːpəˈsɔnɪk] ADJ supersônico

superstar ['suːpəstɑː'] N superstar m/f

superstition [suːpəˈstɪʃən] N superstição f

superstitious [suːpəˈstɪʃəs] ADJ supersticioso

superstore ['suːpəstɔː'] (BRIT) N hipermercado

supertanker ['suːpətæŋkə'] N superpetroleiro

supertax ['suːpətæks] N sobretaxa

supervise ['suːpəvaɪz] VT supervisar, supervisionar

supervision [suːpəˈvɪʒən] N supervisão f; **under medical ~** a critério médico

supervisor ['suːpəvaɪzə'] N supervisor(a) m/f; (academic) orientador(a) m/f

supervisory [suːpəˈvaɪzərɪ] ADJ fiscalizador(a)

supine ['suːpaɪn] ADJ em supinação

supper ['sʌpə'] N jantar m; (late evening) ceia; **to have ~** jantar

supplant [səˈplɑːnt] VT suplantar

supple ['sʌpl] ADJ flexível

supplement [n 'sʌplɪmənt, vt sʌplɪˈmɛnt] N suplemento ▶ VT suprir, completar

supplementary [sʌplɪˈmɛntərɪ] ADJ suplementar

supplementary benefit (BRIT) N auxílio suplementar pago aos da renda baixa

supplier [səˈplaɪə'] N abastecedor(a) m/f, fornecedor(a) m/f; (stockist) distribuidor(a) m/f

supply [sə'plaɪ] VT (*provide*): **to ~ sth (to sb)** fornecer algo (a alguém); (*need*) suprir a; (*equip*): **to ~ (with)** suprir (de) ▶ N fornecimento, provisão *f*; (*stock*) estoque *m*; (*supplying*) abastecimento ▶ ADJ (*teacher etc*) suplente; **supplies** NPL (*food*) víveres *mpl*; (*Mil*) apetrechos *mpl*; **office supplies** material *m* de escritório; **to be in short ~** estar escasso; **the electricity/water/gas ~** o abastecimento de força/água/gás; **~ and demand** oferta e procura

supply teacher (BRIT) N professor(a) *m/f* suplente

support [sə'pɔːt] N (*moral, financial etc*) apoio; (*Tech*) suporte *m* ▶ VT apoiar; (*financially*) manter; (*Tech: hold up*) sustentar; (*theory etc*) defender; (*Sport: team*) torcer por; **to ~ o.s.** (*financially*) ganhar a vida

supporter [sə'pɔːtə^r] N (*Pol etc*) partidário(-a); (*Sport*) torcedor(a) *m/f*

supporting [sə'pɔːtɪŋ] ADJ (*Theatre etc: role*) secundário; (: *actor*) coadjuvante

supportive [sə'pɔːtɪv] ADJ solidário

suppose [sə'pəuz] VT supor; (*imagine*) imaginar; (*duty*): **to be ~d to do sth** dever fazer algo ▶ VI supor; imaginar; **he's ~d to be an expert** dizem que ele é um perito; **I don't ~ she'll come** eu acho que ela não virá

supposedly [sə'pəuzɪdlɪ] ADV supostamente, pretensamente

supposing [sə'pəuzɪŋ] CONJ caso, supondo-se que; **always ~ he comes** caso ele venha

supposition [sʌpə'zɪʃən] N suposição *f*

suppository [sə'pɔzɪtərɪ] N supositório

suppress [sə'prɛs] VT (*information*) suprimir; (*feelings, revolt*) reprimir; (*yawn*) conter; (*scandal*) abafar, encobrir

suppression [sə'prɛʃən] N (*information*) supressão *f*; (*feelings, revolt*) repressão *f*; (*yawn*) controle *m*; (*scandal*) abafamento

suppressor [sə'prɛsə^r] N (*Elec etc*) supressor *m*

supremacy [su'prɛməsɪ] N supremacia

supreme [su'priːm] ADJ supremo

Supreme Court (US) N Corte *f* Suprema

Supt. ABBR (*Police*) = **superintendent**

surcharge ['sɜːtʃɑːdʒ] N sobretaxa

sure [ʃuə^r] ADJ (*gen*) seguro; (*definite*) certo; (*aim*) certeiro ▶ ADV (*inf: esp* US): **that ~ is pretty** é bonito mesmo; **to make ~ of sth/ that** assegurar-se de algo/que; **~!** (*of course*) claro que sim!; **~ enough** efetivamente; **I'm not ~ how/why/when** não tenho certeza como/por que/quando; **to be ~ of sth** ter certeza de alguma coisa; **to be ~ of o.s.** estar seguro de si

sure-footed [-'futɪd] ADJ de andar seguro

surely ['ʃuəlɪ] ADV (*certainly*: US: *also*: **sure**) certamente; **~ you don't mean that!** não acredito que você queira dizer isso

surety ['ʃuərətɪ] N garantia, fiança; (*person*) fiador(a) *m/f*; **to go** *or* **stand ~ for sb** afiançar alguém, prestar fiança por alguém

surf [sɜːf] N (*foam*) espuma; (*waves*) ondas *fpl*, arrebentação *f* ▶ VI fazer surfe, pegar onda (*inf*)

surface ['sɜːfɪs] N superfície *f* ▶ VT (*road*) revestir ▶ VI vir à superfície *or* à tona; (*fig: news, feeling*) vir à tona; **on the ~** (*fig*) à primeira vista

surface area N área da superfície

surface mail N correio comum

surfboard ['sɜːfbɔːd] N prancha de surfe

surfeit ['sɜːfɪt] N: **a ~ of** um excesso de

surfer ['sɜːfə^r] N surfista *m/f*; (*on the Internet*) internauta *m/f*

surfing ['sɜːfɪŋ] N surfe *m*; **to go ~** fazer surfe, pegar onda (*inf*)

surge [sɜːdʒ] N onda; (*Elec*) surto ▶ VI (*sea*) encapelar-se; (*people, vehicles*) precipitar-se; (*feeling*) aumentar repentinamente; **to ~ forward** avançar em tropel

surgeon ['sɜːdʒən] N cirurgião(-giã) *m/f*

Surgeon General (US) N diretor(a) *m/f* nacional de saúde

surgery ['sɜːdʒərɪ] N cirurgia; (BRIT: *room*) consultório; (*also*: **surgery hours**) horas *fpl* de consulta; **to undergo ~** operar-se

surgical ['sɜːdʒɪkl] ADJ cirúrgico

surgical spirit (BRIT) N álcool *m*

surly ['sɜːlɪ] ADJ malcriado, rude

surmise [sə'maɪz] VT conjeturar

surmount [sə'maunt] VT superar, sobrepujar, vencer

surname ['sɜːneɪm] N sobrenome *m* (BR), apelido (PT)

surpass [sɜː'pɑːs] VT superar

surplus ['sɜːpləs] N excedente *m*; (*Comm*) superávit *m* ▶ ADJ excedente, de sobra; **~ to my requirements** que me sobram; **~ stock** estoque *m* excedente

surprise [sə'praɪz] N surpresa; (*astonishment*) assombro ▶ VT surpreender; **to take by ~** (*person*) pegar de surpresa; (*Mil: town, fort*) atacar de surpresa

surprising [sə'praɪzɪŋ] ADJ surpreendente; (*unexpected*) inesperado

surprisingly [sə'praɪzɪŋlɪ] ADV (*easy, helpful*) surpreendentemente; (**somewhat**) **~, he agreed** para surpresa de todos, ele concordou

surrealism [sə'rɪəlɪzm] N surrealismo

surrealist [sə'rɪəlɪst] ADJ, N surrealista *m/f*

surrender [sə'rɛndə^r] N rendição *f*, entrega ▶ VI render-se, entregar-se ▶ VT (*claim, right*) renunciar a

surrender value N valor *m* de resgate

surreptitious [sʌrəp'tɪʃəs] ADJ clandestino, furtivo

surrogate ['sʌrəgɪt] N (BRIT: *substitute*) substituto(-a) ▶ ADJ substituto

surrogate mother N mãe *f* portadora

surround [sə'raund] VT circundar, rodear; (*Mil etc*) cercar

surrounding [sə'raundɪŋ] ADJ circundante, adjacente

S

surroundings [sə'raundɪŋz] NPL arredores *mpl*, cercanias *fpl*

surtax ['sɜːtæks] N sobretaxa

surveillance [sə:'veɪləns] N vigilância

survey [*n* 'sɜːveɪ, *vt* sə:'veɪ] N (*inspection*) inspeção *f*, vistoria; (*investigation: of habits etc*) pesquisa, levantamento; (*of house*) inspeção *f*; (*of land*) levantamento ▶ VT inspecionar, vistoriar; (*look at*) observar, contemplar; (*land*) fazer um levantamento de; (*make inquiries about*) pesquisar, fazer um levantamento de

surveying [sə:'veɪɪŋ] N agrimensura

surveyor [sə:'veɪə*r*] N (*of land*) agrimensor(a) *m/f*; (*of building*) inspetor(a) *m/f*

survival [sə'vaɪvl] N sobrevivência; (*relic*) remanescente *m* ▶ CPD (*course, kit*) de sobrevivência

survive [sə'vaɪv] VI sobreviver; (*custom etc*) perdurar ▶ VT sobreviver a

survivor [sə'vaɪvə*r*] N sobrevivente *m/f*

susceptible [sə'sɛptəbl] ADJ: **~ (to)** (*heat, injury*) suscetível *or* sensível (a); (*flattery, pressure*) vulnerável (a)

suspect [*adj, n* 'sʌspɛkt, *vt* sə'spɛkt] ADJ, N suspeito(-a) ▶ VT suspeitar, desconfiar

suspend [sə'spɛnd] VT suspender

suspended sentence [sə'spɛndɪd-] N condenação *f* condicional

suspender belt [sə'spɛndə*r*-] N cinta-liga

suspenders [sə'spɛndəz] NPL (BRIT) ligas *fpl*; (US) suspensórios *mpl*

suspense [sə'spɛns] N incerteza, ansiedade *f*; (*in film etc*) suspense *m*; **to keep sb in ~** manter alguém em suspense *or* na expectativa

suspension [sə'spɛnʃən] N (*gen, Aut*) suspensão *f*; (*of driving licence*) cassação *f*

suspension bridge N ponte *f* pênsil

suspicion [sə'spɪʃən] N suspeita; (*trace*) traço, vestígio; **to be under ~** estar sob suspeita; **arrested on ~ of murder** preso sob suspeita de homicídio

suspicious [sə'spɪʃəs] ADJ (*suspecting*) suspeitoso; (*causing suspicion*) suspeito; **to be ~ of** *or* **about sb/sth** desconfiar de alguém/algo

suss out [sʌs-] (BRIT *inf*) VT (*discover*) descobrir; (*understand*) sacar

sustain [sə'steɪn] VT sustentar, manter; (*subj: food, drink*) sustenar; (*suffer*) sofrer

sustainable [sə'steɪnəbl] ADJ sustentável

sustained [səs'teɪnd] ADJ (*effort*) contínuo

sustenance ['sʌstɪnəns] N sustento

suture ['su:tʃə*r*] N sutura

SUV N ABBR (= *sports utility vehicle*) SUV *m*

SW ABBR (= *short wave*) OC

swab [swɔb] N (*Med*) mecha de algodão ▶ VT (*Naut: also:* **swab down**) lambazar

swagger ['swægə*r*] VI andar com ar de superioridade

swallow ['swɔləu] N (*bird*) andorinha; (*of food etc*) bocado; (*of drink*) trago ▶ VT engolir, tragar; (*fig: story*) engolir; (*pride*) pôr de lado; (*one's words*) retirar

▶ **swallow up** VT (*savings etc*) consumir

swam [swæm] PT *of* **swim**

swamp [swɔmp] N pântano, brejo ▶ VT atolar, inundar; (*fig: person*) assoberbar

swampy ['swɔmpɪ] ADJ pantanoso

swan [swɔn] N cisne *m*

swank [swæŋk] (*inf*) VI esnobar

swan song N (*fig*) canto do cisne

swap [swɔp] N troca, permuta ▶ VT: **to ~ (for)** trocar (por); (*replace (with)*) substituir (por)

swarm [swɔ:m] N (*of bees*) enxame *m*; (*of people*) multidão *f* ▶ VI enxamear; aglomerar-se; (*place*): **to be ~ing with** estar apinhado de

swarthy ['swɔ:ðɪ] ADJ moreno

swashbuckling ['swɔʃbʌklɪŋ] ADJ (*film*) de capa e espada

swastika ['swɔstɪkə] N suástica

swat [swɔt] VT esmagar ▶ N (BRIT: *also:* **fly swat**) pá *f* para matar mosca

swathe [sweɪð] VT: **to ~ in** (*bandages, blankets*) enfaixar em, envolver em

swatter ['swɔtə*r*] N (*also:* **fly swatter**) pá *f* para matar mosca

sway [sweɪ] VI balançar-se, oscilar ▶ VT (*influence*) influenciar ▶ N (*rule, power*) domínio (sobre); **to hold ~ over sb** dominar alguém

Swaziland ['swɑːzɪlænd] N Suazilândia

swear [swɛə*r*] (*pt* **swore**, *pp* **sworn**) VI (*by oath*) jurar; (*curse*) xingar ▶ VT (*promise*) jurar; **to ~ an oath** prestar juramento; **to ~ to sth** afirmar algo sob juramento

▶ **swear in** VT (*witness*) ajuramentar; (*president*) empossar

swearword ['swɛəwə:d] N palavrão *m*

sweat [swɛt] N suor *m* ▶ VI suar

sweatband ['swɛtbænd] N (*Sport*) tira elástica (para o cabelo)

sweater ['swɛtə*r*] N suéter *m or f* (BR), camisola (PT)

sweatshirt ['swɛtʃə:t] N suéter *m* de malha de algodão

sweatshop ['swɛtʃɔp] N oficina onde os trabalhadores são explorados

sweaty ['swɛtɪ] ADJ suado

Swede [swi:d] N sueco(-a)

swede [swi:d] N *tipo de nabo*

Sweden ['swi:dən] N Suécia

Swedish ['swi:dɪʃ] ADJ sueco ▶ N (*Ling*) sueco

sweep [swi:p] (*pt, pp* **swept**) N (*act*) varredura; (*of arm*) movimento circular; (*range*) extensão *f*, alcance *m*; (*also:* **chimney sweep**) limpador *m* de chaminés ▶ VT varrer; (*with arm*) empurrar; (*subj: current*) arrastar; (: *fashion, craze*) espalhar-se por; (: *disease*) arrasar ▶ VI varrer; (*person*) passar majestosamente

▶ **sweep away** VT varrer; (*rub out*) apagar

▶ **sweep past** VI passar rapidamente; (*brush by*) roçar

▶ **sweep up** VT, VI varrer

sweeping ['swi:pɪŋ] ADJ (*gesture*) dramático; (*reform*) radical; (*statement*) generalizado
sweepstake ['swi:psteɪk] N sweepstake *m*
sweet [swi:t] N (*candy*) bala (BR), rebuçado (PT); (BRIT: *pudding*) sobremesa ▶ ADJ doce; (*sugary*) açucarado; (*fig: air*) fresco; (: *water, smell*) doce; (: *sound*) suave; (: *baby, kitten*) bonitinho; (*kind*) meigo ▶ ADV: **to smell ~** ter bom cheiro; **to taste ~** estar doce; **~ and sour** agridoce
sweetbread ['swi:tbrɛd] N moleja
sweetcorn ['swi:tkɔ:n] N milho
sweeten ['swi:tən] VT pôr açúcar em; (*temper*) abrandar
sweetener ['swi:tnə'] N (*Culin*) adoçante *m*
sweetheart ['swi:thɑ:t] N namorado(-a); (*as address*) amor *m*
sweetly ['swi:tlɪ] ADV docemente; (*gently*) suavemente
sweetness ['swi:tnɪs] N doçura
sweet pea N ervilha-de-cheiro *f*
sweet potato (*irreg: like* **potato**) N batata doce
sweetshop ['swi:tʃɔp] N confeitaria
swell [swɛl] (*pt* **swelled**, *pp* **swollen** *or* **swelled**) VT engrossar ▶ VI (*increase*) aumentar; (*get stronger*) intensificar-se; (*also:* **swell up**) inchar(-se) ▶ N (*of sea*) vaga, onda ▶ ADJ (US inf: *excellent*) bacana
swelling ['swɛlɪŋ] N (*Med*) inchação *f*
sweltering ['swɛltərɪŋ] ADJ (*heat*) sufocante; (*day*) mormacento
swept [swɛpt] PT, PP *of* **sweep**
swerve [swə:v] VI desviar-se
swift [swɪft] N (*bird*) andorinhão *m* ▶ ADJ rápido
swiftly ['swɪftlɪ] ADV rapidamente, velozmente
swiftness ['swɪftnɪs] N rapidez *f*, ligeireza
swig [swɪg] (*inf*) N (*drink*) trago, gole *m*
swill [swɪl] N lavagem *f* ▶ VT (*also:* **swill out, swill down**) lavar, limpar com água
swim [swɪm] (*pt* **swam**, *pp* **swum**) VI nadar; (*head, room*) rodar; (*fig*): **my head/the room is ~ming** estou com a cabeça zonza/sinto o quarto rodar ▶ VT atravessar a nado; (*distance*) percorrer (a nado) ▶ N: **to go for a ~** ir nadar; **to go ~ming** ir nadar; **to ~ a length** nadar uma volta
swimmer ['swɪmə'] N nadador(a) *m/f*
swimming ['swɪmɪŋ] N natação *f*
swimming baths (BRIT) NPL piscina
swimming cap N touca de natação
swimming costume (BRIT) N (*woman's*) maiô *m* (BR), fato de banho (PT); (*man's*) calção *m* de banho (BR), calções *mpl* de banho (PT)
swimming pool N piscina
swimming trunks NPL sunga (BR), calções *mpl* de banho (PT)
swimsuit ['swɪmsu:t] N maiô *m* (BR), fato de banho (PT)
swindle ['swɪndl] N fraude *f* ▶ VT defraudar
swindler ['swɪndlə'] N vigarista *m/f*
swine [swaɪn] N porcos *mpl*; (!) canalha *m*, calhorda *m*

swine flu N gripe *f* suína
swing [swɪŋ] (*pt, pp* **swung**) VT balançar; (*also:* **swing round**) girar, rodar ▶ VI oscilar; (*on swing*) balançar; (*also:* **swing round**) voltar-se bruscamente ▶ N (*in playground*) balanço; (*movement*) balanceio, oscilação *f*; (*change: in opinion*) mudança; (: *of direction*) virada; (*rhythm*) ritmo; **the road ~s south** a estrada vira em direção ao sul; **a ~ to the left** (*Pol*) uma guinada para a esquerda; **to be in full ~** estar a todo vapor; **to get into the ~ of things** familiarizar-se com tudo
swing bridge N ponte *f* giratória
swing door, (US) **swinging door** N porta de vaivém
swingeing ['swɪndʒɪŋ] (BRIT) ADJ esmagador(a); (*cuts*) devastador(a)
swinging ['swɪŋɪŋ] ADJ rítmico; (*person*) badalativo
swipe [swaɪp] N pancada violenta ▶ VT (*hit*) bater com violência; (*inf: steal*) afanar, roubar
swirl [swə:l] VI redemoinhar ▶ N redemoinho
swish [swɪʃ] ADJ (BRIT inf: *smart*) chique ▶ N (*of whip*) silvo; (*of skirt, grass*) ruge-ruge *m* ▶ VI (*tail*) abanar; (*clothes*) fazer ruge-ruge
Swiss [swɪs] ADJ, N INV suíço(-a)
Swiss roll N bolo de rolo, rocambole *m* doce
switch [swɪtʃ] N (*for light, radio etc*) interruptor *m*; (*change*) mudança ▶ VT (*change*) trocar ▶ **switch off** VT apagar; (*engine*) desligar; (BRIT: *gas, water*) fechar
▶ **switch on** VT acender; ligar; abrir
switchback ['swɪtʃbæk] (BRIT) N montanha-russa
switchblade ['swɪtʃbleɪd] N (*also:* **switchblade knife**) canivete *m* de mola
switchboard ['swɪtʃbɔ:d] N (*Tel*) mesa telefônica
switchboard operator N (*Tel*) telefonista *m/f*
Switzerland ['swɪtsələnd] N Suíça
swivel ['swɪvl] VI (*also:* **swivel round**) girar (sobre um eixo), fazer pião
swollen ['swəulən] PP *of* **swell** ▶ ADJ inchado
swoon [swu:n] VI desmaiar
swoop [swu:p] N (*by police etc*) batida; (*of bird*) voo picado ▶ VI (*also:* **swoop down**) precipitar-se, cair
swop [swɔp] N, VT = **swap**
sword [sɔ:d] N espada
swordfish ['sɔ:dfɪʃ] N INV peixe-espada *m*
swore [swɔ:'] PT *of* **swear**
sworn [swɔ:n] PP *of* **swear** ▶ ADJ (*statement*) sob juramento; (*enemy*) declarado
swot [swɔt] VI queimar as pestanas
swum [swʌm] PP *of* **swim**
swung [swʌŋ] PT, PP *of* **swing**
sycamore ['sɪkəmɔ:'] N sicômoro
sycophant ['sɪkəfænt] N bajulador(a) *m/f*
sycophantic [sɪkə'fæntɪk] ADJ (*person*) bajulador(a); (*behaviour*) bajulatório
Sydney ['sɪdnɪ] N Sydney
syllable ['sɪləbl] N sílaba

S

syllabus ['sɪləbəs] N programa m de estudos;
  on the ~ no roteiro
symbol ['sɪmbl] N símbolo
symbolic [sɪm'bɔlɪk], **symbolical** [sɪm'bɔlɪkl]
  ADJ simbólico
symbolism ['sɪmbəlɪzəm] N simbolismo
symbolize ['sɪmbəlaɪz] VT simbolizar
symmetrical [sɪ'mɛtrɪkl] ADJ simétrico
symmetry ['sɪmɪtrɪ] N simetria
sympathetic [sɪmpə'θɛtɪk] ADJ (showing pity)
  compassivo; (understanding) compreensivo;
  (likeable) agradável; (supportive): ~ **to(wards)**
  solidário com
sympathetically [sɪmpə'θɛtɪklɪ] ADV (with
  pity) com compaixão; (understandingly)
  compreensivamente
sympathize ['sɪmpəθaɪz] VI: **to ~ with** (person)
  compadecer-se de; (sb's feelings) compreender;
  (cause) simpatizar com
sympathizer ['sɪmpəθaɪzəʳ] N (Pol)
  simpatizante m/f
sympathy ['sɪmpəθɪ] N (pity) compaixão f;
  sympathies NPL (tendencies) simpatia; **in ~**
  with em acordo com; (strike) em
  solidariedade com; **with our deepest ~**
  com nossos mais profundos pêsames
symphonic [sɪm'fɔnɪk] ADJ sinfônico
symphony ['sɪmfənɪ] N sinfonia
symphony orchestra N orquestra sinfônica
symposia [sɪm'pəuzɪə] NPL of **symposium**
symposium [sɪm'pəuzɪəm] (pl **symposiums** or
  symposia) N simpósio
symptom ['sɪmptəm] N sintoma m; (sign)
  indício
symptomatic [sɪmptə'mætɪk] ADJ sintomático

synagogue ['sɪnəgɔg] N sinagoga
synchromesh ['sɪŋkrəumɛʃ] N (Aut)
  engrenagem f sincronizada
synchronize ['sɪŋkrənaɪz] VT sincronizar ▶ VI:
  to ~ with sincronizar-se com
syncopated ['sɪŋkəpeɪtɪd] ADJ sincopado
syndicate ['sɪndɪkɪt] N sindicato; (of
  newspapers) cadeia
syndrome ['sɪndrəum] N síndrome f
synonym ['sɪnənɪm] N sinônimo
synonymous [sɪ'nɔnɪməs] ADJ: ~ **(with)**
  sinônimo (de)
synopses [sɪ'nɔpsiːz] NPL of **synopsis**
synopsis [sɪ'nɔpsɪs] (pl **synopses**) N sinopse f,
  resumo
syntax ['sɪntæks] N sintaxe f
syntheses ['sɪnθəsiːz] NPL of **synthesis**
synthesis ['sɪnθəsɪs] (pl **syntheses**) N síntese f
synthesizer ['sɪnθəsaɪzəʳ] N (Mus)
  sintetizador m
synthetic [sɪn'θɛtɪk] ADJ sintético ▶ N: ~**s**
  matérias fpl sintéticas
syphilis ['sɪfɪlɪs] N sífilis f
syphon ['saɪfən] = **siphon**
Syria ['sɪrɪə] N Síria
Syrian ['sɪrɪən] ADJ, N sírio(-a)
syringe [sɪ'rɪndʒ] N seringa
syrup ['sɪrəp] N xarope m; (BRIT: also: **golden**
  syrup) melaço
syrupy ['sɪrəpɪ] ADJ xaroposo
system ['sɪstəm] N sistema m; (method)
  método; (Anat) organismo
systematic [sɪstə'mætɪk] ADJ sistemático
system disk N (Comput) disco do sistema
systems analyst N analista m/f de sistemas

Tt

T, t [ti:] N (*letter*) T, t *m*; **T for Tommy** T de
Tereza

TA (*BRIT*) N ABBR = **Territorial Army**

ta [tɑ:] (*BRIT inf*) EXCL obrigado(-a)

tab [tæb] N ABBR = **tabulator** ▶ N lingueta,
aba; (*label*) etiqueta; **to keep ~s on** (*fig*)
vigiar

tabby ['tæbɪ] N (*also:* **tabby cat**) gato malhado
or listrado

table ['teɪbl] N mesa; (*of statistics etc*) quadro,
tabela ▶ VT (*motion etc*) apresentar; **to lay** *or*
set the ~ pôr a mesa; **to clear the ~** tirar a
mesa; **league ~** (*BRIT Football*) classificação *f*
dos times; **~ of contents** índice *m*, sumário

tablecloth ['teɪblklɔθ] N toalha de mesa

table d'hôte [tɑ:bl'dəut] N refeição *f*
comercial

table lamp N abajur *m* (*BR*), candeeiro (*PT*)

tableland ['teɪbllænd] N planalto

table mat N descanso

table salt N sal *m* fino

tablespoon ['teɪblspu:n] N colher *f* de sopa;
(*also:* **tablespoonful:** *as measurement*)
colherada

tablet ['tæblɪt] N (*Med*) comprimido; (*: for
sucking*) pastilha; (*for writing*) bloco; (*also:*
tablet computer) tablet *m*; (*of stone*) lápide *f*;
~ of soap (*BRIT*) sabonete *m*

table tennis N pingue-pongue *m*, tênis *m* de
mesa

table wine N vinho de mesa

tabloid ['tæblɔɪd] N (*newspaper*) tabloide *m*;
the ~s os jornais populares

tabloid press N *ver nota*

> O termo **tabloid press** refere-se aos jornais
> populares de formato meio jornal que
> apresentam muitas fotografias e adotam
> um estilo bastante conciso. O público-
> alvo desses jornais é composto por
> leitores que se interessam pelos fatos do
> dia que contenham um certo toque de
> escândalo; veja **quality (news)papers**.

taboo [tə'bu:] N tabu *m* ▶ ADJ tabu

tabulate ['tæbjuleɪt] VT (*data, figures*) dispor
em forma de tabela

tabulator ['tæbjuleɪtə^r] N tabulador *m*

tachograph ['tækəgrɑ:f] N tacógrafo

tachometer [tæ'kɔmɪtə^r] N tacômetro

tacit ['tæsɪt] ADJ tácito, implícito

taciturn ['tæsɪtə:n] ADJ taciturno

tack [tæk] N (*nail*) tachinha, percevejo; (*BRIT:
stitch*) alinhavo; (*Naut*) amura ▶ VT prender
com tachinha; (*stitch*) alinhavar ▶ VI virar de
bordo; **to change ~** virar de bordo; (*fig*)
mudar de tática; **to ~ sth on to (the end of)
sth** anexar algo a algo

tackle ['tækl] N (*gear*) equipamento; (*also:*
fishing tackle) apetrechos *mpl*; (*for lifting*)
guincho; (*Football*) ato de tirar a bola de
adversário ▶ VT (*difficulty*) atacar; (*challenge:
person*) desafiar; (*grapple with*) atracar-se com;
(*Football*) tirar a bola de

tacky ['tækɪ] ADJ pegajoso, grudento; (*inf:
tasteless*) cafona

tact [tækt] N tato, diplomacia

tactful ['tæktful] ADJ diplomático; **to be ~** ser
diplomata

tactfully ['tæktfulɪ] ADV discretamente, com
tato

tactical ['tæktɪkl] ADJ tático

tactics ['tæktɪks] N, NPL tática

tactless ['tæktlɪs] ADJ sem diplomacia

tactlessly ['tæktlɪslɪ] ADV indiscretamente

tadpole ['tædpəul] N girino

taffy ['tæfɪ] (*US*) N puxa-puxa *m* (*BR*),
caramelo (*PT*)

tag [tæg] N (*label*) etiqueta; **price/name ~**
etiqueta de preço/com o nome
▶ **tag along** VI seguir

Tahiti [tɑ:'hi:tɪ] N Taiti (*no article*)

tail [teɪl] N rabo; (*of bird, comet, plane*) cauda; (*of
shirt, coat*) aba ▶ VT (*follow*) seguir bem de
perto; **to turn ~** dar no pé; *see also* **head**
▶ **tail away** VI (*in size, quality etc*) diminuir
gradualmente
▶ **tail off** VI (*in size, quality etc*) diminuir
gradualmente

tailback ['teɪlbæk] (*BRIT*) N fila (de carros)

tail coat N fraque *m*

tail end N (*of train*) cauda; (*of procession*) parte *f*
final

tailgate ['teɪlgeɪt] N (*Aut*) porta traseira

tailor ['teɪlə^r] N alfaiate *m* ▶ VT: **to ~ sth (to)**
adaptar algo (a); **~'s (shop)** alfaiataria

tailoring ['teɪlərɪŋ] N (*cut*) feitio; (*craft*) ofício
de alfaiate

tailor-made ADJ feito sob medida; (*fig*)
especial

tailwind ['teɪlwɪnd] N vento de popa or de cauda

taint [teɪnt] VT (meat, food) estragar; (fig: reputation) manchar

tainted ['teɪntɪd] ADJ (food) estragado, passado; (water, air) poluído; (fig) manchado

Taiwan ['taɪ'wɑːn] N Taiuan (no article)

take [teɪk] (pt **took**, pp **taken**) VT (gen) tomar; (photo, holiday) tirar; (grab) pegar (em); (gain: prize) ganhar; (require: effort, courage) requerer, exigir; (tolerate) aguentar; (accompany, bring, carry: person) acompanhar, trazer; (: thing) trazer, carregar; (exam) fazer; (hold: passengers etc): **it ~s 50 people** cabem 50 pessoas ▶ VI (dye, fire) pegar ▶ N (Cinema) tomada; **to ~ sth from** (drawer etc) tirar algo de; (person) pegar algo de; **I ~ it that ...** suponho que ...; **I took him for a doctor** eu o tomei por médico; **to ~ sb's hand** pegar a mão de alguém; **to ~ for a walk** levar a passeio; **to be ~n ill** adoecer, ficar doente; **to ~ it upon o.s. to do sth** assumir a responsabilidade de fazer algo; **~ the first (street) on the left** pega a primeira (rua) à esquerda; **it won't ~ long** não vai demorar muito; **I was quite ~n with it/her** gostei muito daquilo/dela
  ▶ **take after** VT FUS parecer-se com
  ▶ **take apart** VT desmontar
  ▶ **take away** VT (extract) tirar; (carry off) levar; (subtract) subtrair ▶ VI: **to ~ away from** diminuir
  ▶ **take back** VT (return) devolver; (one's words) retirar
  ▶ **take down** VT (building) demolir; (dismantle) desmontar; (letter etc) tomar por escrito
  ▶ **take in** VT (deceive) enganar; (understand) compreender; (include) abranger; (lodger) receber; (orphan, stray dog) acolher; (dress etc) apertar
  ▶ **take off** VI (Aviat) decolar; (go away) ir-se ▶ VT (remove) tirar; (imitate) imitar
  ▶ **take on** VT (work) empreender; (employee) empregar; (opponent) desafiar
  ▶ **take out** VT tirar; (extract) extrair; (invite) acompanhar; (licence) tirar; **to ~ sth out of** tirar algo de; **don't ~ it out on me!** não descarregue em cima de mim!
  ▶ **take over** VT (business) assumir; (country) tomar posse de ▶ VI: **to ~ over from sb** suceder a alguém
  ▶ **take to** VT FUS (person) simpatizar com; (activity) afeiçoar-se a; **to ~ to doing sth** criar o hábito de fazer algo
  ▶ **take up** VT (dress) encurtar; (story) continuar; (occupy: time, space) ocupar; (engage in: hobby etc) dedicar-se a; (accept: offer, challenge) aceitar; (absorb: liquids) absorver ▶ VI: **to ~ up with sb** fazer amizade com alguém; **to ~ sb up on a suggestion/offer** aceitar a oferta/sugestão de alguém sobre algo

takeaway ['teɪkəweɪ] (BRIT) ADJ (food) para levar

take-home pay N salário líquido

taken ['teɪkən] PP of **take**

takeoff ['teɪkɔf] N (Aviat) decolagem f

takeout ['teɪkaut] (US) ADJ (food) para levar

takeover ['teɪkəuvəʳ] N (Comm) aquisição f de controle

takeover bid N oferta pública de aquisição de controle

takings ['teɪkɪŋz] NPL (Comm) receita, renda

talc [tælk] N (also: **talcum powder**) talco

tale [teɪl] N (story) conto; (account) narrativa; **to tell ~s** (fig: lie) dizer mentiras; (: sneak) dedurar

talent ['tælənt] N talento

talented ['tæləntɪd] ADJ talentoso

talent scout N caçador(a) m/f de talentos

talk [tɔːk] N conversa, fala; (gossip) mexerico, fofocas fpl; (conversation) conversa, conversação f ▶ VI (speak) falar; (chatter) bater papo, conversar; **talks** NPL (Pol etc) negociações fpl; **to give a ~** dar uma palestra; **to ~ about** falar sobre; **~ing of films, have you seen ...?** por falar em filmes, você viu ...?; **to ~ sb into doing sth** convencer alguém a fazer algo; **to ~ sb out of doing sth** dissuadir alguém de fazer algo; **to ~ shop** falar sobre negócios/ questões profissionais
  ▶ **talk over** VT discutir

talkative ['tɔːkətɪv] ADJ loquaz, tagarela

talker ['tɔːkəʳ] N falador(a) m/f

talking point ['tɔːkɪŋ-] N assunto para discussão

talking-to ['tɔːkɪŋ-] N: **to give sb a good ~** passar um sabão em alguém

talk show N (TV, Radio) programa m de entrevistas

tall [tɔːl] ADJ alto; (tree) grande; **to be 6 feet ~** medir 6 pés, ter 6 pés de altura; **how ~ are you?** qual é a sua altura?

tallboy ['tɔːlbɔɪ] (BRIT) N cômoda alta

tallness ['tɔːlnɪs] N altura

tall story N estória inverossímil

tally ['tælɪ] N conta ▶ VI: **to ~ (with)** conferir (com); **to keep a ~ of sth** fazer um registro de algo

talon ['tælən] N garra

tambourine [tæmbə'riːn] N tamborim m, pandeiro

tame [teɪm] ADJ (animal, bird) domesticado; (mild) manso; (fig: story, style) sem graça, insípido

tamper ['tæmpəʳ] VI: **to ~ with** mexer em

tampon ['tæmpɔn] N tampão m

tan [tæn] N (also: **suntan**) bronzeado ▶ VT bronzear ▶ VI bronzear-se ▶ ADJ (colour) bronzeado, marrom claro; **to get a ~** bronzear-se

tandem ['tændəm] N tandem m; **in ~** junto

tang [tæŋ] N sabor m forte

tangent ['tændʒənt] N (Math) tangente f; **to go off at a ~** (fig) sair pela tangente

tangerine [tændʒə'riːn] N tangerina, mexerica

tangible ['tændʒəbl] ADJ tangível; **~ assets** ativos mpl tangíveis

tangle ['tæŋgl] N emaranhado ▶ VT emaranhar; **to get in(to) a ~** meter-se num rolo

tango ['tæŋgəu] N tango

tank [tæŋk] N (water tank) depósito, tanque m; (for fish) aquário; (Mil) tanque m

tankard ['tæŋkəd] N canecão m

tanker ['tæŋkə^r] N (ship) navio-tanque m; (: for oil) petroleiro; (truck) caminhão-tanque m

tanned [tænd] ADJ (skin) moreno, bronzeado

tannin ['tænɪn] N tanino

tanning ['tænɪŋ] N (of leather) curtimento

tannoy® ['tænɔɪ] (BRIT) N alto-falante m; **over the ~** nos alto-falantes

tantalizing ['tæntəlaɪzɪŋ] ADJ tentador(a)

tantamount ['tæntəmaunt] ADJ: **~ to** equivalente a

tantrum ['tæntrəm] N chilique m, acesso (de raiva); **to throw a ~** ter um chilique or acesso

Tanzania [tænzə'nɪə] N Tanzânia f

Tanzanian [tænzə'nɪən] ADJ, N tanzaniano(-a)

tap [tæp] N (on sink etc) torneira; (gentle blow) palmadinha; (gas tap) chave f ▶ VT dar palmadinha em, bater de leve; (resources) utilizar, explorar; (telephone) grampear; **on ~** (beer) de barril; (resources) disponível

tap-dancing N sapateado

tape [teɪp] N fita; (also: **magnetic tape**) fita magnética; (sticky tape) fita adesiva ▶ VT (record) gravar (em fita); (stick with tape) colar; **on ~** (song etc) em fita

tape deck N gravador m, toca-fitas m inv

tape measure N fita métrica, trena

taper ['teɪpə^r] N círio ▶ VI afilar-se, estreitar-se

tape-record VT gravar (em fita)

tape recorder N gravador m

tape recording N gravação f (em fita)

tapered ['teɪpəd] ADJ afilado

tapering ['teɪpərɪŋ] ADJ afilado

tapestry ['tæpɪstrɪ] N (object) tapete m de parede; (art) tapeçaria

tapeworm ['teɪpwə:m] N solitária

tapioca [tæpɪ'əukə] N tapioca

tappet ['tæpɪt] N (Aut) tucho (BR), ponteiro de válvula (PT)

tar [tɑ:^r] N alcatrão m; (on road) piche m; **low-/middle-~ cigarettes** cigarros com baixo/médio teor de alcatrão

tarantula [tə'ræntjulə] N tarântula

tardy ['tɑ:dɪ] ADJ tardio

target ['tɑ:gɪt] N alvo; (fig: objective) objetivo; **to be on ~** (project) progredir segundo as previsões

target practice N exercício de tiro ao alvo

tariff ['tærɪf] N tarifa

tariff barrier N barreira alfandegária

tarmac ['tɑ:mæk] N (BRIT: on road) macadame m; (Aviat) pista ▶ VT (BRIT) asfaltar

tarnish ['tɑ:nɪʃ] VT empanar o brilho de

tarpaulin [tɑ:'pɔ:lɪn] N lona alcatroada

tarragon ['tærəgən] N estragão m

tart [tɑ:t] N (Culin) torta; (BRIT inf, pej: woman) piranha ▶ ADJ (flavour) ácido, azedo ▶ **tart up** (inf) VT arrumar, dar um jeito em; **to ~ o.s. up** arrumar-se; (pej) empetecar-se

tartan ['tɑ:tn] N pano escocês axadrezado, tartan m ▶ ADJ axadrezado

tartar ['tɑ:tə^r] N (on teeth) tártaro

tartar sauce, tartare sauce ['tɑ:tə^r-] N molho tártaro

task [tɑ:sk] N tarefa; **to take to ~** repreender

task force N (Mil, Police) força-tarefa

taskmaster ['tɑ:skmɑ:stə^r] N: **he's a hard ~** ele é muito exigente

Tasmania [tæz'meɪnɪə] N Tasmânia f

tassel ['tæsl] N borla, pendão m

taste [teɪst] N gosto; (also: **aftertaste**) gosto residual; (sip) golinho; (sample, fig: glimpse, idea) amostra, ideia ▶ VT (get flavour of) provar; (test) experimentar ▶ VI: **to ~ of** or **like** (fish etc) ter gosto or sabor de; **you can ~ the garlic (in it)** sente-se o gosto de alho; **can I have a ~ of this wine?** posso provar o vinho?; **to have a ~ for** sentir predileção por; **in good/bad ~** de bom/mau gosto

taste bud N papila gustativa

tasteful ['teɪstful] ADJ de bom gosto

tastefully ['teɪstfulɪ] ADV com bom gosto

tasteless ['teɪstlɪs] ADJ (food) insípido, insosso; (remark) de mau gosto

tasty ['teɪstɪ] ADJ saboroso, delicioso

tattered ['tætəd] ADJ esfarrapado

tatters ['tætəz] NPL: **in ~** (clothes) em farrapos; (papers etc) em pedaços

tattoo [tə'tu:] N tatuagem f; (spectacle) espetáculo militar ▶ VT tatuar

tatty ['tætɪ] (BRIT inf) ADJ (clothes) surrado; (shop, area) mal-cuidado

taught [tɔ:t] PT, PP de **teach**

taunt [tɔ:nt] N zombaria, escárnio ▶ VT zombar de, mofar de

Taurus ['tɔ:rəs] N Touro

taut [tɔ:t] ADJ esticado

tavern ['tævən] N taverna

tawdry ['tɔ:drɪ] ADJ de mau gosto, espalhafatoso, berrante

tawny ['tɔ:nɪ] ADJ moreno, trigueiro

tax [tæks] N imposto ▶ VT tributar; (fig: test) sobrecarregar; (: patience) esgotar; **before/after ~** antes/depois de impostos; **free of ~** isento de impostos

taxable ['tæksəbl] ADJ (income) tributável

tax allowance N abatimento da renda

taxation [tæk'seɪʃən] N (system) tributação f; (money paid) imposto; **system of ~** sistema fiscal

tax avoidance N evasão f de impostos

tax collector N cobrador(a) m/f de impostos

tax disc (BRIT) N (Aut) ≈ plaqueta

tax evasion N sonegação f fiscal

tax exemption N isenção f de impostos

tax exile N pessoa que se expatria para evitar impostos excessivos

tax-free ADJ isento de impostos
tax haven N refúgio fiscal
taxi ['tæksɪ] N táxi *m* ▸ VI (*Aviat*) taxiar
taxidermist ['tæksɪdə:mɪst] N taxidermista *m/f*
taxi driver N motorista *m/f* de táxi
taximeter ['tæksɪmi:tə^r] N taxímetro
tax inspector (*BRIT*) N fiscal *m/f* de imposto de renda
taxi rank (*BRIT*) N ponto de táxi
taxi stand N ponto de táxi
tax payer N contribuinte *m/f*
tax rebate N devolução *f* de imposto de renda
tax relief N isenção *f* de imposto
tax return N declaração *f* de rendimentos
tax year N ano fiscal, exercício
TB ABBR = **tuberculosis**
TD (*US*) N ABBR = **Treasury Department**; (*Football*) = **touchdown**
tea [ti:] N chá *m*; (*BRIT: meal*) refeição *f* à noite; **high ~** (*BRIT*) ajantarado
tea bag N saquinho (*BR*) *or* carteira (*PT*) de chá
tea break (*BRIT*) N pausa (para o chá)
teacake ['ti:keɪk] (*BRIT*) N pãozinho doce
teach [ti:tʃ] (*pt, pp* **taught**) VT: **to ~ sb sth, ~ sth to sb** ensinar algo a alguém; (*in school*) lecionar ▸ VI ensinar; (*be a teacher*) lecionar; **it taught him a lesson** (*fig*) isto lhe serviu de lição
teacher ['ti:tʃə^r] N professor(a) *m/f*
teacher training college N faculdade *f* de formação de professores
teaching ['ti:tʃɪŋ] N ensino; (*as profession*) magistério
teaching aids NPL recursos *mpl* de ensino
teaching hospital (*BRIT*) N hospital *m* escola
teaching staff (*BRIT*) N corpo docente
tea cosy N coberta do bule, abafador *m*
teacup ['ti:kʌp] N xícara (*BR*) *or* chávena (*PT*) de chá
teak [ti:k] N (madeira de) teca ▸ CPD de teca
tea leaves NPL folhas *fpl* de chá
team [ti:m] N (*Sport*) time *m* (*BR*), equipa (*PT*); (*group*) equipe *f* (*BR*), equipa (*PT*); (*of animals*) parelha
 ▸ **team up** VI: **to ~ up (with)** agrupar-se (com)
team games NPL jogos *mpl* de equipe
teamwork ['ti:mwə:k] N trabalho de equipe
tea party N chá *m* (*reunião*)
teapot ['ti:pɔt] N bule *m* de chá
tear¹ [tɪə^r] N lágrima; **in ~s** chorando, em lágrimas; **to burst into ~s** romper em lágrimas
tear² [tɛə^r] (*pt* **tore**, *pp* **torn**) N rasgão *m* ▸ VT rasgar ▸ VI rasgar-se; **to ~ to pieces** *or* **to bits** *or* **to shreds** despedaçar, estraçalhar; (*fig*) arrasar com
 ▸ **tear along** VI (*rush*) precipitar-se
 ▸ **tear apart** VT rasgar; (*fig*) arrasar
 ▸ **tear away** VT: **to ~ o.s. away (from sth)** desgrudar-se (de algo)
 ▸ **tear out** VT (*sheet of paper, cheque*) arrancar
 ▸ **tear up** VT rasgar

tearaway ['tɛərəweɪ] (*inf*) N bagunceiro(-a)
teardrop ['tɪədrɔp] N lágrima
tearful ['tɪəful] ADJ choroso
tear gas N gás *m* lacrimogênio
tearoom ['ti:ru:m] N salão *m* de chá
tease [ti:z] N implicante *m/f* ▸ VT implicar com
tea set N aparelho de chá
teashop ['ti:ʃɔp] N salão *m* de chá
teaspoon ['ti:spu:n] N colher *f* de chá; (*also:* **teaspoonful:** *as measurement*) (conteúdo de) colher de chá
tea strainer N coador *m* (de chá)
teat [ti:t] N (*of bottle*) bico (de mamadeira)
teatime ['ti:taɪm] N hora do chá
tea towel (*BRIT*) N pano de prato
tea urn N samovar *m*
tech [tɛk] (*inf*) N ABBR = **technology; technical college**
technical ['tɛknɪkl] ADJ técnico
technical college (*BRIT*) N escola técnica
technicality [tɛknɪ'kælɪtɪ] N detalhe *m* técnico
technically ['tɛknɪklɪ] ADV tecnicamente
technician [tɛk'nɪʃn] N técnico(-a)
technique [tɛk'ni:k] N técnica
technocrat ['tɛknəkræt] N tecnocrata *m/f*
technological [tɛknə'lɔdʒɪkl] ADJ tecnológico
technologist [tɛk'nɔlədʒɪst] N tecnólogo(-a)
technology [tɛk'nɔlədʒɪ] N tecnologia
teddy ['tɛdɪ], **teddy bear** N ursinho de pelúcia
tedious ['ti:dɪəs] ADJ maçante, chato
tedium ['ti:dɪəm] N tédio
tee [ti:] N (*Golf*) tee *m*
teem [ti:m] VI abundar, pulular; **to ~ with** abundar em; **it is ~ing (with rain)** está chovendo a cântaros
teenage ['ti:neɪdʒ] ADJ (*fashions etc*) de *or* para adolescentes
teenager ['ti:neɪdʒə^r] N adolescente *m/f*, jovem *m/f*
teens [ti:nz] NPL: **to be in one's ~** estar entre os 13 e 19 anos, estar na adolescência
tee-shirt N = **T-shirt**
teeter ['ti:tə^r] VI balançar-se
teeth [ti:θ] NPL *of* **tooth**
teethe [ti:ð] VI começar a ter dentes
teething ring ['ti:ðɪŋ-] N mastigador *m* para a dentição
teething troubles ['ti:ðɪŋ-] NPL (*fig*) dificuldades *fpl* iniciais
teetotal ['ti:'təutl] ADJ (*person*) abstêmio
teetotaller, (*US*) **teetotaler** ['ti:'təutlə^r] N abstêmio(-a)
TEFL ['tɛfl] N ABBR = **Teaching of English as a Foreign Language**
Teheran [tɛə'rɑ:n] N Teerã (*BR*), Teerão (*PT*)
tel. ABBR (= *telephone*) tel.
Tel Aviv ['tɛlə'vi:v] N Telavive
telecast ['tɛlɪkɑ:st] (*irreg: like* **cast**) VT televisionar, transmitir por televisão
telecommunications [tɛlɪkəmju:nɪ'keɪʃənz] N telecomunicações *fpl*

teleconferencing ['telɪkɔnfərənsɪŋ] N teleconferência f
telegram ['tɛlɪgræm] N telegrama m
telegraph ['tɛlɪgrɑːf] N telégrafo
telegraphic [tɛlɪ'græfɪk] ADJ telegráfico
telegraph pole N poste m telegráfico
telegraph wire N fio telegráfico
telepathic [tɛlɪ'pæθɪk] ADJ telepático
telepathy [tə'lɛpəθɪ] N telepatia
telephone ['tɛlɪfəun] N telefone m ▶ VT (person) telefonar para; (message) telefonar; **to be on the ~** (BRIT), **to have a ~** (subscriber) ter telefone; **to be on the ~** (be speaking) estar falando no telefone
telephone booth, (BRIT) **telephone box** N cabine f telefônica
telephone call N telefonema m
telephone directory N lista telefônica, catálogo (BR)
telephone exchange N estação f telefônica
telephone kiosk (BRIT) N cabine f telefônica
telephone number N (número de) telefone m
telephone operator N telefonista m/f
telephone tapping [-'tæpɪŋ] N escuta telefônica
telephonist [tə'lɛfənɪst] (BRIT) N telefonista m/f
telephoto ['tɛlɪfəutəu] ADJ: **~ lens** teleobjetivo
teleprinter ['tɛlɪprɪntə'] N teletipo
Teleprompter® ['tɛlɪprɔmptə'] (US) N ponto mecânico
telesales ['tɛlɪseɪlz] NPL televendas fpl
telescope ['tɛlɪskəup] N telescópio ▶ VT, VI abrir (or fechar) como um telescópio
telescopic [tɛlɪ'skɔpɪk] ADJ telescópico; (legs, aerial) desmontável
Teletext® ['tɛlətɛks] N (Tel) videotexto
televiewer ['tɛlɪvjuːə'] N telespectador(a) m/f
televise ['tɛlɪvaɪz] VT televisar, televisionar
television ['tɛlɪvɪʒən] N televisão f; **on ~** na televisão
television licence (BRIT) N licença para utilizar um televisor
television programme N programa m de televisão
television set N (aparelho de) televisão f, televisor m
teleworking ['tɛlɪwə:kɪŋ] N teletrabalho m
telex ['tɛlɛks] N telex m ▶ VT (message) enviar por telex, telexar; (person) mandar um telex para ▶ VI enviar um telex
tell [tɛl] (pt, pp told) VT dizer; (relate: story) contar; (distinguish): **to ~ sth from** distinguir algo de ▶ VI (have effect) ter efeito; (talk): **to ~ (of)** falar (de or em); (know how to): **to ~ sb to do sth** dizer para alguém fazer algo; (order) mandar alguém fazer algo; **to ~ sb about sth** falar a alguém de algo; (what happened) contar algo a alguém; **to ~ the time** (know how to) dizer as horas; (clock) marcar as horas; **can you ~ me the time?** pode me dizer a hora?; **(I) ~ you what ...** escuta ...; **I can't ~ them apart** não consigo diferenciar um do outro; **to ~**

the difference sentir a diferença; **how can you ~?** como você sabe?
▶ **tell off** VT repreender
▶ **tell on** VT FUS (inform against) delatar, dedurar
teller ['tɛlə'] N (in bank) caixa m/f
telling ['tɛlɪŋ] ADJ (remark, detail) revelador(a)
telltale ['tɛlteɪl] ADJ (sign) revelador(a)
telly ['tɛlɪ] (BRIT inf) N ABBR = **television**
temerity [tə'mɛrɪtɪ] N temeridade f
temp [tɛmp] (BRIT inf) N temporário(-a) ▶ VI trabalhar como temporário(-a)
temper ['tɛmpə'] N (nature) temperamento; (mood) humor m; (bad temper) mau gênio; (fit of anger) cólera; (of child) birra ▶ VT (moderate) moderar; **to be in a ~** estar de mau humor; **to lose one's ~** perder a paciência or a calma, ficar zangado; **to keep one's ~** controlar-se
temperament ['tɛmprəmənt] N (nature) temperamento
temperamental [tɛmprə'mɛntl] ADJ temperamental
temperance ['tɛmpərəns] N moderação f; (in drinking) sobriedade f
temperate ['tɛmprət] ADJ moderado; (climate) temperado
temperature ['tɛmprətʃə'] N temperatura; **to have** or **run a ~** ter febre
temperature chart N (Med) tabela de temperatura
tempered ['tɛmpəd] ADJ (steel) temperado
tempest ['tɛmpɪst] N tempestade f
tempestuous [tɛm'pɛstjuəs] ADJ (relationship) tempestuoso
tempi ['tɛmpi:] NPL of **tempo**
template ['tɛmplɪt] N molde m
temple ['tɛmpl] N (building) templo; (Anat) têmpora
templet ['tɛmplɪt] N = **template**
tempo ['tɛmpəu] (pl tempos or tempi) N tempo; (fig: of life etc) ritmo
temporal ['tɛmpərəl] ADJ temporal
temporarily ['tɛmpərərɪlɪ] ADV temporariamente; (closed) provisoriamente
temporary ['tɛmpərərɪ] ADJ temporário; (passing) transitório; **~ secretary** secretária temporária; **~ teacher** professor suplente
temporize ['tɛmpəraɪz] VI temporizar
tempt [tɛmpt] VT tentar; **to ~ sb into doing sth** tentar or induzir alguém a fazer algo; **to be ~ed to do sth** ser tentado a fazer algo
temptation [tɛmp'teɪʃən] N tentação f
tempting ['tɛmptɪŋ] ADJ tentador(a)
ten [tɛn] NUM dez ▶ N: **~s of thousands** milhares mpl e milhares; see also **five**
tenable ['tɛnəbl] ADJ sustentável
tenacious [tə'neɪʃəs] ADJ tenaz
tenacity [tə'næsɪtɪ] N tenacidade f
tenancy ['tɛnənsɪ] N aluguel m; (of house) locação f
tenant ['tɛnənt] N inquilino(-a), locatário(-a)
tend [tɛnd] VT (sick etc) cuidar de; (machine) vigiar ▶ VI: **to ~ to do sth** tender a fazer algo

t

tendency ['tɛndənsɪ] N tendência

tender ['tɛndər] ADJ (person, heart, core) terno; (age) tenro; (delicate) delicado; (sore) sensível, dolorido; (meat) macio ▶ N (Comm: offer) oferta, proposta; (money): **legal ~** moeda corrente or legal ▶ VT oferecer; **to ~ one's resignation** pedir demissão; **to put in a ~ (for)** apresentar uma proposta (para); **to put work out to ~** (BRIT) abrir concorrência para uma obra

tenderize ['tɛndəraɪz] VT (Culin) amaciar

tenderly ['tɛndəlɪ] ADV afetuosamente

tenderness ['tɛndənɪs] N ternura; (of meat) maciez f

tendon ['tɛndən] N tendão m

tenement ['tɛnəmənt] N conjunto habitacional

Tenerife [tɛnə'riːf] N Tenerife (no article)

tenet ['tɛnət] N princípio

tenner ['tɛnər] (BRIT inf) N nota de dez libras

tennis ['tɛnɪs] N tênis m ▶ CPD (match, racket etc) de tênis

tennis ball N bola de tênis

tennis court N quadra de tênis

tennis elbow N (Med) sinovite f do cotovelo

tennis player N jogador(a) m/f de tênis

tennis racket N raquete f de tênis

tennis shoes NPL tênis m

tenor ['tɛnər] N (Mus) tenor m; (of speech etc) teor m

tenpin bowling ['tɛnpɪn-] (BRIT) N boliche m com 10 paus

tense [tɛns] ADJ tenso; (muscle) rígido, teso ▶ N (Ling) tempo ▶ VT (tighten: muscles) retesar

tenseness ['tɛnsnɪs] N tensão f

tension ['tɛnʃən] N tensão f

tent [tɛnt] N tenda, barraca

tentacle ['tɛntəkl] N tentáculo

tentative ['tɛntətɪv] ADJ (conclusion) provisório, tentativo; (person) hesitante, indeciso

tenterhooks ['tɛntəhuks] NPL: **on ~** em suspense

tenth [tɛnθ] NUM décimo; see also **fifth**

tent peg N estaca

tent pole N pau m

tenuous ['tɛnjuəs] ADJ tênue

tenure ['tɛnjuər] N (of property) posse f; (of job) estabilidade f

tepid ['tɛpɪd] ADJ tépido, morno

Ter. ABBR = **terrace**

term [təːm] N (Comm) prazo; (word, expression) termo, expressão f; (period) período; (Sch) trimestre m; (Law) sessão f ▶ VT denominar; **terms** NPL (conditions) condições fpl; (Comm) cláusulas fpl, termos mpl; **in ~s of ...** em função de ...; **~ of imprisonment** pena de prisão; **his ~ of office** seu mandato; **in the short/long ~** a curto/longo prazo; **to be on good ~s with sb** dar-se bem com alguém; **to come to ~s with** (person) chegar a um acordo com; (problem) aceitar

terminal ['təːmɪnl] ADJ incurável ▶ N (Elec) borne m; (BRIT: also: **air terminal**) terminal m; (for oil, ore etc, also Comput) terminal m; (BRIT: also: **coach terminal**) estação f rodoviária

terminate ['təːmɪneɪt] VT terminar ▶ VI: **to ~ in** acabar em; **to ~ a pregnancy** fazer um aborto

termination [təːmɪ'neɪʃən] N término; (of contract) rescisão f; **~ of pregnancy** (Med) interrupção da gravidez

termini ['təːmɪnaɪ] NPL of **terminus**

terminology [təːmɪ'nɔlədʒɪ] N terminologia

terminus ['təːmɪnəs] (pl **termini**) N terminal m

termite ['təːmaɪt] N cupim m

Terr. ABBR = **terrace**

terrace ['tɛrəs] N terraço; (BRIT: row of houses) lance m de casas; **the terraces** NPL (BRIT Sport) a arquibancada (BR), a geral (PT)

terraced ['tɛrəst] ADJ (house) ladeado por outras casas; (garden) em dois níveis

terracotta ['tɛrə'kɔtə] N terracota

terrain [tɛ'reɪn] N terreno

terrible ['tɛrɪbl] ADJ terrível, horroroso; (conditions) precário; (inf: awful) terrível

terribly ['tɛrɪblɪ] ADV terrivelmente; (very badly) pessimamente

terrier ['tɛrɪər] N terrier m

terrific [tə'rɪfɪk] ADJ terrível, magnífico; (wonderful) maravilhoso, sensacional

terrify ['tɛrɪfaɪ] VT aterrorizar

territorial [tɛrɪ'tɔːrɪəl] ADJ territorial

territorial waters NPL águas fpl territoriais

territory ['tɛrɪtərɪ] N território

terror ['tɛrər] N terror m

terrorism ['tɛrərɪzəm] N terrorismo

terrorist ['tɛrərɪst] N terrorista m/f

terrorize ['tɛrəraɪz] VT aterrorizar

terse [təːs] ADJ (style) conciso, sucinto; (reply) brusco

tertiary ['təːʃərɪ] ADJ terciário; **~ education** (BRIT) ensino superior

Terylene® ['tɛrɪliːn] (BRIT) N tergal® m

TESL ['tɛsl] N ABBR = **Teaching of English as a Second Language**

test [tɛst] N (trial, check) prova, ensaio; (: of goods in factory) controle m; (of courage etc, Chem) prova; (Med) exame m; (exam) teste m, prova; (also: **driving test**) exame de motorista ▶ VT testar, pôr à prova; **to put sth to the ~** pôr algo à prova

testament ['tɛstəmənt] N testamento; **the Old/New T~** o Velho/Novo Testamento

test ban N (also: **nuclear test ban**) proibição f de testes nucleares

test case N (Law, fig) caso exemplar

test flight N teste m de voo

testicle ['tɛstɪkl] N testículo

testify ['tɛstɪfaɪ] VI (Law) depor, testemunhar; **to ~ to sth** (Law) atestar algo; (gen) testemunhar algo

testimonial [tɛstɪ'məunɪəl] N (reference) carta de recomendação; (gift) obséquio, tributo

testimony ['tɛstɪmənɪ] N (Law) testemunho, depoimento; **to be (a) ~ to** ser uma prova de

testing ['tɛstɪŋ] ADJ (situation, period) difícil

testing ground N campo de provas

test match N (*Cricket, Rugby*) jogo internacional

test paper N (*Sch*) prova escrita

test pilot N piloto de prova

test tube N proveta, tubo de ensaio

test-tube baby N bebê *m* de proveta

testy ['tɛstɪ] ADJ rabugento, irritável

tetanus ['tɛtənəs] N tétano

tetchy ['tɛtʃɪ] ADJ irritável

tether ['tɛðəʳ] VT amarrar ▶ N: **at the end of one's ~** a ponto de perder a paciência *or* as estribeiras

text [tɛkst] N texto; (*message*) mensagem *f* de texto, torpedo (*inf*) ▶ VT mandar uma mensagem de texto *or* (*inf*) um torpedo para

textbook ['tɛkstbuk] N livro didático; (*Sch*) livro escolar

textiles ['tɛkstaɪlz] NPL têxteis *mpl*; (*textile industry*) indústria têxtil

text message N mensagem *f* de texto

texture ['tɛkstʃəʳ] N textura

TGIF (*inf*) ABBR = **thank God it's Friday**

TGWU (*BRIT*) N ABBR (= *Transport and General Workers' Union*) sindicato dos transportadores

Thai [taɪ] ADJ tailandês(-esa) ▶ N tailandês(-esa) *m/f*; (*Ling*) tailandês *m*

Thailand ['taɪlænd] N Tailândia

thalidomide® [θə'lɪdəmaɪd] N talidomida®

Thames [tɛmz] N: **the ~** o Tâmisa (*BR*), o Tamisa (*PT*)

than [ðæn, ðən] CONJ (*in comparisons*) do que; **more ~ 10** mais de 10; **I have more/less ~ you** tenho mais/menos do que você; **she has more apples ~ pears** ela tem mais maçãs do que peras; **she is older ~ you think** ela é mais velha do que você pensa; **more ~ once** mais de uma vez

thank [θæŋk] VT agradecer; **~ you (very much)** muito obrigado(-a); **~ God** graças a Deus; **~s to** graças a; **to ~ sb for sth** agradecer a alguém (por) algo; **to say ~ you** agradecer

thankful ['θæŋkful] ADJ: **~ (for)** agradecido (por); **~ that** (*relieved*) aliviado que

thankfully ['θæŋkfəlɪ] ADV (*gratefully*) agradecidamente; (*fortunately*) felizmente

thankless ['θæŋklɪs] ADJ ingrato

thanks [θæŋks] NPL agradecimentos *mpl*; (*to God etc*) graças *fpl* ▶ EXCL obrigado(-a)!; **~ to** graças a

Thanksgiving ['θæŋksgɪvɪŋ], **Thanksgiving Day** N Dia *m* de Ação de Graças

▎O feriado de Ação de graças
▎(**Thanksgiving Day**) nos Estados Unidos,
▎quarta quinta-feira do mês de novembro,
▎é o dia em que se comemora a boa colheita
▎feita pelos peregrinos originários da
▎Grã-Bretanha em 1621; tradicionalmente,
▎é um dia em que se agradece a Deus e se
▎organiza um grande banquete. Uma festa
▎semelhante é celebrada no Canadá na
▎segunda segunda-feira de outubro.

that [ðæt, ðət] (*pl* **those**) ADJ (*demonstrative*) esse/essa; (*more remote*) aquele/aquela; **that man/woman/book** aquele homem/aquela mulher/aquele livro; **leave these books on the table** deixe aqueles livros na mesa; **that one** esse/essa; **that one over there** aquele lá; **I want this one, not that one** quero este, não esse
▶ PRON **1** (*demonstrative*) esse/essa, aquele/aquela; (*neuter*) isso, aquilo; **who's/what's that?** quem é?/o que é isso?; **is that you?** é você?; **I prefer this to that** eu prefiro isto a aquilo; **that's my house** aquela é a minha casa; **that's what he said** foi isso o que ele disse; **that is (to say)** isto é, quer dizer
2 (*relative: direct: thing, person*) que; (*person*) quem; (*relative: indirect: thing, person*) o/a qual *sg*, os/as quais *pl*; (*person*) quem; **the book (that) I read** o livro que eu li; **the books that are in the library** os livros que estão na biblioteca; **the man (that) I saw** o homem que eu vi; **all (that) I have** tudo o que eu tenho; **the box (that) I put it in** a caixa na qual eu o coloquei; **the man (that) I spoke to** o homem com quem *or* o qual falei
3 (*relative: of time*): **on the day that he came** no dia em que ele veio
▶ CONJ que; **she suggested that I phone you** ela sugeriu que eu telefonasse para você
▶ ADV (*demonstrative*): **I can't work that much** não posso trabalhar tanto; **I didn't realize it was that bad** não pensei que fôsse tão ruim; **that high** dessa altura, até essa altura

thatched [θætʃt] ADJ (*roof*) de sapê; **~ cottage** chalé *m* com telhado de sapê *or* de colmo

thaw [θɔː] N degelo ▶ VI (*ice*) derreter-se; (*food*) descongelar-se ▶ VT (*food*) descongelar; **it's ~ing** (*weather*) degela

the [ðiː, ðə] DEF ART **1** (*gen: singular*) o/a; (*: plural*) os/as; **the history of France** a história da França; **the books/children are in the library** os livros/as crianças estão na biblioteca; **she put it on the table** ela colocou-o na mesa; **he took it from the drawer** ele tirou isto da gaveta; **to play the piano/violin** tocar piano/violino; **I'm going to the cinema** vou ao cinema
2 (*+ adj to form n*): **the rich and the poor** os ricos e os pobres; **to attempt the impossible** tentar o impossível
3 (*in titles*): **Richard the Second** Ricardo II; **Peter the Great** Pedro o Grande
4 (*in comparisons: + adv*): **the more he works, the more he earns** quanto mais ele trabalha, mais ele ganha

theatre, (*US*) **theater** ['θɪətəʳ] N teatro; (*Med: also:* **operating theatre**) sala de operação

t

theatre-goer ['θɪətəgəuə^r] N frequentador(a) *m/f* de teatro
theatrical [θɪ'ætrɪkl] ADJ teatral; **~ company** companhia de teatro
theft [θɛft] N roubo
their [ðɛə^r] ADJ seu/sua, deles/delas
theirs [ðɛəz] PRON (o) seu/(a) sua; **a friend of ~** um amigo seu/deles; **it's ~** é deles
them [ðɛm, ðəm] PRON (*direct*) os/as; (*indirect*) lhes; (*stressed, after prep*) a eles/a elas; **I see ~** eu os vejo; **give ~ the book** dê o livro a eles; **give me some of ~** me dê alguns deles
theme [θiːm] N tema *m*
theme park N *parque de diversões em torno de um único tema*
theme song N tema *m* musical
themselves [ðəm'sɛlvz] PRON (*subject*) eles mesmos/elas mesmas; (*complement*) se; (*after prep*) si (mesmos/as)
then [ðɛn] ADV (*at that time*) então; (*next*) em seguida; (*later*) logo, depois; (*and also*) além disso ▸ CONJ (*therefore*) então, nesse caso, portanto ▸ ADJ: **the ~ president** o então presidente; **by ~** (*past*) até então; (*future*) até lá; **from ~ on** a partir de então; **before ~** antes (disso); **until ~** até lá; **and ~ what?** e então?, e daí?; **what do you want me to do ~?** (*afterwards*) o que você quer que eu faça depois?; (*in that case*) então, o que você quer que eu faça?
theologian [θɪə'ləudʒən] N teólogo(-a)
theological [θɪə'lɔdʒɪkl] ADJ teológico
theology [θɪ'ɔlədʒɪ] N teologia
theorem ['θɪərəm] N teorema *m*
theoretical [θɪə'rɛtɪkl] ADJ teórico
theoretically [θɪə'rɛtɪklɪ] ADV teoricamente
theorize ['θɪəraɪz] VI teorizar, elaborar uma teoria
theory ['θɪərɪ] N teoria; **in ~** em teoria, teoricamente
therapeutic [θɛrə'pjuːtɪk], **therapeutical** [θɛrə'pjuːtɪkl] ADJ terapêutico
therapist ['θɛrəpɪst] N terapeuta *m/f*
therapy ['θɛrəpɪ] N terapia

[KEYWORD]

there [ðɛə^r] ADV **1**: **there is, there are** há, tem; **there are 3 of them** (*people, things*) são três; **there is no-one here/no bread left** não tem ninguém aqui/não tem mais pão; **there has been an accident** houve um acidente
2 (*referring to place*) aí, ali, lá; **put it in/on/up/down there** põe isto lá dentro/cima/em cima/embaixo; **I want that book there** quero aquele livro lá; **there he is!** lá está ele!
3: **there, there!** (*esp to child*) calma!

thereabouts ['ðɛərəbauts] ADV por aí; (*amount*) aproximadamente
thereafter [ðɛər'ɑːftə^r] ADV depois disso
thereby ['ðɛəbaɪ] ADV assim, deste modo

therefore ['ðɛəfɔː] ADV portanto
there's [ðɛəz] = **there is**; **there has**
thereupon [ðɛərə'pɔn] ADV (*at that point*) após o que; (*formal: on that subject*) a respeito
thermal ['θəːml] ADJ térmico; **~ paper/printer** papel térmico/impressora térmica
thermodynamics [θəːmədaɪ'næmɪks] N termodinâmica
thermometer [θə'mɔmɪtə^r] N termômetro
thermonuclear [θəː'məu'njuːklɪə^r] ADJ termonuclear
Thermos® ['θəː'məs] N (*also*: **Thermos flask**) garrafa térmica (BR), termo (PT)
thermostat ['θəː'məustæt] N termostato
thesaurus [θɪ'sɔːrəs] N tesouro, dicionário de sinônimos
these [ðiːz] PL ADJ, PRON estes/estas
theses ['θiːsiːz] NPL *of* **thesis**
thesis ['θiːsɪs] (*pl* **theses**) N tese *f*
they [ðeɪ] PRON PL eles/elas; **~ say that …** (*it is said that*) diz-se que …, dizem que …
they'd [ðeɪd] = **they had**; **they would**
they'll [ðeɪl] = **they shall**; **they will**
they're [ðeɪə^r] = **they are**
they've [ðeɪv] = **they have**
thick [θɪk] ADJ (*in shape*) espesso; (*mud, fog, forest*) denso; (*sauce*) grosso; (*dense*) denso, compacto; (*stupid*) burro ▸ N: **in the ~ of the battle** em plena batalha; **it's 20 cm ~** tem 20 cm de espessura
thicken ['θɪkən] VI (*fog*) adensar-se; (*plot etc*) complicar-se ▸ VT (*sauce etc*) engrossar
thicket ['θɪkɪt] N matagal *m*
thickly ['θɪklɪ] ADV (*spread*) numa camada espessa; (*cut*) em fatias grossas
thickness ['θɪknɪs] N espessura, grossura
thickset [θɪk'sɛt] ADJ troncudo
thick-skinned [-'skɪnd] ADJ (*fig*) insensível, indiferente
thief [θiːf] (*pl* **thieves**) N ladrão/ladra *m/f*
thieves [θiːvz] NPL *of* **thief**
thieving ['θiːvɪŋ] N roubo, furto
thigh [θaɪ] N coxa
thighbone ['θaɪbəun] N fêmur *m*
thimble ['θɪmbl] N dedal *m*
thin [θɪn] ADJ magro; (*slice, line, book*) fino; (*light*) leve; (*hair*) ralo; (*crowd*) pequeno; (*fog*) pouco denso; (*soup, sauce*) aguado ▸ VT (*also*: **thin down**: *sauce, paint*) diluir ▸ VI (*fog*) rarefazer-se; (*also*: **thin out**: *crowd*) dispersar; **his hair is ~** o cabelo dele está caindo
thing [θɪŋ] N coisa; (*object*) negócio; (*matter*) assunto, negócio; (*mania*) mania; **things** NPL (*belongings*) pertences *mpl*; **to have a ~ about sb/sth** ser vidrado em alguém/algo; **the best ~ would be to …** o melhor seria …; **how are ~s?** como vai?, tudo bem?; **first ~ (in the morning)** de manhã, antes de mais nada; **last ~ (at night), he …** logo antes de dormir, ele …; **the ~ is …** é que …, o negócio é o seguinte …; **for one ~** primeiro; **she's got a ~ about …** ela detesta …; **poor ~!** coitadinho(-a)!

think [θɪŋk] (*pt, pp* **thought**) vı pensar; (*believe*) achar ▶ vt pensar, achar; (*imagine*) imaginar; **what did you ~ of them?** o que você achou deles?; **to ~ about sth/sb** pensar em algo/ alguém; **I'll ~ about it** vou pensar sobre isso; **to ~ of doing sth** pensar em fazer algo; **I ~ so/not** acho que sim/não; **to ~ well of sb** fazer bom juízo de alguém; **~ again!** pensa bem!; **to ~ aloud** pensar em voz alta
▶ **think out** vt (*plan*) arquitetar; (*solution*) descobrir
▶ **think over** vt refletir sobre, meditar sobre; **I'd like to ~ things over** eu gostaria de pensar sobre isso com cuidado
▶ **think through** vt considerar todos os aspectos de
▶ **think up** vt inventar, bolar
thinking ['θɪŋkɪŋ] N: **to my (way of) ~** na minha opinião
think tank N comissão f de peritos
thinly ['θɪnlɪ] ADV (*cut*) em fatias finas; (*spread*) numa camada fina
thinness ['θɪnnɪs] N magreza
third [θəːd] ADJ terceiro ▶ N terceiro(-a); (*fraction*) terço; (*Aut*) terceira; (*Sch: degree*) terceira categoria; *see also* **fifth**
third-degree burns NPL queimaduras fpl de terceiro grau
thirdly ['θəːdlɪ] ADV em terceiro lugar
third party insurance N seguro contra terceiros
third-rate ADJ medíocre
Third World N: **the ~** o Terceiro Mundo
thirst [θəːst] N sede f
thirsty ['θəːstɪ] ADJ (*person*) sedento, com sede; (*work*) que dá sede; **to be ~** estar com sede
thirteen ['θəː'tiːn] NUM treze; *see also* **five**
thirteenth [θəː'tiːnθ] NUM décimo terceiro; *see also* **fifth**
thirtieth ['θəːtɪəθ] NUM trigésimo; *see also* **fifth**
thirty ['θəːtɪ] NUM trinta; *see also* **fifty**

(KEYWORD)

this [ðɪs] (*pl* **these**) ADJ (*demonstrative*) este/ esta; **this man/woman/book** este homem/ esta mulher/este livro; **these people/ children/records** estas pessoas/crianças/ estes discos; **this one** este aqui
▶ PRON (*demonstrative*) este/esta; (*neuter*) isto; **who/what is this?** quem é esse?/o que é isso?; **this is where I live** é aqui que eu moro; **this is Mr Brown** (*in photo, introduction*) este é o Sr Brown; (*on phone*) aqui é o Sr Brown
▶ ADV (*demonstrative*): **this high** desta altura; **this long** deste comprimento; **we can't stop now we've gone this far** não podemos parar agora que fomos tão longe

thistle ['θɪsl] N cardo
thong [θɔŋ] N correia, tira de couro
thorn [θɔːn] N espinho
thorny ['θɔːnɪ] ADJ espinhoso

thorough ['θʌrə] ADJ (*search*) minucioso; (*knowledge, research, person: methodical*) metódico, profundo; (*work*) meticuloso; (*cleaning*) completo
thoroughbred ['θʌrəbred] ADJ (*horse*) de puro sangue
thoroughfare ['θʌrəfɛəʳ] N via, passagem f; **"no ~"** "passagem proibida"
thoroughly ['θʌrəlɪ] ADV (*examine, study*) minuciosamente; (*search*) profundamente; (*wash*) completamente; (*very*) muito; **he ~ agreed** concordou completamente
thoroughness ['θʌrənɪs] N (*of person*) meticulosidade f; (*of search etc*) minuciosidade f
those [ðəuz] PRON PL, ADJ esses/essas; (*more remote*) aqueles/aquelas
though [ðəu] CONJ embora, se bem que ▶ ADV no entanto; **even ~** mesmo que; **it's not easy, ~** se bem que não é fácil
thought [θɔːt] PT, PP *of* **think** ▶ N pensamento; (*idea*) ideia; (*opinion*) opinião f; (*reflection*) reflexão f; (*intention*) intenção f; **after much ~** depois de muito pensar; **I've just had a ~** acabei de pensar em alguma coisa; **to give sth some ~** pensar sobre algo
thoughtful ['θɔːtful] ADJ pensativo; (*serious*) sério; (*considerate*) atencioso
thoughtfully ['θɔːtfəlɪ] ADV pensativamente; atenciosamente
thoughtless ['θɔːtlɪs] ADJ (*behaviour*) desatencioso; (*words, person*) inconsequente
thoughtlessly ['θɔːtlɪslɪ] ADV desconsideradamente
thought-provoking [-prə'vəukɪŋ] ADJ instigante
thousand ['θauzənd] NUM mil; **two ~** dois mil; **~s (of)** milhares mpl (de)
thousandth ['θauzənθ] ADJ milésimo
thrash [θræʃ] vt surrar, malhar; (*defeat*) derrotar
▶ **thrash about** vı debater-se
▶ **thrash out** vt discutir exaustivamente
thrashing ['θræʃɪŋ] N: **to give sb a ~** dar uma surra em alguém
thread [θred] N fio, linha; (*of screw*) rosca ▶ vt (*needle*) enfiar; **to ~ one's way between** passar por
threadbare ['θredbɛəʳ] ADJ surrado, puído
threat [θret] N ameaça; **to be under ~ of** estar sob ameaça de
threaten ['θrɛtən] vı ameaçar ▶ vt: **to ~ sb with sth/to do** ameaçar alguém com algo/ de fazer
threatening ['θrɛtnɪŋ] ADJ ameaçador(a)
three [θriː] NUM três; *see also* **five**
three-dimensional ADJ tridimensional, em três dimensões
threefold ['θriːfəuld] ADV: **to increase ~** triplicar
three-piece suit N terno (3 peças) (BR), fato de 3 peças (PT)

t

three-piece suite N conjunto de sofá e duas poltronas

three-ply ADJ (*wool*) triple, com três fios; (*wood*) com três espessuras

three-quarters NPL três quartos *mpl*; **~ full** cheio até os três quartos

three-wheeler N (*car*) carro de três rodas

thresh [θrɛʃ] VT (*Agr*) debulhar

threshing machine ['θrɛʃɪŋ-] N debulhadora

threshold ['θrɛʃhəuld] N limiar *m*; **to be on the ~ of** (*fig*) estar no limiar de

threshold agreement N (*Econ*) acordo sobre a indexação de salários

threw [θruː] PT *of* **throw**

thrift [θrɪft] N economia, poupança

thrifty ['θrɪftɪ] ADJ econômico, frugal

thrill [θrɪl] N (*excitement*) emoção *f*; (*shudder*) estremecimento ▶ VI vibrar ▶ VT emocionar, vibrar; **to be ~ed** (*with gift etc*) estar emocionado

thriller ['θrɪləʳ] N romance *m or* filme *m* de suspense

thrilling ['θrɪlɪŋ] ADJ (*book, play etc*) excitante; (*news, discovery*) emocionante

thrive [θraɪv] (*pt* **thrived** *or* **throve**, *pp* **thrived** *or* **thriven**) VI (*grow*) vicejar; (*do well*) prosperar, florescer; **to ~ on sth** realizar-se ao fazer algo

thriven ['θrɪvn] PP *of* **thrive**

thriving ['θraɪvɪŋ] ADJ próspero

throat [θrəut] N garganta; **to have a sore ~** estar com dor de garganta

throb [θrɔb] N (*of heart*) batida; (*of engine*) vibração *f*; (*of pain*) latejo ▶ VI (*heart*) bater, palpitar; (*pain*) dar pontadas; (*engine*) vibrar; **my head is ~bing** minha cabeça está latejando

throes [θrəuz] NPL: **in the ~ of** no meio de

thrombosis [θrɔm'bəusɪs] N trombose *f*

throne [θrəun] N trono

throng [θrɔŋ] N multidão *f* ▶ VT apinhar, apinhar-se em

throttle ['θrɔtl] N (*Aut*) acelerador *m* ▶ VT estrangular

through [θruː] PREP por, através de; (*time*) durante; (*by means of*) por meio de, por intermédio de; (*owing to*) devido a ▶ ADJ (*ticket, train*) direto ▶ ADV através; **(from) Monday ~ Friday** (*us*) de segunda a sexta; **to let sb ~** deixar alguém passar; **to put sb ~ to sb** (*Tel*) ligar alguém com alguém; **to be ~** (*Tel*) estar na linha; (*have finished*) acabar; **"no ~ traffic"** (*us*) "trânsito proibido"; **"no ~ road"** "rua sem saída"; **I'm halfway ~ the book** estou na metade do livro

throughout [θruː'aut] PREP (*place*) por todo(-a); (*time*) durante todo(-a) ▶ ADV por *or* em todas as partes

throughput ['θruːput] N (*of goods, materials*) quantidade *f* tratada; (*Comput*) capacidade *f* de processamento

throve [θrəuv] PT *of* **thrive**

throw [θrəu] (*pt* **threw**, *pp* **thrown**) N arremesso, tiro; (*Sport*) lançamento ▶ VT jogar, atirar; (*Sport*) lançar; (*rider*) derrubar; (*fig*) desconcertar; (*pot*) afeiçoar; **to ~ a party** dar uma festa

▶ **throw about** VT (*litter etc*) esparramar

▶ **throw around** VT (*litter etc*) esparramar

▶ **throw away** VT (*dispose of*) jogar fora; (*waste*) desperdiçar

▶ **throw in** VT (*Sport*) pôr em jogo

▶ **throw off** VT desfazer-se de; (*habit, cold*) livrar-se

▶ **throw out** VT (*person*) expulsar; (*rubbish*) jogar fora; (*idea*) rejeitar

▶ **throw together** VT (*clothes, meal etc*) arranjar às pressas

▶ **throw up** VI vomitar, botar para fora

throwaway ['θrəuəweɪ] ADJ descartável; (*line, remark*) gratuito

throwback ['θrəubæk] N: **it's a ~ to** é um retrocesso a

throw-in N (*Sport*) lance *m*

thru [θruː] (*us*) PREP, ADJ, ADV = **through**

thrush [θrʌʃ] N (*Zool*) tordo; (*Med*) monília

thrust [θrʌst] VT (*pt, pp* **thrust**) empurrar; (*push in*) enfiar, meter ▶ N impulso; (*Tech*) empuxo

thrusting ['θrʌstɪŋ] ADJ dinâmico

thud [θʌd] N baque *m*, som *m* surdo

thug [θʌg] N (*criminal*) criminoso(-a); (*pej*) facínora *m/f*

thumb [θʌm] N (*Anat*) polegar *m*; (*inf*) dedão *m* ▶ VT: **to ~ a lift** pegar carona (BR), arranjar uma boleia (PT); **to give sb/sth the ~s up** (*approve*) dar luz verde a alguém/ algo

▶ **thumb through** VT FUS folhear

thumb index N índice *m* de dedo

thumbnail ['θʌmneɪl] N unha do polegar

thumbnail sketch N descrição *f* resumida

thumbtack ['θʌmtæk] (*us*) N percevejo, tachinha

thump [θʌmp] N murro, pancada; (*sound*) baque *m* ▶ VT dar um murro em ▶ VI bater

thunder ['θʌndəʳ] N trovão *m*; (*sudden noise*) trovoada; (*of applause etc*) estrondo ▶ VI trovejar; (*train etc*): **to ~ past** passar como um raio

thunderbolt ['θʌndəbəult] N raio

thunderclap ['θʌndəklæp] N estampido do trovão

thunderous ['θʌndərəs] ADJ estrondoso

thunderstorm ['θʌndəstɔːm] N tempestade *f* com trovoada, temporal *m*

thunderstruck ['θʌndəstrʌk] ADJ estupefato

thundery ['θʌndərɪ] ADJ tempestuoso

Thur., Thurs. ABBR (= *Thursday*) qui, 5ª

Thursday ['θəːzdɪ] N quinta-feira; *see also* **Tuesday**

thus [ðʌs] ADV assim, desta maneira; (*consequently*) consequentemente

thwart [θwɔːt] VT frustrar

thyme [taɪm] N tomilho

thyroid ['θaɪrɔɪd] N tireoide *f*

tiara [tɪ'ɑːrə] N tiara, diadema *m*

Tibet [tɪ'bɛt] N Tibete m
Tibetan [tɪ'bɛtən] ADJ tibetano ▶ N
tibetano(-a); (*Ling*) tibetano
tibia ['tɪbɪə] N tíbia
tic [tɪk] N tique m
tick [tɪk] N (*sound: of clock*) tique-taque m;
(*mark*) tique m, marca; (*Zool*) carrapato; (BRIT
inf) **in a ~** num instante; (: *credit*): **to buy sth
on ~** comprar algo a crédito ▶ VI fazer
tique-taque ▶ VT marcar, ticar; **to put a ~
against sth** marcar or ticar algo
▶ **tick off** VT assinalar, ticar; (*person*) dar uma
bronca em
▶ **tick over** (BRIT) VI (*engine*) funcionar em
marcha lenta; (*fig*) ir indo
ticker tape ['tɪkə'-] N fita de teleimpressor;
(US: *in celebrations*) chuva de papel
ticket ['tɪkɪt] N (*for bus, plane*) passagem f; (*for
theatre, raffle*) bilhete m; (*for cinema*) entrada;
(*in shop: on goods*) etiqueta; (: *receipt*) ficha,
nota fiscal; (*for library*) cartão m; (US *Pol*)
chapa; (*also:* **parking ticket:** *fine*) multa; **to
get a (parking) ~** (*Aut*) ganhar uma multa
(por estacionamento ilegal)
ticket agency N agência de ingressos teatrais
ticket barrier (BRIT) N (*Rail*) catraca de
embarque/desembarque
ticket collector N revisor(a) m/f
ticket holder N portador(a) m/f de um bilhete
or ingresso
ticket inspector N revisor(a) m/f
ticket office N bilheteria (BR), bilheteira (PT)
tickle ['tɪkl] N cócegas fpl ▶ VT fazer cócegas
em; (*captivate*) encantar; (*make laugh*) fazer rir
▶ VI fazer cócegas
ticklish ['tɪklɪʃ] ADJ (*person*) coceguento;
(*problem*) delicado; (*which tickles: blanket etc*)
que pica, que faz cócegas; (: *cough*) irritante;
to be ~ (*person*) ter cócegas
tidal ['taɪdl] ADJ de maré
tidal wave N macaréu m, onda gigantesca
tidbit ['tɪdbɪt] (*esp US*) N = **titbit**
tiddlywinks ['tɪdlɪwɪŋks] N jogo de fichas
tide [taɪd] N maré f; (*fig: of events*) curso ▶ VT:
to ~ sb over dar para alguém aguentar;
high/low ~ maré alta/baixa; **the ~ of public
opinion** a corrente da opinião pública
▶ **tide over** VT (*help out*) ajudar num período
difícil
tidily ['taɪdɪlɪ] ADV com capricho
tidiness ['taɪdɪnɪs] N (*good order*) ordem f;
(*neatness*) asseio, limpeza
tidy ['taɪdɪ] ADJ (*room*) arrumado; (*dress, work*)
limpo; (*person*) bem arrumado; (*mind*)
metódico ▶ VT (*also:* **tidy up**) pôr em ordem,
arrumar; **to ~ o.s. up** arrumar-se
tie [taɪ] N (*string etc*) fita, corda; (BRIT: *also:*
necktie) gravata; (*fig: link*) vínculo, laço;
(*Sport: draw*) empate m; (US *Rail*) dormente m
▶ VT amarrar ▶ VI (*Sport*) empatar; **to ~ in a
bow** dar um laço em; **to ~ a knot in sth** dar
um nó em algo; **family ~s** laços de família;
"black/white ~" "smoking/traje a rigor"

▶ **tie down** VT amarrar; (*fig: person: restrict*)
limitar, restringir; (: *to date, price etc*) obrigar
▶ **tie in** VI: **to ~ in (with)** combinar com
▶ **tie on** (BRIT) VT (*label etc*) prender (com
barbante)
▶ **tie up** VT (*parcel*) embrulhar; (*dog*) prender;
(*boat, prisoner etc*) amarrar; (*arrangements*)
concluir; **to be ~d up** (*busy*) estar ocupado
tie-break, tie-breaker N (*Tennis*) tie-break m;
(*in quiz etc*) decisão f de empate
tie-on (BRIT) ADJ (*label*) para atar
tie-pin (BRIT) N alfinete m de gravata
tier [tɪə'] N fileira; (*of cake*) camada
Tierra del Fuego [tɪ'ɛrədɛl'fweɪgəu] N Terra
do Fogo
tie tack (US) N alfinete m de gravata
tie-up (US) N engarrafamento
tiff [tɪf] N briga; (*lover's tiff*) arrufo
tiger ['taɪgə'] N tigre m
tight [taɪt] ADJ (*rope*) esticado, firme; (*money*)
escasso; (*clothes, shoes*) justo; (*bend*) fechado;
(*budget, programme*) rigoroso; (*control*) rigoroso;
(*inf: drunk*) bêbado ▶ ADV (*squeeze*) bem forte;
(*shut*) hermeticamente; **to be packed ~**
(*suitcase*) estar abarrotado; (*people*) estar
apinhado; **everybody hold ~!** segurem
firme!
tighten ['taɪtən] VT (*rope*) esticar; (*screw, grip*)
apertar; (*security*) aumentar ▶ VI esticar-se;
apertar-se
tight-fisted [-'fɪstɪd] ADJ pão-duro
tightly ['taɪtlɪ] ADV (*grasp*) firmemente
tight-rope N corda (bamba)
tight-rope walker N funâmbulo(-a)
tights [taɪts] (BRIT) NPL collant m
tigress ['taɪgrɪs] N tigre fêmea
tilde ['tɪldə] N til m
tile [taɪl] N (*on roof*) telha; (*on floor*) ladrilho;
(*on wall*) azulejo, ladrilho ▶ VT (*floor*)
ladrilhar; (*wall, bathroom*) azulejar
tiled [taɪld] ADJ ladrilhado; (*roof*) de telhas
till [tɪl] N caixa (registradora) ▶ VT (*land*)
cultivar ▶ PREP, CONJ = **until**
tiller ['tɪlə'] N (*Naut*) cana do leme
tilt [tɪlt] VT inclinar ▶ VI inclinar-se ▶ N (*slope*)
inclinação f; (**at) full ~** a toda velocidade
timber ['tɪmbə'] N (*material*) madeira; (*trees*)
mata, floresta
time [taɪm] N tempo; (*epoch: often pl*) época;
(*by clock*) hora; (*moment*) momento; (*occasion*)
vez f; (*Mus*) compasso ▶ VT calcular or medir
o tempo de; (*fix moment for: visit etc*) escolher o
momento para; (*remark etc*): **to ~ sth well/
badly** ser oportuno/não ser oportuno; **a
long ~** muito tempo; **4 at a ~** quatro de uma
vez; **for the ~ being** por enquanto; **from ~
to ~** de vez em quando; **at ~s** às vezes;
~ after ~, ~ and again repetidamente; **in ~
(soon enough)** a tempo; (*after some time*) com o
tempo; (*Mus*) no compasso; **in a week's ~**
dentro de uma semana; **in no ~** num abrir e
fechar de olhos; **any ~** a qualquer hora; **on ~**
na hora; **to be 30 minutes behind/ahead**

t

of ~ estar atrasado/adiantado de 30 minutos; **by the** ~ **he arrived** até ele chegar; **5** ~**s 5 is 25** 5 vezes 5 são 25; **what** ~ **is it? que** horas são?; **what** ~ **do you make it?** que horas você tem?; **to have a good** ~ divertir-se; **we had a hard** ~ foi difícil para nós; **he'll do it in his own (good)** ~ (*without being hurried*) ele vai fazer isso quando tiver tempo; **he'll do it in** (*BRIT*) **or on** (*US*) **his own** ~ (*out of working hours*) ele vai fazer isso fora do expediente; **to be behind the** ~**s** estar antiquado

time-and-motion study N estudo de tempos e movimentos
time bomb N bomba-relógio *f*
time clock N relógio de ponto
time-consuming [-kən'sju:mɪŋ] ADJ que exige muito tempo
time difference N fuso horário
time-honoured, (*US*) **time-honored** [-'ɔnəd] ADJ consagrado pelo tempo
timekeeper ['taɪmki:pəʳ] N (*Sport*) cronometrista *m/f*
time lag (*BRIT*) N defasagem *f*; (*in travel*) fuso horário
timeless ['taɪmlɪs] ADJ eterno
time limit N limite *m* de tempo; (*Comm*) prazo
timely ['taɪmlɪ] ADJ oportuno
time off N tempo livre
timer ['taɪməʳ] N (*in kitchen*) cronômetro; (*switch*) timer *m*
time-saving ADJ que economiza tempo
time scale N prazos *mpl*
time-sharing [-'ʃɛərɪŋ] N (*Comput*) tempo compartilhado
time sheet N folha de ponto
time signal N tope *m*, sinal *m* horário
time switch (*BRIT*) N interruptor *m* horário
timetable ['taɪmteɪbl] N horário; (*of project*) cronograma *m*
time zone N fuso horário
timid ['tɪmɪd] ADJ tímido
timidity [tɪ'mɪdɪtɪ] N timidez *f*
timing ['taɪmɪŋ] N escolha do momento; (*Sport*) cronometragem *f*; **the** ~ **of his resignation** o momento que escolheu para se demitir
timing device N (*on bomb*) dispositivo de retardamento
Timor ['ti:mɔːʳ] N Timor (*no article*)
timpani ['tɪmpənɪ] NPL tímbales *mpl*
tin [tɪn] N estanho; (*also:* **tin plate**) folha-de-flandres *f*; (*BRIT: can*) lata; (*: for baking*) fôrma
tin foil N papel *m* de estanho
tinge [tɪndʒ] N (*of colour*) matiz *m*; (*of feeling*) toque *m* ▸ VT: ~**d with** tingido de
tingle ['tɪŋgl] N comichão *f* ▸ VI formigar
tinker ['tɪŋkəʳ] N funileiro(-a); (*gipsy*) cigano(-a)
▸ **tinker with** VT mexer com
tinkle ['tɪŋkl] VI tilintar, tinir ▸ N (*inf*): **to give sb a** ~ dar uma ligada para alguém
tin mine N mina de estanho

tinned [tɪnd] (*BRIT*) ADJ (*food*) em lata, em conserva
tinny ['tɪnɪ] ADJ metálico
tin opener (*BRIT*) N abridor *m* de latas (*BR*), abre-latas *m inv* (*PT*)
tinsel ['tɪnsl] N ouropel *m*
tint [tɪnt] N matiz *m*; (*for hair*) tintura, tinta ▸ VT (*hair*) pintar
tinted ['tɪntɪd] ADJ (*hair*) pintado; (*spectacles, glass*) fumê *inv*
tiny ['taɪnɪ] ADJ pequenininho, minúsculo
tip [tɪp] N (*end*) ponta; (*gratuity*) gorjeta; (*BRIT: for rubbish*) depósito; (*advice*) dica ▸ VT (*waiter*) dar uma gorjeta a; (*tilt*) inclinar; (*winner*) apostar em; (*overturn: also:* **tip over**) virar, emborcar; (*empty: also:* **tip out**) esvaziar, entornar; **he** ~**ped out the contents of the box** esvaziou a caixa
▸ **tip off** VT avisar
tip-off N (*hint*) aviso, dica
tipped [tɪpt] ADJ (*BRIT: cigarette*) com filtro; **steel-**~ com ponta de aço
Tipp-Ex® ['tɪpɛks] (*BRIT*) N líquido corretor
tipple ['tɪpl] (*BRIT*) VT beberciar ▸ N: **to have a** ~ beber um gole
tipsy ['tɪpsɪ] ADJ embriagado, tocado, alto, alegre
tiptoe ['tɪptəu] N: **on** ~ na ponta dos pés
tiptop ['tɪp'tɔp] ADJ: **in** ~ **condition** em perfeitas condições
tire ['taɪəʳ] N (*US*) = **tyre** ▸ VT cansar ▸ VI cansar-se; (*become bored*) chatear-se
▸ **tire out** VT esgotar, exaurir
tired ['taɪəd] ADJ cansado; **to be** ~ **of sth** estar farto *or* cheio de algo
tiredness ['taɪədnɪs] N cansaço
tireless ['taɪəlɪs] ADJ incansável
tiresome ['taɪəsəm] ADJ enfadonho, chato
tiring ['taɪərɪŋ] ADJ cansativo
tissue ['tɪʃuː] N tecido; (*paper handkerchief*) lenço de papel
tissue paper N papel *m* de seda
tit [tɪt] N (*bird*) passarinho; (*inf: breast*) teta; **to give** ~ **for tat** pagar na mesma moeda
titanium [tɪ'teɪnɪəm] N titânio
titbit ['tɪtbɪt] N (*food*) guloseima; (*news*) boato, rumor *m*
titillate ['tɪtɪleɪt] VT titilar, excitar
titivate ['tɪtɪveɪt] VT arrumar
title ['taɪtl] N título; (*Law: right*): ~ **(to)** direito (a)
title deed N (*Law*) título de propriedade
title page N página de rosto
title role N papel *m* principal
titter ['tɪtəʳ] VI rir-se com riso sufocado
tittle-tattle ['tɪtltætl] N fofocas *fpl* (*BR*), mexericos *mpl* (*PT*)
titular ['tɪtjuləʳ] ADJ (*in name only*) nominal, titular
tizzy ['tɪzɪ] N: **to be in a** ~ estar muito nervoso
T-junction N bifurcação *f* em T
TM N ABBR = **trademark; transcendental meditation**

TN (US) ABBR (*Post*) = **Tennessee**
TNT N ABBR (= *trinitrotoluene*) Tnt *m*, trotil *m*

(KEYWORD)

to [tuː, tə] PREP **1** (*direction*) a, para; (*towards*) para; **to go to France/London/school/the station** ir à França/a Londres/ao colégio/à estação; **to go to Lígia's/the doctor's** ir à casa da Lígia/ao médico; **the road to Edinburgh** a estrada para Edinburgo; **to the left/right** à esquerda/direita
2 (*as far as*) até; **to count to 10** contar até 10; **from 40 to 50 people** de 40 a 50 pessoas
3 (*with expressions of time*): **a quarter to 5** quinze para as 5 (BR), 5 menos um quarto (PT)
4 (*for, or*) de, para; **the key to the front door** a chave da porta da frente; **a letter to his wife** uma carta para a sua mulher
5 (*expressing indirect object*): **to give sth to sb** dar algo a alguém; **to talk to sb** falar com alguém; **I sold it to a friend** vendi isto para um amigo; **to cause damage to sth** causar danos em algo; **to be a danger to sb/sth** ser um perigo para alguém/algo; **to carry out repairs to sth** fazer consertos em algo; **you've done something to your hair** você fêz algo no seu cabelo
6 (*in relation to*) para; **A is to B as C is to D** A está para B assim como C está para D; **3 goals to 2** 3 a 2; **8 apples to the kilo** 8 maçãs por quilo
7 (*purpose, result*) para; **to come to sb's aid** prestar ajuda a alguém; **to sentence sb to death** condenar alguém à morte; **to my surprise** para minha surpresa
▶ WITH VB **1** (*simple infin*): **to go/eat** ir/comer
2 (*following another vb*): **to want/try to do** querer/tentar fazer; **to start to do** começar a fazer
3 (*with vb omitted*): **I don't want to** eu não quero; **you ought to** você deve
4 (*purpose, result*) para; **he did it to help you** ele fez isso para ajudar você
5 (*equivalent to relative clause*) para, a; **I have things to do** eu tenho coisas para fazer; **he has a lot to lose** ele tem muito a perder; **the main thing is to try** o principal é tentar
6 (*after adj etc*) para; **ready to go** pronto para ir; **too old/young to ...** muito velho/jovem para ...
▶ ADV: **pull/push the door to** puxar/empurrar a porta

toad [təud] N sapo
toadstool ['təudstuːl] N chapéu-de-cobra *m*, cogumelo venenoso
toady ['təudɪ] VI ser bajulador(a), puxar saco (*inf*)
toast [təust] N (*Culin*) torradas *fpl*; (*drink, speech*) brinde *m* ▶ VT (*Culin*) torrar; (*drink to*) brindar; **a piece** *or* **slice of ~** uma torrada
toaster ['təustəʳ] N torradeira

toastmaster ['təustmɑːstəʳ] N mestre *m* de cerimônias
toast rack N porta-torradas *m inv*
tobacco [tə'bækəu] N tabaco, fumo (BR)
tobacconist [tə'bækənɪst] N vendedor(a) *m/f* de tabaco; **~'s (shop)** tabacaria, charutaria (BR)
Tobago [tə'beɪgəu] N = **Trinidad and Tobago**
toboggan [tə'bɔgən] N tobogã *m*
today [tə'deɪ] ADV, N (*fig*) hoje *m*; **what day is it ~?** que dia é hoje?; **what date is it ~?** qual é a data de hoje?; **~ is the 4th of March** hoje é dia 4 de março; **a week ago ~** há uma semana atrás; **a fortnight ~** daqui a quinze dias; **~'s paper** o jornal de hoje
toddler ['tɔdləʳ] N criança *que começa a andar*
toddy ['tɔdɪ] N ponche *m* quente
to-do N (*fuss*) rebuliço, alvoroço
toe [təu] N dedo do pé; (*of shoe*) bico ▶ VT: **to ~ the line** (*fig*) conformar-se, cumprir as obrigações; **big ~** dedão *m* do pé; **little ~** dedo mindinho do pé
toehold ['təuhəuld] N apoio
toenail ['təuneɪl] N unha do pé
toffee ['tɔfɪ] N puxa-puxa *m* (BR), caramelo (PT)
toffee apple (BRIT) N maçã *f* do amor
toga ['təugə] N toga
together [tə'gɛðəʳ] ADV juntos; (*at same time*) ao mesmo tempo; **~ with** junto com
togetherness [tə'gɛðənɪs] N companheirismo, camaradagem *f*
toggle button ['tɔgl-] N (*Comput*) botão *m* de alternância
Togo ['təugəu] N Togo
togs [tɔgz] (*inf*) NPL (*clothes*) roupa
toil [tɔɪl] N faina, labuta ▶ VI labutar, trabalhar arduamente
toilet ['tɔɪlət] N (*apparatus*) privada, vaso sanitário; (BRIT: *lavatory*) banheiro (BR), casa de banho (PT) ▶ CPD (*bag, soap etc*) de toalete; **to go to the ~** ir ao banheiro
toilet bag (BRIT) N bolsa de toucador
toilet bowl N vaso sanitário
toilet paper N papel *m* higiênico
toiletries ['tɔɪlɪtrɪz] NPL artigos *mpl* de toalete; (*make-up etc*) artigos de toucador
toilet roll N rolo de papel higiênico
toilet water N água de colônia
to-ing and fro-ing ['tuːɪŋən'frəuɪŋ] (BRIT) N vaivém *m*
token ['təukən] N (*sign*) sinal *m*, símbolo, prova; (*souvenir*) lembrança; (*substitute coin*) ficha; (*voucher*) cupom *m*, vale *m* ▶ CPD (*fee, strike*) simbólico; **by the same ~** (*fig*) pela mesma razão; **book/record ~** (BRIT) vale para comprar livros/discos
Tokyo ['təukjəu] N Tóquio
told [təuld] PT, PP *of* **tell**
tolerable ['tɔlərəbl] ADJ (*bearable*) suportável; (*fairly good*) passável
tolerably ['tɔlərəblɪ] ADV: **~ good** razoável
tolerance ['tɔlərəns] N (*also Tech*) tolerância
tolerant ['tɔlərənt] ADJ: **~ of** tolerante com

t

tolerate ['tɔlǝreɪt] VT suportar; (*Med, Tech*) tolerar

toleration [tɔlǝ'reɪʃǝn] N tolerância

toll [tǝul] N (*of casualties*) número de baixas; (*tax, charge*) pedágio (BR), portagem *f* (PT) ▶ VI (*bell*) dobrar, tanger

tollbridge ['tǝulbrɪdʒ] N ponte *f* de pedágio (BR) *or* de portagem (PT)

tomato [tǝ'mɑːtǝu] (*pl* **tomatoes**) N tomate *m*

tomb [tuːm] N tumba

tombola [tɔm'bǝulǝ] N tômbola

tomboy ['tɔmbɔɪ] N menina moleque

tombstone ['tuːmstǝun] N lápide *f*

tomcat ['tɔmkæt] N gato

tomorrow [tǝ'mɔrǝu] ADV, N amanhã *m*; **the day after ~** depois de amanhã; **~ morning** amanhã de manhã

ton [tʌn] N (BRIT) tonelada; (*Naut: also:* **register ton**) tonelagem *f* de registro; **~s of** (*inf*) um monte de

tonal ['tǝunl] ADJ tonal

tone [tǝun] N tom *m*; (BRIT *Tel*) sinal *m* ▶ VI harmonizar
  ▶ **tone down** VT (*colour, criticism*) suavizar; (*sound*) baixar; (*Mus*) entoar
  ▶ **tone up** VT (*muscles*) tonificar

tone-deaf ADJ que não tem ouvido

toner ['tǝunǝʳ] N (*for photocopier*) tinta

Tonga ['tɔŋgǝ] N Tonga (*no article*)

tongs [tɔŋz] NPL (*for coal*) tenaz *f*; (*for hair*) ferros *mpl* de frisar cabelo

tongue [tʌŋ] N língua; **~ in cheek** ironicamente

tongue-tied [-taɪd] ADJ (*fig*) calado

tongue-twister [-'twɪstǝʳ] N trava-língua *m*

tonic ['tɔnɪk] N (*Med*) tônico; (*Mus*) tônica; (*also:* **tonic water**) (água) tônica

tonight [tǝ'naɪt] ADV, N esta noite, hoje à noite; (**I'll) see you ~!** até a noite!

tonnage ['tʌnɪdʒ] N (*Naut*) tonelagem *f*

tonne [tʌn] (BRIT) N (*metric ton*) tonelada

tonsil ['tɔnsǝl] N amígdala; **to have one's ~s out** tirar as amígdalas

tonsillitis [tɔnsɪ'laɪtɪs] N amigdalite *f*; **to have ~** estar com uma amigdalite

too [tuː] ADV (*excessively*) demais; (*very*) muito; (*also*) também; **~ much** (*adv*) demais; (*adj*) demasiado; **~ many** (*adj*) muitos(-as), demasiados(-as); **~ sweet** doce demais; **I went ~** eu fui também

took [tuk] PT *of* **take**

tool [tuːl] N ferramenta; (*fig: person*) joguete *m* ▶ VT trabalhar

tool box N caixa de ferramentas

tool kit N jogo de ferramentas

toot [tuːt] N (*of horn*) buzinada; (*of whistle*) apito ▶ VI (*with car horn*) buzinar; (*whistle*) apitar

tooth [tuːθ] (*pl* **teeth**) N (*Anat, Tech*) dente *m*; (*molar*) molar *m*; **to have a ~ out** (BRIT) *or* **pulled** (US) arrancar um dente; **to brush one's teeth** escovar os dentes; **by the skin of one's teeth** (*fig*) por um triz

toothache ['tuːθeɪk] N dor *f* de dente; **to have ~** estar com dor de dente

toothbrush ['tuːθbrʌʃ] N escova de dentes

toothpaste ['tuːθpeɪst] N pasta de dentes, creme *m* dental

toothpick ['tuːθpɪk] N palito

tooth powder N pó *m* dentifrício

top [tɔp] N (*of mountain*) cume *m*, cimo; (*of tree*) topo; (*of head*) cocuruto; (*of cupboard, table*) superfície *f*, topo; (*of box, jar, bottle*) tampa; (*of ladder, page*) topo; (*of list etc*) cabeça *m*; (*toy*) pião *m*; (*Dress: blouse etc*) top *m*, blusa; (: *of pyjamas*) paletó *m* ▶ ADJ (*highest: shelf, step*) mais alto; (: *marks*) máximo; (*in rank*) principal, superior; (*best*) melhor ▶ VT (*exceed*) exceder; (*be first in*) estar à cabeça de; **the ~ of the milk** (BRIT) a nata do leite; **at the ~ of the stairs/page/street** no alto da escada/no alto da página/no começo da rua; **on ~ of** (*above*) sobre, em cima de; (*in addition to*) além de; **from ~ to toe** (BRIT) da cabeça aos pés; **from ~ to bottom** de cima abaixo; **at the ~ of the list** à cabeça da lista; **at the ~ of one's voice** aos gritos; **at ~ speed** a toda velocidade; **a ~ surgeon** um dos melhores cirurgiões; **over the ~** (*inf: behaviour etc*) extravagante
  ▶ **top up**, (US) **top off** VT completar; (*mobile phone*) recarregar

topaz ['tǝupæz] N topázio

topcoat ['tɔpkǝut] N sobretudo

topflight ['tɔpflaɪt] ADJ de primeira categoria

top floor N último andar *m*

top hat N cartola

top-heavy ADJ (*object*) desequilibrado

topic ['tɔpɪk] N tópico, assunto

topical ['tɔpɪkl] ADJ atual

topless ['tɔplɪs] ADJ (*bather etc*) topless *inv*, sem a parte superior do biquíni

top-level ADJ (*talks*) de alto nível

topmost ['tɔpmǝust] ADJ o mais alto

topography [tǝ'pɔgrǝfɪ] N topografia

topping ['tɔpɪŋ] N (*Culin*) cobertura

topple ['tɔpl] VT derrubar ▶ VI cair para frente

top-ranking [-'ræŋkɪŋ] ADJ de alto escalão

top-secret ADJ ultrassecreto, supersecreto

top-security (BRIT) ADJ de alta segurança

topsy-turvy ['tɔpsɪ'tǝːvɪ] ADJ, ADV de pernas para o ar, confuso, às avessas

top-up N (*for mobile phone*) recarga; **would you like a ~?** você quer mais?

top-up card N cartão de recarga (para celular)

torch [tɔːtʃ] N tocha, archote *m*; (BRIT: *electric torch*) lanterna

tore [tɔːʳ] PT *of* **tear²**

torment [N 'tɔːment, vt tɔː'ment] N tormento, suplício ▶ VT atormentar; (*fig: annoy*) chatear, aborrecer

torn [tɔːn] PP *of* **tear²** ▶ ADJ: **~ between** (*fig*) dividido entre

tornado [tɔː'neɪdǝu] (*pl* **tornadoes**) N tornado

torpedo [tɔː'piːdǝu] N (*pl* **torpedoes**) torpedo ▶ VT torpedear

torpedo boat N torpedeiro

torpor ['tɔ:pə^r] N torpor *m*
torque [tɔ:k] N momento de torção
torrent ['tɔrənt] N torrente *f*
torrential [tɔ'renʃl] ADJ torrencial
torrid ['tɔrɪd] ADJ tórrido; (*fig*) abrasador(a)
torso ['tɔ:səu] N torso
tortoise ['tɔ:təs] N tartaruga
tortoiseshell ['tɔ:təʃel] CPD de tartaruga
tortuous ['tɔ:tjuəs] ADJ tortuoso; (*argument, mind*) confuso
torture ['tɔ:tʃə^r] N tortura ▶ VT torturar; (*fig*) atormentar
torturer ['tɔ:tʃərə^r] N torturador(a) *m/f*
Tory ['tɔ:rɪ] (BRIT) ADJ, N (Pol) conservador(a) *m/f*
toss [tɔs] VT atirar, arremessar; (*head*) lançar para trás ▶ N (*of head*) meneio; (*of coin*) lançamento ▶ VI: **to ~ and turn in bed** virar de um lado para o outro na cama; **to ~ a coin** tirar cara ou coroa; **to ~ up for sth** (BRIT) jogar cara ou coroa por algo; **to win/lose the ~** ganhar/perder no cara ou coroa; (*Sport*) ganhar/perder o sorteio
tot [tɔt] N (BRIT: *drink*) copinho, golinho; (*child*) criancinha
▶ **tot up** (BRIT) VT (*figures*) somar, adicionar
total ['təutl] ADJ total ▶ N total *m*, soma ▶ VT (*add up*) somar; (*amount to*) montar a; **in ~** em total
totalitarian [təutælɪ'tɛərɪən] ADJ totalitário
totality [təu'tælɪtɪ] N totalidade *f*
totally ['təutəlɪ] ADV totalmente
tote bag [təut-] N sacola
totem pole ['təutəm-] N mastro totêmico
totter ['tɔtə^r] VI cambalear; (*object, government*) vacilar
touch [tʌtʃ] N (*sense, also skill: of pianist etc*) toque *m*; (*contact*) contato; (*Football*): **in ~** fora do campo ▶ VT tocar (em); (*tamper with*) mexer com; (*make contact with*) fazer contato com; (*emotionally*) comover; **the personal ~** o toque pessoal; **to put the finishing ~es to sth** dar os últimos retoques em algo; **a ~ of** (*fig*) um traço de; **to get in ~ with sb** entrar em contato com alguém; **to lose ~** (*friends*) perder o contato; **to be out of ~ with events** não estar a par dos acontecimentos; **no artist in the country can ~ him** nenhum artista no país se compara a ele
▶ **touch on** VT FUS (*topic*) tocar em, fazer menção de
▶ **touch up** VT (*paint*) retocar
touch-and-go ADJ arriscado; **it was ~ whether we did it** por pouco fizemos aquilo
touchdown ['tʌtʃdaun] N aterrissagem *f* (BR), aterragem *f* (PT); (*on sea*) amerissagem *f* (BR), amaragem *f* (PT); (*US Football*) touchdown *m* (*colocação da bola no chão atrás da linha de gol*)
touched [tʌtʃt] ADJ comovido; (*inf*) tocado, muito louco
touching ['tʌtʃɪŋ] ADJ comovedor(a)
touchline ['tʌtʃlaɪn] N (Sport) linha de fundo
touch screen N (*Comput*) touch screen *m*, ecrã táctil (PT)

touch-type VI datilografar sem olhar para as teclas
touchy ['tʌtʃɪ] ADJ (*person*) suscetível, sensível
tough [tʌf] ADJ duro; (*difficult*) difícil; (*resistant*) resistente; (*person: physically*) forte; (*: mentally*) tenaz; (*exam, experience*) brabo; (*firm*) firme, inflexível ▶ N (*gangster etc*) bandido, capanga *m*; **~ luck!** azar!; **they got ~ with the workers** começaram a falar grosso com os trabalhadores
toughen ['tʌfən] VT (*sb's character*) fortalecer; (*glass etc*) tornar mais resistente
toughness ['tʌfnɪs] N dureza; (*difficulty*) dificuldade *f*; (*resistance*) resistência; (*of person*) tenacidade *f*
toupee ['tu:peɪ] N peruca
tour ['tuə^r] N viagem *f*, excursão *f*; (*also: package tour*) excursão organizada; (*of town, museum*) visita; (*by artist*) turnê *f* ▶ VT (*country, city*) excursionar por; (*factory*) visitar; **to go on a ~ of** (*museum, region*) visitar; **to go on ~** fazer turnê
touring ['tuərɪŋ] N viagens *fpl* turísticas, turismo
tourism ['tuərɪzm] N turismo
tourist ['tuərɪst] N turista *m/f* ▶ CPD turístico; **the ~ trade** o turismo
tourist office N (*in country*) escritório de turismo; (*in embassy etc*) departamento de turismo
tournament ['tuənəmənt] N torneio
tourniquet ['tuənɪkeɪ] N (Med) torniquete *m*
tour operator (BRIT) N empresa de viagens
tousled ['tauzld] ADJ (*hair*) despenteado
tout [taut] VI: **to ~ for** angariar clientes para ▶ VT (BRIT): **to ~ sth (around)** tentar vender algo ▶ N (BRIT: *ticket tout*) cambista *m/f*
tow [təu] N: **to give sb a ~** (*Aut*) rebocar alguém ▶ VT rebocar; **"on ~"** (BRIT), **"in ~"** (US) (*Aut*) "rebocado"; **with her husband in ~** com o marido a tiracolo
toward [tə'wɔ:d], **towards** [tə'wɔ:dz] PREP em direção a; (*of attitude*) para com; (*of purpose*) para; **~(s) noon/the end of the year** perto do meio-dia/do fim do ano; **to feel friendly ~(s) sb** sentir amizade em relação a alguém
towel ['tauəl] N toalha; (*also: tea towel*) pano; **to throw in the ~** (*fig*) dar-se por vencido
towelling ['tauəlɪŋ] N (*fabric*) tecido para toalhas
towel rail, (US) **towel rack** N toalheiro
tower ['tauə^r] N torre *f* ▶ VI (*building, mountain*) elevar-se; **to ~ above** *or* **over sb/sth** dominar alguém/algo
tower block (BRIT) N prédio alto, espigão *m*, cortiço (BR)
towering ['tauərɪŋ] ADJ elevado; (*figure*) eminente
towline ['təulaɪn] N cabo de reboque
town [taun] N cidade *f*; **to go to ~** ir à cidade; (*fig*) fazer com entusiasmo, mandar brasa (BR); **in the ~** na cidade; **to be out of ~** (*person*) estar fora da cidade

t

town centre N centro (da cidade)
town clerk N administrador(a) m/f municipal
town council N câmara municipal
town hall N prefeitura (BR), concelho (PT)
town plan N mapa m da cidade
town planner N urbanista m/f
town planning N urbanismo
townspeople ['taunzpi:pl] NPL habitantes mpl da cidade
towpath ['təupɑ:θ] N caminho de sirga
towrope ['təurəup] N cabo de reboque
tow truck (US) N reboque m (BR), pronto socorro (PT)
toxic ['tɔksɪk] ADJ tóxico
toxin ['tɔksɪn] N toxina
toy [tɔɪ] N brinquedo ▶ CPD de brinquedo
▶ **toy with** VT FUS (object, food) brincar com; (idea) contemplar
toy shop N loja de brinquedos
trace [treɪs] N (sign) sinal m; (small amount) traço ▶ VT (through paper) decalcar; (draw) traçar, esboçar; (follow) seguir a pista de; (locate) encontrar; **without ~** (disappear) sem deixar vestígios; **there was no ~ of it** não havia nenhum vestígio disso
trace element N elemento traço
trachea [trə'kɪə] N (Anat) traqueia
tracing paper ['treɪsɪŋ-] N papel m de decalque
track [træk] N (mark) pegada, vestígio; (path: gen) caminho, vereda; (: of bullet etc) trajetória; (: of suspect, animal) pista, rasto; (Rail) trilhos (BR), carris mpl (PT); (on CD) faixa; (Sport) pista; (on record) faixa ▶ VT seguir a pista de; **to keep ~ of** não perder de vista; (fig) manter-se informado sobre; **to be on the right ~** (fig) estar no caminho certo
▶ **track down** VT (prey) seguir a pista de; (sth lost) procurar e encontrar
tracked [trækt] ADJ com lagarta
tracker dog ['trækə-] (BRIT) N cão m policial
track events NPL (Sport) corridas fpl
tracking station ['trækɪŋ-] N (Space) estação f de rastreamento
track record N: **to have a good ~** (fig) ter uma boa folha de serviço
track suit N roupa de jogging
tract [trækt] N (Geo) região f; (pamphlet) folheto; **respiratory ~** (Anat) aparelho respiratório
traction ['trækʃən] N tração f; (Med): **in ~** em tração
tractor ['træktə'] N trator m
tractor feed N (on printer) alimentação f a trator
trade [treɪd] N comércio; (skill, job) ofício ▶ VI negociar, comerciar ▶ VT: **to ~ sth (for sth)** trocar algo (por algo); **to ~ with/in** comerciar com/em; **foreign ~** comércio exterior; **Department of T~ and Industry** (BRIT) Ministério de Indústria e Comércio
▶ **trade in** VT dar como parte do pagamento
trade barrier N barreira comercial

trade deficit N déficit m na balança comercial
Trade Descriptions Act (BRIT) N lei contra a publicidade mentirosa
trade discount N desconto de revendedor
trade fair N feira industrial
trade-in N venda
trade-in price N valor de um objeto usado que se desconta do preço do outro novo
trademark ['treɪdmɑ:k] N marca registrada
trade mission N missão f comercial
trade name N (of product) marca or nome comercial de um produto; (of company) razão f social
trader ['treɪdə'] N comerciante m/f
trade secret N segredo do ofício
tradesman ['treɪdzmən] (irreg: like man) N (shopkeeper) lojista m
trade union N sindicato
trade unionism [-'ju:njənɪzəm] N sindicalismo
trade unionist [-'ju:njənɪst] N sindicalista m/f
trade wind N vento alísio
trading ['treɪdɪŋ] N comércio
trading estate (BRIT) N parque m industrial
trading stamp N selo de bonificação
tradition [trə'dɪʃən] N tradição f
traditional [trə'dɪʃənl] ADJ tradicional
traffic ['træfɪk] N trânsito; (air traffic etc) tráfego; (illegal) tráfico ▶ VI: **to ~ in** (pej: liquor, drugs) traficar com, fazer tráfico com
traffic circle (US) N rotatória
traffic island N refúgio de segurança (para pedestres)
traffic jam N engarrafamento, congestionamento
trafficker ['træfɪkə'] N traficante m/f
traffic lights NPL sinal m luminoso
traffic offence (BRIT) N infração f de trânsito
traffic sign N placa de sinalização
traffic violation (US) N infração f
traffic warden N guarda m/f de trânsito
tragedy ['trædʒədɪ] N tragédia
tragic ['trædʒɪk] ADJ trágico
trail [treɪl] N (tracks) rasto, pista; (path) caminho, trilha; (wake) esteira; (of smoke, dust) rasto, rastro ▶ VT (drag) arrastar; (follow) seguir a pista de; (follow closely) vigiar ▶ VI arrastar-se; (hang loosely) pender; (in game, contest) ficar para trás; **to be on sb's ~** estar no encalço de alguém
▶ **trail away** VI (sound, voice) ir-se perdendo; (interest) diminuir
▶ **trail behind** VI atrasar-se
▶ **trail off** VI (sound, voice) ir-se perdendo; (interest) diminuir
trailer ['treɪlə'] N (Aut) reboque m; (US: caravan) trailer m (BR), rulote f (PT); (Cinema) trailer
trailer truck (US) N caminhão-reboque m
train [treɪn] N trem m (BR), comboio (PT); (of dress) cauda; (series) sequência, série f; (followers) séquito, comitiva ▶ VT (professionals etc) formar; (teach skills to) instruir; (Sport) treinar; (dog) adestrar, amestrar; (point: gun

etc): **to ~ on** apontar para ▶ vɪ (*learn a skill*)
instruir-se; (*Sport*) treinar; (*be educated*) ser
treinado; **to lose one's ~ of thought** perder
o fio; **to go by ~** ir de trem; **to ~ sb to do sth**
treinar alguém para fazer algo

train attendant (*us*) N revisor(a) *m/f*

trained [treɪnd] ADJ (*worker*) especializado;
(*teacher*) formado; (*animal*) adestrado

trainee [treɪ'niː] N estagiário(-a); (*in trade*)
aprendiz *m/f*

trainer ['treɪnə^r] N (*Sport*) treinador(a) *m/f*;
(*of animals*) adestrador(a) *m/f*; **trainers** NPL
(*shoes*) tênis *m*

training ['treɪnɪŋ] N instrução *f*; (*Sport, for
occupation*) treinamento; (*professional*)
formação; **in ~** en treinamento

training college N (*for teachers*) Escola Normal

training course N curso de formação
profissional

training shoes NPL tênis *m*

traipse [treɪps] vɪ perambular

trait [treɪt] N traço

traitor ['treɪtə^r] N traidor(a) *m/f*

trajectory [trə'dʒɛktərɪ] N trajetória

tram [træm] N (*also*: **tramcar**) bonde *m*
(*BR*), eléctrico (*PT*)

tramline ['træmlaɪn] N trilho para bondes

tramp [træmp] N (*person*) vagabundo(-a);
(*inf, pej: woman*) piranha ▶ vɪ caminhar
pesadamente ▶ vᴛ (*walk through: town, streets*)
percorrer, andar por

trample ['træmpl] vᴛ: **to ~ (underfoot)**
calcar aos pés

trampoline ['træmpəliːn] N trampolim *m*

trance [trɑːns] N estupor *m*; (*Med*) transe *m*
hipnótico; **to go into a ~** cair em transe

tranquil ['træŋkwɪl] ADJ tranquilo

tranquillity [træŋ'kwɪlɪtɪ] N tranquilidade *f*

tranquillizer ['træŋkwɪlaɪzə^r] N (*Med*)
tranquilizante *m*

transact [træn'zækt] vᴛ (*business*) negociar

transaction [træn'zækʃən] N transação *f*,
negócio; **transactions** NPL (*minutes*) ata;
cash ~ transação à vista

transatlantic [trænzət'læntɪk] ADJ
transatlântico

transcend [træn'sɛnd] vᴛ transcender,
exceder; (*excel over*) ultrapassar

transcendental [trænsɛn'dɛntl] ADJ:
~ meditation meditação *f* transcendental

transcribe [træn'skraɪb] vᴛ transcrever

transcript ['trænskrɪpt] N cópia, traslado

transcription [træn'skrɪpʃən] N transcrição *f*

transept ['trænsɛpt] N transepto

transfer [*n* 'trænsfə^r, *vt* træns'fəː^r] N
transferência; (*picture, design*) decalcomania
▶ vᴛ transferir; **to ~ the charges** (*BRIT Tel*)
ligar a cobrar; **by bank ~** por transferência
bancária

transferable [træns'fəːrəbl] ADJ transferível;
not ~ intransferível

transfix [træns'fɪks] vᴛ trespassar; (*fig*): **~ed
with fear** paralisado de medo

transform [træns'fɔːm] vᴛ transformar

transformation [trænsfə'meɪʃən] N
transformação *f*

transformer [træns'fɔːmə^r] N (*Elec*)
transformador *m*

transfusion [træns'fjuːʒən] N (*also*: **blood
transfusion**) transfusão *f* (de sangue)

transgress [træns'grɛs] vᴛ transgredir

transient ['trænzɪənt] ADJ transitório

transistor [træn'zɪstə^r] N (*Elec*: *also*:
transistor radio) transistor *m*

transit ['trænzɪt] N: **in ~** em trânsito, de
passagem

transit camp N campo de trânsito

transition [træn'zɪʃən] N transição *f*

transitional [træn'zɪʃənl] ADJ de transição,
transicional

transitive ['trænzɪtɪv] ADJ (*Ling*) transitivo

transit lounge N salão *m* de trânsito

transitory ['trænzɪtərɪ] ADJ transitório

translate [trænz'leɪt] vᴛ traduzir; **to ~ from/
into** traduzir do/para o

translation [trænz'leɪʃən] N tradução *f*

translator [trænz'leɪtə^r] N tradutor(a) *m/f*

translucent [trænz'luːsnt] ADJ translúcido

transmission [trænz'mɪʃən] N transmissão *f*

transmit [trænz'mɪt] vᴛ transmitir

transmitter [trænz'mɪtə^r] N transmissor *m*;
(*station*) emissora

transparency [træns'pɛərnsɪ] N (*of glass etc*)
transparência; (*BRIT Phot*) diapositivo

transparent [træns'pærnt] ADJ transparente

transpire [træns'paɪə^r] vɪ (*turn out*) tornar
sabido; (*happen*) ocorrer, acontecer; (*become
known*): **it finally ~d that ...** no final
soube-se que ...

transplant [*vt* træns'plɑːnt, *n* 'trænsplɑːnt] vᴛ
transplantar ▶ N (*Med*) transplante *m*; **to
have a heart ~** ter um transplante de
coração

transport [*n* 'trænspɔːt, *vt* træns'pɔːt] N
transporte *m* ▶ vᴛ transportar; (*carry*)
acarretar; **public ~** transportes coletivos;
Department of T~ (*BRIT*) ministério dos
Transportes

transportation [trænspɔː'teɪʃən] N
transporte *m*; **Department of T~** (*us*)
ministério da Infraestrutura

transport café (*BRIT*) N lanchonete *f* de
estrada

transpose [træns'pəuz] vᴛ transpor

transverse ['trænzvəːs] ADJ transversal

transvestite [trænz'vɛstaɪt] N travesti *m/f*

trap [træp] N (*snare*) armadilha, cilada; (*trick*)
cilada; (*carriage*) aranha, charrete *f* ▶ vᴛ
(*animal, person*) pegar numa armadilha;
(*immobilize*) bloquear; (*jam*) emperrar; **to be
~ped** (*in bad marriage, fire*) estar preso(-a); **to
set** *ou* **lay a ~ (for sb)** montar uma
armadilha (para alguém); **to shut one's ~**
(*inf*) calar a boca; **to ~ one's finger in the
door** prender o dedo na porta

trap door N alçapão *m*

t

trapeze [trə'piːz] N trapézio
trapper ['træpəʳ] N caçador m de peles
trappings ['træpɪŋz] NPL adornos mpl, enfeites mpl
trash [træʃ] N (pej: goods) refugo, escória; (: nonsense) besteiras fpl; (us: rubbish) lixo
trash can (us) N lata de lixo
trauma ['trɔːmə] N trauma m
traumatic [trɔː'mætɪk] ADJ traumático
travel ['trævl] N viagem f ▶ VI viajar; (sound) propagar-se; (news) levar; (wine): **this wine ~s well** este vinho não sofre alteração ao ser transportado; (move) deslocar-se ▶ VT (distance) percorrer; **travels** NPL (journeys) viagens fpl
travel agency N agência de viagens
travel agent N agente m/f de viagens
travel brochure N prospecto turístico
traveller, (us) **traveler** ['trævələʳ] N viajante m/f; (Comm) caixeiro(-a) viajante
traveller's cheque, (us) **traveler's check** N cheque m de viagem
travelling, (us) **traveling** ['trævəlɪŋ] N as viagens, viajar m ▶ ADJ (circus, exhibition) itinerante; (salesman) viajante ▶ CPD (bag, clock, expenses) de viagem
travelling salesman, (us) **traveling salesman** (irreg: like **man**) N caixeiro viajante
travelogue ['trævəlɔg] N (book) livro de viagem; (film) documentário de viagem
travel sickness N enjoo
traverse ['trævəs] VT atravessar
travesty ['trævəstɪ] N paródia
trawler ['trɔːləʳ] N traineira
tray [treɪ] N bandeja; (on desk) cesta
treacherous ['trɛtʃərəs] ADJ traiçoeiro; (ground, tide) perigoso; **road conditions are ~** as estradas estão perigosas
treachery ['trɛtʃərɪ] N traição f
treacle ['triːkl] N melado
tread [trɛd] (pt **trod,** pp **trodden**) VI pisar ▶ N (step) passo, pisada; (sound) passada; (of stair) piso; (of tyre) banda de rodagem ▶ **tread on** VT FUS pisar (em)
treadle ['trɛdl] N pedal m
treas. ABBR = **treasurer**
treason ['triːzn] N traição f
treasure ['trɛʒəʳ] N tesouro; (person) joia ▶ VT (value) apreciar, estimar; **treasures** NPL (art treasures etc) preciosidades fpl
treasure hunt N caça ao tesouro
treasurer ['trɛʒərəʳ] N tesoureiro(-a)
treasury ['trɛʒərɪ] N tesouraria; (Pol): **the T~** (BRIT) or **T~ Department** (US) ≈ o Tesouro Nacional
treasury bill N letra do Tesouro (Nacional)
treat [triːt] N (present) regalo, deleite m; (pleasure) prazer m ▶ VT tratar; **to ~ sb to sth** convidar alguém para algo; **to give sb a ~** dar um prazer a alguém; **to ~ sth as a joke** não levar algo a sério
treatise ['triːtɪz] N tratado

treatment ['triːtmənt] N tratamento; **to have ~ for sth** (Med) fazer tratamento para algo
treaty ['triːtɪ] N tratado, acordo
treble ['trɛbl] ADJ tríplice ▶ N (Mus) soprano ▶ VT triplicar ▶ VI triplicar(-se)
treble clef N clave f de sol
tree [triː] N árvore f
tree-lined ADJ ladeado de árvores
treetop ['triːtɔp] N copa (de árvore)
tree trunk N tronco de árvore
trek [trɛk] N (long journey) jornada; (walk) caminhada; (as holiday) excursão f (a pé) ▶ VI (as holiday) caminhar
trellis ['trɛlɪs] N grade f de ripas, latada
tremble ['trɛmbl] VI tremer
trembling ['trɛmblɪŋ] N tremor m ▶ ADJ trêmulo, trepidante
tremendous [trɪ'mɛndəs] ADJ tremendo; (enormous) enorme; (excellent) sensacional, fantástico
tremendously [trɪ'mɛndəslɪ] ADV (well, clever etc) extraordinariamente; (very much) muitíssimo; (very well) muito bem
tremor ['trɛməʳ] N tremor m; (also: **earth tremor**) tremor de terra
trench [trɛntʃ] N trincheira
trench coat N capa (de chuva)
trench warfare N guerra de trincheiras
trend [trɛnd] N (tendency) tendência; (of events) curso; (fashion) modismo, tendência; (on social network: also: **trending topic**) trending topic m ▶ VI (on social network) ser compartilhado no Twitter até virar trending topic; **a ~ towards/away from doing** uma tendência a/contra fazer; **to set the ~** dar o tom; **to set a ~** lançar uma moda; **what's ~ing on Twitter?** quais são os trending topics do Twitter?
trendy ['trɛndɪ] ADJ (idea) de acordo com a tendência atual; (clothes) da última moda
trepidation [trɛpɪ'deɪʃən] N trepidação f; (fear) apreensão f
trespass ['trɛspəs] VI: **to ~ on** invadir; **"no ~ing"** "entrada proibida"
trespasser ['trɛspəsəʳ] N intruso(-a); **"~s will be prosecuted"** "aqueles que invadirem esta área serão punidos"
tress [trɛs] N trança
trestle ['trɛsl] N cavalete m
trestle table N mesa de cavaletes
trial ['traɪəl] N (Law) processo; (test: of machine etc) prova, teste m; (hardship) provação f; **trials** NPL (unpleasant experiences) dissabores mpl; (Sport) eliminatórias fpl; **horse ~s** provas fpl de equitação; **by ~ and error** por tentativas; **~ by jury** julgamento por júri; **to be sent for ~** ser levado a julgamento; **to be on ~** ser julgado
trial balance N (Comm) balancete m
trial basis N: **on a ~** em experiência
trial period N período de experiência
trial run N ensaio

triangle ['traɪæŋɡl] N (*Math, Mus*) triângulo

triangular [traɪ'æŋɡjʊlə^r] ADJ triangular

triathlon [traɪ'æθlən] N triatlo

tribal ['traɪbəl] ADJ tribal

tribe [traɪb] N tribo *f*

tribesman ['traɪbzmən] (*irreg: like* **man**) N membro da tribo

tribulation [trɪbju'leɪʃən] N tribulação *f*, aflição *f*

tribunal [traɪ'bju:nl] N tribunal *m*

tributary ['trɪbju:tərɪ] N (*river*) afluente *m*

tribute ['trɪbju:t] N homenagem *f*; (*payment*) tributo; **to pay ~ to** prestar homenagem a, homenagear

trice [traɪs] N: **in a ~** num instante

trick [trɪk] N truque *m*; (*deceit*) fraude *f*, trapaça; (*joke*) peça, brincadeira; (*skill, knack*) habilidade *f*; (*Cards*) vaza ▶ VT enganar; **to play a ~ on sb** pregar uma peça em alguém; **to ~ sb into doing sth** induzir alguém a fazer algo pela astúcia; **to ~ sb out of sth** obter algo de alguém pela astúcia; **it's a ~ of the light** é uma ilusão de ótica; **that should do the ~** (*inf*) isso deveria dar resultado

trickery ['trɪkərɪ] N trapaça, astúcia

trickle ['trɪkl] N (*of water etc*) fio (de água) ▶ VI gotejar, pingar; **to ~ in/out** (*people*) ir entrando/saindo aos poucos

trick question N pergunta capciosa

trickster ['trɪkstə^r] N vigarista *m/f*

tricky ['trɪkɪ] ADJ difícil, complicado

tricycle ['traɪsɪkl] N triciclo

trifle ['traɪfl] N (*small detail*) bobagem *f*, besteira; (*Culin*) *tipo de bolo com fruta e creme* ▶ ADV: **a ~ long** um pouquinho longo ▶ VI: **to ~ with** brincar com

trifling ['traɪflɪŋ] ADJ insignificante

trigger ['trɪɡə^r] N (*of gun*) gatilho ▶ **trigger off** VT desencadear

trigonometry [trɪɡə'nɔmətrɪ] N trigonometria

trilby ['trɪlbɪ] (*BRIT*) N (*also:* **trilby hat**) chapéu *m* de feltro

trill [trɪl] N (*of bird, Mus*) trinado, trilo

trilogy ['trɪlədʒɪ] N trilogia

trim [trɪm] ADJ (*figure*) elegante; (*house*) arrumado; (*garden*) bem cuidado ▶ N (*haircut etc*) aparada; (*on car*) estofamento; (*embellishment*) acabamento, remate *m* ▶ VT (*cut*) aparar, cortar; (*decorate*): **to ~ (with)** enfeitar (com); (*Naut: sail*) ajustar; **to keep in (good) ~** manter em bom estado

trimmings ['trɪmɪŋz] NPL decoração *f*; (*extras: Culin*) acompanhamentos *mpl*

Trinidad and Tobago ['trɪnɪdæd-] N Trinidad e Tobago (*no article*)

Trinity ['trɪnɪtɪ] N: **the ~** a Trindade

trinket ['trɪŋkɪt] N bugiganga; (*piece of jewellery*) berloque *m*, bijuteria

trio ['tri:əu] N trio

trip [trɪp] N viagem *f*; (*outing*) excursão *f*; (*stumble*) tropeção *m* ▶ VI (*also:* **trip up**) tropeçar; (*go lightly*) andar com passos ligeiros ▶ VT fazer tropeçar; **on a ~** de viagem ▶ **trip up** VI tropeçar ▶ VT passar uma rasteira em

tripartite [traɪ'pɑ:taɪt] ADJ (*in three parts*) tripartido; (*Pol*) tripartidário

tripe [traɪp] N (*Culin*) bucho, tripa; (*pej: rubbish*) bobagem *f*

triple ['trɪpl] ADJ triplo, tríplice ▶ ADV: **~ the distance/the speed** três vezes a distância/a velocidade

triplets ['trɪplɪts] NPL trigêmeos(-as) *mpl/fpl*

triplicate ['trɪplɪkət] N: **in ~** em triplicata, em três vias

tripod ['traɪpɔd] N tripé *m*

Tripoli ['trɪpəlɪ] N Trípoli

tripper ['trɪpə^r] (*BRIT*) N excursionista *m/f*

tripwire ['trɪpwaɪə^r] N fio de disparo

trite [traɪt] ADJ gasto, banal

triumph ['traɪʌmf] N (*satisfaction*) satisfação *f*; (*great achievement*) triunfo ▶ VI: **to ~ (over)** triunfar (sobre)

triumphal [traɪ'ʌmfl] ADJ triunfal

triumphant [traɪ'ʌmfənt] ADJ triunfante

trivia ['trɪvɪə] NPL trivialidades *fpl*

trivial ['trɪvɪəl] ADJ insignificante; (*commonplace*) trivial

triviality [trɪvɪ'ælɪtɪ] N trivialidade *f*

trivialize ['trɪvɪəlaɪz] VT banalizar, trivializar

trod [trɔd] PT *of* **tread**

trodden ['trɔdn] PP *of* **tread**

troll [trɔl, trəul] (*inf*) N (*Comput*) troll *m* ▶ VI trollar

trolley ['trɔlɪ] N carrinho; (*table on wheels*) mesa volante

trolley bus N ônibus *m* elétrico (*BR*), trólei *m* (*PT*)

trollop ['trɔləp] N rameira

trombone [trɔm'bəun] N trombone *m*

troop [tru:p] N bando, grupo ▶ VI: **to ~ in/out** entrar/sair em bando; **troops** NPL (*Mil*) tropas *fpl*; (: *men*) homens *mpl*; **~ing the colour** (*BRIT: ceremony*) saudação da bandeira

troop carrier N (*plane*) avião *m* de transporte de tropas; (*Naut: also:* **troopship**) navio-transporte *m*

trooper ['tru:pə^r] N (*Mil*) soldado de cavalaria; (*US: policeman*) ≈ policial *m* militar, PM *m*

troopship ['tru:pʃɪp] N navio-transporte *m*

trophy ['trəufɪ] N troféu *m*

tropic ['trɔpɪk] N trópico; **in the ~s** nos trópicos; **T~ of Cancer/Capricorn** Trópico de Câncer/Capricórnio

tropical ['trɔpɪkl] ADJ tropical

trot [trɔt] N trote *m*; (*fast pace*) passo rápido ▶ VI trotar; (*person*) andar rapidamente; **on the ~** (*fig: inf*) a fio ▶ **trot out** VT (*excuse, reason*) apresentar, dar; (*names, facts*) recitar

trouble ['trʌbl] N problema(s) *m(pl)*, dificuldade(s) *f(pl)*; (*worry*) preocupação *f*; (*bother, effort*) incômodo, trabalho; (*Pol*) distúrbios *mpl*; (*Med*): **stomach ~** *etc* problemas *mpl* gástricos *etc* ▶ VT perturbar;

t

(*worry*) preocupar, incomodar ▶ vi: **to ~ to do
sth** incomodar-se *or* preocupar-se de fazer
algo; **troubles** NPL (*Pol etc*) distúrbios *mpl*; **to
be in ~** (*in difficulty*) estar num aperto; (*for
doing sth wrong*) estar numa encrenca; (*ship,
climber etc*) estar em dificuldade; **to go to the
~ of doing sth** dar-se ao trabalho de fazer
algo; **to have ~ doing sth** ter dificuldade
em fazer algo; **it's no ~!** não tem problema!;
please don't ~ yourself por favor, não se dê
trabalho!; **the ~ is ...** o problema é ...;
what's the ~? qual é o problema?

troubled ['trʌbld] ADJ (*person*) preocupado;
(*epoch, life*) agitado

trouble-free ADJ sem problemas

troublemaker ['trʌblmeɪkəʳ] N criador(a)-de-
casos *m/f*; (*child*) encrenqueiro(-a)

troubleshooter ['trʌblʃuːtəʳ] N (*in conflict*)
conciliador(a) *m/f*; (*solver of problems*)
solucionador(a) *m/f* de problemas

troublesome ['trʌblsəm] ADJ importuno;
(*child, cough*) incômodo

trouble spot N área de conflito

trough [trɔf] N (*also:* **drinking trough**)
bebedouro, cocho; (*also:* **feeding trough**)
gamela; (*depression*) depressão *f*; (*channel*)
canal *m*; **~ of low pressure** (*Meteorology*)
cavado de baixa pressão

trounce [traʊns] VT (*defeat*) dar uma surra *or*
um banho em

troupe [truːp] N companhia teatral

trouser press N passadeira de calças

trousers ['traʊzəz] NPL calça (*BR*), calças *fpl* (*PT*)

trouser suit (*BRIT*) N terninho (*BR*), conjunto
de calças casaco (*PT*)

trousseau ['truːsəu] (*pl* **trousseaux** *or*
trousseaus) N enxoval *m*

trousseaux ['truːsəuz] NPL *of* **trousseau**

trout [traʊt] N INV truta

trowel ['traʊəl] N (*garden tool*) colher *f* de
jardineiro; (*builder's tool*) colher *f* de pedreiro

truancy ['truːənsɪ] N evasão *f* escolar

truant ['truːənt] (*BRIT*) N: **to play ~** matar aula
(*BR*), fazer gazeta (*PT*)

truce [truːs] N trégua, armistício

truck [trʌk] N caminhão *m* (*BR*), camião *m* (*PT*);
(*Rail*) vagão *m*

truck driver N caminhoneiro(-a) (*BR*),
camionista *m/f* (*PT*)

trucker ['trʌkəʳ] (*esp US*) N caminhoneiro (*BR*),
camionista *m/f* (*PT*)

truck farm (*US*) N horta

trucking ['trʌkɪŋ] (*esp US*) N transporte *m*
rodoviário

trucking company (*US*) N transportadora

truck stop (*US*) N bar *m* de estrada

truculent ['trʌkjulənt] ADJ agressivo

trudge [trʌdʒ] VI andar com dificuldade,
arrastar-se

true [truː] ADJ verdadeiro; (*accurate*) exato;
(*genuine*) autêntico; (*faithful*) fiel, leal; (*wall*)
aprumado; (*beam*) nivelado; (*wheel*)
alinhado; **to come ~** realizar-se, tornar-se

realidade; **~ to life** realista, fiel à realidade;
it's ~ é verdade

truffle ['trʌfl] N trufa; (*sweet*) docinho de
chocolate *or* rum

truly ['truːlɪ] ADV (*really*) realmente; (*truthfully*)
verdadeiramente; (*faithfully*) fielmente;
yours ~ (*in letter*) atenciosamente

trump [trʌmp] N trunfo; **to turn** *or* **come up
~s** (*fig*) salvar a pátria

trump card N (*also fig*) trunfo

trumped-up [trʌmpt-] ADJ inventado,
forjado

trumpet ['trʌmpɪt] N trombeta

truncated [trʌŋ'keɪtɪd] ADJ truncado

truncheon ['trʌntʃən] N cassetete *m*

trundle ['trʌndl] VT (*push slowly: trolley etc*)
empurrar lentamente ▶ vi: **to ~ along** rolar
or rodar fazendo ruído

trunk [trʌŋk] N (*of tree, person*) tronco; (*of
elephant*) tromba; (*case*) baú *m*; (*US Aut*) mala
(*BR*), porta-bagagens *m* (*PT*); **trunks** NPL (*also:*
swimming trunks) sunga (*BR*), calções *mpl* de
banho (*PT*)

trunk call (*BRIT*) N (*Tel*) ligação *f* interurbana

trunk road (*BRIT*) N ≈ rodovia nacional

truss [trʌs] N (*Med*) funda ▶ vT: **to ~ (up)** atar,
amarrar

trust [trʌst] N confiança; (*responsibility*)
responsabilidade *f*; (*Comm*) truste *m*; (*Law*)
fideicomisso ▶ vT (*rely on*) confiar em;
(*entrust*): **to ~ sth to sb** confiar algo a
alguém; (*hope*): **to ~ (that)** esperar que; **to
take sth on ~** aceitar algo sem verificação
prévia; **in ~** (*Law*) em fideicomisso

trust company N companhia fiduciária

trusted ['trʌstɪd] ADJ de confiança

trustee [trʌs'tiː] N (*Law*) fideicomissário(-a),
depositário(-a); (*of school etc*)
administrador(a) *m/f*

trustful ['trʌstful] ADJ confiante

trust fund N fundo de fideicomisso

trusting ['trʌstɪŋ] ADJ confiante

trustworthy ['trʌstwɜːðɪ] ADJ digno de
confiança

trusty ['trʌstɪ] ADJ fidedigno, fiel

truth [truːθ, *pl* truːðz] N verdade *f*

truthful ['truːθful] ADJ (*person*) sincero,
honesto; (*account*) verídico

truthfully ['truːθfulɪ] ADV sinceramente

truthfulness ['truːθfulnɪs] N veracidade *f*

try [traɪ] N tentativa; (*Rugby*) ensaio ▶ vT
(*Law*) julgar; (*test: sth new*) provar, pôr à prova;
(*attempt*) tentar; (*food etc*) experimentar;
(*strain*) cansar ▶ vi tentar; **to have a ~** fazer
uma tentativa; **to ~ to do sth** tentar fazer
algo; **to ~ one's (very) best** *or* **one's (very)
hardest** fazer (todo) o possível; **to give sth
a ~** tentar algo

▶ **try on** vT (*clothes*) experimentar, provar

to ~ it on with sb (*fig: test sb's patience*) testar
a paciência de alguém; (*: try to trick*) tentar
engambelar alguém

▶ **try out** vT experimentar, provar

trying ['traɪɪŋ] ADJ (*person, experience*) exasperante

tsar [zɑ:ʳ] N czar *m*

T-shirt N camiseta (BR), T-shirt *f* (PT)

T-square N régua em T

TT ADJ ABBR (BRIT *inf*) = **teetotal** ▶ ABBR (US *Post*) = **Trust Territory**

tub [tʌb] N tina; (*bath*) banheira

tuba ['tju:bə] N tuba

tubby ['tʌbɪ] ADJ gorducho

tube [tju:b] N tubo; (*pipe*) cano; (BRIT: *underground*) metrô *m* (BR), metro(-politano) (PT); (*for tyre*) câmara-de-ar *f*

tubeless ['tju:blɪs] ADJ sem câmara

tuber ['tju:bəʳ] N (*Bot*) tubérculo

tuberculosis [tjubɜ:kju'ləusɪs] N tuberculose *f*

tube station (BRIT) N estação *f* de metrô

tubing ['tju:bɪŋ] N tubulação *f*, encanamento; **a piece of ~** um pedaço de tubo

tubular ['tju:bjuləʳ] ADJ tubular; (*furniture*) tubiforme

TUC (BRIT) N ABBR (= *Trades Union Congress*) ≈ CUT *f*

tuck [tʌk] N (*Sewing*) prega, dobra ▶ VT (*put*) enfiar, meter

▶ **tuck away** VT esconder; **to be ~ed away** estar escondido

▶ **tuck in** VT enfiar para dentro; (*child*) aconchegar ▶ VI (*eat*) comer com apetite

▶ **tuck up** VT (*child*) aconchegar

tuck shop N loja de balas

Tue., Tues. ABBR (= *Tuesday*) ter, 3ª

Tuesday ['tju:zdɪ] N terça-feira; (**the date**) **today is ~ 23rd March** hoje é terça-feira, 23 de março; **on ~** na terça(-feira); **on ~s** nas terças(-feiras); **every ~** todas as terças(-feiras); **every other ~** terça-feira sim, terça-feira não; **last/next ~** na terça-feira passada/na terça-feira que vem; **~ next** na terça-feira que vem; **the following ~** na terça-feira seguinte; **a week on ~** sem ser essa terça, a outra; **the ~ before last** na terça-feira retrasada; **the ~ after next** sem ser essa terça, a outra; **~ morning/ lunchtime/afternoon/evening** na terça-feira de manhã/ao meio-dia/à tarde/à noite; **~ night** na terça-feira à noite; **~'s newspaper** o jornal de terça-feira

tuft [tʌft] N penacho; (*of grass etc*) tufo

tug [tʌg] N (*ship*) rebocador *m* ▶ VT puxar

tug-of-war N cabo-de-guerra *m*; (*fig*) disputa

tuition [tju:'ɪʃən] N ensino; (*private tuition*) aulas *fpl* particulares; (US: *fees*) taxas *fpl* escolares

tulip ['tju:lɪp] N tulipa

tumble ['tʌmbl] N (*fall*) queda ▶ VI cair, tombar ▶ VT derrubar; **to ~ to sth** (*inf*) sacar algo

tumbledown ['tʌmbldaun] ADJ em ruínas

tumble dryer (BRIT) N máquina de secar roupa

tumbler ['tʌmbləʳ] N copo

tummy ['tʌmɪ] (*inf*) N (*belly*) barriga; (*stomach*) estômago

tumour, (US) **tumor** ['tju:məʳ] N tumor *m*

tumult ['tju:mʌlt] N tumulto

tumultuous [tju:'mʌltjuəs] ADJ tumultuado

tuna ['tju:nə] N INV (*also*: **tuna fish**) atum *m*

tune [tju:n] N melodia ▶ VT (*Mus*) afinar; (*Radio, TV*) sintonizar; (*Aut*) regular; **to be in/ out of ~** (*instrument*) estar afinado/ desafinado; (*singer*) cantar afinado/ desafinar; **to be in/out of ~ with** (*fig*) harmonizar-se com/destoar de; **she was robbed to the ~ of £10,000** ela foi roubada em mais de £10,000

▶ **tune in** VI (*Radio, TV*): **to ~ in (to)** sintonizar (com)

▶ **tune up** VI (*musician*) afinar (seu instrumento)

tuneful ['tju:nful] ADJ melodioso

tuner ['tju:nəʳ] N (*radio set*) sintonizador *m*; **piano ~** afinador(a) *m/f* de pianos

tuner amplifier N sintonizador *m* amplificador

tungsten ['tʌŋstən] N tungstênio

tunic ['tju:nɪk] N túnica

tuning ['tju:nɪŋ] N (*of radio*) sintonia; (*Mus*) afinação *f*; (*of car*) regulagem *f*

tuning fork N diapasão *m*

Tunis ['tju:nɪs] N Túnis

Tunisia [tju:'nɪzɪə] N Tunísia

Tunisian [tju:'nɪzɪən] ADJ, N tunisiano(-a)

tunnel ['tʌnl] N túnel *m*; (*in mine*) galeria ▶ VI abrir um túnel (*or* uma galeria)

tunny ['tʌnɪ] N atum *m*

turban ['tɜ:bən] N turbante *m*

turbid ['tɜ:bɪd] ADJ turvo

turbine ['tɜ:baɪn] N turbina

turbojet [tɜ:bəu'dʒɛt] N turbojato (BR), turbojacto (PT)

turboprop [tɜ:bəu'prɔp] N (*engine*) turboélice *m*

turbot ['tɜ:bət] N INV rodovalho

turbulence ['tɜ:bjuləns] N (*Aviat*) turbulência

turbulent ['tɜ:bjulənt] ADJ turbulento

tureen [tə'ri:n] N terrina

turf [tɜ:f] N torrão *m* ▶ VT relvar, gramar; **the T~** o turfe

▶ **turf out** (*inf*) VT (*thing*) jogar fora; (*person*) pôr no olho da rua

turf accountant (BRIT) N corretor *m* de apostas

turgid ['tɜ:dʒɪd] ADJ (*speech*) pomposo

Turk [tɜ:k] N turco(-a)

Turkey ['tɜ:kɪ] N Turquia

turkey ['tɜ:kɪ] N peru(a) *m/f*

Turkish ['tɜ:kɪʃ] ADJ turco(-a) ▶ N (*Ling*) turco

Turkish bath N banho turco

Turkish delight N lokum *m*

turmeric ['tɜ:mərɪk] N açafrão-da-terra *m*

turmoil ['tɜ:mɔɪl] N tumulto, distúrbio, agitação *f*; **in ~** agitado, tumultuado

turn [tɜ:n] N volta, turno; (*in road*) curva; (*go*) vez *f*, turno; (*tendency: of mind, events*) propensão *f*, tendência; (*Theatre*) número; (*Med*) choque *m* ▶ VT dar volta a, fazer girar; (*collar*) virar; (*steak*) virar; (*milk*) azedar;

t

(*shape: wood*) tornear; (*change*): **to ~ sth into**
converter algo em ▸ vi virar; (*person: look back*)
voltar-se; (*reverse direction*) mudar de direção;
(*milk*) (*change*) mudar; (*become*)
tornar-se, virar; **to ~ nasty** engrossar; **to ~
forty** fazer quarenta anos; **to ~ into**
converter-se em; **a good ~** um favor; **it gave
me quite a ~** me deu um susto enorme; **"no
left ~"** (*Aut*) "proibido virar à esquerda"; **it's
your ~** é a sua vez; **in ~** por sua vez; **to take
~s (at)** revezar (em); **at the ~ of the year/
century** no final do ano/século; **to take a ~
for the worse** (*situation, patient*) piorar; **to ~
left** (*Aut*) virar à esquerda; **she has no one
to ~ to** ela não tem a quem recorrer
▸ **turn about** vi dar meia-volta
▸ **turn away** vi virar a cabeça ▸ vt (*reject:
person*) rejeitar; (: *business, applicants*) recusar
▸ **turn back** vi voltar atrás ▸ vt voltar para
trás; (*clock*) atrasar
▸ **turn down** vt (*refuse*) recusar; (*reduce*)
baixar; (*fold*) dobrar, virar para baixo
▸ **turn in** vi (*inf: go to bed*) ir dormir ▸ vt (*fold*)
dobrar para dentro
▸ **turn off** vi (*from road*) virar, sair do caminho
▸ vt (*light, radio etc*) apagar; (*engine*) desligar
▸ **turn on** vt (*light*) acender; (*engine, radio*)
ligar; (*tap*) abrir
▸ **turn out** vt (*light, gas*) apagar; (*produce*)
produzir ▸ vi (*troops*) ser mobilizado; **to ~ out
to be ...** revelar-se (ser) ..., resultar (ser) ...,
vir a ser ...
▸ **turn over** vi (*person*) virar-se ▸ vt (*object*)
virar
▸ **turn round** vi voltar-se, virar-se ▸ vt girar
▸ **turn up** vi (*person*) aparecer, pintar; (*lost
object*) aparecer ▸ vt (*collar*) subir; (*volume,
radio etc*) aumentar
turnabout ['tə:nəbaut] N reviravolta
turnaround ['tə:nəraund] N reviravolta
turncoat ['tə:nkəut] N vira-casaca *m/f*
turned-up [tə:nd-] ADJ (*nose*) arrebitado
turning ['tə:nɪŋ] N (*in road*) via lateral; **the
first ~ on the right** a primeira à direita
turning circle (*BRIT*) N raio de viragem
turning point N (*fig*) momento decisivo,
virada
turning radius (*US*) N raio de viragem
turnip ['tə:nɪp] N nabo
turnout ['tə:naut] N assistência; (*in election*)
comparecimento às urnas
turnover ['tə:nəuvə^r] N (*Comm: amount of
money*) volume *m* de negócios; (: *of goods*)
movimento; (*of staff*) rotatividade *f*; (*Culin*)
espécie de pastel
turnpike ['tə:npaɪk] (*US*) N estrada *or* rodovia
com pedágio (*BR*) *or* portagem (*PT*)
turnstile ['tə:nstaɪl] N borboleta (*BR*),
torniquete *m* (*PT*)
turntable ['tə:nteɪbl] N (*on record player*) prato
turn-up (*BRIT*) N (*on trousers*) volta, dobra
turpentine ['tə:pəntaɪn] N (*also*: **turps**)
aguarrás *f*

turquoise ['tə:kwɔɪz] N (*stone*) turquesa ▸ ADJ
azul-turquesa *inv*
turret ['tʌrɪt] N torrinha
turtle ['tə:tl] N tartaruga, cágado
turtleneck ['tə:tlnɛk], **turtleneck sweater** N
pulôver *m* (*BR*) *or* camisola (*PT*) de gola alta
tusk [tʌsk] N defesa (de elefante)
tussle ['tʌsl] N (*fight*) luta; (*scuffle*) contenda,
rixa
tutor ['tju:tə^r] N professor(a) *m/f*; (*private tutor*)
professor(a) *m/f* particular
tutorial [tju:'tɔ:rɪəl] N (*Sch*) seminário
tuxedo [tʌk'si:dəu] (*US*) N smoking *m*
TV N ABBR (= *television*) TV *f*
TV dinner N comida pronta
twaddle ['twɔdl] N bobagens *fpl*, disparates *mpl*
twang [twæŋ] N (*of instrument*) dedilhado;
(*of voice*) timbre *m* nasal *or* fanhoso ▸ vi vibrar
▸ vt (*guitar*) dedilhar
tweak [twi:k] vt (*nose, ear*) beliscar; (*hair*)
puxar
tweed [twi:d] N tweed *m*, *pano grosso de lã*
tweet [twi:t] N (*on Twitter*) tweet *m* ▸ vt, vi
tuitar
tweezers ['twi:zəz] NPL pinça (pequena)
twelfth [twɛlfθ] NUM décimo segundo; *see
also* **fifth**
Twelfth Night N noite *f* de Reis, Epifania
twelve [twɛlv] NUM doze; **at ~ (o'clock)**
(*midday*) ao meio-dia; (*midnight*) à meia-noite;
see also **five**
twentieth ['twɛntɪɪθ] NUM vigésimo; *see also*
fifth
twenty ['twɛntɪ] NUM vinte; *see also* **five**
twerp [twə:p] (*inf*) N imbecil *m/f*
twice [twaɪs] ADV duas vezes; **~ as much**
duas vezes mais; **~ a week** duas vezes por
semana; **she is ~ your age** ela tem duas
vezes a sua idade
twiddle ['twɪdl] vt, vi: **to ~ (with) sth** mexer
em algo; **to ~ one's thumbs** (*fig*) chupar o
dedo
twig [twɪg] N graveto, varinha ▸ vt, vi (*inf*)
sacar
twilight ['twaɪlaɪt] N crepúsculo, meia-luz *f*;
in the ~ na penumbra
twill [twɪl] N sarja
twin [twɪn] ADJ (*sister, brother, towers*) gêmeo(-a);
(*beds*) separado ▸ N gêmeo(-a) ▸ vt irmanar
twin-bedded room [-'bɛdɪd] N quarto com
duas camas
twin beds NPL camas *fpl* separadas
twin-carburettor ADJ de dois carburadores
twine [twaɪn] N barbante *m* (*BR*), cordel *m* (*PT*)
▸ vi (*plant*) enroscar-se, enrolar-se
twin-engined [-'ɛndʒɪnd] ADJ bimotor;
~ aircraft (avião *m*) bimotor *m*
twinge [twɪndʒ] N (*of pain*) pontada; (*of
conscience*) remorso
twinkle ['twɪŋkl] N cintilação *f* ▸ vi cintilar;
(*eyes*) pestanejar
twin room N quarto com duas camas
twin town N cidade *f* irmã

twirl [twə:l] N giro, volta ▶ VT fazer girar ▶ VI girar rapidamente

twist [twist] N (action) torção f; (in road, coil) curva; (in wire, flex) virada; (in story) mudança imprevista ▶ VT torcer, retorcer; (ankle) torcer; (weave) entrelaçar; (roll around) enrolar; (fig) deturpar ▶ VI serpentear; **to ~ one's ankle/wrist** torcer o tornozelo/pulso

twisted ['twistid] ADJ (wire, rope, ankle) torcido; (fig: mind, logic) deturpado

twit [twit] (inf) N idiota m/f, bobo(-a)

twitch [twitʃ] N puxão m; (nervous) tique m nervoso ▶ VI contrair-se

two [tu:] NUM dois; **~ by ~, in ~s** de dois em dois; **to put ~ and ~ together** (fig) tirar conclusões; see also **five**

two-door ADJ (Aut) de duas portas

two-faced [-feist] (pej) ADJ (person) falso

twofold ['tu:fəuld] ADV: **to increase ~** duplicar ▶ ADJ (increase) em cem por cento; (reply) duplo

two-piece N (also: **two-piece suit**) traje m de duas peças; (also: **two-piece swimsuit**) maiô m de duas peças, biquíni m

two-seater [-'si:tər] N (plane) avião m de dois lugares; (car) carro de dois lugares

twosome ['tu:səm] N (people) casal m

two-stroke N (also: **two-stroke engine**) motor m de dois tempos ▶ ADJ de dois tempos

two-tone ADJ em dois tons

two-way ADJ: **~ radio** rádio emissor-receptor; **~ traffic** trânsito em mão dupla

TX (US) ABBR (Post) = **Texas**

tycoon [tai'ku:n] N: (**business**) ~ magnata m

type [taip] N (category) tipo, espécie f; (model) modelo; (Typ) tipo, letra ▶ VT (letter etc) datilografar, bater (à máquina); **what ~ do you want?** que tipo você quer?; **in bold/ italic ~** em negrito/itálico

typecast ['taipka:st] ADJ que representa sempre o mesmo papel

typeface ['taipfeis] N tipo, letra

typescript ['taipskript] N texto datilografado

typeset ['taipset] (irreg: like **set**) VT compor (para imprimir)

typesetter ['taipsɛtər] N compositor(a) m/f

typewriter ['taipraitər] N máquina de escrever

typewritten ['taipritn] ADJ datilografado

typhoid ['taifɔid] N febre f tifoide

typhoon [tai'fu:n] N tufão m

typhus ['taifəs] N tifo

typical ['tipikl] ADJ típico

typify ['tipifai] VT tipificar, simbolizar

typing ['taipiŋ] N datilografia

typing error N erro de datilografia

typing pool N seção f de datilografia

typist ['taipist] N datilógrafo(-a) m/f

typo ['taipəu] (inf) N ABBR (= typographical error) erro tipográfico

typography [tai'pɔgrəfi] N tipografia

tyranny ['tirəni] N tirania

tyrant ['taiərənt] N tirano(-a)

tyre, (US) **tire** ['taiər] N pneu m

tyre pressure N pressão f dos pneus

Tyrrhenian Sea [ti'ri:niən-] N: **the ~** o mar Tirreno

tzar [zɑ:ʳ] N = **tsar**

Uu

U¹, u [ju:] N (letter) U, u m; **U for Uncle** U de
Úrsula

U² (BRIT) N ABBR (Cinema: = universal) ≈ livre

UAW (US) N ABBR (= United Automobile Workers)
sindicato dos trabalhadores na indústria
automobilística

UB40 (BRIT) N ABBR (= unemployment benefit form
40) carteira que comprova que o portador recebe o
auxílio-desemprego

U-bend N (in pipe) curva em U

ubiquitous [ju:'bɪkwɪtəs] ADJ ubíquo,
onipresente

UDA (BRIT) N ABBR = **Ulster Defence
Association**

UDC (BRIT) N ABBR = **Urban District Council**

udder ['ʌdə'] N ubre f

UDI (BRIT) N ABBR (Pol) = **unilateral declaration
of independence**

UDR (BRIT) N ABBR = **Ulster Defence
Regiment**

UEFA [ju:'eɪfə] N ABBR (= Union of European
Football Associations) UEFA f

UFO ['ju:fəu] N ABBR (= unidentified flying object)
óvni m

Uganda [ju:'gændə] N Uganda (no article)

Ugandan [ju:'gændən] ADJ, N ugandense m/f

ugh [ə:h] EXCL uh!

ugliness ['ʌglɪnɪs] N feiura

ugly ['ʌglɪ] ADJ feio; (dangerous) perigoso

UHF ABBR (= ultra-high frequency) UHF,
freqüência ultra-alta

UHT ADJ ABBR (= ultra-heat treated): ~ **milk**
leite m longa-vida

UK N ABBR = **United Kingdom**

ulcer ['ʌlsə'] N úlcera; **mouth** ~ afta

Ulster ['ʌlstə'] N Ulster m, Irlanda do Norte

ulterior [ʌl'tɪərɪə'] ADJ ulterior; ~ **motive**
segundas intenções fpl

ultimata [ʌltɪ'meɪtə] NPL of **ultimatum**

ultimate ['ʌltɪmət] ADJ último, final;
(authority) máximo ▶ N: **the ~ in luxury** o
máximo em luxo

ultimately ['ʌltɪmətlɪ] ADV (in the end) no final,
por último; (fundamentally) no fundo

ultimatum [ʌltɪ'meɪtəm] (pl **ultimatums** or
ultimata) N ultimato

ultrasonic [ʌltrə'sɔnɪk] ADJ ultrassônico

ultrasound ['ʌltrəsaund] N (Med) ultrassom m

ultraviolet [ʌltrə'vaɪəlɪt] ADJ ultravioleta

umbilical cord [ʌmbɪ'laɪkl-] N cordão m
umbilical

umbrage ['ʌmbrɪdʒ] N: **to take** ~ ofender-se

umbrella [ʌm'brelə] N guarda-chuva m; (for
sun) guarda-sol m, barraca (da praia); (fig):
under the ~ of sob a égide de

umpire ['ʌmpaɪə'] N árbitro ▶ VT arbitrar

umpteen [ʌmp'ti:n] ADJ inúmeros(-as)

umpteenth [ʌmp'ti:nθ] ADJ: **for the ~ time**
pela enésima vez

UMW N ABBR (= United Mineworkers of America)
sindicato dos mineiros

UN N ABBR (= United Nations) ONU f

unabashed [ʌnə'bæʃt] ADJ imperturbado

unabated [ʌnə'beɪtɪd] ADJ sem diminuir

unable [ʌn'eɪbl] ADJ: **to be ~ to do sth** não
poder fazer algo; (be incapable) ser incapaz de
fazer algo

unabridged [ʌnə'brɪdʒd] ADJ integral

unacceptable [ʌnək'sɛptəbl] ADJ (behaviour)
insuportável; (price, proposal) inaceitável

unaccompanied [ʌnə'kʌmpənɪd] ADJ
desacompanhado; (singing, song) sem
acompanhamento

unaccountably [ʌnə'kauntəblɪ] ADV
inexplicavelmente

unaccounted [ʌnə'kauntɪd] ADJ: **two
passengers are ~ for** dois passageiros estão
desaparecidos

unaccustomed [ʌnə'kʌstəmd] ADJ
desacostumado; **to be ~ to** não estar
acostumado a

unacquainted [ʌnə'kweɪntɪd] ADJ: **to be ~
with** (person) não conhecer; (facts etc) não
estar familiarizado com

unadulterated [ʌnə'dʌltəreɪtɪd] ADJ puro,
natural

unaffected [ʌnə'fɛktɪd] ADJ (person, behaviour)
natural, simples inv; (emotionally): **to be ~ by**
não se comover com

unafraid [ʌnə'freɪd] ADJ: **to be ~** não ter medo

unaided [ʌn'eɪdɪd] ADJ sem ajuda, por si só

unanimity [ju:nə'nɪmɪtɪ] N unanimidade f

unanimous [ju:'nænɪməs] ADJ unânime

unanimously [ju:'nænɪməslɪ] ADV
unanimemente

unanswered [ʌn'ɑ:nsəd] ADJ sem resposta

unappetizing [ʌn'æpɪtaɪzɪŋ] ADJ pouco
apetitoso

unappreciative [ʌnə'pri:ʃiətɪv] ADJ (*ungrateful*) ingrato

unarmed [ʌn'ɑ:md] ADJ (*without a weapon*) desarmado; (*defenceless*) indefeso

unashamed [ʌnə'ʃeɪmd] ADJ (*open*) desembaraçado; (*pleasure, greed*) descarado; (*impudent*) descarado

unassisted [ʌnə'sɪstɪd] ADJ, ADV sem ajuda

unassuming [ʌnə'sju:mɪŋ] ADJ modesto, despretencioso

unattached [ʌnə'tætʃt] ADJ (*person*) livre; (*part etc*) solto, separado

unattended [ʌnə'tɛndɪd] ADJ (*car, luggage*) abandonado

unattractive [ʌnə'træktɪv] ADJ sem atrativos; (*building, appearance, idea*) pouco atraente

unauthorized [ʌn'ɔ:θəraɪzd] ADJ não autorizado, sem autorização

unavailable [ʌnə'veɪləbl] ADJ (*article, room, book*) indisponível; (*person*) não disponível

unavoidable [ʌnə'vɔɪdəbl] ADJ inevitável

unavoidably [ʌnə'vɔɪdəblɪ] ADV inevitavelmente

unaware [ʌnə'wɛəʳ] ADJ: **to be ~ of** ignorar, não perceber

unawares [ʌnə'wɛəz] ADV improvisadamente, de surpresa

unbalanced [ʌn'bælənst] ADJ desequilibrado

unbearable [ʌn'bɛərəbl] ADJ insuportável

unbeatable [ʌn'bi:təbl] ADJ (*team*) invencível; (*price*) sem igual

unbeaten [ʌn'bi:tn] ADJ invicto; (*record*) não batido

unbecoming [ʌnbɪ'kʌmɪŋ] ADJ (*unseemly: language, behaviour*) inconveniente; (*unflattering: garment*) que não fica bem

unbeknown [ʌnbɪ'nəun], **unbeknownst** [ʌnbɪ'nəunst] ADV: **~(st) to me** sem eu saber

unbelief [ʌnbɪ'li:f] N incredulidade f

unbelievable [ʌnbɪ'li:vəbl] ADJ inacreditável; (*amazing*) incrível

unbelievingly [ʌnbɪ'li:vɪŋlɪ] ADV incredulamente

unbend [ʌn'bɛnd] (*irreg: like* **bend**) VI relaxar-se ▸ VT (*wire*) desentortar

unbending [ʌn'bɛndɪŋ] ADJ inflexível

unbent [ʌn'bɛnt] PT, PP *of* **unbend**

unbiased [ʌn'baɪəst] ADJ imparcial

unblemished [ʌn'blɛmɪʃt] ADJ imaculado

unblock [ʌn'blɔk] VT (*pipe*) desentupir

unborn [ʌn'bɔ:n] ADJ por nascer

unbounded [ʌn'baundɪd] ADJ ilimitado, infinito, imenso

unbreakable [ʌn'breɪkəbl] ADJ inquebrável

unbridled [ʌn'braɪdld] ADJ (*fig*) desenfreado

unbroken [ʌn'brəukən] ADJ (*seal*) intacto; (*line*) contínuo; (*silence, series*) ininterrupto; (*record*) mantido; (*spirit*) indômito

unbuckle [ʌn'bʌkl] VT desafivelar

unburden [ʌn'bə:dn] VT: **to ~ o.s.** desabafar

unbutton [ʌn'bʌtn] VT desabotoar

uncalled-for [ʌn'kɔ:ld-] ADJ desnecessário, gratuito

uncanny [ʌn'kænɪ] ADJ (*silence, resemblance*) estranho; (*knack*) excepcional

unceasing [ʌn'si:sɪŋ] ADJ contínuo

unceremonious [ʌnsɛrɪ'məunɪəs] ADJ (*abrupt*) incerimonioso; (*rude*) rude

uncertain [ʌn'sə:tn] ADJ incerto; (*character*) indeciso; (*unsure*): **~ about** inseguro sobre; **we were ~ whether ...** não tínhamos certeza se ...; **in no ~ terms** em termos precisos

uncertainty [ʌn'sə:tntɪ] N incerteza; (*also pl: doubts*) dúvidas *fpl*

unchallenged [ʌn'tʃæləndʒd] ADJ incontestado; **to go ~** não ser contestado

unchanged [ʌn'tʃeɪndʒd] ADJ inalterado

uncharitable [ʌn'tʃærɪtəbl] ADJ sem caridade

uncharted [ʌn'tʃɑ:tɪd] ADJ inexplorado

unchecked [ʌn'tʃɛkt] ADV sem controle, descontrolado

uncivilized [ʌn'sɪvəlaɪzd] ADJ (*country, people*) primitivo; (*fig: behaviour*) incivilizado; (: *hour*) de manhã bem cedo

uncle ['ʌŋkl] N tio

unclear [ʌn'klɪəʳ] ADJ (*not obvious*) pouco evidente; (*confused*) confuso; (*indistinct*) indistinto; **I'm still ~ about what I'm supposed to do** ainda não sei exatamente o que devo fazer

uncoil [ʌn'kɔɪl] VT desenrolar ▸ VI desenrolar-se

uncomfortable [ʌn'kʌmfətəbl] ADJ incômodo; (*uneasy*) pouco à vontade; (*situation*) desagradável

uncomfortably [ʌn'kʌmftəblɪ] ADV desconfortavelmente; (*uneasily*) sem graça; (*unpleasantly*) desagradavelmente

uncommitted [ʌnkə'mɪtɪd] ADJ não comprometido

uncommon [ʌn'kɔmən] ADJ raro, incomum, excepcional

uncommunicative [ʌnkə'mju:nɪkətɪv] ADJ reservado

uncomplicated [ʌn'kɔmplɪkeɪtɪd] ADJ descomplicado, simples *inv*

uncompromising [ʌn'kɔmprəmaɪzɪŋ] ADJ intransigente, inflexível

unconcerned [ʌnkən'sə:nd] ADJ indiferente, despreocupado; **to be ~ (about)** não estar preocupado (com)

unconditional [ʌnkən'dɪʃənl] ADJ incondicional

uncongenial [ʌnkən'dʒi:nɪəl] ADJ desagradável

unconnected [ʌnkə'nɛktɪd] ADJ não relacionado

unconscious [ʌn'kɔnʃəs] ADJ sem sentidos, desacordado; (*unaware*): **~ of** inconsciente de ▸ N: **the ~** o inconsciente; **to knock sb ~** pôr alguém nocaute, nocautear alguém

unconsciously [ʌn'kɔnʃəslɪ] ADV inconscientemente

unconstitutional [ʌnkɔnstɪ'tju:ʃənl] ADJ inconstitucional

uncontested [ʌnkən'tɛstɪd] ADJ incontestado

u

uncontrollable [ˌʌnkən'trəuləbl] ADJ (*temper*) ingovernável; (*child, animal, laughter*) incontrolável

uncontrolled [ˌʌnkən'trəuld] ADJ descontrolado

unconventional [ˌʌnkən'vɛnʃənl] ADJ (*person*) inconvencional; (*approach*) heterodoxo

unconvinced [ˌʌnkən'vɪnst] ADJ: **to be ~** não estar convencido

unconvincing [ˌʌnkən'vɪnsɪŋ] ADJ pouco convincente

uncork [ʌn'kɔːk] VT desarrolhar

uncorroborated [ˌʌnkə'rɔbəreɪtɪd] ADJ não confirmado

uncouth [ʌn'kuːθ] ADJ rude, grosseiro

uncover [ʌn'kʌvəʳ] VT descobrir; (*take lid off*) destapar, destampar

unctuous ['ʌŋktjuəs] ADJ untuoso, pegajoso

undamaged [ʌn'dæmɪdʒd] ADJ (*goods*) intacto; (*fig: reputation*) incólume

undaunted [ʌn'dɔːntɪd] ADJ impávido, inabalável

undecided [ˌʌndɪ'saɪdɪd] ADJ (*character*) indeciso; (*question*) não respondido, pendente

undelivered [ˌʌndɪ'lɪvəd] ADJ não entregue

undeniable [ˌʌndɪ'naɪəbl] ADJ inegável

under ['ʌndəʳ] PREP embaixo de (BR), debaixo de (PT); (*fig*) sob; (*in age, price: less than*) menos de; (*according to*) segundo, de acordo com ▶ ADV embaixo; (*movement*) por baixo; **from ~ sth** de embaixo de algo; **~ there** ali embaixo; **in ~ 2 hours** em menos de 2 horas; **~ anaesthetic** sob anestesia; **~ discussion** em discussão; **~ the circumstances** nas circunstâncias; **~ repair** em conserto

under... [ʌndəʳ] PREFIX sub-

under-age ADJ menor de idade; **~ drinking** consumo de bebidas alcoólicas por menores de idade

underarm ['ʌndərɑːm] ADV com a mão por baixo ▶ ADJ (*throw*) com a mão por baixo; (*deodorant*) para as axilas

undercapitalized [ˌʌndə'kæpɪtəlaɪzd] ADJ subcapitalizado

undercarriage ['ʌndəkærɪdʒ] (BRIT) N (*Aviat*) trem *m* de aterrissagem

undercharge [ˌʌndə'tʃɑːdʒ] VT não cobrar o suficiente

underclass ['ʌndəklɑːs] N classe *f* marginalizada

underclothes ['ʌndəkləuðz] NPL roupa de baixo, roupa íntima

undercoat ['ʌndəkəut] N (*paint*) primeira mão *f*

undercover ['ʌndəkʌvəʳ] ADJ secreto, clandestino

undercurrent ['ʌndəkʌrənt] N (*fig*) tendência

undercut [ʌndə'kʌt] (*irreg: like* **cut**) VT (*person*) prejudicar; (*prices*) vender por menos que

underdeveloped [ˌʌndədɪ'vɛləpt] ADJ subdesenvolvido

underdog ['ʌndədɔg] N o mais fraco

underdone [ˌʌndə'dʌn] ADJ (*Culin*) mal passado

under-employment N subemprego

underestimate [ˌʌndər'ɛstɪmeɪt] VT subestimar

underexposed [ˌʌndərɪk'spəuzd] ADJ (*Phot*) sem exposição suficiente

underfed [ˌʌndə'fɛd] ADJ subnutrido

underfoot [ˌʌndə'fut] ADV sob os pés

under-funded ['ʌndə'fʌndɪd] ADJ subfinanciado, sem verbas suficientes

undergo [ˌʌndə'gəu] (*irreg: like* **go**) VT sofrer; (*test*) passar por; (*operation, treatment*) ser submetido a; **the car is ~ing repairs** o carro está sendo consertado

undergraduate [ˌʌndə'grædjuət] N universitário(-a) ▶ CPD: **~ courses** profissões *fpl* universitárias

underground ['ʌndəgraund] N (BRIT) metrô *m* (BR), metro(-politano) (PT); (*Pol*) organização *f* clandestina ▶ ADJ subterrâneo; (*fig*) clandestino ▶ ADV (*work*) embaixo da terra; (*fig*) na clandestinidade

undergrowth ['ʌndəgrəuθ] N vegetação *f* rasteira

underhand [ˌʌndə'hænd], **underhanded** [ˌʌndə'hændɪd] ADJ (*fig*) secreto e desonesto

underinsured [ˌʌndərɪn'ʃuəd] ADJ segurado abaixo do valor corrente

underlie [ˌʌndə'laɪ] (*irreg: like* **lie**) VT (*fig*) ser a base de

underline [ˌʌndə'laɪn] VT sublinhar

underling ['ʌndəlɪŋ] (*pej*) N subalterno(-a)

underlying [ˌʌndə'laɪɪŋ] ADJ: **the ~ cause** a causa subjacente

undermentioned [ˌʌndə'mɛnʃənd] ADJ abaixo mencionado

undermine [ˌʌndə'maɪn] VT minar, solapar

underneath [ˌʌndə'niːθ] ADV embaixo, debaixo, por baixo ▶ PREP embaixo de (BR), debaixo de (PT)

undernourished [ˌʌndə'nʌrɪʃt] ADJ subnutrido

underpaid [ˌʌndə'peɪd] ADJ mal pago

underpants ['ʌndəpænts] (BRIT) NPL cueca (BR), cuecas *fpl* (PT)

underpass ['ʌndəpɑːs] (BRIT) N passagem *f* inferior

underpin [ˌʌndə'pɪn] VT (*argument, case*) sustentar

underplay [ˌʌndə'pleɪ] (BRIT) VT minimizar

underpopulated [ˌʌndə'pɔpjuleɪtɪd] ADJ de população reduzida

underprice [ˌʌndə'praɪs] VT vender abaixo do preço

underprivileged [ˌʌndə'prɪvɪlɪdʒd] ADJ menos favorecido

underrate [ˌʌndə'reɪt] VT depreciar, subestimar

underscore [ˌʌndə'skɔːʳ] VT sublinhar

underseal [ˌʌndə'siːl] (BRIT) VT fazer bronzina em

undersecretary [ˌʌndə'sɛkrətərɪ] N subsecretário(-a)

undersell [ˌʌndə'sɛl] (*irreg: like* **sell**) VT (*competitors*) vender por preço mais baixo que

undershirt ['ʌndəʃəːt] (US) N camiseta
undershorts ['ʌndəʃɔːts] (US) NPL cueca (BR),
cuecas fpl (PT)
underside ['ʌndəsaɪd] N parte f inferior
undersigned ['ʌndəsaɪnd] ADJ, N abaixo
assinado(-a)
underskirt ['ʌndəskəːt] (BRIT) N anágua
understaffed [ʌndə'stɑːft] ADJ com falta de
pessoal
understand [ʌndə'stænd] (irreg: like **stand**) VT
entender, compreender ▶ VI (believe): **to ~
that** acreditar que; **I ~ that ...** (I hear) ouço
dizer que ...; (I sympathize) eu compreendo
que ...; **to make o.s. understood** fazer-se
entender
understandable [ʌndə'stændəbl] ADJ
compreensível
understanding [ʌndə'stændɪŋ] ADJ
compreensivo ▶ N (in relationship)
compreensão f; (knowledge) entendimento;
(agreement) acordo; **to come to an ~** chegar a
um acordo; **on the ~ that ...** sob condição
que ..., contanto que ...
understate [ʌndə'steɪt] VT minimizar
understatement [ʌndə'steɪtmənt] N (quality)
subestimação f; (euphemism) eufemismo; **it's
an ~ to say that ...** é uma subestimação
dizer que ...
understood [ʌndə'stud] PT, PP of **understand**
▶ ADJ entendido; (implied) subentendido,
implícito
understudy ['ʌndəstʌdɪ] N ator m substituto/
atriz f substituta
undertake [ʌndə'teɪk] (irreg: like **take**) VT (job,
project) empreender; (task, duty) incumbir-se
de, encarregar-se de; **to ~ to do sth**
comprometer-se a fazer algo
undertaker ['ʌndəteɪkəʳ] N agente m/f
funerário(-a)
undertaking ['ʌndəteɪkɪŋ] N
empreendimento; (promise) promessa
undertone ['ʌndətəun] N (of criticism etc)
sugestão f; (low voice): **in an ~** em meia voz
undertook [ʌndə'tuk] PT of **undertake**
undervalue [ʌndə'væljuː] VT subestimar
underwater [ʌndə'wɔːtəʳ] ADV sob a água
▶ ADJ subaquático
underwear ['ʌndəwɛəʳ] N roupa de baixo
underweight [ʌndə'weɪt] ADJ de peso inferior
ao normal; (person) magro
underwent [ʌndə'wɛnt] PT of **undergo**
underworld ['ʌndəwəːld] N (of crime) submundo
underwrite [ʌndə'raɪt] (irreg: like **write**) VT
(Comm) subscrever
underwriter ['ʌndəraɪtəʳ] N (Insurance)
subscritor(a) m/f (que faz resseguro)
underwritten [ʌndə'rɪtn] PP of **underwrite**
underwrote [ʌndə'rəut] PT of **underwrite**
undeserving [ʌndɪ'zəːvɪŋ] ADJ: **to be ~ of** não
merecer
undesirable [ʌndɪ'zaɪərəbl] ADJ indesejável
undeveloped [ʌndɪ'vɛləpt] ADJ (land, resources)
não desenvolvido

undid [ʌn'dɪd] PT of **undo**
undies ['ʌndɪz] (inf) NPL roupa de baixo, roupa
íntima
undignified [ʌn'dɪgnɪfaɪd] ADJ sem
dignidade, indecoroso
undiluted [ʌndaɪ'luːtɪd] ADJ não diluído,
puro; (pleasure) puro
undiplomatic [ʌndɪplə'mætɪk] ADJ pouco
diplomático, inábil
undischarged [ʌndɪs'tʃɑːdʒd] ADJ:
~ bankrupt falido(-a) não reabilitado(-a)
undisciplined [ʌn'dɪsɪplɪnd] ADJ
indisciplinado
undisguised [ʌndɪs'gaɪzd] ADJ (dislike etc)
patente
undisputed [ʌndɪ'spjuːtɪd] ADJ incontestável
undistinguished [ʌndɪs'tɪŋgwɪʃt] ADJ
medíocre, regular
undisturbed [ʌndɪs'təːbd] ADJ (sleep)
tranquilo; **to leave sth ~** não mexer em algo
undivided [ʌndɪ'vaɪdɪd] ADJ: **can I have your
~ attention?** quero a sua total atenção
undo [ʌn'duː] (irreg: like **do**) VT (unfasten)
desatar; (spoil) desmanchar
undoing [ʌn'duːɪŋ] N ruína, desgraça
undone [ʌn'dʌn] PP of **undo** ▶ ADJ: **to come ~**
desfazer-se
undoubted [ʌn'dautɪd] ADJ indubitável
undoubtedly [ʌn'dautɪdlɪ] ADV sem dúvida,
indubitavelmente
undress [ʌn'drɛs] VI despir-se, tirar a roupa
▶ VT despir, tirar a roupa de
undrinkable [ʌn'drɪŋkəbl] ADJ (unpalatable)
intragável; (poisonous) impotável
undue [ʌn'djuː] ADJ excessivo
undulating ['ʌndjuleɪtɪŋ] ADJ ondulante
unduly [ʌn'djuːlɪ] ADV excessivamente
undying [ʌn'daɪɪŋ] ADJ eterno
unearned [ʌn'əːnd] ADJ (praise, respect)
imerecido; **~ income** rendimento não
ganho com o trabalho individual
unearth [ʌn'əːθ] VT desenterrar; (fig) revelar
unearthly [ʌn'əːθlɪ] ADJ sobrenatural; **at an ~
hour of the night** na calada da noite
uneasy [ʌn'iːzɪ] ADJ (person) preocupado;
(feeling) incômodo; (peace, truce)
desconfortável; **to feel ~ about doing sth**
estar apreensivo quanto a fazer algo
uneconomic, uneconomical [ʌniːkə'nɔmɪkl]
ADJ antieconômico; (unprofitable) não
rentável
uneducated [ʌn'ɛdjukeɪtɪd] ADJ inculto, sem
instrução, não escolarizado
unemployed [ʌnɪm'plɔɪd] ADJ desempregado
▶ NPL: **the ~** os desempregados
unemployment [ʌnɪm'plɔɪmənt] N
desemprego
unemployment benefit, (US)
unemployment compensation N
auxílio-desemprego
unending [ʌn'ɛndɪŋ] ADJ interminável
unenthusiastic [ʌnɪnθuːzɪ'æstɪk] ADJ sem
entusiasmo

u

unenviable [ʌnˈɛnvɪəbl] ADJ nada invejável
unequal [ʌnˈiːkwəl] ADJ desigual
unequalled, (US) **unequaled** [ʌnˈiːkwəld] ADJ inigualável, sem igual
unequivocal [ʌnəˈkwɪvəkl] ADJ (answer) inequívoco; (person) categórico
unerring [ʌnˈəːrɪŋ] ADJ infalível
UNESCO [juːˈnɛskəu] N ABBR (= United Nations Educational, Scientific and Cultural Organization) UNESCO f
unethical [ʌnˈɛθɪkl] ADJ (methods) imoral; (professional behaviour) contrário à ética
uneven [ʌnˈiːvn] ADJ desigual; (road etc) irregular, acidentado
uneventful [ʌnɪˈvɛntful] ADJ tranquilo, rotineiro
unexceptional [ʌnɪkˈsɛpʃənl] ADJ regular, corriqueiro
unexciting [ʌnɪkˈsaɪtɪŋ] ADJ monótono
unexpected [ʌnɪkˈspɛktɪd] ADJ inesperado
unexpectedly [ʌnɪkˈspɛktɪdlɪ] ADV inesperadamente
unexplained [ʌnɪkˈspleɪnd] ADJ inexplicado
unexploded [ʌnɪkˈspləudɪd] ADJ não explodido
unfailing [ʌnˈfeɪlɪŋ] ADJ inexaurível
unfair [ʌnˈfɛər] ADJ: ~ **(to)** injusto (com); **it's ~ that** ... não é justo que ...
unfair dismissal N demissão f injusta or infundada
unfairly [ʌnˈfɛəlɪ] ADV injustamente
unfaithful [ʌnˈfeɪθful] ADJ infiel
unfamiliar [ʌnfəˈmɪlɪər] ADJ pouco familiar, desconhecido; **to be ~ with sth** não estar familiarizado com algo
unfashionable [ʌnˈfæʃnəbl] ADJ fora da moda
unfasten [ʌnˈfɑːsn] VT desatar; (open) abrir
unfathomable [ʌnˈfæðəməbl] ADJ insondável
unfavourable, (US) **unfavorable** [ʌnˈfeɪvərəbl] ADJ desfavorável
unfavourably, (US) **unfavorably** [ʌnˈfeɪvrəblɪ] ADV: **to look ~ upon** não ser favorável a
unfeeling [ʌnˈfiːlɪŋ] ADJ insensível
unfinished [ʌnˈfɪnɪʃt] ADJ incompleto, inacabado
unfit [ʌnˈfɪt] ADJ (physically) sem preparo físico; (incompetent) incompetente, incapaz; ~ **for work** inapto para trabalhar
unflagging [ʌnˈflægɪŋ] ADJ incansável
unflappable [ʌnˈflæpəbl] ADJ imperturbável, sereno
unflattering [ʌnˈflætərɪŋ] ADJ (dress, hairstyle) que não fica bem; (remark) pouco elogioso
unflinching [ʌnˈflɪntʃɪŋ] ADJ destemido, intrépido
unfold [ʌnˈfəuld] VT desdobrar; (fig) revelar ▶ VI (story, situation) desdobrar-se
unforeseeable [ʌnfɔːˈsiːəbl] ADJ imprevisível
unforeseen [ʌnfɔːˈsiːn] ADJ imprevisto
unforgettable [ʌnfəˈgɛtəbl] ADJ inesquecível
unforgivable [ʌnfəˈgɪvəbl] ADJ imperdoável
unformatted [ʌnˈfɔːmætɪd] ADJ (disk, text) não formatado

unfortunate [ʌnˈfɔːtʃənət] ADJ infeliz; (event, remark) inoportuno
unfortunately [ʌnˈfɔːtʃənətlɪ] ADV infelizmente
unfounded [ʌnˈfaundɪd] ADJ infundado
unfriend [ʌnˈfrɛnd] VT (on social network) excluir (em rede social)
unfriendly [ʌnˈfrɛndlɪ] ADJ antipático
unfulfilled [ʌnfulˈfɪld] ADJ (ambition, prophecy) não realizado; (desire) não satisfeito; (promise, terms of contract) não cumprido; (person) que não se realizou
unfurl [ʌnˈfəːl] VT desfraldar
unfurnished [ʌnˈfəːnɪʃt] ADJ desmobiliado, sem mobília
ungainly [ʌnˈgeɪnlɪ] ADJ desalinhado
ungodly [ʌnˈgɔdlɪ] ADJ ímpio; **at an ~ hour** às altas horas da madrugada
ungrateful [ʌnˈgreɪtful] ADJ mal-agradecido, ingrato
unguarded [ʌnˈgɑːdɪd] ADJ: ~ **moment** momento de inatenção
unhappily [ʌnˈhæpəlɪ] ADV tristemente; (unfortunately) infelizmente
unhappiness [ʌnˈhæpɪnɪs] N infelicidade f
unhappy [ʌnˈhæpɪ] ADJ (sad) triste; (unfortunate) desventurado; (childhood) infeliz; (dissatisfied): ~ **with** (arrangements etc) descontente com, insatisfeito com
unharmed [ʌnˈhɑːmd] ADJ ileso
unhealthy [ʌnˈhɛlθɪ] ADJ insalubre; (person) doentio; (fig) anormal
unheard-of [ʌnˈhəːd-] ADJ insólito; (unknown) desconhecido
unhelpful [ʌnˈhɛlpful] ADJ (person) imprestável; (advice) inútil
unhesitating [ʌnˈhɛzɪteɪtɪŋ] ADJ (loyalty) firme; (reply) imediato
unhook [ʌnˈhuk] VT desenganchar; (from wall) despendurar; (dress) abrir, soltar
unhurt [ʌnˈhəːt] ADJ ileso
unhygienic [ʌnhaɪˈdʒiːnɪk] ADJ anti-higiênico
UNICEF [ˈjuːnɪsɛf] N ABBR (= United Nations International Children's Emergency Fund) Unicef m
unicorn [ˈjuːnɪkɔːn] N licorne m, unicórnio
unidentified [ʌnaɪˈdɛntɪfaɪd] ADJ não-identificado; see also **UFO**
uniform [ˈjuːnɪfɔːm] N uniforme m ▶ ADJ uniforme
uniformity [juːnɪˈfɔːmɪtɪ] N uniformidade f
unify [ˈjuːnɪfaɪ] VT unificar, unir
unilateral [juːnɪˈlætərəl] ADJ unilateral
unimaginable [ʌnɪˈmædʒɪnəbl] ADJ inimaginável, inconcebível
unimaginative [ʌnɪˈmædʒɪnətɪv] ADJ sem imaginação
unimpaired [ʌnɪmˈpɛəd] ADJ inalterado
unimportant [ʌnɪmˈpɔːtənt] ADJ sem importância
unimpressed [ʌnɪmˈprɛst] ADJ indiferente
uninhabited [ʌnɪnˈhæbɪtɪd] ADJ inabitado
uninhibited [ʌnɪnˈhɪbɪtɪd] ADJ sem inibições
uninjured [ʌnˈɪndʒəd] ADJ ileso

uninspired [ʌnɪn'spaɪəd] ADJ insípido

uninstall ['ʌnɪnstɔːl] VT (*Comput*) desinstalar

unintelligent [ʌnɪn'tɛlɪdʒənt] ADJ ininteligente

unintentional [ʌnɪn'tɛnʃənəl] ADJ involuntário, não intencional

unintentionally [ʌnɪn'tɛnʃənəlɪ] ADV sem querer

uninvited [ʌnɪn'vaɪtɪd] ADJ (*guest*) não convidado

uninviting [ʌnɪn'vaɪtɪŋ] ADJ (*place*) pouco convidativo; (*food*) pouco apetitoso

union ['juːnjən] N união *f*; (*also*: **trade union**) sindicato (de trabalhadores) ▶ CPD sindical

unionize ['juːnjənaɪz] VT sindicalizar

Union Jack N bandeira britânica

Union of Soviet Socialist Republics N União *f* das Repúblicas Socialistas Soviéticas

union shop N empresa onde todos os trabalhadores têm que filiar-se ao sindicato

unique [juː'niːk] ADJ único, sem igual

unisex ['juːnɪsɛks] ADJ unissex *inv*

unison ['juːnɪsn] N: **in ~** em harmonia, em uníssono

unit ['juːnɪt] N unidade *f*; (*of furniture etc*) segão *f*; (*team, squad*) equipe *f*; **kitchen ~** armário de cozinha; **sink ~** pia de cozinha; **production ~** unidade de produção

unit cost N custo unitário

unite [juː'naɪt] VT unir ▶ VI unir-se

united [juː'naɪtɪd] ADJ unido; (*effort*) conjunto

United Arab Emirates NPL Emirados *mpl* Árabes Unidos

United Kingdom N Reino Unido

United Nations, United Nations Organization N (Organização *f* das) Nações *fpl* Unidas

United States, United States of America N Estados Unidos *mpl* (da América)

unit price N preço unitário

unit trust (*BRIT*) N (*Comm*) fundo de investimento

unity ['juːnɪtɪ] N unidade *f*

Univ. ABBR = **university**

universal [juːnɪ'vɜːsl] ADJ universal

universe ['juːnɪvɜːs] N universo

university [juːnɪ'vɜːsɪtɪ] N universidade *f*, faculdade *f* ▶ CPD universitário

unjust [ʌn'dʒʌst] ADJ injusto

unjustifiable [ʌndʒʌstɪ'faɪəbl] ADJ injustificável

unjustified [ʌn'dʒʌstɪfaɪd] ADJ injustificado; (*text*) não alinhado

unkempt [ʌn'kɛmpt] ADJ desleixado, descuidado; (*hair*) despenteado; (*beard*) mal tratado

unkind [ʌn'kaɪnd] ADJ maldoso; (*comment etc*) cruel

unkindly [ʌn'kaɪndlɪ] ADV (*treat, speak*) maldosamente

unknown [ʌn'nəʊn] ADJ desconhecido; **~ to me** sem eu saber; **~ quantity** (*Math, fig*) incógnita

unladen [ʌn'leɪdn] ADJ (*ship, weight*) sem carga

unlawful [ʌn'lɔːful] ADJ ilegal

unleaded [ʌn'lɛdɪd] ADJ (*petrol, fuel*) sem chumbo

unleash [ʌn'liːʃ] VT (*fig*) desencadear

unleavened [ʌn'lɛvənd] ADJ sem fermento

unless [ʌn'lɛs] CONJ a menos que, a não ser que; **~ he comes** a menos que ele venha; **~ otherwise stated** salvo indicação contrária; **~ I am mistaken** se não me engano

unlicensed [ʌn'laɪsnst] (*BRIT*) ADJ sem licença para a venda de bebidas alcoólicas

unlike [ʌn'laɪk] ADJ diferente ▶ PREP diferentemente de, ao contrário de

unlikelihood [ʌn'laɪklɪhud] N improbabilidade *f*

unlikely [ʌn'laɪklɪ] ADJ (*not likely*) improvável; (*unexpected*) inesperado

unlimited [ʌn'lɪmɪtɪd] ADJ ilimitado

unlisted [ʌn'lɪstɪd] ADJ (*Stock Exchange*) não cotado na Bolsa de Valores; (*US Tel*): **an ~ number** um número que não consta na lista telefônica

unlit [ʌn'lɪt] ADJ (*room*) sem luz

unload [ʌn'ləʊd] VT descarregar

unlock [ʌn'lɔk] VT destrancar

unlucky [ʌn'lʌkɪ] ADJ infeliz; (*object, number*) de mau agouro; **to be ~** ser azarado, ter azar

unmanageable [ʌn'mænɪdʒəbl] ADJ (*unwieldy: tool*) de difícil manuseio, difícil de manejar; (*situation*) difícil de controlar

unmanned [ʌn'mænd] ADJ não tripulado, sem tripulação

unmarked [ʌn'mɑːkt] ADJ (*unstained*) sem marca; **~ police car** carro policial sem identificação

unmarried [ʌn'mærɪd] ADJ solteiro

unmask [ʌn'mɑːsk] VT desmascarar

unmatched [ʌn'mætʃt] ADJ sem igual, inigualável

unmentionable [ʌn'mɛnʃnəbl] ADJ (*topic*) que não se deve mencionar; (*word*) que não se diz

unmerciful [ʌn'mɜːsɪful] ADJ impiedoso

unmistakable, unmistakeable [ʌnmɪs'teɪkəbl] ADJ inconfundível

unmitigated [ʌn'mɪtɪgeɪtɪd] ADJ não mitigado, absoluto

unnamed [ʌn'neɪmd] ADJ (*nameless*) sem nome; (*anonymous*) anônimo

unnatural [ʌn'nætʃrəl] ADJ antinatural, artificial; (*manner*) afetado; (*habit*) depravado

unnecessary [ʌn'nɛsəsərɪ] ADJ desnecessário, inútil

unnerve [ʌn'nɜːv] VT amedrontar

unnoticed [ʌn'nəʊtɪst] ADJ: **(to go** *or* **pass) ~** (passar) despercebido

UNO ['juːnəʊ] N ABBR (= *United Nations Organization*) ONU *f*

unobservant [ʌnəb'zɜːvənt] N desatento

unobtainable [ʌnəb'teɪnəbl] ADJ inacessível; (*Tel*) ocupado

unobtrusive [ʌnəb'truːsɪv] ADJ discreto

unoccupied [ʌn'ɔkjupaɪd] ADJ (*seat etc*) desocupado, livre; (*house*) desocupado, vazio

unofficial [ʌnə'fɪʃl] ADJ não-oficial, informal; (*strike*) desautorizado

unopened [ʌn'əupənd] ADJ por abrir

unopposed [ʌnə'pəuzd] ADJ incontestado, sem oposição

unorthodox [ʌn'ɔ:θədɔks] ADJ pouco ortodoxo, heterodoxo

unpack [ʌn'pæk] VI desembrulhar ▶ VT desfazer

unpaid [ʌn'peɪd] ADJ (*bill*) a pagar, não pago; (*holiday*) não pago, sem salário; (*work, worker*) não remunerado

unpalatable [ʌn'pælətəbl] ADJ desagradável

unparalleled [ʌn'pærəlɛld] ADJ (*unequalled*) sem paralelo; (*unique*) único, incomparável

unpatriotic [ʌnpætrɪ'ɔtɪk] ADJ (*person*) antipatriota; (*speech, attitude*) antipatriótico

unplanned [ʌn'plænd] ADJ (*visit*) imprevisto; (*baby*) não previsto

unpleasant [ʌn'plɛznt] ADJ (*disagreeable*) desagradável; (*person, manner*) antipático

unplug [ʌn'plʌg] VT desligar

unpolluted [ʌnpə'lu:tɪd] ADJ impoluído

unpopular [ʌn'pɔpjulə^r] ADJ impopular

unprecedented [ʌn'prɛsɪdəntɪd] ADJ sem precedentes

unpredictable [ʌnprɪ'dɪktəbl] ADJ imprevisível

unprejudiced [ʌn'prɛdʒudɪst] ADJ (*not biased*) imparcial; (*having no prejudices*) sem preconceitos

unprepared [ʌnprɪ'pɛəd] ADJ (*person*) despreparado; (*speech*) improvisado

unprepossessing [ʌnpri:pə'zɛsɪŋ] ADJ pouco atraente

unpretentious [ʌnprɪ'tɛnʃəs] ADJ despretensioso

unprincipled [ʌn'prɪnsɪpld] ADJ sem princípios

unproductive [ʌnprə'dʌktɪv] ADJ improdutivo

unprofessional [ʌnprə'fɛʃənl] ADJ (*conduct*) pouco profissional

unprofitable [ʌn'prɔfɪtəbl] ADJ não lucrativo

unprovoked [ʌnprə'vəukt] ADJ sem provocação

unpunished [ʌn'pʌnɪʃt] ADJ ímpune

unqualified [ʌn'kwɔlɪfaɪd] ADJ (*teacher*) não qualificado, inabilitado; (*success*) irrestrito, absoluto

unquestionably [ʌn'kwɛstʃənəblɪ] ADV indubitavelmente

unquestioning [ʌn'kwɛstʃənɪŋ] ADJ (*obedience, acceptance*) incondicional, total

unravel [ʌn'rævl] VT desemaranhar; (*mystery*) desvendar

unreal [ʌn'rɪəl] ADJ irreal, ilusório; (*extraordinary*) extraordinário

unrealistic [ʌnrɪə'lɪstɪk] ADJ pouco realista

unreasonable [ʌn'ri:znəbl] ADJ insensato; (*demand*) absurdo

unrecognizable [ʌnrɛkəg'naɪzəbl] ADJ irreconhecível

unrecognized [ʌn'rɛkəgnaɪzd] ADJ (*talent, genius*) não reconhecido

unrecorded [ʌnrə'kɔ:dɪd] ADJ não registrado

unrefined [ʌnrə'faɪnd] ADJ (*sugar, petroleum*) não refinado

unrehearsed [ʌnrɪ'hə:st] ADJ improvisado

unrelated [ʌnrɪ'leɪtɪd] ADJ sem relação; (*family*) sem parentesco

unrelenting [ʌnrɪ'lɛntɪŋ] ADJ implacável

unreliable [ʌnrɪ'laɪəbl] ADJ (*person*) indigno de confiança; (*machine*) incerto, perigoso

unrelieved [ʌnrɪ'li:vd] ADJ (*monotony*) invariável

unremitting [ʌnrɪ'mɪtɪŋ] ADJ constante, incessante

unrepeatable [ʌnrɪ'pi:təbl] ADJ (*offer*) irrepetível

unrepentant [ʌnrɪ'pɛntənt] ADJ convicto, impenitente

unrepresentative [ʌnrɛprɪ'zɛntətɪv] ADJ pouco representativo *or* característico

unreserved [ʌnrɪ'zə:vd] ADJ (*seat*) não reservado; (*approval, admiration*) total, integral

unreservedly [ʌnrɪ'zə:vɪdlɪ] ADV sem reserva, francamente

unresponsive [ʌnrɪs'pɔnsɪv] ADJ indiferente, impassível

unrest [ʌn'rɛst] N inquietação *f*, desassossego; (*Pol*) distúrbios *mpl*

unrestricted [ʌnrɪ'strɪktɪd] ADJ irrestrito, ilimitado

unrewarded [ʌnrɪ'wɔ:dɪd] ADJ sem sucesso

unripe [ʌn'raɪp] ADJ verde, imaturo

unrivalled, (*US*) **unrivaled** [ʌn'raɪvəld] ADJ sem igual, incomparável

unroll [ʌn'rəul] VT desenrolar

unruffled [ʌn'rʌfld] ADJ (*person*) sereno, imperturbável; (*hair*) liso

unruly [ʌn'ru:lɪ] ADJ indisciplinado; (*hair*) desalinhado

unsafe [ʌn'seɪf] ADJ perigoso; **~ to eat/drink** não comestível/potável

unsaid [ʌn'sɛd] ADJ: **to leave sth ~** deixar algo por dizer

unsaleable, (*US*) **unsalable** [ʌn'seɪləbl] ADJ invendável, invendível

unsatisfactory [ʌnsætɪs'fæktərɪ] ADJ insatisfatório

unsatisfied [ʌn'sætɪsfaɪd] ADJ descontente

unsavoury, (*US*) **unsavory** [ʌn'seɪvərɪ] ADJ (*fig*) repugnante, vil

unscathed [ʌn'skeɪðd] ADJ ileso

unscientific [ʌnsaɪən'tɪfɪk] ADJ não científico

unscrew [ʌn'skru:] VT desparafusar

unscrupulous [ʌn'skru:pjuləs] ADJ inescrupuloso, imoral

unsecured [ʌnsə'kjuəd] ADJ: **~ creditor** credor(a) *m/f* quirografário(-a)

unseemly [ʌn'si:mlɪ] ADJ inconveniente

unseen [ʌn'si:n] ADJ (*person*) despercebido; (*danger*) escondido

unselfish [ʌn'sɛlfɪʃ] ADJ desinteressado

unsettled [ʌn'sɛtld] ADJ (*uncertain*) incerto, duvidoso; (*weather*) instável; (*person*) inquieto

unsettling [ʌn'sɛtlɪŋ] ADJ inquietador(a), inquietante

unshakable, unshakeable [ʌn'ʃeɪkəbl] ADJ inabalável

unshaven [ʌn'ʃeɪvn] ADJ com a barba por fazer

unsightly [ʌn'saɪtlɪ] ADJ feio, disforme

unskilled [ʌn'skɪld] ADJ não-especializado

unsociable [ʌn'səʊʃəbl] ADJ antissocial

unsocial [ʌn'səʊʃl] ADJ (*hours*) fora do horário normal

unsold [ʌn'səʊld] ADJ não vendido

unsolicited [ʌnsə'lɪsɪtɪd] ADJ não solicitado, espontâneo

unsophisticated [ʌnsə'fɪstɪkeɪtɪd] ADJ simples *inv*, natural

unsound [ʌn'saʊnd] ADJ (*health*) mau; (*floor, foundations*) em mau estado; (*policy, advice*) infundado

unspeakable [ʌn'spiːkəbl] ADJ indescritível; (*awful*) inqualificável

unspoken [ʌn'spəʊkən] ADJ (*agreement, approval*) tácito

unstable [ʌn'steɪbl] ADJ (*piece of furniture*) em falso; (*government, mentally*) instável; (*step, voice*) trêmulo; (*ladder*) em falso

unsteady [ʌn'stɛdɪ] ADJ (*hand, person*) trêmulo; (*ladder*) instável

unstinting [ʌn'stɪntɪŋ] ADJ (*support*) irrestrito, total; (*generosity*) ilimitado

unstuck [ʌn'stʌk] ADJ: **to come ~** despregar-se; (*fig*) fracassar

unsubstantiated [ʌnsəb'stænʃɪeɪtɪd] ADJ (*rumour*) que não foi confirmado; (*accusation*) sem provas

unsuccessful [ʌnsək'sɛsful] ADJ (*attempt*) frustrado, vão/vã; (*writer, proposal*) sem êxito; **to be ~** (*in attempting sth*) ser mal sucedido, não conseguir; (*application*) ser recusado

unsuccessfully [ʌnsək'sɛsfulɪ] ADV em vão, debalde

unsuitable [ʌn'suːtəbl] ADJ (*clothes, person*) inadequado; (*time, moment*) inconveniente

unsuited [ʌn'suːtɪd] ADJ: **to be ~ for** *or* **to** ser inadequado *or* impróprio para

unsupported [ʌnsə'pɔːtɪd] ADJ (*claim*) não verificado; (*theory*) não sustentado

unsure [ʌn'ʃuəʳ] ADJ inseguro, incerto; **to be ~ of o.s.** não ser seguro de si

unsuspecting [ʌnsə'spɛktɪŋ] ADJ confiante, insuspeitado

unsweetened [ʌn'swiːtənd] ADJ não adoçado, sem açúcar

unswerving [ʌn'swəːvɪŋ] ADJ inabalável, firme, resoluto

unsympathetic [ʌnsɪmpə'θɛtɪk] ADJ insensível; (*unlikeable*) antipático; **~ to** indiferente a

untangle [ʌn'tæŋgl] VT desemaranhar, desenredar

untapped [ʌn'tæpt] ADJ (*resources*) inexplorado

untaxed [ʌn'tækst] ADJ (*goods*) isento de impostos; (*income*) não tributado

unthinkable [ʌn'θɪŋkəbl] ADJ impensável, inconcebível, incalculável

untidy [ʌn'taɪdɪ] ADJ (*room*) desarrumado, desleixado; (*appearance*) desmazelado, desalinhado

untie [ʌn'taɪ] VT desatar, desfazer; (*dog, prisoner*) soltar

until [ən'tɪl] PREP até ▶ CONJ até que; **~ he comes** até que ele venha; **~ now** até agora; **~ then** até então; **from morning ~ night** de manhã à noite

untimely [ʌn'taɪmlɪ] ADJ inoportuno, intempestivo; (*death*) prematuro

untold [ʌn'təʊld] ADJ (*story*) inédito; (*suffering*) incalculável; (*joy, wealth*) inestimável

untouched [ʌn'tʌtʃt] ADJ (*not used*) intacto; (*safe: person*) ileso; **~ by** indiferente a

untoward [ʌntə'wɔːd] ADJ desfavorável, inconveniente

untrammelled [ʌn'træmld] ADJ sem entraves

untranslatable [ʌntræns'leɪtəbl] ADJ impossível de traduzir, intraduzível

untrue [ʌn'truː] ADJ falso

untrustworthy [ʌn'trʌstwəːðɪ] ADJ indigno de confiança

unusable [ʌn'juːzəbl] ADJ inutilizável, imprestável

unused¹ [ʌn'juːzd] ADJ novo, sem uso

unused² [ʌn'juːst] ADJ: **to be ~ to sth/to doing sth** não estar acostumado com algo/a fazer algo

unusual [ʌn'juːʒuəl] ADJ (*strange*) estranho; (*rare*) incomum; (*exceptional*) extraordinário

unusually [ʌn'juːʒəlɪ] ADV extraordinariamente

unveil [ʌn'veɪl] VT (*statue*) desvelar, descobrir

unwanted [ʌn'wɒntɪd] ADJ não desejado, indesejável

unwarranted [ʌn'wɒrəntɪd] ADJ injustificado

unwary [ʌn'wɛərɪ] ADJ imprudente

unwavering [ʌn'weɪvərɪŋ] ADJ firme

unwelcome [ʌn'wɛlkəm] ADJ (*guest*) inoportuno; (*news*) desagradável; **to feel ~** não se sentir à vontade

unwell [ʌn'wɛl] ADJ: **to be ~** estar doente; **to feel ~** estar indisposto

unwieldy [ʌn'wiːldɪ] ADJ difícil de manejar, pesado

unwilling [ʌn'wɪlɪŋ] ADJ: **to be ~ to do sth** relutar em fazer algo, não querer fazer algo

unwillingly [ʌn'wɪlɪŋlɪ] ADV de má vontade

unwind [ʌn'waɪnd] (*irreg: like* **wind**) VT desenrolar ▶ VI (*relax*) relaxar-se

unwise [ʌn'waɪz] ADJ imprudente

unwitting [ʌn'wɪtɪŋ] ADJ inconsciente, involuntário

unworkable [ʌn'wəːkəbl] ADJ (*plan etc*) inviável, inexequível

unworthy [ʌn'wəːðɪ] ADJ indigno

unwound [ʌn'waund] PT, PP *of* **unwind**

unwrap [ʌn'ræp] VT desembrulhar

u

unwritten [ʌn'rɪtən] ADJ (*agreement*) tácito
unzip [ʌn'zɪp] VT abrir (o fecho ecler de)

(KEYWORD)

up [ʌp] PREP: **to go/be up sth** subir algo/
estar em cima de algo; **we climbed/walked
up the hill** nós subimos/andamos até em
cima da colina; **they live further up the
street** eles moram mais adiante nesta rua;
go up that road and turn left vá por
aquela rua e vire à esquerda
▶ ADV **1** (*upwards, higher*) em cima, para cima;
up in the sky/the mountains lá no céu/nas
montanhas; **up there** lá em cima; **up
above** em cima; **there's a village and up
above, on the hill, a monastery** há uma
aldeia e, mais acima na colina, um
monastério
2: **to be up** (*out of bed*) estar de pé; (*prices, level*)
estar elevado; (*building, tent*) estar erguido
3: **up to** (*as far as*) até; **the water came up to
his knees** a água subiu até os seus joelhos;
up to now até agora
4: **to be up to** (*depending on*): **it is up to you**
você é quem sabe, você decide; **it's not up to
me to decide** não sou eu quem decide
5: **to be up to** (*equal to*) estar à altura de; **he's
not up to it** (*job, task etc*) ele não é capaz de
fazê-lo; **his work is not up to the required
standard** seu trabalho não atende aos
padrões exigidos
6: **to be up to** (*inf: be doing*) estar fazendo (BR)
or a fazer (PT); **what is he up to?** (*showing
disapproval, suspicion*) o que ele está querendo?,
o que ele está tramando?
▶ N: **ups and downs** (*in life, career*) altos *mpl* e
baixos; **we all have our ups and downs**
todos nós temos nossos altos e baixos

up-and-coming ADJ prometedor(a)
upbeat ['ʌpbiːt] ADJ (*Mus*) movimentado;
(*optimistic*) otimista
upbraid [ʌp'breɪd] VT repreender, censurar
upbringing ['ʌpbrɪŋɪŋ] N educação *f*, criação *f*
upcoming ['ʌpkʌmɪŋ] ADJ próximo
update [ʌp'deɪt] VT atualizar, pôr em dia;
(*contract etc*) atualizar
upend [ʌp'ɛnd] VT colocar em pé
upgrade [ʌp'greɪd] VT (*person*) promover; (*job*)
melhorar; (*house*) reformar; (*Comput*) fazer
um upgrade de
upheaval [ʌp'hiːvl] N transtorno; (*unrest*)
convulsão *f*
upheld [ʌp'hɛld] PT, PP *of* **uphold**
uphill [ʌp'hɪl] ADJ ladeira acima; (*fig: task*)
trabalhoso, árduo ▶ ADV: **to go ~** ir morro
acima
uphold [ʌp'həuld] (*irreg: like* **hold**) VT defender,
preservar
upholstery [ʌp'həulstərɪ] N estofamento
upkeep ['ʌpkiːp] N manutenção *f*
upload ['ʌpləud] VT (*Comput*) fazer upload de,
transferir

up-market ADJ (*product*) requintado
upon [ə'pɔn] PREP sobre
upper ['ʌpəʳ] ADJ superior, de cima ▶ N (*of shoe*)
gáspea, parte *f* superior
upper class N: **the ~** a classe alta
upper-class ADJ de classe alta
upper hand N: **to have the ~** ter controle *or*
domínio
uppermost ['ʌpəməust] ADJ mais elevado;
what was ~ in my mind o que me
preocupava mais
Upper Volta [-'vɔltə] N Alto Volta *m*
upright ['ʌpraɪt] ADJ vertical; (*straight*) reto;
(*fig*) honesto ▶ N viga vertical
uprising ['ʌpraɪzɪŋ] N revolta, rebelião *f*,
sublevação *f*
uproar ['ʌprɔːʳ] N tumulto, algazarra
uproot [ʌp'ruːt] VT (*tree*) arrancar; (*fig*)
desarraigar
upset [n 'ʌpsɛt, vt, adj ʌp'sɛt] (*irreg: like* **set**) N (*to
plan etc*) revés *m*, reviravolta; (*stomach upset*)
indisposição *f* ▶ VT (*glass etc*) virar; (*spill*)
derramar; (*plan*) perturbar; (*person: annoy*)
aborrecer; (: *sadden*) afligir ▶ ADJ aborrecido,
contrariado; (*sad*) aflito; (*stomach*)
indisposto
upset price (*US, SCOTLAND*) N preço mínimo
upsetting [ʌp'sɛtɪŋ] ADJ desconcertante
upshot ['ʌpʃɔt] N resultado, conclusão *f*
upside down ['ʌpsaɪd-] ADV de cabeça para
baixo; **to turn a place ~** (*fig*) deixar um
lugar de cabeça para baixo
upstairs [ʌp'stɛəz] ADV (*be*) em cima; (*go*) lá
em cima ▶ ADJ (*room*) de cima ▶ N andar *m* de
cima
upstart ['ʌpstɑːt] (*pej*) N novo-rico, pessoa
sem classe
upstream [ʌp'striːm] ADV rio acima
upsurge ['ʌpsəːdʒ] N (*of enthusiasm etc*)
explosão *f*
uptake ['ʌpteɪk] N: **he is quick on the ~** ele
vê longe; **he is slow on the ~** ele tem
raciocínio lento
uptight [ʌp'taɪt] (*inf*) ADJ nervoso
up-to-date ADJ (*person*) moderno, atualizado;
(*information*) atualizado; **to be ~ with the
facts** estar a par dos fatos
upturn ['ʌptəːn] N (*in luck*) virada; (*in economy*)
retomada
upturned ['ʌptəːnd] ADJ (*nose*) arrebitado
upward ['ʌpwəd] ADJ ascendente, para cima
▶ ADV para cima; (*more than*): **~ of** para cima
de
upwards ['ʌpwədz] ADV = **upward**
URA (*US*) N ABBR = **Urban Renewal
Administration**
Ural Mountains ['juərəl-] NPL: **the ~** (*also:* **the
Urals**) as montanhas Urais, os Urais
uranium [juə'reɪnɪəm] N urânio
Uranus [juə'reɪnəs] N Urano
urban ['əːbən] ADJ urbano, da cidade
urbane [əː'beɪn] ADJ gentil, urbano
urbanization [əːbənaɪ'zeɪʃən] N urbanização *f*

urchin ['ə:tʃɪn] (pej) N moleque m, criança maltrapilha

urge [ə:dʒ] N (force) impulso; (desire) desejo
▸ VT: **to ~ sb to do sth** incitar alguém a fazer algo
▸ **urge on** VT animar, encorajar

urgency ['ə:dʒənsɪ] N urgência; (of tone) insistência

urgent ['ə:dʒənt] ADJ urgente; (tone, plea) insistente

urgently ['ə:dʒəntlɪ] ADV urgentemente

urinal [juə'raɪnl] (BRIT) N (vessel) urinol m; (building) mictório

urinate ['juərɪneɪt] VI urinar, mijar

urine ['juərɪn] N urina

URL ABBR (= uniform resource locator) URL m

urn [ə:n] N urna; (also: **tea urn**) samovar m

Uruguay ['juərəgwaɪ] N Uruguai m

Uruguayan [juərə'gwaɪən] ADJ, N uruguaio(-a)

US N ABBR (= United States) EUA mpl

us [ʌs] PRON nos; (after prep) nós; see also **me**

USA N ABBR (= United States of America) EUA mpl; (Mil) = **United States Army**

usable ['ju:zəbl] ADJ usável, utilizável

USAF N ABBR = **United States Air Force**

usage ['ju:zɪdʒ] N uso

USB ABBR (Comput: = universal serial bus) USB m

USB stick N (Comput) pen drive m

USCG N ABBR = **United States Coast Guard**

USDA N ABBR = **United States Department of Agriculture**

USDAW ['ʌzdɔ:] (BRIT) N ABBR (= Union of Shop, Distributive and Allied Workers) sindicato dos varejistas e distribuidores

USDI N ABBR = **United States Department of the Interior**

use [n ju:s, vt ju:z] N uso, emprego; (usefulness) utilidade f ▸ VT usar, utilizar; (phrase) empregar; **in ~** em uso; **out of ~** fora de uso; **ready for ~** pronto para ser usado; **to be of ~** ser útil; **it's no ~** (pointless) é inútil; (not useful) não serve; **to have ~ of** ter uso de; **to make ~ of** fazer uso de; **to be ~d to** estar acostumado a; **she ~d to do it** ela costumava fazê-lo
▸ **use up** VT esgotar, consumir; (money) gastar

used [ju:zd] ADJ usado

useful ['ju:sful] ADJ útil; **to come in ~** ser útil

usefulness ['ju:sfəlnɪs] N utilidade f

useless ['ju:slɪs] ADJ inútil; (person) incapaz

user ['ju:zər] N usuário(-a) (BR), utente m/f (PT)

user-friendly ADJ de fácil utilização

username N (Comput) nome de usuário m

USES N ABBR = **United States Employment Service**

usher ['ʌʃər] N (in cinema) lanterninha m (BR), arrumador m (PT); (at wedding) oficial m de justiça ▸ VT: **to ~ sb in** fazer alguém entrar

usherette [ʌʃə'rɛt] N (in cinema) lanterninha (BR), arrumadora (PT)

USIA N ABBR = **United States Information Agency**

USM N ABBR = **United States Mail; United States Mint**

USN N ABBR = **United States Navy**

USP N ABBR (= unique selling proposition) proposta única de valor

USPHS N ABBR = **United States Public Health Service**

USPO N ABBR = **United States Post Office**

USS N ABBR = **United States Ship; United States Steamer**

USSR N ABBR (= Union of Soviet Socialist Republics) URSS f

usual ['ju:ʒuəl] ADJ usual, habitual; **as ~** como de habitual, como sempre

usually ['ju:ʒuəlɪ] ADV normalmente

usurer ['ju:ʒərər] N usurário(-a)

usurp [ju:'zə:p] VT usurpar

UT (US) ABBR (Post) = **Utah**

ute [ju:t] (AUST, NZ inf) N ABBR (= utility truck) camioneta

utensil [ju:'tɛnsl] N utensílio; **kitchen ~s** utensílios de cozinha

uterus ['ju:tərəs] N útero

utilitarian [ju:tɪlɪ'tɛərɪən] ADJ utilitário

utility [ju:'tɪlɪtɪ] N utilidade f; (public utility) utilidade f pública

utility room N área de serviço

utilization [ju:tɪlaɪ'zeɪʃən] N utilização f

utilize ['ju:tɪlaɪz] VT utilizar

utmost ['ʌtməust] ADJ maior ▸ N: **to do one's ~** fazer todo o possível; **of the ~ importance** da maior importância

utter ['ʌtər] ADJ total ▸ VT (sounds) emitir; (words) proferir, pronunciar

utterance ['ʌtərəns] N declaração f

utterly ['ʌtəlɪ] ADV completamente, totalmente

U-turn N retorno; (fig) reviravolta

u

Vv

V, v [viː] N *(letter)* V, v *m*; **V for Victor** V de Vera

v ABBR = **verse**; *(= vide: see)* vide; *(= versus)* v; *(= volt)* v

VA *(US)* ABBR *(Post)* = **Virginia**

vac [væk] *(BRIT inf)* N ABBR = **vacation**

vacancy ['veɪkənsɪ] N *(BRIT: job)* vaga; *(room)* quarto livre; **"no vacancies"** "cheio"

vacant ['veɪkənt] ADJ *(house)* vazio; *(post)* vago; *(seat etc)* desocupado, livre; *(expression)* distraído

vacant lot N terreno vago; *(uncultivated)* terreno baldio

vacate [və'keɪt] VT *(house)* desocupar; *(job)* deixar; *(throne)* renunciar a

vacation [və'keɪʃən] *(esp US)* N férias *fpl*; **to take a ~** tirar férias; **on ~** de férias

vacation course N curso de férias

vacationer [və'keɪʃənəʳ] *(US)* N veranista *m/f*

vaccinate ['væksɪneɪt] VT: **to ~ sb (against sth)** vacinar alguém (contra algo)

vaccination [væksɪ'neɪʃən] N vacinação *f*

vaccine ['væksiːn] N vacina

vacuum ['vækjum] N vácuo *m*

vacuum bottle *(US)* N garrafa térmica *(BR)*, termo *(PT)*

vacuum cleaner N aspirador *m* de pó

vacuum flask *(BRIT)* N garrafa térmica *(BR)*, termo *(PT)*

vacuum-packed ADJ embalado a vácuo

vagabond ['vægəbɔnd] N vagabundo(-a)

vagary ['veɪgərɪ] N extravagância, capricho

vagina [və'dʒaɪnə] N vagina

vagrancy ['veɪgrənsɪ] N vadiagem *f*

vagrant ['veɪgrənt] N vagabundo(-a), vadio(-a)

vague [veɪg] ADJ vago; *(blurred: memory)* fraco; **I haven't the ~st idea** não tenho a mínima ideia

vaguely ['veɪglɪ] ADV vagamente

vain [veɪn] ADJ *(conceited)* vaidoso; *(useless)* vão/vã, inútil; **in ~** em vão

valance ['væləns] N sanefa

vale [veɪl] N vale *m*

valedictory [vælɪ'dɪktərɪ] ADJ de despedida

valentine ['væləntaɪn] N *(also: **valentine card**)* cartão *m* do Dia dos Namorados; *(person)* namorado; **V~'s Day** Dia *m* dos Namorados

valet ['vælɪt] N *(of lord)* criado pessoal; *(in hotel)* camareiro

valet parking N estacionamento por manobrista

valet service N *(for clothes)* lavagem *f* a seco; *(for car)* limpeza completa

valiant ['vælɪənt] ADJ carajoso

valid ['vælɪd] ADJ válido

validate ['vælɪdeɪt] VT *(contract, document)* validar, legitimar; *(argument, claim)* confirmar, corroborar

validity [və'lɪdɪtɪ] N validade *f*

valise [və'liːz] N maleta

valley ['vælɪ] N vale *m*

valour, *(US)* **valor** ['væləʳ] N valor *m*, valentia

valuable ['væljuəbl] ADJ *(jewel)* de valor; *(time)* valioso; *(help)* precioso

valuables ['væljuəblz] NPL objetos *mpl* de valor

valuation [vælju'eɪʃən] N avaliação *f*; *(of quality)* apreciação *f*

value ['væljuː] N valor *m*; *(importance)* importância ▶ VT *(fix price of)* avaliar; *(appreciate)* valorizar, estimar; *(cherish)* apreciar; **values** NPL *(principles)* valores *mpl*; **you get good ~ (for money) in that shop** o seu dinheiro rende mais naquela loja; **to lose (in) ~** desvalorizar-se; **to gain (in) ~** valorizar-se; **to be of great ~ to sb** *(fig)* ser de grande utilidade para alguém; **to be ~d at $8** ser avaliado em $8

value added tax [-'ædɪd-] *(BRIT)* N imposto sobre a circulação de mercadorias *(BR)*, imposto sobre valor acrescentado *(PT)*

valued ['væljuːd] ADJ *(appreciated)* valorizado

valuer ['væljuəʳ] N avaliador(a) *m/f*

valve [vælv] N válvula; *(in radio)* lâmpada

vampire ['væmpaɪəʳ] N vampiro(-a)

van [væn] N *(Aut)* camionete *f* *(BR)*, camioneta *(PT)*

V and A *(BRIT)* N ABBR = **Victoria and Albert Museum**

vandal ['vændl] N vândalo(-a)

vandalism ['vændəlɪzəm] N vandalismo

vandalize ['vændəlaɪz] VT destruir, depredar

vanguard ['vængɑːd] N: **in the ~ of** na vanguarda de

vanilla [və'nɪlə] N baunilha ▶ CPD *(ice cream)* de baunilha

vanish ['vænɪʃ] VI desaparecer, sumir
vanity ['vænɪtɪ] N vaidade f
vanity case N bolsa de maquilagem
vantage point ['vɑːntɪdʒ-] N posição f estratégica
vapor ['veɪpəʳ] (US) N = **vapour**
vaporize ['veɪpəraɪz] VT vaporizar ▶ VI vaporizar-se
vapour, (US) **vapor** ['veɪpəʳ] N vapor m
variable ['vɛərɪəbl] ADJ variável ▶ N variável f
variance ['vɛərɪəns] N: **to be at ~ (with)** estar em desacordo (com)
variant ['vɛərɪənt] N variante f
variation [vɛərɪ'eɪʃən] N variação f; (variant) variante f; (in opinion) mudança
varicose ['værɪkəus] ADJ: **~ veins** varizes fpl
varied ['vɛərɪd] ADJ variado
variety [və'raɪətɪ] N variedade f, diversidade f; (type, quantity) variedade; **for a ~ of reasons** por várias or diversas razões
variety show N espetáculo de variedades
various ['vɛərɪəs] ADJ vários(-as), diversos(-as); (several) vários(-as); **at ~ times** (different) em horas variadas; (several) várias vezes
varnish ['vɑːnɪʃ] N verniz m; (nail varnish) esmalte m ▶ VT envernizar; (nails) pintar (com esmalte)
vary ['vɛərɪ] VT variar; (change) mudar ▶ VI variar; (deviate) desviar-se; (become different): **to ~ with** or **according to** variar de acordo com
varying ['vɛərɪɪŋ] ADJ variado
vase [vɑːz] N vaso
vasectomy [væ'sɛktəmɪ] N vasectomia
Vaseline® ['væsɪliːn] N vaselina®
vast [vɑːst] ADJ enorme
vastly ['vɑːstlɪ] ADV (underestimate etc) enormemente; (different) completamente
vastness ['vɑːstnɪs] N imensidão f
VAT [væt] (BRIT) N ABBR (= value added tax) ≈ ICM m (BR), IVA m (PT)
vat [væt] N tina, cuba
Vatican ['vætɪkən] N: **the ~** o Vaticano
vault [vɔːlt] N (of roof) abóbada; (tomb) sepulcro; (in bank) caixa-forte f; (jump) salto ▶ VT (also: **vault over**) saltar (por cima de)
vaunted ['vɔːntɪd] ADJ: **much-~** tão alardeado
VC N ABBR = **vice-chairman**; (BRIT: = Victoria Cross) distinção militar
VCR N ABBR = **video cassette recorder**
VD N ABBR = **venereal disease**
VDU N ABBR = **visual display unit**
veal [viːl] N carne f de vitela
veer [vɪəʳ] VI virar
veg. [vɛdʒ] (BRIT inf) N ABBR = **vegetable**
vegan ['viːgən] N vegetalista m/f
vegetable ['vɛdʒtəbl] N (Bot) vegetal m; (edible plant) legume m, hortaliça ▶ ADJ vegetal; **vegetables** NPL (cooked) verduras fpl
vegetable garden N horta

vegetarian [vɛdʒɪ'tɛərɪən] ADJ, N vegetariano(-a)
vegetate ['vɛdʒɪteɪt] VI vegetar
vegetation [vɛdʒɪ'teɪʃən] N vegetação f
vehemence ['viːɪməns] N veemência, violência
vehement ['viːɪmənt] ADJ veemente; (impassioned) apaixonado; (attack) violento
vehicle ['viːɪkl] N veículo
vehicular [vɪ'hɪkjuləʳ] ADJ: **"no ~ traffic"** "proibido trânsito de veículos automotores"
veil [veɪl] N véu m ▶ VT velar; **under a ~ of secrecy** (fig) sob um manto de sigilo
veiled [veɪld] ADJ velado
vein [veɪn] N veia; (of ore etc) filão m; (on leaf) nervura; (fig: mood) tom m
vellum ['vɛləm] N papel m velino
velocity [vɪ'lɒsɪtɪ] N velocidade f
velvet ['vɛlvɪt] N veludo ▶ ADJ aveludado
vendetta [vɛn'dɛtə] N vendeta
vending machine ['vɛndɪŋ-] N vendedor m automático
vendor ['vɛndəʳ] N vendedor(a) m/f; **street ~** camelô m
veneer [və'nɪəʳ] N capa exterior, folheado; (wood) compensado; (fig) aparência
venerable ['vɛnərəbl] ADJ venerável
venereal [vɪ'nɪərɪəl] ADJ: **~ disease** doença venérea
Venetian blind [vɪ'niːʃən-] N persiana
Venezuela [vɛnɛ'zweɪlə] N Venezuela
Venezuelan [vɛnɛ'zweɪlən] ADJ, N venezuelano(-a)
vengeance ['vɛndʒəns] N vingança; **with a ~** (fig) para valer
vengeful ['vɛndʒful] ADJ vingativo
Venice ['vɛnɪs] N Veneza
venison ['vɛnɪsn] N carne f de veado
venom ['vɛnəm] N veneno; (bitterness) malevolência
venomous ['vɛnəməs] ADJ venenoso; (look, stare) malévolo
vent [vɛnt] N (opening, in jacket) abertura; (also: **air vent**) respiradouro; (in wall) abertura para ventilação ▶ VT (fig: feelings) desabafar, descarregar
ventilate ['vɛntɪleɪt] VT ventilar
ventilation [vɛntɪ'leɪʃən] N ventilação f
ventilation shaft N poço de ventilação
ventilator ['vɛntɪleɪtəʳ] N ventilador m
ventriloquist [vɛn'trɪləkwɪst] N ventríloquo
venture ['vɛntʃəʳ] N empreendimento ▶ VT aventurar; (opinion) arriscar ▶ VI arriscar-se; **business ~** empreendimento comercial; **to ~ to do sth** aventurar-se or arriscar-se a fazer algo
venture capital N capital m de especulação
venue ['vɛnjuː] N local m; (meeting place) ponto de encontro; (theatre etc) espaço
Venus ['viːnəs] N (planet) Vênus f
veracity [və'ræsɪtɪ] N veracidade f
veranda, verandah [və'rændə] N varanda
verb [vəːb] N verbo

v

verbal ['vɜːbəl] ADJ verbal
verbally ['vɜːbəlɪ] ADV verbalmente
verbatim [vɜː'beɪtɪm] ADJ, ADV palavra por palavra
verbose [vɜː'bəʊs] ADJ prolixo
verdict ['vɜːdɪkt] N veredicto, decisão f; (fig) opinião f, parecer m; ~ **of guilty/not guilty** veredicto de culpado/não culpado
verge [vɜːdʒ] N beira, margem f; (on road) acostamento (BR), berma (PT); **"soft ~s"** (BRIT Aut) "acostamento mole"; **to be on the ~ of doing sth** estar a ponto or à beira de fazer algo
▶ **verge on** VT FUS beirar em
verger ['vɜːdʒəʳ] N (Rel) sacristão m
verification [vɛrɪfɪ'keɪʃən] N verificação f
verify ['vɛrɪfaɪ] VT verificar
veritable ['vɛrɪtəbl] ADJ verdadeiro
vermin ['vɜːmɪn] NPL (animals) bichos mpl; (insects, fig) insetos mpl nocivos
vermouth ['vɜːməθ] N vermute m
vernacular [və'nækjʊləʳ] N vernáculo; **in the ~** na língua corrente
versatile ['vɜːsətaɪl] ADJ (person) versátil; (machine, tool etc) polivalente; (mind) ágil, flexível
verse [vɜːs] N verso, poesia; (stanza) estrofe f; (in bible) versículo; **in ~** em verso
versed [vɜːst] ADJ: **(well-)~ in** versado em
version ['vɜːʃən] N versão f
versus ['vɜːsəs] PREP contra, versus
vertebra ['vɜːtɪbrə] (pl **vertebrae**) N vértebra
vertebrae ['vɜːtɪbriː] NPL of **vertebra**
vertebrate ['vɜːtɪbrɪt] N vertebrado
vertical ['vɜːtɪkl] ADJ vertical ▶ N vertical f
vertically ['vɜːtɪklɪ] ADV verticalmente
vertigo ['vɜːtɪgəʊ] N vertigem f; **to suffer from ~** ter vertigens
verve [vɜːv] N garra, pique m
very ['vɛrɪ] ADV muito ▶ ADJ: **the ~ book which** o mesmo livro que; **the ~ thought (of it) ...** só de pensar (nisso) ...; **at the ~ end** bem no final; **the ~ last** o último (de todos), bem o último; **at the ~ least** no mínimo; **~ much** muitíssimo; **~ little** muito pouco, pouquíssimo
vespers ['vɛspəz] NPL vésperas fpl
vessel ['vɛsl] N (Anat) vaso; (Naut) navio, barco; (container) vaso, vasilha
vest [vɛst] N (BRIT) camiseta (BR), camisola interior (PT); (US: waistcoat) colete m ▶ VT: **to ~ sb with sth, to ~ sth in sb** investir alguém de algo, conferir algo a alguém
vested interest ['vɛstɪd-] N: **to have a ~ in doing** ter um interesse em fazer; **vested interests** NPL (Comm) direitos mpl adquiridos
vestibule ['vɛstɪbjuːl] N vestíbulo
vestige ['vɛstɪdʒ] N vestígio
vestry ['vɛstrɪ] N sacristia
Vesuvius [vɪ'suːvɪəs] N Vesúvio
vet [vɛt] N ABBR (= veterinary surgeon) veterinário(-a) ▶ VT examinar

veteran ['vɛtərn] N veterano(-a); (also: **war veteran**) veterano de guerra ▶ ADJ: **she's a ~ campaigner for ...** ela é uma veterana nas campanhas de ...
veteran car N carro antigo
veterinarian [vɛtrɪ'nɛərɪən] (US) N veterinário(-a)
veterinary ['vɛtrɪnərɪ] ADJ veterinário
veterinary surgeon (BRIT) N veterinário(-a)
veto ['viːtəʊ] N (pl **vetoes**) veto ▶ VT vetar; **to put a ~ on** opor seu veto a
vex [vɛks] VT (irritate) irritar, apoquentar; (make impatient) impacientar
vexed [vɛkst] ADJ (question) controvertido, discutido
VFD (US) N ABBR = **voluntary fire department**
VG (BRIT) N ABBR (Sch) = **very good**
VHF ABBR (= very high frequency) VHF, frequência muito alta
VI (US) ABBR (Post) = **Virgin Islands**
via ['vaɪə] PREP por, via
viability [vaɪə'bɪlɪtɪ] N viabilidade f
viable ['vaɪəbl] ADJ viável
viaduct ['vaɪədʌkt] N viaduto
vibrant ['vaɪbrənt] ADJ (lively) entusiasmado; (colour) vibrante; (voice) ressonante
vibrate [vaɪ'breɪt] VI vibrar
vibration [vaɪ'breɪʃən] N vibração f
vicar ['vɪkəʳ] N vigário
vicarage ['vɪkərɪdʒ] N vicariato
vicarious [vɪ'kɛərɪəs] ADJ (pleasure, existence) indireto
vice [vaɪs] N (evil) vício; (Tech) torno mecânico
vice- [vaɪs] PREFIX vice-
vice-chairman (irreg: like **man**) N vice-presidente m/f
vice-chancellor (BRIT) N reitor(a) m/f
vice-president N vice-presidente m/f
vice squad N delegacia de costumes
vice versa ['vaɪsɪ'vɜːsə] ADV vice-versa
vicinity [vɪ'sɪnɪtɪ] N (area: nearness) proximidade f; **in the ~ of** nas proximidades de
vicious ['vɪʃəs] ADJ (violent) violento; (depraved) depravado, vicioso; (cruel) cruel; (bitter) rancoroso
vicious circle N círculo vicioso
viciousness ['vɪʃəsnɪs] N violência; depravação f; crueldade f; rancor m
vicissitudes [vɪ'sɪsɪtjuːdz] NPL vicissitudes fpl
victim ['vɪktɪm] N vítima f
victimization [vɪktɪmaɪ'zeɪʃən] N perseguição f; (in strike) represálias fpl
victimize ['vɪktɪmaɪz] VT (strikers etc) fazer represália contra
victor ['vɪktəʳ] N vencedor(a) m/f
Victorian [vɪk'tɔːrɪən] ADJ vitoriano
victorious [vɪk'tɔːrɪəs] ADJ vitorioso
victory ['vɪktərɪ] N vitória; **to win a ~ over sb** conseguir uma vitória sobre alguém
video ['vɪdɪəʊ] N (video film) vídeo; (pop video) videoclipe m; (also: **video cassette**)

videocassete *m*; (*also*: **video cassette recorder**) videocassete *m* ▶ CPD de vídeo
video camera N filmadora
video cassette N videocassete *m*
video cassette recorder N videocassete *m*
videophone N videofone *m*
video recording N gravação *f* em vídeo
video tape N videoteipe *m*; (*cassette*) videocassete *m*
video wall N painel *m* de vídeo
vie [vaɪ] VI: **to ~ (with sb) (for sth)** competir (com alguém) (por algo)
Vienna [vɪˈɛnə] N Viena
Vietnam, Viet Nam [ˈvjɛtˈnæm] N Vietnã *m* (BR), Vietname *m* (PT)
Vietnamese [vjɛtnəˈmiːz] ADJ vietnamita ▶ N INV vietnamita *m/f*; (*Ling*) vietnamita *m*
view [vjuː] N vista; (*outlook*) perspectiva; (*landscape*) paisagem *f*; (*opinion*) opinião *f*, parecer *m* ▶ VT (*look at, fig*) olhar; (*examine*) examinar; **on ~** (*in museum etc*) em exposição; **in full ~ (of)** à plena vista (de); **an overall ~ of the situation** uma visão geral da situação; **in my ~** na minha opinião; **in ~ of the weather/the fact that** em vista do tempo/do fato de que; **with a ~ to doing sth** com a intenção de fazer algo
viewer [ˈvjuːəʳ] N (*small projector*) visor *m*; (*person*) telespectador(a) *m/f*
viewfinder [ˈvjuːfaɪndəʳ] N visor *m*
viewpoint [ˈvjuːpɔɪnt] N ponto de vista; (*place*) lugar *m*
vigil [ˈvɪdʒɪl] N vigília; **to keep ~** velar
vigilance [ˈvɪdʒɪləns] N vigilância
vigilant [ˈvɪdʒɪlənt] ADJ vigilante
vigor [ˈvɪgəʳ] (US) N = **vigour**
vigorous [ˈvɪgərəs] ADJ vigoroso; (*plant*) vigoso
vigour, (US) **vigor** [ˈvɪgəʳ] N energia, vigor *m*
vile [vaɪl] ADJ (*action*) vil, infame; (*smell*) repugnante, repulsivo; (*temper*) violento
vilify [ˈvɪlɪfaɪ] VT vilipendiar
villa [ˈvɪlə] N (*country house*) casa de campo; (*suburban house*) vila, quinta
village [ˈvɪlɪdʒ] N aldeia, povoado
villager [ˈvɪlɪdʒəʳ] N aldeão/aldeã *m/f*
villain [ˈvɪlən] N (*scoundrel*) patife *m*; (BRIT: in novel etc) vilão *m*; (*criminal*) marginal *m/f*
VIN (US) N ABBR = **vehicle identification number**
vindicate [ˈvɪndɪkeɪt] VT vingar; (*justify*) jusficar
vindication [vɪndɪˈkeɪʃən] N: **in ~ of** em defesa de
vindictive [vɪnˈdɪktɪv] ADJ vingativo
vine [vaɪn] N vinha, videira; (*climbing plant*) planta trepadeira
vinegar [ˈvɪnɪgəʳ] N vinagre *m*
vine grower N vinhateiro(-a), viticultor(a) *m/f*
vine-growing ADJ vitícola ▶ N viticultura
vineyard [ˈvɪnjɑːd] N vinha, vinhedo
vintage [ˈvɪntɪdʒ] N vindima; (*year*) safra, colheita ▶ CPD (*comedy*) de época; (*performance*) clássico; **the 1970 ~** a safra de 1970

vintage car N carro antigo
vintage wine N vinho velho
vinyl [ˈvaɪnl] N vinil *m*
viola [vɪˈəʊlə] N viola
violate [ˈvaɪəleɪt] VT violar
violation [vaɪəˈleɪʃən] N violação *f*; **in ~ of** (*rule, law*) em violação de
violence [ˈvaɪələns] N violência; (*strength*) força
violent [ˈvaɪələnt] ADJ violento; (*intense*) intenso; **a ~ dislike of sb/sth** uma forte aversão a alguém/algo
violently [ˈvaɪələntlɪ] ADV violentemente; (*ill, angry*) extremamente
violet [ˈvaɪələt] ADJ violeta ▶ N (*colour, plant*) violeta
violin [vaɪəˈlɪn] N violino
violinist [vaɪəˈlɪnɪst] N violinista *m/f*
VIP N ABBR (= *very important person*) VIP *m/f*
viper [ˈvaɪpəʳ] N víbora
viral [ˈvaɪərəl] ADJ (*Med*) viral; **to go ~** (*Comput*) propagar-se rapidamente
virgin [ˈvəːdʒɪn] N virgem *m/f* ▶ ADJ virgem; **the Blessed V~** a Virgem Santíssima
virginity [vəːˈdʒɪnɪtɪ] N virgindade *f*
Virgo [ˈvəːgəʊ] N Virgem *f*
virile [ˈvɪraɪl] ADJ viril
virility [vɪˈrɪlɪtɪ] N virilidade *f*
virtual [ˈvəːtjuəl] ADJ (*Comput, Phys*) virtual; (*in effect*): **it's a ~ impossibility** é praticamente impossível; **the ~ leader** o líder na prática
virtually [ˈvəːtjuəlɪ] ADV (*almost*) praticamente
virtual reality [ˈvəːtjuəl-] N (*Comput*) realidade *f* virtual
virtue [ˈvəːtjuː] N virtude *f*; (*advantage*) vantagem *f*; **by ~ of** em virtude de
virtuoso [vəːtjuˈəʊzəʊ] (*pl* **virtuosos** *or* **virtuosi**) N virtuoso(-a)
virtuous [ˈvəːtjuəs] ADJ virtuoso
virulent [ˈvɪrulənt] ADJ virulento
virus [ˈvaɪərəs] N vírus *m*
visa [ˈviːzə] N visto
vis-à-vis [viːzəˈviː] PREP com relação a
viscose [ˈvɪskəʊz] N viscose *f*
viscount [ˈvaɪkaʊnt] N visconde *m*
viscous [ˈvɪskəs] ADJ viscoso
vise [vaɪs] (US) N (*Tech*) = **vice**
visibility [vɪzɪˈbɪlɪtɪ] N visibilidade *f*
visible [ˈvɪzəbl] ADJ visível; **~ exports/imports** exportações *fpl* /importações *fpl* visíveis
visibly [ˈvɪzəblɪ] ADV visivelmente
vision [ˈvɪʒən] N (*sight*) vista, visão *f*; (*foresight, in dream*) visão *f*
visionary [ˈvɪʒənərɪ] N visionário(-a)
visit [ˈvɪzɪt] N visita ▶ VT (*person, US: also*: **visit with**) visitar, fazer uma visita a; (*place*) ir a, ir conhecer; **on a private/official ~** em visita particular/oficial
visiting [ˈvɪzɪtɪŋ] ADJ (*speaker, team*) visitante
visiting card N cartão *m* de visita
visiting hours NPL horário de visita

V

visiting professor N professor(a) m/f de outra faculdade

visitor ['vɪzɪtə'] N visitante m/f; (to a house) visita; (tourist) turista m/f; (tripper) excursionista m/f

visitors' book N livro de visitas

visor ['vaɪzə'] N viseira

VISTA ['vɪstə] N ABBR (= Volunteers in Service to America) programa de assistência às regiões pobres

vista ['vɪstə] N vista

visual ['vɪzjuəl] ADJ visual

visual aid N recurso visual

visual display unit N terminal m de vídeo

visualize ['vɪzjuəlaɪz] VT visualizar; (foresee) prever

visually ['vɪzjuəlɪ] ADV visualmente; ~ **handicapped** deficiente visual

vital ['vaɪtl] ADJ (essential) essencial, indispensável; (important) de importância vital; (crucial) crucial; (person) vivo; (of life) vital; **of ~ importance** de importância vital

vitality [vaɪ'tælɪtɪ] N energia, vitalidade f

vitally ['vaɪtəlɪ] ADV: ~ **important** de importância vital

vital statistics NPL (of population) estatística demográfica; (fig) medidas fpl

vitamin ['vɪtəmɪn] N vitamina

vitiate ['vɪʃɪeɪt] VT viciar

vitreous ['vɪtrɪəs] ADJ vítreo

vitriolic [vɪtrɪ'ɔlɪk] ADJ (fig) mordaz

viva ['vaɪvə] N (also: **viva voce**) exame m oral

vivacious [vɪ'veɪʃəs] ADJ vivaz, animado

vivacity [vɪ'væsɪtɪ] N vivacidade f

vivid ['vɪvɪd] ADJ (account) vívido; (light) claro, brilhante; (imagination, colour) vivo

vividly ['vɪvɪdlɪ] ADV (describe) vividamente; (remember) distintamente

vivisection [vɪvɪ'sɛkʃən] N vivissecção f

vixen ['vɪksn] N raposa; (pej: woman) megera

viz ABBR (= videlicet) a saber

VLF ABBR = **very low frequency**

V-neck N (also: **V-neck jumper, V-neck pullover**) suéter f com decote em V

VOA N ABBR (= Voice of America) voz f da América, emissora que transmite para o estrangeiro

vocabulary [vəu'kæbjulə
rɪ] N vocabulário

vocal ['vəukl] ADJ vocal; (noisy) clamoroso; (articulate) claro, eloquente

vocal cords NPL cordas fpl vocais

vocalist ['vəukəlɪst] N vocalista m/f, cantor(a) m/f

vocals ['vəuklz] NPL vozes fpl

vocation [vəu'keɪʃən] N vocação f

vocational [vəu'keɪʃənl] ADJ vocacional; ~ **guidance/training** orientação f vocacional/ensino profissionalizante

vociferous [və'sɪfərəs] ADJ vociferante

vodka ['vɔdkə] N vodca

vogue [vəug] N voga, moda; **to be in ~** estar na moda

voice [vɔɪs] N voz f ▶ VT (opinion) expressar; **in a low/loud ~** em voz baixa/alta; **to give ~ to** dar voz a

voice mail N (system) correio m de voz; (device) caixa f postal

void [vɔɪd] N vazio; (hole) oco ▶ ADJ (null) nulo; (empty): ~ **of** destituído de

voile [vɔɪl] N voile m

vol. ABBR (= volume) vol.

volatile ['vɔlətaɪl] ADJ volátil; (situation, person) imprevisível

volcanic [vɔl'kænɪk] ADJ vulcânico

volcano [vɔl'keɪnəu] (pl **volcanoes**) N vulcão m

volition [və'lɪʃən] N: **of one's own ~** de livre vontade

volley ['vɔlɪ] N (of gunfire) descarga, salva; (of stones etc) chuva; (of questions etc) enxurrada, chuva; (Tennis etc) voleio

volleyball ['vɔlɪbɔːl] N voleibol m, vôlei m (BR)

volt [vəult] N volt m

voltage ['vəultɪdʒ] N voltagem f; **high/low ~** alta/baixa tensão

voluble ['vɔljubl] ADJ (person) tagarela; (speech) loquaz

volume ['vɔljuːm] N volume m; (of tank) capacidade f; ~ **one/two** tomo um/dois; **his expression spoke ~s** sua expressão disse tudo

volume control N (Radio, TV) controle m de volume

volume discount N (Comm) desconto de volume

voluminous [və'luːmɪnəs] ADJ volumoso

voluntarily ['vɔləntrɪlɪ] ADV livremente, voluntariamente

voluntary ['vɔləntərɪ] ADJ voluntário; (unpaid) (a título) gratuito

voluntary liquidation N (Comm) liquidação f requerida pela empresa

voluntary redundancy (BRIT) N demissão f voluntária

volunteer [vɔlən'tɪə'] N voluntário(-a) ▶ VT oferecer voluntariamente ▶ VI (Mil) alistar-se voluntariamente; **to ~ to do** oferecer-se voluntariamente para fazer

voluptuous [və'lʌptjuəs] ADJ voluptuoso

vomit ['vɔmɪt] N vômito ▶ VT, VI vomitar

vote [vəut] N voto; (votes cast) votação f; (right to vote) direito de votar; (franchise) título de eleitor ▶ VT: **to be ~d chairman** etc ser eleito presidente etc; (propose): **to ~ that** propor que; (in election) votar ▶ VI votar; **to put sth to the ~, to take a ~ on sth** votar algo, submeter algo à votação; **to ~ for sb** votar em alguém; **to ~ for/against a proposal** votar a favor de/contra uma proposta; **to ~ to do sth** votar a favor de fazer algo; **~ of censure** voto de censura; **~ of confidence** voto de confiança; **~ of thanks** agradecimento

voter ['vəutə'] N votante m/f, eleitor(a) m/f

voting ['vəutɪŋ] N votação f

voting paper (BRIT) N cédula eleitoral

voting right N direito de voto

voucher ['vautʃə'] N (also: **luncheon voucher**) vale-refeição m; (with petrol etc) vale m; (gift *voucher*) vale *m* para presente; (*receipt*) comprovante *m*

vouch for [vautʃ-] VT FUS garantir, responder por

vow [vau] N voto ▶ VT: **to ~ to do/that** prometer solenemente fazer/que ▶ VI fazer votos; **to take** *or* **make a ~ to do sth** fazer voto de fazer algo

vowel ['vauəl] N vogal *f*

voyage ['vɔɪɪdʒ] N (*journey*) viagem *f*; (*crossing*) travessia

VP N ABBR = **vice-president**

vs ABBR (= *versus*) x

V-sign (BRIT) N *gesto grosseiro*; **to give a ~ to sb** ≈ dar uma banana para alguém

VSO (BRIT) N ABBR = **Voluntary Service Overseas**

VT (US) ABBR (*Post*) = **Vermont**

vulgar ['vʌlgəʳ] ADJ (*rude*) grosseiro, ordinário; (*in bad taste*) vulgar, baixo

vulgarity [vʌl'gærɪtɪ] N grosseria; (*bad taste*) vulgaridade *f*

vulnerability [vʌlnərə'bɪlɪtɪ] N vulnerabilidade *f*

vulnerable ['vʌlnərəbl] ADJ vulnerável

vulture ['vʌltʃəʳ] N abutre *m*, urubu *m*

V

Ww

W¹, w ['dʌblju:] N (*letter*) W, w *m*; **W for William** W de William

W² ABBR (= *west*) O; (*Elec:* = *watt*) W

WA (*US*) ABBR (*Post*) = **Washington**

wad [wɔd] N (*of cotton wool*) chumaço; (*of paper*) bola; (*of banknotes etc*) maço

wadding ['wɔdɪŋ] N enchimento

waddle ['wɔdl] VI andar gingando *or* bamboleando

wade [weɪd] VI: **to ~ through** andar em; (*fig: a book*) ler com dificuldade ▶ VT vadear, atravessar (a vau)

wafer ['weɪfə^r] N (*biscuit*) bolacha; (*Rel*) hóstia

wafer-thin ADJ fininho, finíssimo

waffle ['wɔfl] N (*Culin*) waffle *m*; (*empty talk*) lengalenga ▶ VI encher linguiça

waffle iron N fôrma para fazer waffles

waft [wɔft] VT levar ▶ VI flutuar

wag [wæg] VT (*tail*) sacudir; (*finger*) menear ▶ VI acenar, abanar; **the dog ~ged its tail** o cachorro abanou o rabo

wage [weɪdʒ] N (*also:* **wages**) salário, ordenado ▶ VT: **to ~ war** empreender *or* fazer guerra; **a day's ~s** uma diária

wage claim N reivindicação *f* salarial

wage differential N desnível *m* salarial, diferença de salário

wage earner [-ə:nə^r] N assalariado(-a)

wage freeze N congelamento de salários

wage packet (*BRIT*) N envelope *m* de pagamento

wager ['weɪdʒə^r] N aposta, parada ▶ VT apostar

waggle ['wægl] VT mover

waggon, wagon ['wægən] N (*horse-drawn*) carroça; (*BRIT Rail*) vagão *m*

wail [weɪl] N lamento, gemido ▶ VI lamentar-se, gemer; (*siren*) tocar

waist [weɪst] N cintura

waistcoat ['weɪskəut] (*BRIT*) N colete *m*

waistline ['weɪstlaɪn] N cintura

wait [weɪt] N espera ▶ VI esperar; **to lie in ~ for** aguardar em emboscada; **I can't ~ to** (*fig*) estou morrendo de vontade de; **to ~ for sb/sth** esperar por alguém/algo; **to keep sb ~ing** deixar alguém esperando; **~ a minute!** espera aí!; **"repairs while you ~"** "conserta-se na hora"

▶ **wait behind** VI ficar para trás

▶ **wait on** VT FUS servir

▶ **wait up** VI esperar, não ir dormir; **don't ~ up for me** vá dormir, não espere por mim

waiter ['weɪtə^r] N garçom *m* (*BR*), empregado (*PT*)

waiting ['weɪtɪŋ] N: **"no ~"** (*BRIT Aut*) "proibido estacionar"

waiting list ['weɪtɪŋ-] N lista de espera

waiting room N sala de espera

waitress ['weɪtrɪs] N garçonete *f* (*BR*), empregada (*PT*)

waive [weɪv] VT abrir mão de

waiver ['weɪvə^r] N desistência

wake [weɪk] (*pt* **woke**, *pp* **woken**) VT (*also:* **wake up**) acordar ▶ VI acordar ▶ N (*for dead person*) velório; (*Naut*) esteira; **to ~ up to sth** (*fig*) abrir os olhos *or* acordar para algo; **in the ~ of** (*fig*) na esteira de; **to follow in sb's ~** (*fig*) seguir a esteira *or* o exemplo de alguém

waken ['weɪkən] VT, VI = **wake**

Wales [weɪlz] N País *m* de Gales; **the Prince of ~** o Príncipe de Gales

walk [wɔːk] N passeio; (*hike*) excursão *f* a pé, caminhada; (*gait*) passo, modo de andar; (*in park etc*) alameda, passeio ▶ VI andar; (*for pleasure, exercise*) passear ▶ VT (*distance*) percorrer a pé, andar; (*dog*) levar para passear; **it's 10 minutes' ~ from here** daqui são 10 minutos a pé; **to go for a ~** (*ir*) dar uma volta; **I'll ~ you home** vou andar com você até a sua casa; **people from all ~s of life** pessoas de todos os níveis

▶ **walk out** VI (*go out*) sair; (*audience*) retirar-se; (*strike*) entrar em greve

▶ **walk out on** VT FUS (*family etc*) abandonar

walker ['wɔːkə^r] N (*person*) caminhante *m/f*

walkie-talkie ['wɔːkɪ'tɔːkɪ] N transmissor-receptor *m* portátil, walkie-talkie *m*

walking ['wɔːkɪŋ] N o andar; **it's within ~ distance** dá para ir a pé

walking holiday N férias *fpl* fazendo excursões a pé

walking shoes NPL sapatos *mpl* de caminhada

walking stick N bengala

Walkman® N Walkman® *m*

walk-on ADJ (*Theatre: part*) de figurante

walkout ['wɔːkaut] N (*of workers*) greve *f* branca

walkover ['wɔːkəuvə^r] (inf) N barbada
walkway ['wɔːkweɪ] N passeio, passadiço
wall [wɔːl] N parede f; (exterior) muro; (city wall etc) muralha; **to go to the ~** (fig: firm etc) falir, quebrar
▶ **wall in** VT (garden etc) cercar com muros
wall cupboard N armário de parede
walled [wɔːld] ADJ (city) cercado por muralhas; (garden) murado, cercado
wallet ['wɔlɪt] N carteira
wallflower ['wɔːlflauə^r] N goivo-amarelo; **to be a ~** (fig) tomar chá de cadeira
wall hanging N tapete m
wallop ['wɔləp] (BRIT inf) VT surrar, espancar
wallow ['wɔləu] VI (in mud) chafurdar; (in water) rolar; (person: in guilt) regozijar-se; **to ~ in one's own grief** regozijar-se na própria dor
wallpaper ['wɔːlpeɪpə^r] N papel m de parede
▶ VT colocar papel de parede em
wall-to-wall ADJ: **~ carpeting** carpete m
walnut ['wɔːlnʌt] N noz f; (tree, wood) nogueira
walrus ['wɔːlrəs] (pl **walrus** or **walruses**) N morsa
waltz [wɔːlts] N valsa ▶ VI valsar
wan [wɔn] ADJ pálido; (smile) amarelo
wand [wɔnd] N (also: **magic wand**) varinha de condão
wander ['wɔndə^r] VI (person) vagar, perambular; (thoughts) divagar; (get lost) extraviar-se ▶ VT perambular
wanderer ['wɔndərə^r] N vagabundo(-a)
wandering ['wɔndərɪŋ] ADJ errante; (thoughts) distraído; (tribe) nômade; (minstrel, actor) itinerante
wane [weɪn] VI diminuir; (moon) minguar
wangle ['wæŋgl] (BRIT inf) VT: **to ~ sth** conseguir algo através de pistolão
wanker ['wæŋkə^r] (!) N babaca m/f
want [wɔnt] VT (wish for) querer; (demand) exigir; (need) precisar de, necessitar; (lack) carecer de ▶ N (poverty) pobreza, miséria; **wants** NPL (needs) necessidades fpl; **for ~ of** por falta de; **to ~ to do** querer fazer; **to ~ sb to do sth** querer que alguém faça algo; **"cook ~ed"** "precisa-se cozinheiro"
want ads (US) NPL classificados mpl
wanted ['wɔntɪd] ADJ (criminal etc) procurado (pela polícia); **you're ~ on the phone** estão querendo falar com você no telefone
wanting ['wɔntɪŋ] ADJ falto, deficiente; **to be found ~** não estar à altura da situação; **to be ~ in** carecer de
wanton ['wɔntən] ADJ (destruction) gratuito, irresponsável; (licentious) libertino, lascivo
war [wɔː^r] N guerra; **to make ~ (on)** fazer guerra (contra); **to go to ~** entrar na guerra; **~ of attrition** guerra de atrição
warble ['wɔːbl] N gorjeio ▶ VI gorjear
war cry N grito de guerra
ward [wɔːd] N (in hospital) ala; (Pol) distrito eleitoral; (Law: child) tutelado(-a), pupilo(-a)
▶ **ward off** VT desviar, aparar; (attack) repelir

warden ['wɔːdn] N (BRIT: of institution) diretor(a) m/f; (of park, game reserve) administrador(a) m/f; (BRIT: also: **traffic warden**) guarda m/f
warder ['wɔːdə^r] (BRIT) N carcereiro(-a)
wardrobe ['wɔːdrəub] N (cupboard) armário; (clothes) guarda-roupa m
warehouse ['wɛəhaus] N armazém m, depósito
wares [wɛəz] NPL mercadorias fpl
warfare ['wɔːfɛə^r] N guerra, combate m
war game N jogo de estrategia militar
warhead ['wɔːhɛd] N ogiva
warily ['wɛərɪlɪ] ADV cautelosamente, com precaução
warlike ['wɔːlaɪk] ADJ guerreiro, bélico
warm [wɔːm] ADJ quente; (thanks, welcome) caloroso, cordial; (supporter) entusiasmado; **it's ~** está quente; **I'm ~** estou com calor; **to keep sth ~** manter algo aquecido
▶ **warm up** VI (person, room) esquentar; (athlete) fazer aquecimento; (discussion) esquentar-se ▶ VT esquentar
warm-blooded [-'blʌdɪd] ADJ de sangue quente
war memorial N monumento aos mortos
warm-hearted [-'hɑːtɪd] ADJ afetuoso
warmly ['wɔːmlɪ] ADV calorosamente, afetuosamente
warmonger ['wɔːmʌŋgə^r] N belicista m/f
warmongering ['wɔːmʌŋgərɪŋ] N belicismo
warmth [wɔːmθ] N calor m; (friendliness) calor humano
warm-up N (Sport) aquecimento
warn [wɔːn] VT prevenir, avisar; **to ~ sb against sth** prevenir alguém contra algo; **to ~ sb that/of/(not) to do** prevenir alguém de que/de/para (não) fazer
warning ['wɔːnɪŋ] N advertência; (in writing) aviso; (signal) sinal m; **without (any) ~** (suddenly) de improviso, inopinadamente; (without notice) sem aviso prévio, sem avisar; **gale ~** (Meteorology) aviso de vendaval
warning light N luz f de advertência
warning triangle N (Aut) triângulo de advertência
warp [wɔːp] N (Textiles) urdidura ▶ VT deformar ▶ VI empenar, deformar-se
warpath ['wɔːpɑːθ] N: **to be on the ~** (fig) estar disposto a brigar
warped [wɔːpt] ADJ (wood) empenado; (fig: sense of humour) pervertido, deformado
warrant ['wɔrnt] N (guarantee) garantia; (voucher) comprovante m; (Law: to arrest) mandado de prisão; (: to search) mandado de busca ▶ VT (justify) justificar
warrant officer N (Mil) subtenente m; (Naut) suboficial m
warranty ['wɔrəntɪ] N garantia; **under ~** (Comm) sob garantia
warren ['wɔrən] N (of rabbits) lura; (house) coelheira; (fig) labirinto
warring ['wɔːrɪŋ] ADJ (nations) em guerra; (interests etc) antagônico

W

warrior ['wɔrɪə'] N guerreiro(-a)
Warsaw ['wɔːsɔː] N Varsóvia
warship ['wɔːʃɪp] N navio de guerra
wart [wɔːt] N verruga
wartime ['wɔːtaɪm] N: **in ~** em tempo de
guerra
wary ['wɛərɪ] ADJ cauteloso, precavido; **to
be ~ about** or **of doing sth** hesitar em fazer
algo
was [wɔz] PT of **be**
wash [wɔʃ] VT lavar; (sweep, carry: sea etc) levar,
arrastar; (: ashore) lançar ▶ VI lavar-se; (sea
etc): **to ~ over/against sth** bater/chocar-se
contra algo ▶ N (clothes etc) lavagem f; (of ship)
esteira; **to have a ~** lavar-se; **to give sth a ~**
lavar algo; **he was ~ed overboard** foi
arrastado do navio pelas águas
  ▶ **wash away** VT (stain) tirar ao lavar; (subj:
  river etc) levar, arrastar
  ▶ **wash down** VT lavar; (food) regar
  ▶ **wash off** VT tirar lavando ▶ VI sair ao lavar
  ▶ **wash up** VI (BRIT) lavar a louça; (US)
  lavar-se
washable ['wɔʃəbl] ADJ lavável
washbasin ['wɔʃbeɪsn] N pia (BR), lavatório (PT)
washbowl ['wɔʃbəul] (US) N = **washbasin**
washcloth ['wɔʃklɔθ] (US) N toalhinha para
lavar o rosto
washer ['wɔʃə'] N (Tech) arruela, anilha
wash-hand basin (BRIT) N pia (BR), lavatório (PT)
washing ['wɔʃɪŋ] (BRIT) N (dirty) roupa suja;
(clean) roupa lavada
washing line (BRIT) N corda de estender roupa,
varal m
washing machine N máquina de lavar roupa,
lavadora
washing powder (BRIT) N sabão m em pó
Washington ['wɔʃɪŋtən] N (city, state)
Washington
washing-up N: **to do the ~** lavar a louça
washing-up liquid (BRIT) N detergente m
wash-out (inf) N fracasso, fiasco
washroom ['wɔʃruːm] (US) N banheiro (BR),
casa de banho (PT)
wasn't ['wɔznt] = **was not**
WASP, Wasp (US inf) N ABBR (= White
Anglo-Saxon Protestant) apelido, muitas vezes
pejorativo, dado aos membros da classe dominante
nos EUA
wasp [wɔsp] N vespa
waspish ['wɔspɪʃ] ADJ irritadiço
wastage ['weɪstɪdʒ] N desgaste m, desperdício;
(loss) perda; **natural ~** desgaste natural
waste [weɪst] N desperdício, esbanjamento;
(wastage) desperdício; (of time) perda; (food)
sobras fpl; (also: **household waste**) detritos
mpl domésticos; (rubbish) lixo ▶ ADJ (material)
de refugo; (left over) de sobra; (land) baldio
  ▶ VT (squander) esbanjar, desperdiçar; (time,
  opportunity) perder; **wastes** NPL ermos mpl;
  it's a ~ of money é jogar dinheiro fora;
  to go to ~ ser desperdiçado; **to lay ~** (destroy)
  devastar

  ▶ **waste away** VI definhar
waste bin (BRIT) N lata de lixo
waste disposal, (BRIT) **waste disposal unit** N
triturador m de lixo
wasteful ['weɪstful] ADJ esbanjador(a);
(process) antieconômico
waste ground (BRIT) N terreno baldio
wasteland ['weɪstlənd] N terra inculta;
(in town) terreno baldio
wastepaper basket ['weɪstpeɪpə'-] N cesta
de papéis
waste pipe N cano de esgoto
waste products N (Industry) resíduos mpl
watch [wɔtʃ] N (clock) relógio; (also:
wristwatch) relógio de pulso; (act of watching)
vigia; (guard: Mil) sentinela; (Naut: spell of
duty) quarto ▶ VT (look at) observar, olhar;
(programme, match) assistir a; (television) ver;
(spy on, guard) vigiar; (be careful of) tomar
cuidado com ▶ VI ver, olhar; (keep guard)
montar guarda; **to keep a close ~ on sb/sth**
vigiar alguém/algo, ficar de olho em
alguém/algo; **~ what you're doing** presta
atenção no que você está fazendo
  ▶ **watch out** VI ter cuidado
watchband ['wɔtʃbænd] (US) N pulseira de
relógio
watchdog ['wɔtʃdɔg] N cão m de guarda; (fig)
vigia m/f
watchful ['wɔtʃful] ADJ vigilante, atento
watchmaker ['wɔtʃmeɪkə'] N relojoeiro(-a)
watchman ['wɔtʃmən] (irreg: like **man**) N
vigia m; (also: **night watchman**) guarda m
noturno; (: in factory) vigia m noturno
watch stem (US) N botão m de corda
watchstrap ['wɔtʃstræp] N pulseira de relógio
watchword ['wɔtʃwəːd] N lema m, divisa
water ['wɔːtə'] N água ▶ VT (plant) regar ▶ VI
(eyes) lacrimejar; (mouth) salivar; **a drink
of ~** um copo d'água; **in British ~s** nas
águas territoriais britânicas; **to pass ~**
urinar; **to make sb's mouth ~** dar água na
boca de alguém
  ▶ **water down** VT (milk) aguar; (fig) diluir
water cannon N tanque de espirrar água para
dispersar multidões
water closet (BRIT) N privada
watercolour, (US) **watercolor** ['wɔːtəkʌlə'] N
aquarela
water-cooled [-kuːld] ADJ refrigerado a água
watercress ['wɔːtəkrɛs] N agrião m
waterfall ['wɔːtəfɔːl] N cascata, cachoeira
waterfront ['wɔːtəfrʌnt] N (seafront) orla
marítima; (docks) zona portuária
water heater N aquecedor m de água, boiler m
water hole N bebedouro, poço
water ice (BRIT) N sorvete de frutas à base de água
watering can ['wɔːtərɪŋ-] N regador m
water level N nível m d'água
water lily N nenúfar m
waterline ['wɔːtəlaɪn] N (Naut) linha d'água
waterlogged ['wɔːtəlɔgd] ADJ alagado
water main N adutora

watermark ['wɔːtəmɑːk] N (on paper) filigrana
watermelon ['wɔːtəmɛlən] N melancia
water polo N polo aquático
waterproof ['wɔːtəpruːf] ADJ impermeável; (watch) à prova d'água
water-repellent ADJ hidrófugo
watershed ['wɔːtəʃɛd] N (Geo) linha divisória das águas; (fig) momento crítico
water-skiing N esqui m aquático
water softener N abrandador m de água
water tank N depósito d'água
watertight ['wɔːtətaɪt] ADJ hermético, à prova d'água
water vapour N vapor m de água
waterway ['wɔːtəweɪ] N hidrovia
waterworks ['wɔːtəwəːks] NPL usina hidráulica
watery ['wɔːtərɪ] ADJ (colour) pálido; (coffee) aguado; (eyes) húmido
watt [wɔt] N watt m
wattage ['wɔtɪdʒ] N wattagem f
wattle ['wɔtl] N caniçada
wave [weɪv] N (on water, Radio, fig) onda; (of hand) aceno, sinal m; (in hair) onda, ondulação f ▶ VI acenar com a mão; (flag, grass, branches) tremular ▶ VT (hand) acenar; (handkerchief) acenar com; (weapon) brandir; (hair) ondular; **to ~ goodbye to sb** despedir-se de alguém com um aceno; **short/medium/long ~** (Radio) ondas curtas/médias/longas; **the new ~** (Cinema, Mus) a nova onda
▶ **wave aside** VT (fig: suggestion, objection) rejeitar; (: doubts) pôr de lado; (person): **to ~ sb aside** fazer sinal para alguém pôr-se de lado
▶ **wave away** VT (fig: suggestion, objection) rejeitar; (: doubts) pôr de lado; (person): **to ~ sb away** fazer sinal para alguém pôr-se de lado
waveband ['weɪvbænd] N faixa de onda
wavelength ['weɪvlɛŋθ] N comprimento de onda; **to be on the same ~ as** ter os mesmos gostos e atitudes que
waver ['weɪvər] VI vacilar; (voice, eyes, love) hesitar
wavy ['weɪvɪ] ADJ (hair) ondulado; (line) ondulante
wax [wæks] N cera ▶ VT encerar; (car) polir ▶ VI (moon) crescer
waxworks ['wækswəːks] N museu m de cera ▶ NPL (models) figuras fpl de cera
way [weɪ] N caminho; (distance) percurso; (direction) direção f, sentido; (manner) maneira, modo; (habit) costume m; (condition) estado; **which ~? — this ~** por onde? — por aqui; **to crawl one's ~ to ...** arrastar-se até ...; **to lie one's ~ out of it** mentir para livrar-se de apuros; **on the ~ (to)** a caminho (de); **to be on one's ~** estar a caminho; **to be in the ~** atrapalhar; **to keep out of sb's ~** evitar alguém; **it's a long ~ away** é muito longe; **the village is rather out of the ~** o lugarejo é um pouco fora de mão; **to go out of one's ~ to do sth** (fig) dar-se ao trabalho

de fazer algo; **to lose one's ~** perder-se; **to be under ~** (work, project) estar em andamento; **to make ~ (for sb/sth)** abrir caminho (para alguém/algo); **to get one's own ~** conseguir o que quer; **to put sth the right ~ up** (BRIT) colocar algo na posição certa; **to be the wrong ~ round** estar às avessas; **he's in a bad ~** ele vai muito mal; **in a ~** de certo modo, até certo ponto; **in some ~s** a certos respeitos; **by the ~** a propósito; **"~ in"** (BRIT) "entrada"; **"~ out"** (BRIT) "saída"; **the ~ back** o caminho de volta; **"give ~"** (BRIT Aut) "dê a preferência"; **in the ~ of** em matéria de; **by ~ of** (through) por, via; (as a sort of) à guisa de; **no ~!** (inf) de jeito nenhum!
waybill ['weɪbɪl] N (Comm) conhecimento
waylay ['weɪleɪ] (irreg: like **lay**) VT armar uma cilada para; (fig): **I got waylaid** alguém me deteve
wayside ['weɪsaɪd] N beira da estrada; **to fall by the ~** (fig) desistir; (morally) corromper-se
way station N (US) (Rail) apeadeiro; (fig) etapa
wayward ['weɪwəd] ADJ (behaviour, child) caprichoso, voluntarioso
WC ['dʌblju'siː] (BRIT) N ABBR (= water closet) privada
WCC N ABBR = **World Council of Churches**
we [wiː] PRON PL nós
weak [wiːk] ADJ fraco, débil; (morally, currency) fraco; (excuse) pouco convincente; (tea) aguado, ralo; **to grow ~(er)** enfraquecer, ficar cada vez mais fraco
weaken ['wiːkən] VI enfraquecer(-se); (give way) ceder; (influence, power) diminuir ▶ VT enfraquecer; (lessen) diminuir
weak-kneed [-niːd] ADJ (fig) covarde
weakling ['wiːklɪŋ] N pessoa fraca or delicada; (morally) pessoa de personalidade fraca
weakly ['wiːklɪ] ADJ fraco ▶ ADV fracamente
weakness ['wiːknɪs] N fraqueza; (fault) ponto fraco; **to have a ~ for** ter uma queda por
wealth [wɛlθ] N (money, resources) riqueza; (of details) abundância
wealth tax N imposto sobre fortunas
wealthy ['wɛlθɪ] ADJ (person, family) rico, abastado; (country) rico
wean [wiːn] VT desmamar
weapon ['wɛpən] N arma; **~s of mass destruction** armas de destruição em massa
wear [wɛər] (pt **wore**, pp **worn**) N (use) uso; (deterioration through use) desgaste m; (clothing): **baby/sports ~** roupa infantil/de esporte ▶ VT (clothes) usar; (shoes) usar, calçar; (put on) vestir; (damage: through use) desgastar; (beard etc) ter ▶ VI (last) durar; (rub through etc) gastar-se; **town/evening ~** traje m de passeio/de gala; **to ~ a hole in sth** fazer um buraco em algo pelo uso
▶ **wear away** VT gastar ▶ VI desgastar-se
▶ **wear down** VT gastar; (strength) esgotar
▶ **wear off** VI (pain etc) passar
▶ **wear on** VI alongar-se

W

▶ **wear out** VT desgastar; (*person, strength*) esgotar

wearable ['wɛərəbl] ADJ que se pode usar

wear and tear N desgaste *m*

wearily ['wɪərɪlɪ] ADV de maneira cansada

weariness ['wɪərɪnɪs] N cansaço, fadiga; (*boredom*) aborrecimento

wearisome ['wɪərɪsəm] ADJ (*tiring*) cansativo; (*boring*) fastidioso

weary ['wɪərɪ] ADJ (*tired*) cansado; (*dispirited*) deprimido ▶ VT aborrecer ▶ VI: **to ~ of** cansar-se de

weasel ['wi:zl] N (*Zool*) doninha

weather ['wɛðər] N tempo ▶ VT (*storm, crisis*) resistir a; **what's the ~ like?** como está o tempo?; **under the ~** (*fig: ill*) doente

weather-beaten ADJ curtido; (*building, stone*) castigado, erodido

weathercock ['wɛðəkɔk] N cata-vento

weather forecast N previsão *f* do tempo

weatherman ['wɛðəmæn] (*irreg: like* **man**: *inf*) N meteorologista *m*

weatherproof ['wɛðəpru:f] ADJ (*garment*) impermeável; (*building*) à prova de intempérie

weather report N boletim *m* meteorológico

weather vane [-veɪn] N = **weathercock**

weave [wi:v] (*pt* **wove**, *pp* **woven**) VT (*cloth*) tecer; (*fig*) compor, criar ▶ VI (*fig: pt, pp* **weaved**: *move in and out*) ziguezaguear

weaver ['wi:vər] N tecelão(-loa) *m/f*

weaving ['wi:vɪŋ] N tecelagem *f*

web [wɛb] N (*of spider*) teia; (*on foot*) membrana; (*network*) rede *f*; **the (World Wide) W~** a (World Wide) Web

web address N endereço web

webbed [wɛbd] ADJ (*foot*) palmípede

webbing ['wɛbɪŋ] N (*on chair*) tira de tecido forte

webcam ['wɛbkæm] N webcam *f*

webinar ['wɛbɪnɑːr] N seminário online, webinar *m*

weblog ['wɛblɔg] N weblog *m*

webmail ['wɛbmeɪl] N (serviço *m* de) webmail *m*

web page N página (da) web

website ['wɛbsaɪt] N site *m*, website *m*

wed [wɛd] (*pt, pp* **wedded**) VT casar ▶ VI casar-se ▶ N: **the newly-~s** os recém-casados

Wed. ABBR (= *Wednesday*) qua., 4ª

we'd [wi:d] = **we had**; **we would**

wedded ['wɛdɪd] PT, PP *of* **wed**

wedding ['wɛdɪŋ] N casamento, núpcias *fpl*; **silver/golden ~** (*anniversary*) bodas *fpl* de prata/de ouro

wedding anniversary N aniversário de casamento; **silver/golden ~** bodas *fpl* de prata/de ouro

wedding day N dia *m* de casamento

wedding dress N vestido de noiva

wedding night N noite *f* de núpcias

wedding present N presente *m* de casamento

wedding ring N anel *m or* aliança de casamento

wedge [wɛdʒ] N (*of wood etc*) cunha, calço; (*of cake*) fatia ▶ VT (*pack tightly*) apinhar; (*door*) pôr calço em

wedge-heeled shoes [-hi:ld-] NPL sapatos *mpl* tipo Annabella

wedlock ['wɛdlɔk] N matrimônio, casamento

Wednesday ['wɛdnzdɪ] N quarta-feira; *see also* **Tuesday**

wee [wi:] (SCOTLAND) ADJ pequeno, pequenino

weed [wi:d] N erva daninha ▶ VT capinar

weedkiller ['wi:dkɪlər] N herbicida *m*

weedy ['wi:dɪ] ADJ (*man*) fraquinho

week [wi:k] N semana; **once/twice a ~** uma vez/duas vezes por semana; **in two ~s' time** daqui a duas semanas; **a ~ today** daqui a uma semana; **Tuesday ~, a ~ on Tuesday** sem ser essa terça-feira, a outra; **every other ~** uma semana sim, uma semana não

weekday ['wi:kdeɪ] N dia *m* de semana; (*Comm*) dia útil; **on ~s** durante a semana

weekend ['wi:kɛnd] N fim *m* de semana

weekend case N maleta

weekly ['wi:klɪ] ADV semanalmente ▶ ADJ semanal ▶ N semanário

weep [wi:p] (*pt, pp* **wept**) VI (*person*) chorar; (*Med: wound*) supurar

weeping willow ['wi:pɪŋ-] N salgueiro chorão

weft [wɛft] N (*Textiles*) trama

weigh [weɪ] VT, VI pesar; **to ~ anchor** levantar ferro; **to ~ the pros and cons** pesar os prós e contras

▶ **weigh down** VT sobrecarregar; (*fig: with worry*) deprimir, acabrunhar

▶ **weigh out** VT (*goods*) pesar

▶ **weigh up** VT ponderar, avaliar

weighbridge ['weɪbrɪdʒ] N báscula automática

weighing machine ['weɪɪŋ-] N balança

weight [weɪt] N peso ▶ VT carregar com peso; (*fig: statistic*) ponderar; **to lose/put on ~** emagrecer/engordar; **sold by ~** vendido por peso; **~s and measures** pesos e medidas

weighting ['weɪtɪŋ] N (*allowance*) indenização *f* de residência

weightlessness ['weɪtlɪsnɪs] N ausência de peso

weightlifter ['weɪtlɪftər] N levantador *m* de pesos

weight training N musculação *f*

weighty ['weɪtɪ] ADJ pesado; (*matters*) importante

weir [wɪər] N represa, açude *m*

weird [wɪəd] ADJ esquisito, estranho

weirdo ['wɪədəu] N (*inf*) esquisitão(-tona) *m/f*

welcome ['wɛlkəm] ADJ bem-vindo ▶ N acolhimento, recepção *f* ▶ VT dar as boas-vindas a; (*be glad of*) saudar; **you're ~** (*after thanks*) de nada; **to make sb ~** dar bom acolhimento a alguém; **you're ~ to try** pode tentar se quiser

welcoming ['wɛlkəmɪŋ] ADJ acolhedor(a); (speech) de boas-vindas

weld [wɛld] N solda ▶ VT soldar, unir

welder ['wɛldəʳ] N (person) soldador(a) m/f

welding ['wɛldɪŋ] N soldagem f, solda

welfare ['wɛlfɛəʳ] N bem-estar m; (social aid) assistência social

welfare state N país auto-financiador da sua assistência social

welfare work N trabalho social

well [wɛl] N poço; (pool) nascente f ▶ ADV bem ▶ ADJ: **to be ~** estar bem (de saúde) ▶ EXCL bem!, então!; **as ~** também; **as ~ as** assim como; **~ done!** muito bem!; **get ~ soon!** melhoras!; **to do ~** ir or sair-se bem; (business) ir bem; **to think ~ of sb** ter um bom conceito a respeito de alguém; **I don't feel ~** não estou me sentindo bem; **you might as ~ tell me** é melhor você me contar logo; **~, as I was saying …** bem, como eu estava dizendo …
▶ **well up** VI brotar

we'll [wi:l] = **we will; we shall**

well-behaved [-bɪ'heɪvd] ADJ bem comportado

well-being N bem-estar m

well-bred ADJ bem educado

well-built ADJ (person) robusto; (house) bem construído

well-chosen ADJ bem escolhido

well-deserved [-dɪ'zə:vd] ADJ bem merecido

well-developed [-dɪ'vɛləpt] ADJ bem desenvolvido

well-disposed ADJ: **~ to(wards)** favorável a

well-dressed [-drɛst] ADJ bem vestido

well-earned ADJ (rest) bem merecido

well-groomed [-gru:md] ADJ bem tratado

well-heeled [-hi:ld] (inf) ADJ (wealthy) rico

well-informed ADJ bem informado, versado

wellingtons ['wɛlɪŋtənz] N (also: **wellington boots**) botas de borracha até os joelhos

well-kept ADJ (house, hands etc) bem tratado; (secret) bem guardado

well-known ADJ conhecido; **it's a ~ fact that …** é sabido que …

well-mannered [-'mænəd] ADJ bem educado

well-meaning ADJ bem intencionado

well-nigh [-naɪ] ADV: **~ impossible** praticamente impossível

well-off ADJ próspero, rico

well-read ADJ lido, versado

well-spoken ADJ (person) bem-falante

well-stocked [-stɔkt] ADJ bem abastecido

well-timed [-taɪmd] ADJ oportuno

well-to-do ADJ abastado

well-wisher [-'wɪʃəʳ] N simpatizante m/f; (admirer) admirador(a) m/f

Welsh [wɛlʃ] ADJ galês/galesa ▶ N (Ling) galês m; **the Welsh** NPL (people) os galeses

Welshman ['wɛlʃmən] (irreg: like **man**) N galês m

Welsh rarebit N torradas com queijo derretido

Welshwoman ['wɛlʃwumən] (irreg: like **woman**) N galesa

welter ['wɛltəʳ] N tumulto

went [wɛnt] PT of **go**

wept [wɛpt] PT, PP of **weep**

were [wə:ʳ] PT of **be**

we're [wɪəʳ] = **we are**

weren't [wə:nt] = **were not**

werewolf ['wɪəwulf] (irreg: like **wolf**) N lobisomem m

west [wɛst] N oeste m ▶ ADJ ocidental, do oeste ▶ ADV para o oeste or ao oeste; **the W~** (Pol) o Oeste, o Ocidente

westbound ['wɛstbaund] ADJ em direção ao oeste

West Country (BRIT) N: **the ~** o sudoeste da Inglaterra

westerly ['wɛstəlɪ] ADJ (situation) ocidental; (wind) oeste

western ['wɛstən] ADJ ocidental ▶ N (Cinema) western m, bangue-bangue (BR inf)

westernized ['wɛstənaɪzd] ADJ ocidentalizado

West German ADJ, N alemão(-ã) m/f ocidental

West Germany N Alemanha Ocidental

West Indian ADJ, N antilhano(-a)

West Indies [-'ɪndɪz] NPL Antilhas fpl

Westminster ['wɛstmɪnstəʳ] N (BRIT Parliament) o Parlamento britânico

westward ['wɛstwəd], **westwards** ['wɛstwədz] ADV para o oeste

wet [wɛt] ADJ molhado; (damp) úmido; (wet through) encharcado; (rainy) chuvoso ▶ N (BRIT Pol) político de tendência moderada ▶ VT (pt, pp **wet** or **wetted**) molhar; **to ~ one's pants** or **o.s.** fazer xixi na calça; **to get ~** molhar-se; **"~ paint"** "tinta fresca"

wet blanket (pej) N (fig) desmancha-prazeres m/f inv

wetness ['wɛtnɪs] N umidade f

wetsuit ['wɛtsu:t] N roupa de mergulho

we've [wi:v] = **we have**

whack [wæk] VT bater

whacked [wækt] (inf) ADJ morto, esgotado

whale [weɪl] N (Zool) baleia

whaler ['weɪləʳ] N baleeiro

whaling ['weɪlɪŋ] N caça a baleias

wharf [wɔ:f] (pl **wharves**) N cais m inv

wharves [wɔ:vz] NPL of **wharf**

(KEYWORD)

what [wɔt] ADJ **1** (in direct/indirect questions) que, qual; **what size is it?** que tamanho é este?; **what colour/shape is it?** qual é a cor/o formato?; **what books do you need?** que livros você precisa?; **he asked me what books I needed** ele me perguntou de quais os livros eu precisava

2 (in exclamations) quê!, como!; **what a mess!** que bagunça!

▶ PRON **1** (interrogative) que, o que; **what are you doing?** o que é que você está fazendo?; **what's happened?** o que aconteceu?; **what's in there?** o que é que tem lá dentro?; **what are you talking about?** sobre o que você está falando?; **what is it called?** como

W

se chama?; **what about me?** e eu?; **what about doing ...?** que tal fazer ...?
2 (*relative*) o que; **I saw what you did/was on the table** eu vi o que você fez/estava na mesa; **he asked me what she had said** ele me perguntou o que ela tinha dito
▸ EXCL (*disbelieving*): **what, no coffee?** ué, não tem café?; **I've crashed the car — what!** bati com o carro — o quê!

whatever [wɔt'ɛvəʳ] ADJ: **~ book you choose** qualquer livro que você escolha ▸ PRON: **do ~ is necessary/you want** faça tudo o que for preciso/o que você quiser; **~ happens** aconteça o que acontecer; **no reason ~** nenhuma razão seja qual for or em absoluto; **nothing ~** nada em absoluto
whatsoever [wɔtsəu'ɛvəʳ] ADJ = **whatever**
wheat [wi:t] N trigo
wheatgerm ['wi:tdʒə:m] N germe *m* de trigo
wheatmeal ['wi:tmi:l] N farinha de trigo
wheedle ['wi:dl] VT: **to ~ sb into doing sth** persuadir alguém a fazer algo; **to ~ sth out of sb** conseguir algo de alguém por meio de agrados
wheel [wi:l] N roda; (*also:* **steering wheel**) volante *m*; (*Naut*) roda do leme ▸ VT (*pram etc*) empurrar ▸ VI (*birds*) dar voltas; (*also:* **wheel round**) girar, dar voltas, virar-se
wheelbarrow ['wi:lbærəu] N carrinho de mão
wheelbase ['wi:lbeɪs] N distância entre os eixos
wheelchair ['wi:ltʃɛəʳ] N cadeira de rodas
wheel clamp N (*Aut*) grampo com que se imobiliza carros estacionados ilegalmente
wheeler-dealer ['wi:lə-] N negocista *m/f*
wheelhouse ['wi:lhaus] N casa do leme
wheeling ['wi:lɪŋ] N: **~ and dealing** negociatas *fpl*
wheeze [wi:z] N respiração *f* difícil, chiado ▸ VI respirar ruidosamente

(KEYWORD)

when [wɛn] ADV quando; **when are you going to Brazil?** quando você vai para o Brasil?
▸ CONJ **1** (*at, during, after the time that*) quando; **she was reading when I came in** ela estava lendo quando eu entrei; **when you've read it, tell me what you think** depois que você tiver lido isto, diga-me o que acha; **that was when I needed you** foi quando eu precisei de você
2 (*on, at which*) quando, em que; **on the day when I met him** no dia em que o conheci; **one day when it was raining** um dia quando estava chovendo
3 (*whereas*) ao passo que; **you said I was wrong when in fact I was right** você disse que eu estava errado quando, na verdade, eu estava certo; **why did you buy it when you can't afford it?** por que você comprou isto se não tinha condições (de fazê-lo)

whenever [wɛn'ɛvəʳ] CONJ quando, quando quer que; (*every time that*) sempre que ▸ ADV quando você quiser
where [wɛəʳ] ADV onde ▸ CONJ onde, aonde; **this is ~ ...** aqui é onde ...; **~ are you from?** de onde você é?
whereabouts ['wɛərəbauts] ADV (por) onde ▸ N: **nobody knows his ~** ninguém sabe o seu paradeiro
whereas [wɛər'æz] CONJ uma vez que, ao passo que
whereby [wɛə'baɪ] ADV (*formal*) pelo qual (or pela qual *etc*)
whereupon [wɛərə'pɔn] ADV depois do que
wherever [wɛər'ɛvəʳ] CONJ onde quer que ▸ ADV (*interrogative*) onde?; **sit ~ you like** sente-se onde quiser
wherewithal ['wɛəwɪðɔ:l] N recursos *mpl*, meios *mpl*
whet [wɛt] VT afiar; (*appetite*) abrir
whether ['wɛðəʳ] CONJ se; **I don't know ~ to accept or not** não sei se aceito ou não; **~ you go or not** quer você vá quer não; **it's doubtful ~ ...** não é certo que ...
whey [weɪ] N soro (de leite)

(KEYWORD)

which [wɪtʃ] ADJ **1** (*interrogative*) que, qual; **which picture do you want?** que quadro você quer?; **which books are yours?** quais são os seus livros?; **which one?** qual?
2: **in which case** em cujo caso; **the train may be late, in which case don't wait up** o trem talvez esteja atrasado e, neste caso, não espere; **by which time** momento em que; **we got there at 8pm, by which time the cinema was full** quando chegamos lá às 8 da noite, o cinema estava lotado
▸ PRON **1** (*interrogative*) qual; **which (of these) are yours?** quais (destes) são seus?; **I don't mind which** não me importa qual
2 (*relative*) que, o que, o qual *etc*; **the apple which you ate** a maçã que você comeu; **the apple which is on the table** a maçã que está sobre a mesa; **the meeting (which) we attended** a reunião da qual participamos; **the chair on which you are sitting** a cadeira na qual você está sentado; **the book of which you spoke** o livro do qual você falou; **he said he knew, which is true** ele disse que sabia, o que é verdade; **after which** depois do que

whichever [wɪtʃ'ɛvəʳ] ADJ: **take ~ book you prefer** pegue o livro que preferir; **~ book you take** qualquer livro que você pegue
whiff [wɪf] N cheiro; **to catch a ~ of sth** tomar o cheiro de algo
while [waɪl] N tempo, momento ▸ CONJ enquanto, ao mesmo tempo que; (*as long as*) contanto que; (*although*) embora; **for a ~** durante algum tempo; **in a ~** daqui a pouco; **all the ~** todo o tempo; **we'll make**

it worth your ~ faremos com que valha a pena para você
▶ **while away** VT (*time*) encher
whilst [waɪlst] CONJ = **while**
whim [wɪm] N capricho, veneta
whimper ['wɪmpə^r] N (*weeping*) choradeira; (*moan*) lamúria ▶ VI choramingar, soluçar
whimsical ['wɪmzɪkl] ADJ (*person*) caprichoso, de veneta; (*look*) excêntrico
whine [waɪn] N (*of pain*) gemido; (*of engine, siren*) zunido ▶ VI (*person, animal*) gemer; zunir; (*fig*) lamuriar-se; (*dog*) ganir
whip [wɪp] N açoite m; (*for riding*) chicote m; (*Pol*) líder m/f da bancada ▶ VT chicotear; (*snatch*) apanhar de repente; (*cream, eggs*) bater; (*move quickly*): **to ~ sth out/off/away** etc arrancar algo
▶ **whip up** VT (*cream*) bater; (*inf: meal*) arrumar; (*stir up: feeling*) atiçar; (*: support*) angariar
whiplash ['wɪplæʃ] N (*Med: also:* **whiplash injury**) golpe m de chicote, chicotinho
whipped cream [wɪpt-] N creme m chantilly
whipping boy ['wɪpɪŋ-] N (*fig*) bode m expiatório
whip-round (BRIT) N coleta, vaquinha
whirl [wə:l] N remoinho ▶ VT fazer girar ▶ VI (*dancers*) rodopiar; (*leaves, water etc*) redemoinhar
whirlpool ['wə:lpu:l] N remoinho
whirlwind ['wə:lwɪnd] N furacão m, remoinho
whirr [wə:^r] VI zumbir
whisk [wɪsk] N (*Culin*) batedeira ▶ VT bater; **to ~ sth away from sb** arrebatar algo de alguém; **to ~ sb away** or **off** levar alguém rapidamente
whiskers ['wɪskəz] NPL (*of animal*) bigodes mpl; (*of man*) suíças fpl
whisky, (US, IRELAND) **whiskey** ['wɪskɪ] N uísque m (BR), whisky m (PT)
whisper ['wɪspə^r] N sussurro, murmúrio; (*rumour*) rumor m ▶ VT, VI sussurrar; **to ~ sth to sb** sussurrar algo para alguém
whispering ['wɪspərɪŋ] N sussurros mpl
whist [wɪst] (BRIT) N uíste m (BR), whist m (PT)
whistle ['wɪsl] N (*sound*) assobio; (*object*) apito ▶ VT, VI assobiar
whistle-stop ADJ: **to make a ~ tour** (*Pol*) fazer uma viagem eleitoral
Whit [wɪt] N Pentecostes m
white [waɪt] ADJ branco; (*pale*) pálido ▶ N branco; (*of egg*) clara; **the whites** NPL (*washing*) a roupa branca; **tennis ~s** traje m de tênis; **to turn** or **go ~** (*person*) ficar branco or pálido; (*hair*) ficar grisalho
whitebait ['waɪtbeɪt] N filhote m de arenque
whiteboard ['waɪtbɔ:d] N quadro branco; **interactive ~** quadro interativo
white coffee (BRIT) N café m com leite
white-collar worker N empregado(-a) de escritório
white elephant N (*fig*) elefante m branco

white goods N eletrodomésticos mpl
white-hot ADJ (*metal*) incandescente
White House N *ver nota*

A Casa Branca (**White House**) é um grande edifício branco situado em Washington D.C. onde reside o presidente dos Estados Unidos. Por extensão, o termo se refere também ao poder executivo americano.

white lie N mentira inofensiva or social
whiteness ['waɪtnɪs] N brancura
white noise N ruído branco
whiteout ['waɪtaut] N resplendor m branco
White Paper N (*Pol*) relatório oficial sobre determinado assunto
whitewash ['waɪtwɔʃ] N (*paint*) cal f ▶ VT caiar; (*fig*) encobrir
whiting ['waɪtɪŋ] N INV pescada-marlonga
Whit Monday N segunda-feira de Pentecostes
Whitsun ['wɪtsn] N Pentecostes m
whittle ['wɪtl] VT aparar; **to ~ away, ~ down** reduzir gradualmente, corroer
whizz [wɪz] VI zunir; **to ~ past** or **by** passar a toda velocidade
whizz kid (*inf*) N prodígio
WHO N ABBR (= *World Health Organization*) OMS f

(KEYWORD)

who [hu:] PRON **1** (*interrogative*) quem?; **who is it?** quem é?; **who's there?** quem está aí?; **who are you looking for?** quem você está procurando?
2 (*relative*) que, o qual *etc*, quem; **my cousin, who lives in New York** meu primo que mora em Nova Iorque; **the man/woman who spoke to me** o homem/a mulher que falou comigo; **those who can swim** aqueles que sabem nadar

whodunit [hu:'dʌnɪt] (*inf*) N romance m (or filme m) policial
whoever [hu:'ɛvə^r] PRON: **~ finds it** quem quer que or seja quem for que o encontre; **ask ~ you like** pergunte a quem quiser; **~ he marries** não importa com quem se case; **~ told you that?** quem te disse isso pelo amor de Deus?
whole [həul] ADJ (*complete*) todo, inteiro; (*not broken*) intacto ▶ N (*all*): **the ~ of the time** o tempo todo; (*entire unit*) conjunto; (*total*) total m; **the ~ lot (of it)** tudo; **the ~ lot (of them)** todos(-as); **the ~ of the town** toda a cidade, a cidade inteira; **~ villages were destroyed** lugarejos inteiros foram destruídos; **on the ~, as a ~** como um todo, no conjunto
wholefood [həul'fu:d] N, **wholefoods** [həul'fu:dz] NPL comida integral
wholehearted [həul'ha:tɪd] ADJ total
wholemeal ['həulmi:l] (BRIT) ADJ (*flour, bread*) integral
whole note (US) N semibreve f

W

wholesale ['həʊlseɪl] N venda por atacado
▶ ADJ por atacado; (*destruction*) em grande
escala ▶ ADV por atacado
wholesaler ['həʊlseɪlə^r] N atacadista *m/f*
wholesome ['həʊlsəm] ADJ saudável, sadio
wholewheat ['həʊlwiːt] ADJ = **wholemeal**
wholly ['həʊlɪ] ADV totalmente,
completamente

KEYWORD

whom [huːm] PRON **1** (*interrogative*) quem?;
whom did you see? quem você viu?; **to
whom did you give it?** para quem você deu
isto?
2 (*relative*) que, quem; **the man whom I saw/
to whom I spoke** o homem que eu vi/com
quem eu falei

whooping cough ['huːpɪŋ-] N coqueluche *f*
whoosh [wuʃ] N chio
whopper ['wɔpə^r] (*inf*) N (*lie*) lorota; (*large
thing*): **it was a ~** era enorme
whopping ['wɔpɪŋ] (*inf*) ADJ (*big*) imenso
whore [hɔː^r] (*inf: pej*) N puta

KEYWORD

whose [huːz] ADJ **1** (*possessive: interrogative*):
whose book is this?, whose is this book?
de quem é este livro?; **I don't know whose
it is** eu não sei de quem é isto
2 (*possessive: relative*): **the man whose son you
rescued** o homem cujo filho você salvou;
**the girl whose sister you were speaking
to** a menina com cuja irmã você estava
falando; **the woman whose car was
stolen** a mulher de quem o carro foi
roubado
▶ PRON de quem; **whose is this?** de quem é
isto?; **I know whose it is** eu seu de quem é;
whose are these? de quem são estes?

Who's Who N Quem é quem (*registro de
notabilidades*)

KEYWORD

why [waɪ] ADV por que (BR), porque (PT); (*at end
of sentence*) por quê (BR), porquê (PT); **why is
he always late?** por que ele está sempre
atrasado?; **I'm not coming — why not?** eu
não vou — por que não?
▶ CONJ por que; **I wonder why he said that**
eu me pergunto por que ele disse isso; **that's
not why I'm here** não é por isso que estou
aqui; **the reason why** a razão por que
▶ EXCL (*expressing surprise, shock, annoyance*) ora
essa!; (*explaining*) bem!; **why, it's you!** ora,
é você!

whyever [waɪˈɛvə^r] ADV mas por que
WI N ABBR (BRIT: = *Women's Institute*) *associação de
mulheres* ▶ ABBR (*Geo*) = **West Indies**; (US Post)
= **Wisconsin**
wick [wɪk] N mecha, pavio

wicked ['wɪkɪd] ADJ (*crime, man, witch*) perverso;
(*smile*) malicioso; (*inf: terrible: prices, waste*)
terrível
wicker ['wɪkə^r] N (*also*: **wickerwork**) (trabalho
de) vime *m* ▶ ADJ de vime
wicket ['wɪkɪt] N (*Cricket*) arco
wicket keeper N (*Cricket*) guarda-meta *m* (no
críquete)
wide [waɪd] ADJ largo; (*broad*) extenso, amplo;
(*area, publicity, knowledge*) amplo ▶ ADV: **to
open ~** abrir totalmente; **to shoot ~** atirar
longe do alvo; **it is 4 metres ~** tem 4 metros
de largura
wide-angle lens N lente *f* grande angular
wide-awake ADJ bem acordado; (*fig*) vivo,
esperto
wide-eyed [-aɪd] ADJ de olhos arregalados;
(*fig*) ingênuo
widely ['waɪdlɪ] ADV (*different*) extremamente;
(*travelled, spaced*) muito; (*believed, known*)
ampliamente; **it is ~ believed that ...** há
uma convicção generalizada de que ...; **to
be ~ read** ser muito lido
widen ['waɪdən] VT (*road, river*) alargar; (*one's
experience*) aumentar ▶ VI alargar-se
wideness ['waɪdnɪs] N largura; (*breadth*)
extensão *f*
wide open ADJ (*eyes*) arregalado; (*door*)
escancarado
wide-ranging [-ˈreɪndʒɪŋ] ADJ (*survey, report*)
abrangente; (*interests*) diversos
widespread ['waɪdspred] ADJ (*belief etc*)
difundido, comum
widget ['wɪdʒɪt] N (*gadget*) pequeno utensílio;
(*Comput*) widget *m*
widow ['wɪdəʊ] N viúva
widowed ['wɪdəʊd] ADJ viúvo
widower ['wɪdəʊə^r] N viúvo
width [wɪdθ] N largura; **it's 7 metres in ~**
tem 7 metros de largura
widthways ['wɪdθweɪz] ADV transversalmente
wield [wiːld] VT (*sword*) brandir, empunhar;
(*power*) exercer
wife [waɪf] (*pl* **wives**) N mulher *f*, esposa
Wi-Fi ['waɪfaɪ] N Wi-Fi *m*
wig [wɪg] N peruca
wigging ['wɪgɪŋ] (BRIT *inf*) N sabão *m*,
descompostura
wiggle ['wɪgl] VT menear, agitar ▶ VI menear,
agitar-se
wiggly ['wɪglɪ] ADJ (*line*) ondulado
wiki ['wiːkiː] N (*Comput*) wiki *f*
wild [waɪld] ADJ (*animal*) selvagem; (*plant*)
silvestre; (*rough*) violento, furioso; (*idea*)
disparatado, extravagante; (*person*)
insensato; (*enthusiastic*): **to be ~ about** ser
louco por ▶ N: **the ~** a natureza; **wilds** NPL
(*remote area*) regiões *fpl* selvagens, terras *fpl*
virgens
wild card N (*Comput*) caractere *m* de
substituição
wildcat ['waɪldkæt] N gato selvagem; (US:
lynx) lince *m*

wildcat strike N *greve espontánea e não autorizada pelo sindicato*
wilderness ['wɪldənɪs] N *ermo*; *(in Brazil)* sertão *m*
wildfire ['waɪldfaɪəʳ] N: **to spread like ~** espalhar-se rapidamente
wild-goose chase N *(fig)* busca inútil
wildlife ['waɪldlaɪf] N *animais mpl (e plantas fpl)* selvagens
wildly ['waɪldlɪ] ADV *(behave)* freneticamente; *(hit, guess)* irrefletidamente; *(happy)* extremamente
wiles [waɪlz] NPL *artimanhas fpl*, *estratagemas mpl*
wilful, *(US)* **willful** ['wɪlful] ADJ *(person)* teimoso, voluntarioso; *(action)* deliberado, intencional; *(crime)* premeditado

(KEYWORD)

will [wɪl] AUX VB **1** *(forming future tense):* **I will finish it tomorrow** vou acabar isto amanhã; **I will have finished it by tomorrow** até amanhã eu terei terminado isto; **will you do it? — yes I will/no I won't** você vai fazer isto? — sim, vou/não eu não vou

2 *(in conjectures, predictions):* **he will come** ele virá; **he will** *or* **he'll be there by now** nesta altura ele está lá; **that will be the postman** deve ser o carteiro; **this medicine will/won't help you** este remédio vai/não vai fazer efeito em você

3 *(in commands, requests, offers):* **will you be quiet!** fique quieto, por favor!; **will you come?** você vem?; **will you help me?** você pode me ajudar?; **will you have a cup of tea?** você vai querer uma xícara de chá *or* um chá?; **I won't put up with it** eu não vou tolerar isto

▶ VT *(pt, pp* **willed**) **to will sb to do sth** desejar que alguém faça algo; **he willed himself to go on** reuniu grande força de vontade para continuar

▶ N *(volition)* vontade *f*; *(testament)* testamento

willful ['wɪlful] *(US)* ADJ = **wilful**
willing ['wɪlɪŋ] ADJ *(with goodwill)* disposto, pronto; *(enthusiastic)* entusiasmado; *(submissive)* complacente ▶ N: **to show ~** mostrar boa vontade; **he's ~ to do it** ele é disposto a fazê-lo
willingly ['wɪlɪŋlɪ] ADV de bom grado, de boa vontade
willingness ['wɪlɪŋnɪs] N boa vontade *f*, disposição *f*
will-o'-the-wisp N fogo-fátuo; *(fig)* quimera
willow ['wɪləu] N salgueiro
willpower ['wɪlpauəʳ] N força de vontade
willy-nilly ['wɪlɪ'nɪlɪ] ADV quer queira ou não
wilt [wɪlt] VI *(flower)* murchar; *(plant)* morrer
Wilts [wɪlts] *(BRIT)* ABBR = **Wiltshire**
wily ['waɪlɪ] ADJ esperto, astuto
wimp [wɪmp] *(inf)* N banana *m*

win [wɪn] *(pt, pp* **won**) N *(in sports etc)* vitória
▶ VT ganhar, vencer; *(obtain)* conseguir, obter; *(support)* alcançar ▶ VI ganhar
▶ **win over** VT conquistar
▶ **win round** *(BRIT)* VT = **win over**
wince [wɪns] VI encolher-se, estremecer ▶ N estremecimento
winch [wɪntʃ] N guincho
wind[1] [wɪnd] N vento; *(Med)* gases *mpl*, flatulência; *(breath)* fôlego ▶ VT *(take breath away from)* deixar sem fôlego; **the ~(s)** *(Mus)* instrumentos *mpl* de sopro; **into** *or* **against the ~** contra o vento; **to get ~ of sth** *(fig)* ter notícia de algo, tomar conhecimento de algo; **to break ~** soltar gases intestinais
wind[2] [waɪnd] *(pt, pp* **wound**) VT enrolar, bobinar; *(wrap)* envolver; *(clock, toy)* dar corda a ▶ VI *(road, river)* serpentear
▶ **wind down** VT *(car window)* abaixar, abrir; *(fig: production, business)* diminuir gradativamente
▶ **wind up** VT *(clock)* dar corda em; *(debate)* rematar, concluir
windbreak ['wɪndbreɪk] N quebra-ventos *m*
windbreaker ['wɪndbreɪkəʳ] *(US)* N anoraque *m*
windcheater ['wɪndtʃiːtəʳ] *(BRIT)* N anoraque *m*
winder ['waɪndəʳ] *(BRIT)* N *(on watch)* botão *m* de corda
windfall ['wɪndfɔːl] N golpe *m* de sorte
wind farm N parque *m* eólico
winding ['waɪndɪŋ] ADJ *(road)* sinuoso, tortuoso; *(staircase)* de caracol, em espiral
wind instrument N *(Mus)* instrumento de sopro
windmill ['wɪndmɪl] N moinho de vento
window ['wɪndəu] N janela; *(in shop etc)* vitrine *f* (BR), montra (PT)
window box N jardineira (no peitoril da janela)
window cleaner N *(person)* limpador(a) *m/f* de janelas
window dressing N decoração *f* de vitrines
window envelope N envelope *m* de janela
window frame N caixilho da janela
window ledge N peitoril *m* da janela
window pane N vidraça, vidro
window-shopping N: **to go ~** ir ver vitrines
windowsill ['wɪndəusɪl] N *(inside)* peitoril *m*; *(outside)* soleira
windpipe ['wɪndpaɪp] N traqueia
windscreen ['wɪndskriːn] *(BRIT)* N para-brisa *m*
windscreen washer *(BRIT)* N lavador *m* de para-brisa
windscreen wiper [-'waɪpəʳ] *(BRIT)* N limpador *m* de para-brisa
windshield ['wɪndʃiːld] *(US)* N = **windscreen**
windswept ['wɪndswɛpt] ADJ varrido pelo vento
wind tunnel N túnel *m* aerodinâmico
wind turbine ['wɪndtɜːbaɪn] N turbina eólica
windy ['wɪndɪ] ADJ com muito vento, batido pelo vento; **it's ~** está ventando (BR), faz vento (PT)

W

wine [waɪn] N vinho ▶ VT: **to ~ and dine sb** levar alguém para jantar
wine bar N bar *m* para degustação de vinhos
wine cellar N adega
wine glass N cálice *m* (de vinho)
wine list N lista de vinhos
wine merchant N negociante *m/f* de vinhos
wine tasting [-'teɪstɪŋ] N degustação *f* de vinhos
wine waiter N garção *m* dos vinhos
wing [wɪŋ] N asa; (*of building*) ala; (*Aut*) aleta, para-lamas *m inv*; **wings** NPL (*Theatre*) bastidores *mpl*
winger ['wɪŋəʳ] N (*Sport*) ponta, extremo
wing mirror (*BRIT*) N espelho lateral
wing nut N porca borboleta
wingspan ['wɪŋspæn] N envergadura
wingspread ['wɪŋspred] N envergadura
wink [wɪŋk] N piscadela ▶ VI piscar o olho; (*light etc*) piscar
winkle ['wɪŋkl] N búzio
winner ['wɪnəʳ] N vencedor(a) *m/f*
winning ['wɪnɪŋ] ADJ (*team*) vencedor(a); (*goal*) decisivo; (*smile*) sedutor(a)
winning post N meta de chegada
winnings ['wɪnɪŋz] NPL ganhos *mpl*
winsome ['wɪnsəm] ADJ encantador(a), cativante
winter ['wɪntəʳ] N inverno ▶ VI hibernar
winter sports NPL esportes *mpl* (*BR*) or desportos *mpl* (*PT*) de inverno
wintry ['wɪntrɪ] ADJ glacial, invernal
wipe [waɪp] N: **to give sth a ~** limpar algo com um pano ▶ VT limpar; (*rub*) esfregar; (*erase: tape*) apagar; **to ~ one's nose** limpar o nariz
▶ **wipe off** VT remover esfregando
▶ **wipe out** VT (*debt*) liquidar; (*memory*) apagar; (*destroy*) exterminar
▶ **wipe up** VT (*mess*) limpar; (*dishes*) enxugar
wire ['waɪəʳ] N arame *m*; (*Elec*) fio (elétrico); (*telegram*) telegrama *m* ▶ VT (*house*) instalar a rede elétrica em; (*also*: **wire up**) conectar; (*telegram*) telegrafar para
wire brush N escova de aço
wire cutters [-'kʌtəz] NPL alicate *m* corta-arame
wireless ['waɪəlɪs] ADJ sem fio (*BR*), sem fios (*PT*) ▶ N (*BRIT*) rádio
wire netting N rede *f* de arame
wire-tapping [-'tæpɪŋ] N escuta telefônica
wiring ['waɪərɪŋ] N instalação *f* elétrica
wiry ['waɪərɪ] ADJ nervoso; (*hair*) grosso
wisdom ['wɪzdəm] N (*of person*) prudência; (*of action, remark*) bom-senso, sabedoria
wisdom tooth (*irreg: like* **tooth**) N dente *m* do siso
wise [waɪz] ADJ (*person*) prudente; (*action, remark*) sensato; **I'm none the ~r** eu não entendi nada
▶ **wise up** (*inf*) VI: **to ~ up to** abrir os olhos para
...wise [waɪz] SUFFIX: **time~** *etc* com relação ao tempo *etc*

wisecrack ['waɪzkræk] N piada
wish [wɪʃ] N desejo ▶ VT desejar; (*want*) querer; **best ~es** (*on birthday etc*) parabéns *mpl*, felicidades *fpl*; **with best ~es** (*in letter*) cumprimentos; **give her my best ~es** dá um abraço para ela; **to ~ sb goodbye** despedir-se de alguém; **he ~ed me well** me desejou boa sorte; **to ~ to do/sb to do sth** querer fazer/que alguém faça algo; **to ~ for** desejar; **to ~ sth on sb** desejar algo a alguém
wishful ['wɪʃful] ADJ: **it's ~ thinking** é doce ilusão
wishy-washy ['wɪʃɪ'wɔʃɪ] (*inf*) ADJ (*colour*) indefinido; (*person*) sem caráter; (*ideas*) aguado
wisp [wɪsp] N mecha, tufo; (*of smoke*) fio
wistful ['wɪstful] ADJ melancólico
wit [wɪt] N (*wittiness*) presença de espírito, engenho; (*intelligence: also*: **wits**) entendimento; (*person*) espirituoso(-a); **to be at one's ~s' end** (*fig*) não saber para onde se virar; **to have one's ~s about one** ter uma presença de espírito; **to ~** a saber
witch [wɪtʃ] N bruxa
witchcraft ['wɪtʃkrɑːft] N bruxaria
witch doctor N médico feiticeiro, pajé *m* (*BR*)
witch-hunt N caça às bruxas

[KEYWORD]

with [wɪð, wɪθ] PREP **1** (*accompanying, in the company of*) com; **I was with him** eu estava com ele; **to stay overnight with friends** dormir na casa de amigos; **we'll take the children with us** vamos levar as crianças conosco; **I'll be with you in a minute** vou vê-lo num minuto; **I'm with you** (*I understand*) compreendo; **to be with it** (*inf*) estar por dentro; (*: aware*) estar a par da situação; (*: up-to-date*) estar atualizado
2 (*descriptive*) com, de; **a room with a view** um quarto com vista; **the man with the grey hat/blue eyes** o homem do chapéu cinza/de olhos azuis
3 (*indicating manner, means, cause*) com, de; **with tears in her eyes** com os olhos cheios de lágrimas; **to walk with a stick** andar com uma bengala; **to tremble with fear** tremer de medo; **to fill sth with water** encher algo de água

withdraw [wɪð'drɔː] (*irreg: like* **draw**) VT tirar, remover; (*offer*) retirar ▶ VI retirar-se; (*go back on promise*) voltar atrás; **to ~ money (from the bank)** retirar dinheiro (do banco); **to ~ into o.s.** introverter-se
withdrawal [wɪð'drɔːəl] N retirada
withdrawal symptoms NPL síndrome *f* de abstinência; **to have ~** ter uma reação
withdrawn [wɪð'drɔːn] PP *of* **withdraw** ▶ ADJ (*person*) reservado, introvertido
wither ['wɪðəʳ] VI murchar
withered ['wɪðəd] ADJ murcho

withhold [wɪð'həuld] (*irreg: like* **hold**) VT (*money*) reter; (*decision*) adiar; (*permission*) negar; (*information*) esconder

within [wɪð'ɪn] PREP dentro de ▶ ADV dentro; **~ reach** ao alcance da mão; **~ sight** à vista; **~ the week** antes do fim da semana; **~ a mile of** a uma milha de; **~ an hour from now** daqui a uma hora; **to be ~ the law** estar dentro da lei

without [wɪð'aut] PREP sem; **~ anybody knowing** sem ninguém saber; **to go** or **do ~ sth** passar sem algo

withstand [wɪð'stænd] (*irreg: like* **stand**) VT resistir a

witness ['wɪtnɪs] N (*person*) testemunha; (*evidence*) testemunho ▶ VT (*event*) testemunhar, presenciar; (*document*) legalizar; **to bear ~ to sth** (*fig*) testemunhar algo; **~ for the prosecution/defence** testemunha para acusação/defesa; **to ~ to sth/having seen sth** testemunhar algo/ter visto algo

witness box, (US) **witness stand** N banco das testemunhas

witticism ['wɪtɪsɪzm] N observação *f* espirituosa, chiste *m*

witty ['wɪtɪ] ADJ espirituoso

wives [waɪvz] NPL *of* **wife**

wizard ['wɪzəd] N feiticeiro, mago

wizened ['wɪznd] ADJ encarquilhado

wk ABBR = **week**

Wm. ABBR = **William**

WO N ABBR = **warrant officer**

wobble ['wɔbl] VI oscilar; (*chair*) balançar

wobbly ['wɔblɪ] ADJ (*table*) balançante, bambo

woe [wəu] N dor *f*, mágoa

woke [wəuk] PT *of* **wake**

woken ['wəukən] PP *of* **wake**

wolf [wulf] (*pl* **wolves**) N lobo

wolves [wulvz] NPL *of* **wolf**

woman ['wumən] (*pl* **women**) N mulher *f*; **~ doctor** médica; **~ teacher** professora; **young ~** mulher jovem; **women's page** (*Press*) página da mulher

womanize ['wumənaɪz] VI paquerar as mulheres

womanly ['wumənlɪ] ADJ feminino

womb [wu:m] N (*Anat*) matriz *f*, útero

women ['wɪmɪn] NPL *of* **woman**

women's lib [-lɪb] (*inf*) N = **women's liberation movement**

women's liberation movement N movimento pela libertação da mulher

won [wʌn] PT, PP *of* **win**

wonder ['wʌndə^r] N maravilha, prodígio; (*feeling*) espanto ▶ VI: **to ~ whether/why** perguntar-se a si mesmo se/por quê; **to ~ at** admirar-se de; **to ~ about** pensar sobre or em; **it's no ~ that** não é de admirar que

wonderful ['wʌndəful] ADJ maravilhoso; (*miraculous*) impressionante

wonderfully ['wʌndəfulɪ] ADV maravilhosamente

wonky ['wɔŋkɪ] (BRIT) ADJ errado, torto

won't [wəunt] = **will not**

woo [wu:] VT (*woman*) namorar, cortejar; (*audience*) atrair

wood [wud] N (*timber*) madeira; (*forest*) floresta, bosque *m*; (*firewood*) lenha ▶ CPD de madeira

wood carving N (*act*) escultura em madeira; (*object*) entalhe *m*

wooded ['wudɪd] ADJ arborizado

wooden ['wudən] ADJ de madeira; (*fig*) inexpressivo

woodland ['wudlənd] N floresta, bosque *m*

woodpecker ['wudpɛkə^r] N pica-pau *m*

wood pigeon N pombo torcaz

woodwind ['wudwɪnd] N (*Mus*) instrumentos *mpl* de sopro de madeira

woodwork ['wudwə:k] N carpintaria

woodworm ['wudwə:m] N carcoma, caruncho

woof [wuf] N (*of dog*) latido ▶ VI latir; **~, ~!** au-au!

wool [wul] N lã *f*; **to pull the ~ over sb's eyes** (*fig*) enganar alguém, vender a alguém gato por lebre

woollen ['wulən] ADJ de lã

woollens ['wulənz] NPL artigos *mpl* de lã

woolly, (US) **wooly** ['wulɪ] ADJ de lã; (*fig: ideas*) confuso

woozy ['wu:zɪ] ADJ (*inf*) zonzo

word [wə:d] N palavra; (*news*) notícia; (*message*) aviso ▶ VT (*express*) expressar; (*document*) redigir; **in other ~s** em outras palavras, ou seja; **to break/keep one's ~** faltar à palavra/cumprir a promessa; **~ for ~** ao pé da letra; **what's the ~ for "pen" in Portuguese?** como se fala "pen" em português?; **to put sth into ~s** expressar algo; **to have a ~ with sb** falar com alguém; **to have ~s with sb** discutir com alguém; **I'll take your ~ for it** acredito em você; **to send ~ that** ... mandar dizer que ...; **to leave ~ that** ... deixar recado dizendo que ...

wording ['wə:dɪŋ] N fraseado

word-perfect ADJ: **he was ~ in his speech** *etc* ele sabia o discurso *etc* de cor

word processing N processamento de textos

word processor [-'prəusɛsə^r] N processador *m* de textos

wordy ['wə:dɪ] ADJ prolixo, verboso

wore [wɔ:^r] PT *of* **wear**

work [wə:k] N trabalho; (*job*) emprego, trabalho; (*Art, Literature*) obra ▶ VI trabalhar; (*mechanism*) funcionar; (*medicine etc*) surtir efeito, ser eficaz; (*plan*) dar certo ▶ VT (*clay*) moldar; (*wood etc*) talhar; (*mine etc*) explorar; (*machine*) fazer trabalhar, manejar; (*effect, miracle*) causar; **road ~s** obras *fpl* (na estrada); **to go to ~** ir trabalhar; **to set to ~, to start ~** começar a trabalhar; **to be at ~ (on sth)** estar trabalhando (em algo); **to be out of ~** estar desempregado; **to ~ hard**

trabalhar muito; **to ~ loose** (*part*) soltar-se;
(*knot*) afrouxar-se
▶ **work on** VT FUS trabalhar em, dedicar-se a;
(*principle*) basear-se em
▶ **work out** VI (*plans etc*) dar certo, surtir efeito
▶ VT (*problem*) resolver; (*plan*) elaborar,
formular; **it ~s out at £100** dá £100
workable ['wə:kəbl] ADJ (*solution*) viável
workaholic [wə:kə'hɔlɪk] N burro de carga
workbench ['wə:kbɛntʃ] N banco, bancada
worked up [wə:kt-] ADJ: **to get ~** ficar
exaltado
worker ['wə:kəʳ] N trabalhador(a) *m/f*,
operário(-a); **office ~** empregado(-a) de
escritório
work force N força de trabalho
work-in (BRIT) N ocupação *f* de fábrica *etc* (*sem
paralisação da produção*)
working ['wə:kɪŋ] ADJ (*day, tools etc, conditions*)
de trabalho; (*wife*) que trabalha; (*population,
partner*) ativo; **a ~ knowledge of English** um
conhecimento prático do inglês
working capital N (*Comm*) capital *m* de giro
working class N proletariado, classe *f*
operária ▶ ADJ: **working-class** do
proletariado, da classe operária
working man (*irreg: like* **man**) N
trabalhador *m*
working model N modelo articulado
working order N: **in ~** em perfeito estado
working party (BRIT) N grupo de trabalho
working week N semana de trabalho
work-in-progress N (*Comm*) produção *f* em
curso
workload ['wə:kləud] N carga de trabalho
workman ['wə:kmən] N (*irreg: like* **man**) N
operário, trabalhador *m*
workmanship ['wə:kmənʃɪp] N (*art*)
acabamento; (*skill*) habilidade *f*
workmate ['wə:kmeɪt] N colega *m/f* de
trabalho
workout ['wə:kaut] N treinamento, treino
work permit N permissão *f* de trabalho
works N (BRIT: *factory*) fábrica, usina; (*of clock,
machine*) mecanismo
works council N comissão *f* de operários
worksheet ['wə:kʃi:t] N (*with exercises*) folha de
exercícios; (*of hours worked*) registro das horas
de trabalho
workshop ['wə:kʃɔp] N oficina; (*practical
session*) aula prática
work station N estação *f* de trabalho
work study N estudo de trabalho
work-to-rule (BRIT) N paralisação *f* de
trabalho extraordinário (*forma de protesto*)
world [wə:ld] N mundo ▶ CPD mundial; **to
think the ~ of sb** (*fig*) ter alguém em alto
conceito; **all over the ~** no mundo inteiro;
what in the ~ is he doing? o que é que ele
está fazendo, pelo amor de Deus?; **to do sb
a ~ of good** fazer muito bem a alguém; **W~
War One/Two** Primeira/Segunda Guerra
Mundial; **out of this ~** sensacional

World Cup N: **the ~** (*Football*) a Copa do Mundo
world-famous ADJ de fama mundial
worldly ['wə:ldlɪ] ADJ mundano;
(*knowledgeable*) experiente
worldwide ['wə:ldwaɪd] ADJ mundial,
universal ▶ ADV no mundo inteiro
worm [wə:m] N verme *m*; (*also:* **earthworm**)
minhoca, lombriga
worn [wɔ:n] PP of **wear** ▶ ADJ gasto
worn-out ADJ (*object*) gasto; (*person*) esgotado,
exausto
worried ['wʌrɪd] ADJ preocupado; **to be ~
about sth** estar preocupado com algo
worrier ['wʌrɪəʳ] N: **he's a ~** ele se preocupa
com tudo
worry ['wʌrɪ] N preocupação *f* ▶ VT preocupar,
inquietar ▶ VI preocupar-se, afligir-se; **to ~
about** *or* **over sth/sb** preocupar-se com
algo/alguém
worrying ['wʌrɪɪŋ] ADJ inquietante,
preocupante
worse [wə:s] ADJ, ADV pior ▶ N o pior; **a change
for the ~** uma mudança para pior, uma
piora; **to get ~** piorar; **he's none the ~ for
it** não lhe fez mal; **so much the ~ for you!**
pior para você!
worsen ['wə:sən] VT, VI piorar
worse off ADJ com menos dinheiro; (*fig*):
you'll be ~ this way assim você ficará pior
que nunca
worship ['wə:ʃɪp] N culto; (*act*) adoração *f* ▶ VT
(*god*) adorar, venerar; (*person, thing*) adorar;
Your W~ (BRIT: *to mayor*) vossa Excelência;
(: *to judge*) senhor Juiz
worshipper ['wə:ʃɪpəʳ] N devoto(-a),
venerador(a) *m/f*
worst [wə:st] ADJ (o/a) pior ▶ ADV pior ▶ N o
pior; **at ~** na pior das hipóteses; **if the ~
comes to the ~** se o pior acontecer
worsted ['wə:stɪd] N: **(wool) ~** lã *f* penteada
worth [wə:θ] N valor *m*, mérito ▶ ADJ: **to be ~**
valer; **it's ~ it** vale a pena; **to be ~ one's
while** (*to do*) valer a pena (fazer); **how
much is it ~?** quanto vale?; **£5 ~ of apples**
maçãs no valor de £5
worthless ['wə:θlɪs] ADJ sem valor; (*person*)
imprestável; (*thing*) inútil
worthwhile [wə:θ'waɪl] ADJ (*activity*) que vale
a pena; (*cause*) de mérito, louvável; **a ~ book**
um livro que vale a pena ler
worthy ['wə:ðɪ] ADJ (*person*) merecedor(a),
respeitável; (*motive*) justo; **~ of** digno de

⎧ **KEYWORD** ⎫

would [wud] AUX VB **1** (*conditional tense*): **if you
asked him, he would do it** se você pedisse,
ele faria isto; **if you had asked him, he
would have done it** se você tivesse pedido,
ele teria feito isto
2 (*in offers, invitations, requests*): **would you like
a biscuit?** você quer um biscoito?; **would
you ask him to come in?** pode pedir a ele
para entrar?; **would you close the door,**

please? quer fechar a porta por favor?
3 (in indirect speech): **I said I would do it** eu disse que eu faria isto; **he asked me if I would go with him** ele me perguntou se eu iria com ele
4 (emphatic): **it WOULD have to snow today!** tinha que nevar logo hoje!; **you WOULD say that, wouldn't you?** é lógico que você vai dizer isso
5 (insistence): **she wouldn't behave** não houve jeito dela se comportar
6 (conjecture): **it would have been midnight** devia ser meia-noite; **it would seem so** parece que sim
7 (indicating habit): **he would go on Mondays** costumava ir nas segundas-feiras

would-be ADJ aspirante, que pretende ser
wouldn't ['wudnt] = **would not**
wound¹ [waund] PT, PP of **wind²**
wound² [wu:nd] N ferida ▶ VT ferir
wove [wəuv] PT of **weave**
woven ['wəuvən] PP of **weave**
WP N ABBR = **word processing; word processor** ▶ ABBR (BRIT inf) = **weather permitting**
WPC (BRIT) N ABBR = **woman police constable**
wpm ABBR (= words per minute) palavras por minuto
WRAC (BRIT) N ABBR = **Women's Royal Army Corps**
WRAF (BRIT) N ABBR = **Women's Royal Air Force**
wrangle ['ræŋgl] N briga ▶ VI brigar
wrap [ræp] N (stole) xale m; (cape) capa ▶ VT (cover) envolver; (also: **wrap up**) embrulhar; **under ~s** (fig: plan, scheme) em sigilo
wrapper ['ræpər] N (on chocolate) invólucro; (BRIT: of book) capa
wrapping paper ['ræpɪŋ-] N papel m de embrulho; (fancy) papel de presente
wrath [rɔθ] N cólera, ira
wreak [ri:k] VT (destruction) causar; **to ~ havoc (on)** causar estragos (em); **to ~ vengeance on** vingar-se em, tirar vingança de
wreath [ri:θ] (pl **wreaths** [ri:ðz]) N (funeral wreath) coroa; (of flowers) grinalda
wreathe [ri:ð] VT trançar, cingir
wreck [rɛk] N (of vehicle) destroços mpl; (ship) restos mpl do naufrágio; (pej: person) caco ▶ VT destruir, danificar; (fig) arruinar, arrasar
wreckage ['rɛkɪdʒ] N (of car, plane) destroços mpl; (of ship) restos mpl; (of building) escombros mpl
wrecker ['rɛkər] (US) N (breakdown van) reboque m (BR), pronto socorro (PT)
WREN [rɛn] (BRIT) N ABBR membro do WRNS
wren [rɛn] N (Zool) carriça
wrench [rɛntʃ] N (Tech) chave f inglesa; (tug) puxão m; (fig) separação f penosa ▶ VT torcer com força; **to ~ sth from sb** arrancar algo de alguém
wrest [rɛst] VT: **to ~ sth from sb** extorquir algo de or a alguém

wrestle ['rɛsl] VI: **to ~ (with sb)** lutar (com or contra alguém); **to ~ with** (fig) lutar com
wrestler ['rɛslər] N lutador m
wrestling ['rɛslɪŋ] N luta (livre)
wrestling match N partida de luta romana
wretch [rɛtʃ] N desgraçado(-a); **little ~!** (often humorous) seu desgraçado!
wretched ['rɛtʃɪd] ADJ desventurado, infeliz; (inf) maldito
wriggle ['rɪgl] N contorção f ▶ VI (also: **wriggle about**) retorcer-se, contorcer-se
wring [rɪŋ] (pt, pp **wrung**) VT (clothes, neck) torcer; (hands) apertar; (fig): **to ~ sth out of sb** arrancar algo de alguém
wringer ['rɪŋər] N máquina de espremer roupa
wringing ['rɪŋɪŋ] ADJ (also: **wringing wet**) encharcado, ensopado
wrinkle ['rɪŋkl] N (on skin) ruga; (on paper) prega ▶ VT franzir ▶ VI enrugar-se; (cloth etc) franzir-se
wrinkled ['rɪŋkld] ADJ (fabric, paper) franzido, pregueado; (surface, skin) enrugado
wrinkly ['rɪŋklɪ] ADJ (fabric, paper) franzido, pregueado; (surface, skin) enrugado
wrist [rɪst] N pulso
wristband ['rɪstbænd] (BRIT) N (of shirt) punho; (of watch) pulseira
wristwatch ['rɪstwɔtʃ] N relógio m de pulso
writ [rɪt] N mandado judicial; **to issue a ~ against sb, serve a ~ on sb** demandar judicialmente alguém
write [raɪt] (pt **wrote**, pp **written**) VT escrever; (cheque, prescription) passar ▶ VI escrever; **to ~ to sb** escrever para alguém
▶ **write away** VI: **to ~ away for** (information) escrever pedindo; (goods) encomendar pelo correio
▶ **write down** VT escrever; (note) anotar; (put on paper) pôr no papel
▶ **write off** VT (debt, plan) cancelar; (capital) reduzir; (smash up: car) destroçar
▶ **write out** VT escrever por extenso; (cheque etc) passar; (fair copy) passar a limpo
▶ **write up** VT redigir
write-off N perda total; **the car is a ~** o carro virou sucata or está destroçado
writer ['raɪtər] N escritor(a) m/f
write-up N crítica
writhe [raɪð] VI contorcer-se
writing ['raɪtɪŋ] N escrita; (handwriting) caligrafia, letra; (of author) obra; **in ~** por escrito; **to put sth in ~** pôr algo no papel; **in my own ~** do próprio punho
writing case N pasta com material de escrita
writing desk N escrivaninha
writing paper N papel m para escrever
written ['rɪtn] PP of **write**
WRNS (BRIT) N ABBR = **Women's Royal Naval Service**
wrong [rɔŋ] ADJ (bad) errado, mau; (unfair) injusto; (incorrect) errado, equivocado; (inappropriate) impróprio ▶ ADV mal, errado ▶ N mal m; (injustice) injustiça ▶ VT ser

w

injusto com; (*hurt*) ofender; **to be ~** estar errado; **you are ~ to do it** você se engana ao fazê-lo; **it's ~ to steal, stealing is ~** é errado roubar; **you are ~ about that, you've got it ~** você está enganado sobre isso; **to be in the ~** não ter razão; **what's ~?** o que é que há?; **there's nothing ~** não há nada de errado, não tem problema; **what's ~ with the car?** qual é o problema com o carro?; **to go ~** (*person*) desencaminhar-se; (*plan*) dar errado; (*machine*) sofrer uma avaria

wrongdoer ['rɔŋduːəʳ] N malfeitor(a) *m/f*

wrongful ['rɔŋful] ADJ injusto; **~ dismissal** demissão *f* injusta

wrongly ['rɔŋlɪ] ADV (*treat*) injustamente; (*incorrectly*) errado

wrong number N (*Tel*): **you have the ~** o número está errado

wrong side N (*of cloth*) avesso

wrote [rəut] PT *of* **write**

wrought [rɔːt] ADJ: **~ iron** ferro forjado

wrung [rʌŋ] PT, PP *of* **wring**

WRVS (*BRIT*) N ABBR (= *Women's Royal Voluntary Service*) *instituição de caridade*

wry [raɪ] ADJ (*humour, expression*) irônico; **to make a ~ face** fazer uma careta

wt. ABBR = **weight**

WV (*US*) ABBR (*Post*) = **West Virginia**

WWW N ABBR = **World Wide Web**; **the ~** a WWW

WY (*US*) ABBR (*Post*) = **Wyoming**

WYSIWYG ['wɪzɪwɪg] ABBR (*Comput*: = *what you see is what you get*) *o documento sairá na impressora exatamente como aparece na tela*

Xx

X, x [ɛks] N (letter) X, x m; (BRIT Cinema: old)
(proibido para menores de) 18 anos;
X for Xmas X de Xavier; **if you have x
dollars a year ...** se você tem x dólares
por ano ...

Xerox® ['zɪərɔks] N (also: **Xerox machine**)
xerox® m; (photocopy) xerox® m ▶ VT xerocar,
tirar um xerox de

XL ABBR = **extra large**

Xmas ['ɛksməs] N ABBR = **Christmas**

X-rated [-'reɪtɪd] (US) ADJ (film) proibido para
menores de 18 anos

X-ray [ɛks'reɪ] N radiografia ▶ VT radiografar,
tirar uma chapa de; **X-rays** NPL raios mpl X;
to have an ~ tirar or bater um raio x

xylophone ['zaɪləfəun] N xilofone m

Yy

Y, y [waɪ] N (*letter*) Y, y *m*; **Y for Yellow** (*BRIT*) *or* **Yoke** (*US*) Y de Yolanda

yacht [jɔt] N iate *m*; (*smaller*) veleiro

yachting ['jɔtɪŋ] N (*sport*) iatismo

yachtsman ['jɔtsmən] (*irreg: like* **man**) N iatista *m*

yam [jæm] N inhame *m*

Yank [jæŋk] (*pej*) N ianque *m/f*

yank [jæŋk] VT arrancar

Yankee ['jæŋkɪ] N = **Yank**

yap [jæp] VI (*dog*) ganir

yard [jɑːd] N pátio, quintal *m*; (*US: garden*) jardim *m*; (*measure*) jarda (*914 mm; 3 feet*); **builder's** ~ depósito de material de construção

yardstick ['jɑːdstɪk] N (*fig*) critério, padrão *m*

yarn [jɑːn] N fio; (*tale*) história inverossímil

yawn [jɔːn] N bocejo ▶ VI bocejar

yawning ['jɔːnɪŋ] ADJ (*gap*) enorme

yd ABBR = **yard**

yeah [jɛə] (*inf*) ADV é

year [jɪəʳ] N ano; **to be 8 ~s old** ter 8 anos; **every** ~ todos os anos, todo ano; **this** ~ este ano; **a** *or* **per** ~ por ano; **~ in, ~ out** entra ano, sai ano; **an eight-~-old child** uma criança de oito anos (de idade)

yearbook ['jɪəbuk] N anuário, almanaque *m*

yearly ['jɪəlɪ] ADJ anual ▶ ADV anualmente; **twice** ~ duas vezes por ano

yearn [jəːn] VI: **to ~ to do/for sth** ansiar fazer/por algo

yearning ['jəːnɪŋ] N ânsia, desejo ardente

yeast [jiːst] N levedura, fermento

yell [jɛl] N grito, berro ▶ VI gritar, berrar

yellow ['jɛləu] ADJ amarelo ▶ N amarelo

yellow fever N febre *f* amarela

yellowish ['jɛləuɪʃ] ADJ amarelado

Yellow Pages® NPL (*Tel*) Páginas Amarelas *fpl*

Yellow Sea N: **the** ~ o mar Amarelo

yelp [jɛlp] N latido ▶ VI latir

Yemen ['jɛmən] N Iêmen *m* (*BR*), Iémene *m* (*PT*)

yen [jɛn] N (*currency*) iene *m*; (*craving*): ~ **for/to do** desejo de/de fazer

yeoman ['jəumən] (*irreg: like* **man**) N: **Y~ of the Guard** membro da guarda real

yes [jɛs] ADV, N sim *m*; **do you speak English?** — **I do** você fala inglês? — falo (sim); **does the plane leave at six?** — ~ o avião sai às seis? — é; **to say** ~ **to sth/sb** (*approve*) dar o sim a algo/alguém

yesterday ['jɛstədɪ] ADV, N ontem *m*; **the day before** ~ anteontem; ~ **morning/evening** ontem de manhã/à noite; **all day** ~ ontem o dia inteiro

yet [jɛt] ADV ainda ▶ CONJ porém, no entanto; **it is not finished** ~ ainda não está acabado; **must you go just** ~? você já tem que ir?; **the best** ~ o melhor até agora; **as** ~ até agora, ainda; **a few days** ~ mais alguns dias; ~ **again** mais uma vez

yew [juː] N teixo

Y-fronts® ['waɪfrʌnts] NPL (*BRIT*) cueca slip (com abertura lateral)

YHA (*BRIT*) N ABBR = **Youth Hostels Association**

Yiddish ['jɪdɪʃ] N (i)ídiche *m*

yield [jiːld] N produção *f*; (*Agr*) colheita; (*Comm*) rendimento ▶ VT (*gen*) produzir; (*profit*) render; (*surrender*) ceder ▶ VI (*give way*) render-se, ceder; (*US Aut*) ceder; **a** ~ **of 5%** um rendimento de 5%

YMCA N ABBR (= *Young Men's Christian Association*) ≈ ACM *f*

yob ['jɔb], **yobbo** ['jɔbəu] (*BRIT inf*) N bagunceiro

yodel ['jəudl] VI cantar tirolesa

yoga ['jəugə] N ioga

yoghurt, yogurt ['jəugət] N iogurte *m*

yoke [jəuk] N canga, cangalha; (*of oxen*) junta; (*on shoulders*) balancim *m*; (*fig*) jugo ▶ VT (*also:* **yoke together**) unir, ligar

yolk [jəuk] N gema (do ovo)

yonder ['jɔndəʳ] ADV além, acolá

Yorks [jɔːks] (*BRIT*) ABBR = **Yorkshire**

KEYWORD

you [juː] PRON **1** (*subj: singular*) tu, você; (: *plural*) vós, vocês; **you French enjoy your food** vocês franceses gostam de comer; **you and I will go** nós iremos

2 (*direct object: singular*) te, o/a; (: *plural*) vos, os/ as; (*indirect object: singular*) te, lhe; (: *plural*) vos, lhes; **I know you** eu lhe conheço; **I gave it to you** dei isto para você

3 (*stressed*) você; **I told YOU to do it** eu disse para você fazer isto

4 (*after prep, in comparisons: singular*) ti, você;

(: *plural*) vós, vocês; (*polite form: singular*) o senhor/a senhora; (: *plural*) os senhores/as senhoras; **it's for you** é para você; **can I come with you?** posso ir com você?; **with you** contigo, com você; convosco, com vocês; com o senhor *etc*; **she's younger than you** ela é mais jovem do que você

5 (*impers: one*): **you never know** nunca se sabe; **apples do you good** as maçãs fazem bem à saúde; **you can't do that!** não se pode fazer isto!

you'd [ju:d] = **you had; you would**
you'll [ju:l] = **you will; you shall**
young [jʌŋ] ADJ jovem ▶ NPL (*of animal*) filhotes *mpl*, crias *fpl*; (*people*): **the ~** a juventude, os jovens; **a ~ man** um jovem; **a ~ lady** (*unmarried*) uma jovem, uma moça; (*married*) uma jovem senhora; **my ~er brother** o meu irmão mais novo
younger ['jʌŋəʳ] ADJ (*brother etc*) mais novo; **the ~ generation** a geração mais jovem
youngish ['jʌŋɪʃ] ADJ bem novo
youngster ['jʌŋstəʳ] N jovem *m/f*, moço(-a)
your [jɔ:ʳ] ADJ teu/tua, seu/sua; (*plural*) vosso, seu/sua; (*formal*) do senhor/da senhora; *see* **my**
you're [juəʳ] = **you are**
yours [jɔ:z] PRON teu/tua, seu/sua; (*plural*) vosso, seu/sua; (*formal*) do senhor/da senhora; **~ is blue** o teu(-a) tua *etc* é azul; **is**

it ~? é teu *etc*?; **~ sincerely** *or* **faithfully** atenciosamente; **a friend of ~** um amigo seu *etc*; *see also* **mine¹**
yourself [jɔ:'sɛlf] PRON (*emphatic*) tu mesmo, você mesmo; (*object, reflexive*) te, se; (*after prep*) ti mesmo, si mesmo; (*formal*) o senhor mesmo/a senhora mesma; **you ~ told me** você mesmo me falou; **(all) by ~** sozinho(-a); *see also* **oneself**
yourselves [jɔ:'sɛlvz] PRON (*emphatic*) vós mesmos, vocês mesmos; (*object, reflexive*) vos, se; (*after prep*) vós mesmos, vôces mesmos; (*formal*) os senhores mesmos/as senhoras mesmas; *see also* **oneself**
youth [ju:θ] (*pl* **youths** [ju:ðz]) N mocidade *f*, juventude *f*; (*young man*) jovem *m*; **in my ~** na minha juventude
youth club N associação *f* de juventude
youthful ['ju:θful] ADJ juvenil
youthfulness ['ju:θfəlnəs] N juventude *f*
youth hostel N albergue *m* da juventude
you've [ju:v] = **you have**
yowl [jaul] N uivo ▶ VI uivar
Yugoslav ['ju:gəuslɑ:v] ADJ, N iugoslavo(-a)
Yugoslavia [ju:gəu'slɑ:vɪə] N Iugoslávia
Yugoslavian [ju:gəu'slɑ:vɪən] ADJ iugoslavo
Yule [ju:l] N: **~ log** acha de Natal
Yuletide ['ju:ltaɪd] N época natalina *or* do Natal
yuppie ['jʌpɪ] (*inf*) ADJ, N yuppie *m/f*
YWCA N ABBR (= *Young Women's Christian Association*) ≈ ACM *f*

y

Zz

Z, z [zɛd, (US) zi:] N (*letter*) Z, z *m*; **Z for Zebra** Z de Zebra
Zaire [zɑːˈiːəʳ] N Zaire *m*
Zambia [ˈzæmbɪə] N Zâmbia
Zambian [ˈzæmbɪən] ADJ, N zambiano(-a)
zany [ˈzeɪnɪ] ADJ tolo, bobo
zeal [ziːl] N entusiasmo; (*religious*) fervor *m*
zealot [ˈzɛlət] N fanático(-a)
zealous [ˈzɛləs] ADJ zeloso, entusiasta
zebra [ˈziːbrə] N zebra
zebra crossing (BRIT) N faixa (para pedestres) (BR), passadeira (PT)
zenith [ˈzɛnɪθ] N (*Astronomy*) zênite *m*; (*fig*) apogeu *m*
zero [ˈzɪərəu] N zero ▶ VI: **to ~ in on** fazer mira em; **5 degrees below ~** 5 graus abaixo de zero
zero hour N hora zero
zero-rated [-ˈreɪtɪd] (BRIT) ADJ isento de IVA
zest [zɛst] N vivacidade *f*, entusiasmo; (*of lemon etc*) zesto
zigzag [ˈzɪgzæg] N ziguezague *m* ▶ VI ziguezaguear
Zimbabwe [zɪmˈbɑːbwɪ] N Zimbábue *m* (BR), Zimbabwe *m* (PT)
Zimbabwean [zɪmˈbɑːbwɪən] ADJ, N zimbabuano(-a) (BR), zimbabweano(-a) (PT)

Zimmer® [ˈzɪməʳ] N (*also:* **Zimmer frame**) andador *m*
zinc [zɪŋk] N zinco
Zionism [ˈzaɪənɪzm] N sionismo
Zionist [ˈzaɪənɪst] ADJ, N sionista *m/f*
zip [zɪp] N (*also:* **zip fastener**) fecho ecler (BR) *or* éclair (PT); (*energy*) vigor *m* ▶ VT (*also:* **zip up**) fechar o fecho ecler de, subir o fecho ecler de
zip code (US) N código postal
zip file N (*Comput*) arquivo zipado
zipper [ˈzɪpəʳ] (US) N = **zip**
zit [zɪt] (*inf*) N espinha
zither [ˈzɪðəʳ] N citara
zodiac [ˈzəudɪæk] N zodíaco
zombie [ˈzɔmbɪ] N (*fig*): **like a ~** como um zumbi
zone [zəun] N zona
zoo [zuː] N (jardim *m*) zoológico
zoological [zuəˈlɔdʒɪkl] ADJ zoológico
zoologist [zuːˈɔlədʒɪst] N zoólogo(-a)
zoology [zuːˈɔlədʒɪ] N zoologia
zoom [zuːm] VI: **to ~ past** passar zunindo; **to ~ in (on sb/sth)** (*Phot, Cinema*) fechar a câmera (em alguém/algo)
zoom lens N zoom *m*, zum *m*
zucchini [zuːˈkiːnɪ] (US) NPL abobrinha
Zulu [ˈzuːluː] ADJ, N zulu *m/f*
Zurich [ˈzjuərɪk] N Zurique

Gramática
Inglesa

Contents

1 Os substantivos e o sintagma nominal

1.1 Substantivos contáveis/incontáveis (countable/uncountable)

Algumas coisas são consideradas elementos individuais, ou seja, podem ser contadas uma a uma. Os substantivos que se referem a elas são chamados contáveis e, portanto, dispõem tanto de uma forma singular como de plural, expresso normalmente pela terminação **-s**. Note que poderão ocorrer mudanças ortográficas decorrentes do acréscimo dos sufixos (→6.1):

> *... one table, ... two cats, ... three hundred pounds*

⚠ Alguns substantivos de uso frequente têm plurais irregulares, que não são formados com o sufixo **-s**:

child → *children*	*foot* → *feet*
man → *men*	*mouse* → *mice*
tooth → *teeth*	*woman* → *women*

Por outro lado, considera-se que existam coisas que podem ser contadas uma a uma; para se referir a estas, são usados os substantivos incontáveis:

> *The donkey needed food and water.*
> *All prices include travel to and from London.*

Estes geralmente fazem referência a:

---
substâncias: **coal • food • ice • iron • rice • steel • water**
qualidades humanas: **courage • cruelty • honesty • patience**
sentimentos: **anger • happiness • joy • pride • relief • respect**
atividades: **aid • help • sleep • travel • work**
ideias abstratas: **beauty • death • freedom • fun • life • luck**

Cuidado: note que, às vezes, no inglês usa-se um substantivo incontável para algo que em português é contável; nesse caso, os elementos são considerados um conjunto em vez de um a um. Por exemplo, *furniture* significa "mobiliário, móveis", mas, para dizer "um móvel", é preciso usar a expressão *a piece of furniture*. O uso dos substantivos incontáveis deve levar em conta as seguintes regras:

1.2 Os substantivos incontáveis têm uma única forma, não dispondo, portanto, de plural:

---
advice • baggage • equipment • furniture
homework • information • knowledge • luggage
machinery • money • news • traffic

> *I needed help with my homework.*
> *The children had great fun playing with the puppets.*
> *We want to spend more money on roads.*

1.3 ⚠ Alguns substantivos incontáveis terminam com **-s** e, assim, parecem ser substantivos contáveis no plural.

Geralmente, referem-se a:

> matérias de estudo: **mathematics** · **physics**
> atividades: **athletics** · **gymnastics**
> jogos: **cards** · **darts** · **skittles**
> enfermidades: **measles** · **mumps**

> *Mathematics is too difficult for me.*

1.4 Os substantivos incontáveis são usados sem o artigo *a(n)*:

> *They resent having to pay money to people like me.*
> *My father started work when he was ten.*

São usados com *the* quando se referem a algo específico ou citado anteriormente:

> *I am interested in the education of young children.*
> *I liked the music in the song, but the words were boring.*

1.5 Muitas vezes, os substantivos incontáveis são usados com vocábulos que expressam uma quantidade aproximada, como *some* (→1.42–45), ou uma locução, como *a loaf of*, *packets of* ou *a piece of*. O uso de *a bit of* é comum na linguagem falada:

> *Please buy some bread when you go to the shop.*
> Quando for à loja, compre pão.
> *Let me give you some advice.*
> Deixe-me dar-lhe um conselho.
> *He gave me a very good piece of advice.*
> Ele me deu um bom conselho.

1.6 Alguns substantivos incontáveis relacionados com comidas ou bebidas podem ser contáveis quando se referem a quantidades concretas:

> *Do you like coffee?* (incontável)
> *We asked for two coffees.* (contável)

1.7 Alguns substantivos são incontáveis quando se referem a algo de modo genérico e contáveis quando se referem a um caso concreto:

> *Victory was now assured.*
> A vitória estava então assegurada.
> *The political party won a convincing victory.*
> O partido político obteve uma vitória convincente.

1.8 Alguns substantivos têm um significado específico quando estão no singular, acompanhadas do determinante *the* (já que se referem a coisas que são únicas), ou no plural, quando não são usadas com esse sentido:

GRAMÁTICA INGLESA

> air • country • countryside • dark • daytime
> end • future • ground • moon • past • sea
> seaside • sky • sun • wind • world

I'm scared of the dark.
My uncle has a farm in the country.

Outros normalmente são usados no singular com *a* porque se referem a atividades concretas:

> bath • chance • drink • fight • go • jog
> move • rest • ride • run • shower • smoke
> snooze • start • try • walk • wash

Why don't we go outside for a smoke?
I went upstairs for a wash.

1.9 Outros substantivos são usados no plural com um significado especial, com ou sem o determinante (como os substantivos contáveis), mas não são usados em singular com esse mesmo significado:

His clothes looked terribly dirty.
Troops are being sent in today.

Alguns desses substantivos são sempre usados com um determinante (→1.26):

> authorities • likes • movies • travels

I went to the pictures with Tina.

Outros, por sua vez, geralmente são usados sem determinante:

> airs • expenses • goods • refreshments • riches

They have agreed to pay for travel and expenses.

1.10 Substantivos coletivos

Os substantivos coletivos (pois se referem a um grupo de pessoas ou de coisas) podem ser acompanhados do verbo no plural ou no singular, já que é possível considerar o grupo tanto como uma unidade quanto como vários indivíduos juntos:

> army • audience • committee • company • crew • enemy
> family • flock • gang • government • group • herd
> navy • press • public • staff • team • data • media

Our family isn't poor any more.
My family are perfectly normal.
The BBC is showing the programme on Saturday.
The BBC are planning to use the new satellite.

No entanto, no inglês americano, é raro usar um verbo no plural após um substantivo coletivo – prefere-se usar o verbo no singular.

1.11 Um substantivo pode vir acompanhado de outras palavras que especificam seu significado e que fazem parte do sintagma nominal. Essas palavras podem ser determinantes (→1.26), adjetivos (→2.1–11), outro substantivo, sintagmas nominais com preposição (→1.13–14) e construções com pronomes relativos ("que...") (→2.12–16):

> *He was eating a cake.*
> *He was using blue ink.*
> *I like chocolate cake.*
> *I spoke to a girl in a dark grey dress.*
> *She wrote to the man who employed me.*
> *The front door of the house was wide open.*

1.12 Quando um substantivo tem seu significado especificado por outro, o que especifica vem logo antes do que é especificado. Note que, às vezes, em português é necessário usar uma construção com a preposição "de", ou às vezes um adjetivo:

> *... a mathematics exam.*
> *... uma prova de matemática.*
> *... chocolate cake.*
> *... bolo de chocolate.*
> *... the oil industry.*
> *... a indústria petrolífera.*

1.13 Usa-se um sintagma nominal com a preposição *of*:

- após substantivos que se referem a uma ação ou um evento para indicar o sujeito ou o objeto de tal ação ou evento:

> *... the arrival of the police.*
> *... the destruction of their city.*

- para definir o material de que algo é feito:

> *... a wall of stone*

- para indicar o tema de um texto ou uma imagem:

> *... a picture of them both in the paper*

1.14 Usa-se um sintagma nominal com outras preposições:

- para descrever algo ou alguém do ponto de vista do lugar com o que se associa, usando a preposição de lugar correspondente:

> *... the house on the prairie*
> *... a casa na pradaria*
> *... the woman in the shop*
> *... a mulher da tenda*

GRAMÁTICA INGLESA

- **with** – quando se quer indicar o que uma pessoa tem:

    ... a girl with red hair.
    ... uma garota de cabelo vermelho.
    ... the man with the gun.
    ... o homem com a pistola.

- **in** – quando se quer indicar o que a pessoa está usando (ou traz com ela):

    ... a man in a raincoat.
    ... the man in dark glasses.

- **to** – com os seguintes substantivos:

alternative • answer • approach • attitude devotion • introduction • invitation • reaction reference • resistance • return

    This was my first real introduction to Africa.

- **for** – com os seguintes substantivos:

admiration • desire • dislike • need • reason • respect responsibility • search • substitute • taste • thirst

    Their need for money is growing fast.

- **on** – com os seguintes substantivos:

agreement • attack • comment • effect • tax

    She had a dreadful effect on me.

- **in** – com os seguintes substantivos:

decrease • difficulty • fall • increase • rise

    They demanded a large increase in wages.

1.15 Para indicar a quem pertence algo, usa-se um substantivo seguido de apóstrofo e "s" (**-'s**):

    Sylvia put her hand on John's arm.
    Sylvia pôs a mão no braço de John.
    Could you give me Charles's address?
    Você poderia me dar o endereço de Charles?
    They have bought Sue and Tim's car.
    Compraram o carro de Sue e Tim.

Se o substantivo é um plural terminando em "s" (→1.1, 6.1), usa-se somente o apóstrofo ('). Se o plural não é indicado pelo sufixo **-s**, são usados apóstrofo e "s":

    It is not his parents' problem.
    Não é problema de seus pais.
    Where are the children's shoes?
    Onde estão os sapatos das crianças?

Esta forma também é usada com frequência para se referir à casa de alguém ou ao lugar em que um profissional especializado atende.

Em inglês britânico, palavras como *house* ou *shop* são geralmente omitidas, ficando subentendidas:

> **He's at David's.**
> *Está na casa de David.*
> **She must go to the chemist's.**
> *Ela tem que ir à farmácia.*

O apóstrofo também é usado quando uma expressão de tempo serve para descrever outro substantivo:

> **They have four weeks' holiday per year.**
> *Têm quatro semanas de férias por ano.*

1.16 Pronomes

Os usos de *this*, *that*, *these*, *those* como pronomes são detalhados em 1.33–35; os de *some* e *any*, em 1.43; finalmente, os pronomes relativos são explicados em 2.12–16. Por outro lado, os pronomes indefinidos que se formam a partir de *some*, *any*, *no* e *every* aparecem nas seções 1.46–48 e 1.55.

Usa-se um pronome pessoal:

- para voltar a se referir a algo ou alguém que já tenha sido mencionado

- para se referir diretamente a coisas ou pessoas que estão presentes ou são implicadas em determinada situação

> **John took the book and opened it.**
> **My father is fat – he weighs over fifteen stone.**
> **He rang Mary and invited her to dinner.**
> **"Have you been to New York?" — "Yes, it was very crowded."**
> **I do the washing, he does the cooking.**

1.17 Estes pronomes podem ter duas formas distintas, dependendo de sua função em relação ao verbo: como sujeito ou objeto.

As formas de objeto são usadas, além de como objeto de um verbo, logo após uma preposição ou após o verbo principal.

Formas de sujeito:

I • you • he • she • it • we • you • they

Formas de objeto:

me • you • him • her • it • us • you • them

> **We were all sitting in a cafe with him.**
> **Did you give it to them?**

> *Who is it? — It's me.*
> *There was only John, Baz and me in the room.*

Cuidado: **you** é usado para "tu", "você", "vós" e "vocês". As diferenças de uso dessas palavras, seja em termos de tratamento ou de número, são identificáveis no inglês pelo contexto.

1.18 *You* e *they* podem ser usados para falar de pessoas em geral:

> *You have to drive on the left side of the road in Britain.*
> *Dirige-se do lado esquerdo da pista na Grã-Bretanha.*
> *They say she's very clever.*
> *Dizem que ela é muito inteligente.*

1.19 *It* pode ser usado como sujeito impessoal em expressões gerais que se referem às horas, às datas ou às condições climáticas, ou ainda para falar de situações em geral:

> *What time is it?*
> *It is January 19th.*
> *It is rainy and cold.*
> *It is too far to walk.*
> *I like it here. Can we stay a bit longer?*

1.20 *They/them* podem fazer referência a:

- *somebody/someone*, *anybody/anyone*, embora estes sempre venham seguidos por um verbo no singular:

> *If anybody comes, tell them I'm not in.*

- substantivos coletivos (→1.10), mesmo que anteriormente tenha sido usado um verbo no singular:

> *His family was waiting in the next room, but they had not yet been informed.*

1.21 Pronomes possessivos

Para dizer a quem algo pertence, usam-se os pronomes possessivos:

mine • yours • his • hers • ours • theirs

> *Is that coffee yours or mine?*
> *Esse café é seu ou meu?*
> *It was his fault, not ours.*
> *A culpa foi dele, não nossa.*

1.22 Pronomes reflexivos

Quando o pronome objeto se refere à mesma pessoa expressada pelo sujeito, usa-se um pronome reflexivo:

singular: **myself** • **yourself** • **himself** • **herself** • **itself** plural: **ourselves** • **yourselves** • **themselves**

> **He should give himself more time.**
> *Ele deveria se dar mais tempo.*

Os pronomes reflexivos também são usados para dar ênfase, e neste caso equivalem a "(alguém) mesmo":

> **I made it myself.**
> *Eu mesmo fiz.*

Também são usados após uma preposição, exceto em expressões adverbiais de lugar e após a preposição **with** significando "em companhia de", contanto que a pessoa mencionada seja a mesma do sujeito:

> **Tell me about yourself.**
> **You should have your notes in front of you.**
> **He would have to bring Judy with him.**

1.23 One

One, ones são pronomes usados para falar de coisas do mesmo tipo, porém com características distintas, para não ser necessário voltar a mencionar o tipo de coisa, citando apenas a característica:

> **My car is the blue one.**
> *Meu carro é o azul.*
> **Don't you have one with buttons instead of a zip?**
> *Você não tem um com botões em vez de um zíper?*
> **Are the new curtains longer than the old ones?**
> *As cortinas novas são mais compridas que as velhas?*

1.24 One, ones são usados juntamente com **this, these, that, those** quando a característica que distingue várias coisas do mesmo tipo é a proximidade:

> **I like this one better.**
> *Gosto mais deste.*
> **We'll have those ones, thank you.**
> *Levaremos aquelas, obrigado.*

Também podem se combinar com **which**, significando "qual" ou "quais":

> **Which ones were damaged?**
> *Quais foram danificados?*

1.25 Em inglês considerado culto, **one** é usado para expressar opiniões de maneira geral, normalmente aquelas que se acredita serem compartilhadas e generalizadas:

> **One has to think of the practical side of things.**
> *É preciso pensar no lado prático das coisas.*
> **One never knows what to say in such situations.**
> *Nunca se sabe o que dizer em situações deste tipo.*

GRAMÁTICA INGLESA

1.26 Determinantes

À frente do substantivo ou de qualquer adjetivo (isto é, no princípio do sintagma nominal), usa-se com frequência um determinante.

Há vários tipos: alguns fazem referência a algo concreto ou já mencionado enquanto outros se referem a algo mais geral ou não mencionado antes.

Muitos deles também podem ser usados como pronomes.

Os determinantes são:

> **the** (→1.27–32)
> **this** • **these** • **that** • **those** (→1.33–35)
> **a/an** (→1.36–41)
>
> **some** • **any** • **no** (→1.42–45)
>
> os quantificadores **much** • **many** • **little** • **few** (→1.49–52) • **all** (→1.53)
> • **most** • **a little** • **a few** • **the whole** • **every** (→1.54–55) • **each** • **both** (→1.57)
> • **half** • **either** (→1.58)
> • **other** (→1.60) • **another** (→1.61) • **more** • **less** • **fewer**
> os adjetivos possessivos **my** • **your** • **his** • **her** • **its** • **our** • **their**
> os determinantes interrogativos **what** • **which** • **whose**
> os numerais **one** • **two** • **three** • **four** ...

I met the two Swedish girls in London.
Conheci duas garotas suecas em Londres.
I don't like this picture.
Não gosto deste quadro.
There was a man in the corridor.
Havia um homem no corredor.
The patients know their rights like any other customer.
Os pacientes conhecem seus direitos como quaisquer outros clientes.
There weren't many people.
Não havia muita gente.
Most people agreed.
A maioria das pessoas concordou.
We need more time.
Precisamos de mais tempo.
We ought to eat less fat.
Deveríamos comer menos gorduras.
Few people like him.
Poucas pessoas gostam dele.
We had a few drinks.
Tomamos algumas bebidas.

1.27 Geralmente usa-se **the** nos mesmos casos que o artigo definido em português:

The girls were not at home.
As meninas não estavam em casa.

> *I don't like using the phone.*
> Não gosto de usar o telefone.
> *My father's favourite flower is the rose.*
> A flor favorita de meu pai é a rosa.
> *We spent our holidays in the Canaries.*
> Passamos nossas férias nas Canárias.

1.28 Exceções

Quando se fala de um tipo de coisa, animal ou pessoa de maneira geral, é usado em inglês somente o substantivo no plural:

> *Many adults don't listen to children.*
> Muitos adultos não escutam as crianças.
> *Dogs are mammals, the same as mice and whales.*
> Os cães são mamíferos, como os camundongos e as baleias.

Note que também é possível falar de um tipo de coisa, animal ou pessoa de maneira geral usando o substantivo no singular. Nesse caso, usa-se *the*:

> *The dog is a mammal, the same as the mouse and the whale.*
> O cão é um mamífero, como o camundongo e a baleia.

1.29 Não se usa em expressões adverbiais de tempo, com *at*, *by*, *on*:

> *on Monday, by night*

1.30 Não se usa com o nome de lagos e montanhas (mas sim com o de cordilheiras):

> *Lake Michigan is in the north of the United States.*
> *Mount Everest is in the Himalayas and Aconcagua in the Andes.*

1.31 Não se usa com direções nem com cifras ou letras:

> *A famous shopping area of London is Oxford Street.*
> *The main post office is at 11, Union Street.*
> *The winning number is three thousand five hundred and forty-five.*
> *Z is the last letter of the alphabet.*

1.32 Usa-se com adjetivos como *rich*, *poor*, *young*, *old* e *unemployed*, além de outros adjetivos de nacionalidade, para falar daquele determinado grupo de indivíduos:

> *They were discussing the problem of the unemployed.*
> *The French are opposed to the idea.*

1.33 This, that, these, those

This significa "este, esta, isto". *These* é a forma de plural ("estes, estas"). *That* significa "esse, essa, isso" ou "aquele, aquela, aquilo", de acordo com o contexto. *Those* é a forma de plural:

> *This book is a present from my mother.*
> *When did you buy that hat?*

Esses determinantes também são usados como pronomes:

> **This is a list of rules.**
> **'I brought you these.' Adam held out a bag of grapes.**
> **That looks interesting.**
> **Those are mine.**

1.34 Em determinadas expressões, o uso de **tha**t com o verbo **be** tem um significado muito próximo daquele do **it** impessoal (→ 3.42); nesse caso, nenhuma das expressões equivalentes em português costuma ser usada:

> **Who's that?**
> *Quem é?*
> **Was that Patrick on the phone?**
> *Era Patrick no telefone?*

1.35 Também são usados para falar de coisas que acabaram de ser mencionadas (ou que estão prestes a ser) sem que acompanhem um substantivo.

É preciso levar em conta que essas expressões nem sempre funcionam como seus equivalentes em português:

> **That was an interesting word you used just now.**
> *Que interesante, essa palavra que você acabou de usar.*
> **These are not easy questions to answer.**
> *Estas perguntas não são fáceis de responder.*
> **This is what I want to say: it wasn't my idea.**
> *É o que quero dizer: não foi ideia minha.*

1.36 **A/an** são usados nos mesmos casos que seus equivalentes em português:

> **I got a postcard from Susan.**
> *Recebi um cartão-postal de Susan.*
> **His brother was a sensitive child.**
> *Seu irmão era uma criança sensível.*
> **I chose a picture that reminded me of my own country.**
> *Escolhi um quadro que me lembrava do meu próprio país.*

Usa-se **an** quando a palavra seguinte começa com um som vocálico:

> **an apple**
> **an honest man** ['ɔnist]
> **an hour** ['auʳ]

⚠ Se o som não é vocálico, mas semivocálico, usa-se **a**:

> **a university** [juni'vəːsiti]
> **a hamster** ['h mstəʳ]

1.37 São usados após o verbo **be** e os demais verbos de ligação quando se deseja citar a profissão de alguém:

> **He became a school teacher.**
> *Ele se tornou professor.*

> *She is a model and an artist.*
> Ela é modelo e artista.

1.38 Note que o numeral **one** é usado quando a intenção é enfatizar a quantidade, ou seja, para dizer que não se trata de dois, três ou quatro, mas sim de um:

> *I got (only) one postcard from Susan (in the three years she was abroad).*
> Recebi (apenas) um cartão-postal de Susan (nos três anos em que ela esteve no exterior).

1.39 Usa-se **a** com **hundred** e **thousand**, que também podem ser usados com **one**:

> *I've just spent a hundred pounds.*
> Acabei de gastar cem libras.
> *I've told you a thousand times!*
> Já lhe disse mil vezes!

1.40 Usam-se **a/an** antes de "e meio(a)" ou "e um quarto" ao falar de quantidades:

> *One and a half sugars in my coffee, please.*
> Uma colher e meia de açúcar no meu café, por favor.
> *A kilo and a quarter is roughly three pounds.*
> Um quilo e um quarto equivalem a aproximadamente três libras.

1.41 Usam-se com "meio, meia" ao falar da metade de algo. Note que é possível que venha antes ou depois de **half**:

> *You'll have to walk for half a mile.*
> Você terá que caminhar meia milha.

1.42 *Some; any; no*

A não tem forma de plural. Para esses casos, usam-se **some** ou **any**:

> *He has bought some plants for the house.*
> Ela comprou umas plantas para a casa.

Some e **any** são usados para se referir a uma quantidade aproximada:

> *There's some chocolate cake over there.*
> Há bolo de chocolate ali.
> *I had some good ideas.*
> Tive algumas boas ideias.

É possível usar **some** em perguntas educadas ou quando se espera uma resposta afirmativa:

> *Would you like some coffee?*
> Gostaria de um café?
> *Could you give me some examples?*
> Poderia nos dar uns exemplos?

Usa-se **any** em perguntas e negações. Também acompanha substantivos no singular com significado de "qualquer":

Are there any apples left?
Sobraram maçãs?
I don't have any money.
Não tenho dinheiro.
Any container will do.
Qualquer recipiente serve.

Não é usado quando há a combinação de **any** com a negação:

I don't see any problem in that/I see no problem in that.
Não vejo problema algum.

1.43 **Some** e **any** podem ser usados para substituir o substantivo, como pronomes.

No caso de **no**, o pronome correspondente é **none**:

You need change? I think I've got some on me.
Precisa de trocado? Acho que tenho algum comigo.
Children? No, I don't have any./No, I have none.
Filhos? Não, não tenho nenhum.

1.44 São usados com substantivos contáveis (→1.1–7) com o significado de "um pouco de", "nada de". Em português, em muitas ocasiões somente o substantivo seria usado:

I have left some food for you in the fridge.
Deixei um pouco de comida para você na geladeira.
Don't you speak any Dutch?
Você não fala nada de holandês?
He's left me with no money.
Ele me deixou sem dinheiro.

1.45 São usados com substantivos no plural com o significado de "algum" ou "nenhum":

Some trains are running late.
Alguns trens estão atrasados.
Are there any jobs men can do but women can't?
Existe algum trabalho que os homens podem fazer, mas as mulheres não?
There weren't any tomatoes left/There were no tomatoes left.
Não havia mais nenhum tomate.

1.46 **Some**, **any**, **no** e **every** (→1.42-45, 1.54-55) são combinados com **-body** ou **-one** para dizer "alguém, qualquer um, nenhum, todo o mundo", com **-thing** para dizer "algo, qualquer coisa, nada, tudo" e com **-where** para dizer "em algum/qualquer/nenhum lugar, por toda a parte":

> anybody · anyone · anything · anywhere
> everywhere · everybody · everyone · everything
> nobody · no one · nothing · nowhere
> somewhere · somebody · someone · something

I was there for an hour before anybody came.
Fiquei ali por uma hora até chegar alguém.
It had to be someone with a car.
Tinha que ser alguém com um carro.
Jane said nothing for a while.
Jane não disse nada por um instante.
Everyone knows that.
Todo mundo sabe disso.

Em inglês americano informal, *anyplace*, *no place* e **someplace** podem substituir *anywhere*, *nowhere* e **somewhere**.

1.47 Se vêm como sujeitos de um verbo, essas expressões recebem uma forma verbal no singular, embora possam se referir a mais de uma pessoa ou coisa:

Everyone knows that.
Todo mundo sabe disso.
Is anybody there?
Há alguém aí?

Depois de uma combinação com *-body* ou *-one*, geralmente é usado o pronome pessoal **they** com o verbo no plural:

Anybody can say what they think.
Qualquer um pode dar sua opinião.

1.48 São usados seguidos de *else* com o significado de "mais, outro, diferente":

I don't want to see anybody else today.
Não quero ver mais ninguém hoje.
I don't like it here. Let's go somewhere else.
Não gosto daqui. Vamos a outro lugar.

1.49 Usa-se *much* para dizer "muito, muita" e *many* para "muitos, muitas".

Da mesma forma, as noções de "pouco, pouca" são expressas por *little* e "poucos, poucas" por *few*:

I haven't got much time.
Não tenho muito tempo.
He wrote many novels.
Escreveu muitos romances.
He has little enthusiasm for the idea.
Tinha pouco entusiasmo pela ideia.
Visitors to our house? There were few.
Visitantes à nossa casa? Houve poucos.

1.50 Usa-se *much* em negações apenas em uma combinação com *very*, *so* e *too* (→1.51–52):

He didn't speak much English.
Ele não falava muito inglês.

GRAMÁTICA INGLESA

No lugar de **much** em uma oração afirmativa, geralmente são usadas outras expressões que também acompanham substantivos contáveis:

> **He needed a lot of attention.**
> *Ele precisava de muita atenção.*
> **I've got plenty of** ou **lots of money.**
> *Tenho muito dinheiro ou dinheiro de sobra.*
> **He remembered a large room with lots of windows.**
> *Ele se lembrou de um quarto grande com muitas cortinas.*

1.51 Usa-se **very** com **much, many, little** e **few**:

> **Very many old people live alone.**
> *Muitos idosos vivem sozinhos.*
> **We have very little time.**
> *Temos pouco tempo.*
> **There are very few cars like these nowadays.**
> *Há muitos poucos carros como estes hoje em dia.*

1.52 **Much/many** são usados somente com o significado de "tanto(s), tanta(s)"; com **little/few**, o sentido é de "tão pouco(s)":

> **They have so much money and we have so little.**
> *Eles têm tanto dinheiro e nós, tão pouco.*

Usa-se **too** com **much/many** com o significado de "muito(s), muita(s)" e com **little/few** significando "muito pouco(s), muito pouca(s)":

> **Too many people still smoke.**
> *Muitas pessoas ainda fumam.*

1.53 Usa-se **all** com substantivos contáveis e incontáveis com o significado de "todos" ou "todo". É possível usar **the** após **all**.

Exatamente como ocorre em português, a ordem em que **all** se coloca pode mudar, dependendo da ênfase que se queira dar:

> **All children should complete the primary course.**
> *Todas as crianças deveriam finalizar a educação primária.*
> **He soon lost all hope of becoming a rock star.**
> *Logo perdeu toda esperança de se tornar uma estrela do rock.*
> **All the items are priced individually.**
> *Todos os artigos recebem seus preços individualmente.*
> **The items are all priced individually.**
> *Os artigos todos recebem seus preços individualmente.*

1.54 Também se usa **every** com o significado de "todos", mas com substantivos contáveis no singular e o verbo também. Note que em português é usado um substantivo no plural:

> **Every child has milk every day.**
> *Todas as crianças bebem leite todos os dias.*

> **She spoke to every person at that party.**
> *Ela falou com todas as pessoas daquela festa.*

1.55 **Every** combina-se com **-body** e **-one** para significar "todos, todo o mundo", com **-thing** para significar "tudo" e com **-where** para significar "por toda parte":

> **Everyone else is downstairs.**
> *Todos os demais estão lá embaixo.*

1.56 Usa-se **each** com ou sem o substantivo com o significado de "cada (um ou uma)". Muitas vezes, esse significado é igual ao de **every**, "todos".

As diferenças são as mesmas que existem entre as expressões equivalentes em português:

> **Each county is subdivided into several districts.**
> *Cada condado é subdividido em vários distritos.*
> **Each applicant has five choices.**
> *Cada candidato tem cinco opções.*
> **Oranges are twenty pence each.**
> *As laranjas são vendidas a vinte centavos cada uma.*

1.57 Usa-se **both** com o significado de "ambos" ou "os dois/as duas":

> **Dennis held his coffee with both hands.**
> *Dennis segurava seu café com ambas as mãos.*
> **Both children were happy with their presents.**
> *As duas crianças estavam felizes com seus presentes.*
> **Both the young men agreed to come.**
> *Ambos os jovens concordaram em vir.*

A expressão **Both... and...** é usada com o significado de "tanto... como..." quando se fala de duas coisas ou pessoas ao mesmo tempo:

> **I am looking for opportunities both in this country and abroad.**
> *Estou buscando oportunidades tanto neste país como no exterior.*

1.58 Usa-se **either** quando se fala de duas coisas ou pessoas com o significado de "qualquer um dos dois" ou também de "ambos".

Neither é a forma negativa. Também são usados em determinado tipo de respostas (→3.54):

> **There were tables on either side of the door.**
> *Havia mesas em ambos os lados da porta.*
> **You can sit at either side of the table.**
> *Você pode sentar em qualquer (um) dos lados da mesa.*
> **Neither man knew what he was doing.**
> *Nenhum dos homens sabia o que estava fazendo.*

1.59 **Either... or...** são usados com o significado de "ou... ou..." para dizer que somente uma das duas possibilidades é válida. **Neither... nor...** é a forma

GRAMÁTICA INGLESA

negativa, usada com o significado de "nem... nem..." para dizer que nenhuma das possibilidades é válida:

> **You either love him or hate him.**
> *Ou você o ama ou o odeia.*
> **I was expecting you neither today nor tomorrow.**
> *Não lhe esperava nem hoje nem amanhã.*

1.60 Usa-se **the other** com o significado de "o outro, a outra" quando se fala de duas coisas ou pessoas. **Other** é usado com substantivos no plural com o significado de "outros, outras":

> **The other man has gone.**
> *O outro homem se foi.*
> **I've got other things to think about.**
> *Tenho outras coisas para pensar.*
> **The other European countries have beaten us.**
> *Os outros países europeus nos derrotaram.*

1.61 Usa-se **another** com substantivos contáveis no singular com o significado de "outro mais, outra mais". É usado com um número e um substantivo contável no plural com o significado de "outros tantos mais, outras tantas mais":

> **Could I have another cup of coffee?**
> *Posso tomar outra xícara de café?*
> **Another four years passed before we met again.**
> *Passaram-se mais quatro anos antes de nos encontrarmos novamente.*

2 O adjetivo

2.1 Em inglês, os adjetivos colocam-se, como regra geral, antes do substantivo, e não depois, como no português:

> **She bought a loaf of white bread.**
> *Ela comprou um pão branco.*
> **There was no clear evidence.**
> *Não havia provas claras.*

2.2 Alguns adjetivos são usados exclusivamente antes do substantivo. Por exemplo, diz-se *an atomic bomb*, mas não **The bomb was atomic**. Entre eles:

> **eastern • northern • southern • western • atomic
> countless • digital • existing • indoor • introductory
> maximum • neighbouring • occasional • outdoor**

> **He sent countless letters to the newspapers.**
> *Ele enviou inúmeras cartas aos jornais.*

Outros são usados somente após um verbo de ligação. Por exemplo, pode-se dizer **She was glad**, mas não *a glad woman*:

> **afraid • alive • alone • asleep • aware • content • due
> glad • ill • ready • sorry • sure • unable • well**

> **I wanted to be alone.**
> *Queria estar sozinho.*
> **I'm not quite sure.**
> *Não tenho certeza.*

2.3 Alguns adjetivos não podem ser usados sozinhos após um verbo de ligação, mas com determinada preposição e um sintagma nominal:

> **aware of • accustomed to • fond of
> unaccustomed to • unaware of • used to**

> **She's very fond of you.**
> **He is unaccustomed to the heat.**

2.4 Alguns adjetivos podem ser usados sozinhos ou seguidos de determinada preposição. São usados sozinhos ou com *of* para especificar a causa do sentimento:

> **afraid • ashamed • convinced • critical • envious
> frightened • jealous • proud • scared • suspicious • tired**

> **They may feel jealous (of your success).**
> **I was terrified (of her).**

• São usados sozinhos ou seguidos de *of* para especificar a pessoa que detém a qualidade:

> **brave** • **careless** • **clever** • **generous** • **good** • **intelligent**
> **kind** • **nice** • **polite** • **sensible** • **silly** • **stupid**
> **thoughtful** • **unkind** • **unreasonable** • **wrong**

That was clever (of you)!
I turned the job down, which was stupid (of me).

- São usados sozinhos ou seguidos de **to** aqueles que geralmente se referem a:

> semelhança: **close** • **equal** • **identical** • **related** • **similar**
> matrimônio: **engaged** • **married**
> lealdade: **devoted** • **loyal**
> classificação: **junior** • **senior**

My problems are very similar (to yours).
He was dedicated (to his job).

- São usados sozinhos ou seguidos de **with** para especificar a causa do sentimento:

> **bored** • **content** • **displeased** • **impatient**
> **pleased** • **satisfied**

I could never be bored (with football).
He was pleased (with her).

- São usados sozinhos ou com **for** para especificar a coisa ou a pessoa a que se refere a qualidade:

> **common** • **difficult** • **easy** • **essential** • **important**
> **necessary** • **possible** • **unnecessary** • **unusual** • **usual**

It's difficult for young people on their own.
It was unusual for them to go away at the weekend.

2.5 Alguns adjetivos podem ser usados sozinhos ou com preposições diferentes.

- São usados sozinhos, ou com sujeito impessoal + **of** + o sujeito da ação, ou ainda com sujeito pessoal + **to** + o objeto da ação:

> **cruel** • **friendly** • **generous** • **good** • **kind** • **mean** • **nasty**
> **nice** • **polite** • **rude** • **unfriendly** • **unkind**

He is very rude.
It was rude of him to leave so suddenly.
She was rude to him for no reason.

- São usados sozinhos ou com **about** para especificar uma coisa ou **with** para especificar uma pessoa:

> **angry** • **annoyed** • **delighted** • **disappointed**
> **fed up** • **furious** • **happy** • **upset**

They looked very angry.
She was still angry about the result.
I'm very angry with you.

2.6 Alguns adjetivos que caracterizam medidas são colocados depois do substantivo de medida:

> deep · high · long · old · tall · thick · wide

He was about six feet tall.
Ele media seis pés (de altura).
The water was several metres deep.
A água tinha vários metros de profundidade.
The baby is nine months old.
O bebê tem nove meses (de idade).

⚠ Note que não se usa *heavy* para falar de peso, mas *in weight*:

This parcel is two kilos in weight.
Esta encomenda pesa dois kilos.

2.7 Quando são usados mais de um adjetivo diante de um substantivo, é colocado primeiro aquele que dá uma opinião própria e em seguida aquele que descreve algo.

Geralmente usa-se *and* entre adjetivos somente quando vão depois de um verbo de ligação:

You live in a nice big house.
Você mora em uma casa grande e legal.
She was wearing a beautiful pink suit.
Ela vestia um lindo traje rosa.
He's tall and slim.
Ele é alto e magro.

2.8 Quando há dois ou mais adjetivos que dão uma opinião própria, o que tem um significado mais geral é colocado primeiro:

I sat in a lovely comfortable armchair in the corner.
Sentei em uma poltrona confortável no canto.
He had a nice cold beer.
Ele bebeu uma cerveja gelada.

2.9 Quando há dois ou mais adjetivos que descrevam características, são colocados na seguinte ordem:

tamanho forma idade cor nacionalidade material

We met some young Chinese girls.
Conhecemos umas jovens chinesas.
There was a large round wooden table in the room.
Havia uma grande mesa redonda de madeira no quarto.

2.10 Quando são usadas as formas comparativas de um adjetivo (→ 2.17–25), são colocadas antes dos demais adjetivos:

> *Some of the better English actors have gone to live in Hollywood.*
> *Alguns dos melhores atores ingleses foram viver em Hollywood.*
> *These are the highest monthly figures on record.*
> *Estas são as cifras mensais mais altas já registradas.*

2.11 Quando se usa um substantivo seguido de outro (→ 1.12), qualquer dos adjetivos é colocado sempre antes do primeiro substantivo, nunca entre os dois:

> *He works in the French film industry.*
> *Ele trabalha na indústria cinematográfica francesa.*
> *He receives a large weekly cash payment.*
> *Ele recebe um grande salário semanal em espécie.*

2.12 As partículas interrogativas podem ser usadas para fazer perguntas (→ 3.55). Os pronomes *who*, *which*, *when*, *where* e *why* podem ser usados também para formar orações subordinadas que funcionam como adjetivo dentro da oração principal especificando as características do substantivo:

> *The woman who lives next door is very friendly.*
> *The car which I wanted to buy was not for sale.*

2.13 Usa-se *who* ao falar de pessoas e *which* ao falar de coisas. Geralmente, é possível usar *that* no lugar de ambos:

> *He was the man who bought my house.*
> *He was the man that bought my house.*
> *There was ice cream which Aunt Jen had made herself.*
> *There was ice cream that Aunt Jen had made herself.*

2.14 Diferentemente do português, se há uma preposição na frase, ela é colocada no final de toda a oração que modifica o substantivo:

> *The house that we lived in was huge.*

Ao contrário do português, *who*, *which* e *that* podem ser omitidos da oração, mas somente quando não funcionam como sujeito:

> *The woman who lives next door is very friendly.*
> *The car I wanted to buy was not for sale.*
> *The house we lived in was huge.*

2.15 *Whose* é o possessivo de *who* e é usado com o significado de "cujo, cuja, cujos, cujas":

> *We have only told the people whose work is relevant to this project.*

2.16 Após palavras que tratam de tempo, usa-se *when*. Após palavras que tratam de lugares, usa-se *where*. Após razões, usa-se *why*:

> *This is the year when profits should increase.*
> *He showed me the place where they worked.*
> *There are several reasons why we can't do that.*

2.17 Comparações

O comparativo **more** pode acompanhar substantivos incontáveis, contáveis (no plural) e também adjetivos e advérbios de mais de duas sílabas e a maioria dos de duas:

> **His visit might do more harm than good.**
> *Sua visita pode causar mais dano que benefício.*
> **He does more hours than I do.**
> *Ele faz mais horas que eu.*
> **Be more careful next time.**
> *Tenha mais cuidado da próxima vez.*

2.18 Os adjetivos e advérbios de uma sílaba ou de duas sílabas que acabam em consoante + **-y** recebem a terminação **-er**. Note que podem ocorrer mudanças ortográficas quando uma terminação é acrescentada (→6.2):

> **angry • busy • dirty • easy • friendly**
> **funny • heavy • lucky • silly • tiny**

> **They worked harder.**
> *Eles trabalharam muito mais.*
> **It couldn't be easier.**
> *Não poderia ser mais fácil.*

Alguns adjetivos de duas sílabas usados com frequência podem seguir qualquer dos dois procedimentos:

> **common • cruel • gentle • handsome • likely**
> **narrow • pleasant • polite • simple • stupid**

2.19 Para comparar substantivos contáveis no singular, é necessário usar **a/an** antes do substantivo:

> **My sister is more of an artist than me.**
> *Minha irmã é mais artista que eu.*

2.20 Usa-se **less** com substantivos incontáveis e com adjetivos e advérbios em geral. Com substantivos contáveis, usa-se **fewer**:

> **This machinery uses less energy.**
> *Este maquinário usa menos energia.*
> **There are fewer trees here.**
> *Há menos árvores aqui.*
> **They were less fortunate than us.**
> *Tivemos menos sorte que nós.*
> **We see him less frequently than we used to.**
> *Nós o vemos com menos frequência que costumávamos.*

2.21 Note que há duas construções comparativas que não são usadas em português:

> **The smaller a parcel is, the cheaper it is to send.**
> *Quanto menor a encomenda, mais barato seu envio.*

> *It's getting harder and harder to find a job.*
> *Está se tornando cada vez mais difícil encontrar um trabalho.*

2.22 *As... (as...)* é usado com o significado de "tão/tanto(s)... (quanto...)" com adjetivos, advérbios e grupos verbais. Com substantivos, é usado seguido de *much/many*:

> *You're as bad as your sister.*
> *Você é tão má quanto sua irmã.*
> *He doesn't get as many calls as I do.*
> *Ele não recebe tantas chamadas quanto eu.*

2.23 *Most* e a terminação *-est* são usados com o significado de "o/a mais, mais..." nos mesmos casos que *more* e a terminação *-er*, respectivamente. Alguns adjetivos e advérbios de uso frequente têm formas irregulares:

good/well n better n best
bad/badly n worse n worst
far → farther/further → farthest/furthest

> *Tokyo is Japan's largest city.*
> *Tóquio é a maior cidade do Japão.*
> *He was the most interesting person there.*
> *Ele era a pessoa mais interessante dos que estavam lá.*
> *She sat near the furthest window.*
> *Ela sentou perto da janela mais distante.*

2.24 Pode-se usar *most* sem estabelecer uma comparação, em cujo caso não se usa *the*:

> *This book is most interesting.*
> *Este livro é interessantíssimo.*
> *This book is most interesting.*
> *Este livro é o mais interessante.*

2.25 *So... (that...)* pode ser usado para fazer uma comparação, o que nem sempre acontece necessariamente. Pode acompanhar um adjetivo, advérbio ou grupo nominal precedido de *many/much/few/little* (→1.52):

> *Science is changing so rapidly (that it's difficult to keep up to date).*
> *A ciência está mudando tão rapidamente (que é difícil manter-se em dia).*
> *I want to do so many different things.*
> *Quero fazer tantas coisas diferentes.*

2.26 Usa-se *such a...* precedendo um substantivo no singular. Em plural, usa-se sem *a (such...)*. Se o substantivo leva um adjetivo, *such* é colocado antes deste:

> *There was such a noise we couldn't hear.*
> *Havia ruído tal que não conseguíamos ouvir.*
> *They said such nasty things about you.*
> *Disseram coisas muito desagradáveis sobre você.*

3 O verbo e o sintagma verbal

3.1 Em inglês, são usadas bem menos flexões que em português para se referir à pessoa ou ao tempo verbal, indicados respectivamente pelo uso obrigatório dos pronomes e dos verbos auxiliares ou modais:

> *We wanted to know what happened.*
> *Did she phone you?*
> *We will see how simple a language can be.*
> *I might not go.*

Exceto no caso do imperativo, em inglês é necessário incluir sempre uma palavra ou um grupo de palavras que faça o papel de sujeito (→3.28–29).

3.2 Para formar os tempos verbais que não sejam o presente simples ou o passado simples na forma afirmativa (→3.8), a forma afirmativa do imperativo (→3.28-29) ou as formas não pessoais de infinitivo (→3.49), gerúndio (→3.45–48) ou particípio (→3.3), é necessário combinar o verbo principal com uma forma de um verbo auxiliar (→3.6), que indica o tempo ou se a voz é ativa ou passiva:

> *I have seen it before.*
> *Had you heard about it?*
> *It could not be done.*
> *They have been robbed.*

3.3 Os verbos aos quais se pode acrescentar a terminação *-ed*, que são a maioria, chamam-se verbos regulares. Há certos verbos que têm uma ou duas formas diferentes em vez desta terminação; são os chamados verbos irregulares.

Os verbos regulares têm quatro formas:

a) a forma base, que é aquela mencionada, por exemplo, em um dicionário, e que é usada para quase todas as pessoas no presente (→3.8-9), com os verbos modais (→3.12–27) e na construção *to...* (→3.49)

b) a forma com *-s*, que é usada somente no presente quando o sujeito está na terceira pessoa do singular.

c) a forma de gerúndio *-ing*

d) a forma de particípio *-ed*

Note que as eventuais mudanças ortográficas produzidas com o acréscimo de terminação (→6.1–2) não fazem com que os verbos sejam irregulares:

> **ask • asks • asking • asked**
> **try • tries • trying • tried**
> **reach • reaches • reaching • reached**
> **dance • dances • dancing • danced**
> **dip • dips • dipping • dipped**

3.4 Os verbos irregulares podem ter três, quatro ou cinco formas diferentes, pois podem ter uma forma diferente para o passado e às vezes outra para o particípio. Todas essas formas aparecem na parte inglês-português do dicionário depois da forma base:

> cost • costs • costing • cost • cost
> think • thinks • thinking • thought • thought
> swim • swims • swimming • swam • swum

3.5 O verbo principal pode ser precedido de:

- um ou dois verbos auxiliares

  > **I had met him in Zermatt.**
  > *Eu o havia conhecido em Zermatt.*
  > **The car was being repaired.**
  > *Estavam consertando o carro.*

- um verbo modal

  > **You can go now.**
  > *Agora você pode ir.*
  > **I would like to ask you a question.**
  > *Queria lhe fazer uma pergunta.*

- um verbo modal e um ou dois auxiliares

  > **I could have spent the whole year on it.**
  > *Podia ter passado o ano todo assim.*
  > **She would have been delighted to see you.**
  > *Ela teria ficado encantada em vê-la.*

3.6 Os verbos auxiliares: *be*, *have*, *do*

Em inglês, há três verbos auxiliares: *be*, *have* e *do*.

	be	have	do
presente	*am/is/are*	*have/has*	*do/does*
-ing	*being*	*having*	*doing*
passado	*was/were*	*had*	*did*
particípio	*been*	*had*	*done*

Como verbo auxiliar, *be* pode ser acompanhado de:

- um verbo com a forma *-ing* para formar os tempos contínuos (→ 3.7):

  > **He is living in Germany.**
  > *Ele está morando na Alemanha.*
  > **They were going to phone you.**
  > *Iam ligar para você.*

- um particípio para formar a voz passiva (→ 3.39–41):

  These cars are made in Japan.
  Estes carros são fabricados no Japão.
  The walls of her house were covered with posters.
  As paredes de sua casa eram cobertas de pôsteres.

Have é usado como verbo auxiliar com um particípio para formar os tempos perfeitos (→ 3.9–10):

  I have changed my mind.
  Mudei de ideia.
  I wish you had met Guy.
  Queria que você tivesse conhecido Guy.

Have e **be** são usados juntos para formar o presente perfeito contínuo (→ 3.7), o passado perfeito contínuo (→ 3.7) e os tempos perfeitos na voz passiva (→ 3.39-41):

  He has been working very hard recently.
  Ele tem trabalhado bastante ultimamente.
  The guest-room window has been repaired.
  A janela do quarto de hóspedes foi consertada.

Do é empregado como auxiliar para:

- a forma negativa ou interrogativa dos verbos no presente simples (→ 3.9) e no passado simples (→ 3.10)

  He doesn't think he can come to the party.
  Ele acha que não poderá vir à festa.
  Do you like her new haircut?
  Você gostou do novo corte de cabelo dela?
  She didn't buy the house.
  Ela não comprou a casa.

- enfatizar o verbo (somente em frases afirmativas):

  People do in fact make mistakes.
  Na verdade, as pessoas cometem erros, sim.

3.7 Os tempos contínuos

Os tempos contínuos são os seguintes:

- presente contínuo = presente do verbo **be** + **-ing**

  They're (= They are) having a meeting.

- futuro continuo = **will** + **be** + **-ing**:

  She'll (= She will) be leaving tomorrow.

- passado continuo = passado de **be** + **-ing**:

  The train was going very fast.

GRAMÁTICA INGLESA

- presente perfeito contínuo = presente de **have** + **been** + **-ing**:

  I've (= I have) been living here since last year.

- passado perfeito contínuo = passado de **have** + **been** + **-ing**:

  I'd (= I had) been walking for hours when I saw the road.

Os tempos contínuos são usados para:

- indicar que uma ação se desenrola sem interrupção antes e depois de um dado momento:

  I'm looking at the photographs my brother sent me.
  Estou vendo as fotografias que meu irmão me mandou.

- indicar que uma ação se desenrola antes e depois de outra ação que interrompe aquela:

  The phone always rings when I'm taking a bath.
  O telefone sempre toca quando estou no banho.
  He was watching television when the doorbell rang.
  Ele estava vendo televisão quando a campainha tocou.

- explicar a duração da ação:

  We had been living in Athens for five years.
  Estávamos morando em Atenas por cinco anos.
  They'll be staying with us for a couple of weeks.
  Ficarão conosco por algumas semanas.

- descrever um estado ou situação temporal:

  I'm living in San Diego at the moment.
  Atualmente estou morando em São Diego.
  He was working at home at the time.
  Ele estava trabalhando em casa naquela hora.
  She's been spending the summer in Europe.
  Ela está passando o verão na Europa.

- indicar que algo está ocorrendo ou que uma ação está se desenrolando:

  The children are growing quickly.
  Os meninos estão crescendo muito rapidamente.
  Her English was improving.
  Seu inglês estava melhorando.

⚠ Os verbos de percepção geralmente são usados mais com o modal **can** do que com a forma contínua:

  I can smell gas.
  Estou sentindo cheiro de gás.

3.8 Os tempos simples

Os tempos simples são assim chamados porque são os únicos usados sem um verbo auxiliar na forma afirmativa. O verbo é colocado logo depois do sujeito, exceto quando determinados advérbios se intercalam entre o sujeito e o verbo (→ 4.3):

> *I live in San Francisco.*
> *George comes every Monday.*
> *I lived in Los Angeles.*
> *George came every Tuesday.*

Os tempos simples são os seguintes:

- presente simples = a forma base do verbo (+ **-s** para *He/She/It*):

> *I live just outside London.*
> *He likes Australia.*

- passado simples (ou pretérito perfeito simples) = a forma base + **-ed** para os verbos regulares:

> *I liked her a lot.*

- e o passado simples, no caso dos verbos irregulares:

> *I bought six CDs.*

⚠ Com a negação **not** e em perguntas, é usado o auxiliar **do** (ou **does**).

> *I don't live in Birmingham.*
> *George doesn't come every Friday.*
> *Do you live near here?*
> *Does your husband do most of the cooking?*
> *George didn't come every Thursday.*
> *Did you see him?*

3.9 Os tempos de presente são:

- o presente simples, o presente contínuo, o presente perfeito e o presente perfeito contínuo.

O presente perfeito (ou pretérito perfeito composto) é formado com o presente de **have** + **-ed**:

> *She's (= She has) often climbed that tree.*
> *I've (= I have) lost my passport.*

O presente simples é usado para:

- falar do presente em geral ou de uma ação habitual ou que acontece com regularidade:

> *George lives in Birmingham.*
> *Do you eat meat?*

- afirmar uma verdade universal:

> *Water boils at 100 degrees centigrade.*

- referir-se ao futuro quando se fala de algo que está programado ou que se espera que ocorra no futuro:

    The next train leaves at two fifteen in the morning.
    It's Tuesday tomorrow.

O presente contínuo é usado para:

- referir-se a algo que está ocorrendo agora mesmo:

    I'm cooking the dinner.
    Estou fazendo o jantar.

- indicar uma situação temporal:

    She's living in a hotel at present.
    Atualmente ela vive em um hotel.

- falar de algo já programado que vai ocorrer. Neste caso, é quase sempre acompanhado de expressões de tempo como **tomorrow**, **next week** ou **later**

    The Browns are having a party next week.
    Os Browns farão uma festa na semana que vem.

O presente perfeito é usado para:

- assinalar as repercussões que algo que ocorreu no passado tem no presente:

    I'm afraid I've forgotten my book.
    Que pena, mas esqueci o livro.
    Have you heard from Jill recently?
    Você teve notícias de Jill ultimamente?
    Karen has just phoned you.
    Karen acabou de ligar para você.

- falar de um período que começou no passado e que se prolonga até o presente:

    Have you really lived here for ten years?
    Você mora mesmo aqui há dez anos?
    He has worked here since 2007.
    Ele trabalha aqui desde 2007.

- referir-se a um momento futuro na oração subordinada de tempo:

    Tell me when you have finished.
    Avise-me quando terminar.
    I'll write to you as soon as I have heard from Jenny.
    Escreverei para você assim que souber de Jenny.

3.10 Os tempos do passado são:

- o passado simples, o passado contínuo, o passado perfeito e o passado perfeito contínuo.

O passado perfeito (ou mais-que-perfeito) é formado com o passado de **have** + particípio passado:

> *He had lived in the same village all his life.*
> *I had forgotten my book.*

O passado simples é usado para:

- referir-se a um evento que ocorreu no passado:

> *I woke up early and got out of bed.*
> *Me desperté temprano y me levanté.*

- falar de uma situação que durou certo período no passado:

> *She lived just outside Los Angeles.*
> *Ela vivia (ou viveu) nos arredores de Los Angeles.*

- referir-se a algo que costumava ocorrer no passado:

> *We usually spent the winter at Aunt Meg's house.*
> *Costumávamos passar (ou passávamos) o inverno na casa de tia Meg.*

O passado contínuo é usado para:

- falar de algo que continuou ocorrendo antes e depois de um dado momento no passado:

> *They were sitting in the kitchen when they heard the explosion.*
> *Eles estavam sentados na cozinha quando ouviram a exposão.*

- referir-se a uma situação temporal:

> *Bill was using my office until I came back from Buenos Aires.*
> *Bill usou meu escritório até eu voltar de Buenos Aires.*

O passado perfeito é usado:

- quando nos referimos a um tempo anterior a um determinado momento do passado:

> *I apologized because I had forgotten my book.*
> *Pedi desculpas porque tinha esquecido o livro.*

- se falamos de um período de tempo que começou em um momento anterior do passado e que se prolongou durante um tempo, usamos a forma contínua:

> *I was about twenty. I had been studying French for a couple of years.*
> *Eu tinha uns vinte anos. Vinha estudando francês havia uns anos.*

Nessas duas orações, a segunda é mais formal ou menos direta. Às vezes, um tempo do passado é preferível a um do presente quando se quer ser mais educado:

> *Do you want to see me now?* ou *Did you want to see me now?*
> *I wonder if you can help me.* ou *I was wondering if you could help me.*

GRAMÁTICA INGLESA

3.11 O uso dos tempos com *for*, *since*, *ago*

Com *ago*, o verbo da frase principal fica sempre no passado simples:

> **We moved into this house five years ago.**
> *Nós nos mudamos para esta casa há cinco anos.*

Com *for*, o verbo da oração principal pode ficar:

- no passado, se a ação ocorre inteiramente no passado:

> **We lived in China for two years.**
> *Vivemos na China por dois anos.*

- no presente perfeito, e geralmente na forma contínua, para indicar que a ação começou no passado e se prolonga no presente:

> **We have been living here for five years.**
> *Estamos morando aqui há cinco anos.*
> **I have been a member of the swimming club for many years.**
> *Sou membro do clube de natação há muitos anos.*

- no passado perfeito ou no passado perfeito contínuo, quando se fala de duas ações que ocorreram no passado:

> **We had been working** ou **We had worked there for nine months when the company closed.**
> *Vínhamos trabalhando ali havia nove meses quando a empresa fechou.*

- no futuro:

> **We will be in Japan for two weeks.**
> *Estaremos no Japão por duas semanas.*
> **I'll be staying with you for a month.**
> *Ficarei na sua casa por um mês.*

Com *since*, o verbo da oração principal pode estar:

- no presente perfeito, e geralmente na forma contínua, para indicar que a ação começou no passado e se prolonga no presente:

> **We have been living here since 2005.**
> *Estamos morando aqui desde 2005.*
> **I've been in politics since I was at the University.**
> *Dedico-me à política desde que estava na universidade.*

- no passado perfeito ou no passado perfeito contínuo, quando se faz referência a duas ações ou situações que ocorreram no passado:

> **I had not seen him since Christmas.**
> *Não o tinha visto desde o Natal.*
> **He hadn't cried since he was a boy of ten.**
> *Ele não havia chorado desde os dez anos de idade.*

3.12 Os verbos modais são:

> *will*, *shall*, *would*, *can*, *could*, *may*, *might*, *must*, *should*, *ought to*

Têm uma única forma e, à exceção de **ought**, são usados com o infinitivo sem **to**.

3.13 Nunca se podem usar dois modais juntos nem podem ser precedidos de um verbo auxiliar. Por exemplo, não se pode dizer **He will can come**. Em vez disso, deve-se dizer **He will be able to come**, usando uma expressão com significado idêntico ao do modal.

3.14 **Will** é um verbo modal que na maioria das vezes é usado para falar do futuro:

> **The weather tomorrow will be warm and sunny.**
> *Amanhã o tempo estará quente e ensolarado.*
> **I'm tired. I think I'll go to bed.**
> *Estou cansado. Acho que vou dormir.*
> **Don't be late. I'll be waiting for you.**
> *Não se atrase. Estarei esperando você.*
> **By the time we arrive, he'll already have left.**
> *Na hora em que chegarmos, ele já terá ido embora.*

3.15 Ao falar de intenções próprias, usa-se **will** ou **be going to**:

> **I'll ring you tonight.**
> **I'm going to stay at home today.**

Ao falar do que outra pessoa decidiu fazer, usa-se **be going to**:

> **They're going to have a party.**

⚠ Note que normalmente não se usa **going to** com o verbo **go**. Geralmente prefere-se dizer **I'm going** em vez de **I'm going to go**:

> **'What are you going to do this weekend?' — 'I'm going to the cinema'.**

3.16 Também se usa **will** para solicitar algo ou fazer um convite:

> **Will you do me a favour?**
> *Você quer me fazer um favor?*
> **Will you come to my party on Saturday?**
> *Você vem à minha festa no sábado?*

3.17 Usa-se **shall** somente com **I** e **we**, principalmente na forma interrogativa para fazer uma sugestão a outra pessoa:

> **Shall we go and see a film?**
> *Vamos ver um filme?*
> **Shall I shut the door?**
> *Fecho a porta?/Quer que eu feche a porta?*

3.18 No inglês falado, usa-se **would** com **you** para fazer um convite a alguém ou pedir de maneira educada que faça algo:

> **Would you tell her Adrian phoned?**
> *Você poderia dizer-lhe que Adrian ligou?*
> **I'd like you to finish this work by Thursday.**
> *Gostaria que você terminasse este trabalho até a quinta-feira.*

> **Would you mind doing the dishes?**
> *Você se importaria de lavar os pratos?*
> **Would you like a drink?**
> *Gostaria de beber um drinque?*

3.19 Usa-se **would** com verbos como **like** para solicitar um serviço, falar do que alguém gostaria e para aceitar algo que tenha sido oferecido:

> **We'd like seats in the non-smoking section, please.**
> *Gostaríamos de sentar na zona de não fumantes, por favor.*
> **I wouldn't like to see something so disgusting.**
> *Não gostaria de ver algo tão desagradável.*
> **I wouldn't mind a cup of tea.**
> *Eu tomaria um chá.*

Quando vem seguido de **rather** ou **sooner** mais a forma base de um verbo (→ 3.3), é usado para falar de preferências:

> **He'd rather be playing golf.**
> *Ele preferiria estar jogando golfe.*
> **I'd sooner walk than take the bus.**
> *Prefiro ir andando a tomar o ônibus.*

3.20 *can, could, be able to*

Can é usado para dizer que algo pode ser ou acontecer:

> **Cooking can be a real pleasure.**
> *Cozinhar pode ser um verdadeiro prazer.*

Usa-se **could** para dizer que algo poderia ter sido ou acontecido:

> **You could have gone to Chicago.**
> *Você poderia ter ido a Chicago.*
> **If I'd been there, I could have helped you.**
> *Se eu estivesse lá, poderia ter ajudado.*
> **There could be a storm.**
> *Poderia haver uma tempestade.*

Can e **could** são usados para falar da capacidade de fazer algo:

> **Anybody can become a qualified teacher.**
> *Qualquer um pode se tornar um professor qualificado.*
> **He could run faster than anybody else.**
> *Ele podia correr mais rápido que qualquer outro.*
> **She couldn't have taken the car, because Jim was using it.**
> *Ela não poderia ter levado o carro porque Jim o estava usando.*

Também são usados para dizer que alguém sabe ou sabia fazer algo, pois aprendeu e pode fazer:

> **He cannot dance.**
> *Ele não sabe dançar.*

GRAMÁTICA INGLESA

A lot of them couldn't read or write.
Muitos deles não sabiam ler nem escrever.

3.21 Para expressar estes significados com formas verbais que não permitem o uso de **can**, são usadas formas da expressão equivalente **be able to**:

Nobody else will be able to read it.
Ninguém mais conseguirá lê-lo.
... the satisfaction of being able to do the job.
... a satisfação de conseguir fazer o trabalho.
Everyone used to be able to have free eye tests.
Todo mundo costumava poder fazer exames de visão gratuitos.

Esta expressão também pode ser usada em formas que permitem o emprego de **can** ou **could**, para descrever quando alguém é capaz de fazer algo:

She was able to tie her own shoelaces.
Ela era capaz de amarrar os próprios cadarços.
She could tie her own shoelaces.
Ela conseguia amarrar os próprios cadarços.

3.22 **Can** e **could** são usados no inglês falado para pedir algo de uma maneira educada ou para alguém se oferecer para fazer algo:

Can I help you with the dishes?
Posso ajudar com os pratos?
Could I help you carry those bags?
Posso ajudar a levar essas bolsas?
We could go to the cinema on Friday.
Poderíamos ir ao cinema na sexta-feira.
Could you do me a favour?
Você poderia me fazer um favor?

3.23 **Can**, **could**, **may** ou **be allowed to** são usados para pedir permissão.

A construção com **may** é a mais formal:

Can I ask a question?
Posso fazer uma pergunta?
Could I just interrupt a minute?
Poderia interromper um minuto?
May I have a cigarette?
Você poderia me dar um cigarro?

Somente **can** e **may** são usados para dar permissão:

You can borrow that pen if you want to.
Você pode tomar essa caneta emprestada se quiser.
You may leave as soon as you have finished.
Você pode sair assim que tiver terminado.

GRAMÁTICA INGLESA

Para expressar permissão, também é possível usar **be allowed to**, mas não quando é a própria pessoa que pede ou dá a permissão:

> **It was only after several months that I was allowed to visit her.**
> *Somente depois de vários meses é que eu consegui visitá-la.*
> **Teachers will be allowed to decide for themselves.**
> *Os professores terão permissão de decidir por si mesmos.*

3.24 **May** e **might** são usados para dizer que existe a possibilidade de que algo aconteça ou tenha acontecido:

> **He might come.**
> *Pode ser que ele venha.*
> **You may have noticed this advertisement.**
> *Pode ser que você tenha notado este anúncio.*

3.25 **Must** e **have to**.

Para dizer que algo deve ser feito, que algo deve acontecer ou que algo deve ser como é, usa-se **must**:

> **The plants must have plenty of sunshine.**
> *As plantas devem receber bastante sol.*
> **You must come to the meeting.**
> *Você tem que vir à reunião.*

3.26 Quando uma pessoa está falando de outras, deve usar **must** para emitir sua própria opinião; se essa afirmação não tem a ver com sua opinião pessoal, deve-se usar **have to**:

> **They have to pay the bill by Thursday.** (porque têm uma dívida)
> **They must pay the bill by Thursday.** (porque têm uma dívida comigo)
> **She has to go now.** (porque tem coisas a fazer)
> **She must go now.** (porque é a minha opinião)

3.27 **Should** e **ought to** são sinônimos e têm os mesmos significados que "deveria" em português:

> **We should send her a postcard.**
> *Deveríamos enviar-lhe um postal.*
> **We ought to have stayed in tonight.**
> *Deveríamos ter ficado em casa esta noite.*
> **You ought not to see him again.**
> *Você não deveria voltar a vê-lo.*

Quando **ought** é usado em uma oração negativa em inglês americano, não há necessidade de usar ‹to› em seguida:

> **We ought not forget that others are listening to us.**
> *Não devemos esquecer que outros estão nos escutando.*

3.28 Imperativos

A forma afirmativa do imperativo é a mesma que a forma base de um verbo, não sendo precedida de um pronome:

> *Come to my place.*
> *Start when you hear the bell.*
> *Sit down and let me get you a drink.*
> *Be careful!*

A forma negativa é formada com o auxiliar *do*:

Do not/Don't/Never + forma BASE

> *Do not write in this book.*
> *Don't go so fast.*
> *Never open the front door to strangers.*

Em inglês, o imperativo é usado com pessoas bem conhecidas ou em situações de perigo ou urgência. Nas várias outras ocasiões, é preferível o uso de verbos modais (→ 3.18–19) ou as construções com *let*, que convertem a ordem em um pedido educado:

> *Would you mind waiting a moment?*

3.29 Let + grupo nominal + forma BASE

A forma de imperativo com *let* é usada para pedir permissão a outra pessoa para fazer algo. Quando a pessoa é a mesma que faz o pedido, é uma maneira de se oferecer para fazer algo por alguém:

> *Let Philip have a look at it.*
> *Let them go to bed late.*
> *Let me take your coat.*

A forma negativa é formada com o auxiliar *do*:

Don't + *let* + grupo nominal + forma BASE

> *Don't let me make you late for your appointment.*

A forma com *let* é usada com *us* quando se aplica a nós, ou seja, quando o falante também se inclui. A forma contraída *let's* é mais frequente – a forma *let us* é usada somente no inglês culto ou escrito. A forma negativa é *let's not* ou *don't let's*:

> *Let's go outside.*
> *Let us consider a very simple example.*
> *Let's not/Don't let's talk about that.*

3.30 Verbos com dois objetos

Alguns verbos levam dois objetos. Nesse caso, o objeto que indica a pessoa pode ser colocado imediatamente depois da forma verbal, ou depois do outro objeto, em cujo caso usa-se *for* ou *to*:

GRAMÁTICA INGLESA

> *They booked me a place.* ou *They booked a place for me.*
> *I had given my cousin books on India.* ou *I had given books on India*
> *to my cousin.*

Se for um pronome ou qualquer outro tipo de grupo nominal (→1.11) de uma ou duas palavras (como um substantivo com *the*), o objeto que indica a pessoa é colocado antes do outro objeto:

> *Dad gave me a car.*
> *You promised the lad a job.*

Se o grupo nominal que funciona como objeto de pessoa for composto de várias palavras, geralmente é colocado depois do outro objeto:

> *She taught physics to pupils at the local school.*

3.31 Usa-se um pronome reflexivo (→1.22) quando se quer indicar que o objeto é a mesma coisa ou pessoa que o sujeito do verbo na mesma oração:

> *Ann poured herself a drink.*
> *The men formed themselves into a line.*
> *Here's the money, go and buy yourself an ice cream.*

3.32 ⚠ Diferentemente do que acontece em português, verbos como *dress*, *shave* e *wash*, que descrevem ações que as pessoas praticam a si mesmas, normalmente não recebem pronomes reflexivos em inglês. Com esses verbos, os pronomes reflexivos têm apenas um caráter enfático:

> *I usually shave before breakfast.*
> *Geralmente me barbeio antes do café da manhã.*
> *He prefers to shave himself, even with that broken arm.*
> *Ele prefere ele mesmo se barbear, mesmo com o braço quebrado.*

Cuidado: usa-se o possessivo, e não um pronome reflexivo, quando se fala de partes do corpo:

> *I hurt my foot on the bike.*
> *Machuquei o pé com a bicicleta.*
> *He cut his nails before going out.*
> *Ele cortou as unhas antes de sair.*

3.33 Quando se quer enfatizar que duas ou várias pessoas ou grupos de pessoas estão implicados da mesma maneira, podem-se usar os pronomes *each other* ou *one another*, "um ao outro/uma à outra/uns aos outros...", como o objeto do verbo. *Each other* ou *one another* geralmente são usados com verbos que se referem a ações em que há contato físico entre pessoas, como *cuddle*, *embrace*, *fight*, *hug*, *kiss*, *touch* etc:

> *We embraced each other.*
> *They fought one another desperately for it.*
> *It was the first time they had touched one another.*

3.34 Alguns verbos são seguidos de um sintagma nominal com preposição (→3.37–38), de modo que outra preposição é usada antes de *each other* ou *one another*:

> *They parted from each other after only two weeks.*
> *We talk to one another as often as possible.*

3.35 Alguns verbos podem ser usados com objeto para mencionar tanto a pessoa que realiza a ação como a coisa que se vê afetada, ou sem objeto para mencionar somente a coisa afetada. Nesse caso, a coisa afetada tem função de sujeito:

> *I broke the glass.*
> *The glass broke all over the floor.*
> *I've boiled an egg.*
> *The rice is boiling.*

Cuidado: note que, em português, muitos desses verbos são usados de forma reflexiva quando a pessoa não é mencionada. Outras vezes, um verbo em inglês que admite as duas construções tem dois equivalentes distintos em português:

> *When I opened the door, there was Laverne.*
> *Ao abrir a porta, me deparei com Laverne.*
> *Suddenly the door opened.*
> *A porta se abriu de repente.*
> *I'm cooking spaghetti.*
> *Estou fazendo espaguete.*
> *The spaghetti is cooking.*
> *O espaguete está cozinhando.*

3.36 Para descrever algumas ações, às vezes são usados verbos que têm pouco significado sozinhos e que tomam como objeto um substantivo que descreve a ação. A construção com verbo e substantivo normalmente permite acrescentar mais informação sobre o objeto, por exemplo usando adjetivos antes do substantivo:

> *I had a nice rest.*
> *Helen went upstairs to rest.*
> *She made a remark about the weather.*
> *I remarked that it surely would be better if I came.*

Os verbos que aparecem mais frequentemente com esse tipo de construção são *have*, *give*, *make*, *take*, *go* e *do*:

> *We usually have lunch at one o'clock.*
> *Mr. Sutton gave a shout of triumph.*
> *He made the shortest speech I've ever heard.*
> *He was taking no chances.*
> *Every morning, he goes jogging with Tommy.*
> *He does all the shopping and I do the washing.*

GRAMÁTICA INGLESA

3.37 Nos **phrasal verbs**, combina-se um verbo com um advérbio ou uma preposição. O significado do verbo às vezes pode mudar radicalmente:

> **Turn right at the next corner.**
> *Vire à direita na próxima esquina.*
> **She turned off the radio.**
> *Ela desligou o rádio.*
> **She broke her arm in the accident.**
> *Ela quebrou o braço no acidente.*
> **They broke out of prison on Thursday night.**
> *Eles escaparam da prisão na noite de quinta-feira.*

3.38 As diferentes composições verbais desse tipo se distribuem em quatro grupos.

Os do primeiro grupo não têm objeto:

> **break out • catch on • check up • come in • get by
> give in • go away • grow up • stand down • start up
> stay up • stop off • watch out • wear off**

> **War broke out in September.**
> **You'll have to stay up late tonight.**

Os do segundo grupo tomam o objeto depois da composição verbal. Embora pareça ser um grupo nominal com uma preposição, esta é considerada parte do verbo porque lhe confere um significado distinto:

> **fall for • bargain for • deal with • look after
> part with • pick on • set about • take after**

> **She looked after her invalid mother.**
> **Peter takes after his father but John is more like me.**

Os do terceiro grupo recebem o objeto logo depois do verbo:

> **bring around • keep up • knock out**

> **They tried to bring her round.**

Alguns verbos pertencem ao segundo e ao terceiro grupo, ou seja, o objeto pode ir depois da composição verbal ou logo depois do verbo:

> **fold up • hand over • knock over • point out
> pull down • put away • put up • rub out • sort out
> take up • tear up • throw away • try out**

> **It took ages to clean up the mess.**
> **It took ages to clean the mess up.**

No entanto, se o objeto é um pronome, é colocado sempre logo depois do verbo.

> **There was such a mess. It took ages to clean it up.**

Os verbos do quarto grupo recebem um objeto com preposição após a preposição ou o advérbio da composição verbal:

verbo + advérbio/preposição + preposição + objeto.

> **come in for • come up against • get on with**
> **lead up to • look forward to • put up with**
> **stick up for • walk out on**

> *I'm looking forward to my holiday.*
> *Children have to learn to stick up for themselves.*

Uma minoria de verbos tem a forma do quarto grupo e também toma outro objeto logo depois do verbo:

verbo + objeto + preposição/advérbio + preposição + objeto.

> **do out of • put down to • put up to**
> **take out on • talk out of**

> *John tried to talk her out of it.*

3.39 Quando se deseja chamar a atenção para a pessoa ou coisa afetada pela ação, mais que na pessoa ou coisa que pratica a ação, usam-se as formas verbais na voz passiva. Somente os verbos que geralmente recebem objeto admitem tais construções:

> *Mr. Smith locks the gate at six o'clock every night.*
> *The gate is locked at six o'clock every night.*
> *The storm destroyed dozens of trees.*
> *Dozens of trees were destroyed.*

3.40 Quando se usa a voz passiva, é normal não mencionar a pessoa ou coisa que executa a ação, porque não se sabe ou não se quer dizer (por ser irrelevante) quem ou o que seja. Caso se queira mencionar, este agente vai depois do verbo, precedido pela preposição **by**:

> *Her boyfriend was shot in the chest.*
> *He was brought up by an aunt.*

A estrutura da voz passiva é a seguinte:

(modal +) forma de **be** + particípio

> *Jobs are still being lost.*
> *What can be done?*
> *We won't be beaten.*
> *He couldn't have been told by Jimmy.*

⚠ **Get** às vezes é usado em inglês coloquial no lugar de **be** para formar a passiva:

> *Our car gets cleaned every weekend.*
> *He got killed in a plane crash.*

GRAMÁTICA INGLESA

3.41 No caso de verbos com dois objetos (→ 3.30), qualquer um deles pode ser o sujeito da oração passiva:

> *The secretary was given the key.* ou *The key was given to the secretary.*
> *The books will be sent to you.* ou *You will be sent the books.*

3.42 Sujeitos impessoais

O pronome *it* pode ser usado como sujeito de uma oração sem que se refira a algo já mencionado. Este uso impessoal de *it* introduz uma nova informação e é usado em particular para falar de horas ou datas:

> *It is nearly one o'clock.*
> *It's the sixth of April today.*

It + verbos que se referem ao estado do tempo

> *It's still raining.*
> *It was pouring with rain.*

Usam-se as construções *it* + forma de *be* + adjetivo (+ substantivo) e *it* + forma de *get* + adjetivo para descrever o estado ou as mudanças de tempo:

> *It's a lovely day.*
> *It was getting cold.*

Usa-se *it* + forma de *be* + adjetivo/grupo nominal para expressar a opinião sobre um lugar, uma situação ou um acontecimento:

> *It was terribly cold outside.*
> *It's fun working for him.*
> *It was a pleasure to be there.*

Usa-se *it* + verbos que expressam sentimentos, como *interest*, *please*, *surprise* ou *upset* + grupo nominal + *that.../to...* para indicar a reação de alguém diante de um feito, uma situação ou um acontecimento:

> *It surprised me that he should want to talk about his work.*
> *It comforted him to know his mother was at home.*

3.43 *There* também pode ser usado como sujeito impessoal de uma oração, tanto quanto um advérbio de lugar (→ 4.1). Após *there*, usa-se uma forma do verbo *be*, *appear to be* ou *seem to be* e um grupo nominal. A forma verbal pode estar contraída:

> *There is work to be done.*
> *There'll be a party tonight.*
> *There appears to be a mistake in the bill.*

3.44 *There is/there are* são usados com uma forma verbal no singular (*is...*, *has...*, *appears...*, *seems...*) se o grupo nominal que segue o verbo (ou o primeiro substantivo, caso haja mais de um) está no singular ou é incontável:

> *There is one point we must add here.*
> *There was a sofa and two chairs.*

Usa-se uma forma verbal no plural se o grupo nominal está no plural e antes de frases como *a number (of)*, *a lot (of)* e *a few (of)*:

> **There were two men in the room.**
> **There were a lot of shoppers in the streets.**

3.45 A forma verbal de gerúndio com **-ing** pode ser usada para formar um adjetivo a partir de um verbo e é colocada logo antes do substantivo:

> **He lives in a charming house just outside the town.**
> *Ele mora em uma casa encantadora nos arredores da cidade.*
> **His novels are always interesting and surprising.**
> *Seus romances são sempre interessantes e surpreendentes.*
> **Britain is an aging society.**
> *A Grã-Bretanha tem uma sociedade em processo de envelhecimento.*
> **Increasing prices are making food very expensive.**
> *O aumento de preço está encarecendo muito a comida.*

A forma verbal de gerúndio com **-ing** é usada depois do substantivo para especificar a ação sendo executada em um momento concreto ou em geral:

> **Most of the people strolling in the park were teenagers.**
> *A maioria das pessoas que passeavam pelo parque era de adolescentes.*
> **The men working there were not very friendly.**
> *Os homens que trabalhavam ali não eram muito simpáticos.*

3.46 A forma verbal de gerúndio com **-ing** é usada depois do verbo principal para falar de uma ação quando o sujeito é o mesmo do verbo principal. Também pode ser usada na forma passiva. Outros verbos são seguidos de uma forma de infinitivo **to**...(→ 3.49), e alguns como **bother**, **try** ou **prefer** admitem as duas construções:

> **I don't mind telling you.**
> *Não me importo de lhe dizer.*
> **I've just finished reading that book.**
> *Acabei de terminar esse livro.*
> **She carried on reading.**
> *Ela continuou lendo.*
> **I dislike being interrupted.**
> *Não gosto de ser interrompido.*
> **I didn't bother answering./I didn't bother to answer.**
> *Não me preocupei em responder.*

3.47 A forma verbal de gerúndio com **-ing** é usada depois de **come** e **go** para indicar uma atividade física ou esportiva:

> **They both came running out.**
> *Os dois saíram correndo.*
> **Did you say they might go camping?**
> *Você falou que eles poderiam acampar?*

3.48 A forma verbal de gerúndio com **-ing** é usada depois de alguns verbos como **catch**, **find**, **imagine**, **leave**, **prevent**, **stop**, **watch** e seu objeto. O objeto do verbo principal é o sujeito da forma **-ing**:

> **He left them making their calculations.**
> *Eles os deixou fazendo seus cálculos.*
> **I found her waiting for me outside.**
> *Eu a encontrei esperando por mim do lado de fora.*

3.49 A forma verbal de infinitivo **to…** é usada depois de alguns verbos para se referir a uma ação quando o sujeito for igual ao do verbo principal. Geralmente equivale ao infinitivo em português:

> **She had agreed to let us use her car.**
> *Ela tinha concordado em nos deixar usar seu carro.*
> **I decided not to go out for the evening.**
> *Decidi não sair esta noite.*
> **England failed to win a place in the finals.**
> *A Inglaterra não conseguiu conquistar uma vaga na final.*

A forma verbal de infinitivo **to…** é usada depois de alguns verbos e seu objeto ou seu grupo nominal com preposição. O equivalente em português é uma forma de subjuntivo precedida de "que":

> **I asked her to explain.**
> *Pedi a ela que desse uma explicação.*
> **I waited for him to speak.**
> *Esperei que ele falasse.*

Cuidado: o verbo **want** é usado com o infinitivo **to…**

> **I want you to help me.**
> *Quero que me ajude.*

3.50 A forma verbal do particípio pode ser usada da mesma maneira que um adjetivo:

> **A bored student complained to his teacher.**
> **The bird had a broken wing.**
> **The man injured in the accident was taken to hospital.**
> **She was wearing a dress bought in Paris.**

3.51 Perguntas

Diferentemente do português, em inglês, a ordem das palavras muda ao se fazer uma pergunta diretamente, mas não quando se faz de maneira indireta. Note que, nesse segundo caso, são usadas formas verbais simples, e não a forma com verbo auxiliar **do**:

> **What will you talk about?**
> **I'd like to know what you will talk about.**
> **Did you have a good flight?**
> **I asked him if he had a good flight.**

3.52 Para as perguntas cuja resposta é simplesmente sim ou não, o verbo auxiliar da forma verbal (n 3.2–3) é colocado no começo, seguido do sujeito e o restante das palavras segue sua ordem habitual. Para responder a uma dessas perguntas, usa-se, após *yes* ou *no*, o auxiliar, o modal ou a forma correspondente de *be* contraída com *not* (→ 3.58), se a resposta for negativa:

> *Is he coming? — Yes, he is./No, he isn't.*
> *Can John swim? — Yes, he can./No, he can't.*
> *Will you have finished by lunchtime? — No, I won't.*
> *Have you finished yet? — Yes, I have./No, I haven't.*
> *Was it lonely without us? — Yes, it was.*

Note que os tempos simples levam *do* como verbo auxiliar em perguntas deste tipo:

> *Do you like wine? — Yes, I do/No, I don't.*
> *Did he go to the theatre? — Yes, he did./No, he didn't.*
> *Do you have any questions? — Yes, we do./No, we don't.*

Quando *have* significa "ter", é possível colocá-lo antes do sujeito sem o uso de um verbo auxiliar, embora esta construção seja menos habitual, especialmente no inglês americano:

> *Has he any idea what it's like?*

3.53 No inglês falado, é muito comum perguntar algo com uma frase seguido de uma *question tag* (pergunta curta) ao final para pedir confirmação do que acaba de ser dito. Essa pequena pergunta repete a forma verbal da oração, mas usando unicamente o verbo auxiliar correspondente seguido do sujeito. A *question tag* leva a negação *not* depois do verbo auxiliar se na frase anterior não há nenhuma negação:

> *They don't live here, do they?*
> *You haven't seen it before, have you?*
> *You will stay in touch, won't you?*
> *It is quite warm, isn't it?*

Se a frase for negativa, no entanto, não se usa *not* na *question tag*:

> *It doesn't work, does it?*
> *He wasn't hungry, was he?*
> *They didn't come, did they?*

Também é possível fazer uma pergunta desse tipo mais para expressar surpresa, chateação ou outros sentimentos do que para necessariamente pedir confirmação. Nesse caso, tanto a frase como a pergunta vão na forma afirmativa:

> *You fell on your back, did you?*
> *You're working late again, are you?*

3.54 Para dizer "nem eu, nem você" etc, são usados *neither/nor* seguido do verbo auxiliar e o sujeito ou o sujeito e a negação do verbo auxiliar seguido de *either*:

> *"I don't know where it is." — "Neither do I"/"Nor do I"/"I don't, either."*

Para dizer "eu também, você também" etc, é usado *so* seguido do verbo auxiliar e o sujeito:

> *"I have been working a lot." — "So have all the others."*

3.55 As partículas interrogativas em inglês são:

> **what · which · when · where · who · whom · whose**
> **why · how · how much · how many · how long**

Note que *whom* é usado somente no inglês culto.

As partículas interrogativas são sempre a primeira palavra nas perguntas em que são usadas.

Com essas partículas, a ordem do verbo auxiliar com o sujeito fica invertida, como em qualquer pergunta:

> *How many are there?*
> *Which do you like best?*
> *When would you be coming down?*
> *Why did you do it?*
> *Where did you get that from?*
> *Whose idea was it?*

A única exceção se dá quando se está perguntando pelo sujeito do verbo. Nesse caso, segue-se a ordem habitual da oração. Note que nesse caso são usadas formas verbais simples, e não a forma com verbo auxiliar *do*:

> *Who could have done it?*
> *What happened?*
> *Which is the best restaurant?*

3.56 Se houver uma preposição, esta é colocada no final. No entanto, com *whom*, ela é sempre posta antes do pronome:

> *What's this for?*
> *What's the book about?*
> *With whom were you talking?*

3.57 Não tendo somente o significado de "como", *how* também pode acompanhar adjetivos e advérbios, ou *many* e *much*:

> *How did you know we were coming?*
> Como você sabia que viríamos?
> *How old are your children?*
> Que idade têm seus filhos?
> *How long have you lived here?*
> Você mora aqui há quanto tempo?
> *How many were there?*
> Quantos havia?

3.58 Negações

A negação das formas verbais é composta da palavra **not** (contraída ou não) após o primeiro verbo. É preciso tomar cuidado com as formas verbais simples que necessitam de um auxiliar na forma negativa (→3.6):

> *They do not need to talk.*
> *I was not smiling.*
> *I haven't been playing football.*

Note que também se usa **do** como auxiliar quando **do** vem como verbo principal:

> *I didn't do it.*

Estas são algumas das contrações mais frequentes:

isn't	haven't	doesn't	mightn't	won't
aren't	hasn't	didn't	mustn't	wouldn't
wasn't	hadn't	—	oughtn't	—
weren't	—	can't	shan't	daren't
—	don't	couldn't	shouldn't	needn't

3.59 Em inglês, não se repetem duas negações como é costume em português, portanto não se usa **not** com os seguintes termos: *no one • nobody • nothing • nowhere* (→1.46) *• none* (→1.43) *• never* (→4.6) *• neither (... nor...)* (→1.59). Caso a partícula **not** seja usada, ou se houver outra negação, os seguintes correspondentes são empregados:

> **anyone • anybody • anything • anywhere**
> **any • ever • either**

There is nothing you can do./There isn't anything you can do.
> Não há nada que você possa fazer.
> *She's never late./She isn't ever late.*
> Ela nunca se atrasa.
> *Nobody wanted anything to eat.*
> Ninguém queria nada de comer.

4 Expressões adverbiais

4.1 As palavras que expressam quando, como, onde ou em que circunstâncias algo acontece são chamadas de advérbios. Essa função também pode ser cumprida por um grupo nominal (→1.11) com ou sem preposição, ou mesmo dois advérbios juntos, e nesse caso são tratados em geral como expressões adverbiais:

> *Sit there quietly, and listen to this music.*
> *Come and see me next week.*
> *The children were playing in the park.*
> *He did not play well enough to win.*

4.2 As expressões adverbiais que respondem às perguntas "como", "onde" ou "quando" (quando se referem a um momento no tempo) são colocadas depois do verbo principal e seu objeto, caso exista:

> *She sang beautifully.*
> *The book was lying on the table.*
> *The car broke down yesterday.*
> *I did learn to play a few tunes very badly.*

Caso se utilizem várias expressões com esses significados, geralmente são colocadas na seguinte ordem: como + onde + quando:

> *She spoke very well at the village hall last night.*

4.3 As expressões adverbiais que indicam com que frequência, probabilidade e imediatismo algo acontece são colocadas logo antes do verbo principal, tanto com formas verbais simples como compostas:

> *She occasionally comes to my house.*
> *You have very probably heard the news by now.*
> *They had already given me the money.*
> *She really enjoyed the party.*

4.4 É possível colocar uma expressão adverbial em uma posição distinta da oração para enfatizá-la:

> *Slowly, he opened his eyes.*
> *In September I travelled to California.*
> *Next to the coffee machine stood a pile of cups.*

Note que depois de expressões de lugar nesta posição, como no último exemplo, o verbo pode ir antes do sujeito.

A expressão adverbial pode ir logo antes do verbo principal, com caráter enfático, se se trata de um advérbio ou dois juntos:

> *He deliberately chose it because it was cheap.*
> *I very much wanted to go with them.*

É possível mudar a ordem habitual dos advérbios para enfatizar alguma expressão em outra posição:

> *They were sitting in the car quite happily.*
> *At the meeting last night, she spoke very well.*

4.5 *Ago* é um advérbio usado com uma forma verbal no passado para dizer há quanto tempo algo aconteceu. É sempre colocado ao final da expressão:

> *We saw him about a month ago.*
> *John's wife died five years ago.*

Cuidado: note que *ago* não é usado com o presente perfeito. Não se diz *We have gone to Spain two years ago*, mas *We went to Spain two years ago*.

4.6 Advérbios de frequência

Algumas expressões adverbiais nos dizem com que frequência algo acontece:

> a lot • always • ever • frequently • hardly ever
> never • normally • occasionally • often
> rarely • sometimes • usually

> *We often swam in the sea.*
> *She never comes to my parties.*

Outras podem ser usadas para dizer qual a probabilidade de algo acontecer:

> certainly • definitely • maybe • obviously
> perhaps • possibly • probably • really

> *I definitely saw her yesterday.*
> *The driver probably knows the best route.*

4.7 Essas expressões adverbiais são colocadas antes de uma forma simples do verbo e geralmente são intercaladas quando usadas com formas verbais compostas:

> *He sometimes works downstairs in the kitchen.*
> *You are definitely wasting your time.*
> *I have never had such a horrible meal!*
> *I shall never forget this day.*

Note que esses advérbios normalmente se colocam após o verbo principal quando este é *be*:

> *He is always careful with his money.*
> *You are probably right.*

Perhaps geralmente é colocado no começo da oração, ao passo que *a lot* sempre é colocado após o verbo principal:

> *Perhaps the beaches are cleaner in the north.*
> *I go swimming a lot in the summer.*

4.8 *Ever* geralmente é usado em perguntas, negações ou orações condicionais. Às vezes, pode ser usado em orações afirmativas, por exemplo após um superlativo:

> *Have you ever been to a football match?*
> *Don't ever do that again!*
> *If you ever need anything, just call me.*
> *She is the best dancer I have ever seen.*

⚠ Note que há duas maneiras de dizer "nunca": usando *never* ou combinando *not* e *ever*:

> *Don't ever do that again!*
> *Never do that again!*

4.9 *Still, yet, already*

Still significa "ainda" em orações afirmativas. Coloca-se antes de uma forma simples do verbo; é intercalado nas formas verbais compostas, seguindo o verbo *be*:

> *My family still lives in India.*
> Minha família ainda mora na Índia.
> *You will still get tickets, if you hurry.*
> Você ainda consegue ingressos, se se apressar.
> *We were still waiting for the election results.*
> Ainda esperávamos os resultados eleitorais.
> *His father is still alive.*
> O pai dele ainda está vivo.

Still pode ser usado depois do sujeito e antes da forma verbal em orações negativas para expressar surpresa ou impaciência:

> *You still haven't given us the keys.*
> Você ainda não nos deu as chaves.

⚠ Note que *still* pode ser usado no começo de uma oração com o significado de "ainda assim":

> *Still, he is my brother, so I'll have to help him.*
> Ainda assim, é meu irmão, então tenho que ajudá-lo.

4.10 *Yet* é usado com o significado de "ainda" ao final de uma oração negativa e de "já" ao final de uma pergunta:

> *We haven't got the tickets yet.*
> Ainda não pegamos os ingressos.
> *Have you joined the swimming club yet?*
> Você já se matriculou no clube de natação?

Note que *yet* também pode ser usado no começo de uma oração com o significado de "no entanto":

> *They know they won't win. Yet they keep on trying.*

4.11 *Any longer* ou *any more* significam "já" em orações negativas e são colocados ao final da oração:

> *I couldn't wait any longer.*
> *Já não conseguia mais esperar.*
> *He's not going to play any more.*
> *Ele não vai mais jogar.*

Already significa "já" em orações afirmativas. Coloca-se antes de uma forma simples do verbo; é intercalado nas formas verbais compostas:

> *I already know her.*
> *I've already seen them.*
> *I am already aware of that problem.*

Também pode ser colocado ao final para ter seu significado enfatizado:

> *I've done it already.*

4.12 Note que, quando usado no começo de uma oração, *really* serve para expressar surpresa, da mesma forma que funciona como um advérbio de modo (→ 4.16) quando vem ao final:

> *Really, I didn't know that!*
> *He wanted it really, but he was too shy to ask.*

4.13 Algumas expressões adverbiais aumentam ou reduzem a intensidade do que é expresso pelo verbo. Esta função é realizada por somente um tipo de palavra, o advérbio:

> *I totally disagree.*
> *Discordo totalmente.*
> *I can nearly reach the top shelf.*
> *Quase alcanço a estante de cima.*

Alguns advérbios de intensidade podem ser colocados antes ou depois do verbo principal, ou depois do objeto, caso exista:

badly · completely · greatly · seriously · strongly · totally

> *I disagree completely* ou *I completely disagree with John Taylor.*
> *That argument doesn't convince me totally* ou *totally convince me.*

Outros são principalmente usados logo antes do verbo principal:

almost · largely · nearly · quite · really

> *He almost crashed into a bus.*
> *I quite like it.*

4.14 *A lot* e *very much* são colocados depois do verbo principal, ou depois do objeto, caso exista. *Very much* pode ser colocado depois do sujeito e antes de verbos como *want*, *prefer* e *enjoy*:

> *She helped a lot.*

> *We liked him very much.*
> *I very much wanted to take it with me.*

4.15 Alguns advérbios de intensidade que modificam o significado de adjetivos ou outros advérbios são colocados antes destes:

> **awfully • extremely • fairly • pretty**
> **quite • rather • really • very**

> *... a fairly large office, with filing space.*

⚠ Note que **rather** pode ser colocado tanto antes como depois de **a** ou **an** quando vem seguido de um adjetivo e um substantivo:

> *Seaford is rather a pleasant town./Seaford is a rather pleasant town.*

4.16 Os advérbios de modo geralmente são formados com o acréscimo da terminação **-ly** a um adjetivo. Em muitas ocasiões, um advérbio com **-ly** equivale a um com "-mente" em português, mas nem sempre:

Adjetivos		Advérbios
bad	→	badly
beautiful	→	beautifully
quick	→	quickly
quiet	→	quietly
soft	→	softly

Cuidado: não é possível formar advérbios a partir de adjetivos que já acabem em **-ly**. Por exemplo, não se pode dizer *He smiled at you friendlily*. Em vez disso, às vezes é possível usar um grupo nominal encabeçado por uma preposição:

> *He smiled at me in a friendly way.*

4.17 Alguns advérbios de modo (como **fast**, **hard** e **late**) têm a mesma forma que os adjetivos correspondentes:

> *I've always been interested in fast cars.*
> *The driver was driving too fast.*
> *It was a hard job.*
> *He works very hard.*
> *The train arrived late as usual.*

4.18 Geralmente não se usam grupos nominais com ou sem preposição como expressões adverbiais de modo. No entanto, às vezes é necessário usá-los, por exemplo, quando não há um advérbio para o significado que se queira expressar. O grupo nominal normalmente inclui um substantivo como **way**, **fashion** ou **manner**, ou ainda um substantivo que faça referência à voz de alguém:

> *She asked me in such a nice manner that I couldn't refuse.*
> *They spoke in angry tones.*

5 Preposições

As seguintes preposições (→ 5.1–7) são usadas para introduzir expressões de lugar:

5.1 *At* é usado para se referir a um lugar como um ponto concreto:

> *She waited at the bus stop for over twenty minutes.*
> *'Where were you last night?' – 'At Mick's house.'*

É usado com palavras como *back*, *bottom*, *end*, *front* e *top* para falar de partes diferentes de um lugar:

> *Mr. Castle was waiting at the bottom of the stairs.*
> *I saw a taxi at the end of the street.*

É usado com lugares públicos e instituições (→ 5.4) e também para dizer "em casa" (*at home*) e "no trabalho" (*at work*):

> *I have to be at the station by ten o'clock.*
> *We landed at a small airport.*
> *She wanted to stay at home.*

Do mesmo modo que é usado para dizer na casa de alguém, também é usado para falar de uma locação ou um serviço especializado:

> *I'll see you at Fred's house.*
> *I buy my bread at the local baker's.*

Para falar de direções, *at* é usado para dar o número do local. Utiliza-se *in*, ou também *on*, no inglês americano, quando somente o nome da rua é dado:

> *They used to live at 5 Weston Road.*
> *She got a job in Oxford Street.*
> *He lived on Fifth Avenue in New York City.*

5.2 *On* é usado quando se considera um lugar como uma superfície:

> *I sat down on the sofa.*
> *She put her keys on the table.*

É usado quando um lugar é considerado um ponto em uma linha, por exemplo, uma estrada, uma linha de trem, um rio ou uma praia ou costa:

> *Scrabster is on the north coast.*
> *Las Cruces is on I-25 between Albuquerque and El Paso.*

5.3 *In* é usado com países, regiões, cidades e povoados:

> *A thousand homes in the east of Scotland suffered power cuts.*
> *I've been teaching at a college in Baltimore.*

Com recipientes de qualquer tipo para falar do que está contido:

> *She kept the cards in a little box.*

Com um local, ao citar as pessoas ou coisas que ali estão (→4.8):

> *They were having dinner in the restaurant.*

5.4 at/in

Muitas vezes, um lugar pode ser considerado de duas maneiras: como instituição ou como locação, razão pela qual é possível usar *at* ou *in*, respectivamente:

> *I had a hard day at the office.*
> *I left my coat behind in the office.*
> *There's a good film at the cinema.*
> *It was very cold in the cinema.*

5.5 Usam-se *on*, *onto* e *off* para se referir à posição ou ao movimento de uma pessoa ou coisa dentro e fora de meios de transporte como ônibus, trens, barcos e aviões. Se a intenção é dar ênfase à posição ou ao movimento para dentro ou fora do veículo como tal mais que como meio de transporte, é possível usar *in*, *into* e *out of* com esses meios de transporte:

> *Why don't you come on the train with me to New York?*
> *Por que você não vem comigo no trem para Nova York?*
> *Peter Hurd was already on the plane from California.*
> *Peter Hurd já estava no avião vindo da Califórnia.*
> *Mr Bixby stepped off the train and walked quickly to the exit.*
> *O senhor Bixby desceu do trem e se apressou em direção à saída.*
> *The passengers in the plane were beginning to panic.*
> *Os passageiros do avião começaram a entrar em pânico.*
> *We jumped out of the bus and ran into the nearest shop.*
> *Descemos do ônibus e entramos correndo na loja mais próxima.*

5.6 Usam-se *in*, *into* e *out of* para se referir à posição ou ao movimento de uma pessoa ou coisa para dentro e fora de carros, vans, caminhões, táxis e ambulâncias (→4.9):

> *I followed them in my car.*
> *Eu os segui no meu carro.*
> *Mr. Ward happened to be getting into his truck.*
> *Por acaso, Sr. Ward estava entrando em seu caminhão.*
> *She was carried out of the ambulance.*
> *Ela foi tirada da ambulância.*

5.7 Para dizer que tipo de veículo ou meio de transporte é usado para ir a algum local, usa-se *by*. Somente para dizer "a pé" é usada a preposição *on*:

by bus · by bicycle · by car · by coach · by plane · by train

> *She had come by car with her husband and her four children.*
> *Ela tinha vindo de carro com seu marido e seus quatro filhos.*

> *I left Escondido in the afternoon and went by bus and train to Santa Monica.*
> Saí de Escondido à tarde e fui de ônibus e de trem a Santa Mônica.
> *Marie decided to continue on foot.*
> Marie decidiu continuar a pé.

5.8 As seguintes preposições são usadas para introduzir expressões de tempo:

At é usado com:

> horas: *at eight o'clock* • *at 3.15*
> festas religiosas: *at Christmas* • *at Easter*
> refeições: *at breakfast* • *at lunchtime*
> períodos específicos: *at night* • *at the weekend* • *at weekends* (inglês britânico)

In é usado com:

> estações do ano: *in autumn* • *in the spring*
> anos e séculos: *in nineteen eighty-five* • *in the year two thousand* • *in the nineteenth century*
> meses: *in July* • *in December*
> partes do dia: *in the morning* • *in the evenings*

Note que também se usa *in* para falar do futuro:

> *I think we'll find out in the next few days.*
> Acho que descobriremos nos próximos dias.

On é usado com:

> dias da semana: *on Monday* • *on Tuesday morning* • *on Sunday evenings*
> datas especiais: *on Christmas day* • *on my birthday* • *on his wedding anniversary*
> datas: *on the twentieth of July* • *on June the twenty-first*
> períodos específicos: *on the weekend* • *on weekends*

5.9 *For* é usado com verbos em qualquer tempo gramatical para dizer quanto tempo algo dura:

> *He is in Italy for a month.*
> Ele fica na Itália por um mês.
> *I remained silent for a long time.*
> Fiquei em silêncio por muito tempo.
> *I will be in Sao Paulo for three months.*
> Estarei três meses em São Paulo.

5.10 **During** e **over** são usados para um período em que algo acontece:

> *I saw him twice during the summer holidays.*
> *Will you stay in Washington over Christmas?*

Cuidado: **during** não é usado para dizer quanto tempo algo dura. Não se pode dizer **I went there during three weeks**. Para esse significado, usa-se **for** (→5.9).

5.11 **By** é usado quando se quer dizer "até":

> **By eleven o'clock, Brody was back in his office.**
> *Até onze horas, Brody já estava de volta ao seu escritório.*
> **Can we get this finished by tomorrow?**
> *Podemos terminar isso até amanhã?*

6 Mudanças ortográficas

6.1 "-S"

A terminação -s serve para formar o plural dos substantivos contáveis (→1.1) e a forma verbal do presente simples para *she*, *he*, *it* (→3.3).

Note que os substantivos contáveis são os únicos a que se acrescenta -s para formar o plural. Outras palavras que têm ou podem ter significado no plural não mudam sua forma.

Às palavras, tanto substantivos como verbos, que terminam em **-ss**, **-ch**, **-s**, **-sh** e **-x**, acrescenta-se **-es**, que se pronuncia [iz]:

class → classes	*gas → gases*
fox → foxes	*watch → watches*
dish → dishes	

Aos substantivos que terminam em **-o**, acrescenta-se **-es**. Alguns substantivos que terminam em **-o** recebem somente **-s**. Em ambos os casos, a pronúncia é [z]:

photo → photos	*hero → heroes*
piano → pianos	*potato → potatoes*

As palavras que terminam em **-y** (precedidas de consoante) trocam o **-y** por **-ies**, que se pronuncia [iz]:

country → countries	*cry → cries*
lady → ladies	*party → parties*
victory → victories	

A terminação **-y** precedida de vogal não muda:

boy → boys	*day → days*
key → keys	*pray → prays*
valley → valleys	

6.2 -ING, -ED, -ER, -EST

As palavras de uma sílaba que terminam em vogal curta ou consoante que não seja **-w**, **-x** ou **-y** duplicam a consoante:

dip → dipping/dipped	*big → bigger/biggest*
fat → fatter/fattest	*thin → thinner/thinnest*
hot → hotter/hottest	*wet → wetter/wettest*
sad → sadder/saddest	

As palavras que terminam com consoante seguida de **-y** trocam essa terminação por **-i**, exceto aquelas com a terminação **-ing**, que não mudam:

happy → happier/happiest

6.3 -LY

Quando se forma um advérbio com **-ly** a partir de um adjetivo, as seguintes mudanças são produzidas:

-le muda para *-ly*	*gentle* →	*gently*
-y muda para *-ily*	*easy* →	*easily*
-ic muda para *-ically*	*automatic* →	*automatically*
-ue muda para *-uly*	*true* →	*truly*
-ful muda para *-fully*	*beautiful* →	*beautifully*

Exceção: **public** → **publicly**

Índice

GRAMÁTICA INGLESA

GRAMÁTICA INGLESA

GRAMÁTICA INGLESA

Portuguese Grammar Guide

Abbreviations used

sing.	singular
plur.	plural
masc.	masculine
fem.	feminine
Coll	colloquial or casual speech
Wr	written; also used to indicate more formal speech
Eur	European Portuguese usage
Br	Brazilian Portuguese usage

Contents

1. Simple tenses: formation

In Portuguese the following are simple tenses: present; preterite; imperfect; future; conditional; imperative; present subjunctive; imperfect subjunctive; future subjunctive.

These simple tenses are formed by adding endings to a verb stem. The endings show the number and person of the subject of the verb:

Eu cant<u>o</u>.	I sing.
N<u>ós</u> cant<u>amos</u>.	We sing.
Ele comer<u>á</u>.	He will eat.
Eles comer<u>ão</u>.	They will eat.

Second-person verb forms

Third-person endings for *você* and *vocês*: even though *você* and *vocês* mean *you* (singular and plural), for historical reasons they are used with third-person verb endings.

Você cant<u>a</u>.	You sing.
Ele cant<u>a</u>.	He sings.
Vocês com<u>em</u>.	You sing. (plural)
Eles com<u>em</u>.	They sing.

In the verb tables these endings will be identified as: **2nd**, **3rd person**.

Traditional second-person endings: these are for subjects *tu* and *vós*, which also mean *you* (singular and plural).

Tu cant<u>as</u>.	You sing.
Vós cant<u>ais</u>.	You sing. (plural)

Singular endings for *tu* will be shown separately in the verb tables, identified as: **2nd person**. Plural endings for *vós* will also appear, but in brackets, as they are no longer in current use.

For information on the different ways of saying *you* in Portuguese see *Tu*, *você*, and *o senhor / a senhora* on pages 107–108.

Regular verbs

The stem and endings of regular verbs are predictable. The verb tables in the following sections show the patterns for regular verbs. For irregular verbs see page 86 onwards.

There are three regular verb patterns (known as conjugations), each identifiable by the ending of the infinitive:

First conjugation verbs end in *-ar*, e.g. ***cantar*** *to sing*.
Second conjugation verbs end in *-er*, e.g. ***comer*** *to eat*.
Third conjugation verbs end in *-ir*, e.g. ***partir*** *to leave*, *depart*.

These three conjugations are explained on the following pages.

Infinitives ending in -ôr and -or

Pôr, meaning to put, place, is irregular even in the infinitive. Its endings are shown in the tables for irregular verbs. These endings also apply to its compounds, e.g. **compor** to compose, organize; **dispor** to arrange; **impor** to impose; **opor** to oppose. Note the absence of written accent ô in the compounds.

2. Simple tenses: first conjugation

For all tenses other than the future, the conditional and the future subjunctive, the stem is formed removing **ar** from the infinitive. To this stem we add the appropriate endings for each person, as shown in the table below. The stem of the future, the conditional and the future subjunctive is the same as the infinitive.

Example

person	(1) present	(2) preterite	(3) imperfect
eu	cant-o	cant-ei	cant-ava
tu	cant-as	cant-aste	cant-avas
você, ele/ela	cant-a	cant-ou	cant-ava
nós	cant-amos	cant-amos(*)	cant-ávamos
vocês, eles/elas	cant-am	cant-aram	cant-avam

(*) alternative spelling: **cantámos**

person	(4) future	(5) conditional	(6) imperative (*)
eu	cantar-ei	cantar-ia	
tu	cantar-ás	cantar-ias	cant-a!
você, ele/ela	cantar-á	cantar-ia	
nós	cantar-emos	cantar-íamos	
vocês, eles/elas	cantar-ão	cantar-iam	

person	(7) present subjunctive	(8) imperfect subjunctive	(9) future subjunctive
eu	cant-e	cant-asse	cantar
tu	cant-es	cant-asses	cantar-es
você, ele/ela	cant-e	cant-asse	cantar
nós	cant-emos	cant-ássemos	cantar-mos
vocês, eles/elas	cant-em	cant-assem	cantar-em

(*) See **The imperative and alternatives**, pages 72–74.

3. Simple tenses: second conjugation

For all tenses other than the future, the conditional and the future subjunctive, the stem is formed removing **ar** from the infinitive. To this stem we add the appropriate endings for each person, as shown in the table below. For all tenses other than the future, the conditional and the future subjunctive, the stem is formed removing **er** from the infinitive. To this stem, we add the appropriate endings for each person, as shown in the table below. The stem of the future, the conditional and the future subjunctive is the same as the infinitive.

Example

person	(1) present	(2) preterite	(3) imperfect
eu	com-o	com-i	com-ia
tu	com-es	com-este	com-ias
você, ele/ela	com-e	com-eu	com-ia
nós	com-emos	com-emos	com-íamos
vocês, eles/elas	com-em	com-eram	com-iam

person	(4) future	(5) conditional	(6) imperative (*)
eu	cantar-ei	cantar-ia	cant-a!
tu	cantar-ás	cantar-ias	
você, ele/ela	cantar-á	cantar-ia	
nós	cantar-emos	cantar-íamos	
vocês, eles/elas	cantar-ão	cantar-iam	

person	(7) present subjunctive	(8) imperfect subjunctive	(9) future subjunctive
eu	com-a	com-esse	com-er
tu	com-as	com-esses	com-eres
você, ele/ela	com-a	com-esse	com-er
nós	com-amos	com-êssemos	com-ermos
vocês, eles/elas	com-am	com-essem	com-erem

(*) See **The imperative and alternatives**, pages 72–74.

4. Simple tenses: third conjugation

For all tenses other than the future, the conditional and the future subjunctive, the stem is formed removing **ar** from the infinitive. To this stem we add the appropriate endings for each person, as shown in the table below. For all tenses other than the future, the conditional and the future subjunctive, the stem is formed removing **ir** from the infinitive. To this stem, we add the appropriate endings for each person, as shown in the table below. The stem of the future, the conditional and the future subjunctive is the same as the infinitive.

Example

person	(1) present	(2) preterite	(3) imperfect
eu	part-o	part-i	part-ia
tu	part-es	part-iste	part-ias
você, ele/ela	part-e	part-iu	part-ia
nós	part-imos	part-imos	part-íamos
vocês, eles/elas	part-em	part-iram	part-iam

person	(4) future	(5) conditional	(6) imperative (*)
eu	part-irei	part-iria	part-e!
tu	part-irás	part-irias	
você, ele/ela	part-irá	part-iria	
nós	part-iremos	part-iríamos	
vocês, eles/elas	part-irão	part-iriam	

person	(7) present subjunctive	(8) imperfect subjunctive	(9) future subjunctive
eu	part-a	part-isse	part-ir
tu	part-as	part-isses	part-ires
você, ele/ela	part-a	part-isse	part-ir
nós	part-amos	part-íssemos	part-irmos
vocês, eles/elas	part-am	part-issem	part-irem

(*) See **The imperative and alternatives**, pages 72–74.

5. Conjugation spelling and stem changes

Before some endings, certain spelling changes have to be made. Some of these are simply to obey Portuguese spelling conventions, while others reflect a change in the pronunciation of the stem. In the latter case, a phonetic symbol is shown in the tables below.

Changes reflecting Portuguese spelling conventions

Conjugation	1st	1st	1st
Infinitive ending	-car	-çar	-gar
Change	-c→-qu before e	-ç→c before e	-g→-gu before e
Model	ficar (to stay)	começar (to begin)	pagar (to pay)
	→Eu fiquei	→Comecem!	→Pague!

Conjugation	2nd	2nd and 3rd	2nd and 3rd
Infinitive ending	-cer	-ger and -gir	-guer and -guir
Change	-c→-ç before a or o	-g→j before a or o	-gu→-g before a or o
Model	descer (to climb down)	eleger (to elect)	erguer (to lift)
	→Desçam!	→... que eles elejam	→... que eles ergam
		fugir (to run away)	conseguir (to manage)
		→Fuja!	→Eu não consigo.

Spelling and sound changes

In certain 3rd conjugation verbs there are some root changes at the core of the stem:

Root vowel	-e-	-e-	-o-	-u-
Change	-e- [e]→-i- [i]	-e- [e]→-i- [i]	-o- [o]→-u- [u]	-u- [u]→-o- [o]
Tenses affected	present (1st person sing.), polite imperative, present subjunctive	present (1st, 2nd, 3rd person sing. and 3rd person plur.), imperative (sing.), polite imperative, present subjunctive	present (1st person sing.), polite imperative, present subjunctive	present (2nd and 3rd person sing. and 3rd person plur.), imperative (sing.)
Model	repetir (to repeat) Eu repito Repitam! ... que ele repita	progredir (to progress) Eu progrido Progride! Progridam! ... que ele progrida	dormir (to sleep) Eu durmo Durmam! ... que ele durma	subir (to climb up) Você sobe Eles sobem Sobe!

PORTUGUESE GRAMMAR GUIDE

In certain 1st, 2nd and 3rd conjugation verbs there are some stem and ending changes:

Infinitive ending	-ear	-oer	-air
Change	**-e-** [e] → **-ei-** [ej]	**-o-** [o] → **-ói-** [oj] stressed	**-a-** [a] → **-ai-** [aj] (*)
Tenses affected	present (1st, 2nd, 3rd person sing. and 3rd person plur.), imperative (sing.), polite imperative, present subjunctive (1st, 2nd, 3rd person sing. and 3rd person plur.)	present (2nd and 3rd person sing.), imperative (sing.)	present (1st, 2nd, 3rd person sing. and 1st person plur.), imperative (sing.), polite imperative, present subjunctive
Model	*passear* (to go for a stroll) *Eu passeio* *Passeiem!* *... que ele passeie*	*roer* (to gnaw, nibble) *(Tu) róis* *Ele rói* *Rói!*	*sair* (to go / come out) *Eu saio* *Você sai* *Saia!* *... que eles saiam*

Infinitive ending	-uir	-uir	-uzir
Change	**-u-** [u] → **-ui-** [uj] (*)	**-u-** [u] → **-ói-** [oj] stressed (*) or **-o-** [o] stressed	**-z-** [z] → **-z-** [z] (Br) / [ʒ] (Eur) (**)
Tenses affected	present (2nd and 3rd person sing. and 1st person plur.), imperative (sing.)	present (2nd and 3rd person sing. and 3rd person plur.), imperative (sing.)	present (3rd person sing.), imperative (sing.)
Model	*incluir* (to include) *Nós incluimos* *Inclui!*	*construir* (to build) *Constrói* *Eles constroem*	*traduzir* (to translate) *Ele traduz* *Traduz!*

(*) The verb endings **-e** and **-es** are dropped: e.g., *Você sai*, *(Tu) sais*; *Inclui!*, *(Tu) incluis*; *Constrói!*, *(Tu) constróis*.

(**) The verb ending **-e** is dropped and the **-z-** stands for a different sound: *Eu traduzo* [z] but *Ele traduz* [z] (Br) / [ʒ] (Eur).

6. The imperative and alternatives

Some verb forms are used to ask or tell someone to do something. They can also be used to give directions or instructions on how to operate a machine, for instance.

Commands, requests and advice

Polite imperative

Cante!	**Coma!**	**Parta!**	talking to one person
Cantem!	**Comam!**	**Partam!**	talking to more than one person
Sing, (please)!	*Eat, (please)!*	*Leave, (please)!*	

These forms are borrowed from the **present subjunctive** and, as such, have an inbuilt element of politeness. However, *por favor*, meaning *please*, can always be added on to them, if you want to be even more polite and respectful.

Talking to one person

Coma, por favor!	*Please eat!*
Venha!	*Come along, please!*
Peça agora!	*Ask for it now, please!*
Vá embora!	*Go away, please!*
Abra a janela, por favor!	*Please open the window!*

Talking to more than one person

Comecem!	*Start, please!*
Vão embora!	*Go away, please!*
Venham, por favor!	*Please will you come!*

Alternative

canta	*come*	*parte*	talking to one person
cantam	*comem*	*partem*	talking to more than one person
(You) sing	*(You) eat*	*(You) leave*	

These forms are borrowed from the **present** (i.e. present indicative) and show the requested or suggested action as a description of what to do. This is heard on both sides of the Atlantic but more so in Brazil.

Talking to one person

Você parte amanhã, por favor.	*You will please leave tomorrow.*
(Você) vira à esquerda na próxima esquina.	*(You) turn left at the next corner.*

Talking to more than one person

Vocês partem amanhã, por favor.	*You will please leave tomorrow.*

The third person singular ending of the present (the form you would use for someone addressed as *você*, *o senhor* or *a senhora*) just happens to coincide with the *tu*-ending of the traditional **imperative**:

Canta!	**Come!**	**Parte!**	talking to one person
Sing!	*Eat!*	*Leave!*	

This approach gives a familiar tone.

Talking to one person

Come tudo!	*Eat it all!*
Sai daí!	*Get out of there!*
Vai embora!	*Go away!*

Let's

The equivalent of the English *let's* + infinitive construction is usually *vamos* + infinitive.

Vamos is also used on its own: *Vamos! Let's go!*

Vamos sair agora!	*Let's get out now!*
Vamos beber alguma coisa!	*Let's have something to drink!*

Don't

To ask or tell someone not to do something, use 'polite' forms from the present subjunctive:

Não cantes!	**Não comas!**	**Não partas!**	familiar form (singular)
Não cante!	**Não coma!**	**Não parta!**	polite form (singular)
Não cantem!	**Não comam!**	**Não partam!**	talking to more than one person (anyone)

Don't sing, (please)! *Don't eat, (please)!* *Don't leave, (please)!*

See also **Tu**, **você** and **o senhor / a senhora**, pages 107–108.

7. Compound tenses: formation

In Portuguese the following are compound tenses: present perfect; pluperfect; future perfect; conditional perfect; present perfect subjunctive; pluperfect subjunctive; future perfect subjunctive.

Compound tenses consist of the past participle of the verb preceded by an auxiliary verb and are formed the same way for both regular and irregular verbs.

The auxiliary verb is normally **ter**.

The past participle may be regular or irregular but remains invariable, i.e. it does not change to agree with the subject in gender or number. For past participle formation see page 80.

Ele tinha cantado.	*He had sung.*
Elas tinham cantado.	*They (fem.) had sung.*

Formation of the different compound tenses

Present Perfect
(Present of the auxiliary verb plus past participle)

Eu tenho cantado.	*I have been singing.*
Tem chovido muito.	*It has been raining a lot.*

Pluperfect
(Imperfect of the auxiliary verb plus past participle)

Eu tinha cantado.	*I had sung.*
Tinha chovido muito.	*It had been raining a lot.*

Future Perfect
(Future of the auxiliary verb plus past participle)

Eu terei cantado.	*I shall have sung (by then).*
Às 20 horas eles já terão partido.	*By 8 pm they will already have left.*

Conditional Perfect
(Conditional of the auxiliary verb plus past participle)

Eu teria cantado.	*I would have sung.*
O avião teria chegado mais cedo.	*The plane would have arrived earlier.*

Present Perfect Subjunctive
(Present subjunctive of the auxiliary verb plus past participle)

...que eu tenha cantado.	*...(that) I have sung.*
Eu espero que ele tenha entendido tudo.	*I hope that he has understood everything.*

Pluperfect Subjunctive
(Imperfect subjunctive of the auxiliary verb plus past participle)

...que eu tivesse cantado.	*...(that) I had sung.*
Eu esperava que ele tivesse entendido tudo.	*I hoped that he had understood everything.*

Future Perfect Subjunctive
(Future subjunctive of the auxiliary verb plus past participle)

...quando eu tiver cantado.	*...(when) I have sung.*
Quando ele tiver entendido tudo.	*When he has understood everything.*

Other auxiliary-plus-verb constructions: formation

Colloquial future

Future
(Present of *ir*, used as an auxiliary verb, plus the infinitive of the main verb)

Eu vou cantar.	*I am going to sing.*
Eu vou comprar uma casa nova daqui a dez anos.	*I am going to buy a new house in ten years' time.*

Future in the past
(Imperfect of *ir*, used as an auxiliary verb, plus the infinitive of the main verb)

Eu ia cantar.	*I was going to sing.*
Nós íamos comprar um presente.	*We were going to buy a present.*

When the main verb is *ir* itself, a simple tense is used:

Eu vou lá.	*I am going there.*
Eu ia lá.	*I was going there.*

Continuous tenses

Present Continuous
(Present of *estar* plus preposition *a* plus the infinitive of the main verb (Eur))
(Present of *estar* plus the present participle of the main verb (Br))

Eu estou a ler um livro. (Eur)	*I am reading a book.*
Eu estou lendo um livro. (Br)	

Past Continuous
(Imperfect of *estar* plus preposition *a* plus the infinitive of the main verb (Eur))
(Imperfect of *estar* plus the present participle of the main verb (Br))

Eu estava a ler um livro. (Eur)	*I was reading a book.*
Eu estava lendo um livro. (Br)	

8. Reflexive verbs

A reflexive verb is one that is accompanied by a reflexive pronoun to show that the subject both *performs* and *receives* the action (e.g. *I washed myself*).

lavar-se   to wash oneself

reflexive pronouns			
	singular		**plural**	
1st person	*me*	*myself*	*nos*	*ourselves*
2nd person	*se (general)* *te (familiar)*	*yourself*	*se (both general and familiar)*	*yourselves*
3rd person	*se*	*him/her/itself*	*se*	*themselves*

Ele ainda não se lavou.   He hasn't washed (himself) yet. or He hasn't had a wash yet.

Elas ainda não se lavaram.   They (fem.) haven't washed (themselves) yet.

When conjugating a reflexive verb, in Brazilian Portuguese the reflexive pronoun comes before the verb; in European Portuguese it also comes before the verb in negative sentences and in sentences with an interrogative word, but it comes after the verb (linked with a hyphen) in affirmative sentences:

Ele lavou-se. (Eur), *Ele se lavou.* (Br)   He washed (himself).
Ele não se lavou. (Eur) (Br)   He didn't wash (himself).
Quando é que ele se lavou? (Eur) (Br)   When did he wash (himself)?

In the first person plural, when the reflexive pronoun comes after the verb, the final **-s** of the verb is dropped:

Nós lavamo-nos. (lavamos + nos) (Eur)   We wash (ourselves).

Portuguese reflexives also express reciprocity:

Eles beijam-se. (Eur), *Eles se beijam.* (Br)   They kiss (each other).
Nós encontramo-nos às quinze. (Eur),   We'll meet at 3 pm.
Nós nos encontramos às quinze. (Br)

In fact, reflexive constructions are used much more extensively in Portuguese than in English, where other constructions tend to be used instead:

Como é que você se chama? (Eur) (Br)   What's your name?
Eu chamo-me... (Eur), *Eu me chamo...* (Br)   My name is.... (literally: I call myself...)

Other common reflexive verbs in Portuguese:

deitar-se, to go to bed • *despedir-se*, to say goodbye • *divertir-se*, to have a nice time
esquecer-se, to forget • *ir-se (embora)*, to go (away) • *lembrar-se*, to remember
levantar-se, to get up • *pentear-se*, to comb one's hair • *sentar-se*, to sit down
vestir-se, to get dressed

9. The passive

In the passive, the subject *receives* the action (e.g. *I was called*) as opposed to *performing* it (e.g. *I called*). The Portuguese passive is formed in very much the same way as the English one, i.e. using a form of the verb **ser** meaning *to be*, and a past participle:

Ele foi recompensado.	*He was rewarded.*
O carro foi vendido.	*The car was sold.*

In the passive in Portuguese, the past participle agrees in gender and number with the subject:

Elas foram recompensadas.	*They (fem.) were recompensed.*
Os carros foram vendidos.	*The cars were sold.*

The Portuguese *se* construction as an alternative to the passive

(It performs similarly to a reflexive verb in the third person)

Fala-se Português.	*Portuguese is spoken.*
Alugam-se bicicletas	*Bicycles for hire (can be hired).*

The *se* construction can also have other English translations (*you, one, we*):

Como se escreve o seu nome?	*How do you spell your name?*
Come-se bem neste restaurante.	*You eat well in this restaurant.*

10. Impersonal verbs

In English, **it** is often used as an impersonal subject. In Portuguese, however, the subject pronoun is omitted in such cases:

Vale a pena.	<u>It</u> *is worthwhile.*

Frequently used impersonal verbs

Verbs for the weather and other natural phenomena:

Choveu ontem.	*It rained yesterday.*
Nevou nestes últimos dias.	*It has rained in the past few days.*
Anoiteceu cedo.	*It has got dark early.*

haver
for talking about existence or events:

Há lojas perto daqui?	*Are there any shops nearby?*
Haverá um desfile de Carnaval.	*There will be a Carnival parade.*

Note: in colloquial Brazilian speech, **tem** is used instead of **há**, e.g. **Tem lojas perto daqui?**

for elapsed time:

Fui lá há quatro anos.	*I went there four years ago.*
Há duas semana que eu cheguei aqui.	*I arrived here two weeks ago.*

fazer
for weather:

Faz muito calor.	*It's very hot.*

for elapsed time:

Faz duas semana que eu cheguei aqui.	*I arrived here two weeks ago.*

estar
for weather:

Está frio hoje.	*It's cold today.*

ser
for weather and seasons:

É verão.	*It is summer.*

for telling the time:

É uma hora.	*It's one o'clock.*
São vinte e uma horas.	*It's 9 pm.*

for distance:

São cinco quilómetros (Eur) /	*It's five km away.*
quilômetros (Br) **daqui até lá.**	

for days of the week and dates:

Ontem foi quarta-feira.	*Yesterday it was Wednesday.*
Hoje é dia seis de outubro. or	*Today it's October 6th.*
Hoje são seis de outubro.	

in impersonal expressions:

É bom.	*It's good.*
É fácil.	*It's easy.*
É importante.	*It's important.*

11. The infinitive

Portuguese has both an infinitive and a personal infinitive. The former is the way a verb usually appears in a dictionary and means *to...*, e.g. *cantar to sing*. The latter takes personal endings, e.g. *cantarmos (us) to sing*.

The infinitive

The dependent infinitive

Some verbs introduce a dependent infinitive directly, without a linking preposition:

conseguir • decidir • desejar • detestar • esperar • evitar • preferir • prometer • querer recear • recusar • saber • tencionar • tentar

Consegui chegar cedo.	*I managed to arrive early.*
Destesto nadar.	*I hate swimming.*
Prefiro ir para a praia.	*I prefer going to the beach.*
Queria comprar um presente para você.	*I wanted to buy a present for you.*

The perfect infinitive

The perfect infinitive is formed using an appropriate form of the auxiliary verb **ter** and the past participle of the verb in question:

Depois de ter tentado acabar o trabalho hoje, desisti. *After having tried to finish my work today, I gave up.*

The personal infinitive

The **inflected** or **personal infinitive** is formed by the addition of personal endings and is regular for all verbs.

To the appropriate infinitive add the following endings:

	1st person	
sing.	2nd perspn	**-es**
	2nd, 3rd person	
pl.	1st person	**-mos**
	2nd person	**-(des)**
	2nd, 3rd person	**-em**

Ele pediu para eu cantar. *He asked (for) me to sing.*
Ele pediu para (nós) cantarmos. *He asked (for) us to sing.*

12. Present and past participles

Present participle

Formation

First, second and third conjugation
Replace the final **-r** of the infinitive with **-ndo**:

cantar to sing → *cantando* singing
comer to eat → *comendo* eating
partir to leave → *partindo* leaving

See also **Irregular verbs**, pages 86–92.

Use

The Portuguese **present participle** (or **gerund**) is not used as much as the English *-ing* forms but has a similar role in two main situations.

To express the circumstances (time, cause, etc) surrounding an action or event:

Partindo agora, chegarei mais cedo. *By leaving now or If I leave now, I'll get there earlier.*

As part of a continuous tense:

Vou indo bem. *I'm keeping well.*

Note that the Portuguese **present participle** (or **gerund**) is invariable.

See also **Modal auxiliary verbs**, page 82 and **Use of tenses**, pages 83–85.

PORTUGUESE GRAMMAR GUIDE

Past participle

Formation

First conjugation
Replace the infinitive ending -*ar* with -*ado*:

> *cantar* to sing → *cantado* sung

Second and third conjugation
Replace the infinitive endings -*er* and -*ir* with -*ido*:

> *comer* to eat → *comido* eaten
> *partir* to leave → *partido* left

Some past participles are irregular, even when the verb is otherwise regular:

> *abrir* to open → *aberto* open(ed)
> *escrever* to write → *escrito* written

Some verbs have two past participles, one regular and one irregular. See below for when to use them.

> *morrer* to die → *morrido* or *morto* died, dead
> *acender* to light → *acendido* or *aceso* lit; switched on

See also **Irregular verbs**, pages 86–92.

Use

The Portuguese **past participle** is used in the following ways.

As part of a perfect tense:

> *Eles tinham cantado muito bem.*   They had sung very well.
> *Ela tinha acendido a luz.*   She had switched on the light.

In the passive voice:

> *O bolo foi comido.*   The cake has been eaten.
> *A luz foi acendida por ela.*   The light was switched on by her.

As an adjective:

> *A luz está acesa.*   The light is (switched) on.
> *Estas contas estão pagas.*   These bills are paid.

Where there are two past participles, one regular and one irregular, the former is used for the perfect tenses and is invariable:

> *Ela tinha acendido a luz.*   She had switched on the light.
> *Os pobres animais tinham morrido.*   The poor animals had died.

When used as an adjective or in a passive construction, the past participle must agree in gender and number with the noun to which it relates:

> *A loja está aberta.*   The shop is open.
> *Este livro está bem escrito.*   This book is well written.
> *A luz foi acendida por ela.*   The light was switched on by her.

13. Ser and estar

Portuguese has two verbs that both correspond to *to be*: *ser* and *estar*. They are not interchangeable, however. To find out how to conjugate them, please see **Irregular verbs**, pages 86–92. Their different meanings and uses are explained below.

Ser

Ser is used for things that are considered inherent to the subject. This includes origin; nationality; kinship; profession; possession; location of non-movable things; geographical location; numbers; time; and impersonal general statements:

Ela é de São Paulo.	She is from São Paulo.
Ela é brasileira.	She is Brazilian.
Elas são irmãs.	They are sisters.
Ele é professor.	He is a teacher.
O lápis é meu.	The pencil is mine.
A sala de estar é no primeiro andar.	The sitting room is on the first floor.
Portugal é na Europa.	Portugal is in Europe.
Três mais três são seis.	3 + 3 = 6
São treze horas.	It is 1 pm.
É verdade.	It is true.

Estar

Estar is used for things that are considered non-inherent to the subject and, as such, often transitory. This includes personal location; location of movable things; temporary conditions; certain expressions of feeling; location of pain; and time span:

Eles estão em casa.	They are at home.
O livro está em cima da mesa.	The book is on the table.
Hoje estou muito cansada.	Today I am very tired.
Estávamos no período de férias.	We were in the holiday period.

Ser versus estar

Sometimes there is a difference in meaning depending on which verb is used:

ser	*Ele é magro.*	He is slim. (slim-built)
estar	*Ele está magro.*	He is looking slim / thin. (lost weight)
ser	*Aquela casa é muito bonita.*	That house is very pretty. (nice building)
estar	*Aquela casa está muito bonita.*	That house is looking very pretty. (after having been repainted, etc)

14. Modal auxiliary verbs

In Portuguese, some modal auxiliary verbs are followed by a verb in the infinitive and others by a verb in the gerund (also known as the present participle). How they are used and what they mean is explained below.

Modals followed directly by a verb in the infinitive

dever *must; should; be predictable*

Devemos telefonar para ele ainda hoje.	*We must phone him before the end of today.*
Você devia ser professor.	*You should be a teacher.*

poder *to be able to, can; may (permission); may (probability)*

Eu posso ir lá amanhã.	*I can go there tomorrow.*
Vocês podem todos entrar.	*You may all come in.*

Modals linked to a following infinitive by a connector (often a preposition)

acabar de *to have just …*

Acabamos de chegar.	*We have just arrived.*

acabar por *to end up (by) …*

Eles acabaram por ficar em casa.	*They ended up staying at home.*

chegar a *to end up …*

Eles chegaram a chorar.	*They ended up crying.*

começar por *to start by …*

Comecei por ler as instruções.	*I started by reading the instructions.*

deixar de *to stop, give up; to fail to*

Ele deixou de estudar.	*He gave up studying.*

haver de *to be determined to, must*

Nós havemos de vencer o jogo.	*We are determined to or must win the game.*

ter que (Coll) / **ter de** (Wr) *to have to*

Nós temos que / de assinar o contrato	*We have to sign the agreement.*

Modals followed by a present participle (or gerund)

acabar *to end up … -ing*

Eles acabaram rindo.	*They ended up laughing.*

começar *to start … -ing*

Ele já começou fazendo o trabalho.	*He has already started doing the work.*
Ele já começou a fazer o trabalho. (Eur)	

continuar *to go on … -ing*

Vocês continuam trabalhando juntos?	*Are you still working together?*
Vocês continuam a trabalhar juntos? (Eur)	

15. Use of tenses

The present

For general truths:

> **A Terra é um planeta.** *The Earth is a planet.*

For things that happen on a regular basis:

> **Eu bebo café todos os dias.** *I drink coffee every day.*

Used to talk about the future, usually with a time expression:

> **Amanhã vou lá.** *I am going / will go there tomorrow.*

With expressions indicating time that has elapsed (e.g. **há**) for something that started in the past and is still continuing:

> **Eu aprendo Português há seis meses.** *I've been learning Portuguese for six months.*

The preterite

For things that were completed in the past:

> **Eu morei em África durante dois anos.** *I lived in Africa for two years.*

The imperfect

When focusing on the unfolding of a past occurrence:

> **Quando eu morava em África** *When I lived / was living / used to live in Africa*
> **trabalhava numa escola.** *I worked / used to work in a school.*

In relaxed speech, instead of the conditional:

> **Nós íamos** (Coll for **iríamos**) **lá, se** *We would go there, if we could.*
> **pudéssemos.**

The present perfect

When focusing on something that has been happening a lot in the recent past:

> **Tem chovido muito nos últimos dias.** *It has rained a lot over the last few days.*

The pluperfect

When focusing on something that had happened in the past before a specific point in time:

> **Tinha chovido muito uns dias antes.** *It had rained a lot a few days before (that day).*

The future

For a future occurrence:

> **O verão chegará daqui a uns meses.** *Summer will be here in a few months' time.*

For conjecture and uncertainty:

> **Quem sabe se ele virá.** *Who knows whether he will come.*

See also **The colloquial future**, below.

The future perfect

For a future occurrence before another future point in time:

Amanhã ele já terá partido.   By tomorrow he will (already) have left.

The colloquial future

As an alternative to the future:

O verão vai chegar daqui a uns meses.   Summer is going to be here in a few months' time.

Continuous tenses

For emphasis on an ongoing occurrence:

Eu estou a trabalhar agora. (Eur)   I am working now.
Eu estou trabalhando agora. (Br)
Eles estavam a trabalhar naquele momento. (Eur)   They were working at that moment.
Eles estavam trabalhando naquele momento. (Br)

The conditional

To voice desires or aspirations:

Eu gostaria de ter um carro novo.   I should / would like to have a new car.

For hypothetical future occurrences:

Nós iríamos lá, se pudéssemos.   We would go there, if we could.

To talk about events that were still to come in the past:

Eu sabia que eles viriam domingo passado. I knew they would come last Sunday.

See also **The imperfect**, above.

The conditional perfect

For things that failed to happen in the past:

Nós teríamos ido lá, se tivéssemos podido. We would have gone there, if we had been able to.

The imperative

See **The imperative and alternatives**, pages 72–74.

The subjunctive

See **The subjunctive: when to use it**, pages 85–86.

The personal infinitive

For clarity over who does what:

É preciso nós completarmos a tarefa.   We need to finish off the task. (literally, It is
                                       necessary we (to) finish off the task.)

as compared with:

É preciso completar a tarefa.   The task needs finishing off. (literally, It is
                                       necessary to finish off the task.)

For tense replacement:

The infinitive is not time-bound (present, past, future) or mood-linked (indicative, subjunctive, etc). As such it is often used as an alternative to tense use and for bypassing more complex constructions:

Ao abrirmos a porta, nós sentimos o frio vindo de fora.	On opening the door, we felt the cold air coming from outside.

instead of:

Quando (nós) abrimos a porta, nós sentimos o frio vindo de fora.	When we opened the door, we felt the cold air coming from outside.
Eles pediram para eu cantar.	They asked (for) me to sing.

instead of:

Eles pediram que eu cantasse.	They asked that I sing / whether I would sing.

16. The subjunctive: when to use it

The subjunctive is used for actions or states seen as dependent on actual events or confirmation, as opposed to being considered definite facts or able be taken for granted.

Present subjunctive

After expressions of doubt or fear:

Duvido que elas cantem hoje.	I doubt that they'll sing today.
Receio que ele volte tarde demais.	I fear he may come back too late.

After expressions of empathy or sorrow:

Lamento que ela não goste do presente.	I am sorry she doesn't like the present.
Tenho pena que ele esteja doente.	I am sorry that he's ill.

For stressing how essential, important or desirable something is:

É essencial que você estude.	It is essential that you study.

In wishes, hopes and requests:

Espero que ela faça boa viagem.	I hope she will have a good journey.
Peço que você estude.	I would ask you to study. (Please study)

For wishing someone well:

Durma bem!	Sleep well!
Faça boa viagem!	Have a good journey!

Present perfect subjunctive

For talking about uncertain occurrences before another past event:

Duvido que elas tenham cantado antes da chegada dele.	I doubt that they would have sung before his arrival.
Receio que ele tenha voltado tarde demais.	I fear he may have come back too late.
É desejável que você tenha estudado o suficiente antes do exame.	It will be beneficial if you put sufficient effort into your studies before taking the exam.

Imperfect subjunctive

For talking about essential or desirable things that have little likelihood of happening:

Seria essencial / desejável que você estudasse. — *It would be essential / desirable that you studied.*

Nós iríamos /íamos (Coll) **lá, se pudéssemos.** *We would go there, if we could.*

For expressing wishes, hopes or requests that are unlikely to be fulfilled:

Pedi que você estudasse. — *I asked you to study. (but you don't appear to be doing so)*

Pluperfect subjunctive

For talking about conditions that were not fulfilled:

Nós teríamos / tínhamos (Coll) **ido lá, se tivéssemos podido.** — *We would have gone there, if we had been able to.*

Future subjunctive

For talking about conditions that, if fulfilled, will enable something else to happen:

Se você estudar, passará no exame. *If you study, you will pass your exam.*

Future perfect subjunctive

For talking about conditions that, if fulfilled by a certain time, will enable a future occurrence:

Se você tiver estudado antes do exame, passará. — *If you've done your revision before the exam, you will pass.*

17. Irregular verb tables

Please note that the following tables only show tenses with irregular verb forms. For tenses not listed here, please use the regular verb endings shown on pages 69–72.

caber (to fit)

person	present	preterite	present subjunctive	imperfect subjunctive	future subjunctive
eu	caibo	coube	caiba	coubesse	couber
tu	cabes	coubeste	caibas	coubesses	couberes
você, ele/ela	cabe	coube	caiba	coubesse	couber
nós	cabemos	coubemos	caibamos	coubéssemos	coubermos
vocês, eles/elas	cabem	couberam	caibam	coubessem	couberem

crer (to believe)

person	present	imperative	present subjunctive
eu	creio		creia
tu	crês	crê	creias
você, ele/ela	crê		creia
nós	cremos		creiamos
vocês, eles/elas	creem		creiam

dar *(to give)*

person	present	preterite	imperative
eu	*dou*	*dei*	
tu	*dás*	*deste*	*dá*
você, ele/ela	*dá*	*deu*	
nós	*damos*	*demos*	
vocês, eles/elas	*dão*	*deram*	

person	present subjunctive	imperfect subjunctive	future subjunctive
eu	*dê*	*desse*	*der*
tu	*dês*	*desses*	*deres*
você, ele/ela	*dê*	*desse*	*der*
nós	*demos*	*déssemos*	*dermos*
vocês, eles/elas	*deem*	*dessem*	*derem*

dizer *(to say)*

person	present	preterite	future	conditional
eu	*digo*	*disse*	*direi*	*diria*
tu	*dizes*	*disseste*	*dirás*	*dirias*
você, ele/ela	*diz*	*disse*	*dirá*	*diria*
nós	*dizemos*	*dissemos*	*diremos*	*diríamos*
vocês, eles/elas	*dizem*	*disseram*	*dirão*	*diriam*

person	present subjunctive	imperfect subjunctive	future subjunctive	imperative
eu	*diga*	*dissesse*	*disser*	
tu	*digas*	*dissesses*	*disseres*	*diz(e)*
você, ele/ela	*diga*	*dissesse*	*disser*	
nós	*digamos*	*disséssemos*	*dissermos*	
vocês, eles/elas	*digam*	*dissessem*	*disserem*	

past participle *dito*

estar *(to be)*

person	present	preterite	imperative
eu	*estou*	*estive*	
tu	*estás*	*estiveste*	*está*
você, ele/ela	*está*	*esteve*	
nós	*estamos*	*estivemos*	
vocês, eles/elas	*estão*	*estiveram*	

person	present subjunctive	imperfect subjunctive	future subjunctive
eu	*esteja*	*estivesse*	*estiver*
tu	*estejas*	*estivesses*	*estiveres*
você, ele/ela	*esteja*	*estivesse*	*estiver*
nós	*estejamos*	*estivéssemos*	*estivermos*
vocês, eles/elas	*estejam*	*estivessem*	*estiverem*

fazer (to do, make)

person	present	preterite	future	conditional
eu	faço	fiz	farei	faria
tu	fazes	fizeste	farás	farias
você, ele/ela	faz	fez	fará	faria
nós	fazemos	fizemos	faremos	faríamos
vocês, eles/elas	fazem	fizeram	farão	fariam

person	imperative	present subjunctive	imperfect subjunctive	future subjunctive
eu		faça	fizesse	fizer
tu	faz(e)	faças	fizesses	fizeres
você, ele/ela		faça	fizesse	fizer
nós		façamos	fizéssemos	fizermos
vocês, eles/elas		façam	fizessem	fizerem

past participle feito

haver (there is/are, etc, to have)

person	present	preterite
eu	hei	houve
tu	hás	houveste
você, ele/ela	há	houve
nós	havemos	houvemos
vocês, eles/elas	hão	houveram

person	present subjunctive	imperfect subjunctive	future subjunctive
eu	haja	houvesse	houver
tu	hajas	houvesses	houveres
você, ele/ela	haja	houvesse	houver
nós	hajamos	houvéssemos	houvermos
vocês, eles/elas	hajam	houvessem	houverem

ir (to go)

person	present	preterite	imperative
eu	vou	fui	
tu	vais	foste	vai
você, ele/ela	vai	foi	
nós	vamos	fomos	
vocês, eles/elas	vão	foram	

person	present subjunctive	imperfect subjunctive	future subjunctive
eu	vá	fosse	for
tu	vás	fosses	fores
você, ele/ela	vá	fosse	for
nós	vamos	fôssemos	formos
vocês, eles/elas	vão	fossem	forem

ler *(to read)*

person	present	imperative	present subjunctive
eu	leio		leia
tu	lês	lê	leias
você, ele/ela	lê		leia
nós	lemos		leiamos
vocês, eles/elas	leem		leiam

ouvir *(to hear)*

person	present	imperative	present subjunctive
eu	ouço		ouça
tu	ouves	ouve	ouças
você, ele/ela	ouve		ouça
nós	ouvimos		ouçamos
vocês, eles/elas	ouvem		ouçam

pedir *(to ask for)*

person	present	imperative	present subjunctive
eu	peço		peça
tu	pedes	pede	peças
você, ele/ela	pede		peça
nós	pedimos		peçamos
vocês, eles/elas	pedem		peçam

perder *(to lose)*

person	present	imperative	present subjunctive
eu	perco		perca
tu	perdes	perde	percas
você, ele/ela	perde		perca
nós	perdemos		percamos
vocês, eles/elas	perdem		percam

poder *(to be able to, can, may)*

person	present	preterite
eu	posso	pude
tu	podes	pudeste
você, ele/ela	pode	pôde
nós	podemos	pudemos
vocês, eles/elas	podem	puderam

person	present subjunctive	imperfect subjunctive	future subjunctive
eu	possa	pudesse	puder
tu	possas	pudesses	puderes
você, ele/ela	possa	pudesse	puder
nós	possamos	pudéssemos	pudermos
vocês, eles/elas	possam	pudessem	puderem

VERBS

pôr (to put)

person	present	preterite	imperfect	imperative
eu	ponho	pus	punha	
tu	pões	puseste	punhas	põe
você, ele/ela	põe	pôs	punha	
nós	pomos	pusemos	púnhamos	
vocês, eles/elas	põem	puseram	punham	

person	present subjunctive	imperfect subjunctive	future subjunctive
eu	ponha	pusesse	puser
tu	ponhas	pusesses	puseres
você, ele/ela	ponha	pusesse	puser
nós	ponhamos	puséssemos	pusermos
vocês, eles/elas	ponham	pusessem	puserem

present participle
pondo

past participle
posto

querer (to want)

person	present	preterite
eu	quero	quis
tu	queres	quiseste
você, ele/ela	quer	quis
nós	queremos	quisemos
vocês, eles/elas	querem	quiseram

person	present subjunctive	imperfect subjunctive	future subjunctive
eu	queira	quisesse	quiser
tu	queiras	quisesses	quiseres
você, ele/ela	queira	quisesse	quiser
nós	queiramos	quiséssemos	quisermos
vocês, eles/elas	queiram	quisessem	quiserem

saber (to know)

person	present	preterite	imperative
eu	sei	soube	
tu	sabes	soubeste	sabe
você, ele/ela	sabe	soube	
nós	sabemos	soubemos	
vocês, eles/elas	sabem	souberam	

person	present subjunctive	imperfect subjunctive	future subjunctive
eu	saiba	soubesse	souber
tu	saibas	soubesses	souberes
você, ele/ela	saiba	soubesse	souber
nós	saibamos	soubéssemos	soubermos
vocês, eles/elas	saibam	soubessem	souberem

ser *(to be)*

person	present	preterite	imperfect	imperative
eu	sou	fui	era	
tu	és	foste	eras	sê
você, ele/ela	é	foi	era	
nós	somos	fomos	éramos	
vocês, eles/elas	são	foram	eram	

person	present subjunctive	imperfect subjunctive	future subjunctive
eu	seja	fosse	for
tu	sejas	fosses	fores
você, ele/ela	seja	fosse	for
nós	sejamos	fôssemos	formos
vocês, eles/elas	sejam	fossem	forem

ter *(to have)*

person	present	preterite	imperfect	imperative
eu	tenho	tive	tinha	
tu	tens	tiveste	tinhas	tem
você, ele/ela	tem	teve	tinha	
nós	temos	tivemos	tínhamos	
vocês, eles/elas	têm	tiveram	tinham	

person	present subjunctive	imperfect subjunctive	future subjunctive
eu	tenha	tivesse	tiver
tu	tenhas	tivesses	tiveres
você, ele/ela	tenha	tivesse	tiver
nós	tenhamos	tivéssemos	tivermos
vocês, eles/elas	tenham	tivessem	tiverem

trazer *(to bring)*

person	present	preterite	imperative
eu	trago	trouxe	
tu	trazes	trouxeste	traz(e)
você, ele/ela	traz	trouxe	
nós	trazemos	trouxemos	
vocês, eles/elas	trazem	trouxeram	

person	future	conditional
eu	trarei	traria
tu	trarás	trarias
você, ele/ela	trará	traria
nós	traremos	traríamos
vocês, eles/elas	trarão	trariam

person	present subjunctive	imperfect subjunctive	future subjunctive
eu	traga	trouxesse	trouxer
tu	tragas	trouxesses	trouxeres
você, ele/ela	traga	trouxesse	trouxer
nós	tragamos	trouxéssemos	trouxermos
vocês, eles/elas	tragam	trouxessem	trouxerem

ver (to see)

person	present	preterite	imperative
eu	vejo	vi	
tu	vês	viste	vê
você, ele/ela	vê	viu	
nós	vemos	vimos	
vocês, eles/elas	veem	viram	

person	present subjunctive	imperfect subjunctive	future subjunctive
eu	veja	visse	vir
tu	vejas	visses	vires
você, ele/ela	veja	visse	vir
nós	vejamos	víssemos	virmos
vocês, eles/elas	vejam	vissem	virem

past participle visto

vir (to come)

person	present	preterite	imperfect	imperative
eu	venho	vim	vinha	
tu	vens	vieste	vinhas	vem
você, ele/ela	vem	veio	vinha	
nós	vimos	viemos	vínhamos	
vocês, eles/elas	vêm	vieram	vinham	

person	present subjunctive	imperfect subjunctive	future subjunctive
eu	venha	viesse	vier
tu	venhas	viesses	vieres
você, ele/ela	venha	viesse	vier
nós	venhamos	viéssemos	viermos
vocês, eles/elas	venham	viessem	vierem

past participle vindo

For the **imperative** see **The imperative and alternatives**, pages 72–74.

18. Gender of nouns

In Portuguese, all nouns are either masculine or feminine. This grammatical gender applies not only to people and animals but also to inanimate objects and abstract concepts:

homem	*man*	(masculine)
vaca	*cow*	(feminine)
carro	*car*	(masculine)
felicidade	*happiness*	(feminine)

Gender guidelines

There are some guidelines that can help you work out whether a noun is masculine or feminine.

By meaning

Generally, males and females are masculine and feminine respectively:

homem (masculine) */ mulher* (feminine)   *man / woman*
cavalo (masculine) */ égua* (feminine)   *horse / mare*
gato (masculine) */ gata* (feminine)   *cat / she-cat*

By word ending

Usually masculine: nouns ending in the vowels *-o* and *-u*, the consonants *-l*, *-r*, and *-z*, and the letters *-ume*:

gato • livro • peru • hotel • mar • rapaz • legume

Usually feminine: nouns ending in the vowel *-a* and the letters *-gem*, *-dade*, *-tude* and *-ão* (when the ending corresponds to *-ion* in the English translation):

gata • escola • garagem • identidade • juventude • atenção

However, since there are exceptions, it is always advisable to learn a noun with its definite article, i.e., the word for *the*, which indicates its gender. Please see **The definite article**, pages 97–98.

Some nouns have only one gender, often feminine, which applies to both male and female. The following nouns are always feminine even when they refer to a male:

pessoa • criança • testemunha • vítima

A masculine plural can cover both genders:

irmão	brother	**irmãos**	*brothers* or *brother(s) and sister(s)*
senhor	gentleman	**senhores**	*gentlemen* or *ladies and gentlemen*

19. Formation of feminines

As in English, males and females are sometimes differentiated by the use of two different words in Portuguese, e.g.:

homem / mulher	*man / woman*
pai / mãe	*father / mother*
boi / vaca	*ox / cow*

However, the male-female distinction is often shown by a change of ending.

Words ending in *-o* (but not *-ão*) in the masculine change to *-a* in the feminine:

menino / menina	*boy / girl*
filho / filha	*son / daughter*
médico / médica	*(male) doctor / (female) doctor*
brasileiro / brasileira	*Brazilian man / Brazilian woman*
pato / pata	*drake / duck*

Some words ending in *-ão* drop the final *-o*:

irmão / irmã	*brother / sister*
cidadão / cidadã	*(male) citizen / (female) citizen*

A few words ending in *-ão* change to *-oa*:

patrão / patroa	*(male) boss / (female) boss*
leão / leoa	*lion / lioness*

A few words ending in *-ão* change to *-ona*:

folião / foliona	*(male) reveller / (female) reveller*
brincalhão / brincalhona	*(male) playful person / (female) playful person*

Words ending in *-or* generally add *a*:

senhor / senhora	*gentleman / lady*
professor / professora	*(male) teacher / (female) teacher*

A few words ending in *-or* substitute *-eira*:

arrumador / arrumadeira	*cleaning man / cleaning lady*
falador / faladeira	*(male) chatterbox / (female) chatterbox*

A few words ending in *-or* substitute *-riz*:

ator / atriz	*actor / actress*
imperador / imperatriz	*emperor / empress*

Words ending in *-ês* normally add **a** and lose their written accent:

português / portuguesa	*Portuguese man / Portuguese woman*
freguês / freguesa	*(male) customer / (female) customer*

Words ending in *-ista* do not change:

dentista	*(male) dentist / (female) dentist*
motorista	*(male) driver / (female) driver*

Most words ending in *-a* or *-e* do not change:

estudante	*(male) student / (female) student*
habitante	*(male) inhabitant / (female) inhabitant*
colega	*(male) colleague / (female) colleague*

Most words ending in *-eu* change to *-eia*:

europeu / europeia	*European man / European woman*

Words ending in *-ô* change to *-ó*:

avô / avó	*grandfather / grandmother*

Words ending in *-ói* change to *-oína*:

herói / heroína	*hero / heroine*

A number of words take *-esa*, *-essa* or *-isa* endings in the feminine:

príncipe / princesa	*prince / princess*
abade / abadessa	*abbot / abbess*
poeta / poetisa	*poet / poetess*

For some animals the gender distinction is expressed by adding the words **macho** (*male*) and **fêmea** (*female*):

jacaré macho / fêmea	*(male) alligator / (female) alligator*
girafa macho / fêmea	*(male) giraffe / (female) giraffe*

When an adjective is used as a noun, sometimes a change in form will not occur:

jovem / jovem	*(male) young person / (female) young person*

20. Formation of plurals

As a general rule, simply add an *-s* to nouns ending in a single vowel:

menino	*little boy*	**meninos**	*little boys*
chave	*key*	**chaves**	*keys*

Specific endings

Words ending in *-m* change to *-ns*:

homem	*man*	**homens**	*men*
nuvem	*cloud*	**nuvens**	*clouds*

Words ending in the consonants *-r*, *-z* and *-n* add *-es*:

mulher	*woman*	**mulheres**	*women*
cor	*colour*	**cores**	*colours*
rapaz	*boy, young man*	**rapazes**	*boys, young men*
luz	*light*	**luzes**	*lights*
espécimen	*specimen*	**espécimens** or **especímenes**	*specimens*

Words ending in *-ês* add *-es* and lose their accent:

freguês	*customer*	**fregueses**	*customers*
mês	*month*	**meses**	*months*

NOUNS

Words ending in **-al** change to **-ais**:

animal	animal	**animais**	animals
carnaval	carnival	**carnavais**	carnivals

Exception: **mal**, **males** evil, evils

Words ending in stressed **-el** change to **-éis** and those ending in unstressed **-el** change to **-eis**:

hotel	hotel	**hotéis**	hotels
papel	paper	**papéis**	papers
nível	level	**níveis**	levels
automóvel	motor car	**automóveis**	motor cars

Words ending in stressed **-il** change to **-is** and those ending in unstressed **-il** change to **-eis**:

barril	barrel	**barris**	barrels
fuzil	rifle	**fuzis**	rifles
réptil	reptile	**répteis**	reptiles
fóssil	fossil	**fósseis**	fossils

Words ending in stressed **-ol** change to **-óis** and those ending in unstressed **-ol** change to **-ois**:

lençol	bed sheet	**lençóis**	bed sheets
farol	lighthouse	**faróis**	lighthouses
álcool	alcohol	**álcoois**	types of alcohol

Words ending in stressed **-ul** change to **-uis** and those ending in unstressed **-ul** add **-es**:

paul	swamp	**pauis**	swamps
cônsul	consul	**cônsules**	consuls

Some words ending in **-ão** add **-s** while others change to **-ões** or **-ães**.

mão	hand	**mãos**	hands
irmão	brother	**irmãos**	brothers
avião	aeroplane	**aviões**	aeroplanes
botão	button	**botões**	buttons
pão	loaf	**pães**	loaves
capitão	captain	**capitães**	captains

Words ending in **-s** have the same form for both singular and plural:

lápis	pencil	**lápis**	pencils
pires	saucer	**pires**	saucers

Some nouns are used only in the plural:

óculos	glasses, spectacles
arredores	suburbs
belas-artes	fine arts

21. The definite article

The Portuguese definite article agrees in gender (i.e. masc. or fem.) and number (i.e. sing. or plur.) with the noun to which it relates. As such, it has the following forms:

o	masculine singular	*os*	masculine plural
a	feminine singular	*as*	feminine plural

o homem	the man	*os homens*	the men
a chave	the key	*as chaves*	the keys

(Please note that Portuguese *a* translates English *the*, not *a/an*.)

Where the noun would otherwise be ambiguous as to gender or number, the article provides clarification:

o estudante	the male student	*a estudante*	the female student
o artista	the male artist	*a artista*	the female artist
o lápis	the pencil	*os lápis*	the pencils

See **Formation of feminines**, pages 94–95, and **Formation of plurals**, pages 95–96.

For nouns that mean different things depending on their gender, it is the article that helps identify the sense in question:

o capital	capital (money)	*a capital*	capital (city)
o guia	guide book	*a guia*	bill of lading; advice slip

See **Gender of nouns**, page 93.

Basically the role of the definite article is much the same in Portuguese as it is in English, but its use is broader in Portuguese.

with nouns when making generalizations

A natureza é linda.	Nature is beautiful.
O ouro é um metal precioso.	Gold is a precious metal.
Os gatos miam.	Cats miaow.

with the names of seasons, days of the week and special dates

Quando começa o verão?	When does summer start?
A segunda-feira é o dia mais ocupado.	Monday is the busiest day.

with the name of continents and several countries – **Portugal** is an exception

O Brasil fica na América e Portugal na Europa.	Brazil is in America and Portugal in Europe.

with the names of some states, regions and cities

O Amazonas é o maior estado do Brasil.	Amazonas is the largest state in Brazil.
A Madeira fica no Oceano Atlântico.	Madeira is in the Atlantic Ocean.
O Rio de Janeiro é a antiga capital do Brasil.	Rio de Janeiro is Brazil's former capital city.

often with the names of languages

O Português é falado em vários países.	Portuguese is spoken in several countries.

with parts of the body, belongings, close relations and friends

Vou lavar o cabelo.	*I am going to wash my hair.*
Não esqueça o guarda-chuva!	*Don't forget your umbrella!*
Ela saiu com os amigos.	*She went out with her friends.*

With possessives:

Este é o meu livro.	*This is my book.*

with a title followed by a name

O doutor Oliveira não está.	*Doctor Oliveira is not in.*

with names of people – in Portugal more so than in Brazil

Comprei um presente para a Lúcia.	*I have bought a present for Lúcia.*

Conversely, unlike in English, the definite article is not used in Portuguese with the names of musical instruments meant in a general sense:

Ela toca piano.	*She plays the piano.*

22. The indefinite article

The Portuguese indefinite article agrees with the noun to which it relates. As such it has a masculine and a feminine form:

um	*masculine*
uma	*feminine*
um homem	*a man*
uma chave	*a key*

The Portuguese indefinite article also has plural forms. These often correspond to *some* and *a few* in English:

uns homens	*some / a few men*
umas chaves	*some / a few keys*

Portuguese **um / uma** sometimes corresponds to the English indefinite article *a / an* and sometimes to the number *one*. See **Cardinal and ordinal numbers**, pages 121–124. Partly as a result of this, usage varies between the two languages.

Unlike in English, the Portuguese indefinite article is not used:

with a classifying noun, denoting someone's job, religion, affiliation, age group, etc

Ela é professora.	*She is a teacher.*
Ela é católica.	*She is a Catholic.*
Ele já é adulto.	*He is an adult.*

with hundreds and thousands

Cem dias é muito tempo.	*A hundred days is a long time.*
Este parqueamento tem capacidade para mil veículos.	*This parking area has space for a thousand vehicles.*

23. Formation of feminines and plurals

Most adjectives agree in gender and number with the noun they modify.

Formation of feminines

Words ending in -o (but not -ão) change to -a:
  alto / alta • *vermelho / vermelha* • *brasileiro / brasileira*

Some words ending in -ão drop the final -o:
  são / sã • *cristão / cristã* • *alemão / alemã*

A few words ending in -ão change to -ona:
  brincalhão / brincalhona • *comilão / comilona*

Words ending in -or generally add -a but some change to -eira:
  trabalhador / trabalhadora • *falador / faladeira*

Words ending in -ês normally add -a (and lose their accent):
  inglês / inglesa • *português / portuguesa*

Exception: **cortês**, *polite*, which stays the same for the feminine.

Words ending in -eu change to -eia:
  europeu / europeia • *hebreu / hebreia*

Words ending in -u add -a:
  cru / crua • *nu / nua*

Exception: **mau / má**, *bad*

Words ending in -e or -a usually do not change:
  grande / grande • *doce / doce* • *belga / belga*

Some words ending in -l, -s, and -z do not change:
  fácil / fácil • *simples / simples* • *capaz / capaz*

Some words ending in -m do not change:
  jovem / jovem • *ruim / ruim*

Exception: **bom / boa**, *good*

ADJECTIVES

Formation of plurals

Most words ending in a single vowel add **-s**:

doce, doces	sweet
elegante, elegantes	elegant
grande, grandes	big, large
vermelha, vermelhas	red
brasileiro, brasileiros	Brazilian

Words ending in **-m** change to **-ns**:

jovem, jovens	young
bom, bons	good

Words ending in **-r** or **-z** add **-es**:

melhor, melhores	better
feliz, felizes	happy

Words ending in **-ês** add **-es** (and lose their accent):

português, portugueses	Portuguese
cortês, corteses	polite

Words ending in **-al** change to **-ais**:

usual, usuais	usual
internacional, internacionais	international

Words ending in **-el** generally change to **-eis**:

amável, amáveis	kind
possível, possíveis	possible

Words ending in stressed **-il** change to **-is** and those ending in unstressed **-il** change to **-eis**:

civil, civis	civil
fácil, fáceis	easy

A small number of words ending in **-ol** and **-ul** change to **-óis**, and **-uis** respectively:

espanhol, espanhóis	Spanish
azul, azuis	blue

Some words ending in **-ão** add **-s**, while others change to **-ões** or **-ães**:

cristão, cristãos	Christian
folgazão, folgazões	fun-loving
alemão, alemães	German

A small number of words ending in **-s** do not change:

simples, simples	simple

For information on the position of adjectives, see **Word order**, pages 118–119.

24. Comparatives and superlatives

Comparatives

These are formed using the following constructions:

mais ... (que)	*more ... /-er ... (than)*
menos ... (que)	*less ... (than)*
tão ... quanto or tão ... como (*)	*as ... as*

(*) Both forms are used east and west of the Atlantic but you are likely to hear **quanto** more often in Brazil and **como** more often in Portugal.

O casaco azul é mais confortável e bonito que o casaco verde.	*The blue coat is more comfortable and prettier than the green coat.*
O chapéu branco é menos bonito que o chapéu amarelo.	*The white hat is not as pretty as (is less pretty than) the yellow hat.*
*O chapéu vermelho é tão bonito quanto (or **como**) o chapéu amarelo.*	*The red hat is as pretty as the yellow hat.*

Superlatives

These are formed using the following constructions:

mais ... (de) ...	*most ... /-est... (of)*
menos (de) ...	*least ... (of)*

Este é o casaco mais confortável e mais bonito (de todos).	*This one is the most comfortable and prettiest coat (of all).*
Este é o casaco menos confortável e menos bonito (de todos).	*This is the least comfortable and least pretty coat (of all).*

Adjectives with irregular comparatives and superlatives

adjective	comparative	superlative
bom	*melhor*	*o melhor*
mau, ruim	*pior*	*o pior*
grande	*maior*	*o maior*
pequeno	*menor* (Br)	*o menor* (Br)
	mais pequeno (Eur)	*o mais pequeno* (Eur)

25. Demonstrative adjectives

Demonstrative adjectives agree with the noun in both gender (i.e. masc. or fem.) and number (i.e. sing. or plur.):

	masculine	**feminine**	
singular	*este, esse, aquele*	*esta, essa, aquela*	*this; that*
plural	*estes, esses, aqueles*	*estas, essas, aquelas*	*these; those*

Este casaco é meu.	*This coat is mine.*
Esse guarda-chuva é teu.	*That umbrella is yours.*
Aquelas malas são deles.	*Those suitcases are theirs.*

este (and its feminine and plural) indicate something or someone close to the speaker, i.e. to the 1st person.
esse (and its feminine and plural) indicate something or someone close to the listener, i.e. to the 2nd person.
aquele (and its feminine and plural) indicate something or someone at a distance from both the 1st and 2nd persons.

The form *aquele* translates *that* and *este* *this*, but *esse* can translate both *that* and *this*. Closeness and distance may refer to space, time or sequence in speech or text.

In Brazil, *este* is not used much in colloquial speech, leaving *esse* to cover both meanings:

Speaker A:	*– Esse livro é bom?*	*– Is that book good?*
Speaker B:	*– Sim, este / esse* (Coll Br) *livro é bom.*	*–Yes, this book is good.*

See also **Demonstrative pronouns**, pages 112–113, and **Prepositions**, pages 115–117.

26. Interrogative adjectives

Que...? can translate both English *What...?* and *Which...?*. It is used when seeking identification or a definition:

Que rua é esta?	*What street is this?*
Que carro é que você comprou?	*Which car did you buy?, What type of car have you bought?*

Qual...? translates English *Which...?*. It implies the notion of choice or selection. It agrees in number with its noun and has the form *Quais...?* for the plural:

Qual livro você vai escolher?	*Which book will you choose?*
Quais calças você vai comprar?	*Which trousers are you going to buy?*

Quanto...?, Quanta...?, Quantos...?, Quantas...? translates English *How much...?* and *How many...?*. It agrees in gender and number with the noun it relates to:

Quanto tempo vai demorar?	*How long is it going to take?*
Quanta paciência será preciso!?	*How much patience will be needed!?*
Quantos livros é que você leu?	*How many books have you read?*

27. Possessive adjectives

Possessor	Possessives		
	Masculine, singular and plural	Feminine, singular and plural	
1st person sing. (I)	o(s) meus(s)	a(s) minha(s)	my
2nd person sing. (you)	o(s) seu(s) (relating to você / o senhor / a senhora) o(s) [noun] de ... o(s) teu(s)	a(s) sua(s) (relating to você, o senhor, a senhora) a(s) [noun] de ... a(s) tua(s)	your
3rd person sing. (he / she / it)	o(s) seu(s) o(s) [noun] dele / dela	a(s) sua(s) a(s) [noun] dele / dela	his / her / its
1st person plur. (we)	o(s) nosso(s)	a(s) nossa(s)	our
2nd person plur. (you)	o(s) seu(s) (relating to vocês etc) o(s) vosso(s) o(s) [noun] de ...	a(s) sua(s) (relating to vocês etc) a(s) vossa(s) a(s) [noun] de ...	your
3rd person plur. (they)	o(s) seu(s) o(s) [noun] deles / delas	a(s) sua(s) a(s) [noun] deles / delas	their

Agreement

Portuguese possessive adjectives agree in gender (i.e. masc. or fem.) and number (i.e. sing. or plur.) with the thing possessed:

o meu chapéu	my hat
o nosso carro	our car
a minha mala	my suitcase
os meus sapatos	my shoes
as nossas luvas	our gloves

Alternative forms for second- and third-person possessors

Since the third-person forms *seu(s) / sua(s)* could mean *his, hers, theirs* or *yours*, alternatives are often used to clarify who the owner is. So, particularly in speech, constructions consisting of the preposition *de* contracted with a third person subject pronoun, *ele(s) / ela(s)*, are frequently used to indicate third-person possessors:

o chapéu dela (= de + ela)	her hat
o carro dele (= de + ele)	his car
as malas delas (= de + elas)	their suitcases

Portuguese usage of possessive adjectives compared with English

Unlike in English, possessive adjectives are not used with parts of the body, articles of clothing or other personal belongings, close relations or friends, etc, when the possessor is also the subject of the sentence and the connection is obvious.

Ela cruzou os braços.	She crossed her arms.
O cachorro abanou o rabo.	The little dog wagged his tail.
Eu perdi os óculos.	I have lost my spectacles.
Ela deixou a bolsa no carro.	She left her purse in the car.
A mãe levou os filhos para a praia.	The mother took her children to the beach.
Eles perderam o juízo.	They have lost their minds.

PORTUGUESE GRAMMAR GUIDE

28. Personal pronouns

Subject pronouns

	singular		plural	
1st person	*eu*	I	*nós*	we
2nd person	*você*	you	*vocês*	you
	tu		(*vós* – no longer in general use)	
3rd person (masc.)	*ele*	he; it	*eles*	they
(fem.)	*ela*	she; it	*elas*	they

você, tu

In today's Portuguese, *você* is a second-person singular subject marker, although it is followed by a verb in the third person. The other subject marker, *tu*, is the traditional second-person singular subject pronoun. Both *você* and *tu* share the same plural, *vocês*. (For the difference in meaning between *você* and *tu* see pages 107–108.)

There is variation in the use of *você* and *tu*. In European Portuguese *tu* is very much alive and well. In Brazil preference is given to *você* at a national level, but some Brazilian speakers use the subject pronoun *tu*, often conjugated with the verb ending for *você*.

Cecília, você gosta de viajar?	Cecília, do you like travelling?
Cecília, tu gostas de viajar? (Eur)	Cecília, do you like travelling?
Cecília, tu gosta de viajar? (Coll Br) (regionally)	Cecília, do you like travelling?

vós

The second-person subject pronoun is the plural counterpart of *tu* in the *tu-vós* duality inherited from Latin, but it is no longer in general use. You may come across it in specific contexts, e.g. in church.

ele / ela; eles / elas

The form of the third-person subject pronoun reflects not only the number but also the gender of the noun(s) it replaces, this being people, animals or things. With inanimate objects the pronoun tends to be omitted.

Ela gosta de viajar.	She likes travelling.
Eles estão deitados no telhado. (os gatos)	They are lying on the roof. (the cats)
(Ela) tem quatro pernas. (a mesa)	It has four legs. (the table)

A masculine plural can refer to both genders:

Eles gostam de viajar. (Cecília e Eduardo)	They like travelling. (Cecília and Eduardo)

Subject marker omission

Where the verb ending indicates the subject clearly, the subject marker can be dropped:

(Eu) telefonei ontem.	I phoned yesterday.
(Nós) vamos à praia amanhã.	We are going to the beach tomorrow.

Direct object pronouns

	singular		plural	
1st person	**me**	me	**nos**	us
2nd person	**o/a**	you	**os/as**, **vos** (Eur)	you
	você		(Wr Br)	
	te		**vocês**	
3rd person (masc.)	**o**	him; it	**os**	them
	ele (Coll Br)		**eles** (Coll Br)	
(fem.)	**a**	her; it	**as**	them
	ela (Coll Br)		**elas** (Coll Br)	

Eu não te vi.   *I didn't see you.*
Eles não nos viram.   *They didn't see us.*

Particularly in speech, subject-marker words are also often used as direct objects:

Eles não viram a gente.   *They didn't see us.*
Eu vi você ontem.   *I saw you yesterday.*
Ele levou o senhor de carro?   *Did he take you by car, sir?*

Object pronouns after a verb

When object pronouns **o(s)** / **a(s)** follow verb forms ending in a nasal sound, they change to **no(s)** / **na(s)**:

O trabalho era muito mas eles fizeram-no   *There was a lot of work but they did it all.*
todo.
As lições eram fáceis. Eles aprenderam-nas   *The lessons were easy. They learned them well.*
bem.

When object pronouns **o(s)** / **a(s)** follow verb forms ending in **-r**, **-s** or **-z**, they change to **lo(s)** / **la(s)** and the verb ending also changes:

Eu vou comprá-lo. (comprar+o)   *I am going to buy it.*
Eu não pude ouvi-la (ouvir+a)   *I couldn't hear her.*
Ele pô-lo ali. (pôs+o)   *He put it there.*
Você fê-lo. (fez+o)   *You did it.*

These constructions are often avoided, particularly in speech, using one of two methods:

by placing the pronoun before the verb

Muito prazer em conhecê-la. or   *Delighted to meet you.*
  Muito prazer em a conhecer.

by using the same words as for subject markers

Muito prazer em conhecê-la. or **Muito**   *Delighted to meet you.*
  prazer em conhecer você. (general)
Muito prazer em conhecer a senhora.
  (courteous)

For position of direct object pronouns, see also **Word order**, page 119.

Indirect object pronouns

	singular		plural	
1st person	*me*	*(to) me*	*nos*	*(to) us*
2nd person	*lhe* *te* *(para) você* (Coll Br)	*(to) you*	*lhes* *vos* (Eur) (Wr Br) *(para) vocês* (Coll Br)	*(to) you*
3rd person (masc.) (fem.)	*lhe* *(para) ele* (Coll Br) *lhe* *(para) ela* (Coll Br)	*(to) him; it* *(to) her; it*	*lhes* *(para) eles* (Coll Br) *lhes* *(para) elas* (Coll Br)	*(to) them* *(to) them*

Particularly in speech, indirect objects can also be indicated using subject-marker words preceded by a preposition. This is much more widely heard in Brazil than in Portugal:

Eu não lhe comprei um presente. or	*I haven't bought her a present.*
Eu não comprei um presente para ela.	
Você já lhes deu o dinheiro? or	*Have you given them the money (yet)?*
Você já deu o dinheiro a eles?	
Eu não lhe telefonei ontem. or	*I didn't phone you yesterday.*
Eu não telefonei para você ontem.	

For position of indirect object pronouns, see also **Word order**, page 119.

Combined forms

Indirect-object pronouns can combine and contract with the direct object pronouns *o(s) / a(s)* in forms such as *mo* (me+o), *to* (te+o), *lho* (lhe+o), etc. Such constructions can be avoided by using a stressed pronoun preceded by a preposition. See **Stressed pronouns** below.

Não lho venda. (lhe+o) or	*Don't sell it to him.*
Não o venda a ele.	
Ele trouxe as chaves e deu-mas. (me+as)	*He brought over the keys and gave them to me.*
or *Ele trouxe as chaves e deu-as a mim.*	

Stressed pronouns

	singular		plural	
1st person	*para mim*	*to me*	*para nós*	*to us*
2nd person	*para você, ti* *para si* (Eur) (Wr Br)	*to you*	*para vocês*	*to you*
3rd person (masc.) (fem.)	*para ele* *para ela*	*to him; it* *to her; it*	*para eles* *para elas*	*to them* *to them*

Personal pronouns take a stressed form after a preposition. In some cases, these are the same words as the subject pronouns:

Eles olharam para nós.	*They looked at us.*
Essa carta for escrita por mim.	*That letter was written by me.*
Ela disse a ti que viria?	*Did she tell you she would come?*
Eu fui com eles.	*I went with them.*
Aquilo era para você. = Aquilo era para si. (Eur) (Wr Br)	*That was for you.*

The preposition *com* (*with*) combines with personal pronouns in the following ways:

comigo	*with me*
contigo	*with you*
connosco (Eur), *conosco* (Br)	*with us*
consigo (Eur) (Wr Br) = *com você*	*with you*
convosco (Eur) (Wr Br) = *com vocês*	*with you*

Reflexive pronouns

These are dealt with under **Reflexive verbs**, page 76.

29. *Tu, você* and *o senhor / a senhora*

Saying *you* in Portuguese

In today's English there is an all-embracing pronoun used for addressing people: *you*.
The closest Portuguese translation is *você*:

Você está de férias?	*Are you on holiday?* (addressing one person)

When talking to someone, in English a courteous tone can be imparted by adding *sir* or *madam*. In Portuguese this effect is achieved by replacing *você* with the nouns *o senhor* (literally, *the gentleman*) and *a senhora* (*the lady*):

O senhor está de férias?	*Are you on holiday, sir?*
A senhora está de férias?	*Are you on holiday, madam?*

A friendly or familiar tone can be obtained in English by adding e.g. *mate* or *dear*.
In Portuguese, the same effect can be achieved by using *tu*, and its related forms *te* and *ti*, but there is variation in practice.

In Portugal, including Madeira and the Azores, as well as in Portuguese-speaking regions of Africa and Asia, *tu* is the main choice for this purpose, along with its related object pronouns, *te* and *ti*:

Tu estás de férias?	*Are you on holiday, dear?*
Eu não te vi na praia. (Eur)	*I didn't see you on the beach.*

In Brazil, there is a general preference for *você* in conjunction with the object pronouns *te* and *ti*, though *tu* can also be heard:

Você está de férias?	*Are you on holiday, dear?*
Eu não te vi na praia. (Br)	*I didn't see you on the beach.*

When talking to more than one person, *você* is pluralized to *vocês*.

Vocês estão de férias?	*Are you on holiday?*

The nouns are pluralized to *os senhores* (*the gentlemen*) or *as senhoras* (*the ladies*).
A masculine plural can refer to a pair or group that includes both genders:

As senhoras estão de férias?	*Are you on holiday, ladies?*
Os senhores estão de férias?	*Are you on holiday, ladies and gentlemen?*

Where *tu* is used in the singular, *vocês* is used in the plural:

Vocês estão de férias?	*Are you on holiday, my dears?*

Verb agreement for *you*

The verb endings used for both *o senhor / a senhora* and *você* are third-person forms:

O senhor está de férias?	*Are you on holiday, sir?*
Você está de férias?	*Are you on holiday?*

In Portugal and the other geographical locations listed above, the subject pronoun *tu* has retained its traditional second-person singular verb endings. Because they are distinctive as a second-person marker, *tu* can be omitted without loss of meaning:

Tu estás de férias? (Eur) or **Estás de férias?**　*Are you on holiday, dear?*

In Brazil, when the subject pronoun *tu* is used, it is often conjugated with third-person verb endings, like *você*. This is particularly the case in the north-east and in some areas on the Atlantic coast:

Tu está de férias (Coll Br) (regionally)　*Are you on holiday, dear?*

When talking to more than one person, third-person plural verb endings are used in modern Portuguese whatever the subject marker, whether it is *vocês* (plural to both *você* and *tu*) or *os senhores / as senhoras*:

Vocês estão de férias?	*Are you on holiday? / Are you on holiday, my dears?*
Os senhores estão de férias?	*Are you on holiday, ladies and gentlemen?*

When unsure which form of address to use, you can just use a third-person verb ending without a subject pronoun or other marker. This is heard on both sides of the Atlantic but more so in Portugal:

Está de férias?	*Are you on holiday?*
	(addressing one person)
Estão de férias?	*Are you on holiday?*
	(addressing more than one person)

30. Indefinite pronouns

Tudo (*all, everything*) is neuter:

É tudo.	*That's all.*
Tudo o que você me disse é verdade.	*Everything you told me is true.*

Nada (*nothing*) is neuter:

Não vi nada.　*I saw nothing.* or *I didn't see anything.*

Alguém (*someone, somebody, anyone, anybody*) is invariable:

Há alguém naquela sala.	*There is somebody in that room.*
Alguém falou com ele sobre o assunto?	*Has anyone discussed the matter with him?*

Ninguém (*nobody, none, no one*) is invariable:

Ninguém veio aqui. or **Não veio ninguém aqui.**　*Nobody came here.*

Todo, toda (*each one, every*), **todos, todas** (*all*) are masculine, feminine and plural forms parallel to **tudo**:

Quantas laranjas você quer?	*How many oranges would you like?*
Todas.	*All (of them).*

Algum, alguma, alguns, algumas (*some, any*) change in gender and number according to the noun they refer to:

Você tem dinheiro?	*Have you got any money on you?*
Algum.	*Some.*

Nenhum, nenhuma, nenhuns, nenhumas (*none*) change in gender and number according to the noun they refer to:

Nenhum deles veio.	*None of them has come.*

Outro, outra (*another*), **outros, outras** (*others*) change in gender and number according to the noun they refer to:

Você quer esta camisa?	*Would you like this shirt?*
Não, prefiro outra.	*No, I would prefer another one.*

Qualquer (*any*) and its plural form **quaisquer** change in number (but not in gender) according to the noun they refer to:

Falarei com qualquer deles.	*I'll talk to any of them.*
Quaisquer servem.	*Any will do. (more than one)*

Ambos, ambas (*both*) are used only in the plural but change in gender according to the noun they refer to:

Gosto de ambos.	*I like both.*

Cada or **cada um, cada uma** (*each, each one*). The use of **um/uma** (which agrees with the noun referred to) is optional:

Os vencedores recebem uma medalha cada (um).	*The winners will receive a medal each.*

For *nada*, *ninguém* and *nenhum*, etc, see also **Negatives**, pages 119–120.

31. Relative pronouns

Que (*that, which, who, whom*) is the most frequently used relative pronoun in Portuguese. It is invariable and can be used both as subject and direct object:

O rapaz que veio aqui é meu aluno.	*The boy who or that came here is a pupil of mine.*
A minha amiga é a pessoa que você vê ali.	*My friend is the person (whom or who or that) you can see over there.*
A caneta que está em cima da mesa é minha.	*The pen that or which is on the table is mine.*
Tenho o livro que você pediu.	*I have the book (which or that) you asked for.*

(Please note that, unlike English, Portuguese never omits the relative pronoun.)

PRONOUNS

Que can be preceded by a preposition, in which case it often translates English *which* and *whom*:

O apartamento em que ela mora é espaçoso.	*The apartment in which she lives or that she lives in is spacious.*
A companhia para que ele trabalhava fica fora da cidade.	*The company for which he worked is out of town.*

Quem (*whom*) is often used in preference to **que** when the relative pronoun refers to a person or people and is the object of the verb. It is invariable:

A senhora a quem entreguei o livro é a minha professora.	*The lady to who or whom I handed the book is my teacher.*
O patrão para quem ele trabalhava já se aposentou.	*The boss who he worked for has now retired.* or *The boss he worked for has now retired.*

O qual, a qual, os quais, as quais (*which, who, whom*) is a relative pronoun that varies in gender and number with the noun it relates to. It is not used much in conversation:

O presidente, o qual também é orador, proferiu um discurso.	*The president, who is also a good speaker, made a speech.*
São quarto as cidades nas quais ele falou.	*There were four cities in which he gave a talk* or *(that) he gave a talk in.*
Um homem, o nome do qual desconheço, dirigiu-se ao presidente.	*A man, whose name I do not know, approached the president.*

Cujo, cuja, cujos, cujas (*whose*) is a relative pronoun that functions as an adjective and agrees in gender and number with the noun it accompanies. It provides an alternative to *do qual*, etc:

Um homem, cujo nome desconheço, dirigiu-se ao presidente.	*A man, whose name I do not know, approached the president.*

O que (*that which*) is a combination of the demonstrative pronoun **o** and the relative pronoun **que**. Used as a neuter pronoun, it is often equivalent to *that*, *what* or *which* in English:

Tudo o que você me disse é verdade.	*Everything (that) you told me is true.*
Só aceitarei o que é justo.	*I will accept only what is fair.*
Somos o que somos.	*We are what we are.*
Ela é professora, o que eu não sabia.	*She is a teacher, which I didn't know.*

O que, a que, os que, as que are also options available. In this case the demonstrative pronoun agrees in gender and number with a specific noun and can translate English *the one(s); this, these, that, those; he/she/it/they who*:

Você prefere os meus livros ou os que estão na mesa?	*Do you prefer my books or the ones / those on the table?*
Na corrida feminina a que chegar primeiro ganhará o troféu.	*In the ladies' race the one or the woman who arrives first will win the trophy.*

The adverbs **onde** (*where*) for place and **como** (*how*) for manner can also be used as relative pronouns:

O apartamento onde ela mora é espaçoso.	*The apartment where she lives is spacious.*

The *onde* and *como* options also provide alternatives to *qual*:

> **São quarto as cidades onde ele falou.**
> instead of
> **São quarto as cidades nas quais ele falou.** (Wr)

There were four cities where he gave a talk.

There were four cities in which he gave a talk.

> **A maneira como ele nos tratou é um escândalo.**
> instead of
> **A maneira pela qual ele nos tratou é um escândalo.** (Wr)

(How) he treated us was scandalous.

The way (in which) he treated us was scandalous.

32. Interrogative pronouns

Quem...? translates English *Who...?* and *Whom...?*, both singular and plural:

> **Quem veio aqui ontem?** Who came here yesterday?

De quem...? translates English *Whose...?*, but, unlike the English construction, it has to be followed by a verb rather than a noun:

> **De quem é este passaporte?** Whose passport is this?

Que...? and *Qual...?* are equivalent to *What?* and *Which?* in English.
Que...? is used when the questioner is expecting an answer that identifies or defines.
Qual...? (plural *Quais...?*) is used when the possible answers are more restricted and there is an implicit idea of choice:

> **Qual você prefere?** Which do you prefer? (choosing one out of two or more options)
> **Quais você prefere?** Which do you prefer? (choosing more than one out of a limited range of possibilities)

Quanto...?, Quanta...?, Quantos...?, Quantas...? corresponds to *How much?, How many?* in English and agrees in gender and number with the noun:

> **Quanto custa?** How much does it cost?
> **Quantas são?** How many are there?

33. Possessive pronouns

Possessor	Possessives		
	Masculine, singular and plural	Feminine, singular and plural	
1st person sing. (I)	*o(s) meu(s)*	*a(s) minha(s)*	mine
2nd person sing. (you)	*o(s) seu(s)* (relating to *você, o senhor, a senhora*) *o(s) de ...* *o(s) teu(s)*	*a(s) sua(s)* (relating to *você, o senhor, a senhora*) *a(s) de ...* *a(s) tua(s)*	yours
3rd person sing. (he / she / it)	*o(s) seu(s)* *o(s) dele / dela*	*a(s) sua(s)* *a(s) dele / dela*	his / hers / its

1st person plur. (we)	o(s) nosso(s)	a(s) nossa(s)	ours
2nd person plur. (you)	o(s) seu(s) (relating to vocês etc) o(s) vosso(s) o(s) de ...	a(s) sua(s) (relating to vocês etc) a(s) vossa(s) a(s) de ...	yours
3rd person plur. (they)	o(s) seu(s) o(s) deles / delas	a(s) sua(s) a(s) deles / delas	theirs

Agreement

Portuguese possessive pronouns agree in gender and number with the thing possessed:

o meu (=chapéu)	mine (= hat)
o nosso (= carro)	ours (= car)
a minha (= mala)	mine (= suitcase)
os meus (= sapatos)	mine (= shoes)
as nossas (= luvas)	ours (= gloves)

Alternative forms for second- and third-person possessors

Since the third-person forms **seu(s) / sua(s)** could mean his, hers, theirs or yours, alternatives are often used to clarify who the owner is. So, particularly in speech, constructions consisting of the preposition **de** contracted with a third person subject pronoun, **ele(s) / ela(s)**, are frequently used to indicate third-person possessors:

o dela (= de + ela)	(*chapéu*, hat)	hers
o dele (= de + ele)	(*carro*, car)	his
as delas (= de + elas)	(*malas*, suitcases)	theirs

(For contracted forms see also pages 115–116.)

This same technique can be applied to the second person, with preposition **de** followed by the subject-marker word(s):

a de você (less heard than a sua)	(*mala*, suitcase)	yours
a do senhor	(*mala*, suitcase)	yours
a do João (Coll Eur)	(*mala*, suitcase)	yours
as das senhoras	(*malas*, suitcases)	yours

Omission of o / a

With one-word possessives (**meu**, **seu**, **teu**, **nosso**, **vosso**, etc), **o(s) / a(s)** is omitted when the possessive stands alone (normally after the verb **ser**) except when being emphatic about who something belongs to:

De quem é aquela mala?	Whose suitcase is that?
É minha. but	It's mine.
Aquela mala é a minha.	That suitcase is mine. (no one else's)

34. Demonstrative pronouns

Demonstrative pronouns have forms that agree in gender (i.e masc. or fem.) and number (i.e. sing. or plur.) with the noun they replace:

	masculine	feminine	
singular	este, esse, aquele	esta, essa, aquela	this; that (one)
plural	estes, esses, aqueles	estas, essas, aquelas	these; those (ones)

There are also invariable neuter forms, for something or someone yet to be identified:

isto, isso, aquilo *this; that (one)*

Este é o meu casaco. This is my coat.
Esse é o teu guarda-chuva. That is your umbrella.
Aquelas são as malas deles. Those are their suitcases.
Aquilo parece ser o meu passaporte. That could be my passport.

isto, este (and their feminine and plural forms) are used to indicate something close to the speaker, i.e. to the 1st person.
isso, esse (and their feminine and plural forms) are used to indicate something close to the listener, i.e. to the 2nd person.
aquilo, aquele (and their feminine and plural forms) are used to indicate something at a distance away from both the 1st and 2nd persons.

Speaker A: *O que é aquilo lá em cima no céu?* What is that up there in the sky?
Speaker B: *É um helicóptero.* It's a helicopter.
Speaker A: *Aquele helicóptero vai muito alto.* That helicopter is flying rather high.

The forms *isso* and *esse* can translate both *that* and *this*:

Speaker A: *O que é isso?* What is that? (you are holding)
Speaker B: *É uma caneta.* It's a pen.

but

Speaker A: *Destes dois livros eu prefiro este.* Out of these two books I prefer this one. (the one closer to A)
Speaker B: *Eu também prefiro esse.* I prefer this / that one too.

In Brazil, *isto* and *este* are not much used in colloquial speech, leaving *isso* and *esse* to cover both.

In the word combination *o que*, *o* is a demonstrative pronoun – see **Relative pronouns**, pages 109–111.

See also **Demonstrative adjectives**, page 102, and **Prepositions**, pages 115–117.

35. Adverbs

Adverbs in -*mente*

In Portuguese a large number of adverbs are formed by adding -*mente* to an adjective, very much in the same way as -*ly* is added to adjectives in English:

forte strong *fortemente* strongly
feliz happy *felizmente* happily

With adjectives that have alternative masculine and feminine endings, -*mente* is added to the feminine form:

lindo beautiful *lindamente* beautifully
sincero sincere *sinceramente* sincerely

ADVERBS

The adjective part of the adverb loses its stress to the **-mente** ending, meaning that written accents disappear:

cortês	*courteous*	**cortesmente**	*courteously*
rápido	*quick, fast*	**rapidamente**	*quickly*

When two adverbs are used together, normally only the second one takes a **-mente** ending:

Ela falou clara e resolutamente.	*She spoke clearly and decisively.*
Ele trabalha lenta mas eficientemente.	*He works slowly but efficiently.*

Other adverbs

Common adverbs of manner include **bem**, *well*; **mal**, *badly, poorly*; **depressa**, *fast, quickly*; **devagar**, *slowly*; **assim**, *like this*:

Tudo correu bem.	*All went well.*
Eles procederam mal.	*They behaved badly.*
Não consigo trabalhar assim.	*I can't work this way.*

Common adverbs of time include **agora**, *now*; **antes**, *before*; **depois**, *after*; **ainda**, *still*; **sempre**, *always*; **nunca**, *never*:

Vou trabalhar agora.	*I am going to work now.*
Farei isso depois.	*I will do that afterwards.*
Eu nunca gostei disso.	*I never liked that.*

Common adverbs of place include **perto**, *near*; **longe**, *far*; **atrás**, *behind*; **debaixo**, *under*; **diante**, *in front, ahead*; **em cima**, *above*; **fora**, *out*; **dentro**, *in*; **aqui**, *here*; **aí**, *there*; **ali**, *there*; **lá**, *there*:

aqui, *here*	close to the speaker, i.e. the 1st person
aí, *there*	close to the listener, i.e. the 2nd person
ali, *there*	away from both the 1st and 2nd person
lá, *there*	far away or cut off from both the 1st and 2nd person

Comparatives and superlatives

Comparatives and superlatives of adverbs are formed with constructions similar to those for adjectives:

João corre depressa.	*João runs fast or quickly.*
João corre mais depressa que Mário.	*João runs faster or more quickly than Mário.*
João é quem corre mais depressa de todos.	*It's João who runs the fastest or the quickest.*

Some adverbs have irregular comparative and superlative forms:

bem	*well*	**melhor**	*better*	**o melhor**	*(the) best*
mal	*badly*	**pior**	*worse*	**o pior**	*(the) worst*
muito	*much, very*	**mais**	*more*	**o mais**	*(the) most*
pouco	*little*	**menos**	*less*	**o menos**	*(the) least*

Ontem o dia correu o melhor possível.	*The day couldn't have gone better yesterday.*
Hoje trabalhei mais que ontem.	*Today I worked harder (more) than yesterday.*

36. Prepositions

Contracted words

Portuguese prepositions often combine and contract with a following word, particularly the **definite article**:

a + o = ao	*a + a = à*	to / at / on the
de + o = do	*de + a = da*	of / from the
em + o = no	*em + a = na*	in / on the
por + o = pelo	*por + a = pela*	by / for the

à uma hora	at one o'clock
às treze horas	at one p.m.
a porta do carro	the car door
A caneta da aluna está aqui.	The (female) student's pen is here.
Ele é dos Estados Unidos.	He is from the United States.
Moro no Recife.	I live in Recife.
O gato fugiu pela janela.	The cat escaped through the window.

Contractions can optionally occur with the **indefinite article** too:

de + um = dum	*de + uma = duma*	of / from a
em + um = num	*em + uma = numa*	in / on a

Eu encontrei o livro duma aluna. or	I found the book belonging to one of the
Eu encontrei o livro de uma aluna.	(female) students.
Eu moro num bairro novo. or	I live in a new area of town.
Eu moro em um bairro novo.	

Particularly in speech, contractions can also occur with a number of other words starting with a vowel. This includes personal pronouns, demonstratives and some adverbs.

With **personal pronouns**

de + ele = dele	*de + ela = dela*	his, her(s), its
em + ele = nele	*em + ela = nela*	in / on him, her, it

O carro dele é grande.	His car is big.
Tenho confiança nele.	I trust him.

With **demonstratives**
(referring to something or someone near you and / or near the person or people you are talking to)

de + esse = desse	*de + essa = dessa*	of / from that / this (one)
de + isso = disso		of / from that / this (thing)
em + esse = nesse	*em + essa = nessa*	in / on that / this (one)
em + isso = nisso		in / on that / this (thing)
de + este = deste	*de + esta = desta*	of / from this (one)
de + isto = disto		of / from this (thing)
em + este = neste	*em + esta = nesta*	in / on this (one)
em + isto = nisto		in / on this (thing)

Ele comeu quase metade desses bolinhos.	He has eaten nearly half of these cakes.
Não gosto disso.	I don't like that.
Nunca você pensou nisto?	Have you never thought about this?

PORTUGUESE GRAMMAR GUIDE

PREPOSITIONS

(referring to something or someone at a distance from both you and the person or people you are talking to)

a + aquele = àquele	*a + aquela = àquela*	to / at / on that (one)
a + aquilo = àquilo		to / at / on that (thing)
de + aquele = daquele	*de + aquela = daquela*	of / from that (one)
de + aquilo = daquilo		of / from that (thing)
em + aquele = naquele	*em + aquela = naquela*	in / on that (one)
em + aquilo = naquilo		in / on that (thing)

Ela foi àquela festa vestida de fada.	She went to that party dressed as a fairy.
As casas daquelas pessoas são bastante grandes.	Those people's houses are quite big.
Você só pensa naquilo.	That's the only thing you ever think about.

With **adverbs** of place and time:

de + aqui = daqui	from here
de + aí = daí	from there / here
de + ali = dali	from there

Perto dali, estavam dois carros.	Nearby (near that place) there were two cars.
Daí a um mês ele voltou.	A month later he came back.

See **Personal pronouns**, pages 104–107, **Demonstrative Pronouns**, pages 112–113, and **Adverbs**, pages 113–114.

Specific cases relating to frequently-used prepositions

There are many subtleties of meaning in the ways prepositions link words together in a language and there are often variations in usage among native speakers from different areas. On top of this, there are differences in how speakers of different languages see connections between words. All this makes prepositions especially prone to mismatches across different languages. For this reason, key distinctions are made below for Portuguese prepositions in relation to English ones. Alternatives are also shown for European usage (Eur), both spoken and written, and for Brazilian usage, spoken (Coll Br) and written (Wr Br), the latter also covering formal speech.

Main roles for *de*

de translates English *from*, in the context of origin or point of departure:

Eles são de Portugal.	They are from Portugal.
Acabei de chegar do Brasil.	I have just arrived from Brazil.

de is used for possession and generally translates English 's and s':

A mala da senhora é aquela preta ali.	The lady's suitcase (suitcase + of + the lady) is the black one over there.
João é o amigo dos rapazes.	John is the boys' friend. (friend + of + the boys).

de is used in noun compounds and similar constructions where a noun is qualified by a word other than an adjective:

Aquela é a minha bagagem de mão.	That over there is my hand luggage (luggage + of + hand).
Eu queria um saco de dormir.	I would like a sleeping bag (bag + of + to sleep).

Different uses of **por** and **para** when translating *for*:

Choose **por** when denoting cause and **para** for direction, purpose or goal:

Ele foi recompensado pelo seu trabalho.	*He was rewarded for his work.*
O Algarve é famoso pelas sua praias.	*The Algarve is famous for its beaches.*
Eu vou estudar para o exame.	*I am going to study for the exam.*
Eu trouxe isso para você.	*I have brought this for you.*

Different uses of **a** and **em** with days and dates:

For isolated events: **em** or nothing (Eur) (Wr Br) (Coll Br)
For habitual events: **a** (Eur) (Wr Br); **em** (Coll Br)

Eu vou lá na quarta-feira. Eu vou lá quarta-feira. (Eur) (Wr Br) (Coll Br)	*I am going there (on) Wednesday.*
Eu tenho aula de Inglês às quartas-feiras. (Eur) (Wr Br)	*I have an English class on Wednesdays.*
Eu tenho aula de Inglês nas quartas-feiras. (Coll Br)	*I have an English class on Wednesdays.*

37. Conjunctions

Generally, Portuguese and English conjunctions are used in much the same way. However, there are some differences to note.

Coordinating conjunctions

As in English, Portuguese coordinating conjunctions join together clauses or groups of words that have a similar status. To talk about alternatives, however, there are two cases in which Portuguese repeats the same connective words whereas English uses different words:

Ou... ou...	*Either... or...*
Nem... nem...	*Neither... nor...*
Ou vocês estudam ou vocês não serão aprovados.	*Either you study or you won't pass your exam.*
Nem ele nem ela vai conseguir isso.	*Neither he nor she is going to get that.*

Subordinating conjunctions

As in English, Portuguese subordinating conjunctions link main and subordinate clauses together.

Conjunctions introducing subordinate clauses

se, *if* or *whether*

Sairei se não chover.	*I'll go out if it doesn't rain.*
Não sei se choverá ou não.	*I don't know whether it will rain or not.*

que, *that* (but often omitted in English)

Eu disse que sim.	*I said yes.*
Você disse que não.	*You said no.*
Soubemos que ia chover.	*We knew (that) it was going to rain.*
Ninguém sabe que o carro foi vendido.	*No one knows (that) the car has been sold.*

The verb in the subordinate clause

After some conjunctions the subjunctive may be needed in the subordinate clause, depending on the time reference and the type of statement involved. This is the case, for instance, with *quando*, *when*, and *que*, *that*:

> **Geralmente faço o café quando eles chegam.** *Usually I make coffee when they arrive.*
> Subordinate clause: present indicative (regular action)
> **Vou fazer o café quando eles chegarem.** *I'll make coffee when they arrive.* (action in
> Subordinate clause: future subjunctive the future)

Some conjunctions are always followed by a subjunctive in the subordinate clause. This is the case, for example, with conjunctions of concession, condition and purpose:

> **Geralmente como isso embora não goste** *Usually I eat that although I don't like it much.*
> **muito.** (concession)
> Subordinate clause: present subjunctive
> **Falei com eles para que tudo se fizesse.** *I talked to them so as to be sure that it would*
> Subordinate clause: imperfect subjunctive *all get done.* (purpose)

See **Use of tenses**, pages 83–85, and **The subjunctive: when to use it**, pages 85–86.

38. Word order

In Portuguese, as in English, the usual order in a declarative sentence is subject + verb + complement (where there is one):

> **Nós somos amigos.** *We're friends.*
> **Eu bebi o chá.** *I've drunk my tea.*
> **Ela riu.** *She laughed.*

Although a subject generally precedes the verb, in Portuguese the subject pronoun (or other subject marker) can be omitted if it is clear from the context or verb form:

> **Somos amigos.** *We're friends.*
> **Bebi o chá.** *I've drunk my tea.*

Inversion occurs:

– with verbs that do not take subjects:

> **Há lojas perto daqui.** *There are shops nearby.*

– when the sentence begins with an adverb:

> **Aqui estão os livros.** *Here are the books.*

– in sentences with the **se** construction:

> **Vendem-se carros aqui.** *Cars are sold here.*

Adjectives

Descriptive adjectives generally follow their nouns:

> **O lápis preto está em cima da mesa.** *The black pencil is on the table.*

Some adjectives have different meanings depending on whether they go before or after the noun:

> **É um simples exercício.** *It is a mere exercise.*
> **É um exercício simples.** *It is an easy exercise.*

Ele é um homem grande.	*He is a big man.*
Ele é um grande homem.	*He is a great man.*

Modifiers such as indefinites, possessives, demonstratives, numerals, etc generally precede their nouns:

Ela preferiu outro vestido.	*She liked another dress better.*
O seu chapéu é bonito.	*Your hat is pretty.*
Aquele livro é bom.	*That book is good.*
A menina tem dois gatos.	*The little girl has two cats.*

Object pronouns

In a simple declarative sentence, the object pronoun goes before the verb in Brazil, particularly in spoken language, and goes after it in Portugal (linked with a hyphen):

Ele ajudou-nos. (Eur) (Wr Br)	*He helped us.*
Ele nos ajudou. (Coll Br)	
Eles cumprimentaram-me. (Eur) (Wr Br)	*They greeted me.*
Eles me cumprimentaram. (Coll Br)	

In other situations, the object pronoun goes before the verb in both Brazil and Portugal. This includes negative and interrogative sentences as well as subordinate clauses:

Ele não nos ajudou.	*He didn't help us.*
Quando é que você me viu?	*When did you see me?*
Eu vi o homem que te telefonou ontem.	*I have seen the man who phoned you yesterday.*

See also **Personal pronouns**, pages 104–107.

Reflexive pronouns

Word order with reflexive pronouns is dealt with under **Reflexive verbs**, page 76.

Negative sentences

For word order in negative sentences, see **Negatives**, pages 119–120.

Interrogative sentences

For word order in interrogative sentences, see **Question forms**, pages 120–121.

39. Negatives

Saying *not* and *no*

Unlike in English, a Portuguese sentence can be made negative just by placing the word *não*, *not*, before the verb. No auxiliary verb is required:

Aquele carro não é novo.	*That car is not new.*
Eu não trabalho aqui.	*I don't work here.*
Eles não querem falar.	*They don't want to talk / won't talk.*

If there is an object pronoun, this will come between *não* and the verb:

Ela não me telefonou.	*She hasn't phoned me.*
Eles não nos deram a notícia.	*They haven't told us the news.*

In addition to translating *not*, *não* also translates *no* as opposed to *yes*:

Sim!	*Yes!*
Não!	*No!*

For yes/no replies, see **Question forms**, pages 120–121.

Other negatives

Other important negatives are:

the coordinating conjunctions *nem... nem....*

Nem ele nem ela trabalha aqui.	*Neither he nor she works here.*

adverbs *nunca* and *nunca mais*

Eu nunca fui lá.	*I have never been there.*
Ele nunca mais trabalhou aqui.	*He has never worked here again.*

indefinite pronouns *nada*, *ninguém*, *nenhum* (*nenhuma*, *nenhuns*, *nenhumas*)

Nada a declarar.	*Nothing to declare.*
Ninguém vem aqui.	*No one comes here.*
Nenhum deles chegou atrasado.	*None of them arrived late.*

40. Question forms

Questions for yes/no replies

Unlike English, in Portuguese there is no subject-verb inversion or auxiliary required. Simply turn a statement into a question by using a rising intonation at the end of the sentence. The normal word order is generally followed and the question is indicated only by the intonation of the voice:

O jantar foi bom?	*Was dinner good?*
Você vai para a praia?	*Are you going to the beach?*
Eles já chegaram?	*Have they arrived yet?*
Você fala Português?	*Do you speak Portuguese?*

For the answer:

You can reply with *Sim*, *Yes*, or *Não*, *No*. However, particularly in affirmative replies, native speakers tend to repeat elements from the question while changing the verb ending as required:

O jantar foi bom?	*Was dinner good?*
Não, não foi.	*No, it wasn't.*
Você fala Português.	*Do you speak Portuguese?*
Falo, sim.	*Yes, I do.*

Questions beginning with an interrogative word

Except for *Como...?*, *How...?* and *Quanto...?*, *How much ...?*, Portuguese question words usually have a *Wh-* word counterpart in English:

Que rua é esta?	*What street is this?*
Quem veio aqui ontem?	*Who came here yesterday?*
De quem é aquele passaporte?	*Whose passport is that?*
Onde estão as chaves?	*Where are the keys?*
Quanto tempo vai demorar?	*How long is it going to take?*
Como se diz isso em Português?	*How do you say that in Portuguese?*

See also **Interrogative adjectives**, page 102, and **Interrogative pronouns**, page 111.

When a subject word is present, inversion may or may not occur without there being any change in meaning, regardless of which side of the Atlantic you are on:

Que livro você comprou? or **What book did you buy?**
Que livro comprou você?

However, if the expression **é que** is used, word order follows a subject + verb sequence:

Que livro é que você comprou? **What book did you buy?**

A special question word in Brazil is **Cadê...?** or **Quedê...?**. It derives from the expression **Que é feito de...?** (What has become of ...?) and is used meaning Where is...?:

Cadê o teu irmão? (Coll Br) **Where's your brother?**
Que é feito do teu irmão? (Eur) (Wr Br) **What has become of your brother?**

Tag questions

To make a tag question, you can leave the sentence as it is and simply repeat the verb at the end:

Ele comprou um computador novo, não **He's bought a new computer, hasn't he?**
comprou?

However, a more widely heard alternative is the use of a phrase like **não?**, **não é?**, **não é verdade?** at the end:

Ele comprou um computador novo, não é? **He's bought a new computer, hasn't he?**

41. Cardinal and ordinal numbers

Cardinal (one, two, etc)		Ordinal (first, second, etc)	
zero	0		
um	1	primeiro	1º
dois	2	segundo	2º
três	3	terceiro	3º
quatro	4	quarto	4º
cinco	5	quinto	5º
seis	6	sexto	6º
sete	7	sétimo	7º
oito	8	oitavo	8º
nove	9	nono	9º
dez	10	décimo	10º
onze	11	décimo primeiro	11º
doze	12	décimo segundo	12º
treze	13	décimo terceiro	13º
quatorze	14	décimo quarto	14º
quinze	15	décimo quinto	15º
dezasseis (Eur), dezesseis (Br)	16	décimo sexto	16º
dezassete (Eur), dezessete (Br)	17	décimo sétimo	17º
dezoito	18	décimo oitavo	18º
dezanove (Eur), dezenove (Br)	19	décimo nono	19º
vinte	20	vigésimo	20º

vinte e um	21	vigésimo primeiro	21°
trinta	30	trigésimo	30°
quarenta	40	quadragésimo	40°
cinquenta	50	quinquagésimo	50°
sessenta	60	sexagésimo	60°
setenta	70	septuagésimo (Eur), setuagésimo (Br)	70°
oitenta	80	octogésimo	80°
noventa	90	nonagésimo	90°
cem	100	centésimo	100°
cento e um	101	centésimo primeiro	101°
duzentos	200	ducentésimo	200°
trezentos	300	trecentésimo	300°
quatrocentos	400	quadringentésimo	400°
quinhentos	500	quingentésimo	500°
seiscentos	600	seiscentésimo	600°
setecentos	700	septingentésimo	700°
oitocentos	800	octingentésimo	800°
novecentos	900	nongentésimo	900°
mil	1,000	milésimo	1,000°
um milhão	1,000,000	milionésimo	1,000,000°

Differences in relation to English

In Portuguese no number or indefinite article precedes the words for 100 or 1,000:

cem carros	one/a hundred cars
mil carros	one/a thousand cars

In Portuguese, the word for 100 (cem) changes form before lower numbers:

cento e dez carros	one hundred and ten cars

Unlike in English, there is a preposition de after the word for million(s):

um milhão de carros	one million cars

Ordinal numbers are often substituted by cardinal numbers, particularly in speech:

O vigésimo carro or O carro número vinte	the twentieth car

Note that hundreds, tens and units are linked together using e (and) but a comma is used for thousands and millions when followed by more than two lower numbers:

vinte e um	twenty-one
cento e vinte e dois	one hundred and twenty-two
mil, cento e vinte e três	one thousand, one hundred and twenty-three
um milhão, cento e vinte e quatro	one million, one hundred and twenty-four

In Portuguese, commas and dots are used in the opposite way to English, since commas are used to show decimal places while the role of dots is to separate out larger numbers (thousands, millions, etc):

zero vírgula cinco	0,5	zero point five	0.5
cinco vírgula dois	5,2	five point two	5.2
mil	1.000	one thousand	1,000
um milhão	1.000.000	one million	1,000,000

Gender and number in numerals

There are masculine and feminine forms for cardinals 1 and 2:

| um carro e uma bicicleta | one car and one bicycle |
| dois carros e duas bicicletas | two cars and two bicycles |

There are masculine and feminine forms for the multiples of 100 (which are expressed in the plural):

| duzentos carros | two hundred cars |
| duzentas bicicletas | two hundred bicycles |

There are masculine and feminine forms for the ordinals:

o primeiro carro	the first car
a segunda bicicleta	the second bicycle
o décimo terceiro carro	the thirteenth car
a vigésima quarta bicicleta	the twenty-fourth bicycle

Fractions

um meio	½	a half	três quartos	¾	three quarters
um terço	⅓	a third	seis e meio	6½	six and a half
um quarto	¼	a quarter			

Other

quatro vírgula cinco (4,5)	4.5
vinte por cento	20%
dois mais dois	2 + 2
seis menos quatro	6 - 4
três vezes três	3×3
oito a dividir por dois	8 ÷ 2

Weight, quantity and measurement

um quilo de laranjas	a kilo of oranges
meio quilo de bananas	half a kilo of bananas
uma dúzia de maçãs	a dozen apples
meia dúzia de ovos	half a dozen eggs
uma dezena de carros	around ten cars
centenas de pessoas	hundreds of people
vinte centímetros	twenty centimetres
meio metro	half a metre
dez quilómetros (Eur), quilômetros (Br)	ten kilometres

Phone numbers

When saying phone numbers, digits tend to be grouped in twos for clarity, and, in Brazil, the word *meia* (from *meia dúzia*, half a dozen) is usually used instead of *seis* for 6: 246 3718 *dois, quarto, seis/meia, trinta e sete, dezoito*.

Miscellaneous

Ele mora no número quinze.	He lives at number 15.
Ela mora no apartamento 7.	She lives in flat 7.
Eles moram no terceiro andar.	They live on the third floor.
Hoje estão trinta graus centígrados.	It's 30° C today.
É na página cento e noventa.	It's on page 190.
É no capítulo três or capítulo terceiro.	It's in chapter 3.

For time, days of the week and months see **Calendar and time**, pages 124–125.

42. Calendar and time

Week

Except for Saturday (*sábado*) and Sunday (*domingo*), in Portuguese the days of the week are expressed using ordinal numbers plus the word *feira*, which in speech is often omitted.

segunda-feira or *segunda*	Monday
terça-feira or *terça*	Tuesday
quarta-feira or *quarta*	Wednesday
quinta-feira or *quinta*	Thursday
sexta-feira or *sexta*	Friday

(For *Tuesday*, **terça** is a shortened form of the ordinal number **terceira**.)

Que dia da semana é hoje?	What day of the week is it today?
É quarta.	It's Wednesday.
Que dia da semana foi ontem?	What day of the week was it yesterday?
Foi terça.	It was Tuesday.

Dates

While English uses ordinal numbers for the days of the month, Portuguese uses cardinals. There is one exception, however; the ordinal number **primeiro** can be used for the first day of the month, though this usage is more common in Brazil than in Portugal:

quinze de setembro	15th of September
o primeiro de janeiro	first of January

While the verb used to talk about dates in English is always in the singular, in Portuguese the verb becomes plural to agree with a plural number in the date:

Que data é hoje? or *Que dia é hoje?*	What's the date today?
São quinze de setembro.	It is the fifteenth of September.

Unlike in English, years are not expressed in hundreds:

dois mil e doze	twenty twelve (2012)

Week and date

Hoje é quinta, dia vinte de setembro de dois mil e doze.	Today it is Thursday, the 20th of September, 2012.

Time

While English always uses the singular form of the verb to talk about time, in Portuguese a plural form is used if the plural noun *horas* is expressed or understood:

Que horas são?	*What time is it?*
São seis horas.	*It is six o'clock.*
É uma hora.	*It is one o'clock.*
É meio dia.	*It is midday.*
É meia-noite.	*It is midnight.*

Time past and to the hour is expressed differently from in English. Minutes are used on both sides of the Atlantic, but, in Portugal, *quarto* (*quarter*) and *meia* (*half*) are also widely used:

É uma e dez.	*It is one ten (ten past one).*
São dez para as duas.	*It is ten to two.*
É uma e quinze. or *É uma e um quarto.*	*It is one fifteen. / It is a quarter past one.*
São seis e trinta. or *São seis e meia.*	*It is six thirty. / It is half past six.*
São quinze para as oito. or	*It is fifteen minutes to eight. /*
É um quarto para as oito.	*It is a quarter to eight.*

Where English uses *a.m.* and *p.m.*, Portuguese adds a time phrase:

sete da manhã (in the morning)	*seven a.m.*
uma da tarde (in the afternoon)	*one p.m.*
dez da noite (in the evening)	*ten p.m.*
três da madrugada (in the early hours of the morning)	*three a.m.*

The 24-hour clock is also frequently used:

A loja fecha às treze horas.	*The shop closes at 13.00.*
A loja fecha à uma da tarde.	*The shop closes at 1 p.m.*
O concerto começa às vinte e duas horas.	*The concert begins at 22.00.*
O concerto começa às dez da noite.	*The concert begins at 10 p.m.*

Calendar and time expressions

no século vinte	*in the twentieth century*
nos anos noventa	*in the nineties*
há dois anos or *dois anos atrás*	*two years ago*
dentro de dois anos	*in two years' time*
há duas horas or *duas horas atrás*	*two hours ago*
dentro de duas horas	*in two hours' time*
São cinco horas em ponto.	*It is five o'clock on the dot.*

See also **Cardinal and ordinal numbers**, pages 121–122, **Formation of plurals**, page 100.

Index

Please note the numbers in the index refer to section numbers, not page numbers.

PORTUGUESE GRAMMAR GUIDE

INDEX

PORTUGUESE GRAMMAR GUIDE

Português – Inglês
Portuguese – English

Aa

A, a [a] (*pl* **as**) M A, a; **A de Antônio** A for Andrew (*BRIT*) *ou* Able (*US*)

(PALAVRA-CHAVE)

a [a] ART DEF the; *ver tb* **o**
▶ PRON (*ela*) her; (*você*) you; (*coisa*) it; *ver tb* **o**
▶ PREP (*a* + *o(s)* = *ao(s)*; *a* + *a(s)* = *à(s)*; *a* + *aquele/a(s)* = *àquele/a(s)*) **1** (*direção*) to; **à direita/ esquerda** to *ou* on the right/left
2 (*distância*): **está a 15 km daqui** it's 15 km from here
3 (*posição*): **ao lado de** beside, at the side of
4 (*tempo*) at; **a que horas?** at what time?; **às 5 horas** at 5 o'clock; **à noite** at night; **aos 15 anos** at 15 years of age
5 (*maneira*): **à francesa** in the French way; **a cavalo/pé** on horseback/foot
6 (*meio, instrumento*): **à força** by force; **a mão** by hand; **a lápis** in pencil; **fogão a gás** gas stove
7 (*razão*): **a R$10 o quilo** at R$10 a kilo; **a mais de 100 km/h** at over 100 km/h
8 (*depois de certos verbos*): **começou a nevar** it started snowing *ou* to snow; **passar a fazer** to become
9 (+ *infin*): **ao vê-lo, reconheci-o imediatamente** when I saw him, I recognized him immediately; **ele ficou muito nervoso ao falar com o professor** he became very nervous while he was talking to the teacher
10 (*PT*: + *infin, gerúndio*): **a correr** running; **estou a trabalhar** I'm working

à [a] = **a** + **a**; *ver* **a**
(a) ABR (= *assinado*) signed
AAB ABR F (= *Aliança Anticomunista Brasileira*) terrorist group
aba ['aba] F (*de chapéu*) brim; (*de casaco*) tail; (*de montanha*) foot
abacate [aba'katʃi] M avocado (pear)
abacaxi [abaka'ʃi] (*BR*) M pineapple; (*col: problema*) problem
abade, ssa [a'badʒi, aba'desa] M/F abbot/abbess
Abadi [aba'dʒi] ABR F = **Associação Brasileira das Administradoras de Imóveis**
abadia [aba'dʒia] F abbey
abafadiço, -a [abafa'dʒisu, a] ADJ stifling; (*ar*) stuffy

abafado, -a [aba'fadu, a] ADJ (*ar*) stuffy; (*tempo*) humid, close; (*ocupado*) (extremely) busy; (*angustiado*) anxious
abafamento [abafa'mẽtu] M fug; (*sufocação*) suffocation
abafar [aba'far] VT to suffocate; (*ocultar*) to suppress; (*som*) to muffle; (*encobrir*) to cover up; (*col*) to pinch ▶ VI (*col: fazer sucesso*) to steal the show
abagunçado, -a [abagũ'sadu, a] ADJ messy
abagunçar [abagũ'sar] VT to make a mess of, mess up
abaixar [abaj'ʃar] VT to lower; (*luz, som*) to turn down; **abaixar-se** VR to stoop
abaixo [a'bajʃu] ADV down ▶ PREP: **~ de** below; **~ o governo!** down with the government!; **morro ~** downhill; **rio ~** downstream; **mais ~** further down; **~ e acima** up and down; **~ assinado** undersigned
abaixo-assinado [-asi'nadu] (*pl* **-s**) M (*documento*) petition
abajur [aba'ʒur] (*BR*) M (*cúpula*) lampshade; (*luminária*) table lamp
abalado, -a [aba'ladu, a] ADJ unstable, unsteady; (*fig*) shaken
abalar [aba'lar] VT to shake; (*fig: comover*) to affect ▶ VI to shake; **abalar-se** VR to be moved
abalizado, -a [abali'zadu, a] ADJ eminent, distinguished; (*opinião*) reliable
abalo [a'balu] M (*comoção*) shock; (*ação*) shaking; **~ sísmico** earth tremor
abalroar [abawro'ar] VT: **o carro foi abalroado pelo caminhão** the car was hit by the lorry
abanar [aba'nar] VT to shake; (*rabo*) to wag; (*com leque*) to fan
abandalhar [abãda'ʎar] VT to debase
abandonar [abãdo'nar] VT (*deixar*) to leave; (*ideia*) to reject; (*estudos*) to abandon; (*esperança*) to give up; (*descuidar*) to neglect; **abandonar-se** VR: **~-se a** to abandon o.s. to
abandono [abã'donu] M (*ato*) desertion; (*estado*) neglect
abarcar [abar'kar] VT (*abranger*) to comprise; (*conter*) to enclose
abarrotado, -a [abaho'tadu, a] ADJ (*gaveta*) crammed full; (*lugar*) packed

abarrotar [abaho'tar] VT: ~ **de** to cram with

abastado, -a [abas'tadu, a] ADJ wealthy

abastança [abas'tãsa] F abundance, surfeit

abastardar [abastar'dar] VT to corrupt

abastecer [abaste'ser] VT to supply; *(motor)* to fuel; *(Auto)* to fill up; *(Aer)* to refuel; **abastecer-se** VR: ~-**se de** to stock up with

abastecimento [abastesi'mētu] M supply; *(comestíveis)* provisions pl; *(ato)* supplying; *(de avião)* refuelling *(BRIT)*, refueling *(US)*; **abastecimentos** MPL *(suprimentos)* supplies

abater [aba'ter] VT *(gado)* to slaughter; *(preço)* to reduce, lower; *(debilitar)* to weaken; *(desalentar)* to upset

abatido, -a [aba'tʃidu, a] ADJ depressed, downcast; *(fisionomia)* haggard

abatimento [abatʃi'mētu] M *(fraqueza)* weakness; *(de preço)* reduction; *(prostração)* depression; **fazer um ~ em** to give a discount on

abaulado, -a [abaw'ladu, a] ADJ convex; *(estrada)* cambered

abaular-se [abaw'larsi] VR to bulge

ABBC ABR F = **Associação Brasileira dos Bancos Comerciais**

ABBR ABR F (= *Associação Brasileira Beneficente de Reabilitação*) charity for the disabled

abcesso [ab'sɛsu] M = **abscesso**

abdicação [abdʒika'sãw] *(pl -ões)* F abdication

abdicar [abdʒi'kar] VT, VI to abdicate

abdômen [ab'domẽ] M abdomen

á-bê-cê [abe'se] M alphabet; *(fig)* rudiments pl

abecedário [abese'darju] M alphabet, ABC

Abeenras ABR F = **Associação Brasileira das Empresas de Engenharia, Reparos e Atividades Subaquáticas**

abeirar [abej'rar] VT to bring near; **abeirar-se** VR: ~-**se de** to draw near to

abelha [a'beʎa] F bee

abelha-mestra *(pl abelhas-mestras)* F queen bee

abelhudo, -a [abe'ʎudu, a] ADJ nosy

abençoar [abẽ'swar] VT to bless

abendiçoar [abẽdʒi'swar] VT to bless

aberração [abeha'sãw] *(pl -ões)* F aberration

aberta [a'bɛrta] F opening; *(clareira)* clearing; *(intervalo)* break

aberto, -a [a'bɛrtu, a] PP *de* **abrir** ▶ ADJ open; *(céu)* clear; *(sinal)* green; *(torneira)* on; *(desprotegido)* exposed; *(liberal)* open-minded

abertura [aber'tura] F opening; *(Foto)* aperture; *(ranhura)* gap, crevice; *(Pol)* liberalization

abestalhado, -a [abesta'ʎadu, a] ADJ stupid

ABH ABR F = **Associação Brasileira da Indústria de Hotéis**

ABI ABR F = **Associação Brasileira de Imprensa**

Abifarma ABR F = **Associação Brasileira da Indústria Farmacêutica**

abilolado, -a [abilo'ladu, a] ADJ crazy

abismado, -a [abiz'madu, a] ADJ astonished

abismo [a'bizmu] M abyss, chasm; *(fig)* depths pl

abjeção [abʒe'sãw] F baseness

abjeto, -a [ab'ʒɛtu, a] ADJ abject, contemptible

abjudicar [abʒudʒi'kar] VT to seize

ABL ABR F = **Academia Brasileira de Letras**

ABMU ABR F = **Associação Brasileira de Mulheres Universitárias**

abnegação [abnega'sãw] F self-denial

abnegado, -a [abne'gadu, a] ADJ self-sacrificing

abnegar [abne'gar] VT to renounce

abóbada [a'bɔbada] F vault; *(telhado)* arched roof

abobalhado, -a [aboba'ʎadu, a] ADJ *(criança)* simple

abóbora [a'bɔbora] F pumpkin

abobrinha [abo'briɲa] F courgette *(BRIT)*, zucchini *(US)*

abocanhar [aboka'ɲar] VT *(apanhar com a boca)* to seize with the mouth; *(morder)* to bite

abolição [aboli'sãw] F abolition

abolir [abo'lir] VT to abolish

abominação [abomina'sãw] *(pl -ões)* F abomination

abominar [abomi'nar] VT to loathe, detest

abominável [abomi'navew] *(pl -eis)* ADJ abominable

abonar [abo'nar] VT to guarantee

abono [a'bonu] M guarantee; *(Jur)* bail; *(louvor)* praise; ~ **de família** child benefit

abordagem [abor'daʒẽ] *(pl -ns)* F approach

abordar [abor'dar] VT *(Náut)* to board; *(pessoa)* to approach; *(assunto)* to broach, tackle

aborígene [abo'riʒeni] ADJ aboriginal ▶ M/F aborigine

aborrecer [abohe'ser] VT *(chatear)* to annoy; *(maçar)* to bore; **aborrecer-se** VR to get upset; to get bored

aborrecido, -a [abohe'sidu, a] ADJ boring; *(chateado)* annoyed

aborrecimento [abohesi'mētu] M boredom; *(chateação)* annoyance

abortar [abor'tar] VI *(Med)* to have a miscarriage; (: *de propósito*) to have an abortion ▶ VT to abort

aborto [a'bortu] M *(Med)* miscarriage; (: *forçado*) abortion; **fazer/ter um ~** to have an abortion/a miscarriage

abotoadura [abotwa'dura] F cufflink

abotoar [abo'twar] VT to button up ▶ VI *(Bot)* to bud

abr. ABR (= *abril*) Apr.

abraçar [abra'sar] VT to hug; *(causa)* to embrace; **abraçar-se** VR to embrace; **ele abraçou-se a mim** he embraced me

abraço [a'brasu] M embrace, hug; **com um ~** *(em carta)* with best wishes

abrandar [abrã'dar] VT to reduce; *(suavizar)* to soften ▶ VI to diminish; *(acalmar)* to calm down

abranger [abrã'ʒer] VT *(assunto)* to cover; *(alcançar)* to reach

abranjo *etc* [a'brãʒu] VB *ver* **abranger**

abrasar [abra'zar] VT to burn; *(desbastar)* to erode ▶ VI to be on fire

abrasileirado, -a [abrazilej'radu, a] ADJ Brazilianized

ABRATES ABR F = **Associação Brasileira de Tradutores**

ABRATT ABR F = **Associação Brasileira dos Transportadores Exclusivos de Turismo**

abre-garrafas ['abri-] (PT) M INV bottle opener

abre-latas ['abri-] (PT) M INV tin (BRIT) *ou* can opener

abreugrafia [abrewgra'fia] F X-ray

abreviação [abrevja'sãw] *(pl* **-ões***)* F abbreviation; *(de texto)* abridgement

abreviar [abre'vjar] VT to abbreviate; *(encurtar)* to shorten; *(texto)* to abridge

abreviatura [abrevja'tura] F abbreviation

abridor [abri'dor] (BR) M opener; **~ (de lata)** tin (BRIT) *ou* can opener; **~ de garrafa** bottle opener

abrigar [abri'gar] VT to shelter; *(proteger)* to protect; **abrigar-se** VR to take shelter

abrigo [a'brigu] M shelter, cover; **~ antiaéreo** air-raid shelter; **~ antinuclear** fall-out shelter

abril [a'briw] M April; *ver tb* **julho**

On 25 April (**25 de abril**) 1974 in Portugal, the MAF (Armed Forces Movement) instigated the bloodless revolution that was to topple the 48-year-old dictatorship presided over until 1968 by António de Oliveira Salazar. The red carnation has come to symbolize the coup, as it is said that the Armed Forces took to the streets with carnations in the barrels of their rifles. 25 April is now a public holiday in Portugal.

abrilhantar [abriʎã'tar] VT to enhance

abrir [a'brir] VT to open; *(fechadura)* to unlock; *(vestuário)* to unfasten; *(torneira)* to turn on; *(buraco, exceção)* to make; *(processo)* to start ▶ VI to open; *(sinal)* to go green; *(tempo)* to clear up; **abrir-se** VR: **~-se com alguém** to confide in sb, open up to sb

ab-rogação [abhoga'sãw] *(pl* **-ões***)* F repeal, annulment

ab-rogar [abho'gar] VT to repeal, annul

abrolho [a'broʎu] M thorn

abrupto, -a [a'bruptu, a] ADJ abrupt; *(repentino)* sudden

abrutalhado, -a [abruta'ʎadu, a] ADJ *(pessoa)* coarse; *(sapatos)* heavy

abscesso [ab'sɛsu] M abscess

absenteísta [absẽte'ista] M/F absentee

absentismo [absẽ'tʃizmu] M absenteeism

abside [ab'sidʒi] F apse; *(relicário)* shrine

absolutamente [absoluta'mẽtʃi] ADV absolutely; *(em resposta)* absolutely not, not at all

absolutismo [absolu'tʃizmu] M absolutism

absolutista [absolu'tʃista] ADJ, M/F absolutist

absoluto, -a [abso'lutu, a] ADJ absolute; **em ~** absolutely not, not at all

absolver [absow'ver] VT to absolve; *(Jur)* to acquit

absolvição [absowvi'sãw] *(pl* **-ões***)* F absolution; *(Jur)* acquittal

absorção [absor'sãw] F absorption

absorto, -a [ab'sortu, a] PP *de* **absorver** ▶ ADJ absorbed, engrossed

absorvente [absor'vẽtʃi] ADJ *(papel etc)* absorbent; *(livro etc)* absorbing

absorver [absor'ver] VT to absorb; **absorver-se** em to concentrate on

abstêmio, -a [abs'temju, a] ADJ abstemious; *(álcool)* teetotal ▶ M/F abstainer; teetotaller (BRIT), teetotaler (US)

abstenção [abstẽ'sãw] *(pl* **-ões***)* F abstention

abstencionista [abstẽsjo'nista] ADJ abstaining ▶ M/F abstainer

abstenções [abstẽ'sõjs] FPL *de* **abstenção**

abster-se [abs'tersi] *(irreg: como* **ter***)* VR: **~ de** to abstain *ou* refrain from

abstinência [abstʃi'nẽsja] F abstinence; *(jejum)* fasting

abstinha *etc* [abs'tʃiɲa] VB *ver* **abster-se**

abstive *etc* [abs'tʃivi] VB *ver* **abster-se**

abstração [abstra'sãw] F abstraction; *(concentração)* concentration

abstrair [abstra'ir] VT to abstract; *(omitir)* to omit; *(separar)* to separate

abstrato, -a [abs'tratu, a] ADJ abstract

absurdo, -a [abi'surdu, a] ADJ absurd ▶ M nonsense

abulia [abu'lia] F apathy

abundância [abũ'dãsja] F abundance

abundante [abũ'dãtʃi] ADJ abundant

abundar [abũ'dar] VI to abound

aburguesado, -a [aburge'zadu, a] ADJ middle-class, bourgeois

abusar [abu'zar] VI *(exceder-se)* to go too far; **~ de** to abuse

abuso [a'buzu] M abuse; *(Jur)* indecent assault; **~ de confiança** breach of trust

abutre [a'butri] M vulture

AC ABR = **Acre**

a.C. ABR *(= antes de Cristo)* B.C.

a/c ABR *(= aos cuidados de)* Attn:

acabado, -a [aka'badu, a] ADJ finished; *(esgotado)* worn out; *(envelhecido)* aged

acabamento [akaba'mẽtu] M finish

acabar [aka'bar] VT *(terminar)* to finish, complete; *(levar a cabo)* to accomplish; *(aperfeiçoar)* to complete; *(consumir)* to use up; *(rematar)* to finish off ▶ VI to finish, end, come to an end; **acabar-se** VR *(terminar)* to be over; *(prazo)* to expire; *(esgotar-se)* to run out; **~ com** to put an end to; *(destruir)* to do away with; *(namorado)* to finish with; **~ de chegar** to have just arrived; **~ por fazer** to end up (by) doing; **acabou-se!** it's all over!; *(basta!)* that's enough!; **ele acabou cedendo** he eventually gave in, he ended up giving in; **... que não acaba mais** no end of ...; **quando acaba** *(no final)* in the end

acabrunhado, -a [akabru'ɲadu, a] ADJ (*abatido*) depressed; (*envergonhado*) embarrassed

acabrunhar [akabru'ɲar] VT (*entristecer*) to distress; (*envergonhar*) to embarrass

acácia [a'kasja] F acacia

academia [akade'mia] F academy; ~ **(de ginástica)** gym

Academia Brasileira de Letras *see note*

> Founded in 1896 in Rio de Janeiro, on the initiative of the author Machado de Assis, the **Academia Brasileira de Letras**, or ABL, aims to preserve and develop the Portuguese language and Brazilian literature. Machado de Assis was its president until 1908. It is made up of forty life members known as the *imortais*. The Academia's activities include publication of reference books, promotion of literary prizes, and running a library, museum and archive.

acadêmico, -a [aka'demiku, a] ADJ, M/F academic

açafrão [asa'frãw] M saffron

acalcanhar [akawka'ɲar] VT (*sapato*) to put out of shape

acalentar [akalẽ'tar] VT to rock to sleep; (*esperanças*) to cherish

acalmar [akaw'mar] VT to calm ▶ VI (*vento etc*) to abate; **acalmar-se** VR to calm down

acalorado, -a [akalo'radu, a] ADJ heated

acalorar [akalo'rar] VT to heat; (*fig*) to inflame; **acalorar-se** VR (*fig*) to get heated

acamado, -a [aka'madu, a] ADJ bedridden

açambarcar [asãbar'kar] VT to monopolize; (*mercado*) to corner

acampamento [akãpa'mẽtu] M camping; (*Mil*) camp, encampment; **levantar ~** to raise camp

acampar [akã'par] VI to camp

acanhado, -a [aka'ɲadu, a] ADJ shy

acanhamento [akaɲa'mẽtu] M shyness

acanhar-se [aka'ɲarsi] VR to be shy

ação [a'sãw] (*pl* **-ões**) F action; (*ato*) act, deed; (*Mil*) battle; (*enredo*) plot; (*Jur*) lawsuit; (*Com*) share; ~ **bonificada** (*Com*) bonus share; ~ **de graças** thanksgiving; ~ **integralizada/diferida** (*Com*) fully paid-in/deferred share; ~ **ordinária/preferencial** (*Com*) ordinary/preference share

acarajé [akara'ʒɛ] M (*Culin*) beans fried in palm oil

acareação [akarja'sãw] (*pl* **-ões**) F confrontation

acarear [aka'rjar] VT to confront

acariciar [akari'sjar] VT to caress; (*fig*) to cherish

acarinhar [akari'ɲar] VT to caress; (*fig*) to treat with tenderness

acarretar [akahe'tar] VT to result in, bring about

acasalamento [akazala'mẽtu] M mating

acasalar [akaza'lar] VT to mate; **acasalar-se** VR to mate

acaso [a'kazu] M chance; **ao ~** at random; **por ~** by chance

acastanhado, -a [akasta'ɲadu, a] ADJ brownish; (*cabelo*) auburn

acatamento [akata'mẽtu] M respect, deference; (*de lei*) observance

acatar [aka'tar] VT (*respeitar*) to respect; (*honrar*) to honour (BRIT), honor (US); (*lei*) to obey

acautelar [akawte'lar] VT to warn; **acautelar-se** VR to be cautious; **~-se contra** to guard against

ACC ABR M = **adiantamento de contratos de câmbio**

acebolado, -a [asebo'ladu, a] ADJ (*Culin*) flavoured (BRIT) ou flavored (US) with onion

aceder [ase'der] VI: **~ a** to agree to, accede to

aceitação [asejta'sãw] F acceptance; (*aprovação*) approval

aceitar [asej'tar] VT to accept; (*aprovar*) to approve; **você aceita uma bebida?** would you like a drink?

aceitável [asej'tavew] (*pl* **-eis**) ADJ acceptable

aceite [a'sejtə] (PT) PP *de* **aceitar** ▶ ADJ accepted ▶ M acceptance

aceito, -a [a'sejtu, a] PP *de* **aceitar** ▶ ADJ accepted

aceleração [aselera'sãw] F acceleration; (*pressa*) haste

acelerado, -a [asele'radu, a] ADJ (*rápido*) quick; (*apressado*) hasty

acelerador [aselera'dor] M accelerator

acelerar [asele'rar] VT, VI to accelerate; **~ o passo** to go faster

acenar [ase'nar] VI (*com a mão*) to wave; (*com a cabeça*) to nod; **~ com** (*oferecer*) to offer, promise

acendedor [asẽde'dor] M lighter

acender [asẽ'der] VT (*cigarro, fogo*) to light; (*luz*) to switch on; (*fig*) to excite, inflame

aceno [a'sɛnu] M sign, gesture; (*com a mão*) wave; (*com a cabeça*) nod

acento [a'sẽtu] M accent; (*de intensidade*) stress; **~ agudo/circunflexo** acute/circumflex accent

acentuação [asẽtwa'sãw] F accentuation; (*ênfase*) stress

acentuado, -a [asẽ'twadu, a] ADJ (*sílaba*) stressed; (*saliente*) conspicuous

acentuar [asẽ'twar] VT (*marcar com acento*) to accent; (*salientar*) to stress, emphasize; (*realçar*) to enhance

acepção [asep'sãw] (*pl* **-ões**) F (*de uma palavra*) sense

acepipe [ase'pipi] M titbit (BRIT), tidbit (US), delicacy; **acepipes** MPL (PT) hors d'œuvres

acerca [a'serka] ADV: **~ de** about, concerning

acercar-se [aser'karsi] VR: **~ de** to approach, draw near to

acérrimo, -a [a'sehimu, a] ADJ SUPERL *de* **acre**: (*acre*) (very) bitter; (*defensor*) staunch

acertado, -a [aser'tadu, a] ADJ (*certo*) right, correct; (*sensato*) sensible

acertar [aser'tar] VT (*ajustar*) to put right; (*relógio*) to set; (*alvo*) to hit; (*acordo*) to reach; (*pergunta*) to get right ▶ VI to get it right, be right; **~ o caminho** to find the right way; **~ com** to hit upon

acervo [a'servu] M heap; (*Jur*) estate; (*de museu etc*) collection; **um ~ de** vast quantities of

aceso, -a [a'sezu, a] PP *de* **acender** ▶ ADJ (*luz, gás, TV*) on; (*fogo*) alight; (*excitado*) excited; (*furioso*) furious

acessar [ase'sar] VT (*Comput*) to access

acessível [ase'sivew] (*pl* **-eis**) ADJ accessible; (*pessoa*) approachable; (*preço*) reasonable, affordable

acesso [a'sɛsu] M access; (*Med*) fit, attack; **um ~ de cólera** a fit of anger; **de fácil ~** easy to get to; **~ à Internet** (*Comput*) internet access

acessório, -a [ase'sɔrju, a] ADJ (*máquina, equipamento*) backup ▶ M accessory

ACET (BR) ABR F = **Agência Central dos Teatros**

acetona [ase'tɔna] F nail varnish remover; (*Quím*) acetone

achacar [aʃa'kar] (*col*) VT (*dinheiro*) to extort

achado [a'ʃadu] ADJ: **não se dar por ~** to play dumb ▶ M find, discovery; (*pechincha*) bargain; (*sorte*) godsend

achaque [a'ʃaki] M ailment

achar [a'ʃar] VT (*descobrir*) to find; (*pensar*) to think; **achar-se** VR (*considerar-se*) to think (that) one is; (*encontrar-se*) to be; **~ de fazer** (*resolver*) to decide to do; **o que é que você acha disso?** what do you think of it?; **acho que ...** I think (that) ...; **acho que sim** I think so; **~ algo bom/estranho** *etc* to find sth good/strange *etc*; **~ ruim** to be cross

achatar [aʃa'tar] VT to squash, flatten; (*fig*) to talk round, convince

achegar-se [aʃe'garsi] VR: **~ a** *ou* **de** to approach, get closer to

acidentado, -a [asidē'tadu, a] ADJ (*terreno*) rough; (*estrada*) bumpy; (*viagem*) eventful; (*vida*) difficult ▶ M/F injured person

acidental [asidē'taw] (*pl* **-ais**) ADJ accidental

acidente [asi'dētʃi] M accident; (*acaso*) chance; **por ~** by accident; **~ de trânsito** road accident

acidez [asi'dez] F acidity

ácido, -a ['asidu, a] ADJ acid; (*azedo*) sour ▶ M acid

acima [a'sima] ADV above; (*para cima*) up ▶ PREP: **~ de** above; (*além de*) beyond; **mais ~** higher up; **rio ~** up river; **passar rua ~** to go up the street; **~ de 1000** more than 1000

acinte [a'sītʃi] M provocation ▶ ADV deliberately, on purpose

acintosamente [asītoza'mētʃi] ADV on purpose

acinzentado, -a [asīzē'tadu, a] ADJ greyish (BRIT), grayish (US)

acionado, -a [asjo'nadu, a] M/F (*Jur*) defendant

acionar [asjo'nar] VT to set in motion; (*máquina*) to operate; (*Jur*) to sue

acionista [asjo'nista] M/F shareholder; **~ majoritário/minoritário** majority/minority shareholder

acirrado, -a [asi'hadu, a] ADJ (*luta, competição*) tough

acirrar [asi'har] VT to incite, stir up

aclamação [aklama'sāw] F acclamation; (*ovação*) applause

aclamar [akla'mar] VT to acclaim; (*aplaudir*) to applaud

aclarado, -a [akla'radu, a] ADJ clear

aclarar [akla'rar] VT to explain, clarify ▶ VI to clear up; **aclarar-se** VR to become clear

aclimatação [aklimata'sāw] F acclimatization

aclimatar [aklima'tar] VT to acclimatize (BRIT), acclimate (US); **aclimatar-se** VR to become acclimatized *ou* acclimated

aclive [a'klivi] M slope, incline

ACM ABR F (= *Associação Cristã de Moços*) YMCA

aço ['asu] M (*metal*) steel; **~ inox** stainless steel

acocorar-se [akoko'rarsi] VR to squat, crouch

acode *etc* [a'kodʒi] VB *ver* **acudir**

ações [a'sōjs] FPL *de* **ação**

acoitar [akoj'tar] VT to shelter, give refuge to

açoitar [asoj'tar] VT to whip, lash

açoite [a'sojtʃi] M whip, lash

acolá [ako'la] ADV over there

acolchoado, -a [akow'ʃwadu, a] ADJ quilted ▶ M quilt

acolchoar [akow'ʃwar] VT (*costurar*) to quilt; (*forrar*) to pad; (*estofar*) to upholster

acolhedor, a [akoʎe'dor(a)] ADJ welcoming; (*hospitaleiro*) hospitable

acolher [ako'ʎer] VT to welcome; (*abrigar*) to shelter; (*aceitar*) to accept; **acolher-se** VR to shelter

acolhida [ako'ʎida] F (*recepção*) reception, welcome; (*refúgio*) refuge

acolhimento [akoʎi'mētu] M = **acolhida**

acometer [akome'ter] VT (*atacar*) to attack; (*suj: doença*) to take hold of

acomodação [akomoda'sāw] (*pl* **-ões**) F accommodation; (*arranjo*) arrangement; (*adaptação*) adaptation

acomodar [akomo'dar] VT (*alojar*) to accommodate; (*arrumar*) to arrange; (*tornar cômodo*) to make comfortable; (*adaptar*) to adapt

acompanhamento [akōpaɲa'mētu] M attendance; (*cortejo*) procession; (*Mús*) accompaniment; (*Culin*) side dish

acompanhante [akōpa'ɲātʃi] M/F companion; (*Mús*) accompanist; (*de idoso, doente*) carer (BRIT), caregiver (US)

acompanhar [akōpa'ɲar] VT to accompany, go along with; (*Mús*) to accompany; (*assistir*) to watch; (*eventos*) to keep up with; **~ alguém até a porta** to show sb to the door

aconchegado, -a [akōʃe'gadu, a] ADJ snug, cosy (BRIT), cozy (US)

aconchegante [akõʃe'gãtʃi] ADJ cosy (BRIT), cozy (US)

aconchegar [akõʃe'gar] VT to bring near; **aconchegar-se** VR (acomodar-se) to make o.s. comfortable; **~-se com** M to snuggle up to

aconchego [akõ'ʃegu] M cuddle

acondicionamento [akõdʒisjona'mẽtu] M packaging

acondicionar [akõdʒisjo'nar] VT to condition; (empacotar) to pack, wrap (up)

aconselhar [akõse'ʎar] VT to advise; (recomendar) to recommend; **aconselhar-se** VR: **~-se com** to consult; **~ alguém a fazer** to advise sb to do

aconselhável [akõse'ʎavew] (pl **-eis**) ADJ advisable

acontecer [akõte'ser] VI to happen

acontecimento [akõtesi'mẽtu] M event

acordar [akor'dar] VT (despertar) to wake (up); (concordar) to agree (on) ▶ VI (despertar) to wake up

acorde [a'kɔrdʒi] M chord

acordeão [akor'dʒjãw] (pl **-ões**) M accordion

acordeonista [akordʒjo'nista] M/F accordionist

acordo [a'kordu] M agreement; **"de ~!"** "agreed!"; **de ~ com** (pessoa) in agreement with; (conforme) in accordance with; **estar de ~** to agree; **~ de cavalheiros** gentlemen's agreement

Açores [a'soris] MPL: **os ~** the Azores

açoriano, -a [aso'rjanu, a] ADJ, M/F Azorean

acorrentar [akohẽ'tar] VT to chain (up)

acorrer [ako'her] VI: **~ a alguém** to come to sb's aid

acossar [ako'sar] VT (perseguir) to pursue; (atormentar) to harass

acostamento [akosta'mẽtu] M hard shoulder (BRIT), berm (US)

acostar [akos'tar] VT to lean against; (Náut) to bring alongside; **acostar-se** VR to lean back

acostumado, -a [akostu'madu, a] ADJ (habitual) usual, customary; **estar ~** to be used to it; **estar ~ a algo** to be used to sth

acostumar [akostu'mar] VT to accustom; **acostumar-se** VR: **~-se a** to get used to

acotovelar [akotove'lar] VT to jostle; **acotovelar-se** VR to jostle

açougue [a'sogi] M butcher's (shop)

açougueiro [aso'gejru] M butcher

acovardado, -a [akovar'dadu, a] ADJ intimidated

acovardar-se [akovar'darsi] VR (desanimar) to lose courage; (amedrontar-se) to flinch, cower

acre ['akri] ADJ (gosto) bitter; (cheiro) acrid; (fig) harsh

acreano, -a [a'krjanu, a] ADJ from Acre ▶ M/F native of Acre

acreditado, -a [akredʒi'tadu, a] ADJ accredited

acreditar [akredʒi'tar] VT to believe; (Com) to credit; (afiançar) to guarantee ▶ VI: **~ em** to

believe in; (ter confiança em) to have faith in; **"acredite na sinalização"** "follow traffic signs"

acreditável [akredʒi'tavew] (pl **-eis**) ADJ credible

acre-doce ADJ (Culin) sweet and sour

acrescentar [akresẽ'tar] VT to add

acrescer [akre'ser] VT (aumentar) to increase; (juntar) to add ▶ VI to increase; **acresce que ...** add to that the fact that ....

acréscimo [a'kresimu] M addition; (aumento) increase; (elevação) rise

acriançado, -a [akrjã'sadu, a] ADJ childish

acrílico [a'kriliku] M acrylic

acrimônia [akri'monja] F acrimony

acrobacia [akroba'sia] F acrobatics pl; **acrobacias** FPL: **~s aéreas** aerobatics pl

acrobata [akro'bata] M/F acrobat

acuar [a'kwar] VT to corner

açúcar [a'sukar] M sugar

açucarado, -a [asuka'radu, a] ADJ sugary

açucarar [asuka'rar] VT to sugar; (adoçar) to sweeten

açucareiro [asuka'rejru] M sugar bowl

açude [a'sudʒi] M dam

acudir [aku'dʒir] VT (ir em socorro) to help, assist ▶ VI (responder) to reply, respond; **~ a** to come to the aid of

acuidade [akwi'dadʒi] F perceptiveness

açular [asu'lar] VT (incitar) to incite; **~ um cachorro contra alguém** to set a dog on sb

acumulação [akumula'sãw] (pl **-ões**) F accumulation

acumulado, -a [akumu'ladu, a] ADJ (Com: juros, despesas) accrued

acumular [akumu'lar] VT to accumulate; (reunir) to collect; (amontoar) to pile up; (funções) to combine

acúmulo [a'kumulu] M accumulation

acusação [akuza'sãw] (pl **-ões**) F accusation, charge; (ato) accusation; (Jur) prosecution

acusado, -a [aku'zadu, a] M/F accused

acusar [aku'zar] VT to accuse; (revelar) to reveal; (culpar) to blame; **~ o recebimento de** to acknowledge receipt of

acústica [a'kustʃika] F (ciência) acoustics sg; (de uma sala) acoustics pl

acústico, -a [a'kustʃiku, a] ADJ acoustic

adaga [a'daga] F dagger

adágio [a'daʒu] M adage; (Mús) adagio

adaptabilidade [adaptabili'dadʒi] F adaptability

adaptação [adapta'sãw] (pl **-ões**) F adaptation

adaptado, -a [adap'tadu, a] ADJ (criança) well-adjusted

adaptar [adap'tar] VT (modificar) to adapt; (acomodar) to fit; **adaptar-se** VR: **~-se a** to adapt to

ADECIF (BR) ABR F = **Associação de Diretores de Empresas de Créditos, Investimentos e Financiamento**

adega [a'dɛga] F cellar

adelgaçado, -a [adewga'sadu, a] ADJ thin; (*aguçado*) pointed

ademais [adʒi'majs] ADV (*além disso*) besides, moreover

ADEMI (BR) ABR F = **Associação de Dirigentes de Empresa do Mercado Imobiliário**

adentro [a'dētru] ADV inside, in; **mata ~** into the woods

adepto, -a [a'dɛptu, a] M/F follower; (*de time*) supporter

adequado, -a [ade'kwadu, a] ADJ appropriate

adequar [ade'kwar] VT to adapt, make suitable

adereçar [adere'sar] VT to adorn, decorate; **adereçar-se** VR to dress up

adereço [ade'resu] M adornment; **adereços** MPL (*Teatro*) stage props

aderência [ade'rēsja] F adherence

aderente [ade'rētʃi] ADJ adhesive, sticky ▶ M/F (*partidário*) supporter

aderir [ade'rir] VI to adhere; (*colar*) to stick; (*a uma moda etc*) to join in

adesão [ade'zãw] F adhesion; (*patrocínio*) support

adesivo, -a [ade'zivu, a] ADJ adhesive, sticky ▶ M adhesive tape; (*Med*) sticking plaster

adestrado, -a [ades'tradu, a] ADJ skilful (BRIT), skillful (US), skilled

adestrador, a [adestra'dor(a)] M/F trainer

adestramento [adestra'mētu] M training

adestrar [ades'trar] VT to train, instruct; (*cavalo*) to break in

adeus [a'dews] EXCL goodbye!; **dizer ~** to say goodbye, bid farewell

adiamento [adʒja'mētu] M postponement; (*de uma sessão*) adjournment

adiantado, -a [adʒjã'tadu, a] ADJ advanced; (*relógio*) fast; **chegar ~** to arrive ahead of time; **pagar ~** to pay in advance

adiantamento [adʒjãta'mētu] M progress; (*dinheiro*) advance (payment)

adiantar [adʒjã'tar] VT (*dinheiro, salário*) to advance, pay in advance; (*relógio*) to put forward; (*trabalho*) to advance; (*dizer*) to say in advance ▶ VI (*relógio*) to be fast; (*conselho, violência etc*) to be of use; **adiantar-se** VR to advance, get ahead; **não adianta reclamar/insistir** there's no point ou it's no use complaining/insisting; **~-se a alguém** to get ahead of sb; **~-se para** to come up to

adiante [a'dʒjãtʃi] ADV (*na frente*) in front; (*para a frente*) forward; **mais ~** further on; (*no futuro*) later on

adiar [a'dʒjar] VT to postpone, put off; (*sessão*) to adjourn

adição [adʒi'sãw] (*pl* **-ões**) F addition; (*Mat*) sum

adicionar [adʒisjo'nar] VT to add

adições [adʒi'sõjs] FPL *de* **adição**

adido, -a [a'dʒidu, a] M/F attaché

adiro *etc* [a'diru] VB *ver* **aderir**

Adis-Abeba [adʒiza'bɛba] N Addis Ababa

adivinhação [adʒiviɲa'sãw] F (*destino*) fortune-telling; (*conjectura*) guessing, guesswork

adivinhar [adʒivi'ɲar] VT to guess; (*ler a sorte*) to foretell ▶ VI to guess; **~ o pensamento de alguém** to read sb's mind

adivinho, -a [adʒi'viɲu, a] M/F fortune-teller

adjacente [adʒa'sētʃi] ADJ adjacent

adjetivo [adʒe'tʃivu] M adjective

adjudicação [adʒudʒika'sãw] (*pl* **-ões**) F grant; (*de contratos*) award; (*Jur*) decision

adjudicar [adʒudʒi'kar] VT to award, grant

adjunto, -a [ad'ʒũtu, a] ADJ joined, attached ▶ M/F assistant

administração [adʒiministra'sãw] (*pl* **-ões**) F administration; (*direção*) management; (*comissão*) board; **~ de empresas** business administration, management; **~ fiduciária** trusteeship

administrador, a [adʒiministra'dor(a)] M/F administrator; (*diretor*) director; (*gerente*) manager

administrar [adʒiminis'trar] VT to administer, manage; (*governar*) to govern; (*remédio*) to administer

admiração [adʒimira'sãw] F (*assombro*) wonder; (*estima*) admiration; **ponto de ~** (PT) exclamation mark

admirado, -a [adʒimi'radu, a] ADJ astonished, surprised

admirador, a [adʒimira'dor(a)] ADJ admiring

admirar [adʒimi'rar] VT to admire; **admirar-se** VR: **~-se de** to be astonished ou surprised at; **não me admiro!** I'm not surprised; **não é de se ~** it's not surprising

admirável [adʒimi'ravew] (*pl* **-eis**) ADJ (*assombroso*) amazing

admissão [adʒimi'sãw] (*pl* **-ões**) F admission; (*consentimento para entrar*) admittance; (*de escola*) intake

admitir [adʒimi'tʃir] VT (*aceitar*) to admit; (*permitir*) to allow; (*funcionário*) to take on

admoestação [admwesta'sãw] (*pl* **-ões**) F admonition; (*repreensão*) reprimand

admoestar [admwes'tar] VT to admonish

adoção [ado'sãw] F adoption

adoçar [ado'sar] VT to sweeten

adocicado, -a [adosi'kadu, a] ADJ slightly sweet

adoecer [adoe'ser] VI to fall ill ▶ VT to make ill; **~ de ou com** to fall ill with

adoidado, -a [adoj'dadu, a] ADJ crazy ▶ ADV (*col*) like mad ou crazy

adolescente [adole'sētʃi] ADJ, M/F adolescent

adoração [adora'sãw] F adoration; (*veneração*) worship

adorar [ado'rar] VT to adore; (*venerar*) to worship; (*col: gostar muito de*) to love

adorável [ado'ravew] (*pl* **-eis**) ADJ adorable

adormecer [adorme'ser] VI to fall asleep; (*entorpecer-se*) to go numb

adormecido, -a [adorme'sidu, a] ADJ sleeping ▶ M/F sleeper

adornar [ador'nar] VT to adorn, decorate

adorno [a'dornu] M adornment
adotar [ado'tar] VT to adopt
adotivo, -a [ado'tʃivu, a] ADJ (filho) adopted
adquirir [adʒiki'rir] VT to acquire; (obter) to obtain
adrede [a'dredʒi] ADV on purpose, deliberately
Adriático, -a [a'drjatʃiku, a] ADJ: **o (mar) ~** the Adriatic (Sea)
adro ['adru] M (church) forecourt; (em volta da igreja) churchyard
aduana [a'dwana] F customs pl, customs house
aduaneiro, -a [adwa'nejru, a] ADJ customs atr ▶ M customs officer
adubação [aduba'sãw] F fertilizing
adubar [adu'bar] VT to manure; (fertilizar) to fertilize
adubo [a'dubu] M (fertilizante) fertilizer
adulação [adula'sãw] F flattery
adulador, a [adula'dor(a)] ADJ flattering ▶ M/F flatterer
adular [adu'lar] VT to flatter
adulteração [aduwtera'sãw] F adulteration; (de contas) falsification
adulterador, a [aduwtera'dor(a)] M/F adulterator
adulterar [aduwte'rar] VT (vinho) to adulterate; (contas) to falsify ▶ VI to commit adultery
adultério [aduw'tɛrju] M adultery
adúltero, -a [a'duwteru, a] M/F adulterer/adulteress
adulto, -a [a'duwtu, a] ADJ, M/F adult
adunco, -a [a'dũku, a] ADJ (nariz) hook
adveio etc [ad'veju] VB ver **advir**
adventício, -a [advẽ'tʃisju, a] ADJ (casual) accidental; (estrangeiro) foreign ▶ M/F foreigner
advento [ad'vẽtu] M advent; **o A~** Advent
advérbio [adʒi'verbju] M adverb
adversário [adʒiver'sarju] M adversary, opponent, enemy
adversidade [adʒiversi'dadʒi] F adversity, misfortune
adverso, -a [adʒi'vɛrsu, a] ADJ adverse, unfavourable (BRIT), unfavorable (US); (oposto): **~ a** opposed to
advertência [adʒiver'tẽsja] F warning; (repreensão) (gentle) reprimand
advertido, -a [adʒiver'tʃidu, a] ADJ prudent; (informado) well-advised
advertir [adʒiver'tʃir] VT to warn; (repreender) to reprimand; (chamar a atenção a) to draw attention to
advier etc [ad'vjer] VB ver **advir**
advindo, -a [ad'vĩdu, a] ADJ: **~ de** resulting from
advir [ad'vir] (irreg: como **vir**) VI: **~ de** to result from
advocacia [adʒivoka'sia] F legal profession, law
advogado, -a [adʒivo'gadu, a] M/F lawyer

advogar [adʒivo'gar] VT (promover) to advocate; (Jur) to plead ▶ VI to practise (BRIT) ou practice (US) law
aéreo, -a [a'ɛrju, a] ADJ air atr; (pessoa) vague
aerobarco [aero'barku] M jetfoil
aeroclube [aero'klubi] M flying club
aerodinâmica [aerodʒi'namika] F aerodynamics sg
aerodinâmico, -a [aerodʒi'namiku, a] ADJ aerodynamic
aeródromo [aero'drɔmu] M airfield
aeroespacial [aeroispa'sjaw] (pl **-ais**) ADJ aerospace atr
aerofagia [aerofa'ʒia] F (Med) hyperventilation
aerofoto [aero'fɔtu] F aerial photograph
aeromoço, -a [aero'mosu, a] (BR) M/F flight attendant
aeromodelismo [aeromode'lizmu] M aeromodelling
aeronauta [aero'nawta] M/F airman/woman
aeronáutica [aero'nawtʃika] F air force; (ciência) ≈ aeronautics sg; **Departamento de A~ Civil** ≈ Civil Aviation Authority
aeronave [aero'navi] F aircraft
aeroporto [aero'portu] M airport
aerossol [aero'sɔw] (pl **-óis**) M aerosol
afã [a'fã] M (entusiasmo) enthusiasm; (diligência) diligence; (ânsia) eagerness; (esforço) effort; (faina) task, job; **no seu ~ de agradar** in his eagerness to please
afabilidade [afabili'dadʒi] F friendliness, kindness
afaço etc [a'fasu] VB ver **afazer**
afagar [afa'gar] VT (acariciar) to caress; (cabelo) to stroke
afamado, -a [afa'madu, a] ADJ renowned
afanar [afa'nar] (col) VT to nick, pinch
afanoso, -a [afa'nozu, ɔza] ADJ laborious; (meticuloso) painstaking
afasia [afa'zia] F aphasia
afastado, -a [afas'tadu, a] ADJ (distante) remote; (isolado) secluded; (pernas) apart; (amigo) distant; **manter-se ~** to keep to o.s.
afastamento [afasta'mẽtu] M removal; (distância) distance; (de emprego solicitado) rejection; (de pessoal) lay-off, sacking
afastar [afas'tar] VT to remove; (amigo) to distance; (separar) to separate; (ideia) to put out of one's mind; (pessoal) to lay off; **afastar-se** VR (ir-se embora) to move away, go away; (de amigo) to distance o.s.; (de cargo) to step down; **~ os olhos de** to take one's eyes off; **~-se do assunto** to stray from the subject
afável [a'favew] (pl **-eis**) ADJ friendly, genial
afazer [afa'zer] (irreg: como **fazer**) VT to accustom; **afazer-se** VR: **~-se a** to get used to
afazeres [afa'zeris] MPL business sg; (dever) duties, tasks; **~ domésticos** household chores
afegã [afe'] F de **afegão**

Afeganistão [afeganis'tãw] M: **o ~** Afghanistan

afegão, -gã [afe'gãw, 'gã] (*pl* **-ões/-s**) ADJ, M/F Afghan

afeição [afej'sãw] F (*amor*) affection, fondness; (*dedicação*) devotion

afeiçoado, -a [afej'swadu, a] ADJ: **~ a** (*amoroso*) fond of; (*devotado*) devoted to ▶ M/F friend

afeiçoar-se [afej'swarsi] VR: **~ a** (*tomar gosto por*) to take a liking to

afeito, -a [a'fejtu, a] PP *de* **afazer** ▶ ADJ: **~ a** accustomed to, used to

afeminado, -a [afemi'nadu, a] ADJ effeminate

aferidor [aferi'dor] M (*de pesos e medidas*) inspector; (*verificador*) checker; (*instrumento*) gauge (BRIT), gage (US)

aferir [afe'rir] VT (*verificar*) to check, inspect; (*comparar*) to compare; (*conhecimentos, resultados*) to assess

aferrado, -a [afe'hadu, a] ADJ obstinate, stubborn

aferrar [afe'har] VT (*prender*) to secure; (*Náut*) to anchor; (*agarrar*) to grasp; **aferrar-se** VR: **~-se a** to cling to

aferrolhar [afeho'ʎar] VT to bolt; (*pessoa*) to imprison; (*coisas*) to hoard

aferventar [afervẽ'tar] VT to bring to the (BRIT) *ou* a (US) boil

afetação [afeta'sãw] F affectation

afetado, -a [afe'tadu, a] ADJ pretentious, affected

afetar [afe'tar] VT to affect; (*fingir*) to feign

afetividade [afetʃivi'dadʒi] F affection

afetivo, -a [afe'tʃivu, a] ADJ affectionate; (*problema*) emotional

afeto [a'fɛtu] M affection

afetuoso, -a [afe'twozu, ɔza] ADJ affectionate

afez *etc* [a'fez] VB *ver* **afazer**

AFI ABR M (= *Alfabeto Fonético Internacional*) IPA

afiado, -a [a'fjadu, a] ADJ sharp; (*pessoa*) well-trained

afiançar [afjã'sar] VT (*Jur*) to stand bail for; (*garantir*) to guarantee

afiar [a'fjar] VT to sharpen

aficionado, -a [afisjo'nadu, a] M/F enthusiast

afigurar-se [afigu'rarsi] VR to seem, appear; **afigura-se-me que ...** it seems to me that ...

afilado, -a [afi'ladu, a] ADJ (*nariz*) thin

afilhado, -a [afi'ʎadu, a] M/F godson/ goddaughter

afiliação [afilja'sãw] (*pl* **-ões**) F affiliation

afiliada [afi'ljada] F affiliate, affiliated company

afiliado, -a [afi'ljadu, a] ADJ affiliated

afiliar [afi'ljar] VT to affiliate; **afiliar-se** VR: **~-se a** to join

afim [a'fĩ] (*pl* **-ns**) ADJ (*semelhante*) similar; (*consanguíneo*) related ▶ M/F relative, relation; **estar ~ de (fazer) algo** to feel like (doing) sth, fancy (doing) sth; **estar ~ de alguém** (*col*) to fancy sb

afinação [afina'sãw] F (*Mús*) tuning

afinado, -a [afi'nadu, a] ADJ in tune

afinal [afi'naw] ADV at last, finally; **~ (de contas)** after all

afinar [afi'nar] VT (*Mús*) to tune ▶ VI (*adelgaçar*) to taper

afinco [a'fĩku] M tenacity, persistence; **com ~** tenaciously

afinidade [afini'dadʒi] F affinity

afins [a'fĩs] PL *de* **afim**

afirmação [afirma'sãw] (*pl* **-ões**) F affirmation; (*declaração*) statement

afirmar [afir'mar] VT, VI to affirm, assert; (*declarar*) to declare

afirmativo, -a [afirma'tʃivu, a] ADJ affirmative

afiro *etc* [a'firu] VB *ver* **aferir**

afivelar [afive'lar] VT to buckle

afixar [afik'sar] VT (*cartazes*) to stick, post

afiz *etc* [a'fiz] VB *ver* **afazer**

afizer *etc* [afi'zer] VB *ver* **afazer**

aflição [afli'sãw] F (*sofrimento*) affliction; (*ansiedade*) anxiety; (*angústia*) anguish

afligir [afli'ʒir] VT to distress; (*atormentar*) to torment; (*inquietar*) to worry; **afligir-se** VR: **~-se com** to worry about

aflijo *etc* [a'fliʒu] VB *ver* **afligir**

aflito, -a [a'flitu, a] PP *de* **afligir** ▶ ADJ distressed, anxious

aflorar [aflo'rar] VI to emerge, appear

afluência [a'flwẽsja] F affluence; (*corrente copiosa*) flow; (*de pessoas*) stream

afluente [a'flwẽtʃi] ADJ copious; (*rico*) affluent ▶ M tributary

afluir [a'flwir] VI to flow; (*pessoas*) to congregate

afobação [afoba'sãw] F fluster; (*ansiedade*) panic

afobado, -a [afo'badu, a] ADJ flustered; (*ansioso*) panicky, nervous

afobamento [afoba'mẽtu] M fluster; (*ansiedade*) panic

afobar [afo'bar] VT to fluster; (*deixar ansioso*) to make nervous *ou* panicky ▶ VI to get flustered; to panic, get nervous; **afobar-se** VR to get flustered

afofar [afo'far] VT to fluff

afogado, -a [afo'gadu, a] ADJ drowned

afogador [afoga'dor] (BR) M (*Auto*) choke

afogar [afo'gar] VT to drown ▶ VI (*Auto*) to flood; **afogar-se** VR to drown, be drowned

afoito, -a [a'fojtu, a] ADJ bold, daring

afonia [afo'nia] F voice loss

afônico, -a [a'foniku, a] ADJ: **estou ~** I've lost my voice

afora [a'fɔra] PREP except for, apart from ▶ ADV: **rua ~** down the street; **pelo mundo ~** throughout the world; **porta ~** out into the street

aforismo [afo'rizmu] M aphorism

aforrar [afo'har] VT (*roupa*) to line; (*poupar*) to save; (*liberar*) to free

afortunado, -a [afortu'nadu, a] ADJ fortunate, lucky

afrescalhado, -a [afreska'ʎadu, a] (*col*) ADJ effeminate, camp

afresco [a'fresku] M fresco

África ['afrika] F: **a ~** Africa; **a ~ do Sul** South Africa

africano, -a [afri'kanu, a] ADJ, M/F African

AFRMM (BR) ABR M (= *Adicional ao Frete para Renovação da Marinha Mercante*) *tax on goods imported by sea*

afro-brasileiro, -a ['afru-] (*pl* **-s**) ADJ Afro-Brazilian

afrodisíaco [afrodʒi'ziaku] M aphrodisiac

afronta [a'frõta] F insult, affront

afrontado, -a [afrõ'tadu, a] ADJ (*ofendido*) offended; (*com má digestão*) too full

afrontar [afrõ'tar] VT to insult; (*ofender*) to offend

afrouxar [afro'ʃar] VT (*desapertar*) to slacken; (*soltar*) to loosen ▶ VI (*soltar-se*) to come loose

afta ['afta] F (mouth) ulcer

afugentar [afuʒẽ'tar] VT to drive away, put to flight

afundar [afũ'dar] VT (*submergir*) to sink; (*cavidade*) to deepen; **afundar-se** VR to sink; (*col: num exame*) to do badly

agá [a'ga] M aitch, h

agachar-se [aga'ʃarsi] VR (*acaçapar-se*) to crouch, squat; (*curvar-se*) to stoop; (*fig*) to cringe

agarração [agaha'sãw] (*col*) F necking

agarrado, -a [aga'hadu, a] ADJ: **~ a** (*preso*) stuck to; (*a uma pessoa*) very attached to

agarramento [agaha'mẽtu] M (*a uma pessoa*) close attachment; (*col: agarração*) necking

agarrar [aga'har] VT to seize, grasp; **agarrar-se** VR: **~-se a** to cling to, hold on to

agasalhado, -a [agaza'ʎadu, a] ADJ warmly dressed, wrapped up

agasalhar [agaza'ʎar] VT to dress warmly, wrap up; **agasalhar-se** VR to wrap o.s. up

agasalho [aga'zaʎu] M (*casaco*) coat; (*suéter*) sweater

ágeis ['aʒejs] PL *de* **ágil**

agência [a'ʒẽsja] F agency; (*escritório*) office; (*de banco etc*) branch; **~ de correio** (BR) post office; **~ de viagens** travel agency; **~ publicitária** advertising agency

agenciar [aʒẽ'sjar] VT (*negociar*) to negotiate; (*obter*) to procure; (*ser agente de*) to act as an agent for

agenda [a'ʒẽda] F diary; **~ eletrônica** personal organizer

agente [a'ʒẽtʃi] M/F agent; (*de polícia*) policeman/woman; **~ de seguros** (insurance) underwriter

agigantado, -a [aʒigã'tadu, a] ADJ gigantic

ágil ['aʒiw] (*pl* **-eis**) ADJ agile

agilidade [aʒili'dadʒi] F agility

agilizar [aʒili'zar] VT: **~ algo** (*dar andamento a*) to get sth moving; (*acelerar*) to speed sth up

ágio ['aʒju] M premium

agiota [a'ʒjɔta] M/F moneylender

agir [a'ʒir] VI to act; **~ bem/mal** to do right/wrong

agitação [aʒita'sãw] (*pl* **-ões**) F agitation; (*perturbação*) disturbance; (*inquietação*) restlessness

agitado, -a [aʒi'tadu, a] ADJ agitated, disturbed; (*inquieto*) restless

agitar [aʒi'tar] VT to agitate, disturb; (*sacudir*) to shake; (*cauda*) to wag; (*mexer*) to stir; (*os braços*) to swing, wave; **agitar-se** VR to get upset; (*mar*) to get rough

aglomeração [aglomera'sãw] (*pl* **-ões**) F gathering; (*multidão*) crowd

aglomerado [aglome'radu] M: **~ urbano** city

aglomerar [aglome'rar] VT to heap up, pile up; **aglomerar-se** VR (*multidão*) to crowd together

AGO ABR F (= *assembleia geral ordinária*) AGM

ago. ABR (= *agosto*) Aug.

agonia [ago'nia] F agony, anguish; (*ânsia da morte*) death throes *pl*; (*indecisão*) indecision

agoniado, -a [ago'njadu, a] ADJ anguished

agonizante [agoni'zãtʃi] ADJ dying ▶ M/F dying person

agonizar [agoni'zar] VI to be dying; (*afligir-se*) to agonize

agora [a'gɔra] ADV now; (*hoje em dia*) now, nowadays; **e ~?** now what?; **~ mesmo** right now; (*há pouco*) a moment ago; **a partir de ~**, **de ~ em diante** from now on; **até ~** so far, up to now; **por ~** for now; **~ que** now that; **eu lhe disse ontem** I told him yesterday; **~, se ele esquecer ...** but if he forgets ...

agorinha [ago'riɲa] ADV just now

agosto [a'gostu] M August; *ver tb* **julho**

agourar [ago'rar] VT to predict, foretell ▶ VI to augur ill

agouro [a'goru] M omen; (*mau agouro*) bad omen

agraciar [agra'sjar] VT (*condecorar*) to decorate

agradabilíssimo, -a [agradabi'lisimu, a] ADJ SUPERL *de* **agradável**

agradar [agra'dar] VT (*deleitar*) to please; (*fazer agrados a*) to be nice to ▶ VI (*ser agradável*) to be pleasing; (*satisfazer: show, piada etc*) to go down well

agradável [agra'davew] (*pl* **-eis**) ADJ pleasant

agradecer [agrade'ser] VT: **~ algo a alguém**, **~ a alguém por algo** to thank sb for sth

agradecido, -a [agrade'sidu, a] ADJ grateful; **mal ~** ungrateful

agradecimento [agradesi'mẽtu] M gratitude; **agradecimentos** MPL (*gratidão*) thanks

agrado [a'gradu] M: **fazer um ~ a alguém** (*afagar*) to be affectionate with sb; (*ser agradável*) to be nice to sb

agrário, -a [a'grarju, a] ADJ agrarian; **reforma agrária** land reform

agravação [agrava'sãw] (PT) F aggravation; (*piora*) worsening

agravamento [agrava'mẽtu] (BR) M aggravation

agravante [agra'vãtʃi] ADJ aggravating ▶ F aggravating circumstance

agravar [agra'var] VT to aggravate, make worse; **agravar-se** VR (*piorar*) to get worse

agravo [a'gravu] M (*Jur*) appeal

agredir [agre'dʒir] VT to attack; (*insultar*) to insult

agregado, -a [agre'gadu, a] M/F (*lavrador*) tenant farmer; (*BR*) lodger ▶ M aggregate, sum total

agregar [agre'gar] VT (*juntar*) to collect; (*acrescentar*) to add

agressão [agre'sãw] (*pl* -**ões**) F aggression; (*ataque*) attack; (*assalto*) assault

agressividade [agresivi'dadʒi] F aggressiveness

agressivo, -a [agre'sivu, a] ADJ aggressive

agressões [agre'sõjs] FPL *de* **agressão**

agressor, a [agre'sor(a)] M/F aggressor

agreste [a'grestʃi] ADJ rural, rustic; (*terreno*) wild, uncultivated

agrião [a'grjãw] M watercress

agrícola [a'grikola] ADJ agricultural

agricultável [agrikuw'tavew] (*pl* -**eis**) ADJ arable

agricultor [agrikuw'tor] M farmer

agricultura [agrikuw'tura] F agriculture, farming

agrido *etc* [a'gridu] VB *ver* **agredir**

agridoce [agri'dosi] ADJ bittersweet

agronegócio [agrone'gɔsju] M agribusiness

agronomia [agrono'mia] F agronomy

agrônomo, -a [a'gronomu, a] M/F agronomist

agropecuária [agrope'kwarja] F farming, agriculture

agropecuário, -a [agrope'kwarju, a] ADJ farming *atr*, agricultural

agrotóxico [agro'tɔksiku] M pesticide

agrupamento [agrupa'mẽtu] M grouping

agrupar [agru'par] VT to group; **agrupar-se** VR to group together

agrura [a'grura] F bitterness

água ['agwa] F water; **águas** FPL (*mar*) waters; (*chuvas*) rain *sg*; (*maré*) tides; ~ **abaixo/acima** downstream/upstream; **até debaixo da ~** (*fig*) one thousand per cent; **dar ~ na boca** (*comida*) to be mouthwatering; **estar na ~** (*bêbado*) to be drunk; **fazer ~** (*Náut*) to leak; **ir nas ~s de alguém** (*fig*) to follow in sb's footsteps; ~ **benta** holy water; ~ **com açúcar** *adj inv* schmaltzy, mushy; ~ **corrente** running water; ~ **de coco** coconut water; ~ **doce** fresh water; ~ **dura/leve** hard/soft water; ~ **mineral** mineral water; ~ **oxigenada** peroxide; ~ **salgada** salt water; ~ **sanitária** household bleach; **jogar ~ na fervura** (*fig*) to put a damper on things; **mudar como da ~ para o vinho** to change radically; **desta ~ não beberei!** that won't happen to me!; ~**s passadas não movem moinhos** it's all water under the bridge

aguaceiro [agwa'sejru] M (*chuva*) (heavy) shower, downpour; (*com vento*) squall

água-de-colônia (*pl* **águas-de-colônia**) F eau-de-cologne

aguado, -a [a'gwadu, a] ADJ watery

água-furtada [-fur'tada] (*pl* **águas-furtadas**) F garret, attic

água-marinha (*pl* **águas-marinhas**) F aquamarine

aguar [a'gwar] VT to water ▶ VI: ~ **por** (*salivar*) to drool over

aguardar [agwar'dar] VT to wait for, await; (*contar com*) to expect ▶ VI to wait

aguardente [agwar'dẽtʃi] M spirit (*BRIT*), liquor (*US*)

aguarrás [agwa'hajs] F turpentine

água-viva (*pl* **águas-vivas**) F jellyfish

açuçado, -a [agu'sadu, a] ADJ pointed; (*espírito, sentidos*) acute

açuçar [agu'sar] VT (*afiar*) to sharpen; (*estimular*) to excite; ~ **a vista** to keep one's eyes peeled

agudeza [agu'deza] F sharpness; (*perspicácia*) perspicacity; (*de som*) shrillness

agudo, -a [a'gudu, a] ADJ sharp; (*som*) shrill; (*intenso*) acute

aguentar [agwẽ'tar] VT (*muro etc*) to hold up; (*dor, injustiças*) to stand, put up with; (*peso*) to withstand; (*resistir a*) to stand up to ▶ VI to last, hold out; (*resistir a peso*) to hold; **aguentar-se** VR (*manter-se*) to remain, hold on; ~ **com** to hold, withstand; ~ **fazer algo** to manage to do sth; **não ~ de** not to be able to stand; ~ **firme** to hold out

aguerrido, -a [age'hidu, a] ADJ warlike, bellicose; (*corajoso*) courageous

águia ['agja] F eagle; (*fig*) genius

agulha [a'guʎa] F (*de coser, tricô*) needle; (*Náut*) compass; (*Ferro*) points *pl* (*BRIT*), switch (*US*); **trabalho de ~** needlework

agulheta [agu'ʎeta] F (*bico*) nozzle

ah [a] EXCL oh!

AI ABR F = **Anistia Internacional** ▶ ABR M (*BR*) = **Ato Institucional**; **AI-5** *measure passed in 1968 suspending congress and banning opposition politicians*

ai [aj] EXCL (*suspiro*) oh!; (*de dor*) ouch! ▶ M (*suspiro*) sigh; (*gemido*) groan; **ai de mim** poor me!

aí [a'i] ADV there; (*então*) then; **por aí** (*em lugar indeterminado*) somewhere over there, thereabouts; **espera aí!** wait!, hang on a minute!; **está aí!** (*col*) right!; **aí é que 'tá!** (*col*) that's just the point; **e por aí afora** *ou* **vai** and so on; **já não está aí quem falou** (*col*) I stand corrected; **e aí?** and then what?; **e aí (como vai)?** (*col*) how are things with you?

aiatolá [ajato'la] M ayatollah

aidético, -a [aj'dɛtʃiku, a] ADJ suffering from AIDS ▶ M/F person with AIDS

AIDS ['ajdʒs] F AIDS

ainda [a'ĩda] ADV still; (*mesmo*) even; ~ **agora** just now; ~ **assim** even so, nevertheless; ~ **bem** just as well; ~ **por cima** on top of all that, in addition; ~ **não** not yet; ~ **que** even if; **maior ~** even bigger

aipim [aj'pĩ] M cassava

aipo ['ajpu] M celery

airado, -a [aj'radu, a] ADJ (*frívolo*) frivolous; (*leviano*) dissolute

airoso, -a [aj'rozu, ɔza] ADJ graceful, elegant

ajantarado [aʒãta'radu] M *lunch and dinner combined*

ajardinar [aʒardʒi'nar] VT to make into a garden

ajeitar [aʒej'tar] VT (*adaptar*) to fit, adjust; (*arranjar*) to arrange, fix; **ajeitar-se** VR to adapt; **aos poucos as coisas se ajeitam** things will gradually sort themselves out

ajo *etc* ['aʒu] VB *ver* **agir**

ajoelhado, -a [aʒwe'ʎadu, a] ADJ kneeling

ajoelhar [aʒwe'ʎar] VI to kneel (down); **ajoelhar-se** VR to kneel down

ajuda [a'ʒuda] F help, aid; (*subsídio*) grant, subsidy; **sem ~** unaided; **dar ~ a alguém** to lend *ou* give sb a hand; **~ de custo** allowance

ajudante [aʒu'dãtʃi] M/F assistant, helper; (*Mil*) adjutant

ajudar [aʒu'dar] VT to help

ajuizado, -a [aʒwi'zadu, a] ADJ (*sensato*) sensible; (*sábio*) wise; (*prudente*) discreet

ajuizar [aʒwi'zar] VT to judge; (*calcular*) to calculate

ajuntamento [aʒũta'mẽtu] M gathering

ajuntar [aʒũ'tar] VT (*unir*) to join; (*documentos*) to attach; (*reunir*) to gather

ajustagem [aʒus'taʒẽ] (*pl* **-ns**) (BR) F (*Tec*) adjustment

ajustagens [aʒus'taʒẽs] FPL *de* **ajustagem**

ajustamento [aʒusta'mẽtu] M adjustment; (*de contas*) settlement

ajustar [aʒus'tar] VT (*regular*) to adjust; (*conta, disputa*) to settle; (*acomodar*) to fit; (*roupa*) to take in; (*contratar*) to contract; (*estipular*) to stipulate; (*preço*) to agree on; **ajustar-se** VR: **~-se a** to conform to; (*adaptar-se*) to adapt to

ajustável [aʒus'tavew] (*pl* **-eis**) ADJ adjustable; (*aplicável*) applicable

ajuste [a'ʒustʃi] M (*acordo*) agreement; (*de contas*) settlement; (*adaptação*) adjustment; **~ final** (*Com*) settlement of account

AL ABR = **Alagoas** ▶ ABR F (BR: = *Aliança Liberal*) *former political party*

al. ABR = **Alameda**

ala ['ala] F (*fileira*) row; (*passagem*) aisle; (*de edifício, exército, ave*) wing

Alá [a'la] M Allah

ALADI ABR F = **Associação Latino-Americana de Desenvolvimento e Intercâmbio**

alagação [alaga'sãw] F flooding

alagadiço, -a [alaga'dʒisu, a] ADJ swampy, marshy ▶ M swamp, marsh

alagamento [alaga'mẽtu] M flooding; (*arrasamento*) destruction

alagar [ala'gar] VT, VI to flood

alagoano, -a [ala'gwanu, a] ADJ from Alagoas ▶ M/F native *ou* inhabitant of Alagoas

alambique [alã'biki] M still

alameda [ala'meda] F (*avenida*) avenue; (*arvoredo*) grove

álamo ['alamu] M poplar

alanhar [ala'ɲar] VT to slash; (*peixe*) to gut

alar [a'lar] VT to haul, heave

alaranjado, -a [alarã'ʒadu, a] ADJ orangey

alarde [a'lardʒi] M (*ostentação*) ostentation; (*jactância*) boasting; **fazer ~ de** to boast about

alardear [alar'dʒjar] VT to show off; (*gabar-se de*) to boast of ▶ VI to boast; **alardear-se** VR to boast; **~ fazer** to boast of doing; **~(-se) valente** to boast of being strong

alargamento [alarga'mẽtu] M enlargement

alargar [alar'gar] VT (*ampliar*) to extend; (*fazer mais largo*) to widen, broaden; (*afrouxar*) to loosen, slacken

alarido [ala'ridu] M (*clamor*) outcry; (*tumulto*) uproar

alarma [a'larma] F alarm; (*susto*) panic; (*tumulto*) tumult; (*vozearia*) outcry; **dar o sinal de ~** to raise the alarm; **~ de roubo** burglar alarm

alarmante [alar'mãtʃi] ADJ alarming

alarmar [alar'mar] VT to alarm; **alarmar-se** VR to be alarmed

alarme [a'larmi] M = **alarma**

alarmista [alar'mista] ADJ, M/F alarmist

Alasca [a'laska] M: **o ~** Alaska

alastrado, -a [alas'tradu, a] ADJ: **~ de** strewn with

alastrar [alas'trar] VT (*espalhar*) to scatter; (*disseminar*) to spread; (*lastrar*) to ballast; **alastrar-se** VR (*epidemia, rumor*) to spread

alavanca [ala'vãka] F lever; (*pé de cabra*) crowbar; **~ de mudanças** gear lever

alavancar [alavã'kar] VT to lever; (*fig: negócios, economia*) to kick-start

albanês, -esa [awba'nes, eza] ADJ, M/F Albanian ▶ M (*Ling*) Albanian

Albânia [aw'banja] F: **a ~** Albania

albergar [awber'gar] VT (*hospedar*) to provide lodging for; (*abrigar*) to shelter

albergue [aw'bɛrgi] M (*estalagem*) inn; (*refúgio*) hospice, shelter; **~ noturno** hotel; **~ para jovens** youth hostel

albino, -a [aw'binu, a] ADJ, M/F albino

albufeira [awbu'fejra] F lagoon

álbum ['awbũ] (*pl* **-ns**) M album; **~ de recortes** scrapbook

alça ['awsa] F strap; (*asa*) handle; (*de fusil*) sight

alcácer [aw'kaser] M fortress

alcachofra [awka'ʃofra] F artichoke

alcaçuz [awka'suz] M liquorice

alçada [aw'sada] F (*jurisdição*) jurisdiction; (*competência*) competence; **isso não é da minha ~** that is beyond my control

alcaguete [awka'gwetʃi] M/F informer

álcali ['awkali] M alkali

alcalino, -a [awka'linu, a] ADJ alkaline

alcançar [awkã'sar] VT to reach; (*estender*) to hand, pass; (*obter*) to obtain, get; (*atingir*) to attain; (*compreender*) to understand; (*desfalcar*): **~ uma firma em $1 milhão** to embezzle $1 million from a firm ▶ VI to reach; **alcançar-se** VR (*fazer um desfalque*) to embezzle funds

alcançável [awkã'savew] (*pl* **-eis**) ADJ (*acessível*) reachable; (*atingível*) attainable

alcance [aw'kãsi] M reach; (*competência*) power, competence; (*compreensão*) understanding; (*de tiro, visão*) range; (*desfalque*) embezzlement; **ao ~ de** within reach *ou* range of; **ao ~ da voz** within earshot; **de grande ~** far-reaching; **fora do ~ da mão** out of reach; **fora do ~ de alguém** beyond sb's grasp

alcantilado, -a [awkãtʃi'ladu, a] ADJ (*íngreme*) steep; (*penhascoso*) craggy

alçapão [awsa'pãw] (*pl* **-ões**) M trapdoor; (*arapuca*) trap

alcaparra [awka'paha] F caper

alçapões [awsa'põjs] MPL *de* **alçapão**

alçaprema [awsa'prɛma] F (*alavanca*) crowbar

alçar [aw'sar] VT to lift (up); (*voz*) to raise; **~ voo** to take off

alcaravia [awkara'via] F: **sementes de ~** caraway seeds

alcateia [awka'teja] F (*de lobos*) pack; (*de ladrões*) gang

alcatra [aw'katra] F rump (steak)

alcatrão [awka'trãw] M tar

álcool ['awkɔw] M alcohol

alcoólatra [aw'kɔlatra] M/F alcoholic

alcoólico, -a [aw'kɔliku, a] ADJ, M/F alcoholic

alcoolismo [awko'lizmu] M alcoholism

Alcorão [awko'rãw] M Koran

alcova [aw'kova] F bedroom

alcoviteiro, -a [awkovi'tejru, a] M/F pimp/procuress

alcunha [aw'kuɲa] F nickname

aldeão, -deã [aw'dʒjãw, jã] (*pl* **-ões/-s**) M/F villager

aldeia [aw'deja] F village

aldeões [aw'dʒjõjs] MPL *de* **aldeão**

aldraba [aw'draba] (PT) F (*tranqueta*) latch; (*de bater*) door knocker

aleatório, -a [alea'tɔrju, a] ADJ random

alecrim [ale'krĩ] M rosemary

alegação [alega'sãw] (*pl* **-ões**) F allegation

alegado [ale'gadu] M (*Jur*) plea

alegar [ale'gar] VT to allege; (*Jur*) to plead

alegoria [alego'ria] F allegory

alegórico, -a [ale'gɔriku, a] ADJ allegorical; **carro ~** float

alegrar [ale'grar] VT (*tornar feliz*) to cheer (up), gladden; (*ambiente*) to brighten up; (*animar*) to liven (up); **alegrar-se** VR to cheer up

alegre [a'lɛgri] ADJ (*jovial*) cheerful; (*contente*) happy, glad; (*cores*) bright; (*embriagado*) merry, tight

alegria [ale'gria] F joy, happiness

aleguei *etc* [ale'gej] VB *ver* **alegar**

aleia [a'lɛja] F (*tree-lined*) avenue; (*passagem*) alley

aleijado, -a [alej'ʒadu, a] ADJ crippled ▶ M/F cripple

aleijão [alej'ʒãw] (*pl* **-ões**) M deformity

aleijar [alej'ʒar] VT (*mutilar*) to maim

aleijões [alej'ʒõjs] MPL *de* **aleijão**

aleitamento [alejta'mẽtu] M breast-feeding

aleitar [alej'tar] VT, VI to breast-feed

além [a'lẽj] ADV (*lá ao longe*) over there; (*mais adiante*) further on ▶ M: **o ~** the hereafter ▶ PREP: **~ de** beyond; (*no outro lado de*) on the other side of; (*para mais de*) over; (*ademais de*) apart from, besides; **~ disso** moreover; **mais ~** further

alemã [ale'mã] F *de* **alemão**

alemães [ale'mãjs] MPL *de* **alemão**

Alemanha [ale'maɲa] F: **a ~** Germany

alemão, -mã [ale'mãw, 'mã] (*pl* **-ães/-s**) ADJ, M/F German ▶ M (*Ling*) German

alentado, -a [alẽ'tadu, a] ADJ (*valente*) valiant; (*grande*) great; (*volumoso*) substantial

alentador, a [alẽta'dor(a)] ADJ encouraging

alentar [alẽ'tar] VT to encourage; **alentar-se** VR to cheer up

alentejano, -a [alẽte'ʒanu, a] ADJ from Alentejo ▶ M/F native *ou* inhabitant of Alentejo

alento [a'lẽtu] M (*fôlego*) breath; (*ânimo*) courage; **dar ~** to encourage; **tomar ~** to draw breath

alergia [aler'ʒia] F: **~ (a)** allergy (to); (*fig*) aversion (to)

alérgico, -a [a'lɛrʒiku, a] ADJ: **~ (a)** allergic (to); **ele é ~ a João/à política** he can't stand João/politics

alerta [a'lɛrta] ADJ alert ▶ ADV on the alert ▶ M alert

alertar [aler'tar] VT to alert; **alertar-se** VR to be alerted

Alf. ABR = **Alferes**

alfabético, -a [awfa'bɛtʃiku, a] ADJ alphabetical

alfabetização [awfabetʃiza'sãw] F literacy

alfabetizado, -a [awfabetʃi'zadu, a] ADJ literate

alfabetizar [awfabetʃi'zar] VT to teach to read and write; **alfabetizar-se** VR to learn to read and write

alfabeto [awfa'bɛtu] M alphabet

alface [aw'fasi] F lettuce

alfaia [aw'faja] F (*móveis*) furniture; (*utensílio*) utensil; (*enfeite*) ornament

alfaiataria [awfajata'ria] F tailor's shop

alfaiate [awfa'jatʃi] M tailor

alfândega [aw'fãdʒiga] F customs *pl*, customs house

alfandegário, -a [awfãde'garju, a] ADJ customs *atr* ▶ M/F customs officer

alfanumérico, -a [awfanu'mɛriku, a] ADJ alphanumeric

alfavaca [awfa'vaka] F basil

alfazema [awfa'zɛma] F lavender

alfena [aw'fɛna] F privet

alfinetada [awfine'tada] F prick; (*dor aguda*) stabbing pain; (*fig*) dig

alfinetar [awfine'tar] VT to prick (with a pin); (*costura*) to pin; (*fig*) to needle

alfinete [awfi'netʃi] M pin; ~ **de chapéu** hat pin; ~ **de fralda** nappy (BRIT) ou diaper (US) pin; ~ **de segurança** safety pin

alfineteira [awfine'tejra] F pin cushion; (caixa) pin box

alga ['awga] F seaweed; (Bot) alga

algarismo [awga'rizmu] M numeral, digit; ~ **arábico/romano** Arabic/Roman numeral

Algarve [aw'garvi] M: **o** ~ the Algarve

algarvio, -a [awgar'viu, a] ADJ from the Algarve ▶ M/F native ou inhabitant of the Algarve

algazarra [awga'zaha] F uproar, racket

álgebra ['awʒebra] F algebra

algemar [awʒe'mar] VT to handcuff

algemas [aw'ʒemas] FPL handcuffs

algibeira [awʒi'bejra] F pocket

algo ['awgu] ADV somewhat, rather ▶ PRON something; (qualquer coisa) anything

algodão [awgo'dãw] M cotton; ~(-**doce**) candy floss; ~ (**hidrófilo**) cotton wool (BRIT), absorbent cotton (US)

algodoeiro, -a [awgo'dwejru, a] ADJ (indústria) cotton atr ▶ M cotton plant

algoritmo [awgo'hitʃimu] M algorithm

algoz [aw'goz] M beast, cruel person

alguém [aw'gẽj] PRON someone, somebody; (em frases interrogativas ou negativas) anyone, anybody; **ser ~ na vida** to be somebody in life

algum, a [aw'gũ, 'guma] ADJ some; (em frases interrogativas ou negativas) any ▶ PRON one; (no plural) some; (negativa): **de modo** ~ in no way; **coisa ~a** nothing; ~ **dia** one day; ~ **tempo** for a while; ~**a coisa** something; ~**a vez** sometime

algures [aw'guris] ADV somewhere

alheio, -a [a'ʎeju, a] ADJ (de outra pessoa) someone else's; (de outras pessoas) other people's; (estranho) alien; (estrangeiro) foreign; (impróprio) irrelevant; ~ **a** foreign to; (desatento) unaware of; ~ **de** (afastado) removed from, far from; (ignorante) unaware of

alho ['aʎu] M garlic; **confundir** ~**s com bugalhos** to get things mixed up

alho-poró [-po'rɔ] (pl **alhos-porós**) M leek

ali [a'li] ADV there; **até** ~ up to there; **por** ~ around there, somewhere there; (direção) that way; ~ **por** (tempo) round about; **de** ~ **por diante** from then on; ~ **dentro** in there

aliado, -a [a'ljadu, a] ADJ allied ▶ M/F ally

aliança [a'ljãsa] F alliance; (anel) wedding ring

aliar [a'ljar] VT to ally; **aliar-se** VR to form an alliance

aliás [a'ljajs] ADV (a propósito) as a matter of fact; (ou seja) rather, that is; (contudo) nevertheless; (diga-se de passagem) incidentally

álibi ['alibi] M alibi

alicate [ali'katʃi] M pliers pl; ~ **de unhas** nail clippers pl

alicerçar [aliser'sar] VT (argumento etc) to base; (consolidar) to consolidate

alicerce [ali'sɛrsi] M (de edifício) foundation; (fig: base) basis

aliciar [ali'sjar] VT (seduzir) to entice; (atrair) to attract

alienação [aljena'sãw] F alienation; (de bens) transfer (of property); ~ **mental** insanity

alienado, -a [alje'nadu, a] ADJ alienated; (demente) insane; (bens) transferred ▶ M/F lunatic

alienar [alje'nar] VT (bens) to transfer; (afastar) to alienate; **alienar-se** VR to become alienated

alienígena [alje'niʒena] ADJ, M/F alien

alijar [ali'ʒar] VT to jettison; (livrar-se de) to get rid of; **alijar-se** VR: ~-**se de** to free o.s. of

alimentação [alimẽta'sãw] F (alimentos) food; (ação) feeding; (nutrição) nourishment; (Elet) supply

alimentar [alimẽ'tar] VT to feed; (fig) to nurture ▶ ADJ (produto) food atr; (hábitos) eating atr; **alimentar-se** VR: ~-**se de** to feed on

alimentício, -a [alimẽ'tʃisju, a] ADJ nourishing; **gêneros** ~**s** foodstuffs

alimento [ali'mẽtu] M food; (nutrição) nourishment

alínea [a'linja] F opening line of a paragraph; (subdivisão de artigo) sub-heading

alinhado, -a [ali'ɲadu, a] ADJ (elegante) elegant; (texto) aligned; ~ **à esquerda/ direita** (texto) ranged left/right

alinhamento [aliɲa'mẽtu] M alignment; ~ **da margem** justification

alinhar [ali'ɲar] VT to align; **alinhar-se** VR (enfileirar-se) to form a line

alinhavar [aliɲa'var] VT (Costura) to tack

alinhavo [ali'ɲavu] M tacking

alinho [a'liɲu] M (alinhamento) alignment; (elegância) neatness

alíquota [a'likwota] F bracket, percentage

alisar [ali'zar] VT (tornar liso) to smooth; (cabelo) to straighten; (acariciar) to stroke

alistamento [alista'mẽtu] M enlistment

alistar [alis'tar] VT (Mil) to recruit; **alistar-se** VR to enlist

aliteração [alitera'sãw] F alliteration

aliviado, -a [ali'vjadu, a] ADJ (pessoa, dor) relieved; (folgado) free; (carga) lightened

aliviar [ali'vjar] VT to relieve; (carga etc) to lighten ▶ VI (diminuir) to diminish; (acalmar) to give relief; **aliviar-se** VR: ~-**se de** (libertar-se) to unburden o.s. of

alívio [a'livju] M relief

Alm. ABR = **Almirante**

alma ['awma] F soul; (entusiasmo) enthusiasm; (caráter) character; **eu daria a ~ para fazer** I would give anything to do; **sua ~, sua palma** don't say I didn't warn you

almanaque [awma'naki] M almanac; **cultura de** ~ superficial knowledge

almejar [awme'ʒar] VT to long for, yearn for
almirantado [awmirã'tadu] M admiralty
almirante [awmi'rãtʃi] M admiral
almoçado, -a [awmo'sadu, a] ADJ: **ele está ~**
he's had lunch
almoçar [awmo'sar] VI to have lunch ▶ VT:
~ peixe to have fish for lunch
almoço [aw'mosu] M lunch; **pequeno ~** (PT)
breakfast
almofada [awmo'fada] F cushion; (PT:
travesseiro) pillow
almofadado, -a [awmofa'dadu, a] ADJ
cushioned
almofadinha [awmofa'dʒiɲa] F pin cushion
almôndega [aw'mõdega] F meat ball
almotolia [awmoto'lia] F oilcan
almoxarifado [awmoʃari'fadu] M storeroom
almoxarife [awmoʃa'rifi] M storekeeper
ALN (BR) ABR F (= Ação Libertadora Nacional)
former group opposed to junta
alô [a'lo] (BR) EXCL (Tel) hello!
alocação [aloka'sãw] (pl -**ões**) F allocation
alocar [alo'kar] VT to allocate
aloirado, -a [aloj'radu, a] ADJ = **alourado**
alojamento [aloʒa'mẽtu] M accommodation
(BRIT), accommodations pl (US); (habitação)
housing; (Mil) billet
alojar [alo'ʒar] VT to lodge; (Mil) to billet;
alojar-se VR to stay
alongamento [alõga'mẽtu] M lengthening;
(prazo) extension; (ginástica) stretching
alongar [alõ'gar] VT (fazer longo) to lengthen;
(prazo) to extend; (prolongar) to prolong;
(braço) to stretch out; **alongar-se** VR (sobre um
assunto) to dwell
aloprado, -a [alo'pradu, a] (col) ADJ nutty
alourado, -a [alo'radu, a] ADJ blondish
alpaca [aw'paka] F alpaca
alpendre [aw'pẽdri] M (telheiro) shed; (pórtico)
porch
alpercata [awper'kata] F sandal
Alpes ['awpis] MPL: **os ~** the Alps
alpinismo [awpi'nizmu] M mountaineering,
climbing
alpinista [awpi'nista] M/F mountaineer,
climber
alq. ABR = **alqueire**
alquebrar [awke'brar] VT to bend; (enfraquecer)
to weaken ▶ VI (curvar) to stoop, be bent
double
alqueire [aw'kejri] M ≈ 4.84 hectares (in São
Paulo = 2.42 hectares)
alqueive [aw'kejvi] M fallow land
alquimia [awki'mia] F alchemy
alquimista [awki'mista] M/F alchemist
Alsácia [aw'sasja] F: **a ~** Alsace
alta ['awta] F (de preços) rise; (de hospital)
discharge; (Bolsa) high; **estar em ~** to be on
the up; **pessoa da ~** high-class ou
high-society person
alta-fidelidade F hi-fi, high fidelity
altaneiro, -a [awta'nejru, a] ADJ (soberbo)
proud

altar [aw'tar] M altar
altar-mor [-'mɔr] (pl **altares-mores**) M high
altar
alta-roda F high society
alta-tensão F high tension
altear [aw'tʃjar] VT to raise; (reputação) to
enhance ▶ VI to spread out; **altear-se** VR to
be enhanced
alteração [awtera'sãw] (pl -**ões**) F alteration;
(desordem) disturbance; (falsificação)
falsification
alterado, -a [awte'radu, a] ADJ (de mau humor)
bad-tempered, irritated
alterar [awte'rar] VT (mudar) to alter; (falsificar)
to falsify; **alterar-se** VR (mudar-se) to change;
(enfurecer-se) to lose one's temper
altercar [awter'kar] VI to have an altercation
▶ VT to argue for, advocate
alter ego [awter-] M alter ego
alternado, -a [awter'nadu, a] ADJ alternate
alternância [awter'nãsja] F (Agr) crop
rotation
alternar [awter'nar] VT, VI to alternate;
alternar-se VR to alternate; (por turnos) to
take turns
alternativa [awterna'tʃiva] F alternative
alternativo, -a [awterna'tʃivu, a] ADJ
alternative; (Elet) alternating
alteroso, -a [awte'rozu, ɔza] ADJ towering;
(majestoso) majestic
alteza [aw'teza] F highness
altissonante [awtʃiso'nãtʃi] ADJ high-
sounding
altista [aw'tʃista] M/F (Bolsa) bull ▶ ADJ
(tendência) bullish; **mercado ~** bull market
altitude [awtʃi'tudʒi] F altitude
altivez [awtʃi'vez] F (arrogância) haughtiness;
(nobreza) loftiness
altivo, -a [aw'tʃivu, a] ADJ (arrogante) haughty;
(elevado) lofty
alto, -a ['awtu, a] ADJ high; (pessoa) tall; (som)
loud; (importância, luxo) great; (Geo) upper
▶ ADV (falar) loudly, loud; (voar) high ▶ EXCL
halt! ▶ M (topo) top, summit; **do ~** from
above; **por ~** superficially; **estar ~** (bêbado)
to be tipsy; **alta fidelidade** high fidelity,
hi-fi; **alta noite** dead of night; **~ lá!** just a
minute!; **~s e baixos** ups and downs
alto-astral (pl **alto-astrais**) ADJ upbeat
alto-falante (pl **-s**) M loudspeaker
altruísmo [awtru'izmu] M altruism
altruísta [awtru'ista] ADJ altruistic
altruístico, -a [awtru'istʃiku, a] ADJ altruistic
altura [aw'tura] F height; (momento) point,
juncture; (altitude) altitude; (de um som)
pitch; (lugar) whereabouts; **em que ~ da Rio
Branco fica a livraria?** whereabouts in Rio
Branco is the bookshop?; **na ~ do banco**
near the bank; **nesta ~** at this juncture;
estar à ~ de (ser capaz de) to be up to; **pôr
alguém nas ~s** (fig) to praise sb to the skies;
ter 1.80 metros de ~ to be 1.80 metres (BRIT)
ou meters (US) tall

alucinação [alusina'sãw] (pl -ões) F
hallucination

alucinado, -a [alusi'nadu, a] ADJ (maluco)
crazy; ~ **por** crazy about

alucinante [alusi'nãtʃi] ADJ (que enlouquece)
mind-boggling; (que irrita) infuriating;
(ritmo, paixão) intoxicating

aludir [alu'dʒir] VI: ~ **a** to allude to, hint at

alugar [alu'gar] VT (tomar de aluguel) to rent,
hire; (dar de aluguel) to let, rent out; **alugar-se**
VR to let

aluguel [alu'gɛw] (pl -**éis**) (BR) M rent; (ação)
renting; ~ **de carro** car hire (BRIT) ou rental
(US)

aluguer [alu'gɛr] (PT) M = **aluguel**

aluir [a'lwir] VT (abalar) to shake; (derrubar) to
demolish; (arruinar) to ruin ▶ VI to collapse;
(ameaçar ruína) to crumble

alumiar [alu'mjar] VT to light (up) ▶ VI to give
light

alumínio [alu'minju] M aluminium (BRIT),
aluminum (US)

alunissagem [aluni'saʒẽ] (pl -**ns**) F moon
landing

alunissar [aluni'sar] VI to land on the moon

aluno, -a [a'lunu, a] M/F pupil, student;
~ **excepcional** pupil with learning
difficulties

alusão [alu'zãw] (pl -ões) F allusion, reference

alusivo, -a [alu'zivu, a] ADJ allusive

alusões [alu'zõjs] FPL de **alusão**

alvará [awva'ra] M permit

alvejante [awve'ʒãtʃi] M bleach

alvejar [awve'ʒar] VT (tomar como alvo) to aim
at; (branquear) to whiten, bleach ▶ VI to
whiten

alvenaria [awvena'ria] F masonry, brickwork;
de ~ brick atr, brick-built

alvéolo [aw'vɛolu] M cavity; (de dentes) socket

alvitrar [awvi'trar] VT to propose, suggest

alvitre [aw'vitri] M opinion

alvo, -a [a'awvu, a] ADJ white ▶ M target;
acertar no ou **atingir o ~** to hit the mark;
ser ~ de críticas etc to be the object of
criticism etc

alvorada [awvo'rada] F dawn

alvorecer [awvore'ser] VI to dawn

alvoroçar [awvoro'sar] VT (agitar) to stir up;
(entusiasmar) to excite; **alvoroçar-se** VR to get
agitated

alvoroço [awvo'rosu] M (agitação) commotion;
(entusiasmo) enthusiasm

alvura [aw'vura] F (brancura) whiteness;
(pureza) purity

AM ABR = **Amazonas**; (Rádio: = amplitude
modulada) AM

Amã [a'mã] N Amman

amabilidade [amabili'dadʒi] F kindness;
(simpatia) friendliness

amabilíssimo, -a [amabi'lisimu, a] ADJ
SUPERL de **amável**

amaciante [ama'sjãtʃi] M: ~ **(de roupa)**
fabric conditioner

amaciar [ama'sjar] VT (tornar macio) to soften;
(carro) to run in

ama de leite ['ama-] (pl **amas de leite**) F
wet-nurse

amado, -a [a'madu, a] M/F beloved,
sweetheart

amador, a [ama'dor(a)] ADJ, M/F amateur

amadorismo [amado'rizmu] M amateur
status

amadorístico, -a [amado'ristʃiku, a] ADJ
amateurish

amadurecer [amadure'ser] VT, VI (frutos) to
ripen; (fig) to mature

âmago ['amagu] M (centro) heart, core;
(medula) pith; (essência) essence

amainar [amaj'nar] VI (tempestade) to abate;
(cólera) to calm down

amaldiçoar [amawdʒi'swar] VT to curse,
swear at

amálgama [a'mawgama] F amalgam

amalgamar [amawga'mar] VT to
amalgamate; (combinar) to fuse (BRIT), fuze
(US), blend

amalucado, -a [amalu'kadu, a] ADJ crazy,
whacky

amamentação [amamẽta'sãw] F breast-
feeding

amamentar [amamẽ'tar] VT, VI to breast-feed

AMAN (BR) ABR F = **Academia Militar das
Agulhas Negras**

amanhã [ama'ɲã] ADV, M tomorrow; ~ **de
manhã** tomorrow morning; ~ **de tarde**
tomorrow afternoon; ~ **à noite** tomorrow
night; **depois de ~** the day after tomorrow

amanhecer [amaɲe'ser] VI (alvorecer) to dawn;
(encontrar-se pela manhã): **amanhecemos em
Paris** we were in Paris at daybreak ▶ M
dawn; **ao ~** at daybreak

amansar [amã'sar] VT (animais) to tame;
(cavalos) to break in; (aplacar) to placate ▶ VI
to grow tame

amante [a'mãtʃi] M/F lover

amanteigado, -a [amãtej'gadu, a] ADJ:
biscoito ~ shortbread

amapaense [amapa'ẽsi] ADJ from Amapá
▶ M/F native ou inhabitant of Amapá

amar [a'mar] VT to love; **eu te amo** I love you

amarelado, -a [amare'ladu, a] ADJ yellowish;
(pele) sallow

amarelar [amare'lar] VT, VI to yellow

amarelinha [amare'liɲa] F (jogo) hopscotch

amarelo, -a [ama'rɛlu, a] ADJ yellow ▶ M
yellow

amarfanhar [amarfa'ɲar] VT to screw up

amargar [amar'gar] VT to make bitter; (fig) to
embitter; (sofrer) to suffer; **ser de ~** to be
murder

amargo, -a [a'margu, a] ADJ bitter

amargura [amar'gura] F bitterness; (fig:
sofrimento) sadness, suffering

amargurado, -a [amargu'radu, a] ADJ sad

amargurar [amargu'rar] VT to embitter,
sadden; (sofrer) to endure

amarração [amaha'sãw] F: **ser uma ~** (col) to be great

amarrado, -a [ama'hadu, a] ADJ (cara) scowling, angry; (col: casado etc) spoken for

amarrar [ama'har] VT to tie (up); (Náut) to moor; **amarrar-se** VR: **~ -se em** to like very much; **~ a cara** to frown, scowl

amarronzado, -a [amahõ'zadu, a] ADJ brownish

amarrotar [amaho'tar] VT to crease

ama-seca ['ama-] (pl **amas-secas**) F nanny

amassado, -a [ama'sadu, a] ADJ (roupa) creased; (papel) screwed up; (carro) smashed in

amassar [ama'sar] VT (pão) to knead; (misturar) to mix; (papel) to screw up; (roupa) to crease; (carro) to dent

amável [a'mavew] (pl **-eis**) ADJ (afável) kind

amazona [ama'zɔna] F horsewoman

Amazonas [ama'zɔnas] M: **o ~** the Amazon

amazonense [amazo'nẽsi] ADJ from Amazonas ▶ M/F native ou inhabitant of Amazonas

Amazônia [ama'zonja] F: **a ~** the Amazon region

> **Amazônia** is the region formed by the basin of the river Amazon (the river with the largest volume of water in the world) and its tributaries. With a total area of almost 7 million square kilometres, it stretches from the Atlantic to the Andes. Most of **Amazônia** is in Brazilian territory, although it also extends into Peru, Colombia, Venezuela and Bolivia. It contains the richest biodiversity and largest area of tropical rainforest in the world.

amazônico, -a [ama'zoniku, a] ADJ Amazonian

âmbar ['ãbar] M amber

ambição [ambi'sãw] (pl **-ões**) F ambition

ambicionar [ãbisjo'nar] VT (ter ambição de) to aspire to; (desejar) to crave for

ambicioso, -a [ãbi'sjozu, ɔza] ADJ ambitious

ambições [ãbi'sõjs] FPL de **ambição**

ambidestro, -a [ãbi'destru, a] ADJ ambidextrous

ambiental [ãbjẽ'taw] (pl **-ais**) ADJ environmental

ambientalista [ãbjẽta'lista] M/F environmentalist

ambientar [ãbjẽ'tar] VT (filme etc) to set; (adaptar): **~ alguém a algo** to get sb used to sth; **ambientar-se** VR to fit in

ambiente [ã'bjẽtʃi] M atmosphere; (meio, Comput) environment; (de uma casa) ambience ▶ ADJ surrounding; **meio ~** environment; **temperatura ~** room temperature

ambiguidade [ambigwi'dadʒi] F ambiguity

ambíguo, -a [ã'bigwu, a] ADJ ambiguous

âmbito ['ãbitu] M (extensão) extent; (campo de ação) scope, range; **no ~ nacional/**

internacional at (the) national/ international level

ambivalência [ãbiva'lẽsja] F ambivalence

ambivalente [ãbiva'lẽtʃi] ADJ ambivalent

ambos, ambas ['ãbus, as] ADJ PL both; **~ nós** both of us; **~ os lados** both sides

ambrosia [ãbro'zia] F egg custard

ambulância [ãbu'lãsja] F ambulance

ambulante [ãbu'lãtʃi] ADJ walking; (errante) wandering; (biblioteca) mobile

ambulatório [ãbula'tɔrju] M outpatient department

ameaça [ame'asa] F threat; **~ de bomba** bomb scare

ameaçador, a [ameasa'dor(a)] ADJ threatening, menacing

ameaçar [amea'sar] VT to threaten

ameba [a'mɛba] F amoeba (BRIT), ameba (US)

amedrontador, a [amedrõta'dor(a)] ADJ intimidating, frightening

amedrontar [amedrõ'tar] VT to scare, intimidate; **amedrontar-se** VR to be frightened

ameia [a'meja] F battlement

ameixa [a'mejʃa] F plum; (passa) prune

amélia [a'mɛlja] (col) F long-suffering wife (ou girlfriend)

amém [a'mẽj] EXCL amen!; **dizer ~ a** (fig) to agree to

amêndoa [a'mẽdwa] F almond

amendoado, -a [amẽ'dwadu, a] ADJ (olhos) almond-shaped

amendoeira [amẽ'dwejra] F almond tree

amendoim [amẽdo'ĩ] (pl **-ns**) M peanut

amenidade [ameni'dadʒi] F wellbeing; **amenidades** FPL (assuntos superficiais) small talk sg

amenizar [ameni'zar] VT (abrandar) to soften; (tornar agradável) to make pleasant; (facilitar) to ease; (briga) to settle

ameno, -a [a'mɛnu, a] ADJ (agradável) pleasant; (clima) mild, gentle

América [a'mɛrika] F: **a ~** America; **a ~ do Norte/do Sul** North/South America; **a ~ Central/Latina** Central/Latin America

americanizado, -a [amerikani'zadu, a] ADJ Americanized

americano, -a [ameri'kanu, a] ADJ, M/F American

amesquinhar [ameski'ɲar] VT to belittle; **amesquinhar-se** VR to belittle o.s.; (tornar-se avarento) to become stingy

amestrar [ames'trar] VT to train

ametista [ame'tʃista] F amethyst

amianto [a'mjãtu] M asbestos

amicíssimo, -a [ami'sisimu, a] ADJ SUPERL de **amigo**

amido [a'midu] M starch

amigar-se [ami'garsi] VR: **~ (com)** to become friends (with)

amigável [ami'gavew] (pl **-eis**) ADJ amicable

amígdala [a'migdala] F tonsil

amigdalite [amigda'litʃi] F tonsillitis

amigo, -a [a'migu, a] ADJ friendly ▶ M/F friend; **ser ~ de** to be friends with; **~ da onça** false friend

amistoso, -a [amis'tozu, ɔza] ADJ friendly, cordial ▶ M (*jogo*) friendly

AMIU (BR) ABR F (= *Assistência Médica Infantil de Urgência*) emergency paediatric service

amiudar [amju'dar] VT, VI to repeat; **~ as visitas** to make frequent visits

amiúde [a'mjudʒi] ADV often, frequently

amizade [ami'zadʒi] F (*relação*) friendship; (*simpatia*) friendliness; **fazer ~s** to make friends; **~ colorida** casual relationship

amnésia [am'nɛzja] F amnesia

amnistia [amnis'tia] (PT) F = **anistia**

amofinar [amofi'nar] VT to trouble; **amofinar-se (com)** VR to fret (over)

amolação [amola'sãw] (*pl* -**ões**) F bother, annoyance; (*desgosto*) upset

amolador, a [amola'dor(a)] M/F knife sharpener

amolante [amo'lãtʃi] (BR) ADJ bothersome

amolar [amo'lar] VT (*afiar*) to sharpen; (*aborrecer*) to annoy, bother ▶ VI to be annoying; **amolar-se** VR (*aborrecer-se*) to get annoyed

amoldar [amow'dar] VT to mould (BRIT), mold (US); **amoldar-se** VR: **~-se a** (*conformar-se*) to conform to; (*acostumar-se*) to get used to

amolecer [amole'ser] VT to soften ▶ VI to soften; (*abrandar-se*) to relent

amolecimento [amolesi'mẽtu] M softening

amônia [a'monja] F ammonia

amoníaco [amo'niaku] M ammonia

amontoado [amõ'twadu] M mass; (*de coisas*) pile

amontoar [amõ'twar] VT to pile up, accumulate; **~ riquezas** to amass a fortune

amor [a'mor] M love; **por ~ de** for the sake of; **fazer ~** to make love; **ela é um ~ (de pessoa)** she's a lovely person; **~ próprio** self-esteem; (*orgulho*) conceit

amora [a'mɔra] F mulberry; (*amora-preta*) blackberry; **~ silvestre** blackberry

amoral [amo'raw] (*pl* -**ais**) ADJ amoral

amora-preta (*pl* **amoras-pretas**) F blackberry

amordaçar [amorda'sar] VT to gag

amoreco [amo'rɛku] M: **ela é um ~** she's a lovely person

amorenado, -a [amore'nadu, a] ADJ darkish

amorfo, -a [a'mɔrfu, a] ADJ (*objeto*) amorphous; (*pessoa*) dull

amornar [amor'nar] VT to warm

amoroso, -a [amo'rozu, ɔza] ADJ loving, affectionate

amor-perfeito (*pl* **amores-perfeitos**) M pansy

amortecedor [amortese'dor] M shock absorber

amortecer [amorte'ser] VT to deaden ▶ VI to weaken, fade

amortecido, -a [amorte'sidu, a] ADJ deadened; (*enfraquecido*) weak

amortização [amortʃiza'sãw] F payment in instalments (BRIT) *ou* installments (US); (Com) amortization

amortizar [amortʃi'zar] VT to pay in instalments (BRIT) *ou* installments (US)

amostra [a'mɔstra] F sample

amostragem [amos'traʒẽ] F sampling

amotinado, -a [amotʃi'nadu, a] ADJ mutinous, rebellious

amotinar [amotʃi'nar] VI to rebel, mutiny; **amotinar-se** VR to rebel, mutiny

amparar [ãpa'rar] VT to support; (*ajudar*) to assist; **amparar-se** VR: **~-se em/contra** (*apoiar-se*) to lean on/against

amparo [ã'paru] M (*apoio*) support; (*auxílio*) help, assistance

ampère [ã'pɛri] (BR) M ampere, amp

ampliação [amplja'sãw] (*pl* -**ões**) F (*aumento*) enlargement; (*extensão*) extension

ampliar [ã'pljar] VT to enlarge; (*conhecimento*) to broaden

amplidão [ãpli'dãw] F vastness

amplificação [ãplifika'sãw] (*pl* -**ões**) F (*aumento*) enlargement; (*de som*) amplification

amplificador [ãplifika'dor] M amplifier

amplificar [ãplifi'kar] VT to amplify

amplitude [ãpli'tudʒi] F (Tec) amplitude; (*espaço*) spaciousness; (*fig: extensão*) extent

amplo, -a ['ãplu, a] ADJ (*sala*) spacious; (*conhecimento, sentido*) broad; (*possibilidade*) ample

ampola [ã'pola] F ampoule (BRIT), ampule (US)

amputação [ãputa'sãw] (*pl* -**ões**) F amputation

amputar [ãpu'tar] VT to amputate

Amsterdã [amister'dã] (BR) N Amsterdam

Amsterdão [amister'dãw] (PT) N = **Amsterdã**

amuado, -a [a'mwadu, a] ADJ sulky

amuar [a'mwar] VI to sulk

amuleto [amu'letu] M charm

amuo [a'muu] M sulkiness

anã [a'nã] F *de* **anão**

anacrônico, -a [ana'kroniku, a] ADJ anachronistic

anacronismo [anakro'nizmu] M anachronism

anagrama [ana'grama] M anagram

anágua [a'nagwa] F petticoat

ANAI ABR F = **Associação Nacional de Apoio ao Índio**

anais [a'najs] MPL annals

analfabetismo [anawfabe'tʃizmu] M illiteracy

analfabeto, -a [anawfa'bɛtu, a] ADJ, M/F illiterate

analgésico, -a [anaw'ʒɛziku, a] ADJ analgesic ▶ M painkiller

analisar [anali'zar] VT to analyse

análise [a'nalizi] F analysis

analista [ana'lista] M/F analyst; **~ de sistemas** systems analyst

analítico, -a [ana'litʃiku, a] ADJ analytical

analogia [analo'ʒia] F analogy
análogo, -a [a'nalogu, a] ADJ analogous
ananás [ana'nas] (pl **ananases**) M (BR) variety of pineapple; (PT) pineapple
anão, anã [a'nãw, a'nã] (pl **-ões/-s**) M/F dwarf
anarquia [anar'kia] F anarchy; (fig) chaos
anárquico, -a [a'narkiku, a] ADJ anarchic
anarquista [anar'kista] M/F anarchist
anarquizar [anarki'zar] VT (povo) to incite to anarchy; (desordenar) to mess up; (ridicularizar) to ridicule
anátema [a'natema] M anathema
anatomia [anato'mia] F anatomy
anatômico, -a [ana'tomiku, a] ADJ anatomical
anavalhar [anava'ʎar] VT to slash
Anbid (BR) ABR F = **Associação Nacional de Bancos de Investimentos e Desenvolvimento**
anca ['ãka] F (de pessoa) hip; (de animal) rump
Ancara [ã'kara] N Ankara
ancestrais [ãses'trajs] MPL ancestors
anchova [ã'ʃova] F anchovy
ancião, anciã [ã'sjãw, ã'sjã] (pl **-ões/-s**) ADJ old ▶ M/F old man/woman; (de uma tribo) elder
ancinho [ã'siɲu] M rake
anciões [a'sjõjs] MPL de **ancião**
âncora ['ãkora] F anchor ▶ M/F (TV, Rádio) anchor man/woman
ancoradouro [ãkora'doru] M anchorage
ancorar [ãko'rar] VT, VI to anchor
andada [ã'dada] F walk; **dar uma ~** to go for a walk
andador [ãda'dor] M (para idoso) Zimmer® frame
andaime [ã'dajmi] M (Arq) scaffolding
Andaluzia [ãdalu'zia] F: **a ~** Andalucia
andamento [ãda'mẽtu] M (progresso) progress; (rumo) course; (Mús) tempo; **em ~** in progress; **dar ~ a algo** to set sth in motion
andanças [ã'dãsas] FPL wanderings
andar [ã'dar] VI (ir a pé) to walk; (máquina) to work; (progredir) to go, to progress; (estar): **ela anda triste** she's been sad lately ▶ M (modo de caminhar) gait; (pavimento) floor, storey (BRIT), story (US); **anda!** hurry up!; **~ com alguém** to have an affair with sb; **~ a cavalo** to ride; **~ de trem/avião/bicicleta** to travel by train/to fly/to ride a bike
andarilho, -a [ãda'riʎu, a] M/F good walker
ANDC (BR) ABR F = **Associação Nacional de Defesa do Consumidor**
Andes ['ãdʒis] MPL: **os ~** the Andes
Andima (BR) ABR F = **Associação Nacional das Instituições de Mercado Aberto**
andorinha [ãdo'riɲa] F (pássaro) swallow
Andorra [ã'doʀa] F Andorra
andrógino, -a [ã'drɔʒinu, a] ADJ androgynous
anedota [ane'dɔta] F anecdote
anedótico, -a [ane'dɔtʃiku, a] ADJ anecdotal
anel [a'nɛw] (pl **-éis**) M ring; (elo) link; (de cabelo) curl; **~ de casamento** wedding ring

anelado, -a [ane'ladu, a] ADJ curly
anemia [ane'mia] F anaemia (BRIT), anemia (US)
anêmico, -a [a'nemiku, a] ADJ anaemic (BRIT), anemic (US)
anestesia [aneste'zia] F anaesthesia (BRIT), anesthesia (US); (anestésico) anaesthetic (BRIT), anesthetic (US)
anestesiar [aneste'zjar] VT to anaesthetize (BRIT), anesthetize (US)
anestésico [anes'tɛziku] M (Med) anaesthetic (BRIT), anesthetic (US)
anestesista [aneste'zista] M/F anaesthetist (BRIT), anesthetist (US)
anexação [aneksa'sãw] (pl **-ões**) F annexation; (de documento) enclosure
anexar [anek'sar] VT to annex; (juntar) to attach; (documento) to enclose
anexo, -a [a'nɛksu, a] ADJ attached ▶ M annexe; (de igreja) hall; (em carta) enclosure; (em e-mail) attachment; **segue em ~** please find enclosed
Anfavea (BR) ABR F = **Associação Nacional dos Fabricantes de Veículos Automotores**
anfetamina [ãfeta'mina] F amphetamine
anfíbio, -a [ã'fibju, a] ADJ amphibious ▶ M amphibian
anfiteatro [ãfi'tʃjatru] M amphitheatre (BRIT), amphitheater (US); (no teatro) dress circle
anfitrião, -triã [ãfi'trjãw, 'trjã] (pl **-ões/-s**) M/F host/hostess
angariar [ãga'rjar] VT (fundos, donativos) to raise; (adeptos) to attract; (reputação, simpatia) to gain; **~ votos** to canvass (for votes)
angelical [ãʒeli'kaw] (pl **-ais**) ADJ angelic
angina [ã'ʒina] F: **~ do peito** angina (pectoris)
anglicano, -a [ãgli'kanu, a] ADJ, M/F Anglican
anglicismo [ãgli'sizmu] M Anglicism
anglo-saxão, anglo-saxôni(c)a [ãglosak'sãw, sak'soni(k)a] (pl **-ões/-s**) M/F Anglo-Saxon
anglo-saxônico, -a [ãglosak'soniku, a] ADJ Anglo-Saxon
Angola [ã'gɔla] F Angola
angolano, -a [ãgo'lanu, a] ADJ, M/F Angolan
angolense [ãgo'lẽsi] ADJ, M/F Angolan
angorá [ãgo'ra] ADJ angora
angra ['ãgra] F inlet, cove
angu [ã'gu] M corn-meal purée
angular [ãgu'lar] ADJ angular
ângulo ['ãgulu] M angle; (canto) corner; (fig) angle, point of view
angústia [ã'gustʃja] F anguish, distress
angustiado, -a [ãgus'tʃjadu, a] ADJ distressed
angustiante [ãgus'tʃjãtʃi] ADJ distressing; (momentos) anxious, nerve-racking
angustiar [ãgus'tʃjar] VT to distress
anil [a'niw] M (cor) indigo
animação [anima'sãw] F (vivacidade) liveliness; (movimento) bustle; (entusiasmo) enthusiasm
animado, -a [ani'madu, a] ADJ (vivo) lively; (alegre) cheerful; **~ com** enthusiastic about

animador, a [anima'dor(a)] ADJ encouraging
▶ M/F (BR TV) presenter; (de festa) entertainer;
~(a) de torcida cheerleader

animal [ani'maw] (pl **-ais**) ADJ, M animal; ~ de
estimação pet (animal)

animalesco, -a [anima'lesku, a] ADJ bestial,
brutish

animar [ani'mar] VT (dar vida) to liven up;
(encorajar) to encourage; **animar-se** VR
(alegrar-se) to cheer up; (festa etc) to liven up;
~-se a to bring o.s. to

ânimo ['animu] M (coragem) courage; ~! cheer
up!; **perder o ~** to lose heart; **recobrar o ~**
to pluck up courage; (alegrar-se) to cheer up

animosidade [animozi'dadʒi] F animosity

aninhar [ani'ɲar] VT to nestle; **aninhar-se** VR
to nestle

aniquilação [anikila'sãw] F annihilation

aniquilar [aniki'lar] VT to annihilate; (destruir)
to destroy; (prostrar) to shatter; **aniquilar-se**
VR to be annihilated; (moralmente) to be
shattered

anis [a'nis] M aniseed

anistia [anis'tʃia] F amnesty

aniversariante [aniversa'rjãtʃi] M/F birthday
boy/girl

aniversário [aniver'sarju] M anniversary; (de
nascimento) birthday; (: festa) birthday party;
~ de casamento wedding anniversary

anjo ['aʒu] M angel; ~ da guarda guardian
angel

ANL (BR) ABR F (= Aliança Nacional Libertadora)
1930's left-wing movement

ano ['anu] M year; **Feliz A~ Novo!** Happy
New Year!; **o ~ passado** last year; **o ~ que
vem** next year; **por ~** per annum; **fazer ~s**
to have a birthday; **ele faz ~s hoje** it's his
birthday today; **ter dez ~s** to be ten (years
old); **dia de ~s** (PT) birthday; ~ **civil** calendar
year; ~ **corrente** current year; ~ **financeiro**
financial year; ~ **letivo** academic year; (da
escola) school year

ano-bom M New Year

anões [a'nõjs] MPL de **anão**

anoitecer [anojte'ser] VI to grow dark ▶ M
nightfall; **ao ~** at nightfall

anomalia [anoma'lia] F anomaly

anômalo, -a [a'nomalu, a] ADJ anomalous

anonimato [anoni'matu] M anonymity

anônimo, -a [a'nonimu, a] ADJ anonymous;
(Com): **sociedade anônima** limited
company (BRIT), stock company (US)

anoraque [ano'raki] M anorak

anorexia [ano'rɛksja] F anorexia

anoréxico, -a [ano'rɛksiku, a] ADJ anorexic

anormal [anor'maw] (pl **-ais**) ADJ abnormal;
(incomum) unusual; (excepcional) handicapped

anormalidade [anormali'dadʒi] F
abnormality

anotação [anota'sãw] (pl **-ões**) F (comentário)
annotation; (nota) note

anotar [ano'tar] VT (tomar nota) to note down;
(esclarecer) to annotate

anseio etc [ã'seju] VB ver **ansiar**

ânsia ['ãsja] F (ansiedade) anxiety; (desejo):
~ **(de)** longing (for); **ter ~s (de vômito)** to
feel sick

ansiado, -a [ã'sjadu, a] ADJ longed for

ansiar [ã'sjar] VI: ~ **por** (desejar) to yearn for;
~ **por fazer** to long to do

ansiedade [ãsje'dadʒi] F anxiety; (desejo)
eagerness

ansioso, -a [ã'sjozu, ɔza] ADJ anxious;
(desejoso) eager

antagônico, -a [ãta'goniku, a] ADJ
antagonistic; (rival) opposing

antagonismo [ãtago'nizmu] M (hostilidade)
antagonism; (oposição) opposition

antagonista [ãtago'nista] M/F antagonist;
(adversário) opponent

antártico, -a [ã'tartʃiku, a] ADJ antarctic ▶ M:
o A~ the Antarctic

ante ['ãtʃi] PREP (na presença de) before; (em vista
de) in view of, faced with

antebraço [ãtʃi'brasu] M forearm

antecedência [ãtese'dẽsja] F: **com ~** in
advance; **3 dias de ~** three days' notice

antecedente [ãtese'dẽtʃi] ADJ (anterior)
preceding ▶ M antecedent; **antecedentes**
MPL (registro) record sg; (passado) background
sg; ~s **criminais** criminal record sg ou past sg

anteceder [ãtese'der] VT to precede

antecessor, a [ãtese'sor(a)] M/F predecessor

antecipação [ãtesipa'sãw] F anticipation;
com um mês de ~ a month in advance;
~ **de pagamento** advance (payment)

antecipadamente [ãtesipada'mẽtʃi] ADV in
advance, beforehand; **pagar ~** to pay in
advance

antecipado, -a [ãtesi'padu, a] ADJ (pagamento)
(in) advance

antecipar [ãtesi'par] VT to anticipate,
forestall; (adiantar) to bring forward;
antecipar-se VR (adiantar-se) to be previous

antegozar [ãtego'zar] VT to anticipate

antemão [ante'mãw] ADV: **de ~** beforehand

antena [ã'tena] F (Bio) antenna, feeler; (Rádio,
TV) aerial; ~ **direcional** directional aerial;
~ **parabólica** satellite dish

anteontem [ãtʃi'õtẽ] ADV the day before
yesterday

anteparo [ãte'paru] M (proteção) screen

antepassado [ãtʃipa'sadu] M ancestor

antepor [ãte'por] (irreg: como **pôr**) VT (pôr antes)
to put before; **antepor-se** VR to anticipate

anteprojeto [ãtepro'ʒɛtu] M outline, draft;
~ **de lei** draft bill

antepunha etc [ãte'puɲa] VB ver **antepor**

antepus etc [ãte'pus] VB ver **antepor**

antepuser etc [ãtepu'zer] VB ver **antepor**

anterior [ãte'rjor] ADJ (prévio) previous; (antigo)
former; (de posição) front

antes ['ãtʃis] ADV before; (antigamente)
formerly; (ao contrário) rather ▶ PREP: ~ **de**
before; **o quanto ~** as soon as possible;
~ **de partir** before leaving; ~ **do tempo**

ahead of time; **~ de tudo** above all; **~ que** before

antessala [āte'sala] F ante-room

antever [āte'ver] (*irreg: como* **ver**) VT to anticipate, foresee

antevisto, -a [āte'vistu, a] PP *de* **antever**

anti- [ātʃi] PREFIXO anti-

antiácido, -a [ã'tʃjasidu, a] ADJ, M antacid

antiaéreo, -a [ātʃja'ɛrju, a] ADJ anti-aircraft

antiamericano, -a [ātʃjameri'kanu, a] ADJ anti-American

antibiótico, -a [ātʃi'bjɔtʃiku, a] ADJ, M antibiotic

anticaspa [ātʃi'kaspa] ADJ INV anti-dandruff

anticiclone [ātʃisi'klɔni] M anticyclone

anticlímax [ātʃi'klimaks] M anticlimax

anticoncepcional [ātʃikõsepsjo'naw] (*pl* **-ais**) ADJ, M contraceptive

anticongelante [ātʃikõʒe'lātʃi] M antifreeze

anticonstitucional [ātʃikõstʃitusjo'naw] (*pl* **-ais**) ADJ unconstitutional

anticorpo [ātʃi'korpu] M antibody

antidemocrático, -a [ātʃidemo'kratʃiku, a] ADJ undemocratic

antidepressivo, -a [ātʃidepre'sivu, a] ADJ, M anti-depressant

antiderrapante [ātʃideha'pātʃi] ADJ (*pneu*) non-skid

antídoto [ã'tʃidotu] M antidote

antiestético, -a [ātʃjes'tetʃiku, a] ADJ tasteless

antiético, -a [ã'tʃjɛtʃiku, a] ADJ unethical

antigamente [ātʃiga'mētʃi] ADV formerly; (*no passado*) in the past

antiglobalização [ātʃiglobaliza'sãw] F antiglobalization

antigo, -a [ã'tʃigu, a] ADJ old; (*histórico*) ancient; (*de estilo*) antique; (*chefe etc*) former; **ele é muito ~ na firma** he's been with the firm for many years; **os ~s** (*gregos etc*) the ancients

Antígua [ã'tʃigwa] F Antigua

antiguidade [ātʃigwi'dadʒi] F antiquity, ancient times *pl*; (*de emprego*) seniority; **antiguidades** FPL (*monumentos*) ancient monuments; (*artigos*) antiques

anti-higiênico, -a ADJ unhygienic

anti-histamínico, -a [-ista'miniku, a] ADJ antihistamine ▸ M antihistamine

anti-horário, -a ADJ anticlockwise

antilhano, -a [ātʃi'ʎanu, a] ADJ, M/F West Indian

Antilhas [ã'tʃiʎas] FPL: **as ~** the West Indies

antílope [ã'tʃilopi] M antelope

antipatia [ātʃipa'tʃia] F antipathy, dislike

antipático, -a [ātʃi'patʃiku, a] ADJ unpleasant, unfriendly

antipatizar [ātʃipatʃi'zar] VI: **~ com alguém** to dislike sb

antipatriótico, -a [ātʃipa'trjɔtʃiku, a] ADJ unpatriotic

antipoluente [ātʃipo'lwētʃi] ADJ non-pollutant

antiquado, -a [ātʃi'kwadu, a] ADJ antiquated; (*fora de moda*) out of date, old-fashioned

antiquário, -a [ātʃi'kwarju, a] M/F antique dealer ▸ M (*loja*) antique shop

antiquíssimo, -a [ātʃi'kisimu, a] ADJ SUPERL *de* **antigo**

antissemita [ātise'mita] ADJ anti-Semitic

antissemitismo [-semi'tʃizmu] M anti-Semitism

antisséptico, -a [āti'sɛpʃtiku, a] ADJ, M antiseptic

antissocial [ātiso'sjaw] (*pl* **-ais**) ADJ antisocial

antiterrorismo [ātʃiteho'rizmu] M counterterrorism

antítese [ã'tʃitezi] F antithesis

antitruste [ātʃi'trustʃi] ADJ: **legislação ~** (*Com*) antitrust legislation

antivírus [ātʃi'virus] M INV (*Comput*) antivirus

antolhos [ã'toʎus] MPL (*pala*) eye-shade *sg*; (*de cavalo*) blinkers

antologia [ātolo'ʒia] F anthology

antônimo [ã'tonimu] M antonym

antro ['ātru] M cave, cavern; (*de animal*) lair; (*de ladrões*) den

antropofagia [ātropofa'ʒia] F cannibalism

antropófago, -a [ātro'pofagu, a] M/F cannibal

antropologia [ātropolo'ʒia] F anthropology

antropólogo, -a [ātro'pologu, a] M/F anthropologist

ANTTUR (BR) ABR F = **Associação Nacional de Transportadores de Turismo e Agências de Viagens**

anual [a'nwaw] (*pl* **-ais**) ADJ annual, yearly

anuário [a'nwarju] M yearbook

anuidade [anwi'dadʒi] F annuity

anuir [a'nwir] VI: **~ a** to agree to; **~ com** to comply with

anulação [anula'sãw] (*pl* **-ões**) F cancellation; (*de contrato, casamento*) annulment

anular [anu'lar] VT to cancel; (*contrato, casamento*) to annul; (*efeito*) to cancel out ▸ M ring finger

anunciante [anũ'sjātʃi] M (*Com*) advertiser

anunciar [anũ'sjar] VT to announce; (*Com: produto*) to advertise

anúncio [a'nũsju] M announcement; (*Com*) advertisement, advert; (*cartaz*) notice; **~ luminoso** neon sign; **~s classificados** small *ou* classified ads

ânus ['anus] M INV anus

anverso [ã'versu] M (*de moeda*) obverse

anzol [ã'zɔw] (*pl* **-óis**) M fish-hook

ao [aw] = **a + o**; *ver a*

aonde [a'õdʒi] ADV where; **~ quer que** wherever

aos [aws] = **a + os**; *ver a*

AP ABR = **Amapá**

Ap. ABR = **apartamento**

apadrinhar [apadri'ɲar] VT (*ser padrinho*) to act as godfather to; (: *de noivo*) to be best man to; (*proteger*) to protect; (*patrocinar*) to support

apagado, -a [apa'gadu, a] ADJ (*fogo*) out; (*luz elétrica*) off; (*indistinto*) faint; (*pessoa*) dull

apagão [apa'gãw] (*pl* **-ões**) M power cut (BRIT), power outage (US)

apagar [apa'gar] VT (*fogo*) to put out; (*luz elétrica*) to switch off; (*vela*) to blow out; (*com borracha*) to rub out, erase; (*quadro-negro*) to clean; **apagar-se** VR to go out; (*desmaiar*) to pass out; (*col: dormir*) to nod off

apaguei *etc* [apa'gej] VB *ver* **apagar**

apaixonado, -a [apajʃo'nadu, a] ADJ (*pessoa*) in love; (*discurso*) impassioned; (*pessoa*): **ele está ~ por ela** he is in love with her; **ele é ~ por tênis** he's mad about tennis

apaixonante [apajʃo'nãtʃi] ADJ captivating

apaixonar-se [apajʃo'narsi] VR: **~ por** to fall in love with

Apalaches [apa'laʃis] MPL: **os ~** the Appalachians

apalermado, -a [apaler'madu, a] ADJ silly

apalpadela [apawpa'dɛla] F touch

apalpar [apaw'par] VT to touch, feel; (*Med*) to examine

apanhado [apa'ɲadu] M (*de flores*) bunch; (*resumo*) summary; (*pregas*) gathering

apanhar [apa'ɲar] VT to catch; (*algo à mão, do chão*) to pick up; (*ir buscar, surra, táxi*) to get; (*flores, frutas*) to pick; (*agarrar*) to grab ▶ VI (*ser espancado*) to get a beating; (*em jogo*) to take a beating; **~ sol/chuva** to sunbathe/get soaked

apaniguado, -a [apani'gwadu, a] M/F (*protegido*) protégé(e)

apapagaiado, -a [apapaga'jadu, a] ADJ loud, garish

apara [a'para] F (*de madeira*) shaving; (*de papel*) clipping

aparador [apara'dor] M sideboard

aparafusar [aparafu'zar] VT to screw

apara-lápis [apara'lapis] (PT) M INV pencil sharpener

aparar [apa'rar] VT (*cabelo*) to trim; (*lápis*) to sharpen; (*algo arremessado*) to catch; (*pancada*) to parry; (*madeira*) to plane

aparato [apa'ratu] M pomp; (*coleção*) array

aparatoso, -a [apara'tozu, ɔza] ADJ grand

aparecer [apare'ser] VI to appear; (*apresentar-se*) to turn up; (*ser publicado*) to be published; **~ em casa de alguém** to call on sb

aparecimento [aparesi'mẽtu] M appearance; (*publicação*) publication

aparelhado, -a [apare'ʎadu, a] ADJ (*preparado*) ready, prepared; (*madeira*) planed

aparelhagem [apare'ʎaʒẽ] F equipment; (*carpintaria*) finishing; (*Náut*) rigging

aparelhar [apare'ʎar] VT (*preparar*) to prepare, get ready; (*Náut*) to rig; **aparelhar-se** VR to get ready

aparelho [apare'reʎu] M apparatus; (*equipamento*) equipment; (*Pesca*) tackle, gear; (*máquina*) machine; (BR: *fone*) telephone; **~ de barbear** electric shaver; **~ de chá** tea set; **~ de rádio/TV** radio/TV set; **~ digestivo** digestive system; **~ doméstico** domestic appliance; **~ sanitário** bathroom suite

aparência [apa'rẽsja] F appearance; (*aspecto*) aspect; **na ~** apparently; **sob a ~ de** under the guise of; **ter ~ de** to look like, seem;

manter as ~s to keep up appearances; **salvar as ~s** to save face; **as ~s enganam** appearances are deceptive

aparentado, -a [aparẽ'tadu, a] ADJ related; **bem ~** well connected

aparentar [aparẽ'tar] VT (*fingir*) to feign; (*parecer*) to give the appearance of

aparente [apa'rẽtʃi] ADJ apparent; (*concreto, madeira*) exposed

aparição [apari'sãw] (*pl* **-ões**) F (*visão*) apparition; (*fantasma*) ghost

aparo [a'paru] (PT) M (*de caneta*) (pen) nib

apartamento [aparta'mẽtu] M apartment, flat (BRIT)

apartar [apar'tar] VT to separate; **apartar-se** VR to separate

aparte [a'partʃi] M (*Teatro*) aside

apartheid [apar'tajd] M apartheid

aparvalhado, -a [aparva'ʎadu, a] ADJ idiotic

apatetado, -a [apate'tadu, a] ADJ sluggish

apatia [apa'tʃia] F apathy

apático, -a [a'patʃiku, a] ADJ apathetic

apátrida [a'patrida] M/F stateless person

apavorado, -a [apavo'radu, a] ADJ terrified

apavoramento [apavora'mẽtu] M terror

apavorante [apavo'rãtʃi] ADJ terrifying

apavorar [apavo'rar] VT to terrify ▶ VI to be terrifying; **apavorar-se** VR to be terrified

apaziguar [apazi'gwar] VT to appease; **apaziguar-se** VR to calm down

apear-se [a'pjarsi] VR: **~ de** (*cavalo*) to dismount from

apedrejar [apedre'ʒar] VT to stone

apegado, -a [ape'gadu, a] ADJ: **ser ~ a** (*gostar de*) to be attached to

apegar-se [ape'garsi] VR: **~ a** (*afeiçoar-se*) to become attached to

apego [a'pegu] M (*afeição*) attachment

apeguei *etc* [ape'gej] VB *ver* **apegar-se**

apelação [apela'sãw] (*pl* **-ões**) F appeal

apelante [ape'lãtʃi] M/F appellant

apelar [ape'lar] VI to appeal; **~ da sentença** (*Jur*) to appeal against the sentence; **~ para** to appeal to; **~ para a ignorância/violência** to resort to abuse/violence

apelidar [apeli'dar] VT (BR) to nickname; (PT) to give a surname to; **apelidar-se** VR: **~-se de** to go by the name of; **Eduardo, apelidado de Dudu** Eduardo, nicknamed Dudu

apelido [ape'lidu] M (PT: *nome de família*) surname; (BR: *alcunha*) nickname; **feio é ~!** (*col*) ugly is not the word for it!

apelo [a'pelu] M appeal

apenas [a'penas] ADV only

apêndice [a'pẽdʒisi] M appendix; (*anexo*) supplement

apendicite [apẽdʒi'sitʃi] F appendicitis

Apeninos [ape'ninus] MPL: **os ~** the Apennines

apenso, -a [a'pẽsu, a] ADJ (*documento*) attached

apequenar [apeke'nar] VT to belittle

aperceber-se [aperse'bersi] VR: **~ de** to notice, see

aperfeiçoamento [aperfejswa'mẽtu] M (*perfeição*) perfection; (*melhoramento*) improvement

aperfeiçoar [aperfej'swar] VT to perfect; (*melhorar*) to improve; **aperfeiçoar-se** VR to improve o.s.

aperitivo [aperi'tʃivu] M aperitif

aperreação [apehja'sãw] F annoyance

aperreado, -a [ape'hjadu, a] ADJ fed up

aperrear [ape'hjar] VT to annoy

apertado, -a [aper'tadu, a] ADJ tight; (*estreito*) narrow; (*sem dinheiro*) hard-up; (*vida*) hard

apertar [aper'tar] VT (*agarrar*) to hold tight; (*roupa*) to take in; (*cinto*) to tighten; (*esponja*) to squeeze; (*botão*) to press; (*despesas*) to limit; (*vigilância*) to step up; (*coração*) to break; (*fig: pessoa*) to put pressure on ▶ VI (*sapatos*) to pinch; (*chuva, frio*) to get worse; (*estrada*) to narrow; **apertar-se** VR (*com roupa*) to corset o.s.; (*reduzir despesas*) to cut down (on expenses); (*ter problemas financeiros*) to feel the pinch; ~ **em** (*insistir*) to insist on, press; ~ **a mão de alguém** (*cumprimentar*) to shake hands with sb

aperto [a'pertu] M (*pressão*) pressure; (*situação difícil*) spot of bother, jam; **um ~ de mãos** a handshake

apesar [ape'zar] PREP: ~ **de** in spite of, despite; ~ **disso** nevertheless; ~ **de que** in spite of the fact that, even though

apetecer [apete'ser] VI (*comida*) to be appetizing; **esse prato não me apetece** I don't fancy that dish

apetecível [apete'sivew] (*pl* **-eis**) ADJ tempting

apetite [ape'tʃitʃi] M appetite; (*desejo*) desire; (*fig: ânimo*) go; **abrir o** ~ to get up an appetite; **bom ~!** enjoy your meal!

apetitoso, -a [apeti'tozu, ɔza] ADJ appetizing

apetrechar [apetre'ʃar] VT to fit out, equip

apetrechos [ape'treʃus] MPL gear sg; (*Pesca*) tackle sg

ápice ['apisi] M (*cume*) summit, top; (*vértice*) apex; **num ~** (PT) in a trice

apicultura [apikuw'tura] F beekeeping, apiculture

apiedar-se [apje'darsi] VR: ~ **de** (*ter piedade*) to pity; (*compadecer-se*) to take pity on

apimentado, -a [apimẽ'tadu, a] ADJ peppery

apimentar [apimẽ'tar] VT to pepper

apinhado, -a [api'ɲadu, a] ADJ crowded

apinhar [api'ɲar] VT to crowd, pack; **apinhar-se** VR (*aglomerar-se*) to crowd together; **~-se de** (*gente*) to be filled *ou* packed with

apitar [api'tar] VI to whistle; (*col*): **ele não apita em nada em casa** he doesn't have a say in anything at home ▶ VT (*jogo*) to referee

apito [a'pitu] M whistle

aplacar [apla'kar] VT to placate ▶ VI to calm down; **aplacar-se** VR to calm down

aplainar [aplaj'nar] VT (*madeira*) to plane; (*nivelar*) to level out

aplanar [apla'nar] VT (*alisar*) to smooth; (*nivelar*) to level; (*dificuldades*) to smooth over

aplaudir [aplaw'dʒir] VT to applaud

aplauso [a'plawzu] M applause; (*apoio*) support; (*elogio*) praise; (*aprovação*) approval; **~s** applause *sg*

aplicação [aplika'sãw] (*pl* **-ões**) F application; (*esforço*) effort; (*Costura*) appliqué; (*da lei*) enforcement; (*de dinheiro*) investment; (*de aluno*) diligence; (PT Comput) application, app (*col*)

aplicado, -a [apli'kadu, a] ADJ hard-working

aplicar [apli'kar] VT to apply; (*lei*) to enforce; (*dinheiro*) to invest; **aplicar-se** VR: **~-se a** to devote o.s. to, apply o.s. to

aplicativo, -a [aplika'tʃivu, a] ADJ: **pacote/ software ~** applications package/software ▶ M (BR Comput) application, app (*col*)

aplicável [apli'kavew] (*pl* **-eis**) ADJ applicable

aplique [a'pliki] M (*luz*) wall light; (*peruca*) hairpiece

apliquei *etc* [apli'kej] VB *ver* **aplicar**

apocalipse [apoka'lipsi] F apocalypse

apócrifo, -a [a'pokrifu, a] ADJ apocryphal

apoderar-se [apode'rarsi] VR: ~ **de** to seize, take possession of

apodrecer [apodre'ser] VT to rot; (*dente*) to decay ▶ VI to rot; to decay

apodrecimento [apodresi'mẽtu] M rottenness, decay; (*de dentes*) decay

apogeu [apo'ʒew] M (*Astronomia*) apogee; (*fig*) height, peak

apoiar [apo'jar] VT to support; (*basear*) to base; (*moção*) to second; **apoiar-se** VR: **~-se em** to rest on

apoio [a'poju] M support; (*financeiro*) backing; ~ **moral** moral support

apólice [a'polisi] F (*certificado*) policy, certificate; (*ação*) share, bond; ~ **de seguro** insurance policy

apologia [apolo'ʒia] F (*elogio*) eulogy; (*defesa*) defence (BRIT), defense (US)

apologista [apolo'ʒista] M/F apologist

apontador [apõta'dor] M pencil sharpener

apontamento [apõta'mẽtu] M (*nota*) note

apontar [apõ'tar] VT (*fusil*) to aim; (*erro*) to point out; (*com o dedo*) to point at *ou* to; (*razão*) to put forward; (*nomes*) to name ▶ VI (*aparecer*) to begin to appear; (*brotar*) to sprout; (*com o dedo*) to point; ~! take aim!; ~ **para** to point to; (*com arma*) to aim at

apoplético, -a [apo'plɛtʃiku, a] ADJ apoplectic

apoquentar [apokẽ'tar] VT to annoy, pester; **apoquentar-se** VR to get annoyed

aporrinhação [apohiɲa'sãw] F annoyance

aporrinhar [apohi'ɲar] VT to pester, annoy

aportar [apor'tar] VI to dock

aportuguesado, -a [aportuge'zadu, a] ADJ made Portuguese

após [a'pojs] PREP after

aposentado, -a [apozẽ'tadu, a] ADJ retired ▶ M/F retired person, pensioner; **ser ~** to be retired

aposentadoria [apozẽtado'ria] F retirement; (*dinheiro*) pension

aposentar [apozẽ'tar] VT to retire; **aposentar-se** VR to retire

aposento [apo'zẽtu] M room

após-guerra M post-war period; **a Alemanha do ~** post-war Germany

apossar-se [apo'sarsi] VR: **~ de** to take possession of, seize

aposta [a'pɔsta] F bet

apostar [apos'tar] VT to bet ► VI: **~ em** to bet on

a posteriori [aposte'rjori] ADV afterwards

apostila [apos'tʃila] F students' notes *pl*, study aid

apóstolo [a'pɔstolu] M apostle

apóstrofo [a'pɔstrofu] M apostrophe

apoteose [apote'ɔzi] F apotheosis

aprazar [apra'zar] VT to allow

aprazer [apra'zer] VI to be pleasing; **~ a alguém** to please sb; **ele faz o que lhe apraz** he does as he pleases; **aprazia-lhe escrever cartas** he liked to write letters

aprazível [apra'zivew] (*pl* **-eis**) ADJ pleasant

apreçar [apre'sar] VT to value, price

apreciação [apresja'sãw] F appreciation

apreciar [apre'sjar] VT to appreciate; (*gostar de*) to enjoy

apreciativo, -a [apresja'tʃivu, a] ADJ appreciative

apreciável [apre'sjavew] (*pl* **-eis**) ADJ appreciable

apreço [a'presu] M (*estima*) esteem, regard; (*consideração*) consideration; **em ~** in question

apreender [aprjẽ'der] VT to apprehend; (*tomar*) to seize; (*entender*) to grasp

apreensão [aprjẽ'sãw] (*pl* **-ões**) F (*percepção*) perception; (*tomada*) seizure, arrest; (*receio*) apprehension

apreensivo, -a [aprjẽ'sivu, a] ADJ apprehensive

apreensões [aprjẽ'sõjs] FPL *de* **apreensão**

apregoar [apre'gwar] VT to proclaim, announce; (*mercadorias*) to cry

aprender [aprẽ'der] VT, VI to learn; **~ a ler** to learn to read; **~ de cor** to learn by heart

aprendiz [aprẽ'dʒiz] M apprentice; (*condutor*) learner

aprendizado [aprendʒi'zadu] M (*num ofício*) apprenticeship; (*numa profissão*) training; (*escolar*) learning

aprendizagem [aprẽdʒi'zaʒẽ] F (*num ofício*) apprenticeship; (*numa profissão*) training; (*escolar*) learning

apresentação [aprezẽta'sãw] (*pl* **-ões**) F presentation; (*de peça, filme*) performance; (*de pessoas*) introduction; (*porte pessoal*) appearance; **~ de contas** (*Com*) rendering of accounts

apresentador, a [aprezẽta'dor(a)] M/F presenter

apresentar [aprezẽ'tar] VT to present; (*pessoas*) to introduce; (*entregar*) to hand; (*trabalho, documento*) to submit; (*queixa*) to lodge; **apresentar-se** VR (*identificar-se*) to introduce o.s.; (*problema*) to present itself; (*à polícia etc*) to report; **quero ~-lhe ...** may I introduce you to ...

apresentável [aprezẽ'tavew] (*pl* **-eis**) ADJ presentable

apressado, -a [apre'sadu, a] ADJ hurried, hasty; **estar ~** to be in a hurry

apressar [apre'sar] VT to hurry, hasten; **apressar-se** VR to hurry (up)

aprestar [apres'tar] VT (*aparelhar*) to equip, fit out; (*aprontar*) to get ready; **aprestar-se** VR to get ready

aprestos [a'prestus] MPL (*preparativos*) preparations

aprimorado, -a [aprimo'radu, a] ADJ (*trabalho*) polished; (*pessoa*) elegant

aprimorar [aprimo'rar] VT to improve; **aprimorar-se** VR (*no vestir*) to make o.s. look nice

a priori [a'prjori] ADV beforehand

aprisionamento [aprizjona'mẽtu] M imprisonment

aprisionar [aprizjo'nar] VT (*cativar*) to capture; (*encarcerar*) to imprison

aprofundado, -a [aprofũ'dadu, a] ADJ (*estudo, discussão*) in-depth

aprofundar [aprofũ'dar] VT to deepen, make deeper; **aprofundar-se** VR: **~-se em** to go deeper into

aprontar [aprõ'tar] VT to get ready, prepare; (*briga*) to pick ► VI (*col*) to play up; **aprontar-se** VR to get ready; **~ alguma** (*col*) to be up to something

apropriação [aproprja'sãw] (*pl* **-ões**) F appropriation; (*tomada*) seizure; **~ de custos** (*Com*) cost appropriation

apropriado, -a [apro'prjadu, a] ADJ appropriate, suitable

apropriar [apro'prjar] VT to appropriate; **apropriar-se** VR: **~-se de** to seize, take possession of

aprovação [aprova'sãw] F approval; (*louvor*) praise; (*num exame*) pass

aprovado, -a [apro'vadu, a] ADJ approved; **ser ~ num exame** to pass an exam; **o índice de ~s** the pass rate

aprovar [apro'var] VT to approve of; (*exame*) to pass ► VI to make the grade, come up to scratch

aproveitador, a [aprovejta'dor(a)] M/F opportunist

aproveitamento [aprovejta'mẽtu] M use, utilization; (*nos estudos*) progress

aproveitar [aprovej'tar] VT (*tirar proveito de*) to take advantage of; (*utilizar*) to use; (*não desperdiçar*) to make the most of; (*oportunidade*) to take; (*fazer bom uso de*) to make good use of ► VI to make the most of it; (*PT*) to be of use; **não aproveita** it's no use; **aproveite!** enjoy yourself!, have a good time!

aproveitável [aprovej'tavew] (*pl* **-eis**) ADJ usable

aprovisionamento [aprovizjona'mētu] M supply, provision

aprovisionar [aprovizjo'nar] VT to supply; (*estocar*) to stock

aproximação [aprosima'sãw] (*pl* **-ões**) F (*estimativa*) approximation; (*chegada*) approach; (*proximidade*) nearness, closeness

aproximado, -a [aprosi'madu, a] ADJ (*cálculo*) approximate; (*perto*) nearby

aproximar [aprosi'mar] VT to bring near; (*aliar*) to bring together; **aproximar-se** VR: **~-se de** (*acercar-se*) to approach

aprumado, -a [apru'madu, a] ADJ vertical; (*altivo*) upright; (*elegante*) well-dressed

aprumo [a'prumu] M vertical position; (*elegância*) elegance; (*altivez*) haughtiness

aptidão [aptʃi'dãw] F aptitude, ability; (*jeito*) knack; **~ física** physical fitness

aptitude [aptʃi'tudʒi] F aptitude, ability; (*jeito*) knack

apto, -a ['aptu, a] ADJ apt; (*capaz*) capable

apto. ABR = **apartamento**

APU (PT) ABR F (= *Aliança Povo Unido*) *political party*

apunhalar [apuɲa'lar] VT to stab

apuração [apura'sãw] F (*de votos*) counting; (*descoberta*) ascertainment; (*averiguação*) investigation; **~ de contas** (*Com*) settlement of accounts; **~ de custos** (*Com*) costing

apurado, -a [apu'radu, a] ADJ refined

apurar [apu'rar] VT (*aperfeiçoar*) to perfect; (*descobrir*) to find out; (*averiguar*) to investigate; (*dinheiro*) to raise, get; (*votos*) to count; **apurar-se** VR (*no trajar*) to dress up

apuro [a'puru] M (*elegância*) refinement, elegance; (*dificuldade*) difficulty; **estar em ~s** to be in trouble

aquarela [akwa'rɛla] F watercolour (BRIT), watercolor (US)

aquário [a'kwarju] M aquarium; **A~** (*Astrologia*) Aquarius

aquartelar [akwarte'lar] VT (*Mil*) to billet, quarter

aquático, -a [a'kwatʃiku, a] ADJ aquatic, water *atr*

aquecedor, a [akese'dor(a)] ADJ warming ▶ M heater

aquecer [ake'ser] VT to heat ▶ VI to heat up; **aquecer-se** VR to heat up

aquecido, -a [ake'sidu, a] ADJ heated

aquecimento [akesi'mētu] M heating; (*da economia*) acceleration; **~ central** central heating; **~ global** global warming

aqueduto [ake'dutu] M aqueduct

aquele, ela [a'keli, ɛla] ADJ (*sg*) that; (*pl*) those ▶ PRON (*sg*) that one; (*pl*) those (ones); **sem mais aquela** (*inesperadamente*) all of a sudden; (*sem cerimônia*) without so much as a "by your leave"; **foi aquela confusão** it was a real mess

àquele, ela [a'keli, ɛla] = **a + aquele**; *ver* **a**

aquém [a'kēj] ADV on this side; **~ de** on this side of

aqui [a'ki] ADV here; **eis ~** here is/are; **~ mesmo** right here; **até ~** up to here; **por ~** hereabouts; (*nesta direção*) this way; **por ~ e por ali** here and there; **estou por ~!** (*col*) I've had it up to here!; *ver tb* **daqui**

aquiescência [akje'sēsja] F consent

aquiescer [akje'ser] VI: **~ (a)** to consent (to)

aquietar [akje'tar] VT to calm, quieten; **aquietar-se** VR to calm down

aquilatar [akila'tar] VT (*metais*) to value; (*avaliar*) to evaluate

aquilo [a'kilu] PRON that; **~ que** what

àquilo [a'kilu] = **a + aquilo**; *ver* **a**

aquisição [akizi'sãw] (*pl* **-ões**) F acquisition

aquisitivo, -a [akizi'tʃivu, a] ADJ: **poder ~** purchasing power

ar [ar] M air; (*aspecto*) look; (*brisa*) breeze; (PT *Auto*) choke; **ares** MPL (*atitude*) airs; (*clima*) climate *sg*; **ao ar livre** in the open air; **ir ao/sair do ar** (*TV, Rádio*) to go on/off the air; **no ar** (*TV, Rádio*) on air; (*fig: planos*) up in the air; **dar-se ares** to put on airs; **ir pelos ares** (*explodir*) to blow up; **tomar ar** to get some air

árabe ['arabi] ADJ, M/F Arab ▶ M (*Ling*) Arabic

Arábia [a'rabja] F: **a ~ Saudita** Saudi Arabia

arado [a'radu] M plough (BRIT), plow (US)

aragem [a'raʒē] (*pl* **-ns**) F breeze

arame [a'rami] M wire; **~ farpado** barbed wire

aranha [a'raɲa] F spider

aranha-caranguejeira [-karãʒe'ʒejra] (*pl* **aranhas-caranguejeiras**) F bird-eating spider

arapuca [ara'puka] F trap; (*truque*) trick

araque [a'raki] M: **de ~** (*col*) phony, bogus

arar [a'rar] VT to plough (BRIT), plow (US)

arara [a'rara] F macaw; **estar/ficar uma ~** (*fig*) to be/get angry

arbitragem [arbi'traʒē] F arbitration; (*Esporte*) refereeing

arbitrar [arbi'trar] VT to arbitrate; (*Esporte*) to referee; (*adjudicar*) to award

arbitrariedade [arbitrarje'dadʒi] F arbitrariness; (*ato*) arbitrary act

arbitrário, -a [arbi'trarju, a] ADJ arbitrary

arbítrio [ar'bitrju] M decision; **ao ~ de** at the discretion of

árbitro ['arbitru] M (*juiz*) arbiter; (*Jur*) arbitrator; (*Futebol*) referee; (*Tênis*) umpire

arborizado, -a [arbori'zadu, a] ADJ green, wooded; (*rua*) tree-lined

arborizar [arbori'zar] VT to plant with trees

arbusto [ar'bustu] M shrub, bush

arca ['arka] F chest, trunk; **~ de Noé** Noah's Ark

arcabouço [arka'bosu] M outline(s)

arcada [ar'kada] F (*série de arcos*) arcade; (*arco*) arch, span; **~ dentária** dental ridge

arcaico, -a [ar'kajku, a] ADJ archaic; (*antiquado*) antiquated

arcanjo [ar'kãʒu] M archangel

arcar [ar'kar] VT: **~ com** (*responsabilidades*) to shoulder; (*despesas*) to handle; (*consequencias*) to take

arcebispo [arse'bispu] M archbishop
arco ['arku] M (*Arq*) arch; (*Mil, Mús*) bow; (*Elet, Mat*) arc; (*de barril*) hoop
arco-da-velha M: **coisa/história do ~** amazing thing/story
arco-íris (*pl* **arcos-íris**) M rainbow
ar-condicionado (*pl* **ares-condicionados**) M (*aparelho*) air conditioner; (*sistema*) air conditioning
ardente [ar'dẽtʃi] ADJ burning; (*intenso*) fervent; (*apaixonado*) ardent
arder [ar'der] VI to burn; (*pele, olhos*) to sting; **~ de febre** to burn up with fever; **~ de raiva** to seethe (with rage)
ardido, -a [ar'dʒidu, a] ADJ (*picante*) hot
ardil [ar'dʒiw] (*pl* **-is**) M trick, ruse
ardiloso, -a [ardʒi'lozu, ɔza] ADJ cunning
ardis [ar'dʒis] MPL *de* **ardil**
ardor [ar'dor] M (*paixão*) ardour (*BRIT*), ardor (*US*), passion
ardoroso, -a [ardo'rozu, ɔza] ADJ ardent
ardósia [ar'dɔzja] F slate
árduo, -a ['ardwu, a] ADJ arduous; (*difícil*) hard, difficult
área ['arja] F area; (*Esporte*) penalty area; (*fig*) field; **~ (de serviço)** balcony (*for hanging washing etc*)
arear [a'rjar] VT to polish
areia [a'reja] F sand; **~ movediça** quicksand
arejado, -a [are'ʒadu, a] ADJ aired, ventilated
arejar [are'ʒar] VT to air ▶ VI to get some air; (*descansar*) to have a breather; **arejar-se** VR to get some air; to have a break
ARENA (*BR*) ABR F (= *Aliança Renovadora Nacional*) *former political party*
arena [a'rɛna] F arena; (*de circo*) ring
arenito [are'nitu] M sandstone
arenoso, -a [are'nozu, ɔza] ADJ sandy
arenque [a'rẽki] M herring
aresta [a'rɛsta] F edge
arfar [ar'far] VI (*ofegar*) to pant, gasp for breath; (*Náut*) to pitch
argamassa [arga'masa] F mortar
argamassar [argama'sar] VT to cement
Argel [ar'ʒɛw] N Algiers
Argélia [ar'ʒɛlja] F: **a ~** Algeria
argelino, -a [arʒe'linu, a] ADJ, M/F Algerian
Argentina [arʒẽ'tʃina] F: **a ~** Argentina
argentino, -a [arʒẽ'tʃinu, a] ADJ, M/F Argentinian
argila [ar'ʒila] F clay
argiloso, -a [arʒi'lozu, ɔza] ADJ (*terreno*) clay
argola [ar'gɔla] F ring; **argolas** FPL (*brincos*) hooped earrings; **~ (de porta)** door-knocker
argúcia [ar'gusja] F (*sutileza*) subtlety; (*agudeza*) astuteness
arguição [argwi'sãw] (*pl* **-ões**) F oral test
arguir [ar'gwir] VT (*examinar*) to test, examine
argumentação [argumẽta'sãw] F line of argument
argumentador, a [argumẽta'dor(a)] ADJ argumentative ▶ M/F arguer
argumentar [argumẽ'tar] VT, VI to argue

argumento [argu'mẽtu] M argument; (*de obra*) theme
arguto, -a [ar'gutu, a] ADJ (*sutil*) subtle; (*astuto*) shrewd
ária ['arja] F aria
ariano, -a [a'rjanu, a] ADJ, M/F Aryan; (*Astrologia*) Arian
aridez [ari'dez] F (*secura*) dryness; (*esterilidade*) barrenness; (*falta de interesse*) dullness
árido, -a ['aridu, a] ADJ (*seco*) arid, dry; (*estéril*) barren; (*maçante*) dull, boring
Áries ['aris] F Aries
arisco, -a [a'risku, a] ADJ unsociable
aristocracia [aristokra'sia] F aristocracy
aristocrata [aristo'krata] M/F aristocrat
aristocrático, -a [aristo'kratʃiku, a] ADJ aristocratic
aritmética [aritʃ'mɛtʃika] F arithmetic
aritmético, -a [aritʃ'mɛtʃiku, a] ADJ arithmetical
arma ['arma] F weapon; **armas** FPL (*nucleares etc*) arms; (*brasão*) coat *sg* of arms; **de ~s e bagagem** with all one's belongings; **depor as ~s** to lay down arms; **passar pelas ~s** to shoot, execute; **~ branca** cold steel; **~ convencional/nuclear** conventional/ nuclear weapon; **~s de destruir** firearm; **~s de destruição em massa** weapons of mass destruction; **~ de fogo** firearm
armação [arma'sãw] (*pl* **-ões**) F (*armadura*) frame; (*Pesca*) tackle; (*Náut*) rigging; (*de óculos*) frames *pl*
armada [ar'mada] F navy
armadilha [arma'dʒiʎa] F trap
armado, -a [ar'madu, a] ADJ armed; **~ até os dentes** armed to the teeth
armador [arma'dor] M (*Náut*) shipowner
armadura [arma'dura] F armour (*BRIT*), armor (*US*); (*Elet*) armature; (*Constr*) framework
armamento [arma'mẽtu] M (*armas*) armaments *pl*, weapons *pl*; (*Náut*) equipment; (*ato*) arming
armar [ar'mar] VT to arm; (*montar*) to assemble; (*barraca*) to pitch; (*um aparelho*) to set up; (*armadilha*) to set; (*maquinar*) to hatch; (*Náut*) to fit out; **armar-se** VR to arm o.s.; **~ uma briga com** to pick a quarrel with; **~ uma confusão** to cause chaos
armarinho [arma'riɲu] M haberdashery (*BRIT*), notions *pl* (*US*)
armário [ar'marju] M cupboard; (*de roupa*) wardrobe
armazém [arma'zẽj] (*pl* **-ns**) M (*depósito*) warehouse; (*loja*) grocery store
armazenagem [armaze'naʒẽ] F storage
armazenamento [armazena'mẽtu] M storage
armazenar [armaze'nar] VT to store; (*provisões*) to stock; (*Comput*) to store
armazéns [arma'zẽs] MPL *de* **armazém**
armeiro [ar'mejru] M gunsmith
Armênia [ar'menja] F: **a ~** Armenia

arminho [ar'miɲu] M ermine

armistício [armis'tʃisju] M armistice

aro ['aru] M (argola) ring; (de óculos, roda) rim; (de porta) frame

aroma [a'roma] M (de comida, café) aroma; (de perfume) fragrance

aromático, -a [aro'matʃiku, a] ADJ (comida) aromatic; (perfume) fragrant

arpão [ar'pãw] (pl -ões) M harpoon

arpejo [ar'peʒu] M arpeggio

arpoar [ar'pwar] VT to harpoon

arpões [ar'põjs] MPL de **arpão**

arqueado, -a [ar'kjadu, a] ADJ arched

arquear [ar'kjar] VT to arch; **arquear-se** VR to bend, arch; (entortar-se) to warp

arquei etc [ar'kej] VB ver **arcar**

arqueiro, -a [ar'kejru, a] M/F archer; (goleiro) goalkeeper

arquejar [arke'ʒar] VI to pant, wheeze

arquejo [ar'keʒu] M panting, gasping

arqueologia [arkjolo'ʒia] F archaeology (BRIT), archeology (US)

arqueológico, -a [arkjo'lɔʒiku, a] ADJ archaeological (BRIT), archeological (US)

arqueólogo, -a [ar'kjɔlogu, a] M/F archaeologist (BRIT), archeologist (US)

arquétipo [ar'ketʃipu] M archetype

arquibancada [arkibã'kada] F terrace

arquipélago [arki'pɛlagu] M archipelago

arquitetar [arkite'tar] VT to think up

arquiteto, -a [arki'tetu, a] M/F architect

arquitetónico, -a [arkite'toniku, a] ADJ architectural

arquitetura [arkite'tura] F architecture

arquivamento [arkiva'mẽtu] M filing; (de projeto) shelving

arquivar [arki'var] VT to file; (projeto) to shelve

arquivista [arki'vista] M/F archivist

arquivo [ar'kivu] M (ger, Comput) file; (lugar) archive; (de empresa) files pl; (móvel) filing cabinet; **abrir/fechar um ~** (Comput) to open/close a file; **nome do ~** (Comput) file name; **~ ativo** (Comput) active file; **~ zipado** (Comput) zip file

arrabaldes [aha'bawdʒis] MPL suburbs

arraia [a'haja] F (peixe) ray

arraial [aha'jaw] (pl -ais) M (povoação) village; (PT: festa) fair

arraia-miúda F masses pl

arraigado, -a [ahaj'gadu, a] ADJ deep-rooted; (fig) ingrained

arraigar [ahaj'gar] VI to root; **arraigar-se** VR (enraizar-se) to take root; (estabelecer-se) to settle

arrancada [ahã'kada] F (puxão) pull, jerk; (partida) start; (investida) charge; (de atleta) burst of speed; **dar uma ~** (em carro) to pull away (suddenly)

arrancar [ahã'kar] VT to pull out; (botão etc) to pull off; (arrebatar) to snatch (away); (fig: confissão) to extract; (: aplausos) to get ▶ VI to start (off); **arrancar-se** VR (partir) to leave; (fugir) to run off

arranco [a'hãku] M (puxão) pull, jerk; (partida) sudden start

arranha-céu [a'haɲa-] (pl -s) M skyscraper

arranhadura [ahaɲa'dura] F scratch

arranhão [aha'ɲãw] (pl -ões) M scratch

arranhar [aha'ɲar] VT to scratch; **~ (n)uma língua** to know a smattering of a language

arranhões [aha'ɲõjs] MPL de **arranhão**

arranjador, a [ahãʒa'dor(a)] M/F (Mús) arranger

arranjar [ahã'ʒar] VT to arrange; (emprego etc) to get, find; (doença) to get, catch; (namorado) to find; (questão) to settle; **arranjar-se** VR (virar-se) to manage; (conseguir emprego) to get a job; **~-se sem** to do without

arranjo [a'hãʒu] M arrangement; (negociata) shady deal; (col: caso) affair

arranque [a'hãki] M ver **motor**

arranquei etc [ahã'kej] VB ver **arrancar**

arrasado, -a [ahaza'do, a] ADJ (col) gutted

arrasador, a [ahaza'dor(a)] ADJ devastating

arrasar [aha'zar] VT to devastate; (demolir) to demolish; (estragar) to ruin; (verbalmente) to lambast; **arrasar-se** VR to be devastated; (destruir-se) to destroy o.s.; (arruinar-se) to lose everything; (nos exames) to do terribly

arrastado, -a [ahas'tadu, a] ADJ (rasteiro) crawling; (demorado) dragging; (voz) drawling

arrastão [ahas'tãw] (pl -ões) M tug, jerk; (rede) dragnet

arrasta-pé [a'hasta-] (pl **arrasta-pés**) (col) M knees-up, shindig

arrastar [ahas'tar] VT to drag; (atrair) to draw ▶ VI to trail; **arrastar-se** VR (rastejar) to crawl; (andar a custo) to drag o.s.; (tempo) to drag; (processo) to drag on

arrasto [a'hastu] M (ação) dragging; (rede) trawl-net; (Tec) drag

arrazoado, -a [aha'zwadu, a] ADJ (argumento) reasoned ▶ M (Jur) defence (BRIT), defense (US)

arrazoar [aha'zwar] VI (discutir) to argue

arrear [a'hjar] VT (cavalo etc) to bridle

arrebanhar [aheba'ɲar] VT (gado) to herd; (juntar) to gather

arrebatado, -a [aheba'tadu, a] ADJ (impetuoso) rash, impetuous; (enlevado) entranced

arrebatador, a [ahebata'dor(a)] ADJ enchanting

arrebatamento [ahebata'mẽtu] M (impetuosidade) impetuosity; (enlevo) ecstasy

arrebatar [aheba'tar] VT (arrancar) to snatch (away); (levar) to carry off; (enlevar) to entrance; (enfurecer) to enrage; **arrebatar-se** VR (entusiasmar-se) to be entranced

arrebentação [ahebẽta'sãw] F (na praia) surf

arrebentado, -a [ahebẽ'tadu, a] ADJ (quebrado) broken; (vaso etc) smashed; (estafado) worn out

arrebentar [ahebẽ'tar] VT to break; (porta) to break down; (corda) to snap, break ▶ VI to break; to snap, break; (guerra) to break out; (bomba) to explode; (ondas) to break

arrebitado, -a [ahebi'tadu, a] ADJ turned-up; (*nariz*) snub

arrebitar [ahebi'tar] VT to turn up

arrecadação [ahekada'sãw] F (*de impostos etc*) collection; (*impostos arrecadados*) tax revenue, taxes *pl*

arrecadar [aheka'dar] VT (*impostos etc*) to collect

arrecife [ahe'sifi] M reef

arredar [ahe'dar] VT to move away, move back; **arredar-se** VR to move away; **não ~ pé** not to budge, to stand one's ground

arredio, -a [ahe'dʒiu, a] ADJ (*pessoa*) withdrawn

arredondado, -a [ahedõ'dadu, a] ADJ round, rounded

arredondar [ahedõ'dar] VT to round (off); (*conta*) to round up

arredores [ahe'dɔris] MPL suburbs; (*cercanias*) outskirts

arrefecer [ahefe'ser] VT to cool; (*febre*) to lower; (*desanimar*) to discourage ▶ VI to cool (off); to get discouraged

arrefecimento [ahefesi'mẽtu] M cooling

ar-refrigerado (*pl* **ares-refrigerados**) M (*aparelho*) air conditioner; (*sistema*) air conditioning

arregaçar [ahega'sar] VT to roll up

arregalado, -a [ahega'ladu, a] ADJ (*olhos*) wide; **com os olhos ~s** pop-eyed

arregalar [ahega'lar] VT: **~ os olhos** to stare in amazement

arreganhar [ahega'ɲar] VT (*dentes*) to bare; (*lábios*) to draw back

arreios [a'hejus] MPL harness *sg*

arrematar [ahema'tar] VT (*dizer concluindo*) to conclude; (*comprar*) to buy by auction; (*vender*) to sell by auction; (*Costura*) to finish off

arremate [ahe'matʃi] M (*Costura*) finishing off; (*conclusão*) conclusion; (*Futebol*) finishing

arremedar [aheme'dar] VT to mimic

arremedo [ahe'medu] M mimicry

arremessar [aheme'sar] VT to throw, hurl; **arremessar-se** VR to hurl o.s.

arremesso [ahe'mesu] M (*lançamento*) throw; **~ de peso** shot-put

arremeter [aheme'ter] VI to lunge; **~ contra** (*acometer*) to attack, assail

arremetida [aheme'tʃida] F attack, onslaught

arrendador, a [ahẽda'dor(a)] M/F landlord/landlady

arrendamento [ahẽda'mẽtu] M (*ação*) leasing; (*contrato*) lease

arrendar [ahẽ'dar] VT to lease

arrendatário, -a [ahẽda'tarju, a] M/F tenant

arrepender-se [ahepẽ'dersi] VR to repent; (*mudar de opinião*) to change one's mind; **~ de** to regret, be sorry for

arrependido, -a [ahepẽ'dʒidu, a] ADJ (*pessoa*) sorry

arrependimento [ahepẽdʒi'mẽtu] M regret; (*Rel, de crime*) repentance

arrepiado, -a [ahe'pjadu, a] ADJ (*cabelo*) standing on end; (*pele, pessoa*) goose-pimply; (*horrorizado*) horrified

arrepiante [ahe'pjãtʃi] ADJ (*que dá medo*) chilling; (*que emociona*) moving

arrepiar [ahe'pjar] VT (*amedrontar*) to horrify; (*cabelo*) to cause to stand on end; **arrepiar-se** VR (*sentir calafrios*) to shiver; (*cabelo*) to stand on end; **isso me arrepia** it gives me goose flesh; (**ser**) **de ~ os cabelos** (to be) hair-raising

arrepio [ahe'piu] M shiver; (*de frio*) chill; **isso me dá ~s** it gives me the creeps

arresto [a'hɛstu] M (*Jur*) seizure, confiscation

arrevesado, -a [aheve'zadu, a] ADJ (*obscuro*) obscure; (*intricado*) intricate

arrevesar [aheve'zar] VT (*complicar*) to complicate

arriado, -a [a'hjadu, a] ADJ (*exausto*) exhausted; (*por doença*) very weak

arriar [a'hjar] VT (*baixar*) to lower; (*depor*) to lay down ▶ VI (*cair*) to drop; (*vergar*) to sag; (*desistir*) to give up; (*fig*) to collapse; (*Auto: bateria*) to go flat

arribação [ahiba'sãw] (*pl* **-ões**) (BR) F (*de aves*) migration

arribar [ahi'bar] VI (*recuperar-se*) to recuperate

arrimo [a'himu] M support; **~ de família** breadwinner

arriscado, -a [ahis'kadu, a] ADJ risky; (*audacioso*) daring

arriscar [ahis'kar] VT to risk; (*pôr em perigo*) to endanger, jeopardize; **arriscar-se** VR to take a risk; **~-se a fazer** to risk doing

arrisquei *etc* [ahis'kej] VB *ver* **arriscar**

arrivista [ahi'vista] M/F upstart; (*oportunista*) opportunist

arroba [a'hoba] F (*peso*) = 15 kg; (*Comput*) @ ('at' symbol)

arrochado, -a [aho'ʃadu, a] ADJ (*vestido*) skin-tight; (*fig*) tough

arrochar [aho'ʃar] VT (*apertar*) to tighten up ▶ VI (*ser exigente*) to be demanding

arrocho [a'hoʃu] M squeeze; (*fig*) predicament; **~ salarial/ao crédito** wage/credit squeeze

arrogância [aho'gãsja] F arrogance, haughtiness

arrogante [aho'gãtʃi] ADJ arrogant, haughty

arrogar-se [aho'garsi] VR (*direitos, privilégios*) to claim

arroio [a'hoju] M stream

arrojado, -a [aho'ʒadu, a] ADJ (*design*) bold; (*temerário*) rash; (*ousado*) daring

arrojar [aho'ʒar] VT (*lançar*) to hurl

arrojo [a'hoʒu] M (*ousadia*) boldness

arrolamento [ahola'mẽtu] M list

arrolar [aho'lar] VT to list

arrolhar [aho'ʎar] VT to cork

arromba [a'hõba] F: **de ~** great

arrombar [ahõ'bar] VT (*porta*) to break down; (*cofre*) to crack

arrotar [aho'tar] VI to belch ▶ VT (*alardear*) to boast of

arroto [a'hotu] M burp

arroubo [a'hobu] M ecstasy, rapture

arroz [a'hoz] M rice; ~ **doce** rice pudding

arrozal [aho'zaw] (*pl* **-ais**) M rice field

arruaça [a'hwasa] F street riot

arruaceiro, -a [ahwa'sejru, a] M/F rioter

arruela [a'hwɛla] F (*Tec*) washer

arruinar [ahwi'nar] VT to ruin; (*destruir*) to destroy; **arruinar-se** VR to be ruined; (*perder a saúde*) to ruin one's health

arrulhar [ahu'ʎar] VI (*pombos*) to coo

arrulho [a'huʎu] M cooing

arrumação [ahuma'sãw] F (*arranjo*) arrangement; (*de um quarto etc*) tidying up; (*de malas*) packing

arrumadeira [ahuma'dejra] F cleaning lady; (*num hotel*) chambermaid

arrumar [ahu'mar] VT (*pôr em ordem*) to put in order, arrange; (*quarto etc*) to tidy up; (*malas*) to pack; (*emprego*) to get; (*vestir*) to dress up; (*desculpa*) to make up, find; (*vida*) to sort out; **arrumar-se** VR (*aprontar-se*) to get dressed, get ready; (*na vida*) to sort o.s. out; (*virar-se*) to manage

arsenal [arse'naw] (*pl* **-ais**) M (*Mil*) arsenal; ~ **de Marinha** naval dockyard

arsênio [ar'senju] M arsenic

arte ['artʃi] F art; (*habilidade*) skill; (*ofício*) trade, craft; **fazer** ~ (*fig*) to get up to mischief; **as** ~**s cênicas** the performing arts

artefato [artʃi'fatu], (*PT*) **artefacto** M (*manufactured*) article; ~**s de couro** leather goods, leatherware *sg*

arteiro, -a [ar'tejru, a] ADJ (*criança*) mischievous

artéria [ar'tɛrja] F (*Anat*) artery

arterial [arte'rjaw] (*pl* **-ais**) ADJ: **pressão** ~ blood pressure

arteriosclerose [arterjoskle'rɔzi] F hardening of the arteries, arteriosclerosis

artesã [arte'zã] F *de* **artesão**

artesanal [arteza'naw] (*pl* **-ais**) ADJ craft *atr*

artesanato [arteza'natu] M craftwork; **artigos de** ~ craft items

artesão, -sã [arte'zãw, zã] (*pl* **-s/-s**) M/F artisan, craftsman/woman

ártico, -a ['artʃiku, a] ADJ Arctic ▶ M: **o Á**~ the Arctic

articulação [artʃikula'sãw] (*pl* **-ões**) F articulation; (*Med*) joint

articulado, -a [artʃiku'ladu, a] ADJ articulated, jointed

articular [artʃiku'lar] VT (*pronunciar*) to articulate; (*ligar*) to join together

artífice [ar'tʃifisi] M/F craftsman/woman; (*inventor*) inventor

artificial [artʃifi'sjaw] (*pl* **-ais**) ADJ artificial; (*pessoa*) affected

artifício [artʃi'fisju] M stratagem, trick

artificioso, -a [artʃifi'sjozu, ɔza] ADJ (*hábil*) skilful (BRIT), skillful (US); (*astucioso*) artful

artigo [ar'tʃigu] M article; (*Com*) item; **artigos** MPL (*produtos*) goods; ~ **definido/**

indefinido (*Ling*) definite/indefinite article; ~ **de fundo** leading article, editorial; ~**s de toucador** toiletries

artilharia [artʃiʎa'ria] F artillery

artilheiro [artʃi'ʎejru] M gunner, artilleryman; (*Futebol*) striker

artimanha [artʃi'maɲa] F (*ardil*) stratagem; (*astúcia*) cunning

artista [ar'tʃista] M/F artist

artístico, -a [ar'tʃistʃiku, a] ADJ artistic

artrite [ar'tritʃi] F (*Med*) arthritis

arvorar [arvo'rar] VT (*bandeira*) to hoist; (*elevar*): ~ **alguém em** to promote *ou* elevate sb to; **arvorar-se** VR: ~**-se em** to set o.s. up as

árvore ['arvori] F tree; (*Tec*) shaft; ~ **de Natal** Christmas tree

arvoredo [arvo'redu] M grove

as [as] ART DEF *ver* **a**

ás [ajs] M ace

às [as] = **a + as**; *ver* **a**

asa ['aza] F wing; (*de xícara etc*) handle; **dar** ~**s à imaginação** to give free rein to one's imagination

asa-delta (*pl* **asas-delta**) F hang-glider

asbesto [az'bɛstu] M asbestos

ascendência [asẽ'dẽsja] F (*antepassados*) ancestry; (*domínio*) ascendancy, sway

ascendente [asẽ'dẽtʃi] ADJ rising, upward

ascender [asẽ'der] VI (*subir*) to rise, ascend

ascensão [asẽ'sãw] (*pl* **-ões**) F ascent; (*fig*) rise; (*Rel*): **dia da A**~ Ascension Day

ascensor [asẽ'sor] M lift (BRIT), elevator (US)

ascensorista [asẽso'rista] M/F lift operator

asceta [a'seta] M/F ascetic

asco ['asku] M loathing, revulsion; **dar** ~ **a** to revolt, disgust

asfaltar [asfaw'tar] VT to asphalt

asfalto [as'fawtu] M asphalt

asfixia [asfik'sia] F asphyxia, suffocation

asfixiar [asfik'sjar] VT to asphyxiate, suffocate

Ásia ['azja] F: **a** ~ Asia

asiático, -a [a'zjatʃiku, a] ADJ, M/F Asian

asilar [azi'lar] VT to give refuge to; **asilar-se** VR to take refuge

asilo [a'zilu] M (*refúgio*) refuge; (*estabelecimento*) home; ~ **político** political asylum

asma ['azma] F asthma

asmático, -a [az'matʃiku, a] ADJ, M/F asthmatic

asneira [az'nejra] F (*tolice*) stupidity; (*ato, dito*) stupid thing

asno ['aznu] M donkey; (*fig*) ass

aspargo [as'pargu] M asparagus

aspas ['aspas] FPL inverted commas; **entre** ~ in inverted commas

aspecto [as'pɛktu] M (*de uma questão*) aspect; (*aparência*) look, appearance; (*característica*) feature; (*ponto de vista*) point of view; **ter bom** ~ to look good; **tomar um** ~ to take on an aspect

aspereza [aspe'reza] F roughness; (*severidade*) harshness; (*rudeza*) rudeness

aspergir [asper'ʒir] VT to sprinkle

áspero, -a ['asperu, a] ADJ rough; (*severo*) harsh; (*rude*) rude

asperso, -a [as'pɛrsu, a] PP *de* **aspergir** ▶ ADJ scattered

aspiração [aspira'sãw] (*pl* -**ões**) F aspiration; (*inalação*) inhalation

aspirador [aspira'dor] M: ~ **(de pó)** vacuum cleaner; **passar o ~ (em)** to vacuum

aspirante [aspi'rãtʃi] ADJ aspiring ▶ M/F candidate; (*Mil*) cadet; (*Náut*) midshipman

aspirar [aspi'rar] VT to breathe in; (*bombear*) to suck up; (*Ling*) to aspirate ▶ VI to breathe; (*soprar*) to blow; (*desejar*): ~ **a algo** to aspire to sth

aspirina [aspi'rina] F aspirin

aspirjo *etc* [as'pirʒu] VB *ver* **aspergir**

asqueroso, -a [aske'rozu, ɔza] ADJ disgusting, revolting

assadeira [asa'dejra] F roasting tin

assado, -a [a'sadu, a] ADJ roasted; (*Culin*) roast ▶ M roast; **carne assada** roast beef

assadura [asa'dura] F rash; (*em bebê*) nappy rash

assalariado, -a [asala'rjadu, a] ADJ salaried ▶ M/F wage-earner

assaltante [asaw'tãtʃi] M/F assailant; (*de banco*) robber; (*de casa*) burglar; (*na rua*) mugger

assaltar [asaw'tar] VT (*atacar*) to attack; (*casa*) to break into; (*banco*) to rob; (*pessoa na rua*) to mug

assalto [a'sawtu] M (*ataque*) attack, raid; (*a um banco etc*) raid, robbery; (*a uma casa*) burglary, break-in; (*a uma pessoa na rua*) mugging; (*Boxe*) round

assanhado, -a [asa'ɲadu, a] ADJ excited; (*criança*) excitable; (*desavergonhado*) brazen; (*namorador*) amorous

assanhar [asa'ɲar] VT to excite; **assanhar-se** VR to get excited

assar [a'sar] VT to roast; (*na grelha*) to grill

assassinar [asasi'nar] VT to murder, kill; (*Pol*) to assassinate

assassinato [asasi'natu] M murder, killing; (*Pol*) assassination

assassínio [asa'sinju] M murder, killing; (*Pol*) assassination

assassino, -a [asa'sinu, a] M/F murderer; (*Pol*) assassin; ~ **em série** serial killer

assaz [a'saz] ADV (*suficientemente*) sufficiently; (*muito*) rather

asseado, -a [a'sjadu, a] ADJ clean

assediar [ase'dʒjar] VT (*sitiar*) to besiege; (*importunar*) to pester

assédio [a'sɛdʒu] M siege; (*insistência*) insistence

assegurar [asegu'rar] VT (*tornar seguro*) to secure; (*garantir*) to ensure; (*afirmar*) to assure; **assegurar-se** VR: ~-**se de** to make sure of

asseio [a'seju] M cleanliness

assembleia [asẽ'blɛja] F assembly; (*reunião*) meeting; ~ **geral (ordinária)** annual

general meeting; ~ **geral extraordinária** extraordinary general meeting

assemelhar [aseme'ʎar] VT to liken; **assemelhar-se** VR (*ser parecido*) to be alike; ~-**se a** to resemble, look like

assenhorear-se [aseɲo'rjarsi] VR: ~ **de** to take possession of

assentado, -a [asẽ'tadu, a] ADJ (*firme*) fixed, secure; (*combinado*) agreed; (*ajuizado*) sensible

assentamento [asẽta'mẽtu] M registration; (*nota*) entry, record

assentar [asẽ'tar] VT (*fazer sentar*) to seat; (*colocar*) to place; (*tijolos*) to lay; (*estabelecer*) to establish; (*decidir*) to decide upon; (*determinar*) to fix, settle; (*soco*) to land ▶ VI (*pó etc*) to settle; **assentar-se** VR to sit down; ~ **com** to go with; ~ **em** *ou* **a** (*roupa*) to suit

assente [a'sẽtʃi] PP *de* **assentar** ▶ ADJ agreed, decided

assentimento [asẽtʃi'mẽtu] M assent, agreement

assentir [asẽ'tʃir] VI to agree; ~ **(em)** to consent *ou* agree (to); ~ **(a)** to accede (to)

assento [a'sẽtu] M seat; (*base*) base; **tomar ~** (*sentar*) to take a seat; (*pó*) to settle

assertiva [aser'tʃiva] F assertion

assessor, a [ase'sor(a)] M/F adviser; (*Pol*) aide; (*assistente*) assistant

assessoramento [asesora'mẽtu] M assistance

assessorar [aseso'rar] VT to advise

assessoria [aseso'ria] F advisory body

assestar [ases'tar] VT to aim, point

asseveração [asevera'sãw] (*pl* -**ões**) F assertion

asseverar [aseve'rar] VT to affirm, assert

assexuado, -a [asek'swadu, a] ADJ asexual

assiduidade [asidwi'dadʒi] F (*às aulas etc*) regular attendance; (*diligência*) assiduity

assíduo, -a [a'sidwu, a] ADJ (*aluno*) who attends regularly; (*diligente*) assiduous; (*constante*) constant; **ser ~ num lugar** to be a regular visitor to a place

assim [a'sĩ] ADV (*deste modo*) like this, in this way, thus; (*portanto*) therefore; (*igualmente*) likewise; ~ ~ so-so; ~ **mesmo** in any case; **e ~ por diante** and so on; ~ **como** as well as; **como ~?** how do you mean?; ~ **que** (*logo que*) as soon as; **nem tanto ~** not as much as that

assimétrico, -a [asi'mɛtriku, a] ADJ asymmetrical

assimilação [asimila'sãw] F assimilation

assimilar [asimi'lar] VT to assimilate; (*apreender*) to take in; (*assemelhar*) to compare

assin. ABR = **assinatura**

assinalado, -a [asina'ladu, a] ADJ (*marcado*) marked; (*notável*) notable; (*célebre*) eminent

assinalar [asina'lar] VT (*marcar*) to mark; (*distinguir*) to distinguish; (*especificar*) to point out

assinante [asi'nãtʃi] M/F (*de jornal etc*) subscriber

assinar [asi'nar] VT to sign
assinatura [asina'tura] F (*nome*) signature; (*de jornal etc*) subscription; (*Teatro*) season ticket; **fazer a ~ de** (*revista etc*) to take out a subscription to
assinto *etc* [a'sĩtu] VB *ver* **assentir**
assistência [asis'tẽsja] F (*presença*) presence; (*público*) audience; (*auxílio*) aid, assistance; **~ médica** medical aid; **~ social** social work; (*serviços*) social services *pl*; **~ técnica** technical back-up
assistente [asis'tẽtʃi] ADJ assistant ▶ M/F (*pessoa presente*) spectator, onlooker; (*ajudante*) assistant; **~ social** social worker
assistir [asis'tʃir] VT, VI: **~ (a)** (*Med*) to attend (to); **~ a** (*auxiliar*) to assist; (*TV, filme, jogo*) to watch; (*reunião*) to attend; (*caber*) to fall to
assoalho [aso'aʎu] M (wooden) floor
assoar [aso'ar] VT: **~ o nariz** to blow one's nose; **assoar-se** VR (*PT*) to blow one's nose
assoberbado, -a [asober'badu, a] ADJ (*pessoa: de serviço*) snowed under with work
assoberbar [asober'bar] VT (*de serviço*) to overload
assobiar [aso'bjar] VI to whistle
assobio [aso'biu] M whistle; (*instrumento*) whistle; (*de vapor*) hiss
associação [asosja'sãw] (*pl* **-ões**) F association; (*organização*) society; (*parceria*) partnership; **~ de moradores** residents' association
associado, -a [aso'sjadu, a] ADJ associate ▶ M/F associate, member; (*Com*) associate; (*sócio*) partner
associar [aso'sjar] VT to associate; **associar-se** VR (*Com*) to form a partnership; **~-se a** to associate with
assolador, a [asola'dor(a)] ADJ devastating
assolar [aso'lar] VT to devastate
assomar [aso'mar] VI (*aparecer*) to appear; **~ a** (*subir*) to climb to the top of
assombração [asõbra'sãw] (*pl* **-ões**) F (*fantasma*) ghost
assombrado, -a [asõ'bradu, a] ADJ astonished, amazed
assombrar [asõ'brar] VT to astonish, amaze; **assombrar-se** VR to be amazed
assombro [a'sõbru] M amazement, astonishment; (*maravilha*) marvel
assombroso, -a [asõ'brozu, ɔza] ADJ (*espantoso*) astonishing, amazing
assoprar [aso'prar] VI to blow ▶ VT to blow; (*velas*) to blow out
assoviar [aso'vjar] VT = **assobiar**
assovio [aso'viu] M = **assobio**
assumir [asu'mir] VT to assume, take on; (*reconhecer*) to accept, admit ▶ VI to take office
Assunção [asũ'sãw] N (*no Paraguai*) Asunción
assuntar [asũ'tar] VT (*prestar atenção*) to pay attention to; (*verificar*) to find out ▶ VI (*meditar*) to cogitate
assunto [a'sũtu] M (*tema*) subject, matter; (*enredo*) plot

assustadiço, -a [asusta'dʒisu, a] ADJ timorous
assustador, a [asusta'dor(a)] ADJ (*alarmante*) startling; (*amedrontador*) frightening
assustar [asus'tar] VT to frighten, scare, startle; **assustar-se** VR to be frightened
asteca [as'tɛka] ADJ, M/F Aztec
asterisco [aste'risku] M asterisk
astigmatismo [astʃigma'tʃizmu] M astigmatism
astral [as'traw] (*pl* **-ais**) M mood; **bom ~** good vibe; **alto ~** upbeat mood; **baixo ~** gloom; **estar de baixo ~** to be feeling glum
astro ['astru] M star
astrologia [astrolo'ʒia] F astrology
astrólogo, -a [as'trologu, a] M/F astrologer
astronauta [astro'nawta] M/F astronaut
astronave [astro'navi] F spaceship
astronomia [astrono'mia] F astronomy
astronômico, -a [astro'nomiku, a] ADJ (*preço*) astronomical
astrônomo, -a [as'tronomu, a] M/F astronomer
astúcia [as'tusja] F cunning
astuto, -a [as'tutu, a] ADJ astute; (*esperto*) cunning
ata ['ata] F (*de reunião*) minutes *pl*
atacadista [ataka'dʒista] ADJ wholesale ▶ M/F wholesaler
atacado, -a [ata'kadu, a] ADJ (*col: pessoa*) in a bad mood ▶ M: **por ~** wholesale
atacante [ata'kãtʃi] ADJ attacking ▶ M/F attacker, assailant ▶ M (*Futebol*) forward
atacar [ata'kar] VT to attack; (*problema etc*) to tackle
atado, -a [a'tadu, a] ADJ (*desajeitado*) clumsy, awkward; (*perplexo*) puzzled
atadura [ata'dura] F bandage
atalaia [ata'laja] F lookout post
atalhar [ata'ʎar] VT (*impedir*) to prevent; (*abreviar*) to shorten ▶ VI (*tomar um atalho*) to take a short cut
atalho [a'taʎu] M (*caminho*) short cut
atapetar [atape'tar] VT to carpet
ataque [a'taki] M attack; **ter um ~ (de raiva)** to have a fit; **ter um ~ de riso** to burst out laughing; **~ aéreo** air raid; **~ suicida** suicide attack
ataquei *etc* [ata'kej] VB *ver* **atacar**
atar [a'tar] VT to tie (up), fasten; **não ~ nem desatar** (*pessoa*) to waver; (*negócio*) to be in the air
atarantado, -a [atarã'tadu, a] ADJ (*pessoa*) flustered, in a flap
atarantar [atarã'tar] VT to fluster
atarefado, -a [atare'fadu, a] ADJ busy
atarracado, -a [ataha'kadu, a] ADJ stocky
atarraxar [ataha'ʃar] VT to screw
ataúde [ata'udʒi] M coffin
ataviar [ata'vjar] VT to adorn, decorate; **ataviar-se** VR to get dressed up
atavio [ata'viu] M adornment
atazanar [ataza'nar] VT to pester

até [a'tɛ] PREP (PT: +a: lugar) up to, as far as;
(tempo etc) until, till ▶ ADV (tb: **até mesmo**)
even; ~ **agora** up to now; ~ **certo ponto** to a
certain extent; ~ **em cima** to the top; ~ **já**
see you soon; ~ **logo** bye!; ~ **onde** as far as;
~ **que** until; ~ **que enfim!** at last!

atear [ate'ar] VT (fogo) to kindle; (fig) to incite,
inflame; **atear-se** VR (fogo) to blaze; (paixões)
to flare up; ~ **fogo a** to set light to

ateia [a'teja] F de **ateu**

ateísmo [ate'izmu] M atheism

ateliê [ate'lje] M studio

atemorizador, a [atemoriza'dor(a)] ADJ
frightening

atemorizar [atemori'zar] VT to frighten;
(intimidar) to intimidate

Atenas [a'tenas] N Athens

atenção [atẽ'sãw] (pl -ões) F attention;
(cortesia) courtesy; (bondade) kindness; ~! be
careful!; **chamar a** ~ to attract attention;
chamar a ~ **de alguém** to tell sb off

atencioso, -a [atẽ'sjozu, ɔza] ADJ considerate

atenções [atẽ'sõjs] FPL de **atenção**

atender [atẽ'der] VT: ~ **(a)** to attend to;
(receber) to receive; (em loja) to serve; (deferir) to
grant; (telefone etc) to answer; (paciente) to see
▶ VI (ao telefone, porta) to answer; (dar atenção)
to pay attention

atendimento [atẽdʒi'mẽtu] M service;
(recepção) reception; **horário de** ~ opening
hours; (em consultório) surgery (BRIT) ou office
(US) hours

atenho etc [a'teɲu] VB ver **ater-se**

atentado [atẽ'tadu] M (ataque) attack; (crime)
crime; (contra a vida de alguém) attempt on sb's
life; ~ **ao pudor** indecent exposure;
~ **suicida** suicide attack

atentar [atẽ'tar] VT (empreender) to undertake
▶ VI to make an attempt; ~ **a** ou **em** ou **para**
to pay attention to; ~ **contra a vida de**
alguém to make an attempt on sb's life;
~ **contra a moral** to offend against morality

atento, -a [a'tẽtu, a] ADJ attentive; (exame)
careful; **estar ~ a** to be aware ou mindful of

atenuação [atenwa'sãw] (pl -ões) F
reduction, lessening

atenuante [ate'nwãtʃi] ADJ extenuating ▶ M
extenuating circumstance

atenuar [ate'nwar] VT (diminuir) to reduce,
lessen

aterrador, a [ateha'dor(a)] ADJ terrifying

aterragem [ate'haʒẽ] (pl -ns) (PT) F (Aer)
landing

aterrar [ate'har] VT (cobrir com terra) to cover
with earth; (praia) to reclaim ▶ VI (PT Aer) to
land

aterrissagem [atehi'saʒẽ] (pl -ns) (BR) F (Aer)
landing

aterrissar [atehi'sar] (BR) VI (Aer) to land

aterrizar [atehi'zar] (BR) VI = **aterrissar**

aterro [a'tehu] M: ~ **sanitário** landfill (site)

aterrorizado, -a [atehori'zadu, a] ADJ
terrified

aterrorizador, a [atehoriza'dor(a)] ADJ
terrifying

aterrorizante [atehori'zãtʃi] ADJ terrifying

aterrorizar [atehori'zar] VT to terrorize

ater-se [a'tersi] (irreg: como **ter**) VR: ~ **a**
(prender-se) to get caught up in; (limitar-se) to
restrict o.s. to

atestado, -a [ates'tadu, a] ADJ certified ▶ M
certificate; (prova) proof; (Jur) testimony;
~ **médico** medical certificate

atestar [ates'tar] VT (certificar) to certify;
(testemunhar) to bear witness to; (provar) to
prove

ateu, ateia [a'tew, a'teja] ADJ, M/F atheist

ateve etc [a'tevi] VB ver **ater-se**

atiçador [atʃisa'dor] M (utensílio) poker

atiçar [atʃi'sar] VT (fogo) to poke; (incitar) to
incite; (provocar) to provoke; (sentimento) to
induce

atilado, -a [atʃi'ladu, a] ADJ (esperto) clever

atinado, -a [atʃi'nadu, a] ADJ (sensato) wise,
sensible

atinar [atʃi'nar] VT (acertar) to guess correctly
▶ VI: ~ **com** (solução) to find; ~ **em** to notice;
~ **a fazer algo** to succeed in doing sth

atingir [atʃi'ʒir] VT to reach; (acertar) to hit;
(afetar) to affect; (objetivo) to achieve;
(compreender) to grasp

atingível [atʃi'ʒivew] (pl -eis) ADJ attainable

atinha etc [a'tʃiɲa] VB ver **ater-se**

atinjo etc [a'tʃiʒu] VB ver **atingir**

atípico, -a [a'tʃipiku, a] ADJ atypical,
untypical

atirador, a [atʃira'dor(a)] M/F marksman/
woman; ~ **de tocaia** sniper

atirar [atʃi'rar] VT (lançar) to throw, fling, hurl
▶ VI (arma) to shoot; **atirar-se** VR: ~-**se a**
(lançar-se a) to hurl o.s. at; ~ **(em)** to shoot
(at)

atitude [atʃi'tudʒi] F attitude; (postura)
posture; **tomar uma** ~ (reagir) to do
something about it

ativa [a'tʃiva] F (Mil) active service

ativar [atʃi'var] VT to activate; (apressar) to
hasten

ative etc [a'tʃivi] VB ver **ater-se**

atividade [atʃivi'dadʒi] F activity

ativo, -a [a'tʃivu, a] ADJ active ▶ M (Com)
assets pl

atlântico, -a [at'lãtʃiku, a] ADJ Atlantic ▶ M:
o (Oceano) A~ the Atlantic (Ocean)

atlas ['atlas] M INV atlas

atleta [at'lɛta] M/F athlete

atlético, -a [at'lɛtʃiku, a] ADJ athletic

atletismo [atle'tʃizmu] M athletics sg

atmosfera [atmos'fɛra] F atmosphere

ato ['atu] M act; (ação) action; (cerimônia)
ceremony; (Teatro) act; **em ~ contínuo**
straight after; **no** ~ on the spot; **no mesmo**
~ at the same time; ~ **falho** Freudian slip;
~ **público** public ceremony

atoalhado, -a [atoa'ʎadu, a] ADJ: **(tecido)** ~
towelling

atolado, -a [ato'ladu, a] ADJ (tb fig) bogged down

atolar [ato'lar] VT to bog down; **atolar-se** VR to get bogged down

atoleiro [ato'lejru] M bog, quagmire; (fig) quandary, fix

atômico, -a [a'tomiku, a] ADJ atomic

atomizador [atomiza'dor] M atomizer

átomo ['atomu] M atom

atônito, -a [a'tonitu, a] ADJ astonished, amazed

ator [a'tor] M actor

atordoado, -a [ator'dwadu, a] ADJ dazed

atordoador, a [atordwa'dor(a)] ADJ stunning

atordoamento [atordwa'mẽtu] M daze

atordoar [ator'dwar] VT to daze, stun

atormentar [atormẽ'tar] VT to torment; (importunar) to plague

atracação [atraka'sãw] (pl -ões) F (Náut) mooring; (briga) fight; (col: agarração) necking

atração [atra'sãw] (pl -ões) F attraction

atracar [atra'kar] VT, VI (Náut) to moor; **atracar-se** VR to grapple; (col: abraçar-se) to neck

atrações [atra'sõjs] FPL de atração

atraente [atra'ẽtʃi] ADJ attractive

atraiçoar [atraj'swar] VT to betray

atrair [atra'ir] VT to attract; (fascinar) to fascinate

atrapalhação [atrapaʎa'sãw] F (confusão) confusion

atrapalhar [atrapa'ʎar] VT (confundir) to confuse; (perturbar) to disturb; (dificultar) to hinder ▶ VI to be a nuisance; to be a hindrance; **atrapalhar-se** VR to get confused

atrás [a'trajs] ADV behind; (no fundo) at the back ▶ PREP: ~ **de** behind; (no tempo) after; (em busca de) after; **um ~ de outro** one after the other; **dois meses ~** two months ago; **não ficar ~** (fig) not to be far behind

atrasado, -a [atra'zadu, a] ADJ late; (país etc) backward; (relógio etc) slow; (pagamento) overdue; (costumes, pessoa) antiquated; (número de revista) back; **estar ~ nos pagamentos** to be in arrears

atrasados [atra'zadus] MPL (Com) arrears

atrasar [atra'zar] VT to delay; (progresso, desenvolvimento) to hold back; (relógio) to put back; (pagamento) to be late with ▶ VI (relógio etc) to be slow; (avião, pessoa) to be late; **atrasar-se** VR (chegar tarde) to be late; (num trabalho) to fall behind; (num pagamento) to get into arrears

atraso [a'trazu] M delay; (de país etc) backwardness; **atrasos** MPL (Com) arrears; **chegar com ~** to arrive late; **com 20 minutos de ~** 20 minutes late; **com um ~ de 6 meses** (Com: pagamento) six months in arrears; **um ~ de vida** a hindrance

atrativo, -a [atra'tʃivu, a] ADJ attractive ▶ M attraction, appeal; (incentivo) incentive; **atrativos** MPL (encantos) charms

atravancar [atravã'kar] VT to block, obstruct; (encher) to fill up

através [atra'vɛs] ADV across; ~ **de** (de lado a lado) across; (pelo centro de) through; (por meio de) through

atravessado, -a [atrave'sadu, a] ADJ (na garganta) stuck; **estar com alguém ~ na garganta** to be peeved with sb

atravessar [atrave'sar] VT (cruzar) to cross; (pôr ao través) to put ou lay across; (traspassar) to pass through; (crise etc) to go through

atrelar [atre'lar] VT (cão) to put on a leash; (cavalo) to harness; (duas viaturas) to couple up

atrever-se [atre'versi] VR: ~ **a** to dare to

atrevido, -a [atre'vidu, a] ADJ (petulante) cheeky, impudent; (corajoso) bold

atrevimento [atrevi'mẽtu] M (ousadia) boldness; (insolência) cheek, insolence

atribuição [atribwi'sãw] (pl -ões) F attribution; **atribuições** FPL (direitos) rights; (poderes) powers

atribuir [atri'bwir] VT: ~ **algo a** to attribute sth to; (prêmios, regalias) to confer sth on

atribulação [atribula'sãw] (pl -ões) F tribulation

atribular [atribu'lar] VT to trouble, distress; **atribular-se** VR to be distressed

atributo [atri'butu] M attribute

átrio ['atrju] M hall; (pátio) courtyard

atrito [a'tritu] M (fricção) friction; (desentendimento) disagreement

atriz [a'triz] F actress

atrocidade [atrosi'dadʒi] F atrocity

atrofia [atro'fia] F atrophy

atrofiar [atro'fjar] VT to atrophy; **atrofiar-se** VR to atrophy

atropeladamente [atropelada'mẽtʃi] ADV haphazardly

atropelamento [atropela'mẽtu] M (de pedestre) accident involving a pedestrian

atropelar [atrope'lar] VT to knock down, run over; (empurrar) to jostle

atropelo [atro'pelu] M bustle, scramble; (confusão) confusion

atroz [a'trɔz] ADJ (cruel) merciless; (crime) heinous; (dor, lembrança, feiura) terrible, awful

attaché [ata'ʃe] M attaché

atuação [atwa'sãw] (pl -ões) F acting; (de ator etc) performance

atuado, -a [a'twadu, a] ADJ (pessoa) in a bad mood

atual [a'twaw] (pl -ais) ADJ current; (pessoa, carro) modern

atualidade [atwali'dadʒi] F present (time); **atualidades** FPL (notícias) news sg

atualização [atwaliza'sãw] (pl -ões) F updating

atualizado, -a [atwali'zadu, a] ADJ up-to-date

atualizar [atwali'zar] VT to update; **atualizar-se** VR to bring o.s. up to date

atualmente [atwaw'mẽtʃi] ADV at present, currently; (hoje em dia) nowadays

atuante [a'twãtʃi] ADJ active

atuar [a'twar] vi to act; **~ para** to contribute to; **~ sobre** to influence

atulhar [atu'ʎar] vt (*encher*) to cram full; (*meter*) to stuff, cram

atum [a'tũ] (*pl* **-ns**) m tuna (fish)

aturar [atu'rar] vt (*suportar*) to endure, put up with

aturdido, -a [atur'dʒidu, a] adj stunned; (*com barulho*) deafened; (*com confusão, movimento*) bewildered

aturdimento [aturdʒi'mẽtu] m bewilderment

aturdir [atur'dʒir] vt to stun; (*suj: barulho*) to deafen; (: *confusão, movimento*) to bewilder

atxim [a'tʃĩ] excl achoo!

audácia [aw'dasja] f boldness; (*insolência*) insolence; **que ~!** what a cheek!

audacioso, -a [awda'sjozu, ɔza] adj daring; (*insolente*) insolent

audaz [aw'daz] adj daring; (*insolente*) insolent

audição [awdʒi'sãw] (*pl* **-ões**) f audition; (*concerto*) recital

audiência [aw'dʒjẽsja] f audience; (*de tribunal*) session, hearing

audiovisual [awdʒjovi'zwaw] (*pl* **-ais**) adj audiovisual

auditar [awdʒi'tar] vt (*Com*) to audit

auditivo, -a [awdʒi'tʃivu, a] adj hearing *atr*, auditory

auditor, a [awdʒi'tor(a)] m/f (*Com*) auditor; (*juiz*) judge; (*ouvinte*) listener

auditoria [awdʒito'ria] f auditing; **fazer a ~ de** to audit

auditório [awdʒi'tɔrju] m (*ouvintes*) audience; (*recinto*) auditorium; **programa de ~** program(me) recorded before a live audience

audível [aw'dʒivew] (*pl* **-eis**) adj audible

auferir [awfe'rir] vt (*lucro*) to derive

auge ['awʒi] m height, peak

augurar [awgu'rar] vt to augur; (*felicidades*) to wish

augúrio [aw'gurju] m omen

aula ['awla] f (*PT: sala*) classroom; (*lição*) lesson, class; **dar ~** to teach

aumentar [awmẽ'tar] vt to increase; (*salários, preços*) to raise; (*sala, casa*) to expand, extend; (*suj: lente*) to magnify; (*acrescentar*) to add ▶ vi to increase; (*preço, salário*) to rise, go up; **~ de peso** (*pessoa*) to put on weight

aumento [aw'mẽtu] m increase; (*de preços*) rise; (*ampliação*) enlargement; (*crescimento*) growth

áureo, -a ['awrju, a] adj golden

auréola [aw'rɛola] f halo

aurora [aw'rɔra] f dawn

auscultar [awskuw'tar] vt (*opinião pública*) to sound out; (*paciente*): **~ alguém** to sound sb's chest

ausência [aw'zẽsja] f absence

ausentar-se [awzẽ'tarsi] vr (*ir-se*) to go away; (*afastar-se*) to stay away

ausente [aw'zẽtʃi] adj absent ▶ m/f missing person

auspiciar [awspi'sjar] vt to augur

auspício [aw'spisju] m: **sob os ~s de** under the auspices of

auspicioso, -a [awspi'sjozu, ɔza] adj auspicious

austeridade [awsteri'dadʒi] f austerity

austero, -a [aws'tɛru, a] adj austere

austral [aws'traw] (*pl* **-ais**) adj southern

Austrália [aws'tralja] f: **a ~** Australia

australiano, -a [awstra'ljanu, a] adj, m/f Australian

Áustria ['awstrja] f: **a ~** Austria

austríaco, -a [aws'triaku, a] adj, m/f Austrian

autarquia [awtar'kia] f autonomous government organization, ≈ quango (*BRIT*)

autárquico, -a [aw'tarkiku, a] adj autonomous

autenticar [awtẽtʃi'kar] vt to authenticate; (*Com, Jur*) to certify

autenticidade [awtẽtʃisi'dadʒi] f authenticity

autêntico, -a [aw'tẽtʃiku, a] adj authentic; (*pessoa*) genuine; (*verdadeiro*) true, real

autismo [aw'tʃizmu] m autism

autista [aw'tʃista] adj autistic ▶ m/f autistic person

auto ['awtu] m (*automóvel*) car; **autos** mpl (*Jur: processo*) legal proceedings; (*documentos*) legal papers

autoadesivo, -a [awtoade'zivu, a] adj self-adhesive

autoafirmação [awtoafirma'sãw] f self-assertion

autobiografia [awtobjogra'fia] f autobiography

autobiográfico, -a [awtobjo'grafiku, a] adj autobiographical

autobronzeador [awtobrõzja'dor] adj self-tanning

autocarro [awto'kahu] (*PT*) m bus

autocontrole [awtokõ'troli] m self-control

autocrata [awto'krata] adj autocratic

autóctone [aw'tɔktoni] adj indigenous ▶ m/f native

autodefesa [awtode'feza] f self-defence (*BRIT*), self-defense (*US*)

autodestruição [awtodes'trwisãw] f self-destruction

autodeterminação [awtodetermina'sãw] f self-determination

autodidata [awtodʒi'data] adj self-taught ▶ m/f autodidact

autodisciplina [awtodʒisi'plina] f self-discipline

autodomínio [awtodo'minju] m self-control

autódromo [aw'tɔdromu] m race track

autoescola [awtois'kɔla] f driving school

autoestrada [awtois'trada] f motorway (*BRIT*), expressway (*US*)

autografar [awtogra'far] vt to autograph

autógrafo [aw'tɔgrafu] m autograph

automação [awtoma'sãw] f automation; **~ de escritórios** office automation

automático, -a [awto'matʃiku, a] ADJ automatic

automatização [awtomatʃiza'sãw] F = **automação**

automatizar [awtomatʃi'zar] VT to automate

autômato [aw'tomatu] M automaton

automedicar-se [awtomedʒi'karsi] VR to treat o.s.

automobilismo [awtomobi'lizmu] M motoring; (*Esporte*) motor car racing

automóvel [awto'mɔvew] (*pl* -**eis**) M motor car (BRIT), automobile (US)

autonomia [awtono'mia] F autonomy

autônomo, -a [aw'tonomu, a] ADJ autonomous; (*trabalhador*) self-employed ▶ M/F self-employed person

autopeça [awto'pɛsa] F car spare

autópsia [aw'tɔpsja] F post-mortem, autopsy

autor, a [aw'tor(a)] M/F author; (*de um crime*) perpetrator; (*Jur*) plaintiff

autoral [awto'raw] (*pl* -**ais**) ADJ: **direitos autorais** copyright *sg*

autoridade [awtori'dadʒi] F authority

autoritário, -a [awtori'tarju, a] ADJ authoritarian

autoritarismo [awtorita'rizmu] M authoritarianism

autorização [awtoriza'sãw] (*pl* -**ões**) F permission, authorization; **dar ~ a alguém para** to give sb permission to, to authorize sb to

autorizar [awtori'zar] VT to authorize

autorretrato [awtohe'tratu] M self-portrait

autosserviço [awtoser'visu] M self-service

autossuficiente [awtosufi'sjẽtʃi] ADJ self-sufficient

autossugestão [awtosuʒes'tãw] F autosuggestion

autuar [aw'twar] VT to sue

auxiliar [awsi'ljar] ADJ auxiliary ▶ M/F assistant ▶ VT to help, assist

auxílio [aw'silju] M help, assistance, aid

auxílio-doença (*pl* **auxílios-doença**) M sickness benefit, sick pay

Av. ABR (= *avenida*) Ave.

avacalhado, -a [avaka'ʎadu, a] ADJ sloppy

avacalhar [avaka'ʎar] (*col*) VT to screw up

aval [a'vaw] (*pl* -**ais**) M guarantee; (*Com*) surety

avalancha [ava'lãʃa] F avalanche

avalanche [ava'lãʃi] F = **avalancha**

avaliação [avalja'sãw] (*pl* -**ões**) F valuation; (*apreciação*) assessment, evaluation

avaliador, a [avalja'dor(a)] M/F: **~ de danos** loss adjuster

avaliar [ava'ljar] VT to value; to assess, evaluate; (*imaginar*) to imagine; **~ algo em $100** to value sth at $100

avalista [ava'lista] M/F guarantor

avalizar [avali'zar] VT to guarantee

avançada [avã'sada] F advance

avançado, -a [avã'sadu, a] ADJ advanced; (*ideias, pessoa*) progressive

avançar [avã'sar] VT to move forward ▶ VI to advance

avanço [a'vãsu] M advancement; (*progresso*) progress; (*melhora*) improvement, advance

avantajado, -a [avãta'ʒadu, a] ADJ (*corpulento*) stout

avante [a'vãtʃi] ADV forward

avarento, -a [ava'rẽtu, a] ADJ mean ▶ M/F miser

avareza [ava'reza] F meanness

avaria [ava'ria] F damage; (*Tec*) breakdown

avariado, -a [ava'rjadu, a] ADJ damaged; (*máquina*) out of order; (*carro*) broken down

avariar [ava'rjar] VT to damage ▶ VI to suffer damage; (*Tec*) to break down

avaro, -a [a'varu, a] ADJ mean ▶ M/F miser

ave ['avi] F bird

aveia [a'veja] F oats *pl*

aveio *etc* [a'veju] VB *ver* **avir-se**

avelã [ave'lã] F hazelnut

aveludado, -a [avelu'dadu, a] ADJ velvety; (*voz*) smooth

avenho *etc* [a'veɲu] VB *ver* **avir-se**

avenida [ave'nida] F avenue

avental [avẽ'taw] (*pl* -**ais**) M apron; (*vestido*) pinafore dress (BRIT), jumper (US)

aventar [avẽ'tar] VT (*ideia etc*) to put forward

aventura [avẽ'tura] F adventure; (*proeza*) exploit

aventurar [avẽtu'rar] VT (*ousar*) to risk, venture; **aventurar-se** VR: **~-se a** to dare to

aventureiro, -a [avẽtu'rejru, a] ADJ adventurous ▶ M/F adventurer

averiguação [averigwa'sãw] (*pl* -**ões**) F investigation, inquiry; (*verificação*) verification

averiguar [averi'gwar] VT (*inquirir*) to investigate; (*verificar*) to verify

avermelhado, -a [averme'ʎadu, a] ADJ reddish

aversão [aver'sãw] (*pl* -**ões**) F aversion

averso, -a [a'versu, a] ADJ: **~ a** averse to

aversões [aver'sõjs] FPL *de* **aversão**

avesso, -a [a'vesu, a] ADJ (*lado*) opposite, reverse ▶ M wrong side, reverse; **ao ~** inside out; **às avessas** (*inverso*) upside down; (*oposto*) the wrong way round; **virar pelo ~** to turn inside out

avestruz [aves'truz] M ostrich

aviação [avja'sãw] F aviation, flying

aviado, -a [a'vjadu, a] ADJ (*executado*) ready; (*apressado*) hurried

aviador, a [avja'dor(a)] M/F aviator, airman/woman

aviamento [avja'mẽtu] M (*Costura*) haberdashery (BRIT), notions *pl* (US); (*de receita médica*) filling; (*Com*) goodwill

avião [a'vjãw] (*pl* -**ões**) M aeroplane; **~ a jato** jet

aviar [a'vjar] VT (*receita médica*) to make up

avicultor, a [avikuw'tor(a)] M/F poultry farmer

avicultura [avikuw'tura] F poultry farming

avidez [avi'dez] F (*cobiça*) greed; (*desejo*) eagerness

ávido, -a ['avidu, a] ADJ (*cobiçoso*) greedy; (*desejoso*) eager

aviltamento [aviwta'mētu] M debasement

aviltar [aviw'tar] VT to debase; **aviltar-se** VR to demean o.s.

avim *etc* [a'vī] VB *ver* **avir-se**

avinagrado, -a [avina'gradu, a] ADJ sour, acid

aviões [a'vjõjs] MPL *de* **avião**

avir-se [a'virsi] (*irreg: como* **vir**) VR (*conciliar-se*) to reach an understanding

avisar [avi'zar] VT (*advertir*) to warn; (*informar*) to tell, let know; **ele avisou que chega amanhã** he said he's arriving tomorrow

aviso [a'vizu] M (*comunicação*) notice; (*advertência*) warning; **~ prévio** notice

avistar [avis'tar] VT to catch sight of; **avistar-se** VR: **~-se com** (*ter entrevista*) to have an interview with

avitaminose [avitami'nɔzi] F vitamin deficiency

avivar [avi'var] VT (*intensificar*) to intensify, heighten; (*memória*) to bring back

avizinhar-se [avizi'ɲarsi] VR (*aproximar-se*) to approach, come near

avo ['avu] M: **um doze ~s** one twelfth

avô, avó [a'vo, a'vɔ] M/F grandfather/mother; **avós** MPL grandparents

avoado, -a [avo'adu, a] ADJ (*pessoa*) absent-minded

avolumar [avolu'mar] VT (*aumentar: em volume*) to swell; (: *em número*) to accumulate; (*ocupar espaço*) to fill; **avolumar-se** VR to increase; to swell

avulso, -a [a'vuwsu, a] ADJ separate, detached ▶ M single copy

avultado, -a [avuw'tadu, a] ADJ large, bulky

avultar [avuw'tar] VT to enlarge, expand ▶ VI (*sobressair*) to stand out; (*aumentar*) to increase

axila [ak'sila] F armpit

axioma [a'sjɔma] M axiom

azáfama [a'zafama] F bustle; (*pressa*) hurry

azaleia [aza'leja] F azalea

azar [a'zar] M bad luck; **~!** too bad!, bad luck!; **estar com ~, ter ~** to be unlucky

azarado, -a [aza'radu, a] ADJ (*desafortunado*) unlucky

azarento, -a [aza'rētu, a] ADJ (*que dá azar*) unlucky

azedar [aze'dar] VT to turn sour; (*pessoa*) to put in a bad mood ▶ VI to turn sour; (*leite*) to go off

azedo, -a [a'zedu, a] ADJ (*sabor*) sour; (*leite*) off; (*fig*) grumpy, bad-tempered

azedume [aze'dumi] M (*sabor*) sourness; (*fig*) grumpiness

azeitar [azej'tar] VT (*untar*) to grease; (*lubrificar*) to oil

azeite [a'zejtʃi] M oil; (*de oliva*) olive oil

azeitona [azej'tɔna] F olive

Azerbaijão [azerbaj'ʒãw] M: **o ~** Azerbaijan

azeviche [aze'viʃi] M (*cor*) jet black

azevinho [aze'viɲu] M holly

azia [a'zia] F heartburn

aziago, -a [a'zjagu, a] ADJ (*de mau agouro*) ominous

azinhaga [azi'ɲaga] F (*country*) lane

azinhavre [azi'ɲavri] M verdigris

azo ['azu] M (*oportunidade*) opportunity; (*pretexto*) pretext; **dar ~ a** to give occasion to

azougue [a'zogi] M quicksilver; (*Quím*) mercury; (*fig: pessoa: inquieta*) live wire; (: *esperta*) sharp person

azucrinar [azukri'nar] VT to bother, pester

azul [a'zuw] (*pl* **-uis**) ADJ blue; **tudo ~** (*fig*) everything's rosy

azular [azu'lar] VI to flee

azulejar [azule'ʒar] VT to tile

azulejo [azu'leʒu] M (*glazed*) tile

azul-marinho ADJ INV navy blue

azul-turquesa ADJ INV turquoise

Bb

B, b [be] (*pl* **bs**) M B, b; **B de Beatriz** B for
  Benjamin (BRIT) *ou* Baker (US)
baba ['baba] F dribble; **~ de moça** *sweet made
  with sugar, coconut milk and eggs*
babá [ba'ba] F nanny
babaca [ba'baka] (!) M wanker (BRIT!), asshole
  (US!)
babado [ba'badu] M frill; (*col*) piece of gossip
babador [baba'dor] M bib
babaquice [baba'kisi] F stupidity; (*ato, dito*)
  stupid thing
babar [ba'bar] VT to dribble on ▶ VI to dribble;
  babar-se VR to dribble; **~(-se) por** to drool
  over
babeiro [ba'bejru] (PT) M bib
babel [ba'bɛw] (*pl* **-éis**) F (*fig*) muddle
baby-sitter ['bejbisiter] (*pl* **-s**) M/F baby-sitter
bacalhau [baka'ʎaw] M (dried) cod
bacalhoada [bakaʎo'ada] F salt cod stew
bacana [ba'kana] (*col*) ADJ great
bacanal [baka'naw] (*pl* **-ais**) M orgy
bacharel [baʃa'rɛw] (*pl* **-éis**) M graduate
bacharelado [baʃare'ladu] M bachelor's
  degree
bacharelar-se [baʃare'larsi] VR to graduate
bacia [ba'sia] F basin; (*sanitária*) bowl; (*Anat*)
  pelvis
background [bɛk'grãwdʒi] (*pl* **-s**) M background
backup [ba'kapi] (*pl* **-s**) M (*Comput*) back-up;
  fazer um ~ de to back up
baço, -a ['basu, a] ADJ dull; (*metal*) tarnished
  ▶ M (*Anat*) spleen
bacon ['bejkõ] M bacon
bactéria [bak'tɛrja] F germ, bacterium;
  bactérias MPL (*germes*) bacteria *pl*
badalado, -a [bada'ladu, a] (*col*) ADJ talked
  about, famous
badalar [bada'lar] VT, VI (*sino*) to ring ▶ VI to
  ring; (*col*) to go out and about
badalativo, -a [badala'tʃivu, a] (*col*) ADJ
  fun-loving
badalo [ba'dalu] M clapper
badejo [ba'deʒu] M sea bass
baderna [ba'dɛrna] F commotion
badulaque [badu'laki] M trinket;
  badulaques MPL (*coisas sem valor*) junk *sg*
bafafá [bafa'fa] (*col*) M kerfuffle
bafejar [bafe'ʒar] VT (*aquecer com o bafo*) to
  blow; (*fortuna*) to smile upon

bafejo [ba'feʒu] M (*sopro*) whiff; **~ da sorte**
  stroke of luck
bafio [ba'fiu] M musty smell
bafo ['bafu] M (*hálito*) (bad) breath; **isso é ~
  dele** (*col*) he's just making it up
bafômetro [ba'fometru] M Breathalyser®
baforada [bafo'rada] F (*fumaça*) puff
bagaço [ba'gasu] M (*de frutos*) pulp; (PT:
  cachaça) brandy; **estar/ficar um ~** (*fig: pessoa*)
  to be/get run down
bagageiro [baga'ʒejru] M (*Auto*) roof rack; (PT)
  porter
bagagem [ba'gaʒẽ] F luggage; (*fig*) baggage,
  luggage; **recebimento de ~** (*Aer*) baggage
  reclaim
bagatela [baga'tɛla] F trinket; (*fig*) trifle
Bagdá [bagi'da] N Baghdad
bago ['bagu] M (*fruto*) berry; (*uva*) grape; (*de
  chumbo*) pellet; (!) ball (!)
bagulho [ba'guʎu] M (*objeto*) piece of junk;
  (*pessoa*): **ser um ~** to be as ugly as sin
bagunça [ba'gũsa] F (*confusão*) mess,
  shambles *sg*
bagunçado, -a [bagũ'sadu, a] ADJ messy
bagunçar [bagũ'sar] VT to mess up
bagunceiro, -a [bagũ'sejru, a] ADJ messy
Bahamas [ba'amas] FPL: **as ~** the Bahamas
baia ['baja] F bail
baía [ba'ia] F bay
baiano, -a [ba'janu, a] ADJ, M/F Bahian
baila ['bajla] F: **trazer/vir à ~** to bring/come up
bailado [baj'ladu] M dance; (*balé*) ballet
bailar [baj'lar] VT, VI to dance
bailarino, -a [bajla'rinu, a] M/F ballet dancer
baile ['bajli] M dance; (*formal*) ball; **dar um ~
  em alguém** to pull sb's leg; **~ à fantasia**
  fancy-dress ball
bainha [ba'iɲa] F (*de arma*) sheath; (*de costura*)
  hem
baioneta [bajo'neta] F bayonet; **~ calada**
  fixed bayonet
bairrista [baj'hista] ADJ loyal to one's
  neighbo(u)rhood ▶ M/F proud local
bairro ['bajhu] M district
baita ['bajta] ADJ huge; (*gripe*) bad
baixa ['bajʃa] F (*abaixamento*) decrease; (*de
  preço*) reduction, fall; (*diminuição*) drop;
  (*Bolsa*) low; (*em combate*) casualty; (*do serviço*)
  discharge; **dar** *ou* **ter ~** to be discharged

baixada [baj'ʃada] F lowland
baixa-mar (pl **baixa-mares**) F low tide
baixar [baj'ʃar] VT to lower; (bandeira) to take down; (ordem) to issue; (lei) to pass; (Comput) to download ▶ VI to go (ou come) down; (temperatura, preço) to drop, fall; (col: aparecer) to show up; ~ **ao hospital** to go into hospital
baixaria [bajʃa'ria] F vulgarity; (ação) cheap trick
baixela [baj'ʃɛla] F serving set
baixeza [baj'ʃeza] F meanness, baseness
baixinho [baj'ʃiɲu] ADV (falar) softly, quietly; (em segredo) secretly
baixio [baj'ʃiu] M sandbank, sandbar
baixista [baj'ʃista] M/F (Bolsa) bear ▶ ADJ bear atr
baixo, -a ['bajʃu, a] ADJ low; (pessoa) short, small; (rio) shallow; (linguagem) common; (olhos) lowered; (atitude) mean, base; (metal) base ▶ ADV low; (em posição baixa) low down; (falar) softly ▶ M (Mús) bass; **em ~** below; (em casa) downstairs; **em voz baixa** in a quiet voice; **para ~** down, downwards; (em casa) downstairs; **por ~ de** under, underneath; **altos e ~s** ups and downs; **estar por ~** to be down on one's luck
baixo-astral (pl **baixo-astrais**) ADJ gloomy
baixote, -a [baj'ʃɔtʃi, ta] ADJ shortish
bajulador, a [baʒula'dor(a)] ADJ obsequious
bajular [baʒu'lar] VT to fawn over
bala ['bala] F bullet; (BR: doce) sweet; **estar em ponto de ~** (fig) to be in tip-top condition; **estar/ficar uma ~** (fig) to be/get furious
balada [ba'lada] F ballad
balaio [ba'laju] M straw basket
balança [ba'lãsa] F scales pl; **B~** (Astrologia) Libra; **~ comercial** balance of trade; **~ de pagamentos** balance of payments
balançar [balã'sar] VT (fazer oscilar) to swing; (pesar) to weigh (up) ▶ VI to swing; (carro, avião) to shake; (navio) to roll; (em cadeira) to rock; **balançar-se** VR to swing
balancear [balã'sjar] VT to balance
balancete [balã'setʃi] M (Com) trial balance
balanço [ba'lãsu] M (movimento) swinging; (brinquedo) swing; (de navio) rolling; (de carro, avião) shaking; (Com: registro) balance (sheet); (: verificação) audit; **fazer um ~ de** (fig) to take stock of
balangandã [balãgã'dã] M bauble
balão [ba'lãw] (pl **-ões**) M balloon; (em história em quadrinhos) speech bubble; (Auto) turning area; **soltar um ~ de ensaio** (fig) to put out feelers; **~ de oxigênio** oxygen tank
balar [ba'lar] VI to bleat
balaustrada [balaws'trada] F balustrade
balaústre [bala'ustri] M ban(n)ister
balbuciar [bawbu'sjar] VT, VI to babble
balbucio [bawbu'siu] M babbling
balbúrdia [baw'burdʒja] F uproar, bedlam
balcão [baw'kãw] (pl **-ões**) M balcony; (de loja) counter; (Teatro) circle; **~ de informações** information desk

balconista [bawko'nista] M/F shop assistant
baldado, -a [baw'dadu, a] ADJ unsuccessful, fruitless
baldar [baw'dar] VT to frustrate, foil
balde ['bawdʒi] M bucket, pail
baldeação [bawdʒja'sãw] (pl **-ões**) F transfer; **fazer ~** to change
baldio, -a [baw'dʒiu, a] ADJ fallow, uncultivated; **(terreno) ~** (piece of) waste ground
balé [ba'lɛ] M ballet
baleeira [bale'ejra] F whaler
baleia [ba'leja] F whale
baleiro, -a [ba'lejru, a] M/F confectioner
balido [ba'lidu] M bleating; (um só) bleat
balística [ba'listʃika] F ballistics sg
balístico, -a [ba'listʃiku, a] ADJ ballistic
baliza [ba'liza] F (estaca) post; (boia) buoy; (luminosa) beacon; (Esporte) goal
balizar [bali'zar] VT to mark out
balneário [baw'njarju] M bathing resort
balões [ba'lõjs] MPL de **balão**
balofo, -a [ba'lofu, a] ADJ (fofo) fluffy; (gordo) plump, tubby
baloiço [ba'lojsu] (PT) M (de criança) swing; (ação) swinging
baloução [balo'sar] (PT) VT, VI to swing
baloiço [ba'losu] (PT) M = **baloiço**
balsa ['bawsa] F raft; (barca) ferry
bálsamo ['bawsamu] M balm
báltico, -a ['bawtʃiku, a] ADJ Baltic ▶ M: **o B~** the Baltic
baluarte [ba'lwartʃi] M rampart, bulwark; (fig) supporter
balzaquiana [bawza'kjana] F woman in her thirties
bamba ['bãba] ADJ, M/F expert
bambear [bã'bjar] VT to loosen ▶ VI to work loose; (pessoa) to grow weak
bambo, -a ['bãbu, a] ADJ slack, loose; (pernas) limp, wobbly
bambolê [bãbo'le] M hula hoop
bamboleante [bãbo'ljãtʃi] ADJ swaying; (sem firmeza) wobbly
bambolear [bãbo'ljar] VT to sway ▶ VI (pessoa) to sway; (coisa) to wobble
bambu [bã'bu] M bamboo
banal [ba'naw] (pl **-ais**) ADJ banal
banalidade [banali'dadʒi] F banality
banana [ba'nana] F banana ▶ M/F (col) wimp; **dar uma ~** ≈ to stick two fingers up
bananada [bana'nada] F banana paste
bananeira [bana'nejra] F banana tree
bananosa [bana'nɔza] (col) F: **estar numa ~** to be in a fix
banca ['bãka] F (de trabalho) bench; (escritório) office; (em jogo) bank; **~ (de jornais)** newsstand; **botar ~** (col) to show off; **botar ~ em** ou **para cima de** (col) to lay down the law to; **~ examinadora** examining body, examination board
bancada [bã'kada] F (banco, Pol) bench; (de cozinha) worktop

bancar [bã'kar] vt (*financiar*) to finance ▶ vi (*fingir*): ~ **que** to pretend that; ~ **o idiota** *etc* to play the fool *etc*; ~ **que** to pretend that

bancário, -a [bã'karju, a] adj bank *atr* ▶ m/f bank employee

bancarrota [bãka'hota] f bankruptcy; **ir à** ~ to go bankrupt

banco ['bãku] m (*assento*) bench; (*Com*) bank; (*de cozinha*) stool; ~ **de areia** sandbank; ~ **de dados** (*Comput*) database

banda ['bãda] f band; (*lado*) side; (*cinto*) sash; **de** ~ sideways; **pôr de** ~ to put aside; **nestas** ~**s** in these parts; ~ **de percussão** steel band; ~ **desenhada** (*PT*) cartoon; ~ **gástrica** (*Med*) gastric band; ~ **larga** (*Tel*) broadband

bandear-se [bãde'arsi] vr: ~ **para** *ou* **a** to go over to

bandeira [bã'dejra] f flag; (*estandarte, fig*) banner; (*de porta*) fanlight; ~ **a meio pau** flag at half mast; **dar uma** ~ **em alguém** (*col*) to give sb the brush-off; **levar uma** ~ to get the brush-off; **dar** ~ (*col*) to give o.s. away

bandeirante [bãdej'rãtʃi] m pioneer ▶ f girl guide

bandeirinha [bãdej'riɲa] m (*Esporte*) linesman

bandeja [bã'deʒa] f tray; **dar algo de** ~ **a alguém** (*col*) to give sb sth on a plate

bandido, -a [bã'dʒidu, a] m bandit ▶ m/f (*fig*) rascal

bando ['bãdu] m band; (*grupo*) group; (*de malfeitores*) gang; (*de ovelhas*) flock; (*de gado*) herd; (*de livros etc*) pile

bandô [bã'do] m pelmet

bandoleiro [bãdo'lejru] m bandit

bandolim [bãdo'lĩ] (*pl* -**ns**) m mandolin

bangalô [bãga'lo] m bungalow

Bangcoc [bãŋ'kɔki] n Bangkok

Bangladesh [bãgla'dɛʃ] m Bangladesh

bangue-bangue [bãgi'bãgi] m: (**filme de**) ~ western

banguela [bã'gɛla] adj toothless

banha ['baɲa] f fat; (*de porco*) lard

banhar [ba'ɲar] vt (*molhar*) to wet; (*mergulhar*) to dip; (*lavar*) to wash, bathe; **banhar-se** vr (*no mar*) to bathe

banheira [ba'ɲejra] f bath

banheiro [ba'ɲejru] m bathroom; (*PT*) lifeguard

banhista [ba'ɲista] m/f bather; (*salva-vidas*) lifeguard

banho ['baɲu] m (*Tec, na banheira*) bath; (*mergulho*) dip; **dar um** ~ **de cerveja** *etc* **em alguém** to spill beer *etc* all over sb; **tomar** ~ to have a bath; (*de chuveiro*) to have a shower; **tomar um** ~ **de** (*fig*) to have a heavy dose of; **vai tomar** ~! (*col*) get lost!; ~ **de chuveiro** shower; ~ **de espuma** bubble bath; **tomar** ~ **de mar** to have a swim (in the sea); ~ **de sol** sunbathing

banho-maria (*pl* **banhos-maria(s)**) m (*Culin*) bain-marie

banimento [bani'mẽtu] m banishment

banir [ba'nir] vt to banish

banjo ['bãʒu] m banjo

banquei *etc* [bã'kej] vb *ver* **bancar**

banqueiro, -a [bã'kejru, a] m/f banker

banqueta [bã'keta] f stool

banquete [bã'ketʃi] m banquet; (*fig*) feast

banquetear [bãke'tʃjar] vt to feast; **banquetear-se** vr: ~-**se com** to feast on

banqueteiro, -a [bãke'tejru, a] m/f caterer

banzé [bã'zɛ] (*col*) m kerfuffle

baque ['baki] m thud, thump; (*contratempo*) setback; (*queda*) fall; **levar um** ~ to be hard hit; ~ **duplo** (*col*) double whammy

baquear [ba'kjar] vi to topple over

bar [bar] m bar

barafunda [bara'fũda] f confusion; (*de coisas*) hotch-potch

barafustar [barafus'tar] vi: ~ **por** to burst through

baralhada [bara'ʎada] f muddle

baralhar [bara'ʎar] vt (*fig*) to mix up, confuse

baralho [ba'raʎu] m pack of cards

barão [ba'rãw] (*pl* -**ões**) m baron

barata [ba'rata] f cockroach; **entregue às** ~**s** (*pessoa*) gone to the dogs; (*plano*) gone out the window

baratear [bara'tʃjar] vt to cut the price of; (*menosprezar*) to belittle

barateiro, -a [bara'tejru, a] adj cheap

baratinado, -a [baratʃi'nadu, a] (*col*) adj in a flap; (*transtornado*) shaken up

baratinar [baratʃi'nar] (*col*) vt to drive crazy; (*transtornar*) to shake up

barato, -a [ba'ratu, a] adj cheap ▶ adv cheaply ▶ m (*col*): **a festa foi um** ~ the party was great

barba ['barba] f beard; **barbas** fpl whiskers; **nas** ~**s de** (*fig*) under the nose of; **fazer a** ~ to shave; **pôr as** ~**s de molho** to take precautions

barbada [bar'bada] (*col*) f cinch, piece of cake; (*Turfe*) favourite

barbado, -a [bar'badu, a] adj bearded

Barbados [bar'badus] m Barbados

barbante [bar'bãtʃi] (*BR*) m string

barbaramente [barbara'mẽtʃi] adv (*muito*) a lot

barbaridade [barbari'dadʒi] f barbarity, cruelty; (*disparate*) nonsense; **que** ~! good heavens!

barbárie [bar'barie] f barbarism

barbarismo [barba'rizmu] m barbarism

bárbaro, -a ['barbaru, a] adj barbaric; (*dor, calor*) terrible; (*maravilhoso*) great

barbatana [barba'tana] f fin

barbeador [barbja'dor] m razor; (*tb*: **barbeador elétrico**) shaver

barbear [bar'bjar] vt to shave; **barbear-se** vr to shave

barbearia [barbja'ria] f barber's (shop)

barbeiragem [barbej'raʒẽ] f bad driving; **fazer uma** ~ to drive badly; (*fig*) to bungle it

barbeiro [bar'bejru] M barber; (*loja*) barber's; (*motorista*) bad driver, Sunday driver
barbitúrico [barbi'turiku] M barbiturate
barbudo, -a [bar'budu, a] ADJ bearded
barca ['barka] F barge; (*de travessia*) ferry
barcaça [bar'kasa] F barge
barco ['barku] M boat; **estar no mesmo ~** (*fig*) to be in the same boat; **deixar o ~ correr** (*fig*) to let things take their course; **tocar o ~ para a frente** (*fig*) to struggle on; **~ a motor** motorboat; **~ a remo** rowing boat; **~ a vela** sailing boat
Barein [ba'rēj] M: **o ~** Bahrain
barganha [bar'gaɲa] F bargain
barganhar [barga'ɲar] VT, VI to negotiate
barítono [ba'ritonu] M baritone
barlavento [barla'vẽtu] M (*Náut*) windward; **a ~** to windward
barman [bar'mã] (*pl* **-men**) M barman
barnabé [barna'bɛ] (*col*) M petty civil servant
barões [ba'rõjs] MPL *de* **barão**
barômetro [ba'rometru] M barometer
baronesa [baro'neza] F baroness
barqueiro [bar'kejru] M boatman
barra ['baha] F bar; (*faixa*) strip; (*traço*) stroke; (*alavanca*) lever; (*col: situação*) scene; (*em endereço web*) forward slash; **aguentar** *ou* **segurar a ~** to hold out; **forçar a ~** (*col*) to force the issue; **ser uma ~** (*pessoa, entrevista*) to be tough; **~ de direção** steering column; **~ fixa** high bar; **~s paralelas** parallel bars
barraca [ba'haka] F (*tenda*) tent; (*de feira*) stall; (*de madeira*) hut; (*de praia*) sunshade
barracão [baha'kãw] (*pl* **-ões**) M (*de madeira*) shed
barraco [ba'haku] M shack, shanty; (*col: confusão*) scene; **armar um** *ou* **fazer ~** to make a scene
barracões [baha'kõjs] MPL *de* **barracão**
barragem [ba'haʒẽ] (*pl* **-ns**) F (*represa*) dam; (*impedimento*) barrier
barranco [ba'hãku] M ravine, gully; (*de rio*) bank
barra-pesada (*pl* **barras-pesadas**) M/F shady character ▶ ADJ INV (*lugar*) rough; (*pessoa*) shady; (*difícil*) difficult
barraqueiro, -a [baha'kejru, a] (*col*) ADJ stroppy (*col*)
barrar [ba'har] VT to bar
barreira [ba'hejra] F barrier; (*cerca*) fence; (*Esporte*) hurdle; **pôr ~s a** to put obstacles in the way of; **~ do som** sound barrier
barrento, -a [ba'hẽtu, a] ADJ muddy
barrete [ba'hetʃi] (*PT*) M cap
barricada [bahi'kada] F barricade
barriga [ba'higa] F belly; **estar de ~** to be pregnant; **falar** *ou* **chorar de ~ cheia** to complain for no reason; **fazer ~** to bulge; **~ da perna** calf
barrigudo, -a [bahi'gudu, a] ADJ paunchy, pot-bellied
barril [ba'hiw] (*pl* **-is**) M barrel, cask
barro ['bahu] M clay; (*lama*) mud

barroco, -a [ba'hoku, a] ADJ baroque; (*ornamentado*) extravagant
barrote [ba'hɔtʃi] M beam
barulhada [baru'ʎada] F racket, din
barulhento, -a [baru'ʎẽtu, a] ADJ noisy
barulho [ba'ruʎu] M (*ruído*) noise; (*tumulto*) din
base ['bazi] F base; (*fig*) basis; **sem ~** groundless; **com ~ em** based on; **na ~ de** (*por meio de*) by means of
baseado, -a [ba'zjadu, a] ADJ well-founded ▶ M (*col*) joint
basear [ba'zjar] VT to base; **basear-se** VR: **~-se em** to be based on
básico, -a ['baziku, a] ADJ basic
basquete [bas'ketʃi] M = **basquetebol**
basquetebol [baskete'bɔw] M basketball
basta ['basta] M: **dar um ~ em** to call a halt to
bastante [bas'tãtʃi] ADJ (*suficiente*) enough; (*muito*) quite a lot (of) ▶ ADV enough; a lot
bastão [bas'tãw] (*pl* **-ões**) M stick
bastar [bas'tar] VI to be enough, be sufficient; **bastar-se** VR to be self-sufficient; **basta!** (that's) enough!; **~ para** to be enough to
bastardo, -a [bas'tardu, a] ADJ, M/F bastard
bastidor [bastʃi'dor] M frame; **bastidores** MPL (*Teatro*) wings; **nos ~es** (*fig*) behind the scenes
basto, -a ['bastu, a] ADJ (*espesso*) thick; (*denso*) dense
bastões [bas'tõjs] MPL *de* **bastão**
bata ['bata] F (*de mulher*) smock; (*de médico*) overall
batalha [ba'taʎa] F battle
batalhador, a [bataʎa'dor(a)] ADJ struggling ▶ M/F fighter
batalhão [bata'ʎãw] (*pl* **-ões**) M battalion
batalhar [bata'ʎar] VI to battle, fight; (*esforçar-se*) to make an effort, try hard ▶ VT (*emprego*) to go after
batalhões [bata'ʎõjs] MPL *de* **batalhão**
batata [ba'tata] F potato; **~ doce** sweet potato; **~ frita** chips *pl* (BRIT), French fries *pl*; (*de pacote*) crisps *pl* (BRIT), (potato) chips *pl* (US)
bate-boca ['batʃi-] (*pl* **-s**) M row, quarrel
bate-bola ['batʃi-] (*pl* **-s**) M kick-around
batedeira [bate'dejra] F beater; (*de manteiga*) churn; **~ elétrica** mixer
batedor [bate'dor] M beater; (*polícia*) escort; (*Críquete*) batsman; **~ de carteiras** pickpocket
bátega ['batega] F downpour
batelada [bate'lada] F: **uma ~ de** a whole bunch of
batente [ba'tẽtʃi] M doorpost; (*col*) job; **no ~** at work
bate-papo ['batʃi-] (*pl* **-s**) (BR) M chat
bater [ba'ter] VT to beat; (*golpear*) to strike; (*horas*) to strike; (*pé*) to stamp; (*foto*) to take; (*datilografar*) to type; (*porta*) to slam; (*asas*) to flap; (*recorde*) to break; (*roupa: usar muito*) to wear all the time ▶ VI (*porta*) to slam; (*sino*) to ring; (*janela*) to bang; (*coração*) to beat; (*sol*)

to beat down; **bater-se** VR: **~-se para fazer/ por** to fight to do/for; **~ (à porta)** to knock (at the door); **~ à maquina** to type; **~ em** to hit; (*lugar*) to arrive in; (*assunto*) to harp on; **~ com o carro** to crash one's car; **~ com a cabeça** to bang one's head; **~ com o pé (em)** to kick; **ele não bate bem** (*col*) he is a bit crazy; **~ a carteira de alguém** (*col*) to nick sb's wallet

bateria [bate'ria] F battery; (*Mús*) drums *pl*; **~ de cozinha** kitchen utensils *pl*

baterista [bate'rista] M/F drummer

batida [ba'tʃida] F beat; (*da porta*) slam; (*à porta*) knock; (*da polícia*) raid; (*Auto*) crash; (*bebida*) cocktail of cachaça, fruit and sugar; **dar uma ~ em** (*polícia*) to raid; (*colidir com*) to bump into; **dar uma ~ com o carro** to crash one's car; **dar uma ~ no carro de alguém** to crash into sb's car

batido, -a [ba'tʃidu, a] ADJ beaten; (*roupa*) worn; (*assunto*) hackneyed ► M: **~ de leite** (PT) milk shake

batina [ba'tʃina] F (*Rel*) cassock

batismal [batʃiz'maw] (*pl* **-ais**) ADJ *ver* **pia**

batismo [ba'tʃizmu] M baptism, christening

batizado [batʃi'zadu] M christening

batizar [batʃi'zar] VT to baptize, christen; (*vinho*) to dilute

batom [ba'tõ] (*pl* **-ns**) M lipstick

batucada [batu'kada] F dance percussion group

batucar [batu'kar] VT, VI to drum

batuque [ba'tuki] M drumming

batuta [ba'tuta] F baton ► ADJ (*col*) clever

baú [ba'u] M trunk

baunilha [baw'niʎa] F vanilla

bazar [ba'zar] M bazaar; (*loja*) shop

bazófia [ba'zɔfja] F boasting, bragging

BB ABR M = **Banco do Brasil**

BBF ABR F = **Bolsa Brasileira de Futuros**

BC ABR M = **Banco Central do Brasil**

BCG ABR M (= *Bacilo Calmette-Guérin*) BCG

bê-á-bá [bea'ba] M ABC

beatitude [beatʃi'tudʒi] F bliss

beato, -a [be'atu, a] ADJ blessed; (*devoto*) overpious

bêbado, -a [ˈbebadu, a] ADJ, M/F drunk

bebê [be'be] M baby

bebedeira [bebe'dejra] F drunkenness; **tomar uma ~** to get drunk

bêbedo, -a [ˈbebedu, a] ADJ, M/F = **bêbado**

bebedor, a [bebe'dor(a)] M/F drinker; (*ébrio*) drunkard

bebedouro [bebe'douru] M drinking fountain

beber [be'ber] VT to drink; (*absorver*) to drink up, to soak up ► VI to drink

bebericar [beberi'kar] VT, VI to sip

bebida [be'bida] F drink

bebum [be'bũ] (*pl* **-ns**) (*col*) ADJ pissed (*col*)

beca [ˈbɛka] F gown

beça [ˈbɛsa] (*col*) F: **à ~** (*com vb*) a lot; (*com n*) a lot of; (*com adj*) really

beco [ˈbeku] M alley, lane; **~ sem saída** cul-de-sac; (*fig*) dead end

bedelho [be'deʎu] M kid; **meter o ~ em** to poke one's nose into

bege [ˈbɛʒi] ADJ INV beige

beicinho [bej'siɲu] M: **fazer ~** to sulk

beiço [ˈbejsu] M lip; **fazer ~** to pout

beiçudo, -a [bej'sudu, a] ADJ thick-lipped

beija-flor [bejʒa'flɔr] (*pl* **-es**) M hummingbird

beijar [bej'ʒar] VT to kiss; **beijar-se** VR to kiss (one another)

beijo [ˈbejʒu] M kiss; **dar ~s em alguém** to kiss sb; **~ de língua** French kiss

beijoca [bej'ʒɔka] F kiss

beijocar [bejʒo'kar] VT to kiss

beira [ˈbejra] F (*borda*) edge; (*de rio*) bank; (*orla*) border; **à ~ de** on the edge of; (*ao lado de*) beside, by; (*fig*) on the verge of; **~ do telhado** eaves *pl*

beirada [bej'rada] F edge

beira-mar F seaside

beirar [bej'rar] VT (*ficar à beira de*) to be at the edge of; (*caminhar à beira de*) to skirt; (*desespero*) to be on the verge of; (*idade*) to approach, near ► VI: **~ com** to border on; **~ por** (*idade*) to approach

Beirute [bej'rutʃi] N Beirut

beisebol [bejsi'bow] M baseball

belas-artes FPL fine arts

beldade [bew'dadʒi] F beauty

beleléu [bele'lɛw] (*col*) M: **ir para o ~** to go wrong

belenense [bele'nẽsi] ADJ from Belém ► M/F native *ou* inhabitant of Belém

beleza [be'leza] F beauty; **que ~!** how lovely!; **ser uma ~** to be lovely; **concurso de ~** beauty contest

belga [ˈbɛwga] ADJ, M/F Belgian

Bélgica [ˈbɛwʒika] F: **a ~** Belgium

Belgrado [bew'gradu] N Belgrade

beliche [be'liʃi] M bunk

bélico, -a [ˈbɛliku, a] ADJ war *atr*

belicoso, -a [beli'kozu, ɔza] ADJ warlike

beligerante [beliʒe'rãtʃi] ADJ belligerent

beliscão [belis'kãw] (*pl* **-ões**) M pinch

beliscar [belis'kar] VT to pinch, nip; (*comida*) to nibble

beliscões [belis'kõjs] MPL *de* **beliscão**

Belize [be'lizi] M Belize

belo, -a [ˈbɛlu, a] ADJ beautiful

belo-horizontino, -a [-orizõ'tʃinu, a] ADJ from Belo Horizonte ► M/F person from Belo Horizonte

bel-prazer [bɛw-] M: **a seu ~** at one's own convenience

beltrano [bew'tranu] M so-and-so

belvedere [bewve'deri] M lookout point

PALAVRA-CHAVE

bem [bẽj] ADV **1** (*de maneira satisfatória, correta etc*) well; **trabalha/come bem** she works/ eats well; **respondeu bem** he answered correctly; **me sinto/não me sinto bem**

I feel fine/I don't feel very well; **tudo bem?** — **tudo bem** how's it going? — fine **2** (*valor intensivo*) very; **um quarto bem quente** a nice warm room; **bem se vê que** ... it's clear that ... **3** (*bastante*) quite, fairly; **a casa é bem grande** the house is quite big **4** (*exatamente*): **bem ali** right there; **não é bem assim** it's not quite like that **5** (*estar bem*): **estou muito bem aqui** I feel very happy here; **está bem! vou fazê-lo** oh all right, I'll do it! **6** (*de bom grado*): **eu bem que iria mas** ... I'd gladly go but ... **7** (*cheirar*) good, nice

▶ M **1** (*bem-estar*) good; **estou dizendo isso para o seu bem** I'm telling you for your own good; **o bem e o mal** good and evil **2** (*posses*): **bens** goods, property *sg*; **bens de consumo** consumer goods; **bens de família** family possessions; **bens móveis/imóveis** moveable property *sg*/real estate *sg*

▶ EXCL **1** (*aprovação*): **bem!** OK!; **muito bem!** well done! **2** (*desaprovação*): **bem feito!** it serves you right!

▶ ADJ INV (*tom depreciativo*): **gente bem** posh people

▶ CONJ **1**: **nem bem** as soon as, no sooner than; **nem bem ela chegou começou a dar ordens** as soon as she arrived she started to give orders, no sooner had she arrived than she started to give orders **2**: **se bem que** though; **gostaria de ir se bem que não tenho dinheiro** I'd like to go even though I've got no money **3**: **bem como** as well as; **o livro bem como a peça foram escritos por ele** the book as well as the play was written by him

bem-agradecido, -a ADJ grateful
bem-apessoado, -a [-ape'swadu, a] ADJ smart, well-groomed
bem-arrumado, -a [-ahu'madu, a] ADJ well-dressed
bem-comportado, -a [-kõpor'tadu, a] ADJ well-behaved
bem-conceituado, -a [-kõsej'twadu, a] ADJ highly regarded
bem-disposto, -a [-dʒis'postu, 'pɔsta] ADJ well, in good form
bem-educado, -a ADJ well-mannered
bem-estar M well-being
bem-humorado, -a [-umo'radu, a] ADJ good-tempered
bem-intencionado, -a ADJ well-intentioned
bem-me-quer (*pl* **-es**) M daisy
bem-sucedido, -a ADJ successful
bem-vindo, -a [-vĩdu] ADJ welcome
bem-visto, -a ADJ well thought of
bênção ['bẽsãw] (*pl* **-s**) F blessing
bendigo *etc* [bẽ'dʒigu] VB *ver* **bendizer**
bendisse *etc* [bẽ'dʒisi] VB *ver* **bendizer**

bendito, -a [bẽ'dʒitu, a] PP *de* **bendizer** ▶ ADJ blessed
bendizer [bẽdʒi'zer] (*irreg: como* **dizer**) VT (*louvar*) to praise; (*abençoar*) to bless
beneficência [benefi'sẽsja] F (*bondade*) kindness; (*caridade*) charity; **obra de ~** charity
beneficente [benefi'sẽtʃi] ADJ (*organização*) charitable; (*feira*) charity *atr*
beneficiado, -a [benefi'sjadu, a] M/F beneficiary
beneficiar [benefi'sjar] VT (*favorecer*) to benefit; (*melhorar*) to improve; **beneficiar-se** VR to benefit
benefício [bene'fisju] M (*proveito*) benefit, profit; (*favor*) favour (BRIT), favor (US); **em ~ de** in aid of; **em ~ próprio** for one's own benefit
benéfico, -a [be'nɛfiku, a] ADJ (*benigno*) beneficial; (*generoso*) generous
Benelux [bene'luks] M Benelux
benemérito, -a [bene'mɛritu, a] ADJ (*digno*) worthy
beneplácito [bene'plasitu] M consent, approval
benevolência [benevo'lẽsja] F benevolence, kindness
benévolo, -a [be'nɛvolu, a] ADJ benevolent, kind
Benfam [bẽ'fami] ABR F = **Sociedade Brasileira de Bem-Estar da Família**
benfazejo, -a [bẽfa'zeʒu, a] ADJ benevolent
benfeitor, a [bẽfej'tor(a)] M/F benefactor/benefactress
benfeitoria [bẽfejto'ria] F improvement
bengala [bẽ'gala] F walking stick
benigno, -a [be'nignu, a] ADJ (*bondoso*) kind; (*agradável*) pleasant; (*Med*) benign
Benin [be'nĩ] M: **o ~** Benin
benquisto, -a [bẽ'kistu, a] ADJ well-loved, well-liked
bens [bẽjs] MPL *de* **bem**
bento, -a ['bẽtu, a] PP *de* **benzer** ▶ ADJ blessed; (*água*) holy
benzedeiro, -a [bẽze'dejru, a] M/F sorcerer/sorceress
benzer [bẽ'zer] VT to bless; **benzer-se** VR to cross o.s.
berçário [ber'sarju] M nursery
berço ['bersu] M (*com balanço*) cradle; (*cama*) cot; (*origem*) birthplace; **nascer em ~ de ouro** (*fig*) to be born with a silver spoon in one's mouth; **ter ~** to be from a good family
berimbau [berĩ'baw] M *percussion instrument*
berinjela [berĩ'ʒɛla] F aubergine (BRIT), eggplant (US)
Berlim [ber'lĩ] N Berlin
berlinda [ber'lĩda] F: **estar na ~** to be in the firing-line
berma ['bɛrma] (*PT*) F hard shoulder (BRIT), berm (US)
bermuda [ber'muda] F Bermuda shorts *pl*
Bermudas [ber'mudas] FPL: **as ~** Bermuda *sg*

Berna ['bɛrna] N Bern

berrante [be'hãtʃi] ADJ flashy, gaudy

berrar [be'har] VI to bellow; (*criança*) to bawl; (*col*) to holler

berreiro [be'hejru] M: **abrir o ~** to burst out crying

berro ['bɛhu] M yell

besouro [be'zoru] M beetle

besta ['bɛsta] ADJ (*tolo*) stupid; (*convencido*) full of oneself; (*pretensioso*) pretentious ▶ F (*animal*) beast; (*pessoa*) fool; **~ de carga** beast of burden; **ficar ~** (*col: supreso*) to be amazed; **fazer alguém de ~** (*col*) to make a fool of sb

bestar [bes'tar] VI to laze around

besteira [bes'tejra] F (*tolice*) foolishness; (*insignificância*) small thing; **dizer ~s** to talk nonsense; **fazer uma ~** to do something silly

bestial [bes'tʃjaw] (*pl* **-ais**) ADJ bestial; (*repugnante*) repulsive

bestialidade [bestʃjali'dadʒi] F bestiality

bestificar [bestʃifi'kar] VT to astonish, dumbfound

best-seller [bɛst'sɛler] (*pl* **-s**) M best seller

besuntar [bezũ'tar] VT to smear, daub

betão [be'tãw] (PT) M concrete

beterraba [bete'haba] F beetroot

betoneira [beto'nejra] F cement mixer

betume [be'tumi] M asphalt

bexiga [be'ʃiga] F (*órgão*) bladder

bezerro, -a [be'zehu, a] M/F calf

BI (PT) ABR M (= *bilhete de identidade*) identity card; *ver tb* **cartão**

bianual [bja'nwaw] (*pl* **-ais**) ADJ biannual, twice yearly

bibelô [bibe'lo] M ornament

Bíblia ['biblja] F Bible

bíblico, -a ['bibliku, a] ADJ biblical

bibliografia [bibljogra'fia] F bibliography

biblioteca [bibljo'tɛka] F library; (*estante*) bookcase

bibliotecário, -a [bibljote'karju, a] M/F librarian

biblioteconomia [bibljotekono'mia] F librarianship

bica ['bika] F tap; (PT) black coffee, espresso; **suar em ~s** to drip with sweat

bicada [bi'kada] F peck

bicama [bi'kama] F pull-out bed

bicar [bi'kar] VT to peck

bicarbonato [bikarbo'natu] M bicarbonate

bíceps ['biseps] M INV biceps

bicha ['biʃa] F (*lombriga*) worm; (PT: *fila*) queue; (BR *col, pej: homossexual*) queer

bichado, -a [bi'ʃadu, a] ADJ eaten away

bicheiro [bi'ʃejru] M (*illegal*) bookie

bicho ['biʃu] M animal; (*inseto*) insect, bug; (*col: pessoa: intratável*) pain (in the neck); (*: feio*): **ela é um ~ (feio)** she's as ugly as sin; **virar ~** (*col*) to get mad; **ver que ~ ~ dá** (*col*) to see what happens; **que ~ te mordeu?** what's got into you?; **um ~ de sete cabeças** a big deal; **~ do mato** shy person

bicho-da-seda (*pl* **bichos-da-seda**) M silk worm

bicho-papão [-pa'pãw] (*pl* **bichos-papões**) M bogeyman

bicicleta [bisi'klɛta] F bicycle; (*col*) bike; **andar de ~** to cycle; **~ ergométrica** exercise bike

bico ['biku] M (*de ave*) beak; (*ponta*) point; (*de chaleira*) spout; (*boca*) mouth; (*de pena*) nib; (*do peito*) nipple; (*de gás*) jet; (*col: emprego*) casual job; (*chupeta*) dummy; **calar o ~** to shut up; **não abrir o ~** not to say a word; **fazer ~** to sulk

bicudo, -a [bi'kudu, a] ADJ pointed; (*difícil*) tricky

BID ABR M = **Banco Interamericano de Desenvolvimento**

bidê [bi'de] M bidet

bidimensional [bidʒimẽsjo'naw] (*pl* **-ais**) ADJ two-dimensional

bidirecional [bidʒiresjo'naw] (*pl* **-ais**) ADJ bidirectional

biela ['bjɛla] F con(necting) rod

bienal [bje'naw] (*pl* **-ais**) ADJ biennial ▶ F (biennial) art exhibition

bife ['bifi] M (*beef*) steak; **~ a cavalo** steak with fried eggs; **~ à milanesa** beef escalope; **~ de panela** beef stew

bifocal [bifo'kaw] (*pl* **-ais**) ADJ bifocal; **óculos bifocais** bifocals

bifurcação [bifurka'sãw] (*pl* **-ões**) F fork

bifurcar-se [bifur'karsi] VR to fork, divide

bigamia [biga'mia] F bigamy

bígamo, -a ['bigamu, a] ADJ bigamous ▶ M/F bigamist

bigode [bi'gɔdʒi] M moustache

bigodudo, -a [bigo'dudu, a] ADJ with a big moustache

bigorna [bi'gɔrna] F anvil

bijuteria [biʒute'ria] F (costume) jewellery (BRIT) *ou* jewelry (US)

bilateral [bilate'raw] (*pl* **-ais**) ADJ bilateral

bilhão [bi'ʎãw] (*pl* **-ões**) M billion

bilhar [bi'ʎar] M (*jogo*) billiards *sg*

bilhete [bi'ʎetʃi] M (*entrada, loteria*) ticket; (*cartinha*) note; **o ~ azul** (*fig*) the sack; **~ eletrônico** e-ticket; **~ de ida** single (BRIT) *ou* one-way ticket; **~ de ida e volta** return (BRIT) *ou* round-trip (US) ticket; **~ de identidade** (PT) identity card; *ver tb* **cartão**

bilheteira [biʎe'tejra] (PT) F ticket office; (*Teatro*) box office

bilheteiro, -a [biʎe'tejru, a] M/F ticket seller

bilheteria [biʎete'ria] F ticket office; box office; **sucesso de ~** box-office success

bilhões [bi'ʎõjs] *pl de* **bilhão**

bilíngue [bi'lĩgwi] ADJ bilingual

bilionário, -a [biljo'narju, a] ADJ, M/F billionaire

bilioso, -a [bi'ljozu, ɔza] ADJ bilious; (*fig*) bad-tempered

bílis ['bilis] M bile

bimensal [bimẽ'saw] (*pl* **-ais**) ADJ twice-monthly

bimestral [bimes'traw] (*pl* **-ais**) ADJ two-monthly

bimotor [bimo'tor] ADJ twin-engined

binário, -a [bi'narju, a] ADJ binary

bingo ['bĩgu] M bingo

binóculo [bi'nɔkulu] M binoculars *pl*; (*para teatro*) opera glasses *pl*

biocombustível [bjokõbus'tʃivew] (*pl* **-eis**) M biofuel

biodegradável [bjodegra'davew] (*pl* **-eis**) ADJ biodegradable

biodiesel [bjo'dʒizew] M biodiesel

biodiversidade [bjodʒiversi'dadʒi] F biodiversity

biografia [bjogra'fia] F biography

biográfico, -a [bjo'grafiku, a] ADJ biographical

biógrafo, -a ['bjɔgrafu, a] M/F biographer

biologia [bjolo'ʒia] F biology

biológico, -a [bjo'lɔʒiku, a] ADJ biological

biólogo, -a ['bjɔlogu, a] M/F biologist

biombo ['bjõbu] M (*tapume*) screen

biônico, -a ['bjoniku, a] ADJ bionic; (*Pol: senador*) non-elected

biópsia ['bjɔpsja] F biopsy

bioquímica [bjo'kimika] F biochemistry

bioterrorismo [bjoteho'rizmu] M bioterrorism

bip [bip] M pager, paging device

bipartidário, -a [bipartʃi'darju, a] ADJ two-party *atr*, bipartite

bipartidarismo [bipartʃida'rizmu] M two-party system

biquíni [bi'kini] M bikini

BIRD ABR M = **Banco Internacional de Reconstrução e Desenvolvimento**

birita [bi'rita] (*col*) F drink

birmanês, -esa [birma'nes, eza] ADJ, M/F Burmese ▶ M (*Ling*) Burmese

Birmânia [bir'manja] F: **a ~** Burma

birosca [bi'roska] F (*small*) shop

birra ['biha] F (*teima*) wilfulness (BRIT), willfulness (US), obstinacy; (*aversão*) aversion; **fazer ~** to have a tantrum; **ter ~ com** to dislike

birrento, -a [bi'hẽtu, a] ADJ stubborn, obstinate

biruta [bi'ruta] ADJ crazy ▶ F windsock

bis [bis] EXCL encore!

bisar [bi'zar] VT (*suj: público*) to ask for an encore of; (*: artista*) to do an encore of

bisavô, -vó [biza'vo, vɔ] M/F great-grandfather/great-grandmother; **bisavós** MPL great-grandparents

bisbilhotar [bizbiʎo'tar] VT to pry into ▶ VI to snoop

bisbilhoteiro, -a [bizbiʎo'tejru, a] ADJ prying ▶ M/F snoop

bisbilhotice [bizbiʎo'tʃisi] F prying

Biscaia [bis'kaja] F: **o golfo de ~** the Bay of Biscay

biscate [bis'katʃi] M odd job

biscateiro, -a [biska'tejru, a] M/F odd-job person

biscoito [bis'kojtu] M biscuit (BRIT), cookie (US)

bisnaga [biz'naga] F (*tubo*) tube; (*pão*) French stick

bisneto, -a [biz'nɛtu, a] M/F great-grandson/great-granddaughter; **bisnetos** MPL (*filhos de neto*) great-grandchildren

bisonho, -a [bi'zoɲu, a] ADJ inexperienced ▶ M/F newcomer

bispado [bis'padu] M bishopric

bispo ['bispu] M bishop

bissemanal [bisema'naw] (*pl* **-ais**) ADJ twice-weekly

bissexto, -a [bi'sestu, a] ADJ: **ano ~** leap year

bissexual [bisek'swaw] (*pl* **-ais**) ADJ, M/F bisexual

bisturi [bistu'ri] M scalpel

bit ['bitʃi] M (*Comput*) bit

bitola [bi'tɔla] F gauge (BRIT), gage (US); (*padrão*) pattern; (*estalão*) standard

bitolado, -a [bito'ladu, a] ADJ narrow-minded

bizarro, -a [bi'zahu, a] ADJ bizarre

blablablá [blabla'bla] (*col*) M chitchat

black-tie ['blɛktaj] M evening dress

blasé [bla'zɛ] ADJ blasé

blasfemar [blasfe'mar] VT to curse ▶ VI to blaspheme

blasfêmia [blas'femja] F blasphemy

blasfemo, -a [blas'femu, a] ADJ blasphemous ▶ M/F blasphemer

blazer ['blejzer] (*pl* **-s**) M blazer

blecaute [ble'kawtʃi] M power cut

blefar [ble'far] VI to bluff

blefe ['blɛfi] M bluff

blindado, -a [blĩ'dadu, a] ADJ armoured (BRIT), armored (US)

blindagem [blĩ'daʒẽ] F armour(-plating) (BRIT), armor(-plating) (US)

blitz [blits] F police road block

bloco ['blɔku] M block; (*Pol*) bloc; (*de escrever*) writing pad; **voto em ~** block vote; **~ de carnaval** carnival troupe; **~ de cilindros** cylinder block

blog ['blɔgi] M blog

blogar [blo'gar] VI to blog

blogosfera [blɔgos'fɛra] F blogosphere

blogue ['blɔgi] M blog

blogueiro, -a [blo'gejru, a] M/F blogger

bloqueador [blokja'dor] M: **~ solar** sunblock

bloquear [blo'kjar] VT to blockade; (*obstruir*) to block

bloqueio [blo'keju] M (*Mil*) blockade; (*obstrução*) blockage; (*Psico*) mental block

blusa ['bluza] F (*de mulher*) blouse; (*de homem*) shirt; **~ de lã** jumper

blusão [blu'zãw] (*pl* **-ões**) M jacket

BMeF (BR) ABR F = **Bolsa Mercantil e de Futuros**

BMSP ABR F = **Bolsa de Mercadorias de São Paulo**

BNDES ABR M (= *Banco Nacional de Desenvolvimento Econômico e Social*) Brazilian development bank

BNH (BR) ABR M (= *Banco Nacional da Habitação*) home-funding bank

boa ['boa] ADJ F *de* **bom** ▶ F boa constrictor
boa-gente ADJ INV nice
boa-pinta (*pl* **boas-pintas**) ADJ handsome
boa-praça (*pl* **boas-praças**) ADJ nice
boate ['bwatʃi] F nightclub
boateiro, -a [bwa'tejru, a] ADJ gossipy ▶ M/F gossip
boato ['bwatu] M rumour (BRIT), rumor (US)
boa-vida (*pl* **boas-vidas**) M/F loafer
bobagem [bo'baʒẽ] (*pl* **-ns**) F silliness, nonsense; (*dito, ato*) silly thing; **deixe de bobagens!** stop being silly!
bobeada [bo'bjada] F slip-up
bobear [bo'bjar] VI to miss out
bobice [bo'bisi] F silliness, nonsense; (*dito, ato*) silly thing
bobina [bo'bina] F reel, bobbin; (*Elet*) coil; (*Foto*) spool; (*de papel*) roll
bobo, -a ['bobu, a] ADJ silly, daft ▶ M/F fool ▶ M (*de corte*) jester; **fazer-se de ~** to act the fool
bobó [bo'bɔ] M *beans, palm oil and manioc*
boboca [bo'bɔka] ADJ silly ▶ M/F fool
boca ['boka] F mouth; (*entrada*) entrance; (*de fogão*) ring; **de ~** orally; **de ~ aberta** open-mouthed, amazed; **bater ~** to argue; **botar a ~ no mundo** (*berrar*) to scream; (*revelar*) to spill the beans; **falar da ~ para fora** to say one thing and mean another; **ser boa ~** to eat anything; **vira essa ~ para lá!** don't tempt providence!; **~ da noite** nightfall; **~ (de fumo)** drug den
boca-de-sino ADJ INV bell-bottomed
bocadinho [boka'dʒiɲu] M: **um ~** (*pouco tempo*) a little while; (*pouquinho*) a little bit
bocado [bo'kadu] M (*quantidade na boca*) mouthful, bite; (*pedaço*) piece, bit; **um ~ de tempo** quite some time
bocal [bo'kaw] (*pl* **-ais**) M (*de vaso*) mouth; (*Mús, de aparelho*) mouthpiece; (*de cano*) nozzle
boçal [bo'saw] (*pl* **-ais**) ADJ ignorant; (*grosseiro*) uncouth
boçalidade [bosali'dadʒi] F coarseness; (*ignorância*) ignorance
boca-livre (*pl* **bocas-livres**) F free meal
bocejar [bose'ʒar] VI to yawn
bocejo [bo'seʒu] M yawn
bochecha [bo'ʃeʃa] F cheek
bochechar [boʃe'ʃar] VI to rinse one's mouth
bochecho [bo'ʃeʃu] M mouthwash
bochechudo, -a [boʃe'ʃudu, a] ADJ puffy-cheeked
boda ['boda] F wedding; **bodas** FPL (*aniversário de casamento*) wedding anniversary *sg*; **~s de prata/ouro** silver/golden wedding *sg*
bode ['bɔdʒi] M goat; **~ expiatório** scapegoat; **vai dar ~** (*col*) there'll be trouble
bodega [bo'dɛga] F piece of rubbish
bodum [bo'dũ] M stink
boêmio, -a [bo'emju, a] ADJ, M/F Bohemian
bofetada [bofe'tada] F slap
bofetão [bofe'tãw] (*pl* **-ões**) M punch
Bogotá [bogo'ta] N Bogota

boi [boj] M ox; **pegar o ~ pelos chifres** (*fig*) to take the bull by the horns
bói [bɔj] M office boy
boia ['bɔja] F buoy; (*col*) grub; (*de braço*) armband, water wing
boiada [bo'jada] F herd of cattle
boia-fria (*pl* **boias-frias**) M/F (itinerant) farm labourer (BRIT) *ou* laborer (US)
boiar [bo'jar] VT to float ▶ VI to float; (*col*) to be lost; **~ em** (*inglês etc*) to be hopeless at
boi-bumbá [-bũ'ba] N *see note*

The **boi-bumbá**, or *bumba-meu-boi*, is a traditional folk dance from north-eastern Brazil, which brings together human, animal and mythological characters in a theatrical performance. The ox, which the dance is named after, is played by a dancer wearing an iron frame covered in pieces of colourful fabric. Eventually the beast is "killed" and its meat is symbolically shared out before it comes back to life in the finale.

boicotar [bojko'tar] VT to boycott
boicote [boj'kɔtʃi] M boycott
boiler ['bɔjlar] (*pl* **-s**) M boiler
boina ['bojna] F beret
bojo ['boʒu] M (*saliência*) bulge
bojudo, -a [bo'ʒudu, a] ADJ bulging; (*arredondado*) rounded
bola ['bɔla] F ball; (*confusão*) confusion; **dar ~ (para)** (*col*) to care (about); (*dar atenção*) to pay attention (to); **dar ~ para** (*flertar*) to flirt with; **não dar ~ para alguém** to ignore sb; **ela não dá a menor ~ (para isso)** she couldn't care less (about it); **pisar na ~** (*fig*) to make a mistake; **ser bom de ~** to be good at football; **não ser certo da ~** (*col*) not to be right in the head; **ser uma ~** (*pessoa: gordo*) to be fat; (: *engraçado*) to be a real character; **~ de futebol** football; **~ de gude** marble; **~ de neve** snowball
bolacha [bo'laʃa] F biscuit (BRIT), cookie (US); (*col: bofetada*) wallop; (*para chope*) beer mat
bolada [bo'lada] F (*dinheiro*) lump sum
bolar [bo'lar] VT to think up; **bem bolado** clever
bole *etc* ['bɔli] VB *ver* **bulir**
boleia [bo'leja] F (*de caminhão*) cab; (PT: *carona*) lift; **dar uma ~ a alguém** (PT) to give sb a lift
boletim [bole'tʃĩ] (*pl* **-ns**) M report; (*publicação*) newsletter; (*Educ*) report; **~ meteorológico** weather forecast
bolha ['boʎa] F (*na pele*) blister; (*de ar, sabão*) bubble ▶ M/F (*col*) fool
boliche [bo'liʃi] M (*jogo*) bowling, skittles *sg*
bolinar [boli'nar] VT: **~ alguém** (*col*) to feel sb up
bolinho [bo'liɲu] M: **~ de carne** meat ball; **~ de arroz/bacalhau** rice/dry cod cake
Bolívia [bo'livja] F: **a ~** Bolivia
boliviano, -a [boli'vjanu, a] ADJ, M/F Bolivian
bolo ['bolu] M cake; (*monte: de gente*) bunch; (: *de papéis*) bundle; **dar o ~ em alguém** to

stand sb up; **vai dar ~** (col) there's going to
be trouble

bolor [bo'lor] M mould (BRIT), mold (US); (nas
plantas) mildew; (bafio) mustiness

bolorento, -a [bolo'rẽtu, a] ADJ mouldy (BRIT),
moldy (US)

bolota [bo'lɔta] F acorn

bolsa ['bowsa] F bag; (Com: tb: **bolsa de
valores**) stock exchange; **~ (de estudos)**
scholarship; **~ de mercadorias** commodities
market; **~ de valores** stock exchange

bolsista [bow'sista] M/F scholarship holder

bolso ['bowsu] M pocket; **de ~** pocket atr;
dicionário de ~ pocket dictionary

PALAVRA-CHAVE

bom, boa [bõ, 'boa] ADJ (pl **bons/boas**) **1**
(ótimo) good; **é um livro bom** ou **um bom
livro** it's a good book; **a comida está boa**
the food is delicious; **o tempo está bom**
the weather's fine; **ele foi muito bom
comigo** he was very nice ou kind to me
2 (apropriado): **ser bom para** to be good for;
acho bom você não ir I think it's better if
you don't go
3 (irônico): **um bom quarto de hora** a good
quarter of an hour; **que bom motorista
você é!** a fine ou some driver you are!; **seria
bom que ...!** a fine thing it would be if ...!;
essa é boa! what a cheek!
4 (saudação): **bom dia!** good morning!; **boa
tarde!** good afternoon!; **boa noite!** good
evening!; (ao deitar-se) good night!; **tudo
bom?** how's it going?
5 (outras frases): **está bom?** OK?
▶ EXCL: **bom!** all right!; **bom, ...** right, ...

bomba ['bõba] F (Mil) bomb; (Tec) pump;
(Culin) éclair; (fig) bombshell; **~ atômica/
relógio/de fumaça** atomic/time/smoke
bomb; **~ de gasolina** petrol (BRIT) ou gas (US)
pump; **~ de incêndio** fire extinguisher;
levar ~ (em exame) to fail

bombada [bõ'bada] F (prejuízo) loss

Bombaim [bõba'ĩ] N Mumbai

bombardear [bõbar'dʒjar] VT to bomb,
bombard; (fig) to bombard

bombardeio [bõbar'deju] M bombing,
bombardment; **~ suicida** suicide bombing

bomba-relógio (pl **bombas-relógio**) F time
bomb

bombástico, -a [bõ'bastʃiku, a] ADJ (pessoa)
pompous

bombear [bõ'bjar] VT to pump

bombeiro [bõ'bejru] M fireman; (BR:
encanador) plumber; **o corpo de ~s** fire
brigade

bombom [bõ'bõ] (pl **-ns**) M chocolate

bombordo [bõ'bɔrdu] M (Náut) port

bonachão, -chona [bona'ʃãw, 'ʃona] (pl
-ões/-s) ADJ simple and kind-hearted

bonança [bo'nãsa] F (no mar) fair weather;
(fig) calm

bondade [bõ'dadʒi] F goodness, kindness;
tenha a ~ de vir would you please come

bonde ['bõdʒi] (BR) M tram

bondoso, -a [bõ'dozu, ɔza] ADJ kind, good

boné [bo'nɛ] M cap

boneca [bo'nɛka] F doll

boneco [bo'neku] M dummy

bonificação [bonifika'sãw] (pl **-ões**) F bonus

bonina [bo'nina] (PT) F daisy

boníssimo, -a [bo'nisimu, a] ADJ SUPERL
de **bom**

bonitão, -tona [boni'tãw, 'tona] (pl **-ões/-s**)
ADJ very attractive; (col) dishy

bonito, -a [bo'nitu, a] ADJ (belo) pretty; (gesto,
dia) nice ▶ M (peixe) tuna (fish), tunny; **fazer
um ~** to do a good deed

bonitões [boni'tõjs] MPL de **bonitão**

bonitona [boni'tona] F de **bonitão**

bônus ['bonus] M INV bonus

boquiaberto, -a [bokja'bɛrtu, a] ADJ
dumbfounded, astonished

borboleta [borbo'leta] F butterfly; (BR: roleta)
turnstile

borboletear [borbole'tʃjar] VI to flutter, flit

borbotão [borbo'tãw] (pl **-ões**) M gush, spurt;
sair aos borbotões to gush out

borbulhante [borbu'ʎãtʃi] ADJ bubbling

borbulhar [borbu'ʎar] VI to bubble; (jorrar) to
gush out

borco ['borku] M: **de ~** (coisa) upside down;
(pessoa) face down

borda ['bɔrda] F edge; (do rio) bank; **à ~ de** on
the edge of

bordado [bor'dadu] M embroidery

bordão [bor'dãw] (pl **-ões**) M staff; (Mús) bass
string; (arrimo) support; (frase) catch phrase

bordar [bor'dar] VT to embroider

bordéis [bor'dɛjs] MPL de **bordel**

bordejar [borde'ʒar] VI (Náut) to tack

bordel [bor'dɛw] (pl **-éis**) M brothel

bordo ['bɔrdu] M (ao bordejar) tack; (de navio)
side; **a ~** on board

bordoada [bor'dwada] F blow

bordões [bor'dõjs] MPL de **bordão**

borla ['bɔrla] F tassel

borocoxô [boroko'ʃo] ADJ dispirited

borra ['boha] F dregs pl

borracha [bo'haʃa] F rubber

borracheiro [boha'ʃejru] M tyre (BRIT) ou tire
(US) specialist

borracho, -a [bo'haʃu, a] ADJ drunk ▶ M/F
drunk(ard)

borrador [boha'dor] M (Com) day book

borrão [bo'hãw] (pl **-ões**) M (rascunho) rough
draft; (mancha) blot

borrar [bo'har] VT to blot; (riscar) to cross out;
(pintar) to daub; (sujar) to dirty

borrasca [bo'haska] F storm; (no mar) squall

borrifar [bohi'far] VT to sprinkle

borrifo [bo'hifu] M spray

borrões [bo'hõjs] MPL de **borrão**

bosque ['bɔski] M wood, forest

bossa ['bɔsa] F (charme) charm; (inchaço)

swelling; (*no crânio*) bump; (*corcova*) hump;
ter ~ para to have an aptitude for
Bossa nova (*Mús*) *see note*

> **Bossa nova** is a type of music invented
> by young, middle-class inhabitants of
> Rio de Janeiro at the end of the 1950s. It
> has an obvious jazz influence, an
> unusual, rhythmic beat and lyrics
> praising beauty and love. **Bossa nova**
> became known around the world
> through the work of the conductor and
> composer Antônio Carlos Jobim, whose
> compositions, working with the poet
> Vinícius de Morais, include the famous
> song "The Girl from Ipanema".

bosta ['bɔsta] F dung; (*de humanos*) excrement
bota ['bɔta] F boot; **~s de borracha**
wellingtons; **bater as ~s** (*col*) to kick the
bucket
bota-fora (*pl* bota-fora) F (*despedida*) send-off
botânica [bo'tanika] F botany; *ver tb* **botânico**
botânico, -a [bo'taniku, a] ADJ botanical
▶ M/F botanist
botão [bo'tãw] (*pl* **-ões**) M button; (*flor*) bud;
dizer com os seus botões (*fig*) to say to o.s.
botar [bo'tar] VT to put; (*PT: lançar*) to throw;
(*roupa, sapatos*) to put on; (*mesa*) to set; (*defeito*)
to find; (*ovos*) to lay; **~ para quebrar** (*col*) to
go for broke, go all out; **~ em dia** to get up
to date
bote ['bɔtʃi] M (*barco*) boat; (*com arma*) thrust;
(*salto*) spring; (*de cobra*) strike
boteco [bo'tɛku] (*col*) M bar
botequim [botʃi'kĩ] (*pl* **-ns**) M bar
boticário, -a [botʃi'karju, a] M/F pharmacist,
chemist (BRIT)
botija [bo'tʃiʒa] F (*earthenware*) jug
botina [bo'tʃina] F ankle boot
botoeira [bo'twejra] F buttonhole
botões [bo'tõjs] MPL *de* **botão**
Botsuana [bot'swana] F: **a ~** Botswana
Bovespa [bo'vɛspa] ABR F = **Bolsa de Valores
do Estado de São Paulo**
bovino, -a [bo'vinu, a] ADJ bovine
boxe ['bɔksi] M boxing
boxeador [boksja'dor] M boxer
boy [bɔj] M = **bói**
brabo, -a ['brabu, a] ADJ (*feroz*) fierce; (*zangado*)
angry; (*ruim*) bad; (*calor*) unbearable; (*gripe*)
bad
braça ['brasa] F (*Náut*) fathom
braçada [bra'sada] F armful; (*Natação*) stroke
braçadeira [brasa'dejra] F armband; (*de
cortina*) tie-back; (*metálica*) bracket; (*Esporte*)
sweatband
braçal [bra'saw] (*pl* **-ais**) ADJ manual
bracejar [brase'ʒar] VI to wave one's arms
about
bracelete [brase'letʃi] M bracelet
braço ['brasu] M arm; (*trabalhador*) hand;
~ direito (*fig*) right-hand man; **a ~s com**
struggling with; **de ~s cruzados** with arms
folded; (*fig*) without lifting a finger; **de ~**

dado arm-in-arm; **cruzar os ~s** (*fig*) to
down tools; **não dar o ~ a torcer** (*fig*) not to
give in; **meter o ~ em** (*col*) to clobber;
receber de ~s abertos (*fig*) to welcome with
open arms
bradar [bra'dar] VT, VI to shout, yell
brado ['bradu] M shout, yell
braguilha [bra'giʎa] F flies *pl*
braile ['brajli] M braille
bramido [bra'midu] M roar
bramir [bra'mir] VI to roar
branco, -a ['brãku, a] ADJ white ▶ M/F white
man/woman ▶ M (*espaço*) blank; **em ~**
blank; **noite em ~** sleepless night; **deu um
~ nele** he drew a blank
brancura [brã'kura] F whiteness
brandir [brã'dʒir] VT to brandish
brando, -a ['brãdu, a] ADJ gentle; (*mole*) soft
brandura [brã'dura] F gentleness; (*moleza*)
softness
branquear [brã'kjar] VT to whiten; (*alvejar*) to
bleach ▶ VI to turn white
brasa ['braza] F hot coal; **em ~** red-hot; **pisar
em ~** to be on tenterhooks; **mandar ~** (*col*) to
go for it; **puxar a ~ para a sua sardinha** (*col*)
to look out for o.s.
brasão [bra'zãw] (*pl* **-ões**) M coat of arms
braseiro [bra'zejru] M brazier
Brasil [bra'ziw] M: **o ~** Brazil
brasileirismo [brazilej'rizmu] M
Brazilianism
brasileiro, -a [brazi'lejru, a] ADJ, M/F Brazilian
Brasília [bra'zilja] N Brasília
brasilianista [brazilja'nista] M/F Brazilianist
brasiliense [brazi'ljẽsi] ADJ from Brasília
▶ M/F person from Brasília
brasões [bra'zõjs] MPL *de* **brasão**
bravata [bra'vata] F bravado, boasting
bravatear [brava'tʃar] VI to boast, brag
bravio, -a [bra'viu, a] ADJ (*selvagem*) wild,
untamed; (*feroz*) ferocious
bravo, -a ['bravu, a] ADJ (*corajoso*) brave;
(*furioso*) angry; (*mar*) rough, stormy ▶ M
brave man; **~!** bravo!
bravura [bra'vura] F courage, bravery
breca ['brɛka] F: **ser levado da ~** to be very
naughty
brecar [bre'kar] VT (*carro*) to stop; (*reprimir*) to
curb ▶ VI to brake
brecha ['brɛʃa] F breach; (*abertura*) opening;
(*dano*) damage; (*meio de escapar*) loophole; (*col*)
chance
brega ['brɛga] (*col*) ADJ tacky, naff (BRIT)
brejeiro, -a [bre'ʒejru, a] ADJ impish
brejo ['brɛʒu] M marsh, swamp; **ir para o ~**
(*fig*) to go down the drain
brenha ['brɛɲa] F (*mata*) dense wood
breque ['brɛki] M (*freio*) brake
breu [brew] M tar, pitch; **escuro como ~**
pitch black
breve ['brɛvi] ADJ short; (*conciso, rápido*) brief
▶ ADV soon; **em ~** soon, shortly; **até ~** see
you soon

brevê [bre've] M pilot's licence (BRIT) *ou* license (US)

brevidade [brevi'dadʒi] F brevity, shortness

bridge ['bridʒi] M bridge

briga ['briga] F (*luta*) fight; (*verbal*) quarrel

brigada [bri'gada] F brigade

brigadeiro [briga'dejru] M brigadier; (*doce*) chocolate truffle

brigão, -gona [bri'gãw, ɔna] (*pl* -**ões/-s**) ADJ quarrelsome ▶ M/F troublemaker

brigar [bri'gar] VI (*lutar*) to fight; (*altercar*) to quarrel

brigões [bri'gõjs] MPL *de* **brigão**

brigona [bri'gɔna] F *de* **brigão**

briguei *etc* [bri'gej] VB *ver* **brigar**

brilhante [bri'ʎãtʃi] ADJ brilliant ▶ M diamond

brilhar [bri'ʎar] VI to shine

brilho ['briʎu] M (*luz viva*) brilliance; (*esplendor*) splendour (BRIT), splendor (US); (*nos sapatos*) shine; (*de metais, olhos*) gleam

brincadeira [brĩka'dejra] F (*divertimento*) fun; (*gracejo*) joke; (*de criança*) game; **deixe de ~s!** stop fooling!; **de ~** for fun; **fora de ~** joking apart; **não é ~** it's no joke

brincalhão, -lhona [brĩka'ʎãw, ɔna] (*pl* -**ões/-s**) ADJ playful ▶ M/F joker, teaser

brincar [brĩ'kar] VI to play; (*gracejar*) to joke; **estou brincando** I'm only kidding; **~ de soldados** to play (at) soldiers; **~ com alguém** (*mexer com*) to tease sb

brinco ['brĩku] M (*joia*) earring; **estar um ~** to be spotless

brindar [brĩ'dar] VT (*beber*) to drink to; (*presentear*) to give a present to

brinde ['brĩdʒi] M (*saudação*) toast; (*presente*) free gift

brinquedo [brĩ'kedu] M toy

brinquei *etc* [brĩ'kej] VB *ver* **brincar**

brio ['briu] M self-respect, dignity

brioso, -a ['brjozu, ɔza] ADJ self-respecting

brisa ['briza] F breeze

britânico, -a [bri'taniku, a] ADJ British ▶ M/F Briton

broca ['brɔka] F drill

broche ['brɔʃi] M brooch

brochura [bro'ʃura] F (*livro*) paperback; (*folheto*) brochure, pamphlet

brócolis ['brɔkolis] MPL broccoli *sg*

brócolos ['brɔkolus] (PT) MPL = **brócolis**

bronca ['brõka] (*col*) F telling off; **dar uma ~ em** to tell off; **levar uma ~** to get told off

bronco, -a ['brõku, a] ADJ (*rude*) coarse; (*burro*) thick

bronquear [brõ'kjar] (*col*) VI to get angry; **~ com** to tell off

bronquite [brõ'kitʃi] F bronchitis

bronze ['brõzi] M bronze

bronzeado, -a [brõ'zjadu, a] ADJ (*da cor do bronze*) bronze *atr*; (*pelo sol*) suntanned ▶ M suntan

bronzear [brõ'zjar] VT to tan; **bronzear-se** VR to get a tan

brotar [bro'tar] VT to produce ▶ VI (*manar*) to flow; (*Bot*) to sprout; (*nascer*) to spring up

brotinho, -a [bro'tʃiɲu, a] M/F teenager

broto ['brotu] M bud; (*fig*) youngster

broxa ['brɔʃa] F (*large*) paint brush

bruços ['brusus] MPL: **de ~** face down

bruma ['bruma] F mist, haze

brumoso, -a [bru'mozu, ɔza] ADJ misty, hazy

brunido, -a [bru'nidu, a] ADJ polished

brunir [bru'nir] VT to polish

brusco, -a ['brusku, a] ADJ brusque; (*súbito*) sudden

brutal [bru'taw] (*pl* -**ais**) ADJ brutal

brutalidade [brutali'dadʒi] F brutality

brutamontes [bruta'mõtʃis] M INV (*corpulento*) hulk; (*bruto*) brute

bruto, -a ['brutu, a] ADJ brutish; (*grosseiro*) coarse; (*móvel*) heavy; (*diamante*) uncut; (*petróleo*) crude; (*peso, Com*) gross; (*aggressivo*) aggressive ▶ M brute; **em ~** raw, unworked; **um ~ resfriado** an awful cold

bruxa ['bruʃa] F witch; (*velha feia*) hag

bruxaria [bruʃa'ria] F witchcraft

Bruxelas [bru'ʃelas] N Brussels

bruxo ['bruʃu] M wizard

bruxulear [bruʃu'ljar] VI to flicker

BTN (BR) ABR M (= *Bônus do Tesouro Nacional*) government bond used to quote prices

Bucareste [buka'rɛstʃi] N Bucharest

bucha ['buʃa] F (*para parafuso*) Rawlplug®; (*para buracos*) bung; **acertar na ~** (*fig*) to hit the nail on the head

bucho ['buʃu] (*col*) M gut; **ela é um ~** (**feio**) she's as ugly as sin

buço ['busu] M down

Budapest [buda'pɛstʃi] N Budapest

budismo [bu'dʒizmu] M Buddhism

budista [bu'dʒista] ADJ, M/F Buddhist

bueiro [bu'ejru] M storm drain

Buenos Aires ['bwɛnuz'ajris] N Buenos Aires

búfalo ['bufalu] M buffalo

bufante [bu'fãtʃi] ADJ (*manga etc*) puffed, full

bufar [bu'far] VI to puff, pant; (*com raiva*) to snort; (*reclamar*) to moan, grumble

bufê [bu'fe] M (*móvel*) sideboard; (*comida*) buffet; (*serviço*) catering service

buffer ['bafer] (*pl* -**s**) M (*Comput*) buffer

bugiganga [buʒi'gãga] F trinket; **bugigangas** FPL (*coisas sem valor*) knick-knacks

bujão [bu'ʒãw] (*pl* -**ões**) M (*Tec*) cap; **~ de gás** gas cylinder

bula ['bula] F (*Rel*) papal bull; (*Med*) directions *pl* for use

bulbo ['buwbu] M bulb

buldôzer [buw'dozer] (*pl* **buldôzeres**) M bulldozer

bule ['buli] M (*de chá*) teapot; (*de café*) coffeepot

Bulgária [buw'garja] F: **a ~** Bulgaria

búlgaro, -a ['buwgaru, a] ADJ, M/F Bulgarian ▶ M (*Ling*) Bulgarian

bulha ['buʎa] F row

bulhufas [bu'ʎufas] (*col*) PRON nothing

bulício [bu'lisju] M (*agitação*) bustle; (*sussurro*) rustling

buliçoso, -a [buli'sozu, ɔza] ADJ (*vivo*) lively; (*agitado*) restless

bulimia [buli'mia] F bulimia

bulir [bu'lir] VT to move ▶ VI to move, stir; **~ com** to tease; **~ em** to touch, meddle with

bumbum [bũ'bũ] (*pl* **-ns**) (*col*) M bottom

bunda ['bũda] (*col*) F bottom, backside

buquê [bu'ke] M bouquet

buraco [bu'raku] M hole; (*de agulha*) eye; (*jogo*) rummy; **ser um ~** (*difícil*) to be tough; **~ da fechadura** keyhole

burburinho [burbu'riɲu] M hubbub; (*murmúrio*) murmur

burguês, -guesa [bur'ges, 'geza] ADJ middle-class, bourgeois

burguesia [burge'zia] F middle class, bourgeoisie

buril [bu'riw] (*pl* **-is**) M chisel

burilar [buri'lar] VT to chisel

buris [bu'ris] MPL *de* **buril**

Burkina [bur'kina] M: **o ~** Burkina Faso

burla ['burla] F trick, fraud; (*zombaria*) mockery

burlar [bur'lar] VT (*enganar*) to cheat; (*defraudar*) to swindle; (*a lei, impostos*) to evade

burlesco, -a [bur'lesku, a] ADJ burlesque

burocracia [burokra'sia] F bureaucracy; (*excessiva*) red tape

burocrata [buro'krata] M/F bureaucrat

burocrático, -a [buro'kratʃiku, a] ADJ bureaucratic

burrice [bu'hisi] F stupidity

burro, -a ['buhu, a] ADJ stupid; (*pouco inteligente*) dim, thick ▶ M/F (*Zool*) donkey; (*pessoa*) fool, idiot; **pra ~** (*col*) a lot; (*com adj*) really; **dar com os ~s n'água** (*fig*) to come a cropper; **~ de carga** (*fig*) hard worker

Burundi [burũ'dʒi] M: **o ~** Burundi

busca ['buska] F search; **em ~ de** in search of; **dar ~ a** to search for

buscador [buska'dor] M search engine

busca-pé [buska'pɛ] (*pl* **busca-pés**) M banger

buscar [bus'kar] VT to fetch; (*procurar*) to look *ou* search for; **ir ~** to fetch, go for; **mandar ~** to send for

busquei *etc* [bus'kej] VB *ver* **buscar**

bússola ['busola] F compass

bustiê [bustʃi'e] M boob tube

busto ['bustu] M bust

butique [bu'tʃiki] M boutique

buzina [bu'zina] F horn

buzinada [buzi'nada] F toot, hoot

buzinar [buzi'nar] VI to sound one's horn, toot the horn ▶ VT to hoot; **~ nos ouvidos de alguém** (*fig*) to hassle sb; **~ algo nos ouvidos de alguém** (*fig*) to drum sth into sb

búzio ['buzju] M (*concha*) conch

BVRJ ABR F = **Bolsa de Valores do Rio de Janeiro**

Cc

C, c [se] (pl **cs**) M C, c; **C de Carlos** C for Charlie

c/ ABR = **com**

cá [ka] ADV here; **de cá** on this side; **para cá** here, over here; **para lá e para cá** back and forth; **de lá para cá** since then; **de um ano para cá** in the last year; **cá entre nós** just between us

caatinga [ka'tʃĩga] (BR) F scrub(-land)

cabal [ka'baw] (pl **-ais**) ADJ (completo) complete; (exato) exact

cabala [ka'bala] F (maquinação) conspiracy, intrigue

cabalar [kaba'lar] VT (votos etc) to canvass (for) ▶ VI to canvass

cabana [ka'bana] F hut

cabaré [kaba're] M (boate) night club

cabeça [ka'besa] F head; (inteligência) brain; (de uma lista) top ▶ M/F (de uma revolta) leader; (de uma organização) brains sg; **cinquenta ~s de gado** fifty head of cattle; **de ~** off the top of one's head; (calcular) in one's head; **de ~ para baixo** upside down; **por ~** per person, per head; **deu-lhe na ~ de** he took it into his head to; **esquentar a ~** (col) to lose one's cool; **não estar com a ~ para fazer** not to feel like doing; **fazer a ~ de alguém** (col) to talk sb into it; **levar na ~** (col) to come a cropper; **meter na ~** to get into one's head; **tirar algo da ~** to put sth out of one's mind; **perder a ~** to lose one's head; **quebrar a ~** to rack one's brains; **subir à ~** (sucesso etc) to go to sb's head; **com a ~ no ar** absent-minded; **~ de porco** (col) tenement building; **~ de vento** m, f scatterbrain; **~ fria** cool-headedness

cabeçada [kabe'sada] F (pancada com cabeça) butt; (Futebol) header; (asneira) blunder; **dar uma ~ (em)** to bang one's head (on); **dar uma ~** (fazer asneira) to make a blunder; **dar uma ~ na bola** (Futebol) to head the ball

cabeçalho [kabe'saʎu] M (de livro) title page; (de página, capítulo) heading

cabecear [kabe'sjar] VT (Futebol) to head ▶ VI to nod; to head the ball

cabeceira [kabe'sejra] F (de cama) head; (de mesa) end; **leitura de ~** bedtime reading

cabeçudo, -a [kabe'sudu, a] ADJ with a big head; (teimoso) headstrong

cabedal [kabe'daw] (pl **-ais**) M wealth

cabeleira [kabe'lejra] F head of hair; (postiça) wig

cabeleireiro, -a [kabelej'rejru, a] M/F hairdresser

cabelo [ka'belu] M hair; **cortar/fazer o ~** to have one's hair cut/done; **ter ~ na venta** to be short-tempered

cabeludo, -a [kabe'ludu, a] ADJ hairy; (difícil) complicated; (obsceno) obscene

caber [ka'ber] VI: **~ (em)** (poder entrar) to fit, go; (roupa) to fit; (ser compatível) to be appropriate (in); **~ a** (em partilha) to fall to; **cabe a alguém fazer** it is up to sb to do; **~ por** to fit through; **não cabe aqui fazer comentários** this is not the time or place to comment; **acho que cabe exigir um explicação** I think it is reasonable to demand an explanation; **são fatos que cabe apurar** they are facts which should be investigated; **tua dúvida cabe perfeitamente** your doubt is perfectly in order; **não ~ em si de** to be beside o.s. with

cabide [ka'bidʒi] M (coat) hanger; (móvel) hat stand; (fixo à parede) coat rack; **~ de empregos** person who has several jobs

cabideiro [kabi'dejru] M hat stand; (na parede) coat rack; (para sapatos) rack

cabimento [kabi'mẽtu] M suitability; **ter ~** to be fitting ou appropriate; **não ter ~** to be inconceivable

cabine [ka'bini] F cabin; (em loja) fitting room; (do piloto) (Aer) cockpit; **~ telefônica** telephone box (BRIT) ou booth

cabisbaixo, -a [kabiz'bajʃu, a] ADJ (deprimido) dispirited, crestfallen; (com a cabeça para baixo) head down

cabível [ka'bivew] (pl **-eis**) ADJ conceivable

cabo ['kabu] M (extremidade) end; (de faca, vassoura etc) handle; (corda) rope; (cabo etc) cable; (Geo) cape; (Mil) corporal; **ao ~ de** at the end of; **de ~ a rabo** from beginning to end; **levar a ~** to carry out; **dar ~ de** to do away with; **~ eleitoral** canvasser

caboclo, -a [ka'boklu, a] (BR) ADJ copper-coloured (BRIT), copper-colored (US) ▶ M/F mestizo

cabotino, -a [kabo'tʃinu, a] ADJ ostentatious ▶ M/F show-off

Cabo Verde M Cape Verde

cabo-verdiano, -a [-ver'dʒjanu, a] ADJ, M/F Cape Verdean

cabra ['kabra] F goat ▶ M (BR: *sujeito*) guy; (: *capanga*) hired gun

cabra-cega F blind man's buff

cabra-macho (*pl* **cabras-machos**) M tough guy

cabreiro, -a [ka'brejru, a] (*col*) ADJ suspicious

cabresto [kab'restu] M (*de cavalos*) halter

cabrito [ka'britu] M kid

cabrocha [ka'brɔʃa] F mulatto girl

caça ['kasa] F hunting; (*busca*) hunt; (*animal*) quarry, game ▶ M (*Aer*) fighter (plane); **~ a baleias** whaling; **à ~ de** in pursuit of

caçada [ka'sada] F (*jornada de caçadores*) hunting trip

caçador, a [kasa'dor(a)] M/F hunter

caçamba [ka'sãba] F (*balde*) bucket

caça-minas M INV minesweeper

caça-níqueis M INV slot machine

cação [ka'sãw] (*pl* **-ões**) M shark

caçapa [ka'sapa] F pocket

caçar [ka'sar] VT to hunt; (*com espingarda*) to shoot; (*procurar*) to seek ▶ VI to hunt, go hunting

cacareco [kaka'rɛku] M piece of junk; **cacarecos** MPL (*coisas sem valor*) junk *sg*

cacarejar [kakare'ʒar] VI (*galinhas etc*) to cluck

cacarejo [kaka'reʒu] M clucking

caçarola [kasa'rɔla] F (sauce)pan

cacau [ka'kaw] M cocoa; (*Bot*) cacao

cacaueiro [kaka'wejru] M cocoa tree

cacetada [kase'tada] F blow (with a stick)

cacete [ka'setʃi] ADJ tiresome, boring ▶ M/F bore ▶ M club, stick ▶ EXCL damn! (*col*); **está quente pra ~** (!) it's bloody hot (!)

caceteação [kasetʃja'sãw] F annoyance

cacetear [kase'tʃjar] VT to annoy

Cacex [ka'sɛks] ABR F (= *Carteira do Comércio Exterior*) part of Banco do Brasil which helps to finance foreign trade

cachaça [ka'ʃasa] F (white) rum

cachaceiro, -a [kaʃa'sejru, a] ADJ drunk ▶ M/F drunkard

cachaço [ka'ʃasu] M neck

cachê [ka'ʃe] M fee

cachecol [kaʃe'kɔw] (*pl* **-óis**) M scarf

cachepô [kaʃe'po] M plant pot

cachimbo [ka'ʃĩbu] M pipe

cacho ['kaʃu] M bunch; (*de cabelo*) curl, lock; (*longo*) ringlet; (*col: caso*) affair

cachoeira [kaʃo'wejra] F waterfall

cachorra [ka'ʃoha] F bitch, (female) puppy; **estar com a ~** (*col*) to be in a foul mood

cachorrada [kaʃo'hada] F pack of dogs; (*sujeira*) dirty trick

cachorrinho, -a [kaʃo'hiɲu, a] M/F puppy ▶ M (*nado*) doggy paddle

cachorro [ka'ʃohu] M dog, puppy; (*filhote de animal*) cub; (*patife*) rascal; **soltar os ~s em cima de alguém** (*fig*) to lash out at sb; **estar matando ~ a grito** (*col*) to be scraping the barrel

cachorro-quente (*pl* **cachorros-quentes**) M hot dog

cacilda [ka'siwda] EXCL wow!, crikey!

cacique [ka'siki] M (Indian) chief; (*mandachuva*) local boss

caco ['kaku] M bit, fragment; (*pessoa velha*) old relic; **chegamos ~s humanos** we arrived dead on our feet

caçoada [ka'swada] F jibe

caçoar [ka'swar] VT to mock, make fun of ▶ VI to mock

cações [ka'sõjs] MPL *de* **cação**

cacoete [ka'kwetʃi] M twitch, tic

cacto ['kaktu] M cactus

caçula [ka'sula] M/F youngest child

cada ['kada] ADJ INV each; (*todo*) every; **$10 ~** $10 each; **~ um** each one; **~ semana** each week; **a ~ 3 horas** every 3 hours; **em ~ 3 crianças, uma já teve sarampo** out of every 3 children, one has already had measles; **~ vez mais** more and more; **~ vez mais barato** cheaper and cheaper; **tem ~ museu em Londres!** there are so many different museums in London; **tem ~ um!** it takes all sorts!

cadafalso [kada'fawsu] M (*forca*) gallows *sg*

cadarço [ka'darsu] M shoelace

cadastrar [kadas'trar] VT to register; **cadastrar-se** VR to register

cadastro [ka'dastru] M (*registro*) register; (*ato*) registration; (*de criminosos*) criminal record; (*de banco etc*) client records *pl*; (*de imóveis*) land registry; **~ bancário** (*de pessoa*) credit rating

cadáver [ka'daver] M corpse, (dead) body; **só passando por cima do meu ~** over my dead body; **ao chegar ao hospital, o motorista já era ~** the driver was dead on arrival at hospital

cadavérico, -a [kada'vɛriku, a] ADJ (*exame*) post-mortem; (*pessoa*) emaciated

CADE (BR) ABR M = **Conselho Administrativo de Defesa Econômica**

cadê [ka'de] (*col*) ADV: **~ ...?** where's/where are ...?, what's happened to ...?

cadeado [ka'dʒjadu] M padlock

cadeia [ka'deja] F chain; (*prisão*) prison; (*rede*) network

cadeira [ka'dejra] F (*móvel*) chair; (*disciplina*) subject; (*Teatro*) stall; (*função*) post; **cadeiras** FPL (*Anat*) hips; **~ cativa** private seat; **~ de balanço** rocking chair; **~ de rodas** wheelchair; **falar de ~** (*fig*) to speak with authority

cadeirudo, -a [kadej'rudu, a] ADJ big-hipped

cadela [ka'dɛla] F (*cão*) bitch

cadência [ka'dẽsja] F cadence; (*ritmo*) rhythm

cadenciado, -a [kadẽ'sjadu, a] ADJ rhythmic; (*pausado*) slow

cadente [ka'dẽtʃi] ADJ (*estrela*) falling

caderneta [kader'neta] F notebook; **~ de poupança** savings account

caderno [ka'dɛrnu] M exercise book; (*de notas*) notebook; (*de jornal*) section

cadete [ka'detʃi] M cadet

cadinho [ka'dʒiɲu] M crucible; (fig) melting pot

caducar [kadu'kar] VI (documentos) to lapse, expire; (pessoa) to become senile

caduco, -a [ka'duku, a] ADJ (nulo) invalid, expired; (senil) senile; (Bot) deciduous

caduquice [kadu'kisi] F senility

cães [kãjs] MPL de **cão**

cafajeste [kafa'ʒɛstʃi] (col) ADJ roguish; (vulgar) vulgar, coarse ▶ M/F rogue; rough customer

café [ka'fɛ] M coffee; (estabelecimento) café ▶ ADJ INV coffee-coloured (BRIT), coffee-colored (US); **~ com leite** white coffee (BRIT), coffee with cream (US); **~ preto** black coffee; **~ da manhã** (BR) breakfast; **~ pequeno** (fig) small potatoes

cafeeiro, -a [kafe'ejru, a] ADJ coffee atr ▶ M coffee plant

cafeicultor [kafejkuw'tor] M coffee-grower

cafeicultura [kafejkuw'tura] F coffee-growing

cafeína [kafe'ina] F caffein(e)

cafetã [kafe'tã] M caftan

cafetão [kafe'tãw] (pl **-ões**) M pimp

cafeteira [kafe'tejra] F (vaso) coffeepot; (máquina) percolator

cafetina [kafe'tʃina] F madam

cafetões [kafe'tõjs] MPL de **cafetão**

cafezal [kafe'zaw] (pl **-ais**) M coffee plantation

cafezinho [kafe'ziɲu] M small black coffee

cafona [ka'fona] ADJ tacky ▶ M/F tacky person

cafonice [kafo'nisi] F tackiness; (coisa) tacky thing

cafundó [kafũ'dɔ] M: **no ~ de judas** out in the sticks

cafuné [kafu'nɛ] M: **fazer ~ em alguém** to stroke sb's hair

cagaço [ka'gasu] (!) M shits pl (!)

cagada [ka'gada] (!) F shit (!); (coisa malfeita) cock-up (!)

cágado ['kagadu] M turtle; **a passos de ~** (fig) at a snail's pace

caganeira [kaga'nejra] (col) F runs pl

cagão, -gona [ka'gãw, 'gɔna] (pl **-ões/-s**) (col) M/F: **ser ~** to be a chicken

cagar [ka'gar] (!) VI to (have a) shit (!) ▶ VT: **~ regras** to tell others what to do; **cagar-se** VR: **~-se de medo** to be shit scared (!); **~ (para)** not to give a shit (about) (!)

cagões [ka'gõjs] MPL de **cagão**

cagona [ka'gɔna] F de **cagão**

caguetar [kagwe'tar] VT to inform on

caguete [ka'gwetʃi] M informer

caiaque [ka'jaki] M kayak

caiar [kaj'ar] VT to whitewash

caiba etc ['kajba] VB ver **caber**

cãibra ['kãjbra] F (Med) cramp

caibro ['kajbru] M joist

caída [ka'ida] F = **queda**

caído, -a [ka'idu, a] ADJ (deprimido) dejected; (derrubado) fallen; (pendente) droopy; **~ por** (apaixonado) in love with

câimbra ['kãjbra] F = **cãibra**

caimento [kaj'mẽtu] M hang, fall

caipira [kaj'pira] ADJ countrified; (sem traquejo social) provincial ▶ M/F yokel

caipirinha [kajpi'riɲa] F cocktail of cachaça, lemon and sugar

cair [ka'ir] VI to fall; (ser vítima de logro) to be taken in; **~ bem/mal** (roupa) to fit well/badly; (col: pessoa) to look good/bad; **~ em si** to come to one's senses; **~ de quatro** to land on all fours; **estou caindo de sono** I'm really sleepy; **~ para trás** (fig) to be taken aback; **ao ~ da noite** at nightfall; **o Natal caiu num domingo** Christmas fell on a Sunday; **essa comida me caiu mal** that food did not agree with me

Cairo ['kajru] M: **o ~** Cairo

cais [kajs] M (Náut) quay; (PT Ferro) platform

caixa ['kajʃa] F box; (cofre) safe; (de uma loja) cash desk ▶ M/F (pessoa) cashier; **~ automática** ou **eletrônico** cash machine; **de alta/baixa ~** (col) well-off/poor; **fazer a ~** (Com) to cash up; **pequena ~** petty cash; **~ acústica** loudspeaker; **~ de correio** letter box; **~ de entrada** (Comput) inbox; **~ de mudanças** (BR) ou **de velocidades** gear box; **~ de saída** (Comput) outbox; **~ econômica** savings bank; **~ postal** P.O. box; **~ registradora** cash register

caixa-alta (pl **caixas-altas**) (col) ADJ rich ▶ M/F fat cat

caixa-d'água (pl **caixas-d'água**) F water tank

caixa-forte (pl **caixas-fortes**) F vault

caixão [kaj'ʃãw] (pl **-ões**) M (ataúde) coffin; (caixa grande) large box

caixa-preta (pl **caixas-pretas**) F (Aer) black box

caixeiro, -a [kaj'ʃejru, a] M/F shop assistant; (entregador) delivery man/woman

caixeiro-viajante, caixeira-viajante (pl **caixeiros-viajantes/caixeiras-viajantes**) M/F commercial traveller (BRIT) ou traveler (US)

caixilho [kaj'ʃiʎu] M (moldura) frame

caixões [kaj'ʃõjs] MPL de **caixão**

caixote [kaj'ʃotʃi] M packing case; **~ do lixo** (PT) dustbin (BRIT), garbage can (US)

caju [ka'ʒu] M cashew fruit

cajueiro [ka'ʒwejru] M cashew tree

cal [kaw] F lime; (na água) chalk; (para caiar) whitewash

calabouço [kala'bosu] M dungeon

calada [ka'lada] F: **na ~ da noite** at dead of night

calado, -a [ka'ladu, a] ADJ quiet

calafetar [kalafe'tar] VT to stop up

calafrio [kala'friu] M shiver; **ter ~s** to shiver

calamar [kala'mar] M squid

calamidade [kalami'dadʒi] F calamity, disaster

calamitoso, -a [kalami'tozu, ɔza] ADJ disastrous

calão [ka'lãw] M: (baixo) **~** (BR) bad language; (PT) slang

calar [ka'lar] vt (*não dizer*) to keep quiet about; (*impor silêncio a*) to silence ▶ vi to go quiet; (*manter-se calado*) to keep quiet; **calar-se** vr to go quiet; to keep quiet; **~ em** (*penetrar*) to mark; **cala a boca!** shut up!

calça ['kawsa] f (*tb*: **calças**) trousers *pl* (BRIT), pants *pl* (US)

calçada [kaw'sada] f (PT: *rua*) roadway; (BR: *passeio*) pavement (BRIT), sidewalk (US)

calçadão [kawsa'dãw] (*pl* **-ões**) m pedestrian precinct (BRIT), pedestrian zone (US)

calçadeira [kawsa'dejra] f shoe-horn

calçado, -a [kaw'sadu, a] adj (*rua*) paved ▶ m shoe; **calçados** mpl (*para os pés*) footwear *sg*

calçadões [kawsa'dõjs] mpl *de* **calçadão**

calçamento [kawsa'mẽtu] m paving

calcanhar [kawka'ɲar] m (*Anat*) heel; **~ de aquiles** Achilles' heel

calção [kaw'sãw] (*pl* **-ões**) m shorts *pl*; **~ de banho** swimming trunks *pl*

calcar [kaw'kar] vt (*pisar em*) to tread on; (*espezinhar*) to trample (on); (*comprimir*) to press; (*reprimir*) to repress

calçar [kaw'sar] vt (*sapatos, luvas*) to put on; (*pavimentar*) to pave; (*pôr calço*) to wedge; **calçar-se** vr to put on one's shoes; **o sapato calça bem?** does the shoe fit?; **ela calça (número) 28** she takes size 28 (in shoes)

calcário, -a [kaw'karju, a] adj (*água*) hard ▶ m limestone

calceiro, -a [kaw'sejru, a] m/f shoe-maker

calcinha [kaw'siɲa] f panties *pl*

cálcio ['kawsju] m calcium

calço ['kawsu] m (*cunha*) wedge

calções [kaw'sõjs] mpl *de* **calção**

calculador [kawkula'dor] m = **calculadora**

calculadora [kawkula'dora] f calculator

calcular [kawku'lar] vt to calculate; (*imaginar*) to imagine ▶ vi to make calculations; **~ que** to reckon that

calculável [kawku'lavew] (*pl* **-eis**) adj calculable

calculista [kawku'lista] adj calculating ▶ m/f opportunist

cálculo ['kawkulu] m calculation; (*Mat*) calculus; (*Med*) stone

calda ['kawda] f (*de doce*) syrup; **caldas** fpl (*águas termais*) hot springs

caldeira [kaw'dejra] f (*Tec*) boiler

caldeirada [kawdej'rada] (PT) f (*guisado*) fish stew

caldeirão [kawdej'rãw] (*pl* **-ões**) m cauldron

caldo ['kawdu] m (*sopa*) broth; (*de fruta*) juice; **~ de carne/galinha** beef/chicken stock; **~ verde** potato and cabbage broth

calefação [kalefa'sãw] f heating

caleidoscópio [kalejdo'skɔpju] m kaleidoscope

calejado, -a [kale'ʒadu, a] adj calloused; (*fig: experiente*) experienced; (: *endurecido*) callous

calejar [kale'ʒar] vt (*mãos*) to callous; (*pessoa*) to harden; **calejar-se** vr (*mãos*) to get

calluses; (*insensibilizar-se*) to become callous; (*tornar-se experiente*) to get experience

calendário [kalē'darju] m calendar

calha ['kaʎa] f (*sulco*) channel; (*para água*) gutter

calhamaço [kaʎa'masu] m tome

calhambeque [kaʎã'bɛki] (*col*) m old banger

calhar [ka'ʎar] vi: **calhou viajarmos no mesmo avião** we happened to travel on the same plane; **calhou que** it so happened that; **ele calhou de chegar** he happened to arrive; **~ a** (*cair bem*) to suit; **vir a ~** to come at the right time; **se ~** (PT) perhaps, maybe

calhau [ka'ʎaw] m stone, pebble

calibrado, -a [kali'bradu, a] adj (*meio bêbado*) tipsy

calibrar [kali'brar] vt to gauge (BRIT), gage (US), calibrate

calibre [ka'libri] m (*de cano*) bore, calibre (BRIT), caliber (US); (*fig*) calibre

cálice ['kalisi] m (*copinho*) wine glass; (*Rel*) chalice

calidez [kali'dez] f warmth

cálido, -a ['kalidu, a] adj warm

caligrafia [kaligra'fia] f (*arte*) calligraphy; (*letra*) handwriting

calista [ka'lista] m/f chiropodist (BRIT), podiatrist (US)

calma ['kawma] f calm; **conservar/perder a ~** to keep/lose one's temper; **~!** take it easy!

calmante [kaw'mãtʃi] adj soothing ▶ m (*Med*) tranquillizer

calmo, -a ['kawmu, a] adj calm, tranquil

calo ['kalu] m callus; (*no pé*) corn; **pisar nos ~s de alguém** (*fig*) to hit a (raw) nerve

calombo [ka'lõbu] m lump; (*na estrada*) bump

calor [ka'lor] m heat; (*agradável*) warmth; (*fig*) warmth; **está** *ou* **faz ~** it is hot; **estar com ~** to be hot

calorento, -a [kalo'rẽtu, a] adj (*pessoa*) sensitive to heat; (*lugar*) hot

caloria [kalo'ria] f calorie

caloroso, -a [kalo'rozu, ɔza] adj warm; (*entusiástico*) enthusiastic; (*protesto*) fervent

calota [ka'lɔta] f (*Auto*) hubcap

calote [ka'lɔtʃi] (*col*) m (*dívida*) bad debt; **dar o ~** to welsh (on one's debts)

caloteiro, -a [kalo'tejru, a] (*col*) adj unreliable ▶ m/f bad payer

calouro, -a [ka'loru, a] m/f (*Educ*) fresher (BRIT), freshman (US); (*noviço*) novice

calúnia [ka'lunja] f slander

caluniador, a [kalunja'dor(a)] adj slanderous ▶ m/f slanderer

caluniar [kalu'njar] vt to slander

calunioso, -a [kalu'njozu, ɔza] adj slanderous

calvície [kaw'visi] f baldness

calvo, -a ['kawvu, a] adj bald

cama ['kama] f bed; **~ de casal** double bed; **~ de solteiro** single bed; **de ~** (*doente*) ill (in bed); **ficar de ~** to take to one's bed

cama-beliche (*pl* **camas-beliche(s)**) f bunk bed

camada [ka'mada] F layer; (de tinta) coat
camafeu [kama'few] M cameo
câmara ['kamara] F chamber; (PT Foto) camera; **~ de ar** inner tube; **~ municipal** (BR) town council; (PT) town hall
câmara-ardente F: **estar exposto em ~** to lie in state
camarada [kama'rada] ADJ friendly, nice; (preço) good ▶ M/F comrade; (sujeito) guy/woman
camaradagem [kamara'daʒẽ] F comradeship, camaraderie; **por ~** out of friendliness
camarão [kama'rãw] (pl **-ões**) M shrimp; (graúdo) prawn
camareiro, -a [kama'rejru, a] M/F cleaner/chambermaid
camarilha [kama'riʎa] F clique
camarim [kama'rĩ] (pl **-ns**) M (Teatro) dressing room
Camarões [kama'rõjs] M: **o ~** Cameroon
camarões [kama'rõjs] MPL de **camarão**
camarote [kama'rɔtʃi] M (Náut) cabin; (Teatro) box
cambada [kã'bada] F bunch, gang
cambaio, -a [kã'baju, a] ADJ (mesa) wobbly, rickety
cambalacho [kãba'laʃu] M scam
cambaleante [kãba'ljãtʃi] ADJ unsteady (on one's feet)
cambalear [kãba'ljar] VI to stagger, reel
cambalhota [kãba'ʎɔta] F somersault
cambar [kã'bar] VI: **~ para** to lean on
cambial [kã'bjaw] (pl **-ais**) ADJ exchange atr
cambiante [kã'bjãtʃi] ADJ changing, variable ▶ M (cor) shade
cambiar [kã'bjar] VT to change; (trocar) to exchange
câmbio ['kãbju] M (dinheiro etc) exchange; (preço de câmbio) rate of exchange; **~ livre** free trade; **~ negro** black market; **~ oficial/paralelo** official/black market
cambista [kã'bista] M (de dinheiro) money changer; (BR: de ingressos) (ticket-)tout
Camboja [kã'bɔʒa] M: **o ~** Cambodia
cambojano, -a [kãbo'ʒanu, a] ADJ, M/F Cambodian
camburão [kãbu'rãw] (pl **-ões**) M police van
camélia [ka'mɛlja] F camellia
camelo [ka'melu] M camel; (fig) dunce
camelô [kame'lo] M street pedlar
câmera ['kamera] (BR) F camera ▶ M/F camera operator; **em ~ lenta** in slow motion; **~ de segurança** security camera, CCTV camera; **~ digital** digital camera
camião [ka'mjãw] (pl **-ões**) (PT) M lorry (BRIT), truck (US)
caminhada [kami'ɲada] F walk
caminhante [kami'ɲãtʃi] M/F walker
caminhão [kami'ɲãw] (pl **-ões**) (BR) M lorry (BRIT), truck (US); **~ do lixo** dustcart (BRIT), garbage truck (US)
caminhar [kami'ɲar] VI (ir a pé) to walk;

(processo) to get under way; (negócios) to go, to progress
caminho [ka'miɲu] M way; (vereda) road, path; **~ de ferro** (PT) railway (BRIT), railroad (US); **a meio ~** halfway (there); **ser meio ~ andado** (fig) to be halfway there; **a ~** on the way, en route; **cortar ~** to take a short cut; **ir pelo mesmo ~** to go the same way; **pôr-se a ~** to set off
caminhões [kami'ɲõjs] MPL de **caminhão**
caminhoneiro, -a [kamiɲo'nejru, a] M/F lorry driver (BRIT), truck driver (US)
caminhonete [kamiɲo'nɛtʃi] M (Auto) van
camiões [ka'mjõjs] MPL de **camião**
camioneta [kamjo'neta] (PT) F (para passageiros) coach; (comercial) van
camionista [kamjo'nista] (PT) M/F lorry driver (BRIT), truck driver (US)
camisa [ka'miza] F shirt; **~ de dormir** nightshirt; **~ de força** straitjacket; **~ esporte/polo/social** sports/polo/dress shirt; **mudar de ~** (Esporte) to change sides
camiseta [kami'zeta] (BR) F T-shirt; (interior) vest
camisinha [kami'ziɲa] (col) F condom
camisola [kami'zɔla] F (BR) nightdress; (PT: pulôver) sweater; **~ interior** (PT) vest
camomila [kamo'mila] F camomile
campa ['kãpa] F (de sepultura) gravestone
campainha [kãpa'iɲa] F bell
campal [kã'paw] (pl **-ais**) ADJ: **batalha ~** pitched battle; **missa ~** open-air mass
campanário [kãpa'narju] M (torre) church tower, steeple
campanha [kã'paɲa] F (Mil etc) campaign; (planície) plain
campeão, -peã [kã'pjãw, 'pjã] (pl **-ões/-s**) M/F champion
campeonato [kãpjo'natu] M championship
campestre [kã'pɛstri] ADJ rural, rustic
campina [kã'pina] F prairie, grassland
camping ['kãpĩ] (pl **-s**) (BR) M camping; (lugar) campsite
campismo [kã'pizmu] M camping; **parque de ~** campsite
campista [kã'pista] M/F camper
campo ['kãpu] M field; (fora da cidade) countryside; (Esporte) ground; (acampamento) camp; (âmbito) field; (Tênis) court
camponês, -esa [kãpo'nes, eza] M/F countryman/woman; (agricultor) farmer
campus ['kãpus] M INV campus
camuflagem [kamu'flaʒẽ] F camouflage
camuflar [kamu'flar] VT to camouflage
camundongo [kamũ'dõgu] (BR) M mouse
camurça [ka'mursa] F suede
CAN (BR) ABR M = **Correio Aéreo Nacional**
cana ['kana] F cane; (col: cadeia) nick; (de açúcar) sugar cane; **ir em ~** to be put behind bars
Canadá [kana'da] M: **o ~** Canada
canadense [kana'dẽsi] ADJ, M/F Canadian

canal [ka'naw] (*pl* **-ais**) M channel; (*de navegação*) canal; (*Anat*) duct

canalha [ka'naʎa] F rabble, mob ▶ M/F wretch, scoundrel

canalização [kanaliza'sãw] F (*de água*) plumbing; (*de gás*) piping

canalizador, a [kanaliza'dor(a)] (PT) M/F plumber

canalizar [kanali'zar] VT (*água, esforços*) to channel; (*colocar canos*) to lay pipes in

canapé [kana'pɛ] M sofa

canapê [kana'pe] M (*Culin*) canapé

canário [ka'narju] M canary

canastra [ka'nastra] F (big) basket; (*jogo*) canasta

canastrão, -trona [kanas'trãw, 'trɔna] (*pl* **-ões/-s**) M/F ham actor/actress

canavial [kana'vjaw] (*pl* **-ais**) M cane field

canavieiro, -a [kana'vjejru, a] ADJ sugar cane *atr*

canção [kã'sãw] (*pl* **-ões**) F song; **~ de ninar** lullaby

cancela [kã'sɛla] F gate

cancelamento [kãsela'mētu] M cancellation

cancelar [kãse'lar] VT to cancel; (*invalidar*) to annul; (*riscar*) to cross out

câncer ['kãser] M cancer; **C~** (*Astrologia*) Cancer

canceriano, -a [kãse'rjanu, a] ADJ, M/F Cancerian

cancerígeno, -a [kãse'riʒenu, a] ADJ carcinogenic

cancerologista [kãserolo'ʒista] M/F cancer specialist, oncologist

canceroso, -a [kãse'rozu, ɔza] ADJ (*célula*) cancerous ▶ M/F cancer sufferer

canções [kã'sõjs] FPL *de* **canção**

cancro ['kãkru] (PT) M cancer

candango, -a [kã'dãgu, a] M/F person from Brasília

candeeiro [kãdʒi'ejru] M (BR: *a óleo*) oil-lamp; (*a gás*) gas-lamp; (PT) lamp

candelabro [kãde'labru] M (*castiçal*) candlestick; (*lustre*) chandelier

candente [kã'dētʃi] ADJ white hot; (*fig*) inflamed

candidatar-se [kãdʒida'tarsi] VR: **~ a** (*vaga*) to apply for; (*presidência*) to stand for

candidato, -a [kãdʒi'datu, a] M/F candidate; (*a cargo*) applicant

candidatura [kãdʒida'tura] F candidature; (*a cargo*) application

cândido, -a ['kãdʒidu, a] ADJ (*ingênuo*) naive; (*inocente*) innocent

candomblé [kãdõ'blɛ] M *see note*

> **Candomblé** is Brazil's most influential Afro-Brazilian religion. Practised mainly in Bahia, it mixes catholicism with Yoruba traditions. According to **candomblé**, believers become possessed by spirits and thus become an instrument of communication between divine and mortal forces. **Candomblé** ceremonies are great spectacles of African rhythm and dance held in *terreiros*.

candura [kã'dura] F (*simplicidade*) simplicity; (*inocência*) innocence

caneca [ka'nɛka] F mug

caneco [ka'nɛku] M tankard; **pintar os ~s** (*col*) to play up

canela [ka'nɛla] F (*especiaria*) cinnamon; (*Anat*) shin

canelada [kane'lada] F kick in the shins; **dei uma ~ na mesa** I hit my shins on the table

caneta [ka'neta] F pen; **~ esferográfica** ballpoint pen; **~ pilot** felt-tip pen

caneta-tinteiro (*pl* **canetas-tinteiro**) F fountain pen

canga ['kãga] F beach wrap

cangaceiro [kãga'sejru] (BR) M bandit

cangote [kã'gotʃi] M (back of the) neck

canguru [kãgu'ru] M kangaroo

cânhamo ['kaɲamu] M hemp

canhão [ka'ɲãw] (*pl* **-ões**) M (*Mil*) cannon; (*Geo*) canyon

canhestro, -a [ka'ɲestru, a] ADJ awkward

canhões [ka'ɲõjs] MPL *de* **canhão**

canhoto, -a [ka'ɲotu, a] ADJ left-handed ▶ M/F left-handed person ▶ M (*de cheque*) stub

canibal [kani'baw] (*pl* **-ais**) M/F cannibal

canibalismo [kaniba'lizmu] M cannibalism

caniço, -a [ka'nisu, a] ADJ (*col*) skinny ▶ M reed

canícula [ka'nikula] F searing heat

canil [ka'niw] (*pl* **-is**) M kennel

caninha [ka'niɲa] (*col*) F rum

canino, -a [ka'ninu, a] ADJ canine; (*fome*) terrible ▶ M canine

canis [ka'nis] MPL *de* **canil**

canivete [kani'vetʃi] M penknife; **nem que chovam ~s** whatever happens, come what may

canja ['kãʒa] F (*sopa*) chicken broth; (*col*) cinch, pushover

canjica [kã'ʒika] F maize porridge

cano ['kanu] M pipe; (*tubo*) tube; (*de arma de fogo*) barrel; (*de bota*) top; **~ de esgoto** sewer; **entrar pelo ~** (*col*) to come off badly

canoa [ka'noa] F canoe

canoagem [ka'nwaʒē] F canoeing

canoeiro, -a [ka'nwejru, a] M/F canoeist

canoísta [kano'ista] M/F canoeist

canonizar [kanoni'zar] VT to canonize

cansaço [kã'sasu] M tiredness

cansado, -a [kã'sadu, a] ADJ tired

cansar [kã'sar] VT (*fatigar*) to tire; (*entediar*) to bore ▶ VI (*ficar cansado*) to get tired; **cansar-se** VR to get tired

cansativo, -a [kãsa'tʃivu, a] ADJ tiring; (*tedioso*) tedious

canseira [kã'sejra] F (*cansaço*) weariness; (*trabalho árduo*) toil; **dar ~ em alguém** to wear sb out

cantada [kã'tada] (*col*) F chat-up line; **dar uma ~ em** to chat up

cantado, -a [kã'tadu, a] ADJ (*missa*) sung; (*sotaque*) sing-song

cantar [kã'tar] VT to sing; (*respostas etc*) to sing out; (*col: seduzir*) to chat up ▶ VI to sing ▶ M song

cantarolar [kãtaro'lar] VT to hum

canteiro [kã'tejru] M stonemason; (*de flores*) flower bed; (*de obra*) site office

cantiga [kã'tʃiga] F ballad; ~ **de ninar** lullaby

cantil [kã'tʃiw] (*pl* -is) M canteen, flask

cantina [kã'tʃina] F canteen

cantis [kã'tʃis] MPL *de* **cantil**

canto ['kãtu] M corner; (*lugar*) place; (*canção*) song

cantor, a [kã'tor(a)] M/F singer

cantoria [kãto'ria] F singing

canudo [ka'nudu] M tube; (*para beber*) straw

cão [kãw] (*pl* **cães**) M dog; (*pessoa*) rascal; **ser ou estar um ~ de ruim** (*col*) to be awful

caolho, -a [ka'oʎu, a] ADJ cross-eyed

caos ['kaos] M chaos

caótico, -a [ka'ɔtʃiku, a] ADJ chaotic

capa ['kapa] F (*roupa*) cape; (*cobertura*) cover; **livro de ~ dura/mole** hardback/paperback (book)

capacete [kapa'setʃi] M helmet

capacho [ka'paʃu] M door mat; (*fig*) toady

capacidade [kapasi'dadʒi] F capacity; (*aptidão*) ability, competence; **ser uma ~** (*pessoa*) to be brilliant; ~ **ociosa** (*Com*) idle capacity

capacíssimo, -a [kapa'sisimu, a] ADJ SUPERL *de* **capaz**

capacitar [kapasi'tar] VT: ~ **alguém a fazer/ para algo** to prepare sb to do/for sth; **capacitar-se** VR: ~-**se de/de que** to convince o.s. of/that

capar [ka'par] VT to castrate, geld

capataz [kapa'taz] M foreman

capaz [ka'paz] ADJ able, capable; **ser ~ de** to be able to (*ou* capable of); **sou ~ de ...** (*talvez*) I might ...; **é ~ de chover hoje** it might rain today

capcioso, -a [kap'sjozu, ɔza] ADJ (*pergunta*) trick; (*pessoa*) tricky

capela [ka'pɛla] F chapel

capelão [kape'lãw] (*pl* -ães) M (*Rel*) chaplain

Capemi [kape'mi] (BR) ABR F (= *Caixa de Pecúlios, Pensões e Montepios dos Militares*) *military pension fund*

capenga [ka'pẽga] ADJ lame ▶ M/F cripple

capengar [kapẽ'gar] VI to limp

Capes (BR) ABR F (*Educ*: = *Coordenação de Aperfeiçoamento de Pessoal de Nível Superior*) *grant-awarding body*

capeta [ka'peta] M devil; **ele é um ~** he's a little devil

capilar [kapi'lar] ADJ hair atr

capim [ka'pĩ] M grass

capinar [kapi'nar] VT to weed ▶ VI to weed; (*col*) to clear off

capitães [kapi'tãjs] MPL *de* **capitão**

capital [kapi'taw] (*pl* -ais) ADJ, M capital ▶ F (*cidade*) capital; ~ **circulante** (*Com*) circulating capital; ~ **de giro** (*Com*) working

capital; ~ **investido** (*Com*) investment capital; ~ **(em) ações** (*Com*) share capital; ~ **imobilizado** *ou* **fixo** (*Com*) fixed capital; ~ **integralizado** (*Com*) paid-up capital; ~ **próprio** *ou* **social** (*Com*) equity capital; ~ **de risco** (*Com*) venture capital

capitalismo [kapita'lizmu] M capitalism

capitalista [kapita'lista] M/F capitalist

capitalizar [kapitali'zar] VT (*tirar proveito de*) to capitalize on; (*Com*) to capitalize

capitanear [kapita'njar] VT to command, head

capitania [kapita'nia] F: ~ **do porto** port authority

capitão [kapi'tãw] (*pl* -ães) M captain

capitulação [kapitula'sãw] F capitulation, surrender

capitular [kapitu'lar] VT (*falhas, causas*) to list; (*descrever*) to characterize; (*rendição*) to fix the terms of ▶ VI to capitulate; ~ **alguém de algo** to brand sb (as) sth

capítulo [ka'pitulu] M chapter; (*de novela*) episode

capô [ka'po] M (*Auto*) bonnet (BRIT), hood (US)

capoeira [ka'pwejra] F (PT) hencoop; (*mata*) brushwood

> **Capoeira** is a fusion of martial arts and dance which originated among African slaves in colonial Brazil. It is danced in a circle to the sound of the *berimbau*, a percussion instrument of African origin. Opposed by the Brazilian authorities until the beginning of the twentieth century, today **capoeira** is regarded as a national sport.

capota [ka'pota] F (*Auto*) hood, top

capotar [kapo'tar] VI to overturn

capote [ka'potʃi] M overcoat

caprichar [kapri'ʃar] VI: ~ **em** to take trouble over

capricho [ka'priʃu] M whim, caprice; (*teimosia*) obstinacy; (*apuro*) care

caprichoso, -a [kapri'ʃozu, ɔza] ADJ capricious; (*com apuro*) meticulous

capricorniano, -a [kaprikor'njanu, a] ADJ, M/F Capricorn

Capricórnio [kapri'kɔrnju] M Capricorn

cápsula ['kapsula] F capsule

captar [kap'tar] VT (*atrair*) to win; (*Rádio*) to pick up; (*águas*) to collect, dam up; (*compreender*) to catch

captura [kap'tura] F capture; ~ **de tela** (*Comput*) screenshot

capturar [kaptu'rar] VT to capture, seize

capuz [ka'puz] M hood

caquético, -a [ka'kɛtʃiku, a] ADJ doddery

caqui [ka'ki] M persimmon

cáqui ['kaki] ADJ khaki

cara ['kara] F (*de pessoa*) face; (*aspecto*) appearance ▶ M (*col*) guy; (*coragem*) courage, heart; ~ **ou coroa?** heads or tails?; **de ~** straightaway; **está na ~** it's obvious; **dar de ~ com** to bump into; **estar com boa ~** to look well; (*comida*) to look good; **não vou com a ~ dele** (*col*) I'm not very keen on him; **meter a ~** (*col*) to put one's back into it; **ser a ~ de** (*col*) to be the spitting image of; **ter ~ de** to look (like)

carabina [kara'bina] F rifle

Caracas [ka'rakas] N Caracas

caracol [kara'kɔw] (*pl* **-óis**) M snail; (*de cabelo*) curl; **escada em ~** spiral staircase

caracteres [karak'tɛris] MPL *de* **caráter**

característica [karakte'ristʃika] F characteristic, feature

característico, -a [karakte'ristʃika, a] ADJ characteristic

caracterização [karakteriza'sãw] F characterization; (*de ator*) make-up

caracterizar [karakteri'zar] VT to characterize, typify; (*ator*) to make up; **caracterizar-se** VR to be characterized; (*ator*) to get into character

cara de pau F cheek ▶ ADJ INV brazen

caraíba [kara'iba] ADJ Carib; (PT) Caribbean

caramanchão [karamã'ʃãw] (*pl* **-ões**) M gazebo

caramba [ka'rãba] EXCL blimey (BRIT), gee (US); **quente pra ~** (*col*) really hot

carambola [karã'bɔla] F carambola (*fruit*)

caramelo [kara'mɛlu] M caramel; (*bala*) toffee

cara-metade (*pl* **caras-metades**) F better half

caranguejo [karã'geʒu] M crab

carão [ka'rãw] (*pl* **-ões**) M telling-off; **passar/levar um ~** to give/get a telling-off

carapuça [kara'pusa] F cap; **enfiar a ~** to take the hint personally

caratê [kara'te] M karate

caráter [ka'rater] (*pl* **caracteres**) M character; **de ~ social** of a social nature; **a ~** in character; **uma pessoa de ~** a person of hono(u)r

caravana [kara'vana] F caravan

carboidrato [karboi'dratu] M carbohydrate

carbônico, -a [kar'boniku, a] ADJ carbon *atr*

carbonizar [karboni'zar] VT to carbonize; (*queimar*) to char

carbono [kar'bonu] M carbon

carburador [karbura'dor] M carburettor (BRIT), carburetor (US)

carcaça [kar'kasa] F (*esqueleto*) carcass; (*armação*) frame; (*de navio*) hull

carcamano, -a [karka'manu, a] M/F Italian-Brazilian

cárcere ['karseri] M prison

carcereiro, -a [karse'rejru, a] M/F jailer, warder

carcomido, -a [karko'midu, a] ADJ worm-eaten; (*rosto*) pock-marked, pitted

cardápio [kar'dapju] M menu

cardeal [kar'dʒjaw] (*pl* **-ais**) ADJ, M cardinal

cardíaco, -a [kar'dʒiaku, a] ADJ cardiac ▶ M/F person with a heart condition; **ataque ~** heart attack; **parada cardíaca** cardiac arrest

cardigã [kardʒi'gã] M cardigan

cardinal [kardʒi'naw] (*pl* **-ais**) ADJ cardinal

cardiológico, -a [kardʒjo'lɔʒiku, a] ADJ heart *atr*

cardiologista [kardʒjolo'ʒista] M/F heart specialist, cardiologist

cardume [kar'dumi] M (*peixes*) shoal

careca [ka'rɛka] ADJ bald ▶ F baldness; **estar ~ de fazer/saber** (*col*) to be used to doing/know full well

carecer [kare'ser] VI: **~ de** (*ter falta*) to lack; (*precisar*) to need

careiro, -a [ka'rejru, a] ADJ expensive

carência [ka'rẽsja] F (*falta*) lack, shortage; (*necessidade*) need; (*privação*) deprivation

carente [ka'rẽtʃi] ADJ wanting; (*pessoa*) needy, deprived; (*de carinho*) in need of affection

carestia [kares'tʃia] F high cost; (*preços altos*) high prices *pl*; (*escassez*) scarcity

careta [ka'reta] ADJ (*col*) straight, square ▶ F grimace; **fazer uma ~** to pull a face

carga ['karga] F load; (*de navio, avião*) cargo; (*ato de carregar*) loading; (*Elet*) charge; (*fig: peso*) burden; (*Mil*) attack, charge; **voltar à ~** to insist; **~ d'água** heavy downpour; **~ horária** workload; **~ aérea** air cargo

cargo ['kargu] M (*responsabilidade*) responsibility; (*função*) post; **a ~ de** in charge of; **ter a ~** to be in charge of; **tomar a ~** to take charge of; **~ honorífico** honorary post; **~ de confiança** position of trust; **~ público** public office

cargueiro [kar'gejru] M cargo ship

cariar [ka'rjar] VT, VI to decay

Caribe [ka'ribi] M: **o ~** the Caribbean (Sea)

caricatura [karika'tura] F caricature

caricatural [karikatu'raw] (*pl* **-ais**) ADJ (*fig*) grotesque

caricaturar [karikatu'rar] VT to caricature

caricaturista [karikatu'rista] M/F caricaturist

carícia [ka'risja] F caress

caridade [kari'dadʒi] F charity; **obra de ~** charity

caridoso, -a [kari'dozu, ɔza] ADJ charitable

cárie ['kari] F tooth decay; (*Med*) caries *sg*

carimbar [karĩ'bar] VT to stamp; (*no correio*) to postmark

carimbo [ka'rĩbu] M stamp; (*postal*) postmark

carinho [ka'riɲu] M affection, fondness; (*carícia*) caress; **fazer ~** to caress; **com ~** affectionately; (*com cuidado*) with care

carinhoso, -a [kari'ɲozu, ɔza] ADJ affectionate

carioca [ka'rjɔka] ADJ of Rio de Janeiro ▶ M/F native of Rio de Janeiro ▶ M (*café*) *type of weak coffee*

carisma [ka'rizma] M charisma

carismático, -a [kariz'matʃiku, a] ADJ charismatic

caritativo, -a [karita'tʃivu, a] ADJ charitable

carnal [kar'naw] (*pl* **-ais**) ADJ carnal; **primo ~** first cousin

carnaval [karna'vaw] (*pl* **-ais**) M carnival

> In Brazil, **Carnaval** is the popular festival held each year in the four days before Lent. It is celebrated in very different ways in different parts of the country. In Rio de Janeiro, for example, the big attraction is the parades of the *escolas de samba*, in Salvador the *trios elétricos*, in Recife the *frevo* and, in Olinda, the giant figures, such as the *Homen da meia-noite* and *Mulher do meio-dia*. In Portugal, **Carnaval** is celebrated on Shrove Tuesday, with street parties and processions taking place throughout the country.

carnavalesco, -a [karnava'lesku, a] ADJ (*festa*) carnival *atr*; (*pessoa*) keen on carnival; (*fig*) grotesque ▶ M/F carnival organizer

carne ['karni] F flesh; (*Culin*) meat; **em ~ e osso** in the flesh; **ser de ~ e osso** to be human; **~ assada** roast beef

carnê [kar'ne] M (*para compras*) payment book

carneiro [kar'nejru] M sheep; (*macho*) ram; **perna/costeleta de ~** leg of lamb/lamb chop

carniça [kar'nisa] F carrion; **pular ~** to play leapfrog

carnificina [karnifi'sina] F slaughter

carnívoro, -a [kar'nivoru, a] ADJ carnivorous ▶ M carnivore

carnudo, -a [kar'nudu, a] ADJ plump, fleshy; (*col*) beefy; (*lábios*) thick; (*fruta*) fleshy

caro, -a ['karu, a] ADJ dear, expensive; (*estimado*) dear; **sair ~** to work out expensive; **cobrar/pagar ~** to charge a lot/pay dearly

carochinha [karo'ʃiɲa] F: **conto da ~** fairy tale

caroço [ka'rosu] M (*de frutos*) stone; (*endurecimento*) lump

carões [ka'rõjs] MPL *de* **carão**

carola [ka'rɔla] (*col*) M/F pious person

carona [ka'rɔna] F lift; **viajar de ~** to hitchhike; **pegar uma ~** to get a lift

carpete [kar'petʃi] M (*fitted*) carpet

carpintaria [karpĩta'ria] F carpentry

carpinteiro [karpĩ'tejru] M carpenter; (*Teatro*) stagehand

carranca [ka'hãka] F frown, scowl

carrancudo, -a [kahã'kudu, a] ADJ (*soturno*) sullen; (*semblante*) scowling

carrapato [kaha'patu] M (*inseto*) tick; (*pessoa*) hanger-on

carrapicho [kaha'piʃu] M (*do cabelo*) bun

carrasco [ka'hasku] M executioner; (*fig*) tyrant

carrear [ka'hjar] VT (*transportar*) to transport; (*arrastar*) to carry; (*acarretar*) to bring on

carreata [kahe'ata] F motorcade

carregado, -a [kahe'gadu, a] ADJ loaded, laden; (*semblante*) sullen; (*céu*) dark; (*ambiente*) tense

carregador [kahega'dor] M porter

carregamento [kahega'mẽtu] M (*ação*) loading; (*carga*) load, cargo

carregar [kahe'gar] VT to load; (*levar*) to carry; (*bateria*) to charge; (PT: *apertar*) to press; (*levar para longe*) to take away ▶ VI: **~ em** (*pôr em demasia*) to overdo, put too much; (*pôr enfase*) to bring out

carreira [ka'hejra] F (*ação de correr*) run, running; (*profissão*) career; (*Turfe*) race; (*Náut*) slipway; (*fileira*) row; **às ~s** in a hurry; **dar uma ~** to go quickly; **fazer ~** to make a career; **arrepiar ~** to abandon one's career

carreirista [kahej'rista] ADJ, M/F careerist

carreta [ka'heta] F cart

carreteiro [kahe'tejru] M cart driver

carretel [kahe'tɛw] (*pl* **-éis**) M spool, reel

carreto [ka'hetu] M freight

carril [ka'hiw] (*pl* **-is**) (PT) M (*Ferro*) rail

carrilhão [kahi'ʎãw] (*pl* **-ões**) M chime

carrinho [ka'hiɲu] M (*para bagagem, compras*) trolley; (*brinquedo*) toy car; **~ (de criança)** pram; **~ de mão** wheelbarrow; **~ de chá** tea trolley; **~ de compras** shopping trolley (BRIT), shopping cart (US)

carris [ka'his] MPL *de* **carril**

carro ['kaho] M (*automóvel*) car; (*de bois*) cart; (*de mão*) handcart, barrow; (*de máquina de escrever*) carriage; **pôr o ~ adiante dos bois** (*fig*) to put the cart before the horse; **~ de corrida** racing car; **~ de passeio** saloon car; **~ de praça** cab; **~ de bombeiro** fire engine; **~ esporte** sports car

carro-bomba (*pl* **carros-bomba**) M car bomb

carroça [ka'hɔsa] F cart, wagon

carroceria [kahose'ria] F (*Auto*) bodywork

carro-chefe (*pl* **carros-chefe(s)**) M (*de desfile*) main float; (*fig*) flagship, centrepiece (BRIT), centerpiece (US)

carrocinha [kaho'siɲa] F wagon

carro-forte (*pl* **carros-fortes**) M security van

carrossel [kaho'sɛw] (*pl* **-éis**) M merry-go-round

carruagem [ka'hwaʒẽ] (*pl* **-ns**) F carriage, coach

carta ['karta] F letter; (*de jogar*) card; (*mapa*) chart; **~ aberta** open letter; **~ aérea** airmail letter; **~ registrada** registered letter; **~ de apresentação** letter of introduction; **~ de crédito/intenção** letter of credit/intent; **~ de condução** (PT) driving licence (BRIT), driver's license (US); **dar as ~s** to deal; **dar/ ter ~ branca** to give/have carte blanche; **pôr as ~s na mesa** (*fig*) to put one's cards on the table; **~ magna** charter; **~ patente** patent

carta-bomba (*pl* **cartas-bomba(s)**) F letter bomb

cartada [kar'tada] F (*fig*) move

cartão [kar'tãw] (*pl* **-ões**) M card; (PT: *material*) cardboard; **~ comercial** business card; **~ de crédito** credit card; **~ de cidadão** (PT) identity card; **~ de débito** debit card; **~ de memória** memory card; **~ de recarga** (*para celular*) top-up card; **~ de visita** (calling) card; **~ telefônico** phone card

All Portuguese citizens are required to carry an identity card. The new smart-card version, issued for the first time in the second half of the 2000s, is known as the **cartão de cidadão**, and will eventually replace the BI or *bilhete de identidade*. As well as providing a photograph and giving standard details such as the owner's name, date of birth, height and names of parents, it includes on the same card electoral, medical and tax-payer identification details. Like the BI, this card can be used instead of a passport for travel within the European Union.

cartão-postal (*pl* **cartões-postais**) M postcard; (*lugar turístico*) sight

cartaz [kar'taz] M poster, bill (*US*); **ter ~** (*ser famoso*) to be well-known; (*ter popularidade*) to be popular; (**estar**) **em ~** (*Teatro, Cinema*) (to be) showing

cartear [kar'tʃjar] VI to play cards ▶ VT to play

carteira [kar'tejra] F (*móvel*) desk; (*para dinheiro*) wallet; (*de ações*) portfolio; **~ de identidade** (*BR*) identity card; **~ de motorista** driving licence (*BRIT*), driver's license (*US*)

The identity card carried by Brazilian citizens is known as the **carteira de identidade** or RG (from *registro geral*). On it are the holder's name (and those of their parents), their photograph, date of birth, signature and right thumb print, as well as their RG identification number and, optionally, their **CPF** (tax-payer's identification number). The card can be used instead of a passport for travel to some Latin American countries.

carteiro [kar'tejru] M postman (*BRIT*), mailman (*US*)

cartel [kar'tɛw] (*pl* **-éis**) M cartel

cartilagem [kartʃi'laʒẽ] (*pl* **-ns**) F (*Anat*) cartilage

cartões [kar'tõjs] MPL *de* **cartão**

cartografia [kartogra'fia] F cartography

cartola [kar'tɔla] F top hat

cartolina [karto'lina] F card

cartomante [karto'mãtʃi] M/F fortune-teller

cartório [kar'tɔrju] M registry office

cartucho [kar'tuʃu] M cartridge; (*saco de papel*) packet

cartum [kar'tũ] (*pl* **-ns**) M cartoon

cartunista [kartu'nista] M/F cartoonist

cartuns [kar'tũs] MPL *de* **cartum**

caruncho [ka'rũʃu] M (*inseto*) woodworm

carvalho [kar'vaʎu] M oak

carvão [kar'vãw] (*pl* **-ões**) M coal; (*de madeira*) charcoal

carvoeiro [karvo'ejru] M *coal merchant*

carvões [kar'võjs] MPL *de* **carvão**

casa ['kaza] F house; (*lar*) home; (*Com*) firm; (*Mat: decimal*) place; **em/para ~** (at) home/home; **~ de botão** buttonhole; **~ de saúde** hospital; **~ da moeda** mint; **~ de banho** (*PT*)

bathroom; **~ e comida** board and lodging; **ser de ~** to be like one of the family; **ter dez anos de ~** (*numa firma*) to have ten years' service behind one; **~ de câmbio** bureau de change; **~ de campo** country house; **~ de cômodos** tenement; **~ de máquinas** engine room; **~ de repouso** old people's home (*BRIT*), retirement home (*US*); **~ popular** ≈ council house

casaca [ka'zaka] F tails *pl*; **virar a ~** to become a turncoat

casação [kaza'kãw] (*pl* **-ões**) M overcoat

casaco [ka'zaku] M coat; (*paletó*) jacket; **~ de peles** fur coat

casacões [kaza'kõjs] MPL *de* **casacão**

casado, -a [ka'zadu, a] ADJ married; **bem ~** happily married

casa-forte (*pl* **casas-fortes**) F vault

casa-grande (*pl* **casas-grandes**) F great house

casal [ka'zaw] (*pl* **-ais**) M couple

casamenteiro, -a [kazamẽ'tejru, a] ADJ wedding *atr*

casamento [kaza'mẽtu] M marriage; (*boda*) wedding; (*fig*) combination

casar [ka'zar] VT to marry; (*combinar*) to match (up); **casar-se** VR to get married; (*harmonizar-se*) to combine well

casarão [kaza'rãw] (*pl* **-ões**) M mansion

casca ['kaska] F (*de árvore*) bark; (*de banana*) skin; (*de ferida*) scab; (*de laranja*) peel; (*de nozes, ovos*) shell; (*de milho etc*) husk; (*de pão*) crust

casca-grossa (*pl* **cascas-grossas**) ADJ coarse, uneducated

cascalho [kas'kaʎu] M gravel; (*na praia*) shingle

cascão [kas'kãw] M crust; (*sujeira*) grime

cascata [kas'kata] F waterfall; (*col: mentira*) tall story

cascateiro, -a [kaska'tejru, a] (*col*) ADJ big-mouthed ▶ M/F storyteller

cascavel [kaska'vɛw] (*pl* **-éis**) M (*serpente*) rattlesnake

casco ['kasku] M (*crânio*) skull; (*de animal*) hoof; (*de navio*) hull; (*para bebidas*) empty bottle; (*de tartaruga*) shell

cascudo [kas'kudu] M rap on the head

casebre [ka'zɛbri] M hovel, shack

caseiro, -a [ka'zejru, a] ADJ (*produtos*) home-made; (*pessoa, vida*) domestic ▶ M/F housekeeper

caserna [ka'zɛrna] F barracks *pl*

casmurro, -a [kaz'muhu, a] ADJ introverted

caso ['kazu] M case; (*tb:* **caso amoroso**) affair; (*estória*) story ▶ CONJ in case, if; **de ~ pensado** deliberately; **no ~ de** in case (of); **em todo ~** in any case; **neste ~** in that case; **~ necessário** if necessary; **criar ~** to cause trouble; **fazer pouco ~ de** to belittle; **não fazer ~** to ignore; **vir ao ~** to be relevant; **~ de emergência** emergency

casório [ka'zɔrju] (*col*) M wedding

caspa ['kaspa] F dandruff

casquinha [kas'kiɲa] F (*de sorvete*) cone; (*pele*) skin

cassação [kasa'sãw] F withholding; *(de políticos)* banning

cassar [ka'sar] VT *(direitos, licença)* to cancel, withhold; *(políticos)* to ban

cassete [ka'sɛtʃi] M cassette

cassetete [kase'tetʃi] M truncheon (*BRIT*), nightstick (*US*)

cassino [ka'sinu] M casino

casta ['kasta] F caste; *(estirpe)* lineage

castanha [kas'taɲa] F chestnut; **~ de caju** cashew nut

castanha-do-pará [-pa'ra] *(pl* **castanhas-do-pará***)* F Brazil nut

castanheiro [kasta'ɲejru] M chestnut tree

castanho, -a [kas'taɲu, a] ADJ brown

castanholas [kasta'ɲɔlas] FPL castanets

castelo [kas'tɛlu] M castle; **fazer ~s no ar** *(fig)* to build castles in the air

castiçal [kastʃi'saw] *(pl* **-ais***)* M candlestick

castiço, -a [kas'tʃisu, a] ADJ pure; *(de boa casta)* of good stock, pedigree *atr*

castidade [kastʃi'dadʒi] F chastity

castigar [kastʃi'gar] VT to punish; *(aperfeiçoar)* to perfect; *(col: tocar)* to play

castigo [kas'tʃigu] M punishment; *(fig: mortificação)* pain; **estar/ficar de ~** *(criança)* to be getting punished/be punished

casto, -a ['kastu, a] ADJ chaste

castor [kas'tor] M beaver

castrar [kas'trar] VT to castrate

casual [ka'zwaw] *(pl* **-ais***)* ADJ chance *atr*, accidental; *(fortuito)* fortuitous

casualidade [kazwali'dadʒi] F chance; *(acidente)* accident; **por casual** by chance, accidentally

casulo [ka'zulu] M *(de sementes)* pod; *(de insetos)* cocoon

cata ['kata] F: **à ~ de** in search of

cataclismo [kata'klizmu] M cataclysm

catacumbas [kata'kũbas] FPL catacombs

catalizador, a [kataliza'dor(a)] ADJ catalytic ▶ M catalyst

catalogar [katalo'gar] VT to catalogue (*BRIT*), catalog (*US*)

catálogo [ka'talogu] M catalogue (*BRIT*), catalog (*US*); **~ (telefônico)** telephone directory

Catalunha [kata'luɲa] F: **a ~** Catalonia

catapora [kata'pɔra] (*BR*) F chickenpox

Catar [ka'tar] M: **o ~** Qatar

catar [ka'tar] VT to pick (up); *(procurar)* to look for, search for; *(arroz)* to clean; *(recolher)* to collect, gather

catarata [kata'rata] F waterfall; *(Med)* cataract

catarro [ka'tahu] M catarrh

catártico, -a [ka'tartʃiku, a] ADJ cathartic

catástrofe [ka'tastrofi] F catastrophe

catastrófico, -a [katas'trɔfiku, a] ADJ catastrophic

catatau [kata'tau] M: **um ~ de** a lot of

cata-vento M weathercock

catecismo [kate'sizmu] M catechism

cátedra ['katedra] F chair

catedral [kate'draw] *(pl* **-ais***)* F cathedral

catedrático, -a [kate'dratʃiku, a] M/F professor

categoria [katego'ria] F category; *(social)* rank; *(qualidade)* quality; **de alta ~** first-rate

categórico, -a [kate'gɔriku, a] ADJ categorical

categorizar [kategori'zar] VT to categorize

catequizar [kateki'zar] VT to talk round; *(Rel)* to catechize

catinga [ka'tʃĩga] F stench, stink

catinguento, -a [katʃi'gẽtu, a] ADJ smelly

catiripapo [katʃiri'papu] M punch

cativante [katʃi'vãtʃi] ADJ captivating; *(atraente)* charming

cativar [katʃi'var] VT *(escravizar)* to enslave; *(fascinar)* to captivate; *(atrair)* to charm

cativeiro [katʃi'vejru] M captivity; *(escravidão)* slavery; *(cadeia)* prison

cativo, -a [ka'tʃivu, a] M/F *(escravo)* slave; *(prisioneiro)* prisoner

catolicismo [katoli'sizmu] M catholicism

católico, -a [ka'tɔliku, a] ADJ, M/F Catholic

catorze [ka'torzi] NUM fourteen; *ver tb* **cinco**

catraca [ka'traka] F turnstile; **~ de embarque/desembarque** *(em estação)* ticket barrier

catucar [katu'kar] VT = **cutucar**

caturrice [katu'hisi] F obstinacy

caução [kaw'sãw] *(pl* **-ões***)* F security, guarantee; *(Jur)* bail; **prestar ~** to give bail; **sob ~** on bail

caucionante [kawsjo'nãtʃi] M/F guarantor

caucionar [kawsjo'nar] VT to guarantee, stand surety for; *(Jur)* to stand bail for

cauções [kaw'sõjs] FPL *de* **caução**

cauda ['kawda] F tail; *(de vestido)* train

caudal [kaw'daw] *(pl* **-ais***)* M torrent

caudaloso, -a [kawda'lozu, ɔza] ADJ torrential

caudilho [kaw'dʒiʎu] M leader, chief

caule ['kauli] M stalk, stem

causa ['kawza] F cause; *(motivo)* motive, reason; *(Jur)* lawsuit, case; **por ~ de** because of; **em ~** in question

causador, a [kawza'dor(a)] ADJ which caused ▶ M cause

causar [kaw'zar] VT to cause, bring about

cáustico, -a ['kawstʃiku, a] ADJ caustic

cautela [kaw'tela] F caution; *(senha)* ticket; *(título)* share certificate; **~ (de penhor)** pawn ticket

cautelar [kawte'lar] ADJ precautionary

cauteloso, -a [kawte'lozu, ɔza] ADJ cautious, wary

cauterizar [kawteri'zar] VT to cauterize

cava ['kava] F *(de manga)* armhole

cavação [kava'sãw] *(col)* F wheeling and dealing

cavaco [ka'vaku] M: **~s do ofício** occupational hazards

cavado, -a [ka'vadu, a] ADJ *(olhos)* sunken; *(roupa)* low-cut

cavador, a [kava'dor(a)] ADJ go-getting ▶ M/F go-getter

cavala [ka'vala] F mackerel

cavalar [kava'lar] ADJ (*descomunal*) enormous, huge

cavalaria [kavala'ria] F (*Mil*) cavalry; (*instituição medieval*) chivalry

cavalariça [kavala'risa] F stable

cavaleiro [kava'lejru] M rider, horseman; (*medieval*) knight

cavalete [kava'letʃi] M stand; (*Foto*) tripod; (*de pintor*) easel; (*de mesa*) trestle; (*do violino*) bridge

cavalgar [kavaw'gar] VT to ride ▶ VI: **~ em** to ride on; **~ (sobre)** to jump over

cavalheiresco, -a [kavaʎej'resku, a] ADJ courteous, gallant, gentlemanly

cavalheiro, -a [kava'ʎejru, a] ADJ courteous, gallant ▶ M gentleman; (*Dança*) partner

cavalinho [kava'liɲu] M: **~ de pau** rocking horse

cavalo [ka'valu] M horse; (*Xadrez*) knight; (*pessoa*): **ser um ~** to be rude; **a ~** on horseback; **50~s(-vapor), 50 ~s de força** 50 horsepower; **quantos ~s tem esse carro?** how many horsepower is that car?; **fazer de algo um ~ de batalha** to make a mountain out of a molehill about sth; **tirar o ~ da chuva** (*fig*) to forget the idea; **~ de corrida** racehorse

cavalo-marinho (*pl* **cavalos-marinhos**) M seahorse

cavanhaque [kava'ɲaki] M goatee (beard)

cavaquinho [kava'kiɲu] M small guitar

cavar [ka'var] VT to dig; (*decote*) to lower; (*esforçar-se para obter*) to try to get ▶ VI to dig; (*fig*) to delve; (*animal*) to burrow; (*esforçar-se*) to try hard; **~ a vida** to earn one's living

cave ['kavi] (*PT*) F wine cellar

caveira [ka'vejra] F skull; **fazer a ~ de alguém** (*col*) to blacken sb's name

caverna [ka'vɛrna] F cavern

cavernoso, -a [kaver'nozu, ɔza] ADJ (*voz*) booming; (*pessoa*) horrible

caviar [ka'vjar] M caviar

cavidade [kavi'dadʒi] F cavity

cavilha [ka'viʎa] F (*de madeira*) peg, dowel; (*de metal*) bolt

cavo, -a ['kavu, a] ADJ (*côncavo*) concave

caxias [ka'ʃias] ADJ INV overdisciplined ▶ M/F INV stickler for discipline

caxumba [ka'ʃũba] F mumps *sg*

CBA ABR F = **Confederação Brasileira de Automobilismo**

CBAt ABR F = **Confederação Brasileira de Atletismo**

CBD ABR F = **Confederação Brasileira de Desportos**

CBF ABR F = **Confederação Brasileira de Futebol**

CBT ABR M = **Código Brasileiro de Telecomunicações**

CBTU ABR F = **Companhia Brasileira de Trens Urbanos**

c/c ABR (= *conta corrente*) c/a

CCT (*BR*) ABR M = **Conselho Científico e Tecnológico**

CD ABR M CD

CDB (*BR*) ABR M = **Certificado de Depósito Bancário**

CDC (*BR*) ABR M = **Conselho de Desenvolvimento Comercial**

CDDPH (*BR*) ABR M = **Conselho de Defesa dos Direitos da Pessoa Humana**

CDI (*BR*) ABR M = **Certificado de Depósito Interbancário; Conselho de Desenvolvimento Industrial**

cê [se] (*col*) PRON = **você**

cear [sjar] VT to have for supper ▶ VI to dine

cearense [sea'rẽsi] ADJ from Ceará ▶ M/F person from Ceará

cebola [se'bola] F onion

cebolinha [sebo'liɲa] F spring onion

Cebrae (*BR*) ABR F = **Centro de Apoio à Pequena e Média Empresa**

Cebrap ABR M = **Centro Brasileiro de Análise e Planejamento**

cecear [se'sjar] VI to lisp

cê-cedilha (*pl* **cês-cedilhas**) M c cedilla

ceceio [se'seju] M lisp

cê-dê-efe [-'ɛfi] (*pl* **cê-dê-efes**) (*col*) M/F swot

ceder [se'der] VT to give up; (*dar*) to hand over; (*emprestar*) to lend ▶ VI to give in, yield; (*porta etc*) to give (way); **~ a** to give in to

cedilha [se'dʒiʎa] F cedilla

cedo ['sedu] ADV early; (*em breve*) soon; **mais ~ ou mais tarde** sooner or later; **o mais ~ possível** as soon as possible

cedro ['sɛdru] M cedar

cédula ['sɛdula] F (*moeda-papel*) banknote; (*eleitoral*) ballot paper

CEE ABR F (= *Comunidade Econômica Europeia*) EEC

CEF (*BR*) ABR F (= *Caixa Econômica Federal*) federal bank

cegar [se'gar] VT to blind; (*ofuscar*) to dazzle; (*tesoura*) to blunt ▶ VI (*ofuscar*) to be dazzling

cego, -a ['segu, a] ADJ blind; (*total*) complete, total; (*tesoura*) blunt ▶ M/F blind man/woman; **às cegas** blindly; **ser ~ por alguém** to be mad about sb

cegonha [se'goɲa] F stork

cegueira [se'gejra] F blindness

CEI (*BR*) ABR F (= *Comissão Especial de Inquérito*) commission of inquiry

ceia ['seja] F supper

ceifa ['sejfa] F harvest; (*fig*) destruction

ceifar [sej'far] VT to reap, harvest; (*vidas*) to destroy

cela ['sɛla] F cell

celebração [selebra'sãw] (*pl* **-ões**) F celebration

celebrar [sele'brar] VT to celebrate; (*exaltar*) to praise; (*acordo*) to seal

célebre ['sɛlebri] ADJ famous, well-known

celebridade [selebri'dadʒi] F celebrity

celebrizar [selebri'zar] VT to make famous; **celebrizar-se** VR to become famous

celeiro [se'lejru] M granary; (*depósito*) barn
célere ['sɛleri] ADJ swift, quick
celeste [se'lɛstʃi] ADJ celestial, heavenly
celeuma [se'lewma] F pandemonium, uproar
celibatário, -a [seliba'tarju, a] ADJ unmarried, single ▶ M/F bachelor/spinster
celibato [seli'batu] M celibacy
celofane [selo'fani] M cellophane; **papel ~** cling film
celta ['sɛwta] ADJ Celtic ▶ M/F Celt
célula ['sɛlula] F (*Bio, Elet*) cell
celular [selu'lar] ADJ cellular ▶ N: **(telefone) ~** mobile (phone) (*BRIT*), cellphone (*US*); **~ com câmera** camera phone
célula-tronco [-'trõku] (*pl* **células-tronco(s)**) F stem cell
celulite [selu'litʃi] F cellulite
celulose [selu'lɔzi] F cellulose
cem [sẽ] NUM hundred; **ser ~ por cento** (*fig*) to be great; *ver tb* **cinquenta**
cemitério [semi'tɛrju] M cemetery, graveyard
cena ['sɛna] F scene; (*palco*) stage; **em ~** on the stage; **levar à ~** to stage; **fazer uma ~** to make a scene
cenário [se'narju] M (*Teatro*) scenery; (*Cinema*) scenario; (*de um acontecimento*) scene, setting; (*panorama*) view
cenho ['sɛɲu] M face
cênico, -a ['seniku, a] ADJ (*Teatro*) stage *atr*; (*Cinema*) set *atr*
cenografia [senogra'fia] F set design
cenógrafo, -a [se'nɔgrafu, a] M/F (*Teatro*) set designer
cenoura [se'nora] F carrot
censo ['sẽsu] M census
censor, a [sẽ'sor(a)] M/F censor
censura [sẽ'sura] F (*Pol etc*) censorship; (*reprovação*) censure, criticism; (*repreensão*) reprimand
censurar [sẽsu'rar] VT (*reprovar*) to censure; (*filme, livro etc*) to censor
censurável [sẽsu'ravew] (*pl* **-eis**) ADJ reprehensible
centavo [sẽ'tavu] M cent; **estar sem um ~** to be penniless
centeio [sẽ'teju] M rye
centelha [sẽ'teʎa] F spark; (*fig*) flash
centena [sẽ'tena] F hundred; **às ~s** in hundreds
centenário, -a [sẽte'narju, a] ADJ centenary ▶ M/F centenarian ▶ M centenary, centennial
centésimo, -a [sẽ'tɛzimu, a] ADJ hundredth ▶ M hundredth (part)
centígrado [sẽ'tʃigradu] M centigrade
centilitro [sẽtʃi'litru] M centilitre (*BRIT*), centiliter (*US*)
centímetro [sẽ'tʃimetru] M centimetre (*BRIT*), centimeter (*US*)
cento ['sẽtu] M: **~ e um** one hundred and one; **por ~** per cent
centopeia [sẽto'peja] F centipede

central [sẽ'traw] (*pl* **-ais**) ADJ central ▶ F (*de polícia etc*) head office; **~ elétrica** (electric) power station; **~ telefônica** telephone exchange
centralização [sẽtraliza'sãw] F centralization
centralizar [sẽtrali'zar] VT to centralize; **centralizar-se** VR to be centralized
centrar [sẽ'trar] VT to centre (*BRIT*), center (*US*)
centro ['sẽtru] M centre (*BRIT*), center (*US*); (*de uma cidade*) town centre; **~ das atenções** centre of attention; **~ de custo/lucro** (*Com*) cost/profit centre; **~ de mesa** centrepiece (*BRIT*), centerpiece (*US*)
centroavante [sẽtroa'vãtʃi] M (*Futebol*) centre forward
CEP ['sɛpi] (*BR*) ABR M (= *Código de Endereçamento Postal*) postcode (*BRIT*), zip code (*US*)
cepo ['sepu] M (*toco*) stump; (*toro*) log
cera ['sera] F wax; **fazer ~** (*fig*) to dawdle, waste time
cerâmica [se'ramika] F pottery; (*arte*) ceramics *sg*
cerâmico, -a [se'ramiku, a] ADJ ceramic
ceramista [sera'mista] M/F potter
cerca ['serka] F (*de madeira, arame*) fence ▶ PREP: **~ de** (*aproximadamente*) around, about; **~ viva** hedge
cercado, -a [ser'kadu, a] ADJ surrounded; (*com cerca*) fenced in ▶ M enclosure; (*para animais*) pen; (*para crianças*) playpen
cercanias [serka'nias] FPL (*arredores*) outskirts; (*vizinhança*) neighbourhood *sg* (*BRIT*), neighborhood *sg* (*US*)
cercar [ser'kar] VT to enclose; (*pôr cerca em*) to fence in; (*rodear*) to surround; (*assediar*) to besiege
cercear [ser'sjar] VT (*liberdade*) to curtail, restrict
cerco ['serku] M encirclement; (*Mil*) siege; **pôr ~ a** to besiege
cereal [se'rjaw] (*pl* **-ais**) M cereal
cerebral [sere'braw] (*pl* **-ais**) ADJ cerebral, brain *atr*
cérebro ['sɛrebru] M brain; (*fig*) intelligence, brains *pl*
cereja [se'reʒa] F cherry
cerejeira [sere'ʒejra] F cherry tree
cerimônia [seri'monja] F ceremony; **de ~** formal; **sem ~** informal; **fazer ~** to stand on ceremony; **~ de posse** swearing-in ceremony, investiture
cerimonial [serimo'njaw] (*pl* **-ais**) ADJ, M ceremonial
cerimonioso, -a [serimo'njozu, ɔza] ADJ ceremonious
cerne ['sɛrni] M kernel
ceroulas [se'rolas] FPL long johns
cerração [seha'sãw] F (*nevoeiro*) fog
cerrado, -a [se'hadu, a] ADJ shut, closed; (*punho*) clenched; (*denso*) dense, thick ▶ M (*vegetação*) scrub(land)

cerrar [se'har] VT to close, shut; **cerrar-se** VR to close, shut

certame [ser'tami] M (concurso) contest, competition

certeiro, -a [ser'tejru, a] ADJ (tiro) accurate, well-aimed; (acertado) correct

certeza [ser'teza] F certainty; **com ~** certainly, surely; (provavelmente) probably; **ter ~ de** to be certain ou sure of; **ter ~ de que** to be sure that; **tem ~?** are you sure?

certidão [sertʃi'dãw] (pl **-ões**) F certificate

certificado [sertʃifi'kadu] M (garantia) certificate

certificar [sertʃifi'kar] VT to certify; (assegurar) to assure; **certificar-se** VR: **~-se de** to make sure of

certo, -a ['sɛrtu, a] ADJ certain, sure; (exato, direito) right; (um, algum) a certain ▶ ADV correctly; **na certa** certainly; **ao ~** for certain; **dar ~** to work; **está ~** okay, all right

cerveja [ser'veʒa] F beer

cervejaria [serveʒa'ria] F (fábrica) brewery; (bar) bar, public house

cervical [servi'kaw] (pl **-ais**) ADJ cervical

cérvice ['sɛrvisi] F cervix

cervo ['sɛrvu] M deer

cerzir [ser'zir] VT to darn

cesariana [seza'rjana] F Caesarian (BRIT), Cesarian (US)

cessação [sesa'sãw] F halting, ceasing

cessão [se'sãw] (pl **-ões**) F (cedência) surrender; (transferência) transfer

cessar [se'sar] VI to cease, stop; **sem ~** continually

cessar-fogo M INV cease-fire

cessões [se'sõjs] FPL de **cessão**

cesta ['sesta] F basket; **~ básica** food parcel

cesto ['sestu] M basket; (com tampa) hamper

ceticismo [setʃi'sizmu] M scepticism (BRIT), skepticism (US)

cético, -a ['sɛtʃiku, a] ADJ sceptical (BRIT), skeptical (US) ▶ M/F sceptic (BRIT), skeptic (US)

cetim [se'tʃĩ] M satin

cetro ['sɛtru] M sceptre (BRIT), scepter (US)

céu [sɛw] M sky; (Rel) heaven; (da boca) roof; **cair do ~** (fig) to come at the right time; **mover ~s e terra** (fig) to move heaven and earth

cevada [se'vada] F barley

cevar [se'var] VT (engordar) to fatten; (alimentar) to feed; (engodar) to bait

CFTV ABR M (= circuito fechado de TV) CCTV

CGC (BR) ABR M (= Cadastro Geral de Contribuintes) roll of tax payers

CGT (BR) ABR F (= Central Geral dos Trabalhadores) trade union

chá [ʃa] M tea; (reunião) tea party; **dar um ~ de sumiço** (col) to disappear; **tomar ~ de cadeira** (fig) to be a wallflower; **~ de bebê** baby shower; **~ de panela** bridal shower

chã [ʃã] F: **~ (de dentro)** topside

chacal [ʃa'kaw] (pl **-ais**) M jackal

chácara ['ʃakara] F (granja) farm; (casa de campo) country house

chacina [ʃa'sina] F slaughter

chacinar [ʃasi'nar] VT (matar) to slaughter

chacoalhar [ʃakwa'ʎar] VT to shake; (col: amolar) to bug ▶ VI to shake about; to be annoying

chacota [ʃa'kɔta] F (zombaria) mockery

chacrinha [ʃa'kriɲa] (col) F get-together

Chade ['ʃadʒi] M: **o ~** Chad

chafariz [ʃafa'riz] M fountain

chafurdar [ʃafur'dar] VI: **~ em** to wallow in; **chafurdar-se** VR: **~-se em** to wallow in

chaga ['ʃaga] F (Med) wound; (fig) disease

chalé [ʃa'lɛ] M chalet

chaleira [ʃa'lejra] F kettle; (bajulador) crawler, toady

chaleirar [ʃalej'rar] VT to crawl to

chama ['ʃama] F flame; **em ~s** on fire

chamada [ʃa'mada] F call; (Mil) roll call; (Educ) register; (no jornal) headline; **dar uma ~ em alguém** (repreender) to tell sb off

chamar [ʃa'mar] VT to call; (convidar) to invite; (atenção) to attract ▶ VI to call; (telefone) to ring; **chamar-se** VR to be called; **chamo-me João** my name is John; **~ alguém de idiota/ Dudu** to call sb an idiot/Dudu; **mandar ~** to summon, send for

chamariz [ʃama'riz] M decoy; (fig) lure

chamativo, -a [ʃama'tʃivu, a] ADJ showy, flashy

chamego [ʃa'megu] M cuddle

chaminé [ʃami'nɛ] F chimney; (de navio) funnel

champanha [ʃã'paɲa] M ou F champagne

champanhe [ʃã'paɲi] M ou F = **champanha**

champu [ʃã'pu] (PT) M shampoo

chamuscar [ʃamus'kar] VT to scorch, singe; **chamuscar-se** VR to scorch o.s.

chance ['ʃãsi] F chance

chancela [ʃã'sɛla] F seal, official stamp

chancelaria [ʃãsela'ria] F chancellery

chanceler [ʃãse'ler] M chancellor

chanchada [ʃã'ʃada] F second-rate film (ou play)

chantagear [ʃãta'ʒjar] VT to blackmail

chantagem [ʃã'taʒẽ] F blackmail

chantagista [ʃãta'ʒista] M/F blackmailer

chão [ʃãw] (pl **chãos**) M ground; (terra) soil; (piso) floor

chapa ['ʃapa] F (placa) plate; (eleitoral) list ▶ M/F (col) mate, friend; **~ de matrícula** (PT Auto) number (BRIT) ou license (US) plate; **bife na ~** grilled steak; **oi, meu ~!** hi, mate!

chapa-branca (pl **chapas-brancas**) M civil service car

chapelaria [ʃapela'ria] F (loja) hat shop

chapeleira [ʃape'lejra] F hat box; ver tb **chapeleiro**

chapeleiro, -a [ʃape'lejru, a] M/F milliner

chapéu [ʃa'pɛw] M hat

chapéu-coco (pl **chapéus-coco(s)**) M bowler (hat) (BRIT), derby (US)

chapinha [ʃa'piɲa] F: **~ (de garrafa)** (bottle) top

chapinhar [ʃapi'ɲar] vi to splash
charada [ʃa'rada] F (*quebra-cabeça*) puzzle
charco ['ʃarku] M marsh, bog
charge ['ʃarʒi] F (political) cartoon
chargista [ʃar'ʒista] M/F (political) cartoonist
charlatão [ʃarla'tãw] (*pl* **-ães**) M charlatan; (*curandeiro*) quack
charme ['ʃarmi] M charm; **fazer ~** to be nice, use one's charm
charmoso, -a [ʃar'mozu, ɔza] ADJ charming
charneca [ʃar'nɛka] F moor, heath
charrete [ʃa'hɛtʃi] F cart
charter ['tʃarter] ADJ INV charter ▶ M (*pl* **-s**) charter flight
charuto [ʃa'rutu] M cigar
chassi [ʃa'si] M (*Auto, Elet*) chassis
chata ['ʃata] F (*embarcação*) barge; *ver tb* **chato**
chateação [ʃatʃja'sãw] (*pl* **-ões**) F bother, hassle; (*maçada*) bore
chatear [ʃa'tʃjar] vt (*aborrecer*) to bother, upset; (*importunar*) to pester; (*entediar*) to bore; (*irritar*) to annoy ▶ vi to be upsetting; to be boring; to be annoying; **chatear-se** vr to get upset; to get bored; to get annoyed
chatice [ʃa'tʃisi] F nuisance
chato, -a ['ʃatu, a] ADJ (*plano*) flat, level; (*pé*) flat; (*tedioso*) boring; (*irritante*) annoying; (*que fica mal*) bad, rude ▶ M/F bore; (*quem irrita*) pain
chatura [ʃa'tura] (*col*) F pain (in the neck)
chauvinismo [ʃawvi'nizmu] M chauvinism
chauvinista [ʃawvi'nista] ADJ chauvinistic ▶ M/F chauvinist
chavão [ʃa'vãw] (*pl* **-ões**) M cliché
chave ['ʃavi] F key; (*Elet*) switch; (*Tip*) curly bracket; **~ de porcas** spanner; **~ inglesa** (monkey) wrench; **~ de fenda** screwdriver
-chave SUFIXO key *atr*
chaveiro [ʃa'vejru] M (*utensílio*) key ring; (*pessoa*) locksmith
chávena ['ʃavena] (*PT*) F cup
checar [ʃe'kar] vt to check
check-up [tʃe'kapi] (*pl* **-s**) M check-up
chefatura [ʃefa'tura] F: **~ de polícia** police headquarters *sg*
chefe ['ʃɛfi] M/F head, chief; (*patrão*) boss; **~ de turma** foreman; **~ de estação** stationmaster
chefia [ʃe'fia] F (*liderança*) leadership; (*direção*) management; (*repartição*) headquarters *sg*; **estar com a ~ de** to be in charge of
chefiar [ʃe'fjar] vt to lead
chega ['ʃega] (*col*) M: **dar um ~ em alguém** to tell sb off ▶ PREP even
chegada [ʃe'gada] F arrival; **dar uma ~** to drop by
chegado, -a [ʃe'gadu, a] ADJ (*próximo*) near; (*íntimo*) close; **ser ~ a** (*bebidas, comidas*) to be keen on
chegar [ʃe'gar] vt (*aproximar*) to bring near ▶ vi to arrive; (*ser suficiente*) to be enough; **chegar-se** vr: **~-se a** to approach; **chega!** that's enough!; **~ a** (*atingir*) to reach; (*conseguir*) to

manage to; **~ algo para cá/para lá** to bring sth closer/move sth over; **chega (mais) para cá/para lá!** come closer!/move over!; **vou chegando** I'm leaving
cheia ['ʃeja] F flood
cheio, -a ['ʃeju, a] ADJ full; (*repleto*) full up; (*col: farto*) fed up; **~ de si** self-important; **~ de dedos** all fingers and thumbs; (*inibido*) awkward; **~ de frescura** (*col*) fussy; **~ da nota** (*col*) rich, loaded; **acertar em ~** to be exactly right, hit the nail on the head; **estar ~ de algo** (*col*) to be fed up with sth
cheirar [ʃej'rar] vt, vi to smell; **~ a** to smell of; **isto não me cheira bem** there's something fishy about this
cheiro ['ʃejru] M smell; **ter ~ de** to smell of
cheiroso, -a [ʃej'rozu, ɔza] ADJ: **ser** *ou* **estar ~** to smell nice
cheiro-verde M bunch of parsley and spring onion
cheque ['ʃɛki] M cheque (*BRIT*), check (*US*); (*Xadrez*) check; **~ cruzado** crossed cheque; **~ de viagem** traveller's cheque (*BRIT*), traveler's check (*US*); **~ em branco** blank cheque; **~ sem fundos** uncovered cheque, rubber cheque (*col*); **~ voador** rubber cheque (*col*)
chequei *etc* [ʃe'kej] vB *ver* **checar**
cherne ['ʃɛrni] M grouper
chiado ['ʃjadu] M squeak(ing); (*de vapor*) hiss(ing)
chiar [ʃjar] vi to squeak; (*porta*) to creak; (*vapor*) to hiss; (*fritura*) to sizzle; (*col: reclamar*) to grumble
chibata [ʃi'bata] F (*vara*) cane
chiclete [ʃi'klɛtʃi] M chewing gum; **~ de bola** bubble gum
chicória [ʃi'kɔrja] F chicory
chicote [ʃi'kɔtʃi] M whip
chicotear [ʃiko'tʃjar] vt to whip, lash
chifrada [ʃi'frada] F (*golpe*) butt
chifrar [ʃi'frar] vt to two-time
chifre ['ʃifri] M (*corno*) horn; **pôr ~ em alguém** (*col*) to be unfaithful to sb, cheat on sb
chifrudo, -a [ʃi'frudu, a] (*col*) ADJ cuckolded
Chile ['ʃili] M: **o ~** Chile
chileno, -a [ʃi'lenu, a] ADJ, M/F Chilean
chilique [ʃi'liki] (*col*) M fit
chilrear [ʃiw'hjar] vi to chirp, twitter
chilreio [ʃiw'heju] M chirping
chimarrão [ʃima'hãw] (*pl* **-ões**) M mate tea *without sugar taken from a pipe-like cup*
chimpanzé [ʃĩpã'zɛ] M chimpanzee
China ['ʃina] F: **a ~** China
chinelo [ʃi'nɛlu] M slipper; **~ (de dedo)** flip-flop; **botar no ~** (*fig*) to put to shame
chinês, -esa [ʃi'nes, eza] ADJ, M/F Chinese ▶ M (*Ling*) Chinese
chinfrim [ʃĩ'frĩ] (*pl* **-ns**) ADJ cheap and cheerful
chino, -a ['ʃinu, a] M/F Chinese
chio ['ʃiu] M squeak; (*de rodas*) screech
chip ['ʃipi] M (*Comput*) chip

Chipre ['ʃipri] F Cyprus

chique ['ʃiki] ADJ stylish, chic

chiqueiro [ʃi'kejru] M pigsty

chispa ['ʃispa] F spark

chispada [ʃis'pada] (BR) F dash

chispar [ʃis'par] VI (correr) to dash

chita ['ʃita] F printed cotton, calico

choça ['ʃɔsa] F shack, hut

chocalhar [ʃoka'ʎar] VT, VI to rattle

chocalho [ʃo'kaʎu] M (Mús, brinquedo) rattle; (para animais) bell

chocante [ʃo'kãtʃi] ADJ shocking; (col) amazing

chocar [ʃo'kar] VT (incubar) to hatch, incubate; (ofender) to shock, offend ▶ VI to shock; **chocar-se** VR to crash, collide; to be shocked

chocho, -a ['ʃoʃu, a] ADJ hollow, empty; (fraco) weak; (sem graça) dull

chocolate [ʃoko'latʃi] M chocolate

chofer [ʃo'fer] M driver

chofre ['ʃofri] M: **de ~** all of a sudden

chongas ['ʃõgas] (col) PRON zilch, bugger all (!)

chopada [ʃo'pada] F drinking session

chope ['ʃopi] M draught beer

choque¹ ['ʃɔki] M (abalo) shock; (colisão) collision; (Med, Elet) shock; (impacto) impact; (conflito) clash, conflict; **~ cultural** culture shock

choque² ['ʃɔki] VB ver **chocar**

choradeira [ʃora'dejra] F fit of crying

chorado, -a [ʃo'radu, a] ADJ (canto) sad; (gol) hard-won

choramingar [ʃoramĩ'gar] VI to whine, whimper

choramingas [ʃora'mĩgas] M/F INV crybaby

choramingo [ʃora'mĩgu] M whine, whimper

chorão, -rona [ʃo'rãw, rɔna] (pl **-ões/-s**) ADJ tearful ▶ M/F crybaby ▶ M (Bot) weeping willow

chorar [ʃo'rar] VT, VI to weep, cry

chorinho [ʃo'riɲu] M type of Brazilian music

choro ['ʃoru] M crying; (Mús) type of Brazilian music

chorões [ʃo'rõjs] MPL de **chorão**

chorona [ʃo'rɔna] F de **chorão**

choroso, -a [ʃo'rozu, ɔza] ADJ tearful

choupana [ʃo'pana] F shack, hut

chouriço [ʃo'risu] M (BR) black pudding; (PT) spicy sausage

chove não molha [ʃovinãw'mɔʎa] (col) M shilly-shallying

chover [ʃo'ver] VI to rain; **~ a cântaros** to rain cats and dogs; **~am cartas** letters poured in

chuchu [ʃu'ʃu] M chayote (vegetable); **ele fala/ está quente pra ~** (col) he talks a lot/it's really hot

chucrute [ʃu'krutʃi] M sauerkraut

chué [ʃu'ɛ] (col) ADJ lousy

chulé [ʃu'lɛ] M foot odour (BRIT) ou odor (US)

chulear [ʃu'ljar] VT to hem

chulo, -a ['ʃulu, a] ADJ vulgar

chumaço [ʃu'masu] M (de papel, notas) wad; (material) wadding

chumbado, -a [ʃũ'badu, a] (col) ADJ (cansado) dog-tired; (doente) laid out

chumbar [ʃũ'bar] VT to fill with lead; (soldar) to solder; (atirar em) to fire at ▶ VI (PT: reprovar) to fail

chumbo ['ʃũbu] M lead; (de caça) gunshot; (PT: de dente) filling; **sem ~ (gasolina)** unleaded; **esta mala está um ~** this case weighs a ton

chupado, -a [ʃu'padu, a] (col) ADJ (cara, pessoa) drawn

chupar [ʃu'par] VT to suck; (absorver) to absorb

chupeta [ʃu'peta] F (para criança) dummy (BRIT), pacifier (US)

churrascaria [ʃuhaska'ria] F barbecue restaurant

churrasco [ʃu'hasku] M barbecue

churrasqueira [ʃuhas'kejra] F barbecue

churrasquinho [ʃuhas'kiɲu] M kebab

chutar [ʃu'tar] VT to kick; (col: adivinhar) to guess at; (: dar o fora em) to dump ▶ VI to kick; to guess; (col: mentir) to lie

chute ['ʃutʃi] M kick; (para o gol) shot; (col: mentira) lie; **dar o ~ em alguém** (col) to give sb the boot

chuteira [ʃu'tejra] F football boot; **pendurar as ~s** (col) to retire

chuva ['ʃuva] F rain; **tomar ~** to get caught in the rain; **estar na ~** (fig) to be drunk; **~ de pedra** hailstorm

chuvarada [ʃuva'rada] F torrential rain

chuveirada [ʃuvej'rada] F shower

chuveiro [ʃu'vejru] M shower

chuviscar [ʃuvis'kar] VI to drizzle

chuvisco [ʃu'visku] M drizzle

chuvoso, -a [ʃu'vozu, ɔza] ADJ rainy

CI (BR) ABR F (= carteira de identidade) identity card; ver tb **carteira**

CIA (BR) ABR F (= Central Intelligence Agency) CIA

Cia. ABR (= companhia) Co

ciberataque [sibera'taki] M cyber attack

cibercafé [siberka'fɛ] M cybercafé

ciberespaço [siberis'pasu] M cyberspace

cibernética [siber'nɛtʃika] F cybernetics sg

cibersegurança [sibersegu'rãsa] F cybersecurity

CIC (BR) ABR M = **Cartão de Identificação do Contribuinte**

cica ['sika] F sharpness

cicatriz [sika'triz] F scar

cicatrização [sikatriza'sãw] F scarring

cicatrizar [sikatri'zar] VT (rosto) to scar; (ferida) to heal; (fig) to cure, heal ▶ VI to heal; (rosto) to scar

cicerone [sise'rɔni] M tourist guide

ciciar [si'sjar] VI to whisper; (rumorejar) to murmur

cíclico, -a ['sikliku, a] ADJ cyclical

ciclismo [si'klizmu] M cycling

ciclista [si'klista] M/F cyclist

ciclo ['siklu] M cycle; **~ básico** foundation year

ciclone [si'klɔni] M cyclone

ciclovia [siklo'via] F cycle path

cidadã [sida'dã] F de **cidadão**

cidadania [sidada'nia] F citizenship

cidadão, cidadã [sida'dãw] (pl **-s/-s**) M/F citizen

cidade [si'dadʒi] F town; (grande) city

cidadela [sida'dɛla] F citadel

cidra ['sidra] F citron

CIE (BR) ABR M = **Centro de Informações do Exército**

ciência ['sjẽsja] F science; (erudição) knowledge; **~s humanas/socias** business studies/social sciences

ciente ['sjẽtʃi] ADJ aware

científico, -a [sjẽ'tʃifiku, a] ADJ scientific

cientista [sjẽ'tʃista] M/F scientist

CIEP (BR) ABR M (= Centro Integrado de Educação Popular) combined school and community centre

cifra ['sifra] F (escrita secreta) cipher; (algarismo) number, figure; (total) sum

cifrão [si'frãw] (pl **-ões**) M money sign

cifrar [si'frar] VT to write in code

cifrões [si'frõjs] MPL de **cifrão**

cigano, -a [si'ganu, a] ADJ, M/F gypsy

cigarra [si'gaha] F cicada; (Elet) buzzer

cigarreira [siga'hejra] F (estojo) cigarette case

cigarrilha [siga'hiʎa] F cheroot

cigarro [si'gahu] M cigarette

cilada [si'lada] F (emboscada) ambush; (armadilha) trap; (embuste) trick

cilíndrico, -a [si'lĩdriku, a] ADJ cylindrical

cilindro [si'lĩdru] M cylinder; (rolo) roller

cílio ['silju] M eyelash

cima ['sima] F: **de ~ para baixo** from top to bottom; **para ~** up; **em ~ de** on, on top of; **por ~ de** over; **de ~** from above; **lá em ~** up there; (em casa) upstairs; **ainda por ~** on top of that; **estar por ~** to be better off; **dar em ~ de alguém** (col) to be after sb; **tudo em ~?** (col) how's it going?

cimeira [si'mejra] (PT) F summit

cimentar [simẽ'tar] VT to cement

cimento [si'mẽtu] M cement; (chão) concrete floor; (fig) foundation; **~ armado** reinforced concrete

cimo ['simu] M top, summit

cinco ['sĩku] NUM five; **somos ~** there are five of us; **ela tem ~ anos** she is five (years old); **aos ~ anos (de idade)** at the age of five; **são ~ horas** it's five o'clock; **às ~ (horas)** at five (o'clock); **hoje é dia ~ de julho** today is the fifth of July; **no dia ~ de julho** on the fifth of July, on July the fifth; **eles moram no número ~/na Barata Ribeiro número ~** they live at number five/number five Barata Ribeiro Street; **~ e um quarto/meio** five and a quarter/a half

Cindacta [sĩ'dakta] (BR) ABR M = **Centro Integrado de Defesa Aérea e Controle de Tráfego Aéreo**

cindir [sĩ'dʒir] VT to split; (cortar) to cut

cineasta [sine'asta] M/F film maker

cinegrafista [sinegra'fista] M/F cameraman/woman

cinema [si'nɛma] F cinema

cinematográfico, -a [sinemato'grafiku, a] ADJ cinematographic

Cingapura [sĩga'pura] F Singapore

cingir [sĩ'ʒir] VT (pôr à cintura) to fasten round one's waist; (prender em volta) to tie round; (cercar) to encircle, ring; (coroa, espada) to put on; **cingir-se** VR: **~-se a** (restringir-se) to restrict o.s. to

cínico, -a ['siniku, a] ADJ cynical ▶ M/F cynic

cinismo [si'nizmu] M cynicism

cinjo etc ['sĩʒu] VB ver **cingir**

cinquenta [sĩ'kwẽta] NUM fifty; **umas ~ pessoas** about fifty people; **ele tem uns ~ anos** he's about fifty; **ele está na casa dos ~ anos** he's in his fifties; **nos anos ~** in the fifties; **ir a ~** (Auto) to do fifty (km/h)

cinquentão, -tona [sĩkwẽ'tãw, 'tona] (pl **-tões/-s**) M/F person in his/her fifties ▶ ADJ in his/her fifties

cinta ['sĩta] F (faixa) sash; (de mulher) girdle

cintado, -a [sĩ'tadu, a] ADJ gathered at the waist

cintilante [sĩtʃi'lãtʃi] ADJ sparkling

cintilar [sĩtʃi'lar] VI to sparkle, glitter

cinto ['sĩtu] M belt; **~ de segurança** safety belt; (Auto) seat belt

cintura [sĩ'tura] F waist; (linha) waistline

cinturão [sĩtu'rãw] (pl **-ões**) M belt; **~ verde** green belt

cinza ['sĩza] ADJ INV grey (BRIT), gray (US) ▶ F ash, ashes pl

cinzeiro [sĩ'zejru] M ashtray

cinzel [sĩ'zɛw] (pl **-éis**) M chisel

cinzelar [sĩze'lar] VT to chisel; (gravar) to carve, engrave

cinzento, -a [sĩ'zẽtu, a] ADJ grey (BRIT), gray (US)

cio [siu] M mating season; **no ~** on heat, in season

cioso, -a ['sjozu, ɔza] ADJ conscientious

CIP (BR) ABR M = **Conselho Interministerial de Preços**

cipreste [si'prɛstʃi] M cypress (tree)

cipriota [si'prjɔta] ADJ, M/F Cypriot

circense [sir'sẽsi] ADJ circus atr

circo ['sirku] M circus

circuito [sir'kwitu] M circuit

circulação [sirkula'sãw] F circulation

circular [sirku'lar] ADJ circular, round ▶ F (carta) circular ▶ VI to circulate; (girar, andar) to go round ▶ VT to circulate; (estar em volta de) to surround; (percorrer em roda) to go round

círculo ['sirkulu] M circle

circunavegar [sirkunave'gar] VT to circumnavigate, sail round

circuncidar [sirkũsi'dar] VT to circumcise

circuncisão [sirkũsi'zãw] F circumcision

circundante [sirkũ'dãtʃi] ADJ surrounding

circundar [sirkũ'dar] VT to surround

circunferência [sirkũfe'rẽsja] F circumference

circunflexo, -a [sirkũ'flɛksu, a] ADJ circumflex ▶ M circumflex (accent)
circunlóquio [sirkũ'lɔkju] M circumlocution
circunscrever [sirkũskre'ver] VT to circumscribe, limit; (*epidemia*) to contain; (*abranger*) to cover; **circunscrever-se** VR to be limited
circunscrição [sirkũskri'sãw] (*pl* -ões) F district; ~ **eleitoral** constituency
circunscrito, -a [sirkũs'kritu, a] PP *de* **circunscrever**
circunspecção [sirkũspe'sãw] F seriousness
circunspeto, -a [sirkũ'spɛtu, a] ADJ serious
circunstância [sirkũ'stãsja] F circumstance; ~**s atenuantes** mitigating circumstances
circunstanciado, -a [sirkũstã'sjadu, a] ADJ detailed
circunstancial [sirkũstã'sjaw] (*pl* -ais) ADJ circumstantial
circunstante [sirkũ'stãtʃi] M/F onlooker, bystander; **circunstantes** MPL (*audiência*) audience *sg*
cirrose [si'hɔzi] F cirrhosis
cirurgia [sirur'ʒia] F surgery; ~ **plástica/ estética** plastic/cosmetic surgery
cirurgião, -giã [sirur'ʒjãw, 'ʒjã] (*pl* -ões/-s) M/F surgeon
cirúrgico, -a [si'rurʒiku, a] ADJ surgical
cirurgiões [sirur'ʒjõjs] MPL *de* **cirurgião**
cirzo *etc* ['sihzu] VB *ver* **cerzir**
cisão [si'zãw] (*pl* -ões) F (*divisão*) split, division; (*desacordo*) disagreement
cisco ['sisku] M speck
cisma ['sizma] M schism ▶ F (*mania*) silly idea; (*suspeita*) suspicion; (*antipatia*) dislike; (*devaneio*) dream
cismado, -a [siz'madu, a] ADJ with fixed ideas
cismar [siz'mar] VI (*pensar*): ~ **em** to brood over; (*antipatizar*): ~ **com** to take a dislike to ▶ VT: ~ **que** to be convinced that; ~ **de** *ou* **em fazer** (*meter na cabeça*) to get into one's head to do; (*insistir*) to insist on doing
cisne ['sizni] M swan
cisões [si'zõjs] FPL *de* **cisão**
cisterna [sis'tɛrna] F cistern, tank
cistite [sis'tʃitʃi] F cystitis
citação [sita'sãw] (*pl* -ões) F quotation; (*Jur*) summons *sg*
citadino, -a [sita'dʒinu, a] ADJ town *atr*
citar [si'tar] VT to quote; (*Jur*) to summon
cítrico, -a ['sitriku, a] ADJ (*fruta*) citrus; (*ácido*) citric
ciumada [sju'mada] F fit of jealousy
ciúme ['sjumi] M jealousy; **ter ~s de** to be jealous of
ciumeira [sju'mejra] (*col*) F = **ciumada**
ciumento, -a [sju'mẽtu, a] ADJ jealous
cívico, -a ['siviku, a] ADJ civic
civil [si'viw] (*pl* -is) ADJ civil ▶ M/F civilian
civilidade [sivili'dadʒi] F politeness
civilização [siviliza'sãw] (*pl* -ões) F civilization
civilizador, a [siviliza'dor(a)] ADJ civilizing

civilizar [sivili'zar] VT to civilize
civis [si'vis] PL *de* **civil**
civismo [si'vizmu] M public spirit
clamar [kla'mar] VT to clamour (*BRIT*) *ou* clamor (*US*) for ▶ VI to cry out, clamo(u)r
clamor [kla'mor] M outcry, uproar
clamoroso, -a [klamo'rozu, ɔza] ADJ noisy
clandestino, -a [klãdes'tʃinu, a] ADJ clandestine; (*ilegal*) underground
clara ['klara] F egg white
claraboia [klara'bɔja] F skylight
clarão [kla'rãw] (*pl* -ões) M (*cintilação*) flash; (*claridade*) gleam
clarear [kla'rjar] VI (*dia*) to dawn; (*tempo*) to clear up, brighten up ▶ VT to clarify
clareira [kla'rejra] F (*na mata*) clearing
clareza [kla'reza] F clarity
claridade [klari'dadʒi] F (*luz*) brightness
clarim [kla'rĩ] (*pl* -ns) M bugle
clarinete [klari'netʃi] M clarinet
clarinetista [klarine'tʃista] M/F clarinet player
clarins [kla'rĩs] MPL *de* **clarim**
clarividente [klarivi'dẽtʃi] ADJ (*prudente*) far-sighted, prudent
claro, -a ['klaru, a] ADJ clear; (*luminoso*) bright; (*cor*) light; (*evidente*) clear, evident ▶ M (*na escrita*) space; (*clareira*) clearing ▶ ADV clearly; ~! of course!; ~ **que sim!/não!** of course!/of course not!; **às claras** openly; (*publicamente*) publicly; **dia ~** daylight; **passar a noite em ~** not to sleep a wink all night; ~ **como água** crystal clear
clarões [kla'rõjs] MPL *de* **clarão**
classe ['klasi] F class; ~ **média/operária** middle/working class; ~ **econômica/ executiva** economy/business class
clássico, -a ['klasiku, a] ADJ classical; (*fig*) classic; (*habitual*) usual ▶ M classic
classificação [klasifika'sãw] (*pl* -ões) F classification; (*Esporte*) place, placing
classificado, -a [klasifi'kadu, a] ADJ (*em exame*) successful; (*anúncio*) classified; (*Esporte*) placed, qualified ▶ M (*anúncio*) classified ad
classificar [klasifi'kar] VT to classify; **classificar-se** VR: ~**-se de algo** to call o.s. sth, describe o.s. as sth
classificatório, -a [klasifika'tɔrju, a] ADJ qualifying
classudo, -a [kla'sudu, a] (*col*) ADJ classy
claudicar [klawdʒi'kar] VI (*mancar*) to limp; (*errar*) to err
claustro ['klawstru] M cloister
claustrofobia [klawstrofo'bia] F claustrophobia
claustrofóbico, -a [klawstro'fɔbiku, a] ADJ claustrophobic
cláusula ['klawzula] F clause
clausura [klaw'zura] F (*recinto*) enclosure; (*vida*) cloistered existence
clave ['klavi] F (*Mús*) clef
clavícula [kla'vikula] F collar bone
clemência [kle'mẽsja] F mercy

clemente [kleˈmẽtʃi] ADJ merciful
cleptomaníaco, -a [kleptomaˈniaku, a] M/F
kleptomaniac
clérigo [ˈklɛrigu] M clergyman
clero [ˈklɛru] M clergy
clicar [kliˈkar] VI (Comput) to click; ~ **duas**
vezes em to double-click on
clichê [kliˈʃe] M (Foto) plate; (chavão) cliché
cliente [ˈkljẽtʃi] M client; (de loja) customer;
(de médico) patient
clientela [kljẽˈtela] F clientele; (de loja)
customers pl; (de médico) patients pl
clima [ˈklima] M climate
climático, -a [kliˈmatʃiku, a] ADJ climatic
clímax [ˈklimaks] M INV climax
clínica [ˈklinika] F clinic; ~ **geral** general
practice; ver tb **clínico**
clinicar [kliniˈkar] VI to have a practice
clínico, -a [ˈkliniku, a] ADJ clinical ▶ M/F
doctor; ~ **geral** general practitioner, GP
clipe [ˈklipi] M clip; (para papéis) paper clip
clique [ˈkliki] M (Comput) click
clitóris [kliˈtɔris] M INV clitoris
clone [ˈkloni] M clone
clorar [kloˈrar] VT to chlorinate
cloro [ˈkloru] M chlorine
clorofórmio [kloroˈfɔrmju] M chloroform
close [ˈklozi] M close-up
clube [ˈklubi] M club
CMB ABR F (= Casa da Moeda do Brasil) Brazilian
National Mint
CMN (BR) ABR M = **Conselho Monetário**
Nacional
CNA ABR M (= Congresso Nacional Africano) ANC;
(BR) = **Conselho Nacional do Álcool**
CNB (BR) ABR M = **Conselho Nacional da**
Borracha
CNBB ABR F = **Confederação Nacional dos**
Bispos do Brasil
CNBV (BR) ABR M = **Comissão Nacional da**
Bolsa de Valores
CND (BR) ABR M = **Conselho Nacional de**
Desportos
CNDC (BR) ABR M = **Conselho Nacional de**
Defesa ao Consumidor
CNDM (BR) ABR M = **Conselho Nacional dos**
Direitos da Mulher
CNDU (BR) ABR M = **Conselho Nacional de**
Desenvolvimento Urbano
CNEN (BR) ABR F (= Comissão Nacional de Energia
Nuclear) ≈ AEA (BRIT), ≈ AEC (US)
CNPq (BR) ABR M (= Conselho Nacional de
Desenvolvimento Científico e Tecnológico)
organization supporting higher education
CNS (BR) ABR M = **Conselho Nacional de**
Saúde
CNT (BR) ABR M = **Conselho Nacional de**
Transportes
CNV (BR) ABR M = **Cadastro Nacional de**
Veículos
coabitar [koabiˈtar] VI to live together,
cohabit
coação [koaˈsãw] F coercion

coadjuvante [koadʒuˈvãtʃi] ADJ supporting
▶ M/F (num crime) accomplice; (Teatro, Cinema)
co-star
coadjuvar [koadʒuˈvar] VT to aid; (Teatro,
Cinema) to support
coador [koaˈdor] M strainer; (de café) filter
bag; (para legumes) colander
coadunar [koaduˈnar] VT to combine;
coadunar-se VR to combine
coagir [koaˈʒir] VT to coerce, compel
coagular [koaguˈlar] VT, VI to coagulate;
(sangue) to clot; **coagular-se** VR to congeal
coágulo [koˈagulu] M clot
coajo etc [koˈaʒu] VB ver **coagir**
coalhada [koaˈʎada] F curd
coalhado, -a [koaˈʎadu, a] ADJ curdled; ~ **de**
gente packed
coalhar [koaˈʎar] VT, VI (leite) to curdle;
coalhar-se VR to curdle
coalizão [koaliˈzãw] (pl **-ões**) F coalition
coar [koˈar] VT (líquido) to strain
coautor, a [koawˈtor(a)] M/F (de livro)
co-author; (de crime) accomplice
coaxar [koaˈʃar] VI to croak ▶ M croaking
COB ABR M = **Comité Olímpico Brasileiro**
cobaia [koˈbaja] F guinea pig
cobalto [koˈbawtu] M cobalt
coberta [koˈbɛrta] F cover, covering; (Náut)
deck
coberto, -a [koˈbɛrtu, a] PP de **cobrir** ▶ ADJ
covered
cobertor [koberˈtor] M blanket
cobertura [koberˈtura] F covering; (telhado)
roof; (apartamento) penthouse; (TV, Rádio,
Jornalismo) coverage; (Seguros) cover; (Tel)
network coverage; **aqui não tem ~** there's
no network coverage here
cobiça [koˈbisa] F greed
cobiçar [kobiˈsar] VT to covet
cobiçoso, -a [kobiˈsozu, ɔza] ADJ covetous
cobra [ˈkɔbra] F snake ▶ M/F (col) expert ▶ ADJ
(col) expert; **dizer ~s e lagartos de alguém**
to say bad things about sb
cobrador, a [kobraˈdor(a)] M/F collector; (em
transporte) conductor; ~ **de ônibus** bus
conductor; ~ **de impostos** tax collector
cobrança [koˈbrãsa] F collection; (ato de cobrar)
charging; ~ **de pênalti/falta** penalty/free
kick
cobrar [koˈbrar] VT to collect; (preço) to charge;
(pênalti) to take; ~ **o prometido** to remind sb
of what they promised; ~ **uma falta** (Futebol)
to take a free kick
cobre [ˈkɔbri] M copper; **cobres** MPL (dinheiro)
money sg
cobrir [koˈbrir] VT to cover; **cobrir-se** VR to
cover o.s.
coca [ˈkɔka] F (arbusto) coca bush
coça [ˈkɔsa] (col) F wallop
cocada [koˈkada] F coconut sweet
cocaína [kokaˈina] F cocaine
coçar [koˈsar] VT to scratch ▶ VI (comichar) to
itch; **coçar-se** VR to scratch o.s.; **não ter**

tempo nem para se ~ to have no time to breathe

cócegas ['kɔsegas] FPL: **fazer ~ em** to tickle; **tenho ~ nos pés** I have tickly feet; **sentir ~** to be ticklish; **estar em ~ para fazer** to be itching to do

coceira [ko'sejra] F itch; (*qualidade*) itchiness

cocheira [ko'ʃejra] F stable

cochichar [koʃi'ʃar] VI to whisper

cochicho [ko'ʃiʃu] M whispering

cochilada [koʃi'lada] F snooze; **dar uma ~** to have a snooze

cochilar [koʃi'lar] VI to snooze, doze

cochilo [ko'ʃilu] M nap

coco ['koku] M coconut

cocô [ko'ko] (*col*) M pooh

cócoras ['kɔkoras] FPL: **de ~** squatting; **ficar de ~** to squat (down)

cocoricar [kokori'kar] VI to crow

cocuruto [koku'rutu] M top

côdea ['kodʒja] F crust

codeína [kode'ina] F codeine

Codici [kodʒi'si] (*BR*) ABR F = **Comissão de Defesa dos Direitos do Cidadão**

codificar [kodʒifi'kar] VT (*leis*) to codify; (*mensagem*) to encode, code

código ['kɔdʒigu] M code; **~ de barras** bar code; **~ de ética profissional** code of practice

codinome [kodʒi'nɔmi] M code name

codorna [ko'dɔrna] F quail

coeditar [koedʒi'tar] VT to co-publish

coeficiente [koefi'sjẽtʃi] M (*Mat*) coefficient; (*fig*) factor

coelho [ko'eʎu] M rabbit; **matar dois ~s de uma cajadada só** (*fig*) to kill two birds with one stone

coentro [ko'ẽtru] M coriander

coerção [koer'sãw] F coercion

coerência [koe'rẽsja] F coherence; (*consequência*) consistency

coerente [koe'rẽtʃi] ADJ coherent; (*consequente*) consistent

coesão [koe'zãw] F cohesion

coeso, -a ['kwɛzu, a] ADJ cohesive

coexistência [koezis'tẽsja] F coexistence

coexistir [koezis'tʃir] VI to coexist

Cofie (*BR*) ABR F = **Comissão de Fusão e Incorporação de Empresas**

cofre ['kɔfri] M safe; (*caixa*) strongbox; **os ~s públicos** public funds

cogitação [koʒita'sãw] F contemplation; **estar fora de ~** to be out of the question

cogitar [koʒi'tar] VT, VI to contemplate

cognitivo, -a [kogni'tʃivu, a] ADJ cognitive

cognominar [kognomi'nar] VT to nickname

cogumelo [kogu'mɛlu] M mushroom; **~ venenoso** toadstool

COHAB (*BR*) ABR F = **Companhia de Habitação Popular**

coibição [koibi'sãw] (*pl* **-ões**) F restraint, restriction

coibir [koi'bir] VT to restrain; **coibir-se** VR: **~-se de** to abstain from; **~ de** to restrain from

coice ['kojsi] M kick; (*de arma*) recoil; **dar ~s em** to kick; (*fig*) to be aggressive with

coincidência [koĩsi'dẽsja] F coincidence

coincidir [koĩsi'dʒir] VI to coincide; (*concordar*) to agree

coisa ['kojza] F thing; (*assunto*) matter; **coisas** FPL (*objetos*) things; (*col: órgãos genitais*) privates; **~ de** about; **ser uma ~** (*col*) to be really something; (*ruim*) to be terrible; **que ~!** gosh!; **não dizer ~ com ~** not to make any sense; **deu uma ~ nele** something strange got into him

coisíssima [koj'zisima] F: **~ nenhuma** (*nada*) nothing; (*de modo algum*) not at all

coitado, -a [koj'tadu, a] ADJ poor, wretched; **~!** poor thing!; **~ do João** poor John

coito ['kojtu] M intercourse, coitus

cola ['kɔla] F glue; (*BR: cópia*) crib

colaboração [kolabora'sãw] (*pl* **-ões**) F collaboration; (*num jornal etc*) contribution

colaborador, a [kolabora'dor(a)] M/F collaborator; (*em jornal*) contributor

colaborar [kolabo'rar] VI to collaborate; (*ajudar*) to help; (*escrever artigos etc*) to contribute

colagem [ko'laʒẽ] F collage

colante [ko'lãtʃi] ADJ (*roupa*) skin-tight

colapso [ko'lapsu] M collapse; **~ cardíaco** heart failure

colar [ko'lar] VT to stick, glue; (*BR: copiar*) to crib ▶ VI to stick; to cheat; (*col: ser acreditado*) to stand up, stick ▶ M necklace; **~ grau** to graduate

colarinho [kola'riɲu] M collar; (*col: na cerveja*) head

colarinho-branco (*pl* **colarinhos-brancos**) M white-collar worker

colateral [kolate'raw] (*pl* **-ais**) ADJ: **efeito ~** side effect

colcha ['kowʃa] F bedspread

colchão [kow'ʃãw] (*pl* **-ões**) M mattress

colcheia [kow'ʃeja] F (*Mús*) quaver

colchete [kow'ʃetʃi] M clasp, fastening; (*parêntese*) square bracket; **~ de gancho** hook and eye; **~ de pressão** press stud, popper

colchões [kow'ʃõjs] MPL *de* **colchão**

colchonete [kowʃo'nɛtʃi] M (*portable*) mattress

coleção [kole'sãw] (*pl* **-ões**) F collection

colecionador, a [kolesjona'dor(a)] M/F collector

colecionar [kolesjo'nar] VT to collect

coleções [kole'sõjs] FPL *de* **coleção**

colega [ko'lɛga] M/F (*de trabalho*) colleague; (*de escola*) classmate; (*amigo*) friend

colegial [kole'ʒjaw] (*pl* **-ais**) ADJ school atr ▶ M/F schoolboy/girl

colégio [ko'lɛʒu] M school; **~ eleitoral** electoral college

coleguismo [kole'gizmu] M loyalty to one's colleagues

coleira [ko'lejra] F collar

cólera ['kɔlera] F (ira) anger; (fúria) rage ▶ M ou F (Med) cholera

colérico, -a [ko'lɛriku, a] ADJ (irado) angry; (furioso) furious ▶ M/F (Med) cholera patient

colesterol [koleste'rɔw] M cholesterol

coleta [ko'lɛta] F collection; (imposto) levy

coletânea [kole'tanja] F collection

coletar [kole'tar] VT to tax; (arrecadar) to collect

colete [ko'letʃi] M waistcoat (BRIT), vest (US); ~ **salva-vidas** life jacket (BRIT), life preserver (US)

coletividade [koletʃivi'dadʒi] F community

coletivo, -a [kole'tʃivu, a] ADJ collective; (transportes) public ▶ M bus

coletor, a [kole'tor(a)] M/F collector

coletoria [koleto'ria] F tax office

colheita [ko'ʎejta] F harvest; (produto) crop

colher [ko'ʎer] VT (recolher) to gather, pick; (dados) to gather ▶ F spoon; ~ **de chá/sopa** teaspoon/tablespoon; **dar uma ~ de chá a alguém** (fig) to do sb a favo(u)r; **de ~** (col) on a silver platter

colherada [koʎe'rada] F spoonful

colibri [koli'bri] M hummingbird

cólica ['kɔlika] F colic

colidir [koli'dʒir] VI: ~ **com** to collide with, crash into

coligação [koliga'sãw] (pl -**ões**) F coalition

coligar [koli'gar] VT to bring together, unite; **coligar-se** VR to join forces

coligir [koli'ʒir] VT to collect

colina [ko'lina] F hill

colírio [ko'lirju] M eyewash

colisão [koli'zãw] (pl -**ões**) F collision

colis postaux [ko'li pos'to] MPL small packets

colite [ko'litʃi] F colitis

collant [ko'lã] (pl -**s**) M tights pl (BRIT), pantihose (US); (blusa) leotard

colmeia [kow'meja] F beehive

colo ['kɔlu] M neck; (regaço) lap; **no ~** on one's lap, in one's arms

colocação [koloka'sãw] (pl -**ões**) F placing; (emprego) job, position; (de pneus, tapete etc) fitting; (de uma questão, ideia) positing; (opinião) position

colocar [kolo'kar] VT to put, place; (empregar) to find a job for, place; (Com) to market; (pneus, tapetes) to fit; (questão, ideia) to put forward, state; **colocar-se** VR to place o.s.; **coloque-se no meu lugar** put yourself in my position

Colômbia [ko'lõbja] F: **a ~** Colombia

colombiano, -a [kolõ'bjanu, a] ADJ, M/F Colombian

cólon ['kɔlõ] M colon

colônia [ko'lonja] F colony; (perfume) cologne

colonial [kolo'njaw] (pl -**ais**) ADJ colonial

colonialismo [kolonja'lizmu] M colonialism

colonização [koloniza'sãw] F colonization

colonizador, a [koloniza'dor(a)] ADJ colonizing ▶ M/F colonist, settler

colonizar [koloni'zar] VT to colonize

colono, -a [ko'lɔnu, a] M/F settler; (cultivador) tenant farmer

coloquei etc [kolo'kej] VB ver **colocar**

coloquial [kolo'kjaw] (pl -**ais**) ADJ colloquial

colóquio [ko'lɔkju] M conversation; (congresso) conference

coloração [kolora'sãw] F colouration (BRIT), coloration (US)

colorido, -a [kolo'ridu, a] ADJ colourful (BRIT), colorful (US) ▶ M colouring (BRIT), coloring (US)

colorir [kolo'rir] VT to colour (BRIT), color (US)

colossal [kolo'saw] (pl -**ais**) ADJ colossal

colosso [ko'losu] M (pessoa) giant; (coisa) extraordinary thing

coluna [ko'luna] F column; (pilar) pillar; ~ **dorsal** ou **vertebral** spine

colunável [kolu'navew] (pl -**eis**) ADJ famous ▶ M/F celebrity

colunista [kolu'nista] M/F columnist

com [kõ] PREP with; **estar ~ fome** to be hungry; ~ **cuidado** carefully; **estar ~ dinheiro/câncer** to have some money on one/have cancer; **"não ultrapasse ~ faixa contínua"** "do not overtake when centre line is unbroken"

coma ['kɔma] F coma

comadre [ko'madri] F (urinol) bedpan; **minha ~** the godmother of my child (ou the mother of my godchild)

comandante [komã'dãtʃi] M commander; (Mil) commandant; (Náut) captain

comandar [komã'dar] VT to command

comando [ko'mãdu] M command

combate [kõ'batʃi] M combat, fight; (fig) battle

combatente [kõba'tẽtʃi] M/F combatant

combater [kõba'ter] VT to fight, combat; (opor-se a) to oppose ▶ VI to fight; **combater-se** VR to fight

combinação [kõbina'sãw] (pl -**ões**) F combination; (Quím) compound; (acordo) arrangement; (plano) scheme; (roupa) slip

combinar [kõbi'nar] VT to combine; (jantar etc) to arrange; (fuga etc) to plan ▶ VI (roupas etc) to go together; **combinar-se** VR to combine; (pessoas) to get on well together; (temperamentos) to go well together; ~ **com** (harmonizar-se) to go with; ~ **de fazer** to arrange to do; **combinado!** agreed!

comboio [kõ'boju] M (PT) train; (de navios, carros) convoy

combustão [kõbus'tãw] (pl -**ões**) F combustion

combustível [kõbus'tʃivew] M fuel

combustões [kõbus'tõjs] FPL de **combustão**

começar [kome'sar] VT, VI to begin, start; ~ **a fazer** to begin ou start to do

começo¹ [ko'mesu] M beginning, start

começo² VB ver **comedir-se**

comédia [ko'mɛdʒja] F comedy

comediante [kome'dʒjãtʃi] M/F (comic) actor/actress

comedido, -a [kome'dʒidu, a] ADJ moderate; (prudente) prudent

comedir-se [kome'dʒirsi] VR to control o.s.
comedorias [komedo'rias] FPL food sg
comemoração [komemora'sãw] (pl **-ões**) F commemoration
comemorar [komemo'rar] VT to commemorate; (celebrar: sucesso etc) to celebrate
comemorativo, -a [komemora'tʃivu, a] ADJ commemorative
comensal [komẽ'saw] (pl **-ais**) M/F diner
comentar [komẽ'tar] VT to comment on; (maliciosamente) to make comments about
comentário [komẽ'tarju] M comment, remark; (análise) commentary; **sem ~** no comment
comentarista [komẽta'rista] M/F commentator
comer [ko'mer] VT to eat; (Damas, Xadrez) to take, capture; (dinheiro) to eat up; (corroer) to eat away ▶ VI to eat; **comer-se** VR: **~-se (de)** to be consumed (with); **dar de ~ a** to feed; **~ por quatro** (fig) to eat like a horse; **~ fogo** (col) to go through hell
comercial [komer'sjaw] (pl **-ais**) ADJ commercial; (relativo ao negócio) business atr ▶ M commercial
comercialização [komersjaliza'sãw] F marketing
comercializar [komersjali'zar] VT to market
comercializável [komersjali'zavew] (pl **-eis**) ADJ marketable
comerciante [komer'sjãtʃi] M/F trader
comerciar [komer'sjar] VI to trade, do business
comerciário, -a [komer'sjarju, a] M/F employee in business
comércio [ko'mɛrsju] M commerce; (tráfico) trade; (negócio) business; (lojas) shops pl; **de fechar o ~** (col) really stunning; **~ eletrônico** e-commerce; **~ justo** fair trade
comes ['kɔmis] MPL: **~ e bebes** food and drink
comestíveis [komes'tʃiveis] MPL foodstuffs, food sg
comestível [komes'tʃivew] (pl **-eis**) ADJ edible
cometa [ko'meta] M comet
cometer [kome'ter] VT to commit
cometimento [kometʃi'mẽtu] M undertaking, commitment
comichão [komi'ʃãw] F itch, itching
comichar [komi'ʃar] VT, VI to itch
comicidade [komisi'dadʒi] F comic quality
comício [ko'misju] M (Pol) rally, meeting; (assembleia) assembly
cômico, -a ['komiku, a] ADJ comic(al) ▶ M comedian; (de teatro) actor
comida [ko'mida] F (alimento) food; (refeição) meal; **~ caseira** home cooking; **~ pronta** ready meal (BRIT), TV dinner (US)
comigo [ko'migu] PRON with me; (reflexivo) with myself
comilança [komi'lãsa] F overeating

comilão, -lona [komi'lãw, 'lɔna] (pl **-ões/-s**) ADJ greedy ▶ M/F glutton
cominho [ko'miɲu] M cumin
comiserar [komize'rar] VT to move to pity; **comiserar-se** VR: **~-se (de)** to sympathize (with)
comissão [komi'sãw] (pl **-ões**) F commission; (comitê) committee
comissário [komi'sarju] M commissioner; (Com) agent; **~ de bordo** (Aer) steward; (Náut) purser
comissionar [komisjo'nar] VT to commission
comissões [komi'sõjs] FPL de **comissão**
comitê [komi'te] M committee
comitiva [komi'tʃiva] F entourage

(PALAVRA-CHAVE)

como ['kɔmu] ADV **1** (modo) as; **ela fez como eu pedi** she did as I asked; **como se** as if; **como quiser** as you wish; **seja como for** be that as it may
2 (assim como) like; **ela tem olhos azuis como o pai** she has blue eyes like her father's; **ela trabalha numa loja, como a mãe** she works in a shop, as does her mother
3 (de que maneira) how; **como?** pardon?; **como!** what!; **como assim?** what do you mean?; **como não!** of course!
▶ CONJ (porque) as, since; **como estava tarde ele dormiu aqui** since it was late he slept here

comoção [komo'sãw] (pl **-ões**) F (abalo) distress; (revolta) commotion
cômoda ['komoda] F chest of drawers (BRIT), bureau (US)
comodidade [komodʒi'dadʒi] F (conforto) comfort; (conveniência) convenience
comodismo [komo'dʒizmu] M complacency
comodista [komo'dʒista] ADJ complacent
cômodo, -a ['komodu, a] ADJ (confortável) comfortable; (conveniente) convenient ▶ M (aposento) room
comovedor, a [komove'dor(a)] ADJ moving, touching
comovente [komo'vẽtʃi] ADJ moving, touching
comover [komo'ver] VT to move ▶ VI to be moving; **comover-se** VR to be moved
comovido, -a [komo'vidu, a] ADJ moved
compacto, -a [kõ'paktu, a] ADJ (pequeno) compact; (espesso) thick; (sólido) solid ▶ M (disco) single
compadecer-se [kõpade'sersi] VR: **~ de** to pity
compadecido, -a [kõpade'sidu, a] ADJ sympathetic
compadecimento [kõpadesi'mẽtu] M sympathy; (piedade) pity
compadre [kõ'padri] M (col: companheiro) buddy, pal, crony; **meu ~** the godfather of my child (ou the father of my godchild)

compaixão [kõpaj'ʃãw] M (*piedade*) compassion, pity; (*misericórdia*) mercy

companheirão, -rona [kõpaɲej'rãw, 'rɔna] (*pl* **-ões/-s**) M/F good friend

companheirismo [kõpaɲej'rizmu] M companionship

companheiro, -a [kõpa'ɲejru, a] M/F companion; (*colega*) friend; (*col*) buddy, mate; **~ de viagem** fellow traveller (BRIT) *ou* traveler (US), travelling (BRIT) *ou* traveling (US) companion

companheirões [kõpaɲej'rõjs] MPL *de* **companheirão**

companheirona [kõpaɲej'rɔna] F *de* **companheirão**

companhia [kõpa'ɲia] F (*Com*) company, firm; (*convivência*) company; **fazer ~ a alguém** to keep sb company; **em ~ de** accompanied by; **dama de ~** companion

comparação [kõpara'sãw] (*pl* **-ões**) F comparison

comparar [kõpa'rar] VT to compare; **comparar-se** VR: **~-se com** to bear comparison with; **~ com** to compare with; **~ a** to liken to

comparativo, -a [kõpara'tʃivu, a] ADJ comparative

comparável [kõpa'ravew] (*pl* **-eis**) ADJ comparable

comparecer [kõpare'ser] VI to appear, make an appearance; **~ a uma reunião** to attend a meeting

comparecimento [kõparesi'mẽtu] M (*presença*) attendance

comparsa [kõ'parsa] M/F (*Teatro*) extra; (*cúmplice*) accomplice

compartilhar [kõpartʃi'ʎar] VT (*partilhar*) to share ▶ VI: **~ de** (*participar de*) to share in, participate in; **~ com alguém** to share with sb

compartimentar [kõpartʃimẽ'tar] VT to compartmentalize

compartimento [kõpartʃi'mẽtu] M compartment; (*aposento*) room

compartir [kõpar'tʃir] VT (*dividir*) to share out ▶ VI: **~ de** to share in

compassado, -a [kõpa'sadu, a] ADJ (*medido*) measured; (*moderado*) moderate; (*cadenciado*) regular; (*pausado*) slow

compassivo, -a [kõpa'sivu, a] ADJ compassionate

compasso [kõ'pasu] M (*instrumento*) pair of compasses; (*Mús*) time; (*ritmo*) beat; **dentro do ~** in time with the music; **fora do ~** out of time

compatibilidade [kõpatʃibili'dadʒi] F compatibility

compatível [kõpa'tʃivew] (*pl* **-eis**) ADJ compatible

compatriota [kõpa'trjɔta] M/F fellow countryman/woman, compatriot

compelir [kõpe'lir] VT to force, compel

compêndio [kõ'pẽdʒju] M (*sumário*) compendium; (*livro de texto*) textbook

compenetração [kõpenetra'sãw] (*pl* **-ões**) F conviction

compenetrar [kõpene'trar] VT to convince; **compenetrar-se** VR to be convinced

compensação [kõpẽsa'sãw] (*pl* **-ões**) F compensation; (*de cheques*) clearance; **em ~** on the other hand

compensado [kõpẽ'sadu] M hardboard

compensador, a [kõpẽsa'dor(a)] ADJ compensatory

compensar [kõpẽ'sar] VT (*reparar o dano*) to make up for, compensate for; (*equilibrar*) to offset, counterbalance; (*cheque*) to clear

competência [kõpe'tẽsja] F competence, ability; (*responsabilidade*) responsibility; **isto é de minha ~** this is my responsibility

competente [kõpe'tẽtʃi] ADJ (*capaz*) competent, able; (*apropriado*) appropriate; (*responsável*) responsible

competição [kõpetʃi'sãw] (*pl* **-ões**) F competition

competidor, a [kõpetʃi'dor(a)] M/F competitor

competir [kõpe'tʃir] VI to compete; **~ a alguém** (*ser da competência de*) to be sb's responsibility; (*caber*) to be up to sb; **~ com** to compete with

competitividade [kõpetʃitʃivi'dadʒi] F competitiveness

competitivo, -a [kõpetʃi'tʃivu, a] ADJ competitive

compilação [kõpila'sãw] (*pl* **-ões**) F compilation

compilar [kõpi'lar] VT to compile

compilo *etc* [kõ'pilu] VB *ver* **compelir**

compito *etc* [kõ'pitu] VB *ver* **competir**

complacência [kõpla'sẽsja] F complaisance

complacente [kõpla'sẽtʃi] ADJ obliging

compleição [kõplej'sãw] (*pl* **-ões**) F build

complementar [kõplemẽ'tar] ADJ complementary ▶ VT to supplement

complemento [kõple'mẽtu] M complement

completamente [kõpleta'mẽtʃi] ADV completely, quite

completar [kõple'tar] VT to complete; (*água, gasolina*) to fill up, top up; **~ dez anos** to be ten

completo, -a [kõ'plɛtu, a] ADJ complete; (*cheio*) full (up); **por ~** completely

complexado, -a [kõplek'sadu, a] ADJ hung-up; **estar/ficar ~** to have/get a complex

complexidade [kõpleksi'dadʒi] F complexity

complexo, -a [kõ'plɛksu, a] ADJ complex ▶ M complex; **~ de Édipo** Oedipus complex

complicação [kõplika'sãw] (*pl* **-ões**) F complication

complicado, -a [kõpli'kadu, a] ADJ complicated

complicar [kõpli'kar] VT to complicate; **complicar-se** VR to become complicated; (*enredo*) to thicken

complô [kõ'plo] M plot, conspiracy

compõe etc [kõ'põj] VB ver **compor**

compomos etc [kõ'pomos] VB ver **compor**

componente [kõpo'nẽtʃi] ADJ, M component

componho etc [kõ'poɲu] VB ver **compor**

compor [kõ'por] (irreg: como **pôr**) VT to compose; (discurso, livro) to write; (arranjar) to arrange; (Tip) to set ▶ VI to compose; **compor-se** VR (controlar-se) to compose o.s.; **~-se de** to consist of

comporta [kõ'pɔrta] F floodgate; (de canal) lock

comportamento [kõporta'mẽtu] M behaviour (BRIT), behavior (US); (conduta) conduct; **mau ~** misbehavio(u)r

comportar [kõpor'tar] VT (suportar) to put up with, bear; (conter) to hold; **comportar-se** VR (portar-se) to behave; **~-se mal** to misbehave, behave badly

compôs [kõ'pos] VB ver **compor**

composição [kõpozi'sãw] (pl **-ões**) F composition; (Tip) typesetting; (conciliação) compromise

compositor, a [kõpozi'tor(a)] M/F composer; (Tip) typesetter

composto, -a [kõ'postu, 'pɔsta] PP de **compor** ▶ ADJ (sério) serious; (de muitos elementos) composite, compound ▶ M compound; **~ de** made up of, composed of

compostura [kõpos'tura] F composure

compota [kõ'pɔta] F fruit in syrup; **~ de laranja** oranges in syrup

compra ['kõpra] F purchase; **fazer ~s** to go shopping

comprador, a [kõpra'dor(a)] M/F buyer, purchaser

comprar [kõ'prar] VT to buy; (subornar) to bribe; **~ briga** to look for trouble; **~ a briga de alguém** to fight sb's battle for him

comprazer-se [kõpra'zersi] VR: **~ com/em fazer** to take pleasure in/in doing

compreender [kõprj 'der] VT (entender) to understand; (constar de) to comprise, consist of, be composed of; (abranger) to cover

compreensão [kõprjẽ'sãw] F understanding, comprehension

compreensível [kõprjẽ'sivew] (pl **-eis**) ADJ understandable, comprehensible

compreensivo, -a [kõprjẽ'sivu, a] ADJ understanding

compressa [kõ'prɛsa] F compress

compressão [kõpre'sãw] (pl **-ões**) F compression

compressor, a [kõpre'sor(a)] ADJ ver **rolo**

comprido, -a [kõ'pridu, a] ADJ long; (alto) tall; **ao ~** lengthways

comprimento [kõpri'mẽtu] M length

comprimido, -a [kõpri'midu, a] ADJ compressed ▶ M (pílula) pill; (pastilha) tablet

comprimir [kõpri'mir] VT to compress; (apertar) to squeeze

comprometedor, a [kõpromete'dor(a)] ADJ compromising

comprometer [kõprome'ter] VT to compromise; (envolver) to involve; (arriscar) to jeopardize; (empenhar) to pledge; **comprometer-se** VR to commit o.s.; **~-se a** to undertake to, promise to; **~-se com alguém** to make a commitment to sb

comprometido, -a [kõprome'tʃidu, a] ADJ (ocupado) busy; (noivo etc) spoken for

compromisso [kõpro'misu] M (promessa) promise; (obrigação) commitment; (hora marcada) appointment, engagement; (acordo) agreement; **sem ~** without obligation

comprovação [kõprova'sãw] (pl **-ões**) F proof, evidence; (Admin) receipts pl

comprovante [kõpro'vãtʃi] ADJ of proof ▶ M receipt; **~ de residência** proof of address

comprovar [kõpro'var] VT to prove; (confirmar) to confirm

compulsão [kõpuw'sãw] (pl **-ões**) F compulsion

compulsivo, -a [kõpuw'sivu, a] ADJ compulsive

compulsões [kõpuw'sõjs] FPL de **compulsão**

compulsório, -a [kõpuw'sɔrju, a] ADJ compulsory

compunção [kõpũ'sãw] F compunction

compungir [kõpũ'ʒir] VT to pain ▶ VI to be painful

compunha etc [kõ'puɲa] VB ver **compor**

compus etc [kõ'pus] VB ver **compor**

compuser etc [kõpu'zer] VB ver **compor**

computação [kõputa'sãw] F computation; (ciência, curso) computer science, computing; **~ em nuvem** cloud computing

computador [kõputa'dor] M computer

computadorizar [kõputadori'zar] VT to computerize

computar [kõpu'tar] VT to compute; (calcular) to calculate; (contar) to count

cômputo ['kõputu] M computation

comum [ko'mũ] (pl **-ns**) ADJ (pessoa) ordinary, common; (habitual) usual ▶ M the usual thing; **em ~** in common; **o ~ é partirmos às 8** we usually set off at 8; **fora do ~** unusual

comuna [ko'muna] (col) M/F communist

comungar [komũ'gar] VI to take communion

comunhão [komu'ɲãw] (pl **-ões**) F communion; (Rel) Holy Communion; **~ de bens** joint ownership

comunicação [komunika'sãw] (pl **-ões**) F communication; (mensagem) message; (curso) media studies sg; (acesso) access

comunicado [komuni'kadu] M notice; (oficial) communiqué

comunicar [komuni'kar] VT to communicate; (unir) to join ▶ VI to communicate; **comunicar-se** VR to communicate; **~ algo a alguém** to inform sb of sth; **~-se com** (entrar em contato) to get in touch with

comunicativo, -a [komunika'tʃivu, a] ADJ communicative; (riso) infectious

comunidade [komuni'dadʒi] F community; **C~ (Econômica) Europeia** European (Economic) Community

comunismo [komu'nizmu] M communism

comunista [komu'nista] ADJ, M/F communist

comunitário, -a [komuni'tarju, a] ADJ community *atr*

comuns [ko'mũs] PL *de* **comum**

comutador [komuta'dor] M switch

comutar [komu'tar] VT (*Jur*) to commute; (*trocar*) to exchange

concatenar [kõkate'nar] VT (*ideias*) to string together

côncavo, -a ['kõkavu, a] ADJ concave; (*cavado*) hollow ▶ M hollow

conceber [kõse'ber] VT to conceive; (*imaginar*) to conceive of, imagine; (*entender*) to understand ▶ VI to conceive, become pregnant

concebível [kõse'bivew] (*pl* **-eis**) ADJ conceivable

conceder [kõse'der] VT (*permitir*) to allow; (*outorgar*) to grant, accord; (*admitir*) to concede; (*dar*) to give ▶ VI: **~ em** to agree to

conceito [kõ'sejtu] M (*ideia*) concept, idea; (*fama*) reputation; (*opinião*) opinion

conceituado, -a [kõsej'twadu, a] ADJ well thought of, highly regarded

conceituar [kõsej'twar] VT to conceptualize

concentração [kõsẽtra'sãw] (*pl* **-ões**) F concentration; (*Esporte*) training camp

concentrado, -a [kõsẽ'tradu, a] ADJ concentrated ▶ M concentrate

concentrar [kõsẽ'trar] VT to concentrate; (*atenção*) to focus; (*reunir*) to bring together; (*molho*) to thicken; **concentrar-se** VR to concentrate; **~-se em** to concentrate on

concepção [kõsep'sãw] (*pl* **-ões**) F (*geração*) conception; (*noção*) idea, concept; (*opinião*) opinion

concernente [kõser'nẽtʃi] ADJ: **~ a** concerning

concernir [kõser'nir] VI: **~ a** to concern

concertar [kõser'tar] VT (*endireitar*) to adjust; (*conciliar*) to reconcile

concerto [kõ'sertu] M concert

concessão [kõse'sãw] (*pl* **-ões**) F concession; (*permissão*) permission

concessionária [kõsesjo'narja] F dealer, dealership

concessionário [kõsesjo'narju] M concessionaire

concessões [kõse'sõjs] FPL *de* **concessão**

concha ['kõʃa] F (*moluscos*) shell; (*para líquidos*) ladle

conchavo [kõ'ʃavu] M conspiracy

conciliação [kõsilja'sãw] (*pl* **-ões**) F reconciliation

conciliador, a [kõsilja'dor(a)] ADJ conciliatory ▶ M/F conciliator

conciliar [kõsi'ljar] VT to reconcile; **~ o sono** to get to sleep

conciliatório, -a [kõsilja'tɔrju, a] ADJ conciliatory

conciliável [kõsi'ljavew] (*pl* **-eis**) ADJ reconcilable

concílio [kõ'silju] M (*Rel*) council

concisão [kõsi'zãw] F concision, conciseness

conciso, -a [kõ'sizu, a] ADJ brief, concise

concitar [kõsi'tar] VT (*estimular*) to stir up, arouse; (*incitar*) to incite

conclamar [kõkla'mar] VT to shout; (*aclamar*) to acclaim; (*convocar*) to call together

Conclat [kõ'klatʃi] (BR) ABR F (= *Conferência Nacional da Classe Trabalhadora*) trade union

conclave [kõ'klavi] M conclave

concludente [kõklu'dẽtʃi] ADJ conclusive

concluir [kõ'klwir] VT (*terminar*) to end, conclude ▶ VI (*deduzir*) to conclude

conclusão [kõklu'zãw] (*pl* **-ões**) F (*término*) end; (*dedução*) conclusion; **chegar a uma ~** to come to a conclusion; **~, ele não veio** (*col*) the upshot is, he didn't come

conclusivo, -a [kõklu'zivu, a] ADJ conclusive

conclusões [kõklu'zõjs] FPL *de* **conclusão**

concomitante [kõkomi'tãtʃi] ADJ concomitant

concordância [kõkor'dãsja] F agreement

concordante [kõkor'dãtʃi] ADJ (*fatos*) concordant

concordar [kõkor'dar] VI, VT to agree; **não concordo!** I disagree!; **~ com** to agree with; **~ em** to agree to

concordata [kõkor'data] F liquidation agreement

concórdia [kõ'kɔrdʒja] F (*acordo*) agreement; (*paz*) peace

concorrência [kõko'hẽsja] F competition; (*a um cargo*) application

concorrente [kõko'hẽtʃi] M/F (*competidor*) contestant; (*candidato*) candidate

concorrer [kõko'her] VI (*competir*) to compete; **~ a** (*candidatar-se*) to apply for; **~ para** (*contribuir*) to contribute to

concorrido, -a [kõko'hidu, a] ADJ popular

concretização [kõkretʃiza'sãw] F realization

concretizar [kõkretʃi'zar] VT to make real; **concretizar-se** VR (*sonho*) to come true; (*ambições*) to be realized

concreto, -a [kõ'kretu, a] ADJ concrete; (*verdadeiro*) real; (*sólido*) solid ▶ M concrete; **~ armado** reinforced concrete

concupiscência [kõkupi'sẽsja] F greed; (*lascívia*) lust

concurso [kõ'kursu] M contest; (*exame*) competition; **~ público** open competition

concussão [kõku'sãw] F concussion; (*desfalque*) embezzlement

condado [kõ'dadu] M county

condão [kõ'dãw] M *ver* **varinha**

conde ['kõdʒi] M count

condecoração [kõdekora'sãw] (*pl* **-ões**) F decoration

condecorar [kõdeko'rar] VT to decorate

condenação [kõdena'sãw] (*pl* **-ões**) F condemnation; (*Jur*) conviction

condenar [kõde'nar] VT to condemn; (*Jur: sentenciar*) to sentence; (: *declarar culpado*) to convict

condenável [kõde'navew] (*pl* **-eis**) ADJ reprehensible

condensação [kõdēsa'sãw] F condensation

condensar [kõdē'sar] VT to condense; **condensar-se** VR to condense

condescendência [kõdesē'dēsja] F acquiescence

condescendente [kõdesē'dētʃi] ADJ condescending

condescender [kõdesē'der] VI to acquiesce; **~ a** *ou* **em** to condescend to, deign to

condessa [kõ'desa] F countess

condição [kõdʒi'sãw] (*pl* **-ões**) F condition; (*social*) status; (*qualidade*) capacity; **com a ~ de que** on condition that, provided that; **ter ~** *ou* **condições para fazer** to be able to do; **em condições de fazer** (*pessoa*) able to do; (*carro etc*) in condition to do; **em sua ~ de líder** in his capacity as leader

condicionado, -a [kõdʒisjo'nadu, a] ADJ conditioned

condicional [kõdʒisjo'naw] (*pl* **-ais**) ADJ conditional

condicionamento [kõdʒisjona'mētu] M conditioning

condições [kõdʒi'sõjs] FPL *de* **condição**

condigno, -a [kõ'dʒignu, a] ADJ (*apropriado*) fitting; (*merecido*) deserved

condigo *etc* [kõ'dʒigu] VB *ver* **condizer**

condimentar [kõdʒimē'tar] VT to season

condimento [kõdʒi'mētu] M seasoning

condisse *etc* [kõ'dʒisi] VB *ver* **condizer**

condito [kõ'dʒitu] PP *de* **condizer**

condizente [kõdʒi'zētʃi] ADJ: **~ com** in keeping with

condizer [kõdʒi'zer] (*irreg: como* **dizer**) VI: **~ com** to match

condoer-se [kõdo'ersi] VR: **~ de** to pity

condolência [kõdo'lēsja] F condolence

condomínio [kõdo'minju] M condominium; (*contribuição*) service charge; **~ fechado** gated community

condução [kõdu'sãw] F (*ato de conduzir*) driving; (*transporte*) transport; (*ônibus*) bus; (*Fís*) conduction

conducente [kõdu'sētʃi] ADJ: **~ a** conducive to

conduta [kõ'duta] F conduct, behaviour (*BRIT*), behavior (*US*); **má ~** misconduct

conduto [kõ'dutu] M (*tubo*) tube; (*cano*) pipe; (*canal*) channel

condutor, a [kõdu'tor(a)] M/F (*de veículo*) driver ▶ M (*Elet*) conductor

conduzir [kõdu'zir] VT (*PT: veículo*) to drive; (*levar*) to lead; (*negócio*) to manage; (*Fís*) to conduct ▶ VI (*PT*) to drive; **conduzir-se** VR to behave; **~ a** to lead to

cone ['kɔni] M cone

conectar [konek'tar] VT to connect

cônego ['konegu] M (*Rel*) canon

conexão [konek'sãw] (*pl* **-ões**) F connection; (*voo*) connecting flight

conexo, -a [ko'nɛksu, a] ADJ connected

conexões [konek'sõjs] FPL *de* **conexão**

confabular [kõfabu'lar] VI to talk; **~ com** to talk to

confecção [kõfek'sãw] (*pl* **-ões**) F (*feitura*) making; (*de um boletim*) production; (*roupa*) ready-to-wear clothes *pl*; (*negócio*) business selling ready-to-wear clothes

confeccionar [kõfeksjo'nar] VT (*fazer*) to make; (*fabricar*) to manufacture

confeccionista [kõfeksjo'nista] M/F *maker of ready-to-wear clothes*

confecções [kõfek'sõjs] FPL *de* **confecção**

confederação [kõfedera'sãw] (*pl* **-ões**) F confederation; (*liga*) league

confederar [kõfede'rar] VT to unite; **confederar-se** VR to form an alliance

confeitar [kõfej'tar] VT (*bolo*) to ice

confeitaria [kõfejta'ria] F patisserie

confeiteiro, -a [kõfej'tejru, a] M/F confectioner

conferência [kõfe'rēsja] F conference; (*discurso*) lecture; **fazer uma ~** to give a lecture

conferencista [kõferē'sista] M/F (*que fala*) speaker

conferente [kõfe'rētʃi] M/F (*verificador*) checker

conferir [kõfe'rir] VT (*verificar*) to check; (*comparar*) to compare; (*outorgar*) to grant; (*título*) to confer ▶ VI (*estar certo*) to tally; **confira!** see for yourself, check it out (*col*)

confessar [kõfe'sar] VT, VI to confess; **confessar-se** VR to confess; **~ alguém** (*Rel*) to hear sb's confession; **~-se culpado** (*Jur*) to plead guilty

confessionário [kõfesjo'narju] M confessional

confessor [kõfe'sor] M confessor

confete [kõ'fetʃi] M confetti; **jogar ~** (*col*) to be flattering

confiabilidade [kõfjabili'dadʒi] F reliability

confiado, -a [kõ'fjadu, a] (*col*) ADJ cheeky

confiança [kõ'fjãsa] F confidence; (*fé*) trust; (*familiaridade*) familiarity; **de ~** reliable; **digno de ~** trustworthy; **ter ~ em alguém** to trust sb; **dar ~ a alguém** (*no tratamento*) to be on informal terms with sb

confiante [kõ'fjãtʃi] ADJ confident; **~ em** confident of

confiar [kõ'fjar] VT to entrust; (*segredo*) to confide ▶ VI: **~ em** to trust; (*ter fé*) to have faith in

confiável [kõ'fjavew] (*pl* **-eis**) ADJ reliable

confidência [kõfi'dēsja] F secret; **em ~** in confidence

confidencial [kõfidē'sjaw] (*pl* **-ais**) ADJ confidential

confidenciar [kõfidē'sjar] VT to tell in confidence

confidente [kõfi'dẽtʃi] M/F confidant(e)

configuração [kõfigura'sãw] (pl **-ões**) F configuration; (forma) shape, form

configurar [kõfigu'rar] VT to shape, form; (representar) to represent; (Comput) to configure

confinamento [kõfina'mẽtu] M confinement

confinar [kõfi'nar] VT (limitar) to limit; (enclausurar) to confine ▶ VI: ~ **com** to border on; **confinar-se** VR: **~-se a** to confine o.s. to

confins [kõ'fĩs] MPL limits, boundaries; **nos ~ de judas** (col) out in the sticks

confirmação [kõfirma'sãw] (pl **-ões**) F confirmation

confirmar [kõfir'mar] VT to confirm; **confirmar-se** VR (Rel) to be confirmed; (realizar-se) to come true

confiro etc [kõ'firu] VB ver **conferir**

confiscar [kõfis'kar] VT to confiscate, seize

confisco [kõ'fisku] M confiscation

confissão [kõfi'sãw] (pl **-ões**) F confession

conflagração [kõflagra'sãw] (pl **-ões**) F conflagration

conflagrar [kõfla'grar] VT to inflame, set alight; (fig) to plunge into turmoil

conflitante [kõfli'tãtʃi] ADJ conflicting

conflito [kõ'flitu] M conflict; **entrar em ~ (com)** to clash (with)

confluente [kõ'flwẽtʃi] M tributary

conformação [kõforma'sãw] (pl **-ões**) F (resignação) resignation; (forma) form

conformado, -a [kõfor'madu, a] ADJ resigned

conformar [kõfor'mar] VT (formar) to form ▶ VI: ~ **com** to conform to; **conformar-se** VR: **~-se com** to resign o.s. to; (acomodar-se) to conform to

conforme [kõ'formi] PREP according to; (dependendo de) depending on ▶ CONJ (logo que) as soon as; (como) as, according to what; (à medida que) as; (dependendo de) depending on; **você vai? — ~** are you going? — it depends

conformidade [kõformi'dadʒi] F agreement; **em ~ com** in accordance with

conformismo [kõfor'mizmu] M conformity

conformista [kõfor'mista] M/F conformist

confortante [kõfor'tãtʃi] ADJ comforting

confortar [kõfor'tar] VT (consolar) to comfort, console

confortável [kõfor'tavew] (pl **-eis**) ADJ comfortable

conforto [kõ'fortu] M comfort

confraria [kõfra'ria] F fraternity

confraternizar [kõfraterni'zar] VI to fraternize

confrontação [kõfrõta'sãw] (pl **-ões**) F (acareação) confrontation; (comparação) comparison

confrontar [kõfrõ'tar] VT (acarear) to confront; (comparar) to compare; **confrontar-se** VR to face each other

confronto [kõ'frõtu] M confrontation; (comparação) comparison

confundir [kõfũ'dʒir] VT to confuse; **confundir-se** VR to get mixed up, get confused

confusão [kõfu'zãw] (pl **-ões**) F confusion; (tumulto) uproar; (problemas) trouble; (barafunda) chaos; **isso vai dar tanta ~** this will cause so much trouble; **fazer ~** (confundir-se) to get mixed up ou confused

confuso, -a [kõ'fuzu, a] ADJ confused; (problema) confusing; **está tudo muito ~ aqui hoje** it's all very chaotic in here today

confusões [kõfu'zõjs] FPL de **confusão**

congelado, -a [kõʒe'ladu, a] ADJ frozen

congelador [kõʒela'dor] M freezer, deep freeze

congelamento [kõʒela'mẽtu] M freezing; (Econ) freeze

congelar [kõʒe'lar] VT to freeze; **congelar-se** VR to freeze

congênere [kõ'ʒeneri] ADJ similar

congênito, -a [kõ'ʒenitu, a] ADJ congenital

congestão [kõʒes'tãw] F congestion

congestionado, -a [kõʒestʃjo'nadu, a] ADJ (trânsito) congested; (olhos) bloodshot; (rosto) flushed

congestionamento [kõʒestʃjona'mẽtu] M congestion; **um ~ (de tráfego)** a traffic jam

congestionar [kõʒestʃjo'nar] VT to congest; **congestionar-se** VR (rosto) to go red

conglomeração [kõglomera'sãw] (pl **-ões**) F conglomeration

conglomerado [kõglome'radu] M conglomerate

conglomerar [kõglome'rar] VT to heap together; **conglomerar-se** VR (unir-se) to join together, group together

Congo ['kõgu] M: **o ~** the Congo

congratular [kõgratu'lar] VT: ~ **alguém por** to congratulate sb on

congregação [kõgrega'sãw] (pl **-ões**) F (Rel) congregation; (reunião) gathering

congregar [kõgre'gar] VT to bring together; **congregar-se** VR to congregate

congressista [kõgre'sista] M/F congressman/woman

congresso [kõ'grɛsu] M congress, conference

conhaque [ko'naki] M cognac, brandy

conhecedor, a [koɲese'dor(a)] ADJ knowing ▶ M/F connoisseur, expert

conhecer [koɲe'ser] VT to know; (travar conhecimento com) to meet; (descobrir) to discover; **conhecer-se** VR (travar conhecimento) to meet; (ter conhecimento) to know each other; ~ **alguém de nome/vista** to know sb by name/sight; **quero ~ sua casa** I'd like to see your house; **você conhece Paris?** have you ever been to Paris?

conhecido, -a [koɲe'sidu, a] ADJ known; (célebre) well-known ▶ M/F acquaintance

conhecimento [koɲesi'mẽtu] M knowledge; (ideia) idea; (conhecido) acquaintance; (Com) bill of lading; **conhecimentos** MPL (informações) knowledge sg; **levar ao ~ de alguém** to bring to sb's notice; **ter ~ de**

to know; **tomar ~ de** to learn about; **não tomar ~ de** (*não dar atenção a*) to take no notice of; **é de ~ geral** it is common knowledge; **~ aéreo** air waybill

cônico, -a ['koniku, a] ADJ conical

conivência [koni'vēsja] F connivance

conivente [koni'vētʃi] ADJ conniving; **ser ~ em** to connive in

conjetura [kõʒe'tura] F conjecture, supposition; **fazer ~ (sobre)** to guess (at)

conjeturar [kõʒetu'rar] VT to guess at ▶ VI to conjecture

conjugação [kõʒuga'sãw] (*pl* -**ões**) F conjugation

conjugado [kõʒu'gadu] M studio

conjugal [kõʒu'gaw] (*pl* -**ais**) ADJ conjugal; **vida ~** married life

conjugar [kõʒu'gar] VT (*verbo*) to conjugate; (*unir*) to join; **conjugar-se** VR to join together

cônjuge ['kõʒuʒi] M spouse

conjunção [kõʒũ'sãw] (*pl* -**ões**) F (*união*) union; (*Ling*) conjunction

conjuntivite [kõʒũtʃi'vitʃi] F conjunctivitis

conjuntivo [kõʒũ'tʃivu] (PT) M (*Ling*) subjunctive

conjunto, -a [kõ'ʒũtu, a] ADJ joint ▶ M (*totalidade*) whole; (*coleção*) collection; (*músicos*) group; (*roupa*) outfit; **em ~** together

conjuntura [kõʒũ'tura] F situation

conluio [kõ'luju] M collusion

conosco [ko'nosku] PRON with us

conotação [konota'sãw] (*pl* -**ões**) F connotation

conotar [kono'tar] VT to connote

conquanto [kõ'kwantu] CONJ although, though

conquista [kõ'kista] F conquest; (*da ciência*) achievement

conquistador, a [kõkista'dor(a)] ADJ conquering ▶ M conqueror; (*namorador*) ladies' man

conquistar [kõkis'tar] VT (*subjugar*) to conquer; (*alcançar*) to achieve; (*ganhar*) to win, gain; (*pessoa*) to win over

consagração [kõsagra'sãw] (*pl* -**ões**) F (*Rel*) consecration; (*aclamação*) acclaim; (*exaltação*) praise; (*dedicação*) dedication; (*de uma expressão*) establishment

consagrado, -a [kõsa'gradu, a] ADJ (*estabelecido*) established

consagrar [kõsa'grar] VT (*Rel*) to consecrate; (*aclamar*) to acclaim; (*dedicar*) to dedicate; (*tempo*) to devote; (*expressão*) to establish; (*exaltar*) to glorify; **consagrar-se** VR: **~-se a** to devote o.s. to

consanguíneo, -a [kõsã'gwinju, a] ADJ related by blood ▶ M/F blood relation

consciência [kõ'sjēsja] F (*moral*) conscience; (*percepção*) awareness; (*senso de responsabilidade*) conscientiousness; **estar com a ~ limpa/ pesada** to have a clear/guilty conscience; **ter ~ de** to be conscious of

consciencioso, -a [kõsjē'sjozu, ɔza] ADJ conscientious

consciente [kõ'sjētʃi] ADJ conscious

conscientizar [kõsjētʃi'zar] VT: **~ alguém** (*politicamente*) to raise sb's awareness; **conscientizar-se** VR to become more aware; **~-se de** to be aware of; **~ alguém de algo** to make sb aware of sth

cônscio, -a ['kõsju, a] ADJ aware

conscrição [kõskri'sãw] F conscription

consecução [kõseku'sãw] F attainment

consecutivo, -a [kõseku'tʃivu, a] ADJ consecutive

conseguinte [kõse'gĩtʃi] ADJ: **por ~** consequently

conseguir [kõse'gir] VT (*obter*) to get, obtain; **~ fazer** to manage to do, succeed in doing; **não consigo abrir a porta** I can't open the door

conselheiro, -a [kõse'ʎejru, a] M/F (*que aconselha*) counsellor (BRIT), counselor (US), adviser; (*Pol*) councillor

conselho [kõ'seʎu] M piece of advice; (*corporação*) council; **conselhos** MPL (*advertência*) advice *sg*; **~ de guerra** court martial; **C~ de ministros** (*Pol*) Cabinet; **C~ de Diretoria** board of directors; **o C~ de Segurança da ONU** the UN Security Council

consenso [kõ'sẽsu] M consensus, agreement

consensual [kõsẽ'swaw] (*pl* -**ais**) ADJ agreed

consentimento [kõsẽtʃi'mẽtu] M consent, permission

consentir [kõsẽ'tʃir] VT (*admitir*) to allow, permit; (*aprovar*) to agree to ▶ VI: **~ em** to agree to

consequência [kõse'kwẽsja] F consequence; **por ~** consequently; **em ~ de** as a consequence of

consequente [kõse'kwẽtʃi] ADJ consequent; (*coerente*) consistent

consertar [kõser'tar] VT to mend, repair; (*remediar*) to put right

conserto [kõ'sertu] M repair

conserva [kõ'serva] F pickle; **em ~** pickled; **fábrica de ~s** cannery

conservação [kõserva'sãw] F conservation; (*de vida, alimentos*) preservation

conservacionista [kõservasjo'nista] ADJ, M/F conservationist

conservado, -a [kõser'vadu, a] ADJ (*pessoa*) well-preserved

conservador, a [kõserva'dor(a)] ADJ conservative ▶ M/F (*Pol*) conservative

conservadorismo [kõservado'rizmu] M conservatism

conservante [kõser'vãtʃi] M preservative

conservar [kõser'var] VT (*preservar*) to preserve, maintain; (*reter, manter*) to keep, retain; **conservar-se** VR to keep; **"conserve-se à direita"** "keep right"

conservatório [kõserva'tɔrju] M conservatory

consideração [kõsidera'sãw] (*pl* -**ões**) F consideration; (*estima*) respect, esteem;

(*reflexão*) thought; **levar em ~** to take into account

considerado, -a [kõside'radu, a] ADJ respected, well thought of

considerar [kõside'rar] VT to consider; (*prezar*) to respect ▶ VI to consider; **considerar-se** VR to consider o.s.

considerável [kõside'ravew] (*pl* -**eis**) ADJ considerable

consignação [kõsigna'sãw] (*pl* -**ões**) F consignment; (*registro*) recording; (*de verbas*) assignment

consignar [kõsig'nar] VT (*mercadorias*) to send, dispatch; (*registrar*) to record; (*verba etc*) to assign

consigo¹ [kõ'sigu] PRON (*m*) with him; (*f*) with her; (*pl*) with them; (*com você*) with you

consigo² VB *ver* **conseguir**

consinto [kõ'sĩtu] VB *ver* **consentir**

consistência [kõsis'tẽsja] F consistency

consistente [kõsis'tẽtʃi] ADJ (*sólido*) solid; (*espesso*) thick

consistir [kõsis'tʃir] VI: **~ em** to be made up of, consist of

consoante [kõso'ãtʃi] F consonant ▶ PREP according to ▶ CONJ as; **~ prometera** as he had promised

consola [kõ'sɔla] F (*Comput*) console

consolação [kõsola'sãw] (*pl* -**ões**) F consolation

consolador, a [kõsola'dor(a)] ADJ consoling

consolar [kõso'lar] VT to console; **consolar-se** VR to console o.s.

console [kõ'sɔli] F (*Comput*) console

consolidar [kõsoli'dar] VT to consolidate; (*fratura*) to knit ▶ VI to become solid; to knit together

consolo [kõ'solu] M consolation

consome *etc* [kõ'somi] VB *ver* **consumir**

consomê [kõso'me] M consommé

consonância [kõso'nãsja] F (*harmonia*) harmony; (*concordância*) agreement

consorciar [kõsor'sjar] VT to join; (*combinar*) to combine ▶ VI: **~ a** to unite with

consórcio [kõ'sɔrsju] M (*união*) partnership; (*Com*) consortium

consorte [kõ'sɔrtʃi] M/F consort

conspícuo, -a [kõ'spikwu, a] ADJ conspicuous

conspiração [kõspira'sãw] (*pl* -**ões**) F plot, conspiracy

conspirador, a [kõspira'dor(a)] M/F plotter, conspirator

conspirar [kõspi'rar] VT to plot ▶ VI to plot, conspire

constância [kõs'tãsja] F constancy; (*estabilidade*) steadiness

constante [kõs'tãtʃi] ADJ constant; (*estável*) steady ▶ F constant

constar [kõs'tar] VI to be in; **consta que** it says that; **~ de** to consist of; **não me constava que ...** I was not aware that ...; **ao que me consta** as far as I know

constatação [kõstata'sãw] (*pl* -**ões**) F observation

constatar [kõsta'tar] VT (*estabelecer*) to establish; (*notar*) to notice; (*evidenciar*) to show up; (*óbito*) to certify; **pudemos ~ que** we could see that

constelação [kõstela'sãw] (*pl* -**ões**) F constellation; (*grupo*) cluster

constelado, -a [kõste'ladu, a] ADJ (*estrelado*) starry

consternação [kõsterna'sãw] F (*desalento*) depression; (*desolação*) distress

consternado, -a [kõster'nadu, a] ADJ (*desalentado*) depressed; (*desolado*) distressed

consternar [kõster'nar] VT (*desolar*) to distress; (*desalentar*) to depress; **consternar-se** VR to be distressed; to be depressed

constipação [kõstʃipa'sãw] (*pl* -**ões**) (PT) F cold

constipado, -a [kõstʃi'padu, a] (PT) ADJ: **estar ~** to have a cold

constipar-se [kõstʃi'parsi] (PT) VR to catch a cold

constitucional [kõstʃitusjo'naw] (*pl* -**ais**) ADJ constitutional

constituição [kõstʃitwi'sãw] (*pl* -**ões**) F constitution

constituinte [kõstʃi'twĩtʃi] ADJ constituent ▶ M/F (*deputado*) member ▶ F: **a C~** the Constituent Assembly

constituir [kõstʃi'twir] VT (*representar*) to constitute; (*formar*) to form; (*estabelecer*) to establish, set up; (*nomear*) to appoint; **constituir-se** VR: **~-se em** to set o.s. up as; (*representar*) to constitute

constrangedor, a [kõstrãʒe'dor(a)] ADJ restricting; (*que acanha*) embarrassing

constranger [kõstrã'ʒer] VT to constrain; (*acanhar*) to embarrass; **constranger-se** VR (*acanhar-se*) to feel embarrassed

constrangimento [kõstrãʒi'mẽtu] M constraint; (*acanhamento*) embarrassment

constranjo *etc* [kõs'trãʒu] VB *ver* **constranger**

construção [kõstru'sãw] (*pl* -**ões**) F building, construction

construir [kõs'trwir] VT to build, construct

construtivo, -a [kõstru'tʃivu, a] ADJ constructive

construtor, a [kõstru'tor(a)] ADJ building *atr*, construction *atr* ▶ M/F builder ▶ F building contractor

cônsul ['kõsuw] (*pl* **cônsules**) M consul

consulado [kõsu'ladu] M consulate

consulesa [kõsu'leza] F (woman) consul; (*esposa*) consul's wife

consulta [kõ'suwta] F consultation; **livro de ~** reference book; **horário de ~** surgery hours *pl* (BRIT), office hours *pl* (US)

consultar [kõsuw'tar] VT to consult; **~ alguém sobre** to ask sb's opinion about

consultivo, -a [kõsuw'tʃivu, a] ADJ advisory

consultor, a [kõsuw'tor(a)] M/F adviser, consultant

consultoria [kõsuwto'ria] F consultancy

consultório [kõsuw'tɔrju] M surgery
consumação [kõsuma'sãw] (*pl* -**ões**) F consummation; (*em restaurante etc*) minimum order
consumado, -a [kõsu'madu, a] ADJ consummate; *ver tb* **fato**
consumar [kõsu'mar] VT to consummate; **consumar-se** VR to be consummated
consumidor, a [kõsumi'dor(a)] ADJ consumer *atr* ► M/F consumer
consumir [kõsu'mir] VT to consume; (*devorar*) to eat away; (*gastar*) to use up; **consumir-se** VR to waste away
consumismo [kõsu'mizmu] M consumerism
consumista [kõsu'mista] ADJ, M/F consumerist
consumo [kõ'sumu] M consumption; **artigos de** ~ consumer goods
conta ['kõta] F (*cálculo*) count; (*em restaurante*) bill; (*fatura*) invoice; (*bancária*) account; (*de colar*) bead; (*responsabilidade*) responsibility; **contas** FPL (*Com*) accounts; **à** ~ **de** to the account of; **ajustar** ~**s com** (*fig*) to settle an account with; **fazer de** ~ **que** to pretend that; **levar** *ou* **ter em** ~ to take into account; **por** ~ **própria** of one's own accord; **trabalhar por** ~ **própria** to work for oneself; **prestar** ~**s de** to account for; **não é da sua** ~ it's none of your business; **tomar** ~ **de** (*criança etc*) to look after; (*encarregar-se de*) to take care of; (*dominar*) to take hold of; **afinal de** ~**s** after all; **dar-se** ~ **de** to realize; (*notar*) to notice; **isso fica por sua** ~ this is for you to deal with; **dar** ~ **de** (*notar*) to notice; (*prestar contas de*) to account for; (*de tarefa*) to handle, cope with; **ficar por** ~ (*furioso*) to get mad; **ser a** ~ to be just enough; **dar** ~ **do recado** (*col*) to deliver the goods; ~ **bancária** bank account; ~ **conjunta** joint account; ~ **corrente** current account; ~ **de e-mail** *ou* **de correio eletrônico** email account
contábil [kõ'tabiw] (*pl* -**eis**) ADJ accounting *atr*
contabilidade [kõtabili'dadʒi] F bookkeeping, accountancy; (*departamento*) accounts department; ~ **de custos** cost accounting
contabilista [kõtabi'lista] (PT) M/F accountant
contabilizar [kõtabili'zar] VT to write up, book; **valor contabilizado** (*Com*) book value
contacto [kõ'tatu] (PT) M = **contato**
contado, -a [kõ'tadu, a] ADJ: **dinheiro de** ~ (PT) cash payment; **estamos com dinheiro** ~ **para só três meses** we've got just enough money for three months
contador, a [kõta'dor(a)] M/F (*Com*) accountant ► M (*Tec: medidor*) meter; ~ **de estórias** story-teller
contadoria [kõtado'ria] F audit department
contagem [kõ'taʒẽ] (*pl* -**ns**) F (*de números*) counting; (*escore*) score; **abrir a** ~ (*Futebol*) to open the scoring
contagiante [kõta'ʒjãtʃi] ADJ (*alegria*) contagious

contagiar [kõta'ʒjar] VT to infect; **contagiar-se** VR to become infected
contágio [kõ'taʒju] M infection
contagioso, -a [kõta'ʒjozu, ɔza] ADJ (*doença*) contagious
conta-gotas M INV dropper
contaminação [kõtamina'sãw] F contamination
contaminar [kõtami'nar] VT to contaminate
contanto que [kõ'tãtu ki] CONJ provided that
conta-quilómetros (PT) M INV speedometer
contar [kõ'tar] VT to count; (*narrar*) to tell; (*pretender*) to intend; (*imaginar*) to think ► VI to count; ~ **com** to count on; (*esperar*) to expect; **ela contava que a fossem ajudar** she expected them to help her; ~ **em fazer** to count on doing, expect to do
contatar [kõta'tar] VT to contact
contato [kõ'tatu] M contact; **entrar em** ~ **com** to get in touch with, contact
contêiner [kõ'tejner] M container
contemplação [kõtẽpla'sãw] F contemplation
contemplar [kõtẽ'plar] VT to contemplate; (*olhar*) to gaze at ► VI to meditate; **contemplar-se** VR to look at o.s.
contemplativo, -a [kõtẽpla'tʃivu, a] ADJ (*pessoa*) thoughtful; (*vida, literatura*) contemplative
contemporâneo, -a [kõtẽpo'ranju, a] ADJ, M/F contemporary
contemporizar [kõtẽpori'zar] VT (*situação*) to ease ► VI to ease the situation
contenção [kõtẽ'sãw] (*pl* -**ões**) F restriction, containment; ~ **de despesas** cutbacks *pl*
contencioso, -a [kõtẽ'sjozu, ɔza] ADJ contentious
contenções [kõtẽ'sõjs] FPL *de* **contenção**
contenda [kõ'tẽda] F quarrel, dispute
contenho *etc* [kõ'teɲu] VB *ver* **conter**
contentamento [kõtẽta'mẽtu] M (*felicidade*) happiness; (*satisfação*) contentment
contentar [kõtẽ'tar] VT (*dar prazer*) to please; (*dar satisfação*) to satisfy; **contentar-se** VR to be satisfied
contente [kõ'tẽtʃi] ADJ (*alegre*) happy; (*satisfeito*) pleased, satisfied
contento [kõ'tẽtu] M: **a** ~ satisfactorily
conter [kõ'ter] (*irreg: como* **ter**) VT (*encerrar*) to contain, hold; (*refrear*) to restrain, hold back; (*gastos*) to curb; **conter-se** VR to restrain o.s.
conterrâneo, -a [kõte'hanju, a] ADJ fellow ► M/F compatriot, fellow countryman/woman
contestação [kõtesta'sãw] (*pl* -**ões**) F challenge; (*negação*) denial
contestar [kõtes'tar] VT (*contrariar*) to dispute, contest, question; (*impugnar*) to challenge
contestável [kõtes'tavew] (*pl* -**eis**) ADJ questionable
conteúdo [kõte'udu] M contents *pl*; (*de um texto*) content
conteve *etc* [kõ'tevi] VB *ver* **conter**

contexto [kõ'testu] M context
contido, -a [kõ'tʃidu, a] PP *de* **conter** ▶ ADJ contained; (*raiva*) repressed
contigo [kõ'tʃigu] PRON with you
contiguidade [kõtʃigwi'dadʒi] F proximity
contíguo, -a [kõ'tʃigwu, a] ADJ: ~ **a** next to
continência [kõtʃi'nẽsja] F (*militar*) salute; **fazer ~ a** to salute
continental [kõtʃinẽ'taw] (*pl* **-ais**) ADJ continental
continente [kõtʃi'nẽtʃi] M continent
contingência [kõtʃĩ'ʒẽsja] F contingency
contingente [kõtʃĩ'ʒẽtʃi] ADJ uncertain ▶ M (*Mil*) contingent; (*Com*) contingency, reserve
continuação [kõtʃinwa'sãw] F continuation
continuar [kõtʃi'nwar] VT to continue ▶ VI to continue, go on; ~ **falando** *ou* **a falar** to go on talking, continue talking *ou* to talk; **continue!** carry on!; **ela continua doente** she is still sick
continuidade [kõtʃinwi'dadʒi] F continuity
contínuo, -a [kõ'tʃinwu, a] ADJ (*persistente*) continual; (*sem interrupção*) continuous ▶ M office boy
contista [kõ'tʃista] M/F story writer
contive *etc* [kõ'tʃivi] VB *ver* **conter**
contiver *etc* [kõtʃi'ver] VB *ver* **conter**
conto ['kõtu] M story, tale; ~ **de fadas** fairy tale; ~ **do vigário** confidence trick
contorção [kõtor'sãw] (*pl* **-ões**) F contortion; (*dos músculos*) twitch
contorcer [kõtor'ser] VT to twist; **contorcer-se** VR to writhe
contorções [kõtor'sõjs] FPL *de* **contorção**
contornar [kõtor'nar] VT (*rodear*) to go round; (*ladear*) to skirt; (*fig: problema*) to get round
contornável [kõtor'navew] (*pl* **-eis**) ADJ avoidable
contorno [kõ'tornu] M outline; (*da terra*) contour; (*do rosto*) profile
contra ['kõtra] PREP against ▶ M: **os prós e os ~s** the pros and cons; **dar o ~ (a)** to be opposed (to); **ser do ~** to be against it
contra-almirante M rear-admiral
contra-argumento M counter-argument
contra-atacar VT to counterattack
contra-ataque M counterattack
contrabaixo [kõtra'bajʃu] M double bass
contrabalançar [kõtrabalã'sar] VT to counterbalance; (*compensar*) to compensate
contrabandear [kõtrabã'dʒjar] VT, VI to smuggle
contrabandista [kõtrabã'dʒista] M/F smuggler
contrabando [kõtra'bãdu] M smuggling; (*artigos*) contraband
contrabarra [kõtra'baha] F (*Comput*) backslash
contração [kõtra'sãw] (*pl* **-ões**) F contraction
contracapa [kõtra'kapa] F inside cover
contracenar [kõtrase'nar] VI: ~ **com** to act alongside, star with

contraceptivo, -a [kõtrasep'tʃivu, a] ADJ contraceptive ▶ M contraceptive
contracheque [kõtra'ʃɛki] M pay slip (*BRIT*), check stub (*US*)
contrações [kõtra'sõjs] FPL *de* **contração**
contradição [kõtradʒi'sãw] (*pl* **-ões**) F contradiction
contradigo *etc* [kõtra'dʒigu] VB *ver* **contradizer**
contradisse *etc* [kõtra'dʒisi] VB *ver* **contradizer**
contradito [kõtra'dʒitu] PP *de* **contradizer**
contraditório, -a [kõtradʒi'tɔrju, a] ADJ contradictory
contradizer [kõtradʒi'zer] (*irreg: como* **dizer**) VT to contradict; **contradizer-se** VR (*pessoa*) to contradict o.s.; (*atitudes*) to be contradictory
contrafazer [kõtrafa'zer] (*irreg: como* **fazer**) VT to forge, counterfeit; (*pessoa*) to imitate, take off
contrafeito, -a [kõtra'fejtu, a] PP *de* **contrafazer** ▶ ADJ constrained
contrafez *etc* [kõtra'fez] VB *ver* **contrafazer**
contrafilé [kõtrafi'lɛ] M rump steak
contrafiz *etc* [kõtra'fiz] VB *ver* **contrafazer**
contrafizer *etc* [kõtrafi'zer] VB *ver* **contrafazer**
contragosto [kõtra'gostu] M: **a ~** against one's will, unwillingly
contraído, -a [kõtra'idu, a] ADJ (*tímido*) timid, shy
contraindicação [kõtraindʒika'sãw] (*pl* **-ões**) F contra-indication
contraindicado, -a [kõtraindʒi'kadu] ADJ contra-indicated
contrair [kõtra'ir] VT to contract; (*doença*) to contract, catch; (*hábito*) to form; **contrair-se** VR to contract; ~ **matrimônio** to get married
contralto [kõ'trawtu] M contralto
contramão [kõtra'mãw] ADJ one-way ▶ F: **na ~** the wrong way down a one-way street
contramestre, -tra [kõtra'mɛstri, tra] M/F (*em fábrica*) supervisor ▶ M (*Náut*) boatswain
Contran [kõ'trã] (*BR*) ABR M = **Conselho Nacional de Trânsito**
contraofensiva [kõtraofẽ'siva] F counteroffensive
contraoferta [kõtrao'fɛrta] F counteroffer
contraparente, -a [kõtrapa'rẽtʃi, ta] M/F distant relative; (*afim*) in-law
contrapartida [kõtrapar'tʃida] F (*Com*) counterentry; (*fig*) compensation; **em ~ a** in the face of
contrapesar [kõtrape'zar] VT to counterbalance; (*fig*) to offset
contrapeso [kõtra'pezu] M counterbalance; (*Tec*) counterweight; (*Com*) makeweight
contrapor [kõtra'por] (*irreg: como* **pôr**) VT (*comparar*) to compare; **contrapor-se** VR: ~**-se a** to be in opposition to; (*atitude*) to go against; ~ **algo a algo** to set sth against sth
contraproducente [kõtraprodu'sẽtʃi] ADJ counterproductive, self-defeating

contrapunha *etc* [kõtra'puɲa] vʙ *ver* **contrapor**

contrapus *etc* [kõtra'pus] vʙ *ver* **contrapor**

contrapuser *etc* [kõtrapu'zer] vʙ *ver* **contrapor**

contrariar [kõtra'rjar] vᴛ (*contradizer*) to contradict; (*aborrecer*) to annoy

contrariedade [kõtrarje'dadʒi] ꜰ (*aborrecimento*) annoyance, vexation

contrário, -a [kõ'trarju, a] ADJ (*oposto*) opposite; (*pessoa*) opposed; (*desfavorável*) unfavourable (ʙʀɪᴛ), unfavorable (ᴜs), adverse ▶ ᴍ opposite; **do ~** otherwise; **pelo ou ao ~** on the contrary; **ao ~** (*do outro lado*) the other way round; **muito pelo ~** on the contrary, quite the opposite

contrarregra [kõtra'hɛgra] ᴍ/ꜰ stage manager

contrarrevolução [kõtrahevolu'sãw] (*pl* -**ões**) ꜰ counter-revolution

contrassenso [kõtra'sẽsu] ᴍ nonsense

contrastante [kõtras'tãtʃi] ADJ contrasting

contrastar [kõtras'tar] vᴛ to contrast

contraste [kõ'trastʃi] ᴍ contrast

contratação [kõtrata'sãw] ꜰ (*de pessoal*) employment

contratante [kõtra'tãtʃi] ADJ contracting ▶ ᴍ/ꜰ contractor

contratar [kõtra'tar] vᴛ (*serviços*) to contract; (*pessoal*) to employ, take on

contratempo [kõtra'tẽpu] ᴍ (*imprevisto*) setback; (*aborrecimento*) upset; (*dificuldade*) difficulty

contrato [kõ'tratu] ᴍ contract; (*acordo*) agreement

contratual [kõtra'twaw] (*pl* -**ais**) ADJ contractual

contravapor [kõtrava'por] (*col*) ᴍ rebuff

contravenção [kõtravẽ'sãw] (*pl* -**ões**) ꜰ contravention, violation

contraventor, a [kõtravẽ'tor(a)] ᴍ/ꜰ offender

contribuição [kõtribwi'sãw] (*pl* -**ões**) ꜰ contribution; (*imposto*) tax

contribuinte [kõtri'bwĩtʃi] ᴍ/ꜰ contributor; (*que paga impostos*) taxpayer

contribuir [kõtri'bwir] vᴛ to contribute ▶ vɪ to contribute; (*pagar impostos*) to pay taxes

contrição [kõtri'sãw] ꜰ contrition

contrito, -a [kõ'tritu, a] ADJ contrite

controlar [kõtro'lar] vᴛ to control; **controlar-se** vʀ to control o.s.

controlável [kõtro'lavew] (*pl* -**eis**) ADJ controllable

controle [kõ'troli] ᴍ control; **~ remoto** remote control; **~ de crédito** (*Com*) credit control; **~ de qualidade** (*Com*) quality control

controvérsia [kõtro'vɛrsja] ꜰ controversy; (*discussão*) debate

controverso, -a [kõtro'vɛrsu, a] ADJ controversial

contudo [kõ'tudu] ᴄᴏɴᴊ nevertheless, however

contumácia [kõtu'masja] ꜰ obstinacy; (*Jur*) contempt of court

contumaz [kõtu'majz] ADJ obstinate, stubborn ▶ ᴍ/ꜰ (*Jur*) defaulter

contundente [kõtũ'dẽtʃi] ADJ bruising; (*argumento*) cutting; **instrumento ~** blunt instrument

contundir [kõtũ'dʒir] vᴛ to bruise; **contundir-se** to bruise o.s.

conturbação [kõturba'sãw] (*pl* -**ões**) ꜰ disturbance, unrest; (*motim*) riot

conturbado, -a [kõtur'badu, a] ADJ disturbed

conturbar [kõtur'bar] vᴛ to disturb; (*amotinar*) to stir up

contusão [kõtu'zãw] (*pl* -**ões**) ꜰ bruise

contuso, -a [kõ'tuzu, a] ADJ bruised

contusões [kõtu'zõjs] ꜰᴘʟ *de* **contusão**

convalescença [kõvale'sẽsa] ꜰ convalescence

convalescer [kõvale'ser] vɪ to convalesce

conveio *etc* [kõ'veju] vʙ *ver* **convir**

convenção [kõvẽ'sãw] (*pl* -**ões**) ꜰ convention; (*acordo*) agreement

convencer [kõvẽ'ser] vᴛ to convince; (*persuadir*) to persuade; **convencer-se** vʀ: **~-se de** to be convinced about

convencido, -a [kõvẽ'sidu, a] ADJ (*convicto*) convinced; (*col: imodesto*) conceited, smug

convencimento [kõvẽsi'mẽtu] ᴍ (*convicção*) conviction; (*col: imodéstia*) conceit, smugness

convencional [kõvẽsjo'naw] (*pl* -**ais**) ADJ conventional

convencionar [kõvẽsjo'nar] vᴛ to agree on; **convencionar-se** vʀ: **~-se em** to agree to

convenções [kõvẽ'sõjs] ꜰᴘʟ *de* **convenção**

convenha *etc* [kõ'veɲa] vʙ *ver* **convir**

conveniência [kõve'njẽsja] ꜰ convenience

conveniente [kõve'njẽtʃi] ADJ convenient, suitable; (*vantajoso*) advantageous

convênio [kõ'venju] ᴍ (*reunião*) convention; (*acordo*) agreement

convento [kõ'vẽtu] ᴍ convent

convergir [kõver'ʒir] vɪ to converge

conversa [kõ'vɛrsa] ꜰ conversation; (*papo*) idle talk; (*promessa falsa*) hot air; **ir na ~ de alguém** (*col*) to be taken in by sb; **~ vai, ~ vem** in the course of conversation; **ele não tem muita ~** he hasn't got a lot to say for himself

conversação [kõversa'sãw] (*pl* -**ões**) ꜰ (*ato*) conversation

conversadeira [kõversa'dejra] ꜰ *de* **conversador**

conversado, -a [kõver'sadu, a] ADJ (*assunto*) talked about; (*pessoa*) talkative, chatty; **estamos ~s** we've said all we had to say

conversador, -deira [kõversa'dor, 'dejra] ADJ talkative, chatty

conversa-fiada (*pl* **conversas-fiadas**) ᴍ/ꜰ: **ser um ~** to be all talk

conversão [kõver'sãw] (*pl* -**ões**) ꜰ conversion

conversar [kõver'sar] vɪ to talk; (*bater papo*) to chat

conversibilidade [kõversibili'daʒi] F
convertibility
conversível [kõver'sivew] (*pl* **-eis**) ADJ
convertible ▸ M (*Auto*) convertible
conversões [kõver'sõjs] FPL *de* **conversão**
converter [kõver'ter] VT to convert;
converter-se VR to be converted
convertido, -a [kõver'tʃidu, a] ADJ converted
▸ M/F convert
convés [kõ'vɛs] (*pl* **-eses**) M (*Náut*) deck
convexo, -a [kõ'vɛksu, a] ADJ convex
convicção [kõvik'sãw] (*pl* **-ões**) F conviction;
(*certeza*) certainty
convicto, -a [kõ'viktu, a] ADJ (*convencido*)
convinced; (*réu*) convicted; (*patriota etc*) staunch
convidado, -a [kõvi'dadu, a] ADJ invited
▸ M/F guest
convidar [kõvi'dar] VT to invite; **convidar-se**
VR to invite o.s.
convidativo, -a [kõvida'tʃivu, a] ADJ inviting
convier *etc* [kõ'vjer] VB *ver* **convir**
convincente [kõvĩ'sẽtʃi] ADJ convincing
convir [kõ'vir] (*irreg: como* **vir**) VI (*ser conveniente*)
to suit, be convenient; (*ficar bem*) to be
appropriate; (*concordar*) to agree; **convém
fazer isso o mais rápido possível** we must
do this as soon as possible; **você há de ~
que ...** you must agree that ....
convirjo *etc* [kõ'virʒu] VB *ver* **convergir**
convite [kõ'vitʃi] M invitation
conviva [kõ'viva] M/F guest
convivência [kõvi'vẽsja] F living together;
(*familiaridade*) familiarity, intimacy
conviver [kõvi'ver] VI: **~ com** (*viver em comum*)
to live with; (*ter familiaridade*) to get on with
convívio [kõ'vivju] M (*viver em comum*) living
together; (*familiaridade*) familiarity
convocar [kõvo'kar] VT to summon, call
upon; (*reunião, eleições*) to call; (*para o serviço
militar*) to call up
convosco [kõ'vosku] ADV with you
convulsão [kõvuw'sãw] (*pl* **-ões**) F
convulsion; (*fig*) upheaval
convulsionar [kõvuwsjo'nar] VT (*abalar*) to
shake; (*excitar*) to stir up
convulsivo, -a [kõvuw'sivu, a] ADJ convulsive
convulsões [kõvuw'sõjs] FPL *de* **convulsão**
cooper ['kuper] M jogging, running; **fazer ~**
to go jogging *ou* running
cooperação [koopera'sãw] F cooperation
cooperante [koope'rãtʃi] ADJ cooperative,
helpful
cooperar [koope'rar] VI to cooperate
cooperativa [koopera'tʃiva] F (*Com*)
cooperative
cooperativo, -a [koopera'tʃivu, a] ADJ
cooperative
coordenação [koordena'sãw] F coordination
coordenada [koorde'nada] F coordinate
coordenar [koorde'nar] VT to coordinate
copa ['kɔpa] F (*de árvore*) top; (*dum chapéu*)
crown; (*compartimento*) pantry; (*torneio*) cup;
copas FPL (*Cartas*) hearts

copeira [ko'pejra] F kitchen maid
Copenhague [kope'nagi] N Copenhagen
cópia ['kɔpja] F copy; **tirar ~ de** to copy
copiadora [kopja'dora] F (*máquina*)
duplicating machine
copiar [ko'pjar] VT to copy
copidesque [kopi'dɛski] M copy editing
▸ M/F copy editor
copiloto [kopi'lotu] M co-pilot
copioso, -a [ko'pjozu, ɔza] ADJ abundant,
numerous; (*refeição*) large; (*provas*) ample
copirraite [kopi'hajtʃi] M copyright
copo ['kɔpu] M glass; **ser um bom ~** (*col*) to be
a good drinker
copyright [kopi'hajtʃi] M = **copirraite**
coque ['kɔki] M (*penteado*) bun
coqueiro [ko'kejru] M (*Bot*) coconut palm
coqueluche [koke'luʃi] F (*Med*) whooping
cough; (*mania*) rage
coquete [ko'kɛtʃi] ADJ coquettish
coquetel [koke'tɛw] (*pl* **-éis**) M cocktail; (*festa*)
cocktail party
cor¹ [kɔr] M: **de ~** by heart
cor² [kor] F colour (BRIT), color (US); **de ~**
colo(u)red
coração [kora'sãw] (*pl* **-ões**) M heart; **de
bom ~** kind-hearted; **de todo o ~**
wholeheartedly
corado, -a [ko'radu, a] ADJ ruddy
coragem [ko'raʒẽ] F courage; (*atrevimento*)
nerve
corais [ko'rajs] MPL *de* **coral**
corajoso, -a [kora'ʒozu, ɔza] ADJ courageous
coral [ko'raw] (*pl* **-ais**) ADJ choral ▸ M (*Mús*)
choir; (*Zool*) coral
corante [ko'rãtʃi] ADJ, M colouring (BRIT),
coloring (US)
corar [ko'rar] VT (*pintar*) to paint; (*roupa*) to
bleach (in the sun) ▸ VI (*ruborizar-se*) to blush;
(*tornar-se branco*) to bleach
corbelha [kor'bɛʎa] F basket
corcova [kor'kɔva] F hump
corcunda [kor'kũda] ADJ hunchbacked ▸ F
hump ▸ M/F (*pessoa*) hunchback
corda ['kɔrda] F (*cabo*) rope, line; (*Mús*) string;
(*varal*) clothes line; (*de relógio*) spring; **dar ~
em** to wind up; **roer a ~** to go back on one's
word; **~s vocais** vocal cords; **estar com
toda a ~** (*pessoa*) to be really wound up; **dar ~
a alguém** (*deixar falar*) to set sb off; (*flertar*) to
flirt with sb
cordão [kor'dãw] (*pl* **-ões**) M string, twine;
(*joia*) chain; (*no carnaval*) group; (*Elet*) lead;
(*fileira*) row; **~ de sapato** shoestring
cordeiro [kor'dejru] M lamb; (*fig*) sheep
cordel [kor'dɛw] (*pl* **-éis**) M string; **literatura
de ~** pamphlet literature
cor-de-rosa ADJ INV pink
cordial [kor'dʒjaw] (*pl* **-ais**) ADJ cordial ▸ M
(*bebida*) cordial
cordialidade [kordʒjali'dadʒi] F warmth,
cordiality
cordilheira [kordʒi'ʎejra] F mountain range

cordões [kor'dõjs] MPL *de* **cordão**

coreano, -a [ko'rjanu, a] ADJ Korean ▸ M/F Korean ▸ M (*Ling*) Korean

Coreia [ko'rɛja] F: **a ~** Korea

coreografia [korjogra'fia] F choreography

coreógrafo, -a [ko'rjɔgrafu, a] M/F choreographer

coreto [ko'retu] M bandstand; **bagunçar o ~ (de alguém)** (*col*) to spoil things (for sb)

corisco [ko'risku] M (*faísca*) flash

corista [ko'rista] M/F chorister ▸ F (*Teatro*) chorus girl

coriza [ko'riza] F runny nose

corja ['kɔrʒa] F (*PT: canalha*) rabble; (*bando*) gang

córnea ['kɔrnja] F cornea

córner ['kɔrner] M (*Futebol*) corner

corneta [kor'neta] F cornet; (*Mil*) bugle

corneteiro [korne'tejru] M bugler

cornetim [korne'tʃĩ] (*pl* **-ns**) M (*Mús*) French horn

coro ['koru] M chorus; (*conjunto de cantores*) choir; **em ~** in chorus

coroa [ko'roa] F crown; (*de flores*) garland ▸ M/F (*BR col*) old timer

coroação [korwa'sãw] (*pl* **-ões**) F coronation

coroar [koro'ar] VT to crown; (*premiar*) to reward

coronel [koro'nɛw] (*pl* **-éis**) M colonel; (*político*) local political boss

coronha [ko'rɔɲa] F (*de um fuzil*) butt; (*de um revólver*) handle

corpete [kor'petʃi] M bodice

corpo ['korpu] M body; (*aparência física*) figure; (: *de homem*) build; (*de vestido*) bodice; (*Mil*) corps *sg*; **de ~ e alma** (*fig*) wholeheartedly; **lutar ~ a ~** to fight hand to hand; **fazer ~ mole** to get out of it; **tirar o ~ fora** (*col*) to duck out; **~ diplomático** diplomatic corps *sg*; **~ docente** teaching staff (*BRIT*), faculty (*US*); **~ estranho** (*Med*) foreign body

corporal [korpo'raw] (*pl* **-ais**) ADJ physical

corpulência [korpu'lẽsja] F stoutness

corpulento, -a [korpu'lẽtu, a] ADJ stout

correção [kohe'sãw] (*pl* **-ões**) F correction; (*exatidão*) correctness; **casa de ~** reformatory; **~ salarial/monetária** wage/monetary correction

corre-corre [kɔhi'kɔhi] (*pl* **-s**) M (*pressa*) scramble; (*de muitas pessoas*) stampede

corrediço, -a [kohe'dʒisu, a] ADJ sliding

corredor, a [kohe'dor(a)] M/F runner ▸ M (*passagem*) corridor, passageway; (*em avião etc*) aisle; (*cavalo*) racehorse; **o ~ da morte** death row

córrego ['kɔhegu] M stream, brook

correia [ko'heja] F strap; (*de máquina*) belt; (*para cachorro*) leash

correio [ko'heju] M mail, post; (*local*) post office; (*carteiro*) postman (*BRIT*), mailman (*US*); **~ aéreo** air mail; **pôr no ~** to post; **pelo ~** by post; **~ eletrônico** email; **~ de voz** voice mail

correlação [kohela'sãw] (*pl* **-ões**) F correlation

correlacionar [kohelasjo'nar] VT to correlate

correlações [kohela'sõjs] FPL *de* **correlação**

correligionário, -a [koheliʒjo'narju, a] M/F (*Pol*) fellow party member

corrente [ko'hẽtʃi] ADJ (*atual*) current; (*águas*) running; (*fluente*) flowing; (*comum*) usual, common ▸ F current; (*cadeia, joia*) chain; **~ de ar** draught (*BRIT*), draft (*US*)

correnteza [kohẽ'teza] F (*de ar*) draught (*BRIT*), draft (*US*); (*de rio*) current

correr [ko'her] VT to run; (*viajar por*) to travel across; (*cortina*) to draw; (*expulsar*) to drive out ▸ VI to run; (*em carro*) to drive fast, speed; (*líquido*) to flow, run; (*o tempo*) to elapse; (*boato*) to go round; (*atuar com rapidez*) to rush; **está tudo correndo bem** everything is going well; **as despesas ~ão por minha conta** I will handle the expenses

correria [kohe'ria] F rush

correspondência [kohespõ'dẽsja] F correspondence

correspondente [kohespõ'dẽtʃi] ADJ corresponding ▸ M correspondent

corresponder [kohespõ'der] VI: **~ a** to correspond to; (*ser igual*) to match (up to); (*retribuir*) to reciprocate; **corresponder-se** VR: **~-se com** to correspond with

corretagem [kohe'taʒẽ] F brokerage

corretivo, -a [kohe'tʃivu, a] ADJ corrective ▸ M punishment

correto, -a [ko'hɛtu, a] ADJ correct; (*conduta*) right; (*pessoa*) straight, honest

corretor, a [kohe'tor(a)] M/F broker ▸ M (*para datilografia*) correction strip; **~ de fundos** *ou* **de bolsa** stockbroker; **~ de imóveis** estate agent (*BRIT*), realtor (*US*); **~ ortográfico** spellchecker

corrida [ko'hida] F (*ato de correr*) running; (*certame*) race; (*de taxi*) fare; **~ de cavalos** horse race; **~ armamentista** arms race

corrido, -a [ko'hidu, a] ADJ (*rápido*) quick; (*expulso*) driven out ▸ ADV quickly

corrigir [kohi'ʒir] VT to correct; (*defeito, injustiça*) to put right

corrimão [kohi'mãw] (*pl* **corrimãos**) M handrail

corriqueiro, -a [kohi'kejru, a] ADJ common; (*problema*) trivial

corroa *etc* [ko'hoa] VB *ver* **corroer**

corroboração [kohobora'sãw] (*pl* **-ões**) F confirmation

corroborar [kohobo'rar] VT to corroborate, confirm

corroer [koho'er] VT (*metais*) to corrode; (*fig*) to eat away; **corroer-se** VR to corrode; to be eaten away

corromper [kohõ'per] VT to corrupt; (*subornar*) to bribe; **corromper-se** VR to be corrupted

corrosão [koho'zãw] F (*de metais*) corrosion; (*fig*) erosion

corrosivo, -a [koho'zivu, a] ADJ corrosive

corrupção [kohup'sãw] F corruption

corrupto, -a [ko'huptu, a] ADJ corrupt

Córsega ['kɔrsega] F: **a ~** Corsica

cortada [kor'tada] F (Esporte) smash; **dar uma ~ em alguém** (fig) to cut sb short

cortado [kor'tadu] M (aperto) tight spot; **trazer alguém num ~** to keep sb under one's thumb

cortadura [korta'dura] F (corte) cut; (entre montes) gap

cortante [kor'tãtʃi] ADJ cutting

cortar [kor'tar] VT to cut; (eliminar) to cut out; (água, telefone etc) to cut off; (efeito) to stop; (Auto) to cut up ▶ VI to cut; (encurtar caminho) to take a short cut; **cortar-se** VR to cut o.s.; **~ o cabelo** (no cabeleireiro) to have one's hair cut; **~ a palavra de alguém** to interrupt sb

corte¹ ['kɔrtʃi] M cut; (gume) cutting edge; (de luz) power cut; **sem ~** (tesoura etc) blunt; **~ de cabelo** haircut

corte² ['kɔrtʃi] F (de um monarca) court; (de uma pessoa) retinue; **cortes** FPL (PT) parliament sg

cortejar [korte'ʒar] VT to court

cortejo [kor'teʒu] M (procissão) procession

cortês [kor'tes] (pl **-eses**) ADJ polite

cortesão, -tesã [korte'zãw, te'zã] (pl **-s/-s**) ADJ courtly ▶ M/F courtier ▶ F courtesan

cortesia [korte'zia] F politeness; (de empresa) free offer

cortiça [kor'tʃisa] F (matéria) cork

cortiço [kor'tʃisu] M (habitação) slum tenement

cortina [kor'tʃina] F curtain; **~ de rolo** roller blind; **~ de voile** net curtain

cortisona [kortʃi'zɔna] F cortisone

coruja [ko'ruʒa] ADJ: **pai/mãe ~** proud father/mother ▶ F owl; **sessão ~** late show

coruscar [korus'kar] VI to sparkle, glitter

corvo ['korvu] M crow

cós [kɔs] M INV waistband; (cintura) waist

cosca ['kɔska] F: **fazer ~** to tickle

coser [ko'zer] VT, VI to sew, stitch

cosmético, -a [koz'mɛtʃiku, a] ADJ cosmetic ▶ M cosmetic

cósmico, -a ['kɔzmiku, a] ADJ cosmic

cosmo ['kɔzmu] M cosmos

cosmonauta [kozmo'nawta] M/F cosmonaut

cosmopolita [kozmopo'lita] ADJ cosmopolitan

cospe etc ['kɔspi] VB ver **cuspir**

costa ['kɔsta] F coast; **costas** FPL (dorso) back sg; **dar as ~s a** to turn one's back on; **ter ~s largas** (fig) to be thick-skinned; **ter ~s quentes** (fig) to have powerful backing, have friends in high places

costado [kos'tadu] M back; **de quatro ~s** through and through

Costa do Marfim F: **a ~** the Ivory Coast

Costa Rica F: **a ~** Costa Rica

costarriquenho, -a [kostahi'keɲu, a] ADJ, M/F Costa Rican

costear [kos'tʃjar] VT (rodear) to go round; (gado) to round up; (Náut) to follow ▶ VI to follow the coast

costela [kos'tɛla] F rib

costeleta [koste'leta] F chop, cutlet; **costeletas** FPL (suíças) side-whiskers

costumar [kostu'mar] VT (habituar) to accustom ▶ VI: **ele costuma chegar às 6.00** he usually arrives at 6.00; **costumava dizer ...** he used to say ...

costume [kos'tumi] M custom, habit; (traje) costume; **costumes** MPL (comportamento) behaviour sg (BRIT), behavior sg (US); (conduta) conduct sg; (de um povo) customs; **de ~** usual; **como de ~** as usual; **ter o ~ de fazer** to have a habit of doing

costumeiro, -a [kostu'mejru, a] ADJ usual, habitual

costura [kos'tura] F sewing, needlework; (sutura) seam; **sem ~** seamless

costurar [kostu'rar] VT, VI to sew

costureira [kostu'rejra] F dressmaker; (móvel) sewing box

cota ['kɔta] F (quinhão) quota, share; (Geo) height

cotação [kota'sãw] (pl **-ões**) F (de preços) list, quotation; (Bolsa) price; (consideração) esteem; **~ bancária** bank rate

cotado, -a [ko'tadu, a] ADJ (Com: ação) quoted; (bem-conceituado) well thought of; (num concurso) fancied

cotar [ko'tar] VT (ações) to quote; **~ algo em** to value sth at

cotejar [kote'ʒar] VT to compare

cotejo [ko'teʒu] M comparison

cotidiano, -a [kotʃi'dʒjanu, a] ADJ daily, everyday ▶ M: **o ~** daily life

cotoco [ko'toku] M (do corpo) stump; (de uma vela etc) stub

cotonete® [koto'nɛtʃi] M cotton bud (BRIT)

cotovelada [kotove'lada] F (pancada) shove; (cutucada) nudge

cotovelo [koto'velu] M (Anat) elbow; (curva) bend; **falar pelos ~s** to talk non-stop

coube etc ['kobi] VB ver **caber**

couraça [ko'rasa] F (para o peito) breastplate; (de navio etc) armour-plate (BRIT), armor-plate (US); (de animal) shell

couraçado [kora'sadu] (PT) M battleship

couro ['koru] M leather; (de um animal) hide; **~ cabeludo** scalp

couve ['kovi] F spring greens pl

couve-de-bruxelas (pl **couves-de-bruxelas**) F Brussels sprout

couve-flor (pl **couves-flor(es)**) F cauliflower

couvert [ku'vɛr] M cover charge

cova ['kɔva] F (escavação) pit; (caverna) cavern; (sepultura) grave

covarde [ko'vardʒi] ADJ cowardly ▶ M/F coward

covardia [kovar'dʒia] F cowardice

coveiro [ko'vejru] M gravedigger

covil [ko'viw] (pl **-is**) M den, lair

covinha [ko'viɲa] F dimple

covis [ko'vis] MPL de **covil**

coxa ['koʃa] F thigh

coxear [ko'ʃjar] vı to limp, hobble
coxia [ko'ʃia] ꜰ (*passagem*) aisle, gangway
coxo, -a ['koʃu, a] ᴀᴅᴊ lame
cozer [ko'zer] ᴠᴛ, vı to cook
cozido [ko'zidu] ᴍ stew
cozinha [ko'ziɲa] ꜰ (*compartimento*) kitchen; (*arte*) cookery; (*modo de cozinhar*) cuisine; **~ americana** open-plan kitchen; **~ planejada** fitted kitchen
cozinhar [kozi'ɲar] ᴠᴛ to cook; (*remanchar*) to put off ▶ vı to cook
cozinheiro, -a [kozi'ɲejru, a] ᴍ/ꜰ cook
CP ᴀʙʀ = **Caminhos de Ferro Portugueses**
CPF (ʙʀ) ᴀʙʀ ᴍ (= *Cadastro de Pessoa Física*) tax-payer's identification number
CPI (ʙʀ) ᴀʙʀ ꜰ = **Comissão Parlamentar de Inquérito**
CPJ (ʙʀ) ᴀʙʀ ᴍ (= *Cadastro de Pessoa Jurídica*) register of companies
CPLP ᴀʙʀ ꜰ *see note*

> The **CPLP** or the *Comunidade de Países de Língua Portuguesa* was set up in 1996 to establish economic and diplomatic links between all countries where the official language is Portuguese. The members are Brazil, Portugal, Angola, Mozambique, Guinea-Bissau, Cape Verde and São Tomé e Príncipe. Portuguese is spoken by around 170 million people around the world today.

crachá [kra'ʃa] ᴍ badge
crânio ['kranju] ᴍ skull; **ser um ~** (*col*) to be a whizz kid
craque ['kraki] ᴍ/ꜰ ace, expert ▶ ᴍ (*jogador de futebol*) soccer star
crasso, -a ['krasu, a] ᴀᴅᴊ crass
cratera [kra'tɛra] ꜰ crater
cravar [kra'var] ᴠᴛ (*prego etc*) to drive (in); (*pedras*) to set; (*com os olhos*) to stare at; **cravar-se** ᴠʀ to penetrate
cravejar [krave'ʒar] ᴠᴛ (*com cravos*) to nail; (*pedras*) to set; **~ alguém de balas** to spray sb with bullets
cravo ['kravu] ᴍ (*flor*) carnation; (*Mús*) harpsichord; (*especiaria*) clove; (*na pele*) blackhead; (*prego*) nail
creche ['krɛʃi] ꜰ crèche, day-care centre
Creci [krɛ'si] (ʙʀ) ᴀʙʀ ᴍ (= *Conselho Regional dos Corretores de Imóveis*) regulatory body of estate agents
credenciais [kredẽ'sjajs] ꜰᴘʟ credentials
credenciar [kredẽ'sjar] ᴠᴛ to accredit; (*habilitar*) to qualify
crediário [kre'dʒjarju] ᴍ credit plan
credibilidade [kredʒibili'dadʒi] ꜰ credibility
creditar [kredʒi'tar] ᴠᴛ to guarantee; (*Com*) to credit; **~ algo a alguém** (*quantia*) to credit sb with sth; (*garantir*) to assure sb of sth; **~ alguém em** to credit sb with; **~ uma quantia numa conta** to deposit an amount into an account
crédito ['krɛdʒitu] ᴍ credit; **a ~** on credit; **digno de ~** reliable

credo ['krɛdu] ᴍ creed; **~!** heavens!
credor, a [kre'dor(a)] ᴀᴅᴊ worthy, deserving; (*Com: saldo*) credit atr ▶ ᴍ/ꜰ creditor
credulidade [kreduli'dadʒi] ꜰ credulity
crédulo, -a ['krɛdulu, a] ᴀᴅᴊ credulous
creio *etc* ['kreju] ᴠʙ *ver* **crer**
cremação [krema'sãw] (*pl* **-ões**) ꜰ cremation
cremalheira [krema'ʎejra] ꜰ ratchet
cremar [kre'mar] ᴠᴛ to cremate
crematório [krema'tɔrju] ᴍ crematorium
creme ['krɛmi] ᴀᴅᴊ ɪɴᴠ cream ▶ ᴍ cream; (*Culin: doce*) custard; **~ dental** toothpaste; **~ de leite** single cream
cremoso, -a [kre'mozu, ɔza] ᴀᴅᴊ creamy
crença ['krẽsa] ꜰ belief
crendice [krẽ'dʒisi] ꜰ superstition
crente ['krẽtʃi] ᴀᴅᴊ believing ▶ ᴍ/ꜰ believer; (*protestante*) Protestant; (*evangélico*) born-again Christian; **estar ~ que** to think (that)
creosoto [kreo'zotu] ᴍ creosote
crepitação [krepita'sãw] ꜰ crackling
crepitante [krepi'tãtʃi] ᴀᴅᴊ crackling
crepitar [krepi'tar] vı to crackle
crepom [kre'põ] ᴀᴅᴊ: **papel ~** crêpe paper
crepuscular [krepusku'lar] ᴀᴅᴊ twilight atr
crepúsculo [kre'puskulu] ᴍ dusk, twilight
crer [krer] ᴠᴛ, vı to believe; **crer-se** ᴠʀ to believe o.s. to be; **~ em** to believe in; **~ que** to think (that); **creio que sim** I think so
crescendo [kre'sẽdu] ᴍ crescendo
crescente [kre'sẽtʃi] ᴀᴅᴊ growing; (*forma*) crescent ▶ ᴍ crescent
crescer [kre'ser] vı to grow; (*Culin: massa*) to rise
crescido, -a [kre'sidu, a] ᴀᴅᴊ (*pessoa*) grown up
crescimento [kresi'mẽtu] ᴍ growth
crespo, -a ['krespu, a] ᴀᴅᴊ (*cabelo*) curly
cretinice [kretʃi'nisi] ꜰ stupidity; (*ato, dito*) stupid thing
cretino [kre'tʃinu] ᴍ cretin, imbecile
cria ['kria] ꜰ (*animal: sg*) baby animal; (: *pl*) young *pl*
criação [krja'sãw] (*pl* **-ões**) ꜰ creation; (*de animais*) raising, breeding; (*educação*) upbringing; (*animais domésticos*) livestock *pl*; **filho de ~** adopted child
criado, -a ['krjadu, a] ᴍ/ꜰ servant
criado-mudo (*pl* **criados-mudos**) ᴍ bedside table
criador, a [krja'dor(a)] ᴍ/ꜰ creator; **~ de gado** cattle breeder
criança ['krjãsa] ᴀᴅᴊ childish ▶ ꜰ child; **ela é muito ~ para entender certas coisas** she's too young to understand certain things
criançada [krjã'sada] ꜰ: **a ~** the kids
criancice [krjã'sisi] ꜰ (*ato, dito*) childish thing; (*qualidade*) childishness
criar [krjar] ᴠᴛ to create; (*crianças*) to bring up; (*animais*) to raise, breed; (*amamentar*) to suckle, nurse; (*planta*) to grow; **criar-se** ᴠʀ: **~-se (com)** to grow up (with); **~ fama/ coragem** to achieve notoriety/pluck up courage; **~ caso** to make trouble

criatividade [kriatʃivi'dadʒi] F creativity
criativo, -a [kria'tʃivu, a] ADJ creative
criatura [kria'tura] F creature; (*indivíduo*) individual
crime ['krimi] M crime; ~ **organizado** organized crime
criminal [krimi'naw] (*pl* **-ais**) ADJ criminal
criminalidade [kriminali'dadʒi] F crime
criminoso, -a [krimi'nozu, ɔza] ADJ, M/F criminal
crina ['krina] F mane
crioulo, -a ['krjolu, a] ADJ creole ▶ M/F creole; (*BR: negro*) Black (person)
criptografar [kriptogra'far] VT (*Comput, Tel*) to encrypt
críquete ['kriketʃi] M cricket
crisálida [kri'zalida] F chrysalis
crisântemo [kri'zãtemu] M chrysanthemum
crise ['krizi] F crisis; (*escassez*) shortage; (*Med*) attack, fit; ~ **de choro** fit of hysterical crying
crisma ['krizma] F (*Rel*) confirmation
crismar [kriz'mar] VT (*Rel*) to confirm; **crismar-se** VR to be confirmed
crista ['krista] F (*de serra, onda*) crest; (*de galo*) cock's comb; **estar na ~ da onda** (*fig*) to enjoy a prominent position
cristal [kris'taw] (*pl* **-ais**) M crystal; (*vidro*) glass; **cristais** MPL (*copos*) glassware *sg*
cristalino, -a [krista'linu, a] ADJ crystal-clear
cristalizar [kristali'zar] VI to crystallize
cristandade [kristã'dadʒi] F Christianity
cristão, -tã [kris'tãw, 'tã] (*pl* **-s/-s**) ADJ, M/F Christian
cristianismo [kristʃja'nizmu] M Christianity
Cristo ['kristu] M Christ
critério [kri'tɛrju] M (*norma*) criterion; (*juízo*) discretion, judgement; **deixo isso a seu ~** I'll leave that to your discretion
criterioso, -a [krite'rjozu, ɔza] ADJ thoughtful, careful
crítica ['kritʃika] F criticism; (*artigo*) critique; (*conjunto de críticos*) critics *pl*; *ver tb* **crítico**
criticar [kritʃi'kar] VT to criticize; (*um livro*) to review
crítico, -a ['kritʃiku, a] ADJ critical ▶ M/F critic
critiquei *etc* [kritʃi'kej] VB *ver* **criticar**
crivar [kri'var] VT (*com balas etc*) to riddle; (*de perguntas, de insultos*) to bombard
crível ['krivew] (*pl* **-eis**) ADJ credible
crivo ['krivu] M sieve; (*fig*) scrutiny
crocante [kro'kãtʃi] ADJ (*pão, alface*) crispy; (*nozes, chocolate*) crunchy
crochê [kro'ʃe] M crochet
crocodilo [kroko'dʒilu] M crocodile
cromo ['krɔmu] M chrome
cromossomo [kromo'sɔmu] M chromosome
crônica ['kronika] F chronicle; (*coluna de jornal*) newspaper column; (*texto jornalístico*) feature; (*conto*) short story
crônico, -a ['kroniku, a] ADJ chronic
cronista [kro'nista] M/F (*de jornal*) columnist; (*historiógrafo*) chronicler; (*contista*) short story writer

cronologia [kronolo'ʒia] F chronology
cronológico, -a [krono'lɔʒiku, a] ADJ chronological
cronometrar [kronome'trar] VT to time
cronômetro [kro'nometru] M stopwatch
croquete [kro'ketʃi] M croquette
croqui [kro'ki] M sketch
crosta ['krosta] F crust; (*Med*) scab
cru, a [kru, 'krua] ADJ raw; (*não refinado*) crude; (*ignorante*) not very good; (*realidade*) harsh, stark
crucial [kru'sjaw] (*pl* **-ais**) ADJ crucial
crucificação [krusifika'sãw] (*pl* **-ões**) F crucifixion
crucificar [krusifi'kar] VT to crucify
crucifixo [krusi'fiksu] M crucifix
crudelíssimo, -a [krude'lisimu, a] ADJ SUPERL *de* **cruel**
cruel [kru'ɛw] (*pl* **-éis**) ADJ cruel
crueldade [kruew'dadʒi] F cruelty
cruento, -a [kru'ẽtu, a] ADJ bloody
crupe ['krupi] M (*Med*) croup
crustáceos [krus'tasjus] MPL crustaceans
cruz [kruz] F cross; (*infortúnio*) undoing; ~ **gamada** swastika; **C~ Vermelha** Red Cross; **estar entre a ~ e a caldeirinha** (*fig*) to be between the devil and the deep blue sea (*BRIT*), be between a rock and a hard place (*US*)
cruzada [kru'zada] F crusade
cruzado, -a [kru'zadu, a] ADJ crossed ▶ M crusader; (*moeda*) cruzado
cruzador [kruza'dor] M (*navio*) cruiser
cruzamento [kruza'mẽtu] M (*de estradas*) crossroads; (*mestiçagem*) cross
cruzar [kru'zar] VT to cross ▶ VI (*Náut*) to cruise; (*pessoas*) to pass each other by; ~ **com** to meet
cruzeiro [kru'zejru] M (*cruz*) (*monumental*) cross; (*moeda*) cruzeiro; (*viagem de navio*) cruise
CSN (*BR*) ABR M = **Conselho de Segurança Nacional**
CTB ABR F = **Companhia Telefônica Brasileira**
cu [ku] (!) M arse (!); **vai tomar no cu** fuck off (!); **cu de ferro** (*m, f: col*) swot
Cuba ['kuba] F Cuba
cubano, -a [ku'banu, a] ADJ, M/F Cuban
cúbico, -a ['kubiku, a] ADJ cubic
cubículo [ku'bikulu] M cubicle
cubismo [ku'bizmu] M cubism
cubo ['kubu] M cube; (*de roda*) hub
cubro *etc* ['kubru] VB *ver* **cobrir**
cuca ['kuka] (*col*) F head; **fundir a ~** (*quebrar a cabeça*) to rack one's brain; (*baratinar*) to boggle the mind; (*perturbar*) to drive crazy
cuca-fresca (*pl* **cucas-frescas**) (*col*) M/F cool customer
cuco ['kuku] M cuckoo
cucuia [ku'kuja] F: **ir para a ~** (*col*) to go down the drain
cueca ['kwɛka] F (*BR*) underpants *pl*; **cuecas** FPL (*PT: para homens*) underpants *pl*; (*para*

mulheres) panties *pl*; ~ **samba-canção** boxer shorts *pl*; ~ **slip** briefs *pl*

cueiro [ku'ejru] M wrap

cuíca ['kwika] F *kind of musical instrument*

cuidado [kwi'dadu] M care; **aos ~s de** in the care of; **ter** ~ to be careful; **~!** watch out!, be careful!; **tomar** ~ (**de**) to be careful (of); **~ para não se cortar** be careful you don't cut yourself

cuidador, -a [kwida'dor(a)] M/F carer (BRIT), caregiver (US)

cuidadoso, -a [kwida'dozu, ɔza] ADJ careful

cuidar [kwi'dar] VI: **~ de** to take care of, look after; **cuidar-se** VR to look after o.s.

cujo, -a ['kuʒu, a] PRON (*de quem*) whose; (*de que*) of which

culatra [ku'latra] F (*de arma*) breech

culinária [kuli'narja] F cookery

culinário, -a [kuli'narju, a] ADJ culinary

culminância [kuwmi'nãsja] F culmination

culminante [kuwmi'nãtʃi] ADJ: **ponto ~** highest point; (*fig*) peak

culminar [kuwmi'nar] VI: **~ (com)** to culminate (in)

culote [ku'lɔtʃi] M (*calça*) jodhpurs *pl*; (*gordura*) flab on the thighs

culpa ['kuwpa] F fault; (*Jur*) guilt; **ter ~ de** to be to blame for; **por ~ de** because of; **pôr a ~ em** to put the blame on; **sentimento de ~** guilty conscience

culpabilidade [kuwpabili'dadʒi] F guilt

culpado, -a [kuw'padu, a] ADJ guilty ▶ M/F culprit

culpar [kuw'par] VT to blame; (*acusar*) to accuse; **culpar-se** VR to take the blame

culpável [kuw'pavew] (*pl* -**eis**) ADJ guilty

cultivar [kuwtʃi'var] VT to cultivate; (*plantas*) to grow

cultivável [kuwtʃi'vavew] (*pl* -**eis**) ADJ cultivable

cultivo [kuw'tʃivu] M cultivation

culto, -a ['kuwtu, a] ADJ cultured ▶ M (*homenagem*) worship; (*religião*) cult

cultura [kuw'tura] F culture; (*da terra*) cultivation

cultural [kuwtu'raw] (*pl* -**ais**) ADJ cultural

cumbuca [kũ'buka] F pot

cume ['kumi] M top, summit; (*fig*) climax

cúmplice ['kũplisi] M/F accomplice

cumplicidade [kũplisi'dadʒi] F complicity

cumpridor, a [kũpri'dor(a)] ADJ punctilious, responsible

cumprimentar [kũprimẽ'tar] VT (*saudar*) to greet; (*dar parabéns*) to congratulate; **cumprimentar-se** VR to greet one another

cumprimento [kũpri'mẽtu] M (*realização*) fulfilment; (*saudação*) greeting; (*elogio*) compliment; **cumprimentos** MPL (*saudações*) best wishes; **~ de uma lei/ordem** compliance with a law/an order

cumprir [kũ'prir] VT (*desempenhar*) to carry out; (*promessa*) to keep; (*lei*) to obey; (*pena*) to serve ▶ VI (*convir*) to be necessary; **cumprir-se** VR to be fulfilled; **~ a palavra** to keep one's word; **fazer ~** to enforce

cumulativo, -a [kumula'tʃivu, a] ADJ cumulative

cúmulo ['kumulu] M height; **é o ~!** that's the limit!

cunha ['kuɲa] F wedge

cunhado, -a [ku'ɲadu, a] M/F brother-in-law/ sister-in-law

cunhar [ku'ɲar] VT (*moedas*) to mint; (*palavras*) to coin

cunho ['kuɲu] M (*marca*) hallmark; (*caráter*) nature

cupê [ku'pe] M coupé

cupim [ku'pĩ] (*pl* -**ns**) M termite

cupincha [ku'pĩʃa] M/F mate, pal

cupins [ku'pĩs] MPL *de* **cupim**

cupom [ku'põ] (*pl* -**ns**) M coupon

cúpula ['kupula] F (*Arq*) dome; (*de abajur*) shade; (*de partido etc*) leadership; (**reunião de**) ~ summit (meeting)

cura ['kura] F (*ato de curar*) cure; (*tratamento*) treatment; (*de carnes etc*) curing, preservation ▶ M priest

curador, a [kura'dor(a)] M/F (*de menores, órfãos*) guardian; (*de instituição*) trustee

curandeiro [kurã'dejru] M (*feiticeiro*) healer, medicine man; (*charlatão*) quack

curar [ku'rar] VT (*doença*) to cure; (*ferida*) to treat; (*carne etc*) to cure, preserve; **curar-se** VR to get well

curativo [kura'tʃivu] M dressing

curável [ku'ravew] (*pl* -**eis**) ADJ curable

curetagem [kure'taʒẽ] F curettage

curinga [ku'rĩga] M wild card

curingão [kurĩ'gãw] (*pl* -**ões**) M joker

curiosidade [kurjozi'dadʒi] F curiosity; (*objeto raro*) curio

curioso, -a [ku'rjozu, ɔza] ADJ curious ▶ M/F snooper, inquisitive person; **curiosos** MPL (*espectadores*) onlookers; **o ~ é ...** the strange thing is ....

curitibano, -a [kuritʃi'banu, a] ADJ from Curitiba ▶ M/F person from Curitiba

curral [ku'haw] (*pl* -**ais**) M pen, enclosure

currar [ku'har] (*col*) VT to rape

currículo [ku'hikulu] M (*profissional*) curriculum vitae, CV, résumé (US); (*programa*) curriculum

curriculum vitae [ku'hikulũ 'vite] M curriculum vitae

cursar [kur'sar] VT (*aulas, escola*) to attend; (*cursos*) to follow; **ele está cursando História** he's studying *ou* doing history

cursivo [kur'sivu] M (*Tip*) script

curso ['kursu] M course; (*direção*) direction; **em ~** (*ano etc*) current; (*processo*) in progress; (*dinheiro*) in circulation; **~ primário/ secundário/superior** primary school/ secondary school/degree course; **~ normal** teacher-training course

cursor [kur'sor] M (*Comput*) cursor

curta ['kurta] M (*Cinema*) short

curta-metragem (pl **curtas-metragens**) M short film

curtição [kurtʃi'sãw] F (col) fun; (de couro) tanning

curtido, -a [kur'tʃidu, a] ADJ (fig) hardened

curtir [kur'tʃir] VT (couro) to tan; (tornar rijo) to toughen up; (padecer) to suffer, endure; (col) to enjoy

curto, -a ['kurtu, a] ADJ short; (inteligência) limited ▶ M (Elet) short (circuit)

curto-circuito (pl **curtos-circuitos**) M short circuit

curva ['kurva] F curve; (de estrada, rio) bend; **~ fechada** hairpin bend

curvar [kur'var] VT to bend, curve; (submeter) to put down; **curvar-se** VR (abaixar-se) to stoop; **~-se a** (submeter-se) to submit to

curvatura [kurva'tura] F curvature

curvo, -a ['kurvu, a] ADJ curved; (estrada) winding

cuscuz [kus'kuz] M couscous

cusparada [kuspa'rada] F spit; **dar uma ~** to spit

cuspe ['kuspi] M spit, spittle

cuspido, -a [kus'pidu, a] ADJ covered in spittle; **ele é o pai ~ e escarrado** (col) he's the spitting image of his father

cuspir [kus'pir] VT, VI to spit; **~ no prato em que se come** to bite the hand that feeds one

custa ['kusta] F: **à ~ de** at the expense of; **custas** FPL (Jur) costs

custar [kus'tar] VI to cost; (ser difícil) to be difficult; (demorar) to take a long time; **~ caro** to be expensive; **~ a fazer** (ter dificuldade) to have trouble doing; (demorar) to take a long time to do; **não custa nada perguntar** there's no harm in asking

custear [kus'tʃar] VT to bear the cost of

custeio [kus'teju] M funding; (relação de custos) costing

custo ['kustu] M cost; **a ~** with difficulty; **a todo ~** at all costs

custódia [kus'tɔdʒja] F custody

CUT (BR) ABR F (= Central Única de Trabalhadores) trade union

cutelaria [kutela'ria] F knife-making

cutelo [ku'tɛlu] M cleaver

cutícula [ku'tʃikula] F cuticle

cútis ['kutʃis] F INV (pele) skin; (tez) complexion

cutucada [kutu'kada] F nudge; (com o dedo) prod

cutucar [kutu'kar] VT (com o dedo) to prod, poke; (com o cotovelo) to nudge

CVV (BR) ABR M (= Centro de Valorização da Vida) Samaritan organization

Cz$ ABR = **cruzado**

czar [kzar] M czar

Dd

D, d [de] M (pl **ds**) D, d ▶ ABR = **dona**; (= direito) R.; (= deve) d; **D de dado** D for David (BRIT) ou dog (US)

d/ ABR = **dia**

da [da] = **de + a**; ver **de**

dá [da] VB ver **dar**

DAC (BR) ABR M = **Departamento de Aviação Civil**

dactilografar etc [datilogra'far] (PT) = **datilografar** etc

dadaísmo [dada'izmu] M Dadaism

dádiva ['dadʒiva] F (donativo) donation; (oferta) gift

dadivoso, -a [dadʒi'vozu, ɔza] ADJ generous

dado, -a ['dadu, a] ADJ given; (sociável) sociable ▶ M (em jogo) die; (fato) fact; (Comput) piece of data; **dados** MPL (em jogo) dice; (fatos, Comput) data sg; **ser ~ a algo** to be prone ou given to sth; **em ~ momento** at a given moment; **~ que** (suposto que) supposing that; (uma vez que) given that

daí [da'ji] ADV (= de + aí) (desse lugar) from there; (desse momento) from then; (col: num relato) then; **~ a um mês** a month later; **~ por** ou **em diante** from then on; **e ~?** (col) so what?

dali [da'li] ADV = **de + ali**; ver **de**

dália ['dalja] F dahlia

daltônico, -a [daw'toniku, a] ADJ colour-blind (BRIT), color-blind (US)

daltonismo [dawto'nizmu] M colour (BRIT) ou color (US) blindness

dama ['dama] F lady; (Xadrez, Cartas) queen; **damas** FPL (jogo) draughts (BRIT), checkers (US); **~ de honra** bridesmaid

Damasco [da'masku] N Damascus

damasco [da'masku] M (fruta) apricot; (tecido) damask

danação [dana'sāw] F damnation; (travessura) mischief, naughtiness

danado, -a [da'nadu, a] ADJ (condenado) damned; (zangado) furious, angry; (menino) mischievous, naughty; **cão ~** mad dog; **ela está com uma fome/dor danada** she's really hungry/got a terrible pain; **uma gripe danada/um susto ~** a really bad case of flu/a hell of a fright; **ele é ~ de bom** (col) he's really good; **ser ~ em algo** to be really good at sth

danar-se [dā'narsi] VR (enfurecer-se) to get furious; **dane-se!** (col) damn it!; **danou-se!** (col) oh, gosh!

dança ['dāsa] F dance; **entrar na ~** to get involved

dançar [dā'sar] VI to dance; (col: pessoa: sair-se mal) to lose out; (: em exame) to fail; (: coisa) to go by the board

dançarino, -a [dāsa'rinu, a] M/F dancer

danceteria [dāsete'ria] F disco(theque)

dancing ['dāsīŋ] M dance hall

danificar [danifi'kar] VT (objeto) to damage

daninho, -a [da'niɲu, a] ADJ harmful; (gênio) nasty

dano ['danu] M (tb: **danos**) damage; (moral) harm; (a uma pessoa) injury

danoso, -a [da'nozu, ɔza] ADJ (a uma pessoa) harmful; (a uma coisa) damaging

dantes ['dātʃis] ADV before, formerly

Danúbio [da'nubju] M: **o ~** the Danube

daquele, -a [da'kele, 'kɛla] = **de + aquele**; ver **de**

daqui [da'ki] ADV (= de + aqui) (deste lugar) from here; **~ a pouco** soon, in a little while; **~ a uma semana** a week from now, in a week's time; **~ em diante** from now on

daquilo [da'kilu] = **de + aquilo**; ver **de**

(PALAVRA-CHAVE)

dar [dar] VT **1** (ger) to give; (festa) to hold; (problemas) to cause; **dar algo a alguém** to give sb sth, give sth to sb; **dar de beber a alguém** to give sb a drink; **dar aula de francês** to teach French

2 (produzir: fruta etc) to produce

3 (notícias no jornal) to publish

4 (cartas) to deal

5 (+ n: perífrase de vb): **me dá medo/pena** it frightens/upsets me

▶ VI **1: dar com** (coisa) to find; (pessoa) to meet

2: dar em (bater) to hit; (resultar) to lead to; (lugar) to come to

3: dá no mesmo it's all the same

4: dar de si (sapatos etc) to stretch, give

5: dar para (impess: ser possível) to be able to; **dá para trocar dinheiro aqui?** can I change money here?; **vai dar para eu ir amanhã** I'll be able to go tomorrow; **dá para você vir amanhã? — não, amanhã**

não vai dar can you come tomorrow? — no,
I can't
6 (*ser suficiente*): **dar para/para fazer** to be
enough for/to do; **dá para todo mundo?** is
there enough for everyone?
dar-se VR **1** (*sair-se*): **dar-se bem/mal** to do
well/badly
2: **dar-se (com alguém)** to be acquainted
(with sb); **dar-se bem (com alguém)** to get
on well (with sb)
3: **dar-se por vencido** to give up

Dardanelos [darda'nɛlus] MPL: **os ~** the
Dardanelles
dardo ['dardu] M dart; (*grande*) spear
das [das] = **de** + **as**; *ver* **de**
data ['data] F date; (*época*) time; **de longa ~** of
long standing
datação [data'sãw] F dating
datar [da'tar] VT to date ▶ VI: **~ de** to date
from
datilografar [datʃilogra'far] VT to type
datilografia [datʃilogra'fia] F typing
datilógrafo, -a [datʃi'lɔgrafu, a] M/F typist
(BRIT), stenographer (US)
dativo, -a [da'tʃivu, a] ADJ dative ▶ M dative
d.C. ABR (= *depois de Cristo*) A.D.
DDD ABR F (= *discagem direta a distância*) *direct
long-distance dialling* ▶ ABR M (*código*) dialling
code (BRIT), area code (US)
DDI ABR F (= *discagem direta internacional*) IDD
▶ ABR M (*código de país*) country code

de [dʒi] (*de* + *o(s)/a(s)* = *do(s)/da(s)*; + *ali* = *dali*; +
ele(s)/a(s) = *dele(s)/a(s)*; + *esse(s)/a(s)* =
desse(s)/a(s); + *isso* = *disso*; + *este(s)/a(s)* =
deste(s)/a(s); + *isto* = *disto*; + *aquele(s)/a(s)* =
daquele(s)/a(s); + *aquilo* = *daquilo*) PREP **1** (*posse*)
of; **a casa de João/da irmã** João's/my
sister's house; **é dele** it's his; **um romance
de** a novel by
2 (*origem, distância, com números*) from; **sou de
São Paulo** I'm from São Paulo; **de 8 a 20**
from 8 to 20; **sair do cinema** to leave the
cinema; **de dois em dois** two by two, two at
a time
3 (*valor descritivo*): **um copo de vinho** a glass
of wine; **um homem de cabelo comprido**
a man with long hair; **o infeliz do homem**
(*col*) the poor man; **um bilhete de avião** an
air ticket; **uma criança de três anos** a
three-year-old (child); **uma máquina de
costurar** a sewing machine; **aulas de
inglês** English lessons; **feito de madeira**
made of wood; **vestido de branco** dressed
in white
4 (*modo*): **de trem/avião** by train/plane; **de
lado** sideways
5 (*hora, tempo*): **às 8 da manhã** at 8 o'clock in
the morning; **de dia/noite** by day/night; **de
hoje a oito dias** a week from now; **de
dois em dois dias** every other day

6 (*comparações*): **mais/menos de cem
pessoas** more/less than a hundred people;
é o mais caro da loja it's the most
expensive in the shop; **ela é mais bonita do
que sua irmã** she's prettier than her sister;
gastei mais do que pretendia I spent more
than I intended
7 (*causa*): **estou morto de calor** I'm boiling
hot; **ela morreu de câncer** she died of
cancer
8 (*adj* + *de* + *infin*): **fácil de entender** easy to
understand

dê *etc* [de] VB *ver* **dar**
deão [dʒi'ãw] (*pl* **deãos**) M dean
debaixo [de'bajʃu] ADV below, underneath
▶ PREP: **~ de** under, beneath
debalde [de'bawdʒi] ADV in vain
debandada [debã'dada] F stampede; **em ~**
in confusion
debandar [debã'dar] VT to put to flight ▶ VI to
disperse
debate [de'batʃi] M (*discussão*) discussion,
debate; (*disputa*) argument
debater [deba'ter] VT to debate; (*discutir*) to
discuss; **debater-se** VR to struggle
débeis ['debejs] PL *de* **débil**
debelar [debe'lar] VT to put down, suppress;
(*crise*) to overcome; (*doença*) to cure
debênture [de'bẽturi] F (*Com*) debenture
debicar [debi'kar] VT (*caçoar*) to make fun of
débil ['debiw] (*pl* **-eis**) ADJ (*pessoa*) weak, feeble;
(*Psico*) retarded ▶ M: **~ mental** mentally
handicapped person; (*col: ofensivo*) moron (!)
debilidade [debili'dadʒi] F weakness;
~ mental mental handicap
debilitação [debilita'sãw] F weakening
debilitante [debili'tãtʃi] ADJ debilitating
debilitar [debili'tar] VT to weaken; **debilitar-
se** VR to become weak, weaken
debiloide [debi'lɔjdʒi] (*col*) ADJ idiotic ▶ M/F
idiot
debique [de'biki] M mockery, ridicule
debitar [debi'tar] VT to debit; **~ a conta de
alguém em $40** to debit sb's account by
$40; **~ $40 à** *ou* **na conta de alguém** to debit
$40 to sb's account
débito ['debitu] M debit
debochado, -a [debo'ʃadu, a] ADJ (*pessoa*)
sardonic; (*jeito, tom*) mocking ▶ M/F sardonic
person
debochar [debo'ʃar] VT to mock ▶ VI: **~ de** to
mock
deboche [de'bɔʃi] M gibe
debruar [de'brwar] VT (*roupa*) to edge; (*desenho*)
to adorn
debruçar [debru'sar] VT to bend over;
debruçar-se VR to bend over; (*inclinar-se*) to
lean over; **~-se na janela** to lean out of the
window
debrum [de'brũ] M edging
debulha [de'buʎa] F (*de trigo*) threshing
debulhar [debu'ʎar] VT (*grão*) to thresh;

(*descascar*) to shell; **debulhar-se** VR: **~-se em lágrimas** to burst into tears

debutante [debu'tãtʃi] F débutante

debutar [debu'tar] VI to appear for the first time, make one's début

década ['dɛkada] F decade

decadência [deka'dẽsja] F decadence

decadente [deka'dẽtʃi] ADJ decadent

decair [deka'ir] VI to decline; (*restaurante etc*) to go downhill; (*pressão, velocidade*) to drop; (*planta*) to wilt

decalcar [dekaw'kar] VT to trace; (*fig*) to copy

decalque [de'kawki] M tracing

decano [de'kanu] M oldest member

decantar [dekã'tar] VT (*líquido*) to decant; (*purificar*) to purify

decapitar [dekapi'tar] VT to behead, decapitate

decatlo [de'katlu] M decathlon

decência [de'sẽsja] F decency

decênio [de'senju] M decade

decente [de'sẽtʃi] ADJ decent; (*apropriado*) proper; (*honrado*) honourable (BRIT), honorable (US); (*trabalho*) neat, presentable

decentemente [desẽtʃi'mẽtʃi] ADV (*com decoro*) decently; (*apropriadamente*) properly; (*honradamente*) honourably (BRIT), honorably (US)

decepar [dese'par] VT to cut off, chop off

decepção [desep'sãw] (*pl* **-ões**) F disappointment; (*desilusão*) disillusionment

decepcionar [desepsjo'nar] VT to disappoint, let down; (*desiludir*) to disillusion; **decepcionar-se** VR to be disappointed; to be disillusioned; **o filme decepcionou** the film was disappointing

decepções [desep'sõjs] FPL *de* **decepção**

decerto [dʒi'sɛrtu] ADV certainly

decidido, -a [desi'dʒidu, a] ADJ (*pessoa*) determined; (*questão*) resolved

decidir [desi'dʒir] VT (*determinar*) to decide; (*solucionar*) to resolve; **decidir-se** VR: **~-se a** to make up one's mind to; **~-se por** to decide on, go for

decíduo, -a [de'sidwu, a] ADJ (*Bot*) deciduous

decifrar [desi'frar] VT to decipher; (*futuro*) to foretell; (*compreender*) to understand

decifrável [desi'fravew] (*pl* **-eis**) ADJ decipherable

decimal [desi'maw] (*pl* **-ais**) ADJ decimal ▶ M (*número*) decimal

décimo, -a ['dɛsimu, a] ADJ tenth ▶ M tenth; **~ nono** nineteenth; **~ oitavo** eighteenth; **~ primeiro** eleventh; **~ quarto** fourteenth; **~ quinto** fifteenth; **~ segundo** twelfth; **~ sétimo** seventeenth; **~ sexto** sixteenth; **~ terceiro** thirteenth; *ver tb* **quinto**

decisão [desi'zãw] (*pl* **-ões**) F decision; (*capacidade de decidir*) decisiveness, resolution; **~ por pênaltis** (*Futebol*) penalty shoot-out

decisivo, -a [desi'zivu, a] ADJ (*fator*) decisive; (*jogo*) deciding

decisões [desi'zõjs] FPL *de* **decisão**

declamação [deklama'sãw] F (*de poema*) recitation; (*pej*) ranting

declamar [dekla'mar] VT (*poemas*) to recite ▶ VI (*pej*) to rant

declaração [deklara'sãw] (*pl* **-ões**) F declaration; (*depoimento*) statement; (*revelação*) revelation; **~ de amor** proposal; **~ de imposto de renda** income tax return; **~ juramentada** affidavit

declarado, -a [dekla'radu, a] ADJ (*intenção*) declared; (*opinião*) professed; (*inimigo*) sworn; (*alcoólatra*) self-confessed; (*cristão etc*) avowed

declarante [dekla'rãtʃi] M/F (*Jur*) witness

declarar [dekla'rar] VT to declare; (*confessar*) to confess

Dec-lei [dek-] ABR M = **decreto-lei**

declinação [deklina'sãw] (*pl* **-ões**) F (*Ling*) declension

declinar [dekli'nar] VT (*recusar*) to decline, refuse; (*nomes*) to give; (*Ling*) to decline ▶ VI (*sol*) to go down; (*terreno*) to slope down

declínio [de'klinju] M decline

declive [de'klivi] M slope, incline

decô [de'ko] ADJ INV Art-Deco

decodificador [dekodʒifika'dor] M (*Comput*) decoder

decodificar [dekodʒifi'kar] VT to decode

decolagem [deko'laʒẽ] (*pl* **-ns**) F (*Aer*) take-off

decolar [deko'lar] VI (*Aer*) to take off

decompor [dekõ'por] (*irreg: como* **pôr**) VT (*analisar*) to analyse; (*apodrecer*) to rot; (*rosto*) to contort; **decompor-se** VR to rot, decompose

decomposição [dekõpozi'sãw] (*pl* **-ões**) F (*apodrecimento*) decomposition; (*análise*) dissection; (*do rosto*) contortion

decomposto, -a [dekõ'postu, a] PP *de* **decompor**

decompunha *etc* [dekõ'puɲa] VB *ver* **decompor**

decompus *etc* [dekõ'pus] VB *ver* **decompor**

decompuser *etc* [dekõpu'zer] VB *ver* **decompor**

decoração [dekora'sãw] F decoration; (*Teatro*) scenery

decorar [deko'rar] VT to decorate; (*aprender*) to learn by heart

decorativo, -a [dekora'tʃivu, a] ADJ decorative

decoro [de'koru] M (*decência*) decency; (*dignidade*) decorum

decoroso, -a [deko'rozu, ɔza] ADJ decent, respectable

decorrência [deko'hẽsja] F consequence, result; **em ~ de** as a result of

decorrente [deko'hẽtʃi] ADJ: **~ de** resulting from

decorrer [deko'her] VI (*tempo*) to pass; (*acontecer*) to take place, happen ▶ M: **no ~ de** in the course of; **~ de** to result from

decotado, -a [deko'tadu, a] ADJ (*roupa*) low-cut

decote [de'kɔtʃi] M (*de vestido*) low neckline

decrépito, -a [de'krɛpitu, a] ADJ decrepit

d

decrescente [dekre'sẽtʃi] ADJ decreasing, diminishing

decrescer [dekre'ser] VI to decrease, diminish

decréscimo [de'krɛsimu] M decrease, decline

decretação [dekreta'sãw] (*pl* **-ões**) F announcement; (*de estado de sítio*) declaration

decretar [dekre'tar] VT to decree, order; (*estado de sítio*) to declare; (*anunciar*) to announce; (*determinar*) to determine

decreto [de'krɛtu] M decree, order; **nem por ~** not for love nor money

decreto-lei (*pl* **decretos-leis**) M act, law

decúbito [de'kubitu] M: **em ~** recumbent

decurso [de'kursu] M (*tempo*) course; **no ~ de** in the course of, during

dedal [de'daw] (*pl* **-ais**) M thimble

dedão [de'dãw] (*pl* **-ões**) M thumb; (*do pé*) big toe

dedetização [dedetʃiza'sãw] F spraying with insecticide

dedetizar [dedetʃi'zar] VT to spray with insecticide

dedicação [dedʒika'sãw] F dedication; (*devotamento*) devotion

dedicado, -a [dedʒi'kadu, a] ADJ (*tb Comput*) dedicated

dedicar [dedʒi'kar] VT (*poema*) to dedicate; (*tempo, atenção*) to devote; **dedicar-se** VR: **~-se a** to devote o.s. to

dedicatória [dedʒika'tɔrja] F (*de obra*) dedication

dedilhar [dedʒi'ʎar] VT (*Mús: no braço*) to finger; (: *nas cordas*) to pluck

dedo ['dedu] M finger; (*do pé*) toe; **dois ~s (de)** a little bit (of); **escolher a ~** to handpick; **~ anular** ring finger; **~ indicador** index finger; **~ mínimo** *ou* **mindinho** little finger; **~ polegar** thumb

dedo-duro (*pl* **dedos-duros**) (*col*) M (*criminoso*) grass; (*criança*) sneak, tell-tale

dedões [de'dõjs] MPL *de* **dedão**

dedução [dedu'sãw] (*pl* **-ões**) F deduction

dedurar [dedu'rar] (*col*) VT: **~ alguém** (*criminoso*) to grass on sb; (*colega etc*) to drop sb in it

dedutivo, -a [dedu'tʃivu, a] ADJ deductive

deduzir [dedu'zir] VT (*concluir*): **~ (de)** to deduce (from), infer (from); (*quantia*) to deduct (from)

defasado, -a [defa'zadu, a] ADJ: **~ (de)** out of step (with)

defasagem [defa'zaʒẽ] (*pl* **-ns**) F discrepancy

defecar [defe'kar] VI to defecate

defecção [defek'sãw] (*pl* **-ões**) F defection; (*deserção*) desertion

defectivo, -a [defek'tʃivu, a] ADJ faulty, defective; (*Ling*) defective

defeito [de'fejtu] M defect, flaw; **pôr ~s em** to find fault with; **com ~** broken, out of order; **para ninguém botar ~** (*col*) perfect

defeituoso, -a [defej'twozu, ɔza] ADJ defective, faulty

defender [defẽ'der] VT (*ger, Jur*) to defend; (*proteger*) to protect; **defender-se** VR to stand up for o.s.; (*numa língua*) to get by; **~-se de** (*de ataque*) to defend o.s. against; (*do frio etc*) to protect o.s. against

defensável [defẽ'savew] (*pl* **-eis**) ADJ defensible

defensiva [defẽ'siva] F defensive; **estar** *ou* **ficar na ~** to be on the defensive

defensor, a [defẽ'sor(a)] M/F defender; (*Jur*) defending counsel

deferência [defe'rẽsja] F (*condescendência*) deference; (*respeito*) respect

deferente [defe'rẽtʃi] ADJ deferential

deferimento [deferi'mẽtu] M (*de dinheiro, pedido, petição*) granting; (*de prêmio, condecoração*) awarding; (*aceitação*) acceptance

deferir [defe'rir] VT (*pedido, petição*) to grant; (*prêmio, condecoração*) to award ▶ VI: **~ a** (*pedido, petição*) to concede to; (*sugestão*) to accept

defesa [de'feza] F defence (BRIT), defense (US); (*Jur*) counsel for the defence ▶ M (*Futebol*) back

deficiência [defi'sjẽsja] F deficiency

deficiente [defi'sjẽtʃi] ADJ (*imperfeito*) defective; (*carente*): **~ (em)** deficient (in)

déficit ['dɛfisitʃi] (*pl* **-s**) M deficit

deficitário, -a [defisi'tarju, a] ADJ in deficit

definhar [defi'ɲar] VT to debilitate ▶ VI (*consumir-se*) to waste away; (*Bot*) to wither

definição [defini'sãw] (*pl* **-ões**) F definition

definir [defi'nir] VT to define; **definir-se** VR (*decidir-se*) to make a decision; (*explicar-se*) to make one's position clear; **~-se a favor de/ contra algo** to come out in favo(u)r of/ against sth; **~-se como** to describe o.s. as

definitivamente [definitʃiva'mẽtʃi] ADV (*finalmente*) definitively; (*permanentemente*) for good; (*sem dúvida*) definitely

definitivo, -a [defini'tʃivu, a] ADJ (*final*) final, definitive; (*permanente*) permanent; (*resposta, data*) definite

definível [defi'nivew] (*pl* **-eis**) ADJ definable

defiro *etc* [de'firu] VB *ver* **deferir**

deflação [defla'sãw] F deflation

deflacionar [deflasjo'nar] VT to deflate

deflacionário, -a [deflasjo'narju, a] ADJ deflationary

deflagração [deflagra'sãw] (*pl* **-ões**) F explosion; (*fig*) outbreak

deflagrar [defla'grar] VI to explode; (*fig*) to break out ▶ VT to set off; (*fig*) to trigger

deflorar [deflo'rar] VT to deflower

deformação [deforma'sãw] (*pl* **-ões**) F loss of shape; (*de corpo*) deformation; (*de imagem, pensamento*) distortion

deformar [defor'mar] VT to put out of shape; (*corpo*) to deform; (*imagem, pensamento*) to distort; **deformar-se** VR to lose shape; to be deformed; to become distorted

deformidade [deformi'dadʒi] F deformity

defraudação [defrawda'sãw] (*pl* **-ões**) F fraud; (*de dinheiro*) embezzlement

defraudar [defraw'dar] VT (*dinheiro*) to embezzle; (*uma pessoa*) to defraud; **~ alguém de algo** to cheat sb of sth

defrontar [defrõ'tar] VT to face ▶ VI: **~ com** to face; (*dar com*) to come face to face with; **defrontar-se** VR to face each other

defronte [de'frõtʃi] ADV opposite ▶ PREP: **~ de** opposite

defumado, -a [defu'madu, a] ADJ smoked

defumar [defu'mar] VT (*presunto*) to smoke; (*perfumar*) to perfume

defunto, -a [de'fũtu, a] ADJ dead ▶ M/F dead person

degelar [deʒe'lar] VT to thaw; (*geladeira*) to defrost ▶ VI to thaw out; to defrost

degelo [de'ʒelu] M thaw

degeneração [deʒenera'sãw] F (*processo*) degeneration; (*estado*) degeneracy

degenerar [deʒene'rar] VI: **~ (em)** to degenerate (into); **degenerar-se** VR to become degenerate

deglutir [deglu'tʃir] VT, VI to swallow

degolação [degola'sãw] (*pl* **-ões**) F beheading, decapitation

degolar [dego'lar] VT to decapitate

degradação [degrada'sãw] F degradation

degradante [degra'dãtʃi] ADJ degrading

degradar [degra'dar] VT to degrade, debase; **degradar-se** VR to demean o.s.

dégradé [degra'de] ADJ INV (*cor*) shaded off

degrau [de'graw] M step; (*de escada de mão*) rung

degredar [degre'dar] VT to exile

degredo [de'gredu] M exile

degringolar [degrĩgo'lar] VI (*cair*) to tumble down; (*fig*) to collapse; (: *deteriorar-se*) to deteriorate; (*desorganizar-se*) to get messed up

degustação [degusta'sãw] (*pl* **-ões**) F tasting, sampling; (*saborear*) savouring (BRIT), savoring (US)

degustar [degus'tar] VT (*provar*) to taste; (*saborear*) to savour (BRIT), savor (US)

dei *etc* [dej] VB *ver* **dar**

deificar [dejfi'kar] VT to deify

deitada [dej'tada] (*col*) F: **dar uma ~** to have a lie-down

deitado, -a [dej'tadu, a] ADJ (*estendido*) lying down; (*na cama*) in bed

deitar [dej'tar] VT to lay down; (*na cama*) to put to bed; (*colocar*) to put, place; (*lançar*) to cast; (PT: *líquido*) to pour; **deitar-se** VR to lie down; to go to bed; **~ sangue** (PT) to bleed; **~ abaixo** to knock down, flatten; **~ a fazer algo** to start doing sth; **~ uma carta** (PT) to post a letter; **~ fora** (PT) to throw away *ou* out; **~ e rolar** (*col*) to do as one likes

deixa ['dejʃa] F clue, hint; (*Teatro*) cue; (*chance*) chance

deixar [dej'ʃar] VT to leave; (*abandonar*) to abandon; (*permitir*) to let, allow ▶ VI: **~ de** (*parar*) to stop; (*não fazer*) to fail to; **não posso ~ de ir** I must go; **não posso ~ de rir** I can't help laughing; **~ cair** to drop; **~ alguém**

louco to drive sb crazy *ou* mad; **~ alguém cansado/nervoso** *etc* to make sb tired/nervous *etc*; **~ a desejar** to leave something to be desired; **deixa disso!** (*col*) come off it!; **deixa para lá!** (*col*) forget it!

dela ['dɛla] = **de + ela**; *ver* **de**

delação [dela'sãw] (*pl* **-ões**) F (*de pessoa: denúncia*) accusation; (: *traição*) betrayal; (*de abusos*) disclosure

delatar [dela'tar] VT (*pessoa*) to inform on; (*abusos*) to reveal; (*à polícia*) to report

delator, a [dela'tor(a)] M/F informer

délavé [dela've] ADJ INV (*jeans*) faded

dele ['deli] = **de + ele**; *ver* **de**

delegação [delega'sãw] (*pl* **-ões**) F delegation

delegacia [delega'sia] F office; **~ de polícia** police station

delegações [delega'sõjs] FPL *de* **delegação**

delegado, -a [dele'gadu, a] M/F delegate, representative; **~ de polícia** police chief

delegar [dele'gar] VT to delegate

deleitar [delej'tar] VT to delight; **deleitar-se** VR: **~-se com** to delight in

deleite [de'lejtʃi] M delight

deleitoso, -a [delej'tozu, ɔza] ADJ delightful

deletar [dele'tar] VT (*Comput*) to delete

deletério, -a [dele'tɛrju, a] ADJ harmful

delével [de'lɛvew] (*pl* **-eis**) ADJ erasable

delgado, -a [dew'gadu, a] ADJ thin; (*esbelto*) slim, slender; (*fino*) fine

Délhi ['deli] N: **(Nova) ~** (New) Delhi

deliberação [delibera'sãw] (*pl* **-ões**) F deliberation; (*decisão*) decision

deliberar [delibe'rar] VT to decide, resolve ▶ VI to deliberate

deliberativo, -a [delibera'tʃivu, a] ADJ (*conselho*) deliberative

delicadeza [delika'deza] F delicacy; (*cortesia*) kindness

delicado, -a [deli'kadu, a] ADJ delicate; (*frágil*) fragile; (*cortês*) polite; (*sensível*) sensitive

delícia [de'lisja] F delight; (*prazer*) pleasure; **esse bolo é uma ~** this cake is delicious; **que ~!** how lovely!

deliciar [deli'sjar] VT to delight; **deliciar-se** VR: **~-se com algo** to take delight in sth

delicioso, -a [deli'sjozu, ɔza] ADJ lovely; (*comida, bebida*) delicious

delimitação [delimita'sãw] F delimitation

delimitar [delimi'tar] VT to delimit

delineador [delinja'dor] M (*de olhos*) eyeliner

delinear [deli'njar] VT to outline

delinquência [delĩ'kwẽsja] F delinquency

delinquente [delĩ'kwẽtʃi] ADJ, M/F delinquent, criminal

delinquir [delĩ'kwir] VI to commit an offence (BRIT) *ou* offense (US)

delir [de'lir] VT to erase

delirante [deli'rãtʃi] ADJ delirious; (*show, atuação*) thrilling

delirar [deli'rar] VI (*com febre*) to be delirious; (*de ódio, prazer*) to go mad, go wild

d

delírio [de'lirju] M (Med) delirium; (êxtase) ecstasy; (excitação) excitement

delirium tremens [de'liriũ 'trɛmẽs] M delirium tremens

delito [de'litu] M (crime) crime; (falta) offence (BRIT), offense (US)

delonga [de'lõga] F delay; **sem mais ~s** without more ado

delongar [delõ'gar] VT to delay; **delongar-se** VR (conversa) to wear on; **~-se em** to dwell on

delta ['dɛwta] F delta

demagogia [demago'ʒia] F demagogy

demagógico, -a [dema'gɔʒiku, a] ADJ demagogic

demagogo [dema'gogu] M demagogue

demais [dʒi'majs] ADV (em demasia) too much; (muitíssimo) a lot, very much ▶ PRON: **os/as ~** the rest (of them); **já é ~!** this is too much!; **é bom ~** it's really good; **foi ~** (col: bacana) it was great

demanda [de'mãda] F (Jur) lawsuit; (disputa) claim; (requisição) request; (Econ) demand; **em ~ de** in search of

demandar [demã'dar] VT (Jur) to sue; (exigir, reclamar) to demand; (porto) to head for

demão [de'mãw] (pl **demãos**) F (de tinta) coat, layer

demarcação [demarka'sãw] F demarcation

demarcar [demar'kar] VT (delimitar) to demarcate; (fixar) to mark out

demarcatório, -a [demarka'tɔrju, a] ADJ: **linha demarcatória** demarcation line

demasia [dema'zia] F excess, surplus; (imoderação) lack of moderation; **em ~** (dinheiro, comida etc) too much; (cartas, problemas etc) too many

demasiadamente [demazjada'mẽtʃi] ADV too much; (com adj) too

demasiado, -a [dema'zjadu, a] ADJ too much; (pl) too many ▶ ADV too much; (com adj) too

demência [de'mẽsja] F dementia

demente [de'mẽtʃi] ADJ insane, demented

demérito, -a [de'mɛritu, a] ADJ unworthy ▶ M demerit

demissão [demi'sãw] (pl **-ões**) F dismissal; **pedido de ~** resignation; **pedir ~** to resign

demissionário, -a [demisjo'narju, a] ADJ resigning, outgoing

demissões [demi'sõjs] FPL de **demissão**

demitir [demi'tʃir] VT to dismiss; (col) to sack, fire; **demitir-se** VR to resign

democracia [demokra'sia] F democracy

democrata [demo'krata] M/F democrat

democrático, -a [demo'kratʃiku, a] ADJ democratic

democratização [demokratʃiza'sãw] F democratization

democratizar [demokratʃi'zar] VT to democratize

démodé [demo'de] ADJ INV old-fashioned

demografia [demogra'fia] F demography

demográfico, -a [demo'grafiku, a] ADJ demographic

demolição [demoli'sãw] (pl **-ões**) F demolition

demolir [demo'lir] VT to demolish, knock down; (fig) to destroy

demoníaco, -a [demo'niaku, a] ADJ devilish

demônio [de'monju] M devil, demon; (col: criança) brat

demonstração [demõstra'sãw] (pl **-ões**) F (lição prática) demonstration; (de amizade) show, display; (prova) proof; **~ de contas** (Com) statement of account; **~ de lucros e perdas** (Com) profit and loss statement

demonstrar [demõs'trar] VT (mostrar) to demonstrate; (provar) to prove; (amizade etc) to show

demonstrativo, -a [demõstra'tʃivu, a] ADJ demonstrative

demonstrável [demõ'stravew] (pl **-eis**) ADJ demonstrable

demora [de'mɔra] F delay; (parada) stop; **sem ~** at once, without delay; **qual é a ~ disso?** how long will this take?

demorado, -a [demo'radu, a] ADJ slow

demorar [demo'rar] VT to delay, slow down ▶ VI (permanecer) to stay; (tardar a vir) to be late; (conserto) to take (a long) time; **demorar-se** VR to stay for a long time, linger; **~ a chegar** to be a long time coming; **vai ~ muito?** will it take long?; **não vou ~** I won't be long

demover [demo'ver] VT: **~ alguém de algo** to talk sb out of sth; **demover-se** VR: **~-se de algo** to be talked out of sth

Denatran [dena'trã] (BR) ABR M (= Departamento Nacional de Trânsito) ≈ Ministry of Transport

dendê [dẽ'de] M (Culin: óleo) palm oil; (Bot) oil palm

denegrir [dene'grir] VT to blacken; (difamar) to denigrate

dengo [dẽgu] M coyness; (choro) whimpering

dengoso, -a [dẽ'gozu, ɔza] ADJ coy; (criança: choraminguento): **ser ~** to be a crybaby

dengue ['dẽgi] F (Med) dengue

denigro etc [de'nigru] VB ver **denegrir**

denodado, -a [deno'dadu, a] ADJ brave, daring

denominação [denomina'sãw] (pl **-ões**) F (Rel) denomination; (título) name; (ato) naming

denominador [denomina'dor] M: **~ comum** (Mat, fig) common denominator

denominar [denomi'nar] VT: **~ algo/alguém ...** to call sth/sb ...; **denominar-se** VR to be called; (a si mesmo) to call o.s.

denotar [deno'tar] VT (indicar) to show, indicate; (significar) to signify

densidade [dẽsi'dadʒi] F density

denso, -a [dẽsu, a] ADJ (cerrado) dense; (espesso) thick; (compacto) compact

dentada [dẽ'tada] F bite

dentado, -a [dẽ'tadu, a] ADJ serrated

dentadura [dẽta'dura] F teeth pl, set of teeth; (artificial) dentures pl

dental [dẽ'taw] (pl **-ais**) ADJ dental

dentário, -a [dẽ'tarju, a] ADJ dental

dente ['dẽtʃi] M tooth; (*de animal*) fang; (*de elefante*) tusk; (*de alho*) clove; **falar entre os ~s** to mutter, mumble; **~ de leite/do siso** milk/wisdom tooth; **~s postiços** false teeth

dente-de-leão (*pl* **dentes-de-leão**) M dandelion

Dentel [dẽ'tɛw] (BR) ABR M = **Departamento Nacional de Telecomunicações**

dentição [dẽtʃi'sãw] F (*formação dos dentes*) teething; (*dentes*) teeth *pl*; **primeira ~** milk teeth; **segunda ~** second teeth

dentifrício [dẽtʃi'frisju] M toothpaste

dentina [dẽ'tʃina] F dentine

dentista [dẽ'tʃista] M/F dentist

dentre ['dẽtri] PREP (from) among

dentro ['dẽtru] ADV inside ▶ PREP: **~ de** inside; (*tempo*) (with)in; **de ~ para fora** inside out; **dar uma ~** (*col*) to get it right; **aí ~** in there; **por ~** on the inside; **estar por ~** (*col: fig*) to be in the know; **estar por ~ de algo** (*col: fig*) to know the ins and outs of sth

dentuça [dẽ'tusa] F buck teeth *pl*; *ver tb* **dentuço**

dentuço, -a [dẽ'tusu, a] ADJ buck-toothed ▶ M/F buck-toothed person; **ser ~** to have buck teeth

denúncia [de'nũsja] F denunciation; (*acusação*) accusation; (*de roubo*) report

denunciar [denũ'sjar] VT (*acusar*) to denounce; (*delatar*) to inform on; (*revelar*) to reveal

deparar [depa'rar] VT (*revelar*) to reveal; (*fazer aparecer*) to present ▶ VI: **~ com** to come across, meet; **deparar-se** VR: **~-se com** to come across, meet

departamental [departamẽ'taw] (*pl* **-ais**) ADJ departmental

departamento [departa'mẽtu] M department; **D~ de Marcas e Patentes** Patent Office

depauperar [depawpe'rar] VT: **~ algo/alguém** to bleed sth/sb dry

depenar [depe'nar] VT to pluck; (*col: roubar*) to clean out

dependência [depẽ'dẽsja] F dependence; (*edificação*) annexe (BRIT), annex (US); (*colonial*) dependency; (*cômodo*) room

dependente [depẽ'dẽtʃi] M/F dependant

depender [depẽ'der] VI: **~ de** to depend on

dependurar [depẽdu'rar] VI to hang

depilação [depila'sãw] (*pl* **-ões**) F depilation

depilador, a [depila'dor(a)] M/F beauty therapist

depilar [depi'lar] VT to wax; **~ as pernas** (*mandar fazer*) to have one's legs done; (*fazer sozinho*) to do one's legs

depilatório [depila'tɔrju] M hair-remover

deplorar [deplo'rar] VT (*lamentar*) to regret; (*morte, perda*) to lament

deplorável [deplo'ravew] (*pl* **-eis**) ADJ deplorable; (*lamentável*) regrettable

depoente [de'pwẽtʃi] M/F witness

depoimento [depoj'mẽtu] M testimony, evidence; (*na polícia*) statement

depois [de'pojs] ADV afterwards ▶ PREP: **~ de** after; **~ de comer** after eating; **~ que** after

depor [de'por] (*irreg: como* **pôr**) VT (*pôr*) to place; (*indicar*) to indicate; (*rei*) to depose; (*governo*) to overthrow ▶ VI (Jur) to testify, give evidence; (*na polícia*) to give a statement; **esses fatos depõem contra/a favor dele** these facts speak against him/in his favo(u)r

deportação [deporta'sãw] (*pl* **-ões**) F deportation

deportar [depor'tar] VT to deport

deposição [depozi'sãw] (*pl* **-ões**) F deposition; (*governo*) overthrow

depositante [depozi'tãtʃi] M/F depositor ▶ ADJ depositing

depositar [depozi'tar] VT to deposit; (*voto*) to cast; (*colocar*) to place; **depositar-se** VR (*líquido*) to form a deposit; **~ confiança em** to place one's confidence in

depositário, -a [depozi'tarju, a] M/F trustee; (*fig*) confidant(e)

depósito [de'pozitu] M deposit; (*armazém*) warehouse, depot; (*de lixo*) dump; (*reservatório*) tank; **~ a prazo fixo** fixed-term deposit; **~ de bagagens** left-luggage office (BRIT), checkroom (US)

depravação [deprava'sãw] F depravity, corruption

depravado, -a [depra'vadu, a] ADJ depraved ▶ M/F degenerate

depravar [depra'var] VT to deprave, corrupt; (*estragar*) to ruin; **depravar-se** VR to become depraved

deprecar [depre'kar] VT to beg for, pray for ▶ VI to plead

depreciação [depresja'sãw] F depreciation

depreciador, a [depresja'dor(a)] ADJ deprecatory

depreciar [depre'sjar] VT (*desvalorizar*) to devalue; (Com) to write down; (*menosprezar*) to belittle; **depreciar-se** VR to depreciate, lose value; (*menosprezar-se*) to belittle o.s.

depredação [depreda'sãw] F depredation

depredador, a [depreda'dor(a)] ADJ destructive ▶ M/F vandal

depredar [depre'dar] VT to wreck

depreender [deprjẽ'der] VT: **~ algo/que ... (de algo)** to gather sth/that ... (from sth)

depressa [dʒi'prɛsa] ADV fast, quickly; **vamos ~** let's get a move on!

depressão [depre'sãw] (*pl* **-ões**) F depression

depressivo, -a [depre'sivu, a] ADJ depressive

depressões [depre'sõjs] FPL *de* **depressão**

deprimente [depri'mẽtʃi] ADJ depressing

deprimido, -a [depri'midu, a] ADJ depressed

deprimir [depri'mir] VT to depress; **deprimir-se** VR to get depressed

depuração [depura'sãw] F purification

depurar [depu'rar] VT to purify; (Comput: *programa*) to debug

deputado, -a [depu'tadu, a] M/F deputy; (*agente*) agent; (Pol) ≈ Member of Parliament (BRIT), ≈ Representative (US)

deputar [depu'tar] VT to delegate

deque ['dɛki] M deck

DER (BR) ABR M (= *Departamento de Estradas de Rodagem*) *state highways department*

der *etc* [der] VB *ver* **dar**

deriva [de'riva] F drift; **ir à ~** to drift; **ficar à ~** to be adrift

derivação [deriva'sãw] (*pl* **-ões**) F derivation

derivar [deri'var] VT (*desviar*) to divert; (*Ling*) to derive ▶ VI (*ir à deriva*) to drift; **derivar-se** VR (*palavra*) to be derived; (*ir à deriva*) to drift; (*provir*): **~(-se) (de)** to derive *ou* be derived (from)

dermatologia [dermatolo'ʒia] F dermatology

dermatologista [dermatolo'ʒista] M/F dermatologist

dernier cri [der'nje 'kri] M last word

derradeiro, -a [deha'dejru, a] ADJ last, final

derramamento [dehama'mẽtu] M spilling; (*de sangue, lágrimas*) shedding

derramar [deha'mar] VT (*sem querer*) to spill; (*entornar*) to pour; (*sangue, lágrimas*) to shed; **derramar-se** VR to pour out

derrame [de'hami] M haemorrhage (BRIT), hemorrhage (US)

derrapagem [deha'paʒẽ] (*pl* **-ns**) F skid; (*ação*) skidding

derrapar [deha'par] VI to skid

derredor [dehe'dor] ADV, PREP: **em ~ (de)** around

derreter [dehe'ter] VT to melt; **derreter-se** VR to melt; (*coisa congelada*) to thaw; (*enternecer-se*) to be touched; **~ alguém** to win sb's heart; **~-se por alguém** to fall for sb

derretido, -a [dehe'tʃidu, a] ADJ melted; (*enternecido*) touched; (*apaixonado*) smitten; **estar ~ por alguém** to be crazy about sb

derrocada [deho'kada] F downfall; (*ruína*) collapse

derrogação [dehoga'sãw] (*pl* **-ões**) F amendment

derrota [de'hɔta] F defeat, rout; (*Náut*) route

derrotar [deho'tar] VT (*vencer*) to defeat; (*em jogo*) to beat

derrubar [dehu'bar] VT to knock down; (*governo*) to bring down; (*suj: doença*) to lay low; (*col: prejudicar*) to put down

desabafar [dʒizaba'far] VT (*sentimentos*) to give vent to ▶ VI: **~ (com)** to unburden o.s. (to); **desabafar-se** VR: **~-se (com)** to unburden o.s. (to)

desabafo [dʒiza'bafu] M confession

desabalado, -a [dʒizaba'ladu, a] ADJ: **correr/ sair ~** to run headlong/rush out

desabamento [dʒizaba'mẽtu] M collapse

desabar [dʒiza'bar] VI (*edifício, ponte*) to collapse; (*chuva*) to pour down; (*tempestade*) to break

desabilitar [dʒizabili'tar] VT: **~ alguém a** *ou* **para (fazer) algo** to bar sb from (doing) sth

desabitado, -a [dʒizabi'tadu, a] ADJ uninhabited

desabituar [dʒizabi'twar] VT: **~ alguém de (fazer) algo** to get sb out of the habit of (doing) sth; **desabituar-se** VR: **~-se de (fazer) algo** to get out of the habit of (doing) sth

desabonar [dʒizabo'nar] VT to discredit; **desabonar-se** VR to be discredited

desabotoar [dʒizabo'twar] VT to unbutton

desabrido, -a [dʒiza'bridu, a] ADJ rude, brusque

desabrigado, -a [dʒizabri'gadu, a] ADJ (*sem casa*) homeless; (*exposto*) exposed

desabrigar [dʒizabri'gar] VT to make homeless

desabrochar [dʒizabro'ʃar] VI (*flores, fig*) to blossom ▶ M blossoming

desabusado, -a [dʒizabu'zadu, a] ADJ (*sem preconceitos*) unprejudiced; (*atrevido*) impudent

desacatar [dʒizaka'tar] VT (*desrespeitar*) to have *ou* show no respect for; (*afrontar*) to defy; (*desprezar*) to scorn ▶ VI (*col*) to be amazing

desacato [dʒiza'katu] M (*falta de respeito*) disrespect; (*desprezo*) disregard; (*col*): **ele é um ~** he's amazing

desaceleração [dʒizaselera'sãw] F (*tb Econ*) slowing down

desacelerar [dʒizasele'rar] VT to slow down

desacerto [dʒiza'sertu] M mistake, blunder

desacomodar [dʒizakomo'dar] VT to move out

desacompanhado, -a [dʒizakõpa'ɲadu, a] ADJ on one's own, alone

desaconselhar [dʒizakõse'ʎar] VT: **~ algo (a alguém)** to advise (sb) against sth

desaconselhável [dʒizakõse'ʎavew] (*pl* **-eis**) ADJ inadvisable

desacordado, -a [dʒizakor'dadu, a] ADJ unconscious

desacordo [dʒiza'kordu] M (*falta de acordo*) disagreement; (*desarmonia*) discord

desacostumado, -a [dʒizakostumadu, a] ADJ: **~ (a)** unaccustomed (to)

desacostumar [dʒizakostu'mar] VT: **~ alguém de algo** to get sb out of the habit of sth; **desacostumar-se** VR: **~-se de algo** to give sth up

desacreditado, -a [dʒizakredʒi'tadu, a] ADJ discredited

desacreditar [dʒizakredʒi'tar] VT to discredit; **desacreditar-se** VR to lose one's reputation

desafeto [dʒiza'fɛtu] M coldness

desafiador, a [dʒizafja'dor(a)] ADJ challenging; (*pessoa*) defiant ▶ M/F challenger

desafiar [dʒiza'fjar] VT (*propor combate a*) to challenge; (*afrontar*) to defy

desafinação [dʒizafina'sãw] F dissonance

desafinado, -a [dʒizafi'nadu, a] ADJ out of tune

desafinar [dʒizafi'nar] VT to put out of tune ▶ VI to play out of tune; (*cantor*) to sing out of tune

desafio [dʒiza'fiu] M challenge; (PT Esporte) match, game

desafivelar [dʒizafive'lar] VT to unbuckle

desafogado, -a [dʒizafo'gadu, a] ADJ (desimpedido) clear; (desembaraçado) free

desafogar [dʒizafo'gar] VT (libertar) to free; (desapertar) to relieve; (desabafar) to give vent to; **desafogar-se** VR to free o.s.; (desabafar-se) to unburden o.s.

desafogo [dʒiza'fogu] M (alívio) relief; (folga) leisure

desaforado, -a [dʒizafo'radu, a] ADJ rude, insolent

desaforo [dʒiza'foru] M insolence, abuse

desafortunado, -a [dʒizafortu'nadu, a] ADJ unfortunate, unlucky

desafronta [dʒiza'frõta] F (satisfação) redress; (vingança) revenge

desagasalhado, -a [dʒizagaza'ʎadu, a] ADJ scantily clad

desagradar [dʒizagra'dar] VT to displease ▶ VI: ~ **a alguém** to displease sb

desagradável [dʒizagra'davew] (pl **-eis**) ADJ unpleasant

desagrado [dʒiza'gradu] M displeasure

desagravar [dʒizagra'var] VT (insulta) to make amends for; (pessoa) to make amends to; **desagravar-se** VR to avenge o.s.

desagravo [dʒiza'gravu] M amends pl

desagregação [dʒizagrega'sãw] F (separação) separation; (dissolução) disintegration

desagregar [dʒizagre'gar] VT (desunir) to break up, split; (separar) to separate; **desagregar-se** VR to break up, split; to separate

desaguar [dʒiza'gwar] VT to drain ▶ VI: ~ **(em)** to flow ou empty (into)

desairoso, -a [dʒizaj'rozu, ɔza] ADJ inelegant

desajeitado, -a [dʒizaʒej'tadu, a] ADJ clumsy, awkward

desajuizado, -a [dʒizaʒwi'zadu, a] ADJ foolish, unwise

desajustado, -a [dʒizaʒus'tadu, a] ADJ (Psico) maladjusted; (peças) in need of adjustment ▶ M/F maladjusted person

desajustamento [dʒizaʒusta'mẽtu] M (Psico) maladjustment

desajustar [dʒizaʒus'tar] VT (peças) to mess up

desajuste [dʒiza'ʒustʃi] M (Psico) maladjustment; (mecânico) problem

desalentado, -a [dʒizalẽ'tadu, a] ADJ disheartened

desalentar [dʒizalẽ'tar] VT to discourage; (deprimir) to depress

desalento [dʒiza'lẽtu] M discouragement

desalinhado, -a [dʒizali'ɲadu, a] ADJ untidy

desalinho [dʒiza'liɲu] M untidiness

desalmado, -a [dʒizaw'madu, a] ADJ cruel, inhuman

desalojar [dʒizalo'ʒar] VT (expulsar) to oust; **desalojar-se** VR to move out

desamarrar [dʒizama'har] VT to untie ▶ VI (Náut) to cast off

desamarrotar [dʒizamaho'tar] VT to smooth out

desamassar [dʒizama'sar] VT (papel) to smooth out; (chapéu etc) to straighten out; (carro) to beat out

desambientado, -a [dʒizãbjẽ'tadu, a] ADJ unsettled

desamor [dʒiza'mor] M dislike

desamparado, -a [dʒizãpa'radu, a] ADJ (abandonado) abandoned; (sem apoio) helpless

desamparar [dʒizãpa'rar] VT to abandon

desamparo [dʒizã'paru] M helplessness

desandar [dʒizã'dar] VI (maionese, clara) to separate; ~ **a fazer** to begin to do; ~ **a correr** to break into a run; ~ **a chorar** to burst into tears

desanimação [dʒizanima'sãw] F dejection

desanimado, -a [dʒizani'madu, a] ADJ (pessoa) fed up, dispirited; (festa) dull; **ser** ~ (pessoa) to be apathetic

desanimar [dʒizani'mar] VT (abater) to dishearten; (desencorajar): ~ **(de fazer)** to discourage (from doing) ▶ VI to lose heart; (ser desanimado) to be discouraging; ~ **de fazer algo** to lose the will to do sth; (desistir) to give up doing sth

desânimo [dʒi'zanimu] M dejection

desanuviado, -a [dʒizanu'vjadu, a] ADJ cloudless, clear

desanuviar [dʒizanu'vjar] VT (céu) to clear; **desanuviar-se** VR to clear; to stop; ~ **alguém** to put sb's mind at rest

desapaixonado, -a [dʒizapajʃo'nadu, a] ADJ dispassionate

desaparafusar [dʒizaparafu'zar] VT to unscrew

desaparecer [dʒizapare'ser] VI to disappear, vanish

desaparecido, -a [dʒizapare'sidu, a] ADJ lost, missing ▶ M/F missing person

desaparecimento [dʒizaparesi'mẽtu] M disappearance; (falecimento) death

desapegado, -a [dʒizape'gadu, a] ADJ indifferent, detached

desapegar [dʒizape'gar] VT to detach; **desapegar-se** VR: **~-se de** to go off

desapego [dʒiza'pegu] M indifference, detachment

desapercebido, -a [dʒizaperse'bidu, a] ADJ unnoticed

desapertar [dʒizaper'tar] VT (afrouxar) to loosen; (livrar) to free

desapiedado, -a [dʒizapje'dadu, a] ADJ pitiless, ruthless

desapontador, a [dʒizapõta'dor(a)] ADJ disappointing

desapontamento [dʒizapõta'mẽtu] M disappointment

desapontar [dʒizapõ'tar] VT to disappoint

desapossar [dʒizapo'sar] VT: ~ **alguém de algo** to take sth away from sb; **desapossar-se** VR: **~-se de algo** to give sth up

desaprender [dʒizaprẽ'der] vт to forget ▶ vι:
~ **a fazer** to forget how to do

desapropriação [dʒizaproprja'sãw] ғ (de bens)
expropriation; (de pessoa) dispossession

desapropriar [dʒizapro'prjar] vт (bens) to
expropriate; (pessoa) to dispossess

desaprovação [dʒizaprova'sãw] ғ
disapproval

desaprovar [dʒizapro'var] vт (reprovar) to
disapprove of; (censurar) to object to

desaproveitado, -a [dʒizaprovej'tadu, a] adj
wasted; (terras) undeveloped

desaquecimento [dʒizakesi'mẽtu] м (Econ)
cooling

desarmamento [dʒizarma'mẽtu] м
disarmament

desarmar [dʒizar'mar] vт to disarm;
(desmontar) to dismantle; (bomba) to defuse

desarmonia [dʒizarmo'nia] ғ discord

desarraigar [dʒizahaj'gar] vт to uproot

desarranjado, -a [dʒizahã'ʒadu, a] adj
(intestino) upset; (Tec) out of order; **estar ~**
(pessoa) to have diarrhoea (вкіт) ou diarrhea (us)

desarranjar [dʒizahã'ʒar] vт (transtornar) to
upset, disturb; (desordenar) to mess up

desarranjo [dʒiza'hãʒu] м (desordem) disorder;
(enguiço) breakdown; (diarreia) diarrhoea
(вкіт), diarrhea (us)

desarregaçar [dʒizahega'sar] vт (mangas) to
roll down

desarrumado, -a [dʒizahu'madu, a] adj
untidy, messy

desarrumar [dʒizahu'mar] vт to mess up;
(mala) to unpack

desarticulado, -a [dʒizartʃiku'ladu, a] adj
dislocated

desarticular [dʒizartʃiku'lar] vт (osso) to
dislocate

desarvorado, -a [dʒizarvo'radu, a] adj
(desorientado) disoriented

desassociar [dʒizaso'sjar] vт to disassociate;
desassociar-se vr: **~-se de algo** to
disassociate o.s. from sth

desassossego [dʒizaso'segu] м (inquietação)
disquiet; (perturbação) restlessness

desastrado, -a [dʒizas'tradu, a] adj clumsy

desastre [dʒi'zastri] м disaster; (acidente)
accident; (de avião) crash

desastroso, -a [dʒizas'trozu, ɔza] adj
disastrous

desatar [dʒiza'tar] vт (nó) to undo, untie ▶ vι:
~ **a fazer** to begin to do; ~ **a chorar** to burst
into tears; ~ **a rir** to burst out laughing

desatarraxar [dʒizataha'ʃar] vт to unscrew

desatencioso, -a [dʒizatẽ'sjozu, ɔza] adj
inattentive; (descortês) impolite

desatender [dʒizatẽ'der] vт (não fazer caso de)
to pay no attention to, ignore ▶ vι: ~ **a** to
ignore

desatento, -a [dʒiza'tẽtu, a] adj inattentive

desatinado, -a [dʒizatʃi'nadu, a] adj crazy,
wild ▶ м/ғ lunatic

desatinar [dʒizatʃi'nar] vι to behave foolishly

desatino [dʒiza'tʃinu] м (loucura) madness;
(ato) folly

desativar [dʒizatʃi'var] vт (firma, usina) to shut
down; (veículos) to withdraw from service;
(bomba) to deactivate, defuse

desatracar [dʒizatra'kar] vт (navio) to
unmoor; (brigões) to separate ▶ vι (navio) to
cast off

desatravancar [dʒizatravã'kar] vт to clear

desatrelar [dʒizatre'lar] vт to unhitch

desatualizado, -a [dʒizatwali'zadu, a] adj out
of date; (pessoa) out of touch

desautorizar [dʒizawtori'zar] vт (prática) to
disallow; (desacreditar) to discredit; ~ **alguém**
(tirar a autoridade de) to undermine sb's
authority

desavença [dʒiza'vẽsa] ғ (briga) quarrel;
(discórdia) disagreement; **em ~** at
loggerheads

desavergonhado, -a [dʒizavergo'ɲadu, a] adj
insolent, impudent, shameless

desavir-se [dʒiza'virsi] (irreg: como vir) vr:
~ **(com alguém em algo)** to quarrel ou
disagree (with sb about sth)

desavisado, -a [dʒizavi'zadu, a] adj careless

desbancar [dʒizbã'kar] vт: ~ **alguém (em**
algo) to outdo sb (in sth)

desbaratar [dʒizbara'tar] vт to ruin;
(desperdiçar) to waste, squander; (vencer) to
crush; (pôr em desordem) to mess up

desbarrigado, -a [dʒizbahi'gadu, a] adj
flat-bellied

desbastar [dʒizbas'tar] vт (cabelo, plantas) to
thin (out); (vegetação) to trim

desbocado, -a [dʒizbo'kadu, a] adj (pessoa)
foul-mouthed, crude

desbotar [dʒizbo'tar] vт to discolour (вкіт),
discolor (us) ▶ vι to fade

desbragadamente [dʒizbragada'mẽtʃi] adv
(beber) to excess; (mentir) blatantly

desbravador, a [dʒizbrava'dor(a)] м/ғ
explorer

desbravar [dʒizbra'var] vт (terras desconhecidas)
to explore

desbundante [dʒizbũ'dãtʃi] (col) adj fantastic

desbundar [dʒizbũ'dar] (col) vт to knock out
▶ vι to flip, freak out

desbunde [dʒiz'bũdʒi] (col) м knockout

desburocratizar [dʒizburokratʃi'zar] vт:
~ **algo** to remove the bureaucracy from sth

descabelar [dʒiskabe'lar] vт: ~ **alguém** to
mess up sb's hair; **descabelar-se** vr to get
one's hair messed up

descabido, -a [dʒiska'bidu, a] adj (impróprio)
improper; (inoportuno) inappropriate

descadeirado, -a [dʒiskadej'radu, a] adj
(cansado) weary; **ficar ~** (com dor) to get
backache

descafeinado, -a [dʒiskafej'nadu, a] adj
decaffeinated ▶ n decaf

descalabro [dʒiska'labru] м disaster

descalçar [dʒiskaw'sar] vт (sapatos) to take
off; **descalçar-se** vr to take off one's shoes

descalço, -a [dʒis'kawsu, a] ADJ barefoot
descambar [dʒiskã'bar] VI: **~ (de algo) para algo** to sink ou deteriorate (from sth) to sth; **~ para** ou **em** to degenerate into
descampado [dʒiskã'padu] M open country
descansado, -a [dʒiskã'sadu, a] ADJ (tranquilo) calm, quiet; (vagaroso) slow; **fique ~** don't worry; **pode ficar ~ que ...** you can rest assured that ...
descansar [dʒiskã'sar] VT to rest; (apoiar) to lean ▶ VI to rest; to lean
descanso [dʒis'kãsu] M (repouso) rest; (folga) break; (para prato) mat; **sem ~** without a break
descapitalização [dʒiskapitaliza'sãw] F (Com) decapitalization
descarado, -a [dʒiska'radu, a] ADJ cheeky, impudent
descaramento [dʒiskara'mẽtu] M cheek, impudence
descarga [dʒis'karga] F unloading; (Mil) volley; (Elet) discharge; (de vaso sanitário): **dar a ~** to flush the toilet
descarnado, -a [dʒiskar'nadu, a] ADJ scrawny, skinny
descaroçar [dʒiskaro'sar] VT (semente) to seed; (fruto) to stone, core; (algodão) to gin
descarregadouro [dʒiskahega'doru] M wharf
descarregamento [dʒiskahega'mẽtu] M (de carga) unloading; (Elet) discharge
descarregar [dʒiskahe'gar] VT (carga) to unload; (Elet) to discharge; (aliviar) to relieve; (raiva) to vent, give vent to; (arma) to fire ▶ VI to unload; (bateria) to run out; **~ a raiva em alguém** to take it out on sb
descarrilhamento [dʒiskahiʎa'mẽtu] M derailment
descarrilhar [dʒiskahi'ʎar] VT to derail ▶ VI to run off the rails; (fig) to go off the rails
descartar [dʒiskar'tar] VT to discard; **descartar-se** VR: **~-se de** to get rid of
descartável [dʒiskar'tavew] (pl -eis) ADJ disposable
descascador [dʒiskaska'dor] M peeler
descascar [dʒiskas'kar] VT (fruta) to peel; (ervilhas) to shell ▶ VI (depois do sol) to peel; (cobra) to shed its skin; **o feijão descascou** the skin came off the beans
descaso [dʒis'kazu] M disregard
descendência [desẽ'dẽsja] F descendants pl, offspring pl
descendente [desẽ'dẽtʃi] ADJ descending, going down ▶ M/F descendant
descender [desẽ'der] VI: **~ de** to descend from
descentralização [dʒisẽtraliza'sãw] F decentralization
descentralizar [dʒisẽtrali'zar] VT to decentralize
descer [de'ser] VT (escada) to go (ou come) down; (bagagem) to take down ▶ VI (saltar) to get off; (baixar) to go (ou come) down; **~ a pormenores** to get down to details

descida [de'sida] F descent; (declive) slope; (abaixamento) fall, drop
desclassificação [dʒisklasifika'sãw] F disqualification
desclassificar [dʒisklasifi'kar] VT (eliminar) to disqualify; (desacreditar) to discredit
descoberta [dʒisko'berta] F discovery; (invenção) invention
descoberto, -a [dʒisko'bertu, a] PP de **descobrir** ▶ ADJ (nu) bare, naked; (exposto) exposed ▶ M overdraft; **a ~** openly; **conta a ~** overdrawn account; **pôr** ou **sacar a ~** (conta) to overdraw
descobridor, a [dʒiskobri'dor(a)] M/F discoverer; (explorador) explorer
descobrimento [dʒiskobri'mẽtu] M discovery
Descobrimentos MPL see note
> Mainly due to the seafaring expertise of Henry the Navigator, Portugal enjoyed a period of unrivalled overseas expansion during the 15th century. He organized and financed several voyages to Africa, which eventually led to the rounding of the Cape of Good Hope in 1488 by Bartolomeu Dias. In 1497, Vasco da Gama became the first European to travel by sea to India, where he established a lucrative spice trade, and a few years later, in 1500, Pedro Álvares Cabral reached Brazil, which he claimed for Portugal. Brazil remained under Portuguese rule until 1822.

descobrir [dʒisko'brir] VT to discover; (tirar a cobertura de) to uncover; (panela) to take the lid off; (averiguar) to find out; (enigma) to solve
descolar [dʒisko'lar] VT to unstick; (col: arranjar) to get hold of; (: dar) to give ▶ VI: **a criança não descola da mãe** the child won't leave its mother's side
descoloração [dʒiskolora'sãw] F discolouration (BRIT), discoloration (US)
descolorante [dʒiskolo'rãtʃi] ADJ bleaching ▶ M bleach
descolorar [dʒiskolo'rar] VT, VI = **descorar**
descolorir [dʒiskolo'rir] VT to discolour (BRIT), discolor (US); (cabelo) to bleach ▶ VI to fade
descomedimento [dʒiskomedʒi'mẽtu] M lack of moderation
descompassado, -a [dʒiskõpa'sadu, a] ADJ (exagerado) out of all proportion; (ritmo) out of step
descompor [dʒeskõ'por] (irreg: como **pôr**) VT to disarrange; (insultar) to abuse; (repreender) to scold, tell off; (fisionomia) to distort, twist; **descompor-se** VR (desordinar-se) to fall into disarray; (fisionomia) to be twisted; (desarrumar-se) to expose o.s.
descomposto, -a [dʒiskõ'postu, 'pɔsta] PP de **descompor** ▶ ADJ (desalinhado) dishevelled; (fisionomia) twisted
descompostura [dʒiskõpos'tura] F (repreensão) dressing-down; (insulto) abuse; **passar uma**

~ **em alguém** to give sb a dressing-down; to hurl abuse at sb

descompressão [dʒiskõpre'sãw] F decompression

descomprometido, -a [dʒiskõprome'tʃidu, a] ADJ (*sem namorado*) unattached

descomunal [dʒiskomu'naw] (*pl* **-ais**) ADJ (*fora do comum*) extraordinary; (*colossal*) huge, enormous

desconcentrar [dʒiskõsẽ'trar] VT to distract; **desconcentrar-se** VR to lose one's concentration

desconcertado, -a [dʒiskõser'tadu, a] ADJ disconcerted

desconcertante [dʒiskõser'tãtʃi] ADJ disconcerting

desconcertar [dʒiskõser'tar] VT (*atrapalhar*) to confuse, baffle; **desconcertar-se** VR to get upset

desconexo, -a [dʒisko'nɛksu, a] ADJ (*desunido*) disconnected, unrelated; (*incoerente*) incoherent

desconfiado, -a [dʒiskõ'fjadu, a] ADJ suspicious, distrustful ▶ M/F suspicious person

desconfiança [dʒiskõ'fjãsa] F suspicion, distrust

desconfiar [dʒiskõ'fjar] VI to be suspicious; ~ **de alguém** (*não ter confiança em*) to distrust sb; (*suspeitar*) to suspect sb; ~ **que ...** to have the feeling that ...

desconforme [dʒiskõ'fɔrmi] ADJ disagreeing, at variance

desconfortável [dʒiskõfor'tavew] (*pl* **-eis**) ADJ uncomfortable

desconforto [dʒiskõ'fortu] M discomfort

descongelar [dʒiskõʒe'lar] VT (*degelar*) to thaw out; **descongelar-se** VR (*derreter-se*) to melt

descongestionante [dʒiskõʒestʃjo'nãtʃi] ADJ, M decongestant

descongestionar [dʒiskõʒestʃjo'nar] VT (*cabeça, trânsito*) to clear; (*rua, cidade*) to relieve congestion in

desconhecer [dʒiskoɲe'ser] VT (*ignorar*) not to know; (*não reconhecer*) not to recognize; (*um benefício*) not to acknowledge; (*não admitir*) not to accept

desconhecido, -a [dʒiskoɲe'sidu, a] ADJ unknown ▶ M/F stranger

desconhecimento [dʒiskoɲesi'mẽtu] M ignorance

desconjuntado, -a [dʒiskõʒũ'tadu, a] ADJ disjointed; (*ossos*) dislocated

desconjuntar [dʒiskõʒũ'tar] VT (*ossos*) to dislocate; **desconjuntar-se** VR to come apart

desconsideração [dʒiskõsidera'sãw] F: ~ (**de algo**) disregard (for sth)

desconsiderar [dʒiskõside'rar] VT: ~ **alguém** to show a lack of consideration for sb; ~ **algo** to fail to take into consideration

desconsolado, -a [dʒiskõso'ladu, a] ADJ miserable, disconsolate

desconsolador, a [dʒiskõsola'dor(a)] ADJ distressing

desconsolar [dʒiskõso'lar] VT to sadden, depress; **desconsolar-se** VR to despair

descontar [dʒiskõ'tar] VT (*abater*) to deduct; (*não levar em conta*) to discount; (*não fazer caso de*) to make light of

descontentamento [dʒiskõtẽta'mẽtu] M discontent; (*desprazer*) displeasure

descontentar [dʒiskõtẽ'tar] VT to displease

descontente [dʒiskõ'tẽtʃi] ADJ discontented, dissatisfied

descontínuo, -a [dʒiskõ'tʃinwu, a] ADJ broken

desconto [dʒis'kõtu] M discount; **com** ~ at a discount; **dar um** ~ (**para**) (*fig*) to make allowances (for)

descontração [dʒiskõtra'sãw] F casualness

descontraído, -a [dʒiskõtra'idu, a] ADJ casual, relaxed

descontrair [dʒiskõtra'ir] VT to relax; **descontrair-se** VR to relax

descontrolar-se [dʒiskõtro'larsi] VR (*situação*) to get out of control; (*pessoa*) to lose one's self-control

descontrole [dʒiskõ'troli] M lack of control

desconversar [dʒiskõver'sar] VI to change the subject

descorar [dʒisko'rar] VT to discolour (BRIT), discolor (US) ▶ VI to pale, fade

descortês, -esa [dʒiskor'tes, teza] ADJ rude, impolite

descortesia [dʒiskorte'zia] F rudeness, impoliteness

descortinar [dʒiskortʃi'nar] VT (*retrato*) to unveil; (*avistar*) to catch sight of; (*notar*) to notice

descoser [dʒisko'zer] VT (*descosturar*) to unstitch; (*rasgar*) to rip apart; **descoser-se** VR to come apart at the seams

descosturar [dʒiskostu'rar] (BR) VT = **descoser**

descrédito [dʒis'krɛdʒitu] M discredit

descrença [dʒis'krẽsa] F disbelief, incredulity

descrente [dʒis'krẽtʃi] ADJ sceptical (BRIT), skeptical (US) ▶ M/F sceptic (BRIT), skeptic (US)

descrer [dʒis'krer] (*irreg: como* **crer**) VT to disbelieve ▶ VI: ~ **de** not to believe in

descrever [dʒiskre'ver] VT to describe

descrição [dʒiskri'sãw] (*pl* **-ões**) F description

descriptografar [dʒizkriptogra'far] VT (*Comput, Tel*) to decrypt

descritivo, -a [dʒiskri'tʃivu, a] ADJ descriptive

descrito, -a [dʒis'kritu, a] PP *de* **descrever**

descubro *etc* [dʒis'kubru] VB *ver* **descobrir**

descuidado, -a [dʒiskwi'dadu, a] ADJ careless

descuidar [dʒiskwi'dar] VT to neglect ▶ VI: ~ **de** to neglect, disregard

descuido [dʒis'kwidu] M (*falta de cuidado*) carelessness; (*negligência*) neglect; (*erro*) oversight, slip; **por** ~ inadvertently

desculpa [dʒis'kuwpa] F (*pretexto, escusa*) excuse; (*perdão*) pardon; **pedir ~s a alguém por** *ou* **de algo** to apologize to sb for sth

desculpar [dʒiskuw'par] VT (*justificar*) to excuse; (*perdoar*) to pardon, forgive; **desculpar-se** VR to apologize; ~ **algo a alguém** to forgive sb for sth; **desculpe!** (I'm) sorry, I beg your pardon

desculpável [dʒiskuw'pavew] (*pl* **-eis**) ADJ forgivable

(PALAVRA-CHAVE)

desde ['dezdʒi] PREP **1** (*lugar*): **desde ... até ...** from ... to ...; **andamos desde a praia até o restaurante** we walked from the beach to the restaurant
2 (*tempo: + adv, n*): **desde então** from then on, ever since; **desde já** (*de agora*) from now on; (*imediatamente*) at once, right now; **desde o casamento** since the wedding
3 (*tempo: + vb*) since; for; **conhecemo-nos desde 1978/há 20 anos** we've known each other since 1978/for 20 years; **não o vejo desde 1983** I haven't seen him since 1983
4 (*variedade*): **desde os mais baratos até os mais luxuosos** from the cheapest to the most luxurious
▶ CONJ: **desde que** since; **desde que comecei a trabalhar não o vi mais** I haven't seen him since I started work; **não saiu de casa desde que chegou** he hasn't been out since he arrived

desdém [dez'dẽ] M scorn, disdain
desdenhar [dezde'ɲar] VT to scorn, disdain
desdenhoso, -a [dezde'ɲozu, ɔza] ADJ disdainful, scornful
desdentado, -a [dʒizdẽ'tadu, a] ADJ toothless
desdigo *etc* [dʒiz'dʒigu] VB *ver* **desdizer**
desdisse *etc* [dʒiz'dʒisi] VB *ver* **desdizer**
desdita [dʒiz'dʒita] F (*desventura*) misfortune; (*infelicidade*) unhappiness
desdizer [dʒizdʒi'zer] (*irreg: como* **dizer**) VT to contradict; **desdizer-se** VR to go back on one's word
desdobramento [dʒizdobra'mẽtu] M (*de aventura, crise*) ramification; (*de obra etc*) spin-off; (*Com: de conta*) breakdown
desdobrar [dʒizdo'brar] VT (*abrir*) to unfold; (*esforços*) to increase, redouble; (*tropas*) to deploy; (*Com: conta*) to break down; (*bandeira*) to unfurl; (*dividir em grupos*) to split up; **desdobrar-se** VR to unfold; (*empenhar-se*) to work hard, make a big effort
deseducar [dʒizedu'kar] VT: ~ **alguém** to neglect sb's education
desejar [dese'ʒar] VT to want, desire; ~ **ardentemente** to long for; **que deseja?** what would you like?; ~ **algo a alguém** to wish sb sth
desejável [dese'ʒavew] (*pl* **-eis**) ADJ desirable
desejo [de'zeʒu] M wish, desire
desejoso, -a [deze'ʒozu, ɔza] ADJ: ~ **de algo** wishing for sth; ~ **de fazer** keen to do
deselegância [dʒizele'gãsja] F lack of elegance

deselegante [dʒizele'gãtʃi] ADJ inelegant
desemaranhar [dʒizimara'ɲar] VT to disentangle
desembainhar [dʒizēbaj'ɲar] VT (*espada*) to draw
desembalar [dʒizēba'lar] VT to unwrap
desembaraçado, -a [dʒizēbara'sadu, a] ADJ (*livre*) free, clear; (*desinibido*) uninhibited, free and easy; (*expedito*) efficient; (*cabelo*) untangled
desembaraçar [dʒizēbara'sar] VT (*livrar*) to free; (*Com: navio, remessa*) to clear; (*cabelo*) to untangle; **desembaraçar-se** VR (*desinibir-se*) to lose one's inhibitions; (*tornar-se expedito*) to show initiative; ~**-se de** to get rid of
desembaraço [dʒizēba'rasu] M liveliness; (*facilidade*) ease; (*confiança*) self-assurance; ~ **alfandegário** customs clearance
desembarcar [dʒizēbar'kar] VT (*carga*) to unload; (*passageiros*) to let off ▶ VI to disembark
desembargador, a [dʒizēbarga'dor(a)] M/F High Court judge
desembarque [dʒizē'barki] M landing, disembarkation; "~" (*no aeroporto*) "arrivals"
desembestado, -a [dʒizēbes'tadu, a] ADJ: **sair ~** to rush off *ou* out
desembocadura [dʒizēboka'dura] F mouth
desembocar [dʒizēbo'kar] VI: ~ **em** (*rio*) to flow into; (*rua*) to lead into
desembolsar [dʒizēbow'sar] VT to spend
desembolso [dʒizē'bowsu] M expenditure
desembrulhar [dʒizēbru'ʎar] VT to unwrap
desembuchar [dʒizēbu'ʃar] (*col*) VT to get off one's chest ▶ VI to get things off one's chest
desempacotar [dʒizēpako'tar] VT to unpack
desempatar [dʒizēpa'tar] VT to decide ▶ VI to decide the match (*ou race etc*)
desempate [dʒizē'patʃi] M: **partida de ~** (*jogo*) play-off, decider
desempenar [dʒizēpe'nar] VT (*endireitar*) to straighten; **desempenar-se** VR to stand up straight
desempenhar [dʒizēpe'ɲar] VT (*cumprir*) to carry out, fulfil (BRIT), fulfill (US); (*papel*) to play
desempenho [dʒizē'peɲu] M performance; (*de obrigações etc*) fulfilment (BRIT), fulfillment (US)
desemperrar [dʒizēpe'har] VT, VI to loosen
desempregado, -a [dʒizēpre'gadu, a] ADJ unemployed ▶ M/F unemployed person
desempregar-se [dʒizēpre'garsi] VR to lose one's job
desemprego [dʒizē'pregu] M unemployment
desencadear [dʒizēka'dʒjar] VT to unleash; (*despertar*) to provoke, trigger off ▶ VI (*chuva*) to pour; **desencadear-se** VR to break loose; (*tempestade*) to break
desencaixado, -a [dʒizēkaj'ʃadu, a] ADJ misplaced
desencaixar [dʒizēkaj'ʃar] VT to put out of joint; (*deslocar*) to dislodge; **desencaixar-se** VR to become dislodged

d

desencaixotar [dʒizēkajʃo'tar] vt to unpack

desencalhar [dʒizēka'ʎar] vt (navio) to refloat ▶ vi to be refloated; (col: moça) to find a husband

desencaminhar [dʒizēkami'ɲar] vt to lead astray; (dinheiro) to embezzle; **desencaminhar-se** vr to go astray

desencantar [dʒizēkã'tar] vt to disenchant; (desiludir) to disillusion

desencardir [dʒizēkar'dʒir] vt to clean

desencargo [dʒizē'kargu] m fulfilment (BRIT), fulfillment (US); **para ~ de consciência** to clear one's conscience

desencarregar-se [dʒizēkahe'garsi] vr (de obrigação) to discharge o.s.

desencavar [dʒizēka'var] vt to unearth

desencontrar [dʒizēkõ'trar] vt to keep apart; **desencontrar-se** vr (não se encontrar) to miss each other; (perder-se um do outro) to lose each other; **~-se de** to miss; to get separated from

desencontro [dʒizē'kõtru] m failure to meet

desencorajar [dʒizēkora'ʒar] vt to discourage

desencostar [dʒizēkos'tar] vt to move away; **desencostar-se** vr: **~-se de** to move away from

desencriptar [dʒizēkrip'tar] vt (Comput, Tel) to decrypt

desenfastiar [dʒizēfas'tʃjar] vt to amuse; **desenfastiar-se** vr to amuse o.s.

desenferrujar [dʒizēfehu'zar] vt (metal) to clean the rust off; (pernas) to stretch; (língua) to brush up

desenfreado, -a [dʒizē'frjadu, a] ADJ wild

desenganado, -a [dʒizēga'nadu, a] ADJ (sem cura) incurable; (desiludido) disillusioned

desenganar [dʒizēga'nar] vt: **~ alguém** to disillusion sb; (de falsas crenças) to open sb's eyes; (doente) to give up hope of curing; **desenganar-se** vr to become disillusioned; (sair de erro) to realize the truth

desengano [dʒizē'ganu] m disillusionment; (desapontamento) disappointment

desengarrafar [dʒizēgaha'far] vt (trânsito) to unblock; (vinho) to pour out

desengatar [dʒizēga'tar] vt to unhitch; (Ferro) to uncouple

desengonçado, -a [dʒizēgõ'sadu, a] ADJ (malseguro) rickety; (pessoa) ungainly

desengrenado, -a [dʒizēgre'nadu, a] ADJ (Auto) out of gear, in neutral

desengrenar [dʒizēgre'nar] vt to disengage; (carro) to put in neutral

desengrossar [dʒizēgro'sar] vt to thin

desenhar [deze'ɲar] vt to draw; (Tec) to design; **desenhar-se** vr (destacar-se) to stand out; (figurar-se) to take shape

desenhista [deze'ɲista] m/f (Tec) designer

desenho [de'zeɲu] m drawing; (modelo) design; (esboço) sketch; (plano) plan; **~ animado** cartoon; **~ industrial** industrial design

desenlace [dʒizē'lasi] m outcome

desenredar [dʒizēhe'dar] vt to disentangle; (mistério) to unravel; (questão) to sort out, resolve; (dúvida) to clear up; (explicação) to clarify; **desenredar-se** vr: **~-se de algo** to extricate o.s. from sth; **~ alguém de algo** to extricate sb from sth

desenrolar [dʒizēho'lar] vt to unroll; (narrativa) to develop; **desenrolar-se** vr to unfold

desentender [dʒizētē'der] vt (não entender) to misunderstand; **desentender-se** vr: **~-se com** to have a disagreement with

desentendido, -a [dʒizētē'dʒidu, a] ADJ: **fazer-se de ~** to pretend not to understand

desentendimento [dʒizētēdʒi'mētu] m misunderstanding

desenterrar [dʒizēte'har] vt (cadáver) to exhume; (tesouro) to dig up; (descobrir) to bring to light

desentoado, -a [dʒizē'twadu, a] ADJ (desafinado) out of tune

desentranhar [dʒizētra'ɲar] vt to disembowel; (raiz) to draw out; (lembranças) to dredge up; (mistério) to fathom

desentrosado, -a [dʒizētro'zadu, a] ADJ unintegrated

desentupir [dʒizētu'pir] vt to unblock

desenvolto, -a [dʒizē'vowtu, a] ADJ (desembaraçado) self-assured, confident; (desinibido) uninhibited

desenvoltura [dʒizēvow'tura] f (desembaraço) self-confidence

desenvolver [dʒizēvow'ver] vt to develop; **desenvolver-se** vr to develop

desenvolvido, -a [dʒizēvow'vidu, a] ADJ developed

desenvolvimento [dʒizēvowvi'mētu] m development; (crescimento) growth; **país em ~** developing country

desenxabido, -a [dʒizēʃa'bidu, a] ADJ dull

desequilibrado, -a [dʒizekili'bradu, a] ADJ unbalanced

desequilibrar [dʒizekili'brar] vt (pessoa) to throw off balance; (objeto) to tip over; (fig) to unbalance; **desequilibrar-se** vr to lose one's balance; to tip over

desequilíbrio [dʒizeki'librju] m imbalance

deserção [dezer'sãw] f desertion

desertar [deser'tar] vt to desert, abandon ▶ vi to desert

deserto, -a [de'zɛrtu, a] ADJ deserted ▶ m desert

desertor, a [dezer'tor(a)] m/f deserter

desesperado, -a [dʒizespe'radu, a] ADJ desperate; (furioso) furious

desesperador, a [dʒizespera'dor(a)] ADJ desperate; (enfurecedor) maddening

desesperança [dʒizespe'rãsa] f despair

desesperançar [dʒizesperã'sar] vt: **~ alguém** to make sb despair

desesperar [dʒizespe'rar] vt to drive to despair; (enfurecer) to infuriate; **desesperar-se** vr to despair; (enfurecer-se) to become infuriated

desespero [dʒizes'peru] M despair, desperation; (*raiva*) fury; **levar ao ~** to drive to despair

desestabilizar [dʒizestabili'zar] VT to destabilize

desestimulador, a [dʒizestʃimula'dor(a)] ADJ discouraging

desestimular [dʒizestʃimu'lar] VT to discourage

desfaçatez [dʒisfasa'tez] F impudence, cheek

desfalcar [dʒisfaw'kar] VT (*dinheiro*) to embezzle; (*reduzir*): **~ (de)** to reduce (by); **~ uma firma em $4000** to embezzle $4000 from a firm; **o jogo está desfalcado** the game is incomplete

desfalecer [dʒisfale'ser] VT (*enfraquecer*) to weaken ▶ VI (*enfraquecer*) to weaken; (*desmaiar*) to faint

desfalecimento [dʒisfalesi'mẽtu] M (*enfraquecimento*) weakening; (*desmaio*) faint

desfalque [dʒis'fawki] M (*de dinheiro*) embezzlement; (*diminuição*) reduction

desfavor [dʒisfa'vor] M disfavour (BRIT), disfavor (US)

desfavorável [dʒisfavo'ravew] (*pl* **-eis**) ADJ unfavourable (BRIT), unfavorable (US)

desfavorecer [dʒisfavore'ser] VT to discriminate against

desfazer [dʒisfa'zer] (*irreg: como* **fazer**) VT (*costura*) to undo; (*dúvidas*) to dispel; (*agravo*) to redress; (*grupo*) to break up; (*contrato*) to dissolve; (*noivado*) to break off ▶ VI: **~ de alguém** to belittle sb; **desfazer-se** VR (*desaparecer*) to vanish; (*tecido*) to come to pieces; (*grupo*) to break up; (*vaso*) to break; **~-se de** (*livrar-se*) to get rid of; **~-se em lágrimas/gentilezas** to burst into tears/go out of one's way to please

desfechar [dʒisfe'ʃar] VT (*disparar*) to fire; (*setas*) to shoot; (*golpe*) to deal; (*insultos*) to hurl

desfecho [dʒis'feʃu] M ending, outcome

desfeita [dʒis'fejta] F affront, insult

desfeito, -a [dʒis'fejtu, a] PP *de* **desfazer** ▶ ADJ (*desmanchado*) undone; (*cama*) unmade; (*contrato*) broken

desferir [dʒisfe'rir] VT (*golpe*) to strike; (*sons*) to emit; (*lançar*) to throw

desfiar [dʒis'fjar] VT (*tecido*) to unravel; (*Culin: galinha*) to tear into thin shreds; **desfiar-se** VR to become frayed; **~ o rosário** to say one's rosary

desfiguração [dʒisfigura'sãw] F distortion

desfigurar [dʒisfigu'rar] VT (*pessoa, cidade*) to disfigure; (*texto*) to mutilate; **desfigurar-se** VR to be disfigured

desfiladeiro [dʒisfila'dejru] M (*de montanha*) pass

desfilar [dʒisfi'lar] VI to parade

desfile [dʒis'fili] M parade, procession

desflorestamento [dʒisfloresta'mẽtu] M deforestation

desflorestar [dʒisflores'tar] VT to clear of forest

desforra [dʒis'fɔha] F (*vingança*) revenge; (*reparação*) redress; **tirar ~** to get even

desfraldar [dʒisfraw'dar] VT to unfurl

desfranzir [dʒisfrã'zir] VT to smooth out

desfrutar [dʒisfru'tar] VT to enjoy ▶ VI: **~ de** to enjoy; **~ de bom conceito** to have a good reputation, be well thought of

desfrute [dʒis'frutʃi] M (*deleite*) enjoyment; (*desplante*): **ter o ~ de fazer algo** to have the nerve to do sth

desgarrado, -a [dʒizga'hadu, a] ADJ stray; (*navio*) off course

desgarrar-se [dʒizga'harsi] VR: **~ de** to stray from

desgastante [dʒizgas'tãtʃi] ADJ (*fig*) stressful

desgastar [dʒizgas'tar] VT to wear away, erode; (*pessoa*) to wear out, get down; **desgastar-se** VR to be worn away; (*pessoa*) to get worn out

desgaste [dʒiz'gastʃi] M wear and tear; (*mental*) stress

desgostar [dʒizgos'tar] VT to upset ▶ VI: **~ de** to dislike; **desgostar-se** VR: **~-se de** to go off; **~-se com** to take offence at

desgosto [dʒiz'gostu] M (*desprazer*) displeasure; (*pesar*) sorrow, unhappiness

desgostoso, -a [dʒizgos'tozu, ɔza] ADJ sad, sorrowful

desgraça [dʒiz'grasa] F (*desventura*) misfortune; (*miséria*) misery; (*desfavor*) disgrace

desgraçado, -a [dʒizgra'sadu, a] ADJ poor; (*col: admirável*) amazing ▶ M/F wretch; **estou com uma gripe desgraçada** (*col*) I've got a hell of a cold

desgraçar [dʒizgra'sar] VT to disgrace

desgraceira [dʒizgra'sejra] F series of misfortunes

desgravar [dʒizgra'var] VT (*música*) to wipe, rub off

desgrenhado, -a [dʒizgre'ɲadu, a] ADJ dishevelled, tousled

desgrenhar [dʒizgre'ɲar] VT to tousle; **desgrenhar-se** VR to get tousled

desgrudar [dʒizgru'dar] VT to unstick ▶ VI: **~ de** to tear o.s. away from; **~ algo de algo** to take sth off sth

desguarnecer [dʒizgwarne'ser] VT to strip

desidratação [dʒizidrata'sãw] F dehydration

desidratante [dʒizidra'tãtʃi] ADJ dehydrating

desidratar [dʒizidra'tar] VT to dehydrate

design [dʒi'zãjn] M design

designação [dezigna'sãw] (*pl* **-ões**) F designation; (*nomeação*) appointment

designar [dezig'nar] VT to designate; (*nomear*) to name, appoint; (*dia, data*) to fix

designer [dʒi'zajner] (*pl* **-s**) M/F designer

desígnio [de'zignju] M (*propósito*) purpose; (*intenção*) intention

desigual [dezi'gwaw] (*pl* **-ais**) ADJ unequal; (*terreno*) uneven

desigualdade [dʒizigwaw'dadʒi] F inequality

desiludir [dʒizilu'dʒir] VT (*desenganar*) to disillusion; (*causar decepção a*) to disappoint; **desiludir-se** VR to lose one's illusions

desilusão [dʒizilu'zãw] F disillusionment, disenchantment

desimpedido, -a [dʒizĩpe'dʒidu, a] ADJ free

desimpedir [dʒizĩpe'dʒir] VT (*desobstruir*) to unblock; (*trânsito*) to ease

desinchar [dʒizĩ'ʃar] VT (*Med*) to get rid of the swelling on ▶ VI: **meu pé desinchou** the swelling in my foot went down

desincumbir-se [dʒizĩkũ'birsi] VR: ~ **de algo** to carry sth out

desinfeccionar [dʒizĩfeksjo'nar] VT to disinfect

desinfetante [dʒizĩfe'tãtʃi] ADJ, M disinfectant

desinfetar [dʒizĩfe'tar] VT to disinfect

desinflamar [dʒizĩfla'mar] VT to remove *ou* get rid of the inflammation on; **desinflamar-se** VR to become less inflamed

desinibido, -a [dʒizini'bidu, a] ADJ uninhibited

desinibir [dʒizini'bir] VT to make less inhibited; **desinibir-se** VR to lose one's inhibitions

desinstalar [dʒizĩsta'lar] VT (*Comput*) to uninstall

desintegração [dʒizĩtegra'sãw] F disintegration, break-up

desintegrar [dʒizĩte'grar] VT to separate; **desintegrar-se** VR to disintegrate, fall to pieces

desinteressado, -a [dʒizĩtere'sadu, a] ADJ disinterested

desinteressar [dʒizĩtere'sar] VT: ~ **alguém de algo** to make sb lose interest in sth; **desinteressar-se** VR to lose interest

desinteresse [dʒizĩte'resi] M (*falta de interesse*) lack of interest

desintoxicar [dʒizĩtoksi'kar] VT to detoxify

desistência [dezis'tẽsja] F giving up; (*cancelamento*) cancellation

desistir [dezis'tʃir] VI to give up; ~ **de fumar** to stop smoking; **ele ia, mas no final desistiu** he was going, but in the end he gave up the idea *ou* he decided not to

desjejum [dʒiʒe'ʒũ] M breakfast

deslanchar [dʒizlã'ʃar] VI (*carro*) to move off; (*projeto*) to get off the ground, take off

deslavado, -a [dʒizla'vadu, a] ADJ (*pessoa, atitude*) shameless; (*mentira*) blatant

desleal [dʒizle'aw] (*pl* **-ais**) ADJ disloyal

deslealdade [dʒizleaw'dadʒi] F disloyalty

desleixado, -a [dʒizlej'ʃadu, a] ADJ sloppy

desleixo [dʒiz'lejʃu] M sloppiness

desligado, -a [dʒizli'gadu, a] ADJ (*eletricidade*) off; (*pessoa*) absent-minded; **estar ~** to be miles away

desligar [dʒizli'gar] VT (*Tec*) to disconnect; (*luz, TV, motor*) to switch off; (*telefone*) to hang up; **desligar-se** VR: **~-se de algo** (*afastar-se*) to leave sth; (*problemas etc*) to turn one's back on sth; **não desligue** (*Tel*) hold the line

deslizante [dʒizli'zãtʃi] ADJ slippery

deslizar [dʒizli'zar] VI to slide; (*por acidente*) to slip; (*passar de leve*) to glide

deslize [dʒiz'lizi] M (*lapso*) lapse; (*escorregadela*) slip

deslocado, -a [dʒizlo'kadu, a] ADJ (*membro*) dislocated; (*desambientado*) out of place

deslocamento [dʒizloka'mẽtu] M moving; (*de membro*) dislocation; (*de funcionário*) transfer

deslocar [dʒizlo'kar] VT (*mover*) to move; (*articulação*) to dislocate; (*funcionário*) to transfer; **deslocar-se** VR to move; to be dislocated; **eu me desloquei até lá à toa** I went all the way there for nothing

deslumbrado, -a [dʒizlũ'bradu, a] ADJ (*ofuscado*) dazzled; (*maravilhado*) amazed ▶ M/F impressionable person

deslumbramento [dʒizlũbra'mẽtu] M dazzle; (*fascinação*) fascination

deslumbrante [dʒizlũ'brãtʃi] ADJ (*ofuscante*) dazzling; (*casa, festa*) amazing

deslumbrar [dʒizlũ'brar] VT (*ofuscar*) to dazzle; (*maravilhar*) to amaze; (*fascinar*) to fascinate ▶ VI to be dazzling; to be amazing; **deslumbrar-se** VR: **~-se com** to be fascinated by

deslustrar [dʒizlus'trar] VT to tarnish

desmaiado, -a [dʒizma'jadu, a] ADJ (*sem sentidos*) unconscious; (*cor*) pale

desmaiar [dʒizma'jar] VI to faint

desmaio [dʒiz'maju] M faint

desmamar [dʒizma'mar] VT to wean

desmancha-prazeres [dʒiz'manʃa-] M/F INV kill-joy, spoilsport

desmanchar [dʒizmã'ʃar] VT (*costura*) to undo; (*contrato*) to break; (*noivado*) to break off; (*penteado*) to mess up; **desmanchar-se** VR (*costura*) to come undone

desmantelar [dʒizmãte'lar] VT (*demolir*) to demolish; (*desmontar*) to dismantle, take apart

desmarcar [dʒizmar'kar] VT (*compromisso*) to cancel

desmascarar [dʒizmaska'rar] VT to unmask

desmatamento [dʒizmata'mẽtu] M deforestation

desmatar [dʒizma'tar] VT to clear the forest from

desmazelado, -a [dʒizmaze'ladu, a] ADJ slovenly, untidy

desmazelar-se [dʒizmaze'larsi] VR to get untidy

desmedido, -a [dʒizme'dʒidu, a] ADJ excessive

desmembramento [dʒizmẽbra'mẽtu] M dismemberment

desmembrar [dʒizmẽ'brar] VT to dismember

desmemoriado, -a [dʒizmemo'rjadu, a] ADJ forgetful

desmentido [dʒizmẽ'tʃidu] M (*negação*) denial; (*contradição*) contradiction

desmentir [dʒizmẽ'tʃir] VT (*contradizer*) to contradict; (*negar*) to deny

desmerecer [dʒizmere'ser] VT (*não merecer*) not to deserve; (*desfazer de*) to belittle

desmesurado, -a [dʒizmezu'radu, a] ADJ immense, enormous

desmilinguido, -a [dʒizmilĩ'gwidu, a] (*col*) ADJ spent

desmiolado, -a [dʒizmjo'ladu, a] ADJ brainless; (*esquecido*) forgetful

desmistificar [dʒizmistʃifi'kar] VT to demystify; **~ alguém** to remove the mystery surrounding sb

desmitificar [dʒizmitʃifi'kar] VT: **~ algo/ alguém** to dispel the myth(s) surrounding sth/sb

desmontar [dʒizmõ'tar] VT (*máquina*) to take to pieces ▶ VI (*do cavalo*) to dismount, get off

desmoralização [dʒizmoraliza'sãw] F demoralization

desmoralizante [dʒizmorali'zãtʃi] ADJ demoralizing

desmoralizar [dʒizmorali'zar] VT to demoralize

desmoronamento [dʒizmorona'mẽtu] M collapse

desmoronar [dʒizmoro'nar] VT to knock down ▶ VI to collapse

desmotivado, -a [dʒizmotʃi'vadu, a] ADJ despondent

desmunhecar [dʒizmuɲe'kar] (*col*) VI (*declarar-se homossexual*) to come out; (*fazer gestos efeminados*) to be camp

desnatado, -a [dʒizna'tadu, a] ADJ (*leite*) skimmed

desnaturado, -a [dʒiznatu'radu, a] ADJ inhumane ▶ M/F monster

desnecessário, -a [dʒiznese'sarju, a] ADJ unnecessary

desnível [dʒiz'nivew] M unevenness; (*fig*) difference

desnorteado, -a [dʒiznor'tʃjadu, a] ADJ (*perturbado*) bewildered, confused; (*desorientado*) off course

desnortear [dʒiznor'tʃjar] VT (*desorientar*) to throw off course; (*perturbar*) to bewilder; **desnortear-se** VR to lose one's way; (*perturbar-se*) to become confused

desnudar [dʒiznu'dar] VT to strip; (*revelar*) to expose; **desnudar-se** VR to undress

desnutrição [dʒiznutri'sãw] F malnutrition

desnutrido, -a [dʒiznu'tridu, a] ADJ malnourished

desobedecer [dʒizobede'ser] VT to disobey

desobediência [dʒizobe'dʒjẽsja] F disobedience

desobediente [dʒizobe'dʒjẽtʃi] ADJ disobedient

desobrigar [dʒizobri'gar] VT: **~ (de)** to free (from); **~ de fazer algo** to free from doing sth

desobstruir [dʒizobis'trwir] VT to unblock

desocupação [dʒizokupa'sãw] F (*de casa*) vacating; (*falta de ocupação*) leisure; (*desemprego*) unemployment

desocupado, -a [dʒizoku'padu, a] ADJ (*casa*) empty, vacant; (*disponível*) free; (*sem trabalho*) unemployed

desocupar [dʒizoku'par] VT (*casa*) to vacate; (*liberar*) to free

desodorante [dʒizodo'rãtʃi], (PT) **desodorizante** [dʒizodori'zãtʃi] M deodorant

desodorizar [dʒizodori'zar] VT to deodorize

desolação [dezola'sãw] F (*consternação*) grief; (*de um lugar*) desolation

desolado, -a [dezo'ladu, a] ADJ (*consternado*) distressed; (*lugar*) desolate

desolar [dezo'lar] VT (*consternar*) to distress; (*lugar*) to devastate

desonestidade [dezonestʃi'dadʒi] F dishonesty

desonesto, -a [dezo'nɛstu, a] ADJ dishonest

desonra [dʒi'zõha] F dishonour (BRIT), dishonor (US); (*descrédito*) disgrace

desonrar [dʒizõ'har] VT (*infamar*) to disgrace; (*mulher*) to seduce; **desonrar-se** VR to disgrace o.s.

desonroso, -a [dʒizõ'hozu, ɔza] ADJ dishonourable (BRIT), dishonorable (US)

desopilar [dʒizopi'lar] VT (*Med*) to flush out; (*mente*) to clear

desoprimir [dʒizopri'mir] VT to relieve; **desoprimir-se** VR to be relieved

desordeiro, -a [dʒizor'dejru, a] ADJ troublemaking ▶ M/F troublemaker, hooligan

desordem [dʒi'zordẽ] F disorder, confusion; **em ~** (*casa*) untidy

desordenar [dʒizorde'nar] VT (*tirar da ordem*) to put out of order; (*desarrumar*) to mess up

desorganização [dʒizorganiza'sãw] F disorganization

desorganizar [dʒizorgani'zar] VT to disorganize; (*dissolver*) to break up; **desorganizar-se** VR to become disorganized; to break up

desorientação [dʒizorjẽta'sãw] F bewilderment, confusion

desorientar [dʒizorjẽ'tar] VT (*desnortear*) to throw off course; (*perturbar*) to confuse; (*desvairar*) to unhinge; **desorientar-se** VR (*perder-se*) to lose one's way; to get confused; to go mad

desossar [dʒizo'sar] VT (*galinha*) to bone

desovar [dʒizo'var] VT to lay; (*peixe*) to spawn

despachado, -a [dʒispa'ʃadu, a] ADJ (*pessoa*) efficient

despachante [dʒispa'ʃãtʃi] M/F (*de mercadorias*) forwarding agent; (*de documentos*) agent (*who handles official bureaucracy*)

despachar [dʒispa'ʃar] VT (*expedir*) to dispatch, send off; (*atender, resolver*) to deal with; (*despedir*) to sack ▶ VI (*funcionário*) to work; **despachar-se** VR to hurry (up)

despacho [dʒis'paʃu] M dispatch; (*de negócios*) handling; (*nota em requerimento*) ruling; (*reunião*) consultation; (*macumba*) witchcraft

desparafusar [dʒisparafu'sar] vt to unscrew
despeço etc [dʒis'pɛsu] vb ver **despedir**
despedaçar [dʒispeda'sar] vt (quebrar) to smash; (rasgar) to tear apart; **despedaçar-se** vr to smash; to tear
despedida [dʒispe'dʒida] f (adeus) farewell; (de trabalhador) dismissal
despedir [dʒispe'dʒir] vt (de emprego) to dismiss, sack; **despedir-se** vr: **~-se (de)** to say goodbye (to)
despeitado, -a [dʒispej'tadu, a] adj spiteful; (ressentido) resentful
despeito [dʒis'pejtu] m spite; **a ~ de** in spite of, despite
despejar [dʒispe'ʒar] vt (água) to pour; (esvaziar) to empty; (inquilino) to evict
despejo [dʒis'peʒu] m (de casa) eviction; **quarto de ~** junk room
despencar [dʒispẽ'kar] vi to fall down, tumble down
despender [dʒispẽ'der] vt (dinheiro) to spend; (energia) to expend
despenhadeiro [dʒispeɲa'dejru] m cliff, precipice
despensa [dʒis'pẽsa] f larder
despentear [dʒispẽ'tʃjar] vt (cabelo: sem querer) to mess up; (: de propósito) to let down; **despentear-se** vr to mess one's hair up; to let one's hair down
despercebido, -a [dʒisperse'bidu, a] adj unnoticed
desperdiçar [dʒisperdʒi'sar] vt to waste; (dinheiro) to squander
desperdício [dʒisper'dʒisju] m waste
despersonalizar [dʒispersonali'zar] vt to depersonalize
despersuadir [dʒisperswa'dʒir] vt: **~ alguém de fazer algo** to dissuade sb from doing sth
despertador [dʒisperta'dor] m (tb: **relógio despertador**) alarm clock
despertar [dʒisper'tar] vt (pessoa) to wake; (suspeitas, interesse) to arouse; (reminiscências) to revive; (apetite) to whet ▶ vi to wake up, awake ▶ m awakening
desperto, -a [dʒis'pɛrtu, a] adj awake
despesa [dʒis'peza] f expense; **despesas** fpl (de uma empresa) expenses, costs; **~s antecipadas** prepayments; **~s gerais** (Com) overheads; **~s mercantis** sales and marketing expenses; **~s não operacionais** non-operating expenses ou costs; **~s operacionais** operating expenses ou costs; **~s tributárias** (de uma empresa) corporation tax sg
despido, -a [dʒis'pidu, a] adj (nu) naked, bare; (livre) free
despir [dʒis'pir] vt (roupa) to take off; (pessoa) to undress; (despojar) to strip; **despir-se** vr to undress
despistar [dʒispis'tar] vt to throw off the scent
desplante [dʒis'plãtʃi] m (fig) nerve

despojado, -a [dʒispo'ʒadu, a] adj (pessoa) unambitious; (lugar) spartan, basic
despojar [dʒispo'ʒar] vt (casas) to loot, sack; (pessoas) to rob; **~ alguém de algo** to strip sb of sth
despojo [dʒis'poʒu] m loot, booty; **despojos** mpl: **~s mortais** (restos) mortal remains
despoluir [dʒispo'lwir] vt to clean up
despontar [dʒispõ'tar] vi to emerge; (sol) to come out; (: ao amanhecer) to come up; **ao ~ do dia** at daybreak
desporto [dʒis'portu] m sport
déspota ['dɛspota] m/f despot
despotismo [despo'tʃizmu] m despotism
despovoado, -a [dʒispo'vwadu, a] adj uninhabited ▶ m wilderness
despovoar [dʒispo'vwar] vt to depopulate
desprazer [dʒispra'zer] m displeasure
desprecavido, -a [dʒispreka'vidu, a] adj unprepared, careless
despregar [dʒispre'gar] vt to take off, detach; **despregar-se** vr to come off; **~ os olhos de algo** to take one's eyes off sth
desprender [dʒisprẽ'der] vt (soltar) to loosen; (desatar) to unfasten; (emitir) to emit; **desprender-se** vr (botão) to come off; (cheiro) to be given off; **~-se dos braços de alguém** to extricate o.s. from sb's arms
desprendido, -a [dʒisprẽ'dʒidu, a] adj (abnegado) disinterested
despreocupado, -a [dʒispreoku'pado, a] adj carefree, unconcerned; **com a notícia ele ficou mais ~** after hearing the news he was less concerned ou worried
despreocupar [dʒispreoku'par] vt: **~ alguém (de algo)** to set sb's mind at rest (about sth); **despreocupar-se** vr: **~-se (de algo)** to stop worrying (about sth)
despreparado, -a [dʒisprepa'radu, a] adj unprepared
desprestigiar [dʒisprestʃi'ʒjar] vt to discredit; **desprestigiar-se** vr to lose prestige
despretensioso, -a [dʒispretẽ'sjozu, ɔza] adj unpretentious, modest
desprevenido, -a [dʒispreve'nidu, a] adj unprepared, unready; **apanhar ~** to catch unawares
desprezar [dʒispre'zar] vt (desdenhar) to despise, disdain; (não dar importância a) to disregard, ignore
desprezível [dʒispre'zivew] (pl **-eis**) adj despicable
desprezo [dʒis'prezu] m scorn, contempt; **dar ao ~** to ignore
desproporção [dʒispropor'sãw] f disproportion
desproporcionado, -a [dʒisproporsjo'nadu, a] adj disproportionate; (desigual) unequal
desproporcional [dʒisproporsjo'naw] adj disproportionate
despropositado, -a [dʒispropozi'tadu, a] adj (absurdo) preposterous

despropósito [dʒispro'pɔzitu] M nonsense

desproteger [dʒisprote'ʒer] VT to leave unprotected

desprover [dʒispro'ver] VT: **~ alguém (de algo)** to deprive sb (of sth)

desprovido, -a [dʒispro'vidu, a] ADJ deprived; **~ de** without

despudorado, -a [dʒispudo'radu, a] ADJ shameless

desqualificar [dʒiskwalifi'kar] VT (Esporte etc) to disqualify; (tornar indigno) to disgrace, lower

desquitar-se [dʒiski'tarsi] VR to get a legal separation

desquite [dʒis'kitʃi] M legal separation

desregrado, -a [dʒizhe'gradu, a] ADJ (desordenado) disorderly, unruly; (devasso) immoderate

desregrar-se [dʒizhe'grarsi] VR to run riot

desregular [dʒizhegu'lar] VT (mercado) to deregulate

desrespeitar [dʒizhespej'tar] VT to have no respect for

desrespeito [dʒizhe'spejtu] M disrespect

desrespeitoso, -a [dʒizhespej'tozu, ɔza] ADJ disrespectful

desse¹, a ['desi, a] = **de + esse, a**; ver **de**

desse² VB ver **dar**

destacado, -a [dʒista'kadu, a] ADJ outstanding; (separado) detached

destacamento [dʒistaka'mẽtu] M (Mil) detachment

destacar [dʒista'kar] VT (Mil) to detail; (separar) to detach; (fazer sobressair) to highlight; (enfatizar) to emphasize ▶ VI to stand out; **destacar-se** VR to stand out; (pessoa) to be outstanding

destampar [dʒistã'par] VT to take the lid off

destapar [dʒista'par] VT to uncover

destaque [dʒis'taki] M distinction; (pessoa, coisa) highlight; (do noticiário) main point; **pessoa de ~** distinguished person

deste, a ['destʃi, a] = **de + este, a**; ver **de**

destemido, -a [deste'midu, a] ADJ fearless, intrepid

destemperar [dʒistẽpe'rar] VT (diluir) to dilute, weaken ▶ VI (perder a cabeça) to go mad

desterrar [dʒiste'har] VT (exilar) to exile; (fig) to banish

desterro [dʒis'tehu] M exile

destilação [destʃila'sãw] F distillation

destilar [destʃi'lar] VT to distil (BRIT), distill (US)

destilaria [destʃila'ria] F distillery

destinação [destʃina'sãw] (pl **-ões**) F destination

destinar [destʃi'nar] VT to destine; (dinheiro): **~ (para)** to set aside (for); **destinar-se** VR: **~-se a** to be intended for; (carta) to be addressed to

destinatário, -a [destʃina'tarju, a] M/F addressee

destino [des'tʃinu] M destiny, fate; (lugar) destination; **com ~ a** bound for; **sem ~** adj aimless; adv aimlessly

destituição [destʃitwi'sãw] (pl **-ões**) F (demissão) dismissal

destituir [destʃi'twir] VT (demitir) to dismiss; **~ de** (privar de) to deprive of; (demitir de) to dismiss from

destoante [dʒisto'ãtʃi] ADJ (som) discordant; (opiniões) diverging

destoar [dʒisto'ar] VI (som) to jar; **~ (de)** (não condizer) to be out of keeping (with); (traje, cor) to clash (with); (pessoa: discordar) to disagree (with)

destorcer [dʒistor'ser] VT to straighten out

destrambelhado, -a [dʒistrãbe'ʎadu, a] ADJ scatterbrained

destrancar [dʒistrã'kar] VT to unlock

destratar [dʒistra'tar] VT to abuse, insult

destravar [dʒistra'var] VT (veículo) to take the brake off; (fechadura) to unlatch

destreza [des'treza] F (habilidade) skill; (agilidade) dexterity

destrinchar [dʒistrĩ'ʃar] VT (desenredar) to unravel; (esmiuçar) to treat in detail; (problema) to solve, resolve

destro, -a ['destru, a] ADJ (hábil) skilful (BRIT), skillful (US); (ágil) agile; (não canhoto) right-handed

destrocar [dʒistro'kar] VT to give back, return

destroçar [dʒistro'sar] VT (destruir) to destroy; (quebrar) to smash, break; (devastar) to ruin, wreck

destroços [dʒis'trɔsus] MPL wreckage sg

destróier [dʒis'trɔjer] M destroyer

destronar [dʒistro'nar] VT to depose

destroncar [dʒistrõ'kar] VT to dislocate

destruição [dʒistrwi'sãw] F destruction

destruidor, a [dʒistrwi'dor(a)] ADJ destructive

destruir [dʒis'trwir] VT to destroy

desumano, -a [dʒizu'manu, a] ADJ inhuman; (bárbaro) cruel

desunião [dʒizu'njãw] F disunity; (separação) separation

desunir [dʒizu'nir] VT (separar) to separate; (Tec) to disconnect; (fig: desavir) to cause a rift between

desusado, -a [dʒizu'zadu, a] ADJ (não usado) disused; (incomum) unusual

desuso [dʒi'zuzu] M disuse; **em ~** outdated

desvairado, -a [dʒizvaj'radu, a] ADJ (louco) crazy, demented; (desorientado) bewildered

desvairar [dʒizvaj'rar] VT to drive mad

desvalido, -a [dʒizva'lidu, a] ADJ (desamparado) helpless; (miserável) destitute

desvalorização [dʒizvaloriza'sãw] (pl **-ões**) F devaluation

desvalorizar [dʒizvalori'zar] VT to devalue; **desvalorizar-se** VR (pessoa) to undervalue o.s.; (carro) to depreciate; (moeda) to lose value

desvanecer [dʒizvane'ser] VT (envaidecer) to make proud; (sentimentos) to dispel; **desvanecer-se** VR (envaidecer-se) to feel proud; (sentimentos) to vanish

desvanecido, -a [dʒizvane'sidu, a] ADJ proud

desvantagem [dʒizvã'taʒē] (*pl* **-ns**) F
disadvantage

desvantajoso, -a [dʒizvãta'ʒozu, ɔza] ADJ
disadvantageous

desvão [dʒiz'vãw] (*pl* **-s**) M loft

desvario [dʒizva'riu] M madness, folly

desvelar [dʒizve'lar] VT (*noiva, estátua*) to
unveil; (*corpo, trama*) to uncover; (*segredo*) to
reveal; (*problema*) to clarify; **desvelar-se** VR:
~-se em fazer algo to go to a lot of trouble
to do sth

desvelo [dʒiz'velu] M (*cuidado*) care; (*dedicação*)
devotion

desvencilhar [dʒizvēsi'ʎar] VT to free,
extricate; **desvencilhar-se** VR to free o.s.,
extricate o.s.

desvendar [dʒizvē'dar] VT (*tirar a venda*) to
remove the blindfold from; (*revelar*) to
disclose; (*mistério*) to solve

desventura [dʒizvē'tura] F (*infortúnio*)
misfortune; (*infelicidade*) unhappiness

desventurado, -a [dʒizvētu'radu, a] ADJ
(*desafortunado*) unfortunate; (*infeliz*) unhappy
▶ M/F wretch

desviar [dʒiz'vjar] VT to divert; (*golpe*) to
deflect; (*dinheiro*) to embezzle; **desviar-se** VR
(*afastar-se*) to turn away; **~-se de** (*evitar*) to
avoid; **~-se do assunto** to digress; **~ os
olhos** to look away; **desviei o carro para a
direita** I pulled the car over to the right;
tentei desviá-lo do assunto I tried to get *ou*
steer him off the subject

desvincular [dʒizvĩku'lar] VT: **~ algo de algo**
to divest sth of sth; **desvincular-se** VR: **~-se
de algo** to disassociate o.s. from sth

desvio [dʒiz'viu] M diversion, detour; (*curva*)
bend; (*fig*) deviation; (*de dinheiro*)
embezzlement; (*de mercadorias*)
misappropriation; (*Ferro*) siding; (*da coluna
vertebral*) dislocation

desvirar [dʒizvi'rar] VT to turn back

desvirginar [dʒizvirʒi'nar] VT to deflower

desvirtuar [dʒizvir'twar] VT (*fatos*) to
misrepresent

detalhadamente [detaʎada'mētʃi] ADV in
detail

detalhado, -a [deta'ʎadu, a] ADJ detailed

detalhar [deta'ʎar] VT to (give in) detail

detalhe [de'taʎi] M detail; **entrar em ~** to go
into detail

detalhista [deta'ʎista] ADJ painstaking,
meticulous

detectar [detek'tar] VT to detect

detector [detek'tor] M detector

detenção [detē'sãw] (*pl* **-ões**) F detention

détente [de'tãtʃi] F détente

detento, -a [de'tētu, a] M/F detainee

detentor, a [detē'tor(a)] M/F (*de título, recorde*)
holder

deter [de'ter] (*irreg: como* **ter**) VT (*fazer parar*) to
stop; (*prender*) to arrest, detain; (*reter*) to
keep; (*conter: riso*) to contain; **deter-se** VR
(*parar*) to stop; (*ficar*) to stay; (*conter-se*) to

restrain o.s.; **~-se em minúcias** *etc* to get
bogged down in details *etc*

detergente [deter'ʒētʃi] M detergent

deterioração [deterjora'sãw] F deterioration

deteriorar [deterjo'rar] VT to spoil, damage;
deteriorar-se VR to deteriorate; (*relações*) to
worsen

determinação [determina'sãw] F (*firmeza*)
determination; (*decisão*) decision; (*ordem*)
order; **por ~ de** by order of

determinado, -a [determi'nadu, a] ADJ
(*resoluto*) determined; (*certo*) certain, given

determinar [determi'nar] VT (*fixar, precisar*) to
determine; (*decretar*) to order; (*resolver*) to
decide (on); (*causar*) to cause; (*fronteiras*) to
mark out

detestar [detes'tar] VT to hate, detest

detestável [detes'tavew] (*pl* **-eis**) ADJ horrible,
hateful

detetive [dete'tʃivi] M/F detective

detidamente [detʃida'mētʃi] ADV carefully,
thoroughly

detido, -a [de'tʃidu, a] ADJ (*preso*) under arrest;
(*minucioso*) thorough ▶ M/F person under
arrest, prisoner

detonação [detona'sãw] (*pl* **-ões**) F explosion

detonar [deto'nar] VI to detonate, go off ▶ VT
to detonate

Detran [de'trã] (BR) ABR M (= *Departamento de
Trânsito*) *state traffic department*

detrás [de'trajs] ADV behind ▶ PREP: **~ de**
behind; **por ~** (*from*) behind

detrimento [detri'mētu] M: **em ~ de** to the
detriment of

detrito [de'tritu] M debris *sg*; (*de comida*)
remains *pl*; (*resíduo*) dregs *pl*

deturpação [deturpa'sãw] F corruption;
(*de palavras*) distortion

deturpar [detur'par] VT to corrupt; (*desfigurar*)
to disfigure; (*palavras*) to twist; **você
deturpou minhas palavras** you twisted
my words

deu [dew] VB *ver* **dar**

deus, a [dews, 'dewza] M/F god/goddess;
D~ me livre! God forbid!; **graças a D~**
thank goodness; **se D~ quiser** God willing;
meu D~! good Lord!; **D~ e o mundo**
everybody; **~ nos acuda** commotion

deus-dará [-da'ra] M: **viver ao ~** to live from
hand to mouth; **estar ao ~** (*casa*) to be
unattended

devagar [dʒiva'gar] ADV slowly ▶ ADJ INV (*col*):
ele é um cara tão ~ he's such an old fogey

devagarinho [dʒivaga'riɲu] ADV nice and
slowly

devanear [deva'njar] VT to imagine, dream of
▶ VI to daydream; (*divagar*) to wander, digress

devaneio [deva'neju] M daydream

devassa [de'vasa] F investigation, inquiry

devassado, -a [deva'sadu, a] ADJ (*casa*)
exposed

devassidão [devasi'dãw] F debauchery

devasso, -a [de'vasu, a] ADJ dissolute

devastar [devas'tar] VT (destruir) to devastate; (arruinar) to ruin

deve ['dɛvi] M (débito) debit; (coluna) debit column

devedor, a [deve'dor(a)] ADJ (pessoa) in debt ▶ M/F debtor; **saldo ~** debit balance

dever [de'ver] M duty ▶ VT to owe ▶ VI (suposição): **deve (de) estar doente** he must be ill; (obrigação): **devo partir às oito** I must go at eight; **você devia ir ao médico** you should go to the doctor; **ele devia ter vindo** he should have come; **que devo fazer?** what shall I do?

deveras [dʒi'vɛras] ADV really, truly

devidamente [devida'mẽtʃi] ADV properly; (preencher formulário etc) duly

devido, -a [de'vidu, a] ADJ (maneira) proper; (respeito) due; **~ a** due to, owing to; **no ~ tempo** in due course

devoção [devo'sãw] F devotion

devolução [devolu'sãw] F devolution; (restituição) return; (reembolso) refund; **~ de impostos** tax rebate

devolver [devow'ver] VT to give back, return; (Com) to refund

devorar [devo'rar] VT to devour; (destruir) to destroy

devotar [devo'tar] VT to devote; **devotar-se** VR: **~-se a** to devote o.s. to

devoto, -a [de'vɔtu, a] ADJ devout ▶ M/F devotee

dez [dɛz] NUM ten; ver tb **cinco**

dez. ABR (= dezembro) Dec.

dezanove [deza'nɔvə] (PT) NUM = **dezenove**

dezasseis [deza'sejs] (PT) NUM = **dezesseis**

dezassete [deza'setə] (PT) NUM = **dezessete**

dezembro [de'zẽbru] M December; ver tb **julho**

dezena [de'zena] F: **uma ~** ten

dezenove [deze'nɔvi] NUM nineteen; ver tb **cinco**

dezesseis [deze'sejs] NUM sixteen; ver tb **cinco**

dezessete [dezi'setʃi] NUM seventeen; ver tb **cinco**

dezoito [dʒi'zojtu] NUM eighteen; ver tb **cinco**

DF (BR) ABR = **Distrito Federal**

dia ['dʒia] M day; (claridade) daylight; **~ a ~** day by day; **~ de folga** day off; **~ santo** holy day; **~ útil** weekday; **estar ou andar em ~ (com)** to be up to date (with); **de ~** in the daytime, by day; **mais ~ menos ~** sooner or later; **todo ~, todos os ~s** every day; **o ~ inteiro** all day (long); **~ sim, ~ não** every other day; **de dois em dois ~s** every two days; **no ~ seguinte** the next day; **~ após ~** day after day; **do ~ para a noite** (fig) overnight; **bom ~** good morning; **um ~ desses** one of these days; **~s a fio** days on end; **~ cheio/morto** busy/quiet ou slow day; **todo santo ~** (col) every single day, day after day; **recebo por ~** I'm paid by the day; **um bebê de ~s** a newborn baby; **ele está com os ~s contados** his days are numbered

dia a dia M daily life, everyday life

diabete, diabetes [dʒia'bɛtʃi(s)] F diabetes sg

diabético, -a [dʒia'bɛtʃiku, a] ADJ, M/F diabetic

diabo ['dʒiabu] M devil; **que ~!** (col) damn it!; **por que ~ ...?** why on earth ...?; **o ~ é que ...** (col) the darnedest thing is that ...; **o ~ do eletricista não apareceu** (col) the damned electricity man didn't turn up; **está um calor do ~** (col) it's damned (ou bloody (!)) hot; **deu um trabalho dos ~s** (col) it was a hell of a job; **quente pra ~** (col) damned hot; **dizer o ~ de alguém** (col) to slag sb off

diabólico, -a [dʒia'bɔliku, a] ADJ diabolical

diabrete [dʒia'bretʃi] M imp

diabrura [dʒia'brura] F prank; **diabruras** FPL (travessura) mischief sg

diacho ['dʒiaʃu] (col) EXCL hell!

diadema [dʒia'dema] M diadem; (joia) tiara

diáfano, -a ['dʒjafanu, a] ADJ (tecido) diaphanous; (águas) clear

diafragma [dʒia'fragma] M diaphragm; (anticoncepcional) diaphragm, cap

diagnosticar [dʒjagnostʃi'kar] VT to diagnose

diagnóstico [dʒjag'nɔstʃiku] M diagnosis

diagonal [dʒjago'naw] (pl **-ais**) ADJ, F diagonal

diagrama [dʒja'grama] M diagram

diagramador, a [dʒjagrama'dor(a)] M/F designer

diagramar [dʒjagra'mar] VT to design

dialética [dʒja'lɛtʃika] F dialectics sg

dialeto [dʒja'lɛtu] M dialect

dialogar [dʒjalo'gar] VI: **~ (com alguém)** to talk (to sb); (Pol) to have ou hold talks (with sb)

diálogo ['dʒjalogu] M dialogue; (conversa) talk, conversation

diamante [dʒja'mãtʃi] M diamond

diâmetro ['dʒjametru] M diameter

diante ['dʒjãtʃi] PREP: **~ de** before; (na frente de) in front of; (problemas etc) in the face of; **e assim por ~** and so on; **para ~** forward

dianteira [dʒjã'tejra] F front, vanguard; **tomar a ~** to get ahead

dianteiro, -a [dʒjã'tejru, a] ADJ front

diapasão [dʒjapa'zãw] (pl **-ões**) M (afinador) tuning fork; (tom) pitch; (extensão de voz ou instrumento) range

diapositivo [dʒjapozi'tʃivu] M (Foto) slide

diária ['dʒjarja] F (de hotel) daily rate

diário, -a ['dʒjarju, a] ADJ daily ▶ M diary; (jornal) (daily) newspaper; (Com) daybook; **~ de bordo** (Aer) logbook

diarista [dʒja'rista] M/F casual worker, worker paid by the day; (em casa) cleaner

diarreia [dʒja'heja] F diarrhoea (BRIT), diarrhea (US)

dica ['dʒika] (col) F hint

dicção [dʒik'sãw] F diction

dicionário [dʒisjo'narju] M dictionary

dicionarista [dʒisjona'rista] M/F lexicographer

dicotomia [dʒikoto'mia] F dichotomy

didata [dʒi'data] M/F teacher

didática [dʒi'datʃika] F education, teaching

didático, -a [dʒi'datʃiku, a] ADJ (*livro*) educational; (*método*) teaching atr; (*modo*) didactic

diesel ['dʒizew] M: **motor a ~** diesel engine

dieta ['dʒjɛta] F diet; **fazer ~** to go on a diet

dietético, -a [dʒje'tɛtʃiku, a] ADJ dietetic

dietista [dʒje'tʃista] M/F dietician

difamação [dʒifama'sãw] F (*falada*) slander; (*escrita*) libel

difamador, a [dʒifama'dor(a)] ADJ defamatory ▶ M/F slanderer

difamar [dʒifa'mar] VT to slander; (*por escrito*) to libel

difamatório, -a [dʒifama'tɔrju, a] ADJ defamatory

diferença [dʒife'rẽsa] F difference; **~ de gols** (*Futebol*) goal difference; **ela tem uma ~ comigo** she's got something against me

diferenciação [dʒiferẽsja'sãw] F (*tb Mat*) differentiation

diferenciar [dʒiferẽ'sjar] VT to differentiate

diferente [dʒife'rẽtʃi] ADJ different; **estar ~ com alguém** to be at odds with sb

diferimento [dʒiferi'mẽtu] M deferment

diferir [dʒife'rir] VI: **~ (de)** to differ (from) ▶ VT (*adiar*) to defer

difícil [dʒi'fisiw] (*pl* **-eis**) ADJ (*trabalho, vida*) difficult, hard; (*problema, situação*) difficult; (*pessoa: intratável*) difficult; (: *exigente*) hard to please; (*improvável*) unlikely; **o ~ é ...** the difficult thing is ...; **acho ~ ela aceitar nossa proposta** I think it's unlikely she will accept our proposal; **falar ~** to use big words; **bancar o ~** to play hard to get

dificílimo, -a [dʒifi'silimu, a] ADJ SUPERL *de* **difícil**

dificilmente [dʒifisiw'mẽtʃi] ADV with difficulty; (*mal*) hardly; (*raramente*) hardly ever; **~ ele poderá ...** it won't be easy for him to ....

dificuldade [dʒifikuw'dadʒi] F difficulty; (*aperto*) trouble; **em ~s** in trouble

dificultar [dʒifikuw'tar] VT to make difficult; (*complicar*) to complicate

difteria [dʒifte'ria] F diphtheria

difundir [dʒifũ'dʒir] VT (*luz*) to diffuse; (*boato, rumor*) to spread; (*notícia*) to spread, circulate; (*ideias*) to disseminate

difusão [dʒifu'zãw] F (*de luz*) diffusion; (*espalhamento*) spreading; (*de notícias*) circulation; (*de ideias*) dissemination

difuso, -a [dʒi'fuzu, a] ADJ diffuse

digerir [dʒiʒe'rir] VT, VI to digest

digestão [dʒiʒes'tãw] F digestion

digital [dʒiʒi'taw] (*pl* **-ais**) ADJ digital; **impressão ~** fingerprint

digitar [dʒiʒi'tar] VT (*Comput: dados*) to key (in)

dígito ['dʒiʒitu] M digit

digladiar [dʒigla'dʒjar] VI to fight, fence; **digladiar-se** VR: **~ (com alguém)** to do battle (with sb)

dignar-se [dʒig'narsi] VR: **~ de** to deign to, condescend to

dignidade [dʒigni'dadʒi] F dignity

dignificar [dʒignifi'kar] VT to dignify

digno, -a ['dʒignu, a] ADJ (*merecedor*) worthy; (*nobre*) dignified

digo *etc* ['dʒigu] VB *ver* **dizer**

digressão [dʒigre'sãw] (*pl* **-ões**) F digression

dilaceração [dʒilasera'sãw] (*pl* **-ões**) F laceration

dilacerante [dʒilase'rãtʃi] ADJ (*dor*) excruciating; (*cruel*) cruel

dilacerar [dʒilase'rar] VT to tear to pieces, lacerate; **dilacerar-se** VR to tear one another to pieces

dilapidação [dʒilapida'sãw] F (*de casas etc*) demolition; (*de dinheiro*) squandering

dilapidar [dʒilapi'dar] VT (*fortuna*) to squander; (*casa*) to demolish

dilatação [dʒilata'sãw] F dilation

dilatar [dʒila'tar] VT to dilate, expand; (*prolongar*) to prolong; (*retardar*) to delay

dilatório, -a [dʒila'tɔrju, a] ADJ dilatory

dilema [dʒi'lɛma] M dilemma

diletante [dʒile'tãtʃi] ADJ, M/F amateur; (*pej*) dilettante

diletantismo [dʒiletã'tʃizmu] M amateurism; (*pej*) dilettantism

diligência [dʒili'ʒẽsja] F diligence; (*pesquisa*) inquiry; (*veículo*) stagecoach

diligenciar [dʒiliʒẽ'sjar] VT to strive for; **~ (por) fazer** to strive to do

diligente [dʒili'ʒẽtʃi] ADJ hardworking, industrious

diluição [dʒilwi'sãw] F dilution

diluir [dʒi'lwir] VT to dilute

dilúvio [dʒi'luvju] M flood

dimensão [dʒimẽ'sãw] (*pl* **-ões**) F dimension; **dimensões** FPL (*medidas*) measurements

dimensionar [dʒimẽsjo'nar] VT: **~ algo** to calculate the size of sth; (*fig*) to assess the extent of sth

diminuição [dʒiminwi'sãw] F reduction

diminuir [dʒimi'nwir] VT to reduce; (*som*) to turn down; (*interesse*) to lessen ▶ VI to lessen, diminish; (*preço*) to go down; (*dor*) to wear off; (*barulho*) to die down

diminutivo, -a [dʒiminu'tʃivu, a] ADJ diminutive ▶ M (*Ling*) diminutive

diminuto, -a [dʒimi'nutu, a] ADJ minute, tiny

Dinamarca [dʒina'marka] F Denmark

dinamarquês, -quesa [dʒinamar'kes, 'keza] ADJ Danish ▶ M/F Dane ▶ M (*Ling*) Danish

dinâmico, -a [dʒi'namiku, a] ADJ dynamic

dinamismo [dʒina'mizmu] M (*fig*) energy, drive

dinamitar [dʒinami'tar] VT to blow up

dinamite [dʒina'mitʃi] F dynamite

dínamo ['dʒinamu] M dynamo

dinastia [dʒinas'tʃia] F dynasty

dinda ['dʒĩda] (*col*) F godmother

dindim [dʒĩ'dʒĩ] (*col*) M (*dinheiro*) cash

dinheirão [dʒinej'rãw] M: **um ~** loads *pl* of money

dinheiro [dʒi'ɲejru] M money; **~ à vista** cash for paying in cash; **sem ~** penniless; **em ~** in cash; **~ em caixa** money in the till; **~ em espécie** cash; **~ vivo** hard cash

dinossauro [dʒino'sawru] M dinosaur

diocese [dʒo'sɛzi] F diocese

dióxido ['dʒɔksidu] M dioxide; **~ de carbono** carbon dioxide

DIP (BR) ABR M = **Departamento de Imprensa e Propaganda**

diploma [dʒip'lɔma] M diploma

diplomacia [dʒiploma'sia] F diplomacy; (fig) tact

diplomando, -a [dʒiplo'mãdu, a] M/F diploma candidate

diplomar [dʒiplo'mar] VT to give a diploma (ou degree) to; **diplomar-se** VR: **~-se (em algo)** to get one's diploma (in sth)

diplomata [dʒiplo'mata] M/F diplomat

diplomático, -a [dʒiplo'matʃiku, a] ADJ diplomatic; (discreto) tactful

dique ['dʒiki] M dam; (Geo) dyke

direção [dʒire'sãw] (pl **-ões**) F direction; (endereço) address; (Auto) steering; (administração) management; (comando) leadership; (diretoria) board of directors; **em ~ a** towards

direi etc [dʒi'rej] VB ver **dizer**

direita [dʒi'rejta] F (mão) right hand; (lado) right-hand side; (Pol) right wing; **à ~** on the right; **"mantenha-se à ~"** "keep right"

direitinho [dʒirej'tʃiɲu] ADV properly, just right; (diretamente) directly

direitista [dʒirej'tʃista] ADJ right-wing ▶ M/F right-winger

direito, -a [dʒi'rejtu, a] ADJ (lado) right-hand; (mão) right; (honesto) honest; (devido) proper; (justo) right, just ▶ M (prerrogativa) right; (Jur) law; (de tecido) right side ▶ ADV (em linha reta) straight; (bem) right; (de maneira certa) properly; **direitos** MPL (humanos) rights; (alfandegários) duty sg; **~ civil** civil law; **~s civis** civil rights; **~s de importação** import duty; **~s humanos** human rights; **livre de ~s** duty-free; **ter ~ a** to have a right to, be entitled to; **minha roupa está direita?/meu cabelo está ~?** are my clothes/is my hair all right?

diretas [dʒi'rɛtas] FPL (Pol) direct elections

direto, -a [dʒi'rɛtu, a] ADJ direct ▶ ADV straight; **transmissão direta** (TV) live broadcast; **ir ~ ao assunto** to get straight to the point

diretor, a [dʒire'tor(a)] ADJ directing, guiding ▶ M/F (Com, de cinema) director; (de jornal) editor; (de escola) head teacher

diretor-gerente, diretora-gerente (pl **diretores-gerentes/diretoras-gerentes**) M/F managing director

diretoria [dʒireto'ria] F (cargo) directorship; (: em escola) headship; (direção: Com) management; (sala) boardroom

diretório [dʒire'tɔrju] M directorate; (Comput) directory; **~ acadêmico** students' union

diretriz [dʒire'triz] F directive

dirigente [dʒiri'ʒẽtʃi] ADJ (classe) ruling ▶ M/F (de país, partido) leader; (diretor) director; (gerente) manager

dirigir [dʒiri'ʒir] VT to direct; (Com) to manage, run; (veículo) to drive; (atenção) to turn ▶ VI to drive; **dirigir-se** VR: **~-se a** (falar com) to speak to, address; (ir, recorrer) to go to; (esforços) to be directed towards

dirimir [dʒiri'mir] VT (dúvida, contenda) to settle, clear up

discagem [dʒis'kaʒẽ] F (Tel) dialling; **~ direta** direct dialling

discar [dʒis'kar] VT to dial

discente [dʒi'sẽtʃi] ADJ: **corpo ~** student body

discernimento [dʒiserni'mẽtu] M discernment

discernir [dʒiser'nir] VT (perceber) to discern, perceive; (diferenciar) to discriminate, distinguish

discernível [dʒiser'nivew] (pl **-eis**) ADJ discernible

disciplina [dʒisi'plina] F discipline

disciplinador, a [dʒisiplina'dor(a)] ADJ disciplinary

disciplinar [dʒisipli'nar] VT to discipline; **disciplinar-se** VR to discipline o.s.

discípulo, -a [dʒi'sipulu, a] M/F disciple; (aluno) pupil

disco ['dʒisku] M disc; (Comput) disk; (Mús) record; (de telefone) dial; **~ rígido** (Comput) hard drive, hard disk; **~ do sistema** system disk; **~ voador** flying saucer

discordância [dʒiskor'dãsja] F disagreement; (de opiniões) difference

discordante [dʒiskor'dãtʃi] ADJ divergent, conflicting

discordar [dʒiskor'dar] VI: **~ de alguém em algo** to disagree with sb on sth; **discordar-se** VR to disagree

discórdia [dʒis'kɔrdʒja] F discord, strife

discorrer [dʒisko'her] VI: **~ (sobre)** (falar) to talk (about)

discoteca [dʒisko'tɛka] F (boate) discotheque, disco (col); (coleção de discos) record library

discotecário, -a [dʒiskote'karju, a] M/F disc jockey, DJ

discrepância [dʒiskre'pãsja] F discrepancy; (desacordo) disagreement

discrepante [dʒiskre'pãtʃi] ADJ conflicting

discrepar [dʒiskre'par] VI: **~ de** to differ from

discreto, -a [dʒis'krɛtu, a] ADJ discreet; (modesto) modest; (prudente) shrewd; (roupa) plain, sober

discrição [dʒiskri'sãw] F discretion, good sense

discricionário, -a [dʒiskrisjo'narju, a] ADJ discretionary

discriminação [dʒiskrimina'sãw] F discrimination; (especificação) differentiation; **~ racial** racial discrimination

discriminar [dʒiskrimi'nar] VT to distinguish ▶ VI: ~ **entre** to discriminate between

discriminatório, -a [dʒiskrimina'tɔrju, a] ADJ discriminatory

discursar [dʒiskur'sar] VI (*em público*) to make a speech; (*falar*) to speak

discurso [dʒis'kursu] M speech; (*Ling*) discourse

discussão [dʒisku'sãw] (*pl* -**ões**) F (*debate*) discussion, debate; (*contenda*) argument

discutir [dʒisku'tʃir] VT to discuss ▶ VI: ~ (**sobre algo**) (*debater*) to talk (about sth); (*contender*) to argue (about sth)

discutível [dʒisku'tʃivew] (*pl* -**eis**) ADJ debatable

disenteria [dʒizẽte'ria] F dysentery

disfarçar [dʒisfar'sar] VT to disguise ▶ VI to pretend; **disfarçar-se** VR: ~-**se em** *ou* **de algo** to disguise o.s. as sth

disfarce [dʒis'farsi] M disguise; (*máscara*) mask

disfasia [dʒisfa'sia] F (*Med*) speech defect

disforme [dʒis'fɔrmi] ADJ deformed; (*monstruoso*) hideous

disfunção [dʒisfũ'sãw] (*pl* -**ões**) F (*Med*) dysfunction

dislético, -a [dʒiz'lɛtʃiku, a] ADJ, M/F dyslexic

dislexia [dʒizlek'sia] F dyslexia

disléxico, -a [dʒiz'lɛksiku, a] ADJ, M/F dyslexic

díspar ['dʒispar] ADJ dissimilar

disparada [dʒispa'rada] F: **dar uma** ~ to surge ahead; **em** ~ at full tilt

disparado, -a [dʒispa'radu, a] ADJ very fast ▶ ADV by a long way

disparar [dʒispa'rar] VT to shoot, fire ▶ VI to fire; (*arma*) to go off; (*correr*) to shoot off, bolt

disparatado, -a [dʒispara'tadu, a] ADJ silly, absurd

disparate [dʒispa'ratʃi] M nonsense, rubbish; (*ação*) blunder

disparidade [dʒispari'dadʒi] F disparity

dispêndio [dʒis'pẽdʒu] M expenditure

dispendioso, -a [dʒispẽ'dʒjozu, ɔza] ADJ costly, expensive

dispensa [dʒis'pẽsa] F exemption; (*Rel*) dispensation

dispensar [dʒispẽ'sar] VT (*desobrigar*) to excuse; (*prescindir de*) to do without; (*conferir*) to grant

dispensário [dʒispẽ'sarju] M dispensary

dispensável [dʒispẽ'savew] (*pl* -**eis**) ADJ expendable

dispepsia [dʒispep'sia] F dyspepsia

dispersão [dʒisper'sãw] F dispersal

dispersar [dʒisper'sar] VT, VI to disperse

dispersivo, -a [dʒisper'sivu, a] ADJ (*pessoa*) scatterbrained

disperso, -a [dʒis'pɛrsu, a] ADJ scattered

displicência [dʒispli'sẽsja] (BR) F (*descuido*) negligence, carelessness

displicente [dʒispli'sẽtʃi] ADJ careless

dispo *etc* ['dʒispu] VB *ver* **despir**

disponibilidade [dʒisponibili'dadʒi] F availability; (*finanças*) liquid *ou* available assets *pl*; ~ **de caixa** cash in hand

disponível [dʒispo'nivew] (*pl* -**eis**) ADJ available

dispor [dʒis'por] (*irreg: como* **pôr**) VT (*arranjar*) to arrange; (*colocar em ordem*) to put in order ▶ VI: ~ **de** (*usar*) to have the use of; (*ter*) to have, own; (*pessoas*) to have at one's disposal; **dispor-se** VR: ~-**se a** (*estar pronto a*) to be prepared to, be willing to; (*decidir*) to decide to; ~ **sobre** to talk about; **não disponho de tempo para …** I can't afford the time to …; **disponha!** feel free!

disposição [dʒispozi'sãw] (*pl* -**ões**) F arrangement; (*humor*) disposition; (*inclinação*) inclination; **à sua** ~ at your disposal

dispositivo [dʒispozi'tʃivu] M (*mecanismo*) gadget, device; (*determinação de lei*) provision; (*conjunto de meios*): ~ **de segurança** security operation; ~ **intrauterino** intra-uterine device

disposto, -a [dʒis'poftu, 'pɔsta] PP *de* **dispor** ▶ ADJ (*arranjado*) arranged; **estar** ~ **a** to be willing to; **estar bem** ~ to look well; **sentir-se** ~ **a fazer algo** to feel like doing sth

disputa [dʒis'puta] F (*contenda*) dispute, argument; (*competição*) contest

disputar [dʒispu'tar] VT to dispute; (*concorrer a*) to compete for; (*lutar por*) to fight over ▶ VI (*discutir*) to quarrel, argue; to compete; ~ **uma corrida** to run a race

disquete [dʒis'ketʃi] M (*Comput*) diskette

dissabor [dʒisa'bor] M (*desgosto*) sorrow; (*aborrecimento*) annoyance

disse *etc* ['dʒisi] VB *ver* **dizer**

dissecar [dʒise'kar] VT to dissect

disseminação [dʒisemina'sãw] F (*de pólen etc*) spread(ing); (*de ideias*) dissemination

disseminar [dʒisemi'nar] VT to disseminate; (*espalhar*) to spread

dissensão [dʒisẽ'sãw] F dissension, discord

dissentir [dʒisẽ'tʃir] VI: ~ **de alguém (em algo)** to be in disagreement with sb (over sth); ~ **de algo** (*não combinar*) to be at variance with sth

disse que disse [dʒisiki'dʒisi] M gossip, tittle-tattle

dissertação [dʒiserta'sãw] (*pl* -**ões**) F dissertation; (*discurso*) lecture

dissertar [dʒiser'tar] VI to speak

dissidência [dʒisi'dẽsja] F (*divergência*) dissension; (*dissidentes*) dissidents *pl*; (*cisão*) difference of opinion

dissidente [dʒisi'dẽtʃi] ADJ, M/F dissident

dissídio [dʒi'sidʒu] M (*Jur*): ~ **coletivo/individual** collective/individual dispute

dissimilar [dʒisimi'lar] ADJ dissimilar

dissimulação [dʒisimula'sãw] F (*fingimento*) pretence (BRIT), pretense (US); (*disfarce*) disguise

dissimular [dʒisimu'lar] VT (*ocultar*) to hide; (*fingir*) to feign ▶ VI to dissemble

dissinto *etc* [dʒi'sĩtu] VB *ver* **dissentir**

dissipação [dʒisipa'sãw] F waste, squandering

dissipar [dʒisi'par] VT (*dispersar*) to disperse, dispel; (*malgastar*) to squander, waste; **dissipar-se** VR to vanish

disso ['dʒisu] = **de + isso**; *ver* **de**

dissociar [dʒiso'sjar] VT: ~ **algo (de/em algo)** to separate sth (from sth)/break sth up (into sth); **dissociar-se** VR: ~-**se de algo** to dissociate o.s. from sth

dissolução [dʒisolu'sãw] F (*dissolvência*) dissolving; (*libertinagem*) debauchery; (*de casamento*) dissolution

dissoluto, -a [dʒiso'lutu, a] ADJ dissolute, debauched

dissolver [dʒisow'ver] VT to dissolve; (*dispersar*) to disperse; (*motim*) to break up

dissonância [dʒiso'nãsja] F dissonance; (*discordância*) discord

dissonante [dʒiso'nãtʃi] ADJ (*som*) dissonant, discordant; (*fig*) discordant

dissuadir [dʒiswa'dʒir] VT to dissuade; ~ **alguém de fazer algo** to talk sb out of doing sth, dissuade sb from doing sth

dissuasão [dʒiswa'zãw] F dissuasion

dissuasivo, -a [dʒiswa'zivu, a] ADJ dissuasive

distância [dʒis'tãsja] F distance; **a grande ~** far away; **a 3 quilômetros de ~** 3 kilometres (BRIT) *ou* kilometers (US) away

distanciamento [dʒistãsja'mẽtu] M distancing

distanciar [dʒistã'sjar] VT (*afastar*) to distance, set apart; (*colocar por intervalos*) to space out; **distanciar-se** VR to move away; (*fig*) to distance o.s.

distante [dʒis'tãtʃi] ADJ distant, far-off; (*fig*) aloof

distar [dʒis'tar] VI to be far away; **o aeroporto dista 10 quilômetros da cidade** the airport is 10 km away from the city

distender [dʒistẽ'der] VT (*estender*) to expand; (*estirar*) to stretch; (*dilatar*) to distend; (*músculo*) to pull; **distender-se** VR to expand; to distend

distinção [dʒistʃĩ'sãw] (*pl* -**ões**) F distinction; **fazer ~** to make a distinction

distinguir [dʒistʃĩ'gir] VT (*diferenciar*) to distinguish, differentiate; (*avistar, ouvir*) to make out; (*enobrecer*) to distinguish; **distinguir-se** VR to stand out; ~ **algo de algo/ entre** to distinguish sth from sth/between

distintivo, -a [dʒistʃĩ'tʃivu, a] ADJ distinctive ► M (*insígnia*) badge; (*emblema*) emblem

distinto, -a [dʒis'tʃĩtu, a] ADJ (*diferente*) different; (*eminente*) distinguished; (*claro*) distinct; (*refinado*) refined

disto ['dʒistu] = **de + isto**; *ver* **de**

distorção [dʒistor'sãw] (*pl* -**ões**) F distortion

distorcer [dʒistor'ser] VT to distort

distorções [dʒistor'sõjs] FPL *de* **distorção**

distração [dʒistra'sãw] (*pl* -**ões**) F (*alheamento*) absent-mindedness; (*divertimento*) pastime; (*descuido*) oversight

distraído, -a [dʒistra'idu, a] ADJ absent-minded; (*não atento*) inattentive

distrair [dʒistra'ir] VT (*tornar desatento*) to distract; (*divertir*) to amuse; **distrair-se** VR to amuse o.s.

distribuição [dʒistribwi'sãw] F distribution; (*de cartas*) delivery

distribuidor, a [dʒistribwi'dor(a)] M/F distributor ► M (*Auto*) distributor ► F (*Com*) distribution company, distributor

distribuir [dʒistri'bwir] VT to distribute; (*repartir*) to share out; (*cartas*) to deliver

distrito [dʒis'tritu] M district; (*delegacia*) police station; ~ **eleitoral** constituency; ~ **federal** federal area

distúrbio [dʒis'turbju] M disturbance; **distúrbios** MPL (*Pol*) riots

ditado [dʒi'tadu] M dictation; (*provérbio*) saying

ditador [dʒita'dor] M dictator

ditadura [dʒita'dura] F dictatorship

ditame [dʒi'tami] M (*da consciência*) dictate; (*regra*) rule

ditar [dʒi'tar] VT to dictate; (*impor*) to impose

ditatorial [dʒitato'rjaw] (*pl* -**ais**) ADJ dictatorial

dito, -a ['dʒitu, a] PP *de* **dizer** ► M: ~ **espirituoso** witticism; ~ **e feito** no sooner said than done

dito-cujo (*pl* **ditos-cujos**) (*col*) M said person

ditongo [dʒi'tõgu] M diphthong

ditoso, -a [dʒi'tozu, ɔza] ADJ (*feliz*) happy; (*venturoso*) lucky

DIU ['dʒiu] ABR M (= *dispositivo intrauterino*) IUD

diurético, -a [dʒju'rɛtʃiku, a] ADJ diuretic ► M diuretic

diurno, -a ['dʒjurnu, a] ADJ daytime *atr*

divã [dʒi'vã] M couch, divan

divagação [dʒivaga'sãw] (*pl* -**ões**) F (*andança*) wandering; (*digressão*) digression; (*devaneio*) rambling

divagar [dʒiva'gar] VI (*vaguear*) to wander; (*falar sem nexo*) to ramble (on); ~ **do assunto** to wander off the subject, digress

divergência [dʒiver'ʒẽsja] F divergence; (*desacordo*) disagreement

divergente [dʒiver'ʒẽtʃi] ADJ divergent

divergir [dʒiver'ʒir] VI to diverge; (*discordar*): ~ **(de alguém)** to disagree (with sb)

diversão [dʒiver'sãw] (*pl* -**ões**) F (*divertimento*) amusement; (*passatempo*) pastime

diversidade [dʒiversi'dadʒi] F diversity

diversificação [dʒiversifika'sãw] F diversification

diversificar [dʒiversifi'kar] VT to diversify ► VI to vary

diverso, -a [dʒi'vɛrsu, a] ADJ (*diferente*) different; (*pl*) various

diversões [dʒiver'sõjs] FPL *de* **diversão**

diversos, -sas [dʒi'vɛrsus, sas] ADJ several ► MPL (*na contabilidade*) sundries

divertido, -a [dʒiver'tʃidu, a] ADJ amusing, funny

d

divertimento [dʒivertʃi'mẽtu] M amusement, entertainment

divertir [dʒiver'tʃir] VT to amuse, entertain; **divertir-se** VR to enjoy o.s., have a good time

dívida ['dʒivida] F debt; (*obrigação*) indebtedness; **contrair ~s** to run into debt; **~ externa** foreign debt

dividendo [dʒivi'dẽdu] M dividend

dividido, -a [dʒivi'dʒidu, a] ADJ divided; **sentir-se ~ entre duas coisas** to feel torn between two things

dividir [dʒivi'dʒir] VT to divide; (*despesas, lucro, comida etc*) to share; (*separar*) to separate ▶ VI (*Mat*) to divide; **dividir-se** VR to divide, split up; **as opiniões se dividem** opinions are divided; **ele tem que se ~ entre a família e o trabalho** he has to divide his time between the family and work; **~ 21 por 7** to divide 21 by 7; **~ algo em 3 partes** to divide sth into 3 parts; **~ algo pela metade** to divide sth in half *ou* in two

divindade [dʒivĩ'dadʒi] F divinity

divino, -a [dʒi'vinu, a] ADJ divine; (*col*) gorgeous ▶ M Holy Ghost

divirjo *etc* [dʒi'virʒu] VB *ver* **divergir**

divisa [dʒi'viza] F (*emblema*) emblem; (*frase*) slogan; (*fronteira*) border; (*Mil*) stripe; **divisas** FPL (*câmbio*) foreign exchange *sg*, foreign currency *sg*

divisão [dʒivi'zãw] (*pl* -**ões**) F division; (*discórdia*) split; (*partilha*) sharing

divisar [dʒivi'zar] VT (*avistar*) to see, make out

divisível [dʒivi'zivew] (*pl* -**eis**) ADJ divisible

divisões [dʒivi'zõjs] FPL *de* **divisão**

divisória [dʒivi'zɔrja] F partition

divisório, -a [dʒivi'zɔrju, a] ADJ (*linha*) dividing

divorciado, -a [dʒivor'sjadu, a] ADJ divorced ▶ M/F divorcé(e)

divorciar [dʒivor'sjar] VT to divorce; **divorciar-se** VR to get divorced

divórcio [dʒi'vɔrsju] M divorce

divulgação [dʒivuwga'sãw] F (*de notícias*) spread; (*de segredo*) divulging; (*de produto*) marketing

divulgar [dʒivuw'gar] VT (*notícias*) to spread; (*segredo*) to divulge; (*produto*) to market; (*livro*) to publish; **divulgar-se** VR to leak out

dizer [dʒi'zer] VT to say ▶ M saying; **dizer-se** VR to claim to be; **diz-se** *ou* **dizem que ...** it is said that ...; **diga-se de passagem** by the way; **~ algo a alguém** (*informar, avisar*) to tell sb sth; (*falar*) to say sth to sb; **~ a alguém que ...** to tell sb that ...; **o que você diz da minha sugestão?** what do you think of my suggestion?; **~ para alguém fazer** to tell sb to do; **o filme não me disse nada** (*não interessou*) the film left me cold; **o nome não me diz nada** (*não significa*) the name means nothing to me; **~ bem com** to go well with; **querer ~** to mean; **quer ~** that is to say; **nem é preciso ~** that goes without saying; **não ~ coisa com coisa** to make no sense; **digo** (*ou seja*) I mean; **diga!** what is it?; **não**

diga! you don't say!; **digamos** let's say; **bem que eu te disse, eu não disse?** I told you so; **ele tem dificuldade em acordar às sete, que dirá às cinco** he finds it difficult to wake at seven, let alone *ou* never mind five; **por assim ~** so to speak; **até ~ chega** as much as possible

dizimar [dʒizi'mar] VT to decimate; (*herança*) to fritter away

Djibuti [dʒibu'tʃi] M: **o ~** Djibouti

DNER (BR) ABR M (= *Departamento Nacional de Estradas de Rodagem*) *national highways department*

DNOCS (BR) ABR M = **Departamento Nacional de Obras contra as Secas**

DNPM (BR) ABR M = **Departamento Nacional de Produção Mineral**

do [du] = **de + o**; *ver* **de**

dó [dɔ] M (*lástima*) pity; (*Mús*) do; **ter dó de** to feel sorry for

doação [doa'sãw] (*pl* -**ões**) F donation, gift

doador, a [doa'dor(a)] M/F donor

doar [do'ar] VT to donate, give

dobra ['dɔbra] F fold; (*prega*) pleat; (*de calças*) turn-up

dobradiça [dobra'dʒisa] F hinge

dobradiço, -a [dobra'dʒisu, a] ADJ flexible

dobradinha [dobra'dʒiɲa] F (*Culin*) tripe stew; (*col: dupla*) pair, partnership

dobrar [do'brar] VT (*duplicar*) to double; (*papel*) to fold; (*joelho*) to bend; (*esquina*) to turn, go round; **~ alguém** to talk sb round ▶ VI to double; (*sino*) to toll; (*vergar*) to bend; **dobrar-se** VR to double (up)

dobro ['dobru] M double

DOC (BR) ABR F = **Diretoria de Obras de Cooperação**

doca ['dɔka] F (*Náut*) dock

doce ['dosi] ADJ sweet; (*terno*) gentle ▶ M sweet; **ele é um ~** he's a sweetie; **fazer ~** (*col*) to play hard to get

doce-de-coco (*pl* **doces-de-coco**) M (*pessoa*) sweetie

doceiro, -a [do'sejru, a] M/F sweet-seller

dóceis ['dɔsejs] ADJ PL *de* **dócil**

docemente [dose'mẽtʃi] ADV gently

docência [do'sẽsja] F teaching *atr*

docente [do'sẽtʃi] ADJ teaching *atr*; **o corpo ~** teaching staff

dócil ['dɔsiw] (*pl* -**eis**) ADJ docile

documentação [dokumẽta'sãw] F documentation; (*documentos*) papers *pl*

documentar [dokumẽ'tar] VT to document

documentário, -a [dokumẽ'tarju, a] ADJ, M documentary

documento [doku'mẽtu] M document; **não é ~** (*col*) it doesn't mean a thing

doçura [do'sura] F sweetness; (*brandura*) gentleness

Dodecaneso [dodeka'nɛzu] M: **o ~** the Dodecanese

dodói [do'dɔj] (*col*) M: **você tem ~?** does it hurt? ▶ ADJ INV ill, under the weather

doença [do'ēsa] F illness
doente [do'ētʃi] ADJ ill, sick ▶ M/F sick person; (*cliente*) patient
doentio, -a [doē'tʃiu, a] ADJ (*pessoa*) sickly; (*clima*) unhealthy; (*curiosidade*) morbid
doer [do'er] VI to hurt, ache; ~ **a alguém** (*pesar*) to grieve sb; **dói ver tanta pobreza** it's sad to see so much poverty
dogma ['dɔgma] M dogma
dogmático, -a [dog'matʃiku, a] ADJ dogmatic
DOI (BR) ABR M (= *Destacamento de Operações Internas*) *military secret police*
Doi-Codi ['dɔi-'kɔdʒi] (BR) ABR M (= *Departamento de Operações e Informações – Centro de Operação e Defesa Interna*) *secret police HQ during the military dictatorship*
doidão, -dona [doj'dãw, 'dɔna] (*pl* **-ões/-s**) ADJ: (**ser**) ~ (*to be*) completely crazy; (**estar**) ~ (*to be*) high
doideira [doj'dejra] F madness, foolishness
doidice [doj'dʒisi] F madness, foolishness
doidivanas [dojdʒi'vanas] M/F INV hothead
doido, -a ['dojdu, a] ADJ mad, crazy ▶ M/F madman/woman; ~ **por** mad *ou* crazy about; ~ **varrido** *ou* **de pedras** (*col*) raving loony
doído, -a [do'idu, a] ADJ sore, painful; (*moralmente*) hurt; (*que causa dor*) painful
doidões [doj'dõjs] MPL *de* **doidão**
doidona [doj'dɔna] F *de* **doidão**
doirar [doj'rar] VT = **dourar**
dois, duas [dojs, 'duas] NUM two; **conversa a** ~ tête-à-tête; *ver tb* **cinco**
dólar ['dɔlar] M dollar; ~ **oficial** dollar at the official rate; ~ **turismo** dollar at the special tourist rate
doleiro, -a [do'lejru, a] M/F (black market) dollar dealer
dolo ['dɔlu] M fraud
dolorido, -a [dolo'ridu, a] ADJ painful, sore; (*fig*) sorrowful
dolorosa [dolo'rɔza] F bill
doloroso, -a [dolo'rozu, ɔza] ADJ painful
dom [dõ] M gift; (*aptidão*) knack; **o** ~ **da palavra** the gift of the gab
dom. ABR (= *domingo*) Sun.
domador, a [domador(a)] M/F tamer
domar [do'mar] VT to tame
doméstica [do'mɛstʃika] F maid
domesticado, -a [domestʃi'kadu, a] ADJ domesticated; (*manso*) tame
domesticar [domestʃi'kar] VT to domesticate; (*povo*) to tame
doméstico, -a [do'mɛstʃiku, a] ADJ domestic; (*vida*) home *atr*
domiciliar [domisi'ljar] ADJ home *atr*
domicílio [domi'silju] M home, residence; **vendas/entrega a** ~ home sales/delivery; "**entregamos a** ~" "we deliver"
dominação [domina'sãw] F domination
dominador, a [domina'dor(a)] ADJ (*pessoa*) domineering; (*olhar*) imposing ▶ M/F ruler

dominante [domi'nātʃi] ADJ dominant; (*predominante*) predominant
dominar [domi'nar] VT to dominate; (*reprimir*) to overcome ▶ VI to dominate, prevail; **dominar-se** VR to control o.s.
domingo [do'mĩgu] M Sunday; *ver tb* **terça-feira**
domingueiro, -a [domĩ'gejru, a] ADJ Sunday *atr*; **traje** ~ Sunday best
Dominica [domi'nika] F Dominica
dominicano, -a [domini'kanu, a] ADJ, M/F Dominican; **República Dominicana** Dominican Republic
domínio [do'minju] M (*poder*) power; (*dominação*) control; (*território*) domain; (*esfera*) sphere; ~ **próprio** self-control
dom-juan [-'ʒwã] M ladies' man, Don Juan
domo ['dɔmu] M dome
dona ['dɔna] F (*proprietária*) owner; (*col: mulher*) lady; ~ **de casa** housewife; **D~ Lígia** Lígia; **D~ Luísa Souza** Mrs Luísa Souza
donatário, -a [dona'tarju, a] M/F recipient
donde ['dõdə] (PT) ADV from where; (*daí*) thus; ~ **vem?** where do you come from?
dondoca [dõ'dɔka] (*col*) F society lady, lady of leisure
dono ['donu] M (*proprietário*) owner
donzela [dõ'zɛla] F (*mulher*) maiden
dopar [do'par] VT (*cavalo*) to dope; **dopar-se** VR (*atleta*) to take drugs
DOPS (BR) ABR M (= *Departamento de Ordem Política e Social*) *internal security agency*
dor [dor] F ache; (*aguda*) pain; (*fig*) grief, sorrow; ~ **de cabeça** headache; ~ **de cotovelo** (*col: ciúmes*) jealousy; (*por decepçao amorosa*) a bruised heart; ~ **de dentes** toothache; ~ **de estômago** stomachache
doravante [dora'vātʃi] ADV henceforth
dormência [dor'mēsja] F numbness
dormente [dor'mētʃi] ADJ numb ▶ M (*Ferro*) sleeper
dormida [dor'mida] F sleep; (*lugar*) place to sleep; **dar uma** ~ to have a sleep
dormideira [dormi'dejra] F drowsiness
dorminhoco, -a [dormi'ɲoku, a] ADJ dozy ▶ M/F sleepyhead
dormir [dor'mir] VI to sleep; ~ **como uma pedra** *ou* **a sono solto** to sleep like a log *ou* soundly; **hora de** ~ bedtime; ~ **no ponto** (*fig*) to miss the boat; ~ **fora** to spend the night away
dormitar [dormi'tar] VI to doze
dormitório [dormi'tɔrju] M bedroom; (*coletivo*) dormitory
dorsal [dor'saw] (*pl* **-ais**) ADJ: **coluna** ~ spine
dorso ['dorsu] M back
dos [dus] = **de + os**; *ver* **de**
dosagem [do'zaʒē] F dosage
dosar [do'zar] VT (*medicamento*) to judge the correct dosage of; (*graduar*) to give in small doses; **você tem que** ~ **bem o que diz para ele** you have to be careful what you say to him

d

dose ['dɔzi] F dose; **~ cavalar** huge dose; **~ excessiva** overdose; **é ~ para leão** *ou* **cavalo** (*col*) it's too much

dossiê [do'sje] M dossier, file

dotação [dota'sãw] (*pl* **-ões**) F endowment, allocation

dotado, -a [do'tadu, a] ADJ gifted; **~ de** endowed with

dotar [do'tar] VT to endow; (*filha*) to give a dowry to; **~ alguém de algo** to endow sb with sth

dote ['dɔtʃi] M dowry; (*fig*) gift

DOU ABR M (= *Diário Oficial da União*) *official journal of Brazilian government*

dou [do] VB *ver* **dar**

dourado, -a [do'radu, a] ADJ golden; (*com camada de ouro*) gilt, gilded ▶ M gilt; (*cor*) golden colour (BRIT) *ou* color (US)

dourar [do'rar] VT to gild

douto, -a ['dotu, a] ADJ learned

doutor, a [do'tor(a)] M/F doctor; **D~** (*forma de tratamento*) Sir; **D~ Eduardo Souza** Mr Eduardo Souza

doutorado [doto'radu] M doctorate

doutrina [do'trina] F doctrine

doze ['dozi] NUM twelve; *ver tb* **cinco**

DP (BR) ABR F = **delegacia de polícia**

DPF (BR) ABR M = **Departamento de Polícia Federal**

DPNRE (BR) ABR M = **Departamento de Parques Nacionais e Reservas Equivalentes**

Dr. ABR (= *Doutor*) Dr

Dra. ABR (= *Doutora*) Dr

draga ['draga] F dredger

dragagem [dra'gaʒẽ] F dredging

dragão [dra'gãw] (*pl* **-ões**) M dragon; (*Mil*) dragoon

dragar [dra'gar] VT to dredge

drágea ['draʒja] F tablet

dragões [dra'gõjs] MPL *de* **dragão**

drama ['drama] M (*teatro*) drama; (*peça*) play; **fazer ~** (*col*) to make a scene; **ser um ~** (*col*) to be an ordeal

dramalhão [drama'ʎãw] (*pl* **-ões**) M melodrama

dramático, -a [dra'matʃiku, a] ADJ dramatic

dramatização [dramatʃiza'sãw] (*pl* **-ões**) F dramatization

dramatizar [dramatʃi'zar] VT, VI to dramatize

dramaturgo, -a [drama'turgu, a] M/F playwright, dramatist

drapeado, -a [dra'pjadu, a] ADJ draped ▶ M hang

drástico, -a ['drastʃiku, a] ADJ drastic

drenagem [dre'naʒẽ] F drainage

drenar [dre'nar] VT to drain

dreno ['drɛnu] M drain

driblar [dri'blar] VT (*Futebol*) to dribble; (*fig*) to get round ▶ VI to dribble

drinque ['drĩki] M drink

drive ['drajvi] M (*Comput*) drive

droga ['drɔga] F drug; (*fig*) rubbish ▶ EXCL: **~!** damn!, blast!; **ser uma ~** (*col: filme, caneta etc*) to be a dead loss; (: *obrigação, atividade*) to be a drag; **~ recreacional** recreational drug

drogado, -a [dro'gadu, a] M/F drug addict

drogar [dro'gar] VT to drug; **drogar-se** VR to take drugs

drogaria [droga'ria] F chemist's shop (BRIT), drugstore (US)

dromedário [drome'darju] M dromedary

duas ['duas] F *de* **dois**

duas-peças M INV two-piece

dúbio, -a ['dubju, a] ADJ dubious; (*vago*) uncertain

dublagem [du'blaʒẽ] F (*de filme*) dubbing

dublar [du'blar] VT to dub

dublê [du'ble] M/F double

ducentésimo, -a [dusẽ'tɛzimu, a] NUM two-hundredth

ducha ['duʃa] F shower; (*Med*) douche

ducto ['duktu] M duct

duelo ['dwɛlu] M duel

duende [du'wẽdʒi] M elf

dueto ['dwetu] M duet

dulcíssimo, -a [duw'sisimu, a] ADJ SUPERL *de* **doce**

dumping ['dãpĩ] M (*Econ*) dumping

duna ['duna] F dune

duodécimo, -a [dwo'dɛsimu, a] NUM twelfth

duodeno [dwo'dɛnu] M duodenum

dupla ['dupla] F pair; (*Esporte*): **~ masculina/ feminina/mista** men's/women's/mixed doubles

dúplex ['dupleks] ADJ INV two-storey (BRIT), two-story (US) ▶ M INV luxury maisonette, duplex

duplicação [duplika'sãw] F (*repetição*) duplication; (*aumento*) doubling

duplicar [dupli'kar] VT (*repetir*) to duplicate ▶ VI (*dobrar*) to double

duplicata [dupli'kata] F (*cópia*) duplicate; (*título*) trade note, bill

duplicidade [duplisi'dadʒi] F (*fig*) duplicity

duplo, -a ['duplu, a] ADJ, M double

duque ['duki] M duke

duquesa [du'keza] F duchess

durabilidade [durabili'dadʒi] F durability

duração [dura'sãw] F duration; **de pouca ~** short-lived

duradouro, -a [dura'doru, a] ADJ lasting

durante [du'rãtʃi] PREP during; **~ uma hora** for an hour

durão, -rona [du'rãw, 'rɔna] (*pl* **-ões/-s**) (*col*) ADJ strict, tough

durar [du'rar] VI to last

durável [du'ravew] (*pl* **-eis**) ADJ lasting

durex® [du'rɛks] ADJ: **fita ~** adhesive tape, Sellotape® (BRIT), Scotch tape® (US)

dureza [du'reza] F hardness; (*severidade*) harshness; (*col: falta de dinheiro*) lack of funds

durmo *etc* ['durmu] VB *ver* **dormir**

duro, -a ['duru, a] ADJ hard; (*severo*) harsh; (*resistente, fig*) tough; (*sentença, palavras*) harsh, tough; (*inverno*) hard, harsh; (*fig: difícil*) hard, tough; **ser ~ com alguém** to be hard on sb;

estar ~ (*col*) to be broke; **dar um ~** (*col: trabalhar*) to work hard; **dar um ~ em alguém** (*col*) to come down hard on sb; **~ de roer** (*fig*) hard to take; **no ~** (*col*) really; **a praia estava dura de gente** the beach was packed

durões [du'rõjs] MPL *de* **durão**

durona [du'rɔna] F *de* **durão**

DUT (BR) ABR M (= *documento único de trânsito*) *vehicle licensing document*

dúvida ['duvida] F doubt; **sem ~** undoubtedly, without a doubt

duvidar [duvi'dar] VT to doubt ▶ VI to have one's doubts; **~ de alguém/algo** to doubt sb/sth; **~ que ...** to doubt that ...; **duvido!** I doubt it!; **duvido que você consiga correr a maratona** I bet you don't manage to run the marathon

duvidoso, -a [duvi'dozu, ɔza] ADJ (*incerto*) doubtful; (*suspeito*) dubious

duzentos, -as [du'zẽtus, as] NUM two hundred

dúzia ['duzja] F dozen; **meia ~** half a dozen

DVD ABR M (= *disco digital versátil*) DVD

dz. ABR = **dúzia**

Ee

E, e [ε] M (pl **es**) E, e ▶ ABR (= *esquerda*) L.;
(= *este*) E; (= *editor*) Ed.; **E de Eliane** E for
Edward (BRIT) *ou* easy (US)

e [i] CONJ and; **e a bagagem?** what about the
luggage?

é [ε] VB *ver* **ser**

EAPAC (BR) ABR F (= *Escola de Aperfeiçoamento e
Preparação Civil*) civil service training school

ébano ['ɛbanu] M ebony

EBN ABR F = **Empresa Brasileira de Notícias**

ébrio, -a ['ɛbrju, a] ADJ drunk ▶ M/F
drunkard

EBTU ABR F = **Empresa Brasileira de
Transportes Urbanos**

ebulição [ebuli'sãw] F boiling; (*fig*) ferment

ebuliente [ebu'ljētʃi] ADJ boiling

ECEME (BR) ABR F (= *Escola de Comando e
Estado-Maior do Exército*) officer training school

eclesiástico, -a [ekle'zjastʃiku, a] ADJ
ecclesiastical, church *atr* ▶ M clergyman

eclético, -a [e'klɛtʃiku, a] ADJ eclectic

eclipsar [eklip'sar] VT (*tb fig*) to eclipse

eclipse [e'klipsi] M eclipse

eclodir [eklo'dʒir] VI (*aparecer*) to emerge;
(*revolução*) to break out; (*flor*) to open

eclusa [e'kluza] F (*de canal*) lock; (*comporta*)
floodgate

eco ['ɛku] M echo; **ter ~** to catch on

ecoar [e'kwar] VT to echo ▶ VI (*ressoar*) to echo;
(*fig: repercutir*) to have repercussions

ecologia [ekolo'ʒia] F ecology

ecológico, -a [eko'lɔʒiku, a] ADJ ecological,
eco-friendly

ecologista [ekolo'ʒista] M/F ecologist

economia [ekono'mia] F economy; (*ciência*)
economics *sg*; **economias** FPL (*poupanças*)
savings; **fazer ~ (de)** to economize (with)

econômico, -a [eko'nomiku, a] ADJ (*barato*)
cheap; (*que consome pouco*) economical;
(*pessoa*) thrifty; (*Com*) economic

economista [ekono'mista] M/F economist

economizar [ekonomi'zar] VT (*gastar com
economia*) to economize on; (*poupar*) to save
(up) ▶ VI to economize; to save up

ecossistema [ekosis'tema] M ecosystem

ecrã [e'krã] (PT) **écran** ['ɛkrã] M screen; **~ tactil**
touch screen

ECT ABR F = **Empresa Brasileira de Correios e
Telégrafos**

ecumênico, -a [eku'meniku, a] ADJ
ecumenical

eczema [eg'zema] M eczema

Ed. ABR = **edifício**

ed. ABR = **edição**

éden ['ɛdẽ] M paradise

edição [edʒi'sãw] (pl **-ões**) F (*publicação*)
publication; (*conjunto de exemplares*) edition;
(*TV, Cinema*) editing; **~ atualizada/revista**
updated/revised edition; **~ extra** special
edition; **~ de imagem** video editing

edicto [e'ditu] (PT) M = **edito**

edificação [edʒifika'sãw] F construction,
building; (*fig: moral*) edification

edificante [edʒifi'kãtʃi] ADJ edifying

edificar [edʒifi'kar] VT (*construir*) to build; (*fig*)
to edify ▶ VI to be edifying

edifício [edʒi'fisju] M building; **~ garagem**
multistorey car park (BRIT), multistory
parking lot (US)

Edimburgo [edʒī'burgu] N Edinburgh

Édipo ['ɛdʒipu] M *ver* **complexo**

edital [edʒi'taw] (pl **-ais**) M announcement

editar [edʒi'tar] VT to publish; (*Comput etc*) to
edit

edito [e'dʒitu] M edict, decree

editor, a [edʒi'tor(a)] ADJ publishing *atr* ▶ M/F
publisher; (*redator*) editor ▶ F publishing
company; **casa ~a** publishing house; **~ de
imagem** video editor; **~ de texto** (*Comput*)
text editor

editoração [edʒitora'sãw] F: **~ eletrônica**
desktop publishing

editoria [edʒito'ria] F section; **~ de esportes**
(*em jornal*) sports desk

editorial [edʒitor'jaw] (pl **-ais**) ADJ publishing
atr ▶ M editorial

edredão [edrə'dãw] (pl **-ões**) (PT) M = **edredom**

edredom [edre'dõ] (pl **-ns**) M eiderdown

educação [eduka'sãw] F (*ensino*) education;
(*criação*) upbringing; (*de animais*) training;
(*maneiras*) good manners *pl*; **é falta de ~ falar
com a boca cheia** it's rude to talk with your
mouth full

educacional [edukasjo'naw] (pl **-ais**) ADJ
education *atr*

educado, -a [edu'kadu, a] ADJ (*bem-educado*)
polite

educador, a [eduka'dor(a)] M/F educator

educandário [edukã'darju] M educational establishment

educar [edu'kar] VT (*instruir*) to educate; (*criar*) to bring up; (*animal*) to train

educativo, -a [eduka'tʃivu, a] ADJ educational

efeito [e'fejtu] M effect; **fazer ~** to work; **levar a ~** to put into effect; **com ~** indeed; **para todos os ~s** to all intents and purposes; **~ estufa** greenhouse effect

efêmero, -a [e'femeru, a] ADJ ephemeral, short-lived

efeminado, -a [efemi'nadu, a] ADJ effeminate ▶ M effeminate man

efervescência [eferve'sēsja] F effervescence; (*fig*) ferment

efervescente [eferve'sētʃi] ADJ fizzy

efervescer [eferve'ser] VI to fizz; (*fig*) to hum

efetivamente [efetʃiva'mētʃi] ADV effectively; (*realmente*) really, in fact

efetivar [efetʃi'var] VT (*mudanças, cortes*) to carry out; (*professor, estagiário*) to take on permanently

efetividade [efetʃivi'dadʒi] F effectiveness; (*realidade*) reality

efetivo, -a [efe'tʃivu, a] ADJ effective; (*real*) actual, real; (*cargo, funcionário*) permanent ▶ M (*Com*) liquid assets *pl*

efetuar [efe'twar] VT to carry out; (*soma*) to do, perform

eficácia [efi'kasja] F (*de pessoa*) efficiency; (*de tratamento*) effectiveness

eficacíssimo, -a [efika'sisimu, a] ADJ SUPERL *de* **eficaz**

eficaz [efi'kaz] ADJ (*pessoa*) efficient; (*tratamento*) effective

eficiência [efi'sjēsja] F efficiency

eficiente [efi'sjētʃi] ADJ efficient, competent

efígie [e'fíʒi] F effigy

efusão [efu'zãw] (*pl* **-ões**) F effusion

efusivo, -a [efu'zivu, a] ADJ effusive; (*sentimentos*) warmest

efusões [efu'zõjs] FPL *de* **efusão**

Egeu [e'ʒew] M: **o (mar) ~** the Aegean (Sea)

EGF (*BR*) ABR M = **empréstimo do governo federal**

égide ['ɛʒidʒi] F: **sob a ~ de** under the aegis (*BRIT*) *ou* egis (*US*) of

egípcio, -a [e'ʒipsju, a] ADJ, M/F Egyptian

Egito [e'ʒitu] M: **o ~** Egypt

ego ['ɛgu] M ego

egocêntrico, -a [ego'sētriku, a] ADJ self-centred (*BRIT*), self-centered (*US*), egocentric

egoísmo [ego'izmu] M selfishness, egoism

egoísta [ego'ista] ADJ selfish, egoistic ▶ M/F egoist ▶ M earplug

egolatria [egola'tria] F self-admiration

egotismo [ego'tʃizmu] M egotism

egotista [ego'tʃista] M/F egotist ▶ ADJ egotistical

egrégio, -a [e'grɛʒju, a] ADJ distinguished

egresso [e'grɛsu] M (*preso*) ex-prisoner; (*frade*) former monk; (*universidade*) graduate

égua ['ɛgwa] F mare

ei [ej] EXCL hey!

ei-lo = **eis + o**

eira ['ejra] (*PT*) F threshing floor; **sem ~ nem beira** down and out

eis [ejs] ADV (*sg*) here is; (*pl*) here are; **~ aí** there is; there are

eivado, -a [ej'vadu, a] ADJ (*fig*) full

eixo ['ejʃu] M (*de rodas*) axle; (*Mat*) axis; (*de máquina*) shaft; **~ de transmissão** drive shaft; **entrar nos ~s** (*pessoa*) to get back on the straight and narrow; (*situação*) to get back to normal; **pôr algo/alguém nos ~s** to set sth/sb straight; **sair dos ~s** to step out of line; **o ~ Rio-São Paulo** the Rio-São Paulo area

ejacular [eʒaku'lar] VT (*sêmen*) to ejaculate; (*líquido*) to spurt ▶ VI to ejaculate

ejetar [eʒe'tar] VT to eject

ela ['ɛla] PRON (*pessoa*) she; (*coisa*) it; (*com prep*) her; it; **elas** FPL they; (*com prep*) them; **~s por ~s** (*col*) tit for tat; **aí é que são ~s** (*col*) that's just the point

elã [e'lã] M enthusiasm, drive

elaboração [elabora'sãw] (*pl* **-ões**) F (*de uma teoria*) working out; (*preparo*) preparation

elaborador, a [elabora'dor(a)] M/F maker

elaborar [elabo'rar] VT (*preparar*) to prepare; (*fazer*) to make

elasticidade [elastʃisi'dadʒi] F elasticity; (*flexibilidade*) suppleness

elástico, -a [e'lastʃiku, a] ADJ elastic; (*flexível*) flexible; (*colchão*) springy ▶ M elastic band

ele ['eli] PRON he; (*coisa*) it; (*com prep*) him; it; **eles** MPL they; (*com prep*) them

elefante, -ta [ele'fãtʃi, ta] M/F elephant; (*col: pessoa gorda*) fatso, fatty; **~ branco** (*fig*) white elephant

elefantino, -a [elefã'tʃinu, a] ADJ elephantine

elegância [ele'gãsja] F elegance

elegante [ele'gãtʃi] ADJ elegant; (*da moda*) fashionable

eleger [ele'ʒer] VT (*por votação*) to elect; (*escolher*) to choose

elegia [ele'ʒia] F elegy

elegibilidade [eleʒibili'dadʒi] F eligibility

elegível [ele'ʒivew] (*pl* **-eis**) ADJ eligible

eleição [elej'sãw] (*pl* **-ões**) F (*por votação*) election; (*escolha*) choice

eleito, -a [e'lejtu, a] PP *de* **eleger** ▶ ADJ (*por votação*) elected; (*escolhido*) chosen

eleitor, a [elej'tor(a)] M/F voter

eleitorado [elejto'radu] M electorate; **conhecer o seu ~** (*fig: col*) to know what one is up against

eleitoral [elejto'raw] (*pl* **-ais**) ADJ electoral

elejo *etc* [e'leʒu] VB *ver* **eleger**

elementar [elemē'tar] ADJ (*simples*) elementary; (*fundamental*) basic, fundamental

elemento [ele'mētu] M element; (*parte*) component; (*recurso*) means; (*informação*)

grounds *pl*; **elementos** MPL (*rudimentos*) rudiments; **ele é mau ~** he's a bad lot
elenco [e'lẽku] M list; (*de atores*) cast
elepê [eli'pe] M LP, album
eletivo, -a [ele'tʃivu, a] ADJ elective
eletricidade [eletrisi'dadʒi] F electricity
eletricista [eletri'sista] M/F electrician
elétrico, -a [e'lɛtriku, a] ADJ electric; (*fig: agitado*) worked up ▶ M tram (BRIT), streetcar (US)
eletrificar [eletrifi'kar] VT to electrify
eletrizar [eletri'zar] VT to electrify; (*fig*) to thrill
eletro [e'lɛtru] M (*Med*) ECG
eletro... [eletru] PREFIXO electro...
Eletrobrás [eletro'bras] ABR F *Brazilian state electricity company*
eletrocutar [eletroku'tar] VT to electrocute
eletrodo [ele'trodu], (PT) **elétrodo** [e'letrodu] M electrode
eletrodomésticos [eletrodo'mɛstʃikus] (BR) MPL (electrical) household appliances
eletrônica [ele'tronika] F electronics *sg*
eletrônico, -a [ele'troniku, a] ADJ electronic
elevação [eleva'sãw] (*pl* **-ões**) F (*Arq*) elevation; (*aumento*) rise; (*ato*) raising; (*altura*) height; (*promoção*) elevation, promotion; (*ponto elevado*) bump
elevado, -a [ele'vadu, a] ADJ high; (*pensamento, estilo*) elevated ▶ M (*via*) elevated road
elevador [eleva'dor] M lift (BRIT), elevator (US); **~ de serviço** service lift
elevar [ele'var] VT (*levantar*) to lift up; (*voz, preço*) to raise; (*exaltar*) to exalt; (*promover*) to elevate, to promote; **elevar-se** VR to rise
eliminação [elimina'sãw] F elimination
eliminar [elimi'nar] VT to remove, eliminate; (*suprimir*) to delete; (*possibilidade*) to rule out; (*Med, banir*) to expel; (*Esporte*) to eliminate
eliminatória [elimina'tɔrja] F (*Esporte*) heat, preliminary round; (*exame*) test
eliminatório, -a [elimina'tɔrju, a] ADJ eliminatory
elipse [e'lipsi] F ellipse; (*Ling*) ellipsis
elite [e'litʃi] F elite
elitismo [eli'tʃizmu] M elitism
elitista [eli'tʃista] ADJ, M/F elitist
elitizar [elitʃi'zar] VT (*arte, ensino*) to make elitist
elixir [elik'sir] M elixir
elo ['ɛlu] M link
elocução [eloku'sãw] F elocution
elogiar [elo'ʒjar] VT to praise; **~ alguém por algo** to compliment sb on sth
elogio [elo'ʒiu] M praise; (*cumprimento*) compliment
elogioso, -a [elo'ʒozu, ɔza] ADJ complimentary
eloquência [elo'kwẽsja] F eloquence
eloquente [elo'kwẽtʃi] ADJ eloquent; (*persuasivo*) persuasive
El Salvador [ew-] N El Salvador
elucidação [elusida'sãw] F elucidation

elucidar [elusi'dar] VT to elucidate, clarify
elucidativo, -a [elusida'tʃivu, a] ADJ elucidatory
elucubração [elukubra'sãw] (*pl* **-ões**) F cogitation, musing

(PALAVRA-CHAVE)

em [ẽ] (*em* + *o(s)/a(s)* = *no(s)/na(s)*; + *ele(s)/a(s)* = *nele(s)/a(s)*; + *esse(s)/a(s)* = *nesse(s)/a(s)*; + *isso* = *nisso*; + *este(s)/a(s)* = *neste(s)/a(s)*; + *isto* = *nisto*; + *aquele(s)/a(s)* = *naquele(s)/a(s)*; + *aquilo* = *naquilo*; + *um* = *num*; + *uma(s)* = *numa(s)*) PREP **1** (*posição*) in; (: *sobre*) on; **está na gaveta/no bolso** it's in the drawer/pocket; **está na mesa/no chão** it's on the table/floor
2 (*lugar*) in; (: *casa, escritório etc*) at; (: *andar, meio de transporte*) on; **no Brasil/em São Paulo** in Brazil/São Paulo; **em casa/no dentista** at home/the dentist; **no avião** on the plane; **no quinto andar** on the fifth floor
3 (*ação*) into; **ela entrou na sala de aula** she went into the classroom; **colocar algo na bolsa** to put sth into one's bag
4 (*tempo*) in; on; **em 1962/em três semanas** in 1962/in three weeks; **no inverno** in the winter; **em janeiro, no mês de janeiro** in January; **nessa ocasião/altura** on that occasion/at that time; **em breve** soon
5 (*diferença*): **reduzir/aumentar em 20%** to reduce/increase by 20%
6 (*modo*): **escrito em inglês** written in English
7 (*após vb que indica gastar etc*): on; **a metade do seu salário vai em comida** he spends half his salary on food
8 (*tema, ocupação*): **especialista no assunto** expert on the subject; **ele trabalha na construção civil** he works in the building industry

emaecer [imae'ser] VI to fade
Emaer [ema'er] (BR) ABR M = **Estado-Maior da Aeronáutica**
emagrecer [imagre'ser] VT to make thin ▶ VI to grow thin; (*mediante regime*) to slim
emagrecimento [imagresi'mẽtu] M (*mediante regime*) slimming
e-mail [i'mew] M email; **mandar um ~ para alguém** to email sb; **mandar algo por ~** to email sth
emanar [ema'nar] VI: **~ de** to come from, emanate from
emancipação [imãsipa'sãw] (*pl* **-ões**) F emancipation; (*atingir a maioridade*) coming of age
emancipar [imãsi'par] VT to emancipate; **emancipar-se** VR (*atingir a maioridade*) to come of age
emaranhado, -a [imara'ɲadu, a] ADJ tangled ▶ M tangle
emaranhar [imara'ɲar] VT to tangle; (*complicar*) to complicate; **emaranhar-se** VR to get entangled; (*fig*) to get mixed up

emassar [ema'sar] VT (*parede*) to plaster; (*janela*) to putty

Emater [ema'ter] (BR) ABR F (= *Empresa de Assistência Técnica e Extensão Rural*) *company giving aid to farmers*

embaçado, -a [ẽba'sadu, a] ADJ (*vidro*) steamed up

embaçar [ẽba'sar] VT to steam up

embaciado, -a [ẽba'sjadu, a] ADJ dull; (*vidro*) misted; (*janela*) steamed up; (*olhos*) misty

embaciar [ẽba'sjar] VT (*vidro*) to steam up; (*olhos*) to cloud ▶ VI to steam up; (*olhos*) to grow misty

embainhar [ẽbaj'ɲar] VT (*espada*) to put away, sheathe; (*calça etc*) to hem

embaixada [ẽbaj'ʃada] F embassy

embaixador, a [ẽbajʃa'dor(a)] M/F ambassador

embaixatriz [ẽbajʃa'triz] F ambassador; (*mulher de embaixador*) ambassador's wife

embaixo [ẽ'bajʃu] ADV below, underneath ▶ PREP: **~ de** under, underneath; (**lá**) **~** (*em andar inferior*) downstairs

embalado, -a [ẽba'ladu, a] ADJ (*acelerado*) fast; (*drogado*) high; **ir ~** to race (along)

embalagem [ẽba'laʒẽ] F packing; (*de produto: caixa etc*) packaging

embalar [ẽba'lar] VT to pack; (*balançar*) to rock

embalo [ẽ'balu] M (*balanço*) rocking; (*impulso*) rush; (*col: com drogas*) high; **aproveitar o ~** to take the opportunity

embalsamar [ẽbawsa'mar] VT (*perfumar*) to perfume; (*cadáver*) to embalm

embananado, -a [ẽbana'nadu, a] (*col*) ADJ (*confuso*) muddled; (*em dificuldades*) in trouble

embananamento [ẽbanana'mẽtu] (*col*) M muddle; (*bananosa*) jam

embananar [ẽbana'nar] (*col*) VT (*tornar confuso*) to muddle up; (*complicar*) to complicate; (*meter em dificuldades*) to get into trouble; **embananar-se** VR to get tied up in knots

embaraçar [ẽbara'sar] VT (*impedir*) to hinder; (*complicar*) to complicate; (*encabular*) to embarrass; (*confundir*) to confuse; (*obstruir*) to block; **embaraçar-se** VR to become embarrassed

embaraço [ẽba'rasu] M (*estorvo*) hindrance; (*cábula*) embarrassment

embaraçoso, -a [ẽbara'sozu, ɔza] ADJ embarrassing

embarafustar [ẽbarafus'tar] VI: **~ por** to burst *ou* barge into

embaralhar [ẽbara'ʎar] VT (*confundir*) to muddle up; (*cartas*) to shuffle; **embaralhar-se** VR to get mixed up

embarcação [ẽbarka'sãw] (*pl* **-ões**) F vessel

embarcadiço [ẽbarka'dʒisu] M seafarer

embarcadouro [ẽbarka'doru] M wharf

embarcar [ẽbar'kar] VT to embark, put on board; (*mercadorias*) to ship, stow ▶ VI to go on board, embark; **~ em algo** (*fig: col*) to fall for sth

embargar [ẽbar'gar] VT (*Jur*) to seize; (*pôr obstáculos a*) to hinder; (*reprimir: voz*) to keep down; (*impedir*) to forbid

embargo [ẽ'bargu] M (*de navio*) embargo; (*Jur*) seizure; (*impedimento*) impediment; **sem ~** nevertheless

embarque [ẽ'barki] M (*de pessoas*) boarding, embarkation; (*de mercadorias*) shipment

embasamento [ẽbaza'mẽtu] M (*Arq*) foundation; (*de coluna*) base; (*fig*) basis

embasbacado, -a [ẽbazba'kadu, a] ADJ gaping, open-mouthed

embasbacar [ẽbazba'kar] VT to leave open-mouthed; **embasbacar-se** VR to be taken aback, be dumbfounded

embate [ẽ'batʃi] M clash; (*choque*) shock

embatucar [ẽbatu'kar] VT to dumbfound ▶ VI to be speechless

embebedar [ẽbebe'dar] VT to make drunk ▶ VI: **o vinho embebeda** wine makes you drunk; **embebedar-se** VR to get drunk

embeber [ẽbe'ber] VT to soak up, absorb; **embeber-se** VR: **~-se em** to become absorbed in

embelezador, a [ẽbeleza'dor(a)] ADJ cosmetic

embelezar [ẽbele'zar] VT to make beautiful; (*casa*) to brighten up; **embelezar-se** VR to make o.s. beautiful

embevecer [ẽbeve'ser] VT to captivate; **embevecer-se** VR to be captivated

embicar [ẽbi'kar] VI (*Náut*) to enter port, dock; (*fig*): **~ para** to head for; **~ com alguém** to quarrel with sb

embirrar [ẽbi'har] VI to sulk; **~ em** to insist on; **~ com** to dislike

emblema [ẽ'blema] M emblem; (*na roupa*) badge

embocadura [ẽboka'dura] F (*de rio*) mouth; (*Mús*) mouthpiece; (*de freio*) bit

emboço [ẽ'bosu] M roughcast, render

embolar [ẽbo'lar] VT (*confundir*) to confuse ▶ VI: **~ com** to grapple with; **embolar-se** VR: **~-se (com)** to grapple (with)

êmbolo ['ẽbolu] M piston

embolorar [ẽbolo'rar] VI to go musty

embolsar [ẽbow'sar] VT to pocket; (*herança etc*) to come into

embonecar [ẽbone'kar] VT to doll up; **embonecar-se** VR to doll o.s. up, get dolled up

embora [ẽ'bɔra] CONJ though, although ▶ EXCL even so, what of it?; **ir(-se) ~** to go away

emborcar [ẽbor'kar] VT to turn upside down

emboscada [ẽbos'kada] F ambush

embotar [ẽbo'tar] VT (*lâmina*) to blunt; (*fig*) to deaden, dull

embrabecer [ẽbrabe'ser] VI = **embravecer**

Embraer [ẽbraer] ABR F (= *Empresa Brasileira de Aeronáutica SA*) *aerospace company*

embranquecer [ẽbrãke'ser] VT, VI to turn white

Embratur [ēbra'tur] ABR F (= *Empresa Brasileira de Turismo*) *state tourist board*

embravecer [ēbrave'ser] VR to get furious; **embravecer-se** VR to get furious

embreagem [ēb'rjaʒē] (*pl* **-ns**) F (*Auto*) clutch

embrear [ē'brjar] VT (*Auto*) to disengage ▶ VI to let in the clutch

embrenhar [ēbre'ɲar] VT to penetrate; **embrenhar-se** VR: **~-se (em/por)** to make one's way (into/through)

embriagante [ēbrja'gãtʃi] ADJ intoxicating

embriagar [ēbrja'gar] VT to make drunk, intoxicate; **embriagar-se** VR to get drunk

embriaguez [ēbrja'gez] F drunkenness; (*fig*) rapture; **~ no volante** drunk(en) driving

embrião [e'brjãw] (*pl* **-ões**) M embryo

embrionário, -a [ēbrjo'narju, a] ADJ (*tb fig*) embryonic

embromação [ēbroma'sãw] (*pl* **-ões**) F stalling; (*trapaça*) con

embromador, a [ēbroma'dor(a)] ADJ (*remanchador*) slow; (*trapaceiro*) dishonest, bent ▶ M/F (*remanchador*) staller; (*trapaçeiro*) con merchant

embromar [ēbro'mar] VT (*adiar*) to put off; (*enganar*) to con, to cheat ▶ VI (*prometer e não cumprir*) to make empty promises, be all talk (and no action); (*protelar*) to stall; (*falar em rodeios*) to beat about the bush

embrulhada [ēbru'ʎada] F muddle, mess

embrulhar [ēbru'ʎar] VT (*pacote*) to wrap; (*enrolar*) to roll up; (*confundir*) to muddle up; (*enganar*) to cheat; (*estômago*) to upset; **embrulhar-se** VR to get into a muddle; **ao contar a estória, ele embrulhou tudo** when he told the story he got everything mixed up

embrulho [ē'bruʎu] M (*pacote*) package, parcel; (*confusão*) mix-up

embrutecer [ēbrute'ser] VT, VI to brutalize; **embrutecer-se** VR to be brutalized

emburrar [ēbu'har] VI to sulk

embuste [ē'bustʃi] M (*engano*) deception; (*ardil*) trick

embusteiro, -a [ēbus'tejru, a] ADJ deceitful ▶ M/F cheat; (*mentiroso*) liar; (*impostor*) impostor

embutido, -a [ēbu'tʃidu, a] ADJ (*armário*) built-in, fitted

embutir [ēbu'tʃir] VT to build in; (*marfim etc*) to inlay

emenda [e'mēda] F correction; (*Jur*) amendment; (*de uma pessoa*) improvement; (*ligação*) join; (*sambladura*) joint; (*Costura*) seam

emendar [emē'dar] VT (*corrigir*) to correct; (*reparar*) to mend; (*injustiças*) to make amends for; (*Jur*) to amend; (*ajuntar*) to put together; **emendar-se** VR to mend one's ways

ementa [e'mēta] (*PT*) F menu

emergência [imer'ʒēsja] F (*nascimento*) emergence; (*crise*) emergency

emergente [imer'ʒētʒi] ADJ emerging

emergir [imer'ʒir] VI to emerge, appear; (*submarino*) to surface

EMFA (BR) ABR M = **Estado-maior das Forças Armadas**

emigração [emigra'sãw] (*pl* **-ões**) F emigration; (*de aves*) migration

emigrado, -a [emi'gradu, a] ADJ emigrant

emigrante [emi'grãtʃi] M/F emigrant

emigrar [emi'grar] VI to emigrate; (*aves*) to migrate

eminência [emi'nēsja] F eminence; (*altura*) height

eminente [emi'nētʃi] ADJ eminent, distinguished; (*Geo*) high

Emirados Árabes Unidos [emi'radus-] MPL: **os ~** the United Arab Emirates

emirjo *etc* [e'mirʒu] VB *ver* **emergir**

emissão [emi'sãw] (*pl* **-ões**) F emission; (*Rádio*) broadcast; (*de moeda, ações*) issue; **emissões de carbono** carbon emissions

emissário, -a [emi'sarju, a] M/F emissary ▶ M outlet

emissões [emi'sõjs] FPL *de* **emissão**

emissor, a [emi'sor(a)] ADJ (*de moeda-papel*) issuing ▶ M (*Rádio*) transmitter ▶ F (*estação*) broadcasting station; (*empresa*) broadcasting company

emitente [emi'tētʃi] ADJ (*Com*) issuing ▶ M/F issuer

emitir [emi'tʃir] VT (*som*) to give out; (*cheiro*) to give off; (*moeda, ações*) to issue; (*Rádio*) to broadcast; (*opinião*) to express ▶ VI (*emitir moeda*) to print money

emoção [emo'sãw] (*pl* **-ões**) F emotion; (*excitação*) excitement

emocional [imosjo'naw] (*pl* **-ais**) ADJ emotional

emocionante [imosjo'nãtʃi] ADJ (*comovente*) moving; (*excitante*) exciting

emocionar [imosjo'nar] VT (*comover*) to move; (*perturbar*) to upset; (*excitar*) to excite, thrill ▶ VI to be exciting; (*comover*) to be moving; **emocionar-se** VR to get emotional

emoções [emo'sõjs] FPL *de* **emoção**

emoldurar [emowdu'rar] VT to frame

emotividade [emotʃivi'dadʒi] F emotions *pl*

emotivo, -a [emo'tʃivu, a] ADJ emotional

empacar [ēpa'kar] VI (*cavalo*) to baulk; (*fig: negócios etc*) to grind to a halt; (*orador*) to dry up; **~ numa palavra** to get stuck on a word

empachado, -a [ēpa'ʃadu, a] ADJ full up

empacotar [ēpako'tar] VT to pack, wrap up ▶ VI (*col: morrer*) to pop one's clogs

empada [ē'pada] F pie

empadão [ēpa'dãw] (*pl* **-ões**) M pie

empalhar [ēpa'ʎar] VT (*animal*) to stuff; (*louça, fruta*) to pack with straw

empalidecer [ēpalide'ser] VT, VI to turn pale

empanar [ēpa'nar] VT (*fig*) to tarnish; (*Culin*) to batter

empanturrar [ēpãtu'har] VT: **~ alguém de algo** to stuff sb full of sth; **empanturrar-se** VR to gorge o.s., stuff o.s. (*col*)

empanzinado, -a [ẽpãzi'nadu, a] ADJ full
empapar [ẽpa'par] VT to soak; **empapar-se** VR
to get soaked
empapuçado, -a [ẽpapu'sadu, a] ADJ (olhos)
puffy; (blusa) full
emparedar [ẽpare'dar] VT to wall in; (pessoa)
to shut up
emparelhar [ẽpare'ʎar] VT to pair; (equiparar)
to match ▶ VI: ~ **com** to be equal to
empastado, -a [ẽpas'tadu, a] ADJ (cabelo)
plastered down
empastar [ẽpas'tar] VT: ~ **algo de algo** to
plaster sth with sth
empatar [ẽpa'tar] VT (embaraçar) to hinder;
(dinheiro) to tie up; (no jogo) to draw;
(corredores) to tie; (tempo) to take up ▶ VI (no
jogo): ~ **(com)** to draw (with)
empate [ẽ'patʃi] M (no jogo) draw; (numa corrida
etc) tie; (Xadrez) stalemate; (em negociações)
deadlock
empatia [ẽpa'tʃia] F empathy
empavonar-se [ẽpavo'narsi] VR to strut
empecilho [ẽpe'siʎu] M obstacle; (col) snag
empedernido, -a [ẽpeder'nidu, a] ADJ
hard-hearted
empedrar [ẽpe'drar] VT to pave
empenar [ẽpe'nar] VT, VI (curvar) to warp
empenhar [ẽpe'ɲar] VT (objeto) to pawn;
(palavra) to pledge; (empregar) to exert;
(compelir) to oblige; **empenhar-se** VR: ~-se
em fazer to strive to do, do one's utmost
to do
empenho [ẽ'peɲu] M (de um objeto) pawning;
(palavra) pledge; (insistência): ~ **(em)**
commitment (to); **ele pôs todo seu ~ neste
projeto** he committed himself
wholeheartedly to this project
emperiquitar-se [ẽperiki'tarsi] VR to get done
up to the nines
emperrar [ẽpe'har] VT (máquina) to jam; (porta,
junta) to make stiff; (fazer calar) to cut short
▶ VI to jam; (gaveta, porta) to stick; (junta) to
go stiff; (calar) to go quiet
empertigado, -a [ẽpertʃi'gadu, a] ADJ
upright
empertigar-se [ẽpertʃi'garsi] VR to stand up
straight
empestar [ẽpes'tar] VT (infetar) to infect;
(tornar desagradável) to pollute, stink out (col)
empetecar [ẽpete'kar] VT to doll up;
empetecar-se VR to doll o.s. up
empilhar [ẽpi'ʎar] VT to pile up
empinado, -a [ẽpi'nadu, a] ADJ (direito)
upright; (cavalo) rearing; (colina) steep
empinar [ẽpi'nar] VT to raise, uplift; (ressaltar)
to thrust out; (papagaio) to fly; (copo) to
empty
empipocar [ẽpipo'kar] VI to come out in spots
empírico, -a [ẽ'piriku, a] ADJ empirical
empistolado, -a [ẽpisto'ladu, a] ADJ
well-connected
emplacar [ẽpla'kar] VT (col: anos, sucessos) to
notch up; (carro) to put number (BRIT) ou

license (US) plates on; ~ **o ano 2050** to make
it to the year 2050
emplastrar [ẽplas'trar] VT to put in plaster
emplastro [ẽ'plaʃtru] M (Med) plaster
empobrecer [ẽpobre'ser] VT to impoverish
▶ VI to become poor
empobrecimento [ẽpobresi'mẽtu] M
impoverishment
empoeirar [ẽpoej'rar] VT to cover in dust
empola [ẽ'pola] F (na pele) blister; (de água)
bubble
empolado, -a [ẽpo'ladu, a] ADJ covered with
blisters; (estilo) pompous, bombastic
empolgação [ẽpowga'sãw] F excitement;
(entusiasmo) enthusiasm
empolgante [ẽpow'gãtʃi] ADJ exciting
empolgar [ẽpow'gar] VT to stimulate, fill
with enthusiasm; (prender a atenção de):
~ **alguém** to keep sb riveted
emporcalhar [ẽporka'ʎar] VT to dirty;
emporcalhar-se VR to get dirty
empório [ẽ'porju] M (mercado) market;
(armazém) department store
empossar [ẽpo'sar] VT to appoint
empreendedor, a [ẽprjẽde'dor(a)] ADJ
enterprising ▶ M/F entrepreneur
empreender [ẽprjẽ'der] VT to undertake
empreendimento [ẽprjẽdʒi'mẽtu] M
undertaking
empregada [ẽpre'gada] F (BR: doméstica) maid;
(PT: de restaurante) waitress; ver tb **empregado**
empregado, -a [ẽpre'gadu, a] M/F employee;
(em escritório) clerk ▶ M (PT: de restaurante)
waiter
empregador, a [ẽprega'dor(a)] M/F employer
empregar [ẽpre'gar] VT (pessoa) to employ;
(coisa) to use; **empregar-se** VR to get a job
empregatício, -a [ẽprega'tʃisju, a] ADJ ver
vínculo
emprego [ẽ'pregu] M (ocupação) job; (uso) use
empreguismo [ẽpre'gizmu] M patronage,
nepotism
empreitada [ẽprej'tada] F (Com) contract job;
(tarefa) enterprise, venture
empreiteira [ẽprej'tejra] F (firma) contractor
empreiteiro [ẽprej'tejru] M contractor
empresa [ẽ'preza] F undertaking; (Com)
enterprise, firm; ~ **pontocom** dotcom
empresariado [ẽpreza'rjadu] M business
community
empresarial [ẽpreza'rjaw] (pl **-ais**) ADJ
business atr
empresário, -a [ẽpre'zarju, a] M/F
businessman/woman; (de cantor, boxeador etc)
manager; ~ **teatral** impresario
emprestado, -a [ẽpres'tadu, a] ADJ on loan;
pedir ~ to borrow; **tomar algo ~** to borrow
sth
emprestar [ẽpres'tar] VT to lend
empréstimo [ẽ'prɛstʃimu] M loan
emproado, -a [ẽpro'adu, a] ADJ arrogant
empulhação [ẽpuʎa'sãw] (pl **-ões**) F (ato)
trickery; (embuste) con

empulhar [ēpu'ʎar] VT to trick, con
empunhar [ēpu'ɲar] VT to grasp, seize
empurrão [ēpu'hãw] (pl **-ões**) M push, shove;
  aos empurrões jostling
empurrar [ēpu'har] VT to push
empurrões [ēpu'hõjs] MPL de **empurrão**
emudecer [emude'ser] VT to silence ▶ VI to
  fall silent, go quiet
emular [emu'lar] VT to emulate
enaltecer [enawte'ser] VT (fig) to elevate
enamorado, -a [enamo'radu, a] ADJ
  (encantado) enchanted; (apaixonado) in love
ENAP (BR) ABR F (= Escola Nacional de
  Administração Pública) civil service training school
encabeçar [ēkabe'sar] VT to head
encabulação [ēkabula'sãw] F (vergonha)
  embarrassment; (acanhamento) shyness
encabulado, -a [ēkabu'ladu, a] ADJ shy
encabular [ēkabu'lar] VT to embarrass ▶ VI
  (fato, situação) to be embarrassing; (pessoa)
  to get embarrassed; **não se encabule!** don't
  be shy!
encaçapar [ēkasa'par] VT (bola) to sink; (col:
  surrar) to bash
encadeamento [ēkadʒja'mētu] M (série)
  chain; (conexão) link
encadear [ēka'dʒjar] VT to chain together,
  link together
encadernação [ēkaderna'sãw] (pl **-ões**) F
  (de livro) binding
encadernado, -a [ēkader'nadu, a] ADJ bound;
  (de capa dura) hardback
encadernador, a [ēkaderna'dor(a)] M/F
  bookbinder
encadernar [ēkader'nar] VT to bind
encafuar [ēka'fwar] VT to hide; **encafuar-se**
  VR to hide
encaixar [ēkaj'ʃar] VT (colocar) to fit in; (inserir)
  to insert ▶ VI to fit
encaixe [ē'kajʃi] M (ato) fitting; (ranhura)
  groove; (buraco) socket
encaixotar [ēkajʃo'tar] VT to pack into boxes
encalacrar [ēkala'krar] VT: **~ alguém** to get
  sb into trouble; **encalacrar-se** VR to get into
  debt
encalço [ē'kawsu] M pursuit; **ir no ~ de** to
  pursue
encalhado, -a [ēka'ʎadu, a] ADJ stranded;
  (mercadoria) unsaleable; (col: solteiro)
  unmarried
encalhar [ēka'ʎar] VI (embarcação) to run
  aground; (fig: processo) to grind to a halt;
  (: mercadoria) to be returned, not to sell; (col:
  ficar solteiro) to be left on the shelf
encalorado, -a [ēkalo'radu, a] ADJ hot
encaminhar [ēkami'ɲar] VT (dirigir) to direct;
  (no bom caminho) to put on the right path;
  (processo) to set in motion; **encaminhar-se** VR:
  ~-se para/a to set out for/to; **eu encaminhei-
  os para a seção devida** I referred them to
  the appropriate department; **~ uma petição
  a alguém** to refer an application to sb; **foi
  minha mãe quem me encaminhou para**

as letras it was my mother who steered me
  towards literature; **as coisas se
  encaminham bem no momento** things
  are going well at the moment
encampar [ēkã'par] VT (empresa) to
  expropriate; (opinião, medida) to adopt
encanador [ēkana'dor] (BR) M plumber
encanamento [ēkana'mētu] (BR) M
  plumbing
encanar [ēka'nar] VT to channel; (BR col:
  prender) to throw in jail
encanecido, -a [ēkane'sidu, a] ADJ grey (BRIT),
  gray (US); (cabelo) white
encantado, -a [ēkã'tadu, a] ADJ (contente)
  delighted; (castelo etc) enchanted; (fascinado)
  ~ (por alguém/algo) smitten (with sb/sth)
encantador, a [ēkãta'dor(a)] ADJ delightful,
  charming ▶ M/F enchanter/enchantress
encantamento [ēkãta'mētu] M (magia) spell;
  (fascinação) charm
encantar [ēkã'tar] VT (enfeitiçar) to bewitch;
  (cativar) to charm; (deliciar) to delight
encanto [ē'kãtu] M (delícia) delight;
  (fascinação) charm
encapar [ēka'par] VT (livro, sofá) to cover;
  (envolver) to wrap
encapelar [ēkape'lar] VT (mar) to swell ▶ VI
  (mar) to turn rough
encapetado, -a [ēkape'tadu, a] ADJ (criança)
  mischievous
encapotar [ēkapo'tar] VT to wrap up;
  encapotar-se VR to wrap o.s. up
encaracolar [ēkarako'lar] VT, VI to curl;
  encaracolar-se VR to curl up
encarangar [ēkarã'gar] VT to cripple ▶ VI
  (pessoa) to be crippled; (reumatismo) to be
  crippling
encarapinhado, -a [ēkarapi'ɲadu, a] ADJ
  (cabelo) frizzy
encarapitar [ēkarapi'tar] VT to perch;
  encarapitar-se VR: **~-se em algo** to climb
  on top of sth; (num cargo etc) to get o.s. fixed
  up in sth
encarar [ēka'rar] VT to face; (olhar) to look at;
  (considerar) to consider
encarcerar [ēkarse'rar] VT to imprison
encardido, -a [ēkar'dʒidu, a] ADJ (roupa, casa)
  grimy; (pele) sallow
encardir [ēkar'dʒir] VT to make grimy ▶ VI to
  get grimy
encarecer [ēkare'ser] VT (subir o preço) to raise
  the price of; (louvar) to praise; (exagerar) to
  exaggerate ▶ VI to go up in price, get dearer
encarecidamente [ēkaresida'mētʃi] ADV
  insistently
encarecimento [ēkaresi'mētu] M (preço)
  increase
encargo [ē'kargu] M (responsabilidade)
  responsibility; (ocupação) job, assignment;
  (oneroso) burden; **dar a alguém o ~ de fazer
  algo** to give sb the job of doing sth
encarnação [ēkarna'sãw] (pl **-ões**) F
  incarnation

encarnado, -a [ēkar'nadu, a] ADJ red, scarlet

encarnar [ēkar'nar] VT to embody, personify; (*Teatro*) to play ▶ VI to be embodied; **encarnar-se** VR to be embodied; **~ em alguém** (*col*) to pick on sb

encarneirado, -a [ēkarnej'radu, a] ADJ (*mar*) choppy

encaroçar [ēkaro'sar] VI (*molho*) to go lumpy; (*pele*) to come up in bumps

encarquilhado, -a [ēkarki'ʎadu, a] ADJ (*fruta*) wizened; (*rosto*) wrinkled

encarregado, -a [ēkahe'gadu, a] ADJ: **~ de** in charge of sth ▶ M/F person in charge ▶ M (*de operários*) foreman; **~ de negócios** chargé d'affaires

encarregar [ēkahe'gar] VT: **~ alguém de algo** to put sb in charge of sth; **encarregar-se** VR: **~-se de fazer** to undertake to do

encarreirar [ēkahej'rar] VT to guide; (*negócios*) to run; (*moralmente*): **~ alguém** to put sb on the right track

encarrilhar [ēkahi'ʎar] VT to put back on the rails; (*fig*) to put on the right track

encartar [ēkar'tar] VT to insert

encarte [ē'kartʃi] M insert

encasacar-se [ēkaza'karsi] VR to put on one's coat

encasquetar [ēkaske'tar] VT: **~ uma ideia** to get an idea into one's head

encatarrado, -a [ēkata'hadu, a] ADJ congested

encenação [ēsena'sãw] (*pl* **-ões**) F (*de peça*) staging, putting on; (*produção*) production; (*fingimento*) play-acting; (*atitude fingida*) put-on, put-up job (*col*); **fazer ~** (*col*) to put it on

encenador, a [ēsena'dor(a)] M/F (*Teatro*) director

encenar [ēse'nar] VT (*Teatro: pôr em cena*) to stage, put on; (: *produzir*) to produce; (*fingir*) to put on

enceradeira [ēsera'dejra] F floor-polisher

encerar [ēse'rar] VT to wax

encerramento [ēseha'mētu] M (*término*) close, end

encerrar [ēse'har] VT (*confinar*) to shut in, lock up; (*conter*) to contain; (*concluir*) to close

encestar [ēses'tar] VT (*Basquete*) to put in the basket ▶ VI to score a basket

encetar [ēse'tar] VT to start, begin

encharcar [ēʃar'kar] VT (*alagar*) to flood; (*ensopar*) to soak, drench; **encharcar-se** VR to get soaked *ou* drenched; **~-se de algo** (*beber muito*) to drink gallons of sth

encheção [ēʃe'sãw] (*col*) F annoyance

enchente [ē'ʃētʃi] F flood

encher [ē'ʃer] VT to fill (up); (*balão*) to blow up; (*tempo*) to fill, take up ▶ VI (*col*) to be annoying; **encher-se** VR to fill up; **~-se (de)** (*col*) to get fed up (with); **~ de** *ou* **com** to fill up with; **~ o saco de alguém** (*col*) to bug sb, piss sb off (!); **ela enche o filho de presentes** she showers her son with presents

enchimento [ēʃi'mētu] M filling

enchova [ē'ʃova] F anchovy

enciclopédia [ēsiklo'pedʒja] F encyclopedia, encyclopaedia (BRIT)

enciumar [ēsju'mar] VT to make jealous; **enciumar-se** VR to get jealous

enclausurar [ēklawzu'rar] VT to shut away; **enclausurar-se** VR to shut o.s. away

encoberto, -a [ēko'bɛrtu, a] PP *de* **encobrir** ▶ ADJ (*escondido*) concealed; (*tempo*) overcast

encobrir [ēko'brir] VT to conceal, hide

encolerizar [ēkoleri'zar] VT to irritate, annoy; **encolerizar-se** VR to get angry

encolher [ēko'ʎer] VT (*pernas*) to draw up; (*os ombros*) to shrug; (*roupa*) to shrink ▶ VI to shrink; **encolher-se** VR (*de frio*) to huddle; (*para dar lugar*) to hunch up

encomenda [ēko'mēda] F order; **feito de ~** made to order, custom-made; **vir de ~** (*fig*) to come just at the right time

encomendar [ēkomē'dar] VT: **~ algo a alguém** to order sth from sb

encompridar [ēkõpri'dar] VT to lengthen

encontrão [ēkõ'trãw] (*pl* **-ões**) M (*esbarrão*) collision, impact; (*empurrão*) shove; **dar um ~ em** to bump into; **ir aos encontrões pela multidão** to jostle one's way through the crowd

encontrar [ēkõ'trar] VT (*achar*) to find; (*inesperadamente*) to come across, meet; (*dar com*) to bump into ▶ VI: **~ com** to bump into; **encontrar-se** VR (*achar-se*) to be; (*ter encontro*): **~-se (com alguém)** to meet (sb)

encontro [ē'kõtru] M (*de pessoas*) meeting; (*Mil*) encounter; **~ marcado** appointment; **ir/vir ao ~ de** to go/come and meet; (*aspirações*) to meet, fulfil(l); **ir de ~ a** to go against, run contrary to; **meu carro foi de ~ ao muro** my car ran into the wall

encontrões [ēkõ'trõjs] MPL *de* **encontrão**

encorajamento [ēkoraʒa'mētu] M encouragement

encorajar [ēkora'ʒar] VT to encourage

encorpado, -a [ēkor'padu, a] ADJ stout; (*vinho*) full-bodied; (*tecido*) closely-woven; (*papel*) thick

encorpar [ēkor'par] VT (*ampliar*) to expand ▶ VI (*criança*) to fill out

encosta [ē'kɔsta] F slope

encostar [ēkos'tar] VT (*cabeça*) to put down; (*carro*) to park; (*pôr de lado*) to put to one side; (*pôr junto*) to put side by side; (*porta*) to leave ajar ▶ VI to pull in; **encostar-se** VR: **~-se em** to lean against; (*deitar-se*) to lie down on; **~ em** to lean against; **~ a mão em** (*bater*) to hit; **ele está sempre se encostando nos outros** he's always depending on others

encosto [ē'kɔstu] M (*arrimo*) support; (*de cadeira*) back

encouraçado, -a [ēkora'sadu, a] ADJ armoured (BRIT), armored (US) ▶ M (*Náut*) battleship

encravado, -a [ēkra'vadu, a] ADJ (*unha*) ingrowing

encravar [ēkra'var] VT: ~ **algo em algo** to stick sth into sth; (*diamante num anel*) to mount sth in sth

encrenca [ē'krēka] (*col*) F (*problema*) fix, jam; (*briga*) fight; **meter-se numa** ~ to get into trouble

encrencar [ēkrē'kar] (*col*) VT (*situação*) to complicate; (*pessoa*) to get into trouble ▶ VI (*complicar-se*) to get complicated; (*carro*) to break down; **encrencar-se** VR to get complicated; to get into trouble; ~ **(com alguém)** to fall out (with sb)

encrenqueiro, -a [ēkrē'kejru, a] (*col*) M/F troublemaker ▶ ADJ troublemaking

encrespado, -a [ēkres'padu, a] ADJ (*cabelo*) curly; (*mar*) choppy; (*água*) rippling

encrespar [ēkres'par] VT (*o cabelo*) to curl; **encrespar-se** VR (*o cabelo*) to curl; (*água*) to ripple; (*o mar*) to get choppy

encriptar [ēkrip'tar] VT (*Comput, Tel*) to encrypt

encruar [ēkru'ar] VI (*negócio*) to grind to a halt

encruzilhada [ēkruzi'ʎada] F crossroads *sg*

encucação [ēkuka'sãw] (*pl* **-ões**) F fixation

encucado, -a [ēku'kadu, a] (*col*) ADJ: ~ **(com)** hung up (about)

encucar [ēku'kar] (*col*) VT: ~ **alguém** to give sb a hang-up ▶ VI: ~ **com** *ou* **em algo/alguém** to be hung up about sth/sb

encurralar [ēkura'lar] VT (*gado, pessoas*) to herd; (*cercar*) to corner

encurtar [ēkur'tar] VT to shorten

endêmico, -a [ē'demiku, a] ADJ endemic

endemoninhado, -a [ēdemoni'ɲadu, a] ADJ (*pessoa*) possessed; (*espírito*) demoniac; (*fig: criança*) naughty

endentar [ēdē'tar] VT to engage

endereçar [ēdere'sar] VT (*carta*) to address; (*encaminhar*) to direct

endereço [ēde'resu] M address; ~ **de e-mail** email address; ~ **web** web address

endeusar [ēdew'zar] VT (*amado*) to deify; (*amado*) to worship

endiabrado, -a [ēdʒja'bradu, a] ADJ devilish; (*travesso*) mischievous

endinheirado, -a [ēdʒiɲej'radu, a] ADJ rich, wealthy, well-off

endireitar [ēdʒirej'tar] VT (*objeto*) to straighten; (*retificar*) to put right; (*fig*) to straighten out; **endireitar-se** VR to straighten up

endividado, -a [ēdʒivi'dadu, a] ADJ in debt

endividamento [ēdʒivida'mētu] M debt

endividar [ēdʒivi'dar] VT to put into debt; **endividar-se** VR to run into debt

endócrino, -a [ē'dɔkrinu, a] ADJ: **glândula endócrina** endocrine gland

endoidecer [ēdojde'ser] VT to madden ▶ VI to go mad

endoscopia [ēdosko'pia] F (*Med*) endoscopy

endossante [ēdo'sãtʃi] M/F endorser

endossar [ēdo'sar] VT to endorse

endossável [ēdo'savew] (*pl* **-eis**) ADJ endorsable

endosso [ē'dosu] M endorsement

endurecer [ēdure'ser] VT, VI to harden

endurecido, -a [ēdure'sidu, a] ADJ hardened

endurecimento [ēduresi'mētu] M hardening

ENE ABR (= *és-nordeste*) ENE

enegrecer [enegre'ser] VT to darken; (*fig: nome*) to blacken ▶ VI to darken

enema [e'nema] M enema

energético, -a [ener'ʒetʃiku, a] ADJ energy *atr* ▶ M energy source; (*tb*: **bebida energética**) energy drink

energia [enɛr'ʒia] F (*vigor*) energy, drive; (*Tec*) power, energy; ~ **solar** solar power

enérgico, -a [e'nɛrʒiku, a] ADJ energetic, vigorous; **ele é ~ com os filhos** he is hard on his children

enervação [enerva'sãw] F annoyance, irritation

enervante [ener'vãtʃi] ADJ annoying

enervar [ener'var] VT to annoy, irritate ▶ VI to be irritating; **enervar-se** VR to get annoyed

enevoado, -a [ene'vwadu, a] ADJ misty, hazy

enfadar [ēfa'dar] VT (*entediar*) to bore; (*incomodar*) to annoy; **enfadar-se** VR: **~-se de** to get tired of; **~-se com** (*aborrecer-se*) to get fed up with

enfado [ē'fadu] M annoyance

enfadonho, -a [ēfa'doɲu, a] ADJ (*cansativo*) tiresome; (*aborrecido*) boring

enfaixar [ēfaj'ʃar] VT (*perna*) to bandage, bind; (*bebê*) to wrap up

enfarte [ē'fartʃi] M (*Med*) coronary

ênfase ['ēfazi] F emphasis, stress

enfastiado, -a [ēfas'tʃjadu, a] ADJ bored

enfastiar [ēfas'tʃjar] VT (*cansar*) to weary; (*aborrecer*) to bore; **enfastiar-se** VR: **~-se de** *ou* **com** to get tired of; to get bored with

enfático, -a [ē'fatʃiku, a] ADJ emphatic

enfatizar [ēfatʃi'zar] VT to emphasize

enfear [ēfe'ar] VT (*pessoa etc*) to make ugly; (*deturpar*) to distort ▶ VI to become ugly

enfeitar [ēfej'tar] VT to decorate; **enfeitar-se** VR to dress up

enfeite [ē'fejtʃi] M decoration

enfeitiçante [ēfejtʃi'sãtʃi] ADJ enchanting, charming

enfeitiçar [ēfejtʃi'sar] VT to bewitch, cast a spell on

enfermagem [ēfer'maʒē] F nursing

enfermaria [ēferma'ria] F ward

enfermeiro, -a [ēfer'mejru, a] M/F nurse

enfermidade [ēfermi'dadʒi] F illness

enfermo, -a [ē'fermu, a] ADJ ill, sick ▶ M/F sick person, patient

enferrujar [ēfehu'ʒar] VT to rust, corrode ▶ VI to go rusty

enfezado, -a [ēfe'zadu, a] ADJ (*irritadiço*) irritable; (*irritado*) angry, mad

enfezar [ēfe'zar] VT (*irritar*) to make angry; **enfezar-se** VR to become angry

enfiada [ē'fjada] F (de pérolas) string; (fila) row
enfiar [ē'fjar] VT (meter) to put; (agulha) to thread; (pérolas) to string together; (vestir) to slip on; **enfiar-se** VR: **~-se em** to slip into
enfileirar [ēfilej'rar] VT to line up
enfim [ē'fĩ] ADV finally, at last; (em suma) in short; **até que ~!** at last!
enfocar [ēfo'kar] VT (assunto) to tackle
enfoque [ē'fɔki] M approach
enforcamento [ēforka'mētu] M hanging
enforcar [ēfor'kar] VT to hang; (trabalho, aulas) to skip; **enforcar-se** VR to hang o.s.; **~ a sexta-feira** to take the Friday off
enfraquecer [ēfrake'ser] VT to weaken ▶ VI to grow weak
enfraquecimento [ēfrakesi'mētu] M weakening
enfrentar [ēfrē'tar] VT (encarar) to face; (confrontar) to confront; (problemas) to face up to
enfronhado, -a [ēfro'ɲadu, a] ADJ: **estar bem ~ num assunto** to be well versed in a subject
enfronhar [ēfro'ɲar] VI: **~ alguém em algo** to instruct sb in sth; **enfronhar-se** VR: **~-se em algo** to learn about sth, become well versed in sth
enfumaçado, -a [ēfuma'sadu, a] ADJ full of smoke, smoky
enfumaçar [ēfuma'sar] VT to fill with smoke
enfurecer [ēfure'ser] VT to infuriate; **enfurecer-se** VR to get furious
enfurnar [ēfur'nar] VT to hide away; (meter) to stow away; **enfurnar-se** VR to hide (o.s.) away
engᵃ ABR (= engenheira) Eng.
engaiolar [ēgajo'lar] (col) VT to jail
engajamento [ēgaʒa'mētu] M (empenho, Pol) commitment; (de trabalhadores) hiring; (Mil) enlistment
engajar [ēga'ʒar] VT (trabalhadores) to take on, hire; **engajar-se** VR to take up employment; (Mil) to enlist; **~-se em algo** to get involved in sth; (Pol) to be committed to sth
engalfinhar-se [ēgawfĩ'ɲarsi] VR (atacar-se) to fight; (discutir) to argue
engambelar [ēgãbe'lar] VT to con, trick
enganado, -a [ēga'nadu, a] ADJ (errado) mistaken; (traído) deceived
enganador, a [ēgana'dor(a)] ADJ (mentiroso) deceitful; (artificioso) fake; (conselho) misleading; (aspecto) deceptive
enganar [ēga'nar] VT to deceive; (desonrar) to seduce; (cônjuge) to be unfaithful to; (fome) to stave off; **enganar-se** VR (cair em erro) to be wrong, be mistaken; (iludir-se) to deceive o.s.; **as aparências enganam** appearances are deceptive
enganchar [ēgã'ʃar] VT: **~ algo (em algo)** to hook sth up (to sth)
engano [ē'gãnu] M (error) mistake; (ilusão) deception; (logro) trick; **é ~** (Tel) I've (ou you've) got the wrong number

engarrafado, -a [ēgaha'fadu, a] ADJ bottled; (trânsito) blocked
engarrafamento [ēgahafa'mētu] M bottling; (de trânsito) traffic jam
engarrafar [ēgaha'far] VT to bottle; (trânsito) to block
engasgar [ēgaz'gar] VT to choke ▶ VI to choke; (máquina) to splutter; **engasgar-se** VR to choke
engasgo [ē'gazgu] M choking
engastar [ēgas'tar] VT (joias) to set, mount
engaste [ē'gasti] M meeting, mounting
engatar [ēga'tar] VT (vagões) to couple, hitch up; (Auto) to put into gear
engatilhar [ēgatʃi'ʎar] VT (revólver) to cock; (fig: resposta etc) to prepare
engatinhar [ēgatʃi'ɲar] VI to crawl; (fig) to be feeling one's way
engavetamento [ēgaveta'mētu] M (de carros) pile-up
engavetar [ēgave'tar] VT (fig: projeto) to shelve; **engavetar-se** VR to crash into one another; **~-se em algo** to crash into (the back of) sth
engelhar [ēʒe'ʎar] VT, VI (pele) to wrinkle
engendrar [ēʒē'drar] VT to dream up
engenharia [ēʒeɲa'ria] F engineering
engenheiro, -a [ēʒe'ɲejru, a] M/F engineer
engenho [ē'ʒeɲu] M (talento) talent; (destreza) skill; (máquina) machine; (moenda) mill; (fazenda) sugar plantation
engenhoso, -a [ēʒe'ɲozu, ɔza] ADJ clever, ingenious
engessar [ēʒe'sar] VT (perna) to put in plaster; (parede) to plaster
englobar [ēglo'bar] VT to include
eng° ABR (= engenheiro) Eng.
engodar [ēgo'dar] VT to lure, entice
engodo [ē'godu] M (para peixe) bait; (para pessoas) lure, enticement
engolir [ēgo'lir] VT to swallow; **até hoje não engoli o que ele me fez** I still haven't forgiven him for what he did to me
engomar [ēgo'mar] VT (roupa) to starch; (passar) to iron
engonço [ē'gõsu] M hinge
engordar [ēgor'dar] VT to fatten ▶ VI to put on weight; **o açúcar engorda** sugar is fattening
engordurado, -a [ēgordu'radu, a] ADJ (comida) fatty; (mãos) greasy
engordurar [ēgordu'rar] VT to cover with grease
engraçado, -a [ēgra'sadu, a] ADJ funny, amusing
engraçar-se [ēgra'sarsi] (col) VR: **~ com alguém** to take advantage of sb
engradado [ēgra'dadu] M crate
engrandecer [ēgrãde'ser] VT to elevate ▶ VI to grow; **engrandecer-se** VR to become great
engravatar-se [ēgrava'tarsi] VR to put on a tie; (vestir-se bem) to dress smartly

engravidar [ẽgravi'dar] VT: ~ **alguém** to get sb pregnant; (*Med*) to impregnate sb ▸ VI to get pregnant

engraxador [ẽgraʃa'dor] (PT) M shoe shiner

engraxar [ẽgra'ʃar] VT to polish

engraxate [ẽgra'ʃatʃi] M shoe shiner

engrenagem [ẽgre'naʒẽ] (*pl* **-ns**) F (*Auto*) gear

engrenar [ẽgre'nar] VT (*Auto*) to put into gear; (*fig: conversa*) to strike up ▸ VI: ~ **com alguém** to get on with sb

engrolado, -a [ẽgro'ladu, a] ADJ (*voz*) slurred

engrossar [ẽgro'sar] VT (*sopa*) to thicken; (*aumentar*) to swell; (*voz*) to raise ▸ VI to thicken; to swell; to rise; (*col: pessoa, conversa*) to turn nasty

engrupir [ẽgru'pir] (*col*) VT to con, trick

enguia [ẽ'gia] F eel

enguiçar [ẽgi'sar] VI (*máquina*) to break down ▸ VT to cause to break down

enguiço [ẽ'gisu] M (*empecilho*) snag; (*desarranjo*) breakdown

engulho [ẽ'guʎu] M nausea

enigma [e'nigima] M enigma; (*mistério*) mystery

enigmático, -a [enigi'matʃiku, a] ADJ enigmatic

enjaular [ẽʒaw'lar] VT (*fera*) to cage, cage up; (*prender: pessoa*) to imprison

enjeitado, -a [ẽʒej'tadu, a] M/F foundling, waif

enjeitar [ẽʒej'tar] VT (*rejeitar*) to reject; (*abandonar*) to abandon; (*condenar*) to condemn

enjoado, -a [ẽ'ʒwadu, a] ADJ sick; (*enfastiado*) bored; (*enfadonho*) boring; (*mal-humorado*) in a bad mood

enjoar [ẽ'ʒwar] VT to make sick; (*enfastiar*) to bore ▸ VI (*pessoa*) to be sick; (*remédio, comida*) to cause nausea; **enjoar-se** VR: ~**-se de** to get sick of; **eu enjoo com o cheiro de fritura** the smell of frying makes me sick; **eu enjoei de ir ao cinema** I'm sick of going to the cinema

enjoativo, -a [ẽʒwa'tʃivu, a] ADJ (*comida*) revolting; (*tedioso*) boring

enjoo [ẽ'ʒou] M sickness; (*em carro*) travel sickness; (*em navio*) seasickness; (*aborrecimento*) boredom; **que ~!** what a bore!

enlaçar [ẽla'sar] VT (*atar*) to tie, bind; (*abraçar*) to hug; (*unir*) to link, join; (*bois*) to hitch; (*cingir*) to wind around; **enlaçar-se** VR to be linked

enlace [ẽ'lasi] M link, connection; (*casamento*) marriage, union

enlamear [ẽla'mjar] VT to cover in mud; (*reputação*) to besmirch

enlatado, -a [ẽla'tadu, a] ADJ tinned (BRIT), canned ▸ M (*pej: filme*) foreign import; **enlatados** MPL (*comida*) tinned (BRIT) ou canned foods

enlatar [ẽla'tar] VT (*comida*) to can

enlevar [ẽle'var] VT (*extasiar*) to enrapture; (*absorver*) to absorb

enlevo [ẽ'levu] M (*êxtase*) rapture; (*deleite*) delight

enlouquecer [ẽloke'ser] VT to drive mad ▸ VI to go mad

enluarado, -a [ẽlua'rado, a] ADJ moonlit

enlutado, -a [ẽlu'tadu, a] ADJ in mourning

enlutar-se [ẽlu'tarsi] VR to go into mourning

enobrecer [enobre'ser] VT to ennoble ▸ VI to be ennobling

enojar [eno'jar] VT to disgust, sicken

enorme [e'nɔrmi] ADJ enormous, huge

enormidade [enormi'dadʒi] F enormity; **uma ~ (de)** (*col*) a hell of a lot (of)

enovelar [enove'lar] VT to wind into a ball; (*enrolar*) to roll up

enquadrar [ẽkwa'drar] VT to fit; (*gravura*) to frame ▸ VI: ~ **com** (*condizer*) to fit ou tie in with

enquanto [ẽ'kwãtu] CONJ while; (*considerado como*) as; ~ **isso** meanwhile; **por ~** for the time being; ~ **ele não vem** until he comes; ~ **que** whereas

enquete [ẽ'kɛtʃi] F survey

enrabichar-se [ẽhabi'ʃarsi] VR: ~ **por alguém** to fall for sb

enraivecer [ẽhajve'ser] VT to enrage

enraizar [ẽhaj'zar] VI to take root; **enraizar-se** VR (*pessoa*) to settle down

enrascada [ẽhas'kada] F tight spot, predicament; **meter-se numa ~** to get into a spot of bother

enrascar [ẽhas'kar] VT to embroil; **enrascar-se** VR to get embroiled

enredar [ẽhe'dar] VT (*emaranhar*) to entangle; (*complicar*) to complicate; **enredar-se** VR to get entangled

enredo [ẽ'hedu] M (*de uma obra*) plot; (*intriga*) intrigue; **ele faz tanto ~** (*fig*) he makes such a fuss

enregelado, -a [ẽheʒe'ladu, a] ADJ (*pessoa, mão*) frozen; (*muito frio*) freezing

enrijecer [ẽhiʒe'ser] VT to stiffen; **enrijecer-se** VR to stiffen; (*fortalecer*) to get stronger

enriquecer [ẽhike'ser] VT to make rich; (*fig*) to enrich ▸ VI to get rich; **enriquecer-se** VR to get rich

enriquecimento [ẽhikesi'mẽtu] M enrichment

enrolado, -a [ẽho'ladu, a] (*col*) ADJ complicated

enrolar [ẽho'lar] VT to roll up; (*agasalhar*) to wrap up; (*col: enganar*) to con ▸ VI (*col*) to waffle; **enrolar-se** VR to roll up; to wrap up; (*col: confundir-se*) to get mixed ou muddled up

enroscar [ẽhos'kar] VT (*torcer*) to twist, wind (round); **enroscar-se** VR to coil up

enrouquecer [ẽhoke'ser] VT to make hoarse ▸ VI to go hoarse

enrubescer [ẽhube'ser] VT to redden, colour (BRIT), color (US) ▸ VI (*por vergonha*) to blush, go red

enrugar [ẽhu'gar] VT (*pele*) to wrinkle; (*testa*) to furrow; (*tecido*) to crease ▶ VI (*pele, mãos*) to go wrinkly; (*pessoa*) to get wrinkles

enrustido, -a [ẽhus'tʃido, a] (*col*) ADJ withdrawn

ensaboar [ẽsa'bwar] VT to wash with soap; **ensaboar-se** VR to soap o.s.

ensaiar [ẽsa'jar] VT (*provar*) to test, try out; (*treinar*) to practise (*BRIT*), practice (*US*); (*Teatro*) to rehearse

ensaio [ẽ'saju] M (*prova*) test; (*tentativa*) attempt; (*treino*) practice; (*Teatro*) rehearsal; (*literário*) essay

ensaísta [ẽsaj'ista] M/F essayist

ensanguentado, -a [ẽsãgwẽ'tadu, a] ADJ bloody

ensanguentar [ẽsãgwẽ'tar] VT to stain with blood

enseada [ẽ'sjada] F inlet, cove; (*baía*) bay

ensebado, -a [ẽse'badu, a] ADJ greasy; (*sujo*) soiled

ensejar [ẽse'ʒar] VT: ~ **algo (a alguém)** to provide (sb with) an opportunity for sth

ensejo [ẽ'seʒu] M chance, opportunity

ensimesmado, -a [ẽsimez'madu, a] ADJ lost in thought

ensimesmar-se [ẽsimez'marsi] VR to be lost in thought; ~ **em** to be lost in

ensinamento [ẽsina'mẽtu] M teaching; (*exemplo*) lesson

ensinar [ẽsi'nar] VT, VI to teach; ~ **alguém a patinar** to teach sb to skate; ~ **algo a alguém** to teach sb sth; ~ **o caminho a alguém** to show sb the way; **você quer ~ o padre a rezar missa?** are you trying to teach your grandmother to suck eggs?

ensino [ẽ'sinu] M teaching, tuition; (*educação*) education; ~ **fundamental** primary education; ~ **médio** secondary education

ensolarado, -a [ẽsola'radu, a] ADJ sunny

ensombrecido, -a [ẽsõbre'sidu, a] ADJ darkened

ensopado, -a [ẽso'padu, a] ADJ soaked ▶ M stew

ensopar [ẽso'par] VT to soak, drench

ensurdecedor, a [ẽsurdese'dor(a)] ADJ deafening

ensurdecer [ẽsurde'ser] VT to deafen ▶ VI to go deaf

entabular [ẽtabu'lar] VT (*negociação*) to start, open; (*empreender*) to undertake; (*assunto*) to broach; (*conversa*) to strike up

entalado, -a [ẽta'ladu, a] ADJ (*apertado*) wedged, jammed; (*enrascado*) embroiled, involved; (*engasgado*) choking

entalar [ẽta'lar] VT (*encravar*) to wedge, jam; (*fig*) to put in a fix; (*encher*): **ela me entalou de comida** she stuffed me full of food

entalhador, a [ẽtaʎa'dor(a)] M/F woodcarver

entalhar [ẽta'ʎar] VT to carve

entalhe [ẽ'taʎi] M groove, notch

entalho [ẽ'taʎu] M woodcarving

entanto [ẽ'tãtu] ADV: **no** ~ yet, however

então [ẽ'tãw] ADV then; **até** ~ up to that time; **desde** ~ ever since; **e ~?** well then?; **para** ~ so that; **pois** ~ in that case; ~, **você vai ou não?** so, are you going or not?

entardecer [ẽtarde'ser] VI to get late ▶ M sunset

ente ['ẽtʃi] M being; ~**s queridos** loved ones

enteado, -a [ẽ'tʃjadu, a] M/F stepson/stepdaughter

entediante [ẽte'dʒjãtʃi] ADJ boring, tedious

entediar [ẽte'dʒjar] VT to bore; **entediar-se** VR to get bored

entendedor, a [ẽtẽde'dor(a)] ADJ knowledgeable ▶ M: **a bom ~ meia palavra basta** a word to the wise is enough

entender [ẽtẽ'der] VT (*compreender*) to understand; (*pensar*) to think; (*ouvir*) to hear; **entender-se** VR (*compreender-se*) to understand one another; **dar a** ~ to imply; **no meu** ~ in my opinion; ~ **de música** to know about music; ~ **de fazer** to decide to do; ~**-se por** to be meant by; ~**-se com alguém** to get along with sb; (*dialogar*) to sort things out with sb

entendido, -a [ẽtẽ'dʒidu, a] ADJ: ~ **(em)** knowledgeable (about) ▶ M/F: ~**/a (em)** authority (on); **bem** ~ that is

entendimento [ẽtẽdʒi'mẽtu] M understanding

enternecedor, a [ẽternese'dor(a)] ADJ touching

enternecer [ẽterne'ser] VT to move, touch; **enternecer-se** VR to be moved

enterrar [ẽte'har] VT to bury; (*faca*) to plunge; (*lever à ruina*) to ruin; (*assunto*) to close; ~ **o chapéu na cabeça** to put one's hat on

enterro [ẽ'tehu] M burial; (*funeral*) funeral

entidade [ẽtʃi'dadʒi] F (*ser*) being; (*corporação*) body; (*coisa que existe*) entity

entoação [ẽtoa'sãw] F singing

entoar [ẽ'twar] VT (*cantar*) to chant

entonação [ẽtona'sãw] (*pl* -**ões**) F intonation

entontecer [ẽtõte'ser] VT to make dizzy; (*enlouquecer*) to drive mad ▶ VI to become *ou* get dizzy; to go mad; **o vinho entontece** wine makes you dizzy

entornar [ẽtor'nar] VT to spill; (*fig: copo*) to drink ▶ VI to drink a lot

entorpecente [ẽtorpe'sẽtʃi] M narcotic

entorpecer [ẽtorpe'ser] VT (*paralisar*) to numb, stupefy; (*retardar*) to slow down

entorpecimento [ẽtorpesi'mẽtu] M numbness; (*torpor*) lethargy

entorse [ẽ'torsi] F sprain

entortar [ẽtor'tar] VT (*curvar*) to bend; (*empenar*) to warp; ~ **os olhos** to squint

entourage [ãtu'raʒi] M entourage

entrada [ẽ'trada] F (*ato*) entry; (*lugar*) entrance; (*Tec*) inlet; (*de casa*) doorway; (*começo*) beginning; (*bilhete*) ticket; (*Culin*) starter, entrée; (*Comput*) input; (*pagamento inicial*) down payment; (*corredor de casa*) hall; **entradas** FPL (*no cabelo*) receding hairline;

~ gratuita admission free; **"~ proibida"** "no entry", "no admittance"; **meia ~** half-price ticket; **dar ~ em** (*requerimento*) to submit; (*processo*) to institute; **~ de serviço** service entrance

entrado, -a [ẽ'tradu, a] ADJ: **~ em anos** (PT) elderly

entra e sai ['ẽtrai'saj] M comings and goings *pl*

entranhado, -a [ẽtra'ɲadu, a] ADJ deep-rooted

entranhar-se [ẽtra'ɲarsi] VR to penetrate

entranhas [ẽ'traɲas] FPL bowels, entrails; (*sentimentos*) feelings; (*centro*) heart *sg*

entrar [ẽ'trar] VI to go (*ou* come) in, enter; (*conseguir entrar*) to get in; **deixar ~** to let in; **~ com** (*Comput: dados etc*) to enter; **eu entrei com £100** I put in £100; **~ de férias/licença** to start one's holiday (BRIT) *ou* vacation (US)/ leave; **~ em** (*casa etc*) to go (*ou* come) into, enter; (*assunto*) to get onto; (*comida, bebida*) to start in on; (*universidade*) to enter; **~ em detalhes** to go into details; **~ em vigor** to come into force; **ele entra às 9 no trabalho** he starts work at 9.00; **o que entra nesta receita?** what goes into this recipe?; **~ para um clube** to join a club; **quando a primavera entra** when spring comes; **~ bem** (*col*) to get into trouble

entravar [ẽtra'var] VT to obstruct, impede

entrave [ẽ'travi] M (*fig*) impediment

entre ['ẽtri] PREP (*dois*) between; (*mais de dois*) among(st); **~ si** amongst themselves

entreaberto, -a [ẽtrja'bɛrtu, a] PP *de* **entreabrir ▸** ADJ half-open; (*porta*) ajar

entreabrir [ẽtrja'brir] VT to half open; **entreabrir-se** VR (*flores*) to open up

entrechocar-se [ẽtriʃo'karsi] VR to collide, crash; (*fig*) to clash

entrecortado, -a [ẽtrikor'tadu, a] ADJ intermittent; **região entrecortada de estradas** region intersected by roads

entrecosto [ẽtri'kostu] M (*Culin*) entrecôte

entrega [ẽ'trega] F (*de mercadorias*) delivery; (*a alguém*) handing over; (*rendição*) surrender; **caminhão/serviço de ~** delivery van/ service; **pronta ~** speedy delivery; **~ rápida** special delivery; **~ a domicílio** home delivery

entregar [ẽtre'gar] VT (*dar*) to hand over; (*mercadorias*) to deliver; (*denunciar*) to hand over; (*confiar*) to entrust; (*devolver*) to return; **entregar-se** VR (*render-se*) to give o.s. up; (*dedicar-se*) to devote o.s.; **~ os pontos** to give up, throw in the towel; **~-se à dor/bebida** to be overcome by grief/take to drink; **~-se a um homem** to sleep with a man

entregue [ẽ'trɛgi] PP *de* **entregar**

entrelaçar [ẽtrila'sar] VT to entwine

entrelinha [ẽtre'liɲa] F line space; **ler nas ~s** to read between the lines

entremear [ẽtri'mjar] VT to intermingle

entremostrar [ẽtrimos'trar] VT to give a glimpse of

entreolhar-se [ẽtrio'ʎarsi] VR to exchange glances

entrepernas [ẽtri'pɛrnas] ADV between one's legs

entrepor [ẽtripor] (*irreg: como* **pôr**) VT to insert; **entrepor-se** VR: **~-se entre** to come between

entressafra [ẽtri'safra] F time between harvests; (*fig*): **as ~s de algo** the periods without sth

entretanto [ẽtri'tãtu] CONJ however

entretela [ẽtri'tɛla] F (*Costura*) interlining, buckram

entretenimento [ẽtriteni'mẽtu] M entertainment; (*distração*) pastime

entreter [ẽtri'ter] (*irreg: como* **ter**) VT (*divertir*) to entertain, amuse; (*ocupar*) to occupy; (*manter*) to keep up; (*esperanças*) to cherish; **entreter-se** VR to amuse o.s.; to occupy o.s.

entrevar [ẽtre'var] VT to paralyse, cripple

entrever [ẽtri'ver] (*irreg: como* **ver**) VT to glimpse, catch a glimpse of

entrevista [ẽtre'vista] F interview; **~ coletiva** (**à imprensa**) press conference

entrevistador, a [ẽtrevista'dor(a)] M/F interviewer

entrevistar [ẽtrevis'tar] VT to interview; **entrevistar-se** VR to have an interview

entrevisto, -a [ẽtre'vistu, a] PP *de* **entrever**

entristecedor, a [ẽtristese'dor(a)] ADJ saddening, sad

entristecer [ẽtriste'ser] VT to sadden, grieve ▸ VI to feel sad; **entristecer-se** VR to feel sad

entroncamento [ẽtrõka'mẽtu] M junction

entrosado, -a [ẽtro'zadu, a] ADJ (*fig*) integrated

entrosamento [ẽtroza'mẽtu] M (*fig*) integration

entrosar [ẽtro'zar] VT (*rodas*) to mesh; (*peças*) to fit; (*fig*) to integrate ▸ VI to mesh; to fit; **~ com** (*fig*) to fit in with; **~ em** (*adaptar-se*) to settle into

entrudo [ẽ'trudu] (PT) M carnival; (*Rel*) Shrovetide

entulhar [ẽtu'ʎar] VT to cram full; (*suj: multidão*) to pack

entulho [ẽ'tuʎu] M rubble, debris *sg*

entupido, -a [ẽtu'pidu, a] ADJ blocked; **estar ~** (*col: congestionado*) to have a blocked-up nose; (*de comida*) to be fit to burst, be full up

entupimento [ẽtupi'mẽtu] M blockage

entupir [ẽtu'pir] VT to block, clog; **entupir-se** VR to become blocked; (*de comida*) to stuff o.s.

entupitivo, -a [ẽtupi'tʃivu, a] ADJ filling

enturmar-se [ẽtur'marsi] VR: **~ (com)** to make friends (with)

entusiasmar [ẽtuzjaz'mar] VT to fill with enthusiasm; (*animar*) to excite; **entusiasmar-se** VR to get excited

entusiasmo [ẽtu'zjazmu] M enthusiasm; (*júbilo*) excitement

entusiasta [ẽtu'zjasta] ADJ enthusiastic ▸ M/F enthusiast

entusiástico, -a [ētu'zjastʃiku, a] ADJ enthusiastic

enumeração [enumera'sãw] (pl **-ões**) F enumeration; (numeração) numbering

enumerar [enume'rar] VT to enumerate; (com números) to number

enunciar [enũ'sjar] VT to express, state

envaidecer [ēvajde'ser] VT to make conceited; **envaidecer-se** VR to become conceited

envelhecer [ēveʎe'ser] VT to age ▶ VI to grow old, age

envelhecimento [ēveʎesi'mētu] M aging

envelope [ēve'lɔpi] M envelope

envenenado, -a [ēvene'nadu, a] ADJ poisoned; (col: festa, roupa) wild, great; (: carro) souped-up

envenenamento [ēvenena'mētu] M poisoning; **~ do sangue** blood poisoning

envenenar [ēvene'nar] VT to poison; (fig) to corrupt; (: declaração, palavras) to distort, twist; (tornar amargo) to sour; (col: carro) to soup up ▶ VI to be poisonous; **envenenar-se** VR to poison o.s.

enverdecer [ēverde'ser] VT to turn green

enveredar [ēvere'dar] VI: **~ por um caminho** to follow a road; **~ para** to head for

envergadura [ēverga'dura] F (asas, velas) spread; (de avião) wingspan; (fig) scope; **de grande ~** large-scale

envergar [ēver'gar] VT (arquear) to bend; (vestir) to wear

envergonhado, -a [ēvergo'ɲadu, a] ADJ ashamed; (tímido) shy

envergonhar [ēvergo'ɲar] VT to shame; (degradar) to disgrace; **envergonhar-se** VR to be ashamed

envernizar [ēverni'zar] VT to varnish

enviado, -a [ē'vjadu, a] M/F envoy, messenger

enviar [ē'vjar] VT to send

envidar [ēvi'dar] VT: **~ esforços (para fazer algo)** to endeavour (BRIT) ou endeavor (US) (to do sth)

envidraçado, -a [ēvidra'sadu, a] ADJ: **varanda envidraçada** conservatory

envidraçar [ēvidra'sar] VT to glaze

enviesado, -a [ēvje'zadu, a] ADJ slanting

envilecer [ēvile'ser] VT to debase, degrade

envio [ē'viu] M sending; (expedição) dispatch; (remessa) remittance; (de mercadorias) consignment

enviuvar [ēvju'var] VI to be widowed

envolto, -a [ē'vowtu, a] PP de **envolver**

envoltório [ēvow'tɔrju] M cover

envolvente [ēvow'vētʃi] ADJ compelling

envolver [ēvow'ver] VT (embrulhar) to wrap (up); (cobrir) to cover; (comprometer, acarretar) to involve; (nos braços) to embrace; **envolver-se** VR (intrometer-se) to become involved; (cobrir-se) to wrap o.s. up

envolvimento [ēvowvi'mētu] M involvement

enxada [ē'ʃada] F hoe

enxadrista [ēʃa'drista] M/F chess player

enxaguada [ēʃa'gwada] F rinse

enxaguar [ēʃa'gwar] VT to rinse

enxame [ē'ʃami] M swarm

enxaqueca [ēʃa'keka] F migraine

enxergão [ēʃer'gãw] (pl **-ões**) M (straw) mattress

enxergar [ēʃer'gar] VT (avistar) to catch sight of; (divisar) to make out; (notar) to observe, see; **enxergar-se** VR: **ele não se enxerga** he doesn't know his place

enxergões [ēʃer'gõjs] MPL de **enxergão**

enxerido, -a [ēʃe'ridu, a] ADJ nosy, interfering

enxertar [ēʃer'tar] VT to graft; (fig) to incorporate

enxerto [ē'ʃertu] M graft

enxó [ē'ʃɔ] M adze

enxofre [ē'ʃofri] M sulphur (BRIT), sulfur (US)

enxota-moscas [ē'ʃota-] (PT) M fly swatter

enxotar [ēʃo'tar] VT (expulsar) to drive out

enxoval [ēʃo'vaw] (pl **-ais**) M (de noiva) trousseau; (de recém-nascido) layette

enxovalhar [ēʃova'ʎar] VT (sujar) to soil; (amarrotar) to crumple; (reputação) to blacken; (insultar) to insult; **enxovalhar-se** VR to disgrace o.s.

enxugador [ēʃuga'dor] M clothes drier

enxugar [ēʃu'gar] VT to dry; (fig: texto) to tidy up; (: organização, quadro de pessoal) to downsize; **~ as lágrimas** to dry one's eyes

enxurrada [ēʃu'hada] F (de água) torrent; (fig) spate

enxuto, -a [ē'ʃutu, a] ADJ dry; (corpo) shapely; (bonito) good-looking

enzima [ē'zima] F enzyme

epicentro [epi'sētru] M epicentre (BRIT), epicenter (US)

épico, -a ['ɛpiku, a] ADJ epic ▶ M epic poet

epidemia [epide'mia] F epidemic

epidêmico, -a [epi'demiku, a] ADJ epidemic

Epifania [epifa'nia] F Epiphany

epilepsia [epile'psia] F epilepsy

epiléptico, -a [epi'lɛptʃiku, a] ADJ, M/F epileptic

epílogo [e'pilogu] M epilogue

episcopado [episko'padu] M bishopric

episódio [epi'zɔdʒu] M episode

epístola [e'pistola] F epistle; (carta) letter

epitáfio [epi'tafju] M epitaph

epítome [e'pitomi] M summary; (fig) epitome

época ['ɛpoka] F time, period; (da história) age, epoch; **~ da colheita** harvest time; **naquela ~** at that time; **fazer ~** to be epoch-making; **fazer segunda ~** to resit one's exams

epopeia [epo'peja] F epic

equação [ekwa'sãw] (pl **-ões**) F equation

equacionar [ekwasjo'nar] VT to set out

equações [ekwa'sõjs] FPL de **equação**

Equador [ekwa'dor] M: **o ~** Ecuador

equador [ekwa'dor] M equator

equânime [e'kwanimi] ADJ fair; (caráter) unbiassed, neutral

equatorial [ekwato'rjaw] (pl **-ais**) ADJ equatorial

equatoriano, -a [ekwato'rjanu, a] ADJ, M/F Ecuadorian

equestre [e'kwɛstri] ADJ equestrian

equidade [ekwi'dadʒi] F equity

equidistante [ekwidʒis'tãtʃi] ADJ equidistant

equilátero, -a [ekwi'lateru, a] ADJ equilateral

equilibrado, -a [ekili'bradu, a] ADJ balanced; (pessoa) level-headed

equilibrar [ekili'brar] VT to balance; **equilibrar-se** VR to balance

equilíbrio [eki'librju] M balance; **perder o ~** to lose one's balance

equino, -a [e'kwinu, a] ADJ equine

equipa [e'kipa] (PT) F team

equipamento [ekipa'mẽtu] M equipment, kit

equipar [eki'par] VT (navio) to fit out; (prover) to equip

equiparação [ekipara'sãw] (pl -ões) F comparison

equiparar [ekiparar] VT (comparar) to equate; **equiparar-se** VR: ~-se a to equal

equiparável [ekipa'ravew] (pl -eis) ADJ comparable, equitable

equipe [e'kipi] (BR) F team

equitação [ekita'sãw] F (ato) riding; (arte) horsemanship

equitativo, -a [ekwita'tʃivu, a] ADJ fair, equitable

equivalência [ekiva'lẽsja] F equivalence

equivalente [ekiva'lẽtʃi] ADJ, M equivalent

equivaler [ekiva'ler] VI: ~ a to be the same as, equal

equivocado, -a [ekivo'kadu, a] ADJ mistaken, wrong

equivocar-se [ekivo'karsi] VR to make a mistake, be wrong

equívoco, -a [e'kivoku, a] ADJ ambiguous ▶ M (engano) mistake

ER ABR (= espera resposta) RSVP

era¹ ['ɛra] F era, age

era² VB ver **ser**

erário [e'rarju] M exchequer

ereção [ere'sãw] (pl -ões) F (tb Fisiol) erection

eremita [ere'mita] M/F hermit

eremitério [eremi'tɛrju] M hermitage

ereto, -a [e'rɛtu, a] ADJ upright, erect

erguer [er'ger] VT (levantar) to raise, lift; (edificar) to build, erect; **erguer-se** VR to rise; (pessoa) to stand up

eriçado, -a [eri'sadu, a] ADJ bristling; (cabelos) (standing) on end

eriçar [eri'sar] VT: ~ o cabelo de alguém to make sb's hair stand on end; **eriçar-se** VR to bristle; (cabelos) to stand on end

erigir [eri'ʒir] VT to erect

ermo, -a ['ermu, a] ADJ (solitário) lonely; (desabitado) uninhabited ▶ M wilderness

erógeno, -a [e'rɔʒenu, a] ADJ erogenous

erosão [ero'zãw] F erosion

erótico, -a [e'rɔtʃiku, a] ADJ erotic

erotismo [ero'tʃizmu] M eroticism

erradicar [ehadʒi'kar] VT to eradicate

errado, -a [e'hadu, a] ADJ wrong; **dar ~** to go wrong

errante [e'hãtʃi] ADJ wandering

errar [e'har] VT (alvo) to miss; (conta) to get wrong ▶ VI (vaguear) to wander, roam; (enganar-se) to be wrong, make a mistake; ~ o caminho to lose one's way

errata [e'hata] F errata

erro ['ehu] M mistake; **salvo ~** unless I am mistaken; ~ de imprensa misprint; ~ de pronúncia mispronunciation

errôneo, -a [e'honju, a] ADJ wrong, mistaken; (falso) false, untrue

erudição [erudʒi'sãw] F erudition, learning

erudito, -a [eru'dʒitu, a] ADJ learned, scholarly ▶ M scholar

erupção [erup'sãw] (pl -ões) F eruption; (na pele) rash; (fig) outbreak

erva ['ɛrva] F herb; ~ daninha weed; (col: dinheiro) dosh; (: maconha) dope

erva-cidreira [-si'drejra] (pl ervas-cidreiras) F lemon verbena

erva-doce (pl ervas-doces) F fennel

erva-mate (pl ervas-mate(s)) F maté

ervilha [er'viʎa] F pea

ES (BR) ABR = **Espírito Santo**

ESAO [e'saw] (BR) ABR F (= Escola Superior de Aperfeiçoamento de Oficiais) officer training school

esbaforido, -a [izbafo'ridu, a] ADJ breathless, panting

esbaldar-se [izbaw'darsi] VR to have a great time, really enjoy o.s.

esbandalhado, -a [izbãda'ʎadu, a] ADJ (pessoa) scruffy; (casa, jardim) untidy

esbanjador, a [izbãʒa'dor(a)] ADJ extravagant, spendthrift ▶ M/F spendthrift

esbanjamento [izbãʒa'mẽtu] M (ato) squandering; (qualidade) extravagance

esbanjar [izbã'ʒar] VT to squander, waste; **estar esbanjando saúde** to be bursting with health

esbarrão [izba'hãw] (pl -ões) M collision

esbarrar [izba'har] VI: ~ em to bump into; (obstáculo, problema) to come up against

esbarrões [izba'hõjs] MPL de **esbarrão**

esbelteza [izbew'tez] F slenderness

esbelto, -a [iz'bewtu, a] ADJ slim, slender

esboçar [izbo'sar] VT to sketch; (delinear) to outline; (plano) to draw up; ~ um sorriso to give a little smile

esboço [iz'bosu] M sketch; (primeira versão) draft; (fig: resumo) outline

esbodegado, -a [izbode'gadu, a] ADJ tatty; (cansado) worn out

esbodegar [izbode'gar] (col) VT to ruin

esbofar [izbo'far] VT to tire out; **esbofar-se** VR to be worn out

esbofetear [izbofe'tʃjar] VT to slap, hit

esbórnia [iz'bɔrnja] F orgy

esborrachar [izboha'ʃar] VT to squash; (esbofetear) to hit; **esborrachar-se** VR to go sprawling

esbranquiçado, -a [izbrãki'sadu, a] ADJ whitish; (*lábios*) pale

esbravejar [izbrave'ʒar] VT, VI to shout

esbregue [iz'brɛgi] (*col*) M (*descompostura*) telling-off, dressing-down (BRIT); (*rolo*) punch-up, brawl

esbugalhado, -a [izbuga'ʎadu, a] ADJ: **olhos ~s** goggle eyes

esbugalhar-se [izbuga'ʎarsi] VR to goggle, boggle

esburacado, -a [izbura'kadu, a] ADJ full of holes, holey; (*rua*) full of potholes

esburacar [izbura'kar] VT to make holes (*ou* a hole) in

escabeche [iska'bɛʃi] M (*Culin*) marinade, *sauce of spiced vinegar and onion*

escabroso, -a [iska'brozu, ɔza] ADJ (*difícil*) tough; (*indecoroso*) indecent

escada [is'kada] F (*dentro da casa*) staircase, stairs *pl*; (*fora da casa*) steps *pl*; (*de mão*) ladder; **~ de incêndio** fire escape; **~ rolante** escalator

escadaria [iskada'ria] F staircase

escafandrista [iskafã'drista] M/F deep-sea diver

escafandro [iska'fãdru] M diving suit

escafeder-se [iskafe'dersi] (*col*) VI to sneak off

escala [is'kala] F scale; (*Náut*) port of call; (*parada*) stop; **fazer ~ em** to call at; **sem ~** non-stop; **~ móvel** sliding scale

escalação [iskala'sãw] F climbing; (*designação*) selection

escalada [iska'lada] F (*de guerra*) escalation

escalafobético, -a [iskalafo'bɛtʃiku, a] (*col*) ADJ weird, strange

escalão [iska'lãw] (*pl* -ões) M step; (*Mil*) echelon; **o primeiro ~ do governo** the highest level of government

escalar [iska'lar] VT (*montanha*) to climb; (*muro*) to scale; (*designar*) to select

escalavrar [iskala'vrar] VT (*pele*) to graze; (*parede*) to damage

escaldado, -a [iskaw'dadu, a] ADJ (*fig*) cautious, wary

escaldar [iskaw'dar] VT to scald; (*Culin*) to blanch; **escaldar-se** VR to scald o.s.

escaler [iska'lɛr] M launch

escalfar [iskaw'far] (PT) VT (*ovos*) to poach

escalões [iska'lõjs] MPL *de* **escalão**

escalonamento [iskalona'mẽtu] M (*Com: de dívida*) scheduling

escalonar [iskalo'nar] VT (*argumentos, opiniões*) to set out; (*dívida*) to spread, schedule

escalope [iska'lɔpi] M escalope (BRIT), cutlet (US)

escama [is'kama] F (*de peixe*) scale; (*de pele*) flake

escamar [iska'mar] VT to scale

escamotear [iskamo'tʃar] VT (*furtar*) to pilfer, pinch (BRIT); (*empalmar*) to make disappear (by sleight of hand)

escancarado, -a [iskãka'radu, a] ADJ wide open

escancarar [iskãka'rar] VT to open wide

escandalizar [iskãdali'zar] VT to shock; **escandalizar-se** VR to be shocked; (*ofender-se*) to be offended

escândalo [is'kãdalu] M scandal; (*indignação*) outrage; **fazer ~** to make a scene

escandaloso, -a [iskãda'lozu, ɔza] ADJ shocking, scandalous

Escandinávia [iskãdʒi'navja] F: **a ~** Scandinavia

escandinavo, -a [iskãdʒi'navu, a] ADJ, M/F Scandinavian

escangalhar [iskãga'ʎar] VT to break, smash (up); **escangalhar-se** VR: **~-se de rir** to split one's sides laughing

escaninho [iska'niɲu] M (*na secretária*) pigeonhole

escanteio [iskã'teju] M (*Futebol*) corner

escapada [iska'pada] F escape; (*ato leviano*) escapade

escapar [iska'par] VI: **~ a** *ou* **de** to escape from; (*fugir*) to run away from; **escapar-se** VR to run away, flee; **deixar ~** (*uma oportunidade*) to miss; (*palavras*) to blurt out; **~ da morte/ de uma incumbência** to escape death/get out of a task; **ele escapou de ser atropelado** he escaped being run over; **o vaso escapou-lhe das mãos** the vase slipped out of his hands; **nada lhe escapa** (*passar despercebido*) nothing escapes him, he doesn't miss a thing; **o nome me escapa no momento** the name escapes me for the moment; **não está bom, mas escapa** it's not good, but it'll do; **~ de boa** (*col*) to have a close shave

escapatória [iskapa'tɔrja] F (*saída*) way out; (*desculpa*) excuse

escape [is'kapi] M (*de gás*) leak; (*Auto*) exhaust

escapismo [iska'pizmu] M escapism

escapulida [iskapu'lida] F escape

escapulir [iskapu'lir] VI: **~ (de)** to get away (from); (*suj: coisa*) to slip (from)

escarafunchar [iskarafũ'ʃar] VT: **~ algo** (*remexer em*) to rummage in sth; (*com as unhas*) to scratch at sth; (*investigar*) to pore over sth

escaramuça [iskara'musa] F skirmish

escaravelho [iskara'veʎu] M beetle

escarcéu [iskar'sɛw] M (*fig*): **fazer um ~** to make a scene

escarlate [iskar'latʃi] ADJ scarlet

escarlatina [iskarla'tʃina] F scarlet fever

escarnecer [iskarne'ser] VT to mock, make fun of ▶ VI: **~ de** to mock, make fun of

escárnio [is'karnju] M mockery; (*desprezo*) derision

escarpa [is'karpa] F steep slope

escarpado, -a [iskar'padu, a] ADJ steep

escarrado, -a [iska'hadu, a] ADJ (*fig*): **ela é o pai ~** she's the spitting image of her father

escarrapachar-se [iskahapa'ʃarsi] VR to sprawl

escarrar [iska'har] VT to spit, cough up ▶ VI to spit

escarro [is'kahu] M phlegm, spit

escasseamento [iskasja'mẽtu] M (*Com*)
shortage
escassear [iska'sjar] VT to skimp on ▶ VI to
become scarce
escassez [iska'sez] F (*falta*) shortage
escasso, -a [is'kasu, a] ADJ scarce
escavação [iskava'sãw] (*pl* **-ões**) F digging,
excavation
escavadeira [iskava'dejra] F digger, JCB®
escavar [iska'var] VT to excavate
esclarecedor, a [isklarese'dor(a)] ADJ
explanatory; (*que alarga o conhecimento*)
informative
esclarecer [isklare'ser] VT (*situação*) to
explain; (*mistério*) to clear up, explain;
esclarecer-se VR: **~-se (sobre algo)** to find
out (about sth); **~ alguém sobre algo** to
explain to sb about sth
esclarecido, -a [isklare'sidu, a] ADJ (*pessoa*)
enlightened
esclarecimento [isklaresi'mẽtu] M
explanation; (*informação*) information
esclerosado, -a [isklero'zadu, a] (*col*) ADJ
(*pessoa*) batty, nutty
esclerótica [iskle'rɔtʃika] F white of the eye
escoadouro [iskoa'doru] M drain; (*cano*)
drainpipe
escoar [isko'ar] VT to drain off ▶ VI to drain
away; **escoar-se** VR to seep out
escocês, -esa [isko'ses, seza] ADJ Scottish,
Scots ▶ M/F Scot, Scotsman/woman
Escócia [is'kɔsja] F Scotland
escoicear [iskoj'sjar] VT to kick; (*fig*) to
ill-treat ▶ VI to kick
escol [is'kɔw] M best; **de ~** of excellence
escola [is'kɔla] F school; **~ de línguas**
language school; **~ de samba** *see note*;
~ naval naval college; **~ primária/
secundária** primary (BRIT) *ou* elementary
(US)/secondary (BRIT) *ou* high (US) school;
~ particular/pública private/state (BRIT) *ou*
public (US) school; **~ superior** college;
fazer ~ to win converts

> **Escolas de samba** are musical and
> recreational associations made up,
> among others, of samba dancers,
> percussionists and carnival dancers.
> Although they exist throughout Brazil,
> the most famous schools are in Rio de
> Janeiro. The schools in Rio rehearse all
> year long for the **carnaval**, when they
> parade along the *Sambódromo*, a
> purpose-built avenue flanked by stands
> for spectators, and compete for the samba
> school championship. Characterized by
> their extravagance, the biggest schools
> have up to 4,000 members and are one of
> Brazil's major tourist attractions.

escolado, -a [isko'ladu, a] ADJ (*esperto*) shrewd;
(*experiente*) experienced
escolar [isko'lar] ADJ school *atr* ▶ M/F
schoolboy/girl; **escolares** MPL (*alunos*)
schoolchildren

escolaridade [iskolari'dadʒi] F schooling
escolarização [iskolariza'sãw] F education,
schooling
escolarizar [iskolari'zar] VT to educate (in
school)
escolha [is'koʎa] F choice
escolher [isko'ʎer] VT to choose, select
escolho [is'koʎu] M (*recife*) reef; (*rocha*) rock
escolta [is'kɔwta] F escort
escoltar [iskow'tar] VT to escort
escombros [is'kõbrus] MPL ruins, debris *sg*
esconde-esconde [iskõdʒis'kõdʒi] M
hide-and-seek
esconder [iskõ'der] VT to hide, conceal;
esconder-se VR to hide; **brincar de ~** to play
hide-and-seek
esconderijo [iskõde'riʒu] M hiding place;
(*de bandidos*) hideout
escondidas [iskõ'dʒidas] FPL: **às ~** secretly
esconjurar [iskõʒu'rar] VT (*o Demônio*) to
exorcize; (*afastar*) to keep off; (*amaldiçoar*) to
curse; **esconjurar-se** VR (*lamentar-se*) to
complain
escopo [is'kopu] M aim, purpose
escora [is'kɔra] F prop, support; (*cilada*)
ambush
escorar [isko'rar] VT to prop (up); (*amparar*) to
support; (*esperar de espreita*) to lie in wait for
▶ VI to lie in wait; **escorar-se** VR: **~-se em**
(*fundamentar-se*) to go by; (*amparar-se*) to live
off
escorbuto [iskor'butu] M scurvy
escore [is'kɔri] M score
escória [is'kɔrja] F (*de metal*) dross; **a ~ da
humanidade** the scum of the earth
escoriação [iskorja'sãw] (*pl* **-ões**) F abrasion,
scratch
escorpiano, -a [iskor'pjanu, a] ADJ, M/F
(*Astrologia*) Scorpio
escorpião [iskorpi'ãw] (*pl* **-ões**) M scorpion;
E~ (*Astrologia*) Scorpio
escorraçar [iskoha'sar] VT (*tratar mal*) to
ill-treat; (*expulsar*) to throw out; **~ alguém
de casa** *ou* **para fora de casa** to throw sb out
of the house
escorrega [isko'hega] F slide
escorregadela [iskohega'dɛla] F slip
escorregadio, -a [iskohega'dʒiu, a] ADJ
slippery
escorregador [iskohega'dor] M slide
escorregão [iskohe'gãw] (*pl* **-ões**) M slip; (*fig*)
slip(-up)
escorregar [iskohe'gar] VI to slip; (*errar*) to
slip up
escorregões [iskohe'gõjs] MPL *de* **escorregão**
escorrer [isko'her] VT (*fazer correr*) to drain
(off); (*verter*) to pour out ▶ VI (*pingar*) to drip;
(*correr em fio*) to trickle
escoteiro [isko'tejru] M scout
escotilha [isko'tʃiʎa] F hatch, hatchway
escova [is'kova] F brush; (*penteado*) blow-dry;
~ de dentes toothbrush; **fazer ~ no cabelo**
to blow-dry one's hair; (*por outra pessoa*) to

have a blow-dry; **~ progressiva** keratin straightening

escovar [isko'var] VT to brush

escovinha [isko'viɲa] F: **cabelo à ~** crew cut

escrachado, -a [iskra'ʃadu, a] (col) ADJ (desleixado) scruffy; **estar** ou **ser ~** (ter ficha na polícia) to have a criminal record

escravatura [iskrava'tura] F (tráfico) slave trade; (escravidão) slavery

escravidão [iskravi'dãw] F slavery

escravização [iskraviza'sãw] F enslavement

escravizar [iskravi'zar] VT to enslave; (cativar) to captivate

escravo, -a [is'kravu, a] ADJ captive ▶ M/F slave; **ele é um ~ do amigo/trabalho** he's a slave to his friend/work

escrete [is'krɛtʃi] M team

escrevente [iskre'vẽtʃi] M/F clerk

escrever [iskre'ver] VT, VI to write; **escrever-se** VR to write to each other; **~ à máquina** to type

escrevinhador, a [iskreviɲa'dor(a)] (col) M/F hack (writer)

escrevinhar [iskrevi'ɲar] VT to scribble

escrita [es'krita] F writing; (pessoal) handwriting; **pôr a ~ em dia** to bring one's correspondence up to date

escrito, -a [es'kritu, a] PP de **escrever** ▶ ADJ written ▶ M piece of writing; **~ à mão** handwritten; **dar por ~** to put in writing; **ela é o pai ~** she's the spitting image of her father

escritor, a [iskri'tor(a)] M/F writer; (autor) author

escritório [iskri'tɔrju] M office; (em casa) study

escritura [iskri'tura] F (Jur) deed; (na compra de imóveis) = exchange of contracts; **as Sagradas E~s** the Scriptures

escrituração [iskritura'sãw] F book-keeping; (de transações, quantias) entering, recording; **~ por partidas simples/dobradas** (Com) single-entry/double-entry book-keeping

escriturar [iskritu'rar] VT (contas) to register, enter up; (documento) to draw up

escriturário, -a [iskritu'rarju, a] M/F clerk

escrivã [iskri'vã] F de **escrivão**

escrivaninha [iskriva'niɲa] F writing desk

escrivão, -vã [iskri'vãw, vã] (pl **-ões/-s**) M/F registrar, recorder

escroque [is'krɔki] M swindler, con man

escroto, -a [is'krotu, a] M scrotum ▶ ADJ (!: pessoa) vile, gross; (: filme etc) crappy (!), shitty (!)

escrúpulo [is'krupulu] M scruple; (cuidado) care; **sem ~** unscrupulous

escrupuloso, -a [iskrupu'lozu, ɔza] ADJ scrupulous; (cuidadoso) careful

escrutinar [iskrutʃi'nar] VI to act as a scrutineer

escrutínio [iskru'tʃinju] M (votação) poll; (apuração de votos) counting; (exame atento) scrutiny; **~ secreto** secret ballot

escudar [isku'dar] VT to shield; **escudar-se** VR to shield o.s.; (apoiar-se): **~-se em algo** to rely on sth

escudeiro [isku'dejru] M squire

escudo [is'kudu] M shield; (moeda) escudo

esculachado, -a [iskula'ʃadu, a] (col) ADJ sloppy

esculachar [iskula'ʃar] (col) VT (bagunçar) to mess up; (espancar) to beat up; (criticar) to get at; (repreender) to tick off

esculacho [isku'laʃu] (col) M mess; (repreensão) telling-off

esculhambação [iskuʎãba'sãw] (pl **-ões**) (!) F mess; (repreensão) telling-off, bollocking (!)

esculhambado, -a [iskuʎã'badu, a] (!) ADJ (descuidado) shabby, slovenly; (estragado) messed up, knackered; (bagunçado) shambolic

esculhambar [iskuʎã'bar] (!) VT to mess up, fuck up (!); **~ alguém** (criticar) to give sb stick; (descompor) to give sb a bollocking (!)

esculpir [iskuw'pir] VT to carve, sculpt; (gravar) to engrave

escultor, a [iskuw'tor(a)] M/F sculptor

escultura [iskuw'tura] F sculpture

escultural [iskuwtu'raw] (pl **-ais**) ADJ sculptural; (corpo) statuesque

escuma [is'kuma] (PT) F foam; (em cerveja) froth

escumadeira [iskuma'dejra] F skimmer

escuna [is'kuna] F (Náut) schooner

escuras [is'kuras] FPL: **às ~** in the dark

escurecer [iskure'ser] VT to darken ▶ VI to get dark; **ao ~** at dusk

escurecimento [iskuresi'mẽtu] M darkening

escuridão [iskuri'dãw] F (trevas) darkness

escuro, -a [is'kuru, a] ADJ (sombrio) dark; (dia) overcast; (pessoa) swarthy ▶ M dark

escuso, -a [is'kuzu, a] ADJ shady

escuta [is'kuta] F listening; **à ~** listening out; **ficar na ~** to stand by; **~ eletrônica/ telefônica** bugging/phone tapping

escutar [isku'tar] VT to listen to; (sem prestar atenção) to hear ▶ VI to listen; to hear; **escuta!** listen!; **ele não escuta bem** he is hard of hearing; **o médico escutou o paciente** the doctor listened to the patient's chest

esdrúxulo, -a [iz'druʃulu, a] ADJ weird, odd

esfacelar [isfase'lar] VT (destruir) to destroy

esfaimado, -a [isfaj'madu, a] ADJ famished, ravenous

esfalfar [isfaw'far] VT to tire out, exhaust; **esfalfar-se** VR to tire o.s. out

esfaquear [isfaki'ar] VT to stab

esfarelar [isfare'lar] VT to crumble; **esfarelar-se** VR to crumble

esfarrapado, -a [isfaha'padu, a] ADJ (roupa) ragged, tattered; (desculpa) lame

esfarrapar [isfaha'par] VT to tear to pieces

esfera [is'fɛra] F sphere; (globo) globe

esférico, -a [is'fɛriku, a] ADJ spherical

esferográfico, -a [isfero'grafiku, a] ADJ:
caneta esferográfica ballpoint pen

esfiapar [isfja'par] VT to fray; **esfiapar-se** VR
to fray

esfinge [is'fĩʒi] F sphinx

esfogueado, -a [isfo'gjadu, a] ADJ impatient

esfolar [isfo'lar] VT to skin; (*arranhar*) to graze;
(*cobrar demais a*) to overcharge, fleece

esfomeado, -a [isfo'mjadu, a] ADJ famished,
starving

esforçado, -a [isfor'sadu, a] ADJ committed,
dedicated

esforçar-se [isfor'sarsi] VR: ~ **para** to try hard
to, strive to

esforço [is'forsu] M effort; **fazer** ~ to try
hard, make an effort

esfregação [isfrega'sãw] F rubbing; (*col*)
necking, petting

esfregaço [isfre'gasu] M smear

esfregar [isfre'gar] VT to rub; (*com água*) to
scrub

esfriamento [isfrja'mẽtu] M cooling

esfriar [is'frjar] VT to cool, chill ▶ VI to get
cold; (*fig*) to cool off

esfumaçar [isfuma'sar] VT to fill with smoke

esfumar [isfu'mar] VT to disperse; **esfumar-
se** VR to fade away

esfuziante [isfu'zjãtʃi] ADJ (*pessoa*) bubbly;
(*alegria*) irrepressible

ESG (BR) ABR F (= *Escola Superior de Guerra*) military
training school

esganado, -a [izga'nadu, a] ADJ (*sufocado*)
choked; (*voraz*) greedy; (*avaro*) grasping

esganar [izga'nar] VT to strangle, choke

esganiçado, -a [izgani'sadu, a] ADJ (*voz*)
shrill

esgaravatar [iʒgarava'tar] VT (*fig*) to delve
into

esgarçar [iʒgar'sar] VT, VI to tear; (*com o uso*) to
wear into a hole

esgazeado, -a [iʒga'zjadu, a] ADJ (*olhos, olhar*)
crazed

esgoelar [izgoe'lar] VT to yell; (*estrangular*) to
choke; **esgoelar-se** VR to yell, scream

esgotado, -a [izgo'tadu, a] ADJ (*exausto*)
exhausted; (*consumido*) used up; (*livros*) out of
print; **os ingressos estão ~s** the tickets are
sold out

esgotamento [izgota'mẽtu] M exhaustion

esgotar [izgo'tar] VT (*vazar*) to drain, empty;
(*recursos*) to use up; (*pessoa, assunto*) to
exhaust; **esgotar-se** VR (*cansar-se*) to become
exhausted; (*mercadorias, edição*) to be sold out;
(*recursos*) to run out

esgoto [iz'gotu] M drain; (*público*) sewer

esgrima [iz'grima] F (*Esporte*) fencing

esgrimir [izgri'mir] VI to fence

esgrouvinhado, -a [izgrovi'ɲadu, a] ADJ
dishevelled

esgueirar-se [izgej'rarsi] VR to slip away,
sneak off

esguelha [iz'geʎa] F slant; **olhar alguém de** ~
to look at sb out of the corner of one's eye

esguichar [izgi'ʃar] VT to squirt ▶ VI to squirt
out

esguicho [iʃ'giʃu] M (*jacto*) jet; (*de mangueira etc*)
spout

esguio, -a [ez'giu, a] ADJ slender

eslavo, -a [iʃ'lavu, a] ADJ Slavic ▶ M/F Slav

esmaecer [izmaje'ser] VI to fade

esmagador, a [izmaga'dor(a)] ADJ crushing;
(*provas*) irrefutable; (*maioria*) overwhelming

esmagar [izma'gar] VT to crush

esmaltado, -a [izmaw'tadu, a] ADJ enamelled
(BRIT), enameled (US)

esmalte [iz'mawtʃi] M enamel; (*de unhas*) nail
polish

esmerado, -a [izme'radu, a] ADJ careful, neat;
(*bem acabado*) polished

esmeralda [izme'rawda] F emerald

esmerar-se [izme'rarsi] VR: ~ **em** to take
great care to

esmero [iz'meru] M (*great*) care

esmigalhar [izmiga'ʎar] VT to crumble;
(*despedaçar*) to shatter; (*esmagar*) to crush;
esmigalhar-se VR (*pão etc*) to crumble; (*vaso*)
to smash, shatter

esmirrado, -a [izmi'hadu, a] ADJ (*roupa*)
skimpy, tight

esmiuçar [izmju'sar] VT (*pão*) to crumble;
(*examinar*) to examine in detail

esmo ['ezmu] M: **a** ~ at random; **andar a** ~
to walk aimlessly; **falar a** ~ to prattle

esmola [iz'mola] F alms pl; (*col: surra*)
thrashing; **pedir ~s** to beg

esmolar [izmo'lar] VT, VI: ~ (**algo a alguém**)
to beg (sth from sb)

esmorecer [izmore'ser] VT to discourage ▶ VI
(*desanimar-se*) to lose heart

esmorecimento [izmoresi'mẽtu] M dismay,
discouragement; (*enfraquecimento*) weakening

esmurrar [izmu'har] VT to punch

Esni [ez'ni] (BR) ABR F (= *Escola Nacional de
Informações*) training school for intelligence services

esnobação [iznoba'sãw] F snobbishness

esnobar [izno'bar] VI to be snobbish ▶ VT:
~ **alguém** to give sb the cold shoulder

esnobe [iz'nɔbi] ADJ snobbish; (*col*) stuck-up
▶ M/F snob

esnobismo [izno'bizmu] M snobbery

esôfago [e'zofagu] M oesophagus (BRIT),
esophagus (US)

esotérico, -a [ezo'teriku, a] ADJ esoteric

esoterismo [ezote'rizmu] M New Age

espaçado, -a [ispa'sadu, a] ADJ spaced out

espaçar [ispa'sar] VT to space out; ~ **visitas/
saídas** etc to visit/go out etc less often

espacejamento [ispaseʃa'mẽtu] M (*Tip*)
spacing; ~ **proporcional** proportional
spacing

espacial [ispa'sjaw] (*pl* -**ais**) ADJ spatial, space
atr; **nave** ~ spaceship

espaço [is'pasu] M space; (*tempo*) period;
(*cultural etc*) venue; ~ **para 3 pessoas** room
for 3 people; **a ~s** from time to time; **sujeito
a** ~ (*em avião*) stand-by

espaçoso, -a [ispa'sozu, ɔza] ADJ spacious, roomy

espada [is'pada] F sword; **espadas** FPL (Cartas) spades; **estar entre a ~ e a parede** to be between the devil and the deep blue sea

espadachim [ispada'ʃĩ] (pl **-ns**) M swordsman

espadarte [ispa'dartʃi] M swordfish

espádua [is'padwa] F shoulder blade

espairecer [ispajre'ser] VT to amuse, entertain ▶ VI to relax; **espairecer-se** VR to relax

espairecimento [ispajresi'mẽtu] M recreation

espaldar [ispaw'dar] M (chair) back

espalha-brasas [ispaʎa'-] M/F INV troublemaker

espalhafato [ispaʎa'fatu] M din, commotion

espalhafatoso, -a [ispaʎafa'tozu, ɔza] ADJ (pessoa) loud, rowdy; (roupa) loud, garish

espalhar [ispa'ʎar] VT to scatter; (boato, medo) to spread; (luz) to shed; **espalhar-se** VR (fogo, boato) to spread; (refestelar-se) to lounge

espanador [ispana'dor] M duster

espanar [ispa'nar] VT to dust

espancamento [ispãka'mẽtu] M beating

espancar [ispã'kar] VT to beat up

espandongado, -a [ispãdõ'gadu, a] ADJ (no vestir) scruffy; (estragado) tatty

Espanha [is'paɲa] F: **a ~** Spain

espanhol, a [ispa'ɲɔw, ɔla] (pl **-óis/-s**) ADJ Spanish ▶ M/F Spaniard ▶ M (Ling) Spanish; **os espanhóis** MPL the Spanish

espantado, -a [ispã'tadu, a] ADJ astonished; (cor) loud, garish

espantalho [ispã'taʎu] M scarecrow

espantar [ispã'tar] VT (causar medo a) to frighten; (admirar) to amaze, astonish; (afugentar) to frighten away ▶ VI to be amazing; **espantar-se** VR to be amazed; (assustar-se) to be frightened

espanto [is'pãtu] M (medo) fright, fear; (admiração) amazement

espantoso, -a [ispã'tozu, ɔza] ADJ amazing

esparadrapo [ispara'drapu] M (sticking) plaster (BRIT), Band-Aid® (US)

espargir [ispar'ʒir] VT (líquido) to sprinkle; (flores) to scatter; (luz) to shed

esparramar [ispaha'mar] VT (líquido) to splash; (espalhar) to scatter

esparso, -a [is'parsu, a] ADJ scattered; (solto) loose

espartano, -a [ispar'tanu, a] ADJ (fig) spartan

espartilho [ispar'tʃiʎu] M corset

espasmo [is'pazmu] M spasm, convulsion

espasmódico, -a [ispaz'mɔdʒiku, a] ADJ spasmodic

espatifar [ispatʃi'far] VT to smash; **espatifar-se** VR to smash; (avião) to crash

espavorir [ispavo'rir] VT to terrify

EsPCEx (BR) ABR F = **Escola Preparatória de Cadetes do Exército**

especial [ispe'sjaw] (pl **-ais**) ADJ special; **em ~** especially

especialidade [ispesjali'dadʒi] F speciality (BRIT), specialty (US); (ramo de atividades) specialization

especialista [ispesja'lista] M/F specialist; (perito) expert

especialização [ispesjaliza'sãw] (pl **-ões**) F specialization

especializado, -a [ispesjali'zadu, a] ADJ specialized; (operário, mão de obra) skilled

especializar-se [ispesjali'zarsi] VR: **~ (em)** to specialize (in)

especiaria [ispesja'ria] F spice

espécie [is'pɛsi] F (Bio) species; (tipo) sort, kind; **causar ~** to be surprising; **pagar em ~** to pay in cash

especificação [ispesifika'sãw] (pl **-ões**) F specification

especificar [ispesifi'kar] VT to specify

específico, -a [ispe'sifiku, a] ADJ specific

espécime [is'pɛsimi] M specimen

espécimen [is'pɛsimẽ] (pl **-s**) M = **espécime**

espectador, a [ispekta'dor(a)] M/F (testemunha) onlooker; (TV) viewer; (Esporte) spectator; (Teatro) member of the audience; **espectadores** MPL audience sg

espectro [is'pɛktru] M spectre (BRIT), specter (US); (Fís) spectrum; (pessoa) gaunt figure

especulação [ispekula'sãw] (pl **-ões**) F speculation

especulador, a [ispekula'dor(a)] ADJ speculating ▶ M/F (na Bolsa etc) speculator; (explorador) opportunist

especular [ispeku'lar] VI: **~ (sobre)** to speculate (on)

especulativo, -a [ispekula'tʃivu, a] ADJ speculative

espelhar [ispe'ʎar] VT to mirror; **espelhar-se** VR to be mirrored; **seus olhos espelham malícia, espelha-se malícia nos seus olhos** there is malice in his eyes

espelho [is'peʎu] M mirror; (fig) model; **~ retrovisor** (Auto) rear-view mirror

espelunca [ispe'lũka] (col) F (bar) dive; (casa) dump, hole

espera [is'pɛra] F (demora) wait; (expectativa) expectation; **à ~ de** waiting for; **à minha ~** waiting for me

espera-marido (pl **espera-maridos**) M (Culin) sweet made with burnt sugar and eggs

esperança [ispe'rãsa] F (confiança) hope; (expectativa) expectation; **dar ~s a alguém** to get sb's hopes up; **que ~!** (col) no chance!

esperançar [isperã'sar] VT: **~ alguém** to give sb hope

esperançoso, -a [isperã'sozu, ɔza] ADJ hopeful

esperar [ispe'rar] VT (aguardar) to wait for; (desejar) to hope for; (contar com, bebê) to expect ▶ VI to wait; to hope; to expect; **espero que sim/não** I hope so/not; **fazer alguém ~** to keep sb waiting; **espera aí!** hold on!; (col: não vem) come off it!

esperável [ispe'ravew] (*pl* **-eis**) ADJ expected, probable

esperma [is'pɛrma] M sperm

espernear [isper'njar] VI to kick out; (*protestar*) to protest

espertalhão, -lhona [isperta'ʎãw, ʎɔna] (*pl* **-ões/-s**) ADJ crafty, shrewd ▶ M/F shrewd operator

esperteza [isper'teza] F cleverness; (*astúcia*) cunning

esperto, -a [is'pɛrtu, a] ADJ clever; (*espertalhão*) crafty; (*col: bacana*) great

espesso, -a [is'pesu, a] ADJ thick

espessura [ispe'sura] F thickness

espetacular [ispetaku'lar] ADJ spectacular

espetáculo [ispe'takulu] M (*Teatro*) show; (*vista*) sight; (*cena ridícula*) spectacle; **dar ~** to make a spectacle of o.s.; **ela/a casa é um ~** (*col*) she/the house is fabulous

espetada [ispe'tada] F prick

espetar [ispe'tar] VT (*carne*) to put on a spit; (*cravar*) to stick; **espetar-se** VR to prick o.s.; **~ algo em algo** to pin sth to sth

espetinho [ispe'tiɲu] M skewer

espeto [is'petu] M spit; (*pau*) pointed stick; (*fig: pessoa magra*) beanpole; **ser um ~** (*ser difícil*) to be awkward

espevitado, -a [ispevi'tadu, a] ADJ (*fig: vivo*) lively

espezinhar [ispezi'ɲar] VT to trample (on); (*humilhar*) to treat like dirt

espia [is'pia] M/F spy

espiã [is'pjã] F *de* **espião**

espiada [is'pjada] F: **dar uma ~** to have a look

espião, -piã [is'pjãw, 'pjã] (*pl* **-ões/-s**) M/F spy

espiar [is'pjar] VT (*espionar*) to spy on; (*uma ocasião*) to watch out for; (*olhar*) to watch ▶ VI to spy; (*olhar*) to peer

espicaçar [ispika'sar] VT to trouble, torment

espichar [ispi'ʃar] VT (*couro*) to stretch out; (*pescoço, pernas*) to stretch ▶ VI (*col: crescer*) to shoot up; **espichar-se** VR to stretch out

espiga [is'piga] F (*de milho*) ear

espigado, -a [ispigadu, a] ADJ (*milho*) fully-grown; (*ereto*) upright

espigueiro [ispi'gejru] M granary

espinafração [ispinafra'sãw] (*pl* **-ões**) (*col*) F telling-off

espinafrar [ispina'frar] (*col*) VT: **~ alguém** (*repreender*) to give sb a telling-off; (*criticar*) to get at sb; (*ridicularizar*) to jeer at sb

espinafre [ispi'nafri] M spinach

espingarda [ispĩ'garda] F shotgun, rifle; **~ de ar comprimido** air rifle

espinha [is'piɲa] F (*de peixe*) bone; (*na pele*) spot, zit (*col*); (*coluna vertebral*) spine

espinhar [ispi'ɲar] VT (*picar*) to prick; (*irritar*) to irritate, annoy

espinheiro [ispi'ɲejru] M bramble bush

espinhento, -a [ispi'ɲẽtu, a] ADJ spotty, pimply

espinho [is'piɲu] M thorn; (*de animal*) spine; (*fig: dificuldade*) snag

espinhoso, -a [ispi'ɲozu, ɔza] ADJ (*planta*) prickly, thorny; (*fig: difícil*) difficult; (: *problema*) thorny

espinotear [ispino'tʃjar] VI (*cavalo*) to buck; (*pessoa*) to leap about

espiões [is'pjõjs] MPL *de* **espião**

espionagem [ispio'naʒẽ] F spying, espionage

espionar [ispjo'nar] VT to spy on ▶ VI to spy, snoop

espiral [ispi'raw] (*pl* **-ais**) ADJ, F spiral

espírita [is'pirita] ADJ, M/F spiritualist

espiritismo [ispiri'tʃizmu] M spiritualism

espírito [is'piritu] M spirit; (*pensamento*) mind; **~ de porco** wet blanket; **~ esportivo** sense of humo(u)r; **~ forte/fraco** (*fig: pessoa*) freethinker/sheep; **E~ Santo** Holy Spirit

espiritual [ispiri'twaw] (*pl* **-ais**) ADJ spiritual

espirituoso, -a [ispiri'twozu, ɔza] ADJ witty

espirrar [ispi'har] VI to sneeze; (*jorrar*) to spurt out ▶ VT (*água*) to spurt

espirro [is'pihu] M sneeze

esplanada [ispla'nada] F esplanade

esplêndido, -a [is'plẽdʒidu, a] ADJ splendid

esplendor [isplẽ'dor] M splendour (BRIT), splendor (US)

espocar [ispo'kar] VI to explode

espoleta [ispo'leta] F (*de arma*) fuse

espoliar [ispo'ljar] VT to plunder

espólio [is'pɔlju] M (*herança*) estate, property; (*roubado*) booty, spoils *pl*

esponja [is'põʒa] F sponge; (*de pó de arroz*) powder puff; (*parasita*) sponger; (*col: ébrio*) boozer

esponjoso, -a [ispõ'ʒozu, ɔza] ADJ spongy

espontaneidade [ispõtanei'dadʒi] F spontaneity

espontâneo, -a [ispõ'tanju, a] ADJ spontaneous; (*pessoa: natural*) straightforward

espora [is'pɔra] F spur

esporádico, -a [ispo'radʒiku, a] ADJ sporadic

esporão [ispo'rãw] (*pl* **-ões**) M (*de galo*) spur

esporear [ispo'rjar] VT (*picar*) to spur on; (*fig*) to incite

esporões [ispo'rõjs] MPL *de* **esporão**

esporte [is'pɔrtʃi] (BR) M sport

esportista [ispor'tʃista] ADJ sporting ▶ M/F sportsman/woman

esportiva [ispor'tʃiva] F sense of humour (BRIT) *ou* humor (US); **perder a ~** to lose one's sense of humo(u)r

esportivo, -a [ispor'tʃivu, a] ADJ sporting

esposa [is'poza] F wife

esposar [ispo'zar] VT to marry; (*causa*) to defend

esposo [is'pozu] M husband

espoucar [ispo'kar] VT = **espocar**

espraiar [ispra'jar] VT, VI to spread; (*dilatar*) to expand; **espraiar-se** VR (*mar*) to wash across the beach; (*rio*) to spread out; (*fig: epidemia*) to spread

espreguiçadeira [ispregisa'dejra] F deck chair; (*com lugar para as pernas*) lounger

espreguiçar-se [ispregi'sarsi] VR to stretch
espreita [is'prejta] F: **ficar à ~** to keep watch
espreitar [isprej'tar] VT (*espiar*) to spy on; (*observar*) to observe, watch
espremedor [ispreme'dor] M squeezer
espremer [ispre'mer] VT (*fruta*) to squeeze; (*roupa molhada*) to wring out; (*pessoas*) to squash; **espremer-se** VR (*multidão*) to be squashed together; (*uma pessoa*) to squash up
espuma [is'puma] F foam; (*de cerveja*) froth, head; (*de sabão*) lather; (*de ondas*) surf; **colchão de ~** foam mattress; **~ de borracha** foam rubber
espumante [ispu'mãtʃi] ADJ frothy, foamy; (*vinho*) sparkling
espumar [ispu'mar] VI to foam; (*fera, cachorro*) to foam at the mouth
espúrio, -a [is'purju, a] ADJ spurious, bogus
esputinique [isputʃi'niki] M satellite, sputnik
esq. ABR (= *esquerdo*) l.; = **esquina**
esq° ABR = **esquerdo**
esquadra [is'kwadra] F (*Náut*) fleet; (PT: *da polícia*) police station
esquadrão [iskwa'drãw] (*pl* -**ões**) M squadron
esquadrilha [iskwa'driʎa] F squadron
esquadrinhar [iskwadri'ɲar] VT (*casa, área*) to search, scour; (*fatos*) to scrutinize
esquadro [is'kwadru] M set square
esquadrões [iskwa'drõjs] MPL *de* **esquadrão**
esqualidez [iskwali'des] F squalor
esquálido, -a [is'kwalidu, a] ADJ squalid, filthy
esquartejar [iskwarte'ʒar] VT to quarter
esquecer [iske'ser] VT, VI to forget; **esquecer-se** VR: **~-se de** to forget; **~-se de fazer algo** to forget to do sth; **~-se (de) que ...** to forget that ...
esquecido, -a [iske'sidu, a] ADJ forgotten; (*pessoa*) forgetful
esquecimento [iskesi'mẽtu] M (*falta de memória*) forgetfulness; (*olvido*) oblivion; **cair no ~** to fall into oblivion
esquelético, -a [iske'lɛtʃiku, a] ADJ (*Anat*) skeletal; (*pessoa*) scrawny
esqueleto [iske'letu] M skeleton; (*arcabouço*) framework; **ser um ~** (*fig: pessoa*) to be just skin and bone
esquema [is'kema] M (*resumo*) outline; (*plano*) scheme; (*diagrama*) diagram, plan; **~ de segurança** security operation
esquemático, -a [iske'matʃiku, a] ADJ schematic
esquematizar [iskematʃi'zar] VT to represent schematically; (*planejar*) to plan
esquentado, -a [iskẽ'tadu, a] ADJ (*fig: irritado*) annoyed; (: *irritadiço*) irritable
esquentar [iskẽ'tar] VT to heat (up), warm (up); (*fig: irritar*) to annoy ▶ VI to warm up; (*casaco*) to be warm; **esquentar-se** VR to get annoyed; **~ a cabeça** (*col*) to get worked up; **não esquenta!** don't worry!
esquerda [is'kerda] F (*tb Pol*) left; **à ~** on the left; **dobrar à ~** to turn left; **políticos de ~**

left-wing politicians; **a ~ festiva** the trendy left
esquerdista [isker'dʒista] ADJ left-wing ▶ M/F left-winger
esquerdo, -a [is'kerdu, a] ADJ left
esquete [is'ketʃi] M (*Teatro, TV*) sketch
esqui [is'ki] M (*patim*) ski; (*esporte*) skiing; **~ aquático** water skiing; **fazer ~** to go skiing
esquiador, a [iskja'dor(a)] M/F skier
esquiar [is'kjar] VI to ski
esquilo [is'kilu] M squirrel
esquina [is'kina] F corner; **fazer ~ com** to join
esquisitão, -ona [iskizi'tãw, ɔna] (*pl* -**ões/-s**) ADJ odd, peculiar
esquisitice [iskizi'tʃisi] F oddity, peculiarity; (*ato, dito*) strange thing
esquisito, -a [iski'zitu, a] ADJ strange, odd
esquisitões [iskizi'tõjs] MPL *de* **esquisitão**
esquisitona [iskizi'tɔna] F *de* **esquisitão**
esquiva [is'kiva] F dodge
esquivar-se [iski'varsi] VR: **~ de** to escape from, get away from; (*deveres*) to get out of
esquivo, -a [is'kivu, a] ADJ aloof, standoffish
esquizofrenia [iskizofre'nia] F schizophrenia
esquizofrênico, -a [iskizo'freniku, a] ADJ, M/F schizophrenic
essa ['esa] PRON: **~ é/foi boa** that is/was a good one; **~ não, sem ~** come off it!; **vamos n~** let's go!; **ainda mais ~!** that's all I need!; **corta ~!** cut it out!; **gostei d~** I like that; **estou n~** count me in, I'm game; **por ~s e outras** for these and other reasons; **~ de fazer ...** this business of doing ...
esse ['esi] ADJ (*sg*) that; (*pl*) those; (BR: *este: sg*) this; (: *pl*) these ▶ PRON (*sg*) that one; (*pl*) those (ones); (BR: *este: sg*) this one; (: *pl*) these (ones)
essência [e'sẽsja] F essence
essencial [esẽ'sjaw] (*pl* -**ais**) ADJ essential; (*principal*) main ▶ M: **o ~** the main thing
Est. ABR (= *Estação*) Stn.; (= *Estrada*) Rd
esta ['esta] F *de* **este²**
estabanado, -a [istaba'nadu, a] ADJ clumsy
estabelecer [istabele'ser] VT to establish; (*fundar*) to set up; **estabelecer-se** VR to establish o.s., set o.s. up; **estabeleceu-se que ...** it was established that ...; **o governo estabeleceu que ...** the government decided that ...
estabelecimento [istabelesi'mẽtu] M establishment; (*casa comercial*) business
estabilidade [istabili'dadʒi] F stability
estabilização [istabiliza'sãw] F stabilization
estabilizar [istabili'zar] VT to stabilize; **estabilizar-se** VR to stabilize
estábulo [is'tabulu] M cow-shed
estaca [is'taka] F post, stake; (*de barraca*) peg; **voltar à ~ zero** to go back to square one
estacada [ista'kada] F (*defensiva*) stockade; (*fileira de estacas*) fencing

estação [ista'sãw] (pl -**ões**) F station; (do ano) season; ~ **de águas** spa; ~ **balneária** seaside resort; ~ **emissora** broadcasting station

estacar [ista'kar] VT to prop up ▶ VI to stop short, halt

estacionamento [istasjona'mẽtu] M (ato) parking; (lugar) car park (BRIT), parking lot (US)

estacionar [istasjo'nar] VT to park ▶ VI to park; (não mover) to remain stationary

estacionário, -a [istasjo'narju, a] ADJ (veículo) stationary; (Com) slack

estações [ista'sõjs] FPL de **estação**

estada [is'tada] F stay

estadia [ista'dʒia] F = **estada**

estádio [is'tadʒu] M stadium

estadista [ista'dʒista] M/F statesman/woman

estado [i'stadu] M state; **E~s Unidos (da América)** United States (of America), USA; ~ **civil** marital status; ~ **de espírito** state of mind; ~ **de saúde** condition; ~ **maior** staff; **em bom** ~ in good condition; **estar em ~ interessante** to be expecting; **estar em ~ de fazer** to be in a position to do

estadual [ista'dwaw] (pl -**ais**) ADJ state atr

estadunidense [istaduni'dẽsi] ADJ (North) American, US atr

estafa [is'tafa] F fatigue; (esgotamento) nervous exhaustion

estafante [ista'fãtʃi] ADJ exhausting

estafar [ista'far] VT to tire out, fatigue; **estafar-se** VR to tire o.s. out

estafermo [ista'fermu] (PT) M scarecrow; (col) nincompoop

estagiar [ista'ʒjar] VI (empregado) to work as a trainee, do a traineeship; (estudante) to work as an intern, do an internship

estagiário, -a [ista'ʒjarju, a] M/F (empregado) trainee; (estudante) intern; (professor) student teacher; (médico) junior doctor

estágio [is'taʒu] M (aprendizado: de empregado) traineeship; (: de estudante) internship; (fase) stage

estagnação [istagna'sãw] F stagnation

estagnado, -a [istag'nadu, a] ADJ stagnant

estagnar [istag'nar] VT to make stagnant; (país) to bring to a standstill ▶ VI to stagnate; **estagnar-se** VR to stagnate

estalagem [ista'laʒẽ] (pl -**ns**) F inn

estalar [ista'lar] VT (quebrar) to break; (os dedos) to snap ▶ VI (fender-se) to split, crack; (crepitar) to crackle; **estou estalando de dor de cabeça** I've got a splitting headache

estaleiro [ista'lejru] M shipyard

estalido [ista'lidu] M pop

estalo [is'talu] M (do chicote) crack; (dos dedos) snap; (dos lábios) smack; (de foguete) bang; ~ **de trovão** thunderclap; **de** ~ suddenly; **me deu um** ~ it clicked, the penny dropped

estampa [is'tãpa] F (figura impressa) print; (ilustração) picture; **ter uma bela** ~ (fig) to be beautiful

estampado, -a [istã'padu, a] ADJ printed ▶ M (tecido) print; (num tecido) pattern; **sua angústia estava estampada no rosto** his anxiety was written on his face

estampar [istã'par] VT (imprimir) to print; (marcar) to stamp

estamparia [istãpa'ria] F (oficina) print shop; (tecido, figura) print

estampido [istã'pidu] M bang

estancar [istã'kar] VT (sangue, água) to staunch; (fazer cessar) to stop; **estancar-se** VR (parar) to stop

estância [is'tãsja] F (fazenda) ranch, farm; (versos) stanza; ~ **hidromineral** spa resort

estandardizar [istãdardʒi'zar] VT to standardize

estandarte [istã'dartʃi] M standard, banner

estande [is'tãdʒi] M stand

estanho [is'taɲu] M (metal) tin

estanque [is'tãki] ADJ watertight

estante [is'tãtʃi] F (armário) bookcase; (suporte) stand

estapafúrdio, -a [istapa'furdʒu, a] ADJ outlandish, odd

(PALAVRA-CHAVE)

estar [is'tar] VI **1** (lugar) to be; (em casa) to be in; (no telefone): **a Lúcia está? — não, ela não está** is Lúcia there? — no, she's not in

2 (estado) to be; **estar doente** to be ill; **estar bem** (de saúde) to be well; (financeiramente) to be well off; **estar calor/frio** to be hot/cold; **estar com fome/sede/medo** to be hungry/thirsty/afraid

3 (ação contínua): **estar fazendo** (BR) ou **a fazer** (PT) to be doing

4 (+ pp: como adj): **estar sentado/cansado** to be sitting down/tired

5 (+ pp: uso passivo): **está condenado à morte** he's been condemned to death; **o livro está emprestado** the book's been borrowed

6: **estar de férias/licença** to be on holiday (BRIT) ou vacation (US)/leave; **ela estava de chapéu** she had a hat on, she was wearing a hat

7: **estar para fazer** to be about to do; **ele está para chegar a qualquer momento** he'll be here any minute; **não estar para conversas** not to be in the mood for talking

8: **estar por fazer** to be still to be done

9: **estar sem dinheiro** to have no money; **estar sem dormir** not to have slept; **estou sem dormir há três dias** I haven't slept for three days; **está sem terminar** it isn't finished yet

10 (frases): **tá (bem)** (col) OK; **estar bem com** to be on good terms with

estardalhaço [istarda'ʎasu] M fuss; (ostentação) ostentation

estarrecer [istahe'ser] VT to petrify ▶ VI to be petrified

estas ['ɛstas] FPL de **este²**

estatal [istaˈtaw] (*pl* **-ais**) ADJ nationalized, state-owned ▶ F state-owned company
estatelado, -a [istateˈladu, a] ADJ (*cair*) sprawling
estatelar [istateˈlar] VT to send sprawling; (*estarrecer*) to stun; **estatelar-se** VR (*cair*) to go sprawling
estática [isˈtatʃika] F (*Tec*) static
estático, -a [isˈtatʃiku, a] ADJ static
estatística [istaˈtʃistʃika] F statistic; (*ciência*) statistics *sg*
estatístico, -a [istaˈtʃistʃiku, a] ADJ statistical
estatização [istatʃizaˈsãw] (*pl* **-ões**) F nationalization
estatizar [istatʃiˈzar] VT to nationalize
estátua [isˈtatwa] F statue
estatueta [istaˈtweta] F statuette
estatura [istaˈtura] F stature
estatuto [istaˈtutu] M (*Jur*) statute; (*de cidade*) bye-law; (*de associação*) rule; **~s sociais** *ou* **da empresa** (*Com*) articles of association
estável [isˈtavew] (*pl* **-eis**) ADJ stable
este¹ [ˈɛstʃi] M east ▶ ADJ INV (*região*) eastern; (*vento, direção*) easterly
este², esta [ˈestʃi, ˈɛsta] ADJ (*sg*) this; (*pl*) these ▶ PRON this one; (*pl*) these; (*a quem/que se referiu por último*) the latter; **esta noite** (*noite passada*) last night; (*noite de hoje*) tonight
esteio [isˈteju] M prop, support; (*Náut*) stay
esteira [isˈtejra] F mat; (*de navio*) wake; (*rumo*) path
esteja *etc* [isˈteʒa] VB *ver* **estar**
estelionato [isteljoˈnatu] M fraud
estêncil [isˈtēsiw] (*pl* **-eis**) M stencil
estender [istēˈder] VT to extend; (*mapa*) to spread out; (*pernas*) to stretch; (*massa*) to roll out; (*conversa*) to draw out; (*corda*) to pull tight; (*roupa molhada*) to hang out; **estender-se** VR (*no chão*) to lie down; (*fila, terreno*) to stretch, extend; **~-se sobre algo** to dwell on sth, expand on sth; **esta lei estende-se a todos** this law applies to all; **o conferencista estendeu-se demais** the speaker went on too long; **~ a mão** to hold out one's hand; **~ uma cadeira para alguém** to offer sb a chair; **~ uma crítica a todos** to extend a criticism to everyone
estenodatilógrafo, -a [istenodatʃiˈlɔgrafu, a] M/F shorthand typist (*BRIT*), stenographer (*US*)
estenografar [istenograˈfar] VT to write in shorthand
estenografia [istenograˈfia] F shorthand
estepe [isˈtɛpi] M spare wheel
esterco [isˈterku] M manure, dung
estéreis [isˈterejs] ADJ PL *de* **estéril**
estereo... [isterju] PREFIXO stereo...
estereofônico, -a [isterjoˈfoniku, a] ADJ stereo(phonic)
estereotipado, -a [isterjotʃiˈpadu, a] ADJ stereotypical
estereotipar [isterjotʃiˈpar] VT to stereotype
estereótipo [isteˈrjɔtʃipu] M stereotype

estéril [isˈtɛriw] (*pl* **-eis**) ADJ sterile; (*terra*) infertile; (*fig*) futile
esterilidade [isteriliˈdadʒi] F sterility; (*de terra*) infertility; (*escassez*) dearth
esterilização [isterilizaˈsãw] F sterilization
esterilizar [isteriliˈzar] VT to sterilize
esterlino, -a [isterˈlinu, a] ADJ sterling ▶ M sterling; **libra esterlina** pound sterling
esteroide [isteˈrɔjdʒi] M steroid
esteta [isˈtɛta] M/F aesthete (*BRIT*), esthete (*US*)
estética [isˈtɛtʃika] F aesthetics *sg* (*BRIT*), esthetics *sg* (*US*)
esteticista [istetʃiˈsista] M/F beautician
estético, -a [isˈtɛtʃiku, a] ADJ aesthetic (*BRIT*), esthetic (*US*)
estetoscópio [istetoˈskɔpju] M stethoscope
esteve [isˈtevi] VB *ver* **estar**
estiagem [isˈtʃjaʒē] (*pl* **-ns**) F (*depois da chuva*) calm after the storm; (*falta de chuva*) dry spell
estiar [isˈtʃjar] VI (*não chover*) to stop raining; (*o tempo*) to clear up
estibordo [istʃiˈbɔrdu] M starboard
esticada [istʃiˈkada] F: **dar uma ~** (*esticar-se*) to stretch, have a stretch; **dar uma ~ numa boate** (*col*) to go on to a nightclub
esticar [istʃiˈkar] VT (*uma corda*) to stretch, tighten; (*a perna*) to stretch; **esticar-se** VR to stretch out; **~ as canelas** (*col*) to pop one's clogs, kick the bucket; **depois da festa esticamos numa boate** (*col*) after the party we went on to a nightclub
estigma [isˈtʃigima] M (*marca*) mark, scar; (*fig*) stigma
estigmatizar [istʃigimatʃiˈzar] VT to brand; **~ alguém de algo** to brand sb (as) sth
estilhaçar [istʃiʎaˈsar] VT to splinter; (*despedaçar*) to shatter; **estilhaçar-se** VR to shatter
estilhaço [istʃiˈʎasu] M fragment; (*de pedra*) chip; (*de madeira, metal*) splinter
estilista [istʃiˈlista] M/F stylist; (*de moda*) designer
estilística [istʃiˈlistʃika] F stylistics *sg*
estilístico, -a [istʃiˈlistʃiku, a] ADJ stylistic
estilizar [istʃiliˈzar] VT to stylize
estilo [isˈtʃilu] M style; (*Tec*) stylus; **~ de vida** way of life; **móveis de ~** stylish furniture; **o vestido não é do meu ~** *ou* **não faz o meu ~** the dress isn't my style
estima [isˈtʃima] F esteem; (*afeto*) affection; **ter ~ a** to have a high regard for
estimação [istʃimaˈsãw] F: **... de ~** favourite (*BRIT*) ..., favorite (*US*) ...
estimado, -a [istʃiˈmadu, a] ADJ respected; (*em cartas*): **E~ Senhor** Dear Sir
estimar [istʃiˈmar] VT (*apreciar*) to appreciate; (*avaliar*) to value; (*ter estima a*) to have a high regard for; (*calcular aproximadamente*) to estimate; **estimar-se** VR: **eles se estimam muito** they have a high regard for one another; **estima-se o número de ouvintes em 3 milhões** the number of listeners is estimated to be 3 million; **~ em** (*avaliar*) to

value at; (*população*) to estimate to be; **estimo que você tenha exito** I wish you success

estimativa [istʃima'tʃiva] F estimate; **fazer uma ~ de algo** to estimate sth; **~ de custo** estimate, costing

estimável [istʃi'mavew] (*pl* **-eis**) ADJ (*digno de estima*) decent; **prejuízo ~ em 3 milhões** loss estimated at 3 million

estimulação [istʃimula'sãw] F stimulation

estimulante [istʃimu'lãtʃi] ADJ stimulating ▶ M stimulant

estimular [istʃimu'lar] VT to stimulate; (*incentivar*) to encourage; **~ alguém a fazer algo** to encourage sb to do sth

estímulo [is'tʃimulu] M stimulus; (*ânimo*) encouragement; **falta de ~** lack of incentive; **ele não tem ~ para nada no momento** he has got no incentive to do anything at the moment

estio [is'tʃiu] M summer

estipêndio [istʃi'pẽdʒu] M pay

estipulação [istʃipula'sãw] (*pl* **-ões**) F stipulation, condition

estipular [istʃipu'lar] VT to stipulate

estirar [istʃi'rar] VT to stretch (out); **estirar-se** VR to stretch

estirpe [is'tʃirpi] F stock, lineage

estivador, a [istʃiva'dor(a)] M/F docker

estive *etc* [is'tʃivi] VB *ver* **estar**

estocada [isto'kada] F stab, thrust

estocado, -a [isto'kadu, a] ADJ (*Com*) in stock

estocagem [isto'kaʒẽ] F (*estocar*) stockpiling; (*estoque*) stock

estocar [isto'kar] VT to stock

Estocolmo [isto'kɔwmu] N Stockholm

estofador, a [istofa'dor(a)] M/F upholsterer

estofar [isto'far] VT to upholster; (*acolchoar*) to pad, stuff

estofo [is'tofu] M (*tecido*) material; (*para acolchoar*) padding, stuffing

estoico, -a [is'tɔjku, a] ADJ stoic(al) ▶ M/F stoic

estojo [is'toʒu] M case; **~ de ferramentas** tool kit; **~ de óculos** glasses case; **~ de tintas** paintbox; **~ de unhas** manicure set

estola [is'tɔla] F stole

estólido, -a [is'tɔlidu, a] ADJ stupid

estômago [is'tomagu] M stomach; **ter ~ para (fazer) algo** to be up to (doing) sth; **estar com o ~ embrulhado** to have an upset stomach; **forrar o ~** to have a little bite to eat

Estônia [is'tonja] F: **a ~** Estonia

estoniano, -a [isto'njanu, a] ADJ, M/F Estonian

estonteante [istõ'tʃjãtʃi] ADJ stunning

estontear [istõ'tʃjar] VT to stun, daze

estoque [is'tɔki] M (*Com*) stock; **em ~** in stock

estore [is'tɔri] M blind

estória [is'tɔrja] F story

estorninho [istor'ninu] M starling

estorricar [istohi'kar] VT, VI = **esturricar**

estorvar [istor'var] VT to hinder, obstruct; (*fig: importunar*) to bother, disturb; **~ alguém de fazer** to prevent sb from doing

estorvo [is'torvu] M hindrance, obstacle; (*amolação*) bother, nuisance

estourado, -a [isto'radu, a] ADJ (*temperamental*) explosive; (*col: cansado*) knackered, worn out

estoura-peito [istora'-] (*pl* **estoura-peitos**) (*col*) M strong cigarette

estourar [isto'rar] VI to explode; (*pneu*) to burst; (*escândalo*) to blow up; (*guerra*) to break out; (*BR: chegar*) to turn up, arrive; **~ (com alguém)** (*zangar-se*) to blow up (at sb); **estou estourando de dor de cabeça** I've got a splitting headache; **eu devo chegar às 9.oo, estourando, 9 e meia** I should get there at 9 o'clock, or 9.30 at the latest

estouro [is'toru] M explosion; **ser um ~** (*col*) to be great; **dar o ~** (*fig: zangar-se*) to blow up, blow one's top

estouvado, -a [isto'vadu, a] ADJ rash, foolhardy

estrábico, -a [is'trabiku, a] ADJ cross-eyed

estrabismo [istra'bizmu] M squint

estraçalhar [istrasa'ʎar] VT (*livro, objeto*) to pull to pieces; (*pessoa*) to tear to pieces; **estraçalhar-se** VR to mutilate one another

estrada [is'trada] F road; **~ de contorno** ring road (BRIT), beltway (US); **~ de ferro** (BR) railway (BRIT), railroad (US); **~ de terra** dirt road; **~ principal** main road (BRIT), state highway (US); **~ secundária** minor road

estrado [is'tradu] M (*tablado*) platform; (*de cama*) base

estragado, -a [istra'gadu, a] ADJ ruined, wrecked; (*saúde*) ruined; (*fruta*) rotten; (*muito mimado*) spoiled, spoilt (BRIT)

estragão [istra'gãw] M tarragon

estraga-prazeres [istraga-] M/F INV spoilsport

estragar [istra'gar] VT to spoil; (*arruinar*) to ruin, wreck; (*desperdiçar*) to waste; (*saúde*) to damage; (*mimar*) to spoil

estrago [is'tragu] M (*destruição*) destruction; (*desperdício*) waste; (*dano*) damage; **os ~s da guerra** the ravages of war

estrangeiro, -a [istrã'ʒejru, a] ADJ foreign ▶ M/F foreigner; **no ~** abroad

estrangulação [istrãgula'sãw] F strangulation

estrangulador [istrãgula'dor] M strangler

estrangular [istrãgu'lar] VT to strangle; **esta suéter está me estrangulando** this sweater is too tight for me

estranhar [istra'ɲar] VT (*surpreender-se de*) to be surprised at; (*achar estranho*): **~ algo** to find sth strange; **estranhei o clima** the climate did not agree with me; **minha filha estranhou a visita/a cama nova** my daughter was shy with the visitor/found it hard to get used to the new bed; **não é de se ~** it's not surprising; **você não quer um**

chocolate? — **estou te estranhando** you don't want a chocolate? — that's not like you

estranho, -a [is'traɲu, a] ADJ strange, odd; (*influências*) outside ▶ M/F (*desconhecido*) stranger; (*de fora*) outsider; **o nome não me é ~** the name rings a bell

Estrasburgo [istraz'burgu] N Strasbourg

estratagema [istrata'ʒema] M (*Mil*) stratagem; (*ardil*) trick

estratégia [istra'tɛʒa] F strategy

estratégico, -a [istra'tɛʒiku, a] ADJ strategic

estratificar-se [istratʃifiʃi'karsi] VR (*fig: ideias, opiniões*) to become entrenched

estrato [is'tratu] M layer, stratum

estratosfera [istratos'fɛra] F stratosphere

estreante [is'trjãtʃi] ADJ new ▶ M/F newcomer

estrear [is'trjar] VT (*vestido*) to wear for the first time; (*peça de teatro*) to perform for the first time; (*veículo*) to use for the first time; (*filme*) to show for the first time, première; (*iniciar*): **~ uma carreira** to embark on *ou* begin a career ▶ VI (*ator, jogador*) to make one's first appearance; (*filme, peça*) to open

estrebaria [istreba'ria] F stable

estrebuchar [istrebu'ʃar] VI to struggle; (*ao morrer*) to shake (in death throes)

estreia [is'treja] F (*de artista*) debut; (*de uma peça*) first night; (*de um filme*) première, opening; **é a ~ do meu carro** it's the first time I've used my car

estreitamento [istrejta'mẽtu] M (*diminuição*) narrowing; (*aperto*) tightening; (*de relações*) strengthening

estreitar [istrej'tar] VT (*reduzir*) to narrow; (*roupa*) to take in; (*abraçar*) to hug; (*laços de amizade*) to strengthen ▶ VI (*estrada*) to narrow; **estreitar-se** VR (*laços de amizade*) to deepen

estreiteza [istrej'teza] F narrowness; (*de regulamento*) strictness; **~ de pontos de vista** narrow-mindedness

estreito, -a [is'trejtu, a] ADJ narrow; (*saia*) straight; (*vínculo, relação*) close; (*medida*) strict ▶ M strait; **ter convivência estreita com alguém** to live at close quarters with sb

estrela [is'trela] F star; **~ cadente** falling star; **~ de cinema** film (BRIT) *ou* movie (US) star; **ter boa ~** to be lucky

estrelado, -a [istre'ladu, a] ADJ (*céu*) starry; (*ovo*) fried; **um filme ~ por Marilyn Monroe** a film starring Marilyn Monroe

estrela-do-mar (*pl* **estrelas-do-mar**) F starfish

estrelar [istre'lar] VT (PT: *ovos*) to fry; (*filme, peça*) to star in; **estrelar-se** VR (*céu*) to fill with stars

estrelato [istre'latu] M: **o ~** stardom

estrelinha [istre'liɲa] F (*fogo de artifício*) sparkler

estrelismo [istre'lizmu] M star quality

estremadura [istrema'dura] F frontier

estremecer [istreme'ser] VT (*sacudir*) to shake; (*amizade*) to strain; (*fazer tremer*): **~ alguém** to make sb shudder ▶ VI (*vibrar*) to shake; (*tremer*) to tremble; (*horrorizar-se*) to shudder; (*amizade*) to be strained; **ela estremeceu de susto, o susto estremeceu-a** the fright made her jump

estremecido, -a [istreme'sidu, a] ADJ (*sacudido*) shaken; (*sobressaltado*) startled; (*amizade*) strained

estremecimento [istremesi'mẽtu] M (*sacudida*) shaking, trembling; (*tremor*) tremor; (*numa amizade*) tension

estremunhado, -a [istremu'ɲadu, a] ADJ half-asleep

estrepar-se [istre'parsi] VR (*fig*) to come unstuck

estrepe [is'trɛpi] (*col*) M (*mulher*) dog

estrépito [is'trɛpitu] M din, racket; **com ~** with a lot of noise, noisily; **fazer ~** to make a din

estrepitoso, -a [istrepitozu, ɔza] ADJ noisy, rowdy; (*fig*) sensational

estressante [istre'sãtʃi] ADJ stressful

estressar [istre'sar] VT to stress

estresse [is'tresi] M stress

estria [is'tria] F groove; (*na pele*) stretch mark

estribar [istri'bar] VT to base; **estribar-se** VR: **~-se em** to be based on

estribeira [istri'bejra] F: **perder as ~s** (*col*) to fly off the handle, lose one's temper

estribilho [istri'biʎu] M (*Mús*) chorus

estribo [is'tribu] M (*de cavalo*) stirrup; (*degrau*) step; (*fig: apoio*) support

estricnina [istrik'nina] F strychnine

estridente [istri'dẽtʃi] ADJ shrill, piercing

estrilar [istri'lar] (*col*) VI (*zangar-se*) to get mad; (*reclamar*) to moan

estrilo [is'trilu] M: **dar um ~** to blow one's top

estripulia [istripu'lia] F prank

estrito, -a [is'tritu, a] ADJ (*rigoroso*) strict; (*restrito*) restricted; **no sentido ~ da palavra** in the strict sense of the word

estrofe [is'trɔfi] F stanza

estrogonofe [istrogo'nɔfi] M (*Culin*) stroganoff

estrompado, -a [istrõ'padu, a] ADJ worn out; (*pessoa*) exhausted

estrondar [istrõ'dar] VI to boom; (*fig*) to resound

estrondo [is'trõdu] M (*de trovão*) rumble; (*de armas*) din; **~ sônico** sonic boom

estrondoso, -a [istrõ'dozu, ɔza] ADJ (*ovação*) tumultuous, thunderous; (*sucesso*) resounding; (*notícia*) sensational

estropiar [istro'pjar] VT (*aleijar*) to maim, cripple; (*fatigar*) to wear out, exhaust; (*texto*) to mutilate; (*pronunciar mal*) to mispronounce

estrumar [istru'mar] VT to spread manure on

estrume [is'trumi] M manure

estrutura [istru'tura] F structure; (*armação*) framework; (*de edifício*) fabric

estrutural [istrutu'raw] (*pl* **-ais**) ADJ structural

estruturalismo [istrutura'lizmu] M structuralism

estruturar [istrutu'rar] VT to structure

estuário [istu'arju] M estuary

estudado, -a [istu'dadu, a] ADJ (*fig*) studied, affected

estudantada [istudã'tada] F students *pl*

estudante [istu'dãtʃi] M/F student

estudantil [istudã'tʃiw] (*pl* **-is**) ADJ student *atr*

estudar [istu'dar] VT, VI to study

estúdio [is'tudʒu] M studio

estudioso, -a [istudʒozu, ɔza] ADJ studious ▶ M/F student

estudo [is'tudu] M study; **~ de caso** case study; **~ de viabilidade** feasibility study

estufa [is'tufa] F (*fogão*) stove; (*de plantas*) greenhouse; (*de fogão*) plate warmer; **efeito ~** greenhouse effect; **este quarto é uma ~** this room is like an oven

estufado [istu'fadu] (PT) M stew

estufar [istu'far] VT (*peito*) to puff up; (*almofada*) to stuff

estulto, -a [is'tuwtu, a] ADJ foolish, silly

estupefação [istupefa'sãw] F amazement, astonishment

estupefato, -a [istupe'fatu, a], (PT) **estupefacto** ADJ dumbfounded; **ele me olhou ~** he looked at me in astonishment

estupendo, -a [istu'pẽdu, a] ADJ wonderful; (*col*) fantastic, terrific

estupidamente [istupida'mẽtʃi] ADV stupidly; **uma cerveja ~ gelada** (*col*) an ice-cold beer

estupidez [istupi'dez] F stupidity; (*ato, dito*) stupid thing; (*grosseria*) rudeness; **que ~!** what a stupid thing to do! (*ou* to say!)

estúpido, -a [is'tupidu, a] ADJ stupid; (*grosseiro*) rude, churlish ▶ M/F idiot; (*grosseiro*) oaf; **calor ~** incredible heat

estupor [istu'por] M stupor; (*fig: pessoa de mau caráter*) bad lot; (: *pessoa feia*) fright

estuporado, -a [istupo'radu, a] ADJ (*estragado*) ruined; (*cansado*) tired out; (*ferido*) seriously injured

estuporar-se [istupo'rarsi] (*col*) VR (*num acidente*) to be seriously injured

estuprador [istupra'dor] M rapist

estuprar [istu'prar] VT to rape

estupro [is'tupru] M rape

estuque [is'tuki] M stucco; (*massa*) plaster

esturricado, -a [istuhi'kadu, a] ADJ (*seco*) shrivelled, dried out; (*roupa*) skimpy, tight

esturricar [istuhi'kar] VT, VI to shrivel, dry out

esvaecer-se [izvaje'sersi] VR to fade away, vanish

esvair-se [izva'jirsi] VR to vanish, disappear; **~ em sangue** to lose a lot of blood

esvaziamento [izvazja'mẽtu] M emptying

esvaziar [izva'zjar] VT to empty; **esvaziar-se** VR to empty

esverdeado, -a [izver'dʒjado, a] ADJ greenish

esvoaçante [izvwa'sãtʃi] ADJ billowing

esvoaçar [izvoa'sar] VI to flutter

ETA ['eta] ABR M (= *Euskadi Ta Askatasuna*) ETA

eta ['eta] (*col*) EXCL: **~ filme chato!** what a boring film!; **~ ferro!** gosh!

etapa [e'tapa] F (*fase*) stage; **por ~s** in stages

etário, -a [e'tarju, a] ADJ age *atr*

etc. ABR (= *et cetera*) etc

éter ['eter] M ether

eternidade [eterni'dadʒi] F eternity

eternizar [eterni'zar] VT (*fazer eterno*) to make eternal; (*nome, pessoa*) to immortalize; (*discussão, processo*) to drag out; **eternizar-se** VR to be immortalized; to drag on

eterno, -a [e'ternu, a] ADJ eternal

ética ['ɛtʃika] F ethics *pl*

ético, -a ['ɛtʃiku, a] ADJ ethical

etimologia [etʃimolo'ʒia] F etymology

etíope [e'tʃiopi] ADJ, M/F Ethiopian

Etiópia [e'tʃjɔpja] F: **a ~** Ethiopia

etiqueta [etʃi'keta] F (*maneiras*) etiquette; (*rótulo, em roupa*) label; (*que se amarra*) tag; **~ adesiva** adhesive *ou* stick-on label

etiquetar [etʃike'tar] VT to label

étnico, -a ['ɛtʃniku, a] ADJ ethnic

etnocêntrico, -a [etʃno'sẽtriku, a] ADJ ethnocentric

etnografia [etʃnogra'fia] F ethnography

etnologia [etʃnolo'ʒia] F ethnology

etos ['ɛtus] M INV ethos

eu [ew] PRON I ▶ M self; **sou eu** it's me; **eu mesmo** I myself; **eu, hein?** I don't know ... (how strange!)

EUA ABR MPL (= *Estados Unidos da América*) USA; **nos ~** in the USA

eucalipto [ewka'liptu] M eucalyptus

eucaristia [ewkaris'tʃia] F Holy Communion

eufemismo [ewfe'mizmu] M euphemism

eufonia [ewfo'nia] F euphony

euforia [ewfo'ria] F euphoria

eunuco [ew'nuku] M eunuch

euro ['ewru] M (*moeda*) euro

Europa [ew'rɔpa] F: **a ~** Europe

europeia [euro'pɛja] F *de* **europeu**

europeizar [ewropeji'zar] VT to Europeanize; **europeizar-se** VR to become Europeanized

europeu, -peia [ewro'peu, 'pɛja] ADJ, M/F European

eutanásia [ewta'nazja] F euthanasia

evacuação [evakwa'sãw] (*pl* **-ões**) F evacuation

evacuar [eva'kwar] VT to evacuate; (*sair de*) to leave; (*Med*) to discharge ▶ VI to defecate

evadir [eva'dʒir] VT to evade; (*col*) to dodge; **evadir-se** VR to escape

evanescente [evane'sẽtʃi] ADJ fading, vanishing

evangelho [evã'ʒeʎu] M gospel

evangélico, -a [evã'ʒɛliku, a] ADJ evangelical ▶ M/F born-again Christian

evaporação [evapora'sãw] F evaporation

evaporar [evapo'rar] VT, VI to evaporate; **evaporar-se** VR to evaporate; (*desaparecer*) to vanish

evasão [eva'zãw] (*pl* **-ões**) F escape, flight; (*fig*) evasion; **~ de impostos** tax avoidance

evasê [eva'ze] ADJ (*saia*) flared

evasiva [eva'ziva] F excuse

evasivo, -a [eva'zivu, a] ADJ evasive

evasões [eva'zõjs] FPL *de* **evasão**

evento [e'vẽtu] M (*acontecimento*) event; (*eventualidade*) eventuality

eventual [evẽ'tuaw] (*pl* **-ais**) ADJ fortuitous, accidental

eventualidade [evẽtwali'dadʒi] F eventuality

evicção [evik'sãw] (*pl* **-ões**) F (*Jur*) eviction

evidência [evi'dẽsja] F evidence, proof

evidenciar [evidẽ'sjar] VT (*comprovar*) to prove; (*mostrar*) to show; **evidenciar-se** VR to be evident, be obvious

evidente [evi'dẽtʃi] ADJ obvious, evident

evitar [evi'tar] VT to avoid; **~ de fazer algo** to avoid doing sth

evitável [evi'tavew] (*pl* **-eis**) ADJ avoidable

evocação [evoka'sãw] (*pl* **-ões**) F evocation; (*de espíritos*) invocation

evocar [evo'kar] VT to evoke; (*espíritos*) to invoke

evolução [evolu'sãw] (*pl* **-ões**) F (*desenvolvimento*) development; (*Mil*) manoeuvre (BRIT), maneuver (US); (*movimento*) movement; (*Bio*) evolution

evoluído, -a [evo'lwidu, a] ADJ advanced; (*pessoa*) broad-minded

evoluir [evo'lwir] VI to evolve; **~ para** to evolve into; **ela não evoluiu com os tempos** she hasn't moved with the times

ex- [es-, ez-] PREFIXO ex-, former

Ex.ª ABR = **excelência**

exacerbação [ezaserba'sãw] F worsening; (*exasperação*) irritation

exacerbante [ezaser'bãtʃi] ADJ exacerbating

exacerbar [ezaser'bar] VT (*irritar*) to irritate, annoy; (*agravar*) to aggravate, worsen; (*revolta, indignação*) to deepen

exagerado, -a [ezaʒe'radu, a] ADJ (*relato*) exaggerated; (*maquilagem etc*) overdone; (*pessoa*): **ele é ~** (*na maneira de falar*) he exaggerates; (*nos gestos*) he overdoes it *ou* things

exagerar [ezaʒe'rar] VT to exaggerate ▶ VI to exaggerate; (*agir com exagero*) to overdo it

exagero [eza'ʒeru] M exaggeration

exalações [ezala'zõjs] FPL fumes

exalar [eza'lar] VT (*odor*) to give off

exaltação [ezawta'sãw] F (*de virtudes etc*) exaltation; (*excitamento*) excitement; (*irritação*) annoyance

exaltado, -a [ezaw'tadu, a] ADJ (*fanático*) fanatical; (*apaixonado*) overexcited

exaltar [ezaw'tar] VT (*elevar: pessoa, virtude*) to exalt; (*louvar*) to praise; (*excitar*) to excite; (*irritar*) to annoy; **exaltar-se** VR (*irritar-se*) to get worked up; (*arrebatar-se*) to get carried away

exame [e'zami] M (*Educ*) examination, exam; (*Med etc*) examination; **fazer um ~** (*Educ*) to take an exam; (*Med*) to have an examination; **~ de direção** driving test; **~ de sangue** blood test; **~ médico** medical (examination); **~ vestibular** university entrance exam

examinador, a [ezamina'dor(a)] M/F examiner ▶ ADJ examining

examinando, -a [ezami'nãdu, a] M/F (*exam*) candidate

examinar [ezami'nar] VT to examine

exangue [e'zãgi] ADJ (*sem sangue*) bloodless

exasperação [ezaspera'sãw] F exasperation

exasperador, a [ezaspera'dor(a)] ADJ exasperating

exasperante [ezaspe'rãtʃi] ADJ exasperating

exasperar [ezaspe'rar] VT to exasperate; **exasperar-se** VR to get exasperated

exatidão [ezatʃi'dãw] F (*precisão*) accuracy; (*perfeição*) correctness

exato, -a [e'zatu, a] ADJ (*certo*) right, correct; (*preciso*) exact; **~!** exactly!

exaurir [ezaw'rir] VT to exhaust, drain; **exaurir-se** VR to become exhausted

exaustão [ezaw'stãw] F exhaustion

exaustar [ezaw'star] VT to exhaust, drain; **exaustar-se** VR to become exhausted

exaustivo, -a [ezaw'stʃivu, a] ADJ (*tratado*) exhaustive; (*trabalho*) exhausting

exausto, -a [e'zawstu, a] PP *de* **exaurir** ▶ ADJ exhausted

exaustor [ezaw'stor] M extractor fan

exceção [ese'sãw] (*pl* **-ões**) F exception; **com ~ de** with the exception of; **abrir ~** to make an exception

excecional (PT) ADJ = **excepcional**

exceções [ese'sõjs] FPL *de* **exceção**

excedente [ese'dẽtʃi] ADJ excess; (*Com*) surplus ▶ M (*Com*) surplus; (**aluno**) ~ *pupil who cannot be given a place because the school is full*

exceder [ese'der] VT to exceed; (*superar*) to surpass; **exceder-se** VR (*cometer excessos*) to go too far; (*cansar-se*) to overdo things; **~ em peso/brilho** to outweigh/outshine

excelência [ese'lẽsja] F excellence; **por ~** par excellence; **Vossa E~** Your Excellency

excelente [ese'lẽtʃi] ADJ excellent

excelentíssimo, -a [eselẽ'tʃisimu, a] ADJ SUPERL *de* **excelente**; (*tratamento*) honourable (BRIT), honorable (US)

excelso, -a [e'sewsu, a] ADJ (*sublime*) sublime; (*excelente*) excellent

excentricidade [esẽtrisi'dadʒi] F eccentricity

excêntrico, -a [e'sẽtriku, a] ADJ, M/F eccentric

excepcional [esepsjo'naw] (*pl* **-ais**) ADJ (*extraordinário*) exceptional; (*especial*) special; (*Med*) handicapped

excepcionalidade [esepsjonali'dadʒi] F exceptional nature

excerto [e'sɛrtu] M fragment, excerpt

excessivo, -a [ese'sivu, a] ADJ excessive

excesso [e'sɛsu] M excess; (*Com*) surplus; **em ~** in excess; **~ de peso** excess weight; **~ de velocidade** excessive speed

exceto [e'sɛtu] PREP except (for), apart from

excetuar [ese'twar] VT to except, make an exception of; **todos, excetuando você** everyone except you

excitação [esita'sãw] F excitement

excitado, -a [esi'tadu, a] ADJ excited; (*estimulado*) aroused

excitante [esi'tãtʃi] ADJ exciting

excitar [esi'tar] VT to excite; (*estimular*) to arouse; **excitar-se** VR to get excited

excitável [esi'tavew] (*pl* **-eis**) ADJ excitable

exclamação [isklama'sãw] (*pl* **-ões**) F exclamation

exclamar [iskla'mar] VI to exclaim

exclamativo, -a [isklama'tʃivu, a] ADJ exclamatory; *ver tb* **ponto**

excluir [is'klwir] VT to exclude, leave out; (*eliminar*) to rule out; (*ser incompatível com*) to preclude

exclusão [isklu'zãw] F exclusion

exclusividade [iskluzivi'dadʒi] F exclusiveness; (*Com*) exclusive rights *pl*; **com ~ no "Globo"** only in the "Globo"

exclusivo, -a [isklu'zivu, a] ADJ exclusive; **para uso ~ de** for the sole use of

excluso, -a [is'kluzu, a] ADJ excluded

excomungar [iskomũ'gar] VT to excommunicate

excremento [iskre'mẽtu] M excrement

excruciante [iskru'sjãtʃi] ADJ excruciating

excursão [iskur'sãw] (*pl* **-ões**) F trip, outing; (*em grupo*) excursion; **~ a pé** hike

excursionar [iskursjo'nar] VI to go on a trip; **~ pela Europa** *etc* to tour Europe *etc*

excursionista [iskursjo'nista] M/F tourist; (*para o dia*) day-tripper; (*a pé*) hiker

excursões [iskur'sõjs] FPL *de* **excursão**

execrável [eze'kravew] (*pl* **-eis**) ADJ execrable, deplorable

execução [izeku'sãw] (*pl* **-ões**) F execution; (*de música*) performance; **~ de hipoteca** (*Com*) foreclosure

executante [izeku'tãtʃi] M/F player, performer

executar [ezeku'tar] VT to execute; (*Mús*) to perform; (*plano*) to carry out; (*papel teatral*) to play; **~ uma hipoteca** (*Com*) to foreclose on a mortgage

executivo, -a [izeku'tʃivu, a] ADJ, M/F executive

executor, a [izeku'tor(a)] M/F executioner

exemplar [ezẽ'plar] ADJ exemplary ▶ M model, example; (*Bio*) specimen; (*livro*) copy; (*peça*) piece

exemplificar [ezẽplifi'kar] VT to exemplify

exemplo [e'zẽplu] M example; **por ~** for example; **dar o ~** to set an example; **servir de ~ a alguém** to be an example to sb; **a ~ de** just like; **a ~ do que** just as; **ela é um ~ de bondade** she's a model of kindness

exéquias [e'zɛkjas] FPL funeral rites

exequível [eze'kwivew] (*pl* **-eis**) ADJ feasible

exercer [ezer'ser] VT to exercise; (*influência, pressão*) to exert; (*função*) to perform; (*profissão*) to practise (BRIT), practice (US); (*obrigações*) to carry out

exercício [ezer'sisju] M (*ginástica, Educ*) exercise; (*de medicina*) practice; (*de direitos*) exercising; (*Mil*) drill; (*Com*) financial year; **em ~** (*funcionário*) in office; (*professor etc*) in service; **em pleno ~ de suas faculdades mentais** in full command of one's mental faculties; **~ anterior/corrente** (*Com*) previous/current (financial) year

exercitar [ezersi'tar] VT (*profissão*) to practise (BRIT), practice (US); (*direitos, músculos*) to exercise; (*adestrar*) to train

exército [e'zɛrsitu] M army

exibição [ezibi'sãw] (*pl* **-ões**) F show, display; (*de filme*) showing

exibicionismo [ezibisjo'nizmu] M flamboyance; (*Psico*) exhibitionism

exibicionista [ezibisjo'nista] ADJ flamboyant; (*Psico*) exhibitionist ▶ M/F flamboyant character; exhibitionist

exibições [ezibi'sõjs] FPL *de* **exibição**

exibido, -a [ezi'bidu, a] ADJ (*exibicionista*) flamboyant ▶ M/F show-off

exibidor, a [ezibi'dor(a)] M/F exhibitor; (*Cinema*) cinema owner

exibir [ezi'bir] VT to show, display; (*alardear*) to show off; (*filme*) to show, screen; **exibir-se** VR to show off; (*indecentemente*) to expose o.s.

exigência [ezi'ʒẽsja] F demand; (*o necessário*) requirement

exigente [ezi'ʒẽtʃi] ADJ demanding; **ser ~ com alguém** to be hard on sb

exigibilidades [eziʒibili'dadʒis] FPL (*Com*) liabilities

exigir [ezi'ʒir] VT to demand; **~ que alguém faça algo** to demand that sb do sth; **o médico exigiu-lhe repouso absoluto** the doctor ordered him to have complete rest

exigível [ezi'ʒivew] (*pl* **-eis**) ADJ (*Com: passivo*): **~ a curto/longo prazo** current/long-term liabilities *pl*

exíguo, -a [e'zigwu, a] ADJ (*diminuto*) small; (*escasso*) scanty

exilado, -a [ezi'ladu, a] ADJ exiled ▶ M/F exile

exilar [ezi'lar] VT to exile; (*pessoa indesejável*) to deport; **exilar-se** VR to go into exile

exílio [e'zilju] M exile; (*forçado*) deportation

exímio, -a [e'zimju, a] ADJ (*eminente*) famous, distinguished; (*excelente*) excellent

eximir [ezi'mir] VT: **~ de** to exempt from; (*obrigação*) to free from; (*culpa*) to clear of; **eximir-se** VR: **~-se de** to avoid, shun

existência [ezis'tẽsja] F existence; (*vida*) life

existencial [ezistẽ'sjaw] (*pl* **-ais**) ADJ existential

existencialismo [ezistẽsja'lizmu] M existentialism

existencialista [ezistēsja'lista] ADJ, M/F existentialist

existente [ezis'tētʃi] ADJ extant; (*vivente*) living

existir [ezis'tʃir] VI to exist; **existe/existem ...** (*há*) there is/are ...; **ela não existe** (*col*) she's incredible

êxito ['ezitu] M (*resultado*) result; (*sucesso*) success; (*música, filme etc*) hit; **ter ~ (em)** to succeed (in), be successful (in); **não ter ~ (em)** to fail (in), be unsuccessful (in)

Exmo, -a (*pl* **-s/-s**) ABR (= *Excelentíssimo*) Dear

êxodo ['ezodu] M exodus

exoneração [ezonera'sãw] (*pl* **-ões**) F dismissal

exonerar [ezone'rar] VT (*demitir*) to dismiss; **~ de uma obrigação** to free from an obligation

exorbitante [ezorbi'tãtʃi] ADJ (*preço*) exorbitant; (*pretensões*) extravagant; (*exigências*) excessive

exorcismo [ezor'sizmu] M exorcism

exorcista [ezor'sista] M/F exorcist

exorcizar [ezorsi'zar] VT to exorcise

exortação [ɛzorta'sãw] (*pl* **-ões**) F exhortation

exortar [ezor'tar] VT: **~ alguém a fazer algo** to urge sb to do sth

exortativo, -a [ezorta'tʃivu, a] ADJ (*tom*) encouraging

exótico, -a [e'zotʃiku, a] ADJ exotic

exotismo [ezo'tʃizmu] M exoticism, exotic nature

expandir [ispã'dʒir] VT to expand; (*espalhar*) to spread; **expandir-se** VR (*dilatar-se*) to expand; **~-se com alguém** to be frank with sb

expansão [ispã'sãw] F expansion, spread; (*de alegria*) effusiveness

expansividade [ispãsivi'dadʒi] F outgoing nature

expansivo, -a [ispã'sivu, a] ADJ (*pessoa*) outgoing

expatriação [ispatrja'sãw] F expatriation

expatriado, -a [ispa'trjadu, a] ADJ, M/F expatriate

expatriar [ispa'trjar] VT to expatriate

expeça *etc* [is'pɛsa] VB *ver* **expedir**

expectativa [ispekta'tʃiva] F (*esperança*) expectation; **na ~ de** in expectation of; **estar na ~** to be expectant; (*em suspense*) to be in suspense; **~ de vida** life expectancy

expectorante [ispekto'rãtʃi] ADJ, M expectorant

expectorar [ispekto'rar] VT to cough up ▶ VI to expectorate

expedição [ispedʒi'sãw] (*pl* **-ões**) F (*viagem*) expedition; (*de mercadorias*) despatch; (*por navio*) shipment; (*de passaporte etc*) issue

expediência [ispe'dʒjēsja] F (*desembaraço*) efficiency

expediente [ispe'dʒjētʃi] M means; (*serviço*) working day; (*correspondência*) correspondence ▶ ADJ expedient; **~ bancário** banking hours *pl*; **~ do escritório** office

hours *pl*; **meio ~** part-time working; **só trabalho meio ~** I only work part-time; **viver de ~s** to live on one's wits; **ser** *ou* **ter ~** (*pessoa*) to be resourceful, have initiative

expedir [ispe'dʒir] VT (*enviar*) to send, despatch; (*bilhete, passaporte, decreto*) to issue

expedito, -a [ispe'dʒitu, a] ADJ prompt, speedy; (*pessoa*) efficient

expelir [ispe'lir] VT (*expulsar*) to expel; (*sangue*) to spit

experiência [ispe'rjēsja] F (*prática*) experience; (*prova*) experiment, test; **em ~** on trial

experienciar [isperjē'sjar] VT to experience

experiente [ispe'rjētʃi] ADJ experienced

experimentação [isperimēta'sãw] F experimentation

experimentado, -a [isperimē'tadu, a] ADJ (*experiente*) experienced; (*testado*) tried; (*provado*) tested

experimental [isperimē'taw] (*pl* **-ais**) ADJ experimental

experimentar [isperimē'tar] VT (*comida*) to taste; (*vestido*) to try on; (*pôr à prova*) to try out, test; (*conhecer pela experiência*) to experience; (*sofrer*) to suffer, undergo; **~ fazer algo** to try doing sth, have a go at doing sth

experimento [isperi'mētu] M (*científico*) experiment

expiar [is'pjar] VT to atone for

expiatório, -a [ispja'tɔrju, a] ADJ *ver* **bode**

expilo *etc* [is'pilu] VB *ver* **expelir**

expiração [ispira'sãw] (*pl* **-ões**) F (*de ar*) exhalation; (*termo*) expiry

expirar [ispi'rar] VT (*ar*) to exhale, breathe out ▶ VI (*morrer*) to die; (*terminar*) to end

explanação [isplana'sãw] (*pl* **-ões**) F explanation

explanar [ispla'nar] VT to explain

explicação [isplika'sãw] (*pl* **-ões**) F explanation; (*PT: lição*) private lesson

explicar [ispli'kar] VT, VI to explain; **explicar-se** VR to explain o.s.; **isto não se explica** this does not make sense

explicável [ispli'kavew] (*pl* **-eis**) ADJ explicable, explainable

explícito, -a [is'plisitu, a] ADJ explicit, clear

explodir [isplo'dʒir] VT (*bomba*) to explode ▶ VI to explode, blow up

exploração [isplora'sãw] F (*de um país*) exploration; (*abuso*) exploitation; (*de uma mina*) running

explorador, a [isplora'dor(a)] ADJ exploitative ▶ M/F (*descobridor*) explorer; (*de outros*) exploiter

explorar [isplo'rar] VT (*região*) to explore; (*mina*) to work, run; (*ferida*) to probe; (*trabalhadores etc*) to exploit

explosão [isplo'zãw] (*pl* **-ões**) F explosion, blast; (*fig*) outburst

explosivo, -a [isplo'zivu, a] ADJ explosive; (*pessoa*) hot-headed ▶ M explosive

explosões [isplo'sõjs] FPL *de* **explosão**

Expoagro [espu'agru] ABR F = **Exposição Agropecuária Internacional do Rio de Janeiro**

expor [is'por] (irreg: como **pôr**) VT to expose; (a vida) to risk; (teoria) to explain; (revelar) to reveal; (mercadorias) to display; (quadros) to exhibit; **expor-se** VR to expose o.s.; **~(-se) a algo** to expose (o.s.) to sth; **seu rosto expõe sinais de cansaço** his face shows signs of tiredness

exportação [isporta'sãw] F (ato) export(ing); (mercadorias) exports pl

exportador, a [isporta'dor(a)] ADJ exporting ▶ M/F exporter

exportar [ispor'tar] VT to export

expôs etc [is'pos] VB ver **expor**

exposição [ispozi'sãw] (pl **-ões**) F (exibição) exhibition; (explicação) explanation; (declaração) statement; (narração) account; (Foto) exposure

expositor, a [ispozi'tor(a)] M/F exhibitor

exposto, -a [is'postu, 'posta] PP de **expor** ▶ ADJ (lugar) exposed; (quadro, mercadoria) on show ou display ▶ M: **o acima ~** the above; **estar ~ a algo** to be open ou exposed to sth

expressão [ispre'sãw] (pl **-ões**) F expression

expressar [ispre'sar] VT to express; **expressar-se** VR to express o.s.

expressividade [ispresivi'dadʒi] F expressiveness

expressivo, -a [ispre'sivu, a] ADJ expressive; (pessoa) demonstrative

expresso, -a [is'prɛsu, a] PP de **exprimir** ▶ ADJ (manifesto) definite, clear; (trem, ordem, carta) express ▶ M express

expressões [ispre'sõjs] FPL de **expressão**

exprimir [ispri'mir] VT to express; **exprimir-se** VR to express o.s.

expropriar [ispro'prjar] VT to expropriate

expugnar [ispugi'nar] VT to take by storm

expulsado, -a [ispuw'sadu, a] PP de **expulsar**

expulsão [ispuw'sãw] (pl **-ões**) F expulsion; (Esporte) sending off

expulsar [ispuw'sar] VT to expel; (de uma festa, clube etc) to throw out; (inimigo) to drive out; (estrangeiro) to expel, deport; (jogador) to send off

expulso, -a [is'puwsu, a] PP de **expulsar**

expulsões [ispuw'sõjs] FPL de **expulsão**

expunha etc [is'puɲa] VB ver **expor**

expurgar [ispur'gar] VT to expurgate

expus etc [is'pus] VB ver **expor**

expuser etc [ispu'zer] VB ver **expor**

êxtase ['estazi] M ecstasy; (transe) trance; **estar em ~** to be in a trance

extasiado, -a [ista'zjadu, a] ADJ entranced

extensão [istẽ'sãw] (pl **-ões**) F (ger, Tel) extension; (de uma empresa) expansion; (terreno) expanse; (tempo) length, duration; (de conhecimentos) extent

extensivo, -a [istẽ'sivu, a] ADJ extensive; **ser ~ a** to extend to

extenso, -a [is'tẽsu, a] ADJ (amplo) extensive, wide; (comprido) long; (conhecimentos) extensive; (artigo) full, comprehensive; **por ~** in full

extensões [istẽ'sõjs] FPL de **extensão**

extenuado, -a [iste'nwadu, a] ADJ (esgotado) worn out

extenuante [iste'nwãtʃi] ADJ exhausting; (debilitante) debilitating

extenuar [iste'nwar] VT to exhaust; (debilitar) to weaken

exterior [iste'rjor] ADJ (de fora) outside, exterior; (aparência) outward; (comércio) foreign ▶ M (da casa) outside; (aspecto) outward appearance; **do ~** (do estrangeiro) from abroad; **no ~** abroad

exteriorizar [isterjori'zar] VT to show, manifest

exteriormente [isterjor'mẽtʃi] ADV on the outside

exterminação [istermina'sãw] F extermination

exterminar [istermi'nar] VT (inimigo) to wipe out, exterminate; (acabar com) to do away with

extermínio [ister'minju] M extermination, wiping out

externato [ister'natu] M day school

externo, -a [is'tɛrnu, a] ADJ external; (aparente) outward; **aluno ~** day pupil; **"para uso ~"** "external use only"

extinção [istʃĩ'sãw] F extinction

extinguir [istʃĩ'gir] VT (fogo) to put out, extinguish; (um povo) to wipe out; **extinguir-se** VR (fogo, luz) to go out; (Bio) to become extinct

extinto, -a [is'tʃĩtu, a] ADJ (fogo) extinguished; (língua) dead; (animal, vulcão) extinct; (associação etc) defunct; (pessoa) dead

extintor [istʃĩ'tor] M (fire) extinguisher

extirpar [istir'par] VT (desarraigar) to uproot; (corrupção) to eradicate; (tumor) to remove

extorquir [istor'kir] VT to extort

extorsão [istor'sãw] F extortion

extorsivo, -a [istor'sivu, a] ADJ extortionate

extra ['ɛstra] ADJ extra ▶ M/F extra person; (Teatro) extra; ver tb **hora**

extração [istra'sãw] (pl **-ões**) F extraction; (de loteria) draw

extraconjugal [estrakõʒu'gaw] (pl **-ais**) ADJ extramarital

extracurricular [estrakuhiku'lar] ADJ extracurricular

extradição [estradʒi'sãw] F extradition

extraditar [estradʒi'tar] VT to extradite

extrafino, -a [estra'finu, a] ADJ extra high-quality

extrair [istra'jir] VT to extract, take out

extrajudicial [estraʒudʒi'sjaw] (pl **-ais**) ADJ out-of-court

extraoficial [estraofi'sjaw] (pl **-ciais**) ADJ unofficial

extraordinário, -a [istraordʒi'narju, a] ADJ extraordinary; (despesa) extra; (reunião) special; **nada de ~** nothing out of the ordinary

extrapolar [istrapo'lar] VT to extrapolate

extraterrestre [estrate'hɛstri] ADJ extraterrestrial

extrato [is'tratu] M extract; (*resumo*) summary; **~ (bancário)** (bank) statement

extravagância [istrava'gãsja] F extravagance

extravagante [istrava'gãtʃi] ADJ extravagant; (*roupa*) outlandish; (*conduta*) wild

extravasar [istrava'zar] VI to overflow

extraviado, -a [istra'vjadu, a] ADJ lost, missing

extraviar [istra'vjar] VT (*perder*) to mislay; (*pessoa*) to lead astray; (*dinheiro*) to embezzle; **extraviar-se** VR to get lost

extravio [istra'viu] M (*perda*) loss; (*roubo*) embezzlement; (*fig*) deviation

extremado, -a [istre'madu, a] ADJ extreme

extremar-se [istre'marsi] VI VR to do one's utmost, make every effort; (*distinguir-se*) to distinguish o.s.; **~ em gentilezas** to show extreme kindness

extrema-unção (*pl* **extrema-unções**) F (*Rel*) extreme unction

extremidade [istremi'dadʒi] F extremity; (*do dedo*) tip; (*ponta*) end; (*beira*) edge

extremo, -a [is'trɛmu, a] ADJ extreme ▶ M extreme; **extremos** MPL (*carinho*) doting *sg*; (*descomedimento*) extremes; **ao ~** extremely; **de um ~ a outro** from one extreme to another

extremoso, -a [istre'mozu, ɔza] ADJ doting

extroversão [estrover'sãw] F extroversion

extroverso, -a [estro'vɛrsu, a] ADJ extrovert

extroverter-se [estrover'tersi] VR to be outgoing

extrovertido, -a [estrover'tʃidu, a] ADJ extrovert, outgoing ▶ M/F extrovert

exu [e'ʃu] M devil (*in voodoo rituals*)

exuberância [ezube'rãsja] F exuberance

exuberante [ezube'rãtʃi] ADJ exuberant

exultação [ezuwta'sãw] F joy, exultation

exultante [ezuw'tãtʃi] ADJ jubilant, exultant

exultar [ezuw'tar] VI to rejoice

exumar [ezu'mar] VT (*corpo*) to exhume; (*fig*) to dig up

ex-voto M votive offering

Ff

F, f ['ɛfi] (*pl* **fs**) M F, f; **F de Francisco** F for Frederick (BRIT) *ou* fox (US)

f ABR = **folha**

F-1 ABR = **Fórmula Um**

fá [fa] M (*Mús*) F

fã [fã] (*col*) M/F fan

FAB ['fabi] ABR F = **Força Aérea Brasileira**

fábrica ['fabrika] F factory; **~ de cerveja** brewery; **~ de conservas** cannery; **~ de papel** paper mill; **a preço de ~** wholesale

fabricação [fabrika'sãw] F manufacture; **de ~ caseira/própria** home-made/own-brand; **~ em série** mass production

fabricante [fabri'kãtʃi] M/F manufacturer

fabricar [fabri'kar] VT to manufacture, make; (*inventar*) to fabricate

fabrico [fa'briku] M production

fabril [fa'briw] (*pl* **-is**) ADJ: **indústria ~** manufacturing industry

fábula ['fabula] F fable; (*conto*) tale; (BR: *grande quantia*) fortune

fabuloso, -a [fabu'lozu, ɔza] ADJ fabulous

faca ['faka] F knife; **é uma ~ de dois gumes** (*fig*) it's a two-edged sword; **entrar na ~** (*col*) to be operated on, to go under the knife; **ter a ~ e o queijo na mão** (*fig*) to have things in hand

facada [fa'kada] F stab, cut; **dar uma ~ em alguém** to stab sb; (*fig: col*) to touch sb for money

façanha [fa'saɲa] F exploit, deed

facão [fa'kãw] (*pl* **-ões**) M carving knife; (*para cortar o mato*) machete

facção [fak'sãw] (*pl* **-ões**) F faction

faccioso, -a [fak'ajozu, ɔza] ADJ factious

facções [fak'sõjs] FPL *de* **facção**

face ['fasi] F (*rosto, de moeda*) face; (*bochecha*) cheek; **em ~ de** in view of; **fazer ~ a** to face up to; **~ a** face to face

faceiro, -a [fa'sejru, a] ADJ (*elegante*) smart; (*alegre*) cheerful

fáceis ['fasejs] ADJ PL *de* **fácil**

faceta [fa'seta] F facet

fachada [fa'ʃada] F façade, front; (*col: rosto*) face, mug (*col*)

facho ['faʃu] M beam

facial [fa'sjaw] (*pl* **-ais**) ADJ facial

fácil ['fasiw] ADJ (*pl* **-eis**) easy; (*temperamento, pessoa*) easy-going; (*mulher*) easy ▶ ADV easily

facilidade [fasili'dadʒi] F ease; (*jeito*) facility; **facilidades** FPL (*recursos*) facilities; **ter ~ para algo** to have a talent *ou* a facility for sth; **com ~** easily

facilimo, -a [fa'silimu, a] ADJ SUPERL *de* **fácil**

facilitação [fasilita'sãw] F facilitation; (*fornecimento*) provision

facilitar [fasili'tar] VT to facilitate, make easy; (*fornecer*): **~ algo a alguém** to provide sb with sth ▶ VI (*agir sem cautela*) to be careless

facinora [fa'sinora] M criminal

fã-clube [fã'klubi] (*pl* **-s**) M fan club

faço *etc* ['fasu] VB *ver* **fazer**

facões [fa'kõjs] FPL *de* **facão**

fac-símile [fak-] (*pl* **fac-símiles**) M (*cópia*) facsimile

factício, -a [fak'tʃisju, a] ADJ unnatural

facto ['faktu] (PT) M = **fato**

factótum [fak'tɔtũ] M factotum

factual [fak'twaw] (*pl* **-ais**) ADJ factual

faculdade [fakuw'dadʒi] F faculty; (*poder*) power; (BR: *escola*) university, college; (*corpo docente*) teaching staff (BRIT), faculty (US); **fazer ~** to go to university *ou* college

facultar [fakuw'tar] VT (*permitir*) to allow; (*conceder*) to grant

facultativo, -a [fakuwta'tʃivu, a] ADJ optional ▶ M/F doctor

fada ['fada] F fairy; **conto de ~s** fairy tale

fadado, -a [fa'dadu, a] ADJ destined

fada-madrinha (*pl* **fadas-madrinhas**) F fairy godmother

fadiga [fa'dʒiga] F fatigue

fadista [fa'dʒista] M/F "fado" singer ▶ M (PT) ruffian

fado ['fadu] M fate; (*canção*) traditional song of Portugal

> The best-known musical form in Portugal is the melancholic **fado**, which is traditionally sung by a soloist (known as a *fadista*) accompanied by the Portuguese *guitarra*. There are two main types of **fado**: Coimbra **fado** is traditionally sung by men, and is considered to be more cerebral than the **fado** from Lisbon, which is sung by both men and women. The theme is nearly always one of deep nostalgia known as *saudade*, and the harsh reality of life.

Faferj [fa'fɛɾʒi] ABR F = **Federação das Associações das Favelas do Estado do Rio de Janeiro**

fagueiro, -a [fa'gejru, a] ADJ (contente) happy; (agradável) pleasant

fagulha [fa'guʎa] F spark

fahrenheit [farē'ajtʃi] ADJ INV Fahrenheit

faia ['faja] F beech (tree)

faina ['fajna] F toil, work; (tarefa) task, job

fair-play ['fɛrplej] M fair play

faisão [faj'zãw] (pl -ões) M pheasant

faísca [fa'iska] F spark; (brilho) flash

faiscante [faj'skãtʃi] ADJ flashing; (fogo) flickering

faiscar [fajs'kar] VI to sparkle; (brilhar) to flash

faisões [faj'zõjs] MPL de **faisão**

faixa ['fajʃa] F (cinto, Judô) belt; (tira) strip; (área) zone; (Auto: pista) lane; (BR: para pedestres) zebra crossing (BRIT), crosswalk (US); (Med) bandage; (num disco) track; **~ etária** age group

faixa-título (pl **faixas-títulos**) F (Mús) title track

fajuto, -a [fa'ʒutu, a] (col) ADJ (pão) rough; (falso: nota) fake

fala ['fala] F speech; **chamar às ~s** to call to account; **sem ~** speechless; **perder a ~** to be struck dumb

falação [fala'sãw] (pl -ões) F (ato) talk; (discurso) speech

falácia [fa'lasja] F fallacy

falações [fala'sõjs] FPL de **falação**

faladeira [fala'dejra] F de **falador**

falado, -a [fa'ladu, a] ADJ (caso etc) talked about, much discussed; (famoso) well-known; (de má fama) notorious; (Cinema) talking

falador, -deira [fala'dor, 'dejra] ADJ talkative ▶ M/F chatterbox

falante [fa'lãtʃi] ADJ talkative

falar [fa'lar] VT (língua) to speak; (besteira etc) to talk; (dizer) to say; (verdade, mentira) to tell ▶ VI to speak, talk; (discursar) to speak; **falar-se** VR to talk to one another; **~ algo a alguém** to tell sb sth; **~ que** to say that; **~ de ou em algo** to talk about sth; **~ com alguém** to talk to sb; **por ~ em** speaking of; **por ~ nisso** by the way; **sem ~ em** not to mention; **~ alto** to talk loudly; **~ alto com alguém** (fig) to give sb a good talking-to; **sua consciência falou mais alto** his conscience got the better of him; **falou!, 'tá falado!** (col) OK!; **falando sério ...** but seriously ...; **~ sozinho** to talk to o.s.; **ele está falando da boca para fora** (col) he's just saying that, he doesn't mean it; **ele falou por ~** he was just saying that; **dar que ~** to cause a stir; **~ para dentro** to talk into one's beard; **~ pelos cotovelos** to talk one's head off; **eles não se falam** (estão de mal) they are not speaking to one another; **nem se fala!** definitely not!

falatório [fala'tɔrju] M (ruído de vozes) voices pl, talking; (falar demorado) diatribe; (maledicência) rumour (BRIT), rumor (US)

falaz [fa'laz] ADJ deceptive, misleading; (falso) false

falcão [faw'kãw] (pl -ões) M falcon

falcatrua [fawka'trua] F (col) scam

falcões [faw'kõjs] MPL de **falcão**

falecer [fale'ser] VI to die

falecido, -a [fale'sidu, a] ADJ dead, late ▶ M/F deceased

falecimento [falesi'mẽtu] M death

falência [fa'lẽsja] F bankruptcy; **abrir ~** to declare o.s. bankrupt; **ir à ~** to go bankrupt; **levar à ~** to bankrupt

falésia [fa'lɛzja] F cliff

falha ['faʎa] F (defeito, Geo etc) fault; (lacuna) omission; (de caráter) flaw

falhar [fa'ʎar] VI to fail; (não acertar) to miss; (errar) to be wrong; (ao telefone) break up; **o motor está falhando** the engine is missing; **sua voz está falhando** you're breaking up

falho, -a ['faʎu, a] ADJ faulty; (deficiente) wanting

fálico, -a ['faliku, a] ADJ phallic

falido, -a [fa'lidu, a] ADJ, M/F bankrupt

falir [fa'lir] VI to fail; (Com) to go bankrupt

falível [fa'livew] (pl -eis) ADJ fallible

falo ['falu] M phallus

falsário, -a [faw'sarju, a] M/F forger

falsear [faw'sjar] VT (forjar) to forge; (falsificar) to falsify; (verdade) to twist; **~ o pé** to blunder

falseta [faw'seta] (col) F dirty trick

falsete [faw'setʃi] M falsetto

falsidade [fawsi'dadʒi] F falsehood; (fingimento) pretence (BRIT), pretense (US); (mentira) lie

falsificação [fawsifika'sãw] (pl -ões) F (ato) falsification; (efeito) forgery; (falsa interpretação) misrepresentation

falsificações [fawsifika'sõjs] FPL de **falsificação**

falsificador, a [fawsifika'dor(a)] M/F forger

falsificar [fawsifi'kar] VT (forjar) to forge; (falsear) to falsify; (adulterar) to adulterate; (desvirtuar) to misrepresent

falso, -a ['fawsu, a] ADJ false; (fraudulento) dishonest; (errôneo) wrong; (joia, moeda, quadro) fake; (pessoa: insincero) two-faced; **pisar em ~** to blunder

falta ['fawta] F (carência) lack; (ausência) absence; (defeito, culpa) fault; (Futebol) foul; **por ou na ~ de** for lack of; **sem ~** without fail; **cometer/cobrar uma ~** (Futebol) to commit a foul/take a free kick; **estar em ~ com alguém** to feel guilty about sb; **fazer ~** to be lacking, be needed; **ela faz ~** she is missed; **este livro não vai te fazer ~?** won't you need this book?; **sentir ~ de alguém/algo** to miss sb/sth; **ter ~ de** to lack, be in need of; **~ de água** water shortage; **~ de ânimo** lack of enthusiasm; **~ de educação** ou **modos** rudeness; **~ de tato** tactlessness

faltar [faw'tar] vi (*escassear*) to be lacking, be wanting; (*pessoa*) to be absent; (*falhar*) to fail; **~ ao trabalho** to be absent from work; **~ à palavra** to break one's word; **falta pouco para ...** it won't be long until ...; **falta uma semana para nossas férias** it's only a week until our holidays; **faltam 10 minutos para as 3** it's ten minutes to three; **faltam 3 páginas (para eu acabar)** there are 3 pages to go (before I finish); **faltam chegar duas pessoas** two people are still to come; **falta fazermos mais algumas coisas** there are still a few things for us to do; **só faltava essa!** that's all I (*ou* we *etc*) needed!; **nada me falta** I have all I need

falto, -a ['fawtu, a] ADJ: **~ de** lacking in, deficient in

faltoso, -a [faw'tozu, ɔza] ADJ (*culpado*) at fault; (*que costuma faltar*) frequently absent

fama ['fama] F (*renome*) fame; (*reputação*) reputation; **ter ~ de (ser) generoso** to be said to be generous; **de ~** famous; **de má ~** notorious, of ill repute

Famerj [fa'mɛrʒi] ABR F = **Federação das Associações de Moradores do Estado do Rio de Janeiro**

famigerado, -a [famiʒe'radu, a] ADJ (*malfeitor*) notorious; (*autor etc*) famous

família [fa'milja] F family ▶ ADJ INV (*col: pessoa*) decent; (: *festa*) well-behaved; **de boa ~** from a good family; **estar em ~** to be one of the family, be among friends; **isso é de ~** this runs in the family, this is a family trait

familiar [fami'ljar] ADJ (*da família*) family *atr*; (*conhecido*) familiar ▶ M/F relation, relative

familiaridade [familjari'dadʒi] F familiarity; (*sem-cerimônia*) informality

familiarização [familjariza'sãw] F familiarization

familiarizar [familjari'zar] VT to familiarize; **familiarizar-se** VR: **~-se com algo** to familiarize o.s. with sth

faminto, -a [fa'mĩtu, a] ADJ hungry; (*fig*): **~ de** eager for

famoso, -a [fa'mozu, ɔza] ADJ famous

fanático, -a [fa'natʃiku, a] ADJ fanatical ▶ M/F fanatic

fanatismo [fana'tʃizmu] M fanaticism

fanhoso, -a [fa'ɲozu, ɔza] ADJ (*pessoa*) with a nasal voice; (*voz*) nasal; **falar** ou **ser ~** to talk through one's nose

faniquito [fani'kitu] (*col*) M attack of nerves

fantasia [fãta'zia] F fantasy; (*imaginação*) imagination; (*capricho*) fancy; (*traje*) fancy dress; **joia (de) ~** (piece of) costume jewellery (BRIT) ou jewelry (US)

fantasiar [fãta'zjar] VT to imagine ▶ VI to daydream; **fantasiar-se** VR to dress up (in fancy dress)

fantasioso, -a [fãta'zjozu, ɔza] ADJ imaginative

fantasista [fãta'zista] ADJ imaginative

fantasma [fã'tazma] M ghost; (*alucinação*) illusion

fantasmagórico, -a [fãtazma'gɔriku, a] ADJ ghostly

fantástico, -a [fã'tastʃiku, a] ADJ fantastic; (*ilusório*) imaginary; (*incrível*) unbelievable

fantoche [fã'tɔʃi] M puppet

fanzoca [fã'zɔka] (*col*) M/F great fan

faqueiro [fa'kejru] M (*jogo de talheres*) set of cutlery; (*pessoa*) cutler

faquir [fa'kir] M fakir

faraó [fara'ɔ] M pharaoh

faraônico, -a [fara'oniku, a] ADJ (*fig: obra*) large-scale

farda ['farda] F uniform

fardar [far'dar] VT to dress in uniform

fardo ['fardu] M bundle; (*carga*) load; (*fig*) burden

farei etc [fa'rej] VB ver **fazer**

farejar [fare'ʒar] VT to sniff around ▶ VI to sniff

farelo [fa'rɛlu] M (*de pão*) crumb; (*de madeira*) sawdust; **~ de trigo** bran

farfalhante [farfa'ʎãtʃi] ADJ rustling

farfalhar [farfa'ʎar] VI to rustle

farfalhudo, -a [farfa'ʎudu, a] ADJ ostentatious

farináceo, -a [fari'nasju, a] ADJ (*alimento*) starchy; (*molho etc*) floury

farináceos [fari'nasjus] MPL (*alimentos*) starchy foods

faringe [fa'rĩʒi] F pharynx

faringite [farĩ'ʒitʃi] F pharyngitis

farinha [fa'riɲa] F: **~ (de mesa)** (manioc) flour; **~ de arroz** rice flour; **~ de osso** bone meal; **~ de rosca** breadcrumbs *pl*; **~ de trigo** plain flour

farmacêutico, -a [farma'sewtʃiku, a] ADJ pharmaceutical ▶ M/F pharmacist, chemist (BRIT)

farmácia [far'masja] F pharmacy, chemist's (shop) (BRIT); (*ciência*) pharmacy

farnel [far'nɛw] (*pl* **-éis**) M (*provisões*) provisions *pl*; (*saco*) food parcel

faro ['faru] M sense of smell; (*fig*) flair

faroeste [fa'rwɛstʃi] M (*filme*) western; (*região*) wild west

farofa [fa'rɔfa] F (*Culin*) side dish based on manioc flour

farofeiro, -a [faro'fejru, a] M/F picnicker (*who comes to the beach from far away*)

farol [fa'rɔw] (*pl* **-óis**) M lighthouse; (*Auto*) headlight; (*col*) bragging; **~ alto** (*Auto*) full (BRIT) ou high (US) beam; **~ baixo** dipped headlights *pl* (BRIT), dimmed beam (US); **contar ~** (*col*) to brag

faroleiro [faro'lejru] M lighthouse keeper; (*col*) braggart

farolete [faro'letʃi] M (*Auto: dianteiro*) sidelight; (*tb:* **farolete traseiro**) tail-light

farpa ['farpa] F barb; (*estilha*) splinter

farpado, -a [far'padu, a] ADJ: **arame ~** barbed wire

farra ['faha] F binge, spree; **cair na ~** to go on the razzle; **só de** *ou* **por ~** just for the fun of it

farrapo [fa'hapu] M rag; **ela parecia um ~** she looked like a tramp; **esta blusa está um ~** this blouse is a sight

farrear [fa'hjar] VI to go on a spree

farripas [fa'hipas] FPL wisps of hair

farrista [fa'hista] ADJ fun-loving ▶ M/F party animal (*col*)

farsa ['farsa] F farce

farsante [far'sãtʃi] M/F joker; (*pessoa sem palavra*) smooth operator

farta ['farta] F: **comer à ~** to eat one's fill

fartar [far'tar] VT (*saciar*) to satiate; (*encher*) to fill up; **fartar-se** VR to gorge o.s.; **~-se de** (*cansar-se*) to get fed up with; **me fartei (de comer)** I'm full up

farto, -a ['fartu, a] ADJ full, satiated; (*abundante*) plentiful; (*aborrecido*) fed up; **cabeleira farta** full head of hair, shock of hair

fartum [far'tũ] (*pl* **-ns**) M stench

fartura [far'tura] F abundance, plenty

fascículo [fa'sikulu] M (*de publicação*) instalment (BRIT), installment (US)

fascinação [fasina'sãw] F fascination; **ter ~ por alguém** to be infatuated with sb

fascinante [fasi'nãtʃi] ADJ fascinating

fascinar [fasi'nar] VT to fascinate; (*encantar*) to charm

fascínio [fa'sinju] M fascination

fascismo [fa'sizmu] M fascism

fascista [fa'sista] ADJ, M/F fascist

fase ['fazi] F phase; (*etapa*) stage

fashion ['fɛʃjõ] (*col*) ADJ trendy

fastidioso, -a [fastʃi'dʒozu, ɔza] ADJ tedious; (*enfadonho*) annoying

fastígio [fas'tʃiʒju] M (*fig*) height

fastio [fas'tʃiu] M lack of appetite; (*tédio*) boredom

fatal [fa'taw] (*pl* **-ais**) ADJ (*mortal*) fatal; (*inevitável*) fateful

fatalidade [fatali'dadʒi] F (*destino*) fate; (*desgraça*) disaster

fatalista [fata'lista] ADJ fatalistic ▶ M/F fatalist

fatalmente [fataw'mẽtʃi] ADV (*de modo fatal*) fatally; (*certamente*) inevitably

fatia [fa'tʃia] F slice

fatídico, -a [fa'tʃidʒiku, a] ADJ fateful

fatigante [fatʃi'gãtʃi] ADJ tiring; (*aborrecido*) tiresome

fatigar [fatʃi'gar] VT to tire; (*aborrecer*) to bore; **fatigar-se** VR to get tired

Fátima ['fatima] F *see note*

> Fátima, situated in central Portugal, is known worldwide as a site of pilgrimage for Catholics. It is said that, in 1917, the Virgin Mary appeared six times to three shepherd children (*os três pastorinhos*). Millions of pilgrims visit Fátima every year.

fato ['fatu] M fact; (*acontecimento*) event; (PT: *traje*) suit; **~ de banho** (PT) swimming costume (BRIT), bathing suit (US); **~ consumado** fait accompli; **de ~** in fact, really; **o ~ é que ...** the fact remains that ...; **chegar às vias de ~** to come to blows

fator [fa'tor] M factor; **~ Rh** (*Med*) Rh *ou* rhesus (BRIT) factor

fátuo, -a ['fatwu, a] ADJ (*vão*) fatuous

fatura [fa'tura] F bill, invoice

faturamento [fatura'mẽtu] M (*Com*: *volume de negócios*) turnover; (*faturar*) invoicing

faturar [fatu'rar] VT to invoice; (*dinheiro*) to make; (*col*: *gol*) to score, notch up ▶ VI (*col*: *ganhar dinheiro*): **~ (alto)** to rake it in; **~ algo a alguém** to invoice sb for sth

fauna ['fawna] F fauna

fausto, -a ['fawstu, a] ADJ lucky ▶ M luxury

fava ['fava] F broad bean; **mandar alguém às ~s** to send sb packing

favela [fa'vɛla] F slum, shanty town

favelado, -a [fave'ladu, a] M/F slum-dweller

favo ['favu] M honeycomb

favor [fa'vor] M favour (BRIT), favor (US); **a ~ de** in favo(u)r of; **em ~ de** on behalf of; **por ~** please; **se faz ~** (PT) please; **fazer um ~ para alguém** to do sb a favo(u)r; **faça** *ou* **faz o ~ de ...** would you be so good as to ..., kindly ...; **faça-me o ~!** (*col*) do me a favo(u)r!; **ter a seu ~** to have to one's credit

favorável [favo'ravew] (*pl* **-eis**) ADJ: **~ (a)** favourable (BRIT) *ou* favorable (US) (to)

favorecer [favore'ser] VT to favour (BRIT), favor (US); (*beneficiar*) to benefit; (*suj: vestido*) to suit; (: *retrato*) to flatter

favoritismo [favori'tʃizmu] M favouritism (BRIT), favoritism (US)

favorito, -a [favo'ritu, a] ADJ, M/F (*tb Comput*) favourite (BRIT), favorite (US)

fax [faks] M (*carta*) fax; (*máquina*) fax (machine); **enviar por ~** to fax

faxina [fa'ʃina] F: **fazer ~** to clean up

faxineiro, -a [faʃi'nejru, a] M/F (*pessoa*) cleaner

faz de conta [fazdʒi'kõta] M: **o ~** make-believe

fazedor, a [faze'dor(a)] M/F maker

fazenda [fa'zẽda] F farm; (*de café*) plantation; (*de gado*) ranch; (*pano*) cloth, fabric; (*Econ*) treasury, exchequer (BRIT)

fazendeiro [fazẽ'dejru] M farmer; (*de café*) plantation-owner; (*de gado*) rancher, ranch-owner

> (**PALAVRA-CHAVE**)

fazer [fa'zer] VT **1** (*fabricar, produzir*) to make; (*construir*) to build; (*pergunta*) to ask; (*poema, música*) to write; **fazer um filme/ruído** to make a film/noise; **eu fiz o vestido** I made the dress

2 (*executar: trabalho etc*) to do; **o que você está**

fazendo? what are you doing?; **fazer a comida** to do the cooking; **fazer o papel de** (*Teatro*) to play
3 (*estudos, alguns esportes*) to do; **fazer medicina/direito** to do *ou* study medicine/law; **fazer ioga/ginástica** to do yoga/keep-fit
4 (*transformar, tornar*): **sair o fará sentir melhor** going out will make him feel better; **sua partida fará o trabalho mais difícil** his departure will make work more difficult
5 (*como sustituto de vb*): **ele bebeu e eu fiz o mesmo** he drank and I did likewise
6: ele faz anos hoje it's his birthday today; **fiz 30 anos ontem** I was 30 yesterday
▶ VI **1** (*portar-se*) to act, behave; **fazer bem/mal** to do the right/wrong thing; **não fiz por mal** I didn't mean it; **faz como quem não sabe** act as if you don't know anything
2: fazer com que alguém faça algo to make sb do sth
▶ VB IMPESS **1: faz calor/frio** it's hot/cold
2 (*tempo*): **faz um ano** a year ago; **faz dois anos que ele se formou** it's two years since he graduated; **faz três meses que ele está aqui** he's been here for three months
3: não faz mal never mind; **tanto faz** it's all the same
fazer-se VR **1: fazer-se de desentendido** to pretend not to understand
2: faz-se com ovos e leite it's made with eggs and milk; **isso não se faz** that's not done

faz-tudo [fajʒ-] M/F INV odd job person
FBI ABR M (= *Federal Bureau of Investigation*) FBI
FC ABR M (= *Futebol Clube*) FC
FDLP ABR F (= *Frente Democrática para a Libertação da Palestina*) PFLP
fé [fɛ] F faith; (*crença*) belief; (*confiança*) trust; **de boa/má fé** in good/bad faith; **dar fé de** to bear witness to; **fazer fé em** to have faith in; **fé em Deus e pé na tábua** go for it
fealdade [feaw'dadʒi] F ugliness
FEB ['fɛbi] ABR F (= *Força Expedicionária Brasileira*) *force sent out in World War II*
FEBEM [fe'bẽ] (BR) ABR F (= *Fundação Estadual do Bem-Estar do Menor*) *reform school*
febrão [fe'brãw] (*pl* -**ões**) M raging fever
febre ['fɛbri] F fever; (*fig*) excitement; ~ **amarela** yellow fever; ~ **de poder** *etc* hunger for power *etc*; ~ **do feno** hay fever
febril [fe'briw] (*pl* -**is**) ADJ feverish
febrões [fe'brõjs] MPL *de* **febrão**
fecal [fe'kaw] (*pl* -**ais**) ADJ *ver* **matéria**
fechada [fe'ʃada] F: **dar uma** ~ **em alguém** (*Auto*) to cut sb up; **levar uma** ~ to be cut up
fechado, -a [fe'ʃadu, a] ADJ shut, closed; (*pessoa*) reserved; (*sinal*) red; (*luz, torneira*) off; (*tempo*) overcast; (*cara*) stern; **noite fechada** well into the night
fechadura [feʃa'dura] F (*de porta*) lock

fechamento [feʃa'mẽtu] M closure
fechar [fe'ʃar] VT to close, shut; (*concluir*) to finish, conclude; (*luz, torneira*) to turn off; (*rua*) to close off; (*ferida*) to close up; (*bar, loja*) to close down; (*negócio*) to make; (*Auto*) to cut up ▶ VI to close (up), shut; (*ferida*) to heal; (*sinal*) to turn red; to close down; (*tempo*) to cloud over; **fechar-se** VR to close, shut; (*pessoa*) to withdraw; ~-**se no quarto** *etc* to shut o.s. away in one's room *etc*; ~ **à chave** to lock; ~ **a cara** to look annoyed; **ser de** ~ **o comércio** (*col*) to be a real show-stopper
fecho ['feʃu] M fastening; (*trinco*) latch; (*término*) close, closing; ~ **ecler** zip fastener (BRIT), zipper (US)
fécula ['fɛkula] F starch
fecundação [fekũda'sãw] F fertilization
fecundar [fekũ'dar] VT to fertilize, make fertile
fecundidade [fekũdʒi'dadʒi] F fertility
fecundo, -a [fe'kũdu, a] ADJ fertile; (*produtivo*) fruitful; (*fig*) prolific
fedelho, -a [fe'deʎu, a] M/F kid
feder [fe'der] VI to stink; **não** ~ **nem cheirar** (*fig*) to be wishy-washy
federação [federa'sãw] (*pl* -**ões**) F federation
federal [fede'raw] (*pl* -**ais**) ADJ federal; (*col: grande*) huge
federativo, -a [federa'tʃivu, a] ADJ federal
fedor [fe'dor] M stench
fedorento, -a [fedo'rẽtu, a] ADJ stinking
FEEM (BR) ABR F (= *Fundação Estadual de Educação do Menor*) *children's home*
Feema [fe'ɛma] (BR) ABR F (= *Fundação Estadual de Engenharia do Meio Ambiente*) *environmental protection agency*
feérico, -a [fe'ɛriku, a] ADJ magical
feição [fej'sãw] (*pl* -**ões**) F form, shape; (*caráter*) nature; (*modo*) manner; **feições** FPL (*face*) features; **à** ~ **de** in the manner of
feijão [fej'ʒãw] (*pl* -**ões**) M bean(s) (*pl*); (*preto*) black bean(s) (*pl*)
feijão-fradinho [-fra'dʒiɲu] (*pl* **feijões-fradinhos**) M black-eyed bean(s) (*pl*)
feijão-mulatinho [-mula'tʃiɲu] (*pl* **feijões-mulatinhos**) M red kidney bean(s) (*pl*)
feijão-preto (*pl* **feijões-pretos**) M black bean(s) (*pl*)
feijão-soja (*pl* **feijões-sojas**) M soya bean(s) (*pl*) (BRIT), soybean(s) (*pl*) (US)
feijão-tropeiro [-tro'pejru] (*pl* **feijões-tropeiros**) M (*Culin*) bean stew
feijoada [fej'ʒwada] F (*Culin*) meat, rice and black beans
feijoeiro [fej'ʒwejru] M bean plant
feijões [fej'ʒõjs] MPL *de* **feijão**
feio, -a ['feju, a] ADJ ugly; (*situação*) grim; (*atitude*) bad; (*tempo*) horrible ▶ ADV (*perder*) badly; **olhar** ~ to give a filthy look; **fazer** ~ to make a bad impression; **ficar** ~ (*dar má impressão*) to look bad; (*situação*) to turn nasty; **quem ama o** ~, **bonito lhe parece** love is blind

feioso, -a [fe'jozu, ɔza] ADJ plain
feira ['fejra] F fair; (*mercado*) market; **fazer a ~** to go to market; **~ livre** market
feirante [fej'rãtʃi] M/F market trader, stallholder
feita ['fejta] F: **certa ~** once, on one occasion; **de uma ~** once and for all
feitiçaria [fejtʃisa'ria] F witchcraft, magic
feiticeira [fejtʃi'sejra] F witch
feiticeiro, -a [fejtʃi'sejru, a] ADJ bewitching, enchanting ▶ M wizard
feitiço [fej'tʃisu] M charm, spell; **virou o ~ contra o feiticeiro** (*fig*) the tables were turned
feitio [fej'tʃiu] M shape, pattern; (*caráter*) nature, manner; (*Tec*) workmanship
feito, -a ['fejtu, a] PP de **fazer** ▶ ADJ (*terminado*) finished, ready ▶ M act, deed; (*façanha*) feat ▶ CONJ like; **~ a mão** hand-made; **homem ~** grown man; **que é ~ dela?** what has become of her?; **bem ~ (por você)!** (it) serves you right!; **dito e ~** no sooner said than done; **estar ~** (*pessoa: ter dinheiro etc*) to have it made
feitor, a [fej'tor(a)] M/F administrator; (*capataz*) supervisor
feitura [fej'tura] F work
feiura [fe'jura] F ugliness
feixe ['fejʃi] M bundle, bunch; (*Tec*) beam
fel [fɛw] M bile, gall; (*fig*) bitterness; **esse remédio é um ~** that medicine is really bitter
felicidade [felisi'dadʒi] F happiness; (*sorte*) good luck; (*êxito*) success; **felicidades** FPL (*congratulações*) congratulations
felicíssimo, -a [feli'sisimu, a] ADJ SUPERL de **feliz**
felicitações [felisita'sõjs] FPL congratulations, best wishes
felicitar [felisi'tar] VT: **~ alguém (por)** to congratulate sb (on)
felino, -a [fe'linu, a] ADJ feline; (*fig: traiçoeiro*) treacherous ▶ M feline
feliz [fe'liz] ADJ happy; (*afortunado*) lucky; (*ideia, sugestão*) timely; (*próspero*) successful; (*expressão*) fortunate; **~ aniversário/Natal!** happy birthday/Christmas!; **dar-se por ~** to think o.s. lucky
felizardo, -a [feli'zardu, a] M/F lucky devil
felizmente [feliz'mẽtʃi] ADV fortunately
felonia [felo'nia] F (*traição*) treachery
felpa ['fewpa] F (*de animais*) down; (*de tecido*) nap
felpudo, -a [few'pudu, a] ADJ (*penujento*) fuzzy; (*peludo*) downy
feltro ['fewtru] M felt
fêmea ['femja] F (*Bio, Bot*) female
feminil [femi'niw] (*pl* **-is**) ADJ feminine
feminilidade [feminili'dadʒi] F femininity
feminino, -a [femi'ninu, a] ADJ feminine; (*sexo*) female; (*equipe, roupa*) women's ▶ M (*Ling*) feminine
feminis [femi'nis] ADJ PL de **feminil**
feminismo [femi'nizmu] M feminism

feminista [femi'nista] ADJ, M/F feminist
fêmur ['femur] M (*Anat*) femur
fenda ['fẽda] F slit, crack; (*Geo*) fissure
fender [fẽ'der] VT, VI to split, crack
fenecer [fene'ser] VI to die; (*terminar*) to come to an end
feno ['fenu] M hay
fenomenal [fenome'naw] (*pl* **-ais**) ADJ phenomenal; (*espantoso*) amazing; (*pessoa*) brilliant
fenômeno [fe'nomenu] M phenomenon
fera ['fɛra] F wild animal; (*fig: pessoa cruel*) beast; (*: pessoa severa*) hothead; **ser ~ em algo** to be brilliant at sth; **ficar uma ~ (com alguém)** (*fig*) to get mad (with sb)
féretro ['fɛretru] M coffin
feriado [fe'rjadu] M (public) holiday (BRIT), vacation (US)
férias ['fɛrjas] FPL holiday(s) (BRIT), vacation *sg* (US); **de ~** on holiday (BRIT), on vacation (US); **tirar ~** to have *ou* take a holiday (BRIT) *ou* vacation (US)
ferida [fe'rida] F wound, injury; **tocar na ~** (*fig*) to hit home; *ver tb* **ferido**
ferido, -a [fe'ridu, a] ADJ injured; (*em batalha*) wounded; (*magoado*) hurt ▶ M/F casualty
ferimento [feri'mẽtu] M injury; (*em batalha*) wound
ferino, -a [fe'rinu, a] ADJ (*cruel*) cruel; (*crítica, ironia*) biting
ferir [fe'rir] VT to injure; (*tb fig*) to hurt; (*em batalha*) to wound; (*ofender*) to offend
fermentar [fermẽ'tar] VT to ferment; (*fig*) to excite ▶ VI to ferment
fermento [fer'mẽtu] M yeast; **~ em pó** baking powder
ferocidade [ferosi'dadʒi] F fierceness, ferocity
ferocíssimo, -a [fero'sisimu, a] ADJ SUPERL de **feroz**
feroz [fe'roz] ADJ fierce, ferocious; (*cruel*) cruel
ferrado, -a [fe'hadu, a] ADJ (*cavalo*) shod; (*col: sem saída*) done for; **~ no sono** sound asleep
ferradura [feha'dura] F horseshoe
ferragem [fe'haʒẽ] (*pl* **-ns**) F (*peças*) hardware; (*guarnição*) metalwork; **loja de ferragens** ironmonger's (BRIT), hardware store (US)
ferramenta [feha'mẽta] F tool; (*caixa de ferramentas*) tool kit
ferrão [fe'hãw] (*pl* **-ões**) M goad; (*de inseto*) sting
ferrar [fe'har] VT to spike; (*cavalo*) to shoe; (*gado*) to brand; **ferrar-se** VR (*col*) to fail
ferreiro [fe'hejru] M blacksmith
ferrenho, -a [fe'heɲu, a] ADJ (*vontade*) iron; (*marxista etc*) staunch
férreo, -a ['fɛhju, a] ADJ iron *atr*; (*Quím*) ferrous; (*vontade*) iron; (*disciplina*) strict; **via férrea** railway (BRIT), railroad (US)
ferrete [fe'hetʃi] M branding iron; (*fig*) stigma
ferro ['fɛhu] M iron; **ferros** MPL (*algemas*) shackles, chains; **~ batido** wrought iron; **~ de passar** iron; **~ fundido** cast iron;

~ ondulado corrugated iron; **a ~ e fogo** at all costs; **ninguém é/não sou de ~** (fig) we're all/I'm only human

ferrões [fe'hõjs] MPL de **ferrão**

ferrolho [fe'hoʎu] M (trinco) bolt

ferro-velho (pl **ferros-velhos**) M (pessoa) scrap metal dealer; (lugar) scrap metal yard

ferrovia [feho'via] F railway (BRIT), railroad (US)

ferroviário, -a [feho'vjarju, a] ADJ railway atr (BRIT), railroad atr (US) ▶ M/F railway ou railroad worker

ferrugem [fe'huʒẽ] F rust; (Bot) blight

fértil ['fɛrtʃiw] (pl **-eis**) ADJ fertile

fertilidade [fertʃili'dadʒi] F fertility; (abundância) fruitfulness

fertilizante [fertʃili'zãtʃi] ADJ fertilizing ▶ M fertilizer

fertilizar [fertʃili'zar] VT to fertilize

fervente [fer'vẽtʃi] ADJ boiling

ferver [fer'ver] VT, VI to boil; **~ de raiva/ indignação** to seethe with rage/indignation; **~ em fogo baixo** (Culin) to simmer

fervilhar [fervi'ʎar] VI (ferver) to simmer; (com atividade) to hum; (pulular): **~ de** to swarm with

fervor [fer'vor] M fervour (BRIT), fervor (US)

fervoroso, -a [fervo'rozu, ɔza] ADJ fervent

fervura [fer'vura] F boiling

festa ['fɛsta] F (reunião) party; (conjunto de ceremônias) festival; **festas** FPL (carícia) embrace; **boas ~s** Merry Christmas and a Happy New Year; **dia de ~** public holiday; **fazer ~ a alguém** to make a fuss of sb; **fazer ~(s) em alguém** to caress sb; **fazer a ~** (fig) to have a ball, have a whale of a time; **~ caipira** hoedown; **~ de arromba** (col) big party; **~ de embalo** (col) wild party

festança [fes'tãsa] F big party

festeiro, -a [fes'tejru, a] ADJ party-loving

festejar [feste'ʒar] VT (celebrar) to celebrate; (acolher) to welcome, greet

festejo [fes'teʒu] M (festividade) festivity; (ato) celebration

festim [fes'tʃĩ] (pl **-ns**) M feast

festival [festʃi'vaw] (pl **-ais**) M festival

festividade [festʃivi'dadʒi] F festivity

festivo, -a [fes'tʃivu, a] ADJ festive

fetiche [fe'tʃiʃi] M fetish

fetichismo [fetʃi'ʒizmu] M fetishism

fetichista [fetʃi'ʃista] ADJ fetishistic ▶ M/F fetishist

fétido, -a ['fɛtʃidu, a] ADJ foul

feto ['fetu] M (Med) foetus (BRIT), fetus (US); (Bot) fern

feudal [few'daw] (pl **-ais**) ADJ feudal

feudalismo [fewda'lizmu] M feudalism

fev. ABR = **fevereiro**

fevereiro [feve'rejru] M February; ver tb **julho**

fez [fez] VB ver **fazer**

fezes ['fɛzis] FPL faeces (BRIT), feces (US)

FGTS (BR) ABR M (= Fundo de Garantia por Tempo de Serviço) pension fund

FGV (BR) ABR F (= Fundação Getúlio Vargas) economic research agency

fiação [fja'sãw] (pl **-ões**) F spinning; (fábrica) textile mill; (Elet) wiring; **fazer a ~ da casa** to rewire the house

fiada ['fjada] F (fileira) row, line

fiado, -a ['fjadu, a] ADJ (a crédito) on credit ▶ ADV: **comprar/vender ~** to buy/sell on credit

fiador, a [fja'dor(a)] M/F (Jur) guarantor; (Com) backer

fiambre ['fjãbri] M cold meat; (presunto) ham

fiança ['fjãsa] F guarantee; (Jur) bail; **prestar ~ por** to stand bail for; **sob ~** on bail

fiapo ['fjapu] M thread

fiar ['fjar] VT (algodão etc) to spin; (confiar) to entrust; (vender a crédito) to sell on credit; **fiar-se** VR: **~-se em** to trust

fiasco ['fjasku] M fiasco

FIBGE ABR F = **Fundação do Instituto Brasileiro de Geografia e Estatística**

fibra ['fibra] F fibre (BRIT), fiber (US); (fig): **pessoa de ~** person of character; **~ ótica** optical fibre ou fiber

(**PALAVRA-CHAVE**)

ficar [fi'kar] VI **1** (permanecer) to stay; (sobrar) to be left; **ficar perguntando/olhando** etc to keep asking/looking etc; **ficar por fazer** to have still to be done; **ficar para trás** to be left behind

2 (tornar-se) to become; **ficar cego/surdo/ louco** to go blind/deaf/mad; **fiquei contente ao saber da notícia** I was happy when I heard the news; **ficar com raiva/ medo** to get angry/frightened; **ficar de bem/mal com alguém** (col) to make up/fall out with sb

3 (posição) to be; **a casa fica ao lado da igreja** the house is next to the church; **ficar sentado/deitado** to be sitting down/lying down

4 (tempo: durar) **ele ficou duas horas para resolver** he took two hours to decide; (: ser adiado): **a reunião ficou para amanhã** the meeting has been postponed until tomorrow

5 (comportamento): **sua atitude não ficou bem** his (ou her etc) behaviour was inappropriate; (cor): **você fica bem em azul** blue suits you, you look good in blue; (roupa): **ficar bem para** to suit

6: **ficar bom** (de saúde) to be cured; (trabalho, foto etc) to turn out well

7: **ficar de fazer algo** (combinar) to arrange to do sth; (prometer) to promise to do sth

8: **ficar de pé** to stand up

ficção [fik'sãw] F fiction

ficcionista [fiksjo'nista] M/F author, fiction writer

ficha ['fiʃa] F (tb: **ficha de telefone**) token; (tb: **ficha de jogo**) chip; (de fichário) (index) card; (*Polícia*) record; (PT *Elet*) plug; (*em loja, lanchonete*) ticket; **dar a ~ de alguém** (*fig: col*) to give the low-down on sb; **ter ~ na polícia** to have a criminal record; **ter ~ limpa** (*col*) to have a clean record; **~ de identidade** means *sg* of identification, ID

fichar [fi'ʃar] VT to file, index

fichário [fi'ʃarju] M (*móvel*) filing cabinet; (*caixa*) card index; (*caderno*) file

ficheiro [fi'ʃejru] (PT) M = **fichário**

fictício, -a [fik'tʃisju, a] ADJ fictitious

FIDA (BR) ABR M = **Fundo Internacional para o Desenvolvimento Agrícola**

fidalgo [fi'dawgu] M nobleman

fidedigno, -a [fide'dʒignu, a] ADJ trustworthy

fidelidade [fideli'dadʒi] F (*lealdade*) fidelity, loyalty; (*exatidão*) accuracy

fidelíssimo, -a [fide'lisimu, a] ADJ SUPERL *de* **fiel**

fiduciário, -a [fidu'sjarju, a] ADJ (*companhia*) trust *atr* ▶ M/F trustee

fiéis [fjɛjs] ADJ PL *de* **fiel** ▶ MPL: **os ~** the faithful

fiel [fjew] (*pl* **-éis**) ADJ (*leal*) faithful, loyal; (*acurado*) accurate; (*que não falha*) reliable

Fiesp [fi'ɛspi] ABR F = **Federação das Indústrias do Estado de São Paulo**

FIFA ['fifa] ABR F (= *Fédération Internationale de Football Association*) FIFA

figa ['figa] F talisman; **fazer uma ~** to make a *figa*, ≈ cross one's fingers; **de uma ~** (*col*) damned

figada [fi'gada] F fig jelly

fígado ['figadu] M liver; **de maus ~s** (*genioso*) bad-tempered; (*vingativo*) vindictive

figo ['figu] M fig

figueira [fi'gejra] F fig tree

figura [fi'gura] F figure; (*forma*) form, shape; (*Ling*) figure of speech; (*aspecto*) appearance; (*Cartas*) face card; (*ilustração*) picture; (*col: pessoa*) character; **fazer ~** to cut a figure; **fazer má ~** to make a bad impression; **mudar de ~** to take on a new aspect; **ser uma ~ difícil** (*col*) to be difficult to get hold of; **ele é uma ~** (*col*) he's a real character

figura-chave (*pl* **figuras-chave**) F key figure

figurado, -a [figu'radu, a] ADJ figurative

figurante [figu'rãtʃi] M/F (*Cinema*) extra

figurão [figu'rãw] (*pl* **-ões**) M big shot

figurar [figu'rar] VI (*ator*) to appear; (*fazer parte*): **~ (entre/em)** to figure ou appear (among/in) ▶ VT (*imaginar*) to imagine; **ela figura ter menos de 30 anos** she looks younger than 30

figurinha [figu'riɲa] F sticker; **~ difícil** (*col*) person who is difficult to get hold of

figurinista [figuri'nista] M/F fashion designer

figurino [figu'rinu] M model; (*revista*) fashion magazine; (*Cinema, Teatro*) costume design; (*exemplo*) example; **como manda o ~** as it should be

figurões [figu'rõjs] MPL *de* **figurão**

Fiji [fi'ʒi] M Fiji

fila ['fila] F row, line; (BR: *fileira de pessoas*) queue (BRIT), line (US); (*num teatro, cinema*) row ▶ M (*cão*) Brazilian mastiff; **em ~** in a row; **fazer ~** to form a line, queue; **~ indiana** single file

Filadélfia [fila'dɛwfja] F Philadelphia

filamento [fila'mẽtu] M filament

filante [fi'lãtʃi] M/F sponger ▶ ADJ sponging

filantropia [filãtro'pia] F philanthropy

filantrópico, -a [filã'trɔpiku, a] ADJ philanthropic

filantropo [filã'tropu] M philanthropist

filão [fi'lãw] (*pl* **-ões**) M (*Jornalismo*) lead

filar [fi'lar] VT (*agarrar*) to seize; (*col: pedir/obter gratuitamente*) to scrounge

filarmônica [filar'monika] F philharmonic

filarmônico, -a [filar'moniku, a] ADJ philharmonic

filatelia [filate'lia] F stamp collecting

filé [fi'lɛ] M (*bife*) steak; (*peixe*) fillet; **~ mignon** filet mignon

fileira [fi'lejra] F row, line; **fileiras** FPL (*serviço militar*) military service *sg*

filete [fi'letʃi] M fillet; (*de parafuso*) thread

filharada [fiʎa'rada] F gang of children

filhinho, -a [fi'ʎiɲu, a] M/F little son/ daughter; **~ de mamãe** mummy's boy; **~ de papai** rich kid

filho, -a ['fiʎu, a] M/F son/daughter; **filhos** MPL children; (*de animais*) young; **minha filha/meu ~** (*col*) dear, darling; **ter um ~** to have a child; (*fig: col*) to have kittens, have a fit; **ele também é ~ de Deus** he is just as good as anyone else; **~ adotivo** adoptive child; **~ da mãe, ~ da puta** (!) wanker (!), bastard (!); **~ de criação** foster child; **~ ilegítimo/natural** illegitimate/natural child; **~ único** only child; **~ único de mãe viúva** (*fig*) one in a million

filhote [fi'ʎotʃi] M (*de leão, urso etc*) cub; (*cachorro*) pup(py)

filiação [filja'sãw] (*pl* **-ões**) F affiliation

filial [fi'ljaw] (*pl* **-ais**) F (*sucursal*) branch ▶ ADJ filial; **gerente de ~** branch manager

filigrana [fili'grana] F filigree

filipeta [fili'peta] F flyer

Filipinas [fili'pinas] FPL: **as ~** the Philippines

filipino, -a [fili'pinu, a] ADJ, M/F Filipino ▶ M (*Ling*) Filipino

filmadora [fiwma'dora] F video camera

filmagem [fiw'maʒẽ] F filming

filmar [fiw'mar] VT, VI to film

filme ['fiwmi] M film (BRIT), movie (US); **~ (de) bangue-bangue** ou **faroeste** western; **~ (de) curta/longa metragem** short/ feature film; **~ de época** period film; **~ de capa e espada** swashbuckling film

filmoteca [fiwmo'tɛka] F (*lugar*) film library; (*coleção*) film collection

filó [fi'lɔ] M tulle

filões [fi'lõjs] MPL *de* **filão**

filologia [filolo'ʒia] F philology

filólogo, -a [fi'lɔlogu, a] M/F philologist
filosofar [filozo'far] VI to philosophize
filosofia [filozo'fia] F philosophy
filosófico, -a [filo'zɔfiku, a] ADJ
philosophical
filósofo, -a [fi'lɔzofu, a] M/F philosopher
filtrar [fiw'trar] VT to filter; **filtrar-se** VR
(líquidos) to filter; (infiltrar-se) to infiltrate
filtro ['fiwtru] M (Tec) filter
fim [fĩ] (pl **-ns**) M end; (motivo) aim, purpose;
(de história, filme) ending; **a ~ de** in order to;
estar a ~ de (fazer) algo to feel like (doing)
sth, fancy (doing) sth; **estar a ~ de alguém**
(col) to fancy sb; **no ~ das contas** after all;
por ~ finally; **sem ~** endless; **ter por ~** to
aim at; **levar ao ~** to carry through; **pôr** ou
dar ~ a to put an end to; **ter ~** to come to an
end; **~ de mundo** (fig) hole; **ele mora no ~
do mundo** he lives miles from anywhere; **é o ~
(do mundo** ou **da picada)** (fig) it's the
pits; **~ de semana** weekend
finado, -a [fi'nadu, a] ADJ, M/F deceased
| The day of **Finados**, 2 November, a
| holiday throughout Brazil, is dedicated
| to remembering the dead. On this day,
| people usually gather in cemeteries to
| remember their family dead, and also to
| worship at the graves of popular figures
| from Brazilian culture and society, such
| as singers, actors and other personalities.
| It is popularly believed that these people
| can work miracles.
final [fi'naw] (pl **-ais**) ADJ final, last ▶ M end;
(Mús) finale ▶ F (Esporte) final
finalista [fina'lista] M/F finalist
finalização [finaliza'sãw] (pl **-ões**) F
conclusion
finalizar [finali'zar] VT to finish, conclude
▶ VI (Futebol) to finish; **finalizar-se** VR to end
Finam [fi'nã] ABR M (= Fundo de Investimento da
Amazônia) regional development fund
Finame [fi'nami] (BR) ABR M = **Agência
Especial de Financiamento Industrial**
finanças [fi'nãsas] FPL finance sg
financeiro, -a [finã'sejru, a] ADJ financial
▶ M/F financier
financiamento [finãsja'mẽtu] M financing
financiar [finã'sjar] VT to finance
financista [finã'sista] M/F financier
finar-se [fi'narsi] VR (consumir-se) to waste
away; (morrer) to die
fincar [fĩ'kar] VT (cravar) to drive in; (fixar) to
fix; (apoiar) to lean
findar [fĩ'dar] VT, VI to end, finish
findo, -a ['fĩdu, a] ADJ (ano) past; (assunto)
closed
fineza [fi'neza] F fineness; (gentileza)
kindness
fingido, -a [fĩ'ʒidu, a] ADJ pretend; (pessoa)
two-faced, insincere ▶ M/F hypocrite
fingimento [fĩʒi'mẽtu] M pretence (BRIT),
pretense (US)
fingir [fĩ'ʒir] VT (simular) to feign ▶ VI to

pretend; **fingir-se** VR: **~-se de** to pretend to
be; **~ fazer/que** to pretend to do/that
finito, -a [fi'nitu, a] ADJ finite
finlandês, -esa [fĩlã'des, eza] ADJ Finnish
▶ M/F Finn ▶ M (Ling) Finnish
Finlândia [fĩ'lãdʒja] F: **a ~** Finland
fino, -a ['finu, a] ADJ fine; (delgado) slender;
(educado) polite; (som, voz) shrill; (elegante)
refined ▶ M: **falar ~** to talk in a high voice;
ser o ~ (col) to be the business; **tirar um ~
em alguém** to almost drive into sb
Finor [fi'nor] (BR) ABR M (= Fundo de Investimento
do Nordeste) regional development fund
finório, -a [fi'nɔrju, a] ADJ crafty, sly
fins [fĩs] MPL de **fim**
Finsocial [fĩso'sjaw] (BR) ABR M = **Fundo de
Investimento Social**
finura [fi'nura] F fineness; (elegância) finesse
fio ['fiu] M thread; (Bot) fibre (BRIT), fiber (US);
(Elet) wire; (Tel) line; (de líquido) trickle;
(gume) edge; (encadeamento) series; **horas/
dias a ~** hours/days on end; **de ~ a pavio**
from beginning to end; **por um ~** (fig:
escapar) by the skin of one's teeth; **bater um
~** (col) to make a call; **estar por um ~** to be
on one's last legs; **perder o ~ (da meada)**
(fig) to lose one's thread; **retomar o ~
perdido** (fig) to take up the thread again;
~ condutor (fig) connecting thread; **sem ~**
(Comput) wireless
fiorde ['fjordʒi] M fjord
firewall [faja'aw] M firewall
Firjan [fir'ʒã] ABR F = **Federação das
Indústrias do Rio do Janeiro**
firma ['firma] F (assinatura) signature; (Com)
firm, company
firmamento [firma'mẽtu] M firmament
firmar [fir'mar] VT (tornar firme) to secure,
make firm; (assinar) to sign; (estabelecer) to
establish; (basear) to base ▶ VI (tempo) to
settle; **firmar-se** VR: **~-se em** (basear-se) to
rest on, be based on
firme ['firmi] ADJ firm; (estável) stable; (sólido)
solid; (tempo) settled ▶ ADV firmly;
aguentar ~ to hang on; **pisar ~** to stride
out
firmeza [fir'meza] F firmness; (estabilidade)
stability; (solidez) solidity
FISA ['fiza] ABR F (= Federação Internacional de
Automobilismo Esportivo) FISA
fiscal [fis'kaw] (pl **-ais**) M/F supervisor;
(aduaneiro) customs officer; (de impostos) tax
inspector
fiscalização [fiskaliza'sãw] (pl **-ões**) F
inspection
fiscalizar [fiskali'zar] VT (supervisionar) to
supervise; (examinar) to inspect, check
fisco ['fisku] M: **o ~** ≈ the Inland Revenue
(BRIT), ≈ the Internal Revenue Service (US)
Fiset [fi'sɛtʃi] (BR) ABR M = **Fundo de
Investimentos Setoriais**
fisgada [fiz'gada] F stabbing pain
fisgar [fiz'gar] VT to catch

física ['fizika] F physics *sg*; ~ **nuclear** nuclear physics; *ver tb* **físico**
físico, -a ['fiziku, a] ADJ physical ▶ M/F (*cientista*) physicist ▶ M (*corpo*) physique
fisiologia [fizjolo'ʒia] F physiology
fisionomia [fizjono'mia] F (*rosto*) face; (*ar*) expression, look; (*aspecto de algo*) appearance; (*conjunto de caracteres*) make-up
fisionomista [fizjono'mista] M/F person with a good memory for faces
fisioterapeuta [fizjotera'pewta] M/F physiotherapist
fisioterapia [fizjotera'pia] F physiotherapy
fissura [fi'sura] F crack; (*col: ansia*) craving
fissurado, -a [fisu'radu, a] ADJ cracked; **estar ~ em** (*col*) to be wild about
fissurar [fisu'rar] VT to crack
fita ['fita] F (*tira*) strip, band; (*de seda, algodão*) ribbon, tape; (*filme*) film; (*para máquina de escrever*) ribbon; (*magnética, adesiva*) tape; ~ **durex**® adhesive tape, Sellotape® (BRIT), Scotch tape® (US); ~ **isolante** insulating tape; ~ **métrica** tape measure; **fazer ~** (*col*) to put on an act; **isso é ~ dela** (*col*) it's just an act
fitar [fi'tar] VT (*com os olhos*) to stare at, gaze at; **fitar-se** VR to stare at each other
fiteiro, -a [fi'tejru, a] ADJ melodramatic
fito, -a ['fitu, a] ADJ fixed ▶ M aim, intention
fivela [fi'vɛla] F buckle
fixação [fiksa'sãw] (*pl* -**ões**) F fixation
fixador [fiksa'dor] M hair gel; (*líquido*) setting lotion
fixar [fik'sar] VT to fix; (*colar, prender*) to stick; (*data, prazo, regras*) to set; (*atenção*) to concentrate; **fixar-se** VR: ~-**se em** (*assunto*) to concentrate on; (*detalhe*) to fix on; (*apegar-se a*) to be attached to; ~ **os olhos em** to stare at; ~ **residência** to set up house, settle down; ~ **algo na memória** to fix sth in one's mind
fixo, -a ['fiksu, a] ADJ fixed; (*firme*) firm; (*permanente*) permanent; (*cor*) fast ▶ M (*tb*: **telefone fixo**) landline
fiz *etc* [fiz] VB *ver* **fazer**
flacidez [flasi'dez] F softness, flabbiness
flácido, -a ['flasidu, a] ADJ flabby
Fla-Flu [fla-] M local derby (*football match between rivals Flamengo and Fluminense*)
flagelado, -a [flaʒe'ladu, a] M/F: **os ~s** the afflicted, the victims
flagrante [fla'grãtʃi] ADJ flagrant; **apanhar em ~** (*delito*) to catch red-handed *ou* in the act
flagrar [fla'grar] VT to catch
flambar [flã'bar] VT (*Culin*) to flambé
flamejante [flame'ʒãtʃi] ADJ flaming
flamejar [flame'ʒar] VI to blaze
flamengo, -a [fla'mẽgu, a] ADJ Flemish ▶ M (*Ling*) Flemish
flamingo [fla'mĩgu] M flamingo
flâmula ['flamula] F pennant
flanco ['flãku] M flank
Flandres ['flãdris] F Flanders

flanela [fla'nɛla] F flannel
flanquear [flã'kjar] VT to flank; (*Mil*) to outflank
flash [flaʃ] M (*Foto*) flash
flashback [flaʃ'baki] (*pl* -**s**) M flashback
flatulência [flatu'lẽsja] F flatulence
flauta ['flawta] F flute; **ele leva tudo na ~** (*col*) he doesn't take anything seriously; ~ **doce** (*Mús*) recorder
flautista [flaw'tʃista] M/F flautist
flecha ['flɛʃa] F arrow
flechada [fle'ʃada] F (*golpe*) shot; (*ferimento*) arrow wound
flertar [fler'tar] VI: ~ (**com alguém**) to flirt (with sb)
flerte ['flertʃi] M flirtation
fleuma ['flewma] F phlegm
flexão [flek'sãw] (*pl* -**ões**) F flexing; (*exercício*) press-up; (*Ling*) inflection
flexibilidade [fleksibili'dadʒi] F flexibility
flexionar [fleksjo'nar] VT, VI (*Ling*) to inflect
flexível [flek'sivew] (*pl* -**eis**) ADJ flexible
flexões [flek'sõjs] FPL *de* **flexão**
fliperama [flipe'rama] M pinball machine
floco ['flɔku] M flake; ~ **de milho** cornflake; ~ **de neve** snowflake; **sorvete de ~s** chocolate chip ice-cream
flor [flor] F flower; (*o melhor*) cream, pick; **em ~** in bloom; **a fina ~** the elite; **à ~ da pele** on edge; **ele não é ~ que se cheire** (*col*) he's a bad lot
flora ['flɔra] F flora
floreado, -a [flo'rjadu, a] ADJ (*jardim*) full of flowers; (*relevo*) ornate; (*estilo*) florid
floreio [flo'reju] M clever turn of phrase
florescente [flore'sẽtʃi] ADJ (*Bot*) in flower; (*próspero*) flourishing
florescer [flore'ser] VI (*Bot*) to flower; (*prosperar*) to flourish
floresta [flo'rɛsta] F forest
florestal [flores'taw] (*pl* -**ais**) ADJ forest *atr*
florianopolitano, -a [florjanopoli'tanu, a] ADJ from Florianópolis ▶ M/F native of Florianópolis
Flórida ['flɔrida] F: **a ~** Florida
florido, -a [flo'ridu, a] ADJ (*jardim*) in flower; (*mesa*) decorated with flowers
florir [flo'rir] VI to flower
flotilha [flo'tʃiʎa] F flotilla
flozô [flo'zo] (*col*) M: **ficar de ~** to lounge around; **viver de ~** to lead a life of leisure
Flu [flu] ABR M = **Fluminense Futebol Clube**
fluência [flu'ẽsja] F fluency
fluente [flu'ẽtʃi] ADJ fluent
fluidez [flui'dez] F fluidity
fluido, -a ['flwidu, a] ADJ fluid ▶ M fluid
fluir [flwir] VI to flow
fluminense [flumi'nẽsi] ADJ from the state of Rio de Janeiro ▶ M/F native *ou* inhabitant of the state of Rio de Janeiro
fluorescente [flwore'sẽtʃi] ADJ fluorescent
flutuação [flutwa'sãw] (*pl* -**ões**) F fluctuation

flutuante [flu'twãtʃi] ADJ floating; (*bandeira*) fluttering; (*fig: vacilante*) hesitant, wavering; (*Com: câmbio*) floating

flutuar [flu'twar] VI to float; (*bandeira*) to flutter; (*fig: vacilar*) to waver

fluvial [flu'vjaw] (*pl* -**ais**) ADJ river *atr*

fluxo ['fluksu] M (*corrente*) flow; (*Elet*) flux; ~ **de caixa** (*Com*) cash flow

fluxograma [flukso'grama] M flow chart

FM ABR (*Rádio: frequencia modulada*) FM ▶ F FM (radio) station

FMI ABR M (= *Fundo Monetário Internacional*) IMF

FMS ABR F = **Federação Mundial dos Sindicatos**

FN (BR) ABR M = **Fuzileiro Naval**

FND (BR) ABR M = **Fundo Nacional de Desenvolvimento**

fobia [fo'bia] F phobia

foca ['fɔka] F (*animal*) seal ▶ M/F (*col: jornalista*) cub reporter

focalização [fokaliza'sãw] F focusing

focalizar [fokali'zar] VT to focus (on)

focinho [fo'siɲu] M snout; (*col: cara*) face, mug (*col*)

foco ['fɔku] M focus; (*Med, fig*) seat, centre (BRIT), center (US); **fora de** ~ out of focus

fofo, -a ['fofu, a] ADJ soft; (*col: pessoa*) cute

fofoca [fo'fɔka] F piece of gossip; **fofocas** FPL (*mexericos*) gossip *sg*; **fazer** ~ to gossip

fofocar [fofo'kar] VI to gossip

fofoqueiro, -a [fofo'kejru, a] ADJ gossipy ▶ M/F gossip

fofura [fo'fura] (*col*) F cutie

fogão [fo'gãw] (*pl* -**ões**) M stove, cooker

fogareiro [foga'rejru] M stove

foge *etc* ['fɔʒi] VB *ver* **fugir**

fogo ['fogu] M fire; (*fig*) ardour (BRIT), ardor (US); **você tem** ~? have you got a light?; ~**s de artifício** fireworks; **a** ~ **lento** on a low flame; **à prova de** ~ fireproof; **abrir** ~ to open fire; **brincar com** ~ (*fig*) to play with fire; **cessar** ~ (*Mil*) to cease fire; **estar com** ~ (*col: pessoa*) to be randy; **estar de** ~ (*col: bêbado*) to be drunk; **pegar** ~ to catch fire; (*estar com febre*) to burn up; **pôr** ~ **a** to set fire to; **ser bom para o** ~ (*fig*) to be useless; **ser** ~ (**na roupa**) (*col: pessoa*) to be a pain; (: *trabalho etc*) to be murder; (: *ser incrível*) to be amazing

fogões [fo'gõjs] MPL *de* **fogão**

fogo-fátuo (*pl* **fogos-fátuos**) M will-o'-the-wisp

fogoso, -a [fo'gozu, ɔza] ADJ fiery; (*libidinoso*) lustful

fogueira [fo'gejra] F bonfire

foguete [fo'getʃi] M rocket; (*pessoa*) live wire; **soltar os** ~**s antes da festa** (*fig*) to jump the gun

foi [foj] VB *ver* **ir, ser**

foice ['fɔjsi] F scythe

folclore [fowk'lɔri] M folklore

folclórico, -a [fowk'lɔriku, a] ADJ (*música etc*) folk *atr*; (*comida, roupa*) ethnic

fole ['fɔli] M bellows *sg*

fôlego ['folegu] M breath; (*folga*) breathing space; **perder o** ~ to get out of breath; **tomar** ~ to pause for breath

folga ['fɔwga] F (*descanso*) rest, break; (*espaço livre*) clearance; (*ócio*) inactivity; (*col: atrevimento*) cheek; **dia de** ~ day off; **que** ~! what a cheek!

folgado, -a [fow'gadu, a] ADJ (*roupa*) loose; (*vida*) leisurely; (*col: atrevido*) cheeky; (: *boa vida*) easy-living ▶ M/F (*col: atrevido*) cheeky devil; (: *boa vida*) loafer

folgar [fow'gar] VT to loosen, slacken ▶ VI (*descansar*) to rest, relax; (*divertir-se*) to have fun, amuse o.s.; ~ **em saber que** ... to be pleased to hear that ...

folgazão, -zona [fowga'zãw, 'zɔna] (*pl* -**ões/-s**) ADJ (*pessoa*) fun-loving; (*gênio*) lively

folha ['foʎa] F leaf; (*de papel, de metal*) sheet; (*página*) page; (*de faca*) blade; (*jornal*) paper; **novo em** ~ brand new; ~ **de estanho** tinfoil (BRIT), aluminum foil (US); ~ **de exercícios** worksheet; ~ **de pagamento** payroll; ~ **de rosto** imprint page

folhagem [fo'ʎaʒẽ] F foliage

folha-seca (*pl* **folhas-secas**) F (*Futebol*) swerving shot

folheado, -a [fo'ʎjadu, a] ADJ veneered; ~ **a ouro** gold-plated

folhear [fo'ʎjar] VT to leaf through

folheto [fo'ʎetu] M booklet, pamphlet

folhinha [fo'ʎiɲa] F tear-off calendar

folhudo, -a [fo'ʎudu, a] ADJ leafy

folia [fo'lia] F revelry, merriment

folião, -liona [fo'ʎjãw, ɔna] (*pl* -**ões/-s**) M/F reveller (*in carnival*)

folículo [fo'likulu] M follicle

foliões [fo'ʎõjs] MPL *de* **folião**

foliona [fo'ʎjona] F *de* **folião**

fome ['fɔmi] F hunger; (*escassez*) famine; (*fig: avidez*) longing; **passar** ~ to go hungry; **estar com** *ou* **ter** ~ to be hungry; **varado de** ~ starving, ravenous

fomentar [fomẽ'tar] VT to instigate, incite; (*discórdia*) to sow, cause

fomento [fo'mẽtu] M (*Med*) fomentation; (*estímulo*) incitement; (*de discórdia, ódio etc*) stirring up

fominha [fo'miɲa] (*col*) ADJ stingy ▶ M/F skinflint

fonador, a [fona'dor(a)] ADJ: **aparelho** ~ vocal track

fone ['fɔni] M telephone, phone; (*peça do telefone*) receiver

fonema [fo'nɛma] M (*Ling*) phoneme

fonética [fo'nɛtʃika] F phonetics *sg*

fonético, -a [fo'nɛtʃiku, a] ADJ phonetic

fonfom [fõ'fõ] (*pl* -**ns**) M toot

fonologia [fonolo'ʒia] F phonology

fonte ['fõtʃi] F (*nascente*) spring; (*chafariz*) fountain; (*origem*) source; (*Anat*) temple; **de** ~ **limpa** from a reliable source; **retido/ tributado na** ~ (*Com*) deducted/taxed at source

footing ['futʃiŋ] M jogging

for [for] VB *ver* **ir, ser**

fora¹ ['fɔra] ADV out, outside ▶ PREP (*além de*) apart from ▶ M: **dar o ~** (*bateria, radio*) to give out; (*pessoa*) to leave, be off; **dar um ~** to slip up; **dar um ~ em alguém** (*namorado*) to chuck sb, dump sb; (*esnobar*) to snub sb; **levar um ~** (*de namorado*) to be given the boot; (*ser esnobado*) to get the brush-off; **~ de** outside; **~ de si** beside o.s.; **estar ~** (*viajando*) to be away; **estar ~ (de casa)** to be out; **lá ~** outside; (*no exterior*) abroad; **jantar ~** to eat out; **com os braços de ~** with bare arms; **ser de ~** to be from out of town; **ficar de ~** not to join in; **lá para ~** outside; **ir para ~** (*viajar*) to go out of town; **com a cabeça para ~ da janela** with one's head sticking out of the window; **costurar/cozinhar para ~** to do sewing/cooking for other people; **por ~** on the outside; **cobrar por ~** to charge extra; **~ de dúvida** beyond doubt; **~ de propósito** irrelevant

fora² VB *ver* **ir, ser**

fora da lei [fɔrada'lej] M/F INV outlaw

foragido, -a [fora'ʒidu, a] ADJ, M/F fugitive; **estar ~** to be on the run

foragir-se [fora'ʒirsi] VR to go on the run

forasteiro, -a [foras'tejru, a] ADJ (*estranho*) alien ▶ M/F outsider, stranger; (*de outro país*) foreigner

forca ['fɔrka] F gallows *sg*

força ['fɔrsa] F (*energia física*) strength; (*Tec, Elet*) power; (*esforço*) effort; (*coerção*) force; **à ~** by force; **à ~ de** by dint of; **com ~** hard; **por ~** of necessity; **dar (uma) ~ a** to back up, encourage; **fazer ~** to try (hard); **como vai essa ~?** (*col*) how's it going?; **F~ Aérea** Air Force; **~ de trabalho** workforce; **~ maior** (*Com*) act of God

forcado [for'kadu] M pitchfork

forçado, -a [for'sadu, a] ADJ forced; (*afetado*) false

forçar [for'sar] VT to force; (*olhos, voz*) to strain; **forçar-se** VR: **~-se a** to force o.s. to

força-tarefa (*pl* **forças-tarefa**) F task force

forcejar [forse'ʒar] VI (*esforçar-se*) to strive; (*lutar*) to struggle

fórceps ['fɔrsips] M INV forceps *pl*

forçoso, -a [for'sozu, ɔza] ADJ (*necessário*) necessary; (*obrigatório*) obligatory

forja ['fɔrʒa] F forge

forjar [for'ʒar] VT to forge; (*pretexto*) to invent

forma ['fɔrma] F form; (*de um objeto*) shape; (*físico*) figure; (*maneira*) way; (*Med*) fitness; **desta ~** in this way; **de (tal) ~ que** in such a way that; **de qualquer ~** anyway; **da mesma ~** likewise; **de outra ~** otherwise; **de ~ alguma** in no way whatsoever; **em ~ de pera/comprimido** pear-shaped/in tablet form; **estar fora de/em ~** (*pessoa*) to be unfit/fit; **manter a ~** to keep fit; **~ de pagamento** means of payment

fôrma ['forma] F (*Culin*) cake tin; (*molde*) mould (BRIT), mold (US); (*para sapatos*) last

formação [forma'sãw] (*pl* **-ões**) F formation; (*antecedentes*) background; (*caráter*) make-up; (*profissional*) training

formado, -a [for'madu, a] ADJ (*modelado*): **ser ~ de** to consist of ▶ M/F graduate; **ser ~ em** to be a graduate in

formal [for'maw] (*pl* **-ais**) ADJ formal

formalidade [formali'dadʒi] F formality

formalizar [formali'zar] VT to formalize

formando, -a [for'mãdu, a] M/F graduating student, graduand

formão [for'mãw] (*pl* **-ões**) M chisel

formar [for'mar] VT to form; (*constituir*) to constitute, make up; (*educar*) to train, educate; (*soldados*) to form up ▶ VI to form up; **formar-se** VR (*tomar forma*) to form; (*Educ*) to graduate

formatar [forma'tar] VT (*Comput*) to format

formato [for'matu] M format; (*de papel*) size

formatura [forma'tura] F (*Mil*) formation; (*Educ*) graduation

fórmica® ['fɔrmika] F Formica®

formidável [formi'davew] (*pl* **-eis**) ADJ tremendous, great

formiga [for'miga] F ant

formigar [formi'gar] VI (*ser abundante*) to abound; (*sentir comichão*) to itch; **~ de algo** to swarm with sth

formigueiro [formi'gejru] M ants' nest; (*multidão*) throng, swarm

formões [for'mõjs] MPL *de* **formão**

Formosa [for'mɔza] F Taiwan

formoso, -a [for'mozu, ɔza] ADJ (*belo*) beautiful; (*esplêndido*) superb

formosura [formo'zura] F beauty

fórmula ['fɔrmula] F formula

formulação [formula'sãw] (*pl* **-ões**) F formulation

formular [formu'lar] VT to formulate; (*queixas*) to voice; **~ votos** to express one's hopes/wishes

formulário [formu'larju] M form; **formulários** MPL: **~s contínuos** (*Comput*) continuous stationery *sg*

fornalha [for'naʎa] F furnace; (*fig: lugar quente*) oven

fornecedor, a [fornese'dor(a)] M/F supplier ▶ F (*empresa*) supplier ▶ ADJ supply *atr*

fornecer [forne'ser] VT to supply, provide; **~ algo a alguém** to supply sb with sth

fornecimento [fornesi'mẽtu] M supply

fornicar [forni'kar] VI to fornicate

forno ['fɔrnu] M (*Culin*) oven; (*Tec*) furnace; (*para cerâmica*) kiln; **alto ~** blast furnace; **cozinheiro/a de ~ e fogão** expert cook

foro ['fɔru] M forum; (*Jur*) Court of Justice; **foros** MPL (*privilégios*) privileges; **de ~ íntimo** personal, private

forra ['fɔha] F: **ir à ~** (*col*) to get one's own back

forragem [fo'haʒẽ] F fodder

forrar [fo'har] VT (*cobrir*) to cover; (: *interior*) to line; (*de papel*) to paper

forro ['fohu] M (*cobertura*) covering; (*interior*) lining; **com ~ de pele** fur-lined

forró [fo'hɔ] M *see note*

> **Forró** is a style of popular music and dance that originated in the north-east of Brazil, but which is now popular all over the country. The instruments which feature in **forró** are the accordion, the bass drum and the triangle, and it is danced with a partner. There are a number of different styles of **forró**, such as the *forró universitário*, which combines various musical genres and has attracted a considerable following among the younger generation in Brazil's cities.

fortalecer [fortale'ser] VT to strengthen

fortalecimento [fortalesi'mẽtu] M strengthening

fortaleza [forta'leza] F (*forte*) fortress; (*força*) strength; (*moral*) fortitude; **ser uma ~** to be as strong as an ox

fortalezense [fortale'zẽsi] ADJ from Fortaleza ▶ M/F native ou inhabitant of Fortaleza

forte ['fɔrtʃi] ADJ strong; (*pancada*) hard; (*chuva*) heavy; (*som*) loud; (*dor*) sharp, strong; (*filme*) powerful; (*pessoa: musculoso*) muscular ▶ ADV strongly; (*som*) loud(ly) ▶ M (*fortaleza*) fort; (*talento*) strength; **ser ~ em algo** (*versado*) to be good at sth ou strong in sth

fortificação [fortʃifika'sãw] (*pl* **-ões**) F fortification; (*fortaleza*) fortress

fortificante [fortʃifi'kãtʃi] ADJ fortifying ▶ M fortifier

fortificar [fortʃifi'kar] VT to fortify; **fortificar-se** VR to build o.s. up

fortuitamente [fortwita'mẽtʃi] ADV (*imprevisivelmente*) by chance, unexpectedly; (*ocasionalmente*) casually

fortuito, -a [for'twitu, a] ADJ accidental

fortuna [for'tuna] F fortune, (good) luck; (*riqueza*) fortune, wealth; **custar uma ~** to cost a fortune

fórum ['forũ] (*pl* **-ns**) M (*Comput*) forum; **~ de discussão** discussion forum, message board

fosco, -a ['fosku, a] ADJ (*sem brilho*) dull; (*opaco*) opaque

fosfato [fos'fatu] M phosphate

fosforescente [fosfore'sẽtʃi] ADJ phosphorescent

fósforo ['fɔsforu] M match; (*Quím*) phosphorus

fossa ['fɔsa] F pit; (*col*) blues *pl*; **estar/ficar na ~** (*col*) to be/get depressed ou down in the dumps; **tirar alguém da ~** (*col*) to cheer sb up; **~ séptica** septic tank

fosse ['fosi] VB *ver* **ir, ser**

fóssil ['fɔsiw] (*pl* **-eis**) M fossil

fosso ['fosu] M trench, ditch; (*de uma fortaleza*) moat

foto ['fɔtu] F photo

fotocópia [foto'kɔpja] F photocopy

fotocopiadora [fotokopja'dora] F photocopier

fotocopiar [fotoko'pjar] VT to photocopy

fotogênico, -a [foto'ʒeniku, a] ADJ photogenic

fotografar [fotogra'far] VT to photograph

fotografia [fotogra'fia] F photography; (*uma foto*) photograph

fotográfico, -a [foto'grafiku, a] ADJ photographic; *ver tb* **máquina**

fotógrafo, -a [fo'tɔgrafu, a] M/F photographer

fotonovela [fotono'vela] F photo story

fotossíntese [foto'sĩtezi] F (*Bio*) photosynthesis

foxtrote [foks'trɔtʃi] M foxtrot

foyer [fua'je] M foyer

foz [fɔz] F mouth (*of river*)

FP-25 ABR FPL (= *Forças Populares do 25 de Abril*) Portuguese terrorist group

fração [fra'sãw] (*pl* **-ões**) F fraction

fracassar [fraka'sar] VI to fail

fracasso [fra'kasu] M failure

fracionar [frasjo'nar] VT to break up; **fracionar-se** VR to break up, fragment

fraco, -a ['fraku, a] ADJ weak; (*sol, som*) faint ▶ M weakness; **estar ~ em algo** to be poor at sth; **ter um ~ por algo** to have a weakness for sth

frações [fra'sõjs] FPL *de* **fração**

frade ['fradʒi] M (*Rel*) friar; (: *monge*) monk

fraga ['fraga] F crag, rock

fragata [fra'gata] F (*Náut*) frigate

frágil ['fraʒiw] (*pl* **-eis**) ADJ (*débil*) fragile; (*Com*) breakable; (*pessoa*) frail; (*saúde*) delicate, poor

fragilidade [fraʒili'dadʒi] F fragility; (*de uma pessoa*) frailty

fragílimo, -a [fra'ʒilimu, a] ADJ SUPERL *de* **frágil**

fragmentar [fragmẽ'tar] VT to break up; **fragmentar-se** VR to break up

fragmento [frag'mẽtu] M fragment

fragrância [fra'grãsja] F fragrance, perfume

fragrante [fra'grãtʃi] ADJ fragrant

frajola [fra'ʒɔla] (*col*) ADJ smart

fralda ['frawda] F (*da camisa*) shirt tail; (*para bebê*) nappy (BRIT), diaper (US); (*de montanha*) foot; **mal saído das ~s** (*fig*) still wet behind the ears

framboesa [frãbo'eza] F raspberry

França ['frãsa] F France

francamente [frãka'mẽtʃi] ADV (*abertamente*) frankly; (*realmente*) really

francês, -esa [frã'ses, eza] ADJ French ▶ M/F Frenchman/woman ▶ M (*Ling*) French

franco, -a ['frãku, a] ADJ (*sincero*) frank; (*isento de pagamento*) free; (*óbvio*) clear ▶ M franc; **entrada franca** free admission

frangalho [frã'gaʎu] M (*trapo*) rag, tatter; (*pessoa*) wreck; **em ~s** in tatters

frango ['frãgu] M chicken; (*Futebol*) easy goal

franja ['frãʒa] F fringe (BRIT), bangs pl (US)

franquear [frã'kjar] VT (*caminho*) to clear; (*isentar de imposto*) to exempt from duties; (*carta*) to frank; **~ algo a alguém** (*facultar*) to make sth available to sb

franqueza [frã'keza] F frankness

franquia [frã'kia] F (Com) franchise; (*isenção*) exemption; **~ de bagagem** baggage allowance; **~ diplomática** diplomatic immunity; **~ postal** Freepost®

franzido [frã'zidu] M pleat

franzino, -a [frã'zinu, a] ADJ skinny

franzir [frã'zir] VT (*preguear*) to pleat; (*enrugar*) to wrinkle, crease; (*lábios*) to curl; **~ as sobrancelhas** to frown

fraque ['fraki] M morning suit

fraquejar [frake'ʒar] VI to grow weak; (*vontade*) to weaken

fraqueza [fra'keza] F weakness

frasco ['frasku] M (*de remédio, perfume*) bottle

frase ['frazi] F sentence; **~ feita** set phrase

fraseado [fra'zjadu] M wording

frasqueira [fras'kejra] F vanity case

fraternal [frater'naw] (*pl* **-ais**) ADJ fraternal, brotherly

fraternidade [fraterni'dadʒi] F fraternity

fraternizar [fraterni'zar] VT to bring together ▶ VI to fraternize

fraterno, -a [fra'tɛrnu, a] ADJ fraternal, brotherly

fratura [fra'tura] F fracture, break

fraturar [fratu'rar] VT to fracture

fraudar [fraw'dar] VT to defraud; (*expectativa, esperanças*) to dash

fraude ['frawdʒi] F fraud

fraudulento, -a [frawdu'lẽtu, a] ADJ fraudulent

freada [fre'ada] (BR) F: **dar uma ~** to slam on the brakes

frear [fre'ar] (BR) VT (*conter*) to curb, restrain; (*veículo*) to stop ▶ VI (*veículo*) to brake

freelance [fri'lãs] M/F freelancer

freezer ['frizer] M freezer

frege ['freʒi] M mess

freguês, -guesa [fre'ges, 'geza] M/F (*cliente*) customer; (PT) parishioner

freguesia [frege'zia] F customers pl; (PT) parish

frei [frej] M friar, monk; (*título*) Brother

freio ['freju] M (BR: *veículo*) brake; (*de cavalo*) bridle; (*bocado do freio*) bit; (*fig*) check; **~ de mão** handbrake

freira ['frejra] F nun

freixo ['frejʃu] M (Bot) ash

Frelimo [fre'limo] ABR F (= *Frente de Libertação de Moçambique*) Frelimo

fremente [fre'mẽtʃi] ADJ (*fig*) rousing

fremir [fre'mir] VI (*bramar*) to roar; (*tremer*) to tremble

frêmito ['fremitu] M (*fig: de alegria etc*) wave

frenesi [frene'zi] M frenzy

frenético, -a [fre'nɛtʃiku, a] ADJ frantic, frenzied

frente ['frẽtʃi] F (*de objeto, Pol, Mil*) front; (*rosto*) face; (*fachada*) façade; **~ a ~** face to face; **à ~ de** at the front of; **de ~ para** facing; **em ~ de** in front of; (*de fronte a*) opposite; **para a ~** ahead, forward; **de trás para ~** from back to front; **porta da ~** front door; **apartamento de ~** apartment at the front; **seguir em ~** to go straight on; **a casa em ~** the house opposite; **na minha** (*ou* sua *etc*) **~** in front of me (*ou* you *etc*); **sair da ~** to get out of the way; **sai da minha ~!** get out of my sight!; **pela ~** ahead, frequently; **pra ~** (*col*) fashionable, trendy; **fazer ~ a algo** to face sth; **ir para a ~** (*progredir*) to progress; **levar à ~** to carry through; **~ de combate** (Mil) front; **~ de trabalho** area of employment; **~ fria/quente** (Meteorologia) cold/warm front

frequência [fre'kwẽsja] F frequency; **com ~** often, frequently

frequentador, a [frekwẽta'dor(a)] M/F regular visitor; (*de restaurante etc*) regular customer

frequentar [frekwẽ'tar] VT to frequent; **~ a casa de alguém** to go to sb's house a lot; **~ um curso** to attend a course

frequente [fre'kwẽtʃi] ADJ frequent

fresca ['freska] F cool breeze

frescão [fres'kãw] (*pl* **-ões**) M air-conditioned coach

fresco, -a ['fresku, a] ADJ fresh; (*vento, tempo*) cool; (*col: efeminado*) camp; (: *afetado*) pretentious; (: *cheio de luxo*) fussy ▶ M (*ar*) fresh air; (Arte) fresco

frescobol [fresko'bɔw] M (kind of) racketball (*played mainly on the beach*)

frescões [fres'kõjs] MPL *de* **frescão**

frescor [fres'kor] M freshness

frescura [fres'kura] F freshness; (*frialdade*) coolness; (*col: luxo*) fussiness; (: *afetaçao*) pretentiousness; **que ~!** how fussy!; how pretentious!

fresta ['frɛsta] F gap, slit

fretar [fre'tar] VT (*avião, navio*) to charter; (*caminhão*) to hire

frete ['frɛtʃi] M (*carregamento*) freight, cargo; (*tarifa*) freightage; **a ~** for hire

freudiano, -a [frɔj'dʒjanu, a] ADJ Freudian

frevo ['frevu] M *improvised Carnival dance*

fria ['fria] F: **dar uma ~ em alguém** to give sb the cold shoulder; **estar/entrar numa ~** (*col*) to be in/get into a mess; **levar uma ~ de alguém** to get the cold shoulder from sb

friagem ['frjaʒẽ] F cold weather

frialdade [frjaw'dadʒi] F coldness; (*indiferença*) indifference, coolness

fricção [frik'sãw] F friction; (*ato*) rubbing; (Med) massage

friccionar [friksjo'nar] VT to rub

fricote [fri'kɔtʃi] (*col*) M finickiness

fricoteiro, -a [fiko'tejru, a] (*col*) ADJ finicky ▶ M/F fusspot

frieira ['frjejra] F chilblain

frieza ['frjeza] F coldness; (*indiferença*) coolness

frigideira [friʒi'dejra] F frying pan

frigidez [friʒi'dez] F frigidity

frígido, -a ['friʒidu, a] ADJ frigid

frigir [fri'ʒir] VT to fry

frigorífico [frigo'rifiku] M refrigerator; (*congelador*) freezer

frincha ['frĩʃa] F chink, slit

frio, -a ['friu, a] ADJ cold; (*col*) forged ▶ M coldness; **frios** MPL (*Culin*) cold meats; **estou com ~** I'm cold; **faz** *ou* **está ~** it's cold

friorento, -a [frjo'rētu, a] ADJ (*pessoa*) sensitive to the cold; (*lugar*) chilly

frisar [fri'zar] VT (*encrespar*) to curl; (*salientar*) to emphasize

Frísia ['frizja] F: **a ~** Frisia

friso ['frizu] M border; (*na parede*) frieze; (*Arq*) moulding (BRIT), molding (US)

fritada [fri'tada] F fry-up; **dar uma ~ em algo** to fry sth

fritar [fri'tar] VT to fry

fritas ['fritas] FPL French fries, chips (BRIT)

frito, -a ['fritu, a] ADJ fried; (*col*): **estar ~** to be done for

fritura [fri'tura] F fried food

frivolidade [frivoli'dadʒi] F frivolity

frívolo, -a ['frivolu, a] ADJ frivolous

fronha ['froɲa] F pillowcase

front [frõ] (*pl* **-s**) M (*Mil, fig*) front

fronte ['frõtʃi] F (*Anat*) forehead, brow

fronteira [frõ'tejra] F frontier, border

fronteiriço, -a [frõtej'risu, a] ADJ frontier *atr*

fronteiro, -a [frõ'tejru, a] ADJ front

frontispício [frõtʃis'pisju] M (*de edifício*) main façade; (*de livro*) frontispiece; (*rosto*) face

frota ['frɔta] F fleet

frouxo, -a ['froʃu, a] ADJ loose; (*corda*) slack; (*fraco*) weak; (*indolente*) slack; (*col: condescendente*) soft

frufru [fru'fru] M (*enfeite*) ruff

frugal [fru'gaw] (*pl* **-ais**) ADJ frugal

fruição [frwi'sãw] F enjoyment

fruir ['frwir] VT to enjoy ▶ VI: **~ de algo** to enjoy sth

frustração [frustra'sãw] F frustration

frustrado, -a [frus'tradu, a] ADJ frustrated; (*planos*) thwarted

frustrante [frus'trãtʃi] ADJ frustrating

frustrar [frus'trar] VT to frustrate

fruta ['fruta] F fruit

fruta-do-conde (*pl* **frutas-do-conde**) F sweetsop

fruta-pão (*pl* **frutas-pães** *ou* **frutas-pão**) F breadfruit

fruteira [fru'tejra] F fruit bowl

frutífero, -a [fru'tʃiferu, a] ADJ (*proveitoso*) fruitful; (*árvore*) fruit-bearing

fruto ['frutu] M (*Bot*) fruit; (*resultado*) result, product; **dar ~** (*fig*) to bear fruit

fubá [fu'ba] M corn meal

fubeca [fu'bɛka] (*col*) F thrashing

fubica [fu'bika] (*col*) F heap, jalopy

fuçar [fu'sar] VI: **~ em algo** (*remexer*) to rummage in sth; (*meter-se*) to meddle in sth

fuças ['fusas] (*col*) FPL face *sg*, chops

fuga ['fuga] F flight, escape; (*de gás etc*) leak; (*da prisão*) escape; (*de namorados*) elopement; (*Mús*) fugue

fugacíssimo, -a [fuga'sisimu, a] ADJ SUPERL *de* **fugaz**

fugaz [fu'gaz] ADJ fleeting

fugida [fu'ʒida] F sortie; **dar uma ~** *ou* **fugidinha** to pop out for a moment

fugir [fu'ʒir] VI to flee, escape; (*prisioneiro*) to escape; (*criança: de casa*) to run away; (*namorados*) to elope; **~ a algo** to avoid sth

fugitivo, -a [fuʒi'tʃivu, a] ADJ, M/F fugitive

fui [fuj] VB *ver* **ir**, **ser**

fulano, -a [fu'lanu, a] M/F so-and-so; **~ de tal** what's-his-name/what's-her-name; **~, beltrano e sicrano** Tom, Dick and Harry

fulcro ['fuwkru] M fulcrum

fuleiro, -a [fu'lejru, a] ADJ tacky; (*col*) crappy

fúlgido, -a ['fuwʒidu, a] ADJ brilliant

fulgir [fuw'ʒir] VI to shine

fulgor [fuw'gor] M brilliance

fuligem [fu'liʒē] F soot

fulminante [fuwmi'nãtʃi] ADJ (*devastador*) devastating; (*palavras*) scathing

fulminar [fuwmi'nar] VT (*ferir, matar*) to strike down; (*petrificar*) to stop dead; (*aniquilar*) to annihilate ▶ VI to flash with lightning; **fulminado por um raio** struck by lightning

fulo, -a ['fulu, a] ADJ: **estar** *ou* **ficar ~ de raiva** to be furious

fumaça [fu'masa] (BR) F (*de fogo*) smoke; (*de gás*) fumes *pl*; **500 e lá vai ~** (*col*) 500 and then some

fumador, a [fuma'dor(a)] (PT) M/F smoker

fumante [fu'mãtʃi] M/F smoker

fumar [fu'mar] VT, VI to smoke

fumê [fu'me] ADJ INV (*vidro*) smoked

fumo ['fumu] M (PT: *de fogo*) smoke; (: *de gás*) fumes *pl*; (BR: *tabaco*) tobacco; (*fumar*) smoking; (BR *col: maconha*) dope; **~ louro** Virginia tobacco; **puxar ~** (*col*) to smoke dope

FUNABEM [funa'bē] (BR) ABR F (= *Fundação Nacional do Bem-Estar do Menor*) children's home

Funai [fu'naj] (BR) ABR F = **Fundação Nacional do Índio**

Funarte [fu'nartʃi] (BR) ABR F = **Fundação Nacional de Arte**

função [fū'sãw] (*pl* **-ões**) F function; (*ofício*) duty; (*papel*) role; (*espetáculo*) performance

Funcep [fū'sɛpi] (BR) ABR F (= *Fundação Centro de Formação do Servidor Público*) civil service training centre

funcho ['fūʃu] M (*Bot*) fennel

funcional [fūsjo'naw] (*pl* **-ais**) ADJ functional

funcionalismo [fūsjona'lizmu] M: **~ público** civil service

funcionamento [fūsjona'mētu] M functioning, working; **pôr em ~** to set going, start

funcionar [fũsjo'nar] vɪ to function; (*máquina*) to work, run; (*dar bom resultado*) to work
funcionário, -a [fũsjo'narju, a] ᴍ/ꜰ official; **~ (público)** civil servant
funções [fũ'sõjs] ꜰᴘʟ *de* **função**
fundação [fũda'sãw] (*pl* **-ões**) ꜰ foundation
fundador, a [fũda'dor(a)] ᴍ/ꜰ founder ▶ ᴀᴅᴊ founding
fundamental [fũdamē'taw] (*pl* **-ais**) ᴀᴅᴊ fundamental, basic
fundamentar [fũdamē'tar] ᴠᴛ (*argumento*) to substantiate; (*basear*): **~ (em)** to base (on)
fundamento [fũda'mẽtu] ᴍ (*fig*) foundation, basis; (*motivo*) motive; **sem ~** groundless
fundar [fũ'dar] ᴠᴛ to establish, found; (*basear*) to base; **fundar-se** ᴠʀ: **~-se em** to be based on
fundear [fũ'dʒjar] ᴠɪ to anchor
fundição [fũdʒi'sãw] (*pl* **-ões**) ꜰ fusing; (*fábrica*) foundry
fundilho [fũ'dʒiʎu] ᴍ (*da calça*) seat
fundir [fũ'dʒir] ᴠᴛ to fuse; (*metal*) to smelt, melt down; (*Com: empresas*) to merge; (*em molde*) to cast; **fundir-se** ᴠʀ (*derreter-se*) to melt; (*juntar-se*) to merge, fuse; (*Com*) to merge; **~ a cuca** to crack up
fundo, -a ['fũdu, a] ᴀᴅᴊ deep; (*fig*) profound; (*col: ignorante*) ignorant; (: *despreparado*) hopeless ▶ ᴍ (*do mar, jardim*) bottom; (*profundidade*) depth; (*base*) basis; (*da loja, casa, do papel*) back; (*de quadro*) background; (*de dinheiro*) fund ▶ ᴀᴅᴠ deeply; **fundos** ᴍᴘʟ (*Com*) funds; (*da casa etc*) back *sg*; **a ~** thoroughly; **ao ~** in the background; **ir ao ~** (*navio*) to sink, go down; **no ~** (*de caixa etc*) at the bottom; (*da casa etc*) at the back; (*de quadro*) in the background; (*fig*) basically, at bottom; **sem ~** (*poço*) bottomless; **dar ~s para** (*casa etc*) to back on to; **~ de contingência** contingency fund; **~ de investimento** investment fund; **F~ Monetário Internacional** International Monetary Fund
fundura [fũ'dura] ꜰ depth; (*col*) ignorance
fúnebre ['funebri] ᴀᴅᴊ funeral *atr*, funereal; (*fig: triste*) gloomy, lugubrious
funeral [fune'raw] (*pl* **-ais**) ᴍ funeral
funerário, -a [fune'rarju, a] ᴀᴅᴊ funeral *atr*; **casa funerária** undertakers *pl*
funesto, -a [fu'nɛstu, a] ᴀᴅᴊ (*fatal*) fatal; (*infausto*) disastrous; (*notícia*) fateful
fungar [fũ'gar] ᴠᴛ, ᴠɪ to sniff
fungo ['fũgu] ᴍ (*Bot*) fungus
funil [fu'niw] (*pl* **-is**) ᴍ funnel
Funrural [fũhu'raw] (ʙʀ) ᴀʙʀ ᴍ = **Fundo de Assistência e Previdência ao Trabalhador Rural**
Funtevê [fũte've] ᴀʙʀ ꜰ = **Fundação Centro-Brasileira de TV Educativa**
fura-bolo ['fura-] (*pl* **fura-bolos**) (*col*) ᴍ index finger
furacão [fura'kãw] (*pl* **-ões**) ᴍ hurricane; **entrar/sair como um ~** to stomp in/out

furado, -a [fu'radu, a] ᴀᴅᴊ perforated; (*pneu*) flat; (*orelha*) pierced; (*col: programa*) crummy
furão, -rona [fu'rãw, 'rɔna] (*pl* **-ões/-s**) ᴍ ferret ▶ ᴍ/ꜰ (*col*) go-getter ▶ ᴀᴅᴊ (*col*) hard-working, dynamic
furar [fu'rar] ᴠᴛ (*perfurar*) to bore, to perforate; (*penetrar*) to penetrate; (*greve*) to break; (*frustrar*) to foil; (*fila*) to jump ▶ ᴠɪ (*col: programa*) to fall through
furdúncio [fur'dũsju] (*col*) ᴍ commotion
furgão [fur'gãw] (*pl* **-ões**) ᴍ van
furgoneta [furgo'neta] (ᴘᴛ) ꜰ van
fúria ['furja] ꜰ fury, rage; **estar uma ~** to be furious
furibundo, -a [furi'bũdu, a] ᴀᴅᴊ furious
furioso, -a [fu'rjozu, ɔza] ᴀᴅᴊ furious
furo ['furu] ᴍ hole; (*num pneu*) puncture; **~ jornalístico** scoop; **dar um ~** (*col*) to make a blunder; **estar muitos ~s acima de algo** (*fig*) to be a cut above sth, be a lot better than sth
furões [fu'rõjs] ᴍᴘʟ *de* **furão**
furona [fu'rɔna] ꜰ *de* **furão**
furor [fu'ror] ᴍ fury, rage; **causar ~** to cause a furore; **fazer ~** to be all the rage
furta-cor ['furta-] (*pl* **furta-cores**) ᴀᴅᴊ iridescent ▶ ᴍ iridescence
furtar [fur'tar] ᴠᴛ, ᴠɪ to steal; **furtar-se** ᴠʀ: **~-se a** to avoid, evade
furtivo, -a [fur'tʃivu, a] ᴀᴅᴊ furtive, stealthy
furto ['furtu] ᴍ theft
furúnculo [fu'rũkulu] ᴍ (*Med*) boil
fusão [fu'zãw] (*pl* **-ões**) ꜰ fusion; (*Com*) merger; (*derretimento*) melting; (*união*) union
fusca ['fuska] (*col*) ᴍ (*VW*) beetle
fusco, -a ['fusku, a] ᴀᴅᴊ dark, dusky
fuselagem [fuze'laʒẽ] (*pl* **-ns**) ꜰ fuselage
fusível [fu'zivew] (*pl* **-eis**) ᴍ (*Elet*) fuse
fuso ['fuzu] ᴍ (*Tec*) spindle; **~ horário** time zone
fusões [fu'zõjs] ꜰᴘʟ *de* **fusão**
fustão [fus'tãw] ᴍ corduroy
fustigar [fustʃi'gar] ᴠᴛ (*açoitar*) to flog, whip; (*suj: vento*) to lash; (*maltratar*) to lash out at
futebol [futʃi'bɔw] ᴍ football; **~ de salão** indoor football; **~ totó** table football; **fazer um ~ de algo** (*col*) to get sth all mixed up
futevôlei [futʃi'volej] ᴍ *see note*

> **Futevôlei** is a type of volleyball in which the ball is allowed to touch only the feet, legs, trunk and head of the players. It is very popular on the beaches of Rio de Janeiro, where tournaments take place during the summer in which many famous footballers take part.

fútil ['futʃiw] (*pl* **-eis**) ᴀᴅᴊ (*pessoa*) superficial, shallow; (*insignificante*) trivial
futilidade [futʃili'dadʒi] ꜰ (*de pessoa*) shallowness; (*insignificância*) triviality; (*coisa fútil*) trivial thing
futurismo [futu'rizmu] ᴍ futurism

futuro, -a [fu'turu, a] ADJ future ▶ M future; **no ~** in the future; **num ~ próximo** in the near future

fuxicar [fuʃi'kar] VI to gossip

fuxico [fu'ʃiku] M piece of gossip

fuxiqueiro, -a [fuʃi'kejru, a] M/F gossip ▶ ADJ gossipy

fuzil [fu'ziw] (*pl* **-is**) M rifle

fuzilamento [fuzila'mẽtu] M shooting

fuzilante [fuzi'lãtʃi] ADJ (*olhos*) blazing

fuzilar [fuzi'lar] VT to shoot ▶ VI (*olhos*) to blaze; (*pessoa*) to fume

fuzileiro, -a [fuzi'lejru, a] M/F: **~ naval** (*Mil*) marine

fuzis [fu'zis] MPL *de* **fuzil**

fuzuê [fu'zwe] M commotion

Gg

G, g [ʒe] (pl **gs**) M G, g; **G de Gomes** G for George

g. ABR (= grama) gr.; (= grau) deg.

Gabão [ga'bãw] M: **o ~** Cabon

gabar [ga'bar] VT to praise; **gabar-se** VR: **~-se de** to boast about

gabardine [gabar'dʒini] F gabardine

gabaritado, -a [gabari'tadu, a] ADJ (pessoa) well-qualified

gabarito [gaba'ritu] M (fig): **ter ~ para** to have the ability to; **de ~** (of) high calibre atr (BRIT) ou caliber atr (US)

gabinete [gabi'netʃi] M (Com) office; (escritório) study; (Pol) cabinet

gado ['gadu] M livestock; (bovino) cattle pl; **~ leiteiro** dairy cattle pl; **~ suíno** pigs pl

gaélico, -a [ga'ɛliku, a] ADJ Gaelic ▶ M (Ling) Gaelic

gafanhoto [gafa'ɲotu] M grasshopper

gafe ['gafi] F gaffe, faux pas; **dar** ou **cometer uma ~** to make a faux pas

gafieira [ga'fjejra] (col) F (lugar) dive; (baile) knees-up

gagá [ga'ga] ADJ senile

gago, -a ['gagu, a] ADJ stuttering ▶ M/F stutterer

gagueira [ga'gejra] F stutter

gaguejar [gage'ʒar] VI to stammer, stutter ▶ VT (resposta) to stammer

gaiato, -a [ga'jatu, a] ADJ funny

gaiola [ga'jɔla] F (para pássaro) cage; (cadeia) jail ▶ M (barco) riverboat

gaita ['gajta] F harmonica; (col: dinheiro) cash, dough; **cheio/a da ~** (col) loaded; **solta a ~!** (col) hand over your cash!; **~ de foles** bagpipes pl

gaivota [gaj'vɔta] F seagull

gajo ['gaʒu] (PT col) M guy, fellow

gala ['gala] F: **traje de ~** evening dress; **festa de ~** gala

galã [ga'lã] M (ator) leading man; (fig) ladies' man

galalau [gala'law] M giant

galante [ga'lãtʃi] ADJ (gracioso) graceful; (gentil) gallant

galanteador [galãtʃja'dor] M suitor, admirer

galantear [galã'tʃjar] VT to court, woo

galanteio [galã'teju] M wooing

galantina [galã'tʃina] F (Culin): **~ de galinha** chicken galantine

galão [ga'lãw] (pl **-ões**) M (Mil) stripe; (medida) gallon; (PT: café) white coffee; (passamanaria) braid

Galápagos [ga'lapagus] N: **(as) Ilhas ~** (the) Galapagos Islands

galardão [galar'dãw] (pl **-ões**) M reward

galardoar [galar'dwar] VT: **~ alguém (com algo)** to reward sb (with sth)

galardões [galar'dõjs] MPL de **galardão**

galáxia [ga'laksja] M galaxy

galé [ga'lɛ] F (Náut) galley ▶ M galley slave

galego, -a [ga'legu, a] ADJ Galician ▶ M/F Galician; (col, pej) Portuguese ▶ M (Ling) Galician

galera [ga'lɛra] F (Náut) galley; (col: pessoas, público) crowd

galeria [gale'ria] F gallery; (Teatro) circle; (para águas pluviais) storm drain

Gales ['galis] M: **País de ~** Wales

galês, -esa [ga'les, eza] ADJ Welsh ▶ M/F Welshman/woman ▶ M (Ling) Welsh; **os galeses** MPL the Welsh

galeto [ga'letu] M spring chicken

galgar [gaw'gar] VT (saltar) to leap over; (subir) to climb up

galgo ['gawgu] M greyhound

galhardia [gaʎar'dʒia] F (elegância) elegance; (bravura, gentileza) gallantry; **com ~** gallantly

galhardo, -a [ga'ʎardu, a] ADJ (elegante) elegant; (bravo, gentil) gallant

galheteiro [gaʎe'tejru] M cruet

galho ['gaʎu] M (de árvore) branch; (col: bico) part-time job; (: problema): **dar o ~** to cause trouble; **quebrar um** ou **o ~** to sort it out

galicismo [gali'sizmu] M Gallicism

galináceos [gali'nasjus] MPL poultry sg

galinha [ga'liɲa] F hen; (Culin, fig: macho) chicken; (fig: puta) slut; **a ~ do vizinho é sempre mais gorda** (fig) the grass is always greener (on the other side of the fence); **matar a ~ dos ovos de ouro** (fig) to kill the goose that lays the golden egg

galinha-d'angola (pl **galinhas-d'angolas**) F guinea fowl

galinha-morta (pl **galinhas-mortas**) (col) F (pechincha) bargain; (coisa fácil) piece of cake ▶ M/F (pessoa) weakling

galinheiro [gali'ɲejru] M (*lugar*) hen-house

galo ['galu] M cock, rooster; (*inchação*) bump; **missa do ~** midnight mass; **ouvir cantar o ~ e não saber onde** (*fig*) to jump to conclusions; **~ de briga** fighting cock; (*fig: pessoa*) troublemaker

galocha [ga'lɔʃa] F (*bota*) Wellington (boot)

galões [ga'lõjs] MPL *de* **galão**

galopante [galo'pãtʃi] ADJ (*fig: inflação*) galloping; (: *doença*) rampant

galopar [galo'par] VI to gallop

galope [ga'lɔpi] M gallop

galpão [gaw'pãw] (*pl* **-ões**) M shed

galvanizar [gawvani'zar] VT to galvanize

gama ['gama] F (*Mús*) scale; (*fig*) range; (*Zool*) doe

gamado, -a [ga'madu, a] (*col*) ADJ: **ser** *ou* **estar ~ por** to be crazy about

gamão [ga'mãw] M backgammon

gamar [ga'mar] (*col*) VI: **~ (por)** to fall in love (with)

gambá [gã'ba] M (*Zool*) opossum; **bêbado como um ~** (*col*) pissed as a newt

Gâmbia ['gãbja] M: **o ~** (the) Gambia

gambito [gã'bitu] M (*Xadrez etc*) gambit; (*col: perna*) pin

game ['geimi] M computer game

gamo ['gamu] M (fallow) deer

Gana ['gana] M Ghana

gana ['gana] F (*desejo*) craving, desire; (*ódio*) hate; **ter ~s de (fazer) algo** to feel like (doing) sth; **ter ~ de alguém** to hate sb

ganância [ga'nãsja] F greed

ganancioso, -a [ganã'sjozu, ɔza] ADJ greedy

gancho ['gãʃu] M hook; (*de calça*) crotch

gandaia [gã'daja] F (*vadiagem*) idling; (*farra*) living it up; **viver na ~** to lead the life of Riley; **cair na ~** to live it up

Ganges ['gãʒis] M: **o ~** the Ganges

gânglio ['gãglju] M (*Med*) ganglion

gangorra [gã'goha] F seesaw

gangrena [gã'grena] F gangrene

gangrenar [gãgre'nar] VI to go gangrenous

gângster ['gãgster] M gangster

gangue ['gãgi] (*col*) F gang

ganhador, a [gaɲa'dor(a)] ADJ winning ▶ M/F winner

ganha-pão ['gaɲa-] (*pl* **-pães**) M living, livelihood

ganhar [ga'ɲar] VT to win; (*salário*) to earn; (*adquirir*) to get; (*lugar*) to reach; (*lucrar*) to gain ▶ VI to win; **~ de alguém** (*num jogo*) to beat sb; **~ a alguém em algo** to outdo sb in sth; **~ tempo** to gain time; **~ a vida** to earn a living; **sair ganhando** to come out better off, come off better; **ganhei o dia** (*fig*) it made my day

ganho ['gaɲu] PP *de* **ganhar** ▶ M (*lucro*) profit, gain; **ganhos** MPL (*ao jogo*) winnings; **~ de capital** (*Com*) capital gain

ganido [ga'nidu] M (*de cão*) yelp; (*de pessoa*) squeal

ganir [ga'nir] VI (*cão*) to yelp; (*pessoa*) to squeal

▶ VT (*gemido, gritos*) to let out

ganso, -a ['gãsu, a] M/F goose

garagem [ga'raʒẽ] (*pl* **-ns**) F garage

garagista [gara'ʒista] M/F garage owner

garanhão [gara'ɲãw] (*pl* **-ões**) M stallion; (*col: homem*) stud

garantia [garã'tʃia] F guarantee; (*de dívida*) surety; **estar na ~** (*compra*) to be under guarantee; **empréstimo sem ~** (*Com*) unsecured loan

garantir [garã'tʃir] VT to guarantee; **garantir-se** VR: **~-se contra algo** to defend o.s. against sth; **~ algo (a alguém)** (*prometer*) to promise (sb) sth; **~ que ...** to maintain that ...; **~ a alguém que ...** to assure sb that ...; **~ alguém contra algo** to defend sb against sth

garatujar [garatu'ʒar] VT to scribble, scrawl

garbo ['garbu] M (*elegância*) elegance; (*distinção*) distinction

garboso, -a [gar'bozu, ɔza] ADJ (*elegante*) elegant; (*distinto*) distinguished

garça ['garsa] F heron

garçom [gar'sõ] (*pl* **-ns**) (BR) M waiter

garçonete [garso'netʃi] (BR) F waitress

garçonnière [garso'njɛr] F love nest

garçons [gar'sõs] MPL *de* **garçom**

garfada [gar'fada] F forkful

garfo ['garfu] M fork; **ser um bom ~** (*fig*) to enjoy one's food

gargalhada [garga'ʎada] F burst of laughter; **rir às ~s** to roar with laughter; **dar** *ou* **soltar uma ~** to burst out laughing; **~ homérica** guffaw

gargalo [gar'galu] M (*tb fig*) bottleneck

garganta [gar'gãta] F (*Anat*) throat; (*Geo*) gorge, ravine ▶ M/F (*col*) braggart, loudmouth ▶ ADJ (*col*) loudmouth(ed); **limpar a ~** to clear one's throat; **molhar a ~** (*col*) to wet one's whistle; **aquilo não me passou pela ~** (*fig*) that stuck in my craw

gargantilha [gargã'tʃiʎa] F choker

gargarejar [gargare'ʒar] VI to gargle

gargarejo [garga'reʒu] M (*ato*) gargling; (*líquido*) gargle

gari [ga'ri] M/F (*na rua*) road sweeper (BRIT), street sweeper (US); (*lixeiro*) dustman (BRIT), garbage man (US)

garimpar [garĩ'par] VI to prospect

garimpeiro [garĩ'pejru] M prospector

garoa [ga'roa] F drizzle

garoar [ga'rwar] VI to drizzle

garotada [garo'tada] F: **a ~** the kids *pl*

garoto, -a [ga'rotu, a] M/F boy/girl ▶ M (BR: *chope*) small beer; (PT: *café*) coffee with milk; **garota de programa** (*col*) prostitute

garoto-propaganda, garota-propaganda (*pl* **garotos-propaganda/garotas-propaganda**) M/F poster boy/girl

garoupa [ga'ropa] F (*peixe*) grouper

garra ['gaha] F claw; (*de ave*) talon; (*fig: entusiasmo*) enthusiasm, drive; **garras** FPL (*fig*) clutches

garrafa [ga'hafa] F bottle
garrafada [gaha'fada] F: **dar uma ~ em alguém** to hit sb with a bottle
garrafão [gaha'fãw] (pl **-ões**) M flagon
garrancho [ga'hãʃu] M scrawl
garrido, -a [ga'hidu, a] ADJ (elegante) smart; (alegre) lively; (vistoso) showy; (gracioso) pretty
garrote [ga'hɔtʃi] M (Med) tourniquet; (tortura) garrote
garupa [ga'rupa] F (de cavalo) hindquarters pl; (de moto) back seat; **andar na ~** (de moto) to ride pillion
gás [gajs] M gas; **gases** MPL (do intestino) wind sg; **~ natural** natural gas; **~ de efeito estufa** greenhouse gas
gaseificar [gazejfi'kar] VT to vaporize; **gaseificar-se** VR to vaporize
gasoduto [gazo'dutu] M gas pipeline
gasóleo [ga'zɔlju] M diesel oil
gasolina [gazo'lina] F petrol (BRIT), gas(oline) (US)
gasômetro [ga'zometru] M gasometer
gasosa [ga'zɔza] F fizzy drink, soda pop (US)
gasoso, -a [ga'zozu, ɔza] ADJ (Quím) gaseous; (água) sparkling; (bebida) fizzy
gáspea ['gaspja] F (de sapato) upper
gastador, -deira [gasta'dor, 'dejra] ADJ, M/F spendthrift
gastar [gas'tar] VT (dinheiro, tempo) to spend; (gasolina, electricidade) to use; (roupa, sapato) to wear out; (salto, piso etc) to wear down; (saúde) to damage; (desperdiçar) to waste ▶ VI to spend; to wear out; to wear down; **gastar-se** VR to wear out; to wear down
gasto, -a ['gastu, a] PP de **gastar** ▶ ADJ (dinheiro, tempo, energias) spent; (frase) trite; (sapato etc, fig: pessoa) worn out; (salto, piso) worn down ▶ M (despesa) expense; **gastos** MPL (Com) expenses, expenditure sg; **~s públicos** public spending sg; **dar para o ~** (col) to do, be OK
gastrenterite [gastrēte'ritʃi] F (Med) gastroenteritis
gástrico, -a ['gastriku, a] ADJ gastric
gastrite [gas'tritʃi] F (Med) gastritis
gastronomia [gastrono'mia] F gastronomy
gastronômico, -a [gastro'nomiku, a] ADJ gastronomic
gata ['gata] F (she-)cat; (col: mulher) sexy lady; **andar de ~s** (PT) to go on all fours; **~ borralheira** Cinderella; (mulher) stay-at-home
gatão [ga'tãw] (pl **-ões**) (col) M (homem) hunk
gatilho [ga'tʃiʎu] M trigger
gatinha [ga'tʃina] (col) F (mulher) sexy lady
gatinhas [ga'tʃinas] FPL: **andar de ~** (BR) to go on all fours
gato ['gatu] M cat; (col: homem) dish, hunk; **ter um ~** (col) to have kittens; **~ escaldado tem medo de água fria** once bitten, twice shy; **~ montês** wild cat
gatões [ga'tõjs] MPL de **gatão**

gato-sapato M: **fazer alguém de ~** to walk all over sb, treat sb like a doormat
gatos-pingados MPL stalwarts
GATT ABR M (= Acordo Geral sobre Tarifas Aduaneiras e Comércio) GATT
gatuno, -a [ga'tunu, a] ADJ thieving ▶ M/F thief
gaúcho, -a [ga'uʃu, a] ADJ from Rio Grande do Sul ▶ M/F native of Rio Grande do Sul
gaveta [ga'veta] F drawer
gavetão [gave'tãw] (pl **-ões**) M big drawer
gavião [ga'vjãw] (pl **-ões**) M hawk
Gaza ['gaza] F: **a faixa de ~** the Gaza Strip
gaza ['gaza] F = **gaze**
gaze ['gazi] F gauze
gazela [ga'zɛla] F gazelle
gazeta [ga'zeta] F (jornal) newspaper, gazette; **fazer ~** to play truant
gazua [ga'zua] F skeleton key
GB ABR (= Guanabara) former state, now Rio de Janeiro
geada ['ʒjada] F frost
geladeira [ʒela'dejra] (BR) F refrigerator, icebox (US)
gelado, -a [ʒe'ladu, a] ADJ frozen; (vento) chilling ▶ M (PT: sorvete) ice cream
gelar [ʒe'lar] VT to freeze; (vinho etc) to chill ▶ VI to freeze
gelatina [ʒela'tʃina] F gelatine; (sobremesa) jelly, Jell-O® (US)
gelatinoso, -a [ʒelatʃi'nozu, ɔza] ADJ gooey
geleia [ʒe'lɛja] F jam
geleira [ʒe'lejra] F (Geo) glacier
gélido, -a ['ʒɛlidu, a] ADJ chill, icy
gelo ['ʒelu] ADJ INV light grey (BRIT) ou gray (US) ▶ M ice; (cor) light grey (BRIT) ou gray (US); **quebrar o ~** (fig) to break the ice; **hoje está um ~** it's freezing today; **dar o ~ em alguém** (col) to give sb the cold shoulder
gelo-seco M dry ice
gema ['ʒema] F (de ovo) yolk; (pedra preciosa) gem; **ser da ~** to be genuine; **ela é paulista da ~** she's a real Paulista
gemada [ʒe'mada] F eggnog
gêmeo, -a ['ʒemju, a] ADJ, M/F twin; **Gêmeos** MPL (Astrologia) Gemini sg
gemer [ʒe'mer] VT (canção) to croon ▶ VI (de dor) to groan, moan; (lamentar-se) to wail, howl; (animal) to whine; (vento) to howl
gemido [ʒe'midu] M groan, moan; (lamento) wail; (de animal) whine
gen. ABR (= general) Gen
gene ['ʒeni] M gene
genealogia [ʒenjalo'ʒia] F genealogy
genealógico, -a [ʒenja'lɔʒiku, a] ADJ genealogical; **árvore genealógica** family tree
Genebra [ʒe'nɛbra] N Geneva
genebra [ʒe'nɛbra] (PT) F gin
general [ʒene'raw] (pl **-ais**) M (Mil) general
generalidade [ʒenerali'dadʒi] F generality; (maioria) majority; **generalidades** FPL (princípios) basics, principles

g

generalização [ʒeneraliza'sãw] (pl **-ões**) F
generalization

generalizar [ʒenerali'zar] VT (*propagar*) to
propagate ▶ VI to generalize; **generalizar-se**
VR to become general, spread

genérico, -a [ʒe'nɛriku, a] ADJ generic

gênero ['ʒeneru] M (*espécie*) type, kind;
(*Literatura*) genre; (*Bio*) genus; (*Ling*) gender;
gêneros MPL (*produtos*) goods; ~**s**
alimentícios foodstuffs; ~**s de primeira**
necessidade essentials; ~ **de vida** way of
life; ~ **humano** humankind, human race;
essa roupa/ele não faz o meu ~ this outfit
is not my style/he is not my type

generosidade [ʒenerozi'dadʒi] F generosity

generoso, -a [ʒene'rozu, ɔza] ADJ generous

gênese ['ʒenezi] F origin, beginning; **G~** (*Rel*)
Genesis

genética [ʒe'nɛtʃika] F genetics *sg*

genético, -a [ʒe'nɛtʃiku, a] ADJ genetic

gengibre [ʒẽ'ʒibri] M ginger

gengiva [ʒẽ'ʒiva] F (*Anat*) gum

genial [ʒe'njaw] (pl **-ais**) ADJ inspired; (*ideia*)
brilliant; (*col*) terrific, fantastic

gênio ['ʒenju] M (*temperamento*) nature;
(*irascibilidade*) temper; (*talento, pessoa*) genius;
de bom ~ good-natured; **de mau** ~
bad-tempered; **um cientista de** ~ a
scientific genius, a genius at science

genioso, -a [ʒe'njozu, ɔza] ADJ short-
tempered

genital [ʒeni'taw] (pl **-ais**) ADJ: **órgãos**
genitais genitals *pl*

genitivo [ʒeni'tʃivu] M (*Ling*) genitive

genitora [ʒeni'tora] F mother

genocídio [ʒeno'sidʒju] M genocide

genoma [ʒe'noma] M genome

genro ['ʒẽhu] M son-in-law

gentalha [ʒẽ'taʎa] F rabble

gente ['ʒẽtʃi] F (*pessoas*) people *pl*; (*col*) folks *pl*;
(*família*) folks *pl*, family; (*col: alguém*): **tem** ~
batendo à porta there's somebody
knocking at the door; **a** ~ (*nós: suj*) we; (*: obj*)
us; ~**!** (*exprime admiração, surpresa*) gosh!; **vai**
com a ~ come with us; **a casa da** ~ our
house; **toda a** ~ everybody; **ficar** ~ to grow
up; **ser** ~ (*ser alguém*) to be somebody;
também ser ~ (*col*) to be as good as anyone
else; **ser** ~ **boa** *ou* **fina** (*col*) to be a nice
person; **a** ~ **bem** the upper crust; ~ **grande**
grown-ups *pl*; **oi/tchau,** ~**!** hi/bye, folks!

gentil [ʒẽ'tʃiw] (pl **-is**) ADJ kind

gentileza [ʒẽtʃi'leza] F kindness; **por** ~ if you
please; **tenha a** ~ **de fazer ...** would you be
so kind as to do ...?

gentinha [ʒẽ'tʃiɲa] F rabble

gentio, -a [ʒẽ'tʃiu, a] ADJ, M/F heathen

gentis [ʒe'tʃis] ADJ PL *de* **gentil**

genuflexão [ʒenuflek'sãw] (pl **-ões**) F (*Rel*)
genuflection

genuíno, -a [ʒe'nwinu, a] ADJ genuine

geofísica [ʒeo'fizika] F geophysics *sg*

geografia [ʒeogra'fia] F geography

geográfico, -a [ʒeo'grafiku, a] ADJ
geographical

geógrafo, -a [ʒe'ɔgrafu, a] M/F geographer

geologia [ʒeolo'ʒia] F geology

geólogo, -a [ʒe'ɔlogu, a] M/F geologist

geometria [ʒeome'tria] F geometry

geométrico, -a [ʒeo'mɛtriku, a] ADJ
geometrical

geopolítico, -a [ʒeopo'litʃiku, a] ADJ
geopolitical

Geórgia ['ʒɔrʒa] F: **a** ~ Georgia

georgiano, -a [ʒor'ʒanu, a] ADJ, M/F Georgian

geração [ʒera'sãw] (pl **-ões**) F (*tb Tec*)
generation; **computadores de quarta** ~
fourth-generation computers

gerador, a [ʒera'dor(a)] ADJ: ~ **de algo**
causing sth ▶ M/F (*produtor*) creator ▶ M (*Tec*)
generator

geral [ʒe'raw] (pl **-ais**) ADJ general ▶ F (*Teatro*)
gallery; (*revisão*) general overhaul; **dar uma**
~ **em algo** (*col*) to have a blitz on sth; **em** ~
in general, generally; **de um modo** ~ on the
whole

geralmente [ʒeraw'mẽtʃi] ADV generally,
usually

gerânio [ʒe'ranju] M geranium

gerar [ʒe'rar] VT (*produzir*) to produce; (*filhos*) to
beget; (*causar: ódios etc*) to engender, cause;
(*eletricidade*) to generate

gerativo, -a [ʒera'tʃivu, a] ADJ generative

gerência [ʒe'rẽsja] F management

gerenciador [ʒerẽsja'dor] M: ~ **de banco de**
dados (*Comput*) database manager

gerencial [ʒerẽ'sjaw] (pl **-ais**) ADJ
management *atr*

gerenciar [ʒerẽ'sjar] VT, VI to manage

gerente [ʒe'rẽtʃi] ADJ managing ▶ M/F
manager

gergelim [ʒerʒe'lĩ] M (*Bot*) sesame

geriatria [ʒerja'tria] F geriatrics *sg*

geriátrico, -a [ʒe'rjatriku, a] ADJ geriatric

geringonça [ʒerĩ'gõsa] F contraption

gerir [ʒe'rir] VT to manage, run

germânico, -a [ʒer'maniku, a] ADJ Germanic

germe ['ʒermi] M (*embrião*) embryo; (*micróbio*)
germ; (*fig*) origin; **o** ~ **de uma ideia** the
germ of an idea

germicida [ʒermi'sida] ADJ germicidal ▶ M
germicide

germinação [ʒermina'sãw] F germination

germinar [ʒermi'nar] VI (*semente*) to
germinate; (*fig*) to develop

gerontologia [ʒerõtolo'ʒia] F gerontology

gerúndio [ʒe'rũdʒju] M (*Ling*) gerund

gesso ['ʒesu] M plaster (of Paris)

gestação [ʒesta'sãw] F gestation

gestante [ʒes'tãtʃi] F pregnant woman

gestão [ʒes'tãw] F management

gesticular [ʒestʃiku'lar] VI to make gestures,
gesture ▶ VT: ~ **um adeus** to wave goodbye

gesto ['ʒestu] M gesture; **fazer** ~**s** to gesture

gibi [ʒi'bi] (*col*) M comic; **não estar no** ~ (*fig*) to
be incredible *ou* amazing

Gibraltar [ʒibraw'tar] F Gibraltar
gigabyte [ʒiga'bajtʃi] M gigabyte
gigante, -a [ʒi'gãtʃi, a] ADJ gigantic, huge ▶ M giant
gigantesco, -a [ʒigã'tesku, a] ADJ gigantic
gigolô [ʒigo'lo] M gigolo
gilete [ʒi'letʃi] (BR) F (*lâmina*) razor blade; (*col*) bisexual, bi
gim [ʒĩ] (*pl* **-ns**) M gin
ginásio [ʒi'nazju] M (*para ginástica*) gymnasium; (*escola*) secondary (BRIT) *ou* high (US) school
ginasta [ʒi'nasta] M/F gymnast
ginástica [ʒi'nastʃika] F (*competitiva*) gymnastics *sg*; (*para fortalecer o corpo*) keep-fit
ginecologia [ʒinekolo'ʒia] F gynaecology (BRIT), gynecology (US)
ginecologista [ʒinekolo'ʒista] M/F gynaecologist (BRIT), gynecologist (US)
ginete [ʒi'netʃi] M thoroughbred
gingar [ʒĩ'gar] VI to sway
ginja ['ʒĩʒa] (PT) F morello cherry
ginjinha [ʒĩ'ʒiɲa] (PT) F cherry brandy
gins [ʒĩs] MPL *de* **gim**
gira ['ʒira] ADJ crazy
gira-discos (PT) M INV record-player
girafa [ʒi'rafa] F giraffe; (*col: pessoa*) giant
girar [ʒi'rar] VT to turn, rotate; (*como pião*) to spin ▶ VI to go round; to spin; (*vaguear*) to wander; **ele não gira bem** (*col*) he's not all there
girassol [ʒira'sɔw] (*pl* **-óis**) M sunflower
giratório, -a [ʒira'tɔrju, a] ADJ revolving; (*cadeira*) swivel *atr*
gíria ['ʒirja] F (*calão*) slang; (*jargão*) jargon
giro¹ ['ʒiru] M turn; **dar um ~** to go for a wander; (*em veículo*) to go for a spin; **que ~!** (PT) great!
giro² VB *ver* **gerir**
giz [ʒiz] M chalk
glacê [gla'se] M icing
glacial [gla'sjaw] (*pl* **-ais**) ADJ icy
gladiador [gladʒja'dor] M gladiator
glamouroso, -a [glamu'rozu, ɔza] ADJ glamorous
glândula ['glãdula] F gland
glandular [glãdu'lar] ADJ glandular
gleba ['glɛba] F field
glicerina [glise'rina] F glycerine
glicose [gli'kɔzi] F glucose
global [glo'baw] (*pl* **-ais**) ADJ (*da terra*) global; (*total*) overall; **quantia ~** lump sum
globalização [globaliza'sãw] F globalization
globo ['globu] M globe; **~ ocular** eyeball
globular [globu'lar] ADJ (*forma*) rounded
glóbulo ['glɔbulu] M (*tb*: **glóbulo sanguíneo**) corpuscle
glória ['glɔrja] F glory
gloriar-se [glo'rjarsi] VR: **~ de** to boast of
glorificar [glorifi'kar] VT to glorify
glorioso, -a [glo'rjozu, ɔza] ADJ glorious
glosa ['glɔza] F comment

glosar [glo'zar] VT to comment on; (*conta*) to cancel
glossário [glo'sarju] M glossary
glote ['glɔtʃi] F (*Anat*) glottis
gluglu [glu'glu] M (*de peru*) gobble-gobble; (*de água*) glug-glug
glutão, -tona [glu'tãw, tɔna] (*pl* **-ões/-s**) ADJ greedy ▶ M/F glutton
glúten ['glutẽ] (*pl* **-s**) M gluten
glutões [glu'tõjs] MPL *de* **glutão**
glutona [glu'tɔna] F *de* **glutão**
gnomo ['gnomu] M gnome
GO ABR = **Goiás**
Goa ['goa] N Goa
godê [go'de] ADJ (*saia*) flared
goela ['gwɛla] F throat
gogó [go'gɔ] (*col*) M Adam's apple
goiaba [go'jaba] F guava
goiabada [goja'bada] F guava jelly
goiabeira [goja'bejra] F guava tree
goianense [goja'n(j)ẽsi] ADJ from Goiânia ▶ M/F native of Goiânia
goiano, -a [go'janu, a] ADJ from Goiás ▶ M/F native of Goiás
gol [gow] (*pl* **-s**) M goal; **marcar um ~** to score a goal
gola ['gɔla] F collar
golaço [go'lasu] M (*Futebol*) great goal
Golan [go'lã] M: **as colinas de ~** the Golan heights
gole ['gɔli] M gulp, swallow; (*pequeno*) sip; **de um só ~** at one gulp; **dar um ~** to have a sip
goleada [go'ljada] F (*Futebol*) convincing win
golear [go'ljar] VT to thrash ▶ VI to win convincingly
goleiro [go'lejru] (BR) M goalkeeper; (*col*) goalie
golfada [gow'fada] F (*jacto*) spurt
golfar [gow'far] VT (*vomitar*) to spit up; (*lançar*) to throw out ▶ VI (*sair*) to spurt out; (*bebê*) to bring up some milk
golfe ['gowfi] M golf; **campo de ~** golf course
golfinho [gow'fiɲu] M (*Zool*) dolphin
golfista [gow'fista] M/F golfer
golfo ['gowfu] M gulf
golinho [go'liɲu] M sip; **beber algo aos ~s** to sip sth
golo ['golu] (PT) M = **gol**
golpe ['gɔwpi] M (*tb fig*) blow; (*de mão*) smack; (*de punho*) punch; (*manobra*) ploy; (*de vento*) gust; **de um só ~** at a stroke; **dar um ~ em alguém** (*golpear*) to hit sb; (*fig: trapacear*) to trick sb; **o ~ é fazer ...** the clever thing is to do ...; **dar o ~ do baú** (*fig*) to marry for money; **~ baixo** (*fig, col*) dirty trick; **~ (de estado)** coup (d'état); **~ de mestre** masterstroke; **~ de vista** (*olhar*) glance; (*de motorista*) eye for distances; **~ mortal** death blow
golpear [gow'pjar] VT to hit; (*com navalha*) to stab; (*com o punho*) to punch
golpista [gow'pista] ADJ tricky
golquíper [gow'kiper] M goalkeeper

g

goma ['gɔma] F (cola) gum, glue; (de roupa) starch; **~ de mascar** chewing gum
gomo ['gomu] M (de laranja) slice
gôndola ['gõdola] F (Náut) gondola; (em supermercado) basket
gondoleiro [gõdo'lejru] M gondolier
gongo ['gõgu] M gong; (sineta) bell
gonorreia [gono'hɛja] F (Med) gonorrhea
gonzo ['gõzu] M hinge
gorar [go'rar] VT to frustrate, thwart ▶ VI (plano) to fail, go wrong
gordo, -a ['gordu, a] ADJ (pessoa) fat; (gordurento) greasy; (carne) fatty; (fig: quantia) considerable, ample ▶ M/F fat man/woman; **nunca vi mais ~** (col) I've never seen him (ou her, them etc) before in my life
gorducho, -a [gor'duʃu, a] ADJ plump, tubby ▶ M/F plump person
gordura [gor'dura] F fat; (derretida) grease; (obesidade) fatness
gordurento, -a [gordu'rẽtu, a] ADJ (ensebado) greasy; (gordo) fatty
gorduroso, -a [gordu'rozu, ɔza] ADJ (pele) greasy; (comida) fatty
gorgolejar [gorgole'ʒar] VI to gurgle
gorila [go'rila] M gorilla
gorjear [gor'ʒjar] VI to chirp, twitter
gorjeio [gor'ʒeju] M twittering, chirping
gorjeta [gor'ʒeta] F tip, gratuity
gororoba [goro'rɔba] (col) F (comida) grub; (comida ruim) muck
gorro ['gohu] M cap; (de lã) hat
gosma ['gɔzma] F spittle; (fig) slime
gosmento, -a [goz'mẽtu, a] ADJ slimy
gostar [gos'tar] VI: **~ de** to like; (férias, viagem etc) to enjoy; **gostar-se** VR to like each other; **~ de fazer algo** to like ou enjoy doing sth; **eu ~ia de ir** I would like to go; **gosto de sua companhia** I enjoy your company; **gosto de nadar** I like ou enjoy swimming; **gostei muito de falar com você** it was very nice talking to you; **~ mais de ...** to prefer ..., to like ... better
gosto ['gostu] M taste; (prazer) pleasure; **falta de ~** lack of taste; **a seu ~** to your liking; **com ~** willingly; (vestir-se) tastefully; (comer) heartily; **de bom/mau ~** in good/bad taste; **para o meu ~** for my liking; **ter ~ de** to taste of; **tenho muito ~ em ...** it gives me a lot of pleasure to ...; **tomar ~ por** to take a liking to
gostosão, -sona [gosto'zaw, 'zɔna] (pl -ões/-s) (col) M/F stunner
gostoso, -a [gos'tozu, ɔza] ADJ (comida) tasty; (agradável) pleasant; (cheiro) lovely; (risada) good; (col: pessoa) gorgeous ▶ M/F (col) cracker; **é ~ viajar** it's really nice to travel
gostosões [gosto'zõjs] MPL de **gostosão**
gostosona [gosto'zɔna] F de **gostosão**
gostosura [gosto'zura] F: **ser uma ~** (comida) to be delicious; (bebê, jogo etc) to be lovely
gota ['gota] F drop; (de suor) bead; (Med) gout; **~ a ~** drop by drop; **ser a ~ d'água** ou **a**

última ~ (fig) to be the last straw; **ser uma ~ d'água no oceano** (fig) to be a drop in the ocean
goteira [go'tejra] F (cano) gutter; (buraco) leak
gotejante [gote'ʒãtʃi] ADJ dripping
gotejar [gote'ʒar] VT to drip ▶ VI to drip; (telhado) to leak
gótico, -a ['gɔtʃiku, a] ADJ Gothic
gotícula [go'tʃikula] F droplet
gourmet [gur'me] (pl -s) M/F gourmet
governador, a [governador(a)] M/F governor
governamental [governamẽ'taw] (pl -ais) ADJ government atr
governanta [gover'nãta] F (de casa) housekeeper; (de criança) governess
governante [gover'nãtʃi] ADJ ruling ▶ M/F ruler ▶ F governess
governar [gover'nar] VT (Pol) to govern, rule; (barco) to steer
governista [gover'nista] ADJ pro-government ▶ M/F government supporter
governo [go'vernu] M government; (controle) control; (Náut) steering; **para o seu ~** (col) for the record, for your information
gozação [goza'sãw] (pl -ões) F (desfrute) enjoyment; (zombaria) teasing; (uma gozação) joke
gozada [go'zada] F: **dar uma ~ em alguém** to pull sb's leg
gozado, -a [go'zadu, a] ADJ funny; (estranho) strange, odd
gozador, a [goza'dor(a)] ADJ (caçoador) comical; (boa-vida) happy-go-lucky ▶ M/F joker; loafer
gozar [go'zar] VT to enjoy; (col: rir de) to make fun of ▶ VI to enjoy o.s.; (ao fazer sexo) to have an orgasm; **~ de** to enjoy; to make fun of
gozo ['gozu] M (prazer) pleasure; (uso) enjoyment, use; (orgasmo) orgasm; **estar em pleno ~ de suas faculdades mentais** to be in full possession of one's faculties; **ser um ~** (ser engraçado) to be a laugh
G/P ABR (Com) = **ganhos e perdas**
GPS ABR M (= global positioning system) GPS
gr. ABR = **grátis**; (= grau) deg.; (= gross) gr.
Grã-Bretanha [grã-bre'taɲa] F Great Britain
graça ['grasa] F (Rel) grace; (charme) charm; (gracejo) joke; (Jur) pardon; **de ~** (grátis) for nothing; (sem motivo) for no reason; **sem ~** dull, boring; **fazer** ou **ter ~** to be funny; **ficar sem ~** to be embarrassed; **~s a** thanks to; **não tem ~ fazer** (é chato) it's no fun to do; (não é certo) it's not right to do; **deixa de ~** don't be cheeky; **não sei que ~ você vê nele/nisso** I don't know what you see in him/it; **ser uma ~** to be lovely
gracejar [grase'ʒar] VI to joke
gracejo [gra'seʒu] M joke
gracinha [gra'siɲa] F: **ser uma ~** to be sweet ou cute; **que ~!** how sweet!
gracioso, -a [gra'sjozu, ɔza] ADJ (pessoa) charming; (gestos) gracious
gradação [grada'sãw] (pl -ões) F gradation
gradativo, -a [grada'tʃivu, a] ADJ gradual

grade ['gradʒi] F (*no chão*) grating; (*grelha*) grill; (*na janela*) bars pl; (*col: cadeia*) prison

gradear [gra'dʒjar] VT (*janela*) to put bars up at; (*jardim*) to fence off

grado, -a ['gradu, a] ADJ (*importante*) important ▶ M: **de bom/mau ~** willingly/unwillingly

graduação [gradwa'sãw] (*pl* -**ões**) F gradation; (*classificação*) grading; (*Educ*) graduation; (*Mil*) rank; **curso de ~** degree course

graduado, -a [gra'dwadu, a] ADJ (*dividido em graus*) graduated; (*diplomado*) graduate; (*eminente*) highly thought of

gradual [gra'dwaw] (*pl* -**ais**) ADJ gradual

graduando, -a [gra'dwandu, a] M/F graduating student, graduand

graduar [gra'dwar] VT (*termômetro*) to graduate; (*classificar*) to grade; (*luz, fogo*) to regulate; **graduar-se** VR to graduate; **~ alguém em algo** (*Educ*) to confer a degree in sth on sb; **~ alguém em coronel** etc (*Mil*) to make sb a colonel etc

graduável [gra'dwavew] (*pl* -**eis**) ADJ adjustable

grafia [gra'fia] F (*escrita*) writing; (*ortografia*) spelling

gráfica ['grafika] F (*arte*) graphics sg; (*estabelecimento*) printer's; (*seção: de jornal etc*) production department; *ver tb* **gráfico**

gráfico, -a ['grafiku, a] ADJ graphic ▶ M/F printer ▶ M (*Mat*) graph; (*diagrama*) diagram, chart; **gráficos** MPL (*Comput*) graphics; **~ de barras** bar chart

grã-finagem [grãfi'naʒẽ] F: **a ~** the upper crust

grã-finismo [grãfi'nizmu] M (*qualidade*) poshness; (*ato*) thing which posh people do; **o ~** (*pessoas*) the upper crust

grã-fino, -a [grã'finu, a] (*col*) ADJ posh ▶ M/F nob, toff

grafite [gra'fitʃi] F (*lápis*) lead; (*pichação*) (piece of) graffiti

grafologia [grafolo'ʒia] F graphology

grama ['grama] M (*peso*) gramme ▶ F (*BR: capim*) grass

gramado [gra'madu] (*BR*) M lawn; (*Futebol*) pitch

gramar [gra'mar] VT to plant *ou* sow with grass; (*PT col*) to be fond of ▶ VI (*PT col*) to cry out

gramática [gra'matʃika] F grammar; *ver tb* **gramático**

gramatical [gramatʃi'kaw] (*pl* -**ais**) ADJ grammatical

gramático, -a [gra'matʃiku, a] ADJ grammatical ▶ M/F grammarian

gramofone [gramo'fɔni] M gramophone

grampeador [grãpja'dor] M stapler

grampear [grã'pjar] VT to staple; (*BR Tel*) to tap; (*col: prender*) to nick

grampo ['grãpu] M staple; (*no cabelo*) hairgrip; (*de carpinteiro*) clamp; (*de chapéu*) hatpin

grana ['grana] (*col*) F cash

Granada [gra'nada] F Grenada

granada [gra'nada] F (*Mil*) shell; (*pedra*) garnet; **~ de mão** hand grenade

grandalhão, -lhona [grãda'ʎãw, 'ʎɔna] (*pl* -**ões/-s**) ADJ enormous

grandão, -dona [grã'dãw, 'dɔna] (*pl* -**ões/-s**) ADJ huge

grande ['grãdʒi] ADJ big, large; (*alto*) tall; (*notável, intenso*) great; (*longo*) long; (*adulto*) grown-up; **mulher ~** big woman; **~ mulher** great woman; **a G~ Londres** Greater London

grandessíssimo, -a [grãdʒi'sisimu, a] ADJ SUPERL *de* **grande**

grandeza [grã'deza] F (*tamanho*) size; (*fig*) greatness; (*ostentação*) grandeur; **ter mania de ~** to have delusions of grandeur

grandiloquente [grãdʒilo'kwẽtʃi] ADJ grandiloquent

grandiosidade [grãdʒjozi'dadʒi] F grandeur, magnificence

grandioso, -a [grã'dʒjozu, ɔza] ADJ magnificent, grand

grandíssimo, -a [grã'dʒisimu, a] ADJ SUPERL *de* **grande**

grandões [grã'dõjs] MPL *de* **grandão**

grandona [grã'dɔna] F *de* **grandão**

granel [gra'nɛw] M: **a ~** (*Com*) in bulk; **compra a ~** bulk buying

granfa ['grãfa] (*col*) ADJ posh ▶ M/F nob, toff

granito [gra'nitu] M (*Geo*) granite

granizo [gra'nizu] M hailstone; **chover ~** to hail; **chuva de ~** hailstorm

granja ['grãʒa] F farm; (*de galinhas*) chicken farm

granjear [grã'ʒjar] VT (*simpatia, amigos*) to win, gain; (*bens, fortuna*) to procure; **~ algo a** *ou* **para alguém** to win sb sth

granulado, -a [granu'ladu, a] ADJ grainy; (*açúcar*) granulated

grânulo ['granulu] M granule

grão ['grãw] (*pl* **grãos**) M grain; (*semente*) seed; (*de café*) bean

grão-de-bico (*pl* **grãos-de-bico**) M chickpea

grapefruit [greip'frutʃi] (*pl* -**s**) M grapefruit

grasnar [graz'nar] VI (*corvo*) to caw; (*pato*) to quack; (*rã*) to croak

gratidão [gratʃi'dãw] F gratitude

gratificação [gratʃifika'sãw] (*pl* -**ões**) F (*gorjeta*) gratuity, tip; (*bônus*) bonus; (*recompensa*) reward

gratificado, -a [gratʃifi'kadu, a] ADJ (*grato*) grateful

gratificante [gratʃifi'kãtʃi] ADJ gratifying

gratificar [gratʃifi'kar] VT (*dar gorjeta a*) to tip; (*dar bônus a*) to give a bonus to; (*recompensar*) to reward

gratinado, -a [gratʃi'nadu, a] ADJ (*Culin*) au gratin ▶ M (*prato*) gratin; (*crosta*) crust

grátis ['gratʃis] ADJ free

grato, -a ['gratu, a] ADJ (*agradecido*) grateful; (*agradável*) pleasant; **ficar ~ a alguém por** to be grateful to sb for

gratuidade [gratwi'dadʒi] F gratuity

gratuito, -a [gra'twitu, a] ADJ (*grátis*) free; (*infundado*) gratuitous

grau [graw] M degree; (*nível*) level; (*Educ*) class; **a temperatura é de 38 ~s** the temperature is 38 degrees; **primo/a em segundo ~** second cousin; **em alto ~** to a high degree; **primeiro/segundo ~** (*Educ*) primary/secondary level; **ensino de primeiro/segundo ~** primary (BRIT) *ou* elementary (US) /secondary education; **estar no 1°/2° ~** (*Educ*) to be at primary/ secondary (BRIT) *ou* elementary/high (US) school

graúdo, -a [gra'udu, a] ADJ (*grande*) big; (*pessoa: influente*) important ▶ M/F bigwig

gravação [grava'sãw] F (*em madeira*) carving; (*em disco, fita*) recording

gravador, a [grava'dor(a)] M tape recorder ▶ M/F engraver ▶ F (*empresa*) record company; **~ de CD/DVD** CD/DVD burner, CD/DVD writer

gravame [gra'vami] M (*imposto*) duty; (*Jur*) lien

gravar [gra'var] VT (*madeira*) to carve; (*metal, pedra*) to engrave; (*na memória*) to fix; (*disco, fita*) to record; **~ algo/alguém com impostos** to mark sth up/burden sb with taxes; **aquele dia ficou gravado na minha mente/memória** that day remained fixed in my mind/memory

gravata [gra'vata] F tie; **dar** *ou* **aplicar uma ~ em alguém** to get sb in a stranglehold; **~ borboleta** bow tie

grave ['gravi] ADJ (*situação, falta*) serious, grave; (*doença*) serious; (*tom*) deep; (*Ling*) grave

gravemente [grave'mẽtʃi] ADV (*doente, ferido*) seriously

graveto [gra'vetu] M piece of kindling

grávida ['gravida] ADJ pregnant

gravidade [gravi'dadʒi] F (*Fís*) gravity; (*de doença, situação*) seriousness

gravidez [gravi'dez] F pregnancy

gravitação [gravita'sãw] F gravitation

gravura [gra'vura] F (*em madeira*) engraving; (*estampa*) print

graxa ['graʃa] F (*para sapatos*) polish; (*lubrificante*) grease

Grécia ['grɛsja] F: **a ~** Greece

grega ['grega] F (*galão*) braid; *ver tb* **grego**

gregário, -a [gre'garju, a] ADJ gregarious

grego, -a ['gregu, a] ADJ, M/F Greek ▶ M (*Ling*) Greek

grei [grej] F flock

grelar [gre'lar] VT to stare at

grelha ['grɛʎa] F grill; (*de fornalha*) grate; **bife na ~** grilled steak

grelhado, -a [gre'ʎadu, a] ADJ grilled ▶ M (*prato*) grill

grelhar [gre'ʎar] VT to grill

grêmio ['gremju] M (*associação*) guild; (*clube*) club

grená [gre'na] ADJ, M dark red

greta ['greta] F crack

gretado, -a [gre'tadu, a] ADJ cracked

greve ['grɛvi] F strike; **fazer ~** to go on strike; **~ de fome** hunger strike; **~ branca** go-slow

grevista [gre'vista] M/F striker

grifado, -a [gri'fadu, a] ADJ in italics

grifar [gri'far] VT to italicize; (*sublinhar*) to underline; (*fig*) to emphasize

griffe ['grifi] M designer label

grifo ['grifu] M italics pl

grilado, -a [gri'ladu, a] (*col*) ADJ full of hang-ups; **estar ~ com algo** to be hung up about sth

grilar [gri'lar] (*col*) VT: **~ alguém** to get sb worked up; **grilar-se** VR to get worked up

grilhão [gri'ʎãw] (*pl* -**ões**) M chain; **grilhões** MPL (*fig*) fetters

grilo ['grilu] M cricket; (*Auto*) squeak; (*col: de pessoa*) hang-up; **qual é o ~?** what's the matter?; **dar ~** (*col*) to cause problems; **se der ~** (*impess*) if there's a problem; **não tem ~!** (*col*) (there's) no problem!

grimpar [grĩ'par] VI to climb

grinalda [gri'nawda] F garland

gringada [grĩ'gada] F (*grupo*) bunch of foreigners; (*gringos*) foreigners pl

gringo, -a ['grĩgu, a] (*col: pej*) M/F foreigner

gripado, -a [gri'padu, a] ADJ: **estar/ficar ~** to have/get a cold

gripar-se [gri'parsi] VR to catch flu

gripe ['gripi] F flu, influenza; **~ aviária** bird flu; **~ suína** swine flu

grisalho, -a [gri'zaʎu, a] ADJ (*cabelo*) grey (BRIT), gray (US)

grita ['grita] F uproar

gritante [gri'tãtʃi] ADJ (*hipocrisia*) glaring; (*desigualdade*) gross; (*mentira*) blatant; (*cor*) loud, garish

gritar [gri'tar] VT to shout, yell ▶ VI to shout; (*de dor, medo*) to scream; (*protestar*) to speak out; **~ com alguém** to shout at sb

gritaria [grita'ria] F shouting, din

grito ['gritu] M shout; (*de medo*) scream; (*de dor*) cry; (*de animal*) call; **dar um ~** to cry out; **falar/protestar aos ~s** to shout/shout protests; **no ~** (*col*) by force

Groenlândia [grwẽ'lãdʒja] F: **a ~** Greenland

grogue ['grɔgi] ADJ groggy

groom [grũ] (*pl* -**s**) M groom

grosa ['grɔza] F gross

groselha [gro'zɛʎa] F (red)currant

grosseiro, -a [gro'sejru, a] ADJ (*pessoa, comentário*) rude; (*piada*) crude; (*modos*) coarse; (*tecido*) coarse, rough; (*móvel*) roughly-made

grosseria [grose'ria] F rudeness; (*ato*): **fazer uma ~** to be rude; (*dito*): **dizer uma ~** to be rude, say something rude

grosso, -a ['grosu, 'grɔsa] ADJ (*tamanho, consistência*) thick; (*áspero*) rough; (*voz*) deep; (*col: pessoa, piada*) rude ▶ M: **o ~ de** the bulk of ▶ ADV: **falar ~** to talk in a deep voice; **falar ~ com alguém** (*fig*) to get tough with sb; **a ~ modo** roughly

grossura [gro'sura] F thickness
grotão [gro'tãw] (*pl* **-ões**) M gorge
grotesco, -a [gro'tesku, a] ADJ grotesque
grotões [gro'tõjs] MPL *de* **grotão**
grua ['grua] F (*Constr*) crane
grudado, -a [gru'dadu, a] ADJ (*fig*): **ser ~ com**
ou **em alguém** to be very attached to sb
grudar [gru'dar] VT to glue, stick ▶ VI to stick
grude ['grudʒi] F glue; (*col: comida*) grub;
(*ligação entre pessoas*): **ficar numa ~** to cling
to sb
grudento, -a [gru'dẽtu, a] ADJ sticky
gruja ['gruʒa] (*col*) F tip
grunhido [gru'nidu] M grunt
grunhir [gru'nir] VI (*porco*) to grunt; (*tigre*) to
growl; (*resmungar*) to grumble
grupo ['grupu] M group; (*Tec*) unit, set
gruta ['gruta] F grotto
guache ['gwaʃi] M gouache
guapo, -a ['gwapu, a] ADJ beautiful
guaraná [gwara'na] M guarana; (*bebida*) *soft*
drink flavoured with guarana
guarani [gwara'ni] ADJ, M/F Guarani ▶ M
(*Ling*) Guarani; (*moeda*) guarani
guarda ['gwarda] M/F policeman/woman
▶ F (*vigilância*) guarding; (*de objeto*)
safekeeping ▶ M (*Mil*) guard; **estar de ~** to
be on guard; **pôr-se em ~** to be on one's
guard; **a velha ~** the old guard; **a G~ Civil**
the Civil Guard
guarda-chuva (*pl* **-s**) M umbrella
guarda-civil (*pl* **guardas-civis**) M/F civil guard
guarda-costas M INV (*Náut*) coastguard boat;
(*capanga*) bodyguard
guardador, a [gwarda'dor(a)] M/F car
attendant
guardados [gwar'dadus] MPL keepsakes,
valuables
guarda-florestal (*pl* **guardas-florestais**) M/F
forest ranger
guarda-fogo (*pl* **-s**) M fireguard
guarda-louça [gwarda'losa] (*pl* **-s**) M
sideboard
guarda-marinha (*pl* **guardas-marinha(s)**) M
naval ensign
guarda-mor [-mɔr] (*pl* **guardas-mores**) M
inspector of customs
guardamoria [gwardamo'ria] F customs
authorities *pl*
guarda-móveis M INV furniture storage
warehouse
guardanapo [gwarda'napu] M napkin
guarda-noturno (*pl* **guardas-noturnos**) M
night watchman
guardar [gwar'dar] VT (*pôr em algum lugar*) to
put away; (*zelar por*) to guard; (*lembrança,
segredo*) to keep; (*vigiar*) to watch over; (*gravar
na memória*) to remember; **guardar-se** VR
(*defender-se*) to protect o.s.; **~ silêncio** to keep
quiet; **~ o lugar para alguém** to keep sb's
seat; **vou ~ este resto de bolo para ele** I'll
keep this last piece of cake for him; **~-se de**
(*acautelar-se*) to guard against

guarda-redes (PT) M INV goalkeeper
guarda-roupa (*pl* **-s**) M wardrobe
guarda-sol (*pl* **-sóis**) M sunshade, parasol
guardião, -diã [gwar'dʒjãw, 'dʒjã] (*pl* **-ães/-s**)
M/F guardian
guarida [gwa'rida] F refuge
guarita [gwa'rita] F (*casinha*) sentry box;
(*torre*) watch tower
guarnecer [gwarne'ser] VT (*Mil: fronteira*) to
garrison; (*comida*) to garnish; (*Náut: tripular*)
to crew; **~ alguém (de algo)** to equip sb
(with sth); **~ a despensa** *etc* **(de algo)** to
stock the pantry *etc* (with sth)
guarnição [gwarni'sãw] (*pl* **-ões**) F (*Mil*)
garrison; (*Náut*) crew; (*Culin*) garnish
Guatemala [gwate'mala] F: **a ~** Guatemala
guatemalteco, -a [gwatemaw'teku, a] ADJ,
M/F Guatemalan
gude ['gudʒi] M: **bola de ~** marble; (*jogo*)
marbles *pl*
gueixa ['gejʃa] F geisha
guelra ['gewha] F (*de peixe*) gill
guerra ['gɛha] F war; **em ~** at war;
declarar ~ (a alguém) to declare war (on
sb); **estar em pé de ~ (com)** (*países, facções*)
to be at war (with); (*vizinhos, casal*) to be at
loggerheads (with); **fazer ~** to wage war;
~ atômica *ou* **nuclear** nuclear war; **~ civil**
civil war; **~ de nervos** war of nerves; **~ fria**
cold war; **~ mundial** world war; **~ santa**
holy war
guerrear [ge'hjar] VI to wage war
guerreiro, -a [ge'hejru, a] ADJ (*espírito*)
fighting; (*belicoso*) warlike ▶ M warrior
guerrilha [ge'hiʎa] F (*luta*) guerrilla warfare;
(*tropa*) guerrilla band
guerrilhar [gehi'ʎar] VI to engage in guerrilla
warfare
guerrilheiro, -a [gehi'ʎejru, a] ADJ guerrilla
atr ▶ M/F guerrilla
gueto ['getu] M ghetto
guia ['gia] F (*orientação*) guidance; (*Com*)
permit, bill of lading; (*formulário*) advice slip
▶ M (*livro*) guide(book) ▶ M/F (*pessoa*) guide;
para que lhe sirva de ~ as a guide
Guiana ['gjana] F: **a ~** Guyana; **a ~ Francesa**
French Guyana
guiar [gjar] VT (*orientar*) to guide; (*Auto*) to
drive; (*cavalos*) to steer ▶ VI (*Auto*) to drive;
guiar-se VR: **~-se por** to go by
guichê [gi'ʃe] M ticket window; (*em banco,
repartição*) window, counter
guidão [gi'dãw] (*pl* **-ões**) M = **guidom**
guidom [gi'dõ] (*pl* **-ns**) M handlebar
guilder [giw'der] M guilder
guilhotina [giʎo'tʃina] F guillotine
guimba ['gĩba] (*col*) F (*cigarette*) butt
guinada [gi'nada] F (*Náut*) lurch; (*virada*)
swerve; **dar uma ~** (*com o carro*) to swerve;
(*fig: governo* etc) to do a U-turn
guinchar [gĩ'ʃar] VT (*carro*) to tow
guincho ['gĩʃu] M (*de animal, rodas*) squeal;
(*de pessoa*) shriek

guindar [gĩ'dar] vt to hoist, lift; (*fig*):
~ **alguém a** to promote sb to
guindaste [gĩ'dastʃi] m hoist, crane
Guiné [gi'nɛ] f: **a** ~ Guinea
Guiné-Bissau [-bi'saw] f: **a** ~ Guinea-Bissau
guisa ['giza] f: **à** ~ **de** like, by way of
guisado [gi'zadu] m stew
guisar [gi'zar] vt to stew
guitarra [gi'taha] f (electric) guitar
guitarrista [gita'hista] m/f guitarist; (*col*)
forger (*of money*)
guizo ['gizu] m bell

gula ['gula] f gluttony, greed
gulodice [gulo'dʒisi] f greed
guloseima [gulo'zejma] f delicacy, titbit
guloso, -a [gu'lozu, ɔza] ADJ greedy
gume ['gumi] m cutting edge; (*fig*)
sharpness
guri, a [gu'ri(a)] m/f kid ▶ f (*namorada*)
girlfriend
gurizote [guri'zɔtʃi] m lad
guru [gu'ru] m/f guru
gustação [gusta'sãw]˙ f tasting
gutural [gutu'raw] (*pl* **-ais**) ADJ guttural

Hh

H, h [a'ga] (*pl* **hs**) M H, h; **H de Henrique** H for Harry (BRIT) *ou* How (US)

h. (*pl* **hs.**) ABR (= *hora*) o'clock

há [a] VB *ver* **haver**

hã [ã] EXCL aha!

habeascorpus ['abjas 'kɔrpus] M habeas corpus

hábil ['abiw] (*pl* **-eis**) ADJ (*competente*) competent, capable; (*com as mãos*) clever; (*astucioso, esperto*) clever, shrewd; (*sutil*) diplomatic; (*Jur*) qualified; **em tempo ~** in reasonable time

habilidade [abili'dadʒi] F (*aptidão, competência*) skill, ability; (*astúcia, esperteza*) shrewdness; (*tato*) discretion; (*Jur*) qualification; **ele não teve a menor ~ com ela** (*tato*) he wasn't at all tactful with her; **ela não tem a menor ~ com crianças** (*jeito*) she's hopeless with children; **ter ~ manual** to be good with one's hands

habilidoso, -a [abili'dozu, ɔza] ADJ skilful (BRIT), skillful (US), clever

habilitação [abilita'sãw] (*pl* **-ões**) F (*aptidão*) competence; (*ato*) qualification; (*Jur*) attestation; **habilitações** FPL (*conhecimentos*) qualifications

habilitado, -a [abili'tadu, a] ADJ qualified; (*manualmente*) skilled

habilitar [abili'tar] VT (*tornar apto*) to enable; (*dar direito a*) to qualify, entitle; (*preparar*) to prepare; (*Jur*) to qualify

habitação [abita'sãw] (*pl* **-ões**) F dwelling, residence; (*Pol: alojamento*) housing

habitacional [abitasjo'naw] (*pl* **-ais**) ADJ housing *atr*

habitações [abita'sõjs] FPL *de* **habitação**

habitante [abi'tãtʃi] M/F inhabitant

habitar [abi'tar] VT (*viver em*) to live in; (*povoar*) to inhabit ▶ VI to live

hábitat ['abitatʃi] M habitat

habitável [abi'tavew] (*pl* **-eis**) ADJ (in)habitable

hábito ['abitu] M habit; (*social*) custom; (*Rel: traje*) habit; **adquirir/perder o ~ de (fazer) algo** to get into/out of the habit of (doing) sth; **ter o ~ de (fazer) algo** to be in the habit of (doing) sth; **por força do ~** by force of habit

habituação [abitwa'sãw] F acclimatization

(BRIT), acclimation (US), adjustment

habituado, -a [abi'twadu, a] ADJ: **~ a (fazer) algo** used to (doing) sth

habitual [abi'twaw] (*pl* **-ais**) ADJ usual

habituar [abi'twar] VT: **~ alguém a** to get sb used to, accustom sb to; **habituar-se** VR: **~-se a** to get used to

habitué [abi'twe] M habitué

hacker ['haker] (*pl* **-s**) M (*Comput*) hacker

hadoque [a'dɔki] M haddock

Haia ['aja] N the Hague

Haiti [aj'tʃi] M: **o ~** Haiti

haitiano, -a [aj'tʃjanu, a] ADJ, M/F Haitian

haja *etc* ['aʒa] VB *ver* **haver**

hálito ['alitu] M breath; **mau ~** bad breath

halitose [ali'tɔzi] F halitosis

hall [hɔw] (*pl* **halls**) M hall; (*de teatro, hotel*) foyer; **~ de entrada** entrance hall

halo ['alu] M halo

haltere [aw'teri] M dumbbell

halterofilismo [awterofi'lizmu] M weightlifting

halterofilista [awterofi'lista] M/F weightlifter

hambúrguer [ã'burger] (*pl* **-s**) M hamburger

handicap [ãdʒi'kapi] M handicap

hangar [ã'gar] M hangar

hão [ãw] VB *ver* **haver**

haras ['aras] M INV stud

hardware ['hadwer] M (*Comput*) hardware

harém [a'rẽ] (*pl* **-ns**) M harem

harmonia [armo'nia] F harmony

harmônica [ar'monika] F concertina

harmonioso, -a [armo'njozu, ɔza] ADJ harmonious

harmonizar [armoni'zar] VT (*Mús*) to harmonize; (*conciliar*): **~ algo (com algo)** to reconcile sth (with sth); **harmonizar-se** VR: **~(-se) (com algo)** (*ideias etc*) to coincide (with sth); (*pessoas*) to be in agreement (with sth); (*música*) to fit in (with sth); (*tapete*) to match (sth)

harpa ['arpa] F harp

harpista [ar'pista] M/F harpist

hashtag [haʃ'tagi] F hashtag

hasta ['asta] F: **~ pública** auction

haste ['astʃi] F (*de bandeira*) flagpole; (*Tec*) shaft, rod; (*Bot*) stem

hastear [as'tʃjar] VT to raise, hoist

Havaí [avaj'i] M: **o ~** Hawaii
havaiano, -a [avaj'anu, a] ADJ, M/F Hawaiian
▶ M (*Ling*) Hawaiian
Havana [a'vana] N Havana
havana [a'vana] ADJ INV light brown ▶ M
(*charuto*) Havana cigar

(PALAVRA-CHAVE)

haver [a'ver] VB AUX **1** (*ter*) to have; **ele havia
saído/comido** he had left/eaten
2: quem haveria de dizer que ... who
would have thought that ...
▶ VB IMPESS **1** (*existência*): **há** (*sg*) there is; (*pl*)
there are; **o que é que há?** what's the
matter?; **o que é que houve?** what
happened?, what was that?; **não há de quê**
don't mention it, you're welcome; **haja o
que houver** come what may
2 (*tempo*): **há séculos/cinco dias que não
o vejo** I haven't seen him for ages/five days;
há um ano que ela chegou it's a year since
she arrived; **há cinco dias (atrás)** five days
ago
haver-se VR: **haver-se com alguém** to sort
things out with sb
▶ M (*Com*) credit
haveres MPL (*pertences*) property *sg*,
possessions; (*riqueza*) wealth *sg*

haxixe [a'ʃiʃi] M hashish
hebraico, -a [e'brajku, a] ADJ, M/F Hebrew
▶ M (*Ling*) Hebrew
hebreu, -breia [e'brew, 'breja] M/F Hebrew
Hébridas ['ɛbridas] FPL: **as (ilhas) ~** the
Hebrides
hecatombe [eka'tõbi] F (*fig*) massacre
hectare [ek'tari] M hectare
hectograma [ekto'grama] M hectogram
hectolitro [ekto'litru] M hectolitre (*BRIT*),
hectoliter (*US*)
hediondo, -a [e'dʒjõdu, a] ADJ (*repulsivo*) vile,
revolting; (*crime*) heinous; (*horrendo*) hideous
hedonista [edo'nista] ADJ hedonistic ▶ M/F
hedonist
hegemonia [eʒemo'nia] F hegemony
hei [ej] VB *ver* **haver**
hein [ẽj] EXCL eh?; (*exprimindo indignação*) hmm
hélice ['ɛlisi] F propeller
helicóptero [eli'kɔpteru] M helicopter
hélio ['ɛlju] M helium
heliporto [eli'portu] M heliport
Helsinque [ew'sĩki] N Helsinki
hem [ẽj] EXCL = **hein**
hematologia [ematolo'ʒia] F haematology
(*BRIT*), hematology (*US*)
hematoma [ema'toma] M bruise
hemisférico, -a [emis'fɛriku, a] ADJ
hemispherical
hemisfério [emis'fɛrju] M hemisphere
hemofilia [emofi'lia] F haemophilia (*BRIT*),
hemophilia (*US*)
hemofílico, -a [emo'filiku, a] ADJ, M/F
haemophiliac (*BRIT*), hemophiliac (*US*)

hemoglobina [emoglo'bina] F haemoglobin
(*BRIT*), hemoglobin (*US*)
hemograma [emo'grama] M blood count
hemorragia [emoha'ʒia] F haemorrhage
(*BRIT*), hemorrhage (*US*); **~ nasal** nosebleed
hemorróidas [emo'hɔjdas] FPL haemorrhoids
(*BRIT*), hemorrhoids (*US*), piles
hena ['ɛna] F henna
henê [e'ne] M = **hena**
hepatite [epa'tʃitʃi] F hepatitis
heptágono [ep'tagonu] M heptagon
hera ['ɛra] F ivy
heráldica [e'rawdʒika] F heraldry
herança [e'rãsa] F inheritance; (*fig*) heritage
herbáceo, -a [er'basju, a] ADJ herbaceous
herbicida [erbi'sida] M weedkiller, herbicide
herbívoro, -a [er'bivoru, a] ADJ herbivorous
▶ M/F herbivore
herdade [er'dadʒi] (*PT*) F large farm
herdar [er'dar] VT: **~ algo (de)** to inherit sth
(from); **~ a** to bequeath to
herdeiro, -a [er'dejru, a] M/F heir(ess)
hereditário, -a [eredʒi'tarju, a] ADJ
hereditary
herege [e'reʒi] M/F heretic
heresia [ere'zia] F heresy
herético, -a [e'rɛtʃiku, a] ADJ heretical
hermafrodita [ermafro'dʒita] M/F
hermaphrodite
hermético, -a [er'mɛtʃiku, a] ADJ airtight; (*fig*)
obscure, impenetrable
hérnia ['ɛrnja] F hernia; **~ de hiato** hiatus
hernia
herói [e'rɔj] M hero
heroico, -a [e'rɔjku, a] ADJ heroic
heroína [ero'ina] F heroine; (*droga*) heroin
heroísmo [ero'izmu] M heroism
herpes ['ɛrpis] M INV herpes *sg*
herpes-zóster [-'zɔster] M (*Med*) shingles *sg*
hertz ['ɛrtzi] M INV hertz
hesitação [ezita'sãw] (*pl* **-ões**) F hesitation
hesitante [ezi'tãtʃi] ADJ hesitant
hesitar [ezi'tar] VI to hesitate; **~ em (fazer)
algo** to hesitate in (doing) sth
heterodoxo, -a [etero'dɔksu, a] ADJ
unorthodox
heterogêneo, -a [etero'ʒenju, a] ADJ
heterogeneous
heterônimo [ete'ronimu] M pen name, nom
de plume
heterossexual [eterosek'swaw] (*pl* **-ais**) ADJ,
M/F heterosexual
heterossexualidade [eterosekswali'dadʒi] F
heterosexuality
hexagonal [eksago'naw] (*pl* **-ais**) ADJ
hexagonal
hexágono [ek'sagonu] M hexagon
hiato ['jatu] M hiatus
hibernação [iberna'sãw] F hibernation
hibernar [iber'nar] VI to hibernate
hibisco [i'bisku] M (*Bot*) hibiscus
híbrido, -a ['ibridu, a] ADJ hybrid
hidramático, -a [idra'matʃiku, a] ADJ

(*mudança*) hydraulic; (*carro*) with hydraulic transmission

hidratante [idra'tãtʃi] ADJ moisturizing ▶ M moisturizer

hidratar [idra'tar] VT to hydrate; (*pele*) to moisturize

hidrato [i'dratu] M: ~ **de carbono** carbohydrate

hidráulica [i'drawlika] F hydraulics *sg*

hidráulico, -a [i'drawliku, a] ADJ hydraulic; **força hidráulica** hydraulic power

hidrelétrica [idre'lɛtrika] F (*usina*) hydroelectric power station; (*empresa*) hydroelectric power company

hidreletricidade [idreletrisi'dadʒi] F hydroelectric power

hidrelétrico, -a [idre'lɛtriku, a] ADJ hydroelectric

hidro... [idru] PREFIXO hydro..., water... *atr*

hidroavião [idrua'vjãw] (*pl* **-ões**) M seaplane

hidrocarboneto [idrokarbo'netu] M hydrocarbon

hidrófilo, -a [i'drɔfilu, a] ADJ absorbent; **algodão** ~ cotton wool (BRIT), absorbent cotton (US)

hidrofobia [idrofo'bia] F rabies *sg*

hidrogênio [idro'ʒenju] M hydrogen

hidroginástica [idroʒi'nastʃika] F aquaerobics

hidroterapia [idrotera'pia] F hydrotherapy

hidrovia [idro'via] F waterway

hiena ['jena] F hyena

hierarquia [jerar'kia] F hierarchy

hierárquico, -a [je'rarkiku, a] ADJ hierarchical

hierarquizar [jerarki'zar] VT to place in a hierarchy

hieroglífico, -a [jero'glifiku, a] ADJ hieroglyphic

hieróglifo [je'rɔglifu] M hieroglyph(ic)

hífen ['ifẽ] (*pl* **-s**) M hyphen

higiene [i'ʒjeni] F hygiene; ~ **mental** (mental) rest

higiênico, -a [i'ʒjeniku, a] ADJ hygienic; (*pessoa*) clean; **papel** ~ toilet paper

hilariante [ila'rjãtʃi] ADJ hilarious

Himalaia [ima'laja] M: **o** ~ the Himalayas *pl*

hímen ['imẽ] (*pl* **-s**) M (*Anat*) hymen

hindi [ĩ'dʒi] M (*Ling*) Hindi

hindu [ĩ'du] ADJ, M/F Hindu; (*indiano*) Indian

hinduísmo [ĩ'dwizmu] M Hinduism

hino ['inu] M hymn; ~ **nacional** national anthem

hinterlândia [ĩter'lãdʒja] F hinterland

hiper... [iper] PREFIXO hyper...; (*col*) really

hipérbole [i'pɛrboli] F hyperbole

hipermercado [ipermer'kadu] M hypermarket

hipersensível [ipersẽ'sivew] (*pl* **-eis**) ADJ hypersensitive

hipertensão [ipertẽ'sãw] F high blood pressure

hípico, -a ['ipiku, a] ADJ riding *atr*; **clube** ~ riding club

hipismo [i'pizmu] M (*turfe*) horse racing; (*equitação*) (horse) riding

hipnose [ip'nɔzi] F hypnosis

hipnótico, -a [ip'nɔtʃiku, a] ADJ hypnotic; (*substância*) sleep-inducing ▶ M sleeping drug

hipnotismo [ipno'tʃizmu] M hypnotism

hipnotizador, a [ipnotʃizador(a)] M/F hypnotist

hipnotizar [ipnotʃi'zar] VT to hypnotize

hipocondríaco, -a [ipokõ'driaku, a] ADJ, M/F hypochondriac

hipocrisia [ipokri'zia] F hypocrisy

hipócrita [i'pɔkrita] ADJ hypocritical ▶ M/F hypocrite

hipodérmico, -a [ipo'dɛrmiku, a] ADJ hypodermic

hipódromo [i'pɔdromu] M racecourse

hipopótamo [ipo'pɔtamu] M hippopotamus

hipoteca [ipo'tɛka] F mortgage

hipotecar [ipote'kar] VT to mortgage

hipotecário, -a [ipote'karju, a] ADJ mortgage *atr*; **credor/devedor** ~ mortgagee/mortgager

hipotermia [ipoter'mia] F hypothermia

hipótese [i'pɔtezi] F hypothesis; **na** ~ **de** in the event of; **em** ~ **alguma** under no circumstances; **na melhor/pior das** ~**s** at best/worst

hipotético, -a [ipo'tɛtʃiku, a] ADJ hypothetical

hirsuto, -a [ir'sutu, a] ADJ (*cabeludo*) hairy, hirsute; (*barba*) spiky; (*fig*: *ríspido*) harsh

hirto, -a ['irtu, a] ADJ stiff, rigid; **ficar** ~ (*pessoa*) to stand stock still

hispânico, -a [is'paniku, a] ADJ Hispanic

hispanista [ispa'nista] M/F Hispanist

hispano-americano, -a [is'pano-] ADJ Spanish American

histamina [ista'mina] F histamine

histerectomia [isterekto'mia] F hysterectomy

histeria [iste'ria] F hysteria; ~ **coletiva** mass hysteria

histérico, -a [is'tɛriku, a] ADJ hysterical

histerismo [iste'rizmu] M hysteria

história [is'tɔrja] F (*estudo, ciência*) history; (*conto*) story; **histórias** FPL (*chateação*) bother *sg*, fuss *sg*; **a mesma** ~ **de sempre** the same old story; **isso é outra** ~ that's a different matter; **é tudo** ~ **dela** she's making it all up; **deixe de** ~! come off it!; **que** ~ **é essa?** what's going on?; **essa** ~ **de ...** (*col*: *troço*) this business of ...; ~ **antiga/natural** ancient/natural history; ~ **da carochinha** fairy story

historiador, a [istorja'dor(a)] M/F historian

historiar [isto'rjar] VT to recount

histórico, -a [is'tɔriku, a] ADJ (*personagem, pesquisa etc*) historical; (*fig*: *notável*) historic ▶ M history

historieta [isto'rjeta] F anecdote, very short story

histrionismo [istrjoˈnizmu] M histrionics pl

hobby [ˈhɔbi] (pl **-bies**) M hobby

hodierno, -a [oˈdʒjɛrnu, a] ADJ today's, present

hoje [ˈoʒi] ADV today; (atualmente) now(adays); **~ à noite** tonight; **de ~ a uma semana** in a week's time; **de ~ em diante** from now on; **~ em dia** nowadays; **~ faz uma semana** a week ago today; **ainda ~** (before the end of) today; **de ~ para amanhã** in one day; **por ~ é só** that's all for today

Holanda [oˈlãda] F: **a ~** Holland

holandês, -esa [olãˈdes, eza] ADJ Dutch ▶ M/F Dutchman/woman ▶ M (Ling) Dutch

holding [ˈhowdiŋ] (pl **-s**) M holding company

holocausto [oloˈkawstu] M holocaust

holofote [oloˈfɔtʃi] M searchlight; (em campo de futebol etc) floodlight

holograma [oloˈgrama] M hologram

homem [ˈomẽ] (pl **-ns**) M man; (a humanidade) mankind; **uma conversa de ~ para ~** a man-to-man talk; **ser o ~ da casa** (fig) to wear the trousers; **ser outro ~** (fig) to be a changed man; **~ de ação** man of action; **~ de bem** honest man; **~ de empresa** ou **negócios** businessman; **~ de estado** statesman; **~ da lei** lawyer; **~ de letras** man of letters; **~ de palavra** man of his word; **~ de peso** influential man; **~ da rua** man in the street; **~ de recursos** man of means; **~ público** public servant

homem-bomba (pl **homens-bomba**) M suicide bomber

homem-feito (pl **homens-feitos**) M grown man

homem-rã (pl **homens-rã(s)**) M frogman, diver

homem-sanduíche (pl **homens-sanduíche(s)**) M sandwich board man

homenageado, -a [omenaˈʒjadu, a] ADJ honoured (BRIT), honored (US) ▶ M/F person hono(u)red

homenageante [omenaˈʒjãtʃi] ADJ respectful

homenagear [omenaˈʒjar] VT (pessoa) to pay tribute to, honour (BRIT), honor (US)

homenagem [omeˈnaʒẽ] F tribute; (Rel) homage; **prestar ~ a alguém** to pay tribute to sb; **em ~ a** in honour (BRIT) ou honor (US) of

homens [ˈomẽs] MPL de **homem**

homenzarrão [omẽzaˈhãw] (pl **-ões**) M hulk (of a man)

homenzinho [omẽˈziɲu] M little man; (jovem) young man

homeopata [omjoˈpata] M/F homoeopath(ic) doctor (BRIT), homeopath(ic doctor) (US)

homeopatia [omjopaˈtʃia] F homoeopathy (BRIT), homeopathy

homeopático, -a [omjoˈpatʃiku, a] ADJ homoeopathic (BRIT), homeopathic (US); (fig): **em doses homeopáticas** in tiny quantities

homérico, -a [oˈmɛriku, a] ADJ (fig) phenomenal

homicida [omiˈsida] ADJ (pessoa) homicidal ▶ M/F murderer

homicídio [omiˈsidʒju] M murder; **~ involuntário** manslaughter

homiziado, -a [omiˈzjadu, a] ADJ in hiding ▶ M/F fugitive

homiziar [omiˈzjar] VT (esconder) to hide; **homiziar-se** VR to hide

homogeneidade [omoʒenejˈdadʒi] F homogeneity

homogeneizado, -a [omoʒenejˈzadu, a] ADJ: **leite ~** homogenized milk

homogêneo, -a [omoˈʒenju, a] ADJ homogeneous; (Culin) blended

homologar [omoloˈgar] VT to ratify

homólogo, -a [oˈmɔlogu, a] ADJ homologous; (fig) equivalent ▶ M/F opposite number

homônimo [oˈmonimu] M (de pessoa) namesake; (Ling) homonym

homossexual [omosekˈswaw] (pl **-ais**) ADJ, M/F homosexual

homossexualismo [omosekswaˈlizmu] M homosexuality

Honduras [õˈduras] F Honduras

hondurenho, -a [õduˈreɲu, a] ADJ, M/F Honduran

honestidade [onestʃiˈdadʒi] F honesty; (decência) decency; (justeza) fairness

honesto, -a [oˈnɛstu, a] ADJ honest; (decente) decent; (justo) fair, just

Hong Kong [oŋˈkoŋ] F Hong Kong

honorário, -a [onoˈrarju, a] ADJ honorary

honorários [onoˈrarjus] MPL fees

honorífico, -a [onoˈrifiku, a] ADJ honorific

honra [ˈõha] F honour (BRIT), honor (US); **honras** FPL: **~s fúnebres** funeral rites; **convidado de ~** guest of hono(u)r; **em ~ de** in hono(u)r of; **por ~ da firma** (por obrigação) out of a sense of duty; (para salvar as aparências) to save face; **fazer as ~s da casa** to do the hono(u)rs, attend to the guests

honradez [õhaˈdez] F honesty; (de pessoa) integrity

honrado, -a [õˈhadu, a] ADJ honest; (respeitado) honourable (BRIT), honorable (US)

honrar [õˈhar] VT to honour (BRIT), honor (US); **honrar-se** VR: **~-se em fazer** to be hono(u)red to do

honraria [õhaˈria] F honour (BRIT), honor (US)

honroso, -a [õˈhozu, ɔza] ADJ honourable (BRIT), honorable (US)

hóquei [ˈhɔkej] M hockey; **~ sobre gelo** ice hockey

hora [ˈɔra] F (60 minutos) hour; (momento) time; **a que ~s?** (at) what time?; **que ~s são?** what time is it?; **são duas ~s** it's two o'clock; **você tem as ~s?** have you got the time?; **isso são ~s?** what time do you call this?; **dar as ~s** (relógio) to strike the hour; **fazer ~** to kill time; **fazer ~ com alguém** (col) to tease sb; **marcar ~** to make an appointment; **perder a ~** to be late; **não vejo a ~ de ...** I can't wait to ...; **às altas ~s da noite** *ou* **da madrugada** in the small hours; **de ~ em ~** every hour; **em boa/má ~** at the right/wrong time; **chegar em cima da ~** to arrive just in time *ou* on the dot; **fora de ~** at the wrong moment; **na ~** *(no ato, em seguida)* on the spot; *(em boa hora)* at the right moment; *(na hora H)* at the moment of truth; **na ~ H** *(no momento certo)* in the nick of time; *(na hora crítica)* at the moment of truth, when it comes (*ou* came) to it; **está na ~ de ...** it's time to ...; **bem na ~** just in time; **chegar na ~** to be on time; **de última ~** *adj* last-minute; **de última ~** *adv* at the last minute; **~ de dormir** bedtime; **do almoço** lunch hour; **meia ~** half an hour; **~ local** local time; **~s extras** overtime *sg*; **trabalhei 2 ~s extras** I worked 2 hours overtime; **você recebe por ~ extra?** do you get paid overtime?; **~s vagas** spare time *sg*

horário, -a [o'rarju, a] ADJ: **100 km ~s** 100 km an hour ▶ M *(tabela)* timetable; *(hora)* time; **~ de expediente** working hours *pl*; *(de um escritório)* office hours *pl*; **~ de verão** summer time; **~ integral** full time; **~ nobre** (TV) prime time

horda ['ɔrda] F horde

horista [o'rista] ADJ paid by the hour ▶ M/F hourly-paid worker

horizontal [orizõ'taw] *(pl* **-ais**) ADJ horizontal ▶ F: **estar na ~** *(col)* to be lying down

horizonte [ori'zõtʃi] M horizon

hormonal [ormo'naw] *(pl* **-ais**) ADJ hormonal

hormônio [or'monju] M hormone

horóscopo [o'rɔskopu] M horoscope

horrendo, -a [o'hẽdu, a] ADJ horrendous, frightful

horripilante [ohipi'lātʃi] ADJ horrifying, hair-raising; *(sorriso)* chilling

horripilar [ohipi'lar] VT to horrify; **horripilar-se** VR to be horrified

horrível [o'hivew] *(pl* **-eis**) ADJ awful, horrible

horror [o'hor] M horror; **que ~!** how awful!!; **ser um ~** to be awful; **ter ~ a algo** to hate sth; **um ~ de** *(porção)* a lot of; **dizer/fazer ~es** to say/do terrible things; **~es de** *(muitos)* loads of; **ele está faturando ~es** he's raking it in, he's making a fortune

horrorizar [ohori'zar] VT to horrify, frighten ▶ VI: **cenas de ~** horrifying scenes; **horrorizar-se** VR to be horrified

horroroso, -a [oho'rozu, ɔza] ADJ horrible, ghastly

horta ['ɔrta] F vegetable garden

hortaliças [orta'lisas] FPL vegetables

hortelã [orte'lã] F mint; **~ pimenta** peppermint

hortelão, -loa [orte'lãw, 'loa] *(pl* **-s** *ou* **-ões/-s)** *(PT)* M/F (market) gardener

hortênsia [or'tẽsja] F hydrangea

horticultor, a [ortʃikuw'tor(a)] M/F market gardener *(BRIT)*, truck farmer *(US)*

horticultura [ortʃikuw'tura] F horticulture

hortifrutigranjeiros [ortʃifrutʃigrã'ʒejrus] MPL fruit and vegetables

hortigranjeiros [ortʃigrã'ʒejrus] MPL garden vegetables

horto ['ortu] M market garden *(BRIT)*, truck farm *(US)*

hospedagem [ospe'daʒẽ] F guest house

hospedar [ospe'dar] VT to put up; **hospedar-se** VR to stay, lodge

hospedaria [ospeda'ria] F guest house

hóspede ['ɔspedʒi] M *(amigo)* guest; *(estranho)* lodger

hospedeira [ospe'dejra] F landlady; *(PT: de bordo)* stewardess, air hostess *(BRIT)*

hospedeiro, -a [ospe'dejru, a] ADJ hospitable ▶ M *(dono)* landlord

hospício [os'pisju] M mental hospital

hospital [ospi'taw] *(pl* **-ais**) M hospital

hospitalar [ospita'lar] ADJ hospital *atr*

hospitaleiro, -a [ospita'lejru, a] ADJ hospitable

hospitalidade [ospitali'dadʒi] F hospitality

hospitalização [ospitaliza'sãw] *(pl* **-ões**) F hospitalization

hospitalizar [ospitali'zar] VT to hospitalize, admit to hospital

hostess ['ɔstes] *(pl* **hostesses**) F hostess

hóstia ['ɔstʃia] F Host, wafer

hostil [os'tʃiw] *(pl* **-is**) ADJ hostile

hostilidade [ostʃili'dadʒi] F hostility

hostilizar [ostʃili'zar] VT to antagonize; *(Mil)* to wage war on

hostis [os'tʃis] PL *de* **hostil**

hotel [o'tew] *(pl* **-éis**) M hotel; **~ de alta rotatividade** motel for sexual encounters

hotelaria [otela'ria] F *(curso)* hotel management; *(conjunto de hotéis)* hotels *pl*

hoteleiro, -a [ote'lejru, a] ADJ hotel *atr* ▶ M/F hotelier; **rede hoteleira** hotel chain

houve *etc* ['ovi] VB *ver* **haver**

hui [wi] EXCL *(de dor)* ow!!; *(de susto, surpresa)* ah!!; *(de repugnância)* ugh!

humanidade [umani'dadʒi] F *(os homens)* man(kind); *(compaixão)* humanity; **humanidades** FPL *(Educ)* humanities

humanismo [uma'nizmu] M humanism

humanista [uma'nista] ADJ, M/F humanist

humanitário, -a [umani'tarju, a] ADJ humanitarian; *(benfeitor)* humane ▶ M/F humanitarian

humanizar [umani'zar] VT to humanize; **humanizar-se** VR to become more human

humano, -a [u'manu, a] ADJ human; *(bondoso)* humane

humanos [u'manus] MPL humans

humildade [umiw'dadʒi] F humility; *(pobreza)* poverty

humilde [u'miwdʒi] ADJ humble; *(pobre)* poor

humildes [u'miwdʒis] MPL/FPL: **os** *(ou* **as)** ~ the poor

humilhação [umiʎa'sãw] F humiliation

humilhante [umi'ʎãtʃi] ADJ humiliating

humilhar [umiˈʎar] vᴛ to humiliate ▶ vɪ to be humiliating; **humilhar-se** vʀ to humble o.s.

humor [uˈmor] ᴍ (*disposição*) mood, temper; (*graça*) humour (ʙʀɪᴛ), humor (ᴜs); **de bom/ mau ~** in a good/bad mood

humorismo [umoˈrizmu] ᴍ humour (ʙʀɪᴛ), humor (ᴜs)

humorista [umoˈrista] ᴍ/ꜰ (*escritor*) humorist; (*na TV, no palco*) comedian

humorístico, -a [umoˈristʃiku, a] ᴀᴅᴊ humorous

húmus [ˈumus] ᴍ ɪɴᴠ humus

húngaro, -a [ˈũgaru, a] ᴀᴅᴊ, ᴍ/ꜰ Hungarian

Hungria [ũˈgria] ꜰ: **a ~** Hungary

hurra [ˈuha] ᴍ cheer ▶ ᴇxᴄʟ hurrah!

Hz ᴀʙʀ (= *hertz*) Hz

Ii

I, i [i] (pl **is**) M I, i; **I de Irene** I for Isaac (BRIT) ou item (US)
ia etc ['ia] VB ver **ir**
IAB ABR M = **Instituto dos Advogados do Brasil; Instituto dos Arquitetos do Brasil**
ialorixá [jalori'ʃa] F macumba priestess
IAPAS (BR) ABR M = **Instituto de Administração da Previdência e Assistência Social**
iate ['jatʃi] M yacht; **~ clube** yacht club
iatismo [ja'tʃizmu] M yachting
iatista [ja'tʃista] M/F yachtsman/woman
IBAM ABR M = **Instituto Brasileiro de Administração Municipal**
IBDF ABR M = **Instituto Brasileiro de Desenvolvimento Florestal**
ibérico, -a [i'bɛriku, a] ADJ, M/F Iberian
ibero, -a [i'bɛru, a] ADJ, M/F Iberian
ibero-americano, -a [iberu-] ADJ, M/F Ibero-American
IBGE ABR M = **Instituto Brasileiro de Geografia e Estatística**
IBMC ABR M = **Instituto Brasileiro do Mercado de Capitais**
Ibope [i'bɔpi] ABR M = **Instituto Brasileiro de Opinião Pública e Estatística; dar ibope** (TV) to get high ratings; (fig) to be popular
IBV ABR M = **Índice da Bolsa de Valores (do Rio de Janeiro)**
içar [i'sar] VT to hoist, raise
iceberg [ajs'bɛrgi] (pl **-s**) M iceberg
ICMS (BR) ABR M (= Imposto sobre Circulação de Mercadorias e Prestação de Serviços) ≈ VAT
icone ['ikoni] M (ger, Comput) icon
iconoclasta [ikono'klasta] ADJ iconoclastic ▶ M/F iconoclast
icterícia [ikte'risja] F jaundice
ida ['ida] F going, departure; **~ e volta** round trip, return; **a (viagem de) ~** the outward journey; **na ~** on the way there; **~s e vindas** comings and goings; **comprei só a ~** I only bought a single ou one-way (US) (ticket)
idade [i'dadʒi] F age; **ter cinco anos de ~** to be five (years old); **de meia ~** middle-aged; **qual é a ~ dele?** how old is he?; **na minha ~** at my age; **ser menor/maior de ~** to be under/of age; **pessoa de ~** elderly person; **estar na ~ de trabalhar** to be (of) working age; **já não estou mais em ~ de fazer** I'm

past doing; **~ atômica** atomic age; **~ da pedra** Stone Age; **I~ Média** Middle Ages pl
ideação [idea'sãw] (pl **-ões**) F conception
ideal [ide'jaw] (pl **-ais**) ADJ, M ideal
idealismo [idea'lizmu] M idealism
idealista [idea'lista] ADJ idealistic ▶ M/F idealist
idealização [idealiza'sãw] (pl **-ões**) F idealization; (planejamento) creation
idealizar [ideali'zar] VT to idealize; (planejar) to devise, create
idear [ide'ar] VT (imaginar) to imagine, think up; (idealizar) to create
ideário [i'dʒarju] M ideas pl, thinking
ideia [i'deja] F idea; (mente) mind; **mudar de ~** to change one's mind; **não ter a mínima ~** to have no idea; **não faço ~** I can't imagine; **estar com ~ de fazer** to plan to do; **fazer uma ~ errada de algo** to get the wrong idea about sth; **~ fixa** obsession; **~ genial** brilliant idea
idem ['idẽ] PRON ditto
idêntico, -a [i'dẽtʃiku, a] ADJ identical
identidade [idẽtʃi'dadʒi] F identity; **carteira de ~** identity (BRIT) ou identification (US) card
identificação [idẽtʃifika'sãw] F identification
identificar [idẽtʃifi'kar] VT to identify; **identificar-se** VR: **~-se com** to identify with
ideologia [ideolo'ʒia] F ideology
ideológico, -a [ideo'lɔʒiku, a] ADJ ideological
ideólogo, -a [ide'ɔlogu, a] M/F ideologue
ídiche ['idiʃi] M = **iídiche**
idílico, -a [i'dʒiliku, a] ADJ idyllic
idílio [i'dʒilju] M idyll
idioma [i'dʒoma] M language
idiomático, -a [idʒo'matʃiku, a] ADJ idiomatic
idiossincrasia [idʒosĩkra'zia] F character
idiota [i'dʒɔta] ADJ idiotic ▶ M/F idiot
idiotice [idʒo'tʃisi] F idiocy
ido, -a ['idu, a] ADJ past
idólatra [i'dɔlatra] ADJ idolatrous ▶ M/F idolater/tress
idolatrar [idola'trar] VT to idolize
idolatria [idola'tria] F idolatry
ídolo ['idolu] M idol
idoneidade [idonej'dadʒi] F suitability; (competência) competence; **~ moral** moral probity

idôneo, -a [i'donju, a] ADJ (*adequado*) suitable, fit; (*pessoa*) able, capable

idos ['idus] MPL bygone days

idoso, -a [i'dozu, ɔza] ADJ elderly, old

Iemanjá [jemã'ʒa] F Iemanjá (*Afro-Brazilian sea goddess*)

Iêmen ['jemẽ] M: **o ~** Yemen

iemenita [jeme'nita] ADJ, M/F Yemeni

iene ['jɛni] M yen

IGC (BR) ABR M = **imposto sobre ganhos de capital**

iglu [i'glu] M igloo

ignaro, -a [igi'naru, a] ADJ ignorant

ignição [igni'sãw] (*pl* **-ões**) F ignition

ignóbil [ig'nɔbiw] (*pl* **-eis**) ADJ ignoble

ignomínia [igno'minja] F disgrace, ignominy

ignominioso, -a [ignomi'njozu, ɔza] ADJ ignominious

ignorado, -a [igno'radu, a] ADJ unknown

ignorância [igno'rãsja] F ignorance; **apelar para a ~** (*col*) to lose one's rag

ignorante [igno'rãtʃi] ADJ ignorant, uneducated ▶ M/F ignoramus

ignorar [igno'rar] VT not to know; (*não dar atenção a*) to ignore

ignoto, -a [ig'nɔtu, a] ADJ (*formal*) unknown

IGP (BR) ABR M = **Índice Geral de Preços**

igreja [i'greʒa] F church

igual [i'gwaw] (*pl* **-ais**) ADJ equal; (*superfície*) even ▶ M/F equal; **em partes iguais** in equal parts; **ser ~** to be the same; **ser ~ a** to be the same as, be like; **~ se ... as if ...**; **por ~** equally; **sem ~** unequalled, without equal; **de ~ para ~** on equal terms; **tratar alguém de ~ para ~** to treat sb as an equal; **nunca vi coisa ~** I've never seen anything like it

igualar [igwa'lar] VT (*ser igual a*) to equal; (*fazer igual*) to make equal; (*nivelar*) to level ▶ VI: **~ a ou com** to be equal to, be the same as; (*ficar no mesmo nível*) to be level with; **igualar-se** VR: **~-se a alguém** to be sb's equal; **~ algo com ou a algo** to equal sth to sth; **~ algo com algo** (*terreno etc*) to level sth with sth

igualdade [igwaw'dadʒi] F (*paridade*) equality; (*uniformidade*) uniformity

igualitário, -a [igwali'tarju, a] ADJ egalitarian

igualmente [igwaw'mẽtʃi] ADV equally; (*também*) likewise, also; **~!** (*saudação*) the same to you!

iguana [i'gwana] M iguana

iguaria [igwa'ria] F (*Culin*) delicacy

ih [i:] EXCL (*de admiração, surpresa*) cor (BRIT), gee (US); (*de perigo próximo*) eek!

iídiche ['jidiʃi] M (*Ling*) Yiddish

ilação [ila'sãw] (*pl* **-ões**) F inference, deduction

I.L. Ano (BR) ABR (*Com*) = **Índice de Lucratividade no Ano**

ilegal [ile'gaw] (*pl* **-ais**) ADJ illegal

ilegalidade [ilegali'dadʒi] F illegality

ilegítimo, -a [ile'ʒitʃimu, a] ADJ illegitimate; (*ilegal*) unlawful

ilegível [ile'ʒivew] (*pl* **-eis**) ADJ illegible

ileso, -a [i'lɛzu, a] ADJ unhurt; **sair ~** to escape unhurt

iletrado, -a [ile'tradu, a] ADJ, M/F illiterate

ilha ['iʎa] F island

ilhar [i'ʎar] VT to cut off, isolate

ilharga [i'ʎarga] F (*Anat*) side

ilhéu, ilhoa [i'ʎɛw, i'ʎoa] M/F islander

ilhós [i'ʎɔs] (*pl* **ilhoses**) M eyelet

ilhota [i'ʎɔta] F small island

ilícito, -a [i'lisitu, a] ADJ illicit

ilimitado, -a [ilimi'tadu, a] ADJ unlimited

ilógico, -a [i'lɔʒiku, a] ADJ illogical; (*absurdo*) absurd

iludir [ilu'dʒir] VT to delude; (*enganar*) to deceive; (*a lei*) to evade; **iludir-se** VR to delude o.s.

iluminação [ilumina'sãw] (*pl* **-ões**) F lighting; (*fig*) enlightenment

iluminado, -a [ilumi'nadu, a] ADJ illuminated, lit; (*estádio*) floodlit; (*fig*) enlightened

iluminante [ilumi'nãtʃi] ADJ bright

iluminar [ilumi'nar] VT to light up; (*estádio etc*) to floodlight; (*fig*) to enlighten

ilusão [ilu'zãw] (*pl* **-ões**) F illusion; (*quimera*) delusion; **~ de ótica** optical illusion; **viver de ilusões** to live in a dream-world

ilusionista [iluzjo'nista] M/F conjurer; (*que escapa*) escapologist

ilusões [ilu'zõjs] FPL *de* **ilusão**

ilusório, -a [ilu'zɔrju, a] ADJ (*enganoso*) deceptive

ilustração [ilustra'sãw] (*pl* **-ões**) F (*figura, exemplo*) illustration; (*saber*) learning

ilustrado, -a [ilus'tradu, a] ADJ (*com gravuras*) illustrated; (*instruído*) learned

ilustrador, a [ilustra'dor(a)] M/F illustrator

ilustrar [ilus'trar] VT (*com gravuras*) to illustrate; (*instruir*) to instruct; (*exemplificar*) to illustrate; **ilustrar-se** VR (*distinguir-se*) to excel; (*instruir-se*) to inform o.s.

ilustrativo, -a [ilustra'tʃivu, a] ADJ illustrative

ilustre [i'lustri] ADJ famous, illustrious; **um ~ desconhecido** a complete stranger

ilustríssimo, -a [ilus'trisimu, a] ADJ SUPERL *de* **ilustre**; (*tratamento*): **~ senhor** dear Sir

ímã ['imã] M magnet

imaculado, -a [imaku'ladu, a] ADJ immaculate

imagem [i'maʒẽ] (*pl* **-ns**) F image; (*semelhança*) likeness; (*TV*) picture; **imagens** FPL (*Literatura*) imagery *sg*; **ela é a ~ do pai** she's the image of her father

imaginação [imaʒina'sãw] (*pl* **-ões**) F imagination

imaginar [imaʒi'nar] VT to imagine; (*supor*) to suppose; **imaginar-se** VR to imagine o.s.; **imagine só!** just imagine!; **obrigado — imagina!** thank you — don't worry about it!

imaginário, -a [imaʒi'narju, a] ADJ imaginary

imaginativo, -a [imaʒina'tʃivu, a] ADJ imaginative

imaginável [imaʒi'navew] (*pl* **-eis**) ADJ imaginable

imaginoso, -a [imaʒi'nozu, ɔza] ADJ (*pessoa*) imaginative

íman ['imã] (PT) M = **ímã**

imanente [ima'nẽtʃi] ADJ: ~ **(a)** inherent (in)

imantar [imã'tar] VT to magnetize

imaturidade [imaturi'dadʒi] F immaturity

imaturo, -a [ima'turu, a] ADJ immature

imbatível [ĩba'tʃivew] (*pl* -**eis**) ADJ invincible

imbecil [ĩbe'siw] (*pl* -**is**) ADJ stupid ▶ M/F imbecile, half-wit

imbecilidade [ĩbesili'dadʒi] F stupidity

imbecis [ĩbe'sis] PL *de* **imbecil**

imberbe [ĩ'bɛrbi] ADJ (*sem barba*) beardless; (*jovem*) youthful

imbricar [ĩbri'kar] VT to overlap; **imbricar-se** VR to overlap

imbuir [ĩ'bwir] VT: ~ **alguém de** (*sentimentos*) to imbue sb with

IME (BR) ABR M = **Instituto Militar de Engenharia**

imediações [imedʒa'sõjs] FPL vicinity *sg*, neighbourhood *sg* (BRIT), neighborhood *sg* (US)

imediatamente [imedʒata'mẽtʃi] ADV immediately, right away

imediato, -a [ime'dʒatu, a] ADJ immediate; (*seguinte*) next ▶ M second-in-command; ~ **a** next to; **de** ~ straight away

imemorial [imemo'rjaw] (*pl* -**ais**) ADJ immemorial

imensidade [imẽsi'dadʒi] F immensity

imensidão [imẽsi'dãw] F hugeness, enormity

imenso, -a [i'mẽsu, a] ADJ immense, huge; (*ódio, amor*) great

imensurável [imẽsu'ravew] (*pl* -**eis**) ADJ immeasurable

imerecido, -a [imere'sidu, a] ADJ undeserved

imergir [imer'ʒir] VT to immerse; (*fig*) to plunge ▶ VI to be immersed; to plunge

imersão [imer'sãw] (*pl* -**ões**) F immersion

imerso, -a [i'mɛrsu, a] ADJ (*tb fig*) immersed

imersões [imer'sõjs] FPL *de* **imersão**

imigração [imigra'sãw] (*pl* -**ões**) F immigration

imigrante [imi'grãtʃi] ADJ, M/F immigrant

imigrar [imi'grar] VI to immigrate

iminência [imi'nẽsja] F imminence

iminente [imi'nẽtʃi] ADJ imminent

imiscuir-se [imis'kwirsi] VR: ~ **em** to meddle (in), interfere (in)

imitação [imita'sãw] (*pl* -**ões**) F imitation, copy; **joia de** ~ imitation jewel

imitador, a [imita'dor(a)] ADJ imitative ▶ M/F imitator

imitar [imi'tar] VT to imitate; (*assinatura*) to copy

imobiliária [imobi'ljarja] F estate agent's (BRIT), real estate broker's (US)

imobiliário, -a [imobi'ljarju, a] ADJ property *atr*, real estate *atr*

imobilidade [imobili'dadʒi] F immobility

imobilizar [imobili'zar] VT to immobilize; (*fig: economia, progresso*) to bring to a standstill; (*Com: capital*) to tie up

imoderação [imodera'sãw] F lack of moderation

imoderado, -a [imode'radu, a] ADJ immoderate

imodéstia [imo'dɛstʃja] F immodesty

imodesto, -a [imo'dɛstu, a] ADJ immodest

imódico, -a [i'mɔdʒiku, a] ADJ exorbitant

imolar [imo'lar] VT (*sacrificar*) to sacrifice; (*prejudicar*) to harm

imoral [imo'raw] (*pl* -**ais**) ADJ immoral

imoralidade [imorali'dadʒi] F immorality

imortal [imor'taw] (*pl* -**ais**) ADJ immortal ▶ M/F (*membro da ABL*) member of the Brazilian Academy of Letters

imortalidade [imortali'dadʒi] F immortality

imortalizar [imortali'zar] VT to immortalize

imóvel [i'mɔvew] (*pl* -**eis**) ADJ (*parado*) motionless, still; (*não movediço*) immovable ▶ M property; (*edifício*) building; **imóveis** MPL (*propriedade*) real estate *sg*, property *sg*

impaciência [ĩpa'sjẽsja] F impatience

impacientar-se [ĩpasjẽ'tarsi] VR to lose one's patience

impaciente [ĩpa'sjẽtʃi] ADJ impatient; (*inquieto*) anxious

impacto [ĩ'paktu], (PT) **impacte** M impact

impagável [ĩpa'gavew] (*pl* -**eis**) ADJ (*fig*) priceless

impaludismo [ĩpalu'dʒizmu] M malaria

ímpar ['ĩpar] ADJ (*número*) odd; (*sem igual*) unique, unequalled

imparcial [ĩpar'sjaw] (*pl* -**ais**) ADJ fair, impartial

imparcialidade [ĩparsjali'dadʒi] F impartiality

impasse [ĩ'pasi] M impasse, deadlock

impassível [ĩpa'sivew] (*pl* -**eis**) ADJ impassive

impávido, -a [ĩ'pavidu, a] ADJ (*formal*) fearless, intrepid

impecável [ĩpe'kavew] (*pl* -**eis**) ADJ perfect, impeccable

impeço *etc* [ĩ'pɛsu] VB *ver* **impedir**

impedido, -a [ĩpe'dʒidu, a] ADJ (*estrada*) blocked; (*Futebol*) offside; (PT*Tel*) engaged (BRIT), busy (US)

impedimento [ĩpedʒi'mẽtu] M impediment; (*Futebol*) offside; (*Pol*) impeachment

impedir [ĩpe'dʒir] VT to obstruct; (*estrada, passagem, tráfego*) to block; (*movimento, execução, progresso*) to impede; ~ **alguém de fazer algo** to prevent sb from doing sth; (*proibir*) to forbid sb to do sth; ~ **(que aconteça) algo** to prevent sth (happening)

impelir [ĩpe'lir] VT (*tb fig*) to drive (on); (*obrigar*) to force

impenetrável [ĩpene'travew] (*pl* -**eis**) ADJ impenetrable

impenitente [ĩpeni'tẽtʃi] ADJ unrepentant

impensado, -a [ĩpẽ'sadu, a] ADJ (*imprevidente*) thoughtless; (*não calculado*) unpremeditated; (*imprevisto*) unforeseen

impensável [ĩpẽ'savew] (*pl* -**eis**) ADJ unthinkable

imperador [ĩpera'dor] M emperor

imperar [ĩpe'rar] VI to reign; *(fig: prevalecer)* to prevail

imperativo, -a [ĩpera'tʃivu, a] ADJ *(tb Ling)* imperative ▶ M absolute necessity; imperative

imperatriz [ĩpera'triz] F empress

imperceptível [ĩpersep'tʃivew] *(pl -eis)* ADJ imperceptible

imperdível [ĩper'dʒivew] *(pl -eis)* ADJ *(eleição)* that cannot be lost; *(filme)* unmissable; *(questão)*: **o ordem pública é uma questão ~ para o partido** the party's onto a winner with law and order

imperdoável [ĩper'dwavew] *(pl -eis)* ADJ unforgivable, inexcusable

imperecível [ĩpere'sivew] *(pl -eis)* ADJ imperishable

imperfeição [ĩmperfej'sãw] *(pl -ões)* F imperfection; *(falha)* flaw

imperfeito, -a [ĩper'fejtu, a] ADJ imperfect ▶ M *(Ling)* imperfect (tense)

imperial [ĩpe'rjaw] *(pl -ais)* ADJ imperial

imperialismo [ĩperja'lizmu] M imperialism

imperialista [ĩperja'lista] ADJ, M/F imperialist

imperícia [ĩpe'risja] F *(inabilidade)* inability; *(inexperiência)* inexperience

império [ĩ'pɛrju] M empire

imperioso, -a [ĩpe'rjozu, ɔza] ADJ *(dominador)* domineering; *(necessidade)* pressing, urgent; *(tom, olhar)* imperious

impermeabilidade [ĩpermjabili'dadʒi] F imperviousness

impermeabilizar [ĩpermjabili'zar] VT to waterproof

impermeável [ĩper'mjavew] *(pl -eis)* ADJ: **~ a** *(tb fig)* impervious to; *(à água)* waterproof ▶ M raincoat

impertinência [ĩpertʃi'nẽsja] F impertinence; *(irrelevância)* irrelevance

impertinente [ĩpertʃi'nẽtʃi] ADJ *(alheio)* irrelevant; *(insolente)* impertinent

imperturbável [ĩpertur'bavew] *(pl -eis)* ADJ imperturbable; *(impassível)* impassive

impessoal [ĩpe'swaw] *(pl -ais)* ADJ impersonal

impetigo [ĩpe'tʃigo] M impetigo

ímpeto ['ĩpetu] M *(Tec: força)* impetus; *(movimento súbito)* start; *(de cólera)* fit; *(de emoção)* surge; *(de chamas)* fury; **agir com ~** to act on impulse; **levantar-se num ~** to get up with a start; **senti um ~ de sair correndo** I felt an urge to run away

impetrante [ĩpe'trãtʃi] M/F *(Jur)* petitioner

impetrar [ĩpe'trar] VT *(Jur)*: **~ algo** to petition for sth

impetuosidade [ĩpetwozi'dadʒi] F impetuosity

impetuoso, -a [ĩpe'twozu, ɔza] ADJ *(pessoa)* headstrong, impetuous; *(ato)* rash, hasty; *(rio)* fast-moving

impiedade [ĩpje'dadʒi] F irreverence; *(crueldade)* cruelty

impiedoso, -a [ĩpje'dozu, ɔza] ADJ merciless, cruel

impilo *etc* [ĩ'pilu] VB *ver* **impelir**

impingir [ĩpĩ'ʒir] VT: **~ algo a alguém** *(mentiras, mercadorias)* to palm sth off on sb; **~ algo em alguém** *(bofetada, pontapé etc)* to land sth on sb

implacável [ĩpla'kavew] *(pl -eis)* ADJ *(pessoa)* unforgiving; *(destino, doença, perseguição)* relentless

implantação [ĩplãta'sãw] *(pl -ões)* F introduction; *(Med)* implant

implantar [ĩplã'tar] VT to introduce; *(Med)* to implant

implante [ĩ'plãtʃi] M *(Med)* implant

implausível [ĩplaw'zivew] *(pl -eis)* ADJ implausible

implementação [ĩplemẽta'sãw] *(pl -ões)* F implementation

implementar [ĩplemẽ'tar] VT to implement

implemento [ĩple'mẽtu] M implement

implicação [ĩplika'sãw] *(pl -ões)* F implication; *(envolvimento)* involvement

implicância [ĩpli'kãsja] F *(ato de chatear)* teasing; *(antipatia)* nastiness; **estar de ~ com alguém** to pick on sb, have it in for sb

implicante [ĩpli'kãtʃi] ADJ bullying ▶ M/F stirrer

implicar [ĩpli'kar] VT *(envolver)* to implicate; *(pressupor)* to imply ▶ VI: **~ com alguém** *(antipatizar)* to be horrible to sb; *(chatear)* to tease sb, pick on sb; **implicar-se** VR *(envolver-se)* to get involved; **~ (em) algo** to involve sth

implícito, -a [ĩ'plisitu, a] ADJ implicit

impliquei *etc* [ĩpli'kej] VB *ver* **implicar**

implodir [ĩplo'dʒir] VI to implode

imploração [ĩplora'sãw] F begging

implorar [ĩplo'rar] VT: **~ (algo a alguém)** to beg *ou* implore (sb for sth)

impõe *etc* [ĩ'põj] VB *ver* **impor**

impoluto, -a [ĩpo'lutu, a] ADJ immaculate; *(pessoa)* beyond reproach

impomos [ĩ'pomos] VB *ver* **impor**

imponderado, -a [ĩpõde'radu, a] ADJ rash

imponderável [ĩpõde'ravew] *(pl -eis)* ADJ imponderable

imponência [ĩpo'nẽsja] F impressiveness

imponente [ĩpo'nẽtʃi] ADJ impressive, imposing

imponho *etc* [ĩ'poɲu] VB *ver* **impor**

impontual [ĩpõ'twaw] *(pl -ais)* ADJ unpunctual

impopular [ĩpopu'lar] ADJ unpopular

impopularidade [ĩpopulari'dadʒi] F unpopularity

impor [ĩ'por] *(irreg: como* **pôr***)* VT to impose; *(respeito)* to command; **impor-se** VR to assert o.s.; **~ algo a alguém** to impose sth on sb

importação [importa'sãw] *(pl -ões)* F *(ato)* importing; *(mercadoria)* import

importador, a [ĩporta'dor(a)] ADJ import *atr* ▶ M/F importer ▶ F *(empresa)* import company; *(loja)* shop selling imported goods

importância [ĩpor'tãsja] F importance; (*de dinheiro*) sum, amount; **dar ~ a algo/alguém** to attach importance to sth/show consideration for sb; **não dê ~ ao que ele disse** take no notice of what he said; **não tem ~** it doesn't matter, never mind; **ter ~** to be important; **de certa ~** of some importance; **sem ~** unimportant

importante [ĩpor'tãtʃi] ADJ important; (*arrogante*) self-important ▶ M: **o (mais) ~** the (most) important thing

importar [ĩpor'tar] VT (*Com*) to import; (*trazer*) to bring in; (*causar: prejuízos etc*) to cause; (*implicar*) to imply, involve ▶ VI to matter, be important; **importar-se** VR: **~-se com algo** to mind sth; **não ou pouco importa!** it doesn't matter!; **~ em** (*preço*) to add up to, amount to; (*resultar*) to lead to; **não me importo** I don't care; **eu pouco me importo que ela venha ou não** I don't care whether she comes or not

importe [ĩ'pɔrtʃi] M (*soma*) amount; (*custo*) cost

importunação [ĩportuna'sãw] (*pl* **-ões**) F annoyance

importunar [ĩportu'nar] VT to bother, annoy

importuno, -a [ĩpor'tunu, a] ADJ (*maçante*) annoying; (*inoportuno*) inopportune ▶ M/F nuisance

impôs [ĩ'pos] VB *ver* **impor**

imposição [ĩpozi'sãw] (*pl* **-ões**) F imposition

impossibilidade [ĩposibili'dadʒi] F impossibility

impossibilitado, -a [ĩposibili'tadu, a] ADJ: **~ de fazer** unable to do

impossibilitar [ĩposibili'tar] VT: **~ algo** to make sth impossible; **~ alguém de fazer, ~ a alguém fazer** to prevent sb doing; **~ algo a alguém, ~ alguém para algo** to make sth impossible for sb

impossível [ĩpo'sivew] (*pl* **-eis**) ADJ impossible; (*insuportável: pessoa*) insufferable; (*incrível*) incredible

impostação [ĩposta'sãw] F (*da voz*) diction, delivery

impostar [ĩpos'tar] VT (*voz*) to throw

imposto [ĩ'postu] PP *de* **impor** ▶ M tax; **antes/depois de ~s** before/after tax; **~ ambiental** green tax, environmental tax; **~ de renda** (*BR*) income tax; **~ predial** rates *pl*; **~ sobre ganhos de capital** capital transfer tax (*BRIT*), inheritance tax (*US*); **~ sobre os lucros** profits tax; **~ sobre transferência de capital** capital transfer tax; **I~ sobre Circulação de Mercadorias (e Serviços)**(*BR*), **~ sobre valor agregado** value added tax (*BRIT*), sales tax (*US*)

impostor, a [ĩpos'tor(a)] M/F impostor

impostura [ĩpos'tura] F deception

impotência [ĩpo'tẽʒja] F impotence

impotente [ĩpo'tẽtʃi] ADJ powerless; (*Med*) impotent

impraticabilidade [ĩpratʃikabili'dadʒi] F impracticability

impraticável [ĩpratʃi'kavew] (*pl* **-eis**) ADJ impracticable; (*rua, rio etc*) impassable

imprecisão [ĩpresi'zãw] (*pl* **-ões**) F inaccuracy

impreciso, -a [ĩpre'sizu, a] ADJ vague; (*falto de rigor*) inaccurate

imprecisões [ĩpresi'zõjs] FPL *de* **imprecisão**

impregnar [ĩpreg'nar] VT to impregnate; **~ algo de** to impregnate sth with; (*fig: mente etc*) to fill sth with

imprensa [ĩ'prẽsa] F (*a arte*) printing; (*máquina, jornais*) press; **~ marrom** tabloid press, gutter press

imprensar [ĩprẽ'sar] VT (*no prelo*) to stamp; (*apertar*) to squash; (*fig*): **~ alguém (contra a parede)** to press sb

imprescindível [ĩpresĩ'dʒivew] (*pl* **-eis**) ADJ essential, indispensable

impressão [ĩpre'sãw] (*pl* **-ões**) F impression; (*de livros*) printing; (*marca*) imprint; **causar boa ~** to make a good impression; **ficar com/ter a ~ (de) que** to get/have the impression that; **ter má ~ de algo** to have a bad impression of sth; **~ digital** fingerprint

impressionante [ĩpresjo'nãtʃi] ADJ impressive; (*abalador*) amazing

impressionar [ĩpresjo'nar] VT to impress; (*abalar*) to affect ▶ VI to be impressive; . (*pessoa*) to make an impression; **impressionar-se** VR: **~-se (com algo)** (*comover-se*) to be moved (by sth)

impressionável [ĩpresjo'navew] (*pl* **-eis**) ADJ impressionable

impressionismo [ĩpresjo'nizmu] M impressionism

impressionista [ĩpresjo'nista] ADJ, M/F impressionist

impresso, -a [ĩ'prɛsu, a] PP *de* **imprimir** ▶ ADJ printed ▶ M (*para preencher*) form; (*folheto*) leaflet; **impressos** MPL (*formulário*) printed matter *sg*

impressões [ĩpre'sõjs] FPL *de* **impressão**

impressor [ĩpre'sor] M printer

impressora [ĩpre'sora] F (*Comput*) printer; **~ jato de tinta** ink-jet printer; **~ laser** laser printer

imprestável [ĩpres'tavew] (*pl* **-eis**) ADJ (*inútil*) useless; (*pessoa*) unhelpful

impreterível [ĩprete'rivew] (*pl* **-eis**) ADJ (*compromisso*) essential; (*prazo*) final

imprevidente [ĩprevi'dẽtʃi] ADJ short-sighted

imprevisão [ĩprevi'zãw] F lack of foresight, short-sightedness

imprevisível [ĩprevi'zivew] (*pl* **-eis**) ADJ unforeseeable

imprevisto, -a [ĩpre'vistu, a] ADJ unexpected, unforeseen ▶ M: **um ~** something unexpected

imprimir [ĩpri'mir] VT to print; (*marca*) to stamp; (*infundir*) to instil (*BRIT*), instill (*US*); **imprimir-se** VR to be stamped, be impressed; **~-se na memória** to impress o.s. on the memory; **~ algo a algo** to stamp sth on sth

improbabilidade [ĩprobabili'daʒi] F
improbability

improcedente [ĩprose'dētʃi] ADJ groundless,
unjustified

improdutivo, -a [ĩprodu'tʃivu, a] ADJ
unproductive

improfícuo, -a [impro'fikwu, a] ADJ useless,
futile

impropério [ĩpro'pɛrju] M insult; **dizer ~s** to
swear

impropriedade [ĩproprje'daʒi] F
inappropriateness; (*moral*) impropriety

impróprio, -a [ĩ'prɔprju, a] ADJ (*inadequado*)
inappropriate; (*indecente*) improper; **filme ~
para menores de 18 anos** X-certificate *ou*
X-rated film

improrrogável [ĩproho'gavew] (*pl* **-eis**) ADJ
non-extendible

improvável [ĩpro'vavew] (*pl* **-eis**) ADJ unlikely

improvidência [ĩprovi'dẽsja] F lack of
foresight

improvidente [ĩprovi'dētʃi] ADJ short-sighted

improvisação [ĩproviza'sãw] (*pl* **-ões**) F
improvisation

improvisado, -a [ĩprovi'zadu, a] ADJ
improvised, impromptu

improvisar [ĩprovi'zar] VT, VI to improvise;
(*Teatro*) to ad-lib

improviso [ĩpro'vizu] M impromptu talk;
de ~ (*de repente*) suddenly; (*sem preparação*)
without preparation; **falar de ~** to talk off
the cuff

imprudência [ĩpru'dẽsja] F rashness;
(*descuido*) carelessness

imprudente [ĩpru'dētʃi] ADJ (*irrefletido*) rash;
(*motorista*) careless

impudico, -a [ĩpu'dʒiku, a] ADJ shameless

impugnar [ĩpug'nar] VT (*refutar*) to refute;
(*opor-se a*) to oppose

impulsionar [ĩpuwsjo'nar] VT (*impelir*) to
drive, impel; (*fig: estimular*) to urge

impulsividade [ĩpuwsivi'daʒi] F
impulsiveness

impulsivo, -a [ĩpuw'sivu, a] ADJ impulsive

impulso [ĩ'puwsu] M impulse; (*fig: estímulo*)
urge, impulse; **tomar ~** (*fig: empresa, negócio*)
to take off; **compra por ~** (*ato*) impulse
buying

impune [ĩ'puni] ADJ unpunished

impunemente [ĩpune'mētʃi] ADV with
impunity

impunha *etc* [ĩ'puɲa] VB *ver* **impor**

impunidade [ĩpuni'daʒi] F impunity

impureza [ĩpu'reza] F impurity

impuro, -a [ĩ'puru, a] ADJ impure

impus *etc* [ĩ'pus] VB *ver* **impor**

impuser *etc* [ĩpu'zer] VB *ver* **impor**

imputação [ĩputa'sãw] (*pl* **-ões**) F
accusation

imputar [ĩpu'tar] VT: **~ algo a** (*atribuir*) to
attribute sth to; **~ algo a alguém** to blame
sb for sth

imputável [ĩpu'tavew] (*pl* **-eis**) ADJ attributable

imundice [imũ'dʒisi] F = **imundície**

imundície [imũ'dʒisje] F filth

imundo, -a [i'mũdu, a] ADJ filthy; (*obsceno*)
dirty

imune [i'muni] ADJ: **~ a** immune to

imunidade [imuni'daʒi] F immunity

imunizar [imuni'zar] VT: **~ alguém (contra
algo)** (*Med*) to immunize sb (against sth);
(*fig*) to protect sb (from sth)

imutável [imu'tavew] (*pl* **-eis**) ADJ (*ideia*) fixed;
(*decisão: firme*) firm; (: *irreversível*) irreversible;
(*pessoa*): **ele tem um comportamento ~**
he's very set in his ways

inabalável [inaba'lavew] (*pl* **-eis**) ADJ
unshakeable

inábil [i'nabiw] (*pl* **-eis**) ADJ (*incapaz*) incapable;
(*desajeitado*) clumsy

inabilidade [inabili'daʒi] F (*incompetência*)
incompetence; (*falta de destreza*) clumsiness

inabilidoso, -a [inabili'dozu, ɔza] ADJ clumsy,
awkward

inabilitação [inabilita'sãw] (*pl* **-ões**) F
disqualification

inabilitar [inabili'tar] VT (*incapacitar*) to
incapacitate; (*em exame*) to disqualify

inabitado, -a [inabi'tadu, a] ADJ uninhabited

inabitável [inabi'tavew] (*pl* **-eis**) ADJ
uninhabitable

inacabado, -a [inaka'badu, a] ADJ unfinished

inacabável [inaka'bavew] (*pl* **-eis**) ADJ
interminable, unending

inação [ina'sãw] F (*inércia*) inactivity;
(*irresolução*) indecision

inaceitável [inasej'tavew] (*pl* **-eis**) ADJ
unacceptable

Inacen [ina'sẽ] (*BR*) ABR M = **Instituto
Nacional de Artes Cênicas**

inacessível [inase'sivew] (*pl* **-eis**) ADJ
inaccessible

inacreditável [inakredʒi'tavew] (*pl* **-eis**) ADJ
unbelievable, incredible

inadaptado, -a [inadap'tadu, a] ADJ
maladjusted

inadequação [inadekwa'sãw] (*pl* **-ões**) F
inadequacy; (*impropriedade*) unsuitability

inadequado, -a [inade'kwadu, a] ADJ
inadequate; (*impróprio*) unsuitable

inadiável [ina'dʒjavew] (*pl* **-eis**) ADJ pressing

inadimplência [inadʒĩ'plẽsja] F (*Jur*) breach of
contract, default

inadimplente [inadʒĩ'plẽtʃi] ADJ (*Jur*) in
breach of contract, at fault

inadimplir [inadʒĩ'plir] VT, VI: **~ (algo)** to
default (on sth)

inadmissível [inadʒimi'sivew] (*pl* **-eis**) ADJ
inadmissible

inadquirível [inadʒiki'rivew] (*pl* **-eis**) ADJ
unobtainable

inadvertência [inadʒiver'tẽsja] F oversight;
por ~ by mistake

inadvertido, -a [inadʒiver'tʃidu, a] ADJ
inadvertent

inalação [inala'sãw] (*pl* **-ões**) F inhalation

inalador [inala'dor] M inhaler
inalar [ina'lar] VT to inhale, breathe in
inalcançável [inawkã'savew] (pl **-eis**) ADJ out of reach; (*sucesso, ambição*) unattainable
inalterado, -a [inawte'radu, a] ADJ unchanged; (*sereno*) unperturbed
inalterável [inawte'ravew] (pl **-eis**) ADJ unchangeable; (*impassível*) imperturbable
Inamps [i'nãps] (BR) ABR M = **Instituto Nacional de Assistência Médica e Previdência Social**
inanição [inani'sãw] (pl **-ões**) F starvation
inanimado, -a [inani'madu, a] ADJ inanimate
inapetência [inape'tẽsja] F loss of appetite
inapetente [inape'tẽtʃi] ADJ off one's food
inaplicado, -a [inapli'kadu, a] ADJ (*aluno*) idle, lazy
inaplicável [inapli'kavew] (pl **-eis**) ADJ inapplicable
inapreciável [inapre'sjavew] (pl **-eis**) ADJ invaluable
inaproveitável [inaprovej'tavew] (pl **-eis**) ADJ useless
inaptidão [inaptʃi'dãw] (pl **-ões**) F inability
inapto, -a [i'naptu, a] ADJ (*incapaz*) unfit, incapable; (*inadequado*) unsuited
inarticulado, -a [inartʃiku'ladu, a] ADJ inarticulate
inatacável [inata'kavew] (pl **-eis**) ADJ unassailable
inatenção [inatẽ'sãw] F inattention
inatingido, -a [inatʃi'ʒidu, a] ADJ unconquered
inatingível [inatʃi'ʒivew] (pl **-eis**) ADJ unattainable
inatividade [inatʃivi'dadʒi] F inactivity; (*aposentadoria*) redundancy (BRIT), dismissal (US); (*Mil: reforma*) retirement (on health grounds)
inativo, -a [ina'tʃivu, a] ADJ inactive; (*aposentado, reformado*) retired
inato, -a [i'natu, a] ADJ innate, inborn
inaudito, -a [inaw'dʒitu, a] ADJ unheard-of
inaudível [inaw'dʒivew] (pl **-eis**) ADJ inaudible
inauguração [inawgura'sãw] (pl **-ões**) F inauguration; (*de exposição*) opening; (*de estátua*) unveiling
inaugural [inawgu'raw] (pl **-ais**) ADJ inaugural
inaugurar [inawgu'rar] VT to inaugurate; (*exposição*) to open; (*estátua*) to unveil
inca ['ĩka] ADJ, M/F Inca
incabível [ĩka'bivew] (pl **-eis**) ADJ unacceptable
incalculável [ĩkawku'lavew] (pl **-eis**) ADJ incalculable
incandescente [ĩkãde'sẽtʃi] ADJ incandescent
incansável [ĩkã'savew] (pl **-eis**) ADJ tireless, untiring
incapacidade [ĩkapasi'dadʒi] F incapacity; (*incompetência*) incompetence; **~ de fazer** inability to do

incapacitado, -a [ĩkapasi'tadu, a] ADJ (*inválido*) disabled, handicapped ▶ M/F handicapped person; **estar ~ de fazer** to be unable to do
incapacitar [ĩkapasi'tar] VT: **~ alguém (para)** to make sb unable (to)
incapaz [ĩka'pajz] ADJ, M/F incompetent; **~ de fazer** incapable of doing; **~ para** unfit for
incauto, -a [ĩ'kawtu, a] ADJ (*imprudente*) rash
incendiar [ĩsẽ'dʒjar] VT to set fire to; (*fig*) to inflame; **incendiar-se** VR to catch fire
incendiário, -a [ĩsẽ'dʒjarju, a] ADJ incendiary; (*fig*) inflammatory ▶ M/F arsonist; (*agitador*) agitator
incêndio [ĩ'sẽdʒju] M fire; **~ criminoso** *ou* **premeditado** arson
incenso [ĩ'sẽsu] M incense
incentivador, a [ĩsẽtʃiva'dor(a)] ADJ stimulating, encouraging
incentivar [ĩsẽtʃi'var] VT to stimulate, encourage
incentivo [ĩsẽ'tʃivu] M incentive; **~ fiscal** tax incentive
incerteza [ĩser'teza] F uncertainty
incerto, -a [ĩ'sɛrtu, a] ADJ uncertain
incessante [ĩse'sãtʃi] ADJ incessant
incesto [ĩ'sɛstu] M incest
incestuoso, -a [ĩses'twozu, ɔza] ADJ incestuous
inchação [ĩʃa'sãw] (pl **-ões**) F swelling
inchado, -a [ĩ'ʃadu, a] ADJ swollen; (*fig*) conceited
inchar [ĩ'ʃar] VT, VI to swell; **inchar-se** VR to swell (up); (*fig*) to become conceited
incidência [ĩsi'dẽsja] F incidence, occurrence
incidente [ĩsi'dẽtʃi] M incident
incidir [ĩsi'dʒir] VI: **~ em erro** to go wrong; **~ em** *ou* **sobre algo** (*luz*) to fall on sth; (*influir*) to affect sth; (*imposto*) to be payable on sth
incinerar [ĩsine'rar] VT to burn
incipiente [ĩsi'pjẽtʃi] ADJ incipient
incisão [ĩsi'zãw] (pl **-ões**) F cut; (*Med*) incision
incisivo, -a [ĩsi'zivu, a] ADJ cutting, sharp; (*fig*) incisive ▶ M incisor
incisões [ĩsi'zõjs] FPL *de* **incisão**
incitação [ĩsita'sãw] (pl **-ões**) F incitement
incitamento [ĩsita'mẽtu] M incitement
incitar [ĩsi'tar] VT to incite; (*pessoa, animal*) to drive on; (*instigar*) to rouse; **~ alguém a (fazer) algo** to urge sb on to (do) sth, incite sb to (do) sth
incivil [ĩsi'viw] (pl **-is**) ADJ rude, ill-mannered
incivilidade [ĩsivili'dadʒi] F rudeness
incivilizado, -a [ĩsivili'zadu, a] ADJ uncivilized
incivis [ĩsi'vis] ADJ PL *de* **incivil**
inclemência [ĩkle'mẽsja] F harshness, rigour (BRIT), rigor (US); (*tempo*) inclemency
inclemente [ĩkle'mẽtʃi] ADJ severe, harsh; (*tempo*) inclement
inclinação [ĩklina'sãw] (pl **-ões**) F inclination; (*da terra*) slope; (*simpatia*) liking; **~ da cabeça** nod

inclinado, -a [īkli'nadu, a] ADJ (*terreno, estrada*) sloping; (*corpo, torre*) leaning; **estar ~/pouco ~ a** to be inclined/loath to

inclinar [īkli'nar] VT (*objeto*) to tilt; (*cabeça*) to nod ▶ VI (*terra*) to slope; (*objeto*) to tilt; **inclinar-se** VR (*objeto*) to tilt; (*dobrar o corpo*) to bow, stoop; **~ para** (*propensão*) to lean towards; **~-se sobre algo** (*debruçar-se*) to lean over sth; **~(-se) para trás** to lean back

ínclito, -a [ˈīklitu, a] ADJ illustrious, renowned

incluir [ī'klwir] VT to include; (*em carta*) to enclose; **incluir-se** VR to be included; **tudo incluído** (*Com*) all in

inclusão [īklu'zāw] F inclusion

inclusive [īklu'zivi] PREP including ▶ ADV inclusive; (*até mesmo*) even; **de segunda à sexta ~** from Monday to Friday inclusive; **e ~ falou que ...** and furthermore he said that ....

incluso, -a [ī'kluzu, a] ADJ included; (*em carta*) enclosed

incobrável [īko'bravew] (*pl* **-eis**) ADJ (*Com*): **dívida ~** bad debt

incoercível [īkoer'sivew] (*pl* **-eis**) ADJ uncontrollable

incoerência [īkoe'rēsja] F incoherence; (*contradição*) inconsistency

incoerente [īkoe'rētʃi] ADJ incoherent; (*contraditório*) inconsistent

incógnita [ī'kɔgnita] F (*Mat*) unknown; (*fato incógnito*) mystery

incógnito, -a [ī'kɔgnitu, a] ADJ unknown ▶ ADV incognito

incolor [īko'lor] ADJ colourless (BRIT), colorless (US)

incólume [ī'kɔlumi] ADJ safe and sound; (*ileso*) unharmed

incomensurável [īkomēsu'ravew] (*pl* **-eis**) ADJ immense

incomodada [īkomo'dada] ADJ (*menstruada*) having one's period

incomodar [īkomo'dar] VT (*importunar*) to bother, trouble; (*aborrecer*) to annoy ▶ VI to be bothersome; **incomodar-se** VR to bother, put o.s. out; **~-se com algo** to be bothered by sth, mind sth; **não se incomode!** don't worry!; **você se incomoda se eu abrir a janela?** do you mind if I open the window?

incômodo, -a [ī'komodu, a] ADJ (*desconfortável*) uncomfortable; (*incomodativo*) troublesome; (*inoportuno*) inconvenient ▶ M (*menstruação*) period; (*maçada*) nuisance, trouble; (*amolação*) inconvenience

incomparável [īkōpa'ravew] (*pl* **-eis**) ADJ incomparable

incompatibilidade [īkōpatʃibili'dadʒi] F incompatibility

incompatibilizar [īkōpatʃibili'zar] VT: **~ alguém (com alguém)** to alienate sb (from sb); **incompatibilizar-se** VR: **~-se (com alguém)** to alienate o.s. (from sb)

incompatível [īkōpa'tʃivew] (*pl* **-eis**) ADJ incompatible

incompetência [īkōpe'tēsja] F incompetence

incompetente [īkōpe'tētʃi] ADJ, M/F incompetent

incompleto, -a [īkō'plɛtu, a] ADJ incomplete, unfinished

incompreendido, -a [īkōprjē'dʒidu, a] ADJ misunderstood

incompreensão [īkōprjē'sāw] F incomprehension

incompreensível [īkōprjē'sivew] (*pl* **-eis**) ADJ incomprehensible

incompreensivo, -a [īkōprjē'sivu, a] ADJ uncomprehending

incomum [īko'mū] ADJ uncommon

incomunicável [īkomuni'kavew] (*pl* **-eis**) ADJ cut off; (*privado de comunicação, fig*) incommunicado; (*preso*) in solitary confinement

inconcebível [īkōse'bivew] (*pl* **-eis**) ADJ inconceivable; (*incrível*) incredible

inconciliável [īkōsi'ljavew] (*pl* **-eis**) ADJ irreconcilable

inconcludente [īkōklu'dētʃi] ADJ inconclusive

inconcluso, -a [īkō'kluzu, a] ADJ unfinished

incondicional [īkōdʒisjo'naw] (*pl* **-ais**) ADJ unconditional; (*apoio*) wholehearted; (*partidário*) staunch; (*amizade, fã*) loyal

inconfesso, -a [īkō'fɛsu, a] ADJ closet atr

inconfidência [īkōfi'dēsja] F disloyalty; (*Jur*) treason

inconfidente [īkōfi'dētʃi] ADJ disloyal ▶ M conspirator

inconformado, -a [īkōfor'madu, a] ADJ bitter; **~ com** unreconciled to

inconfundível [īkōfū'dʒivew] (*pl* **-eis**) ADJ unmistakeable

incongruência [īkō'grwēsja] F: **ser uma ~** to be incongruous

incongruente [īkō'grwētʃi] ADJ incongruous

incôngruo, -a [ī'kōgrwu, a] ADJ incongruous

inconsciência [īkō'sjēsja] F (*Med*) unconsciousness; (*irreflexão*) thoughtlessness

inconsciente [īkō'sjētʃi] ADJ (*Med, Psico*) unconscious; (*involuntário*) unwitting; (*irresponsável*) irresponsible ▶ M (*Psico*) unconscious ▶ M/F (*irresponsável*) irresponsible person

inconsequência [īkōse'kwēsja] F (*irresponsabilidade*) irresponsibility; (*incoerência*) inconsistency

inconsequente [īkōse'kwētʃi] ADJ (*incoerente*) inconsistent; (*contraditório*) illogical; (*irresponsável*) irresponsible

inconsistência [īkōsis'tēsja] F inconsistency; (*falta de solidez*) runny consistency

inconsistente [īkōsis'tētʃi] ADJ inconsistent; (*sem solidez*) runny

inconsolável [īkōso'lavew] (*pl* **-eis**) ADJ inconsolable

inconstância [ĩkõs'tãsja] F fickleness; (*do tempo*) changeability

inconstante [ĩkõs'tãtʃi] ADJ fickle; (*tempo*) changeable

inconstitucional [ĩkõstʃitusjo'naw] (*pl* **-ais**) ADJ unconstitutional

incontável [ĩkõ'tavew] (*pl* **-eis**) ADJ countless

incontestável [ĩkõtes'tavew] (*pl* **-eis**) ADJ undeniable

incontinência [ĩkõtʃi'nẽsja] F (*Med*) incontinence; (*sensual*) licentiousness

incontinente [ĩkõtʃi'nẽtʃi] ADJ (*Med*) incontinent; (*sensual*) licentious

incontinenti [ĩkõtʃi'nẽtʃi] ADV immediately

incontrolável [ĩkõtro'lavew] (*pl* **-eis**) ADJ uncontrollable

incontroverso, -a [ĩkõtro'vɛrsu, a] ADJ incontrovertible

inconveniência [ĩkõve'njẽsja] F (*inadequação*) inconvenience; (*impropriedade*) inappropriateness; (*descortesia*) impoliteness; (*ato, dito*) indiscretion

inconveniente [ĩkõve'njẽtʃi] ADJ (*incômodo*) inconvenient; (*inoportuno*) awkward; (*grosseiro*) rude; (*importuno*) annoying ▶ M (*desvantagem*) disadvantage; (*obstáculo*) difficulty, problem

Incor [ĩ'kor] ABR M (= *Instituto do Coração*) hospital in São Paulo

incorporação [ĩkorpora'sãw] (*pl* **-ões**) F (*tb Com*) incorporation; (*no espiritismo*) embodiment, incorporation

incorporado, -a [ĩkorpo'radu, a] ADJ (*Tec*) built-in

incorporar [ĩkorpo'rar] VT to incorporate; (*juntar*) to add; (*Com*) to merge; **incorporar-se** VR (*espírito*) to be embodied; **~-se a** *ou* **em** to join

incorreção [ĩkohe'sãw] (*pl* **-ões**) F (*erro*) inaccuracy

incorrer [ĩko'her] VI: **~ em** to incur

incorreto, -a [ĩko'hɛtu, a] ADJ incorrect; (*desonesto*) dishonest

incorrigível [ĩkohi'ʒivew] (*pl* **-eis**) ADJ incorrigible

incorruptível [ĩkohup'tʃivew] (*pl* **-eis**) ADJ incorruptible

incorrupto, -a [ĩko'huptu, a] ADJ incorrupt

INCRA [ĩ'kra] (*BR*) ABR M = **Instituto Nacional de Colonização e Reforma Agrária**

incredulidade [ĩkreduli'dadʒi] F incredulity; (*ceticismo*) scepticism (*BRIT*), skepticism (*US*)

incrédulo, -a [ĩ'krɛdulu, a] ADJ incredulous; (*cético*) sceptical (*BRIT*), skeptical (*US*) ▶ M/F sceptic (*BRIT*), skeptic (*US*)

incrementado, -a [ĩkremẽ'tadu, a] ADJ (*indústria*) well-developed; (*col: festa*) lively; (: *roupa*) trendy; (: *carro*) expensive

incrementar [ĩkremẽ'tar] VT (*agricultura, economia, turismo*) to develop; (*aumentar*) to increase; (*col: festa, roupa*) to liven up

incremento [ĩkre'mẽtu] M (*desenvolvimento*) growth; (*aumento*) increase

incriminação [ĩkrimina'sãw] F criminalization

incriminar [ĩkrimi'nar] VT to criminalize; **~ alguém de algo** to accuse sb of sth

incrível [ĩ'krivew] (*pl* **-eis**) ADJ incredible

incrustar [ĩkrus'tar] VT to encrust; (*móveis etc*) to inlay

incubadora [ĩkuba'dora] F incubator

incubar [ĩku'bar] VT (*ovos, doença*) to incubate; (*plano*) to hatch ▶ VI (*ovos*) to incubate

inculpar [ĩkuw'par] VT: **~ alguém de algo** (*culpar*) to blame sb for sth; (*acusar*) to accuse sb of sth; **inculpar-se** VR: **~-se de algo** to blame o.s. for sth

inculto, -a [ĩ'kuwtu, a] ADJ (*pessoa*) uncultured, uneducated; (*terreno*) uncultivated

incumbência [ĩkũ'bẽsja] F task, duty; **não é da minha ~** it is not part of my duty

incumbir [ĩkũ'bir] VT: **~ alguém de algo** *ou* **algo a alguém** to put sb in charge of sth ▶ VI: **~ a alguém** to be sb's duty; **incumbir-se** VR: **~-se de** to undertake, take charge of

incurável [ĩku'ravew] (*pl* **-eis**) ADJ incurable

incúria [ĩ'kurja] F carelessness

incursão [ĩkur'sãw] (*pl* **-ões**) F (*invasão*) raid, attack; (*penetração*) foray

incursionar [ĩkursjo'nar] VI: **~ por algo** to make forays into sth

incursões [ĩkur'sõjs] FPL *de* **incursão**

incutir [ĩku'tʃir] VT: **~ algo (em** *ou* **a alguém)** to instil (*BRIT*) *ou* instill (*US*) *ou* inspire sth (in sb)

inda [ĩda] ADV = **ainda**

indagação [ĩdaga'sãw] (*pl* **-ões**) F (*investigação*) investigation; (*pergunta*) inquiry, question

indagar [ĩda'gar] VT (*investigar*) to investigate, inquire into ▶ VI to inquire; **indagar-se** VR: **~-se a si mesmo** to ask o.s.; **~ algo de alguém** to ask sb about sth; **~ (de alguém) sobre** *ou* **de algo** to inquire (of sb) about sth

indébito, -a [ĩ'dɛbitu, a] ADJ undue; (*queixa*) unfounded

indecência [ĩde'sẽsja] F indecency; (*ato, dito*) vulgar thing

indecente [ĩde'sẽtʃi] ADJ indecent, improper; (*obsceno*) rude, vulgar

indecifrável [ĩdesi'fravew] (*pl* **-eis**) ADJ indecipherable; (*pessoa*) inscrutable

indecisão [ĩdesi'zãw] F indecision

indeciso, -a [ĩde'sizu, a] ADJ undecided; (*hesitante*) indecisive; (*indistinto*) vague; (*hesitante*) hesitant, indecisive

indeclinável [ĩdekli'navew] (*pl* **-eis**) ADJ indeclinable

indecoroso, -a [ĩdeko'rozu, ɔza] ADJ indecent, improper

indefensável [ĩdefẽ'savew] (*pl* **-eis**) ADJ indefensible

indeferido, -a [ĩdefe'ridu, a] ADJ refused, rejected

indeferir [ĩdefe'rir] VT (*desatender*) to reject; (*requerimento*) to turn down

indefeso, -a [īde'fezu, a] ADJ undefended; (população) defenceless (BRIT), defenseless (US)

indefinição [īdefini'sãw] (pl **-ões**) F (de pessoa) vague stance

indefinido, -a [īdefi'nidu, a] ADJ indefinite; (vago) vague, undefined; **por tempo ~** indefinitely

indefinível [īdefi'nivew] (pl **-eis**) ADJ indefinable

indefiro etc [īde'firu] VB ver **indeferir**

indelével [īde'lɛvew] (pl **-eis**) ADJ indelible

indelicadeza [īdelika'deza] F impoliteness; (ação, dito) rude thing

indelicado, -a [īdeli'kadu, a] ADJ impolite, rude

indene [ī'dɛni], (PT) **indemne** ADJ (pessoa) unharmed; (objeto) undamaged

indenização [indeniza'sãw], (PT) **indemnização** (pl **-ões**) F compensation; (Com) indemnity; (de demissão) redundancy (BRIT) ou severance (US) payment

indenizar [īdeni'zar], (PT) **indemnizar** VT: **~ alguém por** ou **de algo** (compensar) to compensate sb for sth; (por gastos) to reimburse sb for sth

independência [īdepẽ'dẽsja] F independence

independente [īdepẽ'dẽtʃi] ADJ independent; (autossuficiente) self-sufficient; **quarto ~** room with private entrance

independer [īdepẽ'der] VI: **~ de algo** not to depend on sth

indescritível [īdeskri'tʃivew] (pl **-eis**) ADJ indescribable

indesculpável [īdʒiskuw'pavew] (pl **-eis**) ADJ inexcusable

indesejável [īdeze'ʒavew] (pl **-eis**) ADJ undesirable

indestrutível [īdʒistru'tʃivew] (pl **-eis**) ADJ indestructible

indeterminado, -a [īdetermi'nadu, a] ADJ indeterminate

indevassável [īdeva'savew] (pl **-eis**) ADJ impenetrable

indevido, -a [īde'vidu, a] ADJ (imerecido) unjust; (impróprio) inappropriate

índex ['īdeks] (pl **índices**) M = **índice**

indexar [īdek'sar] VT to index

Índia ['īdʒa] F: **a ~** India; **as ~s Ocidentais** the West Indies

indiano, -a [ī'dʒanu, a] ADJ, M/F Indian

indicação [indʒika'sãw] (pl **-ões**) F indication; (de termômetro) reading; (para um cargo, prêmio) nomination; (recomendação) recommendation; (de um caminho) directions pl

indicado, -a [īdʒi'kadu, a] ADJ (apropriado) appropriate

indicador, a [īdʒika'dor(a)] ADJ: **~ de** indicative of ▶ M indicator; (Tec) gauge; (dedo) index finger; (ponteiro) pointer; **~ econômico** economic indicator

indicar [īdʒi'kar] VT (mostrar) to indicate; (apontar) to point to; (temperatura) to register; (recomendar) to recommend; (para um cargo)

to nominate; (determinar) to determine; **~ o caminho a alguém** to give sb directions; **ao que tudo indica ...** by the looks of things ....

indicativo, -a [īdʒika'tʃivu, a] ADJ (tb Ling) indicative ▶ M indicative

índice ['īdʒisi] M (de livro) index; (dedo) index finger; (taxa) rate; **~ do custo de vida** cost of living index; **~ de audiência** (TV) rating

índices ['īdʒisis] MPL de **índex**

indiciado, -a [īdʒi'sjadu, a] M/F defendant

indiciar [īdʒi'sjar] VT (Jur: acusar) to charge; (submeter a inquérito) to investigate

indício [ī'dʒisju] M (sinal) sign; (vestígio) trace; (Jur) clue

indiferença [īdʒife'rẽsa] F indifference

indiferente [īdʒife'rẽtʃi] ADJ: **~ (a)** indifferent (to); **isso me é ~** it's all the same to me

indígena [ī'dʒiʒena] ADJ, M/F native; (índio: da América) Indian

indigência [īdʒi'ʒẽsja] F poverty; (fig) lack, need

indigente [īdʒi'ʒẽtʃi] ADJ destitute, indigent

indigestão [īdʒiʒes'tãw] F indigestion

indigesto, -a [ī'dʒiʒestu, a] ADJ indigestible; (fig: aborrecido) dull, boring; (: obscuro) turgid

indignação [īdʒigna'sãw] F indignation

indignado, -a [īdʒig'nadu, a] ADJ indignant

indignar [īdʒig'nar] VT to anger, incense; **indignar-se** VR to get angry; **~-se com** to get indignant about

indignidade [īdʒigni'dadʒi] F indignity; (ultraje) outrage

indigno, -a [ī'dʒignu, a] ADJ (não merecedor) unworthy; (desprezível) disgraceful, despicable

índio, -a ['īdʒju, a] ADJ, M/F (da América) Indian; **o Oceano Í~** the Indian Ocean

indiquei etc [īdʒi'kej] VB ver **indicar**

indireta [īdʒi'rɛta] F insinuation; **dar uma ~** to drop a hint

indireto, -a [īdʒi'rɛtu, a] ADJ indirect; (olhar) sidelong; (procedimento) roundabout

indisciplina [īdʒisi'plina] F indiscipline

indisciplinado, -a [īdʒisipli'nadu, a] ADJ undisciplined

indiscreto, -a [īdʒis'krɛtu, a] ADJ indiscreet

indiscrição [īdʒiskri'sãw] (pl **-ões**) F indiscretion

indiscriminado, -a [īdʒiskrimi'nadu, a] ADJ indiscriminate

indiscutível [īdʒisku'tʃivew] (pl **-eis**) ADJ indisputable

indispensável [īdʒispẽ'savew] (pl **-eis**) ADJ essential, vital ▶ M: **o ~** the essentials pl

indispõe etc [īdʒis'põj] VB ver **indispor**

indispomos etc [īdʒis'pomos] VB ver **indispor**

indisponho etc [īdʒis'poɲu] VB ver **indispor**

indisponível [īdʒispo'nivew] (pl **-eis**) ADJ unavailable

indispor [īdʒis'por] (irreg: como **pôr**) VT (de saúde) to make ill; (aborrecer) to upset; **indispor-se** VR: **~-se com alguém** to fall out with sb; ~ **alguém com** *ou* **contra alguém** to turn sb against sb; ~-**se com** *ou* **contra alguém** (*governo etc*) to turn against sb

indisposição [ĩdʒispozi'sãw] (*pl* -**ões**) F illness

indisposto, -a [ĩdʒis'postu, 'pɔsta] *pp de* **indispor** ▶ ADJ (*doente*) unwell, poorly

indispunha *etc* [ĩdʒis'puɲa] VB *ver* **indispor**

indispus *etc* [ĩdʒis'pus] VB *ver* **indispor**

indispuser *etc* [ĩdʒispu'zer] VB *ver* **indispor**

indisputável [ĩdʒispu'tavew] (*pl* -**eis**) ADJ indisputable

indissolúvel [ĩdʒiso'luvew] (*pl* -**eis**) ADJ (*material*) insoluble; (*contrato*) indissoluble

indistinguível [ĩdʒistʃĩ'givew] (*pl* -**eis**) ADJ indistinguishable

indistinto, -a [ĩdʒis'tʃĩtu, a] ADJ indistinct

individual [ĩdʒivi'dwaw] (*pl* -**ais**) ADJ individual

individualidade [ĩdʒividwali'dadʒi] F individuality

individualismo [ĩdʒividwa'lizmu] M individualism

individualista [ĩdʒividwa'lista] ADJ individualist(ic) ▶ M/F individualist

individualizar [ĩdʒividwali'zar] VT to individualize

indivíduo [ĩdʒi'vidwu] M individual; (*col: sujeito*) person

indivisível [ĩdʒivi'zivew] (*pl* -**eis**) ADJ indivisible

indiviso, -a [ĩdʒi'vizu, a] ADJ undivided; (*propriedade*) joint

indizível [ĩdʒi'zivew] (*pl* -**eis**) ADJ unspeakable; (*indescritível*) indescribable

Ind. Lucr. (BR) ABR (*Com*) = **Índice de Lucratividade**

indóceis [ĩ'dɔsejs] ADJ PL *de* **indócil**

Indochina [ĩdo'ʃina] F: **a ~** Indochina

indócil [ĩ'dɔsiw] (*pl* -**eis**) ADJ (*rebelde*) unruly, wayward; (*impaciente*) restless

indo-europeu, -peia [ĩdu-] ADJ Indo-European

índole [ˈĩdoli] F (*temperamento*) nature; (*tipo*) sort, type

indolência [ĩdo'lẽsja] F laziness, indolence; (*apatia*) apathy

indolente [ĩdo'lẽtʃi] ADJ indolent; (*apático*) apathetic

indolor [ĩdo'lor] ADJ painless

indomável [ĩdo'mavew] (*pl* -**eis**) ADJ (*animal*) untameable; (*coragem*) indomitable; (*criança*) unmanageable; (*paixão*) consuming

indômito, -a [ĩ'domitu, a] ADJ untamed, wild

Indonésia [ĩdo'nɛzja] F: **a ~** Indonesia

indonésio, -a [ĩdo'nɛzju, a] ADJ, M/F Indonesian

indoor [ĩ'dor] ADJ INV (*Esporte*) indoor

indubitável [ĩdubi'tavew] (*pl* -**eis**) ADJ indubitable

indução [ĩdu'sãw] (*pl* -**ões**) F induction; (*persuasão*) inducement

indulgência [ĩduw'ʒẽsja] F indulgence; (*tolerância*) leniency; (*Jur*) clemency

indulgente [ĩduw'ʒẽtʃi] ADJ (*juiz, atitude*) lenient; (*atitude*) indulgent

indultar [ĩduw'tar] VT (*Jur*) to reprieve

indulto [ĩ'duwtu] M (*Jur*) reprieve

indumentária [ĩdumẽ'tarja] F costume

indústria [ĩ'dustrja] F industry; **"~ brasileira"** "made in Brazil"; **~ automobilística** car industry; **~ de consumo** *ou* **de ponta** *ou* **leve** light industry; **~ de base** key industry; **~ pesada** heavy industry; **~ de transformação** process industry

industrial [ĩdus'trjaw] (*pl* -**ais**) ADJ industrial ▶ M/F industrialist

industrialização [ĩdustrjaliza'sãw] F industrialization

industrializado, -a [ĩdustrjali'zadu, a] ADJ (*país*) industrialized; (*produto*) manufactured; (*gêneros*) processed; (*pão*) sliced

industrializar [ĩdustrjali'zar] VT (*país*) to industrialize; (*aproveitar*) to process; **industrializar-se** VR to become industrialized

industriar [ĩdus'trjar] VT (*orientar*) to instruct; (*amestrar*) to train

industrioso, -a [ĩdus'trjozu, ɔza] ADJ (*trabalhador*) hard-working, industrious; (*hábil*) clever, skilful (BRIT), skillful (US)

indutivo, -a [ĩdu'tʃivu, a] ADJ inductive

induzir [ĩdu'zir] VT to induce; (*persuadir*): **~ alguém a fazer** to persuade sb to do; **~ alguém em erro** to mislead sb; **~ (algo de algo)** to infer (sth from sth)

inebriante [ine'brjãtʃi] ADJ intoxicating

inebriar [ine'brjar] VT (*fig*) to intoxicate; **inebriar-se** VR to be intoxicated

inédito, -a [i'nɛdʒitu, a] ADJ (*livro*) unpublished; (*incomum*) unheard-of, rare

inefável [ine'favew] (*pl* -**eis**) ADJ indescribable

ineficácia [inefi'kasja] F (*de remédio, medida*) ineffectiveness; (*de empregado, máquina*) inefficiency

ineficaz [inefi'kajz] ADJ (*remédio, medida*) ineffective; (*empregado, máquina*) inefficient

ineficiência [inefi'sjẽsja] F inefficiency

ineficiente [inefi'sjẽtʃi] ADJ inefficient

inegável [ine'gavew] (*pl* -**eis**) ADJ undeniable

inelutável [inelu'tavew] (*pl* -**eis**) ADJ inescapable

inépcia [i'nɛpsja] F ineptitude

inepto, -a [i'nɛptu, a] ADJ inept, incompetent

inequívoco, -a [ine'kivoku, a] ADJ (*evidente*) clear; (*inconfundível*) unmistakeable

inércia [i'nɛrsja] F (*torpor*) lassitude, lethargy; (*Fís*) inertia

inerente [ine'rẽtʃi] ADJ: **~ a** inherent in *ou* to

inerme [i'nɛrmi] ADJ (*formal: não armado*) unarmed; (*indefeso*) defenceless (BRIT), defenseless (US)

inerte [i'nɛrtʃi] ADJ lethargic; (*Fís*) inert

INES (BR) ABR M = **Instituto Nacional de Educação dos Surdos**

inescrupuloso, -a [ineskrupu'lozu, ɔza] ADJ unscrupulous

inescrutável [ineskru'tavew] (pl -eis) ADJ
inscrutable

inescusável [inesku'zavew] (pl -eis) ADJ
(indesculpável) inexcusable; (indispensável)
essential

inesgotável [inezgo'tavew] (pl -eis) ADJ
inexhaustible; (superabundante) boundless

inesperado, -a [inespe'radu, a] ADJ
unexpected, unforeseen ▶ M: **o ~** the
unexpected

inesquecível [ineske'sivew] (pl -eis) ADJ
unforgettable

inestimável [inestʃi'mavew] (pl -eis) ADJ
invaluable

inevitável [inevi'tavew] (pl -eis) ADJ
inevitable

inexatidão [inezatʃi'dãw] (pl -ões) F
inaccuracy

inexato, -a [ine'zatu, a] ADJ inaccurate

inexaurível [inezaw'rivew] (pl -eis) ADJ
inexhaustible

inexcedível [inese'dʒivew] (pl -eis) ADJ
unsurpassed

inexequível [ineze'kwivew] (pl -eis) ADJ
impracticable, unworkable

inexistência [inezis'tẽsja] F lack

inexistente [inezis'tẽtʃi] ADJ non-existent

inexistir [inezis'tʃir] VI not to exist

inexorável [inezo'ravew] (pl -eis) ADJ
implacable

inexperiência [inespe'rjẽsja] F inexperience,
lack of experience

inexperiente [inespe'rjẽtʃi] ADJ
inexperienced; (ingênuo) naive

inexplicável [inespli'kavew] (pl -eis) ADJ
inexplicable

inexplorado, -a [inesplo'radu, a] ADJ
unexplored

inexpressivo, -a [inespre'sivu, a] ADJ
expressionless

inexpugnável [inespug'navew] (pl -eis) ADJ
(fortaleza) impregnable; (invencível) invincible

inextinto, -a [ines'tʃĩtu, a] ADJ
unextinguished

inextricável [inestri'kavew] (pl -eis) ADJ
inextricable

infalível [ĩfa'livew] (pl -eis) ADJ infallible;
(sucesso) guaranteed

infame [ĩ'fami] ADJ (pessoa, procedimento) mean,
nasty; (comida, trabalho) awful

infâmia [ĩ'famja] F (desonra) disgrace; (vileza)
vicious behaviour; (dito) nasty thing

infância [ĩ'fãsja] F childhood; **primeira ~**
infancy, early childhood

infantaria [ĩfãta'ria] F infantry

infante, -a [ĩ'fãtʃi, a] M/F (filho dos reis) prince/
princess ▶ M (soldado) foot soldier

infanticídio [ĩfãtʃi'sidʒu] M infanticide

infantil [ĩfã'tʃiw] (pl -is) ADJ (ingênuo) childlike;
(pueril) childish; (para crianças) children's

infantilidade [ĩfãtʃili'dadʒi] F childishness;
(dito, ação) childish thing

infantis [ĩfã'tʃis] ADJ PL de **infantil**

infantojuvenil [ĩfãtodʒuve'niw] (pl -is) ADJ
children's

infarto [ĩ'fartu] M heart attack

infatigável [ĩfatʃi'gavew] (pl -eis) ADJ
untiring

infausto, -a [ĩ'fawstu, a] ADJ unlucky

infecção [ĩfek'sãw] (pl -ões) F infection;
(contaminação) contamination

infeccionar [ĩfeksjo'nar] VT (ferida) to infect;
(contaminar) to contaminate

infeccioso, -a [ĩfek'sjozu, ɔza] ADJ infectious

infecções [ĩfek'sõjs] FPL de **infecção**

infelicidade [ĩfelisi'dadʒi] F unhappiness;
(desgraça) misfortune

infelicíssimo, -a [ĩfeli'sisimu, a] ADJ SUPERL
de **infeliz**

infeliz [ĩfe'liz] ADJ (triste) unhappy; (infausto)
unlucky; (ação, medida) unfortunate;
(sugestão, ideia) inappropriate ▶ M/F unhappy
person; **como um ~** (col) like there's no
tomorrow

infelizmente [ĩfeliz'mẽtʃi] ADV unfortunately

infenso, -a [ĩ'fẽsu, a] ADJ adverse

inferior [ĩfe'rjor] ADJ: **~ (a)** (em valor, qualidade)
inferior (to); (mais baixo) lower (than) ▶ M/F
inferior, subordinate

inferioridade [ĩferjori'dadʒi] F inferiority

inferiorizar [ĩferjori'zar] VT to put down;
inferiorizar-se VR to become inferior

inferir [ĩfe'rir] VT to infer, deduce

infernal [ĩfer'naw] (pl -ais) ADJ infernal; (col:
excepcional) amazing

inferninho [ĩfer'niɲu] M club

infernizar [ĩferni'zar] VT: **~ a vida de alguém**
to make sb's life hell

inferno [ĩ'fɛrnu] M hell; **é um ~** (fig) it's hell;
vá pro ~! (col) piss off! (!)

infértil [ĩ'fɛrtʃiw] (pl -eis) ADJ infertile

infertilidade [ĩfertʃili'dadʒi] F infertility

infestar [ĩfes'tar] VT to infest

infetar [ĩfe'tar] VT to infect; (contaminar) to
contaminate

infidelidade [ĩfideli'dadʒi] F infidelity,
unfaithfulness; (Rel) disbelief; **~ conjugal**
marital infidelity

infidelíssimo, -a [ĩfide'lisimu, a] ADJ SUPERL
de **infiel**

infiel [ĩ'fjɛw] (pl -éis) ADJ (desleal) disloyal;
(marido) unfaithful; (texto) inaccurate ▶ M/F
(Rel) non-believer

infiltração [ĩfiwtra'sãw] (pl -ões) F
infiltration

infiltrar [ĩfiw'trar] VT to permeate;
infiltrar-se VR (água, luz, odor) to permeate;
~-se em algo (pessoas) to infiltrate sth

ínfimo, -a ['ĩfimu, a] ADJ lowest; (qualidade)
poorest

infindável [ĩfĩ'davew] (pl -eis) ADJ unending,
constant

infinidade [ĩfini'dadʒi] F infinity; **uma ~ de**
countless

infinitesimal [ĩfinitezi'maw] (pl -ais) ADJ
infinitesimal

infinitivo, -a [ĩfini'tʃivu, a] ADJ, M (*Ling*) infinitive

infinito, -a [ĩfi'nitu, a] ADJ infinite ▶ M infinity

infiro *etc* [ĩ'firu] VB *ver* **inferir**

inflação [ĩfla'sãw] F inflation

inflacionar [ĩflasjo'nar] VT (*Econ*) to inflate

inflacionário, -a [ĩflasjo'narju, a] ADJ inflationary

inflacionista [ĩflasjo'nista] ADJ, M/F inflationist

inflamação [ĩflama'sãw] (*pl* **-ões**) F (*Med*) inflammation; (*de madeira etc*) combustion

inflamado, -a [ĩfla'madu, a] ADJ (*Med*) inflamed; (*discurso*) heated

inflamar [ĩfla'mar] VT (*madeira, pólvora*) to set fire to; (*Med, fig*) to inflame; **inflamar-se** VR to catch fire; (*fig*) to get worked up; **~-se de algo** to be consumed with sth

inflamatório, -a [ĩflama'tɔrju, a] ADJ inflammatory

inflamável [ĩfla'mavew] (*pl* **-eis**) ADJ inflammable

inflar [ĩ'flar] VT to inflate, blow up; **inflar-se** VR to swell (up); **~ algo de algo** to inflate sth (*ou* fill sth up) with sth

inflexibilidade [ĩfleksibili'dadʒi] F inflexibility

inflexível [ĩflek'sivew] (*pl* **-eis**) ADJ stiff, rigid; (*fig*) unyielding

infligir [ĩfli'ʒir] VT: **~ algo (a alguém)** to inflict sth (upon sb)

influência [ĩ'flwẽsja] F influence; **sob a ~ de** under the influence of

influenciar [ĩflwẽ'sjar] VT to influence ▶ VI: **~ em algo** to influence sth, have an influence on sth; **influenciar-se** VR: **~-se por** to be influenced by

influenciável [ĩflwẽ'sjavew] (*pl* **-eis**) ADJ easily influenced

influente [ĩ'flwẽtʃi] ADJ influential

influir [ĩ'flwir] VI (*importar*) to matter, be important; **~ em** *ou* **sobre** to influence, have an influence on

influxo [ĩ'fluksu] M influx; (*maré-cheia*) high tide

informação [ĩforma'sãw] (*pl* **-ões**) F (piece of) information; (*notícia*) news; (*Mil*) intelligence; (*Jur*) inquiry; (*instrução*) instruction; **informações** FPL (*detalhes*) information *sg*; **Informações** FPL (*Tel*) directory enquiries (BRIT), information (US); **pedir informações sobre** to ask about, inquire about; **serviço de ~** intelligence service

informado, -a [ĩfor'madu, a] ADJ informed

informal [ĩfor'maw] (*pl* **-ais**) ADJ informal

informalidade [ĩformali'dadʒi] F informality

informante [ĩfor'mãtʃi] M informant; (*Jur*) informer

informar [ĩfor'mar] VT: **~ alguém (de/sobre algo)** to inform sb (of/about sth) ▶ VI to inform, be informative; **informar-se** VR:

~-se de to find out about, inquire about; **~ de** to report on; **~ algo a alguém** to tell sb sth

informática [ĩfor'matʃika] F IT, information technology

informativo, -a [ĩforma'tʃivu, a] ADJ informative

informatização [ĩformatʃiza'sãw] F computerization

informatizar [ĩformatʃi'zar] VT to computerize

informe [ĩ'fɔrmi] M (piece of) information; (*Mil*) briefing; **informes** MPL (*informações*) information *sg*

infortúnio [ĩfor'tunju] M misfortune

infração [ĩfra'sãw] (*pl* **-ões**) F breach, infringement; (*Esporte*) foul; **~ de trânsito** traffic offence (BRIT) *ou* violation (US)

infraestrutura [ĩfraistru'tura] F infrastructure

infrator, a [ĩfra'tor(a)] M/F offender

infravermelho, -a [ĩfraver'meʎu, a] ADJ infra-red

infrequente [ĩfre'kwẽtʃi] ADJ infrequent

infringir [ĩfrĩ'ʒir] VT to infringe, contravene

infrutífero, -a [ĩfru'tʃiferu, a] ADJ fruitless

infundado, -a [ĩfũ'dadu, a] ADJ groundless, unfounded

infundir [ĩfũ'dʒir] VT to infuse; (*terror*) to strike; (*incutir*) to instil (BRIT), instill (US)

infusão [ĩfu'zãw] (*pl* **-ões**) F infusion

ingenuidade [ĩʒenwi'dadʒi] F ingenuousness

ingênuo, -a [ĩ'ʒenwu, a] ADJ ingenuous, naïve; (*comentário*) harmless ▶ M/F naïve person

ingerência [ĩʒe'rẽsja] F interference

ingerir [ĩʒe'rir] VT to ingest; (*engolir*) to swallow; **ingerir-se** VR: **~-se em algo** to interfere in sth

Inglaterra [ĩgla'tɛha] F: **a ~** England

inglês, -esa [ĩ'gles, eza] ADJ English ▶ M/F Englishman/woman ▶ M (*Ling*) English; **os ingleses** MPL the English; **(só) para ~ ver** (*col*) (just) for show

inglesar [ĩgle'zar] VT to Anglicize; **inglesar-se** VR to become Anglicized

inglório, -a [ĩ'glɔrju, a] ADJ inglorious

ingovernável [ĩgover'navew] (*pl* **-eis**) ADJ ungovernable

ingratidão [ĩgratʒi'dãw] F ingratitude

ingrato, -a [ĩ'gratu, a] ADJ ungrateful

ingrediente [ĩgre'dʒẽtʃi] M ingredient

íngreme ['ĩgremi] ADJ steep

ingressar [ĩgre'sar] VI: **~ em** to enter, go into; (*um clube*) to join

ingresso [ĩ'grɛsu] M (*entrada*) entry; (*admissão*) admission; (*bilhete*) ticket

inhaca [i'ɲaka] (*col*) F (*fedor*) stink

inhame [i'ɲami] M yam

inibição [inibi'sãw] (*pl* **-ões**) F inhibition

inibido, -a [ini'bidu, a] ADJ inhibited

inibidor, a [inibi'dor(a)] ADJ inhibiting

inibir [ini'bir] VT to inhibit; **inibir-se** VR: ~-se (de fazer) to be inhibited (from doing); ~ alguém de fazer to inhibit sb from doing

iniciação [inisja'sãw] (pl -ões) F initiation

iniciado, -a [ini'sjadu, a] M/F initiate

iniciador, a [inisja'dor(a)] ADJ initiating ▶ M/F initiator

inicial [ini'sjaw] (pl -ais) ADJ initial, first ▶ F initial

inicializar [inisjali'zar] VT (Comput) to initialize

iniciar [ini'sjar] VT, VI (começar) to begin, start; ~ alguém em algo (arte, seita) to initiate sb into sth

iniciativa [inisja'tʃiva] F initiative; tomar a ~ to take the initiative; por ~ própria on one's own initiative, off one's own bat (BRIT); a ~ privada (Econ) private enterprise; não ter ~ to lack initiative

início [i'nisju] M beginning, start; no ~ at the start

inigualável [inigwa'lavew] (pl -eis) ADJ unequalled

inimaginável [inimaʒi'navew] (pl -eis) ADJ unimaginable

inimigo, -a [ini'migu, a] ADJ, M/F enemy

inimizade [inimi'zadʒi] F enmity, hatred

inimizar [inimi'zar] VT: ~ alguém com alguém to set sb against sb; **inimizar-se** VR: ~-se com to fall out with

ininteligível [inĩteli'ʒivew] (pl -eis) ADJ unintelligible

ininterrupto, -a [inĩte'huptu, a] ADJ continuous; (esforço) unstinting; (voo) non-stop; (serviço) 24-hour

iniquidade [inikwi'dadʒi] F iniquity

iníquo, -a [i'nikwu, a] ADJ iniquitous

injeção [inʒe'sãw] (pl -ões) F injection

injetado, -a [ĩʒe'tadu, a] ADJ (olhos) bloodshot

injetar [ĩʒe'tar] VT to inject

injunção [ĩʒũ'sãw] (pl -ões) F (ordem) order; (pressão) pressure

injúria [ĩ'ʒurja] F (insulto) insult

injuriar [ĩʒu'rjar] VT to insult

injurioso, -a [ĩʒu'rjozu, ɔza] ADJ insulting; (ofensivo) offensive

injustiça [ĩʒus'tʃisa] F injustice

injustiçado, -a [ĩʒustʃi'sadu, a] ADJ wronged ▶ M/F victim of injustice

injustificável [ĩʒustʃifi'kavew] (pl -eis) ADJ unjustifiable

injusto, -a [ĩ'ʒustu, a] ADJ unfair, unjust

INM (BR) ABR M = **Instituto Nacional de Meteorologia**

inobservado, -a [inobizer'vadu, a] ADJ unobserved; (nunca visto) never witnessed

inobservância [inobizer'vãsja] F non-observance

inobservante [inobizer'vãtʃi] ADJ inobservant

inocência [ino'sẽsja] F innocence

inocentar [inosẽ'tar] VT: ~ alguém (de algo) to clear sb (of sth)

inocente [ino'sẽtʃi] ADJ innocent ▶ M/F innocent man/woman; os ~s the innocent

inoculação [inokula'sãw] (pl -ões) F inoculation

inocular [inoku'lar] VT to inoculate

inócuo, -a [i'nɔkwu, a] ADJ harmless

inodoro, -a [ino'dɔru, a] ADJ odourless (BRIT), odorless (US)

inofensivo, -a [inofẽ'sivu, a] ADJ harmless, inoffensive

inolvidável [inowvi'davew] (pl -eis) ADJ unforgettable

inoperante [inope'rãtʃi] ADJ inoperative

inopinado, -a [inopi'nadu, a] ADJ unexpected

inoportuno, -a [inopor'tunu, a] ADJ inconvenient, inopportune

inorgânico, -a [inor'ganiku, a] ADJ inorganic

inóspito, -a [i'nɔspitu, a] ADJ inhospitable

inovação [inova'sãw] (pl -ões) F innovation

inovar [ino'var] VT to innovate

inoxidável [inoksi'davew] (pl -eis) ADJ: aço ~ stainless steel

INPC (BR) ABR M (= Índice Nacional de Preços ao Consumidor) RPI

inqualificável [ĩkwalifi'kavew] (pl -eis) ADJ incalculable; (vil) unacceptable

inquebrantável [ĩkebrã'tavew] (pl -eis) ADJ unbreakable; (fig) unshakeable

inquérito [ĩ'kɛritu] M inquiry; (Jur) inquest

inquestionável [ĩkestʃjo'navew] (pl -eis) ADJ unquestionable

inquietação [ĩkjeta'sãw] F (preocupação) anxiety, uneasiness; (agitação) restlessness

inquietador, a [ĩkjeta'dor(a)] ADJ worrying, disturbing

inquietante [ĩkje'tãtʃi] ADJ worrying, disturbing

inquietar [ĩkje'tar] VT to worry, disturb; **inquietar-se** VR to worry, bother

inquieto, -a [ĩ'kjetu, a] ADJ (ansioso) anxious, worried; (agitado) restless

inquietude [ĩkje'tudʒi] F (preocupação) anxiety, uneasiness; (agitação) restlessness

inquilino, -a [ĩki'linu, a] M/F tenant

inquirição [ĩkiri'sãw] (pl -ões) F investigation; (Jur) cross-examination

inquirir [ĩki'rir] VT (investigar) to investigate; (perguntar) to question; (Jur) to cross-examine ▶ VI to enquire

inquisição [ĩkizi'sãw] (pl -ões) F: a I~ the Inquisition

inquisitivo, -a [ĩkizi'tʃivu, a] ADJ inquisitive

insaciável [ĩsa'sjavew] (pl -eis) ADJ insatiable

insalubre [ĩsa'lubri] ADJ unhealthy

insanidade [ĩsani'dadʒi] F madness, insanity

insano, -a [ĩ'sanu, a] ADJ insane; (fig: trabalho) exhaustive

insatisfação [ĩsatʃisfa'sãw] F dissatisfaction

insatisfatório, -a [ĩsatʃisfa'tɔrju, a] ADJ unsatisfactory

insatisfeito, -a [ĩsatʃis'fejtu, a] ADJ dissatisfied, unhappy

inscrever [ĩskre'ver] VT (*gravar*) to inscribe; (*aluno*) to enrol (BRIT), enroll (US); (*em registro*) to register; **inscrever-se** VR to enrol(l); to register

inscrição [ĩskri'sãw] (*pl* **-ões**) F (*legenda*) inscription; (*Educ*) enrolment (BRIT), enrollment (US); (*em lista etc*) registration

inscrito, -a [ĩ'skritu, a] PP *de* **inscrever**

insegurança [ĩsegu'rãsa] F insecurity

inseguro, -a [ĩse'guru, a] ADJ insecure

inseminação [ĩsemina'sãw] F: ~ **artificial** artificial insemination

inseminar [ĩsemi'nar] VT to inseminate

insensatez [ĩsẽsa'tez] F folly, madness

insensato, -a [ĩsẽ'satu, a] ADJ unreasonable, foolish

insensibilidade [ĩsẽsibili'dadʒi] F insensitivity; (*dormência*) numbness

insensível [ĩsẽ'sivew] (*pl* **-eis**) ADJ insensitive; (*dormente*) numb

inseparável [ĩsepa'ravew] (*pl* **-eis**) ADJ inseparable

inserção [ĩser'sãw] (*pl* **-ões**) F insertion; (*Comput*) entry

inserir [ĩse'rir] VT to insert, put in; (*Comput: dados*) to enter; **inserir-se** VR: ~**-se em** to become part of

inseticida [ĩsetʃi'sida] M insecticide

inseto [ĩ'sɛtu] M insect

insidioso, -a [ĩsi'dʒjozu, ɔza] ADJ insidious

insigne [ĩ'signi] ADJ distinguished, eminent

insígnia [ĩ'signia] F (*sinal distintivo*) badge; (*emblema*) emblem

insignificância [ĩsignifi'kãsja] F insignificance

insignificante [ĩsignifi'kãtʃi] ADJ insignificant

insinceridade [ĩsĩseri'dadʒi] F insincerity

insincero, -a [ĩsĩ'sɛru, a] ADJ insincere

insinuação [ĩsinwa'sãw] (*pl* **-ões**) F insinuation; (*sugestão*) hint

insinuante [ĩsi'nwãtʃi] ADJ ingratiating

insinuar [ĩsi'nwar] VT to insinuate, imply ▶ VI to make insinuations; **insinuar-se** VR: ~**-se por** *ou* **entre** to slip through; ~**-se na confiança de alguém** to worm one's way into sb's confidence

insípido, -a [ĩ'sipidu, a] ADJ insipid; (*fig*) dull

insiro *etc* [ĩ'siru] VB *ver* **inserir**

insistência [ĩsis'tẽsja] F: ~ **(em)** insistence (on); (*obstinação*) persistence (in)

insistente [ĩsis'tẽtʃi] ADJ (*pessoa*) insistent; (*apelo*) urgent

insistir [ĩsis'tʃir] VI: ~ **(em)** (*exigir*) to insist (on); (*perseverar*) to persist (in); ~ **por algo** to stand up for sth; ~ **sobre algo** to dwell on sth; ~ **(para) que alguém faça** to insist that sb do *ou* on sb doing; ~ **(em) que** to insist that

insociável [ĩso'sjavew] (*pl* **-eis**) ADJ unsociable, antisocial

insofismável [ĩsofiz'mavew] (*pl* **-eis**) ADJ simple

insofrido, -a [ĩso'fridu, a] ADJ impatient, restless

insolação [ĩsola'sãw] F sunstroke; **pegar uma ~** to get sunstroke

insolência [ĩso'lẽsja] F insolence

insolente [ĩso'lẽtʃi] ADJ insolent

insólito, -a [ĩ'sɔlitu, a] ADJ unusual

insolúvel [ĩso'luvew] (*pl* **-eis**) ADJ insoluble

insolvência [ĩsow'vẽsja] F insolvency

insolvente [ĩsow'vẽtʃi] ADJ insolvent

insondável [ĩsõ'davew] (*pl* **-eis**) ADJ unfathomable

insone [ĩ'sɔni] ADJ (*pessoa*) insomniac; (*noite*) sleepless

insônia [ĩ'sonja] F insomnia

insosso, -a [ĩ'sosu, a] ADJ unsalted; (*sem sabor*) tasteless; (*pessoa*) uninteresting, dull

inspeção [ĩspe'sãw] (*pl* **-ões**) F inspection, check; (*departamento*) inspectorate

inspecionar [ĩspesjo'nar] VT to inspect

inspeções [ĩspe'sõjs] FPL *de* **inspeção**

inspetor, a [ĩspe'tor(a)] M/F inspector

inspetoria [ĩspeto'ria] F inspectorate

inspiração [ĩspira'sãw] (*pl* **-ões**) F inspiration; (*nos pulmões*) inhalation

inspirador, a [ĩspira'dor(a)] ADJ inspiring

inspirar [ĩspi'rar] VT to inspire; (*Med*) to inhale; **inspirar-se** VR to be inspired; **ele não me inspira confiança** he does not inspire me with confidence

INSS (BR) ABR M (= *Instituto Nacional do Seguro Social*) ≈ DSS (BRIT), ≈ Welfare Dept (US)

instabilidade [ĩstabili'dadʒi] F instability

instalação [ĩstala'sãw] (*pl* **-ões**) F installation; ~ **elétrica** (*de casa*) wiring; ~ **hidráulica** waterworks *sg*

instalar [ĩsta'lar] VT (*equipamento*) to install; (*estabelecer*) to set up; (*alojar*) to accommodate, put up; (*num cargo*) to place; **instalar-se** VR (*numa cadeira*) to settle down; (*alojar-se*) to settle in; (*num cargo*) to take up office

instância [ĩs'tãsja] F (*insistência*) persistence; (*súplica*) entreaty; (*legislativa*) authority; (*Jur*): **tribunal de primeira ~** ≈ magistrates' court (BRIT), ≈ district court (US); **em última ~** as a last resort

instantâneo, -a [ĩstã'tanju, a] ADJ instant, instantaneous; (*café*) instant ▶ M (*Foto*) snap

instante [ĩs'tãtʃi] ADJ urgent ▶ M moment; **nesse ~** just a moment ago; **num ~** in an instant, quickly; **a cada ~** (at) any moment; **só um ~!** just a moment!

instar [ĩs'tar] VT to urge ▶ VI to insist; ~ **com alguém para que faça algo** to urge sb to do sth

instauração [ĩstawra'sãw] F setting-up; (*de processo, inquérito*) institution

instaurar [ĩstaw'rar] VT to establish, set up; (*processo, inquérito*) to institute

instável [ĩs'tavew] (*pl* **-eis**) ADJ unstable; (*tempo*) unsettled

instigação [ĩstʃiga'sãw] F instigation; **por ~ de alguém** at sb's instigation

instigante [ĩstʃi'gãtʃi] ADJ thought-provoking

instigar [ĩstʃi'gar] VT (*incitar*) to urge; (*provocar*) to provoke; **~ alguém contra alguém** to set sb against sb

instilar [ĩstʃi'lar] VT: **~ algo em algo** (*veneno*) to inject sth into sth; **~ algo em alguém** (*fig: ódio etc*) to instil (BRIT) *ou* instill (US) sth in sb

instintivo, -a [ĩstʃĩ'tʃivu, a] ADJ instinctive

instinto [ĩs'tʃĩtu] M instinct; **por ~** instinctively; **~ de conservação** survival instinct

institucional [ĩstʃitusjo'naw] (*pl* -**ais**) ADJ institutional

instituição [ĩstʃitwi'sãw] (*pl* -**ões**) F institution

instituir [ĩstʃi'twir] VT to institute; (*fundar*) to establish, found; (*prazo*) to set

instituto [ĩstʃi'tutu] M (*escola*) institute; (*instituição*) institution; **~ de beleza** beauty salon; **I~ de Pesos e Medidas** ≈ British Standards Institution

instrução [ĩstru'sãw] (*pl* -**ões**) F education; (*erudição*) learning; (*diretriz*) instruction; (*Mil*) training; **instruções** FPL (*para o uso*) instructions (for use); **manual de instruções** instruction manual

instruído, -a [ĩs'trwidu, a] ADJ educated

instruir [ĩs'trwir] VT to instruct; (*Mil*) to train; (*Jur: processo*) to prepare; **instruir-se** VR: **~-se em algo** to learn sth; **~ alguém de** *ou* **sobre algo** to inform sb about sth

instrumentação [ĩstrumẽta'sãw] F (*Mús*) instrumentation

instrumental [ĩstrumẽ'taw] (*pl* -**ais**) ADJ instrumental ▶ M instruments *pl*

instrumentar [ĩstrumẽ'tar] VT (*Mús*) to score

instrumentista [ĩstrumẽ'tʃista] M/F instrumentalist

instrumento [ĩstru'mẽtu] M instrument; (*ferramenta*) implement; (*Jur*) deed, document; **~ de cordas/percussão/sopro** stringed/percussion/wind instrument; **~ de trabalho** tool

instrutivo, -a [ĩstru'tʃivu, a] ADJ instructive

instrutor, a [ĩstru'tor(a)] M/F instructor; (*Esporte*) coach

insubordinação [ĩsubordʒina'sãw] F rebellion; (*Mil*) insubordination

insubordinado, -a [ĩsubordʒi'nadu, a] ADJ unruly; (*Mil*) insubordinate

insubordinar-se [ĩsubordʒi'narsi] VR to rebel; (*Náut*) to mutiny

insubstituível [ĩsubistʃi'twivew] (*pl* -**eis**) ADJ irreplaceable

insucesso [ĩsu'sesu] M failure

insuficiência [ĩsufi'sjẽsja] F inadequacy; (*carência*) shortage; (*Med*) deficiency; **~ cardíaca** heart failure

insuficiente [ĩsufi'sjẽtʃi] ADJ (*não bastante*) insufficient; (*Educ: nota*) ≈ fail; (*pessoa*) incompetent

insuflar [ĩsu'flar] VT to blow up, inflate; (*ar*) to blow; (*fig*): **~ algo (em ou a alguém)** to instil (BRIT) *ou* instill (US) sth (in sb)

insular [ĩsu'lar] ADJ insular ▶ VT (*Tec*) to insulate

insulina [ĩsu'lina] F insulin

insultar [ĩsuw'tar] VT to insult

insulto [ĩ'suwtu] M insult

insultuoso, -a [ĩsuw'twozu, ɔza] ADJ insulting

insumo [ĩ'sumu] M raw materials *pl*; (*Econ*) input

insuperável [ĩsupe'ravew] (*pl* -**eis**) ADJ (*dificuldade*) insuperable; (*qualidade*) unsurpassable

insuportável [ĩsupor'tavew] (*pl* -**eis**) ADJ unbearable

insurgente [ĩsur'ʒẽtʃi] ADJ rebellious ▶ M/F rebel

insurgir-se [ĩsur'ʒirsi] VR to rebel, revolt

insurreição [ĩsuhej'sãw] (*pl* -**ões**) F rebellion, insurrection

insurreto, -a [ĩsu'hɛtu, a] ADJ rebellious ▶ M/F insurgent

insuspeito, -a [ĩsus'pejtu, a] ADJ unsuspected; (*imparcial*) impartial

insustentável [ĩsustẽ'tavew] (*pl* -**eis**) ADJ untenable

intacto, -a [ĩ'tatu, a] (PT) ADJ = **intato**

intangível [ĩtã'ʒivew] (*pl* -**eis**) ADJ intangible

intato, -a [ĩ'tatu, a] ADJ intact; (*ileso*) unharmed; (*fig*) pure

íntegra ['ĩtegra] F: **na ~** in full

integração [ĩtegra'sãw] F integration

integral [ĩte'graw] (*pl* -**ais**) ADJ whole ▶ F (*Mat*) integral; **arroz ~** brown rice; **pão ~** wholemeal (BRIT) *ou* wholewheat (US) bread

integralismo [ĩtegra'lizmu] M Brazilian fascism

integralmente [ĩtegraw'mẽtʃi] ADV in full, fully

integrante [ĩte'grãtʃi] ADJ integral ▶ M/F member

integrar [ĩte'grar] VT to unite, combine; (*completar*) to form, make up; (*Mat, raças*) to integrate; **integrar-se** VR to become complete; **~-se em** *ou* **a algo** (*juntar-se*) to join sth; (*adaptar-se*) to integrate into sth

integridade [ĩtegri'dadʒi] F (*totalidade*) entirety; (*fig: de pessoa*) integrity

íntegro, -a ['ĩtegru, a] ADJ entire; (*honesto*) upright, honest

inteiramente [ĩtejra'mẽtʃi] ADV completely

inteirar [ĩtej'rar] VT (*completar*) to complete; **inteirar-se** VR: **~-se de** to find out about; **~ alguém de** to inform sb of

inteireza [ĩtej'reza] F entirety; (*moral*) integrity

inteiriçado, -a [ĩtejri'sadu, a] ADJ stiff

inteiriço, -a [ĩtej'risu, a] ADJ (*pedaço de pano*) single; (*vestido*) one-piece

inteiro, -a [ĩ'tejru, a] ADJ (*todo*) whole, entire; (*ileso*) unharmed; (*não quebrado*) undamaged;

(completo, ilimitado) complete; *(vestido)*
one-piece; *(fig: caráter)* upright
intelecto [īte'lɛktu] M intellect
intelectual [ītelek'twaw] *(pl* **-ais***)* ADJ, M/F
intellectual
intelectualidade [ītelektwali'dadʒi] F
(qualidade) intellect; *(pessoas)* intellectuals *pl*
inteligência [īteli'ʒēsja] F intelligence;
(interpretação) interpretation; *(pessoa)*
intellect, thinker; **~ artificial** artificial
intelligence
inteligente [īteli'ʒētʃi] ADJ *(pessoa)* intelligent,
clever; *(decisão, romance, filme etc)* clever
inteligível [īteli'ʒivew] *(pl* **-eis***)* ADJ intelligible
intempérie [ītē'pɛri] F bad weather
intempestivo, -a [ītēpes'tʃivu, a] ADJ
ill-timed
intenção [ītē'sāw] *(pl* **-ões***)* F intention;
segundas intenções ulterior motives; **ter
a ~ de** to intend to; **com boa ~** with good
intent; **com má ~** maliciously; *(Jur)* with
malice aforethought
intencionado, -a [ītēsjo'nadu, a] ADJ: **bem ~**
well-meaning; **mal ~** spiteful
intencional [ītēsjo'naw] *(pl* **-ais***)* ADJ
intentional, deliberate
intencionar [ītēsjo'nar] VT to intend; **~ fazer**
to intend to do
intenções [ītē'sōjs] FPL *de* **intenção**
intendência [ītē'dēsja] *(PT)* F management,
administration
intendente [ītē'dētʃi] M/F manager; *(Mil)*
quartermaster
intensidade [ītēsi'dadʒi] F intensity
intensificação [ītēsifika'sāw] F
intensification
intensificar [ītēsifi'kar] VT to intensify;
intensificar-se VR to intensify
intensivo, -a [ītē'sivu, a] ADJ intensive
intenso, -a [ī'tēsu, a] ADJ intense; *(emoção)*
deep; *(impressão)* vivid; *(vida social)* full
intentar [ītē'tar] VT *(obra)* to plan; *(assalto)* to
commit; *(tentar)* to attempt; **~ fazer** to
intend to do; **~ uma ação contra** *(Jur)* to sue
intento [ī'tētu] M aim, purpose
intentona [ītē'tɔna] F *(Pol)* plot, conspiracy
interação [ītera'sāw] F interaction
interagir [ītera'ʒir] VI: **~ (com)** to interact
(with)
interamericano, -a [īterameri'kanu, a] ADJ
inter-American
interativo, -a [ītera'tʃivu, a] ADJ *(Comput)*
interactive
intercalar [īterka'lar] VT to insert; *(Comput:
arquivos)* to merge
intercâmbio [īter'kābju] M exchange
interceder [īterse'der] VI: **~ por** to intercede
on behalf of
interceptar [ītersep'tar] VT to intercept;
(fazer parar) to stop; *(ligação telefônica)* to cut
off; *(ser obstáculo a)* to hinder
intercessão [īterse'sāw] *(pl* **-ões***)* F
intercession

interconexão [īterkonek'sāw] *(pl* **-ões***)* F
interconnection
intercontinental [īterkōtʃinē'taw] *(pl* **-ais***)*
ADJ intercontinental
intercostal [īterkos'taw] *(pl* **-ais***)* ADJ *(Med)*
intercostal
interdependência [īterdepē'dēsja] F
interdependence
interdição [īterdʒi'sāw] *(pl* **-ões***)* F *(de estrada,
porta)* closure; *(Jur)* injunction; **~ de direitos
civis** removal of civil rights
interdisciplinar [īterdʒisipli'nar] ADJ
interdisciplinary
interditado, -a [īterdʒi'tadu, a] ADJ closed,
sealed off
interditar [īterdʒi'tar] VT *(importação etc)* to
ban; *(estrada, praia)* to close off; *(cinema etc)* to
close down; *(Jur)* to interdict
interdito, -a [īter'dʒitu, a] ADJ *(Jur)* interdicted
▶ M *(Jur: interdição)* injunction
interessado, -a [ītere'sadu, a] ADJ interested;
(amizade) self-seeking ▶ M/F interested party
interessante [ītere'sātʃi] ADJ interesting;
estar em estado ~ to be expecting *ou*
pregnant
interessar [ītere'sar] VT to interest, be of
interest to ▶ VI to be interesting;
interessar-se VR: **~-se em** *ou* **por** to take
an interest in, be interested in; **a quem
possa ~** to whom it may concern
interesse [īte'resi] M interest; *(próprio)*
self-interest; *(proveito)* advantage; **no ~ de**
for the sake of; **por ~ (próprio)** for one's
own ends
interesseiro, -a [ītere'sejru, a] ADJ self-
seeking
interestadual [īteresta'dwaw] *(pl* **-ais***)* ADJ
interstate
interface [īter'fasi] F *(Comput)* interface
interferência [īterfe'rēsja] F interference
interferir [īterfe'rir] VI: **~ em** to interfere in;
(rádio) to jam
interfone [īter'fɔni] M intercom
ínterim ['īterī] M interim; **nesse ~** in the
meantime
interino, -a [īte'rinu, a] ADJ temporary,
interim
interior [īte'rjor] ADJ inner, inside; *(vida)*
inner; *(Com)* domestic, internal ▶ M inside,
interior; *(coração)* heart; *(do país)*: **no ~**
inland; **Ministério do I~** = Home Office
(BRIT), ≈ Department of the Interior *(US)*;
Ministro do I~ ≈ Home Secretary *(BRIT)*,
≈ Secretary of the Interior *(US)*; **na parte ~**
inside
interiorizar [īterjori'zar] VT to internalize
interjeição [īterʒej'sāw] *(pl* **-ões***)* F
interjection
interligar [īterli'gar] VT to interconnect;
interligar-se VR to be interconnected
interlocutor, a [īterloku'tor(a)] M/F speaker;
meu ~ the person I was speaking to
interlúdio [īter'ludʒu] M interlude

intermediário, -a [ĩterme'dʒjarju, a] ADJ intermediary ▶ M/F (*Com*) middleman; (*mediador*) intermediary, mediator

intermédio [ĩter'mɛdʒu] M: **por ~ de** through

interminável [ĩtermi'navew] (*pl* **-eis**) ADJ endless

interministerial [ĩterministe'rjaw] (*pl* **-ais**) ADJ interministerial

intermissão [ĩtermi'sãw] (*pl* **-ões**) F interval

intermitente [ĩtermi'tẽtʃi] ADJ intermittent

internação [ĩterna'sãw] (*pl* **-ões**) F (*de doente*) admission; (*de aluno*) sending to boarding school

internacional [ĩternasjo'naw] (*pl* **-ais**) ADJ international

internacionalismo [ĩternasjona'lizmu] M internationalism

internacionalizar [ĩternasjonali'zar] VT to internationalize; **internacionalizar-se** VR to become international

internações [ĩterna'sõjs] FPL *de* **internação**

internar [ĩter'nar] VT (*aluno*) to put into boarding school; (*doente*) to take into hospital; (*Mil, Pol*) to intern

internato [ĩter'natu] M boarding school

internauta [ĩter'nawta] M/F internet user, web *ou* net surfer (*col*)

Internet [ĩter'netʃi] F internet

interno, -a [ĩ'tɛrnu, a] ADJ internal, interior; (*Pol*) domestic ▶ M/F (*tb*: **aluno interno**) boarder; (*Med: estudante*) houseman (BRIT), intern (US); **de uso ~** (*Med*) for internal use

interpelação [ĩterpela'sãw] (*pl* **-ões**) F questioning; (*Jur*) summons *sg*

interpelar [ĩterpe'lar] VT: **~ alguém sobre algo** to question sb about sth; (*pedir explicações*) to challenge sb about sth

interplanetário, -a [ĩterplane'tarju, a] ADJ interplanetary

interpõe *etc* [ĩter'põj] VB *ver* **interpor**

interpolar [ĩterpo'lar] VT to interpolate

interpor [ĩter'por] (*irreg: como* **pôr**) VT to put in, interpose; **interpor-se** VR to intervene; **~-se a algo** (*contrapor-se*) to militate against sth; **~ A (a B)** (*argumentos etc*) to counter (B) with A

interposto, -a [ĩter'postu, 'pɔsta] PP *de* **interpor**

interpretação [ĩterpreta'sãw] (*pl* **-ões**) F interpretation; (*Teatro*) performance; **má ~** misinterpretation

interpretar [ĩterpre'tar] VT to interpret; (*um papel*) to play; **~ mal** to misinterpret

intérprete [ĩ'tɛrpretʃi] M/F (*Ling*) interpreter; (*Teatro*) performer, artist

interpunha *etc* [ĩter'puɲa] VB *ver* **interpor**

interpus *etc* [ĩter'pus] VB *ver* **interpor**

interpuser *etc* [ĩterpu'zer] VB *ver* **interpor**

inter-racial [ĩter-] (*pl* **-ais**) ADJ interracial

interrogação [ĩtehoga'sãw] (*pl* **-ões**) F questioning, interrogation; **ponto de ~** question mark

interrogador, a [ĩtehoga'dor(a)] M/F interrogator

interrogar [ĩteho'gar] VT to question, interrogate; (*Jur*) to cross-examine

interrogativo, -a [ĩtehoga'tʃivu, a] ADJ interrogative

interrogatório [ĩtehoga'tɔrju] M cross-examination

interromper [ĩtehõ'per] VT to interrupt; (*parar*) to stop; (*Elet*) to cut off

interrupção [ĩtehup'sãw] (*pl* **-ões**) F interruption; (*intervalo*) break

interruptor [ĩtehup'tor] M (*Elet*) switch

interseção [ĩterse'sãw] (*pl* **-ões**) F intersection

interstício [ĩters'tʃisju] M gap

interurbano, -a [ĩterur'banu, a] ADJ (*Tel*) long-distance ▶ M long-distance *ou* trunk call

intervalado, -a [ĩterva'ladu, a] ADJ spaced out

intervalo [ĩter'valu] M interval; (*descanso*) break; **a ~s** every now and then

interveio *etc* [ĩter'veju] VB *ver* **intervir**

intervenção [ĩtervẽ'sãw] (*pl* **-ões**) F intervention; **~ cirúrgica** (*Med*) operation

interventor, a [ĩtervẽ'tor(a)] M/F inspector ▶ M *ou* F (*Pol*) caretaker governor

intervir [ĩter'vir] (*irreg: como* **vir**) VI to intervene; (*sobrevir*) to come up

intestinal [ĩtestʃi'naw] (*pl* **-ais**) ADJ intestinal

intestino [ĩtes'tʃinu] M intestine; **~ delgado/ grosso** small/large intestine; **~ solto** diarrhoea (BRIT), diarrhea (US)

inti [ĩ'tʃi] M inti (*Peruvian currency*)

intimação [ĩtʃima'sãw] (*pl* **-ões**) F (*ordem*) order; (*Jur*) summons

intimar [ĩtʃi'mar] VT (*Jur*) to summon; **~ alguém a fazer** *ou* **a alguém que faça** to order sb to do

intimidação [ĩtʃimida'sãw] F intimidation

intimidade [ĩtʃimi'dadʒi] F intimacy; (*vida privada*) private life; (*familiaridade*) familiarity; **ter ~ com alguém** to be close to sb; **ela é pessoa de minha ~** she's a close friend of mine

intimidar [ĩtʃimi'dar] VT to intimidate; **intimidar-se** VR to be intimidated

íntimo, -a [ĩ'tʃimu, a] ADJ intimate; (*sentimentos*) innermost; (*amigo*) close; (*vida*) private ▶ M/F close friend; **no ~** at heart; **festa íntima** small gathering

intitular [ĩtʃitu'lar] VT (*livro*) to title; **intitular-se** VR to be called; (*livro*) to be entitled; (*a si mesmo*) to call oneself; **~ algo de algo** to call sth sth

intocável [ĩto'kavew] (*pl* **-eis**) ADJ untouchable

intolerância [ĩtole'rãsja] F intolerance

intolerante [ĩtole'rãtʃi] ADJ intolerant

intolerável [ĩtole'ravew] (*pl* **-eis**) ADJ intolerable, unbearable

intoxicação [ĩtoksika'sãw] F poisoning; **~ alimentar** food poisoning

intoxicar [ĩtoksi'kar] VT to poison

intraduzível [ītradu'zivew] (*pl* -**eis**) ADJ untranslatable

intragável [ītra'gavew] (*pl* -**eis**) ADJ unpalatable; (*pessoa*) unbearable

intranet [ītra'nɛtʃi] F intranet

intranquilidade [ītrãkwili'dadʒi] F disquiet

intranquilo, -a [ītrã'kwilu, a] ADJ (*aflito*) worried; (*desassossegado*) restless

intransferível [ītrãsfe'rivew] (*pl* -**eis**) ADJ non-transferable

intransigência [ītrãsi'ʒẽsja] F intransigence

intransigente [ītrãsi'ʒẽtʃi] ADJ uncompromising; (*fig: rígido*) strict

intransitável [ītrãsi'tavew] (*pl* -**eis**) ADJ impassable

intransitivo, -a [ītrãsi'tʃivu, a] ADJ intransitive

intransponível [ītrãspo'nivew] (*pl* -**eis**) ADJ (*rio*) impossible to cross; (*problema*) insurmountable

intratável [ītra'tavew] (*pl* -**eis**) ADJ (*pessoa*) contrary, awkward; (*doença*) untreatable; (*problema*) insurmountable

intrauterino, -a [ītraute'rinu, a] ADJ: **dispositivo** ~ intra-uterine device

intravenoso, -a [ītrave'nozu, ɔza] ADJ intravenous

intrepidez [ītrepi'dez] F courage, bravery

intrépido, -a [ī'trɛpidu, a] ADJ daring, intrepid

intriga [ī'triga] F intrigue; (*enredo*) plot; (*fofoca*) piece of gossip; **intrigas** FPL (*fofocas*) gossip *sg*; ~ **amorosa** (PT) love affair

intrigante [ītri'gãtʃi] M/F troublemaker ▶ ADJ intriguing

intrigar [ītri'gar] VT to intrigue ▶ VI to be intriguing

intrincado, -a [ītrĩ'kadu, a] ADJ intricate

intrínseco, -a [ī'trĩseku, a] ADJ intrinsic

introdução [ītrodu'sãw] (*pl* -**ões**) F introduction

introdutório, -a [ītrodu'tɔrju, a] ADJ introductory

introduzir [ītrodu'zir] VT to introduce; (*prego*) to insert

intróito [ī'trɔjtu] M beginning; (*Rel*) introit

intrometer-se [ītrome'tersi] VR to interfere, meddle

intrometido, -a [ītrome'tʃidu, a] ADJ interfering; (*col*) nosey ▶ M/F busybody

intromissão [ītromi'sãw] (*pl* -**ões**) F interference, meddling

introspecção [ītrospek'sãw] F introspection

introspectivo, -a [ītrospek'tʃivu, a] ADJ introspective

introversão [ītrover'sãw] F introversion

introvertido, -a [ītrover'tʃidu, a] ADJ introverted ▶ M/F introvert

intrujão, -jona [ītru'ʒãw, 'ʒona] (*pl* -**ões/intrujãos**) M/F swindler

intrujar [ītru'ʒar] VT to trick, swindle

intrujões [ītru'ʒõjs] MPL *de* **intrujão**

intrujona [ītru'ʒona] F *de* **intrujão**

intruso, -a [ī'truzu, a] M/F intruder

intuição [ītwi'sãw] (*pl* -**ões**) F intuition; (*pressentimento*) feeling; **por** ~ by intuition, intuitively

intuir [ī'twir] VT, VI to intuit

intuitivo, -a [ītwi'tʃivu, a] ADJ intuitive

intuito [ī'tuito] M (*intento*) intention, aim

intumescência [ītume'sẽsja] F swelling

intumescer-se [ītume'sersi] VR to swell (up)

intumescido, -a [ītume'sidu, a] ADJ swollen

inumano, -a [inu'manu, a] ADJ inhuman

inumerável [inume'ravew] (*pl* -**eis**) ADJ countless, innumerable

inúmero, -a [i'numeru, a] ADJ countless, innumerable

inundação [inũda'sãw] (*pl* -**ões**) F (*enchente*) flood; (*ato*) flooding

inundar [inũ'dar] VT to flood; (*fig*) to inundate ▶ VI (*rio*) to flood

inusitado, -a [inuzi'tadu, a] ADJ unusual

inútil [i'nutʃiw] (*pl* -**eis**) ADJ useless; (*esforço*) futile; (*desnecessário*) pointless ▶ M/F good-for-nothing; **ser** ~ to be of no use, be no good

inutilidade [inutʃili'dadʒi] F uselessness

inutilizar [inutʃili'zar] VT to make useless, render useless; (*incapacitar*) to put out of action; (*danificar*) to ruin; (*esforços*) to thwart; **inutilizar-se** VR (*pessoa*) to become incapacitated

inutilizável [inutʃili'zavew] (*pl* -**eis**) ADJ unusable

inutilmente [inutʃiw'mẽtʃi] ADV in vain

invadir [īva'dʒir] VT to invade; (*suj: água*) to overrun; (*: sentimento*) to overcome

invalidação [īvalida'sãw] F invalidation

invalidar [īvali'dar] VT to invalidate; (*pessoa*) to make an invalid

invalidez [īvali'dez] F disability

inválido, -a [ī'validu, a] ADJ, M/F invalid; ~ **de guerra** wounded war veteran

invariável [īva'rjavew] (*pl* -**eis**) ADJ invariable

invasão [īva'zãw] (*pl* -**ões**) F invasion

invasor, a [īva'zor(a)] ADJ invading ▶ M/F invader

inveja [ī'vɛʒa] F envy

invejar [īve'ʒar] VT to envy; (*cobiçar: bens*) to covet ▶ VI to be envious

invejável [īve'ʒavew] (*pl* -**eis**) ADJ enviable

invejoso, -a [īve'ʒozu, ɔza] ADJ envious ▶ M/F envious person

invenção [īvẽ'sãw] (*pl* -**ões**) F invention

invencível [īvẽ'sivew] (*pl* -**eis**) ADJ invincible

invenções [īvẽ'sõjs] FPL *de* **invenção**

inventado, -a [īvẽ'tadu, a] ADJ (*história, personagem*) made-up

inventar [īvẽ'tar] VT to invent; (*história, desculpa*) to make up; (*nome*) to think up ▶ VI to make things up; ~ **de fazer** to take it into one's head to do

inventariação [īvẽtarja'sãw] (*pl* -**ões**) F (*Com*) stocktaking

inventariar [ĩvẽta'rjar] VT: ~ **algo** to make an inventory of sth
inventário [ĩvẽ'tarju] M inventory
inventiva [ĩvẽ'tʃiva] F inventiveness
inventivo, -a [ĩvẽ'tʃivu, a] ADJ inventive
inventor, a [ĩvẽ'tor(a)] M/F inventor
inverdade [ĩver'dadʒi] F untruth
inverificável [ĩverifi'kavew] (pl -eis) ADJ impossible to verify
invernada [ĩver'nada] F winter pasture
invernar [ĩver'nar] VI to spend the winter
inverno [ĩ'vɛrnu] M winter
inverossímil [ĩvero'simiw], (PT) **inverosímil** (pl -eis) ADJ (improvável) unlikely, improbable; (inacreditável) implausible
inversão [ĩver'sãw] (pl -ões) F reversal, inversion
inverso, -a [ĩ'vɛrsu, a] ADJ inverse; (oposto) opposite; (ordem) reverse ▶ M opposite, reverse; **ao ~ de** contrary to
inversões [ĩver'sõjs] FPL de **inversão**
invertebrado, -a [ĩverte'bradu, a] ADJ invertebrate ▶ M invertebrate
inverter [ĩver'ter] VT (mudar) to alter; (ordem) to invert, reverse; (colocar às avessas) to turn upside down, invert
invés [ĩ'vɛs] M: **ao ~ de** instead of
investida [ĩves'tʃida] F attack; (tentativa) attempt
investidura [ĩvestʃi'dura] F investiture
investigação [ĩvestʃiga'sãw] (pl -ões) F investigation; (pesquisa) research
investigar [ĩvestʃi'gar] VT to investigate; (examinar) to examine; (pesquisar) to research into
investimento [ĩvestʃi'mẽtu] M investment
investir [ĩves'tʃir] VT (dinheiro) to invest ▶ VI to invest; ~ **contra** ou **para alguém** (atacar) to attack sb; ~ **alguém no cargo de presidente** to install sb in the presidency; ~ **para algo** (atirar-se) to rush towards sth
inveterado, -a [ĩvete'radu, a] ADJ (mentiroso) inveterate; (criminoso) hardened; (hábito) deep-rooted
inviabilidade [ĩvjabili'dadʒi] F impracticality
inviabilizar [ĩvjabili'zar] VT: ~ **algo** to make sth impracticable
inviável [ĩ'vjavew] (pl -eis) ADJ impracticable
invicto, -a [ĩ'viktu, a] ADJ unconquered; (invencível) unbeatable
inviolabilidade [ĩvjolabili'dadʒi] F inviolability; (Jur) immunity
inviolável [ĩvjo'lavew] (pl -eis) ADJ inviolable; (Jur) immune
invisível [ĩvi'zivew] (pl -eis) ADJ invisible
invisto etc [ĩ'vistu] VB ver **investir**
invocado, -a [ĩvo'kadu, a] ADJ: **estar/ficar ~ com alguém** to dislike/take a dislike to sb
invocar [ĩvo'kar] VT to invoke; (col: irritar) to provoke; (: impressionar) to have a profound effect on ▶ VI: ~ **com alguém** (col: antipatizar) to take a dislike to sb

invólucro [ĩ'vɔlukru] M (cobertura) covering; (envoltório) wrapping; (caixa) box
involuntário, -a [ĩvolũ'tarju, a] ADJ (movimento) involuntary; (ofensa) unintentional
invulnerável [ĩvuwne'ravew] (pl -eis) ADJ invulnerable
iodo ['jodu] M iodine
IOF (BR) ABR M = **Imposto sobre Operações Financeiras**
ioga ['jɔga] F yoga
iogurte [jo'gurtʃi] M yogurt
ioiô [jo'jo] M yoyo
íon ['iõ] (pl -s) M ion
iônico, -a ['joniku, a] ADJ ionic
IPC (BR) ABR M (= Índice de Preços ao Consumidor) RPI
IPEA (BR) ABR M = **Instituto de Planejamento Econômico Social**
ipecacuanha [ipeka'kwaɲa] F ipecac
IPI (BR) ABR M = **Imposto sobre Produtos Industrializados**
IPM (BR) ABR M = **Inquérito Policial-Militar**
IPT (BR) ABR M = **Instituto de Pesquisas Tecnológicas**
IPTU (BR) ABR M (= Imposto Predial e Territorial Urbano) ≈ rates pl (BRIT), ≈ property tax (US)
IPVA (BR) ABR M (= Imposto Sobre Veículos Automóveis) road (BRIT) ou motor-vehicle (US) tax
IR (BR) ABR M = **imposto de renda**

⸤PALAVRA-CHAVE⸥

ir [ir] VI **1** to go; (a pé) to walk; (a cavalo) to ride; (viajar) to travel; **ir caminhando** to walk; **fui de trem** I went ou travelled by train; **vamos (embora)!**, **vamos nessa!** (col) let's go!; **já vou!** I'm coming!; **ir atrás de alguém** (seguir) to follow sb; (confiar) to take sb's word for it
2 (progredir: pessoa, coisa) to go; **o trabalho vai muito bem** work is going very well; **como vão as coisas?** how are things going?; **vou muito bem** I'm very well; (na escola etc) I'm getting on very well
▶ VB AUX **1** (+ infin): **vou fazer** I will do, I am going to do
2 (+ gerúndio): **ir fazendo** to keep on doing
ir-se VR to go away, leave

IRA ABR M (= Irish Republican Army) IRA
ira ['ira] F anger, rage
Irã [i'rã] M: **o ~** Iran
irado, -a [i'radu, a] ADJ angry, irate
iraniano, -a [ira'njanu, a] ADJ, M/F Iranian
Irão [i'rãw] (PT) M = **Irã**
Iraque [i'raki] M: **o ~** Iraq
iraquiano, -a [ira'kjanu, a] ADJ, M/F Iraqi
irascibilidade [irasibili'dadʒi] F irritability
irascível [ira'sivew] (pl -eis) ADJ irritable, short-tempered
ir e vir M INV comings and goings pl
íris ['iris] F INV iris

Irlanda [ir'lãda] F: **a ~** Ireland; **a ~ do Norte** Northern Ireland

irlandês, -esa [irlã'des, eza] ADJ Irish ▶ M/F Irishman/woman ▶ M (*Ling*) Irish

irmã [ir'mã] F sister ▶ ADJ (*empresa etc*) sister; **almas ~s** kindred souls; **~ Paula** (*fig*) good Samaritan; **~ gêmea** twin sister; **~ de criação** adoptive sister

irmanar [irma'nar] VT to join together, unite

irmandade [irmã'dadʒi] F (*associação*) brotherhood; (*confraternidade*) fraternity

irmão [ir'mãw] (*pl* **irmãos**) M brother; (*fig: similar*) twin; (*col: companheiro*) mate; **~ de criação** adoptive brother; **~ gêmeo** twin brother; **~s siameses** Siamese twins

ironia [iro'nia] F irony; (*sarcasmo*) sarcasm; **com ~** ironically; (*com sarcasmo*) sarcastically; **por ~ do destino** by a quirk of fate

irônico, -a [i'roniku, a] ADJ ironic(al); (*sarcástico*) sarcastic

ironizar [ironi'zar] VT to be ironic about ▶ VI to be ironic

IRPF (BR) ABR M (= *Imposto de Renda Pessoa Física*) personal income tax

IRPJ (BR) ABR M (= *Imposto de Renda Pessoa Jurídica*) corporation tax

irra! ['iha] (PT) EXCL damn!

irracional [ihasjo'naw] (*pl* **-ais**) ADJ irrational

irracionalidade [ihasjonali'dadʒi] F irrationality

irradiação [ihadʒja'sãw] (*pl* **-ões**) F (*de luz*) radiation; (*espalhamento*) spread; (*Rádio*) broadcasting; (*Med*) radiation treatment

irradiar [iha'dʒjar] VT (*luz*) to radiate; (*espalhar*) to spread; (*Rádio*) to broadcast, transmit; (*simpatia*) to radiate, exude ▶ VI to radiate; (*Rádio*) to be on the air; **irradiar-se** VR to spread; to be transmitted

irreais [ihe'ajs] ADJ PL *de* **irreal**

irreajustável [iheaʒus'tavew] (*pl* **-eis**) ADJ fixed

irreal [ihe'aw] (*pl* **-ais**) ADJ unreal

irrealizado, -a [iheali'zadu, a] ADJ (*pessoa*) unfulfilled; (*sonhos*) unrealized

irrealizável [iheali'zavew] (*pl* **-eis**) ADJ unrealizable

irreconciliável [ihekõsi'ljavew] (*pl* **-eis**) ADJ irreconcilable

irreconhecível [ihekõɲe'sivew] (*pl* **-eis**) ADJ unrecognizable

irrecorrível [iheko'hivew] (*pl* **-eis**) ADJ (*Jur*) unappealable

irrecuperável [ihekupe'ravew] (*pl* **-eis**) ADJ irretrievable

irrecusável [iheku'zavew] (*pl* **-eis**) ADJ (*incontestável*) irrefutable; (*convite*) which cannot be turned down

irrefletido, -a [ihefle'tʃidu, a] ADJ rash; **de maneira irrefletida** rashly

irrefreável [ihe'frjavew] (*pl* **-eis**) ADJ uncontrollable

irrefutável [ihefu'tavew] (*pl* **-eis**) ADJ irrefutable

irregular [ihegu'lar] ADJ irregular; (*vida*) unconventional; (*feições*) unusual; (*aluno, gênio*) erratic

irregularidade [ihegulari'dadʒi] F irregularity

irrelevância [ihele'vãsja] F irrelevance

irrelevante [ihele'vãtʃi] ADJ irrelevant

irremediável [iheme'dʒjavew] (*pl* **-eis**) ADJ irremediable; (*sem remédio*) incurable

irreparável [ihepa'ravew] (*pl* **-eis**) ADJ irreparable

irrepreensível [iheprjẽ'sivew] (*pl* **-eis**) ADJ irreproachable, impeccable

irreprimível [ihepri'mivew] (*pl* **-eis**) ADJ irrepressible

irrequietação [ihekjeta'sãw] F restlessness

irrequieto, -a [ihe'kjetu, a] ADJ restless

irresgatável [ihezga'tavew] (*pl* **-eis**) ADJ (*Com*) irredeemable

irresistível [ihezis'tʃivew] (*pl* **-eis**) ADJ irresistible; (*desejo*) overwhelming

irresoluto, -a [ihezo'lutu, a] ADJ (*pessoa*) irresolute, indecisive; (*problema*) unresolved

irresponsabilidade [ihespõsabili'dadʒi] F irresponsibility

irresponsável [ihespõ'savew] (*pl* **-eis**) ADJ irresponsible

irrestrito, -a [ihes'tritu, a] ADJ unrestricted

irreverente [iheve'rẽtʃi] ADJ irreverent

irreversível [ihever'sivew] (*pl* **-eis**) ADJ irreversible

irrevogável [ihevo'gavew] (*pl* **-eis**) ADJ irrevocable

irrigação [ihiga'sãw] F irrigation

irrigar [ihi'gar] VT to irrigate

irrisório, -a [ihi'zɔrju, a] ADJ derisory, ludicrous; (*quantia*) derisory, paltry

irritabilidade [ihitabili'dadʒi] F irritability

irritação [ihita'sãw] (*pl* **-ões**) F irritation

irritadiço, -a [ihita'dʒisu, a] ADJ irritable

irritante [ihi'tãtʃi] ADJ irritating, annoying

irritar [ihi'tar] VT to irritate, annoy; (*Med*) to irritate; **irritar-se** VR to get angry, get annoyed

irritável [ihi'tavew] (*pl* **-eis**) ADJ irritable

irromper [ihõ'per] VI (*epidemia*) to break out; (*surgir*) to emerge; (*lágrimas*) to well; (*voz*) to be heard; (*entrar subitamente*): **~ (em)** to burst in(to)

irrupção [ihup'sãw] (*pl* **-ões**) F invasion; (*de ideias*) emergence; (*de doença*) outbreak

isca ['iska] F (*Pesca*) bait; (*fig*) lure, bait

iscambau [iskã'baw] (*col*) M: **e o ~** and what not

isenção [izẽ'sãw] (*pl* **-ões**) F exemption; **~ de impostos** tax exemption

isentar [izẽ'tar] VT (*dispensar*) to exempt; (*livrar*) to free

isento, -a [i'zẽtu, a] ADJ (*dispensado*) exempt; (*livre*) free; **~ de taxas** duty-free; **~ de impostos** tax-free

Islã [iz'lã] M Islam

islâmico, -a [iz'lamiku, a] ADJ Islamic

islamismo [izla'mizmu] M Islam
islamita [izla'mita] ADJ, M/F Muslim
islandês, -esa [izlã'des, eza] ADJ Icelandic
▶ M/F Icelander ▶ M (*Ling*) Icelandic
Islândia [iz'lãdʒa] F: **a ~** Iceland
isolado, -a [izo'ladu, a] ADJ (*separado*) isolated;
(*solitário*) lonely; (*Elet*) insulated
isolamento [izola'mẽtu] M isolation; (*Med*)
isolation ward; (*Elet*) insulation; **~ acústico**
soundproofing
isolante [izo'lãtʃi] ADJ (*Elet*) insulating
isolar [izo'lar] VT to isolate; (*Elet*) to insulate
▶ VI (*afastar mau agouro*) to touch wood (BRIT),
knock on wood (US); **isolar-se** VR to isolate
o.s., cut o.s. off
isonomia [izono'mia] F equality
isopor® [izo'por] M polystyrene, Styrofoam®
(US)
isotônico, -a [izo'toniku, a] ADJ isotonic ▶ M
isotonic drink
isqueiro [is'kejru] M (cigarette) lighter
Israel [izha'ɛw] M Israel
israelense [izhae'lẽsi] ADJ, M/F Israeli
israelita [izhae'lita] ADJ, M/F Israelite
ISS (BR) ABR M = **Imposto Sobre Serviços**
isso ['isu] PRON that; (*col: isto*) this; **~ mesmo**
exactly; **por ~** therefore, so; **por ~ mesmo**
for that very reason; **só ~?** is that all?; **~!**
that's it!; **é ~, é ~ aí** (*col: você tem razão*) that's
right; (*é tudo*) that's it, that's all; **é ~ mesmo**
exactly, that's right; **não seja por ~** that's

no big deal; **eu não tenho nada com ~** it's
got nothing to do with me; **que é ~?** (*exprime
indignação*) what's going on?, what's all this?;
~ de fazer … this business of doing ….
Istambul [istã'buw] N Istanbul
istmo ['istʃimu] M isthmus
isto ['istu] PRON this; **~ é** that is, namely
ITA (BR) ABR M = **Instituto Tecnológico da
Aeronáutica**
Itália [i'talja] F: **a ~** Italy
italiano, -a [ita'ljanu, a] ADJ, M/F Italian ▶ M
(*Ling*) Italian
itálico [i'taliku] M italics *pl*
Itamarati [itamara'tʃi] M: **o ~** the Brazilian
Foreign Ministry

> The Palace of **Itamarati** was built in 1855
> in Rio de Janeiro. It became the seat of
> government when Brazil became a
> republic in 1889, and was later the
> Foreign Ministry. It ceased to be this
> when the Brazilian capital was
> transferred to Brasília, but **Itamarati** is
> still used to refer to the Foreign Ministry.

item ['itẽ] (*pl* **-ns**) M item
iterar [ite'rar] VT to repeat
itinerante [itʃine'rãtʃi] ADJ, M/F itinerant
itinerário [itʃine'rarju] M (*plano*) itinerary;
(*caminho*) route
Iugoslávia [jugoz'lavja] F: **a ~** Yugoslavia
iugoslavo, -a [jugoz'lavu, a] ADJ, M/F
Yugoslav(ian)

Jj

J, j ['ʒɔta] (*pl* **js**) M J, j; **J de José** J for Jack (*BRIT*) *ou* jig (*US*)

já [ʒa] ADV already; (*em perguntas*) yet; (*agora*) now; (*imediatamente*) right away; (*agora mesmo*) right now ▶ CONJ on the other hand; **até já** bye; **desde já** from now on; **desde já lhe agradeço** thanking you in anticipation; **é para já** it won't be a minute; **já esteve na Inglaterra?** have you ever been to England?; **já não** no longer; **ele já não vem mais aqui** he doesn't come here any more; **já que** as, since; **já se vê** of course; **já vou** I'm coming; **já até** even; **já, já** right away; **já era** (*col*) it's been and gone; **você já viu o filme? — já** have you seen the film? — yes

jabaculê [ʒabaku'le] (*col*) M backhander
jabota [ʒa'bɔta] F giant tortoise
jabuti [ʒabu'tʃi] M giant tortoise
jabuticaba [ʒabutʃi'kaba] F jaboticaba (*type of berry*)
jaca ['ʒaka] F jack fruit
jacarandá [ʒakarã'da] M jacaranda
jacaré [ʒaka'rɛ] (*BR*) M alligator; **fazer** *ou* **pegar ~** to body-surf
Jacarta [ʒa'karta] N Jakarta
jacente [ʒa'sẽtʃi] ADJ lying; (*herança*) unclaimed
jacinto [ʒa'sĩtu] M hyacinth
jactância [ʒak'tãsja] F boasting
jactar-se [ʒak'tarsi] VR: **~ de** to boast about
jade ['ʒadʒi] M jade
jaez [ʒa'ez] M harness; (*fig: categoria*) sort
jaguar [ʒa'gwar] M jaguar
jaguatirica [ʒagwatʃi'rika] F leopard cat
jagunço [ʒa'gũsu] M hired gun(man)
jaleco [ʒa'lɛku] M jacket
Jamaica [ʒa'majka] F: **a ~** Jamaica
jamaicano, -a [ʒamaj'kanu, a] ADJ, M/F Jamaican
jamais [ʒa'majs] ADV never; (*com palavra negativa*) ever; **ninguém ~ o tratou assim** nobody ever treated him like that
jamanta [ʒa'mãta] F juggernaut (*BRIT*), truck-trailer (*US*)
jamegão [ʒame'gãw] (*pl* **-ões**) (*col*) M signature
jan. ABR = **janeiro**
janeiro [ʒa'nejru] M January; *ver tb* **julho**
janela [ʒa'nɛla] F window; **(~) basculante** louvre (*BRIT*) *ou* louver (*US*) window

janelão [ʒane'lãw] (*pl* **-ões**) M picture window
jangada [ʒã'gada] F raft
jangadeiro [ʒãga'dejru] M *jangada* fisherman
janota [ʒa'nɔta] ADJ foppish ▶ M dandy
janta ['ʒãta] (*col*) F dinner
jantar [ʒã'tar] M dinner ▶ VT to have for dinner ▶ VI to have dinner; **~ americano** buffet dinner; **~ dançante** dinner dance
jantarado [ʒãta'radu] M tea
Japão [ʒa'pãw] M: **o ~** Japan
japona [ʒa'pona] F (*casaco*) three-quarter length coat ▶ M/F (*col*) Japanese
japonês, -esa [ʒapo'nes, eza] ADJ, M/F Japanese ▶ M (*Ling*) Japanese
jaqueira [ʒa'kejra] F jack tree
jaqueta [ʒa'keta] F jacket
jaquetão [ʒake'tãw] (*pl* **-ões**) M double-breasted coat
jararaca [ʒara'raka] F (*cobra*) jararaca (*snake*); (*fig: mulher*) shrew
jarda ['ʒarda] F yard
jardim [ʒar'dʒĩ] (*pl* **-ns**) M garden; **~ de infância** kindergarten; **~ de inverno** conservatory; **~ zoológico** zoo
jardinagem [ʒardʒi'naʒẽ] F gardening
jardinar [ʒardʒi'nar] VT to cultivate ▶ VI to garden
jardineira [ʒardʒi'nejra] F (*móvel*) plant-stand; (*caixa*) trough; (*ônibus*) open bus; (*calça*) dungarees *pl*; (*vestido*) pinafore dress (*BRIT*), jumper (*US*); *ver tb* **jardineiro**
jardineiro, -a [ʒardʒi'nejru, a] M/F gardener
jardins [ʒar'dʒĩs] MPL *de* **jardim**
jargão [ʒar'gãw] M jargon
jarra ['ʒaha] F pot
jarro ['ʒahu] M jug
jasmim [ʒaz'mĩ] M jasmine
jato ['ʒatu] M jet; (*de luz*) flash; (*de ar*) blast; **a ~** at top speed
jaula ['ʒawla] F cage
Java ['ʒava] F Java
javali [ʒava'li] M wild boar
jazer [ʒa'zer] VI to lie
jazida [ʒa'zida] F deposit
jazigo [ʒa'zigu] M grave; (*monumento*) tomb; **~ de família** family tomb
jazz [dʒɛz] M jazz
jazzista [dʒa'zista] M/F (*músico*) jazz artist; (*fã*) jazz fan

jazzístico, -a [dʒa'zistʃiku, a] ADJ jazzy

JB ABR M = **Jornal do Brasil**

JEC (BR) ABR F = **Juventude Estudantil Católica**

jeca ['ʒɛka] ADJ rustic; (*cafona*) tacky ▶ M/F Brazilian hillbilly

jeca-tatu (*pl* **jecas-tatus**) M/F Brazilian hillbilly

jeitão [ʒej'tãw] (*pl* **-ões**) (*col*) M (*aspecto*) look; (*modo de ser*) style, way

jeitinho [ʒej'tʃiɲu] M knack

jeito ['ʒejtu] M (*maneira*) way; (*aspecto*) appearance; (*aptidão, habilidade*) skill, knack; (*modos pessoais*) manner; **falta de ~** clumsiness; **ter ~ de** to look like; **ter** *ou* **levar ~ para** to have a gift for, be good at; **não ter ~** (*pessoa*) to be awkward; (*situação*) to be hopeless; **dar um ~ em algo** (*pé*) to twist sth; (*quarto, casa, papéis*) to tidy sth up; (*consertar*) to fix sth; **dar um ~ em alguém** to sort sb out; **dar um ~** to find a way; **tomar ~** to pull one's socks up; **o ~ é ...** the thing to do is ...; **é o ~** it's the best way; **ao ~ de** in the style of; **com ~** tactfully; **daquele ~** (in) that way; (*col: em desordem, mal*) anyhow; **de qualquer ~** anyway; **de ~ nenhum!** no way!; **ficar sem ~** to feel awkward

jeitões [ʒej'tõjs] MPL *de* **jeitão**

jeitoso, -a [ʒej'tozu, ɔza] ADJ (*hábil*) skilful (BRIT), skillful (US); (*elegante*) handsome; (*apropriado*) suitable

jejuar [ʒe'ʒwar] VI to fast

jejum [ʒe'ʒũ] (*pl* **-ns**) M fast; **em ~** fasting

Jeová [ʒeo'va] M: **testemunha de ~** Jehovah's witness

jequice [ʒe'kisi] F country ways *pl*; (*cafonice*) tackiness

jerico [ʒe'riku] M donkey; **ideia de ~** stupid idea

jérsei ['ʒɛrsej] M jersey

Jerusalém [ʒeruza'lẽ] N Jerusalem

jesuíta [ʒe'zwita] M Jesuit

Jesus [ʒe'zus] M Jesus ▶ EXCL heavens!

jetom [ʒe'tõ] (*pl* **-ns**) M (*ficha*) token; (*remuneração*) fee

jiboia [ʒi'bɔja] F boa (constrictor)

jiboiar [ʒibo'jar] VI to let one's dinner go down

jiló [ʒi'lɔ] M *kind of vegetable*

jingle ['dʒĩgew] M jingle

jipe ['ʒipi] M jeep

jirau [ʒi'raw] M (*na cozinha*) rack; (*palanque*) platform

jiu-jítsu [ʒu'ʒitsu] M jiu-jitsu

joalheiro, -a [ʒoa'ʎejru, a] M/F jeweller (BRIT), jeweler (US)

joalheria [ʒoaʎe'ria] F jeweller's (shop) (BRIT), jewelry store (US)

joanete [ʒwa'netʃi] M bunion

joaninha [ʒwa'niɲa] F ladybird (BRIT), ladybug (US)

joão-ninguém (*pl* **joões-ninguém**) M nobody

JOC (BR) ABR F = **Juventude Operária Católica**

joça ['ʒɔsa] (*col*) F thing, contraption

jocoso, -a [ʒo'kozu, ɔza] ADJ jocular, humorous

joelhada [ʒoe'ʎada] F: **dar uma ~ em alguém** to knee sb

joelheira [ʒoe'ʎejra] F (*Esporte*) kneepad

joelho [ʒo'eʎu] M knee; **de ~s** kneeling; **ficar de ~s** to kneel down

jogada [ʒo'gada] F (*num jogo*) move; (*lanço*) throw; (*negócio*) scheme; (*col: modo de agir*) move; **a ~ é a seguinte** (*col*) this is the situation; **morar na ~** (*col*) to catch on

jogado, -a [ʒo'gadu, a] ADJ (*prostrado*) flat out; (*abandonado*) abandoned

jogador, a [ʒoga'dor(a)] M/F player; (*de jogo de azar*) gambler; **~ de futebol** footballer

jogão [ʒo'gãw] (*pl* **-ões**) M great game

jogar [ʒo'gar] VT to play; (*em jogo de azar*) to gamble; (*atirar*) to throw; (*indiretas*) to drop ▶ VI to play; to gamble; (*barco*) to pitch; **jogar-se** VR to throw o.s.; **~ fora** to throw away; **~ na Bolsa** to play the markets; **~ no bicho** to play the numbers game; **~ com** (*combinar*) to match

jogatina [ʒoga'tʃina] F gambling

jogging ['ʒɔgĩ] M jogging; (*roupa*) track suit; **fazer ~** to go jogging, jog

jogo ['ʒogu] M game; (*jogar*) play; (*de azar*) gambling; (*conjunto*) set; (*artimanha*) trick; **abrir o ~** (*fig*) to lay one's cards on the table, come clean; **esconder o ~** to play one's cards close to one's chest; **estar em ~** (*fig*) to be at stake; **fazer o ~ de alguém** to play sb's game, go along with sb; **ter ~ de cintura** (*fig*) to be flexible; **~ da velha** noughts and crosses *sg*; **~ de armar** construction set; **~ de cartas** card game; **~ de computador** computer game; **~ de damas** draughts *sg* (BRIT), checkers *sg* (US); **~ de luz** lighting effects *pl*; **~ de salão** indoor game; **~ do bicho** (illegal) numbers game; **J~s Olímpicos** Olympic Games; **~ limpo/sujo** fair play/dirty tricks *pl*; **o ~ político** political manoeuvring (BRIT) *ou* maneuvering (US)

jogões [ʒo'gõjs] MPL *de* **jogão**

joguei *etc* [ʒo'gej] VB *ver* **jogar**

joguete [ʒo'getʃi] M plaything; **fazer alguém de ~** to toy with sb

joia ['ʒɔja] F jewel; (*taxa*) entry fee ▶ ADJ (*col*) great; **tudo ~?** (*col*) how's things?

jóquei ['ʒɔkej] M (*clube*) jockey club; (*cavaleiro*) jockey

jóquei-clube (*pl* **jóqueis-clubes**) M jockey club

Jordânia [ʒor'danja] F: **a ~** Jordan

jordaniano, -a [ʒorda'njanu, a] ADJ, M/F Jordanian

Jordão [ʒor'dãw] M: **o (rio) ~** the Jordan (River)

jornada [ʒor'nada] F (*viagem*) journey; (*percurso diário*) day's journey; **~ de trabalho** working day

jornal [ʒor'naw] (*pl* **-ais**) M newspaper; (*TV, Rádio*) news *sg*

jornaleiro, -a [ʒorna'lejru, a] M/F newsagent (BRIT), newsdealer (US)

jornalismo [ʒorna'lizmu] M journalism

jornalista [ʒorna'lista] M/F journalist

jornalístico, -a [ʒorna'listʃiku, a] ADJ journalistic

jorrante [ʒo'hãtʃi] ADJ gushing

jorrar [ʒo'har] VI to gush, spurt out

jorro [ʒohu] M jet; (de sangue) spurt; (fig) stream, flood

jovem ['ʒovẽ] (pl -ns) ADJ young; (aspecto) youthful; (música) youth atr ▶ M/F young person

jovial [ʒo'vjaw] (pl -ais) ADJ jovial, cheerful

jovialidade [ʒovjali'dadʒi] F joviality

JPCCC (BR) ABR F = **Justiça de Pequenas Causas Civis e Criminais**

Jr ABR = **Júnior**

JT (BR) ABR M = **Jornal da Tarde**

juba ['ʒuba] F (de leão) mane; (col: cabelo) mop

jubilação [ʒubila'sãw] F (aposentadoria) retirement; (de estudante) sending down

jubilar [ʒubi'lar] VT (aposentar) to retire, pension off; (aluno) to send down

jubileu [ʒubi'lew] M jubilee; ~ **de prata** silver jubilee

júbilo ['ʒubilu] M rejoicing; **com** ~ jubilantly

jubiloso, -a [ʒubi'lozu, ɔza] ADJ jubilant

JUC (BR) ABR F = **Juventude Universitária Católica**

judaico, -a [ʒu'dajku, a] ADJ Jewish

judaísmo [ʒuda'izmu] M Judaism

judas ['ʒudas] M (fig) Judas; (boneco) effigy; **onde J~ perdeu as botas** (col) at the back of beyond

judeu, judia [ʒu'dew, ʒu'dʒia] ADJ Jewish ▶ M/F Jew

judiação [ʒudʒja'sãw] F ill-treatment

judiar [ʒu'dʒjar] VI: ~ **de alguém/algo** to ill-treat sb/sth

judiaria [ʒudʒja'ria] F ill-treatment; **que** ~! how cruel!

judicatura [ʒudʒika'tura] F (cargo) office of judge; (magistratura) judicature

judicial [ʒudʒi'sjaw] (pl -ais) ADJ judicial

judiciário, -a [ʒudʒi'sjarju, a] ADJ judicial; **o (poder)** ~ the judiciary

judicioso, -a [ʒudʒi'sjozu, ɔza] ADJ judicious, wise

judô [ʒu'do] M judo

jugo ['ʒugu] M yoke

juiz, juíza [ʒwiz, -'iza] M/F judge; (em jogos) referee; ~ **de menores** juvenile judge; ~ **de paz** justice of the peace

juizado [ʒwi'zado] M court; **J~ de Menores** Juvenile Court; **J~ de Pequenas Causas** small claims court

juízo ['ʒwizu] M judgement; (parecer) opinion; (siso) common sense; (foro) court; **J~ Final** Day of Judgement, doomsday; **perder o** ~ to lose one's mind; **não ter** ~ to be foolish; **tomar** ou **criar** ~ to come to one's senses; **chamar/levar a** ~ to

summon/take to court; ~! behave yourself!

jujuba [ʒu'ʒuba] F (Bot) jujube; (bala) jujube sweet

jul. ABR = **julho**

julgador, a [ʒuwga'dor(a)] ADJ judging ▶ M/F judge

julgamento [ʒuwga'mẽtu] M judgement; (audiência) trial; (sentença) sentence

julgar [ʒuw'gar] VT to judge; (achar) to think; (Jur: sentenciar) to sentence; **julgar-se** VR: ~-se **algo** to consider o.s. sth, think of o.s. as sth

julho ['ʒuʎu] M July; **dia primeiro de** ~ the first of July (BRIT), July first (US); **dia dois/onze de** ~ the second/eleventh of July (BRIT), July second/eleventh (US); **ele chegou no dia cinco de** ~ he arrived on 5th July ou July 5th; **em** ~ in July; **no começo/fim de** ~ at the beginning/end of July; **em meados de** ~ in mid July; **todo ano em** ~ every July; **em** ~ **do ano que vem/do ano passado** next/last July

jumento, -a [ʒu'mẽtu, a] M/F donkey

jun. ABR = **junho**

junção [ʒũ'sãw] (pl -ões) F (ato) joining; (junta) join

junco ['ʒũku] M reed, rush

junções [ʒũ'sõjs] FPL de **junção**

junho ['ʒunu] M June; ver tb **julho**

junino, -a [ʒu'ninu, a] ADJ June; **festa junina** St John's day party

júnior ['ʒunjor] (pl **juniores**) ADJ younger, junior ▶ M/F (Esporte) junior; **Eduardo Autran J~** Eduardo Autran Junior

junta ['ʒũta] F (comissão) board, committee; (Pol) junta; (articulação, juntura) joint; ~ **comercial** board of trade; ~ **médica** medical team

juntar [ʒũ'tar] VT (por junto) to join; (reunir) to bring together; (aglomerar) to gather together; (recolher) to collect up; (acrescentar) to add; (dinheiro) to save up ▶ VI to gather; **juntar-se** VR to gather; (associar-se) to join up; ~-se **a alguém** to join sb; ~-se **com alguém** to (go and) live with sb

junto, -a ['ʒũtu, a] ADJ joined; (chegado) near; **ir** ~**s** to go together; ~ **a/de** near/next to; **segue** ~ (Com) please find enclosed

juntura [ʒũ'tura] F join; (articulação) joint

Júpiter ['ʒupiter] M Jupiter

jura ['ʒura] F vow

jurado, -a [ʒu'radu, a] ADJ sworn ▶ M/F juror

juramentado, -a [ʒuramẽ'tadu, a] ADJ accredited, legally certified

juramento [ʒura'mẽtu] M oath

jurar [ʒu'rar] VT, VI to swear; **jura?** really?

júri ['ʒuri] M jury

jurídico, -a [ʒu'ridʒiku, a] ADJ legal

jurisconsulto, -a [ʒuriskõ'suwtu, a] M/F legal advisor

jurisdição [ʒuriʃdʒi'sãw] F jurisdiction

jurisprudência [ʒurispru'dẽsja] F jurisprudence

jurista [ʒu'rista] M/F jurist

juros ['ʒurus] MPL (*Econ*) interest *sg*; **a/sem ~** at interest/interest-free; **render ~** to yield *ou* bear interest; **~ fixos/variáveis** fixed/variable interest; **~ simples/compostos** simple/compound interest

jururu [ʒuru'ru] ADJ melancholy, wistful

jus [ʒus] M: **fazer ~ a algo** to live up to sth

jusante [ʒu'zãtʃi] F: **a ~ (de)** downstream (from)

justamente [ʒusta'mẽtʃi] ADV (*com justiça*) fairly, justly; (*precisamente*) exactly

justapor [ʒusta'por] (*irreg: como* **pôr**) VT to juxtapose; **justapor-se** VR to be juxtaposed; **~ algo a algo** to juxtapose sth with sth

justaposição [ʒustapozi'sãw] (*pl* **-ões**) F juxtaposition

justaposto [ʒusta'postu] PP *de* **justapor**

justapunha *etc* [ʒusta'puɲa] VB *ver* **justapor**

justapus *etc* [ʒusta'pus] VB *ver* **justapor**

justapuser *etc* [ʒustapu'zer] VB *ver* **justapor**

justeza [ʒus'teza] F fairness; (*precisão*) precision

justiça [ʒus'tʃisa] F justice; (*poder judiciário*) judiciary; (*equidade*) fairness; (*tribunal*) court; **com ~** justly, fairly; **ir à ~** to go to court; **fazer ~ a** to do justice to; **J~ Eleitoral** Electoral Court; **J~ do Trabalho** ≈ industrial tribunal (BRIT), ≈ labor relations board (US)

justiceiro, -a [ʒustʃi'sejru, a] ADJ righteous; (*inflexível*) inflexible

justificação [ʒustʃifika'sãw] (*pl* **-ões**) F justification

justificar [ʒustʃifi'kar] VT to justify; **justificar-se** VR to justify o.s.

justificativa [ʒustʃifika'tʃiva] F (*Jur*) justification

justificável [ʒustʃifi'kavew] (*pl* **-eis**) ADJ justifiable

justo, -a ['ʒustu, a] ADJ just, fair; (*legítimo: queixa*) legitimate, justified; (*exato*) exact; (*apertado*) tight ▶ ADV just

juta ['ʒuta] F jute

juvenil [ʒuve'niw] (*pl* **-is**) ADJ (*ar*) youthful; (*roupa*) young; (*livro*) for young people; (*Esporte: equipe, campeonato*) youth *atr*, junior ▶ M (*Esporte*) junior championship

juventude [ʒuvẽ'tudʒi] F youth; (*jovialidade*) youthfulness; (*jovens*) young people *pl*, youth

Kk

K, k [ka] (*pl* **ks**) M K, k; **K de Kátia** K for king
kanga ['kãga] F beach wrap
karaokê [karao'ke] M karaoke; (*lugar*) karaoke
  bar
kart ['kartʃi] (*pl* **-s**) M go-kart
ketchup [ke'tʃupi] M ketchup
kg ABR (= *quilograma*) kg
KGB ABR F KGB
kHz ABR (= *quilohertz*) kHz
kibutz [ki'butz] M INV kibbutz
kilt ['kiwtʃi] (*pl* **-s**) M kilt
kirsch [kirs] M kirsch

kit ['kitʃi] (*pl* **-s**) M kit; **~ de sobrevivência**
  survival kit
kitchenette [kitʃe'nɛtʃi] F studio flat
kitsch [kits] ADJ INV, M kitsch
kl ABR (= *quilolitro*) kl
km ABR (= *quilômetro*) km
km/h ABR (= *quilômetros por hora*) km/h
know-how ['now'haw] M know-how
Kremlin [krẽ'lĩ] M: **o ~** the Kremlin
Kuweit [ku'wejtʃi] M: **o ~** Kuwait
kW ABR (= *quilowatt*) kW
kwh ABR (= *quilowatt-hora*) kwh

k

Ll

L¹, l ['eli] (pl **ls**) M L, l; **L de Lúcia** L for Lucy (BRIT) ou love (US)

L² ABR (= *Largo*) Sq.

lá [la] ADV there ▸ M (*Mús*) A; **lá fora** outside; **lá em baixo** down there; **por lá** (*direção*) that way; (*situação*) over there; **até lá** (*no espaço*) there; (*no tempo*) until then; **lá pelas tantas** in the small hours; **para lá de** (*mais do que*) more than; **diga lá ...** come on and say ...; **sei lá!** don't ask me!; **ela sabe lá** she's got no idea; **ele pode lá pagar um aluguel tão caro** there's no way he can pay such a high rent; **o apartamento não é lá essas coisas** the apartment is nothing special; **estar mais para lá do que para cá** (*de cansaço*) to be dead on one's feet; (*prestes a morrer*) to be at death's door

lã [lã] F wool; **de lã** woollen (BRIT), woolen (US); **de pura lã** pure wool; **lã de camelo** camel hair

-la [la] PRON her; (*você*) you; (*coisa*) it

labareda [laba'reda] F flame; (*fig*) ardour (BRIT), ardor (US)

labia ['labja] F (*astúcia*) cunning; **ter ~** to have the gift of the gab

labial [la'bjaw] (pl **-ais**) ADJ lip atr; (*Ling*) labial ▸ F (*Ling*) labial

lábio ['labju] M lip

labirinto [labi'rĩtu] M labyrinth, maze

labor [la'bor] M work, labour (BRIT), labor (US)

laborar [labo'rar] VI: **~ em erro** to labour (BRIT) ou labor (US) under a misconception

laboratório [labora'tɔrju] M laboratory

laborioso, -a [labo'rjozu, ɔza] ADJ (*diligente*) hard-working; (*árduo*) laborious

LABRE ABR F = **Liga de Amadores Brasileiros de Rádio Emissão**

labuta [la'buta] F toil, drudgery

labutar [labu'tar] VI to toil; (*esforçar-se*) to struggle, strive

laca ['laka] F lacquer

laçada [la'sada] F (*nó*) slipknot; (*no tricô*) loop

laçar [la'sar] VT to bind, tie; (*boi*) to rope

laçarote [lasa'rɔtʃi] M big bow

laço ['lasu] M bow; (*de gravata*) knot; (*armadilha*) snare; (*fig*) bond, tie; **dar um ~** to tie a bow; **~s de família** family ties

lacônico, -a [la'koniku, a] ADJ laconic

lacraia [la'kraja] F centipede

lacrar [la'krar] VT to seal (with wax)

lacre ['lakri] M sealing wax

lacrimal [lakri'maw] (pl **-ais**) ADJ (*canal*) tear atr

lacrimejante [lakrime'ʒãtʃi] ADJ weeping

lacrimejar [lakrime'ʒar] VI (*olhos*) to water; (*chorar*) to weep

lacrimogêneo, -a [lakrimo'ʒenju, a] ADJ tear-jerking; **gás ~** tear gas

lacrimoso, -a [lakri'mozu, ɔza] ADJ tearful

lactação [lakta'sãw] F lactation; (*amamentação*) breastfeeding

lácteo, -a ['laktju, a] ADJ milk atr; **Via Láctea** Milky Way

lacticínio [laktʃi'sinju] M dairy product

lactose [lak'tɔzi] F lactose

lacuna [la'kuna] F gap; (*omissão*) omission; (*espaço em branco*) blank

ladainha [lada'iɲa] F litany; (*fig*) rigmarole

ladear [la'dʒjar] VT to flank; (*problema*) to get round; **o rio ladeia a estrada** the river runs by the side of the road

ladeira [la'dejra] F slope

ladino, -a [la'dʒinu, a] ADJ cunning, crafty

lado ['ladu] M side; (*Mil*) flank; (*rumo*) direction; **ao ~** (*perto*) close by; **a casa ao ~** the house next door; **ao ~ de** beside; **de ~** sideways; **deixar de ~** to set aside; (*fig*) to leave out; **de um ~ para outro** back and forth; **do ~ de dentro/fora** on the inside/ outside; **do ~ de cá/lá** on this/that side; **no outro ~ da rua** across the road; **ela foi para aqueles ~s** she went that way; **por um ~ ... por outro ~** on the one hand ... on the other hand; **por todos os ~s** all around; **~ a ~** side by side; **o meu ~** (*col: interesses*) my interests

ladra ['ladra] F thief, robber; (*picareta*) crook

ladrão, -ona [la'drãw, ɔna] (pl **-ões/-s**) ADJ thieving ▸ M/F thief, robber; (*picareta*) crook ▸ M (*tubo*) overflow pipe; **pega ~!** stop thief!

ladrar [la'drar] VI to bark

ladrilhar [ladri'ʎar] VT, VI to tile

ladrilheiro, -a [ladri'ʎejru, a] M/F tiler

ladrilho [la'driʎu] M tile; (*chão*) tiled floor, tiles pl

ladro ['ladru] M (*latido*) bark; (*ladrão*) thief

ladroagem [la'drwaʒẽ] (pl **-ns**) F robbery

ladroeira [la'drwejra] F robbery

ladrões [la'drõjs] MPL *de* **ladrão**

ladrona [la'drona] F *de* **ladrão**

lagarta [la'garta] F caterpillar
lagartixa [lagar'tʃiʃa] F gecko
lagarto [la'gartu] M lizard; (*carne*) silverside
lago ['lagu] M lake; (*de jardim*) pond; (*de sangue*) pool
lagoa [la'goa] F pool, pond; (*lago*) lake
lagosta [la'gosta] F lobster
lagostim [lagos'tʃi] (*pl* **-ns**) M crayfish
lágrima ['lagrima] F tear; **~s de crocodilo** crocodile tears; **chorar ~s de sangue** to cry bitterly
laguna [la'guna] F lagoon
laia ['laja] F kind, sort, type
laico, -a ['lajku, a] ADJ (*pessoa*) lay; (*ensino etc*) secular
laivos ['lajvus] MPL hints, traces
laje ['laʒi] F paving stone, flagstone
lajear [la'ʒjar] VT to pave
lajedo [la'ʒedu] M rock
lajota [la'ʒota] F paving stone
lama ['lama] F mud; **tirar alguém da ~** (*fig*) to rescue sb from poverty
lamaçal [lama'saw] (*pl* **-ais**) M quagmire; (*pântano*) bog, marsh
lamaceiro [lama'sejru] M = **lamaçal**
lamacento, -a [lama'sẽtu, a] ADJ muddy
lambança [lã'bãsa] F mess
lambão, -bona [lã'bãw, 'bona] (*pl* **-ões/-s**) ADJ (*guloso*) greedy; (*no trabalho*) sloppy; (*lambuzado*) messy; (*tolo*) idiotic
lamber [lã'ber] VT to lick; **de ~ os beiços** (*comida*) delicious
lambida [lã'bida] F lick; **dar uma ~ em algo** to lick sth
lambido, -a [lã'bidu, a] ADJ (*cara*) without make-up; (*cabelo*) plastered down
lambiscar [lãbis'kar] VT, VI to nibble
lambisgoia [lãbiz'gɔja] F haggard person
lambões [lã'bõjs] MPL *de* **lambão**
lambona [lã'bona] F *de* **lambão**
lambreta [lã'breta] F scooter
lambri [lã'bri] M, **lambris** [lã'bris] MPL panelling *sg* (BRIT), paneling *sg* (US)
lambuja [lã'buʒa] F start, advantage
lambujem [lã'buʒẽ] (*pl* **-ns**) F start, advantage
lambuzar [lãbu'zar] VT to smear
lambuzeira [lãbu'zejra] F sticky mess
lamentação [lamẽta'sãw] (*pl* **-ões**) F lamentation
lamentar [lamẽ'tar] VT to lament; (*sentir*) to regret; **lamentar-se** VR: **~-se (de algo)** to lament (sth); **~ (que)** to be sorry (that)
lamentável [lamẽ'tavew] (*pl* **-eis**) ADJ regrettable; (*deplorável*) deplorable
lamentavelmente [lamẽtavew'mẽtʃi] ADV regrettably
lamento [la'mẽtu] M lament; (*gemido*) moan
lamentoso, -a [lamẽ'tozu, ɔza] ADJ (*voz, som*) sorrowful; (*lamentável*) lamentable
lâmina ['lamina] F (*chapa*) sheet; (*placa*) plate; (*de faca*) blade; (*de persiana*) slat
laminado, -a [lami'nadu, a] ADJ laminated ▶ M laminate

laminar [lami'nar] VT to laminate
lâmpada ['lãpada] F lamp; (*tb:* **lâmpada elétrica**) light bulb; **~ de mesa** table lamp; **~ fluorescente** fluorescent light
lamparina [lãpa'rina] F lamp
lampejante [lãpe'ʒãtʃi] ADJ flashing, glittering
lampejar [lãpe'ʒar] VI to glisten, flash ▶ VT to give off
lampejo [lã'peʒu] M flash
lampião [lã'pjãw] (*pl* **-ões**) M lantern; (*de rua*) street lamp
lamúria [la'murja] F whining, lamentation; (*col, pej*) sob story
lamuriante [lamu'rjãtʃi] ADJ whining
lamuriar-se [lamu'rjarsi] VR: **~ de algo** to moan about sth
lança ['lãsa] F lance, spear
lançadeira [lãsa'dejra] F shuttle
lançador, a [lãsa'dor(a)] M/F (*Esporte*) thrower; (*em leilão*) bidder; (*Com*) company or person launching a product
lançamento [lãsa'mẽtu] M throwing; (*Com: em livro*) entry; (*Náut, Com: de produto, campanha*) launch; (*Com: de disco, filme*) release; **novo ~** (*livro*) new title; (*filme, disco*) new release; (*produto*) new product; **~ do dardo** (*Esporte*) javelin; **~ do disco** (*Esporte*) discus; **~ do martelo** (*Esporte*) hammer
lança-perfume (*pl* **lança-perfumes**) M ether spray (*used as a drug in carnival*)
lançar [lã'sar] VT to throw; (*navio, produto, campanha*) to launch; (*disco, filme*) to release; (*Com: em livro*) to enter; (*em leilão*) to bid; (*imposto*) to assess; **lançar-se** VR to throw o.s.; **~ ações no mercado** to float shares on the market; **~ mão de algo** to make use of sth
lance ['lãsi] M (*arremesso*) throw; (*incidente*) incident; (*história*) story; (*situação*) position; (*fato*) fact; (*Esporte: jogada*) shot; (*em leilão*) bid; (*de escada*) flight; (*de casas*) row; (*episódio*) moment; (*de muro, estrada*) stretch
lancha ['lãʃa] F launch; (*col: sapato, pé*) clodhopper; **~ torpedeira** torpedo boat
lanchar [lã'ʃar] VI to have a snack ▶ VT to have as a snack
lanche ['lãʃi] M snack
lanchonete [lãʃo'netʃi] (BR) F snack bar
lancinante [lãsi'nãtʃi] ADJ (*dor*) stabbing; (*grito*) piercing
langanho [lã'gaɲu] M rake
languidez [lãgi'dez] F languor, listlessness
lânguido, -a ['lãgidu, a] ADJ languid, listless
lanhar [la'ɲar] VT to slash, gash; (*peixe*) to gut; **lanhar-se** VR to cut o.s.
lanho ['laɲu] M slash, gash
LAN house [lã'hawzi] F internet café
lanígero, -a [la'niʒeru, a] ADJ (*gado*) wool-producing; (*planta*) downy
lanolina [lano'lina] F lanolin
lantejoula [lãte'ʒola] F sequin
lanterna [lã'terna] F lantern; (*portátil*) torch (BRIT), flashlight (US)

lanternagem [lāter'naʒē] (pl **-ns**) F (Auto) panel-beating; (oficina) body shop
lanterneiro, -a [lāter'nejru, a] M/F panel-beater
lanterninha [lāter'niɲa] (BR) M/F usher(ette)
lanugem [la'nuʒē] F down, fluff
Laos ['laws] M: **o ~** Laos
lapão, -pona [la'pãw, 'pɔna] (pl **-ões/-s**) ADJ, M/F Lapp
lapela [la'pɛla] F lapel
lapidador, a [lapida'dor(a)] M/F cutter
lapidar [lapi'dar] VT (joias) to cut; (fig) to polish, refine ▶ ADJ (fig) masterful
lápide ['lapidʒi] F (tumular) tombstone; (comemorativa) memorial stone
lápis ['lapis] M INV pencil; **escrever a ~** to write in pencil; **~ de cor** coloured (BRIT) ou colored (US) pencil, crayon; **~ de olho** eyebrow pencil
lapiseira [lapi'zejra] F propelling (BRIT) ou mechanical (US) pencil; (caixa) pencil case
lápis-lazúli [-la'zuli] M lapis-lazuli
lapões [la'põjs] MPL de **lapão**
lapona [la'pɔna] F de **lapão**
Lapônia [la'ponja] F: **a ~** Lappland
lapso ['lapsu] M lapse; (de tempo) interval; (erro) slip
laquê [la'ke] M lacquer
laquear [la'kjar] VT to lacquer
lar [lar] M home
laranja [la'rãʒa] ADJ INV orange ▶ F orange ▶ M (cor) orange
laranjada [larã'ʒada] F orangeade
laranjal [larã'ʒaw] (pl **-ais**) M orange grove
laranjeira [larã'ʒejra] F orange tree
larápio [la'rapju] M thief
lardo ['lardu] M bacon
lareira [la'rejra] F hearth, fireside
larga ['larga] F: **à ~** lavishly; **dar ~s a** to give free rein to; **viver à ~** to lead a lavish life
largada [lar'gada] F start; **dar a ~** to start; (fig) to make a start
largado, -a [lar'gadu, a] ADJ spurned; (no vestir) scruffy
largar [lar'gar] VT (soltar) to let go of, release; (deixar) to leave; (deixar cair) to drop; (risada) to let out; (velas) to unfurl; (piada) to tell; (pôr em liberdade) to let go ▶ VI (Náut) to set sail; **largar-se** VR (desprender-se) to free o.s.; (ir-se) to go off; (pôr-se) to proceed; **ele não a larga** ou **não larga dela um instante** he won't leave her alone for a moment; **me larga!** leave me alone!; **~ a mão em alguém** to wallop sb; **~ de fazer** to stop doing; **largue de besteira** stop being stupid
largo, -a ['largu, a] ADJ wide, broad; (amplo) extensive; (roupa) loose, baggy; (conversa) long ▶ M (praça) square; (alto-mar) open sea; **ao ~** at a distance, far off; **fazer-se ao ~** to put out to sea; **passar de ~ sobre um assunto** to gloss over a subject; **passar ao ~ de algo** (fig) to sidestep sth
larguei etc [lar'gej] VB ver **largar**

largueza [lar'geza] F largesse
largura [lar'gura] F width, breadth
laringe [la'rĩʒi] F larynx
laringite [larĩ'ʒitʃi] F laryngitis
larva ['larva] F larva, grub
lasanha [la'zaɲa] F lasagna
lasca ['laska] F (de madeira, metal) splinter; (de pedra) chip; (fatia) slice
lascado, -a [las'kadu, a] (col) ADJ in a hurry ou rush
lascar [las'kar] VT to chip; (pergunta) to throw in; (tapa) to let go ▶ VI to chip; **ser** ou **estar de ~** to be horrible
lascívia [la'sivja] F lewdness
lascivo, -a [la'sivu, a] ADJ lewd; (movimentos) sensual
laser ['lejzer] M laser; **raio ~** laser beam
lassidão [lasi'dãw] F lassitude, weariness
lassitude [lasi'tudʒi] F lassitude, weariness
lasso, -a ['lasu, a] ADJ lax; (cansado) weary
lástima ['lastʃima] F pity, compassion; (infortúnio) misfortune; **é uma ~ (que)** it's a shame (that)
lastimar [lastʃi'mar] VT to lament; **lastimar-se** VR to complain, feel sorry for o.s.
lastimável [lastʃi'mavew] (pl **-eis**) ADJ lamentable
lastimoso, -a [lastʃi'mozu, ɔza] ADJ (lamentável) pitiful; (plangente) mournful
lastro ['lastru] M ballast
lata ['lata] F can, tin (BRIT); (material) tin-plate; **~ de lixo** rubbish bin (BRIT), garbage can (US); **~ velha** (col: carro) old banger (BRIT) ou clunker (US)
latada [la'tada] F trellis
latão [la'tãw] M brass
lataria [lata'ria] F (Auto) bodywork; (enlatados) canned food
látego ['lategu] M whip
latejante [late'ʒãtʃi] ADJ throbbing
latejar [late'ʒar] VI to throb
latejo [la'teʒu] M throbbing, beat
latente [la'tẽtʃi] ADJ latent, hidden
lateral [late'raw] (pl **-ais**) ADJ side, lateral ▶ F (Futebol) sideline ▶ M (Futebol) throw-in
látex ['lateks] M INV latex
laticínio [latʃi'sinju] M = **lacticínio**
latido [la'tʃidu] M bark(ing), yelp(ing)
latifundiário, -a [latʃifũ'dʒjarju, a] ADJ land-owning ▶ M/F landowner
latifúndio [latʃi'fũdʒju] M large estate
latim [la'tʃi] M (Ling) Latin; **gastar o seu ~** to waste one's breath
latino, -a [la'tʃinu, a] ADJ Latin
latino-americano, -a ADJ, M/F Latin-American
latir [la'tʃir] VI to bark, yelp
latitude [latʃi'tudʒi] F latitude; (largura) breadth; (fig) scope
lato, -a ['latu, a] ADJ broad
latrina [la'trina] F latrine
latrocínio [latro'sinju] M armed robbery
lauda ['lawda] F page

laudatório, -a [lawda'tɔrju, a] ADJ laudatory
laudo ['lawdu] M (Jur) decision; (resultados) findings pl; (peça escrita) report
laureado, -a [law'rjadu, a] ADJ honoured (BRIT), honored (US) ▶ M laureate
laurear [law'rjar] VT to honour (BRIT), honor (US)
laurel [law'rɛw] (pl **-éis**) M laurel wreath; (fig) prize, reward
lauto, -a ['lawtu, a] ADJ sumptuous; (abundante) lavish, abundant
lava ['lava] F lava
lavabo [la'vabu] M toilet
lavadeira [lava'dejra] F washerwoman
lavadora [lava'dora] F washing machine
lavadouro [lava'doru] M washing place
lavagem [la'vaʒẽ] F washing; **~ a seco** dry cleaning; **~ cerebral** brainwashing; **dar uma ~ em alguém** (col: Esporte) to thrash sb
lavanda [la'vãda] F (Bot) lavender; (colônia) lavender water; (para lavar os dedos) finger bowl
lavanderia [lavãde'ria] F laundry; (aposento) laundry room
lavar [la'var] VT to wash; (culpa) to wash away; **~ a seco** to dry clean; **~ a égua** (col: Esporte) to win hands down; **~ as mãos de algo** (fig) to wash one's hands of sth
lavatório [lava'tɔrju] M washbasin; (aposento) toilet
lavoura [la'vora] F tilling; (agricultura) farming; (terreno) plantation
lavra ['lavra] F ploughing (BRIT), plowing (US); (de minerais) mining; (mina) mine; **ser da ~ de** to be the work of
lavradio, -a [lavra'dʒiu, a] ADJ workable, arable ▶ M farming
lavrador, a [lavra'dor(a)] M/F farmhand, farm labourer (BRIT) ou laborer (US)
lavrar [la'vrar] VT to work; (esculpir) to carve; (redigir) to draw up
laxante [la'ʃãtʃi] ADJ, M laxative
laxativo, -a [laʃa'tʃivu, a] ADJ, M laxative
lazer [la'zer] M leisure
LBA ABR F (= Legião Brasileira de Assistência) charity
LBC (BR) ABR F = **Letra do Banco Central**
leal [le'aw] (pl **-ais**) ADJ loyal
lealdade [leaw'dadʒi] F loyalty
leão [le'ãw] (pl **-ões**) M lion; **L~** (Astrologia) Leo; **o L~** (BR: fisco) ≈ the Inland Revenue (BRIT), the IRS (US); **~ de chácara** bouncer
lebre ['lɛbri] F hare
lecionar [lesjo'nar] VT, VI to teach
lecitina [lesi'tʃina] F lecithin
legação [lega'sãw] (pl **-ões**) F legation
legado [le'gadu] M envoy, legate; (herança) legacy, bequest
legal [le'gaw] ADJ legal, lawful; (col) fine; (: pessoa) nice ▶ ADV (col) well; **(tá) ~!** OK!
legalidade [legali'dadʒi] F legality, lawfulness
legalização [legaliza'sãw] F legalization; (de documento) authentication

legalizar [legali'zar] VT to legalize; (documento) to authenticate
legar [le'gar] VT to bequeath, leave
legatário, -a [lega'tarju, a] M/F legatee
legenda [le'ʒẽda] F inscription; (texto explicativo) caption; (Cinema) subtitle; (Pol) party
legendado, -a [leʒẽ'dadu, a] ADJ (filme) subtitled
legendário, -a [leʒẽ'darju, a] ADJ legendary
legião [le'ʒjãw] (pl **-ões**) F legion; **a L~ Estrangeira** the Foreign Legion
legionário, -a [leʒjo'narju, a] ADJ legionary ▶ M legionary
legislação [leʒizla'sãw] F legislation
legislador, a [leʒizla'dor(a)] M/F legislator
legislar [leʒiz'lar] VI to legislate ▶ VT to pass
legislativo, -a [leʒizla'tʃivu, a] ADJ legislative ▶ M legislature
legislatura [leʒizla'tura] F legislature; (período) term of office
legista [le'ʒista] ADJ: **médico ~** expert in medical law ▶ M/F legal expert; (médico) expert in medical law
legitimar [leʒitʃi'mar] VT to legitimize; (justificar) to legitimate; (filho) to legally adopt
legitimidade [leʒitʃimi'dadʒi] F legitimacy
legítimo, -a [le'ʒitʃimu, a] ADJ legitimate; (justo) rightful; (autêntico) genuine; **legítima defesa** self-defence (BRIT), self-defense (US)
legível [le'ʒivew] ADJ legible, readable; **~ por máquina** machine readable
légua ['lɛgwa] F league
legume [le'gumi] M vegetable
lei [lej] F law; (regra) rule; (metal) standard; **prata de ~** sterling silver; **ditar a ~** to lay down the law
leiaute [lej'awtʃi] M layout
leigo, -a ['lejgu, a] ADJ (Rel) lay, secular ▶ M layman; **ser ~ em algo** (fig) to be no expert at sth, be unversed in sth
leilão [lej'lãw] (pl **-ões**) M auction; **vender em ~** to sell by auction, auction off
leiloamento [lejlwa'mẽtu] M auctioning
leiloar [lej'lwar] VT to auction
leiloeiro, -a [lej'lwejru, a] M/F auctioneer
leilões [lej'lõjs] MPL de **leilão**
leio etc ['leju] VB ver **ler**
leitão, -toa [lej'tãw, 'toa] (pl **-ões/-s**) M/F sucking (BRIT) ou suckling (US) pig
leite ['lejtʃi] M milk; **~ em pó** powdered milk; **~ desnatado** ou **magro** skimmed milk; **~ de magnésia** milk of magnesia; **~ condensado/evaporado** condensed/evaporated milk; **~ de onça** milk with cachaça; **~ de vaca** cow's milk; **~ semidesnatado** semi-skimmed milk
leiteira [lej'tejra] F (para ferver) milk pan; (para servir) milk jug; ver tb **leiteiro**
leiteiro, -a [lej'tejru, a] ADJ (vaca, gado) dairy; (trem) milk atr ▶ M/F milkman/woman
leiteria [lejte'ria] F dairy

leito ['lejtu] M bed
leitoa [lej'toa] F *de* **leitão**
leitões [lej'tõjs] MPL *de* **leitão**
leitor, a [lej'tor(a)] M/F (*pessoa*) reader; (*professor*) lector ▶ M (*objeto*) reader; **~ de livros digitais** e-reader
leitoso, -a [lej'tozu, ɔza] ADJ milky
leitura [lej'tura] F reading; (*livro etc*) reading matter; **pessoa de muita ~** well-read person; **~ dinâmica** speed reading
lelé [le'lɛ] (*col*) ADJ nuts, crazy; **~ da cuca** out of one's mind
lema ['lɛma] M motto; (*Pol*) slogan
lembrança [lẽ'brãsa] F recollection, memory; (*presente*) souvenir; **lembranças** FPL (*recomendações*): **~s a sua mãe!** regards to your mother!
lembrar [lẽ'brar] VT, VI to remember; **lembrar-se** VR: **~(-se) de** to remember; **~(-se) (de) que** to remember that; **~ algo a alguém, ~ alguém de algo** to remind sb of sth; **~ alguém de que, ~ a alguém que** to remind sb that; **esta rua lembra a rua onde eu ...** this street reminds me of the street where I ...; **ele lembra meu irmão** he reminds me of my brother, he is like my brother
lembrete [lẽ'bretʃi] M reminder
leme ['lɛmi] M rudder; (*Náut*) helm; (*fig*) control
lenço ['lẽsu] M handkerchief; (*de pescoço*) scarf; (*de cabeça*) headscarf; **~ de papel** tissue; **~ umedecido** baby wipe
lençol [lẽ'sɔw] (*pl* **-óis**) M sheet; **estar em maus lençóis** to be in a fix; **~ de água** water table
lenda ['lẽda] F legend; (*fig: mentira*) lie
lendário, -a [lẽ'darju, a] ADJ legendary
lengalenga [lẽga'lẽga] F rigmarole
lenha ['lɛɲa] F firewood; **fazer ~** (*de carro*) to have a race; **meter a ~ em alguém** (*col: surrar*) to give sb a beating; (: *criticar*) to run sb down; **ser uma ~** (*col*) to be tough; **botar ~ na fogueira** (*fig*) to fan the flames, make things worse
lenhador [leɲa'dor] M woodcutter
lenho ['lɛɲu] M (*tora*) log; (*material*) timber
leninista [leni'nista] ADJ, M/F Leninist
lenitivo, -a [leni'tʃivu, a] ADJ soothing ▶ M palliative; (*fig: alívio*) relief
lenocínio [leno'sinju] M living off immoral earnings
lente ['lẽtʃi] F lens *sg*; **~ de aumento** magnifying glass; **~s de contato** contact lenses
lentidão [lẽtʃi'dãw] F slowness
lentilha [lẽ'tʃiʎa] F lentil
lento, -a ['lẽtu, a] ADJ slow
leoa [le'oa] F lioness
leões [le'õjs] MPL *de* **leão**
leopardo [ljo'pardu] M leopard
lépido, -a ['lɛpidu, a] ADJ (*alegre*) sprightly, bright; (*ágil*) nimble, agile

leporino, -a [lepo'rinu, a] ADJ: **lábio ~** hare lip
lepra ['lɛpra] F leprosy
leprosário [lepro'zarju] M leprosy hospital
leproso, -a [le'prozu, ɔza] ADJ leprous ▶ M/F leper
leque ['lɛki] M fan; (*fig*) array
LER ABR F (= *lesão por esforço repetitivo*) RSI
ler [ler] VT, VI to read; **~ a sorte de alguém** to tell sb's fortune; **~ nas entrelinhas** (*fig*) to read between the lines
lerdeza [ler'deza] F sluggishness
lerdo, -a ['lɛrdu, a] ADJ slow, sluggish
lero-lero [lɛru'lɛru] (*col*) M chit-chat, idle talk
lés [lɛs] (PT) M: **de ~ a ~** from one end to the other
lesão [le'zãw] (*pl* **-ões**) F harm, injury; (*Jur*) violation; (*Med*) lesion; **~ corporal** (*Jur*) bodily harm; **~ por esforço repetitivo** repetitive strain injury
lesar [le'zar] VT to harm, damage; (*direitos*) to violate; **~ alguém** (*financeiramente*) to leave sb short; **~ o fisco** to withhold one's taxes
lesbianismo [lezbja'nizmu] M lesbianism
lésbica ['lɛzbika] F lesbian
lesco-lesco [lɛsku'lɛsku] (*col*) M daily grind; **estar no ~** to be on the go *ou* hard at it
leseira [le'zejra] F lethargy
lesionar [lezjo'nar] VT to injure
lesivo, -a [le'zivu, a] ADJ harmful
lesma ['lezma] F slug; (*fig: pessoa*) slowcoach
lesões [le'zõjs] FPL *de* **lesão**
Lesoto [le'zotu] M: **o ~** Lesotho
lesse *etc* ['lesi] VB *ver* **ler**
leste ['lɛstʃi] M east
letal [le'taw] (*pl* **-ais**) ADJ lethal
letargia [letar'ʒia] F lethargy
letárgico, -a [le'tarʒiku, a] ADJ lethargic
letivo, -a [le'tʃivu, a] ADJ school *atr*; **ano ~** academic year
Letônia [le'tonja] F: **a ~** Latvia
letra ['letra] F letter; (*caligrafia*) handwriting; (*de canção*) lyrics *pl*; **Letras** FPL (*curso*) language and literature; **à ~** literally; **seguir à ~** to follow to the letter; **ao pé da ~** literally, word for word; **fazer** *ou* **tirar algo de ~** (*col*) to take sth in one's stride; **~ de câmbio** (*Com*) bill of exchange; **~ de forma** block letter; **~ de imprensa** print; **~ de médico** (*fig*) scrawl; **~ maiúscula/minúscula** capital/small letter
letrado, -a [le'tradu, a] ADJ learned, erudite ▶ M/F scholar; **ser ~ em algo** to be well-versed in sth
letreiro [le'trejru] M sign, notice; (*inscrição*) inscription; (*Cinema*) subtitle; **~ luminoso** neon sign
leu *etc* [lew] VB *ver* **ler**
léu [lɛw] M: **ao ~** (*à toa*) aimlessly; (*à mostra*) uncovered
leucemia [lewse'mia] F leukaemia (BRIT), leukemia (US)

leva ['lɛva] F (*de pessoas*) group
levadiço, -a [leva'dʒisu, a] ADJ: **ponte levadiça** drawbridge
levado, -a [le'vadu, a] ADJ mischievous; (*criança*) naughty; **~ da breca** naughty
leva e traz [lɛvai'trajz] M/F INV gossip, stirrer
levantador, a [levãta'dor(a)] ADJ lifting
▶ M/F: **~ de pesos** weightlifter
levantamento [levãta'mẽtu] M lifting, raising; (*revolta*) uprising, rebellion; (*arrolamento*) survey; **~ de pesos** weightlifting
levantar [levã'tar] VT to lift, raise; (*voz, capital*) to raise; (*apanhar*) to pick up; (*suscitar*) to arouse; (*ambiente*) to brighten up ▶ VI to stand up; (*da cama*) to get up; (*dar vida*) to brighten; **levantar-se** VR to stand up; (*da cama*) to get up; (*rebelar-se*) to rebel; **~ voo** to take off; **~ a mão** to raise *ou* put up one's hand
levante [le'vãtʃi] M east; (*revolta*) revolt
levar [le'var] VT to take; (*portar*) to carry; (*tempo*) to pass, spend; (*roupa*) to wear; (*lidar com*) to handle; (*induzir*) to lead; (*filme*) to show; (*peça teatral*) to do, put on; (*vida*) to lead ▶ VI to get a beating; **~ a** to lead to; **~ a mal** to take amiss; **~ a cabo** to carry out; **~ adiante** to go ahead with; **~ uma vida feliz** to lead a happy life; **~ a melhor/pior** to get a good/raw deal; **~ pancadas/um susto/uma bronca** to get hit/a fright/told off; **~ a educação a todos** to bring education to all; **deixar-se ~ por** to be carried along by
leve ['lɛvi] ADJ light; (*insignificante*) slight; **de ~** lightly, softly
levedo [le'vedu] M yeast
levedura [leve'dura] F = **levedo**
leveza [le'veza] F lightness
levezinho [leve'ziɲu] ADJ: **de ~** very lightly
leviandade [levjã'dadʒi] F frivolity
leviano, -a [le'vjanu, a] ADJ frivolous
levitação [levita'sãw] F levitation
levitar [levi'tar] VI to levitate
lexical [leksi'kaw] (*pl* -**ais**) ADJ lexical
léxico, -a ['lɛksiku, a] ADJ lexical ▶ M lexicon
lexicografia [leksikogra'fia] F lexicography
lexicógrafo, -a [leksi'kɔgrafu, a] M/F lexicographer
lezíria [le'zirja] (PT) F marshland
LFT (BR) ABR F = **Letra Financeira do Tesouro**
lha [ʎa] = **lhe + a**
lhama ['ʎama] M llama
lhaneza [ʎa'neza] F amiability
lhano, -a ['ʎanu, a] ADJ amiable
lhas [ʎas] = **lhe + as**
lhe [ʎi] PRON (*a ele*) to him; (*a ela*) to her; (*a você*) to you
lhes [ʎis] PRON PL (*a eles/elas*) to them; (*a vocês*) to you
lho [ʎu] = **lhe + o**
lhos [ʎus] = **lhe + os**
lhufas ['ʎufas] (*col*) PRON nothing, bugger all (!)

li *etc* [li] VB *ver* **ler**
lia ['lia] F dregs *pl*, sediment
liame ['ljami] M tie, bond
libanês, -esa [liba'nes, eza] ADJ Lebanese
Líbano ['libanu] M: **o ~** Lebanon
libelo [li'bɛlu] M satire, lampoon; (*Jur*) formal indictment
libélula [li'bɛlula] F dragonfly
liberação [libera'sãw] F liberation
liberal [libe'raw] (*pl* -**ais**) ADJ, M/F liberal
liberalidade [liberali'dadʒi] F liberality
liberalismo [libera'lizmu] M liberalism
liberalização [liberaliza'sãw] F liberalization
liberalizante [liberali'zãtʃi] ADJ liberalizing
liberalizar [liberali'zar] VT to liberalize
liberar [libe'rar] VT to release; (*permitir*) to allow
liberdade [liber'dadʒi] F freedom; **liberdades** FPL (*direitos*) liberties; **estar em ~** to be free; **pôr alguém em ~** to set sb free; **tomar a ~ de fazer** to take the liberty of doing; **tomar ~s com alguém** to take liberties with sb; **~ condicional** probation; **~ de cultos** freedom of worship; **~ de expressão** freedom of expression; **~ de imprensa** press freedom; **~ de palavra** freedom of speech; **~ de pensamento** freedom of thought; **~ sob palavra** parole
Libéria [li'bɛrja] F: **a ~** Liberia
líbero ['liberu] M (*Futebol*) sweeper
libérrimo, -a [li'bɛhimu, a] ADJ SUPERL *de* **livre**
libertação [liberta'sãw] F release
libertador, a [liberta'dor(a)] M/F liberator
libertar [liber'tar] VT to free, release
libertinagem [libertʃi'naʒẽ] F licentiousness, loose living
libertino, -a [liber'tʃinu, a] ADJ loose-living ▶ M/F libertine
liberto, -a [li'bɛrtu, a] PP *de* **libertar**
Líbia ['libja] F: **a ~** Libya
libidinoso, -a [libidʒi'nozu, ɔza] ADJ lecherous, lustful
libido [li'bidu] F libido
líbio, -a ['libju, a] ADJ, M/F Libyan
libra ['libra] F pound; **L~** (*Astrologia*) Libra; **~ esterlina** pound sterling
librar [li'brar] VT to support
libreto [li'bretu] M libretto
libriano, -a [li'brjanu, a] ADJ, M/F Libran
lição [li'sãw] (*pl* -**ões**) F lesson; **que isto lhe sirva de ~** let this be a lesson to you
licença [li'sẽsa] F licence (BRIT), license (US); (*permissão*) permission; (*do trabalho: Mil*) leave; **com ~** excuse me; **estar de ~** to be on leave; **sob ~** under licence; **dá ~?** may I?; **tirar ~** to take leave; **~ poética** poetic licence
licença-prêmio (*pl* **licenças-prêmio**) F long paid leave
licenciado, -a [lisẽ'sjadu, a] M/F graduate
licenciar [lisẽ'sjar] VT to license; **licenciar-se** VR (*Educ*) to graduate; (*ficar de licença*) to take leave; **~ alguém** to give sb leave

licenciatura [lisẽsja'tura] F (*título*) degree; (*curso*) degree course

licencioso, -a [lisẽ'sjozu, ɔza] ADJ licentious

liceu [li'sew] (*PT*) M secondary (*BRIT*) *ou* high (*US*) school

licitação [lisita'sãw] (*pl* -ões) F auction; (*concorrência*) tender; **abrir ~** to put out to tender

licitante [lisi'tãtʃi] M/F bidder

licitar [lisi'tar] VT (*pôr em leilão*) to put up for auction ▶ VI to bid

lícito, -a ['lisitu, a] ADJ (*Jur*) lawful; (*justo*) fair, just; (*permissível*) permissible

lições [li'sõjs] FPL *de* **lição**

licor [li'kor] M liqueur

licoroso, -a [liko'rozu, ɔza] ADJ (*vinho*) fortified

lida ['lida] F toil; (*col: leitura*): **dar uma ~ em** to have a read of

lidar [li'dar] VI: **~ com** (*ocupar-se*) to deal with; (*combater*) to struggle against; **~ em algo** to work in sth

lide ['lidʒi] F (*trabalho*) work, chores *pl*; (*luta*) fight; (*Jur*) case

líder ['lider] M/F leader

liderança [lide'rãsa] F leadership; (*Esporte*) lead

liderar [lide'rar] VT to lead

lido, -a ['lidu, a] PP *de* **ler** ▶ ADJ (*pessoa*) well-read

lifting ['liftĩŋ] (*pl* -s) M face lift

liga ['liga] F league; (*de meias*) suspender (*BRIT*), garter (*US*); (*metal*) alloy

ligação [liga'sãw] (*pl* -ões) F connection; (*fig: de amizade*) bond; (*Tel*) call; (*relação amorosa*) liaison; **fazer uma ~ para alguém** to call sb; **não consigo completar a ~** (*Tel*) I can't get through; **caiu a ~** (*Tel*) I (*ou* he *etc*) was cut off

ligada [li'gada] F (*Tel*) ring, call; **dar uma ~ para alguém** (*col*) to give sb a ring

ligado, -a [li'gadu, a] ADJ (*Tec*) connected; (*luz, rádio etc*) on; (*metal*) alloy; **estar ~ (em)** (*col: absorto*) to be wrapped up (in); (*: em droga*) to be hooked (on); (*afetivamente*) to be attached (to)

ligadura [liga'dura] F bandage; (*Mús*) ligature

ligamento [liga'mẽtu] M ligament

ligar [li'gar] VT to tie, bind; (*unir*) to join, connect; (*luz, TV*) to switch on; (*afetivamente*) to bind together; (*carro*) to start (up) ▶ VI (*telefonar*) to ring; **ligar-se** VR to join; **~-se com alguém** to join with sb; **~-se a algo** to be connected with sth; **~ para alguém** to ring sb up; **~ para fora** to ring out; **~ para** *ou* **a algo** (*dar atenção*) to take notice of sth; (*dar importância*) to care about sth; **eu nem ligo** it doesn't bother me; **não ligo a mínima (para)** I couldn't care less (about)

ligeireza [liʒej'reza] F lightness; (*rapidez*) swiftness; (*agilidade*) nimbleness

ligeiro, -a [li'ʒejru, a] ADJ light; (*ferimento*) slight; (*referência*) passing; (*conhecimentos*) scant; (*rápido*) quick, swift; (*ágil*) nimble ▶ ADV swiftly, nimbly

liguei *etc* [li'gej] VB *ver* **ligar**

lilás [li'las] ADJ, M lilac

lima ['lima] F (*laranja*) type of orange; (*ferramenta*) file; **~ de unhas** nailfile

limão [li'mãw] (*pl* -ões) M lime; (*tb:* **limão-galego**) lemon

limar [li'mar] VT to file

limbo ['lĩbu] M: **estar no ~** to be in limbo

limeira [li'mejra] F lime tree

limiar [li'mjar] M threshold

liminar [limi'nar] F (*Jur*) preliminary verdict

limitação [limita'sãw] (*pl* -ões) F limitation, restriction

limitado, -a [limi'tadu, a] ADJ limited; **ele é meio** *ou* **bem ~** he's not very bright

limitar [limi'tar] VT to limit, restrict; **limitar-se** VR: **~-se a** to limit o.s. with; **~(-se) com** to border on; **ele limitava-se a dizer ...** he did nothing more than say ....

limite [li'mitʃi] M (*de terreno etc*) limit, boundary; (*fig*) limit; **passar dos ~s** to go too far; **~ de crédito** credit limit; **~ de idade** age limit

limo ['limu] M (*Bot*) water weed; (*lodo*) slime

limoeiro [li'mwejru] M lemon tree

limões [li'mõjs] MPL *de* **limão**

limonada [limo'nada] F lemonade (*BRIT*), lemon soda (*US*)

limpa ['lĩpa] (*col*) F clean; (*roubo*): **fazer uma ~ em** to clean out

limpação [lĩpa'sãw] F cleaning

limpador [lĩpa'dor] M: **~ de para-brisa** windscreen wiper (*BRIT*), windshield wiper (*US*)

limpa-pés M INV shoe scraper

limpar [lĩ'par] VT to clean; (*lágrimas, suor*) to wipe away; (*polir*) to shine, polish; (*fig*) to clean up; (*arroz, peixe*) to clean; (*roubar*) to rob

limpa-trilhos M INV cowcatcher

limpeza [lĩ'peza] F cleanliness; (*esmero*) neatness; (*ato*) cleaning; (*fig*) clean-up; (*roubo*): **fazer uma ~ em** to clean out; **~ de pele** facial; **~ pública** rubbish (*BRIT*) *ou* garbage (*US*) collection, sanitation

límpido, -a ['lĩpidu, a] ADJ limpid

limpo, -a ['lĩpu, a] PP *de* **limpar** ▶ ADJ clean; (*céu, consciência*) clear; (*Com*) net, clear; (*fig*) pure; (*col: pronto*) ready; **passar a ~** to make a fair copy; **tirar a ~** to find out the truth about, clear up; **estar ~ com alguém** (*col*) to be in with sb

limusine [limu'zini] F limousine

lince ['lĩsi] M lynx; **ter olhos de ~** to have eyes like a hawk

linchar [lĩ'ʃar] VT to lynch

lindeza [lĩ'deza] F beauty

lindo, -a ['lĩdu, a] ADJ lovely; **~ de morrer** (*col*) stunning

linear [li'njar] ADJ linear

linfático, -a [lĩ'fatʃiku, a] ADJ lymphatic

lingerie [lĩʒe'ri] M lingerie

lingote [lĩ'gɔtʃi] M ingot
língua ['lĩgwa] F tongue; (*linguagem*)
language; **botar a ~ para fora** to stick out
one's tongue; **dar com a ~ nos dentes** to let
the cat out of the bag; **dobrar a ~** to bite
one's tongue; **estar na ponta da ~** to be on
the tip of one's tongue; **ficar de ~ de fora**
(*exausto*) to be pooped; **pagar pela ~** to live to
regret one's words; **saber algo na ponta da
~** to know sth inside out; **ter uma ~
comprida** (*fig*) to have a big mouth; **em ~ da
gente** (*col*) ≈ in plain English; **~ franca**
lingua franca; **~ materna** mother tongue
linguado [lĩ'gwadu] M (*peixe*) sole
linguagem [lĩ'gwaʒẽ] (*pl* **-ns**) F (*tb Comput*)
language; **~ de alto nível** (*Comput*)
high-level language; **~ de máquina** (*Comput*)
machine language; **~ de montagem**
(*Comput*) assembly language; **~ de
programação** (*Comput*) programming
language; **~ corporal** body language
linguajar [lĩgwa'ʒar] M speech, language
linguarudo, -a [lĩgwa'rudu, a] ADJ gossiping
▶ M/F gossip
lingueta [lĩ'gweta] F (*fechadura*) bolt; (*balança*)
pointer
linguiça [lĩ'gwisa] F sausage; **encher ~** (*col*)
to waffle on
linguista [lĩ'gwista] M/F linguist
linguística [lĩ'gwistʃika] F linguistics *sg*
linguístico, -a [lĩ'gwistʃiku, a] ADJ linguistic
linha ['liɲa] F line; (*para costura*) thread;
(*barbante*) string, cord; (*fila*) row; **linhas** FPL
(*carta*) letter *sg*; **as ~s gerais de um projeto**
the outlines of a project; **em ~** in line, in a
row; (*Comput*) on line; **fora de ~** out of
production; **andar na ~** (*fig*) to toe the line;
sair da ~ (*fig*) to step out of line; **comportar-
se com muita ~** to behave very correctly;
manter/perder a ~ to keep/lose one's cool;
o telefone não deu ~ the line was dead;
~ aérea airline; **~ de apoio** (*PT*) helpline;
~ de ataque (*Futebol*) forward line, forwards
pl; **~ de conduta** course of action; **~ de
crédito** (*Com*) credit line; **~ de fogo** firing
line; **~ de mira** sights *pl*; **~ de montagem**
assembly line; **~ de partido** party line; **~ de
saque** (*Tênis*) baseline; **~ férrea** railway
(*BRIT*), railroad (*US*)
linhaça [li'ɲasa] F linseed
linha-dura (*pl* **linhas-duras**) M/F hardliner
linhagem [li'ɲaʒẽ] F lineage
linho ['liɲu] M linen; (*planta*) flax
linóleo [li'nɔlju] M linoleum
lipoaspiração [lipuaspira'sãw] F liposuction
liquefazer [likefa'zer] (*irreg: como* **fazer**) VT to
liquefy
líquen ['likẽ] M lichen
liquidação [likida'sãw] (*pl* **-ões**) F liquidation;
(*em loja*) (clearance) sale; (*de conta*)
settlement; **em ~** on sale; **entrar em ~** to
go into liquidation
liquidante [liki'dãtʃi] M/F liquidator

liquidar [liki'dar] VT to liquidate; (*conta*) to
settle; (*mercadoria*) to sell off; (*assunto*) to lay
to rest ▶ VI (*loja*) to have a sale; **liquidar-se** VR
(*destruir-se*) to be destroyed; **~ (com) alguém**
(*fig: arrasar*) to destroy sb; (: *matar*) to do away
with sb
liquidez [liki'deʒ] F (*Com*) liquidity
liquidificador [likwidʒifika'dor] M liquidizer
liquidificar [likwidʒifi'kar] VT to liquidize
líquido, -a ['likidu, a] ADJ liquid, fluid; (*Com*)
net ▶ M liquid
lira ['lira] F lyre; (*moeda*) lira
lírica ['lirika] F (*Mús*) lyrics *pl*; (*poesia*) lyric
poetry
lírico, -a ['liriku, a] ADJ lyric(al)
lírio ['lirju] M lily
lírio-do-vale (*pl* **lírios-do-vale**) M lily of the
valley
lirismo [li'rizmu] M lyricism
Lisboa [liʒ'boa] N Lisbon
lisboeta [liʒ'bweta] ADJ Lisbon *atr* ▶ M/F
inhabitant *ou* native of Lisbon
liso, -a ['lizu, a] ADJ smooth; (*tecido*) plain;
(*cabelo*) straight; (*col: sem dinheiro*) broke;
estar ~, leso e louco (*col*) to be flat broke
lisonja [li'zõʒa] F flattery
lisonjeador, a [lizõʒja'dor(a)] ADJ flattering
▶ M/F flatterer
lisonjear [lizõ'ʒjar] VT to flatter
lisonjeiro, -a [lizõ'ʒejru, a] ADJ flattering
lista ['lista] F list; (*listra*) stripe; (*PT: menu*)
menu; **~ civil** civil list; **~ negra** blacklist;
~ telefônica telephone directory
listado, -a [li'stadu, a] ADJ = **listrado**
listagem [lis'taʒẽ] (*pl* **-ns**) F (*Comput*) listing
listar [lis'tar] VT to list
listra ['listra] F stripe
listrado, -a [lis'tradu, a] ADJ striped
literal [lite'raw] (*pl* **-ais**) ADJ literal
literário, -a [lite'rarju, a] ADJ literary
literato [lite'ratu] M man of letters
literatura [litera'tura] F literature
Literatura de cordel *see note*

> **Literatura de cordel** is a type of
> literature typical of the north-east of
> Brazil, and published in the form of
> cheaply printed booklets. Their authors
> hang these booklets from wires attached
> to walls in the street so that people can
> look at them. While they do this, the
> authors sing their stories aloud.
> **Literatura de cordel** deals both with
> local events and people, and with
> everyday public life, almost always in
> an irreverent manner.

litigante [litʃi'gãtʃi] M/F (*Jur*) litigant
litigar [litʃi'gar] VT to contend ▶ VI to go to law
litígio [li'tʃiʒju] M (*Jur*) lawsuit; (*contenda*)
dispute
litigioso, -a [litʃi'ʒozu, ɔza] ADJ (*Jur*) disputed
litografia [litogra'fia] F (*processo*) lithography;
(*gravura*) lithograph
litogravura [litogra'vura] F lithograph

litoral [lito'raw] (*pl* **-ais**) ADJ coastal ▶ M coast, seaboard

litorâneo, -a [lito'ranju, a] ADJ coastal

litro ['litru] M litre (*BRIT*), liter (*US*)

Lituânia [li'twanja] F: **a ~** Lithuania

liturgia [litur'ʒia] F liturgy

litúrgico, -a [li'turʒiku, a] ADJ liturgical

lívido, -a ['lividu, a] ADJ livid

living ['livĩ] (*pl* **-s**) M living room

livramento [livra'mẽtu] M release; **~ condicional** parole

livrar [li'vrar] VT to release, liberate; (*salvar*) to save; **livrar-se** VR to escape; **~-se de** to get rid of; (*compromisso*) to get out of; **Deus me livre!** Heaven forbid!

livraria [livra'ria] F bookshop (*BRIT*), bookstore (*US*)

livre ['livri] ADJ free; (*lugar*) unoccupied; (*desimpedido*) clear, open; **~ de impostos** tax-free; **estar ~ de algo** to be free of sth; **de ~ e espontânea vontade** of one's own free will

livre-arbítrio M free will

livreiro, -a [li'vrejru, a] M/F bookseller

livresco, -a [li'vresku, a] ADJ book *atr*; (*pessoa*) bookish

livrete [li'vretʃi] M booklet

livro ['livru] M book; **~ brochado** paperback; **~ caixa** (*Com*) cash book; **~ de bolso** pocket-sized book; **~ de cabeceira** favo(u)rite book; **~ de cheques** cheque book (*BRIT*), check book (*US*); **~ de consulta** reference book; **~ de cozinha** cookery book (*BRIT*), cookbook (*US*); **~ de mercadorias** stock book; **~ de registro** catalogue (*BRIT*), catalog (*US*); **~ de texto** *ou* **didático** text book; **~ eletrônico** e-book; **~ encadernado** *ou* **de capa dura** hardback

lixa ['liʃa] F sandpaper; (*de unhas*) nailfile; (*peixe*) dogfish

lixadeira [liʃa'dejra] F sander

lixar [li'ʃar] VT to sand; **lixar-se** VR (*col*): **estou me lixando com isso** I couldn't care less about it

lixeira [li'ʃejra] F dustbin (*BRIT*), garbage can (*US*)

lixeiro [li'ʃejru] M dustman (*BRIT*), garbage man (*US*)

lixo ['liʃu] M rubbish, garbage (*US*); **ser um ~** (*col*) to be rubbish; **~ atômico** nuclear waste

Lj. ABR = **loja**

lj. ABR = **loja**

-lo [lu] PRON him; (*você*) you; (*coisa*) it

lobby ['lɔbi] (*pl* **-ies**) M (*Pol*) lobby

lóbi ['lɔbi] M = **lobby**

lobinho [lo'biɲu] M (*Zool*) wolf cub; (*escoteiro*) cub

lobisomem [lobi'somẽ] (*pl* **-ns**) M werewolf

lobista [lo'bista] M/F lobbyist

lobo ['lobu] M wolf; **~ do mar** old sea dog

lobo-marinho (*pl* **lobos-marinhos**) M sea lion

lobrigar [lobri'gar] VT to glimpse

lóbulo ['lɔbulu] M lobe

locação [loka'sãw] (*pl* **-ões**) F lease; (*de vídeo etc*) rental

locador, a [loka'dor(a)] M/F (*de casa*) landlord; (*de carro, filme*) rental agent ▶ F rental company; **~a de vídeo** video rental shop

local [lo'kaw] (*pl* **-ais**) ADJ local ▶ M site, place ▶ F (*notícia*) story

localidade [lokali'dadʒi] F (*lugar*) locality; (*povoação*) town

localização [lokaliza'sãw] (*pl* **-ões**) F location

localizar [lokali'zar] VT to locate; (*situar*) to place; **localizar-se** VR (*estabelecer-se*) to be located; (*orientar-se*) to get one's bearings

loção [lo'sãw] (*pl* **-ões**) F lotion; **~ após-barba** aftershave (lotion)

locatário, -a [loka'tarju, a] M/F (*de casa*) tenant; (*de carro, filme*) hirer

locaute [lo'kawtʃi] M lockout

loções [lo'sõjs] FPL *de* **loção**

locomoção [lokomo'sãw] (*pl* **-ões**) F locomotion

locomotiva [lokomo'tʃiva] F railway (*BRIT*) *ou* railroad (*US*) engine, locomotive

locomover-se [lokomo'versi] VR to move around

locução [loku'sãw] (*pl* **-ões**) F (*Ling*) phrase; (*dicção*) diction

locutor, a [loku'tor(a)] M/F (*TV, Rádio*) announcer

lodacento, -a [loda'sẽtu, a] ADJ muddy

lodo ['lodu] M (*lama*) mud; (*limo*) slime

lodoso, -a [lo'dozu, ɔza] ADJ (*lamacento*) muddy; (*limoso*) slimy

logaritmo [loga'ritʃimo] M logarithm

lógica ['lɔʒika] F logic

lógico, -a ['lɔʒiku, a] ADJ logical; **(é) ~!** of course!

logística [lo'ʒistʃika] F logistics *sg*

logo ['lɔgu] ADV (*imediatamente*) right away, at once; (*em breve*) soon; (*justamente*) just, right; (*mais tarde*) later; **~, ~** in no time; **~ mais** later; **~ no começo** right at the start; **~ que, tão ~** as soon as; **até ~!** bye!; **~ antes/depois** just before/shortly afterwards; **~ de saída** *ou* **de cara** straightaway, right away

logopedia [logope'dʒia] F speech therapy

logopedista [logope'dʒista] M/F speech therapist

logotipo [logo'tʃipu] M logo

logradouro [logra'doru] M public area

lograr [lo'grar] VT (*alcançar*) to achieve; (*obter*) to get, obtain; (*enganar*) to cheat; **~ fazer** to manage to do

logro ['logru] M fraud

loiro, -a ['lojru, a] ADJ = **louro**

loja ['lɔʒa] F shop; (*maçônica*) lodge; **~ de antiguidades** antique shop; **~ de brinquedos** toy shop; **~ de departamentos** department store; **~ de presentes** gift shop (*BRIT*), gift store (*US*); **~ de produtos naturais** health food shop

lojista [lo'ʒista] M/F shopkeeper

lomba ['lõba] F ridge; (*ladeira*) slope

lombada [lõ'bada] F (de animal) back; (de livro) spine; (na estrada) ramp
lombar [lõ'bar] ADJ lumbar
lombeira [lõ'bejra] F listlessness
lombinho [lõ'biɲu] M (carne) tenderloin
lombo ['lõbu] M back; (carne) loin
lombriga [lõ'briga] F ringworm
lona ['lɔna] F canvas; **estar na última ~** (col) to be broke
Londres ['lõdris] N London
londrino, -a [lõ'drinu, a] ADJ London atr ▶ M/F Londoner
longa-metragem (pl longas-metragens) M: **(filme de) ~** feature (film)
longe ['lõʒi] ADV far, far away ▶ ADJ distant; **ao ~** in the distance; **de ~** from far away; (sem dúvida) by a long way; **~ dos olhos, ~ do coração** out of sight, out of mind; **~ de** a long way ou far from; **~ disso** far from it; **ir ~ demais** (fig) to go too far; **essa sua mania vem de ~** he's had this habit for a long time; **ver ~** (fig) to have vision
longevidade [lõʒevi'dadʒi] F longevity
longínquo, -a [lõ'ʒĩkwu, a] ADJ distant, remote
longíquo, -a [lõ'ʒikwu, a] ADJ = **longínquo**
longitude [lõʒi'tudʒi] F (Geo) longitude
longitudinal [lõʒitudʒi'naw] (pl **-ais**) ADJ longitudinal
longo, -a ['lõgu, a] ADJ long ▶ M (vestido) long dress, evening dress; **ao ~ de** along, alongside
lontra ['lõtra] F otter
loquacidade [lokwasi'dadʒi] F loquacity
loquaz [lo'kwaz] ADJ talkative
lorde ['lɔrdʒi] M lord
lorota [lo'rɔta] (col) F fib
losango [lo'zãgu] M lozenge, diamond
lotação [lota'sãw] F capacity; (vinho) blending; (de funcionários) complement; (BR: ônibus) bus; **~ completa** ou **esgotada** (Teatro) sold out
lotado, -a [lo'tadu, a] ADJ (Teatro) full; (ônibus) full up; (bar, praia) packed, crowded
lotar [lo'tar] VT to fill, pack; (funcionário) to place ▶ VI to fill up
lote ['lɔtʃi] M (porção) portion, share; (em leilão) lot; (terreno) plot; (de ações) parcel, batch
loteamento [lotʃja'mẽtu] M division into lots
lotear [lo'tʃjar] VT to divide into lots
loteca [lo'tɛka] (col) F pools pl (BRIT), lottery (US)
loteria [lote'ria] F lottery; **ganhar na ~** to win the lottery; **~ esportiva** football pools pl (BRIT), lottery (US)
loto¹ ['lɔtu] M lotus
loto² ['lɔtu] M bingo
lótus ['lɔtus] M INV lotus
louça ['losa] F china; (conjunto) crockery; (tb: **louça sanitária**) bathroom suite; **de ~** china atr; **~ de barro** earthenware; **~ de jantar** dinner service; **lavar a ~** to do the washing up (BRIT) ou the dishes

louçaria [losa'ria] F china; (loja) china shop
louco, -a ['loku, a] ADJ crazy, mad; (sucesso) runaway; (frio) freezing ▶ M/F lunatic; **~ varrido** raving mad; **~ de fome/raiva** ravenous/hopping mad; **~ por** crazy about; **deixar alguém ~** to drive sb crazy; **ser uma coisa de ~** (col) to be really something; **estar/ficar ~ da vida (com)** to be/get mad (at); **~ de pedra** (col) stark staring mad; **deu uma louca nele e ...** something strange came over him and ...; **cada ~ com sua mania** whatever turns you on
loucura [lo'kura] F madness; (ato) crazy thing; **ser ~ (fazer)** to be crazy (to do); **ser uma ~** to be crazy; (col: ser muito bom) to be fantastic; **ter ~ por** to be crazy about
louquice [lo'kisi] F madness; (ato, dito) crazy thing
louro, -a ['loru, a] ADJ blond, fair ▶ M laurel; (Culin) bay leaf; (cor) blondness; (papagaio) parrot; **louros** MPL (fig) laurels
lousa ['loza] F flagstone; (tumular) gravestone; (quadro-negro) blackboard
louva-a-deus ['lova-] M INV praying mantis
louvação [lova'sãw] (pl **-ões**) F praise
louvar [lo'var] VT, VI: **~ (a)** to praise
louvável [lo'vavew] (pl **-eis**) ADJ praiseworthy
louvor [lo'vor] M praise
LP ABR M LP (record)
lpm ABR (= linhas por minuto) lpm
Ltda. ABR (= Limitada) Ltd
lua ['lua] F moon; **estar** ou **viver no mundo da ~** to have one's head in the clouds; **estar de ~** (col) to be in a mood; **ser de ~** (col) to be moody; **~ cheia/nova** full/new moon; **~ de mel** honeymoon
Luanda ['lwãda] N Luanda
luar ['lwar] M moonlight; **banhado de ~** moonlit
luarento, -a [lwa'rẽtu, a] ADJ moonlit
lubrificação [lubrifika'sãw] (pl **-ões**) F lubrication
lubrificante [lubrifi'kãtʃi] M lubricant ▶ ADJ lubricating
lubrificar [lubrifi'kar] VT to lubricate
lucidez [lusi'dez] F lucidity, clarity
lúcido, -a ['lusidu, a] ADJ lucid
lúcio ['lusju] M (peixe) pike
lucrar [lu'krar] VT (tirar proveito) to profit from ou by; (dinheiro) to make; (gozar) to enjoy ▶ VI to make a profit; **~ com** ou **em** to profit by
lucratividade [lukratʃivi'dadʒi] F profitability
lucrativo, -a [lukra'tʃivu, a] ADJ lucrative, profitable
lucro ['lukru] M gain; (Com) profit; **~ bruto/líquido** (Com) gross/net profit; **participação nos ~s** (Com) profit-sharing; **~s e perdas** (Com) profit and loss
lucubração [lukubra'sãw] (pl **-ões**) F meditation, pondering
ludibriar [ludʒi'brjar] VT (enganar) to dupe, deceive; (escarnecer) to mock, deride

lúdico, -a ['ludʒiku, a] ADJ playful
lufada [lu'fada] F gust (of wind)
lugar [lu'gar] M place; (*espaço*) space, room; (*para sentar*) seat; (*emprego*) job; (*ocasião*) opportunity; **em ~ de** instead of; **dar ~ a** (*causar*) to give rise to; **~ comum** commonplace; **em primeiro ~** in the first place; **em algum/nenhum/todo ~** somewhere/nowhere/everywhere; **em outro ~** somewhere else, elsewhere; **ter ~** (*acontecer*) to take place; **ponha-se em meu ~** put yourself in my place; **ponha-se no seu ~** don't get ideas above your station; **ele foi no meu ~** he went instead of me *ou* in my place; **tirar o primeiro ~** to come first; **conhecer o seu ~** to know one's place; **~ de nascimento** place of birth
lugarejo [luga'reʒu] M village
lúgubre ['lugubri] ADJ mournful; (*escuro*) gloomy
lula ['lula] F squid
lumbago [lũ'bagu] M lumbago
lume ['lumi] M fire; (*luz*) light
luminária [lumi'narja] F lamp; **luminárias** FPL (*iluminações*) illuminations
luminosidade [luminozi'dadʒi] F brightness
luminoso, -a [lumi'nozu, ɔza] ADJ luminous; (*fig: raciocínio*) clear; (: *ideia, talento*) brilliant; (*letreiro*) illuminated
lunar [lu'nar] ADJ lunar ▶ M (*na pele*) mole
lunático, -a [lu'natʃiku, a] ADJ mad
luneta [lu'neta] F eye-glass; (*telescópio*) telescope
lupa ['lupa] F magnifying glass
lúpulo ['lupulu] M (*Bot*) hop
lusco-fusco ['lusku-] M twilight
lusitano, -a [luzi'tanu, a] ADJ Portuguese, Lusitanian
luso, -a ['luzu, a] ADJ Portuguese
luso-brasileiro, -a (*pl* **luso-brasileiros**) ADJ Luso-Brazilian
lustra-móveis ['lustra-] M INV furniture polish
lustrar [lus'trar] VT to polish, clean
lustre ['lustri] M gloss, sheen; (*fig*) lustre (*BRIT*), luster (*US*); (*luminária*) chandelier

lustroso, -a [lus'trozu, ɔza] ADJ shiny
luta ['luta] F fight, struggle; **~ armada** armed combat; **~ de boxe** boxing; **~ de classes** class struggle; **~ livre** wrestling; **foi uma ~ convencê-lo** it was a struggle to convince him
lutador, a [luta'dor(a)] M/F fighter; (*atleta*) wrestler
lutar [lu'tar] VI to fight, struggle; (*luta livre*) to wrestle ▶ VT (*caratê, judô*) to do; **~ contra/por algo** to fight against/for sth; **~ para fazer algo** to fight *ou* struggle to do sth; **~ com** (*dificuldades*) to struggle against; (*competir*) to fight with
luto ['lutu] M mourning; (*tristeza*) grief; **de ~** in mourning; **pôr ~** to go into mourning
luva ['luva] F glove; **luvas** FPL (*pagamento*) payment *sg*; (*ao locador*) fee *sg*; **caber como uma ~** to fit like a glove
luxação [luʃa'sãw] (*pl* **-ões**) F dislocation
luxar [lu'ʃar] VI to show off
Luxemburgo [luʃē'burgu] M: **o ~** Luxembourg
luxento, -a [lu'ʃētu, a] ADJ fussy, finicky
luxo ['luʃu] M luxury; **de ~** luxury *atr*; **dar-se ao ~ de** to allow o.s. to; **poder dar-se ao ~ de** to be able to afford to; **cheio de ~** (*col*) prissy, finicky; **deixe de ~** (*col*) don't come it; **fazer ~** (*col*) to play hard to get; **com ~** luxurious(ly); (*vestir-se*) fancily
luxuosidade [luʃwozi'dadʒi] F luxuriousness
luxuoso, -a [lu'ʃwozu, ɔza] ADJ luxurious
luxúria [lu'ʃurja] F lust
luxuriante [luʃu'rjãtʃi] ADJ lush
luz [luz] F light; (*eletricidade*) electricity; **à ~ de** by the light of; (*fig*) in the light of; **a meia ~** with subdued lighting; **dar à ~ (um filho)** to give birth (to a son); **deu-me uma ~** I had an idea; **~ artificial/natural** artificial/natural light; **~ de vela** candlelight; **pessoa de muita ~** enlightened person
luzidio, -a [luzi'dʒiu, a] ADJ shining, glossy
luzir [lu'zir] VI to shine, gleam; (*fig*) to be successful
Lx.a ABR = **Lisboa**
Lycra® ['lajkra] F Lycra®

Mm

M, m ['emi] (*pl* **ms**) M M, m; **M de Maria** M for Mike
MA ABR = **Maranhão**
ma [ma] PRON = **me + a**
má [ma] ADJ F *de* **mau**
maca ['maka] F stretcher
maçã [ma'sã] F apple; **~ do rosto** cheekbone
macabro, -a [ma'kabru, a] ADJ macabre
macaca [ma'kaka] F: **estar com a ~** (*col*) to be in a foul mood; *ver tb* **macaco**
macacada [maka'kada] F (*turma*): **a ~** (*família, amigos*) the gang
macacão [maka'kãw] (*pl* **-ões**) M (*de trabalhador*) overalls *pl* (BRIT), coveralls *pl* (US); (*da moda*) jump-suit
macaco, -a [ma'kaku, a] M/F monkey ▶ M (*Mecânica*) jack; (*fato*) ~ (PT) overalls *pl* (BRIT), coveralls *pl* (US); (*pessoa feia*) ugly mug; (*tb:* **macaco de imitação**) copycat; **~ velho** (*fig*) old hand; **~s me mordam** (*col*) blow me down
macacões [maka'kõjs] MPL *de* **macacão**
maçada [ma'sada] F bore
macadame [maka'dami] M asphalt, tarmac (BRIT)
maçador, a [masa'dor(a)] (PT) ADJ boring
macambúzio, -a [makã'buzju, a] ADJ sullen
maçaneta [masa'neta] F knob
maçante [ma'sãtʃi] (BR) ADJ boring
macaquear [maka'kjar] VT to ape
macaquice [maka'kisi] F: **fazer ~s** to clown around
maçar [ma'sar] VT to bore
maçarico [masa'riku] M (*tubo*) blowpipe; (*ave*) curlew
maçaroca [masa'rɔka] F wad
macarrão [maka'hãw] M pasta; (*em forma de canudo*) spaghetti
macarronada [makaho'nada] F pasta with cheese and tomato sauce
macarrônico, -a [maka'honiku, a] ADJ (*francês etc*) broken, halting
Macau [ma'kaw] N Macao
maceioense [masej'wẽsi] ADJ from Maceió ▶ M/F person from Maceió
macerado, -a [mase'radu, a] ADJ (*rosto*) haggard
macerar [mase'rar] VT (*amolecer*) to soften;

(*fig: mortificar*) to mortify; (*: rosto*) to make haggard
macérrimo, -a [ma'sɛhimu, a] ADJ SUPERL *de* **magro**
macete [ma'setʃi] M mallet; (*col*) trick; **dar o ~ a alguém** (*col*) to show sb the way
maceteado, -a [mase'tʃjadu, a] (*col*) ADJ (*plano*) clever; (*casa*) well-designed
machadada [maʃa'dada] F blow with an axe (BRIT) ou ax (US)
machado [ma'ʃadu] M axe (BRIT), ax (US)
machão, -ona [ma'ʃãw, ɔ] (*pl* **-ões/-s**) ADJ tough; (*mulher*) butch ▶ M macho man; (*valentão*) tough guy
machê [ma'ʃe] ADJ: **papel ~** papier-mâché
machete [ma'ʃetʃi] M machete
machismo [ma'ʃizmu] M male chauvinism, machismo; (*col*) toughness
machista [ma'ʃista] ADJ chauvinistic, macho ▶ M male chauvinist
macho [ma'ʃu] ADJ male; (*fig*) virile, manly; (*valentão*) tough ▶ M male; (*Tec*) tap
machões [ma'ʃõjs] MPL *de* **machão**
machona [ma'ʃona] ADJ F *de* **machão** ▶ F butch woman; (*col: ofensivo: lésbica*) dyke (!)
machucado, -a [maʃu'kadu, a] ADJ hurt; (*pé, braço*) bad ▶ M injury; (*área machucada*) sore patch
machucar [maʃu'kar] VT to hurt; (*produzir contusão*) to bruise ▶ VI to hurt; **machucar-se** VR to hurt o.s.; (*col: estrepar-se*) to come a cropper
maciço, -a [ma'sisu, a] ADJ solid; (*espesso*) thick; (*quantidade*) massive ▶ M (*Geo*) massif; **ouro ~** solid gold; **uma dose maciça** a massive dose
macieira [ma'sjejra] F apple tree
maciez [ma'sjez] F softness
macilento, -a [masi'lẽtu, a] ADJ gaunt, haggard
macio, -a [ma'siu, a] ADJ soft; (*liso*) smooth
maciota [ma'sjɔta] F: **na ~** without problems
maço ['masu] M (*de folhas, notas*) bundle; (*de cigarros*) packet
maçom [ma'sõ] (*pl* **-ns**) M (*free*)mason
maçonaria [masona'ria] F (*free*)masonry
maconha [ma'kɔɲa] F dope; **cigarro de ~** joint

maconhado, -a [mako'ɲadu, a] ADJ stoned
maconheiro, -a [mako'ɲejru, a] (col) M/F
(viciado) dope fiend; (vendedor) dope peddler
maçônico, -a [ma'soniku, a] ADJ masonic;
loja maçônica masonic lodge
maçons [ma'sõs] MPL de **maçom**
má-criação (pl -ões) F rudeness; (ato, dito)
rude thing
macrobiótica [makro'bjɔtʃika] F (dieta)
macrobiotic diet
macrobiótico, -a [makro'bjɔtʃiku, a] ADJ
macrobiotic
macroeconomia [makroekono'mia] F
macroeconomics sg
mácula ['makula] F stain, blemish
macumba [ma'kũba] F ≈ voodoo; (despacho)
macumba offering
macumbeiro, -a [makũ'bejru, a] ADJ ≈ voodoo
atr ▶ M/F follower of macumba
madama [ma'dama] F = **madame**
madame [ma'dami] F (senhora) lady; (col: dona
de casa) lady of the house; (: esposa) missus;
(: de bordel) madame
Madeira [ma'dejra] F: **a ~** Madeira
madeira [ma'dejra] F wood ▶ M Madeira
(wine); **de ~** wooden; **bater na ~** (fig) to
touch (BRIT) ou knock on (US) wood;
~ compensada plywood; **~ de lei** hardwood
madeira-branca (pl **madeiras-brancas**) F
softwood
madeiramento [madejra'mẽtu] M woodwork
madeirense [madej'rẽsi] ADJ, M/F Madeiran
madeiro [ma'dejru] M (lenho) log; (viga) beam
madeixa [ma'dejʃa] F (de cabelo) lock
madona [ma'dɔna] F madonna
madrasta [ma'drasta] F stepmother; (fig)
heartless mother
madre ['madri] F (freira) nun; (superiora)
mother superior
madrepérola [madre'pɛrola] F mother of
pearl
madressilva [madre'siwva] F honeysuckle
Madri [ma'dri] N Madrid
Madrid [ma'drid] (PT) N Madrid
madrinha [ma'driɲa] F godmother; (fig:
patrocinadora) patron
madrugada [madru'gada] F (early) morning;
(alvorada) dawn, daybreak; **duas horas da ~**
two in the morning
madrugador, a [madruga'dor(a)] M/F early
riser; (fig) early bird ▶ ADJ early-rising
madrugar [madru'gar] VI to get up early;
(aparecer cedo) to be early
madurar [madur'ar] VT, VI (fruta) to ripen; (fig)
to mature
madureza [madu'reza] F (de pessoa) maturity
maduro, -a [ma'duro, a] ADJ (fruta) ripe; (fig)
mature; (: prudente) prudent
mãe [mãj] F mother; **~ adotiva** ou **de criação**
adoptive mother; **~ de família** wife and
mother; **~ de santo** voodoo priestess
mãe-benta (pl **mães-bentas**) F (Culin) coconut
cookie

MAer (BR) ABR M = **Ministério da Aeronáutica**
maestria [majs'tria] F mastery; **com ~** in a
masterly way
maestro, -trina [ma'ɛstru, 'trina] M/F
conductor
má-fé F malicious intent
máfia ['mafja] F mafia
mafioso, -a [ma'fjozu, ɔza] ADJ gangsterish
▶ M mobster
mafuá [ma'fwa] M fair; (bagunça) mess
magarefe [maga'refi] (PT) M butcher
magazine [maga'zini] M magazine; (loja)
department store
magia [ma'ʒia] F magic; **~ negra** black
magic
mágica ['maʒika] F magic; (truque) magic
trick; ver tb **mágico**
mágico, -a ['maʒiku, a] ADJ magic ▶ M/F
magician
magistério [maʒis'tɛrju] M (ensino) teaching;
(profissão) teaching profession; (professorado)
teachers pl
magistrado [maʒis'tradu] M magistrate
magistral [maʒis'traw] (pl -ais) ADJ
magisterial; (fig) masterly
magistratura [maʒistra'tura] F magistracy
magnanimidade [magnanimi'dadʒi] F
magnanimity
magnânimo, -a [mag'nanimu, a] ADJ
magnanimous
magnata [mag'nata] M magnate, tycoon
magnésia [mag'nɛzja] F magnesia
magnésio [mag'nɛzju] M magnesium
magnético, -a [mag'nɛtʃiku, a] ADJ magnetic
magnetismo [magne'tʃizmu] M magnetism
magnetizar [magnetʃi'zar] VT to magnetize;
(fascinar) to mesmerize
magnificência [magnifi'sẽsja] F
magnificence, splendour (BRIT), splendor (US)
magnífico, -a [mag'nifiku, a] ADJ splendid,
magnificent
magnitude [magni'tudʒi] F magnitude
magno, -a ['magnu, a] ADJ (grande) great;
(importante) important
magnólia [mag'nɔlja] F magnolia
mago ['magu] M magician; **os reis ~s** the
Three Wise Men, the Three Kings
mágoa ['magwa] F (tristeza) sorrow, grief;
(fig: desagrado) hurt
magoado, -a [ma'gwadu, a] ADJ hurt
magoar [ma'gwar] VT, VI to hurt; **magoar-se**
VR: **~-se com algo** to be hurt by sth
MAgr (BR) ABR M = **Ministério da Agricultura**
magreza [ma'greza] F slimness; (de carne)
leanness; (fig) meagreness (BRIT),
meagerness (US)
magricela [magri'sɛla] ADJ skinny
magrinho, -a [ma'griɲu, a] ADJ thin
magro, -a ['magru, a] ADJ (pessoa) slim; (carne)
lean; (fig: parco) meagre (BRIT), meager (US);
(leite) skimmed; **ser ~ como um palito** to be
like a beanpole
mai. ABR = **maio**

mainframe [mēj'frejm] M mainframe
maio ['maju] M May; *ver tb* **julho**
maiô [ma'jo] (*BR*) M swimsuit
maionese [majo'nɛzi] F mayonnaise
maior [ma'jɔr] ADJ (*compar: de tamanho*) bigger; (*: de importância*) greater; (*superl: de tamanho*) biggest; (*: de importância*) greatest ▶ M/F adult; **tive a ~ discussão com ela** I had a real argument with her; **foi o ~ barato** (*col*) it was really great; **você não sabe da ~** you'll never guess what; **~ de idade** of age, adult; **~ de 21 anos** over 21; **ser de ~** (*col*) to be of age *ou* grown up; **ser ~ e vacinado** (*col*) to be one's own master
maioral [majo'raw] (*pl* **-ais**) M boss; **o ~** the greatest
Maiorca [maj'ɔrka] F Majorca
maioria [majo'ria] F majority; **a ~ de** most of; **~ absoluta** absolute majority
maioridade [majori'dadʒi] F adulthood; **atingir a ~** to come of age

(PALAVRA-CHAVE)

mais [majs] ADV **1** (*compar*): **mais magro/ inteligente (do que)** thinner/more intelligent (than); **ele trabalha mais (do que eu)** he works more (than me)
2 (*superl*): **o mais ...** the most ...; **o mais magro/inteligente** the thinnest/most intelligent
3 (*negativo*): **ele não trabalha mais aqui** he doesn't work here any more; **nunca mais** never again
4 (*+ adj: valor intensivo*): **que livro mais chato!** what a boring book!
5: **por mais que** however much; **por mais que se esforce ...** no matter how hard you try ...; **por mais que eu quisesse ...** much as I should like to ...
6: **a mais: temos um a mais** we've got one extra
7 (*tempo*): **mais cedo ou mais tarde** sooner or later; **a mais tempo** sooner; **logo mais** later on; **no mais tardar** at the latest
8 (*frases*): **mais ou menos** more or less; **mais uma vez** once more; **cada vez mais** more and more; **sem mais nem menos** out of the blue
▶ ADJ **1** (*compar*): **mais (do que)** more (than); **ele tem mais dinheiro (do que o irmão)** he's got more money (than his brother)
2 (*superl*): **ele é quem tem mais dinheiro** he's got most money
3 (*+ números*): **ela tem mais de dez bolsas** she's got more than ten bags
4 (*negativo*): **não tenho mais dinheiro** I haven't got any more money
5 (*adicional*) else; **mais alguma coisa?** anything else?; **nada/ninguém mais** nothing/no-one else
▶ PREP: **2 mais 2 são 4** 2 and 2 *ou* plus 2 is 4
▶ M: **o mais** the rest

maisena [maj'zena] F cornflour (*BRIT*), corn starch (*US*)
mais-valia (*pl* **mais-valias**) F added value
maître ['mɛtri] M head waiter
maiúscula [ma'juskula] F capital letter
majestade [maʒes'tadʒi] F majesty; **Sua/ Vossa M~** His (*ou* Her)/Your Majesty
majestoso, -a [maʒes'tozu, ɔza] ADJ majestic
major [ma'ʒɔr] M (*Mil*) major
majoritário, -a [maʒori'tarju, a] ADJ majority *atr*
mal [maw] M (*pl* **males**) harm; (*Med*) illness ▶ ADV badly; (*quase não*) hardly ▶ CONJ hardly; **~ desliguei o fone, a campainha tocou** I had hardly put the phone down when the doorbell rang; **o bem e o ~** good and bad; **o ~ é que ...** the problem is that ...; **falar ~ de alguém** to speak ill of sb, run sb down; **desejar ~ a alguém** to wish sb ill; **fazer ~ a alguém** to harm sb; (*deflorar*) to deflower sb; **fazer ~ à saúde de alguém** to damage sb's health; **fazer ~ em fazer** to be wrong to do; **não faz ~** never mind; **não fiz por ~** I meant no harm, I didn't mean it; **levar algo a ~** to take offence (*BRIT*) *ou* offense (*US*) at sth; **querer ~ a alguém** to wish sb ill; **estar ~** (*doente*) to be ill; **passar ~** to be sick; **estar ~ da vida** to be in a bad way; **viver ~ com alguém** not to get on with sb; **~ e porcamente** in a slapdash way; **estar de ~ com alguém** not to be speaking to sb; **dos ~es o menor** the lesser of two evils; **~ de Alzheimer** Alzheimer's (disease); **~ de Parkinson** Parkinson's (disease)
mal- [maw] PREFIXO badly, mis-
mala ['mala] F suitcase; (*BR Auto*) boot, trunk (*US*); **malas** FPL (*bagagem*) luggage *sg*; **fazer as ~s** to pack; **~ aérea** air courier; **~s de mão** hand luggage *sg*; **~ direta** (*Com*) direct mail; **~ postal** mail bag
malabarismo [malaba'rizmu] M juggling; (*fig*) shrewd manoeuvre (*BRIT*) *ou* maneuver (*US*)
malabarista [malaba'rista] M/F juggler; (*fig*) smooth operator
mal-acabado, -a ADJ badly finished; (*pessoa*) deformed
mal-acostumado, -a ADJ maladjusted
mal-afamado, -a ADJ notorious; (*malvisto*) of ill repute
malagradecido, -a [malagrade'sidu, a] ADJ ungrateful
malagueta [mala'geta] F chilli (*BRIT*) *ou* chili (*US*) pepper
malaio, -a [ma'laju, a] ADJ, M/F Malay ▶ M (*Ling*) Malay
Malaísia [mala'izja] F: **a ~** Malaysia
malaísio, -a [mala'izju, a] ADJ, M/F Malaysian
mal-ajambrado, -a [-aʒã'bradu, a] ADJ scruffy
mal-amada ADJ unloved ▶ F spinster
malandragem [malã'draʒē] F (*patifaria*) double-dealing; (*preguiça*) idleness; (*esperteza*) cunning

malandrear [malã'drjar] vi to loaf about ou
around

malandrice [malã'drisi] f = **malandragem**

malandro, -a [ma'lãdru, a] adj (patife)
double-dealing; (preguiçoso) idle; (esperto)
wily, cunning ▶ m/f crook; layabout;
streetwise person

mal-apanhado, -a adj unpleasant-looking

mal-apessoado, -a [-ape'swadu, a] adj
unpleasant-looking

malária [ma'larja] f malaria

mal-arrumado, -a [-ahu'madu, a] adj untidy

mal-assombrado, -a adj haunted

Malavi [mala'vi] m: **o ~** Malawi

mal-avisado, -a [-avi'zadu, a] adj rash

malbaratar [mawbara'tar] vt (dinheiro) to
squander, waste

malcasado, -a [mawka'zadu, a] adj
unhappily married; (com pessoa inferior)
married to sb below one's class

malcheiroso, -a [mawʃej'rozu, ɔza] adj
evil-smelling

malcomportado, -a [mawkõpor'tadu, a] adj
badly behaved

malconceituado, -a [mawkõsej'twadu, a] adj
badly thought of

malcriado, -a [maw'krjadu, a] adj rude ▶ m/f
slob

maldade [maw'dadʒi] f cruelty; (malícia)
malice; **é uma ~** it is cruel

maldição [mawdʒi'sãw] (pl **-ões**) f curse

maldigo etc [maw'dʒigu] vb ver **maldizer**

maldisposto, -a [mawdʒis'postu, 'pɔsta] adj
indisposed

maldisse etc [maw'dʒisi] vb ver **maldizer**

maldito, -a [maw'dʒitu, a] pp de **maldizer**
▶ adj damned

Maldivas [maw'dʒivas] fpl: **as (ilhas) ~** the
Maldives

maldiz etc [maw'dʒiz] vb ver **maldizer**

maldizente [mawdʒi'zẽtʃi] m/f slanderer

maldizer [mawdʒi'zer] (irreg: como **dizer**) vt to
curse

maldoso, -a [maw'dozu, ɔza] adj wicked;
(malicioso) malicious

maldotado, -a [mawdo'tadu, a] adj
untalented

maleável [ma'ljavew] (pl **-eis**) adj malleable

maledicência [maledʒi'sẽsja] f slander

maledicente [maledʒi'sẽtʃi] m/f slanderer

mal-educado, -a adj rude ▶ m/f slob

malefício [male'fisju] m harm

maléfico, -a [ma'lɛfiku, a] adj (pessoa)
malicious; (prejudicial) harmful

mal-empregado, -a adj wasted

mal-encarado, -a [-ẽka'radu, a] adj shady,
shifty

mal-entendido, -a adj misunderstood ▶ m
misunderstanding

mal-estar m (indisposição) indisposition,
discomfort; (embaraço) awkward situation

maleta [ma'leta] f small suitcase, grip

malevolência [malevo'lẽsja] f malice, spite

malevolente [malevo'lẽtʃi] adj malicious,
spiteful

malévolo, -a [ma'lɛvolu, a] adj malicious,
spiteful

malfadado, -a [mawfa'dadu, a] adj unlucky;
(viagem) ill-fated

malfeito, -a [maw'fejtu, a] adj (roupa) poorly
made; (corpo) misshapen; (fig: injusto) wrong,
unjust

malfeitor, -a [mawfej'tor(a)] m/f wrongdoer

malgastar [mawgas'tar] vt to waste

malgasto, -a [maw'gastu, a] adj wasted

malgrado [maw'gradu] prep despite

malha ['maʎa] f (de rede) mesh; (tecido) jersey;
(suéter) sweater; (de ginástica) leotard; **fazer ~**
(pt) to knit; **artigos de ~** knitwear;
~ perdida ladder (brit), run (us); **vestido
de ~** jersey dress

malhado, -a [ma'ʎadu, a] adj mottled; (roque)
heavy

malhar [ma'ʎar] vt (bater) to beat; (cereais) to
thresh; (col: criticar) to knock, run down ▶ vi
(col: fazer ginástica) to work out

malharia [maʎa'ria] f (fábrica) mill; (artigos de
malha) knitted goods pl

malho ['maʎu] m (maço) mallet; (grande)
sledgehammer

mal-humorado, -a [-umo'radu, a] adj
grumpy, sullen

Mali [ma'li] m: **o ~** Mali

malícia [ma'lisja] f malice; (astúcia) slyness;
(esperteza) cleverness; **pôr ~ em algo** to give
sth a double meaning

maliciar [mali'sjar] vt (ação) to see malice in;
(palavras) to misconstrue

malicioso, -a [mali'sjozu, ɔza] adj malicious;
(astuto) sly; (esperto) clever; (mente suja)
dirty-minded

malignidade [maligni'dadʒi] f malice, spite;
(Med) malignancy

maligno, -a [ma'lignu, a] adj (maléfico) evil,
malicious; (danoso) harmful; (Med)
malignant

má-língua (pl **más-línguas**) f backbiting
▶ m/f backbiter

mal-intencionado, -a adj malicious

malmequer [mawme'ker] m marigold

maloca [ma'lɔka] f (casa) communal hut;
(aldeia) (Indian) village; (esconderijo) bolt hole

malocar [malo'kar] (col) vt to hide

malogrado, -a [malo'gradu, a] adj (plano)
abortive, frustrated; (sem êxito) unsuccessful

malograr [malo'grar] vt (planos) to upset;
(frustrar) to thwart, frustrate ▶ vi (planos) to
fall through; (fracassar) to fail; **malograr-se**
vr to fall through; to fail

malogro [ma'logru] m failure

malote [ma'lɔtʃi] m pouch; (serviço) express
courier

malpassado, -a [mawpa'sadu, a] adj
underdone; (bife) rare

malproporcionado, -a [mawproporsjo'nadu,
a] adj ill-proportioned

malquerença [mawke'rẽsa] F ill will, enmity

malquisto, -a [maw'kistu, a] ADJ disliked

malsão, -sã [maw'sãw, 'sã] (*pl* **malsãos**) ADJ (*insalubre*) unhealthy; (*nocivo*) harmful

malsucedido, -a [mawsuse'dʒidu, a] ADJ unsuccessful

Malta ['mawta] F Malta

malta ['mawta] (PT) F gang, mob

malte ['mawtʃi] M malt

maltês, -esa [maw'tes, eza] ADJ, M/F Maltese

maltrapilho, -a [mawtra'piʎu, a] ADJ in rags, ragged ▶ M/F ragamuffin

maltratar [mawtra'tar] VT to ill-treat; (*com palavras*) to abuse; (*estragar*) to ruin, damage

maluco, -a [ma'luku, a] ADJ crazy, daft ▶ M/F madman/woman

maluquice [malu'kisi] F madness; (*ato, dito*) crazy thing

malvadez [mawva'dez] F = **malvadeza**

malvadeza [mawva'deza] F wickedness; (*ato*) wicked thing

malvado, -a [maw'vadu, a] ADJ wicked

malversação [mawversa'sãw] F (*de dinheiro*) embezzlement; (*má administração*) mismanagement

malversar [mawver'sar] VT (*administrar mal*) to mismanage; (*dinheiro*) to embezzle

Malvinas [maw'vinas] FPL: **as (ilhas)** ~ the Falklands, the Falkland Islands

MAM (BR) ABR M (*in Rio*) = **Museu de Arte Moderna**

mama ['mama] F breast

mamada [ma'mada] F breastfeeding

mamadeira [mama'dejra] (BR) F feeding bottle

mamãe [ma'mãj] F mum, mummy

mamão [ma'mãw] (*pl* **-ões**) M papaya

mamar [ma'mar] VT to suck; (*dinheiro*) to extort, get; (*empresa*) to milk (dry) ▶ VI (*bebê*) to be breastfed; ~ **numa empresa** to get a rake-off from a company; **dar de** ~ **a um bebê** to (breast)feed a baby

mamata [ma'mata] F (*negociata*) racket; (*boa vida*) cushy number

mambembe [mã'bẽbi] M/F amateur thespian ▶ ADJ shoddy, second-rate

mameluco, -a [mame'luku, a] M/F half-breed (*of Indian and white*)

mamífero [ma'miferu] M mammal

mamilo [ma'milu] M nipple

mamoeiro [ma'mwejru] M papaya tree

mamões [ma'mõjs] MPL *de* **mamão**

mana ['mana] F sister

manada [ma'nada] F herd, drove

Manágua [ma'nagwa] N Managua

manancial [manã'sjaw] (*pl* **-ais**) M spring; (*fig: fonte*) source; (: *abundância*) wealth

manar [ma'nar] VT, VI to pour

manauense [manaw'ẽsi] ADJ from Manaus ▶ M/F person from Manaus

mancada [mã'kada] F (*erro*) mistake; (*gafe*) blunder; **dar uma** ~ to blunder

mancar [mã'kar] VT to cripple ▶ VI to limp; **mancar-se** VR (*col*) to get the message, take the hint

manceba [mã'seba] F young woman; (*concubina*) concubine

mancebo [mã'sebu] M young man, youth

Mancha ['mãʃa] F: **o canal da** ~ the English Channel

mancha ['mãʃa] F (*nódoa*) stain; (*na pele*) mark, spot; (*em pintura*) blotch; **sem ~s** (*reputação*) spotless

manchado, -a [mã'ʃadu, a] ADJ (*sujo*) soiled; (*malhado*) mottled, spotted

manchar [mã'ʃar] VT to stain, mark; (*reputação*) to soil

manchete [mã'ʃetʃi] F headline; **virar** ~ to make *ou* hit (*col*) the headlines

manco, -a ['mãku, a] ADJ crippled, lame ▶ M/F cripple

mancomunar [mãkomu'nar] VT to contrive; **mancomunar-se** VR: ~**-se (com)** to conspire (with)

mandachuva [mãda'ʃuva] M (*figurão*) big shot; (*chefe*) boss

mandado [mã'dadu] M (*ordem*) order; (*Jur*) writ; (: *tb*: **mandado de segurança**) injunction; ~ **de arresto** repossession order; ~ **de prisão/busca** arrest/search warrant; ~ **de segurança** injunction

mandamento [mãda'mẽtu] M order, command; (*Rel*) commandment

mandante [mã'dãtʃi] M/F instigator; (*dirigente*) person in charge; (*Com*) principal

mandão, -dona [mã'dãw, 'dɔna] (*pl* **-ões/-s**) ADJ bossy, domineering ▶ M/F bossy person

mandar [mã'dar] VT (*ordenar*) to order; (*enviar*) to send ▶ VI to be in charge; **mandar-se** VR (*col: partir*) to make tracks, get going; (*fugir*) to take off; ~ **buscar** *ou* **chamar** to send for; ~ **dizer** to send word; ~ **embora** to send away; ~ **fazer um vestido** to have a dress made; ~ **que alguém faça**, ~ **alguém fazer** to tell sb to do; ~ **alguém passear** (*fig*) to send sb packing; ~ **alguém para o inferno** to tell sb to go to hell; **o que é que você manda?** (*col*) what can I do for you?; ~ **em alguém** to boss sb around; **manda!** (*col*) fire away!; ~ **ver** (*col*) to go to town; ~ **a mão**, ~ **um soco (em alguém)** to hit (sb); **aqui quem manda sou eu** I give the orders around here

mandarim [mãda'rĩ] (*pl* **-ns**) M (*Ling*) Mandarin; (*fig*) mandarin

mandatário, -a [mãda'tarju, a] M/F (*delegado*) delegate; (*representante*) representative, agent

mandato [mã'datu] M (*autorização*) mandate; (*ordem*) order; (*Pol*) term of office

mandíbula [mã'dʒibula] F jaw

mandinga [mã'dʒĩga] F witchcraft

mandioca [mã'dʒɔka] F cassava, manioc

mando ['mãdu] M (*comando*) command; (*poder*) power; **a** ~ **de** by order of

m

mandões [mã'dõjs] MPL *de* **mandão**
mandona [mã'dɔna] F *de* **mandão**
mandrião, -driona [mã'drjãw, 'drjɛna]
(*pl* **-ões/-s**) (PT) ADJ lazy ► M/F idler,
lazybones *sg*
mandriar [mã'drjar] VI to idle, loaf about
mandriões [mã'drjõjs] MPL *de* **mandrião**
mandriona [mã'drjɔna] F *de* **mandrião**
maneira [ma'nejra] F (*modo*) way; (*estilo*) style,
manner; **maneiras** FPL (*modos*) manners;
à ~ de like; **de ~ que** so that; **de ~ alguma**
ou **nenhuma** not at all; **desta ~** in this way;
de qualquer ~ anyway; **não houve ~ de**
convencê-lo it was impossible to convince
him
maneirar [manej'rar] (*col*) VT to sort out, fix
► VI to sort things out; **maneira!** take it
easy!
maneiro, -a [ma'nejru, a] ADJ (*ferramenta*) easy
to use; (*roupa*) attractive; (*trabalho*) easy;
(*pessoa*) capable; (*col: bacana*) great, brilliant
manejar [mane'ʒar] VT (*instrumento*) to handle;
(*máquina*) to work
manejável [mane'ʒavew] (*pl* **-eis**) ADJ
manageable
manejo [ma'neʒu] M handling
manequim [mane'kĩ] (*pl* **-ns**) M (*boneco*)
dummy ► M/F model
maneta [ma'neta] ADJ one-handed ► M/F
one-handed person
manga ['mãga] F sleeve; (*fruta*) mango; (*filtro*)
filter; **em ~s de camisa** in (one's) shirt
sleeves
manganês [mãga'nes] M manganese
mangue ['mãgi] M mangrove swamp;
(*planta*) mangrove; (*col: zona*) red-light
district
mangueira [mã'gejra] F hose(pipe); (*árvore*)
mango tree
manguinha [mã'giɲa] F: **botar as ~s de fora**
(*col*) to let one's hair down
manha ['maɲa] F (*malícia*) guile, craftiness;
(*destreza*) skill; (*ardil*) trick; (*birra*) tantrum;
fazer ~ to have a tantrum
manhã [ma'ɲã] F morning; **de** *ou* **pela ~** in
the morning; **amanhã/hoje de ~**
tomorrow/this morning; **de ~ cedo** early in
the morning; **4 hs da ~** 4 o'clock in the
morning
manhãzinha [maɲã'ziɲa] F: **de ~** early in the
morning
manhoso, -a [ma'ɲozu, ɔza] ADJ (*ardiloso*)
crafty, sly; (*criança*) whining
mania [ma'nia] F (*Med*) mania; (*obsessão*)
craze; **ela é cheia de ~s** she's very
compulsive; **estar com ~ de ...** to have a
thing about ...; **~ de grandeza** delusions *pl*
of grandeur; **~ de perseguição** persecution
complex
maníaco, -a [ma'niaku, a] ADJ manic ► M/F
maniac
maníaco-depressivo (*pl* **maníaco-**
depressivos) ADJ, M/F manic depressive

manicômio [mani'komju] M asylum, mental
hospital
manicura [mani'kura] F (*tratamento*)
manicure; (*pessoa*) manicurist
manicure [mani'kuri] F = **manicura**
manifestação [manifesta'sãw] (*pl* **-ões**) F
show, display; (*expressão*) expression,
declaration; (*política*) demonstration
manifestante [manifes'tãtʃi] M/F
demonstrator
manifestar [manifes'tar] VT (*revelar*) to show,
display; (*declarar*) to express, declare;
manifestar-se VR to manifest o.s.;
(*pronunciar-se*) to express an opinion
manifesto, -a [mani'fɛstu, a] ADJ obvious,
clear ► M manifesto
manilha [ma'niʎa] F (ceramic) drainpipe
manipulação [manipula'sãw] F handling;
(*fig*) manipulation
manipular [manipu'lar] VT to manipulate;
(*manejar*) to handle
manivela [mani'vela] F (*ferramenta*) crank
manjado, -a [mã'ʒadu, a] (*col*) ADJ well-known
manjar [mã'ʒar] M (*iguaria*) delicacy, titbit
(BRIT), tidbit (US) ► VT (*col: conhecer*) to know;
(: *entender*) to grasp; (: *observar*) to check out
► VI (*col*) to catch on; **~ de algo** to know
about sth; **manjou?** (*col*) get it?, see?
manjar-branco M blancmange
manjedoura [mãʒe'dora] F manger, crib
manjericão [mãʒeri'kãw] M basil
mano ['manu] M brother
manobra [ma'nɔbra] F (*de carro, barco*)
manoeuvre (BRIT), maneuver (US); (*de*
mecanismo) operation; (*de trens*) shunting;
(*fig*) move; (: *artimanha*) manoeuvre *ou*
maneuver, trick; **manobras** FPL (*Mil*)
manoeuvres *ou* maneuvers
manobrar [mano'brar] VT to manoeuvre
(BRIT), maneuver (US); (*mecanismo*) to operate,
work; (*governar*) to take charge of; (*manipular*)
to manipulate ► VI to manoeuvre *ou*
maneuver; (*tomar medidas*) to make moves
manobreiro, -a [mano'brejru, a] M/F operator
manobrista [mano'brista] M/F parking
attendant
manquejar [mãke'ʒar] VI to limp
mansão [mã'sãw] (*pl* **-ões**) F mansion
mansidão [mãsi'dãw] F gentleness,
meekness; (*do mar*) calmness; (*de animal*)
tameness
mansinho [mã'siɲu] ADV: **de ~** (*devagar*)
slowly; (*de leve*) gently; (*sorrateiramente*): **sair/**
entrar de ~ to creep out/in
manso, -a ['mãsu, a] ADJ (*brando*) gentle; (*mar*)
calm; (*animal*) tame
mansões [ma'sõjs] FPL *de* **mansão**
manta ['mãta] F (*cobertor*) blanket; (*xale*)
shawl; (*agasalho*) cloak; (*de viajar*) travelling
rug
manteiga [mã'tejga] F butter; **~ derretida**
(*fig, col*) cry-baby; **~ de cacau** cocoa butter
manteigueira [mãtej'gejra] F butter dish

mantém *etc* [mã'tẽ] vʙ *ver* **manter**

mantenedor, a [mãtene'dor(a)] ᴍ/ꜰ (*da família*) breadwinner; (*de opinião, princípio*) holder; (*de ordem, Esporte*) retainer

manter [mã'ter] (*irreg: como* **ter**) vᴛ to maintain; (*num lugar*) to keep; (*uma família*) to support; (*a palavra*) to keep; (*princípios*) to abide by; **manter-se** vʀ (*sustentar-se*) to support o.s.; (*permanecer*) to remain; **~-se firme** to stand firm

mantilha [mã'tʃiʎa] ꜰ mantilla; (*véu*) veil

mantimento [mãtʃi'mẽtu] ᴍ maintenance; **mantimentos** ᴍᴘʟ (*alimentos*) provisions

mantinha *etc* [mã'tʃiɲa] vʙ *ver* **manter**

mantive *etc* [mã'tʃivi] vʙ *ver* **manter**

mantiver *etc* [mãtʃi'ver] vʙ *ver* **manter**

manto ['mãtu] ᴍ cloak; (*de cerimônia*) robe

mantô [mã'to] ᴍ coat

manual [ma'nwaw] (*pl* **-ais**) ᴀᴅᴊ manual ▶ ᴍ handbook, manual; **ter habilidade ~** to be good with one's hands

manufatura [manufa'tura] ꜰ manufacture

manufaturados [manufatu'radus] ᴍᴘʟ manufactured products

manufaturar [manufatu'rar] vᴛ to manufacture

manuscrever [manuskre'ver] vᴛ to write by hand

manuscrito, -a [manus'kritu, a] ᴀᴅᴊ handwritten ▶ ᴍ manuscript

manusear [manu'zjar] vᴛ (*manejar*) to handle; (*livro*) to leaf through

manuseio [manu'zeju] ᴍ handling

manutenção [manutẽ'sãw] ꜰ maintenance; (*da casa*) upkeep

mão [mãw] (*pl* **mãos**) ꜰ hand; (*de animal*) paw; (*de pintura*) coat; (*de direção*) flow of traffic; **à ~** by hand; (*perto*) at hand; **feito à ~** handmade; **de ~s dadas** hand in hand; **de** *ou* **em primeira ~** first-hand; **de segunda ~** second-hand; **em ~** by hand; **fora de ~** out of the way; **abrir ~ de algo** (*fig*) to give sth up; **aguentar a ~** (*col: suportar*) to hold out; (*: esperar*) to hang on; **dar a ~ à palmatória** to admit one's mistake; **dar a ~ a alguém** to hold sb's hand; (*cumprimentar*) to shake hands with sb; **dar uma ~ a alguém** to give sb a hand, help sb out; **ficar na ~** (*col*) to be stood up; **forçar a ~** to go overboard; **lançar ~ de algo** to have recourse to sth; **largar algo de ~** to give sth up; **uma ~ lava a outra** (*fig*) one good turn deserves another; **meter a ~ em alguém** to hit sb; **meter** *ou* **passar a ~ em algo** (*col*) to nick sth; **passar a ~ pela cabeça de alguém** (*fig*) to let sb off; **pôr a ~ no fogo por alguém** (*fig*) to vouch for sb; **pôr ~s à obra** to set to work; **ser uma ~ na roda** (*fig*) to be a great help; **ter ~ leve** (*bater facilmente*) to be violent; (*ser ladrão*) to be light-fingered; **ter a ~ pesada** to be heavy-handed; **ter uma boa ~ para** to be good at; **vir com as ~s abanando** (*fig*) to come back empty-handed; **~ única/dupla** one-way/two-way traffic; **esta rua dá ~ para o centro** this street goes to the centre (ʙʀɪᴛ) *ou* center (ᴜs); **rua de duas ~s** two-way street; **~s ao alto!** hands up!; **de ~ beijada** (*fig*) for nothing; **~ de obra** labour (ʙʀɪᴛ), labor (ᴜs); **~ de obra especializada** skilled labo(u)r

mão-aberta (*pl* **mãos-abertas**) ᴀᴅᴊ generous ▶ ᴍ/ꜰ generous person

mão-cheia ꜰ: **de ~** first-rate

maoísta [maw'ista] ᴀᴅᴊ, ᴍ/ꜰ Maoist

mão-leve (*pl* **mãos-leves**) ᴍ/ꜰ pilferer

mãozinha [mãw'ziɲa] ꜰ: **dar uma ~ a alguém** to give sb a hand, help sb out

mapa ['mapa] ᴍ map; (*gráfico*) chart; **não estar no ~** (*fig, col*) to be extraordinary; **sair do ~** (*col*) to disappear

mapa-múndi [-'mũdʒi] (*pl* **mapas-múndi**) ᴍ world map

Maputo [ma'putu] ɴ Maputo

maquete [ma'kɛtʃi] ꜰ model

maquiador, a [makja'dor(a)] ᴍ/ꜰ make-up artist

maquiagem [ma'kjaʒẽ] ꜰ = **maquilagem**

maquiar [ma'kjar] vᴛ to make up; (*fig*) to touch up; **maquiar-se** vʀ to make o.s. up, put on one's make-up

maquiavélico, -a [makja'vɛliku, a] ᴀᴅᴊ Machiavellian

maquilagem [maki'laʒẽ], (ᴘᴛ) **maquilhagem** ꜰ make-up; (*ato*) making up

maquilar [makilar], (ᴘᴛ) **maquilhar** vᴛ to make up; **maquilar-se** vʀ to make o.s. up, put on one's make-up

máquina ['makina] ꜰ machine; (*de trem*) engine; (*de relógio*) movement; (*fig*) machinery; **~ a vapor** steam engine; **~s agrícolas** agricultural machinery; **~ de calcular** adding machine; **~ de costura** sewing machine; **~ fotográfica** camera; **~ de escrever** typewriter; **~ de lavar (roupa)** washing machine; **~ de lavar louça** dishwasher; **~ de tricotar** knitting machine; **costurar/escrever à ~** to machine-sew/type; **escrito à ~** typewritten; **preencher um formulário à ~** to fill in a form on the typewriter

maquinação [makina'sãw] (*pl* **-ões**) ꜰ machination, plot

maquinal [maki'naw] (*pl* **-ais**) ᴀᴅᴊ mechanical, automatic

maquinar [maki'nar] vᴛ to plot ▶ vɪ to conspire

maquinaria [makina'ria] ꜰ machinery

maquinismo [maki'nizmu] ᴍ mechanism; (*máquinas*) machinery; (*Teatro*) stage machinery

maquinista [maki'nista] ᴍ (*Ferro*) engine driver; (*Náut*) engineer

mar [mar] ᴍ sea; **por ~** by sea; **cair no ~** to fall overboard; **fazer-se ao ~** to set sail; **~ aberto** open sea; **pleno ~, ~ alto** high sea; **um ~ de** (*fig*) a sea of; **~ de rosas** calm sea;

m

(*fig*) bed of roses; **nem tanto ao ~ nem tanto à terra** (*fig*) somewhere in between; **o ~ Cáspio** the Caspian Sea; **o ~ Morto** the Dead Sea; **o ~ Negro** the Black Sea; **o ~ Vermelho** the Red Sea

maraca [ma'raka] F maraca

maracujá [maraku'ʒa] M passion fruit; **pé de ~** passion flower

maracujazeiro [marakuʒa'zejru] M passion-fruit plant

maracutaia [maraku'taja] F dirty trick; (*col*) scam

marafa [ma'rafa] (*col*) F loose living

marafona [mara'fɔna] (*col*) F whore

marajá [mara'ʒa] M maharaja; (*BR Pol*) civil service fat-cat

maranhense [mara'ɲɛsi] ADJ from Maranhão ▶ M/F person from Maranhão

marasmo [ma'raʒmu] M (*inatividade*) stagnation; (*apatia*) apathy

maratona [mara'tona] F marathon

maratonista [marato'nista] M/F marathon runner

maravilha [mara'viʎa] F marvel, wonder; **às mil ~s** wonderfully

maravilhar [maravi'ʎar] VT to amaze, astonish ▶ VI to be amazing; **maravilhar-se** VR: **~-se** to be astonished *ou* amazed at

maravilhoso, -a [maravi'ʎozu, ɔza] ADJ wonderful, marvellous (*BRIT*), marvelous (*US*)

marca ['marka] F mark; (*Com*) make, brand; (*carimbo*) stamp; (*da prata*) hallmark; (*fig: categoria*) calibre (*BRIT*), caliber (*US*); **de ~ maior** (*fig*) of the first order; **~ de fábrica** trademark; **~ registrada** registered trademark

marcação [marka'sãw] (*pl* -**ões**) F marking; (*em jogo*) scoring; (*de instrumento*) reading; (*Teatro*) action; (*PT Tel*) dialling; **estar de ~ com alguém** (*col*) to pick on sb constantly

marcador [marka'dor] M marker; (*de livro*) bookmark; (*Esporte: quadro*) scoreboard; (*: jogador*) scorer

marcante [mar'kãtʃi] ADJ outstanding

marca-passo [marka'pasu] (*pl* -**s**) M (*Med*) pacemaker

marcar [mar'kar] VT to mark; (*hora, data*) to fix, set; (*PT Tel*) to dial; (*animal*) to brand; (*delimitar*) to demarcate; (*observar*) to keep an eye on; (*gol, ponto*) to score; (*Futebol: jogador*) to mark; (*produzir impressão em*) to leave one's mark on ▶ VI (*impressionar*) to make one's mark; **~ uma consulta, ~ hora** to make an appointment; **~ um encontro com alguém** to arrange to meet sb; **~ uma reunião/um jantar para sexta-feira** to arrange a meeting/a dinner for Friday; **~ época** to make history; **~ o ponto** to punch the clock; **ter hora marcada com alguém** to have an appointment with sb; **~ o tempo de algo** to time sth

marcenaria [marsena'ria] F joinery; (*oficina*) joiner's

marceneiro [marse'nejru] M cabinet-maker, joiner

marcha ['marʃa] F march; (*ato*) marching; (*de acontecimentos*) course; (*passo*) pace; (*Auto*) gear; (*progresso*) progress; **~ à ré** (*BR*), **~ atrás** (*PT*) reverse (gear); **primeira (~)** first (gear); **pôr-se em ~** to set off

marchar [mar'ʃar] VI (*ir*) to go; (*andar a pé*) to walk; (*Mil*) to march

marcha-rancho (*pl* **marchas-rancho**) F carnival march

marchetar [marʃe'tar] VT to inlay

marcial [mar'sjaw] (*pl* -**ais**) ADJ martial; **corte ~** court martial; **lei ~** martial law

marciano, -a [mar'sjanu, a] ADJ, M Martian

marco ['marku] M landmark; (*de janela*) frame; (*fig*) frontier; (*moeda*) mark

março ['marsu] M March; *ver tb* **julho**

maré [ma'rɛ] F tide; (*fig: oportunidade*) chance; **~ alta/baixa** high/low tide; **estar de boa ~ ou de ~ alta** to be in a good mood; **remar contra a ~** (*fig*) to swim against the tide

marear [ma'rjar] VT to make seasick; (*oxidar*) to dull, stain ▶ VI to be seasick

marechal [mare'ʃaw] (*pl* -**ais**) M marshal

marejar [mare'ʒar] VT to wet ▶ VI to get wet

maremoto [mare'mɔtu] M tidal wave

maresia [mare'zia] F smell of the sea, sea air

marfim [mar'fĩ] M ivory

margarida [marga'rida] F daisy

margarina [marga'rina] F margarine

margear [mar'ʒjar] VT to border

margem ['marʒẽ] (*pl* -**ns**) F (*borda*) edge; (*de rio*) bank; (*litoral*) shore; (*de impresso*) margin; (*fig: tempo*) time; (*: lugar*) space; (*: oportunidade*) chance; **à ~ de** alongside; **dar ~ a alguém** to give sb a chance; **~ de erro** margin of error; **~ de lucro** profit margin

marginal [marʒi'naw] (*pl* -**ais**) ADJ marginal ▶ M/F delinquent

marginalidade [marʒinali'dadʒi] F delinquency

marginalizar [marʒinali'zar] VT to marginalize

maria-fumaça [ma'ria-] (*pl* **marias-fumaças**) F steam train

maria-sem-vergonha [ma'ria-] (*pl* **marias-sem-vergonha**) F (*Bot*) busy lizzie

maria vai com as outras M/F INV sheep, follower

maricas [ma'rikas] (*ofensivo*) M INV queer (!), poof (!)

marido [ma'ridu] M husband

marimbondo [marĩ'bõdu] M hornet

marina [ma'rina] F marina

marinha [ma'riɲa] F (*tb:* **marinha de guerra**) navy; (*pintura*) seascape; **~ mercante** merchant navy

marinheiro [mari'ɲejru] M seaman, sailor; **~ de primeira viagem** (*fig*) beginner

marinho, -a [ma'riɲu, a] ADJ sea *atr*, marine

marionete [marjo'netʃi] F puppet

mariposa [mari'poza] F moth

marisco [ma'risku] M shellfish
marital [mari'taw] (pl **-ais**) ADJ marital
maritalmente [maritaw'mētʃi] ADV: **viver ~ (com alguém)** to live (with sb) as man and wife
marítimo, -a [ma'ritʃimu, a] ADJ sea atr, maritime; **pesca marítima** sea fishing
marketing ['marketʃiŋ] M marketing
marmanjo [mar'māʒu] M grown man
marmelada [marme'lada] F quince jam; (col) double-dealing
marmelo [mar'mɛlu] M quince
marmita [mar'mita] F (vasilha) pot
mármore ['marmori] M marble
marmóreo, -a [mar'mɔrju, a] ADJ marble atr; (fig) cold
marola [ma'rɔla] F wave, roller
maroto, -a [ma'rotu, a] M/F rogue, rascal; (criança) naughty boy/girl ▶ ADJ roguish; naughty
marquei etc [mar'kej] VB ver **marcar**
marquês, -quesa [mar'kes, 'keza] M/F marquis/marchioness
marqueteiro, -a [marke'tejru, a] M/F (col) spin doctor
marquise [mar'kizi] F awning, canopy
marra ['maha] F: **na ~** (à força) forcibly; (a qualquer preço) whatever the cost
marreco [ma'hɛku] M duck
Marrocos [ma'hɔkus] M: **o ~** Morocco
marrom [ma'hõ] (pl **-ns**) ADJ, M brown
marroquino, -a [maho'kinu, a] ADJ, M/F Moroccan
Marte ['martʃi] M Mars
martelada [marte'lada] F (pancada) blow (with a hammer); (ruído) hammering sound
martelar [marte'lar] VT to hammer; (amolar) to bother ▶ VI to hammer; (insistir): **~ (em algo)** to keep ou harp on (about sth)
martelo [mar'tɛlu] M hammer
martíni® [mar'tʃini] M **martini**®
Martinica [martʃi'nika] F: **a ~** Martinique
mártir ['martʃir] M/F martyr
martírio [mar'tʃirju] M martyrdom; (fig) torment
martirizante [martʃiri'zātʃi] ADJ agonizing
martirizar [martʃiri'zar] VT to martyr; (atormentar) to afflict; **martirizar-se** VR to agonize
marujo [ma'ruʒu] M sailor
marulhar [maru'ʎar] VI (mar) to surge; (ondas) to lap; (produzir ruído) to roar
marulho [ma'ruʎu] M (do mar) surge; (das ondas) lapping
marxismo [mar'ksizmu] M Marxism
marxista [mar'ksista] ADJ, M/F Marxist
marzipã [mahzi'pã] M marzipan
mas [ma(j)s] CONJ but ▶ PRON = **me + as**
mascar [mas'kar] VT to chew
máscara ['maskara] F mask; (para limpeza de pele) face pack; **sob a ~ de** under the guise of; **tirar a ~ de alguém** (fig) to unmask sb;

baile de ~s masked ball; **~ de oxigênio** oxygen mask
mascarado, -a [maska'radu, a] ADJ masked; (convencido) conceited
mascarar [maska'rar] VT to mask; (disfarçar) to disguise; (encobrir) to cover up
mascate [mas'katʃi] M peddler, hawker (BRIT)
mascavo, -a [mas'kavu, a] ADJ: **açúcar ~** brown sugar
mascote [mas'kɔtʃi] F mascot
masculinidade [maskulini'dadʒi] F masculinity
masculino, -a [masku'linu, a] ADJ masculine; (Bio) male ▶ M (Ling) masculine; **roupa masculina** men's clothes pl
másculo, -a ['maskulu, a] ADJ masculine; (viril) manly
masmorra [maz'mɔha] F dungeon; (fig) black hole
masoquismo [mazo'kizmu] M masochism
masoquista [mazo'kista] ADJ masochistic ▶ M/F masochist
MASP ABR M = **Museu de Arte de São Paulo**
massa ['masa] F (Fís: fig) mass; (de tomate) paste; (Culin: de pão) dough; (: macarrão etc) pasta; **as ~s** the masses; **em ~** en masse; **~ de vidraceiro** putty; **estar com as mãos na ~** (fig) to be about ou at it
massacrado, -a [masa'kradu, a] ADJ (povo, sociedade) hard-pressed
massacrante [masa'krātʃi] ADJ annoying
massacrar [masa'krar] VT to massacre; (fig: chatear) to annoy; (: torturar) to tear apart
massacre [ma'sakri] F massacre; (fig) annoyance
massagear [masa'ʒjar] VT to massage ▶ VI to do massage
massagem [ma'saʒē] (pl **-ns**) F massage
massagista [masa'ʒista] M/F masseur/masseuse
massificar [masifi'kar] VT to influence (through mass communication)
massudo, -a [ma'sudu, a] ADJ bulky; (espesso) thick; (com aspecto de massa) doughy
mastectomia [mastekto'mia] F mastectomy
mastigado, -a [mastʃi'gadu, a] ADJ (fig) well-planned
mastigar [mastʃi'gar] VT to chew; (pronunciar mal) to mumble, mutter; (fig: refletir) to mull over
mastim [mas'tʃĩ] (pl **-ns**) M watchdog
mastodonte [masto'dõtʃi] M (fig: pessoa gorda) hulk, lump
mastro ['mastru] M (Náut) mast; (para bandeira) flagpole
masturbação [masturba'sãw] F masturbation
masturbar-se [mastur'barsi] VR to masturbate
mata ['mata] F forest, wood; **~ virgem** virgin forest
mata-bicho M tot of brandy, snifter
mata-borrão M blotting paper

matacão [mata'kãw] (*pl* **-ões**) M lump; (*pedra*) boulder

matado, -a [ma'tadu, a] ADJ (*trabalho*) badly done

matador, a [mata'dor(a)] M/F killer ▶ M (*em tourada*) matador

matadouro [mata'doru] M slaughterhouse

matagal [mata'gaw] (*pl* **-ais**) M bush; (*brenha*) thicket, undergrowth

mata-moscas M INV fly-killer

mata-mosquito (*pl* **mata-mosquitos**) M mosquito exterminator

matança [ma'tãsa] F massacre; (*de reses*) slaughter(ing)

mata-piolho (*pl* **mata-piolhos**) (*col*) M thumb

matar [ma'tar] VT to kill; (*sede*) to quench; (*fome*) to satisfy; (*aula*) to skip; (*trabalho: não aparecer*) to skive off; (: *fazer rápido*) to dash off; (*tempo*) to kill; (*adivinhar*) to guess, get ▶ VI to kill; **matar-se** VR to kill o.s.; (*esfalfar-se*) to wear o.s. out; **um calor/uma dor de ~** stifling heat/excruciating pain; **~ saudades** to catch up

mata-rato (*pl* **mata-ratos**) M (*veneno*) rat poison; (*cigarro*) throat-scraper

mate ['matʃi] ADJ matt ▶ M (*chá*) maté tea; (*xeque-mate*) checkmate

matelassê [matela'se] ADJ quilted ▶ M quilting

matemática [mate'matʃika] F mathematics *sg*, maths *sg* (BRIT), math (US); *ver tb* **matemático**

matemático, -a [mate'matʃiku, a] ADJ mathematical ▶ M/F mathematician

matéria [ma'tɛrja] F matter; (*Tec*) material; (*Educ: assunto*) subject; (*tema*) topic; (*jornalística*) story, article; **em ~ de** on the subject of; **~ fecal** faeces *pl* (BRIT), feces *pl* (US); **~ plástica** plastic

material [mate'rjaw] (*pl* **-ais**) ADJ material; (*físico*) physical ▶ M material; (*Tec*) equipment; (*col: corpo*) body; **~ humano** manpower; **~ bélico** armaments *pl*; **~ de construção** building supplies *pl*; **~ de limpeza** cleaning supplies *pl*; **~ escolar** school supplies *pl*

materialismo [materja'lizmu] M materialism

materialista [materja'lista] ADJ materialistic ▶ M/F materialist

materializar [materjali'zar] VT to materialize; **materializar-se** VR to materialize

matéria-prima (*pl* **matérias-primas**) F raw material

maternal [mater'naw] (*pl* **-ais**) ADJ motherly, maternal; **escola ~** nursery (school)

maternidade [materni'dadʒi] F motherhood, maternity; (*hospital*) maternity hospital

materno, -a [ma'ternu, a] ADJ motherly, maternal; (*língua*) native; (*avô*) maternal

matilha [ma'tʃiʎa] F (*cães*) pack; (*fig: corja*) rabble

matina [ma'tʃina] F morning

matinal [matʃi'naw] (*pl* **-ais**) ADJ morning *atr*

matinê [matʃi'ne] F matinée

matiz [ma'tʃiz] M (*de cor*) shade; (*fig: de ironia*) tinge; (*cor política*) colouring (BRIT), coloring (US)

matizar [matʃi'zar] VT (*colorir*) to tinge, colour (BRIT), color (US); (*combinar cores*) to blend; **~ algo de algo** (*fig*) to tinge sth with sth

mato ['matu] M scrubland, bush; (*plantas agrestes*) scrub; (*o campo*) country; **ser ~** (*col*) to be there for the taking; **estar num ~ sem cachorro** (*col*) to be up the creek without a paddle

mato-grossano, -a [-gro'sanu, a] ADJ, M/F = **mato-grossense**

mato-grossense [-gro'sẽsi] ADJ from Mato Grosso ▶ M/F person from Mato Grosso

matraca [ma'traka] F rattle; (*pessoa*) chatterbox; **falar como uma ~** to talk nineteen to the dozen (BRIT) *ou* a blue streak (US)

matraquear [matra'kjar] VI to rattle, clatter; (*tagarelar*) to chatter, rabbit on

matreiro, -a [ma'trejru, a] ADJ cunning, crafty

matriarca [ma'trjarka] F matriarch

matriarcal [matrjar'kaw] (*pl* **-ais**) ADJ matriarchal

matrícula [ma'trikula] F (*lista*) register; (*inscrição*) registration; (*pagamento*) enrolment (BRIT) *ou* enrollment (US) fee; (*PT Auto*) registration number (BRIT), license number (US); **fazer a ~** to enrol (BRIT), enroll (US)

matricular [matriku'lar] VT to enrol (BRIT), enroll (US), register; **matricular-se** VR to enrol(l), register

matrimonial [matrimo'njaw] (*pl* **-ais**) ADJ marriage *atr*, matrimonial

matrimônio [matri'monju] M marriage; **contrair ~ (com alguém)** to be joined in marriage (with sb)

matriz [ma'triz] F (*Med*) womb; (*fonte*) source; (*molde*) mould (BRIT), mold (US); (*Com*) head office; (*col*) wife; **igreja ~** mother church

matrona [ma'trona] F matron

maturação [matura'sãw] F maturing; (*de fruto*) ripening

maturidade [maturi'dadʒi] F maturity

matusquela [matus'kɛla] (*col*) M/F lunatic

matutar [matu'tar] VT (*planejar*) to plan ▶ VI: **~ em** *ou* **sobre algo** to turn sth over in one's mind

matutino, -a [matu'tʃina, a] ADJ morning *atr* ▶ M morning paper

matuto, -a [ma'tutu, a] ADJ, M/F (*caipira*) rustic; (*provinciano*) provincial

mau, má [maw, ma] ADJ bad; (*malvado*) evil, wicked ▶ M bad; (*Rel*) evil; **os ~s** bad people; (*num filme*) the baddies

mau-caráter (*pl* **maus-caracteres**) ADJ shady ▶ M bad lot

mau-olhado [-o'ʎadu] M evil eye

Maurício [maw'risju] M Mauritius

Mauritânia [mawri'tanja] F: **a ~** Mauritania

mausoléu [mawzo'lɛw] M mausoleum

maus-tratos MPL ill-treatment *sg*

mavioso, -a [ma'vjozu, ɔza] ADJ tender, soft; (*som*) sweet

máx. ABR (= *máximo*) max

máxi ['maksi] ADJ INV (*saia*) maxi

maxidesvalorização [maksidʒizvaloriza'sãw] (*pl* **-ões**) F large-scale devaluation

maxila [mak'sila] F jawbone

maxilar [maksi'lar] ADJ jaw *atr* ▶ M jawbone

máxima ['masima] F maxim, saying

máxime ['maksimɛ] ADV especially

maximizar [masimi'zar] VT to maximize; (*superestimar*) to play up

máximo, -a ['masimu, a] ADJ (*maior que todos*) greatest; (*o maior possível*) maximum ▶ M maximum; (*o cúmulo*) peak; (*temperature*) high; **o ~ cuidado** the greatest of care; **no ~** at most; **ao ~** to the utmost; **chegar ao ~** (*fig*) to reach a peak; **ele se acha o ~** (*col*) he thinks he's the greatest

maxixe [ma'ʃiʃi] M gherkin; (BR: *dança*) 19th-century dance

mazela [ma'zɛla] F (*ferida*) sore spot; (*doença*) illness; (*fig*) blemish

MCom (BR) ABR M = **Ministério das Comunicações**

MCT (BR) ABR M = **Ministério de Ciência e Tecnologia**

MD (BR) ABR M = **Ministério da Desburocratização**

MDB ABR M (*antes*) = **Movimento Democrático Brasileiro**

me [mi] PRON (*direto*) me; (*indireto*) (to) me; (*reflexivo*) (to) myself

meada ['mjada] F skein, hank

meado ['mjadu] M middle; **em** *ou* **nos ~s de julho** in mid-July

meandro ['mjãdru] M meander; **os ~s** (*fig*) the ins and outs

MEC (BR) ABR M = **Ministério de Educação e Cultura**

Meca ['mɛka] N Mecca

mecânica [me'kanika] F (*ciência*) mechanics *sg*; (*mecanismo*) mechanism; *ver tb* **mecânico**

mecânico, -a [me'kaniku, a] ADJ mechanical ▶ M/F mechanic; **broca mecânica** power drill

mecanismo [meka'nizmu] M mechanism

mecanização [mekaniza'sãw] F mechanization

mecanizar [mekani'zar] VT to mechanize

mecenas [me'sɛnas] M INV patron

mecha ['mɛʃa] F (*de vela*) wick; (*cabelo*) tuft; (*no cabelo*) highlight; (*Med*) swab; **fazer ~ no cabelo** to put highlights in one's hair, to highlight one's hair

mechado, -a [me'ʃadu, a] ADJ highlighted

meço *etc* ['mɛsu] VB *ver* **medir**

méd. ABR (= *médio*) av

medalha [me'daʎa] F medal

medalhão [meda'ʎãw] (*pl* **-ões**) M medallion; (*fig: figurão*) big name; (*joia*) locket

média ['mɛdʒja] F average; (*café*) coffee with milk; **em ~** on average; **fazer ~** to ingratiate o.s.

mediação [medʒja'sãw] F mediation; **por ~ de** through

mediador, a [medʒja'dor(a)] M/F mediator

mediano, -a [me'dʒjanu, a] ADJ medium; (*médio*) average; (*medíocre*) mediocre

mediante [me'dʒjãtʃi] PREP by (means of), through; (*a troco de*) in return for

mediar [me'dʒjar] VT to mediate (for) ▶ VI (*ser mediador*) to mediate; **a distância que medeia entre** the distance between

medicação [medʒika'sãw] (*pl* **-ões**) F treatment; (*medicamentos*) medication

medicamento [medʒika'mẽtu] M medicine

medição [medʒi'sãw] (*pl* **-ões**) F measurement

medicar [medʒi'kar] VT to treat ▶ VI to practise (BRIT) *ou* practice (US) medicine; **medicar-se** VR to take medicine, doctor o.s. up

medicina [medʒi'sina] F medicine; **~ legal** forensic medicine

medicinal [medʒisi'naw] (*pl* **-ais**) ADJ medicinal

médico, -a ['mɛdʒiku, a] ADJ medical ▶ M/F doctor; **receita médica** prescription

médico-cirurgião, médica-cirurgiã (*pl* **médicos-cirurgiões/médicas-cirurgiãs**) M/F surgeon

medições [medʒi'sõjs] FPL *de* **medição**

médico-hospitalar (*pl* **-es**) ADJ hospital and medical

médico-legal (*pl* **-ais**) ADJ forensic

médico-legista, médica-legista (*pl* **médicos-legistas/médicas-legistas**) M/F forensic expert (BRIT), medical examiner (US)

medida [me'dʒida] F measure; (*providência*) step; (*medição*) measurement; (*moderação*) prudence; **à ~ que** while, as; **na ~ em que** in so far as; **feito sob ~** made to measure; **software sob ~** bespoke software; **encher as ~s** (*satisfazer*) to fit the bill; **encher as ~s de alguém** (*chatear*) to get on sb's wick; **ir além da ~** to go too far; **tirar as ~s de alguém** to take sb's measurements; **tomar ~s** to take steps; **tomar as ~s de** to measure; **~ de emergência/urgência** emergency/ urgent measure

medidor [medʒi'dor] M: **~ de pressão** pressure gauge; **~ de gás** gas meter

medieval [medʒje'vaw] (*pl* **-ais**) ADJ medieval

médio, -a ['mɛdʒju, a] ADJ (*dedo, classe*) middle; (*tamanho, estatura*) medium; (*mediano*) average; **a ~ prazo** in the medium term; **ensino ~** secondary education; **o brasileiro ~** the average Brazilian

medíocre [me'dʒjɔkri] ADJ mediocre

mediocridade [medʒjokri'dadʒi] F mediocrity

m

mediocrizar [medʒjokri'zar] vt to make mediocre

medir [me'dʒir] vt to measure; (atos, palavras) to weigh; (avaliar: consequências, distâncias) to weigh up ▶ vi to measure; **medir-se** vr to measure o.s.; **~-se (com alguém)** (comparar-se) to be on a par (with sb); **quanto você mede? — meço 1.60 m** how tall are you? — I'm 1.60 m (tall); **a saia mede 80 cm de comprimento** the skirt is 80 cm long; **meça suas palavras!** watch your language!; **~ alguém dos pés à cabeça** (fig) to eye sb up; **não ter mãos a ~** (fig) to have one's hands full

meditação [medʒita'sãw] (pl -ões) F meditation

meditar [medʒi'tar] vi to meditate; **~ sobre algo** to ponder (on) sth

meditativo, -a [medʒita'tʃivu, a] ADJ thoughtful, reflective

mediterrâneo, -a [medʒite'hanju, a] ADJ Mediterranean ▶ M: **o M~** the Mediterranean

médium ['mɛdʒjũ] (pl -ns) M (pessoa) medium

mediunidade [medʒjuni'dadʒi] F second sight

médiuns ['mɛdʒjũs] MPL de **médium**

medo ['medu] M fear; **com ~** afraid; **com ~ que** for fear that; **ficar com ~** to get frightened; **meter ~** to be frightening; **meter ~ em alguém** to frighten sb; **ter ~ de** to be afraid of; **ter um ~ que se pela** (fig) to be frightened out of one's wits

medonho, -a [me'doɲu, a] ADJ terrible, awful

medrar [me'drar] vi to thrive, flourish; (col: ter medo) to get frightened

medroso, -a [me'drozu, ɔza] ADJ (com medo) frightened; (tímido) timid

medula [me'dula] F marrow

megabyte [mega'bajtʃi] M megabyte

megalomania [megaloma'nia] F megalomania

megalomaníaco, -a [megaloma'niaku, a] ADJ, M/F megalomaniac

megaton [mega'tõ] M megaton

megera [me'ʒɛra] F shrew; (mãe) cruel mother

meia ['meja] F stocking; (curta) sock; (meia-entrada) half-price ticket ▶ NUM six; **(ponto de)~** stocking stitch

meia-calça (pl **meias-calças**) F tights pl (BRIT), panty hose (US)

meia-direita (pl **meias-direitas**) F (Futebol) inside right ▶ M (jogador) inside right

meia-entrada (pl **meias-entradas**) F half-price ticket

meia-esquerda (pl **meias-esquerdas**) F (Futebol) inside left ▶ M (jogador) inside left

meia-estação F: **roupa de ~** spring ou autumn clothing

meia-idade F middle age; **pessoa de ~** middle-aged person

meia-lua F half moon; (formato) semicircle

meia-luz F half light

meia-noite F midnight

meia-tigela F: **de ~** two-bit

meia-volta (pl **meias-voltas**) F (tb Mil) about-turn (BRIT), about-face (US)

meigo, -a ['mejgu, a] ADJ sweet

meiguice [mej'gisi] F sweetness

meio, -a ['meju, a] ADJ half ▶ ADV a bit, rather ▶ M (centro) middle; (recurso) means; (social, profissional) environment; (tb: **meio ambiente**) environment; **meios** MPL (recursos) means pl; **~ quilo** half a kilo; **um mês e ~** one and a half months; **cortar ao ~** to cut in half; **deixar algo pelo ~** to leave sth half-finished; **dividir algo ~ a ~** to divide sth in half ou fifty-fifty; **o quarto do ~** the middle room, the room in the middle; **em ~ a** amid; **no ~ (de)** in the middle (of); **nos ~s financeiros** in financial circles; **~s de comunicação (de massa)** (mass) media pl; **~s de comunicação social** social media pl; **~s de produção** means pl of production; **~ de transporte** means sg of transport; **por ~ de** through; **por todos os ~s** by all available means; **não há ~ de chover/de ela chegar cedo** there is no way it's going to rain/she will arrive early; **embolar o ~ de campo** (fig) to foul things up

meio-campo (pl **meios-campos**) M (Futebol: jogador) midfielder; (: posição) midfield

meio-dia M midday, noon

meio-feriado (pl **meios-feriados**) M half-day holiday

meio-fio (pl **meios-fios**) M kerb (BRIT), curb (US)

meio-termo (pl **meios-termos**) M (fig) compromise

meio-tom (pl **meios-tons**) M (Mús) semitone; (nuança) half-tone

mel [mɛw] M honey

melaço [me'lasu] M treacle (BRIT), molasses sg (US)

melado, -a [me'ladu, a] ADJ (pegajoso) sticky ▶ M (melaço) treacle (BRIT), molasses sg (US)

melancia [melã'sia] F watermelon

melancieira [melã'sjejra] F watermelon plant

melancolia [melãko'lia] F melancholy, sadness

melancólico, -a [melã'kɔliku, a] ADJ melancholy, sad

Melanésia [mela'nɛzja] F: **a ~** Melanesia

melão [me'lãw] (pl -ões) M melon

melar [me'lar] vt to dirty ▶ vi (gorar) to flop; **melar-se** vr to get messy

meleca [me'lɛka] (col) F snot; (uma meleca) bogey; **tirar ~** to pick one's nose; **que ~!** (col) what crap! (!)

meleira [me'lejra] F sticky mess

melena [me'lena] F long hair

melhor [me'ʎɔr] ADJ, ADV (compar) better; (superl) best; **~ que nunca** better than ever; **quanto mais ~** the more the better; **seria ~**

começarmos we had better begin; **tanto ~** so much the better; **~ ainda** even better; **bem ~** much better; **o ~ é ...** the best thing is ...; **levar a ~** to come off best; **ou ~ ...** (*ou antes*) or rather ...; **fiz o ~ que pude** I did the best I could; **no ~ da festa** (*fig: no melhor momento*) when things are (*ou* were) in full swing; (*: inesperadamente*) all of a sudden

melhora [me'ʎɔra] F improvement; **~s!** get well soon!

melhorada [meʎo'rada] (*col*) F: **dar uma ~** to get better

melhoramento [meʎora'mẽtu] M improvement

melhorar [meʎo'rar] VT to improve, make better; (*doente*) to cure ▶ VI to improve, get better; **~ de vida** to improve one's circumstances; **~ no emprego** to get better at one's job

meliante [me'ljãtʃi] M scoundrel; (*vagabundo*) tramp

melindrar [melĩ'drar] VT to offend, hurt; **melindrar-se** VR to take offence (BRIT) *ou* offense (US), be hurt

melindre [me'lĩdri] M sensitivity

melindroso, -a [melĩ'drozu, ɔza] ADJ (*sensível*) sensitive, touchy; (*problema, situação*) tricky; (*operação*) delicate

melodia [melo'dʒia] F melody; (*composição*) tune

melódico, -a [me'lɔdʒiku, a] ADJ melodic

melodrama [melo'drama] M melodrama

melodramático, -a [melodra'matʃiku, a] ADJ melodramatic

meloeiro [me'lwejru] M melon plant

melões [me'lõjs] MPL *de* **melão**

meloso, -a [me'lozu, ɔza] ADJ sweet; (*voz*) mellifluous; (*fig: pessoa*) sweet-talking

melro ['mɛwhu] M blackbird

membrana [mẽ'brana] F membrane

membro ['mẽbru] M member; (*Anat: braço, perna*) limb

membrudo, -a [mẽ'brudu, a] ADJ big; (*fig*) robust

memento [me'mẽtu] M reminder; (*caderneta*) jotter

memorando [memo'rãdu] M (*aviso*) note; (*Com: comunicação*) memorandum

memorável [memo'ravew] (*pl* **-eis**) ADJ memorable

memória [me'mɔrja] F memory; **memórias** FPL (*de autor*) memoirs; **de ~** by heart; **em ~ de** in memory of; **~ fraca** bad memory; **falta de ~** loss of memory; **digno de ~** memorable; **vir à ~** to come to mind; **varrer da ~** (*fig*) to wipe sth from one's memory; **~ RAM** RAM memory; **~ não volátil** non-volatile memory

memorial [memo'rjaw] (*pl* **-ais**) M memorial; (*Jur*) brief

memorizar [memori'zar] VT to memorize

menção [mẽ'sãw] (*pl* **-ões**) F mention, reference; **~ honrosa** honours (BRIT),

honors (US), distinction; **fazer ~ de algo** to mention sth; **fazer ~ de sair** to make as if to leave, begin to leave

mencionar [mẽsjo'nar] VT to mention; **para não ~ ...** not to mention ...; **sem ~ ...** let alone ...

menções [mẽ'sõjs] FPL *de* **menção**

mendicância [mẽdʒi'kãsja] F begging

mendicante [mẽdʒi'kãtʃi] ADJ mendicant ▶ M/F beggar

mendigar [mẽdʒi'gar] VT to beg for ▶ VI to beg

mendigo, -a [mẽ'dʒigu, a] M/F beggar

menear [me'njar] VT (*corpo, cabeça*) to shake; (*quadris*) to swing; **~ a cabeça de modo afirmativo** to nod (one's head)

meneio [me'neju] M (*balanço*) swaying

menina [me'nina] F: **~ do olho** pupil; **ser a ~ dos olhos de alguém** (*fig*) to be the apple of sb's eye; *ver tb* **menino**

meninada [meni'nada] F kids *pl*

meningite [menĩ'ʒitʃi] F meningitis

meninice [meni'nisi] F (*infância*) childhood; (*modos de criança*) childishness; (*ato, dito*) childish thing

menino, -a [me'ninu, a] M/F boy/girl; **seu sorriso de ~** his boyish smile

meninote, -a [meni'nɔtʃi, ta] M/F boy/girl

menopausa [meno'pawza] F menopause

menor [me'nɔr] ADJ (*mais pequeno: compar*) smaller; (*: superl*) smallest; (*mais jovem: compar*) younger; (*: superl*) youngest; (*o mínimo*) least, slightest; (*tb*: **menor de idade**) under age ▶ M/F juvenile, young person; (*Jur*) minor; **~ abandonado** abandoned child; **proibido para ~es** over 18s only; (*filme*) X-certificate (BRIT), X-rated (US); **um ~ de 10 anos** a child of ten; **não tenho a ~ ideia** I haven't the slightest idea

menoridade [menori'dadʒi] F under-age status

(PALAVRA-CHAVE)

menos ['menus] ADJ **1** (*compar*): **menos (do que)** (*quantidade*) less (than); (*número*) fewer (than); **com menos entusiasmo** with less enthusiasm; **menos gente** fewer people

2 (*superl*) least; **é o que tem menos culpa** he is the least to blame

▶ ADV **1** (*compar*): **menos (do que)** less (than); **gostei menos do que do outro** I liked it less than the other one

2 (*superl*): **é o menos inteligente da classe** he is the least bright in his class; **de todas elas é a que menos me agrada** out of all of them she's the one I like least; **pelo menos** at (the very) least

3 (*frases*): **temos sete a menos** we are seven short; **não é para menos** it's no wonder; **isso é o de menos** that's nothing

▶ PREP (*exceção*) except; (*números*) minus; **todos menos eu** everyone except (for) me; **5 menos 2** 5 minus 2

▶ CONJ: **a menos que** unless; **a menos que ele venha amanhã** unless he comes tomorrow
▶ M: **o menos** the least

menosprezar [menuspre'zar] VT (*subestimar*) to underrate; (*desprezar*) to despise, scorn
menosprezível [menuspre'zivew] (*pl* **-eis**) ADJ despicable
menosprezo [menus'prezu] M contempt, disdain
mensageiro, -a [mēsa'ʒejru, a] ADJ messenger *atr* ▶ M/F messenger
mensagem [mē'saʒē] (*pl* **-ns**) F message; **~ de erro** (*Comput*) error message; **~ de texto** text (message); **mandar uma ~ de texto para alguém** to text sb; **~ instantânea** instant message
mensal [mē'saw] (*pl* **-ais**) ADJ monthly; **ele ganha £2000 mensais** he earns £2000 a month
mensalidade [mēsali'dadʒi] F monthly payment
mensalmente [mēsaw'mētʃi] ADV monthly
menstruação [mēstrwa'sāw] F period; (*Med*) menstruation
menstruada [mēs'trwada] ADJ having one's period; (*Med*) menstruating
menstrual [mēs'trwaw] (*pl* **-ais**) ADJ menstrual
menstruar [mēs'trwar] VI to menstruate, have a period
mênstruo ['mēstru] M period, menstruation
menta ['mēta] F mint
mental [mē'taw] (*pl* **-ais**) ADJ mental
mentalidade [mētali'dadʒi] F mentality
mentalizar [mētali'zar] VT (*plano*) to conceive; **~ alguém de algo** to make sb realize sth
mente ['mētʃi] F mind; **de boa ~** willingly; **ter em ~** to bear in mind
mentecapto, -a [mētʃi'kaptu, a] ADJ mad, crazy ▶ M/F fool, idiot
mentir [mē'tʃir] VI to lie; **minto!** (I) tell a lie!
mentira [mē'tʃira] F lie; (*ato*) lying; **parece ~ que** it seems incredible that; **de ~** not for real; **~!** (*acusação*) that's a lie!, you're lying; (*de surpresa*) you don't say!, no!
mentiroso, -a [mētʃi'rozu, ɔza] ADJ lying; (*enganoso*) deceitful; (*falso*) deceptive ▶ M/F liar
mentol [mē'tɔw] (*pl* **-óis**) M menthol
mentolado, -a [mēto'ladu, a] ADJ mentholated
mentor [mē'tor] M mentor
menu [me'nu] M (*tb Comput*) menu
mercadinho [merka'dʒiɲu] M local market
mercado [mer'kadu] M market; **~ à vista** spot market; **M~ Comum** Common Market; **~ de capitais** capital market; **~ das pulgas** flea market; **~ de trabalho** labo(u)r market; **~ externo/interno** foreign/domestic *ou* home market; **~ negro** *ou* **paralelo** black market

mercadologia [merkadolo'ʒia] F marketing
mercador [merka'dor] M merchant, trader
mercadoria [merkado'ria] F commodity; **mercadorias** FPL (*produtos*) goods
mercante [mer'kātʃi] ADJ merchant *atr*
mercantil [merkā'tʃiw] (*pl* **-is**) ADJ mercantile, commercial
mercê [mer'se] F (*favor*) favour (*BRIT*), favor (*US*); (*perdão*) mercy; **à ~ de** at the mercy of
mercearia [mersja'ria] F grocer's (shop) (*BRIT*), grocery store
merceeiro [mer'sjejru] M grocer
mercenário, -a [merse'narju, a] ADJ mercenary ▶ M mercenary
mercúrio [mer'kurju] M mercury; **M~** Mercury
merda ['mɛrda] (!) F shit (!) ▶ M/F (*pessoa*) jerk; **a ~ do carro** the bloody (*BRIT*) *ou* goddamn (*US*) car (!); **mandar alguém à ~** to tell sb to piss off (!); **estar numa ~** to be fucked up (!); **~ nenhuma** fuck all (!); **ser uma ~** (*viagem, filme*) to be crap (!)
merecedor, a [merese'dor(a)] ADJ deserving
merecer [mere'ser] VT to deserve; (*consideração*) to merit; (*valer*) to be worth ▶ VI to be worthy
merecido, -a [mere'sidu, a] ADJ deserved; (*castigo, prêmio*) just
merecimento [meresi'mētu] M desert; (*valor, talento*) merit
merenda [me'rēda] F packed lunch; **~ escolar** free school meal
merendar [merē'dar] VI to have school dinner
merendeira [merē'dejra] F (*maleta*) lunch-box; (*funcionária*) dinner-lady
merengue [me'rēgi] M meringue
meretrício [mere'trisju] M prostitution
meretriz [mere'triz] F prostitute
mergulhador, a [merguʎa'dor(a)] ADJ diving ▶ M/F diver
mergulhar [mergu'ʎar] VI (*para nadar*) to dive; (*penetrar*) to plunge ▶ VT: **~ algo em algo** (*num líquido*) to dip sth into sth; (*na terra etc*) to plunge sth into sth; **~ no trabalho/na floresta** to immerse o.s. in one's work/go deep into the forest
mergulho [mer'guʎu] M dip(ping), immersion; (*em natação*) dive; (*voo*) nose-dive; **dar um ~** (*na praia*) to go for a dip
meridiano [meri'dʒjanu] M meridian
meridional [meridʒjo'naw] (*pl* **-ais**) ADJ southern
mérito ['mɛritu] M merit
meritório, -a [meri'tɔrju, a] ADJ meritorious
merluza [mer'luza] F hake
mero, -a ['mɛru, a] ADJ mere
mertiolate® [mertʃjo'latʃi] M antiseptic
mês [mes] M month; **pago por ~** paid by the month; **duas vezes ao ~** twice a month; **~ corrente** this month
mesa ['meza] F table; (*de trabalho*) desk; (*comitê*) board; (*numa reunião*) panel; **pôr/tirar a ~** to lay/clear the table; **à ~** at the

table; **por baixo da ~** (tb fig) under the table; **~ de bilhar** billiard table; **~ de cabeceira** bedside table; **~ de centro** coffee table; **~ de cozinha/jantar** kitchen/dining table; **~ de jogo** card table; **~ de toalete** dressing table; **~ telefônica** switchboard

mesada [me'zada] F monthly allowance; (de criança) pocket money

mesa-redonda (pl **mesas-redondas**) F round table (discussion)

mescla ['mɛskla] F mixture, blend

mesclar [mes'klar] VT to mix (up); (cores) to blend

meseta [me'zeta] F plateau, tableland

mesmice [mez'misi] F sameness

mesmo, -a ['mezmu, a] ADJ same; (enfático) very ▶ ADV (exatamente) right; (até) even; (realmente) really ▶ M/F: **o ~/a mesma** the same (one); **o ~** (a mesma coisa) the same (thing); **eu ~** I myself; **este ~ homem** this very man; **ele ~ o fez** he did it himself; **o Rei ~** the King himself; **continuar na mesma** to be just the same; **dá no** ou **na mesma** it's all the same; **aqui/agora/hoje ~** right here/right now/this very day; **~ que** even if; **é ~** it's true; **é ~?** really?; **(é) isso ~!** exactly!, that's right!; **por isso ~** that's why; **~ assim** even so; **nem ~** not even; **~ quando** even when; **só ~** only; **por si ~** by oneself; **..., e estive com o ~ ontem** (referindo-se a pessoa já mencionada) ..., and I was with him yesterday; **ficar na mesma** (não entender) to be none the wiser; **isto para mim é o ~** it's all the same to me; **o ~, por favor!** (num bar etc) the same again, please

mesquinharia [meskiɲa'ria] F meanness; (ato, dito) mean thing

mesquinho, -a [mes'kiɲu, a] ADJ mean

mesquita [mes'kita] F mosque

messias [me'sias] M Messiah

mestiçar-se [mestʃi'sarsi] VR: **~ (com)** to interbreed (with)

mestiço, -a [mes'tʃisu, a] ADJ half-caste, of mixed race; (animal) crossbred ▶ M/F half-caste; half-breed

mestrado [mes'tradu] M master's degree; **fazer/tirar o ~** to do/get one's master's (degree)

mestre, -a ['mɛstri, a] ADJ (chave, viga) master; (linha, estrada) main; (qualidade) masterly ▶ M/F master/mistress; (professor) teacher; **de ~** masterly; **obra mestra** masterpiece; **ele é ~ em mentir** he's an expert liar; **~ de cerimônias** MC, master of ceremonies; **~ de obras** foreman

mestre-cuca (pl **mestres-cucas**) (col) M chef

mestria [mes'tria] F mastery; (habilidade) expertise; **com ~** to perfection

mesura [me'zura] F (cumprimento) bow; (cortesia) courtesy; **cheio de ~s** cap in hand

meta ['mɛta] F (em corrida) finishing post; (regata) finishing line; (gol) goal; (objetivo) aim, goal

metabolismo [metabo'lizmu] M metabolism

metade [me'tadʒi] F half; (meio) middle; **~ de uma laranja** half an orange; **pela ~** halfway through

metafísica [meta'fizika] F metaphysics sg

metafísico, -a [meta'fiziku, a] ADJ metaphysical

metáfora [me'tafora] F metaphor

metafórico, -a [meta'fɔriku, a] ADJ metaphorical

metal [me'taw] (pl **-ais**) M metal; **metais** MPL (Mús) brass sg

metálico, -a [me'taliku, a] ADJ metallic; (de metal) metal atr

metalinguagem [metalī'gwaʒē] (pl **-ns**) F metalanguage

metalizado, -a [metali'zadu, a] ADJ (papel etc) metallic

metalurgia [metalur'ʒia] F metallurgy

metalúrgica [meta'lurʒika] F metal works sg; ver tb **metalúrgico**

metalúrgico, -a [meta'lurʒiku, a] ADJ metallurgical ▶ M/F metalworker

metamorfose [metamor'fɔzi] F metamorphosis

metamorfosear [metamorfo'zjar] VT: **~ alguém em algo** to transform sb into sth

metano [me'tanu] M methane

meteórico, -a [mete'ɔriku, a] ADJ meteoric

meteorito [meteo'ritu] M meteorite

meteoro [me'tjɔru] M meteor

meteorologia [meteorolo'ʒia] F meteorology

meteorológico, -a [meteoro'lɔʒiku, a] ADJ meteorological

meteorologista [meteorolo'ʒista] M/F meteorologist; (TV, Rádio) weather forecaster

meter [me'ter] VT (colocar) to put; (envolver) to involve; (introduzir) to introduce; **meter-se** VR (esconder-se) to hide; (retirar-se) to closet o.s.; **~-se a fazer algo** to decide to have a go at sth; **~-se a médico** to fancy oneself as a doctor; **~-se com** (provocar) to pick a quarrel with; (associar-se) to get involved with; **meta-se com a sua vida** mind your own business; **~-se em** to get involved in; (intrometer-se) to interfere in; **~ na cabeça** to take it into one's head; **~-se na cama** to get into bed; **~-se onde não é chamado** to poke one's nose in(to other people's business)

meticulosidade [metʃikulozi'dadʒi] F meticulousness

meticuloso, -a [metʃiku'lozu, ɔza] ADJ meticulous

metido, -a [me'tʃidu, a] ADJ (envolvido) involved; (intrometido) meddling; **~ (a besta)** snobbish

metódico, -a [me'tɔdʒiku, a] ADJ methodical

metodismo [meto'dʒizmu] M (Rel) Methodism

metodista [meto'dʒista] ADJ, M/F Methodist

método ['mɛtodu] M method

metodologia [metodolo'ʒia] F methodology

m

metragem [me'traʒẽ] F length (in metres
(BRIT) ou meters (US)); (Cinema) footage,
length; **filme de longa/curta ~** feature ou
full-length/short film
metralhadora [metraʎa'dora] F machine
gun
metralhar [metra'ʎar] VT (ferir, matar) to shoot;
(fazer fogo contra) to spray with machine-gun
fire
métrica ['mɛtrika] F (em poesia) metre (BRIT),
meter (US)
métrico, -a ['mɛtriku, a] ADJ metric
metro ['mɛtru] M metre (BRIT), meter (US);
(PT: metropolitano) underground (BRIT),
subway (US); **~ quadrado/cúbico** square/
cubic metre
metrô [me'tro] (BR) M underground (BRIT),
subway (US)
metrópole [me'trɔpoli] F metropolis; (capital)
capital
metropolitano, -a [metropoli'tanu, a] ADJ
metropolitan ▶ M (PT) underground (BRIT),
subway (US)
metroviário, -a [metro'vjarju, a] ADJ
underground atr (BRIT), subway atr (US) ▶ M/F
underground (BRIT) ou subway (US) worker
meu, minha [mew, 'miɲa] ADJ my ▶ PRON
mine; **os meus** MPL (minha família) my family
ou folks (col); **um amigo ~** a friend of mine;
este livro é ~ this book is mine; **estou na
minha** I'm minding my own business
MEx (BR) ABR M = **Ministério do Exército**
mexer [me'ʃer] VT (mover) to move; (cabeça:
dizendo sim) to nod; (: dizendo não) to shake;
(misturar) to stir; (ovos) to scramble ▶ VI
(mover) to move; **mexer-se** VR to move;
(apressar-se) to get a move on; **~ com algo**
(trabalhar) to work with sth; (comerciar) to deal
in sth; **~ com alguém** (provocar) to tease sb;
(comover) to have a profound effect on sb, get
to sb (col); **~ em algo** to touch sth; **mexa-se!**
get going!, move yourself!
mexerica [meʃe'rika] F tangerine, satsuma
mexericar [meʃeri'kar] VI to gossip
mexerico [meʃe'riku] M piece of gossip;
mexericos MPL (fofocas) gossip sg
mexeriqueiro, -a [meʃeri'kejru, a] ADJ
gossiping ▶ M/F gossip, busybody
mexicano, -a [meʃi'kanu, a] ADJ, M/F Mexican
México ['mɛʃiku] M: **o ~** Mexico; **a Cidade
do ~** Mexico City
mexida [me'ʃida] F mess, disorder
mexido, -a [me'ʃidu, a] ADJ (papéis) mixed up;
(ovos) scrambled
mexilhão [meʃi'ʎãw] (pl -ões) M mussel
mezanino [meza'ninu] M mezzanine (floor)
MF (BR) ABR M = **Ministério da Fazenda**
MG (BR) ABR = **Minas Gerais**
mg ABR (= miligrama) mg
mi [mi] M (Mús) E
miado ['mjadu] M miaow
miar [mjar] VI to miaow; (vento) to whistle
miasma ['mjazma] M (fig) decay

miau [mjaw] M miaow
MIC (BR) ABR M = **Ministério de Indústria e
Comércio**
miçanga [mi'sãga] F beads pl
micção [mik'sãw] F urination
michê [mi'ʃe] M (col) rent boy
mico ['miku] M capuchin monkey
micose [mi'kɔzi] F mycosis
micro... [mikru] PREFIXO micro...
micróbio [mi'krɔbju] M germ, microbe
microblog, microblogue [mikro'blɔgi] M
microblog
microcirurgia [mikrosirur'ʒia] F
microsurgery
microcosmo [mikro'kɔzmu] M microcosm
microempresa [mikroẽ'preza] F small
business
microfilme [mikro'fiwmi] M microfilm
microfone [mikro'fɔni] M microphone
Micronésia [mikro'nɛzja] F: **a ~** Micronesia
micro-onda [mikro'õda] F microwave
micro-ondas [mikro'õdas] M INV microwave
micro-ônibus [mikro'onibus] M INV minibus
microprocessador [mikroprosesa'dor] M
microprocessor
microrganismo [mikrorga'nizmu] M
microorganism
microscópico, -a [mikro'skɔpiku, a] ADJ
microscopic
microscópio [mikro'skɔpju] M microscope
mídi ['midʒi] ADJ INV midi
mídia ['midʒja] F media pl; **~s sociais** social
media pl
migalha [mi'gaʎa] F crumb; **migalhas** FPL
(restos, sobras) scraps
migração [migra'sãw] (pl -ões) F migration
migrar [mi'grar] VI to migrate
migratório, -a [migra'tɔrju, a] ADJ migratory;
aves migratórias birds of passage
miguel [mi'gɛw] (pl -eis) (col) M (banheiro) loo
(BRIT), john (US)
mijada [mi'ʒada] (col) F pee; **dar uma ~** to
have a pee
mijar [mi'ʒar] (col) VI to pee; **mijar-se** VR to
wet o.s.
mijo ['miʒu] (col) M pee
mil [miw] NUM thousand; **dois ~** two
thousand; **estar a ~** (col) to be buzzing
milagre [mi'lagri] M miracle; **por ~**
miraculously
milagroso, -a [mila'grozu, ɔza] ADJ
miraculous
milenar [mile'nar] ADJ thousand-year-old;
(fig) ancient
milênio [mi'lenju] M millennium
milésimo, -a [mi'lɛzimu, a] NUM thousandth
mil-folhas F INV (massa) millefeuille pastry;
(doce) cream slice
milha ['miʎa] F mile; (col: mil cruzeiros): **dez ~s**
ten grand; **~ marítima** nautical mile
milhão [mi'ʎãw] (pl -ões) M million; **um ~ de
vezes** hundreds of times; **adorei milhões!**
(col) I loved it!

milhar [mi'ʎar] M thousand; **turistas aos ~es** tourists in their thousands
milharal [miʎa'raw] (pl **-ais**) M maize (BRIT) ou corn (US) field
milho ['miʎu] M maize (BRIT), corn (US)
milhões [mi'ʎõjs] MPL de **milhão**
miliardário, -a [miljar'darju, a] ADJ, M/F billionaire
milícia [mi'lisja] F (Mil) militia; (: vida) military life; (: força) military force
milico [mi'liku] (col) M military type
miligrama [mili'grama] M milligram(me)
mililitro [mili'litru] M millilitre (BRIT), milliliter (US)
milímetro [mi'limetru] M millimetre (BRIT), millimeter (US)
milionário, -a [miljo'narju, a] ADJ, M/F millionaire
milionésimo, -a [miljo'nɛzimu, a] NUM millionth
militância [mili'tãsja] F militancy
militante [mili'tãtʃi] ADJ, M/F militant
militar [mili'tar] ADJ military ▶ M soldier ▶ VI to fight; **~ em** (Mil: regimento) to serve in; (Pol: partido) to belong to, be active in; (profissão) to work in
militarismo [milita'rizmu] M militarism
militarista [milita'rista] ADJ, M/F militarist
militarizar [militari'zar] VT to militarize
mil-réis M INV former unit of currency in Brazil and Portugal
mim [mĩ] PRON me; (reflexivo) myself; **de ~ para ~** to myself
mimado, -a [mi'madu, a] ADJ spoiled, spoilt (BRIT)
mimar [mi'mar] VT to pamper, spoil
mimeógrafo [mime'ografu] M duplicating machine
mimetismo [mime'tʃizmu] M (Bio) mimicry
mímica ['mimika] F mime; (jogo) charades; ver tb **mímico**
mímico, -a ['mimiku, a] M/F mime artist
mimo ['mimu] M (presente) gift; (pessoa, coisa encantadora) delight; (carinho) tenderness; (gentileza) kindness; **cheio de ~s** (criança) spoiled, spoilt (BRIT)
mimoso, -a [mi'mozu, ɔza] ADJ (delicado) delicate; (carinhoso) tender, loving; (encantador) delightful
MIN (BR) ABR M = **Ministério do Interior**
min. ABR (= mínimo) min.
mina ['mina] F mine; (fig: de riquezas) gold mine; (: de informações) mine of information; (col: garota) girl; **~ de carvão** coal mine; **~ de ouro** (tb fig) gold mine
minar [mi'nar] VT to mine; (fig) to undermine
minarete [mina'retʃi] M minaret
Minc (BR) ABR M = **Ministério da Cultura**
mindinho [mĩ'dʒiɲu] M (tb: **dedo mindinho**) little finger
mineiro, -a [mi'nejru, a] ADJ mining atr; (de Minas Gerais) from Minas Gerais ▶ M/F miner; person from Minas Gerais

mineração [minera'sãw] F mining
mineral [mine'raw] (pl **-ais**) ADJ, M mineral
mineralogia [mineralo'ʒia] F mineralogy
minerar [mine'rar] VT, VI to mine
minério [mi'nerju] M ore; **~ de ferro** iron ore
mingau [mĩ'gaw] M (tb: **mingau de aveia**) porridge; (fig) slop
míngua ['mĩgwa] F lack; **à ~ de** for want of; **viver à ~** to live in poverty
minguado, -a [mĩ'gwadu, a] ADJ scant; (criança) stunted; **~ de algo** short of sth
minguante [mĩ'gwãtʃi] ADJ waning; **(quarto) ~** (Astronomia) last quarter
minguar [mĩ'gwar] VI (diminuir) to decrease, dwindle; (faltar) to run short
minha ['miɲa] F de **meu**
minhoca [mi'ɲɔka] F (earth)worm; (col: bobagem) daft idea; **~ da terra** (fig: caipira) country person
míni ['mini] ADJ INV mini ▶ M minicomputer
mini... [mini] PREFIXO mini...
miniatura [minja'tura] ADJ, F miniature
minicomputador [minikõputa'dor] M minicomputer
mínima ['minima] F (temperatura) low; (Mús) minim
minimalista [minima'lista] ADJ (fig) stark
minimizar [minimi'zar] VT to minimize; (subestimar) to play down
mínimo, -a ['minimu, a] ADJ minimum ▶ M minimum; (tb: **dedo mínimo**) little finger; **não dou ou ligo a mínima para isso** I couldn't care less about it; **a mínima importância/ ideia** the slightest importance/idea; **o ~ que podem fazer** the least they can do; **no ~** at least; **no ~ às 11 horas** at 11.00 at the earliest
minissaia [mini'saja] F miniskirt
ministerial [ministe'rjaw] (pl **-ais**) ADJ ministerial
ministeriável [ministe'rjavew] (pl **-eis**) ADJ eligible to be a minister
ministério [mini'sterju] M ministry; **M~ da Fazenda** ≈ Treasury (BRIT), ≈ Treasury Department (US); **M~ do Interior** ≈ Home Office (BRIT), ≈ Department of the Interior (US); **M~ da Marinha/Educação/Saúde** ≈ Admiralty/Ministry of Education/Health; **M~ das Relações Exteriores** ≈ Foreign Office (BRIT), ≈ State Department (US); **M~ do Trabalho** ≈ Department of Employment (BRIT) ou Labor (US); **~ público** public prosecution service
ministrar [minis'trar] VT (dar) to supply; (remédio) to administer; (aulas) to give ▶ VI to serve as a minister
ministro, -a [mi'nistru, a] M/F minister; **~ da Fazenda** ≈ Chancellor of the Exchequer (BRIT), ≈ Head of the Treasury Department (US); **~ do Interior** ≈ Home Secretary (BRIT); **~ das Relações Exteriores** ≈ Foreign Secretary (BRIT), ≈ Head of the State Department (US); **~ sem pasta** minister without portfolio

m

minorar [mino'rar] vt to lessen, reduce
Minorca [mi'nɔrka] F Menorca
minoria [mino'ria] F minority
minoritário, -a [minori'tarju, a] ADJ minority atr
minto etc ['mĩtu] VB ver **mentir**
minúcia [mi'nusja] F detail
minucioso, -a [minu'sjozu, ɔza] ADJ (indivíduo, busca) thorough; (explicação) detailed
minúsculo, -a [mi'nuskulu, a] ADJ minute, tiny; **letra minúscula** lower case letter
minuta [mi'nuta] F (rascunho) draft; (Culin) dish cooked to order; **~ de contrato** draft contract
minutar [minu'tar] vt to draft
minuto [mi'nutu] M minute
miolo ['mjolu] M inside; (polpa) pulp; (de maçã) core; **miolos** MPL (cérebro, inteligência) brains
míope ['mjopi] ADJ short-sighted ▶ M/F myopic
miopia [mjo'pia] F short-sightedness, myopia
miosótis [mjo'zɔtʃis] M INV (Bot) forget-me-not
mira ['mira] F (de fuzil) sight; (pontaria) aim; (fig) aim, purpose; **à ~ de** on the lookout for; **ter em ~** to have one's eye on
mirabolante [mirabo'lãtʃi] ADJ (roupa) showy, loud; (plano) ambitious; (surpreendente) amazing
mirada [mi'rada] F look
miradouro [mira'doru] M viewpoint, belvedere
miragem [mi'raʒẽ] (pl -ns) F mirage
miramar [mira'mar] M sea view
mirante [mi'rãtʃi] M viewpoint, belvedere
mirar [mi'rar] vt to look at; (observar) to watch; (apontar para) to aim at ▶ VI: **~ em** to aim at; **mirar-se** VR to look at o.s.; **~ para** to look onto
miríade [mi'riadʒi] F myriad
mirim [mi'rĩ] (pl -ns) ADJ little
mirrado, -a [mi'hadu, a] ADJ (planta) withered; (pessoa) haggard
mirrar-se [mi'harsi] VR (planta) to wither, dry up; (pessoa) to waste away
misantropo, -a [mizã'tropu, a] ADJ misanthropic ▶ M/F misanthrope
miscelânea [mise'lanja] F miscellany; (confusão) muddle
miscigenação [misiʒena'sãw] F interbreeding
mise-en-plis [mizã'pli] M shampoo and set
miserável [mize'ravew] (pl -eis) ADJ (digno de compaixão) wretched; (pobre) impoverished; (avaro) stingy, mean; (insignificante) paltry; (lugar) squalid; (infame) despicable ▶ M (indigente) wretch; (coitado) poor thing; (pessoa infame) rotter
miserê [mize're] (col) M poverty, pennilessness
miséria [mi'zɛrja] F (estado lastimável) misery; (pobreza) poverty; (avareza) stinginess;

chorar ~ to complain that one is hard up; **fazer ~s** (col) to do wonders; **ganhar/custar uma ~** to earn/cost a pittance; **ser uma ~** (col) to be awful
misericórdia [mizeri'kɔrdʒja] F (compaixão) pity, compassion; (graça) mercy
misógino, -a [mi'zɔʒinu, a] ADJ misogynistic ▶ M misogynist
missa ['misa] F (Rel) mass; **não saber da ~ a metade** (col) not to know the half of it
missal [mi'saw] (pl -ais) M missal
missão [mi'sãw] (pl -ões) F mission; (dever) duty; (incumbência) job
misse ['misi] F beauty queen
míssil ['misiw] (pl -eis) M missile; **~ balístico/guiado** ballistic/guided missile; **~ de curto/médio/longo alcance** short-/medium-/long-range missile
missionário, -a [misjo'narju, a] M/F missionary
missiva [mi'siva] F missive
missões [mi'sõjs] FPL de **missão**
mister [mis'ter] M (ocupação) occupation; (trabalho) job; **ser ~** to be necessary; **ter-se ~ de algo** to need sth; **não há ~ de** there's no need for
mistério [mis'tɛrju] M mystery; **fazer ~ de algo** to make a mystery of sth; **não ter ~** to be straightforward
misterioso, -a [miste'rjozu, ɔza] ADJ mysterious
misticismo [mistʃi'sizmu] M mysticism
místico, -a ['mistʃiku, a] ADJ, M/F mystic
mistificar [mistʃifi'kar] VT, VI to fool
misto, -a ['mistu, a] ADJ mixed; (confuso) mixed up; (escola) mixed ▶ M mixture
misto-quente (pl **mistos-quentes**) M toasted cheese and ham sandwich
mistura [mis'tura] F mixture; (ato) mixing
misturada [mistu'rada] F jumble
misturar [mistu'rar] VT to mix; (confundir) to mix up; **misturar-se** VR: **~-se com** to mingle with
mítico, -a ['mitʃiku, a] ADJ mythical
mitificar [mitʃifi'kar] VT to mythicize; (mulher, estrela) to idolize
mitigar [mitʃi'gar] VT (raiva) to temper; (dor) to relieve; (sede) to lessen
mito ['mitu] M myth
mitologia [mitolo'ʒia] F mythology
mitológico, -a [mito'lɔʒiku, a] ADJ mythological
miudezas [mju'dezas] FPL minutiae; (bugigangas) odds and ends; (objetos pequenos) trinkets
miúdo, -a ['mjudu, a] ADJ (pequeno) tiny, minute ▶ M/F (PT: criança) youngster, kid; **miúdos** MPL (dinheiro) change sg; (de aves) giblets; **dinheiro ~** small change; **trocar em ~s** (fig) to spell it out
mixa ['miʃa] (col) ADJ (insignificante) measly; (de má qualidade) crummy; (festa) dull
mixagem [mik'saʒẽ] F mixing

mixar¹ [mi'ʃar] ᴠᴛ to mess up ▶ ᴠɪ (*gorar*) to go down the drain; (*acabar*) to finish

mixar² [mik'sar] ᴠᴛ (*sons*) to mix

mixaria [miʃa'ria] (*col*) ꜰ (*coisa sem valor*) trifle; (*insignificância*) trivial matter

mixórdia [mi'ʃɔrdʒja] ꜰ mess, jumble

MJ ᴀʙʀ ᴍ = **Ministério da Justiça**

MM ᴀʙʀ ᴍ = **Ministério da Marinha**

mm ᴀʙʀ (= *milímetro*) mm

MME (*BR*) ᴀʙʀ ᴍ = **Ministério de Minas e Energia**

mnemônico, -a [mne'moniku, a] ᴀᴅᴊ mnemonic

mo [mu] ᴘʀᴏɴ = **me + o**

mó [mɔ] ꜰ (*de moinho*) millstone; (*para afiar*) grindstone

moa *etc* ['moa] ᴠʙ *ver* **moer**

moagem ['mwaʒẽ] ꜰ grinding

móbil ['mɔbiw] (*pl* **-eis**) ᴀᴅᴊ = **móvel**

mobilar [mobi'lar] (*PT*) ᴠᴛ to furnish

móbile ['mɔbili] ᴍ mobile

mobília [mo'bilja] ꜰ furniture

mobiliar [mobi'ljar] (*BR*) ᴠᴛ to furnish

mobiliária [mobi'ljarja] ꜰ furniture shop

mobiliário [mobi'ljarju] ᴍ furnishings *pl*

mobilidade [mobili'dadʒi] ꜰ mobility; (*fig: de espírito*) changeability

mobilização [mobiliza'sãw] ꜰ mobilization

mobilizar [mobili'zar] ᴠᴛ to mobilize; (*movimentar*) to move

Mobral [mo'braw] ᴀʙʀ ᴍ = **Movimento Brasileiro de Alfabetização**

moça ['mosa] ꜰ girl, young woman

moçada [mo'sada] ꜰ (*moços*) boys *pl*; (*moças*) girls *pl*

moçambicano, -a [mosãbi'kanu, a] ᴀᴅᴊ, ᴍ/ꜰ Mozambican

Moçambique [mosã'biki] ᴍ Mozambique

moção [mo'sãw] (*pl* **-ões**) ꜰ motion

mocassim [moka'sĩ] (*pl* **-ns**) ᴍ moccasin; (*sapato esporte*) slip-on

mochila [mo'ʃila] ꜰ rucksack

mochilão [moʃi'lãw] ᴍ backpacking trip; **fazer um ~** to go backpacking

mocidade [mosi'dadʒi] ꜰ youth; (*os moços*) young people *pl*

mocinho, -a [mo'siɲu, a] ᴍ/ꜰ little boy/girl ▶ ᴍ (*herói*) hero, good guy

moço, -a ['mosu, a] ᴀᴅᴊ young ▶ ᴍ young man, lad; **~ de bordo** ordinary seaman; **~ de cavalariça** groom

moções [mo'sõjs] ꜰᴘʟ *de* **moção**

mocorongo, -a [moko'rõgu, a] (*col*) ᴍ/ꜰ country bumpkin

moda ['mɔda] ꜰ fashion; **estar na ~** to be in fashion, be all the rage; **fora da ~** old-fashioned; **sair da** *ou* **cair de ~** to go out of fashion; **a última ~** the latest fashion; **à ~ brasileira** in the Brazilian way; **ele faz tudo à sua ~** he does everything his own way; **fazer ~** to make up stories

modalidade [modali'dadʒi] ꜰ kind; (*Esporte*) event

modelagem [mode'laʒẽ] ꜰ modelling; **~ do corpo** bodybuilding

modelar [mode'lar] ᴠᴛ to model; (*assinalar os contornos de*) to shape, highlight; **modelar-se** ᴠʀ: **~(-se) a algo** to model (o.s.) on sth

modelista [mode'lista] ᴍ/ꜰ designer

modelo [mo'delu] ᴍ model; (*criação de estilista*) design; (*pessoa admirada*) role-model ▶ ᴍ/ꜰ (*manequim*) model

modem ['modẽ] (*pl* **-ns**) ᴍ modem

moderação [modera'sãw] (*pl* **-ões**) ꜰ moderation

moderado, -a [mode'radu, a] ᴀᴅᴊ moderate; (*clima*) mild

moderar [mode'rar] ᴠᴛ to moderate; (*violência*) to control, restrain; (*velocidade*) to reduce; (*voz*) to lower; (*gastos*) to cut down; **moderar-se** ᴠʀ to control o.s.

modernidade [moderni'dadʒi] ꜰ modernity

modernismo [moder'nizmu] ᴍ modernism

modernização [moderniza'sãw] (*pl* **-ões**) ꜰ modernization

modernizar [moderni'zar] ᴠᴛ to modernize; **modernizar-se** ᴠʀ to modernize

moderno, -a [mo'dɛrnu, a] ᴀᴅᴊ modern; (*atual*) present-day

modernoso, -a [moder'nozu, ɔza] ᴀᴅᴊ newfangled

módess® ['mɔdes] (*col*) ᴍ ɪɴᴠ sanitary towel (*BRIT*) *ou* napkin (*US*)

modéstia [mo'dɛstʃja] ꜰ modesty

modesto, -a [mo'dɛstu, a] ᴀᴅᴊ modest; (*simples*) simple, plain; (*vida*) frugal

módico, -a ['mɔdʒiku, a] ᴀᴅᴊ moderate; (*preço*) reasonable; (*bens*) scant

modificação [modʒifika'sãw] (*pl* **-ões**) ꜰ modification

modificar [modʒifi'kar] ᴠᴛ to modify, alter

modinha [mo'dʒiɲa] ꜰ popular song, tune

modismo [mo'dʒizmu] ᴍ idiom

modista [mo'dʒista] ꜰ dressmaker

modo ['mɔdu] ᴍ (*maneira*) way, manner; (*método*) way; (*Ling*) mood; (*Mús*) mode; **modos** ᴍᴘʟ (*comportamento*) manners; **~ de pensar** way of thinking; **de (tal) ~ que** so (that); **de ~ nenhum** in no way; **de qualquer ~** anyway, anyhow; **tenha ~s!** behave yourself!; **de ~ geral** in general; **~ de andar** way of walking, walk; **~ de escrever** style of writing; **~ de emprego** instructions *pl* for use; **~ de ser** way (of being), manner; **~ de vida** way of life

modorra [mo'doha] ꜰ (*sonolência*) drowsiness; (*letargia*) lethargy

modulação [modula'sãw] (*pl* **-ões**) ꜰ modulation; **~ de frequência** frequency modulation

modular [modu'lar] ᴠᴛ to modulate ▶ ᴀᴅᴊ modular

módulo ['mɔdulu] ᴍ module; **~ lunar** lunar module

moeda ['mwɛda] ꜰ (*uma moeda*) coin; (*dinheiro*) currency; **uma ~ de 50p** a 50p piece;

m

~ corrente currency; **pagar na mesma ~** to give tit for tat; **Casa da M~** ≈ the (Royal) Mint (BRIT), ≈ the (US) Mint (US); **~ falsa** forged money; **~ forte** hard currency

moedor [moe'dor] M (de café) grinder; (de carne) mincer

moenda ['mwẽda] F grinding equipment

moer [mwer] VT (café) to grind; (cana) to crush; (bater) to beat; (cansar) to tire out

mofado, -a [mo'fadu, a] ADJ mouldy (BRIT), moldy (US)

mofar [mo'far] VI to go mouldy (BRIT) ou moldy (US); (na prisão) to rot; (ficar esperando) to hang around; (zombar) to mock, scoff ▶ VT to cover in mo(u)ld

mofo ['mofu] M (Bot) mould (BRIT), mold (US); **cheiro de ~** musty smell

mogno ['mɔgnu] M mahogany

mói etc [mɔj] VB ver **moer**

moía etc [mo'ia] VB ver **moer**

moído, -a [mo'idu, a] PP de **moer** ▶ ADJ (café) ground; (carne) minced; (cansado) tired out; (corpo) aching

moinho ['mwĩɲu] M mill; (de café) grinder; **~ de vento** windmill

moisés [moj'zɛs] M INV carry-cot

moita ['mɔjta] F thicket; **~!** mum's the word!; **na ~** (fig) on the quiet; **ficar na ~** (fazer segredo) to keep quiet, not say a word; (ficar na expectativa) to stand by

mola ['mɔla] F (Tec) spring; (fig) motive, motivation

molambo [mo'lãbu] M rag

molar [mo'lar] M molar (tooth)

moldar [mow'dar] VT to mould (BRIT), mold (US); (metal) to cast; (fig) to mo(u)ld, shape

Moldávia [mow'davja] F: **a ~** Moldavia

molde ['mɔwdʒi] M mould (BRIT), mold (US); (de papel) pattern; (fig) model; **~ de vestido** dress pattern

moldura [mow'dura] F (de pintura) frame; (ornato) moulding (BRIT), molding (US)

moldurar [mowdu'rar] VT to frame

mole ['mɔli] ADJ (macio, fofo) soft; (sem energia) listless; (carnes) flabby; (col: fácil) easy; (pessoa: sentimental) soft; (lento) slow; (preguiçoso) sluggish ▶ ADV (facilmente) easily; (lentamente) slowly

moleca [mo'lɛka] F urchin; (menina) youngster

molecada [mole'kada] F urchins pl

molecagem [mole'kaʒẽ] (pl **-ns**) F (de criança) prank; (sujeira) dirty trick; (brincadeira) joke

molécula [mo'lɛkula] F molecule

molecular [moleku'lar] ADJ molecular

molejo [mo'leʒu] M (de carro) suspension; (col: de pessoa) wiggle

moleque [mo'leki] M (de rua) urchin; (menino) youngster; (pessoa sem palavra) unreliable person; (canalha) scoundrel ▶ ADJ (levado) mischievous; (brincalhão) funny

molestar [moles'tar] VT (ofender) to upset; (enfadar) to annoy; (importunar) to bother

moléstia [mo'lɛstʃja] F illness

molesto, -a [mo'lɛstu, a] ADJ tiresome; (prejudicial) unhealthy

moletom [mole'tõ] (pl **-ns**) M (de lã) fleece; (de algodão) sweatshirt material; **blusa de ~** sweatshirt

moleza [mo'leza] F softness; (falta de energia) listlessness; (falta de força) weakness; **ser (uma) ~** (col) to be easy; **na ~** without exerting oneself

molhada [mo'ʎada] F soaking

molhado, -a [mo'ʎadu, a] ADJ wet, damp

molhar [mo'ʎar] VT to wet; (de leve) to moisten; dampen; (mergulhar) to dip; **molhar-se** VR to get wet; (col: urinar) to wet o.s.

molhe ['moʎi] (PT) M jetty; (cais) wharf, quay

molheira [mo'ʎejra] F sauce boat; (para carne) gravy boat

molho¹ ['mɔʎu] M (de chaves) bunch; (de trigo) sheaf

molho² ['moʎu] M (Culin) sauce; (: de salada) dressing; (: de carne) gravy; **pôr de ~** to soak; **estar/deixar de ~** (roupa etc) to be/leave to soak; **estar/ficar de ~** (fig) to be/stay in bed; **~ branco** white sauce; **~ inglês** Worcester sauce

molinete [moli'netʃi] M reel; (caniço) fishing rod

moloide [mo'lɔjdʒi] (col) ADJ slow ▶ M/F lazy-bones

molusco [mo'lusku] M mollusc (BRIT), mollusk (US)

momentâneo, -a [momẽ'tanju, a] ADJ momentary

momento [mo'mẽtu] M moment; (Tec) momentum; **a todo ~** constantly; **de um ~ para outro** suddenly; **no ~ em que** just as; **no/neste ~** at the/this moment; **a qualquer ~** at any moment

Mônaco ['monaku] M Monaco

monarca [mo'narka] M/F monarch, ruler

monarquia [monar'kia] F monarchy

monarquista [monar'kista] ADJ, M/F monarchist

monastério [monas'tɛrju] M monastery

monástico, -a [mo'nastʃiku, a] ADJ monastic

monção [mõ'sãw] (pl **-ões**) F monsoon

mondar [mõ'dar] (PT) VT (ervas daninhas) to pull up; (árvores) to prune; (fig) to weed out

monetário, -a [mone'tarju, a] ADJ monetary; **correção monetária** currency adjustment

monetarismo [moneta'rizmu] M monetarism

monetarista [moneta'rista] ADJ, M/F monetarist

monge ['mõʒi] M monk

mongol [mõ'gɔw] (pl **-óis**) ADJ, M/F Mongol, Mongolian

Mongólia [mõ'gɔlja] F: **a ~** Mongolia

mongolismo [mõgo'lizmu] M (Med) mongolism

mongoloide [mõgo'lɔjdʒi] ADJ, M/F (ofensivo) mongol

monitor [moni'tor] M monitor
monitorar [monito'rar] VT to monitor
monitorizar [monitori'zar] VT = **monitorar**
monja ['mõʒa] F nun
monocromo, -a [mono'krɔmu, a] ADJ monochrome
monóculo [mo'nɔkulu] M monocle
monocultura [monokuw'tura] F monoculture
monogamia [monoga'mia] F monogamy
monogâmico, -a [mono'gamiku, a] ADJ monogamous
monógamo, -a [mo'nɔgamu, a] ADJ monogamous
monograma [mono'grama] M monogram
monologar [monolo'gar] VI to talk to o.s.; (Teatro) to speak a monologue ▶ VT to say to o.s.
monólogo [mo'nɔlogu] M monologue
monoplano [mono'planu] M monoplane
monopólio [mono'pɔlju] M monopoly
monopolizar [monopoli'zar] VT to monopolize
monossilábico, -a [monosi'labiku, a] ADJ monosyllabic
monossílabo [mono'silabu] M monosyllable; **responder por ~s** to reply in monosyllables
monotonia [monoto'nia] F monotony
monótono, -a [mo'nɔtonu, a] ADJ monotonous
monotrilho [mono'triʎu] M monorail
monóxido [mo'nɔksidu] M: **~ de carbono** carbon monoxide
monsenhor [mõse'ɲor] M monsignor
monstro, -a ['mõstru, a] ADJ INV giant ▶ M (tb fig) monster; **~ sagrado** superstar
monstruosidade [mõstrwozi'dadʒi] F monstrosity
monstruoso, -a [mõ'strwozu, ɔza] ADJ monstrous; (enorme) gigantic, huge
monta ['mõta] F: **de pouca ~** trivial, of little account
montador, a [mõta'dor(a)] M/F (Cinema) editor
montagem [mõ'taʒẽ] (pl **-ns**) F assembly; (Arq) erection; (Cinema) editing; (Teatro) production
montanha [mõ'taɲa] F mountain
montanha-russa F roller coaster
montanhês, -esa [mõta'ɲes, eza] ADJ mountain atr ▶ M/F highlander
montanhismo [mõta'ɲizmu] M mountaineering
montanhista [mõta'ɲista] M/F mountaineer ▶ ADJ mountaineering
montanhoso, -a [mõta'ɲozu, ɔza] ADJ mountainous
montante [mõ'tãtʃi] M amount, sum ▶ ADJ (maré) rising; **a ~** (nadar) upstream
montão [mõ'tãw] (pl **-ões**) M heap, pile
montar [mõ'tar] VT (cavalo) to mount, get on; (colocar em) to put on; (cavalgar) to ride; (peças) to assemble, put together; (loja, máquina) to

set up; (casa) to put up; (peça teatral) to put on ▶ VI to ride; **~ a** ou **em** (animal) to get on; (cavalgar) to ride; (despesa) to come to
montaria [mõta'ria] F (cavalgadura) mount
monte ['mõtʃi] M hill; (pilha) heap, pile; **um ~ de** (muitos) a lot of, lots of; **gente aos ~s** loads of people
montepio [mõtʃi'piu] M (pensão) pension; (fundo) trust fund
montês [mõ'tes] ADJ: **cabra ~** mountain goat
Montevidéu [mõtʃivi'dɛw] N Montevideo
montoeira [mõ'twejra] F stack
montões [mõ'tõjs] MPL de **montão**
montra ['mõtra] (PT) F shop window
monumental [monumẽ'taw] (pl **-ais**) ADJ monumental; (fig) magnificent, splendid
monumento [monu'mẽtu] M monument
moqueca [mo'kɛka] F fish or seafood simmered in coconut cream and palm oil; **~ de camarão** prawn moqueca
morada [mo'rada] F home, residence; (PT: endereço) address
moradia [mora'dʒia] F home, dwelling
morador, a [mora'dor(a)] M/F (de casa, bairro) resident; (de casa alugada) tenant
moral [mo'raw] (pl **-ais**) ADJ moral ▶ F (ética) ethics pl; (conclusão) moral ▶ M (de pessoa) sense of morality; (ânimo) morale; **levantar o ~** to raise morale; **estar de ~ baixa** to be demoralized; **~ da história** moral of the story
moralidade [morali'dadʒi] F morality
moralista [mora'lista] ADJ moralistic ▶ M/F moralist
moralizar [morali'zar] VI to moralize ▶ VT to preach at
morango [mo'rãgu] M strawberry
morangueiro [morã'gejru] M strawberry plant
morar [mo'rar] VI to live, reside; (col: entender) to catch on; **~ em algo** (col) to grasp sth; **morou?** got it?, see?
moratória [mora'tɔrja] F moratorium
morbidez [morbi'dez] F morbidness
mórbido, -a ['mɔrbidu, a] ADJ morbid
morcego [mor'segu] M (Bio) bat
morcela [mor'sela] (PT) F black pudding (BRIT), blood sausage (US)
mordaça [mor'dasa] F (de animal) muzzle; (fig) gag
mordaz [mor'daz] ADJ scathing
morder [mor'der] VT to bite; (corroer) to corrode; **morder-se** VR to bite o.s.; **~ a língua** to bite one's tongue; **~-se de inveja** to be green with envy
mordida [mor'dʒida] F bite
mordomia [mordo'mia] F (de executivos) perk; (col: regalia) luxury, comfort
mordomo [mor'dɔmu] M butler
morenaço, -a [more'nasu, a] M/F dark beauty
moreno, -a [mo'renu, a] ADJ dark(-skinned); (de cabelos) dark(-haired); (de tomar sol) brown

m

▶ M/F dark person; **ela é loura ou morena?** is she a blonde or a brunette?

morfina [mor'fina] F morphine

morfologia [morfolo'ʒia] F morphology

morgada [mor'gada] (PT) F heiress

morgado [mor'gadu] (PT) M (*herdeiro*) heir; (*filho mais velho*) eldest son; (*propriedade*) entailed estate

moribundo, -a [mori'būdu, a] ADJ dying

morigerado, -a [moriʒe'radu, a] ADJ upright

moringa [mo'rīga] F water-cooler

mormacento, -a [morma'sētu, a] ADJ sultry

mormaço [mor'masu] M sultry weather

mormente [mor'mētʃi] ADV chiefly, especially

mórmon ['mɔrmõ] M/F Mormon

morno, -a ['mornu, 'mɔrna] ADJ lukewarm, tepid

morosidade [morozi'dadʒi] F slowness

moroso, -a [mo'rozu, ɔza] ADJ slow, sluggish

morrer [mo'her] VI to die; (*luz, cor*) to fade; (*fogo*) to die down; (*Auto*) to stall; ~ **de rir** to kill o.s. laughing; **estou morrendo de fome/inveja/medo/saudades** I'm starving/ green with envy/scared stiff/really missing you (*ou* him, home *etc*); ~ **de amores por alguém** to be mad about sb; **estou morrendo de vontade de fazer** I'm dying to do; ~ **atropelado/afogado** to be knocked down and killed/drown; **lindo de ~** (*col*) stunning; ~ **em** (*col: pagar*) to fork out

morrinha [mo'hiɲa] F (*fedor*) stench ▶ M/F (*col: chato*) pain (in the neck) ▶ ADJ (*col*) boring

morro ['mohu] M hill; (*favela*) shanty town, slum

mortadela [morta'dɛla] F salami

mortal [mor'taw] (*pl* **-ais**) ADJ mortal; (*letal, insuportável*) deadly ▶ M mortal; **restos mortais** mortal remains

mortalha [mor'taʎa] F shroud

mortalidade [mortali'dadʒi] F mortality; ~ **infantil** infant mortality

mortandade [mortã'dadʒi] F slaughter

morte ['mɔrtʃi] F death; **pena de ~** death penalty; **ser de ~** (*fig*) to be impossible; **estar às portas da ~** to be at death's door; **pensar na ~ da bezerra** (*fig*) to be miles away

morteiro [mor'tejru] M mortar

mortiço, -a [mor'tʃisu, a] ADJ (*olhar*) dull; (*desanimado*) lifeless; (*luz*) dimming

mortífero, -a [mor'tʃiferu, a] ADJ deadly, lethal

mortificar [mortʃifi'kar] VT (*torturar*) to torture; (*afligir*) to annoy, torment

morto, -a ['mortu, 'mɔrta] PP *de* **matar, morrer** ▶ ADJ dead; (*cor*) dull; (*exausto*) exhausted; (*inexpressivo*) lifeless ▶ M/F dead man/woman; **cem/os ~s** a hundred/the dead; **estar ~** to be dead; **ser ~** to be killed; **estar ~ de inveja** to be green with envy; **estar ~ de vontade de** to be dying to;

~ **de medo/cansaço** scared stiff/dead tired; **nem ~!** not on your life!, no way!; ~ **da silva** (*col*) dead as a doornail

mos [mus] PRON = **me** + **os**

mosaico [mo'zajku] M mosaic

mosca ['moska] F fly; **estar às ~s** (*bar etc*) to be deserted

mosca-morta (*pl* **moscas-mortas**) (*col*) M/F (*pessoa*) stiff

Moscou [mos'kow] (BR) N Moscow

Moscovo [mos'kovu] (PT) N Moscow

mosquitada [moski'tada] F load of mosquitos

mosquiteiro [moski'tejru] M mosquito net

mosquito [mos'kitu] M mosquito

mossa ['mɔsa] F dent; (*fig*) impression

mostarda [mos'tarda] F mustard

mosteiro [mos'tejru] M monastery; (*de monjas*) convent

mosto ['mostu] M (*do vinho*) must

mostra ['mɔstra] F (*exibição*) display; (*sinal*) sign, indication; **dar ~s de** to show signs of

mostrador [mostra'dor] M (*de relógio*) face, dial

mostrar [mos'trar] VT to show; (*mercadorias*) to display; (*provar*) to demonstrate, prove; **mostrar-se** VR to show o.s. to be; (*exibir-se*) to show off

mostruário [mos'trwarju] M display case

mote ['mɔtʃi] M motto

motéis [mo'tɛjs] MPL *de* **motel**

motejar [mote'ʒar] VI: ~ **de** (*zombar*) to jeer at, make fun of

motejo [mo'teʒu] M mockery, derision

motel [mo'tɛw] (*pl* **-éis**) M motel

motilidade [motʃili'dadʒi] F mobility

motim [mo'tʃĩ] (*pl* **-ns**) M riot, revolt; (*militar*) mutiny

motivação [motʃiva'sãw] (*pl* **-ões**) F motivation

motivado, -a [motʃi'vadu, a] ADJ (*causado*) caused; (*pessoa*) motivated

motivar [motʃi'var] VT (*causar*) to cause, bring about; (*estimular*) to motivate

motivo [mo'tʃivu] M (*causa*): ~ (**de** *ou* **para**) cause (of), reason (for); (*fim*) motive; (*Arte, Mús*) motif; **ser ~ de riso** *etc* to be a cause of laughter *etc*; **dar ~ de algo a alguém** to give sb cause for sth; **por ~ de** because of, owing to; **sem ~** for no reason

moto ['mɔtu] F motorbike ▶ M (*lema*) motto; **de ~ próprio** of one's own accord

motoboy [moto'bɔj] M motorcycle courier

motoca [mo'tɔka] (*col*) F motorbike, bike

motocicleta [motosi'kleta] F motorcycle, motorbike

motociclismo [motosi'klizmu] M motorcycling

motociclista [motosi'klista] M/F motorcyclist

motociclo [moto'siklu] (PT) M = **motocicleta**

motoneta [moto'neta] F (motor-)scooter

motoniveladora [motonivela'dora] F bulldozer

motoqueiro, -a [moto'kejru, a] (col) M/F
biker, motorcyclist
motor, motriz [mo'tor, mo'triz] ADJ (Tec)
driving; (Anat) motor ▸ M motor; (de carro,
avião) engine; **força motriz** driving force;
~ de arranque starter (motor); **~ de
explosão** internal combustion engine;
~ de popa outboard motor; **~ diesel** diesel
engine; **com ~** motorized; **~ de pesquisa**
(PT Comput) search engine
motorista [moto'rista] M/F driver
motorizado, -a [motori'zadu, a] ADJ
motorized; (col: com carro) motorized, driving
motorizar [motori'zar] VT to motorize;
motorizar-se VR to get a car
motorneiro, -a [motor'nejru, a] M/F tram
(BRIT) ou streetcar (US) driver
motosserra [moto'sɛha] F chain-saw
motriz [mo'triz] F de **motor**
mouco, -a ['moku, a] ADJ deaf, hard of
hearing; **fazer ouvido ~** to pretend not to
hear
movediço, -a [move'dʒisu, a] ADJ easily
moved; (instável) unsteady; ver tb **areia**
móvel ['mɔvew] (pl **-eis**) ADJ movable ▸ M (peça
de mobília) piece of furniture; **móveis** MPL
(mobília) furniture sg; **bens móveis** personal
property; **móveis e utensílios** (Com)
fixtures and fittings
mover [mo'ver] VT to move; (cabeça) to shake;
(mecanismo: acionar) to drive; (campanha) to
start (up); **mover-se** VR to move; **~ uma ação**
to start a lawsuit; **~ alguém a fazer** to move
sb to do
movido, -a [mo'vidu, a] ADJ moved; (impelido)
powered; (causado) caused; **~ a álcool**
alcohol-powered
movimentação [movimēta'sãw] (pl **-ões**) F
movement; (na rua) bustle
movimentado, -a [movimē'tadu, a] ADJ (rua,
lugar) busy; (pessoa) active; (show, música)
up-tempo
movimentar [movimē'tar] VT to move;
(animar) to liven up
movimento [movi'mētu] M movement; (Tec)
motion; (na rua) activity, bustle; **de muito ~**
(loja, rua etc) busy; **pôr algo em ~** to set sth in
motion
movível [mo'vivew] (pl **-eis**) ADJ movable
MPAS (BR) ABR M = **Ministério da Previdência
e Assistência Social**
MPB ABR F = **Música Popular Brasileira**
MPlan (BR) ABR M = **Ministério do
Planejamento**
MRE (BR) ABR M = **Ministério das Relações
Exteriores**
MS (BR) ABR = **Mato Grosso do Sul** ▸ ABR M
= **Ministério da Saúde**
MST (BR) ABR M (= Movimento dos Trabalhadores
Rurais Sem Terra) pressure group for land reform
MT (BR) ABR = **Mato Grosso** ▸ ABR M
= **Ministério dos Transportes**
MTb (BR) ABR M = **Ministério do Trabalho**

muamba ['mwãba] (col) F (contrabando)
contraband; (objetos roubados) loot
muambeiro, -a [mwã'bejru, a] M/F smuggler;
(de objetos roubados) fence
muar [mwar] M/F mule
muco ['muku] M mucus
mucosa [mu'kɔza] F (Anat) mucous
membrane
muçulmano, -a [musuw'manu, a] ADJ, M/F
Moslem
muda ['muda] F (planta) seedling; (vestuário)
outfit; **~ de roupa** change of clothes
mudança [mu'dãsa] F change; (de casa) move;
(Auto) gear; **~s climáticas** climate change
mudar [mu'dar] VT to change; (deslocar) to
move ▸ VI to change; (ave) to moult (BRIT),
molt (US); **mudar-se** VR (de casa) to move
(away); **~ de roupa/de assunto** to change
clothes/the subject; **~ de casa** to move
(house); **~ de ideia** to change one's mind
mudez [mu'dez] F muteness; (silêncio) silence
mudo, -a ['mudu, a] ADJ dumb; (calado, filme)
silent; (telefone) dead ▸ M/F mute
mugido [mu'ʒidu] M moo
mugir [mu'ʒir] VI (vaca) to moo, low
mugunzá [mugũ'za] M = **munguzá**

(PALAVRA-CHAVE)

muito, -a ['mwĩtu, a] ADJ (quantidade) a lot of;
(em frase negativa ou interrogativa) much;
(número) lots of, a lot of, many; **muito
esforço** a lot of effort; **faz muito calor** it's
very hot; **muito tempo** a long time;
muitas amigas lots ou a lot of friends;
muitas vezes often
▸ PRON a lot; (em frase negativa ou interrogativa:
sg) much; (: pl) many; **tenho muito que
fazer** I've got a lot to do; **muitos dizem
que ...** a lot of people say that ...
▸ ADV **1** a lot; (+adj) very; (+compar): **muito
melhor** much ou far ou a lot better; **gosto
muito disto** I like it a lot; **sinto muito** I'm
very sorry; **muito interessante** very
interesting
2 (resposta) very; **está cansado? — muito** are
you tired? — very
3 (tempo): **muito depois** long after; **há
muito** a long time ago; **não demorou
muito** it didn't take long

mula ['mula] F mule
mulato, -a [mu'latu, a] ADJ, M/F mulatto
muleta [mu'leta] F crutch; (fig) support
mulher [mu'ʎer] F woman; (esposa) wife; **~ da
vida** prostitute
mulheraço [muʎe'rasu] M fantastic woman
mulherão [muʎe'rãw] (pl **-ões**) M
= **mulheraço**
mulher-bomba (pl **mulheres-bomba**) F
suicide bomber
mulherengo [muʎe'rẽgu] M womanizer ▸ ADJ
womanizing
mulherio [muʎe'riu] M women pl

multa ['muwta] F fine; **levar uma ~** to be fined

multar [muw'tar] VT to fine; **~ alguém em $1000** to fine sb $1000

multi... [muwtʃi] PREFIXO multi...

multicolor [muwtʃiko'lor] ADJ multicoloured (BRIT), multicolored (US)

multidão [muwtʃi'dãw] (pl **-ões**) F crowd; **uma ~ de** (muitos) lots of

multiforme [muwtʃi'fɔrme] ADJ manifold, multifarious

multilateral [muwtʃilate'raw] (pl **-ais**) ADJ multilateral

multimídia [muwtʃi'midʒja] ADJ multimedia

multimilionário, -a [muwtʃimiljo'narju, a] ADJ, M/F multimillionaire

multinacional [muwtʃinasjo'naw] (pl **-ais**) ADJ, F multinational

multiplicação [muwtʃiplika'sãw] F multiplication

multiplicar [muwtʃipli'kar] VT (Mat) to multiply; (aumentar) to increase

multiplicidade [muwtʃiplisi'dadʒi] F multiplicity

múltiplo, -a ['muwtʃiplu, a] ADJ, M multiple; **múltipla escolha** multiple choice

multirracial [muwtʃiha'sjaw] (pl **-ais**) ADJ multiracial

multiusuário, -a [muwtʃju'zwarju, a] ADJ (Comput) multiuser

múmia ['mumja] F mummy; (fig) plodder

mundano, -a [mũ'danu, a] ADJ worldly

mundial [mũ'dʒjaw] (pl **-ais**) ADJ worldwide; (guerra, recorde) world atr ▶ M (campeonato) world championship; **o ~ de futebol** the World Cup

mundo ['mũdu] M world; **todo o ~** everybody; **um ~ de** lots of, a great many; **correr ~** to see the world; **vir ao ~** to come into the world; **como este ~ é pequeno!** (what a) small world!; **desde que o ~ é ~** since time immemorial; **~s e fundos** (quantia altíssima) the earth; **prometer ~s e fundos** to promise the earth; **tinha meio ~ no comício** there were loads of people at the rally; **com esta notícia meu ~ veio abaixo** the news shattered my world; **abarcar o ~ com as pernas** (fig) to take on too much; **Novo/Velho/Terceiro M~** New/Old/Third World

munguzá [mũgu'za] M corn meal

munheca [mu'ɲeka] F wrist

munição [muni'sãw] (pl **-ões**) F (de armas) ammunition; (chumbo) shot; (Mil) munitions pl, supplies pl

municipal [munisi'paw] (pl **-ais**) ADJ municipal

municipalidade [munisipali'dadʒi] F local authority

município [muni'sipju] M local authority; (cidade) town; (condado) county

munições [muni'sõjs] FPL de **munição**

munir [mu'nir] VT: **~ de** to provide with, supply with; **munir-se** VR: **~-se de** (provisões) to equip o.s. with; (paciência) to arm o.s. with

mural [mu'raw] (pl **-ais**) ADJ, M mural

muralha [mu'raʎa] F (de fortaleza) rampart; (muro) wall

murchar [mur'ʃar] VT (Bot) to wither; (sentimentos) to dull; (pessoa) to sadden ▶ VI (Bot) to wither, wilt; (fig) to fade; (: pessoa) to grow sad

murcho, -a ['murʃu, a] ADJ (planta) wilting; (esvaziado) shrunken; (fig) languid, resigned

murmuração [murmura'sãw] F muttering; (maledicência) gossiping

murmurante [murmu'rãtʃi] ADJ murmuring

murmurar [murmu'rar] VI (segredar) to murmur, whisper; (queixar-se) to mutter, grumble; (água) to ripple; (folhagem) to rustle ▶ VT to murmur

murmurinho [murmu'riɲu] M (de vozes) murmuring; (som confuso) noise; (de folhas) rustling; (de água) trickling

murmúrio [mur'murju] M murmuring, whispering; (queixa) grumbling; (de água) rippling; (de folhagem) rustling

muro ['muru] M wall

murro ['muhu] M punch, sock; **dar um ~ em alguém** to punch sb; **levar um ~ de alguém** to be punched by sb; **dar ~ em ponta de faca** (fig) to bang one's head against a brick wall

musa ['muza] F muse

musculação [muskula'sãw] F weight training

muscular [musku'lar] ADJ muscular

musculatura [muskula'tura] F musculature

músculo ['muskulu] M muscle

musculoso, -a [musku'lozu, ɔza] ADJ muscular

museu [mu'zew] M museum; (de pintura) gallery

musgo ['muzgu] M moss

musgoso, -a [muz'gozu, ɔza] ADJ mossy

música ['muzika] F music; (canção) song; **dançar conforme a ~** (fig) to play the game; **~ de câmara** chamber music; **~ de fundo** background music; **~ erudita** classical music; ver tb **músico**

musicado, -a [muzi'kadu, a] ADJ set to music

musical [muzi'kaw] (pl **-ais**) ADJ, M musical; **fundo ~** background music

musicalidade [muzikali'dadʒi] F musicality

músico, -a ['muziku, a] ADJ musical ▶ M/F musician

musse ['musi] F mousse

musselina [muse'lina] F muslin

mutação [muta'sãw] (pl **-ões**) F change, alteration; (Bio) mutation

mutável [mu'tavew] (pl **-eis**) ADJ changeable

mutilação [mutʃila'sãw] F mutilation; (de texto) cutting

mutilado, -a [mutʃi'ladu, a] ADJ mutilated; (*pessoa*) maimed ▶ M/F cripple

mutilar [mutʃi'lar] VT to mutilate; (*pessoa*) to maim; (*texto*) to cut; (*árvore*) to strip

mutirão [mutʃi'rãw] (*pl* **-ões**) M collective effort

mútua ['mutwa] F loan company

mutuante [mu'twãtʃi] M/F lender

mutuário, -a [mu'twarju, a] M/F borrower

mútuo, -a ['mutwu, a] ADJ mutual

muxiba [mu'ʃiba] F (*pelancas*) wrinkled flesh; (*carne para cães*) dog meat; (*seios*) drooping breasts *pl*

muxoxo [mu'ʃoʃu] M tutting; **fazer ~** to tut

MVR (BR) ABR M = **Maior Valor de Referência**

m

Nn

N', n ['eni] (*pl* **ns**) M N, n; **N de Nair** N for
Nelly (*BRIT*) *ou* Nan (*US*)
N² ABR (= *norte*) N
ñ ABR = **não**
n. ABR (= *nascido*) b; (= *nome*) name
na [na] = **em + a**; *ver* **em**
-na [na] PRON her; (*coisa*) it
nabo ['nabu] M turnip
nac. ABR (= *nacional*) nat
nação [na'sãw] (*pl* **-ões**) F nation; **as Nações
Unidas** the United Nations
nácar ['nakar] M mother-of-pearl; (*cor*) pink
nacional [nasjo'naw] (*pl* **-ais**) ADJ national;
(*carro, vinho etc*) domestic, home-produced
nacionalidade [nasjonali'dadʒi] F nationality
nacionalismo [nasjona'lizmu] M
nationalism
nacionalista [nasjona'lista] ADJ, M/F
nationalist
nacionalização [nasjonaliza'sãw] (*pl* **-ões**) F
nationalization
nacionalizar [nasjonali'zar] VT to nationalize
naco ['naku] M piece, chunk
nações [na'sõjs] FPL *de* **nação**
nada ['nada] PRON nothing ▶ M nothingness;
(*pessoa*) nonentity ▶ ADV at all; **não dizer ~**
to say nothing, not to say anything; **antes
de mais ~** first of all; **não é ~ difícil** it's not
at all hard, it's not hard at all; **~ mais**
nothing else; **quase ~** hardly anything;
~ de novo nothing new; **~ feito** nothing
doing; **~ mau** not bad (at all); **obrigado --
de ~** thank you -- not at all *ou* don't mention
it; **(que) ~!**, **~ disso!** nonsense!, not at all!;
não foi ~ it was nothing; **por ~ nesse
mundo** (not) for love nor money; **ele fez o
que você pediu? -- fez ~!** did he do as you
asked? -- no, he did not!; **não ser de ~** (*col*) to
be a dead loss; **é uma coisinha de ~** it's
nothing; **discutimos por um ~** we argued
over nothing
nadada [na'dada] F swim; **dar uma ~** to go
for a swim
nadadeira [nada'dejra] F (*de peixe*) fin; (*de
golfinho, foca, mergulhador*) flipper
nadador, a [nada'dor(a)] ADJ swimming
▶ M/F swimmer
nadar [na'dar] VI to swim; **~ em** to be
dripping with; **estar** *ou* **ficar nadando** (*fig*)

to be out of it, be out of one's depth; **ele está
nadando em dinheiro** he's rolling in
money
nádegas ['nadegas] FPL buttocks
nadinha [na'dʒiɲa] PRON absolutely
nothing
nado ['nadu] M: **a ~** swimming; **atravessar
a ~** to swim across; **~ borboleta** butterfly
(stroke); **~ de cachorrinho** doggy paddle;
~ de costas backstroke; **~ de peito**
breaststroke; **~ livre** freestyle
naftalina [nafta'lina] F naphthaline
náilon ['najilõ] M nylon
naipe ['najpi] M (*cartas*) suit; (*fig: categoria*)
order
Nairobi [naj'rɔbi] N Nairobi
namoradeira [namora'dejra] ADJ flirtatious
▶ F flirt
namorado, -a [namo'radu, a] M/F boyfriend/
girlfriend
namorador, a [namora'dor(a)] ADJ flirtatious
▶ M ladies' man
namorar [namo'rar] VT (*ser namorado de*) to be
going out with; (*cobiçar*) to covet; (*fitar*) to
stare longingly at ▶ VI (*casal*) to go out
together; (*homem, mulher*) to have a boyfriend
(*ou* girlfriend)
namoricar [namori'kar] VT to flirt with ▶ VI
to flirt
namoro [na'moru] M relationship
nanar [na'nar] (*col*) VI to sleep, kip
nanico, -a [na'niku, a] ADJ tiny
nanquim [nã'kĩ] M Indian ink
não [nãw] ADV not; (*resposta*) no ▶ M no; **~ sei**
I don't know; **~ muito** not much; **~ só ...
mas também** not only ... but also; **agora ~**
not now; **~ tem de quê** don't mention it;
~ é? isn't it?, won't you?; **eles são
brasileiros, ~ é?** they're Brazilian, aren't
they?
não... [nãw] PREFIXO non-
não agressão F: **pacto de ~** non-aggression
treaty
não alinhado, -a ADJ non-aligned
não conformista ADJ, M/F non-conformist
não intervenção F non-intervention
napa ['napa] F napa leather
naquele(s), naquela(s) [na'keli(s), na'kɛla(s)]
= **em + aquele(s), aquela(s)**; *ver* **em**

naquilo [na'kilu] = **em** + **aquilo**; ver **em**
narcisismo [narsi'zizmu] M narcissism
narcisista [narsi'zista] ADJ narcissistic
narciso [nar'sizu] M (*Bot*) narcissus; ~ **dos prados** daffodil
narcótico, -a [nar'kɔtʃiku, a] ADJ narcotic ▶ M narcotic
narcotizar [narkotʃi'zar] VT to drug; (*fig*) to bore
narigudo, -a [nari'gudu, a] ADJ with a big nose; **ser** ~ to have a big nose
narina [na'rina] F nostril
nariz [na'riz] M nose; ~ **adunco/arrebitado** hook/snub nose; **meter o** ~ **em** to poke one's nose into; **torcer o** ~ **para** to turn one's nose up at; **ser dono/a do seu** ~ to know one's own mind; **dar com o** ~ **na porta** (*fig*) to find (the) doors closed to one
narração [naha'sãw] (*pl* **-ões**) F narration; (*relato*) account
narrador, a [naha'dor(a)] M/F narrator
narrar [na'har] VT to narrate, recount
narrativa [naha'tʃiva] F narrative; (*história*) story
narrativo, -a [naha'tʃivu, a] ADJ narrative
nas [nas] = **em** + **as**; ver **em**
-nas [nas] PRON them
NASA ['naza] ABR F NASA
nasal [na'zaw] (*pl* **-ais**) ADJ nasal
nasalado, -a [naza'ladu, a] ADJ nasalized, nasal
nasalização [nazaliza'sãw] F nasalization
nascença [na'sẽsa] F birth; **de** ~ by birth; **ele é surdo de** ~ he was born deaf
nascente [na'sẽtʃi] ADJ nascent ▶ M East, Orient ▶ F (*fonte*) spring
nascer [na'ser] VI to be born; (*plantas*) to sprout; (*o sol*) to rise; (*ave*) to hatch; (*dente*) to come through; (*fig: ter origem*) to come into being ▶ M: ~ **do sol** sunrise; ~ **de** (*descender*) to be born of; (*fig: originar-se*) to be born out of; ~ **de novo** (*fig*) to have a narrow escape, escape with one's life; **não nasci ontem** I wasn't born yesterday; ~ **em berço de ouro** to be born with a silver spoon in one's mouth; **ele nasceu para médico** *etc* he was born to be a doctor *etc*; **não nasci para fazer isto** I wasn't cut out to do this
nascido, -a [na'sidu, a] ADJ born; **bem** ~ from a good family
nascimento [nasi'mẽtu] M birth; (*fig*) origin; (*estirpe*) descent
Nassau [na'saw] N Nassau
nata ['nata] F (*Culin*) cream; (*elite*) élite
natação [nata'sãw] M swimming
natais [na'tajs] ADJ PL *de* **natal**
Natal [na'taw] M Christmas; **Feliz** ~! Merry Christmas!
natal [na'taw] (*pl* **-ais**) ADJ (*relativo ao nascimento*) natal; (*país*) native; **cidade** ~ home town
natalício, -a [nata'lisju, a] ADJ: **aniversário** ~ birthday ▶ M birthday

natalidade [natali'dadʒi] F: (**índice de**) ~ birth rate
natalino, -a [nata'linu, a] ADJ Christmas *atr*
natividade [natʃivi'dadʒi] F nativity
nativo, -a [na'tʃivu, a] ADJ, M/F native
NATO ['natu] ABR F NATO
nato, -a ['natu, a] ADJ born
natural [natu'raw] (*pl* **-ais**) ADJ natural; (*nativo*) native ▶ M/F (*nativo*) native; **de tamanho** ~ life-size; **ao** ~ (*Culin*) fresh, uncooked
naturalidade [naturali'dadʒi] F naturalness; **falar com** ~ to talk openly; **agir com a maior** ~ to act as if nothing had happened; **de** ~ **paulista** *etc* born in São Paulo *etc*
naturalismo [natura'lizmu] M naturalism
naturalista [natura'lista] ADJ, M/F naturalist
naturalização [naturaliza'sãw] F naturalization
naturalizado, -a [naturali'zadu, a] ADJ naturalized ▶ M/F naturalized citizen
naturalizar [naturali'zar] VT to naturalize; **naturalizar-se** VR to become naturalized
naturalmente [naturaw'mẽtʃi] ADV naturally; ~! of course!
natureza [natu'reza] F nature; (*espécie*) kind, type; ~ **morta** still life; **por** ~ by nature
naturismo [natu'rizmu] M naturism
naturista [natu'rista] ADJ, M/F naturist
nau [naw] F (*literário*) ship
naufragar [nawfra'gar] VI (*navio*) to be wrecked; (*marinheiro*) to be shipwrecked; (*fig: malograr-se*) to fail
naufrágio [naw'fraʒu] M shipwreck; (*fig*) failure
náufrago, -a ['nawfragu, a] M/F castaway
náusea ['nawzea] F nausea; **dar** ~**s a alguém** to make sb feel sick; **sentir** ~**s** to feel sick
nauseabundo, -a [nawzja'būdu, a] ADJ nauseating, sickening
nauseante [naw'zjãtʃi] ADJ nauseating, sickening
nausear [naw'zjar] VT to nauseate, sicken ▶ VI to feel sick
náutica ['nawtʃika] F seamanship
náutico, -a ['nawtʃiku, a] ADJ nautical
naval [na'vaw] (*pl* **-ais**) ADJ naval; **construção** ~ shipbuilding
navalha [na'vaʎa] F (*de barba*) razor; (*faca*) knife
navalhada [nava'ʎada] F cut (*with a razor*)
navalhar [nava'ʎar] VT to cut *ou* slash with a razor
nave ['navi] F (*de igreja*) nave; ~ **espacial** spaceship
navegação [navega'sãw] F navigation, sailing; ~ **aérea** air traffic; ~ **costeira** coastal shipping; ~ **fluvial** river traffic; **companhia de** ~ shipping line
navegador, a [navega'dor(a)] M/F navigator
navegante [nave'gãtʃi] M seafarer
navegar [nave'gar] VT to navigate; (*mares*) to sail ▶ VI to sail; (*dirigir o rumo*) to navigate

navegável [nave'gavew] (*pl* **-eis**) ADJ navigable

navio [na'viu] M ship; ~ **cargueiro** cargo ship, freighter; ~ **de carreira** liner; ~ **de guerra** warship; ~ **escola** training ship; ~ **fábrica** factory ship; ~ **mercante** merchant ship; ~ **petroleiro** oil tanker; ~ **tanque** tanker; **ficar a ver ~s** to be left high and dry

Nazaré [naza'rɛ] N Nazareth

nazi [na'zi] (PT) ADJ, M/F = **nazista**

nazismo [na'zizmu] M Nazism

nazista [na'zista] (BR) ADJ, M/F Nazi

NB ABR (= *note bem*) NB

n/c ABR (= *nossa carta*) our letter; (= *nossa conta*) our account; (= *nossa casa*) our firm

N da R ABR = **nota da redação**

N do A ABR = **nota do autor**

N do E ABR = **nota do editor**

N do T ABR = **nota do tradutor**

NE ABR (= *nordeste*) NE

neblina [ne'blina] F fog, mist

nebulosa [nebu'lɔza] F (*Astronomia*) nebula

nebulosidade [nebulozi'dadʒi] F cloud

nebuloso, -a [nebu'lozu, ɔza] ADJ foggy, misty; (*céu*) cloudy; (*fig*) vague

neca ['nɛka] (*col*) PRON nothing ▶ EXCL nope

necessaire [nese'sɛr] M toilet bag

necessário, -a [nese'sarju, a] ADJ necessary ▶ M: **o ~** the necessities *pl*; **se for ~** if necessary

necessidade [nesesi'dadʒi] F need, necessity; (*o que se necessita*) need; (*pobreza*) poverty, need; **ter ~ de** to need; **não há ~ de algo/de fazer algo** there is no need for sth/to do sth; **em caso de ~** if need be

necessitado, -a [nesesi'tadu, a] ADJ needy, poor ▶ M/F person in need; **os necessitados** MPL the needy *pl*; ~ **de** in need of

necessitar [nesesi'tar] VT to need, require ▶ VI to be in need; ~ **de** to need

necrológio [nekro'lɔʒu] M obituary

necrópole [ne'krɔpoli] F cemetery

necrose [ne'krɔzi] F necrosis

necrotério [nekro'tɛrju] M mortuary, morgue (US)

néctar ['nɛktar] M nectar

nectarina [nekta'rina] F nectarine

nédio, -a ['nɛdʒu, a] ADJ (*luzidio*) glossy, sleek; (*rechonchudo*) plump

neerlandês, -esa [neerlã'des, eza] ADJ Dutch ▶ M/F Dutchman/woman

Neerlândia [neer'lãdʒa] F the Netherlands *pl*

nefando, -a [ne'fãdu, a] ADJ atrocious, heinous

nefasto, -a [ne'fastu, a] ADJ (*de mau agouro*) ominous; (*trágico*) tragic

negaça [ne'gasa] F lure, bait; (*engano*) deception; (*recusa*) refusal; (*desmentido*) denial

negação [nega'sãw] (*pl* **-ões**) F negation; (*recusa*) refusal; (*desmentido*) denial; **ele é uma ~ em matéria de cozinha** he's hopeless at cooking

negacear [nega'sjar] VT (*atrair*) to entice; (*enganar*) to deceive; (*recusar*) to refuse ▶ VI (*cavalo*) to balk; (*Hipismo*) to refuse

negações [nega'sõjs] FPL *de* **negação**

negar [ne'gar] VT (*desmentir, não permitir*) to deny; (*recusar*) to refuse; **negar-se** VR: **~-se a** to refuse to

negativa [nega'tʃiva] F (*Ling*) negative; (*recusa*) denial

negativo, -a [nega'tʃivu, a] ADJ negative ▶ M (*Tec, Foto*) negative ▶ EXCL (*col*) nope!

negável [ne'gavew] (*pl* **-eis**) ADJ deniable

negligé [negli'ge] M negligee

negligência [negli'ʒẽsja] F negligence, carelessness

negligenciar [negliʒẽ'sjar] VT to neglect

negligente [negli'ʒẽtʃi] ADJ negligent, careless

nego, -a ['negu, a] (*col*) M/F (*negro*) Black; (*camarada*): **tudo bem, (meu) ~?** how are you, mate?; (*querido*): **tchau, (meu) ~** bye, dear *ou* darling

negociação [negosja'sãw] (*pl* **-ões**) F negotiation; (*transação*) transaction

negociador, a [negosja'dor(a)] ADJ negotiating ▶ M/F negotiator

negociante [nego'sjãtʃi] M/F businessman/woman; (*comerciante*) merchant

negociar [nego'sjar] VT (*Pol etc*) to negotiate; (*Com*) to trade ▶ VI: ~ **(com)** to trade *ou* deal (in); to negotiate (with)

negociata [nego'sjata] F crooked deal; **negociatas** MPL (*negócios escusos*) wheeling and dealing *sg*

negociável [nego'sjavew] (*pl* **-eis**) ADJ negotiable

negócio [ne'gɔsju] M (*Com*) business; (*transação*) deal; (*questão*) matter; (*col: troço*) thing; (*assunto*) affair, business; **homem de ~s** businessman; **a ~s** on business; **fazer um bom ~** (*pessoa*) to get a good deal; (*loja etc*) to do good business; **fechar um ~** to make a deal; ~ **fechado!** it's a deal!; **isso não é ~** it's not worth it; **a casa dela é um ~** (*col*) her house is really something; **tenho um ~ para te contar** I've got something to tell you; **aconteceu um ~ estranho comigo** something strange happened to me; **mas que ~ é esse?** (*col*) what's the big idea?; **meu ~ é outro** (*col*) this isn't my thing; **o ~ é o seguinte ...** (*col*) the thing is ...

negocista [nego'sista] ADJ crooked ▶ M/F wheeler-dealer

negridão [negri'dãw] F blackness

negrito [ne'gritu] M (*Tip*) bold (face)

negritude [negri'tudʒi] F (*Pol etc*) Black awareness

negro, -a ['negru, a] ADJ black; (*fig: lúgubre*) black, gloomy ▶ M/F black man/woman; **a situação está negra** the situation is bad; **humor ~** black humo(u)r; **magia negra** black magic

negrume [ne'grumi] M black, darkness

negrura [ne'grura] F blackness

neguei *etc* [ne'gej] VB *ver* **negar**

nele(s), nela(s) ['neli(s), 'nɛla(s)] = **em +
ele(s), ela(s);** *ver* **em**

nem [nẽj] CONJ nor, neither; **~ (sequer)** not
even; **~ que** even if; **~ bem** hardly; **~ um só**
not a single one; **~ estuda ~ trabalha** he
neither studies nor works; **~ eu** nor me;
sem ~ without even; **~ todos** not all;
~ tanto not so much; **~ sempre** not always;
~ por isso nonetheless; **ele fala português
que ~ brasileiro** he speaks Portuguese like
a Brazilian; **~ vem (que não tem)** (*col*) don't
give me that

nenê [ne'ne] M/F baby

neném [ne'nẽj] (*pl* **-ns**) M/F = **nenê**

nenhum, a [ne'ɲũ, 'ɲuma] ADJ no, not any
▶ PRON (*nem um só*) none, not one; (*de dois*)
neither; **~ professor** no teacher; **não vi
professor ~** I didn't see any teachers; **~ dos
professores** none of the teachers; **~ dos
dois** neither of them; **~ lugar** nowhere; **ele
não fez ~ comentário** he didn't make any
comments, he made no comments; **não vou
a ~ lugar** I'm not going anywhere; **estar a ~**
(*col*) to be flat broke

neofascismo [neofa'sizmu] M neofascism

neolatino, -a [neola'tʃinu, a] ADJ: **línguas
neolatinas** Romance languages

neolítico, -a [neo'litʃiku, a] ADJ neolithic

neologismo [neolo'ʒizmu] M neologism

néon ['nɛõ] M neon

neônio [ne'onju] M = **néon**

neorrealismo [neohea'lizmu] M new realism

neozelandês, -esa [neozelã'des, deza] ADJ
New Zealand *atr* ▶ M/F New Zealander

Nepal [ne'paw] M: **o ~** Nepal

nepotismo [nepo'tʃizmu] M nepotism

nervo ['nervu] M (*Anat*) nerve; (*fig*) energy,
strength; (*em carne*) sinew; **ser** *ou* **estar uma
pilha de ~s** to be a bundle of nerves

nervosismo [nervo'zizmu] M (*nervosidade*)
nervousness; (*irritabilidade*) irritability

nervoso, -a [ner'vozu, ɔza] ADJ nervous;
(*irritável*) touchy, on edge; (*exaltado*) worked
up; **isso/ele me deixa ~** he gets on my
nerves; **sistema ~** nervous system

nervudo, -a [ner'vudu, a] (*PT*) ADJ (*robusto*)
robust

nervura [ner'vura] F rib; (*Bot*) vein

néscio, -a ['nɛsju, a] ADJ (*idiota*) stupid;
(*insensato*) foolish

nesga ['nezga] F (*Costura*) gore; (*porção: de
comida*) portion; (: *de mesa, terra*) corner, patch

nesse(s), nessa(s) ['nesi(s), 'nɛsa(s)] = **em +
esse(s), essa(s);** *ver* **em**

neste(s), nesta(s) ['nestʃi(s), 'nɛsta(s)] = **em
+ este(s), esta(s);** *ver* **em**

neto, -a ['nɛtu, a] M/F grandson/daughter;
netos MPL grandchildren

neuralgia [newraw'ʒia] F neuralgia

neurastênico, -a [newras'teniku, a] ADJ (*Psico*)
neurasthenic; (*col: irritadiço*) irritable

neurite [new'ritʃi] F (*Med*) neuritis

neurocirurgião, -giã [newrosirur'ʒjãw, ʒjã] (*pl*
-ões/-s) M/F neurosurgeon

neurologia [newrolo'ʒia] F neurology

neurológico, -a [newro'lɔʒiku, a] ADJ
neurological

neurologista [newrolo'ʒista] M/F neurologist

neurose [new'rɔzi] F neurosis

neurótico, -a [new'rɔtʃiku, a] ADJ, M/F
neurotic

neutralidade [newtrali'dadʒi] F neutrality

neutralização [newtraliza'sãw] F
neutralization

neutralizar [newtrali'zar] VT to neutralize;
(*anular*) to counteract

neutrão [new'trãw] (*pl* **-ões**) (*PT*) M = **nêutron**

neutro, -a ['newtru, a] ADJ (*Ling*) neuter;
(*imparcial*) neutral

neutrões [new'trõjs] MPL *de* **neutrão**

nêutron ['newtrõ] (*pl* **-s**) M neutron; **bomba
de ~s** neutron bomb

nevada [ne'vada] F snowfall

nevado, -a [ne'vadu, a] ADJ snow-covered;
(*branco*) snow-white

nevar [ne'var] VI to snow

nevasca [ne'vaska] F snowstorm

neve ['nɛvi] F snow; **clara em ~** (*Culin*) beaten
egg-white

névoa ['nɛvoa] F fog

nevoeiro [nevo'ejru] M thick fog

nevralgia [nevraw'ʒia] F neuralgia

nexo ['nɛksu] M connection, link; **sem ~**
disconnected, incoherent

nhenhenhém [ɲeɲe'ɲẽj] M (*conversa fiada*) idle
talk; (*reclamação*) whingeing

nhoque ['ɲɔki] M (*Culin*) gnocchi

Nicarágua [nika'ragwa] F: **a ~** Nicaragua

nicaraguense [nikara'gwẽsi] ADJ, M/F
Nicaraguan

nicho ['niʃu] M niche

Nicósia [ni'kɔzja] N Nicosia

nicotina [niko'tʃina] F nicotine

Níger ['niʒer] M: **o ~** Niger

Nigéria [ni'ʒɛrja] F: **a ~** Nigeria

nigeriano, -a [niʒe'rjanu, a] ADJ, M/F Nigerian

niilista [nii'lista] ADJ nihilistic ▶ M/F nihilist

Nilo ['nilu] M: **o ~** the Nile

nimbo ['nĩbu] M (*nuvem*) rain cloud; (*Geo*) halo

ninar [ni'nar] VT to sing to sleep; **ninar-se** VR:
~-se para algo to ignore sth

ninfeta [nĩ'feta] F nymphette

ninfomaníaca [nĩfoma'niaka] F
nymphomaniac

ninguém [nĩ'gẽj] PRON nobody, no-one;
~ o conhece no-one knows him; **não vi ~**
I saw no-one, I didn't see anybody; **~ mais**
nobody else

ninhada [ni'ɲada] F brood

ninharia [niɲa'ria] F trifle

ninho ['niɲu] M (*de aves*) nest; (*toca*) lair; (*lar*)
home; **~ de rato** (*col*) mess, tip

níquel ['nikew] M nickel; **estar sem um ~**
to be penniless

niquelar [nike'lar] vт (*Tec*) to nickel-plate
nirvana [nir'vana] ғ nirvana
nisei [ni'zej] ADJ, M/F second-generation Japanese Brazilian
nisso ['nisu] = **em + isso**
nisto ['nistu] = **em + isto**
nitidez [nitʃi'dez] ғ (*clareza*) clarity; (*brilho*) brightness; (*imagem*) sharpness
nítido, -a ['nitʃidu, a] ADJ clear, distinct; (*brilhante*) bright; (*imagem*) sharp, clear
nitrato [ni'tratu] м nitrate
nítrico, -a ['nitriku, a] ADJ: **ácido ~** nitric acid
nitrogênio [nitro'ʒenju] м nitrogen
nitroglicerina [nitroglise'rina] ғ nitroglycerine
nível ['nivew] (*pl* **-eis**) м level; (*fig: padrão*) level, standard; (*: ponto*) point, pitch; **~ de vida** standard of living; **~ do mar** sea level; **a ~ de** in terms of; **ao ~ de** level with
nivelamento [nivela'mētu] м levelling (BRIT), leveling (US)
nivelar [nive'lar] vт (*terreno etc*) to level ▶ vı: **~ com** to be level with; **nivelar-se** vR: **~-se com** to be equal to; **a morte nivela os homens** death is the great leveller (BRIT) *ou* leveler (US)
NO ABR (= *nordoeste*) NW
no PRON = **em + no**; *ver* **em**
n° ABR (= *número*) no.
nó [nɔ] м knot; (*de uma questão*) crux; **nó corredio** slipknot; **nó na garganta** lump in the throat; **nós dos dedos** knuckles; **dar um nó** to tie a knot
n/o ABR = **nossa ordem**
-no [nu] PRON him; (*coisa*) it
nobilíssimo, -a [nobi'lisimu, a] ADJ SUPERL *de* **nobre**
nobilitar [nobili'tar] vт to ennoble
nobre ['nɔbri] ADJ noble; (*bairro etc*) exclusive ▶ M/F noble; **horário ~** prime time
nobreza [no'breza] ғ nobility
noção [no'sãw] (*pl* **-ões**) ғ notion; **noções** FPL (*rudimentos*) rudiments, basics; **~ vaga** inkling; **não ter a menor ~ de algo** not to have the slightest idea about sth
nocaute [no'kawtʃi] м knockout; (*soco*) knockout blow ▶ ADV: **pôr alguém ~** to knock sb out
nocautear [nokaw'tʃjar] vт to knock out
nocivo, -a [no'sivu, a] ADJ harmful
noções [no'sõjs] FPL *de* **noção**
nódoa ['nɔdwa] ғ spot; (*mancha*) stain
nódulo ['nɔdulu] м nodule
nogueira [no'gejra] ғ (*árvore*) walnut tree; (*madeira*) walnut
noitada [noj'tada] ғ (*noite inteira*) whole night; (*noite de divertimento*) night out
noite ['nojtʃi] ғ night; (*início da noite*) evening; **à** *ou* **de ~** at night, in the evening; **ontem/hoje/amanhã à ~** last night/tonight/tomorrow night; **boa ~** good evening; (*despedida*) good night; **da ~ para o dia** overnight; **tarde da ~** late at night; **passar**

a ~ em claro to have a sleepless night; **a ~ carioca** Rio nightlife; **~ de estreia** opening night
noitinha [noj'tʃiɲa] ғ: **à ~s** at nightfall
noivado [noj'vadu] м engagement
noivar [noj'var] vı: **~ (com)** (*ficar noivo*) to get engaged (to); (*ser noivo*) to be engaged (to)
noivo, -a ['nojvu, a] M/F (*prometido*) fiancé/fiancée; (*no casamento*) bridegroom/bride; **os noivos** MPL (*prometidos*) the engaged couple; (*no casamento*) the bride and groom; (*recém-casados*) the newly-weds
nojeira [no'ʒejra] ғ disgusting thing; (*trabalho*) filthy job
nojento, -a [no'ʒẽtu, a] ADJ disgusting
nojo ['noʒu] м (*náusea*) nausea; (*repulsão*) disgust, loathing; **ela é um ~** she's horrible; **este trabalho está um ~** this work is messy
no-la(s) = **nos + a(s)**
no-lo(s) = **nos + o(s)**
nômade ['nomadʒi] ADJ nomadic ▶ M/F nomad
nome ['nɔmi] м name; (*fama*) fame; **de ~** by name; **escritor de ~** famous writer; **um restaurante de ~** a restaurant with a good reputation; **em ~ de** in the name of; **dar ~ aos bois** to call a spade a spade; **esse ~ não me é estranho** the name rings a bell; **~ comercial** trade name; **~ completo** full name; **~ de batismo** Christian name; **~ de família** family name; **~ de guerra** nickname; **~ feio** swearword; **~ próprio** (*Ling*) proper name
nomeação [nomja'sãw] (*pl* **-ões**) ғ nomination; (*para um cargo*) appointment
nomeada [no'mjada] ғ fame
nomeadamente [nomjada'mẽtʃi] ADV namely
nomear [no'mjar] vт to nominate; (*conferir um cargo a*) to appoint; (*dar nome a*) to name
nomenclatura [nomẽkla'tura] ғ nomenclature
nominal [nomi'naw] (*pl* **-ais**) ADJ nominal
nonagésimo, -a [nona'ʒɛzimu, a] NUM ninetieth
nono, -a ['nonu, a] NUM ninth; *ver tb* **quinto**
nora ['nɔra] ғ daughter-in-law
nordeste [nor'dɛstʃi] м, ADJ northeast; **o N~** the Northeast
nordestino, -a [nordes'tʃinu, a] ADJ north-eastern ▶ M/F North-easterner
nórdico, -a ['nɔrdʒiku, a] ADJ, M/F Nordic
norma ['nɔrma] ғ standard, norm; (*regra*) rule; **como ~** as a rule
normal [nor'maw] (*pl* **-ais**) ADJ normal; (*habitual*) usual; **escola ~** = teacher training college; **curso ~** primary (BRIT) *ou* elementary (US) school teacher training; **está um calor que não é ~** it's incredibly hot
normalidade [normali'dadʒi] ғ normality
normalista [norma'lista] M/F trainee primary (BRIT) *ou* elementary (US) school teacher

normalização [normaliza'sãw] F normalization

normalizar [normali'zar] VT to bring back to normal; (Pol: relações etc) to normalize; **normalizar-se** VR to return to normal

normativo, -a [norma'tʃivu, a] ADJ prescriptive

noroeste [nor'wɛstʃi] ADJ northwest, northwestern ▶ M northwest

norte ['nɔrtʃi] ADJ northern, north; (vento, direção) northerly ▶ M north; **ao ~ de** to the north of

norte-africano, -a ADJ, M/F North African

norte-americano, -a ADJ, M/F (North) American

nortear [nor'tʃjar] VT to orientate; **nortear-se** VR to orientate o.s.

norte-coreano, -a ADJ, M/F North Korean

norte-vietnamita ADJ, M/F North Vietnamese

nortista [nor'tʃista] ADJ northern ▶ M/F Northerner

Noruega [nor'wɛga] F Norway

norueguês, -esa [norwe'ges, geza] ADJ, M/F Norwegian ▶ M (Ling) Norwegian

nos¹ [nus] = **em + os**; ver **em**

nos² [nus] PRON (direto) us; (indireto) us, to us, for us; (reflexivo) (to) ourselves; (recíproco) (to) each other

nós [nɔs] PRON we; (depois de prep) us; **~ mesmos** we ourselves; **para ~** for us; **~ dois** we two, both of us; **cá entre ~** between the two (ou three etc) of us

-nos [nus] PRON them

nossa ['nɔsa] EXCL **~!** my goodness!

nosso, -a ['nɔsu, a] ADJ our ▶ PRON ours; **um amigo ~** a friend of ours; **Nossa Senhora** (Rel) Our Lady; **os ~s** (família) our family sg

nostalgia [nostaw'ʒia] F nostalgia

nostálgico, -a [nos'tawʒiku, a] ADJ nostalgic

nota ['nɔta] F note; (Educ) mark; (conta) bill; (cédula) banknote; **digno de ~** noteworthy; **cheio de ~** (col) flush; **custar uma ~ (preta)** (col) to cost a bomb; **tomar ~** to make a note; **~ de venda** sales receipt; **~ fiscal** receipt; **(~) promissória** promissory note

notabilidade [notabili'dadʒi] F notability; (pessoa) notable

notabilizar [notabili'zar] VT to make known; **notabilizar-se** VR to become known

notação [nota'sãw] (pl **-ões**) F notation

notadamente [notada'mẽtʃi] ADV especially

notar [no'tar] VT (reparar em) to notice, note; **notar-se** VR to be obvious; **é de ~ que** it is to be noted that; **fazer ~** to call attention to

notável [no'tavew] (pl **-eis**) ADJ notable, remarkable

notícia [no'tʃisja] F (uma notícia) piece of news; (TV etc) news item; **notícias** FPL (informações) news sg; **pedir ~s de** to inquire about; **ter ~s de** to hear from

noticiar [notʃi'sjar] VT to announce, report

noticiário [notʃi'sjarju] M (de jornal) news section; (Cinema) newsreel; (TV, Rádio) news bulletin

noticiarista [notʃisja'rista] M/F news writer, reporter; (TV, Rádio) newsreader, newscaster

noticioso, -a [notʃi'sjozu, ɔza] ADJ news atr

notificação [notʃifika'sãw] (pl **-ões**) F notification

notificar [notʃifi'kar] VT to notify, inform

notívago, -a [no'tʃivagu, a] ADJ nocturnal ▶ M/F sleepwalker; (pessoa que gosta da noite) night bird

notoriedade [notorje'dadʒi] F renown, fame

notório, -a [no'tɔrju, a] ADJ well-known

noturno, -a [no'turnu, a] ADJ nocturnal, nightly; (trabalho) night atr ▶ M (trem) night train

nov. ABR (= novembro) Nov.

nova ['nɔva] F piece of news; **novas** FPL (novidades) news sg

novamente [nova'mẽtʃi] ADV again

novato, -a [no'vatu, a] ADJ inexperienced, raw ▶ M/F (principiante) beginner, novice; (Educ) fresher

nove ['nɔvi] NUM nine; ver tb **cinco**

novecentos, -tas [nove'sẽtus, tas] NUM nine hundred

novela [no'vɛla] F short novel, novella; (Rádio, TV) soap opera

novelista [nove'lista] M/F novella writer

novelo [no'velu] M ball of thread

novembro [no'vẽbru] M November; ver tb **julho**

novena [no'vena] F (Rel) novena

noventa [no'vẽta] NUM ninety; ver tb **cinquenta**

noviciado [novi'sjadu] M (Rel) novitiate

noviço, -a [no'visu, a] M/F (Rel, fig) novice

novidade [novi'dadʒi] F novelty; (notícia) piece of news; **novidades** FPL (notícias) news sg; **sem ~** without incident

novidadeiro, -a [novida'dejru, a] ADJ chatty ▶ M/F gossip

novilho, -a [no'viʎu, a] M/F young bull/heifer

novo, -a ['novu, 'nɔva] ADJ new; (jovem) young; (adicional) further; **de ~** again; **~ em folha** brand new; **o que há de ~?** what's new?; **~ rico** nouveau riche

noz [nɔs] F (de várias árvores) nut; (da nogueira) walnut; **~ moscada** nutmeg

nu, a [nu, 'nua] ADJ (corpo, pessoa) naked; (braço, arvore, sala, parede) bare ▶ M nude; **a olho nu** with the naked eye; **a verdade nua e crua** the stark truth ou reality; **pôr a nu** (fig) to expose

nuança [nu'ãsa] F nuance

nubente [nu'bẽtʃi] ADJ, M/F betrothed

nublado, -a [nu'bladu, a] ADJ cloudy, overcast

nublar [nu'blar] VT to darken; **nublar-se** VR to cloud over

nuca ['nuka] F nape (of the neck)

nuclear [nu'kljar] ADJ nuclear; **energia/ usina ~** nuclear energy/power station

núcleo ['nuklju] M nucleus *sg*; *(centro)* centre (BRIT), center (US)

nudez [nu'dez] F nakedness, nudity; *(de paredes etc)* bareness

nudismo [nu'dʒizmu] M nudism

nudista [nu'dʒista] ADJ, M/F nudist

nulidade [nuli'dadʒi] F nullity, invalidity; *(pessoa)* nonentity

nulo, -a ['nulu, a] ADJ *(Jur)* null, void; *(nenhum)* non-existent; *(sem valor)* worthless; *(esforço)* vain, useless; **ele é ~ em matemática** he's useless at maths (BRIT) *ou* math (US)

num¹ [nũ] = **em** + **um**; *ver* **em**

num² [nũ] ADV *(col: não)* not

numa(s) ['numa(s)] = **em** + **uma(s)**; *ver* **em**

numeração [numera'sãw] F *(ato)* numbering; *(números)* numbers *pl*; *(de sapatos etc)* sizes *pl*

numerado, -a [nume'radu, a] ADJ numbered; *(em ordem numérica)* in numerical order

numeral [nume'raw] *(pl* **-ais)** M numeral
▶ ADJ numerical

numerar [nume'rar] VT to number

numerário [nume'rarju] M cash, money

numérico, -a [nu'mɛriku, a] ADJ numerical

número ['numeru] M number; *(de jornal)* issue; *(Teatro etc)* act; *(de sapatos, roupa)* size; **sem ~** countless; **um sem ~ de vezes** hundreds *ou* thousands of times; **amigo/escritor ~ um** number one friend/writer; **fazer ~** to make up the numbers; **ele é um ~** *(col)* he's a riot; **~ cardinal/ordinal** cardinal/ordinal number; **~ de matrícula** registration (BRIT) *ou* license plate (US) number; **~ primo** prime number

numeroso, -a [nume'rozu, ɔza] ADJ numerous

nunca ['nũka] ADV never; **~ mais** never again; **como ~** as never before; **quase ~** hardly ever; **mais que ~** more than ever

nuns [nũs] = **em** + **uns**

nupcial [nup'sjaw] *(pl* **-ais)** ADJ wedding *atr*

núpcias ['nupsjas] FPL nuptials, wedding *sg*

nutrição [nutri'sãw] F nutrition

nutricionista [nutrisjo'nista] M/F nutritionist

nutrido, -a [nu'tridu, a] ADJ *(bem alimentado)* well-nourished; *(robusto)* robust

nutrimento [nutri'mẽtu] M nourishment

nutrir [nu'trir] VT *(sentimento)* to harbour (BRIT), harbor (US); *(alimentar-se)*: **~ (de)** to nourish (with), feed (on); *(fig)* to feed (on) ▶ VI to be nourishing

nutritivo, -a [nutri'tʃivu, a] ADJ nourishing; **valor ~** nutritional value

nuvem ['nuvẽj] *(pl* **-ns)** F cloud; *(de insetos)* swarm; **cair das nuvens** *(fig)* to be astounded; **estar nas nuvens** to be daydreaming, be miles away; **pôr nas nuvens** to praise to the skies; **o aniversário passou em brancas nuvens** the birthday went by without any celebration

Oo

O, o [ɔ] (pl **os**) M O, o; **O de Osvaldo** O for
Oliver (BRIT) ou oboe (US)

o, a [u, a] ART DEF **1** the; **o livro/a mesa/os
estudantes** the book/table/students
2 (com n abstrato: não se traduz): **o amor/a
juventude** love/youth
3 (posse: traduz-se muitas vezes por adj possessivo):
quebrar o braço to break one's arm; **ele
levantou a mão** he put his hand up; **ela
colocou o chapéu** she put her hat on
4 (valor descritivo): **ter a boca grande/os olhos
azuis** to have a big mouth/blue eyes
▶ PRON DEMONSTRATIVO: **meu livro e o seu**
my book and yours; **as de Pedro são
melhores** Pedro's are better; **não a(s)
branca(s) mas a(s) verde(s)** not the white
one(s) but the green one(s)
▶ PRON RELATIVO: **o que** (etc) **1** (indef): **os que
quiserem podem sair** anyone who wants
to can leave; **leve o que mais gostar** take
the one you like best
2 (def): **o que comprei ontem** the one
I bought yesterday; **os que sairam** those
who left
3: **o que** what; **o que eu acho/mais gosto**
what I think/like most
▶ PRON PESSOAL **1** (pessoa: m) him; (: f) her;
(: pl) them; **não consigo vê-lo(s)** I can't see
him/them; **vemo-la todas as semanas** we
see her every week
2 (animal, coisa: sg) it; (: pl) them; **não consigo
vê-lo(s)** I can't see it/them; **acharam-nos
na praia** they found them on the beach

ó [ɔ] EXCL oh!; (olha) look!; **ó Pedro** hey Pedro
ô [o] EXCL oh!; **ô Pedro** hey Pedro; **ô de casa!**
anyone at home?; **ô criança difícil!** oh,
what an awkward child!
OAB ABR F = **Ordem dos Advogados do Brasil**
oásis [oˈasis] M INV oasis
oba [ˈoba] EXCL wow!, great!; (saudação) hi!
obcecado, -a [obiseˈkadu, a] ADJ obsessed
obcecar [obiseˈkar] VT to obsess
obedecer [obedeˈser] VI: **~ a** to obey;
obedeça! (a criança) do as you're told!
obediência [obeˈdʒĕsja] F obedience
obediente [obeˈdʒĕtʃi] ADJ obedient

obelisco [obeˈlisku] M obelisk
obesidade [obeziˈdadʒi] F obesity
obeso, -a [oˈbɛzu, a] ADJ obese
óbice [ˈɔbisi] M obstacle
óbito [ˈɔbitu] M death; **atestado de ~** death
certificate
obituário [obiˈtwarju] M obituary
objeção [obʒeˈsãw] (pl **-ões**) F objection;
(obstáculo) obstacle; **fazer** ou **pôr objeções a**
to object to
objetar [obʒeˈtar] VT to object ▶ VI: **~ (a algo)**
to object (to sth)
objetiva [obʒeˈtʃiva] F lens; **sem ~** aimlessly
objetivar [obʒetʃiˈvar] VT (visar) to aim at;
~ fazer to aim to do, set out to do
objetividade [obʒetʃiviˈdadʒi] F objectivity
objetivo, -a [obʒeˈtʃivu, a] ADJ objective ▶ M
objective, aim
objeto [obˈʒɛtu] M object; **~ de uso pessoal**
personal effect
oblíqua [oˈblikwa] F oblique
oblíquo, -a [oˈblikwu, a] ADJ oblique, slanting;
(olhar) sidelong; (Ling) oblique
obliterar [obliteˈrar] VT to obliterate; (Med) to
close off
oblongo, -a [obˈlõgu, a] ADJ oblong
oboé [oˈbwɛ] M oboe
oboísta [oˈbwista] M/F oboe player
obra [ˈɔbra] F work; (Arq) building,
construction; (Teatro) play; **~s** (na estrada)
roadworks; **em ~s** under repair; **ser ~ de
alguém** to be the work of sb; **ser ~ de algo**
to be the result of sth; **~ de arte** work of art;
~ de caridade charity; **~s completas**
complete works; **~s públicas** public works
obra-mestra (pl **obras-mestras**) F
masterpiece
obra-prima (pl **obras-primas**) F masterpiece
obreiro, -a [oˈbrejru, a] ADJ working ▶ M/F
worker
obrigação [obrigaˈsãw] (pl **-ões**) F
obligation, duty; (Com) bond; **cumprir
(com) suas obrigações** to fulfil(l) one's
obligations; **dever obrigações a alguém**
to owe sb favo(u)rs; **~ ao portador** bearer
bond
obrigado, -a [obriˈgadu, a] ADJ (compelido)
obliged, compelled ▶ EXCL thank you;
(recusa) no, thank you

o

obrigar [obri'gar] VT to oblige, compel;
  obrigar-se VR: ~-**se a fazer algo** to
  undertake to do sth
obrigatoriedade [obrigatorje'dadʒi] F
  compulsory nature
obrigatório, -a [obriga'tɔrju, a] ADJ
  compulsory, obligatory
obscenidade [obiseni'dadʒi] F obscenity
obsceno, -a [obi'sɛnu, a] ADJ obscene
obscurecer [obiskure'ser] VT to darken;
  (*entendimento, verdade etc*) to obscure; (*prestígio*)
  to dim ▸ VI to get dark
obscuridade [obiskuri'dadʒi] F (*falta de luz*)
  darkness; (*fig*) obscurity
obscuro, -a [obi'skuru, a] ADJ dark; (*fig*)
  obscure
obsequiar [obse'kjar] VT (*presentear*) to give
  presents to; (*tratar com agrados*) to treat
  kindly
obséquio [ob'sɛkju] M favour (BRIT), favor
  (US), kindness; **faça o ~ de ...** would you be
  kind enough to ....
obsequioso, -a [obse'kjozu, ɔza] ADJ obliging,
  courteous
observação [obiserva'sãw] (*pl* -**ões**) F
  observation; (*comentário*) remark, comment;
  (*de leis, regras*) observance
observador, a [obiserva'dor(a)] ADJ observant
  ▸ M/F observer
observância [obiser'vãsja] F observance
observar [obiser'var] VT to observe; (*notar*) to
  notice; (*replicar*) to remark; ~ **algo a alguém**
  to point sth out to sb
observatório [observa'tɔrju] M observatory
obsessão [obise'sãw] (*pl* -**ões**) F obsession
obsessivo, -a [obise'sivu, a] ADJ obsessive
obsessões [obise'sõjs] FPL *de* **obsessão**
obsoleto, -a [obiso'lɛtu, a] ADJ obsolete
obstáculo [obi'stakulu] M obstacle;
  (*dificuldade*) hindrance, drawback
obstante [obi'stãtʃi] ADV: **não ~** (*conj*)
  nevertheless, however; (*prep*) in spite of,
  notwithstanding
obstar [obi'star] VI: ~ **a** to hinder; (*opor-se*) to
  oppose
obstetra [obi'stɛtra] M/F obstetrician
obstetrícia [obiste'trisja] F obstetrics *sg*
obstétrico, -a [obi'stɛtriku, a] ADJ obstetric
obstinação [obistʃina'sãw] F obstinacy
obstinado, -a [obistʃi'nadu, a] ADJ obstinate,
  stubborn
obstinar-se [obistʃi'narsi] VR to be obstinate;
  ~ **em** (*insistir em*) to persist in
obstrução [obistru'sãw] (*pl* -**ões**) F
  obstruction
obstruir [obi'strwir] VT to obstruct; (*impedir*)
  to impede
obtêm *etc* [obi'tẽ] VB *ver* **obter**
obtemperar [obitẽpe'rar] VT to reply
  respectfully ▸ VI: ~ (**a algo**) to demur (at sth)
obtenção [obitẽ'sãw] (*pl* -**ões**) F acquisition;
  (*consecução*) attainment
obtenho *etc* [ob'teɲu] VB *ver* **obter**

obtenível [obite'nivew] (*pl* -**eis**) ADJ
  obtainable
obter [obi'ter] (*irreg: como* **ter**) VT to obtain, get;
  (*alcançar*) to gain
obturação [obitura'sãw] (*pl* -**ões**) F (*de dente*)
  filling
obturador [obitura'dor] M (*Foto*) shutter
obturar [obitu'rar] VT to stop up, plug; (*dente*)
  to fill
obtuso, -a [obi'tuzu, a] ADJ (*ger*) obtuse; (*fig:
  pessoa*) thick, slow
obviedade [obvje'dadʒi] F obviousness; (*coisa
  óbvia*) obvious fact
óbvio, -a ['ɔbvju, a] ADJ obvious; (**é**) ~! of
  course!; **é o ~ ululante** it's glaringly *ou*
  screamingly (*col*) obvious
OC ABR (= *onda curta*) SW
ocasião [oka'zjãw] (*pl* -**ões**) F (*oportunidade*)
  opportunity, chance; (*momento, tempo*)
  occasion, time
ocasional [okazjo'naw] (*pl* -**ais**) ADJ chance *atr*
ocasionar [okazjo'nar] VT to cause, bring
  about
ocaso [o'kazu] M (*do sol*) sunset; (*ocidente*)
  west; (*decadência*) decline
Oceania [osja'nia] F: **a ~** Oceania
oceânico, -a [o'sjaniku, a] ADJ ocean *atr*
oceano [o'sjanu] M ocean; **O~ Atlântico/
  Pacífico/Índico** Atlantic/Pacific/Indian
  Ocean
oceanografia [osjanogra'fia] F oceanography
ocidental [osidẽ'taw] (*pl* -**ais**) ADJ western
  ▸ M/F westerner
ocidente [osi'dẽtʃi] M west; **o O~** (*Pol*) the
  West
ócio ['ɔsju] M (*lazer*) leisure; (*inação*) idleness
ociosidade [osjozi'dadʒi] F idleness
ocioso, -a [o'sjozu, ɔza] ADJ idle; (*vaga*)
  unfilled
oco, -a ['oku, a] ADJ hollow, empty
ocorrência [oko'hẽsja] F incident, event;
  (*circunstância*) circumstance
ocorrer [oko'her] VI to happen, occur; (*vir ao
  pensamento*) to come to mind; ~ **a alguém** to
  happen to sb; (*vir ao pensamento*) to occur to sb
ocre ['ɔkri] ADJ, M ochre (BRIT), ocher (US)
octogenário, -a [oktoʒe'narju, a] ADJ
  eighty-year-old ▸ M/F octogenarian
octogésimo, -a [okto'ʒɛzimu, a] NUM
  eightieth
octogonal [oktogo'naw] (*pl* -**ais**) ADJ
  octagonal
octógono [ok'tɔgonu] M octagon
ocular [oku'lar] ADJ ocular; **testemunha ~**
  eye witness
oculista [oku'lista] M/F optician
óculo ['ɔkulu] M spyglass; **óculos** MPL glasses,
  spectacles; ~**s de proteção** goggles
ocultar [okuw'tar] VT to hide, conceal
ocultas [o'kuwtas] FPL: **às ~** in secret
oculto, -a [o'kuwtu, a] ADJ hidden;
  (*desconhecido*) unknown; (*secreto*) secret;
  (*sobrenatural*) occult

ocupação [okupa'sãw] (pl **-ões**) F occupation

ocupacional [okupasjo'naw] (pl **-ais**) ADJ occupational

ocupações [okupa'sõjs] FPL de **ocupação**

ocupado, -a [oku'padu, a] ADJ (pessoa) busy; (lugar) taken, occupied; (BR Tel) engaged (BRIT), busy (US); **sinal de ~** (BR Tel) engaged tone (BRIT), busy signal (US)

ocupar [oku'par] VT to occupy; (tempo) to take up; (pessoa) to keep busy; **ocupar-se** VR to keep o.s. occupied; **~-se com** ou **de** ou **em algo** (dedicar-se a) to deal with sth; (cuidar de) to look after sth; (passar seu tempo com) to occupy o.s. with sth; **posso ~ esta mesa/cadeira?** can I take this table/chair?

ode ['ɔdʒi] F ode

odiar [o'dʒjar] VT to hate

odiento, -a [o'dʒjẽtu, a] ADJ hateful

ódio ['ɔdʒju] M hate, hatred; **que ~!** (col) I'm (ou was) furious!

odioso, -a [o'dʒjozu, ɔza] ADJ hateful

odontologia [odõtolo'ʒia] F dentistry

odor [o'dor] M smell

OEA ABR F (= Organização dos Estados Americanos) OAS

oeste ['wɛstʃi] M west ▶ ADJ INV (região) western; (direção, vento) westerly; **ao ~ de** to the west of; **em direção ao ~** westwards

ofegante [ofe'gãtʃi] ADJ breathless, panting

ofegar [ofe'gar] VI to pant, puff

ofender [ofẽ'der] VT to offend; **ofender-se** VR to take offence (BRIT) ou offense (US)

ofensa [o'fẽsa] F insult; (à lei, moral) offence (BRIT), offense (US)

ofensiva [ofẽ'siva] F (Mil) offensive; **tomar a ~** to go on to the offensive

ofensivo, -a [ofẽ'sivu, a] ADJ offensive; (agressivo) aggressive; **~ à moral** morally offensive

oferecer [ofere'ser] VT to offer; (dar) to give; (jantar) to give; (propor) to propose; (dedicar) to dedicate; **oferecer-se** VR (pessoa) to offer o.s., volunteer; (oportunidade) to present itself, arise; **~-se para fazer** to offer to do

oferecido, -a [ofere'sidu, a] ADJ (intrometido) pushy

oferecimento [oferesi'mẽtu] M offer

oferenda [ofe'rẽda] F (Rel) offering

oferta [o'fɛrta] F (oferecimento) offer; (dádiva) gift; (Com) bid; (em loja) special offer; **a ~ e a demanda** (Econ) supply and demand; **em ~** (numa loja) on special offer

ofertar [ofer'tar] VT to offer

office boy [ɔfis'bɔj] (pl **office boys**) M messenger

oficial [ofi'sjaw] (pl **-ais**) ADJ official ▶ M/F official; (Mil) officer; **~ de justiça** bailiff

oficializar [ofisjali'zar] VT to make official

oficiar [ofi'sjar] VI (Rel) to officiate ▶ VT: **~ (algo) a alguém** to report (sth) to sb

oficina [ofi'sina] F workshop; **~ mecânica** garage

ofício [o'fisju] M (profissão) trade; (Rel) service; (carta) official letter; (função) function; (encargo) job, task; **bons ~s** good offices; **~ de notas** notary public

oficioso, -a [ofi'sjozu, ɔza] ADJ (não oficial) unofficial

ofsete [of'sɛtʃi] M offset printing

oftálmico, -a [of'tawmiku, a] ADJ ophthalmic

oftalmologia [oftawmolo'ʒia] F ophthalmology

ofuscante [ofus'kãtʃi] ADJ dazzling

ofuscar [ofus'kar] VT (obscurecer) to blot out; (deslumbrar) to dazzle; (entendimento) to colour (BRIT), color (US); (suplantar em brilho) to outshine ▶ VI to be dazzling

OGM ABR M (= organismo geneticamente modificado) GMO

ogro ['ɔgru] M ogre

ogum [o'gũ] M Afro-Brazilian god of war

oh [ɔ] EXCL oh

oi [ɔj] EXCL oh; (saudação) hi; (resposta) yes?

oitava [oj'tava] F: **~s de final** round before the quarter finals

oitavo, -a [oj'tavu, a] NUM eighth; ver tb **quinto**

oitenta [oj'tẽta] NUM eighty; ver tb **cinquenta**

oito ['ojtu] NUM eight; **ou ~ ou oitenta** all or nothing; ver tb **cinco**

oitocentos, -tas [ojtu'sẽtus, tas] NUM eight hundred; **os O~** the nineteenth century

ojeriza [oʒe'riza] F dislike; **ter ~ a alguém** to dislike sb

o.k. [o'ke] EXCL, ADV OK, okay

olá [o'la] EXCL hello!

olaria [ola'ria] F (fábrica: de louças de barro) pottery; (: de tijolos) brickworks sg

oleado [o'ljadu] M oilcloth

oleiro, -a [o'lejru, a] M/F potter; (de tijolos) brick maker

óleo ['ɔlju] M (lubricante) oil; **pintura a ~** oil painting; **tinta a ~** oil paint; **~ combustível** fuel oil; **~ de bronzear** suntan oil; **~ diesel** diesel oil

oleoduto [oljo'dutu] M (oil) pipeline

oleoso, -a [o'ljozu, ɔza] ADJ oily; (gorduroso) greasy

olfato [ow'fatu] M sense of smell

olhada [o'ʎada] F glance, look; **dar uma ~** to have a look

olhadela [oʎa'dɛla] F peep

olhar [o'ʎar] VT to look at; (observar) to watch; (ponderar) to consider; (cuidar de) to look after ▶ VI to look ▶ M look; **olhar-se** VR to look at o.s.; (duas pessoas) to look at each other; **olha!** look!; **~ fixamente** to stare at; **~ para** to look at; **~ por** to look after; **~ alguém de frente** to look sb straight in the eye; **e olha lá** (col) and that's pushing it; **olha lá o que você vai me arranjar!** careful you don't make things worse for me!; **~ fixo** stare

olheiras [o'ʎejras] FPL dark rings under the eyes

olho ['oʎu] M (Anat, de agulha) eye; (vista) eyesight; (de queijo) hole; **~ nele!** watch him!; **~ vivo!** keep your eyes open!; **a ~** (*medir, calcular etc*) by eye; **a ~ nu** with the naked eye; **a ~s vistos** visibly; **abrir os ~s de alguém** (*fig*) to open sb's eyes; **andar** *ou* **estar de ~ em algo** to have one's eyes on sth; **custar/pagar os ~s da cara** to cost/pay the earth; **ficar de ~** to keep an eye out; **ficar de ~ em algo** to keep an eye on sth; **ficar de ~ comprido em algo** to look longingly at sth; **passar os ~s por algo** to scan over sth; **pôr alguém nos ~s da rua** to put sb on the street; (*de emprego*) to fire sb; **não pregar o ~** not to sleep a wink; **ter bom ~ para** to have a good eye for; **ver com bons ~s** to approve of; **~ clínico** sharp *ou* keen eye; **~ de lince** sharp eye; **ter ~ de peixe morto** to be glassy-eyed; **~ grande** (*fig*) envy; **estar de ~ grande em algo** to covet sth; **ter ~ grande** to be envious; **~ mágico** (*na porta*) peephole, magic eye; **~ roxo** black eye; **~ por ~** an eye for an eye; **num abrir e fechar de ~s** in a flash; **longe dos ~s, longe do coração** out of sight, out of mind; **ele tem o ~ maior que a barriga** his eyes are bigger than his belly

oligarquia [oligar'kia] F oligarchy
olimpíada [olī'piada] F: **as O~s** the Olympics
olimpicamente [olīpika'mētʃi] ADJ blissfully
olímpico, -a [o'līpiku, a] ADJ (*jogos, chama*) Olympic
olival [oli'vaw] (*pl* **-ais**) M olive grove
olivedo [oli'vedu] M = **olival**
oliveira [oli'vejra] F olive tree
olmeiro [ow'mejru] M = **olmo**
olmo ['ɔwmu] M elm
OLP ABR F (= *Organização para a Libertação da Palestina*) PLO
OM ABR (= *onda média*) MW
Omã [o'mã] M: **(o) ~** Oman
ombreira [ō'brejra] F (*de porta*) doorpost; (*de roupa*) shoulder pad
ombro ['ōbru] M shoulder; **encolher os ~s, dar de ~s** to shrug one's shoulders; **chorar no ~ de alguém** to cry on sb's shoulder
omelete [ome'letʃi] F omelette (*BRIT*), omelet (*US*)
omissão [omi'sãw] (*pl* **-ões**) F omission; (*negligência*) negligence; (*ato de não se manifestar*) failure to appear
omisso, -a [o'misu, a] ADJ omitted; (*negligente*) negligent; (*que não se manifesta*) absent
omissões [omi'sõjs] FPL *de* **omissão**
omitir [omi'tʃir] VT to omit; **omitir-se** VR to fail to appear
OMM ABR F (= *Organização Meteorológica Mundial*) WMO
omnipotente *etc* [omnipo'tētə] (*PT*) = **onipotente** *etc*
omnipresente [omnipre'zētə] (*PT*) ADJ = **onipresente**
omnisciente [omni'sjētə] (*PT*) ADJ = **onisciente**

omnívoro, -a [om'nivoru, a] (*PT*) ADJ = **onívoro**
omoplata [omo'plata] F shoulder blade
OMS ABR F (= *Organização Mundial da Saúde*) WHO
ON ABR (*Com: de ações*) = **ordinária nominativa**
onça ['ōsa] F (*peso*) ounce; (*animal*) jaguar; **ser do tempo da ~** to be as old as the hills; **ficar uma** *ou* **virar ~** (*col*) to get furious; **estou numa ~ danada** (*col*) I'm flat broke
onça-parda (*pl* **onças-pardas**) F puma
onda ['ōda] F wave; (*moda*) fashion; (*confusão*) commotion; **~ sonora/luminosa** sound/light wave; **~ curta/média/longa** short/medium/long wave; **~ de calor** heat wave; **pegar ~** to go surfing; **ir na ~** (*col*) to follow the crowd; **ir na ~ de alguém** (*col*) to be taken in by sb; **estar na ~** to be in fashion; **fazer ~** (*col*) to make a fuss; **deixa de ~!** (*col*) cut the crap! (!); **isso é ~ dela** (*col*) that's just something she's made up; **tirar uma ~ de algo** to act like sth
onde ['ōdʒi] ADV where ▶ CONJ where, in which; **de ~ você é?** where are you from?; **por ~** through which; **por ~?** which way?; **~ quer que** wherever; **não ter ~ cair morto** (*fig*) to have nothing to call one's own; **fazer por ~** to deserve it
ondeado, -a [ō'dʒjadu, a] ADJ wavy ▶ M (*de cabelo*) wave
ondeante [ō'dʒjātʃi] ADJ waving, undulating
ondear [ō'dʒjar] VT to wave ▶ VI to wave; (*água*) to ripple; (*serpear*) to meander, wind
ondulação [ōdula'sãw] (*pl* **-ões**) F undulation
ondulado, -a [ōdu'ladu, a] ADJ wavy
ondulante [ōdu'lātʃi] ADJ wavy
onerar [one'rar] VT to burden; (*Com*) to charge
oneroso, -a [one'rozu, ɔza] ADJ onerous; (*dispendioso*) costly
ONG [oŋ] ABR F (= *Organização Não-Governamental*) NGO
ônibus ['onibus] (*BR*) M INV bus; **ponto de ~** bus stop
onipotência [onipo'tēsja] F omnipotence
onipotente [onipo'tētʃi] ADJ omnipotent
onipresente [onipre'zētʃi] ADJ omnipresent, ever-present
onírico, -a [o'niriku, a] ADJ dreamlike
onisciente [oni'sjētʃi] ADJ omniscient
onívoro, -a [o'nivoru, a] ADJ omnivorous
ônix ['oniks] M onyx
onomástico, -a [ono'mastʃiku, a] ADJ: **índice ~** index of proper names; **dia ~** name day
onomatopeia [onomato'peja] F onomatopoeia
ontem ['ōtẽ] ADV yesterday; **~ à noite** last night; **~ à tarde/de manhã** yesterday afternoon/morning
ONU ['onu] ABR F (= *Organização das Nações Unidas*) UNO
ônus ['onus] M INV onus; (*obrigação*) obligation; (*Com*) charge; (*encargo desagradável*) burden; (*imposto*) tax burden

onze ['õzi] NUM eleven; *ver tb* **cinco**

OP ABR (*Com: ações*) = **ordinária ao portador**

opa ['opa] EXCL (*de admiração*) wow!; (*de espanto*) oops!; (*saudação*) hi!

opacidade [opasi'dadʒi] F opaqueness; (*escuridão*) blackness

opaco, -a [o'paku, a] ADJ opaque; (*obscuro*) dark

opala [o'pala] F opal; (*tecido*) fine muslin

opalino, -a [opa'linu, a] ADJ bluish white

opção [op'sãw] (*pl* **-ões**) F option, choice; (*preferência*) first claim, right

open market ['opẽ'markitʃ] M open market

OPEP [o'pɛpi] ABR F (= *Organização dos Países Exportadores de Petróleo*) OPEC

ópera ['ɔpera] F opera; ~ **bufa** comic opera

operação [opera'sãw] (*pl* **-ões**) F operation; (*Com*) transaction

operacional [operasjo'naw] (*pl* **-ais**) ADJ operational; (*sistema, custos*) operating

operações [opera'sõjs] FPL *de* **operação**

operado, -a [ope'radu, a] ADJ (*Med*) who has (*ou* have) had an operation ▶ M/F person who has had an operation

operador, a [opera'dor(a)] M/F operator; (*cirurgião*) surgeon; (*num cinema*) projectionist

operante [ope'rãtʃi] ADJ effective

operar [ope'rar] VT to operate; (*produzir*) to effect, bring about; (*Med*) to operate on ▶ VI to operate; (*agir*) to act, function; **operar-se** VR (*suceder*) to take place; (*Med*) to have an operation

operariado [opera'rjadu] M: **o** ~ the working class

operário, -a [ope'rarju, a] ADJ working ▶ M/F worker; **classe operária** working class

opereta [ope'reta] F operetta

opinar [opi'nar] VT (*julgar*) to think ▶ VI (*dar o seu parecer*) to give one's opinion

opinião [opi'njãw] (*pl* **-ões**) F opinion; **na minha** ~ in my opinion; **ser de ou da** ~ **(de) que** to be of the opinion that; **ser da** ~ **de alguém** to think the same as sb, share sb's view; **mudar de** ~ to change one's mind; ~ **pública** public opinion

ópio ['ɔpju] M opium

opíparo, -a [o'piparu, a] ADJ (*formal*) splendid, lavish

opõe *etc* [o'põj] VB *ver* **opor**

opomos [o'pomos] VB *ver* **opor**

oponente [opo'nẽtʃi] ADJ opposing ▶ M/F opponent

opor [o'por] (*irreg: como* **pôr**) VT to oppose; (*resistência*) to put up, offer; (*objeção, dificuldade*) to raise; **opor-se** VR: ~**-se a** (*fazer objeção*) to object to; (*resistir*) to oppose; ~ **algo a algo** (*colocar em contraste*) to contrast sth with sth

oportunamente [oportuna'mẽtʃi] ADV at an opportune moment

oportunidade [oportuni'dadʒi] F opportunity; **na primeira** ~ at the first opportunity

oportunismo [oportu'nizmu] M opportunism

oportunista [oportu'nista] ADJ, M/F opportunist

oportuno, -a [opor'tunu, a] ADJ (*momento*) opportune, right; (*oferta de ajuda*) well-timed; (*conveniente*) convenient, suitable

opôs [o'pos] VB *ver* **opor**

oposição [opozi'sãw] F opposition; **em** ~ **a** against; **fazer** ~ **a** to oppose

oposicionista [opozisjo'nista] ADJ opposition *atr* ▶ M/F member of the opposition

oposto, -a [o'postu, 'pɔsta] PP *de* **opor** ▶ ADJ (*contrário*) opposite; (*em frente*) facing, opposite; (*opiniões*) opposing, opposite ▶ M opposite

opressão [opre'sãw] (*pl* **-ões**) F oppression; (*sufocação*) feeling of suffocation, tightness in the chest

opressivo, -a [opre'sivu, a] ADJ oppressive

opressões [opre'sõjs] FPL *de* **opressão**

opressor, a [opre'sor(a)] M/F oppressor

oprimido, -a [opri'midu, a] ADJ oppressed ▶ M: **os** ~**s** the oppressed

oprimir [opri'mir] VT to oppress; (*comprimir*) to press ▶ VI to be oppressive

opróbrio [o'prɔbrju] M (*infâmia*) ignominy; (*formal: desonra*) shame

optar [op'tar] VI to choose; ~ **por** to opt for; ~ **por fazer** to opt to do; ~ **entre** to choose between

optativo, -a [opta'tʃivu, a] ADJ optional; (*Ling*) optative

opulência [opu'lẽsja] F opulence

opulento, -a [opu'lẽtu, a] ADJ opulent

opunha *etc* [o'puɲa] VB *ver* **opor**

opus *etc* [o'pus] VB *ver* **opor**

opúsculo [o'puskulu] M (*livreto*) booklet; (*pequena obra*) pamphlet

opuser *etc* [opu'zer] VB *ver* **opor**

ora ['ɔra] ADV now ▶ CONJ well; **por** ~ for the time being; ~ ..., ~ ... one moment ..., the next ...; ~ **sim**, ~ **não** first yes, then no; ~ **essa!** the very idea!, come off it!; ~ **bem** now then; ~ **viva!** hello there!; ~, **que besteira!** well, how stupid!; ~ **bolas!** (*col*) for heaven's sake!

oração [ora'sãw] (*pl* **-ões**) F (*reza*) prayer; (*discurso*) speech; (*Ling*) clause

oráculo [o'rakulu] M oracle

orador, a [ora'dor(a)] M/F (*aquele que fala*) speaker

oral [o'raw] (*pl* **-ais**) ADJ oral ▶ F oral (exam)

orangotango [orãgu'tãgu] M orang-utan

orar [o'rar] VI (*Rel*) to pray

oratória [ora'tɔrja] F public speaking, oratory

oratório, -a [ora'tɔrju, a] ADJ oratorical ▶ M (*Mús*) oratorio; (*Rel*) oratory

orbe ['ɔrbi] M globe

órbita ['ɔrbita] F orbit; (*do olho*) socket; **entrar/colocar em** ~ to go/put into orbit; **estar em** ~ to be in orbit

orbital [orbi'taw] (*pl* **-ais**) ADJ orbital

O

Órcades ['ɔrkadʒis] FPL: **as ~** the Orkneys
orçamentário, -a [orsamē'tarju, a] ADJ
budget *atr*
orçamento [orsa'mētu] M *(do estado etc)*
budget; *(avaliação)* estimate; **~ sem
compromisso** estimate with no obligation
orçar [or'sar] VT to value, estimate ▸ VI: **~ em**
(gastos etc) to be valued at, be put at; **~ a** to
reach, go up to; **ele orça por 20 anos** he is
around 20; **um projeto orçado em $10
bilhões** a project valued at $10 billion
ordeiro, -a [or'dejru, a] ADJ orderly
ordem ['ordē] *(pl* **-ns)** F order; **às suas ordens**
at your service; **um lucro da ~ de $60
milhões** a profit in the order of $60 million;
até nova ~ until further notice; **de
primeira ~** first-rate; **estar em ~** to be tidy;
pôr em ~ to arrange, tidy; **tudo em ~?** *(col)*
everything OK?; **por ~** in order, in turn;
dar/receber ordens to give/take orders;
dar uma ~ na casa to tidy the house;
~ alfabética/cronológica alphabetical/
chronological order; **~ bancária** banker's
order; **~ de grandeza** order of magnitude;
~ de pagamento *(Com)* banker's draft; **~ de
prisão** *(Jur)* prison order; **~ do dia** agenda;
O~ dos Advogados Bar Association;
~ pública public order, law and order;
~ social social order
ordenação [ordena'sãw] *(pl* **-ões)** F *(Rel)*
ordination; *(ordem)* order; *(arrumação)*
tidiness, orderliness
ordenado, -a [orde'nadu, a] ADJ *(posto em
ordem)* in order; *(metódico)* orderly; *(Rel)*
ordained ▸ M salary, wages *pl*
ordenança [orde'nãsa] M *(Mil)* orderly ▸ F
(regulamento) ordinance
ordenar [orde'nar] VT to arrange, put in order;
(determinar) to order; *(Rel)* to ordain;
ordenar-se VR *(Rel)* to be ordained; **~ que
alguém faça** to order sb to do; **~ algo a
alguém** to order sth from sb
ordenhar [orde'ɲar] VT to milk
ordens ['ordēs] FPL *de* **ordem**
ordinariamente [ordʒinarja'mēte] ADV
ordinarily, usually
ordinário, -a [ordʒi'narju, a] ADJ ordinary;
(comum) usual; *(medíocre)* mediocre; *(grosseiro)*
coarse, vulgar; *(de má qualidade)* inferior; *(sem
caráter)* rough; **de ~** usually
orégano [o'reganu] M oregano
orelha [o'reʎa] F *(Anat)* ear; *(aba)* flap; **de ~s
em pé** *(col)* on one's guard; **endividado até
as ~s** up to one's ears in debt; **~s de abano**
flappy ears
orelhada [ore'ʎada] *(col)* F: **de ~** through the
grapevine
orelhão [ore'ʎãw] *(pl* **-ões)** M payphone
órfã ['ɔrfã] F *de* **órfão**
orfanato [orfa'natu] M orphanage
órfão, -fã ['ɔrfãw, fã] *(pl* **-s/-s)** ADJ, M/F
orphan; **~ de pai** with no father; **~ de** *(fig)*
starved of

orfeão [or'fjãw] *(pl* **-ões)** M choral society
orgânico, -a [or'ganiku, a] ADJ organic
organismo [orga'nizmu] M organism;
(entidade) organization
organista [orga'nista] M/F organist
organização [organiza'sãw] *(pl* **-ões)** F
organization; **~ de caridade** charity; **~ de
fachada** front; **~ sem fins lucrativos**
non-profit-making organization
organizador, a [organiza'dor(a)] M/F
organizer ▸ ADJ *(comitê)* organizing
organizar [organi'zar] VT to organize
organograma [organo'grama] M flow chart
órgão ['ɔrgãw] *(pl* **-s)** M organ; *(governamental
etc)* institution, body; **~ de imprensa** news
publication
orgasmo [or'gazmu] M orgasm
orgia [or'ʒia] F orgy
orgulhar [orgu'ʎar] VT to make proud;
orgulhar-se VR: **~-se de** to be proud of
orgulho [or'guʎu] M pride
orgulhoso, -a [orgu'ʎozu, ɔza] ADJ proud
orientação [orjēta'sãw] F *(direção)* guidance;
(de tese) supervision; *(posição)* position;
(tendência) tendency; **~ educacional**
training, guidance; **~ vocacional** careers
guidance
orientador, a [orjēta'dor(a)] M/F advisor;
(de tese) supervisor ▸ ADJ guiding;
~ profissional careers advisor
oriental [orjē'taw] *(pl* **-ais)** ADJ eastern;
(do Extremo Oriente) oriental ▸ M/F oriental
orientar [orjē'tar] VT *(situar)* to orientate;
(indicar o rumo) to direct; *(aconselhar)* to guide;
orientar-se VR to get one's bearings; **~-se
por algo** to follow sth
oriente [o'rjētʃi] M: **o O~** the East; **Extremo
O~** Far East; **O~ Médio** Middle East
orifício [ori'fisju] M orifice
origem [o'riʒē] *(pl* **-ns)** F origin; *(ascendência)*
lineage, descent; **lugar de ~** birthplace;
pessoa de ~ brasileira/humilde person of
Brazilian origin/of humble origins; **dar ~ a**
to give rise to; **país de ~** country of origin;
ter ~ to originate
original [oriʒi'naw] *(pl* **-ais)** ADJ original;
(estranho) strange, odd ▸ M original; *(na
datilografia)* top copy
originalidade [oriʒinali'dadʒi] F originality;
(excentricidade) eccentricity
originar [oriʒi'nar] VT to give rise to, start;
originar-se VR to arise; **~-se de** to originate
from
originário, -a [oriʒi'narju, a] ADJ *(natural)* native;
~ de *(proveniente)* originating from; **um
pássaro ~ do Brasil** a bird native to Brazil
oriundo, -a [o'rjũdu, a] ADJ: **~ de** *(procedente)*
arising from; *(natural)* native of
orixá [ori'ʃa] M *Afro-Brazilian deity*
orla ['ɔrla] F *(borda)* edge, border; *(de roupa)*
hem; *(faixa)* strip; **~ marítima** seafront
orlar [or'lar] VT: **~ algo de algo** to edge sth
with sth

ornamentação [ornamẽta'sãw] F
ornamentation

ornamental [ornamẽ'taw] (*pl* **-ais**) ADJ
ornamental

ornamentar [ornamẽ'tar] VT to decorate, adorn

ornamento [orna'mẽtu] M adornment,
decoration

ornar [or'nar] VT to adorn, decorate

ornato [or'natu] M adornment, decoration

ornitologia [ornitolo'ʒia] F ornithology

ornitologista [ornitolo'ʒista] M/F
ornithologist

orquestra [or'kɛstra], (PT) **orquesta** F
orchestra; **~ sinfônica/de câmara**
symphony/chamber orchestra

orquestração [orkestra'sãw], (PT)
orquestação F (*Mús*) orchestration; (*fig*)
harmonization

orquestrar [orkes'trar], (PT) **orquestar** VT
(*Mús*) to orchestrate; (*fig*) to harmonize

orquídea [or'kidʒja] F orchid

ortodoxia [ortodok'sia] F orthodoxy

ortodoxo, -a [orto'dɔksu, a] ADJ orthodox

ortografia [ortogra'fia] F spelling

ortopedia [ortope'dʒia] F orthopaedics *sg*
(BRIT), orthopedics *sg* (US)

ortopédico, -a [orto'pɛdʒiku, a] ADJ
orthopaedic (BRIT), orthopedic (US)

ortopedista [ortope'dʒista] M/F orthopaedic
(BRIT) *ou* orthopedic (US) specialist

orvalhar [orva'ʎar] VT to sprinkle with dew

orvalho [or'vaʎu] M dew

os [us] ART DEF *ver* **o**

Osc. ABR (= *oscilação*) *change in price from previous
day*

oscilação [osila'sãw] (*pl* **-ões**) F (*movimento*)
oscillation; (*flutuação*) fluctuation; (*hesitação*)
hesitation

oscilante [osi'lãtʃi] ADJ oscillating; (*fig:
hesitante*) hesitant

oscilar [osi'lar] VI to oscillate; (*balançar-se*) to
sway, swing; (*variar*) to fluctuate; (*hesitar*) to
hesitate

ossatura [osa'tura] F skeleton, frame

ósseo, -a ['ɔsju, a] ADJ bony; (*Anat: medula etc*)
bone *atr*

osso ['osu] M bone; (*dificuldade*) predicament;
um ~ duro de roer a hard nut to crack; **~s
do ofício** occupational hazards

ossudo, -a [o'sudu, a] ADJ bony

ostensivo, -a [ostẽ'sivu, a] ADJ ostensible,
apparent; (*com alarde*) ostentatious

ostentação [ostẽta'sãw] (*pl* **-ões**) F
ostentation; (*exibição*) display, show

ostentar [ostẽ'tar] VT to show; (*alardear*) to
show off, flaunt

ostentoso, -a [ostẽ'tozu, ɔza] ADJ
ostentatious, showy

osteopata [ostʃjo'pata] M/F osteopath

ostra ['ostra] F oyster

ostracismo [ostra'sizmu] M ostracism

OTAN ['otã] ABR F (= *Organização do Tratado do
Atlântico Norte*) NATO

otário [o'tarju] (*col*) M fool, idiot

OTE (BR) ABR F = **Obrigação do Tesouro
Estadual**

ótica ['ɔtʃika] F optics *sg*; (*loja*) optician's; (*fig:
ponto de vista*) viewpoint; *ver tb* **ótico**

ótico, -a ['ɔtʃiku, a] ADJ optical ▶ M/F optician

otimismo [otʃi'mizmu] M optimism

otimista [otʃi'mista] ADJ optimistic ▶ M/F
optimist

otimizar [otʃimi'zar] VT to optimize

ótimo, -a ['ɔtʃimu, a] ADJ excellent, splendid
▶ EXCL great!, super!

OTN (BR) ABR F = **Obrigação do Tesouro
Nacional**

otorrino [oto'hinu] M/F ear, nose and throat
specialist

ou [o] CONJ or; **ou este ou aquele** either this
one or that one; **ou seja** in other words

OUA ABR F (= *Organização da Unidade Africana*)
OAU

ouço *etc* ['osu] VB *ver* **ouvir**

ourela [o'rela] F edge, border

ouriçado, -a [ori'sadu, a] (*col*) ADJ excited

ouriçar [ori'sar] VT (*col: animar*) to liven up;
(: *excitar*) to excite; **ouriçar-se** VR to bristle;
(*col*) to get excited

ouriço [o'risu] M (*europeu*) hedgehog; (*casca*)
shell; (*col: animação*) riot

ouriço-do-mar (*pl* **ouriços-do-mar**) M sea
urchin

ourives [o'rivis] M/F INV (*fabricante*)
goldsmith; (*vendedor*) jeweller (BRIT),
jeweler (US)

ourivesaria [oriveza'ria] F (*arte*) goldsmith's
art; (*loja*) jeweller's (shop) (BRIT), jewelry
store (US)

ouro ['oru] M gold; **ouros** MPL (*Cartas*)
diamonds; **de ~** golden; **nadar em ~** to be
rolling in money; **valer ~s** to be worth one's
weight in gold

ousadia [oza'dʒia] F daring; (*lance ousado*)
daring move; **ter a ~ de fazer** to have the
cheek to do

ousado, -a [o'zadu, a] ADJ daring, bold

ousar [o'zar] VT, VI to dare

out. ABR (= *Outubro*) Oct.

outdoor [awt'dɔr] (*pl* **-s**) M billboard

outeiro [o'tejru] M hill

outonal [oto'naw] (*pl* **-ais**) ADJ autumnal

outono [o'tonu] M autumn

outorga [o'tɔrga] F granting, concession

outorgante [otor'gãtʃi] M/F grantor

outorgar [otor'gar] VT to grant

outrem [o'trẽ] PRON (*sg*) somebody else; (*pl*)
other people

(PALAVRA-CHAVE)

outro, -a ['otru, a] ADJ **1** (*distinto: sg*) another;
(: *pl*) other; **outra coisa** something else; **de
outro modo, de outra maneira** otherwise;
no outro dia the next day; **ela está outra**
(*mudada*) she's changed

2 (*adicional*): **quer outro café?** would you

like another coffee?; **outra vez** again
▶ PRON **1: o outro** the other one; **(os) outros** (the) others; **de outro** somebody else's
2 (*recíproco*): **odeiam-se uns aos outros** they hate one another *ou* each other
3: outro tanto the same again; **comer outro tanto** to eat the same *ou* as much again; **ele recebeu uma dezena de telegramas e outras tantas chamadas** he got about ten telegrams and as many calls

outrora [o'trɔra] ADV formerly
outrossim [otro'sĩ] ADV likewise, moreover
outubro [o'tubru] M October; *ver tb* **julho**
ouvido [o'vidu] M (*Anat*) ear; (*sentido*) hearing; **de ~** by ear; **dar ~s a** to listen to; **entrar por um ~ e sair pelo outro** to go in one ear and out the other; **fazer ~s moucos** *ou* **de mercador** to turn a deaf ear, pretend not to hear; **ser todo ~s** to be all ears; **ter bom ~ para música** to have a good ear for music; **se isso chegar aos ~s dele, ...** if he gets to hear about it, ...
ouvinte [o'vĩtʃi] M/F listener; (*estudante*) auditor
ouvir [o'vir] VT to hear; (*com atenção*) to listen to; (*missa*) to attend ▶ VI to hear; to listen; (*levar descompostura*) to catch it; **~ dizer que ...** to hear that ...; **~ falar de** to hear of
ova ['ɔva] F roe; **uma ~!** (*col*) my eye!, no way!
ovação [ova'sãw] (*pl* -**ões**) F ovation, acclaim
ovacionar [ovasjo'nar] VT to acclaim; (*pessoa no palco*) to give a standing ovation to
ovações [ova'sõjs] FPL *de* **ovação**
oval [o'vaw] (*pl* -**ais**) ADJ, F oval
ovalado, -a [ova'ladu, a] ADJ oval
ovário [o'varju] M ovary

ovelha [o'veʎa] F sheep; **~ negra** (*fig*) black sheep
over ['over] ADJ overnight ▶ M overnight market
overnight [over'najtʃi] = **over**
óvni ['ɔvni] M (= *objeto voador não identificado*) UFO
ovo ['ovu] M egg; **~ cozido duro** hard-boiled egg; **~ pochê** (BR) *ou* **escalfado** (PT) poached egg; **~ estrelado** *ou* **frito** fried egg; **~s mexidos** scrambled eggs; **~ cozido** *ou* **quente** boiled egg; **~s de granja** free-range eggs; **~ de Páscoa** Easter egg; **estar/ acordar de ~ virado** (*col*) to be/wake up in a bad mood; **pisar em ~s** (*fig*) to tread carefully; **ser um ~** (*apartamento etc*) to be a shoebox
ovulação [ovula'sãw] F ovulation
óvulo ['ɔvulu] M egg, ovum
oxalá [oʃa'la] EXCL let's hope ...; **~ a situação melhore em breve** let's hope the situation improves soon
oxidação [oksida'sãw] F (*Quím*) oxidation; (*ferrugem*) rusting
oxidado, -a [oksi'dadu, a] ADJ rusty; (*Quím*) oxidized
oxidar [oksi'dar] VT to rust; (*Quím*) to oxidize; **oxidar-se** VR to rust, go rusty; to oxidize
óxido ['ɔksidu] M oxide
oxigenado, -a [oksiʒe'nadu, a] ADJ (*cabelo*) bleached; (*Quím*) oxygenated; **água oxigenada** peroxide; **uma loura oxigenada** a peroxide blonde
oxigenar [oksiʒe'nar] VT to oxygenate; (*cabelo*) to bleach
oxigênio [oksi'ʒenju] M oxygen
oxum [o'ʃũ] M *Afro-Brazilian river god*
ozônio [o'zonju] M ozone; **camada de ~** ozone layer

Pp

P, p [pe] (*pl* **ps**) M P, p; **P de Pedro** P for Peter
P. ABR (= *Praça*) Sq.; (= *Padre*) Fr.
p. ABR (= *página*) p.; (= *parte*) pt; = **por**;
próximo
p/ ABR = **para**
PA ABR = **Pará** ▶ ABR (*Com: de ações*)
= **preferencial, classe A**
pá [pa] F shovel; (*de remo, hélice*) blade; (*de
moinho*) sail ▶ M (PT) pal, mate; **pá de lixo**
dustpan; **pá mecânica** bulldozer; **uma pá
de** lots of; **da pá virada** (*col*) wild
p.a. ABR (= *por ano*) p.a.
paca ['paka] F (*Zool*) paca ▶ M/F fool ▶ ADJ
stupid ▶ ADV (*col*): **'tá quente ~** it's bloody
hot (!)
pacatez [paka'tez] F (*de pessoa*) quietness;
(*de lugar, vida*) peacefulness
pacato, -a [pa'katu, a] ADJ (*pessoa*) quiet;
(*lugar*) peaceful
pachorra [pa'ʃoha] F phlegm, impassiveness;
ter a ~ de fazer to have the gall to do
pachorrento, -a [paʃo'hẽtu, a] ADJ slow,
sluggish
paciência [pa'sjẽsja] F patience; (*Cartas*)
patience; **ter ~** to be patient; **~!** we'll (*ou*
you'll *etc*) just have to put up with it!;
perder a ~ to lose one's patience
paciente [pa'sjẽtʃi] ADJ, M/F patient
pacificação [pasifika'sãw] F pacification
pacificador, a [pasifika'dor(a)] ADJ calming
▶ M/F peacemaker
pacificar [pasifi'kar] VT to pacify, calm
(down); **pacificar-se** VR to calm down
pacífico, -a [pa'sifiku, a] ADJ (*pessoa*) peace-
loving; (*aceito sem discussão*) undisputed;
(*sossegado*) peaceful; **o (Oceano) P~** the
Pacific (Ocean); **ponto ~** undisputed point
pacifismo [pasi'fizmu] M pacifism
pacifista [pasi'fista] M/F pacifist
paço ['pasu] M palace; (*fig*) court
paçoca [pa'sɔka] F (*doce*) peanut fudge; (*fig:
misturada*) jumble, hotchpotch; (: *coisa
amassada*) crumpled mess
pacote [pa'kɔtʃi] M packet; (*embrulho*) parcel;
(*Econ, Comput, Turismo*) package
pacto ['paktu] M pact; (*ajuste*) agreement;
~ de não agressão non-aggression treaty;
~ de sangue blood pact; **P~ de Varsóvia**
Warsaw Pact

pactuar [pak'twar] VT to agree on ▶ VI:
~ (com) to make a pact *ou* an agreement
with
padaria [pada'ria] F bakery, baker's (shop)
padecer [pade'ser] VT to suffer; (*suportar*) to
put up with, endure ▶ VI: **~ de** to suffer from
padecimento [padesi'mẽtu] M suffering;
(*dor*) pain
padeiro [pa'dejru] M baker
padiola [pa'dʒjola] F stretcher
padrão [pa'drãw] (*pl* **-ões**) M standard;
(*medida*) gauge; (*desenho*) pattern; (*fig: modelo*)
model; **~ de vida** standard of living
padrasto [pa'drastu] M stepfather
padre ['padri] M priest; **O Santo P~** the Holy
Father
padrinho [pa'driɲu] M (*Rel*) godfather; (*de
noivo*) best man; (*patrono*) sponsor; (*paraninfo*)
guest of honour
padroeiro, -a [pa'drwejru, a] M/F patron;
(*santo*) patron saint
padrões [pa'drõjs] MPL *de* **padrão**
padronização [padroniza'sãw] F
standardization
padronizado, -a [padroni'zadu, a] ADJ
standardized, standard
padronizar [padroni'zar] VT to standardize
pães [pãjs] MPL *de* **pão**
paetê [pae'te] M sequin
pág. ABR (= *página*) p
paga ['paga] F payment; (*salário*) pay; **em ~ de**
in return for
pagã [pa'gã] F *de* **pagão**
pagador, a [paga'dor(a)] ADJ paying ▶ M/F
(*quem paga*) payer; (*de salário*) pay clerk; (*de
banco*) teller
pagadoria [pagado'ria] F payment office
pagamento [paga'mẽtu] M payment; **~ a
prazo** *ou* **em prestações** payment in
instal(l)ments; **~ à vista** cash payment;
~ contra entrega (*Com*) COD, cash on delivery
pagão, -gã [pa'gãw, 'gã] (*pl* **-s/-s**) ADJ, M/F
pagan
pagar [pa'gar] VT to pay; (*compras, pecados*) to
pay for; (*o que devia*) to pay back; (*retribuir*) to
repay ▶ VI to pay; **~ por algo** (*tb fig*) to pay for
sth; **~ a prestações** to pay in instal(l)ments;
~ à vista (BR), **~ a pronto** to pay on the spot,
pay at the time of purchase; **~ de contado** (PT)

to pay cash; **a ~** unpaid; **~ caro** (*fig*) to pay a high price; **~ a pena** to pay the penalty; **~ na mesma moeda** (*fig*) to give tit for tat; **~ para ver** (*fig*) to call sb's bluff, demand proof; **você me paga!** you'll pay for this!

página ['paʒina] F page; **~ de rosto** frontispiece, title page; **~ em branco** blank page; **~ (da) web** web page; **~ inicial** home page; **P~s Amarelas** Yellow Pages®

paginação [paʒinaˈsãw] F pagination

paginar [paʒiˈnar] VT to paginate

pago, -a ['pagu, a] PP *de* **pagar** ▶ ADJ paid; (*fig*) even ▶ M pay

pagode [paˈɡɔdʒi] M pagoda; (*fig*) fun, high jinks *pl*; (*festa*) knees-up

pagto. ABR = **pagamento**

paguei *etc* [paˈɡej] VB *ver* **pagar**

pai [paj] M father; **pais** MPL parents; **~ adotivo** adoptive father; **~ de família** family man; **~ de santo** voodoo priest; **~ de todos** (*col*) middle finger; **~ dos burros** (*col*) dictionary; **um idiota de ~ e mãe** (*col*) a complete idiot

painel [pajˈnɛw] (*pl* **-éis**) M (*numa parede*) panel; (*quadro*) picture; (*Auto*) dashboard; (*de avião*) instrument panel; (*reunião de especialistas*) panel (of experts); **~ de vídeo** video wall; **~ solar** solar panel

paio ['paju] M pork sausage

paiol [paˈjɔw] (*pl* **-óis**) M storeroom; (*celeiro*) barn; (*de pólvora*) powder magazine; **~ de carvão** coal bunker

pairar [pajˈrar] VI to hover ▶ VT (*embarcação*) to lie to

país [paˈjis] M country; (*região*) land; **~ encantado** fairyland; **~ natal** native land

paisagem [pajˈzaʒẽ] (*pl* **-ns**) F scenery, landscape; (*pintura*) landscape

paisano, -a [pajˈzanu, a] ADJ civilian ▶ M/F (*não militar*) civilian; (*compatriota*) fellow countryman; **à paisana** (*soldado*) in civvies; (*policial*) in plain clothes

Países Baixos MPL: **os ~** the Netherlands

paixão [pajˈʃãw] (*pl* **-ões**) F passion

paixonite [pajʃoˈnitʃi] (*col*) F: **~ (aguda)** crush, infatuation

pajé [paˈʒɛ] M medicine man

pajear [paˈʒjar] VT (*cuidar*) to look after; (*paparicar*) to mollycoddle

pajem ['paʒẽ] (*pl* **-ns**) M (*moço*) page

pala ['pala] F (*de boné*) peak; (*em automóvel*) sun visor; (*de vestido*) yoke; (*de sapato*) strap; (*col: dica*) tip

palacete [palaˈsetʃi] M small palace

palácio [paˈlasju] M palace; **~ da justiça** courthouse; **~ real** royal palace

Palácio do Planalto *see note*

> **Palácio de Planalto** is the seat of the Brazilian government, in Brasília. The name comes from the fact that the Brazilian capital is situated on a plateau. It has come to be a byword for central government.

paladar [palaˈdar] M taste; (*Anat*) palate

paladino [palaˈdʒinu] M (*medieval, fig*) champion

palafita [palaˈfita] F (*estacaria*) stilts *pl*; (*habitação*) stilt house

palanque [paˈlãki] M (*estrado*) stand

palatável [palaˈtavew] (*pl* **-eis**) ADJ palatable

palato [paˈlatu] M palate

palavra [paˈlavra] F word; (*fala*) speech; (*promessa*) promise; (*direito de falar*) right to speak; **~!** honestly!; **pessoa de/sem ~** reliable/unreliable person; **em outras ~s** in other words; **em poucas ~s** briefly; **cumprir a/faltar com a ~** to keep/break one's word; **dar a ~ a alguém** to give sb the chance to speak; **não dar uma ~** not to say a word; **dirigir a ~ a** to address; **estar com a ~ na boca** to have the word on the tip of one's tongue; **pedir a ~** to ask permission to speak; **ter ~** (*pessoa*) to be reliable; **tirar a ~ da boca de alguém** to take the words right out of sb's mouth; **tomar a ~** to take the floor; **a última ~** (*tb fig*) the last word; **~ de honra** word of honour; **~ de ordem** slogan; **~s cruzadas** crossword (puzzle) *sg*

palavra-chave (*pl* **palavras-chave(s)**) F key word

palavrão [palaˈvrãw] (*pl* **-ões**) M (*obsceno*) swearword

palavreado [palaˈvrjadu] M babble, gibberish; (*loquacidade*) smooth talk

palavrões [palaˈvrõjs] MPL *de* **palavrão**

palco ['pawku] M (*Teatro*) stage; (*fig: local*) scene

paleontologia [paljõtoloˈʒia] F palaeontology (BRIT), paleontology (US)

palerma [paˈlɛrma] ADJ silly, stupid ▶ M/F fool

Palestina [palesˈtʃina] F: **a ~** Palestine

palestino, -a [palesˈtʃinu, a] ADJ, M/F Palestinian

palestra [paˈlɛstra] F (*conversa*) chat, talk; (*conferência*) lecture, talk

palestrar [palesˈtrar] VI to chat, talk

paleta [paˈleta] F palette

paletó [paleˈtɔ] M jacket; **abotoar o ~** (*col*) to kick the bucket

palha ['paʎa] F straw; **chapéu de ~** straw hat; **não mexer** *ou* **levantar uma ~** (*col*) not to lift a finger

palhaçada [paʎaˈsada] F (*ato, dito*) joke; (*cena*) farce

palhaço [paˈʎasu] M clown

palheiro [paˈʎejru] M hayloft; (*monte de feno*) haystack

palheta [paˈʎeta] F (*de veneziana*) slat; (*de turbina*) blade; (*de pintor*) palette

palhoça [paˈʎɔsa] F thatched hut

paliar [paˈljar] VT (*disfarçar*) to disguise, gloss over; (*atenuar*) to mitigate, extenuate

paliativo, -a [paljaˈtʃivu, a] ADJ palliative

paliçada [paliˈsada] F fence; (*militar*) stockade; (*para torneio*) enclosure

palidez [pali'deʒ] F paleness

pálido, -a ['palidu, a] ADJ pale

pálio ['palju] M canopy

palitar [pali'tar] VT to pick ▶ VI to pick one's teeth

paliteiro [pali'tejru] M toothpick holder

palito [pa'litu] M stick; *(para os dentes)* toothpick; *(col: pessoa)* beanpole; *(: perna)* pin

palma ['pawma] F *(folha)* palm leaf; *(da mão)* palm; **bater ~s** to clap; **conhecer algo como a ~ da mão** to know sth like the back of one's hand; **trazer alguém nas ~s da mão** *(fig)* to pamper sb

palmada [paw'mada] F slap

palmatória [pawma'tɔrja] F: **~ do mundo** self-righteous person; *ver tb* **mão**

palmeira [paw'mejra] F palm tree

palmilha [paw'miʎa] F inner sole

palmilhar [pawmi'ʎar] VT, VI to walk

palmito [paw'mitu] M palm heart

palmo ['pawmu] M span; **~ a ~** inch by inch; **não enxerga um ~ adiante do nariz** he can't see further than the nose on his face

palpável [paw'pavew] *(pl* **-eis)** ADJ tangible; *(fig)* obvious

pálpebra ['pawpebra] F eyelid

palpitação [pawpita'sãw] *(pl* **-ões)** F beating, throbbing; **palpitações** FPL *(batimentos cardíacos)* palpitations

palpitante [pawpi'tãtʃi] ADJ beating, throbbing; *(fig: emocionante)* thrilling; *(: de interesse atual)* sensational

palpitar [pawpi'tar] VI *(coração)* to beat; *(comover-se)* to shiver; *(dar palpite)* to stick one's oar in

palpite [paw'pitʃi] M *(intuição)* hunch; *(Jogo, Turfe)* tip; *(opinião)* opinion; **dar ~** to give one's two cents' worth, stick one's oar in

palpiteiro, -a [pawpi'tejru, a] ADJ meddling ▶ M/F meddler

palude [pa'ludʒi] M marsh, swamp

paludismo [palu'dʒizmu] M malaria

palustre [pa'lustri] ADJ *(terra)* marshy; *(aves)* marsh-dwelling

pamonha [pa'moɲa] ADJ idiotic ▶ M/F nitwit

pampa ['pãpa] F pampas; **às ~s** (+ *n: col)* loads of; *(+ adj, adv)* really

panaca [pa'naka] ADJ stupid ▶ M/F fool

panaceia [pana'seja] F panacea

Panamá [pana'ma] M: **o ~** Panama; **o canal do ~** the Panama Canal

panamenho, -a [pana'meɲu, a] ADJ, M/F Panamanian

pan-americano, -a [pan-] ADJ Pan-American

pança ['pãsa] F belly, paunch

pancada [pã'kada] F *(no corpo)* blow, hit; *(choque)* knock; *(de relógio)* stroke ▶ M/F *(col)* loony ▶ ADJ crazy; **~ d'água** downpour; **dar uma ~ com a cabeça** to bang one's head; **dar ~ em alguém** to hit sb; **levar uma ~** to get hit

pancadaria [pãkada'ria] F *(surra)* beating; *(tumulto)* fight

pâncreas ['pãkrjas] M INV pancreas

pançudo, -a [pã'sudu, a] ADJ fat, potbellied

panda ['pãda] F panda

pandarecos [pãda'rɛkus] MPL: **em ~** in pieces; *(fig: exausto)* worn out; *(: moralmente)* devastated

pândega ['pãdega] F merrymaking, good time

pândego, -a ['pãdegu, a] ADJ *(farrista)* merrymaking; *(engraçado)* jolly ▶ M/F merrymaker; joker

pandeiro [pã'dejru] M tambourine

pandemia [pãde'mia] F pandemic

pandemônio [pãde'monju] M pandemonium

pane ['pani] F breakdown

panegírico [pane'ʒiriku] M panegyric

panejar [pane'ʒar] VI to flap

panela [pa'nɛla] F *(de barro)* pot; *(de metal)* pan; *(de cozinhar)* saucepan; *(no dente)* large cavity, hole; **~ de pressão** pressure cooker

panelinha [pane'liɲa] F clique

panfletar [pãfle'tar] VI to distribute pamphlets

panfleto [pã'fletu] M pamphlet

pangaré [pãga'rɛ] M *(cavalo)* nag

pânico ['paniku] M panic; **em ~** panic-stricken; **entrar em ~** to panic

panificação [panifika'sãw] *(pl* **-ões)** F *(fabricação)* bread-making; *(padaria)* bakery

panificadora [panifika'dora] F baker's

pano ['panu] M cloth; *(Teatro)* curtain; *(largura de tecido)* width; *(vela)* sheet, sail; **~ de chão** floor cloth; **~ de pratos** tea towel; **~ de pó** duster; **~ de fundo** *(tb fig)* backdrop; **a todo o ~** at full speed; **por baixo do ~** *(fig)* under the counter; **dar ~ para mangas** *(fig)* to give food for thought; **pôr ~s quentes em algo** *(fig)* to dampen sth down

panorama [pano'rama] M *(vista)* view; *(fig: observação)* survey

panorâmica [pano'ramika] F *(exposição)* survey

panorâmico, -a [pano'ramiku, a] ADJ panoramic

panqueca [pã'kɛka] F pancake

pantalonas [pãta'lonas] FPL baggy trousers

pantanal [pãta'naw] *(pl* **-ais)** M swampland

pântano [pã'tanu] M marsh, swamp

pantanoso, -a [pãta'nozu, ɔza] ADJ marshy, swampy

panteão [pã'tjãw] *(pl* **-ões)** M pantheon

pantera [pã'tɛra] F panther

pantomima [pãto'mima] F pantomime

pantufa [pã'tufa] F slipper

pão [pãw] *(pl* **pães)** M bread; **o P~ de Açúcar** *(no Rio)* Sugarloaf Mountain; **~ árabe** pitta *(BRIT)* ou pita *(US)* bread; **~ de carne** meat loaf; **~ de centeio** rye bread; **~ de fôrma** sliced loaf; **~ caseiro** home-made bread; **~ de ló** sponge cake; **~ francês** French bread; **~ integral** wholemeal *(BRIT)* ou wholewheat *(US)* bread; **~ preto** black bread; **~ torrado** toast; **ganhar o ~** to earn

a living; ~ **dormido** day-old bread; **dizer ~,
~, queijo, queijo** (*col*) to call a spade a spade,
pull no punches; **comer o ~ que o diabo
amassou** (*fig*) to have it tough; **tirar o ~ da
boca de alguém** (*fig*) to take the food out of
sb's mouth

pão-durismo [-du'rizmu] (*col*) M meanness,
stinginess

pão-duro (*pl* **pães-duros**) (*col*) ADJ mean,
stingy ▶ M/F miser

pãozinho [pãw'ziɲu] M roll

papa ['papa] M Pope; (*fig*) spiritual leader ▶ F
mush, pap; (*mingau*) porridge; **não ter ~s na
língua** to be outspoken, not to mince one's
words

papada [pa'pada] F double chin

papagaiada [papagaj'ada] (*col*) F showing off

papagaio [papa'gaju] M parrot; (*pipa*) kite;
(*Com*) accommodation bill; (*Auto*)
provisional licence (*BRIT*), student driver's
license (*US*) ▶ EXCL (*col*) heavens!

papai [pa'paj] M dad, daddy; **P~ Noel** Santa
Claus, Father Christmas; **o ~ aqui** (*col*) yours
truly

papal [pa'paw] (*pl* **-ais**) ADJ papal

papa-moscas F INV (*Bio*) flycatcher

papar [pa'par] (*col*) VT (*comer*) to eat; (*extorquir*):
~ algo a alguém to get sth out of sb ▶ VI to
eat

paparicar [papari'kar] VT to pamper

paparicos [papa'rikus] MPL (*mimos*)
pampering *sg*

papear [pa'pjar] VI to chat

papel [pa'pɛw] (*pl* **-éis**) M paper; (*Teatro*) part;
(*função*) role; **fazer o ~ de** to play the part of;
fazer ~ de idiota *etc* to play the fool *etc*;
~ aéreo airmail paper; **~ de embrulho**
wrapping paper; **~ de escrever/de
alumínio** writing paper/tinfoil; **~ de
parede** wallpaper; **~ de seda/transparente**
tissue paper/tracing paper; **~ filme**
Clingfilm® (*BRIT*), Saran Wrap® (*US*);
~ higiênico toilet paper; **~ laminado** *ou*
lustroso coated paper; **~ ofício** foolscap;
~ pardo brown paper; **~ timbrado** headed
paper; **~ usado** waste paper; **~ yes®** tissue,
kleenex®; **ficar no ~** (*fig*) to stay on the
drawing board; **pôr no ~** to put down on
paper *ou* in writing; **de ~ passado** officially

papelada [pape'lada] F pile of papers;
(*burocracia*) paperwork, red tape

papelão [pape'lãw] M cardboard; (*fig*) fiasco;
fazer um ~ to make a fool of o.s.

papelaria [papela'ria] F stationer's (shop)

papel-carbono M carbon paper

papeleta [pape'leta] F (*cartaz*) notice; (*papel
avulso*) piece of paper; (*Med*) chart

papel-moeda (*pl* **papéis-moeda(s)**) M paper
money, banknotes *pl*

papel-pergaminho M parchment

papelzinho [papew'ziɲu] M scrap of paper

papinha [pa'piɲa] F: **~ de bebê** baby food

papiro [pa'piru] M papyrus

papo ['papu] M (*de ave*) crop; (*col: de pessoa*)
double chin; (: *conversa*) chat; (: *papo furado*)
hot air; **ele é um bom ~** (*col*) he's a good
talker; **bater** *ou* **levar um ~** (*col*) to have a
chat; **bater ~** (*col*) to chat (*also Internet*); **ficar
de ~ para o ar** (*fig*) to laze around; **~ firme**
(*col: verdade*) gospel (truth); (: *pessoa*) straight
talker; **~ de anjo** *sweet made of egg yolks*

papo-firme (*pl* **papos-firmes**) (*col*) ADJ reliable
▶ M/F reliable sort

papo-furado (*pl* **papos-furados**) (*col*) ADJ
unreliable ▶ M/F: **ele é um ~** he never
comes up with the goods

papoula [pa'pola] F poppy

páprica ['paprika] F paprika

Papua Nova Guiné [pa'pua-] F Papua New
Guinea

papudo, -a [pa'pudu, a] ADJ fat in the face,
double-chinned

paqueração [pakera'sãw] (*pl* **-ões**) (*col*) F
pick-up

paquerador, a [pakera'dor(a)] (*col*) ADJ
flirtatious ▶ M/F flirt

paquerar [pake'rar] (*col*) VI to flirt ▶ VT to
chat up

paquete [pa'ketʃi] M steamship

paquistanês, -esa [pakista'nes, eza] ADJ, M/F
Pakistani

Paquistão [pakis'tãw] M: **o ~** Pakistan

par [par] ADJ (*igual*) equal; (*número*) even ▶ M
pair; (*casal*) couple; (*pessoa na dança*) partner;
~ a ~ side by side, level; **ao ~** (*Com*) at par;
sem ~ incomparable; **abaixo de ~** (*Com,
Golfe*) below par; **estar/ficar a ~ de algo** to
be/get up to date with sth

para ['para] PREP for; (*direção*) to, towards;
bom ~ comer good to eat; **~ não ser ouvido**
so as not to be heard; **~ que** so that, in order
that; **~ quê?** what for?, why?; **ir ~ São Paulo**
to go to São Paulo; **ir ~ casa** to go home;
~ com (*atitude*) towards; **de lá ~ cá** since
then; **~ a semana** next week; **estar ~** to be
about to; **é ~ nós ficarmos aqui?** should we
stay here?

parabenizar [parabeni'zar] VT: **~ alguém por
algo** to congratulate sb on sth

parabéns [para'bẽjs] MPL congratulations;
(*no aniversário*) happy birthday; **dar ~ a** to
congratulate; **você está de ~** you are to be
congratulated

parábola [par'rabola] F parable; (*Mat*)
parabola

para-brisa ['para-] (*pl* **-s**) M windscreen (*BRIT*),
windshield (*US*)

para-choque ['para-] (*pl* **-s**) M (*Auto*) bumper

parada [pa'rada] F stop; (*Com*) stoppage;
(*militar, colegial*) parade; (*col: coisa difícil*) ordeal;
ser uma ~ (*col: pessoa: difícil*) to be awkward;
(: *ser bonito*) to be gorgeous; **aguentar a ~** (*col*)
to stick it out; **topar a ~** (*col*) to accept the
challenge; **topar qualquer ~** (*col*) to be
game for anything; **~ cardíaca** heart failure

paradeiro [para'dejru] M whereabouts

paradigma [para'dʒigma] M paradigm
paradisíaco, -a [paradʒi'ʒiaku, a] ADJ (fig) idyllic
parado, -a [pa'radu, a] ADJ (pessoa: imóvel) standing still; (: sem vida) lifeless; (carro) stationary; (máquina) out of action; (olhar) fixed; (trabalhador, fábrica) idle; **fiquei ~ uma hora no ponto de ônibus** I stood for an hour at the bus stop; **não fique aí ~!** don't just stand there!
paradoxal [paradok'saw] (pl **-ais**) ADJ paradoxical
paradoxo [para'dɔksu] M paradox
paraense [para'ẽsi] ADJ from Pará ▶ M/F person from Pará
parafernália [parafer'nalja] F (de uso pessoal) personal items pl; (equipamento) equipment; (tralha) paraphernalia
parafina [para'fina] F paraffin
paráfrase [pa'rafrazi] F paraphrase
parafrasear [parafra'zjar] VT to paraphrase
parafusar [parafu'zar] VT to screw in ▶ VI (meditar) to ponder
parafuso [para'fuzu] M screw; **entrar em ~** (col) to get into a state; **ter um ~ de menos** (col) to have a screw loose
paragem [pa'raʒẽ] (pl **-ns**) F (PT) stop; **paragens** FPL (lugares) parts; **~ de elétrico** (PT) tram (BRIT) ou streetcar (US) stop
parágrafo [pa'ragrafu] M paragraph
Paraguai [para'gwaj] M: **o ~** Paraguay
paraguaio, -a [para'gwaju, a] ADJ, M/F Paraguayan
paraíba [para'iba] (col) M (operário) labourer (BRIT), laborer (US) ▶ F (mulher macho) butch woman
paraibano, -a [paraj'banu, a] ADJ from Paraíba ▶ M/F person from Paraíba
paraíso [para'izu] M paradise
para-lama ['para-] (pl **-s**) M wing (BRIT), fender (US); (de bicicleta) mudguard
paralela [para'lɛla] F parallel line; **paralelas** FPL (Esporte) parallel bars
paralelamente [paralela'mẽtʃi] ADV in parallel; (ao mesmo tempo) at the same time
paralelepípedo [paralele'pipedu] M cobblestone
paralelo, -a [para'lɛlu, a] ADJ (tb Comput) parallel ▶ M (Geo, comparação) parallel
paralisação [paraliza'sãw] (pl **-ões**) F (suspensão) stoppage
paralisar [parali'zar] VT to paralyse; (trabalho) to bring to a standstill; **paralisar-se** VR to become paralysed; (fig) to come to a standstill
paralisia [parali'zia] F paralysis
paralítico, -a [para'litʃiku, a] ADJ, M/F paralytic
paramédico, -a [para'mɛdʒiku, a] ADJ paramedical
paramentado, -a [paramẽ'tadu, a] ADJ smart
paramento [para'mẽtu] M (adorno) ornament; **paramentos** MPL (vestes) vestments; (de igreja) hangings

parâmetro [pa'rametru] M parameter
paramilitar [paramili'tar] ADJ paramilitary
paranaense [parana'ẽsi] ADJ from Paraná ▶ M/F person from Paraná
paraninfo [para'nĩfu] M patron; (pessoa homenageada) guest of honour (BRIT) ou honor (US)
paranoia [para'nɔja] F paranoia
paranoico, -a [para'nɔjku, a] ADJ, M/F paranoid
paranormal [paranor'maw] (pl **-ais**) ADJ paranormal
parapeito [para'pejtu] M (muro) wall, parapet; (da janela) windowsill
parapente [para'pẽtʃi] M (Esporte) paragliding; (equipamento) paraglider
paraplégico, -a [para'plɛʒiku, a] ADJ, M/F paraplegic
paraquedas [para'kɛdas] M INV parachute; **saltar de ~** to parachute
paraquedismo [parake'dʒizmu] M parachuting, sky-diving
paraquedista [parake'dʒista] M/F parachutist ▶ M (Mil) paratrooper
parar [pa'rar] VI to stop; (ficar) to stay ▶ VT to stop; **fazer ~** (deter) to stop; **~ na cadeia** to end up in jail; **~ de fazer** to stop doing
para-raios ['para-] M INV lightning conductor
parasita [para'zita] ADJ parasitic ▶ M parasite
parasitar [parazi'tar] VI to sponge ▶ VT: **~ alguém** to sponge off sb
parasito [para'zitu] M parasite
parceiro, -a [par'sejru, a] ADJ matching ▶ M/F partner
parcela [par'sɛla] F piece, bit; (de pagamento) instalment (BRIT), installment (US); (de terra) plot; (do eleitorado etc) section; (Mat) item
parcelado, -a [parse'ladu, a] ADJ (pagamento) in instalments (BRIT) ou installments (US)
parcelar [parse'lar] VT (pagamento, dívida) to schedule in instalments (BRIT) ou installments (US)
parceria [parse'ria] F partnership
parcial [par'sjaw] (pl **-ais**) ADJ (incompleto) partial; (feito por partes) in parts; (pessoa) biased; (Pol) partisan
parcialidade [parsjali'dadʒi] F bias, partiality; (Pol) partisans pl
parcimonioso, -a [parsimo'njozu, ɔza] ADJ parsimonious
parco, -a ['parku, a] ADJ (escasso) scanty; (econômico) thrifty; (refeição) frugal
pardal [par'daw] (pl **-ais**) M sparrow
pardieiro [par'dʒjejru] M ruin, heap
pardo, -a ['pardu, a] ADJ (cinzento) grey (BRIT), gray (US); (castanho) brown; (mulato) mulatto
parecença [pare'sẽsa] F resemblance
parecer [pare'ser] M (opinião) opinion ▶ VI (ter a aparência de) to look, seem; **parecer-se** VR to look alike, resemble each other; **~ de auditoria** (Com) auditors' report; **~-se com alguém** to look like sb; **~ alguém/algo** to look like sb/sth; **ao que parece** apparently;

P

parece-me que I think that, it seems to me that; **que lhe parece?** what do you think?; **parece que** (*pelo visto*) it looks as if; (*segundo dizem*) apparently

parecido, -a [pare'sidu, a] ADJ alike, similar; **~ com** like

paredão [pare'dãw] (*pl* **-ões**) M (*de serra*) face

parede [pa'redʒi] F wall; **imprensar** *ou* **pôr alguém contra a ~** to put sb on the spot, buttonhole sb; **~ divisória** partition wall

paredões [pare'dõjs] MPL *de* **paredão**

parelha [pa'reʎa] F (*de cavalos*) team; (*par*) pair

parente [pa'rẽtʃi] M/F relative, relation; **ser ~ de alguém** to be related to sb

parentela [parẽ'tɛla] F relations pl

parentesco [parẽ'tesku] M relationship; (*fig*) connection

parêntese [pa'rẽtezi] M parenthesis; (*na escrita*) bracket; (*fig: digressão*) digression

páreo ['parju] M race; (*fig*) competition; **ser um ~ duro** to be a hard nut to crack

pareô [pa'rjo] M beach wrap

pária ['parja] M pariah

paridade [pari'dadʒi] F (*igualdade*) equality; (*de câmbio, remuneração*) parity; **abaixo/acima da ~** below/above par

parir [pa'rir] VT to give birth to ▶ VI to give birth; (*mulher*) to have a baby

Paris [pa'ris] N Paris

parisiense [pari'zjẽsi] ADJ, M/F Parisian

parlamentar [parlamẽ'tar] ADJ parliamentary ▶ M/F member of parliament, MP ▶ VI to parley

parlamentarismo [parlamẽta'rizmu] M parliamentary democracy

parlamentarista [parlamẽta'rista] ADJ in favo(u)r of parliamentary democracy ▶ M/F supporter of the parliamentary system

parlamento [parla'mẽtu] M parliament

parmesão [parme'zãw] ADJ: **(queijo) ~** Parmesan (cheese)

pároco ['paroku] M parish priest

paródia [pa'rɔdʒja] F parody

parodiar [paro'dʒjar] VT (*fazer paródia de*) to parody; (*imitar*) to mimic, copy

paróquia [pa'rɔkja] F (*Rel*) parish; (*col: localidade*) neighbourhood (BRIT), neighborhood (US)

paroquial [paro'kjaw] (*pl* **-ais**) ADJ parochial

paroquiano, -a [paro'kjanu, a] M/F parishioner

paroxismo [parok'sizmu] M fit, attack; **paroxismos** MPL (*de moribundo*) death throes

parque ['parki] M park; **~ industrial** industrial estate; **~ infantil** children's playground; **~ nacional** national park; **~ de diversões** amusement park

parqueamento [parkja'mẽtu] M parking

parquear [par'kjar] VT to park

parreira [pa'hejra] F trellised vine

parrudo, -a [pa'hudu, a] ADJ muscular, well-built

part. ABR (= *particular*) priv.

parte ['partʃi] F part; (*quinhão*) share; (*lado*) side; (*ponto*) point; (*Jur*) party; (*papel*) role; **~ interna** inside; **a maior ~ de** most of; **a maior ~ das vezes** most of the time; **à ~** aside; (*separado*) separate; (*separadamente*) separately; (*além de*) apart from; **da ~ de alguém** on sb's part; **de ~ a ~** each other; **em ~** in part, partly; **em grande ~** to a great extent; **em alguma/qualquer ~** somewhere/anywhere; **em ~ alguma** nowhere; **por toda (a) ~** everywhere; **por ~s** in parts; **por ~ da mãe** on one's mother's side; **pôr de ~** to set aside; **tomar ~ em** to take part in; **dar ~ de alguém à polícia** to report sb to the police; **fazer ~ de algo** to be part of sth; **mandar alguém àquela ~** (!) to tell sb to go to hell

parteira [par'tejra] F midwife

partição [partʃi'sãw] F division; (*Pol*) partition

participação [partʃisipa'sãw] F participation; (*Com*) stake, share; (*comunicação*) announcement, notification

participante [partʃisi'pãtʃi] M/F participant ▶ ADJ participating

participar [partʃisi'par] VT to announce, notify of ▶ VI: **~ de** *ou* **em** (*tomar parte*) to participate in, take part in; (*compartilhar*) to share in

particípio [partʃi'sipju] M participle

partícula [par'tʃikula] F particle

particular [partʃiku'lar] ADJ (*especial*) particular, special; (*privativo, pessoal*) private ▶ M particular; (*indivíduo*) individual; **particulares** MPL (*pormenores*) details; **em ~** in private

particularidade [partʃikulari'dadʒi] F peculiarity

particularizar [partʃikulari'zar] VT (*especificar*) to specify; (*detalhar*) to give details of; **particularizar-se** VR (*privativo, pessoal*) to distinguish o.s.

particularmente [partʃikular'mẽtʃi] ADV privately; (*especialmente*) particularly

partida [par'tʃida] F (*saída*) departure; (*Esporte*) game, match; (*Com: quantidade*) lot; (*: remessa*) shipment; (*em corrida*) start; **dar ~ em** to start; **perder a ~** to lose

partidário, -a [partʃi'darju, a] ADJ supporting ▶ M/F supporter, follower

partido, -a [par'tʃidu, a] ADJ (*dividido*) divided; (*quebrado*) broken ▶ M (*Pol*) party; (*em jogo*) handicap; **tirar ~ de** to profit from; **tomar o ~ de** to side with

partilha [par'tʃiʎa] F share; **~ de ficheiros** file sharing

partilhar [partʃi'ʎar] VT to share; (*distribuir*) to share out

partir [par'tʃir] VT (*quebrar*) to break; (*dividir*) to split ▶ VI (*pôr-se a caminho*) to set off, set out; (*ir-se embora*) to leave, depart; **partir-se** VR (*quebrar-se*) to break; **~ de** (*começar, tomar por base*) to start from; (*originar*) to arise from; **a ~ de** (*starting*) from; **a ~ de agora** from now on, starting from now; **~ ao meio** to split down the middle; **eu parto do princípio que ...** I am working on the principle that ...; **~ para** (col: recorrer a) to resort to; **~ para outra** (col) to move on

partitura [part∫i'tura] F score

parto ['partu] M (child)birth; **estar em trabalho de ~** to be in labour (BRIT) ou labor (US); **~ induzido** induced labo(u)r; **~ prematuro** premature birth

parturiente [partu'rjēt∫i] F woman about to give birth

parvo, -a ['parvu, a] ADJ stupid, silly ▶ M/F fool, idiot

parvoíce [par'vwisi] F silliness, stupidity

Pasart [pa'zart∫i] (BR) ABR M = **Partido Socialista Agrário e Renovador Trabalhista**

Páscoa ['paskwa] F Easter; (dos judeus) Passover; **a ilha da ~** Easter Island

Pasep [pa'zεpi] (BR) ABR M = **Programa de Formação do Patrimônio do Servidor Público**

pasmaceira [pazma'sejra] F (apatia) indolence

pasmado, -a [paz'madu, a] ADJ amazed, astonished

pasmar [paz'mar] VT to amaze, astonish; **pasmar-se** VR: **~-se com** to be amazed at

pasmo, -a ['pazmu, a] ADJ astonished ▶ M amazement

paspalhão, -lhona [paspa'ʎãw, 'ʎɔna] (pl -ões/-s) ADJ stupid ▶ M/F fool

paspalho [pas'paʎu] M simpleton

paspalhões [paspa'ʎõjs] MPL de **paspalhão**

paspalhona [paspa'ʎɔna] F de **paspalhão**

pasquim [pas'kī] (pl **-ns**) M (jornal) satirical newspaper

passa ['pasa] F raisin

passada [pa'sada] F (passo) step; **dar uma ~ em** to call in at

passadeira [pasa'dejra] F (tapete) stair carpet; (mulher) ironing lady; (PT: para peões) zebra crossing (BRIT), crosswalk (US)

passadiço, -a [pasa'dʒisu, a] ADJ passing ▶ M walkway; (Náut) bridge

passado, -a [pa'sadu, a] ADJ (decorrido) past; (antiquado) old-fashioned; (fruta) bad; (peixe) off ▶ M past; **o ano ~** last year; **bem ~** (carne) well done; **ficar ~** (encabulado) to be very embarrassed

passageiro, -a [pasa'ʒejru, a] ADJ (transitório) passing ▶ M/F passenger

passagem [pa'saʒē] (pl **-ns**) F passage; (preço de condução) fare; (bilhete) ticket; **~ de ida e volta** return ticket, round trip ticket (US); **~ de nível** level (BRIT) ou grade (US) crossing; **~ de pedestres** pedestrian crossing (BRIT), crosswalk (US); **~ subterrânea** underpass, subway (BRIT); **de ~** in passing; **estar de ~** to be passing through

passamanaria [pasamana'ria] F trimming

passamento [pasa'mētu] M (morte) passing

passaporte [pasa'pɔrt∫i] M passport

passar [pa'sar] VT to pass; (ponte, rio) to cross; (exceder) to go beyond, exceed; (coar: farinha) to sieve; (: líquido) to strain; (: café) to percolate; (a ferro) to iron; (tarefa) to set; (telegrama) to send; (o tempo) to spend; (bife) to cook; (a outra pessoa) to pass on; (pomada) to put on; (contrabandear) to smuggle ▶ VI to pass; (na rua) to go past; (tempo) to go by; (dor) to wear off; (terminar) to be over; (ser razoável) to pass, be passable; (mudar) to change; **passar-se** VR (acontecer) to go on, happen; (desertar) to go over; (tempo) to go by; **~ bem** (de saúde) to be well; **como está passando?** how are you?; **~ a** (questão) to move on to; (suj: propriedade) to pass to; **~ a fazer** to start to do; **~ a ser** to become; **passava das dez horas** it was past ten o' clock; **ele passa dos 50 anos** he's over 50; **não ~ de** to be nothing more than; **~ na frente** to go ahead; **~ alguém para trás** to con sb; (cônjuge) to cheat on sb; **~ pela casa de** to call in on; **~ pela cabeça de** to occur to; **~ por algo** (sofrer) to go through sth; (transitar: estrada) to go along sth; (ser considerado como) to be thought of as sth; **~ por cima de algo** to overlook sth; **~ algo por algo** to put ou pass sth through sth; **~ sem** to do without

passarela [pasa'rεla] F footbridge; (para modelos) catwalk

pássaro ['pasaru] M bird

passatempo [pasa'tēpu] M pastime; **como ~** for fun

passável [pa'savew] (pl **-eis**) ADJ passable

passe ['pasi] M (licença) pass; (Futebol: ato) pass; (: contrato) contract; **~ de mágica** sleight of hand

passear [pa'sjar] VT to take for a walk ▶ VI (a pé) to go for a walk; (sair) to go out; **~ a cavalo/de carro** to go for a ride/a drive; **não moro aqui, estou passeando** I don't live here, I'm on holiday (BRIT) ou vacation (US); **mandar alguém ~** (col) to send sb packing

passeata [pa'sjata] F (marcha coletiva) protest march; (passeio) stroll

passeio [pa'seju] M walk; (de carro) drive, ride; (excursão) outing; (calçada) pavement (BRIT), sidewalk (US); **dar um ~** to go for a walk; (de carro) to go for a drive ou ride; **~ público** promenade

passional [pasjo'naw] (pl **-ais**) ADJ passionate; **crime ~** crime of passion

passista [pa'sista] M/F dancer (in carnival parade)

passível [pa'sivew] (pl **-eis**) ADJ: **~ de** (dor etc) susceptible to; (pena, multa) subject to

passividade [pasivi'dadʒi] F passivity

passivo, -a [pa'sivu, a] ADJ passive ▶ M (Com) liabilities pl

passo ['pasu] M step; (medida) pace; (modo de andar) walk; (ruído dos passos) footstep; (sinal de pé) footprint; **~ a ~** one step at a time; **a cada ~** constantly; **a um ~ de** (fig) on the verge of; **a dois ~s de** (perto de) a stone's throw away from; **ao ~ que** while; **apertar o ~** to hurry up; **ceder o ~ a** to give way to; **dar um ~** to take a step; **dar um mau ~** to slip up; **marcar ~** (*fig*) to mark time; **seguir os ~s de alguém** (*fig*) to follow in sb's footsteps; **~ de cágado** snail's pace

pasta ['pasta] F paste; (*de couro*) briefcase; (*de cartolina*) folder; (*de ministro*) portfolio; **~ dentifrícia** *ou* **de dentes** toothpaste; **~ de galinha** chicken pâté

pastagem [pas'taʒẽ] (*pl* **-ns**) F pasture

pastar [pas'tar] VT to graze on ▶ VI to graze

pastel [pas'tɛw] (*pl* **-éis**) ADJ INV (*cor*) pastel ▶ M samosa; (*desenho*) pastel drawing

pastelão [paste'lãw] M (*comédia*) slapstick

pastelaria [pastela'ria] F (*loja*) cake shop; (*comida*) pastry

pasteurizado, -a [pastewri'zadu, a] ADJ pasteurized

pastiche [pas'tʃiʃi] M pastiche

pastilha [pas'tʃiʎa] F (*Med*) tablet; (*doce*) pastille

pastio [pas'tʃiu] M pasture; (*ato*) grazing

pasto ['pastu] M (*erva*) grass; (*terreno*) pasture; **casa de ~** (*PT*) cheap restaurant, diner

pastor, a [pas'tor(a)] M/F shepherd(ess) ▶ M (*Rel*) clergyman, pastor

pastoral [pasto'raw] (*pl* **-ais**) ADJ pastoral

pastorear [pasto'rjar] VT (*gado*) to watch over

pastoril [pasto'riw] (*pl* **-is**) ADJ pastoral

pastoso, -a [pas'tozu, ɔza] ADJ pasty

pata ['pata] F (*pé de animal*) foot, paw; (*ave*) duck; (*col: pé*) foot; **meter a ~** to put one's foot in it

pata-choca (*pl* **patas-chocas**) F lump

patada [pa'tada] F kick; **dar uma ~** to kick; (*fig: col*) to behave rudely; **levar uma ~** (*fig*) to be treated rudely

Patagônia [pata'gonja] F: **a ~** Patagonia

patamar [pata'mar] M (*de escada*) landing; (*fig*) level

patavina [pata'vina] PRON nothing, (not) anything

patê [pa'te] M pâté

patente [pa'tẽtʃi] ADJ obvious, evident ▶ F (*Com*) patent; (*Mil: título*) commission; **altas ~s** high-ranking officers

patentear [patẽ'tʃjar] VT to show, reveal; (*Com*) to patent; **patentear-se** VR to be shown, be evident

paternal [pater'naw] (*pl* **-ais**) ADJ paternal, fatherly

paternalista [paterna'lista] ADJ paternalistic

paternidade [paterni'dadʒi] F paternity

paterno, -a [pa'tɛrnu, a] ADJ paternal, fatherly; **casa paterna** family home

pateta [pa'tɛta] ADJ stupid, daft ▶ M/F idiot

patetice [pate'tʃisi] F stupidity; (*ato, dito*) daft thing

patético, -a [pa'tɛtʃiku, a] ADJ pathetic, moving

patíbulo [pa'tʃibulu] M gallows *sg*

patifaria [patʃifa'ria] F roguishness; (*ato*) nasty thing

patife [pa'tʃifi] M scoundrel, rogue

patim [pa'tʃĩ] (*pl* **-ns**) M skate; **~ de rodas** roller skate; **patins em linha** Rollerblades®

patinação [patʃina'sãw] (*pl* **-ões**) F skating; (*lugar*) skating rink

patinador, a [patʃinador(a)] M/F skater

patinar [patʃi'nar] VI to skate; (*Auto: derrapar*) to skid

patinete [patʃi'nɛtʃi] F skateboard

patinhar [patʃi'nar] VI (*como um pato*) to dabble; (*em lama*) to splash about, slosh

patinho [pa'tʃiɲu] M duckling; (*carne*) leg of beef; (*urinol*) bedpan; **cair como um ~** to be taken in

patins [pa'tʃĩs] MPL *de* **patim**

pátio ['patʃju] M (*de uma casa*) patio, backyard; (*espaço cercado de edifícios*) courtyard; (*tb*: **pátio de recreio**) playground; (*Mil*) parade ground

pato ['patu] M duck; (*macho*) drake; (*col: otário*) sucker; **pagar o ~** (*col*) to carry the can

patologia [patolo'ʒia] F pathology

patológico, -a [pato'lɔʒiku, a] ADJ pathological

patologista [patolo'ʒista] M/F pathologist

patota [pa'tɔta] (*col*) F gang

patrão [pa'trãw] (*pl* **-ões**) M (*Com*) boss; (*dono de casa*) master; (*proprietário*) landlord; (*Náut*) skipper; (*col: tratamento*) sir

pátria ['patrja] F homeland; **lutar pela ~** to fight for one's country; **salvar a ~** (*fig*) to save the day

patriarca [pa'trjarka] M patriarch

patriarcal [patrjar'kaw] (*pl* **-ais**) ADJ patriarchal

patrício, -a [pa'trisju, a] ADJ, M/F patrician

patrimonial [patrimo'njaw] (*pl* **-ais**) ADJ (*bens*) family *atr*; (*imposto*) wealth *atr*

patrimônio [patri'monju] M (*herança*) inheritance; (*fig*) heritage; (*bens*) property; **~ líquido** equity

patriota [pa'trjɔta] M/F patriot

patriótico, -a [pa'trjɔtʃiku, a] ADJ patriotic

patriotismo [patrjo'tʃizmu] M patriotism

patroa [pa'troa] F (*mulher do patrão*) boss's wife; (*dona de casa*) lady of the house; (*proprietária*) landlady; (*col: esposa*) missus, wife; (*: tratamento*) madam

patrocinador, a [patrosina'dor(a)] ADJ sponsoring ▶ M/F sponsor, backer

patrocinar [patrosi'nar] VT to sponsor; (*proteger*) to support

patrocínio [patro'sinju] M sponsorship, backing; (*proteção*) support

patrões [pa'trõjs] MPL *de* **patrão**

patrono [pa'trɔnu] M patron; (*advogado*) counsel

patrulha [pa'truʎa] F patrol

patrulhar [patru'ʎar] VT, VI to patrol

pau [paw] M (*madeira*) wood; (*vara*) stick; (*col: briga*) punch-up; (*: real*) real; (*!: pênis*) cock (!); **paus** MPL (*Cartas*) clubs; **~ a ~** neck and neck; **a meio ~** (*bandeira*) at half-mast; **o ~ comeu** (*col*) all hell broke loose; **estar/ ficar ~ da vida** (*col*) to be/get mad; **ir ao** *ou* **levar ~** (*em exame*) to fail; **meter o ~ em alguém** (*col: espancar*) to beat sb up; (*: criticar*) to run sb down; **mostrar a alguém com quantos ~s se faz uma canoa** (*fig*) to teach sb a lesson; **ser ~** (*col: maçante*) to be a drag; **ser ~ para toda obra** to be a jack of all trades; **comida a dar com um ~** tons of food; **~ a pique** wattle and daub; **~ de arara** (*caminhão*) open truck; **~ de bandeira** flagpole; **~ de cabeleira** chaperon

pau-d'água (*pl* **paus-d'água**) M drunkard
paulada [paw'lada] F blow (with a stick)
paulatinamente [pawlatʃina'mẽtʃi] ADV gradually
paulatino, -a [pawla'tʃinu, a] ADJ slow, gradual
Pauliceia [pawli'sɛja] F: **a ~** São Paulo
paulificante [pawlifi'kãtʃi] ADJ annoying
paulificar [pawlifi'kar] VT to annoy, bother
paulista [paw'lista] ADJ from (the state of) São Paulo ▶ M/F person from São Paulo
paulistano, -a [pawliʃi'tanu, a] ADJ from (the city of) São Paulo ▶ M/F person from São Paulo
pau-mandado (*pl* **paus-mandados**) M yes man
paupérrimo, -a [paw'pɛhimu, a] ADJ poverty-stricken
pausa ['pawza] F pause; (*intervalo*) break; (*descanso*) rest
pausado, -a [paw'zadu, a] ADJ (*lento*) slow; (*sem pressa*) leisurely; (*cadenciado*) measured ▶ ADV (*falar*) in measured tones
pauta ['pawta] F (*linha*) (guide)line; (*Mús*) stave; (*lista*) list; (*folha*) ruled paper; (*de programa de TV*) line-up; (*ordem do dia*) agenda; (*indicações*) guidelines *pl*; **sem ~** (*papel*) plain; **em ~** on the agenda
pautado, -a [paw'tadu, a] ADJ (*papel*) ruled
pautar [paw'tar] VT (*papel*) to rule; (*assuntos*) to put in order, list; (*conduta*) to regulate
pauzinho [paw'ziɲu] M: **mexer os ~s** to pull strings
pavão, -voa [pa'vãw, 'voa] (*pl* **-ões/-s**) M/F peacock/peahen
pavê [pa've] M (*Culin*) cream cake
pavilhão [pavi'ʎãw] (*pl* **-ões**) M (*tenda*) tent; (*de madeira*) hut; (*no jardim*) summerhouse; (*em exposição*) pavilion; (*bandeira*) flag; **~ de isolamento** isolation ward
pavimentação [pavimẽta'sãw] F (*da rua*) paving; (*piso*) flooring
pavimentar [pavimẽ'tar] VT to pave
pavimento [pavi'mẽtu] M (*chão, andar*) floor; (*da rua*) road surface
pavio [pa'viu] M wick
pavoa [pa'voa] F *de* **pavão**
pavões [pa'võjs] MPL *de* **pavão**

pavonear [pavo'njar] VT (*ostentar*) to show off ▶ VI (*caminhar*) to strut; **pavonear-se** VR to show off
pavor [pa'vor] M dread, terror; **ter ~ de** to be terrified of
pavoroso, -a [pavo'rozu, ɔza] ADJ dreadful, terrible
paz [pajz] F peace; **fazer as ~es** to make up, be friends again; **estar em ~** to be at peace; **deixar alguém em ~** to leave sb alone; **ser de boa ~** to be easy-going
PB ABR F = **Paraíba** ▶ ABR (*Com: de ações*) = **preferencial, classe B**
PC ABR M (= *Partido Comunista*) PC
Pça. ABR (= *Praça*) Sq.
PCB ABR M = **Partido Comunista Brasileiro**
PCBR ABR M = **Partido Comunista Brasileiro Revolucionário**
PCC ABR M = **Partido Comunista Chinês**
PC do B ABR M = **Partido Comunista do Brasil**
PCN (*BR*) ABR M = **Partido Comunitário Nacional**
PCUS ABR M = **Partido Comunista da União Soviética**
PDC (*BR*) ABR M = **Partido Democrata-Cristão**
PDI (*BR*) ABR M = **Partido Democrático Independente**
PDS (*BR*) ABR M = **Partido Democrático Social**
PDT (*BR*) ABR M = **Partido Democrático Trabalhista**
PE ABR M = **Pernambuco**
pé [pɛ] M foot; (*da mesa*) leg; (*fig: base*) footing; (*de alface*) head; (*de milho, café*) plant; **ir a ~** to walk, go on foot; **ao pé de** near, by; **ao pé da letra** literally; **ao pé do ouvido** in secret; **pé ante pé** on tip-toe; **com um pé nas costas** (*com facilidade*) standing on one's head; **estar de pé** (*festa etc*) to be on; **estar de pé no chão** to be barefoot; **em** *ou* **de pé** standing (up); **em pé de guerra/igualdade** on a war/an equal footing; **dar no pé** (*col*) to run away, take off; **pôr-se em pé, ficar de pé** to stand up; **arredar pé** to move; **bater o pé** (*fig*) to dig one's heels in; **não chegar aos pés de** (*fig*) to be nowhere near as good as; **a água dá pé** (*Natação*) you can touch the bottom; **ficar com o pé atrás** to be wary; **ficar no pé de alguém** to keep on at sb; **larga meu pé!** leave me alone!; **levantar-se** *ou* **acordar com o pé direito/esquerdo** to wake up in a good mood/get out of bed on the wrong side; **meter os pés pelas mãos** to mess up; **perder o pé** (*no mar*) to get out of one's depth; **pôr os pés em** to set foot in; **não ter pé nem cabeça** (*fig*) to make no sense; **ter os pés na terra** (*fig*) to be down-to-earth, have one's feet firmly on the ground; **pé de atleta** athlete's foot; **pés de galinha** (*rugas*) crow's feet; **pé de moleque** peanut brittle; **pé de pato** (*para nadar*) flipper; **pé de vento** gust of wind
peão [pjãw] (*pl* **-ões**) M (*PT*) pedestrian; (*Mil*) foot soldier; (*Xadrez*) pawn; (*trabalhador*) farm labourer (*BRIT*) *ou* laborer (*US*)

P

peça ['pɛsa] F (*pedaço*) piece; (*Auto*) part; (*aposento*) room; (*Teatro*) play; (**serviço**) **pago por ~** piecework; **~ de reposição** spare part; **~ de roupa** garment; **pregar uma ~ em alguém** to play a trick on sb

pecado [pe'kadu] M sin; **~ mortal** deadly sin

pecador, a [peka'dor(a)] M/F sinner, wrongdoer

pecaminoso, -a [pekami'nozu, ɔza] ADJ sinful

pecar [pe'kar] VI to sin; (*cometer falta*) to do wrong; **~ por excesso de zelo** to be over-zealous

pechincha [pe'ʃiʃa] F (*vantagem*) godsend; (*coisa barata*) bargain

pechinchar [peʃi'ʃar] VI to bargain, haggle

pechincheiro, -a [peʃi'ʃejru, a] M/F bargain hunter

peço *etc* ['pɛsu] VB *ver* **pedir**

peçonha [pe'soɲa] F poison

pectina [pek'tʃina] F pectin

pecuária [pe'kwarja] F cattle-raising

pecuário, -a [pe'kwarju, a] ADJ cattle *atr*

pecuarista [pekwa'rista] M/F cattle farmer

peculiar [peku'ljar] ADJ (*especial*) special, peculiar; (*particular*) particular

peculiaridade [pekuljari'dadʒi] F peculiarity

peculio [pe'kulju] M (*acumulado*) savings *pl*; (*bens*) wealth

pecuniário, -a [peku'njarju, a] ADJ money *atr*, financial

pedaço [pe'dasu] M piece; (*fig: trecho*) bit; **aos ~s** in pieces; **caindo aos ~s** (*objeto, carro*) tatty, broken-down; (*casa*) tumbledown; (*pessoa*) worn out

pedágio [pe'daʒju] (*BR*) M (*pagamento*) toll; (*posto*) tollbooth

pedagogia [pedago'ʒia] F pedagogy; (*curso*) education

pedagógico, -a [peda'gɔʒiku, a] ADJ educational, teaching *atr*

pedagogo, -a [peda'gogu, a] M/F educationalist

pé-d'água (*pl* **pés-d'água**) M shower, downpour

pedal [pe'daw] (*pl* **-ais**) M pedal

pedalada [peda'lada] F turn of the pedals; **dar uma ~** to pedal

pedalar [peda'lar] VT, VI to pedal

pedalinho [peda'liɲu] M pedalo (boat)

pedante [pe'dãtʃi] ADJ pretentious ▶ M/F pseud

pedantismo [pedã'tʃizmu] M pretentiousness

pé-de-meia (*pl* **pés-de-meia**) M nest egg, savings *pl*

pederneira [peder'nejra] F flint

pedestal [pedes'taw] (*pl* **-ais**) M pedestal

pedestre [pe'dɛstri] (*BR*) M pedestrian

pediatra [pe'dʒjatra] M/F paediatrician (*BRIT*), pediatrician (*US*)

pediatria [pedʒja'tria] F paediatrics *sg* (*BRIT*), pediatrics *sg* (*US*)

pedicuro, -a [pedʒi'kuru, a] M/F chiropodist (*BRIT*), podiatrist (*US*)

pedida [pe'dʒida] F: **boa ~** (*col*) good idea

pedido [pe'dʒidu] M (*solicitação*) request; (*Com*) order; **a ~ de alguém** at sb's request; **~ de casamento** proposal (of marriage); **~ de demissão** resignation; **~ de desculpa** apology; **~ de informação** inquiry

pedigree [pedʒi'gri] M pedigree

pedinte [pe'dʒĩtʃi] ADJ begging ▶ M/F beggar

pedir [pe'dʒir] VT to ask for; (*Com, comida*) to order; (*exigir*) to demand ▶ VI to ask; (*num restaurante*) to order; **~ algo a alguém** to ask sb for sth; **~ a alguém que faça, ~ para alguém fazer** to ask sb to do; **~ $100 por algo** to ask $100 for sth; **~ alguém em casamento** *ou* **a mão de alguém** to ask for sb's hand in marriage, propose to sb

pedófilo, -a [pe'dɔfilu, a] M/F paedophile (*BRIT*), pedophile (*US*)

pedra ['pɛdra] F stone; (*rochedo*) rock; (*de granizo*) hailstone; (*de açúcar*) lump; (*quadro-negro*) slate; **~ de amolar** grindstone; **~ de gelo** ice cube; **~ preciosa** precious stone; **~ falsa** (*Med*) stone; **~ de toque** (*fig*) touchstone, benchmark; **doido de ~s** raving mad; **dormir como uma ~** to sleep like a log; **pôr uma ~ em cima de algo** (*fig*) to consider sth dead and buried; **ser de ~** (*fig*) to be hard-hearted; **ser uma ~ no sapato de alguém** (*fig*) to be a thorn in sb's side; **vir** *ou* **responder com quatro ~s na mão** (*fig*) to be aggressive; **uma ~ no caminho** (*fig*) a stumbling block, a hindrance

pedrada [pe'drada] F blow with a stone; **dar ~s em** to throw stones at

pedra-mármore F polished marble

pedra-pomes [-'pɔmis] F pumice stone

pedregal [pedre'gaw] (*pl* **-ais**) M stony ground

pedregoso, -a [pedre'gozu, ɔza] ADJ stony, rocky

pedregulho [pedre'guʎu] M gravel

pedreira [pe'drejra] F quarry

pedreiro [pe'drejru] M stonemason

pedúnculo [pe'dũkulu] M stalk

pê-eme [pe'emi] (*pl* **pê-emes**) M military policeman

pé-frio (*pl* **pés-frios**) (*col*) M jinx

pega¹ ['pɛga] M (*briga*) quarrel

pega² ['pega] F magpie; (*PT col: moça*) bird; (: *meretriz*) tart

pegada [pe'gada] F (*de pé*) footprint; (*Futebol*) save; **ir nas ~s de alguém** (*fig*) to follow in sb's footsteps; **~ de carbono** carbon footprint

pegado, -a [pe'gadu, a] ADJ (*colado*) stuck; (*unido*) together; **a casa pegada** the house next door

pega-gelo (*pl* **pega-gelos**) M ice tongs *pl*

pegajoso, -a [pega'ʒozu, ɔza] ADJ sticky

pega pra capar [pɛgapraka'par] (*col*) M INV scuffle

pegar [pe'gar] VT to catch; (*selos*) to stick (on); (*segurar*) to take hold of; (*hábito, mania*) to get into; (*compreender*) to take in; (*trabalho*) to take on; (*estação de rádio*) to pick up, get ▶ vi (*aderir*) to stick; (*planta*) to take; (*moda*) to catch on; (*doença*) to be catching; (*motor*) to start; (*vacina*) to take; (*mentira*) to stand up, stick; (*fogueira*) to catch; **pegar-se** vr (*brigar*) to have a fight, quarrel; **~ com** (*casa*) to be next door to; **~ em** (*começar*) to start on; (*segurar*) to grab, pick up; **ir ~** (*buscar*) to go and get; **~ um emprego** to get a job; **~ uma rua** to take a street; **~ fogo a algo** to set fire to sth; **~ 3 anos de cadeia** to get 3 years in prison; **~ alguém fazendo** to catch sb doing; **pega, ladrão!** stop thief!; **~ no sono** to get to sleep; **ele pegou e disse ...** he upped and said ...; **pegue e pague** cash and carry; **~ bem/mal** (*col*) to go down well/badly

pega-rapaz (*pl* **pega-rapazes**) M kiss curl
pego, -a ['pɛgu, a] PP *de* **pegar**
peguei *etc* [pe'gej] VB *ver* **pegar**
peidar [pej'dar] (!) VI to fart (!)
peido ['pejdu] (!) M fart (!)
peitilho [pej'tʃiʎu] M shirt front
peito ['pejtu] M (*Anat*) chest; (*de ave, mulher*) breast; (*fig*) courage; **dar o ~ a um bebê** to breastfeed a baby; **largar o ~** to be weaned; **meter os ~s** (*col*) to put one's heart into it; **no ~ (e na raça)** (*col*) whatever it takes; **~ do pé** instep; **amigo do ~** bosom pal, close friend
peitoril [pejto'riw] (*pl* **-is**) M windowsill
peitudo, -a [pej'tudu, a] ADJ big-chested; (*valente*) feisty
peixada [pej'ʃada] F *fish cooked in a seafood sauce*
peixaria [pejʃa'ria] F fish shop, fishmonger's (BRIT)
peixe ['pejʃi] M fish; **Peixes** MPL (*Astrologia*) Pisces *sg*; **como ~ fora d'água** like a fish out of water; **filho de ~, peixinho é** like father, like son; **não ter nada com o ~** (*fig*) to have nothing to do with the matter; **vender seu ~** (*ver seus interesses*) to feather one's nest; (*falar*) to say one's piece, have one's say
peixeira [pej'ʃejra] F fishwife; (*faca*) fish knife
peixeiro [pej'ʃejru] M fishmonger
pejar-se [pe'ʒarsi] VR to be ashamed
pejo [pe'ʒu] M shame; **ter ~** to be ashamed
pejorativo, -a [peʒora'tʃivu, a] ADJ pejorative
pela ['pɛla] = *por + a*; *ver* **por**
pelada [pe'lada] F football game

> **Pelada** is an improvised and generally short game of football. In the past it might have been played with an inflatable ball or a ball made of socks. It is still played today wherever there are pieces of open ground and even on the streets.

pelado, -a [pe'ladu, a] ADJ (*sem pele*) skinned; (*sem pelo, cabelo*) shorn; (*nu*) naked, in the nude; (*sem dinheiro*) broke

pelanca [pe'lãka] F fold of skin; (*de carne*) lump
pelancudo, -a [pelã'kudu, a] ADJ (*pessoa*) flabby
pelar [pe'lar] VT (*tirar a pele*) to skin; (*tirar o pelo*) to shear; (*col*) to fleece; **pelar-se** VR: **~-se por** to be crazy about, adore; **~-se de medo** to be scared stiff
pelas ['pɛlas] = *por + as*; *ver* **por**
pele ['pɛli] F (*de pessoa, fruto*) skin; (*couro*) leather; (*como agasalho*) fur; (*de animal*) hide; **cair na ~ de alguém** (*col*) to pester sb; **arriscar/salvar a ~** (*col*) to risk one's neck/save one's skin; **sentir algo na ~** (*fig*) to feel sth at first hand; **estar na ~ de alguém** (*fig*) to be in sb's shoes; **ser** *ou* **estar ~ e osso** to be nothing but skin and bone
peleja [pe'leʒa] F (*luta*) fight; (*briga*) quarrel
pelejar [pele'ʒar] VI (*lutar*) to fight; (*discutir*) to quarrel; **~ pela paz** to fight for peace; **~ para fazer/para que alguém faça** to fight to do/to fight to get sb to do
pelerine [pele'rini] F cape
peleteiro, -a [pele'tejru, a] M/F furrier
peleteria [pelete'ria] F furrier's
pele-vermelha (*pl* **peles-vermelhas**) M/F redskin
pelica [pe'lika] F kid (leather)
pelicano [peli'kanu] M pelican
película [pe'likula] F film; (*de pele*) film of skin
pelintra [pe'lĩtra] (PT) ADJ shabby; (*pobre*) penniless
pelo[1] ['pɛlu] = *por + o*; *ver* **por**
pelo[2] ['pelu] M hair; (*de animal*) fur, coat; **nu em ~** stark naked; **montar em ~** to ride bareback
Peloponeso [pelopo'nɛzu] M: **o ~** the Peloponnese
pelos ['pɛlus] = *por + os*; *ver* **por**
pelota [pe'lɔta] F ball; (*num molho*) lump; (*na pele*) bump; **dar ~ para** (*col*) to pay attention to
pelotão [pelo'tãw] (*pl* **-ões**) M platoon
pelúcia [pe'lusja] F plush
peludo, -a [pe'ludu, a] ADJ hairy; (*animal*) furry
pélvico, -a ['pɛwviku, a] ADJ pelvic
pélvis ['pɛwvis] F INV pelvis
pena ['pena] F (*pluma*) feather; (*de caneta*) nib; (*escrita*) writing; (*Jur*) penalty, punishment; (*sofrimento*) suffering; (*piedade*) pity; **que ~!** what a shame!; **a duras ~s** with great difficulty; **sob ~ de** under penalty of; **cumprir ~** to serve a term in jail; **dar ~** to be upsetting; **é uma ~ que ...** it is a pity that ...; **ter ~ de** to feel sorry for; **valer a ~** to be worthwhile; **não vale a ~** it's not worth it; **~ de morte** death penalty
penacho [pe'naʃu] M plume; (*crista*) crest
penal [pe'naw] (*pl* **-ais**) ADJ penal
penalidade [penali'dadʒi] F (*Jur*) penalty; (*castigo*) punishment; **impor uma ~ a** to penalize

P

penalizar [penali'zar] VT (*causar pena a*) to trouble; (*castigar*) to penalize

pênalti ['penawtʃi] M (*Futebol*) penalty (kick); **cobrar um ~** to take a penalty

penar [pe'nar] VT to grieve ▶ VI to suffer

penca ['pẽka] F bunch; **gente em ~** lots of people

pence ['pẽsi] F dart

pendão [pẽ'dãw] (*pl* **-ões**) M pennant; (*fig*) banner; (*do milho*) blossom

pendência [pẽ'dẽsja] F dispute, quarrel

pendente [pẽ'dẽtʃi] ADJ (*pendurado*) hanging; (*por decidir*) pending; (*inclinado*) sloping; (*dependent*): **~ de** dependent on ▶ M pendant

pender [pẽ'der] VT to hang ▶ VI to hang; (*estar para cair*) to sag, droop; **~ de** (*depender de*) to depend on, hang on; (*estar pendurado*) to hang from; **~ para** (*inclinar*) to lean towards; (*ter tendência para*) to tend towards; **~ a** (*estar disposto a*) to be inclined to

pendões [pẽ'dõjs] MPL *de* **pendão**

pendor [pẽ'dor] M inclination, tendency

pêndulo ['pẽdulu] M pendulum

pendura [pẽ'dura] F: **estar na ~** (*col*) to be broke

pendurado, -a [pẽdu'radu, a] ADJ hanging; (*col: compra*) on tick

pendurar [pẽdu'rar] VT to hang; (*col: conta*) to put on tick ▶ VI: **~ de** to hang from; **não estou com dinheiro hoje, posso ~?** (*col*) I haven't got any money today, can I pay you later?

penduricalho [pẽduri'kaʎu] M pendant

pendurucalho [pẽduru'kaʎu] M = **penduricalho**

penedo [pe'nedu] M rock, boulder

peneira [pe'nejra] F (*de cozinha*) sieve

peneirar [penej'rar] VT to sift, sieve ▶ VI (*chover*) to drizzle

penetra [pe'nɛtra] (*col*) M/F gatecrasher; **entrar de ~** to gatecrash

penetração [penetra'sãw] F penetration; (*perspicácia*) insight, sharpness

penetrante [pene'trãtʃi] ADJ (*olhar*) searching; (*ferida*) deep; (*frio*) biting; (*som, análise*) penetrating, piercing; (*dor, arma*) sharp; (*inteligência, ideias*) incisive

penetrar [pene'trar] VT to get into, penetrate; (*em segredo*) to steal into; (*compreender*) to understand ▶ VI: **~ em** *ou* **por** *ou* **entre** to penetrate

penha ['pẽɲa] F (*rocha*) rock; (*penhasco*) cliff

penhasco [pe'ɲasku] M cliff, crag

penhoar [pe'ɲwar] M dressing gown

penhor [pe'ɲor] M pledge; **casa de ~es** pawnshop; **dar em ~** to pawn

penhora [pe'ɲɔra] F (*Jur*) seizure

penhoradamente [peɲorada'mẽtʃi] ADV gratefully

penhorado, -a [peɲo'radu, a] ADJ pawned

penhorar [peɲo'rar] VT (*dar em penhor*) to pledge, pawn; (*apreender*) to confiscate; (*fig*) to put under an obligation; **a ajuda do**

amigo penhorou-a bastante she was very grateful for her friend's help

pêni ['peni] M penny

penicilina [penisi'lina] F penicillin

penico [pe'niku] M (*col*) potty; **pedir ~** (*col*) to chicken out

Peninos [pe'ninus] MPL: **os ~** the Pennines

península [pe'nĩsula] F peninsula

peninsular [penĩsu'lar] ADJ peninsular

pênis ['penis] M INV penis

penitência [peni'tẽsja] F (*contrição*) penitence; (*expiação*) penance

penitenciar [penitẽ'sjar] VT to impose penance on; (*crime etc*) to pay for; **penitenciar-se** VR to castigate o.s.

penitenciária [penitẽ'sjarja] F prison; *ver tb* **penitenciário**

penitenciário, -a [penitẽ'sjarju, a] ADJ prison atr ▶ M/F prisoner, inmate

penitente [peni'tẽtʃi] ADJ repentant ▶ M/F penitent

penosa [pe'nɔza] (*col*) F chicken

penoso, -a [pe'nozu, ɔza] ADJ (*assunto, tratamento*) painful; (*trabalho*) hard

pensado, -a [pẽ'sadu, a] ADJ deliberate, intentional

pensador, a [pẽsa'dor(a)] M/F thinker

pensamento [pẽsa'mẽtu] M thought; (*ato*) thinking; (*mente*) mind; (*opinião*) way of thinking; (*ideia*) idea

pensante [pẽ'sãtʃi] ADJ thinking

pensão [pẽ'sãw] (*pl* **-ões**) F (*pequeno hotel: tb:* **casa de pensão**) boarding house; (*comida*) board; **~ completa** full board; **~ de aposentadoria** (retirement) pension; **~ alimentícia** alimony, maintenance; **~ de invalidez** disability allowance

pensar [pẽ'sar] VI to think; (*imaginar*) to imagine ▶ VT to think about; (*ferimento*) to dress; **~ em** to think of *ou* about; **~ fazer** (*ter intenção*) to intend to do, be thinking of doing; **~ sobre** (*meditar*) to ponder over; **pensando bem** on second thoughts; **~ alto** to think out loud; **~ melhor** to think better of it

pensativo, -a [pẽsa'tʃivu, a] ADJ thoughtful, pensive

Pensilvânia [pẽsiw'vanja] F: **a ~** Pennsylvania

pensionato [pẽsjo'natu] M boarding school

pensionista [pẽsjo'nista] M/F pensioner; (*que mora em pensão*) boarder

penso, -a ['pẽsu, a] ADJ leaning ▶ M (*curativo*) dressing

pensões [pẽ'sõjs] FPL *de* **pensão**

pentágono [pẽ'tagonu] M pentagon; **o P~** the Pentagon

pentatlo [pẽ'tatlu] M pentathlon

pente ['pẽtʃi] M comb

penteadeira [pẽtʃja'dejra] F dressing table

penteado, -a [pẽ'tʃjadu, a] ADJ (*cabelo*) in place; (*pessoa*) smart ▶ M hairdo, hairstyle

pentear [pẽ'tʃjar] VT to comb; (*arranjar o cabelo*)

to do, style; **pentear-se** VR to comb one's hair; to do one's hair

Pentecostes [pētʃi'kɔstʃis] M Whitsun

pente-fino [pētʃi'finu] (*pl* **pentes-finos**) M fine-tooth comb

penugem [pe'nuʒē] F (*de ave*) down; (*pelo*) fluff

penúltimo, -a [pe'nuwtʃimu, a] ADJ last but one, penultimate

penumbra [pe'nũbra] F (*ao cair da tarde*) twilight, dusk; (*sombra*) shadow; (*meia-luz*) half-light

penúria [pe'nurja] F poverty

peões [pjõjs] MPL *de* **peão**

pepino [pe'pinu] M cucumber

pepita [pe'pita] F (*de ouro*) nugget

pequena [pe'kena] F girl; (*namorada*) girlfriend

pequenez [peke'nez] F smallness; (*fig: mesquinhez*) meanness; ~ **de sentimentos** pettiness

pequenininho, -a [pekeni'niɲu, a] ADJ tiny

pequenino, -a [peke'ninu, a] ADJ little

pequeninos [peke'ninus] MPL: **os** ~ the little children

pequeno, -a [pe'kenu, a] ADJ small; (*mesquinho*) petty ▶ M boy; **em ~ eu fazia ...** when I was small I used to do ....

pequeno-burguês, -esa (*pl* **-eses/-esas**) ADJ petty bourgeois

pequerrucho, -a [peke'huʃu, a] ADJ tiny ▶ M thimble

Pequim [pe'kĩ] N Beijing

pequinês [peki'nes] M (*cão*) Pekinese

pera ['pera] F pear

peralta [pe'rawta] ADJ naughty ▶ M/F (*menino*) naughty child

perambular [perãbu'lar] VI to wander

perante [pe'rãtʃi] PREP before, in the presence of

pé-rapado [-ha'padu] (*pl* **pés-rapados**) M nobody

percalço [per'kawsu] M (*de uma tarefa*) difficulty; (*de profissão, matrimônio etc*) pitfall

per capita [pɛr'kapita] ADV, ADJ per capita

perceber [perse'ber] VT (*notar*) to realize; (*por meio dos sentidos*) to perceive; (*compreender*) to understand; (*ver*) to see; (*ouvir*) to hear; (*ver ao longe*) to make out; (*dinheiro: receber*) to receive

percentagem [persē'taʒē] F percentage

percentual [persē'twaw] (*pl* **-ais**) ADJ percentage *atr* ▶ M percentage

percepção [persep'sãw] F perception; (*compreensão*) understanding

perceptível [persep'tʃivew] (*pl* **-eis**) ADJ perceptible, noticeable; (*som*) audible

perceptividade [perseptʃivi'dadʒi] F perceptiveness, perception

perceptivo, -a [persep'tʃivu, a] ADJ perceptive

percevejo [perse'veʒu] M (*inseto*) bug; (*prego*) drawing pin (BRIT), thumbtack (US)

perco *etc* ['perku] VB *ver* **perder**

percorrer [perko'her] VT (*viajar por*) to travel (across *ou* over); (*passar por*) to go through, traverse; (*investigar*) to search through

percurso [per'kursu] M (*espaço percorrido*) distance (covered); (*trajeto*) route; (*viagem*) journey; **fazer o ~ entre** to travel between

percussão [perku'sãw] F (*Mús*) percussion

percussionista [perkusjo'nista] M/F percussionist, percussion player

percutir [perku'tʃir] VT to strike ▶ VI to reverberate

perda ['perda] F loss; (*desperdício*) waste; ~ **de tempo** waste of time; **~s e danos** damages, losses

perdão [per'dãw] M pardon, forgiveness; **~!** sorry!, I beg your pardon!; **pedir ~ a alguém** to ask sb for forgiveness; **~ da dívida** cancellation of the debt; **~ da pena** (*Jur*) pardon

perder [per'der] VT to lose; (*tempo*) to waste; (*trem, show, oportunidade*) to miss ▶ VI to lose; **perder-se** VR (*extraviar-se*) to get lost; (*arruinar-se*) to be ruined; (*desaparecer*) to disappear; (*em reflexões*) to be lost; (*num discurso*) to lose one's thread; **~-se de alguém** to lose sb; **~ algo de vista** to lose sight of sth; **a ~ de vista** (*fig*) as far as the eye can see; **pôr tudo a ~** to risk losing everything; **saber ~** to be a good loser

perdição [perdʒi'sãw] F perdition, ruin; (*desonra*) depravity; **ser uma ~** (*col*) to be irresistible

perdido, -a [per'dʒidu, a] ADJ lost; (*pervertido*) depraved; **~ por** (*apaixonado*) desperately in love with; **~s e achados** lost and found, lost property

perdigão [perdʒi'gãw] (*pl* **-ões**) M (*macho*) partridge

perdigueiro [perdʒi'gejru] M (*cachorro*) gundog

perdiz [per'dʒiz] F partridge

perdoar [per'dwar] VT (*desculpar*) to forgive; (*pena*) to lift; (*dívida*) to cancel; **~ (algo) a alguém** to forgive sb (for sth)

perdoável [per'dwavew] (*pl* **-eis**) ADJ forgivable

perdulário, -a [perdu'larju, a] ADJ wasteful ▶ M/F spendthrift

perdurar [perdu'rar] VI (*durar muito*) to last a long time; (*continuar a existir*) to still exist

pereba [pe'rɛba] F (*ferida pequena*) scratch

perecer [pere'ser] VI to perish; (*morrer*) to die; (*acabar*) to come to nothing

perecível [pere'sivew] (*pl* **-eis**) ADJ perishable

peregrinação [peregrina'sãw] (*pl* **-ões**) F (*viagem*) travels *pl*; (*Rel*) pilgrimage

peregrinar [peregri'nar] VI (*viajar*) to travel; (*Rel*) to go on a pilgrimage

peregrino, -a [pere'grinu, a] ADJ (*beleza*) rare ▶ M/F pilgrim

pereira [pe'rejra] F pear tree

peremptório, -a [perēp'tɔrju, a] ADJ (*final*) final; (*decisivo*) decisive

P

perene [pe'rɛni] ADJ (*perpétuo*) everlasting; (*Bot*) perennial

perereca [pere'rɛka] F tree frog

perfazer [perfa'zer] (*irreg: como* **fazer**) VT (*completar o número de*) to make up; (*concluir*) to complete

perfeccionismo [perfeksjo'nizmu] M perfectionism

perfeccionista [perfeksjo'nista] ADJ, M/F perfectionist

perfeição [perfej'sãw] F perfection; **à ~** to perfection

perfeitamente [perfejta'mẽtʃi] ADV perfectly ▶ EXCL exactly!

perfeito, -a [per'fejtu, a] ADJ perfect; (*carro etc*) in perfect condition ▶ M (*Ling*) perfect

perfez [per'fez] VB *ver* **perfazer**

perfídia [per'fidʒja] F treachery

pérfido, -a ['pɛrfidu, a] ADJ treacherous

perfil [per'fiw] (*pl* **-is**) M (*do rosto, fig*) profile; (*silhueta*) silhouette, outline; (*Arq*) (cross) section; **de ~** in profile

perfilar [perfi'lar] VT (*soldados*) to line up; (*aprumar*) to straighten up; **perfilar-se** VR to stand to attention

perfilhar [perfi'ʎar] VT (*Jur*) to legally adopt; (*princípio, teoria*) to adopt

perfis [per'fis] MPL *de* **perfil**

perfiz [per'fiz] VB *ver* **perfazer**

perfizer *etc* [perfi'zer] VB *ver* **perfazer**

performance [per'formãs] F performance

perfumado, -a [perfu'madu, a] ADJ sweet-smelling; (*pessoa*) wearing perfume

perfumar [perfu'mar] VT to perfume; **perfumar-se** VR to put perfume on

perfumaria [perfuma'ria] F perfumery; (*col*) idle talk

perfume [per'fumi] M perfume; (*cheiro*) scent

perfunctório, -a [perfũk'tɔrju, a] ADJ perfunctory

perfurado, -a [perfu'radu, a] ADJ (*cartão*) punched

perfurador [perfura'dor] M punch

perfurar [perfu'rar] VT (*o chão*) to drill a hole in; (*papel*) to punch (a hole in)

perfuratriz [perfura'triz] F drill

pergaminho [perga'miɲu] M parchment; (*diploma*) diploma

pérgula ['pɛrgula] F arbour (BRIT), arbor (US)

pergunta [per'gũta] F question; **fazer uma ~ a alguém** to ask sb a question

perguntador, a [pergũta'dor(a)] ADJ inquiring, inquisitive ▶ M/F questioner

perguntar [pergũ'tar] VT to ask; (*interrogar*) to question ▶ VI: **~ por alguém** to ask after sb; **perguntar-se** VR to wonder; **~ algo a alguém** to ask sb sth

perícia [pe'risja] F (*conhecimento*) expertise; (*destreza*) skill; (*exame*) investigation; **~ (criminal)** criminal investigation; (*os peritos criminais*) criminal investigators *pl*

pericial [peri'sjaw] (*pl* **-ais**) ADJ expert

periclitante [perikli'tãtʃi] ADJ (*situação*) perilous; (*saúde*) shaky

periclitar [perikli'tar] VI to be in danger; (*negócio etc*) to be at risk

periculosidade [perikulozi'dadʒi] F dangerousness; (*Jur*) risk factor

peridural [peridu'raw] (*pl* **-ais**) F (*Med*) epidural

periferia [perife'ria] F periphery; (*da cidade*) outskirts *pl*

periférico, -a [peri'fɛriku, a] ADJ peripheral ▶ M (*Comput*) peripheral; **estrada periférica** ring road

perífrase [pe'rifrazi] F circumlocution

perigar [peri'gar] VI to be at risk; **~ ser ...** to risk being ..., be in danger of being ....

perigo [pe'rigu] M danger; **correr ~** to be in danger; **fora de ~** safe, out of danger; **pôr em ~** to endanger; **o carro dele é um ~** his car is a deathtrap; **ser um ~** (*col: pessoa*) to be a tease; **estar a ~** (*col: sem dinheiro*) to be broke; (: *em situação difícil*) to be in a bad way

perigoso, -a [peri'gozu, ɔza] ADJ dangerous; (*arriscado*) risky

perímetro [pe'rimetru] M perimeter; **~ urbano** city limits *pl*

periódico, -a [pe'rjɔdʒiku, a] ADJ periodic; (*chuvas*) occasional; (*doença*) recurrent ▶ M (*revista*) magazine, periodical; (*jornal*) (news)paper

período [pe'riodu] M period; (*estação*) season; **~ letivo** term

peripécia [peri'pɛsja] F (*aventura*) adventure; (*incidente*) turn of events

periquito [peri'kitu] M parakeet

periscópio [peris'kɔpju] M periscope

perito, -a [pe'ritu, a] ADJ expert ▶ M/F expert; (*quem faz perícia*) investigator; **~ em** (*atividade*) expert at, clever at; (*matéria*) highly knowledgeable in; **~ em matéria de** expert in

peritonite [perito'nitʃi] F peritonitis

perjurar [perʒu'rar] VI to commit perjury

perjúrio [per'ʒurju] M perjury

perjuro, -a [per'ʒuru, a] M/F perjurer

permanecer [permane'ser] VI to remain; (*num lugar*) to stay; (*continuar a ser*) to remain, keep; **~ parado** to keep still

permanência [perma'nẽsja] F permanence; (*estada*) stay

permanente [perma'nẽtʃi] ADJ (*dor*) constant; (*cor*) fast; (*residência, pregas*) permanent ▶ M (*cartão*) pass ▶ F perm; **fazer uma ~** to have perm

permeável [per'mjavew] (*pl* **-eis**) ADJ permeable

permeio [per'meju] ADV: **de ~** in between

permissão [permi'sãw] F permission, consent

permissível [permi'sivew] (*pl* **-eis**) ADJ permissible

permissivo, -a [permi'sivu, a] ADJ permissive

permitir [permi'tʃir] vт to allow, permit; (*conceder*) to grant; **~ a alguém fazer** to let sb do, allow sb to do

permuta [per'muta] ꜰ exchange; (*Com*) barter

permutação [permuta'sãw] (*pl* **-ões**) ꜰ (*Mat*) permutation; (*troca*) exchange

permutar [permu'tar] vт to exchange; (*Com*) to barter

perna ['pɛrna] ꜰ leg; **de ~(s) para o ar** upside down, topsy turvy; **em cima da ~** (*col*) sloppily, in a slapdash way; **bater ~s** (*col*) to wander; **passar a ~ em alguém** (*col*) to put one over on sb; **trocar as ~s** (*col*) to stagger; **~ de pau** wooden leg; **~ mecânica** artificial leg; **~s tortas** bow legs

perna de pau m/ꜰ (*Futebol*) bad player

pernambucano, -a [pernãbu'kanu, a] ADJ from Pernambuco ▶ m/ꜰ person from Pernambuco

perneira [per'nejra] ꜰ (*de dançarina etc*) legwarmer

perneta [per'neta] m/ꜰ one-legged person

pernicioso, -a [perni'sjozu, ɔza] ADJ pernicious; (*Med*) malignant

pernil [per'niw] (*pl* **-is**) м (*de animal*) haunch; (*Culin*) leg

pernilongo [perni'lõgu] м mosquito

pernis [per'nis] мᴘʟ *de* **pernil**

pernoitar [pernoj'tar] vɪ to spend the night

pernóstico, -a [per'nɔstʃiku, a] ADJ pedantic ▶ m/ꜰ pedant

pérola ['pɛrola] ꜰ pearl

perpassar [perpa'sar] vɪ (*tempo*) to go by; **~ (por)** to pass (by); **~ a mão em/por** to run one's hand through/over

perpendicular [perpẽdʒiku'lar] ADJ, ꜰ perpendicular; **ser ~ a** to be at right angles to

perpetração [perpetra'sãw] ꜰ perpetration

perpetrar [perpe'trar] vт to perpetrate, commit

perpetuar [perpe'twar] vт to perpetuate

perpetuidade [perpetwi'dadʒi] ꜰ eternity

perpétuo, -a [per'pɛtwu, a] ADJ perpetual; (*eterno*) eternal; **prisão perpétua** life imprisonment

perplexidade [perpleksi'dadʒi] ꜰ confusion, bewilderment

perplexo, -a [per'plɛksu, a] ADJ (*confuso*) bewildered, puzzled; (*indeciso*) uncertain; **ficar ~** (*atônito*) to be taken aback

perquirir [perki'rir] vт to probe, investigate

persa ['pɛrsa] ADJ, m/ꜰ Persian

perscrutar [perskru'tar] vт to scrutinize, examine

perseguição [persegi'sãw] ꜰ pursuit; (*Rel, Pol*) persecution

perseguidor, a [persegi'dor(a)] m/ꜰ pursuer; (*Rel, Pol*) persecutor

perseguir [perse'gir] vт (*seguir*) to pursue; (*correr atrás*) to chase (after); (*Rel, Pol*) to persecute; (*importunar*) to harass, pester

perseverança [perseve'rãsa] ꜰ (*insistência*) persistence; (*constância*) perseverance

perseverante [perseve'rãtʃi] ADJ persistent

perseverar [perseve'rar] vɪ to persevere; **~ em** (*conservar-se firme*) to persevere in, persist in; **~ corajoso** to keep one's courage up; **~ em erro** to persist in doing wrong

Pérsia ['pɛrsja] ꜰ: **a ~** Persia

persiana [per'sjana] ꜰ blind

Pérsico, -a ['pɛrsiku, a] ADJ: **o golfo ~** the Persian Gulf

persignar-se [persig'narsi] vʀ to cross o.s.

persigo *etc* [per'sigu] vʙ *ver* **perseguir**

persistência [persis'tẽsja] ꜰ persistence

persistente [persis'tẽtʃi] ADJ persistent

persistir [persis'tʃir] vɪ to persist; **~ em** to persist in; **~ calado** to keep quiet

personagem [perso'naʒẽ] (*pl* **-ns**) m/ꜰ famous person, celebrity; (*num livro, filme*) character

personalidade [personali'dadʒi] ꜰ personality; **~ dupla** dual personality

personalizado, -a [personali'zadu, a] ADJ personalized; (*móveis etc*) custom-made

personalizar [personali'zar] vт to personalize; (*personificar*) to personify; (*nomear*) to name

personificação [personifika'sãw] ꜰ personification

personificar [personifi'kar] vт to personify

perspectiva [perspek'tʃiva] ꜰ (*na pintura*) perspective; (*panorama*) view; (*probabilidade*) prospect; (*ponto de vista*) point of view; **em ~** in prospect

perspicácia [perspi'kasja] ꜰ insight, perceptiveness

perspicaz [perspi'kajz] ADJ (*que observa*) perceptive; (*sagaz*) shrewd

persuadir [perswa'dʒir] vт to persuade; **persuadir-se** vʀ to convince o.s.; **~ alguém de que/alguém a fazer** to persuade sb that/sb to do

persuasão [perswa'zãw] ꜰ persuasion; (*convicção*) conviction

persuasivo, -a [perswa'zivu, a] ADJ persuasive

pertencente [pertẽ'sẽtʃi] ADJ belonging; **~ a** (*pertinente*) pertaining to

pertencer [pertẽ'ser] vɪ: **~ a** to belong to; (*referir-se*) to concern

pertences [per'tẽsis] мᴘʟ (*de uma pessoa*) belongings

pertinácia [pertʃi'nasja] ꜰ (*persistência*) persistence; (*obstinação*) obstinacy

pertinaz [pertʃi'najz] ADJ (*persistente*) persistent; (*obstinado*) obstinate

pertinência [pertʃi'nẽsja] ꜰ relevance

pertinente [pertʃi'nẽtʃi] ADJ relevant; (*apropriado*) appropriate

perto, -a ['pɛrtu, a] ADJ nearby ▶ ADV near; **~ de** near to; (*em comparação com*) next to; **~ da casa** near *ou* close to the house; **~ de 100 dólares** around 100 dollars; **estar ~ de fazer** (*a ponto de*) to be close to doing; **de ~** closely; (*ver*) close up; (*conhecer*) very well

perturbação [perturba'sãw] (*pl* **-ões**) F disturbance; (*desorientação*) perturbation; (*Med*) trouble; (*Pol*) disturbance; **~ da ordem** breach of the peace

perturbado, -a [pertur'badu, a] ADJ perturbed; (*desvairado*) unbalanced

perturbador, a [perturba'dor(a)] ADJ (*pessoa*) disruptive; (*notícia*) perturbing, disturbing

perturbar [pertur'bar] VT to disturb; (*abalar*) to upset, trouble; (*atrapalhar*) to put off; (*andamento, trânsito*) to disrupt; (*envergonhar*) to embarrass; (*alterar*) to affect; **não perturba!** do not disturb!; **~ a ordem** to cause a breach of the peace

Peru [pe'ru] M: **o ~** Peru

peru, a [pe'ru(a)] M/F turkey ▶ M (*!: pênis*) cock (*!*)

perua [pe'rua] F (*carro*) estate (car) (BRIT), station wagon (US)

peruada [pe'rwada] (*col*) F (*palpite*) tip

peruano, -a [pe'rwanu, a] ADJ, M/F Peruvian

peruar [pe'rwar] VT (*jogo*) to watch ▶ VI to hang around

peruca [pe'ruka] F wig

perversão [perver'sãw] (*pl* **-ões**) F perversion

perversidade [perversi'dadʒi] F perversity

perverso, -a [per'vɛrsu, a] ADJ perverse; (*malvado*) wicked

perversões [perver'sõjs] FPL *de* **perversão**

perverter [perver'ter] VT (*corromper*) to corrupt, pervert; **perverter-se** VR to become corrupt

pervertido, -a [perver'tʃidu, a] ADJ perverted ▶ M/F pervert

pesada [pe'zada] F weighing

pesadelo [peza'delu] M nightmare

pesado, -a [pe'zadu, a] ADJ heavy; (*ambiente*) tense; (*trabalho*) hard; (*estilo*) dull, boring; (*andar*) slow; (*piada*) coarse; (*comida*) stodgy; (*tempo*) sultry ▶ ADV heavily; **pegar no ~** (*col*) to work hard; **da pesada** (*col: legal*) great; (: *barra-pesada*) rough, violent

pesagem [pe'zaʒẽ] F weighing

pêsames ['pezamis] MPL condolences, sympathy *sg*

pesar [pe'zar] VT to weigh; (*fig*) to weigh up ▶ VI to weigh; (*ser pesado*) to be heavy; (*influir*) to carry weight; (*causar mágoa*): **~ a** to hurt, grieve ▶ M grief; **~ sobre** (*recair*) to fall upon; **em que pese a** despite; **apesar dos ~es** despite everything

pesaroso, -a [peza'rozu, ɔza] ADJ (*triste*) sorrowful, sad; (*arrependido*) regretful, sorry

pesca ['pɛska] F (*ato*) fishing; (*os peixes*) catch; **ir à ~** to go fishing; **~ submarina** skin diving

pescada [pes'kada] F whiting

pescado [pes'kadu] M fish

pescador, a [peska'dor(a)] M/F fisherman/ woman; **~ à linha** angler

pescar [pes'kar] VT (*peixe*) to catch; (*tentar apanhar*) to fish for; (*retirar da água*) to fish out; (*um marido*) to catch, get ▶ VI to fish; (BR *col*) to understand; **~ de algo** (*col*) to know about sth; **pescou?** got it?, see?

pescoçada [pesko'sãw] (*pl* **-ões**) M slap

pescoço [pes'kosu] M neck; **até o ~** (*endividado*) up to one's neck

pescoções [pesko'sõjs] MPL *de* **pescoção**

pescoçudo, -a [pesko'sudu, a] ADJ bull-necked

peso ['pezu] M weight; (*fig: ônus*) burden; (*importância*) importance; **pessoa/ argumento de ~** important person/weighty argument; **de pouco ~** lightweight; **em ~** in full force; **~ atômico** atomic weight; **~ bruto/líquido** gross/net weight; **~ morto** dead weight; **ter dois ~s e duas medidas** (*fig*) to have double standards

pespontar [pespõ'tar] VT to backstitch

pesponto [pes'põtu] M backstitch

pesquei *etc* [pes'kej] VB *ver* **pescar**

pesqueiro, -a [pes'kejru, a] ADJ fishing *atr*

pesquisa [pes'kiza] F research; **uma ~** a study; **~ de campo** field work; **~ de mercado** market research; **~ e desenvolvimento** research and development

pesquisador, a [peskiza'dor(a)] M/F researcher

pesquisar [peski'zar] VT, VI to research

pêssego ['pesegu] M peach

pessegueiro [pese'gejru] M peach tree

pessimismo [pesi'mizmu] M pessimism

pessimista [pesi'mista] ADJ pessimistic ▶ M/F pessimist

péssimo, -a ['pɛsimu, a] ADJ very bad, awful; **estar ~** (*pessoa*) to be in a bad way

pessoa [pe'soa] F person; **pessoas** FPL people; **em ~** personally; **~ de bem** honest person; **~ física/jurídica** (*Jur*) private individual/ legal entity

pessoal [pe'swaw] (*pl* **-ais**) ADJ personal ▶ M personnel *pl*, staff *pl*; (*col*) people *pl*, folks *pl*; **oi, ~!** (*col*) hi, everyone!, hi, folks!

pestana [pes'tana] F eyelash; **tirar uma ~** (*col*) to have a nap

pestanejar [pestane'ʒar] VI to blink; **sem ~** (*fig*) without batting an eyelid

peste ['pɛstʃi] F (*epidemia*) epidemic; (*bubônica*) plague; (*fig*) pest, nuisance

pesticida [pestʃi'sida] M pesticide

pestífero, -a [pes'tʃiferu, a] ADJ (*fig*) pernicious

pestilência [pestʃi'lẽsja] F plague; (*epidemia*) epidemic; (*fedor*) stench

pestilento, -a [pestʃi'lẽtu, a] ADJ pestilential, plague *atr*; (*malcheiroso*) putrid

pétala ['pɛtala] F petal

peteca [pe'tɛka] F (kind of) shuttlecock; **fazer alguém de ~** to make a fool of sb; **não deixar a ~ cair** (*col*) to keep the ball rolling

peteleco [pete'lɛku] M flick; **dar um ~ em algo** to flick sth

petição [petʃi'sãw] (*pl* **-ões**) F (*rogo*) request; (*documento*) petition; **em ~ de miséria** in a terrible state

peticionário, -a [petʃisjoˈnarju, a] M/F
petitioner; (*Jur*) plaintiff
petições [petʃiˈsõjs] FPL *de* **petição**
petiscar [petʃisˈkar] VT to nibble at, peck at
▶ VI to have a nibble
petisco [peˈtʃisku] M savoury (BRIT), savory (US),
titbit (BRIT), tidbit (US)
petit-pois [petʃiˈpwa] M INV pea
petiz [peˈtʃiz] (PT) M boy
petrechos [peˈtreʃus] MPL equipment *sg*; (*Mil*)
stores, equipment *sg*; (*de cozinha*) utensils
petrificar [petrifiˈkar] VT to petrify;
(*empedernir*) to harden; (*assombrar*) to stun;
petrificar-se VR to be petrified; to be
stunned; to become hard
Petrobrás [petroˈbrajs] ABR F Brazilian state oil
company
petrodólar [petroˈdɔlar] M petrodollar
petroleiro, -a [petroˈlejru, a] ADJ oil *atr*,
petroleum *atr* ▶ M (*navio*) oil tanker
petróleo [peˈtrɔlju] M oil, petroleum; ~ **bruto**
crude oil
petrolífero, -a [petroˈliferu, a] ADJ oil-
producing
petroquímica [petroˈkimika] F
petrochemicals *pl*; (*ciência*) petrochemistry
petroquímico, -a [petroˈkimiku, a] ADJ
petrochemical
petulância [petuˈlãsja] F impudence
petulante [petuˈlãtʃi] ADJ impudent
petúnia [peˈtunja] F petunia
peúga [peˈjuga] (PT) F sock
pevide [peˈvidʒi] (PT) F (*de melão*) seed; (*de
maçã*) pip
p. ex. ABR (= *por exemplo*) e.g.
pexote [peˈʃotʃi] M/F (*criança*) little kid;
(*novato*) beginner, novice
PF (BR) ABR F = **Polícia Federal**
PFL (BR) ABR M = **Partido da Frente Liberal**
PH (BR) ABR M = **Partido Humanitário**
PI ABR = **Piauí**
pia [ˈpia] F wash basin; (*da cozinha*) sink;
~ **batismal** font
piada [ˈpjada] F joke
piadista [pjaˈdʒista] M/F joker
pianista [pjaˈnista] M/F pianist
piano [ˈpjanu] M piano; ~ **de cauda** grand
piano
pião [pjãw] (*pl* -**ões**) M (*brinquedo*) top
piar [pjar] VI (*pinto*) to cheep; (*coruja*) to hoot;
não ~ not to say a word
piauiense [pjawˈjẽsi] ADJ from Piauí ▶ M/F
person from Piauí
PIB ABR M (= *Produto Interno Bruto*) GNP
picada [piˈkada] F (*de agulha etc*) prick; (*de
abelha*) sting; (*de mosquito, cobra*) bite; (*de avião*)
dive; (*de navalha*) stab; (*atalho*) path, trail;
(*de droga*) shot
picadeiro [pikaˈdejru] M (*circo*) ring
picadinho [pikaˈdʒiɲu] M stew
picado, -a [piˈkadu, a] ADJ (*por agulha*)
pricked; (*por abelha*) stung; (*por cobra,
mosquito*) bitten; (*papel*) shredded; (*carne*)

minced; (*legumes*) chopped
picante [piˈkãtʃi] ADJ (*tempero*) hot; (*piada*)
risqué, blue; (*comentário*) saucy; (*cena, filme*)
raunchy
pica-pau [ˈpika-] (*pl* **pica-paus**) M
woodpecker
picape [piˈkapi] (BR) F pickup (truck)
picar [piˈkar] VT (*com agulha*) to prick; (*suj:
abelha*) to sting; (: *mosquito*) to bite; (: *pássaro*)
to peck; (*um animal*) to goad; (*carne*) to mince;
(*papel*) to shred; (*fruta*) to chop up; (*comichar*)
to prickle ▶ VI (*a isca*) to take the bait;
(*comichar*) to prickle; (*avião*) to dive; **picar-se**
VR to prick o.s.
picardia [pikarˈdʒia] F (*implicância*)
spitefulness; (*esperteza*) craftiness
picaresco, -a [pikaˈresku, a] ADJ comic,
ridiculous
picareta [pikaˈreta] F pickaxe (BRIT), pickax
(US) ▶ M crook
picaretagem [pikareˈtaʒẽ] (*pl* -**ns**) F con
pícaro, -a [ˈpikaru, a] ADJ crafty, cunning
pichação [piʃaˈsãw] (*pl* -**ões**) F (*ato*) spraying;
(*grafite*) piece of graffiti
pichar [piˈʃar] VT (*dizeres, muro*) to spray; (*aplicar
piche em*) to cover with pitch; (*col: espinafrar*) to
run down ▶ VI (*col*) to criticize
piche [ˈpiʃi] M pitch
piclés [ˈpiklis] MPL pickles
pico [ˈpiku] M (*cume*) peak; (*ponta aguda*) sharp
point; (PT: *um pouco*) a bit; **mil e** ~ just over a
thousand; **meio-dia e** ~ just after midday
picolé [pikoˈlɛ] M lolly
picotar [pikoˈtar] VT to perforate; (*bilhete*) to
punch
picote [piˈkɔtʃi] M perforation
pictórico, -a [pikˈtɔriku, a] ADJ pictorial
picuinha [piˈkwiɲa] F: **estar de** ~ **com
alguém** to have it in for sb
piedade [pjeˈdadʒi] F (*devoção*) piety;
(*compaixão*) pity; **ter** ~ **de** to have pity on
piedoso, -a [pjeˈdozu, ɔza] ADJ (*Rel*) pious;
(*compassivo*) merciful
piegas [ˈpjɛgas] ADJ INV sentimental; (*col*)
soppy ▶ M/F INV softy
pieguice [pjeˈgisi] F sentimentality
píer [ˈpier] M pier
piercing [ˈpirsĩ] (*pl* -**s**) M piercing
pifa [ˈpifa] (*col*) M booze-up; **tomar um** ~ to
get smashed
pifado, -a [piˈfadu, a] (*col*) ADJ (*carro*) broken
down; (*TV etc*) broken
pifar [piˈfar] (*col*) VI (*carro*) to break down;
(*rádio etc*) to go wrong; (*plano, programa*) to fall
through
pigarrear [pigaˈhjar] VI to clear one's throat
pigarro [piˈgahu] (*col*) M frog in the throat
pigmeia [pigˈmeja] F *de* **pigmeu**
pigmentação [pigmẽtaˈsãw] F pigmentation,
colouring (BRIT), coloring (US)
pigmento [pigˈmẽtu] M pigment
pigmeu, -meia [pigˈmew, ˈmeja] ADJ, M/F
pigmy

P

pijama [pi'ʒama] M pyjamas pl (BRIT),
pajamas pl (US)
pilantra [pi'lãtɾa] (col) M/F crook
pilantragem [pilã'tɾaʒẽ] (pl **-ns**) (col) F
rip-off (!)
pilão [pi'lãw] (pl **-ões**) M mortar
pilar [pi'laɾ] VT to pound, crush ▶ M pillar
pilastra [pi'lastɾa] F pilaster
pileque [pi'lɛki] (col) M booze-up (!); **tomar
um ~** to get smashed (!) ou plastered (!);
estar de ~ to be smashed (!) ou plastered (!)
pilha ['piʎa] F (Elet) battery; (monte) pile, heap;
às ~s in vast quantities; **estar uma ~ (de
nervos)** to be a bundle of nerves
pilhagem [pi'ʎaʒẽ] F (ato) pillage; (objetos)
plunder, booty
pilhar [pi'ʎaɾ] VT (saquear) to plunder, pillage;
(roubar) to rob; (surpreender) to catch
pilhéria [pi'ʎɛɾja] F joke
pilheriar [piʎe'ɾjaɾ] VI to joke, jest
pilões [pi'lõjs] MPL de **pilão**
pilotagem [pilo'taʒẽ] F flying; **escola de ~**
flying school
pilotar [pilo'taɾ] VT (avião) to fly; (carro de
corrida) to drive ▶ VI to fly
pilotis [pilo'tʃis] MPL stilts
piloto [pi'lotu] M (de avião) pilot; (de navio) first
mate; (motorista) (racing) driver; (bico de gás)
pilot light ▶ ADJ INV (usina, plano) pilot; (peça)
sample atr; **~ automático** automatic pilot;
~ de prova test pilot
pílula ['pilula] F pill; **a ~ (anticoncepcional)**
the pill
pimba ['pĩba] EXCL wham!
pimenta [pi'mẽta] F (Culin) pepper; **~ de
Caiena** cayenne pepper
pimenta-do-reino F black pepper
pimenta-malagueta (pl **pimentas-
malagueta**) F chilli (BRIT) ou chili (US) pepper
pimentão [pimẽ'tãw] (pl **-ões**) M (Bot) pepper;
~ verde green pepper
pimenteira [pimẽ'tejɾa] F (Bot) pepper plant;
(à mesa) pepper pot; (: moedor) pepper mill
pimpão, -pona [pĩ'pãw, 'pɔna] (PT) (pl **-ões/-s**)
ADJ smart, flashy ▶ M/F show-off
pimpolho [pĩ'poʎu] M (criança) youngster
pimpona [pĩ'pɔna] F de **pimpão**
PIN (BR) ABR M = **Plano de Integração
Nacional**
pinacoteca [pinako'tɛka] F art gallery;
(coleção de quadros) art collection
pináculo [pi'nakulu] M (tb fig) pinnacle
pinça ['pĩsa] F (de sobrancelhas) tweezers pl; (de
casa) tongs pl; (Med) callipers pl (BRIT),
calipers pl (US)
pinçar [pĩ'saɾ] VT to pick up; (sobrancelhas) to
pluck; (fig: exemplos, defeitos) to pick out
pincaro ['pĩkaɾu] M summit, peak
pincel [pĩ'sɛw] (pl **-éis**) M brush; (para pintar)
paintbrush; **~ de barba** shaving brush
pincelada [pĩse'lada] F (brush) stroke
pincelar [pĩse'laɾ] VT to paint
pincenê [pĩse'ne] M pince-nez

pindaíba [pĩda'iba] F: **estar na ~** (col) to be
broke
pinel [pi'nɛw] (pl **-éis**) (col) M/F: **ser/ficar ~** to
be/go crazy
pinga ['pĩga] F (cachaça) rum; (PT: trago) drink
pingado, -a [pĩ'gadu, a] ADJ: **~ de** covered in
drops of
pingar [pĩ'gaɾ] VI to drip; (começar a chover) to
start to rain
pingente [pĩ'ʒẽtʃi] M pendant
pingo ['pĩgu] M (gota) drop; (pingo do i) dot;
~ de gente (col) slip of a child; **um ~ de**
(comida etc) a spot of; (educação etc) a scrap of
pingue-pongue [pĩgi-'põgi] M ping-pong
pinguim [pĩ'gwĩ] (pl **-ns**) M penguin
pinguinho [pĩ'giɲu] M little drop; (pouquinho):
um ~ a tiny bit
pinguins [pĩ'gwĩs] MPL de **pinguim**
pinha ['piɲa] F pine cone
pinheiral [piɲej'ɾaw] (pl **-ais**) M pine wood
pinheiro [pi'ɲejɾu] M pine (tree)
pinho ['piɲu] M pine
pinicada [pini'kada] F (beliscão) pinch;
(cutucada) poke; (de pássaro) peck
pinicar [pini'kaɾ] VT (pele) to prickle; (como
bico) to peck; (beliscar) to pinch; (cutucar) to
poke
pinimba [pi'nĩba] (col) F: **estar de ~ com
alguém** to have it in for sb
pino ['pinu] M (peça) pin; (Auto: na porta) lock;
a ~ upright; **sol a ~** noon-day sun; **bater ~**
(Auto) to knock; (col) to be in a bad way
pinoia [pi'nɔja] (col) F piece of trash; **que ~!**
what a drag!
pinote [pi'nɔtʃi] M buck
pinotear [pino'tʃjaɾ] VI to buck
pinta ['pĩta] F (mancha) spot; (col: aparência)
appearance, looks pl; (: sujeito) guy; **dar na ~**
(col) to give o.s. away; **ela tem ~ de (ser)
inglesa** she looks English; **está com ~ de
chover** it looks like rain
pinta-braba [pĩta'bɾaba] (pl **pintas-brabas**)
M/F hoodlum, shady character
pintado, -a [pĩ'tadu, a] ADJ painted; (cabelo)
dyed; (olhos, lábios) made up; **é o avô ~** he's
the image of his grandfather; **não querer
ver alguém nem ~** (col) to hate the sight
of sb
pintar [pĩ'taɾ] VT to paint; (cabelo) to dye;
(rosto) to make up; (descrever) to describe;
(imaginar) to picture ▶ VI to paint; (col:
aparecer) to appear, turn up; (: problemas,
oportunidade) to crop up; **pintar-se** VR to
make o.s. up; **~ (o sete)** to paint the town
red
pintarroxo [pĩta'hoʃu] M (BR) linnet; (PT)
robin
pinto ['pĩtu] M chick; (!) prick (!); **como um ~
(molhado)** like a drowned rat; **ser ~** to be a
piece of cake
pintor, a [pĩ'toɾ(a)] M/F painter
pintura [pĩ'tuɾa] F painting; (maquiagem)
make-up; **~ a óleo** oil painting

pio, -a ['piu, a] ADJ (*devoto*) pious; (*caridoso*) charitable ▶ M cheep, chirp; **não dar um ~** not to make a sound

piões [pjõjs] MPL *de* **pião**

piolho ['pjoʎu] M louse

pioneiro, -a [pjo'nejru, a] ADJ pioneering ▶ M/F pioneer

piopio [pju'pju] (*col*) M birdie, dicky bird

pior ['pjɔr] ADJ, ADV (*compar*) worse; (*superl*) worst ▶ M: **o ~** worst of all ▶ F: **estar na ~** (*col*) to be in a jam

piora ['pjɔra] F worsening

piorar [pjo'rar] VT to make worse, worsen ▶ VI to get worse

pipa ['pipa] F barrel, cask; (*de papel*) kite

piparote [pipa'rɔtʃi] M (*com o dedo*) flick

pipi [pi'pi] (*col*) M (*urina*) pee; **fazer ~** to have a pee, pee

pipilar [pipi'lar] VI to chirp

pipoca [pi'pɔka] F popcorn; (*col: na pele*) blister; **~s!** blast!

pipocar [pipo'kar] VI to pop up; (*aparecer*) to spring up

pipoqueiro, -a [pipo'kejru, a] M/F popcorn seller

pique ['piki] M (*corte*) nick; (*auge*) peak; (*grande disposição*) keenness, enthusiasm; **a ~** vertically, steeply; **a ~ de** on the verge of; **ir/pôr a ~** to sink; **perder o ~** to lose one's momentum; **estou no maior ~ no momento** I'm really in the mood *ou* keen at the moment

piquei *etc* [pi'kej] VB *ver* **picar**

piquenique [piki'niki] M picnic; **fazer ~** to have a picnic

piquete [pi'ketʃi] M (*Mil*) squad; (*em greve*) picket

pira ['pira] (*col*) F: **dar o ~** to take off

pirado, -a [pi'radu, a] (*col*) ADJ crazy

pirâmide [pi'ramidʒi] F pyramid

piranha [pi'raɲa] F piranha (fish); (*col: mulher*) tart

pirão [pi'rãw] M manioc meal

pirar [pi'rar] (*col*) VI to go mad; (*com drogas*) to get high; (*ir embora*) to take off

pirata [pi'rata] M pirate; (*namorador*) lady-killer; (*vigarista*) crook ▶ ADJ pirate

pirataria [pirata'ria] F piracy; (*patifaria*) crime

pires ['piris] M INV saucer

pirilampo [piri'lãpu] M glow worm

Pirineus [piri'news] MPL: **os ~** the Pyrenees

piriri [piri'ri] (*col*) M (*diarreia*) the runs *pl*

pirotecnia [pirotek'nia] F pyrotechnics *sg*, art of making fireworks

pirraça [pi'hasa] F spiteful thing; **fazer ~** to be spiteful

pirracento, -a [piha'sẽtu, a] ADJ (*vingativo*) spiteful; (*perverso*) bloody-minded

pirralho, -a [pi'haʎu, a] M/F child

pirueta [pi'rweta] F pirouette

pirulito [piru'litu] (*BR*) M lollipop

PISA (*BR*) ABR F = **Papel de Imprensa SA**

pisada [pi'zada] F (*passo*) footstep; (*rastro*) footprint

pisar [pi'zar] VT (*andar por cima de*) to tread on; (*uvas*) to tread, press; (*esmagar, subjugar*) to crush; (*café*) to grind; (*assunto*) to harp on ▶ VI (*andar*) to step, tread; (*acelerar*) to put one's foot down; **~ em** (*grama, pé*) to step *ou* tread on; (*casa de alguém, pátria*) to set foot in; **"não pise na grama"** "do not walk on the grass"; **~ forte** to stomp; **pisa mais leve!** don't stamp your feet!

piscadela [piska'dɛla] F (*involuntária*) blink; (*sinal*) wink

pisca-pisca [piska-'piska] (*pl* **-s**) M (*Auto*) indicator

piscar [pis'kar] VT to blink; (*dar sinal*) to wink; (*estrelas*) to twinkle ▶ M: **num ~ de olhos** in a flash

piscicultor, a [pisikuw'tor(a)] M/F fish farmer

piscicultura [pisikuw'tura] F fish farming

piscina [pi'sina] F swimming pool; (*para peixes*) fish pond

piscoso, -a [pis'kozu, ɔza] ADJ rich in fish

piso ['pizu] M floor; **~ salarial** wage floor, lowest wage

pisotear [pizo'tʃjar] VT to trample (on); (*fig*) to ride roughshod over

pisquei *etc* [pis'kej] VB *ver* **piscar**

píssico, -a ['pisiku, a] ADJ crazy, mad

pista ['pista] F (*vestígio*) trace; (*indicação*) clue; (*de corridas*) track; (*Aer*) runway; (*de equitação*) ring; (*de estrada*) lane; (*de dança*) (dance) floor

pistache [pis'taʃi] M pistachio (nut)

pistacho [pis'taʃu] M = **pistache**

pistão [pis'tãw] (*pl* **-ões**) M = **pistom**

pistola [pis'tɔla] F (*arma*) pistol; (*para tinta*) spray gun

pistolão [pisto'lãw] (*pl* **-ões**) M contact

pistoleiro [pisto'lejru] M gunman

pistolões [pisto'lõjs] MPL *de* **pistolão**

pistom [pis'tõ] (*pl* **-ns**) M piston

pitada [pi'tada] F (*porção*) pinch

pitanga [pi'tãga] F Surinam cherry

pitar [pi'tar] VT, VI to smoke

piteira [pi'tejra] F cigarette-holder

pito ['pitu] M (*cachimbo*) pipe; (*col: repreensão*) telling-off; **sossegar o ~** to calm down

pitonisa [pito'niza] F fortune-teller

pitoresco, -a [pito'resku, a] ADJ picturesque

pituitário, -a [pitwi'tarju, a] ADJ (*glândula*) pituitary

pivete [pi'vɛtʃi] M child thief

pivô [pi'vo] M (*Tec*) pivot; (*fig*) central figure, prime mover

pixaim [piʃa'ĩ] ADJ (*cabelo*) frizzy ▶ M frizzy hair

pixote [pi'ʃɔtʃi] M/F = **pexote**

pizza ['pitsa] F pizza

pizzaria [pitsa'ria] F pizzeria

PJ (*BR*) ABR M = **Partido da Juventude**

PL (*BR*) ABR M = **Partido Liberal**

plá [pla] (*col*) M (*dica*) tip; (*papo*) chat

placa ['plaka] F plate; (*Auto*) number plate (*BRIT*), license plate (*US*); (*comemorativa*)

P

plaque; (*Comput*) board; (*na pele*) blotch; **~ de memória** (*Comput*) memory card; **~ de sinalização** road sign; **~ fria** false number *ou* license plate

placar [pla'kar] M scoreboard; **abrir o ~** to open the scoring

placebo [pla'sɛbu] M placebo

placenta [pla'sēta] F placenta

placidez [plasi'deʒ] F peacefulness, serenity

plácido, -a ['plasidu, a] ADJ (*sereno*) calm; (*manso*) placid

plagiador, a [plaʒja'dor(a)] M/F = **plagiário**

plagiar [pla'ʒjar] VT to plagiarize

plagiário, -a [pla'ʒjarju, a] M/F plagiarist

plágio ['plaʒu] M plagiarism

plaina ['plajna] F (*instrumento*) plane

plana ['plana] F: **de primeira ~** first-class

planador [plana'dor] M glider

planalto [pla'nawtu] M tableland, plateau

planar [pla'nar] VI to glide

planear [pla'njar] (*PT*) VT = **planejar**

planejador, a [planeʒa'dor(a)] M/F planner

planejamento [planeʒa'mētu] M planning; (*Arq*) design; **~ familiar** family planning

planejar [plane'ʒar] (*BR*) VT to plan; (*edifício*) to design

planeta [pla'neta] M planet

planetário, -a [plane'tarju, a] ADJ planetary ▶ M planetarium

plangente [plã'ʒētʃi] ADJ plaintive, mournful

planície [pla'nisi] F plain

planificar [planifi'kar] VT (*programar*) to plan out; (*uma região*) to make a plan of

planilha [pla'niʎa] F spreadsheet

plano, -a ['planu, a] ADJ (*terreno*) flat, level; (*liso*) smooth ▶ M plan; (*Mat*) plane; **~ de saúde** health insurance; **~ diretor** master plan; **em primeiro/em último ~** in the foreground/background

planta ['plãta] F (*Bio*) plant; (*de pé*) sole; (*Arq*) plan

plantação [plãta'sãw] F (*ato*) planting; (*terreno*) planted land; (*safra*) crops *pl*

plantado, -a [plã'tadu, a] ADJ: **deixar alguém/ficar ~ em algum lugar** (*col*) to leave sb/be left standing somewhere

plantão [plã'tãw] (*pl* **-ões**) M duty; (*noturno*) night duty; (*plantonista*) person on duty; (*Mil: serviço*) sentry duty; (*: pessoa*) sentry; **estar de ~** to be on duty; **médico/farmácia de ~** duty doctor/pharmacy *ou* chemist's (*BRIT*)

plantar [plã'tar] VT to plant; (*semear*) to sow; (*estaca*) to drive in; (*estabelecer*) to set up; **plantar-se** VR to plant o.s.

plantio [plã'tʃiu] M planting; (*terreno*) planted land

plantões [plã'tõjs] MPL *de* **plantão**

plantonista [plãto'nista] M/F person on duty

planura [pla'nura] F plain

plaquê [pla'ke] (*PT*) M gold plate

plaqueta [pla'keta] F plaque; (*Auto*) licensing badge (*attached to number plate*)

plasma ['plazma] M plasma

plasmar [plaz'mar] VT to mould (*BRIT*), mold (*US*), shape

plástica ['plastʃika] F (*cirurgia*) piece of plastic surgery; (*do corpo*) build; **fazer uma ~** to have plastic surgery

plástico, -a ['plastʃiku, a] ADJ, M plastic

plastificado, -a [plastʃifi'kadu, a] ADJ plastic-coated

plataforma [plata'fɔrma] F platform; **~ de exploração de petróleo** oil rig; **~ de lançamento** launch pad

plátano ['platanu] M plane tree

plateia [pla'tɛja] F (*Teatro etc*) stalls *pl* (*BRIT*), orchestra (*US*); (*espectadores*) audience

platina [pla'tʃina] F platinum

platinado, -a [platʃi'nadu, a] ADJ platinum *atr*; **loura platinada** platinum blonde

platinados [platʃi'nadus] MPL (*Auto*) points

platinar [platʃi'nar] VT (*cabelo*) to dye platinum blonde

platô [pla'to] M plateau

platônico, -a [pla'toniku, a] ADJ platonic

plausibilidade [plawzibili'dadʒi] F plausibility

plausível [plaw'zivew] (*pl* **-eis**) ADJ credible, plausible

playboy [plej'bɔj] (*pl* **-s**) M playboy

playground [plej'grãwdʒi] (*pl* **-s**) M play area

PLB ABR M = **Partido Liberal Brasileiro**

plebe ['plɛbi] F common people *pl*, populace

plebeu, -beia [ple'bew, 'bɛja] ADJ plebeian ▶ M/F pleb

plebiscito [plebi'situ] M referendum, plebiscite

plectro ['plɛktru] M (*Mús*) plectrum

pleitear [plej'tʃjar] VT (*Jur: causa*) to plead; (*contestar*) to contest; (*tentar conseguir*) to go after; (*concorrer a*) to compete for

pleito ['plejtu] M lawsuit, case; (*fig*) dispute; **~ (eleitoral)** election

plenamente [plena'mētʃi] ADV fully, completely

plenário, -a [ple'narju, a] ADJ plenary ▶ M plenary session; (*local*) chamber

plenipotência [plenipo'tēsja] F full powers *pl*

plenipotenciário, -a [plenipotē'sjarju, a] ADJ, M/F plenipotentiary

plenitude [pleni'tudʒi] F plenitude, fullness

pleno, -a ['plenu, a] ADJ full; (*completo*) complete; **em ~ dia** in broad daylight; **em plena rua/Londres** in the middle of the street/London; **em ~ inverno** in the middle *ou* depths of winter; **em ~ mar** out at sea; **ter plena certeza** to be completely sure; **~s poderes** full powers

pleonasmo [pljo'nazmu] M pleonasm

pletora [ple'tɔra] F plethora

pleurisia [plewri'zia] F pleurisy

plinto ['plĩtu] M plinth

plissado, -a [pli'sadu, a] ADJ pleated

pluma ['pluma] F feather

plumagem [plu'maʒē] F plumage

plural [plu'raw] (*pl* **-ais**) ADJ, M plural

pluralismo [plura'lizmu] M pluralism
pluralista [plura'lista] ADJ, M/F pluralist
Plutão [plu'tãw] M Pluto
plutocrata [pluto'krata] M/F plutocrat
plutônio [plu'tonju] M plutonium
pluvial [plu'vjaw] (*pl* -**ais**) ADJ pluvial, rain *atr*
PM (*BR*) ABR F, M = **polícia militar**
PMB ABR M = **Partido Municipalista Brasileiro**
PMC (*BR*) ABR M = **Partido Municipalista Comunitário**
PMDB ABR M = **Partido do Movimento Democrático Brasileiro**
PMN (*BR*) ABR M = **Partido da Mobilização Nacional**
PN ABR M (*BR*) = **Partido Nacionalista** ▶ ABR F (*Com: de ações*) = **preferencial nominativa**
PNA (*BR*) ABR M = **Plano Nacional de Álcool**
PNB ABR M (= *Produto Nacional Bruto*) GNP
PNC (*BR*) ABR M = **Partido Nacionalista Comunitário**
PND ABR M = **Plano Nacional de Desenvolvimento; Partido Nacionalista Democrático**
pneu ['pnew] M tyre (*BRIT*), tire (*US*)
pneumático, -a [pnew'matʃiku, a] ADJ pneumatic ▶ M tyre (*BRIT*), tire (*US*)
pneumonia [pnewmo'nia] F pneumonia
PNR (*BR*) ABR M = **Partido da Nova República**
pó [pɔ] M (*partículas*) powder; (*sujeira*) dust; (*col: cocaína*) coke; **pó de arroz** face powder; **sabão em pó** soap powder; **ouro em pó** gold dust; **tirar o pó (de algo)** to dust (sth)
pô [po] (*col*) EXCL (*dando ênfase*) blimey; (*mostrando desagrado*) damn it!
pobre ['pɔbri] ADJ poor ▶ M/F poor person; **os ~s** the poor; **~ de espírito** simple, dull; **um Sinatra dos ~s** a poor man's Sinatra
pobre-diabo (*pl* **pobres-diabos**) M poor devil
pobretão, -tona [pobre'tãw, 'tɔna] (*pl* -**ões/-s**) M/F pauper
pobreza [po'breza] F poverty; **~ de espírito** simplicity
poça ['pɔsa] F puddle, pool; **~ de sangue** pool of blood
poção [po'sãw] (*pl* -**ões**) F potion
pocilga [po'siwga] F pigsty
poço ['posu] M well; (*de mina, elevador*) shaft; **ser um ~ de ciência/bondade** (*fig*) to be a fount of knowledge/kindness; **~ de petróleo** oil well
poções [po'sõjs] FPL *de* **poção**
poda ['pɔda] F pruning
podadeira [poda'dejra] F pruning knife
podar [po'dar] VT to prune
pôde *etc* ['podʒi] VB *ver* **poder**

(PALAVRA-CHAVE)

poder [po'der] VI **1** (*capacidade*) can, be able to; **não posso fazê-lo** I can't do it, I'm unable to do it

2 (*ter o direito de*) can, may, be allowed to; **posso fumar aqui?** can I smoke here?; **pode entrar?** (*posso?*) can I come in?

3 (*possibilidade*) may, might, could; **pode ser** maybe; **pode ser que** it may be that; **ele poderá vir amanhã** he might come tomorrow

4: **não poder com: não posso com ele** I cannot cope with him

5 (*col: indignação*): **pudera!** no wonder!; **como é que pode?** you're joking!

▶ M power; (*autoridade*) authority; **poder aquisitivo** purchasing power; **estar no poder** to be in power; **em poder de alguém** in sb's hands

poderio [pode'riu] M might, power
poderoso, -a [pode'rozu, ɔza] ADJ powerful
pódio ['pɔdʒju] M podium
podre ['podri] ADJ rotten, putrid; (*fig*) rotten, corrupt; (*col: exausto*) knackered; **sentir-se ~** (*col: mal*) to feel grotty; **~ de rico/cansaço** filthy rich/dog tired
podres ['podris] MPL faults
podridão [podri'dãw] F decay, rottenness; (*fig*) corruption
põe *etc* [põj] VB *ver* **pôr**
poeira [po'ejra] F dust; **~ radioativa** fall-out
poeirada [pwej'rada] F pile of dust
poeirento, -a [pwej'rẽtu, a] ADJ dusty
poema ['pwema] M poem
poente ['pwẽtʃi] M west; (*do sol*) setting
poesia [poe'zia] F poetry; (*poema*) poem
poeta ['pwɛta] M poet
poética ['pwetʃika] F poetics *sg*
poético, -a ['pwetʃiku, a] ADJ poetic
poetisa [pwe'tʃiza] F (woman) poet
poetizar [pwetʃi'zar] VT to set to poetry ▶ VI to write poetry
pogrom [po'grõ] (*pl* -**s**) M pogrom
pois [pojs] ADV (*portanto*) so; (*PT: assentimento*) yes ▶ CONJ as, since, because; (*mas*) but; **~ bem** well then; **~ é** that's right; **~ não!** (*BR*) of course!; **~ não?** (*BR: numa loja*) what can I do for you?; (*PT: em interrogativas*) is it?, are you?, did they? etc; **~ sim!** certainly not!; **~ (então)** then
polaco, -a [po'laku, a] ADJ Polish ▶ M/F Pole ▶ M (*Ling*) Polish
polainas [po'lajnas] FPL gaiters
polar [po'lar] ADJ polar
polaridade [polari'dadʒi] F polarity
polarizar [polari'zar] VT to polarize
polca ['pɔwka] F polka
poldro, -a ['powdru, a] M/F colt/filly
polegada [pole'gada] F inch
polegar [pole'gar] M (*tb*: **dedo polegar**) thumb
poleiro [po'lejru] M perch
polêmica [po'lemika] F controversy
polêmico, -a [po'lemiku, a] ADJ controversial
polemista [pole'mista] ADJ argumentative ▶ M/F debater
polemizar [polemi'zar] VI to debate, argue
pólen ['polẽ] M pollen
polia [po'lia] F pulley

P

poliamida [polja'mida] F polyamide
polichinelo [poliʃi'nɛlu] M Mr Punch
polícia [po'lisja] F police, police force ▶ M/F
policeman/woman; **agente de ~** police
officer; **~ aduaneira** border police;
~ militar military police; **~ rodoviária**
traffic police
policial [poli'sjaw] (pl **-ais**) ADJ police atr ▶ M/F
(BR) policeman/woman; **novela** ou **romance**
~ detective novel
policial-militar (pl **policiais-militares**) ADJ
military police atr
policiamento [polisja'mẽtu] M policing
policiar [poli'sjar] VT to police; (instintos,
modos) to control, keep in check; **policiar-se**
VR to watch o.s.
policlínica [poli'klinika] F general hospital
policultura [polikuw'tura] F mixed farming
polidez [poli'dez] F good manners pl,
politeness
polido, -a [po'lidu, a] ADJ (lustrado) polished,
shiny; (cortês) well-mannered, polite
poliéster [po'ljɛster] M polyester
poliestireno [poljestʃi'renu] M polystyrene
polietileno [poljetʃi'lɛnu] M polythene (BRIT),
polyethylene (US)
poligamia [poliga'mia] F polygamy
polígamo, -a [po'ligamu, a] ADJ polygamous
poliglota [poli'glɔta] ADJ, M/F polyglot
polígono [po'ligonu] M polygon
polimento [poli'mẽtu] M (lustração) polishing;
(finura) refinement
Polinésia [poli'nɛzja] F: **a ~** Polynesia
polinésio, -a [poli'nɛzju, a] ADJ, M/F
Polynesian
polinização [poliniza'sãw] F pollination
polinizar [polini'zar] VT, VI to pollinate
pólio [ˈpɔlju] F polio
poliomielite [poljomje'litʃi] F poliomyelitis
pólipo [ˈpɔlipu] M polyp
polir [po'lir] VT to polish
polissílabo, -a [poli'silabu, a] ADJ polysyllabic
▶ M polysyllable
politécnica [poli'tɛknika] F (Educ)
polytechnic
política [po'litʃika] F politics sg; (programa)
policy; (diplomacia) tact; (astúcia) cunning;
ver tb **político**
politicagem [politʃi'kaʒẽ] F politicking
politicar [politʃi'kar] VI to be involved in
politics; (discorrer) to talk politics
político, -a [po'litʃiku, a] ADJ political; (astuto)
crafty ▶ M/F politician
politiqueiro, -a [politʃi'kejru, a] M/F political
wheeler-dealer ▶ ADJ politicking
politizar [politʃi'zar] VT to politicize;
(trabalhadores) to mobilize politically;
politizar-se VR to become politically aware
polo [ˈpɔlu] M pole; (Esporte) polo; **~ aquático**
water polo; **~ petroquímico** petrochemical
complex; **P~ Norte/Sul** North/South Pole
polonês, -esa [polo'nes, eza] ADJ Polish ▶ M/F
Pole ▶ M (Ling) Polish

Polônia [po'lonja] F: **a ~** Poland
polpa [ˈpowpa] F pulp
polpudo, -a [pow'pudu, a] ADJ (fruta) fleshy;
(negócio) profitable, lucrative; (quantia)
sizeable, considerable
poltrão, -trona [pow'trãw, 'trɔna] (pl **-ões/-s**)
ADJ cowardly ▶ M/F coward
poltrona [pow'trɔna] F armchair; (em teatro,
cinema) upholstered seat; ver tb **poltrão**
poluente [po'lwẽtʃi] ADJ, M pollutant
poluição [polwi'sãw] F pollution
poluidor, a [polwi'dor(a)] ADJ pollutant
poluir [po'lwir] VT to pollute
polvilhar [powvi'ʎar] VT to sprinkle, powder
polvilho [pow'viʎu] M powder; (farinha)
manioc flour
polvo [ˈpowvu] M octopus
pólvora [ˈpɔwvora] F gunpowder
polvorosa [powvo'rɔza] (col) F uproar; **em ~**
(apressado) in a flap; (desarrumado) in a mess
pomada [po'mada] F ointment
pomar [po'mar] M orchard
pomba [ˈpõba] F dove; **~(s)!** for heaven's
sake!
pombal [põ'baw] (pl **-ais**) M dovecote
pombo [ˈpõbu] M pigeon
pombo-correio (pl **pombos-correios**) M
carrier pigeon
pomo [ˈpomu] M: **~ de Adão** (BR) Adam's
apple; **~ de discórdia** bone of contention
pomos [ˈpomos] VB ver **pôr**
pompa [ˈpõpa] F pomp
Pompeia [põ'peja] N Pompeii
pompom [põ'põ] (pl **-ns**) M pompom
pomposo, -a [põ'pozu, ɔza] ADJ ostentatious,
pompous
ponche [ˈpõʃi] M punch
poncheira [põ'ʃejra] F punchbowl
poncho [ˈpõʃu] M poncho
ponderação [põdera'sãw] F consideration,
meditation; (prudência) prudence
ponderado, -a [põde'radu, a] ADJ prudent
ponderar [põde'rar] VT to consider, weigh up
▶ VI to meditate, muse; **~ que** (alegar) to point
out that
pônei [ˈponej] M pony
ponho etc [ˈpoɲu] VB ver **pôr**
ponta [ˈpõta] F tip; (de faca) point; (de sapato)
toe; (extremidade) end; (Teatro, Cinema)
walk-on part; (Futebol: posição) wing;
(: jogador) winger; **uma ~ de** (um pouco) a
touch of; **~ de cigarro** cigarette end; **~ do**
dedo fingertip; **na ~ da língua** on the tip of
one's tongue; **na(s) ~(s) dos pés** on tiptoe;
de ~ a ~ from one end to the other; (do
princípio ao fim) from beginning to end; **~ de**
lança (fig) spearhead; **~ de terra** point;
de ~ (tecnologia) cutting-edge; **estar de ~**
com alguém to be at odds with sb;
aguentar as ~s (col) to hold on
ponta-cabeça F: **de ~** upside down; (cair)
head first
pontada [põ'tada] F (dor) twinge

ponta-direita (pl **pontas-direitas**) M (Futebol) right winger

ponta-esquerda (pl **pontas-esquerdas**) M (Futebol) left winger

pontal [põ'taw] (pl **-ais**) M (de terra) point, promontory

pontão [põ'tãw] M pontoon

pontapé [põta'pε] M kick; **dar ~s em alguém** to kick sb

pontaria [põta'ria] F aim; **fazer ~** to take aim

ponte ['põtʃi] F bridge; **~ aérea** air shuttle, airlift; **~ de safena** (heart) bypass operation; **~ móvel** swing bridge; **~ suspensa** ou **pênsil** suspension bridge

ponteado, -a [põ'tʃjadu, a] ADJ stippled, dotted ▶ M stipple

pontear [po'tʃjar] VT (pontilhar) to dot, stipple; (dar pontos) to sew, stitch

ponteira [põ'tejra] F ferrule, tip

ponteiro [põ'tejru] M (indicador) pointer; (de relógio) hand; (Mús: plectro) plectrum

pontiagudo, -a [põtʃja'gudu, a] ADJ sharp, pointed

pontificado [põtʃifi'kadu] M pontificate

pontificar [põtʃifi'kar] VI to pontificate

pontífice [põ'tʃifisi] M pontiff, Pope

pontilhado, -a [põtʃi'ʎadu, a] ADJ dotted ▶ M dotted area

pontilhar [põtʃi'ʎar] VT to dot, stipple

pontinha [põ'tʃiɲa] F: **uma ~ de** a bit ou touch of

ponto ['põtu] M point; (Med, Costura, Tricô) stitch; (pequeno sinal, do i) dot; (na pontuação) full stop (BRIT), period (US); (na pele) spot; (Teatro) prompter; (de ônibus) stop; (de táxi) rank (BRIT), stand (US); (tb: **ponto cantado**) macumba chant; (matéria escolar) subject; (boca de fumo) drug den; **estar a ~ de fazer** to be on the point of doing; **ao ~** (bife) medium; **até certo ~** to a certain extent; **às cinco em ~** at five o'clock on the dot; **em ~ de bala** (col) all set; **assinar o ~** to sign in; (fig) to put in an appearance; **dar ~s** (Med) to put in stitches; **não dar ~ sem nó** (fig) to look out for one's own interests; **entregar os ~s** (fig) to give up; **fazer ~ em** to hang out at; **pôr um ~ em algo** (fig) to put a stop to sth; **dois ~s** colon sg; **~ cardeal** cardinal point; **~ de admiração** (PT) exclamation mark; **~ de equilíbrio** (Com) break-even point; **~ de exclamação/interrogação** exclamation/question mark; **~ de meia/de tricô** stocking/plain stitch; **~ de mira** bead; **~ de partida** starting point; **~ de referência** point of reference; **~ de venda** point of sale; **~ de vista** point of view, viewpoint; **~ e vírgula** semicolon; **~ facultativo** optional day off; **~ final** (fig) end; (de ônibus) terminus; **~ fraco** weak point

pontuação [põtwa'sãw] F punctuation

pontual [põ'twaw] (pl **-ais**) ADJ punctual

pontualidade [põtwali'dadʒi] F punctuality

pontuar [põ'twar] VT to punctuate

pontudo, -a [põ'tudu, a] ADJ pointed

poodle ['pudw] M poodle

pool [puw] M pool

popa ['popa] F stern, poop; **à ~** astern, aft

popelina [pope'lina] F poplin

população [popula'sãw] (pl **-ões**) F population

populacional [populasjo'naw] (pl **-ais**) ADJ population atr

populações [popula'sõjs] FPL de **população**

popular [popu'lar] ADJ popular

popularidade [populari'dadʒi] F popularity

popularizar [populari'zar] VT to popularize, make popular; **popularizar-se** VR to become popular

populista [popu'lista] ADJ populist

populoso, -a [popu'lozu, ɔza] ADJ populous

pôquer ['poker] M poker

(PALAVRA-CHAVE)

por [por] (por + o(s)/a(s) = pelo(s)/a(s)) PREP **1** (objetivo) for; **lutar pela pátria** to fight for one's country

2 (+ infin): **está por acontecer** it is about to happen, it is yet to happen; **está por fazer** it is still to be done

3 (causa) out of, because of; **por falta de fundos** through lack of funds; **por hábito/natureza** out of habit/by nature; **faço isso por ela** I do it for her; **por isso** therefore; **a razão pela qual ...** the reason why ...; **pelo amor de Deus!** for Heaven's sake!

4 (tempo): **pela manhã** in the morning; **por volta das duas horas** at about two o'clock; **ele vai ficar por uma semana** he's staying for a week

5 (lugar): **por aqui** this way; **viemos pelo parque** we came through the park; **passar por São Paulo** to pass through São Paulo; **por fora/dentro** outside/inside

6 (troca, preço) for; **trocar o velho pelo novo** to change old for new; **comprei o livro por dez libras** I bought the book for ten pounds

7 (valor proporcional): **por cento** per cent; **por hora/dia/semana/mês/ano** hourly/daily/weekly/monthly/yearly; **por cabeça** a ou per head; **por mais difícil etc que seja** however difficult etc it is

8 (modo, meio) by; **por correio/avião** by post/air; **por sí** by o.s.; **por escrito** in writing; **entrar pela entrada principal** to go in through the main entrance

9: por que why; **por quê?** why?

10: por mim tudo bem as far as I'm concerned that's OK

(PALAVRA-CHAVE)

pôr [por] VT **1** (colocar) to put; (roupas) to put on; (objeções, dúvidas) to raise; (ovos, mesa) to lay; (defeito) to find; **põe mais forte** turn it up; **você põe açúcar?** do you take sugar?; **pôr de lado** to set aside

2 (+ adj) to make; **você está me pondo**

nervoso you're making me nervous
pôr-se VR **1** (*sol*) to set
2 (*colocar-se*): **pôr-se de pé** to stand up;
ponha-se no meu lugar put yourself in my
position
3: **pôr-se a** to start to; **ela pôs-se a chorar**
she started crying
▶ M: **o pôr do sol** sunset

porão [po'rãw] (*pl* **-ões**) M (*Náut*) hold; (*de casa*)
basement; (: *armazém*) cellar
porca ['pɔrka] F (*animal*) sow; (*Tec*) nut
porcalhão, -lhona [porka'ʎãw, 'ʎɔna] (*pl*
-ões/-s) ADJ filthy ▶ M/F pig
porção [por'sãw] (*pl* **-ões**) F portion, piece;
uma ~ de a lot of
porcaria [porka'ria] F filth; (*dito sujo*)
obscenity; (*coisa ruim*) piece of junk ▶ EXCL
damn!; **o filme era uma ~** the film was a
load of rubbish
porcelana [porse'lana] F porcelain, china
porcentagem [porsẽ'taʒẽ] (*pl* **-ns**) F
percentage
porco, -a ['porku, 'pɔrka] ADJ filthy ▶ M
(*animal*) pig, hog (US); (*carne*) pork;
~ chauvinista male chauvinist pig
porções [por'sõjs] FPL *de* **porção**
porco-espinho (*pl* **porcos-espinhos**) M
porcupine
porco-montês [-mõ'tes] (*pl* **porcos-
monteses**) M wild boar
porejar [pore'ʒar] VT to exude ▶ VI to be
exuded
porém [po'rẽ] CONJ however
porfia [por'fia] F (*altercação*) dispute, wrangle;
(*rivalidade*) rivalry
pormenor [porme'nor] M detail
pormenorizar [pormenori'zar] VT to detail
pornô [por'no] (*col*) ADJ INV porn ▶ M (*filme*)
porn film
pornochanchada [pornoʃã'ʃada] F (*filme*) soft
porn movie
pornografia [pornogra'fia] F pornography
pornográfico, -a [porno'grafiku, a] ADJ
pornographic
poro ['pɔru] M pore
porões [po'rõjs] MPL *de* **porão**
pororoca [poro'rɔka] F bore
poroso, -a [po'rozu, ɔza] ADJ porous
porquanto [por'kwãtu] CONJ since, seeing
that
porque [por'ke] CONJ because; (*interrogativo:*
PT) why
porquê [por'ke] ADV (*PT*) why ▶ M reason,
motive; **~?** (*PT*) why?
porquinho-da-índia [por'kiɲu-] (*pl*
porquinhos-da-índia) M guinea pig
porra ['poha] (!) F come (!), spunk (!) ▶ EXCL
fuck (!), fucking hell (!); **para quê ~?** what
the fuck for? (!)
porrada [po'hada] F (*col: pancada*) beating;
(: *confusão*) aggro; **uma ~ de** (!) fucking loads
of (!)

porra-louca (*pl* **porras-loucas**) (!) M/F
headcase (*col*) ▶ ADJ crazy
porre ['pɔhi] (*col*) M booze-up (!); **tomar um ~**
to get plastered (!); **estar de ~** to be
plastered (!); **ser um ~** (*ser chato*) to be boring,
be a drag
porretada [pohe'tada] F clubbing
porrete [po'hetʃi] M club
porta ['pɔrta] F door; (*vão da porta*) doorway;
(*de um jardim*) gate; (*Comput*) port; **a ~s
fechadas** behind closed doors; **de ~ em ~**
from door to door; **~ corrediça** sliding door;
~ da rua/da frente/dos fundos street/
front/back door; **~ de entrada** entrance
door; **~ de vaivém** swing door; **~ giratória**
revolving door; **~ sanfonada** folding door
porta-aviões M INV aircraft carrier
porta-bandeira (*pl* **porta-bandeiras**) M/F
standard-bearer
porta-chaves M INV keyring
portador, a [porta'dor(a)] M/F bearer; **ao ~**
(*Com*) payable to the bearer
porta-espada (*pl* **porta-espadas**) M sheath
porta-estandarte (*pl* **porta-estandartes**)
M/F standard-bearer
porta-fólio [-'fɔlju] (*pl* **porta-fólios**) M
portfolio
portagem [por'taʒẽ] (*pl* **-ns**) (*PT*) F toll
porta-joias M INV jewellery (*BRIT*) *ou* jewelry
(*US*) box
portal [por'taw] (*pl* **-ais**) M doorway
porta-lápis M INV pencil box
portaló [porta'lɔ] M (*Náut*) gangway
porta-luvas M INV (*Auto*) glove compartment
porta-malas M INV (*Auto*) boot (*BRIT*), trunk (*US*)
porta-moedas (*PT*) M purse
porta-níqueis M INV purse
portanto [por'tãtu] CONJ so, therefore
portão [por'tãw] (*pl* **-ões**) M gate
porta-partituras (*pl* **porta-partituras**) M
music stand
portar [por'tar] VT to carry; **portar-se** VR to
behave
porta-retrato (*pl* **porta-retratos**) M photo
frame
porta-revistas M INV magazine rack
portaria [porta'ria] F (*de um edifício*) entrance
hall; (*recepção*) reception desk; (*do governo*)
edict, decree; **baixar uma ~** to issue a decree
porta-seios M INV bra, brassiere
portátil [por'tatʃiw] (*pl* **-eis**) ADJ portable
porta-toalhas M INV towel rail
porta-voz (*pl* **-es**) M/F (*pessoa*) spokesman,
spokesperson
porte ['pɔrtʃi] M (*transporte*) transport; (*custo*)
freight charge, carriage; (*Náut*) tonnage,
capacity; (*atitude*) bearing; **~ pago** post paid;
de grande ~ far-reaching, important;
empresa de ~ medio medium-sized
enterprise; **um autor do ~ de ...** an author
of the calibre (*BRIT*) *ou* caliber (*US*) of ....
porteiro, -a [por'tejru, a] M/F caretaker;
~ eletrônico entry phone

portenho, -a [por'teɲu, a] ADJ from Buenos Aires ▶ M/F person from Buenos Aires

portento [por'tẽtu] M wonder, marvel

portentoso, -a [portẽ'tozu, ɔza] ADJ amazing, marvellous (BRIT), marvelous (US)

pórtico ['pɔrtʃiku] M porch, portico

portinhola [portʃi'ɲɔla] F small door; (de carruagem) door

porto ['portu] M (do mar) port, harbour (BRIT), harbor (US); (vinho) port; **o P~** Oporto; **~ de escala** port of call; **~ franco** freeport

porto-alegrense [-ale'grẽsi] ADJ from Porto Alegre ▶ M/F person from Porto Alegre

portões [por'tõjs] MPL de **portão**

Porto Rico M Puerto Rico

porto-riquenho, -a [portuhi'keɲu, a] ADJ, M/F Puerto Rican

portuense [por'twẽsi] ADJ from Oporto ▶ M/F person from Oporto

portuga [por'tuga] (pej) M/F Portuguese

Portugal [portu'gaw] M Portugal

português, -guesa [portu'ges, 'geza] ADJ Portuguese ▶ M/F Portuguese inv ▶ M (Ling) Portuguese; **~ de Portugal/do Brasil** European/Brazilian Portuguese

portunhol [portu'ɲɔw] M mixture of Spanish and Portuguese

porventura [porvẽ'tura] ADJ by chance; **se ~ você...** if you happen to ...

porvir [por'vir] M future

pôs [pos] VB ver **pôr**

pós- [pɔjʃ-] PREFIXO post-

posar [po'zar] VI (Foto) to pose

pós-datado, -a [-da'tadu, a] ADJ post-dated

pós-datar VT to postdate

pose ['pozi] F pose

pós-escrito M postscript

pós-graduação F postgraduation; **curso de ~** postgraduate course

pós-graduado, -a ADJ, M/F postgraduate

pós-guerra M post-war period; **o Brasil do ~** post-war Brazil

posição [pozi'sãw] (pl -ões) F position; (social) standing, status; (de esportista no mundo) ranking; **tomar uma ~** to take a stand

posicionar [pozisjo'nar] VT to position; **posicionar-se** VR to position o.s.; (tomar atitude) to take a position

positivo, -a [pozi'tʃivu, a] ADJ positive ▶ M positive ▶ EXCL (col) yeah!, sure!

posologia [pozolo'ʒia] F dosage

pós-operatório, -a [-opera'tɔrju, a] ADJ post-operative

pospor [pos'por] (irreg: como **pôr**) VT to put after; (adiar) to postpone

possante [po'sãtʃi] ADJ powerful, strong; (carro) flashy

posse ['pɔsi] F possession, ownership; (investidura) swearing in; **posses** FPL (pertences) possessions, belongings; **tomar ~** to take office; **tomar ~ de** to take possession of; **cerimônia de ~** swearing in ceremony; **pessoa de ~s** person of means; **viver de**

acordo com suas ~s to live according to one's means

posseiro, -a [po'sejru, a] ADJ leaseholding ▶ M/F leaseholder

possessão [pose'sãw] F possession

possessivo, -a [pose'sivu, a] ADJ possessive

possesso, -a [po'sɛsu, a] ADJ possessed; (furioso) furious

possibilidade [posibili'dadʒi] F possibility; (oportunidade) chance; **possibilidades** FPL (recursos) means

possibilitar [posibili'tar] VT to make possible, permit

possível [po'sivew] (pl -eis) ADJ possible; **fazer todo o ~** to do one's best; **não é ~!** (col) you're joking!

posso etc ['posu] VB ver **poder**

possuidor, a [poswi'dor(a)] M/F (de casa, livro etc) owner; (de dinheiro, talento etc) possessor; **ser ~ de** to be the owner/possessor of

possuir [po'swir] VT (casa, livro etc) to own; (dinheiro, talento) to possess; (dominar) to possess, grip; (sexualmente) to take, have

post [post] (pl -s) M (Comput) post

posta ['pɔsta] F (pedaço) piece, slice

postal [pos'taw] (pl -ais) ADJ postal ▶ M postcard

postar [pos'tar] VT to place, post; (Comput) to post; **postar-se** VR to position o.s.

posta-restante (pl **postas-restantes**) F poste-restante (BRIT), general delivery (US)

poste ['pɔstʃi] M pole, post

pôster ['poster] M poster

postergar [poster'gar] VT (adiar) to postpone; (amigos) to pass over; (interesse pessoal) to set ou put aside; (lei, norma) to disregard

posteridade [posteri'dadʒi] F posterity

posterior [poste'rjor] ADJ (mais tarde) subsequent, later; (traseiro) rear, back ▶ M (col) posterior, bottom

posteriormente [posterjor'mẽtʃi] ADV later, subsequently

postiço, -a [pos'tʃisu, a] ADJ false, artificial

postigo [pos'tʃigu] M (em porta) peephole

posto, -a ['postu, 'pɔsta] PP de **pôr** ▶ M post, position; (emprego) job; (de diplomata: local) posting; **~ de comando** command post; **~ de gasolina** service ou petrol station; **~ que** although; **a ~s** at action stations; **~ do corpo de bombeiros** fire station; **~ de saúde** health centre ou center

posto-chave (pl **postos-chave(s)**) M key post

postulado [postu'ladu] M postulate, assumption

postulante [postu'lãtʃi] M/F petitioner; (candidato) candidate

postular [postu'lar] VT (pedir) to request; (teoria) to postulate

póstumo, -a ['pɔstumu, a] ADJ posthumous

postura [pos'tura] F (posição) posture, position; (aspecto físico) appearance; (fig) posture

posudo, -a [po'zudu, a] ADJ poseurish

P

potassa [po'tasa] F potash
potássio [po'tasju] M potassium
potável [po'tavew] (*pl* **-eis**) ADJ drinkable;
água ~ drinking water
pote ['pɔtʃi] M jug, pitcher; (*de geleia*) jar; (*de creme*) pot; **chover a ~s** (*PT*) to rain cats and dogs; **dinheiro aos ~s** (*fig*) pots of money
potência [po'tẽsja] F power; (*força*) strength; (*nação*) power; (*virilidade*) potency
potencial [potẽ'sjaw] (*pl* **-ais**) ADJ potential, latent ▶ M potential; **riquezas** *etc* **em ~** potential wealth *etc*
potentado [potẽ'tadu] M potentate
potente [po'tẽtʃi] ADJ powerful, potent
pot-pourri [popu'hi] M (*Mús*) medley; (*fig*) pot-pourri
potro, -a ['potru, a] M/F (*cavalo*) colt/filly, foal
pouca-vergonha (*pl* **poucas-vergonhas**) F (*ato*) shameful act, disgrace; (*falta de vergonha*) shamelessness

(PALAVRA-CHAVE)

pouco, -a ['poku, a] ADJ **1** (*sg*) little, not much; **pouco tempo** little *ou* not much time; **de pouco interesse** of little interest, not very interesting; **pouca coisa** not much
2 (*pl*) few, not many; **uns poucos** a few, some; **poucas vezes** rarely; **poucas crianças comem o que devem** few children eat what they should
▶ ADV **1** little, not much; **custa pouco** it doesn't cost much; **dentro em pouco**, **daqui a pouco** shortly; **pouco antes** shortly before
2 (+ *adj: negativo*): **ela é pouco inteligente/simpática** she's not very bright/friendly
3: **por pouco eu não morri** I almost died
4: **pouco a pouco** little by little
5: **aos poucos** gradually
▶ M: **um pouco** a little, a bit; **nem um pouco** not at all

pouco-caso M scorn
poupador, a [popa'dor(a)] ADJ thrifty
poupança [po'pãsa] F thrift; (*economias*) savings *pl*; (*tb*: **caderneta de poupança**) savings bank
poupar [po'par] VT to save; (*vida*) to spare; ~ **alguém** (*de sofrimentos*) to spare sb; ~ **algo a alguém**, ~ **alguém de algo** (*trabalho etc*) to save sb sth; (*aborrecimentos*) to spare sb sth
pouquinho [po'kiɲu] M: **um ~ (de)** a little
pouquíssimo, -a [po'kisimu, a] ADJ, ADV SUPERL *de* **pouco**
pousada [po'zada] F (*hospedagem*) lodging; (*hospedaria*) inn
pousar [po'zar] VT to place; (*mão*) to rest, place ▶ VI (*avião, pássaro*) to land; (*pernoitar*) to spend the night
pouso ['pozu] M landing; (*lugar*) resting place
povão [po'vãw] M ordinary people *pl*
povaréu [pova'rɛw] M crowd of people
povo ['povu] M people; (*raça*) people *pl*, race;

(*plebe*) common people *pl*; (*multidão*) crowd
povoação [povwa'sãw] (*pl* **-ões**) F (*aldeia*) village, settlement; (*habitantes*) population; (*ato de povoar*) settlement, colonization
povoado [po'vwadu] M village
povoamento [povwa'mẽtu] M settlement
povoar [po'vwar] VT (*de habitantes*) to people, populate; (*de animais etc*) to stock
poxa ['poʃa] EXCL gosh!
PP ABR (*Com: de ações*) = **preferencial ao portador**
PPB ABR M = **Partido do Povo Brasileiro**
PR (*BR*) ABR = **Paraná** ▶ ABR F = **polícia rodoviária**
pra [pra] (*col*) PREP = **para a**; *ver* **para**
praça ['prasa] F (*largo*) square; (*mercado*) marketplace; (*soldado*) soldier; (*cidade*) town ▶ M (*Mil*) private; (*polícia*) constable; **sentar ~** to enlist; **~ de touros** bullring; **~ forte** stronghold
praça-d'armas (*pl* **praças-d'armas**) M officers' mess
pracinha [pra'siɲa] M GI
prado ['pradu] M meadow, grassland; (*BR*: *hipódromo*) racecourse
pra-frente (*col*) ADJ INV trendy
prafrentex [prafrē'tɛks] (*col*) ADJ INV trendy
Praga ['praga] N Prague
praga ['praga] F (*coisa, pessoa importuna*) nuisance; (*maldição*) curse; (*desgraça*) misfortune; (*erva daninha*) weed; **rogar ~ a alguém** to curse sb
pragmático, -a [prag'matʃiku, a] ADJ (*prático*) pragmatic
pragmatismo [pragma'tʃizmu] M pragmatism
pragmatista [pragma'tʃista] ADJ, M/F pragmatist
praguejar [prage'ʒar] VT, VI to curse
praia ['praja] F beach, seashore
pralina [pra'lina] F praline
prancha ['prãʃa] F plank; (*Náut*) gangplank; (*de surfe*) board
prancheta [prã'ʃeta] F (*mesa*) drawing board
prantear [prã'tʃjar] VT to mourn ▶ VI to weep
pranto ['prãtu] M weeping; **debulhar-se em ~** to weep bitterly
Prata ['prata] F: **o rio da ~** the River Plate
prata ['prata] F silver; (*col: cruzeiro*) ≈ quid (*BRIT*), ≈ buck (*US*); **de ~** silver *atr*; **~ de lei** sterling silver
prataria [prata'ria] F silverware; (*pratos*) crockery
pratarrão [prata'hãw] (*pl* **-ões**) M large plate
prateado, -a [pra'tʃjadu, a] ADJ silver-plated; (*brilhante*) silvery; (*cor*) silver ▶ M (*cor*) silver; (*de um objeto*) silver-plating; **papel ~** silver paper
pratear [pra'tʃjar] VT to silver-plate; (*fig*) to turn silver
prateleira [prate'lejra] F shelf
prática ['pratʃika] F (*ato de praticar*) practice; (*experiência*) experience, know-how; (*costume*) habit, custom; **na ~** in practice; **pôr em ~**

to put into practice; **aprender com a ~** to learn with practice; *ver tb* **prático**

praticagem [pratʃi'kaʒẽ] F (*Náut*) pilotage

praticante [pratʃi'kātʃi] ADJ practising (BRIT), practicing (US) ▶ M/F apprentice; (*de esporte*) practitioner

praticar [pratʃi'kar] VT to practise (BRIT), practice (US); (*profissão, medicina*) to practise *ou* practice; (*roubo, operação*) to carry out

praticável [pratʃi'kavew] (*pl* **-eis**) ADJ practical, feasible

prático, -a ['pratʃiku, a] ADJ practical ▶ M/F expert ▶ M (*Náut*) pilot

prato ['pratu] M (*louça*) plate; (*comida*) dish; (*de uma refeição*) course; (*de toca-discos*) turntable; **pratos** MPL (*Mús*) cymbals; **~ raso/fundo/de sobremesa** dinner/soup/dessert plate; **~ do dia** dish of the day; **cuspir no ~ em que comeu** (*fig*) to bite the hand that feeds one; **pôr algo em ~s limpos** to get to the bottom of sth; **~ de resistência** pièce de résistance

praxe ['praʃi] F custom, usage; **de ~** usually; **ser de ~** to be the norm

> Student life in Portugal follows the traditions set out in a written set of rules known as the 'código da **praxe**'. It begins in freshers' week, where freshers are jeered at by their seniors, and are subjected to a number of humiliating practical jokes, such as having their hair cut against their will and being made to walk around town in fancy dress.

prazenteiro, -a [prazẽ'tejru, a] ADJ cheerful, pleasant

prazer [pra'zer] M pleasure ▶ VI: **~ a alguém** to please sb; **muito ~ em conhecê-lo** pleased to meet you

prazeroso, -a [praze'rozu, ɔza] ADJ (*pessoa*) pleased; (*viagem*) pleasurable

prazo ['prazu] M term, period; (*vencimento*) expiry date, time limit; **a curto/médio/longo ~** in the short/medium/long term; **comprar a ~** to buy on hire purchase (BRIT) *ou* on the installment plan (US); **último ~** *ou* **~ final** deadline

pré- [prɛ-] PREFIXO pre-

preamar [prea'mar] (BR) F high tide water

preâmbulo [pre'ãbulu] M preamble, introduction; **sem mais ~s** without further ado

preaquecer [prjake'ser] VT to preheat

pré-aviso M (*prior*) notice

precário, -a [pre'karju, a] ADJ precarious, insecure; (*escasso*) failing; (*estado de saúde*) delicate

precatado, -a [preka'tadu, a] ADJ cautious

precatar-se [preka'tarsi] VR to take precautions; **~ contra** to be wary of; **precate-se para o pior** prepare yourself for the worst

precatória [preka'tɔrja] F (*Jur*) writ, prerogative order

precaução [prekaw'sãw] (*pl* **-ões**) F precaution

precaver-se [preka'versi] VR: **~ (contra** *ou* **de)** to be on one's guard (against); **~ para algo/fazer algo** to prepare o.s. for sth/be prepared to do sth

precavido, -a [preka'vidu, a] ADJ cautious

prece ['prɛsi] F prayer; (*súplica*) entreaty

precedência [prese'dẽsja] F precedence; **ter ~ sobre** to take precedence over

precedente [prese'dẽtʃi] ADJ preceding ▶ M precedent; **sem ~(s)** unprecedented

preceder [prese'der] VT, VI to precede; **~ a algo** to precede sth; (*ter primazia*) to take precedence over sth

preceito [pre'sejtu] M precept, ruling

preceituar [presej'twar] VT to set down, prescribe

preceptor [presep'tor] M mentor

preciosidade [presjozi'dadʒi] F (*qualidade*) preciousness; (*coisa*) treasure

preciosismo [presjo'zizmu] M preciosity

precioso, -a [pre'sjozu, ɔza] ADJ precious; (*de grande importância*) invaluable

precipício [presi'pisju] M precipice; (*fig*) abyss

precipitação [presipita'sãw] F haste; (*imprudência*) rashness

precipitado, -a [presipi'tadu, a] ADJ hasty; (*imprudente*) rash

precipitar [presipi'tar] VT (*atirar*) to hurl; (*acontecimentos*) to precipitate ▶ VI (*Quím*) to precipitate; **precipitar-se** VR (*atirar-se*) to hurl o.s.; (*contra, para*) to rush; (*agir com precipitação*) to be rash, act rashly; **~ alguém/~-se em** (*situação*) to plunge sb/be plunged into; (*aventuras, perigos*) to sweep sb/be swept into

precisado, -a [presi'zadu, a] ADJ needy, in need

precisamente [presiza'mẽtʃi] ADV precisely

precisão [presi'zãw] F (*exatidão*) precision, accuracy; **ter ~ de** to need

precisar [presi'zar] VT to need; (*especificar*) to specify ▶ VI to be in need; **precisar-se** VR: **"precisa-se"** "needed"; **~ de** to need; **não precisa você se preocupar** you needn't worry; **precisa de um passaporte** a passport is necessary *ou* needed; **preciso ir** I have to go; **~ que alguém faça** to need sb to do

preciso, -a [pre'sizu, a] ADJ (*exato*) precise, accurate; (*necessário*) necessary; (*claro*) concise; **é ~ você ir** you must go

preclaro, -a [pre'klaru, a] ADJ famous, illustrious

preço ['presu] M price; (*custo*) cost; (*valor*) value; **por qualquer ~** at any price; **a ~ de banana** (BR) *ou* **de chuva** (PT) dirt cheap; **não ter ~** (*fig*) to be priceless; **~ por atacado/a varejo** wholesale/retail price; **~ de custo** cost price; **~ de venda** sale price; **~ de fábrica/de revendedor** factory/trade price; ~ **à vista** cash price; (*de commodities*) spot price; ~ **pedido** asking price

precoce [pre'kɔsi] ADJ precocious; (*antecipado*) early; (*calvície*) premature

precocidade [prekosi'dadʒi] F precociousness

preconcebido, -a [prekõse'bidu, a] ADJ preconceived

preconceito [prekõ'sejtu] M prejudice

preconizar [prekoni'zar] VT to extol; (*aconselhar*) to advocate

precursor, a [prekur'sor(a)] M/F (*predecessor*) precursor, forerunner; (*mensageiro*) herald

predador [preda'dor] M predator

pré-datado, -a [-da'tadu, a] ADJ predated

pré-datar VT to predate

predatório, -a [preda'tɔrju, a] ADJ predatory

predecessor [predese'sor] M predecessor

predestinado, -a [predestʃi'nadu, a] ADJ predestined

predestinar [predestʃi'nar] VT to predestine

predeterminado, -a [predetermi'nadu, a] ADJ predetermined

predeterminar [predetermi'nar] VT to predetermine

predial [pre'dʒjaw] (*pl* **-ais**) ADJ property *atr*, real-estate *atr*; **imposto** ~ domestic rates

prédica ['predʒika] F sermon

predicado [predʒi'kadu] M predicate

predição [predʒi'sãw] (*pl* **-ões**) F prediction, forecast

predigo *etc* [pre'dʒigu] VB *ver* **predizer**

predileção [predʒile'sãw] (*pl* **-ões**) F preference, predilection

predileto, -a [predʒi'lɛtu, a] ADJ favourite (BRIT), favorite (US)

prédio ['predʒju] M building; ~ **de apartamentos** block of flats (BRIT), apartment house (US)

predispor [predʒis'por] (*irreg: como* **pôr**) VT: ~ **alguém contra** to prejudice sb against; **predispor-se** VR: ~**-se a/para** to get o.s. in the mood to/for; **a natação me predispõe para o trabalho** swimming puts me in the mood for work; **a notícia os predispôs para futuros problemas** the news prepared them for future problems

predisposição [predʒispozi'sãw] F predisposition

predisposto, -a [predʒis'postu, 'posta] PP *de* **predispor** ▶ ADJ predisposed

predispunha *etc* [predʒis'puɲa] VB *ver* **predispor**

predispus *etc* [predʒis'pus] VB *ver* **predispor**

predispuser *etc* [predʒispu'zer] VB *ver* **predispor**

predizer [predʒi'zer] (*irreg: como* **dizer**) VT to predict, forecast

predominância [predomi'nãsja] F predominance, prevalence

predominante [predomi'nãtʃi] ADJ predominant

predominar [predomi'nar] VI to predominate, prevail

predomínio [predo'minju] M predominance, supremacy

pré-eleitoral (*pl* **-ais**) ADJ pre-election

preeminência [preemi'nẽsja] F pre-eminence, superiority

preeminente [preemi'nẽtʃi] ADJ pre-eminent, superior

preencher [preẽ'ʃer] VT (*formulário*) to fill in (BRIT) *ou* out, complete; (*requisitos*) to fulfil (BRIT), fulfill (US), meet; (*espaço, vaga, tempo, cargo*) to fill; ~ **à máquina** (*formulário*) to complete on a typewriter

preenchimento [preẽʃi'mẽtu] M completion; (*de requisitos*) meeting; (*de vaga*) filling

pré-escolar ADJ pre-school

preestabelecer [preestabele'ser] VT to prearrange

pré-estreia F preview

preexistir [preezis'tʃir] VI to preexist; ~ **a algo** to exist before sth

pré-fabricado, -a [-fabri'kadu, a] ADJ prefabricated

prefaciar [prefa'sjar] VT to preface

prefácio [pre'fasju] M preface

prefeito, -a [pre'fejtu, a] M/F mayor

prefeitura [prefej'tura] F town hall

preferência [prefe'rẽsja] F preference; (*Auto*) priority; **de** ~ preferably; **ter** ~ **por** to have a preference for

preferencial [preferẽ'sjaw] (*pl* **-ais**) ADJ (*rua*) main; (*ação*) preference *atr* ▶ F main road (*with priority*)

preferido, -a [prefe'ridu, a] ADJ favourite (BRIT), favorite (US)

preferir [prefe'rir] VT to prefer; ~ **algo a algo** to prefer sth to sth

preferível [prefe'rivew] (*pl* **-eis**) ADJ: ~ **(a)** preferable (to)

prefigurar [prefigu'rar] VT to prefigure

prefiro *etc* [pre'firu] VB *ver* **preferir**

prefixo [pre'fiksu] M (*Ling*) prefix; (*Tel*) code

prega ['prega] F pleat, fold

pregado, -a [pre'gadu, a] ADJ exhausted

pregador [prega'dor] M preacher; (*de roupa*) peg

pregão [pre'gãw] (*pl* **-ões**) M proclamation, cry; **o** ~ (*na Bolsa*) trading; (*em leilão*) bidding

pregar¹ [pre'gar] VT (*sermão*) to preach; (*anunciar*) to proclaim; (*ideias, virtude*) to advocate ▶ VI to preach

pregar² [pre'gar] VT (*com prego*) to nail; (*fixar*) to pin, fasten; (*cosendo*) to sew on ▶ VI to give out; ~ **uma peça** to play a trick; ~ **os olhos em** to fix one's eyes on; **não** ~ **olho** not to sleep a wink; ~ **mentiras em alguém** to fob sb off with lies; ~ **um susto em alguém** to give sb a fright

prego ['pregu] M nail; (*col: casa de penhor*) pawn shop; **dar o** ~ (*pessoa, carro*) to give out; **pôr algo no** ~ to pawn sth; **não meter** ~ **sem estopa** (*fig*) to be out for one's own advantage

pregões [pre'gõjs] MPL *de* **pregão**

pré-gravado, -a [-gra'vadu, a] ADJ prerecorded

pregresso, -a [pre'grɛsu, a] ADJ past, previous

preguear [pre'gjar] VT to pleat, fold

preguiça [pre'gisa] F laziness; (animal) sloth; **estar com ~** to feel lazy; **estou com ~ de cozinhar** I can't be bothered to cook

preguiçar [pregi'sar] VI to laze around

preguiçoso, -a [pregi'sozu, ɔza] ADJ lazy ▶ M/F lazybones

pré-história F prehistory

pré-histórico, -a ADJ prehistoric

preia ['prɛja] F prey

preia-mar (PT) F high tide

preito ['prejtu] M homage, tribute; **render ~ a** to pay homage to

prejudicar [preʒudʒi'kar] VT to damage; (atrapalhar) to hinder; **prejudicar-se** VR (pessoa) to do o.s. no favours (BRIT) ou favors (US)

prejudicial [preʒudʒi'sjaw] (pl **-ais**) ADJ damaging; (à saúde) harmful

prejuízo [pre'ʒwizu] M (dano) damage, harm; (em dinheiro) loss; **com ~** (Com) at a loss; **em ~ de** to the detriment of

prejulgar [preʒuw'gar] VT to prejudge

prelado [pre'ladu] M prelate

preleção [prele'sãw] (pl **-ões**) F lecture

preliminar [prelimi'nar] ADJ preliminary ▶ F (partida) preliminary ▶ M (condição) preliminary; **preliminares** FPL foreplay

prelo ['prɛlu] M (printing) press; **no ~** in the press

prelúdio [pre'ludʒju] M prelude

prematuro, -a [prema'turu, a] ADJ premature

premeditação [premedʒita'sãw] F premeditation

premeditado, -a [premedʒi'tadu, a] ADJ premeditated

premeditar [premedʒi'tar] VT to premeditate

premência [pre'mẽsja] F urgency, pressing nature

pré-menstrual (pl **-ais**) ADJ premenstrual

premente [pre'mẽtʃi] ADJ pressing

premer [pre'mer] VT to press

premiado, -a [pre'mjadu, a] ADJ prizewinning; (bilhete) winning ▶ M/F prizewinner

premiar [pre'mjar] VT to award a prize to; (recompensar) to reward

premiê [pre'mje] M (Pol) premier

premier [pre'mje] M = **premiê**

prêmio ['premju] M prize; (recompensa) reward; (Seguros) premium; **Grande P~** Grand Prix; **~ de consolação** consolation prize

premir [pre'mir] VT = **premer**

premissa [pre'misa] F premise

pré-moldado, -a [-mow'dadu, a] ADJ precast ▶ M breeze block

premonição [premoni'sãw] (pl **-ões**) F premonition

premonitório, -a [premoni'tɔrju, a] ADJ premonitory

pré-natal [prɛ-] (pl **-ais**) ADJ antenatal (BRIT), prenatal (US)

prenda ['prẽda] F gift, present; (em jogo) forfeit; **prendas** FPL (aptidões) talents; **~s domésticas** housework sg

prendado, -a [prẽ'dadu, a] ADJ gifted, talented; (homem: em afazeres domésticos) domesticated

prendedor [prẽde'dor] M fastener; (de cabelo, gravata) clip; **~ de roupa** clothes peg; **~ de papéis** paper clip

prender [prẽ'der] VT (pregar) to fasten, fix; (roupa) to pin; (cabelo) to tie back; (capturar) to arrest; (atar, ligar) to tie; (atenção) to catch; (afetivamente) to tie, bind; (reter: doença, compromisso) to keep; (movimentos) to restrict; **prender-se** VR to get caught, stick; **~-se a alguém** (por amizade) to be attached to sb; (casar-se) to tie o.s. down to sb; **~-se a algo** (detalhes, maus hábitos) to get caught up in sth; **~-se com algo** to be connected with sth

prenhe ['prɛɲi] ADJ pregnant

prenhez [pre'ɲez] F pregnancy

prenome [pre'nɔmi] M first name, Christian name

prensa ['prẽsa] F (ger) press

prensar [prẽ'sar] VT to press, compress; (fruta) to squeeze; (uvas) to press; **~ alguém contra a parede** to push sb up against the wall

prenunciar [prenũ'sjar] VT to predict, foretell; **as nuvens prenunciam chuva** the clouds suggest rain

prenúncio [pre'nũsju] M forewarning, sign

preocupação [preokupa'sãw] (pl **-ões**) F (ideia fixa) preoccupation; (inquietação) worry, concern

preocupante [preoku'pãtʃi] ADJ worrying

preocupar [preoku'par] VT (absorver) to preoccupy; (inquietar) to worry; **preocupar-se** VR: **~-se com** to worry about, be worried about

preparação [prepara'sãw] (pl **-ões**) F preparation

preparado [prepa'radu] M preparation

preparar [prepa'rar] VT to prepare; **preparar-se** VR to get ready; **~-se para algo/para fazer** to prepare for sth/to do

preparativos [prepara'tʃivus] MPL preparations, arrangements

preparo [pre'paru] M preparation; (instrução) ability; **~ físico** physical fitness

preponderância [prepõde'rãsja] F preponderance, predominance

preponderante [prepõde'rãtʃi] ADJ predominant

preponderar [prepõde'rar] VI: **~ (sobre)** to prevail (over)

preposição [prepozi'sãw] (pl **-ões**) F preposition

preposto, -a [pre'postu, 'pɔsta] M/F person in charge; (representante) representative

prepotência [prepo'tẽsja] F superiority; (*despotismo*) absolutism

prepotente [prepo'tẽtʃi] ADJ (*poderoso*) predominant; (*despótico*) despotic; (*atitude*) overbearing

prerrogativa [prehoga'tʃiva] F prerogative, privilege

presa ['preza] F (*na guerra*) spoils *pl*; (*vítima*) prey; (*dente de animal*) fang

presbiteriano, -a [prezbite'rjanu, a] ADJ, M/F Presbyterian

presbitério [prezbi'terju] M presbytery

presciência [pre'sjẽsja] F foreknowledge, foresight

presciente [pre'sjẽtʃi] ADJ far-sighted, prescient

prescindir [presĩ'dʒir] VI: ~ **de algo** to do without sth

prescindível [presĩ'dʒivew] (*pl* **-eis**) ADJ dispensable

prescrever [preskre'ver] VT to prescribe; (*prazo*) to set ▶ VI (*Jur: crime, direito*) to lapse; (*cair em desuso*) to fall into disuse

prescrição [preskri'sãw] (*pl* **-ões**) F order, rule; (*Med*) instruction; (: *de um remédio*) prescription; (*Jur*) lapse

prescrito, -a [pres'kritu, a] PP *de* **prescrever**

presença [pre'zẽsa] F presence; (*frequência*) attendance; ~ **de espírito** presence of mind; **ter boa** ~ to be presentable; **na** ~ **de** in the presence of

presenciar [prezẽ'sjar] VT to be present at; (*testemunhar*) to witness

presente [pre'zẽtʃi] ADJ present; (*fig: interessado*) attentive; (: *evidente*) clear, obvious ▶ M present ▶ F (*Com: carta*): **a** ~ this letter; **os presentes** MPL (*pessoas*) those present; **ter algo** ~ to bear sth in mind; **dar/ganhar de** ~ to give/get as a present; ~ **de grego** undesirable gift, mixed blessing; **anexamos à** ~ we enclose herewith; **pela** ~ hereby

presentear [prezẽ'tʃjar] VT: ~ **alguém (com algo)** to give sb (sth as) a present

presentemente [prezẽtʃe'mẽtʃi] ADV at present

presepada [preze'pada] F (*fanfarrice*) boasting; (*atitude, espetáculo ridículo*) joke

presépio [pre'zɛpju] M Nativity scene, crib

preservação [prezerva'sãw] F preservation

preservar [prezer'var] VT to preserve, protect

preservativo [prezerva'tʃivu] M preservative; (*anticoncepcional*) condom

presidência [prezi'dẽsja] F (*de um país*) presidency; (*de uma assembleia*) chair, presidency; **assumir a** ~ (*Pol*) to become president

presidencial [prezidẽ'sjaw] (*pl* **-ais**) ADJ presidential

presidencialismo [prezidẽsja'lizmu] M presidential system

presidenciável [prezidẽ'sjavew] (*pl* **-eis**) ADJ eligible for the presidency ▶ M/F presidential candidate

presidente, -a [prezi'dẽtʃi, ta] M/F (*de um país*) president; (*de uma assembleia, Com*) chair, president; **o P~ da República** the President (of Brazil)

presidiário, -a [prezi'dʒjarju, a] M/F convict

presídio [pre'zidʒju] M prison

presidir [prezi'dʒir] VT, VI: ~ **(a)** to preside over; (*reunião*) to chair; (*suj: leis, critérios*) to govern

presilha [pre'ziʎa] F fastener; (*para o cabelo*) slide

preso, -a ['prezu, a] ADJ (*em prisão*) imprisoned; (*capturado*) under arrest, captured; (*atado*) bound, tied; (*moralmente*) bound ▶ M/F prisoner; **ficar** ~ **a detalhes** to get bogged down in detail(s); **ficar** ~ **em casa** (*com filhos pequenos etc*) to be stuck at home; **estar** ~ **a alguém** to be attached to sb; **você está** ~**!** you're under arrest!; **com a greve dos ônibus, fiquei** ~ **na cidade** with the bus strike I got stuck in town

pressa ['prɛsa] F haste, hurry; (*rapidez*) speed; (*urgência*) urgency; **às** ~**s** hurriedly; **estar com** ~ to be in a hurry; **sem** ~ unhurriedly; **não tem** ~ there's no hurry; **ter** ~ **de** ou **em fazer** to be in a hurry to do

pressagiar [presa'ʒjar] VT to foretell, presage

presságio [pre'saʒu] M omen, sign; (*pressentimento*) premonition

pressago, -a [pre'sagu, a] ADJ (*comentário*) portentous

pressão [pre'sãw] (*pl* **-ões**) F pressure; (**colchete de**) ~ press stud, popper; **fazer** ~ **(sobre alguém/algo)** to put pressure on (sb/sth); ~ **arterial** ou **sanguínea** blood pressure

pressentimento [presẽtʃi'mẽtu] M premonition, presentiment

pressentir [presẽ'tʃir] VT (*pressagiar*) to foresee; (*suspeitar*) to sense; (*inimigo*) to preempt

pressionar [presjo'nar] VT (*botão*) to press; (*coagir*) to pressure ▶ VI to press, put on pressure

pressões [pre'sõjs] FPL *de* **pressão**

pressupor [presu'por] (*irreg: como* **pôr**) VT to presuppose

pressuposto, -a [presu'postu, 'pɔsta] PP *de* **pressupor** ▶ M (*conjetura*) presupposition

pressupunha *etc* [presu'puɲa] VB *ver* **pressupor**

pressupus *etc* [presu'pus] VB *ver* **pressupor**

pressupuser *etc* [presu'puzer] VB *ver* **pressupor**

pressurização [presuriza'sãw] F pressurization

pressurizado, -a [presuri'zadu, a] ADJ pressurized

pressuroso, -a [presu'rozu, ɔza] ADJ (*apressado*) hurried, in a hurry; (*zeloso*) keen, eager

prestação [presta'sãw] (*pl* **-ões**) F instalment (BRIT), installment (US); (*por uma casa*) repayment; **à** ~, **a prestações** in instal(l)ments; ~ **de contas/serviços** accounts/services rendered

prestamente [presta'mẽtʃi] ADV promptly

prestamista [presta'mista] M/F
moneylender; (*comprador*) person paying
hire purchase (BRIT) *ou* on the installment
plan (US)

prestar [pres'tar] VT (*cuidados*) to give; (*favores,
serviços*) to do; (*contas*) to render; (*informações*)
to supply; (*uma qualidade a algo*) to lend ▶ VI:
~ a alguém para algo to be of use to sb for
sth; **prestar-se** VR: **~-se a** (*servir*) to be
suitable for; (*admitir*) to lend o.s. to; (*dispor-se*)
to be willing to; **~ atenção** to pay attention;
~ juramento to take an oath; **isto não
presta para nada** it's absolutely useless;
ele não presta he's good for nothing;
~ homenagem/culto a to pay tribute to/
worship

prestativo, -a [presta'tʃivu, a] ADJ helpful,
obliging

prestável [pres'tavew] (*pl* **-eis**) ADJ serviceable

prestes ['prɛstʃis] ADJ INV (*pronto*) ready; (*a ponto
de*): **~ a partir** about to leave

presteza [pres'teza] F (*prontidão*) promptness;
(*rapidez*) speed; **com ~** promptly

prestidigitação [prestʃidiʒiʒita'sãw] F sleight
of hand, conjuring, magic tricks *pl*

prestidigitador [prestʃidiʒiʒita'dor] M
conjurer, magician

prestigiar [prestʃi'ʒjar] VT to give prestige to

prestígio [pres'tʃiʒu] M prestige

prestigioso, -a [prestʃi'ʒozu, ɔza] ADJ
prestigious, eminent

préstimo ['prestʃimu] M use, usefulness;
préstimos MPL (*obséquios*) favours (BRIT),
favors (US), services; **sem ~** useless,
worthless

presto, -a ['prɛstu, a] ADJ swift

presumido, -a [prezu'midu, a] ADJ vain,
self-important

presumir [prezu'mir] VT to presume

presunção [prezũ'sãw] (*pl* **-ões**) F (*suposição*)
presumption; (*vaidade*) conceit, self-
importance

presunçoso, -a [prezũ'sozu, ɔza] ADJ vain,
self-important

presunto [pre'zũtu] M ham; (*col: cadáver*) stiff

pret-à-porter [prɛtapor'te] ADJ INV ready-to-
wear

pretendente [pretẽ'dẽtʃi] M/F claimant;
(*candidato*) candidate, applicant ▶ M (*de uma
mulher*) suitor

pretender [pretẽ'der] VT to claim; (*cargo,
emprego*) to go for; **~ fazer** to intend to do

pretensamente [pretẽsa'mẽtʃi] ADV
supposedly

pretensão [pretẽ'sãw] (*pl* **-ões**) F (*reivindicação*)
claim; (*vaidade*) pretension; (*propósito*) aim;
(*aspiração*) aspiration; **pretensões** FPL
(*presunção*) pretentiousness

pretensioso, -a [pretẽ'sjozu, ɔza] ADJ
pretentious

pretenso, -a [pre'tẽsu, a] ADJ alleged,
supposed

pretensões [pretẽ'sõjs] FPL *de* **pretensão**

preterir [prete'rir] VT (*desprezar*) to ignore;
(*deixar de promover*) to pass over; (*ocupar cargo
de*) to displace; (*ser usado em lugar de*) to usurp;
(*omitir*) to disregard

pretérito [pre'tɛritu] M (*Ling*) preterite

pretextar [pretes'tar] VT to give as an excuse

pretexto [pre'testu] M pretext, excuse; **a ~ de**
on the pretext of

preto, -a ['pretu, a] ADJ black; **pôr o ~ no
branco** to put it down in writing

preto e branco ADJ INV (*filme, TV*) black and
white

pretume [pre'tumi] M blackness

prevalecente [prevale'sẽtʃi] ADJ prevalent

prevalecer [prevale'ser] VI to prevail;
prevalecer-se VR: **~-se de** (*aproveitar-se*) to
take advantage of; **~ sobre** to outweigh

prevaricar [prevari'kar] VI (*faltar ao dever*) to
fail in one's duty; (*proceder mal*) to behave
badly; (*cometer adultério*) to commit adultery

prevê *etc* [pre've] VB *ver* **prever**

prevejo *etc* [pre'veʒu] VB *ver* **prever**

prevenção [prevẽ'sãw] (*pl* **-ões**) F (*ato de evitar*)
prevention; (*preconceito*) prejudice; (*cautela*)
caution; **estar de ~ com** *ou* **contra alguém**
to be bias(s)ed against sb

prevenido, -a [preve'nidu, a] ADJ (*cauteloso*)
cautious, wary; (*avisado*) forewarned;
estar ~ (*com dinheiro*) to have cash on one

prevenir [preve'nir] VT (*evitar*) to prevent;
(*avisar*) to warn; (*preparar*) to prepare;
prevenir-se VR: **~-se contra** (*acautelar-se*) to
be wary of; **~-se de** (*equipar-se*) to equip o.s.
with; **~-se para** to prepare (o.s.) for

preventivo, -a [prevẽ'tʃivu, a] ADJ
preventive

prever [pre'ver] (*irreg: como* **ver**) VT to predict,
foresee; (*pressupor*) to presuppose

pré-vestibular [-vestʃibu'lar] ADJ (*curso*)
preparing for university entry ▶ M
preparation for university entry

previa *etc* [pre'via] VB *ver* **prever**

prévia ['prɛvja] F opinion poll

previamente [prevja'mẽtʃi] ADJ previously

previdência [previ'dẽsja] F (*previsão*)
foresight; (*precaução*) precaution; **~ social**
social welfare; (*instituição*) = DSS (BRIT),
= Welfare Department (US)

previdente [previ'dẽtʃi] ADJ: **ser ~** to show
foresight

previno *etc* [pre'vinu] VB *ver* **prevenir**

prévio, -a ['prɛvju, a] ADJ prior; (*preliminar*)
preliminary

previr *etc* [pre'vir] VB *ver* **prever**

previsão [previ'zãw] (*pl* **-ões**) F (*antevisão*)
foresight; (*prognóstico*) prediction, forecast;
~ do tempo weather forecast

previsível [previ'zivew] (*pl* **-eis**) ADJ
predictable

previsões [previ'zõjs] FPL *de* **previsão**

previsto, -a [pre'vistu, a] PP *de* **prever** ▶ ADJ
predicted; (*na lei etc*) prescribed

p

prezado, -a [pre'zadu, a] ADJ esteemed; (*numa carta*) dear

prezar [pre'zar] VT (*amigos*) to value highly; (*autoridade*) to respect; (*gostar de*) to appreciate; **prezar-se** VR (*ter dignidade*) to have self-respect; **~-se de** (*orgulhar-se*) to pride o.s. on

primado [pri'madu] M (*primazia*) primacy

prima-dona (*pl* **prima-donas**) F leading lady

primar [pri'mar] VI to excel, stand out

primário, -a [pri'marju, a] ADJ primary; (*elementar*) basic, rudimentary; (*primitivo*) primitive ▶ M (*curso*) elementary education

primata [pri'mata] M (*Zool*) primate

primavera [prima'vɛra] F spring; (*planta*) primrose

primaveril [primave'riw] (*pl* -**is**) ADJ spring atr; (*pessoa*) youthful, young

primaz [pri'majz] M primate

primazia [prima'zia] F primacy; (*prioridade*) priority; (*superioridade*) superiority

primeira [pri'mejra] F (*Auto*) first (gear)

primeira-dama (*pl* **primeiras-damas**) F (*Pol*) first lady

primeiranista [primejra'nista] M/F first-year (student)

primeiro, -a [pri'mejru, a] ADJ first; (*fundamental*) prime ▶ ADV first; **de primeira** (*pessoa, restaurante*) first-class; (*carne*) prime; **viajar de primeira** to travel first class; **à primeira vista** at first sight; **em ~ lugar** first of all; **de ~** first; **primeira página** (*de jornal*) front page; **ele foi o ~ que disse isso** he was the first to say this

primeiro-time (*col*) ADJ INV top-notch, first-rate

primitivo, -a [primi'tʃivu, a] ADJ primitive; (*original*) original

primo, -a ['primu, a] M/F cousin; **~ irmão** first cousin; **~ em segundo grau** second cousin; (*número*) **~** prime number

primogênito, -a [primo'ʒenitu, a] ADJ, M/F first-born

primor [pri'mor] M excellence, perfection; (*beleza*) beauty; **com ~** to perfection; **é um ~** it's perfect

primordial [primor'dʒjaw] (*pl* -**ais**) ADJ (*primitivo*) primordial, primeval; (*principal*) principal, fundamental

primórdio [pri'mɔrdʒju] M origin

primoroso, -a [primo'rozu, ɔza] ADJ (*excelente*) excellent; (*belo*) exquisite

princesa [prĩ'seza] F princess

principado [prĩsi'padu] M principality

principal [prĩsi'paw] (*pl* -**ais**) ADJ principal; (*entrada, razão, rua*) main ▶ M (*chefe*) head, principal; (*essencial, de dívida*) principal ▶ F (*Ling*) main clause

príncipe ['prĩsipi] M prince

principiante [prĩsi'pjãtʃi] M/F beginner

principiar [prĩsi'pjar] VT, VI to begin; **~ a fazer** to begin to do

princípio [prĩ'sipju] M (*começo*) beginning, start; (*origem*) origin; (*legal, moral*) principle; **princípios** MPL (*de matéria*) rudiments; **em ~** in principle; **no ~** in the beginning; **por ~** on principle; **do ~ ao fim** from beginning to end; **uma pessoa de ~s** a person of principle

prior [prjor] M (*sacerdote*) parish priest; (*de convento*) prior

prioridade [prjori'dadʒi] F priority; **ter ~ sobre** to have priority over

prioritário, -a [prjori'tarju, a] ADJ priority atr

prisão [pri'zãw] (*pl* -**ões**) F (*encarceramento*) imprisonment; (*cadeia*) prison, jail; (*detenção*) arrest; **ordem de ~** arrest warrant; **~ perpétua** life imprisonment; **~ preventiva** protective custody; **~ de ventre** constipation

prisioneiro, -a [prizjo'nejru, a] M/F prisoner

prisma ['prizma] M prism; **sob esse ~** (*fig*) in this light, from this angle

prisões [pri'zõjs] FPL *de* **prisão**

privação [priva'sãw] (*pl* -**ões**) F deprivation; **privações** FPL (*penúria*) hardship *sg*

privacidade [privasi'dadʒi] F privacy

privações [priva'sõjs] FPL *de* **privação**

privada [pri'vada] F toilet

privado, -a [pri'vadu, a] ADJ (*particular*) private; (*carente*) deprived

privar [pri'var] VT to deprive; **privar-se** VR: **~-se de algo** to deprive o.s. of sth, go without sth; **~ alguém de algo** to deprive sb of sth

privativo, -a [priva'tʃivu, a] ADJ (*particular*) private; **~ de** peculiar to

privatização [privatʃiza'sãw] (*pl* -**ões**) F privatization

privatizar [privatʃi'zar] VT to privatize

privilegiado, -a [privile'ʒjadu, a] ADJ privileged; (*excepcional*) unique, exceptional

privilegiar [privile'ʒjar] VT to privilege; (*favorecer*) to favour (BRIT), favor (US)

privilégio [privi'lɛʒu] M privilege

pro [pru] (*col*) = **para + o**

pró [prɔ] ADV for, in favour (BRIT) *ou* favor (US) ▶ M advantage; **os ~s e os contras** the pros and cons; **em ~ de** in favo(u)r of

pró- [prɔ] PREFIXO pro-; **~americano** pro-American

proa ['proa] F prow, bow

proativo, -a [proa'tʃivu, a] ADJ pro-active

probabilidade [probabili'dadʒi] F probability, likelihood; **probabilidades** FPL (*chances*) odds; **segundo todas as ~s** in all probability

probabilíssimo, -a [probabi'lisimu, a] ADJ SUPERL *de* **provável**

problema [prob'lɛma] M problem

problemática [proble'matʃika] F problematics *sg*; (*problemas*) problems *pl*

problemático, -a [proble'matʃiku, a] ADJ problematic

procedência [prose'dẽsja] F (*origem*) origin, source; (*lugar de saída*) point of departure

procedente [prose'dẽtʃi] ADJ (*oriundo*) derived, rising; (*lógico*) logical

proceder [prose'der] VI (*ir adiante*) to proceed; (*comportar-se*) to behave; (*agir*) to act; (*Jur*) to take legal action ▶ M conduct; **~ a** to carry out; **~ de** (*originar-se*) to originate from; (*descender*) to be descended from

procedimento [prosedʒi'mẽtu] M (*comportamento*) conduct, behaviour (BRIT), behavior (US); (*processo*) procedure; (*Jur*) proceedings pl

procela [pro'sɛla] F storm, tempest

proceloso, -a [prose'lozu, ɔza] ADJ stormy

prócer ['prɔser] M chief, leader

processador [prosesa'dor] M processor; **~ de texto** word processor

processamento [prosesa'mẽtu] M (*de requerimentos, dados*) processing; (*Jur*) prosecution; (*verificação*) verification; (*de depoimentos*) taking down; **~ de dados** data processing; **~ por lotes** batch processing; **~ de texto** word processing

processar [prose'sar] VT (*Jur*) to take proceedings against, prosecute; (*verificar*) to check, verify; (*depoimentos*) to take down; (*requerimentos, dados*) to process

processo [pro'sɛsu] M process; (*procedimento*) procedure; (*Jur*) lawsuit, legal proceedings pl; (: *autos*) record; (*conjunto de documentos*) documents pl; (*de uma doença*) course, progress; **abrir um ~ (contra alguém)** to start legal proceedings (against sb); **~ inflamatório** (*Med*) inflammation

procissão [prosi'sãw] (*pl* **-ões**) F procession

proclamação [proklama'sãw] (*pl* **-ões**) F proclamation

Proclamação da República *see note*

> Commemorated on 15 November, which is a Brazilian holiday, the proclamation of the republic in 1889 was a military coup, led by Marshal Deodoro da Fonseca. It brought down the empire which had been established after independence and installed a federal republic in Brazil.

proclamar [prokla'mar] VT to proclaim

proclamas [pro'klamas] MPL banns

procrastinar [prokrastʃi'nar] VT to put off ▶ VI to procrastinate

procriação [prokrja'sãw] F procreation

procriar [pro'krjar] VT, VI to procreate

procura [pro'kura] F search; (*Com*) demand; **em ~ de** in search of

procuração [prokura'sãw] (*pl* **-ões**) F power of attorney; (*documento*) letter of attorney; **por ~** by proxy

procurado, -a [proku'radu, a] ADJ sought after, in demand

procurador, a [prokura'dor(a)] M/F (*advogado*) attorney; (*mandatário*) proxy; **P~ Geral da República** Attorney General

procurar [proku'rar] VT to look for, seek; (*emprego*) to apply for; (*ir visitar*) to call on, go

and see; (*contatar*) to get in touch with; **~ fazer** to try to do

prodigalizar [prodʒigali'zar] VT (*gastar excessivamente*) to squander; (*dar com profusão*) to lavish

prodígio [pro'dʒiʒu] M prodigy

prodigioso, -a [prodʒi'ʒozu, ɔza] ADJ prodigious, marvellous (BRIT), marvelous (US)

pródigo, -a ['prɔdʒigu, a] ADJ (*perdulário*) wasteful; (*generoso*) lavish; **filho ~** prodigal son

produção [produ'sãw] (*pl* **-ões**) F production; (*volume de produção*) output; (*produto*) product; **~ em massa** *ou* **série** mass production

produtividade [produtʃivi'dadʒi] F productivity

produtivo, -a [produ'tʃivu, a] ADJ productive; (*rendoso*) profitable

produto [pro'dutu] M product; (*renda*) proceeds pl, profit; **~s alimentícios** foodstuffs; **~s agrícolas** agricultural produce sg; **ser ~ de** to be a product of; **~ nacional bruto** gross national product; **~s acabados/semiacabados** finished/semi-finished products

produtor, a [produ'tor(a)] ADJ producing ▶ M/F producer

produzido, -a [produ'zidu, a] ADJ trendy

produzir [produ'zir] VT to produce; (*ocasionar*) to cause, bring about; (*render*) to bring in ▶ VI to be productive; (*Econ*) to produce

proeminência [proemi'nẽsja] F prominence; (*protuberância*) protuberance; (*elevação de terreno*) elevation

proeminente [proemi'nẽtʃi] ADJ prominent

proeza [pro'eza] F achievement, feat

profanação [profana'sãw] F sacrilege, profanation

profanar [profa'nar] VT to desecrate, profane

profano, -a [pro'fanu, a] ADJ profane; (*secular*) secular ▶ M/F layman/woman

profecia [profe'sia] F prophecy

proferir [profe'rir] VT to utter; (*sentença*) to pronounce; **~ um discurso** to make a speech

professar [profe'sar] VT to profess; (*profissão*) to practise (BRIT), practice (US) ▶ VI (*Rel*) to take religious vows

professo, -a [pro'fɛsu, a] ADJ (*católico etc*) confirmed; (*político etc*) seasoned

professor, a [profe'sor(a)] M/F teacher; (*universitário*) lecturer; **~ titular** *ou* **catedrático** (university) professor; **~ associado** reader

professorado [profeso'radu] M (*professores*) teachers pl; (*magistério*) teaching profession

profeta, -tisa [pro'fɛta, profe'tʃiza] M/F prophet

profético, -a [pro'fɛtʃiku, a] ADJ prophetic

profetisa [profe'tʃiza] F *de* **profeta**

profetizar [profetʃi'zar] VT, VI to prophesy, predict

proficiência [profi'sjẽsja] F proficiency, competence

proficiente [profi'sjẽtʃi] ADJ proficient, competent

profícuo, -a [pro'fikwu, a] ADJ useful, advantageous

profiro etc [pro'firu] VB ver **proferir**

profissão [profi'sãw] (pl **-ões**) F (ofício) profession; (de fé) declaration; ~ **liberal** liberal profession

profissional [profisjo'naw] (pl **-ais**) ADJ, M/F professional

profissionalizante [profisjonali'zãtʃi] ADJ (ensino) vocational

profissionalizar [profisjonali'zar] VT to professionalize; **profissionalizar-se** VR to turn professional; (atividade) to become professional

profissões [profi'sõjs] FPL de **profissão**

profundas [pro'fũdas] FPL depths

profundidade [profũdʒi'dadʒi] F depth; (fig) profoundness, depth; **tem 4 metros de ~** it is 4 metres ou meters deep

profundo, -a [pro'fũdu, a] ADJ deep; (fig) profound

profusão [profu'zãw] F profusion, abundance

profuso, -a [pro'fuzu, a] ADJ (abundante) profuse, abundant

progênie [pro'ʒeni] F (ascendência) lineage; (prole) offspring, progeny

progenitor, a [proʒeni'tor(a)] M/F ancestor; (pai/mãe) father/mother

prognosticar [prognostʃi'kar] VT to predict, forecast ▶ VI (Med) to make a prognosis

prognóstico [prog'nɔstʃiku] M prediction, forecast; (Med) prognosis

programa [pro'grama] M programme (BRIT), program (US); (Comput) program; (plano) plan; (diversão) thing to do; (de um curso) syllabus; **fazer um ~** to go out; ~ **de índio** (col) boring thing to do

programação [programa'sãw] F planning; (TV, Rádio, Comput) programming; ~ **visual** graphic design

programador, a [programa'dor(a)] M/F programmer; ~ **visual** graphic designer

programar [progra'mar] VT to plan; (Comput) to program

programável [progra'mavew] (pl **-eis**) ADJ programmable

progredir [progre'dʒir] VI to progress, make progress; (avançar) to move forward; (infecção) to progress

progressão [progre'sãw] F progression

progressista [progre'sista] ADJ, M/F progressive

progressivo, -a [progre'sivu, a] ADJ progressive; (gradual) gradual

progresso [pro'grɛsu] M progress

progrido etc [pro'gridu] VB ver **progredir**

proibição [proibi'sãw] (pl **-ões**) F prohibition, ban

proibir [proi'bir] VT to prohibit, forbid; (livro, espetáculo) to ban; **"é proibido fumar"** "no smoking"; ~ **alguém de fazer**, ~ **que alguém faça** to forbid sb to do

proibitivo, -a [proibi'tʃivu, a] ADJ prohibitive

projeção [proʒe'sãw] (pl **-ões**) F projection; (arremesso) throwing; (proeminência) prominence; **tempo de ~** (de filme) running time

projetar [proʒe'tar] VT to project; (arremessar) to throw; (planejar) to plan; (Arq, Tec) to design; **projetar-se** VR (lançar-se) to hurl o.s.; (sombra etc) to fall; (delinear-se) to jut out; ~ **fazer** to plan to do

projétil [pro'ʒetʃiw] (pl **-eis**) M projectile, missile; (Mil) missile

projetista [proʒe'tʃista] ADJ design atr ▶ M/F designer

projeto [pro'ʒɛtu] M (empreendimento) project; (plano) plan; (Tec) design; (de tese etc) draft; ~ **de lei** bill; ~ **assistido por computador** computer-aided design

projetor [proʒe'tor] M (Cinema) projector; (holofote) searchlight

prol [prɔw] M advantage; **em ~ de** on behalf of, for the benefit of

pró-labore [-la'bɔri] M remuneration, wage

prolapso [pro'lapsu] M (Med) prolapse

prole ['prɔli] F offspring, progeny

proletariado [proleta'rjadu] M proletariat

proletário, -a [prole'tarju, a] ADJ, M/F proletarian

proliferação [prolifera'sãw] F proliferation

proliferar [prolife'rar] VI to proliferate

prolífico, -a [pro'lifiku, a] ADJ prolific

prolixo, -a [pro'liksu, a] ADJ long-winded, tedious

prólogo ['prɔlogu] M prologue

prolongação [prolõga'sãw] F extension

prolongado, -a [prolõ'gadu, a] ADJ (demorado) prolonged; (alongado) extended

prolongamento [prolõga'mẽtu] M extension

prolongar [prolõ'gar] VT (tornar mais longo) to extend, lengthen; (decisão etc) to postpone; (vida) to prolong; **prolongar-se** VR to extend; (durar) to last

promessa [pro'mɛsa] F promise; (compromisso) pledge

prometedor, a [promete'dor(a)] ADJ promising

prometer [prome'ter] VT to promise ▶ VI to promise; (ter potencial) to show promise; ~ **fazer/que** to promise to do/that

prometido, -a [prome'tʃidu, a] ADJ promised ▶ M: **o ~** what one promised; **cumprir o ~** to keep one's promise

promiscuidade [promiskwi'dadʒi] F (sexual) promiscuity; (desordem) untidiness

promiscuir-se [promis'kwirsi] VR: ~ **(com)** to mix (with)

promíscuo, -a [pro'miskwu, a] ADJ (misturado) disorderly, mixed up; (comportamento sexual) promiscuous

promissor, a [promi'sor(a)] ADJ promising
promissório, -a [promi'sɔrju, a] ADJ, F: **(nota)**
promissória promissory note
promoção [promo'sãw] (*pl* **-ões**) F promotion;
fazer ~ de alguém/algo to promote sb/sth
promontório [promõ'tɔrju] M headland,
promontory
promotor, a [promo'tor(a)] ADJ promoting
▶ M/F promoter; (*Jur*) prosecutor; **~ público**
public prosecutor
promover [promo'ver] VT (*dar impulso a*) to
promote; (*causar*) to bring about; (*elevar a
cargo superior*) to promote; (*reunião, encontro*) to
arrange
promulgação [promuwga'sãw] F
promulgation
promulgar [promuw'gar] VT (*lei etc*) to
promulgate; (*tornar público*) to declare
publicly
pronome [pro'nɔmi] M pronoun
pronta-entrega (*pl* **pronta-entregas**) F
immediate delivery department
prontidão [prõtʃi'dãw] F (*estar preparado*)
readiness; (*rapidez*) promptness, speed;
estar de ~ to be at the ready
prontificar [prõtʃifi'kar] VT to have ready;
prontificar-se VR: **~-se a fazer/para algo** to
volunteer to do/for sth
pronto, -a [prõtu, a] ADJ ready; (*rápido*) quick,
speedy; (*imediato*) prompt; (*col: sem dinheiro*)
broke ▶ ADV promptly; **de ~** promptly; **estar
~ a ...** to be prepared *ou* willing to ...; **(e) ~!**
(and) that's that!
pronto-socorro (*pl* **prontos-socorros**) M (*BR*)
casualty (*BRIT*), emergency room (*US*); (*PT:
reboque*) tow truck
prontuário [prõ'twarju] M (*manual*)
handbook; (*policial*) record
pronúncia [pro'nũsja] F pronunciation; (*Jur*)
indictment
pronunciação [pronũsja'sãw] (*pl* **-ões**) F
pronouncement; (*Ling*) pronunciation
pronunciamento [pronũsja'mẽtu] M
proclamation, pronouncement
pronunciar [pronũ'sjar] VT to pronounce;
(*discurso*) to make, deliver; (*Jur: réu*) to indict;
(*: sentença*) to pass; **pronunciar-se** VR (*expressar
opinião*) to express one's opinion; **~ mal** to
mispronounce
propagação [propaga'sãw] F propagation;
(*fig: difusão*) dissemination
propaganda [propa'gãda] F (*Pol*) propaganda;
(*Com*) advertising; (*: uma propaganda*) advert,
advertisement; **fazer ~ de** to advertise
propagar [propa'gar] VT to propagate; (*fig:
difundir*) to disseminate
propender [propẽ'der] VI to lean; **~ para algo**
(*fig*) to incline *ou* tend towards sth
propensão [propẽ'sãw] (*pl* **-ões**) F inclination,
tendency
propenso, -a [pro'pẽsu, a] ADJ: **~ a** inclined
to; **ser ~ a** to be inclined to, have a
tendency to

propensões [propẽ'sõjs] FPL *de* **propensão**
propiciar [propi'sjar] VT (*tornar favorável*) to
favour (*BRIT*), favor (*US*); (*permitir*) to allow;
(*proporcionar*) to provide
propício, -a [pro'pisju, a] ADJ (*favorável*)
favourable (*BRIT*), favorable (*US*), propitious;
(*apropriado*) appropriate
propina [pro'pina] F (*gorjeta*) tip; (*PT: cota*) fee
propor [pro'por] (*irreg: como* **pôr**) VT to propose;
(*oferecer*) to offer; (*um problema*) to pose; (*Jur:
ação*) to start, move; **propor-se** VR: **~-se (a)
fazer** (*pretender*) to intend to do; (*visar*) to aim
to do; (*dispor-se*) to decide to do; (*oferecer-se*) to
offer to do; **~-se a** *ou* **para governador** *etc* to
stand for governor *etc*
proporção [propor'sãw] (*pl* **-ões**) F proportion;
proporções FPL (*dimensões*) dimensions; **à ~
que** as
proporcionado, -a [proporsjo'nadu, a] ADJ
proportionate
proporcional [proporsjo'naw] (*pl* **-ais**) ADJ
proportional
proporcionar [proporsjo'nar] VT (*dar*) to
provide, give; (*adaptar*) to adjust, adapt
proporções [propor'sõjs] FPL *de* **proporção**
propôs [pro'pos] VB *ver* **propor**
proposição [propozi'sãw] (*pl* **-ões**) F
proposition, proposal
propositado, -a [propozi'tadu, a] ADJ
intentional
proposital [propozi'taw] (*pl* **-ais**) ADJ
intentional
propósito [pro'pɔzitu] M (*intenção*) purpose;
(*objetivo*) aim; **a ~** by the way; (*oportunamente*)
at an opportune moment; **a ~ de** with
regard to; **com o ~ de** with the purpose of;
de ~ on purpose; **fora de ~** irrelevant
proposta [pro'pɔsta] F proposal; (*oferecimento*)
offer
proposto, -a [pro'postu, 'pɔsta] PP *de* **propor**
propriamente [proprja'mẽtʃi] ADV properly,
exactly; **~ falando** *ou* **dito** strictly speaking;
a Igreja ~ dita the Church proper
propriedade [proprje'dadʒi] F property;
(*direito de proprietário*) ownership; (*o que é
apropriado*) appropriateness, propriety;
~ imobiliária real estate
proprietário, -a [proprje'tarju, a] M/F owner,
proprietor; (*de casa alugada*) landlord/lady;
(*de jornal*) publisher
próprio, -a ['prɔprju, a] ADJ (*possessivo*) own, of
one's own; (*mesmo*) very, selfsame; (*hora,
momento*) opportune, right; (*nome*) proper;
(*característico*) characteristic; (*sentido*) proper,
true; (*depois de pronome*) -self; **~ (para)**
suitable (for); **eu ~** I myself; **ele ~** he
himself; **mora em casa própria** he lives in
a house of his own; **por si ~** of one's own
accord; **o ~ homem** the very man; **ele é o ~
inglês** he's a typical Englishman; **é o ~** it's
him himself
propulsão [propuw'sãw] F propulsion; **~ a
jato** jet propulsion

propulsor, a [propuw'sor(a)] ADJ propelling ▶ M propellor

propus *etc* [pro'pus] VB *ver* **propor**

propuser *etc* [propu'zer] VB *ver* **propor**

prorrogação [prohoga'sãw] (*pl* -**ões**) F extension; (*Com*) deferment; (*Jur*) stay; (*Futebol*) extra time

prorrogar [proho'gar] VT to extend, prolong

prorrogável [proho'gavel] (*pl* -**eis**) ADJ extendible

prorromper [prohõ'per] VI (*águas, lágrimas*) to burst forth, break out; ~ **em choro/ gargalhadas** to burst into tears/burst out laughing

prosa ['prɔza] F prose; (*conversa*) chatter; (*fanfarrice*) boasting, bragging ▶ ADJ full of oneself; **ter boa ~** to have the gift of the gab

prosador, a [proza'dor(a)] M/F prose writer

prosaico, -a [pro'zajku, a] ADJ prosaic

proscênio [pro'senju] M proscenium

proscrever [proskre'ver] VT to prohibit, ban; (*expulsar*) to ban, exile; (*vícios, usos*) to do away with

proscrição [proskri'sãw] (*pl* -**ões**) F proscription; (*proibição*) prohibition, ban; (*desterro*) exile; (*abolição*) abolition

proscrito, -a [pros'kritu, a] PP *de* **proscrever** ▶ M/F (*desterrado*) exile

prosear [pro'zjar] VI to chat

prosélito [pro'zɛlitu] M convert

prosódia [pro'zɔdʒja] F prosody

prosopopeia [prozopo'pɐja] F (*fig*) diatribe; (*col: pose*) pose

prospecto [pros'pɛktu] M (*desdobrável*) leaflet; (*em forma de livro*) brochure

prospector [prospek'tor] M prospector

prosperar [prospe'rar] VI to prosper, thrive

prosperidade [prosperi'dadʒi] F prosperity; (*bom êxito*) success

próspero, -a ['prɔsperu, a] ADJ prosperous; (*bem sucedido*) successful; (*favorável*) favourable (*BRIT*), favorable (*US*)

prosseguimento [prosegi'mẽtu] M continuation

prosseguir [prose'gir] VT to continue ▶ VI to continue, go on; ~ **em** to continue (with)

próstata ['prɔstata] F prostate

prostíbulo [pros'tʃibulu] M brothel

prostituição [prostʃitwi'sãw] F prostitution

prostituir [prostʃi'twir] VT to prostitute; (*fig: desonrar*) to debase; **prostituir-se** VR (*tornar-se prostituta*) to become a prostitute; (*ser prostituta*) to be a prostitute; (*no trabalho*) to prostitute o.s.; (*corromper-se*) to be corrupted; (*desonrar-se*) to debase o.s.

prostituta [prostʃi'tuta] F prostitute

prostração [prostra'sãw] F (*cansaço*) exhaustion; (*moral*) desolation

prostrado, -a [pros'tradu, a] ADJ prostrate

prostrar [pros'trar] VT (*derrubar*) to knock down, throw down; (*extenuar*) to tire out; (*abater*) to lay low; **prostrar-se** VR to prostrate o.s.

protagonista [protago'nista] M/F protagonist

protagonizar [protagoni'zar] VT to play the lead role in; (*fig*) to be at the centre (*BRIT*) *ou* center (*US*) of

proteção [prote'sãw] F protection; (*amparo*) support, backing

protecionismo [protesjo'nizmu] M protectionism

proteger [prote'ʒer] VT to protect

protegido, -a [prote'ʒidu, a] ADJ protected ▶ M/F protégé(e)

proteína [prote'ina] F protein

protejo *etc* [pro'teʒu] VB *ver* **proteger**

protelar [prote'lar] VT to postpone, put off

PROTERRA (*BR*) ABR M = **Programa de Redistribuição da Terra e de Estímulo Agroindustrial do Norte e Nordeste**

protestante [protes'tãtʃi] ADJ, M/F Protestant

protestantismo [protestã'tʃizmu] M Protestantism

protestar [protes'tar] VT to protest; (*declarar*) to declare, affirm ▶ VI to protest

protesto [pro'tɛstu] M protest; (*declaração*) affirmation

protetor, a [prote'tor(a)] ADJ protective ▶ M/F protector; ~ **solar** sunscreen; ~ **de tela** (*Comput*) screensaver

protocolar [protoko'lar] ADJ protocol *atr* ▶ VT to record

protocolo [proto'kɔlu] M protocol; (*recibo*) record slip

protótipo [pro'tɔtʃipu] M prototype

protuberância [protube'rãsja] F bump

protuberante [protube'rãtʃi] ADJ sticking out

prova ['prɔva] F proof; (*Tec: teste*) test, trial; (*Educ: exame*) examination; (*sinal*) sign; (*de comida, bebida*) taste; (*de roupa*) fitting; (*Esporte*) competition; (*Tip*) proof; **prova(s)** F(PL) (*Jur*) evidence *sg*; **à ~** on trial; **à ~ de bala/fogo/água** bulletproof/fireproof/ waterproof; **pôr à ~** to put to the test; ~ **circunstancial/documental** (piece of) circumstantial/documentary evidence

provação [prova'sãw] F (*sofrimento*) trial

provado, -a [pro'vadu, a] ADJ proven

provar [pro'var] VT to prove; (*comida*) to taste, try; (*roupa*) to try on ▶ VI to try

provável [pro'vavew] (*pl* -**eis**) ADJ probable, likely; **é ~ que não venha** he probably won't come

provê *etc* [pro've] VB *ver* **prover**

provedor, a [prove'dor(a)] M/F provider; ~ **de acesso à Internet** internet service provider

proveio *etc* [pro'veju] VB = **provir**

proveito [pro'vejtu] M (*vantagem*) advantage; (*ganho*) profit; **em ~ de** for the benefit of; **fazer ~ de** to make use of; **tirar ~ de** to benefit from

proveitoso, -a [provej'tozu, ɔza] ADJ profitable, advantageous; (*útil*) useful

provejo *etc* [pro'veʒu] VB *ver* **prover**

proveniência [prove'njẽsja] F source, origin

proveniente [prove'njẽtʃi] ADJ: ~ **de** originating from; (que resulta de) arising from

proventos [pro'vẽtus] MPL proceeds pl

prover [pro'ver] (irreg: como **ver**) VT (fornecer) to provide, supply; (vaga) to fill ▶ VI: ~ **a** to take care of, see to; **prover-se** VR: ~-**se de algo** to provide o.s. with sth; ~ **alguém de algo** to provide sb with sth; (dotar) to endow sb with sth

provérbio [pro'vɛrbju] M proverb

proveta [pro'veta] F test tube; **bebê de** ~ test-tube baby

provi etc [pro'vi] VB ver **prover**

provia etc [pro'via] VB ver **prover**

providência [provi'dẽsja] F providence; **providências** FPL (medidas) measures, steps; **tomar** ~**s** to take steps

providencial [providẽ'sjaw] (pl -**ais**) ADJ opportune

providenciar [providẽ'sjar] VT (prover) to provide; (tomar providências) to arrange ▶ VI (tomar providências) to make arrangements, take steps; (prover): ~ **a** to make provision for; ~ **para que** to see to it that

providente [provi'dẽtʃi] ADJ provident; (prudente) prudent, careful

provido, -a [pro'vidu, a] ADJ (fornecido) supplied, provided; (cheio) full up, fully stocked

provier etc [pro'vjer] VB = **provir**

provim etc [pro'vĩ] VB = **provir**

provimento [provi'mẽtu] M provision; **dar** ~ (Jur) to grant a petition

província [pro'vĩsja] F province

provinciano, -a [provĩ'sjanu, a] ADJ provincial

provindo, -a [pro'vĩdu, a] PP = **provir** ▶ ADJ: ~ **de** coming from, originating from

provir¹ [pro'vir] (irreg: como **vir**) VI: ~ **de** to come from, derive from

provir² etc VB ver **prover**

provisão [provi'zãw] (pl -**ões**) F provision, supply; **provisões** FPL (suprimentos) provisions

provisoriamente [provizorja'mẽtʃi] ADV provisionally

provisório, -a [provi'zɔrju, a] ADJ provisional, temporary

provisto, -a [pro'vistu, a] PP de **prover**

provocação [provoka'sãw] (pl -**ões**) F provocation

provocador, a [provoka'dor(a)] ADJ provocative ▶ M/F provoker

provocante [provo'kãtʃi] ADJ provocative

provocar [provo'kar] VT to provoke; (ocasionar) to cause; (atrair) to tempt, attract; (estimular) to rouse, stimulate ▶ VI to provoke, be provocative

proximidade [prosimi'dadʒi] F proximity, nearness; (iminência) imminence; **proximidades** FPL (vizinhança) neighbourhood sg (BRIT), neighborhood sg (US), vicinity sg

próximo, -a ['prɔsimu, a] ADJ (no espaço) near, close; (no tempo) close; (seguinte) next; (amigo, parente) close; (vizinho) neighbouring (BRIT), neighboring (US) ▶ ADV near ▶ M fellow man; ~ **a** ou **de** near (to), close to; **futuro** ~ near future; **até a próxima!** see you again soon!

PRP (BR) ABR M = **Partido Renovador Progressista**

PRT (BR) ABR M = **Partido Reformador Trabalhista**

prudência [pru'dẽsja] F (comedimento) care, prudence; (cautela) care, caution

prudente [pru'dẽtʃi] ADJ sensible, prudent; (cauteloso) cautious

prumo ['prumu] M plumb line; (Náut) lead; **a** ~ perpendicularly, vertically

prurido [pru'ridu] M itch

Prússia ['prusja] F: **a** ~ Prussia

PS (BR) ABR M = **Partido Socialista**

PSB ABR M = **Partido Socialista Brasileiro**

PSC (BR) ABR M = **Partido Social Cristão**

PSD (BR) ABR M = **Partido Social Democrático**

PSDB ABR M = **Partido Social-Democrata Brasileiro**

pseudônimo [psew'donimu] M pseudonym

psicanálise [psika'nalizi] F psychoanalysis

psicanalista [psikana'lista] M/F psychoanalyst

psicanalítico, -a [psikana'litʃiku, a] ADJ psychoanalytic(al)

psicodélico, -a [psiko'dɛliku, a] ADJ psychedelic

psicologia [psikolo'ʒia] F psychology

psicológico, -a [psiko'lɔʒiku, a] ADJ psychological

psicólogo, -a [psi'kɔlogu, a] M/F psychologist

psicopata [psiko'pata] M/F psychopath

psicose [psi'kɔzi] F psychosis; **estar com** ~ **de** to be obsessed with ou by

psicossomático, -a [psikoso'matʃiku, a] ADJ psychosomatic

psicoterapeuta [psikotera'pewta] M/F psychotherapist

psicoterapia [psikotera'pia] F psychotherapy

psicótico, -a [psi'kɔtʃiku, a] ADJ psychotic

psique ['psiki] F psyche

psiquiatra [psi'kjatra] M/F psychiatrist

psiquiatria [psikja'tria] F psychiatry

psiquiátrico, -a [psi'kjatriku, a] ADJ psychiatric

psíquico, -a ['psikiku, a] ADJ psychological

psiu [psiw] EXCL hey!

PST (BR) ABR M = **Partido Social Trabalhista**

PT (BR) ABR M = **Partido dos Trabalhadores**

PTN (BR) ABR M = **Partido Tancredista Nacional**

PTR (BR) ABR M = **Partido Trabalhista Renovador**

PUA (BR) ABR M (= Pacto de Unidade e Ação) workers' movement

pua ['pua] F (de broca) bit; **sentar a** ~ **em alguém** (col) to give sb a beating

p

puberdade [puber'dadʒi] F puberty
púbere ['puberi] ADJ pubescent
púbis ['pubis] M INV pubis
publicação [publika'sãw] F publication
publicar [publi'kar] VT (editar) to publish;
(divulgar) to divulge; (proclamar) to announce
publicidade [publisi'dadʒi] F publicity; (Com)
advertising
publicitário, -a [publisi'tarju, a] ADJ publicity
atr; (Com) advertising atr ▶ M/F (Com)
advertising executive
público, -a ['publiku, a] ADJ public ▶ M public;
(Cinema, Teatro etc) audience; **em ~** in public;
o grande ~ the general public
PUC (BR) ABR F = **Pontifícia Universidade
Católica**
púcaro ['pukaru] (PT) M jug, mug
pude etc ['pudʒi] VB ver **poder**
pudera etc [pu'dɛra] VB ver **poder**
pudicícia [pudi'sisja] F modesty
pudico, -a [pu'dʒiku, a] ADJ bashful,
prudish
pudim [pu'dʒĩ] (pl **-ns**) M pudding;
~ crème caramel
pudim-flã [pudĩ'flã] M crème caramel
pudins [pu'dʒĩs] M ver **pudim**
pudor [pu'dor] M bashfulness, modesty;
(moral) decency; **atentado ao ~** indecent
assault
puerícia [pwe'risja] F childhood
puericultura [pwerikuw'tura] F child care
pueril [pwe'riw] (pl **-is**) ADJ puerile
puerilidade [pwerili'dadʒi] F childishness,
foolishness
pueris [pwe'ris] ADJ PL de **pueril**
pufe ['pufi] M pouf(fe)
pugilismo [puʒi'lizmu] M boxing
pugilista [puʒi'lista] M boxer
pugna ['pugna] F fight, struggle
pugnar [pug'nar] VI to fight
pugnaz [pug'najz] ADJ pugnacious
puído, -a ['pwidu, a] ADJ worn
puir [pwir] VT to wear thin
pujança [pu'ʒãsa] F vigour (BRIT), vigor (US),
strength; (de vegetação) lushness; **na ~ da
vida** in the prime of life
pujante [pu'ʒãtʃi] ADJ powerful; (saúde) robust
pular [pu'lar] VI to jump; (no Carnaval) to
celebrate ▶ VT (muro) to jump (over); (páginas,
trechos) to skip; **~ de alegria** to jump for joy;
~ Carnaval to celebrate Carnival; **~ corda**
to skip
pulga ['puwga] F flea; **estar/ficar com a ~
atrás da orelha** to smell a rat
pulgão [puw'gãw] (pl **-ões**) M greenfly
pulha ['puʎa] (col) M rat, creep
pulmão [puw'mãw] (pl **-ões**) M lung
pulmonar [puwmo'nar] ADJ pulmonary,
lung atr
pulo¹ ['pulu] M jump; **dar ~s (de contente)**
to be delighted; **dar um ~ em** to stop off at;
aos ~s by leaps and bounds; **a um ~ de** a
stone's throw away from; **num ~** in a flash

pulo² etc VB ver **polir**
pulôver [pu'lover] (BR) M pullover
púlpito ['puwpitu] M pulpit
puisação [puwsa'sãw] F pulsation, beating;
(Med) pulse
pulsar [puw'sar] VI (palpitar) to pulsate, throb
pulseira [puw'sejra] F bracelet; (de sapato)
strap
pulso ['puwsu] M (Anat) wrist; (Med) pulse;
(fig) vigour (BRIT), vigor (US), energy; **obra
de ~** work of great importance; **homem
de ~** energetic man; **tomar o ~ de alguém**
to take sb's pulse; **tomar o ~ de algo** (fig) to
look into sth, sound sth out; **a ~** by force
pulular [pulu'lar] VI to abound; (surgir) to
spring up; **~ de** to teem with; (de turistas,
mendigos) to be crawling with
pulverizador [puwveriza'dor] M (para líquidos
etc) spray, spray gun
pulverizar [puwveri'zar] VT to pulverize;
(líquido) to spray; (polvilhar) to dust
pum [pũ] EXCL bang! ▶ M (col) fart (!)
pumba ['pũba] EXCL zoom!
punção [pũ'sãw] (pl **-ões**) M (instrumento)
punch ▶ F (Med) puncture
Pundjab [pũ'dʒabi] M: **o ~** the Punjab
pundonor [pũdo'nor] M dignity, self-respect
pungente [pũ'ʒẽtʃi] ADJ painful
pungir [pũ'ʒir] VT to afflict ▶ VI to be painful
punguear [pũ'gjar] (col) VT (bolso) to pick;
(bolsa) to snatch
punguista [pũ'gista] M pickpocket
punha etc ['puɲa] VB ver **pôr**
punhado [pu'ɲadu] M handful
punhal [pu'ɲaw] (pl **-ais**) M dagger
punhalada [puɲa'lada] F stab
punho ['puɲu] M (Anat) fist; (de manga) cuff;
(de espada) hilt; **de (seu) próprio ~** in one's
own hand(writing)
punição [puni'sãw] (pl **-ões**) F punishment
punir [pu'nir] VT to punish
punitivo, -a [puni'tʃivu, a] ADJ punitive
punja etc ['pũʒa] VB ver **pungir**
pupila [pu'pila] F (Anat) pupil; ver tb **pupilo**
pupilo, -a [pu'pilu, a] M/F (tutelado) ward;
(aluno) pupil
purê [pu're] M purée; **~ de batatas** mashed
potatoes
pureza [pu'reza] F purity
purgação [purga'sãw] (pl **-ões**) F purge;
(purificação) purification
purgante [pur'gãtʃi] M purgative; (col: pessoa)
bore
purgar [pur'gar] VT to purge; (purificar) to purify
purgativo, -a [purga'tʃivu, a] ADJ purgative
▶ M purgative
purgatório [purga'tɔrju] M purgatory
purificação [purifika'sãw] F purification
purificar [purifi'kar] VT to purify
purista [pu'rista] M/F purist
puritanismo [purita'nizmu] M puritanism
puritano, -a [puri'tanu, a] ADJ (atitude)
puritanical; (seita) puritan ▶ M/F puritan

puro, -a ['puru, a] ADJ pure; (*uísque etc*) neat; (*verdade*) plain; (*intenções*) honourable (BRIT), honorable (US); (*estilo*) clear; **isto é pura imaginação sua** it's pure imagination on your part, you're just imagining it; **~ e simples** pure and simple

puro-sangue (*pl* **puros-sangues**) ADJ, M thoroughbred

púrpura ['purpura] F purple

purpúreo, -a [pur'purju, a] ADJ (*cor*) crimson

purpurina [purpu'rina] F metallic paint

purulento, -a [puru'lētu, a] ADJ festering, suppurating

pus¹ [pus] M pus

pus² *etc* [pujs] VB *ver* **pôr**

puser *etc* [pu'zer] VB *ver* **pôr**

pusilânime [puzi'lanimi] ADJ fainthearted; (*covarde*) cowardly

pústula ['pustula] F pustule; (*fig*) rotter

puta ['puta] (*!*) F whore; **~ que pariu!** fucking hell! (*!*); **mandar alguém para a ~ que (o) pariu** to tell sb to fuck off (*!*); *ver tb* **puto**

putativo, -a [puta'tʃivu, a] ADJ supposed

puto, -a ['putu, a] (*!*) M/F (*sem-vergonha*) bastard ▶ ADJ (*zangado*) furious; (*incrível*): **um ~ ...** a hell of a ...; **o ~ de ...** the bloody ...

putrefação [putrefa'sãw] F rotting, putrefaction

putrefato, -a [putre'fatu, a] ADJ rotten

putrefazer [putrefa'zer] (*irreg: como* **fazer**) VT to rot ▶ VI to putrefy, rot; **putrefazer-se** VR to putrefy, rot

pútrido, -a ['putridu, a] ADJ putrid, rotten

puxa ['puʃa] EXCL gosh; **~ vida!** gosh!

puxada [pu'ʃada] F pull; (*puxão*) tug; **dar uma ~** (*nos estudos*) to make an effort

puxado, -a [pu'ʃadu, a] ADJ (*col: aluguel*) steep, high; (*: curso*) tough; (*: trabalho*) hard

puxador [puʃa'dor] M handle, knob

puxão [pu'ʃãw] (*pl* **-ões**) M tug, jerk

puxa-puxa (*pl* **puxa-puxas**) M toffee

puxar [pu'ʃar] VT to pull; (*sacar*) to pull out; (*assunto*) to bring up; (*conversa*) to strike up; (*briga*) to pick ▶ VI: **~ de uma perna** to limp; **~ a** to take after; **~ por** (*alunos etc*) to push; **uma coisa puxa a outra** one thing leads to another; **os paulistas puxam pelo esse** the s is very pronounced in São Paulo

puxa-saco (*pl* **puxa-sacos**) M creep, crawler

puxo ['puʃu] M (*em parto*) push

puxões [pu'ʃõjs] MPL *de* **puxão**

Qq

Q, q [ke] (*pl* **qs**) M Q, q; **Q de Quintela** Q for Queen

q. ABR (= *quartel*) barracks

QG ABR M (= *Quartel-General*) HQ

QI ABR M (= *Quociente de Inteligência*) IQ

ql. ABR (= *quilate*) ct

qtd. ABR (= *quantidade*) qty

qua. ABR (= *quarta-feira*) Weds

quadra ['kwadra] F (*quarteirão*) block; (*de tênis etc*) court; (*período*) time, period; (*jogos*) four; (*estrofe*) quatrain

quadrado, -a [kwa'dradu, a] ADJ square; (*col: antiquado*) square ▶ M square ▶ M/F (*col*) square

quadragésimo, -a [kwadra'ʒɛzimu, a] NUM fortieth; *vertb* **quinto**

quadrangular [kwadrãgu'lar] ADJ quadrangular

quadrângulo [kwa'drãgulu] M quadrangle

quadrar [kwa'drar] VT to square, make square ▶ VI: **~ a** (*ser conveniente*) to suit; **~ com** (*condizer*) to square with

quadriculado, -a [kwadriku'ladu, a] ADJ checked; **papel ~** squared paper

quadril [kwa'driw] (*pl* **-is**) M hip

quadrilátero, -a [kwadri'lateru, a] ADJ quadrilateral

quadrilha [kwa'driʎa] F gang; (*dança*) square dance

quadrimotor [kwadrimo'tor] ADJ four-engined ▶ M four-engined plane

quadrinho [kwa'driɲu] M (*de tira*) frame; **história em ~s** (BR) cartoon, comic strip

quadris [kwa'dris] MPL *de* **quadril**

quadro ['kwadru] M (*pintura*) painting; (*gravura, foto*) picture; (*lista*) list; (*tabela*) chart, table; (*Tec: painel*) panel; (*pessoal*) staff; (*time*) team; (*Teatro, fig*) scene; (*fig: Med*) patient's condition; **~ de avisos** bulletin board; **~ de reserva** (*Mil*) reserve list; **~ branco** whiteboard; **~ clínico** clinical picture; **~ interativo** interactive whiteboard; **o ~ político** (*fig*) the political scene; **~ social** (*de um clube*) members *pl*; (*de uma empresa*) partners *pl*

quadro-negro (*pl* **quadros-negros**) M blackboard

quadrúpede [kwa'drupedʒi] ADJ, M quadruped ▶ M/F (*fig*) blockhead

quadruplicar [kwadrupli'kar] VT, VI to quadruple

quádruplo, -a ['kwadruplu, a] ADJ quadruple ▶ M quadruple ▶ M/F (*quadrigêmeo*) quad

qual [kwaw] PRON (*pl* **-ais**) which ▶ CONJ as, like ▶ EXCL what!; **~ deles** which of them; **~ é o problema/o seu nome?** what's the problem/your name?; **o ~** which; (*pessoa: suj*) who; (: *objeto*) whom; **seja ~ for** whatever *ou* whichever it may be; **cada ~** each one; **~ é? ou ~ é a tua?** (*col*) what are you up to?; **~ seja** such as; **tal ~** just like; **~ nada!, ~ o quê!** no such thing!

qual. ABR (= *qualidade*) qual

qualidade [kwali'dadʒi] F quality; **na ~ de** in the capacity of; **produto de ~** quality product

qualificação [kwalifika'sãw] (*pl* **-ões**) F qualification

qualificado, -a [kwalifi'kadu, a] ADJ qualified; **não ~** unqualified

qualificar [kwalifi'kar] VT to qualify; (*avaliar*) to evaluate; **qualificar-se** VR to qualify; **~ de** *ou* **como** to classify as

qualificativo, -a [kwalifika'tʃivu, a] ADJ qualifying ▶ M qualifier

qualitativo, -a [kwalita'tʃivu, a] ADJ qualitative

qualquer [kwaw'ker] (*pl* **quaisquer**) ADJ, PRON any; **~ pessoa** anyone, anybody; **~ um dos dois** either; **~ outro** any other; **~ dia** any day; **~ que seja** whichever it may be; **um disco ~** any record at all, any record you like; **a ~ momento** at any moment; **a ~ preço** at any price; **de ~ jeito** *ou* **maneira** anyway; (*a qualquer preço*) no matter what; (*sem cuidado*) anyhow; **um(a) ~** (*pej*) any old person

quando ['kwãdu] ADV when ▶ CONJ when; (*interrogativo*) when?; (*ao passo que*) whilst; **~ muito** at most; **~ quer que** whenever; **de ~ em ~, de vez em ~** now and then; **desde ~?** since when?; **~ mais não seja** if for no other reason; **~ de** on the occasion of; **~ menos se esperava** when we (*ou* they, I *etc*) least expected (it)

quant. ABR (= *quantidade*) quant

quantia [kwã'tʃia] F sum, amount

quantidade [kwãtʃi'dadʒi] F quantity, amount; **uma ~ de** a large amount of; **em ~** in large amounts

quantificar [kwãtʃifi'kar] VT to quantify

quantitativo, -a [kwãtʃita'tʃivu, a] ADJ quantitative

(PALAVRA-CHAVE)

quanto, -a ['kwãtu, a] ADJ **1** *(interrogativo: sg)* how much?; (: *pl*) how many?; **quanto tempo?** how long?
2 *(o que for necessário)* all that, as much as; **daremos quantos exemplares ele precisar** we'll give him as many copies as *ou* all the copies he needs
3: **tanto/tantos ... quanto** as much/ many ... as
▶ PRON **1** how much?; how many?; **quanto custa?** how much is it?; **a quanto está o jogo?** what's the score?
2: **tudo quanto** everything that, as much as
3: **tanto/tantos quanto ...** as much/as many as ...
4: **um tanto quanto** somewhat, rather
▶ ADV **1**: **quanto a** as regards; **quanto a mim** as for me
2: **quanto antes** as soon as possible
3: **quanto mais** *(principalmente)* especially; *(muito menos)* let alone; **quanto mais cedo melhor** the sooner the better
4: **tanto quanto possível** as much as possible; **tão ... quanto ...** as ... as ...
▶ CONJ: **quanto mais trabalha, mais ele ganha** the more he works, the more he earns; **quanto mais, (tanto) melhor** the more, the better

quão [kwãw] ADV how

quarenta [kwa'rẽta] NUM forty; *ver tb* **cinquenta**

quarentão, -tona [kwarẽ'tãw, 'tɔna] *(pl* **-ões/-s)** ADJ in one's forties ▶ M/F man/ woman in his/her forties

quarentena [kwarẽ'tena] F quarantine

quarentões [kwarẽ'tõjs] MPL *de* **quarentão**

quarentona [kwarẽ'tɔna] F *de* **quarentão**

quaresma [kwa'rezma] F Lent

quart. ABR = **quarteirão**

quarta ['kwarta] F (*tb*: **quarta-feira**) Wednesday; *(parte)* quarter; *(Auto)* fourth (gear); *(Mús)* fourth; **~ de final** quarter final

quarta-feira ['kwarta-'fejra] *(pl* **quartas- feiras)** F Wednesday; **~ de cinzas** Ash Wednesday; *ver tb* **terça-feira**

quartanista [kwarta'nista] M/F fourth-year

quarteirão [kwartej'rãw] *(pl* **-ões)** M *(de casas)* block

quartel [kwar'tɛw] *(pl* **-éis)** M barracks *sg*

quartel-general *(pl* **quartéis-generais)** M headquarters *pl*

quarteto [kwar'tetu] M *(Mús)* quartet(te); **~ de cordas** string quartet

quarto, -a ['kwartu, a] NUM fourth ▶ M *(quarta parte)* quarter; *(aposento)* bedroom; *(Mil)* watch; *(anca)* haunch; **~ de banho** bathroom; **~ de dormir** bedroom; **~ de casal** double bedroom; **~ de solteiro** single room; **~ crescente/minguante** *(Astronomia)* first/last quarter; **três ~s de hora** three quarters of an hour; **passar um mau ~ de hora** *(fig)* to have a rough time; *ver tb* **quinto**

quarto e sala *(pl* **quarto e salas)** M two-room apartment

quartzo ['kwartsu] M quartz

quase ['kwazi] ADV almost, nearly; **~ nada** hardly anything; **~ nunca** hardly ever; **~ sempre** nearly always

quaternário, -a [kwater'narju, a] ADJ quaternary

quatorze [kwa'torzi] NUM fourteen; *ver tb* **cinco**

quatro ['kwatru] NUM four ▶ M: **~ por ~** four-by-four; **estar/ficar de ~** to be/get down on all fours; *ver tb* **cinco**

quatrocentos, -tas [kwatro'sẽtus, tas] NUM four hundred

(PALAVRA-CHAVE)

que [ki] CONJ **1** *(com oração subordinada: muitas vezes não se traduz)* that; **ele disse que viria** he said (that) he would come; **não há nada que fazer** there's nothing to be done; **espero que sim/não** I hope so/not; **dizer que sim/não** to say yes/no
2 *(consecutivo: muitas vezes não se traduz)* that; **é tão pesado que não consigo levantá-lo** it's so heavy (that) I can't lift it
3 *(comparações)*: **(do) que** than; *ver tb* **mais, menos, mesmo**
▶ PRON **1** *(coisa)* which, that; *(+ prep)* which; **o chapéu que você comprou** the hat (that *ou* which) you bought
2 *(pessoa: suj)* who, that; *(: complemento)* whom, that; **o amigo que me levou ao museu** the friend who took me to the museum; **a moça que eu convidei** the girl (that *ou* whom) I invited
3 *(interrogativo)* what?; **o que você disse?** what did you say?
4 *(exclamação)* what!; **que pena!** what a pity!; **que lindo!** how lovely!

quê [ke] M *(col)* something ▶ PRON what; **~!** what!; **não tem de ~** don't mention it; **para ~?** what for?; **por ~?** why?; **sem ~ nem por ~** for no good reason, all of a sudden

Quebec [ke'bɛk] N Quebec

quebra ['kɛbra] F break, rupture; *(falência)* bankruptcy; *(de energia elétrica)* cut; *(de disciplina)* breakdown; **de ~** in addition; **~ de página** *(Comput)* page break

quebra-cabeça *(pl* **quebra-cabeças)** M puzzle, problem; *(jogo)* jigsaw puzzle

quebrada [ke'brada] F *(vertente)* slope; *(barranco)* ravine, gully

q

quebradiço, -a [kebra'dʒisu, a] ADJ fragile, breakable

quebrado, -a [ke'bradu, a] ADJ broken; *(cansado)* exhausted; *(falido)* bankrupt; *(carro, máquina)* broken down; *(telefone)* out of order; *(col: pronto)* broke

quebrados [ke'bradus] MPL loose change *sg*

quebra-galho *(pl* **quebra-galhos)** *(col)* M lifesaver

quebra-gelos M INV *(Náut)* icebreaker

quebra-mar *(pl* **quebra-mares)** M breakwater, sea wall

quebra-molas M INV speed bump, sleeping policeman

quebra-nozes M INV nutcrackers *pl* (BRIT), nutcracker (US)

quebrantar [kebrã'tar] VT to break; *(entusiasmo, ânimo)* to dampen; *(debilitar)* to weaken, wear out; **quebrantar-se** VR *(tornar-se fraco)* to grow weak

quebranto [ke'brãtu] M *(fraqueza)* weakness; *(mau-olhado)* evil eye

quebra-pau *(pl* **quebra-paus)** *(col)* M row

quebra-quebra *(pl* **quebra-quebras)** M riot

quebrar [ke'brar] VT to break; *(entusiasmo)* to dampen; *(espancar)* to beat; *(dobrar)* to bend ▶ VI to break; *(carro)* to break down; *(Com)* to go bankrupt; *(ficar sem dinheiro)* to go broke

quebra-vento *(pl* **quebra-ventos)** M *(Auto)* fanlight

quéchua ['kɛʃwa] M *(Ling)* Quechua

queda ['kɛda] F fall; *(fig: ruína)* downfall; **ter ~ para algo** to have a bent for sth; **ter uma ~ por alguém** to have a soft spot for sb; **~ de barreira** landslide; **~ de braço** arm wrestling; *(fig)* stand-off

queda-d'água *(pl* **quedas-d'água)** F waterfall

queijada [kej'ʒada] F cheesecake

queijadinha [kejʒa'dʒiɲa] F coconut sweet

queijeira [kej'ʒejra] F cheese dish

queijo ['kejʒu] M cheese; **~ de minas** ≈ Cheshire cheese; **~ do reino** ≈ Edam cheese; **~ prato** ≈ cheddar cheese; **~ ralado** grated cheese

queima ['kejma] F burning; *(Com)* clearance sale

queimada [kej'mada] F burning (of forests)

queimado, -a [kej'madu, a] ADJ burnt; *(de sol: machucado)* sunburnt; *(: bronzeado)* brown, tanned; *(plantas, folhas)* dried up; **cheiro/ gosto de ~** smell of burning/burnt taste

queimadura [kejma'dura] F burn; *(de sol)* sunburn; **~ de primeiro/terceiro grau** first-/third-degree burn

queimar [kej'mar] VT to burn; *(roupa)* to scorch; *(com líquido)* to scald; *(bronzear a pele)* to tan; *(planta, folha)* to wither; *(calorias)* to burn off ▶ VI to burn; *(estar quente)* to be burning hot; *(lâmpada, fusível)* to blow; **queimar-se** VR *(pessoa)* to burn o.s.; *(bronzear-se)* to tan; *(zangar-se)* to get angry

queima-roupa F: **à ~** point-blank, at point-blank range

queira *etc* ['kejra] VB *ver* **querer**

queixa ['kejʃa] F complaint; *(lamentação)* lament; **fazer ~ de alguém** to complain about sb; **ter ~ de alguém** to have a problem with sb

queixa-crime *(pl* **queixas-crime(s))** F *(Jur)* citation

queixada [kej'ʃada] F *(de animal)* jaw; *(queixo grande)* prominent chin

queixar-se [kej'ʃarsi] VR to complain; **~ de** to complain about; *(dores etc)* to complain of

queixo ['kejʃu] M chin; *(maxilar)* jaw; **ficar de ~ caído** to be open-mouthed; **bater o ~** to shiver

queixoso, -a [kej'ʃozu, ɔza] ADJ complaining; *(magoado)* doleful ▶ M/F *(Jur)* plaintiff

queixume [kej'ʃumi] M complaint; *(lamentação)* lament

quem [kẽj] PRON who; *(como objeto)* who(m); **~ quer que** whoever; **seja ~ for** whoever it may be; **de ~ é isto?** whose is this?, ~ é? who is it?; **a pessoa com ~ trabalha** the person he works with; **para ~ você deu o livro?** who did you give the book to?; **convi... ce quiser** invite whoever you want; **~ disse isso, se enganou** whoever said that was wrong; **~ fez isso fui eu** it was me who did it, the person who did it was me; **~ diria!** who would have thought (it)!; **~ me dera ser rico** if only I were rich; **~ me dera que isso não fosse verdade** I wish it weren't true; **~ sabe** *(talvez)* perhaps; **~ sou eu para negar?** who am I to deny it?

Quênia ['kenja] M: **o ~** Kenya

queniano, -a [ke'njanu, a] ADJ, M/F Kenyan

quentão [kẽ'tãw] M ≈ mulled wine

quente ['kẽtʃi] ADJ hot; *(roupa)* warm; *(notícia)* reliable, solid; **o ~ agora é ...** *(col)* the big thing now is ...

quentinha [kẽ'tʃiɲa] F heatproof carton *(for food)*; *(de restaurante)* doggy bag

quentura [kẽ'tura] F heat, warmth

quer¹ [ker] CONJ: **~ ... ~ ...** whether ... or ...; **~ chova ~ não** whether it rains or not; **~ você queira, ~ não** whether you like it or not; **onde/quando/quem ~ que** wherever/ whenever/whoever; **o que ~ que seja** whatever it is; **~ chova, ~ faça sol** come rain or shine

quer² VB *ver* **querer**

querela [ke'rɛla] F dispute; *(Jur)* complaint, accusation

querelado [kere'ladu] M *(Jur)* defendant

querelador, a [kerela'dor(a)] M/F *(Jur)* plaintiff

querelante [kere'lãtʃi] M/F *(Jur)* plaintiff

querelar [kere'lar] VT *(Jur)* to prosecute, sue ▶ VI: **~ contra** *ou* **de** *(queixar-se)* to lodge a complaint against

(PALAVRA-CHAVE)

querer [ke'rer] VT **1** *(desejar)* to want; **quero mais dinheiro** I want more money; **queria**

um chá I'd like a cup of tea; **quero ajudar/ que vá** I want to help/you to go; **você vai querer sair amanhã?** do you want to go out tomorrow?; **eu vou querer uma cerveja** (*num bar etc*) I'd like a beer; **por/sem querer** intentionally/unintentionally; **como queira** as you wish
2 (*perguntas para pedir algo*): **você quer fechar a janela?** will you shut the window?; **quer me dar uma mão?** can you give me a hand?
3 (*amar*) to love
4 (*convite*): **quer entrar/sentar** do come in/ sit down
5: **querer dizer** (*significar*) to mean; (*pretender dizer*) to mean to say; **quero dizer** I mean; **quer dizer** (*com outras palavras*) in other words
▶ vɪ: **querer bem a** to be fond of
querer-se vʀ to love one another
▶ ᴍ (*vontade*) wish; (*afeto*) affection

querido, -a [ke'ridu, a] ADJ dear ▶ ᴍ/ꜰ darling; **~ no grupo/por todos** prized in the group/by all; **o ator ~ das mulheres** the women's favo(u)rite actor; **Q~ João** Dear John
quermesse [ker'mɛsi] ꜰ fête
querosene [kero'zɛni] ᴍ kerosene
querubim [keru'bī] (*pl* **-ns**) ᴍ cherubim
quesito [ke'zitu] ᴍ (*questão*) query, question; (*requisito*) requirement
questão [kes'tāw] (*pl* **-ões**) ꜰ (*pergunta*) question; (*problema*) issue, question; (*Jur*) case; (*contenda*) dispute, quarrel; **fazer ~ (de)** to insist (on); **em ~** in question; **há ~ de um ano** about a year ago; **~ de tempo/de vida ou morte** question of time/matter of life and death; **~ de ordem** point of order; **~ fechada** point of principle
questionar [kestʃjo'nar] vɪ to question ▶ vᴛ to question, call into question
questionário [kestʃjo'narju] ᴍ questionnaire
questionável [kestʃjo'navew] (*pl* **-eis**) ADJ questionable
questões [kes'tōjs] ꜰᴘʟ *de* **questão**
qui. ABR (= *quinta-feira*) Thurs
quiabo ['kjabu] ᴍ okra
quibe ['kibi] ᴍ *deep-fried mince with flour and mint*
quibebe [ki'bɛbi] ᴍ pumpkin purée
quicar [ki'kar] vᴛ (*bola*) to bounce ▶ vɪ to bounce; (*col: pessoa*) to go mad
quiche ['kiʃi] ꜰ quiche
quieto, -a ['kjɛtu, a] ADJ quiet; (*imóvel*) still; **fica ~!** be quiet!
quietude [kje'tudʒi] ꜰ calm, tranquillity
quilate [ki'latʃi] ᴍ carat; (*fig*) calibre (BRIT), caliber (US)
quilha ['kiʎa] ꜰ (*Náut*) keel
quilo ['kilu] ᴍ kilo
quilobyte [kilo'bajtʃi] ᴍ kilobyte
quilograma [kilo'grama] ᴍ kilogram
quilohertz [kilo'hɛrts] ᴍ kilohertz

quilometragem [kilome'traʒē] ꜰ number of kilometres *ou* kilometers travelled, = mileage
quilometrar [kilome'trar] vᴛ to measure in kilometres *ou* kilometers
quilométrico, -a [kilo'mɛtriku, a] ADJ (*distância*) in kilometres *ou* kilometers; (*fig: fila etc*) = mile-long
quilômetro [ki'lometru] ᴍ kilometre (BRIT), kilometer (US)
quilowatt [kilo'watʃi] ᴍ kilowatt
quimbanda [kī'bāda] ᴍ (*ritual*) macumba ceremony; (*feiticeiro*) medicine man; (*local*) macumba site
quimera [ki'mɛra] ꜰ chimera
quimérico, -a [ki'meriku, a] ADJ fantastic
química ['kimika] ꜰ chemistry; *ver tb* **químico**
químico, -a ['kimiku, a] ADJ chemical ▶ ᴍ/ꜰ chemist
quimioterapia [kimjotera'pia] ꜰ chemotherapy
quimono [ki'mɔnu] ᴍ kimono; (*penhoar*) robe
quina ['kina] ꜰ (*canto*) corner; (*de mesa etc*) edge; **de ~** edgeways (BRIT), edgewise (US)
quindim [kī'dʒī] ᴍ *sweet made of egg yolks, coconut and sugar*
quinhão [ki'ɲāw] (*pl* **-ões**) ᴍ share, portion
quinhentista [kiɲe'tʃista] ADJ sixteenth century *atr*
quinhentos, -as [ki'ɲētus, as] NUM five hundred; **isso são outros ~** (*col*) that's a different matter, that's a different kettle of fish
quinhões [ki'ɲōjs] ᴍᴘʟ *de* **quinhão**
quinina [ki'nina] ꜰ quinine
quinquagésimo, -a [kwīkwa'ʒɛzimu, a] NUM fiftieth
quinquilharias [kīkiʎa'rias] ꜰᴘʟ odds and ends; (*miudezas*) knick-knacks, trinkets
quinta ['kīta] ꜰ (*tb*: **quinta-feira**) Thursday; (*propriedade*) estate; (ᴘᴛ) farm
quinta-essência (*pl* **quinta-essências**) ꜰ quintessence
quinta-feira ['kīta-'fejra] (*pl* **quintas-feiras**) ꜰ Thursday; *ver tb* **terça-feira**
quintal [kī'taw] (*pl* **-ais**) ᴍ back yard
quintanista [kīta'nista] ᴍ/ꜰ fifth-year
quinteiro [kī'tejru] (ᴘᴛ) ᴍ farmer
quinteto [kī'tetu] ᴍ quintet(te)
quinto, -a ['kītu, a] NUM fifth; **ele tirou o ~ lugar** he came fifth; **eu fui o ~ a chegar** I was the fifth to arrive, I arrived fifth; (*numa corrida*) I came fifth
quíntuplo, -a [kī'tuplu, a] ADJ, ᴍ quintuple ▶ ᴍ/ꜰ: **~s** (*crianças*) quins, quintuplets
quinze ['kīzi] NUM fifteen; **duas e ~ a** quarter past (BRIT) *ou* after (US) two; **~ para as sete** a quarter to (BRIT) *ou* of (US) seven; *ver tb* **cinco**
quinzena [kī'zɛna] ꜰ two weeks, fortnight (BRIT); (*salário*) two weeks' wages
quinzenal [kīze'naw] (*pl* **-ais**) ADJ fortnightly
quinzenalmente [kīzenaw'mētʃi] ADV fortnightly

q

quiosque ['kjɔski] M kiosk; (de jardim) gazebo

quiproquó [kwipro'kwɔ] M
misunderstanding, mix-up

quiromante [kiro'mãtʃi] M/F palmist,
fortune teller

quis etc [kiz] VB ver **querer**

quiser etc [ki'zer] VB ver **querer**

quisto ['kistu] M cyst

quitação [kita'sãw] (pl -ões) F (remissão)
discharge, remission; (pagamento)
settlement; (recibo) receipt

quitanda [ki'tãda] F (loja) grocer's (shop)
(BRIT), grocery store (US)

quitandeiro, -a [kitã'dejru, a] M/F grocer;
(vendedor de hortaliças) greengrocer (BRIT),
produce dealer (US)

quitar [ki'tar] VT (dívida: pagar) to pay off;
(: perdoar) to cancel; (devedor) to release

quite ['kitʃi] ADJ (livre) free; (com um credor)
squared up; (igualado) even; **estar ~ (com
alguém)** to be quits (with sb)

quitute [ki'tutʃi] M titbit (BRIT), tidbit (US)

quizumba [ki'zũba] (col) F punch-up, brawl

quociente [kwo'sjẽtʃi] M quotient; **~ de
inteligência** intelligence quotient

quorum ['kwɔrũ] M quorum

quota ['kwɔta] F quota; (porção) share, portion

quotidiano, -a [kwotʃi'dʒjanu, a] ADJ
everyday

q.v. ABR (= queira ver) q.v.

Rr

R¹, r ['ɛhi] (*pl* **rs**) M R, r; **R de Roberto** R for Robert (BRIT) *ou* Roger (US)

R² ABR (= *rua*) St

R$ ABR = **real**

rã [hã] F frog

rabada [ha'bada] F (*rabo*) tail; (*fig*) tail end; (*Culin*) oxtail stew

rabanada [haba'nada] F (*Culin*) cinnamon toast; (*golpe*) blow with the tail; **dar uma ~ em alguém** (*col*) to give sb the brush-off

rabanete [haba'netʃi] M radish

rabear [ha'bjar] VI (*cão*) to wag its tail; (*navio*) to wheel around; (*carro*) to skid round

rabecão [habe'kãw] (*pl* **-ões**) M mortuary wagon

rabicho [ha'biʃu] M ponytail

rabino, -a [ha'binu, a] M/F rabbi

rabiscar [habis'kar] VT (*escrever*) to scribble; (*papel*) to scribble on ▶ VI to scribble; (*desenhar*) to doodle

rabisco [ha'bisku] M scribble

rabo ['habu] M (*cauda*) tail; (*!*) arse (*!*); **meter o ~ entre as pernas** (*fig*) to be left with one's tail between one's legs; **olhar alguém com o ~ do olho** to look at sb out of the corner of one's eye; **pegar em ~ de foguete** (*col*) to stick one's neck out; **ser ~ de foguete** (*col*) to be a minefield; **~ de cavalo** ponytail; **não poder ver um ~ de saia** to be a womanizer

rabugento, -a [habu'ʒẽtu, a] ADJ grumpy

rabugice [habu'ʒisi] F grumpiness

rabujar [habu'ʒar] VI to be grumpy; (*criança*) to have a tantrum

raça ['hasa] F breed; (*grupo étnico*) race; **cão/ cavalo de ~** pedigree dog/thoroughbred horse; **(no peito e) na ~** (*col*) by sheer effort; **ter ~** to have guts; (*ter ascendência africana*) to be of African origin

ração [ha'sãw] (*pl* **-ões**) F ration; (*para animal*) food; **~ de cachorro** dog food

racha ['haʃa] F (*fenda*) split; (*greta*) crack ▶ M (*col*) scrap

rachadura [haʃa'dura] F crack

rachar [ha'ʃar] VT to crack; (*objeto, despesas*) to split; (*lenha*) to chop ▶ VI to split; (*cristal*) to crack; **rachar-se** VR to split; to crack; **frio de ~** bitter cold; **sol de ~** scorching sun; **ou vai ou racha** it's make or break

racial [ha'sjaw] (*pl* **-ais**) ADJ racial; **preconceito ~** racial prejudice

raciocinar [hasjosi'nar] VI to reason

raciocínio [hasjo'sinju] M reasoning

racional [hasjo'naw] (*pl* **-ais**) ADJ rational

racionalização [hasjonaliza'sãw] F rationalization

racionalizar [hasjonali'zar] VT to rationalize

racionamento [hasjona'mẽtu] M rationing

racionar [hasjo'nar] VT (*distribuir*) to ration out; (*limitar a venda de*) to ration

racismo [ha'sizmu] M racism

racista [ha'sista] ADJ, M/F racist

rações [ha'sõjs] FPL *de* **ração**

radar [ha'dar] M radar

radiação [hadʒja'sãw] (*pl* **-ões**) F radiation; (*raio*) ray

radiador [hadʒja'dor] M radiator

radialista [hadʒja'lista] M/F radio announcer; (*na produção*) radio producer

radiante [ha'dʒjãtʃi] ADJ radiant; (*de alegria*) overjoyed

radical [hadʒi'kaw] (*pl* **-ais**) ADJ radical ▶ M radical; (*Ling*) root

radicalismo [hadʒika'lizmu] M radicalism

radicalizar [hadʒikali'zar] VT to radicalize; **radicalizar-se** VR to become radical

radicar-se [hadʒi'karsi] VR to take root; (*fixar residência*) to settle

rádio ['hadʒju] M radio; (*Quím*) radium ▶ F radio station

radioamador, a [hadʒjuama'dor(a)] M/F radio ham

radioatividade [hadʒjuatʃivi'dadʒi] F radioactivity

radioativo, -a [hadʒjua'tʃivu, a] ADJ radioactive

radiodifusão [hadʒjodʒifu'zãw] F broadcasting

radiodifusora [hadʒjodʒifu'zora] F radio station

radioemissora [hadʒjuemi'sora] F radio station

radiografar [hadʒjogra'far] VT (*Med*) to X-ray; (*notícia*) to radio

radiografia [hadʒjogra'fia] F X-ray

radiograma [hadʒjo'grama] M cablegram

radiogravador [hadʒjograva'dor] M radio cassette

radiojornal [hadʒjoʒor'naw] (*pl* -**ais**) M radio news *sg*

radiologia [hadʒjolo'ʒia] F radiology

radiologista [hadʒjolo'ʒista] M/F radiologist

radionovela [hadʒjono'vɛla] F radio serial

radiopatrulha [hadʒjopa'truʎa] F (*viatura*) patrol car

radioperador, a [hadʒjopera'dor(a)] M/F radio operator

radiorrepórter [hadʒjohe'pɔrter] M/F radio reporter

radioso, -a [ha'dʒjozu, ɔza] ADJ radiant, brilliant

radiotáxi [hadʒjo'taksi] M radio taxi *ou* cab

radioterapia [hadʒjotera'pia] F radiotherapy

radiouvinte [hadʒjo'vītʃi] M/F (radio) listener

ragu [ha'gu] M stew, ragoût

raia [ˈhaja] F (*risca*) line; (*fronteira*) boundary; (*limite*) limit; (*de corrida*) lane; (*peixe*) ray; **chegar às ~s** to reach the limit

raiado, -a [ha'jadu, a] ADJ striped

raiar [ha'jar] VI (*brilhar*) to shine; (*madrugada*) to dawn; (*aparecer*) to appear

rainha [ha'ina] F queen; **ela é a ~ da preguiça** (*col*) she's the world's worst for laziness

rainha-mãe (*pl* **rainhas-mães**) F queen mother

raio [ˈhaju] M (*de sol*) ray; (*de luz*) beam; (*de roda*) spoke; (*relâmpago*) flash of lightning; (*distância*) range; (*Mat*) radius; **~s X** X-rays; **~ de ação** range; **onde está o ~ da chave?** (*col*) where's the blasted key?

raiva [ˈhajva] F rage, fury; (*Med*) rabies *sg*; **estar/ficar com ~ (de)** to be/get angry (with); **estar morto de ~** to be furious; **ter ~ de** to hate; **tomar ~ de** to begin to hate; **que ~!** I am (*ou* was *etc*) furious!

raivoso, -a [haj'vozu, ɔza] ADJ furious; (*Med*) rabid, mad

raiz [ha'iz] F root; (*origem*) source; **~ quadrada** square root; **criar raízes** to put down roots

rajada [ha'ʒada] F (*vento*) gust; (*de tiros*) burst

ralado, -a [ha'ladu, a] ADJ grated; (*esfolado*) grazed

ralador [hala'dor] M grater

ralar [ha'lar] VT to grate; (*esfolar*) to graze

ralé [ha'lɛ] F common people *pl*, rabble

ralhar [ha'ʎar] VI to scold; **~ com alguém** to tell sb off

rali [ha'li] M rally

ralo, -a [ˈhalu, a] ADJ (*cabelo*) thinning; (*tecido*) thin, flimsy; (*vegetação*) sparse; (*sopa*) thin, watery; (*café*) weak ▶ M (*de regador*) rose, nozzle; (*de pia, banheiro*) drain

rama [ˈhama] F branches *pl*, foliage; **algodão em ~** raw cotton; **pela ~** superficially

ramagem [ha'maʒẽ] F branches *pl*, foliage; (*num tecido*) floral pattern

ramal [ha'maw] (*pl* -**ais**) M (*Ferro*) branch line; (*Tel*) extension; (*Auto*) side road

ramalhete [hama'ʎetʃi] M bouquet, posy

rameira [ha'mejra] F prostitute

ramerrão [hame'hãw] (*pl* -**ões**) M routine, round

ramificar-se [hamifi'karsi] VR to branch out

ramo [ˈhamu] M branch; (*profissão, negócios*) line; (*de flores*) bunch; **Domingo de R~s** Palm Sunday; **um perito do ~** an expert in the field

rampa [ˈhãpa] F ramp; (*ladeira*) slope

rançar [hã'sar] VI to go rancid

rancheiro [hã'ʃejru] M cook

rancho [ˈhãʃu] M (*grupo*) group, band; (*cabana*) hut; (*refeição*) meal

rancor [hã'kor] M (*ressentimento*) bitterness; (*ódio*) hatred

rancoroso, -a [hãko'rozu, ɔza] ADJ bitter, resentful; (*odiento*) hateful

rançoso, -a [hã'sozu, ɔza] ADJ rancid; (*cheiro*) musty

randevu [hãde'vu] M brothel

ranger [hã'ʒer] VI to creak ▶ VT: **~ os dentes** to grind one's teeth

rangido [hã'ʒidu] M creak

rango [ˈhãgu] (*col*) M grub

Rangum [hã'gũ] N Rangoon

ranheta [ha'neta] ADJ sullen, surly

ranhetice [hane'tʃisi] F sullenness; (*ato*) surly thing

ranho [ˈhanu] (*col*) M snot

ranhura [ha'nura] F groove; (*para moeda*) slot

ranjo *etc* [ˈhãju] VB *ver* **ranger**

ranzinza [hã'ziza] ADJ peevish

rapa [ˈhapa] M (*de comida*) remains *pl*; (*carro*) illegal trading patrol car; (*policial*) policeman concerned with illegal street trading

rapadura [hapa'dura] F (*doce*) raw brown sugar

rapagão [hapa'gãw] (*pl* -**ões**) M hunk

rapapé [hapa'pɛ] M touch of the forelock; **rapapés** MPL (*bajulação*) bowing and scraping; (*lisonja*) flattery *sg*; **fazer ~s a alguém** to bow and scrape to sb

rapar [ha'par] VT to scrape; (*a barba*) to shave; (*o cabelo*) to shave off; **~ algo a alguém** (*roubar*) to steal sth from sb

rapariga [hapa'riga] F girl

rapaz [ha'pajz] M boy; (*col*) lad; **ô, ~, tudo bem?** hi, mate, how's it going?

rapaziada [hapa'zjada] F (*grupo*) lads *pl*

rapazote [hapa'zɔtʃi] M little boy

rapé [ha'pɛ] M snuff

rapidez [hapi'dez] F speed, rapidity; **com ~** quickly, fast

rápido, -a [ˈhapidu, a] ADJ quick, fast ▶ ADV fast, quickly ▶ M (*trem*) express

rapina [ha'pina] F robbery; **ave de ~** bird of prey

raposo, -a [ha'pozu, ɔza] M/F fox/vixen; (*fig*) crafty person

rapsódia [hap'sɔdʒja] F rhapsody

raptado, -a [hap'tadu, a] M/F kidnap victim

raptar [hap'tar] VT to kidnap

rapto [ˈhaptu] M kidnapping

raptor [hap'tor] M kidnapper

raqueta [ha'keta] (PT) F = **raquete**

raquetada [hake'tada] F stroke with a (*ou the*) racquet

raquete [ha'ketʃi] F (*de tênis*) racquet; (*de pingue-pongue*) bat

raquidiana [haki'dʒjana] F (*anestesia*) epidural

raquítico, -a [ha'kitʃiku, a] ADJ (*Med*) suffering from rickets; (*franzino*) puny; (*vegetação*) poor

raquitismo [haki'tʃizmu] M (*Med*) rickets *sg*

raramente [hara'mẽtʃi] ADV rarely, seldom

rarear [ha'rjar] VT to make rare; (*diminuir*) to thin out ▶ VI to become rare; (*cabelos*) to thin; (*casas etc*) to thin out

rarefazer [harefa'zer] (*irreg: como* **fazer**) VT, VI to rarefy; (*nuvens*) to disperse, blow away; (*multidão*) to thin out

rarefeito, -a [hare'fejtu, a] PP *de* **rarefazer** ▶ ADJ rarefied; (*multidão, população*) sparse

rarefez [hare'fez] VB *ver* **rarefazer**

rarefizer *etc* [harefi'zer] VB *ver* **rarefazer**

raridade [hari'dadʒi] F rarity

raro, -a ['haru, a] ADJ rare ▶ ADV rarely, seldom; **não ~** often

rasante [ha'zãtʃi] ADJ (*avião*) low-flying; (*voo*) low

rascunhar [hasku'ɲar] VT to draft, make a rough copy of

rascunho [has'kuɲu] M rough copy, draft

rasgado, -a [haz'gadu, a] ADJ (*roupa*) torn, ripped; (*cumprimentos, elogio, gesto*) effusive

rasgão [haz'gãw] (*pl* **-ões**) M tear, rip

rasgar [haz'gar] VT to tear, rip; (*destruir*) to tear up, rip up; **rasgar-se** VR to split

rasgo ['hazgu] M (*rasgão*) tear, rip; (*risco*) stroke; (*ação*) feat; (*ímpeto*) burst; (*da imaginação*) flight

rasgões [haz'gõjs] MPL *de* **rasgão**

rasguei *etc* [haz'gej] VB *ver* **rasgar**

raso, -a ['hazu, a] ADJ (*liso*) flat, level; (*sapato*) flat; (*não fundo*) shallow; (*baixo*) low; (*colher: como medida*) level ▶ M: **o ~** the shallow water; **soldado ~** private

raspa ['haspa] F (*de madeira*) shaving; (*de metal*) filing

raspadeira [haspa'dejra] F scraper

raspão [has'pãw] (*pl* **-ões**) M scratch, graze; **tocar de ~** to graze

raspar [has'par] VT (*limpar, tocar*) to scrape; (*alisar*) to file; (*tocar de raspão*) to graze; (*arranhar*) to scratch; (*pelos, cabeça*) to shave; (*apagar*) to rub out ▶ VI: **~ em** to scrape; **passar raspando (num exame)** to scrape through (an exam)

raspões [has'põjs] MPL *de* **raspão**

rasteira [has'tejra] F (*pernada*) trip; **dar uma ~ em alguém** to trip sb up

rasteiro, -a [has'tejru, a] ADJ (*que se arrasta*) crawling; (*planta*) creeping; (*a pouca altura*) low-lying; (*ordinário*) common

rastejante [haste'ʒãtʃi] ADJ trailing; (*arrastando-se*) creeping; (*voz*) slurred

rastejar [haste'ʒar] VI to crawl; (*furtivamente*) to creep; (*fig: rebaixar-se*) to grovel ▶ VT (*fugitivo etc*) to track

rastilho [has'tʃiʎu] M (*de pólvora*) fuse

rasto ['hastu] M (*pegada*) track; (*de veículo*) trail; (*fig*) sign, trace; **de ~s** crawling; **andar de ~s** to crawl; **levar de ~s** to drag along

rastrear [has'trjar] VT to track; (*investigar*) to scan ▶ VI to track

rastro ['hastru] M = **rasto**

rasura [ha'zura] F deletion

rasurar [hazu'rar] VT to delete items from

rata ['hata] F rat; (*pequena*) mouse; **dar uma ~** to slip up

ratão [ha'tãw] (*pl* **-ões**) M rat

rataplã [hata'plã] M drum roll

ratazana [hata'zana] F rat

ratear [ha'tʃjar] VT (*dividir*) to share ▶ VI (*motor*) to miss

rateio [ha'teju] M (*de custos*) sharing, spreading

ratificação [hatʃifika'sãw] F ratification

ratificar [hatʃifi'kar] VT to ratify

rato ['hatu] M rat; (*rato pequeno*) mouse; **~ de biblioteca** bookworm; **~ de hotel/praia** hotel/beach thief

ratoeira [ha'twejra] F rat trap; (*pequena*) mousetrap

ratões [ha'tõjs] MPL *de* **ratão**

ravina [ha'vina] F ravine

ravióli [ha'vjɔli] M ravioli

razão [ha'zãw] (*pl* **-ões**) F reason; (*bom senso*) common sense; (*argumento*) reasoning, argument; (*conta*) account; (*Mat*) ratio ▶ M (*Com*) ledger; **à ~ de** at the rate of; **com/sem ~** with good reason/for no reason; **em ~ de** on account of; **dar ~ a alguém** to support sb; **ter/não ter ~** to be right/wrong; **ter toda ~ (em fazer)** to be quite right (to do); **estar coberto de ~** to be quite right; **a ~ pela qual ...** the reason why ...; **~ demais para você ficar aqui** all the more reason for you to stay here; **~ de Estado** reason of State

razoável [ha'zwavew] (*pl* **-eis**) ADJ reasonable

razões [ha'zõjs] FPL *de* **razão**

r/c (PT) ABR = **rés do chão**

RDA ABR F (*antes: = República Democrática Alemã*) GDR

ré [hɛ] F (*Auto*) reverse (gear); **dar (marcha à) ré** to reverse, back up; *ver tb* **réu**

reabastecer [heabaste'ser] VT (*avião*) to refuel; (*carro*) to fill up; **reabastecer-se** VR: **~-se de** to replenish one's supply of

reabastecimento [heabastesi'mẽtu] M (*de avião*) refuelling; (*de uma cidade*) reprovisioning

reaberto, -a [hea'bɛrtu, a] PP *de* **reabrir**

reabertura [heaber'tura] F reopening

reabilitação [heabilita'sãw] F rehabilitation; **~ motora** physiotherapy

reabilitar [heabili'tar] VT to rehabilitate; (*falido*) to discharge, rehabilitate

reabrir [hea'brir] VT to reopen

reaça [he'asa] (col) M/F reactionary
reação [hea'sãw] (pl -**ões**) F reaction; ~ **em cadeia** chain reaction
reacender [heasẽ'der] VT to relight; (fig) to rekindle
reacionário, -a [heasjo'narju, a] ADJ reactionary
reações [hea'sõjs] FPL de **reação**
readaptar [headap'tar] VT to readapt
readmitir [headʒimi'tʃir] VT to readmit; (funcionário) to reinstate
readquirir [headʒiki'rir] VT to reacquire
reafirmar [heafir'mar] VT to reaffirm
reagir [hea'ʒir] VI to react; (doente, time perdedor) to fight back; ~ **a** (resistir) to resist; (protestar) to rebel against
reais [he'ajs] ADJ PL de **real**
reaja etc [he'aʒa] VB ver **reagir**
reajustar [heaʒus'tar] VT to readjust; (Mecânica) to regulate; (salário, preço) to adjust (in line with inflation)
reajuste [hea'ʒustʃi] M adjustment; ~ **salarial/de preços** wage/price adjustment (in line with inflation)
real [he'aw] (pl -**ais**) ADJ real; (relativo à realeza) royal ▶ M (moeda) real

> The Brazilian currency, the **real**, was introduced in 1994 as part of a comprehensive economic stabilization package known as the **Plano Real**. This brought an end to some thirty years of hyperinflation which saw successive devaluations and name-changes to the Brazilian currency, from cruzeiro to cruzado (1986), to cruzado novo (1989), back to cruzeiro (1990), to cruzeiro real (1993) and finally to real (1994). The real is subdivided into 100 centavos. The currency symbol is R$ and a comma is used to separate reais and centavos, e.g. R$ 2,40 (two reais and forty centavos).

realçar [heaw'sar] VT to highlight
realce [he'awsi] M (destaque) emphasis; (mais brilho) highlight; **dar ~ a** to enhance
realejo [hea'leʒu] M barrel organ
realeza [hea'leza] F royalty
realidade [heali'dadʒi] F reality; **na ~** actually, in fact; ~ **virtual** virtual reality
realimentação [healimẽta'sãw] F (Elet) feedback
realismo [hea'lizmu] M realism
realista [hea'lista] ADJ realistic ▶ M/F realist
reality show [healitʃi'ʃow] M reality show
realização [healiza'sãw] F fulfilment (BRIT), fulfillment (US), realization; (de projeto) execution, carrying out; (transformação em dinheiro) conversion into cash
realizado, -a [heali'zadu, a] ADJ (pessoa) fulfilled
realizador, a [healiza'dor(a)] ADJ (pessoa) enterprising
realizar [heali'zar] VT (um objetivo) to achieve; (projeto) to carry out; (ambições, sonho) to fulfil

(BRIT), fulfill (US), realize; (negócios) to transact; (perceber, convertir en dinheiro) to realize; **realizar-se** VR (acontecer) to take place; (ambições) to be realized; (sonhos) to come true; (pessoa) to fulfil(l) o.s.; **o congresso será realizado em Lisboa** the conference will be held in Lisbon
realizável [heali'zavew] (pl -**eis**) ADJ realizable
realmente [heaw'mẽtʃi] ADV really; (de fato) actually
reanimar [heani'mar] VT to revive; (encorajar) to encourage; **reanimar-se** VR (pessoa) to cheer up
reaparecer [heapare'ser] VI to reappear
reaprender [heaprẽ'der] VT to relearn
reapresentar [heaprezẽ'tar] VT (espetáculo) to put on again
reaproximação [heaprosima'sãw] (pl -**ões**) F (entre pessoas, países) rapprochement
reaproximar [heaprosi'mar] VT to bring back together; **reaproximar-se** VR to be brought back together
reaquecer [heake'ser] VT to reheat
reassumir [heasu'mir] VT, VI to take over again
reatar [hea'tar] VT (continuar) to resume, take up again; (nó) to retie
reativar [heatʃi'var] VT to reactivate; (organização, lei) to revive
reator [hea'tor] M reactor
reavaliação [heavalja'sãw] F revaluation
reaver [hea'ver] VT to recover, get back
reavivar [heavi'var] VT (cor) to brighten up; (lembrança) to revive; (sofrimento, dor) to bring back
rebaixa [he'bajʃa] F reduction
rebaixar [hebaj'ʃar] VT (tornar mais baixo) to lower; (reduzir) to reduce; (time) to relegate; (funcionário) to demote; (humilhar) to put down ▶ VI to drop; **rebaixar-se** VR to demean o.s.
rebanho [he'baɲu] M (de carneiros, fig) flock; (de gado, elefantes) herd
rebarbar [hebar'bar] VT (opor-se a) to oppose ▶ VI (reclamar) to complain
rebarbativo, -a [hebarba'tʃivu, a] ADJ (pessoa) disagreeable, unpleasant
rebate [he'batʃi] M (sinal) alarm; (Com) discount; ~ **falso** false alarm
rebater [heba'ter] VT (golpe) to ward off; (acusações, argumentos) to refute; (bola) to knock back; (à máquina) to retype
rebelar-se [hebe'larsi] VR to rebel
rebelde [he'bewdʒi] ADJ rebellious; (indisciplinado) unruly, wild ▶ M/F rebel
rebeldia [hebew'dʒia] F rebelliousness; (fig: obstinação) stubbornness; (: oposição) defiance
rebelião [hebe'ljãw] (pl -**ões**) F rebellion
rebentar [hebẽ'tar] VI (guerra) to break out; (louça) to smash; (corda) to snap; (represa) to burst; (ondas) to break ▶ VT (louça) to smash; (corda) to snap; (porta, ponte) to break down

rebento [he'bẽtu] M *(filho)* offspring
rebite [he'bitʃi] M *(Tec)* rivet
reboar [he'bwar] VI to resound, echo
rebobinar [hebobi'nar] VT *(vídeo)* to rewind
rebocador [heboka'dor] M *(Náut)* tug(boat)
rebocar [hebo'kar] VT *(paredes)* to plaster;
(veículo mal estacionado) to tow away; *(dar reboque a)* to tow
reboco [he'boku] M plaster
rebolar [hebo'lar] VT to swing ▶ VI to sway;
(fig) to work hard; **rebolar-se** VR to sway
rebolo [he'bolu] M *(mó)* grindstone; *(cilindro)* cylinder
reboque¹ [he'bɔki] M *(ato)* tow; *(veículo: tb:* **carro reboque**) trailer; *(cabo)* towrope; *(BR: de socorro)* tow truck; **a ~** on ou in *(US)* tow
reboque² *etc* VB *ver* **rebocar**
rebordo [he'bordu] M rim, edge; **~ da lareira** mantelpiece
rebordosa [hebor'dɔza] F *(situação difícil)* difficult situation; *(doença grave)* serious illness; *(reincidência de moléstia)* recurrence; *(pancadaria)* commotion
rebu [he'bu] *(col)* M commotion, rumpus
rebuçado [hebu'sadu] *(PT)* M sweet, candy *(US)*
rebuliço [hebu'lisu] M commotion, hubbub
rebuscado, -a [hebus'kadu, a] ADJ affected
recado [he'kadu] M message; **menino de ~s** errand boy; **dar o ~, dar conta do ~** *(fig)* to deliver the goods; **deixar ~** to leave a message; **mandar ~** to send word
recaída [heka'ida] F relapse
recair [heka'ir] VI *(doente)* to relapse; **~ em erro** ou **falta** to go wrong again; **a culpa recaiu nela** she got the blame; **o acento recai na última sílaba** the accent falls on the last syllable
recalcado, -a [hekaw'kadu, a] ADJ repressed
recalcar [hekaw'kar] VT to repress
recalcitrante [hekawsi'trãtʃi] ADJ recalcitrant
recalque¹ [he'kawki] M repression
recalque² *etc* VB *ver* **recalcar**
recamado, -a [heka'madu, a] ADJ embroidered
recambiar [hekã'bjar] VT to send back
recanto [he'kãtu] M *(lugar aprazível)* corner, nook; *(esconderijo)* hiding place
recapitulação [hekapitula'sãw] F *(resumo)* recapitulation; *(rememorar)* revision
recapitular [hekapitu'lar] VT *(resumir)* to sum up, recapitulate; *(fatos)* to review; *(matéria escolar)* to revise
recarga [he'karga] F *(de celular)* top-up; **preciso fazer a ~ do meu celular** I need to top up my mobile
recarregar [hekahe'gar] VT *(celular)* to top up; *(bateria)* to recharge; *(cartucho)* to refill
recatado, -a [heka'tadu, a] ADJ *(modesto)* modest; *(reservado)* reserved
recatar-se [heka'tarsi] VR to become withdrawn; *(ocultar-se)* to hide
recato [he'katu] M *(modéstia)* modesty

recauchutado, -a [hekawʃu'tadu, a] ADJ *(fig)* revamped; *(col: pessoa)* having had cosmetic surgery; **pneu ~** *(Auto)* retread, remould *(BRIT)*
recauchutagem [hekawʃu'taʒẽ] *(pl* **-ns**) F *(de pneu)* retreading; *(fig)* face-lift
recauchutar [hekawʃu'tar] VT *(pneu)* to retread; *(fig)* to give a face-lift to
recear [he'sjar] VT to fear ▶ VI: **~ por** to fear for; **~ fazer/que** to be afraid to do/that
recebedor, a [hesebe'dor(a)] M/F recipient; *(de impostos)* collector
receber [hese'ber] VT to receive; *(ganhar)* to earn, get; *(hóspedes)* to take in; *(convidados)* to entertain; *(acolher bem)* to welcome ▶ VI *(receber convidados)* to entertain; *(ser pago)* to be paid; **a ~** *(Com)* receivable
recebimento [hesebi'mẽtu] *(BR)* M reception; *(de uma carta)* receipt; **acusar o ~ de** to acknowledge receipt of
receio [he'seju] M fear; **não tenha ~** never fear; **ter ~ de que** to fear that
receita [he'sejta] F *(renda)* income; *(do Estado)* revenue; *(Med)* prescription; *(culinária)* recipe; **~ pública** tax revenue; **R~ Federal** ≈ Inland Revenue *(BRIT)*, ≈ IRS *(US)*
receitar [hesej'tar] VT to prescribe ▶ VI to write prescriptions
recém [he'sẽ] ADV recently, newly
recém-casado, -a [he'sẽ] ADJ newly-married; **os ~s** the newlyweds
recém-chegado, -a M/F newcomer
recém-nascido, -a M/F newborn child
recém-publicado, -a ADJ newly ou recently published
recender [hesẽ'der] VT: **~ um cheiro** to give off a smell ▶ VI to smell; **~ a** to smell of
recenseamento [hesẽsja'mẽtu] M census
recensear [hesẽ'sjar] VT to take a census of
recente [he'sẽtʃi] ADJ recent; *(novo)* new ▶ ADV recently
recentemente [hesẽtʃi'mẽtʃi] ADV recently
receoso, -a [he'sjozu, ɔza] ADJ *(medroso)* frightened, fearful; *(apreensivo)* afraid; **estar ~ de (fazer)** to be afraid of (doing)
recepção [hesep'sãw] *(pl* **-ões**) F reception; *(PT: de uma carta)* receipt; **acusar a ~ de** *(PT)* to acknowledge receipt of
recepcionar [hesepsjo'nar] VT to receive
recepcionista [hesepsjo'nista] M/F receptionist
recepções [hesep'sõjs] FPL *de* **recepção**
receptáculo [hesep'takulu] M receptacle
receptador, a [hesepta'dor(a)] M/F fence, receiver of stolen goods
receptar [hesep'tar] VT to fence, receive
receptivo, -a [hesep'tʃivu, a] ADJ receptive; *(acolhedor)* welcoming
receptor [hesep'tor] M *(Tec)* receiver
recessão [hese'sãw] *(pl* **-ões**) F recession
recesso [he'sɛsu] M recess
recessões [hese'sõjs] FPL *de* **recessão**
rechaçar [heʃa'sar] VT *(ataque)* to repel; *(ideias, argumentos)* to oppose; *(oferta)* to turn down

r

réchaud [he'ʃo] (pl **-s**) M plate-warmer

recheado, -a [he'ʃjadu, a] ADJ (ave, carne) stuffed; (empada, bolo) filled; (cheio) full, crammed

rechear [he'ʃjar] VT to fill; (ave, carne) to stuff

recheio [he'ʃeju] M (para carne assada) stuffing; (de empada, de bolo) filling; (o conteúdo) contents pl

rechonchudo, -a [heʃõ'ʃudu, a] ADJ chubby, plump

recibo [he'sibu] M receipt

reciclagem [hesi'klaʒẽ] F (de papel etc) recycling; (de professores, funcionários) retraining

reciclar [hesi'klar] VT (papel etc) to recycle; (professores, funcionários) to retrain

reciclável [hesi'klavew] (pl **-eis**) ADJ recyclable

recidiva [hesi'dʒiva] F recurrence

recife [he'sifi] M reef

recifense [hesi'fẽsi] ADJ from Recife ▸ M/F person from Recife

recinto [he'sĩtu] M (espaço fechado) enclosure; (lugar) area

recipiente [hesi'pjẽtʃi] M container, receptacle

recíproca [he'siproka] F reverse

reciprocar [hesipro'kar] VT to reciprocate

reciprocidade [hesiprosi'dadʒi] F reciprocity

recíproco, -a [he'siproku, a] ADJ reciprocal

récita ['hɛsita] F (teatral) performance

recitação [hesita'sãw] (pl **-ões**) F recitation

recital [hesi'taw] (pl **-ais**) M recital

recitar [hesi'tar] VT (declamar) to recite

reclamação [heklama'sãw] (pl **-ões**) F (queixa) complaint; (Jur) claim

reclamante [hekla'mãtʃi] M/F claimant

reclamar [hekla'mar] VT (exigir) to demand; (herança) to claim ▸ VI: **~ (de)** (comida etc) to complain (about); (dores etc) to complain (of); **~ contra** to complain about

reclame [he'klami] M advertisement

reclinado, -a [hekli'nadu, a] ADJ (inclinado) leaning; (recostado) lying back

reclinar [hekli'nar] VT to rest, lean; **reclinar-se** VR to lie back; (deitar-se) to lie down

reclinável [hekli'navew] (pl **-eis**) ADJ (cadeira) reclinable

reclusão [heklu'zãw] F (isolamento) seclusion; (encarceramento) imprisonment

recluso, -a [he'kluzu, a] ADJ reclusive ▸ M/F recluse; (prisioneiro) prisoner

recobrar [heko'brar] VT to recover, get back; **recobrar-se** VR to recover

recolher [heko'ʎer] VT to collect; (gado, roupa do varal) to bring in; (juntar) to collect up; (abrigar) to give shelter to; (notas antigas) to withdraw; (encolher) to draw in; **recolher-se** VR (ir para casa) to go home; (deitar-se) to go to bed; (ir para o quarto) to retire; (em meditações) to meditate; **~ alguém a algum lugar** to take sb somewhere

recolhido, -a [heko'ʎidu, a] ADJ (lugar) secluded; (pessoa) withdrawn

recolhimento [hekoʎi'mẽtu] M (vida retraída) retirement; (arrecadação) collection; (ato de levar) taking

recomeçar [hekome'sar] VT, VI to restart; **~ a fazer** to start to do again

recomeço [heko'mesu] M restart

recomendação [hekomẽda'sãw] (pl **-ões**) F recommendation; **recomendações** FPL (cumprimentos) regards; **carta de ~** letter of recommendation

recomendar [hekomẽ'dar] VT to recommend; (confiar) to entrust; **~ alguém a alguém** (enviar cumprimentos) to remember sb to sb, give sb's regards to sb; (pedir favor) to put in a word for sb with sb; **~ algo a alguém** (confiar) to entrust sth to sb; **~ que alguém faça** to recommend that sb do; (lembrar, pedir) to urge that sb do

recomendável [hekomẽ'davew] (pl **-eis**) ADJ advisable

recompensa [hekõ'pẽsa] F (prêmio) reward; (indenização) recompense

recompensar [hekõpẽ'sar] VT (premiar) to reward; **~ alguém de algo** (indenizar) to compensate sb for sth

recompor [hekõ'por] (irreg: como **pôr**) VT (reorganizar) to reorganize; (restabelecer) to restore

recôncavo [he'kõkavu] M (enseada) bay area

reconciliação [hekõsilja'sãw] (pl **-ões**) F reconciliation

reconciliar [hekõsi'ljar] VT to reconcile; **reconciliar-se** VR to become reconciled

recondicionar [hekõdʒisjo'nar] VT to recondition

recôndito, -a [he'kõdʒitu, a] ADJ (escondido) hidden; (lugar) secluded

reconfortar [hekõfor'tar] VT to invigorate; **reconfortar-se** VR to be invigorated

reconhecer [hekoɲe'ser] VT to recognize; (admitir) to admit; (Mil) to reconnoitre (BRIT), reconnoiter (US); (assinatura) to witness

reconhecido, -a [hekoɲe'sidu, a] ADJ recognized; (agradecido) grateful, thankful

reconhecimento [hekoɲesi'mẽtu] M recognition; (admissão) admission; (gratidão) gratitude; (Mil) reconnaissance; (de assinatura) witnessing

reconhecível [hekoɲe'sivew] (pl **-eis**) ADJ recognizable

reconquista [hekõ'kista] F reconquest

reconsiderar [hekõside'rar] VT, VI to reconsider

reconstituinte [hekõstʃi'twĩtʃi] M tonic

reconstituir [hekõstʃi'twir] VT to reconstitute; (doente) to build up; (crime) to piece together

reconstrução [hekõstru'sãw] F reconstruction

reconstruir [hekõs'trwir] VT to rebuild, reconstruct

recontar [hekõ'tar] vt (*objetos, pessoas*) to
recount; (*história*) to retell
recordação [hekorda'sãw] (*pl* -**ões**) F
(*reminiscência*) memory; (*objeto*) memento
recordar [hekor'dar] vt to remember;
recordar-se vr: ~-**se de** to remember; ~ **algo**
a alguém to remind sb of sth
recorde [he'kɔrdʒi] ADJ INV record *atr* ▶ M
record; **em tempo** ~ in record time; **bater**
um ~ to break a record
recordista [hekor'dʒista] ADJ record-breaking
▶ M/F record-breaker; (*quem detém o recorde*)
record-holder; ~ **mundial** world record-
holder
recorrer [heko'her] vi: ~ **a** (*para socorro*) to turn
to; (*valer-se de*) to resort to; ~ **da sentença/**
decisão to appeal against the sentence/
decision
recortar [hekor'tar] vt to cut out
recorte [he'kɔrtʃi] M (*ato*) cutting out; (*de*
jornal) cutting, clipping
recostar [hekos'tar] vt to lean, rest;
recostar-se vr to lean back; (*deitar-se*) to
lie down
recosto [he'kostu] M back(rest)
recreação [hekrja'sãw] F recreation
recrear [he'krjar] vt to entertain, amuse;
recrear-se vr to have fun
recreativo, -a [hekrja'tʃivu, a] ADJ
recreational
recreio [he'kreju] M recreation; (*Educ*)
playtime; **viagem de** ~ trip, outing; **hora**
do ~ break
recriar [he'krjar] vt to recreate
recriminação [hekrimina'sãw] (*pl* -**ões**) F
recrimination
recriminador, a [hekrimina'dor(a)] ADJ
reproving
recriminar [hekrimi'nar] vt to reproach,
reprove
recrudescência [hekrude'sẽsja] F
= **recrudescimento**
recrudescer [hekrude'ser] vi to grow worse,
worsen
recrudescimento [hekrudesi'mẽtu] M
worsening
recruta [he'kruta] M/F recruit
recrutamento [hekruta'mẽtu] M
recruitment
recrutar [hekru'tar] vt to recruit
récua ['hɛkwa] F (*de mulas*) pack, train; (*de*
cavalos) drove
recuado, -a [he'kwadu, a] ADJ (*prédio*) set back
recuar [he'kwar] vt to move back ▶ vi to move
back; (*exército*) to retreat; (*num intento*) to back
out; (*num compromisso*) to backpedal; (*ciência*)
to regress; ~ **a** *ou* **para** (*no tempo*) to return *ou*
regress to; (*numa decisão, opinião*) to back down
to; ~ **de** (*lugar*) to move back from; (*intenções,*
planos) to back out of
recuo [he'kuu] M retreat; (*de ciência*)
regression; (*de intento*) climbdown; (*de um*
prédio) frontage

recuperação [h... ...ery
recuperar [heku... ...ı, ... to... . (*tempo*
perdido) to make up for; (*reabilitar*) to
rehabilitate; **recuperar-se** vr to recover;
~-**se de** to recover *ou* recuperate from
recurso [he'kursu] M (*meio*) resource; (*Jur*)
appeal; **recursos** MPL (*financeiros*)
resources; **em último** ... a last resort; **o** ~
à violência resorting ... violence; **não há**
outro ~ **contra a fome** there is no other
solution to famine; ~**s próprios** (*Com*) own
resources
recusa [he'kuza] F refusal; (*negação*) denial
recusar [heku'zar] vt to refuse; (*negar*) to
deny; **recusar-se** vr: ~-**se a** to refuse to;
~ **fazer** to refuse to do; ~ **algo a alguém** to
refuse *ou* deny sb sth
redação [heda'sãw] (*pl* -**ões**) F (*ato*) writing;
(*Educ*) composition, essay; (*redatores*)
editorial staff; (*lugar*) editorial office
redarguir [hedar'gwir] vi to retort
redator, a [heda'tor(a)] M/F editor
redator-chefe, redatora-chefe (*pl* redatores-
chefes/redatoras-chefes) M/F (*de jornal,*
revista) editor
rede ['hedʒi] F net; (*de salvamento*) safety net;
(*de cabelos*) hairnet; (*de dormir*) hammock;
(*Ferro, Tec, Comput, TV, fig*) network; **a** ~ (*a Internet*)
the web; ~ **bancária** banking system; ~ **de**
esgotos drainage system; ~ **de área local**
local area network; ~ **sem fio** wireless
network; ~ **social** social network, social
networking site; **comunicar-se em** ~ (**com**)
(*Comput*) to network (with); **operação em** ~
(*Comput*) networking
rédea ['hɛdʒja] F rein; **dar** ~ **larga a** to give
free rein to; **tomar as** ~**s** (*fig*) to take control,
take over; **falar à** ~ **solta** to talk nineteen to
the dozen
redenção [hedẽ'sãw] F redemption
redentor, a [hedẽ'tor(a)] ADJ redeeming
▶ M/F redeemer
redigir [hedʒi'ʒir] vt, vi to write
redime *etc* [he'dʒimi] vb *ver* **remir**
redimir [hedʒi'mir] vt (*livrar*) to free; (*Rel*) to
redeem
redobrar [hedo'brar] vt (*dobrar de novo*) to fold
again; (*aumentar*) to increase; (*esforços*) to
redouble; (*sinos*) to ring ▶ vi to increase;
(*intensificar*) to intensify; to ring out
redoma [he'doma] F glass dome
redondamente [hedõda'mẽtʃi] ADV
(*completamente*) completely
redondeza [hedõ'deza] F roundness;
redondezas FPL (*arredores*) surroundings
redondo, -a [he'dõdu, a] ADJ round; (*gordo*)
plump
redor [he'dor] M: **ao** *ou* **em** ~ (**de**) around,
round about
redução [hedu'sãw] (*pl* -**ões**) F reduction;
(*conversão: de moeda*) conversion
redundância [hedũ'dãsja] F redundancy
redundante [hedũ'dãtʃi] ADJ redundant

redundar [hedũ'dar] vi: ~ **em** (*resultar em*) to result in

reduto [he'dutu] M stronghold; (*refúgio*) haven

reduzido, -a [hedu'zidu, a] ADJ reduced; (*limitado*) limited; (*pequeno*) small; **ficar ~ a** to be reduced to

reduzir [hedu'zir] vt to reduce; (*converter: dinheiro*) to convert; (*abreviar*) to abridge; **reduzir-se** vr: ~**-se a** to be reduced to; (*fig: resumir-se em*) to come down to; **"reduza a velocidade"** "reduce speed now"

reedificar [heedʒifi'kar] vt to rebuild

reeditar [heedʒi'tar] vt (*livro*) to republish; (*repetir*) to repeat

reeducar [heedu'kar] vt to reeducate

reeleger [heele'ʒer] vt to re-elect; **reeleger-se** vr to be re-elected

reeleição [heelej'sãw] F re-election

reelejo *etc* [hee'leʒu] vb *ver* **reeleger**

reembolsar [heẽbow'sar] vt (*reaver*) to recover; (*restituir*) to reimburse; (*depósito*) to refund; ~ **alguem de algo** *ou* **algo a alguém** to reimburse sb for sth

reembolso [heẽ'bowsu] M (*de depósito*) refund; (*de despesa*) reimbursement; ~ **postal** cash on delivery

reencarnação [heẽkarna'sãw] F reincarnation

reencarnar [heẽkar'nar] vi to be reincarnated

reencontrar [heẽkõ'trar] vt to meet again; **reencontrar-se** vr: ~**-se (com)** to meet up (with)

reencontro [heẽ'kõtru] M reunion

reentrância [heẽ'trãsja] F recess

reescalonamento [heeskalona'mẽtu] M rescheduling

reescalonar [heeskalo'nar] vt (*dívida*) to reschedule

reescrever [heeskre'ver] vt to rewrite

reestruturação [heestrutura'sãw] F restructuring

reestruturar [heestrutu'rar] vt to restructure

reexaminar [heezami'nar] vt to re-examine

refaço *etc* [he'fasu] vb *ver* **refazer**

refastelado, -a [hefaste'ladu, a] ADJ stretched out

refastelar-se [hefaste'larsi] vr to stretch out, lounge

refazer [hefa'zer] (*irreg: como* **fazer**) vt (*trabalho*) to redo; (*consertar*) to repair, fix; (*forças*) to restore; (*finanças*) to recover; (*vida*) to rebuild; **refazer-se** vr (*Med etc*) to recover; ~**-se de despesas** to recover one's expenses

refeição [hefej'sãw] (*pl* **-ões**) F meal; **na hora da ~** at mealtimes

refeito, -a [he'fejtu, a] PP *de* **refazer**

refeitório [hefej'tɔrju] M dining hall, refectory

refém [he'fẽ] (*pl* **-ns**) M hostage

referência [hefe'rẽsja] F reference; **referências** FPL (*informaçoes para emprego*) references; **com ~ a** with reference to,

about; **fazer ~ a** to make reference to, refer to

referendar [heferẽ'dar] vt to countersign, endorse; (*aprovar: tratado etc*) to ratify

referendum [hefe'rẽdũ] M (*Pol*) referendum

referente [hefe'rẽtʃi] ADJ: ~ **a** concerning, regarding

referido, -a [hefe'ridu, a] ADJ aforesaid, already mentioned

referir [hefe'rir] vt (*contar*) to relate, tell; **referir-se** vr: ~**-se a** to refer to

REFESA [he'fesa] F (= *Rede Ferroviária SA*) Brazilian rail network

refastelar-se [hefeste'larsi] vr = **refastelar-se**

refez [he'fez] vb *ver* **refazer**

refil [he'fiw] (*pl* **-is**) M refill

refilmagem [hefiw'maʒẽ] (*pl* **-ns**) F (*Cinema*) remake

refinado, -a [hefi'nadu, a] ADJ refined

refinamento [hefina'mẽtu] M refinement

refinanciamento [hefinãsja'mẽtu] M refinancing

refinanciar [hefinã'sjar] vt to refinance

refinar [hefi'nar] vt to refine

refinaria [hefina'ria] F refinery

refiro *etc* [he'firu] vb *ver* **referir**

refis [he'fis] MPL *de* **refil**

refiz [he'fiz] vb *ver* **refazer**

refizer *etc* [hefi'zer] vb *ver* **refazer**

refletido, -a [hefle'tʃidu, a] ADJ reflected; (*prudente*) thoughtful; (*ação*) prudent, shrewd

refletir [hefle'tʃir] vt (*espelhar*) to reflect; (*som*) to echo; (*fig: revelar*) to reveal ▶ vi: ~ **em** *ou* **sobre** (*pensar*) to consider, think about; **refletir-se** vr to be reflected; ~**-se em** (*repercutir-se*) to have implications for

refletor, a [hefle'tor(a)] ADJ reflecting ▶ M reflector

reflexão [heflek'sãw] (*pl* **-ões**) F reflection; (*meditação*) thought, reflection

reflexivo, -a [heflek'sivu, a] ADJ reflexive

reflexo, -a [he'flɛksu, a] ADJ (*luz*) reflected; (*ação*) reflex ▶ M reflection; (*Anat*) reflex; (*no cabelo*) streak

reflexões [heflek'sõjs] FPL *de* **reflexão**

reflito *etc* [he'flitu] vb *ver* **refletir**

refluxo [he'fluksu] M ebb

refogado, -a [hefo'gadu, a] ADJ sautéed ▶ M (*molho*) tomatoes, onion, garlic and herbs fried together; (*prato*) stew

refogar [hefo'gar] vt to sauté

reforçado, -a [hefor'sadu, a] ADJ reinforced; (*pessoa*) strong; (*café da manhã, jantar*) hearty

reforçar [hefor'sar] vt to reinforce; (*revigorar*) to invigorate

reforço [he'forsu] M reinforcement

reforma [he'fɔrma] F reform; (*Arq*) renovation; (*Rel*) reformation; (*Mil*) retirement; **fazer ~s em casa** to have building work done in the house; **o banheiro está em ~** the bathroom is being done up; ~ **agrária** land reform; ~ **ministerial** cabinet reshuffle

reformado, -a [hefor'madu, a] ADJ reformed; (*Arq*) renovated; (*Mil*) retired

reformar [hefor'mar] VT to reform; (*Arq*) to renovate; (*Mil*) to retire; (*sentença*) to commute; **reformar-se** VR (*militar*) to retire; (*criminoso*) to reform, mend one's ways

reformatar [heforma'tar] VT to reformat

reformatório [heforma'tɔrju] M reformatory, approved school (BRIT)

refrão [he'frãw] (*pl* -**ões**) M (*cantado*) chorus, refrain; (*provérbio*) saying

refratário, -a [hefra'tarju, a] ADJ (*rebelde*) difficult, unmanageable; (*Tec*) heat-resistant; (*Culin*) ovenproof; **ser ~ a** (*admoestações etc*) to be impervious to

refrear [hefre'ar] VT (*cavalo*) to rein in; (*inimigo*) to contain, check; (*paixões, raiva*) to control; **refrear-se** VR to restrain o.s.; **~ a língua** to mind one's language

refrega [he'frɛga] F fight

refrescante [hefres'kãtʃi] ADJ refreshing

refrescar [hefres'kar] VT (*ar, ambiente*) to cool; (*pessoa*) to refresh ▶ VI to cool down; **refrescar-se** VR to refresh o.s.

refresco [he'fresku] M cool fruit drink, squash; **refrescos** MPL (*refrigerantes*) refreshments

refrigeração [hefriʒera'sãw] F cooling; (*de alimentos*) refrigeration; (*de casa*) air conditioning

refrigerado, -a [hefriʒe'radu, a] ADJ cooled; (*casa*) air-conditioned; (*alimentos*) refrigerated; **~ a ar** air-cooled

refrigerador [hefriʒera'dor] M refrigerator, fridge (BRIT)

refrigerante [hefriʒe'rãtʃi] M soft drink

refrigerar [hefriʒe'rar] VT to keep cool; (*com geladeira*) to refrigerate; (*casa*) to air-condition

refrigério [hefri'ʒɛrju] M solace, consolation

refugar [hefu'gar] VT (*alimentos*) to reject; (*proposta, conselho*) to reject, dismiss ▶ VI (*cavalo*) to balk; (*Hipismo*) to refuse

refugiado, -a [hefu'ʒjadu, a] ADJ, M/F refugee

refugiar-se [hefu'ʒjarsi] VR to take refuge; **~ na leitura** *etc* to seek solace in reading *etc*

refúgio [he'fuʒju] M refuge

refugo [he'fugu] M rubbish, garbage (US); (*mercadoria*) reject

refulgência [hefuw'ʒẽsja] F brilliance

refulgir [hefuw'ʒir] VI to shine

refutação [hefuta'sãw] (*pl* -**ões**) F refutation

refutar [hefu'tar] VT to refute

reg ABR = **regimento; regular**

rega ['hɛga] F watering; (PT: *irrigação*) irrigation

regaço [he'gasu] M (*colo*) lap

regador [hega'dor] M watering can

regalado, -a [hega'ladu, a] ADJ (*encantado*) delighted; (*confortável*) comfortable ▶ ADV comfortably

regalar [hega'lar] VT (*causar prazer*) to delight; **regalar-se** VR (*divertir-se*) to enjoy o.s.;

(*alegrar-se*) to be delighted; **~ alguém com algo** to give sb sth, present sb with sth

regalia [hega'lia] F privilege

regalo [he'galu] M (*presente*) present; (*prazer*) pleasure, treat

regar [he'gar] VT (*plantas, jardim*) to water; (*umedecer*) to sprinkle; **~ o jantar a vinho** to wash one's dinner down with wine

regata [he'gata] F regatta

regatear [hega'tʃjar] VT (*o preço*) to haggle over, bargain for ▶ VI to haggle

regateio [hega'teju] M haggling

regato [he'gatu] M brook, stream

regência [he'ʒẽsja] F regency; (*Ling*) government; (*Mús*) conducting

regeneração [heʒenera'sãw] F regeneration; (*de criminosos*) reform

regenerar [heʒene'rar] VT to regenerate; (*criminoso*) to reform; **regenerar-se** VR to regenerate; to reform

regente [he'ʒẽtʃi] M (*Pol*) regent; (*de orquestra*) conductor; (*de banda*) leader

reger [he'ʒer] VT to govern, rule; (*regular, Ling*) to govern; (*orquestra*) to conduct; (*empresa*) to run ▶ VI (*governar*) to rule; (*maestro*) to conduct; **~ uma cadeira** (*Educ*) to hold a chair

região [he'ʒjãw] (*pl* -**ões**) F region; (*de uma cidade*) area

regime [he'ʒimi] M (*Pol*) regime; (*dieta*) diet; (*maneira*) way; **meu ~ agora é levantar cedo** my routine now is to get up early; **fazer ~** to diet; **estar de ~** to be on a diet; **o ~ das prisões/dos hospitais** the prison/hospital system; **~ de vida** way of life

regimento [heʒi'mẽtu] M regiment; (*regras*) regulations *pl*, rules *pl*; **~ interno** (*de empresa*) company rules *pl*

régio, -a ['hɛʒju, a] ADJ (*real*) royal; (*digno do rei*) regal; (*suntuoso*) princely

regiões [he'ʒjõjs] FPL *de* **região**

regional [heʒjo'naw] (*pl* -**ais**) ADJ regional

registrador, a [heʒis'tra'dor(a)], (PT) **registador, a** M/F registrar, recorder ▶ F: **(caixa) ~a** cash register, till

registrar [heʒis'trar], (PT) **registar** VT to register; (*anotar*) to record; (*com máquina registradora*) to ring up

registro [he'ʒistru], (PT) **registo** M (*ato*) registration; (: *anotação*) recording; (*livro, Ling*) register; (*histórico, Comput*) record; (*relógio*) meter; (*Mús*) range; (*torneira*) stopcock; **~ civil** registry office

rego ['hegu] M (*para água*) ditch; (*de arado*) furrow; (!) crack

reg° ** ABR = **regulamento

regozijar [hegozi'ʒar] VT to gladden; **regozijar-se** VR to be delighted, rejoice

regozijo [hego'ziʒu] M joy, delight

regra ['hegra] F rule; **regras** FPL (*Med*) periods; **sair da ~** to step out of line; **em ~** as a rule, usually; **por via de ~** as a rule

regrado, -a [he'gradu, a] ADJ (*sensato*) sensible

regravável [hegra'vavew] (*pl* **-eis**) ADJ rewritable

regredir [hegre'dʒir] VI to regress; (*doença*) to retreat

regressão [hegre'sãw] F regression

regressar [hegre'sar] VI to come (*ou* go) back, return

regressivo, -a [hegre'sivu, a] ADJ regressive; **contagem regressiva** countdown

regresso [he'grɛsu] M return

regrido *etc* [he'gridu] VB *ver* **regredir**

régua ['hɛgwa] F ruler; **~ de calcular** slide rule

regulador, a [hegula'dor, a] ADJ regulating ▶ M regulator

regulagem [hegu'laʒẽ] F (*de motor, carro*) tuning

regulamentação [hegulamẽta'sãw] F regulation; (*regras*) regulations *pl*

regulamento [hegula'mẽtu] M rules *pl*, regulations *pl*

regular [hegu'lar] ADJ regular; (*estatura*) average, medium; (*tamanho*) normal; (*razoável*) not bad ▶ VT to regulate; (*reger*) to govern; (*máquina*) to adjust; (*carro, motor*) to tune; (*relógio*) to put right ▶ VI to work, function; **regular-se** VR: **~-se por** to be guided by; **ele não regula (bem)** he's not quite right in the head; **~ por** to be about; **~ com alguém** to be about the same age as sb

regularidade [hegulari'dadʒi] F regularity

regularizar [hegulari'zar] VT to regularize

regurgitar [hegurʒi'tar] VT, VI to regurgitate

rei [hej] M king; **ele é o ~ da bagunça** (*col*) he's the world's worst for untidiness; **ter o ~ na barriga** to be full of oneself; **Dia de R-s** Epiphany; **R~ Momo** carnival king

reimprimir [heĩpri'mir] VT to reprint

reinado [hej'nadu] M reign

reinar [hej'nar] VI to reign; (*fig*) to reign, prevail

reincidência [heĩsi'dẽsja] F backsliding; (*de criminoso*) recidivism

reincidir [heĩsi'dʒir] VI to relapse; (*criminoso*) to re-offend; **~ em erro** to do wrong again

reingressar [heĩgre'sar] VI: **~ (em)** to re-enter

reiniciar [hejni'sjar] VT to restart

reino ['hejnu] M kingdom; (*fig*) realm; **~ animal** animal kingdom; **o R~ Unido** the United Kingdom

reintegrar [heĩte'grar] VT (*em emprego*) to reinstate; (*reconduzir*) to return, restore

reiterar [heite'rar] VT to reiterate, repeat

reitor, a [hej'tor(a)] M/F (*de uma universidade*) vice-chancellor (BRIT), president (US) ▶ M (PT: *pároco*) rector

reitoria [hejto'ria] F (*de universidade: cargo*) vice-chancellorship (BRIT), presidency (US); (*gabinete*) vice-chancellor's (BRIT) *ou* president's (US) office

reivindicação [hejvĩdʒika'sãw] (*pl* **-ões**) F claim, demand

reivindicar [hejvĩdʒi'kar] VT to claim; (*aumento salarial, direitos*) to demand

rejeição [heʒej'sãw] (*pl* **-ões**) F rejection

rejeitar [heʒej'tar] VT to reject; (*recusar*) to refuse

rejo *etc* ['heju] VB *ver* **reger**

rejubilar [heʒubi'lar] VT to fill with joy ▶ VI to rejoice; **rejubilar-se** VR to rejoice

rejuvenescedor, a [heʒuvenese'dor(a)] ADJ rejuvenating

rejuvenescer [heʒuvene'ser] VT to rejuvenate ▶ VI to be rejuvenated; **rejuvenescer-se** VR to be rejuvenated

relação [hela'sãw] (*pl* **-ões**) F relation; (*conexão*) connection, relationship; (*relacionamento*) relationship; (*Mat*) ratio; (*lista*) list; **com** *ou* **em ~ a** regarding, with reference to; **ter relações com alguém** to have intercourse with sb; **relações públicas** public relations

relacionado, -a [helasjo'nadu, a] ADJ (*listado*) listed; (*ligado*) related, connected; **uma pessoa bem** *ou* **muito relacionada** a well-connected person

relacionamento [helasjona'mẽtu] M relationship

relacionar [helasjo'nar] VT (*listar*) to make a list of; (*ligar*): **~ algo com algo** to connect sth with sth, relate sth to sth; **relacionar-se** VR to be connected *ou* related; **~ alguém com alguém** to bring sb into contact with sb; **~-se com** (*ligar-se*) to be connected with, have to do with; (*conhecer*) to become acquainted with

relações [hela'sõjs] FPL *de* **relação**

relações-públicas M/F INV PR person

relâmpago [he'lãpagu] M flash of lightning ▶ ADJ INV (*visita*) lightning *atr*; **relâmpagos** MPL (*clarões*) lightning *sg*; **passar como um ~** to flash past; **como um ~** like lightning, as quick as a flash

relampejar [helãpe'ʒar] VI to flash; **relampejou** the lightning flashed

relance [he'lãsi] M glance; **olhar de ~** to glance at

relapso, -a [he'lapsu, a] ADJ (*reincidente*) recidivous; (*negligente*) negligent

relatar [hela'tar] VT to give an account of

relativo, -a [hela'tʃivu, a] ADJ relative

relato [he'latu] M account

relator, a [hela'tor(a)] M/F storyteller

relatório [hela'tɔrju] M report; **~ anual** (*Com*) annual report

relaxado, -a [hela'ʃadu, a] ADJ relaxed; (*desleixado*) slovenly, sloppy; (*relapso*) negligent

relaxamento [helaʃa'mẽtu] M relaxation; (*de moral, costumes*) debasement; (*desleixo*) slovenliness; (*de relapsos*) negligence

relaxante [hela'ʃãtʃi] ADJ relaxing ▶ M tranquillizer

relaxar [hela'ʃar] VT to relax; (*moral, costumes*) to debase ▶ VI to relax; (*tornar-se negligente*):

~ (em) to grow complacent (in); **~ com** (*transigir*) to acquiesce in
relaxe [heˈlaʃi] M relaxation
relê [heˈle] VB *ver* **reler**
relegar [heleˈgar] VT to relegate
releio *etc* [heˈleju] VB *ver* **reler**
relembrar [helẽˈbrar] VT to recall
relento [heˈlẽtu] M: **ao ~** out of doors
reler [heˈler] (*irreg: como* **ler**) VT to reread
reles [ˈhɛlis] ADJ INV (*gente*) common, vulgar; (*comportamento*) despicable; (*mero*) mere
relevância [heleˈvãsja] F relevance
relevante [heleˈvãtʃi] ADJ relevant
relevar [heleˈvar] VT (*tornar saliente*) to emphasize; (*atenuar*) to relieve; (*desculpar*) to pardon, forgive
relevo [heˈlevu] M relief; (*fig*) prominence, importance; **pôr em ~** to emphasize
reli [heˈli] VB *ver* **reler**
relicário [heliˈkarju] M reliquary, shrine
relido, -a [heˈlidu, a] PP *de* **reler**
religião [heliˈʒãw] (*pl* **-ões**) F religion
religioso, -a [heliˈʒozu, ɔza] ADJ religious; (*casamento*) church *atr* ▶ M/F religious person; (*frade/freira*) monk/nun ▶ M (*casamento*) church wedding
relinchar [helĩˈʃar] VI to neigh
relincho [heˈlĩʃu] M (*som*) neigh; (*ato*) neighing
relíquia [heˈlikja] F relic; **~ de família** family heirloom
relógio [heˈlɔʒu] M clock; (*de gás*) meter; **~ de pé** grandfather clock; **~ de ponto** time clock; **~ (de pulso)** (wrist)watch; **~ de sol** sundial; **corrida contra o ~** race against the clock
relojoaria [heloʒwaˈria] F watchmaker's, watch shop
relojoeiro, -a [heloˈʒwejru, a] M/F watchmaker, clockmaker
relutância [heluˈtãsja] F reluctance
relutante [heluˈtãtʃi] ADJ reluctant
relutar [heluˈtar] VI: **~ (em fazer)** to be reluctant (to do); **~ contra algo** to be reluctant to accept sth
reluzente [heluˈzẽtʃi] ADJ brilliant, shining
reluzir [heluˈzir] VI to gleam, shine
relva [ˈhewva] F grass; (*terreno gramado*) lawn
relvado [hewˈvadu] (*PT*) M lawn
rem ABR (= *remetente*) sender
remador, a [hemaˈdor(a)] M/F rower, oarsman/woman
remanchar [hemãˈʃar] VI to delay, take one's time
remanescente [hemaneˈsẽtʃi] ADJ remaining ▶ M remainder; (*excesso*) surplus
remanescer [hemaneˈser] VI to remain
remanso [heˈmãsu] M (*pausa*) pause, rest; (*sossego*) stillness, quiet; (*água*) backwater
remar [heˈmar] VT to row; (*canoa*) to paddle ▶ VI to row; **~ contra a maré** (*fig*) to swim against the tide

remarcação [hemarkaˈsãw] F (*de preços*) changing; (*de artigos*) repricing; (*artigos remarcados*) repriced goods *pl*
remarcar [hemarˈkar] VT (*preços*) to adjust; (*artigos*) to reprice
rematado, -a [hemaˈtadu, a] ADJ (*concluído*) completed
rematar [hemaˈtar] VT to finish off
remate [heˈmatʃi] M (*fim*) end; (*acabamento*) finishing touch; (*Arq*) coping; (*fig: cume*) peak; (*de piada*) punch line
remedeio *etc* [hemeˈdeju] VB *ver* **remediar**
remediado, -a [hemeˈdʒjadu, a] ADJ comfortably off
remediar [hemeˈdʒjar] VT (*corrigir*) to put right, remedy
remediável [hemeˈdʒjavew] (*pl* **-eis**) ADJ rectifiable
remédio [heˈmɛdʒju] M (*medicamento*) medicine; (*recurso, solução*) remedy; (*Jur*) recourse; **não tem ~** there's no way; **que ~?** what else can one do?; **~ caseiro** home remedy
remela [heˈmɛla] F (*nos olhos*) sleep
remelento, -a [hemeˈlẽtu, a] ADJ bleary-eyed
remelexo [hemeˈleʃu] M (*requebro*) swaying
rememorar [hememoˈrar] VT to remember
rememorável [hememoˈravew] (*pl* **-eis**) ADJ memorable
remendar [hemẽˈdar] VT to mend; (*com pano*) to patch
remendo [heˈmẽdu] M repair; (*de pano*) patch
remessa [heˈmɛsa] F (*Com*) shipment; (*de dinheiro*) remittance
remetente [hemeˈtẽtʃi] M/F (*de carta*) sender; (*Com*) shipper
remeter [hemeˈter] VT (*expedir*) to send, dispatch; (*dinheiro*) to remit; (*entregar*) to hand over; **remeter-se** VR: **~-se a** (*referir-se*) to refer to
remexer [hemeˈʃer] VT (*papéis*) to shuffle; (*sacudir: braços*) to wave; (*folhas*) to shake; (*revolver: areia, lama*) to stir up ▶ VI: **~ em** to rummage through; **remexer-se** VR (*mover-se*) to move around; (*rebolar-se*) to sway
remição [hemiˈsãw] F redemption
reminiscência [heminiˈsẽsja] F reminiscence
remir [heˈmir] VT (*coisa penhorada, Rel*) to redeem; (*livrar*) to free; (*danos, perdas*) to make good; **remir-se** VR (*pecador*) to redeem o.s.
remissão [hemiˈsãw] (*pl* **-ões**) F (*Com, Rel*) redemption; (*compensação*) payment; (*num livro*) cross-reference
remisso, -a [heˈmisu, a] ADJ remiss; **~ em fazer** (*lento*) slow to do
remissões [hemiˈsõjs] FPL *de* **remissão**
remível [heˈmivew] (*pl* **-eis**) ADJ redeemable
remo [ˈhemu] M oar; (*de canoa*) paddle; (*Esporte*) rowing
remoa *etc* [heˈmoa] VB *ver* **remoer**
remoção [hemoˈsãw] F removal
remoçar [hemoˈsar] VT to rejuvenate ▶ VI to be rejuvenated

remoer [he'mwer] vt (*café*) to regrind; (*no pensamento*) to turn over in one's mind; (*amofinar*) to eat away; **remoer-se** vr (*amofinar-se*) to be consumed *ou* eaten away

remoinho [hemo'iɲu] m = **rodamoinho**

remontar [hemõ'tar] vt (*elevar*) to raise; (*tornar a armar*) to re-assemble ▶ vi (*em cavalo*) to remount; **~ ao passado** to return to the past; **~ ao século XV** *etc* to date back to the 15th century *etc*; **~ o voo** to soar

remoque [he'mɔki] m gibe, taunt

remorso [he'mɔrsu] m remorse

remoto, -a [he'mɔtu, a] adj remote, far off; (*controle, Comput*) remote

remover [hemo'ver] vt (*mover*) to move; (*transferir*) to transfer; (*demitir*) to dismiss; (*retirar, afastar*) to remove; (*terra*) to churn up

remuneração [hemunera'sãw] (*pl* -**ões**) f remuneration; (*salário*) wage

remunerador, a [hemunera'dor(a)] adj remunerative; (*recompensador*) rewarding

remunerar [hemune'rar] vt to remunerate; (*premiar*) to reward

rena ['hena] f reindeer

renal [he'naw] (*pl* -**ais**) adj renal, kidney *atr*

Renamo [he'namu] abr f = **Resistência Nacional Moçambicana**

Renascença [hena'sẽsa] f: **a ~** the Renaissance

renascer [hena'ser] vi to be reborn; (*fig*) to revive

renascimento [henasi'mẽtu] m rebirth; (*fig*) revival; **o R~** the Renaissance

Renavam (br) abr m = **Registro Nacional de Veículos Automotores**

renda ['hẽda] f income; (*nacional*) revenue; (*de aplicação, locação*) yield; (*tecido*) lace; **~ bruta/líquida** gross/net income; **imposto de ~** (br) income tax; **~ per capita** per capita income

rendado, -a [hẽ'dadu, a] adj lace-trimmed; (*com aspecto de renda*) lacy ▶ m lacework

rendeiro, -a [hẽ'dejru, a] m/f lacemaker

render [hẽ'der] vt (*lucro, dinheiro*) to bring in, yield; (*preço*) to fetch; (*homenagem*) to pay; (*graças*) to give; (*serviços*) to render; (*armas*) to surrender; (*guarda*) to relieve; (*causar*) to bring ▶ vi (*dar lucro*) to pay; (*trabalho*) to be productive; (*comida*) to go a long way; (*conversa, caso*) to go on, last; **render-se** vr to surrender

rendez-vous [hãde'vu] m inv = **randevu**

rendição [hẽdʒi'sãw] f surrender

rendido, -a [hẽ'dʒidu, a] adj subdued

rendimento [hẽdʒi'mẽtu] m (*renda*) income; (*lucro*) profit; (*juro*) yield, interest; (*produtividade*) productivity; (*de máquina*) efficiency; (*de um produto*) value for money; **~ por ação** (Com) earnings per share, earnings yield; **~ de capital** (Com) return on capital

rendoso, -a [hẽ'dozu, ɔza] adj profitable

renegado, -a [hene'gadu, a] adj, m/f renegade

renegar [hene'gar] vt (*crença*) to renounce; (*detestar*) to hate; (*trair*) to betray; (*negar*) to deny; (*desprezar*) to reject

renhido, -a [he'ɲidu, a] adj hard-fought; (*batalha*) bloody

renitência [heni'tẽsja] f obstinacy

renitente [heni'tẽtʃi] adj obstinate, stubborn

Reno ['henu] m: **o ~** the Rhine

renomado, -a [heno'madu, a] adj renowned

renome [he'nɔmi] m fame, renown; **de ~** renowned

renovação [henova'sãw] (*pl* -**ões**) f renewal; (*Arq*) renovation

renovar [heno'var] vt to renew; (*Arq*) to renovate; (*ensino, empresa*) to revamp ▶ vi to be renewed

renque ['hẽki] m row

rentabilidade [hẽtabili'dadʒi] f profitability

rentável [hẽ'tavew] (*pl* -**eis**) adj profitable

rente ['hẽtʃi] adj (*cabelo*) close-cropped; (*casa*) nearby ▶ adv close; (*muito curto*) very short; **~ a** close by

renúncia [he'nũsja] f renunciation; (*de cargo*) resignation; **~ a um direito** waiver (of a right)

renunciar [henũ'sjar] vt to give up, renounce ▶ vi to resign; (*abandonar*): **~ a algo** to give sth up; (*direito*) to surrender sth; (*fé, crença*) to renounce sth

reorganizar [heorgani'zar] vt to reorganize

reouve *etc* [he'ovi] vb *ver* **reaver**

reouver *etc* [heo'ver] vb *ver* **reaver**

reparação [hepara'sãw] (*pl* -**ões**) f (*conserto*) mending, repairing; (*de mal, erros*) remedying; (*de prejuízos, ofensa*) making amends; (*fig*) amends *pl*, reparation

reparar [hepa'rar] vt (*consertar*) to repair; (*forças*) to restore; (*mal, erros*) to remedy; (*prejuízo, danos, ofensa*) to make amends for; (*notar*) to notice ▶ vi: **~ em** to notice; **não repare em** pay no attention to; **repare em** (*olhe*) look at

reparo [he'paru] m (*conserto*) repair; (*crítica*) criticism; (*observação*) observation

repartição [hepartʃi'sãw] (*pl* -**ões**) f (*ato*) distribution; (*seção*) department; (*escritório*) office; **~ (pública)** government department

repartir [hepar'tʃir] vt (*distribuir*) to distribute; (*dividir entre vários*) to share out; (*dividir em várias porções*) to divide up; (*cabelo*) to part; **repartir-se** vr (*dividir-se*) to divide

repassar [hepa'sar] vt (*ponte, fronteira*) to go over again; (*lição*) to revise, go over ▶ vi to go by again; **passar e ~** to go back and forth

repasto [he'pastu] m (*refeição*) meal, repast; (*banquete*) feast

repatriar [hepa'trjar] vt to repatriate; **repatriar-se** vr to go back home

repelão [hepe'lãw] (*pl* -**ões**) m push, shove; **de ~** brusquely

repelente [hepe'lẽtʃi] adj, m repellent

repelir [hepe'lir] vt to repel; (*curiosos*) to drive away; (*ideias, atitudes*) to reject, repudiate;

seu estômago repele certos alimentos
his stomach cannot take certain foods
repelões [hepe'lõjs] FPL *de* **repelão**
repensar [hepẽ'sar] VT to reconsider, rethink
repente [he'pẽtʃi] M outburst; **de ~** suddenly; (*col: talvez*) maybe
repentino, -a [hepẽ'tʃinu, a] ADJ sudden
repercussão [heperku'sãw] (*pl* **-ões**) F repercussion
repercutir [heperku'tʃir] VT (*som*) to echo ▶ VI (*som*) to reverberate, echo; (*fig*): **~ (em)** to have repercussions (on)
repertório [heper'tɔrju] M (*lista*) list; (*coleção*) collection; (*Mús*) repertoire
repetição [hepetʃi'sãw] (*pl* **-ões**) F repetition
repetidamente [hepetʃida'mẽtʃi] ADV repeatedly
repetido, -a [hepe'tʃidu, a] ADJ repeated; **repetidas vezes** repeatedly, again and again
repetir [hepe'tʃir] VT to repeat; (*vestido*) to wear again ▶ VI (*ao comer*) to have seconds; **repetir-se** VR (*acontecer de novo*) to happen again; (*pessoa*) to repeat o.s.
repetitivo, -a [hepetʃi'tʃivu, a] ADJ repetitive
repicar [hepi'kar] VT (*sinos*) to ring ▶ VI to ring (out)
repilo *etc* [he'pilu] VB *ver* **repelir**
repimpado, -a [hepĩ'padu, a] ADJ (*refestelado*) lolling; (*satisfeito*) full up
repique¹ [he'piki] M (*de sinos*) peal; **~ falso** false alarm
repique² *etc* VB *ver* **repicar**
repisar [hepi'zar] VT (*repetir*) to repeat; (*uvas*) to tread ▶ VI: **~ em** (*assunto*) to keep on about, harp on
repito *etc* [he'pitu] VB *ver* **repetir**
replay [he'plei] (*pl* **-s**) M (*TV*) (action) replay
repleto, -a [he'plɛtu, a] ADJ replete, full up
réplica ['hɛplika] F (*cópia*) replica; (*contestação*) reply, retort
replicar [hepli'kar] VT to answer, reply to ▶ VI to reply, answer back
repõe *etc* [he'põj] VB *ver* **repor**
repolho [he'poʎu] M cabbage
repomos [he'pomos] VB *ver* **repor**
reponho *etc* [he'poɲu] VB *ver* **repor**
repontar [hepõ'tar] VI (*aparecer*) to appear
repor [he'por] (*irreg: como* **pôr**) VT to put back, replace; (*restituir*) to return; **repor-se** VR (*pessoa*) to recover
reportagem [hepor'taʒẽ] (*pl* **-ns**) F (*ato*) reporting; (*notícia*) report; (*repórteres*) reporters *pl*
reportar [hepor'tar] VT: **~ a** (*o pensamento*) to take back to; (*atribuir*) to attribute to; **reportar-se** VR: **~-se a** to refer to; (*relacionar-se a*) to be connected with
repórter [he'pɔrter] M/F reporter
repôs [he'pos] VB *ver* **repor**
reposição [hepozi'sãw] (*pl* **-ões**) F replacement; (*restituição*) return; **~ salarial** wage adjustment
repositório [hepozi'tɔrju] M repository

reposto, -a [he'postu, 'pɔsta] PP *de* **repor**
repousar [hepo'zar] VI to rest
repouso [he'pozu] M rest
repreender [heprjẽ'der] VT to reprimand
repreensão [heprjẽ'sãw] (*pl* **-ões**) F rebuke, reprimand
repreensível [heprjẽ'sivew] (*pl* **-eis**) ADJ reprehensible
repreensões [heprjẽ'sõjs] FPL *de* **repreensão**
represa [he'preza] F dam
represália [hepre'zalja] F reprisal
representação [heprezẽta'sãw] (*pl* **-ões**) F representation; (*representantes*) representatives *pl*; (*Teatro*) performance; (*atuação do ator*) acting
representante [heprezẽ'tãtʃi] M/F representative
representar [heprezẽ'tar] VT to represent; (*Teatro: papel*) to play ▶ VI (*ator*) to act; (*tb Jur*) to make a complaint
representativo, -a [heprezẽta'tʃivu, a] ADJ representative
repressão [hepre'sãw] (*pl* **-ões**) F repression
repressivo, -a [hepre'sivu, a] ADJ repressive
repressões [hepre'sõjs] FPL *de* **repressão**
reprimido, -a [hepri'midu, a] ADJ repressed
reprimir [hepri'mir] VT to repress; (*lágrimas*) to keep back
reprise [he'prizi] F reshowing
réprobo, -a ['hɛprobu, a] ADJ, M/F reprobate
reprodução [heprodu'sãw] (*pl* **-ões**) F reproduction
reprodutor, a [heprodu'tor(a)] ADJ reproductive
reproduzir [heprodu'zir] VT to reproduce; (*repetir*) to repeat; **reproduzir-se** VR to breed, multiply; to be repeated
reprovação [heprova'sãw] (*pl* **-ões**) F disapproval; (*em exame*) failure
reprovado, -a [hepro'vadu, a] M/F failed candidate, failure; **taxa de ~s** failure rate
reprovador, a [heprova'dor(a)] ADJ (*olhar*) disapproving, reproving
reprovar [hepro'var] VT (*condenar*) to disapprove of; (*aluno*) to fail
réptil ['hɛptʃiw] (*pl* **-eis**) M reptile
repto ['hɛptu] M challenge, provocation
república [he'publika] F republic; **~ de estudantes** students' house; **~ popular** people's republic
republicano, -a [hepubli'kanu, a] ADJ, M/F republican
repudiar [hepu'dʒjar] VT to repudiate, reject; (*abandonar*) to disown
repúdio [he'pudʒju] M rejection, repudiation
repugnância [hepug'nãsja] F repugnance; (*por comida etc*) disgust; (*aversão*) aversion; (*moral*) abhorrence
repugnante [hepug'nãtʃi] ADJ repugnant, repulsive
repugnar [hepug'nar] VT to oppose ▶ VI to be repulsive; **~ a alguém** to disgust sb; (*moralmente*) to be repugnant to sb

r

repulsa [hɛ'puwsa] F *(ato)* rejection; *(sentimento)* repugnance; *(física)* repulsion

repulsão [hepuw'sãw] *(pl* **-ões)** F repulsion; *(rejeição)* rejection

repulsivo, -a [hepuw'sivu, a] ADJ repulsive

repulsões [hepuw'sõjs] FPL *de* **repulsão**

repunha *etc* [he'puɲa] VB *ver* **repor**

repus *etc* [he'pus] VB *ver* **repor**

repuser [hepu'zer] VB *ver* **repor**

reputação [reputa'sãw] *(pl* **-ões)** F reputation

reputado, -a [hepu'tadu, a] ADJ renowned

reputar [hepu'tar] VT to consider, regard as

repuxado, -a [hepu'ʃadu, a] ADJ *(pele)* tight, firm; *(olhos)* slanted

repuxar [hepu'ʃar] VT *(puxar)* to tug; *(esticar)* to pull tight

repuxo [he'puʃu] M *(de água)* fountain; **aguentar o ~** *(col)* to bear up

requebrado [reke'bradu] M *(rebolado)* swing, sway

requebrar [heke'brar] VT to wiggle, swing; **requebrar-se** VR to wiggle, swing

requeijão [hekej'ʒãw] M cheese spread

requeira *etc* [he'kejra] VB *ver* **requerer**

requentar [hekẽ'tar] VT to reheat, warm up

requer [he'ker] VB *ver* **requerer**

requerente [heke'rẽtʃi] M/F *(Jur)* petitioner

requerer [heke'rer] VT *(emprego)* to apply for; *(pedir)* to request, ask for; *(exigir)* to require; *(Jur)* to petition for

requerimento [hekeri'mẽtu] M application; *(pedido)* request; *(petição)* petition

réquiem ['hɛkjẽ] *(pl* **-ns)** M requiem

requintado, -a [hekĩ'tadu, a] ADJ refined, elegant

requintar [hekĩ'tar] VT to refine ▶ VI: **~ em** to be refined in

requinte [he'kĩtʃi] M refinement, elegance; *(cúmulo)* height

requisição [hekizi'sãw] *(pl* **-ões)** F request, demand

requisitado, -a [hekizi'tadu, a] ADJ *(requerido)* required; *(muito procurado)* sought after

requisitar [hekizi'tar] VT to make a request for; *(Mil)* to requisition

requisito [heki'zitu] M requirement

rês [hes] F head of cattle; **reses** FPL *(gado)* cattle, livestock *sg*

rescindir [hesĩ'dʒir] VT *(contrato)* to rescind

rescrever [heskre'ver] VT = **reescrever**

rés do chão [hɛzdu'ʃãw] *(PT)* M INV *(andar térreo)* ground floor *(BRIT)*, first floor *(US)*

resenha [he'zeɲa] F *(relatório)* report; *(resumo)* summary; *(de livro)* review; **fazer a ~ de** *(livro)* to review

reserva [he'zɛrva] F reserve; *(para hotel, fig: ressalva)* reservation; *(discrição)* discretion ▶ M/F *(Esporte)* reserve; **~ de mercado** *(Com)* protected market; **~ de petróleo** oil reserve; **~ natural** nature reserve; **~ em dinheiro** cash reserve

reservado, -a [hezer'vadu, a] ADJ reserved; *(pej: retraído)* standoffish

reservar [hezer'var] VT to reserve; *(guardar de reserva)* to keep; *(forças)* to conserve; **reservar-se** VR to save o.s.; **~-se o direito de fazer** to reserve the right to do; **ele não sabe o que o futuro lhe reserva** he does not know what the future has in store for him

reservatório [hezerva'tɔrju] M *(lago)* reservoir

reservista [hezer'vista] M/F *(Mil)* member of the reserves

resfolegar [hesfole'gar] VI to pant

resfriado, -a [hes'frjadu, a] *(BR)* ADJ: **estar ~** to have a cold ▶ M cold, chill; **ficar ~** to catch (a) cold

resfriar [hes'frjar] VT to cool, chill ▶ VI *(pessoa)* to catch (a) cold; **resfriar-se** VR to catch (a) cold

resgatar [hezga'tar] VT *(salvar)* to rescue; *(retomar)* to get back, recover; *(dívida)* to pay off; *(Com: ação, coisa penhorada)* to redeem

resgatável [hezga'tavew] *(pl* **-eis)** ADJ redeemable

resgate [hez'gatʃi] M *(salvamento)* rescue; *(para livrar reféns)* ransom; *(Com: de ações, coisa penhorada)* redemption; *(retomada)* recovery

resguardar [hezgwar'dar] VT to protect; **resguardar-se** VR: **~-se de** to guard against

resguardo [hez'gwardu] M protection; *(cuidado)* care; *(convalescência)* estar *ou* ficar de ~ to take *ou* be taking things easy

residência [hezi'dẽsja] F residence

residencial [hezidẽ'sjaw] *(pl* **-ais)** ADJ *(zona, edifício)* residential; *(computador, telefone etc)* home *atr*

residente [hezi'dẽtʃi] ADJ, M/F resident

residir [hezi'dʒir] VI to live, reside; *(achar-se)* to reside

resíduo [he'zidwu] M residue

resignação [hezigna'sãw] *(pl* **-ões)** F resignation

resignadamente [hezignada'mẽtʃi] ADJ with resignation

resignado, -a [hezig'nadu, a] ADJ resigned

resignar-se [hezig'narsi] VR: **~ com** to resign o.s. to

resiliente [hezi'ljẽtʃi] ADJ resilient

resina [he'zina] F resin

resistência [hezis'tẽsja] F resistance; *(de atleta)* stamina; *(de material, objeto)* strength; *(moral)* morale

resistente [hezis'tẽtʃi] ADJ resistant; *(material, objeto)* hard-wearing, strong; **~ a traças** mothproof

resistir [hezis'tʃir] VI *(suporte)* to hold; *(pessoa)* to hold out; **~ a** *(não ceder)* to resist; *(sobreviver)* to survive; **~ ao uso** to wear well; **~ (ao tempo)** to endure, stand the test of time

resma ['hezma] F ream

resmungar [hezmũ'gar] VT, VI to mutter, mumble

resmungo [hez'mũgu] M grumbling

resolução [hezolu'sãw] *(pl* **-ões)** F resolution; *(coragem)* courage; *(de um problema)* solution; **de alta ~ (gráfica)** *(Comput)* high-resolution

resoluto, -a [hezo'lutu, a] ADJ decisive; ~ **a fazer** resolved to do

resolver [hezow'ver] VT to sort out; (*problema*) to solve; (*questão*) to resolve; (*decidir*) to decide; **resolver-se** VR: ~-**se (a fazer)** to make up one's mind (to do), decide (to do); **chorar não resolve** crying doesn't help, it's no use crying; ~-**se por** to decide on

resolvido, -a [hezow'vidu, a] ADJ (*pessoa*) decisive

respaldo [hes'pawdu] M (*de cadeira*) back; (*fig*) support, backing

respectivo, -a [hespek'tʃivu, a] ADJ respective

respeitador, a [hespejta'dor(a)] ADJ respectful

respeitante [hespej'tãtʃi] ADJ: ~ **a** concerning, with regard to

respeitar [hespej'tar] VT to respect

respeitável [hespej'tavew] (*pl* -**eis**) ADJ respectable; (*considerável*) considerable

respeito [hes'pejtu] M: ~ **a** (ou **por**) respect (for); **respeitos** MPL (*cumprimentos*) regards; **a** ~ **de, com** ~ **a** as to, as regards; (*sobre*) about; **dizer** ~ **a** to concern; **faltar ao** ~ **a** to be rude to; **em** ~ **a** with respect to; **dar-se ao** ~ to command respect; **pessoa de** ~ respected person; **ela não me disse nada a seu** ~ she didn't tell me anything about you; **não sei nada a** ~ (**disso**) I know nothing about it

respeitoso, -a [hespej'tozu, ɔza] ADJ respectful

respingar [hespĩ'gar] VT, VI to splash, spatter

respingo [hes'pĩgu] M splash

respiração [hespira'sãw] F breathing; (*Med*) respiration

respirador [hespira'dor] M respirator

respirar [hespi'rar] VT to breathe; (*revelar*) to reveal, show ▶ VI to breathe; (*descansar*) to have a respite

respiratório, -a [hespira'tɔrju, a] ADJ respiratory

respiro [hes'piru] M breath; (*descanso*) respite; (*abertura*) vent

resplandecente [hesplãde'sẽtʃi] ADJ resplendent

resplandecer [hesplãde'ser] VI to gleam, shine (out)

resplendor [hesplẽ'dor] M brilliance; (*fig*) glory

respondão, -dona [hespõ'dãw, 'dɔna] (*pl* -**ões/-s**) ADJ cheeky, insolent

responder [hespõ'der] VT to answer ▶ VI to answer; (*ser respondão*) to answer back; ~ **a** (*tratamento, agressão*) to respond to; (*processo, inquérito*) to undergo; ~ **por** to be responsible for, answer for; (*Com*) to be liable for

respondões [hespõ'dõjs] MPL *de* **respondão**

respondona [hespõ'dɔna] F *de* **respondão**

responsabilidade [hespõsabili'dadʒi] F responsibility; (*Jur*) liability

responsabilizar [hespõsabili'zar] VT: ~ **alguém (por algo)** to hold sb responsible (for sth); **responsabilizar-se** VR: ~-**se por** to take responsibility for

responsável [hespõ'savew] (*pl* -**eis**) ADJ: ~ (**por**) responsible (for) ▶ M person responsible *ou* in charge; ~ **a** answerable to, accountable to

resposta [hes'pɔsta] F answer, reply

resquício [hes'kisju] M (*vestígio*) trace

ressabiado, -a [hesa'bjadu, a] ADJ (*desconfiado*) wary; (*ressentido*) resˈentful

ressaca [he'saka] F (*refluxo*) undertow; (*mar bravo*) rough sea; (*fig: de quem bebeu*) hangover; **estar de** ~ (*mar*) to be rough; (*pessoa*) to have a hangover

ressaibo [he'sajbu] M (*mau sabor*) unpleasant taste; (*fig: indício*) trace; (: *ressentimento*) ill feeling

ressaltar [hesaw'tar] VT to emphasize ▶ VI to stand out

ressalva [he'sawva] F (*proteção*) safeguard; (*Mil*) exemption certificate; (*correção*) correction; (*restrição*) reservation, proviso; (*exceção*) exception

ressarcir [hesar'sir] VT (*pagar*) to compensate; (*compensar*) to compensate for; ~ **alguém de** to compensate sb for

ressecado, -a [hese'kadu, a] ADJ (*terra, lábios*) parched; (*pele, planta*) very dry

ressecar [hese'kar] VT, VI to dry up

resseguro [hese'guru] M reinsurance

ressentido, -a [hesẽ'tʃidu, a] ADJ resentful

ressentimento [hesẽtʃi'mẽtu] M resentment

ressentir-se [hesẽ'tʃirsi] VR: ~ **de** (*ofender-se*) to resent; (*magoar-se*) to be hurt by; (*sofrer*) to suffer from, feel the effects of

ressequido, -a [hese'kidu, a] ADJ = **ressecado**

ressinto *etc* [he'sĩtu] VB *ver* **ressentir-se**

ressoar [he'swar] VI to resound; (*ecoar*) to echo

ressonância [heso'nãsja] F resonance; (*eco*) echo

ressonante [heso'nãtʃi] ADJ resonant

ressurgimento [hesurʒi'mẽtu] M resurgence, revival

ressurreição [hesuhej'sãw] (*pl* -**ões**) F resurrection

ressuscitar [hesusi'tar] VT to revive, resuscitate; (*costumes etc*) to revive ▶ VI to revive

restabelecer [hestabele'ser] VT to re-establish; (*ordem, forças*) to restore; (*doente*) to restore to health; **restabelecer-se** VR to recover, recuperate

restabelecimento [hestabelesi'mẽtu] M re-establishment; (*da ordem*) restoration; (*Med*) recovery

restante [hes'tãtʃi] ADJ remaining ▶ M rest

restar [hes'tar] VI to remain, be left; (*esperança, dúvida*) to remain; **não lhe resta nada** he has nothing left; **resta-me fechar o negócio** I still have to close the deal; **não resta dúvida de que** there is no longer any doubt that

restauração [hestawra'sãw] (*pl* -**ões**) F restoration; (*de doente*) restoring to health; (*de costumes, usos*) revival

restaurante [heʃtaw'rātʃi] M restaurant
restaurar [heʃtaw'rar] VT to restore;
(*recuperar: doente*) to restore to health;
(*costumes, usos*) to revive, restore
réstia ['hɛʃtʃja] F (*de cebolas*) string; (*luz*) ray
restinga [hes'tʃīga] F spit
restituição [heʃtʃitwi'sãw] (*pl* -**ões**) F
restitution, return; (*de dinheiro*) repayment;
(*a cargo*) reinstatement
restituir [heʃtʃi'twir] VT to return; (*dinheiro*) to
repay; (*forças, saúde*) to restore; (*usos*) to
revive; (*reempossar*) to reinstate
resto ['hɛʃtu] M rest; (*Mat*) remainder; **restos**
MPL (*sobras*) remains; (*de comida*) scraps; ~**s**
mortais mortal remains; **de ~** apart from
that
restrição [heʃtri'sãw] (*pl* -**ões**) F restriction
restringir [heʃtrī'ʒir] VT to restrict;
restringir-se VR: ~-**se a** to be restricted to;
(*pessoa*) to restrict o.s. to
restrito, -a [hes'tritu, a] ADJ restricted
resultado [hezuw'tadu] M result; **dar** ~ to
work, be effective; ~ ... (*col*) the upshot
being ...
resultante [hezuw'tātʃi] ADJ resultant; ~ **de**
resulting from
resultar [hezuw'tar] VI: ~ (**de/em**) to result
(from/in) ▶ VI (*vir a ser*) to turn out to be
resumido, -a [hezu'midu, a] ADJ abbreviated,
abridged; (*curto*) concise
resumir [hezu'mir] VT to summarize; (*livro*) to
abridge; (*reduzir*) to reduce; (*conter em resumo*)
to sum up; **resumir-se** VR: ~-**se a** *ou* **em** to
consist in *ou* of
resumo [he'zumu] M summary, résumé;
em ~ in short, briefly
resvalar [hezva'lar] VT to slide, slip
resvés [heʃ'vɛs] ADJ tight ▶ ADV closely; ~ **a**
right by; (*na conta*) just
reta ['hɛta] F (*linha*) straight line; (*trecho de
estrada*) straight; ~ **final** *ou* **de chegada**
home straight; **na** ~ **final** (*tb fig*) on the
home straight
retaguarda [heta'gwarda] F rearguard;
(*posição*) rear
retalhar [heta'ʎar] VT to cut up; (*separar*) to
divide; (*despedaçar*) to shred; (*ferir*) to slash
retalho [he'taʎu] M (*de pano*) scrap, remnant;
vender a ~ (*PT*) to sell retail; **colcha de ~s**
patchwork quilt
retaliação [hetalja'sãw] (*pl* -**ões**) F
retaliation
retaliar [heta'ljar] VT to repay ▶ VI to
retaliate
retangular [hetāgu'lar] ADJ rectangular
retângulo [he'tāgulu] M rectangle
retardado, -a [hetar'dadu, a] ADJ (*Psico*)
retarded
retardar [hetar'dar] VT to hold up, delay;
(*adiar*) to postpone
retardatário, -a [hetarda'tarju, a] M/F
latecomer
retardo [he'tardu] M (*Psico*) retardedness

retenção [hetē'sãw] F retention
reter [he'ter] (*irreg: como* **ter**) VT (*guardar, manter*)
to keep; (*deter*) to stop, detain; (*segurar*) to
hold; (*ladrão, suspeito*) to detain, hold; (*na
memória*) to retain; (*lágrimas, impulsos*) to hold
back; (*impedir de sair*) to keep back; **reter-se**
VR to restrain o.s.
retesado, -a [hete'zadu, a] ADJ taut
retesar [hete'zar] VT (*músculo*) to flex; (*corda*)
to pull taut
reteve [he'tevi] VB *ver* **reter**
reticência [hetʃi'sēsja] F reticence, reserve;
reticências FPL (*Ling*) suspension points
reticente [hetʃi'sētʃi] ADJ reticent
retidão [hetʃi'dãw] F (*integridade*) rectitude;
(*de linha*) straightness
retificar [hetʃifi'kar] VT to rectify
retinha *etc* [he'tʃiɲa] VB *ver* **reter**
retinir [hetʃi'nir] VI (*ferros*) to clink;
(*campainha*) to ring, jingle; (*ressoar*) to
resound
retirada [hetʃi'rada] F (*Mil*) withdrawal,
retreat; (*salário, saque*) withdrawal; **bater em**
~ to beat a retreat
retirado, -a [hetʃi'radu, a] ADJ (*vida*) solitary;
(*lugar*) isolated
retirante [hetʃi'rātʃi] M/F migrant (*from the NE
of Brazil*)
retirar [hetʃi'rar] VT to withdraw; (*tirar*) to
take out; (*afastar*) to take away, remove;
(*fazer sair*) to get out; (*ganhar*) to make;
retirar-se VR to withdraw; (*de uma festa etc*) to
leave; (*da política etc*) to retire; (*recolher-se*) to
retire, withdraw; (*Mil*) to retreat
retiro [he'tʃiru] M retreat
retitude [hetʃi'tudʒi] F rectitude
retive *etc* [he'tʃivi] VB *ver* **reter**
retiver *etc* [he'tʃiver] VB *ver* **reter**
reto, -a ['hɛtu, a] ADJ straight; (*fig: justo*) fair;
(: *honesto*) honest, upright ▶ M (*Anat*) rectum
retocar [heto'kar] VT (*pintura*) to touch up;
(*texto*) to tidy up
retomar [heto'mar] VT to take up again;
(*reaver*) to get back
retoque¹ [he'tɔki] M finishing touch
retoque² *etc* VB *ver* **retocar**
retorcer [hetor'ser] VT to twist; **retorcer-se**
VR to wriggle, writhe; ~-**se de dor** to writhe
in pain
retórica [he'tɔrika] F rhetoric; (*pej*)
affectation
retórico, -a [he'tɔriku, a] ADJ rhetorical; (*pej*)
affected
retornar [hetor'nar] VI to return, go back
retorno [he'tornu] M return; (*Com*) barter,
exchange; (*em rodovia*) turning area; **dar** ~
to do a U-turn; ~ **sobre investimento**
return on investment
retorquir [hetor'kir] VT to answer, say in reply
▶ VI to retort, reply; **ela não retorquiu nada**
she said nothing in reply
retraído, -a [hetra'idu, a] ADJ retracted;
(*tímido*) reserved, timid

retraimento [hetraj'mẽtu] M withdrawal; (contração) contraction; (fig: de pessoa) timidity, shyness

retrair [hetra'ir] VT to withdraw; (contrair) to contract; (pessoa) to make reserved; **retrair-se** VR to withdraw; (encolher-se) to retract

retrasado, -a [hetra'zadu, a] ADJ: **a semana retrasada** the week before last

retratação [hetrata'sãw] (pl -ões) F retraction

retratar [hetra'tar] VT to portray, depict; (mostrar) to show; (dito) to retract; **retratar-se** VR: **~-se (de algo)** to retract (sth)

retrátil [he'tratʃiw] (pl -eis) ADJ retractable; **cinto de segurança ~** inertia-reel seat belt

retratista [hetra'tʃista] M/F portrait painter

retrato [he'tratu] M portrait; (Foto) photo; (fig: efígie) likeness; (: representação) portrayal; **ela é o ~ da mãe** she's the image of her mother; **tirar um ~ (de alguém)** to take a photo (of sb); **~ a meio corpo/de corpo inteiro** half/full-length portrait; **~ falado** Identikit® picture

retribuição [hetribwi'sãw] (pl -ões) F reward, recompense; (pagamento) remuneration; (de hospitalidade, favor) return, reciprocation

retribuir [hetri'bwir] VT (recompensar) to reward, recompense; (pagar) to remunerate; (hospitalidade, favor, sentimento, visita) to return

retroagir [hetroa'ʒir] VI (lei) to be retroactive; (modificar o que está feito) to change what has been done

retroativo, -a [hetroa'tʃivu, a] ADJ retroactive; (pagamento): **~ (a)** backdated (to)

retroceder [hetrose'der] VI to retreat, fall back; (decair) to decline; (num intento) to back down

retrocesso [hetro'sɛsu] M retreat; (ao passado) return; (decadência) decline; (tecla) backspace (key); (da economia) slowdown

retrógrado, -a [he'trɔgradu, a] ADJ retrograde; (reacionário) reactionary

retroprojetor [hetroproʒe'tor] M overhead projector

retrospectiva [hetrospek'tʃiva] F retrospective

retrospectivamente [hetrospektʃiva'mẽtʃi] ADV in retrospect

retrospectivo, -a [hetrospek'tʃivu, a] ADJ retrospective

retrospecto [hetro'spɛktu] M retrospective look; **em ~** in retrospect

retrovisor [hetrovi'zor] ADJ, M: **(espelho) ~** rear-view mirror

retrucar [hetru'kar] VT to answer ▶ VI to retort, reply

retumbância [hetũ'bãsja] F resonance

retumbante [hetũ'bãtʃi] ADJ (tb fig) resounding

retumbar [hetũ'bar] VI to resound, echo; (ribombar) to rumble, boom

returco etc [he'turku] VB ver **retorquir**

réu, ré [hɛw, hɛ] M/F defendant; (culpado) culprit, criminal; **~ de morte** condemned man

reumático, -a [hew'matʃiku, a] ADJ rheumatic

reumatismo [hewma'tʃizmu] M rheumatism

reumatologista [hewmatolo'ʒista] M/F rheumatologist

reunião [heu'njãw] (pl -ões) F meeting; (ato, reencontro) reunion; (festa) get-together, party; **~ de cúpula** summit (meeting); **~ de diretoria** board meeting

reunir [heu'nir] VT (pessoas) to bring together; (partes) to join, unite; (qualidades) to combine; **reunir-se** VR to meet; (amigos) to meet, get together; **~-se a** to join

reutilizar [heutʃili'zar] VT to re-use

revalorizar [hevalori'zar] VT (moeda) to revalue

revanche [he'vãʃi] F revenge; (Esporte) return match

revê etc [he've] VB ver **rever**

reveillon [heve'jõ] M New Year's Eve

revejo etc [he'veʒu] VB ver **rever**

revelação [hevela'sãw] (pl -ões) F revelation; (Foto) development; (novo cantor, ator etc) promising newcomer

revelar [heve'lar] VT to reveal; (mostrar) to show; (Foto) to develop; **revelar-se** VR to turn out to be; **ela se revelou nessa crise** she showed her true colo(u)rs in this crisis

revelia [heve'lia] F default; **à ~** by default; **à ~ de** without the knowledge ou consent of

revendedor, a [hevẽde'dor(a)] M/F dealer

revender [hevẽ'der] VT to resell

rever [he'ver] (irreg: como **ver**) VT to see again; (examinar) to check; (revisar) to revise; (provas tipográficas) to proofread

reverberar [heverbe'rar] VT (luz) to reflect ▶ VI to be reflected

reverdecer [heverde'ser] VT, VI to turn green again

reverência [heve'rẽsja] F reverence, respect; (ato) bow; (: de mulher) curtsey; **fazer uma ~** to bow; to curtsey

reverenciar [heverẽ'sjar] VT to revere, venerate; (obedecer) to obey

reverendo, -a [heve'rẽdu, a] ADJ reverend ▶ M priest, clergyman

reverente [heve'rẽtʃi] ADJ reverential

reversão [hever'sãw] (pl -ões) F reversion

reversível [hever'sivew] (pl -eis) ADJ reversible

reverso [he'vɛrsu] M reverse; **o ~ da medalha** (fig) the other side of the coin

reversões [hever'sõjs] FPL de **reversão**

reverter [hever'ter] VT to revert; (a questão) to return; **~ em benefício de** to benefit

revertério [hever'tɛrju] M: **dar o ~** (col) to go wrong

revés [he'vɛs] M reverse; (infortúnio) setback, mishap; **ao ~** (roupa) inside out; **de ~** (olhar) askance

revestimento [hevestʃi'mẽtu] M (da parede)
covering; (de sofá) cover; (de caixa) lining
revestir [heves'tʃir] VT (traje) to put on;
(cobrir: paredes etc) to cover; (interior de uma
caixa etc) to line; **revestir-se** VR: **~-se de**
(poderes) to assume, take on; (paciência) to
arm o.s. with; (coragem) to take, pluck up;
~ alguém de poderes etc to invest sb with
powers etc
revezamento [heveza'mẽtu] M alternation
revezar [heve'zar] VT to take turns with ▶ VI
to take turns; **revezar-se** VR to take it in
turns
revi [he'vi] VB ver **rever**
revia etc [he'via] VB ver **rever**
revidar [hevi'dar] VT (soco, insulto) to return;
(retrucar) to answer; (crítica) to rise to, respond
to ▶ VI to hit back; (retrucar) to respond
revide [he'vidʒi] M response
revigorar [hevigo'rar] VT to reinvigorate ▶ VI
to regain one's strength; **revigorar-se** VR to
regain one's strength
revir etc [he'vir] VB ver **rever**
revirado, -a [hevi'radu, a] ADJ (casa) untidy,
upside-down
revirar [hevi'rar] VT to turn round; (gaveta)
to turn out, go through; **revirar-se** VR (na
cama) to toss and turn; **~ os olhos** to roll
one's eyes
reviravolta [hevira'vɔwta] F about-turn,
U-turn; (mudança da situação) turn
revisão [hevi'zãw] (pl **-ões**) F revision; (de
máquina) overhaul; (de carro) service; (Jur)
appeal; **~ de provas** proofreading
revisar [hevi'zar] VT to revise; (prova tipográfica)
to proofread
revisões [hevi'zõjs] FPL de **revisão**
revisor, a [hevi'zor(a)] M/F (Ferro etc) ticket
inspector; (de provas) proofreader
revista [he'vista] F (busca) search; (Mil, exame)
inspection; (publicação) magazine;
(: profissional, erudita) journal; (Teatro) revue;
passar ~ a to review; (Mil) to inspect, review;
~ em quadrinhos comic; **~ literária**
literary review; **~ para mulheres** women's
magazine
revistar [hevis'tar] VT to search; (tropa) to
review; (examinar) to examine
revisto' etc [he'vistu] VB ver **revestir**
revisto², -a [he'vistu, a] PP de **rever**
revitalizar [hevitali'zar] VT to revitalize
reviu [he'viu] VB ver **rever**
reviver [hevi'ver] VT to relive; (costumes,
palavras) to revive ▶ VI to revive; (doente) to
pick up
revocar [hevo'kar] VT (o passado) to evoke;
(mandar voltar) to recall; **~ alguém a/de** to
bring sb back to/from
revogação [hevoga'sãw] (pl **-ões**) F (de lei)
repeal; (de ordem) reversal
revogar [hevo'gar] VT to revoke
revolta [he'vɔwta] F revolt; (fig: indignação)
disgust

Revolta da vacina F see note
▌ This was a popular movement of
▌ opposition to the government which
▌ took place in Rio de Janeiro in 1904,
▌ following the passing of a law which
▌ made vaccination against smallpox
▌ compulsory. It was the culmination of
▌ general dissatisfaction with health
▌ reforms undertaken at that time by the
▌ scientist Osvaldo Cruz, and the relocation
▌ programme of the prefect Pereira Passos,
▌ as a result of which part of the population
▌ of Rio had been moved from the slums
▌ and shanty towns of the central region to
▌ suburbs much further out.

revoltado, -a [hevow'tadu, a] ADJ in revolt;
(indignado) disgusted; (amargo) bitter
revoltante [hevow'tãtʃi] ADJ disgusting;
(repugnante) revolting
revoltar [hevow'tar] VT to disgust; (insurgir) to
incite to revolt ▶ VI to cause indignation;
revoltar-se VR to rebel, revolt; (indignar-se) to
be disgusted
revolto, -a [he'vowtu, a] PP de **revolver** ▶ ADJ
(década) turbulent; (mundo) troubled; (cabelo)
dishevelled; (mar) rough; (desarrumado)
untidy
revoltoso, -a [hevow'tozu, ɔza] ADJ in revolt
revolução [hevolu'sãw] (pl **-ões**) F revolution
revolucionar [hevolusjo'nar] VT to
revolutionize
revolucionário, -a [hevolusjo'narju, a] ADJ,
M/F revolutionary
revoluções [hevolu'sõjs] FPL de **revolução**
revolver [hevow'ver] VT (terra) to turn over,
dig over; (gaveta) to rummage through;
(olhos) to roll; (suj: vento) to blow around ▶ VI
(girar) to revolve, rotate
revólver [he'vɔwver] M revolver, gun
reza ['hɛza] F prayer
rezar [he'zar] VT (missa, prece) to say ▶ VI to
pray; **~ (que)** (contar, dizer) to state (that)
RFA ABR F (antes: = República Federal Alemã) FRG
RFFSA (BR) ABR F = **Rede Ferroviária Federal
SA**
RG (BR) ABR M (= Registro Geral) identity document;
ver tb **carteira**
rh ABR: **factor rh** Rh. ou rhesus (BRIT) factor;
rh negativo/positivo rhesus negative/
positive
riacho ['hjaʃu] M stream, brook
ribalta [hi'bawta] F footlights pl; (fig)
boards pl
ribanceira [hibã'sejra] F (margem) steep river
bank; (rampa) steep slope; (precipício) cliff
ribeira [hi'bejra] F riverside; (riacho) river
ribeirão [hibej'rãw] (BR) (pl **-ões**) M stream
ribeirinho, -a [hibej'riɲu, a] ADJ riverside atr
ribeiro [hi'bejru] M brook, stream
ribeirões [hibej'rõjs] MPL de **ribeirão**
ribombar [hibõ'bar] VI (trovão) to rumble,
boom; (ressoar) to resound
ricaço [hi'kasu] M plutocrat, very rich man

rícino ['hisinu] M castor-oil plant; **óleo de ~** castor oil

rico, -a ['hiku, a] ADJ rich; (PT: *lindo*) beautiful; (: *excelente*) splendid ▶ M/F rich man/woman

ricochetear [hikoʃe'tʃjar] VI to ricochet

ricota [hi'kɔta] F cream cheese

ridicularizar [hidʒikulari'zar] VT to ridicule

ridículo, -a [hi'dʒikulu, a] ADJ ridiculous

rifa ['hifa] F raffle

rifão [hi'fãw] (*pl* **-ões** *ou* **-ães**) M proverb, saying

rifar [hi'far] VT to raffle; (*col*: *abandonar*) to dump

rififi [hifi'fi] (*col*) M fight, brawl

rifle ['hifli] M rifle

rifões [hi'fõjs] MPL *de* **rifão**

rigidez [hiʒi'dez] F rigidity, stiffness; (*austeridade*) severity, strictness; (*inflexibilidade*) inflexibility

rígido, -a ['hiʒidu, a] ADJ rigid, stiff; (*fig*) strict

rigor [hi'gor] M rigidity; (*meticulosidade*) rigour (BRIT), rigor (US); (*severidade*) harshness, severity; (*exatidão*) precision; **a ~** strictly speaking; **vestido a ~** in full evening dress; **ser de ~** to be essential *ou* obligatory; **no ~ do inverno** in the depths of winter

rigoroso, -a [higo'rozu, ɔza] ADJ rigorous, strict; (*severo*) strict; (*exigente*) demanding; (*minucioso*) precise, accurate; (*inverno*) hard, harsh

rijo, -a ['hiʒu, a] ADJ tough, hard; (*severo*) harsh, severe; (*músculos, braços*) firm

rim [hĩ] (*pl* **-ns**) M kidney; **rins** MPL (*parte inferior das costas*) small *sg* of the back

rima ['hima] F rhyme; (*poema*) verse, poem

rimar [hi'mar] VT, VI to rhyme; **~ com** (*condizer*) to agree with, tally with

rímel® ['himew] (*pl* **-eis**) M mascara

rinçagem [hĩ'saʒẽ] (*pl* **-ns**) F rinse

rinçar [hĩ'sar] VT to rinse

rinchar [hĩ'ʃar] VI to neigh, whinny

rincho ['hĩʃu] M neigh(ing)

ringue ['hĩgi] M ring

rinha ['hiɲa] F cock-fight

rinoceronte [hinose'rõtʃi] M rhinoceros

rinque ['hĩki] M rink

rins [hĩs] MPL *de* **rim**

Rio ['hiu] M: **o ~ (de Janeiro)** Rio (de Janeiro)

rio ['hiu] M river

ripa ['hipa] F lath, slat

riqueza [hi'keza] F wealth, riches *pl*; (*qualidade*) richness; (*fartura*) abundance; (*fecundidade*) fertility

rir [hir] VI to laugh; **~ de** to laugh at; **morrer de ~** to laugh one's head off

risada [hi'zada] F (*riso*) laughter; (*gargalhada*) guffaw

risca ['hiska] F stroke; (*listra*) stripe; (*no cabelo*) parting; **à ~** to the letter, exactly

riscar [his'kar] VT (*papel*) to draw lines on; (*marcar*) to mark; (*apagar*) to cross out; (*desenhar*) to outline; (*fósforo*) to strike;

(*expulsar: sócios*) to expel, throw out; (*eliminar*) to do away with; (*amigo*) to write off

risco ['hisku] M (*marca*) mark, scratch; (*traço*) stroke; (*desenho*) drawing, sketch; (*perigo*) risk; **sob o ~ de** at the risk of; **correr o ~ de** to run the risk of; **correr ~s** to take risks; **pôr em ~** to put at risk, risk

risível [hi'zivew] (*pl* **-eis**) ADJ laughable, ridiculous

riso ['hizu] M laughter; **não ser motivo de ~** to be no laughing matter

risonho, -a [hi'zoɲu, a] ADJ smiling; (*contente*) cheerful; **estar muito ~** to be all smiles

risoto [hi'zotu] M risotto

rispidez [hispi'dez] F brusqueness; (*aspereza*) harshness

ríspido, -a ['hispidu, a] ADJ brusque; (*áspero*) harsh

risquei *etc* [his'kej] VB *ver* **riscar**

rissole [hi'sɔli] M rissole

riste ['histʃi] M: **em ~** (*dedo*) pointing; (*orelhas*) pointed

rítmico, -a ['hitʃmiku, a] ADJ rhythmic(al)

ritmo ['hitʃmu] M rhythm

rito ['hitu] M rite; (*seita*) cult

ritual [hi'twaw] (*pl* **-ais**) ADJ, M ritual

rival [hi'vaw] (*pl* **-ais**) ADJ, M/F rival

rivalidade [hivali'dadʒi] F rivalry

rivalizar [hivali'zar] VT to rival ▶ VI: **~ com** to compete with, vie with

rixa ['hiʃa] F quarrel, fight

RJ ABR = **Rio de Janeiro**

RN ABR = **Rio Grande do Norte**

RNVA (BR) ABR M = **Registro Nacional de Veículos Automotores**

RO ABR = **Rondônia**

roa *etc* ['hoa] VB *ver* **roer**

robalo [ho'balu] M snook (*type of fish*)

robô [ho'bo] M robot

robustecer [hobuste'ser] VT to strengthen ▶ VI to become stronger; **robustecer-se** VR to become stronger

robustez [hobus'tez] F strength

robusto, -a [ho'bustu, a] ADJ strong, robust

roça ['hɔsa] F plantation; (*no mato*) clearing; (*campo*) country

roçado [ho'sadu] M clearing

rocambole [hokã'bɔli] M roll

roçar [ho'sar] VT (*terreno*) to clear; (*tocar de leve*) to brush against ▶ VI: **~ em** *ou* **por** to brush against

roceiro, -a [ho'sejru, a] M/F (*lavrador*) peasant; (*caipira*) country bumpkin

rocha ['hɔʃa] F rock; (*penedo*) crag

rochedo [ho'ʃedu] M crag, cliff

rock ['hɔki] M = **roque**

rock-and-roll [-ã'hɔw] M rock and roll

roda ['hɔda] F wheel; (*círculo, grupo de pessoas*) circle; (*de saia*) width, fullness; **~ dentada** cog(wheel); **alta ~** high society; **em** *ou* **à ~ de** round, around; **~ de direção** steering wheel; **~ do leme** ship's wheel, helm; **brincar de ~** to play in the round

r

rodada [ho'dada] F (de bebidas, Esporte) round
roda-d'água (pl **rodas-d'água**) F water wheel
rodado, -a [ho'dadu, a] ADJ (saia) full, wide; **o
carro tem 5000 km ~s** the car has 5000 km
on the clock
rodagem [ho'daʒẽ] (pl **-ns**) F: **estrada de ~**
(trunk) road (BRIT)
roda-gigante (pl **rodas-gigantes**) F big wheel
rodamoinho [hodamo'iɲu] M (na água)
whirlpool; (de vento) whirlwind; (no cabelo)
swirl
Ródano ['hɔdanu] M: **o ~** the Rhône
rodapé [hoda'pɛ] M skirting board (BRIT),
baseboard (US); (de página) foot
rodar [ho'dar] VT (fazer girar) to turn, spin;
(viajar por) to tour, travel round; (quilômetros)
to do; (filme) to make; (imprimir) to print;
(Comput: programa) to run ▶ VI (girar) to turn
round; (Auto) to drive around; (col: ser
reprovado) to fail; (: sair) to make o.s. scarce;
(: ser excluído) to be ruled out; **~ por** (a pé) to
wander around; (de carro) to drive around
roda-viva (pl **rodas-vivas**) F bustle, commotion;
estou numa ~ danada I'm in a real flap
rodear [ho'dʒjar] VT to go round; (circundar) to
encircle, surround; (pessoa) to surround
rodeio [ho'deju] M (em discurso)
circumlocution; (subterfúgio) subterfuge; (de
gado) round-up; **fazer ~s** to beat about the
bush; **sem ~s** plainly, frankly
rodela [ho'dɛla] F (pedaço) slice
rodízio [ho'dʒizju] M rota; **à ~** (em restaurante)
at discretion; **em ~** on a rota basis
rodo ['hodu] M rake; (para puxar água) water
rake; **a ~** in abundance
rododendro [hodo'dẽdru] M rhododendron
rodoferroviário, -a [hodofeho'vjarju, a] ADJ
road and rail atr
rodopiar [hodo'pjar] VI to whirl around, swirl
rodopio [hodo'piu] M spin
rodovia [hodo'via] F highway, ≈ motorway
(BRIT), ≈ interstate (US)
rodoviária [hodo'vjarja] F (tb: **estação
rodoviária**) bus station; ver tb **rodoviário**
rodoviário, -a [hodo'vjarju, a] ADJ road atr;
(polícia) traffic atr ▶ M/F roadworker
roedor, a [hwe'dor(a)] ADJ gnawing ▶ M
rodent
roer [hwer] VT to gnaw, nibble; (enferrujar) to
corrode; (afligir) to eat away; **ser duro de ~**
to be a hard nut to crack
rogado [ho'gadu] ADJ: **fazer-se de ~** to play
hard to get
rogar [ho'gar] VI to ask, request; **~ a alguém
que faça** to beg sb to do
rogo ['hogu] M request; **a ~ de** at the request
of
rói [hɔj] VB ver **roer**
roía etc [ho'ia] VB ver **roer**
róis [hɔjs] MPL de **rol**
rojão [ho'ʒãw] (pl **-ões**) M (foguete) rocket; (fig:
ritmo intenso) hectic pace; **aguentar o ~** (fig) to
stick it out

rol [hɔw] (pl **róis**) M roll, list
rolagem [ho'laʒẽ] F (de uma dívida)
snowballing
rolar [ho'lar] VT to roll; (dívida) to run up ▶ VI
to roll; (na cama) to toss and turn; (col: vinho
etc) to flow; (: estender-se) to roll on
roldana [how'dana] F pulley
roleta [ho'leta] F roulette; (borboleta) turnstile
roleta-paulista F: **fazer uma ~** (Auto) to go
through a red light
roleta-russa F Russian roulette
rolha ['hoʎa] F cork; (fig) gag (on free speech)
roliço, -a [ho'lisu, a] ADJ (pessoa) plump,
chubby; (objeto) round, cylindrical
rolo ['holu] M (de papel etc) roll; (para nivelar o
solo, para pintura) roller; (almofada) bolster;
(para cabelo) curler; (col: briga) brawl, fight;
cortina de ~ roller blind; **~ compressor**
steamroller; **~ de massa** ou **pastel** rolling
pin
Roma ['homa] N Rome
romã [ho'mã] F pomegranate
romance [ho'mãsi] M (livro) novel; (caso
amoroso) romance; (fig: história) complicated
story; **~ policial** detective story; **fazer um ~
(de algo)** (exagerar) to dramatize (sth)
romanceado, -a [homã'sjadu, a] ADJ (biografia)
in the style of a novel; (exagerado)
exaggerated, fanciful
romancear [homã'sjar] VT (biografia) to write
in the style of a novel; (exagerar) to
exaggerate, embroider ▶ VI (inventar histórias)
to tell tales
romancista [homã'sista] M/F novelist
românico, -a [ho'maniku, a] ADJ (Ling)
Romance; (Arq) romanesque
romano, -a [ho'manu, a] ADJ, M/F Roman
romântico, -a [ho'mãtʃiku, a] ADJ romantic
romantismo [homã'tʃizmu] M romanticism;
(romance) romance
romaria [homa'ria] F (peregrinação)
pilgrimage; (festa) festival
rombo ['hõbu] M (buraco) hole; (Mat)
rhombus; (fig: desfalque) embezzlement;
(: prejuízo) loss, shortfall
rombudo, -a [hõ'budu, a] ADJ very blunt
romeiro, -a [ho'mejru, a] M/F pilgrim
Romênia [ho'menja] F: **a ~** Romania
romeno, -a [ho'mɛnu, a] ADJ, M/F Rumanian
▶ M (Ling) Rumanian
romeu e julieta [ho'mewiʒu'ljeta] M (Culin)
guava jelly with cheese
rompante [hõ'pãtʃi] M outburst
romper [hõ'per] VT to break; (rasgar) to tear;
(relações) to break off ▶ VI: **~ com** to break
with; **~ de** (jorrar) to well up from; **~ em
pranto** ou **lágrimas** to burst into tears;
~ em soluços to sob
rompimento [hõpi'mẽtu] M (ato) breakage;
(fenda) break; (de relações) breaking off
roncar [hõ'kar] VI to snore
ronco ['hõku] M snore; (de motor) roar; (de
porco) grunt

ronda ['hõda] F patrol, beat; **fazer a ~** to go the rounds

rondar [hõ'dar] VT to patrol, go the rounds of; (*espreitar*) to prowl, hang around; (*rodear*) to go round ▶ VI to prowl, lurk; (*fazer a ronda*) to patrol, do the rounds; **a inflação ronda os 10% ao ano** inflation is in the region of 10% a year

rondoniano, -a [hõdo'njanu, a] ADJ from Rondônia ▶ M/F person from Rondônia

ronquei *etc* [hõ'kej] VB *ver* **roncar**

ronqueira [hõ'kejra] F wheeze

ronrom [hõ'hõ] M purr

ronronar [hõho'nar] VI to purr

roque ['hɔki] M (*Xadrez*) rook, castle; (*Mús*) rock

roqueiro, -a [ho'kejru, a] M/F rock musician

roraimense [horaj'mẽsi] ADJ from Roraima ▶ M/F person from Roraima

rosa ['hɔza] ADJ INV pink ▶ F rose; **a vida não é feita de ~s** life is not a bed of roses; **~ dos ventos** compass

rosado, -a [ho'zadu, a] ADJ rosy, pink

rosário [ho'zarju] M rosary

rosa-shocking [-ʃɔkĩŋ] ADJ INV shocking pink

rosbife [hoz'bifi] M roast beef

rosca ['hoska] F spiral, coil; (*de parafuso*) thread; (*pão*) ring-shaped loaf

roseira [ho'zejra] F rosebush

róseo, -a ['hɔzju, a] ADJ rosy

roseta [ho'zeta] F rosette

rosetar [hoze'tar] VI to loaf around

rosnar [hoz'nar] VI (*cão*) to growl, snarl; (*murmurar*) to mutter, mumble

rossio [ho'siu] (PT) M large square

rosto ['hostu] M (*cara*) face; (*frontispício*) title page

rota ['hɔta] F route, course

rotação [hota'sãw] (*pl* **-ões**) F rotation; **~ de estoques** turnover of stock

rotativa [hota'tʃiva] F rotary printing press

rotatividade [hotatʃivi'dadʒi] F rotation; **hotel de alta ~** hotel renting rooms by the hour, love hotel

rotativo, -a [hota'tʃivu, a] ADJ rotary

roteirista [hotej'rista] M/F scriptwriter

roteiro [ho'tejru] M (*itinerário*) itinerary; (*ordem*) schedule; (*guia*) guidebook; (*de filme*) script; (*de discussão, trabalho escrito*) list of topics; (*fig: norma*) norm

rotina [ho'tʃina] F (*tb Comput*) routine

rotineiro, -a [hotʃi'nejru, a] ADJ routine

roto, -a ['hotu, a] ADJ broken; (*rasgado*) torn; (*maltrapilho*) scruffy; **o ~ rindo do esfarrapado** the pot calling the kettle black

rótula ['hɔtula] F (*Anat*) kneecap

rotular [hotu'lar] VT (*tb fig*) to label; **~ alguém/algo de** to label sb/sth as

rótulo ['hɔtulu] M label, tag; (*fig*) label

rotunda [ho'tũda] F (*Arq*) rotunda

rotundo, -a [ho'tũdu, a] ADJ (*redondo*) round; (*gorducho*) rotund

roubalheira [hoba'ʎejra] F (*do Estado, de empresa*) embezzlement

roubar [ho'bar] VT to steal; (*loja, casa, pessoa*) to rob ▶ VI to steal; (*em jogo, no preço*) to cheat; **~ algo a alguém** to steal sth from sb

roubo ['hobu] M theft, robbery; **$100 é ~** $100 is daylight robbery; **~ de identidade** identity theft

rouco, -a ['roku, a] ADJ hoarse

round ['hãwdʒi] (*pl* **-s**) M (*Boxe*) round

roupa ['hopa] F clothes *pl*, clothing; **~ de baixo** underwear; **~ de cama** bedclothes *pl*, bed linen

roupagem [ho'paʒẽ] (*pl* **-ns**) F clothes *pl*, apparel; (*fig*) appearance

roupão [ho'pãw] (*pl* **-ões**) M dressing gown

rouquidão [hoki'dãw] F hoarseness

rouxinol [hoʃi'nɔw] (*pl* **-óis**) M nightingale

roxo, -a ['hoʃu, a] ADJ purple, violet; **~ por** (*col*) mad about; **~ de saudades** pining away

royalty ['hɔjawtʃi] (*pl* **-ies**) M royalty

RR ABR = **Roraima**

RS ABR = **Rio Grande do Sul**

rua ['hua] F street ▶ EXCL: **~!** get out!, clear off!; **botar alguém na ~** to put sb out on the street; **ir para a ~** to go out; (*ser despedido*) to get the sack; **viver na ~** to be out all the time; **estar na ~ da amargura** to be going through hell; **~ principal** main street; **~ sem saída** no through road, cul-de-sac

Ruanda ['hwãda] F Rwanda

rubéola [hu'bɛola] F (*Med*) German measles

rubi [hu'bi] M ruby

rublo ['hublu] M rouble (BRIT), ruble (US)

rubor [hu'bor] M blush; (*fig*) shyness, bashfulness

ruborizar-se [hubori'zarsi] VR to blush

rubrica [hu'brika] F (*signed*) initials *pl*

rubricar [hubri'kar] VT to initial

rubro, -a ['hubru, a] ADJ ruby-red; (*faces*) rosy, ruddy

rubro-negro, -a ADJ of Flamengo FC

ruço, -a ['husu, a] ADJ grey (BRIT), gray (US), dun; (*desbotado*) faded; (*col*) tough, tricky

rúcula ['hukula] F rocket (BRIT), arugula (US)

rude ['hudʒi] ADJ (*povo*) simple, primitive; (*ignorante*) simple; (*grosseiro*) rude

rudeza [hu'deza] F simplicity; (*grosseria*) rudeness

rudimentar [hudʒimẽ'tar] ADJ rudimentary

rudimento [hudʒi'mẽtu] M rudiment; **rudimentos** MPL (*noções básicas*) rudiments, first principles

ruela ['hwela] F lane, alley

rufar [hu'far] VT (*tambor*) to roll ▶ M roll

rufião [hu'fjãw] (*pl* **-ães** *ou* **-ões**) M pimp

ruflar [huf'lar] VT, VI to rustle

ruga ['huga] F (*na pele*) wrinkle; (*na roupa*) crease

rúgbi ['hugbi] M rugby

ruge ['huʒi] M rouge

rugido [hu'ʒidu] M roar

rugir [hu'ʒir] VI to roar, bellow

ruibarbo [hwi'barbu] M rhubarb
ruído ['hwidu] M noise, din; (*Elet, Tec*) noise
ruidoso, -a [hwi'dozu, ɔza] ADJ noisy
ruim [hu'ĩ] (*pl* **-ns**) ADJ bad; (*defeituoso*)
defective; **achar ~** (*col*) to get upset
ruína ['hwina] F ruin; (*decadência*) downfall;
levar alguém à ~ to ruin sb, be sb's downfall
ruindade [hwĩ'dadʒi] F wickedness, evil;
(*ação*) bad thing
ruins [hu'ĩs] ADJ PL *de* **ruim**
ruir ['hwir] VI to collapse, go to ruin
ruivo, -a ['hwivu, a] ADJ red-haired ▶ M/F
redhead
rujo *etc* ['huju] VB *ver* **rugir**
rulê [hu'le] ADJ: **gola ~** polo neck
rum [hũ] M rum
rumar [hu'mar] VT (*barco*) to steer ▶ VI: **~ para**
to head for
rumba ['hũba] F rumba
ruminação [humina'sãw] (*pl* **-ões**) F
rumination

ruminante [humi'nãtʃi] ADJ, M ruminant
ruminar [humi'nar] VT to chew; (*fig*) to
ponder ▶ VI (*tb fig*) to ruminate
rumo ['humu] M course, bearing; (*fig*) course;
~ a bound for; **sem ~** adrift
rumor [hu'mor] M (*ruído*) noise; (*notícia*)
rumour (*BRIT*), rumor (*US*), report
rumorejar [humore'ʒar] VI to murmur;
(*folhas*) to rustle; (*água*) to ripple
rupia [hu'pia] F rupee
ruptura [hup'tura] F break, rupture
rural [hu'raw] (*pl* **-ais**) ADJ rural
rusga ['huzga] F (*briga*) quarrel, row
rush ['haʃi] M rush; (**a hora do**) **~** rush hour;
o ~ imobiliário the rush to buy property
Rússia ['husja] F: **a ~** Russia
russo, -a ['husu, a] ADJ, M/F Russian ▶ M (*Ling*)
Russian
rústico, -a ['hustʃiku, a] ADJ rustic; (*pessoa*)
simple; (*utensílio, objeto*) rough; (*casa*)
rustic-style; (*lugar*) countrified

Ss

S, s [ˈɛsi] (*pl* **ss**) M S, s; **S de Sandra** S for Sugar
S. ABR (= *Santo/a, São*) St
SA ABR (= *Sociedade Anônima*) plc (BRIT), Inc. (US)
sã [sã] F *de* **são**
Saara [saˈara] M: **o ~** the Sahara
sáb. ABR (= *sábado*) Sat.
sábado [ˈsabadu] M Saturday; (*dos judeus*)
Sabbath; **~ de aleluia** Easter Saturday; *ver tb*
terça-feira
sabão [saˈbãw] (*pl* **-ões**) M soap;
(*descompostura*): **passar um ~ em alguém/
levar um ~** to give sb a telling-off/get a
telling-off; **~ de coco** coconut soap; **~ em pó**
soap powder
sabatina [sabaˈtʃina] F revision test
sabedor, a [sabeˈdo(a)] ADJ informed
sabedoria [sabedoˈria] F wisdom; (*erudição*)
learning
saber [saˈber] VT, VI to know; (*descobrir*) to find
out ▶ M knowledge; **a ~** namely; **~ fazer** to
know how to do, be able to do; **ele sabe
nadar?** can he swim?; **~ de cor (e salteado)**
to know off by heart; **que eu saiba** as far as
I know; **sei** (*col*) I see; **sei lá** (*col*) I've got no
idea, heaven knows; **sabe de uma coisa?**
(*col*) you know what?; **você é quem sabe,
você que sabe** (*col*) it's up to you
Sabesp [saˈbɛspi] ABR M = **Saneamento
Básico do Estado de São Paulo**
sabiá [saˈbja] M/F thrush
sabichão, -chona [sabiˈʃãw, ˈʃona] (*pl* **-ões/-s**)
M/F know-it-all, smart aleck
sabido, -a [saˈbidu, a] ADJ (*versado*)
knowledgeable; (*esperto*) shrewd, clever
sábio, -a [ˈsabju, a] ADJ wise; (*erudito*) learned
▶ M/F wise person; (*erudito*) scholar
sabões [saˈbõjs] MPL *de* **sabão**
sabonete [saboˈnetʃi] M toilet soap
saboneteira [saboneˈtejra] F soap dish
sabor [saˈbor] M taste, flavour (BRIT), flavor (US);
ao ~ de at the mercy of
saborear [saboˈrjar] VT to taste, savour (BRIT),
savor (US); (*fig*) to relish
saboroso, -a [saboˈrozu, ɔza] ADJ tasty,
delicious
sabotador, a [sabotaˈdo(a)] M/F saboteur
sabotagem [saboˈtaʒẽ] F sabotage
sabotar [saboˈtar] VT to sabotage
saburrento, -a [sabuˈhẽtu, a] ADJ (*língua*) furry

SAC [ˈsaki] ABR M (= *serviço de atendimento ao
cliente*) customer service
saca [ˈsaka] F sack
sacada [saˈkada] F balcony; *ver tb* **sacado**
sacado, -a [saˈkadu, a] M/F (*Com*) drawee
sacador, a [sakaˈdo(a)] M/F (*Com*) drawer
sacal [saˈkaw] (*pl* **-ais**) (*col*) ADJ boring; **ser ~**
to be a pain
sacana [saˈkana] (!) ADJ (*canalha*) crooked;
(*lascivo*) randy
sacanagem [sakaˈnaʒẽ] (*pl* **-ns**) (*col*) F (*sujeira*)
dirty trick; (*libidinagem*) screwing; **fazer
uma ~ com alguém** (*sujeira*) to screw sb;
filme de ~ blue movie
sacanear [sakaˈnjar] (!) VT: **~ alguém** (*fazer
sujeira*) to screw sb; (*amolar*) to take the piss
out of sb (!)
sacar [saˈkar] VT to take out, pull out;
(*dinheiro*) to withdraw; (*arma, cheque*) to draw;
(*Esporte*) to serve; (*col: entender*) to understand
▶ VI (*col: entender*) to understand; (: *mentir*) to
tell fibs; (: *dar palpites*) to talk off the top of
one's head; **~ de um revólver** to pull a gun
saçaricar [sasariˈkar] VI to have fun, fool
around
sacarina [sakaˈrina] F saccharine (BRIT),
saccharin (US)
saca-rolhas M INV corkscrew
sacerdócio [saserˈdɔsju] M priesthood
sacerdote [saserˈdɔtʃi] M priest
sachê [saˈʃe] M sachet
saci [saˈsi] M (*personagem folcórica*) one-legged
Black man who ambushes travellers
saciar [saˈsjar] VT (*fome etc*) to satisfy; (*sede*) to
quench
saco [ˈsaku] M bag; (*enseada*) inlet; (*col:
testículos*) balls *pl* (!); **~!** (BR col) damn!; **que ~!**
(BR col) how annoying!; **encher o ~ de
alguém** (BR col) to annoy sb, get on sb's
nerves; **estar de ~ cheio (de)** to be fed up
(with); **haja ~!** give me strength!; **puxar o ~
de alguém** (*col*) to suck up to sb; **ser um ~**
(*col*) to be a drag; **ter ~** (*col*) to have patience;
ter ~ de fazer algo to be bothered to do sth;
~ de água quente hot water bottle; **~ de
café** coffee filter; **~ de dormir** sleeping bag
sacode *etc* [saˈkɔdʒi] VB *ver* **sacudir**
sacola [saˈkɔla] F bag
sacolejar [sakoleˈʒar] VT, VI to shake

sacramentar [sakramē'tar] VT (*documento etc*) to legalize

sacramento [sakra'mẽtu] M sacrament

sacrificar [sakrifi'kar] VT to sacrifice; (*consagrar*) to dedicate; (*submeter*) to subject; (*animal*) to have put down; **sacrificar-se** VR to sacrifice o.s.

sacrifício [sakri'fisju] M sacrifice

sacrilégio [sakri'lɛʒju] M sacrilege

sacrílego, -a [sa'krilegu, a] ADJ sacrilegious

sacristão [sakri'stãw] (**-ões**) M sacristan, sexton

sacristia [sakris'tʃia] F sacristy

sacristões [sakris'tõjs] MPL *de* **sacristão**

sacro, -a ['sakru, a] ADJ sacred; (*santo*) holy; (*música*) religious

sacrossanto, -a [sakro'sãtu, a] ADJ sacrosanct

sacudida [saku'dʒida] F shake

sacudidela [sakudʒi'dɛla] F shake, jolt

sacudido, -a [saku'dʒidu, a] ADJ shaken; (*movimento*) rapid, quick; (*robusto*) sturdy

sacudir [saku'dʒir] VT to shake; **sacudir-se** VR to shake

sádico, -a ['sadʒiku, a] ADJ sadistic ▶ M/F sadist

sadio, -a [sa'dʒiu, a] ADJ healthy

sadismo [sa'dʒizmu] M sadism

sadomasoquista [sadomazo'kista] ADJ sadomasochistic ▶ M/F sadomasochist

safadeza [safa'deza] F (*vileza*) meanness; (*imoralidade*) crudity; (*travessura*) mischief

safado, -a [sa'fadu, a] ADJ (*descarado*) shameless, barefaced; (*imoral*) dirty; (*travesso*) mischievous ▶ M rogue; **estar/ ficar ~ (da vida) com** to be/get furious with

safanão [safa'nãw] (*pl* **-ões**) M (*puxão*) tug; (*tapa*) slap

safári [sa'fari] M safari

safira [sa'fira] F sapphire

safo, -a ['safu, a] ADJ (*livre*) clear; (*col: esperto*) quick, clever

safra ['safra] F harvest; (*fig: de músicos etc*) crop

saga ['saga] F saga

sagacidade [sagasi'dadʒi] F sagacity, shrewdness

sagaz [sa'gajʒ] ADJ sagacious, shrewd

sagitariano, -a [saʒita'rjanu, a] ADJ, M/F Sagittarian

Sagitário [saʒi'tarju] M Sagittarius

sagrado, -a [sa'gradu, a] ADJ sacred, holy

saguão [sa'gwãw] (*pl* **-ões**) M (*pátio*) yard, patio; (*entrada*) foyer, lobby; (*de estação*) entrance hall

saia ['saja] F skirt; (*col: mulher*) woman; **viver agarrado às ~s de alguém** (*fig*) to be tied to sb's apron strings; **~ escocesa** kilt

saia-calça (*pl* **saias-calças**) F culottes *pl*

saiba *etc* ['sajba] VB *ver* **saber**

saibro ['sajbru] M gravel

saída [sa'ida] F (*porta*) exit, way out; (*partida*) departure; (*ato: de pessoa*) going out; (*fig: solução*) way out; (*Comput: de programa*) exit; (*: de dados*) output; **de ~** (*primeiro*) first; (*de cara*)

straight away; **estar de ~** to be on one's way out; **na ~ do cinema** on the way out of the cinema; **(não) ter boa ~** (*produto*) (not) to sell well; **uma mercadoria de muita ~** a commodity which sells well; **dar uma ~** to go out; **ter boas ~s** (*réplicas*) to be witty; **não tem ~** (*fig*) there is no escaping it; **~ de emergência** emergency exit

saideira [saj'dejra] F last drink

saidinha [saj'dʒinha] F: **dar uma ~** to pop out

saiote [sa'jɔtʃi] M short skirt

sair [sa'ir] VI to go (*ou* come) out; (*partir*) to leave; (*realizar-se*) to turn out; (*Comput*) to exit; **sair-se** VR: **~-se bem/mal de** to be successful/unsuccessful in; **~-se com** (*dito*) to come out with; **~ caro/barato** to work out expensive/cheap; **~ ganhando/ perdendo** to come out better/worse off; **~ a alguém** (*parecer-se*) to take after sb; **~ de** (*casa etc*) to leave; (*situação difícil*) to get out of; (*doença*) to come out of; **a notícia saiu na TV/no jornal** the news was on TV/in the paper

sal [saw] (*pl* **sais**) M salt; **sem ~** (*comida*) salt-free; (*pessoa*) lacklustre (BRIT), lackluster (US); **~ de banho** bath salts *pl*; **~ de cozinha** cooking salt

sala ['sala] F room; (*num edifício público*) hall; (*classe, turma*) class; **fazer ~ a alguém** to entertain sb; **~ de audiências** (*Jur*) courtroom; **~ (de aula)** classroom; **~ de bate-papo** (*Internet*) chatroom; **~ de conferências** conference room; **~ de embarque** departure lounge; **~ de espera** waiting room; **~ de espetáculo** concert hall; **~ (de estar)** living room, lounge; **~ de jantar** dining room; **~ de operação** (*Med*) operating theatre (BRIT) *ou* theater (US); **~ de parto** delivery room

salada [sa'lada] F salad; (*fig*) confusion, jumble; **~ de frutas** fruit salad; **~ russa** (*Culin*) Russian salad; (*fig*) hotchpotch

saladeira [sala'dejra] F salad bowl

sala e quarto (*pl* **salas e quartos** *ou* **salas e quarto**) M two-room flat (BRIT) *ou* apartment (US)

salafra [sa'lafra] (*col*) M/F rat

salafrário [sala'frarju] (*col*) M crook

salame [sa'lami] M (*Culin*) salami

salaminho [sala'miɲu] M pepperoni (sausage)

salão [sa'lãw] (*pl* **-ões**) M large room, hall; (*exposição*) show; (*cabeleireiro*) hairdressing salon; **de ~** (*jogos*) proper, (*anedota*) acceptable; **~ de baile** dance studio; **~ de beleza** beauty salon

salarial [sala'rjaw] (*pl* **-ais**) ADJ wage *atr*, pay *atr*

salário [sa'larju] M wages *pl*, salary; **~ mínimo** minimum wage

salário-família (*pl* **salários-família**) M family allowance

saldar [saw'dar] VT (*contas*) to settle; (*dívida*) to pay off

saldo ['sawdu] M balance; (*sobra*) surplus; (*fig: resultado*) result; ~ **anterior/credor/devedor** opening balance/credit balance/debit balance

saleiro [sa'lejru] M salt cellar; (*moedor*) salt mill

salgadinho [sawga'dʒiɲu] M savoury (*BRIT*), savory (*US*), snack

salgado, -a [saw'gadu, a] ADJ salty, salted; (*preço*) exorbitant

salgar [saw'gar] VT to salt

salgueiro [saw'gejru] M willow; ~ **chorão** weeping willow

saliência [sa'ljẽsja] F projection; (*assanhamento*) forwardness

salientar [saljẽ'tar] VT to point out; (*acentuar*) to stress, emphasize; **salientar-se** VR (*pessoa*) to distinguish o.s.

saliente [sa'ljẽtʃi] ADJ jutting out, prominent; (*evidente*) clear, conspicuous; (*importante*) outstanding; (*assanhado*) forward

salina [sa'lina] F salt bed; (*empresa*) salt company

salino, -a [sa'linu, a] ADJ saline

salitre [sa'litri] M saltpetre (*BRIT*), saltpeter (*US*), nitre (*BRIT*), niter (*US*)

saliva [sa'liva] F saliva; **gastar** ~ (*col*) to waste one's breath

salivar [sali'var] VI to salivate

salmão [saw'mãw] (*pl* **-ões**) M salmon ▶ ADJ INV salmon-pink

salmo ['sawmu] M psalm

salmões [saw'mõjs] MPL *de* **salmão**

salmonela [sawmo'nɛla] F salmonella

salmoura [saw'mora] F brine

salobro, -a [sa'lobru, a] ADJ salty, brackish

salões [sa'lõjs] MPL *de* **salão**

saloio [sa'lɔju] (*PT*) M (*camponês*) country bumpkin

Salomão [salo'mãw] N: (**as**) **ilhas (de)** ~ (the) Solomon Islands

salpicão [sawpi'kãw] (*pl* **-ões**) M (*paio*) pork sausage; (*prato*) fricassee

salpicar [sawpi'kar] VT to splash; (*polvilhar, fig*) to sprinkle

salpicões [sawpi'kõjs] MPL *de* **salpicão**

salsa ['sawsa] F parsley

salsicha [saw'siʃa] F sausage

salsichão [sawsi'ʃãw] (*pl* **-ões**) M sausage

saltado, -a [saw'tadu, a] ADJ (*saliente*) protruding

saltar [saw'tar] VT to jump (over), leap (over); (*omitir*) to skip ▶ VI to jump, leap; (*sangue*) to spurt out; (*de ônibus, cavalo*): ~ **de** to get off; ~ **à vista** *ou* **aos olhos** to be obvious

salteado, -a [saw'tʃjadu, a] ADJ broken up; (*Culin*) sautéed

salteador [sawtʃja'dor] M highwayman

saltear [saw'tʃjar] VT (*trechos de um livro*) to skip; (*Culin*) to sauté

saltimbanco [sawtʃĩ'bãku] M travelling (*BRIT*) *ou* traveling (*US*) player

saltitante [sawtʃi'tãtʃi] ADJ: ~ **de alegria** as pleased as punch

saltitar [sawtʃi'tar] VI (*pássaros*) to hop; (*fig: de um assunto a outro*) to skip

salto ['sawtu] M jump, leap; (*de calçado*) heel; **dar um** ~ to jump, leap; **dar -s de alegria** *ou* **de contente** to jump for joy; ~ **de vara** pole vault; ~ **em altura** high jump; ~ **em distância** long jump; ~ **quântico** quantum leap

salto-mortal (*pl* **saltos-mortais**) M somersault

salubre [sa'lubri] ADJ healthy, salubrious

salutar [salu'tar] ADJ salutary, beneficial

salva ['sawva] F salvo; (*bandeja*) tray, salver; (*Bot*) sage; ~ **de palmas** round of applause; ~ **de tiros** round of gunfire

salvação [sawva'sãw] F salvation; ~ **da pátria** *ou* **da lavoura** (*col*) lifesaver

salvador [sawva'dor] M saviour (*BRIT*), savior (*US*)

salvados [saw'vadus] MPL salvage *sg*; (*Com*) salvaged goods

salvaguarda [sawva'gwarda] F protection, safeguard

salvaguardar [sawvagwar'dar] VT to safeguard

salvamento [sawva'mẽtu] M rescue; (*de naufrágio*) salvage

salvar [saw'var] VT (*tb Comput*) to save; (*resgatar*) to rescue; (*objetos, de ruína*) to salvage; (*honra*) to defend; **salvar-se** VR to escape

salva-vidas M INV (*boia*) lifebuoy ▶ M/F INV (*pessoa*) lifeguard; **barco** ~ lifeboat

salve ['sawvi] EXCL hooray (for)!

salvo, -a ['sawvu, a] ADJ safe ▶ PREP except, save; **a** ~ in safety; **pôr-se a** ~ to run to safety; **todos** ~ **ele** all except him

salvo-conduto (*pl* **salvo-condutos** *ou* **salvos-condutos**) M safe-conduct

samambaia [samã'baja] F fern

samaritano [samari'tanu] M: **bom** ~ good Samaritan; (*pej*) do-gooder

samba ['sãba] M samba

> The greatest form of musical expression of the Brazilian people, the **samba** is a type of music and dance of African origin. It embraces a number of rhythmic styles, such as *samba de breque*, *samba-enredo*, *samba-canção* and *pagode*, among others. Officially, the first samba, entitled *Pelo telefone*, was written in Rio in 1917.

samba-canção (*pl* **sambas-canção**) M slow samba; **cueca** ~ boxer shorts *pl*

sambar [sã'bar] VI to dance the samba

sambista [sã'bista] M/F (*dançarino*) samba dancer; (*compositor*) samba composer

sambódromo [sã'bɔdromu] M carnival parade ground

Samoa [sa'moa] M: ~ **Ocidental** Western Samoa

samovar [samo'var] M tea urn

SAMU (BR) ABR M (= *Serviço de Atendimento Móvel de Urgência*) emergency ambulance service

sanar [sa'nar] VT to cure; (*remediar*) to remedy

sanatório [sana'tɔrju] M sanatorium (BRIT), sanitarium (US)

sanável [sa'navew] (*pl* **-eis**) ADJ curable; (*remediável*) remediable

sanca ['sãka] F cornice, moulding (BRIT), molding (US)

sanção [sã'sãw] (*pl* **-ões**) F sanction

sancionar [sãsjo'nar] VT to sanction; (*autorizar*) to authorize

sanções [sã'sõjs] FPL *de* **sanção**

sandália [sã'dalja] F sandal

sândalo ['sãdalu] M sandalwood

sandes ['sãdəʃ] (PT) F INV sandwich

sanduíche [sand'wiʃi] (BR) M sandwich;
~ **americano** ham and egg sandwich;
~ **misto** ham and cheese sandwich;
~ **natural** wholemeal sandwich

saneamento [sanja'mẽtu] M sanitation; (*de governo etc*) clean-up

sanear [sa'njar] VT to clean up; (*pântanos*) to drain

sanfona [sã'fɔna] F (*Mús*) accordion; (*Tricô*) ribbing

sanfonado, -a [sãfo'nadu, a] ADJ (*porta*) folding; (*suéter*) ribbed

sangrar [sã'grar] VT, VI to bleed; ~ **alguém** (*fig*) to bleed sb dry

sangrento, -a [sã'grẽtu, a] ADJ bloody; (*ensanguentado*) bloodstained; (*Culin: carne*) rare

sangria [sã'gria] F bloodshed; (*extorsão*) extortion; (*bebida*) sangria

sangue ['sãgi] M blood; ~ **pisado** bruise

sangue-frio M cold-bloodedness

sanguessuga [sãgi'suga] F leech

sanguinário, -a [sãgi'narju, a] ADJ bloodthirsty, cruel

sanguíneo, -a [sã'ginju, a] ADJ blood *atr*; **grupo** ~ blood group; **pressão sanguínea** blood pressure; **vaso** ~ blood vessel

sanha ['sana] F rage, fury

sanidade [sani'dadʒi] F (*saúde*) health; (*mental*) sanity

sanita [sa'nita] (PT) F toilet, lavatory

sanitário, -a [sani'tarju, a] ADJ sanitary; **vaso** ~ toilet, lavatory (bowl)

sanitários [sani'tarjus] MPL toilets

sanitarista [sanita'rista] M/F health worker

Santiago [sã'tʃjagu] F: ~ **(do Chile)** Santiago (de Chile)

santidade [sãtʃi'dadʒi] F holiness, sanctity; **Sua S~** His Holiness (the Pope)

santificar [sãtʃifi'kar] VT to sanctify, make holy

santinho [sã'tʃiɲu] M (*imagem*) holy picture; (*col: pessoa*) saint

santista [sã'tʃista] ADJ from Santos ▶ M/F person from Santos

santo, -a ['sãtu, a] ADJ holy, sacred; (*pessoa*) saintly; (*remédio*) effective ▶ M/F saint; **todo**

~ **dia** every single day; **ter** ~ **forte** (*col*) to have good backing

santuário [sã'twarju] M shrine, sanctuary

São [sãw] M Saint

são, sã [sãw, sã] (*pl* **-s/-s**) ADJ healthy; (*conselho*) sound; (*atitude*) wholesome; (*mentalmente*) sane; ~ **e salvo** safe and sound

São Lourenço [-lo'rẽsu] M: **o (rio)** ~ the St. Lawrence river

São Marinho M San Marino

São Paulo [-'pawlu] N São Paulo

são-tomense [-to'mẽsi] ADJ from São Tomé e Príncipe ▶ M/F native *ou* inhabitant of São Tomé e Príncipe

sapata [sa'pata] M (*do freio*) shoe

sapatão [sapa'tãw] (*pl* **-ões**) M big shoe; (*col: lésbica*) lesbian

sapataria [sapata'ria] F shoe shop

sapateado [sapa'tʃjadu] M tap dancing

sapateador, a [sapatʃja'dor(a)] M/F tap dancer

sapatear [sapa'tʃjar] VI to tap one's feet; (*dançar*) to tap-dance

sapateiro [sapa'tejru] M shoemaker; (*vendedor*) shoe salesman; (*que conserta*) shoe repairer; (*loja*) shoe repairer's

sapatilha [sapa'tʃiʎa] F (*de balé*) shoe; (*sapato*) pump; (*de atleta*) running shoe

sapato [sa'patu] M shoe

sapatões [sapa'tõjs] MPL *de* **sapatão**

sapé [sa'pɛ] M = **sapê**

sapê [sa'pe] M thatch; **teto de** ~ thatched roof

sapeca [sa'pɛka] ADJ flirtatious; (*criança*) cheeky

sapecar [sape'kar] VT (*tapa, pontapé*) to land ▶ VI (*flertar*) to flirt

sapiência [sa'pjẽsja] F wisdom, learning

sapiente [sa'pjẽtʃi] ADJ wise

sapinho [sa'piɲu] M (*Med*) thrush

sapo ['sapu] M toad; **engolir** ~**s** (*fig*) to sit back and take it

saque¹ ['saki] M (*de dinheiro*) withdrawal; (*Com*) draft, bill; (*Esporte*) serve; (*pilhagem*) plunder, pillage; (*col: mentira*) fib; ~ **a descoberto** (*Com*) overdraft

saque² *etc* VB *ver* **sacar**

saquear [sa'kjar] VT to pillage, plunder

saracotear [sarako'tʃjar] VI to wiggle one's hips; (*vaguear*) to wander around ▶ VT to shake

Saragoça [sara'gɔsa] N Zaragoza

saraiva [sa'rajva] F hail

saraivada [sarai'vada] F hailstorm; **uma** ~ **de** (*fig*) a hail of

saraivar [sarai'var] VI to hail; (*fig*) to spray

sarampo [sa'rãpu] M measles *sg*

sarapintado, -a [sarapĩ'tadu, a] ADJ spotted, speckled

sarar [sa'rar] VT to cure; (*ferida*) to heal ▶ VI to recover, be cured

sarau [sa'raw] M soirée

sarcasmo [sar'kazmu] M sarcasm

sarcástico, -a [sar'kastʃiku, a] ADJ sarcastic

sarda ['sarda] F freckle

Sardenha [sar'dɛɲa] F: **a ~** Sardinia

sardento, -a [sar'dẽtu, a] ADJ freckled, freckly

sardinha [sar'dʒiɲa] F sardine; **como ~ em lata** (apertado) like sardines

sardônico, -a [sar'doniku, a] ADJ sardonic, sarcastic

sargento [sar'ʒẽtu] M sergeant

sári ['sari] M sari

sarjeta [sar'ʒeta] F gutter

sarna ['sarna] F scabies sg

sarrafo [sa'hafu] M: **baixar o ~ em alguém** (col) to let sb have it

sarro ['sahu] M (de vinho, nos dentes) tartar; (na língua) fur, coating; (col) laugh; **tirar um ~** (col) to pet, neck

Satã [sa'tã] M Satan, the Devil

Satanás [sata'nas] M Satan, the Devil

satânico, -a [sa'taniku, a] ADJ satanic; (fig) devilish

satélite [sa'tɛlitʃi] ADJ satellite atr ▶ M satellite

sátira ['satʃira] F satire

satírico, -a [sa'tʃiriku, a] ADJ satirical

satirizar [satʃiri'zar] VT to satirize

satisfação [satʃisfa'sãw] (pl **-ões**) F satisfaction; (recompensa) reparation; **dar uma ~ a alguém** to give sb an explanation; **ela não dá satisfações a ninguém** she answers to no-one; **tomar satisfações de alguém** to ask sb for an explanation

satisfaço etc [satʃis'fasu] VB ver **satisfazer**

satisfações [satʃisfa'sõjs] FPL de **satisfação**

satisfatório, -a [satʃisfa'tɔrju, a] ADJ satisfactory

satisfazer [satʃisfa'zer] (irreg: como **fazer**) VT to satisfy; (dívida) to pay off ▶ VI (ser satisfatório) to be satisfactory; **satisfazer-se** VR to be satisfied; (saciar-se) to fill o.s. up; **~ a** to satisfy; **~ com** to fulfil (BRIT), fulfill (US)

satisfeito, -a [satʃis'fejtu, a] PP de **satisfazer** ▶ ADJ satisfied; (alegre) content; (saciado) full; **dar-se por ~ com algo** to be content with sth; **dar alguém por ~** to make sb happy

satisfez [satʃis'fez] VB ver **satisfazer**

satisfiz etc [satʃis'fiz] VB ver **satisfazer**

saturado, -a [satu'radu, a] ADJ (de comida) full; (aborrecido) fed up; (Com: mercado) saturated

saturar [satu'rar] VT to saturate; (de comida, aborrecimento) to fill

Saturno [sa'turnu] M Saturn

saudação [sawda'sãw] (pl **-ões**) F greeting

saudade [saw'dadʒi] F (desejo ardente) longing, yearning; (lembrança nostálgica) nostalgia; **deixar ~s** to be greatly missed; **matar as ~s de alguém/algo** to catch up with sb/cure one's nostalgia for sth; **ter ~s de** (desejar) to long for; (sentir falta de) to miss; **~s (de casa** ou **da família** ou **da pátria)** homesickness sg

saudar [saw'dar] VT (cumprimentar) to greet; (dar as boas vindas) to welcome; (aclamar) to acclaim

saudável [saw'davew] (pl **-eis**) ADJ healthy; (moralmente) wholesome

saúde [sa'udʒi] F health; (brinde) toast; **~!** (brindando) cheers!; (quando se espirra) bless you!; **à sua ~!** your health!; **beber à ~ de** to drink to, toast; **estar bem/mal de ~** to be well/ill; **não ter mais ~ para fazer** not to be up to doing; **vender ~** to be bursting with health; **~ pública** public health; (órgão) health service

saudosismo [sawdo'zizmu] M nostalgia

saudoso, -a [saw'dozu, ɔza] ADJ (nostálgico) nostalgic; (da família ou terra natal) homesick; (de uma pessoa) longing; (que causa saudades) much-missed

sauna ['sawna] F sauna; **fazer ~** to have ou take a sauna

saveiro [sa'vejru] M sailing boat

saxofone [sakso'fɔni] M saxophone

saxofonista [saksofo'nista] M/F saxophonist

sazonado, -a [sazo'nadu, a] ADJ ripe, mature

sazonal [sazo'naw] (pl **-ais**) ADJ seasonal

SBPC ABR F = **Sociedade Brasileira para o Progresso da Ciência**

SBT ABR M (= Sistema Brasileiro de Televisão) television station

SC ABR = **Santa Catarina**

scanner ['skaner] M scanner

SCDF ABR F = **Sagrada Congregação para a Doutrina da Fé**

SE ABR = **Sergipe**

(PALAVRA-CHAVE)

se [si] PRON **1** (reflexivo: impess) oneself; (: m) himself; (: f) herself; (: coisa) itself; (: você) yourself; (: pl) themselves; (: vocês) yourselves; **ela está se vestindo** she's getting dressed **2** (uso recíproco) each other, one another; **olharam-se** they looked at each other **3** (impess): **come-se bem aqui** you can eat well here; **sabe-se que ...** it is known that ...; **vende(m)-se jornais naquela loja** they sell newspapers in that shop ▶ CONJ if; (em pergunta indireta) whether; **se bem que** even though

sé [sɛ] F cathedral; **Santa Sé** Holy See

sê [se] VB ver **ser**

Seade [se'adʒi] (BR) ABR M = **Sistema Estadual de Análise de Dados**

seara ['sjara] F (campo de cereais) wheat (ou corn) field; (campo cultivado) tilled field

sebe ['sɛbi] (PT) F fence; **~ viva** hedge

sebento, -a [se'bẽtu, a] ADJ greasy; (sujo) dirty, filthy

sebo ['sebu] M tallow; (livraria) secondhand bookshop

seborreia [sebo'hɛja] F seborrhoea (BRIT), seborrhea (US)

seboso, -a [se'bozu, ɔza] ADJ greasy; (sujo) dirty; (col) stuck-up

seca ['seka] F (estiagem) drought

S

secador [seka'dor] M dryer; **~ de cabelo/ roupa** hairdryer/clothes horse

secagem [se'kaʒẽ] F drying

seção [se'sãw] (pl **-ões**) F section; (em loja, repartição) department; **~ rítmica** rhythm section

secar [se'kar] VT to dry; (planta) to parch; (rio) to dry up ▶ VI to dry; to wither; (fonte) to dry up

seccionar [seksjo'nar] VT to split up

secessão [sese'sãw] (pl **-ões**) F secession

seco, -a ['seku, a] ADJ dry; (árido) arid; (fruta, carne) dried; (ríspido) curt, brusque; (pancada, ruído) dull; (magro) thin; (pessoa: frio) cold; (: sério) serious; **em ~** (barco) aground; **estar ~ por algo/para fazer algo** (col) to be dying for sth/to do sth

seções [se'sõjs] FPL de **seção**

secreção [sekre'sãw] (pl **-ões**) F secretion

secretaria [sekreta'ria] F (escritório geral) general office; (de secretário) secretary's office; (ministério) ministry

secretária [sekre'tarja] F (mesa) writing desk; **~ eletrônica** answering machine; ver tb **secretário**

secretariar [sekreta'rjar] VT to work as a secretary to ▶ VI to work as a secretary

secretário, -a [sekre'tarju, a] M/F secretary; **~ particular** private secretary; **S~ de Estado de ...** Secretary of State for ...

secretário-geral, secretária-geral (pl **secretários-gerais/secretárias-gerais**) M/F secretary-general

secreto, -a [se'krɛtu, a] ADJ secret

sectário, -a [sek'tarju, a] ADJ sectarian ▶ M/F follower

sectarismo [sekta'rizmu] M sectarianism

secular [seku'lar] ADJ (leigo) secular, lay; (muito antigo) age-old

secularizar [sekulari'zar] VT to secularize

século ['sɛkulu] M (cem anos) century; (época) age; **há ~s** (fig) for ages (: atrás) ages ago

secundar [sekũ'dar] VT (apoiar) to second, support; (ajudar) to help; (pedido) to follow up

secundário, -a [sekũ'darju, a] ADJ secondary

secura [se'kura] F dryness; (fig) coldness; (col: desejo) keenness

seda ['seda] F silk; **ser** ou **estar uma ~** to be nice; **bicho da ~** silkworm

sedã [se'dã] M (Auto) saloon (car) (BRIT), sedan (US)

sedativo, -a [seda'tʃivu, a] ADJ sedative ▶ M sedative

SEDE (BR) ABR M = **Sistema Estadual de Empregos**

sede[1] ['sɛdʒi] F (de empresa, instituição) headquarters sg; (de governo) seat; (Rel) see, diocese; **~ social** head office

sede[2] ['sedʒi] F thirst; (fig): **~ (de)** craving (for); **estar com** ou **ter ~** to be thirsty; **matar a ~** to quench one's thirst

sedentário, -a [sedẽ'tarju, a] ADJ sedentary

sedento, -a [se'dẽtu, a] ADJ thirsty; (fig): **~ (de)** eager (for)

sediar [se'dʒjar] VT to base

sedição [sedʒi'sãw] F sedition

sedicioso, -a [sedʒi'sjozu, ɔza] ADJ seditious

sedimentar [sedʒimẽ'tar] VI to silt up

sedimento [sedʒi'mẽtu] M sediment

sedoso, -a [se'dozu, ɔza] ADJ silky

sedução [sedu'sãw] (pl **-ões**) F seduction; (atração) allure, charm

sedutor, a [sedu'tor(a)] ADJ seductive; (oferta etc) tempting ▶ M/F seducer

seduzir [sedu'zir] VT to seduce; (fascinar) to fascinate; (desencaminhar) to lead astray

Sefiti [sefi'tʃi] (BR) ABR M = **Serviço de Fiscalização de Trânsito Interestadual e Internacional**

seg. ABR (= segunda-feira) Mon

segmentar [segmẽ'tar] VT to segment

segmento [seg'mẽtu] M segment

segredar [segre'dar] VT, VI to whisper

segredo [se'gredu] M secret; (sigilo) secrecy; (de fechadura) combination; **em ~** in secret; **~ de estado** state secret

segregação [segrega'sãw] F segregation

segregar [segre'gar] VT to segregate, separate

seguidamente [segida'mẽtʃi] ADV (sem parar) continuously; (logo depois) soon afterwards

seguido, -a [se'gidu, a] ADJ following; (contínuo) continuous, consecutive; **~ de** ou **por** followed by; **três dias ~s** three days running; **horas seguidas** for hours on end; **em seguida** next; (logo depois) soon afterwards; (imediatamente) immediately, right away

seguidor, a [segi'dor(a)] M/F follower

seguimento [segi'mẽtu] M continuation; **dar ~ a** to proceed with; **em ~ de** after

seguinte [se'gĩtʃi] ADJ following, next; (o negócio) é o ~ (col) the thing is; **eu lhe disse o ~** this is what I said to him; **pelo ~** hereby

seguir [se'gir] VT to follow; (continuar) to continue ▶ VI to follow; (continuar) to continue, carry on; (ir) to go; **seguir-se** VR: **~-se (a)** to follow; **logo a ~** next; **~-se (de)** to result (from); **ao jantar seguiu-se uma reunião** the dinner was followed by a meeting

segunda [se'gũda] F (tb: **segunda-feira**) Monday; (Mús) second; (Auto) second (gear); **de ~** second-rate

segunda-feira (pl **segundas-feiras**) F Monday; ver tb **terça-feira**

segundanista [segũda'nista] M/F second year (student)

segundo, -a [se'gũdu, a] ADJ second ▶ PREP according to ▶ CONJ as, from what ▶ ADV secondly ▶ M second; **de segunda mão** second-hand; **de segunda (classe)** second-class; **~ ele disse** according to what he said; **~ dizem** apparently; **~ me consta** as far as I know; **~ se afirma** according to what is said, from what is said; **segundas intenções** ulterior motives; **~ tempo** (Futebol) second half; ver tb **quinto**

segundo-time ADJ INV (*pessoa*) second-rate
segurado, -a [segu'radu, a] ADJ, M/F (*Com*) insured
segurador, a [segura'dor(a)] M/F insurer ▶ F insurance company
seguramente [segura'mētʃi] ADV (*com certeza*) certainly; (*muito provavelmente*) surely
segurança [segu'rãsa] F security; (*ausência de perigo*) safety; (*confiança*) confidence; (*convicção*) assurance ▶ M/F security guard; **com ~** assuredly; **~ nacional** national security
segurar [segu'rar] VT to hold up; (*amparar*) to hold up; (*Com: bens*) to insure ▶ VI: **~ em** to hold; **segurar-se** VR (*Com: fazer seguro*) to insure o.s.; **~-se em** to hold on to
seguro, -a [se'guru, a] ADJ (*livre de perigo*) safe; (*livre de risco, firme*) secure; (*certo*) certain, assured; (*confiável*) reliable; (*de si mesmo*) secure, confident; (*tempo*) settled ▶ ADV confidently ▶ M (*Com*) insurance; **~ de si** self-assured; **~ morreu de velho** better safe than sorry; **estar ~ de/de que** to be sure of/that; **fazer ~** to take out an insurance policy; **companhia de ~s** insurance company; **~ contra acidentes/incêndio** accident/fire insurance; **~ de vida/automóvel** life/car insurance
seguro-saúde (*pl* **seguros-saúde**) M health insurance
SEI (BR) ABR F = **Secretaria Especial da Informática**
sei [sej] VB *ver* **saber**
seio ['seju] M breast, bosom; (*âmago*) heart; **~ paranasal** sinus; **no ~ de** in the heart of
seis [sejs] NUM six; *ver tb* **cinco**
seiscentos, -tas [sej'sētus, tas] NUM six hundred
seita ['sejta] F sect
seiva ['sejva] F sap; (*fig*) vigour (BRIT), vigor (US), vitality
seixo ['sejʃu] M pebble
seja *etc* ['seʒa] VB *ver* **ser**
SELA ABR M = **Sistema Econômico Latino-Americano**
sela ['sɛla] F saddle
selagem [se'laʒē] F (*de cartas*) franking; **máquina de ~** franking machine
selar [se'lar] VT (*carta*) to stamp; (*documento oficial, pacto*) to seal; (*cavalo*) to saddle; (*fechar*) to shut, seal; (*concluir*) to conclude
seleção [sele'sãw] (*pl* **-ões**) F selection; (*Esporte*) team
selecionado [selesjo'nadu] M (*Esporte*) team
selecionador, a [selesjona'dor(a)] M/F selector
selecionar [selesjo'nar] VT to select
seleções [sele'sõjs] FPL *de* **seleção**
seleta [se'lɛta] F anthology
seletivo, -a [sele'tʃivu, a] ADJ selective
seleto, -a [se'lɛtu, a] ADJ select
selim [se'lĩ] (*pl* **-ns**) M saddle
selo ['selu] M stamp; (*carimbo, sinete*) seal; (*fig*) stamp, mark

selva ['sɛwva] F jungle
selvagem [sew'vaʒē] (*pl* **-ns**) ADJ (*silvestre*) wild; (*feroz*) fierce; (*povo*) savage; (*fig: indivíduo, maneiras*) coarse
selvageria [sewvaʒe'ria] F savagery
sem [sē] PREP without ▶ CONJ: **~ que eu peça** without my asking; **a casa está ~ limpar há duas semanas** the house hasn't been cleaned for two weeks; **estar/ficar ~ dinheiro/gasolina** to have no/have run out of money/petrol; **~ quê nem para quê** for no apparent reason
SEMA (BR) ABR F = **Secretaria Especial do Meio Ambiente**
semáforo [se'maforu] M (*Auto*) traffic lights *pl*; (*Ferro*) signal
semana [se'mana] F week
semanada [sema'nada] F (*weekly*) wages *pl*; (*mesada*) weekly allowance
semanal [sema'naw] (*pl* **-ais**) ADJ weekly; **ganha $200 semanais** he earns $200 a week
semanário [sema'narju] M weekly (*publication*)
semântica [se'mãtʃika] F semantics *sg*
semântico, -a [se'mãtʃiku, a] ADJ semantic
semblante [sē'blãtʃi] M face; (*fig*) appearance, look
semeadura [semja'dura] F sowing
semear [se'mjar] VT to sow; (*fig*) to spread; (*espalhar*) to scatter
semelhança [seme'ʎãsa] F similarity, resemblance; **a ~ de** like; **ter ~ com** to resemble
semelhante [seme'ʎãtʃi] ADJ similar; (*tal*) such ▶ M fellow creature
semelhar [seme'ʎar] VI: **~ a** to look like, resemble ▶ VT to look like, resemble; **semelhar-se** VR to be alike
sêmen ['semē] M semen
semente [se'mētʃi] F seed
sementeira [semē'tejra] F sowing, spreading
semestral [semes'traw] (*pl* **-ais**) ADJ half-yearly, bi-annual
semestralmente [semestraw'mētʃi] ADV every six months
semestre [se'mɛstri] M six months; (*Educ*) semester
sem-fim M: **um ~ de perguntas** *etc* endless questions *etc*
semi... [semi] PREFIXO semi..., half...
semiaberto, -a [semia'bɛrtu, a] ADJ half-open
semianalfabeto, -a [semianawfa'bɛtu, a] ADJ semiliterate
semibreve [semi'brɛvi] F (*Mús*) semibreve
semicírculo [semi'sirkulu] M semicircle
semicondutor [semikõdu'tor] M semiconductor
semiconsciente [semikõ'sjētʃi] ADJ semiconscious
semifinal [semi'finaw] (*pl* **-ais**) F semi-final
semifinalista [semifina'lista] M/F semi-finalist

S

semi-internato M day school
semi-interno, -a M/F (*tb*: **aluno semi-interno**)
day pupil
seminal [semi'naw] (*pl* **-ais**) ADJ seminal
seminário [semi'narju] M (*Educ, congresso*)
seminar; (*Rel*) seminary
seminarista [semina'rista] M seminarist
seminu, a [semi'nu(a)] ADJ half-naked
semiótica [se'mjɔtʃika] F semiotics *sg*
semiprecioso, -a [semipre'sjozu, ɔza] ADJ
semi-precious
semita [se'mita] ADJ Semitic
semítico, -a [se'mitʃiku, a] ADJ Semitic
semitom [semi'tõ] M (*Mús*) semitone
sem-lar M/F INV homeless person
sem-número M: **um ~ de coisas** loads of
things
semolina [semo'lina] F semolina
sem-par ADJ INV unequalled, unique
sempre ['sẽpri] ADV always; **você ~ vai?** (*PT*)
are you still going?; **~ que** whenever;
como ~ as usual; **a comida/hora** *etc* **de ~**
the usual food/time *etc*; **a mesma história
de ~** the same old story; **para ~** forever;
para todo o ~ for ever and ever; **quase ~**
nearly always
sem-sal ADJ INV insipid
sem-terra M/F INV landless ▶ M/F INV landless
labourer (*BRIT*) *ou* laborer (*US*)
sem-teto ADJ INV homeless ▶ M/F INV
homeless person; **os ~** the homeless
sem-vergonha ADJ INV shameless ▶ M/F INV
(*pessoa*) rogue
Sena ['sɛna] M: **o ~** the Seine
Senac [se'naki] (*BR*) ABR M = **Serviço Nacional
de Aprendizagem Comercial**
senado [se'nadu] M senate
senador, a [sena'dor(a)] M/F senator
Senai [se'naj] (*BR*) ABR M = **Serviço Nacional
de Aprendizagem Industrial**
senão [se'nãw] CONJ (*do contrário*) otherwise;
(*mas sim*) but, but rather ▶ PREP (*exceto*) except
▶ M (*pl* **-ões**) flaw, defect; **~ quando**
suddenly
Senav [se'navi] (*BR*) ABR F = **Superintendência
Estadual de Navegação**
senda ['sẽda] F path
Senegal [sene'gaw] M: **o ~** Senegal
senha ['sɛɲa] F (*sinal*) sign; (*palavra de passe,
Comput*) password; (*de caixa eletrônico*) PIN
number; (*recibo*) receipt; (*bilhete*) ticket,
voucher; (*passe*) pass
senhor, a [se'ɲor(a)] M (*homem*) man; (*formal*)
gentleman; (*homem idoso*) elderly man; (*Rel*)
lord; (*dono*) owner; (*tratamento*) Mr(.);
(*tratamento respeitoso*) sir ▶ F (*mulher*) lady;
(*esposa*) wife; (*mulher idosa*) elderly lady; (*dona*)
owner; (*tratamento*) Mrs(.), Ms(.); (*tratamento
respeitoso*) madam ▶ ADJ marvellous (*BRIT*),
marvelous (*US*); **uma ~a gripe** a bad case of
flu; **o ~/a ~a** (*você*) you; **nossa ~a!** (*col*) gosh;
sim, ~(a)! yes indeed; **estar ~ de si** to be
cool *ou* collected; **estar ~ da situação** to be

in control of the situation; **ser ~ do seu
nariz** to be one's own boss; **~ de engenho**
plantation owner
senhoria [seɲo'ria] F (*proprietária*) landlady;
Vossa S~ (*em cartas*) you
senhoril [seɲo'riw] (*pl* **-is**) ADJ (*roupa etc*)
gentlemen's/ladies'; (*distinto*) lordly
senhorio [seɲo'riu] M (*proprietário*) landlord;
(*posse*) ownership
senhoris [seɲo'ris] ADJ PL *de* **senhoril**
senhorita [seɲo'rita] F young lady;
(*tratamento*) Miss, Ms(.); **a ~** (*você*) you
senil [se'niw] (*pl* **-is**) ADJ senile
senilidade [senili'dadʒi] F senility
senilizar [senili'zar] VT to age
senis [se'nis] ADJ PL *de* **senil**
senões [se'nõjs] MPL *de* **senão**
sensação [sẽsa'sãw] (*pl* **-ões**) F sensation; **a ~
de que/uma ~ de** the feeling that/a feeling
of; **causar ~** to cause a sensation
sensacional [sẽsasjo'naw] (*pl* **-ais**) ADJ
sensational
sensacionalismo [sẽsasjona'lizmu] M
sensationalism
sensacionalista [sẽsasjona'lista] ADJ
sensationalist
sensações [sẽsa'sõjs] FPL *de* **sensação**
sensatez [sẽsa'tez] F good sense
sensato, -a [sẽ'satu, a] ADJ sensible
sensibilidade [sẽsibili'dadʒi] F sensitivity;
(*artística*) sensibility; (*física*) feeling; **estou
com muita ~ neste dedo** this finger is very
sensitive
sensibilizar [sẽsibili'zar] VT to touch, move;
(*opinião pública*) to influence; **sensibilizar-se**
VR to be moved
sensitivo, -a [sẽsi'tʃivu, a] ADJ sensory;
(*pessoa*) sensitive
sensível [sẽ'sivew] (*pl* **-eis**) ADJ sensitive;
(*visível*) noticeable; (*considerável*) considerable;
(*dolorido*) tender
sensivelmente [sẽsivew'mẽtʃi] ADV
perceptibly, markedly
senso ['sẽsu] M sense; (*juízo*) judgement;
~ comum *ou* **bom ~** common sense; **~ de
humor/responsabilidade** sense of humour
(*BRIT*) *ou* humor (*US*) /responsibility
sensorial [sẽso'rjaw] (*pl* **-ais**) ADJ sensory
sensual [sẽ'swaw] (*pl* **-ais**) ADJ sensual,
sensuous; (*voz, pessoa, pose*) sexy
sensualidade [sẽswali'dadʒi] F sensuality,
sensuousness
sentado, -a [sẽ'tadu, a] ADJ sitting; (*almoço*)
sit-down
sentar [sẽ'tar] VT to seat ▶ VI to sit; **sentar-se**
VR to sit down
sentença [sẽ'tẽsa] F (*Jur*) sentence; **~ de
morte** death sentence
sentenciar [sẽtẽ'sjar] VT (*julgar*) to pass
judgement on; (*condenar por sentença*) to
sentence ▶ VI to pass judgement; to pass
sentence
sentidamente [sẽtʃida'mẽtʃi] ADV (*chorar*)

bitterly; (*desculpar-se*) abjectly

sentido, -a [sē'tʃidu, a] ADJ (*magoado*) hurt; (*choro, queixa*) heartfelt ▶ M sense; (*significação*) sense, meaning; (*direção*) direction; (*atenção*) attention; (*aspecto*) respect; ~! (*Mil*) attention!; **em certo ~** in a sense; **sem ~** meaningless; **fazer ~** to make sense; **perder/recobrar os ~s** to lose/ recover consciousness; **(não) ter ~** (not) to be acceptable; **~ figurado** figurative sense; **"~ único"** (PT: *sinal*) "one-way"

sentimental [sē'tʃimē'taw] (*pl* **-ais**) ADJ sentimental; **aventura ~** romance; **vida ~** love life

sentimentalismo [sētʃimēta'lizmu] M sentimentality

sentimento [sētʃi'mētu] M feeling; (*senso*) sense; **sentimentos** MPL (*pêsames*) condolences; **fazer algo com ~** to do sth with feeling; **ter bons ~s** to be good-natured

sentinela [sētʃi'nɛla] F sentry, guard; **estar de ~** to be on guard duty; **render ~** to relieve the guard

sentir [sē'tʃir] VT to feel; (*perceber, pressentir*) to sense; (*ser afetado por*) to be affected by; (*magoar-se*) to be upset by ▶ VI to feel; (*sofrer*) to suffer; **sentir-se** VR to feel; (*julgar-se*) to consider o.s. (to be); **~ (a) falta de** to miss; **~ cheiro/gosto (de)** to smell/taste; **~ tristeza** to feel sad; **~ vontade de** to feel like; **você sente a diferença?** can you tell the difference?; **sinto muito** I am very sorry

senzala [sē'zala] F slave quarters *pl*

separação [separa'sāw] (*pl* **-ões**) F separation

separado, -a [sepa'radu, a] ADJ separate; (*casal*) separated; **em ~** separately, apart

separar [sepa'rar] VT to separate; (*dividir*) to divide; (*pôr de lado*) to put aside; **separar-se** VR to separate; to be divided; **~-se de** to separate from

separata [sepa'rata] F offprint

separatismo [separa'tʃizmu] M separatism

séptico, -a ['sɛptʃiku, a] ADJ septic

septuagésimo, -a [septwa'ʒɛzimu, a] NUM seventieth; *ver tb* **quinto**

sepulcro [se'puwkru] M tomb

sepultamento [sepuwta'mētu] M burial

sepultar [sepuw'tar] VT to bury; (*esconder*) to hide, conceal; (*segredo*) to keep quiet

sepultura [sepuw'tura] F grave, tomb

sequei *etc* [se'kej] VB *ver* **secar**

sequela [se'kwɛla] F sequel; (*consequência*) consequence; (*Med*) after-effect

sequência [se'kwēsja] F sequence

sequencial [sekwē'sjaw] (*pl* **-ais**) ADJ (*Comput*) sequential

sequer [se'kɛr] ADV at least; **(nem) ~** not even

sequestrador, a [sekwestra'dor(a)] M/F (*raptor*) kidnapper; (*de avião etc*) hijacker

sequestrar [sekwes'trar] VT (*bens*) to seize, confiscate; (*raptar*) to kidnap; (*avião etc*) to hijack

sequestro [se'kwɛstru] M seizure; (*rapto*) abduction, kidnapping; (*de avião etc*) hijack

sequidão [seki'dāw] F dryness; (*de pessoa*) coldness

sequioso, -a [se'kjozu, ɔza] ADJ (*sedento*) thirsty; (*fig: desejoso*) eager

séquito ['sɛkitu] M retinue

PALAVRA-CHAVE

ser [ser] VI **1** (*descrição*) to be; **ela é médica/ muito alta** she's a doctor/very tall; **é Ana (Tel)** Ana speaking *ou* here; **ela é de uma bondade incrível** she's incredibly kind; **ele está é danado** he's really angry; **ser de mentir/briga** to be the sort to lie/fight
2 (*horas, datas, números*): **é uma hora** it's one o'clock; **são seis e meia** it's half past six; **é dia 1° de junho** it's the first of June; **somos/são seis** there are six of us/them
3 (*origem, material*): **ser de** to be *ou* come from; (*feito de*) to be made of; (*pertencer*) to belong to; **sua família é da Bahia** his (*ou* her *etc*) family is from Bahia; **a mesa é de mármore** the table is made of marble; **é de Pedro** it's Pedro's, it belongs to Pedro
4 (*em orações passivas*): **já foi descoberto** it had already been discovered
5 (*locuções com subjun*): **ou seja** that is to say; **seja quem for** whoever it may be; **se eu fosse você** if I were you; **se não fosse você,** ... if it hadn't been for you ...
6 (*locuções*): **a não ser** except; **a não ser que** unless; **é** (*resposta afirmativa*) yes; **..., não é?** isn't it?, don't you? *etc*; **ah, é?** really?; **que foi?** (*o que aconteceu?*) what happened?; (*qual é o problema?*) what's the problem?; **será que ...?** I wonder if ...?
▶ M being

seres MPL (*criaturas*) creatures

serão [se'rāw] (*pl* **-ões**) M (*trabalho noturno*) night work; (*horas extraordinárias*) overtime; **fazer ~** to work late; (*dormir tarde*) to go to bed late

sereia [se'reja] F mermaid

serelepe [sere'lɛpi] ADJ frisky

serenar [sere'nar] VT to calm ▶ VI (*pessoa*) to calm down; (*mar*) to grow calm; (*dor*) to subside

serenata [sere'nata] F serenade

serenidade [sereni'dadʒi] F serenity, tranquillity

sereno, -a [se'rɛnu, a] ADJ calm; (*olhar*) serene; (*tempo*) fine, clear ▶ M (*relento*) damp night air; **no ~** in the open

seresta [se'rɛsta] F serenade

SERFA (BR) ABR M = **Serviço de Fiscalização Agrícola**

sergipano, -a [serʒi'panu, a] ADJ from Sergipe ▶ M/F person from Sergipe

seriado, -a [se'rjadu, a] ADJ (*número*) serial; (*publicação, filme*) serialized

serial [se'rjaw] (*pl* **-ais**) ADJ (*Comput*) serial

série ['sɛri] F series; (*sequência*) sequence, succession; (*Educ*) grade; (*categoria*) category; **fora de ~** out of order; (*fig*) extraordinary; **fabricar em ~** to mass-produce

seriedade [serje'dadʒi] F seriousness; (*honestidade*) honesty

seringa [se'rĩga] F syringe

seringal [serĩ'gaw] (*pl* **-ais**) M rubber plantation

seringalista [serĩga'lista] M rubber plantation owner

seringueira [serĩ'gejra] F rubber tree; *ver tb* **seringueiro**

seringueiro, -a [serĩ'gejru, a] M/F rubber tapper

sério, -a ['sɛrju, a] ADJ serious; (*honesto*) honest, decent; (*responsável*) responsible; (*confiável*) reliable; (*roupa*) sober ▶ ADV seriously; **a ~** seriously; **falando ~ ...** seriously ...; **~?** really?

sermão [ser'mãw] (*pl* **-ões**) M sermon; (*fig*) telling-off; **levar um ~ de alguém** to get a telling-off from sb; **passar um ~ em alguém** to give sb a telling-off

serões [se'rõjs] MPL *de* **serão**

serpeante [ser'pjãtʃi] ADJ wriggling; (*fig: caminho, rio*) winding, meandering

serpear [ser'pjar] VI (*como serpente*) to wriggle; (*fig: caminho, rio*) to wind, meander

serpente [ser'pētʃi] F snake; (*pessoa*) snake in the grass

serpentear [serpē'tʃjar] VI = **serpear**

serpentina [serpē'tʃina] F (*conduto*) coil; (*fita de papel*) streamer

serra ['sɛha] F (*montanhas*) mountains *pl*; (*Tec*) saw; **~ circular** circular saw; **~ de arco** hacksaw; **~ de cadeia** chain saw; **~ tico-tico** fret saw

serrado, -a [se'hadu, a] ADJ serrated

serragem [se'haʒē] F (*pó*) sawdust

Serra Leoa F Sierra Leone

serralheiro, -a [seha'ʎejru, a] M/F locksmith

serrania [seha'nia] F mountain range

serrano, -a [se'hanu, a] ADJ highland *atr* ▶ M/F highlander

serrar [se'har] VT to saw

serraria [seha'ria] F sawmill

serrote [se'hɔtʃi] M handsaw

sertanejo, -a [serta'neʒu, a] ADJ rustic, country ▶ M/F inhabitant of the *sertão*

sertão [ser'tãw] (*pl* **-ões**) M backwoods *pl*, bush (country)

servente [ser'vētʃi] M/F (*criado*) servant; (*operário*) labourer (BRIT), laborer (US); **~ de pedreiro** bricklayer's mate

serventuário, -a [servē'twarju, a] M/F (*Jur*) legal official

serviçal [servi'saw] (*pl* **-ais**) ADJ obliging, helpful ▶ M/F (*criado*) servant; (*trabalhador*) wage earner

serviço [ser'visu] M service; (*de chá etc*) set; **o ~** (*emprego*) work; **um ~** (*trabalho*) a job; **não brincar em ~** not to waste time; **dar o ~**

(*col: confessar*) to blab; **estar de ~** to be on duty; **matar o ~** to cut corners; **prestar ~** to help; **~ doméstico** housework; **~ ativo** (*Mil*) active duty; **~ de informações** (*Mil*) intelligence service; **~ militar** military service; **S~ Nacional de Saúde** National Health Service; **S~ Público** Civil Service; **~s públicos** public utilities

servidão [servi'dãw] F servitude, serfdom; (*Jur: de passagem*) right of way

servidor, a [servi'dor(a)] M/F (*criado*) servant; (*funcionário*) employee ▶ M (*Comput*) server; **~ público** civil servant

servil [ser'viw] (*pl* **-is**) ADJ servile

servir [ser'vir] VT to serve ▶ VI to serve; (*ser útil*) to be useful; (*ajudar*) to help; (*roupa: caber*) to fit; **servir-se** VR: **~-se (de)** (*comida, café*) to help o.s. (to); **~-se de** (*meios*) to use, make use of; **~ de** (*prover*) to supply with, provide with; **você está servido?** (*num bar*) are you all right for a drink?; **~ de algo** to serve as sth; **para que serve isto?** what is this for?; **ele não serve para trabalhar aqui** he's not suitable to work here; **qualquer ônibus serve** any bus will do

servis [ser'vis] ADJ PL *de* **servil**

servível [ser'vivew] (*pl* **-eis**) ADJ serviceable; (*roupa*) wearable

servo, -a ['sɛrvu, a] M/F (*feudal*) serf; (*criado*) servant

servo-croata [sɛrvu'krwata] M (*Ling*) Serbo-Croat

Sesc ['sɛski] (BR) ABR M = **Serviço Social do Comércio**

Sesi [sɛ'zi] (BR) ABR M = **Serviço Social da Indústria**

sessão [se'sãw] (*pl* **-ões**) F (*do parlamento etc*) session; (*reunião*) meeting; (*de cinema*) showing; **primeira/segunda ~** first/second show; **~ coruja** late show; **~ da tarde** matinée

sessenta [se'sēta] NUM sixty; *ver tb* **cinquenta**

sessões [se'sõjs] FPL *de* **sessão**

sesta ['sɛsta] F siesta, nap

set ['sɛtʃi] M (*Tênis*) set

set. ABR (= *setembro*) Sept.

seta ['sɛta] F arrow

sete ['sɛtʃi] NUM seven; **pintar o ~** (*fig*) to get up to all sorts; *ver tb* **cinco**

setecentos, -as [sete'sētus, as] NUM seven hundred

setembro [se'tēbru] M September; *ver tb* **julho**

Brazil's independence from Portugal is commemorated on 7 September (**7 de setembro**). Independence was declared in 1822 by the Portuguese prince regent, Dom Pedro, who rebelled against several orders from the Portuguese crown, among them the order to swear loyalty to the Portuguese constitution. It is a national holiday and the occasion for processions and military parades through the main cities.

setenta [se'tẽta] NUM seventy; ver tb **cinquenta**

setentrional [setẽtrjo'naw] (pl **-ais**) ADJ northern

sétima ['sɛtʃima] F (Mús) seventh

sétimo, -a ['sɛtʃimu, a] NUM seventh; ver tb **quinto**

setor [se'tor] M sector

seu, sua [sew, 'sua] ADJ (dele) his; (dela) her; (de coisa) its; (deles, delas) their; (de você, vocês) your ▶ PRON (dele) his; (dela) hers; (deles, delas) theirs; (de você, vocês) yours ▶ M (senhor) Mr(.); **um homem de ~s 60 anos** a man of about sixty; **~ idiota!** you idiot!

Seul [se'uw] N Seoul

severidade [severi'dadʒi] F severity, harshness

severo, -a [se'vɛru, a] ADJ severe, harsh

seviciar [sevi'sjar] VT to ill-treat; (mulher, criança) to batter

sevícias [se'visjas] FPL (maus tratos) ill treatment sg; (desumanidade) inhumanity sg, cruelty sg

Sevilha [se'viʎa] N Seville

sex. ABR (= sexta-feira) Fri

sexagésimo, -a [seksa'ʒɛzimu, a] NUM sixtieth; ver tb **quinto**

sexo ['sɛksu] M sex; **de ~ feminino/masculino** female/male

sexta ['sesta] F (tb: **sexta-feira**) Friday; (Mús) sixth

sexta-feira (pl **sextas-feiras**) F Friday; **S~ Santa** Good Friday; ver tb **terça-feira**

sexto, -a ['sestu, a] NUM sixth; ver tb **quinto**

sexual [se'kswaw] (pl **-ais**) ADJ sexual; (vida, ato) sex atr

sexualidade [sekswali'dadʒi] F sexuality

sexy ['sɛksi] (pl **-s**) ADJ sexy

Seychelles [sej'ʃɛlis] F ou FPL: **a(s) ~** the Seychelles

sezão [se'zãw] (pl **-ões**) F (febre) (intermittent) fever; (malária) malaria

s.f.f. (PT) ABR = **se faz favor**

SFH (BR) ABR M = **Sistema Financeiro de Habitação**

shopping center ['ʃopĩŋ'sɛter] M shopping centre (BRIT), (shopping) mall (US)

short ['ʃortʃi] M (pair of) shorts pl

show [ʃow] (pl **-s**) M show; (de cantor, conjunto) concert, gig; **dar um ~** (fig) to put on a real show; (dar escândalo) to make a scene; **ser um ~** (col) to be a sensation

showroom [ʃow'rũ] (pl **-s**) M showroom

si [si] PRON oneself; (ele) himself; (ela) herself; (coisa) itself; (PT: de você) yourself, you; (: vocês) yourselves; (eles, elas) themselves; **em si** in itself; **fora de si** beside oneself; **cheio de si** full of oneself; **voltar a si** to come round

siamês, -esa [sja'mes, eza] ADJ Siamese

Sibéria [si'bɛrja] F: **a ~** Siberia

sibilar [sibi'lar] VI to hiss

sicário [si'karju] M hired assassin

Sicília [si'silja] F: **a ~** Sicily

sicrano [si'kranu] M: **fulano e ~** so-and-so

SIDA ['sida] (PT) ABR F (= síndrome de deficiência imunológica adquirida) AIDS

siderúrgica [side'rurʒika] F steel industry

siderúrgico, -a [side'rurʒiku, a] ADJ iron and steel atr; (usina) **siderúrgica** steelworks sg

sidra ['sidra] F cider

SIF (BR) ABR M = **Serviço de Inspeção Federal**

sifão [si'fãw] (pl **-ões**) M syphon

sífilis ['sifilis] F syphilis

sifões [si'fõjs] MPL de **sifão**

sigilo [si'ʒilu] M secrecy; **guardar ~ sobre algo** to keep quiet about sth

sigiloso, -a [siʒi'lozu, ɔza] ADJ secret

sigla ['sigla] F acronym; (abreviação) abbreviation

signatário, -a [signa'tarju, a] M/F signatory

significação [signifika'sãw] F significance

significado [signifi'kadu] M meaning

significante [signifi'kãtʃi] ADJ significant

significar [signifi'kar] VT to mean, signify

significativo, -a [signifika'tʃivu, a] ADJ significant

signo ['signu] M sign; **~ do zodíaco** sign of the zodiac, star sign

sigo etc ['sigu] VB ver **seguir**

sílaba ['silaba] F syllable

silenciar [silẽ'sjar] VT (pessoa) to silence; (escândalo) to hush up ▶ VI to remain silent

silêncio [si'lẽsju] M silence, quiet; **~!** silence!; **ficar em ~** to remain silent

silencioso, -a [silẽ'sjozu, ɔza] ADJ silent, quiet ▶ M (Auto) silencer (BRIT), muffler (US)

silhueta [si'ʎweta] F silhouette

silício [si'lisju] M silicon; **plaqueta de ~** silicon chip

silicone [sili'koni] M silicone

silo ['silu] M silo

silvar [siw'var] VI to hiss; (assobiar) to whistle

silvestre [siw'vestri] ADJ wild

silvícola [siw'vikola] ADJ wild

silvicultura [siwvikuw'tura] F forestry

sim [sĩ] ADV yes; **creio que ~** I think so; **isso ~** that's it!; **pelo ~, pelo não** just in case; **dar ou dizer o ~** to consent, say yes

simbólico, -a [sĩ'bɔliku, a] ADJ symbolic

simbolismo [sĩbo'lizmu] M symbolism

simbolizar [sĩboli'zar] VT to symbolise

símbolo ['sĩbolu] M symbol

simetria [sime'tria] F symmetry

simétrico, -a [si'mɛtriku, a] ADJ symmetrical

similar [simi'lar] ADJ similar

similaridade [similari'dadʒi] F similarity

símile ['simili] M simile

similitude [simili'tudʒi] F similarity

simpatia [sĩpa'tʃia] F (por alguém, algo) liking; (afeto) affection; (afinidade, solidariedade) sympathy; **simpatias** FPL (inclinações) sympathies; **com ~** sympathetically; **ser uma ~** to be very nice; **ter ou sentir ~ por** to like

simpático, -a [sĩ'patʃiku, a] ADJ (pessoa, decoração etc) nice; (lugar) pleasant, nice;

(*amável*) kind ▶ M (*Anat*) nervous system; **ser ~ a** to be sympathetic to
simpatizante [sĩpatʃi'zãtʃi] ADJ sympathetic ▶ M/F sympathizer
simpatizar [sĩpatʃi'zar] VI: **~ com** (*pessoa*) to like; (*causa*) to sympathize with
simples ['sĩplis] ADJ INV simple; (*único*) single; (*fácil*) easy; (*mero*) mere; (*ingênuo*) naïve ▶ ADV simply
simplicidade [sĩplisi'dadʒi] F simplicity; (*ingenuidade*) naïvety; (*modéstia*) plainness; (*naturalidade*) naturalness
simplicíssimo, -a [sĩpli'sisimu, a] ADJ SUPERL de **simples**
simplificação [sĩplifika'sãw] (*pl* **-ões**) F simplification
simplificar [sĩplifi'kar] VT to simplify
simplíssimo, -a [sĩ'plisimu, a] ADJ SUPERL de **simples**
simplista [sĩ'plista] ADJ simplistic
simplório, -a [sĩ'plɔrju, a] ADJ simple ▶ M/F simple person
simpósio [sĩ'pɔzju] M symposium
simulação [simula'sãw] (*pl* **-ões**) F simulation; (*fingimento*) pretence (*BRIT*), pretense (*US*), sham
simulacro [simu'lakru] M (*imitação*) imitation; (*fingimento*) pretence (*BRIT*), pretense (*US*)
simulado, -a [simu'ladu, a] ADJ simulated
simular [simu'lar] VT to simulate
simultaneamente [simuwtanja'mẽtʃi] ADV simultaneously
simultâneo, -a [simuw'tanju, a] ADJ simultaneous
sina ['sina] F fate, destiny
sinagoga [sina'gɔga] F synagogue
Sinai [sina'i] M Sinai
sinal [si'naw] (*pl* **-ais**) M (*ger*) sign; (*gesto, Tel*) signal; (*na pele*) mole; (: *de nascença*) birthmark; (*depósito*) deposit; (*tb*: **sinal de tráfego luminoso**) traffic light; **~ rodoviário** road sign; **dar de ~** to give as a deposit; **em ~ de** (*fig*) as a sign of; **por ~** (*por falar nisso*) by the way; (*aliás*) as a matter of fact; **avançar o ~** (*Auto*) to jump the lights; (*fig*) to jump the gun; **dar ~ de vida** to show up; **fazer ~** to signal; **~ da cruz** sign of the cross; **~ de alarma** alarm; **~ de chamada** (*Tel*) ringing tone; **~ de discar** (*BR*) *ou* **de marcar** (*PT*) dialling tone (*BRIT*), dial tone (*US*); **~ de ocupado** (*BR*) *ou* **de impedido** (*PT*) engaged tone (*BRIT*), busy signal (*US*); **~ de mais/menos** (*Mat*) plus/minus sign; **~ de perigo** danger signal; **~ de pontuação** punctuation mark; **~ verde** *ou* **aberto/vermelho** *ou* **fechado** green/red light
sinaleiro [sina'lejru] M (*Ferro*) signalman; (*aparelho*) traffic lights *pl*
sinalização [sinaliza'sãw] F (*ato*) signalling; (*para motoristas*) traffic signs *pl*; (*Ferro*) signals *pl*
sinalizar [sinali'zar] VI to signal

sinceridade [sĩseri'dadʒi] F sincerity
sincero, -a [sĩ'sɛru, a] ADJ sincere; (*opinião, confissão*) honest
sincopado, -a [sĩko'padu, a] ADJ (*Mús*) syncopated
síncope ['sĩkɔpi] F fainting fit
sincronizar [sĩkroni'zar] VT to synchronize
sindical [sĩdʒi'kaw] (*pl* **-ais**) ADJ (trade) union *atr*
sindicalismo [sĩdʒika'lizmu] M trade unionism
sindicalista [sĩdʒika'lista] M/F trade unionist
sindicalizar [sĩdʒikali'zar] VT to unionize; **sindicalizar-se** VR to become unionized
sindicância [sĩdʒi'kãsja] F inquiry, investigation
sindicato [sĩdʒi'katu] M (*de trabalhadores*) trade union; (*financeiro*) syndicate
síndico, -a ['sĩdʒiku, a] M/F (*de condomínio*) manager; (*de massa falida*) receiver
síndrome ['sĩdromi] F syndrome; **~ de Down** Down's syndrome; **~ de deficiência imunológica adquirida** acquired immune deficiency syndrome
SINE (*BR*) ABR M = **Sistema Nacional de Empregos**
sinecura [sine'kura] F sinecure
sineta [si'neta] F bell
sinfonia [sĩfo'nia] F symphony
sinfônica [sĩ'fonika] F (*tb*: **orquestra sinfônica**) symphony orchestra
sinfônico, -a [sĩ'foniku, a] ADJ symphonic
singeleza [sĩʒe'leza] F simplicity
singelo, -a [sĩ'ʒɛlu, a] ADJ simple
singular [sĩgu'lar] ADJ singular; (*extraordinário*) exceptional; (*bizarro*) odd, peculiar
singularidade [sĩgulari'dadʒi] F peculiarity
singularizar [sĩgulari'zar] VT (*distinguir*) to single out; **singularizar-se** VR to stand out, distinguish o.s.
sinistrado, -a [sinis'tradu, a] ADJ damaged
sinistro, -a [si'nistru, a] ADJ sinister ▶ M disaster, accident; (*prejuízo*) damage
sino ['sinu] M bell
sinônimo, -a [si'nonimu, a] ADJ synonymous ▶ M synonym
sinopse [si'nɔpsi] F synopsis
sintático, -a [sĩ'tatʃiku, a] ADJ syntactic
sintaxe [sĩ'tasi] F syntax
síntese ['sĩtezi] F synthesis; **em ~** in short
sintético, -a [sĩ'tɛtʃiku, a] ADJ synthetic; (*resumido*) brief
sintetizar [sĩtetʃi'zar] VT to synthesize; (*resumir*) to summarize
sinto *etc* ['sĩtu] VB *ver* **sentir**
sintoma [sĩ'tɔma] M symptom
sintomático, -a [sĩto'matʃiku, a] ADJ symptomatic
sintonizador [sĩtoniza'dor] M tuner
sintonizar [sĩtoni'zar] VT (*Rádio*) to tune ▶ VI to tune in; **~ (com)** (*pessoa*) to get on (with); (*opinião*) to coincide (with)
sinuca [si'nuka] F snooker; (*mesa*) snooker table; **estar numa ~** (*col*) to be snookered

sinuoso, -a [si'nwozu, ɔza] ADJ (caminho) winding; (linha) wavy

sinusite [sinu'zitʃi] F sinusitis

sionismo [sjo'nizmu] M Zionism

sionista [sjo'nista] ADJ, M/F Zionist

sirena [si'rɛna] F siren

sirene [si'rɛni] F = **sirena**

siri [si'ri] M crab; **casquinha de ~** (Culin) crab au gratin

Síria ['sirja] F: **a ~** Syria

sirigaita [siri'gajta] (col) F floozy

sírio, -a ['sirju, a] ADJ, M/F Syrian

sirvo etc ['sirvu] VB ver **servir**

sísmico, -a ['sizmiku, a] ADJ seismic

sismógrafo [siz'mɔgrafu] M seismograph

siso ['sizu] M good sense; **dente de ~** wisdom tooth

sistema [sis'tɛma] M system; (método) method; **~ imunológico** immune system; **~ operacional** (Comput) operating system; **~ solar** solar system

sistemático, -a [siste'matʃiku, a] ADJ systematic

sistematizar [sistematʃi'zar] VT to systematize

sisudo, -a [si'zudu, a] ADJ serious, sober

site ['sajtʃi] M (na Internet) website; **~ de relacionamentos** social networking site

sitiar [si'tʃjar] VT to besiege

sítio ['sitʃju] M (Mil) siege; (propriedade rural) small farm; (PT: lugar) place; **estado de ~** state of siege

situação [sitwa'sãw] (pl **-ões**) F situation; (posição) position; (social) standing

situado, -a [si'twadu, a] ADJ situated; **estar** ou **ficar ~** to be situated

situar [si'twar] VT (pôr) to place, put; (edifício) to situate, locate; **situar-se** VR (pôr-se) to position o.s.; (estar situado) to be situated

SL ABR = **sobreloja**

sl ABR = **SL**

slogan [iz'lɔgã] (pl **-s**) M slogan

smoking [iz'mokĩs] (pl **-s**) M dinner jacket (BRIT), tuxedo (US)

SMTU (BR) ABR F = **Superintendência Municipal de Transportes Urbanos**

SNI (BR) ABR M (antes: = Serviço Nacional de Informações) state intelligence service

só [sɔ] ADJ alone; (único) single; (solitário) solitary ▶ ADV only; **um só** only one; **a sós** alone; **por si só** by himself (ou herself, itself); **é só!** that's all!; **é só discar** all you have to do is dial; **veja/imagine só** just look/imagine; **não só ... mas também ...** not only ... but also ...; **que** ou **como só ele** etc like nobody else; **é isso?** is that all?

soalho ['swaʎu] M = **assoalho**

soar [swar] VI to sound; (cantar) to sing; (sinos, clarins) to ring; (apito) to blow; (boato) to go round ▶ VT (horas) to strike; (instrumento) to play; **~ a** to sound like; **~ bem/mal** (fig) to go down well/badly

sob [sob] PREP under; **~ emenda** subject to correction; **~ juramento** on oath; **~ medida** (roupa) made to measure; (software) bespoke; **~ minha palavra** on my word; **~ pena de** on pain of

sobe etc ['sɔbi] VB ver **subir**

sobejar [sobe'ʒar] VI (superabundar) to abound; (restar) to be left over

sobejos [so'beʒus] MPL remains, leftovers

soberania [sobera'nia] F sovereignty

soberano, -a [sobe'ranu, a] ADJ sovereign; (fig: supremo) supreme; (: altivo) haughty ▶ M/F sovereign

soberba [so'berba] F haughtiness, arrogance

soberbo, -a [so'berbu, a] ADJ (arrogante) haughty, arrogant; (magnífico) magnificent, splendid

sobra ['sɔbra] F surplus, remnant; **sobras** FPL remains; (de tecido) remnants; (de comida) leftovers; **ter algo de ~** to have sth extra; (tempo, comida, motivos) to have plenty of sth; **ficar de ~** to be left over

sobraçar [sobra'sar] VT (levar debaixo do braço) to carry under one's arm; (meter debaixo do braço) to put under one's arm

sobrado [so'bradu] M (andar) floor; (casa) house (of two or more storeys)

sobranceiro, -a [sobrã'sejru, a] ADJ (que está acima de) lofty, towering; (proeminente) prominent; (arrogante) haughty, arrogant

sobrancelha [sobrã'seʎa] F eyebrow

sobrar [so'brar] VI to be left; **ficar sobrando** (pessoa) to be left out; (: não ter parceiro) to be the odd one out; **sobram-me cinco** I have five left; **isto dá e sobra** this is more than enough

sobre ['sobri] PREP on; (por cima de) over; (acima de) above; (a respeito de) about; **ser meio ~ o chato** (col) to be a bit boring

sobreaviso [sobrja'vizu] M warning; **estar de ~** to be alert, be on one's guard

sobrecapa [sobri'kapa] F cover

sobrecarga [sobri'karga] F overload

sobrecarregar [sobrikahe'gar] VT to overload

sobre-estimar [sobrjestʃi'mar] VT to overestimate

sobre-humano, -a ADJ superhuman

sobrejacente [sobriʒa'sẽtʃi] ADJ: **~ a** over

sobreloja [sobri'lɔʒa] F mezzanine (floor)

sobremaneira [sobrema'nejra] ADV exceedingly

sobremesa [sobri'meza] F dessert

sobremodo [sobri'mɔdu] ADV exceedingly

sobrenatural [sobrinatu'raw] (pl **-ais**) ADJ supernatural; (esforço) superhuman ▶ M: **o ~** the supernatural

sobrenome [sobri'nɔmi] (BR) M surname, family name

sobrepairar [sobripaj'rar] VI: **~ a** to hover above; (crise) to rise above

sobrepor [sobri'por] (irreg: como **pôr**) VT: **~ algo a algo** (pôr em cima) to put sth on top of sth; (adicionar) to add sth to sth; (dar preferência) to put sth before sth; **sobrepor-se** VR: **~-se a** (pôr-se sobre) to cover, go on top of; (sobrevir) to succeed

sobrepujar [sobripu'ʒar] VT (*exceder em altura*) to rise above; (*superar*) to surpass; (*obstáculos, perigos*) to overcome; (*inimigo*) to overwhelm

sobrepunha *etc* [sobri'puɲa] VB *ver* **sobrepor**

sobrepus *etc* [sobri'pujs] VB *ver* **sobrepor**

sobrepuser *etc* [sobripu'zer] VB *ver* **sobrepor**

sobrescritar [sobreskri'tar] VT to address

sobrescrito [sobres'kritu] M address

sobressair [sobrisa'ir] VI to stand out; **sobressair-se** VR to stand out

sobressalente [sobrisa'lẽtʃi] ADJ, M spare

sobressaltado, -a [sobrisaw'tadu, a] ADJ: **viver ~** to live in fear; **acordar ~** to wake up with a start

sobressaltar [sobrisaw'tar] VT to startle, frighten; **sobressaltar-se** VR to be startled

sobressalto [sobri'sawtu] M (*movimento brusco*) start; (*temor*) trepidation; **de ~** suddenly; **o seu ~ com aquele estrondo/aquela notícia** his fright at that noise/his shock at that news; **ter um ~** to get a fright

sobretaxa [sobri'taʃa] F surcharge

sobretudo [sobri'tudu] M overcoat ▶ ADV above all, especially

sobrevir [sobri'vir] (*irreg: como* **vir**) VI to occur, arise; **~ a** (*seguir*) to follow (on from); **sobreveio-lhe uma doença** he was struck down by illness

sobrevivência [sobrivi'vẽsja] F survival

sobrevivente [sobrivi'vẽtʃi] ADJ surviving ▶ M/F survivor

sobreviver [sobrivi'ver] VI: **~ (a)** to survive

sobrevoar [sobrivo'ar] VT, VI to fly over

sobriedade [sobrje'dadʒi] F soberness; (*comedimento*) moderation, restraint

sobrinho, -a [so'briɲu, a] M/F nephew/niece

sóbrio, -a ['sɔbrju, a] ADJ sober; (*moderado*) moderate, restrained

socado, -a [so'kadu, a] ADJ (*alho*) crushed; (*escondido*) hidden; (*pessoa*) stout

socador [soka'dor] M crusher; **~ de alho** garlic press

soçaite [so'sajtʃi] (*col*) M high society

socapa [so'kapa] F: **à ~** furtively, on the sly

socar [so'kar] VT (*esmurrar*) to hit, strike; (*calcar*) to crush, pound; (*massa de pão*) to knead

social [so'sjaw] (*pl* **-ais**) ADJ social; (*entrada, elevador*) private; (*camisa*) dress *atr*

socialismo [sosja'lizmu] M socialism

socialista [sosja'lista] ADJ, M/F socialist

socialite [sosja'lajtʃi] M/F socialite

socializar [sosjali'zar] VT to socialize

sociável [so'sjavew] (*pl* **-eis**) ADJ sociable

sociedade [sosje'dadʒi] F society; (*Com: empresa*) company; (*: de sócios*) partnership; (*associação*) association; **~ anônima** limited company (*BRIT*), incorporated company (*US*); **~ anônima aberta/fechada** public/private limited company

sócio, -a ['sɔsju, a] M/F (*Com*) partner, associate; (*de clube*) member; **~ comanditário** (*Com*) silent partner

socioeconômico, -a [sɔsjueko'nomiku, a] ADJ socioeconomic

sociolinguística [sosjolĩ'gwistʃika] F sociolinguistics *sg*

sociologia [sosjolo'ʒia] F sociology

sociológico, -a [sosjo'lɔʒiku, a] ADJ sociological

sociólogo, -a [so'sjɔlogu, a] M/F sociologist

sociopolítico, -a [sɔsjupo'litʃiku, a] ADJ socio-political

soco ['soku] M punch; **dar um ~ em** to punch

soçobrar [soso'brar] VT (*afundar*) to sink ▶ VI to sink; (*esperanças*) to founder; **~ em** (*fig: no vício etc*) to sink into

soco-inglês (*pl* **socos-ingleses**) M knuckleduster

socorrer [soko'her] VT (*ajudar*) to help, assist; (*salvar*) to rescue; **socorrer-se** VR: **~-se de** to resort to, have recourse to

socorro [so'kohu] M help, assistance; (*reboque*) breakdown (*BRIT*) *ou* tow (*US*) truck; **~!** help!; **ir em ~ de** to come to the aid of; **primeiros ~s** first aid *sg*; **equipe de ~** rescue team

soda ['sɔda] F soda (water); **pedir ~** (*col*) to back off, back down; **~ cáustica** caustic soda

sódio ['sɔdʒju] M sodium

sodomia [sodo'mia] F sodomy

sofá [so'fa] M sofa, settee

sofá-cama (*pl* **sofás-camas**) M sofa-bed

Sófia ['sɔfja] N Sofia

sofisma [so'fizma] M sophism; (*col*) trick

sofismar [sofiz'mar] VT (*fatos*) to twist; (*enganar*) to swindle, cheat

sofisticação [sofistʃika'sãw] F sophistication

sofisticado, -a [sofistʃi'kadu, a] ADJ sophisticated; (*afetado*) pretentious

sofisticar [sofistʃi'kar] VT to refine

sôfrego, -a ['sofregu, a] ADJ (*ávido*) keen; (*impaciente*) impatient; (*no comer*) greedy

sofreguidão [sofregi'dãw] F keenness; (*impaciência*) impatience; (*no comer*) greed

sofrer [so'frer] VT to suffer; (*acidente*) to have; (*aguentar*) to bear, put up with; (*experimentar*) to undergo, experience ▶ VI to suffer; **~ de reumatismo/do fígado** to suffer from rheumatism/with one's liver

sofrido, -a [so'fridu, a] ADJ long-suffering

sofrimento [sofri'mẽtu] M suffering

sofrível [so'frivew] (*pl* **-eis**) ADJ bearable; (*razoável*) reasonable

soft ['sɔftʃi] (*pl* **softs**) M (*Comput*) piece of software, software package

software [sof'twer] (*pl* **softwares**) M (*Comput*) software; **um ~** a piece of software

sogro, -a ['sogru, 'sɔgra] M/F father-in-law/mother-in-law

sóis [sɔjs] MPL *de* **sol**

soja ['sɔʒa] F soya (*BRIT*), soy (*US*); **leite de ~** soya *ou* soy milk

sol [sɔw] (*pl* **sóis**) M sun; (*luz*) sunshine, sunlight; **ao** *ou* **no ~** in the sun; **fazer ~** to be sunny; **pegar ~** to get the sun; **tomar (banho de) ~** to sunbathe

sola ['sɔla] F sole
solado, -a [so'ladu, a] ADJ (*bolo*) flat
solão [so'lãw] M very hot sun
solapar [sola'par] VT (*escavar*) to dig into; (*abalar*) to shake; (*fig: arruinar*) to destroy
solar [so'lar] ADJ solar ▶ M manor house ▶ VT (*sapato*) to sole ▶ VI (*bolo*) not to rise; (*cantor, músico*) to sing (*ou* play) solo; **energia/painel** ~ solar energy/panel
solavanco [sola'vãku] M jolt, bump; **andar aos ~s** to jog along
solda ['sɔwda] F solder
soldado [sow'dadu] M soldier; ~ **de chumbo** toy soldier; ~ **raso** private soldier
soldador, a [sowda'dor(a)] M/F welder
soldadura [sowda'dura] F (*ato*) welding; (*parte soldada*) weld
soldagem [sow'daʒē] F welding
soldar [sow'dar] VT to weld; (*fig*) to unite, amalgamate
soldo ['sowdu] M (*Mil*) pay
soleira [so'lejra] F doorstep
solene [so'lɛni] ADJ solemn
solenidade [soleni'dadʒi] F solemnity; (*cerimônia*) ceremony
solenizar [soleni'zar] VT to solemnize
solércia [so'lɛrsja] F ploy
soletração [soletra'sãw] F spelling
soletrar [sole'trar] VT to spell; (*ler devagar*) to read out slowly
solicitação [solisita'sãw] (*pl* -**ões**) F request; **solicitações** FPL (*apelo*) appeal *sg*
solicitar [solisi'tar] VT to ask for; (*requerer: emprego etc*) to apply for; (*amizade, atenção*) to seek; ~ **algo a alguém** to ask sb for sth
solícito, -a [so'lisitu, a] ADJ helpful
solicitude [solisi'tudʒi] F (*zelo*) care; (*boa vontade*) concern, thoughtfulness; (*empenho*) commitment
solidão [soli'dãw] F solitude, isolation; (*sensação*) loneliness; (*de lugar*) desolation; **sentir** ~ to feel lonely
solidariedade [solidarje'dadʒi] F solidarity
solidário, -a [soli'darju, a] ADJ (*pessoa*) supportive; (*a uma causa etc*) sympathetic; (*Jur: obrigação*) mutually binding; (*: devedores*) jointly liable; **ser** ~ **a** *ou* **com** (*pessoa*) to stand by; (*causa*) to be sympathetic to, sympathize with
solidarizar [solidari'zar] VT to bring together; **solidarizar-se** VR to join forces
solidez [soli'dez] F solidity, strength
solidificar [solidʒifi'kar] VT to solidify; (*fig*) to consolidate; **solidificar-se** VR to solidify; to be consolidated
sólido, -a ['sɔlidu, a] ADJ solid
solilóquio [soli'lɔkju] M soliloquy
solista [so'lista] M/F soloist
solitária [soli'tarja] F (*verme*) tapeworm; (*cela*) solitary confinement
solitário, -a [soli'tarju, a] ADJ lonely, solitary ▶ M hermit; (*joia*) solitaire
solo ['sɔlu] M ground, earth; (*Mús*) solo

soltar [sow'tar] VT (*tornar livre*) to set free; (*desatar*) to loosen, untie; (*afrouxar*) to slacken, loosen; (*largar*) to let go of; (*emitir*) to emit; (*grito, risada*) to let out; (*foguete, fogos de artifício*) to set *ou* let off; (*cabelo*) to let down; (*freio, animais*) to release; (*piada*) to tell; **soltar-se** VR (*desprender-se*) to come loose; (*desinibir-se*) to let o.s. go; ~ **palavrão** to swear
solteirão, -rona [sowtej'rãw, rona] (*pl* -**ões/-s**) ADJ unmarried ▶ M/F bachelor/spinster
solteiro, -a [sow'tejru, a] ADJ single ▶ M/F single man/woman
solteirões [sowtej'rõjs] MPL *de* **solteirão**
solto, -a ['sowtu, a] PP *de* **soltar** ▶ ADJ loose; (*livre*) free; (*sozinho*) alone; (*arroz*) fluffy; **à solta** freely
soltura [sow'tura] F looseness; (*liberdade*) release, discharge
solução [solu'sãw] (*pl* -**ões**) F solution
soluçar [solu'sar] VI (*chorar*) to sob; (*Med*) to hiccup
solucionar [solusjo'nar] VT to solve; (*decidir*) to resolve
soluço [so'lusu] M (*pranto*) sob; (*Med*) hiccup
soluções [solu'sõjs] FPL *de* **solução**
solúvel [so'luvew] (*pl* -**eis**) ADJ soluble
solvência [sow'vēsja] F solvency
solvente [sow'vētʃi] ADJ, M solvent
som [sõ] (*pl* -**ns**) M sound; (*Mús*) tone; (*BR: equipamento*) hi-fi, stereo; (*: música*) music; **ao** ~ **de** (*Mús*) to the accompaniment of; ~ **cd** compact disc player
soma ['sɔma] F sum
Somália [so'malja] F: **a** ~ Somalia
somar [so'mar] VT (*adicionar*) to add (up); (*chegar a*) to add up to, amount to ▶ VI to add up
somatório [soma'tɔrju] M sum; (*fig*) sum total
sombra ['sõbra] F shadow; (*proteção*) shade; (*indício*) trace, sign; **à** ~ **de** in the shade of; (*fig*) under the protection of; **sem** ~ **de dúvida** without a shadow of a doubt; **querer** ~ **e água fresca** (*fig*) to want the good things in life
sombreado, -a [sõ'brjadu, a] ADJ shady ▶ M shading
sombrear [sõ'brjar] VT to shade
sombreiro [sõ'brejru] M (*chapéu*) sombrero
sombrinha [sõ'briɲa] F parasol, sunshade; (*BR*) lady's umbrella
sombrio, -a [sõ'briu, a] ADJ (*escuro*) shady, dark; (*triste*) gloomy; (*rosto*) grim
some *etc* ['sɔmi] VB *ver* **sumir**
somenos [so'menus] ADJ inferior, poor; **de** ~ **importância** unimportant
somente [sɔ'mētʃi] ADV only; **tão** ~ only
somos ['somos] VB *ver* **ser**
sonambulismo [sonãbu'lizmu] M sleepwalking
sonâmbulo, -a [so'nãbulu, a] ADJ sleepwalking ▶ M/F sleepwalker
sonante [so'nãtʃi] ADJ: **moeda** ~ cash
sonata [so'nata] F sonata

sonda ['sõda] F (Náut) plummet, sounding lead; (Med) probe; (de petróleo) drill; (de alimentação) drip; ~ **espacial** space probe

sondagem [sõ'daʒẽ] (pl **-ns**) F (Náut) sounding; (de terreno, opinião) survey; (para petróleo) drilling; (para minerais) boring; (atmosférica) testing

sondar [sõ'dar] VT to probe; (opinião etc) to sound out

soneca [so'nɛka] F nap, snooze; **tirar uma ~** to have a nap

sonegação [sonega'sãw] F withholding; (furto) theft; ~ **de impostos** tax evasion

sonegar [sone'gar] VT (dinheiro, valores) to conceal, withhold; (furtar) to steal, pilfer; (impostos) to dodge, evade; (informações, dados) to withhold

soneto [so'netu] M sonnet

sonhador, a [soɲa'dor(a)] ADJ dreamy ▶ M/F dreamer

sonhar [so'ɲar] VT, VI to dream; ~ **com** to dream about; ~ **em fazer** to dream of doing; ~ **acordado** to daydream; **nem sonhando** ou ~! (col) no way!

sonho ['soɲu] M dream; (Culin) doughnut

sono ['sonu] M sleep; **estar caindo de ~** to be half-asleep; **estar com** ou **ter ~** to be sleepy; **estar sem ~** not to be sleepy; **ferrar no ~** to fall into a deep sleep; **pegar no ~** to fall asleep; **ter o ~ leve/pesado** to be a light/heavy sleeper

sonolência [sono'lẽsja] F drowsiness

sonolento, -a [sono'lẽtu, a] ADJ sleepy, drowsy

sonoridade [sonori'dadʒi] F sound quality

sonoro, -a [so'nɔru, a] ADJ resonant; (consoante) voiced

sonoterapia [sonotera'pia] F hypnotherapy

sons [sõs] MPL de **som**

sonso, -a ['sõsu, a] ADJ sly, artful

sopa ['sopa] F soup; (col) pushover, cinch; **dar ~** (abundar) to be plentiful; (estar disponível) to go spare; (descuidar-se) to be careless; **essa ~ vai acabar** (col) all good things come to an end; ~ **de legumes** vegetable soup

sopapear [sopa'pjar] VT to slap

sopapo [so'papu] M slap, cuff; **dar um ~ em** to slap

sopé [so'pɛ] M foot, bottom

sopeira [so'pejra] F (Culin) soup dish

sopitar [sopi'tar] VT (conter) to curb, repress

soporífero, -a [sopo'riferu, a] ADJ soporific ▶ M sleeping drug

soporífico, -a [sopo'rifiku, a] ADJ, M = **soporífero**

soprano [so'pranu] ADJ, M/F soprano

soprar [so'prar] VT to blow; (balão) to blow up; (vela) to blow out; (dizer em voz baixa) to whisper ▶ VI to blow

sopro ['sopru] M blow, puff; (de vento) gust; (no coração) murmur; **instrumento de ~** wind instrument

soquei etc [so'kej] VB ver **socar**

soquete [so'kɛtʃi] F ankle sock

sordidez [sordʒi'dez] F sordidness; (imundície) squalor

sórdido, -a ['sɔrdʒidu, a] ADJ sordid; (imundo) squalid; (obsceno) indecent, dirty

soro ['soru] M (Med) serum; (do leite) whey

sóror ['sɔror] F (Rel) sister

sorrateiro, -a [soha'tejru, a] ADJ sly, sneaky

sorridente [sohi'dẽtʃi] ADJ smiling

sorrir [so'hir] VI to smile

sorriso [so'hizu] M smile; ~ **amarelo** forced smile

sorte ['sɔrtʃi] F luck; (casualidade) chance; (destino) fate, destiny; (condição) lot; (espécie) sort, kind; **de ~** (pessoa etc) lucky; **desta ~** so, thus; **de ~ que** so that; **por ~** luckily; **dar ~** (trazer sorte) to bring good luck; (ter sorte) to be lucky; **estar com** ou **ter ~** to be lucky; **tentar a ~** to try one's luck; **ter a ~ de** to be lucky enough to; **tirar a ~** to draw lots; **tirar a ~ grande** (tb fig) to hit the jackpot; ~ **grande** big prize

sorteado, -a [sor'tʃjadu, a] ADJ (pessoa, bilhete) winning; (Mil) conscripted

sortear [sor'tʃjar] VT to draw lots for; (rifar) to raffle; (Mil) to draft

sorteio [sor'teju] M draw; (rifa) raffle; (Mil) draft

sortido, -a [sor'tʃidu, a] ADJ (abastecido) supplied, stocked; (variado) assorted; (loja) well-stocked

sortilégio [sortʃi'lɛʒu] M (bruxaria) sorcery; (encantamento) charm, fascination

sortimento [sortʃi'mẽtu] M assortment, stock

sortir [sor'tʃir] VT (abastecer) to supply, stock; (variar) to vary, mix

sortudo, -a [sor'tudu, a] (col) ADJ lucky ▶ M/F lucky beggar

sorumbático, -a [sorũ'batʃiku, a] ADJ gloomy, melancholy

sorvedouro [sorve'doru] M whirlpool; (abismo) chasm; **um ~ de dinheiro** (fig) a drain on resources

sorver [sor'ver] VT (beber) to sip; (inalar) to inhale; (tragar) to swallow up; (absorver) to soak up, absorb

sorvete [sor'vetʃi] (BR) M (feito com leite) ice cream; (feito com água) sorbet; ~ **de chocolate/creme** chocolate/dairy ice cream

sorveteiro [sorve'tejru] M ice-cream man

sorveteria [sorvete'ria] F ice-cream parlour (BRIT) ou parlor (US)

sorvo ['sorvu] M sip

SOS ABR SOS

sósia ['sɔzja] M/F double

soslaio [soz'laju] M: **de ~** (adv) sideways, obliquely; **olhar algo de ~** to squint at sth

sossegado, -a [sose'gadu, a] ADJ peaceful, calm

sossegar [sose'gar] VT to calm, quieten ▶ VI to quieten down

sossego [so'segu] M peace (and quiet)

sotaina [so'tajna] F cassock, soutane

sótão ['sɔtãw] (pl **-s**) M attic, loft

sotaque [so'taki] M accent
sotavento [sota'vētu] M (*Náut*) lee; **a ~ to leeward**
soterrar [sote'haʁ] VT to bury
soturno, -a [so'turnu, a] ADJ sad, gloomy
sou [so] VB *ver* **ser**
soube *etc* ['sobi] VB *ver* **saber**
soutien [su'tʃjã] M = **sutiã**
sova ['sɔva] F beating, thrashing; **dar uma ~ em alguém** to beat sb up; **levar uma ~ (de alguém)** to be beaten up (by sb)
sovaco [so'vaku] M armpit
sovaqueira [sova'kejra] F body odour (*BRIT*) *ou* odor (*US*)
sovar [so'var] VT (*surrar*) to beat, thrash; (*massa*) to knead; (*uva*) to tread; (*roupa*) to wear out; (*couro*) to soften up
soviético, -a [so'vjetʃiku, a] ADJ, M/F Soviet
sovina [so'vina] ADJ mean, stingy ▶ M/F miser, skinflint
sovinice [sovi'nisi] F meanness
sozinho, -a [sɔ'ziɲu, a] ADJ (all) alone, by oneself; (*por si mesmo*) by oneself
SP ABR = **São Paulo**
spam [is'pã] (*pl* **-s**) M (*Comput*) spam
SPI (*BR*) ABR M = **Serviço de Proteção ao Índio**
spot [is'pɔtʃi] (*pl* **-s**) M spotlight
spray [is'prej] (*pl* **-s**) M spray
spread [is'prɛdʒi] M (*Com*) spread
SPU (*BR*) ABR M = **Serviço de Patrimônio da União; Serviço Psiquiátrico de Urgência**
squash [is'kwɛʃ] M squash
Sr. ABR (= *senhor*) Mr
Sra. (*BR*), (*PT*) **Sr.a** ABR (= *senhora*) Mrs
Sri Lanka [ʃri'lãka] M: **o ~** Sri Lanka
Srta. (*BR*), (*PT*) **Sr.ta** ABR (= *senhorita*) Miss
SSP (*BR*) ABR F = **Secretaria de Segurança Pública**
staff [is'tafi] M staff
standard [is'tãdardʒi] ADJ INV standard
status [is'tatus] M status
STF (*BR*) ABR M = **Supremo Tribunal Federal**
STM (*BR*) ABR M = **Supremo Tribunal Militar**
sua ['sua] F *de* **seu**
suado, -a ['swadu, a] ADJ sweaty; (*fig: dinheiro etc*) hard-earned
suadouro [swa'doru] M sweat; (*lugar*) sauna
suar [swar] VT, VI to sweat; (*fig*): **~ por algo/para conseguir algo** to sweat blood for sth/to get sth; **~ em bicas** to sweat buckets; **~ frio** to come out in a cold sweat
suástica ['swastʃika] F swastika
suave ['swavi] ADJ gentle; (*música, voz*) soft; (*sabor, vinho*) smooth; (*cheiro*) delicate; (*dor*) mild; (*trabalho*) light; (*prestações*) easy
suavidade [suavi'dadʒi] F gentleness; (*de voz*) softness
suavizar [swavi'zar] VT to soften; (*dor, sofrimento*) to alleviate
subalimentado, -a [subalimẽ'tadu, a] ADJ undernourished
subalterno, -a [subaw'tɛrnu, a] ADJ inferior, subordinate ▶ M/F subordinate

subalugar [subalu'gar] VT to sublet
subarrendar [subahẽ'dar] (*PT*) VT = **subalugar**
subconsciência [subkõ'sjẽsja] F subconscious
subconsciente [subkõ'sjẽtʃi] ADJ, M subconscious
subdesenvolvido, -a [subdʒizẽvow'vidu, a] ADJ underdeveloped ▶ M/F (*pej*) degenerate
subdesenvolvimento [subdʒizẽvowvi'mẽtu] M underdevelopment
súbdito ['subditu] (*PT*) M = **súdito**
subdividir [subdʒivi'dʒir] VT to subdivide; **subdividir-se** VR to subdivide
subeditor, a [subedʒi'tor(a)] M/F subeditor
subemprego [subẽ'pregu] M low-paid unskilled job
subentender [subẽtẽ'der] VT to understand, assume
subentendido, -a [subẽtẽ'dʒidu, a] ADJ implied ▶ M implication
subestimar [subestʃi'mar] VT to underestimate
subfinanciado, -a [subfinã'sjadu, a] ADJ under-funded
subida [su'bida] F ascent, climb; (*ladeira*) slope; (*de preços*) rise
subido, -a [su'bidu, a] ADJ high
subir [su'bir] VI to go up; (*preço, de posto etc*) to rise ▶ VT (*levantar*) to raise; (*ladeira, escada, rio*) to climb, go up; **~ em** (*morro, árvore*) to climb, go up; (*cadeira, palanque*) to climb onto, get up onto; (*ônibus*) to get on
súbito, -a [su'subitu, a] ADJ sudden ▶ ADV (*tb*: **de súbito**) suddenly
subjacente [subʒa'sẽtʃi] ADJ (*tb fig*) underlying
subjetivo, -a [subʒe'tʃivu, a] ADJ subjective
subjugar [subʒu'gar] VT to subjugate, subdue; (*inimigo*) to overpower; (*moralmente*) to dominate
subjuntivo, -a [subʒũ'tʃivu, a] ADJ, M subjunctive
sublevação [subleva'sãw] (*pl* **-ões**) F (up)rising, revolt
sublevar [suble'var] VT to stir up (to revolt), incite (to revolt); **sublevar-se** VR to revolt, rebel
sublimar [subli'mar] VT (*pessoa*) to exalt; (*desejos*) to sublimate
sublime [su'blimi] ADJ sublime; (*nobre*) noble; (*música, espetáculo*) marvellous (*BRIT*), marvelous (*US*)
sublinhado [subli'ɲadu] M underlining
sublinhar [subli'ɲar] VT (*pôr linha debaixo de*) to underline; (*destacar*) to emphasize, stress
sublocar [sublo'kar] VT, VI to sublet
sublocatário, -a [subloka'tarju, a] M/F sub-tenant
submarino, -a [subma'rinu, a] ADJ underwater ▶ M submarine
submergir [submer'ʒir] VT to submerge; **submergir-se** VR to submerge
submerso, -a [sub'mersu, a] ADJ submerged; (*absorto*): **~ em** immersed *ou* engrossed in

S

submeter [subme'ter] VT (*povos, inimigo*) to subdue; (*plano*) to submit; (*sujeitar*): **~ a** to subject to; **submeter-se** VR: **~-se a** to submit to; (*operação*) to undergo

submirjo etc [sub'mihju] VB ver **submergir**

submissão [submi'sãw] F submission

submisso, -a [sub'misu, a] ADJ submissive, docile

submundo [sub'mũdu] M underworld

subnutrição [subnutri'sãw] F malnutrition

subnutrido, -a [subnu'tridu, a] ADJ undernourished

subordinar [subordʒi'nar] VT to subordinate

subornar [subor'nar] VT to bribe

suborno [su'bornu] M bribery

subproduto [subpro'dutu] M by-product

sub-reptício, -a [subhep'tʃisju, a] ADJ surreptitious

subscrever [subskre'ver] VT to sign; (*opinião, Com: ações*) to subscribe to; (*contribuir*) to put in ▶ VI: **~ a** to endorse; **subscrever-se** VR to sign one's name; **~ para** to contribute to; **subscrevemo-nos ...** (*Com: em cartas*) ≈ we remain ...

subscrição [subskri'sãw] (*pl* **-ões**) F subscription; (*contribuição*) contribution

subscritar [subskri'tar] VT to sign

subscrito, -a [sub'skritu, a] PP *de* **subscrever**

subsecretário, -a [subsekre'tarju, a] M/F under-secretary

subsequente [subse'kwẽtʃi] ADJ subsequent

subserviente [subser'vjẽtʃi] ADJ obsequious, servile

subsidiar [subsi'dʒjar] VT to subsidize

subsidiária [subsi'dʒjarja] F (*Com*) subsidiary (company)

subsidiário, -a [subsi'dʒjarju, a] ADJ subsidiary

subsídio [sub'sidʒu] M subsidy; (*ajuda*) aid; **subsídios** MPL (*informações*) data *sg*, information *sg*

subsistência [subsis'tẽsja] F (*sustento*) subsistence; (*meio de vida*) livelihood

subsistir [subsis'tʃir] VI (*existir*) to exist; (*viver*) to subsist, live; (*estar em vigor*) to be in force; (*perdurar*) to remain, survive

subsolo [sub'sɔlu] M subsoil; (*de prédio*) basement

substabelecer [subistabele'ser] VT to delegate

substância [sub'stãsja] F substance

substancial [substã'sjaw] (*pl* **-ais**) ADJ substantial

substantivo, -a [substã'tʃivu, a] ADJ substantive ▶ M noun

substituição [substʃitwi'sãw] (*pl* **-ões**) F substitution, replacement

substituir [substʃi'twir] VT to substitute, replace

substituto, -a [substi'tutu, a] ADJ, M/F substitute

subterfúgio [subter'fuʒu] M subterfuge

subterrâneo, -a [subite'hanju, a] ADJ subterranean, underground

subtil etc [sub'tiw] (PT) = **sutil** etc

subtítulo [subi'tʃitulu] M subtitle

subtrair [subtra'ir] VT (*furtar*) to steal; (*deduzir*) to subtract ▶ VI to subtract

subumano, -a [subu'manu, a] ADJ subhuman; (*desumano*) inhuman

suburbano, -a [subur'banu, a] ADJ suburban; (*pej*) uncultivated

subúrbio [su'burbju] M suburb

subvenção [subvẽ'sãw] (*pl* **-ões**) F subsidy, grant

subvencionar [subvẽsjo'nar] VT to subsidize

subvenções [subvẽ'sõjs] FPL *de* **subvenção**

subversivo, -a [subver'sivu, a] ADJ, M/F subversive

subverter [subver'ter] VT to subvert; (*povo*) to incite (to revolt); (*planos*) to upset

Sucam ['sukã] (BR) ABR F = **Superintendência da Campanha de Saúde Pública**

sucata [su'kata] F scrap metal

sucatar [suka'tar] VT to scrap

sucção [suk'sãw] F suction

sucedâneo, -a [suse'danju, a] ADJ substitute ▶ M (*substância*) substitute

suceder [suse'der] VI to happen ▶ VT to succeed; **suceder-se** VR to succeed one another; **~ a** (*num cargo*) to succeed; (*seguir*) to follow; **~ com** to happen to; **~-se a** to follow

sucedido [suse'dʒidu] M event, occurrence

sucessão [suse'sãw] (*pl* **-ões**) F succession

sucessivo, -a [suse'sivu, a] ADJ successive

sucesso [su'sɛsu] M success; (*música, filme*) hit; **com/sem ~** successfully/unsuccessfully; **de ~** successful; **fazer** *ou* **ter ~** to be successful

sucessor, a [suse'sor(a)] M/F successor

súcia ['susja] F gang, band

sucinto, -a [su'sĩtu, a] ADJ succinct

suco ['suku] (BR) M juice; **~ de laranja** orange juice

suculento, -a [suku'lẽtu, a] ADJ succulent, juicy; (*substancial*) substantial

sucumbir [sukũ'bir] VI (*render*) to succumb, yield; (*morrer*) to die, perish

sucursal [sukur'saw] (*pl* **-ais**) F (*Com*) branch

Sudam ['sudã] ABR F = **Superintendência de Desenvolvimento da Amazônia**

Sudão [su'dãw] M: **o ~** (the) Sudan

Sudeco [su'dɛku] (BR) ABR F = **Superintendência de Desenvolvimento do Centro-Oeste**

Sudene [su'dɛni] (BR) ABR F = **Superintendência de Desenvolvimento do Nordeste**

Sudepe [su'dɛpi] (BR) ABR F = **Superintendência de Desenvolvimento da Pesca**

sudeste [su'dɛstʃi] ADJ southeast ▶ M south-east

Sudhevea [sude'vɛa] (BR) ABR F = **Superintendência da Borracha**

súdito ['sudʒitu] M (*de rei* etc) subject

sudoeste [sud'wɛstʃi] ADJ southwest ▶ M south-west

Suécia ['swɛsja] F: **a ~** Sweden

sueco, -a ['swɛku, a] ADJ Swedish ▶ M/F Swede ▶ M (*Ling*) Swedish

suéter ['swɛter] (*BR*) M *ou* F sweater

Suez [swɛz] M: **o canal de ~** the Suez canal

suficiência [sufi'sjẽsja] F sufficiency

suficiente [sufi'sjẽtʃi] ADJ sufficient, enough; **o ~** enough

sufixo [su'fiksu] M suffix

suflê [su'fle] M soufflé

sufocante [sufo'kãtʃi] ADJ suffocating; (*calor*) sweltering, oppressive

sufocar [sufo'kar] VT to suffocate; (*revolta*) to put down ▶ VI to suffocate

sufoco [su'foku] M (*afã*) eagerness; (*ansiedade*) anxiety; (*dificuldade*) hassle

sufrágio [su'fraʒu] M (*direito de voto*) suffrage; (*voto*) vote; **~ universal** universal suffrage

sugar [su'gar] VT to suck; (*fig*) to extort

sugerir [suʒe'rir] VT to suggest

sugestão [suʒes'tãw] (*pl* **-ões**) F suggestion; **dar uma ~** to make a suggestion

sugestionar [suʒestʃjo'nar] VT to influence; **sugestionar-se** VR to be influenced

sugestionável [suʒestʃjo'navew] (*pl* **-eis**) ADJ impressionable

sugestivo, -a [suʒes'tʃivu, a] ADJ suggestive

sugestões [suʒes'tõjs] FPL *de* **sugestão**

sugiro *etc* [su'ʒiru] VB *ver* **sugerir**

suguei *etc* [su'gej] VB *ver* **sugar**

Suíça ['swisa] F: **a ~** Switzerland

suíças ['swisas] FPL sideburns; *ver tb* **suíço**

suicida [swi'sida] ADJ suicidal ▶ M/F suicidal person; (*morto*) suicide

suicidar-se [swisi'darsi] VR to commit suicide

suicídio [swi'sidʒju] M suicide

suíço, -a ['swisu, a] ADJ, M/F Swiss

sui generis [swi'ʒɛneris] ADJ INV in a class of one's own, unique

suíno ['swinu] M pig, hog ▶ ADJ *ver* **gado**

Suipa ['swipa] (*BR*) ABR F = **Sociedade União Internacional Protetora dos Animais**

suíte ['switʃi] F (*Mús, em hotel*) suite; (*em residência*) maid's quarters *pl*

sujar [su'ʒar] VT to dirty; (*fig: honra*) to sully ▶ VI to make a mess; **sujar-se** VR to get dirty; (*fig*) to sully o.s.

sujeição [suʒej'sãw] F subjection

sujeira [su'ʒejra] F dirt; (*estado*) dirtiness; (*col*) dirty trick; **fazer uma ~ com alguém** to do the dirty on sb

sujeitar [suʒej'tar] VT to subject; **sujeitar-se** VR to submit

sujeito, -a [su'ʒejtu, a] ADJ: **~ a** subject to ▶ M (*Ling*) subject ▶ M/F man/woman; **~ a espaço** (*Aer*) stand-by

sujidade [suʒi'dadʒi] (*PT*) F dirt; (*estado*) dirtiness

sujo, -a ['suʒu, a] ADJ dirty; (*fig: desonesto*) nasty, dishonest ▶ M dirt; **estar/ficar ~ com alguém** to be/get into sb's bad books

sul [suw] ADJ INV south, southern ▶ M: **o ~** the south

sul-africano, -a ADJ, M/F South African

sul-americano, -a ADJ, M/F South American

sulcar [suw'kar] VT to plough (*BRIT*), plow (*US*); (*rosto*) to line, furrow

sulco [suw'ku] M furrow

sulfato [suw'fatu] M sulphate (*BRIT*), sulfate (*US*)

sulfúrico, -a [suw'furiku, a] ADJ: **ácido ~** sulphuric (*BRIT*) *ou* sulfuric (*US*) acid

sulista [su'lista] ADJ Southern ▶ M/F Southerner

sultão, -tana [suw'tãw, 'tana] (*pl* **-ões/-s**) M/F sultan(a)

suma ['suma] F: **em ~** in short

sumamente [suma'mẽtʃi] ADV extremely

sumário, -a [su'marju, a] ADJ (*breve*) brief, concise; (*Jur*) summary; (*biquíni*) brief, skimpy ▶ M summary

sumiço [su'misu] M disappearance; **dar ~ a** *ou* **em** to do away with; (*comida*) to put away

sumidade [sumi'dadʒi] F (*pessoa*) genius

sumido, -a [su'midu, a] ADJ (*apagado*) faint, indistinct; (*voz*) low; (*desaparecido*) vanished; (*escondido*) hidden; **ela anda sumida** she's not around much

sumir [su'mir] VI to disappear, vanish

sumo, -a ['sumu, a] ADJ (*importância*) extreme; (*qualidade*) supreme ▶ M (*PT*) juice

sumptuoso, -a (*PT*) ADJ = **suntuoso**

Sunab [su'nabi] (*BR*) ABR F = **Superintendência Nacional de Abastecimento**

Sunamam [suna'mami] (*BR*) ABR F = **Superintendência Nacional da Marinha Mercante**

sundae ['sãdej] M sundae

sunga ['sũga] F swimming trunks *pl*

sungar [sũ'gar] VT to hitch up

suntuoso, -a [sũ'twozu, ɔza] ADJ sumptuous

suor [swɔr] M sweat; (*fig*): **com o meu ~** by the sweat of my brow

super... [super-] PREFIXO super-, over-; (*col*) really

superabundante [superabũ'dãtʃi] ADJ overabundant

superado, -a [supe'radu, a] ADJ (*ideias*) outmoded

superalimentar [superalimẽ'tar] VT to overfeed

superaquecer [superake'ser] VT to overheat

superar [supe'rar] VT (*rival*) to surpass; (*inimigo, dificuldade*) to overcome; (*expectativa*) to exceed

superávit [supe'ravitʃi] M (*Com*) surplus

superdose [super'dɔzi] F overdose

superdotado, -a [superdo'tadu, a] ADJ exceptionally gifted

superestimar [superestʃi'mar] VT to overestimate

superestrutura [superestru'tura] F superstructure

S

superficial [superfi'sjaw] (*pl* **-ais**) ADJ superficial; (*pessoa*) shallow

superfície [super'fisi] F (*parte externa*) surface; (*extensão*) area; (*fig: aparência*) appearance

superfino, -a [super'finu, a] ADJ (*de largura*) extra fine; (*de qualidade*) excellent quality

supérfluo, -a [su'pɛrflwu, a] ADJ superfluous, unnecessary

super-homem (*pl* **-ns**) M superman

superintendência [superĩtẽ'dẽsja] F (*órgão*) bureau

superintendente [superĩtẽ'dẽtʃi] M superintendent; (*de empresa*) chief executive

superintender [superĩtẽ'der] VT to superintend

superior [supe'rjor] ADJ superior; (*mais elevado*) higher; (*quantidade*) greater; (*mais acima*) upper ▶ M superior; (*Rel*) superior, abbot; **~ a** superior to; **um número ~ a 10** a number greater *ou* higher than 10; **curso/ensino ~** degree course/higher education; **lábio ~** upper lip

superiora [supe'rjora] ADJ, F: **(madre) ~** mother superior

superioridade [superjori'dadʒi] F superiority

superlativo, -a [superla'tʃivu, a] ADJ superlative ▶ M superlative

superlotação [superlota'sãw] F overcrowding

superlotado, -a [superlo'tadu, a] ADJ (*cheio*) crowded; (*excessivamente cheio*) overcrowded

supermercado [supermer'kadu] M supermarket

superpor [super'por] (*irreg: como* **pôr**) VT: **~ algo a algo** to put sth before sth

superpotência [superpo'tẽsja] F superpower

superpovoado, -a [superpo'vwadu, a] ADJ overpopulated

superprodução [superprodu'sãw] F overproduction

superproteger [superprote'ʒer] VT to overprotect

superpunha *etc* [super'puɲa] VB *ver* **superpor**

superpus *etc* [super'pus] VB *ver* **superpor**

superpuser *etc* [superpu'zer] VB *ver* **superpor**

supersecreto, -a [superse'krɛtu, a] ADJ top secret

supersensível [supersẽ'sivew] (*pl* **-eis**) ADJ oversensitive

supersimples [super'sĩplis] ADJ INV extremely simple

supersônico, -a [super'soniku, a] ADJ supersonic

superstição [superstʃi'sãw] (*pl* **-ões**) F superstition

supersticioso, -a [superstʃi'sjozu, ɔza] ADJ superstitious

superstições [superstʃi'sõjs] FPL *de* **superstição**

supervisão [supervi'zãw] F supervision

supervisionar [supervizjo'nar] VT to supervise

supervisor, a [supervi'zor(a)] M/F supervisor

supetão [supe'tãw] M: **de ~** all of a sudden

suplantar [suplã'tar] VT to supplant, supersede

suplementar [suplemẽ'tar] ADJ supplementary ▶ VT to supplement

suplemento [suple'mẽtu] M supplement

suplente [su'plẽtʃi] M/F substitute

súplica ['suplika] F supplication, plea

suplicante [supli'kãtʃi] M/F supplicant; (*Jur*) plaintiff

suplicar [supli'kar] VT, VI to plead, beg; **~ algo a** *ou* **de alguém** to beg sb for sth; **~ a alguém que faça** to beg sb to do

suplício [su'plisju] M torture; (*experiência penosa*) trial

supor [su'por] (*irreg: como* **pôr**) VT to suppose; (*julgar*) to think; **suponhamos que** let us suppose that; **vamos ~** let us suppose *ou* say; **suponho que sim** I suppose so; **era de ~ que** one could assume that

suportar [supor'tar] VT to hold up, support; (*tolerar*) to bear, tolerate

suportável [supor'tavew] (*pl* **-eis**) ADJ bearable, tolerable

suporte [su'pɔrtʃi] M support, stand; **~ atlético** athletic support, jockstrap

suposição [supozi'sãw] (*pl* **-ões**) F supposition, presumption

supositório [supozi'tɔrju] M suppository

supostamente [suposta'mẽtʃi] ADV supposedly

suposto, -a [su'postu, 'pɔsta] PP *de* **supor** ▶ ADJ supposed ▶ M assumption, supposition

supracitado, -a [suprasi'tadu, a] ADJ foregoing ▶ M foregoing

suprassumo [supra'sumu] M: **o ~ da beleza** *etc* the pinnacle of beauty *etc*

supremacia [suprema'sia] F supremacy

supremo, -a [su'premu, a] ADJ supreme ▶ M: **o S~** the Supreme Court; **S~ Tribunal Federal** (BR) Federal Supreme Court

supressão [supre'sãw] (*pl* **-ões**) F suppression; (*omissão*) omission; (*abolição*) abolition

suprimento [supri'mẽtu] M supply

suprimir [supri'mir] VT to suppress; (*frases de um texto*) to delete; (*abolir*) to abolish

suprir [su'prir] VT (*fazer as vezes de*) to take the place of; **~ alguém de** to provide *ou* supply sb with; **~ algo por algo** to substitute sth with sth; **~ uma quantia** to make up an amount; **~ a falta de alguém/algo** to make up for sb's absence/the lack of sth; **~ as necessidades/uma família** to provide for needs/a family

supunha *etc* [su'puɲa] VB *ver* **supor**

supurar [supu'rar] VI to go septic, suppurate

supus *etc* [su'pus] VB *ver* **supor**

supuser *etc* [supu'zer] VB *ver* **supor**

surdez [sur'dez] F deafness; **aparelho para a ~** hearing aid

surdina [sur'dʒina] F (*Mús*) mute; **em ~** stealthily, on the quiet

surdo, -a ['surdu, a] ADJ deaf; (*som*) muffled, dull; (*consoante*) voiceless ▶ M/F deaf person; **~ como uma porta** as deaf as a post

surdo-mudo, surda-muda ADJ deaf and dumb ▶ M/F deaf-mute

surfe ['surfi] M surfing

surfista [sur'fista] M/F surfer

surgir [sur'ʒir] VI to appear; (*problema, dificuldade*) to arise, crop up; (*oportunidade*) to arise, come up; **~ de** (*proceder*) to come from; **~ à mente** to come ou spring to mind

Suriname [suri'nami] M: **o ~** Surinam

surjo *etc* ['surʒu] VB *ver* **surgir**

surpreendente [surprjẽ'dẽtʃi] ADJ surprising

surpreender [surprjẽ'der] VT to surprise; (*pegar de surpresa*) to take unawares ▶ VI to be surprising; **surpreender-se** VR: **~-se (de)** to be surprised (at)

surpresa [sur'preza] F surprise; **de ~** by surprise

surpreso, -a [sur'prezu, a] PP *de* **surpreender** ▶ ADJ surprised

surra ['suha] F (*ger, Esporte*) thrashing; **dar uma ~ em** to thrash; **levar uma ~ (de)** to get thrashed (by)

surrado, -a [su'hadu, a] ADJ (*espancado*) beaten up; (*roupa*) worn out

surrar [su'har] VT to beat, thrash; (*roupa*) to wear out

surrealismo [suhea'lizmu] M surrealism

surrealista [suhea'lista] ADJ, M/F surrealist

surrupiar [suhu'pjar] VT to steal

sursis [sur'si] M INV (*Jur*) suspended sentence

surtar [sur'tar] VI to freak out

surte *etc* ['surtʃi] VB *ver* **sortir**

surtir [sur'tʃir] VT to produce, bring about ▶ VI: **~ bem** to turn out well; **~ efeito** to have an effect

surto ['surtu] M (*de doença*) outbreak; (*ataque*) outburst; (*de progresso*) surge

SUS [sus] (BR) ABR M (= *Sistema Único de Saúde*) national health service

suscetibilidade [susetʃibili'dadʒi] F susceptibility; (*sensibilidade*) sensitivity

suscetível [suse'tʃivew] (*pl* **-eis**) ADJ susceptible; **~ de** liable to

suscitar [susi'tar] VT to arouse; (*admiração*) to cause; (*dúvidas*) to raise; (*obstáculos*) to throw up

suspeição [suspej'sãw] (*pl* **-ões**) F suspicion

suspeita [sus'pejta] F suspicion

suspeitar [suspej'tar] VT to suspect ▶ VI: **~ de algo** to suspect sth; **~ de alguém** to be suspicious of sb

suspeito, -a [sus'pejtu, a] ADJ suspect, suspicious ▶ M/F suspect

suspeitoso, -a [suspej'tozu, ɔza] ADJ suspicious

suspender [suspẽ'der] VT (*levantar*) to lift; (*pendurar*) to hang; (*trabalho, pagamento etc*) to suspend, stop; (*funcionário, aluno*) to suspend; (*jornal*) to suspend publication of; (*encomenda*) to cancel; (*sessão*) to adjourn, defer; (*viagem*) to put off

suspensão [suspẽ'sãw] (*pl* **-ões**) F (*ger, Auto*) suspension; (*de trabalho, pagamento*) stoppage; (*de viagem, sessão*) deferment; (*de encomenda*) cancellation

suspense [sus'pẽsi] M suspense; **filme de ~** thriller

suspenso, -a [sus'pẽsu, a] PP *de* **suspender**

suspensões [suspẽ'sõjs] FPL *de* **suspensão**

suspensórios [suspẽ'sɔrjus] MPL braces (BRIT), suspenders (US)

suspicácia [suspi'kasja] F distrust, suspicion

suspicaz [suspi'kajz] ADJ (*suspeito*) suspect; (*desconfiado*) suspicious

suspirar [suspi'rar] VI to sigh; **~ por algo** to long for sth

suspiro [sus'piru] M sigh; (*doce*) meringue

sussurrar [susu'har] VT, VI to whisper

sussurro [su'suhu] M whisper

sustância [sus'tãsja] F (*força*) strength; (*de comida*) nourishment

sustar [sus'tar] VT, VI to stop

sustenho *etc* [sus'teɲu] VB *ver* **suster**

sustentabilidade [sustẽtabili'dadʒi] F sustainability

sustentáculo [sustẽ'takulu] M (*tb fig*) support

sustentar [sustẽ'tar] VT to sustain; (*prédio*) to hold up; (*padrão*) to maintain; (*financeiramente, acusação*) to support; **sustentar-se** VR (*alimentar-se*) to sustain o.s.; (*financeiramente*) to support o.s.; (*equilibrar-se*) to balance; **~ que** to maintain that

sustentável [sustẽ'tavew] (*pl* **-eis**) ADJ sustainable

sustento [sus'tẽtu] M sustenance; (*subsistência*) livelihood; (*amparo*) support

suster [sus'ter] (*irreg: como* **ter**) VT to support, hold up; (*reprimir*) to restrain, hold back

susto ['sustu] M fright, scare; **tomar** ou **levar um ~** to get a fright; **que ~!** what a fright!

sutiã [su'tʃjã] M bra(ssiere)

sutil [su'tʃiw] (*pl* **-is**) ADJ subtle; (*fino*) fine, delicate

sutileza [sutʃi'leza] F subtlety; (*finura*) fineness, delicacy

sutilizar [sutʃili'zar] VT to refine

sutis [su'tʃis] ADJ PL *de* **sutil**

sutura [su'tura] F (*Med*) suture

suturar [sutu'rar] VT, VI to suture

S

Tt

T, t [te] (*pl* **ts**) M T, t; **T de Tereza** T for Tommy
ta [ta] = **te** + **a**
tá [ta] (*col*) EXCL (= *está*) OK; **tá bom** OK, fine
tabacaria [tabaka'ria] F tobacconist's (shop)
tabaco [ta'baku] M tobacco
tabefe [ta'bɛfi] (*col*) M slap
tabela [ta'bɛla] F table, chart; (*lista*) list; **por ~** indirectly; **estar caindo pelas ~s** (*fig*) to be feeling low; **~ de preços** price table
tabelado, -a [tabe'ladu, a] ADJ (*produto*) price-controlled; (*preço*) controlled
tabelar [tabe'lar] VT (*produto*) to fix the price of; (*preço*) to fix; (*dados*) to tabulate
tabelião [tabe'ljãw] (*pl* **-ães**) M notary public
taberna [ta'bɛrna] F tavern, bar
tabique [ta'biki] M partition
tablado [ta'bladu] M platform; (*para espectadores*) grandstand
tablet ['tablitʃ] (*pl* **-s**) M (*Comput*) tablet
tablete [ta'blɛtʃi] M (*de chocolate*) bar; (*de manteiga*) pat
tabloide [ta'blɔjdʒi] M tabloid
tabu [ta'bu] ADJ, M taboo
tábua ['tabwa] F (*de madeira*) plank, board; (*Mat*) list, table; (*de mesa*) leaf; (*de passar roupa*) ironing board; **~ de salvação** (*fig*) last resort
tabuada [ta'bwada] F times table; (*livro*) tables book
tabulador [tabula'dor] M tab(ulator key)
tabular [tabu'lar] VT to tabulate
tabuleiro [tabu'lejru] M tray; (*Xadrez*) board
tabuleta [tabu'leta] F (*letreiro*) sign, signboard
taça ['tasa] F cup; **~ de champanhe** champagne glass *ou* flute
tacada [ta'kada] F shot; **de uma ~** in one go
tacanho, -a [ta'kaɲu, a] ADJ mean; (*de ideias curtas*) narrow-minded; (*baixo*) small
tacar [ta'kar] VT (*bola*) to hit; (*col: jogar*) to chuck; **~ a mão** *ou* **um soco em alguém** to punch sb
tacha ['taʃa] F (*prego*) tack; (*em calça jeans*) stud
tachar [ta'ʃar] VT: **~ algo de** to brand sth as
tachinha [ta'ʃiɲa] F drawing pin (BRIT), thumb tack (US)
tácito, -a ['tasitu, a] ADJ tacit, implied
taciturno, -a [tasi'turnu, a] ADJ taciturn, reserved

taco ['taku] M (*Bilhar*) cue; (*Golfe*) club; (*Hóquei*) stick; (*bucha*) plug, wad; (*de assoalho*) parquet block
táctil (PT) ADJ = **tátil**
tadinho, -a [ta'dʒiɲu, a] (*col*) EXCL poor thing!; **~ dele!** poor him!
tafetá [tafe'ta] M taffeta
tagarela [taga'rɛla] ADJ talkative ▶ M/F chatterbox
tagarelar [tagare'lar] VI to chatter
tagarelice [tagare'lisi] F chat, chatter, gossip
tailandês, -esa [tajlã'des, eza] ADJ, M/F Thai ▶ M (*Ling*) Thai
Tailândia [taj'lãdʒja] F: **a ~** Thailand
tailleur [taj'ɛr] M suit
tainha [ta'iɲa] F mullet
taipa ['tajpa] F: **parede de ~** mud wall
tais [tajs] ADJ PL *de* **tal**
Taiti [taj'tʃi] M: **o ~** Tahiti
tal [taw] (*pl* **tais**) ADJ such; **~ e coisa** this and that; **um ~ de Sr. X** a certain Mr. X; **que ~?** what do you think?; (PT) how are things?; **que ~ um cafezinho?** what about a coffee?; **que ~ nós irmos ao cinema?** what about (us) going to the cinema?; **~ pai, ~ filho** like father, like son; **~ como** such as; (*da maneira que*) just as; **~ qual** just like; **o ~ professor** that teacher; **a ~ ponto** to such an extent; **de ~ maneira** in such a way; **e ~** and so on; **o/a ~** (*col*) the greatest; **o Pedro de ~** Peter what's-his-name; **na rua ~** in such and such a street; **foi um ~ de gente ligar lá para casa** there were people ringing home non-stop
tala ['tala] F (*Med*) splint
talão [ta'lãw] (*pl* **-ões**) M (*de recibo*) stub; **~ de cheques** cheque book (BRIT), check book (US)
talco ['tawku] M talcum powder; **pó de ~** (PT) talcum powder
talento [ta'lẽtu] M talent; (*aptidão*) ability
talentoso, -a [talẽ'tozu, ɔza] ADJ talented
talha ['taʎa] F (*corte*) carving; (*vaso*) pitcher; (*Náut*) tackle
talhado, -a [ta'ʎadu, a] ADJ (*apropriado*) appropriate, right; (*leite*) curdled
talhar [ta'ʎar] VT to cut; (*esculpir*) to carve ▶ VI (*coalhar*) to curdle
talharim [taʎa'rĩ] M tagliatelle
talhe [ta'ʎi] M cut, shape; (*de rosto*) line

talher [ta'ʎer] M set of cutlery; **talheres** MPL cutlery *sg*

talho ['taʎu] M (*corte*) cutting, slicing; (PT: *açougue*) butcher's (shop)

talismã [taliz'mã] M talisman

talo ['talu] M stalk, stem; (*Arq*) shaft

talões [ta'lõjs] MPL *de* **talão**

talude [ta'ludʒi] M slope, incline

taludo, -a [ta'ludu, a] ADJ stocky

talvez [taw'vez] ADV perhaps, maybe; ~ **tenha razão** maybe you're right

tamanco [ta'mãku] M clog, wooden shoe

tamanduá [tamã'dwa] M anteater

tamanho, -a [ta'maɲu, a] ADJ such (a) great ▶ M size; **em ~ natural** life-size; **de que ~ é?** what size is it?; **uma casa que não tem ~** (*col*) a huge house; **do ~ de um bonde** (*col*) enormous

tamanho-família ADJ INV family-size; (*fig*) giant-size

tamanho-gigante ADJ INV giant-size

tâmara ['tamara] F date

tamarindo [tama'rĩdu] M tamarind

também [tã'bẽj] ADV also, too, as well; (*além disso*) besides; ~ **não** not ... either, nor; **eu ~ me too**; **eu ~ não** nor me, neither do (*ou* did *ou* am *ou* have *etc*) I

tambor [tã'bor] M drum

tamborilar [tãbori'lar] VI (*com os dedos*) to drum; (*chuva*) to pitter-pat

tamborim [tãbo'rĩ] (*pl* **-ns**) M tambourine

Tâmisa [ta'miza] M: **o ~** the Thames

tampa ['tãpa] F lid; (*de garrafa*) cap

tampão [tã'pãw] (*pl* **-ões**) M tampon; (*para curativos*) compress; (*rolha*) stopper, plug

tampar [tã'par] VT (*lata, garrafa*) to put the lid on; (*cobrir*) to cover

tampinha [tã'piɲa] F lid, top ▶ M/F (*col*) shorty

tampo ['tãpu] M lid; (*Mús*) sounding board

tampões [tã'põjs] MPL *de* **tampão**

tampouco [tã'poku] ADV nor, neither

tanga ['tãga] F loincloth; (*biquíni*) bikini

tangente [tã'ʒẽtʃi] F tangent; (*trecho retilíneo*) straight section; **pela ~** (*fig*) narrowly

tanger [tã'ʒer] VT (*Mús*) to play; (*sinos*) to ring; (*cordas*) to pluck ▶ VI (*sinos*) to ring; ~ **a** (*dizer respeito a*) to concern; **no que tange a** as regards, with respect to

tangerina [tãʒe'rina] F tangerine

tangerineira [tãʒeri'nejra] F tangerine tree

tangível [tã'ʒivew] (*pl* **-eis**) ADJ tangible

tango ['tãgu] M tango

tanjo *etc* ['tãʒu] VB *ver* **tanger**

tanque ['tãki] M (*reservatório, Mil*) tank; (*de lavar roupa*) sink

tanquinho [tã'kiɲu] (*col*) M (*musculatura*) six-pack

tantã [tã'tã] (*col*) ADJ crazy

tanto, -a ['tãtu, a] ADJ, PRON (*sg*) so much; (: + *interrogativa/negativa*) as much; (*pl*) so many; (: + *interrogativa/negativa*) as many ▶ ADV so much; ~ **melhor/pior** so much the better/more's the pity; ~ **... como ...** both ... and ...; ~ **mais ... quanto mais ...** the more ... the more ...; ~ **... quanto ...** as much ... as ...; ~**s ... quanto ...** as many ... as ...; ~ **tempo** so long; **quarenta e ~s anos** forty-odd years; **vinte e tantas pessoas** twenty-odd people; ~ **a Lúcia, quanto o Luís** both Lúcia and Luís; ~ **faz** it's all the same to me, I don't mind; **um ~ de vinho** some wine; **um outro ~ de vinho** a little more wine; **um ~ (quanto)** (*como adv*) rather, somewhat; **as tantas** the small hours; **lá para as tantas** late, in the small hours; **um médico e ~** quite a doctor; **não é para ~** it's not such a big deal; **não** *ou* **nem ~ assim** not as much as all that; ~ **(assim) que** so much so that

Tanzânia [tã'zanja] F: **a ~** Tanzania

tão [tãw] ADV so; ~ **rico quanto** as rich as; ~ **só** only

tapa ['tapa] M slap; **no ~** (*col*) by force

tapado, -a [ta'padu, a] ADJ (*col: bobo*) stupid

tapar [ta'par] VT to cover; (*garrafa*) to cork; (*caixa*) to put the lid on; (*ouvidos*) to block; (*orifício*) to block up; (*encobrir*) to block out

tapeação [tapja'sãw] F cheating

tapear [ta'pjar] VT, VI to cheat

tapeçaria [tapesa'ria] F tapestry; (*loja*) carpet shop

tapetar [tape'tar] VT to carpet

tapete [ta'petʃi] M carpet, rug

tapioca [ta'pjɔka] F tapioca

tapume [ta'pumi] M fencing, boarding

taquicardia [takikar'dʒia] F palpitations *pl*

taquigrafar [takigra'far] VT, VI to write in shorthand

taquigrafia [takigra'fia] F shorthand

taquígrafo, -a [ta'kigrafu, a] M/F shorthand typist (*BRIT*), stenographer (*US*)

tara ['tara] F fetish, mania; (*Com*) tare

tarado, -a [ta'radu, a] ADJ, M/F sex maniac; **ser ~ por** to be mad about

tarar [ta'rar] VI: ~ **(por)** to be smitten (with)

tardança [tar'dãsa] F delay, slowness

tardar [tar'dar] VI to delay, be slow; (*chegar tarde*) to be late ▶ VT to delay; **sem mais ~** without delay; ~ **a** *ou* **em fazer** to take a long time to do; **o mais ~** at the latest

tarde ['tardʒi] F afternoon ▶ ADV late; **ele chegou ~ (demais)** he got there too late; **mais cedo ou mais ~** sooner or later; **antes ~ do que nunca** better late than never; **boa ~!** good afternoon!; **hoje à ~** this afternoon; **à** *ou* **de ~** in the afternoon; **às três da ~** at three in the afternoon; ~ **da noite** late at night; **ontem/sexta à ~** yesterday/(on) Friday afternoon

tardinha [tar'dʒiɲa] F late afternoon; **de ~** late in the afternoon

tardio, -a [tar'dʒiu, a] ADJ late

tarefa [ta'refa] F task, job; (*faina*) chore

tarifa [ta'rifa] F tariff; (*para transportes*) fare; (*lista de preços*) price list; ~ **alfandegária**

customs duty; **~ de embarque** (*Aer*) airport tax

tarimba [ta'rĩba] F bunk; (*fig*) army life; (: *experiência*) experience; **ter ~** to be an old hand

tarimbado, -a [tarĩ'badu, a] ADJ experienced

tartamudear [tartamu'dʒjar] VI, VT to mumble; (*gaguejar*) to stammer, stutter

tartamudo, -a [tarta'mudu, a] M/F mumbler; (*gago*) stammerer, stutterer

tártaro ['tartaru] M tartar

tartaruga [tarta'ruga] F turtle; **pente de ~** tortoiseshell comb

tasca ['taska] (*PT*) F cheap eating place

tascar [tas'kar] VT (*tapa, beijo*) to plant

tasco ['tasku] (*col*) M bit, mouthful

Tasmânia [taz'manja] F: **a ~** Tasmania

tatear [ta'tʃjar] VT to touch, feel; (*fig*) to sound out ▸ VI to feel one's way

táteis ['tatejs] ADJ PL *de* **tátil**

tática ['tatʃika] F tactics *pl*

tático, -a ['tatʃiku, a] ADJ tactical

tátil ['tatʃiw] (*pl* **-eis**) ADJ tactile

tato ['tatu] M touch; (*fig: diplomacia*) tact

tatu [ta'tu] M armadillo

tatuador, a [tatwa'dor(a)] M/F tattooist

tatuagem [ta'twaʒẽ] (*pl* **-ns**) F tattoo

tatuar [ta'twar] VT to tattoo

tauromaquia [tawroma'kia] F bullfighting

tautologia [tawtolo'ʒia] F tautology

tautológico, -a [tawto'lɔʒiku, a] ADJ tautological

taxa ['taʃa] F (*imposto*) tax; (*preço*) fee; (*índice*) rate; **~ de câmbio** exchange rate; **~ de juros** interest rate; **~ bancária** bank rate; **~ de desconto** discount rate; **~ de matrícula** *ou* **inscrição** enrol(l)ment *ou* registration fee; **~ de exportação** export duty; **~ rodoviária** road tax; **~ fixa** (*Com*) flat rate; **~ de retorno** (*Com*) rate of return; **~ de crescimento** growth rate

taxação [taʃa'sãw] F taxation; (*de preços*) fixing

taxar [ta'ʃar] VT (*fixar o preço de*) to fix the price of; (*lançar impostos sobre*) to tax

taxativo, -a [taʃa'tʃivu, a] ADJ categorical, firm

táxi ['taksi] M taxi, cab; **~ aéreo** air taxi

taxímetro [tak'simetru] M taxi meter

taxista [tak'sista] M/F taxi driver, cab driver; (*col*) cabbie, cabby

tchã [tʃã] (*col*) M (*toque*) special touch; (*charme*) charm

tchau [tʃaw] EXCL bye!

tcheco, -a ['tʃɛku, a] ADJ, M/F Czech; **a República Tcheca** the Czech Republic

TCU (*BR*) ABR M = **Tribunal de Contas da União**

te [tʃi] PRON you; (*para você*) (to) you

té [tɛ] ABR *de* **até**

tear [tʃjar] M loom

teatral [tʃja'traw] (*pl* **-ais**) ADJ theatrical; (*grupo*) theatre *atr* (*BRIT*), theater *atr* (*US*); (*obra, arte*) dramatic

teatralizar [tʃjatrali'zar] VT to dramatize

teatro ['tʃjatru] M theatre (*BRIT*), theater (*US*); (*obras*) plays *pl*, dramatic works *pl*; (*gênero, curso*) drama; **peça de ~** play; **fazer ~** (*fig*) to be dramatic; **~ de arena** theatre-in-the-round; **~ de bolso** small theatre; **~ de marionetes** puppet theatre; **~ de variedades** vaudeville theatre; **~ rebolado** burlesque theatre

teatrólogo, -a [tʃja'trɔlogu, a] M/F playwright, dramatist

teatro-revista (*pl* **teatros-revista**) M review theatre (*BRIT*) *ou* theater (*US*)

tecelão, -lã [tese'lãw, 'lã] (*pl* **-ões/-s**) M/F weaver

tecer [te'ser] VT to weave; (*fig: intrigas*) to weave; (*disputas*) to cause ▸ VI to weave

tecido [te'sidu] M cloth, material; (*Anat*) tissue

tecla ['tɛkla] F key; **bater na mesma ~** (*fig*) to harp on the same subject; **~ de controle** (*Comput*) control key; **~ de função** (*Comput*) function key; **~ de saída** (*Comput*) escape key

tecladista [tekla'dʒista] M/F (*Mús*) keyboards player

teclado [tek'ladu] M keyboard; **~ complementar** (*Comput*) keypad

teclar [tek'lar] VT (*dados*) to key (in)

técnica ['teknika] F technique; *ver tb* **técnico**

tecnicalidade [teknikali'dadʒi] F technicality

técnico, -a ['tekniku, a] ADJ technical ▸ M/F technician; (*especialista*) expert

tecnicolor [tekniko'lor] ADJ Technicolor® ▸ M: **em ~** in technicolo(u)r

tecnocrata [tekno'krata] M/F technocrat

tecnologia [teknolo'ʒia] F technology; **~ de ponta** leading edge technology; **~ limpa** clean technology

tecnológico, -a [tekno'lɔʒiku, a] ADJ technological

teco ['tɛku] M hit; (*tiro*) shot; (*peteleco*) flick

teco-teco (*pl* **teco-tecos**) M small plane, light aircraft

tédio ['tɛdʒju] M tedium, boredom

tedioso, -a [te'dʒjozu, ɔza] ADJ tedious, boring

Teerã [tee'rã] N Teheran

teia ['teja] F web; (*fig: enredo*) intrigue, plot; (: *série*) series; **~ de aranha** cobweb; **~ de espionagem** spy ring, web of espionage

teima ['tejma] F insistence

teimar [tej'mar] VI to insist, keep on; **~ em** to insist on

teimosia [tejmo'zia] F stubbornness; **~ em fazer** insistence on doing

teimoso, -a [tej'mozu, ɔza] ADJ obstinate; (*criança*) wilful (*BRIT*), willful (*US*)

teixo ['tejʃu] M yew

Tejo ['teʒu] M: **o (rio) ~** the (river) Tagus

tel. ABR (= *telefone*) tel.

tela ['tɛla] F (*tecido*) fabric, material; (*de pintar*) canvas; (*Cinema, TV*) screen

telão [te'lãw] (*pl* **-ões**) M big screen

Telavive [tela'vivi] N Tel Aviv

tele... ['tele] PREFIXO tele...
telecomandar [telekomã'dar] VT to operate by remote control
telecomando [teleko'mãdu] M remote control
telecomunicações [telekomunika'sõjs] FPL telecommunications
teleconferência [telekõfe'rẽsja] F teleconference
teleférico [tele'fɛriku] M cable car
telefonar [telefo'nar] VI to (tele)phone, phone; **~ para alguém** to (tele)phone sb
telefone [tele'fɔni] M phone, telephone; (*número*) (tele)phone number; (*telefonema*) phone call; **estar/falar no ~** to be/talk on the phone; **~ celular** cellphone, mobile phone; **~ de carro** carphone; **~ fixo** landline; **~ público** public phone; **~ sem fio** cordless (tele)phone
telefonema [telefo'nɛma] M phone call; **dar um ~** to make a phone call
telefônico, -a [tele'foniku, a] ADJ telephone *atr*
telefonista [telefo'nista] M/F telephonist; (*na companhia telefônica*) operator
telegrafar [telegra'far] VT, VI to telegraph, wire
telegrafia [telegra'fia] F telegraphy
telegráfico, -a [tele'grafiku, a] ADJ telegraphic
telegrafista [telegra'fista] M/F telegraph operator
telégrafo [te'lɛgrafu] M telegraph
telegrama [tele'grama] M telegram, cable; **passar um ~** to send a telegram; **~ fonado** telemessage
teleguiado, -a [tele'gjadu, a] ADJ remote-controlled
teleguiar [tele'gjar] VT to operate by remote control
teleimpressor [teleĩpre'sor] M teleprinter
telejornal [teleʒor'naw] (*pl* **-ais**) M television news *sg*
telêmetro [te'lemetru] M rangefinder
telemóvel [tele'mɔvel] (*pl* **-eis**) (*PT*) M mobile (phone) (*BRIT*), cellphone (*US*); **~ com câmara** camera phone
telenovela [teleno'vɛla] F (TV) soap opera
teleobjetiva [teleobʒe'tʃiva] F telephoto lens
telepatia [telepa'tʃia] F telepathy
telepático, -a [tele'patʃiku, a] ADJ telepathic
teleprocessamento [teleprosesa'mẽtu] M teleprocessing
Telerj [te'lɛrʒi] ABR F *Rio telephone company*
telescópico, -a [tele'skɔpiku, a] ADJ telescopic
telescópio [tele'skɔpju] M telescope
Telesp [te'lɛspi] ABR F *São Paulo telephone company*
telespectador, a [telespekta'dor(a)] M/F viewer ▶ ADJ (*público*) viewing
teletexto [tele'testu] M teletext
teletipista [teletʃi'pista] M/F teletypist
teletipo [tele'tʃipu] M teletype
teletrabalho [teletra'baʎu] M teleworking

televendas [tele'vẽdas] FPL telesales
televisão [televi'zãw] F television; **~ por assinatura** pay television; **~ a cabo** cable television; **~ a cores** colo(u)r television; **~ digital** digital television; **~ via satélite** satellite television; **aparelho de ~** television set
televisar [televi'zar] VT = **televisionar**
televisionar [televizjo'nar] VT to televise
televisivo, -a [televi'zivu, a] ADJ television *atr*
televisor [televi'zor] M (*aparelho*) television (set), TV (set)
telex [te'lɛks] M telex; **enviar por ~** to telex
telexar [telɛks'ar] VT to telex
telha ['teʎa] F tile; (*col: cabeça*) head; **ter uma ~ de menos** to have a screw loose; **não estar bom da ~** not to be right in the head; **deu-lhe na ~ (de) viajar** he got it into his head to go travel(l)ing
telhado [te'ʎadu] M roof
telões [te'lõjs] MPL *de* **telão**
tema ['tɛma] M theme; (*assunto*) subject
temática [te'matʃika] F theme
temático, -a [te'matʃiku, a] ADJ thematic
temer [te'mer] VT to fear, be afraid of ▶ VI to be afraid; **~ por** to fear for; **~ que** to be afraid that; **~ fazer** to be afraid of doing
temerário, -a [teme'rarju, a] ADJ reckless; (*arriscado*) risky; (*juízo*) unfounded
temeridade [temeri'dadʒi] F recklessness
temeroso, -a [teme'rozu, ɔza] ADJ fearful, afraid; (*pavoroso*) dreadful
temido, -a [te'midu, a] ADJ fearsome, frightening
temível [te'mivew] (*pl* **-eis**) ADJ = **temido**
temor [te'mor] M fear
tempão [tẽ'pãw] (*col*) M: **um ~** a long time, ages *pl*
têmpera ['tẽpera] F (*de metais*) tempering; (*caráter*) temperament; (*pintura*) distemper, tempera
temperado, -a [tẽpe'radu, a] ADJ (*metal*) tempered; (*clima*) temperate; (*comida*) seasoned
temperamental [tẽperamẽ'taw] (*pl* **-ais**) ADJ temperamental
temperamento [tẽpera'mẽtu] M temperament, nature
temperança [tẽpe'rãsa] F temperance
temperar [tẽpe'rar] VT (*metal*) to temper, harden; (*comida*) to season
temperatura [tẽpera'tura] F temperature
tempero [tẽ'peru] M seasoning, flavouring (*BRIT*), flavoring (*US*)
tempestade [tẽpes'tadʒi] F storm, tempest; **fazer uma ~ em copo de água** to make a mountain out of a molehill
tempestuoso, -a [tẽpes'twozu, ɔza] ADJ stormy; (*fig*) tempestuous
templo ['tẽplu] M temple; (*igreja*) church
tempo ['tẽpu] M time; (*meteorológico*) weather; (*Ling*) tense; **o ~ todo** the whole time; **a ~** on time; **ao mesmo ~** at the same time; **a um ~**

at once; **a ~ e a hora** at the appropriate
time; **antes do ~** before time; **com ~** in
good time; **de ~ em ~** from time to time;
nesse ~ at that time; **nesse meio ~** in the
meantime; **em ~ de fazer** about to do; **em ~
recorde** in record time; **em seu devido ~**
in due course; **quanto ~?** how long?;
muito/pouco ~ a long/short time; **mais ~**
longer; **ganhar/perder ~** to gain/waste
time; **já era ~** it's about time; **não dá ~**
there isn't time; **dar ~ ao ~** to bide one's
time, wait and see; **matar o ~** to kill time;
nos bons ~s in the good old days; **o maior
de todos os ~s** the greatest of all time; **há
~s** for ages; (*atrás*) ages ago; **~ livre** spare
time; **com o passar do ~** in time;
primeiro/segundo ~ (*Esporte*) first/second
half; **~ integral** full time; **~ real** (*Comput*)
real time

tempo-quente M fight, set-to
têmpora ['tɛpora] F (*Anat*) temple
temporada [tɛpo'rada] F season; (*tempo*)
spell; **~ de ópera** opera season
temporal [tɛpo'raw] (*pl* **-ais**) ADJ worldly ▶ M
storm, gale
temporário, -a [tɛpo'rarju, a] ADJ temporary,
provisional
tenacidade [tenasi'dadʒi] F tenacity
tenaz [te'najz] ADJ tenacious ▶ F tongs *pl*
tenção [tɛ'sãw] (*pl* **-ões**) F intention; **fazer ~
de fazer** to decide to do
tencionar [tɛsjo'nar] VT to intend, plan
tenções [tɛ'sõjs] FPL *de* **tenção**
tenda ['tɛda] F (*barraca*) tent; **~ de oxigênio**
oxygen tent
tendão [tɛ'dãw] (*pl* **-ões**) M tendon; **~ de
Aquiles** Achilles tendon
tendência [tɛ'dɛsja] F tendency; (*da moda etc*)
trend; **a ~ de** *ou* **em** *ou* **a fazer** the tendency
to do
tendencioso, -a [tɛdɛ'sjozu, ɔza] ADJ
tendentious, bias(s)ed
tendente [tɛ'dɛtʃi] ADJ: **~ a** tending to
tender [tɛ'der] VI: **~ para** to tend towards;
~ a fazer to tend *ou* have a tendency to do;
(*encaminhar-se*) to head towards doing; (*visar*)
to aim to do
tendinha [tɛ'dʒiɲa] F (*botequim*) bar; (*birosca*)
(small) shop
tendões [tɛ'dõjs] MPL *de* **tendão**
tenebroso, -a [tene'brozu, ɔza] ADJ dark,
gloomy; (*fig*) horrible
tenente [te'nɛtʃi] M lieutenant
tenho *etc* ['tɛɲu] VB *ver* **ter**
tênis ['tenis] M INV (*jogo*) tennis; (*sapatos*)
training shoes *pl*; (*um sapato*) training shoe;
~ de mesa table tennis
tenista [te'nista] M/F tennis player
tenor [te'nor] ADJ, M (*Mús*) tenor
tenro, -a ['tɛɦu, a] ADJ tender; (*macio*) soft;
(*delicado*) delicate; (*novo*) young
tensão [tɛ'sãw] F tension; (*pressão*) pressure,
strain; (*rigidez*) tightness; (*Tec*) stress; (*Elet*:

voltagem) voltage; **~ nervosa** nervous
tension; **~ pré-menstrual** premenstrual
tension
tenso, -a ['tɛsu, a] ADJ tense; (*sob pressão*)
under stress, strained
tentação [tɛta'sãw] F temptation
tentáculo [tɛ'takulu] M tentacle
tentado, -a [tɛ'tadu, a] ADJ (*pessoa*) tempted;
(*crime*) attempted
tentador, a [tɛta'dor(a)] ADJ tempting;
(*sedutor*) inviting ▶ M/F tempter/temptress
tentar [tɛ'tar] VT to try; (*seduzir*) to tempt,
entice ▶ VI to try; **~ fazer** to try to do
tentativa [tɛta'tʃiva] F attempt; **~ de fazer**
attempt to do; **~ de homicídio/suicídio/
roubo** (*Jur*) attempted murder/suicide/
robbery; **por ~s** by trial and error
tentativo, -a [tɛta'tʃivu, a] ADJ tentative
tentear [tɛ'tʃjar] VT (*tentar*) to try
tênue ['tenwi] ADJ tenuous; (*fino*) thin;
(*delicado*) delicate; (*luz, voz*) faint;
(*pequeníssimo*) minute
tenuidade [tenwi'dadʒi] F tenuousness
teologia [teolo'ʒia] F theology
teológico, -a [teo'lɔʒiku, a] ADJ theological
teólogo, -a [te'ɔlogu, a] M/F theologian
teor [te'or] M (*conteúdo*) tenor; (*sentido*)
meaning, drift; (*fig: norma*) system; (: *modo*)
way; (*Quím*) grade; **~ alcoólico** alcoholic
content; **baixo ~ de nicotina** low tar
teorema [teo'rema] M theorem
teoria [teo'ria] F theory
teoricamente [teorika'mɛtʃi] ADV
theoretically, in theory
teórico, -a [te'ɔriku, a] ADJ theoretical ▶ M/F
theoretician
teorizar [teori'zar] VI to theorize
tépido, -a ['tɛpidu, a] ADJ tepid, lukewarm

(PALAVRA-CHAVE)

ter [ter] VT **1** (*possuir, ger*) to have; (*na mão*) to
hold; **você tem uma caneta?** have you got
a pen?; **ela vai ter neném** she is going to
have a baby
2 (*idade, medidas, estado*) to be; **ela tem 7 anos**
she's 7 (years old); **a mesa tem 1 metro de
comprimento** the table is 1 metre long; **ter
fome/sorte** to be hungry/lucky; **ter frio/
calor** to be cold/hot
3 (*conter*) to hold, contain; **a caixa tem um
quilo de chocolates** the box holds one kilo
of chocolates
4: **ter que** *ou* **de fazer** to have to do
5: **ter a ver com** to have to do with
6: **ir ter com** to (go and) meet
▶ VB IMPESS **1**: **tem** (*sg*) there is; (*pl*) there are;
tem 3 dias que não saio de casa I haven't
been out for 3 days
2: **não tem de quê** don't mention it

ter. ABR (= *terça-feira*) Tues
terapeuta [tera'pewta] M/F therapist
terapêutica [tera'pewtʃika] F therapeutics *sg*

terapêutico, -a [tera'pewtʃiku, a] ADJ therapeutic

terapia [tera'pia] F therapy; **~ ocupacional** occupational therapy; **~ de reposição hormonal** hormone replacement therapy

terça ['tersa] F (tb: **terça-feira**) Tuesday

terça-feira (pl **terças-feiras**) F Tuesday; **~ gorda** Shrove Tuesday; **~ que vem** next Tuesday; **~ passada/retrasada** last Tuesday/Tuesday before last; **hoje é ~ dia 12 de junho** today is Tuesday the 12th of June; **na ~** on Tuesday; **nas terças-feiras** on Tuesdays; **todas as terças-feiras** every Tuesday; **~ sim, ~ não** every other Tuesday; **na ~ de manhã** on Tuesday morning; **o jornal da ~** Tuesday's newspaper

terceiranista [tersejra'nista] M/F third-year

terceiro, -a [ter'sejru, a] NUM third ▶ M (Jur) third party; **terceiros** MPL (os outros) outsiders; **o T~ Mundo** the Third World; ver tb **quinto**

terciário, -a [ter'sjarju, a] ADJ tertiary

terço ['tersu] M third (part)

terçol [ter'sɔw] (pl **-óis**) M stye

tergal® [ter'gaw] M Terylene®

tergiversar [terʒiver'sar] VI to prevaricate, evade the issue

termal [ter'maw] (pl **-ais**) ADJ thermal

termas ['termas] FPL bathhouse sg

térmico, -a ['termiku, a] ADJ thermal; **garrafa térmica** (Thermos®) flask

terminação [termina'sãw] (pl **-ões**) F (Ling) ending

terminal [termi'naw] (pl **-ais**) ADJ terminal ▶ M (de rede, Elet, Comput) terminal ▶ F terminal; **~ (de vídeo)** monitor, visual display unit

terminante [termi'nãtʃi] ADJ final; (categórico) categorical, firm; (decisivo) decisive

terminantemente [terminãtʃi'mẽtʃi] ADV categorically, expressly

terminar [termi'nar] VT to finish ▶ VI (pessoa) to finish; (coisa) to end; **~ de fazer** to finish doing; (ter feito há pouco) to have just done; **~ por algo/fazer algo** to end with sth/end up doing sth

término ['terminu] M (fim) end, termination

terminologia [terminolo'ʒia] F terminology

termo ['termu] M term; (fim) end, termination; (limite) limit, boundary; (prazo) period; (PT: garrafa) (Thermos®) flask; **pôr ~ a** to put an end to; **meio ~** compromise; **em ~s (de)** in terms (of)

termodinâmica [termodʒi'namika] F thermodynamics sg

termômetro [ter'mometru] M thermometer

termonuclear [termonukle'ar] ADJ thermonuclear ▶ F nuclear power station

termostato [termos'tatu] M thermostat

terninho [ter'niɲu] M trouser suit (BRIT), pantsuit (US)

terno, -a ['ternu, a] ADJ gentle, tender ▶ M (BR: roupa) suit

ternura [ter'nura] F gentleness, tenderness

terra ['tɛha] F (mundo) earth, world; (Agr, propriedade) land; (pátria) country; (chão) ground; (Geo) soil, earth; (pó) dirt; (Elet) earth; **~ firme** dry land; **por ~** on the ground; **nunca viajei por essas ~s** I've never been to those parts; **ela não é da ~** she's not from these parts; **caminho de ~ batida** dirt road; **de ninguém** no man's land; **~ natal** native land; **~ prometida** promised land; **a T~ Santa** the Holy Land; **~ vegetal** black earth; **soltar em ~** to disembark

terraço [te'hasu] M terrace

terracota [teha'kɔta] F terracotta

Terra do Fogo F Tierra del Fuego

terramoto [teha'mɔtu] (PT) M = **terremoto**

Terra Nova F: **a ~** Newfoundland

terraplenagem [tehaple'naʒẽ] F earth-moving

terreiro [te'hejru] M yard, square; (de macumba) shrine

terremoto [tehe'mɔtu] M earthquake

terreno, -a [te'hɛnu, a] M ground, land; (porção de terra) plot of land; (Geo) terrain ▶ ADJ earthly; **ganhar/perder ~** (fig) to gain/lose ground; **sondar o ~** (fig) to test the ground

térreo, -a ['tɛhju, a] ADJ ground level atr; **andar ~** (BR) ground floor (BRIT), first floor (US)

terrestre [te'hɛstri] ADJ land atr; **globo ~** globe, Earth

terrificante [tehifi'kãtʃi] ADJ terrifying

terrífico, -a [te'hifiku, a] ADJ terrifying

terrina [te'hina] F tureen

territorial [tehito'rjaw] (pl **-ais**) ADJ territorial

território [tehi'tɔrju] M territory; (distrito) district, region

terrível [te'hivew] (pl **-eis**) ADJ terrible, dreadful

terror [te'hor] M terror, dread

terrorismo [teho'rizmu] M terrorism

terrorista [teho'rista] ADJ, M/F terrorist; **~ suicida** suicide bomber

tertúlia [ter'tulja] F gathering (of friends)

tesão [te'zãw] (pl **-ões**) (!) M randiness; (pessoa, coisa) turn-on; (ereção) hard-on; **sentir ~ por alguém** to fancy sb; **estar de ~** to feel randy; (ter ereção) to have a hard-on

tese ['tɛzi] F proposition, theory; (Educ) thesis; **em ~** in theory

teso, -a ['tezu, a] ADJ (cabo) taut; (rígido) stiff; **estar ~** (col) to be broke ou skint

tesões [te'zõjs] MPL de **tesão**

tesoura [te'zora] F scissors pl; (fig) backbiter; **uma ~** a pair of scissors

tesourar [tezo'rar] VT to cut; (col) to run down

tesouraria [tezora'ria] F treasury

tesoureiro, -a [tezo'rejru, a] M/F treasurer

tesouro [te'zoru] M treasure; (erário) treasury, exchequer; (livro) thesaurus; **um ~ (de informações)** a treasure trove of information

testa ['tɛsta] F brow, forehead; **à ~ de** at the head of; **~ de ferro** figurehead

testamentário, -a [testamẽ'tarju, a] ADJ of a will

testamento [testa'mẽtu] M will, testament; (Rel): **Velho/Novo T~** Old/New Testament; **~ em vida** living will

testar [tes'tar] VT to test; (deixar em testamento) to bequeath

teste ['tɛstʃi] M test; **~ de aptidão** aptitude test

testemunha [teste'muɲa] F witness; **~ ocular** eyewitness; **~ de acusação** prosecution witness; **~s de Jeová** Jehovah's witnesses

testemunhar [testemu'ɲar] VI to testify ▶ VT to give evidence about; (presenciar) to witness; (confirmar) to demonstrate

testemunho [teste'muɲu] M evidence, testimony; (prova) evidence; **dar ~** to give evidence

testículo [tes'tʃikulu] M testicle

testificar [testʃifi'kar] VT to testify to; (comprovar) to attest; (assegurar) to maintain

testudo, -a [tes'tudu, a] ADJ big-headed

teta ['tɛta] F teat, nipple

tétano ['tɛtanu] M tetanus

tête-à-tête [tɛtʃia'tɛtʃi] M tête-à-tête

teteia [te'tɛja] F (pessoa) gem

teto ['tɛtu] M ceiling; (telhado) roof; (habitação) home; (para preço etc) ceiling; **~ solar** sun roof

tetracampeão [tetrakã'pjãw] (pl -ões) M four-time champion

tétrico, -a ['tɛtriku, a] ADJ (lúgubre) gloomy, dismal; (horrível) horrible

teu, tua [tew, 'tua] ADJ your ▶ PRON yours

teve ['tevi] VB ver **ter**

tevê [te've] F telly (BRIT), TV

têxtil ['testʃiw] (pl -eis) M textile

texto ['testu] M text

textual [tes'twaw] (pl -ais) ADJ textual; **estas são suas palavras textuais** these are his exact words

textualmente [testwaw'mẽtʃi] ADV (exatamente) exactly, to the letter

textura [tes'tura] F texture

texugo [te'ʃugu] M badger

tez [tez] F complexion; (pele) skin

TFR (BR) ABR M = **Tribunal Federal de Recursos**

thriller ['triler] (pl -s) M thriller

ti [tʃi] PRON you

tia ['tʃia] F aunt

tia-avó (pl **tias-avós**) F great aunt

tiara ['tʃjara] F tiara

Tibete [tʃi'bɛtʃi] M: **o ~** Tibet

tíbia ['tʃibja] F shinbone

TIC [tʃik] ABR F (= Tecnologia de Informação e Comunicação) ICT

ticar [tʃi'kar] VT to tick

tico ['tʃiku] M: **um ~ (de)** a little bit (of)

tido, -a ['tʃidu, a] PP de **ter** ▶ ADJ: **~ como** ou **por** considered to be

tiete ['tʃjetʃi] (col) M/F fan

tifo ['tʃifu] M typhus

tifoide [tʃi'ɔidʒi] ADJ: **febre ~** typhoid (fever)

tigela [tʃi'ʒɛla] F bowl; **de meia ~** (fig, col) second-rate, small-time

tigre ['tʃigri] M tiger

tigresa [tʃi'greza] F tigress

tijolo [tʃi'ʒolu] M brick; **~ furado** air brick

til [tʃiw] (pl **tis**) M tilde

tilintar [tʃiliĩ'tar] VT, VI to jingle ▶ M jingling

timaço [tʃi'masu] (col) M great team

timão [tʃi'mãw] (pl **-ões**) M (Náut) helm, tiller; (time) great team

timbre ['tʃibri] M insignia, emblem; (selo) stamp; (Mús) tone, timbre; (de voz) tone; (Ling: de vogal) quality; (em papel de carta) heading

time ['tʃimi] (BR) M team; **de segundo ~** (fig) second-rate; **tirar o ~ de campo** (col) to get going

timer ['tajmer] (pl **-s**) M timer

timidez [tʃimi'dez] F shyness, timidity

tímido, -a ['tʃimidu, a] ADJ shy, timid

timões [tʃi'mõjs] MPL de **timão**

timoneiro [tʃimo'nejru] M helmsman, coxswain

tímpano ['tʃipanu] M eardrum; (Mús) kettledrum

tina ['tʃina] F vat

tingimento [tʃiʒi'mẽtu] M dyeing

tingir [tʃi'ʒir] VT to dye; (fig) to tinge

tinha etc ['tʃiɲa] VB ver **ter**

tinhoso, -a [tʃi'ɲozu, ɔza] ADJ single-minded

tinido [tʃi'nidu] M jingle

tinir [tʃi'nir] VI to jingle, tinkle; (ouvidos) to ring; (de frio, febre) to shiver; (de raiva, fome) to tremble; **estar tinindo** (carro, atleta) to be in tip-top condition

tinjo etc ['tʃiʒu] VB ver **tingir**

tino ['tʃinu] M (juízo) discernment, judgement; (intuição) intuition; (prudência) prudence; **perder o ~** to lose one's senses; **ter ~ para algo** to have a flair for sth

tinta ['tʃita] F (de pintar) paint; (de escrever) ink; (para tingir) dye; (fig: vestígio) shade, tinge; **carregar nas ~s** (fig) to exaggerate, embroider; **~ de impressão** printing ink

tinteiro [tʃi'tejru] M inkwell

tintim [tʃi'tʃi] EXCL cheers! ▶ M: **~ por ~** blow by blow

tinto, -a ['tʃitu, a] ADJ dyed; (fig) stained; **vinho ~** red wine

tintura [tʃi'tura] F dye; (ato) dyeing; (fig) tinge, hint

tinturaria [tʃitura'ria] F (lavanderia a seco) dry-cleaner's

tintureiro, -a [tʃitu'rejru, a] (col) M/F dry cleaner ▶ M police van

tio ['tʃiu] M uncle; **meus ~s** my uncle and aunt

tio-avô (pl **tios-avôs**) M great uncle

tipa ['tʃipa] (col pej) F dolly bird

tipão [tʃi'pãw] (pl **-ões**) (col) M good looker

típico, -a ['tʃipiku, a] ADJ typical
tipificar [tʃipifi'kar] VT to typify
tipo ['tʃipu] M type; (*de imprensa*) print; (*de impressora*) typeface; (*classe*) kind; (*col: sujeito*) guy, chap; (*pessoa*) person
tipões [tʃi'põjs] MPL *de* **tipão**
tipografia [tʃipogra'fia] F printing, typography; (*estabelecimento*) printer's
tipógrafo, -a [tʃi'pɔgrafu, a] M/F printer
tipoia [tʃi'pɔja] F (*tira de pano*) sling
tique ['tʃiki] M (*Med*) twitch, tic; (*sinal*) tick
tique-taque [-'taki] (*pl* **tique-taques**) M ticking
tíquete ['tʃiketʃi] M ticket
tiquinho [tʃi'kiɲu] M: **um ~ (de)** a little bit (of)
tira ['tʃira] F strip ▶ M (*BR col*) cop
tiracolo [tʃira'kɔlu] M: **a ~** slung from the shoulder; **com o marido a ~** with her husband in tow
tirada [tʃi'rada] F (*dito*) tirade
tiragem [tʃi'raʒē] F (*de livro*) print run; (*de jornal, revista*) circulation; (*de chaminé*) draught (*BRIT*), draft (*US*)
tira-gosto (*pl* **-s**) M snack, savoury (*BRIT*)
tira-manchas M INV stain remover
tirania [tʃira'nia] F tyranny
tirânico, -a [tʃi'raniku, a] ADJ tyrannical
tiranizar [tʃirani'zar] VT to tyrannize
tirano, -a [tʃi'ranu, a] ADJ tyrannical ▶ M/F tyrant
tirante [tʃi'rātʃi] M (*de arreio*) brace; (*Mecânica*) driving rod; (*viga*) tie beam ▶ PREP except; **uma cor ~ a vermelho** *etc* a reddish *etc* colo(u)r
tirar [tʃi'rar] VT to take away; (*de dentro*) to take out; (*de cima*) to take off; (*roupa, sapatos*) to take off; (*arrancar*) to pull out; (*férias*) to take, have; (*boas notas*) to get; (*salário*) to earn, get; (*curso*) to do, take; (*mancha*) to remove; (*foto, cópia*) to take; (*radiografia*) to have; (*mesa*) to clear; (*música, letra*) to take down; (*libertar*) to get out; **~ algo a alguém** to take sth from sb; **sem ~ nem pôr** exactly, precisely; **~ proveito/conclusões de** to benefit/draw conclusions from; **~ alguém para dançar** to ask sb to dance; **~ a tampa de** to take the lid off
tiririca [tʃiri'rika] (*col*) ADJ hopping mad
tiritante [tʃiri'tātʃi] ADJ shivering
tiritar [tʃiri'tar] VI to shiver
tiro ['tʃiru] M (*disparo*) shot; (*ato de disparar*) shooting, firing; **~ ao alvo** target practice; **trocar ~s** to fire at one another; **o ~ saiu pela culatra** (*fig*) the plan backfired; **dar um ~ no escuro** (*fig*) to take a shot in the dark; **ser ~ e queda** (*fig*) to be a dead cert
tirocínio [tʃiro'sinju] M apprenticeship, training
tiroteio [tʃiro'teju] M shooting, exchange of shots
tis [tʃis] MPL *de* **til**
tísica ['tʃizika] F consumption; *ver tb* **tísico**
tísico, -a ['tʃiziku, a] ADJ, M/F consumptive

tisnar [tʃiz'nar] VT (*enegrecer*) to blacken; (*tostar*) to brown
titânico, -a [tʃi'taniku, a] ADJ titanic
titânio [tʃi'tanju] M titanium
títere ['tʃiteri] M (*tb fig*) puppet
titia [tʃi'tʃia] F aunty; **ficar para ~** to be left on the shelf
titica [tʃi'tʃika] (*col*) F (piece of) junk ▶ M/F good-for-nothing
titio [tʃi'tʃiu] M uncle
tititi [tʃitʃi'tʃi] M (*tumulto*) hubbub; (*falatório*) gossip, talk
titubeante [tʃitu'bjātʃi] ADJ tottering; (*vacilante*) hesitant
titubear [tʃitu'bjar] VI (*cambalear*) to totter, stagger; (*vacilar*) to hesitate
titular [tʃitu'lar] ADJ titular ▶ M/F holder; (*Pol*) minister ▶ VT to title
título ['tʃitulu] M title; (*Com*) bond; (*universitário*) degree; **a ~ de** by way of, as; **a ~ de que você fez isso?** what was your reason for doing that?; **a ~ de curiosidade** out of curiosity; **~ ao portador** (*Com*) bearer bond; **~ de propriedade** title deed; **~ de câmbio** (*Com*) bill of exchange
tive *etc* ['tʃivi] VB *ver* **ter**
TJ (*BR*) ABR M = **Tribunal do Júri; Tribunal de Justiça**
tlim [tʃlī] M ring
TO ABR = **Tocantins**
to [tu] = **te + o**
toa ['toa] F towrope; **à ~** (*sem reflexão*) at random; (*sem motivo*) for no reason; (*inutilmente*) for nothing; (*sem ocupação*) with nothing to do; (*sem mais nem menos*) out of the blue; **andar à ~** to wander aimlessly; **não é à ~ que** it is not for nothing *ou* without reason that
toada [to'ada] F tune, melody
toalete [twa'letʃi] M (*banheiro*) toilet ▶ F washing and dressing; **fazer a ~** to have a wash
toalha [to'aʎa] F towel; **~ de mesa** tablecloth; **~ de banho** bath towel; **~ de rosto** hand towel
toar [to'ar] VI to sound, resound
tobogã [tobo'gã] M toboggan
toca ['tɔka] F burrow, hole; (*fig: refúgio*) bolt-hole; (: *casebre*) hovel
toca-discos (*BR*) M INV record-player
tocado, -a [to'kadu, a] ADJ (*col: alegre*) tipsy; (*expulso*) thrown out
tocador [toka'dor] M player; **~ MP3** MP3 player
toca-fitas M INV cassette player
tocaia [to'kaja] F ambush
tocante [to'kātʃi] ADJ moving, touching; **no ~ a** regarding, concerning
tocar [to'kar] VT to touch; (*Mús*) to play; (*campainha*) to ring; (*comover*) to touch; (*programa, campanha*) to conduct; (*ônibus, gado*) to drive; (*expulsar*) to drive out; (*chegar a*) to reach ▶ VI to touch; (*Mús*) to play; (*campainha,*

t

sino, telefone) to ring; (*em carro*) to drive;
tocar-se VR to touch (each other); (*ir-se*) to
head off; (*perceber*) to realize; ~ **a** (*dizer respeito
a*) to concern, affect; ~ **em** to touch; (*assunto*)
to touch upon; (*Náut*) to call at; ~ **para
alguém** (*telefonar*) to ring sb (up), call sb (up);
~ **(o bonde) para frente** (*fig*) to get going,
get a move on; **pelo que me toca** as far as
I am concerned

tocha ['tɔʃa] F torch

toco ['toku] M (*de cigarro*) stub; (*de árvore*)
stump

todavia [toda'via] ADV yet, still, however

(PALAVRA-CHAVE)

todo, -a ['todu, 'tɔda] ADJ **1** (*com artigo sg*) all;
toda a carne all the meat; **toda a noite** all
night, the whole night; **todo o Brasil** the
whole of Brazil; **a toda (velocidade)** at full
speed; **todo o mundo** (BR), **toda a gente**
(PT) everybody, everyone; **em toda (a) parte**
everywhere
2 (*com artigo pl*) all; (: *cada*) every; **todos os
livros** all the books; **todos os dias/todas as
noites** every day/night; **todos os que
querem sair** all those who want to leave;
todos nós all of us
▶ ADV: **ao todo** altogether; (*no total*) in all;
de todo completely
▶ PRON: **todos** everybody *sg*, everyone *sg*

todo-poderoso, -a ADJ almighty, all-powerful
▶ M: **o T~** the Almighty
tofe ['tɔfi] M toffee
toga ['tɔga] F toga; (*Educ, de magistrado*) gown
toicinho [toj'siɲu] M bacon fat
toldo ['towdu] M awning, sun blind
toleima [to'lɛjma] F folly, stupidity
tolerância [tole'rãsja] F tolerance
tolerante [tole'rãtʃi] ADJ tolerant
tolerar [tole'rar] VT to tolerate
tolerável [tole'ravew] (*pl* -**eis**) ADJ tolerable,
bearable; (*satisfatório*) passable; (*falta*)
excusable
tolher [to'ʎer] VT to impede, hinder; (*voz*) to
cut off; ~ **alguém de fazer** to stop sb doing
tolice [to'lisi] F stupidity, foolishness; (*ato,
dito*) stupid thing
tolo, -a ['tolu, a] ADJ foolish, silly, stupid
▶ M/F fool; **fazer alguém/fazer-se de** ~ to
make a fool of sb/o.s.
tom [tõ] (*pl* -**ns**) M tone; (*Mús: altura*) pitch;
(: *escala*) key; (*cor*) shade; **ser de bom** ~ to be
good manners; ~ **agudo/grave** high/low
note; ~ **maior/menor** (*Mús*) major/minor
key
tomada [to'mada] F capture; (*Elet*) socket;
(*Cinema*) shot; ~ **de posse** investiture; ~ **de
preços** tender
tomar [to'mar] VT to take; (*capturar*) to capture,
seize; (*decisão*) to make; (*bebida*) to drink;
tomar-se VR: ~-**se de** to be overcome with;
~ **alguém por algo** to take sb for sth; ~ **algo**

como to take sth as; **toma!** here you are!;
quer ~ **alguma coisa?** do you want something
to drink?; ~ **café** (*de manhã*) to have
breakfast; **toma lá, dá cá** give and take
tomara [to'mara] EXCL: ~! if only!; ~ **que
venha hoje** I hope he comes today
tomara que caia ADJ INV: (*vestido*) ~
strapless dress
tomate [to'matʃi] M tomato
tombadilho [tõba'dʒiʎu] M deck
tombar [tõ'bar] VI to fall down, tumble down
▶ VT to knock down, knock over; (*conservar:
edifício*) to list
tombo ['tõbu] M (*queda*) tumble, fall; (*registro*)
archives *pl*, records *pl*
tomilho [to'miʎu] M thyme
tomo ['tɔmu] M tome, volume
tona ['tɔna] F surface; **vir à** ~ to come to the
surface; (*fig*) to emerge; **trazer à** ~ to bring
up; (*recordações*) to bring back
tonalidade [tonali'dadʒi] F (*de cor*) shade;
(*Mús*) tonality; (: *tom*) key
tonel [to'nɛw] (*pl* -**éis**) M cask, barrel
tonelada [tone'lada] F ton; **uma** ~ **de** (*fig*)
tons of
tonelagem [tone'laʒẽ] F tonnage
toner ['toner] M toner
tônica ['tonika] F (*água*) tonic (water); (*Mús*)
tonic; (*Ling*) stressed syllable; (*fig*) keynote
tônico, -a ['toniku, a] ADJ tonic; (*sílaba*)
stressed ▶ M tonic; **acento** ~ stress
tonificante [tonifi'kãtʃi] ADJ invigorating
tonificar [tonifi'kar] VT to tone up
tons [tõs] MPL *de* **tom**
tontear [tõ'tʃjar] VT: ~ **alguém** to make sb
dizzy; (*suj: barulheira*) to get sb down, give sb
a headache; (: *alvoroço, notícia*) to stun sb ▶ VI
(*pessoa: com bebida*) to get dizzy; (: *com barulho*)
to get a headache; (: *com alvoroço*) to be dazed;
(*barulho*) to be wearing; (*alvoroço*) to be
upsetting; ~ **de sono** to be half-asleep
tonteira [tõ'tejra] F dizziness
tontice [tõ'tʃisi] F stupidity, nonsense
tonto, -a ['tõtu, a] ADJ (*tolo*) stupid, silly;
(*zonzo*) dizzy, lightheaded; (*atarantado*)
flustered; **às tontas** impulsively
tontura [tõ'tura] F dizziness, light-
headedness
topada [to'pada] F trip; **dar uma** ~ **em** to
stub one's toe on
topar [to'par] VT to agree to ▶ VI: ~ **com** to
come across; **topar-se** VR (*duas pessoas*) to run
into one another; ~ **em** (*tropeçar*) to stub
one's toe on; (*esbarrar*) to run into; (*tocar*) to
touch; **você topa ir ao cinema?** do you
fancy going to the cinema?; ~ **que alguém
faça** to agree that sb should do
topa-tudo ['tɔpa-] M INV person who is up for
anything
topázio [to'pazju] M topaz
tope ['tɔpi] M top
topete [to'petʃi] M quiff; **ter o** ~ **de fazer** (*fig*)
to have the cheek to do

tópico, -a ['tɔpiku, a] ADJ topical ▶ M topic
topless [tɔp'lɛs] ADJ INV topless ▶ M INV (*na praia*) topless bikini
topo ['topu] M top; (*extremidade*) end, extremity
topografia [topogra'fia] F topography
topográfico, -a [topo'grafiku, a] ADJ topographical
topônimo [to'ponimu] M place name, toponym
toque¹ ['tɔki] M touch; (*de instrumento musical*) playing; (*de campainha*) ring; (*fig: vestígio*) touch; (*de celular*) ringtone; (*retoque*) finishing touch; **os últimos ~s** the finishing touches; **dar um ~ em alguém** (*col: avisar*) to let sb know; (: *falar com*) to have a word with sb; **a ~ de caixa** in all haste
toque² *etc* VB *ver* **tocar**
Tóquio ['tɔkju] N Tokyo
tora ['tɔra] F (*pedaço*) piece; (*de madeira*) log; (*sesta*) nap; **tirar uma ~** to have a nap
toranja [to'rāʒa] F grapefruit
tórax ['tɔraks] M INV thorax
torção [tor'sāw] (*pl* **-ões**) M twist, twisting; (*Med*) sprain
torcedor, a [torse'dor(a)] M/F supporter, fan
torcedura [torse'dura] F twist; (*Med*) sprain
torcer [tor'ser] VT to twist; (*Med*) to sprain; (*desvirtuar*) to distort, misconstrue; (*roupa: espremer*) to wring; (: *na máquina*) to spin; (*vergar*) to bend ▶ VI: **~ por** (*time*) to support; (*amigo etc*) to keep one's fingers crossed for; **torcer-se** VR (*contorcer-se*) to squirm, writhe; **~ para** *ou* **por** to cheer for; **~ para que tudo dê certo** to keep one's fingers crossed that everything works out right
torcicolo [torsi'kɔlu] M stiff neck
torcida [tor'sida] F (*pavio*) wick; (*Esporte: ato de torcer*) cheering; (: *torcedores*) supporters *pl*; **dar uma ~ em algo** to twist sth; (*roupa*) to wring sth out
torções [tor'sōjs] MPL *de* **torção**
tormenta [tor'mēta] F storm; (*fig*) upset
tormento [tor'mētu] M torment, torture; (*angústia*) anguish
tormentoso, -a [tormē'tozu, ɔza] ADJ stormy, tempestuous
tornado [tor'nadu] M tornado
tornar [tor'nar] VI (*voltar*) to return, go back ▶ VT: **~ algo em algo** to turn *ou* make sth into sth; **tornar-se** VR to become; **~ a fazer algo** to do sth again
torneado, -a [tor'njadu, a] ADJ: **bem ~** (*pernas, pescoço*) shapely
tornear [tor'njar] VT to turn (on a lathe), shape
torneio [tor'neju] M tournament
torneira [tor'nejra] F tap (BRIT), faucet (US)
torniquete [torni'ketʃi] M (*Med*) tourniquet; (PT: *roleta*) turnstile
torno ['tornu] M lathe; (*Cerâmica*) wheel; **em ~ de** (*ao redor de*) around; (*sobre*) about; **em ~ de 5 milhões** around 5 million

tornozeleira [tornoze'lejra] F ankle support
tornozelo [torno'zelu] M ankle
toró [to'rɔ] M (*chuva*) downpour, shower; **caiu um ~** there was a sudden downpour
torpe ['torpi] ADJ vile
torpedear [torpe'dʒjar] VT to torpedo
torpedo [tor'pedu] M (*bomba*) torpedo; (*col: mensagem*) text (message)
torpeza [tor'peza] F vileness
torpor [tor'por] M torpor; (*Med*) numbness
torrada [to'hada] F toast; **uma ~** a piece of toast
torradeira [toha'dejra] F toaster
torrão [to'hāw] (*pl* **-ões**) M turf, sod; (*terra*) soil, land; (*de açúcar*) lump; **~ natal** native land
torrar [to'har] VT (*pão*) to toast; (*café*) to roast; (*plantação*) to parch; (*dinheiro*) to blow, squander; (*vender*) to sell off cheap; **~ (alguém)** (*col*) to get on sb's nerves; **~ a paciência** *ou* **o saco** (*col*) **de alguém** to try sb's patience
torre ['tohi] F tower; (*Xadrez*) castle, rook; (*Elet*) pylon; **~ de celular** mobile-phone mast (BRIT), cell tower (US); **~ de controle** (*Aer*) control tower; **~ de vigia** watchtower
torreão [to'hjāw] (*pl* **-ões**) M turret
torrefação [tohefa'sāw] (*pl* **-ões**) F coffee-roasting house
torrencial [tohē'sjaw] (*pl* **-ais**) ADJ torrential
torrente [to'hētʃi] F (*tb fig*) torrent
torreões [to'hjōjs] MPL *de* **torreão**
torresmo [to'hezmu] M crackling
tórrido, -a ['tɔhidu, a] ADJ torrid
torrinha [to'hiɲa] F (*Teatro*) gallery; **as ~s** the gods
torrões [to'hōjs] MPL *de* **torrão**
torrone [to'hɔni] M nougat
torso ['torsu] M torso, trunk
torta ['tɔrta] F pie, tart; **~ de maçã** apple pie
torto, -a ['tortu, 'tɔrta] ADJ twisted, crooked; **a ~ e a direito** indiscriminately; **cometer erros a ~ e a direito** to make mistakes left, right and centre
tortuoso, -a [tor'twozu, ɔza] ADJ winding
tortura [tor'tura] F torture; (*fig*) anguish, agony
torturador, a [tortura'dor(a)] M/F torturer
torturante [tortu'rātʃi] ADJ (*sonhos*) haunting; (*dor*) excruciating
torturar [tortu'rar] VT to torture; (*fig: afligir*) to torment
torvelinho [torve'liɲu] M (*de vento*) whirlwind; (*de água*) whirlpool; (*fig: de pensamentos*) swirl
tos [tus] = **te + os**
tosão [to'zāw] (*pl* **-ões**) M fleece
tosar [to'zar] VT (*ovelha*) to shear; (*cabelo*) to crop
tosco, -a ['tosku, a] ADJ rough, unpolished; (*grosseiro*) coarse, crude
tosões [to'zōjs] MPL *de* **tosão**
tosquiar [tos'kjar] VT (*ovelha*) to shear, clip

t

tosse ['tɔsi] F cough; **~ de cachorro**
whooping cough; **~ seca** dry ou tickly cough
tossir [to'sir] vi to cough ▶ vт to cough up
tosta ['tɔsta] (PT) F toast; **~ mista** toasted
cheese and ham sandwich
tostado, -a [tos'tadu, a] ADJ toasted; (pessoa)
tanned; (carne) browned
tostão [tos'tãw] M (dinheiro) cash; **estar sem
um ~** to be completely penniless
tostar [tos'tar] vт to toast; (pele, pessoa) to tan;
(carne) to brown; **tostar-se** vʀ to get tanned
total [to'taw] (pl **-ais**) ADJ, M total
totalidade [totali'dadʒi] F totality, entirety;
em sua ~ in its entirety; **a ~ da população/
dos políticos** the entire population/all
politicians
totalitário, -a [totali'tarju, a] ADJ totalitarian
totalitarismo [totalita'rizmu] M
totalitarianism
totalizar [totali'zar] vт to total up
totalmente [totaw'mẽtʃi] ADV totally,
completely
touca ['toka] F bonnet; (de freira) veil; **~ de
banho** bathing cap
toucador [toka'dor] M (penteadeira) dressing
table
toucinho [to'siɲu] M = **toicinho**
toupeira [to'pejra] F mole; (fig) numbskull,
idiot
tourada [to'rada] F bullfight
tourear [to'rjar] vi to fight bulls
toureiro [to'rejru] M bullfighter
touro ['toru] M bull; **T~** (Astrologia) Taurus;
pegar o ~ à unha to take the bull by the
horns
toxemia [tokse'mia] F blood poisoning
tóxico, -a ['tɔksiku, a] ADJ poisonous, toxic
▶ M (veneno) poison; (droga) drug
toxicômano, -a [toksi'komanu, a] M/F drug
addict
toxina [tok'sina] F toxin
TPM ABR F (= tensão pré-menstrual) PMT
trabalhadeira [trabaʎa'dejra] F: **ela é ~** she's
a hard worker
trabalhador, a [trabaʎa'dor(a)] ADJ (laborioso)
hard-working, industrious; (Pol: classe)
working ▶ M/F worker; **~ braçal** manual
worker
trabalhão [traba'ʎãw] (pl **-ões**) M big job
trabalhar [traba'ʎar] vi to work; (Teatro) to act
▶ vт (terra) to till, work; (madeira, metal) to
work; (texto) to work on; **~ com** (comerciar) to
deal in; **~ de** ou **como** to work as
trabalheira [traba'ʎejra] F big job
trabalhista [traba'ʎista] ADJ labour atr (BRIT),
labor atr (US) ▶ M/F Labour Party member
(BRIT); **Partido T~** (Pol) Labour Party (BRIT)
trabalho [tra'baʎu] M work; (emprego, tarefa)
job; (Econ) labour (BRIT), labor (US); (Educ:
tarefa) assignment; **~ braçal** manual work;
~s forçados hard labo(u)r, forced labo(u)r;
estar sem ~ to be out of work; **dar ~** to need
work; **dar ~ a alguém** to cause sb trouble;

dar-se o ~ de fazer to take the trouble to do;
um ~ ingrato a thankless task;
~ doméstico housework; **~ de parto**
labo(u)r
trabalhões [traba'ʎõjs] MPL de **trabalhão**
trabalhoso, -a [traba'ʎozu, ɔza] ADJ laborious,
arduous
traça ['trasa] F moth
traçado [tra'sadu] M sketch, plan
tração [tra'sãw] F traction
traçar [tra'sar] vт to draw; (determinar) to set
out, outline; (limites, fronteiras) to mark out;
(planos) to draw up; (escrever) to compose; (col:
comer, beber) to guzzle down
traço ['trasu] M (linha) line, dash; (de lápis)
stroke; (vestígio) trace, vestige; (aspecto)
feature, trait; **traços** MPL (do rosto) features;
~ (de união) hyphen; (entre frases) dash
tradição [tradʒi'sãw] (pl **-ões**) F tradition
tradicional [tradʒisjo'naw] (pl **-ais**) ADJ
traditional
tradições [tradʒi'sõjs] FPL de **tradição**
tradução [tradu'sãw] (pl **-ões**) F translation
tradutor, a [tradu'tor(a)] M/F translator;
~ juramentado legally recognized
translator
traduzir [tradu'zir] vт to translate;
traduzir-se vʀ to come across; **~ do inglês
para o português** to translate from English
into Portuguese
trafegar [trafe'gar] vi to move, go
trafegável [trafe'gavew] (pl **-eis**) ADJ (rua)
open to traffic
tráfego ['trafegu] M (trânsito) traffic; **~ aéreo/
marítimo** air/sea traffic
traficante [trafi'kãtʃi] M/F trafficker, dealer;
~ de drogas drug trafficker, pusher (col)
traficar [trafi'kar] vi: **~ (com)** to deal (in),
traffic (in)
tráfico ['trafiku] M traffic; **~ de drogas** drug
trafficking
tragada [tra'gada] F (em cigarro) drag, puff
tragar [tra'gar] vт to swallow; (fumaça) to
inhale; (suportar) to tolerate ▶ vi to inhale
tragédia [tra'ʒɛdʒja] F tragedy; **fazer ~ de
algo** to make a drama out of sth
trágico, -a ['traʒiku, a] ADJ tragic; (dado a fazer
tragédia) dramatic
tragicomédia [traʒiko'mɛdʒja] F
tragicomedy
tragicômico, -a [traʒi'komiku, a] ADJ
tragicomic
trago¹ ['tragu] M mouthful; (em cigarro) drag,
puff; **tomar um ~** to have a mouthful; to
have a drag; **de um ~** in one gulp
trago² etc vв ver **trazer**
traguei etc [tra'gej] vв ver **tragar**
traição [traj'sãw] (pl **-ões**) F treason,
treachery; (deslealdade) treachery;
(infidelidade) infidelity; **alta ~** high treason
traiçoeiro, -a [traj'swejru, a] ADJ treacherous;
(infiel) disloyal
traições [traj'sõjs] FPL de **traição**

traidor, a [traj'dor(a)] M/F traitor
trailer ['trejler] (pl **-s**) M trailer; (tipo casa) caravan (BRIT), trailer (US)
traineira [traj'nejra] F trawler
training ['trejnĩŋ] (pl **-s**) M track suit
trair [tra'ir] VT to betray; (mulher, marido) to be unfaithful to; (esperanças) not to live up to; **trair-se** VR to give o.s. away
trajar [tra'ʒar] VT to wear; **trajar-se** VR: **~-se de preto** to be dressed in black
traje ['traʒi] M dress, clothes pl; **~ de banho** swimsuit; **~ de noite** evening gown; **~ a rigor** evening dress; **~ de passeio** smart dress; **em ~s de Adão** in one's birthday suit; **~s menores** smalls, underwear sg
trajeto [tra'ʒɛtu] M course, path
trajetória [traʒe'tɔrja] F trajectory, path; (fig) course
tralha ['traʎa] F fishing net; (col) junk
trama ['trama] F (tecido) weft (BRIT), woof (US); (enredo, conspiração) plot
tramar [tra'mar] VT (tecer) to weave; (maquinar) to plot ▶ VI: **~ contra** to conspire against
trambicar [trãbi'kar] (col) VT to con
trambique [trã'biki] (col) M con
trambiqueiro, -a [trãbi'kejru, a] M/F con merchant ▶ ADJ slippery
trambolhão [trãbo'ʎãw] (pl **-ões**) M tumble; **andar aos trambolhões** to stumble along
trambolho [trã'boʎu] M encumbrance
trambolhões [trãbo'ʎõjs] MPL de **trambolhão**
tramitar [trami'tar] VI to go through the procedure
trâmites ['tramitʃis] MPL procedure sg, channels
tramoia [tra'mɔja] F (fraude) swindle, trick; (trama) plot, scheme
trampolim [trãpo'lĩ] (pl **-ns**) M trampoline; (de piscina) diving board; (fig) springboard
trampolinagem [trãpoli'naʒẽ] (pl **-ns**) F trick, swindle
trampolineiro, -a [trãpoli'nejru, a] M/F trickster, swindler
trampolinice [trãpoli'nisi] F trick, swindle
trampolins [trãpo'lĩs] MPL de **trampolim**
tranca ['trãka] F (de porta) bolt; (de carro) lock
trança ['trãsa] F (cabelo) plait; (galão) braid
trançado, -a [trã'sadu, a] ADJ (cesto) woven
trancafiar [trãka'fjar] VT to lock up
trancão [trã'kãw] (pl **-ões**) M bump
trancar [trã'kar] VT to lock; (matrícula) to suspend; (Futebol) to shove; **trancar-se** VR (mostrar-se fechado) to clam up; **~-se no quarto** to lock o.s. (away) in one's room
trançar [trã'sar] VT to weave; (cabelo) to plait, braid ▶ VI (col) to wander around
tranco ['trãku] M (solavanco) jolt; (esbarrão) bump; (de cavalo) walk; (col: admoestação) put-down; **aos ~s** jolting; **aos ~s e barrancos** with great difficulty; (aos saltos) jolting

trancões [trã'kõjs] MPL de **trancão**
tranquilamente [trãkwila'mẽtʃi] ADV calmly; (facilmente) easily; (seguramente) for sure
tranquilidade [trãkwili'dadʒi] F tranquillity; (paz) peace
tranquilizador, a [trãkwiliza'dor(a)] ADJ reassuring; (música) soothing
tranquilizante [trãkwili'zãtʃi] ADJ = **tranquilizador** ▶ M (Med) tranquillizer
tranquilizar [trãkwili'zar] VT to calm, quieten; (despreocupar): **~ alguém** to reassure sb, put sb's mind at rest; **tranquilizar-se** VR to calm down; (pessoa preocupada) to be reassured
tranquilo, -a [trã'kwilu, a] ADJ peaceful; (mar, pessoa) calm; (criança) quiet; (consciência) clear; (seguro) sure, certain ▶ ADV with no problems
transa ['trãza] (BR col) F (sexo) lovemaking; (transada) sexual encounter
transação [trãza'sãw] (pl **-ões**) F (Com) transaction
transada [trã'zada] (BR col) F sexual encounter; **dar uma ~** (col) to have sex
transado, -a [trã'zadu, a] (BR col) ADJ (casa, bairro, roupa) stylish
Transamazônica [trãzama'zonika] F: **a ~** the trans-Amazonian highway
transamazônico, -a [trãzama'zoniku, a] ADJ trans-Amazonian
transar [trã'zar] (BR col) VI (ter relação sexual) to have sex
transatlântico, -a [trãzat'lãtʃiku, a] ADJ transatlantic ▶ M (transatlantic) liner
transbordar [trãzbor'dar] VI to overflow; **~ de alegria** to burst with happiness
transbordo [trãz'bordu] M (de viajantes) change, transfer
transcendental [trãsẽdẽ'taw] (pl **-ais**) ADJ transcendental
transcender [trãsẽ'der] VT, VI: **~ (a)** to transcend
transcorrer [trãsko'her] VI to elapse, go by; (evento) to pass off
transcrever [trãskre'ver] VT to transcribe
transcrição [trãskri'sãw] (pl **-ões**) F transcription
transcrito, -a [trãs'kritu, a] PP de **transcrever** ▶ M transcript
transe ['trãzi] M ordeal; (lance) plight; (hipnótico) trance; **a todo ~** at all costs
transeunte [trã'zjũtʃi] M/F passer-by
transferência [trãsfe'rẽsja] F transfer; (Jur) conveyancing
transferir [trãsfe'rir] VT to transfer; (adiar) to postpone
transferível [trãsfe'rivew] (pl **-eis**) ADJ transferable
transfigurar [trãsfigu'rar] VT to transfigure, transform; **transfigurar-se** VR to transform
transfiro etc [trãs'firu] VB ver **transferir**
transformação [trãsforma'sãw] (pl **-ões**) F transformation

t

transformador [trãsforma'dor] M (*Elet*) transformer

transformar [trãsfor'mar] VT to transform, turn; **transformar-se** VR to turn; ~ **algo em algo** to turn *ou* transform sth into sth

trânsfuga ['trãsfuga] M (*desertor*) deserter; (*político*) turncoat; (*da Rússia etc*) defector

transfusão [trãsfu'zãw] (*pl* **-ões**) F transfusion; ~ **de sangue** blood transfusion

transgênico, -a [trãz'ʒeniku, a] ADJ (*planta, alimento*) genetically modified, GM

transgredir [trãzgre'dʒir] VT to infringe

transgressão [trãzgre'sãw] (*pl* **-ões**) F transgression, infringement

transgrido *etc* [trãz'gridu] VB *ver* **transgredir**

transição [trãzi'sãw] (*pl* **-ões**) F transition; **período** *ou* **fase de** ~ transition period

transicional [trãzisjo'naw] (*pl* **-ais**) ADJ transitional

transições [trãzi'sõjs] FPL *de* **transição**

transido, -a [trã'zidu, a] ADJ numb

transigente [trãzi'ʒẽtʃi] ADJ willing to compromise

transigir [trãzi'ʒir] VI to compromise, make concessions; ~ **com alguém** to compromise with sb, meet sb halfway

transistor [trãzis'tor] M transistor

transitar [trãzi'tar] VI: ~ **por** to move through; (*rua*) to go along

transitável [trãzi'tavew] (*pl* **-eis**) ADJ (*caminho*) passable

transitivo, -a [trãzi'tʃivu, a] ADJ (*Ling*) transitive

trânsito ['trãzitu] M (*ato*) transit, passage; (*na rua: veículos*) traffic; (: *pessoas*) flow; **em** ~ in transit; **sinal de** ~ traffic signal

transitório, -a [trãzi'tɔrju, a] ADJ transitory, passing; (*período*) transitional

transladar [trãzla'dar] VT = **trasladar**

translado [trãz'ladu] M = **traslado**

translúcido, -a [trãz'lusidu, a] ADJ translucent

transmissão [trãzmi'sãw] (*pl* **-ões**) F transmission; (*Rádio, TV*) transmission, broadcast; (*transferência*) transfer; ~ **ao vivo** live broadcast; ~ **de dados** data transmission

transmissível [trãzmi'sivew] (*pl* **-eis**) ADJ transmittable

transmissões [trãzmi'sõjs] FPL *de* **transmissão**

transmissor, a [trãzmi'sor(a)] ADJ transmitting ▶ M transmitter

transmitir [trãzmi'tʃir] VT to transmit; (*Rádio, TV*) to broadcast, transmit; (*transferir*) to transfer; (*recado, notícia*) to pass on; (*aroma, som*) to carry; **transmitir-se** VR (*doença*) to be transmitted; ~ **algo a alguém** (*paz etc*) to bring sb sth

transparecer [trãspare'ser] VI to be visible, appear; (*revelar-se*) to be apparent

transparência [trãspa'rẽsja] F transparency; (*de água*) clarity

transparente [trãspa'rẽtʃi] ADJ transparent; (*roupa*) see-through; (*água*) clear; (*evidente*) clear, obvious

transpassar [trãspa'sar] VT = **traspassar**

transpiração [trãspira'sãw] F perspiration

transpirar [trãspi'rar] VI (*suar*) to perspire; (*divulgar-se*) to become known; (*verdade*) to come out ▶ VT to exude

transplantar [trãsplã'tar] VT to transplant

transplante [trãs'plãtʃi] M transplant

transpor [trãs'por] (*irreg: como* **pôr**) VT to cross; (*inverter*) to transpose

transportação [trãsporta'sãw] F transportation

transportadora [trãsporta'dora] F haulage company

transportar [trãspor'tar] VT to transport; (*levar*) to carry; (*enlevar*) to entrance, enrapture; (*fig: remontar*) to take back; **transportar-se** VR to be entranced; (*remontar*) to be transported back; **a** ~ (*Com: quantia*) carry forward, c/f

transporte [trãs'pɔrtʃi] M transport; (*Com*) haulage; (*em contas*) amount carried forward; (*fig: êxtase*) rapture, delight; **despesas de** ~ transport costs; **Ministério dos T-s** Ministry of Transport (BRIT), Department of Transportation (US); ~ **rodoviário** road transport; ~**s coletivos** public transport *sg*

transpôs [trãs'pos] VB *ver* **transpor**

transposição [trãspozi'sãw] F transposition; (*de rio*) crossing

transposto, -a [trãs'postu, 'pɔsta] PP *de* **transpor**

transpunha *etc* [trãs'puɲa] VB *ver* **transpor**

transpus *etc* [trãs'pus] VB *ver* **transpor**

transpuser *etc* [trãspu'zer] VB *ver* **transpor**

transtornar [trãstor'nar] VT to upset; (*rotina, reunião*) to disrupt; **transtornar-se** VR to get upset; to be disrupted

transtorno [trãs'tornu] M upset, disruption; (*contrariedade*) hardship; (*mental*) distraction

transversal [trãzver'saw] (*pl* **-ais**) ADJ transverse, cross; (**rua**) ~ cross street

transverso, -a [trãz'vɛrsu, a] ADJ transverse, cross

transviado, -a [trãz'vjadu, a] ADJ wayward, erring

transviar [trãz'vjar] VT to lead astray; **transviar-se** VR to go astray

trapaça [tra'pasa] F swindle, fraud

trapacear [trapa'sjar] VT, VI to swindle

trapaceiro, -a [trapa'sejru, a] ADJ crooked, cheating ▶ M/F swindler, cheat

trapalhada [trapa'ʎada] F confusion, mix-up

trapalhão, -lhona [trapa'ʎãw, 'ʎɔna] (*pl* **-ões/-s**) M/F bungler, blunderer

trapézio [tra'pɛzju] M trapeze; (*Mat*) trapezium

trapezista [trape'zista] M/F trapeze artist

trapo ['trapu] M rag; **ser** *ou* **estar um** ~ (*pessoa*) to be washed up

traqueia [tra'kɛja] F windpipe
traquejo [tra'keʒu] M experience
traqueotomia [trakjoto'mia] F tracheotomy
traquinas [tra'kinas] ADJ INV mischievous
trarei etc [tra'rej] VB ver **trazer**
trás [trajs] PREP, ADV: **para** ~ backwards; **por**
~ **de** behind; **de** ~ from behind; **a luz de** ~
the back light; **de** ~ **para frente** back to
front; **ano** ~ **ano** year after year; **dar para** ~
(fig: pessoa) to go wrong
traseira [tra'zejra] F rear; (Anat) bottom
traseiro, -a [tra'zejru, a] ADJ back, rear ▶ M
(Anat) bottom, behind
trasladar [trazla'dar] VT to remove, transfer;
(copiar) to transcribe
traslado [traz'ladu] M (cópia) transcript;
(deslocamento) removal, transference
traspassar [traspa'sar] VT (rio etc) to cross;
(penetrar) to pierce, penetrate; (exceder) to
exceed, overstep; (transferir) to transmit,
transfer; (PT: sublocar) to sublet
traspasse [tras'pasi] M transfer; (sublocação)
sublease
traste ['trastʃi] M thing; (coisa sem valor) piece
of junk; (patife) rogue, rascal; **estar** ou **ficar**
um ~ to be devastated
tratado [tra'tadu] M treaty; (Literatura)
treatise; ~ **de paz** peace treaty
tratador, a [trata'dor(a)] M/F: ~ **de cavalos**
groom
tratamento [trata'mētu] M treatment;
(título) title; **forma de** ~ form of address;
~ **de choque** shock treatment
tratante [tra'tãtʃi] M/F rogue
tratar [tra'tar] VT to treat; (tema) to deal with,
cover; (combinar) to agree ▶ VI: ~ **com** to deal
with; (combinar) to agree with; **tratar-se** VR
(Med) to take treatment; (cuidar-se) to take
care of o.s.; ~ **de** to deal with; ~ **por** ou **de** to
address as; **de que se trata?** what is it
about?; **trata-se de** it is a question of; ~ **de**
fazer (esforçar-se) to try to do; (resolver) to
resolve to do; **trate da sua vida!** mind your
own business!; ~**se a pão e água** to live on
bread and water
tratável [tra'tavew] (pl -**eis**) ADJ treatable;
(afável) approachable, amenable
trato ['tratu] M (tratamento) treatment;
(contrato) agreement, contract; **tratos** MPL
(relações) dealings; **maus** ~**s** ill-treatment;
pessoa de fino ~ refined person; **dar** ~**s à**
bola to rack one's brains
trator [tra'tor] M tractor
traulitada [trawli'tada] F beating
trauma ['trawma] M trauma
traumático, -a [traw'matʃiku, a] ADJ
traumatic
traumatizante [trawmatʃi'zãtʃi] ADJ
traumatic, harrowing
traumatizar [trawmatʃi'zar] VT to traumatize
travada [tra'vada] F: **dar uma** ~ to put on the
brake
travão [tra'vãw] (pl -**ões**) (PT) M brake

travar [tra'var] VT (roda) to lock; (iniciar) to
engage in; (conversa) to strike up; (luta) to
wage; (carro) to stop; (passagem) to block;
(movimentos) to hinder ▶ VI (PT) to brake;
~ **amizade com** to become friendly with,
make friends with
trave ['travi] F beam, crossbeam; (Esporte)
crossbar; **foi na** ~ (col: resposta etc) (it was)
close
través [tra'vɛs] M slant, incline; **de** ~ across,
sideways; **olhar de** ~ to look sideways (at)
travessa [tra'vɛsa] F crossbeam, crossbar;
(rua) lane, alley; (prato) dish; (para o cabelo)
comb, slide
travessão [trave'sãw] (pl -**ões**) M (de balança)
bar, beam; (pontuação) dash
travesseiro [trave'sejru] M pillow; **consultar**
o ~ to sleep on it
travessia [trave'sia] F (viagem) journey,
crossing
travesso¹, -a [tra'vɛsu, a] ADJ cross, transverse
travesso², -a [tra'vesu, a] ADJ mischievous,
naughty
travessões [trave'sõjs] MPL de **travessão**
travessura [trave'sura] F mischief, prank;
fazer ~**s** to get up to mischief
travesti [traves'tʃi] M/F transvestite; (artista)
drag artist
travões [tra'võjs] MPL de **travão**
trazer [tra'zer] VT to bring; (roupa) to wear;
(nome, marcas) to bear; ~ **à memória** to bring
to mind; **o jornal traz uma notícia sobre**
isso the newspaper has an item about that;
~ **de volta** to bring back
TRE (BR) ABR M = **Tribunal Regional Eleitoral**
trecho ['treʃu] M passage; (de rua, caminho)
stretch; (espaço) space
treco ['trɛku] (col) M (tralha) thing;
(indisposição) bad turn; **trecos** MPL (bugigangas)
stuff sg; **ter um** ~ (sentir-se mal) to be taken
bad; (zangar-se) to have a fit
trégua ['trɛgwa] F truce; (descanso) respite,
rest; **não dar** ~ **a** to give no respite to
treinado, -a [trej'nadu, a] ADJ (atleta) fit;
(animal) trained; (acostumado) practised
(BRIT), practiced (US)
treinador, a [trejna'dor(a)] M/F trainer
treinamento [trejna'mētu] M training
treinar [trej'nar] VT to train; **treinar-se** VR to
train; ~ **seu inglês** to practise (BRIT) ou
practice (US) one's English
treino ['trejnu] M training
trejeito [tre'ʒejtu] M (gesto) gesture; (careta)
grimace, face
trela ['trɛla] F (correia) lead, leash; (col: conversa)
chat; **dar** ~ **a** (col: conversar) to chat with;
(encorajar) to lead on
treliça [tre'lisa] F trellis
trem [trēj] (pl -**ns**) M train; (PT: carruagem)
carriage, coach; **trens** MPL (col: coisas, objetos)
gear sg, belongings; **ir de** ~ to go by train;
mudar de ~ to change trains; **pegar um** ~
to catch a train; **puxar o** ~ (col) to make

t

tracks; **~ de carga/passageiros** freight/
passenger train; **~ correio** mail train; **~ de
aterrissagem** (*avião*) landing gear; **~ da
alegria** (*Pol*) jobs *pl* for the boys, nepotism
trema ['trema] M di(a)eresis
tremedeira [treme'dejra] F trembling
tremelicante [tremeli'kãtʃi] ADJ trembling
tremelicar [tremeli'kar] VI to tremble, shiver
tremelique [treme'liki] M trembling
tremeluzir [tremelu'zir] VI to twinkle, glimmer
tremendo, -a [tre'mẽdu, a] ADJ tremendous;
(*terrível*) terrible, awful
tremer [tre'mer] VI to shudder, quake; (*terra*)
to shake; (*de frio, medo*) to shiver
tremor [tre'mor] M tremor, trembling; **~ de
terra** (earth) tremor
tremular [tremu'lar] VI (*bandeira*) to flutter,
wave; (*luz*) to glimmer, flicker
trêmulo, -a ['tremulu, a] ADJ shaky,
trembling; (*voz*) faltering
trena ['trena] F tape measure
trenó [tre'nɔ] M sledge, sleigh (*BRIT*), sled (*US*)
trens [trẽjs] MPL *de* **trem**
trepada [tre'pada] (!) F screw, fuck (!)
trepadeira [trepa'dejra] F (*Bot*) creeper
trepar [tre'par] VT to climb ▶ VI: **~ em** to
climb; **~ (com alguém)** (!) to screw (sb)
trepidação [trepida'sãw] F shaking
trepidar [trepi'dar] VI to tremble, shake
trépido, -a ['trepidu, a] ADJ fearful
três [tres] NUM three; **a ~ por dois** every five
minutes, all the time; *ver tb* **cinco**
tresloucado, -a [trezlo'kadu, a] ADJ crazy,
deranged
trespassar [trespa'sar] VT = **traspassar**
trespasse [tres'pasi] M = **traspasse**
três-quartos ADJ INV (*saia, manga*) three-
quarter-length ▶ M INV (*apartamento*)
three-room flat (*BRIT*) *ou* apartment
trevas ['trevas] FPL darkness *sg*
trevo ['trevu] M clover; (*de vias*) intersection
treze ['trezi] NUM thirteen; *ver tb* **cinco**
trezentos, -tas [tre'zẽtus, tas] NUM three
hundred
TRH ABR F (= *terapia de reposição hormonal*) HRT
tríade ['triadʒi] F triad
triagem ['trjaʒẽ] F selection; (*separação*)
sorting; **fazer uma ~ de** to make a selection
of, sort out
triangular [trjãgu'lar] ADJ triangular
triângulo ['trjãgulu] M triangle
triatlo [tri'atlu] M triathlon
tribal [tri'baw] (*pl* **-ais**) ADJ tribal
tribo ['tribu] F tribe
tribulação [tribula'sãw] (*pl* **-ões**) F tribulation,
affliction
tribuna [tri'buna] F platform, rostrum; (*Rel*)
pulpit
tribunal [tribu'naw] (*pl* **-ais**) M court;
(*comissão*) tribunal; **~ de apelação** *ou* **de
recursos** court of appeal; **T~ de Justiça/
Contas** Court of Justice/Accounts; **T~ do
Trabalho** Industrial Tribunal

tributação [tributa'sãw] F taxation
tributar [tribu'tar] VT (*impor impostos a*) to tax;
(*pagar*) to pay
tributário, -a [tribu'tarju, a] ADJ tax *atr* ▶ M
(*de rio*) tributary
tributável [tribu'tavew] (*pl* **-eis**) ADJ taxable
tributo [tri'butu] M tribute; (*imposto*) tax
tricampeão, -peã [trikã'pjãw, 'pjã] (*pl* **-ões/-s**)
M/F three-time champion
tricô [tri'ko] M knitting; **artigos de ~** knitted
goods, knitwear *sg*; **ponto de ~** plain stitch
tricolor [triko'lor] ADJ three-coloured (*BRIT*),
three-colored (*US*)
tricotar [triko'tar] VT, VI to knit
tridimensional [tridimẽsjo'naw] (*pl* **-ais**) ADJ
three-dimensional
triênio ['trjenju] M three-year period
trigal [tri'gaw] (*pl* **-ais**) M wheat field
trigêmeo, -a [tri'ʒemju, a] M/F triplet
trigésimo, -a [tri'ʒezimu, a] ADJ thirtieth; *ver
tb* **quinto**
trigo ['trigu] M wheat
trigonometria [trigonome'tria] F
trigonometry
trigueiro, -a [tri'gejru, a] ADJ dark, swarthy
trilátero, -a [tri'lateru, a] ADJ trilateral
trilha ['triʎa] F (*caminho*) path; (*rasto*) track,
trail; (*Comput*) track; **~ sonora** soundtrack
trilhado, -a [tri'ʎadu, a] ADJ (*pisado*)
well-worn, well-trodden; (*percorrido*) covered
trilhão [tri'ʎãw] (*pl* **-ões**) M billion (*BRIT*),
trillion (*US*)
trilhar [tri'ʎar] VT (*vereda*) to tread, wear
trilho ['triʎu] M (*BR Ferro*) rail; (*vereda*) path,
track
trilhões [tri'ʎõjs] MPL *de* **trilhão**
trilíngue [tri'lĩgwi] ADJ trilingual
trilogia [trilo'ʒia] F trilogy
trimestral [trimes'traw] (*pl* **-ais**) ADJ
quarterly
trimestralidade [trimestrali'dadʒi] F
quarterly payment
trimestralmente [trimestraw'mẽtʃi] ADV
quarterly
trimestre [tri'mestri] M (*Educ*) term; (*Com*)
quarter
trinca ['trĩka] F set of three; (*col: trio*)
threesome
trincar [trĩ'kar] VT to crunch; (*morder*) to bite;
(*dentes*) to grit ▶ VI to crunch
trinchar [trĩ'ʃar] VT to carve
trincheira [trĩ'ʃejra] F trench
trinco ['trĩku] M latch
trindade [trĩ'dadʒi] F: **a T~** the Trinity;
trindades FPL (*sino*) angelus *sg*
Trinidad e Tobago [trinidadʒito'bagu] M
Trinidad and Tobago
trinta ['trĩta] NUM thirty; *ver tb* **cinquenta**
trio ['triu] M trio; **~ elétrico**; *see note*

> **Trios elétricos** are lorries, carrying floats
> equipped for sound and/or live music,
> which parade through the streets during
> *carnaval*, especially in Bahia. Bands and

popular performers on the floats draw crowds by giving frenzied performances of various types of music.

tripa ['tripa] F gut, intestine; **tripas** FPL (*intestinos*) bowels; (*vísceras*) guts; (*Culin*) tripe *sg*; **fazer das ~s coração** to make a great effort

tripé [tri'pɛ] M tripod

tríplex ['tripleks] ADJ INV three-storey (*BRIT*), three-story (*US*) ▶ M INV three-stor(e)y apartment

triplicar [tripli'kar] VT, VI to treble; **triplicar-se** VR to treble

Trípoli ['tripoli] N Tripoli

tripulação [tripula'sãw] (*pl* **-ões**) F crew

tripulante [tripu'lãtʃi] M/F crew member

tripular [tripu'lar] VT to man

trisavô, -vó [triza'vo, 'vɔ] M/F great-great-grandfather/mother

triste ['tristʃi] ADJ sad; (*lugar*) depressing

tristeza [tris'teza] F sadness; (*de lugar*) gloominess; **esse professor é uma ~** (*col*) this teacher is awful

tristonho, -a [tris'tɔɲu, a] ADJ sad, melancholy

triturar [tritu'rar] VT (*moer*) to grind; (*espancar*) to beat to a pulp; (*afligir*) to beset

triunfal [trjũ'faw] (*pl* **-ais**) ADJ triumphal

triunfante [trjũ'fãtʃi] ADJ triumphant

triunfar [trjũ'far] VI to triumph

triunfo ['trjũfu] M triumph

trivial [tri'vjaw] (*pl* **-ais**) ADJ (*comum*) common(place), ordinary; (*insignificante*) trivial, trifling ▶ M (*pratos*) everyday food

trivialidade [trivjali'dadʒi] F triviality; **trivialidades** FPL (*futilidades*) trivia *sg*

triz [triz] M: **por um ~** by a hair's breadth; **escapar por um ~** to have a narrow escape

troca ['trɔka] F exchange, swap; **em ~ de** in exchange for

troça ['trɔsa] F ridicule, mockery; **fazer ~ de** to make fun of

trocadilho [troka'dʒiʎu] M pun, play on words

trocado [tro'kadu] M: **~(s)** (small) change

trocador, a [troka'dor(a)] M/F (*em ônibus*) conductor

trocar [tro'kar] VT to exchange, swap; (*mudar*) to change; (*inverter*) to change *ou* swap round; (*confundir*) to mix up; **trocar-se** VR to change; **~ dinheiro** to change money; **~ algo por algo** to exchange *ou* swap sth for sth; **~ algo de lugar** to move sth; **~ de roupa/lugar** to change (clothes)/places; **~ de bem/mal** to make up/fall out

troçar [tro'sar] VI: **~ de** to ridicule, make fun of

troca-troca (*pl* **troca-trocas**) M swap

trocista [tro'sista] M/F joker

troco ['trɔku] M (*dinheiro*) change; (*revide*) retort, rejoinder; **a ~ de** at the cost of; (*por causa de*) because of; **em ~ de** in exchange for; **dar o ~ a alguém** (*fig*) to pay sb back

troço ['trɔsu] (*BR col*) M (*coisa inútil*) piece of junk; (*coisa*) thing; **ser ~** (*pessoa*) to be a big-shot; **ser um ~** to be amazing; **ter um ~** (*sentir-se mal*) to be taken bad; (*zangar-se*) to get mad; **senti** *ou* **me deu um ~** I felt bad; **ele é um ~ de feio** he's incredibly ugly; **meus ~s** my things

troféu [tro'fɛw] M trophy

tromba ['trõba] F (*do elefante*) trunk; (*de outro animal*) snout; (*col*) poker face; **estar de ~** (*col*) to be poker-faced

trombada [trõ'bada] F crash; **dar uma ~** to have a crash

tromba-d'água (*pl* **trombas-d'água**) F waterspout; (*chuva*) downpour

trombadinha [trõba'dʒiɲa] F child thief

trombeta [trõ'beta] F (*Mús*) trumpet

trombone [trõ'bɔni] M (*Mús*) trombone; **botar a boca no ~** (*fig: col*) to tell the world

trombose [trõ'bɔzi] F thrombosis

trombudo, -a [trõ'budu, a] ADJ (*fig*) poker-faced

trompa ['trõpa] F (*Mús*) horn; **~ de Falópio** (*Anat*) Fallopian tube

tronchar [trõ'ʃar] VT to cut off, chop off

troncho, -a ['trõʃu, a] ADJ (*torto*) crooked; **~ de uma perna** one-legged

tronco ['trõku] M (*caule*) trunk; (*ramo*) branch; (*de corpo*) torso, trunk; (*de família*) lineage; (*Tel*) trunk line

troncudo, -a [trõ'kudu, a] ADJ stocky

trono ['trɔnu] M throne

tropa ['trɔpa] F troop, gang; (*Mil*) troop; (*exército*) army; **ir para a ~** (*PT*) to join the army; **~ de choque** riot police, riot squad

tropeção [trope'sãw] (*pl* **-ões**) M trip-up; (*fig*) faux pas, slip-up; **dar um ~ (em)** to stumble (on)

tropeçar [trope'sar] VI to stumble, trip; (*fig*) to blunder; **~ em dificuldades** to meet with difficulties

tropeço [tro'pesu] M stumbling block

tropeções [trope'sõjs] MPL *de* **tropeção**

trôpego, -a ['tropegu, a] ADJ shaky, unsteady

tropel [tro'pɛw] (*pl* **-éis**) M (*ruído*) uproar, tumult; (*confusão*) confusion; (*estrépito de pés*) stamping of feet; (*turbamulta*) mob

tropical [tropi'kaw] (*pl* **-ais**) ADJ tropical

trópico ['trɔpiku] M tropic; **T~ de Câncer/Capricórnio** Tropic of Cancer/Capricorn

troquei *etc* [tro'kej] VB *ver* **trocar**

trotar [tro'tar] VI to trot

trote ['trɔtʃi] M trot; (*por telefone etc*) hoax call; (*: obsceno*) obscene call; (*em calouro*) trick; **passar um ~** to play a hoax

trottoir [tro'twar] M: **fazer ~** to go on the streets (as a prostitute)

trouxa ['troʃa] ADJ (*col*) gullible ▶ F bundle of clothes ▶ M/F (*col: pessoa*) sucker

trouxe *etc* ['trosi] VB *ver* **trazer**

trova ['trɔva] F ballad, folksong

trovador [trova'dor] M troubadour, minstrel

trovão [tro'vãw] (*pl* **-ões**) M clap of thunder; (*trovoada*) thunder

t

trovejar [trove'ʒar] vɪ to thunder
trovoada [tro'vwada] ꜰ thunderstorm
trovoar [tro'vwar] vɪ to thunder
trovões [tro'võjs] ᴍᴘʟ *de* **trovão**
TRT (*ʙʀ*) ᴀʙʀ ᴍ = **Tribunal Regional do Trabalho**
TRU (*ʙʀ*) ᴀʙʀ ꜰ = **Taxa Rodoviária Única**
trucidar [trusi'dar] vᴛ to butcher, slaughter
truculência [truku'lẽsja] ꜰ cruelty, barbarism
truculente [truku'lẽtʃi] ᴀᴅᴊ cruel, barbaric
trufa ['trufa] ꜰ (*Bot*) truffle
truísmo [tru'izmu] ᴍ truism
trumbicar-se [trũbi'karsi] (*col*) vʀ to come a cropper
truncar [trũ'kar] vᴛ to chop off, cut off; (*texto*) to garble
trunfo ['trũfu] ᴍ trump (card)
truque ['truki] ᴍ trick; (*publicitário*) gimmick
truste ['trustʃi] ᴍ trust, monopoly
truta ['truta] ꜰ trout
TSE (*ʙʀ*) ᴀʙʀ ᴍ = **Tribunal Superior Eleitoral**
TST (*ʙʀ*) ᴀʙʀ ᴍ = **Tribunal Superior do Trabalho**
tu [tu] ᴘʀᴏɴ you
tua ['tua] ꜰ *de* **teu**
tuba ['tuba] ꜰ tuba
tubarão [tuba'rãw] (*pl* **-ões**) ᴍ shark
tubário, -a [tu'barju, a] ᴀᴅᴊ: **gravidez tubária** ectopic pregnancy
tubarões [tuba'rõjs] ᴍᴘʟ *de* **tubarão**
tuberculose [tuberku'lɔzi] ꜰ tuberculosis, TB
tuberculoso, -a [tuberku'lozu, ɔza] ᴀᴅᴊ suffering from tuberculosis ▶ ᴍ/ꜰ TB sufferer
tubinho [tu'biɲu] ᴍ tube dress
tubo ['tubu] ᴍ tube, pipe; **~ de ensaio** test tube; **gastar/custar os ~s** (*col*) to spend/cost a bomb
tubulação [tubula'sãw] ꜰ piping, plumbing; **entrar pela ~** to come a cropper
tubular [tubu'lar] ᴀᴅᴊ tubular
tucano [tu'kanu] ᴍ toucan
tudo ['tudu] ᴘʀᴏɴ everything; **~ quanto** everything that; **antes de ~** first of all; **apesar de ~** despite everything; **acima de ~** above all; **depois de ~** after all; **~ ou nada** all or nothing; **estar com ~** to be sitting pretty
tufão [tu'fãw] (*pl* **-ões**) ᴍ typhoon
tugúrio [tu'gurju] ᴍ (*cabana*) hut, shack; (*refúgio*) shelter
tuitar [twi'tar] vᴛ, vɪ to tweet
tulipa [tu'lipa] ꜰ tulip; (*copo*) tall glass
tumba ['tũba] ꜰ (*sepultura*) tomb; (*lápide*) tombstone
tumido, -a [tu'midu, a] ᴀᴅᴊ (*inchado*) swollen
tumor [tu'mor] ᴍ tumour (*ʙʀɪᴛ*), tumor (*us*); **~ benigno/maligno** benign/malignant tumo(u)r; **~ cerebral** brain tumo(u)r
tumular [tumu'lar] ᴀᴅᴊ (*pedra*) tomb *atr*; (*silêncio*) like the grave
túmulo ['tumulu] ᴍ tomb; (*sepultura*) burial; **ser um ~** (*pessoa*) to be very discreet

tumulto [tu'muwtu] ᴍ (*confusão*) uproar, trouble; (*grande movimento*) bustle; (*balbúrdia*) hubbub; (*motim*) riot
tumultuado, -a [tumuw'twadu, a] ᴀᴅᴊ riotous, heated
tumultuar [tumuw'twar] vᴛ (*fazer tumulto em*) to disrupt; (*amotinar*) to rouse, incite
tumultuoso, -a [tumuw'twozu, ɔza] ᴀᴅᴊ tumultuous; (*revolto*) stormy
tunda ['tũda] ꜰ thrashing, beating; (*fig*) dressing-down
túnel ['tunew] (*pl* **-eis**) ᴍ tunnel
túnica [tu'nika] ꜰ tunic
Tunísia [tu'nizja] ꜰ: **a ~** Tunisia
tupi [tu'pi] ᴍ Tupi (tribe); (*Ling*) Tupi ▶ ᴍ/ꜰ Tupi Indian
tupi-guarani [-gwara'ni] ᴍ *see note*

> **Tupi-guarani** is an important branch of indigenous languages from the tropical region of South America. It takes in thirty indigenous peoples and includes Tupi, Guarani, and other languages. Before Brazil was discovered by the Portuguese it had 1,300 indigenous languages, 87% of which are now extinct due to the extermination of indigenous peoples and the loss of territory.

tupiniquim [tupini'kĩ] (*pl* **-ns**) (*pej*) ᴀᴅᴊ Brazilian (Indian)
turba ['turba] ꜰ throng; (*em desordem*) mob
turbamulta [turba'muwta] ꜰ mob
turbante [tur'bãtʃi] ᴍ turban
turbar [tur'bar] vᴛ (*escurecer*) to darken, cloud; (*perturbar*) to perturb; **turbar-se** vʀ to be perturbed
turbilhão [turbi'ʎãw] (*pl* **-ões**) ᴍ (*de vento*) whirlwind; (*de água*) whirlpool; **um ~ de** a whirl of
turbina [tur'bina] ꜰ turbine; **~ eólica** wind turbine
turbulência [turbu'lẽsja] ꜰ turbulence
turbulento, -a [turbu'lẽtu, a] ᴀᴅᴊ turbulent, stormy; (*pessoa*) disorderly
turco, -a ['turku, a] ᴀᴅᴊ Turkish ▶ ᴍ/ꜰ Turk ▶ ᴍ (*Ling*) Turkish
turfa ['turfa] ꜰ peat
turfe ['turfi] ᴍ horse-racing
túrgido, -a [tur'ʒidu, a] ᴀᴅᴊ swollen, bloated
turíbulo [tu'ribulu] ᴍ incense-burner
turismo [tu'rizmu] ᴍ tourism; (*indústria*) tourist industry; **fazer ~** to go sightseeing; **agência de ~** travel agency
turista [tu'rista] ᴍ/ꜰ tourist; (*aluno*) persistent absentee ▶ ᴀᴅᴊ (*classe*) tourist *atr*
turístico, -a [tu'ristʃiku, a] ᴀᴅᴊ tourist *atr*; (*viagem*) sightseeing *atr*
turma ['turma] ꜰ group; (*Educ*) class; **a ~ da pesada** (*col*) the in crowd
turnê [tur'ne] ꜰ tour
turnedô [turne'do] ᴍ (*Culin*) tournedos
turno ['turnu] ᴍ shift; (*vez*) turn; (*Esporte, de eleição*) round; **por ~s** alternately, by turns, in turn; **~ da noite** night shift

turquesa [tur'keza] ADJ INV turquoise
Turquia [tur'kia] F: **a ~** Turkey
turra ['tuha] F (*disputa*) argument, dispute;
andar *ou* **viver às ~s** to be at loggerheads
turvar [tur'var] VT to cloud; (*escurecer*) to
darken; **turvar-se** VR to become clouded;
to darken
turvo, -a ['turvu, a] ADJ clouded
tusso *etc* ['tusu] VB *ver* **tossir**
tusta ['tusta] (*col*) M: **nem um ~** not a penny
tutano [tu'tanu] M (*Anat*) marrow
tutela [tu'tɛla] F protection; (*Jur*)
guardianship; **estar sob a ~ de** (*fig*) to be

under the protection of
tutelar [tute'lar] ADJ protective; (*Jur*)
guardian ▶ VT to protect; to act as a
guardian to
tutor, a [tu'tor(a)] M/F guardian
tutu [tu'tu] M (*Culin*) *beans, bacon and manioc
flour*; (*de balé*) tutu; (*col: dinheiro*) cash
TV [te've] ABR F (= *televisão*) TV
TVE (BR) ABR F (= *Televisão Educativa*) *educational
television station*
TVS (BR) ABR F = **Televisão Stúdio Sílvio
Santos**
tweed ['twidʒi] M tweed

Uu

U, u [u] (*pl* **us**) M U, u; **U de Úrsula** U for Uncle

uai [waj] EXCL ah

UBE ABR F = **União Brasileira de Empresários**

úbere ['uberi] ADJ fertile ▶ M udder

ubérrimo, -a [u'bɛhimu, a] ADJ SUPERL *de* **úbere**

ubiquidade [ubikwi'dadʒi] F ubiquity

ubíquo, -a [u'bikwu, a] ADJ ubiquitous

Ucrânia [u'kranja] F: **a ~** the Ukraine

UD (BR) ABR F = **Feira de Utilidades Domésticas**

UDN ABR F (= *União Democrática Nacional*) *former Brazilian political party*

UE ABR F (= *União Europeia*) EU

ué [wɛ] EXCL what?, just a minute!

UERJ ['wɛrʒi] ABR F = **Universidade Estadual do Rio de Janeiro**

ufa ['ufa] EXCL phew!

ufanar-se [ufa'narsi] VR: **~ de** to take pride in, pride o.s. on

ufanismo [ufa'nizmu] (BR) M boastful nationalism, chauvinism

Uferj [u'fɛrʒi] ABR F = **Unidade Fiscal do Estado do Rio de Janeiro**

UFF ABR F = **Universidade Federal Fluminense**

UFMG ABR F = **Universidade Federal de Minas Gerais**

UFPE ABR F = **Universidade Federal de Pernambuco**

UFRJ ABR F = **Universidade Federal do Rio de Janeiro**

Uganda [u'gãda] M Uganda

ugandense [ugã'dẽsi] ADJ, M/F Ugandan

uh [uh] EXCL ooh!; (*de repugnância*) ugh!

ui [ui] EXCL (*de dor*) ouch, ow; (*de surpresa*) oh; (*de repugnância*) ugh

uísque ['wiski] M whisky (BRIT), whiskey (US)

uisqueria [wiske'ria] F whisk(e)y bar

uivada [wi'vada] F howl

uivante [wi'vãtʃi] ADJ howling

uivar [wi'var] VI to howl; (*berrar*) to yell

uivo ['wivu] M howl; (*fig*) yell

úlcera ['uwsera] F ulcer

ulceração [uwsera'sãw] F ulceration

ulcerar [uwse'rar] VT, VI to ulcerate; **ulcerar-se** VR to ulcerate

ulceroso, -a [uwse'rozu, ɔza] ADJ ulcerous

ulterior [ulte'rjor] ADJ (*além*) further, farther; (*depois*) later, subsequent

ulteriormente [uwterior'mẽtʃi] ADV later on, subsequently

ultimamente [uwtʃima'mẽtʃi] ADV lately

ultimar [uwtʃi'mar] VT to finish; (*negócio, compra*) to complete

ultimato [uwtʃi'matu] M ultimatum

ultimátum [uwtʃi'matũ] M = **ultimato**

último, -a ['uwtʃimu, a] ADJ last; (*mais recente*) latest; (*qualidade*) lowest; (*fig*) final; **por ~** finally; **fazer algo por ~** to do sth last; **nos ~s anos** in recent years; **em ~ caso** if the worst comes to the worst; **pela última vez** (for) the last time; **a última** (*notícia*) the latest (news); (*absurdo*) the latest folly; **dizer as últimas a alguém** to insult sb; **estar nas últimas** (*na miséria*) to be down and out; (*agoniando*) to be on one's last legs

ultra... [uwtra-] PREFIXO ultra-

ultracheio, -a [uwtra'ʃeju, a] ADJ packed

ultrajante [uwtra'ʒãtʃi] ADJ outrageous; (*que insulta*) insulting

ultrajar [uwtra'ʒar] VT to outrage; (*insultar*) to insult, offend

ultraje [uw'traʒi] M outrage; (*insulto*) insult, offence (BRIT), offense (US)

ultraleve [uwtra'lɛvi] ADJ ultralight ▶ M microlite

ultramar [uwtra'mar] M overseas

ultramarino, -a [uwtrama'rinu, a] ADJ overseas

ultramoderno, -a [uwtramo'dɛrnu, a] ADJ ultramodern

ultrapassado, -a [uwtrapa'sadu, a] ADJ (*ideias etc*) outmoded

ultrapassagem [uwtrapa'saʒẽ] F overtaking (BRIT), passing (US)

ultrapassar [uwtrapa'sar] VT (*atravessar*) to cross, go beyond; (*ir além de*) to exceed; (*transgredir*) to overstep; (*Auto*) to overtake (BRIT), pass (US); (*ser superior a*) to surpass ▶ VI (*Auto*) to overtake (BRIT), pass (US)

ultrassecreto, -a [uwtrase'krɛtu, a] ADJ top secret

ultrassensível [uwtrasẽ'sivew] (*pl* **-eis**) ADJ hypersensitive

ultrassom [uwtra'sõ] M ultrasound

ultrassônico, -a [uwtra'soniku, a] ADJ ultrasonic; (*Med*) ultrasound *atr*

ultrassonografia [uwtrasonogra'fia] F ultrasound scanning

ultravioleta [uwtravjo'leta] ADJ ultraviolet
ululante [ulu'lãtʃi] ADJ howling; (*mentira, óbvio*) blatant
ulular [ulu'lar] VI to howl, wail ▶ M howling, wailing

(PALAVRA-CHAVE)

um, a [ũ, 'uma] (*pl* **uns/umas**) NUM one; **um e outro** both; **um a um** one by one; **à uma (hora)** at one (o'clock)
▶ ADJ: **uns cinco** about five; **uns poucos** a few
▶ ART INDEF **1** (*sg*) a; (: *antes de vogal ou 'h' mudo*) an; (*pl*) some; **um livro** a book; **uma maçã** an apple
2 (*dando ênfase*): **estou com uma fome!** I'm so hungry!; **ela é de uma beleza incrível** she's incredibly beautiful
3: **um ao outro** one another; (*entre dois*) each other

umbanda [ũ'bãda] M umbanda (*Afro-Brazilian cult*)
umbigo [ũ'bigu] M navel
umbilical [ũbili'kaw] (*pl* **-ais**) ADJ: **cordão ~** umbilical cord
umbral [ũ'braw] (*pl* **-ais**) M (*limiar*) threshold
umedecer [umede'ser] VT to moisten, wet; **umedecer-se** VR to get wet
umedecido, -a [umede'sidu, a] ADJ damp
umidade [umi'dadʒi] F dampness; (*clima*) humidity
úmido, -a ['umidu, a] ADJ wet, moist; (*roupa*) damp; (*clima*) humid
unânime [u'nanimi] ADJ unanimous
unanimidade [unanimi'dadʒi] F unanimity
unção [ũ'sãw] F anointing; (*Rel*) unction
UNE (BR) ABR F = **União Nacional de Estudantes**
UNESCO [u'nɛsku] ABR F UNESCO
ungir [ũ'ʒir] VT to rub with ointment; (*Rel*) to anoint
unguento [ũ'gwẽtu] M ointment
unha ['uɲa] F nail; (*garra*) claw; **com ~s e dentes** tooth and nail; **ser ~ e carne (com)** to be hand in glove (with); **fazer as ~s** to do one's nails; (*por outra pessoa*) to have one's nails done; **~ encravada** (*no pé*) ingrowing toenail
unhada [u'ɲada] F scratch
unha de fome (*pl* **unhas de fome**) ADJ mean ▶ M/F miser
unhar [u'ɲar] VT to scratch
união [u'ɲãw] (*pl* **-ões**) F union; (*ato*) joining; (*unidade, solidariedade*) unity; (*casamento*) marriage; (*Tec*) joint; **a U~ Soviética** the Soviet Union; **a ~ faz a força** unity is strength; **a U~** (*no Brasil*) the Union, the Federal Government; **a U~ Europeia** the European Union
unicamente [unika'mẽtʃi] ADV only
único, -a ['uniku, a] ADJ only; (*sem igual*) unique; (*um só*) single; **ele é o ~ que ...** he is

the only one who ...; **ela é filha única** she's an only child; **um caso ~** a one-off; **preço ~** one price
unicórnio [uni'kɔrnju] M unicorn
unidade [uni'dadʒi] F unity; (*Tec*, *Com*) unit; **~ central de processamento** (*Comput*) central processing unit; **~ de disco** (*Comput*) disk drive
unido, -a [u'nidu, a] ADJ joined, linked; (*fig*) united; **manter-se ~s** to stick together
Unif [u'nifi] (BR) ABR F = **Unidade Fiscal**
unificação [unifika'sãw] F unification
unificar [unifi'kar] VT to unite; **unificar-se** VR to join together
uniforme [uni'fɔrmi] ADJ uniform; (*semelhante*) alike, similar; (*superfície*) even ▶ M uniform; **de ~** uniformly
uniformidade [uniformi'dadʒi] F uniformity
uniformizado, -a [uniformi'zadu, a] ADJ (*uniforme*) uniform, standardized; (*vestido de uniforme*) in uniform
uniformizar [uniformi'zar] VT to standardize; (*pessoa*) to put into uniform; **uniformizar-se** VR to put on one's uniform
unilateral [unilate'raw] (*pl* **-ais**) ADJ unilateral
unilíngue [uni'lĩgwi] ADJ monolingual
uniões [u'njõjs] FPL *de* **união**
unir [u'nir] VT (*juntar*) to join together; (*ligar*) to link; (*pessoas, fig*) to unite; (*misturar*) to mix together; (*atar*) to tie together; **unir-se** VR to come together; (*povos etc*) to unite; **~-se a alguém** to join forces with sb
unissex [uni'sɛks] ADJ INV unisex
uníssono [u'nisonu] M: **em ~** in unison
Unita [u'nita] ABR F (= *União Nacional pela Libertação de Angola*) Unita
unitário, -a [uni'tarju, a] ADJ (*preço*) unit atr; (*Pol*) unitarian ▶ M/F (*Pol, Rel*) unitarian
universal [univer'saw] (*pl* **-ais**) ADJ universal; (*geral*) general; (*mundial*) worldwide; (*espírito*) broad
universalidade [universali'dadʒi] F universality
universalizar [universali'zar] VT to universalize
universidade [universi'dadʒi] F university
universitário, -a [universi'tarju, a] ADJ university atr ▶ M/F (*professor*) lecturer; (*aluno*) university student
universo [uni'vɛrsu] M universe; (*mundo*) world
unjo *etc* ['ũʒu] VB *ver* **ungir**
uno, -a ['unu, a] ADJ one
uns [ũs] MPL *de* **um**
untar [ũ'tar] VT (*esfregar*) to rub; (*com óleo, manteiga*) to grease
upa ['upa] EXCL (*quando algo cai*) whoops!; (*para animar a se levantar*) up you get!; (*de espanto*) wow!
UPC (BR) ABR F = **Unidade Padrão de Capital**
Urais [u'rajs] MPL: **os ~** the Urals
urânio [u'ranju] M uranium
Urano [u'ranu] M Uranus

u

urbanidade [urbani'dadʒi] F courtesy, politeness

urbanismo [urba'nizmu] M town planning

urbanista [urba'nista] M/F town planner

urbanístico, -a [urba'nistʃiku, a] ADJ town planning atr

urbanização [urbaniza'sãw] F urbanization

urbanizado, -a [urbani'zadu, a] ADJ (zona) built-up

urbanizar [urbani'zar] VT to urbanize; (pessoa) to refine

urbano, -a [ur'banu, a] ADJ (da cidade) urban; (fig) urbane

urbe ['urbi] F city

urdir [ur'dʒir] VT to weave; (fig: maquinar) to weave, hatch

urdu [ur'du] M (Ling) Urdu

uretra [u'retra] F urethra

urgência [ur'ʒẽsja] F urgency; **com toda** ~ as quickly as possible; **de** ~ urgent; **pedir algo com** ~ to ask for sth insistently

urgente [ur'ʒẽtʃi] ADJ urgent

urgir [ur'ʒir] VI to be urgent; (tempo) to be pressing ▶ VT to require urgently; **são providências que urge sejam tomadas** they are steps which urgently need to be taken; **urge fazermos** we must do

urina [u'rina] F urine

urinado, -a [uri'nadu, a] ADJ (molhado) soaked with urine; (manchado) urine-stained

urinar [uri'nar] VI to urinate ▶ VT (sangue) to pass; (cama) to wet; **urinar-se** VR to wet o.s.

urinário, -a [uri'narju, a] ADJ urinary

urinol [uri'nɔw] (pl **-óis**) M chamber pot

urna ['urna] F urn; **urnas** FPL (eleições): **as ~s** the polls; ~ **eleitoral** ballot box

urologia [urolo'ʒia] F urology

urologista [urolo'ʒista] M/F urologist

URP (BR) ABR F = **Unidade de Referência de Preços**

URPE (BR) ABR FPL = **Urgências Pediátricas**

urrar [u'har] VT, VI to roar; (de dor) to yell

urro ['uhu] M roar; (de dor) yell

ursa ['ursa] F bear; **U~ Maior/Menor** Ursa Major/Minor

urso ['ursu] M bear

urso-branco (pl **ursos-brancos**) M polar bear

URSS ABR F (= União das Repúblicas Socialistas Soviéticas): **a** ~ the USSR

urticária [urtʃi'karja] F nettle rash

urtiga [ur'tʃiga] F nettle

urubu [uru'bu] M vulture

urubusservar [urubuser'var] (col) VT, VI to watch

urucubaca [uruku'baka] F bad luck; **estar com uma** ~ to be unlucky

Uruguai [uru'gwaj] M: **o** ~ Uruguay

uruguaio, -a [uru'gwaju, a] ADJ, M/F Uruguayan

urze ['urzi] M heather

usado, -a [u'zadu, a] ADJ used; (comum) common; (roupa) worn; (gasto) worn out; (de segunda mão) second-hand; ~ **a** (acostumado) accustomed to

usar [u'zar] VT (servir-se de) to use; (vestir) to wear; (gastar com o uso) to wear out; (barba, cabelo curto) to have, wear ▶ VI: ~ **de** to use; ~ **fazer** to be in the habit of doing; **modo de** ~ directions pl

usina [u'zina] F (fábrica) factory; (de energia) plant; ~ **de açúcar** sugar mill; ~ **de aço** steelworks; ~ **hidrelétrica** hydroelectric power station; ~ **termonuclear** nuclear power plant

usineiro, -a [uzi'nejru, a] ADJ plant atr ▶ M/F sugar mill owner

uso ['uzu] M (emprego) use; (utilização) usage; (prática) practice; (moda) fashion; (costume) custom; (vestir) wearing; ~ **e desgaste normal** (Com) fair wear and tear

USP ['uspi] ABR F = **Universidade de São Paulo**

usual [u'zwaw] (pl **-ais**) ADJ usual; (comum) common

usuário, -a [u'zwarju, a] M/F user; ~ **do telefone** telephone subscriber

usucapião [uzuka'pjãw] M (Jur) prescription

usufruir [uzu'frwir] VT to enjoy ▶ VI: ~ **de** to enjoy

usufruto [uzu'frutu] M (Jur) usufruct

usura [u'zura] F (juro) interest; (avareza) avarice

usurário, -a [uzu'rarju, a] M/F (avaro) miser; (col: agiota) loan shark ▶ ADJ avaricious

usurpar [uzur'par] VT to usurp

úteis ['utejs] PL de **útil**

utensílio [utẽ'silju] M utensil

uterino, -a [ute'rinu, a] ADJ uterine

útero ['uteru] M womb, uterus

UTI ['utʃi] ABR F (= Unidade de Terapia Intensiva) intensive care (unit), ICU

útil ['utʃiw] (pl **-eis**) ADJ useful; (vantajoso) profitable, worthwhile; (tempo) working; (prazo) stipulated; **dias úteis** weekdays, working days; **em que lhe posso ser** ~? how can I be of assistance (to you)?

utilidade [utʃili'dadʒi] F usefulness; (vantagem) advantage; (utensílio) utility

utilitário, -a [utʃili'tarju, a] ADJ utilitarian, practical; (pessoa) matter-of-fact, pragmatic; (veículo) general purpose atr; **programa** ~ (Comput) utilities program

utilização [utʃiliza'sãw] F use

utilizador, a [utʃiliza'dor(a)] (PT) M/F user

utilizar [utʃili'zar] VT to use; **utilizar-se** VR: ~~**-se de** to make use of

utilizável [utʃili'zavew] (pl **-eis**) ADJ usable

utopia [uto'pia] F Utopia

utópico, -a [u'tɔpiku, a] ADJ Utopian

uva ['uva] F grape; (col: mulher) peach; (: coisa) lovely thing; **ser uma** ~ (pessoa, objeto) to be lovely; **uma** ~ **de pessoa/broche** a lovely person/brooch

úvula ['uvula] F uvula

Vv

V, v [ve] (*pl* **vs**) M V, v; **V de Vera** V for Victor
v ABR (= *volt*) v
vá *etc* [va] VB *ver* **ir**
vã [vã] F *de* **vão²**
vaca ['vaka] F COW; **carne de** ~ beef; **tempo das ~s magras** (*fig*) lean period; **a ~ foi para o brejo** (*fig*) everything went wrong; **voltar à ~ fria** to get back to the subject
vacância [va'kãsja] F vacancy
vacante [va'kãtʃi] ADJ vacant
vaca-preta (*pl* **vacas-pretas**) F *coca-cola with ice cream*
vacilação [vasila'sãw] F (*hesitação*) hesitation; (*balanço*) swaying
vacilada [vasi'lada] F slip-up; **dar uma ~** (*col*) to slip up
vacilante [vasi'lãtʃi] ADJ (*hesitante*) hesitant; (*pouco firme*) unsteady; (*luz*) flickering
vacilar [vasi'lar] VI (*hesitar*) to hesitate; (*balançar*) to sway; (*cambalear*) to stagger; (*luz*) to flicker; (*col*) to slip up
vacina [va'sina] F vaccine
vacinação [vasina'sãw] (*pl* **-ões**) F vaccination
vacinar [vasi'nar] VT to vaccinate; (*fig*) to immunize; **vacinar-se** VR to take vaccine
vacuidade [vakwi'dadʒi] F emptiness
vacum [va'kũ] ADJ: **gado** ~ cattle
vácuo ['vakwu] M vacuum; (*fig*) void; (*espaço*) space; **empacotado a** ~ vacuum-packed
vadear [va'dʒjar] VT to wade through
vadiação [vadʒja'sãw] F vagrancy
vadiagem [va'dʒjaʒẽ] F = **vadiação**
vadiar [va'dʒjar] VI to lounge about; (*não trabalhar*) to idle about; (*não estudar*) to skive; (*perambular*) to wander
vadio, -a [va'dʒiu, a] ADJ (*ocioso*) idle, lazy; (*vagabundo*) vagrant ▸ M/F idler; vagabond, vagrant
vaga ['vaga] F (*onda*) wave; (*em hotel, trabalho*) vacancy; (*em estacionamento*) parking place; **ser bom de** ~ to be good at parking
vagabundear [vagabũ'dʒjar] VI to wander about, roam about; (*vadiar*) to laze around
vagabundo, -a [vaga'bũdu, a] ADJ (*vadio*) lazy, idle; (*de má qualidade*) shoddy; (*canalha*) rotten; (*mulher*) easy ▸ M/F tramp; (*canalha*) bum
vagalhão [vaga'ʎãw] (*pl* **-ões**) M big wave, breaker

vaga-lume [vaga'lumi] (*pl* **vaga-lumes**) M (*Zool*) glow-worm; (*no cinema*) usher
vagão [va'gãw] (*pl* **-ões**) M (*de passageiros*) carriage; (*de cargas*) wagon
vagão-leito (*pl* **vagões-leitos**) (PT) M sleeping car
vagão-restaurante (*pl* **vagões-restaurantes**) M buffet car
vagar [va'gar] VI to wander about, roam about; (*barco*) to drift; (*ficar vago*) to be vacant ▸ M slowness; **fazer algo com mais** ~ to do sth at a more leisurely pace
vagareza [vaga'reza] F slowness; **com** ~ slowly
vagaroso, -a [vaga'rozu, ɔza] ADJ slow
vagem ['vaʒẽ] (*pl* **-ns**) F green bean
vagido [va'ʒidu] M wail
vagina [va'ʒina] F vagina
vaginal [vaʒi'naw] (*pl* **-ais**) ADJ vaginal
vago, -a ['vagu, a] ADJ (*indefinido*) vague; (*desocupado*) vacant, free; **tempo** ~, **horas vagas** spare time
vagões [va'gõjs] MPL *de* **vagão**
vaguear [va'gjar] VI to wander, roam; (*passear*) to ramble
vai *etc* [vaj] VB *ver* **ir**
vaia ['vaja] F booing
vaiar [va'jar] VT, VI to boo, hiss
vaidade [vaj'dadʒi] F vanity; (*futilidade*) futility
vai da valsa M: **ir no** ~ to take life as it comes, go with the flow
vaidoso, -a [vaj'dozu, ɔza] ADJ vain
vai e vem M INV = **vaivém**
vai não vai M INV shilly-shallying
vaivém [vaj'vẽj] M to-ing and fro-ing
vala ['vala] F ditch; ~ **comum** pauper's grave
vale ['vali] M valley; (*poético*) vale; (*escrito*) voucher; (*reconhecimento de dívida*) I O U; ~ **postal** postal order
valentão, -tona [valẽ'tãw, 'tɔna] (*pl* **-ões/-s**) ADJ tough ▸ M/F tough nut
valente [va'lẽtʃi] ADJ brave
valentia [valẽ'tʃia] F courage, bravery; (*proeza*) feat
valentões [valẽ'tõjs] MPL *de* **valentão**
valentona [valẽ'tɔna] F *de* **valentão**
valer [va'ler] VI to be worth; (*ser válido*) to be

V

valid; (ter influência) to carry weight; (servir) to serve; (ser proveitoso) to be useful; **valer-se** VR: **~-se de** to use, make use of; **~ a pena** to be worthwhile; **não vale a pena** it isn't worth it; **vale a pena fazer** it is worth doing; **~ a** (ajudar) to help; **~ por** (equivaler) to be worth the same as; **para ~** (muito) very much, a lot; (realmente) for real, properly; **vale dizer** in other words; **vale examinar os seus direitos** to stand up for one's rights; **vale examinar os detalhes** we should examine the details; **mais vale ... (do que ...)** it would be better to ... (than ...); **não vale empurrar** (Esporte etc) you're not allowed to push; **assim não vale!** that's not fair!; **vale tudo** anything goes; **ser para ~** (col) to be for real; **ou coisa que o valha** or something like it; **valeu!** (col) you bet!

valeta [va'leta] F gutter

valete [va'letʃi] M (Cartas) jack

vale-tudo M INV (Esporte) all-in wrestling; (fig) "anything goes" principle

valha etc ['vaʎa] VB ver **valer**

valia [va'lia] F value; **de grande ~** valuable

validação [valida'sãw] F validation

validade [vali'dadʒi] F validity; (de cartão de crédito) expiry date (BRIT), expiration date (US); (de alimento) best-before date

validar [vali'dar] VT to validate, make valid

válido, -a ['validu, a] ADJ valid

valioso, -a [va'ljozu, ɔza] ADJ valuable

valise [va'lizi] F case, grip

valor [va'lor] M value; (mérito) merit; (coragem) courage; (preço) price; (importância) importance; **valores** MPL (morais) values; (num exame) marks; (Com) securities; **dar ~ a** to value; **sem ~** worthless; **no ~ de** to the value of; **objetos de ~** valuables; **~ nominal** face value; **~ contábil** ou **contabilizado** (Com) book value; **~ ao par** (Com) par value

valorização [valoriza'sãw] F increase in value

valorizar [valori'zar] VT to value; (aumentar o valor) to raise the value of; **valorizar-se** VR to go up in value; (pessoa) to value o.s.

valoroso, -a [valo'rozu, ɔza] ADJ brave

valsa ['vawsa] F waltz

válvula ['vawvula] F valve

vampe ['vãpi] F vamp, femme fatale

vampiro, -a [vã'piru, a] M/F vampire

vandalismo [vãda'lizmu] M vandalism

vândalo, -a ['vãdalu, a] M/F vandal

vangloriar-se [vãglo'rjarsi] VR: **~ de** to boast of ou about

vanguarda [vã'gwarda] F vanguard, forefront; (arte) avant-garde; **artista de ~** avant-garde artist

vantagem [vã'taʒẽ] (pl **-ns**) F advantage; (ganho) profit, benefit; **contar ~** (col) to brag, boast; **levar ~** to get the upper hand; **tirar ~ de** to take advantage of

vantajoso, -a [vãta'ʒozu, ɔza] ADJ advantageous; (lucrativo) profitable; (proveitoso) beneficial

vão¹ [vãw] VB ver **ir**

vão², vã [vãw, vã] (pl **-s/-s**) ADJ vain; (fútil) futile ▶ M (intervalo) space; (de porta etc) opening; (Arq) empty space; **em ~** in vain

vapor [va'por] M steam; (navio) steamer; (de gas) vapour (BRIT), vapor (US); **cozer no ~** to steam; **ferro a ~** steam iron; **a todo o ~** at full speed

vaporizador [vaporiza'dor] M vaporizer; (de perfume) spray

vaporizar [vapori'zar] VT to vaporize; (perfume) to spray

vaporoso, -a [vapo'rozu, ɔza] ADJ steamy, misty; (transparente) transparent, see-through

vaqueiro [va'kejru] M cowboy, cowhand

vaquinha [va'kiɲa] F: **fazer uma ~** to have a whip-round

vara ['vara] F (pau) stick; (Tec) rod; (Jur) jurisdiction; (de porcos) herd; **salto de ~** pole vault; **~ de condão** magic wand

varal [va'raw] (pl **-ais**) M clothes line

varanda [va'rãda] F verandah; (balcão) balcony

varão, -roa [va'rãw, 'roa] (pl **-ões/-s**) ADJ male ▶ M man, male; (de ferro) rod

varapau [vara'paw] (col) M (pessoa) beanpole

varar [va'rar] VT (furar) to pierce; (passar) to cross ▶ VI to beach, run aground

varejar [vare'ʒar] VT (com vara) to beat; (revistar) to search

varejeira [vare'ʒejra] F bluebottle

varejista [vare'ʒista] (BR) M/F retailer ▶ ADJ (mercado) retail

varejo [va'reʒu] (BR) M (Com) retail trade; **loja de ~** retail store; **a ~** retail; **preço no ~** retail price

variação [varja'sãw] (pl **-ões**) F variation, change

variado, -a [va'rjadu, a] ADJ varied; (sortido) assorted

variante [va'rjãtʃi] ADJ, F variant

variar [va'rjar] VT, VI to vary; **para ~** for a change

variável [va'rjavew] (pl **-eis**) ADJ variable; (tempo, humor) changeable ▶ F variable

varicela [vari'sɛla] F chickenpox

variedade [varje'dadʒi] F variety; **variedades** FPL (Teatro) variety sg; **espetáculo/teatro de ~s** variety show/theatre (BRIT) ou theater (US)

Varig ['varigi] ABR F (= Viação Aérea Rio-Grandense) Brazilian national airline

varinha [va'riɲa] F wand; **~ de condão** magic wand

vário, -a ['varju, a] ADJ (diverso) varied; (pl) various, several; (Com) sundry

varíola [va'riola] F smallpox

varizes [va'rizis] FPL varicose veins

varoa [va'roa] F de **varão**

varões [va'rõjs] MPL de **varão**

varonil [varo'niw] (pl **-is**) ADJ manly, virile

VAR-Palmares ABR F (= Vanguarda Armada Revolucionária) former Brazilian terrorist movement

varredor, a [vahe'dor(a)] ADJ sweeping ▶ M/F sweeper; **~ de rua** road sweeper

varrer [va'her] VT to sweep; (*sala*) to sweep out; (*folhas*) to sweep up; (*fig*) to sweep away

varrido, -a [va'hidu, a] ADJ: **um doido ~** a raving lunatic

Varsóvia [var'sɔvja] N Warsaw; **pacto de ~** Warsaw Pact

várzea ['vahzja] F meadow, field

vascular [vasku'lar] ADJ vascular

vasculhar [vasku'ʎar] VT (*pesquisar*) to research; (*remexer*) to rummage through

vasectomia [vazekto'mia] F vasectomy

vaselina® [vaze'lina] F Vaseline®; (*col: pessoa*) smooth talker

vasilha [va'ziʎa] F (*para líquidos*) jug; (*para alimentos*) dish, container; (*barril*) barrel

vaso ['vazu] M pot; (*para flores*) vase; **~ (sanitário)** toilet (bowl); **~ sanguíneo** blood vessel

Vasp ['vaspi] ABR F (= *Viação Aérea de São Paulo*) Brazilian internal airline

vassoura [va'sora] F broom

vastidão [vastʃi'dãw] F vastness, immensity

vasto, -a ['vastu, a] ADJ vast

vatapá [vata'pa] M *fish or chicken with coconut milk, shrimps, peanuts, palm oil and spices*

Vaticano [vatʃi'kanu] M: **o ~** the Vatican; **a Cidade do ~** the Vatican City

vaticinar [vatʃisi'nar] VT to foretell, prophesy

vaticínio [vatʃi'sinju] M prophecy

vau [vaw] M ford, river crossing; (*Náut*) beam

vazamento [vaza'mẽtu] M leak

vazante [va'zãtʃi] F ebb tide

vazão [va'zãw] (*pl* **-ões**) F flow; (*venda*) sale; **dar ~ a** (*expressar*) to give vent to; (*Com*) to clear; (*atender*) to deal with; (*resolver*) to attend to

vazar [va'zar] VT (*tornar vazio*) to empty; (*derramar*) to spill; (*verter*) to pour out ▶ VI to leak; (*maré*) to go out; (*notícia*) to leak; **ser vazado em** (*moldado*) to be modelled on

vazio, -a [va'ziu, a] ADJ empty; (*pessoa*) empty-headed, frivolous; (*cidade*) deserted ▶ M (*tb fig*) emptiness; (*deixado por alguém/algo*) void; **~ de** (*fig: sem*) devoid of

vazões [va'zõjs] FPL *de* **vazão**

VBC (*BR*) ABR M = **Valor Básico de Custeio**

vê *etc* [ve] VB *ver* **ver**

veado ['vjadu] M deer; (*BR col: ofensivo*) poof (*BRIT !*), fag (*US !*); **carne de ~** venison

vedado, -a [ve'dadu, a] ADJ (*proibido*) forbidden; (*fechado*) enclosed

vedar [ve'dar] VT (*proibir*) to ban, prohibit; (*sangue*) to stop (the flow of); (*buraco*) to stop up; (*garrafa*) to cork; (*entrada, passagem*) to block; (*terreno*) to close off

vedete [ve'dɛtʃi] F star

veemência [vje'mẽsja] F vehemence

veemente [vje'mẽtʃi] ADJ vehement

vegetação [veʒeta'sãw] F vegetation

vegetal [veʒe'taw] (*pl* **-ais**) ADJ vegetable *atr*; (*reino, vida*) plant *atr* ▶ M vegetable; **medicamento ~** herbal remedy

vegetalista [veʒeta'lista] ADJ, M/F vegan

vegetar [veʒe'tar] VI to vegetate

vegetariano, -a [veʒeta'rjanu, a] ADJ, M/F vegetarian

vegetativo, -a [veʒeta'tʃivu, a] ADJ: **vida vegetativa** (*fig*) insular life

veia ['veja] F (*Med, Bot*) vein; (*fig: pendor*) bent

veicular [vejku'lar] VT (*em TV, rádio*) to broadcast; (*em jornal*) to carry

veículo [ve'ikulu] M (*tb fig*) vehicle; **~ de propaganda** advertising medium

veio¹ ['veju] M (*de rocha*) vein; (*na mina*) seam; (*de madeira*) grain; (*eixo*) shaft

veio² VB *ver* **vir¹**

vejo *etc* ['veʒu] VB *ver* **ver**

vela ['vɛla] F candle; (*Auto*) spark plug; (*Náut*) sail; **fazer-se à** *ou* **de ~** to set sail; **segurar a ~** (*col*) to play gooseberry; **barco à ~** sailing boat; **~ mestra** mainsail

velar [ve'lar] VT (*cobrir*) to veil; (*ocultar*) to hide; (*vigiar*) to keep watch over; (*um doente*) to sit up with ▶ VI (*não dormir*) to stay up; (*vigiar*) to keep watch; **~ por** to look after

veleidade [velej'dadʒi] F (*capricho*) whim, fancy; (*inconstância*) fickleness

veleiro [ve'lejru] M (*barco*) sailing boat

velejar [vele'ʒar] VI to sail

velhaco, -a [ve'ʎaku, a] ADJ crooked ▶ M/F crook

velha-guarda F old guard

velharia [veʎa'ria] F (*os velhos*) old people *pl*; (*coisa*) old thing

velhice [ve'ʎisi] F old age

velho, -a ['vɛʎu, a] ADJ old ▶ M/F old man/ woman; (*col: pai/mãe*) old man/lady; **meus ~s** (*col: pais*) my folks; **meu ~!** (*col*) old chap

velhote, -ta [ve'ʎɔtʃi, ta] ADJ elderly ▶ M/F elderly man/woman

velocidade [velosi'dadʒi] F speed, velocity; (*PT Auto*) gear; **a toda ~** at full speed; **trem de alta ~** high-speed train; **"diminua a ~"** "reduce speed now"; **~ máxima** (*em estrada*) speed limit; **~ de processamento** (*Comput*) processing speed

velocímetro [velo'simetru] M speedometer

velocíssimo, -a [velo'sisimu, a] ADJ SUPERL *de* **veloz**

velocista [velo'sista] M/F sprinter

velódromo [ve'lɔdromu] M cycle track

velório [ve'lɔrju] M wake

veloz [ve'lɔz] ADJ fast

velozmente [veloz'mẽtʃi] ADV fast

veludo [ve'ludu] M velvet; **~ cotelê** corduroy

vem [vẽj] VB *ver* **vir¹**

vêm [vẽj] VB *ver* **vir¹**

vencedor, a [vẽse'dor(a)] ADJ winning ▶ M/F winner

vencer [vẽ'ser] VT (*num jogo*) to beat; (*competição*) to win; (*inimigo*) to defeat; (*exceder*) to surpass; (*obstáculos*) to overcome; (*percorrer*) to pass ▶ VI (*num jogo*) to win; **vencer(-se)** VR (*prazo*) to run out; (*promissória*) to become due; (*apólice*) to mature

V

vencido, -a [vẽ'sidu, a] ADJ: **dar-se por ~** to give in

vencimento [vẽsi'mẽtu] M (Com) expiry; (: de letra, dívida) maturation; (data) expiry date; (: de promissória) due date; (salário) salary; (de gêneros alimentícios etc) sell-by date; **vencimentos** MPL (ganhos) earnings

venda ['vẽda] F sale; (pano) blindfold; (mercearia) general store; **à ~** on sale, for sale; **pôr algo à ~** to put sth up for sale; **preço de ~** selling price; **~ a crédito** credit sale; **~ a prazo** ou **prestação** sale in instal(l)ments; **~ à vista** cash sale; **~ por atacado** wholesale; **~ pelo correio** mail-order

vendar [vẽ'dar] VT to blindfold

vendaval [vẽda'vaw] (pl **-ais**) M gale

vendável [vẽ'davew] (pl **-eis**) ADJ marketable

vendedor, a [vẽde'dor(a)] M/F seller; (em loja) sales assistant; (de imóvel) vendor; **~ ambulante** street vendor

vender [vẽ'der] VT, VI to sell; **vender-se** VR (pessoa) to allow o.s. to be bribed; **~ por atacado/a varejo** to sell wholesale/retail; **~ fiado/a prestações** ou **a prazo** to sell on credit/in instal(l)ments; **~ à vista** to sell for cash; **ela está vendendo saúde** she's bursting with health

vendeta [vẽ'deta] F vendetta

vendinha [vẽ'diɲa] F corner shop

veneno [ve'nɛnu] M poison; (fig, de serpente) venom; **ser um ~ para** (fig) to be very bad for

venenoso, -a [vene'nozu, ɔza] ADJ poisonous; (fig) venomous

veneração [venera'sãw] F reverence

venerar [vene'rar] VT to revere; (Rel) to worship

venéreo, -a [ve'nɛrju, a] ADJ: **doença venérea** venereal disease

veneta [ve'neta] F: **ser de ~** (pessoa) to be moody; **deu-lhe na ~ (que)** he got it into his head (that)

Veneza [ve'neza] N Venice

veneziana [vene'zjana] F (porta) louvre (BRIT) ou louver (US) door; (janela) louvre ou louver window

Venezuela [vene'zwɛla] F: **a ~** Venezuela

venezuelano, -a [venezwe'lanu, a] ADJ, M/F Venezuelan

venha etc ['veɲa] VB ver **vir¹**

vênia ['venja] F (desculpa) forgiveness; (licença) permission

venial [ve'njaw] (pl **-ais**) ADJ venial, forgiveable

venta ['vẽta] F nostril; **ventas** FPL (nariz) nose sg

ventania [vẽta'nia] F gale

ventar [vẽ'tar] VI: **está ventando** it is windy

ventarola [vẽta'rɔla] F fan

ventilação [vẽtʃila'sãw] F ventilation

ventilador [vẽtʃila'dor] M ventilator; (elétrico) fan

ventilar [vẽtʃi'lar] VT to ventilate; (roupa, sala) to air; (fig) to discuss; (: hipótese, possibilidade) to entertain

vento ['vẽtu] M wind; (brisa) breeze; **de ~ em popa** (fig) swimmingly, very well

ventoinha [vẽ'twiɲa] F (cata-vento) weathercock, weather vane; (PT Auto) fan

ventoso, -a [vẽ'tozu, ɔza] ADJ windy

ventre ['vẽtri] M belly; (literário: útero) womb

ventríloquo, -a [vẽ'trilokwu, a] M/F ventriloquist

ventura [vẽ'tura] F fortune; (felicidade) happiness; **se por ~** if by any chance

venturoso, -a [vẽtu'rozu, ɔza] ADJ happy

Vênus ['venus] F Venus

ver [ver] VT to see; (olhar para, examinar) to look at; (resolver) to see to; (televisão) to watch ▶ VI to see ▶ M: **a meu ~** in my opinion; **ver-se** VR (achar-se) to be, find o.s.; (no espelho) to see o.s.; (duas pessoas) to see each other; **vai ~ que ...** maybe ...; **viu?** (col) OK?; **deixa eu ~** let me see; **ele tem um carro que só vendo** (col) he's got a car like you wouldn't believe; **não tem nada a ~ (com)** it has nothing to do (with); **não tenho nada que ~ com isto** it is nothing to do with me, it is none of my concern; **~-se com** to settle accounts with; **bem se vê que** it's obvious that; **já se vê** of course; **pelo que se vê** apparently

veracidade [verasi'dadʒi] F truthfulness

veranear [vera'njar] VI to spend the summer; (tirar férias) to take summer holidays (BRIT) ou a summer vacation (US)

veraneio [vera'neju] M summer holidays pl (BRIT) ou vacation (US)

veranista [vera'nista] M/F holidaymaker (BRIT), (summer) vacationer (US)

verão [ve'rãw] (pl **-ões**) M summer

veraz [ve'rajz] ADJ truthful

verba ['vɛrba] F allowance; **verba(s)** F(PL) (recursos) funds pl

verbal [ver'baw] (pl **-ais**) ADJ verbal

verbalizar [verbali'zar] VT, VI to verbalize

verbete [ver'betʃi] M (num dicionário) entry

verbo ['vɛrbu] M verb; **deitar o ~** (col) to say a few words; **soltar o ~** (col) to start talking

verborragia [verboha'ʒia] F verbiage, waffle

verboso, -a [ver'bozu, ɔza] ADJ wordy, verbose

verdade [ver'dadʒi] F truth; **na ~** in fact; **é ~** it's true; **é ~?** (col) really?; **uma princesa de ~** a real princess; **de ~** (falar) truthfully; (ameaçar etc) really; **dizer umas ~s a alguém** to tell sb a few home truths; **a ~ nua e crua** the plain truth; **para falar a ~** to tell the truth; **..., não é ~?** (col) ..., isn't that so?

verdadeiramente [verdadejra'mẽtʃi] ADV really

verdadeiro, -a [verda'dejru, a] ADJ true; (genuíno) real; (pessoa) truthful; **foi um ~ desastre** it was a real disaster

verde ['verdʒi] ADJ green; (fruta) unripe; (fig) inexperienced ▶ M green; (plantas etc) greenery; **~ de medo** pale with fear; **~ de fome/raiva** terribly hungry/angry; **jogar ~ (para colher maduro)** to fish, ask leading questions; **Partido V~** Green Party

verde-abacate ADJ INV avocado (green)
verde-garrafa ADJ INV bottle-green
verdejar [verde'ʒar] VI to turn green
verdor [ver'dor] M greenness; (Bot) greenery; (fig) inexperience
verdugo [ver'dugu] M executioner; (fig) beast
verdura [ver'dura] F (hortaliça) greens pl; (Bot) greenery; (cor verde) greenness
verdureiro, -a [verdu'rejru, a] M/F greengrocer (BRIT), produce dealer (US)
vereador, a [verja'dor(a)] M/F councillor (BRIT), councilor (US)
vereda [ve'reda] F path
veredicto [vere'dʒiktu] M verdict
verga ['verga] F (vara) stick; (de metal) rod
vergão [ver'gãw] (pl -ões) M weal
vergar [ver'gar] VT (curvar) to bend ▶ VI to bend; (com um peso) to sag
vergões [ver'gõjs] MPL de **vergão**
vergonha [ver'gɔɲa] F shame; (timidez) embarrassment; (humilhação) humiliation; (ato indecoroso) indecency; (brio) self-respect; **é uma ~** it's disgraceful; **ter ~** to be ashamed; (tímido) to be shy; **ter ~ de fazer** to be ashamed of doing; (ser tímido) to be too shy to do; **não ter ~ na cara** to have a cheek, have no shame
vergonhoso, -a [vergo'ɲozo, ɔza] ADJ (infame) shameful; (indecoroso) disgraceful
verídico, -a [ve'ridʒiku, a] ADJ true, truthful
verificação [verifika'sãw] F (exame) checking; (confirmação) verification
verificar [verifi'kar] VT to check; (confirmar, Comput) to verify; **verificar-se** VR (acontecer) to happen; (realizar-se) to come true; **~ se ...** to check that ...
verme ['vermi] M worm
vermelhidão [vermeʎi'dãw] F redness; (da pele) rosiness
vermelho, -a [ver'meʎu, a] ADJ red ▶ M red; **estar no ~** to be in the red; **ficar ~** to go red
vermute [ver'mutʃi] M vermouth
vernáculo, -a [ver'nakulu, a] ADJ: **língua vernácula** vernacular ▶ M vernacular
vernissage [verni'saz] M opening, vernissage
verniz [ver'niz] M varnish; (couro) patent leather; (fig) whitewash; (: polidez) veneer; **sapatos de ~** patent shoes
verões [ve'rõjs] MPL de **verão**
verossímil [vero'simiw], (PT) **verosímil** (pl -eis) ADJ (provável) likely, probable; (crível) credible
verossimilhança [verosimi'ʎãsa], (PT) **verosimilhança** F probability
verruga [ve'huga] F wart
versado, -a [ver'sadu, a] ADJ: **~ em** clever at, good at
versão [ver'sãw] (pl -ões) F version; (tradução) translation
versar [ver'sar] VI: **~ sobre** to be about, concern
versátil [ver'satʃiw] (pl -eis) ADJ versatile
versatilidade [versatʃili'dadʒi] F versatility

versículo [ver'sikulu] M (Rel) verse; (de artigo) paragraph
verso ['versu] M verse; (linha) line of poetry; (da página) other side, reverse; **vide ~** see over; **~ solto** blank verse; **~s brancos** blank verse sg
versões [ver'sõjs] FPL de **versão**
vértebra ['vertebra] F vertebra
vertebrado, -a [verte'bradu, a] ADJ vertebrate ▶ M vertebrate
vertebral [verte'braw] (pl -ais) ADJ: **coluna ~** spine
vertente [ver'tẽtʃi] F slope
verter [ver'ter] VT to pour; (por acaso) to spill; (traduzir) to translate; (lágrimas, sangue) to shed ▶ VI: **~ de** to spring from; **~ em** (rio) to flow into
vertical [vertʃi'kaw] (pl -ais) ADJ vertical; (de pé) upright, standing ▶ F vertical
vértice ['vertʃisi] M apex
vertigem [ver'tʃiʒẽ] F (medo de altura) vertigo; (tonteira) dizziness
vertiginoso, -a [vertʃiʒi'nozu, ɔza] ADJ dizzy, giddy; (velocidade) frenetic
verve ['vervi] F verve
vesgo, -a ['vezgu, a] ADJ cross-eyed
vesícula [ve'zikula] F: **~ (biliar)** gall bladder
vespa ['vespa] F wasp
véspera ['vespera] F: **a ~ (de)** the day before; **vésperas** FPL (Rel) vespers; **a ~ de Natal** Christmas Eve; **nas ~s de** on the eve of; (de eleição etc) in the run-up to; **estar nas ~s de** to be about to
vesperal [vespe'raw] (pl -ais) ADJ afternoon atr ▶ F matinée
vespertino, -a [vesper'tʃinu, a] ADJ evening atr
veste ['vestʃi] F garment; (Rel) vestment, robe
vestiário [ves'tʃjarju] M (em casa, teatro) cloakroom; (Esporte) changing room (BRIT), locker-room (US); (de ator) dressing room
vestibular [vestʃibu'lar] M college entrance exam
vestíbulo [ves'tʃibulu] M hall(way), vestibule; (Teatro) foyer
vestido, -a [ves'tʃidu, a] ADJ: **~ de branco** etc dressed in white etc ▶ M dress; **~ de baile** ball gown; **~ de noiva** wedding dress
vestidura [vestʃi'dura] F (Rel) robe
vestígio [ves'tʃiʒju] M (rastro) track; (fig) sign, trace
vestimenta [vestʃi'mẽta] F (roupa) garment; (Rel) vestment
vestir [ves'tʃir] VT (uma criança) to dress; (pôr sobre si) to put on; (trajar) to wear; (comprar, dar roupa para) to clothe; (fazer roupa para) to make clothes for; **vestir-se** VR to dress; (pôr roupa) to get dressed; **~-se de algo** to dress up as sth; **ela se veste naquela butique** she buys her clothes in that boutique; **~-se de preto** etc to dress in black etc; **este terno veste bem** this suit is a good fit
vestuário [ves'twarju] M clothing
vetar [ve'tar] VT to veto; (proibir) to forbid

V

veterano, -a [vete'ranu, a] ADJ, M/F veteran

veterinário, -a [veteri'narju, a] ADJ veterinary ▶ M/F vet(erinary surgeon)

veto ['vɛtu] M veto

véu [vɛw] M veil; **~ do paladar** (Anat) soft palate, velum

vexame [ve'ʃami] F (vergonha) shame, disgrace; (tormento) affliction; (humilhação) humiliation; (afronta) insult; **passar um ~** to be disgraced; **dar um ~** to make a fool of o.s.

vexaminoso, -a [veʃami'nozu, ɔza] ADJ shameful, disgraceful

vexar [ve'ʃar] VT (atormentar) to upset; (envergonhar) to put to shame; **vexar-se** VR to be ashamed

vez [vez] F time; (turno) turn; **uma ~** once; **duas ~es** twice; **alguma ~** ever; **algumas ~es, às ~es** sometimes; **~ por outra** sometimes; **cada ~ (que)** every time; **cada ~ mais/menos** more and more/less and less; **desta ~** this time; **de ~** once and for all; **de uma ~** (ao mesmo tempo) at once; (de um golpe) in one go; **de ~ em quando** from time to time; **em ~ de** instead of; **fazer as ~es de** (pessoa) to stand in for; (coisa) to replace; **mais uma ~, outra ~** again, once more; **raras ~es** seldom; **uma ~ que** since; **3 ~es 6** 3 times 6; **de uma ~ por todas** once and for all; **ter ~** (pessoa) to have a chance; (argumento etc) to apply; **muitas ~es** many times; (frequentemente) often; **mais ~es** more often; **na maioria das ~es** most times; **toda ~ que** every time; **um de cada ~** one at a time; **repetidas ~es** repeatedly; **uma ~ ou outra** once in a while; **uma ~ na vida, outra na morte** once in a blue moon; **era uma ~ ...** once upon a time there was ....

vi [vi] VB ver **ver**

via¹ ['via] F road, route; (meio) way; (documento) copy; (conduto) channel ▶ PREP via, by way of; **~ aérea** airmail; **~ de acesso** access road; **V~ Láctea** Milky Way; **primeira ~** (de documento) top copy; **chegar às ~s de fato** to come to blows; **em ~s de** in the process of; **por ~ aérea** by airmail; **por ~ das dúvidas** just in case; **por ~ de regra** generally, as a rule; **por ~ terrestre/marítima** by land/sea

via² etc VB ver **ver**

viabilidade [vjabili'dadʒi] F feasibility, viability

viação [vja'sāw] (pl -ões) F transport; (companhia de ônibus) bus (ou coach) company; (conjunto de estradas) roads pl

viaduto [vja'dutu] M viaduct

viageiro, -a [vja'ʒejru, a] ADJ travelling (BRIT), traveling (US)

viagem ['vjaʒē] (pl -ns) F journey, trip; (o viajar) travel; (Náut) voyage; (com droga) trip; **viagens** FPL (jornadas) travels; **~ de ida e volta** return trip, round trip; **~ de núpcias** honeymoon; **~ de ida** outward trip; **~ de negócios** business trip; **~ inaugural** (Náut) maiden voyage; **boa ~!** bon voyage!, have a good trip!

viajado, -a [vja'ʒadu, a] ADJ well-travelled (BRIT), well-traveled (US)

viajante [vja'ʒãtʃi] ADJ travelling (BRIT), traveling (US) ▶ M traveller (BRIT), traveler (US); (Com) commercial travel(l)er

viajar [vja'ʒar] VI to travel; **~ por** to travel, tour

viário, -a ['vjarju, a] ADJ road atr

viatura [vja'tura] F vehicle

viável ['vjavew] (pl -eis) ADJ feasible, viable

víbora ['vibora] F viper; (fig: pessoa) snake in the grass

vibração [vibra'sāw] (pl -ões) F vibration; (fig) thrill

vibrante [vi'brātʃi] ADJ vibrant; (discurso) stirring

vibrar [vi'brar] VT (brandir) to brandish; (fazer estremecer) to vibrate; (cordas) to strike ▶ VI to vibrate; (som) to echo; (col) to be thrilled

vice ['visi] M/F deputy

vice- [visi-] PREFIXO vice-

vice-campeão, -peã (pl -ões/-s) M/F runner-up

vicejar [vise'ʒar] VI to flourish

vice-presidente, -a M/F vice president

vice-rei M viceroy

vice-reitor, a M/F deputy head

vice-versa [-'vɛrsa] ADV vice versa

viciado, -a [vi'sjadu, a] ADJ addicted; (ar) foul ▶ M/F addict; **um ~ em entorpecentes** a drug addict; **~ em algo** addicted to sth

viciar [vi'sjar] VT (criar vício em) to make addicted; (falsificar) to falsify; (taxímetro etc) to fiddle; **viciar-se** VR to become addicted; **~-se em algo** to become addicted to sth

vicinal [visi'naw] (pl -ais) ADJ local

vício ['visju] M vice; (defeito) failing; (costume) bad habit; (em entorpecentes) addiction

vicioso, -a [vi'sjozu, ɔza] ADJ corrupt, defective; **círculo ~** vicious circle

vicissitude [visisi'tudʒi] F vicissitude; **vicissitudes** FPL ups and downs

viço ['visu] M vigour (BRIT), vigor (US); (da pele) freshness

viçoso, -a [vi'sozu, ɔza] ADJ (plantas) luxuriant; (fig) exuberant

vida ['vida] F life; (duração) lifetime; (fig) vitality; **com ~** alive; **ganhar a ~** to earn one's living; **modo de ~** way of life; **para toda a ~** forever; **sem ~** dull, lifeless; **na ~ real** in real life; **cair na ~** (col) to go on the game; **dar ~ a** (festa, ambiente) to liven up; **dar a ~ por algo/por fazer algo** to give one's right arm for sth/to do sth; **estar bem de ~** to be well off; **estar entre a ~ e a morte** to be at death's door; **mete-se com a sua ~** mind your own business; **é a ~!** that's life!; **danado/feliz da ~** really angry/happy; **siga essa rua toda a ~** follow this street as far as you can go; **ele trabalha que não é ~** (col) he works really hard; **a ~ mansa** the

easy life; **~ civil/privada/pública/
sentimental/sexual/social** civilian/
private/public/love/sex/social life;
~ conjugal/doméstica married/home life;
~ útil (*Com*) useful life

vidão [vi'dãw] M good life

vide ['vidʒi] VT see; **~ verso** see over

videira [vi'dejra] F grapevine

vidente [vi'dẽtʃi] M/F clairvoyant; (*no mundo
antigo*) seer

vídeo ['vidʒju] M video; (*televisão*) TV; (*tela*)
screen

videocâmara [vidʒju'kamara] F video camera

videocassete [vidʒjuka'sɛtʃi] M (*fita*) video
cassette *ou* tape; (*aparelho*) video (recorder)

videoclipe [vidʒju'klipi] M video

videoclube [vidʒju'klubi] M video club

videodisco [vidʒju'dʒisku] M video disk

vídeo game [-'gejmi] (*pl* **vídeo games**) M
video game

videoteipe [vidʒju'tejpi] M (*fita*) video tape;
(*processo*) (video-)taping

videotexto [vidʒju'testu] M Teletext®

vidraça [vi'drasa] F window pane

vidraçaria [vidrasa'ria] F glazier's; (*fábrica*)
glass factory; (*conjunto de vidraças*) glasswork

vidraceiro [vidra'sejru] M glazier

vidrado, -a [vi'dradu, a] ADJ glazed; (*porta*)
glass *atr*; (*olhos*) glazed, glassy; **estar** *ou* **ser ~
em** *ou* **por** (*col*) to be crazy about

vidrar [vi'drar] VT to glaze ▶ VI: **~ em** *ou* **por**
(*col*) to fall in love with

vidreiro [vi'drejru] M glazier, glassmaker

vidro ['vidru] M glass; (*frasco*) bottle; **fibra
de ~** fibreglass (BRIT), fiberglass (US); **~ fosco**
frosted glass; **~ fumê** tinted glass; **~ de
aumento** magnifying glass

viela ['vjɛla] F alley

Viena ['vjɛna] N Vienna

vier *etc* [vjer] VB *ver* **vir¹**

viés [vjes] M slant; (*Costura*) bias strip; **ao** *ou*
de ~ diagonally

vieste ['vjestʃi] VB *ver* **vir¹**

Vietnã [vjet'nã] (BR) M: **o ~** Vietnam

vietnamita [vjetna'mita] ADJ, M/F
Vietnamese

viga ['viga] F beam; (*de ferro*) girder

vigarice [viga'risi] F swindle

vigário [vi'garju] M vicar

vigarista [viga'rista] M swindler, confidence
trickster

vigência [vi'ʒẽsja] F validity; **durante a ~ da
lei** while the law is in force

vigente [vi'ʒẽtʃi] ADJ in force, valid

viger [vi'ʒer] VI to be in force

vigésimo, -a [vi'ʒɛzimu, a] NUM twentieth;
ver tb **quinto**

vigia [vi'ʒia] F (*ato*) watching; (*Náut*) porthole
▶ M night watchman; **de ~** on watch

vigiar [vi'ʒjar] VT to watch, keep an eye on;
(*ocultamente*) to spy on; (*velar por*) to keep
watch over; (*presos, fronteira*) to guard ▶ VI to
be on the lookout

vigilância [viʒi'lãsja] F vigilance

vigilante [viʒi'lãtʃi] ADJ vigilant; (*atento*) alert

vigília [vi'ʒilja] F (*falta de sono*) wakefulness;
(*vigilância*) vigilance

vigor [vi'gor] M energy; **em ~** in force;
entrar/pôr em ~ to take effect/put into
effect

vigorar [vigo'rar] VI to be in force; **a ~ a partir
de** effective as of

vigoroso, -a [vigo'rozu, ɔza] ADJ vigorous

vil [viw] (*pl* **vis**) ADJ vile, low

vila ['vila] F town; (*casa*) villa; (*conjunto de
casas*) group of houses round a courtyard; **~ militar**
military base

vilã [vi'lã] F *de* **vilão**

vilania [vila'nia] F villainy

vilão, -lã [vi'lãw, 'lã] (*pl* **-ões/-s**) M/F villain

vilarejo [vila'reʒu] M village

vileza [vi'leza] F vileness; (*ação*) mean trick

vilipendiar [vilipẽ'dʒjar] VT to revile;
(*desprezar*) to despise

vim [vĩ] VB *ver* **vir¹**

vime ['vimi] M wicker

vinagre [vi'nagri] M vinegar

vinagrete [vina'grɛtʃi] M vinaigrette

vincar [vĩ'kar] VT to crease; (*produzir sulco em*)
to furrow; (*rosto*) to line

vinco ['vĩku] M crease; (*sulco*) furrow; (*no rosto*)
line

vincular [vĩku'lar] VT to link, tie; **vincular-se**
VR to be linked *ou* tied

vínculo ['vĩkulu] M bond, tie; (*relação*) link;
~ de parentesco blood tie; **~ empregatício**
contract of employment

vinda ['vĩda] F arrival; (*ato de vir*) coming;
(*regresso*) return; **dar as boas ~s a** to welcome

vindicar [vĩdʒi'kar] VT to vindicate

vindima [vĩ'dʒima] F grape harvest

vindique *etc* [vĩ'dʒiki] VB *ver* **vindicar**

vindouro, -a [vĩ'doru, a] ADJ future, coming

vingador, a [vĩga'dor(a)] ADJ avenging ▶ M/F
avenger

vingança [vĩ'gãsa] F vengeance, revenge

vingar [vĩ'gar] VT to avenge ▶ VI (*ter êxito*) to be
successful; (*planta*) to grow; **vingar-se** VR:
~-se de to take revenge on

vingativo, -a [vĩga'tʃivu, a] ADJ vindictive

vingue *etc* ['vĩgi] VB *ver* **vingar**

vinha¹ ['viɲa] F vineyard; (*planta*) vine

vinha² *etc* VB *ver* **vir¹**

vinha-d'alho (*pl* **vinhas d'alho**) F marinade

vinhedo [vi'ɲedu] M vineyard

vinho ['viɲu] M wine ▶ ADJ INV maroon;
~ branco/rosado/tinto white/rosé/red
wine; **~ seco/doce** dry/sweet wine;
~ espumante/de mesa sparkling/table
wine; **~ do Porto** port

vinícola [vi'nikola] ADJ INV wine-producing

vinicultor, a [vinikuw'tor(a)] M/F wine
grower

vinicultura [vinikuw'tura] F wine growing,
viticulture

vinil [vi'niw] M vinyl

V

vinte ['vĩtʃi] NUM twenty; **o século ~** the twentieth century; **as ~** (col: de cigarro, bebida) the last bit; ver tb **cinquenta**

vintém [vĩ'tẽj] M: **sem um ~** penniless

vintena [vĩ'tɛna] F: **uma ~** twenty, a score

viola ['vjɔla] F viola

violação [vjola'sãw] (pl **-ões**) F violation; **~ da lei** lawbreaking; **~ de domicílio** housebreaking

violão [vjo'lãw] (pl **-ões**) M guitar

violar [vjo'lar] VT to violate; (a lei) to break

violência [vjo'lẽsja] F violence

violentar [vjolẽ'tar] VT to force; (mulher) to rape; (fig: sentido) to distort

violento, -a [vjo'lẽtu, a] ADJ violent; (furioso) furious

violeta [vjo'leta] F violet ▶ ADJ INV violet

violinista [vjoli'nista] M/F violinist, violin player

violino [vjo'linu] M violin

violões [vjo'lõjs] MPL de **violão**

violoncelista [vjolõse'lista] M/F cellist

violoncelo [vjolõ'sɛlu] M cello

VIP ['vipi] M/F VIP ▶ ADJ (sala) VIP atr

vir¹ [vir] VI to come; **~ a ser** to turn out to be; **a semana que vem** next week; **~ abaixo** to collapse; **mandar ~** to send for; **~ fazendo algo** to have been doing sth; **~ fazer** to come to do; **~ buscar** to come for; **~ com** (alegar) to come up with; **isso não vem ao caso** that's irrelevant; **veio-lhe uma ideia** he had an idea, an idea came to him; **~ a saber** to come to know; **venha o que vier** come what may; **vem cá!** come here!; (col: escuta) listen!; **não vem que não tem!** (col) come off it!

vir² etc VB ver **ver**

viração [vira'sãw] (pl **-ões**) F breeze

vira-casaca ['vira-] (pl **vira-casacas**) M/F turncoat

virada [vi'rada] F turning; (guinada) swerve; (Esporte) turnaround; **dar uma ~** (col) to put on a last burst

virado, -a [vi'radu, a] ADJ (às avessas) upside down ▶ M (Culin): **~ (de feijão)** fried beans with sausage and eggs; **~ para** facing

viral [vi'raw] ADJ viral

vira-lata ['vira-] (pl **vira-latas**) M (cão) mongrel; (pessoa) bum

virar [vi'rar] VT to turn; (página, disco, barco) to turn over; (esquina) to turn; (bolsos) to turn inside out; (copo) to empty; (despejar) to tip; (opinião) to turn round; (transformar-se em) to become ▶ VI to turn; (barco) to capsize, turn over; (mudar) to change; **virar-se** VR to turn; (voltar-se) to turn round; (defender-se) to fend for o.s.; **~ de cabeça para baixo** to turn upside down; **~ do avesso** to turn inside out; **~ para** to face; **vira e mexe** every so often; **~(-se) contra** to turn against; **~-se para** (recorrer a) to turn to; **~-se de bruços** to turn onto one's stomach

viravolta [vira'vɔwta] F (fig) turnabout; (volta completa) complete turn; (giro sobre si mesmo) about-turn; (cambalhota) somersault

virgem ['virʒẽj] (pl **-ns**) ADJ (puro) pure; (mata) virgin; (não usado) unused; (: fita) blank ▶ F virgin; **V~** (Astrologia) Virgo; **~ de** free of

virgindade [virʒĩ'dadʒi] F virginity

vírgula ['virgula] F comma; (decimal) point; **uma ~!** (col) my eye!

virgular [virgu'lar] VT: **~ com** ou **de** (entremear) to punctuate with

viril [vi'riw] (pl **-is**) ADJ virile

virilha [vi'riʎa] F groin

virilidade [virili'dadʒi] F virility

víris [vi'ris] ADJ PL de **víril**

virose [vi'rɔzi] F viral illness

virtual [vir'twaw] (pl **-ais**) ADJ virtual; (potencial) potential

virtualmente [virtwaw'mẽtʃi] ADV virtually

virtude [vir'tudʒi] F virtue; **em ~ de** owing to, because of

virtuosidade [virtwozi'dadʒi] F virtuosity

virtuosismo [virtwo'zizmu] M = **virtuosidade**

virtuoso, -a [vir'twozu, ɔza] ADJ virtuous ▶ M virtuoso

virulência [viru'lẽsja] F virulence

virulento, -a [viru'lẽtu, a] ADJ virulent

vírus ['virus] M INV virus

vis [vis] ADJ PL de **vil**

visado, -a [vi'zadu, a] ADJ stamped; (pessoa: pela polícia, imprensa) under observation

visão [vi'zãw] (pl **-ões**) F vision; (Anat) eyesight; (vista) sight; (maneira de perceber) view; **~ de conjunto** overall view

visar [vi'zar] VT (alvo) to aim at; (ter em vista) to have in view; (ter como objetivo) to aim for; (passaporte, cheque) to stamp ▶ VI: **~ a** to have in view; to aim for; **~ fazer** to aim to do

Visc. ABR = **visconde**

vísceras ['viseras] FPL innards, bowels; (fig) heart sg

visconde [vis'kõdʒi] M viscount

viscondessa [viskõ'desa] F viscountess

viscoso, -a [vis'kozu, ɔza] ADJ sticky, viscous

viseira [vi'zejra] F visor

visibilidade [vizibili'dadʒi] F visibility

visionário, -a [vizjo'narju, a] ADJ, M/F visionary

visita [vi'zita] F visit, call; (pessoa) visitor; (na Internet) hit; **fazer uma ~ a** to visit; **ter ~s** to have company; **~ guiada** guided tour; **~ de médico** (col) flying visit; **horário de ~s** visiting hours pl

visitante [vizi'tãtʃi] ADJ visiting ▶ M/F visitor

visitar [vizi'tar] VT to visit; (inspecionar) to inspect

visível [vi'zivew] (pl **-eis**) ADJ visible

vislumbrar [vizlũ'brar] VT to glimpse, catch a glimpse of

vislumbre [viz'lũbri] M glimpse

visões [vi'zõjs] FPL de **visão**

visom [vi'zõ] (pl **-ns**) M mink; **casaco de ~** mink coat

visor [vi'zor] M (*Foto*) viewfinder

visse *etc* ['visi] VB *ver* **ver**

vista ['vista] F sight; (*Med*) eyesight; (*panorama*) view; (*braguilha*) fly, flies *pl*; **à** *ou* **em ~ de** in view of; **conhecer de ~** to know by sight; **dar na ~** to attract attention; **dar uma ~ de olhos em** to glance at; **fazer ~ grossa (a)** to turn a blind eye (to); **pôr à ~** to show; **ter em ~** to have in mind; **à primeira ~** at first sight; **à ~** visible, showing; (*Com*) in cash; **até a ~!** see you!; **na ~ de todos** in view of everyone; **perder de ~** to lose sight of; **a perder de ~** as far as the eye can (*ou* could) see; (*pagamento*) over a long period; **saltar à ~** to be obvious; **fazer ~** to look nice; **~ cansada/curta** eye strain/shortsightedness

vista-d'olhos F glance, quick look; **dar uma ~ em** to have a quick look at

visto¹, -a ['vistu, a] PP *de* **ver** ▶ ADJ seen ▶ M (*em passaporte*) visa; (*em documento*) stamp; **pelo ~** by the looks of things

visto² VB *ver* **vestir**

vistoria [visto'ria] F inspection

vistoriar [visto'rjar] VT to inspect

vistoso, -a [vis'tozu, ɔza] ADJ eye-catching

visual [vi'zwaw] (*pl* **-ais**) ADJ visual ▶ M (*col: de pessoa*) look; (*aparência*) appearance; (*vista*) view

visualizar [vizwali'zar] VT to visualize

vital [vi'taw] (*pl* **-ais**) ADJ vital; (*essencial*) essential

vitalício, -a [vita'lisju, a] ADJ for life

vitalidade [vitali'dadʒi] F vitality

vitalizar [vitali'zar] VT to revitalize

vitamina [vita'mina] F vitamin; (*para beber*) fruit crush

vitaminado, -a [vitami'nadu, a] ADJ with added vitamins

vitamínico, -a [vita'miniku, a] ADJ vitamin *atr*

vitela [vi'tɛla] F calf; (*carne*) veal

viticultura [vitʃikuw'tura] F wine growing

vítima ['vitʃima] F victim; **fazer-se de ~** to play the martyr

vitimar [vitʃi'mar] VT to sacrifice; (*matar*) to kill, claim the life of; (*danificar*) to damage

vitória [vi'tɔrja] F victory; (*Esporte*) win

vitória-régia (*pl* **vitórias-régias**) F giant water lily

vitorioso, -a [vito'rjozu, ɔza] ADJ victorious; (*time*) winning

vitral [vi'traw] (*pl* **-ais**) M stained glass window

vítreo, -a ['vitrju, a] ADJ (*feito de vidro*) glass *atr*; (*com o aspecto de vidro*) glassy; (*água*) clear

vitrina [vi'trina] F = **vitrine**

vitrine [vi'trini] F shop window; (*armário*) display case

vitrola [vi'trɔla] F record player

viuvez [vju'vez] F widowhood

viúvo, -a ['vjuvu, a] ADJ widowed ▶ M/F widower/widow

viva ['viva] M cheer; **~!** hurray!; **~ o rei!** long live the king!

vivacidade [vivasi'dadʒi] F vivacity; (*energia*) vigour (BRIT), vigor (US)

vivalma [vi'vawma] F: **não ver ~** not to see a (living) soul

vivamente [viva'mētʃi] ADV animatedly; (*descrever, sentir*) vividly; (*protestar*) loudly

vivar [vi'var] VT, VI to cheer

viva-voz [viva'vɔz] M (BR *Tel: em telefone*) speakerphone; (*para celular*) hands-free kit

vivaz [vi'vajz] ADJ (*animado*) lively

viveiro [vi'vejru] M nursery

vivência [vi'vẽsja] F existence; (*experiência*) experience

vivenda [vi'vẽda] F (*casa*) residence

vivente [vi'vẽtʃi] ADJ living ▶ M/F living being; **os ~s** the living

viver [vi'ver] VI to live; (*estar vivo*) to be alive ▶ VT (*vida*) to live; (*experimentar*) to have, experience ▶ M life; **~ de** to live on; **~ à custa de** to live off; **ela vive viajando/cansada** she's always travel(l)ing/tired; **ele vive resfriado/com dor de estômago** he's always got a cold/stomach ache; **vivendo e aprendendo** live and learn

víveres ['viveres] MPL provisions

vivido, -a [vi'vidu, a] ADJ experienced in life

vívido, -a ['vividu, a] ADJ vivid

vivificar [vivifi'kar] VT to bring to life

vivissecção [vivisek'sãw] F vivisection

vivo, -a ['vivu, a] ADJ living; (*esperto*) clever; (*cor*) bright; (*criança, debate*) lively ▶ M: **os ~s** the living; **televisionar ao ~** to televise live; **estar ~** to be alive

vizinhança [vizi'ɲãsa] F neighbourhood (BRIT), neighborhood (US)

vizinho, -a [vi'ziɲu, a] ADJ neighbouring (BRIT), neighboring (US); (*perto*) nearby ▶ M/F neighbour (BRIT), neighbor (US)

vó [vɔ] (*col*) F gran

vô [vo] (*col*) M grandad, grandpa

voador, a [vwa'dor(a)] ADJ flying

voar [vo'ar] VI to fly; (*explodir*) to blow up, explode; **fazer ~ (pelos ares)** (*dinamitar*) to blow up, blast; **~ para cima de alguém** to fly at sb; **estar voando** (*col*) to be in the dark; **~ alto** (*fig*) to aim high; **fazer algo voando** to do sth in a hurry

vocabulário [vokabu'larju] M vocabulary

vocábulo [vo'kabulu] M word

vocação [voka'sãw] (*pl* **-ões**) F vocation

vocacional [vokasjo'naw] (*pl* **-ais**) ADJ vocational; (*orientação*) careers *atr*

vocações [voka'sõjs] FPL *de* **vocação**

vocal [vo'kaw] (*pl* **-ais**) ADJ vocal

você [vo'se] PRON you

vocês [vo'ses] PRON PL you

vociferação [vosifera'sãw] (*pl* **-ões**) F shouting; (*censura*) harangue

vociferar [vosife'rar] VT, VI to shout, yell; **~ contra** to decry

vodca ['vɔdʒka] F vodka

V

voga ['vɔga] F (*Náut*) rowing; (*moda*) fashion; (*popularidade*) popularity; **em ~** popular, fashionable

vogal [vo'gaw] (*pl* **-ais**) F (*Ling*) vowel ▶ M/F (*votante*) voting member

vogar [vo'gar] VI to sail; (*boiar*) to float; (*importar*) to matter; (*estar na moda*) to be popular; (*lei*) to be in force; (*palavra*) to be in use

voile ['vwali] M voile; **cortina de ~** net curtain

vol. ABR (= *volume*) vol.

volante [vo'lãtʃi] M (*Auto*) steering wheel; (*piloto*) racing driver; (*impresso para apostas*) betting slip; (*roda*) flywheel

volátil [vo'latʃiw] (*pl* **-eis**) ADJ volatile

vôlei ['volej] M volleyball

voleibol [volej'bɔw] M = **vôlei**

volt ['vɔwtʃi] (*pl* **-s**) M volt

volta ['vɔwta] F turn; (*regresso*) return; (*curva*) bend, curve; (*circuito*) lap; (*resposta*) retort; **passagem de ida e ~** return ticket (BRIT), round trip ticket (US); **dar uma ~** (*a pé*) to go for a walk; (*de carro*) to go for a drive; **dar ~s** *ou* **uma ~ (a)** to go round; **estar de ~** to be back; **na ~ do correio** by return (post); **por ~ de** about, around; **à** *ou* **em ~ de** around; **na ~** (*no caminho de volta*) on the way back; **vou resolver isso na ~** I'll sort this out when I get back; **estar** *ou* **andar às ~s com** to be tied up with; **fazer a ~, dar meia ~** (*Auto*) to do a U-turn; **dar meia ~** (*Mil*) to do an about-turn; **dar a ~ por cima** (*fig*) to get over it, pick o.s. up; **~ e meia** every so often

voltado, -a [vow'tadu, a] ADJ: **estar ~ para** to be concerned with

voltagem [vow'taʒẽ] F voltage

voltar [vow'tar] VT to turn ▶ VI to return, go (*ou* come) back; **voltar-se** VR to turn round; **~ uma arma contra** to turn a weapon on; **~ a fazer** to do again; **~ a si** to come to; **~ atrás** (*fig*) to backtrack; **~-se para** to turn to; **~-se contra** to turn against

voltear [vow'tʃjar] VT to go round; (*manivela*) to turn ▶ VI to spin; (*borboleta*) to flit around

volubilidade [volubili'dadʒi] F fickleness

volume [vo'lumi] M volume; (*tamanho*) bulk; (*pacote*) package

volumoso, -a [volu'mozu, ɔza] ADJ bulky, big; (*som*) loud

voluntário, -a [volũ'tarju, a] ADJ voluntary ▶ M/F volunteer

voluntarioso, -a [volũta'rjozu, ɔza] ADJ headstrong

volúpia [vo'lupja] F pleasure, ecstasy

voluptuoso, -a [volup'twozu, ɔza] ADJ voluptuous

volúvel [vo'luvew] (*pl* **-eis**) ADJ fickle, changeable

volver [vow'ver] VT to turn ▶ VI to go (*ou* come) back

vomitar [vomi'tar] VT, VI to vomit; (*fig*) to pour out

vômito ['vomitu] M (*ato*) vomiting; (*efeito*) vomit

vontade [võ'tadʒi] F will; (*desejo*) wish; **boa/má ~** good/ill will; **de boa/má ~** willingly/grudgingly; **frutas à ~** fruit galore; **coma à ~** eat as much as you like; **fique** *ou* **esteja à ~** make yourself at home; **não estar à ~** to be uncomfortable *ou* ill at ease; **com ~** (*com prazer*) with pleasure; (*com gana*) with gusto; **estar com** *ou* **ter ~ de fazer** to feel like doing; **dar ~ a alguém de fazer** to make sb want to do; **essa música dá ~ de bailar** this music makes you want to dance; **fazer a ~ de alguém** to do what sb wants; **de livre e espontânea ~** of one's own free will; **por ~ própria** off one's own bat; **força de ~** will power; **ser cheio de ~s** to be spoilt

voo ['vou] M flight; **levantar ~** to take off; **~ cego** flying blind, instrument flying; **~ livre** (*Esporte*) hang-gliding; **~ picado** nose dive

voragem [vo'raʒẽ] (*pl* **-ns**) F abyss, gulf; (*de águas*) whirlpool; (*fig: de paixões*) maelstrom

voraz [vo'rajz] ADJ voracious, greedy

vórtice ['vɔrtʃisi] M vortex

vos [vus] PRON you

vós [vɔs] PRON you

vosso, -a ['vɔsu, a] ADJ your ▶ PRON: **(o) ~** yours

votação [vota'sãw] (*pl* **-ões**) F vote, ballot; (*ato*) voting; **submeter algo a ~** to put sth to the vote; **~ secreta** secret ballot

votado, -a [vo'tadu, a] ADJ: **o deputado mais ~** the MP (BRIT) *ou* Member of Congress (US) with the highest number of votes

votante [vo'tãtʃi] M/F voter

votar [vo'tar] VT (*eleger*) to vote for; (*aprovar*) to pass; (*submeter a votação*) to vote on; (*dedicar*) to devote ▶ VI to vote; **votar-se** VR: **~-se a** to devote o.s. to; **~ em** to vote for; **~ por/contra** to vote for/against

voto ['vɔtu] M vote; (*promessa*) vow; **votos** MPL (*desejos*) wishes; **fazer ~s por** to wish for; **fazer ~s que** to hope that; **fazer ~ de castidade** to take a vow of chastity; **~ nulo** *ou* **em branco** blank vote; **~ de confiança** vote of confidence; **~ secreto** secret ballot

vou [vo] VB *ver* **ir**

vovó [vo'vɔ] F grandma

vovô [vo'vo] M grandad

voz [vɔz] F voice; (*clamor*) cry; **a meia ~** in a whisper; **dar ~ de prisão a alguém** to tell sb he is under arrest; **de viva ~** orally; **ter ~ ativa** to have a say; **em ~ baixa** in a low voice; **em ~ alta** aloud; **levantar a ~ para alguém** to raise one's voice to sb; **~ de cana rachada** (*col*) screeching voice; **~ de comando** command, order

vozearia [vozja'ria] F = **vozerio**

vozeirão [vozej'rãw] (*pl* **-ões**) M loud voice

vozerio [voze'riu] M hullabaloo

VPR ABR F (= *Vanguarda Popular Revolucionária*) *former Brazilian revolutionary movement*

vulcânico, -a [vuw'kaniku, a] ADJ volcanic
vulcão [vuw'kãw] (pl **-ões**) M volcano
vulgar [vuw'gar] ADJ (comum) common; (reles) cheap; (pej: pessoa etc) vulgar
vulgaridade [vuwgari'dadʒi] F commonness; (pej) vulgarity
vulgarizar [vuwgari'zar] VT to popularize; (abandalhar) to cheapen
vulgarmente [vuwgar'mētʃi] ADV commonly, popularly
vulgo ['vuwgu] M common people pl ▶ ADV commonly known as

vulnerabilidade [vuwnerabili'dadʒi] F vulnerability
vulnerável [vuwne'ravew] (pl **-eis**) ADJ vulnerable
vulto ['vuwtu] M figure; (volume) mass; (fig) importance; (pessoa importante) important person; **obras de ~** important works; **tomar ~** to take shape
vultoso, -a [vuw'tozu, ɔza] ADJ bulky; (importante) important; (quantia) considerable
vulva ['vuwva] F vulva
vupt ['vuptʃi] EXCL wham!

V

W, w ['dablju] (*pl* **ws**) M W, w; **W de William**
W for William

w. ABR (= *watt*) w

walkie-talkie [wɔki'tɔki] (*pl* **-s**) M walkie-talkie

watt ['wɔtʃi] (*pl* **-s**) M watt

watt-hora (*pl* **watts-horas**) M watt-hour

web ['wɛbi] F, ADJ (*Comput*) web

webcam [wɛb'kã] F webcam

western ['wɛstern] (*pl* **-s**) M western

windsurfe [wĩ'surfi] M windsurfing

windsurfista [wĩsur'fista] M/F windsurfer

WWW ABR F (= *World Wide Web*) WWW

X, x [ʃis] (pl **xs**) M X, x; **o X do problema** the crux of the problem; **X de Xavier** X for Xmas

xá [ʃa] M shah

xadrez [ʃa'drez] M (jogo) chess; (tabuleiro) chessboard; (tecido) checked cloth; (col: cadeia) clink ▶ ADJ INV check(ered); **tecido de ~** check material

xale ['ʃali] M shawl

xampu [ʃã'pu] M shampoo

Xangai [ʃã'gaj] N Shanghai

xangô [ʃã'go] M (orixá) Afro-Brazilian deity; (culto) Afro-Brazilian religion

xará [ʃa'ra] M/F namesake; (companheiro) mate

xaropada [ʃaro'pada] (col) F bore; (conversa) boring talk

xarope [ʃa'rɔpi] M syrup; (para a tosse) cough syrup

xavante [ʃa'vãtʃi] ADJ, M/F Shavante Indian

xaveco [ʃa'vɛku] M (coisa sem valor) piece of junk

xaxim [ʃa'ʃĩ] M plant fibre (BRIT) ou fiber (US) (used to plant indoor plants)

xelim [ʃe'lĩ] (pl **-ns**) M shilling

xenofobia [ʃenofo'bia] F xenophobia

xenófobo, -a [ʃe'nɔfobu, a] ADJ xenophobic ▶ M/F xenophobe

xepa ['ʃepa] (col) F leftovers pl

xepeiro, -a [ʃe'pejru, a] M/F rubbish (BRIT) ou garbage (US) picker

xeque ['ʃɛki] M (Xadrez) check; (soberano) sheikh; **pôr em ~** (fig) to call into question

xeque-mate (pl **xeques-mate**) M checkmate

xereta [ʃe'reta] M/F busybody ▶ ADJ nosy

xeretar [ʃere'tar] VI to poke one's nose in

xerez [ʃe'rez] M sherry

xerife [ʃe'rifi] M sheriff

xerocar [ʃero'kar] VT to photocopy, Xerox®

xerocópia [ʃero'kɔpja] F photocopy

xerocopiar [ʃeroko'pjar] VT = **xerocar**

xerox® [ʃe'rɔks] M (copia) photocopy; (máquina) photocopier

xexelento, -a [ʃeʃe'lẽtu, a] (col) ADJ scruffy ▶ M/F scruff

xexéu [ʃe'ʃew] M stink

xi [ʃi] EXCL cor! (BRIT), gee! (US)

xícara ['ʃikara] (BR) F cup

xicrinha [ʃi'kriɲa] (BR) F little cup

xiita [ʃi'ita] ADJ, M/F Shiite

xilindró [ʃili'drɔ] (col) M clink

xilofone [ʃilo'fɔni] M xylophone

xilografia [ʃilogra'fia] F woodcut

xingação [ʃĩga'sãw] (pl **-ões**) F curse

xingamento [ʃĩga'mẽtu] M = **xingação**

xingar [ʃĩ'gar] VT to swear at ▶ VI to swear; **~ alguém de algo** to call sb sth

xingatório [ʃĩga'tɔrju] M stream of invectives

Xingu [ʃĩ'gu] M see note

> The **Xingu** National Park was created in 1961 by the federal government and directed by the brothers Orlando and Cláudio Vilasboas, who were known internationally for their efforts to preserve Brazil's indigenous people. Situated in the north of the state of Mato Grosso, it aims to preserve indigenous culture. It brings together sixteen communities, a total of two thousand Indians.

xinxim [ʃĩ'ʃĩ] M (tb: **xinxim de galinha**) chicken ragout

xixi [ʃi'ʃi] (col) M wee, pee; **fazer ~** to wee, have a wee

xô [ʃo] EXCL shoo

xodó [ʃo'dɔ] M (pessoa) sweetheart; (coisa) passion; **ter ~ por alguém/algo** to have a soft spot for sb/sth

Zz

Z, z [ze] (*pl* **zs**) M Z, z; **Z de Zebra** Z for Zebra
zaga ['zaga] F (*Futebol*) fullback position
zagueiro [za'gejru] M (*Futebol*) fullback
Zaire ['zajri] M: **o ~** Zaire
Zâmbia ['zãbja] F Zambia
zanga ['zãga] F (*raiva*) anger; (*irritação*) annoyance
zangado, -a [zã'gadu, a] ADJ angry; (*irritado*) annoyed; (*irritadiço*) bad-tempered; **ele está ~ comigo** (*de relações cortadas*) he's not speaking to me
zangão [zã'gãw] (*pl* **-ões**) M (*inseto*) drone
zangar [zã'gar] VT to annoy, irritate ▶ VI to get angry; **zangar-se** VR (*aborrecer-se*) to get annoyed; **~-se com** to get cross with
zangões [zã'gõjs] MPL *de* **zangão**
zanzar [zã'zar] VI to wander
zarolho, -a [za'roʎu, a] ADJ blind in one eye
zarpar [zar'par] VI (*navio*) to set sail; (*ir-se*) to set off; (*fugir*) to run away
Zé [ze] ABR (= *José*) Joe
zebra ['zebra] F zebra; (*col: pessoa*) silly ass; (*jogo*) upset, turn-up for the books; **deu ~** (*col*) there was an upset
zebrar [ze'brar] VI to be a turn-up for the books
zelador, a [zela'dor(a)] M/F caretaker ▶ ADJ caring
zelar [ze'lar] VT, VI: **~ (por)** to look after
zelo ['zelu] M devotion, zeal; **~ por alguém/ algo** devotion to sb/sth
zeloso, -a [ze'lozu, ɔza] ADJ zealous; (*diligente*) hard-working
zen-budismo [zẽ-] M Zen (Buddhism)
zênite ['zenitʃi] M zenith
zé-povinho [-po'viɲu] (*pl* **zé-povinhos**) M the man in the street; (*o povo*) the masses *pl*; (*ralé*) riff raff
zerar [ze'rar] VT (*conta, inflação*) to reduce to zero; (*déficit*) to pay off, wipe out; (*aluno*) to give no marks to ▶ VI: **~ em** (*aluno*) to get no marks in
zerinho, -a [ze'riɲu, a] (*col*) ADJ brand new
zero ['zeru] M zero; (*Esporte*) nil; **ser um ~ à esquerda** to be useless; **8 graus abaixo/ acima de ~** 8 degrees below/above zero; **reduzir alguém a ~** to clean sb out; **ficar a ~** to lose everything; **começar do ~** (*fig*) to start from nothing

zero-quilômetro ADJ INV brand new ▶ M INV brand new car
ziguezague [zigi'zagi] M zigzag
ziguezagueante [zigiza'gjãtʃi] ADJ zigzag
ziguezaguear [zigiza'gjar] VI to zigzag
Zimbábue [zĩ'babwi] M: **o ~** Zimbabwe
zinco ['zĩku] M zinc; **folha de ~** corrugated iron
-zinho, -a [-'ziɲu, a] SUFIXO little; **florzinha** little flower
zipe ['zipi] M = **zíper**
zíper ['ziper] M zip (BRIT), zipper (US)
ziquizira [ziki'zira] (*col*) F lurgy
zoada ['zwada] F = **zoeira**
zodíaco [zo'dʒiaku] M zodiac
zoeira ['zwejra] F din
zombador, a [zõba'dor(a)] ADJ mocking ▶ M/F mocker
zombar [zõ'bar] VI to mock; **~ de** to make fun of
zombaria [zõba'ria] F mockery, ridicule
zona ['zona] F area; (*de cidade*) district; (*Geo*) zone; (*col: local de meretrício*) red-light district; (: *confusão*) mess; (: *tumulto*) free-for-all; **fazer a ~** to be on the game; **fazer uma ~** to raise hell, make a fuss; **~ eleitoral** electoral district, constituency; **~ franca** free-trade area; **Z~ Norte/Sul** (*do Rio, São Paulo etc*) Northern/Southern District; **a Z~ Sul carioca** *the fashionable middle-class suburbs along the beaches in Rio*
zonear [zo'njar] VT to divide into districts; (*col*) to make a mess in ▶ VI (*col*) to raise hell
zonzeira [zõ'zejra] F dizziness; **dar/sentir ~** to make/feel dizzy
zonzo, -a ['zõzu, a] ADJ dizzy; (*fraco*) woozy
zoo ['zou] M zoo
zoologia [zolo'ʒia] F zoology
zoológico, -a [zo'lɔʒiku, a] ADJ zoological; **jardim ~** zoo
zoólogo, -a [zo'ɔlogu, a] M/F zoologist
zoom [zũ] M = **zum**
zorra ['zoha] (*col*) F mess
zuarte ['zwartʃi] M denim
zulu [zu'lu] ADJ, M/F Zulu ▶ M (*Ling*) Zulu
zum [zũ] M zoom lens
zumbido [zũ'bidu] M buzz(ing); (*de tráfego*) hum; **um ~ no ouvido** a ringing in one's ear
zumbir [zũ'bir] VI to buzz; (*ouvido*) to ring ▶ M buzzing; ringing

zunido [zu'nidu] M (*de vento*) whistling; (*de inseto*) buzz

zunir [zu'nir] VI (*vento*) to whistle; (*seta*) to whizz; (*bala*) to zip; (*inseto*) to buzz

zunzum [zũ'zũ] M buzz(ing); (*boato*) rumour (BRIT), rumor (US)

zunzunzum [zũzũ'zũ] M rumour (BRIT), rumor (US)

zura ['zura] M/F INV miser ▶ ADJ INV mean, stingy

zureta [zu'reta] (*col*) M/F loony

Zurique [zu'riki] N Zurich

zurrapa [zu'hapa] F rough wine, plonk (*col*)

zurrar [zu'har] VI to bray

zurro ['zuhu] M bray

Z